THE OFFICIAL ENCYCLOPEDIA OF BRIDGE

NEWLY REVISED, FIFTH EDITION

Published by American Contract Bridge League, Inc., 2990 Airways Boulevard, Memphis, Tennessee 38116-3875. Manufactured in the United States of America.

Library of Congress Cataloging in Publication Data

Main entry under title:

The Official Encyclopedia of Bridge

ISBN   0-943855-48-9

CONTRIBUTING EDITORS

To this edition	To earlier editions
Phillip Alder	Jean Besse
Carlos Cabanne	Eric Crowhurst
Larry N. Cohen	Albert Dormer
Gabriel Chagas	Robert Ewen
Hugh Darwen	*M. Harrison-Gray
Sue Emery	*Monroe Ingberman
Albert Field	*Fred Karpin
Santanu Ghose	Sami Kehela
Richard Grenside	*Rhoda Barrow Lederer
Olof Hanner	Marshall Miles
Diane Hayward	*Victor Mollo
Per Jannersten	Jeff Rubens
Jared Johnson	Alec Traub
Patrick Jourdain	*Roy Telfer
Edgar Kaplan	
Phillip Martin	**PROOFREADERS**
Svend Novrup	
David Parry	Jack Bridges
R. Anthony Priday	Peter Filandro
Bill Sachen	James Fitzgerald
Ton Schipperheyn	
Frank Stewart	
Jess Stuart	
Dorothy Truscott	
Sol Weinstein	

Deceased

THE OFFICIAL ENCYCLOPEDIA OF BRIDGE

Newly revised Fifth Edition

*Authorized by the American Contract Bridge League
and prepared under its supervision*

HENRY G. FRANCIS
Editor-in-Chief

ALAN F. TRUSCOTT
Executive Editor

DORTHY A. FRANCIS
Editor, Fifth Edition

FOREWORD

This Encyclopedia was the brainchild of the late Richard L. Frey, who suggested the project to the American Contract Bridge League in 1962. His aim was to "Provide an official and authoritative answer to any question a reader might ask about the game of contract bridge and its leading players." He brought me from England to do the work. The book was completed in the of 18 months and published in 1964.

The new book included much new technical, biographical and bibliographical material, and one *tour de force*: the suit combinations section by Eric Crowhurst was remarkable in its depth and accuracy. It has continued virtually unchanged in subsequent editions. The late Albert Morehead, who had a deep knowledge of the history of the game, contributed greatly as chairman of the Advisory Board.

A British edition with a European focus, prepared by Rhoda Barrow Lederer, appeared in 1967. The second American edition (1971) was supervised by Thomas M. Smith, and the third (1976) by Amalya L. Kearse, now a Justice of the Federal Court of Appeals in New York. Mr. Frey continued as Editor Emeritus, with Henry G. Francis as editor-in-chief of the third fourth and fifth editions. The editor of the fourth edition (1984) was Diane Hayward.

This fifth edition, with Mr. Francis again in overall control, has been prepared largely by me (technical and foreign) and by Dorthy Francis (American biographies and updated tournament results). Frank Stewart contributed much new material to the technical section, and William Sachen prepared the Bibliography. Many others made lesser contributions, and some of these are listed as contributing editors. A complete list is impossible, but our thanks go to all who have helped in any way.

Note that in earlier editions some technical entries gave credit to an author. Since these credits were incomplete, and many entries have been substantially modified, there are no such credits in this edition.

The listings of regional winners have been excised in order to make room for additional technical material. The changes in the technical section have been far greater than in any of the earlier editions, reflecting the many theoretical advances in the past decade.

The first four editions were published by Crown Publishers Inc. of New York City. The fifth is being published by the American Contract Bridge League under the authority of its Board of Directors and its Chief Executive Officer, Roy G. Green.

— ALAN TRUSCOTT
Executive Editor

How to use this Encyclopedia

For easy reference, this book has been divided into four main parts: I. General information (technical - bidding and play; historical; procedural - organization, laws, etc.; geographical; and terminological); II. Biographies; III. International and national results; IV. Bibliography.

I. General Information.

Technical. When more than one name is in use for a specific system, convention, etc., the major entry is usually under the name most commonly used in North America. Other names are provided with a cross-reference.

The reader who wishes to study a particular field is advised to consult one of the following group headings: BIDDING; BIDDING SYSTEMS; COLLOQUIALISMS; DEFENSE; DEFENSE TO ONE NOTRUMP; DOUBLES; DUMMY PLAY; DUPLICATE BRIDGE; LEADS; MATHEMATICS OF BRIDGE; OPENING BID; REBIDS; RESPONSE; SIGNALS; SLAM CONVENTIONS; SQUEEZE; SUIT COMBINATIONS; TROPHIES; TRUMP PLAY; VALUATION.

Historical. Every effort has been made to record the history of the American Contract Bridge League and other national and international organizations. Information of importance, some of which was uncovered since the fourth edition, will be found under HISTORY OF BRIDGE and HISTORY OF PLAYING CARDS. (Also see the biographical entries of historical figures.)

Procedural. The Laws of Contract Bridge (1993) and the Laws of Duplicate Contract Bridge (1987) are presented in full. Various aspects of tournament organization are dealt with or cross-referenced under the heading DUPLICATE BRIDGE.

Geographical. National bridge organizations throughout the world are listed, often with some description and history.

Terminological. An effort has been made to list and define all terms and colloquialisms in common use in the English-speaking world.

II. Biographies.
More than 2,800 bridge personalities from around the world are listed. Stricter criteria have been used for inclusion.

III. Championship results.
Here are listed winners of world championships, zonal championships, ACBL and ABA championships, European Championships and many others.

IV. Bibliography.
Significant books on all aspects of bridge are listed by subject.

The American Contract Bridge League, P.O. Box 161192, Memphis, TN 38186 will endeavor to render library service to owners of this Encyclopedia who send a request for information with a self-addressed stamped envelope.

A

ABA. See AMERICAN BRIDGE ASSOCIATION.

ABL. See AMERICAN BRIDGE LEAGUE.

ABTA. See AMERICAN BRIDGE TEACHERS ASSOCIATION.

ACBL. See AMERICAN CONTRACT BRIDGE LEAGUE.

ACBL BULLETIN. See BULLETIN, THE CONTRACT BRIDGE.

ACBL CHARITY FOUNDATION. See CHARITY PROGRAM OF THE ACBL.

ACBL EDUCATIONAL FOUNDATION. The foundation was created to raise funds to be used for bridge educational purposes. The foundation has made many grants to educational projects including the special courses offered at the New York Foundation for the Hard of Hearing and by the ACBL Education Department. It also gives a $500 prize to the winner of the Youth Division of the ACBL Instant Matchpoints Game.

1994 Foundation officers:
President: Jayne Thomas
17751A Lake Carlton Drive
FL 33549
Also P.O.Box 271687
Tampa FL 33688
Home phone 813-961-1172
FAX 813-265-1373
Vice President: John Gustafson
Secretary-Treasurer: Aileen Osofsky
860 UN Plazza #19C
New York NY 10017
Home phone 212-421-5405
or
9475 E. Mariposa Grande
Scottsdale AZ 85155
Home phone 602-585-0408
FAX 602-585-4900

Board of directors: Harriette Hirsch-Buckman, Michael Jones, Dr. Eugene Kales, Shirley Pagan, Bernard Warshauer and Charles Wilkinson. Advisers: Dr. Patricia Cayne, Joan Levy Gerard, Barbara Nudelman and Chris Wilson. President emeritus: Thomas Sanders.

ACBL HANDBOOK. A handbook that includes the regulations and practices followed by the American Contract Bridge League in several important phases of its activities. Covered in detail are the regulations and practices involving membership, clubs, units, districts, tournaments and discipline. Interested persons or groups may secure copies from ACBL HEADQUARTERS.

ACBL HEADQUARTERS. 2990 Airways Boulevard, Memphis, Tennessee 38116-3847. Phone — 901-332-5586. FAX — 901-398-7754. Membership Assistance numbers: U.S. 1-800-467-1623; Canada 1-800-467-2623. Sales Department numbers: U.S. 1-800-264-2743; Canada 1-800-264-8786.

ACBL LAWS COMMISSION. See LAWS COMMISSION OF THE ACBL.

ACBL PLAYER NUMBER. See PLAYER NUMBER.

ACBL PLAYER OF THE YEAR. Awarded to the ACBL member who earns the most masterpoints during a calendar year in nationally-rated events. For winners see Appendix II.

ACBLSCORE. The computer program devised by the American Contract Bridge League to score bridge tournaments and club games, compute masterpoint awards, compile personnel records, prepare monthly club reports and provide reports on tournament events for publications.

ACBL TEACHING SERIES. The ACBL teaching series consists of four textbooks designed to make bridge easy to learn and fun to play. Each text has a coordinated teacher manual which offers lesson plans for teachers. These books, written for the ACBL by Audrey Grant, follow a spiral curriculum and each one contains eight two-hour lessons. The first book, *The Club Series*, focuses on bidding; the second book, *The Diamond Series*, focuses on the play of the hand; the third book, *The Heart Series*, focuses on defense; the fourth book, *The Spade Series*, introduces competitive bridge (duplicate). *The Notrump Series* has been approved as the fifth step in the beginning bridge courses. *The Notrump Series* will focus on basic conventions and is scheduled to be published in 1995.

ACBL has developed E-Z Deal decks of cards for each of the four basic courses. These cards are coded so that a student can deal the lesson hands found at the end of each chapter. The E-Z Deal cards eliminate the need for a teacher to pre-duplicate hands used in the classroom. There are in addition E-Z Deal booklets for the series which offer the chapter summaries for each text in a format that students can use for easy reference

ACBL has developed a television series, *The Bridge Class*, based on *The Club Series* text. This program contains 13 half-hour shows and is distributed by PBS. ACBL has developed a second series for television known as *Play Bridge with Audrey Grant*. This program contains 13 half-hour shows based on *The Diamond Series* and 13 half-hour shows based on *The Heart Series*. The next series of 13 shows based on *The Spade Series* will be produced in 1995. See also TELEVISION.

Interest in the ACBL Teaching Series is widespread. Foreign translations of these books into Spanish, French Canadian and Japanese have been authorized by ACBL.

ACBL-WIDE CHARITY PAIRS. Special one-session games staged twice a year to raise money for the ACBL Charity Foundation and the Canadian Bridge Federation Charitable Fund. All ACBL clubs are offered the opportunity to run a section of these games. Results are funneled to ACBL where overall and district winners are determined. For results see Appendix IV.

ACBL-WIDE GAMES. Many special games are played across the entire American Contract Bridge League. Included are charity games, International Fund games, Senior games, Epson Pairs and Instant Matchpoint games. Special hand records are distributed to all clubs, units and districts running such games so that all the competitors play exactly the same set of hands. Analysis sheets prepared by experts are distributed to all players at the conclusion of each game. Proceeds from the charity games go to the ACBL Charity Foundation or the Canadian Bridge Federation Charitable Fund. Proceeds from International Fund games are used to help cover the expenses of those selected to participate in world championship events. See CHARITY PROGRAM OF THE ACBL, ACBL-WIDE CHARITY PAIRS, ACBL-WIDE INSTANT MATCHPOINT GAMES, ACBL-WIDE INTERNATIONAL FUND PAIRS, ACBL-WIDE SENIOR GAMES AND EPSON PAIRS. For results see Appendix IV.

ACBL-WIDE INSTANT MATCHPOINT PAIRS. This event was inaugurated in 1987 as part of the ACBL Golden Anniversary celebration. Royal Viking Cruise Lines sponsored the event in that year and in four of the six years that followed. This is the only event on the ACBL calendar where gold points are available at clubs. In the open contest the first point of the award for a section top is gold. ACBL-wide winners earn special prizes. Winners of a special Youth contest earn a $500 scholarship provided by the ACBL Educational Foundation. For winners, see Appendix IV.

ACBL-WIDE INTERNATIONAL FUND PAIRS. Special one-session games staged three times a year on an ACBL-wide basis by the American Contract Bridge League. All ACBL clubs are offered the opportunity to run a section of these games. Results are funneled to ACBL where overall and district winners are determined. These games raise funds that are used to help those qualifying for international play to cover their expenses while representing the ACBL in international competition. For winners see Appendix IV.

ACBL-WIDE SENIOR GAMES. Once a year the American Contract Bridge League stages a one-session game for Seniors (55 years or older) on an ACBL-wide basis. All ACBL clubs are offered the opportunity to run a section of this game. Results are funneled to ACBL where overall and district winners are determined. For winners see Appendix IV.

AWL. See AMERICAN WHIST LEAGUE.

A POSTERIORI PROBABILITIES. See PROBABILITIES, A POSTERIORI.

A PRIORI PROBABILITIES. See PROBABILITIES, A PRIORI.

ABOVE THE LINE. A phrase denoting all scores in rubber bridge entered above a horizontal line on the scoresheet, including penalties and the premiums for honors, slams, rubbers, overtricks, and fulfilling a doubled or redoubled contract. See PREMIUM SCORE.

ABSOLUTE FORCE. A bid which makes it incumbent on partner to guarantee that another bid can be made by the player making the absolute force. Unless the bid is overcalled or doubled immediately, the partner is under conventional obligation to make some call other than a pass. See DEMAND BID, FORCING BID.

ACCIDENTS. From time to time a player may suffer from some misfortune. He may miscount his points, missort his hand, mishear the bidding, or pull out a wrong card. In such circumstances he should be particularly careful not to react in any way when he discovers his error.

ACCORDING TO HOYLE. A phrase indicating that a procedure is sanctioned both legally and ethically; in addition, that it has the backing of custom. The prestige of EDMOND HOYLE was so great that the phrase "according to Hoyle" came to mean correct procedure in general.

ACCREDITED TEACHERS. Accredited Teachers earn the title by successfully completing the ACBL's Teacher Accreditation Program (TAP). The TAP was created in 1986 as part of the ACBL's new BRIDGE EDUCATION PROGRAM. It is a ten-hour seminar designed by Audrey Grant, a Canadian educator, to develop new bridge teachers and to introduce them to the ACBL's TEACHING SERIES. Many established bridge teachers have participated in the TAP as a form of continuing education and are also ACCREDITED TEACHERS. Interested ACBL members and volunteer workers have taken the TAP course and have earned the title of ACBL Accredited Teacher.

Special programs for Accredited Teachers are offered at each ACBL NABC. These include dinner meetings and special workshops/seminars. A quarterly newsletter, *The Bridge Teacher*, is published by ACBL and contains news of the organization's activities, teaching tips, special funded teaching programs and general information of interest to this group.

ACE. The suit card with only a single pip. In most games, including all those of the bridge family, it is the highest ranking card; hence, a top performer in any field.

In England, the ace of spades was the card which indicated that the duty had been paid and its printing was controlled by the government. Ever since the wrapper carried the duty or tax notation, the card has remained ornate in England and the United States, where each manufacturer developed an individual design to serve as a trademark.

In other countries, other aces have served to carry the trademarks: clubs in France, hearts in Germany. See: ACE-SHOWING RESPONSES; HONOR TRICKS; OPENING LEADS; POINT-COUNT.

ACE FROM ACE-KING. The traditional lead of the king from an ace-king holding has been abandoned by many players in favor of the ace lead. Some players lead the ace against notrump contracts only, because an ace lead against notrump is unlikely to be attractive if the king is not held.

The argument in favor of leading the ace is that it avoids certain ambiguities which arise if the king is led:

(1) After the lead of the king against a suit contract, the opening leader's partner is unsure whether to indicate a small doubleton combination. He would wish to do so if the lead is from ace-king, but not if it is from king-queen. The same would apply if the leader's partner holds a doubleton jack.

(2) After the lead of the king against any contract, the opening leader's partner is uncertain whether to signal

with his second card holding the jack and two small cards. In this situation he would wish to signal if the lead was from king-queen but not if it was from ace-king. (It is assumed in all cases that dummy holds three worthless cards.)

Against this, the proponents of the king lead point out that the lead of an unsupported ace is not uncommon against a suit contract, and the leader's partner may wish to know whether the king is held.

Holding a doubleton ace-king, this special procedure is reversed: the king is led followed by the ace.

Whatever convention is being used, the ace lead is tactically advisable against a slam contract: the king is too revealing when the opposing hands have a singleton opposite a combination headed by queen-jack.

For an alternative method of avoiding the ambiguity arising from the king lead, see RUSINOW LEADS.

ACE AND KING SHOWING RESPONSES. A method of showing aces and kings in response to an opening two bid. Some combinations can be shown in one bid; others require more rounds of bidding. With no aces and no kings, the responder bids 2 NT. With one king and no aces, the first response is 2 NT, and then if partner makes a bid below the game level, responder bids the suit with the king.

If responder has one ace and no kings, he bids the suit in which he has the ace. If he has two kings and no aces, he jumps to 3 NT. If he has two aces and no kings, he jumps to 4 NT. If he has one ace and one king, he first bids the suit in which he has the ace and later bids the suit in which he has the king.

ACE-ASKING BIDS. See BLACKWOOD, GERBER.

ACE-GRABBER. A player who leads or takes his aces at his first opportunity, often making the play easier for the opponents.

ACE-HIGH. (1) A term dating from whist days indicating that the ace is the highest card in the suit or the cut. Obsolescent in bridge because the alternative procedures associated with other games have been generally forgotten. (2) Descriptive of a suit held by one player in which the ace is the top card.

ACE IDENTIFICATION. An extension of the GERBER CONVENTION, devised by Norman Squire of England, to discover which ace a partnership is missing.

When responder has shown one or two aces in response to 4♣, 4 NT asks for further information. If responder has one ace, he bids the suit of the ace. If he has two aces, he bids:

5 ♣ with aces of the same color
5 ♦ with aces of the same rank
5 ♥ with mixed aces

This may assist in deciding whether to bid a small slam, and possibly a grand slam if the 4 NT bidder has a void. See also ROMAN GERBER.

ACE LEAD. Against notrump, by a convention of long standing, this lead requires partner to play his highest card of the suit led. This may be helpful if the opening leader has A-K-J-10-x-x, and his partner holds the queen, but these situations are not common. This is not applicable if a partnership uses ACE FROM ACE-KING as a

standard lead.

ACE OF CLUBS. For a variety of reasons, the vast majority of ACBL members play mostly in club games, seldom venturing out to tournaments. Many are fine players who simply do not like to, or cannot afford to, travel — or who simply prefer the intimate atmosphere of the club.

To recognize achievement at the club level, the Ace of Clubs competition was created in 1984. As with the winners in the MINI-McKENNEY races, the Ace of Clubs champions are recognized at the Unit level as well as ACBL-wide.

All points won at the club level are counted except for North American Open Pairs and Grand National Teams. For winners, see Appendix IV.

ACE SHOWING. See CUEBIDS TO SHOW CONTROLS.

ACE-SHOWING RESPONSES. Answers to forcing opening bids that are based on the theory that the opener with a powerful unbalanced hand is more interested in his partner's first-round controls than in his long suit or general strength.

This is sometimes employed over FORCING TWO-BIDS, but is also common in conjunction with conventional TWO CLUBS STRONG ARTIFICIAL OPENINGS, especially in Europe. A minimum response, other than a negative one, shows the ace of the suit bid. The responses to a conventional 2♣ bid would be:

2 ♦	negative
2 ♥ or 2 ♠	ace-showing
2 NT	8 points at least, but aceless
3 ♣ or 3 ♦	ace-showing
3 NT	two aces

Some French experts vary this scheme in two ways. A 2 NT response is permitted with two kings; and a hand holding two aces can make a more precise response:

3 ♥	two mixed aces (♠ and ♦, or ♥ and ♣)
3 ♠	two aces of the same color
3 NT	two aces, both major or both minor

The opening bidder can subsequently ask for kings by using the bid normally employed to ask for aces — 4 NT or 4♣ at choice.

An alternative scheme is to respond according to the step principle, showing aces and kings simultaneously. See STEP RESPONSES. See also BLUE TEAM CLUB; CAB SYSTEM; DYNAMIC NOTRUMP; SCHENKEN SYSTEM.

ACE VALUES. A method of distributional valuation developed as part of the BARON SYSTEM.

When valuing a hand for a raise, the HONOR TRICK value of the hand is added to the following distributional values:

	with 3 trumps	with 4 trumps
void	2	3
singleton	1	2
doubleton	°	1

(But a second shortage counts at half value unless five trumps are held.)

The total is the level to which responder should raise playing LIMIT RAISES. For example:

♠ Q J 3 2   ♥ K Q 6   ♦ K 6 5 2   ♣ 9 6

In response to a 1♠ opening bid, this hand counts three

ace values (two for honor tricks plus one for the club doubleton) and therefore justifies a raise to 3♠.

If the opening bidder is planning to raise his partner's response, he subtracts two from his ace values and raises to the level of the answer: i.e., with four ace values he raises to the two level, with five to the three level, and so on. See DISTRIBUTIONAL COUNTS.

ACES OVER TWO-BIDS. See ACE-SHOWING RESPONSES.

ACES SCIENTIFIC SYSTEM. A detailed system formulated by the ACES TEAM with the aid of a computer for research and experimentation. Precise standards are set for all phases of bidding, including detailed methods for dealing with opponents' interference in constructive auctions. The main features of the system, as described by Bobby Goldman, are:

(1) 15° to 18 point notrump openings. Responses of 2♦ and 2♥ are JACOBY TRANSFERS; 2♠ promises both minor suits and is a mild slam try; 3♣ and 3♦ are weak; 3♥ and 3♠, both artificial, are mild slam tries in clubs and diamonds respectively.

2♣ is non-forcing STAYMAN, following which responder may: rebid 3♣ to seek a 4-4 minor suit fit; or rebid 3♦ (artificial) to show a long minor suit and slam interest; or rebid three of the other major suit to show four-card support for opener's major, an unidentified singleton and slam interest.

(2) Major suit openings promise at least five cards; a 1NT response is forcing for one round; two-level responses are virtually forcing to game. Jump raises are limit, and forcing raises may be made in one of six ways to show specific point ranges and hands with and without singletons. See UNBALANCED SWISS, VALUE SWISS.

Jump shifts into minor suits show solid suits with at least 6° playing tricks; opener 's rebids below 3 NT show stoppers rather than suits.

(3) Minor suit openings promise at least three-card suits. Immediate jump raises are limit; jumps to three of the *other* minor suit are forcing raises. These jump shifts and delayed jump raises are forcing to 3 NT or four of a minor. Jump shift responses into major suits promise either a solid suit, an excellent suit in a notrump type hand, or a strong suit with strong support for opener.

(4) 2♣ openings (strong and artificial) are usually forcing to game. Responses of 2♦ are neutral; other suits are natural with good values in the suit; 2 NT and 3 NT deny any aces and show balanced hands with no suit worse than J-x-x. Two-level openings other than clubs are WEAK TWO-BIDS.

(5) Slam conventions include modern Roman responses to Blackwood, plus a fifth step to show two aces and a useful void, and additional steps to show one ace and a useful void. Further slam tries may be made after the ace-asking response. 5 NT, even after Blackwood, asks about trump quality whenever a fit has been agreed. See also GERBER and SUPER GERBER.

ACES TEAM. A full-time professional bridge team, organized in 1968 by Dallas financier Ira Corn for the express purpose of returning the world team championship to the United States.

Corn selected six players from among America's leading young experts, paying each a salary, plus tournament expenses, to undertake a full-time career of studying and playing bridge. He started with James Jacoby and Bobby Wolff, and shortly thereafter added Billy Eisenberg, Bobby Goldman and Michael Lawrence. Robert Hamman joined the team in 1969. Monroe Ingberman, mathematician and bridge writer, worked with the Aces as their first coach. In mid-1968 retired Air Force Colonel Joseph Musumeci was added as trainer and coach. The team was incorporated as the U.S. Aces, but was popularly known as the Dallas Aces and later simply as the Aces.

Using a computer to analyze results and to generate specific sets of hands to provide practice in given areas of the game — slam hands, preemptive openings, etc. — the Aces spent 50 to 60 hours a week perfecting the bidding systems and discussing problems encountered at the table. Complete records of all hands played were compiled for critical analysis. From the intensive study and analysis emerged various bidding styles including the ORANGE CLUB, used by Wolff and Jacoby; the similar BLACK CLUB, used by Hamman and Eisenberg; and the ACES SCIENTIFIC SYSTEM, used by Goldman and Lawrence. Besides competing in North American Championships and Regional knockout team-of-four contests, the Aces also engaged many of America's top experts in practice matches in Dallas and staged a series of exhibition matches. See SHARIF BRIDGE CIRCUS.

In 1969, the team achieved the first major goal set by Corn by winning the Spingold Knockout Teams and later a playoff match that earned the Aces the right to represent North America in the 1970 BERMUDA BOWL in Stockholm, Sweden. With the BLUE TEAM retired, the Aces returned the Bermuda Bowl to North America for the first time since 1954. The Aces successfully defended their world title in 1971. See WORLD CHAMPIONSHIPS.

In 1971 Eisenberg left the team and was replaced by Paul Soloway. By June of 1972 the team had become a part-time effort, with the players being paid only their expenses rather than salaries. Thereafter the makeup of the Aces began to change. In 1972 the Aces were runner-up to Italy in the Team Olympiad. Jacoby-Wolff played the Orange Club; Hamman-Soloway, the Green Club and Goldman-Lawrence, Standard American with special treatments. In early 1973 Soloway was replaced by Mark Blumenthal. The Aces were second to Italy in the Bermuda Bowl, playing as two threesomes: Wolff-Hamman-Jacoby playing Aces Club and Goldman-Lawrence-Blumenthal playing Standard American with special treatments. Soon thereafter Lawrence and Jacoby left the team and were replaced by Eric Murray and Sami Kehela. In 1974 the Aces were second to Italy with Hamman-Wolff playing the Aces Club, Blumenthal-Goldman, Aces Scientific, and Kehela-Murray, Colonial Acol.

In 1975 Eddie Kantar and John Swanson made their first appearances in international play with the Aces and Soloway-Eisenberg were back on the team. The Aces were second to Italy in the Bermuda Bowl and the team was Hamman-Wolff (Aces Club); Eisenberg-Kantar, Soloway-Swanson (Standard American with special treatments).

In 1976 North America did not fare well in the Team Olympiad, but won the Bermuda Bowl. On the team were two former Aces — Soloway and Eisenberg.

The Aces won the 1977 Bermuda Bowl as Zone 2 representatives, and another team from North America finished second. Playing for the Aces once again were Hamman-Wolff, Soloway-Swanson and Eisenberg-

Kantar. In 1979 four ex-Aces won the Bermuda Bowl in Rio on a team captained by Malcolm Brachman (Eisenberg, Goldman, Kantar, Soloway). The next year, in the 1980 World Team Olympiad, Corn captained the Aces to second place behind France. His team was Hamman-Wolff, still playing the Aces Club; Soloway-Ira Rubin (Standard American with special treatments) and Fred Hamilton-Mike Passell (five-card majors, two-over-one game force). In 1981 for the first time in many years no Ace or former Ace was present on the U.S. international team.

In the fall of 1981 Corn put together one more Aces team. He had great hopes for Hamman-Wolff (the only players to remain constantly with the Aces throughout a 13-year period), Alan Sontag-Peter Weichsel and Mike Becker-Ronnie Rubin. Just three months after Corn's sudden death of a heart attack in April, 1982, the Aces won the Spingold in Albuquerque and qualified for the International Team Trials in Minneapolis that November.

Hamman, in summing up the history and the victory of this Aces team, reported, "Just say that we won one for big Ira." The Aces name stuck with them. In the Minneapolis trials, which they won, they were known as the Aces and their non-playing captain was Joe Musumeci.

From that point on the Aces Team as such disappeared into history. But members of the team continued to have many successes. Hamman and Wolff headed the WBF rankings in 1992. Lawrence and Kantar are prolific bridge authors. Soloway became the first player to break the 40,000-point barrier in 1994, Jacoby was a syndicated bridge columnist.

ACOL DIRECT KING CONVENTION. A bid of 4NT to ask for kings by a player whose partner has already made a bid specifically showing the number of aces he holds (which might be zero). This convention may be used after an ACOL TWO-BID has been raised directly to the game level, or after the GAMBLING 3NT if this opening denies a side-suit ace but may include side-suit kings, or after STEP RESPONSES TO STRONG, ARTIFICIAL TWO-BIDS.

ACOL 4NT OPENING. A specialized bid asking for aces. The responses are:

5 ♣ = no ace	5 ♠ = ♠ A
5 ♦ = ♦ A	5 NT = two aces
5 ♥ = ♥ A	6 ♣ = ♣ A

ACOL SYSTEM. The system which is standard in British tournament play and widely used in other parts of the world. The originators were a group of players which included Maurice Harrison-Gray, Iain Macleod, J. C. H. Marx, Terence Reese and S.J. Simon. It was called Acol because it was first played in 1934 in the small North London bridge club on the street of the same name. Many of the ideas were derived from the early writings of Ely Culbertson. The chief features of the system are:

(1) The weak notrump not vulnerable and the strong notrump vulnerable. The original ranges were 13-15 and 16-18, but 12-14 has become standard for the weak range, and 15-17 is often preferred to 16-18. The system is frequently used with a weak or strong notrump at all vulnerabilities (see also THREE-QUARTER NOTRUMP).

(2) LIMIT RAISES and notrump responses. Raises and notrump responses are never forcing in their own right.

After an opening bid of 1♣, a response of 2 NT or 3♣ is encouraging but not forcing, showing about 11 points or the distributional equivalent.

(3) Jump rebids are not forcing unless in a new suit.

(4) Opening suit bids tend to be slightly weaker than in American methods, especially if a six-card major suit is held.

(5) Two-over-one responses were made very freely, perhaps with 8 points, in the early days of the system but now correspond to traditional Standard American. Some play this response as forcing to 2NT.

(6) Fourth-suit bids are used conventionally by most Acol experts. See FOURTH SUIT FORCING.

(7) 2♣, artificial strong opening, forcing to 2 NT.

(8) ACOL TWO-BID, forcing for one round.

(9) GAMBLING 3 NT. A long strong minor suit with at least two other suits protected.

(10) 4 NT opening asks for specific aces. See ACOL 4 NT OPENING.

Other regular features of the system are listed separately: CULBERTSON 4-5 NT or BLACKWOOD; STAYMAN CONVENTION; GRAND SLAM FORCE; TRIAL BID. Optional features of Acol listed separately include: ACOL DIRECT KING CONVENTION; BARON SLAM TRY; BENJAMIN; CROWHURST; FLINT; GERBER CONVENTION; INTEREST-SHOWING BIDS; KOCK-WERNER REDOUBLE; RESPONSIVE DOUBLE; ROMAN BLACKWOOD; ROMAN 2♦; SHARPLES; SHORT-SUIT GAME TRY; STRONG NOTRUMP AFTER PASSING; SWISS; TEXAS; UNUSUAL NO-TRUMP; VOID-SHOWING BIDS; WEISSBERGER.

ACOL TWO-BID. A type of intermediate two-bid, strong and forcing for one round. A strong distributional hand is required with at least eight playing tricks:

(a)	(b)
♠ A K Q 8 7 5 4	♣ 8
♥ A J 4	♥ A Q J 10 5 4
♦ 9 6	♦ A K 9 8 5
♣ 2	♣ 9
Bid: 2♠	Bid: 2♥

A suit of six or more cards is normal, but the bid can be used with two strong five-card suits.

The negative response is traditionally 2 NT but the modern style is to use the next highest suit, a Herbert negative. After the negative, a simple rebid or a bid of a lower-ranking suit at the three level is non-forcing.

A suit takeout response approximates to a standard two-over-one takeout, but can be weaker at the level of two. A single raise is highly constructive, suggesting a slam. A double raise shows about 10 points but no ace. If responder has moderate strength but no marked distributional feature and no slam ambitions, he can make a negative response and then bid game. See BENJAMIN.

ACORNS. One of the suits in old-time PLAYING CARDS. See also PACK.

ACTIVE DEFENSE. A risky defensive policy aiming to develop or cash tricks quickly, usually because dummy has a suit that will provide discards for declarer's losers.

ACTIVE ETHICS. Actions to enable all players to have equal access to methods and understandings used by their opponents. The concept was first broached by Bobby Wolff during his tenure as president of the American Contract Bridge League. According to Wolff, Active Ethics has nothing to do with such items as score corrections — players are supposed to make sure they have the right scores whether or not the adjustment favors them. Instead Wolff characterizes Active Ethics as the desire to not take advantage — the desire to make sure that the opponents are privy to all of a partnership's conventions, treatments, habits and idiosyncrasies. "The game itself is more important than winning" says Wolff, subsequently president of the World Bridge Federation.

ADEQUATE TRUMP SUPPORT. See TRUMP SUPPORT.

ADJUSTED SCORE. There are two types of Adjusted Score: (1) Artificial, when no result can be estimated. The score will normally be 40%, 50% or 60% according to circumstances. The total is not necessarily 100%.(2) Assigned Adjusted Score. The non-offending side gets the most favorable result that was likely; the offending side gets the most unfavorable at all probable. See Law 12.

The application of an adjusted score will affect other scores. See FOULED BOARD.

ADVANCE, ADVANCER. The first action by the partner of the player who makes the first move for the defensive side, and the player who makes it. An example is a response to an overcall. See RUBENS ADVANCES.

ADVANCE CUEBID. A cuebid of a first-round control (in rare cases, a second-round control) made before the cuebidder's partner knows the agreed trump suit. The purpose of this cuebid is to distinguish between a normal raise and a raise based on controls plus a good distributional fit that offers some hope for slam if partner has the right distribution or high-card structure.

For example the bidding goes:

SOUTH	NORTH
1 ♠	2 ♥
3 ♠	4 ♣

North holds:

 ♠ J 6 5
 ♥ A Q 9 7 3
 ♦ 9 2
 ♣ A 10 4

If South holds a solid spade suit, the ♥K and a diamond control, slam at spades will be a reasonable undertaking, but might not be reached unless North shows his slam interest by cuebidding the ♣A before supporting spades. From South's seat, however, the 4♣ bid is ambiguous. North could have a heart-club two-suiter or be making an advance cuebid.

The cuebid might also be used after a jump shift:

SOUTH	NORTH
1 ♠	1 NT
3 ♦	4 ♣

North holds:

 ♠ 7
 ♥ Q 10 6 4
 ♦ K 8 7 3 2
 ♣ A 5 2

North's hand has grown to slam proportions after South's jump shift, so he makes a slam try by cuebidding the ♣A before raising diamonds. Here also South is not yet certain whether North has a legitimate club suit or is

cuebidding in support of diamonds or possibly spades.

Variations of this cuebid occur in many notrump sequences, but cannot be considered true advance cuebids because the trump suit is set by implication.

For example:

SOUTH	NORTH	SOUTH	NORTH	SOUTH	NORTH
1 NT	3 ♠	2NT	3 ♥	1 ♣	1 ♠
4 ♦		4 ♣		2 NT	3 ♥
				4 ♦	

The logical interpretation of South's last bid in each of these auctions is that he has strong support for partner's last named suit, a maximum for his previous bid(s), a wealth of first- and second-round controls, usually a ruffing value, and the ace of the cuebid suit. Without these features, South would support North's suit or rebid 3 NT, as North's bidding requested. See also RESPONSES TO 1 NT AND 2 NT.

Certain "impossible" bids can logically be interpreted as advance cuebids.

NORTH	SOUTH
3 ♣	3 ♥
4 ♦	

South's 3♥ response is forcing; North will usually rebid 4♣ or raise to 4♥. Since North is unlikely to have a diamond suit worth suggesting as trumps, he can bid 4♦ on:

 ♠ 9 5
 ♥ Q 7 4
 ♦ 3
 ♣ A Q 9 8 5 3 2

After North has opened 3♣, he can hardly hold a better hand in support of hearts. See also ADVANCE SAVE, SACRIFICE.

ADVANCED LEBENSOHL. Variant of Lebensohl over 1NT interference, invented by Glenn McIntyre of Boston. Bids from 2NT through 3♥ are transfers showing invitational or better values. Opener may accept the transfer to deny game interest or make another bid to force to game. 2NT, the club transfer, may also be the start of slow Stayman or a prelude to a signoff in 3♦ or 3♥ if those suits were not available at the two level. See LEBENSOHL.

ADVANCE SAVE. A sacrifice bid made before the opponents have reached their probable optimum contract. The ploy is also known as a premature or anticipatory save. The opponents will usually know that the sacrificer does not expect to make his bid; hence, his objective is to make them guess at a high level without giving them full opportunity to exchange information.

For example, East-West are vulnerable, and the bidding goes:

WEST	NORTH	EAST	SOUTH
1 ♣	2 ♥	3 ♥	6 ♥

South holds:

 ♠ J 10 7 4
 ♥ K 10 7 5 3
 ♦ 7 4 2
 ♣ 6

North's 2♥ bid is preemptive. East-West are probably headed for slam in clubs, so South wants to set them a problem. South is prepared to concede a penalty of 1100 or thereabouts, which may be an accurate sacrifice and may also goad East-West into attempting an impossible contract.

Dlr: North
Vul: N-S

```
                ♠ A K 5 4 2
                ♥ A 10 6
                ♦ 9
                ♣ A K J 6
  ♠ 6                          ♠ J 9 8 7
  ♥ 9 4                        ♥ 5 3
  ♦ Q 10 7 5 4 2               ♦ A J 8 6
  ♣ Q 10 7 2                   ♣ 9 8 5
                ♠ Q 10 3
                ♥ K Q J 8 7 2
                ♦ K 3
                ♣ 4 3
```

WEST	NORTH	EAST	SOUTH
	1♠	Pass	2♥
Pass	4♦(1)	Dbl	4NT
7♦	7♥	All Pass	

(1) Heart fit, diamond shortness

In the 1980 U.S. International Team Trials, East's double of 4♦ was turned into an advance save by West. North, with massive extra strength, guessed wrong by bidding 7♥.

An advance sacrificer must have a hand that will limit the size of a penalty; else, he will not welcome a penalty double

Dlr: East
Vul: N-S

```
                ♠ 9 8 3
                ♥ 9
                ♦ A Q J 10 6 3
                ♣ 9 7 6
  ♠ Q 10 4 2                   ♠ 5
  ♥ A J 8                      ♠ 7 5 3
  ♦ 8 7 4                      ♦ 9 5 2
  ♣ A 8 5                      ♣ K Q J 4 3 2
                ♠ A K J 7 6
                ♥ K Q 10 6 4 2
                ♦ K
                ♣ 10
```

WEST	NORTH	EAST	SOUTH
		3♣	4♣
5♣	Dbl	All Pass	

In the 1980 Olympiad Teams final, West's 5♣ bid was poorly judged. West had balanced distribution and enough high cards for a possible plus on defense against a major-suit game. North doubled 5♣ for +500, while 4♠ went down at the other table.

The scoring changes in the 1987 edition of *Laws of Duplicate Bridge* make violent advance saves less desirable. Indeed, the possibility of quixotic results at IMP scoring was a catalyst for those changes. With pre-1987 scoring, if North-South could make 7♣ for +2140, East-West stood to gain 6 IMPs by going down ten at 7♦ for −1900.

Tactics

An advance sacrificer must avoid pushing the opponents into a cold contract. On the deal below, East had to preempt just enough: high enough to keep North-South from learning they had a slam, low enough to give them room to stop at game.

Dlr: West
Vul: N-S

```
                ♠ K 5
                ♥ Q 5 3
                ♦ 8 5 3
                ♣ K J 10 3 2
  ♠ J 9 8 7 6 4                ♠ A Q 3 2
  ♥ J 9 7 2                    ♥ 10 8 6 4
  ♦ J                          ♦ 10 9
  ♣ 7 5                        ♣ Q 9 8
                ♠ 10
                ♥ A K
                ♦ A K Q 7 6 4 2
                ♣ A 6 4
```

Table 1

WEST	NORTH	EAST	SOUTH
3♠	Pass	5♠	6♦
All Pass			

Table 2

WEST	NORTH	EAST	SOUTH
3♠	Pass	4♠	5♦
All Pass			

At Table 1, East's strenuous efforts goaded South into the cold slam, and then East failed to save at 6♠ for −900 (old scoring). At Table 2, East beat par with a restrained raise to 4♠.

ADVANCED SENIOR MASTER. A rank once used by ACBL to denote a player just below Life Master rank. This rank is now known as NABC Master.

ADVERSARY. Either opponent of declarer, or, during the auction, a player on the other side. The laws of 1963 use opponent for the latter and defender for the former. Senior adversary was synonymous with declarer's left-hand opponent, and junior adversary with his right-hand opponent.

AFRICA. There is no African zone in the World Bridge Federation, although the return of South Africa to active international participation in 1992 made it more likely that one would be formed eventually. Several African countries are members of the Bridge Federation of Asia and the Middle East.

AGGREGATE SCORE. See TOTAL POINT SCORING.

ALCATRAZ COUP. A coup in contract bridge is a term applied to any strategic play. A few situations can come up which are not covered by the rules. The Alcatraz Coup is one of these; as the name suggests, it is considered a form of robbery that almost warrants a prison term for the perpetrator. The following is an example:

DUMMY
A J 10

DECLARER
K x

Declarer, to make three tricks in the suit, calls the jack from dummy and, receiving a small card from right-hand opponent, fails to follow suit. Fourth hand either produces the queen or a small card. If a small card, declarer corrects his revoke by substituting the small card, leads to his king, and has the ace in dummy for the third trick. If fourth hand produces the queen, declarer corrects his revoke by producing the king, sweetly permitting his left-hand opponent to change his play, and finesses the located queen on the next play.

Whenever the coup occurs, the defenders are entitled to redress and should receive an adjusted score in accordance with LAWS OF DUPLICATE (Laws 12A, 47F). No director would permit a declarer to gain an advantage of this type, and any such swindle attempted deliberately should meet with a serious penalty on ethical charges.

Coincidentally, bridge was played at Alcatraz. See BRIDGE IN PRISONS.

ALERT. The word used by a player to call attention to the opponents that partner has made a bid that has a conventional or unusual meaning. See ALERTING.

ALERTING. A method of drawing opponents' attention to the fact that a particular bid has a conventional or unusual meaning. In 1971 the ACBL adopted a CONVENTION CARD that provided boxes for a partnership to check off its basic bidding agreements, thereby eliminating the need to list all partnership understandings. The revised 1994 card had a similar configuration. The recommended procedure is that when such a bid occurs, the player announces to his right-hand opponent, "Alert." The opponent can request an explanation at that time by saying, "Please explain," or can reserve the right to inquire at any later time when it is his turn to call or play. See EXPLANATION OF CONVENTIONAL CALL OR PLAY. A player must use the Alert procedure unless his opponents specifically request him not to do so before the auction begins. See CONVENTION.

A player who gains information from his partner's Alert is not permitted to use this information to his advantage. If it is determined that this has happened, the director is empowered to award an adjusted score and to impose a penalty if he thinks the situation calls for it.

If a player Alerts in error, fails to Alert or gives a wrong explanation of the Alert, his partner cannot correct the error immediately, nor can he indicate in any way that a mistake has occurred. At the conclusion of the auction, the declarer or the dummy should clarify any necessary points concerning that side's Alerts. However, the defending side must wait until the conclusion of play before making any statements of correction — an earlier explanation could easily give partner information to which he is not entitled. If declarer believes he has been damaged by the Alert mistake, and the director agrees, the director is empowered to adjust the score.

Use of diagonal bidding screens makes it necessary for a player to Alert his own bid. The recommended procedure is to place the Alert card on the bidding tray. Some players simply point to the Alert card, which can lead to arguments.

ALLIGATOR COUP. See CROCODILE COUP.

ALL-STAR GAMES. In the late Eighties and early Nineties, considerable attention was given to promotion of bridge with the aim of reawakening the kind of widespread interest the game enjoyed in the Forties and Fifties. One strategy for accomplishing this goal was to attract the attention of the news media by conducting competitions patterned after the professional tennis tour. Thus was born the all-star circuit. Matthew Granovetter, editor of *Bridge Today Magazine*, developed the concept and executed several successful all-star tournaments — with cash prizes for the winners — in the early Nineties. The schedule was sporadic, however, and Granovetter's ulti-

mate goal was to secure a major sponsor so that the tournaments could be conducted on a regular basis. The all-star games — usually individual movements with about 20 participants — were held in such varied locations as Albany NY, Novato CA and Boca Raton FL. Sponsors included a health club, a shopping mall and Perrier, the French bottler of mineral water. For winners see Appendix IV.

ALPHA ASKING BIDS. (1) Asking bids in the ROMAN SYSTEM concerned with controls in a side suit. See ROMAN ASKING BIDS. (2) Asking bids in the SUPER PRECISION system concerned with responder's support for the suit opened at the one level. See SUPER PRECISION ASKING BIDS.

ALTERNATE THREAT SQUEEZE. See COMPOUND SQUEEZE.

ALTERNATIVE SQUEEZE. (Either-Or Squeeze). A simple squeeze played as a double squeeze.

♠ A K Q x
♥ K
♦ —
♣ —

♠ x x x
♥ x
♦ K
♣ A

Suppose West has the ♥A, and East has the ♦A. Spades cannot be guarded by both opponents, so North's small spade technically cannot be a DOUBLE MENACE because it is not possible for opponents to hold four spades each. However, when South leads the ♣A, whichever opponent is actually guarding spades must unguard that suit in order to keep his ace. If West keeps his ♥A, North discards the ♥K. If West started with four or more spades the squeeze has worked on him. Alternatively, if West started with fewer than four spades, East is now squeezed.

AMBER. British colloquialism for describing the situation if both sides are vulnerable. Similarly "game all."

AMBIGUOUS BIDS. See PARTNERSHIP MISUNDERSTANDINGS.

AMBULANCE SERVICE. Rescuing partner from an impending large penalty.

AMERICAN AUCTION BRIDGE LEAGUE. See AMERICAN BRIDGE LEAGUE.

AMERICAN AUCTION BRIDGE LEAGUE GOLDEN ANNIVERSARY. In 1977 the AMERICAN CONTRACT BRIDGE LEAGUE observed the Golden Anniversary of the founding of the first bridge league in 1927. That year the *Bulletin* noted the 50th birthday with a series of monthly articles which were eventually expanded into the ACBL publication *No Passing Fancy*, authored by Sue Emery. These told the story of the founding of the American Auction Bridge League, and which, two years later, became the AMERICAN BRIDGE LEAGUE which, in 1937, merged with the UNITED STATES BRIDGE ASSOCIATION to form the American Contract Bridge League. The story was told of how the new game of contract swept auction aside, of the tremendous challenge matches of the Thirties, of the amalgamation of warring bridge organizations, of the birth of the masterpoint, of the giants of the early days and of the tremendous growth of bridge at the club and tournament level.

AMERICAN BRIDGE ASSOCIATION. This national organization was founded in 1932 to encourage duplicate bridge among African-American players. It continued to develop steadily, reaching a total membership of about 8,000 in 1993. It conducts two annual National tournaments, a Spring National, usually held in April since 1968 and a Summer National, usually held in August since 1934. There are open, mixed, men's and women's pairs, an individual and team championships for open, mixed, men's and women's teams. The premier event is the knockout teams. The earliest National championships were held in New York City. Now they are held in many major cities in the United States, Canada and the Islands. For past results of the ABA Open Teams and Open Pairs, See Appendix I.

In the early days of contract bridge, African-Americans were excluded from most major tournaments. In 1932, a small group of African-American tennis players at Buckroe Beach, Virginia, decided to foster and promote duplicate bridge among African-Americans. To that end, they conceived the idea of establishing a national organization and made contact with similar groups in other parts of the country. The result was the founding of the American Bridge Association by Dr. M.E. DuBissette (president, 1932-35), Horace R. Miller (president, 1936) and L.C. Collins with John W, Cromwell, Jr., of Washington D.C.

In 1936 the ABA merged with the Eastern Bridge League, a group of New York City clubs headed by Morgan S. Jensen. There followed a period of steady expansion under the presidency of Dr. E.T. Belsaw (1936-49). Four geographical sections were formed. These were subsequently expanded to eight, which conducted Sectional tournaments equivalent to ACBL Regional tournaments. A masterpoint system was established for rating players. The quarterly *ABA Bulletin*, edited by W. R. Tatem from 1944-53, became an outstanding publication. Its high standards were maintained under succeeding editors, Clarence Farmer (1953-70), Bobbye Caldwell (1970-1976 and 1979-81), Wilma Snell (1977-1978) , and Dr. William Furr (1982-).

Official recognition of the growing acceptance of African-American participation in tournaments came in 1952, when the ACBL passed an amendment proposed by Gen. Robert Gill by which each unit became the sole judge of membership qualifications in its territory.

Enactment of federal legislation which forbade the exclusion of African-Americans from hotels, etc., was speedily followed in 1964 by an ACBL regulation ensuring the right of any ACBL member to play in any National tournament no matter where held.

The last barrier to ACBL membership for African-Americans was removed in 1967 when the ACBL included in its by-laws the proviso that "no person shall be denied membership because of race, color, or creed."

An outstanding achievement of the ABA administration under Victor R. Daly, Washington, D.C. (president, 1949-64) was the conduct of negotiations leading to the building of mutual rapport and respect between the ACBL

and the ABA. Hundreds of ABA members joined the ACBL. Many have become Life Masters. The first African-American Life Master was Marion Wildy (1956). The first ABA Life Master to achieve Life Master ranking in the ACBL was Leo Benson (1962).

The close association of the ACBL and the ABA continued under the ABA presidency of Maurice Robinson, New York City (president 1964-1969). At the suggestion of the ABA, representatives of the ABA and the Greater New York BA, a unit of the ACBL, met in two exhibition matches in New York in 1969. This resulted in one win for each organization.

Pauline Taylor was the first woman president of the ABA, assuming the office in 1972. Later presidents were:

Dr. Arnold P. Jones
Dr. A. Jacqueline Sheppard
Arthur J. Reid, Jr.
George Johnson
Geraldine Wilson
Thelma Woodson
Robert J. Price
Anita Troy

Negotiations with the Northwest Bridge Association in 1977-79 by George Johnson, treasurer, culminated in the association joining the ABA.

Since 1977 Robert J. Price, Chicago, has been the number one player in the ABA. His partner, Joyce Williams, also of Chicago, has been the leading woman player. Sara Pearson is the leading player on the West Coast.

Other notably successful partnerships have been: Reginald Chapman, Washington DC and Roscoe Rigmaiden, Philadelphia PA; Lionel Barton, Missouri City TX and Dwight Galley, Houston TX; Chester Johnson and Herbert Taylor, Chicago IL; Sara Pearson of Culver City CA and Mae Clark of Arlington TX; Naomi and Heyward Ballard, Detroit MI; George Johnson, Charlotte NC, and Edna Cravanas, Oakland CA; Bill and Berry Thompson, Detroit MI; Willis M. Troy, Henderson NV and Colonel Robert Friend, Irvine CA; Worth and Gloria Christler, Atlanta GA; Beverly and Samuel Lucas, Yellow Springs OH; Dr. Clarice Reid, Bethesda MD, and Dorothy Sides, Cincinnati OH; Dr. Milton and Bessie Haley, Dayton OH; John Washington and Julius Field, New York NY; Lawrence Berkley, New York NY, and George Hudson, St. Louis MO; Melvin Rhone, Chicago IL, and Harold Bickham, Indianapolis IN; Allie Raines and J.T. McGhee, Detroit MI; and Lee Pennington, Nashville TN and Mary E. Moragne, New York NY.

The William Friend Award is won by the top-point winner in a calendar year. Roscoe Rigmaiden was the first winner. The 1992 winner was Lionel Barton. In 1987 the Powder Puff, an award for the top woman point winner, was renamed "The Joyce Williams Derby" in honor of the woman who has been the top female player in the association for more than 10 years. Joyce was the first, and frequent, winner of the award. The 1992 winner was Sara Pearson of Culver City CA.

Top 25 players in the ABA by masterpoints as of March 1993:

1. Robert Price, Chicago IL
2. Lionel Barton, Missouri City TX
3. Chester Johnson, Chicago IL
4. Reginald Chapman, Washington DC
5. Joyce Williams, Chicago IL
6. Roscoe Rigmaiden, Philadelphia PA
7. Dwight Galley, Houston TX

8.   Julius Fields, New York NY
9.   Lee Pennington, Nashville TX
10.   John Jordan III, Washington DC
11.   Lawrence Berkley, New York NY
12.   Dr. Arnold Jones Jr., Hilton Head SC
13.   George Johnson, Charlotte NC
14.   Luis Pietri, Philadelphia PA
15.   Arthur Reid Jr., Bethesda MD
16.   John Washington, New York NY
17.   Arthur Wills, Southfield MI
18.   Beverly Lucas, Yellow Springs OH
19.   Sandra Stevenson, Springfield OH
20.   Leonard Jefferson, Arlington TX
21.   Samuel Lucas, Yellow Springs OH
22.   Louis Sutherland, Louisville KY
23.   Naomi Ballard, Detroit MI
24.   Mary E. Moragne, New York NY
25.   Mae Clark, Arlington TX

Officers: 1993
  President: Anita Troy, Henderson NV
  Executive Vice-President: Kenneth Cox, Riverdale NY
  Executive Secretary: Gloria Christler,
    2798 Lakewood Ave. SW, Atlanta GA 30315
    Tel: 404-768-5517.

AMERICAN BRIDGE LEAGUE. An organization founded in 1927 at Hanover NH (see HISTORY OF BRIDGE). The original title was "American Auction Bridge League," but the word "Auction" was dropped in 1929. The League amalgamated with UNITED STATES BRIDGE ASSOCIATION in 1937 to form the AMERICAN CONTRACT BRIDGE LEAGUE. ABL presidents are listed under PRESIDENTS, and ABL results are listed in Appendix I.

AMERICAN BRIDGE OLYMPICS. American winners of the WORLD PAR CONTESTS are listed in Appendix III.

The Culbertson organization staged a national Olympic in 1932, distinct from the world event. The winners were: North-South, Dr. and Mrs. Monte F. Meyer; East-West, James M. Magner, Jr., and William C. Campbell.

AMERICAN BRIDGE TEACHERS' ASSOCIATION. A nonprofit professional organization composed primarily of bridge teachers, but also includes tournament directors and bridge writers, dedicated to promoting higher standards of bridge teaching and playing.

The ABTA was founded in 1957 by a charter membership of 150. At the initial meeting, held in New York City, the 14 members attending, including Deborah N. Glover, the organizing secretary, and George S. Coffin, the organizing treasurer, proposed that the goal of the organization be "to provide and protect the standards of bridge teaching and its practitioners, to establish a code of ethics and minimal fees insofar as is practical, and to make known in the public and professional interest any information in the bridge profession."

The association is divided into ten regions, each headed by a vice president, who, with the assistance of state chairmen, arrange frequent meetings where teachers learn new techniques and have an opportunity to examine the latest teaching equipment. In addition, there is an annual meeting, usually held in conjunction with the Summer North American Championships of the ACBL, where several days are spent listening to outstanding bridge teachers and players. Most of the leading bridge personalities have addressed this convention at least once and many have appeared on several occasions.

Applicants for membership have to submit information to an ABTA committee regarding their professional bridge teaching experience, bridge affiliations, experience and knowledge for acceptance in the organization. After five years a member can apply for designation as a Master Bridge Teacher. 1992 membership was 600.

Honorary Members: Charles Goren (1960); Oswald Jacoby (1977); Howard Schenken, Richard Frey, Easley Blackwood (1978); Sam Stayman (1980); Alfred Sheinwold (1980); Fred Karpin (1982).

The ABTA *Quarterly Magazine* has been edited and published since 1969 by Frank Thomas Jr. (939 Riverside Drive, Sherman Oaks CA 91423). Earlier editors were George Coffin and Harold Shaw.

Presidents of the ABTA have been:

1958-59	Jo Woods
1960-61	Margaret M. Wales
1962	Deborah N. Glover
1963	George S. Gooden
1964	Dorothy Jane Cook
1965	Kenneth B. Turner
1966	Nellie Harrington
1967	Helen D. Albano
1968-69	Thelma Smith
1970-71	Helen Cale
1972-73	Effie Lindsay Long White
1974-75	Edward L. Gordy
1976-77	Eloene Griggs
1978-79	Antha Mallander
1980-81	Dr. T. B. Lyons
1982-83	Frank Thomas Jr.
1984-85	Antha Mallander
1986-87	Bert Gilliken
1988-89	Ruth De More
1990-91	Roberta Salob
1992-93	Harry Lampert
1993-94	Ginny Schuett

Officers 1994:
  President: Ginny Schuett, Riverwoods IL
  1st Vice President: Bill Sachen, Waukegan IL
  2nd Vice President: Norma Sands, Denver CO
  ABTA Bulletin Editor: Frank Perkins
  Business Secretary: Lorna W. Wise
                1509 21st Avenue North
                Texas City, TX 77590
                Tel: 409-948-2401

AMERICAN CONTRACT BRIDGE LEAGUE. The governing body for organized bridge activities and promotion on the North American continent. Duplicate bridge in the United States, Canada, Mexico and Bermuda is managed by ACBL, by far the largest bridge organization in the world. ACBL traces its history from the organization of the American Auction Bridge League in Hanover NH at the 1927 congress (tournament) of the American Whist League, by a group sparked by Ralph R. Richards, including E. J. Tobin, Robert W. Halpin, Henry P. Jaeger and Clayton W. Aldrich. Tobin was named executive secretary. Contract bridge was introduced at the second congress held in Cleveland in 1928, during which year the infant organization acquired the services of William E. McKenney, whose originality, drive and organizational ability did much to establish ACBL.

The increased popularity of contract bridge led to the name change to American Bridge League in 1929. A merger of this group with the United States Bridge Association was effected in 1937, with McKenney, first named executive secretary in 1929, remaining at the helm of the organization until 1947, shortly before his death in 1950.

In 1948-49 a major reorganization of the ACBL was carried out by Waldemar von Zedtwitz, as president and chairman, aided by the steering committee of Robert J. Gill, Ralph Gresham, Lee Hazen, Bertram Lebhar Jr., Raymond J. McGrover, and Albert H. Morehead and the Bylaws Committee headed by Lawrence Weiss of Boston.

McKenney was succeeded by Russell J. Baldwin, who was business manager until his recall to active duty with the U. S. Army in 1951, at which time Alvin Landy was named acting business manager. In 1952, Landy was advanced to the position of executive secretary, remaining in that post until his death in 1967. Tom Stoddard, then executive administrator, served briefly as executive secretary pro tem until Easley Blackwood was appointed to that post in 1968. Blackwood retired after three years, as he had planned, on March 1, 1971. Richard Goldberg, assistant executive secretary under both Landy and Blackwood, was named as Blackwood's successor. Goldberg served as executive secretary until he retired in 1984. His successor was Ralph Cohen, who served for two and a half years. Cohen had served as Goldberg's assistant from 1971 to 1984. He was succeeded by William Gross, a former member of the Board of Directors who also had served a term as ACBL president. Gross held this position until he retired in 1991. He was replaced by Stephen Signiago, a Memphis businessman. Signiago's successor was Denis Howard of Australia, former president of the World Bridge Federation. Howard served as pro tem chief executive officer for six months in 1992, at which time Roy G. Green became the chief executive officer. Green's background was in banking and real estate.

ACBL membership grew spectacularly from the 270 who joined the American Auction Bridge League to more than 15,000 at its 20th birthday in 1947. Following the 1956 merger with the Pacific Bridge League, which became the ACBL's Western Division, growth accelerated to 170,000 in 1970 and approached 200,000 in 1993.

During these years, the ACBL moved to New York from the Midwest in 1934; then to its own building in Greenwich CT in 1967. This became sole national headquarters in 1968 when the Western office was closed. In 1972 ACBL erected its own building in Memphis TN, opened in late November at 2200 Democrat Road, with adequate space for its needs at that time. Because of additional member services and programs, ACBL outgrew these quarters in 1989 and moved into a four-story building at 2990 Airways Blvd., only a few blocks away from their previous quarters.

In addition to the growth in membership, there has been a substantial increase in ACBL's scope and influence. Beyond the authorization and supervision of bridge tournament activities from the level of North American and Regional Championship tournaments to the games run in some 4,200 duplicate clubs, ACBL activities include: formulation and publication of the Laws, both of Contract (Rubber) Bridge and of Duplicate Contract Bridge; conduct of charity games and other activities which have

raised millions of dollars for hundreds of charitable purposes; publication of a monthly magazine on bridge activities around the world; cooperation with other national bridge organizations through membership in the World Bridge Federation; hosting three World Team Olympiads (1964, 1972 and 1984), three World Pair Olympiads (1978, 1986 and 1994), two Venice Cups (1978 and 1981) and eight world championships for the Bermuda Bowl.

Two major forces in ACBL's growth are the MASTERPOINT PLAN and the RANKING OF PLAYERS, both of which were important considerations in ACBL's consolidation with USBA and the Pacific Bridge League. In 1961, the huge task of issuing and recording members' masterpoints was computerized. In 1975, when this service had grown to require mailing some 38,000 notification postcards per semi-monthly cycle, it was streamlined to a once-a-month operation. In 1992 the ACBL inaugurated a system whereby the masterpoint notifications were included in a polybag with the monthly ACBL publication, the *Bulletin*. Many other jobs formerly done manually now are done by the computer — *Bulletin* mailing labels, new member welcome cards, membership cards, membership renewal notices, Unit report forms, special lists such as new Life Masters and Top 500 leaders, club sanction renewal forms, transaction journals, newsletters, masterpoint updating, scoring at tournaments, inventory control, sales, cash receipts, accounts payable, etc. The *Bulletin* is the most widely distributed and one of the most highly respected publications in its field. ACBL also compiled and published records and selected hands of all world championships and team Olympiads from 1953 to 1989.

An additional service was added to ACBL in 1993 — the MAD (Member Assistance Department) line. This is two 800 telephone lines, one for the United States and one for Canada, that members can call to get answers to their questions, to offer suggestions and to make complaints. ACBL also is very much into the business of bridge education. The Education Department staff actively supports bridge programs in colleges, high schools and grade schools; trains bridge teachers; provides special publications for teachers and students; prepares special videotapes for public television, and runs special competitions such as college championships. The teacher and student texts used in classes sponsored by ACBL were written by Audrey Grant.

In 1993 Memphis headquarters for ACBL employed approximately 90 persons. In addition there were more than 200 tournament directors of various ranks on staff. Members of the ACBL Board of Directors and Board of Governors are chosen by the membership. The Board of Directors elects the presidents and Honorary Members of the ACBL. Copies of the Bylaws and ACBL Handbook are available to members on request from ACBL Headquarters.

AMERICAN CONTRACT BRIDGE LEAGUE CHAMPIONSHIPS. Three North American Bridge Championships (NABCs) are staged annually by the American Contract Bridge League, one each in the spring, summer and fall. The NABCs are divided among the three sections of North America — west, central and east — so that as many members as possible will have an opportunity to play in at least one. The basic tournament lasts for 10 days, starting on a Friday and lasting through the second Sunday. Special knockout and pair events also are held on the Thursday evening prior to the start of the NABC, with the proceeds going to the ACBL Charity Foundation and the Canadian Bridge Federation Charitable Trust. Other special events such as the finals of Flight A of the North American Pairs (Spring) and the Grand National Teams (Summer) also are staged just prior to the start of an NABC.

An NABC contains events for players of every level. There are several North American Championships consisting of at least four sessions at each NABC. At least one two-session regionally-rated event is held daily — usually there are several as the result of flighting and stratification. Multi-session regionally-rated knockout teams also are scheduled throughout the NABC. These knockouts, which draw large numbers of teams, often are flighted or bracketed. For those who are not interested in major events, there are continuous pairs — a series of single-session events where the winner is the player who has the best two sessions over a series of sessions. There are also side games — one-session events. In addition there is a wide-ranging program of events for new and less experienced players, with a special directing staff available for them. Games held in this area include Bridge Plus+ for absolute newcomers plus games for those with 0-5, 0-20, 0-50, 0-100, 0-200 and 0-300 masterpoints.

Major North American Championships at the various NABCs are as follows. Spring — Vanderbilt Knockout Teams, North American Pairs Flights A and B, North American Non-Life Master Pairs, Open Pairs I, Open Pairs II, Womens Pairs, Mixed Pairs, Silver Ribbon Pairs, Swiss Teams, Womens Swiss Teams. Summer — Spingold Knockout Teams, Grand National Teams Flights A, B and C, Life Master Pairs, Womens Knockout Teams, IMP (International Matchpoint) Pairs, Master Mixed Teams, Red Ribbon Pairs, Non-Life Master Swiss Teams, Junior Pairs. Fall — Reisinger Board-a-Match Teams, Blue Ribbon Pairs, North American Swiss Teams, Life Master Open Pairs, Life Master Womens Pairs, Open Board-a-Match Teams, Womens Board-a-Match Teams, Non-Life Master Pairs, North American 49er Pairs. For results see Appendix I.

Winners of major womens events and womens teams that qualify as the result of other varied criteria qualify to play in the North American Womens Bridge Championship in years when it is necesary to qualify teams for the Venice Cup or the World Womens Team Olympiad. Teams seeking berths in the Bermuda Bowl or the World Team Olympiad compete in the special International Team Trials that will be inaugurated in 1995.

Players attending an NABC receive a publication each morning detailing the results of the previous day, the schedule for the next two days, special announcements and an assortment of feature articles, including many reports of deals of special interest. Half-hour lectures are provided twice a day for newcomers and less experienced players. Many other seminars and entertainments are staged throughout each NABC.

AMERICAN CONTRACT BRIDGE LEAGUE GOLDEN ANNIVERSARY.
In 1987 the ACBL held a year-long celebration of its golden anniversary, commemorating the 1937 merger of Ely Culbertson's UNITED STATES BRIDGE ASSOCIATION and Bill McKenney's AMERICAN BRIDGE LEAGUE. Features of the Golden Anniversary Year were (1) a series of stories on the first 50 years of the ACBL printed in the *Bul-*

letin (which had progressed from a four-page leaflet to a full-sized monthly magazine of 132 pages); (2) a slick Golden Anniversary edition of the *Bulletin* published in 1988, sketching features of the anniversary and highlighting events and personalities of the half century; (3) the first ACBLwide Instant Matchpoint Pairs was inaugurated as part of the Golden Anniversary observance — for the first time, gold points were awarded to section winners at club games; (4) ACBL celebrated its own Jubilee by winning both the Bermuda Bowl and the Venice Cup at the World Championships in Jamaica; (5) the Golden Anniversary Year was culminated with a Golden Jubilee Gala held at the Anaheim NABC in November. It was a fitting finale. The total of 13,948 tables broke all previous Fall records for attendance. From the opening earthquakes to an unprecdented four-nation win in the Reisinger, it was a scintillating tournament. The Jubilee Gala was a full dress affair with thousands of players taking part in the festivities.

AMERICAN LEADS. Leads devised at whist to give partner a count when a solid suit was being led. The lead of the jack followed by the queen, for example, showed a solid seven-card suit. The inventors were Cavendish of London and Nicholas Browse Trist of New Orleans. Although they have long been obsolete, American leads were a milestone in the development of defensive signals.

AMERICAN WHIST LEAGUE. The AWL was founded in Milwaukee in 1891 as a central organization to control and promulgate the laws of WHIST. Its sponsorship of tournaments between representatives of member clubs did much to stimulate the competitive aspects of games of the bridge family. Within the first few years of the life of this league its members worked out official laws, rules, a code of ethics, boards, methods of scoring, and movements of boards and players for all sorts of games up to teams of sixteen.

By the end of the Thirties, the League existed in name only, although whist congresses, attended by a few lifelong devotees, continued into the Fifties. The careers of many of the players prominent in whist continued into auction bridge and contract, including such names listed in this *Encyclopedia* as Robert F. Foster, Robert W. Halpin, Nathan Kelly, Sidney S. Lenz, Winfield S. Liggett Jr., Andrew J. Mouat, Charles L. Patton, Ralph R. Richards, P. Hal Sims, Charlton Wallace, Wilbur C. Whitehead and Milton C. Work.

The AWL prolonged its life by adding an Auction Team event in 1924 and an Auction Pair event in 1930. A Contract Whist event in 1934 did not prove popular and was dropped, but the Contract Pair event began in 1930 and the Team event in 1932 continued through 1937.

AMERICAN WHIST MOVEMENT. A schedule for conducting duplicate contests between teams-of-four originated for tournaments at whist, later adapted to auction and contract bridge.

The movement is primarily designed for an odd number of teams. The contest starts with one team and one set of boards at each table. The N-S pairs are stationary and the E-W pairs move. Before the first round the E-W pairs skip one table in the lower direction and the boards are dealt (at this moment only). The progression between the rounds is regular: the moving pairs skip down one table and the boards are moved down one table. If you want a shorter movement you may omit an even number of rounds, either in the beginning and the end, or in the middle.

The movement may be adopted to an even number of teams with two irregularities in the progression. At the first irregularity the moving pairs skip an extra table (the E-W pairs move down three tables), at the second irregularity both the pairs and the boards skip an extra table (the boards are then moved down two tables). The time for the irregularities are given under SIX TABLES, EIGHT TABLES, etc.

In this adaption for an even number of teams each team will miss one team. To avoid this, a round may be added, in which each match has it own boards, shared between the two tables in the match. See TEAM-OF-FOUR MOVEMENTS.

AMSTERDAM CLUB SYSTEM. Bidding system used mainly in the Netherlands. The main features of the system's opening bids:

1♣—17 or more HCP.
1♦—12-16 HCP with fewer than four hearts.
1♥—12-16 HCP, canapé with clubs or diamonds possible.
1♠—12-16 HCP, canapé with clubs possible.
1 NT—15-17 HCP.
2♣—12-16 HCP, solid suit, second suit possible.
2♦—Multi.
2♥ or 2♠—Roman.
2 NT —Minors.
3♣ or 3♦ —in first or second position shows a strong, solid six-card suit with outside stoppers.
3 NT —Solid suit, no outside entries.
4♣ and 4♦—Transfers respectively to 4♥ and 4♠.

In this system, many relays are used to get the opening bidder to clarify his holding.

ANALYSIS. The appraisal of a bidding or playing situation. It is generally used in reference to the play of the cards. A good analyst will recognize the possibilities inherent in a particular deal and act accordingly, so as to give his side the best mathematical or psychological chance in either dummy play or defense.

ANALYSIS SHEETS. Printed matter giving analyses of deals played in a specific contest, such as an ACBL-WIDE game. Since the hands are computer dealt, and since they are the same at all sites, it is possible to arrange for an expert to be given a set of the deals months in advance. The expert then makes a thorough study of each deal before writing a short synopsis of what is likely to happen and what should happen. This material is typeset and printed in advance and sent to the persons in charge at each site where the deals will be played. The package of analysis sheets is opened immediately after the game and each player receives a copy, enabling him to check his results against what the expert considers to be par.

ANCHOR SUIT. When a two-suited bid specifies one suit but leaves the other unspecified, (See ASTRO and MICHAELS) the specified suit is called the anchor suit.

ANGLO-AMERICAN MATCHES. Teams representing Great Britain (or England) and the United States (or North America) have met on many occasions. The official meetings in World Championship competition are given under WORLD CHAMPIONSHIP with these headings: WORLD TEAM OLYMPIAD, BERMUDA BOWL, VENICE TROPHY TEAMS, ROSENBLUM CUP TEAMS. See Appendix V for results. For results of semi-official and unofficial matches, see Appendix IV. See also JOSHUA CRANE.

ANTICIPATION. See PREPAREDNESS, PRINCIPLE OF.

ANTI-FRAGMENT BIDS. See SPLINTER BIDS.

ANTIGUA CONTRACT BRIDGE ASSOCIATION.
1992 President:
Sydney Christian
P.O.Box 20
St. Mary's Street,
St. Johns, Antigua.
Tel and fax: 809 462 11136 or 2413

ANTI-SPLINTER BIDS. Various bids used in responding to an opening of a major to show opening values but no short suit. See SPLINTER BID.

APPEAL. An appeal is of, or for, a director's ruling. (See Laws 92 and 93, and Law 79C for expiration period). Any ruling by a director may be appealed, but an Appeals Committee does not have the authority to overrule the Director on a point of Law. In team events, the captain must concur in the appeal.

APPENDIX MOVEMENTS. Frequently it is necessary to alter various game movements for various reasons — late arriving pairs, a desire to have all pairs play exactly the same boards, etc. See APPENDIX PAIR, APPENDIX TABLE and ROVER.

APPENDIX PAIR. A method of adding an extra pair in a movement. The appendix pair will be stationary at some point, replacing the pair scheduled for that position who sit out for a round. A pair cannot be appended at a table which already has a stationary pair. See also ROVER.

APPENDIX TABLE. A method of expanding sections to accommodate extra tables without increasing the number of boards in play; particularly useful for adding late pairs or tables to HOWELL MOVEMENTS. The result of adding appendix tables to the seven-table Howell game has led to the THREE-QUARTER MOVEMENT for eight, nine, and up to 12 tables.

Appendix tables in Mitchell movements are used when it is necessary for all the pairs to play all the boards. The method is ideally suited for 7, 11 and 13 tables. A further use is to append a Novice table to a regular game where inexperienced players may be accommodated without delaying the regular game. The application of the appendix table principle by former National Tournament Director Paul Marks has made the RAINBOW INDIVIDUAL MOVEMENT adaptable for numbers of tables one or even two greater than prime numbers such as 7, 11, 13, 17, etc.

The technique of handling an appendix table is simple. In a Howell movement, a table (or tables) may be appended to any table where there are two moving pairs. The North-South pair at the base table is instructed to remain stationary as is the East-West pair at the appended table. Boards are constantly relayed from the base table to the appended table, and as moving pairs arrive at the base table to sit North-South, they are instructed to play at the appended table, then to resume their regular progression. In a Mitchell game, a table (or tables) may be appended to any section that consists of a prime number of tables. Boards are placed on the base table (or tables) and are relayed with the appended table (or tables). Throughout the game the boards move regularly to the next lower table within the prime section. The East-West pair at the base table remains stationary, as does the North-South pair at the appended table. All other pairs move each round; East-West moves to the next higher table and North-South skips one table to the next higher table.

APPROACH-FORCING SYSTEM. A term applicable to most standard methods of bidding, including GOREN or STANDARD AMERICAN. The CULBERTSON SYSTEM was the earliest of these, and was the basis on which many other systems were built. The original objective of Ely Culbertson was to emphasize the need for slow suit exploration, in preference to an early excursion into notrump. See APPROACH PRINCIPLE.

APPROACH PRINCIPLE. The precept of Ely Culbertson favoring opening suit-bids and a slow exchange of information in preference to notrump opening bids and responses. He described it this way:

"In view of the fact that in making an opening bid, the player is venturing into unknown territory, it is wise for him to proceed cautiously, to feel his way, and thus, protected by a network of approach suit-bids of one, act with care until he learns something about the distribution of honor strength held by his partner and his adversaries.

"The Approach Principle, as applied to contract, may be stated as follows: *Whenever a hand contains a biddable suit, even a shaded four-card minor, that suit and not notrump should usually first be bid.* The *notrump complex*, which suggests that the opening bid on a hand should be notrump even when the hand contains a biddable suit, is a disease especially prevalent among advanced players. The logical place for notrump bidding is after information has been exchanged as to suit lengths and distribution. Notrump bids in the early stages crowd the bidding too much and eliminate many valuable suit-bids, while the bid of a suit always leaves the alternative of notrump without increasing the contract. The use of the Approach Principle does not decrease, but, as a matter of fact, increases the number of safe notrump contracts undertaken."

Culbertson's dislike of indiscriminate notrump bids stemmed from experience. Too many of his contemporaries carried over from auction the phobia created by the scoring table (where if the opponents held three honors in a suit they might outscore the declarer who made only two-odd or three-odd). Thus they tended to bid 1NT with almost any hand lacking a suit headed by three honors. Hampered by lack of a Stayman convention to discover a 4-4 fit after the notrump opening, far too often the wrong contract was reached. In support of the approach idea, Culbertson quoted the following hands:

WEST (dealer)	EAST
♠ A Q x x	♠ J x x x
♥ A x	♥ x
♦ A J x	♦ K x x x
♣ A 10 x x	♣ K x x x

Culbertson's suggested bidding was:

WEST	EAST
1 ♠	2 ♠
3 NT	4 ♠
Pass	

A few years later, most good players — including Culbertsonites — would open with 1♣, and arrive at the same final contract. But in citing this example, he was shooting at the flaw of opening a notrump with more than the desirable strength, as well as the danger of missing the spade fit.

In the beginning, Culbertson recommended notrump openings on a range of three honor tricks not vulnerable to four-plus honor tricks vulnerable. His zeal for approach principles caused him to limit the bid to 4-3-3-3 distribution with an occasional exception for 4-4-3-2, including a strong doubleton not less than Q-x.

Thus, analysis of the 1937 prototype World Championship reveals that the Culbertson team did not use a single opening bid of 1 NT. As methods of responding to 1 NT were improved so as to discover suit fits after the notrump opening, Culbertson gradually relaxed his strictures against opening notrumps on hands of the wrong distribution in order to use the bid on more hands of the right high-card strength. Thus, by 1949, 4-4-3-2 and 5-3-3-2 distributions (but not five-card majors) were officially included in the notrump family — no longer as exceptions. But while the distributional range was spread, the high-card range was narrowed, standardized at three and one-half to four-plus honor tricks which were later interpreted — by Culbertson as well as by others — as 16-18 high-card points, with even 6-3-2-2 distributions admitted to the notrump family on hands of proper high-card strength and strong doubletons.

In spite of these changes, over a span of more than 30 years the Culbertson Approach Principle remained, with but little alteration, a basic principle of bidding. A few more hands containing biddable suits were opened with 1 NT; the standards for biddable suits in the responder's hand were shaded down. But it remained standard practice to avoid indiscriminate notrump openings, and especially to avoid responses of 1 NT to partner's suit bid if a response could be given at the one level in another suit. The notrump response may result in a suit fit being missed, and may lead to the weak hand becoming the declarer at notrump. Many experts play that a response of 1 NT to 1♦, for example, absolutely denies holding a four-card major suit. Others, however, would not choose to respond in a worthless four-card suit. See BIDDABLE SUITS.

ARABIAN BRIDGE FEDERATION. Founded originally in 1969 by Candy Baker and Maxine Moats as the Saudi Arabian Bridge League. Revived in 1989 by Robert Grover, the Federation has more than 350 members in Saudi Arabia and holds kingdom-wide competitions. Officers 1992:

President, Robert D. Grover.
Secretary, Kathleen M. Grover.
Box 5660, Dhahran 31311, Saudi Arabia.

ARGENTINE BRIDGE ASSOCIATION. (Asociación del Bridge Argentina). This association was founded in 1934, the first on the South American continent. It is a member of the South American Bridge Confederation, with a membership that grew from 750 in 1969 to 2,800 in 1992. It is sponsor of the team that has won the South American Championships 15 times. Until Venezuela triumphed in 1965, Argentina was the only country to represent South America in the Bermuda Bowl, doing so on nine occasions, beginning in 1958. National competitions include Open Teams, Open Pairs, and Master Individual; also the GABARRET CUP, given for the most masterpoints in a year.

Officers 1992:
President: Dr. Alberto Piccioli
Secretary: Antonio De Marco, Maipu 934, 1006, Buenos Aires, Argentina.
Tel: 54 1 312 6704
Fax: 54 1 454805

ARNO. See LITTLE ROMAN.

ARRANGEMENT OF CARDS. The act of sorting the cards in one's own hand or (by the declarer) in the dummy's hand, which includes the conventional placing of trumps to the declarer's left in the dummy's hand. Most players sort their cards into suits, red and black alternately, and place the cards in each suit according to rank. It is regarded as an offense against the proprieties of bridge for any player to draw inferences about another player's hand by noting the position of the cards. But some players split suits and avoid singletons at the end of the hand to protect themselves against players with better eyesight than ethics.

ARRANGEMENT OF TABLES. At a duplicate tournament, the arrangement of tables depends on the size and shape of the playing space and the expected number of tables which must be accommodated (see TABLE SPACING). A hairpin type arrangement is more desirable than a straight line arrangement for sections in order to bring the last table into proximity with the first in each section.

ARRANGEMENT OF TRICKS. In duplicate bridge, the act of turning a card face down on the edge of the table immediately in front of a player after four cards have been played to a trick, with the long axis of the card pointing to the players who won the trick; in rubber bridge, the act of collecting the cards played to a trick by a member of the side that won the trick and then turning them face down on the table so that the tricks are identifiable in proper sequence. See LAWS (Law 65); LAWS OF DUPLICATE (Law 65).

ARRANGING. (1) A term having reference to the aligning of the cards of the dummy as that hand is being spread on the table just after the opening lead has been made. The declarer may arrange the cards to his own satisfaction when he states that he is doing so.

(2) A statement by a player before he has bid in the first round of bidding meaning that he has been lax in picking up his hand or looking at it, and is not in a position to act when it becomes his turn. A call of some sort should follow this remark with reasonable dispatch.

(3) The act of sorting one's own cards. See ARRANGEMENT OF CARDS.

ARROW. The symbol on the duplicate board which in

dicates the alignment required so that the North player receives the hand designated for him. Table cards have the compass points printed on the edges; the boards have the arrow symbol pointing to the North hand; the arrow point and the printed direction coinciding, each player's hand is directly in front of him in the board. See: ARROW SWITCH; SCRAMBLED MITCHELL MOVEMENT.

ARROW SWITCH. The right-angle switch of the boards in some rounds to get increased balance. In a Mitchell movement, the arrow switch is used to obtain a single winner. See SCRAMBLED MITCHELL MOVEMENT.

ARTIFICIAL CALL. An arbitrary call which can be correctly interpreted by partner only if agreement has been reached about its meaning in advance.

Certain artificial bids are now so standard that their apparent normal meaning would be considered as an artificial convention. For example: a takeout double; a 2 NT negative response to an opening two-bid, etc.

At the extreme of artificiality are cipher bids which bear no relation to the suit named or to any other suit. The most common examples are the Stayman responses of 2♣ and 3♣ over 1 NT and 2 NT respectively, and the responses to Blackwood.

Cipher bids are developed to the maximum by a RELAY SYSTEM, in which one player can make a series of artificial bids to discover the details of his partner's hand. In extreme cases, an original pass can be used artificially. See WEAK OPENING SYSTEMS.

The proliferation of artificial bids of all kinds in the postwar years led to some objections. The AMERICAN CONTRACT BRIDGE LEAGUE, the FRENCH BRIDGE FEDERATION, and the ENGLISH BRIDGE UNION, among others, restrict the use of artificial systems and conventions, such as the Italian systems and others of similar complexity, in normal tournament play. It is considered that the users of such systems gain an unfair advantage against opponents unfamiliar with the methods employed. This is particularly true in pair tournaments and other events in which a small number of boards are played in each round.

Defensive bids take on a different meaning against artificial systems, and the meanings of doubles, notrump bids, and bids in the opponent's suit have to be carefully considered. A further point is that a defender can afford to pass over an artificial forcing bid holding a strong hand, knowing that he will get a further opportunity to bid.

At the international level the use of artificial bids and systems is restricted by the WBF.

In the early Thirties there was some doubt about the legality of certain artificial bids. In 1933 the Portland Club in London, one of the law-making bodies, ruled that the Culbertson 4-5 NT convention and others that could indicate the possession of specific cards were illegal. The decision was based on the idea that a bid that showed possession of a particular card amounted to the exposure of that card.

This ruling was quickly challenged in America, and the Whist Club gave an opposite verdict.

ARTIFICIAL CLUB BIDS. See ONE CLUB SYSTEMS.

ARTIFICIAL RESPONSES AND REBIDS AFTER

NATURAL NOTRUMP. See NOTRUMP BIDDING.

ARUBA BRIDGE FEDERATION. The Federation was founded in 1986, after separating from the Netherlands Antilles Bridge Association. Its Aruba club organized CAC Championships in 1977 and 1988. 50 players were members in 1992.

Officers 1993:
    President: Geert Van Eyck
    Secretary: Adeline Eilers
    17 Beaujonstraat, Oranjestad, Aruba, Dutch Caribbean.
    Tel. 297 8 24953.

ASBURY PARK. The scene of many of the most important national championships in the early years of contract bridge. The nine-day Summer championships of the ABL and later of the ACBL were held there from 1930 to 1941 inclusive, making it the focal point of the bridge tournament year. In the early Forties the Asbury Park Convention Hall became too small to accommodate a national championship.

ASEAN BRIDGE CLUB CHAMPIONSHIPS. Contested annually since 1979 in October-November between Brunei, Indonesia, Malaysia, Philippines, Singapore and Thailand. Indonesia had an unbroken string of successes in the Open Series 1979-91.

ASIA. Countries of Asia are divided into two zones. See FAR EAST BRIDGE FEDERATION and BRIDGE FEDERATION OF ASIA AND THE MIDDLE EAST.

ASKING BIDS. A method by which one player can discover specific information about distribution, controls or trump quality held by his partner. These bids usually are used when exploring for a slam contract, but sometimes are used when checking the feasibility of a game contract. The original Asking Bids were devised by Albert Morehead and developed by Ely Culbertson.

Responses and rebids that would not be considered SPLINTER BIDS ask about the suit named, with a sign-off in the trump suit to deny control.

For many years Asking Bids fell into disuse. They were not a part of Standard American or any of the major systems used. However, in recent years various forms of Asking Bids have very much returned to favor. Many of the leading Italian players who consistently won world championships in the Fifties, Sixties and Seventies employed Asking Bids. All of the RELAY SYSTEMS now in vogue all over the world rely heavily on Asking Bids. Most of these relay systems have one member of a partnership asking a long series of questions by making relay bids and the other partner responding in a predetermined pattern. Using these sophisticated methods, it often is possible for the asking partner to announce his partner's exact distribution plus the location of all honor cards.

Several Asking Bids are commonly used by most partnerships. The 5 NT GRAND SLAM FORCE is an Asking Bid as are ace-asking bids like BLACKWOOD and GERBER. The WESTERN CUEBID is an Asking Bid, attempting to ferret out the possibility of a notrump game. A raise to five of a suit after an opponent has overcalled usually asks partner to bid the slam if he has first-round or second-round control of the opponents' suit. Even the

Stayman 2♣ response to 1 NT is an Asking Bid.

However, the Asking Bids used by those employing relay methods go far beyond these simple applications.

Various Asking Bids can be used in responding to a major-suit preemptive openings. Possible are:

(1) In response to 3♥ or 3♠, 4♣ can be used to ask for suit quality. Rebids are: 4♦ denies ace or king; 4♥ promises ace or king; 4♠ promises ace and king; 4 NT shows solid suit.

(2) Combined with (1), 4♦ can ask for a short suit. Then opener signs off in his suit to deny a short suit; bids a singleton; bids 4 NT with an unidentified void, and 5♣ asks for its location (after 3♠ - 4♦; 4 NT - 5♣, 5♠ is a club void.)

(3) New-suit response to a three or four of a major suit can ask about the suit bid. First step by opener shows at least two losers in the suit; second step shows second-round control; third step shows first-round control.

See also AUSTRALIAN ASKING BIDS, BETA ASKING BIDS and SUPER-PRECISION ASKING BIDS.

ASOCIACION. National organizations with names beginning in this way are listed under the name of the country.

ASPRO. A method of defending against 1 NT openings based on ASTRO, devised by Terence Reese. (The name is borrowed from a popular British brand of aspirin.)

The term *astronaut* is used to designate the overcaller, and the term *relay* to describe the responses in the neutral suit. Aspro is varied in three respects:

(1) *Major two-suiters* are bid differently. With five spades and four or five hearts, the astronaut bids 2♣ and follows with 2♠ over the 2♦ relay.

With four spades and five hearts the treatment varies with the strength of the overcaller's hand. Normally he bids 2♣ followed by 2♥ giving responder the opportunity to show spades. With a stronger hand he bids 2♦ followed by 2 NT.

(2) *Pronounced two-suiters* (6-5 or 6-6 distribution). Specific bids are laid down for each two-suited hand:

2 NT	black suits
3 ♣	minor suits
3 ♦	red suits
3 ♥	major suits

With the odd two-suiters (spades-diamonds or hearts-clubs), bid two of the minor suit and follow with a jump in a six-card suit.

(3) *A redouble* by the astronaut or the responder is an SOS. For alternative methods of defending against 1 NT, see DEFENSE TO ONE NOTRUMP.

ASPTRO. A defense to 1 NT which takes an element from ASPRO and ASTRO. 2♣ shows hearts and another suit and 2♦ shows spades and another suit.

ASSETS. A method of distributional valuation originated by Alan Truscott and described by him in several books. It provides for automatic re-evaluation by opener and responder as the bidding develops.

    For a long suit (5 or more cards), count one asset
    For a singleton, count one asset
    For a void, count two assets

Each asset, or distributional point, is counted at the start, and may bring the high-card points up to the 13 points required for an opening. This gives a sound result, for it distinguishes between 4-3-3-3 and 4-4-4-1, which the long-suit method does not, and between 5-4-2-2 and 5-4-3-1, which neither the long-suit method nor the short-suit method does.

Both opener and responder adjust their assets in the light of the auction:

If there appears to be no fit, assets disappear
If there is an 8-card fit, assets count normally
If there is a 9-card fit, assets double
If there is a 10-card fit, assets triple

Suppose that after a 1♠ opening showing a five-card suit responder holds:

> ♠ J x x x x
> ♥ x x x x x
> ♦ —
> ♣ x x x

Four assets triple, and the jack gives a total of 13 for a bid of 4 ♠ .

ASSIGNMENT OF SEATS. Methods of assigning seats vary from country to country. The following is the ACBL practice. At a duplicate tournament the seating assignments are made on the entry blank which is purchased by the contestants. In the second session of pair events, when there has been a qualifying session, this may be done by giving GUIDE CARDS to the players which show their seating assignment for all rounds. See SEED, SEEDING.

ASSIST. To raise a suit first bid by partner. See RAISE.

ASSOCIATION. National organizations with names beginning in this way are listed under the names of the countries.

ASSUMPTIONS IN PLAY. Assumption is a basic element of dummy play and defense. Any finesse, for example, may be taken on the assumption that it will win. In planning the play or defense of an entire deal, declarers and defenders must often assume that the cards lie so the contract can be made or defeated; they proceed on the assumption that such a lie of the cards exists.

> ♠ 10 6 4 2
> ♥ A 3
> ♦ A Q 5 4
> ♣ K 9 3
>
> ♠ Q
> ♥ K J 9 6 4 2
> ♦ K 3 2
> ♣ 6 4 2

South plays at 4♥ after opening a weak 2♥ bid. West leads the ♠3. East wins the ace and shifts to a club, and West takes the ace and returns the ♣Q. East ruffs dummy's king and leads a low spade. South ruffs and leads a heart to the ace, West following with the ten. Should South finesse the jack on the next heart or put up the king?

South knows that West held six clubs and at least three spades, and South must assume a 3-3 diamond break, since he needs a discard for his losing club. South should therefore play West for 3-1-3-6 distribution and finesse the ♥J.

> ♠ K 9 5
> ♥ K J 10 8 5
> ♦ A J 3
> ♣ 7 3

> ♠ 8 2   ♠ 7 3
> ♥ A 3 2   ♥ 9 7 4
> ♦ Q 8 6 5   ♦ K 10 2
> ♣ Q J 10 2   ♣ A 9 8 5 4

> ♠ A Q J 10 6 4
> ♥ Q 6
> ♦ 9 7 4
> ♣ K 6

WEST	NORTH	EAST	SOUTH
			1 ♠
Pass	2 ♥	Pass	2 ♠
Pass	4 ♠	All Pass	

West leads the ♣Q, and East wins the ace. East knows that the defense cannot prevail if South has solid trumps and the ♥A. East must assume that West has one major-suit trick, but it is too much to expect him to have two. Hence, East must assume that West has the ♦Q. It is essential to shift to a diamond at the second trick, giving declarer no time to draw trumps and set up the hearts for discards.

When a contract depends on the position of two or three key cards, it often helps to make a definite assumption about one of them. If you can afford to have it wrong, assume that it is wrong; if you must have it right, assume that it is right and build up your picture of the opposing hands on that basis.

Here is a difficult example of a second-degree assumption, quoted from *The Expert Game* by Terence Reese.

> ♠ A K 10 6 3
> ♥ Q 5
> ♦ Q 4
> ♣ K Q 6 2
>
> ♠ Q J 9 4 2
> ♥ 7
> ♦ A J 6 3
> ♣ 8 7 4

West deals at game all and the bidding goes:

WEST	NORTH	EAST	SOUTH
1 ♥	Dbl	2 ♥	3 ♠
Pass	4 ♠	All Pass	

West leads the ♥K and continues with the ♥A. South ruffs and draws trumps in two rounds. What should he play next? The contract will fail only if South loses two tricks in clubs and one in diamonds. Suppose that he leads a club, which looks obvious. If East holds the ♣A, then surely West will hold the ♦K and South will be defeated. Playing a diamond first, on the other hand, South is completely safe. If West holds the ♦K, and puts it up, there will be two club discards on declarer's ♦A-J. But if East holds the ♦K, then assuredly West will hold the ♣A. It is a puzzling but instructive hand. This is the distribution against which South has to guard:

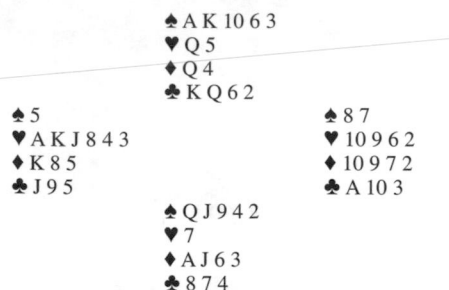

```
            ♠ A K 10 6 3
            ♥ Q 5
            ♦ Q 4
            ♣ K Q 6 2
♠ 5                        ♠ 8 7
♥ A K J 8 4 3              ♥ 10 9 6 2
♦ K 8 5                    ♦ 10 9 7 2
♣ J 9 5                    ♣ A 10 3
            ♠ Q J 9 4 2
            ♥ 7
            ♦ A J 6 3
            ♣ 8 7 4
```

ASSUMPTIONS, MATHEMATICAL. See MATH-
EMATICAL ASSUMPTIONS.

ASTRO. Over 1 NT, a specialized use of minor-suit over
calls to show two-suited hands. The name of the convention is derived from the initial letters of the inventors'
names: Allinger-STern-ROsler. After a strong or a weak
notrump, in the direct or the reopening position:

2♣ shows *hearts* and a minor suit

2♦ shows *spades* and another suit

The Astro bidder promises at least nine cards in two suits,
and his suits must have some solidity if he is vulnerable.

The Astro bidder's partner has a choice of these actions:

(1) Two of the anchor major (i.e., the particular major
suit guaranteed by the overcaller): shows at least three
cards in the suit and no game ambitions.

(2) Three of the anchor major: a game invitation with
at least four-card support. The strength depends mainly
on the vulnerability situation, and to a lesser extent on
the strength of the notrump opening.

(3) Four of the anchor major: natural.

(4) Pass: a weak hand and a long suit (probably of six
cards) in the minor bid by partner.

(5) Two of the neutral suit (i.e., the next suit above the
Astro bid): a negative action, denying the ability to make
any other response. Indicates at least a doubleton in the
neutral suit and usually fewer than three cards in the anchor suit.

(6) 2 NT: artificial and forcing. Shows some support
for the anchor major, and suggests game prospects without guaranteeing a further bid.

(7) New suit takeout or jump (including a jump in the
neutral suit and a raise of the takeout bid): shows a six-
card or longer suit.

The Astro bidder has a choice of rebids after a neutral
response. He may pass with five cards in the neutral suit,
or show five cards in the anchor suit by bidding it. He
may show his second suit at the level of three, indicating
a probable six-card suit and more than minimum playing
strength.

In most sequences, 2 NT by either player is artificial
and forcing. As responder's second bid, it is likely to be
weak:

	WEST		EAST
	♠ A 5 2		♠ Q 4 3
	♥ A J 10 5 4		♥ 6
	♦ 6		♦ Q 8 5 3 2
	♣ K 10 8 5		♣ Q 9 6 4

WEST	NORTH	EAST	SOUTH
			1 NT
2 ♣	Pass	2 ♦	Pass
2 ♥	Pass	2 NT	Pass
3 ♣	All pass		

Astro Variations

Some partnerships use a variation of Astro similar to
the BROZEL convention, called Pinpoint Astro, which
is more explicit as to the two suits held.

2 ♣ shows hearts and clubs

2 ♦ shows hearts and diamonds

2 ♥ shows hearts and spades

2 ♠ shows spades and a minor suit

A modification adopted by many Roth-Stone players
uses both two-level and three-level overcalls in order to
show precisely which suits are held:

2 ♣ shows clubs and spades

2 ♦ shows diamonds and spades

3 ♥ shows clubs and hearts

3 ♠ shows diamonds and hearts

Double shows hearts and spades

Yet another variation, devised by Matthew Granovetter,
uses a double to show spades and another suit. 2♣ shows
clubs and hearts; 2♦ shows diamonds and hearts.

Defense

The opening bidder's partner has several choices if his
side appears to have the balance of strength. He can
double with a defensive hand, usually with a good holding in the anchor major and the suit he doubles; cuebid
the anchor major when his hand is unsuited to defense;
or pass to await developments (remembering that there
might not be any). A non-jump new-suit bid (including a
raise in the Astro bidder's minor) would be unconstructive. 2 NT would be natural. For an alternative defense to Astro, see LEBENSOHL CONVENTION.

For alternative defensive conventions against notrump
openings, see DEFENSE TO ONE NOTRUMP.

ASTRO CUEBID. Devised by the authors of the ASTRO
convention, these are used to show certain two-suited
hands.

An immediate cuebid in the suit bid by the opener shows
a long minor together with a shorter major suit. The bid
shows clubs and hearts unless one of these suits has been
bid, in which case the next-higher suit is assumed.

(a)	(b)
♠ 5 3	♠ 5
♥ A K J 6	♥ K 10 6 5 2
♦ 7	♦ Q 10 9 7 4 3
♣ A Q 10 8 5 2	♣ 6

With hand (a), the cuebid would be used over 1♦ or
1♠. This is an inconvenient hand to bid with standard
methods. Note that the problem is less acute if the minor
suits are reversed. Over 1♠, for example, a double would
then be appropriate, followed by a diamond bid over a
club response.

With hand (b), 2♣ can be bid over 1♣ at favorable vulnerability. As clubs have been bid, the cuebid must show
the red suits.

ATTACK. To take the initiative in bidding or play at some
risk. Used particularly with reference to the opening lead.

ATTACKING LEADS. A risky lead from a high-card
combination such as A-Q, K-J or an unsupported high
honor in an active attempt to win or establish fast tricks.
This is common against a notrump contract, but less common against a suit contract when a passive lead is often
called for. See OPENING LEADS.

The term *attacking lead* used to be applied to a lead
from an honor sequence, but this meaning is obsolete.

Several situations deserve special mention:

(1) An attacking lead is desirable when the leader holds four or more trumps or can deduce that his partner holds four or more trumps.

(2) An attacking lead is desirable when the opponents have reached a suit game tentatively after bidding three suits. For example:

WEST	EAST
	1 ♣
1 ♥	1 ♠
3 ♣	4 ♣
5 ♣	

The opening leader can expect his partner to have any missing high diamond honor because both West and East have avoided notrump. It is probably desirable to take diamond tricks before declarer can get discards.

(3) An attacking lead has to be considered against a contract at a high level, either in a suit or notrump, if the bidding suggests that declarer will have a long suit in his hand or the dummy.

(4) An attacking lead should not be made against a grand slam.

ATTITUDE. The interest or lack of interest of a defender in having a suit led or continued by his partner. The usual method of encouraging the lead or continuation of a suit is a HIGH-LOW SIGNAL. See also ODD-EVEN DISCARDS and UPSIDE-DOWN SIGNALS.

AUCTION. The bidding by the four players for the contract. The dealer is the first bidder after the cards are dealt. He may pass or bid. The bidding proceeds clockwise around the table. Each player may pass, make a bid or raise a preceding bid, or double or redouble. The bidding ends when three players have passed in succession (or four players on the first round of bidding).

In the American Midwest *auction* is sometimes used as a synonym for *final contract*. "4♠ was a fine auction."

AUCTION BRIDGE. The third step in the evolution of the general game of bridge. Its predecessors were WHIST and BRIDGE WHIST. The great innovation in auction bridge was the introduction of competitive bidding. It was first played in 1903 or 1904, but the precise circumstances are disputed. The first code of laws governing the play of auction was set forth in 1908, the product of a joint committee of the Bath Club and the Portland Club. The popularity of auction bridge increased enormously, and the activity in whist and bridge whist decreased proportionately. After the introduction of contract bridge in 1926, auction bridge lost favor rapidly.

In auction bridge the aim was to keep the contract as low as possible because the declarer's side was credited with the number of tricks won, whether contracted for or not. For example, the declarer may have bid 2♠ and actually won six tricks over his book. He was credited with making a small slam. Penalties and premiums in auction are the same without regard to vulnerability. Honor scoring in auction bridge is different from contract bridge — so important, in fact, that it may distort the bidding, especially in duplicate auction.

Auction bridge scoring is as follows:

Scoring. Provided declarer has won at least the number of odd tricks named in his contract, declarer's side scores for each odd trick won:

	Undoubled	Doubled	Redoubled
With notrump	10	20	40
With spades trump	9	18	36
With hearts trump	8	16	32
With diamonds trump	7	14	28
With clubs trump	6	12	24

Game and Rubber. When a side scores, in one or more deals, 30 points or more for odd tricks, it has won a game and both sides start fresh on the next game. When a side has won two games, it wins the rubber and adds to its score 250 points.

Doubles and Redoubles. If a doubled contract is fulfilled, declarer's side scores 50 points bonus plus 50 points for each odd trick in excess of his contract. If a redoubled contract is fulfilled, declarer's side scores 100 points bonus plus 100 points for each odd trick in excess of his contract. These bonuses are additional to the score for odd tricks, but do not count toward game.

Undertricks. For every trick by which declarer falls short of his contract, his opponents score 50 points; if the contract is doubled, 100 points; if it is redoubled, 200 points.

Honors. The side which holds the majority of the trump honors (A, K, Q, J, 10), or of the aces at notrump, scores:

For 3 trump honors (or aces) 30
For 4 aces in one hand at notrump 100
For 5 trump honors in one hand 100
For 4 trump honors in one hand 80
For 4 trump honors in one hand, 5th in partner's hand 90

Slams. A side which wins 12 of the 13 tricks, regardless of the contract, scores 50 points for a small slam. A side which wins all 13 tricks, regardless of the contract, scores 100 points for a grand slam.

Points for overtricks, undertricks, honors and slams do not count toward game. Only odd tricks count toward game, and only when declarer fulfills his contract.

Contract Bridge for Auction Players by Ely Culbertson gives the complete details of auction bidding contrasted, in parallel columns, with contract bidding. See also *Auction Bridge Complete* by Milton C. Work.

AUGUST CONVENTION. See TWO-WAY STAYMAN.

AUSTRALIAN ASKING BIDS. A slight modification of the original CULBERTSON ASKING BIDS. Holding a singleton in the asked suit and two aces, a jump is made in the suit of the lower-ranking ace. In some cases the asking bid can be made below the four level: 2♠ in response to 1♥, for example, is used as an asking bid.

AUSTRALIAN BRIDGE. An independent magazine with six issues a year founded by Denis Howard in 1970. It was managed and edited by Ron Klinger 1972-84, and since then by Richard Brightling and Stephen Lester. Address: P.O. Box 654, Split Junction, NSW 2088, Australia.

AUSTRALIAN BRIDGE FEDERATION. The Federation was founded in 1934 as the Australian Bridge Council with New South Wales, Victoria and South Australia as members. It now covers all Australia, and membership has risen from 2,000 in 1970 to 23,000 in 1992. Australia competes in Far East Championships and hosted the event in 1971 and 1985. Its teams have won the open title twice and the women's title seven times. Australia is a member of Zone 7, the South Pacific, and has represented the zone in many world championships, finishing third in two Bermuda Bowls. Australia hosted the Bermuda Bowl and Venice Cup in Perth in 1989. There are four major Australian tournaments. The 1992 National Open Teams attracted 226 entries, and the Grand National Teams 600.

Officers 1993:
President: John Brockwell
Secretary: John Scudder
PO 3322, Manuka, ACT 2603 Australia
Tel: 06 258 5647
Fax: 06 259 2912

AUSTRALIAN TRUMP-ASKING BID. A trump-asking bid initiated by either partner's use of the cheapest bid in notrump immediately after a major suit has been agreed. The inquiry, which could be made as low as the two level, focuses on the king and queen of trumps. Lacking both king and queen, the partner of the asking bidder signs off in the trump suit. The other responses are in steps, not counting the trump suit as a step:

1st step	queen
2nd step	king
3rd step	king and extra length
4th step	king and queen
5th step	king and queen and extra length

For alternative methods see TRUMP ASKING BID.

AUSTRIAN BRIDGE FEDERATION (ÖSTERREICHISCHER BRIDGE SPORT VERBAND). The Federation was founded in 1929 by Dr. Paul Stern, inventor of the Vienna (Austrian) System, and he became its first president. In 1992 it had 1800 members.

Austrian teams were extremely successful before World War II, with these victories: European Open Teams, 1932, 1933 and 1936, European Women's Teams, 1935 and 1936, and the Open and Women's Teams World Championships, 1937.

Austrians have had several victories since World War II: World Pairs, 1970; European Junior Teams, 1976; European Open Pairs, 1981; European Open Teams, 1985; European Team Cup, 1988; European Women's Teams, 1991; European Junior Pairs, 1991; European Women's Individual, 1992. The Federation organizes Open Team, Open Pair and Mixed Pair Championships, and numerous tournaments.

Officers 1993:
President: Dr. Franz Kriftner
Secretary: Peter Zimmerl
A 1010 Wien
Reischachstrasse 3
Tel. 43-222/712 25 17

AUSTRIAN SYSTEM. See VIENNA SYSTEM.

AUTOBRIDGE. A commercial device, invented in the Thirties and still popular. Lesson hands can be used for self-teaching bidding and play. A deal sheet is inserted in a special board so that only the player's own cards are shown. As the deal progresses, the player finds that his own bids and plays are automatically corrected, and that the bids and plays of the other players are automatically revealed. The board and deal sheets are accompanied by a booklet, in which the hands are set out and the bidding and play explained by experts.

Experts who have composed *Autobridge* hands include

Ely and Josephine Culbertson, Albert Morehead, Richard Frey, Charles Goren, Alfred Sheinwold, and Alan Truscott.

AUTOMATIC HAND REGISTERS. In original duplicate whist before 1883 each hand was written on a *register* (hand-record slip), then tricks were scooped in as usual. So the players had to reconstruct their hands from registers for replay at the next table. The four loose hands were carefully piled atop each other crosswise into a small box, a device too unstable to move without mixing up or scrambling the cards. So after every round *all* players had to move to new tables.

In 1883 James Alison invented the automatic hand register simply by having players keep all their played cards face down in front of themselves as today we still do. Each perpendicular card marked a trick won, a *live* soldier; else it was placed horizontally. But players still put their played hands in the little box *in stasis* on the table.

In order to correct this second problem special card trays were introduced, each equipped with rubber bands to hold each hand more securely for passing the boards to the next table. Soon a company in Kalamazoo MI manufactured the world's first duplicate board with card pockets sold as Paine's Whist Trays. These were cumbersome, but at least they aided the growing popularity of duplicate whist, especially in the great whist tournaments held 1894 through 1936 by the AMERICAN WHIST LEAGUE.

AUTOMATIC SQUEEZE. A simple squeeze which will operate against either opponent.

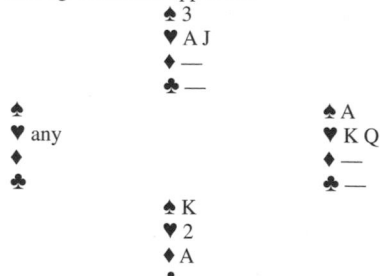

The lead of South's ♦A squeezes East, and would also squeeze West if the defenders' hands were exchanged. Whatever West discards, the ♠3 is thrown from dummy.

This situation contrasts with a POSITIONAL SQUEEZE, when only the player who plays immediately after the squeeze card is under pressure, and the declarer's discard from the third hand varies with the defender's discard. See also SQUEEZE.

AUTOMATIC TWO DIAMONDS RESPONSE. See TWO DIAMONDS ARTIFICIAL RESPONSE TO FORCING TWO CLUBS OPENER.

AUTOMATON CONTRACT BRIDGE PLAYER. An obsolete electric machine designed by William Patzer to play a specific bridge hand against anyone who would put a coin into the machine to start the proceedings. The machine would make winning plays against various stratagems used by the declarer — i.e., the paying customer. See also ROBOT BRIDGE PLAYER.

In the days of whist there were several very popular machines which, it was claimed, were able to play whist.

The first, invented by an American named Balcom and adapted for exhibition by Maelzel, was exhibited circa 1829-31. An automaton called "Psycho" was exhibited by John Maskelyne at the Egyptian Hall, Piccadilly, London for several decades starting in 1875. The *New York Journal* exhibited an automaton whist player, named the "Yellow Kid," in New York in 1896.

AVERAGE EXPECTANCY. The term applied to the expected holding of the partner of the opening bidder; it may refer to one-third of the missing cards of a suit or one-third of the missing honor strength. The fraction will vary as the bidding progresses. It was much used in the CULBERTSON SYSTEM in his arguments for preemptive bids.

AVERAGE HAND. A hand that contains ten high-card points. An ace, king, queen, and a jack, or one-fourth of all the high honors, is the average expectation of each player before the hands are seen. This basic assumption furnishes the player with a simple yardstick for measuring the relative high-card strength of a given hand, and may assist materially in estimating the game potential or penalty expectancy of any bid. Hence, two or three points added to an average hand is the valuation of a hand with a minimum opening bid.

AVERAGE SCORE. One half the matchpoints possible on a given deal or in a particular session of a matchpoint pairs tournament.

In IMP pair games average on a given board is the arithmetical mean of all scores on that board, usually excluding the highest and the lowest. This constructed average is called a *datum.* See INTERNATIONAL MATCHPOINTS.

The average score is usually the basis on which adjusted scores are awarded when a particular deal cannot be properly played. When the deal cannot be played through no fault of one pair, the adjustment is usually 20% of the average score added to the average score. Deduction from the average score is made by the tournament director when one of the pairs is at fault. These are referred to as Average-plus and Average-minus.

AVOIDANCE. A plan of play designed to prevent a particular opponent from gaining the lead.

There are two main reasons for pursuing such a plan. First, it may be necessary to prevent a defender with established winners from gaining the lead, especially at notrump. Second, declarer may have a suit combination which is vulnerable to a lead from a particular side. Both aspects of avoidance arise if either of these suit combinations is held:

(a)	(b)
DUMMY	DUMMY
3 2	2
DECLARER	DECLARER
A J 4	K J 4 3

In each case South is playing 3 NT and West leads the 5 to East's queen. If South wins the trick, East becomes the dangerous hand, but if South holds up twice, West becomes the opponent to be feared. South's play at the first trick must therefore be determined by an examination of the whole hand to discover which opponent is more likely to secure the lead. If a vital king or queen is missing in a side suit, it is usually obvious which opponent may gain the lead. If the missing card is an ace, there will often be an inference available from the bidding. In the examples above, West would be likely to have a side ace if he has volunteered a bid, and unlikely to have one if he has passed throughout.

The suit combination which most commonly indicates the need for an avoidance play is a guarded king or the equivalent: a guarded queen when one top honor has been played, or, as in the examples above, a guarded jack when two top honors have been played; a guarded 10 would operate in the same way if three honors have been played.

But if declarer may have to lose the lead twice, the danger suit may be one in which he has one sure guard and a partial guard:

(a)	(b)	(c)
DUMMY	DUMMY	DUMMY
J 4 3 2	A 3 2	K 3 2
DECLARER	DECLARER	DECLARER
A 10	Q 4	Q 4

In each case the right-hand opponent is the danger hand. In (a) and (b) there is a certainty of two stoppers if the suit is led from the left. In (c), suppose that the left-hand opponent holds the ace. Declarer then has two tricks if the suit is led from his left, but only one trick if it is led from the right.

The danger hand may suddenly change. Suppose that in (a) the danger hand secures the lead and plays a low card. The 10 loses to an honor, and the ace is knocked out. The left-hand opponent has suddenly become the danger hand: he may have one small card remaining, which he can lead to allow his partner to score two tricks.

Similarly, in (c), the right-hand opponent may gain the lead and play a low card. Declarer puts up the queen, which holds the trick. It is obvious that the left-hand opponent must not be permitted to gain the lead.

Avoidance play may require unusual handling of a suit which needs development.

(d)	(e)	(f)
DUMMY	DUMMY	DUMMY
K J 8	K 9 2	K 9
DECLARER	DECLARER	DECLARER
A 10 9 5 2	A J 4 3	A Q 4 3 2

The left-hand opponent is the danger hand. In (d) declarer runs the 10 or 9: it would be quite wrong to play the ace first, because the queen may have three guards. In (e) a deep finesse of the 9 is taken if South is trying for three tricks. The danger hand can secure the lead only if it has both the missing honors. In (f) the 9 is finessed with the virtual certainty that it will lose. (If the danger hand held both honors, he would play one.) This ensures four tricks against any normal break, and keeps the danger hand from the lead unless it has J-10-x-x.

Another type of avoidance play is possible in this situation:

```
          A K 3 2
Q 8 7               J 10 9
          6 5 4
```

South needs three tricks in this suit, but must not permit East to gain the lead. Declarer leads twice from his hand, permitting West to win a trick with the queen if he plays it at any stage. If West is able to make a discard on the suit led from dummy back to declarer's hand, he can thwart South's plan by the spectacular discard of his queen.

Avoidance play can also be effected by LOSER-ON-LOSER technique or by DUCKING.

B

BA. Bridge Association.

BL. Bridge League.

BABY BLACKWOOD. The use of a 3 NT bid conventionally to discover the number of aces held by partner. The convention was originally used after a forcing double raise in a major suit but can be used after a limit raise. For example:

SOUTH	NORTH
1 ♥	3 ♥ (forcing)
3 NT	

South's 3 NT bid is a request for aces. North bids 4♣ with no aces (or four aces), 4♦ with one ace, and so on. Similarly, an immediate jump to 3 NT in response to a 1♥ or 1♠ opening may be used as Baby Blackwood. Those using Bergen Raises and similar methods which locate a fit below 3 NT can use Baby Blackwood.

An alternative proposal is to have 2 NT to uncover the number of aces partner holds. Whenever either player bids 2 NT, partner bids 3♣ with no aces, 3♦ with one ace, etc. Subsequent bids of 3 NT, 4 NT and 5 NT can then be used to locate the number of kings, queens and jacks, respectively held by partner. See BLACKWOOD.

BACK IN. To make the first bid for one's side, after passing on a previous round, in the face of opposing bidding. See BALANCING.

BACK SCORE. The summary sheet on which the results of each rubber are credited to the winners and debited against the losers, in rubber bridge or Chicago. Results are entered in hundreds of points, with 50 points ignored in England but counted as 100 in the United States. The back score is referred to by more colorful names in England, as "flogger" or "washing list," while many American clubs refer to it as a "ledger."

BACKWARD FINESSE. An unnatural finessing maneuver which may sometimes be made for special reasons.

(a)

```
                ♠ A 3 2
♠ Q 5 4                    ♠ 10 8 7 6
                ♠ K J 9
```

(b)

```
                ♠ K 3 2
♠ A J 4                    ♠ 9 7 6 5
                ♠ Q 10 8
```

In (a), the normal play is to finesse the jack, which is an even chance. As the cards lie, it is easy to see that the winning play is to lead the jack. If this is covered, South finesses the 9 on the way back.

Similarly in (b), the normal play is to finesse the 10 after leading to the king, but the lead of the 10 is essential in the position given, with a finesse of the 8 to follow. (The position of the ace is irrelevant.)

There are three possible reasons for selecting the backward finesse. First, there may be a good reason to believe that the natural finesse will fail, based on an inference from an opening bid, for example, or a failure to open the bidding.

Second, the backward finesse may be an AVOIDANCE play. Suppose that in both of the above cases the declarer has an extra small card in his own hand and in the dummy, and needs three tricks without allowing West to gain the lead. His best play is the jack in (a) and the 10 in (b). It is doubtful whether this should be classified as a backward finesse, because South may well reject the finesse on the way back.

Third, the play may be selected when SHOOTING for a top in a pair event or playing for a SWING in a team-of-four match.

In defense the backward finesse can be a natural play dictated by cards visible in dummy. See SANDWICH DEFENSE.

BACKWASH SQUEEZE. A unique type of TRUMP SQUEEZE in which both menaces are in the same hand and the player sitting behind the hand with the menaces holds both guards plus a losing trump, and is caught in the backwash of a squeeze by means of a ruff taken in the hand holding the menaces. Analyzed and described by Geza Ottlik in the February 1974 issue of *The Bridge World*, the backwash squeeze can have any of a number of other end-game characteristics. Three of his hands are used here by permission of *The Bridge World*.

Occasionally the backwash squeeze can be used as a DISCOVERY play. The following example requires a VIENNA COUP for the execution of the squeeze.

```
                    ♠ A 10 8 5 4 2
                    ♥ 10 7 3
                    ♦ 9 2
                    ♣ K J
♠ 3                                      ♠ K Q J 9 7
♥ A 9 6 5                                ♥ 4 2
♦ J 6 4 3                                ♦ A 8 7
♣ Q 7 6 5                                ♣ 8 4 2
                    ♠ 6
                    ♥ K Q J 8
                    ♦ K Q 10 5
                    ♣ A 10 9 3
```

South plays in 4♥ after East doubled 3NT for a spade lead. West leads a heart and East plays low. South wins with the 8 and leads a club to the jack, which holds. So far, so good. Declarer leads a diamond to the king, which wins, a club to the king, and another diamond. East plays the ♦A and leads a trump. West plays the ace and another trump while East throws a spade. The lead is in the South hand, and declarer needs five of the last six tricks, in this position:

```
                    ♠ A 10 8 5 4 2
                    ♥ —
                    ♦ —
                    ♣ —
♠ 3                                      ♠ K Q J 9
♥ 9                                      ♥ —
♦ J 6                                    ♦ 8
♣ Q 7                                    ♣ 8
                    ♠ 6
                    ♥ K
                    ♦ Q 10
                    ♣ A 10
```

If either minor-suit honor were unguarded the contract could be made by guessing which, dropping it, and drawing the last trump. But the bidding suggests that West has the hand shown. The solution is to lead a spade to the ace, and ruff a losing spade with the master trump, setting up an unnecessary trump trick for West (Vienna Coup), but squeezing him in the process. When the spade is ruffed, West is backwash-squeezed. South may, of course, misguess the position — he still has to read West's holding correctly. But he is no worse off than before; he will have seen another card played before making the decision and will have confirmed the exact spade count. No other play will work in the above ending.

The backwash squeeze can be used to strip a defender of his exit cards preparatory to a throw-in play.

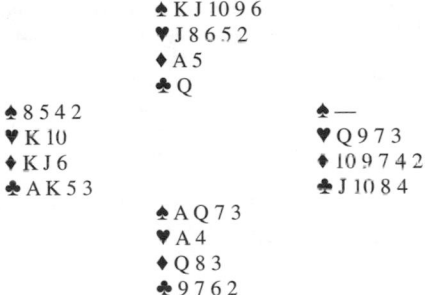

```
            ♠ K J 10 9 6
            ♥ J 8 6 5 2
            ♦ A 5
            ♣ Q
♠ 8 5 4 2                    ♠ —
♥ K 10                       ♥ Q 9 7 3
♦ K J 6                      ♦ 10 9 7 4 2
♣ A K 5 3                    ♣ J 10 8 4
            ♠ A Q 7 3
            ♥ A 4
            ♦ Q 8 3
            ♣ 9 7 6 2
```

South has arrived in 4♠ after a 13-15 notrump opening by West and an Astro 2♦ bid by North, showing spades and another suit. West led the ♣K and forced dummy with a second club. Planning to set up dummy, declarer led ace and another heart. West won and forced dummy again in clubs. Declarer ruffed a heart high, then led a low spade to dummy and discovered the unfortunate spade division. Suddenly a simple hand had become complicated. North was on lead, with declarer needing five of the last six tricks:

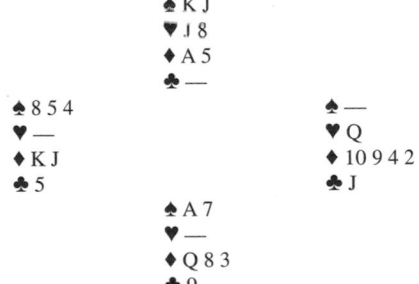

```
            ♠ K J
            ♥ J 8
            ♦ A 5
            ♣ —
♠ 8 5 4                      ♠ —
♥ —                          ♥ Q
♦ K J                        ♦ 10 9 4 2
♣ 5                          ♣ J
            ♠ A 7
            ♥ —
            ♦ Q 8 3
            ♣ 9
```

Declarer ruffed a heart with the ♠A — and the backwash caught West in its undertow. An underruff would let declarer draw trumps; and a diamond pitch would allow South to cash the ♦A and then lead the ♥J, throwing a club. Thus, West had to part with his club — his only exit card. South cashed the ♠K-J and led the last heart. West ruffed, but was endplayed.

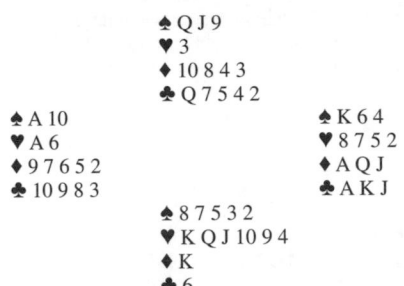

```
            ♠ Q J 9
            ♥ 3
            ♦ 10 8 4 3
            ♣ Q 7 5 4 2
♠ A 10                       ♠ K 6 4
♥ A 6                        ♥ 8 7 5 2
♦ 9 7 6 5 2                  ♦ A Q J
♣ 10 9 8 3                   ♣ A K J
            ♠ 8 7 5 3 2
            ♥ K Q J 10 9 4
            ♦ K
            ♣ 6
```

South has arrived in 2♠ doubled after a strong 1♣ opening by East showing 17 or more points, and a CARD-SHOWING DOUBLE by West promising 6-8 points. Clubs were led and continued, with South ruffing the second round. South tried to slip the ♥9 through, but West took his ace and shifted to the ace and another spade. When East won his trump king he cashed the ♦A and continued with the queen. Declarer had lost five tricks and apparently had one more to lose — if he drew the last trump he could not return to the closed hand to run the hearts. Because of the blockage in the North-South spades, East's ♣6 prevented ordinary suit-establishment. However, South ruffed the ♦Q and cashed three top hearts, East being forced to follow suit, leaving this position:

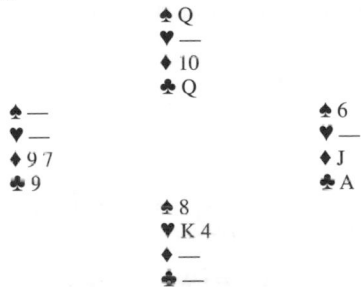

```
            ♠ Q
            ♥ —
            ♦ 10
            ♣ Q
♠ —                          ♠ 6
♥ —                          ♥ —
♦ 9 7                        ♦ J
♣ 9                          ♣ A
            ♠ 8
            ♥ K 4
            ♦ —
            ♣ —
```

South led a heart, ruffed it with dummy's Q and East was squeezed. If he underruffed, the South hand would be high. If he discarded a plain suit he would promote one of dummy's cards which would be led, forcing East to ruff and allowing South to overruff.

BAD CARD HOLDER. A player who seems consistently to hold less than his fair share of honor cards at rubber bridge. Although many losing players explain their losses by claiming to be bad card holders, lack of skill is a more likely explanation. Both mathematics and practical tests suggest that any given player and any given partnership will hold close to an average holding over a long period in terms of percentage.

BAD CARDS. (1) Consistently inferior cards in a session of rubber bridge. (2) Cards that are expected, on the basis of the bidding, to be of little or no value to partner. If partner shows an unbalanced distribution with one very long suit or two long suits, minor honors in the other suits are unlikely to be of value to him. Similarly, tenace holdings or single honors other than the ace deteriorate if the suit is bid by the left-hand opponent.

See WORKING CARDS.

BAD HANDS. Hands containing little or no honor strength.

S. J. Simon pointed out that underbidding with a bad hand is a common error of the average player. He gave this spectacular example of the need to bid with a weak hand:

EAST
♠ 4 3 2
♥ K 2
♦ 5 4 3 2
♣ 5 4 3 2

The bidding:

WEST	NORTH	EAST	SOUTH
	1 ♦	Pass	2 ♣
2 ♦	3 ♣	Pass	3 ♦
4 ♣	4 ♦	Pass	5 ♣
5 ♦	Pass	5 ♠	Pass
6 ♠	Pass	?	

East has been forced to express a choice between the major suits, and has shown no strength whatever. He has the vital ♥K, and West must be confident of making 12 tricks without that card. Therefore the ♥K must be the 13th trick, and East should bid the grand slam.

If partner shows great strength, a player should always ask himself whether his hand is better than it might be in the light of his earlier bidding.

BAD POINTS. See BAD CARDS (2).

BAHAMAS CONTRACT BRIDGE CLUB.
Organized in 1965 by the late Fred Rubbra.
1992 Club Manager: Noreen Wurdemann
P.O. Box CB-11070, Nassau, Bahamas.
Tel: 809 327 7455

BALANCE OF POWER. A concept first put forth by S. Garton Churchill involving the calculation of the safety of entering the auction based on actions taken by the opponents. See BALANCING.

BALANCE OF STRENGTH. The concept of calculating which side holds the majority of the high-card points. If a player adds his own point-count to the minimum shown by his partner, and the total is more than 20, he knows his side has the balance of strength. Sometimes he can infer that his side is likely to have the balance of strength by relying on the normal expectation of strength in his partner's hand.

BALANCED COMPARISONS. A principle embodied in most types of duplicate movement. A movement is perfectly balanced if any two competing pairs are compared (i.e. play in the same direction) on the same number of boards, independent of which two competing pairs are being compared.

Any full MITCHELL MOVEMENT is automatically balanced because the players do not change direction, and the stationary players, like the moving players, compare with each other throughout.

A Scrambled Mitchell, giving one winner among all pairs, cannot be completely balanced. This is a general phenomenon when the number of rounds is much less than the number of competing pairs.

The original HOWELL MOVEMENTS were not balanced, nor were the later schedules prepared by Col. Russell J. Baldwin and William C. McKenney. The first balanced Howell schedules were prepared by Jacques Ach and Charles Kennedy in 1935.

BALANCED DISTRIBUTION (or pattern). A hand that appears suitable for notrump rather than trump contracts. Standard types are 4-4-3-2, 4-3-3-3, and 5-3-3-2; 5-4-2-2 and 6-3-2-2 are borderline cases. See EXPECTED NUMBER OF CONTROLS IN BALANCED HANDS. The completely balanced 4-3-3-3 distribution can be described colloquially as flat, square or round, an example of the strangeness of bridge geometry.

Balanced distribution can also refer to an even division of one suit around the table.

BALANCING. (Or protection, which is the normal term in England). Reopening with a bid or double when the opposing bidding has stopped at a low level.

After a suit opening

WEST	NORTH	EAST	SOUTH
1 ♦	Pass	Pass	?

East's hand is known to be extremely weak, so South can balance with a hand of medium strength on the assumption that his partner has unrevealed strength.

The normal range for a simple suit bid by South in this situation would be 8-13 points in high cards. The spade suit is particularly significant: possession of spades favors balancing action, and lack of spades counts against it.

In more general terms, a shortage in an unbid suit, especially a major, militates against balancing, and a shortage in the opponent's suit favors it.

♠ 3
♥ A Q 6 4
♦ K J 5 3
♣ Q 6 4 2

South has sufficient strength to bid 1♥, but that would be dangerous. The opponents almost certainly have a spade fit, which they are likely to discover if given the opportunity. It is perhaps better policy to allow them to play 1♦, which may be a poor contract for them.

But if the opening bid had been 1♠, balancing action (in this case a double) would be automatic. It is now probable that East-West are in their best denomination, that North-South have a fit somewhere, and that North has some strength. North will frequently pass a strong hand with length and strength in the opponent's suit, but South can discount that possibility if he himself has the opponent's suit.

If South jumps in a new suit, he shows a hand too good for a simple balancing bid, probably a six-card or strong five-card suit and about 12-16 points.

A balancing double closely resembles a takeout double by the second player: there is virtually no upper limit, but with only moderate strength it should usually indicate a shortage in the opponent's suit and at least three-card support for each unbid suit. A balancing double may be slightly weaker (a minimum of about 9 points with ideal distribution) than an immediate takeout double. A balancing double is unattractive with a void in the opponent's suit and 5-4-4-0 distribution because the doubler's partner will often pass for penalties. Marshall Miles suggests that the cuebid in the opponent's suit should be used freely in this position: it would not guarantee a game or even a second bid, and cuebidder's partner bids as he would in response to a takeout double.

A balancing bid of 1 NT is a weakish action, but exactly how weak is a matter of opinion. Standard treatment suggests the equivalent of a weak notrump opening, with about 11-14 points. KAPLAN-SHEINWOLD indicates an 8-10 point range, because a stronger hand would double. Others advise a 12-16 point range, because hands of this strength may otherwise present problems: a double may not be convenient with three or four cards in the opponent's suit and a doubleton in an unbid suit.

After a suit opening and response

The most important consideration is whether the opening side seems to have a fit. If the opening bid is raised to the two-level and the opener passes, balancing action is strongly indicated, especially if the opening bid was in a minor suit.

WEST	NORTH	EAST	SOUTH
1♣	Pass	2♣	Pass
Pass	?		

In this situation North should almost invariably balance. Holding:

♠ A J 5 3
♥ K J 4 2
♦ J 3
♣ 6 4 2

he doubles. If South bids 2♦, North passes or perhaps corrects to 2♥, leaving South the option of continuing with 2♠.

When one side has a fit, their opponents are almost sure to have a fit also. If the opening bid was 1♦ raised to 2♦, balancing is usually called for. For this reason many players, as opener, continue to three of the minor suit as a preemptive maneuver to forestall balancing action.

WEST	NORTH	EAST	SOUTH
1♣	Pass	2♣	Pass
3♣			

or

WEST	NORTH	EAST	SOUTH
1♦	Pass	2♦	Pass
3♦			

See PREEMPTIVE RE-RAISE.

Balancing action is desirable in theory but more difficult in practice if a major suit has been opened and raised. The player who balances must be prepared for his side to land at the three-level, although a balancing bid of 2♠ over 2♥ can occasionally be risked with a four-card suit. Partner will suspect a four-card suit because of the failure to make an immediate overcall.

There is a case for "balancing" in the live position with minimal values:

WEST	NORTH	EAST	SOUTH
1♥	Pass	2♥	2♠

If the opponents have a fit, you are likely to have a fit. Marty Bergen recommends this action with:

♠ K Q J 10 3
♥ 5
♦ 8 7 6 2
♣ 9 4 3

This has lead-directing value, and solves the problem that partner may be unable to balance because he has heart length.

When an opening bid is raised directly, the opening side usually has a combined eight-card or better fit (though pairs that employ FOUR-CARD MAJORS may sometimes land in a 4-3 fit). The same applies if the responder's suit is raised. Balancing action is indicated after:

WEST	NORTH	EAST	SOUTH
1♣	Pass	1♥	Pass
2♥	Pass	Pass	?

South may benefit, however, from a knowledge of his opponents' style: If East-West often raise a response with three-card support, South cannot be sure that East-West have an eight-card fit.

There are other situations in which the opening side probably has an eight-card fit:

	(a)		(b)	
	WEST	EAST	WEST	EAST
	1♥	1NT	1♦	1♥
	2♥		2♦	

In both cases, North-South are likely to have a spade fit and should usually try to contest the auction, either with a spade bid or balancing double.

Balancing actions need not be restricted to the pass-out position:

	(c)	
	WEST	EAST
	1NT	2♥

East's 2♥ bid is natural and non-forcing. Both West and East have limited their strength, and West will normally pass. Therefore, either North or South may be obliged to take balancing action. If South holds:

♠ K J 10 7 5 3
♥ 7 4
♦ Q 7 4
♣ 6 3

he should bid 2♠. If South passes, North may decline to balance because he lacks length in spades and is reluctant to compete at the three level.

Similarly, on auctions (a) and (b), above, both North and South are in a position to balance. East-West are probably about to drop the auction at the two-level.

If the opening side fails to locate a trump suit (perhaps after bidding three suits) or stops at 1NT, balancing is less attractive.

WEST	NORTH	EAST	SOUTH
1♣	Pass	1♥	Pass
2♣	Pass	2♥	Pass
Pass	?		

North cannot act safely. East-West may have substantial high-card strength; they may have retired only because the hands fit poorly. If the deal is a misfit, North probably does better to defend.

WEST	NORTH	EAST	SOUTH
1♥	Pass	1NT	Pass
Pass	Dbl		

or

WEST	NORTH	EAST	SOUTH
1♥	Pass	1♠	Pass
1NT	Dbl		

In these sequences, North is implying that he passed originally on a strong hand because he holds strength and length in the opener's heart suit. He is hoping for a penalty, although South might choose to bid if his hand is very weak and he has a long suit.

Balancing actions need not be confined to low levels.

Dlr: East
Vul: E-W

	♠ K Q 7 2	
	♥ K J 8 5 4 3 2	
	♦ 7	
	♣ 2	
♠ 8 6 4 3		♠ —
♥ 10		♥ Q 6
♦ A K 6 3		♦ J 10 9 5 4 2
♣ A Q 9 8		♣ K 10 7 6 5
	♠ A J 10 9 5	
	♥ A 9 7	
	♦ Q 8	
	♣ J 4 3	

WEST	NORTH	EAST	SOUTH
		Pass	1 ♠
Pass	4NT	Pass	5 ♥
Pass	5 ♠	Pass	Pass
Pass			

In the 1968 Olympiad Open Teams final, West's final pass came only after long study. The winning decision — easier with all four hands in view — was to balance with 5NT, unusual for the minor suits.

After a 1NT opening

A 1NT bid passed by the opener's partner produces a situation in which balancing is often not expedient. The probabilities are that the opening side has no good fit, and therefore that the defending side also has no good fit. The best policy, therefore, generally is to remain silent. To bid a five-card suit in the pass-out position may produce a double from opener's partner and a singleton trump in the dummy. However, some risks may have to be taken at board-a-match or pair scoring; conventional machinery such as ASTRO HAMILTON (Cappelletti) OR LANDY can prove helpful. See also UNUSUAL NOTRUMP.

BAMBERGER POINT-COUNT. See ROBERTSON POINT-COUNT and VIENNA SYSTEM.

BANGKOK CLUB. A system devised by Somboon Nandhabiwat and used by Thailand in world championships in 1966, 1967 and 1969. It is a relative of the VIENNA SYSTEM.

1 ♣ opening is a one-round force, showing 12-20 points and denying a 5-card suit outside clubs. 1 ♦ is a negative response, 1NT is an artificial game-forcing response, and other responses are semi-positive.

1♦, 1♥ and 1♠ show 11-17 points with a 5-card suit. 1NT is artificial and strong with 18+ points. Two-bids are natural and game-forcing.

BAR, BARRED. (1) The penalty for certain types of infractions sometimes calls for the partner of the offender to make a forced pass on his next turn. At other times the partner of the offender must pass whenever it is his turn to bid for the rest of the auction. Such situations arise when a player bids out of turn, corrects an insufficient bid in various permissible ways, and exposes a card during the auction.

(2) An ethical player, when his partner has hesitated and then passed at some point during the auction, is expected to bar himself from taking any action on his cards that is in any way questionable; that is, he will lean over backwards to avoid taking advantage of his partner's hesitation.

(3) A player may be technically *barred* from further bidding, especially if he has limited his hand previously. See, e.g., PREEMPTIVE RE-RAISE, SIGN-OFF BID.

(4) A player may be prohibited by the methods he is using from making a certain bid. For example, pairs using psychic responses to WEAK TWO-BIDS may agree that opener is barred from rebidding past three of his own suit. The opponents are entitled to know if this is the case, so such a sequence calls for an Alert.

BARBADOS BRIDGE LEAGUE. The League was founded in 1966 by the late E.L. "Jimmy" Cozier. It hosts an annual international tournament at the end of October.

Officers 1993:
  President: Hyacinth, Lady Burton
  Secretary: Arden Clarke
  23 Pine Road, Belleville, St. Michael, Barbados
  Tel: 809 427 4839

BARCO SQUEEZE. A triple-double squeeze, exerting pressure on both opponents in three suits. The most famous example was played by Edward T. Barco, and described by him in *The Bridge World* (Dec. 1935).

```
              ♠ A 5 4
              ♥ K J 3
              ♦ A J 8
              ♣ A 10 7 2
♠ Q 10 3 2              ♠ J 9 8
♥ 8 4                  ♥ 2
♦ 10 9 5 3 2           ♦ Q 6 4
♣ K 8                  ♣ J 9 6 5 4 3
              ♠ K 7 6
              ♥ A Q 10 9 7 6 5
              ♦ K 7
              ♣ Q
```

West led a trump against South's contract of 7♥, and declarer ran five trump tricks to reach this ending:

```
              ♠ A 5 4
              ♥ —
              ♦ A J 8
              ♣ A 10
♠ Q 10 3 2              ♠ J 9 8
♥ —                    ♥ —
♦ 10 9 5               ♦ Q 6 4
♣ K                    ♣ J 9
              ♠ K 7 6
              ♥ 7 6
              ♦ K 7
              ♣ Q
```

South led a further heart, on which West and North discarded a spade. East was squeezed, and had to discard a spade also. The last trump squeezed West in three suits. However, if he had discarded a diamond, declarer would have had to make the double-dummy play of entering dummy and leading the ♦J. See HEXAGON SQUEEZE and OCTAGONAL TWO-TRICK SQUEEZE.

BAROMETER. A method originated in Sweden in which all groups of boards are played simultaneously. Running scores are posted on the Barometer shortly after the conclusion of each round, thus heightening the interest for both players and spectators. Toward the end of an event, the known positions of the pairs in contention often will influence the tactics they choose in attempting to win. A Barometer contest can be arbitrarily split into a number of sessions.

The best movement for a Barometer for pairs is Barometer Howell (or Endless Howell) where the pairs each time move to the next table, up or down, in the way described for FLOWER MOVEMENT.

For individual contests there are barometer movements (for up to 13 tables) in which each player has every other player as a partner once and as an opponent twice.

BARON-BARCLAY BRIDGE SUPPLIES. The world's biggest bridge supply company. Baron was founded in 1975 by Randy and Mary Baron of Shelbyville KY and merged in 1990 with its chief rival, Barclay Bridge Supplies. Its business is shared about equally between US mail order, tournament sales, and wholesale foreign trade. Address: 3600 Chamberlain Lane Suite 230, Louisville KY. 40241. Tel 1-800-274-2221.

BARON COROLLARY. An adjunct to TWO-WAY STAYMAN, of increasing popularity in Canada, that is designed to discover 4-4 minor suit fits. After responder has bid 2♦ (forcing to game), and opener has bid 2 NT, denying a four-card major or a five-card minor, a 3♣ rebid by responder asks opener's precise distribution. Opener rebids 3♦ with 3-3-4-3, 3 NT with 3-3-3-4, or three of his longer major if he has two four-card minors.

BARON NOTRUMP OVERCALL. An equivalent to a weak takeout double. It is usually made with a singleton or void in the opponent's suit, and the most likely distribution is 4-4-4-1. The maximum strength is 13 points, and the minimum depends on vulnerability. It has achieved little popularity because 1 NT is valuable as a natural overcall. For an alternative method of making a weak takeout double, see MICHAELS CUEBID.

BARON SLAM TRY. An invitation to a slam contract if partner holds good trumps. A bid of the suit next below the agreed suit at the five or six level specifically asks partner whether he holds good trumps. So if spades are agreed, 5♥ invites 6♠, and 6♥ invites 7♠. What constitutes good trumps depends on the previous auction. Partner must ask himself how much worse his trump holding might be in the light of his previous calls.

BARON SYSTEM. An English system developed in the Forties by Leo Baron, Adam Meredith and others. Its exponents have had considerable success in British tournament play, and many of the system ideas have taken root in the general theory of the game. Examples are: (1) the weak notrump opening bid combined with a 1 NT constructive rebid; (2) bidding UP THE LINE with four-card suits; (3) relaxed requirements for BIDDABLE SUITS; (4) the five-card suit requirement for a response of 2♥ to an opening of 1♠; (5) the lead of ACE FROM ACE-KING.

Other distinctive features of the system are: (6) A bid of the third suit by the opener is forcing (e.g., 1♣-1♥-1♠). Some experts using standard methods follow this theory when the response is at the level of two. (7) An immediate raise requires at least four-card trump support. (8) Suit opening bids are highly prepared, with a four-card spade suit being opened ahead of a five-card heart suit regardless of quality. (9) Simple overcalls are strong and jump overcalls weak. See also: ACE VALUES; BARON NOTRUMP OVERCALL; BARON SLAM TRY; 2 NT OPENING; 2 NT RESPONSE.

BARON TWO NOTRUMP RESPONSE. See TWO NOTRUMP RESPONSE.

BARRAGE. The French term for PREEMPTIVE BID. Sometimes used by English writers to describe a series of obstructive bids.

BARRED. Forbidden to bid, for one round of bidding or for a complete auction. This usually occurs following an infraction by partner.

BARRICADE. An obsolete term for PREEMPTIVE BID

or BARRAGE, coined by P. Hal Sims.

BARRY CRANE TOP 500. This trophy is presented to the ACBL member who has accumulated the most masterpoints during the calendar year. Originally the McKenney Trophy, it was put into play by William E. McKenney, ACBL executive secretary. It was known as the McKenney Trophy contest from 1937-1981. When the list was expanded to include the leading 500 players it was called the Top 500 from 1982-1985. It became the Barry Crane Top 500 in 1986. Crane, who was murdered in July 1985, was ACBL's top masterpoint holder and was acknowledge by his peers to be unequalled as a masterpoint winner and a matchpoint player. His influence on the race was dominant for more than three decades. For winners see Appendix II.

BART. An artificial forcing two-diamond bid used in this sequence:

Opener	Responder
1♠	1 NT
2♣	2♦

This shows various hands, many of them including a five-card heart suit. The opener makes that assumption, and will often bid two hearts with a doubleton, perhaps ending the bidding.

The responder may continue with: (a) 2♠, with a doubleton spade and 8-9 points; (b) 2 NT with four-card club support and 10-11 points; (c) 3♣ with five-card club support and 10-11 points; (d) t3♦ ,t o play.

Immediate bids of 2♠ or 3♣ by responder are similar but weaker.

BASE III. A powerful computer program, created by Fred Gitelman of Toronto, for creating, storing and analyzing bridge problems, which may be complete deals or end-positions. A unique feature is the program's ability to take a 52-card diagram and decide whether a given contract can or cannot be made, and show how. This procedure may, however, take a long time. End-positions are solved very quickly. Another feature helps in the analysis of suit combinations and the calculation of percentages. The user can input his own hands, or he can create hands for bidding practice or simulations in a similar fashion to BOREL.

The creator of the program hopes eventually to produce a high-level program that will bid, play and defend, but formidable obstacles must be faced. It is not easy to teach a computer to draw inferences from opposing bids that may be artificial, stylistic or psychic.

BATH COUP. A simple hold-up of the ace when the jack is also held:

(a)
```
              4 3 2
K Q 10 9 6              7 5
              A J 8
```
(b)
```
              A 3 2
K Q 10 9 6              7 5
              J 8 4
```

In each case the king is led and is allowed to win. If declarer holds two small cards, as in (b), he should generally play the higher one. This play may cause West to think that East has begun a high-low, and induce him to continue the suit to South's advantage.

The play dates from the days of whist, and is presumably named after the English watering place of Bath.

BATTLE, SARAH. A character invented by Charles Lamb to embody his idea of what a perfect whist player should be. In his *Essays of Elia* he wrote: "She loved a thorough-paced partner, a determined enemy. She took and gave no concessions. She never made a revoke nor even passed it over in her adversary without exacting the utmost forfeiture. She fought a good fight — cut and thrust.

"She sat bolt upright, and neither showed you her cards, nor desired to see yours. I never in my life — and I knew Sarah Battle many of the best years of it — saw her take out her snuffbox when it was her turn to play, or snuff a candle in the midst of a game or ring for a servant until it was fairly over. She never introduced or connived at miscellaneous conversation during its progress. As she emphatically observed, 'cards are cards,' and if I ever saw mingled distaste in her fine last-century countenance, it was at the airs of a young gentleman of a literary turn, who had been with difficulty persuaded to take a hand, and who, in his excess of candor, declared that he thought there was no harm in unbending the mind now and then, after serious studies, in recreations of that kind! She could not bear to have her noble occupation, to which she wound up her faculties, considered in that light. It was her business, her duty, the thing she came into the world to do — and she did it. She unbent her mind afterwards over a book."

BATTLE OF THE CENTURY. See CULBERTSON-LENZ MATCH.

BATTLE OF THE SEXES. A marathon trans-Atlantic match played April 1 to April 15 1989. This was the first transatlantic match, and more than 1000 players took part, playing 24 hours a day with a pair of men against a pair of women. The companion table, in Paris, had the opposite seating. A record number of boards, 2352, were played, and after seesaw exchanges the men won by 196 imps, a small margin in view of the length of the match. The match was conceived and organized by Alan Truscott, with Claire Tornay in charge in New York, at the Cavendish Club, and José Damiani in charge in Paris.

On the following deal Damiani as East was the victim of fine play by Danielle Gaviard.

```
                ♠ Q 4
                ♥ A K 9 4
                ♦ A Q
                ♣ A 10 8 7 5
♠ K J 10 8 6 3              ♠ A 9 7 5
♥ Q 8 3                     ♥ J 10 6 2
♦ K 7 3                     ♦ 8
♣ 6                        ♣ Q J 4 2
                ♠ 2
                ♥ 7 5
                ♦ J 10 9 6 5 4 2
                ♣ K 9 3
```

Both sides were vulnerable. The bidding:

West	North	East	South
2 ♠	Dbl	4 ♠	5 ♦
Pass	Pass	Pass	

Gaviard landed in 5♦ as shown, after a weak opening two-bid on her left. It might seem that she was due to lose a trump trick, a spade trick and a club trick, but she

took advantage of a subtle defensive error.

West led his singleton club, South played low from dummy and captured East's jack with the king. She finessed the ♦Q successfully, cashed the ace, and led a spade. East put up the ace, and continued with a spade ruffed by the declarer.

A diamond was surrendered to West, who routinely played another spade and gave Gaviard her chance. She ruffed and reached this ending:

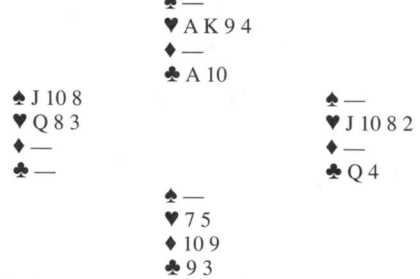

```
        ♠ —
        ♥ A K 9 4
        ♦ —
        ♣ A 10
♠ J 10 8        ♠ —
♥ Q 8 3         ♥ J 10 8 2
♦ —             ♦ —
♣ —             ♣ Q 4
        ♠ —
        ♥ 7 5
        ♦ 10 9
        ♣ 9 3
```

On the next trump lead the ♣10 was thrown from the dummy and Damiani, in the East seat, was subjected to a trump squeeze. He had to choose between throwing a heart and allowing South to establish a heart winner in the dummy, and throwing a club and permitting the ♣9 to score.

West was left to discover that he should have shifted to a heart after winning the ♦K. And the women gained 10 imps: in the replay the men with the North-South cards in New York, played 3♣ and scored 110.

BECKER. Over an opponent's 1NT opening, a simple conventional method of showing certain two-suited hands. A 2♣ overcall promises length in both minor suits, and a 2♦ overcall promises length in both major suits. The overcaller suggests limited high-card strength, since a penalty double is available with a strong hand. Overcaller also suggests at least five cards in each suit, but players often employ Becker, as well as other two-suited overcalls, with 4-5 distribution, especially at matchpoint duplicate.

For alternative defenses to an opposing 1NT opening, see DEFENSE TO ONE NOTRUMP.

BED. See GO TO BED.

BELATED SUPPORT. Support for the opener's original suit on the second round after opener has rebid 2 NT (as distinguished from PREFERENCE and JUMP PREFERENCE).

WEST	EAST
1 ♥	1 ♠
2 NT	3 ♥

Many players consider this a forcing sequence, which would show exactly three-card support if LIMIT RAISES are being used. If the opener then bids 3♠ he also shows three-card support.

BELGIAN BRIDGE FEDERATION. (Fédération Belge de Bridge; Belgische Bridge Federatie). The Federation was founded in 1932 by a group of 13 clubs. In 1978 it divided into two leagues, the Flemish Bridge League and the League of the Belgian French Community. The League hosted European Championships in 1935, 1965 and 1973, and four Common Market Championships. In 1992 there were about 7,500 members. Officers 1993:

President: Paul Magerman
Secretary-Treasurer: Albert Van Escote
Avenue Louis Lepoutre 49/2, 1060 Brussels, Belgium. Tel. 32 2 345 79 37

BELONG. An expression to indicate which side can legitimately expect to buy the contract. A player who says he knew that "the hand belonged to the opponents" indicates that he judged the opposition could make the highest positive score on the deal. In such circumstances, it may pay to take an ADVANCE SAVE or other preemptive action. Alternatively, a player who judges that he will be outgunned in high cards may prefer to remain silent on the theory that he will end up as a defender and does not wish to give information that may help the declarer.

An alternative meaning of the word in modern bridge jargon, especially in a POST-MORTEM, is to indicate the most desirable contract for a side: "We belong in 5♦".

BELOW THE LINE. Points at RUBBER BRIDGE entered below the horizontal line on the score sheet. These points are solely those made by bidding and making partscores, games or slams. All other points are scored above the line only. Points scored below the line count toward winning a game or rubber. At DUPLICATE BRIDGE or CHICAGO, the term may be used loosely to refer to trick score. See SCORING.

BENJAMIN. Convention permitting an Acol player to use weak WEAK TWO-BIDS in the major suits; invented by Albert Benjamin (Scotland). Opening bids of 2♠ and 2♥ are weak. An opening bid of 2♦ is equivalent to an Acol bid of 2♣ and almost guarantees game. The negative response is 2♥ and the sequence 2♦-2♥-2 NT, showing 23-24 points, can be passed.

An opening bid of 2♣ shows a normal Acol one-round forcing two-bid in an unspecified suit and promises at least eight playing tricks. The negative response is 2♦ and any positive response is forcing to game. With this method it is possible to use an Acol two-bid when clubs is the primary suit. See ACOL SYSTEM.

BENNETT MURDER. A historic tragedy which took place in Kansas City KS in 1931. The victim was John S. Bennett, a prosperous perfume salesman, who met his death as a result of a game of contract in which he played with his wife against another married couple. His wife became so infuriated at her husband's play that she shot him following a bitter quarrel. She was tried for murder later the same year, and acquitted.

The following account of the episode appeared in the *New York Evening Journal*:

"As the game went on," Mrs. Hoffman said, "the Bennetts' criticism of each other grew more and more caustic. Finally a spade hand was bought by them in the following manner: Bennett bid a spade. My husband overcalled with 2♦. Mrs. Bennett promptly boosted the original spade bid to four. I passed. Mrs. Bennett, as dummy, laid down a rather good hand. But her husband was set. This seemed to infuriate his wife and she began goading him with remarks about 'bum bridge players.' He came right back at her. I don't remember the exact words. This kept up for several minutes. We tried to stop the argu-

ment by demanding cards, but by this time the row had become so pronounced that Bennett, reaching across the table, grabbed Myrtle's arm and slapped her several times. We tried to intervene, but it was futile. While Mrs. Bennett repeated over and over in a strained singsong tone, 'Nobody but a bum would hit a woman,' her husband jumped up and shouted, 'I'm going to spend the night at a hotel. And tomorrow I'm leaving town.' His wife said to us: 'I think you folks had better go.' Of course, we started to do so."

While the Hoffmans were putting on their things Mrs. Bennett dashed into the bedroom of her mother, Mrs. Alice B. Adkins, and snatched the family automatic from a dresser drawer. "John's going to St. Joseph," she explained to the older woman, "and wants to be armed." Bennett had gone to his "den," near the bathroom, to pack for the intended trip. Hoffman, adjusting his muffler, turned back and saw his friend alone for the moment. While Mrs. Hoffman waited in the doorway, her husband advanced toward Bennett, hoping to say a word or two that would dispel this angry depression. The two men were in conversation as Mrs. Bennett darted in, pistol in hand. Bennett saw her, ran to the bathroom, slammed the door just as two bullets pierced the wooden paneling. Hoffman, rigid with astonishment, remained in the den. His wife, hearing the shots, ran down the hall and began pounding on the door of the next apartment. It is thought Bennett died from two bullets fired as he neared the door leading to the street. He staggered to a chair — the Hoffmans agree — moaning, "She got me." Then he slumped, unconscious, to the floor. Mrs. Bennett was standing at the other side of the living room, the gun dangling loosely from her fingers. As Bennett fell, her daze broke. She ran toward him. Police found her bent over him, giving vent to wild sobs.

The alleged hand was as follows.

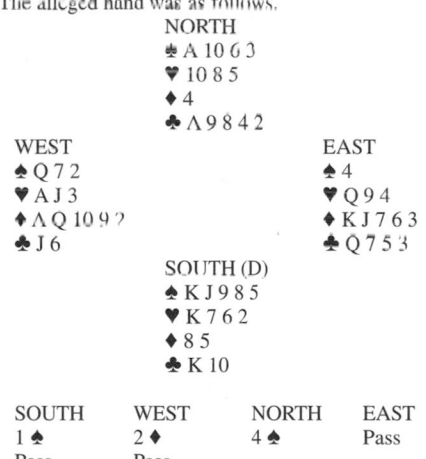

```
                    NORTH
                    ♣ A 10 6 3
                    ♥ 10 8 5
                    ♦ 4
                    ♣ A 9 8 4 2
WEST                                        EAST
♠ Q 7 2                                     ♠ 4
♥ A J 3                                     ♥ Q 9 4
♦ A Q 10 9 2                                ♦ K J 7 6 3
♣ J 6                                       ♣ Q 7 5 3
                    SOUTH (D)
                    ♠ K J 9 8 5
                    ♥ K 7 6 2
                    ♦ 8 5
                    ♣ K 10
```

SOUTH	WEST	NORTH	EAST
1♠	2♦	4♠	Pass
Pass	Pass		

Mr. Bennett opened the bidding without sufficient values for an opening bid, and suffered an unusually heavy penalty. However, 4♠ was not an impossible contract, and Ely Culbertson analyzed the deal as follows:

We have heard of lives depending on the play of a card. It is not often that we find that figure of speech literally true. Here is a case in point. Mr. Bennett had overbid his hand. Of that there can be no doubt, but even with this, so kind were the gods of distribution that he might have saved his life had he played his cards a little better. Mr. Hoffman opened the ♦A, then shifted to the club suit when he saw the dummy void of diamonds, and led the ♣ J. This Mr. Bennett won with his king and started to pull the adverse trumps. Here again he flirted with death, as people so frequently do when they fail to have a plan either in the game of bridge or the game of life. He still could make his contract and save his life. The proper play before drawing the trumps would have been to establish the club suit after ruffing the last diamond. Suppose Mr. Bennett, when he took the club trick with his king, had led his last diamond and trumped it with one of dummy's small trumps. He could then lead a trump and go up with the king. Now he would lead the ♣ 10, and, when Mr. Hoffman followed suit, his troubles would be over. He would play the ♣ A and lead the nine or eight. If Mrs. Hoffman put up the queen, Mr. Bennett should trump and let Mr. Hoffman overtrump if he pleased. If Mr. Hoffman, after winning this trick, led a heart, the contract and a life would be saved. If he led a diamond the same would be true. A lead of the trump might still have permitted the fatal dénouement but at least Mr. Bennett would have had the satisfaction of knowing that he had played the cards dealt him by fate to the very best of his ability.

The episode was entertainingly described at length by Alexander Woollcott in *While Rome Burns*.

BERGEN OVER NOTRUMP.

Devised by Marty Bergen, and sometimes known as D.O.N.T., or Disturbing Opponent's Notrump. Like BROZEL, which it somewhat resembles, it is based on the idea that a penalty double of a strong notrump is rarely profitable. The structure is:

Dbl. = a one-suiter, usually not spades

  (Partner responds 2♣, and doubler can show his suit)

2 ♣ = ♣ and another suit

2 ♦ = ♦ and a major

2 ♥ = ♥ and ♠

2 ♠ = natural

The same structure can be used in other situations, such as: (a) they double our 1NT (then redouble is a one-suiter); and (b) they overcall 1NT. See DEFENSE TO ONE NOTRUMP.

BERGEN RAISES.

A method devised by Marty Bergen to give responder more ways to raise opening bidder's major suit. This method enables responder to distinguish among raises of various strengths with either three- or four-card support.

WEST   EAST

1 ♠   2 ♠ = three trumps, 7 to 10 points

        3 ♣ = four trumps, 7 to 10 points

        3 ♦ = four trumps, a limit raise

        3 ♠ = four or more trumps, 0 to 7 points, preemptive

The responses are similar if the opening bid is 1♥.

In Bergen's original writeup (April 1982 ACBL *Bulletin*), the meanings of the 3♦ and 3♥/3♠ responses were interchanged.

This is based on the idea that it is "safe" to go to the three-level with a 9-card fit. See LAW OF TOTAL TRICKS. For the schedule of Bergen Raises following a takeout double, see RESPONSES OVER OPPONENT'S TAKEOUT DOUBLE.

In defense, following a response of 3♣ or 3♦, double is usually lead-directing, but may be the first move with a major-minor two-suiter, with the major suit to be bid later; a cuebid of opener's major shows the other major and

the unbid minor; pass and double is takeout.

BERMUDA.

ACBL Unit 198. Bermuda hosted the first BERMUDA BOWL in 1950, hence the name of the trophy. Bermuda also was the host for the 25th anniversary Bermuda Bowl in 1975, at which the BERMUDA INCIDENT took place. The Bermuda Unit conducts a regional championship every winter, usually in late January. Bermuda plans to make application for the 50th Anniversary Bermuda Bowl. This will take place in 2001 because Bermuda Bowls are held in odd-numbered years only.

BERMUDA BOWL.

The annual World Team Championship; the trophy at stake therein.

The first postwar world contract bridge team championship was played in Bermuda in 1950 on the initiative of Norman M. Bach. The contest was a three-cornered match among teams representing the United States, Great Britain (the European champion), and Europe (a combined Sweden-Iceland team).

The next six Bermuda Bowl contests were two-team events between the United States and the winners of the European Championships.

In 1958, the contest became a three-cornered event with the inclusion of the South American champions.

In 1960, 1964, 1968 and 1972, which were Team Olympiad years, there was no Bermuda Bowl competition. In 1974 the WORLD BRIDGE FEDERATION voted to conduct the Bermuda Bowl in odd-number years only. To provide a transition, the Bermuda Bowl and the World Team Olympiad were played consecutively in Monte Carlo in 1976.

Starting in 1961, the defending champion was invited to compete. This practice was discontinued after the 1977 Bermuda Bowl, when two teams from the United States met in the final. One was the team that qualified through the Trials method, the other was the defending champion. The Executive Council of the WBF decided it was not good for two teams from the same zone to compete in the final.

From 1950 to 1963 inclusive, the Bermuda Bowl was organized under the auspices of the ACBL and the EBL, with the collaboration of the South American Bridge Confederation starting in 1958. Since 1963, the Bermuda Bowl has been conducted by the WBF. In 1965 the WBF voted to expand the event to a five-team contest by including the Far East champions, who became eligible for the first time in 1966. The Bermuda Bowl became a six-sided affair for the first time in 1971 when Australia exercised its right to represent the South Pacific Zone. The Central American-Caribbean Zone was represented for the first time in the 1979 championship. And the Bridge Federation of Asia and the Middle East fielded a representative in the Bermuda Bowl for the first time in 1981. The European Zone was allotted a second spot in the competition in 1981.

The pattern for Bermuda Bowl competition was changed radically, starting with the 1983 competition. The winners of the North American Team Trials and the European champions advanced automatically to the semifinals. The North American runner-up and the second-place European team also qualified for Bermuda Bowl play, but they had to take part in a round-robin with the winners of the other zones to determine the other two semifinalists. Also eligible to play in the round-robin were the victors from South America, Far East, Central

America-Caribbean, Australia-New Zealand and Asia-Middle East. In addition, the host country has the right to enter a team if that country has not already qualified as a Zonal representative.

In order to insure that two teams from the same Zone do not meet in the final, the WBF stipulated that if two teams from the same Zone reach the semifinals, they must oppose each other in a semifinal.

The WBF also decided in 1981 that future Bermuda Bowls, starting in 1985, would not be held in either Europe or North America. World Team Olympiads and World Pair Championships would be held in even years in either North America or Europe, while Bermuda Bowls would be held elsewhere in odd years.

The pattern changed again in Yokohama, Japan, in 1991. The number of teams was enlarged to permit the inclusion of four teams from Europe, three from North America, one from the South Pacific, two from all other zones plus one from the host country. The policy of exempting one European team and one North American team from the qualifying stage was abandoned, as was the restriction which required the final to be between two teams from different zones. (However, a final between two teams from the same country was not permitted, a restriction affecting only ACBL). Teams were in two qualifying groups, with four from each advancing to quarterfinal playoffs.

For a full listing of Bermuda Bowl results, see Appendix V.

BERMUDA INCIDENT. In 1975, the Bermuda Bowl was played in Bermuda in celebration of the 25th anniversary of the Bermuda Bowl. During the early qualifying stages, Gianfranco Facchini, a member of the Italian team, was observed apparently giving foot signals to his partner, Sergio Zucchelli.

The first person to notice unusual foot movements was Bruce Keidan, an American news correspondent monitoring the match between Italy and France. Keidan reported his observation to the North American npc, Alfred Sheinwold, and to Edgar Kaplan, a member of the WBF Appeals Committee. Kaplan informed WBF President Julius Rosenblum. Rosenblum observed for a time, then assigned special observers from the Appeals Committee, Johannes Hammerich of Venezuela and James O'Sullivan of Australia, to monitor the Italian pair.

According to Keidan, Hammerich and O'Sullivan, Facchini reached out with his feet on several occasions during auctions and before opening leads, and apparently touched Zucchelli on the toes once or more; Zucchelli's feet remained completely immobile, and Facchini did not move his feet at other times. Rosenblum, Hammerich and WBF Vice President Jaime Ortiz-Patiño of Switzerland therefore decided to monitor Italy's next qualifying match, using European observers. Before this plan could be implemented, however, the WBF was informed that the North American team would refuse to play against Zucchelli and Facchini in the next scheduled match. This, plus the fact that rumors of the foot movement accusation were already rampant, caused the WBF to inform all team captains of what had transpired, to postpone the Italy-North American match, and to convene a hearing immediately.

The WBF Appeals Committee heard testimony from observers Keidan, Hammerich, O'Sullivan, Rosenblum and Tracy Deninger of Bermuda. Facchini did not deny moving his feet, but attributed his movements to nervous tension. Zucchelli testified that he was unaware of any foot actions by his partner. Oswald Jacoby, who had analyzed some of the hands, was called as a witness, but the Committee was unable to find specific correlation between the foot movements observed and the bidding or play of the hands — a factor usually considered essential to conclusive proof of cheating. The WBF therefore resolved that Facchini and Zucchelli "... be severely reprimanded for improper conduct with respect to the actions of Mr. Facchini moving his feet unnaturally and touching his partner's feet during the auction and before the opening lead". Coffee tables were thereafter placed beneath the card tables to block any possibility of further such movements.

Sheinwold promptly issued a statement: "The North American team endorses the verdict of *guilty* but deplores the failure of the World Bridge Federation to bar this pair from further international competitions." The word guilty had not appeared in the original verdict, but a later statement from Rosenblum corrected this omission by declaring that the accused pair "had been found guilty only of improper foot movements." The first meeting between the Italian and North American teams, postponed from Sunday afternoon, was played that evening. Italian npc Sandro Salvetti kept the suspect pair out of the lineup, saying that their nerves were frayed by the accusations. Two days later, the pair also sat out the second qualifying match against North America, although they had played in other matches in the interim.

On the morning of the first session of the final between Italy and North America, when Sheinwold learned that Facchini and Zucchelli were listed in Italy's starting lineup, he announced that the North American team would not play against this pair unless instructed to do so by the ACBL. ACBL representatives in Bermuda unanimously ordered the team to play. Italy fared poorly with the accused pair in the lineup, and it was only after they had been benched at the request of Benito Garozzo and Giorgio Belladonna that Italy staged an "impossible" rally to retain the world title.

The partnership of the accused players was broken up and the WBF advised Italian bridge officials that it would not welcome the nomination of either player to any event it conducted in the immediately foreseeable future. See BUENOS AIRES AFFAIR; CAPTAIN; CHEATING; CHEATING ACCUSATIONS.

BETA ASKING BIDS. (1) Asking bids in the ROMAN and SUPER PRECISION SYSTEMS concerned with responder's support for the suit bid by the 1♣ opener. After the negative response of 1♦, opener initiates the inquiry by jumping in a major suit (or, in Roman, by simply rebidding a minor suit). The responses are as set out in ROMAN ASKING BIDS.

(2) Asking bids in the SUPER PRECISION system concerned with the quality of a side suit after responder has made a positive response in notrump are also sometimes called Beta Asking Bids, although the difference in schedule of responses has led them to be designated Delta Asking bids in the version of Super Precision used by Giorgio Belladonna and Benito Garozzo. See SUPER PRECISION ASKING BIDS.

BETS. Betting is illegal in tournament play sanctioned by the American Contract Bridge League or any of its affiliated groups.

Occasionally rather sizable bets have been made on the results of challenge bridge matches, notably the CULBERTSON-LENZ MATCH of 1931-32 and the CULBERTSON-SIMS MATCH of 1935.

Bets on the outcome of a rubber or match are based on the side winning the larger number of points rather than the rubber bonus or bonuses, and are thus distinguished from STAKES, which are based on the difference in points earned at so much per point.

BIBLIOGRAPHY. See the last section of this *Encyclopedia*.

BID. A call by which a player proposes a contract that his side will win at least as many odd tricks (one to seven) as his bid specifies, provided the hand is played at the denomination named. See LAWS (Laws 17 through 40).

BID BOXES. See BIDDING BOXES.

BID OF MORE THAN SEVEN. A call by a player contracting for more than seven-odd tricks, and one which is, therefore, inadmissible. See LAWS (Law #38).

BID OUT OF ROTATION. A call by a player, not in turn. See LAWS (Law #31).

BID WHIST. An outgrowth of whist somewhat similar to auction bridge in method of bidding but differing considerably in method of scoring. The bidding is opened by the player to the left of the dealer; highest bidder leads after he has named the trump suit. Seventeen points is the maximum score on a deal, each trick counting one and the four face cards of the trump suit counting one each to the player who takes them in a trick. Sometimes confused with BRIDGE WHIST, this game, now obsolete, was not a direct link in the chain between whist and contract. See HISTORY OF BRIDGE.

BIDDABLE SUIT. The minimum requirements for a bid in terms of the length and strength of the suit.

In the Thirties, the CULBERTSON SYSTEM laid down Q-J-3-2 as a minimum biddable suit, but permitted this to be shaded slightly in certain circumstances. Modern writers tend to reject a generalized rule for biddable suits, recognizing that the requirements must depend on the circumstances in which the bid is made. Four main situations can be listed.

Opening bid.

The higher the rank of the suit, the higher the suit requirements tend to be. 1♣ is often used as a prepared bid with 4-3-3-3, 3-4-3-3 or 4-4-2-3 distribution. (The advent of FIVE-CARD MAJORS has seen this tendency grow.) Some authorities require that a three-card suit be headed by an honor, but this is not always possible:

♠ A J 8 5
♥ A K J
♦ 5 4 2
♣ 8 5 3

Many players using standard methods would bid 1♣ and hope for the best.

If the red suits were reversed in this example, some experts would open 1♦, regarding the quality of the suit as of greater importance than the convenience of rebid provided by an opening of 1♣. But this is an exceptional

case. A bid of 1♦ usually shows at least a four-card suit, but no guarantee is made about the quality of the suit. Four small cards may be sufficient in certain circumstances.

Standards are generally higher for major-suit openings (not taking into account players who favor FIVE-CARD MAJORS). Using standard methods, few experts are prepared to open with 1♥ or 1♠ unless the suit is biddable in the original Culbertson sense. A few players distinguish between hearts and spades, opening four-card heart suits more readily than four-card spade suits.

Responses to suit bids.

A similar principle applies: the most economical bid may sometimes be made with a three-card suit, especially a minor suit, while the most space-consuming bid usually indicates a five-card or longer suit.

(a)	(b)	(c)
♠ K 7 5	♠ 9 7 5	♠ 9 7 5
♥ A 5 2	♥ A 5 4 2	♥ A K 4
♦ A 6 3	♦ K 6 3	♦ 6 4 3
♣ 9 6 4 3	♣ A 6 3	♣ 8 7 4 3

With hand (a), most experts would select a response of 1♦ to an opening bid of 1♣. This is a waiting bid which can come to little harm, and there is no good alternative unless a 2 NT response is being used as a limit bid.

Hand (b) presents a problem when responding to an opening bid of 1♠ if a 1 NT response is not forcing. 2♥ is clearly ruled out because nearly all experts reserve this space-consuming response for hands containing a five-card or longer heart suit. The hand is not strong enough for 2 NT (unless this is played as limit). So the general expert choice would be 2♣.

It is usually dangerous to bid a three-card major suit, but Pierre Jais of France, used to recommend 1♥ in response to 1♦ with hand (c), or 1♠ in response to 1♥ if the major suits are reversed. This is an extreme treatment, but illustrates the general principle of striving to make the most economical bid.

Conversely, a response at the two-level in the suit ranking immediately below the opener's almost always shows a minimum of five cards, as with the response of 2♥ to 1♠.

The most controversial problem concerning biddable suits is whether a weak four-card major suit should be bid at the one-level in preference to 1 NT.

The authorities who favor five-card majors require a four-card suit of any strength to be shown at the level of one, but other leading writers are divided or noncommittal on this point. See WALSH SYSTEM.

Rebids.

This is similarly controversial when the choice lies between showing a weak four-card major suit and rebidding 1 NT. In 1959, a panel of American experts were asked whether they subscribed to the idea of "giving highest priority to finding a major-suit fit." There were 29 panelists who answered yes, without reservations; 38 panelists answered yes, with reservations; 17 replied that they would bid the four-card major suit only if it was worth showing. On this specific hand:

♠ 7 4 3 2
♥ 5 3
♦ A Q 7
♣ A Q J 7

the panelists were asked to choose between a rebid of 1♠ and a rebid of 1 NT after opening 1♣ and receiving a response of 1♥. There were 49 votes for 1♠ and 43 for

1 NT.

In a survey conducted by *The Bridge World* magazine in 1967, 90 leading experts were asked whether a 1NT rebid after an opening bid of 1♣ and a response of 1♥ denied a four-card spade suit. Sixty-five percent replied yes, indicating that the tendency at that time favored rebidding major suits regardless of quality.

In 1984, *The Bridge World* asked experts whether they approved of the 1♠ rebid on these hands:

(a)	(b)	(c)
♠ A J 6 4	♠ A K J 6	♠ J 5 3 2
♥ J 4 3	♥ K 4 3	♥ K 6 4
♦ K 6 4	♦ 10 4 2	♦ A Q 10
♣ A J 4	♣ Q 4 3	♣ K 10 3

Fifty-nine percent approved on (a), 66 percent on (b), but only 47 percent on (c). On such hands, therefore, it seems that experts are increasingly willing to use judgment and rebid 1NT to give a general picture of their strength and pattern. This is affected by the increasing number of players who use the Walsh idea of responding in a major suit and concealing a diamond suit of any length unless the hand is strong.

The problem is different at the level of two, when the choice lies between rebidding a five-card suit and introducing a weak four-card suit. Almost all experts would prefer to show the four-card suit, if lower ranking.

Overcalls.

In most situations, the overcaller can apply the standards of a rebiddable suit (see OPENER'S REBID), but standards must vary widely in accordance with such factors as vulnerability, level of the auction, and preemptive effect. See OVERCALL.

BIDDER. A player who states or indicates a bid. Occasionally the term is used to indicate a player who is prone to overbid, or one who will prefer trying a doubtful contact rather than defending in a competitive bidding situation. Also, any player during the auction period.

BIDDING. The period following the deal and ending after the third successive pass of any bid, double or redouble. Aspects of this phase of the game are listed under the following group headings: COMPETITIVE BIDDING; CUE-BID; COMPETITIVE; DEFENSE TO ONE NOTRUMP; DEFENSIVE BIDDING; DOUBLES; FOUR CLUB CONVENTIONS; FOUR NOTRUMP CONVENTIONS; NOTRUMP BIDDING; OPENING BID; OVERCALLS; REBIDS; RESPONSE; SLAM BIDDING; TWO-SUITER CONVENTIONS; VALUATION.

Other articles include: APPROACH PRINCIPLE; BIDDABLE SUIT; BIDDING SPACE; CANAPÉ; CAPTAINCY; COMMAND BID; CONVENTIONS; DISCOURAGING BID; ENCOURAGING; FORCING; HERBERT NEGATIVE; IDLE BIDS; IMP TACTICS; IMPOSSIBLE BIDS; INFERENCE; LAW OF TOTAL TRICKS; LEAD-INHIBITING BID; LIMIT BID; MATCHPOINT BIDDING; PARTNERSHIP BIDDING; PARTSCORE BIDDING; PSYCHIC BIDDING; PSYCHIC CONTROLS; RUBBER BRIDGE TACTICS; RULE OF TWO AND THREE; SAFETY LEVEL; SIGN-OFF BID; THREE-SUITER; WEAK SUIT.

BIDDING BOX. A device to permit silent bidding, first used in Scandinavian countries. To make a bid, the player takes the appropriate card from a box attached to the corner of the table on his right and places it in front of him on the table. All bidding cards remain on the table until the auction is concluded, thus avoiding the need for a review of the bidding. The possibility of mishearing or misunderstanding a bid also is eliminated. Bidding boxes were used for the first time in World Championships during the World Pair Championships in Sweden in 1970. Beginning in the World Championships at Las Palmas in 1974, bidding boxes have been used exclusively at World Championships. Bidding boxes also are used during late rounds of ACBL championships. The consensus of those who have used bidding boxes is that they are a great improvement over verbal bidding, especially in international matches.

In March 1994, the ACBL Board of Directors passed a regulation that, effective with the Fall NABC, bidding-boxes would be used in all events except Intermediate/Novice games where their use would be optional. Units and districts were encouraged to use bidding-boxes in their games. Also, handicapped players requiring bidding-boxes have preference when availability is limited. Non-handicapped players may use bidding-boxes, if available, in games in which such use is not mandated as long as no player at the table objects.

BIDDING CHALLENGE. Feature of some bridge magazines, providing readers with pairs of hands to bid and a comparison with the efforts of a panel of experts. Called "Challenge the Champs" in *The Bridge World*.

BIDDING CONTESTS. See INTERNATIONAL BRIDGE ACADEMY.

BIDDING SCREEN. See SCREEN.

BIDDING SPACE. The amount of room used in terms of bids which have been skipped. A response of 1♥ to 1♦, for example, uses no bidding space, but a response of 2♣ would use up all the possible bidding space. The general theory is that the length of a suit tends to increase as the bidding space consumed in bidding it increases.

(1) In opening the bidding, 1♣ is not infrequently a three-card suit, and the length expectancy increases up the line. 1♠ is usually a five-card suit, even for players who do not require five-card majors.

(2) Similarly in responding, a response using no bidding space, e.g., 1♣-1♦, may occasionally be a three-card suit. A response using all the bidding space (e.g. 1♠-2♥) is nearly always a five-card suit.

(3) In rebidding by the opener, a rebid in the original suit is most likely to be a five-card suit if it consumes no space (1♥-2♦-2♥), but almost sure to be a six-card suit if all the bidding space has been used (1♥-1♠-2♥).

(4) Overcalls represent exceptions, for tactical reasons. 1♠ over an opposing bid of 1♣ is slightly more likely to be a four-card suit than it would be over 1♥. In the former case the overcaller may be taking a calculated risk in the hope of shutting the opponents out of a heart fit.

BIDDING SYSTEMS. Specific methods of bidding are discussed under the following headings:

ACES SCIENTIFIC; ACOL; AMSTERDAM CLUB; APPROACH-FORCING; BANGKOK CLUB; BARON; BIG DIAMOND; BISSELL; BLUE TEAM CLUB; BRIDGE WORLD STANDARD; CAB; CANARY CLUB; CARROT CLUB; CHURCHILL STYLE; COLO-

NIAL ACOL; CULBERTSON; DUTCH SPADE; EAST-ERN SCIENTIFIC; EFOS; FOUR ACES; GOREN; HUM SYSTEMS; KAPLAN-SHEINWOLD; LEGHORN DIA-MOND; LITTLE MAJOR; LITTLE ROMAN CLUB; MARMIC; MOSCITO; NEW SOUTH WALES; OFFI-CIAL; ORANGE CLUB; PRECISION CLUB; PRO SYS-TEM; REITH'S ONE-OVER-ONE; RELAY SYSTEMS; ROMAN; ROMEX; ROTH-STONE; SCHENKEN; SIM-PLIFIED CLUB; SIMPLIFIED PRECISION; SIMS; STANDARD AMERICAN; STONE-AGE ACOL WITH PAKISTANI PREEMPTS; SUPER PRECISION; SYM-METRIC RELAY; TWO OVER ONE; ULTIMATE CLUB; WEAK OPENING SYSTEMS; WESTERN SCI-ENTIFIC; VANDERBILT CLUB; VIENNA; WALSH; WINSLOW.

BIDDING TO THE SCORE. See PARTSCORE BID-DING.

BIDDING TRAY. See TRAY.

BIFF. Colloquial for trumping the led suit, particularly a winning card on an early lead.

BIG CLUB. See SCHENKEN SYSTEM.

BIG DIAMOND SYSTEM. A method introduced by G. Robert Nail and Robert Stucker, the cornerstone of which is a forcing 1♦ opening, promising an unbalanced hand with at least 17 points. 1♥ is the negative response (0-9), and 1NT is an artificial positive response in hearts.

Other openings: 1♣, forcing, showing a balanced hand not suitable for a 1NT opening (14-16) or 2NT opening (20-21). A 1♦ response is negative (0-10); 2♣, non-forc-ing, showing 12-15 points with 4-4 or longer in the mi-nor suits; 2♦, showing 14-16 points and 4-4 or 5-4 in the major suits.

BIG TOP. The highest matchpoint score on a board when two or more sections are scored together. Common big tops are 25 and 38. See SCORING ACROSS THE FIELD.

BIOGRAPHIES. See Section II.

BIONIC BRIDGE. A plan to use computers to play bridge without cards. It was conceived by C.C. Wei and developed in Taiwan by Patrick Huang and others. It was a forerunner of more sophisticated methods now avail-able. See COMPUTER PLAY

BIRITCH, or Russian Whist. The historic four-page pamphlet, thought to be the earliest publication of the rules of bridge. Authorship has now been traced to John Collinson of London, in whose name copyright was en-tered July 14, 1886. A reproduction, made available through the courtesy of Cambridge University Library, is in the ACBL library. The principal innovations from short whist are described as follows:

No card is turned up for trumps.

The dealer, after the cards have been looked at, has the option of declaring the suit he elects for trumps, or of saying "Pass," in which latter case his partner must de-clare trumps.

In either case, the one declaring may, instead of declar-ing trumps, say "BIRITCH," which means that the hands shall be played without trumps.

Either of the adversaries may say "Contre," in which case the value of all tricks taken is doubled, the dealer or his partner may however thereupon say "Surcontre," in which latter case the value of all tricks taken is quadrupled, and so on ad infinitum.

The person to the left of the dealer leads a card. Then the partner of the dealer exposes all his cards, on the table, which are played by the dealer as at Dummy Whist.
GAMES AND RUBBERS

A game is won by the first side which scores in play 30 points. The honors do not score towards the game.

The Rubber consists of two games out of three.
SCORING

The odd tricks count as follows:

If "Biritch" is declared	each 10 points
If "Hearts" are made trumps	" 8 "
If "Diamonds" are made trumps	" 6 "
If "Clubs" are made trumps	" 4 "
If "Spades" are made trumps	" 2 "

If all the tricks are taken by one side they add 40 extra points. This is called "GRAND SLAMM."

If all the tricks but one are taken by one side they add 20 extra points. This is called "PETIT SLAMM."

The winners of each rubber add 40 points to their score. This is called "CONSOLATION."

There are four honors if "BIRITCH" is declared, which are the four aces.

Equality in aces counts nothing.

3 aces	3 tricks
4 aces	4 tricks
4 aces in one hand	8 tricks

There are five honors, viz: Ace, King, Queen, Knave, and Ten, if trumps are declared.

Simple honors (3)	2 tricks
4 simple honors	4 tricks
4 simple honors in one hand	8 tricks
5 simple honors in one hand	1 trick additional to the score for four honors

If one hand has no trumps (trumps having been declared), his side, in case of it scoring honors, adds the value of simple honors to its honor score, or, in case of the other side scor-ing honors, the value of simple honors is deducted from the latter's honor score.

This is called "CHICANE."

Despite existence of the historic pamphlet, derivation of the name *bridge* from *Biritch* was long disputed on the ground that no such word existed in Russian. Research by Robert True in the early Seventies found that earlier Russian dictionaries did include the term, defined as *her-ald*, town crier, announcer, making it a logical name for a game which introduced the new idea of announcing the declaration at which the hand was to be played. It is in-teresting to observe the designation of Biritch for the dec-laration of notrump, a feature never part of whist. Use in the pamphlet of the French terms for double and redouble would tend to confirm that bridge was played earlier in France, or in those diplomatic circles where French was the prevailing language. See also HISTORY OF BRIDGE.

BISSELL. An original method for showing distribution with the first bid, devised by Harold Bissell of New York and published in 1936. It attracted favorable attention from B. Jay Becker, Louis Watson and Edward Hymes, and anticipated some modern European systems, such as ROMAN and RELAY.

Valuation. This was by a distributional point-count which ingeniously took into account the strength of com-bined honors as well as suit lengths. Honor cards were valued at 3, 2 and 1 point respectively if there were 0, 1

or 2 higher honors missing in the same suit.

To these were added distributional points: 1 for the fourth card in any suit; and 4 for the fifth and succeeding cards in any suit.

The grand total bore a direct relation to the playing-trick strength of a hand (three times the number of playing tricks) and was therefore an accurate measure of the power of the hand.

BIT. British colloquialism for a small card. "Ace-bit" means a doubleton ace.

BLACK POINTS. Points won at club games and Unit championships. See GOLD POINTS; RANKING OF PLAYERS; RED POINTS; REGIONAL AND NATIONAL POINTS; SILVER POINTS.

BLACK AND RED GERBER. A variation of the GERBER convention devised by Irving Cowan which uses 4♣ as the ace-asking bid only when a red suit has been agreed on as trumps. When clubs or spades are to be trumps, the ace-asking bid is 4♦. This modification retains a lower-level ace-asking bid than BLACKWOOD, while avoiding the ambiguity of using 4♣ as Gerber, with clubs as the agreed suit.

BLACKPOOL MOVEMENT. A movement popular in England in which 10 tables play 24 boards. Two boards are played in each round, and bye stands are placed between tables 1 and 10, and between 5 and 6. Players and boards move as in a normal MITCHELL MOVEMENT for 11 rounds, so that in the eleventh round original opponents are again in opposition. For the twelfth round East-West pairs deduct their pair number from 11 and move to the indicated table.

BLACKWOOD. A convention in which a 4 NT bid is used to discover the number of aces held by partner. It was invented by Easley Blackwood in 1933 and has attained worldwide popularity.

The conventional responses to the 4 NT bid are:

5 ♣	no ace or four aces
5 ♦	one ace
5 ♥	two aces
5 ♠	three aces

If the 4NT bidder continues by bidding 5NT, he asks for kings in a similar fashion. As this must be an attempt to reach a grand slam, the 5NT bid guarantees that the partnership holds all four aces. (At matchpoint duplicate scoring, this idea might be disregarded in the interest of seeking a contract of 6NT.)

Some players use the next meaningless bid, instead of 5NT, to ask for kings. This is called ROLLING BLACKWOOD.

Requirements.

There are no specific requirements, but the 4 NT bidder should feel safe at the level of five and have an expectation of 12 playing tricks in the combined hands. He should expect to be able to make a successful decision on the basis of his partner's response and should therefore usually be well provided with second- and third-round playing tricks in the combined hands.

It is seldom wise to use the convention when holding a void suit or worthless doubleton in an unbid suit, or when matters such as trump quality remain unresolved.

If the intent is to play in a minor-suit slam, a Blackwood

bidder must use discretion if he has fewer than two aces. He may use Blackwood if the intended trump suit is diamonds, but not if it is clubs. (One variation of responses when clubs is the agreed trump suit caters to this difficulty: the 4NT bidder assumes that his partner has at least one ace; hence, there is no response to show no aces. A 5♣ response shows one, 5♦ shows two, etc.)

In some circumstances it may be possible to play in 5NT. If the Blackwood bidder next bids an unbid suit at the five-level, he is requesting responder to bid 5 NT. However, this is rarely necessary since a Blackwood bidder is normally intending to play in a suit.

Void suits.

Void suits may not be counted as aces, but there are several methods in which voids can be indicated.

(1) Make the normal response, but at the level of six, to show the indicated number of aces and an unspecified void. Thus 6♣ shows no ace and a void; 6♦ shows one ace and a void, etc.

(2) Bid 6♣ to show one ace and a void; 6♦ to show two aces and a void.

(3) Bid 5 NT to show two aces and a void; six of a suit ranking below the agreed trump suit to show a void in that suit and one ace; six of the agreed trump suit to show one ace and a higher-ranking void.

(4) Holding two aces, make the response that normally shows no aces; holding three aces, make the response that normally shows one ace. When the 4 NT bidder signs off, the responder does not pass, but now bids the suit of his void. Responses at the six level show one ace and a void, as in (3) above.

(5) Using a three-step set of normal responses to Blackwood in which 5♣ shows 0 or 3 aces, 5♦ shows 1 or 4, and 5♥ shows two aces, make a bid higher than 5♥ to show a void. 5♠ shows a spade void and one ace; other responses are as in (3) above.

Interference bidding.

See BLACKWOOD AFTER INTERFERENCE.

Non-conventional.

There are a number of situations in which 4 NT should be treated as a natural bid. Experts sometimes disagree on specific situations, but there is general agreement on the following rule:

A 4 NT bid is a natural bid whenever the partnership has not bid a suit genuinely. For example:

SOUTH	NORTH	SOUTH	NORTH	SOUTH	NORTH
1 NT	4 NT	2 ♣	2 ♦	1 NT	2 ♣
		2 NT	4 NT	2 ♦	4 NT
		(using an			
		artificial			
		2♣ bid)			

But there are other circumstances in which the 4 NT bid should be treated as natural. Careful partnership agreement is needed. The following rule is generally valid: If, during the auction, one player bids 3 NT and his partner bids four of a minor suit as a slam suggestion, a subsequent 4 NT bid by either player should be a natural sign-off bid. For example:

SOUTH	NORTH		SOUTH	NORTH
1 ♠	2 ♥		1 ♠	2 ♣
3 NT	4 ♦		3 NT	4 ♣
4 NT			4 NT	

In these sequences the final bid rejects the slam invitations and expresses a desire to play in 4 NT.

A more general rule is recommended by Terence Reese; 4 NT is natural when no suit has been agreed, either directly or by inference. This covers a wide range.

For example:

SOUTH	NORTH
1 ♠	2 ♥
3 NT	4 NT

Many players would regard this as conventional, but on Reese's rule it would be natural.

SOUTH	NORTH
1 ♥	2 NT
4 NT	

This type of 4 NT bid is listed as conventional by Blackwood himself, but would be natural on Reese's rule. If South wishes to bid 4 NT conventionally, he can make a forcing bid at the level of three and follow with 4 NT the next round.

By agreement, a raise from 2 NT to 4 NT at any stage can be regarded as natural: a conventional 4 NT can always be postponed. But judgment may be required when 3 NT is followed by 4 NT.

SOUTH	NORTH
1 ♠	3 ♥
3 NT	4 NT

This is clearly conventional. North may be planning to play in either major suit, but has had no opportunity to fix a suit below game level.

Also, any sudden jump from a suit bid to 4 NT is of necessity conventional. See also: BABY BLACKWOOD; BYZANTINE BLACKWOOD; CULBERTSON 4-5 NT; DECLARATIVE-INTERROGATIVE 4 NT; GERBER CONVENTION; KEY CARD BLACKWOOD; KICK-BACK; NORMAN 4 NT; ROLLING BLACKWOOD; ROMAN BLACKWOOD; ROMAN GERBER; RO-MAN KEY CARD BLACKWOOD; SUPER BLACKWOOD; SUPER GERBER; and SUPPRESSING THE BID ACE.

BLACKWOOD AFTER INTERFERENCE. The traditional method for dealing with opponents who overcall a Blackwood bid has been to double whenever the size of the prospective penalty is attractive, and otherwise to pass with no aces and bid the cheapest suit with one ace, and so forth up the line. Modern conventions recognize that the penalty will rarely be sufficiently lucrative to warrant a double, and therefore give that call an artificial meaning related to the number of aces held by the Blackwood responder. The most common such conventions are:

(1) DEPO, which stands for Double Even, Pass Odd. A double shows zero, two, or four aces; a pass shows one or three.

(2) DOPI, which stands for Double Zero, Pass 1. A double shows no aces, pass shows 1, and two or more aces are shown by bidding up the line.

(3) PODI, which stands for Pass Zero, Double 1. The double and the pass have the reverse of the meanings they have using DOPI; other bids are the same. Similarly, DOPE is the reverse of DEPO.

DOPI is more widely used than PODI. A number of experts agree to use DOPI when the overcall is below the trump suit at the five-level, allowing room for bidding two or more aces up the line, and to use DEPO when the overcall is at five of the trump suit or higher and space is scarce.

It is also possible to use Roman responses with DOPI or PODI. The first step shows 0 or 3 aces, the second step shows 1 or 4 while the first bid other than pass or double shows 2. Pairs that play KEY CARD BLACKWOOD

would be well advised to discuss whether or not the trump king counts in responding after interference.

Some experts play a variation of DOPI when 4 NT is doubled. ROPI (redouble zero, pass one) or its reverse, RIPO can be used. This can lead to occasional misunderstandings, and the more popular choice is to act as if the double had not taken place.

BLACKWOOD THEORY OF DISTRIBUTION. A formula applied when missing four cards including the queen.

$$♠ K J 10 7 4$$
$$♠ A 8 6 2$$

South lays down the ace and both defenders play low. On the second round West plays low, and South has to decide whether to finesse or play for the drop.

Mathematically it is extremely close. Easley Blackwood suggested a rule based on the LAW OF SYMMETRY: If the combined North-South holding in their shortest suit is:

(a) five cards, or four cards divided 2-2: play for the drop;

(b) four cards divided 3-1 or 4-0, or fewer than four cards: finesse. This formula was tested on a large number of published hands and produced excellent results. However, it can apply only when there are no indications from the bidding and play, which is rarely the case.

BLANCHARD CASE. Just after the 1984 Fall NABC in San Diego, Robert and Jill Blanchard of New York City filed suit against the ACBL in Los Angeles. The Blanchards' claim was that gender-based events such as the Men's Pairs violated California's Unruh Act, an anti-discrimination statute. Five years later, the Los Angeles Superior Court, in which the suit was filed, dismissed the suit for lack of prosecution. As part of a settlement with the Blanchards, in which they agreed not to appeal, the ACBL's insurance carrier paid $15,000 toward the couple's legal expenses. The insurance carrier paid all of ACBL's legal expenses.

Beginning in 1990, three nationally-rated events formerly restricted to men were changed to open events. The Life Master Men's Pairs at the Spring NABC is now one of two Open Pairs; the Men's Swiss Teams, also contested in the Spring, is now the Open Swiss Teams; and the Men's Board-a-Match Teams, contested in the Fall, is now the Open Board-a-Match Teams.

Around the time of the Blanchards' suit — and in response to complaints by the couple — the ACBL also eliminated gender-based events from those used to qualify ACBL pairs for WBF competition. The Blanchards claimed that they could not qualify together in events restricted to men or women. The ACBL Board of Directors agreed and changed the qualifying policy.

BLANK. A void. Used as an adjective, it indicates lack of a protecting small card for an honor, as a blank king. As a verb, it means to discard a protecting small card, as to blank a king.

Blank honors, whether singleton or doubleton, are slightly devalued in most POINT-COUNT methods.

BLANK HAND. A hand with seemingly no trick-taking potential (see YARBOROUGH).

BLANK SUIT. See VOID.

BLIND LEAD. The first lead on any hand, so called because the opening leader has not seen the dummy. This term is particularly applied when the leader's partner has not bid, and the declarer's side has bid only one denomination. Terence Reese is quoted as saying "Blind leads are for deaf players." See OPENING LEAD.

BLIND PLAYERS. Blindness is not an insurmountable obstacle to bridge playing. The cards are marked with Braille symbols, and sighted players in turn call the card played to each trick. A blind player may at any time ask that the remaining cards in the dummy be called out. Early Braille markings were not standardized and often players could not read one another's Braille.

    J. Patrick Dunne and Dr. Arthur Dye were the first blind players to participate in major American Contract Bridge League tournaments. Dr. Lois Zwart (later Wiley) commenced playing a few years later, accompanied by her seeing eye dog. Dr. Dye and Dr. Wiley both earned Life Master rating as have other blind players — John Larsen of Minneapolis, Anne Cunningham of Charlotte NC, Sarah Howard of Newport News VA, and Michael Andrew Levinson of Daly City CA who, though legally blind, won the Life Master Men's Pairs at the Fall 1981 North American Championships.

BLITZ. To crush your opponents, usually in a session of team play in which their score is zero.

BLIZZARD. British colloquialism for a worthless hand, probably a yarborough.

BLOCK. A situation in which entry problems within a particular suit make it difficult or impossible to cash winners or possible winners in that suit. This occurs when both members of a partnership (the declaring side or the defense) hold significant honor cards, and one of them has no accompanying small cards. For example:

NORTH	NORTH
K Q J 10	Q J 3 2
SOUTH	SOUTH
A	A K

In these cases the block is complete, and the honor cards in dummy cannot be utilized unless a side entry is available. Sometimes the block may be less embarrassing:

NORTH	NORTH
A J 4 3 2	A 4 3 2
SOUTH	SOUTH
K Q	K Q J

If there is no side entry to dummy, South must overtake his last honor with dummy's ace. He needs a 3-3 division of the defenders' cards to make more than three tricks.

    The general rule for resolving blocked situations, or for avoiding unnecessary blocks, is that high cards must be played from the shorter hand as quickly as possible. See also UNBLOCKING and INTERNAL BLOCK.

BLOCKBUSTER. A bridge hand of seemingly tremendous trick-taking potential. Frequently, however, these hands have a weakness and give rise to very large sets when the partner's hand contains no protective features and the trump suit divides unfavorably. See also MONSTER and ROCK-CRUSHER.

BLOCKED SQUEEZE. See CRISS-CROSS SQUEEZE, under SIMPLE SQUEEZE. For other types of blocked squeeze, see ENTRY SQUEEZE and STEPPINGSTONE SQUEEZE.

BLOCKING. Playing so as to create a block in the opponent's suit. For example:

$$♠ A 5 2$$
$$♠ K 10 8 6 3 \qquad ♠ Q 9$$
$$♠ J 7 4$$

West leads the ♠6 against 3 NT. The normal play is to hold up the ace twice, but this is useless if West rather than East is likely to gain the lead. In that case South should put up dummy's ace, abandoning the chance that the lead is from king-queen. Whenever East holds a doubleton honor the spade suit is blocked for the defense.

    Notice that if the defensive entry was held by East, he would need to unblock with the queen on the first trick. Other positions:

$$♠ A 6 4$$
$$♠ Q 9 8 5 3 \qquad ♠ K J$$
$$♠ 10 7 2$$

In this position West leads the five and South puts up dummy's ace, hoping for East to hold two honors doubleton. When the defenders gain the lead, they can cash only one spade trick.

$$♠ 8 6$$
$$♠ A 9 4 3 2 \qquad ♠ K J 10$$
$$♠ Q 7 5$$

When East wins the lead of the three with the king, and returns the jack, South should cover and thus block the suit. He assumes that West's three is an honest fourth-best lead, in which case West cannot have six spades, and East cannot have a doubleton.

If there were two small spot cards missing, suggesting a six-card suit with West, South should play low on the jack.

$$♠ A 3$$
$$♠ K J 7 5 4 \qquad ♠ Q 8$$
$$♠ 10 9 6 2$$

On the lead of the five, South blocks the suit by putting up dummy's ace. This permits a triumph for the rare player who underleads K Q J x x (see OPENING LEADS).

$$♠ 7 5$$
$$♠ Q 6 2 \qquad ♠ A 10 9 8 4$$
$$♠ K J 3$$

West leads the two to East's ace, and the 10 is returned. If South judges that West had led from an honor, he puts up the king and achieves a block. See also UNBLOCKING.

BLUE PETER. A humorous term for a high-low signal invented in 1834 by Lord Henry Bentinck. This was probably the first defensive signal in any game of the whist family. The name is nautical in origin, referring to a signal hoisted in harbor to denote that a ship is ready to sail. Bentinck's signal was used in a side suit to indicate to partner a desire to have trumps led. For uses of the high-low or echo in contract, see SIGNALS, SIGNALING and PETER.

BLUE RIBBON PAIRS, NORTH AMERICAN CHAMPIONSHIP. A championship event contested annually at the Fall NABC, under which heading past results are listed. Entry is limited to (1) players who, within a specified period of time, have finished high in North American Championship events, or have finished first or second in regionally rated events, (2) the top 100 masterpoint holders, (3) members of current official teams representing the ACBL or any of its member countries in international competition, and (4) winners of Grand National District championships. For winners, see Appendix I.

BLUE TEAM. The popular name of the Italian international bridge team which gained a remarkable series of successes beginning in 1956. The name is apparently derived from the 1956 Italian Trials, when the Blue Team defeated the Red Team.

Federico Rosa, the late Secretary of the Italian Bridge Federation, explained that the successes of the Blue Team were closely connected with the name of Carl' Alberto Perroux, the Technical Commissioner of the Italian Bridge Federation. He undertook this duty in 1950, and scored his first success in the following year when the team which he had selected won the European Championship in Venice. But the subsequent World Championship encounter with the United States at Naples showed that the young Italian champions were lacking in experience and team discipline.

But this did not cause Perroux to lose heart. He wrote then that the Italians had wished to reach the moon too quickly. This was a promise and a threat. From that day, two groups of enthusiasts, under the paternal leadership of the Technical Commissioner, dedicated themselves to a profound and detailed study of the game. As a result the two schools — the Neapolitan and the Roman — gave birth not only to two of the most accurate bidding systems ever devised, NEAPOLITAN and ROMAN, plus LITTLE ROMAN, but also to the great story of the Blue Team, made up of men such as Walter Avarelli, Giorgio Belladonna, Eugenio Chiaradia, Massimo D'Alelio, Pietro Forquet, Benito Garozzo, Camillo Pabis-Ticci, and Guglielmo Siniscalco.

The Italians did not have to wait too long before avenging the 1951 defeat. From 1956 the Blue Team, captained by Perroux through 1966, then by others, went from victory to victory, and finally reached the moon. They set an international record which will probably never be equalled: four consecutive European Championship wins, ten consecutive World Championship victories in the Bermuda Bowl, and three consecutive World Team Olympiad victories.

With the universe theirs, the Blue Team announced its retirement after winning the 1969 World Championship. After the Aces' victories in the 1970 and 1971 Bermuda Bowls, the Blue Team briefly returned to world competition for the 1972 World Team Olympiad. Using modifications of the Precision Club system, the Blue Team won the round-robin and went on to defeat the Aces in the finals 203-138. Italy continued its domination of the Bermuda Bowl in 1973, 1974, and 1975 but with only two or three members of the traditional Blue Team in the lineup.

BLUE TEAM CLUB. An increasingly popular offspring of the NEAPOLITAN system, developed principally by Benito Garozzo. See BIBLIOGRAPHY C. The chief features of the Blue Team Club are:

1♣ opening is forcing and normally shows 17 or more points (4-3-2-1 count). Occasionally distributional factors may dictate a 1♣ bid with slightly less than 17, or a weaker opening with exactly 17.

Responses show controls by steps, counting an ace as 2 controls and a king as 1. 1♦ shows 0-2 controls, less than 6 points; 1♥ shows 0-2 controls, 6 points or more; 1♠ shows 3 controls, and so on up to 2♦, which shows 6 controls and 2 NT showing 7. Jump responses of two of a major show a six-card suit headed by two honors but less than 6 points.

If 1♦ is overcalled at the one-level, a pass is equivalent to the first step response and a double to the second. Other responses are control-showing, except that two hearts and two spades retain the same meaning as if there were no intervention. After a jump overcall the responses follow a similar pattern: pass is the weakest bid, double shows 6 or more points, suit responses are forcing for a round, a response in notrump shows 3 or 4 controls, and a cuebid shows 5 or more controls.

1♣ is generally forcing to 1 NT if the response is one diamond, or to 2 NT if the response is 1♥. The partnership is committed to game after any other control-showing response.

The opener can force to game by a jump rebid in a suit. If he rebids 1 NT or 2 NT, the responder can use Stayman. Responder usually makes his first rebid in his best suit, and subsequently shows significant features.

1♦, 1♥, and 1♠ openings are natural limited bids, showing 12-16 points and at least a four-card suit. Occasionally 1♦ may be opened on a three-card suit. With two suits of equal length, opener bids the higher-ranking. With two suits of unequal length, the shorter suit is bid first unless the hand is a minimum and the long suit is higher-ranking.

Most responses are normal. Jump raises are limited. A 2 NT jump response is invitational, showing 11-12 points and 4-3-3-3 distribution. Jump shifts show solid or near-solid suits and 13 points or more. Strong hands are bid according to the Canapé principle. Responder's first suit may not be a real suit if his second is higher-ranking.

A response at the two-level is forcing for one round, or to 2 NT. Opener must rebid a five-card suit if he has one. After a 1♥ or 1♠ opening, a second-round jump by responder to 4♣ or 4♦ agrees opener's suit is trump and shows a control in the bid suit. See BLUE TEAM FOUR CLUBS-FOUR DIAMONDS CONVENTION.

If opener has a maximum opening, usually 14-16 points, he may make a jump rebid or reverse. Concentration of points in the bid suits favors the selection of a strong rebid.

1NT opening shows a balanced hand, either 13-15 points with a club suit and exactly three cards in each major, or 16-17 points. Minor-suit responses are artificial. 2♣ normally shows 8-11 points and requests opener conventionally to rebid 2♠ with the strong notrump, or make some other two-level bid to describe the strength and club length of the 13-15 notrump. After a 2♠ rebid, 2 NT by responder asks for majors; minor-suit rebids are non-forcing. After any other rebid by opener, responder's rebids are mostly non-forcing, though encouraging in some cases.

A 2♦ response shows a minimum of 12 points and is forcing to game. With a strong notrump, opener bids a four-card major or bids 3♣ with no major, after which 3♦ by responder inquires about the minors. With a weak notrump, opener rebids 2 NT, after which 3♦ by responder requests opener to describe his strength and number of clubs in four steps.

Jump responses to the three-level show six-card suits

headed by two of the top three honors with 6-7 points. Jump responses of 4♣ and 4♦ are transfers to 4♥ and 4♠ respectively.

2♣ opening shows a good club suit of at least five cards and 12-16 points. If a second suit is held, opener will usually have a minimum of 15. A response of 2♦ is artificial and asks opener to bid a secondary suit. If he does not have one, he rebids either 2 NT with stoppers in two of the outside suits, or 3♣ with a stopper in only one outside suit. 3♦ by responder then requests opener to pinpoint his stoppers. Other two-level responses are natural and non-forcing. Jump responses are forcing to game. 2♦ opening shows a powerful three-suited hand (4-4-4-1) with 17-24 points. See BLUE TEAM TWO DIAMONDS. 2♥ and 2♠ openings are WEAK TWO-BIDS with a normal range of 8-11. 2 NT is the only forcing response.

3♣ opening is a natural preempt and shows a minimum of seven playing tricks, including one outside the club suit.

GAMBLING 3 NT.

Other opening bids are standard.

Blackwood is used on the first and second rounds of bidding, or in later rounds if a jump bid. Responses are ROMAN BLACKWOOD style, with 5♣ showing one ace or four, and 5♦ showing none or three. In other situations 4 NT is a natural slam invitation. Partner can cooperate by showing an additional feature. He may pass, but more often signs off in the agreed suit. See DECLARATIVE INTERROGATIVE FOUR NOTRUMP.

Defensive bidding is normal, but overcalls are made freely, especially at the one-level. Jump overcalls are intermediate. In response to takeout double, the cheapest bid may be a HERBERT NEGATIVE.

BLUE TEAM FOUR CLUB-FOUR DIAMOND CONVENTION.

A delayed game raise used in the BLUE TEAM CLUB system to describe responder's minor suit controls. When opener bids and rebids a major suit or opens a major suit and rebids in notrump and responder has excellent support for opener's suit, he responds as follows:

(1) 2♣ followed by 4♣ shows first- or second-round control of clubs and denies first- or second-round control of diamonds;

(2) 2♦ followed by 4♦ shows first- or second-round control of diamonds and denies first- or second-round control of clubs;

(3) 2♣ followed by 4♦ shows either first-round control of both clubs and diamonds or second-round control of both suits;

(4) 2♦ followed by 4♣ shows first-round control of one minor and second-round control of the other.

See also NEAPOLITAN FOUR DIAMONDS CONVENTION.

BLUE TEAM TWO DIAMONDS.

An opening bid showing a hand worth 17-24 high-card points, with 4-4-4-1 distribution.

An integral part of the BLUE TEAM CLUB system, this convention can also be used with standard methods. Responses fall into one of four categories:

(1) *Immediate sign-off:* with a very weak hand (about 0-5 points) and three or more spades, responder bids 2♠. Opener will normally pass unless he has either a singleton spade or a maximum hand with four spades. With a

singleton spade, opener rebids 2 NT, allowing responder to select one of the other three suits.

(2) *Discouraging response with long broken suit:* with a hand worth 5-6 points containing a broken six-card suit, responder bids three of his suit. If that suit is opener's singleton he will pass unless he has a maximum. If opener has four cards in responder's suit he may either bid game or try for slam by cuebidding his singleton. After the cuebid, responder bids in steps to show whether he has the ace or king of his suit, and whether or not he has any singleton.

(3) *Encouraging response with long good suit:* with a hand worth about 6-7 points containing a six-card suit headed by any three honors or two of the top three honors, responder bids 2 NT. This bid asks opener to bid the suit below his singleton. At his next turn responder bids his suit (or bids 3 NT if his suit is clubs and opener has shown a singleton club by rebidding 3♠). If opener's singleton is in responder's long suit, opener may pass with a minimum, or may bid game in notrump or in responder's suit with a maximum. If opener has four cards in responder's suit the partnership is committed to game, and opener may try for slam by cuebidding. Responder then cuebids a singleton if he has one.

(4) *Relay response:* with a hand unsuitable for any of the above responses, responder bids 2♥, an artificial bid that asks opener for information. With a minor suit singleton and/or a maximum (21-24), opener bids the denomination below his singleton; rebids of 2 NT and 3♣ show minimum hands and rebids of 3♦ through 3 NT show maximums. If opener has instead a minimum (17-20) and a major suit singleton, he rebids 2♠; responder then rebids 2 NT asking opener to bid 3♣ with a singleton heart, 3♦ with a singleton spade and 17-18 HCP, or 3♥ with a singleton spade and 19-20. Responder may then cuebid opener's known singleton to ask about various features of opener's hand such as point count, controls, and queens.

BLUFF. A bid or play made with deceptive intent. See PSYCHIC BID and DECEPTIVE PLAY.

BLUFF FINESSE. See CHINESE FINESSE.

BOARD. (1) A duplicate board. (2) The table on which the cards are played. (3) The dummy's hand, so called because it lies on the table. See LAWS OF DUPLICATE (Law #2).

BOARD, DUPLICATE. An oblong or square board used in various forms of duplicate bridge, slotted with four sections, each deep enough to hold one quarter of a standard deck of playing cards.

The face, or top, of each board has listings appropriate to the board's use, as follows: numbered so that it can be quickly distinguished from companion boards of the same set, one slot marked to indicate the dealer, vulnerability conditions marked both in the slot itself (usually in red) and on the face of the board.

Sometimes the cards to be placed in the slots are shuffled by the players and dealt at the beginning of each contest, but for larger tournaments organizers usually obtain preshuffled or machine-prepared hands to be put into play instead of player-dealt hands.

As adapted for use in contract bridge, the boards are usually packed in sets of 32 or 36 in a carrying case designed for them. Dealer and vulnerability follow a standardized pattern, with North dealing the first board, East the second, South the third, and West the fourth with the same rotation repeated for every subsequent set of four. Vulnerability is arranged in a 16-board pattern as follows:

Board	1	2	3	4	5	6	7	8
Dealer	N	E	S	W	N	E	S	W
Vulnerability	No	N-S	E-W	Both	N-S	E-W	Both	No

Board	9	10	11	12	13	14	15	16
Dealer	N	E	S	W	N	E	S	W
Vulnerability	E-W	Both	No	N-S	Both	No	N-S	E-W

Thus every player deals in each of the four possible vulnerability situations. George Beynon noted that this pattern can be put into a magic square, in which N means N-S vulnerable; E, E-W; B means Both; and O for no vulnerability thus:

O N E B

N E B O

E B O N

B O N E

The first duplicate boards (then called trays) were devised by Cassius M. Paine and J. L. Sebring in 1891. They were square boards, called Kalamazoo after the company that manufactured them. The first oblong boards were produced by William McKenney in 1928 using paper, and the first metal boards were manufactured in 1931 by F. Dudley Courtenay. The first plastic boards were used by the ACBL at the North American Championships in Salt Lake City in 1976. The ACBL now uses plastic boards exclusively.

Square and circular boards are also used, and paper, cardboard, wood, and plastic are alternative materials. Wallets made of plastic and foldable when not in use are popular in Europe and South America.

BOARD OF DIRECTORS OF THE ACBL. The body that manages and controls the business and activities of the ACBL. The Board is composed of one director elected by each DISTRICT for a three-year term. The terms of the directors are staggered, with approximately one-third of the directors being elected each year. Each year the Board of Directors elects from among incumbent members a president of the ACBL to serve for one year. Usually the Board meets three times a year, usually just before the Spring, Summer and Fall NABCs.

BOARD OF GOVERNORS OF THE ACBL. A body that has the power to make recommendations to the BOARD OF DIRECTORS OF THE ACBL, to propose amendments to the BYLAWS OF THE ACBL and to receive reports from and to ratify certain actions taken by that Board. The Board of Governors is composed of five members from each DISTRICT and members-at-large. Two of the five representatives from each District are designated First Alternate Director and Second Alternate Director from such District during their terms of office. The members-at-large, who have full voting rights, consist of past presidents of the ACBL and past chairmen of the Board of Governors. They are permanent members of the Board of Governors. Three regular meetings a year are held, usually during the North American Bridge Championships.

BOARD-A-MATCH. A method of playing multiple team matches in which each team plays against a variety of opponents and each board has exactly the value of 1 point. Although this method used to be prevalent in North America, it has been replaced in large part by INTERNATIONAL MATCHPOINTS with SWISS MOVEMENT pairing.

The movement is so arranged that if the North-South pair of a given team plays a board against the East-West pair of an opposing team, the East-West pair of the given team plays the same board against the North-South pair of the same opposing team. If the total of a team's North-South and East-West scores on the same board is positive, that team receives 1 point. If it is negative, the team receives 0 points. If the total is exactly zero (that is, if both teams achieve the same score), both teams receive point.

Some National events are still played in this fashion: the REISINGER TEAMS; the OPEN BOARD-A-MATCH TEAMS; the WOMEN'S TEAMS; and the MASTER MIXED TEAMS. It is occasionally scheduled at the regional and sectional levels.

Top-flight players claim board-a-match is the toughest type of bridge event, requiring intense concentration for every card played. The event's popularity diminished over the years when it became apparent that the skill involved is so high that the same teams were winning almost all the time.

Board-a-match is virtually unknown in Europe, where it is sometimes termed "point-a-board." For movements employed see AMERICAN WHIST; NEW ENGLAND RELAY; PATTON.

BODY. A term used to describe a hand with useful intermediate cards such as 10s, 9s, and 8s. Some authorities advocate counting a 10 as half a point, sometimes only for notrump purposes. The 10 is of greatest value in combination with one or two higher honors, such as K-10-x, Q-10-x, or K-Q-10. It has least value when isolated (10-x-x) or in a solid suit (A-K-Q-J-10). Similarly a 9 may be valuable in combination (Q-10-9) but almost worthless in isolation.

Body may be a decisive factor in making a bidding decision:

♠ K 10 5 4

♥ A Q 9

♦ Q 10 9

♣ K J 8

This hand counts 15 points in high cards, but the intermediate cards make it a "good" 15, and most experts would treat it as a 16-point hand and open with a standard 16-18 notrump.

Body is a factor to consider when making BORDERLINE OPENING BIDS. As the bidding proceeds, a player can often revalue his intermediate cards. A holding of 10-9-x is certainly worthless if the bidding marks partner with a singleton or a void, and very probably worthless opposite a doubleton. But there is a good chance that the 10-9 will be valuable opposite a probable three card suit: partner may have something like A-J-x, K-J-x, or Q-8-x.

BOLIVIAN BRIDGE ASSOCIATION. (Asociacion Boliviana de Bridge)

The Association was founded in 1968, has 98 members in three clubs, and conducts five national championships. It hosted the 40th South American Championships in Santa Cruz de la Sierra. Its players have won two South American Pairs titles.

Officers 1992:
President: Solange Bozzo de Bottega
Secretary: Patrizia Milone Di Fabio
            Casilla 2918,
            Cochabamba Bolivia
            Tel. 42926

BOLS BRIDGE TIPS. A series of annual contests invented by the late Herman Filarski and subsidized by the Bols Company of The Netherlands. Players of international stature submitted bridge tips for publication in periodicals all over the world. A panel of judges voted each year to decide the winner. The tips were distributed to members of the INTERNATIONAL BRIDGE PRESS ASSOCIATION and became a popular feature in most bridge magazines and many newspaper columns worldwide. The articles appeared in 19 languages. Later the tips were gathered together, expanded and made into a book, Bridge Tips by World Masters, with Terence Reese as editor.

The contest was suspended from 1978 to 1986. Winners:

1974-5	Terence Reese
1975-6	Jean Besse
1976-7	Jeff Rubens
1987	Steen Moller
1988	Michael Lawrence
1989	Zia Mahmood
1990	Gabriel Chagas
1991	Chip Martel
1992	Eric Crowhurst
1993	Larry Cohen

BOLS BRILLIANCY AWARDS. Outstanding writeups of spectacular plays. The Bols Company of The Netherlands offers prizes annually to the writers who chronicle the most brilliant plays and to the players who perform the brilliancies. Journalists from all over the world compete, and winners are chosen by an international panel of experts.

The contest was organized by the International Bridge Press Association. The winners were:

1976	Ron Klinger
1977	Anders Morath
1978	Gilles Cohen
1979	Dano de Falco
1980	Dick Cummings
1981	John Collings
1982	Jean Besse
1983	Marvin Rosenblatt
1984	Jeff Rothstein
1985	Anders Brunzell
1986	Ed Manfield

BONNEY'S SQUEEZE. A triple squeeze against one opponent combined with a simple squeeze against the other. Analyzed by Norman Bonney of Boston.

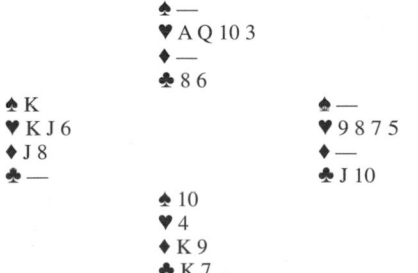

South leads the ♦K on which he throws a club from dummy. East is squeezed and must discard a heart. Now the lead of the ♦K squeezes West in three suits. At the start South has all but two of the remaining tricks, but he manages to win all six by means of the squeeze.

BONUS. A term used in all types of bridge to describe various premiums given under the scoring rules to sides or partnerships who accomplish specified aims.

In rubber bridge, bonuses are awarded for the winning of the rubber by scoring two games before the opponents have scored two games. A bonus of 700 points is credited to the side winning a two-game rubber before the opponents have won even one game. If the opponents have won a game, the bonus becomes 500 points. A bonus of 50 points is paid any side scoring a successful doubled contract, and similarly 100 for making a redoubled contract. A bonus is scored above the scoring line for a side which, in the given hand, has held honors in trump, or all the aces in one hand at notrump. This bonus is either 100 or 150 points. (See HONORS.) Bonus scores are given to sides who successfully bid and make any slam contract. (See SLAM.) If a rubber of bridge has to be terminated before its regular conclusion, a bonus of 300 points is given to a side that is a game ahead, and a partscore earns a 100-point bonus.

In CHICAGO bridge, bonuses can occur on each of the four hands, inasmuch as in this type of contest each deal is really almost a separate game of itself. A non-vulnerable side scoring a game in Chicago is credited with 300 points immediately, and a vulnerable side, 500. Slam bonuses are the same as in rubber bridge, and honors are likewise scored. A partial score achieved on the fourth or final deal, however, acquires an extra bonus of 100 points. This bonus, however, is awarded only for partials actually acquired on the last deal — there is no premium for a partial remaining open at the conclusion of a four-deal chukker.

In duplicate bridge, a bonus is awarded for the making of any partial score (a below-game score) on a given deal. The bonus is 50 points. The regular slam premiums apply in duplicate scoring as explained above, but there are no bonuses for honors, except in total-point scoring. In duplicate, the regular Chicago bonuses for games bid and made apply, e.g., 300 for making a non-vulnerable game and 500 for making a vulnerable game.

BOOK. The tricks won by a side which have no value in the score; a whist term with little significance at contract bridge. For the declarer, the first six tricks taken constitute his book; for the adversaries, the amount of the declarer's bid subtracted from seven, or the maximum number of tricks the adversaries may take without defeating declarer's contract. The origin of the term apparently lies in the old practice of forming the first six tricks into a "book" by placing them all in one stack.

BOOK GAME. Style of a player who is acquainted with the situations described in the books about bridge, and rigorously follows this pattern of bidding and play. It features theoretical knowledge, but implies lack of skill from practice and lack of versatility.

BOOK PLAYER. A player who plays a BOOK GAME. "The book player is a safe partner, but is not very dangerous as an adversary." (A. W. Drayton: *Art of Practical*

Whist).

BOOKS. See BIBLIOGRAPHY.

BORDERLINE OPENING BIDS. When the decision seems to be close between opening the bidding with one of a suit and passing, a number of considerations may influence a good player.

Position at the table.

The third player can open relatively freely, with a point or two fewer than normally required. This may inconvenience the fourth player, who is likely to have the best hand at the table. The third player can open light because there is no necessity to rebid. Indeed, to do so would suggest a sound opening; hence, a desirable feature of a light opening is the ability to pass any response in comfort. A light opening should still contain acceptable defensive values. It should be based on a good suit, since lead direction is a principal reason to risk such an opening.

Vulnerability.

This may sway a borderline decision, especially at matchpoints. With a 5-3-3-2 hand, for example, when the five-card suit is weak, there is a distinct possibility of playing a part-score down two to save an opposing part-score. The vulnerability would then make the difference between a good score and a bad one.

Quality and location of honors.

In general, a hand with honors in its long suits is well placed in attack, while a hand with honors in its short suits is more effective in defense. This factor is allowed for to some extent in most point-count systems, which devalue singleton kings, queens, and jacks, and doubleton queens and jacks.

Consider the following two hands:

(a)	(b)
♠ 9 4 3	♠ A J 4
♥ A J 7 5 3	♥ J 7 5 3 2
♦ A Q 5 4	♦ J 5 4 3
♣ 3	♣ A

The distribution and point-count are the same, but hand (a) has a sound opening bid, and hand (b) does not — although it could have an acceptable opening bid in some situations. The difference lies in the location of the honor cards. Hands with supporting honors are generally stronger than hands with scattered honors.

(a)	(b)
♠ A 8 6 4	♠ A K 5 3
♥ K 5 3	♥ 6 4 2
♦ K 4	♦ 8 5
♣ Q 7 4 2	♣ K Q 4 2

More players would open hand (b) than hand (a).

Hands that contain PRIMARY HONORS (aces and kings) are more attractive to open than hands filled with queens and jacks. Aces and kings will win tricks on defense if the opponents compete and obtain the contract. See PRIMARY HONORS and SECONDARY HONORS.

Rebid prospects.

The ease or difficulty of the rebid will often be a determining factor.

♠ 6
♥ A Q J
♦ K 9 4 2
♣ Q 8 6 4 2

If this hand is opened 1♣, the likely 1♠ response leaves opener with no attractive rebid; nor it is desirable to open

1♦ and rebid 2♣ with minimum values and weak suits. An original pass avoids these difficulties.

Majors or minors.

The possession of a major suit, and particularly spades, favors an opening bid. An opening bid in a major has some obstructive value, and the prospects of outbidding the opponents and of scoring a game are slightly improved.

Playing tricks and body.

The prospect of winning tricks, regardless of how many high-card points are held, is a logical argument for opening the bidding. In 1984, *The Bridge World* magazine polled experts on their standards for opening bids. Ninety percent said they would open:

♠ 8 6
♥ 7
♦ A Q 4 2
♣ A J 10 8 4 2

as dealer, neither vulnerable. Fifty-one percent would open:

♠ 8 6
♥ 7
♣ A J 10 3
♣ A J 10 8 4 2

However, experts also pay attention to body, or the presence of intermediate cards. Only 16 percent would open:

♠ 8 6
♥ 7
♦ A J 8 3
♣ A J 8 7 4 2

Presumably, for the reasons given earlier, more experts would open if the long suits were spades and hearts.

Pearson point count

This is a method used by many players to determine whether or not to open a borderline hand in fourth position. The count works this way: the number of high-card points is added to the number of spades. If the total is 15 or more, the recommendation is to open the bidding. The spade suit often is the key when bidding for pluses on partials.

BOREL. A powerful computer program designed by John Lowenthal. It generates deals which can be specified in any desired way. This permits hands to be printed out for partnership practice in a given area. As an example, the program could give South a 15-17 point notrump opening facing a hand with at least five spades and at least 6 points. It is also used by theorists for simulations to test the desirability of a particular bidding action, or to compare opening lead choices in a given situation. See BASE III.

BOSTON CHESS CLUB. This, club, founded in 1857 in Boston MA, was the oldest club devoted to games in the United States. In 1926, bridge-playing replaced chess as the chief activity at the club. In modern times contract was played almost exclusively. When the club encountered severe difficulties in 1981 due to a split over acceptance of a player who once had been expelled from ACBL for cheating, the interests in the club were sold to the Cavendish Club in Brookline MA.

BOTSWANA BRIDGE FEDERATION. Founded 1990. Officers 1993:
  Chairman: Dr. Justice Simon Moeti
  Secretary: Mrs. J.P. Crowe

P.O. Box 802, Gaborone Botswana
Tel. 267 371 381
Fax 267 352 490

BOTTOM. In tournament play, the lowest score on a particular hand in the group in direct competition. It is extended, in conversation, to indicate an excruciatingly bad result.

BOUGHT. See BUY.

BOX A CARD. To place a hand in a duplicate board with a card, usually not the top card, turned face up.

BRACKETED KNOCKOUTS. A method of conducting knockout events for a large number of teams with a limited number of sessions for matches available. The teams are divided into groups, usually of 8, 16 or 32, and each group competes in a separate event with its own set of winners. The criterion for deciding which teams go into which brackets usually is masterpoints.

BRAZILIAN BRIDGE CONFEDERATION (CONFEDERAÇAO BRASILEIRA DE BRIDGE). the Confederation was founded in 1955, joining the bridge leagues of seven states. By 1992 it had a membership of 4200. Brazilian players have won the Bermuda Bowl, the World Teams, and the World Pairs twice. They have won the South American Teams 21 times and the South American Women's Teams 15 times.
Officers 1992:
President: Ernesto D'Orsi
Avenida Brigadeiro Faria Lima 1237 #101
01451 Sao Paulo S.P. Brazil.
Phone 55-11 212 5355
Fax 55-11 814 1518

BREAK. The distribution of the outstanding cards in a suit in a manner favorable to the declarer. This may imply that a suit was divided evenly or nearly so, or that an adversely held honor was positioned so that it did not develop into a winning trick. The term "break" is also used to indicate the actual distribution of the cards outstanding in the suit; or with the adjective "bad" to indicate unfavorable distribution from the declarer's standpoint.

In most contexts, "split" may be used as a synonym for "break," both as a noun and a verb: "the suit split (or broke) badly (or well)." "There was a bad split (or break) in spades." For expectations as to how a suit will break, see MATHEMATICAL TABLES 4, 4A.

BREAKAGE. A rubber bridge term for rounding off the score to the nearest 100 points.

BREAKING TIES. The breaking of ties in duplicate contests, when it is a question of the winner, is done for the purpose of awarding of trophies when it is not feasible to award duplicates to the tying pairs or teams. Masterpoint awards in ACBL tournaments are awarded equally to each tying group, the amount being one-half the sum of the awards for first and second places. The main occasion for breaking of ties during the course of the competition is to determine which of two or more pairs, tied for the last qualifying position or positions, is entered into the final session. In either case, for pair events, the method

is similar. All boards played by all tying groups are considered, and 1 point is awarded for an above average score and ° point for an average score if the board or boards were not played in direct comparison. If the tying pairs are in direct comparison on any board, 1 point is awarded to the pair with the better matchpoint result on that board, ° point if their matchpoint result is a tie. In team events, the result of the match between the two tying teams is used with Board-a-Match scoring. In head-to-head team competition, such as knockout events, additional boards are played. In Swiss Teams, ties usually are broken by means of Swiss Points. The total of scores of all opponents are tallied for the tied teams, and the winner is the team with the highest total. Sometimes only matches played in the second half of the event are used to compute Swiss Points. The method of breaking ties should be approved by the Sponsoring Organization or announced in the Conditions of Contest, before being used.

Ties are now much rarer in ACBL events. Until 1992, two pairs were considered tied if the difference in score was less than half a matchpoint; two teams in board-a-match events were considered tied if the difference in score was less than a quarter of a matchpoint. The Board of Directors passed a regulation changing this so that only an exact tie is considered a tie in board-a-match team events. In pair events pairs are not considered to be tied unless the difference between their scores is less than .01 matchpoints. The same is true in individual events.

BRIDGE. A partnership game of cards derived from WHIST and played by four persons. The term can refer to three distinct games, which are listed under BRIDGE WHIST, AUCTION BRIDGE, and CONTRACT.

All these games have been referred to simply as *bridge* during their periods of dominance, and the term "bridge whist" was not used when the game was in vogue (1894-1904). It was coined subsequently to distinguish the game from its successors.

The earliest printed mention of *bridge* appears to be in a pamphlet published in 1886 entitled "Biritch, or Russian Whist." Although there is no certainty that the game is Russian, the fact that it was christened "Russian Whist" gave weight to the idea that it originated in Russia. It does, as a matter of fact, bear a close resemblance to Vint, Preference, and similar games; and Vint certainly is of Russian origin. See also BIRITCH; HISTORY OF BRIDGE.

BRIDGE FOR BEGINNERS. A special form of duplicate for players with little playing experience and no experience with duplicate. The play is informal, with instructors ready to offer advice at all times.

BRIDGE BATTLE OF THE CENTURY. See CULBERTSON-LENZ MATCH.

BRIDGE BUFFS' BULLETIN. A bulletin published quarterly since 1973 by Bill Sachen in the interests of bridge book collectors. New and old books and periodicals are reviewed, master lists of all known bridge and whist books have been published, and subscribers can publicize lists of books they wish to purchase or sell. See BIBLIOGRAPHY.

BRIDGE COLUMNS. Ever since the game of auction bridge became popular, newspapers and periodicals have had columns in which bridge is featured. These columns are quite varied, frequently containing local bridge news including results of local duplicate contests, anecdotes, interesting results; other columns are of a didactic nature such as quizzes and problems; while others feature outstanding and unusual bridge hands with explanations of bidding and play and sidelights on the personalities involved. Some are distributed to newspapers through national syndicates, appearing in hundreds of papers; others are produced locally for one, two or three papers.

The popularity of bridge columns is attested to by the fact that very few papers have ever dropped one permanently because every such attempt met with violent protest from the readers of the paper.

BRIDGE D'ITALIA. A beautifully produced magazine published by the Italian Bridge Federation. Edited by Riccardo Vandoni, earlier by Guido Barbone and Dino Mazza. Address: Via Orti 3, 20122 Milan Italy.

BRIDGE EDUCATION PROGRAM. ACBL established a Bridge Education Program in 1986. The goal of this new program was ultimately to ensure the future of the organization. Faced with an aging membership and a general decline in the popularity of bridge, the ACBL designed the Bridge Education Program (1) to teach new people to play the game, and (2) to lead these new players to ACBL membership.

ACBL's Bridge Education Program has grown into a strong arm of the organization. It supports many successful programs including: (1) The development of four textbooks and teacher manuals which compose the ACBL TEACHING SERIES and produce considerable income for the ACBL through sales and foreign translations; (2) a bridge teaching program for schools (SBLS - School Bridge Lesson Series), administered by ACBL and funded by the ACBL EDUCATIONAL FOUNDATION, which led to the development of the ACBL Junior Program and many new young ACBL members; (3) new player membership programs such as the Reduced Price Membership program which make ACBL membership meaningful for the new player.

BRIDGE FEDERATION. NCBOs with names starting in this way are listed under the country name.

BRIDGE FEDERATION OF ASIA AND THE MIDDLE EAST (BFAME). This Federation was founded in 1979 with 5 NCBOs by Mazhar Jafri of Pakistan, who became its Secretary, Treasurer and WBF Delegate, and by Prem Chandra Goenka of India, who became president. Zonal championships have been staged biennially since 1981. (For results, see Appendix.) The best zonal results in World Championships were by Pakistan, which finished second in the Bermuda Bowl in 1981 and second in the Rosenblum Cup in 1986. In 1992 the zone had 15 members: Bangladesh, India, Nepal, Pakistan and Sri Lanka from South Asia; Egypt, Jordan, Kuwait and Saudi Arabia from the Middle East; Botswana, Kenya, Mauritius, Reunion, Tanzania and Tunisia from Africa and the Indian Ocean.
Officers 1992:
 President: Prem Chandra Goenka
 Secretary: Mazhar Jafri
   Shaukat Law Associates
   217-218 Central Hotel Annexe
   Abdullah Haroon Road, Karachi.

BRIDGE GOLF. See GOLF.

BRIDGE HISTORY. See HISTORY OF BRIDGE.

BRIDGE IN PRISON CAMPS. The absorbing character of duplicate bridge to such an extent that one is unaware of the passage of time has made it an ideal activity for prisoners of war confined in military prison camps.

The Hanoi Duplicate Club. When Lt. Col. William Means was returned to the U.S. from Vietnam, he gave an extraordinary account of how he and the prisoners on his cellblock were able to conquer boredom and other afflictions — at least part of the time — with a duplicate bridge game.

It was six years and seven months from the time his plane was shot down in July 1966 until his release with the first contingent of freed POWs in February 1973. During the last three years of that time, Means was in charge of entertainment for his cell block. He had been part of a group that played party bridge at Shaw Air Force Base in Sumter SC in 1963 and had a brief exposure to duplicate. In prison in Hanoi, one of his fellow prisoners had experienced duplicate and was able to help in setting up and scoring the games.

There were only five decks of cards. There were no duplicate boards, no traveling score sheets, no table cards, no tables. So the same five decks of cards were played at each table, then shuffled and played over again. Duplicate boards were porcelain covered metal plates that often served as the duplicate board and the traveling score. When there were no pencils for scoring on the plates, toilet paper was used for score sheets with scores entered by use of cotton-tipped bamboo sticks dipped in homemade ink. For tables they used their POW blankets, folded into the shape of a table. The hands, each wrapped with a scrap of paper showing its compass position, were stacked atop an upside down plate for passing from one "table" to another.

These duplicate contests were held regularly on Wednesday and Sunday nights and pairs stayed intact for one month. Session scores for each pair were accumulated and at the end of a month, North-South and East-West winners were declared. In lieu of masterpoints, the players put up candy and cigarettes from their personal ration and these were awarded the winners. At the beginning of a new month partners were redrawn and a fresh series of games began.

Duplicate games of from three to six tables were a regular semi-weekly feature the last three years before the POWs were released. Ground rules were established and administered according to bridge laws as they were remembered from the old days at Shaw, with Col. Means either directing the games himself or appointing a substitute.

Hostages played bridge too. While American hostages were being held in Iran (Nov. 4, 1979-Jan. 20, 1981) many of them learned to play bridge to help pass the time. One hostage in solitary confinement dealt out thousands of hands and got quite upset because East-West were getting most of the high cards — he identified with North-South.

BRIDGE IN PRISONS. In 1972, recognizing that bridge is such an absorbing and constructive activity that it might assist in the rehabilitation of prisoners, the ACBL Board of Directors and the ACBL Charity Foundation instituted a policy of encouraging the playing of duplicate bridge in penal institutions.

The ACBL and various member units have donated cards, boards, bridge books, and other instructional materials to prison duplicate clubs. In 1973 the ACBL Charity Foundation made a $5,000 contribution to the Foundation for the Advancement of Inmate Rehabilitation and Recreation. The American Bridge Teachers' Association has assisted the program by waiving its initiation fees and dues for prison inmates who qualify as bridge teachers and pass the ABTA examination. Local clubs have encouraged their players to participate in prison duplicate games. By early 1982 there were some two dozen duplicate clubs in penal institutions.

It is perhaps fitting that bridge be encouraged in prisons since the idea of playing with one hand exposed as the dummy may have originated in Newgate Prison, where whist was played in this manner as a three-handed game prior to 1820.

A remarkable account of bridgeplaying in Alcatraz was provided in 1992 by Morton Sobell of San Francisco, who was an inmate there from 1952 to 1958 as a result of his involvement in the Rosenberg espionage case.

"It was the only card game. We used a special deck of dominoes, rather than cards. They came in four colors to denote suits and the values were denoted by the number of dots: jack was 11 etc. And we had a wooden board with a ledge for holding the dominoes so that they could not be seen by others.

"Play was out in the small yard, behind the first and third base lines, so that on frequent occasions a softball would land in the middle of the table, which was a blanket-covered folding-leg bridge table cut down to about 20 inches in height. We sat on hassocks.

"With a population of 250 men it was not unusual to have 20 games going on weekends. It was a sight to behold: The men all bent over in their thin pea coats in the foggy drizzly cold, playing all weekend long, about five or six hours each day.

"Usually the men arranged the game Friday night for a 25,000 or 50,000 point series. Whoever reached the figure first won. The bets were usually the moth-eaten stale Wings cigarettes which were distributed, three packs a week to each of the men.

"I am not a card player, but for want of anything else to do I played some. What amazed me was that each night, on returning to the cellhouse, many of the men would replay each of the hands from memory, discussing the bidding and the play. These were men who had never played bridge until they came to the Rock, but obviously they had card-sense which I didn't.

"The bridge was not very sophisticated, and as I recall nobody engaged in any artificial bids. Nor was there any real intensity in the play. It was just something to pass the time." See TURGENEV.

BRIDGE JOURNAL, THE. A bimonthly magazine intended for the edification of and exchange of ideas by serious players, founded in 1963 by Paul Heitner and Jeff Rubens and aimed at improving technical and mechanical aspects of the game, especially at tournament level. Some of the regular features of this publication were a *Spotlight on Bidding* match between experts, a problem forum on bidding and play, and a *Systems Corner*. When Rubens became associate editor of *The Bridge World* in 1967, the *Journal* ceased independent publication and merged with *The Bridge World*. See BIBLIOGRAPHY.

BRIDGE MAGAZINE. An English monthly with an international reputation published in Leeds. It was founded in 1926 by A. E. Manning-Foster, and is therefore the oldest bridge periodical. Publication was suspended, however, during the war years, and in number of issues *Bridge Magazine* is therefore exceeded by *The Bridge World*. Ewart Kempson became the editor when publication was resumed in 1946, and continued in that capacity after the merger with the *British Bridge World* in 1964. After Kempson's death in 1966 Eric C. Milnes assumed the post of editor.

Phillip Alder was editor 1980-85 and Alan Hiron 1985-90. Glyn Liggins took over as editor in 1990. During Hiron's editorship the name was changed to *Bridge International*. "International" was dropped in 1990 and the original name was resumed in 1992. Address: London Road, Wheatley, Oxford, OX91YR England.

BRIDGE MAGAZINE IMP. Dutch magazine for the better players, founded in 1990 by Jan van Cleeff. 8 issues annually: PO Box 93326, 2509 AH The Hague, Netherlands.

BRIDGE MATHEMATICS. See MATHEMATICS OF BRIDGE.

BRIDGE-O-RAMA. A method of displaying bridge competition to a large audience. The technique was devised in Italy and first used in the 1958 Bermuda Bowl. The forerunner of this development was used in the Thirties when an electric display board was used in exhibitions in department stores. The features of Bridge-O-Rama include a large display board on which the hands can be placed in frames, so that the representations of the actual cards are lighted, along with devices for indicating the winning card, tricks won by declarer or defender, the contract, and other information. In addition to the display board there is a console, or bank of light switches, by which the lights of the display board are controlled. Explanations and comments on the bidding and play are provided by an expert panel.

The largest audience for a Bridge-O-Rama showing was the crowd of 1,500 that attended the finals of the 1964 Olympiad in the Hotel Americana in New York City. The size of the crowd made necessary the simultaneous vugraph screening of the hands for spectators too far away to see the Bridge-O-Rama board.

Because setting up the deals for Bridge-O-Rama slowed up the play and required a large staff, exhibitions since the 1971 Bermuda Bowl in Taiwan have been almost exclusively by means of vugraph. Usually the Vugraph show also features closed circuit television of the play in the open room, often with a camera focused on each of the players. See VUGRAPH.

BRIDGE OLYMPICS. See WORLD PAR CONTESTS and Appendix IV.

BRIDGE PLUS. A special form of duplicate play devised for students. It is patterned after the students' classroom experience. The games usually last two hours, allowing the students to play 10-14 hands. The games are supervised by accredited teachers.

BRIDGE TODAY. A major magazine, with six yearly issues, published in Ballston Lake N.Y. Matthew and Pamela Granovetter are founders, editors and publishers. Some of the world's best player-writers, including Zia, Marty Bergen, Alvin Roth, Mike Lawrence, Eddie Kantar and Chip Martel, are frequent contributors. Address: Granovetter Books, 3838 Catalina St., Los Alamitos CA 90720 USA.

BRIDGE TOURNAMENT FOR CLUBS IN COPENHAGEN. The world's oldest yearly bridge event, played every year since 1927. Invitations are issued to all clubs in Copenhagen, of any sort, including clubs promoting relations between countries, clubs of doctors, engineers, women's liberation, etc. Each year the tournament is played on the second Monday of each month from November through April.

BRIDGE WHIST. The game which succeeded WHIST in popularity until AUCTION BRIDGE became the vogue early in the twentieth century. Chief differences between bridge whist and whist are the manner of selection of the trump suit, the introduction of play at notrump, the exposure of the dummy hand, and the innovation of the double and redouble calls, which could continue indefinitely. This endless redoubling feature introduced the element of gambling for very high stakes into the staid game of whist, which caused a storm of disapproval. The *Whist Reference Book*, published in 1898, called doubling "the most objectionable feature of the game." Instead of the trump suit being selected by the turn of the last card dealt, the dealer or his partner has the privilege of naming the trump suit or notrump. It was a requirement of the game that the leader ask, "Partner, may I lead?" to which his partner, if he did not plan to double, was required to respond, "Pray do." The play then proceeded as in auction or contract bridge.

The scoring is different from whist, in which each trick counted only one point. In bridge whist, the four suits and notrump have varying values. Spades are the lowest of the suits in value, followed in ascending order by clubs, diamonds, hearts, and notrump. Honors, games, rubbers, and slams are also scored. The greatest exponent of the strategy and tactics of bridge whist was Joseph B. Elwell, who wrote many books on the subject, chief among them, *Advanced Bridge*, published in 1904.

Contemporary players and writers referred to the game simply as "bridge." As the shorter term was also used later to refer to auction bridge and contract bridge, card historians invented the term "bridge whist" to identify the original form of bridge.

BRIDGE WORLD, THE. The oldest *continuously* published magazine dealing with contract bridge, founded and first published by Ely Culbertson in October, 1929. Published monthly, it was a comparative success from the start, and such events as the Culbertson-Lenz Match of 1931-1932 and the Culbertson-Sims match later did much to further interest.

Culbertson, who held the post of editor-in-chief until September, 1943, founded the magazine with the idea of making it a widely popular publication, and for a short time it was placed on newsstand sale. However, this proved uneconomical. It soon became what it has remained — a magazine for better than average players and a sounding board for new and improved theories.

The magazine was the first to present such ideas as the Stayman Convention, the Roth-Stone and Kaplan-Sheinwold systems, Lavinthal suit-preference signals, Unusual Notrump bids, Key Card Blackwood, many modern uses of transfers and doubles, etc. The Master Solvers Club features a panel of experts who vote for and explain why they chose what they consider to be the correct bid in a monthly series of problems. This idea has been copied by bridge publications all over the world.

Publication was taken over from Culbertson in 1943 by Albert H. Morehead, who edited it in association with Richard L. Frey, Josephine Culbertson, Alphonse Moyse Jr. and others until 1946 when it was taken over by Moyse. Moyse ran it under the Culbertson aegis until the death of the Culbertsons — December 1955 and March 1956, when he became sole owner and editor.

In November 1963 the magazine was bought by the McCall Corporation, with Moyse retained as editor. When Moyse retired in 1966, McCall's divested itself of the magazine. Edgar Kaplan and Jeff Rubens became sole owners, with Kaplan assuming the role of editor and Rubens co-editor. Much of the material that Rubens had been publishing in *Bridge Journal* appeared in *The Bridge World*, including a highly popular series of bidding matches between expert partnerships.

The list of sometime editors and contributing editors includes many famous bridge writers — B. Jay Becker, Sam Fry Jr., Charles Goren, William Huske, Oswald Jacoby, Theodore Lightner, Walter Malowan, Geoffrey Mott-Smith, Alfred Sheinwold, Alexander Sobel, Alan Truscott, Bobby Wolff, Waldemar von Zedtwitz, Edwin Kantar, Eric Kokish, Kit Woolsey and others.

BRIDGE WORLD STANDARD. A consensus system developed in 1967 and periodically revised, most recently in 1993. It was based on the majority preferences of 125 leading experts and thousands of *Bridge World* readers. The methods used in the system were determined by polls: A clear expert preference determined the treatment, while close questions were decided by the readers' vote.

Because it is a consensus system, BWS is rarely used by regular partnerships. It is, however, valuable in forming casual partnerships. If both partners know the system, they need only discuss areas in which they wish to diverge from it.

Opening Bids and Responses

Minimum requirement with balanced hand: good 12.

1NT: good 15 to bad 18. Jacoby transfers (splinter rebids; game raise is slam try; 2♦ plus 2♠ forcing only one round); 2♠ shows minors; Texas transfers; Stayman (2♠ rebid invitational; 2♥ rebid weak; minor rebid forcing); Smolen; three of a minor invitational; Gerber.

2NT: good 20 to bad 22 (small doubleton acceptable). Jacoby transfers; 3♠ shows minors; Texas transfers; Gerber; High Gerber.

2♣ artificial, strong: Natural responses (positive response requires good suit); 2♦ neutral; second negative = cheaper minor to 3♦.

Preempts: 2NT (asks for feature if maximum and new-suit responses forcing). Weak "gambling" three-bids; new-suit response to game-level opening asking bid (step responses).

3 NT: gambling (little outside strength); 4♦ response artificial.

Five-card majors in first and second position: 1NT response forcing; two-over-one promises rebid; limit jump raises (four trumps; cheapest rebid asks shortness); 2NT strong raise (asks shortness); 3NT natural, 16-17; passed hand responses: 1NT 6-12, 2♣ a strong raise, 3♣ natural.

Responses to minor-suit openings: Single raise strong, 10 pts. up, denies major; jump raise weak; 1NT 8-10 after 1♣ , 6-10 after 1♦; 2NT natural, game force: up the line may be ignored with moderate hand; 2♣ response to 1♦ does not promises a rebid after 2♦.

Partnership Bidding

Splinter raises: Double-jump shift responses; single jump in fourth suit if one level above a reverse; single jump in third suit if four level, or reverse; double jump in fourth suit; four of opener's minor after new-suit rebid; jump-shift by 2♦ responder to 2♣; new-suit jump after single major raise; double new-suit jump after 1NT response.

Slam methods: Roman Key-Card Blackwood with trump-queen ask; DOPI; 5NT (2 keys) or higher response with void; 5NT response invites seven, asks king cue-bidding. Cheapest-weakest responses to grand-slam force. Gerber after 1NT or 2NT opening or rebid. Picture jumps in forcing situations.

Other methods: Fourth-suit bidding: non-forcing by passed hand unless reverse; 1♠ may be weak; promises another bid at two-level; game force if reverse or at three-level. Third-suit bidding (e.g. 1♣-1♦-2♣-2♥); game force if reverse or at three-level, otherwise does not promise rebid. Opener's suit-over-suit reverse promises rebid; responder's cheaper of 2NT and fourth suit neutral. All non-jump-shift secondary jumps by one-over-one responder invitational. Opener's jump rebid to four of original minor is strong raise. Unbid minor forcing and artificial after 1NT rebid, requests support. 3♣ artificial, may be prelude to sign-off, after 2NT jump by opener. Reraise to three of major preemptive.

Competitive Bidding

Negative doubles: After suit opening, through 3♠ (including opener's suit); after 1NT opening, at the three level, unlimited; suggests length in unbid major: of 1♥ shows 4♠; of 1♠ after minor opening shows four or more hearts. Repeat same-suit double by negative doubler for takeout.

Weak jump responses after overcall of minor opening. Over overcall: jump raise preemptive, cue-bid is at least limit raise, jump cue-bid is splinter. Over two-suited overcalls: cheapest cue = raise; next cue = unbid suit; unbid suit non-forcing. Over minor Michaels: unbid suit non-forcing; major suit shows stopper. Over major Michaels: cue-bid in enemy major is limit raise or better; new suit forcing. Support doubles and redoubles when a raise to two is available, except 1♣ -pass-1♦-1♠ -double shows hearts.

Over a double of partner's suit bid: new suit forcing at the one level only; jump shift nonforcing; 2NT limit raise or better; double jump in new suit splinter.

Lebensohl after two-level overcalls of 1NT. Jump cue-bid by opener is splinter raise. Pass and pull strong in forcing situation.

Defensive Bidding

Michaels cue-bids (in minor: majors; in major: other major plus unspecified minor) in direct position over suit one-bids and over 1NT response; weak or quite strong.

Direct jump cue-bid natural over minor, asks stopper over major. Takeout doubles of preemptive openings through 4♥; otherwise for penalty. Maximal overcall

double of raised suit. Reopenings: 1NT 10-14; 2 NT 18-19. In fourth seat over a response: 1NT and cuebids natural. After 1NT overcall: 2♣ Stayman; jumps invitational. Double of free new-suit bid by responder shows fourth suit plus tolerance.

Cappelletti (Hamilton) over 1NT (all situations). Direct 2NT unusual for lower unbid suits; weak or quite strong. Take-out doubles may be light with shape; new-suit rebid very strong. Preemptive jump overcalls and jump raises of overcalls. Responsive and extended responsive doubles after takeout doubles, at the two level after an overcall, after a preempt. Cue-bid by advancer forcing until a suit is bid twice, or game. Lebensohl after double of weak two-bid, either position by unpassed hand, and following 1NT overcall.

Opening Leads

Against suit contracts: third from even: low from odd. All other leads old-fashioned.

BRIDGE WORLD TEAM. A name applied to several teams in the early Thirties whose members were particularly associated with *The Bridge World*. The most famous of these teams comprised Ely and Josephine Culbertson, Waldemar von Zedtwitz, and Theodore Lightner. Their successes included the VANDERBILT CUP of 1930 and the first of the ANGLO-AMERICAN MATCHES.

BRIDGERAMA. The European term for BRIDGE-O-RAMA.

BRIDGETTE. A bridge game for two players invented by Prince Joli Kansil (the former Joel D. Gaines), with the assistance of Waldemar von Zedtwitz. It is played with a 55-card deck — the standard pack plus three extra cards called *colons*. The colons are used in the play to force the opponent to discontinue the suit he is leading. In an advanced version of Bridgette, *cuebids* are used to elicit specific information about the opponent's distribution.

BRILLIANCY. Exceptional play or defense that qualifies the player for honor awards. See BOLS BRILLIANCY AWARDS.

BRING IN. To establish a suit and make effective use of the established winners. The ability to bring in a suit may be affected by considerations of ENTRIES, TEMPO, CONTROLS, or DUCKING, or by the SUIT COMBINATION in the suit being established.

BRITISH BRIDGE. Direct methods of bidding advocated in the Thirties by a group of English players headed by Walter Buller and Ewart Kempson, as opposed to the approach-forcing methods popularized by Ely Culbertson.

BRITISH BRIDGE LEAGUE. The League was founded in 1931 by A.E. Manning-Foster, and reorganized in 1938 as a federal body. The members are ENGLISH BRIDGE UNION, NORTHERN IRELAND BRIDGE UNION, SCOTTISH BRIDGE UNION, AND WELSH BRIDGE UNION, with a combined membership of 30,000. India, New Zealand and South Africa were formerly affiliated.

The League selects British teams for European Championships and world events. Their successes include wins in the 1955 Bermuda Bowl, 1981 and 1985 Venice Trophy, 1989 World Junior Championship, and many European titles.

The League was host to the 1989 World Junior Championships in Nottingham, and has staged many European Championships.

The League organizes the CAMROSE TROPHY for home international competition, the GOLD CUP for open teams, the Portland Cup for Mixed Pairs, and the Lady Milne Cup for Women's Teams.

Officers 1993:
    President: Tom Workman
    Secretary, Anna Gudge
    13 Chaucer Road, Sudbury,
    Suffolk CO1O 6LN   England
    Tel. 44 787 881920
    Fax: 44 787 881339

BRITISH BRIDGE WORLD. An English monthly publication (1932-1939) founded by Hubert Phillips. It was revived in 1956 as a successor to the *Contract Bridge Journal*, and continued until 1964 when it merged with *Bridge Magazine*. See BIBLIOGRAPHY.

BRITISH PARLIAMENT MATCHES. Matches between the House of Commons and the House of Lords held annually since 1975. This unique event was founded by Rixi Markus with the assistance of the Right Honourable Harold Lever, MP, and is staged by *The Guardian*, national daily newspaper for which Markus was bridge editor. The matches are played under the conditions of rubber duplicate: that is, the same hands are played at each of the two tables in the match but the scoring is rubber-bridge scoring. After the 1992 match the House of Lords led in the series 10-8, having won in 1975, 1979-83, and 1987-1990.

BROKEN SEQUENCE. A combination of at least three high cards (A, K, Q, J, 10, 9) which has at least two cards in sequence and at least one higher card almost in sequence. Examples: A Q J; K J 10 9; A K J 10; Q 10 9; but not K Q 10 or Q J 9. Similar is INTERIOR SEQUENCE.

BROKEN SUIT. A suit containing no honor cards in sequence.

BROZEL. Developed by Bernard Zeller as a defense against an opposing 1NT opening, and may be used either in the direct or balancing position.

A double shows a one-suited hand. If partner does not wish to defend, he bids 2♣ and passes the doubler's next bid. All overcalls on the two-level show two suits as follows:

2 ♣	shows hearts and clubs
2 ♦	shows hearts and diamonds
2 ♥	shows hearts and spades
2 ♠	shows spades and a minor
2 NT	shows clubs and diamonds

An overcall on the three-level shows a singleton or void in the bid suit and support for the other three suits.

After a weak response to a 1NT opening, a double again describes a one-suited hand. Without suitable defense, partner bids the next higher-ranking suit, then passes the doubler's next bid. All simple overcalls shows the bid suit and the next higher-ranking unbid suit. 2NT is a takeout for the three unbid suits, and a cuebid is a stronger takeout, implying game possibilities.

For alternative defensive conventions against notrump openings, see DEFENSE TO ONE NOTRUMP.

BUENOS AIRES AFFAIR. In 1965, the international bridge world was rocked by a widely publicized charge that Terence Reese and Boris Schapiro, representing Great Britain in the Bermuda Bowl at Buenos Aires, Argentina, had transmitted information about the heart suit by finger signals.

The original observations were made by B. Jay Becker and Dorothy Hayden, members of the North American team, and Alan Truscott, bridge editor for *The New York Times*. They testified that the British pair were observed to be holding their cards in a varying manner, with a different number of fingers, either closed or spread, showing at the back of their hands from deal to deal. After comparing findings, it was suggested that Reese and Schapiro were signaling the number of hearts they held (two fingers for two or five hearts, depending on whether the fingers were closed or spread, three fingers for three or six hearts, and so forth). The evidence was presented to John Gerber (npc, North American team), who in turn brought it to the attention of Ralph Swimer (npc, British team) and Geoffrey Butler, chairman of the British Bridge League and member of the World Bridge Federation Executive Committee and chairman of its Appeals Committee. After an independent investigation, Butler called a meeting of the Appeals Committee to present his observations, to study the evidence further, and to inform Reese and Schapiro of the charges against them. Both denied the allegations. The matter was then brought to the attention of the WBF Executive Committee. On the last day of the World Championship, by a vote of 10-0 (Carl'Alberto Perroux abstaining, one absentee), the Executive Committee found Reese and Schapiro guilty of using illegal signals, and the evidence was turned over to the British Bridge League for final disposition. Swimer conceded the Great Britain-Argentine match, which Great Britain had won 380-184, and the Great Britain-North American match, in which Great Britain was leading 288-242 with twenty boards to play.

After receiving the WBF report, the British Bridge League set up an independent inquiry to study the charges, headed by Sir John Foster, Queens Counsel, and General Lord Bourne, assisted on the technical aspects of the case by Alan Hiron and Richard Anthony Priday. The Foster report, released after more than ten months' consideration, found Reese and Schapiro "not guilty" of the cheating allegation. In the opinion of Sir John Foster, who required the highest standard of proof, the technical evidence appeared to indicate that Reese and Schapiro had not profited in the bidding or play from a foreknowledge of the heart suit, and thus failed to substantiate the testimony of the prosecution's witnesses.

After learning of this verdict, which was released after the 1966 WBF meeting, WBF President Charles Solomon stated, "It is doubtful that the WBF can accept the decision of the London hearing . . ." His position was that the WBF had rendered the verdict in Buenos Aires and had submitted its report to the British Bridge League to determine what punitive action would be taken.

At its annual meeting in 1967, the WBF Executive Committee reaffirmed its earlier guilty verdict and passed a resolution that the chairman of the Credentials Committee refer applications of any player found guilty of irregular practices in WBF-sponsored tournaments to the Executive Council. The implication was that applications by Reese and Schapiro would not be accepted, and the implication became fact in 1968 when the Executive Council so answered a query from the British Bridge League concerning possible entry of Reese and Schapiro in the 1968 World Team Olympiad. As a result, the British Bridge League elected not to participate in the Olympiad.

In 1968, the Executive Council restored Reese and Schapiro to good standing on the ground that the three-year ban that had been in effect since 1965 constituted adequate punishment.

The repercussions of the episode during the years of controversy spanned the American and European continents. An article by Rixi Markus defending Reese that appeared in *The Bridge World* resulted in a libel suit by Swimer, and the reluctance of Reese and Swimer to play against each other created problems in the 1968 British Team Trials. The evidence for both sides was presented in books by two of the controversy's leading figures: Reese's *Story of an Accusation* and Truscott's *The Great Bridge Scandal*. See BIBLIOGRAPHY, P. See also BERMUDA INCIDENT, CHEATING ACCUSATIONS.

BULGARIAN BRIDGE FEDERATION. Founded in 1979 as part of the Bulgarian National All-Sports Union and had 600 members in 1992. Organizes annual team, pair and mixed championships, and tournaments in Sofia, Plovdiv and Varna. Hosted 1988 European Junior Championships. Bulgarian women players have won the European Women's Pairs and bronze medals in 1988 World Team Olympiad.

Officers 1992:

President: Christo Drumev

Secretary, Trayan Christov, 1000 Sofia, 18 Levsky Boulevard.

Telex 22723. Fax 65 70 53.

BULLETIN, THE. A monthly magazine that is the official organ of the American Contract Bridge League. It has by far the largest circulation of any bridge periodical, since it goes to all ACBL members, totaling approximately 200,000. It was published originally as *The Bulletin of the American Bridge League* in 1934. The word "Contract" was added when the name of the organization was changed in 1937. It became *The Contract Bridge Bulletin* in 1962. Because of postal regulations, the name reverted to *The Bulletin* in 1993.

Earliest issues, edited by Geoffrey Mott-Smith and William Huske, consisted of a four-page tabloid newspaper listing tournament results and facts concerning upcoming tournaments. In subsequent years it was edited by George Beynon and then Alfred Sheinwold.

In May 1958, editorship was assumed by Richard L. Frey, who instituted radical changes in format and content. In June of 1958 the directory of bridge clubs was included in the *Bulletin* for the first time. In June 1959, increasing circulation made possible a switch to offset printing. In 1960, the publication went from 10 issues a year to a full 12-issue monthly. Pages jumped from 408 in 1958 to 968 in 1969. A Master Pointers section was begun in February 1964. Frey also instituted the insert plan by which various ACBL districts and units could have their own publication inserted into the *Bulletin* and mailed with it.

In 1970, Frey retired and his duties were assumed by three of his assistants. Steven Becker was appointed executive editor; Tannah Hirsch became the editor; and Thomas Smith was named business manager.

Major changes in the top editorial positions took place again in 1972, when the ACBL moved its headquarters to Memphis. Late in 1972 Henry G. Francis became executive editor; Sue Emery was appointed editor; Richard Oshlag became business and advertising manager. Oshlag became head of the ACBL computer department in 1983 and Frank Stewart became managing editor. Stewart resigned in 1989, at which time Brent Manley took over as managing editor.

Under Francis, the *Bulletin* again made major strides. In addition to extensive coverage of major bridge events around the world, the Master Pointers section was expanded, in-depth personal interviews were introduced, a new department for New Players was added, and The Mailbox became the springboard for all sorts of high-spirited discussions, from smoking to Gold Points, from Alerts to professionalism. In addition, the *Bulletin* increased its insert department which was geared to specific geographic areas — Mid-Atlantic, Midwest, Midsouth, Northwest, Canada, New York, etc. The *Bulletin* has continued its growth: in 1981 *Bulletin* pages numbered 1304; in 1994 this number had climbed to 1712, with a minimum of 132 pages per issue. See Bibliography, O.

BULLETINS. Daily Bulletins, introduced at the 1955 European Championships in Amsterdam, are issued at all World Championships and at most international championships. Daily Bulletins at World Championships are enhanced by contests which draw interesting contributions from outstanding journalists present at the tournament. Daily Bulletins also are issued at all ACBL North American Championships and at many ACBL regionals. Daily Bulletins from the World Championships and from the ACBL are available on subscription. In addition, many ACBL Districts and Units issue Bulletins on a regular basis giving local news and including some technical material.

BUMBLEDOG AND BUMBLEPUPPY. Humorous terms applied to bad players or bad play in whist.

BUMP MITCHELL. An adaptation of the MITCHELL MOVEMENT invented by Forrest Sharpe for the accommodation of a half table. The game is set up as if there were no half table (extra pair) and boards are distributed to all the full tables only. If the number of full tables is even, a skip at the normal time will be necessary.

The extra pair plays North-South, sitting out the first round and taking the highest North-South number. At round two this pair replaces the North-South pair at Table 1 and stays at Table 1 for the rest of the session. The North-South pair originally at Table 1 sits out the second round and bumps the North-South pair originally at Table 2 on the third round, remaining at Table 2 for the rest of the session. In like fashion pair 2 bumps pair 3, pair 3 bumps pair 4, etc., until the end of the session. It is convenient and logical, but not necessary, to actually change the number of a table to match the number of the North-South pair that is sitting there. It also is not necessary for the pair that was sitting out to physically supplant another pair. The pair with the highest North-South number keeps their own table.

At round 2 the North-South pair at Table 1 sit with no opponents and no boards (as if they did not exist). On round 3 the North-South pair at Table 2 sit with no opponents and no boards, etc.

The pairs that sit out must be factored up the proper amount so that their scores may be compared with those of the ones who did not sit out.

All boards are in play every round, so all have the same matchpoint top, no matter how many rounds are played. A complete movement is not required.

The total number of rounds possible is one fewer than the number of full tables. For example: nine rounds are possible with $10°$ tables.

This movement is not acceptable if $7°$, $9°$ or $13°$ tables are in play and one desires to play seven rounds of four boards, nine rounds of three boards and 13 rounds of two boards, respectively. Now rarely used.

BURNER. A colloquialism used in bridge tournaments to refer to a photocopy of raw scores (i.e., not matchpointed) made available to players a few minutes after the end of a session or the machine used to produce it. Now made obsolete by computer scoring.

BUSINESS DOUBLE. See PENALTY DOUBLE.

BUSINESS PASS. See PENALTY PASS.

BUST. Bridge slang term for a seemingly valueless hand. See YARBOROUGH.

BUSY CARD AND IDLE CARD. These terms were originated by Ely Culbertson, and used in his *Red Book on Play* (see BIBLIOGRAPHY). His definitions are:

A busy card is one which will have a definite duty in the play of the hand, either as a trick winner or as a guard to a card which will or may eventually win a trick. The idle cards have no such function; they serve the holder only in that he may discard them and save his busy cards for a better purpose.

If a suit is distributed as shown in the diagram, then West's small card is idle, but both the king and queen are busy.

```
                    A J 10
        K Q x                   x x x x
                     x x x
```

The terms arise in connection with squeeze play, whose object is to force the discard of a busy card by an opponent.

BUTCHER. Colloquialism to indicate a bad misplay: "He butchered the hand." An alternative term is 'misere'.

BUTLER SCORING. See IMP PAIR SCORING.

BUY. In a competitive auction, to make a bid that the opponents do not contest. "He bought it for three hearts."

BYE. (1) In team-of-four competition, an advance to a later round without the necessity of winning or playing a match. This occurs at some point in the play in order to reduce the field to a power of two.

(2) In pair contests, a BYESTAND is used as a temporary resting place for boards not in play during a particular round.

(3) In pair matches, when an uneven number of pairs compete, there is one table, a bye table, at which traveling pairs find no opponents, or where a stationary pair has no opponents come to them.

(4) A slang term, unsanctioned by law, for "I pass". Sometimes also "Bye me," or "I go bye". Such terms are to be avoided since, unless they are always used, they infringe the warning against different designations for the same call.

BYESTAND. A stand (it may be a chair or small side table) where one or more sets of boards rest during rounds in which they are not in play. The byestand is usually placed in such position that the boards will be conveniently available to the table where they will be in play next.

The most common use of a byestand is described under MITCHELL MOVEMENT. A pamphlet (available on request from the ACBL office) instructs the tournament director what procedure to follow to correct the omission or misplacement of the byestand in a Mitchell movement. The use of a byestand in a Mitchell game is necessary only when it is desired to play all the boards. (See EIGHT TABLES; TWELVE TABLES.) If one or more sets of boards are not to be played, the SKIP MOVEMENT eliminates the need for the byestand.

Byestands also are common in all HOWELL and THREE-QUARTER movements as well as some team movements.

BYLAWS. Regulations by which national organizations, clubs and other bridge entities govern their membership and activities.

BYLAWS OF THE ACBL. The ACBL Bylaws govern principally such matters as elections; meetings; powers of the Board of Directors, Board of Governors and officers; structure; membership; standing and special committees, and the Laws Commission. With respect to membership in the ACBL, the Bylaws provide as follows:

Any person is eligible for membership in the ACBL. There shall be the following categories of membership:

1. *Member.*

Upon application and payment of annual dues as established by the Board of Directors, an applicant shall become and remain a member unless:

a. The member has failed to pay dues in accordance with regulations established by the Board of Directors; or

b. The member has been censured or expelled in accordance with regulations established by the Board of Directors; or

c. The member has been reclassified as an honorary or life member.

2. *Life Member.*

A member who meets the qualifications and requirements as established by the Board of Directors shall be reclassified as a life member upon ratification by a majority vote of the Board of Governors. Life members shall not be required to pay dues but may be required, in order to maintain an active status and receive services from the ACBL, to pay such annual service charges as may be established by the Board of Directors.

3. *Honorary Member.*

The Board of Directors may elect honorary members according to guidelines adopted by the Board of

Directors. Honorary members shall be exempt from the payment of dues or annual service charges, shall retain an active status and shall receive services from the ACBL.

Any member, including a life member, shall be a member of the Unit within whose jurisdiction he or she resides unless there are District regulations creating exceptions. Any member or life member of the ACBL may be censured, suspended, expelled or otherwise disciplined in accordance with regulations established by the Board of Directors. Every member in each category of membership shall be subject to regulations established by the Board of Directors establishing binding and compulsory arbitration to settle disputes involving the ACBL and its members.

BYZANTINE BLACKWOOD. A complex variation of the 4 NT ace-asking convention, devised by J.C.H.Marx of Great Britain, in which the responses are given in the style of ROMAN BLACKWOOD and may be based on a key-suit king instead of one of the aces normally shown. Key suits include the trump suit, any genuine side suit that has been bid and supported, and any suit bid by a player whose partner's first bid was in notrump. Byzantine is not used when there are more than two key suits. If there is only one key suit, a king of a half-key suit, i.e., a genuine suit that has been bid but not supported, may be shown.

For example, when there is only one key suit, a Byzantine 5♣ response shows no aces, or three aces, or two aces plus the key-suit king.

C

CAC or CACBF. See CENTRAL AMERICAN AND CARIBBEAN BRIDGE FEDERATION.

CBA. CONTRACT BRIDGE ASSOCIATION.

CBL. CONTRACT BRIDGE LEAGUE.

CAB. A British system of bidding that incorporates some features of STANDARD AMERICAN: a strong 1NT opening with GLADIATOR responses (but responses of 2♦, 2♥ and 2♠ are constructive though non-forcing); forcing jump raises and 2NT response (except in competition); a conventional 2♣ opening with ace-showing responses; ACOL TWO-BIDS; opening bids of 3♣ and 3♦ that suggest a solid or nearly solid suit and invite 3NT. The initials CAB stand for Two Clubs, Ace-asking and Blackwood. Leslie Dodds was the principal contributor to the development of CAB, now virtually obsolete.

CADDY. An assistant at a bridge tournament. Duties of the caddy are to dress the tables (putting pickup slips, pencils and private scores on the tables); picking up the completed entry blanks; assembling the boards at the conclusion of play, and otherwise making himself useful. In pair events or team events scored by BOARD-A-MATCH, the caddy picks up the scoreslips at the completion of each round and assists the scorer in checking doubtful slips. In a KNOCKOUT TOURNAMENT or a team game with a SWISS MOVEMENT there are no scoreslips to be picked up, and the caddy's chief duty during the session is to transport the boards played at

one table of each match to the other table of the same match.

Assignment of caddies to work various sessions of a duplicate tournament is the responsibility of the local tournament committee. Generally selection is made from interested high-school boys and girls. Some caddies become expert players.

CALCUTTA. A duplicate tournament with a feature making possible a fair-sized financial gain to any player or other participant. After the entries have been made, an auction is held at which players, spectators and others bid for and buy the contesting pairs. The total of the moneys bid for the players is put into a pool which is distributed to the purchasers of the winning entries. In addition, cash prizes or other worthwhile stimuli are provided so that the contestants themselves have a stake in the results. It is usually a proviso that a contestant may purchase from the buyer up to a 50% interest in his own partnership at the original price.

The most famous Calcutta, attracting many of the world's best players, is that staged each May by New York's Cavendish Club, and continued after that famous body closed its doors in 1991. See CAVENDISH.

Because of the gambling feature involved in the auctioning of the participants, the AMERICAN CONTRACT BRIDGE LEAGUE does not sanction a Calcutta, and masterpoints are not awarded. See GAMBLING AT BRIDGE.

CALIFORNIA CUEBID. See WESTERN CUEBIDS; CUEBIDS IN OPPONENT'S SUIT.

CALIFORNIA SCORING. A method of computing the East-West pairs' matchpoint score by assigning them the same score as their North-South opponents, rather than the reciprocal. Using this method the East-West pair with the lowest score is then the winner. Alternatively, each East-West score may be subtracted from the maximum possible matchpoint total to produce the same score that would have been achieved using regular matchpoint scoring methods. California Scoring derived its name from its popularity primarily in California and other Western clubs. Computer scoring has made it obsolescent. See TRAVELING SCORESLIP.

CALL. Any bid, double, redouble or pass. See LAWS.

CALL AFTER THE FINAL PASS. See LAWS (Law 35).

CALL IN ROTATION AFTER AN ILLEGAL CALL. See LAWS (Law 34).

CALL OUT OF TURN. See LAWS (Laws 28-35).

CALLING A CARD OR A SUIT. The privilege of compelling an opponent to lead or play a certain card or a certain suit, to play his highest or lowest, or to win or lose a trick. See LAWS (Laws 26, 27c, 30b, 31b, 32, 36a, 37, 38, 39b, 50, 52, 52, 55b, 56, 57, 73). See LAWS OF DUPLICATE (Laws 46, 51).

CAMROSE TROPHY. The Home International series competed for annually among England, Scotland, Wales and Northern Ireland under the auspices of the British

Bridge League. The trophy was presented by Lord Camrose in 1936. Two series, 1937 and 1938, which included the Irish Free State, were completed before war curtailed the 1939 event. The series restarted in 1946, including what was then Eire until 1951, and celebrated its 50th season in 1993. England has won on 38 occasions, Scotland 10 times, and those two countries tied in 1972 and 1973. The Scottish wins were in 1964, 1965, 1967, 1970, 1971, 1974, 1976, 1977, 1979 and 1989.

CANADIAN BRIDGE FEDERATION. Although Canada is part of the American Contract Bridge League, the nation also has its own national contract bridge organization, the Canadian Bridge Federation (CBF). The CBF deals with its own national championships, its own charity organization and representation in world championships. The CBF was founded in 1967 in order to promote a national identity and union of Canadian players. It stages annual open and women's championships. The CBF determines which teams will represent Canada in the World Olympiads. It also determines the teams that compete with Mexico and Bermuda in odd-numbered years to decide which of the three countries will compete in Bermuda Bowl and Venice Cup world competition. The CBF publishes a magazine, the *Canadian Bridge Digest*, and has its own charity organization, the Canadian Charitable Fund.

1994 officers: Doug Heron, president; George Holland, vice-president; Janice Anderson, executive secretary and treasurer; Gary Westfall, charity; Katie Thorpe, Gim Ong, Gary Mitchell, Aidan Ballantyne, directors; George Retek, Jonathan Steinberg, Dick Anderson, ex-officio directors.

CANADIAN NATIONAL TEAMS. Until 1980 teams representing Canada competed in the Grand National Teams. In 1980 Canada separated from the Grand National Teams and staged its own national championship, a practice that has continued since that time. The format calls for grass-roots contests at clubs in the fall, with succeeding qualifications leading to the national finals. The winning team qualifies to represent Canada in the World Team Olympiad in Olympic years and in the tri-country playoffs for a berth in the Bermuda Bowl with Bermuda and Mexico in odd-numbered years. In the fourth year the winners represent Canada in the Rosenblum Teams. See Appendix I.

CANAPÉ. A bidding method in which the long suit is usually bid on the second round. This was developed by Pierre Albarran (1894-1960) in France, where it has had a considerable following. By contrast, standard methods are described in France as la longue d'abord (long suit first).

Canapé has influenced Italian bidding theory; it is incorporated in both the ROMAN and BLUE TEAM CLUB systems, and in offspring systems such as the ORANGE CLUB, as played by Bob Hamman-Bobby Wolff, and the SIMPLIFIED CLUB, which is a total canapé system.

Albarran's definition of canapé was: "With a two-suited hand of more than minimum strength, the higher-ranking suit must be bid on the first round if it has four cards, and on the second round if it has more than four cards."

Four-card major suits are usually bid ahead of any minor suit; five-card major suits are bid on the first round if the hand is a minimum. Normal reverse sequences are inverted (inversé):

♠ A Q 10 x x
♥ K Q x x
♦ K x
♣ x x

Using canapé, the opening bid is 1♥, and 2♠ is bid on the next round. A heart preference is highly improbable, so the canapé player can stay safely at the level of two.

Canapé is admittedly in difficulty with certain minimum hands, such as those with four spades and five clubs. 1♠ followed by 3♣ would exaggerate the strength, and 1♣ followed by 1♠ would imply a five-card spade suit.

A modified version called "canapé tendency" (tendance canapé) was used successfully in international competition by Pierre Jaïs and Roger Trézel. They bid minimum hands in normal fashion, but adopt the canapé principle for hands of maximum strength and some hands of intermediate strength.

CANARY CLUB. An artificial bidding system, now obsolete, developed in 1964 by John Lowenthal and the Paul Heitner. The name of the system is derived from its chief features: Canapé, Relay and 1♣ forcing.

CANNIBAL SQUEEZE. See SUICIDE SQUEEZE.

CANSINO. A defense to 1NT in which an overcall of 2♣- shows clubs and two other suits, and 2♦ shows both majors. See DEFENSE TO ONE NOTRUMP.

CAP GEMINI PANDATA WORLD TOP TOURNAMENT. Played annually in The Hague, Netherlands, the invitational event routinely has one of the strongest fields in international competition.

The tournament debuted in 1987 as the Staten Bank Invitational. It underwent two name changes before Cap Gemini, a computer company, took on sponsorship in 1991 after co-sponsoring the tournament with Staten Bank the year before.

In the tournament, 16 pairs play 15 head-to-head matches in round-robin style. Scoring originally was by IMPs converted to Victory Points. In later tournaments, scoring was by IMPs compared to a datum derived from scores across the field. See Appendix III.

CAP VOLMAC WORLD TOP TOURNAMENT. See CAP GEMINI PANDATA WORLD TOP TOURNAMENT. See Appendix III.

CAPPELLETTI CUEBIDS. When the opponents have bid two suits, the lower-level cuebid shows both unbid suits with greater length in the lower-ranking suit. The higher-level cuebid shows both unbid suits with greater length in the higher-ranking suit.

CAPPELLETTI. (Also called Hamilton, and in Britain, Pottage). A defense against a 1NT opening devised by A. Michael Cappelletti. Over an opponent's 1NT opening, in either the direct or balancing seat, 2♥/2♠ shows that suit plus a minor; 2♦ shows both majors; 2♣ shows any one-suited hand.

All these overcalls suggest fewer than 15 good points; better hands usually double, although a 2NT overcall is available to show a strong distributional hand. Overcalls at the three level or higher are natural.

The structure may be played soundly or aggressively.

A conservative pair would probably require a good six-card suit or better to bid 2♣, 5-5 in the majors to bid 2♦, and a five-card major to overcall in a major, all with substantial high-card values. Active pairs may frequently bid 2♦ with 4-4 in the majors, 2♥/2♠ with any four-card major and a five-card minor, and 2♣ on hands that would have opened a weak two-bid (including good five-card suits).

Responses (in an active style) are:

(i) After 2♣: Pass, possible, with at least six clubs; 2♦, the normal response, allowing the 2♣ bidder to pass or bid his suit; 2♥/2♠, possible, with at least a strong five-card suit; 2NT: 11 or more points, plus support for all four suits. The 2♣ bidder is invited to bid game with a maximum.

(ii) After 2♦: Pass, requires at least six strong diamonds; 2♥/2♠ choice of suit, unconstructive; 2NT, asks for the 2♦ bidder's better minor; 3♣, requires at least six strong clubs; 3♥/3♠: invitational, promising four or more trumps. It is possible, however, to play this bid as preemptive.

(iii) After 2♥/2♠: New suit, natural, non-forcing; Raise, 7 to 10 points; 2NT, asks for the minor, but if followed by three of the major, promises 10 to 12 points and invites game.

After 1NT-2♣-Dbl, a redouble shows 7 or more high-card points with some support for all suits; it invites the 2♣ bidder to compete to the three-level.

It is also possible to play Cappelletti after 1NT overcalls of partner's minor-suit opening. See DEFENSE TO ONE NOTRUMP; TRANSFER OVERCALLS OF ONE NOTRUMP.

CAPTAIN. Teams representing major bridge countries in international play normally have a nonplaying captain (although Great Britain won three successive European Championships 1948-50 with Maurice Harrison-Gray as playing captain). The captain's chief function is to decide who shall play at each stage in the contest, taking into account such factors as the ability and stamina of the players at his command, the caliber of the opposition, the closed and open room, and VUGRAPH. In addition, the captain represents the team in discussions relating to the conditions of play, and in protests and appeals. He also acts as the team's spokesman on all social occasions.

The importance of the captain's role has been recognized in recent years, and it is usual for a World Championship contestant to appoint an experienced player whose decisions will be respected and accepted by the players in his charge. At one time the president of the ACBL was automatically designated nonplaying captain of its international team, but this practice was discontinued after 1961.

With the inception of the playoff method of ACBL selection from the winners of the four major team championships, each team was required to select a nonplaying captain from a panel of eligible captains selected by the ACBL Board of Directors, and the captain of the winning team was virtually an automatic selection for the World Championship, although subject to Board confirmation.

Carl'Alberto Perroux, of Italy, who made a considerable contribution to the remarkable series of victories compiled by the BLUE TEAM, earned a reputation as one of the most powerful and successful nonplaying captains in the history of bridge.

Dan Morse has been a highly successful captain of American teams. He was the American captain when North America finally ended Italy's Blue Team reign in the Bermuda Bowl in 1976. He also was captain of the United States team in 1988 when the U.S. won the World Team Olympiad for the first time.

Alfred Sheinwold also has been an active captain for North America. He was captain of the American team in the 1975 Bermuda Bowl when the foot-tapping incident took place. Rather than have his team play against the foot-tappers, who were allowed to continue playing, Sheinwold withdrew his team from the competition. However, the ACBL tournament committee on hand at the tournament overruled him and sent the American team back into action.

CAPTAINCY. The control of the auction assumed by one partner in certain situations. The classical approach to constructive bidding is that each partner fully describes his hand; then the two partners act together to choose a contract.

WEST	EAST
1♠	2♥
3♣	3♠
4♦	4♥
4♠	5♣
6♣	

The above auction is a dialogue between equals: both players participate in the search for the best contract; both can use their judgment.

In many auctions, however, one player's bidding narrowly defines his strength and suggests a trump suit (or notrump); he is said to limit his hand. The basis of the limit approach is that the auction is easier if one player limits his hand quickly. His partner then becomes captain of the partnership and must place the contract at the proper level.

WEST	NORTH	EAST	SOUTH
3♠	4♥	Dbl	Pass
4♠			

West has violated captaincy, his descriptive 3♠ opening put East in charge.

In Blackwood auctions the 4NT bidder is captain, and his partner merely follows instructions in making the agreed responses. But captaincy may shift from one partner to another in a single auction. For example, if the Blackwood bidder continues with 5NT, indicating his side's possession of all the aces, in some circumstances responder may bid a grand slam.

The idea of captaincy is best seen in relay systems: one player makes meaningless bids (relays) to obtain information about his partner's strength and distribution; he then places the contract all by himself.

The term also applies to the player in charge of the affairs of a team. The captain can be either a player or a non-player. The captain makes the key decisions for his team — who will sit out, who will play with whom, what table which players will sit at, whether to appeal a director's decision, etc.

CARD COMBINATIONS. See SUIT COMBINA-TIONS.

CARD COMMITTEE. In private clubs it is customary that a committee of two or more members is charged with the responsibility of order and decorum in the club's card room. Referred to this committee are disputes which arise in the play that cannot be settled by reference to the rules of the game in question. Also under the jurisdiction of this committee come such questions as what games will be permitted, rules of procedure for forming tables, maximum stakes and unpaid wagers. With respect to contract bridge tournaments, see COMMITTEE.

CARD, DAMAGED OR MARKED. See DAMAGED CARD.

CARD FEE. See ENTRIES.

CARD PLAYED. See PLAYED CARD.

CARD READING. Drawing correct inferences about the nature of the opponent's holdings and distribution from information disclosed by the fall of the cards.

    ♠ A 8
    ♥ K Q J 7 6
    ♦ J 8 7
    ♣ 6 5 3

    ♠ Q J 10 4 3 2
    ♥ A 5 3
    ♦ A K
    ♣ 10 7

South plays in 4♠ after East has opened the bidding with 1♣. West leads the ♣2 and East wins with the ace, and shifts to the ♥9. A seemingly secure contract is now in some jeopardy. East clearly has a singleton heart, and very likely three trumps including the king. Obviously his play is to win the second trump lead and put partner in with a club honor for a heart ruff. Declarer can foil this defense by playing East for the ♦Q (not unlikely on the bidding). Winning the heart in dummy, he plays off the ♦A-K before crossing to the ♠A. The ♦J is led from dummy, East covering and South discarding his last club, thus effectively severing communication between the defenders. The complete deal:

    ♠ A 5
    ♥ K Q J 7 6
    ♦ J 8 7
    ♣ 6 5 3

♠ 7 6   ♠ K 9 5
♥ 10 8 4 2   ♥ 9
♦ 9 5 4 2   ♦ Q 10 6 3
♣ K 8 2   ♣ A Q J 9 4

    ♠ Q J 10 4 3 2
    ♥ A 5 3
    ♦ A K
    ♣ 10 7

Combining accurate card-reading with counting often provides valuable clues for the defense. Careful examination of the evidence provided East with the opportu-

nity to defeat the contract on this hand:

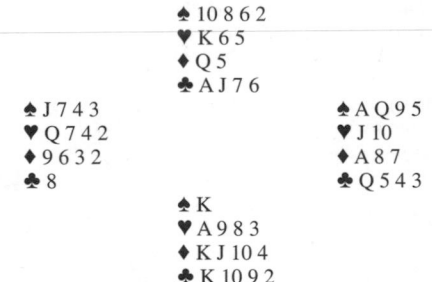

    ♠ 10 8 6 2
    ♥ K 6 5
    ♦ Q 5
    ♣ A J 7 6

♠ J 7 4 3   ♠ A Q 9 5
♥ Q 7 4 2   ♥ J 10
♦ 9 6 3 2   ♦ A 8 7
♣ 8   ♣ Q 5 4 3

    ♠ K
    ♥ A 9 8 3
    ♦ K J 10 4
    ♣ K 10 9 2

The bidding has been:

SOUTH	NORTH
1♣	1♠
1 NT	2 NT
3 NT	

West leads the ♥ 2, and East's 10 loses to declarer's ace. A club is led to dummy's ace, and the jack run, West discarding the ♦ 2. The ♦ Q is taken by East, and he reviews the situation.

He knows that South has four club tricks, and at least two in hearts. What about the diamonds? West's diamond discard on the second club is revealing: he is unlikely to have parted with one from 10-x-x-x or J-x-x-x. Could West have started with five diamonds? Not very likely, for in that case he might have led one. South can therefore be assumed to have three diamond tricks, enough for his contract, should he regain the lead. The only hope for the defense seems to lie in spades. If East's estimate of the situation is correct, then West had started with a 4-4-4-1 distribution, marking declarer with a singleton spade — very likely the king, considering his bidding.

Declarer's play of the club suit seems to bear this out; having a two-way finesse, he chose to take it into the hand that was less likely to shift to spades, if it lost. On this reasoning East lays down the ♠A, dropping declarer's king, and continues with a small card to his partner's jack. A third round of spades permits East to score the Q-9 to defeat the contract. See also COUNTING THE HAND and INFERENCE.

For full discussions of card reading, see: *Card Reading* by Eric Jannersten; *The Art of Card Reading at Bridge* by Fred Karpin; *Bridge Logic* by Hugh Kelsey; *All 52 Cards* by Marshall Miles; *How To Read Your Opponent's Cards* by Mike Lawrence. See BIBLIOGRAPHY D.

CARD SENSE. A special aptitude for playing card games, specifically (in this context) bridge.

Until psychological research and Army selection procedures satisfactorily demonstrated the existence of special aptitudes, there was considerable controversy about whether card sense existed.

Although he changed his mind later, Ely Culbertson was originally among the skeptics, commenting as follows: "One hears a good deal about that elusive something called 'card sense.' It is spoken of as though it were some mysterious, deeply inborn faculty which cannot be taught. Lack of 'card sense' is always said to be the great bugaboo blocking the prospective bridge player's path to improvement. As a matter of fact, 'card sense' - whatever those who use the term mean - is a certain facility at cards shown by some players and entirely lacking in others. "

Among good bridge players, it is virtually impossible to distinguish between what is the result of card sense and what is the result of experience. Card sense is more easily distinguishable among beginners, where it appears to be a compound of various elements: intelligence, interest and youth.

There is probably a high correlation between ability to learn the elements of bridge and mathematical aptitude, and a somewhat lower correlation with intelligence quotient. See also INTUITION.

CARD-SHOWING DOUBLE. A double that does not promise any particular distribution but instead shows general high-card strength. The amount of strength promised by a double that shows cards obviously varies according to the circumstances in which the double is made. For example, the DOUBLE OF TWO CLUBS RESPONSE to a WEAK NOTRUMP would show strength equivalent to that of a double of a 1 NT opening; the double of interference with a PRECISION CLUB opening bid, however, promises about 5-8 points.

CARDS. Used in a colloquial sense, usually in describing the meaning of certain doubles, to mean high-card strength. See CARD-SHOWING DOUBLE.

CARDS, NEUTRAL AND POSITIVE. The only information disclosed by the play of a neutral card is the obvious point that the player has that particular card. The essence of this is that the player is not void of the suit, and even this knowledge will generally have little or no effect on problems of probability.

A card may be said to have positive value when:

(1) the holder was deemed certain to have played it, or;

(2) it indicates the position of one or more other specified cards, or suggests their probable location, or;

(3) it indicates the distribution of all the outstanding cards of a suit.

```
                NORTH
                ♠ 5 4 3
                ♥ A K 2
                ♦ A J 8 6 5
                ♣ K 3

                SOUTH
                ♠ A J 2
                ♥ Q 8 4 3
                ♦ K 10 7
                ♣ A J 5
```

South plays in notrump, and West leads the ♠K. South assumes that West holds the ♠ K-Q-10. If he also assumes that West was certain to make this lead, there will be odds of 13 to 10 that East has the ♦Q:

(a) If East follows with a low spade, these odds are only very slightly altered. East's card is neutral, and indicates only that West does not have seven spades. The elimination of all distributions where West holds seven spades removes more cases favorable to East's holding the ♦Q than unfavorable cases. The odds are a very little less than 13 to 10, and the difference may be disregarded.

(b) If East plays a heart at trick one, there will be positive significance in the fact that he has played a non-spade, though the card itself is neutral. The odds are 13 to 6 that East holds the ♦Q. We know now that East is not void of hearts, but we cannot say that he was certain to play a heart whatever cards he holds.

(c) If East discards a club at trick one, the odds are again 13 to 6 that he has the ♦Q.

CARDS OF A SUIT IN OPPONENT'S HAND. See SUIT, NUMBER OF CARDS IN.

CARIBBEAN CHAMPIONSHIPS. Organized in 1964 as an informal international championship for countries in the Caribbean area. The first Caribbean Championship was held in Curaçao, Netherlands Antilles, and the two subsequent tournaments were staged in Barranquilla, Colombia, and Caracas, Venezuela, respectively. Venezuela won the first two events and Colombia won the championship in 1968. See CENTRAL AMERICAN AND CARIBBEAN CHAMPIONSHIPS. See Appendix III.

CARROT CLUB. A forcing club system invented by Hans Göthe of Sweden.

CARRYOVER SCORES. Methods for determining carryover scores are the responsibility of the sponsoring organization.

Under the regulations of the AMERICAN CONTRACT BRIDGE LEAGUE, certain events in tournaments of sectional or higher rating are conducted in more than one session. These events may or may not involve elimination of some of the contestants from the main event (see CONSOLATION EVENT).

If no players are eliminated from the event, their matchpoint score is carried over from one session to the succeeding session, and the event decided upon the total score in all sessions. Regulations require that if a later session of a playthrough multi-session event has a different top score on a board, provision is made for adjusting to the top score in the first session. See FACTORING.

When the original starting field is reduced for later sessions, regulations provide that scores in the early (qualifying) round or rounds be carried over into the final session on the basis of this formula:

$$\text{carryover} = \frac{M \times QFD \times A \times B}{E \times S}$$

where M represents the number of matchpoints in the qualifying round or rounds which a contestant scores, QFD is the square of the number of pairs in the final session, A is the average on a board in the finals, B is the number of boards in the qualifying round or rounds, E is the number of pairs entered in the event, and S is the sum of all qualifying scores of pairs eligible for the finals.

If there is one qualifying round and one final, the total spread from top to bottom score is reduced to twice the top score on a board in the finals; if there are two qualifying rounds and one final, the total is reduced to three boards; and for two qualifying rounds and two final rounds, four boards. The formula may give a smaller spread.

The carryover method also is used in some ACBL team events. In board-a-match events at North American Championships, such as the Reisinger Teams, a carryover formula along lines similar to the ones outlined above is applied. In the North American Swiss Teams event, different carryover formulas are applied from qualifying to semifinal and from semifinal to final. Half of any score greater than 5 is carried over from qualifying to semifinal. However, Victory Points are used in the final. Each finalist is given a carryover equivalent to 1 Victory Point for each full quarter over 5 a team scores in the semifinal.

At the world level, a special carryover formula has been applied in some Bermuda Bowl contests. Half the IMP difference from the round-robin is carried over to the final or semifinal if the team that finished higher in the round-robin has the plus; only one-third of the IMP difference is carried over if the team that finished lower in the round-robin has the plus.

Carryover also is applied from the qualifying to the semifinal and from the semifinal to the final of the World Open Pairs and from the qualifying to the final of the World Women's Pairs. A special carryover formula also is used in the Swiss Teams portion of the Rosenblum Teams. Another special carryover plan was used in the semifinals of the 1980 World Team Olympiad.

CARVE. To badly misplay, or butcher, a hand (British).

CASH. To play a winning card and win the trick.

CASH IN (also CASH OUT). To take a series of tricks by playing winning cards one after another. The term is usually applied to a situation where a player realizes that he is on lead for what is probably going to be the last time during that particular hand, and while in control, he will now take his tricks. The term can be applied to a declarer as well as defenders.

CAVALIER. A fourth COAT CARD, which is still maintained in some playing cards as an alternative to the JACK. See PACK.

CAVENDISH CLUB (New York City). Founded in 1925 by Wilbur C. Whitehead, in association with Gratz M. Scott, and Edwin A. Wetzlar, the Club was housed for the first eight years at the Mayfair House, and then moved to the Ambassador Hotel. It was at the Ritz Tower Hotel 1950-65 and occupied premises on Central Park South 1965-74. In 1974 it moved to the Carlton House, stayed until 1983, and after a brief stop on 48th Street, ended in a townhouse on 73rd. St. Rent escalations and falling membership forced the Club to cease operations on May 31, 1991.

From 1941 the Cavendish Club was a not-for-profit membership corporation, managed by B. Jay Becker 1941 to 1947 and Rudolf Muhsam 1947 to 1973, who were also club secretary, Thomas M. Smith from 1973 to 1987, Thomas L. Snow, 1987 to 1990 and Richard Reisig, 1990 to 1991.

In 1975, the Club inaugurated the CAVENDISH INVITATIONAL PAIRS, which became one of the strongest and most prestigious invitational events in the world. Presidents were: Gratz M. Scott 1925-35; Frank Crowninshield 1935-47; Nate Spingold 1948-58; Samuel Stayman 1958-61 and 1981-82; Howard Schenken 1961-64; Harold Ogust 1964-67; Leonard Hess 1967-70; Edward Loewenthal 1970-73; Roy V. Titus 1973-76 and 1980-81; Archie A. Brauer, 1976-79; Yehuda Koppel 1979-80 and 1985-86; William Roberts 1982-85; Sidney Rosen 1986-87; Claire Tornay 1987-90; and Thomas M. Smith 1990-91.

Members included many players of international reputation.

CAVENDISH INVITATIONAL CHARITY PAIRS. The first invitational event in North America offering significant cash prizes, organized by Michael Moss and Thomas M. Smith and approved by the Cavendish Club Board of Directors in 1975. From its inception, the event featured a then unique IMPs-across-the-field scoring format and a Calcutta Auction Pool of the pairs, which often exceeded $250,000. A portion of the pool was donated to charity, chiefly the Children's Cancer Fund of America, but after a change in the tax laws, the Club dropped "charity" from its event and earmarked funds to beneficiaries of its own choosing. Before the Cavendish Club's demise, the Cavendish Invitational Pairs was established as a separate corporation in an effort to assure its continuation. See Appendix IV.

CELEBRITIES. Many persons who are outstanding in their own spheres of activity also find much enjoyment playing bridge. Heads of state whose bridge-playing activities have received considerable publicity include U.S. President Dwight D. Eisenhower and Chinese Premier Deng Xiaoping. Many top-flight performers of stage, screen and television have been and are avid players. Omar Sharif has played in top-level competition and is acknowledged world-wide as an accomplished competitor. Telly Savalas, TV's Kojak who was a look-alike of ACBL tournament director Bill Schoder, enjoyed a strong rubber or two, as do Elizabeth Taylor, Ronnie Cox, Dick Yarmy, Cara Williams, Don Addams, Robert Quarry and Ray Walker. George Burns finds the game exciting, and playwright George S. Kaufman has even contributed magazine articles about the game. The Marx Brothers also were bridge players. Movie and TV cameraman George Clemmens met his wife while they were playing in a bridge game on the movie lot.

The sports world has many bridge enthusiasts — it is one of the favorite games when clubs are making long trips. The list includes the likes of Tom Seaver, Jim Bunning, Tim McCarver, Richie Ashburn, Pinky Higgins, Norm Cash and Dizzy Dean. Life Master Pauline Betz Addie, the former tennis great, also enjoys a good game of duplicate, and chess experts Bent Larsen and Anatoly Karpov have considerable bridge talent. See IRINA LEVITINA.

Folks in the world of music also find relaxation playing bridge. Sonya LaUnica, a world-famous singer, once said "It's easier to sing than to bid these computer hands!" Concert pianist Leonard Pennario has achieved Life Master rating even though he constantly hears great pieces of music while trying to concentrate on a hand. Beverly Sills and Robert Helps have also turned to bridge for relaxation. Ignace Paderewski and opera conductor Walter Herbert had great appreciation for the intricacies of bridge.

Carl Albert, former speaker of the House of Representatives, and Justice John Stevens of the U.S. Supreme Court find pleasure in a good bridge game. Federal Judge Carl Rubin is a former president of the American Contract Bridge League, and Federal Judge Amalya Kearse not only is a bridge expert — she also was editor of the Third Edition of the *Bridge Encyclopedia*, won a Women's Pairs World Championship and is a bridge author. Bridge enthusiast Abe Drasin is mayor of Grand Rapids MI.

In the world of literature, Somerset Maugham not only played the game — he managed to inject bridge situations into some of his works, as did Ian Fleming, creator of James Bond, and Agatha Christie. C.S. Forester and Charles Dickens dealt with whist. Author Terry Quinn is much interested in the game, and one of his works, *The Great Bridge Conspiracy*, is entirely about bridge. Novelist Don Von Elsner is the well-known creator of the bridge character, Jake Winkman.

In the world of business, Lawrence Tisch, CEO of the CBS television network, and Warren Buffett, head of Berkshire Hathaway, are enthusiastic players who have taken part in matches alongside the late Malcolm Forbes. They represented the corporate world in several matches against the U.S.Congress and the British Parliament. Every year there is a bridge match in Great Britain between members of the House of Lords and the House of Commons.

This should in no way be construed to be a complete list of celebrities interested in bridge — it is only the tip of the iceberg. However, it gives an indication of how bridge is part of the life of folks in all professions and vocations.

CENTRAL AMERICAN AND CARIBBEAN BRIDGE FEDERATION. Founded in 1971, with E.L. Cozier as president, the Federation was recognized in 1976 as Zone 5 of the World Bridge Federation. Member countries in 1992 were: Antigua; Aruba; Bahamas; Barbados; Colombia; Costa Rica; Dominica; Dominican Republic; French Guiana; Guadeloupe; Guyana; Haiti; Jamaica; Martinique; Netherlands Antilles; Panama; St. Kitts and Nevis; Suriname; Trinidad and Tobago; Venezuela; Virgin Islands. Biennial Championships are staged, with winners listed in Appendix III.

Officers 1992:
President:
Brigitte Mavromichalis,
Sea Breeze, Maxwell Coast Road,
Christchurch, Barbados.
Tel: 1 809 428 2825
Fax: 1 809 428 2872
Secretary, Vaughn Theobalds
22 Trafalgar Road,
Kingston 10, Jamaica.

CENTRAL AMERICAN-CARIBBEAN CHAMPIONSHIPS. Formerly CARIBBEAN CHAMPIONSHIPS. Held annually for the member nations of the CENTRAL AMERICAN AND CARIBBEAN BRIDGE FEDERATION. For results, see APPENDIX III.

CHAIRMAN. The chief elected official of the AMERICAN CONTRACT BRIDGE LEAGUE prior to the reorganization in 1949. Subsequently the title was revived, in the form of Chairman of the BOARD OF DIRECTORS. Since 1963 the title has regularly been accorded to the immediate past-president of the ACBL. Chairmen before that date were:

1938-42	*Nate Spingold	1955	*Charles Solomon
1943-45	*Albert H. Morehead	1956	*J.G. Ripstra
1946-47	*Brig. Gen. Robert J. Gill	1957	*Charles Solomon
1948-49	* Waldemar von Zedtwitz	1958	*Winslow H. Randall
1950-52	*Curt Reisinger	1959	*Frank T. Westcott
1953	Peter Leventritt	1960-61	*Max Manchester
1954	*Julius Rosenblum	1962`	*Jerry Lewis

*deceased.

See PRESIDENT.

Chairmen also can be the head of a committee, such as a tournament appeals committee. The leading planner for a tournament frequently is referred to as the tournament chairman.

CHALLENGE. A declaration proposed by Sidney Lenz

in 1929 to replace the Takeout Double. It was used experimentally in one New York club, but received little support.

In the Fifties the term was revived in a different sense, as an attempt to check artificial bidding. When any one player has made two bids, a positive bid can be *challenged*. The bidding then ends, and the contract reached is played redoubled. This plan, originated by Col. Cyril Rocke, also received little support.

CHAMPIONSHIP TOURNAMENTS. The principal function of the ACBL and other governing bodies is to provide interesting bridge competitions for its members, and to record accurately the achievements made by each member in competitive play. To this end the ACBL sponsors and conducts more than 1000 tournaments a year at which masterpoints are awarded. These tournaments are divided into several classes depending on the importance of the event, the territory represented, the movement employed, the conditions of sponsorship and the number of entries. Classification of each event is published in advance, and masterpoints are awarded according to formulas that take into consideration various factors.

(1) *North American Championships (NABC).* These championships are conducted by the ACBL. Each major event is held only once a year, split among the three ten-day tournaments — a spring date in March, a summer date late in July or August, and a fall date late in November or December. To facilitate entry by players in various parts of the country, it is customary to hold one championship in the Eastern, one in the Central, and one in the Western part of the country. Colloquially, these are often referred to by their original names: Spring Nationals, Summer Nationals and Fall Nationals. For results, see Appendix I.

(2) *Regional Championships.* ACBL membership is divided into 25 geographical districts, each strictly limited as to territory. Regional championships are conducted by ACBL districts under the supervision of a rated director appointed by the ACBL. These tournaments offer the players of the area an opportunity to earn a substantial number of gold and red points, awards that are necessary to achieve the rank of Life Master. In addition, at each NABC a large number of secondary events, most of which are flighted or stratified, are conducted, all with regional championship status.

(3) *Sectional Championships.* These events are conducted by ACBL units under the supervision of a rated director appointed by the ACBL. Each unit is expected to conduct at least one Sectional tournament a year. Additional tournaments are allocated on the basis of membership and history of previous sectional tournament scheduling. The points awarded at Sectionals are silver, a very important fact for those interested in becoming Life Masters. A would-be Life Master must win at least 50 silver points, and silver points are available only at Sectionals.

(4) *Unit Championships.* Each unit may conduct 16 sessions of Unit Championship-rated events annually.

Further information is contained in the *ACBL Handbook*, latest copies of which are available from ACBL Headquarters.

Championship tournaments are staged in countries throughout the world. Many determine national championships, and many decide area or continental championships, such as the South American Championships, the

European Championships, etc. Tournaments also are held at the world level: Bermuda Bowl, Venice Cup, Team Olympiad, etc. For results, see Appendices III, IV and V.

CHANCE. The element of luck or hazard present in almost all card games but materially reduced in potency as a feature in bridge. Chance in bridge is usually concerned with the quality of the cards dealt one in rubber contests, but even this should become relatively equal to both sides over a long period of time. The number of points held by a player or partnership tends to approach the theoretical expectation over a long period, although the absolute difference may increase. In play situations chance can be a factor, but the expert player will tend to be able to reduce its influence by applying skill and mathematical deliberation to situations where a lesser player would merely play on and attribute any failure to bad luck.

In duplicate, chance can be a considerable factor in the short run. Good contracts fail and bad contracts succeed; hands which represent borderline games and slams are likely to favor one side at the expense of the other. Less obvious, but equally important, is the chance of playing the right opponents at the right moment. With luck you will play against good opponents when they have no control of the bidding and play, and against weaker players when the bidding and play are slightly too difficult for them. See also FORTUNE.

CHANGE OF SUIT. The first mention of a suit not previously bid by any player; used on a wide variety of hands in which exploration is called for. In standard methods, the general rule is that a change of suit by the responder is forcing for one round; a change of suit by the opener is nonforcing. This is subject to many exceptions.

Changes of suit by the responder are nonforcing in the following cases:

(1) If responder passed originally. But a jump shift by a passed hand is a doubtful case. Most authorities treat this bid as forcing for one round, implying a fit with the opener's suit. But some players reserve the right to pass, especially if the jump is from a minor suit to a major.

(2) If the second player doubled (but some play a change of suit over a double as forcing, or vary their treatment according to the level at which responder acts).

(3) If the second player overcalls 1NT. Similarly, when the second player overcalls with a conventional bid, such as a Michaels Cuebid, responder can double to show strength; a bid in a new suit is non-forcing.

(4) If the opener rebid 1NT; for example:

WEST	EAST
1 ♣	1 ♠
1NT	2 ♦

(But in some systems this sequence retains its forcing character; see also UNBID MINOR FORCING.)

(5) In response to a 1NT opening, at the level of two.

(6) After a 1NT response and a two-level rebid by opener:

WEST	EAST
1 ♠	1 NT
2 ♣	2 ♥

Changes of suit by the opener are forcing in the following cases:

(1) A jump shift below the game level.
(2) A reverse below the game level.
(3) After a single raise by responder:

WEST	EAST
1 ♥	2 ♥
3 ♦	

(4) After responder has shown strength:

WEST	EAST		WEST	EAST
1 ♥	2 NT		1 ♥	2 ♠
3 ♦			3 ♣	

WEST	EAST
1 ♠	2 ♣
2 ♥	

CHANGING A CALL. The act of substituting a call for a call made previously at the same turn. See LAWS (Law 25).

CHANGING PROBABILITIES DURING PLAY. See PROBABILITIES A POSTERIORI and PROBABILITIES A PRIORI.

CHARITY FOUNDATION. See CHARITY PROGRAM OF THE ACBL.

CHARITY PROGRAM OF THE ACBL. The ACBL devotes a substantial part of its effort and activity to its charity program. Charity funds are turned over to the ACBL Charity Foundation, which is administered by an elected Board of Trustees. Under approved Bylaws, the Trustees may make grants to any local or national charity deemed worthy.

It is the policy of the Trustees to select, as beneficiaries, national organizations functioning in many areas, and to devote a large part of their funds to medical research from which lasting benefits can be expected. The charity program has two purposes. The first is to make an important contribution to worthy charities. The second is to foster good public relations for ACBL and to provide units and clubs with a promotional tool with which they can stimulate interest and extend their activities. The program includes many types of games at the club, unit, regional and national levels.

The earliest charity games began in 1934 on the initiative of William McKenney, and these efforts were continued in subsequent years, especially in New York City. The chief beneficiaries were various children's organizations, including the Children's Cancer Fund, Inc., and the War Orphans Scholarship, Inc.

From 1951 to 1964 one or two charities were nominated annually as the beneficiaries of the ACBL's national charity program.

The desire to aid less well-known but thoroughly worthwhile causes with smaller contributions, rather than to make one or two very large contributions, to a national group each year, led the Board of Directors of the ACBL to establish its own Charity Foundation on July 1, 1964.

The Charity Foundation donates approximately $250,000 per year to charities which includes the Charity of the Year program. Recent charities that have been ACBL's Charity of the Year:

1982-1983 -- National Kidney Foundation
1984-1985 -- National Committee for the Prevention of Child Abuse
1986-1987 -- Arthritis Foundation
1988-1989 -- American Foundation for AIDS Research
1990-1991 -- National Hospice Organization (primary charity -- $100,000 annual grant)

1990-1991 -- National Committee for the Prevention of Child Abuse (secondary charity -- $50,000 annual grant)

1992-1993 -- National Multiple Sclerosis Society

1994-1995 -- Alzheimer's Disease and Related Disorders

The League appointed as original trustees of the Foundation a group composed of: General Alfred M. Gruenther (President), Benjamin O. Johnson, John E. Simon, Jerry M. Lewis, and Sidney B. Fink.

The following have been honored as trustees emeriti of the foundation: *Percy Bean, Richard Hewitt, Ruth McConnell, John Norwood, Abner Parker, Carl Rubin, *Leo Seewald, *Nate Silverstein, *Sam Stayman, *Edgar Theus, Kathie Wei-Sender and Joseph Weintraub. (*-deceased)

Presidents following Gruenther's retirement in 1965 have been Fink (1965-1967), Johnson (1968-1973), Joseph J. Stedem (1973-1974) Bean (1975-1980), Jerome R. Silverman (1981-1982), McConnell (1983), Silverstein (1984), Wei-Sender (1985-1986), Hewitt (1987), Joan DeWitt McKean (1988-1989), Bean (1990), Hewitt (1991), McKean (1992-1993).

CHARLES GOREN FOUNDATION. See INTERCOLLEGIATE BRIDGE TOURNAMENT. Also see Appendix IV.

CHEAPER MINOR. See DEFENSE TO OPENING THREE-BID; SECOND NEGATIVE RESPONSE AFTER ARTIFICIAL FORCING OPENING.

CHEAPEST BID. The most economical bid available at any particular point in the auction, such as 1♦ in response to 1♣. Many conventional bids and systems make use of this principle of economy by attaching special meanings to club bids at various levels, and occasionally to diamond bids. The same principle of economy is followed in making natural opening bids and responses. See CHOICE OF SUIT and UP THE LINE.

CHEATING. Throughout history, card cheats have always been held in contempt. It is so with bridge.

The Laws of Contract Bridge are not designed to prevent cheating or to provide redress. The lawgivers have taken the view that it would be wrong to accord cheats a status by providing legal remedies against their activities. This also is the policy of the ACBL: exclusion from membership is the penalty for premeditated cheating, but cases of momentary weakness often are dealt with by temporary suspension. ("The penalty of cheating is exclusion from society," wrote the great whist authority, Cavendish.)

Cheating at Rubber Bridge. At rubber bridge, cheating is not a problem. Short of actually manipulating or marking the cards, it is impracticable for a lone player to cheat effectively. The fact that good bridge is so exact an art militates against cheating, for a player who makes bids or plays which are against the odds but which prove consistently successful soon excites suspicion. Cheating in clubs is therefore rare.

Traditional forms of cardsharping are unrewarding in bridge because each deal is almost equally important. A sharper can hardly make a killing by awaiting a suitable opening as in such games as poker, and if he just happened to pick up good cards every time he dealt, his career would be shortlived.

The dealing of seconds, therefore, the classic technique of the cardsharping aristocracy, is not an effective means of winning. (An accomplished sharp, dealing from a marked pack, sees when a high card is about to go to an opponent, and deals that opponent the next card instead, keeping the high card for himself or his partner.) For the same reason, another time-honored device of sharps, ringing in a cold deck, will not yield a reward commensurate with the risk.

Cheating at Duplicate. The fact that duplicate is a game for fixed partnerships as opposed to the cut-in style of rubber bridge makes dishonesty more practicable. Fortunately, in duplicate there is a powerful safeguard; success gained otherwise than by fair combat is empty to a true bridge player, and cheating presents no attraction to a normal person. It is happily true that to most competitors their own self respect is at least as important as the kudos to be gained from tournament successes.

Cheating at duplicate is by no means easy to define. Although the Laws do not recognize cheats, the section called *The Proprieties* defines two main types of improper conduct: breaches of ethics and breaches of etiquette. Breaches of ethics are commonly thought of as unfair practices which fall short of deliberate cheating, but it is possible for the difference to be one of degree only. For example, a pair who take note of inflections in bidding would be considered unethical, while a pair who set out to impart similar information by secret signals would be considered cheats. (See also ETHICS, ETIQUETTE and PROPRIETIES.)

The following are some examples of infringements peculiar to the tournament world. By their aggravated nature they can be classified as cheating and have been dealt with as such by the ACBL.

Spying on upcoming boards. Disciplinary action has been taken against players who have been observed taking note of play at other tables. One player who cheated too discreetly to be detected by ordinary surveillance was found out when an observant tournament director noticed he seemed to score consistently better on even-numbered boards than on odd numbered boards. Observation over a period of time proved he made a practice of listening to conversations at adjoining tables when he had finished a set of boards, making notes on his private scorecard.

Secret signals. Various forms of signaling, usually by the defenders, have been attempted. Generally the purpose is either to suggest an opening lead or to convey the hand pattern held — i.e., 4-5-3-1, etc. The result of such cheating, if attended by any degree of success, is that the suspicions of competent players are aroused and the offenders are marked men.

Many tournament procedures have been devised that are unobtrusive but effective safeguards against cheating. Thus, in the Laws of Duplicate, some of the examples cited as irregularities are anticheating safeguards. These are:

90 B.3. Any discussion of the bidding, play or result of a board, which may be overheard at another table.

90 B.4. Any comparison of scores with another contestant during a session.

90 B.5. Any touching or handling of cards belonging to another player.

See BERMUDA INCIDENT, BUENOS AIRES AFFAIR, CHEATING ACCUSATIONS, HOUSTON AFFAIR, SION-COKIN AFFAIR.

CHEATING ACCUSATIONS. Accusations of cheating are rare in serious tournament bridge, and substantiated accusations are even rarer. It is generally recognized that an allegation that is not supported by solid evidence should not be made, and that accusation by rumor is highly improper.

At the international level there have been very few cases of charges being brought. Most of these were disposed of, without widespread publicity, by the national or international committees concerned. The notable exceptions occurred in the 1965 and 1975 BERMUDA BOWL. See BERMUDA INCIDENT, BUENOS AIRES AFFAIR.

Several suggestions have been made, aimed at preventing cheating and forestalling accusations of cheating. Screens called FRANCO BOARDS were introduced in Italian events years ago, but did not find general acceptance. In 1974, the proposal of WBF President Julius Rosenblum to use BIDDING SCREENS in the 1975 Bermuda Bowl in order to eliminate accusations of cheating met with a sharp division of opinion, with many taking the position that such screens would be demeaning to the players and to bridge itself. Nevertheless, in 1975 bidding screens were used for the first time in World Championship play, and their use in combination with bidding boxes virtually eliminated any problems relating to the inadvertent exchange of unauthorized information and the ethical problems resulting from hesitations. The response of the players to the screens and boxes was overwhelmingly positive. The irony of the 1975 Bermuda Bowl was, however, that while the screens designed to eliminate cheating accusations were being enthusiastically received, an Italian pair were accused of cheating by using foot signals under the tables. See BERMUDA INCIDENT.

Another accusation of cheating was leveled at two members of Italy's 1973 and 1974 Bermuda Bowl champions. Leandro Burgay, who was passed over by the Italian Bridge Federation as a choice for the 1976 Bermuda Bowl and World Team Olympiad team, presented a tape to the FIB. Burgay claimed the tape contained a telephone conversation between him and Benito Bianchi in which Bianchi had openly discussed illegal signaling methods. According to the tape, Bianchi explained how he and Pietro Forquet had used cigarettes to convey signals during the 1973 and 1974 Bermuda Bowl contests The case came to the attention of the WBF, but nothing ever came of it because it was never proved that the tapes were authentic. See also HOUSTON AFFAIR and SION-COKIN AFFAIR.

CHECKBACK STAYMAN. A common conventional agreement following a 1 NT rebid, searching for an unbid major suit or a preference to responder's major.

Opener	Responder
1 ♣	1 ♥
1NT	2 ♣

This asks opener to give preference to hearts, or show an unbid four-card spade suit. With neither he bids 2♦. 2♣ followed by 2♥ or 2♠ is invitational, whereas those bids made directly would be weak.

Some use 2♦ as a game-forcing Stayman, and 2♣ as a weak Stayman. If the latter, responder has invitational values if he bids again.

See CROWHURST and NEW MINOR FORCING.

CHESS PLAYERS. Nobody has ever reached the highest levels at both chess and bridge, but many have been expert at one game and near-expert at the other. High-ranking bridge players who are also classed as strong chess players include Alan Truscott and Louis Levy. Sol Rubinow and Oswald Jacoby also were fine chess players. Among chess players, two former world champions, Emanuel Lasker and José Raoul Capablanca, once were contributing editors to *The Bridge World*.

Guillaume le Breton Deschapelles of France was acknowledged as the finest player of his day at both chess and whist. A modern Frenchman has done even better. Pierre Ghestem won two world bridge team titles, was world champion at dames (i.e. checkers or draughts), and was French chess champion, an astonishing triple.

When living in St. Petersburg, then Leningrad, Irina Levitina reached the final of the World Women's Chess Championship in 1984 and continued to contend at the highest levels. She was also Russia's best woman bridge-player. She became a United States resident in 1991, and quickly made a mark by winning the 1993 North American Women's Knockout Teams.

CHEST YOUR CARDS. Hold your cards close to your chest, so that they are not visible to an opponent. Usually a request by another player. The culprit may have a vision problem, or simply be careless. An alternative solution is to "lap the cards" — hold them in the lap where they are hidden by the table.

CHICAGO (Four-Deal Bridge). A form of the game much played in clubs and well suited to home play. Its effect is to avoid long rubbers of uncertain duration; a member never need wait longer than the time (about twenty minutes) required to complete four deals. The game is called "Chicago" for the city in which it originated, and sometimes "club bridge."

Basic rules. The LAWS OF CONTRACT BRIDGE and rules for CLUB PROCEDURE are followed, except as modified by the following rules.

The rubber. A rubber, sometimes called a chukker, consists of a series of four deals that have been bid and played. If a deal is passed out, the same player deals again and the deal passed out does not count as one of the four deals.

A fifth deal is void if attention is drawn to it at any time before there has been a new cut for partners or the game has terminated; if the error is not discovered in time for correction, the score stands as recorded. A sixth or subsequent deal is unconditionally void and no score for such a deal is ever permissible.

In case fewer than four deals are played, the score shall stand for the incomplete series and the fourth deal need not be played unless attention is drawn to the error before there has been a new cut for partners or the game has terminated.

When the players are pivoting, the fact that the players have taken their proper seats for the next rubber shall be considered a cut for partners. (In a pivot game, partnerships for each rubber follow a fixed rotation.)

Vulnerability. Vulnerability is not determined by previous scores but by the following schedule:

First deal: neither side vulnerable.

Second and third deals: dealer's side vulnerable, the other side non-vulnerable.

Fourth deal: both sides vulnerable.

Premiums. For making or completing a game (100 or more trick points), a side receives a premium of 300 points if on that deal it is not vulnerable or 500 points if on that deal it is vulnerable. There is no additional premium for winning two or more games, each game premium being scored separately.

The score. As a reminder of vulnerability in Four Deal Bridge, two intersecting diagonal lines should be drawn near the top of the score pad, as follows:

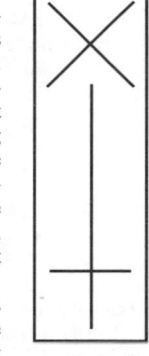

The numeral "1" should be inserted in that one of the four angles thus formed that faces the first dealer. After play of the first deal is completed, "2" is inserted in the next angle in clockwise rotation, facing the dealer of the second deal. The numerals "3" and "4" are subsequently inserted at the start of the third and fourth deals, respectively, each in the angle facing the current dealer.

A correctly numbered diagram is conclusive as to vulnerability. There is no redress for a bid influenced by the scorer's failure to draw the diagram or for an error or omission in inserting a numeral or numerals in the diagram. Such error or omission should, upon discovery, be immediately corrected, and the deal or deals should be scored or rescored as though the diagram and the number or numbers thereon had been properly inserted.

Partscores. Partscores made previously may be combined with a partscore made in the current deal to complete a game of 100 or more trick points. The game premium is determined by the vulnerability of the side that completes the game. When a side makes or completes a game, no previous partscore of either side may thereafter be counted toward game.

A side that makes a partscore in the fourth deal, if the partscore is not sufficient to complete a game, receives a premium of 100 points. This premium is scored whether or not the same side or the other side has an uncompleted partscore. There is no separate premium for making a partscore in any other circumstances.

Deal out of turn. When a player deals out of turn, and there is no right to a redeal, the player who should have dealt retains his right to call first, but such right is lost if it is not claimed before the actual dealer calls. If the actual dealer calls before attention is drawn to the deal out of turn, each player thereafter calls in rotation. Vulnerability and scoring values are determined by the position of the player who should have dealt, regardless of which player actually dealt or called first. Neither the rotation of the deal nor the scoring is affected by a deal out of turn. The next dealer is the player who would have dealt next if the deal had been in turn.

Optional rules and customs. The following practices, not required, have proved acceptable in some clubs and games.

(i) Since the essence of the game is speed, if a deal is passed out, the pack that has been shuffled for the next deal should be used by the same dealer.

(ii) The net score of a rubber should be translated into even hundreds (according to American custom) by crediting as 100 points any fraction thereof amounting to 50 or more points: e.g., 750 points count as 800; 740 points count as 700 points.

(iii) No two players may play a second consecutive rubber as partners at the same table. If two players draw each other again, the player who has drawn the highest card should play with the player who has drawn the third-highest, against the other two players.

(iv) To avoid confusion as to how many deals have been played: Each deal should be scored, even if there is no net advantage to either side (for example, when one side is entitled to 100 points for undertrick penalties and the other side is entitled to 100 points for honors). In a result that completes a game, premiums for overtricks, game, slam, or making a doubled contract should be combined with the trick score to produce one total, which is entered below the line; for example, if a side makes 2♠ doubled and vulnerable with an overtrick, 870 should be scored below the line, not 120 below the line and 50, 500, and 200 above the line.

In some clubs, particularly in New York City, the vulnerability on the second and third deals is reversed. The objective is to give the non-vulnerable side an opportunity to preempt as dealer.

Tactics. Suppose that on the fourth deal, South is declarer at 4♠ with:

♠ Q J 8 3
♥ 8 5 4 3
♦ A J 6
♣ 8 5

♠ A K 10 7 5 2
♥ A 2
♦ K 3
♣ K 6 4

West leads the ♣Q. East wins the ace and shifts to a heart. South checks the score; his side is ahead by 190 points. South can take the ♥A, draw trumps and claim 11 tricks for +650 and victory by 840 points; N-S will win an 8-point chukker. If South makes an extra overtrick, however, N-S will win a 9-point rubber, and if South takes only ten tricks for +620, N-S will still win an 8-point rubber. South should therefore win the ♥A, draw trumps and finesse the ♦J in pursuit of a second overtrick.

In the auction, overbidding the score has the same significance as at rubber bridge: if N-S have a 60 partial, an auction such as 1♠-2♠-3♠ suggests slam. At Chicago, however, the changing vulnerability affects tactics. Suppose that on the third deal, there are three passes to South, who holds:

♠ J 7 5
♥ A Q 10 7 2
♦ K 7 5
♣ J 5

If South passes, E-W get a redeal and retain their vulnerability. South should open 1♥ to deprive the opponents of their chance to make a vulnerable game or slam.

Suppose that on the third deal South holds:

♠ 8 4
♥ K 7 4
♦ A J 9 5 2
♣ K J 4

N-S are vulnerable. After two passes, South should pass. Since North has passed, game is unlikely. South hopes the deal will be passed out, giving N-S another chance to take advantage of their vulnerable status.

Rubber is a misnomer, because it should refer to the traditional best-of-three games format. Alternative words that have some currency are "chukker", originally a period of polo, and "wheel" from the X diagram used to track the dealer on the scorepad. Curiously and coincidentally, chukker is derived from a word meaning "wheel". See COMPENSATION.

CHICAGO TROPHY. Awarded for the North American Open Team Championship (board-a-match scoring) until 1965 when it was replaced by the REISINGER MEMORIAL TROPHY; contested at the Fall NABC (under which heading past results are listed). The Chicago Trophy was donated by the Auction Bridge Club of Chicago in 1929. (In 1928, the open team competition was for the Harold S. Vanderbilt Cup.) See Appendix I for results.

CHICANE. A term from BRIDGE WHIST referring to a hand that is void of trumps. It was scored the same as three honors. In contract bridge, the term is obsolete in its original sense, though it is occasionally used to describe a void suit, as "chicane in hearts."

CHICO TWO DIAMONDS. A simplified version of the MULTI TWO DIAMONDS. An opening bid of 2♦ shows either a weak two-bid in a major or a strong (20+) 4-4-4-1.

CHILEAN BRIDGE FEDERATION (Federacion Chilena de Bridge). The Federation was founded in 1951, and hosted the South American Championships in 1951, -1957, 1965, 1972 and 1984 in Santiago. Chile also hosted the 1993 Bermuda Bowl and Venice Cup championships in Santiago.
President 1993:
Roberto Garcia,
Federacion Chilena de Bridge,
Isadora Goyanechea 2990,
Depto. 111-Santiago,
Chile.

CHINESE BRIDGE ASSOCIATION. Founded in 1980. In 1992 there were 66 groups, organized by province and city. The Association hosted the Far East Championships in 1987 and 1991, and is scheduled to host the 1995 Bermuda Bowl. Its teams have won one open and two women's zonal team titles.
Officers 1992:
Honorary President: Deng Xiaoping
President Emeritus: Wan Li
President: Rong Gaotang
9 Tiyugan Road
Beijing, China.
Tel. 701 33 77
Fax: 701 55 88

CHINESE FINESSE. An attempt to win a trick by leading an unsupported honor.

```
            ♣ A 5
♠ K 8 6 2              ♠ J 10 7
            ♠ Q 9 4 3
```

If South needs to avoid a loser in this suit, he may dismiss the remote chance of dropping the singleton king and try the effect of leading the queen from his hand. In the diagrammed situation West may well decide to duck, fearing that South has Q-J-10, with or without the 9.

CHINESE TAIPEI. See TAIWAN.

CHOICE, RESTRICTED. See RESTRICTED CHOICE.

CHOICE OF PACKS AND SEATS. The winner (or highest card) of the cut for first deal has the choice of which seat he will take and which of the two packs he wishes to deal. Presumably, unless the wrong player deals at some subsequent point, the cards will continue to be dealt by this player and his partner, the other pack by their opponents.

CHOICE OF SUIT. In opening the bidding and responding, a long suit is normally bid ahead of a short one, but a few exceptions should be noted:
(1) A three-card minor suit, particularly clubs, is often bid ahead of a four-card major suit. Using FIVE-CARD MAJORS, the prepared minor-suit bid is made in all situations. In standard methods the major suit will usually be preferred if the suit is biddable and there will not be any rebid difficulty. In practice a four-card major is rarely bid with a 4-3-3-3 distribution: a minimum hand needs to keep the bidding at a low level; a hand of medium strength normally opens 1 NT; and a maximum hand bids 1♣ in order to make it easy for partner to respond.
(2) A strong four-card suit is often bid ahead of a five-card suit that ranks immediately beneath it. (However, with strong hands, a REVERSE from the long suit into the short suit becomes possible.) An acute problem can arise if both suits are of poor quality:

```
♠ A 6 4 2
♥ A 8 5 4 3
♦ A J 6
♣ 8
```

To bid 1♠ followed by 2♥ would be risky. One solution is to open 1♥ and improvise a 2♦ rebid if responder bids 2♣.

```
♠ Q
♥ A J 4
♦ K 7 5 2
♣ A 10 8 5 2
```

Since the diamond suit is weak, the best plan may be to open 1♣ and rebid 1NT over the likely 1♠ response. This sequence does not accurately describe opener's pattern, but neither does a 1♦ opening followed by 2♣; furthermore, a 1NT rebid better limits opener's strength.

```
♠ 4
♥ A K 4
♦ K Q 9 5
♣ K J 7 5 3
```

A 1♦ opening is desirable. If the response is 1♠, opener rebids 2♣. If responder then returns to 2♦, opener has enough extra strength to act again by bidding 2NT.

```
♠ 7 5
♥ A K 5 4
♦ A K 6 5 4
♣ Q 6
```

Players whose style allows a reverse on hands of this strength can open 1♦. If a reverse promises more strength, opener must start with 1♥ or, more likely, 1NT.
Cases are on record in world-championship play where players opened in a strong four-card minor suit ahead of

a weak five-card major, as a U.S. player did when he bid 1♦ on:

♠ 10 7 5 3 2
♥ 8
♦ A K J 10
♣ K 4 3

(3) A five-card suit may be bid ahead of a six-card suit ranking immediately below it if the hand is a minimum:

♠ x
♥ A J x x x
♦ A Q x x x x
♣ x

1♦ followed by a heart bid would not be justified by the strength of the hand, and opposing bidding might shut out the heart suit. Most players will bid 1♥, treating the hand as a 5-5 distribution.

(4) In response to 1♠, a three-card club or diamond suit is sometimes bid in preference to a four-card heart suit.

(5) In response to an opening bid in a red suit, a major suit is sometimes bid at the one-level in preference to a five- or six-card minor suit at the two-level. This may be because the hand is not strong enough to bid at the level of two, or to avoid concealing the major suit when the hand is not worth two constructive bids.

See also BIDDABLE SUITS; CANAPÉ; THREE-CARD SUITS, BIDS IN; WALSH.

With two or three suits of equal length, the choice is more complicated:

(6) With five-card suits (or six-card suits), the opener normally bids the higher-ranking.

With two five-card black suits, expert opinion is divided: a 1♣ opening leaves room for a response at the one level and an easy 1♠ rebid; a 1♠ opening immediately announces possession of the major suit, avoids some rebid problems and has preemptive value. Experts often exercise judgment in the matter, considering the quality of the suits and the strength of the hand. Most experts would open 1♣ with a powerful hand such as:

♠ A Q 8 6 4
♥ A 5
♦ 7
♣ A K J 7 4

to make it easier for partner — or the opponents — to keep the auction alive. With:

♠ A K 8 5 2	or	♠ A K J 10 3
♥ Q 5		♥ A 5
♦ 3		♠ 4
♣ A K 6 4 2		♣ 10 8 6 4 2

most would open 1♠ — in the first case because they are willing to rebid clubs at the level of three; in the second because they treat the club holding as a four-card suit.

A rare exception can arise when a player holds a minimum hand and a void. With 5-0-5-3 or 3-5-0-5, some players bid the minor suit for reasons of preparedness.

(7) With two or three four-card suits, opener at one time would usually begin with the suit below the shortage, or most nearly below it, to prepare an economical rebid after the expected response in his short suit.

♠ 6 5 2	♠ 5 4
♥ A K 6 4	♥ A K 6 4
♦ 5 4	♦ 6 5 2
♣ A Q 7 5	♣ A Q 7 5

Opener would start with 1♣ on the first hand and 1♥ on the second. But with hands containing two strong four-card major suits, such as:

♠ A Q 10 6
♥ A K 10 5
♦ 5 4 3
♣ J 3

experts disagree on the better opening bid. And if the "rule" dictated opening in a weak four-card major suit, most players would search for another bid.

(a)	(b)	(c)
♠ 7 5	♠ 7 4	♠ 6 4 3
♥ Q 8 6 4	♥ J 5 4 3	♥ K 10 5 3
♦ A 4 2	♦ A Q 6 4	♦ A Q 7 5
♣ A K 6 4	♣ A K 4	♣ A 4
1♣	1♦	1♦

In all three cases, opener could comfortably rebid 1NT over a response of 1♠.

The advent of FIVE-CARD MAJORS further eroded the "rule"; pairs using this style found the choice of a suit limited by system. However, the five-card-major style is not trouble-free. On hand (c), above, and on the two hands below,

♠ J 5 4 3	♠ J 7 5 3
♥ J 7 4 2	♥ A K 5
♦ A K 3	♦ J 8 5 3
♣ A 10	♣ A 10

opener has a doubleton club; he therefore used to have a problem after a response of 2♣ to a 1♦ opening. In the modern style there is no difficulty, since opener's 2NT rebid after a two-over-one response suggests no extra strength.

If the opener's hand is extremely strong, he rarely has a rebid problem. In that case, a minor suit is often bid in preference to a major, with the idea of keeping the bidding low and giving partner maximum opportunity to respond if his hand is weak.

If the opener holds both minor suits, he often has a free choice and may be guided by tactical or lead-inhibiting (or lead-directing) considerations. Since opener will seldom wish to bid both suits, he need not open 1♦ to prepare a 2♣ rebid. However, 1♦ may be preferable holding a worthless tripleton heart:

♠ A J
♥ 10 6 4
♦ K J 10 3
♣ K J 5 3

A 1♣ opening would leave opener with an awkward rebid after an overcall of 1♥ and a response of 1♠.

♠ 6 5
♥ J 6 4
♦ A Q 7 5
♣ A K 6 5

Here, opener must plan his rebid after a 1♥ response. If he is willing to raise to 2♥ or rebid 1NT, he can start with 1♣; otherwise, he must open 1♦, planning to rebid 2♣.

Hands with three four-card suits are often difficult to describe. To open in the "middle" suit may sometimes fare better than the traditional "suit below the shortage":

♠ K Q 9 4
♥ K Q 10 4
♦ A 9 5 3
♣ 3

A 1♥ opening avoids the awkward rebid that opener faces if he opens 1♠ and receives a response of 1NT or 2♣. (Again, a 1♦ opening is required in a FIVE-CARD MAJOR style.)

♠ Q
♥ K J 9 3
♦ K 7 6 4
♣ A J 7 3

If opener expects a 1♠ response and is willing to rebid 1NT, he can open 1♣. To open 1♦, keeping a 2♣ rebid in reserve, would work well if the response were 1NT. A 1♥ opening might lose if the response were 1NT; opener would have to guess which minor suit to bid next.

(8) With five-card suits, responder invariably prefers the higher-ranking for his response. For responder's choice with four-card suits, see UP THE LINE.

CHUKKER. A term for four deals of CHICAGO. It is also used in a long team match for a group of boards followed by comparison of scores. The term is borrowed from polo.

CHURCHILL STYLE. The methods of bidding advocated by S. Garton Churchill of New York. The main features are:

(1) A weak notrump opening. Churchill was among the first leading American theorists to advocate this bid and his followers were the exclusive advocates of it for many years.

(2) A "utility" 1NT response with a wide variety of weak hands. This was the forerunner of the forcing ROTHSTONE 1NT response.

(3) Light opening bids with distributional patterns such as 5-4-3-1, 5-4-4-0, 4-4-4-1, 6-4-3-0, 5-5-3-0, 6-5-1-1, etc.

(4) Frequent bids in short suits; Churchill was well before his time in using such bids as all-purpose bids for exploring for games and slams, or steering the contract into a particular hand, etc.

(5) Constructive overcalls; forcing jump overcalls.

(6) Four-card openings in suits of any strength.

(7) "Picture Bidding"; jump rebids and responses used essentially to describe solid or near-solid suits as well as slam aspirations.

(8) No strength-showing forcing opening bid.

(9) Sparing use of preemptive bids.

(10) Balance of Power bidding (see BALANCING).

CIPHER BID. See ARTIFICIAL BID.

CIRCUS. See SHARIF BRIDGE CIRCUS.

C.I.S. or Commonwealth of Independent States. An Association of Russia and Belorussia for international representation. See RUSSIA.

CLAIM OR CONCESSION. A suggestion that play be curtailed; a statement to the effect that a player will win (claim) or lose (concession) a specific number of tricks. The definition is the same for both duplicate and social bridge, but the procedure following a claim or concession is quite different.

In social bridge, the player who claims, or concedes, must put his cards open upon the table, and then make a comprehensive statement of his intentions. If the claim is disputed, play continues with claimer's cards exposed. Claimer is restricted by the statement he made: He may not take an unannounced finesse, except one proven or

virtually proven; If he may have been unaware that a trump remained out, his opponents may require him to draw, or not to draw, trump; He may adopt only a routine line of play, not an unannounced unusual line.

If claimer is declarer, either defender (or both) may face his cards for partner's inspection without penalty. If claimer is a defender, declarer may prohibit the other defender from making a play that could be suggested by seeing partner's cards.

In duplicate bridge a claim or concession ends play. When there is any dispute the Director is called to hear the claimer repeat his statement and to adjudicate the result. In adjudicating, the Director restricts claimer's proposed line of play as in rubber bridge.

A concession may be withdrawn if the player has conceded a trick he has already won, or must win on any possible play of the remaining cards. In rubber bridge this right lapses when all players have called on a subsequent deal. In duplicate it lapses with the expiration of the normal protest period. If a conceded trick cannot be lost by any probable play, the concession may be withdrawn: in rubber bridge until the cards are mixed together; in duplicate until the conceding side calls on a susequent deal or the round ends. In duplicate, agreeing to an opponent's claim, "acquiescing", is not conceding: an acquiescence may be withdrawn within the normal protest period. In either game, a concession by one defender is withdrawn if the other objects immediately.

In both codes of law this general principle is established: After any disputed claim, the objective is to settle the issue as equitably as possible to both sides, but any doubtful point should be resolved in favor of the claimer's opponents.

CLARAC SLAM TRY. A feature of the PRO SYSTEM based principally on a 4♣ bid to ask about aces and other controls. The name CLARAC is an acronym for Club Asking, Respond Aces and Controls.

Responses to 4♣ vary according to whether responder has previously shown a good hand. If his hand is limited, a 4♥ response (for example) shows one ace plus first- or second-round control in hearts. If responder has shown a strong hand, the responses to 4♣ show one ace more than they do by a limited hand.

After any response to 4♣ (except 4♦, which denies an ace or K-Q combination), a suit bid by the 4♣ bidder is an asking bid in that suit. More asking bids may follow.

CLASH SQUEEZE. A squeeze in three suits, distinguished by the presence of a special type of long menace called a clash menace, analyzed and named by Chien-Hwa Wang (in *Bridge Magazine* articles 1956-57).

A 2
K   J 10
        Q

South's queen is a clash menace against West's king.

        A x x
Q J   9 x x
        K 10

South's 10 is a clash menace against West's queen and jack.

The following are the basic positions for a clash squeeze.

(1) Simple Squeeze-Positional

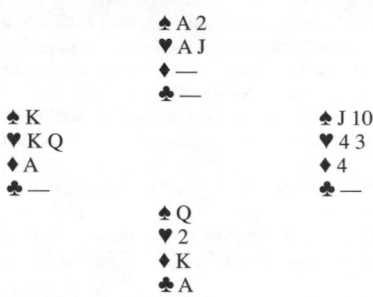

```
            ♠ A 2
            ♥ A J
            ♦ —
            ♣ —
♠ K                    ♠ J 10
♥ K Q                  ♥ 4 3
♦ A                    ♦ 4
♣ —                    ♣ —
            ♠ Q
            ♥ 2
            ♦ K
            ♣ A
```

South leads the ♣A, which squeezes West in three suits (if West discards a spade, South cashes the queen and then crosses to the ♥A in order to take the ♠A).

Delayed (secondary)

```
            ♠ A 2
            ♥ K 10
            ♦ K 4
            ♣ —
♠ K                    ♠ J 10
♥ Q J                  ♥ A 3
♦ Q 6 5                ♦ 8 7
♣ —                    ♣ —
            ♠ Q
            ♥ 2
            ♦ A 3 2
            ♣ A
```

South leads the ♣A, which squeezes West in three suits. West must discard a heart, and North throws a spade. Now South can lead a heart and establish a trick in that suit. See also VICE SQUEEZE.

(2) Double Squeeze (nonsimultaneous and positional). A double clash squeeze consists of two parts: a clash squeeze against one opponent, then a simple squeeze against the other.

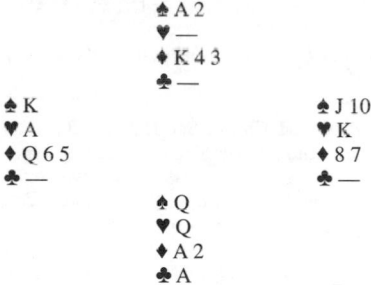

```
            ♠ A 2
            ♥ —
            ♦ K 4 3
            ♣ —
♠ K                    ♠ J 10
♥ A                    ♥ K
♦ Q 6 5                ♦ 8 7
♣ —                    ♣ —
            ♠ Q
            ♥ Q
            ♦ A 2
            ♣ A
```

South leads the ♣A, and West is clash squeezed. He must discard a heart, after which South plays the ♦K then ♦A to squeeze East in the majors.

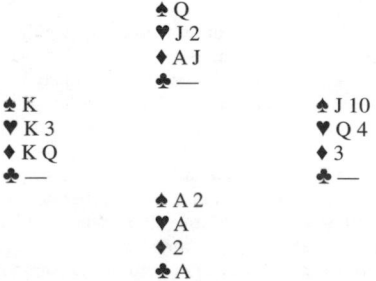

```
            ♠ Q
            ♥ J 2
            ♦ A J
            ♣ —
♠ K                    ♠ J 10
♥ K 3                  ♥ Q 4
♦ K Q                  ♦ 3
♣ —                    ♣ —
            ♠ A 2
            ♥ A
            ♦ 2
            ♣ A
```

The ♣A lead by South clash squeezes West, and forces him to discard a heart. South cashes the ♥A (VIENNA COUP), then crosses to the ♦A, squeezing East in the majors.

(3) Double Squeeze (simultaneous)

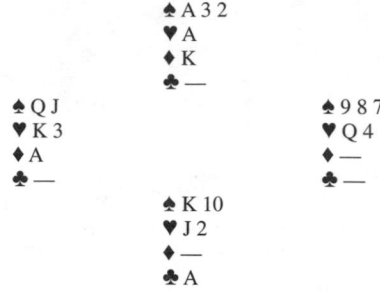

```
            ♠ A 3 2
            ♥ A
            ♦ K
            ♣ —
♠ Q J                  ♠ 9 8 7
♥ K 3                  ♥ Q 4
♦ A                    ♦ —
♣ —                    ♣ —
            ♠ K 10
            ♥ J 2
            ♦ —
            ♣ A
```

On the lead of the ♣A West must discard a heart, North throws a diamond, and East is squeezed in the majors. This is a positional squeeze.

Secondary

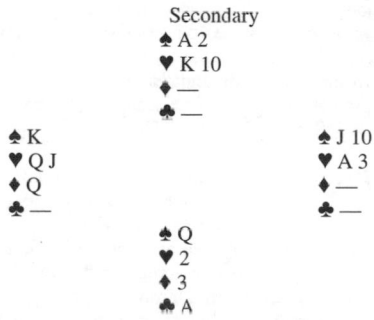

```
            ♠ A 2
            ♥ K 10
            ♦ —
            ♣ —
♠ K                    ♠ J 10
♥ Q J                  ♥ A 3
♦ Q                    ♦ —
♣ —                    ♣ —
            ♠ Q
            ♥ 2
            ♦ 3
            ♣ A
```

South leads the ♣A. If West discards a heart , North throws a spade, and East throws a spade. South leads a heart to establish a trick in that suit, with the ♠A for an entry. If West throws a spade, North throws a heart as does East. South cashes the ♠Q and leads a heart to throw in East who must give the last trick to North's ♠A.

(4) Trump Squeeze

Single

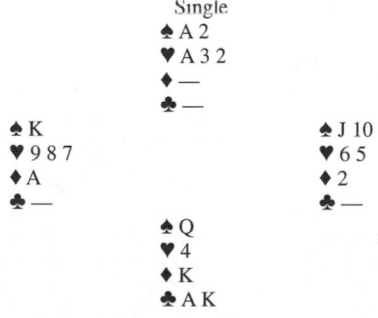

```
            ♠ A 2
            ♥ A 3 2
            ♦ —
            ♣ —
♠ K                    ♠ J 10
♥ 9 8 7                ♥ 6 5
♦ A                    ♦ 2
♣ —                    ♣ —
            ♠ Q
            ♥ 4
            ♦ K
            ♣ A K
```

With clubs as trumps, South leads the king of that suit. West can do no better than discard a heart, but now South can ruff out that suit, using the ♠A as a re-entry. This squeeze is positional.

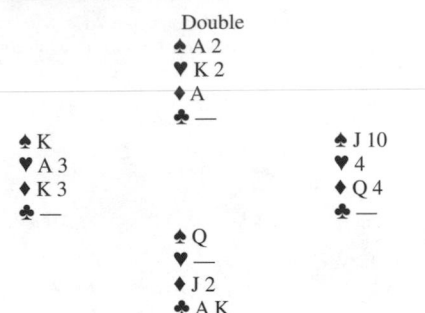

Double
♠ A 2
♥ K 2
♦ A
♣ —

♠ K   ♠ J 10
♥ A 3   ♥ 4
♦ K 3   ♦ Q 4
♣ —   ♣ —

♠ Q
♥ —
♦ J 2
♣ A K

Clubs are trumps. South leads the trump king, and West must throw a diamond. North and East discard hearts. South cashes the ♦A and ruffs a heart, squeezing East in spades and diamonds. See HEDGEHOG SQUEEZE.

CLEAR A SUIT. At notrump play, to clear a suit is to force out, by continued leads of the suit, adversely held high cards so that the remainder of the cards in that suit are winners. At suit play, the term is used also to indicate a line of play which cashes winners in one side suit and trumps out the balance of the cards in that suit so as to eliminate all cards of the suit from both the declarer's and dummy's hand. Then if a trick is lost to the defense later, a further lead of this suit gives declarer the option of trumping in one hand while discarding a potential loser in the other. See also ELIMINATION.

CLOCKS. Devices used at tournaments to indicate to the players how much time is left in the round and when the round is ended. The clocks usually are large display boxes with the time indicated by lights. A sound usually is emitted when two minutes remain in the round, and a second sound occurs when the round is over.

Clocks also are used to time pairs in a team event. Since there are penalties for slow play, it becomes necessary to determine who was responsible for the slow play. The only realistic way to do this is to time the individual pairs with clocks such as chess clocks.

CLOSED HAND. The hand of the declarer, as distinct from the OPEN HAND, which is now legally referred to as the DUMMY. The term dates from BRIDGE WHIST, which introduced the idea of an exposed hand visible to the other players.

CLOSED ROOM. In team-of-four matches, particularly in knockout matches, the two pairs of a team play in different rooms or different areas of the same room. One of these rooms is designated the open room, one the closed room. Normally, spectators are permitted in the open room, and these spectators are free to come and go, without hindrance. However, if spectators are permitted in the closed room, they are restricted to one table and are not permitted to leave until the match they are watching is terminated. As soon as one of the matches in the closed room has been terminated, the original open room becomes a closed room to which no other spectators are permitted entrance, and to which no contestant or spectator may be readmitted after leaving until the last open room contest has terminated.

In important matches where arrangements are made for play-by-play relaying of information to a large group of spectators, the boards are originally played in a closed room with a starting time appreciably earlier than that for the replay. Thus information may be kept from the players in the replay but made available to spectators, who can contrast the results of the first play with what is going on in the replay. Spectators thus are more fully informed of what has gone on than are any of the actual contestants.

In some major events such as the European Championship, the open room is always open, but players are not permitted to leave the closed room until the open half of their match is completed. See BRIDGE-O-RAMA.

CLOTHESLINE. An arrangement by which traveling scoreslips can be displayed for study by the players when the recapitulation sheet does not show information beyond the matchpoint score itself.

CLUB. (1) The symbol ♣, which appears on the 13 cards of the lowest ranking of the four suits in a bridge deck, stems from the French (trefle), but the name seems to be of Spanish or Italian origin as a translation of basto or bastone. (2) The club suit consists of the 13 cards bearing this symbol. Since the club suit as trump is the least likely final declaration when a choice of trump suits is available, many systems make use of the naming of this suit to show conventional holdings. See CLUB CONVENTIONS.

CLUB BRIDGE. See CHICAGO.

CLUB CHARITY GAMES. See CHARITY PROGRAM OF THE ACBL.

CLUB CONVENTIONS. The low-ranking club suit is particularly well suited for conventional uses of various kinds. The VANDERBILT CLUB was the original "club convention" and has had many successors (see ONE CLUB SYSTEMS and TWO CLUB SYSTEMS). Conventional club bids at higher levels include TWO CLUBS STRONG ARTIFICIAL OPENING, STAYMAN and GERBER.

CLUB PROCEDURES. See HOUSE RULES. Each bridge club will find that there are situations in its operation that are not covered by the Laws or where the Laws do not agree with the desire of the members of the club on such points as precedence in entering a table, complement of a table, personal dislikes of certain players, methods of settling games for stakes and like problems. Procedures used in such cases should always be consistent and definitely formulated for future reference.

CLUB SYSTEMS. See ONE CLUB SYSTEMS, TWO CLUB SYSTEMS.

CLUBS. Organizations or groups of bridge players who form units acting as centers of interest for players in a particular community. All over the world may be found clubs catering to the needs and wishes of people in all walks of life who have one common interest, contract bridge.

Clubs are today so diversified as to type of premises and rules of membership that a comprehensive description is impossible. Large cities all over the world have at least one and often many more such clubs. Those who prefer to play for stakes can usually be accommodated, providing they pass whatever standards are set up. Those who prefer duplicate can usually find an open-game club devoted to such purposes. In smaller towns throughout America, the emphasis has shifted to duplicate bridge, and a club for that purpose is almost always available to the players of the community. The ACBL issues directories of the 4000-plus clubs that operate games approved by ACBL. Games usually occur at regular periods, with specially scheduled club championship events every calendar quarter. Fees are charged for each participation, and in some cases annual dues as well. In North America, many owners have banded together into the Club Owners Association for the group's mutual benefit. See OLDEST CLUBS.

CLUBS FOR TAKEOUT. A variation of CHEAPER MINOR TAKEOUT. The bid for takeout is always made in clubs. Even when the preempt is in clubs, the next higher club bid shows a hand worth a takeout double.

COAT CARDS. The original term in English for the three cards of each suit which represent costumed human figures: the king, queen and jack. In some countries a fourth coat card, variously the valet or courtier, is included in the deck. The term has been superseded by a corruption, "court cards." See FACE CARDS.

COFFEEHOUSE BRIDGE. Card playing in European coffee houses frequently featured conversational or other gambits designed to mislead opponents, and the term "coffeehouse bridge" became a synonym for legal but unethical gambits. Such questions as "Did you bid a *spade?*" with a rising inflection to inform partner of a sound spade holding in one's own cards, or "What did you bid first over 1♦?" to right-hand opponent when one wants his partner to lead that suit against a notrump contract, are gambits that are easily caught. Such a player is ostracized at rubber bridge, and the offense is adjudicated in duplicate bridge when a director is present. Action on a doubtful hand after a slow pass by partner is somewhat harder to classify, but the ethical player will pass all such doubtful hands after such a slow pass by partner.

Conversational gambits, even when made without any devious intent, have no place at the bridge table among serious, ethical players.

COFFEEHOUSING. Indulging in unethical actions with full intent to mislead opponents.

```
              K J
     Q 2              A 5
              4 3
```

The 4 is led from the closed hand, and West hesitates before playing the obvious 2. This is coffeehousing — an attempt to make the declarer believe that West was thinking of playing the ace. If this happens in tournament play, South should call the director and is likely to get redress under Law 73D2. See COFFEEHOUSE BRIDGE.

C.O.I. See COMMITTEE FOR AN OPEN AND IMPROVED ACBL.

COLD. Bridge slang term describing an easily makable contract. In post-mortem heat, players tend to exaggerate the degrees of coldness. Frigid and icy are similar terms. A colorful variation is "colder than a creek rock" or "crick rock."

COLLECTION AND ARRANGEMENT OF TRICKS. See LAWS OF CONTRACT BRIDGE (Law 65); LAWS OF DUPLICATE (Law 65).

COLLECTIONS OF PLAYING CARDS. Collections, public and private, are fairly numerous; quite a few museums have cards as part of their material on graphic arts.

The largest collection in the United States, a gift of the United States Playing Card Company to the Museum of Art, is in Cincinnati OH. In New York City, the Morgan Library has a few of the oldest and most valuable cards. Yale University has a collection of more than 3000 packs, uncut sheets, and card printers' woodblocks acquired by the late Melbert and Mary Cary and willed to Yale University in 1967.

The French collection is in the Bibliotheque Nationale in Paris; London has a collection in the Guildhall; others are in Vienna, Nuremberg, Dresden, Munich, and Budapest. The Deutschspielkarten Museum in Leinfelden, Germany, south of Stuttgart, is a research center and an exhibition. The Museo "Fournier" de Naipes in Vitoria, Spain, has a collection of 6,000 packs and more than 12,000 books. The largest private collection, belonging to Albert Field, Astoria N.Y., has been willed to Columbia University.

COLLEGE BRIDGE. See INTERCOLLEGIATE BRIDGE TOURNAMENT. Also see Appendix IV for results.

COLLOQUIALISMS. Bridge has evolved or adopted its share of colloquialisms. For example, see the following: BIFF; BLOCKBUSTER; DEATH HOLDING; DUB; FIXED; FRAME; GAME HOG; GOULASH; HOOK; HORSE AND HORSE; JUNK; KIBITZ; KICK IT; KILLED; LAY-DOWN; LOCK; MAMA-PAPA BRIDGE; MAYONNAISE; PALOOKA; PHANTOM SACRIFICE; PIANOLA; PUMP; PUNCH; QUACK; RAGS; RIDE; SHAKE; SOCK; STIFF; SUCKER'S DOUBLE; TANK; UNDER THE GUN; and UPPERCUT.

COLOMBIAN BRIDGE FEDERATION. (Federación Colombiana de Bridge). The Federation was founded in 1963 by clubs in Bogotá, Medellín, Barranquilla, Cali and Pereira. The Federation hosted the Central American and Caribbean Championships in 1980 and 1989, and won both Open Team and Women's Team title in 1989. 1992 Officers:
  President: Jorge Barrera Carrasquilla
  Secretary: Mónica Durán de Luna
  C11 77 No. 9-76 (104)
  Santa Fé de Bogotá
  Colombia.
  Tel. 2368774.

COLONIAL ACOL. A version of ACOL popular in Canada; its basic elements were used by all three Canadian pairs in the 1972 World Team Olympiad.

Major features include four-card major suit openings (1♣ opening may be prepared). Jump raises are usually limit, with either SWISS, JACOBY 2 NT or SPLINTERS used to show a strong raise. 1 NT opening is 16-18, although some shade it to 15-17, with TWO-WAY STAYMAN. Opening bids of 2♦, 2♥, or 2♠ are ACOL

TWO-BIDS; some partnerships use FLANNERY 2♦.

COLOR. A term occasionally used to distinguish suit-play as opposed to notrump play. In the bidding, to "change the color" means to bid a new suit. The term is virtually synonymous with "suit."

COLORFUL CUEBID. An immediate overcall in the opponent's major suit to show two unbid suits of the same color. Devised by Dorothy Hayden Truscott. See also CUEBIDS IN OPPONENT'S SUIT; MICHAELS CUE-BID.

COLUMNS. See BRIDGE COLUMNS.

COMBINATION FINESSE. See DOUBLE FINESSE and INTRA-FINESSE.

COMBINATION TEAM SCORING. A method of scoring team-of-four events that permits comparison of pair scores as well as team scores. After award of team scores on a win-half-loss basis, the North-South scores are matchpointed on the basis of the number of times the board was played, and the East-West scores are matchpointed on the same basis.

In theory this combination team scoring permits a team to analyze its game as to which of the pairs contributed to the winning or losing of boards by securing a less-than-average result.

This is also the method by which team scores are computed on a board that has been fouled between the times that the two halves of the team play it. The fields resulting from the fouling are matchpointed separately, and the combination of the percentages of the possible matchpoints totaled for the two team halves. Such a total of less than 70 loses the board, exceeding 130 wins the board, and between these percentages a half on the board is awarded.

COMBINATIONS. The idea of a combination is fundamental to bridge calculations. Examples where this conception is used are in calculating the probability of a specified hand pattern or the division of a suit among the four players. It is also frequently used in calculating the respective probabilities of (or the ratio between) the division of the combined holding of the defenders in a specified suit or with specified honor holdings.

Our general expression for a combination is nCr, which we read as 'the number of combinations of n things taken r at a time'. For example, 4C2 means the number of ways in which we can select two articles out of a total of four articles.

We note that if r=n we can write nCn in place of nCr. Whatever the number n represents nCn is equal to 1. After all, there is only one way in which we can select n articles out of a total of n articles. There is also only one way in which we can select no (0) articles.

The values of a selected number of combinations are given in Mathematical Tables, Table 5.

If we wish to calculate the value of a combination we need to understand the concept of the 'factorial'. For bridge purposes the factorial of a number is the product of all numbers from 1 up to and including the specified number, e. g., five factorial (written 5!) is 1 x 2 x 3 x 4 x 5. When using factorials in our calculations we often find it simpler to reverse the above order, setting out 5! as 5 x 4 x 3 x 2 x 1.

Conventionally the value of 0! is taken as 1.

Consider the number of ways in which 13 cards can be selected from a pack of 52 cards. Our first can be any one of the 52 cards, our second any one of 51 cards, etc. We have the following calculation:

$$52 \times 51 \times 50 \ldots 41 \times 40$$

which is the same as multiplying all the numbers from 52 down to 1 and dividing the answer by the product of all the numbers from 39 down to 1. We can express this calculation in mathematical shorthand as:

$$\frac{52!}{39!}$$

However, this is not the whole story. The answer we obtain would be correct if we were interested in the order in which we select the 13 cards. This is not the case. The order in which the cards are selected is irrelevant for our purpose. Let us take one of the 13 cards at random. It could have been selected on any one of our 13 draws. A second of these cards could have been selected on any one of the remaining twelve draws, and so on. In other words, we have 13 x 12 x 11 .... x 1 (or 13!) ways in which those 13 cards could be selected. This means that the total number of ways in which 13 cards can be selected from a pack of 52 cards is

$$\frac{52!}{39! \; 13!}$$

(See NUMBER OF POSSIBLE HANDS, DEALS).

Our general formula for this type of calculation is

$$\frac{n!}{r! \times (n-r)!}$$

Let us now look at a simple example where the defenders have a combined holding of four cards in a specified suit. This means that they hold 22 cards in the other three suits. A named player can have a holding in the specified suit of

0 cards in 4C0 x 22C13 ways.
1 card in 4C1 x 22C12 ways.
2 cards in 4C2 x 22C11 ways.
3 cards in 4C3 x 22C10 ways.
4 cards in 4C4 x 22C9 ways.

Bearing in mind that 26 cards can be divided between the two defenders in 26C13 (or 10,400,600) ways, we obtain the following table

		%.
4C0 x 22C13	= 1 x 497,420	
	= 497,420 =	4.782 6
4C1 x 22C12	= 4 x 646,646	
	= 2,586,584 =	24.869 6
4C2 x 22C11	= 6 x 705,432	
	= 4,232,592 =	40.695 7
4C3 x 22C10	= 4 x 646,646	
	= 2,586,584 =	24.869 6
4C4 x 22C9	= 1 x 497,420	
	= 497,420 =	4.782 6
TOTAL	10,400,600	100.000 1

The extra 0.0001% is, of course, due to approximating.

We note that nCr = nC(n-r). In other words, 4C1 is equal to 4C3. This is obvious, for if one player can hold r cards in a specified number of ways his partner must be able to hold the remainder of the partnership cards in exactly the same number of ways.

Now let us examine the problem of a holding of specified cards. Let us assume that the four cards held by the defense in a named suit consist of K-Q-x-x. What is the probability that a named defender, e.g., West, holds both the king and the queen? He can hold

$$K\text{-}Q\text{-}x\text{-}x = 4C4 \times 22C9$$
$$= 1 \times 497{,}420$$
$$= 497{,}420$$
$$K\text{-}Q\text{-}x = 2C2 \times 2C1 \times 22C10$$
$$= 1 \times 2 \times 646{,}646$$
$$= 1{,}293{,}292$$
$$K\text{-}Q = 2C2 \times 22C11$$
$$= 1 \times 705{,}432$$
$$= \underline{705{,}432}$$
$$2{,}496{,}144 \text{ Total}$$

The respective percentages are: 4.7826; 12.4348; 6.7826. The total is exactly 24%.

When we compare the probability of his holding the doubleton K-Q with the probability of his holding the singleton K half our work is already done. We have

$$K\text{-}Q = 2C2 \times 22C11 = 1 \times 705{,}432$$
$$= 705{,}432 = 6.782\ 6\%$$
$$K = 1C1 \times 22C12 = 1 \times 646{,}646$$
$$= 646{,}646 = 6.2174\%$$

We find that 705,432 and 646,646 have a highest common factor (HCF) of 58,786 giving us a ratio of 12:11.

As 2C2 and 1C1 are both equal to 1 we are really comparing 22C11 and 22C12. This comparison can be made without the above calculations if we note that

$$nC(r+1) = \frac{nCr \times (n-r)}{r+1}$$

In our above example we have n = 22 and r = 11, so

$$22C12 = \frac{22C11 \times (22-11)}{11+1} \text{ or } \frac{22C11 \times 11}{12}$$

giving us a ratio of 22C12 to 22C11 or 11:12. Alternatively we can use the formula

$$nC(r-1) = \frac{nCr \times r}{n\ (r-1)} \text{ or } 22C11 = \frac{22C12 \times 12}{22\ (12-1)}$$

giving us the ratio of 22C11 to 22C12 as 12:11. This method may be used to draw other comparisons, e.g., which has the greater probability, and by how much, that a named player will hold two out of four missing cards or that he will hold three of such cards? We have a comparison between

$$4C2 \times 22C11 \text{ and } 4C3 \times 22C10.$$

We know that

$$22C11 = 22C10 \times 12/11$$

and that

$$4C2 = 4C3 \times 3/2$$

so

$$4C2 \times 22C11 = \left(4C3 \times \frac{3)}{2} \right) \left(22C10 \times \frac{12)}{11} \right)$$

The ratio is thus

$$4C2 \times 22C11 : 4C3 \times 22C10 :: 18 : 11$$

This means that the chance of a named player holding two of four missing cards is higher than his chance of holding three of such cards. However, the overall chance of a 3-1 or 1-3 break is 22 : 18 (or 11 : 9) as there are two different (and equal) ways in which the defenders' cards can be divided so that one of them holds three cards, but only one way in which each of them holds two cards.

There are many other problems in which we can use this method of calculating the ratios between two (or more) different probabilities.

COME-ON, COME-ON SIGNAL. A defensive maneuver by which one player indicates to his partner that he wishes a suit, led by his partner, to be continued. The usual come-on is a HIGH-LOW SIGNAL, called also an "echo," and in England, a PETER. An alternative is the UPSIDE-DOWN SIGNAL.

COMIC NOTRUMP OVERCALL. An overcall of 1 NT to show a weak hand with a long suit. Partner bids 2♣ to locate the long suit. See also GARDENER NOTRUMP OVERCALL.

COMMAND BID. A term suggested by George Rosenkranz to describe a bid that commands partner to make a specific response, but: (a) does not promise a holding in the commanded suit (compare TRANSFER BID); (b) promises no particular strength (compare DEMAND BID); (c) does not ask about the holding in any suit (compare ASKING BID). For example:

WEST	NORTH	EAST	SOUTH
2 ♠	Dbl	Pass	2 NT

By partnership agreement, South's bid of 2NT is LEBENSOHL. North is forced to bid 3♣, after which South has several options.

With the advent of conventions such as PUPPET STAYMAN, the alternative term "puppet bid" has come into use.

COMMITTEE. In tournaments of the American Contract Bridge League of sectional or higher rating, a committee from the sponsoring organization is charged with the responsibility of making necessary arrangements. This is known as the tournament committee. The work of this committee is divided into two parts, before and during the tournament. Among the pretournament duties are arrangements for location, dates, securing of sanctions, arrangements for services to the players, prizes, obtaining the services of a director, publicity and financing.

During the course of a tournament, the director may be called on to make a ruling where he is unable to secure agreement on the facts under question. In such cases, and in cases where the director uses his discretionary powers, a player may, through the director, appeal to the tournament committee. Such an appeal is based on questions of fact, not of law. See Chapter XI, LAWS OF DUPLICATE CONTRACT BRIDGE.

Appeals to the national authority on matters of conduct, deportment or ethics can be taken to the National Conduct, Deportment and Ethics Committee, and on questions of law to the National Laws Commission.

Occasionally, the tournament committee delegates to a subcommittee (known as an appeals committee) its duties at a particular tournament. See NATIONAL APPEALS COMMITTEE.

At world championships, a specially appointed appeals committee is on duty during and after every session of play.

COMMITTEE FOR AN OPEN AND IMPROVED ACBL (COI). Organized in 1990 by a group of ACBL members interested in promoting openness in Board and Management functions and offering constructive criticisms. Besides the concentration on communications, the group focused specifically on cost containment, efficiency at headquarters, reducing the size of the Board of Directors and the costs of Board meetings, honorariums and expenses. They advocated Bylaw revision and redistricting. At the Boston NABC in the summer of 1990, the annual membership meeting was reconvened five times (probably the longest in history) as amendments to Bylaws were initiated. Four months later at the Fall NABC in San Francisco the membership and the Board of Governors voted in favor of four of five recommended Bylaws. Also at San Francisco COI participated in formation of the President's Advisory Committee on Policies and Procedures (PACPP) composed of three members each from the Board of Directors, the Board of Governors and the general membership with Jack Feagin, head of COI, as spokesman for membership. Four years later the *COI Newsletter* agreed that PACPP —presented as an alternative to the "war being waged by some of the members hoping to achieve changes in the ACBL government and management" — proved to be a flop.

At the Spring NABC in Atlantic City in 1991 the Bylaws changes were transformed into "Special Standing Rules" (a supplement to ACBL Bylaws) subject to cancellation by a simple majority vote of the Board of Directors. In Las Vegas in the Summer of 1991 COI endorsed Board of Governors recommendations and passed pertinent resolutions to save money and improve existing Bylaws. However, the annual membership meeting was declared a non-meeting because of lack of a quorum so none of the resolutions could be brought up or voted upon. At the COI meeting in Washington DC in July 1993 the topics of discussion were the new club plan and alternate methods of reducing the size of the Board of Directors.

Leaders of the COI and editors of its Newsletter are Jack Feagin, Nadine Wood and Jim Wood. In 1994 the secretary was Barbara Heller of Decatur GA, and Betty Dudka of Alexandria VA was treasurer.

COMMON MARKET CHAMPIONSHIPS. See EUROPEAN COMMUNITY CHAMPIONSHIPS. For results, see Appendix IV.

COMMONSENSE SYSTEM. See CRANE SYSTEM.

COMMUNICATION BETWEEN PARTNERS. The act of conveying information within a partnership. It is a breach of ethics when information is conveyed intentionally by a remark, gesture or mannerism. See LAWS (Proprieties, 1). Information can of course be conveyed legitimately by bids and defensive plays.

COMMUNICATION PLAY. A play intended to preserve or establish communication (transfer of the lead) between partnership hands to make it possible at a strategic time to lead from a certain hand; or a play to destroy such means of communication between the opponents. Various plays of this nature are discussed in the following articles: DESCHAPELLES COUP; DUCKING; ENTRY; ENTRY-KILLING PLAY; HOLDUP; MERRIMAC COUP; SCISSORS COUP.

COMMUNICATIONS. The ability to transfer the lead from one hand to the opposite hand.

COMMUTER BRIDGE. A set-to at bridge on trains, popular in Boston, Chicago, New York, Philadelphia and other cities. Players who regularly use the same train for commuting arrange to have the first player to enter the train reserve a double seat, and the other players use the same car, joining the game as soon as they board the train. In New York, the cards are dealt as the last player boards, and play is continued until the train reaches the Newark or 125th Street station, after which no further hands are dealt.

Originally, running scores in the form of rubbers prevailed, continuing from day to day with settlement of the wagers made monthly, but in the Sixties four-deal bridge (CHICAGO) gained ground. In some groups it is common to make a Tunnel Bid: A wild action aimed at recovering lost ground as the train runs into the terminal.

COMPARING SCORES. Discussion of results already achieved by contestants in a duplicate competition. Making such comparisons with other contestants playing the same board in tournament play before the session's play has been completed has long been held to be unethical. Since 1963 these comparisons have been declared illegal, and the director is authorized to assess penalties for such actions..

The private scores kept by many tournament players furnish material for long and involved discussions of what might have been, and are very useful for later study and as a reminder of holdings.

In club games where traveling scoreslips are used to facilitate the scoring of the game, knowledge of previous results on an individual board is legitimately available to the players after the board has been played. Courtesy requires that the player responsible for scoring the result make the slip available to the other players who are entitled to see it; discussion of previous results should be held in abeyance until both (or all) the boards of the current round have been completed. Score comparison is not regarded with disfavor in Europe. Players may compare scores on boards already played by both partnerships unless specifically instructed to the contrary. See ESTIMATION.

COMPARISONS. At duplicate, comparisons are made between pairs (or players) who played a board in the same direction, and consequently under similar conditions of dealer, vulnerability, and holding. See BALANCED COMPARISONS.

COMPASS POINTS. In discussing bridge hands, columnists describe the four players by using the points of the compass to distinguish the players. Thus North and South compete against East and West. In tournament play, too, the table markers designate the seating of the players for the original deals by compass directions at designated tables. In the usual Mitchell type of tournament competition, the North and South players remain in the same seats throughout, doing the scoring and passing the boards, while the East and West players move from table to table in a direction opposite that in which the boards are passed. In other types of competition, a pair of players may occupy either the North-South or the East-West seats for a portion of the session.

COMPENSATION. A method of playing a one-table game with the luck of the deal virtually eliminated. It was devised by players in Kharkov in the Ukraine and was developed by players in Moscow.

By analyzing thousands of deals with the aid of a computer, they calculated the scoring expectation with a given number of high-card points in the partnership hands. This established a table so that players can measure at the end of a deal whether they have met, fallen short or surpassed expectations.

Their table is: 20 points, 0; 21, 50; 22, 70; 23, 110. For higher point counts the expectation varies with vulnerability: 24 points, 200 not vulnerable, 290 vulnerable; 25, 300, 440; 26, 350, 520; 27, 400, 630; 28, 430, 630; 29, 460, 660; 30, 490, 690; 31, 600, 900; 32, 700, 1050; 33, 900, 1350; 34, 1000, 1500; 35, 1100, 1650; 36, 1200, 1800; 37+, 1300, 1950.

An example of how the scoring works: a vulnerable partnership that bids and makes 3NT for 600 with 24 points collects 600 - 290 = 310.

COMPETITION. (1) Any duplicate bridge contest. See TOURNAMENT. (2) A bidding situation in which both sides are active.

COMPETITIVE BIDDING. Bidding sequences in which both partnerships enter the auction. Grouped articles dealing with competitive bidding include DEFENSE TO ONE NOTRUMP; DEFENSIVE BIDDING; DOUBLES; OVERCALLS; TWO-SUITER CONVENTIONS. Other separate entries are: ADVANCE SAVE; BALANCING; CLUBS FOR TAKEOUT; DEATH HOLDING; DEFENSE TO OPENING FOUR-BIDS; DEFENSE TO OPENING THREE BIDS; DEFENSE TO STRONG ARTIFICIAL OPENINGS; DEFENSE TO TWO-SUITED INTERFERENCE; DOUBLE FOR SACRIFICE; ESCAPE, ESCAPE SUIT; EXCLUSION BID; FORCING PASS; KOCK-WERNER REDOUBLE; LEAD-DIRECTING BID; LEBENSOHL APPLICATIONS; REDOUBLE; RESCUE; SACRIFICE; SCRAMBLING; SOS REDOUBLE; TRANSFERS OVER DOUBLES OF OPENING PREEMPTIVE BIDS; TRAP PASS; WRIGGLE.

COMPETITIVE DOUBLE. A double in a competitive auction which invites partner to bid game but gives him the option of signing off in a partscore or passing for penalties. One increasingly popular example is the MAXIMAL OVERCALL DOUBLE. Competitive doubles can be useful in contested auctions where the enemy suit has been bid and raised at a low level:

WEST	NORTH	EAST	SOUTH
			1 ♥
2 ♣	2 ♥	3 ♣	Pass
Pass	?		

North may hold

♠ A 7 4 3   ♥ J 6 2   ♦ A 10 9 4   ♣ 8 3

He is too strong to pass and his holding in clubs is too weak to make either a penalty double or a cooperative double, but his aces are useful for either offense or defense. Since South will usually not have sufficient values in the opponents' suit to double for penalties in such an auction, and since any unilateral action could easily be wrong, some experts prefer to use this double as competitive. It says: "Partner, I have a good hand with two-way values and don't know what to do; *you* decide."

Another typical competitive double occurs when the doubler's previous bidding shows that he cannot possibly be strong in the suit he is doubling.

WEST	NORTH	EAST	SOUTH
			1 ♦
Pass	1 NT	2 ♠	Pass
Pass	?		

North cannot have as many as four good spades in view of his original 1 NT response, and his location in front of the spade bidder is hardly ideal for defensive purposes. Thus a double is competitive, showing a hand such as:

♠ A 6 3   ♥ J 6 4   ♦ A 6   ♣ 10 9 7 4 3

Partner is asked to decide whether to play for the penalty, or bid on in notrump.

COMPLEMENTARY SCORES. When two contestants play against each other in a matchpoint contest, their combined matchpoint scores add up to the matchpoint top available on that board, and the two scores are complements of each other. For example, if top score is 12 points and the North-South pair earns 8 points, the opposing East-West pair earns 4 points. Similarly if one pair earns 2° points, the opposing pair earns 9 ° points.

COMPLETE THE CUT. See CUT (2).

COMPLETE TABLE. In rubber bridge, four or more players. In club bridge, club rules sometimes specify six players as constituting a complete table. When a table is complete, no other player may cut in until or unless one of the players withdraws.

The alternative procedure, common in England, is for players to cut into any table which has completed a rubber, provided only that three players may not cut in unless there is only one table in play. This arrangement produces a greater circulation of players.

COMPOUND GUARD SQUEEZE. A squeeze in three suits, in which two suits are stopped by both opponents and the third suit holding requires a defender to retain certain cards to prevent declarer from taking a winning finesse.

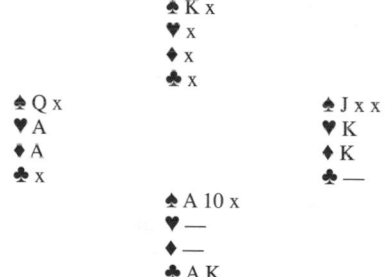

```
                    ♠ K x
                    ♥ x
                    ♦ x
                    ♣ x
♠ Q x                              ♠ J x x
♥ A                                ♥ K
♦ A                                ♦ K
♣ x                                ♣ —
                    ♠ A 10 x
                    ♥ —
                    ♦ —
                    ♣ A K
```

South leads the ♣A to squeeze East, who must discard a red card. On the continuation of the ♣K, West must discard the red suit which East has retained. North discards the suit which West has kept, and East is squeezed in spades and the red suit he has saved.

See COMPOUND SQUEEZE, COMPOUND TRUMP GUARD SQUEEZE, GUARD SQUEEZE.

COMPOUND SQUEEZE. A preparatory triple squeeze, followed by a double squeeze, analyzed exhaustively by Clyde E. Love. This ending requires two double menaces (guarded by both opponents) and a one-card menace. The one-card menace must be placed to the left of the opponent threatened. Declarer has all remaining tricks but one.

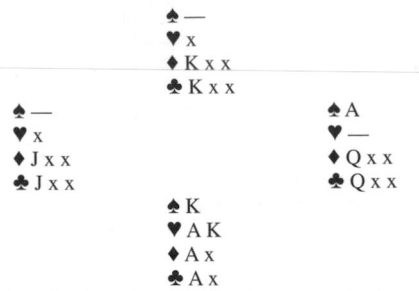

♠ —
♥ x
♦ K x x
♣ K x x

♠ —   ♠ A
♥ x   ♥ —
♦ J x x   ♦ Q x x
♣ J x x   ♣ Q x x

♠ K
♥ A K
♦ A x
♣ A x

South leads the ♥A, and East is squeezed in three suits. In order to avoid giving declarer a trick directly, East must unguard a minor suit. South cashes the king and ace of that suit, leaving West with the sole guard in that suit. Now the lead of South's remaining heart effects a double squeeze. Each of the double menaces must be accompanied by a winner in its suit to provide an entry.

The alternate threat squeeze is a hybrid form of compound squeeze with very special requirements.

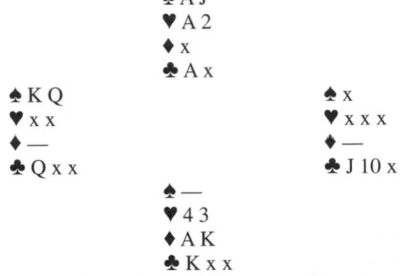

♠ A J
♥ A 2
♦ x
♣ A x

♠ K Q   ♠ x
♥ x x   ♥ x x x
♦ —   ♦ —
♣ Q x x   ♣ J 10 x

♠ —
♥ 4 3
♦ A K
♣ K x x

South leads the ♦A, and West must discard one of his guards. Since a spade would give up a trick directly, West must throw a heart or a club. If he chooses a heart, the low heart is discarded by North on the ♦K continuation. Meanwhile, East has thrown a heart and a spade. Now a heart lead squeezes West (in spades and clubs), and the ♠A which follows squeezes East (in hearts and clubs). If West chooses to discard a club on the ♦A, declarer leads a club to the ace, cashes the ♠A and returns to his hand with the ♣K. Now the lead of the ♦K brings about a simultaneous double squeeze.

From this, the special requirements for this squeeze are: (1) a one-card menace accompanied by a winner and placed to the left of the threatened opponent; (2) a double menace (the alternate threat suit) accompanied by a winner and any two cards of that suit in the hand opposite.

In addition, the usual requirements for a compound squeeze must be present.

COMPOUND TRUMP GUARD SQUEEZE. A compound guard squeeze with a trump element.

♠ A J 10
♥ A x
♦ A x
♣ —

♠ K x   ♠ Q x x
♥ K x   ♥ Q x
♦ K x   ♦ Q x
♣ x   ♣ —

♠ —
♥ x x
♦ x x
♣ A K Q

Clubs are trumps. On the lead of the ♣A North throws a red-suit loser. East is squeezed in three suits and must discard a red card. On the next club lead West abandons the suit East has retained and the other red-suit loser is thrown from the dummy. East discards from the red suit he has already unguarded, and is trump squeezed by a lead to that ace. See COMPOUND SQUEEZE; COMPOUND GUARD SQUEEZE; GUARD SQUEEZE; TRUMP SQUEEZE.

COMPOUND TRUMP SQUEEZE. A compound squeeze in which at least one opponent is subject to a trump squeeze. The following ending was posed is a double-dummy problem by William Whitfeld before 1900.

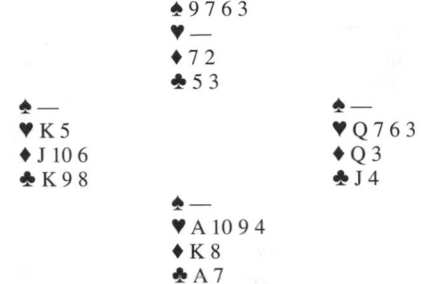

♠ 9 7 6 3
♥ —
♦ 7 2
♣ 5 3

♠ —   ♠ —
♥ K 5   ♥ Q 7 6 3
♦ J 10 6   ♦ Q 3
♣ K 9 8   ♣ J 4

♠ —
♥ A 10 9 4
♦ K 8
♣ A 7

South has the lead with spades as trumps and needs all the tricks.

South leads a low heart and trumps in dummy. A trump is led from dummy and East must discard a club or a diamond to avoid letting declarer establish an extra heart trick by ruffing. South discards whichever suit East discards, and leads that suit from dummy, winning in his hand. Declarer now cashes the ♥A, discarding a diamond from dummy, and leads a small heart, ruffing. When dummy's last trump is led, East obviously must keep his last heart and discard whichever minor suit he has retained. South discards his heart and West is squeezed in the minor suits.

COMPUTER GAMES. Several manufacturers have produced bridge games that are powered by computers. Some have deals preprogrammed into them, others require cassettes. See COMPUTER PLAY.

COMPUTER HANDS. First used in the Eastern States Regional tournament in 1963 on the initiative of Martin Scheinberg. Hand records prepared from the computer's random shuffle provide a practical, quick, inexpensive method of producing twinned hands in a multi-section event.

The rules of Contract Bridge require that a precise series of operations be performed in dealing a hand. This process is specified (1) to guarantee that any particular deal is completely random and (2) to ensure that no player has any clue as to the nature of the deal before he picks up his cards. The computer is capable of dealing in the same manner as humans, but it is hardly practical. Instead the computer is programmed to use a very simple technique. In the computer memory, 52 locations are set aside, each one representing a card. The sequence in which the cards are initially arranged is immaterial. Let us assume the order to be spades, hearts, diamonds and clubs each arranged in natural order. For the first card (♠A) the computer selects a series of eight random digits. The same random generation process is used to fill the remainder of the 52 positions. This process generates a completely unpredictable and unrelated sequence of digits. The computer now arranges or sorts these random numbers into arithmetic sequence. After this is done, the first 13 cards are assigned to North, the second 13 to East, etc. Other methods of distributing the cards could be used, but this works as well as any. After this is done, the computer must arrange the hands in suits in sequence and prepare to have them printed out.

The use of computer hands has become widespread at tournaments from the Sectional level up. In addition to the usual hand records, where one hand is printed per sheet, the computer now also produces a printed record on which as many as 18 hands appear. These can be used as a master for printing at tournaments, so that at the end of each session a set of hand records is available to every contestant.

Computer hands cause no problems in the conduct of the game. Of course the players who actually duplicate hands from a hand record cannot play those particular hands, so the movement cannot be complete. But this is a small price to pay for the ability to have the same hands played at every table throughout a large tournament.

Over the years, there have been frequent complaints concerning the distribution and unusual or unfortunate suit breaks. These are regularly blamed on computer hands. However, many studies have been made in an attempt to determine whether the random deals performed by the computer match the odds for distribution. The patterns of the 3,080 computer hands used in the round-robin qualifying rounds of the 1972 World Team Olympiad were analyzed by *The Bridge World*, and the incidence of each hand pattern was found to be very close to mathematical expectations (see MATHEMATICAL TABLES, Table 1). Suits were found to have broken evenly slightly more often than would be expected. Tournament Director Sid Kilsheimer decided to do a similar check of computer hands. He chose the hands that have been played from 1964 through 1981 in the ACBL-Wide Charity, Olympiad Fund and International Fund games. These are hands that were played all over the American Contract Bridge League. He checked 60 sets of hand records (8,024 hands), and the predicted occurrence of various distributions was extremely close to the expected occurrence. Said Kilsheimer in an article in the *ACBL Bulletin* (November 1981), " I for one as a director and player am firmly convinced that the computer hands do represent a truly fair set of deals."

COMPUTER PLAY. Three networks are available that permit a player to sit at his computer and play a bridge game with others around the country, or the world. Kibitzing is possible. This concept is under development as this *Encyclopedia* is being prepared. It seems to offer possibilities for a general development of bridge, bringing in players who cannot easily gain access to other players for any normal form of the game. International competition with players staying at home will become possible.

(1) OKBridge. Used largely by students and academics with access to Internet. Contact: Matthew Clegg, Tel. 619 558 3408.

(2) ImagiNation. Offers rubber bridge and other games. Tel: 1 800 SIERRA 1.

(3) Tel-a-Bridge. Offers rubber bridge, and also duplicate, probably ACBL sponsored with masterpoint awards. Tel: 619 459 0327.

COMPUTER PROGRAMS. Many software programs have been written that relate to technical aspects of bridge. Programs that have the ambitious aim of having the computer bid, play and defend have not yet been perfected, although an IBM executive used a mainframe computer in the Eighties and produced a high-level performance in all three areas. At the 1980 world championships in Valkenburg, the Netherlands, a Volmac program for constructive bidding was demonstrated and did about as well as the human experts. It used artificial bidding methods designed by Benito Garozzo.

A number of programs have been designed for commercial distribution, but perform on a rather lower level. The best-known is the Bridge Baron, created by Tom Throop and later renamed the Micro Bridge Companion. An independent device, not requiring the use of a computer, is the Bridge Challenger. See COMPUTER PLAY.

For two other major technical programs with other purposes see BASE III and BOREL.

COMPUTER SCORING. Almost all tournaments today are scored with the help of a computer. Many excellent programs have been devised that enable a game to be scored almost instantly once the last board has been played. The program used by the American Contract Bridge League is called ACBLScore. This and other programs are in use all over the world. Even most club games are scored by computer.

Computer scoring has made scoring across the field an easy process. When scoring was done manually, scoring across an entire field was an arduous process, requiring many hours and with the results prone to error. With computer scoring, the results are available almost instantaneously. And if an error is found, a couple of simple keystrokes usually is enough to make the correction.

Until the advent of computers, all scoring was done manually. The scorer would enter all results on a large recap sheet, do the necessary matchpointing (figuring the point score for each recorded result), add the scores for each pair and rank the fields.

The first serious attempt to score a tournament with computer assistance occurred in Ostend, Belgium, in the early Fifties. The players used sensitized pencils to enter the scores on punched cards that were fed directly into a machine. Besides calculating the overall standings, the machine furnished each pair with a virtual reproduction of their personal scorecard complete with the matchpoints on each board.

CONCEDE. To yield one or more of the remaining tricks to the opponents. See Laws (Laws 68, 69, 70, 71); LAWS OF DUPLICATE (Laws 68, 69, 70, 71).

CONCESSION. See CLAIM OR CONCESSION.

CONDITIONS OF CONTEST. A statement governing the competition in an event. In general there should be a preliminary statement as to the masterpoint requirements or other prerequisites for entry into the event, the number of sessions the event will run, the entry fee, how many qualifying sessions and how many final (or semifinal) sessions. In knockout team games there should also be a statement as to such matters as the number of boards to be played in each match; the seeding rights, i.e.., the rights exercisable by the higher-ranked team with respect to the choice of seats and opponents; any restrictions on the right to have two pairs who played each other in the first half of the match play against each other in the second half; the method of resolution of the match in the event of a tie, and so forth. In Swiss team games the conditions of contest must include statements as to the form of scoring used, including the scale of victory points, if any. In a pair event a final statement, made up after the event is under way, includes the setup of the game, number to be qualified and method of qualification, whether at-large pairs will be qualified, and computation of the carryover, and the setup of the final (or semifinal) session(s).

Under Law 78D and Law 80, all such conditions become Law, and therefore have the full backing of Law.

CONDONING. An action immediately following an irregularity by the opposition which would have been a proper one if the preceding action had been proper.

At rubber bridge, an irregular bid can be condoned in this way unless the non-offending side has drawn attention to the irregularity. In duplicate such a bid can be condoned as a matter of law. In both forms of the game an irregular lead can be condoned in all circumstances. If a declarer leads from the wrong hand, a defender may follow in proper sequence, either on his own initiative or if his partner so requires. See LAWS 34, 53, 60; LAWS OF DUPLICATE (Laws 27, 53, 60).

CONDUCT. See ETHICS AND CONDUCT.

CONFERENCE. A voluntary association of neighboring ACBL units or districts organized to further the purposes of the ACBL and of its member units. The powers of a Conference are limited to those delegated to it by the member units. Among the reasons for organizing an ACBL Conference are the promotion of matters of mutual interest, such as tournament attendance and the reduction of inter-unit and inter-district frictions.

CONGLOMERATE MAJOR RAISES. An extension of the SWISS CONVENTION designed to allow responder to make a forcing raise of a major suit opening while specifying whether it is based on a singleton somewhere in the hand, on great high card strength, on very good trumps or merely on general strength. Using the bids just beyond a jump raise (starting with 3♠ over 1♥, or 3 NT over 1♠), responder bids as follows:

First step	shows a singleton (unidentified)
Second step	shows 17-18 HCP
Third step	shows four trumps headed by at least two of the top three honors, or more than four trumps headed by at least the ace or king
Fourth step	shows any hand worth a strong raise that does not meet the above criteria.

After responder has shown a singleton, opener can ask where it is by making the cheapest bid. Responder bids the suit of his singleton if he can do so without going past four of the trump suit; otherwise he bids four of the trump suit.

For alternative methods see SUPER SWISS, UNBALANCED SWISS RAISE, VALUE SWISS RAISES.

CONGRESS. Term for tournament, dating back to the days of whist. The term no longer is used in North America but still is common as a synonym for tournament in other parts of the world.

CONGRESS, UNITED STATES. A team of players from the United States Congress played matches against CORPORATE AMERICA 1989, 1990 and 1993. Corporate America, made up of major business executives, defeated Congress in all three matches. Playing in 1989 were Rep. Arlan Stangeland (R-Minnesota), captain; Sen. Bob Packwood (R-Oregon); Sen. Rudy Boschwitz (R-Minnesota), Rep. Hank Brown (R-Colorado); Rep. Robert Kastenmeier (D-Wisconsin); Sen. Bob Kerrey (D-Nebraska); Rep. Jim Leach (R-Iowa); Rep. Lynn Martin (R-Illinois); Rep. Howard Nielson (R-Utah); Rep. Robert Zion (R-Wisconsin). On the 1990 team were Stangeland; Boschwitz; Brown; Rep. Jim Bunning (R-Kentucky); Sen. James Jeffords (R-Vermont); Kastenmeier; Leach; Nielson; Packwood; Rep. Robert Smith (R-Oregon); Zion. The 1993 team was made up of Leach; Stangeland; Brown; Bunning; Jeffords; Kastenmeier; Packwood; Judge Melvin Welles, and Zion.

CONSOLATION EVENT. In most sectional and higher-rated tournaments, the open pair event and occasionally other events were held in two or more sessions, with one or two qualifying sessions. The players who do not qualify for the last session or sessions were eligible for competition in a secondary event played at the same time as the final of the main event, known as a Consolation. These events are now very rare: Players who fail to qualify play in an entirely new event that includes new participants.

CONSTRUCTIVE. A description applied to a bid that suggests game prospects but is not forcing. The partner will take further action more often than not. See ENCOURAGING (1).

CONSTRUCTIVE BIDDING. Auctions in which one side attempts to locate its best contract without interference from the opponents.

CONSTRUCTIVE RAISES. The use of an immediate raise from 1♠ to 2♠ or 1♥ to 2♥ to show 8-10 points. Weaker raises are shown by bidding 1NT forcing and then reverting to spades. This is a slightly weakened version of the Roth-Stone treatment, in which the raise was virtually forcing.

CONSULTATION. This practice between partners regarding a penalty is forbidden under Law 10C2, LAWS OF DUPLICATE, and any such discussion cancels the right to penalize.

CONTESTANT. One or more players competing for a combined score. In an individual contest, each player enters as an individual, changing partners as the movement requires and receiving credit for his own score on each board he plays. In a pair contest, players enter as pairs, playing with the same partner throughout for a common score on all boards played. In a team contest, players enter as a team of four or more, changing partners among their own teammates as permitted by the CONDITIONS OF CONTEST, but competing for a common score. In WBF events it is usual to classify the non-playing captain as a contestant.

CONTESTED AUCTION. See COMPETITIVE BIDDING.

CONTINENTAL CLUB of Amsterdam. Founded in 1889 as a meeting point for Amsterdam businessmen and their American colleagues to play whist and other card games. The Continental is the world's second-oldest bridge club after London's Portland Club. It was prominent in Dutch (and European) bridge in the Thirties but the Nazi holocaust in World War II deprived it of many Jewish members. Afterward the membership included the top echelon of Dutch bridge: the brothers Ernst and Frits Goudsmit, Martijn Cats, Herman Filarski, Bob Slavenburg, Jut Kramer, Kees Kaiser and, later, Jaap Kokkes, Arie van Heusden and Max Rebattu. Another member, Maurits Caransa, founded the tournament named after him. He was kidnapped in 1978 after a visit to the club and released after payment of 8,000,000 guilders. During the 100th anniversary celebrations in 1989, the club burned down and moved to another building.

CONTINUOUS PAIRS. A multi-session event in which a pair or a player may compete as often as he wishes. The final standings are determined by comparing the two best percentage games for all players. The player with the highest total percentage for two games is adjudged the winner, and lower placings are determined in the same way.

CONTRACT. (1) The undertaking by declarer's side to win, at the denomination named, the number of odd tricks specified in the final bid, whether undoubled, doubled or redoubled. (2) The game of contract bridge, loosely. See TRUMP SUIT.

CONTRACT BRIDGE. Fourth in the succession of partnership card games that began with WHIST and continued with BRIDGE WHIST and AUCTION BRIDGE. The essential point of difference from its predecessor is that no tricks won in the play are counted toward game except those which are contracted for in the bidding. A declarer contracting for and making 100 points in trick score has made a game and becomes vulnerable. Game contracts are: 3 NT (first trick worth 40, and subsequent tricks 30 each); four of a major suit, hearts or spades, worth 30 each; five of a minor suit, diamonds or clubs, worth 20 each. See SCORING, MAJORITY CALLING.

Sides may be predetermined if two partnerships are pre-established. Otherwise the cards are cut to establish partnerships and, in any case, to determine the first dealer. Partners face each other in seats arbitrarily named for compass points, North and South opposing East and West. The player at the dealer's left shuffles the cards and presents them to the dealer, who offers them to the player at his right for a cut. Normally, two decks of 52 cards are used, the dealer's partner shuffling the second deck and placing them after shuffling at his right, from where the next dealer offers the cards to the previous dealer for a cut. The dealer distributes the cards one at a time to each player in a clockwise manner beginning with the player on his left, and taking the last card himself, ending with each player having before him a hand of 13 cards. The players study their hands, and the bidding period begins.

The dealer has the opportunity to open the bidding, or he may pass. During the bidding, correct procedure requires that bids be made in a uniform manner, as, "pass," "1♠," "double," etc. Any variation from the standard formula is improper, as also are any gestures, remarks, mannerisms or grimaces. See PROPRIETIES. The auction proceeds until three players have passed in succession following the last bid, double or redouble. If all four players pass, the deal is abandoned and the next player deals. (In CHICAGO, the same dealer redeals.) At the end of the bidding, the declarer is determined as that player of the partnership who first named the denomination, suit or notrump, of the final bid. This completes the bidding phase of the hand.

The player to the left of the declarer has the duty of making the opening lead. After he has led a card, declarer's partner places his hand face up on the table, and the play of his cards is at the management of the declarer. See ARRANGING.

The play consists of 13 tricks, to each of which each player contributes one card in proper clockwise sequence. To each trick each player must play a card of the suit led, if able. If unable, he may play any card. Any trick containing a trump is won by the highest trump; any trick not containing a trump is won by the highest card of the suit led. The winner of each trick has the right and duty of leading to the next trick.

The declarer then attempts to make his contract, by taking as many tricks in excess of six as his final contract specified he would take. If he succeeds, he enters his trick points BELOW THE LINE and any extra tricks or bonuses he may have earned ABOVE THE LINE. When a partnership's total of trick points exceeds 100, that partnership is vulnerable, and a new game is started from a zero trick score on each side. The side first winning two games gets the bonus for winning the rubber. See SCORING.

If the declarer fails to make his contract, his opponents score points above the line for each undertrick. These points are increased if the contract has been doubled or redoubled during the period of the auction.

See HISTORY OF BRIDGE.

CONTRACT BRIDGE FORUM. The monthly bridge publication published for four districts of the Western Conference of the American Contract Bridge League. The publication, which appears in a newspaper format, was originated by Tom Stoddard as a private enterprise and later was the official publication of the Pacific Bridge League. The editor is Ken Monzingo, P.O. Box 33567, San Diego CA 92163.

CONTRACT BRIDGE GOLDEN ANNIVERSARY. The invention of contract bridge by Harold Vanderbilt in 1925 was celebrated at a Golden Anniversary party during International Team Trials in Palo Alto CA on Halloween weekend in 1975. Lew Mathe, ACBL president at the time, and Alan Truscott, *New York Times* bridge editor, paid tribute to Harold Vanderbilt whose ideas and talent brought us the game as we know it today. Appropriately, the party was held in the Bay Area where Vanderbilt's cruise ship *Finland* set sail in October 1925. On that cruise Vanderbilt put the finishing touches to his new scoring table with its concept of vulnerability, and contract was born.

The 60th anniversary was observed in Winnipeg, Manitoba, at the NABC in November 1985. The 60th birthday of contract bridge was celebrated with a 235-pound birthday cake designed to serve 1200 people. The *Bulletin* cover took note of the 60th anniversary with pictures naming "Stars of the Decades" -- Harold Vanderbilt in the Twenties, Ely Culbertson in the Thirties, Charles Goren in the Forties, Howard Schenken in the Fifties, Oswald Jacoby in the Sixties, Bob Hamman in the Seventies and Barry Crane in the Eighties. See HISTORY OF BRIDGE

CONTRACT BRIDGE LAWS. For rubber bridge, see LAWS OF CONTRACT BRIDGE; for duplicate bridge, see LAWS OF DUPLICATE CONTRACT BRIDGE; for Chicago, see CHICAGO.

CONTRACT WHIST. A cross between WHIST and CONTRACT BRIDGE. The four players bid in turn for the contract, but the play is that of whist, with all four hands concealed. The principles of the game were set forth in *Contract Whist*, by HUBERT PHILLIPS, published in 1932. Although played only occasionally, it is considered by some to be a game requiring high skill.

CONTRACTING. A word which signifies the act of agreeing to take a certain number of tricks in a deal of bridge.

CONTRACTING SIDE. Declarer and his partner. The opponents are the defending side.

CONTROL ASKING BIDS. See ASKING BIDS.

CONTROL MAINTENANCE. A strategy aimed at preventing a defender from gaining the mastery of a particular suit. In notrump hands, HOLD-UP PLAY is the key to control. In trump play, control usually refers to the struggle against a defender holding trump length. The following example is from *Reese On Play* by Terence Reese.

A fairly well-known stratagem to avoid losing control of trumps is to refuse to ruff until dummy can cope with the suit which the opponents have led:

```
              ♠ Q 10 8
              ♥ 9 8
              ♦ Q J 8 7
              ♣ K 9 8 7
♠ 7 6                        ♠ 5 4 3 2
♥ Q J 10 7 6                 ♥ K 5 4 3 2
♦ A 9 4                      ♦ 10 5
♣ J 6 3                      ♣ 10 2
              ♠ A K J 9
              ♥ A
              ♦ K 6 3 2
              ♣ A Q 5 4
```

The ♥Q is led against 4♠. If declarer draws three or four rounds of trumps, the 4-2 split is fatal for him. The right play is to draw two rounds of trumps and then clear diamonds. West wins with the ace and plays a second heart; South discards a club from his hand and any further heart leads can be dealt with in dummy.

In the play of this hand declarer used two stratagems to protect himself from losing control; one was to clear the side suit before drawing trumps, and the other was to refuse to ruff the second heart.

CONTROLLED PSYCHICS. See PSYCHIC CONTROLS.

CONTROLS. (1) Generally, holdings that prevent the opponents' winning one, two or conceivably three immediate tricks in a specified suit.
First-round control: ace, or a void in a trump contract.
Second-round control: king, or a singleton in a trump contract.
Third-round control: queen, or a doubleton in a trump contract.
Controls may be discovered or revealed by means of ASKING BIDS or CUEBIDS.
(2) Specifically, aces and kings. An ace is normally counted as two "controls," and a king as one. See BLUE TEAM CLUB, SYMMETRIC RELAY SYSTEM and EXPECTED NUMBER OF CONTROLS IN BALANCED HAND.

CONVENIENT MINOR. See SHORT CLUB.

CONVENTION. A call or play with a defined meaning, which may be artificial. The oldest convention is the fourth-best lead, which dates back to Hoyle about 1740. The oldest bidding convention is the takeout double, which was not as obvious when it originated about 1912 as it is today.

CONVENTION CARD. A printed card listing commonly used conventions. It is used by players in duplicate bridge to indicate to opponents the conventions and special understandings a pair has. A pair must fill out a set of convention cards before beginning play that lists offensive style and conventions, defensive conventions and understandings and lead agreements.

The card used by the American Contract Bridge League lists offensive bids on the front, defensive bids and lead understandings on the back. The common conventions are printed on the card so that players merely have to make checkmarks. Open areas also are provided so that players can write in any conventions or understandings that are not in the printed matter.

The card used by the World Bridge Federation is more complicated than the ACBL card. Pairs planning to play in major world events must submit their cards in advance for WBF approval. Failure to do so can result in penalties. Pairs competing in world events often have to submit additional pages reflecting their unusual methods.

Sponsoring organizations have a right to regulate conventions under Law 40E.

CONVENTIONS, ACBL. Following are the conventions permitted in ACBL tournaments. There are three lists — a general list that must be allowed in almost all ACBL tournaments, a limited list for use in games that have an upper masterpoint limit of 20, and a superchart that lists conventions that require a pre-Alert and can be used in all certain specific North American Championship events.

GENERAL CONVENTION CHART

The conventions listed below must be allowed in all ACBL-sanctioned tournament play (other than in events with an upper restriction of 20 or fewer masterpoints and events for which the ACBL conditions of contest state otherwise) and at club-level events with multiple-site overall masterpoint awards. However, club managers have full authority to regulate conventions in games conducted solely at their clubs. Conventions listed on the ACBL Limited Convention Chart are marked with an *.

Opening Bids

*1♣ artificial forcing opening bid indicating a minimum of 10 HCP (a negative 1♦ response may be used)

*1♦ may be used as an all-purpose opening bid when played in conjunction with a forcing 1♣ (15+ HCP) and 5-card major(s)

1NT forcing opening bid indicating a balanced or unbalanced hand and minimum of 16 HCP

2♣ artificial opening bid indicating one of:
    *a) a strong hand, balanced or unbalanced
    b) a three-suiter with a minimum of 10 HCP

2♦ artificial opening bid showing one of:
    a) both majors with a minimum of 10 HCP
    b) a strong hand, balanced or unbalanced
    c) a three-suiter with a minimum of 10 HCP

Opening suit bid at the two level or higher indicating the bid suit, another known suit, a minimum of 10 HCP and at least 5-4 distribution in the suits

Opening notrump bid at the two level or higher indicating at least 5-4 distribution in the minors

Opening 3NT bid indicating
    *a) a solid suit
    b) a broken minor

Opening four-level bid transfers to a known suit

Responses and Rebids

1♦ in response to 1♣ to deny
    a) a four-card major(s)
    b) a five-card major

1NT response to a major suit opening bid or 1♣ response to a 1♥ opening bid forcing one round; cannot guarantee game invitational or better values

1NT response to a 1♥ opening bid to indicate at least four spades and at least 6 HCP

2♣ or 2♦ response to 3rd or 4th seat major suit opener asking the quality of opening bid

*Single or higher jump shifts (including into notrump) to indicate a raise or to force to game

Relay systems are not allowed over artificial bids. All other bids are allowed over artificial bids

All constructive calls made during the second and subsequent rounds of bidding

*Calls that ask for aces, kings, queens, singletons, voids, trump quality and responses thereto

*Responses and rebids after natural notrump including those that have two non-consecutive ranges neither of which exceeds 3 HCP. No conventional responses are allowed over notrump bids with a lower limit of fewer than 10 HCP or with a range of greater than 5 HCP

*Responses and rebids after opening bids of 2♣ or higher (for this classification, by partnership agreement, weak 2 bids must not have fewer than 5 HCP, must be within a range of 7 HCP and the suit must contain at least five cards).

Competitive Auctions

Conventional balancing calls

*Conventional doubles and redoubles

Notrump overcall for
    *a) two-suit takeout showing at least 5-4 distribution and at least one known suit
    b) three-suit takeout

Jump overcalls into a suit to indicate at least 5-4 distribution in two suits, at least one of which is known

*Cuebid of an opponent's suit

*Defenses to:
    *a) conventional calls;
    *b) notrump bids;

*c) opening bids of 2♣ or higher

Disallowed

Conventions and/or agreements whose primary purpose is to destroy the opponents' methods

Psyching of artificial opening bids

Psyching of conventional responses to artificial opening bids

Psychic controls

Relay (tell me more) systems

Opening one bids which by partnership agreement could show fewer than 8 high-card points (not applicable to a psych)

Carding

Dual-message carding strategies are not approved except on each defender's first discard. Only right-side-up or upside-down card ordering strategies are approved. Encrypted signals are not approved

LIMITED CONVENTIONS

(May be used in games with an upper limit of 20 or fewer MPs)

Clubs. Club management shall determine the conventions permitted in club games with an upper limit of 20 or fewer masterpoints.

Local and Higher Events. The sponsoring organization of local and higher-rated tournaments may determine the conventions permitted in games with an upper limit of 20 or fewer masterpoints.

Opening bids

A 1♣ opening bid may be both artificial (says nothing about clubs) and forcing (partner must respond at least once), but opener must have at least 10 HCP. A negative 1♦ response may be used.

When a forcing 1♣ opening to show at least 15 HCP is combined with a five-card major opening bid structure, a 1♦ opening may be used to show an opening hand not meeting the requirements for any other bid.

A 2♣ opening bid may be artificial and strong. It may be balanced (a hand stronger than a traditional 2NT opening) or unbalanced (a hand with which you would open a strong two-bid if playing that way.) Further bidding will describe the hand.

A 3NT opening bid may show a hand with a long solid suit (Gambling).

Responses and rebids

A jump shift of one or more levels (into a suit or into notrump) may be used either to force to game or to show a raise of partner's suit.

Any meaning may be given to the responses and rebids after an opening bid of 1NT. Exception: if the 1NT opening has an agreed lower limit of fewer than 10 HCP, responses and rebids may not be conventional   they must be natural.

Any meaning may be given to the response to and rebids after an opening bid of 2♣ or higher. Exception: if the opening bid is a weak two-bid with (a) an agreed point range of more than 7 HCP, (b) an agreement that the bid suit can contain fewer than five cards, or (c) an agreement that the hand can contain fewer than 5 HCP, responses and rebids may not be conventional   they must be natural.

Any call may be used to ask partner or to respond to partner about aces, kings, queens, singletons, voids or trump quality with the exceptions noted above.

Competitive auctions

Any meaning may be given to a double or a redouble.

A notrump overcall or jump overcall may be used to show a two-suited hand (at least 5-4 distribution in the two suits). At least one of the suits must be known. The second suit may be known or unknown.

Any meaning may be given to the cuebid of an opponent's suit.

Any meaning may be given to calls used to defend against opponents' conventional calls, notrump bids and opening bids of 2♣ or higher.

Disallowed

Conventions and/or agreements with a primary purpose of destroying the opponents' methods are not allowed (e.g., a bid telling nothing about the bidder's hand, made simply to use up bidding space).

Agreements allowing the partnership to open the bidding at the one level with fewer than 8 HCP are not allowed. This does not preclude a psychic opening bid.

Psyching of artificial opening bids or conventional responses to artificial opening bids is not allowed.

Psychic controls (bids designed to determine whether partner has psyched or to clarify the nature of the psych) are not allowed.

Relay systems (one player tells nothing about his own hand while interrogating partner about his hand through a series of conventional calls) are not allowed.

Carding

A discard (a card played while not following suit) can convey a message to partner. The message can pertain to the length of the discarded suit, to the attitude toward the suit (desire to have partner lead that suit) or to another suit (no information about the discarded suit). A pair may decide to attribute the attitude message (good-bad) to the cards on either higher-to-lower basis (a higher card is more positive than a lower card) or a lower-to-higher basis (a low card is more positive than a higher card).

A discard may carry more than one message, but only at each defender's first discard of the hand. Dual-message discards are not permitted as second or subsequent discards. Encrypted signals (the order and/or message is based on information known to the other defender but not yet to declarer) are not allowed at any time.

ACBL SUPER CHART

Pre-Alerts are required for all conventional methods not permitted on the ACBL General Convention Chart. Descriptions of, and suggested defenses to, such methods must be made available in writing.

This chart applies to:

Vanderbilt Knockout Teams	All sessions
Spingold Knockout Teams	All sessions
Women's Knockout Teams	All sessions
Reisinger Board-A-Match Teams	All sessions
Grand National Open Teams	All sessions played at the NABC

All other nationally-rated events with no upper masterpoint limit.

All sessions after the first two masterpoint restrictions qualifying sessions (the ACBL General Conventions Chart applies to the first two qualifying sessions).

Allowed: Any non-destructive treatment or method.

Disallowed: Forcing pass systems, encrypted signals, psychic controls, psyching of artificial opening bid and/or conventional responses thereto.

CONVERSATION. Conversation is carried on at the bridge table in the language of the bidding and the play of cards. Any other conversation during the bidding or play of the hand is either distracting (and therefore discourteous), revealing (and therefore improper and even illegal), or misleading. (See COFFEEHOUSING, legal at poker but not at bridge.) Although bridge is a social game, any socializing or gossiping should be confined to the short period of the deal, or prior to the start of the game or during a refreshment intermission. See BATTLE, SARAH.

COOPERATIVE DOUBLE. A double that leaves partner the option of passing for penalties or bidding further. (A special type is the OPTIONAL DOUBLE.) Originally used by Ely Culbertson to describe a double of an opening three-bid, the term is now better reserved for some more complicated situations:

WEST	NORTH	EAST	SOUTH
Pass	Pass	1 ♥	Dbl
1 ♠	2 ♦	Pass	Pass
2 ♥	Pass	Pass	Dbl

Since South's first double suggested support for the unbid suits, he cannot be well-stocked in hearts. South's second double suggests a hand such as:

♠ A 10 6 3
♥ Q 5
♦ K 7 5
♣ A Q 10 6

South has good defensive values, a doubleton heart honor and moderate support for diamonds. The double is a suggestion that leaves the final decision to North.

WEST	NORTH	EAST	SOUTH
			1 ♣
Pass	Pass	Dbl	1 ♠
2 ♦	Pass	Pass	Dbl

In the light of his previous bidding, South can hardly have any positive assurance of defeating 2♦. He obviously has a maximum one-bid, perhaps 20 high-card points and 4-3-1-5 distribution. North has to consider whether he can contribute anything to the defense, and may decide to bid 2♠, 3♣, 2♥ or pass.

This type of double can occur in many disguises, but the doubler has always limited his hand in such a way that he cannot be in a position to guarantee a penalty. See also COMPETITIVE DOUBLE; DOUBLE; MAXIMAL OVERCALL DOUBLE; OPTIONAL DOUBLE.

COPENHAGEN CLUBS, Bridge Tournament of the. The world's oldest regularly played event, founded in November 1927. It has been played every year since then, even during World War II, on the second Monday of each winter month.

COPENHAGEN CONVENTION. A defensive scheme devised by John Trelde and Gert Lenk of Denmark and popular there. After an opening bid of one of a suit, 2NT shows the low unbid suits, 3♣ shows the high and low unbid suits, and 3♦ shows the high unbid suits. See PENALTY.

CORPORATE AMERICA. A Corporate America team, made up of major corporate executives, was formed in 1989 to play a challenge match against a team made up of members of Congress. Matches were held in Washington DC in May of 1989, 1990 and 1993, and Corporate America was the victor in all three matches.

Playing for Corporate America in 1989 were Laurence Tisch, president and chief executive officer of the Columbia Broadcasting System, captain; Alan "Ace" Greenberg, chairman and chief executive officer of The Bear Stearns Companies; James Cayne, president of Bear Stearns; Warren Buffett, chief executive officer of Berkshire Hathaway; George Gillespie III, partner in Cravath, Swaine and Moore; the late Malcolm Forbes, chairman and editor-in-chief of *Forbes Magazine*. The 1990 team: Tisch; Buffett; Greenberg; Cayne; Gillespie; Jack Dreyfus, founder of the Dreyfus Fund and president of the Dreyfus Medical Foundation; Milton Petrie, chief executive officer of Petrie Stores Corporation. The 1993 team: Buffett; Gillespie; Cayne; Rita Shugart, president of the Monterey Airplane Co.; Nick Nickell, president of Kelso and Co., and Warren Spector, former KING OF BRIDGE.

Corporate America played a challenge match against the British Parliament team in February, 1990, at the London home of Forbes. Corporate America lost to the Lords but defeated the House of Commons. Playing for Corporate America were Tisch, Forbes, Gillespie, Cayne, Greenberg, Petrie and Buffett.

CORRECT THE COUNT. See RECTIFYING THE COUNT.

CORRECTION PERIOD. The time specified by the sponsoring organization during which corrections to the score may be sought.

Scoring errors may be made by a director (as when he wrongly transcribes a score) or by players at the table. The former must be corrected immediately if attention is drawn to them before the conclusion of the correction period. The latter require evidence that an error was in fact made, the director will often check the private scorecards of the players involved before changing a score.

The correction period's expiration is specified in the Conditions of Contest. (Before the advent of scoring by computer, it often appeared on the RECAPITULATION SHEET or, in a knockout event, on the bracket sheet.) Law 79C of the Laws of Duplicate Bridge states that, unless the sponsoring organization specifies a different time, the correction period expires a minimum of 30 minutes after the official score has been completed and made available for inspection.

Great latitude is allowed in handling scoring correction, in part because of the varying nature of tournament events. For instance, in the case of a club that meets once a week, the correction period may extend until the next weekly session. At a tournament, the correction period for a one-session event usually does not expire until 24 hours after the event (except on the last day of the tournament).

In a multi-session playthrough event, however, the correction period expires about an hour before the end of the next session. In an event with a qualifying stage, the correction period may be shorter; although the scores in a qualifying session — and the masterpoint awards — may be changed until the end of the tournament, the qualifying field must be determined at least 15 minutes prior to the beginning of the next stage of the event.

In a Swiss Teams, the result of each match must be reported quickly so assignments for the next match can be made. (In case of an appeal of a director's ruling in a Swiss Teams, pairings for the next match are made on the assumption that both sides win the appeal.) In an event such as the Vanderbilt Knockout Teams, the correction period may expire at the announced starting time of the next session of an ongoing match, or one hour before the announced starting time for the next match for the last two sessions of a completed match, or 30 minutes after the end of the match for the last two sessions of a final match.

A noted instance of a belated scoring appeal came in the 1990 World Knockout Teams in Geneva. In the third quarter of one semifinal match, a board was scored as down five doubled, -1100, when the actual result was down six. The error affected the result of the match, but was not brought before the tournament committee until the next day. Still, the losing team had a chance, since the Conditions of Contest permitted the committee to correct a manifestly incorrect score. The committee judged, however, that the error lay in what had been agreed to at the table. Had the deal been scored as down six, -1100, that would have been obviously — manifestly — incorrect. But the agreed result, though mistaken, had been scored correctly, so the outcome of the match stood. See PROTEST PERIOD and SCORE CORRECTIONS.

COUNT. A term used in three distinct senses, referring to: (1) the number of cards held in a suit, see COUNTING THE HAND, COUNT SIGNALS, FOSTER ECHO, TRUMP ECHO; (2) the strength of a hand, see DISTRIBUTIONAL COUNTS, POINT-COUNT; (3) the number of tricks that must be lost for the operation of a squeeze; See RECTIFYING THE COUNT, SQUEEZE WITHOUT THE COUNT.

COUNT SIGNALS. (also called Length Signals.) A method by which one defender indicates to his partner the length held in a particular suit. The standard procedure is to play high low with an even number of cards and to play the lowest with an odd number of cards.

The converse procedure, upside down count signals, originated long ago in Sweden and became popular in North America in the Eighties. The advantage of this is that the defender is not in difficulty with some doubletons. One may not be able to spare the higher card, for signalling purposes, when it is a jack, a ten or a nine. With three cards one can normally spare the middle card if the top card would be extravagant.

The normal application occurs when declarer attacks a suit in which he is strong, but a signal can be made in a suit which is both led and dominated by the defenders. (See FOSTER ECHO.) In a high-level contract, the opening leader may need to know his partner's length in order to judge which tricks can be cashed quickly.

Accurate suit-length signals are the key to a golden treasury of defensive plays, seemingly brilliant, but in fact within the compass of everyone who is willing to count the cards. After a few tricks have been played, good defensive signalers may know nearly all about the unseen hands and should be able to play just as accurately as declarer.

Everyone agrees that when a defender does echo, he shows an even number of cards. When he does not, that does necessarily indicate an odd number. A defender may decide not to echo for fear of giving information to declarer. Conversely he may echo with an even number in an attempt to fool declarer.

When following a suit played by the declarer, always echo to show an even number of cards unless it appears that this may help declarer, in which case do not echo at all. However, occasional false signals should be made in situations where it will not matter that partner is misled. See also TRUMP SIGNAL.

In this connection, there are two valid psychological points. First, it is not wise to try to outsmart declarer continually by making false signals. Declarer usually comes out of a guessing game better than the defenders. When declarer has the lead, he has command of the play. He can come out of a huddle and play in a manner that leaves the defenders no time for thought and, of course, a false signal must be made smoothly and urbanely — otherwise it is likely to boomerang. Therefore, false signals should be avoided unless the play has been thought out well in advance. However, some false signals must be

made. It is essential not to become typed as a player whose echoes are always dependable.

The second psychological point arises when a defender is afraid to signal for fear of tipping his hand. If it seems a borderline case, it is better to signal. Declarers are desperately afraid of looking silly in a situation like this:

K 9 5 3
10 8 6 2   J 7
A Q 4

South plays the ace and queen, and West, caught on the wrong foot, echoes with the 6 and 2. Vain declarers, and those with critical partners, will not finesse dummy's 9 on the third round (although the finesse is the percentage play — see RESTRICTED CHOICE.) They would rather be wrong five times in a situation like this than suffer the ignominy of letting East make a trick with J-10-x. In a world of bluff and double-bluff, this human failing is something tangible to hold onto. Notice that South does slightly better to play the queen before the ace, letting West think that his partner may have the ace. In that case a signal is more plausible, although still wrong.

Usually the defenders must cooperate to lead declarer astray. In a situation such as the following, declarer is more likely to go wrong if both players falsecard.

♠ J 10 2
♥ J 9 8 3
♦ 9 3
♣ 9 5 4 3

♠ A 9 4   ♠ 3
♥ A 10 7   ♥ K 6 5 4 2
♦ Q J 6 2   ♦ 10 7 4
♣ K Q 10   ♣ J 8 6 2

♠ K Q 8 7 6 5
♥ Q
♦ A K 8 5
♣ A 7

West's 1♦ opening is passed to South, who lands in 4♠. West leads the ♣K and South holds off in order to create a ruffing communication between dummy and the closed hand. South wins the second club and plays diamonds, intending to ruff the third round low and the fourth high. If East is awake, he will try to persuade declarer to ruff both diamonds high and rely on a 2-2 trump break. When South plays the ♦A and ♦K, East plays high-low with the 10 and 4. But West must keep up with the ball too and

withhold his normal suit-length signal; he should play the 2 followed by the 6, supporting the theory that the diamonds are 5-2.

For a method by which declarer can play to take advantage of length signals, see DISCOVERY.

COUNT SQUEEZE. A squeeze that operates on a player who does not guard a crucial suit in such a way as to give declarer a count of the suit, allowing him to drop an honor offside instead of taking a losing finesse.

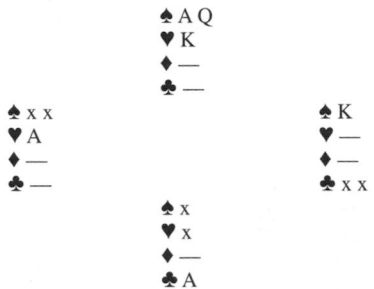

Suppose that West is known to have the ♥A, South leads the ♣A and West discards a spade. North can safely discard the ♥K. South leads a spade, and West follows low. North's ace must be played for it is known that West's remaining card is the ♥A. If West had guarded spades, he would have been caught in a SHOW-UP SQUEEZE.

COUNTING CARDS. It is each player's responsibility to determine that the hand he is about to play contains exactly 13 cards. This determination should be made before he looks at the face of any card. The Laws of Duplicate Bridge also require that 13 cards be replaced in the pocket of the board. (There is no longer a requirement to actually count the cards.)

COUNTING THE HAND. Deducing the distribution of the hidden hands from information gained during the bidding and early stages of play.

On many hands, the crucial play depends on the distribution of one particular suit. By observing or projecting the distributions of the other three suits, a player may be able to deduce how the key suit splits, *even if that suit has not yet been led.*

The procedure used is simple arithmetic, based on two facts: each suit has 13 cards; each player started with 13 cards in his hand.

The following is an elementary illustration of the basic technique of counting the hand: A decision which at first glance is a pure guess reduces to a certainty as a result of the play of the other suits.

WEST	EAST
♠ A Q 7	♠ K 5 3
♥ K Q 6	♥ A 4 2
♦ A K J 3	♦ Q 8 4 2
♣ A J 5	♣ K 10 3

West plays 7 NT, with the ♠J led. He should delay his decision in clubs to the very end, by first cashing all his winners. South follows twice to each major, but discards clubs on the third round of each. He then follows to three rounds of diamonds, while North discards a heart on the third round. Now, by subtraction, North is known to have started with five cards in each major and two diamonds, hence only one club. So West cashes dummy's ♣K, and (unless North drops the queen) finesses through South with certainty.

In the above example, counting the hand made declarer's final play a sure thing. More often, counting will indicate which play has the highest probability of success.

Suppose South had followed to four diamonds. Now it would be known that he started with five clubs, and North with two clubs. Then West should finesse through South as before, this time with odds of five to two that South has the missing queen. (When declarer finally takes the finesse, each defender has only one unknown card, but the odds determined from the count of the *initial* distribution are unchanged.) See PROBABILITIES, A POSTERIORI and A PRIORI.

In the illustration above, declarer's problem was simply which way to take a finesse. Sometimes counting the hand will help declarer decide between a squeeze and a finesse. Sometimes it will point up the necessity to handle a problem suit in a way radically different from what he would otherwise have attempted.

WEST	EAST
♠ A K Q	♠ 7 5 3
♥ A K Q	♥ 6 4 2
♦ A Q 8	♦ K 7 3
♣ K Q 7 3	♣ A 10 4 2

Again West plays 7 NT, with the ♣J led. Apparently West must cash king and queen of clubs, hoping that North has two or more clubs or that the jack is singleton. But before playing clubs, West should cash his major-suit winners. On the third round of each, South discards diamonds. West then cashes the ♦A-Q, and both opponents follow. Counting North's hand — five spades, five hearts, and two diamonds — shows that he has at most one club, which must be the 8, 9, or jack if West is to make the contract. So West abandons the normal play in clubs, and instead leads the 3 to dummy's ace. If North follows with the 8 or 9, declarer leads a club from dummy and covers South's card, using the carefully preserved ♦K as a re-entry for a second finesse if South splits his holding.

The preceding examples were played at notrump, so declarer could count the hand by cashing his winners and noting when the opponents showed out. In a suit contract, this type of play runs the risk of the opponents gaining a ruff. However, in a suit contract, declarer may be able to count the hand by using his own trumps for ruffing. For example, if dummy has A-K-x-x in a side suit, and declarer has two small, declarer may be able to ruff the suit twice in his hand. He does not gain any tricks by doing this, as his long trumps were winners anyhow. In fact, in the process of ruffing he destroys any squeeze or throw-in threat in the suit. But he is sure to obtain the count of the suit, if that is the crucial factor in the play of the rest of the hand.

So far, we have considered only cases where declarer's information on the count was gained during the play. Inferences about suit lengths may also be drawn from the opponents' bidding (or failure to bid), from the opening lead, or from defenders' plays or signals (see DISCOVERY). These inferences are, of course, not as firm as when a player fails to follow suit.

Defensive Play. Counting the hand is as important for the defenders as for the declarer.

NORTH (Dummy)
♠ K J
♥ 10 5 3
♦ A 8 6 3
♣ A 8 7 2

               EAST
               ♠ A Q 6
               ♥ J 9 7 6
               ♦ Q J 10
               ♣ J 9 5

South plays in 5♦, no other suits having been bid. West leads the ♠5. East wins and leads a second high spade, which South ruffs. South cashes ♦ K-A; West follows once, then discards a spade. South now cashes the ♥ A-K-Q (West following three times), then leads a diamond. East wins and counts declarer's hand — one spade, three hearts, five diamonds, therefore four clubs. So East does not fall for declarer's trap, and by returning a club, jeopardizing West's doubleton king or queen. Instead he leads a major, yielding a useless ruff and sluff, and eventually sets the hand with a club trick.

In addition to absolute counts, as in the above example, and inferential counts from the bidding, the defenders have a counting aid not available to the declarer — the COUNT SIGNAL. Most experts use such signals sparingly, to help partner in the play of one specific suit. The policy of some experts is to signal length in all suits when they think partner will profit more than declarer from a complete count of the hand.

In general, when partner is unlikely to be misled, a defender should make it as difficult as possible for declarer to count the hand. For instance, if a suit has gone around three times, the defender should retain the thirteenth card as long as possible, to keep declarer in doubt as to its location. It is usually wrong for a defender's first discard to be a worthless card in a suit where he has five cards and dummy has four cards — an astute declarer may be able to use this inference in counting the hand.

For a full discussion of counting, see *All Fifty-Two Cards* by Marshall Miles (BIBLIOGRAPHY, D). See also CARD READING.

COUNTING TRUMPS. This does not present problems for the expert, but the inexperienced player sometimes has trouble. There are three methods, which in increasing order of efficiency are:

(1) Wait until you need to know and then add the cards played to the cards remaining in view and subtract from 13 — a lot of effort that often produces the wrong result.

(2) a. As declarer, note at the start how many trumps the defenders have, and mentally reduce that total as the cards appear.

    b. As defender, make a guess from the bidding about the length of declarer's trumps. See how many this gives your partner. Then adjust your thinking if required.

(3) Think in terms of distributional patterns, which are of course the same as the patterns of a particular hand. If you have a 4-4 trump fit you are thinking of the patterns 4-4-3-2 or 4-4-4-1. If one defender shows out on the second round you know automatically that the other defender began with four and has two more. Players who are used to thinking in terms of patterns are able without difficulty to count all the suits. Two elements of the pattern are known at the start. When the bidding or play reveals a third, the fourth element is known automatically.

This is the expert method, and intermediate players should take the trouble to acquire the knack. A conscious effort to note the pattern of any 13-card hand improves familiarity with the patterns.

COUP. A special play maneuver by declarer. More specifically, without further designation, it refers to an endplay situation in which a defender's finessable trumps are trapped without a finesse. This may arise when there is no entry to take a finesse, or when there is no trump to lead for a finesse. Often the coup has to be prepared by shortening the trump length, reducing it to not more than.the same length as the defender's. For example:

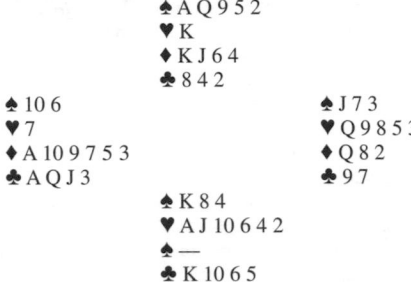

```
              ♠ A Q 9 5 2
              ♥ K
              ♦ K J 6 4
              ♣ 8 4 2
♠ 10 6                        ♠ J 7 3
♥ 7                          ♥ Q 9 8 5 3
♦ A 10 9 7 5 3                ♦ Q 8 2
♣ A Q J 3                    ♣ 9 7
              ♠ K 8 4
              ♥ A J 10 6 4 2
              ♦ —
              ♣ K 10 6 5
```

South plays in 4♥ after West has shown minor suits by an unusual notrump overcall. The ♦A is led and ruffed, and a heart is led to the king. South cashes the ♦K, ruffs a diamond, and plays three rounds of spades ending in dummy. A spade is ruffed, and a club is played. South must eventually make his two remaining trumps.

When the preparation of the coup makes it necessary to ruff a winner, the term GRAND COUP is used. Single, double and triple grand coups refer to situations in which one, two, and three winners are ruffed respectively.

For the term coup applied in other special contexts, including some unusual defense maneuvers, see ALCATRAZ; BATH COUP; COUP EN PASSANT; CROCODILE COUP; DESCHAPELLES COUP; DEVIL'S COUP; GRAND COUP; IDIOT COUP; MERRIMAC COUP; MORTON'S FORK COUP; PITT COUP; ROBERT COUP; SCISSORS COUP; SERPENT'S COUP; VIENNA COUP.

COUP EN BLANC. A term formerly used by some writers instead of DUCK.

COUP EN PASSANT. The lead of a plain suit card to promote a low trump behind a higher trump to a winning position. The term is taken from chess. See also ELOPEMENT.

In the following position, spades are trump. The lead is in the North hand.

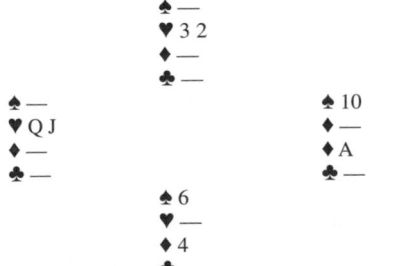

```
              ♠ —
              ♥ 3 2
              ♦ —
              ♣ —
♠ —                          ♠ 10
♥ Q J                        ♦ —
♦ —                          ♦ A
♣ —                          ♣ —
              ♠ 6
              ♥ —
              ♦ 4
              ♣ —
```

Declarer (South) holds no more winning cards. How-

ever, when a heart is led from the North hand, South makes a trick with the ♠6. If East discards, South ruffs the heart. If East ruffs with his master trump, the ♠6 wins the final trick. In the above example, if East held ♠ 10-5, South would score the ♠6 en passant in a similar manner, overruffing if East ruffed low and discarding if East ruffed high.

COUP WITHOUT A NAME. See SCISSORS COUP.

COURT CARDS. The king, queen and jack of each suit are represented by coated figures rather than pips, giving rise to the expression coat card. This term was corrupted to court card, probably due to the association with the figures in a royal court, and sometimes, wrongly, extended to include the ace.

COURTESY. See Proprieties, Law 74.

COURTESY BID. A response made on a very weak hand to allow for the possibility that the opener has great strength. The courtesy response is never made in response to a major suit, partly because partner's next action may be a game bid and partly because the contract of 1♥ or 1♠ will be playable. The courtesy response with a very weak hand is often indicated if the opening bid is 1♣ and responder is short in clubs. If he is 4-4-4-1, for example, a 1♦ response is likely to improve the contract with little risk and avoids the danger of playing in a 3-1 fit. This situation illustrates a weakness of standard bidding vis-à-vis strong-club methods.

COURTESY OF THE TABLE. A feature of the laws of auction bridge and the first laws of contract bridge. If dummy left the table, the defenders were required to take over dummy's duty of guarding declarer against the possibility of revoking. No penalty could be exacted against a declarer who revoked if the defenders had failed to ask the routine question, "Having no more?"

It was customary, although not legally necessary, for the dummy to ask for the Courtesy of the Table on leaving the table. This served to remind the defenders of their obligation in the matter.

This requirement was omitted from the first International edition of Laws, published in 1932.

COVER CARDS. A method of valuation devised by George Rosenkranz as part of the ROMEX SYSTEM, but applicable in any method.

Aces and kings are cover cards — also queens if they are likely to be effective. If the opener's hand is measured in terms of losers, responder can judge how many of the losers he covers:

```
              RESPONDER
              ♠ Q x
              ♥ K Q x x
              ♦ K x x x
              ♣ x x x
OPENER                 RESPONDER
1 ♠                    1 NT
2 ♥                    4 ♥
```

The opening bidder should have at most seven losers, and responder has four cover cards: ♠Q, ♥K-Q and ♦K. Four of opener's losers are covered, leaving three, and game can be bid. If the ♠Q were the ♣Q it could not be counted as a cover card, and a raise to 3♥ would be sufficient. See LOSING TRICK COUNT.

COVERING HONORS. When an honor is led and the next player follows with a higher honor, he is said to have covered an honor with an honor. Second hand should usually cover an honor if he might establish a trick in that suit for himself or partner in the process.

If an honor is led from a sequence of touching honors, it is seldom proper to cover until the last of the sequentials is led. The following examples are typical:

(a)
           A x x
K x x   10 x x
           Q J 9 x

The queen is led. If West covers, then South can take a finesse against the 10. West must duck the first honor lead but cover at the second opportunity.

If West does cover, he can be expected to hold K, K-x, or K-10.

(b)
           K x x
Q x x   A 9 x x
           J 10 8

South leads the jack and makes two tricks if West covers. If West ducks, East can win or duck, and South is held to one trick provided the defenders avoid leading the suit subsequently.

(c)
           A x x
Q 9 x   K 8 x x
           J 10 x

If West covers the jack he gives South two tricks.

The decision about whether to cover is generally more difficult when the honor is led by declarer. Generally, if dummy does not have the honor directly below declarer's card, it should be assumed that declarer has it, and the defender should wait and cover the next honor. If dummy has the honor below the card led by declarer, it is often proper to cover unless declarer is believed to have a TWO-WAY FINESSE. When in doubt, the best policy is usually to duck quickly. An exception to the rule about not covering a sequence occurs when the opposing suit can be blocked:

(d)
           A K x x x
Q 9 x   x x x
           J 10

If dummy has no entry, West must cover the jack or 10 to prevent declarer from making five tricks.

(e)
           Q J 10 9 x
x x x   K x x x
           A

If the queen is led and covered, the remainder of the suit is established in the North hand.

(f)
           A x
K x x   x x x
           Q J 10 x x

If the queen is led West must not cover. He can ensure a trick in the suit because the ace must be played on the second round.

There are numerous exceptions to this rule, and a clever declarer can pose the defenders many problems, as in the following examples:

(g)
           A x
K x x   J 10 x x
           Q x x x

If South needs to steal a trick in the suit, he can lead the queen — West may duck.

(h)
           A x x
K x   10 9 x
           Q J x x x

If South leads the queen, West must cover with a doubleton king; otherwise South can continue with a small card and drop the king.

(i)
           Q J 10 8 x
A x x x   K 9 x
           x

At a trump contract, North leads the queen in a side suit. East must play the king. If he ducks, the king may be ruffed out eventually.

CRACK. An expert player, partnership or team. As a verb, there are three meanings: (1) to obtain bad results after a period of success; (2) to double; (3) to open a new suit during the play of the hand. The latter two meanings are bridge colloquialisms.

CRANE SYSTEM. An obsolete bidding system devised by Joshua Crane in which the full value of the hand was bid immediately in accordance with its point-count. A hand counting to 12-15 was bid at the one level; a hand worth 16-19 was bid at the two level, etc. This may have been the earliest published system to include a distributional point-count: both opener and responder counted three points for a singleton and six points for a void once the trump suit had been agreed. Also called, somewhat optimistically, the *commonsense system*.

CRASH. A method of bidding defensively against an artificial forcing 1♣ opening bid developed by Kit Woolsey and Steve Robinson. The word CRASH is an acronym for Color-RAnk-SHape. After an opening 1♣ forcing bid, a double or an overcall of 1♦ or 1 NT show various types of two-suited hands. Double shows color — both suits are red or both are black. 1♦ shows rank — both suits are majors or both are minors. 1 NT shows shape — both suits are pointed (spades and diamonds) or both are rounded. These bids are usually made on weak distributional hands — usually at least nine cards in the suits pinpointed. Bids of 1♥, 1♠, 2♣ and 2♦ show single-suited hands. Partner of the CRASH bidder usually responds as high as possible in the lowest suit possible. Overcaller passes if this is one of his suits, but bids the next higher suit in his own two-suiter if the overcaller has chosen the wrong pair of suits. For example:

WEST	NORTH	EAST	SOUTH
1♣	Dbl	Pass	3♣
Pass	3♦	Pass	?

If South is 4-4 in clubs and hearts, he will correct to hearts because he knows partner has a heart-diamond hand. If North had a black hand, he would have passed 3♣.

The original version of this convention had 1♦ for color, 1♥ for rank and 1 NT for shape, with a double reserved to show a hand of some strength and with all two-level overcalls showing one-suited hands.

The original writeup by Woolsey appeared in *The Bridge World* magazine in March 1976. Short articles in the March 1983 and August 1986 issues elaborated on CRASH.

CRASHING HONORS. The deceptive play of a suit by declarer resulting in the defense wasting two high honors on one trick.

The most common situation in which the declarer can crash honors occurs when the declarer holds concealed length in his own hand. The lead of an honor from dummy may cause second hand to cover with an honor, crashing still a third honor in the other defender's hand. For example:

♠ J 8 5 3
♠ A   ♠ K 4
♠ Q 10 9 7 6 2

If the ♠ J is led from dummy (North), East may play the king in the hope that West holds ♠ 10-x, 10-9, or 10-x-x.

Declarer may also crash honors with a lead from his own hand toward the dummy. This play is most likely to work if dummy is apparently (or actually) short of entries, as the defenders may believe declarer did not have the option of taking a finesse. Thus:

♥ 9 8 7 6
♥ K 4   ♥ A
♥ Q J 10 5 3 2

With dummy (North) barren of entries, South leads the ♥ Q. If West believes declarer is trying to avoid a loser in the suit by leading the queen from A-Q-J, he may play the king.

More subtle examples of crashing honors can be found in holdings in which the declarer is missing several top cards. The choice of card to lead might not seem too important in this suit:

♦ J 8 5 3

♦ 10 9 7 6 4

If possible, declarer (South) should start the diamond suit by leading the jack from dummy. East may play the ace from A-Q-2, or may split honors from K-Q-2.

Sometimes, it helps declarer's plan if the defenders know about his length in a suit. In the example below, South has indicated a six-card club suit.

♣ J 8
♣ Q 5 3   ♣ A K
♣ 10 9 7 6 4 2

South leads the ♣ 2 toward dummy's jack. As he would make the same play with A-K-7-6-4-2 of clubs in his hand, West is faced with a guess. If West takes the wrong view, the defense will crash honors in clubs.

In a slightly different sense, declarer may sometimes crash a single honor by making it fall on a trick with low cards, so it will not interfere with the trick-taking potential of declarer's honor cards.

♠ —
♠ A 5   ♠ J 10 9
♠ K Q 8 7 6 4 3 2

South, who has opened with 4♠, can afford to lose only one spade trick. His only chance is to lead the ♠ Q from the closed hand. West may suspect that South has an even longer suit than he actually holds (or may make a mistake), and so play low. South can now crash the A with one of East's minor honors by leading a low spade, preserving his king for the third round of the suit.

CRISSCROSS RAISE. Players using limit raises in response to minor-suit openings have a problem with opening values and balanced distribution. One solution is the criss-cross jump shift: 1♣ – 2♦ shows a forcing raise in clubs, and 1♦ – 3♣ shows a forcing raise in diamonds. With an unbalanced hand a SPLINTER is usually available, and many players avoid the problem by using INVERTED MINOR SUIT RAISES.

CRISSCROSS SQUEEZE. A blocked squeeze described under SIMPLE SQUEEZE.

CROATIAN BRIDGE FEDERATION (Hrvatski Bridge Savez). Founded in 1991 after the disintegration of the former Yugoslav NCBO, the Federation has a membership of about 350, principally in the Zagreb and Rijeka areas. Officers 1992:
President: Davor Rase
Foreign Relations: Fred Kulenovic
Kuhaceva 13, 41107 Zagreb, Croatia.
Tel: 003841217159
Fax: 003841232106

CROCKFORD'S CLUB. In London, England, a famous proprietary club descending from a gambling club founded by William Crockford in 1827. In modern times it has been primarily a bridge club. In December 1961, Crockford's reverted to its gambling traditions by becoming the headquarters of chemin-de-fer in England.

CROCKFORD'S CLUB. Founded by Ely Culbertson in New York in 1932 and named after the English club of the same name. The club was famous for its high-quality cuisine and for its luxurious appointments, as was its sister club in Chicago. Many famous American players of the Thirties were members of Crockford's. Many members were drawn from high society rather than from the tournament bridge world. The club was in operation from 1932 to 1938.

CROCODILE COUP. A defensive maneuver to foil an impending endplay. Like a crocodile opening his jaws, a defender in second seat wins a trick with an unnecessarily high card, preventing his partner from being thrown in.

Dlr: West   ♠ Q 9 8 3
Vul: E-W   ♥ K 6 4
           ♦ 7 4 2
           ♣ Q 7 4

♠ 10   ♠ 7 5
♥ Q J 3   ♥ A 10 9 8 5 2
♦ A Q J 9 8 6   ♦ K
♣ 9 3 2   ♣ J 10 8 6

           ♠ A K J 6 4 2
           ♥ 7
           ♦ 10 5 3
           ♣ A K 5

WEST	NORTH	EAST	SOUTH
2 ♦	Pass	Pass	3 ♠
Pass	4 ♠	All Pass	

West leads the ♥ Q and ♥ J. South ruffs, draws trumps, ruffs dummy's last heart and cashes his club tricks. He then leads a low diamond from his hand. If West plays the nine, East must win and concede a ruff-and-discard. West must count declarer's distribution, realize that the defense needs three diamond tricks to defeat the contract, and rise with the ♦ A — a Crocodile Coup.

Similar but less spectacular plays occur frequently. Suppose this suit is trumps:

           6 4 2
K J 3   Q 8
           A 10 9 7 5

South, the declarer, leads the ace and a low trump. West can infer that East has the queen, since South took no finesse. West can therefore rise with the king, capturing East's queen. West then has the option of drawing a third round of trumps.

A deal in the 1969 U.S International Team Trials produced a comic sequence of plays that Oswald Jacoby called the "Reverse Crocodile Coup." The contract was 1NT, and the heart suit was:

```
                 J 4
    A 9 5 3 2               Q 7 6
                K 10 8
```

West led the ♥3, dummy played the 4 and East smoothly contributed the 6 (the correct technical play). South won the 8 and was convinced that West had the ♥AQ. With no more attractive play, South returned the ♥10, hoping the defenders would break a new suit. West, equally deceived about the heart situation, placed South with the K-Q-10-8; he put up the ♥A and shifted!

Declarers have been known to steal a trick with an "anti-crocodile coup" — inducing a defender to try for a Crocodile Coup when none was required.

CROSS-IMP. See IMP PAIR GAMES.

CROSSRUFF. A method of play whereby ruffing tricks are made in each of a partnership's hands, thus using the trumps separately.

When a crossruff is played, ruffing tricks are being taken in two side suits. It is usually a good idea to cash winners in the remaining suit at an early stage.

```
                 ♠ A Q 5
                 ♥ 3
                 ♦ A J 8 5 3
                 ♣ K Q 10 5
    ♠ 6 4 3 2                 ♠ 10 9 8
    ♥ K Q 10 6 4              ♥ J 9
    ♦ 4                       ♦ K Q 10 7 6 2
    ♣ 6 4 3                   ♣ 7 2
                 ♠ K J 7
                 ♥ A 8 7 5 2
                 ♦ 9
                 ♣ A J 9 8
```

After East opens 3♦, West leads a trump against South's 6♣ contract. South can count only five top tricks outside of clubs and must therefore make all his remaining trumps separately. He must be careful to cash his three spade tricks immediately, else the defenders will discard spades when failing to follow to red-suit tricks. If this happens, declarer will lose his good spades to opposing ruffs. If the spades cannot be cashed at once, there is no hope for the contract.

CROWHURST. A secondary Stayman inquiry after a 1NT rebid by opener, devised by Eric Crowhurst and widely used by British tournament players. Opener is assumed to have 12-16 HCP; the 2♣ rebid by responder asks for further clarification. If opener has 15-16 he rebids 2 NT (game forcing) regardless of his distribution; with 12-14 opener either (1) rebids a five-card major suit, (2) shows three-card support for responder's major suit, (3) shows an unbid four-card major suit, or (4) bids 2♦. See also STAYMAN ON SECOND ROUND.

CROWNINSHIELD TROPHY. Presented by Frank Crowninshield for British-American competition. It was contested only once, in 1949, when an unofficial U.S. team (John Crawford, Peter Leventritt, George Rapee,

Samuel Stayman) played matches against two British teams. The result was a win for Britain by 330 aggregate points. See ANGLO-AMERICAN MATCHES. For results see Appendix IV.

CUDGELS. The club suit.

CUEBID. A forcing bid in a suit in which the bidder cannot wish to play. It is applied to (1) bids in the opponents' suit at any level; (2) bids to show controls at a high level after a suit has been agreed directly or by inference.

Cuebids are discussed under the following headings: ADVANCE CUEBID; ASTRO CUEBID; CAPPELLETTI CUEBIDS; COLORFUL CUEBID; CUEBID AS A LIGHT TAKEOUT; CUEBIDS IN OPPONENTS SUITS; CUEBIDS TO SHOW CONTROLS; DIRECTIONAL ASKING BID; JUMP CUEBID; KANTAR CUEBID; MICHAELS CUEBID; UNASSUMING CUEBID; WESTERN CUEBID.

CUEBID AS A LIGHT TAKEOUT. An immediate cuebid of an opponent's opening bid is a weak takeout bid for the other three suits. This method reserves the takeout double for stronger hands having greater defensive values.

CUEBIDS IN OPPONENT'S SUIT. When a player bids a suit which has originally been called by his opponents, he is said to make a cuebid. A cuebid is not made in the expectation of actually playing in the relevant suit; it is made for exploratory or control-showing purposes.

In the early days of contract bridge, a cuebid could be made in only two situations: the immediate overcall in the opponent's suit guaranteed a void (or at any rate, no losers) in the suit. This was later extended to strong hands with a singleton in the suit. At later stages in the auction, opposite a partner who had already bid, the cuebid in the opponent's suit was used to show control of the suit, and suggest slam

In the above form, the opportunity to make a cuebid rarely occurred. Theorists, particularly in England and California, developed the idea that any cuebid below game is simply forcing, and this idea eventually prevailed. It made use of many idle bids.

Cuebids are used much more extensively by experts than by others. In studying the meaning of various cuebids, the subject is considered (1) from opener's viewpoint, (2) from responder's viewpoint, and (3) from defenders' viewpoint.

Cuebids by Opener

The level at which the cuebid is made is a vital consideration. The meaning changes according to whether game has been reached.

Above the game level, there can be no doubt that the cuebid is a slam try. The same is true in this sort of situation:

WEST	NORTH	EAST	SOUTH
			1♠
2♥	3♠	Pass	4♥

North-South are already committed to playing in at least a game in spades, so 4♥ must be a slam try, showing control of the heart suit. First-round control of hearts (ace or void) is virtually guaranteed.

But when partnership is still searching for the safest game contract, the cuebid by opener is much less precise. He may or may not have slam ambitions. He may or may not have a control in the cuebid suit. Time will tell:

WEST	NORTH	EAST	SOUTH
			1 ♣
1 ♥	1 ♠	Pass	2 ♥

All North can tell at this stage is that South has an enormous hand, and wants to be in at least a game. North must make the most helpful bid he can think of, which is likely to be notrump if he has a heart stopper. If he has a double heart stopper and a weak hand he should jump to 3 NT. This should serve as a warning to South that duplication is present. South may have any of the following hands:

(a)
♠ A Q 7 4
♥ 6
♦ A 6 3
♣ A K J 5 4

South's hand offers good slam prospects, and it would be wrong to raise immediately to 4♠. He plans to bid 4♠ on the next round, whatever rebid he gets from North. A delayed raise to game always promises more than an immediate game bid. See FAST ARRIVAL, PRINCIPLE OF.

(b)
♠ A 4
♥ 7 5
♦ A J 5
♣ A K Q J 5 4

Here the cuebid is made, not as in slam try, but as a means of reaching the best game contract.

Although he has no spade fit and no heart control, South must insist on reaching game. He is too strong to bid 3♣, which could be passed. If North bids 2NT, South raises to 3NT. If North rebids 2♠, South simply bids 3♣, and awaits developments.

(c)	(d)
♠ A J 6	♠ A 6 5
♥ 5	♥ 5 4
♦ A J 7	♦ K Q J 6 4
♣ A K Q 9 5 4	♣ A K Q J

On both these hands South will bid 3♠ if North bids 2NT in response to South's 2♥ cuebid. In each case, the best contract may turn out to be 4♠, which North will bid if he has a five-card suit or a strong four-card suit.

Notice that in no case is South void in hearts. With a void it will usually be better to make a jump cuebid. This pinpoints a void specifically.

In some circumstances, a cuebid is not even completely forcing to game. Consider the following:

WEST	NORTH	EAST	SOUTH
			1 ♣
Pass	Pass	1 ♥	2 ♥

or

WEST	NORTH	EAST	SOUTH
			1 ♣
1 ♥	Pass	2 ♥	3 ♥

South cannot be insisting on game here because he did not open with a forcing bid, and his partner's hand may be completely worthless. He may have either of these hands:

♠ A Q 5 4　　　　♠ A K 3
♥ —　　　　　　 ♥ —
♦ A K 7 2　　　　♦ A J 8 4
♣ A Q J 8 6　　　♣ K Q J 8 7 3 2

This particular cuebid, even without a jump, suggests a void in hearts. (With a singleton heart, a takeout double would be the normal action: South would then be less

reluctant to hear his partner pass the double for penalties.)

The following example shows the advantage of playing the low-level cuebid as a vague forcing bid, without any guarantee of control in the suit.

WEST	NORTH	EAST	SOUTH
			1 ♣
2 ♠*	3 ♥	Pass	3 ♠

*weak

South holds:

♠ 7 5
♥ J 3
♦ Q 8 3
♣ A K Q 7 4 3

This use of the cuebid to ask about stoppers first became popular on the West Coast of the United States. Hence it is called a WESTERN CUEBID and it has since become standard. It is the only way for South to steer the contract into 3NT if North has a spade guard. (If South had a spade stopper he could simply bid 3NT himself.) Unless the partnership has this understanding, South is forced to bid 4♣, or even 4♥, when the notrump game may easily be best (see DIRECTIONAL ASKING BID).

A cuebid must always be considered within the framework of the bidding. If the cuebidder and his partner have limited their hands by the earlier auction, the cuebid may be made even in a partscore situation, when there is no intention of reaching game. This is illustrated by the following example:

WEST	NORTH	EAST	SOUTH
			1 ♣
1 ♦	Pass	1 NT	Pass
Pass	Dbl	Pass	2 ♦

South's hand was:

♠ Q J 10 6
♥ A 7 5 4
♦ 6
♣ K J 8 4

As he had passed over 1NT and then refused to stand the double, it was clear that South was weak. With North also limited by his original pass, the cuebid was simply a useful maneuver to find a major-suit fit.

Cuebids by Responder

WEST	NORTH	EAST	SOUTH
			1 ♣
1 ♠	2 ♠		

Classically this would have shown a club fit with no losers in spades, and a desire to reach at least game. In the modern style North could have any of the following hands:

(a)	(b)	(c)
♠ A 6	♠ 7 4 2	♠ K J
♥ A K J	♥ K J 7 3	♥ A J 7 4
♦ 9 6 5 3 2	♦ A 10 5	♦ A J 6
♣ J 4 2	♣ K Q 7	♣ 10 6 4 2

All three hands would present problems without the use of the cuebid. A bid of 2♥ on (b) or (c) would suggest a five-card suit, and a bid of 2♦ on (a) is misleading with such a weak suit. In each case North raises to 3NT if South's rebid is 2NT, showing a spade stopper.

This usage in no way bars responder from making the cuebid with its classical meaning. He follows with a club raise or a clear-cut slam move, and the situation becomes clear to opener.

When North has a spade void, he can show this unequivocally by a jump cuebid of 3♠. (Unusual jump bids which have no normal meaning can often be useful to show a specific void.)

A modern alternative meaning for the jump cuebid in this situation requires opener to bid 3NT. The cuebidder will have opening values, balanced distribution and a spade stopper, probably A x x or K x x. Perhaps:

    ♠ A 3 2
    ♥ K 7 4
    ♦ Q 8 5
    ♣ K J 7 2

This permits 3NT to be played from the right side when the opening bidder has Q x or J x x. (Suggested by Marty Bergen.)

The responder can cuebid with great freedom on the second round of bidding:

WEST	NORTH	EAST	SOUTH
			1 ♣
Pass	1 ♦	1 ♠	Pass
Pass	2 ♠		

North holds:

    ♠ Q 8
    ♥ A 10 5
    ♦ A J 8 7 4
    ♣ J 5 2

In this case South is limited by his failure to bid over 1♠, which strongly suggests that his hand is minimum. North intends to pass if he gets a discouraging bid of 3♣ or 3♦ from South. This is one case in which the bidding can die short of game after a cuebid. If South has any game ambitions, he must make some more constructive bid.

Counter-cues and redoubles. If South has ♠ A-x-x or ♠ K-x-x, for example, he can make a countercuebid of ♠3, which steers 3NT into the North hand.

Having the contract played from the right side of the table is a consideration also on this deal:

Dlr: S   ♠ Q 5
Vul: N-S   ♥ 6 2
            ♦ K Q 3
            ♣ A Q 8 7 6 4

♠ J 10 9 8 6 2   ♠ K 7 4
♥ A K 10 3   ♥ 9 8
♦ 7 4   ♦ J 9 8 5
♣ 5   ♣ J 10 9 2

        ♠ A 3
        ♥ Q J 7 5 4
        ♦ A 10 6 2
        ♣ K 3

WEST	NORTH	EAST	SOUTH
			1 ♥
Pass	2 ♣	Pass	2 ♦
2 ♠	3 ♠	Dbl	Redbl
Pass	3 NT	All Pass	

If the cuebid were not available, North would be in trouble over 2♠. 3♣ or 3♦ would be substantial underbids, likely to lead to a missed game.

East's double of 3♠ strongly suggests that he has a top spade honor, so North-South are able to play 3NT from the North position. When a cuebid (in the opponent's suit or otherwise) is doubled, a redouble shows control of the suit; whether it is first or second-round control is a matter for partnership agreement.

There are often opportunities for using the cuebid after an original pass by the cuebidder:

WEST	NORTH	EAST	SOUTH
	Pass	Pass	1 ♦
1 ♠	2 ♠		

This shows a near opening bid, a balanced distribution, and insufficient spade strength to bid 2 NT. For example:

(a)	(b)
♠ 7 4 3 2	♠ A 6 4
♥ A Q 6	♥ A K 9
♦ Q 8 5	♦ 10 9 8
♣ K 10 7	♣ 10 9 7 3

Holding a fit with the opener's suit, the responder will rarely wish to look further than a raise of partner's suit. With the hands given, North would have an impossible bid to make. In each case he is hoping for 3 NT, but with his partner to play it.

In the event of North wishing to make a cuebid because he has a powerful diamond fit, he can still do so. But until North clarifies the situation on the next round, South must bid on the assumption that North's hand is balanced. Any simple bid by South on the second round, such as 3♣ or 3♦, may be passed. So if South wants to be in game he must make a counter-cuebid of 3♠ or take some other strong action.

A cuebid in notrump. A cuebid in notrump is both rare and rarely understood. Suppose the bidding goes:

WEST	NORTH	EAST	SOUTH
			1 ♦
1 NT	2 NT		

What does North's bid mean? It cannot be a balanced hand trying for a notrump game, because any such hand would simply double 1NT and take a penalty. 2NT in this situation should be regarded as a cuebid, simply forcing to game or perhaps forcing to four of a minor. It shows an unbalanced hand which does not wish to defend against notrump. A two-suiter is likely, such as:

    ♠ A Q 6 5 4 2
    ♥ A J 6 5 3
    ♦ 9
    ♣ 4

There should be game in one of the major suits, but a double will not work out well if, as is likely, West has a strong club suit.

Once the game level has been reached, the cuebid becomes simply control-showing. Almost invariably it will show the ace or a void, but might occasionally be made with a second-round control. This can be ventured if the cuebidder's trump holding is strong, as there is then no danger that partner will race for a grand slam missing a trick in the enemy suit.

Negative inferences. The failure to cuebid can be very significant:

WEST		EAST
♠ A Q 7 5 4 3		♠ K J 8 5
♥ A K J 6 3		♥ 7 2
♦ —		♦ A Q 10 8 3
♣ 9 4		♣ 10 6

WEST	NORTH	EAST	SOUTH
1 ♠	4 ♣	4 ♠	Pass
5 ♠	Pass	Pass	

This asks only for control of clubs. If West had any other worries he would make a suitable cuebid.

Similarly, a player who holds

    ♠ 5 2
    ♥ A Q 7 6 4 2
    ♦ —
    ♣ A K 8 7 3

can bid 5♥ when his partner's 1♥ has been overcalled with 1♠.

There are numerous possibilities for cuebidding after partner's opening bid of 1NT. Frequently the cuebid has to take the place of a STAYMAN inquiry which has been frustrated by the intervening bid.

♠ A K 7 3
♥ Q 6
♦ A 10 6 2
♣ K J 6

South holds this hand and the bidding goes:

WEST	NORTH	EAST	SOUTH
			1 NT
2 ♥	3 ♥	Pass	3 ♠
Pass	3 NT	Pass	?

North's bid of 3♥ could have any of three meanings. He could be paving the way for a slam; he could be trying to find a 4-4 spade fit to play in 4♠; or he could be worrying about the presence of a heart guard for 3NT.

The 3NT bid makes it clear that he does not have spades, nor is he seeking a slam. His only reason for not bidding 3NT directly was because he has no heart guard.

In these circumstances, West would enjoy 3NT, so South must bid 4♦. He expects to play a game in spades, diamonds, or clubs. (But see LEBENSOHL).

Another curious cuebid can arise after a NT opening bid:

WEST	NORTH	EAST	SOUTH
			1 NT
Dbl	2 NT		

This cannot be a natural bid, because a hand which is ready to suggest 3NT would prefer to redouble. The redouble is almost sure to produce a good score, probably from a penalty when the opponents play in some doubled contract at the two-level. So 2NT must be a forcing bid with a very unbalanced distribution — probably a two-suiter on which game seems feasible. Over West's double, a jump to 3♠ for example, should be preemptive, not forcing, so 2NT is the only forcing bid at North's disposal.

Cuebids by the Defender

Cuebids by the side which did not open the bidding are considered under two headings; cuebids by second hand and cuebids by fourth hand.

Cuebids by second hand. The immediate overcall in the opponent's suit has been the subject of experiment in recent years. There are no fewer than five varieties:

(1) *Classical* (Culbertson-Goren). The equivalent of an opening forcing bid, guaranteeing a game. Goren insists that the cuebid shows first-round control in the cuebid suit, without explaining what to do if that feature is not present. Culbertson is less rigid, permitting the cuebid with a singleton, and allowing for the possibility that the bidding may die short of game if the responding hand is very weak. Modern bidders contend that these interpretations weaken the value of the bid, since there is so rarely an opportunity to use it.

(2) *Modern* (Reese and Dormer). Here the cuebid is used for most powerful hands with game prospects when a takeout double is unsuitable because a penalty pass would be unwelcome. *Blueprint for Bidding* gives these three examples of 2♦ after an opening 1♦:

(a)   (b)
♠ A K 10 8 4 3 2   ♠ A Q 10 7 4
♥ K 4   ♥ K J 8 7 5
♦ 7   ♦ —
♣ A J 6   ♣ A Q 5

(c)
♠ K Q 9 5 4
♥ A
♦ 9
♣ A K J 8 3 2

In (a), the spades are bid and rebid, and the bidding can die at 3♠. If (b) gets a 3♣ response, a repeat cuebid of 3♦ is used to ask for a major suit. The bidding can stop at 3♥ or 3♠. If (c) gets a 2♥ response, which is likely, the rebid is 3♣, which can be passed.

(3) *Hypermodern* (the MICHAELS CUEBID). Here there is a two-suited hand, usually less than opening bid strength. Over a minor suit it shows major suits; over a major suit it shows the unbid major and an unspecified minor. In the latter case the hand may be stronger. See also KANTAR CUEBID.

It is generally true that two-suited hands are difficult to bid in defense, and this has given rise to various attempts, such as the unusual notrump, to show two suits with one bid.

(4) *Artificial* (the ASTRO CUEBID). This method is described by its inventors, Larry Rosler, Roger Stern and Paul Allinger. It shows a minor-major two-suiter — the lower unbid minor and the lower unbid major. The minor suit is always long, and the distribution is likely to be 6-5, 6-4, or 5-4. The strength will vary wildly. At favorable vulnerability, it might be a 5-point hand hoping for a sacrifice, while at unfavorable vulnerability the cuebidder must have a sound hand able to play safely at the three-level. See also COLORFUL CUEBID.

(5) *Natural.* There is a strong argument for playing an immediate overcall in an opponent's minor suit as a natural bid to show a suit, especially if the opponents do not open four-card major suits. In that case they will frequently bid a three-card minor suit, and the second player may want to bid the suit naturally.

Against opponents who open freely with weak four-card major suits, or even three-card major suits, the cuebid may be used naturally at all times.

Of the five different methods listed above, the most popular, in expert circles, is the third method, i.e., Michaels Cuebid.

The second player may make delayed cuebid in a variety of circumstances. A common situation, when the second hand is strong, follows a takeout double:

WEST	NORTH	EAST	SOUTH
			1 ♥
Dbl	Pass	2 ♣	Pass
2 ♥			

Many years ago this bid was used as a natural bid to show a strong heart suit, and it was not forcing. This treatment has been abandoned, partly because such hands usually pass the opening heart bid, and partly because it is needed as a cuebid with a variety of strong hands.

The precise meaning of the cuebid is influenced by the type of immediate cuebid being used. If this has the traditional strong meaning, then the delayed cuebid is certain to be less than a game-forcing hand. Using a specialized cuebid — (3), (4), or (5) above — the delayed cuebid has no upward limit. In either case the minimum should be a hand with about 20 points.

A cuebid following partner's double is, of course, very different:

WEST	NORTH	EAST	SOUTH
			1 ♠
Pass	Pass	Dbl	Pass
2 ♠			

It would be unprofitable to reserve this cuebid for a hand which can guarantee game because West's original pass makes it unlikely that he has such a hand. The cuebid here simply suggests a game, and West could have as little as:

♠ 8 7 4
♥ J 10 8 5
♦ A Q 10
♣ K 9 2

If East's next bid is 3♣ or 3♦, West can and should pass. Over 3♥, he can just afford to continue to game, because all his points are *working*. If East has a good sound double, he will either bid a game directly or make a further cuebid of 3♠.

A pass followed by a bid in the opponent's suit may need a little study. Usually it is a natural bid, based on a

strong suit which the opponent has stolen. For example:

WEST	NORTH	EAST	SOUTH
			1 ♠
Pass	1 NT	Pass	Pass
2 ♠			

This indicates a good six-card spade suit. South and North may well have only four spades and one spade respectively, so West cannot allow himself to be talked out of playing in spades. He would be less inclined to bid 2♠, perhaps, if the opening bid promised a five-card suit. See OVERCALL IN OPPONENT'S MAJOR SUIT.

The same would apply if the opening bid was in hearts, but the situation is different when the opening bid was in a minor suit:

WEST	NORTH	EAST	SOUTH
			1 ♦
Pass	1 NT	Pass	Pass
2 ♦			

Now it is much less likely that West will want to bid 2♦ naturally, because North-South will almost always have six diamonds between them and usually more. It is more useful, therefore, to use the bid in the opponent's minor suit as a cuebid for a major-suit takeout on this type of hand:

♠ K 8 5 3
♥ A 10 6 3
♦ 7 5 4
♣ K 2

West could not afford to make an original double with this hand, partly because his strength is insufficient, and partly because he is not prepared for a club response. It is highly probable after this auction that East-West have a 4-4 fit or better in one of the major suits, and the 2♦ cuebid is an effective way for East-West to balance themselves into a major suit.

If West makes a cuebid of this type, and East is in any doubt about its significance, he can usually come to the right conclusion by considering his own holding in the cuebid suit. If he has a misfit in the cuebid suit, the bid is likely to be natural. If not, it is likely to be for a takeout.

To complete the picture as far as cuebids by the second player are concerned, there is the rare notrump cuebid. A bid of 2NT over an opening bid of 1NT can, by agreement, be either: (a) an unusual notrump showing minor-suit length; or (b) a freak two-suited hand of any kind.

Cuebids by Fourth Hand. Here there is much more variety. Six common cases need consideration.

(1) *After two passes.* If South bids 1♦ and East bids 2♦ in the pass-out position, the cuebid should mean the same as if made by second hand. East bears in mind that West

and North are limited by their original passes.

(2) *After a pass and a suit response.*

WEST	NORTH	EAST	SOUTH
			1 ♦
Pass	1 ♠	2 ♦ or 2 ♠	

This requires partnership agreement. Many, particularly in Britain, would consider one or both of these as natural, indicating a good 6-card suit or better. Others consider them strong and forcing, which is the traditional American interpretation. The same problem arises when second-hand has overcalled.

(3) *After an overcall and a pass*

WEST	NORTH	EAST	SOUTH
			1 ♦
1 ♠	Pass	2 ♦	

This is back to the earlier pattern: a strong hand which expects to go to game but does not know where to go. East might hold:

♠ K 3
♥ Q J 6 2
♦ 10 3
♣ A K 7 5 4

East expects to reach game, but this could be in any denomination except diamonds. West may show any additional feature: a second suit if he has one; a diamond guard by bidding notrump; or a good overcall including a six-card spade suit by jumping to 3♠. If he can do no more than rebid 2♠, East raises to 3♠, which can be passed. If East-West are vulnerable, East might go to 4♠ over 2♠. This depends on the partnership's overcalling standards.

Alternatively, East may hold a hand which is worth a raise to 4♠, but offers some slam chances. If he bids 2♦, and follows with 4♠ West may be able to continue.

Another treatment that has become increasingly popular among modern players is to use this cuebid as responder's only strong bid, usually equivalent to a limit raise of the overcaller's suit.

For example, the bidding goes:

WEST	NORTH	EAST	SOUTH
1 ♥	1 ♠	Pass	2 ♥

South holds:

♠ K 9 5
♥ A 7 2
♦ K J 9 8 3
♣ 10 6

In standard methods, South would express the value of his hand by jump raising to 3♠, but this may get his side too high. Employing the cuebid as an invitational measure permits South to explore accurately for game without endangering the partial contract. If North rebids 2♠, South passes, while if North shows additional values above a minimum overcall by jumping to 3♠ or introducing a new suit, South supports spades as cheaply as possible to describe the limited nature of his cuebid. With a stronger hand, South would again cuebid, but would take some further action over a minimum rebid by North. As a corollary, a double raise of an overcall is freed for use as a preemptive tactic.

Consider also the jump cuebid:

WEST	NORTH	EAST	SOUTH
1 ♥	1 ♠	Pass	3 ♥

This is commonly used as a limit raise in spades, leaving 3♠ available as a preemptive move. Some prefer to use this as a good preemptive raise, with 7-9 points, spade length and a singleton. Stronger hands must start with a cuebid at the two-level, a scheme known as Mixed Raises.

See also RESPONDING TO OVERCALLS and UNAS-SUMING CUEBID.

(4) *After a double and a pass*

This is very common:

WEST	NORTH	EAST	SOUTH
			1♦
Dbl	Pass	2♦	

East can hold any hand on which he expects to get to game, but does not know where. A typical hand would be:

♠ K 7 6 3
♥ K 7 6 3
♦ 9 3 2
♣ A K

Over 2♦, West is almost sure to bid a major, which East raises to game. A raise to 3♠ (or 3♥) would not be forcing. It would be appropriate if the ♣K were turned into the jack or a small card.

This last point involves an important principle. In general, a cuebid is not completely forcing to game. It loses its forcing quality when a limited position is reached. A raise is always limited, so the bidding can die below game. A minimum double and a minimum cuebid may not have enough combined values for game. This allows East to make the cuebid freely on hands which would otherwise present a problem.

(5) *After a double and a bid*

WEST	NORTH	EAST	SOUTH
1♦	Dbl	1♥	2♥

This is similar to (2), in that the opponents have bid two suits. 2♥ is a normal cuebid, with no interest in a heart contract. Holding four hearts or more, he would certainly double. But the only way to show diamonds at this point is to bid them, so 2♦ should simply mean a desire to play in that contract.

(6) *After a notrump overcall*

WEST	NORTH	EAST	SOUTH
1♦	1 NT	Pass	2♦

There are two schools of thought about this position. The normal interpretation is that it is a cuebid, which can be used as a Stayman substitute.

Alternatively, 2♣ can be retained as a Stayman bid, in which case 2♦ is a weak hand that wants to play in diamonds. This is not too unlikely because the notrump bidder has promised a good diamond holding.

The situation changes to some degree when the opening bid is 1♣.

WEST	NORTH	EAST	SOUTH
1♣	1 NT	Pass	2♣

Obviously this presents a dilemma. If 2♣ indicates a weak hand that should play in clubs, how does the partnership look for a major suit fit? Many players use CHEAPER MINOR, which means that 2♣ would show the weak club hand while 2♦ would probe for the major suit fit.

Jump cuebids

Another form of cuebid that has been adopted by many players. A jump cuebid is used to show a strong raise in the overcaller's suit. When this is used, a simple cuebid usually indicates a limit raise, while a jump in the overcaller's suit is preemptive. The use of the regular and jump cuebids also can be reversed, with the jump cuebid showing the limit raise and the immediate cue the strong raise. The jump cuebid also can be used to show a singleton in the opponent's suit.

Conclusion

Cuebidding is an extremely broad subject. There are hundreds of situations in which low-level cuebids can be used effectively, and most of them are impossible to classify because they occur on the second or third round of bidding. In these situations, cuebids may provide an answer to bidding problems which would otherwise be insoluble.

Other cuebid situations are listed under CUEBID and CUEBIDS TO SHOW CONTROLS.

CUEBIDS TO SHOW CONTROLS (see also CUEBIDS IN OPPONENT'S SUIT). A bid in a suit in which the partnership cannot wish to play is usually a control-showing cuebid if the partnership is already committed to a game contract. A slam invitation is implied:

(a)		(b)	
NORTH	SOUTH	NORTH	SOUTH
1♠	3♠	1♣	1♥
4♦		3♥	4♦

In each case the side is committed to game, and a suit has been firmly agreed. The final bid is a slam suggestion, and the cuebidder's partner acts accordingly. If his hand is completely unsuitable for slam purposes, he signs off in the agreed trump suit at the lowest level. If he is willing to cooperate in a slam venture, he can bid a slam directly or take some other strong action which would take the bidding past the game level. When in doubt, he can sometimes make a further cuebid below the game level; in case (a), South can make a cuebid of 4♥ in his turn without taking the bidding past 4♠.

The first cuebid is assumed to show first-round control (usually the ace, but occasionally a void), although a hand which is known to be very weak might make a cuebid with a king. Later cuebids by either player may show second-round controls.

It is usual (and in some systems compulsory) to make the cheapest possible cuebid. Therefore in case (a) above, North denies first-round club control, and in case (b), South denies first-round spade control.

An alternative recommended by Jeremy Flint is to cuebid first the higher ranking of two touching aces and the lower of two nontouching aces. (The trump suit is excluded in determining which suits are touching.) The intent is to create extra room for the partnership to show all its controls. A hand given in illustration by Hugh Kelsey in his book on Slam Bidding (see BIBLIOGRAPHY, C) is:

WEST	EAST
♠ A 7	♠ 3
♥ A 5 4	♥ K 8 6
♦ J 10 9 6 5 2	♦ A K Q 7
♣ K 4	♣ A Q 8 5 3

Using standard methods of bidding all controls as cheaply as possible, the auction would start:

WEST	EAST
1♦	3♣
3♦	4♦
4♥	5♣
5♠	?

East cannot be sure his partner has the ♣K and cannot find out without committing himself one way or not. Using the Flint style, however, the auction would be:

WEST	EAST
1♦	3♣
3♦	4♦
4♠	5♣
5♥	5♠
6♣	7♦

West's cuebid of his aces in reverse order has created just one bit of extra space, but that one step is enough. The Flint method has its disadvantages, however, when the hand that initiates the cuebidding has only one ace, for there will be second-round controls that the hand cannot show without promising first-round control.

A bluff cuebid is made not infrequently to inhibit a lead:

NORTH	SOUTH
1 ♠	3 ♠
4 ♣	4 ♠
6 ♠	Pass

It is possible that North had a grand slam in mind, but abandoned that possibility when South made the discouraging return to 4♠. But it is more likely, if North is a good player, that he was bent on 6♠ and bid 4♣ on the way to inhibit a club lead. If East is also a good player he will see through the maneuver and lead a club, which opens the way for a double-cross genuine cuebid.

Certain bids may at first sight appear to be cuebids, but on inspection do not conform to the definition:

(a)		(b)	
NORTH	SOUTH	NORTH	SOUTH
1 ♥	2 ♣	1 ♥	2 ♣
3 ♣	3 ♠	4 ♣	4 ♥

In case (a), North-South are not committed to a game contract, because the bidding can die in 4♣. 3♠ is not a cuebid suggesting a slam, but a STRENGTH-SHOWING BID suggesting 3NT, the spade holding could be Q-J-x.

In case (b), South's bid of 4♥ is quite unconstructive. It simply suggests that 4♥ may be a better contract than 5♣, and the heart support may be as little as a doubleton honor.

The above treatment should be regarded as standard unless a partnership agrees otherwise. For alternative treatments see: ASKING BID; INTEREST-SHOWING BID; and ROMAN ASKING BID. For related topics see also: DOUBLE OF A CUEBID; GENERAL PURPOSE CUEBID; OUT-OF-THE-BLUE CUEBID; SPLINTER BID; TRIAL BID; and VOID-SHOWING BID.

In the early years of contract, various authorities, including Robert F. Foster, Sidney Lenz, George Reith, and E. V. Shepard, devised complex systems of cuebidding. These were intended to offer alternatives to the CULBERTSON 4-5 NT CONVENTION and other devices for locating aces, but they did not achieve any popularity.

CULBERTSON ASKING BID. See ASKING BID.

CULBERTSON FOUR-FIVE NOTRUMP. A slam convention showing aces and kings as well as asking for them. The 4NT bid promises either: three aces or two aces and a king of a suit genuinely bid by the partnership.

The responses: Holding two aces, or one ace and all the kings of genuinely bid suits, bid: 5 NT. Holding no ace, bid: five of lowest genuinely bid suit. Holding one ace, usually bid the ace suit (but if this is the lowest bid suit, a jump to six is necessary).

Notice that the signoff is not in the agreed trump suit, but in the lowest suit which the partnership has genuinely bid. Responder can exercise some discretion when he holds one ace and no additional values. If his normal esponse wou

d take the bidding above the five level in the agreed trump suit, he may invent some lower bid.

Holding two aces *and* a king, the responder is often interested in a grand slam. Provided his king is not in the agreed trump suit, he may bid the suit in which he holds a king. This may be temporarily misleading, but he can clarify the situation by making a constructive bid on the next round.

This convention was generally superseded by Blackwood and other conventions, but retained popularity among some leading British players. See BYZANTINE BLACKWOOD.

CULBERTSON-LENZ MATCH. The *Bridge Battle of the Century*, as it was called when it took place between December 1931 and January 1932, was a genuine milestone in the history of the development and promotion of bridge as it is known today. Combining as it did every feature designed to capture and hold the interest of the then bridge-mad multitudes, and starring the greatest celebrities then prominent in bridge, it was predestined to be an exciting and long-remembered event. These were the years when bridge was making its impact felt keenly in the United States for the first time.

During the previous decade, many new styles of bidding and play had come to the forefront, and most prominent among these was the CULBERTSON SYSTEM. Conceived and popularized by a man who was a born molder of opinions and customs, and who was a superbly able practical psychologist as well, the Culbertson System took the nation by storm, and was indeed original in concept and, as practiced by its leading exponents, a successful and highly practical method of bidding in bridge. Naturally its success caused many rivalries and feuds among those players who were at the very top rungs of the bridge ability ladder. This resulted in a strange war — a Systemic War in which 12 leading authorities (including Sidney Lenz, Milton Work, Wilbur C. Whitehead and Edward V. Shepard) got together and organized a corporation, Bridge Headquarters — all forces joined to combat Culbertson's domination of contract bridge.

The principal leader of the various groups in opposition to the Culbertson methods was Lenz, a veteran of auction bridge. In his camp were other great luminaries of the game who also felt that their methods were superior to the Culbertson System. The name by which the Lenz forces' system was called was the Official System. A book on this system, which acknowledged its debt to Culbertson in that much of it was derived from his c ncepts, was later to be written by Work. The actual m tch was the result of a challenge made earlier in 1931 y Culbertson to the Lenz faction. There were many complications to be ironed out before agreement as to conditions could actually be achieved, but essentially the match was finally played on a pair-against-pair basis, with Culbertson wagering $5,000 against Lenz's $ 1,000 on the outcome, with the money going to charity no matter who won. Culbertson promoted the match as the struggle of a young, loving married couple against the forces of adversity — 12 jealous authorities, the establishment, combined against them. Of course it was also billed as a grudge fight and a battle of systems. As a result the match was a topic of conversation at every bridge table and at many dinner tables long before it began. In all, 150 rubbers were played, and during 88 of them Culbertson played with his wife, Josephine. His partners for the balance of the encounter were Theodore A. Lightner, Waldemar Von Zedtwitz, Howard Schenken, and Michael Gottlieb. Lenz played the first 103 rubbers with Oswald

Jacoby, who then resigned because of a difference of opinion on the play of a defensive situation. Lenz's partner for the remainder of the session was Cmdr. Winfield Liggett Jr. Alfred Gruenther, then a lieutenant instructor at West Point, was chief referee of the match.

The Culbertson team won by 8,980 points. Careful and accurate records of cards held for each deal were kept, and at the conclusion it was determined that each side had held fairly much the same number of high cards as the other. The first half of the match was held at New York's Chatham Hotel, and the second part at the newly opened Waldorf-Astoria. The conditions of play and of protocol in general were governed by an agreement to which both Culbertson and Lenz were signatory, and the bridge laws under which the match was conducted were those published by the Whist Club of New York.

Coverage by the press of the nation was stupendous. Stories about the match were on the front pages of newspapers all over America. Regular correspondents were dispatched to the scenes of play, and some of the great newspaper personalities of the time wrote articles for their papers and for syndicates. The Associated Press laid heavy cables right into the Culbertson apartment at the Chatham Hotel, assigned reporters to the match and gave play-by-play coverage while Western Union and Postal Telegraph established branches in a spare room.

A continuous line of the rich and famous moved into the drawing room and out of it, viewing the action through cracks in a large leather screen, and trying to catch a glimpse of the players' faces or the flash of a card being played. Culbertson called it the greatest peep-show in history. A 438-page book *(Famous Hands of the Culbertson-Lenz Match)* was published in three sections with bidding and play analyzed by Culbertson and his partners, Jacoby, and Lt. Gruenther. Complete statistics were collated, and records of every phase of the match carefully kept. However, the single most significant feature of the entire proceedings was the enormous impetus it gave bridge when the game's popularity was already great.

	Culbertson	Lenz
Points won	122,925	113,945
Rubbers won	77	73
Number of two-game rubbers	37	32
Size of average rubber won		934
866		
Largest rubber won	2,590	2,825
Games	195	186
Small slams bid and made	9	8
Small slams defeated		
(not including sacrifices)		9
5		
Grand slams defeated	0	1
Opening suit bids of one	366	289
Opening 1 NT bids	43	45
Opening forcing bids	5	5
Small slams made but not bid		
(many owing to lucky breaks)	20	19
Games made but not bid		
(many owing to lucky breaks)	15	13
Successful contracts	273	273
Defeated contracts	142	162
Number of (exact) game contracts		
voluntarily bid and defeated	48	49
Number of penalties of 600 plus	7	14
Points lost in penalties of 600 plus	5,900	11,500
Aces	1,745	1,771
Kings	1,775	1,741
Honor tricks	3,649°	3,648

Points (4-3-2-1)	18,091	17,898
Value of average rubber	899	
Hands dealt	879	
Hands passed out	25	

CULBERTSON NATIONAL STUDIOS. An organization of bridge teachers which flourished in the Thirties. Some 4,000 bridge teachers passed examinations in the CULBERTSON SYSTEM and were granted certificates attesting their fitness to teach the Culbertson methods. A similar organization was developed later by Charles Goren. See also AMERICAN BRIDGE TEACHERS ASSOCIATION.

CULBERTSON-SIMS MATCH. A 150-rubber pair match held in March and April of 1935 with Ely and Josephine Culbertson on one side against P. Hal and Dorothy Sims. On the next-to-last day of the match, Culbertson played with Albert H. Morehead and Sims with B. Jay Becker, while the ladies took a holiday. The match was won by the Culbertsons by a margin of 16,130 points. In this match, which took place as a result of a challenge issued by Sims, accurate records were kept of the proceedings and of the cards and deals held by the participants. Publicity for the contest was not as widespread as in the CULBERTSON-LENZ MATCH three years earlier, but the nation's interest was aroused. Both sides took to the airwaves on weekly radio broadcasts to describe various features of the games, and hands of particular merit were discussed. The match served to whet the public's already keen appetite for bridge and anything about it, as well as to reinforce the position of authority held by the Culbertson group.

CULBERTSON SYSTEM. The system of bidding developed by Ely Culbertson, revised periodically to incorporate new developments. For example, in 1930 Culbertson regarded a response in a new suit as nonforcing, which was a departure from his 1925 auction principles. He adhered to this in the 1933 *Blue Book*, which listed a one-over-one response as "99 44/100% forcing", but abandoned the idea in 1935 when it became clear that the mass of bridge players would not be converted.

Other nonforcing bids were featured in the early Blue Books, abandoned shortly afterward, and revived by others as "modern" innovations. Examples are: LIMIT RAISES; limit 2 NT response; and WEAK NOTRUMP openings, nonvulnerable. All these became features of the ACOL style; and limit raises and weak notrumps regained some popularity among American tournament players in the Sixties. The 1933 *Blue Book* also included the WEAK JUMP OVERCALL.

The Culbertson System, influenced both by the methods of the successful FOUR ACES and by pressure of public opinion, was crystallized in the 1936 *Gold Book*. The bidding set out in the *Gold Book*, with one notable exception, became standard practice in America for the next 15 years, and was only slightly modified by the GOREN SYSTEM, which won the allegiance of the bridge-playing masses in the Fifties. The chief features were:

(1) Valuation by HONOR TRICKS.

(2) Uniform standards for BIDDABLE SUITS, with Q-J-x-x a minimum four-card suit. This applied to the opening bidder, irrespective of whether the suit was a major or a minor. The responder could bid a shaded or

conditional biddable suit.

(3) The APPROACH PRINCIPLE, emphasizing suit opening bids and responses in preference to notrump bids.

(4) The FORCING-TWO-BID; any opening suit bid of two requiring the partnership to reach game. (Later modified, 1952-53, so that responder could pass after a sequence such as 2♠-2 NT-3♠.)

(5) The forcing takeout (or jump shift) showed 3° honor tricks (or about 16 points). This requirement was raised by Goren and later authorities.

(6) STRONG NOTRUMP (4-4 1/2 honor tricks) preferably limited to 4-3-3-3 distribution in accordance with the approach principle.

(7) Jump rebids by opener or responder (see OPENER'S REBIDS) not forcing unless in a new suit. (This principle was modified by later writers: see GOREN SYSTEM and STANDARD AMERICAN.)

(8) ASKING BIDS were introduced in 1936, and reintroduced in 1953 with amplifications, but never gained substantial support.

In 1952-53 Culbertson also introduced his own DISTRIBUTIONAL COUNT.

CULBERTSON TROPHY. Any of a number of trophies donated by Ely and Josephine Culbertson, all of them for minor events. In 1962 the name was given to the World Pair Championship trophy, first contested at Cannes, France.

CUMBERLAND HAND. See DUKE OF CUMBERLAND HAND.

CUMULATIVE SCORE. In tournament bridge, when an event is scheduled for more than one session of play and there is no elimination of players from the event, the winner of the event is decided by cumulative score, that is, the total of the scores made in each of the sessions. However, should there be a different average score for the two or more sessions (owing to playing a different number of boards, a no-show for the second session, or other reason), the later sessions' scores are factored by a multiplier that makes the sessions comparable to the first session, so that a particularly high score in any session would carry the same weight as in any other session.

In rubber bridge, where the partnerships change from rubber to rubber, a cumulative score of points won or lost in each rubber is kept so that each player's status of winnings or losses is shown at the termination of each rubber.

In progressive or party bridge, the cumulative score is the totality of points won at all tables at which the player played. Generally, only plus scores are considered, and losses are not deducted before being entered onto the cumulative scoresheet.

In knockout team-of-four matches, all points are scored both plus and minus for both pairs of both teams, and the team with a greater plus total than minus total is the winner. This is referred to as AGGREGATE SCORE or TOTAL-POINT SCORING and has been almost completely supplanted in head-to-head matches by International Match Points.

CUPS, SWORDS, MONEY, WANDS. Names of suits in Tarot. Tarot was a special deck of cards used in ancient Italy and elsewhere for various games and for fortunetelling. Tarot cards are still in use today, mostly for parlor games.

CURAÇAO. See Netherlands Antilles.

CURIOSITIES. See FREAK HANDS.

CURSE OF SCOTLAND. A term applied to the ♦9, for which various explanations are given, none completely authoritative. The *Bridge Magazine* once listed six possible origins for the term as follows:

1. That in the once popular round game *Pope Joan*, the ♦9 was called the Pope, the antichrist of Scottish Reformers.

2. That the ♦9 was the chief card in the game *cornette*, introduced into Scotland by the unhappy Queen Mary.

3. That "Butcher" Cumberland wrote the orders for the Battle of Culloden, 1746, on the back of the card. This is very doubtful.

4. That the order for the Massacre of Glencoe (1692) was signed on the back of this card.

5. That the dispositions for the fatal field of Flodden (1513) were drawn up on it by James IV of Scotland. Both these last have only the slightest authority.

6. That it is derived from the nine lozenges that formed the arms of the Earl of Stair, who was especially loathed for his connection with the Massacre of Glencoe and the union with England (1707).

CURTAILING MOVEMENT DURING PLAY. A method of terminating a game at a given time, without playing all the boards scheduled according to the movement in use. It is accomplished by omitting one or more of the rounds normally scheduled by the movement.

In general, any movement in which all boards in play at each round may be terminated at the end of any round, with no other defect than disturbance of balanced comparisons.

In a pair or individual movement involving either bye boards or relays, early termination also disrupts the scoring, for some boards will be played more often than others. This will result in a different top on certain boards, and a different possible score for some or all contestants. See REDUCED HOWELL.

CURTAIN CARD. A record of a hand in a duplicate board. The curtain card is placed in the tray with the hand; the player is thus able to determine that the hand he has taken from the board is the one that was to have been there. Use of curtain cards is rare in the United States, but still found elsewhere. An advantage of curtain cards is that fouled boards are discovered immediately. See FOULED BOARD; HAND RECORD; MISSING CARD; TRUSCOTT CARD.

CUT. (1) At the commencement of rubber bridge play, a pack of cards is spread out, face downward, and each player draws one, turning it face up. Rank and suit of these cards determine the makeup of the first partnerships, and the original dealer. (2) At the conclusion of each hand, the cards are gathered together and reshuffled for the next deal. The new dealer presents the shuffled deck to the right-hand opponent, who cuts the pack by removing more than four but fewer than 48 cards from the top of the deck, and places the cards removed alongside the balance of the deck, nearer to the dealer. The dealer then completes the cut by placing the part of the pack which was originally on the bottom above the part originally on the top. (3) A colloquial term for the verbs "trump" or "ruff," used commonly in Scotland. (4) To terminate a movement before the scheduled completion.

CUT IN. To assert the right to become a member of an incomplete table, or to become a member of a complete table at such time as it may become incomplete.

CUTTHROAT BRIDGE. 1. A name applied to a traditional three-handed game (described under THREE-HANDED BRIDGE) and to a four-handed game with flexible partnerships.

In the four-handed version originated by S.B. Fishburne, Tulsa OK, and sometimes called "Reject" or "Let's Pick Partners," the opening bid must be natural and honest (at least 13 points in high cards, and at least four cards in the suit bid). The auction closes when a bid is followed by three passes; doubling and redoubling takes place later. No partscore contracts are played: the cards are thrown in, and the deal passes.

The player who makes the final bid is always declarer, and after the final pass he nominates one of the other three players as his partner. That player becomes the dummy, and moves into the seat opposite the declarer. Declarer's partner has the option of rejecting the partnership, in which case he scores with the defenders instead of with the declarer. Either defender may double and declarer (or dummy if he has not rejected) may redouble.

A separate score is kept for each player, using normal contract scoring as far as possible. The rubber bonus is only 500 if either defender has a game. Only plus scores are recorded, so no entry is made on the score of the one, two, or three players who are on the losing end of a deal. In the final scoring, each player has a reckoning with each other player.

Honors are scored only by the player holding them. A player becomes vulnerable in the usual way. A non-vulnerable player scores 300 if his vulnerable partner scores rubber points.

A weak point in this version of the game was the rejection of partscores. 3NT was seldom played, because a player with a weak hand could bid 4♣ or 4♦ without risk; unless someone made a higher bid, the hands were thrown in.

This gave rise to another version which gained considerable popularity in New York clubs: After the (natural) opening bid, the next player must make a bid of 4 NT or higher. Some games include a GOULASH feature. For a variation including a nullo feature, see RAZZLE-DAZZLE.

2. A term used to describe the manner in which some bridge players play: To go after every possible trick, whether as declarer or defender.

CUTTING FOR DEAL, PARTNERS. At the beginning of each rubber, in order to establish partnerships and determine the original dealer, the four participating players each draw a card from an unfaced deck. The two players drawing the highest ranking cards play as partners, and the player with the higher of these two is the dealer on the first hand. An alternative method of determining deal and partners for second and subsequent rubbers is pivoting (see PIVOT BRIDGE).

At CHICAGO, a method combining both the cut and the pivot is frequently used, the cut establishing partner-

ships and deal for the first round, the highest cut card determining the pivot player. After the first round, the pivot player remains stationary and plays with his original right-hand opponent for the second round, and then with his original left-hand opponent for the third round. The pivot player, who deals the first hand of each of the three rounds, is often termed the wheel. See LAWS (Law 3).

CUTTING OUT. It is frequently impractical to have exactly four players. When five players form a table, an order of omission from the table is established by drawing. The player with the lowest card sits out the first rubber, and other players sit out in their turn in the order thus established.

Alternatively, a fresh draw can be made after each rubber, with the lowest to sit out; only players who have not sat out participate in the draw. This is a matter of club procedure.

The draw for participation in the rubber is usually quite distinct from the draw, or cut, for partners. But see PIVOT BRIDGE.

CYCLIC MOVEMENT. A movement in which contestants follow each other in a regular sequence or series. When a move is called, each contestant moves to a position previously occupied by a given other contestant, whose name or number is known in advance. The HOWELL MOVEMENT for pairs is a typical cyclic movement. Many other movements for pairs, teams or individuals use the cyclic feature in some form.

D

D.I. See DECLARATIVE-INTERROGATIVE FOUR NOTRUMP.

DAB. See DIRECTIONAL ASKING BID.

DAMAGED CARD. According to the LAWS OF CONTRACT BRIDGE, Law 7: A pack containing a card so damaged or marked that it may be identified from its back. It must be replaced if attention is drawn to the imperfection before the first card of the current deal is dealt.

DANGER HAND. The declarer often strives to prevent one opponent, the danger hand, from obtaining the lead. This may be because that player has established winners, or because he will be able to make a damaging lead through a vulnerable honor holding. See AVOIDANCE.

DANISH BRIDGE LEAGUE (Danmarks Bridgeforbund) was founded 1939 when Dansk Bridge Liga and Dansk Bridge Union, both founded 1933, were unified. For many years the two lesser organizations continued separately, and the nationwide body only organized the finals of the Danish Championships, and selected teams for international events. The first international event in Denmark was a match against Great Britain in 1932, won by Denmark. In 1933 Denmark joined the EBL and came third in its first European Championship. After World War II Denmark restarted the European Championships in Copenhagen in 1948, and the Nordic Championships began a year earlier. Danish ladies were Europe's most successful from 1938-1959 winning six European Championships. In the Eighties a new generation made its way to the top and won Olympiad gold in Venice 1988. One of the pairs, Bettina Kalkerup - Charlotte Palmund, is the most winning Danish pair ever, also taking silver in the World Ladies Pairs 1984 in addition to many other international and national titles. Denmark won bronze medals in 1948 and 1961 while the silver medals in 1979 and bronze medals in the Olympiad 1984 were highlights in modern days. In World Championships Denmark won a gold medal for Otto Kaalund-Jorgensen 1937 together with Elna Friberg in the mixed pairs, and the Danish Junior team qualified for the World Championship 1991 but did not qualify for the semifinals. The best junior result was winning the European Championship 1970. The Danish Bridge league had only 4,000 members in the beginning of the Seventies but with the election of Gunnar Zabel as chairman a fruitful period began, and soon a masterpoint scheme was made. The Federation had its own publishing firm, book store, secretariat, and in the end a full time general secretary. As a result the membership grew rapidly and in 1992 had passed 20,000. All towns of moderate size have their bridge clubs and/or bridge schools, and participation in the federation activities is huge. The most common systems in Denmark are all inspired by Standard American and Acol, very often mixed to some extent. The official magazine of the bridge league, *Dansk Bridge*, goes to all members and has existed since 1941. See COPENHAGEN BRIDGE CLUB. Officers 1993:

President, Bent Haestrup
Secretary, Ib Lundby,
Skovledet 95 A
3400 Hillerod
Denmark
Tel: 45 42 255329
Fax: 45 42 266789

DATUM. A reference score from which the number of IMPs won or lost in an IMP pair game can be computed. See AVERAGE SCORE.

DEAD. Bridge jargon to describe a player in a hopeless situation. It usually refers to the play of the hand, as in, "North made a killing shift, and I was dead." Also said of a hand, especially dummy, which has been robbed of (or never had) an entry.

DEAL. (1) To distribute the 52 cards at contract; (2) the privilege of thus distributing the cards; (3) the act of dealing; (4) the cards themselves when distributed.

The dealer distributes the cards face down, one at a time in rotation into four separate hands of 13 cards each, the first card to the player on his left and the last card to himself. If he deals two cards simultaneously or consecutively to the same player, or fails to deal a card to a player, he may rectify the error, provided he does so immediately and to the satisfaction of the other players. The dealer must not allow the face of any card to be seen while he is dealing. Until the deal is completed, no player but the dealer may touch any card except to correct or prevent an irregularity.

In duplicate, the cards may be placed into any pocket. If the sponsoring organization wishes, the dealing may be from computer printouts or by dealing machine.

See LAWS (Laws 8, 9, 10), LAWS OF DUPLICATE BRIDGE (Law 6).

DEALER. The player who distributes the cards at a hand of bridge. At the start of a rubber of regular bridge or of CHICAGO, a cut is made for partners and for the deal privilege. The player who receives the highest card becomes dealer. The entire deck is given out one by one in turn to each player starting at the left of the dealer, each fourth card going to the dealer himself. The dealer speaks first in the auction by either bidding or passing. Subsequent calls proceed normally in a clockwise direction.

The term *dealer* is also a specialized slang word applying to a person who knows how to cheat at cards by arranging or stacking the pack in such fashion as to give himself and/or his partner by far the best of the cards continuously.

DEALING DEVICE. (1) A crank-operated machine which distributes the cards. (2) An electrically operated card table which accepts the used pack, shuffles it, and distributes the cards for the next deal. Neither has gained wide acceptance. (3) Various electronic devices, in Sweden, United States and France, intended to solve the problem of pre-dealing large numbers of identical hands. All use special bar coding on the cards. The French device even places the cards into a specially designed board after the sorting procedure. See DUPLIMATE.

DEATH HOLDING. A holding in a suit which seems an *a priori* certainty to kill the partnership's chances of playing or defending successfully. The most common examples are (1) a holding of x-x in the opponents' suit in a hand with slam possibilities; with a small doubleton in one hand it is likely that neither partner can adequately control the opponents' suit for slam play; (2) a defensive holding of Q-x in front of a long suit headed by A K in the dummy's or declarer's hand; such a holding gives little hope of a trick on power, and no hope that declarer will misplay or misguess.

DECEPTION, MATHEMATICS OF. The rule of multiplication of probabilities (see PROBABILITY OF SUCCESSIVE EVENTS) is applicable when declarer has to decide whether a card is a DECEPTIVE PLAY. The probability that a suspected card is true is the probability that the player holds a distribution that leaves him no choice but to play it. The probability that it is false is the probability that he has a distribution from which the deceptive play would be attractive, multiplied by the probability that he would in fact decide to play the falsecard.

A 8 3 2

K Q 10 4

After winning the opening lead, South plays the king. West follows low, and East plays the 9. The probability that this is a singleton is approximately 2.8%. However, East may hold J-9-x-x, and the probability of this holding is about 8.4%. Consequently, if the probability that East would play the 9 from J-9-x-x is greater than 1/2, that distribution would be more likely than the singleton 9. Albert Dormer and Terence Reese have postulated that the play of the 9 from J-9-x-x is obligatory, in order to present South with a choice of plays on the second round. If South accepts this view, he must play the ace next time. (For simplicity, the assumption has been made that, if West held J-7-6-5, he would play the low cards indiscriminately.)

The problem should be pursued a little further. Suppose that the only deception envisaged is the play of the 9 from J-9-x-x, that is to say that East holds either J-9-x-x or the singleton 9 when he plays the 9. With a side entry to dummy, South can now give himself a better chance. He enters dummy and leads low toward the Q-10. If East shows out, South plays the queen, and has a marked finesse against West.

To counteract this, East must not merely play the 9 from J-9-x-x, but also from 9-x-x and 9-x. If he is deemed capable of this, there is little attraction for declarer in the play just described, since if East follows to a low card from dummy, declarer will have to guess whether to finesse the 10 or play the queen. As 9-x-x and 9-x each have a probability of about 10.2%, South would do better to play dummy's ace on the second round, unless he estimates only a very small probability of the 9 being played from a doubleton or tripleton.

A detailed explanation of this case is as follows: It is assumed that East will always play the 9 from J-9-x-x. The possible plans for South are:

A. Low to the ace, so as to be able to finesse against East if West shows out.

B. Enter dummy with a side-suit, lead toward Q-10, and finesse the 10 if East follows.

C. Enter dummy with a side-suit, lead toward Q-10, and play the queen if East follows:

The probabilities that the relevant distributions were dealt to East are: 9-x or 9-x-x, 64%; J-9-x-x, 27%; singleton 9, 9%. Let p = the probability that East will play the 9 if he has 9-x or 9-x-x. Then the chance of plan A succeeding is .64 times p + .27, and of plan B succeeding, .09 + .27. Therefore if p is less than 14%, plan A is preferable. That is, plan A should be preferred unless it is thought that West would not play the 9 from 9-x or 9-x-x at least seven times in fifty. The chance of plan C succeeding is .64 times p + .09, and plan C is thus clearly inferior to plan A. If entries permit, the two should be led from North's hand on the first round of that suit. It is now more difficult for East to play the 9 from J-9-x-x. West may hold the 10 and the play of the 9 could concede a trick unnecessarily.

DECEPTIVE BID. See LEAD-INHIBITING BID and PSYCHIC BIDDING.

DECEPTIVE LEAD. See OPENING LEAD.

DECEPTIVE OPENING LEAD. See FALSE-CARDING and OPENING LEAD.

DECEPTIVE PLAY. The term deceptive play could well be used of any play that aims to mislead an opponent. Discriminating writers, however, tend to restrict the use of the term to plays by the declarer. Deceptive play by the defenders is more suitably described as FALSECARDING, and is dealt with under that title.

Deceptive plays by the declarer are analyzed under these headings:

(1) Weakness-concealing plays. Bluff is the basis of most of these plays; the declarer deliberately does something which is not correct technique, in the hope that the deceptive effect of his play will outweigh its mathematical shortcoming.

♠ 8 6 3
♥ 9 2
♦ Q J 10 6 4
♣ K Q 7

♠ A K 9 4
♥ A J
♦ K 9 8 3
♣ A 8 2

West leads a small heart against South's 3 NT contract, and East puts up the queen. If perfect defense were to be assumed, South's best play would be to duck. After winning the next trick he would play diamonds, hoping that the defender with the ♦A had no more hearts to play.

This plan has a slight but legitimate chance of success. In practice it is very much better to win the first trick, and drive out the ♦A. If West has it, and the ♥K as well, he may not find the right continuation. East's play of the ♥Q on the opening lead has made it plain to West that declarer has the jack, but he does not know that it is bare. West may conclude that h' best chance of defeating the contract is to find East ' .th a black ace, so that he can lead hearts through de .arer's jack.

On other occasior , the declarer tries to bluff his way through by openi·.g up a weak suit himself.

♠ J 6 2
♥ A K 10
♦ 8 6 3
♣ A 10 9 7

♠ Q 7 3
♥ Q 8 3
♦ A 10 2
♣ K Q 4 3

West leads the ♥4 against South's 3 NT contract.

Declarer's ninth trick can come only from spades, and then only if both ace and king are in one hand. Further, if declarer attacks spades himself, and is lucky enough to find the cards suitably placed, the defender will probably shift to diamonds.

Declarer's best plan is to take the opening lead in dummy and lead diamonds himself, inserting the 10 if East plays low and ducking if East puts up an honor. There is a reasonable chance that the defenders will attack spades.

Many weakness-concealing plays involve releasing a high card earlier than need be. Against a notrump contract, West leads the two of a suit in which dummy holds J-x-x and declarer Q-x. If East plays the ace, it can do no harm for declarer to drop the queen. East will probably recognize that this is not a singleton, and he may assume that declarer's other card is the king. There are many variations of this theme.

Sometimes bluff is needed to extract tricks from an unpromising holding. A declarer who is reduced to the necessity of attempting to make two tricks with K-x-x in dummy and J-x-x in the closed hand does best to lead the king from the table. If the cards are distributed as follows:

```
              K x x
   A 10 x              Q x x x
              J x x
```

West may conclude that South is trying to establish a suit headed by the queen and jack in the closed hand. If

West seeks to molest declarer's communications by holding up the ace, South has every chance of two tricks, for East is unlikely to put up the queen on the second round and West may hold up the ace a second time.

(2) Strength-concealing plays. These are resorted to most frequently in notrump contracts. The usual occasion is when declarer wants the defenders to continue a suit which they have opened, rather than shift to a suit which he fears more.

♠ K J 7 3
♥ 10 7 2
♦ Q J 10 5
♣ 8 7

♠ A Q 2
♥ J 8
♦ A 9 7 4 3
♣ A Q 6

West leads a small club against 3 NT and East plays the jack. Declarer can afford to win with the ace rather than the queen. He crosses to dummy with a spade and takes the diamond finesse, hoping that if it loses West will continue clubs rather than shift to hearts. The stratagem is a familiar one but can be effective.

Following is a play to conceal strength which can occur equally at a suit contract or at notrump:

Q 5 2

A 10 9 8

South needs to develop a second trick in the suit, but entry difficulties make it necessary to lead from the closed hand. He has no indication of where the king is located.

Some players will lead the 10 in the hope of putting pressure on West, but actually the 8 is better, especially if West can be expected to realize that South has the ace. By leading the 8, declarer conceals the fact that he has a possible finesse against the jack. Hence, if West has the king, he is more likely to put it up, for from his viewpoint the declarer may have no option but to play dummy's queen. It is, therefore, sound psychology to lead the 8, and run it if West plays low.

(3) Honor-crashing plays. Plays aimed at persuading the defenders to spend two honors — usually trumps — on one trick range from the simple to the subtle. Some examples are given under the title CRASHING HONORS, but others are more deceptive in flavor.

Q 7 x x

10 8 x x x

The usual way of playing this suit is by leading small toward the queen. Declarer loses only two tricks provided that the suit divides evenly, that West has the lone jack, or that West has A-K-x or A-K-J.

The fact that the defenders would expect declarer to play thus can make the lead of the queen from dummy effective. If the bidding rules out the possibility that East has a singleton, the queen lead cannot cost and may tempt a cover from East if he has K-J-x or A-J-x.

Sometimes the best way of crashing the defenders' honors is to induce them to ruff with a small trump before the trump suit has been touched.

♠ Q 9 8 6
♥ A K 8
♦ K Q 7 6 4
♣ A

♠ K   ♠ A 2
♥ J 10 9 7 5 4 3   ♥ 6 2
♦ 10   ♦ 9 8 3 2
♣ Q J 9 6   ♣ 7 5 4 3 2

♠ J 10 7 5 4 3
♥ Q
♦ A J 5
♣ K 10 8

In a pairs contest South plays 4♠ after West has made a preemptive bid in hearts. When West opens the ♥J, South's best deceptive play is to win in hand, cross to the ♣A, and continue hearts, throwing a diamond from hand. If East ruffs in small on the third round, South overruffs and drops the enemy trumps together for a high matchpoint score.

(4) Scrambling plays. When the declarer has pronounced views as to whether he wants the defenders to continue a suit or shift, he may be able to cut in on their signals. The general rule for declarer is to put out the same signals as he would if he were defending — a high card to encourage a continuation, a low card to discourage. The following is a basic position:

974
A K J 3   10 8 5
Q 6 2

When West leads the king against a suit contract, South drops the 6 to make East's 5 look like the beginning of an echo.

If the declarer has more than two cards to signal with, it does not necessarily follow that he should play the highest.

932
A K J   10 8 5
Q 7 6 4

When West leads the king and East plays the 5, South should drop the 6, not the 7. If he played the 7, West would realize that some deception was afoot, for it is a basic rule of defensive signaling that encouraging signals should be as high as is safely possible. East, therefore, would not start an echo with the 5 if he also held the 6. So, if South dropped the 7 in the above diagram, West would suspect that he held the 6 as well. Similarly:

8 3
Q J 10 5   9 7
A K 6 4 2

South is playing a notrump contract, having concealed this suit in the bidding. West leads the queen, and South, needing to develop the suit, encourages in the hope that West will continue. In this diagram, both the 4 and the 6 are apt to be effective, but against players who themselves always falsecard as high as possible the 4 is best; if West reasons that South would play the 6 to encourage, West will be all the more convinced that East's 7 is the beginning of a signal.

It can be good policy for declarer to scramble the signals even when he has no immediate objective in mind.

K Q 4
J 9 5 2   10 8 6
A 7 3

Suppose South wants to enter dummy to lead another suit. By leading the 7, rather than the 3, he may confuse West's count of the hand. East's 6 may appear to West as the beginning of an echo; it may even suggest to him that East is holding up the ace.

There are some more advanced situations where the declarer has not only to play the right card — he has to know also which hand to lead from.

KQJ82

965 A 10 4

7 3

South is playing a notrump contract, and has no entries to dummy. He needs two tricks from the suit.

If South starts by playing the 3 toward dummy's king, West will play the 5, and East will know that his partner has either three cards in the suit or a singleton. In neither case can it cost East to play his ace on the second round, so South will be thwarted in his endeavor.

Suppose instead that South leads the 7 from hand; now, from East's angle his partner's 5 could be the beginning of an echo, showing a doubleton. In any case, East allows dummy to win the first trick, but the critical point comes on the second round: provided that the second lead comes from dummy, East will have to make his decision without any sure guidance from partner.

On other occasions it can be better to make both leads from the closed hand:

KQJ2

A 8 6 10 9 4

7 5 3

This time South is playing a suit contract, and will be inconvenienced if the ace is held up until the third round. He leads the 5 from hand and dummy wins. Now he must re-enter the closed hand in another suit and lead the 7; West may place his partner with two or four cards, and in either event may release the ace. The principle followed is to make the defender with the stop card play second to the vital trick.

Also coming broadly under the heading of scrambling plays are those where the declarer has to follow suit with a particular card in order to make it more difficult for the defenders to gauge his holding.

K J 6

8 5 A Q 10 7 4 2

9 3

South is playing a suit contract, and West leads the 8 of this side suit, which East has bid. Dummy plays the jack, East the queen, and South drops the 9. If he plays the 3 instead, East knows that it is safe to continue with ace and another (unless the partnership is playing MUD leads). After the play of the 9, however, East has to take account of the possibility that declarer has a singleton.

In general, in such situations as above, the declarer follows suit with a card higher than the one led, but sometimes only a certain card will do.

K 7 4 3

2 A Q 8 6 5

J 10 9

Again West leads a suit bid by his partner, and this time declarer wants to lose only one trick. (Discards are available elsewhere.) His best chance is to play low from dummy and drop the 10 from hand. East may still read the situation correctly, but his task would be easier if declarer played either the jack or the 9; he would then be able to infer that partner would not have opened the 2 from either J-10-2 or 10-9-2.

(5) Miscellaneous deceptive plays. One group of situations which does not fall readily under any other heading, and which has been little explored is the following:

	WEST	EAST
(a)	10 7 3 2	A K Q 6 4
(b)	J 6 5 4	A K 10 7 3
(c)	10 5 4 3	A K 8 6 2

In each case East is declarer, and these are his trump holdings. It costs nothing to lead the high card from West each time, intending, if North plays low, to overtake and play normally for the drop. Occasionally the deceptive precaution will pay dividends, as where North covers the 10 with the jack from J-9-8-5 in example (a), enabling his cards to be picked up by subsequent finesses. Example (b) is similar, while in (c) East improves his chances not only when North has all four outstanding cards but also when he covers from J-9-7 or Q-9-7.

There are many similar positions, and the field is widened when account is taken of bidding inferences.

WEST EAST

10 4 3 2 A K 8 6

The 10 lead costs only when North has the lone queen or jack. If the bidding precludes this possibility, the 10 is liable to prove doubly effective, since North will be expecting declarer to play him for trump length. Further, North may not care to outbluff the declarer by playing low from a holding headed by queen and jack, since declarer may well run the 10 in this situation.

The basis of another group of miscellaneous plays is that the lead should be made from dummy toward the closed hand:

A Q x x

x x x

South has to develop this suit at notrump but does not need immediate tricks. Best play is to lead small from dummy on the first round. East may put up the king from a variety of holdings which would have ruined the declarer had he played any other way. Similarly:

K x x x

Q x

At a suit contract, South leads from dummy on the first round, and the queen holds. Ordinary technique is to play low from both hands on the next round, and hope to ruff out the ace on the third. Entries permitting, however, it is better to re-enter dummy after the queen, and to lead again toward the closed hand. East may put up the ace, fearing that declarer started with both queen and jack.

DECK. (1) The pack; a synonym used regularly in America but not in England. (2) A colloquial term for a big hand. "Holding the deck" refers to a hand with a disproportionate number of high cards, or to a session in which a player holds a number of such hands. See PACK.

DECLARATION. (1) Contract, e.g., a heart declaration. (2) A statement of intent as to further line of play made by the declarer at some point previous to the play of the last trick of any given hand. See also CALL.

DECLARATIVE-INTERROGATIVE (D.I.) FOUR NOTRUMP. The use of 4NT as a general slam investigation, rarely as BLACKWOOD; developed originally as part of the NEAPOLITAN system. 4 NT is Blackwood if it is a jump bid, or bid at the first opportunity after a sudden leap to game. Otherwise, it promises two aces if bid by an unlimited hand, or one ace by a limited hand,

and requests partner to show an undisclosed feature (a first- or second-round control, or even a key queen) by bidding the suit containing the feature. The reply does not promise extra values unless it goes past five of the agreed trump suit. Responder may also answer by jumping to six of the agreed suit to deny interest in a grand slam, or by bidding 5 NT to announce a complete maximum and strong interest in a grand slam. Over any normal five-level reply, a rebid of 5 NT again asks for additional features in an effort to reach a grand slam and promises one more ace than originally guaranteed.

In several systems such as KAPLAN-SHEINWOLD and BLUE TEAM CLUB, D.I. 4NT asks for features without promising a specific number of aces. In Blue Team when 4NT is bid in the course of a series of cuebids it is a generalized slam try indicating that all suits are controlled, unless the player who bids a 4NT bypasses a suit in which control has not been shown. Some expert partnerships have agreed that after a Blackwood 4NT and the ace-showing response, 5NT is always declarative-interrogative, asking for features rather than for the number of kings.

DECLARER.

The player who first bid the denomination of the final bid. If the final bid is hearts, the player on the side making the final bid that first named hearts is the declarer. He becomes the declarer when the opening lead is faced, and controls the play of the dummy and his own hand as a unit.

DECLARER'S CLAIM OR CONCESSION OF TRICKS.

See CLAIM OR CONCESSION and LAWS (Law 68); LAWS OF DUPLICATE (Laws 68-71).

DEEP FINESSE.

A finesse when three or more cards are missing higher in rank than the card finessed. This is often made in order to execute a DUCK or AVOIDANCE play, but can be a genuine play necessary to achieve the best result. Well-known situations are:

(a)	(b)	(c)
Q 10 x	A J 9	A Q 9
x x x	x x x	x x x

With (a) the 10 is finessed, although it might be right to put up the queen if West leads a low card: it would be unusual to lead from A-J or K J with Q-10-x visible in dummy.

With (b) and (c) the 9 is finessed to give the maximum chance.

A rarer deep finesse can occur when a singleton is held opposite a five-card suit including J-10-8:

(d)	(e)	(f)
A J 10 8 x	K J 10 8 x	Q J 10 8 x
x	x	x

In each case the best chance of developing three tricks is to finesse the 8 on the first round. See also FINESSE and SUIT COMBINATIONS.

DEFEAT THE CONTRACT.

To prevent the declaring side from making as many tricks as required by the final contract.

DEFECTIVE TRICK.

A trick that contains fewer or more than four legally played cards. See LAWS (Law 67); LAWS OF DUPLICATE (Law 67).

DEFENDER.

An opponent of the declarer; one who attempts to prevent the declarer from making his contract. The secondary objective of preventing overtricks is of major importance at duplicate.

DEFENDER'S CLAIM OR CONCESSION OF TRICKS.

See CLAIM OR CONCESSION and LAWS (Law 70); LAWS OF DUPLICATE (Laws 68, 69, 70, 71).

DEFENDING HAND.

Either opponent of the declarer; occasionally used in the bidding to refer to an opponent of the player who opened the bidding.

DEFENSE, DEFENSIVE PLAY.

The play by the opponents of the declarer. The primary object of defensive play is normally to defeat the contract, even at the expense of presenting declarer with overtricks if the chosen line of defense is unsuccessful.

At duplicate, however, particularly at matchpoint play, holding declarer to a minimum number of tricks can be important, indeed. Articles dealing with defensive play that should be consulted are: COVERING HONORS; DEFENSE TO A SQUEEZE; DESCHAPELLES COUP; DISCARDING; DISCOVERY; DUCK; ENTRY-KILLING PLAY; FALSECARDING; FORCING DECLARER TO RUFF; JETTISON; MATCHPOINT DEFENSE; MERRIMAC COUP; OPTIMUM STRATEGY; OVERRUFF, PLAY FROM EQUALS; RUFF AND DISCARD; RULE OF ELEVEN; SECOND HAND PLAY; SPOT CARDS; THIRD HAND PLAY; THROUGH STRENGTH; TRUMP PROMOTION; UNDERRUFF; UP TO WEAKNESS; UPPERCUT. For all topics relating to LEADS, OPENING LEADS, SIGNALS, see those headings.

DEFENSE TO DOUBLE OF 1NT.

In standard practice the double of a 1NT opening bid is for penalties. The usual means of escape is for opener's partner to bid a suit, and the traditional meaning of a redouble is to penalize the doubler. See DOUBLES OF NOTRUMP BIDS (Third hand problems). However, several alternatives are designed either to locate the partnership's best escape suit, or to place the notrump opener as declarer, or both.

One suggested method is to use TRANSFER BIDS. Responder bids the suit next below his long suit. If responder's suit is clubs he redoubles to ask opener to bid clubs. If responder has no long suit but has seven or eight cards in the major suits, he can redouble, ostensibly transferring to clubs; but, after opener bids 2♣, responder bids 2♦, asking opener to choose between hearts and spades.

In a simpler method, suggested by Martin J. Cohn of Atlanta, suit bids by responder remain natural, and the redouble itself is used as a Stayman-type inquiry for the majors.

A third possibility is to use a response of 2♦ to ask opener to bid his better major suit, and to redouble to ask him to bid his better minor suit. In this method, responder's immediate run-out to 2♥ or 2♠ would be natural, and his bid of 2♣ would promise a long minor suit. If responder's suit is diamonds he runs to that suit over the double of 2♣ that will presumably be forthcoming.

Finally, a method proposed by Alan Truscott. A redouble forces 2♣ and may show club length. If the redoubler follows with two of a red suit he shows a four-card suit with at least one other four-card suit higher in rank. A direct 2♣ bid shows a four-card club suit with at least one other four-card suit in reserve. Direct bids of 2♦ and higher are natural. Unlike other methods, this enables the partnerships to find 4-4 fits in the minor suits with assurance. The method works equally well when a 1NT overcall is doubled. See SWINE.

DEFENSE TO INTERFERENCE WITH BLACK-WOOD. See BLACKWOOD AFTER INTERFERNCE.

DEFENSE TO 1NT. Specialized actions after an opposing opening bid of 1NT are discussed under other headings: ASPRO; ASPTRO; ASTRO; BECKER; BERGEN OVER NOTRUMP; BROZEL; CANSINO; CAPPELLETTI OVER NOTRUMP; DOUBLES OF NOTRUMP BIDS; EXCLUSION BID; HAMILTON; GRANO-ASTRO; LANDY; RIPSTRA; SUCTION.

The general rule of the defenders is to pass when in doubt. An overcall is far more dangerous after a notrump opening than after a suit opening because the opening bidder has defined his hand precisely. The opener's partner is therefore in a position to judge the defensive prospects accurately.

This caution applies equally in the pass-out position. Although the fourth player has the advantage of knowing that the opposing strength has an upward limit of about 23 points, he should be discouraged by knowing that his side is unlikely to have a good suit fit. The opening bid and the pass by the opener's partner imply that those two hands are balanced. If the fourth player has a long suit, his partner is likely to be short in the same suit.

An overcall should therefore be assumed to be a six-card suit, although a nonvulnerable player might sometimes venture into the auction with a strong five-card suit. Even with a six-card suit and a good hand, it may be advisable to pass if the distribution is defensive (e.g., 6-3-2-2) rather than attacking (say, 6-4-2-1).

If the opening bid is a strong notrump, the opponents are unlikely to head for game and make it. But this is not so against a weak notrump, and responding to an overcall needs consideration. Some experts regard a bid of 2 NT by the overcaller's partner as a forcing bid — a type of cuebid in the opener's denomination. Suit takeouts of the overcall are then nonforcing.

DEFENSE TO OPENING FOUR-BID. Against an opponent's opening bid at the four level it is standard to use the calls of double and 4NT in a variety of ways, depending on the suit of the opening bid.

Against an opening preempt of 4♣ or 4♦, a double is for takeout. Some partnerships use a bid of 4NT as a natural bid; some use it as BLACKWOOD.

Against a 4♥ opening, a double is for takeout and guarantees spade support. The prevailing agreement is that a 4NT bid is takeout for the minor suits.

Against a 4♠ opening a double is used for penalties. Hence a 4NT bid is for takeout.

DEFENSE TO OPENING THREE-BID. The following methods can be used as a defense against Weak Two-bids also:

(1) *Standard.* A double is primarily for takeout, but is sometimes described as "cooperative" or "optional" because the doubler's partner may sometimes decide to pass

in the expectation of a penalty.

A normal minimum for the double would be 16 points in high cards, or 13 points in the pass-out seat. The double implies support for the unbid major or majors unless the doubler has considerable reserve strength.

Other bids would be natural, including 3 NT, which would be a minimum of 17 points. Desirable features for this bid would be a double stopper in the opener's suit and a good minor suit.

(2) *Fishbein.* Devised by Harry Fishbein. A double of a three-bid is for penalties, and the doubler's partner should rarely take any action. A bid in the cheapest available suit is a conventional bid to replace a takeout double. 3♥ over 3♦, for example, would show a minimum of 16 points in high cards and a three-suited hand, or possibly a two-suited hand. The Fishbein takeout bid over 3♠ would be 4♣. The takeout bid is unconditionally forcing because it might be based on a two-suited hand. The convention does not apply in the pass-out position.

(3) *Cheaper (or lower) minor.* The use of the cheaper available minor suit as a takeout bid: 3♦ over 3♣, and 4♣ over other three-bids. As in the Fishbein convention, a double is for penalties, and the convention does not apply sitting under the three-bidder (although it can apply by partnership agreement).

This convention is standard among English tournament players. A variation is known in America as the SMITH CONVENTION, devised by Curtis Smith. He recommends the use of 4♣ as the takeout bid in all circumstances, even over 3♣.

(4) *Optional double.* A double that promises a balanced hand with both support for the unbid suits and some strength in the opener's suit. It invites the doubler's partner to pass for penalties.

(5) *Weiss.* The use of the cheaper minor for takeout as in (3) above, with the double used as an optional double as in (4).

(6) *3 NT for takeout.* Rare in America, but combined with a double for penalties, this is standard procedure in England at rubber bridge. A disadvantage is that 3 NT is often needed as a natural bid.

(7) *Reese.* 3 NT for a takeout over major-suit three-bids only, with a double for penalties. Double for takeout over minor suits and in fourth seat.

(8) *Two-suiter takeouts.* Overcalls of four in a minor suit after a major-suit three-bid can be used to show that suit and the unbid major. In combination with standard takeout doubles, this solves some difficult two-suiter problems. The single-suited minor-suit hand is often suitable for a 3NT overcall or a jump to the five-level. The two-suiter bids can be applied in both second and fourth seats. (A minor two-suiter can be shown by a jump to an "unusual" 4NT.)

(9) *Cheaper minor over the blacks.* 3♦ over 3♣ and 4♣ over 3♠ are for takeout. Double over these bids is therefore for penalties. Double over 3♦ and 3♥ is cooperative.

(10) *FILO* (British). A combination of *Fi*shbein over red suits and *lo*wer minor, or cheaper minor, over black suits. All doubles suggest a penalty.

DEFENSE TO PREEMPTIVE BIDS. See DEFENSE TO OPENING FOUR-BID; DEFENSE TO OPENING THREE-BID and WEAK TWO-BIDS.

DEFENSE TO A SQUEEZE. The prerequisites for a true squeeze are: menace cards, properly located and oriented; sufficient entries to these menaces; and correct timing. Unless all these elements are present, the squeeze will not be effective unless the opponents misdefend. There are several principles which can assist the defenders to discard correctly.

(1) *Two-card menace.* If one defender guards a two-card menace and two isolated menaces, then he should unguard the long menace when a choice must be made among the three suits.

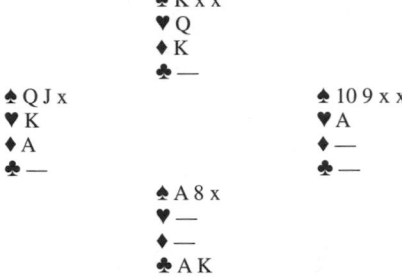

The lead of the ♣A squeezes West in three suits. If he discards a diamond, North's king becomes established. If he discards a heart, the ending leads to a twin-entry DOUBLE SQUEEZE. West must discard a spade, his guard to the long menace.

(2) *Unguarding a menace.* When a defender guards two long menaces and one isolated menace, then he should unguard the long menace placed to his left.

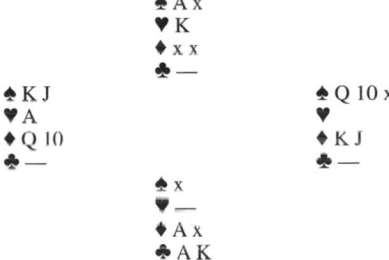

South leads the ♣A, which squeezes West in three suits. If he discards the ♥A, then North's king becomes established. If he discards a diamond, then South cashes the ace of that suit, which leads to a positional double squeeze. West must discard a spade, the guard to the long menace situated to his left.

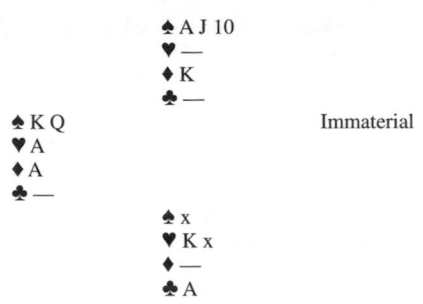

This resembles an automatic REPEATED SQUEEZE position, but it is faulty in that a one-card menace (the ♦K) is misplaced in the North hand. When South leads the ♣A, West must discard the ♦A. Otherwise South can win all the remaining tricks.

(4) *Underruff.* On rare occasions an UNDERRUFF proves to be a defender's only safe play. The following hand from a par contest illustrates the point. (Romanet).

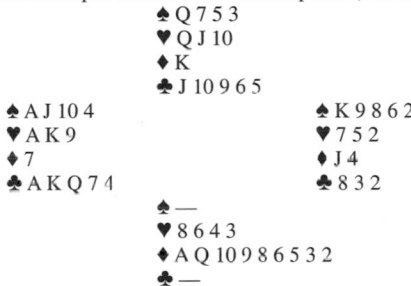

East is declarer in 6♠. South leads the ♦A, followed by the queen. West ruffs the second diamond with the ace and North must underruff. Any other discard would enable declarer to establish a trick. When the trumps are run off, North cannot be squeezed since he discards after West, the hand which contains all the menace cards.

Sometimes correct discarding will not save the defenders; an early attack against one of the basic elements of the squeeze may be the only means to break it up.

(5) *Destruction of the menace.* This can be effected in two ways: (1) by leading the suit at every opportunity, thus forcing declarer to play the menace card prematurely; and (2) by making it impossible to ISOLATE THE MENACE. This latter occurs usually at a trump contract. Terence Reese provides this example to illustrate the attack on menace cards.

```
              ♠ A 10 6 2
              ♥ 8 6 4 3
              ♦ 8 6
              ♣ A 6 3
♠ K J 3                      ♠ 9 8 7 4
♥ A K Q 10 7                 ♥ J 9 2
♦ J 7                        ♦ 9 5
♣ 10 9 5                     ♣ J 8 4 2
              ♠ Q 5
              ♥ 5
              ♦ A K Q 10 4 3 2
              ♣ K Q 7
```

South is declarer at 6♦. West leads the ♥K. If West continues with another heart, South ruffs, and after drawing trumps, enters dummy with the ♣A to ruff a third heart,

---

(3) *PROGRESSIVE SQUEEZE defense.* In this example, South leads the ♣A, which squeezes East in three suits. Any discard costs a trick, so East's primary objective is to protect himself from a progressive squeeze, which would cost him two tricks. A heart is the only discard that will achieve this end.

thus leaving West alone with the burden of guarding that suit as well as the spade suit. However, if West refrains from leading the second heart, then the heart menace cannot be isolated; East's jack cannot be ruffed out, West can discard all his hearts, relying on East to guard that suit.

(6) *Attack on entries.* This defense consists of playing the suit where declarer has a long menace. In this way a two-card menace may become an isolated menace, a twin-entry menace may be transformed into an ordinary two-card menace, etc.

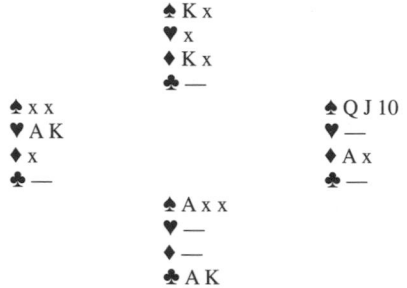

Clubs are trumps, and West has the lead. If West leads a heart or a diamond, South can ruff and play his last trump, and East will be squeezed in diamonds and spades. The ending is a twin-entry simple squeeze. However, if West leads a spade, the twin-entry menace is reduced to a two-card menace of the usual sort and the squeeze must fail.

(7) *Failure to rectify the count.* Many times declarer must lose one or two tricks to the opponents in RECTIFYING THE COUNT for a squeeze. Defenders can withhold their cooperation in this maneuver, either by failure to cash established winners or by refusing to win a trick offered by the declarer. The example below, if permitted to succeed, is known as a SUICIDE SQUEEZE.

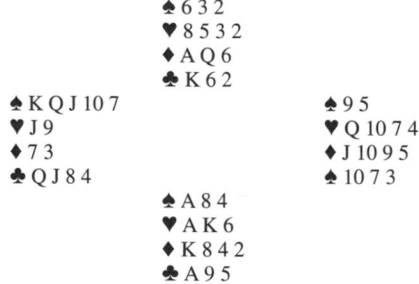

South is declarer at 3 NT, and West leads a spade.

South wins the second round and returns the suit. If West cooperates with declarer and cashes all his spades, then East can discard his clubs, but the second club lead won in dummy later squeezes him in the red suits. West cannot even cash the fourth spade without putting pressure on his partner. East can let go of two clubs on the third and fourth spades, but when declarer cashes his ♣A-K, East must either unguard the diamonds or discard a heart, whereupon declarer will be able to set up dummy's fourth heart for his ninth trick. West can cash only two spades, but then he must switch and declarer cannot make his contract.

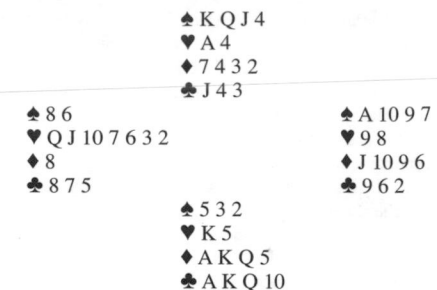

South is declarer at 6NT after West opens 3♥. West leads the ♥Q. South takes the king and leads a spade to the king. If East wins the first or second spade lead, South can execute a spade-diamond squeeze against East. If East ducks two rounds of spades, however, the contract is unmakable. See also *Killing Defense at Bridge* by Hugh Kelsey.

DEFENSE TO MULTI. See MULTI.

DEFENSE TO STRONG, ARTIFICIAL BIDS. Since systems based on a strong, artificial opening bid (usually 1♣) have become increasingly popular, the defending side needs new ways to enter the auction, both to prepare for a sacrifice and to obstruct the opponents. Several methods are in current use; they are based on the premise that the defending side can most profitably act with one long suit or a two-suiter.

A majority of tournament players employ a simple defense: a double to show length in both major suits, 1NT to show length in both minors. (MATHE). Other overcalls are natural; jump overcalls are preemptive. This method applies directly over a forcing 1♣ opening and an artificial 1♦ response.

The same defense can in theory be used over an artificial, forcing 2♣ opening. Pairs seldom have this agreement, however, since (1) they must enter the auction a level higher; (2) a 2♣ opening suggests massive defensive values; hence, the chance of finding a paying sacrifice decreases, while the chance of giving the opening side information to use in the play increases.

Few pairs, in fact, have any special agreements over an opposing 2♣ opening: in the absence of any agreements, a double of 2♣ is logically lead-directing, promising club strength; 2NT shows length in the minor suits; suit overcalls are natural.

More sophisticated schemes are discussed under their own headings: See EXCLUSION BIDS, CRASH, IDAK, ROBINSON and WONDER BIDS.

Alan Truscott devised a method by which the defending side can show all possible one- and two-suited hands. A jump overcall is natural; a simple overcall shows length in the bid suit and the suit that ranks just above it. Hence, over 1♣, 1♦ = diamonds and hearts; 1♥ = hearts and spades; 1♠ = spades and clubs; 2♣ = clubs and diamonds. The two non-touching suit combinations are shown by double (clubs and hearts) and 1NT (spades and diamonds). Over a negative 1♦ response, the only change is that double shows diamonds and spades, 1NT shows clubs and hearts.

A modified version, preferred later by the author of the method, uses minimum actions to show one-suiters and jump bids, starting with 2♦, to show two-suiters. When defender has a balanced strong hand he should pass on the first round.

DEFENSE TO TWO-SUITED INTERFERENCE.

When an opponent conventionally shows a two-suited hand, as with a MICHAELS CUEBID or an UNUSUAL 2NT OVERCALL, the opening bidder's partner has several countermeasures: a double, a raise, at least one cuebid and a bid of a new suit not shown by the opponent's interference.

A double and a cuebid are strength-showing actions. A double suggests a hand that would have been worth a redouble of a takeout double. Responder should avoid this action, however, unless he seeks to penalize the opponents. A double may goad the opponents into further preemption, and if responder has a strong hand with several offensive features, he should begin to describe his hand.

A cuebid in a suit shown by the interference is a general force that begins investigation for the best contract; by partnership agreement, it may promise support for opener's suit or length in the fourth suit (see below).

A single raise in opener's suit is equivalent to a normal single raise. Responder needs no extra high-card values, but he should be careful of raising with poor trumps; the opponent's overcall increases the chance of a bad trump split.

WEST	NORTH	EAST	SOUTH
1 ♥	2 ♥(1)	?	

(1) Spades and a minor

Neither side vulnerable. East should bid 3♥ with:

♠ 5 4   ♥ Q 10 6 2   ♦ A 9 6 4 2   ♣ J 4.

East could not raise to 3♥ (as a LIMIT RAISE) if North had passed, but he must stretch to compete over North's interference.

A bid in a new suit is natural and non-forcing. If the opponent's action shows two suits, but one is unspecified, responder can cuebid only in the known suit.

WEST	NORTH	EAST	SOUTH
1 ♠	2 ♠ (1)	?	

(1) Hearts and a minor

A 3♥ bid by East is a cuebid; both 3♣ and 3♦ are natural and non-forcing, since North's minor suit is unknown.

Practice varies among experts. This problem was presented to an expert panel in *The Bridge World* magazine:

IMP scoring, neither side vulnerable:

WEST	NORTH	EAST	SOUTH
	1 ♣	2 ♣ (1)	?

(1) Michaels; both majors

What should South call with:

♠ 3   ♥ K 8 3   ♦ A K 10 6 3   ♣ K J 10 3

Sixteen of 30 panelists doubled despite the prospect of a leap in spades by West. Eight bid 2♦; some considered the bid forcing. One cuebid 2♠, and one jumped to 3♦.

Edgar Kaplan suggested a cuebid of 2♥. In Kaplan's style, 2♥ suggests a club fit, a stopper or control in hearts and unbalanced distribution; hence, it implies spade shortness. Ira Rubin preferred 3♠, a splinter bid suggesting spade shortness and club support. Marty Bergen uses a method over Michaels similar to Unusual over Unusual (see below): his 2♥ cuebid shows a good club raise; a 2♠ cuebid would show a strong hand with diamonds.

When the opponents interfere with an Unusual 2NT overcall, many pairs employ the method known as Unusual over Unusual. They retain the strength-showing message of a double and the competitive nature of a single raise, but assign a specific meaning to each cuebid. Each

cuebid shows the strength of a limit raise or better, plus length in a suit not promised by the overcall.

In Bergen's method, for example, the lower cuebid shows support for partner's suit; the higher cuebid shows a good hand with the fourth suit.

WEST	NORTH	EAST	
1 ♠	2NT	3 ♣	= limit raise or better in spades
		3 ♦	= good hand with hearts
		3 ♥	= natural, non-forcing
		3 ♠	= weak, competitive

WEST	NORTH	EAST	
1 ♣	2NT (1)	3 ♣	= weak, competitive
		3 ♦	= limit raise or better in clubs
		3 ♥	= good hand with spades
		3 ♠	= natural, non-forcing

(1) Hearts and diamonds

The alternative is to play that the lower cue-bid shows the lower of the possible suits, and the higher the higher. Thus after a major opening 3♣ shows hearts and 3♦ shows spades, irrespective of the opening bid.

For a convention dealing in part with two-suited interference over 1NT openings, see LEBENSOHL.

DEFENSIVE BIDDING.

All the bidding by a side after the opponents have opened the auction. (However, the bidding by the opener's side can sometimes be "defensive.") The following main headings should be consulted: COMPETITIVE BIDDING; CUEBID; DOUBLES; OVERCALLS. Some specialized defensive methods are listed under various systems, such as ROTH-STONE and KAPLAN-SHEINWOLD.

Accurate defensive bidding requires considerable judgment and experience. In this department of the game, the expert has a much greater advantage over the average player than he has in normal constructive bidding. Some of the many factors which have to be taken into account are:

(1) *The risk involved.* Is there a real danger of being doubled and losing more than the opponents could score if left to their own devices? This may vary with the type of scoring, and with a psychological estimate of the opponents. Are they likely to be quick doublers?

(2) *The prospects of achieving something by action.* Possible goals are: (a) bidding and making a part-score, game, or slam; (b) saving effectively against a contract the opponents could make (see SAVE); (c) pushing the opponents to a level at which the defense may have a chance; (d) disrupting the opponents' bidding so that they reach the wrong contract. In general, the holding in the opponent's suit is a determining factor: a shortage favors action, and length and/or strength indicate passivity.

(3) *Vulnerability,* a paramount factor. Favorable vulnerability often generates aggressive action by the defenders, especially at duplicate. Both sides are very conscious of the fact that a three-trick defeat is a triumph for the defenders if it saves a vulnerable game, with the extra possibility that the opening side may permit itself to be pushed to a dangerous level.

This situation becomes exaggerated at the slam level: a nonvulnerable pair can afford to go down six tricks to save a vulnerable small slam in a major, and eight tricks to save a vulnerable grand slam.

(4) *Level of the auction.* If a bid has to be made at a higher level, it is obviously more dangerous, and it may also offer poorer prospects. A side that bids 1♠ over an opposing 1♦ is more likely to buy the final contract than

a player who bids 2♦ over 1♠. For both these reasons a bid at a higher level indicates a better hand. Similarly a double of 1♣ can be made more freely than a double of 1♠, because the latter offers fewer prospects and is less safe.

(5) *Estimate of partner's hand.* Simple addition of the minimum point-counts shown by the opponents and the points held by a defender will often reveal that partner's hand is virtually worthless. If you hold 16 points and a balanced hand, and an opening bid of 1♠ on your left gets a response of 2♦, partner's probable range is 0-3 points, and the lower end of that scale is the more likely. To bid in such a situation, which the Europeans call "in sandwich," is clearly dangerous. It would be less dangerous if the response was 1 NT, and least dangerous if the opener's suit had been raised. If the opener's side has established a fit, the chance that the defending side has a good fit is increased.

(6) *Honor wastage.* Queens and jacks in suits bid by the opponents are not only worthless for attacking purposes but should be rated as a minus quantity: they increase the defensive prospects, and therefore the danger of a PHANTOM SAVE. Conversely, queens and jacks in a suit held by the defending side are probably worthless in defense. Queens and jacks in side-suits are likely to play a part in any contract.

(7) *Honor position.* Most honor holdings increase in value when the suit is bid by the right-hand opponent, and decrease in value when the suit is bid on the left. (The exceptions are solid sequences such as king-queen-jack, and an ace not backed by another honor.) Similarly, three small cards is a poor holding if the suit was bid on the right, but rather better if the suit was bid on the left; any honor holding which partner may have has lost or gained value as a result of the bidding.

(8) *Length of suit.* An immediate overcall of an opening suit bid is normally at least five cards. In most other situations, a suit bid by the defending side is likely to be based on six-card length; e.g., after a notrump opening, or after two suit bids by the opener's side.

(9) *Raise your partner.* The need to support partner freely increases as the auction becomes more competitive. For example, if both sides are vulnerable and the bidding goes:

WEST	NORTH	EAST	SOUTH
			1♥
1♠	4♥	?	

If East has some honor strength, it might be right for him to bid 4♠ holding a singleton spade honor: the chance that West has a very substantial spade suit is greatly increased by the North-South bidding.

(10) *Preparation.* The defending side may have to prepare its bidding in the same way that the opener does. A minimum takeout double would be unprepared if the doubler has a doubleton in an unbid suit. Consider this hand after right-hand opponent has bid 1♥:

♠ A Q 6 4 3
♥ 7
♦ 5
♣ A 10 9 8 6 3

At favorable vulnerability there are excellent chances of an effective save over an opposing 4♥ bid, so 2♣ followed by a spade bid at the lowest available level on the next round is the indicated procedure. At unfavorable

vulnerability, it is sufficient to overcall 1♠. Unless partner can support spades there is no great future, and it would be too dangerous to make a second bid at a high level. At equal vulnerability the decision would be closer. (This assumes that a Michaels Cuebid is not available.)

(11) *Fit in side-suit.* When a good fit has been established in one suit, the degree of fit in another suit may be an important consideration. In a competitive auction a player who has overcalled and found a fit should sometimes bid a second suit in order to help his partner judge the right action at a high level. If the overcaller's partner bids a side-suit after finding a fit, it is more likely to be for lead-directing purposes.

(12) *Holding in the opponent's suit.* Three small cards in the opponent's suit is usually a bad holding, but it becomes better than a doubleton if the suit has been strongly bid and supported: partner can be expected to have a singleton or void.

(13) *Push.* The defenders frequently have to make "push" bids:

WEST	NORTH	EAST	SOUTH
			1♠
2♣	2♠	3♣	

East's club support may be only a doubleton honor. The bid is worthwhile if he thinks that each side can make about eight tricks. The risk is not great, and East gives his side the chance of a plus score if the opponents allow themselves to be pushed to 3♠.

DEFENSIVE TRICK. A card or card combination that may be expected to win a trick if an opponent becomes the declarer.

In some situations a player with a solitary defensive trick may need to take positive action. If 6♥ is reached voluntarily and the bidding has indicated that 6♠ is a possible SACRIFICE, a hand that is known to be very weak should usually double if it has one defensive trick. This should help partner to make the right decision (which may still be to bid 6♠), and avoid a PHANTOM SACRIFICE. For artificial uses of doubles and passes to reveal whether or not the partnership has enough defensive tricks to defeat the slam, see DOUBLE FOR SACRIFICE.

DELAYED DUCK SQUEEZE. A particular form of SECONDARY SQUEEZE.

DELAYED GAME RAISE. A bidding sequence equivalent to a standard jump raise.

♠ K J 5 4
♥ A 5 3
♦ 8 2
♣ A Q 9 7

This hand is too strong to raise an opening 1♠ to 4♠ in any normal bidding style. Using LIMIT RAISES, a substitute for the forcing double raise is necessary, and 2♣ followed by 4♠ is the usual device. This is not completely satisfactory if the opener's rebid is 2♠ because the nature of responder's hand is not clarified; but in that case the slam prospects are remote.

For alternative solutions to this problem, see SWISS, THREE NOTRUMP RESPONSE, and TWO NOTRUMP RESPONSE. These devices would be used on relatively balanced hands, in which case the delayed game raise can be reserved for markedly two-suited hands.

In modern bidding styles, a bid of 1NT, forcing, following by a jump to game in opener's suit, shows a balanced hand with 13-15 points and three-card support.

DELAYED RAISE. See BELATED SUPPORT; PREFERENCE.

DELAYED STAYMAN. See STAYMAN ON SECOND ROUND.

DELTA ASKING BIDS. See SUPER PRECISION ASKING BIDS.

DEMAND BID. A forcing bid. A term used occasionally to refer to a FORCING TWO-BID but otherwise obsolete.

DENIAL BID. A bid that indicates lack of support for partner's bid (an obsolescent term).

DENIAL CUEBIDS. A method of showing honor-location in the later stages of the auction. It was first used in several relay systems, in differing formats. The procedure developed by Roy Kerr and others in New Zealand as part of SYMMETRIC RELAYS has been adopted by some standard bidders.

The method assumes that one player has already described his distribution, approximate strength, and controls (or possibly key-cards). He shows his high cards by: bidding one step to deny a high honor in his primary suit; two steps to deny in his second suit, etc. If two suits are (or could be) equal in length, the higher-ranking is inspected first.

Here is an example based on a Flannery opening:

WEST	EAST
♠ K 6 5 3	♠ A Q 4
♥ K Q 8 7 5	♥ A
♦ A	♦ 6 5 3
♣ 6 5 4	♣ Q J 9 8 7 2

WEST	EAST
2 ♦ (1)	2 NT (2)
3 ♣ (3)	3 ♦ (4)
3 NT (5)	4 ♣ (6)
4 ♠ (7)	5 ♣ (8)
Pass	

(1) Flannery, four spades, five hearts, 11-16 points
(2) The normal inquiry. In effect a relay.
(3) Tripleton club, so 4-5-3-1.
(4) Relay asking for controls.
(5) Four controls. (Two are assumed for the opening bid.)
(6) Relay, asking for denial cue-bids.
(7) The third step, promising a high heart, a high spade but no high clubs. (The next relay would ask again about hearts. Suits known to be singleton or void are ignored.)
(8) Knowing ♣AK are missing.

If the opener has a similar hand with ♣AK and neither the king nor queen of hearts, he will show six working controls (a singleton king does not count) and no top honor in hearts. Responder will bid 7♣, knowing that the six controls are the ♠K, ♦A and ♣AK.

The denial cuebid concept can be applied in many situations, including sequences that follow Roman Key-card Blackwood.

DENMARK. See DANISH BRIDGE LEAGUE.

DENOMINATION. The suit or notrump specified in a bid. See LAWS (Law 18).

DEPO. See BLACKWOOD AFTER INTERFERENCE.

DESCENDING ORDER. The order of the rank of the denominations: notrump, spades, hearts, diamonds and clubs.

DESCHAPELLES COUP. The lead of an unsupported high honor in order to establish an entry to partner's hand. This sacrificial play was invented by GUILLAUME DESCHAPELLES at whist.

	♠ A Q 10 4	
	♥ A J	
	♦ 8 7 5 4	
	♣ 8 6 3	

♠ 3 2		♠ 9 8 7 6 5
♥ Q 8 6		♥ K 10 7 5
♦ K Q J 9 6 3		♦ A
♣ 7 5		♣ A 4 2

	♠ K J	
	♥ 9 4 3 2	
	♦ 10 2	
	♣ K Q J 10 9	

The blocked diamond position makes it very difficult for the defense to defeat South's highly optimistic 3 NT contract. East overtakes the ♦K lead with his ace, and must hope that his partner has a queen outside diamonds. If West has the ♣Q, the contract will be defeated automatically, so East assumes that his partner holds the ♥Q. The return of the ♥K is the key play. Whether or not South ducks, West's ♥Q is established as an entry, and South can be held to five tricks. Any other play by East at the second trick permits South to make his contract. Note that the play of the ♥K cannot give South his contract if West has the ♣Q; South's maximum would then be four spade tricks, three heart tricks, and one club trick.

For a similar defensive play aimed at destroying an entry instead of creating one, see MERRIMAC COUP.

DESPERATION LEAD OR PLAY. A lead or play made in defiance of the dictates of safety when defensive prospects seem poor. A tactic usually reserved for rubber bridge, not duplicate. For example, after this bidding:

WEST	NORTH	EAST	SOUTH
	Pass	1 ♠	Pass
3 ♠	Pass	4 ♠	All Pass

South has to lead from:

♠ 8 7
♥ K 4
♦ J 8 5 4 2
♣ 9 7 4 3

The lead of the ♥K is a desperation lead trying to promote a heart ruff in South's hand. North may hold ♥A, or ♥Q and ♠A.

DEUCE. Another name for the 2, the card of lowest rank in a suit.

DEVIL'S BEDPOSTS. The ♣4.

DEVIL'S COUP. Often called the disappearing trump trick; defenders' seemingly certain trump winner vanishes owing to a certain lie of the cards:

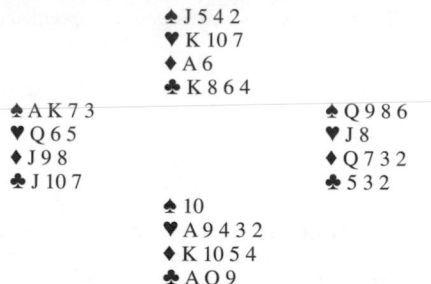

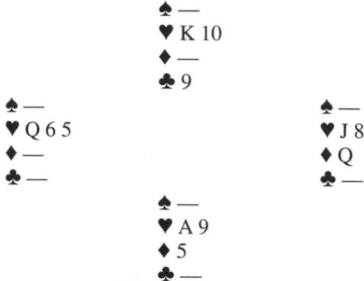

Declarer (South) reaches an optimistic ♥6 contract, apparently off a spade and a trump trick. However, West leads two rounds of spades. South ruffs the second, plays three rounds of clubs ending in dummy, and ruffs a spade. Ace, king, and a small diamond ruffed in dummy is followed by a ruff of dummy's last spade, arriving at the following end position:

South leads his diamond and East-West are helpless to prevent him from taking the remainder of the tricks. If West trumps low, North overtrumps and makes the last two tricks with high trumps. If West ruffs with the queen, dummy overruffs with the king, and East's jack is finessed on the return.

For another type of disappearing trump trick, see SMOTHER PLAY.

DEVIL'S PICTURE BOOK, DEVIL'S TICKETS.

Names given to playing cards by New England Puritans. From the time of their introduction in Europe, gambling at cards had been opposed: in 1397, John 1, King of Castille, forbade dice and cards; in 1397, the Provost of Paris forbade playing at dice or cards on workdays; in 1404, the Synod of Langres forbade clergymen to play at dice or cards; in 1423, St. Bernardino preached against cards and persuaded the people of Bologna to throw their cards into a fire; and in 1541, the Parliament of Paris forbade play at dice or cards in the homes of the town and suburbs.

The objections were usually against gambling or against working-men wasting their time; but the Puritans, for example, held that the Second Commandment (graven images) was violated by face cards. Hence, some churches permitted games using decks without court cards.

The opposition to cards has dwindled steadily, and the term is used humorously today except in a few isolated communities.

DEVYN PRESS.

A publishing firm specializing in bridge books, some new and some reissues of out-of-print works. It was founded in 1979 by Randy Baron, with Andrew Bernstein who later withdrew.

DIAMOND. (1) The suit second lowest in rank, next above the club suit, represented by the symbol ♦; (2) the symbol. The suit originated in France in the sixteenth century; its name obviously comes from the diamond-shaped lozenge used for the pips.

DIAMOND LIFE MASTER. An ACBL Life Master who has more than 5000 masterpoints. Also an ABA Life Master with more than 1000 masterpoints.

DINK. To shorten the trumps of either dummy or declarer by forcing him to ruff; a rarely used colloquialism.

DIRECT COMPETITION. Such competition exists between two contestants when they play hands which are identical with respect to cards, relative location, dealer, and vulnerability. See BALANCED COMPARISONS.

DIRECTION. The designation of North, South, East, West, or the hand held by these players.

DIRECTIONAL ASKING BID. A specialized use of a low-level CUEBID IN OPPONENT'S SUIT to invite partner to bid notrump. Partner must bid notrump if he holds Q-x, J-x-x, or better in the opponent's suit. The directional asking bidder may have two objectives. First, he may wish to discover whether his side has a combined stopper in the opponent's suit when he himself holds Q-x, J-x-x, or a singleton king. Second, he may wish to steer the contract into his partner's hand. A player with A-x-x or K-x-x should wish to be dummy if the right-hand opponent has bid the suit. The lead should come up to partner's possible Q-x or J-x-x.

However, the low-level cuebid is regularly used on the West Coast and in England as a general-purpose forcing bid (or Western cuebid). The cuebidder will often have no stopper of any kind in the opponent's suit, and his partner bids notrump if, and only if, he has a full stopper in his own right. (In general, the Western cuebid "asks" if opponents have bid only one suit, but shows a stopper if they have bid more than one.)

Each partnership must decide whether the low-level cuebid shows a guard (East Coast style), no guard (West Coast style), or half a guard (directional asking bid).

Players who use the West Coast style, who are the great majority of American players, can sometimes use a repeat cuebid below the game level as a directional asking bid:

WEST	NORTH	EAST	SOUTH
			1 ♣
Pass	1 ♦	1 ♥	2 ♥
Pass	3 ♣	Pass	3 ♥

South holds:

    ♠ A 4
    ♥ J 7 3
    ♦ 9
    ♣ A K Q 9 7 6 2

2♥ is a Western Cue-bid asking for a stopper. 3♥ is a directional asking bid, asking for half a stopper. 3NT can still be reached if North has as little as a singleton heart king or queen.

DIRECTOR. (1) Tournament director, the person designated to supervise a bridge tournament and to apply and interpret the LAWS OF DUPLICATE BRIDGE. These duties are outlined in Laws 81-91, and his responsibilities set forth. (2) Director of ACBL governing body at national or lower level. Throughout this *Encyclopedia*, Director (capitalized) is used in sense (2). Tournament director is not capitalized.

DIRECTOR CLASSIFICATION. See TOURNAMENT DIRECTORS.

DIRECTOR'S INSTRUCTIONS. See INSTRUCTIONS, DIRECTOR'S.

DISAPPEARING TRUMP TRICK. See DEVIL'S COUP; SMOTHER PLAY.

DISCARD. (1) To play a card which is neither of the suit led, or of the trump suit, or (2) the card so played. Colloquialisms for discard include ditch, pitch and shake. Defenders can and do convey information to each other by the specific nature of certain discards. See DEFENSE; DISCARDING; SIGNALING.

DISCARDING. Deciding what cards to keep in the later stages of the play is one of the basic arts of the game. Although each case must be considered on its own merits, several general considerations are worth remembering.

(1) *It is desirable to keep parity with a useful side suit in dummy.*

NORTH
♠ A K Q 7 4

WEST
♠ 10 8 5 3 2

West should avoid a spade discard. If South held the singleton jack or J-x, he would then win five tricks, if South held a low singleton, he could establish dummy's fifth spade.

NORTH
♠ A K 8 2

WEST
♠ 9 7 6 4

If South has a doubleton queen, West's holding constitutes a stopper. To retain his spades, West should not hesitate, for example, to unguard a queen in another suit in which dummy is weak. Even if declarer has A-K-J, he may finesse.

West's spade holding could be significant with the 5 instead of the 9; if South held J-9-3 or 10-9-3, he would need a side entry to dummy to take four tricks.

The same consideration applies when declarer is known to have or may have a long suit.

(2) *A defender who pays attention to the bidding can often reconstruct declarer's hand and decide whether his bidding would be consistent with or without a particular honor.*

Suppose this is the position:

NORTH
♣ K J 5

EAST
♣ Q 8 6 3

When discarding, East must make up his mind who holds the ♣A. If South holds it, East must retain three clubs; if West has the ace, East needs only to keep a doubleton.

If in the same situation East holds only low clubs, he should be careful to retain three clubs if he believes declarer holds the ace.

(3) *Many discards are informative and contribute to accurate defense.* The defenders should seldom worry

about giving away information to declarer; declarers dislike being deceived, and many place no reliance on the defenders' plays.

A valuable rule is to signal with the highest card you can spare. Hence, a high encouraging discard denies the next higher card and promises the next lower.

NORTH
♣ 4 3 2

WEST
♣ A 8 5

If East discards the ♣K, West can lead the suit happily. If East throws the jack, West can lead the 5; East must have started with K-J-10-9 or J-10-9-x. But if East throws the queen, West must leave clubs alone; South's king can be trapped later.

A player discarding from a worthless hand should try to help his partner, who may need information. If a defender has worthless holdings in two suits, he should normally discard from both suits as soon as possible. To discard low cards from only one suit would suggest that he has something to look after in the other.

If partner may be interested in length rather than strength, a possible maneuver is to discard one suit completely. Alternatively, it is possible to give COUNT SIGNALS at each stage. With 9-7-5-3-2, the sequence would be 2, 7, 3, 9, 5. The first discard is discouraging; subsequently, a low card indicates a odd number of cards remaining, a high card indicates an even number. See PRESENT COUNT.

	♠ K 4 3	
	♥ 8 3	
	♦ K 10 7 6 3	
	♣ K 4 3	
♠ J 10 6		♠ Q 9 8 2
♥ A 10 7 6 5		♥ Q 9 4 2
♦ Q 8 4		♦ 2
♣ J 10		♣ Q 9 8 5
	♠ A 7 5	
	♥ K J	
	♦ A J 9 5	
	♣ A 7 6 2	

West leads the ♥6 against South's 3NT. South takes East's queen with the king, leads a diamond to the king and returns a diamond. East should discard the ♥2, suggesting an original holding of four hearts, and West will know to lay down the ♥A when he gets in with the ♦Q.

	♠ A 7 5 3	
	♥ 7 6	
	♦ 10 3 2	
	♣ K Q 7 6	
♠ Q 10 8 2		♠ K 9
♥ 10 4 3		♥ J 9
♦ J 4		♦ K 9 8 7 6
♣ A 8 5 2		♣ J 10 9 3
	♠ J 6 4	
	♥ A K Q 8 5 2	
	♦ A Q 5	
	♣ 4	

WEST	NORTH	EAST	SOUTH
			1 ♥
Pass	1 ♠	Pass	3 ♥
Pass	4 ♥	All Pass	

West leads the ♠2. East wins the king and returns the ♠9: jack, queen, ace. South finesses the ♦Q and draws trumps. On the third trump, East should discard the ♣J to signal an even number. If South holds the ♣A, he has the rest of the tricks; if West has the ♣A, East wants him to take it at the right time. If West wins the first club and continues spades, South goes down.

Here is another example of an informative discard:

```
              ♠ K Q 3 2
              ♥ 9 8
              ♦ Q J 4
              ♣ K 7 5 2
♠ 8 7                        ♠ J 10 9 6 5
♥ A 10 7 6 4                 ♥ Q J 3
♦ K 8 6 3                    ♦ 7
♣ J 8                        ♣ Q 10 9 6
              ♠ A 4
              ♥ K 5 2
              ♦ A 10 9 5 2
              ♣ A 4 3
```

WEST	NORTH	EAST	SOUTH
			1NT
Pass	2♣	Pass	2♦
Pass	3NT	All Pass	

West leads the ♥6: 8, jack, king. South goes to the ♣K and passes the ♦Q, winning. When he leads the ♦J next, East should discard the ♥Q. The RULE OF ELEVEN tells East that South has no more hearts higher than the 6, so West's suit is ready to cash. But West may not know; from his point of view, South's hand could be,

   ♠ J x   ♥ K Q x   ♦ A 10 9 x x   ♣ A Q x

making a spade switch necessary.

```
              ♠ 10 8 7 3
              ♥ 6 3
              ♦ K 6
              ♣ K J 10 7 3
♠ A J 4                      ♠ Q 9 6 2
♥ Q 10 8 5 4                 ♥ 9 7
♦ 10 8 4                     ♦ J 9 7 5
♣ 8 5                        ♣ A 6 4
              ♠ K 5
              ♥ A K J 2
              ♦ A Q 3 2
              ♣ Q 9 2
```

WEST	NORTH	EAST	SOUTH
			1♦
Pass	1♠	Pass	2NT
Pass	3NT	All Pass	

West leads the ♥5: 3, 9, J. South attacks clubs, and East holds off. On the third club, West can discard the ♥Q, disavowing interest in hearts, and East should shift to spades.

(4) *A taxing situation arises when declarer forces discards by cashing a long suit, and a defender has more than one suit to guard.*

Even if no squeeze threatens, cooperative discarding may be needed to prevent the loss of a trick. In this situation, a defender cannot and should not try to guard every suit; he must guard one and leave the other to his partner. The deal below is given by Marshall Miles.

```
              ♠ Q 5
              ♥ 10 9 6 3 2
              ♦ Q
              ♣ A Q 9 8 2
♠ J 9 7 6 3                  ♠ K 10 8
♥ K 5                        ♥ J 8 7 4
♦ K 8 5                      ♦ 10 9 7 2
♣ 7 6 3                      ♣ 5 4
              ♠ A 4 2
              ♥ A Q
              ♦ A J 6 4 3
              ♣ K J 10
```

WEST	NORTH	EAST	SOUTH
Pass	1♥	Pass	1♦ 2NT
Pass	3♣	Pass	3NT
All Pass			

West leads the ♠6. South wins the third spade and runs the clubs. On the third club, East must decide which red suit to guard; suppose he judges to keep diamonds and therefore throws three hearts. West must discard twice; if he pitches a winning spade to guard both red kings, South is safe by passing the ♦Q. Hence, West must cooperate with East by keeping ♥K5 and blanking the ♦K. South must then guess well to make his game.

(5) *A defender can safely discard winners for which he has no entry. An exception arises in this common position:*

```
              NORTH
              ♣ A Q
                              EAST
                              ♣ K 2
```

At the 12th trick South can try for an overtrick by taking a club finesse. If East has kept two clubs, South can take the finesse safely. But if East has kept one club and a winner, South may choose not to jeopardize his contract.

Another type of tactical discard may be necessary when a defender is threatened with a strip-squeeze:

```
              ♠ J 4
              ♥ 5 2
              ♦ A Q 8 6 3
              ♣ K J 6 4
♠ K 8 5 2                    ♠ 10 9 7 3
♥ K Q 10 7 3                 ♥ 9 8 6
♦ 7 2                        ♦ 10 9 4
♣ 9 3                        ♣ 8 7 5
              ♠ A Q 6
              ♥ A J 4
              ♦ K J 5
              ♣ A Q 10 2
```

WEST	NORTH	EAST	SOUTH
			2NT
Pass	6NT	All Pass	

West leads the ♥K. South takes the ace and cashes nine tricks in the minor suits. If West's last three cards are the ♥Q and the guarded ♠K, South can lead a heart for an endplay. To mislead declarer, West does best to discard three low spades early, then the ♥3 and ♥10.

It will often be clear that unless partner has certain cards, nothing can be done. A defender can then discard on the assumption that partner has those cards.

```
              ♠ K J 6 3
              ♥ 8 7 3
              ♦ 9 6 5 2
              ♣ 6 5
♠ 5                          ♠ 9 8 4
♥ Q 10 6 2                   ♥ J 9 5 4
♦ Q 10 8 4                   ♦ J 7
♣ Q J 10 4                   ♣ A 9 3 2
              ♠ A Q 10 7 2
              ♥ A K
              ♦ A K 3
              ♣ K 8 7
```

WEST	NORTH	EAST	SOUTH
			2♣
Pass	2♦	Pass	2♠
Pass	4♠	All Pass	

West leads the ♣Q. East takes the ace and returns a club. South wins, ruffs a club in dummy and runs his trumps, forcing West to unguard a red queen.

West knows that South held five spades and three clubs. If South had four diamonds, East would have switched to his singleton at the second trick. If South had four hearts, he would have led hearts earlier so to ruff his fourth heart in dummy if necessary. Assuming South has three cards in one red suit and two in the other, West should keep diamonds. The reason is simple: If South has a diamond loser, only West can guard diamonds.

(6) *A tactical discard may be used to create an entry*

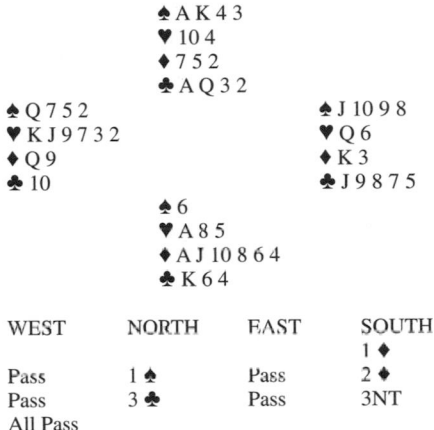

```
              ♠ A K 4 3
              ♥ 10 4
              ♦ 7 5 2
              ♣ A Q 3 2
♠ Q 7 5 2                    ♠ J 10 9 8
♥ K J 9 7 3 2                ♥ Q 6
♦ Q 9                        ♦ K 3
♣ 10                         ♣ J 9 8 7 5
              ♠ 6
              ♥ A 8 5
              ♦ A J 10 8 6 4
              ♣ K 6 4
```

WEST	NORTH	EAST	SOUTH
			1 ♦
Pass	1 ♠	Pass	2 ♦
Pass	3 ♣	Pass	3NT
All Pass			

West leads the ♥7 against South's 3NT, and South holds up the ace twice. On the third heart, East should discard the ♦K. If South's diamonds are headed by A-Q-J, the king is worthless; if West has the ♦Q, East must unblock; otherwise, South can set up the diamonds without letting West gain the lead.

(7) *The so-called IDLE FIFTH CARD in a suit is always an attractive discard — so much so that declarer can often infer that a defender's first discard comes from a five-card suit.*

```
              ♠ Q 6 3
              ♥ K Q 9 4
              ♦ K 9 3 2
              ♣ 9 7
♠ A K 9 7 4 2                ♠ 8
♥ 6                          ♥ J 8 7 5 2
♦ 6 4                        ♦ J 10 8 5
♣ K 10 8 6                   ♣ Q 5 4
              ♠ J 10 5
              ♥ A 10 3
              ♦ A Q 7
              ♣ A J 3 2
```

WEST	NORTH	EAST	SOUTH
			1NT
2 ♠	3NT	All Pass	

West led the ♠K and continued with the ace, on which East discarded the ♥2. South drew the inference, and after winning the third spade, he cashed the ♥K and led a heart to the ten to make the contract. East could lose nothing by throwing clubs on the spade leads.

(8) *Declarer also has occasions for delicate discarding.*

```
              ♠ A 7
              ♥ 8 6 3 2
              ♦ K Q J 6
              ♣ K 9 4
♠ Q J 10                     ♠ 8
♥ K 10 5                     ♥ A Q 9
♦ A 9 5 2                    ♦ 10 8 7 4 3
♣ J 6 2                      ♣ 10 8 5 3
              ♠ K 9 6 5 4 3 2
              ♥ J 7 4
              ♦ —
              ♣ A Q 7
```

WEST	NORTH	EAST	SOUTH
	1 ♦	Pass	1 ♠
Pass	1NT	Pass	4 ♠
All Pass			

West led the ♠Q. South won with dummy's ace and led the ♦K, throwing a club. When West took the ♦A he naturally shifted to the ♣J, and South made his game. See DEFENSE TO A SQUEEZE. See also *More Killing Defense* by Hugh Kelsey.

DISCIPLINARY CODE. The ACBL Disciplinary Code, approved in 1975, provides that every member charged should have a fair hearing. Disciplinary bodies in the ACBL are Units, Districts, the National Board of Directors and Tournament Committees. The jurisdiction of these bodies, grounds for discipline, sanctions which may be imposed, appeal procedures and procedural principles for the conduct of hearings are covered by the Code.

DISCIPLINE. The ability of both members of a partnership to follow an agreed system when partnership action is called for.

The ROTH-STONE SYSTEM was the first to stress partnership discipline as a requirement for use of the system, although all systems had implied its necessity without actually stressing it. Selection committees for teams in international competition have more and more stressed the importance of discipline under the heading of established partnerships.

DISCOURAGING BID. A bid indicating that game is unlikely but not impossible. Examples are: responder's raise of opener's suit from one to two, as a first response or as a rebid; responder's bid of 1NT as a first response or as a rebid; opener's minimum rebid of his suit after a one-round forcing response at the two level; and in some styles a suit takeout in response to an overcall.

The bidder expects a combined point-count in the range of 18-22, or the distributional equivalent, and partner continues only if he has considerable additional strength in terms of high cards, distribution or fit.

DISCOURAGING CARD. A card which denotes a lack of interest in a suit being continued or led. Usually a low card, the 6 or lower, it may be played either when following suit or when discarding upon another suit. See also DISCARD and SIGNALS.

DISCOVERY. The process of maneuvering the play in order to learn vital information about the hidden hands.

Terence Reese gives this example in *The Expert Game*.

```
            ♠ 10 8 4 2                    ♠ 9 3
            ♥ K 9 8 3                     ♥ A 8 7 2
            ♦ A Q 4 3                     ♦ 7 6 4 2
            ♣ Q                           ♣ K J 7
♣9 led                        ♠ A Q 10 7              ♠ 8 4
            ♠ A Q J 9 7 5     ♥ K Q 9 4               ♥ J 10 6 3
            ♥ —               ♦ Q J 3                 ♦ K 10
            ♦ 6 5 2           ♣ A 2                   ♣ 10 8 6 5 3
            ♣ A K 7 4                     ♠ K J 6 5 2
                                          ♥ 5
                                          ♦ A 9 8 5
                                          ♣ Q 9 4
```

With neither vulnerable, South opens 1♠ in fourth seat. North raises to 4♠, and South bids 6♠.

South will look first to see if there is any reason for cashing the ♣A and play for some elimination position. The chances of this are obscure, so he may judge that the hand depends on one of two finesses and lead a spade for a finesse of the queen.

It is possible to improve on that play. At the second trick declarer should lead the ♥K from dummy. If East covers with the ace, South ruffs and finesses the ♦Q. East wins with the king and leads the ♣6. Now South has discovered for sure that East holds the ♥A and ♦K. Since West opened the ♣9 it is probable also that East holds ♣J-10; if South wants to look further, he can place East with intermediate cards in both hearts and diamonds, for had West held a solid sequence in either suit he would presumably have led it.

In short, South has built up for East a hand on which, if it contained the ♠K as well, he might well have opened the bidding third hand. Having reached this point, South may decline the spade finesse and play for the drop of the singleton king.

A different type of discovery play can be aimed at determining a suit division.

```
            ♠ Q 8 3
            ♥ 8 4
            ♦ 8 7 2
            ♣ K Q 8 4 3
♥3 led                        ♥10 played
            ♠ A K 5
            ♥ K 9 6
            ♦ K Q J 10 5
            ♣ A 6
```

South opens 2 NT and is raised to 3 NT. He wins the first trick with the ♥K, and has to choose between playing diamonds and clubs. The diamond play wins if the heart suit is split 4-4; the club play wins if the clubs split 3-3.

The even club split is slightly more likely mathematically, and the heart lead increases the chance that West has a five-card suit. But instead of plunging on clubs, South can give himself both chances if the defenders are good players. At the second trick he leads the ♣6 to dummy's king, followed by a low club to the ace. West is likely to signal his club length (see COUNT SIGNALS) by playing low from a three-card holding or high from two or four. if West's club plays indicate that the suit will not break, South abandons clubs and tries diamonds. This preserves the chance of making the contract if the hearts are split evenly and avoids a possible two-trick defeat.

Discovery plays by the defenders are very rare. The following example is from the 1961 British International Trials.

Both sides vulnerable; dealer East.

WEST	NORTH	EAST	SOUTH
		Pass	Pass
1 ♥	Pass	2 ♥	2 ♠
Dbl	2 NT	Pass	3 ♦
Dbl	All Pass		

West led the ♥K, captured by dummy's ace. South led a spade to his jack, and West won with the queen. It was clearly necessary for the defenders to lead trumps, but the lead of the queen would have blocked the suit, and prevented the defenders from playing three rounds advantageously. West judged that his partner must have a high diamond honor or the ♣Q. To learn which, he led the ♣A to get an attitude signal. When East dropped the ♣3 it was clear that he did not hold the ♣Q, so West shifted to the ♦3. South was held to six tricks, losing 800.

DISCRETIONARY POWERS. See ADJUSTED SCORE and Duplicate Law 12.

DISQUALIFICATION. Law 91, LAWS OF DUPLICATE BRIDGE, provides that a director is specifically empowered to suspend a player for the balance of a session, or subject to the approval of the tournament committee or the sponsoring organization, to disqualify a player, pair or team for cause in order to maintain discipline or order.

DISTRIBUTION. The manner in which the cards of a suit are dispersed among the four hands of a deal, or the manner in which the number of cards in the four suits are distributed in one hand. Variations in distribution are the basis of various bidding systems in use. See BIDDING.

DISTRIBUTIONAL COUNTS. Distributional points added to high-card points are used to arrive at an overall hand valuation. There are various ways in which the standard 4-3-2-1 point-count can be supplemented:
Goren Count, devised by William Anderson of Toronto, and adopted and developed by Charles Goren.

void	counts 3 points
singleton	counts 2 points
doubleton	counts 1 point

This applies to the opener's hand, and these points are added to the high-card point-count (subject to the usual corrections).

If the responding hand plans to raise the opener's suit, he applies a different count:

void	counts 5 points
singleton	counts 3 points
doubleton	counts 1 point

In addition, the responder makes certain corrections, deducting a point for each of the following; (a) a raise with 3 trumps; (b) a 4-3-3-3 distribution; (c) an insufficiently guarded high card. Also, a point is added for a king, queen, or jack in the trump suit provided this does not bring the total number of high-card points in the trump suit to more than 4.

Karpin Count, popularized by Fred Karpin, who was the first to achieve a large following with a distributional point-count method.

Distributional points are assigned for length, one point for each card over four in any suit. Thus any five-card suit counts 1 point, any six-card suit 2 points, and so on.

Short suits are counted in raising partner according to the following schedule:

	with 4 or more trumps	with 3 trumps
void counts:	3	2
singleton counts:	2	1
doubleton counts:	1	0

These are in addition to points for length.

A simple version of the Karpin idea was published in 1947 by Richard Miller. An even earlier pioneer of distributional point-count was Victor Porter of Boston. His method, published in 1938, allowed 4 points for each singleton and void, and 2 points for a doubleton in both hands.

Culbertson Count, published by Ely Culbertson in 1952. For an opening suit bid, count each card over three in any suit as one point except that the fourth card does not count in the trump suit. When declarer's opening bid has been raised, he counts the fourth trump as a point, and adds 2 points when he holds six or more trumps. Responder also counts 2 points for holding six or more trumps when giving a raise and makes some minor correction: (a) 1 point is deducted for three-card trump support or 4-3-3-3 distribution; (b) 1 point is added for holding a void or two singletons.

Prior to Culbertson's adoption of point-count, he advocated a distributional count. Honor winners and long-suit winners were added, and the total of the combined hands represented the level to which the side could bid. A supporting hand counted ruffing values, but did not count length in side suits.

Roth Count, devised by Alvin Roth to quantify the point-count adjustments in hand evaluation which experts make in light of the bidding. The Roth system retains the 4-3-2-1 Work point-count for honor cards and the basic 3-2-1 Goren count for shortness. It adds points for long suits: 1 point for any six-card major or for a good six-card minor; 2 points for any seven-card major or for a good seven-card minor.

Adjustments to shortness and length points are made in light of the degree of fit shown by one's partner's bidding. With 0-2 cards in partner's suit, no points are counted for shortness in a side suit; with 3 cards in partner's suit, the normal 3-2-1 scale of shortness count should be used; with 4 cards in partner's suit one extra point should be added for each singleton, plus one extra point if there are any doubletons. If one's own suit is raised by partner or if partner makes a notrump bid showing a balanced hand, one point is added for each card in the suit in excess of four.

Combination count, devised in England, uses lengths and shortages immediately. Karpin length points are supplemented by 2 for a void and 1 for a singleton. This is applied to both opener and responder in all situations with two provisos: (a) the opening bidder may not count more than 3 distributional points; (b) in responses and

rebids no player may count more distributional points than he has cards in his partner's suit.

All distributional counts are an attempt to reach by formula the bid which an expert will make on the basis of experience. Their chief value is in giving guidance to inexperienced players; experts seldom make any conscious calculation of distributional points. See VALUATION and ASSETS.

DISTRIBUTIONAL POINT-COUNT. For the distributional value of certain short suit holdings translated into point-count, see DISTRIBUTIONAL COUNTS, DISTRIBUTIONAL VALUES.

DISTRIBUTIONAL VALUES. The trick-taking possibilities of a hand that depend on the distribution of the cards in the other three hands rather than on the rank of the cards in their respective suits; low-card tricks in general, including long-suit tricks and ruffing tricks (short-suit tricks).

The classic example of the power of distribution versus points is the DUKE OF CUMBERLAND'S HAND. A slight variation, given below, has been immortalized by Ian Fleming in his *Moonraker*.

The famous James Bond, sitting North and partnering M, sets out to teach a lesson to the cheat Drax.

Having prearranged the pack, Bond sees to it that the evil Drax gets the West hand and it will be clear that, no matter which of his three suits East chooses to lead, the final contract of 7♣ doubled and redoubled by Bond cannot be defeated. Playing for enormous stakes, this costs Drax something like 15,000 pounds — a salutary lesson indeed!

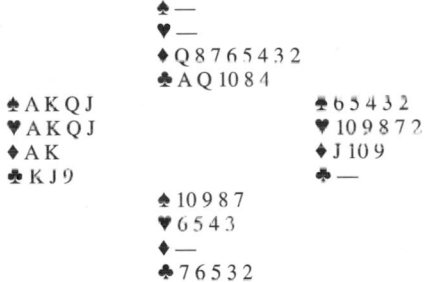

DISTINGUISHED MEMBER. A special award set up by the ACBL Board of Directors. No time schedule for awarding the honor was established, nor were there specific criteria set out for selecting the recipient except that the person should be a truly distinguished member of ACBL. The first and only recipient through 1992 was Lou Bluhm of Atlanta, who was singled out for his personal attributes and contributions to bridge, particularly in the area of ethics and courtesy.

DISTRICT, DISTRICT ORGANIZATION. One of 25 sectors of the American Contract Bridge League. Each district is represented on the ACBL Board of Director by a director, elected by the unit boards of the district. Each district also is allotted five representatives on the ACBL Board of Governors. Each district is governed by a district organization whose functions include the organization of regional tournaments, staging a district-wide contest to determine the district's representative in the Grand National Teams (United States districts only), staging a district-wide contest to determine the district's representatives in the three flights of the North American Pairs, staging a district-wide contest to determine the pair that will represent the district in the North American 49er Pairs, coordinating sectional tournaments with neighboring districts and handling special cases by means of an appointed district judiciary committee.

DISTRICT CHAMPIONSHIP. See GRAND NATIONALS CHAMPIONSHIPS (2).

DISTRICT JUDICIARY COMMITTEE. A committee of the DISTRICT ORGANIZATION whose rights and responsibilities include hearing appeals from disciplinary action imposed on a member by a unit board of directors, and conducting disciplinary hearings *ab initio*, which may result in censure, suspension or expulsion of a player.

DITCH. A colloquialism for DISCARD.

DOG. A very poor hand. (Colloq.)

DOMINICA BRIDGE ASSOCIATION.
Officers 1993:
  President, Dr. Don McIntyre
  Secretary, Henry Volney
  19A Munro St.
  Goodwill, Com. of Dominica W.I.
  Tel. 809 44 84111
  Fax: 809 44 83124

D.O.N.T. See BERGEN OVER NOTRUMP.

DOOP. A device developed by Ronald Andersen which permits "one table duplicate games," so that hands previously played in tournaments can be played in the home.

DOPE. See BLACKWOOD AFTER INTERFERENCE.

DOPI. See BLACKWOOD AFTER INTERFERENCE.

DOUBLE. A call that increases the scoring value of odd tricks or undertricks on an opponent's bid. See LAWS (Law 19).

DOUBLE ACTION. In some bidding situations, a player will pass after some hesitation, squirming, gesture or other mannerism that will alert his partner to the idea that he has some other possible action than a pass in mind. Such a hesitation on the part of one's partner should not deter a player from taking whatever action his own holdings might justify. However, it is unethical to re-open the bidding with a double to encourage partner to take whatever action he was considering. For a player who has so hesitated to take action after a double by his partner is highly questionable ethically.

DOUBLE AGAINST SLAM. See DOUBLE FOR SACRIFICE; LIGHTNER DOUBLE.

DOUBLE-BARRELED STAYMAN. A method of combining forcing and non-forcing STAYMAN. See TWO-WAY STAYMAN.

DOUBLE COUP. A trump coup in which two ruffs are necessary to achieve the required end position.

DOUBLE DUMMY. (1) Play of a hand that could not be improved upon, as though declarer were looking at all four hands as in DOUBLE DUMMY PROBLEMS. It can also be used to refer to perfect play by the defenders.

Originally, Double Dummy was a two-handed form of whist in which each player had a dummy. Some players exposed all four hands, thus giving rise to the modern usage.

(2) Trademark of a two-hand contract game, introduced in 1975, in which each player has a dummy. Since each player already sees two hands, no dummy hand is put down on the table.

DOUBLE DUMMY PROBLEMS. Problems in the play of the hand in which the solver knows the holdings in all four hands. The contract and the opening lead are specified. Like chess problems, they are for the solitary analyst, and require great skill in construction.

Double dummy problems have a long history, and were constructed in the 19th Century before bridge challenged the popularity of whist. They were often appended to bridge columns, usually in a setting in which each player has played most of his cards. See WHITFELD SIX.

The most common double dummy problem has a full 52-card lay-out. There is usually an unusual twist, perhaps involving a squeeze or endplay, and the solver needs to explore several variations. The opponents are assumed to play perfectly.

The genre thrived in the United States in the first half of this century. Since then it has been largely confined to British magazines, particularly *Bridge Magazine* (and its successors) which has had a continuous double dummy solving contest with high quality problems. It was directed until 1965 by Ernest Pawle and subsequently by Hugh Darwen. The following is a classic Darwen construction:

MAMMOTH ON A SEESAW

```
                ♠ 7 6 5 4 3 2
                ♥ A K
                ♦ A
                ♣ K J 3 2
   ♠ —                        ♠ Q J 10 9 8
   ♥ —                        ♥ Q J 10 9 8
   ♦ J 10 9 8 7 6 5 4 3 2     ♦ Q
   ♣ 10 9 8                   ♣ 7 6
                ♠ A K
                ♥ 7 6 5 4 3 2
                ♦ K
                ♣ A Q 5 4
```

South is required to make 10 tricks in notrump. The lead is the ♣10.

The solution is astonishing, and superficially ludicrous: South must allow West to win the first trick with the ♣10. South wins the next two tricks in the dummy with the ♣J and ♦A, with the order depending on West's play to the second trick.

The lead of the ♣2 then squeezes East out of two tricks. If he throws a heart, South wins with the ♣Q and works on hearts. If he throws a spade, South wins with the ♣A and works on spades.

There are three major original collections of problems: *Sure Tricks* by George Coffin, based on work by Ivar Andersson. *Double Dummy Bridge* by George Coffin. *Bridge Magic* by Hugh Darwen. See SINGLE DUMMY PROBLEMS and INFERENTIAL PROBLEM.

DOUBLE ELIMINATION. A method used in the VANDERBILT and SPINGOLD knockout team events in the annual ACBL spring and summer tournaments from the mid-Fifties until 1966 and 1965 respectively, and occasionally in other knockout team events.

As is implied in the name, a knockout tournament is one in which a team that loses a head-on match is eliminated from further competition. In a double knockout, the usual procedure is modified to provide that no team is eliminated until it has lost two matches.

The first competition between teams thus results in a group of losers and a group of winners (usually termed winners' bracket and losers' bracket). Matches continue in the winners' bracket, with half the competing teams continuing in the winners' bracket in the next round, the balance joining the losers' bracket. Eventually there is one surviving team from the winners' bracket.

In the losers' bracket, head-on play continues between one-time losers. Winners of these matches continue play in the next round, with losers in this bracket being eliminated as they have then lost their second match. In each round of the losers' bracket, the winners of the previous round are joined for the next round by the losers in the preceding round from the winners' bracket. This can often lead to a possible rematch between two teams that have previously competed against each other, and the CONDITIONS OF CONTEST are usually designed to provide as few as possible of such rematches.

Special provisions must usually be made in the conditions for the last few matches, depending on whether the losers' bracket ends up in a round of two, three, four, or five. See REPECHAGE.

DOUBLE FINESSE. A finesse against two outstanding honors. The classic situation is:

A Q 10

x x x

The only serious chance of making three tricks is to finesse the 10. A more difficult situation is:

A J 4 3 2

10 9 6 5

With this holding some players would play the ace, hoping for an honor to fall or for a 2-2 division. But the better percentage play is to take two finesses. See also DEEP FINESSE, FINESSE, and SUIT COMBINATIONS.

DOUBLE FOR SACRIFICE. A double of an opponent's voluntary slam bid after the doubler's side has bid and raised a suit preemptively, designed to help the defenders decide whether they have enough tricks to defeat the slam or should sacrifice. The double indicates how many tricks the doubler expects to take. There are two variations of the convention.

One method, called the Negative Slam Double, or Unpenalty Double, requires the left-hand opponent of the slam bidder to double only if he has no defensive tricks. If his partner has fewer than two such tricks, he sacrifices. If the slam bidder's LHO has one or two tricks he passes and his partner doubles only if he has no tricks, allowing the slam to be played doubled if the pass was made with two tricks, or the sacrifice to be taken if the pass was made with one trick. For obvious reasons, Richard L. Frey originally christened this convention the "Undouble."

An alternative method, called the Positive Slam Double, requires the slam bidder's LHO to double only if he has two defensive tricks. If instead he passes, his partner will sacrifice with no tricks, pass with two tricks, or double with one trick, allowing the slam to be played doubled if the pass was made with one trick, or the sacrifice to be taken if the pass was made with no tricks.

These sacrificial maneuvers became less frequent with the introduction of increased penalties for non-vulnerable partnerships.

DOUBLE GRAND COUP. A play by which declarer twice ruffs winning cards in order to reduce the hand which is long in trumps to the same length as that of an opponent, in preparation for a coup.

DOUBLE IN SLAM-GOING AUCTION. See DEFENSE TO INTERFERENCE WITH BLACKWOOD; DOUBLE FOR SACRIFICE; DOUBLE OF A CUEBID; LEAD DIRECTING DOUBLE; LIGHTNER DOUBLE.

DOUBLE JUMP. A bid two levels higher than necessary. This may refer to a RAISE (1♥-4♥), a RESPONSE (1♥-3♠) or an OVERCALL (1♥-3♠ or 4♣). The term is obsolescent, partly because it is frequently misunderstood or misused by inexperienced players who confuse a DOUBLE RAISE (1♥-3♥) with a DOUBLE JUMP RAISE (1♥-4♥).

DOUBLE JUMP OVERCALL. A preemptive jump after an opposing opening bid. As with all preemptive actions, the bidder must allow for the vulnerability and the level at which he has to bid. The bid normally requires a suit of at least seven cards, but some liberties may be taken at favorable vulnerability. Over 1♣, a jump to 3♠ may be tried with a hand as weak as:

♠ K Q J 10 3 2
♥ 3
♦ 10 9 7 5
♣ 8 4

This offers a definite possibility of shutting out the heart suit. In other situations the RULE OF TWO AND THREE should be applied. See PREEMPTIVE BID; PREEMPTIVE OVERCALL; and WEAK JUMP OVERCALL.

DOUBLE JUMP RAISE. A triple raise, such as 1♥-4♥; sometimes confused with a jump raise such as 1♥-3♥. See TRIPLE RAISE.

DOUBLE JUMP SHIFT REBID. See OPENER'S REBID.

DOUBLE JUMP TAKEOUT. A preemptive response one level higher than a JUMP SHIFT, such as 1♥-3♠, or 1♠-4♥. See PREEMPTIVE RESPONSES.

DOUBLE KNOCKOUTS. See DOUBLE ELIMINATION.

DOUBLE MENACE. In a double squeeze situation, the threat card in the suit guarded by both opponents.

DOUBLE MITCHELL. A form of duplicate tournament competition to permit comparison between a greater number of pairs that can be had in direct competition in a single section. The boards are carefully twinned (either at the table or beforehand) and a MITCHELL MOVEMENT used. In scoring the event, all North-South scores from both sections are entered on the same recapitulation sheet, and the matchpoints are awarded across the pairs in both sections as one field. Similar treatment is accorded the East-West scores. Thus top score is increased from 12 to 25 on a board.

Double Mitchell is also used to describe a movement for two small sections which can be linked together to permit half of the boards to be played by the midway point. For example, suppose two parallel six-table sections in which the tables are numbered 1 through 6 and 11 through 16, are sharing boards, 1 with 11 etc. on each round. Both sections move within themselves for three rounds using the normal Mitchell progression. The moving pairs then move to the adjoining section without progressing, i.e., from table 1 to 11, 2 to 12, etc. After a further three rounds of normal Mitchell progressions, all pairs have played all the boards then in play. New boards are then introduced in play and twinned. Players then take their positions for what would normally be the fourth round (add three or subtract three from their original pair number in the section they started in), and play three rounds in that section. After these three rounds, they make a move similar to that after the third round, and complete the last three rounds in the adjacent section. If all sections in a big tournament are thus subdivided, it becomes possible to commence the matchpointing in the middle of the play. In Europe, where all sections are matchpointed against the whole field, with top score occasionally in the hundreds, this is a distinct advantage.

DOUBLE NEGATIVE. A bid or rebid by responder after opener has opened with a strong two-bid or an artificial strong 2♣ bid, that denies a hand worth more than 0-3 points. Several such double negatives are in current use:

(1) HERBERT NEGATIVE (touching suit) rebid after a negative response has previously been made to the forcing opening.

(2) Cheaper minor rebid after a negative response has previously been made to the forcing opening.

This is sometimes called a SECOND NEGATIVE.

See also STEP RESPONSE and ACE-SHOWING RESPONSES.

DOUBLE OF A CUEBID. At a high level, a double of a suit bid in which there is no intention of playing can be used for lead-directing purposes, or perhaps to suggest a save. It is an indiscreet action if there is no positive purpose other than intimidation, because it gives the left-hand opponent the possibility of a pass or a redouble. There is no general agreement about the meaning of a redouble in this situation: in one style the redouble shows second-round control of the suit.

A double of a cuebid at a low level would be lead-directing by a side which is on the defensive. But a double of a normally preemptive cuebid such as a MICHAELS CUEBID would, in standard practice, show a strong defensive hand. See DEFENSE TO TWO-SUITED INTERFERENCE.

DOUBLE OF THREE NOTRUMP. See LEAD-DIRECTING DOUBLE.

DOUBLE OF TWO CLUB RESPONSE TO NO-TRUMP. The 2♣ response to an opening bid of 1NT is almost invariably the STAYMAN convention. When 2♣

is bid in response to a strong notrump, a double by the LHO of the 2♣ bidder is normally a lead-directing bid showing length and strength in clubs, but not promising overall strength. See DOUBLES OF ARTIFICIAL BIDS FOR PENALTIES.

When the opening notrump bid is of the weak variety, however, the responder sometimes has a very weak hand with which he wishes to escape into a suit. See WEAK NOTRUMP. The escape is frequently initiated by a 2♣ response. Consequently for most expert partnerships the double of the 2♣ response to a weak opening notrump simply shows general strength. The double does not promise any particular distribution, but suggests that the doubler has a hand with which it would have been appropriate for him to double the notrump opening had he been sitting over the opener.

DOUBLE OUT OF ROTATION. See LAWS OF DUPLICATE, Law 32.

DOUBLE RAISE. A jump raise of opener's suit from one to three (1♠-3♠ or 1♦-3♦).

In the Goren style, a double raise promised 13 to 15 points with at least four-card trump support and forced to game. Most modern tournament players have abandoned this treatment. If opener's suit is a major, many pairs play a double raise as game-invitational but not forcing (see LIMIT JUMP RAISE); a few pairs use preemptive double raises; most pairs play a double raise as preemptive after the second player doubles (see TWO NOTRUMP RESPONSE OVER OPPONENT'S TAKEOUT DOUBLE), and some do so if the second player overcalls.

Many pairs also use limit double raises in the minor suits, but INVERTED MINOR-SUIT RAISES are an alternate treatment; in this method, a single raise is strong and forcing, a double raise is weak and preemptive. See also CRISS-CROSS RAISES.

Any partnership that uses limit double raises should adopt a conventional forcing raise. See BERGEN RAISES; DELAYED GAME RAISE; JACOBY TWO NOTRUMP; SPLINTER BIDS; SWISS CONVENTION; TWO NOTRUMP RESPONSE and THREE NOTRUMP RESPONSE.

DOUBLE RAISE IN MINOR, PREEMPTIVE. See INVERTED MINOR SUIT RAISES.

DOUBLE SHOWING ACES. See DEFENSE TO INTERFERENCE WITH BLACKWOOD.

DOUBLE SQUEEZE. A squeeze of both opponents. It involves three suits, which may be labeled A, B, and C; then one opponent is squeezed in suits A and B while the other is squeezed in suits B and C. Thus a double squeeze is a combination of two simple squeezes, one against each opponent. Every double squeeze requires a squeeze card, a double menace, and two isolated menaces, guarded by only one opponent. Declarer must have all but one of the remaining tricks. The following classifications are based on analysis by Bertrand Romanet.

(1) *Simultaneous.* In a simultaneous double squeeze both opponents are squeezed on the same trick. There are three basic positions:

(a) Balanced

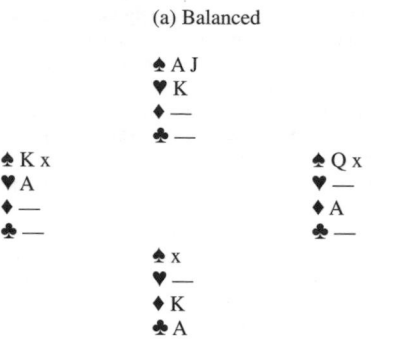

South leads the squeeze card, the ♣A. West is squeezed in the majors, and he must discard a spade. North throws a heart, and East is squeezed in spades and diamonds. This is a positional squeeze.

(b) Automatic

    ♠ A K x
    ♥ —
    ♦ —
    ♣ x
♠ Q 10 x   ♠ J 9 x
♥ A   ♥ —
♦ —   ♦ A
♣ —   ♣ —
    ♠ x
    ♥ K
    ♦ K
    ♣ A

South leads the ♣A, squeezing West in the majors. West must discard a spade, and now East is squeezed in spades and diamonds.

(c) Twin Entry

    ♠ K x
    ♥ K
    ♦ K
    ♣ —
♠ Q 10 x   ♠ J 9 x
♥ A   ♥ —
♦ —   ♦ A
♣ —   ♣ —
    ♠ A x x
    ♥ —
    ♦ —
    ♣ A

South leads the ♣A, West must throw a spade, North discards a heart, and East is squeezed in spades and diamonds. This is a positional squeeze.

(2) *Non-simultaneous.* In a non-simultaneous double squeeze there are two separate squeeze cards. Declarer's last established trick in the fourth suit squeezes one opponent; a trick or more thereafter, the second squeeze card disposes of the other opponent. The second squeeze card lies opposite the first squeeze card, and it accompanies the isolated menace guarded by the opponent who was squeezed initially. There are four basic positions (Romanet):

(a) Inverted Left

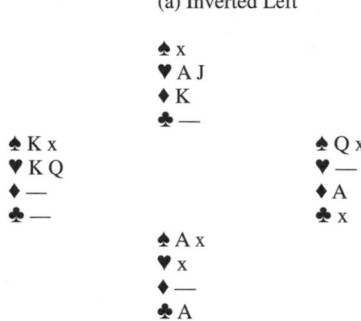

South leads the ♣A, forcing West to discard a spade, and North throws a low heart. Now South leads a heart to the ace which squeezes East in spades and diamonds. This is a positional squeeze.

The term *inverted* refers to the fact that the double menace accompanies the squeeze card, which is unusual since the double menace ordinarily lies opposite the squeeze card. Left indicates that the isolated menace guarded on the left is accompanied by a winner.

(b) Inverted Right

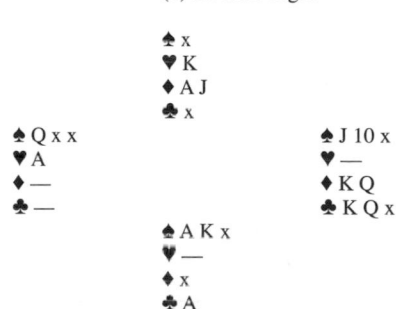

South leads the ♣A, forcing East to discard a spade. Now North wins the ♦A, squeezing West in spades and hearts. This is an automatic squeeze. For this squeeze an ordinary two-card menace against both opponents does not suffice; a recessed menace is required.

(c) Twin Entry Left

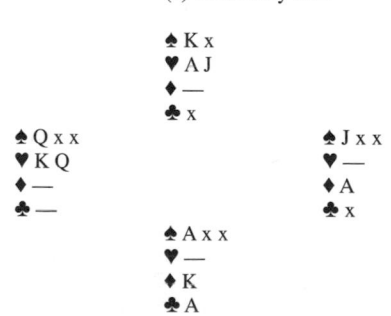

South leads the ♣A, which forces West to discard a spade. Now a lead to the ♠K, followed by the ♥A squeezes East in spades and diamonds. This is a positional squeeze.

It combines elements of the balanced and twin-entry positions discussed above.

(d) Inverted Left Recessed

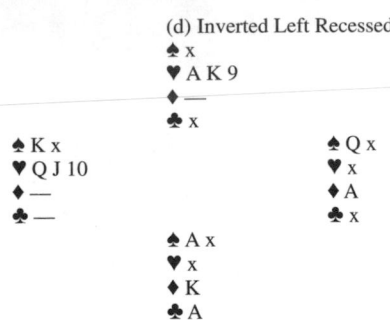

♠ x
♥ A K 9
♦ —
♣ x

♠ K x   ♠ Q x
♥ Q J 10   ♥ x
♦ —   ♦ A
♣ —   ♣ x

♠ A x
♥ x
♦ K
♣ A

South leads the ♣A, which forces West to discard a spade. Now North wins two top hearts, the last of which squeezes East in spades and diamonds. This is a positional squeeze.

The isolated menaces are arranged as in a balanced double squeeze, but the double menace is inverted. As compensation, North must have two winners, one of which is an entry. The last two positions illustrate the available endings. See also BARCO SQUEEZE; BONNEY'S SQUEEZE; CLASH SQUEEZE; HEXAGON SQUEEZE; OCTAGON SQUEEZE; RECIPROCAL SQUEEZE.

DOUBLE TENACE. A tenace in which the sequence is broken in two places, such as A-Q-10, K-J-9.

DOUBLE TOP. In some individual tournaments it is not practical to maintain direct comparison within a group on all of the boards played. Thus every score will be duplicated to each of the two players who were partners on the board. In matchpointing the scores, thus, there are two identical entries for each score, and each award is entered twice, once to each of the players. Thus there are two top scores on each board; and a game so scored is referred to as scored with a double top.

The term is also used to refer to a scoring method more in use in other continents, whereby each matchpoint score is obtained by counting two points for each poorer score and one point for each equal score. This eliminates the half points in matchpointing. Thus with 13 pairs in competition, top score would be 24 rather than 12, amounting to a double top. See STANZA MOVEMENT.

DOUBLED INTO GAME. Making a doubled contract and collecting a game bonus that would not have been scored without the double. So it is any doubled contract, except 3NT, between 2♥ and 4♦.

It is certainly undesirable to be the defenders in this situation, but one must accept such results occasionally. Players who never double the opponents into game are certainly letting many good penalty opportunities escape.

DOUBLER. A player who has doubled.

DOUBLES. The two main categories are PENALTY DOUBLES and TAKEOUT DOUBLES, which are listed separately. Distinguishing between the two types is not always easy. The following is a sound general rule: A double of a suit bid below the game level is for takeout if partner has not bid. Conversely, a double is for penalties if:
(1) The bidding is at the game level or above; or
(2) The bid doubled is in notrump; or

(3) The doubler's partner has already bid. But these generalities require some qualification in particular cases.

(1) Even at the game level, a double may have a takeout flavor. If the bidding goes 1♥-pass-4♥-double, the doubler is unlikely to be loaded with hearts. He indicates a hand with considerable high-card strength, and expects a takeout, although partner will often exercise his option of passing for penalties. If the suit were spades, the penalty aspect would be more dominant.

(2) A double of a response of 1NT is a special case (1♥-pass-1NT-double). This is primarily for takeout, although responder may exercise his option to pass.

(3) Doubles on the second round have to be considered on their merits, and are sometimes ambiguous. The old theory was that a double of a suit rebid is for penalties when the same suit could have been doubled on the first round. This is true in cases like:

WEST	NORTH	EAST	SOUTH
			1♠
Pass	2♣/1 NT	Pass	2♠
Dbl			

West must have spade length and strength, and was lying in wait. The situation would not be so clear in a minor suit:

WEST	NORTH	EAST	SOUTH
			1♦
Pass	1 NT	Pass	2♦
Dbl			

West may have diamond strength, but equally, since both opponents are limited, he may be looking for a major suit. East's diamond length will usually enable him to interpret the double correctly.

If another takeout action is available, a double is clearly for penalties. The following sequences only look similar:

(a)

WEST	NORTH	EAST	SOUTH
			1♣
Pass	1♦	Pass	2♣
Dbl			

(b)

WEST	NORTH	EAST	SOUTH
			1♦
Pass	2♣	Pass	2♦
Dbl			

Sequence (a) is clearly for penalties: West would make a cuebid of 2♦ holding the majors. (The same would apply to the sequence 1♦-pass-1 NT-pass-2♣-double.)

In sequence (b) the cuebid is not available, so the double is ambiguous: it is likely to be for a takeout, but East must inspect his hand.

Experts disagree about the meaning of this rare sequence:

WEST	NORTH	EAST	SOUTH
			1♥
Pass	1 NT	Pass	2♣
Dbl			

The doubler can be expected to have some heart strength, but whether he has clubs is not clear.

Other delayed doubles are also rare, and tend to have length and strength in the opener's suit. For example

WEST	NORTH	EAST	SOUTH
			1♣
Pass	1♥	Pass	1♠
Dbl			

West presumably has a hand worth a take-out double

of one spade, with 1-4-4-4 a possible distribution.

WEST	NORTH	EAST	SOUTH
			1 ♣
Pass	1 ♥	Pass	1 NT
Dbl			

This has a penalty flavor. West has a strong hand with club length and strength. He is likely to be short in hearts.

A double is in principle for penalties if three suits have been bid around the table: there are no longer two or more suits between which the responder can choose. However, if made at a low level, some expert partnerships nevertheless use such doubles as takeout, and some treat the double as a COOPERATIVE DOUBLE. See NEGATIVE DOUBLES, SNAPDRAGON.

Doubles other than penalty doubles and takeout doubles may be used in a variety of situations to give information. In slam auctions, for example, doubles may be used offensively as a DEFENSE TO INTERFERENCE WITH BLACKWOOD. Defensively, doubles may be used to exchange information as to when to sacrifice against a slam. See DOUBLE FOR SACRIFICE.

Other doubling situations are discussed under: BALANCING; CARDSHOWING DOUBLE; COMPETITIVE DOUBLE; COOPERATIVE DOUBLE; DEFENSE TO DOUBLE OF ONE NOTRUMP; DOUBLE OF ARTIFICIAL BID FOR PENALTIES; DOUBLE OF CUE-BID; DOUBLE OF TWO CLUB RESPONSE TO ONE NOTRUMP; DOUBLES OF NOTRUMP BIDS; FISHER DOUBLE; FREE DOUBLE; INHIBITORY DOUBLE; LEAD-DIRECTING DOUBLE; LIGHTNER DOUBLE; MAXIMAL OVERCALL DOUBLE; NEGATIVE DOUBLE; OPTIONAL DOUBLE; PENALTY PASS; RESCUE; RESPONSES OVER OPPONENT'S TAKEOUT DOUBLE; RESPONSIVE DOUBLE; SNAPDRAGON; STRIPED-TAILED APE DOUBLE; SUPPORT DOUBLE; SUCKER'S DOUBLE; TRANSFERS OVER DOUBLES OF ONE NOTRUMP; TWO NOTRUMP OVER TAKEOUT DOUBLE; WRIGGLE; as well as PENALTY DOUBLES and TAKEOUT DOUBLES

DOUBLES OF ARTIFICIAL BIDS FOR PENALTIES.

At a high level the situation is clear-cut. A player who doubles a response to BLACKWOOD, or a GERBER 4♣ bid, for example, is showing strength in the suit he has doubled in the hope of directing his partner to the right opening lead. There is a negative inference which is sometimes overlooked: the player who does not double a conventional bid on his right usually does not want that suit led.

At a low level, other considerations come into play. The double for business is the standard treatment when the hand seems sure to belong to the side that is doubled. This would apply if the bid doubled is: a conventional 2♣; a conventional response (negative or ace-showing) to a conventional 2♣; or a Stayman response to 2 NT or a standard (strong) notrump. See also FISHER DOUBLE.

When the doubling side may well have the majority of the high-card strength, the double may be put to better use by partnership agreement — either to show general strength or in some more specialized way. Each situation needs examination in relation to the convention used by the opponent. See DOUBLE OF TWO CLUB RESPONSE TO NOTRUMP; JACOBY TRANSFER BIDS; ONE CLUB SYSTEMS; ROMAN SYSTEM; TEXAS; and WEAK NOTRUMP. For an alternative treatment of

all such situations, see TWO-SUITER conventions.

DOUBLES OF NOTRUMP BIDS.

In principle, such doubles are for penalties, and partner is not expected to take out the double unless he has a very poor defensive hand with a long suit. There is one important exception:

WEST	NORTH	EAST	SOUTH
1 ♥	Pass	1 NT	Dbl

It is probably more useful to reserve South's double for a hand which would make a takeout double of 1♥ than for the rarer hand which would wish to punish 1 NT, although North may often choose to pass for penalties.

A number of situations deserve separate comment:

(1) *Doubles of strong notrump openings.* A very rare action, seldom justified unless a long strong suit is held together with side entries. Partner should hardly ever take out the double. A player with a balanced 17-point hand should usually pass a notrump opening, because the likely losses from doubling exceed the likely profits. The meaning of the double does not vary in fourth seat, and the opening leader tends to lead a short suit. For alternative treatments, see DEFENSE TO ONE NOTRUMP.

(2) *Doubles of weak notrump openings.* A double by second hand should be at least as strong as the opening bid, and a good suit to lead is desirable but not essential. To pass a weak notrump with a balanced 15-point hand runs a serious risk of missing a game; to double with less leads to trouble when the opener's side has the balance of strength.

The double by fourth hand is a theoretical problem. Apparently the fact that opener's partner has passed should encourage the fourth player, but this is deceptive. Experienced players do not pass very weak hands when their partners have opened with 1NT, instead they scramble out into a suit at the level of two in an attempt to avert disaster. So when 1NT has been passed, the opener's side is more likely than not to hold the balance of strength, and the fourth player should be cautious about doubling. (But this sort of thinking might permit the third player to try a doublecross by passing with a near-yarborough.) Conversely, the fourth player should double a two level suit takeout by third hand with any hand he would have doubled an opening weak notrump on his right. Many players extend this treatment to a double of a Stayman response to allow for the possibility that third hand is taking evasive action (see DOUBLE OF TWO CLUBS RESPONSE TO NOTRUMP); this gives up the lead-directing double of a Stayman bid based on clubs.

The doubler's partner should take out only with a long suit and a very weak hand.

(3) *Double of a 1NT overcall.* By third player this is a simple indication that he has at least 8-9 points and therefore expects his side to have the balance of strength. This principle applies to most notrump doubles: the double is made when the doubler thinks it more likely than not that his side has more than 20 high-card points. If the opener doubles 1 NT, either by second or fourth hand, he shows a maximum one-bid, probably 19-21 in high cards.

(4) *Doubles of 3 NT are often lead-directing.* See LEAD-DIRECTING DOUBLE.

(5) *Double of a notrump rebid.*

WEST	NORTH	EAST	SOUTH
			1 ♣
Pass	1 ♥	Pass	1 NT
Dbl			

or

WEST	NORTH	EAST	SOUTH
			1 ♣
Pass	1 ♥	Pass	1 NT
Pass	Pass	Dbl	

In both sequences the double is intended for penalties. In the first case West has club strength, and in the second case East has heart strength.

(6) *Third hand problems.* When an opening 1NT bid is doubled, the opening bidder's partner has four standard options.

(a) *Redouble.* A call indicating that the opener's side has the majority of the high-card strength, and that a penalty should be available if the doubling side escapes into a suit. A frequent action holding 9 points or more opposite a weak (12-14) notrump. Opposite a standard (16-18) notrump, 5 points is theoretically sufficient, but slightly more is desirable in view of the likelihood that the doubler has a good suit to lead.

(b) *Two notrump.* A bid with no natural meaning, because a strong balanced hand would always redouble. It is therefore treated as a type of cuebid, and is likely to be based on a strong two-suited hand.

(c) *Two clubs.* Not Stayman after a double. It is normally a natural bid with a long club suit, and should be assumed to be so by the opener. However, the bid is often made on a weak unbalanced hand with the intention of making an SOS redouble when doubled. This would be an appropriate action with a 4-4-4-1 distribution, for example.

(d) *Three of a suit.* An unlikely action opposite a standard notrump. Opposite a weak notrump it would be preemptive, with a six-card suit and no game ambitions.

For other options available to the partner of the opening notrump bidder, see DEFENSE TO DOUBLE OF ONE NOTRUMP.

DOUBLETON. An original holding of two cards in a suit. If an opening lead is made from a doubleton, the top card is customarily led first. (A low lead from a doubleton is normal in Poland.) For evaluation of a doubleton, see DISTRIBUTIONAL POINT-COUNT.

DOUBLY IMPROPER CALL. A call which is irregular in two respects, such as an insufficient bid out of rotation. See LAWS (Law 31).

DOWN. Defeated; said of a declarer who has failed to make a contract. The term is used in various ways, such as "We are down two" or "down 800," meaning the side has failed to make a contract by two tricks or has incurred a penalty of 800 points.

DRAW FOR PARTNERS. See LAWS (Law 3).

DRAWING TRUMPS. The action of removing the trumps from the opponents' hands. When he first gains the lead, declarer tends to draw trumps, but must be careful not to remove cards from his own hand or dummy which are necessary for some other purposes. There are various considerations which may persuade declarer to postpone drawing trumps.

Ruffs. Declarer may need to ruff some of his losers in the dummy. It may be necessary to give the lead to the opponents in the process of establishing and taking the ruffs, and they may lead trumps at every opportunity. Declarer must leave at least enough trumps in dummy to

take care of his losers while allowing for such trump leads by the defense (see CROSSRUFF).

Entries. Often declarer can use dummy's trumps as entries. These entries may be required for finesses or development of a side suit in declarer's hand. If no other entries are available, these plays must be made while drawing trumps.

Sometimes declarer plans to establish dummy's suit. Once it has been established, the trump suit may provide the only entry to dummy. If this delayed entry would not be available after drawing trumps and taking ruffs in dummy, then either play must be postponed, and dummy's suit established first. Eventually the dummy may be entered by drawing the last trump, or by means of a ruff.

Stoppers. Dummy's trumps may serve as stoppers in a certain suit. However, it may not be expedient for declarer to ruff all his losers in that suit; instead he plans to establish discards, which may entail losing the lead to the opponents. Declarer seeks to leave one trump in dummy (to stop the opponents' suit) for each time he must lose the lead in this fashion.

Declarer may be able to use his trumps or dummy's trumps as stoppers. He may be unable to ruff in his hand lest he lose trump control. Therefore he must leave enough trumps in the dummy to cope with the opponents' suit while he proceeds with the development of the hand.

Timing. Declarer may put off drawing trumps because his play for the hand as a whole requires him to deal first with other matters:

(1) Declarer may seek to establish a quick discard for a potential loser before the defenders can establish and cash their trick in that suit.

(2) Declarer has a side-suit which is not solid. Unless he has abundant trumps it is best to test the side-suit before all the trumps are drawn. This is important if the trump suit is broken.

(3) Declarer has a choice between the ruffing game and the long suit plan (particularly if the long suit is in dummy). By leading the long suit at once, declarer can vary his plan according to circumstances.

Weakness. If the trump length and strength is shared about equally between the two sides, declarer should usually avoid trump leads:

NORTH
J 5 4

SOUTH
K 9 7 2

In such situations South can hope to collect two or three trump tricks by leaving his holding intact for the end game.

But with extreme weakness in trumps, declarer is on the defensive. He may need to lead trumps to avoid opposing ruffs.

Master Trump. Declarer usually ceases to draw trumps when one defender has one or two master trumps. But a trump continuation may still be desirable to achieve a throw-in, or simply to get rid of the lead; and it may be necessary to drive out a master trump which would otherwise interrupt the run of dummy's established suit at a time when dummy has no remaining entry.

DRIVE OUT. To force the play of a high card, i.e., to lead or play a card sufficiently high in rank to force the play of an adverse commanding card to win the trick, or to continue until this result is achieved.

DROP. To capture an adverse potential winning card by the direct lead of a higher card or series of higher cards, as to drop an unguarded king by the play of an ace; also, the play which endeavors to capture an adverse card, as to "play for the drop," instead of finessing.

Whether to finesse or play for the drop is generally a case of determining the correct mathematical probabilities. However, this preference is considerably modified by information derived from the bidding and play, and it is the policy of good players to obtain as much information as possible, inferential as well as exact, before committing themselves. For example:

WEST	NORTH	EAST	SOUTH
1♣	Pass	Pass	1 NT
Pass	3 NT	All Pass	

If during the play, East shows up with an ace or king, it is highly unlikely that he will hold another high honor, since he passed his partner in 1♣. It would therefore be indicated for South to disregard the mathematical probabilities and confidently place all missing honors in the West hand.

DRURY. A conventional 2♣ response by a PASSED HAND after partner's major-suit opening.

WEST	EAST
Pass	1♠
2♣	

The 2♣ bid asks opener to clarify his strength. West might hold:

♠ Q 9 2		♠ J 10 5
♥ 10 6 4	or	♥ A 5 4 2
♦ A K 7 4		♦ A J 8 5
♣ Q 4 3		♣ 9 3

Without Drury, West has no attractive action: a single raise is an underbid; a double raise with only three trumps and poor distribution is inappropriate; a natural response of 2♣ might be passed, and even if opener bid again, responder might have to go to the three level to show the spade support.

The convention works similarly after a 1♥ opening, though its frequency of use may be slightly lower because responder often bids 1♠.

Douglas Drury devised Drury, so the story goes, as protection from the feather-light third-hand openings of his partner Eric Murray. The convention as employed by most modern pairs differs in some respects from Drury's original version.

In the original, a 2♦ rebid by opener suggested a subminimum opening. Responder could then sign off at two of opener's major. However, a 1984 poll of experts showed a preference — by a margin of more than two to one — for a rebid of the major suit as opener's weak action. Any other rebid suggests a sound opening. Hence, the variation once known as REVERSE DRURY is now standard.

A few partnerships play Drury in competition:

WEST	NORTH	EAST	SOUTH
			Pass
Pass	1♥	1♠	2♣

Some players use 2♦ additionally, showing 4-card support, with 2♣ showing exactly 3-card support. This is useful to the opener if he has a distributional hand. (Suggested by Marty Bergen.) See STRONG NOTRUMP AFTER PASSING.

DUB. At bridge, a dub is a player whose game is below the standards of the players with whom he competes.

DUCK. To play a small card, and surrender a trick which could be won, with the object of preserving an ENTRY. When the suit has been led by an opponent, the duck is mechanically identical to a HOLD-UP, in that a master card (or cards) is retained, but the objective is different. A player ducks in order to pursue his own aims, but holds up in order to thwart the opponents.

A *COUP EN BLANC* is a ducking play for the purpose of winning a later trick.

Apart from a considerable number of situations listed under SAFETY PLAY, ducking plays may be listed under five main headings:

(1) *Suit combinations.* To make the maximum number of tricks in notrump with no side entry to dummy:

(a)	(b)
A K x x x	A Q x x x
x x or x x x	x x or x x x

In (a) the first trick is ducked and the declarer hopes for an even split to make four tricks; with three small, he may duck once to score four tricks, twice to insure making three tricks against a 4-1 split.

The situation in (b) is similar, but declarer finesses on the second round; if declarer has three small cards, the first-round duck is slightly better than a finesse followed by a duck because right-hand opponent might hold a singleton king.

(c)	(d)
K Q 10 7 x x	K J 8 x x x x
x x	x x

These are harder, and declarer needs more optimism. In each case he must duck the first trick completely in the hope of finding the right-hand opponent with a singleton ace. If the required situation does exist, it would be brilliant play for the left-hand opponent to play his highest card in an attempt to deflect declarer from his purpose.

(2) *Trap combination.* In notrump with no side entry in dummy:

(e)	(f)	(g)
A Q J x x x	A Q J x x	A Q 10 x x x
x x	x x x	x x x

In each case a small card is led, and left-hand opponent plays the king. A duck ensures the loss of only one trick, and is essential in (e): if left-hand opponent has brilliantly played the king from a doubleton or tripleton, he has gained a trick for his side.

In (f) and (g) declarer does slightly better to win the first trick, return to his hand, and plan to duck the second round if the king was singleton; but he requires a convenient entry, and there may be an AVOIDANCE consideration.

(h)	(i)
A K x x x	A Q x x x
J 10	J 10

If declarer's lead is covered, he must duck and hope for a 3-3 division. The only hope of five tricks is for left-hand opponent to fail to cover holding Q-x-x (or K-x-x). It is therefore better to lead the 10, following the principle of leading low from a sequence when you wish to avoid a cover.

(j)   (k)
A x x x x   A x x x x

Q J x   J 10 9

In both cases declarer leads a high card and must duck if left-hand opponent covers. In (k) the jack is the best lead: declarer plans to follow with the 9. If left-hand opponent is left with a doubleton honor, he may make the mistake of playing low, and declarer makes four tricks.

(3) *Double and triple.* Again in notrump with no side entry to dummy:

(l)   (m)
A x x x x   A 9 x x x

x x x   x x x x

With (l) two ducks and a 3-2 split are needed to make three tricks. (m) requires one duck if the suit splits 2-2, giving four tricks; a 3-1 split requires two ducks, and gives three tricks; a 4-0 split requires three ducks and gives two tricks. This is the only possible situation for a triple duck.

(4) *Control.* In a trump contract:

(n)   (o)   (p)
x x   A x   A x x

A x x   x x x   x x x

Declarer usually ducks with (n) unless there is a possibility of a 7-1 division. This prepares for a ruff in dummy without the need for a side entry, and retains control of the suit if the opponents shift: this may be most important if they are able to draw dummy's trumps.

Declarer would not duck with (o) if a ruff is the only consideration, but it may be right to duck for control reasons. If the defenders can prevent a ruff, declarer is better placed with the ace still in dummy.

The duck with (p) could also be described as a hold-up. It interferes with the defensive communications, and may prevent the defense taking a second trick if the suit is divided 5-2.

(5) *Defensive.* A defender in a trump contract often ducks to prepare for a ruff by his side or in order to prevent a ruff by declarer:

(q)   (r)
WEST   EAST   WEST   EAST
x x   A x x x   x x   A x x

In (q) West leads a doubleton in a side suit in the hope of getting a ruff. East ducks if he can judge that the lead is more likely to be a doubleton than a singleton, and if he thinks that West is more likely to secure the lead.

The objective is reversed in (r), although the mechanics are the same. West leads a doubleton trump aiming to prevent a ruff in the dummy. Again East ducks if he judges that West has a doubleton and the likely entry.

The suit combination plays described above for the declarer are also available for the defenders, almost always in notrump contracts. Some ducks that are simple for the declarer are very much harder for the defense:

(s)   (t)
x x   J x x
K x x   A x x x x   K x x x x   A x x
Q J 10   Q x

In (s) West leads low and an entryless East must duck. In (t) the duck can be on the first or second round. The first-round duck may have the advantage of depriving dummy of an entry, because declarer can drop the queen under the ace. This would only lose if the lead was from

Q-x-x-x specifically. See also THIRD-HAND PLAY.

DUEL. A two-handed form of bridge invented by Norman B. Hasselriis, and described by him in *The Bridge World* magazine for February 1950. See HONEYMOON BRIDGE.

DUFFER. A bridge player of inferior ability.

DUKE OF CUMBERLAND HAND. A phenomenal hand at whist. The Duke of Cumberland, son of George III, King of England, was an inveterate gambler for high stakes. One day, at the notorious gaming rooms in Bath, it is said that he was dealt the following hand:

♠ A K Q   ♥ A K Q J   ♦ A K   ♣ K J 9 7

The game being whist, the last card, a club, was turned to set the trump suit. The Duke, sitting at dealer's left, had the opening lead. In accordance with sound whist precepts, he opened the ♣7. Obviously it was to his interest to knock out all the opponents' trumps as quickly as possible to avoid the ruffing of any of his solid top cards.

The Duke's opponents proceeded to assert that he would not win a single trick, and to infuriate him into a bet. The complete deal was:

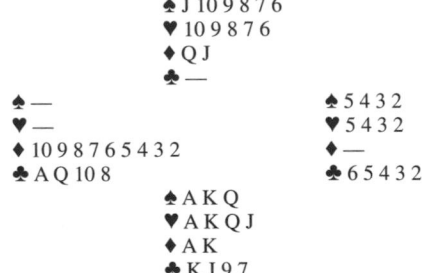

West won the ♣ 7 with the 8, and led a diamond which was trumped by his partner. East returned a club, the Duke's 9 being taken by the 10, and a second diamond was trumped by East. East led his last trump into his partner's tenace over the Duke, and West won and led the final trump from his hand, felling the Duke's king. West's seven established diamonds won the last seven tricks.

This display of virtuosity by East-West allegedly cost the Duke the sum of 20,000 pounds or nearly $100,000.

Such is the story of the Duke of Cumberland's Hand as related by Professor Richard A. Proctor in *How to Play Whist* (1885). One wonders why the Duke, an experienced whist player, did not speculate on how his opponents could foretell the outcome. (Remember that no hand is exposed in whist.) A more plausible version of this legendary episode suggests that the South hand was given to the Duke, who knew that it was manufactured and ventured to bet in the face of that knowledge.

The victim may have been an earlier duke, "Butcher" Cumberland, son of George II, but the scant evidence favors the later duke. See DISTRIBUTIONAL VALUES.

DUMB BIDDER. A British device to permit silent bidding. It consists of a small board placed in the center of the table on which the four suits, notrump, numbers from 1 to 7, double, redouble, and pass are inscribed. Each player makes his bid by tapping the appropriate sections with a pencil. This avoids any possible revealing inflections. For alternative silent methods see BIDDING BOX,

SLIDING BOX, WRITTEN BIDDING.

DUMMY. (1) The declarer's partner after he has placed his cards face up on the table, which is done immediately after the opening lead is faced by the opponent on the declarer's left; (2) the cards held by the declarer's partner, also called the dummy's hand. The name originated in dummy whist, in which there were only three players, the fourth hand being exposed as the "dummy," an imaginary and silent player (see HISTORY OF BRIDGE). The dummy in bridge takes no part in the play; he may not suggest by word or gesture any lead or play, but at the conclusion of play he may call attention to errors of play or violations of law. The dummy may ask his partner if he has any or none of the suit led, to prevent a revoke. If the dummy looks at his partner's hand or the hand of either adversary, he forfeits his right to protect his partner from revoking. See LAWS (Laws 42, 43).

DUMMY BRIDGE. A form of bridge for three. Player cutting low plays as dummy's partner for the entire game or rubber. Usually only single games are played before a new cut, the winner scoring a bonus of 50 points. Dealer or his partner names the trump suit. Dummy deals first and partner declares, having looked only at the dummy hand. When an opponent deals, however, he may pass to his partner the right to name trumps. Dealer's left-hand opponent is the only player who may double. The dummy is not exposed until after the opening lead. Otherwise, play is as in BRIDGE WHIST.

One theory of the origin of AUCTION BRIDGE attributes it to a game in which three British officers in a post in India remote from any fourth player evolved the idea of bidding for the dummy.

DUMMY PLAY. The management of the assets of the declarer and the dummy; synonymous with "declarer's play." The subject is dealt with under the following general headings: COUP; ENDPLAY; FINESSE; MATHEMATICS OF BRIDGE; SQUEEZE; TRUMP PLAY. Also under the following particular titles: ASSUMPTIONS IN PLAY; AVOIDANCE; BACKWARD FINESSE; BLACKWOOD THEORY OF DISTRIBUTION; BLOCK; BLOCKING; CARD READING; CARDS, NEUTRAL AND POSITIVE; CONTROL; COUNTING THE HAND; CRASHING HONORS; CROSSRUFF; DECEPTION, MATHEMATICS OF; DECEPTIVE PLAY; DEEP FINESSE; DESPERATION LEAD OR PLAY; DISCOVERY; DRAWING TRUMPS; DROP; DUCK; DUMMY REVERSAL; DUMMY'S FIRST TRICK PLAY; ECONOMY OF HONORS; ENTRY; EXIT PLAY; EXPECTATION; FALSECARDING; GAMBIT; GROSVENOR GAMBIT; HOLD UP; IMP TACTICS; INFERENCE; JETTISON; LOSER ON LOSER; MATCHPOINT PLAY; NEGATIVE INFERENCE; OBLIGATORY FINESSE; OPTIONS; OVERTAKE; PERCENTAGE PLAY; PLAY FROM EQUALS; PROBABILITIES; RESTRICTED CHOICE; RUFF AND DISCARD; RUFF AND RUFF; RUFFING FINESSE; RULE OF ELEVEN; SAFETY PLAY; SHOOTING; SINGLE-DUMMY PROBLEMS; SINGLETON KING; SMOTHER PLAY; SPOT CARDS; SUIT COMBINATIONS; THROW-IN; TRUMP PICK-UP; TRUMP SUIT MANAGEMENT; TWO-WAY FINESSE; UNBLOCKING; UNDERRUFF.

DUMMY REVERSAL. A procedure by which the dummy is made the master hand. Generally speaking, it is advantageous to ruff only in the hand that contains shorter trumps, but in a dummy reversal extra tricks may sometimes be developed by ruffing in the long hand and later using dummy's trumps to extract those of the opponents.

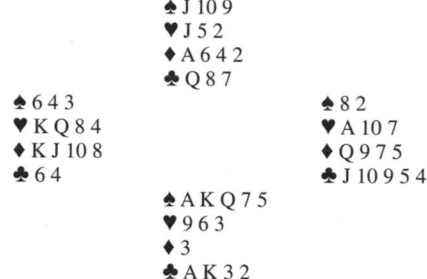

South plays in 4♠, and the defense cash their three heart tricks before shifting to a diamond. Superficially it seems that declarer must bank on an even division in clubs or alternatively draw two rounds of trumps and then attempt to ruff the fourth club in dummy in case they divide unevenly. Both these lines are inferior to the dummy reversal which requires only a 3-2 break in trumps. Dummy wins the diamond, and a low diamond is ruffed with the ♠A. Dummy is re-entered twice in spades — declarer conserving his small trumps for that purpose — to ruff the remaining diamonds with the king and queen, leaving this position:

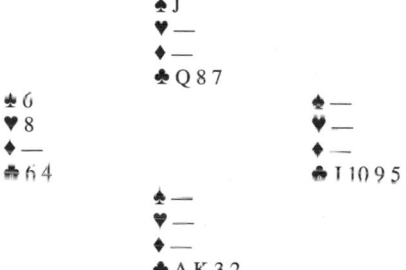

Declarer now crosses to dummy's ♣Q, and leads the ♠J, extracting the last trump upon which he discards his losing club, and takes the last two tricks with the ♣A-K.

Sometimes the decision to "reverse," or establish the dummy in preference to his hand, is forced upon declarer by the character of his trump suit.

♠ A K J
♥ 10 2
♦ A J 8 7 3
♣ A 9 8

♠ 3 2   ♠ 10 9 4
♥ 7 5 4   ♥ Q J 9 3
♦ Q 9 5 4   ♦ K 10 6
♣ Q J 10 2   ♣ 6 5 4

♠ Q 8 7 6 5
♥ A K 8 6
♦ 2
♣ K 7 3

The contract is 6♠, and West leads the ♣Q. If declarer attempts to ruff his losing hearts in dummy he will promote a trump trick for East which together with the club loser will spell defeat. However, by ruffing three of dummy's diamonds in his hand — establishing the fifth diamond in the process — he can utilize dummy's trumps for drawing purposes. That way he makes his slam, losing only a club trick.

DUMMY WHIST. A variety of WHIST for three. The player who draws the lowest card plays with the dummy as his partner. The last card dealt is turned as trumps. Dummy is not exposed until after the opening lead is made. Each trick over book (6) counts as one point. Seven points are game.

DUMMY'S FIRST TRICK PLAY. Most of the problems concerning the choice of plays from dummy at the first trick relate to doubleton honors. An interesting rule, suggested by M. D. Macdonald of Greenboro NC, covers the play with Q-x and J-x when declarer has at least one honor:

Play low from dummy if the opponents have *exactly* two significant honors. In table form:

| | doubleton queen | |
declarer has	significant honors	play
A-10-x	K-J	low
K-10-x	A-J	low
J-x-x	A-K	low
A-x-(x)	K	high
A-9-x	K-J-10	high
10-x-x	A-K-J	high
A-J-x	K	high
K-x-(x)	A	high

(doubtful case K-9-x, in which the right play varies with circumstances.)

| | doubleton jack | |
declarer has	significant honors	play
A-10-x	K-Q	low
Q-x-x	A-K	low
K-10-x	A-Q	low
A-K-x	Q	high
A-Q-x	K	high
A-9-x	K-Q-10	high
K-9-x	A-Q-10	high

(Two obvious exceptions: A-x-x and K-x-x).

When dummy has more than two cards, it is usually right to play low at the first trick, but there are some obvious exceptions. Play high, for example, with Q-x-x facing nothing, or J-x-x facing A-K-x.

Special circumstances may call for special plays:

(a)	(b)
A-x-x	K-10-x
J-x-x	Q-x-x

In (a) the play of the ace may block the suit. East would have to have a doubleton king or queen. But if he has a quick entry he can unblock effectively.

In (b) it is sometimes right to play the king from dummy. If East has A-J-9-x-x he will have to win and cannot continue. If dummy plays low East can play the 9, ready to run the suit if West gains the lead.

DUMMY'S FORFEITURE OF RIGHTS. This is invoked if the player whose hand is the dummy intentionally looks at his partner's or an opponent's hand. He then forfeits his privileges as far as protecting his partner against revokes or leading from the wrong hand. See LAWS (Laws 42, 43).

DUMMY'S HAND. It is the responsibility of all the

players equally that dummy's hand shall be a proper one. No revoke can be claimed as a result of an improper play from the dummy. See DUMMY.

DUMMY'S RIGHTS AND LIMITATIONS. Dummy has certain absolute and limited rights as described in LAWS OF DUPLICATE (Laws 42, 43). In a rubber bridge game, particularly under social conditions in the home, the old rule of *courtesy of the table* required that the opponents inquire of the declarer whether a play to a trick constituted a revoke, and failure to so inquire waived the right to a penalty for such a revoke.

DUOBRIDGE. A four-handed bridge game for two players invented by Art Kaplan of Merrick NY in 1977. The game is played with a regular 52-card deck. It is unique as a two-player bridge game in that the players play as partners against imaginary opponents. The key to the game is the DuoBridge Deal, a semi-random deal of the cards based on mathematical principles that enable the players to feel they are actually participating in a four-handed game. See HONEYMOON BRIDGE.

DUPLICATE. A term applied to the playing of the same deal of cards by more than one table of players; successively applied to whist, auction bridge and contract bridge. See DUPLICATE BRIDGE and HISTORY OF BRIDGE.

DUPLICATE, MATHEMATICS OF MATCHPOINT. See MATHEMATICS OF MATCHPOINT PLAY.

DUPLICATE BOARD. See BOARD, DUPLICATE.

DUPLICATE BRIDGE. The form of bridge in which the same hand is played more than once. Each competing unit (which may be an individual, pair or team) seeks to perform better than one or more other units playing the identical deals in similar circumstances. The luck of the deal, so important in rubber bridge, is therefore eliminated to a large extent, and bridge becomes a satisfactory test of skill. (But see CHANCE.)

Cavendish, the great whist authority, organized what amounted to a duplicate whist match by getting four experts, sitting North-South at one table and East-West at the other, against four ordinary players. As he predicted, the experts won far more than half the tricks available.

The first application of the duplicate idea dates from whist. The pioneer in this field was JOHN T. MITCHELL, who invented the first pair movement and whose book on duplicate whist was published in 1891. The long series of American Whist League Championships began in the same year. (See HISTORY OF BRIDGE.)

The duplicate principle was never applied to the original game of bridge (see BRIDGE WHIST) which flourished in the decade 1894-1904. It was generally believed that bridge, unlike whist, was not a suitable game for serious competition. This was perhaps partly because at this stage of its development bridge permitted unlimited redoubles, which emphasized the gambling element in the game and gave it a poker-like character.

The first games of duplicate auction bridge were apparently held in 1914 under the auspices of the American Whist League, but another 10 years elapsed before a national auction tournament was staged.

The application of duplicate to contract bridge was a rapid development, and the first national championship was held in 1928, when the game was less than three years old, under the auspices of the AMERICAN (auction) BRIDGE LEAGUE.

The most popular form of duplicate is the weekly club game. This usually consists of a pair event of 21 to 28 boards, lasting some 3° hours. The number of tables varies widely. Usually the players pay a card fee. Many clubs run several games a week, and a few clubs in large metropolitan areas run games each afternoon and evening throughout the year.

North American players wishing to join a club can obtain free copies of a booklet entitled "Easy Guide to Duplicate" and of a Directory of Clubs by applying to ACBL HEADQUARTERS. In other nations interested persons should apply to the national contract bridge organization. Most such organizations are listed in this book under the name of the country.

Duplicate bridge can be a satisfying home game for eight players. (See TWO TABLES.) It is also very popular as part of the recreation program of commercial and industrial organizations.

For the more complex organization of tournaments above the club level, see AMERICAN CONTRACT BRIDGE LEAGUE and CHAMPIONSHIP TOURNAMENTS.

The mechanics of play at duplicate are covered in LAWS OF DUPLICATE BRIDGE, Laws 2-8. In order to make replay of the hand possible, some modification of the mechanics of the deal, shuffle and gathering of tricks from those of RUBBER BRIDGE or CHICAGO is necessary.

Essentially, the mechanics of duplicate require the following steps:

(1) Getting the right boards and correct opponents to the table. See MOVEMENTS.

(2) Withdrawal of the hand to be played from the board, counting the cards to ascertain the correctness of the hand.

(3) Determination of vulnerability and dealer on the board (see BOARD, DUPLICATE). The bidding then proceeds as in rubber bridge.

(4) The play to the trick. Instead of playing to the center of the table, each player faces his contribution or lead face up, in front of him, in turn. When the four cards have been played to the trick, each player turns his card face down, in a line, in front of him. The card is pointed toward his partner if they have won the trick, but placed with the length from right to left if the trick was won by the opposition.

(5) Determination of and agreement about the result. All four players should, as a result of the preceding paragraph, agree as to the number of tricks won by the declarer. If disagreement exists, the cards should not be disturbed, but the result should be determined by the director, who should be summoned.

(6) Recounting the cards and replacing them in the pockets of the duplicate board.

At duplicate every deal is scored separately. Neither partscores nor games bid and made carry over to the next deal. Whenever one side scores a game or a partscore they collect, in addition to the trick score, an immediate bonus:

For making a vulnerable game   500
For making a nonvulnerable game   300
For making a part score   50

Honors do not count at duplicate. In all other respects the scoring is the same as at rubber bridge.

Articles dealing with various aspects of handling duplicate tournaments are: TWO, THREE, FOUR, etc., to FIFTEEN TABLES; MOVEMENT: AMERICAN WHIST, BARCLAY, BLACKPOOL, BUMP MITCHELL, CYCLIC, HOWELL, INDIVIDUAL, MCKENNEY-BALDWIN, RAINBOW INDIVIDUAL, ROVER, SCRAMBLED MITCHELL, SHORT HOWELL, SWISS, TEAM-OF-FOUR MOVEMENTS, BOARD-A-MATCH TEAMS, THREE-QUARTER HOWELL; ADJUSTED SCORE, APPENDIX TABLE, ARROW, ARROW SWITCH, ASSIGNMENT OF SEATS, BALANCED COMPARISONS, BREAKING TIES, BYESTAND, CALIFORNIA SCORING, CARRY-OVER SCORES, CONVENTION CARD, CURTAILING, MOVEMENT DURING PLAY, DUPLICATE SCORING, ENTRIES, FACTORING, FOULED BOARD, HALF TABLE, HAND RECORDS, HYBRID SCORING, INTERNATIONAL MATCHPOINTS, TABLE, COMPUTER HANDS, MATCHPOINT, POSTING THE SCORE, PRIVATE SCORECARD, RECTIFICATION, ROUND-ROBIN, SCORING CORRECTIONS, SEED/SEEDING, SLOW PLAY, STARTING TIME, SUBSTITUTE, SUSPENSION, TRAVELING SCORE, TOURNAMENT DIRECTOR.

DUPLICATE BRIDGE LAWS. See LAWS OF DUPLICATE.

DUPLICATE SCORING. The scoring of each deal is covered by the provisions of Laws 77 and 78 of the LAWS OF DUPLICATE. The following scoring table lists all possible duplicate results:

		Not Vulnerable			Vulnerable	
Bid Made		Undbl	Dbl	Rdbl	Undbl	Dbl	Rdbl
1♣ - 1♦	1	70	140	230	70	140	230
	2	90	240	430	90	340	630
	3	110	340	630	110	540	1030
	4	130	440	830	130	740	1430
	5	150	540	1030	150	940	1830
	6	170	640	1230	170	1140	2230
	7	190	740	1430	190	1340	2630
1♥ - 1♠	1	80	160	520	80	160	720
	2	110	260	720	110	360	1120
	3	140	360	920	140	560	1520
	4	170	460	1120	170	760	1920
	5	200	560	1320	200	960	2320
	6	230	660	1520	230	1160	2720
	7	260	760	1720	260	1360	3120
1 NT	1	90	180	560	90	180	760
	2	120	280	760	120	380	1160
	3	150	380	960	150	580	1560
	4	180	480	1160	180	780	1960
	5	210	580	1360	210	980	2360
	6	240	680	1560	240	1180	2760
	7	270	780	1760	270	1380	3160
2♣ - 2♦	2	90	180	560	90	180	760
	3	110	280	760	110	380	1160
	4	130	380	960	130	580	1560
	5	150	480	1160	150	780	1960
	6	170	580	1360	170	980	2360
	7	190	680	1560	190	1180	2760
2♥ - 2♠	2	110	470	640	110	670	840
	3	140	570	840	140	870	1240
	4	170	670	1040	170	1070	1640
	5	200	770	1240	200	1270	2040
	6	230	870	1440	230	1470	2440

	7	260	970	1640	260	1670	2840

2 NT							
	2	120	490	680	120	690	880
	3	150	590	880	150	890	1280
	4	180	690	1080	180	1090	1680
	5	210	790	1280	210	1290	2080
	6	240	890	1480	240	1490	2480
	7	270	990	1680	270	1690	2880

3♣ - 3♦							
	3	110	470	640	110	670	840
	4	130	570	840	130	870	1240
	5	150	670	1040	150	1070	1640
	6	170	770	1240	170	1270	2040
	7	190	870	1440	190	1470	2440

3♥ - 3♠							
	3	140	530	760	140	730	960
	4	170	630	960	170	930	1360
	5	200	730	1160	200	1130	1760
	6	230	830	1360	230	1330	2160
	7	260	930	1560	260	1530	2560

3 NT							
	3	400	550	800	600	750	1000
	4	430	650	1000	630	950	1400
	5	460	750	1200	660	1150	1800
	6	490	850	1400	690	1350	2200
	7	520	950	1600	720	1550	2600

4♣ - 4♦							
	4	130	510	720	130	710	920
	5	150	610	920	150	910	1320
	6	170	710	1120	170	1110	1720
	7	190	810	1320	190	1310	2120

4♥ - 4♠							
	4	420	590	880	620	790	1080
	5	450	690	1080	650	990	1480
	6	480	790	1280	680	1190	1880
	7	510	890	1480	710	1390	2280

4 NT							
	4	430	610	920	630	810	1120
	5	460	710	1120	660	1010	1520
	6	490	810	1320	690	1210	1920
	7	520	910	1520	720	1410	2320

5♣ - 5♦							
	5	400	550	800	600	750	1000
	6	420	650	1000	620	950	1400
	7	440	750	1200	640	1150	1800

5♣ - 5♦							
	5	450	650	1000	650	850	1200
	6	480	750	1200	680	1050	1600
	7	510	850	1400	710	1250	2000

5 NT							
	5	460	670	1040	660	870	1240
	6	490	770	1240	690	1070	1640
	7	520	870	1440	720	1270	2040

6♣ - 6♦							
	6	920	1090	1380	1370	1540	1830
	7	940	1190	1580	1390	1740	2230

6♥ - 6♠							
	6	980	1210	1620	1430	1660	2070
	7	1010	1310	1820	1460	1860	2470

6 NT							
	6	990	1230	1660	1440	1680	2110
	7	1020	1330	1860	1470	1880	2510

7♣ - 7♦							
	7	1440	1630	1960	2140	2330	2660

7♥ - 7♠							
	7	1510	1770	2240	2210	2470	2940

7 NT							
	7	1520	1790	2280	2220	2490	2980

DEFEATED CONTRACTS

	Not Vulnerable			Vulnerable		
Down	Undbl	Dbl	Rdbl	Undbl	Dbl	Rdbl
1	50	100	200	100	200	400
2	100	300	600	200	500	1000

3	150	500	1000	300	800	1600
4	200	800	1600	400	1100	2200
5	250	1100	2200	500	1400	2800
6	300	1400	2800	600	1700	3400
7	350	1700	3400	700	2000	4000
8	400	2000	4000	800	2300	4600
9	450	2300	4600	900	2600	5200
10	500	2600	5200	1000	2900	5800
11	550	2900	5800	1100	3200	6400
12	600	3200	6400	1200	3500	7000
13	650	3500	7000	1300	3800	7600

After the score on any hand has been determined according to this table, a comparison of results becomes possible.

Most pair events and all individual events are scored on a matchpoint basis. After all the scores have been determined on a board, 1 matchpoint is awarded to a team, pair or individual for every score that they have bettered, and ° matchpoint for every score that they have duplicated. Totaling of the matchpoint scores determines the winner for the session. When an event is held in two or more sessions without elimination, the total score is carried forward. The event winner determined by the largest total score.

Scores for a multi-session event where elimination is involved, however, do not carry over totals from the qualifying round. Carryover depends on the number of qualifying rounds and the number of final rounds and is provided for by conditions of contest. For details of the formula used in ACBL tournaments, see CARRYOVER SCORES.

For team-of-four play, there are three methods of scoring in use: BOARD-A-MATCH; TOTAL POINTS, and INTERNATIONAL MATCHPOINTs. (Other methods in use in Europe include COMBINATION TEAM SCORING and QUOTIENT SCORING.)

In board-a-match, the most common type of team competition in the United States until the introduction of the enormously popular SWISS MOVEMENT in 1967, each board is scored as 1, ° or 0 match points, depending on whether the total score on the two plays is greater than zero, zero, or less than zero. This system of scoring overemphasizes the extra trick, the notrump versus suit play, the hair-trigger partscore double. An alternative, particularly in longer matches, is total-point scoring, which, however, has the defect of being able to determine the outcome of a match on two or so major SWING hands. The International Matchpoint method, which has gained almost universal currency, is designed to eliminate the defects of both board-a-match and total-point scoring methods. In the present IMP scale (see Law 78), the small swings are rewarded with fewer points than larger swings, but the award to a large swing hand is still great in comparison.

IMP scoring may be used for pair events, where a pair's score on a board is determined by its reference to a mean score on the board (by averaging all except the upper and lower scores made) with an IMP award based on the difference. (See INTERNATIONAL MATCHPOINTS; INTERNATIONAL OPEN TEAM SELECTION.)

In Swiss Teams, scoring is based on International Matchpoints. Sometimes the win-tie-loss method is used; sometimes the IMP total is converted to Victory Points.

DUPLICATE TECHNIQUE. See IMP TACTICS; MATCHPOINT BIDDING; MATCHPOINT PLAY.

DUPLICATE TOURNAMENT. See DUPLICATE BRIDGE and CHAMPIONSHIP TOURNAMENTS.

DUPLICATE TRAY. See BOARD, DUPLICATE.

DUPLICATE WHIST. The oldest form of duplicate competition, in which movements such as the MITCHELL and HOWELL were developed.

DUPLICATING BOARDS. See TWINNING.

DUPLICATION OF DISTRIBUTION. This occurs where the suit lengths in a partnership's hands are evenly matched. A distributional flaw that limits the trick-taking potential of a pair of hands, it manifests itself in the absence of a long suit that can be developed.

♠ A Q 10	♠ K J 9
♥ K Q J 9	♥ A 10 6 2
♦ A 10 3	♦ 9 7 6
♣ 6 4 2	♣ Q 7 3

The presence of a long card in either hand would permit the development of an additional trick, but with the above distribution, no game contract is likely to be fulfilled, though sufficient values are held. Also called mirror distribution.

DUPLICATION OF VALUES. A concentration of strength and control in the same suit between two partners. When too much of the combined strength of the partnership is concentrated at one point there are likely to be serious weaknesses elsewhere and an unsound contract is often reached.

WEST	EAST
♠ A K	♠ Q J
♥ K Q J 10 4	♥ A 9 7 5
♦ A 7 5	♦ K 6 4 3
♣ 4 3 2	♣ 8 6 5

The above hands contain sufficient values to warrant a game contract in hearts, which has to fail owing to the poor division of strength in the black suits.

Another form of duplication:

WEST	EAST
♠ 6 4	♠ A K Q 8 7
♥ A J 10 4 3	♥ K Q 7 6
♦ K Q 8 5	♦ 9
♣ 9 7 5	♣ 6 4 2

A contract of 4♥ would be almost impossible to avoid, though declarer has four quick losers. Both hands contain, in effect, second-round control in spades and diamonds, leaving a glaring weakness in clubs. If West's ♦K-Q (5 points) were changed to the ace (4 points), the game would be a laydown, for now East's singleton diamond would be pulling its weight.

Certain sequences have been devised to identify duplication of values at the slam level — for example, keeping out of six where there is a prospect of two immediate losers in a suit:

WEST	EAST
1♠	3♠
4♦	4♥
5♠	

Here the opener's last bid asks partner to bid a slam if he has as good as a second-round control in the unbid suit, clubs.

In a general way, duplication can be detected when a player has a void or singleton in a suit in which his partner has indicated some strength. For example:

| WEST | NORTH | EAST |
| 1♥ | 1♠ | 1 NT |

West holds:

♠ —
♥ K Q 8 6 2
♦ A Q 9 3
♣ K J 7 4

and must tread warily, for his partner's values (in spades) seem to be misplaced for purposes of a suit contract.

DUPLIMATE. A machine that duplicates deals rapidly for use in duplicate tournaments. The machine reads bar-coded playing cards, automatically dropping the cards into the correct pockets of a duplicate board. The machines are produced by Per Jannersten of Sweden.

DUTCH BRIDGE LEAGUE. See NETHERLANDS BRIDGE LEAGUE.

DUTCH SPADE. A transfer system, developed by Max Rebattu of the Netherlands. The opening shows the next higher suit: Pass = 1♣, 1♣ = 1♦, 1♦ = 1♥, 1♥ = 1♠. The 1♠ opening is used as random, 0-10 points, any distribution. The inventor and his partner, Anton Maas, used it in finishing second in the 1982 World Pairs.

DYNAMIC NOTRUMP. A 1NT opening bid to show an unbalanced hand with 18-21 points. Developed by George Rosenkranz as a cornerstone of the ROMEX SYSTEM.

Responses are control-showing as in the BLUE TEAM style, counting an ace as two controls and a king as one. 2♣ shows no more than one control with 0-6 points; 2♦ shows less than two controls with 7 or more points; 2♥ shows two controls; 2♠ shows three controls, etc.

Opener's rebids are natural except that after a 2♣ response, 2♦ asks responder to bid a major. A notrump rebid describes a minor two-suiter.

With a balanced hand of less than 19 points, opener opens in a suit, then rebids either 1 NT with 12-16 points or 2 NT with 17-18 points.

E

EBL. See EUROPEAN BRIDGE LEAGUE.

EFOS. Economical Forcing System. See EFOS SYSTEM.

EAST. One of the four hands at the bridge table. East is the partner of West and the left-hand opponent of North.

EASTERN CUEBID. A low-level cuebid in an opponent's suit, showing a stopper in the suit. The converse, a WESTERN CUEBID, asks partner for a stopper.

EASTERN SCIENTIFIC. A style of bidding in which the principal features are strong notrump openings with non-forcing Stayman and Jacoby Transfer bids, five-card major-suit openings with a forcing 1 NT response and limit raises. Two-over-one responses are strong but not necessarily forcing to game. Other elements are weak two-bids, with a strong artificial 2♣ opening forcing to 2 NT or three of a major suit; also negative and responsive doubles. See STANDARD AMERICAN and BRIDGE WORLD STANDARD.

EASY ACES. In auction bridge, at notrump, no honors were scored when aces were divided 2-2 among the pairs.

Also, the name of a popular radio show in the Thirties associated with Goodman Ace and his wife Jane. It was a comedy series which began with a bridge theme.

ECHO. See HIGH-LOW SIGNAL.

ECONOMY OF HONORS. A playing technique intended to preserve honor cards from capture by opposing honors or trumps. The opponents can sometimes be encouraged to give up their high cards in exchange for low ones.

K Q x x

J x x

South leads twice from his own hand in order to make three tricks when West holds A-x. See ACE GRABBER , which illustrates the opposite principle.

Michael Sullivan gave these examples of economy of honors.

(1)

```
                    ♠ 10 6 3 2
                    ♥ K 6
                    ♦ K 9 6
                    ♣ 8 6 4 3
♠ K J 9 4                            ♠ Q 7
♥ Q J 8 5                            ♥ 10 4 3 2
♦ J 8 5 2                            ♦ Q 10 3
♣ A                                 ♣ J 10 9 7
                    ♠ A 8 5
                    ♥ A 9 7
                    ♦ A 7 4
                    ♣ K Q 5 2
```

South plays 1 NT and receives the lead of the ♦2 from West. Needing two club tricks and holding actual or potential stoppers in all other suits, South wins the ♦A and, as insurance against the bare ♣A in the West hand, leads a low club. The ace drops and all is well, but even if it had not, the entries and tempos are available for two subsequent leads toward the ♣K-Q-x.

(2)

```
                    ♠ K 9 6 3
                    ♥ A 10
                    ♦ A 5
                    ♣ A 6 5 3 2
♠ J                                 ♠ 10
♥ Q 8 3                             ♥ K J 7 6 4 2
♦ 10 8 4 2                          ♦ K Q 9 7 6 3
♣ K Q J 9 7                         ♣ —
                    ♠ A Q 8 7 5 4 2
                    ♥ 9 5
                    ♦ J
                    ♣ 10 8 4
```

West leads the ♣K against South's contract of 4♠. Unless the ♣A is ruffed, South has 10 certain tricks. To guard against that lone possibility, declarer ducks the first round of clubs and subsequent club leads until West either shifts to another suit or permits South to ruff the fourth round of clubs. Eventually declarer gets to discard his losing heart on the carefully preserved ♣A.

ECUADOR BRIDGE ASSOCIATION (Federacion Ecuatoriana de Bridge).

Secretary 1992:
Ernesto Salgado Burbano
Rep. del Salvador 750 y Portugal
Quito, Ecuador
Fax: 593 2 437881

EDUCATIONAL FOUNDATION. Foundations established by the American Contract Bridge League and the World Bridge Federation to foster the spread of bridge awareness through education. See ACBL EDUCATIONAL FOUNDATION and WORLD BRIDGE FEDERATION.

EFOS SYSTEM. The "economical forcing system" used in international championships by leading Swedish players such as Jan Wohlin, Nils Olaf Lilliehook, and Gunnar Anulf. A minimum suit response, such as 1♠ in reply to 1♥, is treated artificially. The object is to give the opener every opportunity to make a natural descriptive rebid. A single raise of responder's artificial suit response is a strong bid indicating reversing values. For a similar idea, see RELAY SYSTEM.

EGYPTIAN BRIDGE FEDERATION. The Federation was founded in 1934 as the Association Egyptienne de Bridge. Its women's team, as United Arab Republics, won the 1960 world title and BFAME titles in 1987 and 1991. Its open team won the BFAME title in 1989.

Nayer Nashed
8 Gawad Hosni Street
Cairo, Egypt
Fax: 20 2 393 8950.

EHAA (Every Hand An Adventure). A highly natural system developed in the early Sixties, which became quite popular during the Seventies and is still in widespread use today. Its salient features are four-card majors, sound opening bids, weak two-bids in all four suits and an opening bid of 1 NT that shows less than an opening bid of one of a suit (most players use a 10-12 HCP range). In general, EHAA players tend to use a minimal number of conventions, relying heavily on bidding judgment rather than a scientific approach. Most forego the use of any artificial forcing opening bid, although some use a 3♣ opening as an artificial game force.

The heart of the system is an undisciplined weak two-bid, showing almost any kind of hand pattern, promising 6-12 HCP and a minimum of five cards, possibly as little as x-x-x-x-x, in the suit bid. All responses and rebids are natural, with a single raise or 2 NT response played as constructive but not forcing.

EIGHT or EIGHT-SPOT. The seventh highest ranking card in each suit, having eight pips of the suit to which it belongs on the face. See: DISCARD; HIGH-LOW SIGNALS; OPENING LEADS; RULE OF ELEVEN.

EIGHT TABLES. At duplicate, eight tables provide for competition among 32 players as individuals, 16 pairs or eight teams-of-four. See IRREGULAR RAINBOW.

An eight-table individual movement can be constructed, based on a seven-table RAINBOW MOVEMENT, with the addition of stationary players numbered 29, 30, 31 and 32.

As a pair game, eight tables may be either a MITCHELL of a THREE-QUARTER MOVEMENT. Two possibilities exist if the game is a Mitchell. In the first a relay is set up between tables 1 and 2 and a byestand is placed between tables 5 and 6. The full eight rounds always should be played because difficult factoring is involved otherwise. In the second type of Mitchell, four boards are played per round and a skip is called after the fourth round. Each pair plays 28 boards. If the 16-pair Three-Quarter Movement is used, there are three stationary pairs, and each pair plays 26 boards. It is also possible to play an 11-round Three-Quarter Movement, often called a Short Howell. There are five stationary pairs, and each pair plays 22 boards.

As a team-of-four contest the choice is between a THURNER movement and a SWISS TEAM movement. Alternatively, you may start the game with four boards on each table and let the moving (E-W) pairs skip down one table. Following the first round the boards move to the next lower table but the East-West pairs skip two tables instead of one. East-West 1 skips from table 7 to table 4; East-West 2 skips from 8 to 5; etc.

Following the second, third and fourth rounds the East-West pairs skip a table in the lower direction and the boards move to the next lower table. After the fifth round the East-West pairs skip two tables and the boards skip one table. East-West pair 1 skips from 6 to 3; East-West 2 skips from 7 to 4; etc. To save confusion the director can pick up the boards, put them in order, and redistribute them, four to a table, starting with 25 to 28 on table 1.

If a seventh round is advisable, have East-West pairs 1 to 4 add 4 to their number and go to that table. East-West 5 to 8 will subtract 4 from their number and go to that table. Boards in play will be reshuffled. This is the only time during the game the boards are reshuffled. Tables 1 and 5 will relay boards 1 to 4, tables 2 and 6 will relay boards 5 to 8, tables 3 and 7 will relay 9 to 12 and 4 and 8 will relay 13 to 16.

For 7° or 8° tables, see HALF TABLE MOVEMENTS.

EIRE. See IRELAND.

EITHER-OR SQUEEZE. See ALTERNATIVE SQUEEZE.

ELEVEN, RULE OF. See RULE OF ELEVEN.

ELEVEN TABLES. At duplicate, 11 tables afford excellent competition for either 44 individuals, 22 pairs or 11 teams-of-four.

As an individual tournament, 11-table games are conducted under the RAINBOW MOVEMENT. Twenty-two boards are in play for 11 rounds, and top is 10, average 110. It is also possible to extend the number of partnerships and boards to 24 or 27 by playing eight or nine rounds of three boards each. An interchange of partnerships by an exchange of seats between East and South, for two-board rounds, or by a counterclockwise movement by West in a three-board round, increases the number of partnerships, but usually slows down the speed with which the game can be conducted.

As a pair contest, a MITCHELL is usually the choice. Three boards are given out at each table, and each pair plays either 27 or 24 boards, depending on the number of rounds. It is also possible to give out two boards to a table, in which case each pair meets every pair playing in the opposite direction for a total of 22 boards. It is possible to play a THREE-QUARTER MOVEMENT — nine stationary pairs and 26 boards — but this is rarely chosen.

Standard teams-of-four movement requires 10 rounds. At 30 boards, it is too long, at 20 boards, too short for most sessions. Usually 24 boards are played, with the two middle rounds eliminated. After four rounds, traveling pairs return the boards just played to their home table and subtract three (or add eight) to their number to get their fifth-round assignment. If it is advisable to play 10 rounds of three boards each, distribute three boards to a table with 1-3 on table 1, 4-6 on table 2, going around to 31-33 on table 11. The boards are shuffled before the first round and not shuffled again during the game. To start the game have the East-West pairs skip a table in the lower direction. East-West 1 skips to 10, East-West 2 skips to 11, etc. After each round the East-West players skip a table in the lower direction and the boards move one table in the lower direction.

A method that permits each team to play 26 boards works as follows. The movement is the same as for the 30-board game listed above. The teams play three boards a round for the first three rounds. At this point the director removes the highest numbered board from each table, and the teams play two boards per round for the next four rounds. The director then returns the third board to each set and the final four rounds are three-board rounds. This method allows each team to play every other team, albeit not the same number of boards against each.

For 10° tables or 11° tables, see HALF TABLE MOVEMENTS.

ELIMINATION. A type of endplay in which (1) neutral suits are all played from both declarer's and dummy's hand, the last of such plays (2) saddling a defender with the lead in order to force the defender to make a lead desired by the declarer. The play of the neutral cards is referred to as a STRIP PLAY, the saddling of a defender with the lead as a THROW-IN PLAY. See the latter for a discussion of various types and illustrations. See also PARTIAL ELIMINATION.

ELOPEMENT. A term coined by Geza Ottlik of Budapest, Hungary, in a series of *Bridge World* articles to describe coups by which a player scores a trick with a trump that would not ordinarily have sufficient rank to take a trick. The simplest type of elopement is a COUP EN PASSANT. In the following elopement, spades are trump:

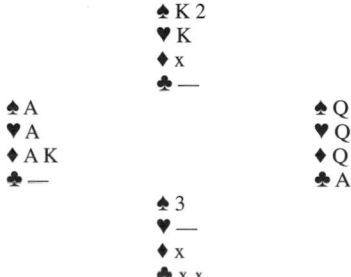

South leads a club and, remarkably, takes three tricks. If West ruffs, a diamond is discarded from dummy. If West throws a diamond, the club is ruffed in dummy and a heart is ruffed in the South hand, and the lead of South's last club is a coup en passant. If West instead throws the ♥A, the club is ruffed and the ♥K provides a discard for South's losing diamond while West ruffs with his master trump.

EMPTY. A colloquial term indicating that the spot cards in a suit are of no value. "King empty fourth" means a four-card suit headed by the king with the spot cards unimportant.

ENCRYPTED SIGNALS. Devised by Peter Winkler. Using such signals, information can be passed both covertly and legally between partners, adding a new dimension to the theory of the game. They are banned by the ACBL and many other official bodies.

Suppose that in the course of bidding toward a slam South wishes to tell his partner (North) that he holds the ♣A. He can usually do this by making an appropriate bid (e.g., a cuebid of 4♣), but the opponents also may benefit from this information.

Nonetheless, the information that South has the ♣A is sometimes passed to North in unwittingly covert fashion; if North, holding the other three aces, employs an ace-asking convention (such as Blackwood) and South gives the one-ace reply, North can then see that his partner's ace is in clubs, but no law requires North to reveal to the opponents what he can deduce from looking at his own hand.

Once one piece of information has been passed covertly, it can be used as key for another; e.g., conceivably South's next bid might carry the message "I hold the king of the suit ranking one below the suit in which I hold the ace."

To clarify the situation consider the following gross simplification. Suppose that there are only three players, A, B and C, and each is randomly dealt a card from a deck which consists only of the three cards x, y and z. A wishes to communicate a single bit of information (e.g., whether or not he dyes his hair) to B but not to C. Suppose that A holds x and he "guesses" that B holds y; A then makes the following public announcement: "I hold either x or y." If B responds "So do I," then key is established. If A dyes his hair he is now in a position to say "I dye my hair if my card is x, otherwise I do not." C remains in the dark.

On the other hand if A misguesses and B holds z, B will respond "Sorry; I have neither x nor y"; the key is now blown and A cannot attain his objective. It thus appears that the situation is worth, on the average, 1/2 bit of key to A and B. It should be noted, however, that if C had for some reason revealed his holding, then no guessing by A would have been necessary.

Using a similar strategy at the bridge table, with four players and 52 cards, suggests an average of 4 1/3 bits of key available for covert partnership communication. That may not sound like much to a cryptographer, but to a bridge player the ability to transfer even a single bit of information covertly to his partner could be crucial.

Of course, the guessing needed to establish key at the bridge table has to be coded by legal bids. Since there are barely enough of these for sufficient communication to arrive at a good contract, bids cannot be wasted solely for the purpose of establishing key. Hence we attempt to establish key only when the attempt simultaneously passes information valuable in the selection of a contract. Key established in this manner will be termed active key.

When the opponents are doing the bidding we must be content to listen; frequently they will reveal a piece of information which establishes our key "for free." This passive key can then be used to encrypt defensive signals.

Here is a simple example of an active crypto-convention. A jump raise of partner's opening suit traditionally shows a strong hand with trump support; suppose we require in addition either the ace or king of trumps. (With both or neither some other response, e.g., 3 NT, can be employed.) This is useful by itself, since trump quality is important in slam bidding, but it is also an attempt to establish key. If opener is missing both top trumps he rebids 3 NT and key is lost, but otherwise, if interested in slam, he rebids as follows: with the ace of trumps, he cuebids normally (i.e., bids a suit in which he has control); but with the king of trumps, he cuebids a suit in which he lacks control. Responder can tell which by looking at his own top trump, but the opponents have not been tipped off as to the killing opening lead.

Certain modern conventions which guarantee specific holdings make key establishment an easy second step. An example is disciplined weak two-bids, in which an opening two-bid in first or second position guarantees two of the top three honors in the trump suit. Why not have some response (say, 2 NT) guarantee the missing honor? This provides key for a three-way encryption of opener's "feature" rebid; e. g. the sequence 2♠ - 2 NT - 3♥ might be used to show "either A-K of trumps and a high heart or A-Q of trumps and a high club or K-Q of trumps and a high diamond." Only partner knows for sure.

To take advantage of passive key one needs at least two different opening lead agreements (e.g., fourth-best, and third/fifth best) and at least two signaling systems (e.g., low card encourages, high card encourages.) One of the systems is selected for use whenever no key is obtained.

Key is obtainable whenever the opponent who eventually becomes declarer gives an exact count of some quantity. Examples: declarer answers the Stayman convention, showing four cards of a certain suit, or uses the splinter convention, showing one card; declarer shows his aces or kings in a Blackwood reply; declarer shows his exact pointcount in a notrump sequence; declarer shows out of a suit early in the play. In each case the exposure of the dummy will enable each defender to count the number of the objects in question that his partner holds. The opening leader can, for example, use one lead agreement when holding an odd number of "objects" and the other when holding an even number. His partner can "read" the lead as soon as dummy is spread, but hopefully the declarer cannot until too late in the play.

When key is obtained because declarer has shown out of a suit, it is too late to encrypt the opening lead but perhaps not too late to encrypt the defensive signals. Here a fancy encryption scheme can be used because the defenders may have a lot of key; they, and only they, know the exact spot-card distribution of the suit in question.

It should be noted that although passive key is more easily obtained than active key, it must be used with discretion. Some forms are not completely reliable (e.g. Stayman, point-count). Worse, it may occasionally happen that the key can be "turned" - declarer determines during the play what system is in use and deduces the location of cards involved in the key. On balance, though, most forms of passive key are safe and effective.

EN PASSANT. See COUP EN PASSANT.

ENCOURAGING. (1) A term applied to a bid which strongly urges partner to continue to game. The bid is usually one trick short of game (2 NT, 3♥ or 3♠), and indicates that the combined hands are known to total 23-24 points (or the distributional equivalent), and that therefore game is in view. If partner has an unpromising hand with no values in reserve for his previous bidding, he may pass, but will usually continue to game.

The following bids are all encouraging in standard theory:

SOUTH	NORTH	SOUTH	NORTH
1♣	1♥	1♣	1♥
2 NT		3♥	

WEST	NORTH	EAST	SOUTH
			1♣
1♥	Pass	3♥	

The last sequence, with a jump raise of an overcall, is treated as preemptive by some theorists.

In many other sequences, opinions are divided. For example, a jump bid by responder was always treated as forcing in traditional methods, especially as interpreted on the East Coast. But a jump by responder in notrump or in a suit already bid by the partnership is simply encouraging in the style of experts in other areas such as the West Coast, the Midwest, Texas, and England. The number of traditionalists dwindled, and the encouraging style became standard in tournament play in the 80s. See JUMP REBIDS BY RESPONDER.

CONSTRUCTIVE and *forward-going* are almost synonymous terms for encouraging.

(2) A term applied to a defensive signal by which a player urges his partner to continue playing the suit led. See COME-ON, HIGH-LOW SIGNAL, ODD-EVEN SIGNALS, UPSIDE-DOWN SIGNALS.

ENDLESS HOWELL. A Howell Movement in which all pairs play all other pairs no matter how many pairs there are in the field. There is one stationary pair North-South at Table 1. Pairs playing East-West move down one table each round; pairs playing North-South move up one table each round. After a pair plays East-West at Table 1, it switches to North-South. At the highest-numbered table, the pair moving in as North-South switches to East-West at the same table in the following round.

ENDPLAY. A play taking place usually toward the end of the hand, though sometimes earlier. The preparation for an endplay may begin as early as the first or second trick; its object is to win an additional trick. They are essentially of three types; the forced lead or throw-in play, the coup or trump-reducing play, and the squeeze play. Many variations of each type occur. Endplay is often given a restricted meaning, as a synonym for throw-in: "East was now endplayed." Articles dealing with various endplays are listed under the general headings COUP and SQUEEZE, and under the particular headings RUFF AND DISCARD, RUFF AND RUFF, SMOTHER PLAY, THROW-IN, TRUMP PICK-UP, UNDERRUFF.

ENGLISH BRIDGE UNION. The Union was founded in 1938 as the successor to the Duplicate Bridge Control Board. It is a member of the British Bridge League, and its players have achieved many international successes representing Great Britain. The EBU was host to European Championships in 1950, 1961, 1975 and 1981. In 1992 it had a membership of about 28,000 in 900 clubs. Officers, 1992:

Chairman, Gerald Faulkner
General Manager, Raymond Brock
Broadfields, Bicester Road
Aylesbury, Bucks. HP19 3BG England.

ENTRIES. Sold for events at a bridge tournament to provide a control of seating assignments. Each entry blank designates an individual's, pair's or team's original seating assignment as to table number (and direction if appropriate) and section.

Particular seating assignments are usually separated from others at multi-sectioned events for assignment to known expert players to distribute such players equitably throughout the field. See SEED, SEEDING and ASSIGNMENT OF SEATS.

ENTRY. A means of securing the lead in a particular hand. Careful and effective use of entries is one of the basic arts of card play. In most situations it is sound strategy to maintain entries in both hands, which means preserving entries in the weaker hand where possible.

When both hands hold high cards, and there are more high cards than tricks, declarer should try to preserve a flexible entry situation:

♠ A Q 10

♠ K J 9

Suppose the first spade trick is won with the ace. If South will need entries to dummy, he should drop his king; if he needs entries to his hand, he should drop the 9. The jack is definitely a bad play. Declarer should aim to have the sequence of cards alternate from hand to hand: dropping the jack would leave dummy's Q 10 in effective sequence.

Similarly when drawing trumps, declarer may leave himself with two low trumps in one hand and one in the other. He should try to arrange that the single trump ranks between the trumps in the opposite hand.

A 4-4 fit will often provide an entry with a spot card if the suits divides 3-2.

A Q 10 3

K J 9 2

If dummy needs every possible entry, South should start by overtaking any high card as economically as possible. Later he repeats the process, and if the suit splits 3-2, he does so a third time, giving dummy a fourth-round entry with the three.

The same is true if the defenders have one, two, or three winners in the suit. If declarer has four small cards in each hand, he can arrange to win the fourth round in either hand, except in the rare case when the spot cards do not overlap at all.

Some special situations involving entries are dealt with under the following headings. DESCHAPELLES COUP; ENTRY-SHIFTING SQUEEZE; ENTRY SQUEEZE; GAMBIT; HOLD UP; MERRIMAC COUP; SCISSORS COUP; STEPPINGSTONE SQUEEZE; UNBLOCKING; UNBLOCKING SQUEEZE.

ENTRY-KILLING PLAY. A play made with the object of cutting the opponents' entry to a particular hand. Special varieties of this are discussed under MERRIMAC COUP (by the defense) and SCISSORS COUP (by the declarer).

The following are typical maneuvers by second hand when dummy is entryless:

♠ A J 10 x x
♠ Q x x   ♠ K x x
♠ x x

When South leads the suit, West must play the queen to hold South to one trick in the suit. If he plays low, East must allow the 10 or jack to hold to prevent South making four tricks.

♠ A J 9 x
♠ K 10 x   ♠ Q 8 x x
♠ x x

When South leads, West must again play high. If he plays low, South can make a second trick in the suit by finessing the nine.

Similarly, plays can be made by the declarer. If East were declarer in these two cases, he would play high from dummy on a lead from South if he could judge the situation accurately.

ENTRY-SHIFTING SQUEEZE. An entry-shifting squeeze is a positional squeeze in which the squeeze card is a winner accompanied by additional winners in the same suit that provide communication between declarer's hand and dummy. Declarer manages his entries in the suit of the squeeze card so that he can take advantage of the discards chosen by the defender under pressure.

I. Trumps

A. One opponent guards two suits

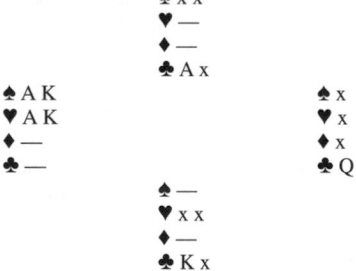

Clubs are trumps, and South leads. If East's trump were the deuce, declarer could claim the remaining tricks on a crossruff. In the actual end position, South leads the ♣K and West is squeezed in the majors: If West discards a heart, South retains the lead, and a heart ruff establishes a long card in that suit; if West discards a spade, declarer overtakes with dummy's ♣A, and he ruffs a spade to establish a winner in dummy.

B.One opponent guards three suits

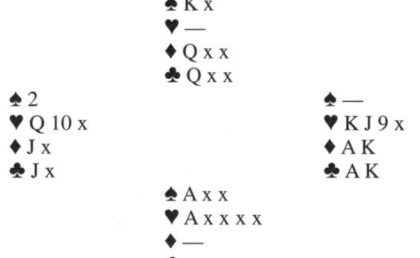

With spades as trumps, North leads the ♠K, and East is squeezed in three suits: If he discards a club or a diamond, North retains the lead to ruff out the remaining honor in that suit; if he discards a heart, then South overtakes with the ♠A in order to establish hearts.

The two-suit squeezes require a balanced trump holding (equal length in both hands) when declarer has all but one of the remaining tricks, but they require an unbalanced trump holding if a trick must be lost after the squeeze.

The three-suit squeezes require an unbalanced trump holding, unless a throw-in menace is involved, in which case a balanced trump holding is needed.

II. Notrump

A. One opponent guards two suits

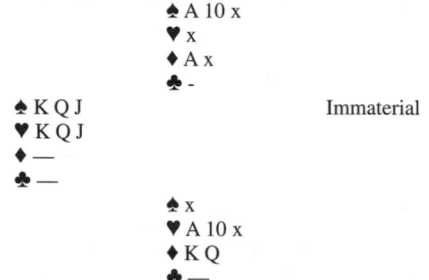

South is declarer in a notrump contract. When the ♦K is led, West is squeezed in the majors: If West discards a heart, declarer overtakes with the ♦A and then plays ace and another heart, establishing the long heart in his hand, with the ♦Q as entry to cash it; if West discards a spade, dummy's low diamond is played, retaining the ♦A as entry to the long spade, established by playing ace and another.

B. One opponent guards three suits

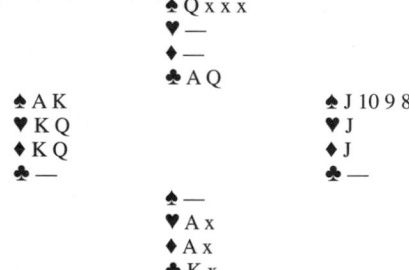

In a notrump contract, South leads a low club, squeezing West in three suits: If West unguards a red suit, North wins the ♣A, and returns a club to the K, allowing South to cash the red aces, and the long card in the suit unguarded by West; after a spade discard by West, North wins the ♣Q, concedes a spade to West, wins the forced return of a red suit, cashes the other red ace, and returns a club to the ♣A in order to cash the ♠Q.

Stepping-Stone:

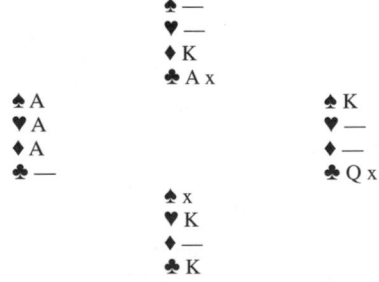

Needing two tricks at notrump, South leads the ♣K, and West is squeezed in three suits: discarding a red ace establishes the corresponding king for declarer, so West discards the ♠A. (If South held the ♠K, this discard would concede a trick directly.) South retains the lead and exits with a spade to East's K, forcing him to lead a club to North's ♣A.

ENTRY SQUEEZE. A squeeze that is aimed at forcing a defender, or both defenders, to discard from a seemingly worthless holding so that declarer can create an extra entry to one hand or the other by overtaking a card of winning rank. Analyzed and described by Geza Ottlik in the December 1967 issue of Bridge World. His article, entitled "The Quest," won the first International Bridge Academy "Article of the Year" award in 1968, and two of the hands from this article follow.

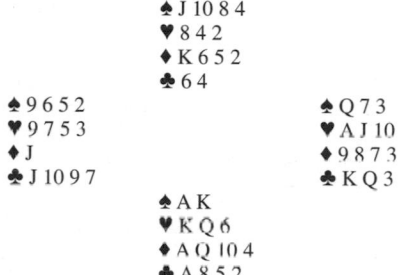

```
              ♠ J 10 8 4
              ♥ 8 4 2
              ♦ K 6 5 2
              ♣ 6 4
♠ 9 6 5 2                    ♠ Q 7 3
♥ 9 7 5 3                    ♥ A J 10
♦ J                         ♦ 9 8 7 3
♣ J 10 9 7                  ♣ K Q 3
              ♠ A K
              ♥ K Q 6
              ♦ A Q 10 4
              ♣ A 8 5 2
```

South declares 3 NT after East has opened the bidding, and West leads the ♣J. East overtakes with the queen and continues with the king and a third club as declarer holds up the ace until the third round. The ♦A-Q reveal the 4-1 division, but South can still get home if he concedes a club to West, which crushes East in three suits. Clearly East cannot let go of a spade, and if he discards a heart, one heart lead from dummy suffices to establish two tricks in that suit for declarer. So East is forced to discard one of his "useless" diamonds. Now declarer has two diamond entries to dummy by overtaking the 10 with the king and can lead twice toward his heart honors. As Ottlik noted in his article: "Those silly little diamonds in East's hand have a function after all. Nondescript, irrelevant, or immaterial as they may be called, by their sheer existence they also serve. They stand and wait, in the way, blocking traffic, hindering enemy lines of communication. And having this value, however silent, taciturn and hidden, they are subject to the pressure of a squeeze."

The entry squeeze can also operate against both opponents in the form of a double squeeze.

```
              ♠ A 6 4
              ♥ 10 6 5
              ♦ J 8 7 4
              ♣ 9 4 2
♠ J 10 8                     ♠ 9 7 5 2
♥ Q 7 4 2                    ♥ K 8 3
♦ 10 6 5 2                   ♦ Q 9 3
♣ 7 6                       ♣ 10 8 5
              ♠ K Q 3
              ♥ A J 9
              ♦ A K
              ♣ A K Q J 3
```

West leads the ♠J against South's contract of 6 NT. Rather than bank everything on finding East with both heart honors, or guessing which opponent might hold a doubleton honor, declarer wins the spade in hand and

cashes five rounds of clubs, discarding a diamond and a heart from dummy. On the last club West is in some difficulty. If he holds fewer than three hearts, South can lead a heart from his hand to establish two tricks in that suit. Alternatively, if West comes down to fewer than three diamonds, declarer can cash the ♦A-K, the ♠K-A, then take the heart finesse; West, marooned with nothing but hearts, must then return a heart into declarer's tenace. So West is "squeezed" down to a singleton spade. East, in turn, is squeezed on the last club, for he must also hold three cards in each red suit and can hold no more than one spade. South has thus squeezed both opponents in a suit in which he started with three top winners and now makes his slam by overtaking the ♠K with the ace for a heart finesse. The ♠6 provides entry to dummy for the second heart finesse. See also ENTRY-SHIFTING SQUEEZE, OVERTAKING SQUEEZE, STEPPING-STONE SQUEEZE, and UNBLOCKING SQUEEZE.

EPSON WORLDWIDE BRIDGE CONTEST. Advanced by the World Bridge Federation and sponsored by Seiko Epson Corporation of Japan, the first world simultaneous pairs contest was held in June 1986. Organized by José Damiani of France, the format was for a single-session 24-board event to be conducted in heats throughout the world on the same day at roughly the same time. All contestants played the same hands and at the end of the session received souvenir booklets containing hand analyses prepared by Omar Sharif. In the 1986 contest 80 countries participated at some 1000 sites. In the second year nearly 75,000 players took part in the event, held simultaneously in 85 countries around the world, gaining a place in *The Guinness Book of Records 1988* as the biggest tournament. Beginning in 1990, an association with the World Federation of Great Towers added interest when games were presented live by satellite from famous towers across the globe. In 1991 about 90,000 people from 95 countries participated in the tournament. In 1992 the contest saw another innovation when two sessions were organized, allowing a choice of playing on Friday evening or Saturday afternoon. Attendance grew to 100,000 through 1993. Games were scored by instant matchpoints with 100 top, 1200 average. For results see Appendix IV.

EQUALS. Cards that are in sequence, or cards that are in effect in sequence because all cards of intervening rank have been played. See PLAY FROM EQUALS.
EQUITY. The equity rule for adjusting scores. See LAWS OF DUPLICATE (Law 12).

ERRORS IN SCORING. See LAWS OF DUPLICATE (Law 79) and SCORING CORRECTIONS.

ESCAPE MECHANISM. See SOS REDOUBLE and WRIGGLE.

ESCAPE SUIT. A long suit held in reserve by a player making a gambling or psychic bid. An overcall of 1 NT by a player with a weak hand and a long broken suit is a well-worn tactic. It is not difficult to expose the maneuver by doubling and forcing the overcaller to escape into his suit, but the tactic has some positive value: a weak hand with a long suit might otherwise be shut out of the auction unless WEAK JUMP OVERCALLS are being used.

Psychic bids in a short suit with an escape suit in reserve are seldom met with because they tend to be more dangerous to partner than to the opponents.

For a regular systemic use of a bid with an escape suit, see GAMBLING THREE NOTRUMP.

ESTABLISH. To make a suit or an individual card good by forcing out the opponent's guards or winners. Thus one may establish K-Q-J-10-9 of a suit for four tricks after conceding one to the ace.

ESTABLISHED CARD. A card that has been promoted to winning rank after all higher-ranking cards in the other hands have been played.

ESTABLISHED ENTRY. An entry developed by driving out a higher card.

ESTABLISHED REVOKE. A revoke which may not be corrected. A revoke becomes established as soon as the revoking player or his partner leads or plays to the next trick, or, if the revoke is made in leading, as soon as the revoking player's partner plays to the trick on which the revoke is made; or by the act of making a claim. A revoke made on the 12th trick may be corrected, even if established. See LAWS (Law 62D).

ESTABLISHED SUIT. A long suit in which a player holds all the remaining high cards, which at notrump or after trumps have been drawn at a suit contract will all be winners when the suit is led and run. The object of notrump play is essentially to establish one or more long suits by drawing or forcing out whatever high cards the opponents may hold in that suit.

ESTIMATION. The attempt to judge the score that one is likely to have earned in a duplicate game. Generally a player estimates by comparing his result on a hand with those likely to be obtained elsewhere. As a result of this procedure, one can often alter one's tactics toward the end of a session, playing a somewhat chancier game if one is behind and needs "tops" to win, or playing "down the middle" if one is way ahead and can afford to coast. See SHOOTING.

ETHICS AND CONDUCT. The term "ethics" is commonly used in relation to the observance of fair play. Breaches of ethics are generally thought of as unfair practices which fall short of deliberate cheating.

The Laws deal with the whole question of proper behavior at bridge under the general heading, "Proprieties." See Laws of Duplicate #72-4. This includes ETIQUETTE. In the Laws of Contract Bridge the Proprieties are in a separate section following Law #81.

ETIQUETTE. Much of the popularity of contract bridge is attributable to the high standards of etiquette which are observed by the players. No other modern game leans so heavily on the expectation that participants will conduct themselves in a highly civilized manner.

In tournament bridge, violations of proper etiquette are to be expected from inexperienced players, either through ignorance or inadvertence. A well-mannered opponent who is the victim of such a violation will, if he considers that comment is called for, be at pains to make it clear that his comment is intended to be helpful rather than admonitory.

At the other end of the scale is the noxious violation by the experienced player who complains loudly - but unofficially — of a violation of ethics or etiquette committed against him. "I wuz robbed!" is never heard from a player of high standards of etiquette; he either makes an official protest or says nothing.

The LAWS OF CONTRACT BRIDGE deal with the whole question of proper behavior under the heading, "Proprieties." Matters of etiquette, as distinct from questions of ethics, are dealt with in Part III of the Proprieties.

Among the breaches of good manners frequently observed are the following: discussion between two partners of a board just played when there is another board to play; looking at an opponent's hand after it has been placed in the board without asking permission; criticism of an opponent's bidding or any implication of bad faith on the part of the opponents without having previously called the director to the table. Appearing at a bridge tournament dressed carelessly or sloppily is an insult to the ladies and gentlemen against whom such a player competes.

Among the examples of good manners at the table are these items summed up by J. S. Weller, printed in the *Bridge Bulletin* of Johannesburg, South Africa.

(1) Good temper. Bring pleasure with you to this amusement. Take every event in good humor, and by no means incite ill humor.

(2) Silence. Never talk or twitch when someone is thinking - most rigidly enforced during the auction when no questions are to be tolerated.

(3) Smooth action. Smooth flow of action without aggravating chitchat enhances the joy of the game and gets hands finished faster. Have your bid ready before it is your turn.

(4) Advice. Don't give advice. Just think.

(5) Visitors. Visitors must remain still in one place until the hand is completed. They are bound by all proprieties even more strictly than the players. They are not even allowed to be careless, such as leaving a hand they feel is dull. They may never point out any infraction or impulsively correct a player.

(6) Sportsmanship. Feel that others are doing the best they can, considering the effect on them of your presence. No grown person, much less a bridge player, ever makes a condescending, belittling or humiliating remark. Once in a while you will be gratified to observe an act deserving of a compliment. Give it.

(7) Winning. Winning makes a prize player feel very good indeed. It makes a child exult.

(8) Losing. Losing is accompanied by a grim, cheerful, determined, hopeful, anxious, patient demeanor; never by a complaint or a grumble.

(9) Facts. When two cannot agree on what has occurred, the child is right. The bridge player will agree that he possibly could be. If a referee gives a decision, be gracious; don't talk back.

(10) Women. Women do not exist in a bridge game, nor do men; only bridge players. All are equally bound by etiquette. Courtesy exists, favors because of sex do not.

EUROPEAN BRIDGE LEAGUE. Founded in 1947 at Copenhagen, by delegates from the bridge federations of eight countries (Belgium, Denmark, Finland, France,

Great Britain, The Netherlands, Norway, and Sweden). All were members of the INTERNATIONAL BRIDGE LEAGUE, which they voted to dissolve to form a new league, in a new setting, Denmark. A. J. E. Lucardie was elected President, and Herman Dedichen (at whose instigation the meeting was called) was named Honorary Secretary. Congresses of the league have always been combined with the European Championships. In 1948 the League was a member of the group of three, with the Portland Club and ACBL, that issued the International Laws of Bridge. Membership of the EBL numbers a total of 35 countries, the original eight plus Austria, Bulgaria, Croatia, Estonia, Georgia, Germany, Greece, Hungary, Iceland, Ireland, Israel, Italy, Latvia, Lebanon, Liechtenstein, Lithuania, Luxembourg, Monaco, Poland, Portugal, Russia, San Marino, Slovenia, Spain, Switzerland, Turkey and Yugoslavia.

The European Championship results, listed in Appendix II, include the prewar events held under the auspices of the International Bridge League. Similarly, there were no European Championships in 1960, 1964, 1968, 1972 and 1976 because World Team Olympiads took place in those years. When the WBF decided to hold the BERMUDA BOWL Competition in the odd-numbered years only, starting in 1977, the European Championships also became a biennial event, to be held shortly prior to each Bermuda Bowl.

Some of the many contributions of the European Bridge League and its constituent bodies to bridge on the international level include: European Match Points (later called INTERNATIONAL MATCH POINTS); procedure for recording in detail a large number of matches played simultaneously; the development of BRIDGE-O-RAMA; and the custom of using English as the international bridge language.

Considerable contributions to the development of international bridge in Europe have been made by:
A. J. E. Lucardie (IBL President 1933-34 and 1938-39); Sir A. Noël Mobbs of England (EBL President 1948-50); Baron Robert De Nexon (EBL President 1950-65); Count Carl Bonde (EBL President 1965-69), Marchese Silvio Carina-Mazzaccara (EBL President 1969-73); André Lemaitre (EBL President 1973-80); Nils Jensen (EBL President 1981-87); Herman Dedichen (EBL Secretary 1947-58); Ernst Heldring (EBL Secretary 1958-71); Wolf Achterberg (EBL Secretary 1971-79); David Bardach (EBL Secretary 1979-1993). Because of their impressive contributions to the EBL, the following have been elected President Emeritus: Baron de Nexon (1965); Geoffrey Butler (1974); Nils Jensen (1987).
Officers 1992:
President
José Damiani,
2 Rue de Lyautey,
75016 Paris, France.
Fax 33 1 45 27 21 17
Vice Presidents: André Boekhorst
                 William Pencharz
For results of EBL Championships, see Appendix III.

EUROPEAN BRIDGE REVIEW. See BIBLIOGRAPHY, O.

EUROPEAN COMMUNITY CHAMPIONSHIPS. These championships, also known as the European Common Market Championships, are held every two years.

Over the years Italy has had the best record, winning the overall championship in 1967, 1971, 1973, 1977, 1979, 1981, 1985 and 1993. France has been the overall champion four times. Championships are played for Open Teams, Womens Teams, Mixed Teams, Junior Teams, Open Pairs, Womens Pairs, Mixed Pairs and Junior Pairs. For results see Appendix IV.

EUROPEAN JUNIOR CHAMPIONSHIPS. A biennial team event for players under the age of 25, first staged in 1968 and officially, under EBL auspices, from 1972. Winners are listed in Appendix IV.

EVEN. A term applying to the equal distribution of the outstanding cards in a suit, as a 3-3 division of six outstanding cards.

EVENT. A contest of one or more sessions in duplicate bridge played to determine a winner.

EXCESS POINTS. When cumulative scoring was used in pair competition, the limit placed on the number of points that could be scored was, for the defenders, 600 if not vulnerable, 900 if vulnerable; for the declarer, 800 if not vulnerable, 1,000 if vulnerable. No limitation was placed if the contract was for a slam. Losers lost total points, winners were credited only with the maximum and the balance carried to a special "excess points" column used only for breaking ties. In England, the 600 maximum for defenders was 700. Since matchpoint scoring has almost totally replaced total-point scoring, this provision was omitted from the Laws of 1943 and subsequently.

EXCLUSION. A Unit board of directors may vote to exclude a member of another Unit from its tournaments for cause. See also SUSPENSION.

EXCLUSION BID. A bid which shows a holding in every suit except the one named. This is a feature of the ROMAN SYSTEM. After an opening bid of 2♣ or 2♦, showing a three-suited hand, the opener rebids in his short suit if he receives the conventional positive response of 2 NT (see ROMAN TWO DIAMONDS). Similarly, the Roman System prescribes a bid in the shortest unbid suit in response to a takeout double; this has a transfer effect, permitting the stronger hand to become declarer. A takeout double is itself an exclusion call in a wide sense: it implies support for all suits except the one already bid.

Exclusion bids have been adopted by some partnerships as a defense against strong artificial opening bids. This device is useful for competing on three-suited hands in which no suit has been bid naturally. An extension of this convention devised by Andrew Bernstein, which he calls the "Super Convention," is to use an overcall of an opponent's notrump opening as a two-way exclusion bid. The overcall thus shows either length in the suit bid, or shortness in the suit bid and support for all other suits. The partner of the overcaller is expected to treat the overcall as natural if he has fewer than three cards in the suit. Otherwise he is expected to take his choice of the other suits.

EXHAUST. To draw all cards of a suit from the hand of any player. A player becoming void of a suit during the play is said to be exhausted of that suit, as distinguished from holding no cards of that suit originally.

EXHIBITION MATCHES. At certain major championship tournaments, advance arrangements are made for exhibition matches before a considerable audience. In such events, all contestants must agree, as a condition of entry, that they will, if required, participate in the exhibition matches at the announced time and place. The right of the governing body to impose this condition has been vigorously contested by some players, but without success. Since a considerable number of spectators are involved, the starting time must be rigidly observed, taking precedence over the convenience of the contestants. See BRIDGE-O-RAMA and VUGRAPH.

EXIT. To "get out of one's hand," particularly when it is undesirable to lead from one's hand, usually by making a lead which is not likely to jeopardize the value of any partnership holding.

EXIT CARD. A card by which one can exit from one's hand, offering an escape from an opponent's attempted throw-in or elimination play.

EXIT PLAY. A defensive unblocking maneuver executed in order to avoid a throw-in.

```
              ♠ K Q 10 9
              ♥ Q 10 3
              ♦ K 4 2
              ♣ 9 4 3
♠ 7 2                        ♠ 6 5
♥ A K 8 5                    ♥ 7 6 2
♦ Q J 9                      ♦ 10 8 7 5
♣ K J 8 6                    ♣ 10 7 5 2
              ♠ A J 8 4 3
              ♥ J 9 4
              ♦ A 6 3
              ♣ A Q
```

South is in 4♠ after an opening bid on his left, and West leads three rounds of hearts. Declarer wins, draws trumps, and plays ace, king, and another diamond, hoping to throw West in for a favorable club lead. West, however, makes an exit play, disembarrassing himself of the queen and jack on the first two diamond leads, and retaining the 9, which his partner overtakes on the third round to play a club, defeating the contract.

EXODUS. A method of responding after partner's opening 1 NT bid has been doubled. A redouble forces opener to rebid 2♣. The redouble indicates that responder has a suit he wishes to play at the two level. If it is clubs he passes partner's forced 2♣. If he bids another suit, declarer passes.

If responder bids a suit at the two level over the double, he is asking opener to choose between the suit bid and the suit immediately higher, i.e., opener's choice over 2♥ would be either hearts or spades. If responder's suits are not touching, he bids two of his lower-ranking suit. If opener bids the next higher suit, responder bids his higher-ranking suit, allowing opener to make a choice.

If responder, after redoubling, bids 2 NT over opener's forced 2♣, he is using a form Of FORCING STAYMAN. If responder bids 2♠ over the double, opener must rebid 2 NT, and responder now bids his minor, guaranteeing a hand good enough for 3 NT or at least four of the minor. See DEFENSE TO DOUBLE OF ONE NOTRUMP and

DOUBLES OF NOTRUMP BIDS.

EXPANDED MITCHELL (or HESITATION MITCHELL). A way to play one, or more than one, extra rounds in a MITCHELL MOVEMENT introduced by E. E. Blandon. The expansion is obtained by decreasing the number of stationary pairs and letting the moving pairs visit not only EW places but also the NS places at some table or tables. See also REDUCED HOWELL.

EXPECTANCY. What a player is entitled to expect in various circumstances governed by mathematical probabilities. (1) In the deal, a player's expectancy is one ace, one king, one queen and one jack. (2) After looking at his hand and before any bidding has taken place, a player may expect his partner to hold one-third of the outstanding honor cards. (3) In some bidding situations, a player's expectation of partner's strength may be clear-cut. If a player with 17 points hears a bid of 1 NT (16-18) bid on his right, the expectation of his partner's hand is three points. (4) In the play, expectancy depends on more complex mathematical calculations. (See MATHEMATICAL TABLES.) The trick expectancy from the most promising line of play in many situations is given under SUIT COMBINATIONS. See also EXPECTATION.

EXPECTATION. The average result which would be achieved over a long trial period. In order to compute the expectation of a particular play, it is necessary to consider not only the frequency of gain or loss but also the amount that is being risked. For example, let us compute the expectation of a pair that reaches a contract of 4♠, not vulnerable, at rubber bridge. This contract, we will say, depends on winning one of two finesses (a 75% chance). Assuming the contract will either make or fail by one trick and that the pair will receive 300 points for making the game. The pair's expectation is:

(75%)	↔	(+ 420)	+	(25%)	↔	(-50)
chance		result		chance		result
of		of		of		of
success		success		failure		failure

This sum is 315 - 12.5 = 302.5. In making this computation we take into account that 75% of the time the pair will score + 420 and 25 % of the time the pair will score - 50.

Let us contrast this expectation with that of a pair with the same cards that stops in 3♠. The expectation of the latter is (assuming 50 points for a part score):

(75%)	↔	(+ 170)	+	(25%)	↔	(+ 140)
chance		result		chance		result
of an		of		of		when just
overtrick		overtrick		making		making

This sum is 127.5 + 35.0 = 162.5. Thus, the expectation of the pair bidding game is higher. This indicates that it is favorable to attempt the game under these conditions. By bidding the game, a pair will win an average of 302.5 points whereas by stopping short it will win an average of only 162.5 points. A similar calculation will indicate that it is not profitable (in the long run) to bid such a game which depends on two successful finesses (only a 25% chance).

In the play of the hand, the declarer may sometimes be unable to determine the correct play without resorting to (at least a rough) calculation of the expectation of different lines.

EXPECTED NUMBER OF CONTROLS IN BALANCED HANDS

hcp	Relative Freq.	0	1	2	3	4	5	6	7	8	9	10	11	12
3	1216	67	33											
4	1891	40	39	21										
5	2505	23	48	29										
6	3129	12	41	47										
7	3795	5	30	46	19									
8	4192	2	19	44	28	7								
9	4377	*	10	35	44	11								
10	4379	*	5	24	44	27								
11	4179	*	2	14	40	33	11							
12	3755	*	1	8	30	42	17	2						
13	3242		*	3	20	39	34	4						
14	2687		*	1	11	33	38	17						
15	2115		*	*	5	24	42	23	6					
16	1596			*	2	14	36	37	10	1				
17	1155			*	1	8	27	39	24	1				
18	799			*	*	3	18	39	30	10				
19	526				*	1	10	32	40	15	2			
20	333				*	*	5	22	38	31	4			
21	201				*	*	2	13	35	35	15			
22	115					*	1	6	26	43	20	4		
23	62.9					*	*	3	17	38	35	7		
24	32.6					*	*	1	9	31	38	21		
25	16.0						*	*	4	21	43	26	6	
26	7.32							*	1	12	37	41	9	
27	3.21							*	*	6	28	41	25	
28	1.28							*	*	2	18	44	32	4
29	0.48								*	1	9	35	49	6

WEST	EAST
♠ A K 6 2	♠ 5 4
♥ A K 6 2	♥ 5 4
♦ A K 2	♦ 5 4
♣ 3 2	♣ A K Q 7 6 5 4

West plays 6 NT against the opening lead of the ♦ Q. East-West are vulnerable. How should West play?

A safety play for the contract is available. West needs only six club tricks for his contract. By ducking the first round of clubs he ensures his contract without an overtrick (+ 1440). By trying to run the clubs, he will make an overtrick (+ 1470) unless North holds all four clubs. If declarer fails to make the safety play and North has four clubs, he will be down three tricks 300).

The expectation of the safety play is:
$$(100\%) \times + 1440 = 1440$$
The expectation of trying to split the clubs is:

(5%) ↔ (-300) + (90%) ↔ (+1470)
chance / chance
North has / clubs are
four clubs / not 4-0
+ (5%) ↔ (1440)
chance
South has
four clubs

This expectation is only 1380. Therefore, the safety play is the superior play.

WEST	EAST
♠ Q 5 4 3	♠ J 2
♥ Q 5 4 3	♥ J 2
♦ A K 2	♦ 5 4
♣ 3 2	♣ A K Q 7 6 5 4

West plays in 1 NT against an opening lead of the ♦ Q. East-West are not vulnerable. Once again the safety play guarantees the contract (with an overtrick) for + 120. If West fails to employ the safety play and North has all four clubs, he will be set two tricks for –100.

The expectation of the safety play is
$$(100\%) \times + 120 = 120$$
while the expectation of trying to run the clubs without loss is
(5%) ↔ (−100) + (90%) ↔ (+ 150)
+ (5%) ↔ (+ 120) = 136
(assuming the defenders will discard correctly on the run of clubs)

In this case, the safety play is not the superior play. (This does not take into account the fact that if the clubs were 4-0 there might have been some North-South bidding. Such a consideration makes the safety play even less desirable.)

EXPECTED NUMBER OF CONTROLS IN BALANCED HANDS. A table of the number of controls statistically predictable in balanced hands of varying strength was analyzed and described by GEORGE ROSENKRANZ in the December 1974 issue of *The Bridge World* (see tabulation below). Knowledge of the average expectations of numbers of aces and kings for the strength pointcount already shown is useful in determining whether or not to bid aggressively.

The table shows the approximate frequencies of specific numbers of controls (Ace = 2, King = 1) in all hands with 4-3-3-3, 4-4-3-2 or 5-3-3-2 distribution. Blanks indicate zero frequency; asterisks indicate less than one-half of 1 percent frequency.

EXPERT. A player of conceded skill. The caliber of the player accorded this title will vary with the circles in which he regularly plays; expertise cannot be measured by Masterpoints or in any other mechanical way, such as by having won one tournament or even by having played in international competition.

The title of expert will probably be recognized as valid only when it has been awarded by a verdict of the expert's peers. It is, however, loosely used to characterize anyone who plays better than the usual level of the game in which the player plays.

EXPLANATION OF ANY CALL OR PLAY. Whenever a player makes a conventional call that is not a Class A Convention, his partner should alert the opponents so that they may inquire as to its meaning. See ALERTING, PRIVATE CONVENTION. During the auction and before the final pass any player may, at his own turn to call, ask for a full explanation of any call made by an opponent. After the final pass and throughout the play, any player except dummy may, at his own turn to play, ask for an explanation of opposing calls or card play conventions. See FACE DOWN LEADS; LAWS OF DUPLICATE (Laws 20, 41.).

A player who asks for an explanation of a bid should beware of giving information to his partner by his question. For example, a player who asks the meaning of a normal 1♣ opening bid when he holds great club strength may be subject to penalty under Law 16. It is better to ask a question in general terms, rather than draw attention to one particular suit-bid and so expose oneself to the suggestion that the question may be lead-directing.

When the auction is over, it is recommended that dummy volunteer any explanation about his side's bidding which he may think necessary. Voluntary explanations during the auction are not advisable because they may enlighten partner (or appear to enlighten him). If a player gains information as a result of his partner's explanation, he must carefully avoid taking advantage of it. However, it would be improper to offer an immediate correction of partner's incorrect explanation of the partnership understanding. More often than not, this would give unauthorized information to partner. If the offending side is also the declaring side, the mistaken information should be corrected before the opening lead is made. If the offending side is the defending side, no correction can be offered until the completion of the hand — again to correct earlier could result in unauthorized information for partner. If the non-offending side feels they have been injured by the incorrect information given, they have the right to seek adjudication of the board by the director, and failing that, by the Appeals Committee. See LAWS OF DUPLICATE (Laws 73,75).

A tournament director may direct a player to leave the table while his partner gives an explanation; and it may be proper for him to depart voluntarily (at his partner's request or of his own volition) if a possibility of a misunderstanding exists.

EXPOSED CARD. For cards exposed during the bidding, see Law 24. Cards exposed during the play are covered by Laws 48, 49, and 68; LAWS OF DUPLICATE (Laws 48, 49, 68).

EXPOSED HAND. A hand placed in full view of all the players. This usually refers to dummy's hand, but it may also apply to the hand of declarer or a defender, which may become exposed by accident or in the process of making a claim. See Laws 48, 49, 62, 64, 68; LAWS OF DUPLICATE (Laws 48, 49, 62, 64, 68).

EXTENDED GERBER. A method of pinpointing certain key cards in slam bidding, devised by Jerold A. Fink of Cincinnati.

After a trump suit is established, a bid of 4♣ requests partner to show controls (ace-2 controls, king-1 control). 4♦ shows 0 or 1; 4♥ shows 2; 4♠ shows 3; 4 NT shows 4. With 5 or more controls, responder subtracts 5 and bids accordingly. After the conventional 4♦ response, a 4♥ bid asks responder to clarify whether he holds 0 or 1 controls by bidding 4♠ with 0 controls (or 5 or 10), or 4 NT with 1 control (or 6 or 11).

Other four-level bids by the asking bidder are sign-offs. The asking bidder may also sign off by bidding 5♣ and passing partner's forced 5♦ response, or by bidding 5♦ and passing partner's forced 5♥ response or correcting it to 5♠. Other combinations of rebids on the five level are conventional, asking partner to show points (king-2 points, queen-1 point) in two specific suits by seven steps, ranging from 0 points for the first step to 6 points for the seventh step.

EXTENDED LANDY. The Landy convention is a 2♣ takeout for the major suits over an opponent's notrump opening. An extension was proposed by Ira Rubin in 1947, using a two-club bid as a takeout request after a response or rebid of one notrump after a suit opening. It implies more distribution and less strength than a double. It also applies in the passout seat.

WEST	NORTH	EAST	SOUTH
1♦	Pass	1♠	Pass
1NT	2♣		

This shows five or more clubs and exactly four hearts, based on North's failure to overcall immediately.

Other similar uses were developed later by Martin Cohn.

EXTRA TRICK. A trick scored in excess of the number of tricks required to fulfill a contract. Such tricks are scored above the line and do not count toward game at their trick value. Extra tricks carry premium values if the contract has been doubled or redoubled. See OVERTRICK and SCORING.

F

FACE (of a card). The front of a playing card, containing the suit and rank of the card.

FACE CARDS. The cards which have a representation of a human figure, called originally coat cards, later court cards. Their design is virtually the same for all manufacturers in America and Britain, deriving from eighteenth century French patterns.

Earlier designs depended on the skill of the artists who carved the wood blocks, and gradually degenerated from representation of recognizable people and objects into meaningless figures. It has been said that Henry VIII was the model for all four kings; the oldest extant English cards have the same curling moustache and divided beard on the four kings, and legend has it that the queens were likenesses of Elizabeth of York, Henry VII's queen. The remainder of the design is clearly derived from cards made in Rouen, France; the faces differ, but the costumes, position of the hands, and weapons all show similarities.

The French packs developed along their own lines until 1813, when an official design was promulgated; the cards were all named, and even today the names appear on many packs:

	SPADES	HEARTS	DIAMONDS	CLUBS
KING	David	Charles	César	Alexandre
QUEEN	Pallas	Judith	Rachel	Argine
JACK	Hogier	Lahire	Hector	Lancelot

All represent real or mythical figures except Argine, an anagram of Regina.

In the Hungarian pack, eight of the face cards represent characters in Schiller's drama, *Wilhelm Tell*, set in Switzerland:

SUITS	OBER	UNTER
Acorns	Wilhelm Tell	Reszö Harras
Leaves	Ulrich Ruden	Walter Fürst
Bells	Vadász Stüssi	Itel Reding
Hearts	Herman Gezler	Pásztor Kuoni

But an oddity exists; the cards were never used in Switzerland.

The usual German packs do not have a queen, but have two jacks (or knaves), the Ober and the Unter. Some German packs, however, have four face cards, king-queen-jack-jack. The trappola pack (Italo-Spanish) uses a cavalier in place of a queen.

FACE-DOWN LEADS. A procedure first introduced experimentally by the WBF in 1972 and adopted by the ACBL in 1975, recommending that the opening leader place his opening lead face down on the table, after which his partner may ask questions about the auction. This ensures that the partner of the leader will have the opportunity to ask questions about the auction before dummy is tabled, and that his questions will not influence the opening leader in his choice.

However, a face-up lead does not deprive the leader's partner of the right to ask questions. The face-down lead has a secondary purpose: If the lead is out of turn, the card can be retrieved without penalty.

This is now a requirement under Law 41 but there is no penalty for failure to lead face down. Sponsoring organizations may opt for face-up leads.

FACED CARD. A card exposed to all the players, which may be a card in the dummy, a penalty card, or a card exposed by a player making a claim or his opponent. No revoke penalty can be exacted for failure to play a faced card. See also PLAYED CARD.

FACT. A happening at a bridge table. When the facts are in dispute, or their interpretation is a matter of judgment, the matter may be referred to the tournament committee. This includes the significance or otherwise of hesitations. The committee may not overrule the director on a point of law, although an appeal may lie to the NATIONAL LAWS COMMISSION.

FACTORING. The process of adjusting matchpoint scores to the same base to make them comparable for ranking purposes.

When scores are to be compared for ranking within a group of contestants, it is necessary that the comparison be on the same base. For instance, in a 12° table Mitchell game, the usual procedure is to have a phantom pair 13 in one of the two fields. Consequently all the pairs in one direction have a bye round, playing only 24 boards, while the pairs in the other direction play all 26 boards. Top on a board in such a case is 11. The pairs that did not sit out have a possible of 286, but those who sat out have a possible of only 264. To make the scores comparable,

the scores of the pairs that sat out must be multiplied by the fraction 286/264 (13/12). To facilitate the computation, add 1/12 of the score obtained to the scores of the pairs that sat out..

Some half-table movements are more complicated. For instance, with 15° tables, there would be 16 pairs in one direction and 15 in the other, but only 13 rounds would be played. The best method of handling this situation is to set up a ROVER movement — one pair successively replaces pairs sitting in their direction after sitting out the first round according to a formula set up to guarantee that no pair plays another pair twice and that no pair plays the same set of boards twice. All pairs in the direction in which the rover pair is not playing would play 13 rounds — 26 boards — with a 12 top for a 312 possible. In the other direction, the rover pair plus all of the pairs that the rover replaced for a round would play only 24 boards, a possible of only 288. The pairs sitting in the rover's direction who were not bumped would play 26 boards for a 312 possible. To determine a winner it is necessary to factor the scores of those who had the lower possible up to the possible of the rest of the field, or 312/288, which reduces to 13/12.

In all half-table games it is possible to set up a movement where top on a board is the same for all boards. Whenever possible, the director should attempt to set up such a movement. However, from time to time a situation arises where certain boards are played more or less frequently than other boards, resulting in a higher top score on certain boards. When this happens, it is necessary to factor all boards with a lower top by a fraction that will make those boards have a top equivalent to the top of the boards with the higher top. If some boards have a top of six and others have a top of five, then it is necessary to multiply the matchpoint scores on the boards with the five top by 6/5.

For one-session events in more than one section where there is a different top score in each section (an example would be one 14-table Mitchell section, top 12, average 156, and one 7-table three-quarters movement, top 6, average 78), the scores in the section with the lower top score must be factored up to those of the larger section (in this case, by simply doubling, 312/156 or 2 being the factor applied).

If the smaller section were an 11-table game with a three-quarters movement, 10 top, 130 average, the factor would be 312/260 or 6/5.

In two-session events (without elimination) in which there are more or fewer contestants in the second session, and consequently the top score on a board is different, the second session is always adjusted to the score of the first session.

If a half-table movement winds up with different tops on some boards, then it is necessary to do a double factoring. First the tops on the boards should be factored so that there is the same top on all boards. Then a second factoring should equalize the scores based on the number of boards each pair played.

FAILURE TO COMPLY WITH A LEAD OR PLAY PENALTY. The act of playing an INCORRECT CARD when a player is able to lead or play from an unfaced hand a card or suit required by law or specified by an opponent in accordance with an agreed penalty. See LAWS OF DUPLICATE, Law 52.

FALL, FALL OF THE CARDS. The play of a card or cards on a trick; the order in which they are played.

FALL NATIONALS. See FALL NORTH AMERICAN BRIDGE CHAMPIONSHIPS.

FALL NORTH AMERICAN BRIDGE CHAMPIONSHIPS. Formerly called the Winter Nationals or the Fall Nationals. This annual tournament held since 1927 takes place in November or early December. These championships were originally under the auspices of the American Bridge League, and since 1937 have been controlled by the American Contract Bridge League. The Fall NABC began as a four-day tournament and was enlarged to eight days four years later. Nine-day tournaments became standard in postwar years. In 1963, the addition of the International Fund Pairs lengthened the tournament to nine and one-half days. It became a full ten-day tournament when ACBL rescheduled major events in 1969. In 1981 a pre-tournament Charity Gala was added. The Thursday evening Charity game took various forms, and by 1992 was a substantial bridge event with 177 tables in play in Charity Pairs games and first rounds of Charity Knockout Teams.

In 1928 the major event of the ABL's "Winter Congress" was the Open Pairs played for the Cavendish Trophy. The Chicago Trophy (now the Reisinger) for the Board-a-Match Teams-of-Four was put in play in 1929. The Reisinger Teams and the Blue Ribbon Pairs (inaugurated in 1963) are the premier (six-session) events at the Fall NABC along with the North American Swiss Teams event which was added to the schedule in 1977. The four-session Life Master Women's Pairs, formerly held simultaneously with the Life Master Men's Pairs, has, since 1990, played opposite a new Life Master Open Pairs. The four-session Women's Board-a-Match Teams, formerly held simultaneously with the Men's Board-a-Match Teams, has, since 1990, played opposite an Open Board-a-Match Teams. For past results of Fall Championships, see Appendix I.

Fall North American Championships Attendance (an asterisk indicates the record was broken that year; table counts not available until 1952)

Year	Site	Tables
1927	Chicago	
1928	Cleveland	
1929	Chicago	
1930	Cleveland	
1931	Philadelphia	
1932	New York	
1933	Cincinnati	
1934	New York	
1935	Chicago	
1936	Chicago	
1937	Washington	
1938	Cleveland	
1939	Pittsburgh	
1940	Philadelphia	
1941	Richmond	
1942	Syracuse	
1943	New York	
1944	Atlantic City	
1945	Atlantic City	
1946	Hollywood FL	
1947	Atlantic City	
1948	Philadelphia	
1949	Philadelphia	
1950	New Orleans	
1951	Detroit	
1952	Miami	2,017
1953	Dallas	1,798
1954	Atlanta	1,775
1955	Miami	2,359*
1956	New Orleans	2,777*
1957	Los Angeles	6,154*
1958	Detroit	4,046
1959	Coronado CA	5,838
1960	New York City	6,391*
1961	Houston	4,967
1962	Phoenix	6,468*
1963	Bal Harbour FL	7,129*
1964	Dallas	8,686*
1965	San Francisco	11,198*
1966	Pittsburgh	8,896
1967	New Orleans	8,904
1968	Coronado CA	7,858
1969	Bal Harbour FL	9,069
1970	Houston	7,994
1971	Phoenix	7,080
1972	Lancaster PA	11,545*
1973	Las Vegas	13,464*
1974	San Antonio	8,419
1975	New Orleans	11,705
1976	Pittsburgh	8,787
1977	Atlanta	10,701
1978	Denver	9,467
1979	Cincinnati	9,262
1980	Lancaster PA	13,521*
1981	San Francisco	11,377
1982	Minneapolis	7,465
1983	Bal Harbour FL	10,555
1984	San Diego	12,072
1985	Winnipeg MB	5,534
1986	Atlanta	11,285
1987	Anaheim CA	13,948*
1988	Nashville	13,214
1989	Lancaster PA	12,580
1990	San Francisco	13,239
1991	Indianapolis	9,298
1992	Orlando FL	14,980*
1993	Seattle	11,456
1994	Minneapolis	
1995	Atlanta	
1996	San Francisco	

FALSECARDING. A defender is said to falsecard when he plays a card other than his lowest with the intention of deceiving the declarer. (Thus, a high card played as the beginning of an echo is not a falsecard because there is no intention to deceive.)

The term falsecard derives from the fact that defenders normally play true cards in order to provide each other with information. The declarer, with no partner to worry about, is not obliged to play true cards, so for him there is no such thing as a falsecard.

Deceptive play by the declarer may extend to the conduct of the whole hand, whereas in practical play the defenders are usually limited to the play of a single falsecard to one trick. It is, therefore, convenient to treat the subject of deceptive play by the defenders under the title "Falsecarding," dealing with declarer play under the title DECEPTIVE PLAY.

The defenders' advantage

Although the defenders are usually restricted to the choice of a single card, rather than a complete tactical play, they have many more opportunities for skillful deception than the declarer, a fact which is not generally realized. Consider this situation:

```
              K 7 3
J 9 6 2                A Q 4
              10 8 5
```

East is the declarer, and clearly there is no way for him to bring in the suit without loss. If dummy's jack is led, North covers and South's 10 is promoted.

Now suppose instead that the declarer is South and that West is on lead. If West leads the jack, the declarer cannot be sure whether or not it is right to cover; he cannot see the defenders' cards. In the diagram, the king must be put on to make the 10 a guard; but it may turn out that West has made a clever play from the Q-J, the true position being:

```
              K 7 3
Q J 9 2                A 6 4
              10 8 5
```

Now if the king is played on the first lead from West, East wins with the ace and returns the suit through South's 10; the defenders take all the tricks.

Suppose that in the second diagram the declarer is East once more, and that he again leads an honor from dummy. If North covers, he allows declarer all the tricks, but North has no difficulty in playing low; seeing the Q-J in dummy, he ducks the first lead, following the maxim that a defender should cover the last of touching honors - a complete answer to problems of this sort.

Clever falsecarding aims at exploiting the defenders' advantage in situations of that kind. Falsecarding is analyzed under these headings: Playing a Known Card; Trump Suit Falsecarding; Random Falsecards Which Cannot Deceive Partner; False Signals; Deceptive Opening Leads; Falsecarding in the Middle or End Game.

Playing a known card

A well-established principle of defensive play is that in a critical position a defender should play a card he is known to hold or will soon be known to hold, if he can do so without sacrificing a trick. Example:

```
              A J 5
Q 10 3                8 6 2
              K 9 7 4
```

South leads low, finesses dummy's jack, and continues with ace and another. When the ace is played, West can follow suit with two cards of equal value, the queen and 10. He should play the card he is known to hold, the queen, offering declarer the possibility of finessing the 9 on the third round.

Such maneuvers are common in a keen game, even when the defender has no specific objective in mind.

```
              A K J 6
Q 5 4                10 8 3 2
              9 7
```

South finesses dummy's jack. West should play the queen on the next round, for until he releases the queen, declarer knows that the suit cannot possibly be ruffed on his left. Similarly:

```
              A Q 7 5
K J 10 3                8 6 4 2
              9
```

Playing a crossruff, South finesses dummy's queen and

continues with ace and another, ruffing. Until West parts with the card he is known to hold, the king, declarer can safely ruff low.

More difficult to gauge is the early release of a high card whose position is not marked but soon will be.

```
              A K J 3 2
Q 8 4                10 9 6 5
              7
```

At a trump contract, this is a side suit. South cashes the ace and ruffs a low card. West, who can see that his queen will fall under the king next, plays it on the second round, and South will think only three tricks are available.

It may be necessary to have a grasp of the strategy of the entire hand before this sort of play is safe.

```
                    ♠ Q 4
                    ♥ K J 10 8 3
                    ♦ Q 8 6
                    ♣ A 3 2
♠ 9 2                           ♠ J 3
♥ 9 6 4                         ♥ A Q 7 5
♦ 10 7 5 2                      ♦ A K J 4
♣ J 10 6 4                      ♣ K 7 5
                    ♠ A K 10 8 7 6 5
                    ♥ 2
                    ♦ 9 3
                    ♣ Q 9 8
```

South plays in 4♠ after East has opened the bidding. Diamonds are led and South ruffs the third round. Needing to establish two heart tricks, he finesses dummy's 10.

East wins with the ace, not the queen, and returns a trump. East judges that declarer will expect him to have the ace for his opening bid, so if he wins the first trick with the queen, declarer will take a ruffing finesse against the ace on the next round and make his contract. After East's deceptive play of the ace, however, declarer may try to bring down the queen in West by ruffing the second round. If he tries that, shortage of entries prevents him establishing a second heart trick.

The following hand illustrates a different reason for releasing a high card whose location will soon be known to the declarer.

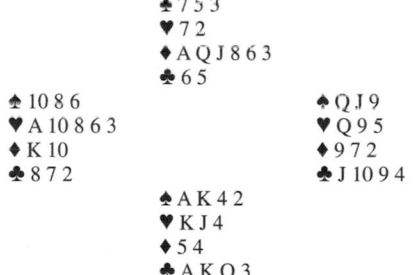

```
                    ♠ 7 5 3
                    ♥ 7 2
                    ♦ A Q J 8 6 3
                    ♣ 6 5
♠ 10 8 6                        ♠ Q J 9
♥ A 10 8 6 3                    ♥ Q 9 5
♦ K 10                          ♦ 9 7 2
♣ 8 7 2                         ♣ J 10 9 4
                    ♠ A K 4 2
                    ♥ K J 4
                    ♦ 5 4
                    ♣ A K Q 3
```

In a pairs contest, West leads a small heart against 3 NT, and the queen is topped by the king. South returns a diamond, and West, knowing that his king is lost, plays it immediately. Now South has a problem, even if he knows West as a guileful player. If he takes the trick and it turns out that the king is singleton, he may take only nine tricks; by ducking, he could have won 11 tricks by establishing the long cards without letting East gain the lead.

Trump suit falsecarding

The suit combinations illustrated in the following can exist in any suit, whether trumps or not, but it is best to consider them as being trump. The fact that in every case the declarer has the majority of cards means that the suit usually will be trumps; also, the deceptive maneuvers require an exact appreciation of the layout of the suit, and in practical play this condition is seldom met unless the suit is trumps.

The essence of most of the following plays is that a falsecard is obligatory; failure to falsecard leaves declarer no option but to adopt the winning line of play. The falsecard presents him with the possibility of following an alternative line, which will lose. This type of falsecard is still purposeful even if the declarer is unlikely to fall into the trap set for him. Had the falsecard not been played, there would have been no possibility of declarer's going wrong; after the falsecard there is such a possibility, however slight.

<pre>
        A J 8 3
  K 2   10 9 6
        Q 7 5 4
</pre>

South leads small and finesses dummy's jack. If East plays the 6, declarer has no choice but to play the ace on the next round, making all the tricks. If East plays the 9 or 10, declarer may enter the closed hand to lead the queen, which would be the winning play if East had 10-9 doubleton or a singleton.

There are some plays which appear dangerous at first sight but which in fact are obligatory if a high standard of play is to be assumed.

<pre>
        A Q 6 2
  4   K 10 8 3
        J 9 7 5
</pre>

When declarer leads small and finesses dummy's queen, only the 8 from East offers hope of a second trick. If East wins with the king, the ace will be played on the next round, and a third-round finesse will pick up the suit. After the play of the 8, declarer may come to hand and lead the jack, which would be a good play if East held 10-8 alone, but costs a trick in the actual diagram. Following is one of many variations of the theme.

<pre>
        K Q 9 4
  10 8 6 3   A
        J 7 5 2
</pre>

Unless West plays the 8 when a low trump is led toward dummy's king, he has no chance of a second trick.

Many falsecarding positions are associated with the holding of J-9 doubleton and related holdings:

<pre>
        Q 8 3
  A 7 6   J 9
        K 10 5 4 2
</pre>

South attacks this suit by leading low from dummy. East follows with the jack, and South's king loses to West's ace. South is likely to finesse the 8 next, playing West for A-9-7-6.

<pre>
        K 8 3
  7 6 5   A J 9
        Q 10 4 2
</pre>

If South leads low from dummy, East may gain by playing the jack.

This next position also has variations:

<pre>
        J 9 3
  8 5 4   Q 10
        A K 7 6 2
</pre>

Whether South lays down the ace from hand or leads the 3 from dummy, East can probably read the position well enough to gauge that it is safe to drop the queen.

The following play is liable to score:

<pre>
        Q 2
  J 10   A 7 3
        K 9 8 6 5 4
</pre>

When South leads small to the queen, East ducks smoothly and the declarer probably continues by finessing the 9 in his own hand. Had East taken the queen with the ace, South would have played to drop the jack on the next round, recognizing that there would be no purpose in finessing against A-J-7-3 in East's hand. A similar position:

<pre>
        7
  J 10 6   A 5
        K Q 9 8 4 3 2
</pre>

Dummy's 7 is led and the king wins. Unless West plays the 10 or jack, declarer has no choice but to lead a low card to the next trick.

Many falsecards have a better chance of succeeding in a pairs contest, where declarers are willing to take measured risks for an extra trick.

<pre>
        J 8 6 2
  Q 10 9 5   3
        A K 7 4
</pre>

When South plays the ace, West drops the 9 or 10. If declarer can afford to lose one trick, he does best to play small toward the jack, which preserves the position against any lie of the defenders' cards, but in a pairs contest he may decide instead to cross to dummy and lead the jack. This is equally safe against four cards in East's hand, and nets a big matchpoint score if West holds 10-9 alone.

Occasionally it is possible to forestall these defensive wiles.

<pre>
        Q 8 4 2
  3   J 9 6 5
        A K 10 7
</pre>

When declarer plays the ace from hand, the standard falsecard for East is the 9. If he fails to play the 9, declarer is bound to continue by leading toward the queen, discovering the finesse against the jack. After the play of the 9, declarer may continue with the king from hand, with the idea of finessing against West if he has J-6-5-3.

Entries permitting, declarer in the above situation should make the first lead from dummy. Now it is dangerous for East to drop the 9, for partner could have the singleton 10.

There is another type of falsecard which, though not occurring in the trump suit, is associated with suit contracts. This is the play of a high card perhaps setting up winners for declarer - to dissuade declarer from following a line of play which the defender knows must win. A bold player may sacrifice a high card in this way even though he may be unable to envisage the likely effect; it is sufficient for him that the declarer must be deflected from the course which he has apparently set. A classic hand of this kind was defended by the British player, Terence Reese, in his Oxford days.

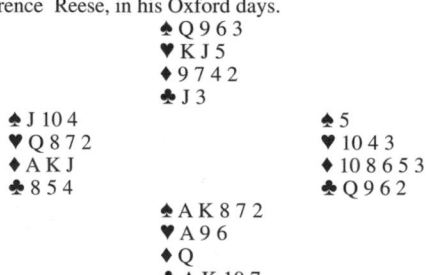

West led diamonds against South's 6♠ contract.

Having ruffed the second round, South played three rounds of clubs, ruffing in dummy. Since it was evident that the fourth club could be ruffed with impunity, Reese dropped the queen on the third round.

The declarer continued with the ♠Q-A. When East showed out on the second trump, it appeared safe to lead the ♣10, intending to discard a heart in dummy and subsequently ruff a heart. When the ♣10 was led, West made his trump jack to defeat a contract which would have been made routinely had not East falsecarded.

Random falsecards which cannot deceive partner

The previous situations have been mainly those where an immediate purpose could be discerned, justifying the defender in breaching his duty to play true cards. There are, however, situations where it is permissible for a defender to falsecard with the more general aim of harrying the declarer, and spoiling his count of the hand. The most common is where declarer has shown out of a suit; now, since both defenders know the exact distribution of the suit, they may falsecard with no specific aim in mind.

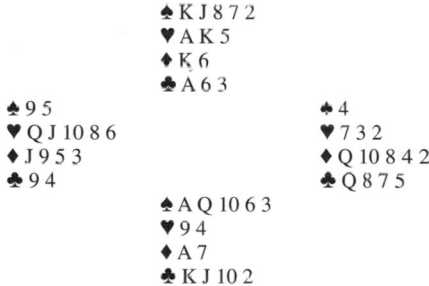

```
              ♠ K J 8 7 2
              ♥ A K 5
              ♦ K 6
              ♣ A 6 3
  ♠ 9 5                        ♠ 4
  ♥ Q J 10 8 6                 ♥ 7 3 2
  ♦ J 9 5 3                    ♦ Q 10 8 4 2
  ♣ 9 4                        ♣ Q 8 7 5
              ♠ A Q 10 6 3
              ♥ 9 4
              ♦ A 7
              ♣ K J 10 2
```

West leads the ♥Q against 6♠. South's only problem is to locate the ♣Q for the overtrick and, though the hand does not lend itself to maneuver, declarer should endeavor to extract what information he can before putting himself to the club guess. After drawing trumps, he plays a second and third round of hearts, ruffing. West must play his cards circumspectly; if he follows thoughtlessly with the 6 and 8, declarer will reflect that West probably had a five-card heart suit, since the lead of the queen is more attractive when both jack and 10 are behind it. So slight a consideration as this would be enough to sway declarer's play of the clubs; South would play East for the ♣Q since, holding shorter hearts than West, he may hold longer clubs.

On the second and third round of hearts, West does best to play the 10 and jack, seeking to create the impression that East is the player with long hearts, but if declarer notices that East has played the 7 on the third round although the 6 is still missing, he may begin to wonder.

If, in a situation like that, West really held the doubleton ♣Q, it is doubtful whether he would be well advised to play his hearts in such a way as to give declarer a true count of the suit, in the expectation that declarer would take the losing play in clubs. Such maneuvers fall into the category of pure bluff rather than tactics, and in a keen game the defenders usually do best to play accurately and let declarer guess.

Falsecards of that type are more effective if made before declarer actually shows out of the suit, since he is then more inclined to take them at face value.

```
              ♠ K 10 7
              ♥ A 5
              ♦ K 4 3 2
              ♣ 10 8 6 5
  ♠ Q 9 8                      ♠ 6 5 3 2
  ♥ Q 10 4 3                   ♥ J 6 2
  ♦ 9 5                        ♦ J 6
  ♣ J 9 7 3                    ♣ A K Q 2
              ♠ A J 4
              ♥ K 9 8 7
              ♦ A Q 10 8 7
              ♣ 4
```

South plays 6♦ after East has dealt and passed. When West leads the ♣3, East falsecards, winning with the king rather than the queen. (If the ace stands up on the next round, West will not be critical of the falsecard; if it doesn't, West knows all.) Declarer ruffs the ace, and has to guess the spade position to make his contract. Had East won the opening lead with the queen, South would have reflected (after finding the red jacks in East) that East might have opened the bidding had he held the ♠Q and 13 points in all.

False Signals

The defenders labor under the disadvantage that most of their signals are sent "in clear" and so are liable to enemy interception. On a hand like the following, the declarer's task is easier if his opponents are known as conscientious signalers.

```
              ♠ 8 7
              ♥ K 8 7 5 4
              ♦ 8 6 2
              ♣ A 9 5


              ♠ A K Q 10 6 5
              ♥ A 2
              ♦ A Q J
              ♣ K 7
```

South plays 6♠ in a pairs contest. Having won the club lead with the king and drawn trumps, South's problem is whether to try to ruff out the hearts for two discards or to finesse diamonds; shortage of entries means that he cannot try both. But, if the defenders echo to show two or four cards, declarer knows what to do after playing ace and another heart.

Best results are obtained by defenders who keep up with the game and at a given time are conscious whether a false signal could mislead partner. Very often it can be recognized that partner will not be misled. In such cases, defenders should vary their signals between true and falsecards rather than try to outsmart the declarer.

False signals can be used to persuade the declarer to ruff unnecessarily, or to ruff high, in a critical trump situation.

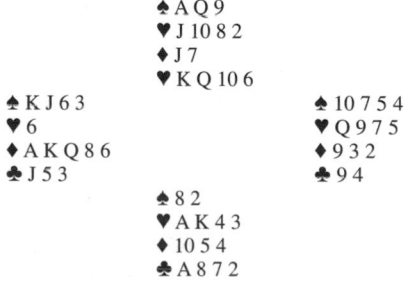

```
              ♠ A Q 9
              ♥ J 10 8 2
              ♦ J 7
              ♥ K Q 10 6
  ♠ K J 6 3                    ♠ 10 7 5 4
  ♥ 6                          ♥ Q 9 7 5
  ♦ A K Q 8 6                  ♦ 9 3 2
  ♣ J 5 3                      ♣ 9 4
              ♠ 8 2
              ♥ A K 4 3
              ♦ 10 5 4
              ♣ A 8 7 2
```

South plays 4♥ after West has opened 1♦. On the ♦A-K, East echoes with the 9 and 2. Since it is quite possible that East has a doubleton diamond, declarer may judge to ruff with the 10 when West plays the third round. If he does so, he loses two trump tricks instead of one.

A defender must occasionally falsecard his partner to direct the defense. This is an example deal from a pairs event:

```
                      ♠ Q 7 5
                      ♥ K Q 10 3 2
                      ♦ K 6
                      ♣ 9 5 4
        ♠ 9 3                         ♠ J 4
        ♥ A 9 7                       ♥ 8 6 4
        ♦ 9 8 7 5 4                   ♦ A Q
        ♣ 10 7 2                      ♣ K Q J 8 6 3
                      ♠ A K 10 8 6 2
                      ♥ J 5
                      ♦ J 10 3 2
                      ♣ A
```

WEST	NORTH	EAST	SOUTH
		1 ♣	1 ♠
Pass	2 ♦	Pass	3 ♠
Pass	4 ♠	All Pass	

West leads the ♣2. East can see that his defense is moot unless West has a trump trick or the ♥A. Even then, West must shift to diamonds. East therefore plays the ♣K at the first trick, denying the queen. When West takes the ♥A, he will find the diamond switch. (No doubt West should lead a diamond in any case, but East can make the winning play easier.)

Deceptive Opening Leads

Defenders should seldom depart from the accepted conventional leads. To underlead an ace against a suit contract, or to lead an honor from the middle of a sequence, may score on a particular hand, but if it is done frequently, the loss in partnership accuracy will outweigh the gain thus made.

Because that is generally recognized as true, the occasional deceptive lead can be all the more effective. Some leads, such as the jack from Q-J doubleton, are so well known as to lack any element of surprise. The following is also far from fresh:

```
              J 6 4
    10 9 2               Q 3
              A K 8 7 5
```

Left to himself, the declarer loses no tricks in this trump suit when he plays to drop the doubleton queen. Some authorities have commended the opening lead of the 9, the theory being that declarer may put on the jack and play East for Q-10-3-2 or Q-10-x.

Declarer's protection against being duped too often is the knowledge that a good defender seldom leads a trump other than his lowest. To lead the 9 from 9-2, for example, can never gain as compared with leading the 2, and can cost in more than one way. Since most defenders are averse to leading a singleton trump, the declarer should look suspiciously at the lead of a 9 or card of similar rank; particularly when, as in the preceding diagram, he himself holds the card of next lower rank, and knows that the card led cannot be the top of a sequence.

The deceptive lead of fifth-best instead of fourth-best against notrump is a more persuasive maneuver. It is liable to gain in many situations like the following:

```
                      ♠ K 9 8
                      ♥ Q 6
                      ♦ J 10 3 2
                      ♣ K Q 8 5
        ♠ A 5                         ♠ J 10 7 6 3
        ♥ A 10 8 4 2                  ♥ 9 7 5
        ♦ K 9 6                       ♦ 5 4
        ♣ J 9 3                       ♣ 10 6 2
                      ♠ Q 4 2
                      ♥ K J 3
                      ♦ A Q 8 7
                      ♣ A 7 4
```

West's own wealth of high cards makes it unlikely that his partner can contribute to the defense, so he leads the ♥2 against 3 NT. Dummy wins, the ♦J runs to West's king, and a small heart comes back. Declarer cashes his diamonds, and both defenders discard spades. Now South has to decide whether to set up a spade or to seek his ninth trick in clubs. After cashing two rounds of clubs he is none the wiser and, taking the opening lead at its face value, he may think that hearts are 4-4 and that it is safe to play a spade.

No less effective is the lead of third-best in an attempt to create the impression that a five-card suit is held. This is the other side of the picture from the previous deal:

```
                      ♠ Q 10 9
                      ♥ Q 6 2
                      ♦ A K 6
                      ♣ Q 9 7 5
        ♠ A 7 3 2                     ♠ 8 5 4
        ♥ A 9                         ♥ 7 5 4 3
        ♦ J 10 5 3                    ♦ 7 4
        ♣ A 8 4                       ♣ J 6 3 2
                      ♠ K J 6
                      ♥ K J 10 8
                      ♦ Q 9 8 2
                      ♣ K 10
```

Again West knows that partner has little to fight with, so he leads the ♠3 against South's 3 NT contract. After driving out the ♥A and receiving the return of the ♠2, South has only eight tricks, and has to decide whether to play a club or test diamonds. If he knew that West had only four spades, he could safely play a club; after the deceptive lead, however, he may decide to try for the diamond break, in which case he establishes a setting trick for the defenders.

Other opportunities for a deceptive lead are sometimes missed. Suppose the declarer in a notrump contract opened the bidding with 1 NT, and subsequently showed a spade suit in response to Stayman; since both defenders have a count of the spades, expecting declarer to have precisely four, there is no reason why the defender, if he decides to open up the suit, should give declarer free information by leading a conventional fourth-best; he can simply lead his lowest card.

Falsecarding in the Middle or End Game

At the opening lead, the defender is restricted in his deceptive maneuvers by the necessity of not misleading partner, and by a general lack of information. In the middle game, however, it is possible for both defenders to know the exact lie of the cards while declarer is still in doubt. When this is the case, defenders can deceive declarer without deceiving each other.

The position illustrated under the heading The Defenders' Advantage is a basic one to which there are many variations. Example:

```
              K 7 3
  A Q 8                  J 9 6 2
              10 5 4
```

Judging in the middle game that three tricks are needed from this suit, West leads the queen. Declarer may duck twice, playing him for Q-J.

```
              A J 9 4
  Q 10 5                 K 8 6
              7 3 2
```

South leads low, intending to follow the percentages by finessing the 9 the first time and the jack the second. By putting up the queen, West may persuade declarer that he has the king as well, and deflect him from his course. Similar positions arise when West is on lead:

```
              J 9 6
  K 10 5 2               Q 8 3
              A 7 4
```

If circumstances compel West to open this suit, the king is the card. Conversely, in a position such as the following, it may be best to lead small:

```
              J 9 7
  K Q 3                  10 6 5 2
              A 8 4
```

There are a number of miscellaneous positions in the middle game where the play of a high card may alter declarer's whole plan of campaign:

```
              A Q 10 9
  7 4 3                  K J 8
              6 5 2
```

When declarer finesses dummy's 10, East wins with the king instead of the jack. If declarer assumes that the jack is with West, and that he has three certain tricks by finessing the 9 on the next round, he may fall into indiscretion.

In the end game there are occasions when a desperate lead offers the only hope of escaping from an elimination.

```
              A 9 7
  Q 8 2                  J 6 4 3
              K 10 5
```

If South has staged an elimination which compels West to open this suit, the queen is best, offering declarer the possibility of winning in hand, and finessing against the jack. If West leads small instead, declarer can play only for split honors. Similarly:

```
              Q 9 7
  J 8 4                  K 10 6 2
              A 5 3
```

If West leads small, declarer may play low in dummy, and capture the 10 with the ace; on the next round he probably finesses the 9. If West leads the jack on the first round, declarer may cover on the assumption that the 9 sits behind the 10.

Suppose that in the above example the declarer is on lead, and plays small toward the table. Suppose also that East is marked with the king, and the declarer intends to insert dummy's 9, forcing East to lead away from the king or concede a ruff-sluff. On South's lead, West puts in the jack to make it appear that he has the 10 as well, in which case declarer's play would be to duck in dummy.

For declarer's counter-weapon, see DECEPTION, MATHEMATICS OF. See also *Deceptive Play at Bridge* by Hugh Kelsey; *Falsecards* by Mike Lawrence.

FALSE PREFERENCE. A return to partner's original suit at the lowest level when holding greater length in the second suit. See PREFERENCE BIDS.

FAMILY (bridge playing). Perhaps the world's biggest bridge-playing family is anchored by Gail Greenberg of New York, a WBF Grand Master who has won four world titles. Her first and third husbands, Steve Shane and Jack Greenberg, are strong players while her second husband, Mike Moss, was second in the 1990 World Team Olympiad. Two of her children, Jill Blanchard and Brad Moss, have won NABC titles. In addition, Brad was the 1989 *King of Bridge* and his brother Andrew was the 1991 *King of Bridge.*

The first siblings to be named *King of Bridge* were brothers Marc Franklin in 1977 and Matthew Franklin in 1978.

Brothers David, Bill and Doug Hsieh all achieved early success — and Life Master status — playing with father George and others. Bill, the 1983 *King of Bridge,* became the youngest Life Master at age 13 in 1980 and Doug won the title in 1981 at age 11.

Powerful family combinations of yesteryear were brothers B. Jay and Simon Becker and B. Jay's sons, Steve and Michael, all with North American championships. Michael became a world champion when he won the Bermuda Bowl in 1983. His wife Judith won the NABC Swiss Teams in 1980.

The Jacoby family of Dallas featured two world champions, Oswald and son Jim. Both Oswald's wife Mary Zita and Jim's wife Judy won Life Master status.

Another two-generational bridge-playing family is the Seamon family of Miami. William Seamon and his sister Anne Burnstein, both champion players, are deceased but the rest of the family — sister Edith Freilich, wife Rita, son Michael and daughter Janice — continue to be frequent winners in regional and NABC events.

The Cohen family is headed by father Ralph, who won the NABC IMP Pairs in 1990 and who has represented Canada and ACBL in international competition. Son Billy won the 1978 Swiss, the 1987 Reisinger Board-a-Match Teams and the 1993 Open Swiss. Wife Joan, son Jordan and Jordan's wife Fran are also Life Masters.

The Hamman family includes Bob Hamman, regarded by many as the best bridge player in the world; wife Petra, who won the Women's Board a Match Teams in 1989; former wife Barbara, who won the Womens KO Teams in 1985; son Chris, a Bronze Life Master who began playing with his dad in 1993; and Chris' wife Gigi. Gigi, the former Gigi Geiger, is also a member of a bridge-playing family which includes mother Gen Geiger and sister Kathryn Slaats.

Among the more successful of the parent-child pairs are the Cappellettis — Mike Sr. and Mike Jr. The Mikes finished second in the Reisinger Board-a-Match Teams at the Fall NABC in Indianapolis in 1991 and have had half a dozen top-10 finishes in the 20 North American championships they've played in together. Mike Sr.'s wife, Susan Green, won the Women's KO Teams in 1991 and former wife Kathie Walvick is a WBF World Master.

Another successful father-son combination is Richard Pavlicek Sr. and Richard Pavlicek Jr. The two have fourth-place finishes in the Blue Ribbon Pairs at the Fall NABC in Indianapolis in 1991 and the Open Pairs at the Pan American Games in Corpus Christi TX in 1992. Wife/mother Mabel is a Gold Life Master.

A successful mother-son combination is Jill Wooldridge and son Joel, who first gained notice when they won the Mixed Pairs at the Toronto regional in 1990. At the time, Joel was 10 years old. He subsequently became ACBL's youngster Life Master at age 11.

Sam Hirschman, the 1994 *King of Bridge,* was the youngest Life Master before Joel. His teacher and principal partner was father Martin Hirschman, who was co-editor of the NEC World Junior Team Championships *Daily Bulletin* in 1991. A second Hirschman son, Dan, won his first regional title at the All-American Regional in Cleveland OH in May 1994 at age 9. Mother Marcy Abramson is also a Life Master.

Steve Weinstein has had great success playing with his stepfather Fred Stewart. The two won the Life Master Pairs at the Summer NABC in Boston in 1981 — when Weinstein was 17 and the youngest player ever to win an NABC title. They won the Reisinger Board-a-Match Teams at the San Diego NABC in 1984, the Blue Ribbon Pairs at the Anaheim NABC in 1987 and the 1993 Cavendish Invitational Pairs.

The Crossleys are a three-generation family whose youngest generation includes 1974 Vanderbilt winners David and Robert.

The Kasle family includes Gaylor, 1994 Vanderbilt winner who is #9 on the list of ACBL members with the most masterpoints; wife Barbara, a Gold Life Master; and mother Lee, who was a national champion in 1959. Sidney Kasle, Gaylor's father, was LM #525 with many wins and a record for service to the Central Indiana Unit of the ACBL.

Powerful bridge families in Europe include the Gardeners of Great Britain, the Bianchis and Valentis of Italy and the Shaltzes of Denmark. Dorthe Shaltz advanced to the quarterfinals of the 1993 Bermuda Bowl, the first woman to reach the playoff stage in many years. In Australia, both Peter Gill and his sister, Barbara Travis, have represented their country in major world championships. Gabino Cintra, World Pairs Champion in 1978, and his wife Lia have been mainstays for Brazil in world competition.

FAR EAST BRIDGE FEDERATION. The Far East Bridge Federation was formed in 1957 and began regular zonal championships in that year. Australia and New Zealand have competed frequently, although not members of the zone. Members of the zone in 1992 were: China; Hong Kong; Indonesia; Japan; Macao; Malaysia; Philippines; Singapore; Thailand; Taiwan. Far East teams reached the final of the Bermuda Bowl in 1969 and 1970. President 1992:

Khunying Ester Chodchoy Sophonpanich
P.O.Box 2588,
Bangkok 10501
Thailand
Fax: 6 2 275 5314

For results of Far East Championships, see Appendix III.

FAST ARRIVAL. The idea that the faster a contract is reached, the weaker the hand that places the contract; and, conversely, the slower the approach, the stronger the suggestion that a higher contract may be appropriate.

(a)		(b)	
WEST	EAST	WEST	EAST
1 ♠	2 ♣	1 ♠	2 ♣
2 ♠	4 ♠	2 ♠	3 ♦
		3NT	4 ♠

East's bidding is more encouraging in (b) than in (a).

For decades, constructive bidding was based on the idea that the better your hand, the higher you bid. In the Fifties and Sixties, a minimum-bidding style arose that espoused slow, scientific investigation for the best contract. The principle of Fast Arrival was a logical product of this style. Since jumps to game left less room for slam investigation, they implied an absence of slammish values and discouraged more bidding.

The significance of the two auctions above is indisputable, but the implications of other auctions are less clear and a matter for partnership discussion.

WEST	EAST
1 ♥	2 ♦
2 ♠	4 ♠

After East's response at the two-level and West's reverse, East-West are assured of game. In the classical approach, East's raise to 4♠ promises excellent spade support and willingness to hear West bid again. In Fast Arrival, East's 4♠ promises minimum values, trumps that may be only fair and no slam aspirations. If East wanted to leave room for slam investigation, he would raise to 3♠.

WEST	EAST
1 ♥	2 ♦
2 ♠	3 ♠

In the classical approach, East promises spade support, but the rest of his hand is not clearly defined. Using Fast Arrival, East implies interest in slam.

Though Fast Arrival often shows to advantage, a jump bid may be needed to emphasize a crucial feature. For example, trump quality is a major factor in slam bidding, and a jump in trumps should promise strong support.

WEST	EAST
♠ A 9 4	♠ J 10 8 7
♥ A	♥ K 9 5 4
♦ A Q J 9 4	♦ K 10 8 2
♣ A 9 7 3	♣ K

1 ♦	1 ♥
3 ♣	3 ♦
3 ♠	4 ♣
4 ♦	5 ♦
Pass	

This auction occurred in a U.S. Team Trials. At the other three tables, East followed his first response with a jump preference in diamonds, promising strong support, and reached the excellent slam.

Fast Arrival auctions also sustain a loss when they end in the wrong contract.

WEST	EAST
♠ A 8 5	♠ J 6 3
♥ J 9 6 4 2	♥ A 7 3
♦ A Q 5	♦ K 10 9 6 2
♣ K 2	♣ A 7

Table 1

WEST	EAST
1 ♥	2 ♦
2NT	4 ♥

Table 2

1 ♥	2 ♦
2NT	3 ♥
3NT	

The auction at Table 1 was Fast Arrival. A spade opening lead sank 4♥, while 3NT made at Table 2.

See an article in the *The Bridge World,* Dec. 1978. See

also TWO OVER ONE GAME FORCE.

FAST PASS. A lightning action which may improperly convey weakness. The prevention of a fast pass is one of the reasons for the SKIP-BID WARNING. See also RHYTHM.

FEATURE, FEATURE SHOWING. A feature is a particular holding of an ace or king (occasionally a queen) which may be of particular importance in a given hand. Showing of features in a hand through the bidding commences only when a suit is agreed on and a game is assured. Among the conventions that are in common use to determine features are ACE-SHOWING RESPONSES, ASKING BIDS, GERBER, BLACKWOOD, and other 4 NT bids, the GRAND SLAM FORCE, CUEBIDS, and various combinations or modifications thereof. See also WEAK TWO-BIDS.

FEDERATION, FEDERACION, FEDERACAO. See country name.

FERT. The weak opening in strong pass systems, called a "bid of misery" by Edgar Kaplan. The usual range is 0-7, and a variety of one-level suit-bids are used. A major-suit fert is more risky than a minor-suit fert, but more difficult to handle.

A fert at unfavorable vulnerability is decidedly risky, but only if the opponents are prepared to take advantage of it. They must decide whether action over a strong pass is equivalent to an overcall or an opening bid. If the former, it is possible to make an overcall of one club. One aggressive counter-measure is fert over fert: A minimum suit bid announces that the next player has a fert range. This allows him to pass with moderate balanced hands and double with strong hands, maximizing the chance of emerging with a big penalty. Some fert users therefore abandon them at unfavorable vulnerability.

The fert causes great confusion for the opponents, who seldom get an opportunity for a normal constructive auction. But the purpose is not simply destructive: The strong pass gains a step when compared with a strong club method. See WEAK OPENING SYSTEMS.

FICTION. See LITERATURE AND BRIDGE.

FIELD. All the players entered in an event.

FIELD REPRESENTATIVE. An ACBL tournament director assigned to supervise bridge activity at the tournament and club level in one of the ACBL's seven areas.

FIELDING A PSYCHIC. An abnormal or unexpected action by the partner of a psychic bidder which protects the partnership and makes it appear that the player is aware of the psychic before it can legitimately be shown to have been exposed by the course of events. For example:

SOUTH	WEST	NORTH	EAST
1 ♠	Pass	2 ♥	3 ♦
Pass	Pass	Pass	

If South has opened with a psychic bid and North has 12 points, the psychic has been fielded and the partner will face action by a director and perhaps a committee. But if East does not act and South passes, the psychic has been exposed and North can take any action he pleases.

See PSYCHIC BIDDING.

FIFTEEN TABLES. At duplicate, 15 tables provide for competition among 60 players, 30 pairs, or 15 teams-of-four. It is a very good movement for 15 teams-of-four for board-a-match. It is inconvenient for 15 tables of Swiss Teams, but a board-a-match type movement can be used with imp scoring.

As an Individual tournament, a group of 60 players used to be extremely awkward. The movement usually used was a 52-player RAINBOW with a double appendix. However, Tournament Director Maury Braunstein devised a movement that allows for 26 boards to be played in 13 rounds, with a top of 12. The movement through most rounds is similar to that used in other Individuals: South up one table, East up two tables, West down two tables, boards down one table, North stationary. After Rounds 5 and 7, East and West skip an extra table. After Round 12, South, West, East and the boards all move an extra table. If hand record duplication is used, the duplication round is counted as the first round and only 24 boards are played, with a top of 11. This duplication round counts as a playing round as far as the irregular moves are concerned.

As a pair game, a MITCHELL, either straight or scrambled is used. There are guide cards available for treating 14 to 20 tables as appendix movements using only 26 boards. This is standard in many countries where direct comparison on all the boards in play is desired. It is also sometimes used as the last session of multi-session events, although twinned seven-, eight-, or nine-table sections give comparable results with proper seeding of the sections.

As a team game, 28 boards are required to complete the movement. When 24 boards are desired, either the middle two, or the first and last rounds, can be omitted.

For 14½ or 15½ tables see HALF TABLE MOVEMENTS.

FIFTH ACE. See KEY CARD BLACKWOOD and ROMAN KEY CARD BLACKWOOD.

FIFTH HONOR. The ten-spot of the trump suit.

FILM. See DEFENSE TO OPENING THREE BIDS.

FINAL BID. The last bid in the auction, followed by three consecutive passes. There can be no further bidding. The final bid becomes the contract.

FINESSE. The attempt to gain power for lower-ranking cards by taking advantage of the favorable position of higher-ranking cards held by the opposition.
The most common uses of the finesse are:
(1) *To avoid losing a trick.*

♣ A Q

♣ 3 2

South cannot afford to lose a club trick. He therefore leads a club to North's queen, finessing against the king. If West has the king, the queen will win, and South will avoid a club loser.

♠ Q 10 6 2

♠ J 9 3   ♠ K 8 7 5

♠ A 4

West leads the ♠3, and South must avoid a spade loser. If South reads the position correctly, he will play the ♠10 from dummy, finessing against the ♠J. This enables South to avoid a spade loser.

(2) *To gain a trick with low-ranking cards*

♥ A 3 2

♥ Q 6 5

Needing two heart tricks, South cashes North's ace and leads toward his queen. If East holds the king, the queen will score a trick for South.

♦ Q 3 2

♦ 7 6 5

South needs one diamond trick. His best chance is to find West with both the A-K. He therefore leads toward the queen in the North hand, in an attempt to finesse against the A-K, thereby creating a trick for the queen.

(3) *To prepare for a second finesse in the same suit.* A finesse can often be used to create a second finesse. When this is done successfully, the second finesse usually results in the direct gain of a trick.

♣ A J 10

♣ 4 3 2

Needing two club tricks, South leads low to dummy's 10. If this finesse loses to an honor in the East hand, declarer is in position to take two tricks via a second finesse if West has the remaining high honor.

♠ A J 9

♠ 4 3 2

Needing two spade tricks, South leads low toward the North hand. When West follows low, he finesses the 9. If West started with K-10 or Q-10, this will drive a high honor from the East hand and a second finesse of the jack will result in two tricks for South.

(4) *To prepare for a pinning play in the same suit.* A finesse can also be preparatory to a different form of trick-gaining play in a suit. By taking an early finesse, it may be possible to reduce the length of the suit in one enemy hand.

♥ Q 9 8 7

♥ J 5   ♥ K 10 6

♥ A 4 3 2

Needing three heart tricks, South leads low, and finesses dummy's 7. East wins with the 10, but declarer later enters the North hand, and pushes the queen through East, blotting out the entire defensive holding. This combination of plays is now called an INTRA-FINESSE.

♦ Q 10 8 3 2

♦ J 9 4   ♦ A K 7 6

♦ 5

With some other suit as trump, South must develop two diamond tricks. He leads low from his hand, finessing North's 8. Later, the queen is led from the North hand to ruff away East's remaining honor. The suit will now fall after the second ruff (see FALSECARDING).

(5) *As an avoidance play.* A finesse may prove useful for keeping a particular opponent off lead.

♠ Q J 9
♥ A 10 9
♦ 10 7 5 4 2
♣ 3 2

♠ 3   ♠ A 6 5
♥ 5 4 3 2   ♥ 8 7 6
♦ Q 9 8   ♦ K J 6 3
♣ A Q 10 9 5   ♣ J 7 6

♠ K 10 8 7 4 2
♥ K Q J
♦ A
♣ K 8 4

Against South's 4♠ contract, West leads the ♠3. East plays two round of spades.

South now leads a club from dummy. If East follows low, South should finesse the 8! This is an avoidance play, designed to keep East off lead and avoid the killing play of the third trump.

If East has the ♣A, the next club lead will score the ♣K, and produce the game-going trick. However, if West has the ace, East can be prevented from leading the third round of trump. South later enters dummy with a heart, and leads a club to his king. This loses to West's ace, but declarer cannot be prevented from ruffing his third club in dummy.

(6) *As a safety play.* A finesse is often part of a safety play.

♠ K 9 2

♠ A J 5 4 3

South wishes to avoid losing two spade tricks. He cashes the ace and then leads toward dummy. If West follows with a small card, he finesses dummy's 9 to guard against West having started with Q-10-x-x (See SAFETY PLAY).

♠ A 10 9 8

♠ K 7 6 5 4

South wishes to avoid losing two spade tricks. He leads from either hand, and finesses by playing low from the opposite hand. In this way, Q-J-x-x in either hand can be picked up with only one loser.

(7) *To gain one or more entries*

♠ K 7 4
♥ J 8 7
♦ A 9 7 6 5
♣ J 10

♠ 8 5 2   ♠ —
♥ A K 10 9   ♥ Q 6 5 4 2
♦ Q 2   ♦ J 10 3
♣ A Q 9 8   ♣ 7 6 5 3 2

♠ A Q J 10 9 6 3
♥ 3
♦ K 8 4
♣ K 4

This hand demonstrates many techniques in the play of the cards. With best play on both sides, it hinges on repeated finesses to gain entries. South opens 4♠ in third position, and all pass. West leads the ♥K which holds. West cannot continue with the ♥A, for declarer will discard a diamond from his hand, later establishing the diamond suit by ruffing (see LOSER-ON-LOSER), preventing a lead through the ♣K. If West leads a lower heart, declarer will play the ♥J to force East's queen. He will later pass the ♥8 to West while discarding a diamond and will thereby make his contract (see AVOIDANCE).

Nor can West profitably shift to diamonds. If West leads the ♦Q, declarer lets him hold the trick; if West leads the ♦2, declarer wins the king, draws trumps, leads a diamond and ducks West's queen. (Declarer cannot succeed in this deal if he leads diamonds himself. He can lead to the ♦A and play a low diamond from both hands next, forcing West to win, but declarer cannot then unblock the ♦K before he draws trumps.)

Since West cannot profitably lead clubs, his only chance is to shift to a trump. Because of the recurring finesse for entry position in the trump suit, it makes no difference which trump West plays.

Suppose West leads the ♠2. Declarer finesses dummy's

4, which holds. The ♥J is played from dummy, East covers with the queen, and declarer ruffs with an honor. Now the ♦K and ♦A are cashed, West unblocking the ♦Q under the ♦K to avoid being thrown in with that card. The ♥8 is played. When East cannot cover, declarer's last diamond is discarded.

West wins and cannot lead a club or a heart, so he plays another trump. Declarer finesses the 7 (or wins the king while unblocking from his hand if West plays the 8), underplaying with his 6, ruffs a diamond to establish the suit, re-enters dummy with the remaining spade, and runs the diamonds.

On this deal, two finesses were taken against West's trump cards to obtain a third entry to dummy. Notice that if South must lead spades himself, he can enter dummy only twice against best defense by West.

See also BACKWARD FINESSE; CHINESE FINESSE; DEEP FINESSE; DOUBLE FINESSE; INTRA-FINESSE; OBLIGATORY FINESSE; RESTRICTED CHOICE; RUFFING FINESSE; SAFETY PLAY; SUIT COMBINATIONS; TWO-WAY FINESSE.

FINESSE, OBLIGATORY. see OBLIGATORY FINESSE.

FINESSING AGAINST PARTNER. See THIRD-HAND PLAY.

FINESSING PROBABILITIES. These and all finessing situations are listed under SUIT COMBINATIONS.

FINLAND, BRIDGE LEAGUE OF (Suomen Bridgeliitto Finlands Bridgeförbund). The League was founded in 1936 by the Helsingfors Bridge Club and Bridge Club Spades, the two clubs then in existence. It now has about 1850 members and 52 clubs. The League hosted European Championships in 1953 and 1989, and Nordic Championships in 1957, 1971 and 1982.
Officers 1993:
President: Olli Manni
Executive Secretary: Leo Nelimo
Linnustajunkuja 6 G 39
02940 Espoo, Finland.
Tel. 358 0 4371346
Fax 358 0 464305

FIRST HAND. The dealer, who is the first player to have the opportunity to bid or pass, has the first hand. Should the first hand make a call other than a pass, he becomes the opening bidder. If the first hand passes, the opportunity to become the opening bidder passes to the opponent on his left.

FIRST UP. A bidding system devised by Berl Stallard of the United States. The system called for the opening bidder to bid his lowest four-card suit, and the responder then bid his lowest four-card suit. Fit was all-important, suit quality was less so. Although several experiments with the system proved moderately successful, First Up never achieved wide usage.

FISHBEIN CONVENTION. See DEFENSE TO OPENING THREE-BID.

FISHBEIN TROPHY. This trophy is awarded every year to the player with the best overall individual performance

record in the American Contract Bridge League Summer North American Bridge Championships. The trophy, in memory of Sally Fishbein, was donated by ACBL in recognition of the untiring efforts of Harry Fishbein who served as Treasurer of ACBL and refused to accept the customary compensation. For winners see Appendix II.

FISHBOWL. A sealed, soundproofed room with space for one table and four players. It has a one-way glass front, permitting a Bridgerama audience to see in but preventing the players from seeing out. It was used in some world and European Championships in the sixties, and was later replaced by closed-circuit television monitors to permit the spectators to see the players more clearly.

FISHER DOUBLE. A lead directing double of a notrump contract asking for a minor-suit lead, developed by Dr. John Fisher. After an opening bid of 1 or 2 NT, if there have been no legitimate suit bids, a double of the final notrump contract asks for a club lead if Stayman has not been used and a diamond lead if it has.

A slightly simpler version is to play that a double always asks for a diamond lead, making the use of Stayman irrelevant.

FIT. A term referring to the effectiveness or ineffectiveness of two partnership hands in combination commonly used to refer specifically to the TRUMP SUIT, under which heading various trump fits are discussed.

When the hand as a whole is considered, the fit may be distributional. With a sound trump fit, a shortage in each hand in different suits is likely to lead to an effective CROSSRUFF. (For an unsatisfactory fit, see DUPLICATION OF DISTRIBUTION.)

Fit can also be considered in terms of honor cards, which may or may not be effective in play (see GOOD CARDS).

FIT-SHOWING JUMPS. With the opponents silent throughout, you pass, your partner opens in third or fourth position and you make a jump-shift response; perhaps:

West	North	East	South
	Pass	Pass	1 ♦
Pass	2 ♥		

What does this jump shift signify?

The normal expert agreement is that it is a fit-showing jump. It describes a hand with the following characteristics:

a. a maximum pass: 9-11 points
b. at least nine cards (5-4 or 4-5) in the two suits bid
c. virtually all the points concentrated in the two suits.

An ideal hand for the auction given above would look something like this:

♠ 5 3 ♥ A Q J 8 7 ♦ K 10 7 6 ♣ 6 2

That, in essence, is the fit-showing jump in action. But there are some other situations worth considering.

Suppose your partner's third-seat opening bid was 1♥. What do you respond with each of these hands?

1. ♠ K 3 ♥ Q 7 6 4 ♦ K Q 6 5 ♣ 7 6 2
2. ♠ 5 3 ♥ 6 2 ♦ A 7 3 ♣ K Q J 8 7 2
3. ♠ A K 8 5 4 ♥ Q J 7 4 3 ♦ 5 4 ♣ 2
4. ♠ 2 ♥ Q J 7 4 3 ♦ 5 4 ♣ A K 8 5 4

Assuming that you are using the REVERSE DRURY convention, 2♣ would be your choice with the first hand. If you do not employ Drury, you would make a limit raise of 3♥.

Because 2♣ is an artificial bid when using Drury, you

must make a jump response of 3♣ with the second hand. This shows a maximum pass with six respectable clubs. (Or you bid a simple 2♣ if not using Drury.)

The third hand is an ideal fit-showing jump: you bid 2♠. (You could make a splinter bid, but the second suit is a more important feature of your hand. You can cue-bid the shortage later if partner is interested in a slam.)

The problem comes with the fourth hand. If 2♣ is Drury and 3♣ natural, how do you make a fit-showing jump in clubs? Most experts keep the 2NT response for this hand.

However, there are alternative agreements. Some pairs ignore the possibility altogether! They normally use the 2NT response for a maximum minor two-suiter. And others, a small minority, use the jump raise to three of the agreed major for the fit-showing jump in clubs.

Finally, suppose you pick up this hand:
♠4 ♥K J 10 4 ♦8 3 ♣K Q J 7 6 3
The vulnerability is unfavorable for your side. The auction begins like this:

West	North	East	South
			1 ♥
2 ♠ (a)	?		

(a) Weak

What would you do?

You could bid a simple 4♥, but will you or your partner be able to judge the auction correctly when East bids 4♠?

You could bid 3♣, but that commits you to bidding 5♥ over 4♠. You can hardly ignore your heart support for the whole auction.

The ideal answer is a bid of 4♣ as a fit-showing jump. You tell partner that you have a hand worth 4♥ with a good side suit as well. Now he should be able to make an intelligent decision over 4♠. (True, for most pairs this jump would be treated as a SPLINTER BID, but perhaps that isn't such a wise agreement in this sort of situation unless the jump is in the opponent's suit.)

It is even possible to use this type of fit-showing jump at a lower level.

West	North	East	South
			1 ♥
1 ♠	3 ♣/4 ♣		

The 3♣ response shows a hand worth a limit raise in hearts with a reasonable club suit. The 4♣ jump shows the same hand except that it is worth game in hearts. (Here, some pairs who treat 3♣ as fit-showing play that 4♣ is a splinter bid. For these pairs, 3♣ shows a hand worth *at least* a limit raise in hearts.)

FIVE or FIVE-SPOT. The tenth ranking card in a suit, having five pips of the suit to which it belongs.

FIVE-ACE BLACKWOOD. See KEYCARD BLACKWOOD.

FIVE-BID. Any bid at the five level, to take 11 tricks if it becomes the final contract. As an opening bid, it indicates a hand of unusual power. As a bid made during the auction, it may be a slam invitation or part of a specialized slam convention. To play voluntarily 5♠ or 5♥ and fail is one of the most ignominious results possible at the bridge table. Experts prefer to estimate slam possibilities below the game level. See: ADVANCE SAVE; BLACKWOOD; FIVE OF A MAJOR OPENING; 5 NT OPENING; PREEMPTIVE BID; SUPER GERBER.

FIVE-CARD MAJORS. The concept according to which an opening bid of 1♠ or 1♥ guarantees at least a five-card suit. This is standard in American tournament play, but European methods vary. It is not usually applied after partner has passed. There are arguments for and against this procedure.

The knowledge that the opening bidder has a five-card suit often simplifies responder's problems, especially if there is competitive bidding. If the opening bid promises a five-card suit, a jump raise to three (either forcing or limit) can be made readily with three-card support, and a single raise can even be made with a doubleton. With this hand:

♠ K 2
♥ 8
♦ 10 8 6 4 3
♣ K 8 5 4 2

there is no sensible response to an opening bid of 1♠ (assuming that 1 NT is not forcing). But 2♠ is attractive if the spade bidder has promised a five-card suit, and it may help to shut out an opposing heart contract.

There are two main arguments against the five-card rule. First, it forces the opening bidder to make frequent prepared, and slightly unnatural, bids in minor suits. Problems arise especially with two four-card majors and a club shortage (4-4-4-1 or 4-4-3-2 distributions) when the opening bid has to be 1♦, and a response of 2♣ causes difficulty. It is true that a major-suit fit can always be found if the opponents are silent; but a heart fit often remains undiscovered if there is an overcall of 1♠.

Second, the extended use of the minor-suit opening gives more freedom to the opposition. A major-suit opening has distinct preemptive value, and may make it difficult for the opponents to enter the auction.

A possible compromise worth consideration is to bid four-card heart suits but not four-card spade suits. It is the 1♠ opening which commonly sets responder problems, and a spade fit, unlike a heart fit, seldom goes undiscovered after a minor-suit opening.

Grafting the five-card requirement onto otherwise traditional methods creates bidding problems with certain kinds of hands, most notably those with 4-4-4-1 distribution, those with two four-card majors and three bad diamonds, and those with a good four-card major ranking directly above a bad five-card suit. Those who opt for five-card majors tend to be most successful when playing a system which integrates that factor with forcing notrump responses and negative doubles.

The five-card major guideline was introduced into North American tournament bidding in the fifties by the ROTH-STONE and KAPLAN-SHEINWOLD systems. It gradually became standard, displacing the traditional four-card major openings which were part of the Culbertson and Goren Systems.

In the 70s and 80s American tournament players moved strongly toward five-card majors, reducing the practitioners of four-card majors to a small minority. See BRIDGE WORLD STANDARD, EASTERN SCIENTIFIC, WALSH SYSTEM.

FIVE OF A MAJOR OPENING. Shows a hand missing both top honors in the trump suit, but with no outside losers. Partner is invited to raise accordingly with one or both of the missing key cards. Probably the rarest bid in bridge.

FIVE NOTRUMP OPENING. A very rare opening bid, showing a balanced hand which can guarantee 11 tricks. Responder is asked to raise the bidding one level for each ace, king or queen he holds.

FIVE-ODD. A term indicating five tricks over the book, or 11 tricks in all.

FIVE OR SEVEN. A phrase indicating the type of partnership holdings on which a successful play makes a grand slam, but if the play is not successful, the opponents can cash a second trick immediately, holding the result to five-odd. For a hand of this type, see MATCHPOINT BIDDING. In rubber bridge, probably the grand slam contract should be preferred, but there may be situations at duplicate where a six-odd contract is tactically better, even though this is neither the maximum nor the safest contract.

FIVE-CARD SPADES. Some systems, mainly in Britain, require that a 1♠ opening must have at least five cards, while four-card heart openings are acceptable.

FIVE-CARD STAYMAN. See PUPPET STAYMAN.

FIVE-SUIT BRIDGE. This game, devised in 1937 by Dr. Walter H. W. Marseille, a Viennese psychologist and mathematician, used a special 65-card deck. There were five suits of 13 cards and each of the four players was dealt 16 cards. The remaining card was called the "widow" and placed face upwards on the table. After the dummy was exposed the declarer was entitled to exchange any card in his own hand or the dummy for the widow.

The fifth suit was green in color (except in England where it was blue) and was called "leaves" in Austria, "crowns" or "royals" in England and "eagles" in America. Public interest was aroused when George VI bought some decks at an exhibition and several books were written about the game, but it did not achieve lasting popularity. One authority gives the inventor's name as Dr. Marculis.

FIVE TABLES. At duplicate five tables provide competition for 20 players, 10 pairs, or five teams-of-four.

As an Individual, the 20-player RAINBOW Movement is recommended. Begin the game by putting five boards on each table. 1-5 go on table 1, 6-10 go on table 2, right around to 21-25 on table 5. The boards are shuffled before the first round only.

As a pair event, a Mitchell of five rounds of five boards can be used. However, the HOWELL MOVEMENT with nine rounds of three boards is preferable.

For team-of-four contests, see TEAM-OF-FOUR MOVEMENTS; the standard team-of-four progression (pairs skip a table down while boards move one table down) completes the game in four rounds, usually of six boards each. TOTAL POINT, BOARD-A-MATCH, or IMP scoring can be used.

For 4° tables or 5° tables, see HALF TABLE MOVEMENTS.

FIXED. A colloquial term to designate a pair (or a team) that has received a bad score through no fault of its own. Usually applied to a situation in which an opposing player has made a technical error or suffered a legal misadventure, and gained a good result thereby. His innocent opponents, who suffered, but probably not in silence, can say that they have been fixed.

FLAG-FLYING. An obsolete colloquialism for a bid made with full consciousness of its failure if allowed to stand, in the hope of avoiding a greater loss if the opponents are permitted to play the contract. The term was used to describe a bid made after the opponents had apparently reached their final contract, rather than one interjected during the auction. In this way it is distinguished from preemptive action (see PREEMPTIVE BID). *Sacrifice* and *save* are the modern terms.

FLANNERY TWO DIAMONDS. Developed by William Flannery to show an 11-15 point hand with five hearts and four spades.

Major-suit responses on the two-level are signoffs, though opener may raise with a maximum and a minor-suit void. Jump responses in the majors are invitational, and jumps to 4♣ and 4♦ are transfers to 4♥ and 4♠ respectively. If responder bids a minor on the three-level, opener bids 3 NT with a fit (ace or king doubleton, or queen third). A 2 NT response asks opener to clarify his strength and distribution. Opener rebids 3 ♥ with 11-13 points or 3 ♠ with 14-15 points and two cards in each minor (or 3 NT with 14-15 if his strength is concentrated in his minor suit doubletons), 3♣ or 3♦ with three cards in the bid suit, or 4♣ or 4♦ with four cards in the bid suit.

The standard defense to Flannery 2♦ is to play that a 2♥ overcall is a three-suited takeout (with shortness in hearts). Double of 2♦ shows the equivalent of a strong notrump opener and is penalty oriented. A 2 NT overcall is unusual for the minors, while suit overcalls other than 2♥ are natural.

An alternative is to play that a double shows a balanced hand in the 13-16 range, and 2 NT shows a stronger balanced hand. See also FLANNERY TWO HEARTS.

FLANNERY TWO HEARTS. An opening bid of 2♥ to show a hand worth 11-15 points with five hearts and four spades. Responses and rebids are the same as for the FLANNERY 2♦ convention, except that to sign off in hearts responder simply passes.

The Flannery 2♥ bid is not as easy to defend against as its 2♦ counterpart. The usual practice is to play that the double of 2♥ shows the strong notrump and that 2♠ shows a three-suited takeout. The assumption (not always valid) is that the long spade suit is the least likely hand one might hold.

Here also it is possible to use a double and a 2 NT overcall to show moderate and strong balanced hands.

FLAT. (1) Hand: A hand without distributional values, particularly one with 4-3-3-3 distribution. "Square" and "round" are also used to describe this type of hand.

(2) Board: A deal on which no variations in result are expected in the replays. In team play, a board in which the two scores are identical and therefore do not affect the score. Also called a PUSH.

FLIGHT. A division of a game in which competitors are separated according to the number of masterpoints held. Usually the top flight is open to all comers, while lower flights have an upper masterpoint limit.

FLIGHTED PAIRS. A pair event that is broken down into two or more fields based on masterpoints. Each field competes as a separate event. The flight for which a pair is eligible is determined by the masterpoint holding of the player with the more points. Pairs may play in a higher classification but cannot play in a lower one. A common breakdown for flighting in American Contract Bridge League events is 0 to infinity, Flight A; 0-750, Flight B; 0-300, Flight C.

FLIGHTED TEAMS. A team event that is broken down into two or more fields based on masterpoints. Each field competes as a separate event. The flight for which a team is eligible is determined by the masterpoint holding of the player with the most points. Teams may play in a higher classification but cannot play in a lower one. A common breakdown for flighting in American Contract Bridge League events is 0 to infinity, Flight A; 0-750, Flight B; 0-300, Flight C.

FLINT. An artificial 3♦ response to a 2NT opening, devised by the Jeremy Flint of England to permit a partnership to stop below game. (Though this author is credited with other conventions — see below — the 3♦ convention is the one known simply as Flint.)

Opener is forced to rebid 3♥. Responder passes if his long suit is hearts; otherwise, he bids 3♠, 4♣ or 4♦. Opener is then expected to pass, but may continue to game if his hand is particularly suitable.

Responder can still bid 3♦ in a natural sense if he follows with any action other than a minimum suit bid. If responder next bids 3NT, for instance, he shows a diamond suit and mild slam interest.

A modification, the Flint 3♣, allows a partnership to rest in 3♦ or three of a major suit after a 2NT opening. A 3♣ response forces opener to bid 3♦, and responder then passes or signs off in a major suit. A 3♦ response is used as a Stayman inquiry for a major suit.

Another convention, the Flint 2♦, is used to investigate game in notrump or a minor suit after a WEAK NOTRUMP opening. A 2♦ response shows either a hand with a solid minor suit or an unbalanced hand with at least four cards in each minor. Opener rebids a four-card major suit if he has one or bids 2NT otherwise. Responder's next bid clarifies his hand.

The popularity of transfer bidding has made these Flint conventions obsolescent.

FLIP-FLOP. A reversal of the usual meaning of a 2 NT response when a minor-suit opening is doubled. The idea is to use it preemptively, reserving the jump raise to show invitational values. See TWO NOTRUMP RESPONSE (Over opponent's take-out double).

FLOAT. A colloquialism meaning that three passes follow. "1NT float" means 1NT - pass - pass - pass. A similar term is Swish.

FLOGGER. See BACK SCORE.

FLOWER MOVEMENT. The Flower movement is an adaptation of the HOWELL MOVEMENT so that the apparently haphazard movement of the players is replaced by an orderly progression. One pair (North-South at table

1) remains stationary throughout. All other pairs progress, East-West moving toward the higher-numbered table, until they reach the highest-numbered table. After that round they merely switch directions at that table and thereafter move to the next lower-numbered table. As the players reach table 2, North-South, their next progression is to table 1, where they will sit East-West, then to table 2, East-West.

The movement has simple player moves. There are two disadvantages, however. One is that the movement cannot be made as balanced as an ordinary Howell. The other is that board progression is irregular, which is why the movement is best played with a central table for all idle boards. Board movement should be by the director. See also BAROMETER.

FLUKE. A fortuitous profit. An extreme case would be represented by a player dropping a card that appears disastrous but produces a brilliant result.

FOLLOWING SUIT. The legal obligation of each player to play a card of the suit led if possible.

FORBES, Malcolm, magazine publisher. On bridge: "Playing bridge reflects intelligence. It's one of the really great pleasures of life. I think anybody who's missing bridge is missing so much in life. Don't make the mistake of missing out on the fun of bridge."

FORCE. (1) Noun: Any bid making it incumbent upon the bidder's partner to bid at least once more. (2) Verb: To cause to ruff; to cause a player to use a high card.

FORCED BID. When a player makes a FORCING BID, his partner is required systemically to make some sort of response. The response may be a WEAKNESS RESPONSE, or a STRENGTH-SHOWING BID. It is possible that a PASS is a correct response (see PENALTY PASS) to a bid normally forcing.

In some conventions, a specific minimum bid is sometimes forced or virtually forced. See GLADIATOR and LEBENSOHL.

FORCING BID. A bid which, because of system or convention, requires the partner to "keep the bidding open," by making some call other than a pass if there is no intervening call. Examples can be found under FORCING SEQUENCES and FORCING PASS.

Perhaps the most widely used forcing bids are the JUMP SHIFT by an unpassed hand and the ONE-OVER-ONE or TWO-OVER-ONE responses by an unpassed hand.

FORCING CLUB. See ONE CLUB, ARTIFICIAL AND FORCING.

FORCING DECLARER TO RUFF. A method of defensive play, usually sound strategy when other forms of defense seem inadvisable or doubtful. When a defender, by the play of an established side suit, forces declarer to use his valuable trumps, it sometimes causes the declarer to lose control of the play. This is sometimes called "pumping" declarer. In the following deal the insistent forcing of the declarer's strong trump hand enabled the defending partnership to defeat an otherwise sure game contract:

```
                    ♠ 6 4 3 2
                    ♥ K 10 8
                    ♦ A Q J
                    ♣ A J 10
  ♠ K Q 10 9 5                    ♠ A 7
  ♥ A 5 4 3                       ♥ 7
  ♦ 10 3                          ♦ 7 6 5 4 2
  ♣ 7 2                           ♣ 9 6 5 4 3
                    ♠ J 8
                    ♥ Q J 9 6 2
                    ♦ K 9 8
                    ♣ K Q 8
```

With West the dealer, the bidding went:

WEST	NORTH	EAST	SOUTH
1 ♠	Dbl	Pass	3 ♥
Pass	4 ♥	All Pass	

West's opening lead was the ♠K, which East won with the ace to unblock his partner's suit. East returned the ♠7, which West won with the queen. West continued the suit, forcing South to ruff. South now led a heart, and when West won with the ace he led another spade, forcing South to ruff a second time. South led a second round of hearts. At this point, it is obvious that South could not make his contract, for West's greater length in trumps gave him a trump winner. This was brought about by West's continued forcing, which battered down the declarer's trump fortress.

FORCING LEADS. Plays by the opening leader aimed at weakening the declarer's trump suit. The lead is most effective when the leader has four trumps, and can visualize the declarer being forced to ruff prematurely and perhaps lose trump control.

Generally a forcing lead is made from a long suit, as in notrump, for should the attack succeed, the declarer may have to exhaust his attenuated trump suit in extracting the defender's trumps. Subsequently, if the defense regains the lead, they will be, in a position to cash the established cards in their suit, for the hand will have been reduced to notrump.

```
                    ♠ 7 6 5
                    ♥ A 9 8 4
                    ♦ K 8 6 3
                    ♣ A 10
  ♠ A 9 3 2                       ♠ 8
  ♥ K Q 10 7                      ♥ J 6 5 2
  ♦ 7                             ♦ A 5 4 2
  ♣ 8 7 6 5                       ♣ J 9 4 3
                    ♠ K Q J 10 4
                    ♥ 3
                    ♦ Q J 10 9
                    ♣ K Q 2
```

The contract is 4♠ by South. If the singleton diamond is led, the declarer has an easy ride, but holding four trumps, West should resist this temptation and attack in hearts. Declarer wins and forces out the ♠A. West continues hearts, reducing South's trump length to his own. Declarer is now in a cleft stick: if he draws West's trumps and plays diamonds, East wins, and the defense secures two heart tricks. Alternatively, if he abandons trumps after discovering the bad break, West will score two of his small trumps.

Often the opening leader can diagnose the proper occasion for a forcing lead from the auction:

SOUTH	NORTH
1 ♠	2 ♣
2 ♦	2 NT
3 ♣	3 ♠
4 ♠	

West holds:
```
  ♠ 9 8
  ♥ K J 6
  ♦ 10 5 3 2
  ♣ Q 7 6 3 2
```

South's bidding has pinpointed a singleton or void in hearts; East almost certainly has at least four trumps. A forcing game should be initiated by leading the ♥K (pinning a possible singleton queen in the South hand). See also ATTACKING LEADS.

FORCING ONE NOTRUMP RESPONSE. See ONE NOTRUMP RESPONSE TO MAJOR, FORCING

FORCING PASS. A pass which forces partner to take action. Such a pass may be made in the following situations:

(1) The opponents have taken an obvious sacrifice. A forcing pass denotes the desire to bid toward a higher contract if partner is willing.

(2) The opportunity for a sacrifice has arisen. A forcing pass denotes the desire to sacrifice, and asks partner to do so if he cannot double the opponents, and defeat their contract.

(3) A safety level has been established below which the contract cannot be sold. A forcing pass denotes inability to find a suitable call, or the desire to see if partner can double the enemy bid.

(4) After a slam-level sacrifice, a forcing pass sometimes denotes control of the enemy suit, and requests partner to bid a slam if he has the necessary outside values.

An important situation arises at a high level:

WEST	NORTH	EAST	SOUTH
1 ♥	2 ♦	3 ♦	5 ♦
Pass	Pass	Dbl.	Pass
5 ♥			

Most experts have an agreement that this sequence is strong, inviting 6♥, and that a direct 5♥ bid is weaker. But the converse agreement is possible. This conforms to the principle of FAST ARRIVAL.

(5) Some bidding systems employ a forcing pass as a form of opening bid. If the bidder opens the bidding by bidding a suit or notrump, he is indicating that his hand is lower than opening-bid range. Usually each bid has a special conventional meaning. If the opener has a full opening bid, he must pass, and it is up to partner to open the bidding, knowing that his partner has good values. The system causes serious disruption to opposition bidding. Most players do not know how to cope with this method that is the reverse of the usual. Such systems are not permitted in ACBL play or in world pair tournaments. Such systems are allowed, however, in major world team championships such as the Bermuda Bowl. In the past, pairs from New Zealand, Brazil and Poland, among others, have used forcing pass systems. The ACBL does not allow them because the ACBL has a policy against destructive systems — systems aimed at disrupting the opponents rather than at arriving at the correct contract.

FORCING RAISE. Perhaps nothing in bidding has changed as much in recent years as the way in which responder makes a forcing raise of opener's suit. Until recently, a DOUBLE RAISE was practically the only way to indicate a forcing raise. Today, however, the double raise usually is a LIMIT BID. Diverse methods of showing the forcing raise have been developed, including JACOBY 2 NT, MINISPLINTERS, SPLINTERS, THREE CLUBS RESPONSE AS A MAJOR RAISE, THREE NOTRUMP RESPONSE, and various forms of SWISS. See also INVERTED MINOR SUIT RAISE and CRISS-CROSS RAISE.

FORCING REBID. See OPENER'S REBID and RESPONDER'S REBID.

FORCING SEQUENCES. A series of bids that requires the bidding to continue. Some sequences cannot be passed because the last bid showed strength; in such cases, the bidding may be forcing for one round only. Other sequences are forcing because the partnership has established that they have the values for game or slam; they are committed to continue until they reach game (or extract a worthwhile penalty).

Examples of forcing sequences follow. No unanimity of opinion exists as to the nature of many sequences. With the plethora of bidding systems and styles, sequences admit to varying interpretations, not only from system to system, but from pair to pair.

Sequences that are forcing for one round:
1. A new suit by responder:
   - (a) 1 ♥ 1 ♠
   - (b) 1 ♣ 1 ♠
       2 ♣ 2 ♥
   - (c) 1 ♣ 1 ♥
       1 ♠ 2 ♦
     (See FOURTH SUIT ARTIFICIAL.)
   - (d) 1 ♣ 1 ♦
       1NT 2 ♥ (but not 1 ♣-1 ♥-1NT-2 ♦)
   - (e) 1 ♠ 2 ♦
       2 ♠ 3 ♣
   - (f) 3 ♣ 3 ♠
2. A reverse by opener:
   - (a) 1 ♣ 1 ♠
       2 ♥ (but not forcing for traditionalists)
   - (b) 1 ♠ 2 ♦
       3 ♣ (sometimes called a high reverse)
3. A new suit by opener after a two-over-one response:
     1 ♠ 2 ♣
     2 ♥
4. A new suit bid after the trump suit is agreed:
   - (a) 1 ♥ 2 ♥
       3 ♣
   - (b) 1 ♠ 3 ♠
       4 ♣
   - (c) 1 ♦ 1 ♠
       2 ♠ 3 ♣
5. A strength-showing sequence by opener:
     1 ♦ 1 ♠
     2 ♣ 2NT
     3 ♦ (but not 1 ♦-1 ♠-2 ♦-2NT-3 ♣)

6. A new suit bid by responder after responder redoubles on his first turn:

WEST	NORTH	EAST	SOUTH
	1 ♦	Dbl	Redbl
Pass	Pass	1 ♥	1 ♠

7. A passed-hand jump shift after a major suit opening:
     Pass 1 ♥
     3 ♦

The 3 ♦ bid by the passed hand implies a heart fit, so most pairs treat it as forcing. See DRURY and FIT-SHOWING JUMPS.

Game-forcing sequences
1. A first-round jump by responder:
   - (a) 1 ♠ 2NT (natural)
   - (b) 1 ♥ 2NT (an artificial forcing raise)
   - (c) 1 ♥ 2 ♠ (See WEAK JUMP-SHIFT RESPONSE.)
2. A jump rebid by opener after a two-level response:
     1 ♥ 2 ♣
     3 ♥ or 4 ♣
3. A jump shift by opener:
     1 ♥ 1 ♠
     3 ♣
4. Miscellaneous sequences:
   - (a) 1 ♥ 1 ♠
       3 ♥ 3 ♠
   - (b) 1 ♥ 2 ♦
       2NT 3 ♥

However, if opener's 2NT rebid suggests no extra strength, this sequence also could be played as invitational, according to partnership agreement.
   - (c) 1 ♦ 1 ♥
       3 ♦ 4 ♦

The modern style is to play this as forcing, perhaps inviting the start of a cuebid sequence. However, there are still many pairs who play this sequence as merely invitational to game. (If opener's 2NT rebid suggests no extra strength, this sequence may be played as invitational.)
   - (d) 1 ♠ 2 ♥
       3 ♦ 3NT
       4 ♣

Many modern pairs use a style in which a response in a new suit at the two-level usually commits the partnership to game. An advantage of this style is to create more forcing sequences and permit leisurely investigation for the best contract. In this style, the sequence:
     1 ♠ 2 ♣
     2 ♠ 3 ♣

is forcing to game. (See TWO OVER ONE GAME FORCE; and FAST ARRIVAL.)

The above discussion centers on forcing sequences after opening bids of one of a suit. For other forcing sequences, see FORCING TWO-BID and 1NT OPENING. Furthermore, JUMP REBIDS BY RESPONDER, a controversial topic, is treated separately.

FORCING STAYMAN. See STAYMAN.

FORCING TAKEOUT. See JUMP SHIFT.

FORCING TWO-BID. The traditional use of an opening two-bid in a suit to show a hand which can virtually guarantee game, or even slam. (Also referred to as

Culbertson two-bid, DEMAND BID or STRONG TWO). It was a cornerstone of the CULBERTSON system and remained standard practice in the U.S. and many other parts of the world. In postwar years virtually all experts abandoned the Forcing Two in favor of the WEAK TWO-BID, the ACOL TWO-BID, and other treatments. A variety of formulas have been put forward to determine whether a hand is worth a forcing two. Goren gives this schedule:

With a good five-card suit	25 high-card points.
With a good six-card suit	23 high-card points
With a good seven-card suit	21 high-card points.

With a second good five-card suit, one point less is needed. If the game is to be in a minor suit, two points more are needed. Two more formulae were devised by Hy Lavinthal: (a) More honor tricks than possible losers. (This rule was incorporated into the Culbertson System.) (b) Rule of 24: add to the high-card point count two points for every card over four in any suit; then subtract a point for any king or queen not in sequence with a next-ranking honor; bid two if the answer is 24 or more. However, the expert does not normally use such rules; he employs the forcing two-bid if he has reasonable game prospects opposite a worthless or nearly worthless hand.

Another consideration is that a hand may be slightly too weak for a forcing two, but at the same time distinctly too strong for an opening bid of one in a suit. In such circumstances, a slightly shaded two bid may be a lesser evil than an over-strength one-bid.

However, the likelihood that a one-bid may be passed out is a further consideration. Highly distributional hands may safely be opened with a bid of only one, because if opener's partner passes it is most unlikely that both opponents will do so. Lacking controls of three suits therefore, the expert will tend to open with a one-bid and jump later to show distribution.

Culbertson later modified the unconditionally game-forcing character of the bid to permit partner to pass a bust hand if opener's call after a 2 NT response was a simple rebid of his first suit, i.e.:

2♥-2 NT-3♥

Responses. The conventional negative response is 2 NT. Other responses are positive and natural, showing at least 7-8 points and seldom less than one quick trick (i.e., an ace, a king-queen, or two kings)

However, other responding treatments are used, including ACE-SHOWING RESPONSES and HERBERT NEGATIVE.

FORESIGHT. Looking ahead in the bidding or play. Examples of this are the prepared minor-suit opening bid to provide a convenient rebid over partner's or opponents' action, the early loss of a trick in order to set up a squeeze position, and a switch by defenders to a new suit in order to break up a possible throw-in play. See BIDDING; ENDPLAY; PREPAREDNESS, PRINCIPLE OF.

FORFEIT. To cancel a right or turn to call. See LAWS OF CONTRACT BRIDGE (Law 15), LAWS OF DUPLICATE (Law 11).

FORK. See FOURCHETTE.

FORTUNE. Chance may play an important role at the card table, but fortune can be significant in bridge events away from the table. There are three recorded instances of players achieving international honors as a result of fortuitous circumstances.

In 1937 the United States Women's team at the World Championship at Budapest found itself one short. An American lady whose name has not been recorded was brought in to complete the team. She was a player with social bridge experience only who happened to be staying in Budapest at the time.

In 1961 at the Fall North American Championships in Houston, Robert Stucker and Jack Blair formed an impromptu partnership in order to complete a section in the Open Pairs and oblige the tournament director. They finished second in the event and subsequently represented the United States in the World Open Pairs in Cannes in consequence of their success.

Mary Edwards of Esher, England, was brought in as a substitute in the 1959 British international women's trials to replace a player who had fallen ill. From an apparently hopeless position, trailing the rest of the field by a substantial margin, she qualified for the British team in partnership with Mrs. G. R. Higginson, St. Annes-on-Sea, England. Subsequently they became European champions when their team won in Palermo, Italy.

FORTUNE TELLING. Predicting the future of an individual by giving significance to a pattern of playing cards spread before him. Standard packs can, of course, be used, but the TAROTS, with their individuality, provide a greater opportunity for imaginative divination.

FORWARD GOING. See CONSTRUCTIVE.

FOSTER ECHO. A third-hand unblocking play against notrump, intended at the same time to show count. With a four-card holding, the first play is the second highest, followed by the third highest, with the lowest saved for last. With a three-card holding, the first play is second highest and the second is the highest, again saving the lowest for last.

FOULED BOARD. A board into which a card or cards or hands have been interchanged to incorrect pockets. Usually a fouled board occurs when the board is being discussed after the play, and various hands are interchanged across the table.

Fouling a board is a major misdemeanor in bridge competition, because the scores prior to and after the fouling cannot be compared. When a board has been reported as fouled, the director must determine at what point in the competition the fouling occurred, and must matchpoint the results in some fair manner in the two fields thus created.

The WBF formula for scoring fouled boards and those needing adjusted scores was adopted by the ACBL in 1990. It is:

$$M = \frac{(N \times S)}{n} + \frac{(N - n)}{2n}$$

M = Final matchpoints on the board
N = Number of scores on the board
S = Matchpoint score in the group
n = number of scores in the group
Specifications:

The formula applies to groups of 3 or more scores on a fouled board.

The formula applies to a group of 3 scores when it is the larger group, otherwise the scores in a group of 3 are awarded matchpoint scores of 70%, 60% and 50%.

The scores in a group of 2 are awarded matchpoint scores of 65% and 55%.

Equal scores in groups of 3 and 2 share the arbitrary matchpoint awards.

A single score is awarded a matchpoint score of 60% in each direction.

Matchpoint scores are rounded to the nearest 100th with .005 rounded up.

ACBL clubs that score by hand are permitted to use the earlier formula, not obsolete.

To guard against the possibility of fouling a board, no more than one hand should be removed from the board at a time during discussions. This is particularly true when the opponents are not at the table.

In board-a-match team play, the correct manner of handling a fouled board is a matter of regulation, which has been changed from time to time. Under 1976 regulations of the ACBL, the scores, both North-South and East-West, are divided into two fields, before and after the fouling, each field is matchpointed independently, and the percentage of possible match points for each pair then is determined. For each team that played the board in different positions, the percentages are added and the board is won if the total is 120 or more, halved from 80 to 120, and lost with 80 or less. Results for teams that played the board in identical form are computed in the usual way, since the fouling occurred either before both halves of the teams had played it, or after both halves of the teams had played it.

A board with two hands having an incorrect number of cards, for example 12-14 is not fouled since no result can be achieved on this deal. The Law: "Incorrect Number of Cards" applies and the pair(s) who looked at their incorrect hands should receive average minus.

ACBL policy provides that the players who created the fouled board and made it necessary to apply the formula should be penalized one full board. (A foul in duplication that applies to one section only, and does not invoke the formula, is not so penalized.)

FOUR or FOUR-SPOT. The eleventh ranking card of each suit, designated by four pips of the suit symbol on the face.

FOUR ACES SYSTEM. Methods used by the FOUR ACES TEAM in winning many championships during the Thirties. The main features of the system were:

(1) Point count of ace = 3; king = 2; queen = 1; jack = 1/2. This makes a total of 26 points in the pack, and 6° represent an average hand; 9° points represent a mandatory opening bid.

(2) Limited 1 NT opening with a range of 11°-13 points. (Hands with less than seven honor cards are devalued by ° point for each honor, and hands with more than seven honors similarly increased in value.) Establishment of this notrump range solved major rebidding headaches; in combination with point-count and rigidly prescribed responses, it precluded many of the notrump bidding faults that plagued inexpert players.

(3) Minor-suit bids, if need be in a three-card suit, as exploring maneuvers, either by the opener or the responder.

(4) WEAK JUMP OVERCALLS.

(5) PSYCHIC BIDS by third hand and occasionally first hand showing some high-card strength in the suit bid and little else.

(6) JUMP SHIFT to the level of two or three as a psychic control. The opener rebids 2 NT with a psychic, and with any other rebid a slam is reached.

The Four Aces' book included a number of other original ideas, many of which have become standard practice.

FOUR ACES TEAM. The team that dominated tournament competition in the mid-Thirties. The first appearance of this team was at the Summer NAC in Asbury Park in 1933, when David Burnstine (Bruce), Richard Frey, Oswald Jacoby, and Howard Schenken won the forerunner of the Spingold Teams. Michael Gottlieb joined the team immediately afterward, and during 1934 the Four Aces' major wins included the Vanderbilt, the Spingold, the Grand National and the forerunner of the Reisinger. They successfully defended the Grand National 1935, and also repeated in the Vanderbilt, with Sherman Stearns replacing Frey, who had resigned. Burnstine, Jacoby, Schenken and Gottlieb defeated France in the first world championship match, played in Madison Square Garden. Gottlieb retired in 1936 and was replaced by Merwin D. Maier. B. Jay Becker and other experts played occasionally as members of the team, which did not play after Dec. 1941 but continued as an entity for purposes of book and newspaper publication until 1945.

The Four Aces played their own system, and wrote a book, *The Four Aces System of Contract Bridge* (see BIBLIOGRAPHY, C) which presented their original expert methods. Though the system was widely followed by tournament players, the book was not a commercial success.

FOUR-BID. A bid at the four-level, to take 10 tricks if it becomes the final contract.

FOUR-CARD MAJORS. Opening bids of 1♠ or 1♥ holding a four-card suit. The old auction bridge idea of requiring a five-card suit for an opening bid has found a place in several modern systems such as ROTH-STONE and KAPLAN-SHEINWOLD. In the Seventies the pendulum swung so far that a majority of experts and tournament players were using five-card majors. To what extent they have been followed by the bridge public at large remains doubtful, but the tendency has been for bridge teachers to recommend the five-card style. (see BIDDABLE SUITS). By 1993 four-card majors had become obsolescent in North America but were alive and well in Europe.

FOUR-CARD SUIT BIDS. See BIDDABLE SUITS.

FOUR CLUB CONVENTIONS. See CLARAC SLAM TRY, NAMYATS, RUBIN TRANSFERS, SOUTH AFRICAN TEXAS, SWISS CONVENTION. See also SPLINTER BID, VOID-SHOWING BIDS.

An alternative usage, devised by Howard Robinson of New York City, is to use 4♣ as a three-stage asking bid to determine singletons, aces, and trump honors.

When 4♣ is a jump bid, or immediately follows a jump raise of another suit, partner is requested to bid a suit in which he holds a singleton or revert to the agreed trump suit with no singleton. The next ranking suit by the asking bidder then requests partner to show the number of aces he holds. If the asking bidder again bids the next ranking suit, responder shows his trump honors (ace, king, or queen) by three steps. The asking bidder signs off whenever he bypasses the asking denomination or reverts to the agreed trump suit.

FOUR CLUBS AND FOUR DIAMONDS OPENING PREEMPTS. Such bids usually are based on an eight-card minor in a poor hand. If the partnership is using a GAMBLING THREE NOTRUMP to show a solid minor, then an opening of 4♣ or 4♦ would show a broken suit.

FOUR CLUBS AND FOUR DIAMONDS OPENING TRANSFERS. See NAMYATS.

FOUR-DEAL BRIDGE. See CHICAGO.

FOUR DIAMOND CONVENTIONS. See BLUE TEAM 4♣-4♦ CONVENTION; NAMYATS; NEAPOLITAN FOUR DIAMONDS CONVENTION; RUBIN TRANSFERS; SOUTH AFRICAN TEXAS; TEXAS.

FOUR-FIVE NOTRUMP CONVENTION. See CULBERTSON FOUR-FIVE NOTRUMP.

FOUR HORSEMEN. A champion team of the early Thirties. It was formed by P. Hal Sims in 1931 to challenge the earlier success of the Culbertson team. The other "horsemen" were Willard S. Karn, David Burnstine (Bruce) and Oswald Jacoby. They won the two major team championships in 1932, the Vanderbilt and the Asbury Park, by large margins, and won the Reisinger convincingly in 1933. Sims' efforts to develop and promote his own system in opposition to Culbertson did not suit Jacoby and Bruce, who successively left the team (See FOUR ACES TEAM).

FOUR NOTRUMP CONVENTIONS. Since a 4 NT bid is the lowest bid possible above the major-suit game level, it is a bid that is frequently used to initiate inquiries to lead either to a slam bid, or to stay below the slam level if the partnership hands cannot make a slam. Among the specialized uses of this bid are the following, dealt with in the following articles: ACOL FOUR NOTRUMP OPENING, BLACKWOOD, BYZANTINE BLACKWOOD, CULBERTSON FOUR-FIVE NOTRUMP, DECLARATIVE-INTERROGATIVE FOUR NOTRUMP, DEFENSE TO OPENING FOUR-BID, KEY-CARD BLACKWOOD, KING CONVENTION, NORMAN, ROMAN BLACKWOOD, SAN FRANCISCO, SUPPRESSING THE BID ACE.

For a discussion of the distinction between the quantitative and conventional uses of 4 NT, see BLACKWOOD.

FOUR NOTRUMP OPENING. In standard methods, shows a balanced hand too strong to open 3 NT. It should be a ten-trick hand with perhaps 28-30 points. This rare bid is in disuse in standard practice, because an opening 2♣ bid followed by 4 NT will serve equally well. For alternative treatments, see ACOL FOUR NOTRUMP OPENING; FOUR NOTRUMP OPENING PREEMPT; RUBIN TRANSFERS.

FOUR NOTRUMP OPENING PREEMPT. Devised by Terence Reese and Jeremy Flint as part of the Little Major System and subsequently adopted by several American experts to distinguish between a strong and weak minor-suit game preempt.

An opening bid of 4 NT shows a weak preempt of 5♣ or 5♦ with fewer than five controls, counting an ace or void as two controls and a king or singleton as one control. Consequently, an opening bid of 5♣ or 5♦ would show a stronger preempt, five or more controls. For an alternative treatment see RUBIN TRANSFERS.

FOUR NOTRUMP OVERCALL. A bid of 4 NT after an opposing opening bid is usually a form of the UNUSUAL NOTRUMP, calling for a minor suit. This could not apply after an opening bid of 3♣, 3♦, or a weak 2♦, in which case the bid would be Blackwood. For treatment of 4 NT overcall after an opening bid at the four level see DEFENSE TO OPENING FOUR-BID.

FOUR-ODD. Four tricks over book, or ten tricks in all.

FOUR OF A SUIT OPENING. A natural opening bid of four to show a long, strong suit with little side strength. A typical hand would contain a seven- or eight-card suit, but a six-card suit is possible.

$$♠ —$$
$$♥ K Q J 6 5 4$$
$$♦ K Q J 8 7$$
$$♣ 3 2$$

If this is the dealer's hand, 4♥ has a lot to recommend it. An opening four in a minor would seldom be based on a solid suit, because of the possibility of 3 NT. For alternative treatments, see NAMYATS, LITTLE MAJOR, RUBIN TRANSFERS.

FOUR-SUIT TRANSFER BIDS. Transfer bids into all four suits achieved some popularity in tournament play in the 80s. The usual plan, in response to 1NT, is:

2 ♦ shows heart length
2 ♥ shows spade length
2 ♠ shows club length
2NT shows diamond length

After 2♠ and 2NT, the opener should accept the transfer if he has a fit with responder's suit and make the intermediate bid if he does not. If responder has a good minor suit, perhaps A Q x x x x, he can play 3NT with a fit and three of his suit without one. And if responder has a weak minor two-suiter he can bid two notrump and pass the rebid.

The responder will often have a strong hand and will continue bidding. The meaning of a subsequent major-suit bid needs agreement.

Using this method, a direct 2NT bid by responder is not available as a natural invitation. To give such a message, the responder must use Stayman and follow with 2 NT, which does not, therefore, imply possession of a four-card major suit.

FOUR TABLES. At duplicate, four tables provide for competition among 16 (or 17) players as individuals, eight pairs of players, or four teams of four.

A full individual tournament, with all possible partnerships, has the difficulty of being very short (15 or 17 boards) or very long (30 or 34 boards). A reduced tournament in 12 or 13 rounds, 24 or 26 boards, is usually preferable. See INDIVIDUAL MOVEMENTS.

As a pair game, the HOWELL MOVEMENT, with seven rounds, is preferable to the MITCHELL MOVEMENT, with only four rounds. Either three or four boards may be played per round.

If the Mitchell movement is used, Tables 1 and 4 should relay boards throughout, with a byestand between tables 2 and 3. Boards move from 4 to 3 to byestand to 2 to 1 where they are shared with 4. East-West pairs move up.

The board-sharing can be avoided by using this schedule:

	Table 1			Table 2			Table 3			Table 4		
Round	NS	EW	B	NS	EW	B	NS	EW	B	NS	EW	B
1	1	5	1	2	6	2	3	7	3	4	8	4
2	1	6	4	2	5	3	3	8	2	4	7	1
3	1	7	2	2	8	1	3	5	4	4	6	3
4	1	8	3	2	7	4	3	6	1	4	5	2

As a team-of-four event, three stanzas are required; in the first stanza, traveling pairs of teams 1 and 2 exchange places, as do the traveling pairs of 3 and 4; boards are relayed between tables 1 and 2 and between tables 3 and 4; in the second stanza, traveling pairs of teams 1 play at 3 and of team 3 at 1; similarly with teams 2 and 4; in the third stanza, teams 1 and 4 and teams 2 and 3 interchange traveling pairs, and relay the boards. Boards are reshuffled at the end of each stanza, and the six matches are scored individually. BOARD-A-MATCH, TOTAL POINT, or INTERNATIONAL MATCHPOINT SCORING can be used, and ties broken with summation from the three matches at board-a-match or total point or by quotient of points won divided by points lost at International Match Points. You may instead use the following way of playing, where 1-4 are the teams and a and b denotes the two pairs in each team:

	Table 1			Table 2			Table 3			Table 4		
Round	NS	EW	B	NS	EW	B	NS	EW	B	NS	EW	B
1	1a	2b	1	2a	3b	2	3a	4a	4	4b	1b	5
2	2a	1b	1	3a	2b	2	4b	3b	4	1a	4a	5
3	4a	3b	1	3a	1b	3	1a	2a	4	2b	4b	6
4	3a	4b	1	1a	3b	3	2b	1b	4	4a	2a	6
5	1a	4b	2	4a	2b	3	2a	3a	5	3b	1b	6
6	4a	1b	2	2a	4b	3	3b	2b	5	1a	3a	6

For 3° and 4° tables, see HALF TABLE MOVEMENTS.

FOURCHETTE. An obsolete term for a tenace such as A-Q, K-J or Q-10.

FOUR-THREE-TWO-ONE COUNT. See POINTCOUNT.

FOURTEEN TABLES. At duplicate, 14 tables provide competition among 56 players, as individuals, 28 pairs, or 14 teams. The team-of-four can be board-a-match or Swiss team competition — either is a good contest.

As an individual tournament, twinned RAINBOW sections of seven tables can be used with a 13 top. This provides 21 boards with the same number of partnerships. Also possible is an Appendix Rainbow as described in TWELVE TABLES, where the bumped players will play boards 27 and 28 at table 14, with all other players moving and all players playing 13 rounds, 26 boards, top 12, average 156. The Appendix Rainbow movement could be cut at 11 or 12 rounds if desired.

As a pair game, 14 tables has become the basic unit for a section where there are many sections. When it is desired to preduplicate the hands from prepared hand records, the players who do the duplicating do not play the hand they duplicate; therefore it is necessary to have at least 14 tables in each section in order to play the standard 26 boards.

A possibility is to duplicate, let the board set be moved down one table, and have the EW pairs remain. Play a Skip Mitchell. After seven rounds of play (the duplication rounds is not counted), the moving pairs will skip the boards they duplicated.

As a team contest the THURNER MOVEMENT with two boards a round is available. Alternatively,you may start by having East-West skip a table in the lower direction and the boards are shuffled. After the first and second round the boards move to the next lower table and the East-West pairs skip a table in the lower direction. After the third round the boards move normally but the moving pairs skip an extra table. The East-West pairs move normally for the next six rounds. After the ninth round the moving pairs skip an extra table and the boards skip a table. For the remaining rounds the moving pairs make the regular team-of-four move.

If a 13th round is advisable the moving pairs 1 to 7 add 7 to their table number and go to that table. Moving pairs 8 to 14 subtract 7 from their table number and go to that table. Tables 1 and 8, 2 and 9, 3 and 10, 4 and 11, 5 and 12, 6 and 13, and 7 and 14 relay boards for that round. For the 13th round the boards are reshuffled.

A stagger movement is possible, similar to the one described under EIGHT TABLES and TWELVE TABLES.

For 13° or 14° tables see HALF TABLE MOVEMENTS.

FOURTEEN THIRTY. A variation of Roman Key Card Blackwood in which the normal responses in a minor suit are inverted: 5♣ shows one key card or four, and 5♦ three or zero. The name is 1430, rather than 1403, because that is a familiar score. The advantage arises when hearts are trumps and responder has one ace: A five-diamond relay bid is then available to ask for the trump queen. Some partnerships invert only if hearts are trump.

FOURTH BEST. See FOURTH HIGHEST.

FOURTH HAND. The fourth player to have the opportunity to make a call, the player to the dealer's right.

FOURTH-HAND BIDS. For a discussion of minimum openings in fourth seat, see BORDERLINE OPENING BIDS.

The idea that the fourth player must have additional strength to open the bidding is now quite obsolete, and at duplicate a player may open slightly light in the hope of snatching a partscore.

Opening three-bids and weak two-bids in fourth position show maximum values, close to an opening bid, but rarely occur. Other opening bids are not affected by the positional factor. See also PASSED HAND.

FOURTH HIGHEST. Traditionally the fourth-highest card of a long suit is led to develop long card tricks in a suit or to give partner the count in the suit led. The application of the RULE OF ELEVEN when the card led is the fourth highest is a determining factor in play by third-hand and declarer. This is the oldest convention in the game, dating to Edmund Hoyle's *A Short Treatise on Whist* and perhaps earlier.

FOURTH-SUIT ARTIFICIAL. A convention, introduced by Norman Squire, England, in which the bid of the only unbid suit by responder at his second turn is a waiting move promising nothing about the suit named. This is popularly called "fourth-suit forcing", but this is an unsatisfactory term since nobody plays such a bid as nonforcing.

The question is whether or not the bid shows length and/or strength in the fourth suit. When used artificially, as it is by a majority of experts, the responder usually has two or three losers in the fourth suit. The opener should not bid notrump unless he has a stopper in the fourth suit, which is in effect an unbid suit. Examples of the bid are:

NORTH	NORTH	NORTH
♠ 7 5 4	♠ A 3	♠ 8 4
♥ A 6 2	♥ 7 5 4	♥ K 6
♦ A K Q 4	♦ 9 7 2	♦ A K Q 6 4 2
♣ 8 4 3	♣ A K J 6 5	♣ 7 5 3
(a)	(b)	(c)

SOUTH	NORTH	SOUTH	NORTH	SOUTH	NORTH
1 ♣	1 ♦	1 ♠	2 ♣	1 ♠	2 ♦
1 ♥	1 ♠	2 ♦	2 ♥	2 ♥	3 ♣

The fourth suit is forcing for one round only, and promises a minimum of 10-11 points if made at the two-level or higher. Responder seldom wishes to bid the fourth suit in a natural sense, because he would then be able to bid notrump.

Sequence (a) is forcing for one round, but may be natural and weak to provide for the possibility that opener's distribution is 4-4-1-4 or 4-4-0-5. Some players would bid two spades with the hand shown, to suggest general strength but spade weakness.

Three-level fourth-suit bids are considered game-forcing, and some would treat two-level bids, such as (b) similarly. This affected by the two-over-one style being used. See OUT-OF-THE-BLUE CUEBID.

FOURTH-SUIT FORCING. A popular misdescription of FOURTH-SUIT ARTIFICIAL.

FRACTIONAL MASTERPOINT CERTIFICATES. See RATING POINTS.

FRAGMENT. A term describing a suit of two or more cards that is not long enough to bid naturally; usually a three card holding. The bid of a fragment is designed to imply shortness in an unbid suit. See FRAGMENT BID.

FRAGMENT BID. An unusual bid — usually a double jump — in a new suit on the second round of bidding, showing a fit with partner's suit and a shortage in the fourth suit (devised by Monroe Ingberman). The last bid in each of the following sequences is a fragment bid:

(a)		(b)		(c)	
NORTH	SOUTH	NORTH	SOUTH	NORTH	SOUTH
1 ♣	1 ♥	1 ♣	1 ♥	1 ♣	1 ♥
3 ♠		1 ♠	4 ♦	1 ♠	4 ♣

The fragment bidder usually has two or three cards in the fragment suit, and must have a singleton or void in the fourth suit — clubs in (b).

The fragment idea can be extended to this situation:

NORTH	SOUTH
1 ♥	2 ♣
2 ♦	3 ♠

Here the bid shows a fit with hearts and a diamond shortage. (The more orthodox treatment is to use this sequence to show a fit with diamonds, because South's hand has

been improved by North's rebid.)

For alternative treatments of such sequences, see ASK-ING BIDS, SPLINTER BIDS, SWISS CONVENTION, and VOID-SHOWING BIDS.

Although fragment bids were originally devised as a use for the double jump shift, which was otherwise usually an idle bid, when a player has made a bid that denies a two-suited hand, a fragment bid may be made in a suit without jumping. The implication of the fragment bid is that the bidder has support for his partner's suit and a singleton in the remaining suit. See Soloway theory of JUMP SHIFTS.

FRAME. A colloquialism for a game. The term probably came from the appearance of the scoring pad used in rubber bridge: the vertical and horizontal lines, the edge of the single column pad, and the line drawn underneath the score when the game is completed "frame" the trick-score constituting the game.

FRANCE. See FRENCH BRIDGE FEDERATION.

FRANCO-AMERICAN MATCHES. Teams representing France and the United States (or North America) have met on many occasions. For results, see Appendix IV.

FREAK. A single hand or a complete deal, of abnormally unbalanced distribution. Usually a hand in which one player has more than seven cards in one suit, or more than eleven cards in two suits.

FREAK HANDS. In the field of bidding, there is no doubt that the expert has a tremendous advantage over the great majority of bridge players, for he has come across virtually every conceivable bidding situation, and has learned how to handle it. There is one type of bidding situation, however, that even the veriest of tyros handles as well (or as badly) as the expert. This is in the field of freak hands, hands that contain eight, nine or ten-card suits, plus a void or two. (See DUKE OF CUMBERLAND'S HAND, HEARTBREAKER, MISSISSIPPI HEART HAND, and SWING HAND.) These hands defy scientific evaluation, and past experiences are of no help in appraising these anomalies. So the expert, like the average player, has to guess what he should bid; and when it comes to guessing, anybody is as good as anybody else.

Consider a few freak hands. The three deals which follow were all taken from North American Championships events. The first one arose in the Master Mixed Teams Championship of 1961.

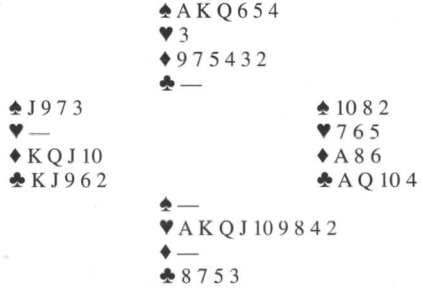

As is readily apparent, South can take 13 tricks at hearts

against any defense. When the board was played, East, as dealer, passed, and South either passed, bid 1♥, bid 4♥, or bid 6♥. As to what the proper bid on the South hand was, there is no answer.

How freak hands can wreck the stoutest plans is evidenced in the following deal, which came up in the Master Mixed Teams Championship of 1949.

```
                ♠ K Q J 5 4 3 2
                ♥ 3
                ♦ —
                ♣ A Q 10 7 4
  ♠ 9                              ♠ A 8 7
  ♥ 10 8 6 5                       ♥ K Q 9 4
  ♦ Q 10 8 4 2                     ♦ A K J
  ♣ 9 8 3                          ♣ K 5 2
                ♠ 10 6
                ♥ A J 7 2
                ♦ 9 7 6 5 3
                ♣ J 6
```

Neither side vulnerable. North dealer. The bidding at every table was identical.

WEST	NORTH	EAST	SOUTH
	1♠	Dbl	Pass
2♦	4♠	Dbl	All Pass

Eleven tricks were made at every table, declarer's only losers being the ace of trumps and the ♣K. Is there an authority, an expert, or an average player, who would dare to say that East's business double of 4♠ was an improper bid?

We have all run into situations comparable to the one contained in this final deal, and there is not a thing we can do about it in preparing ourselves to handle it in the future.

```
                ♠ 5
                ♥ 7 4
                ♦ 10 8 4
                ♣ J 10 7 6 4 3 2
  ♠ K Q J 7 6 3 2                  ♠ 10 9 8 4
  ♥ K Q 3                          ♥ A J 10 9 5 2
  ♦ —                              ♦ 6 5 3
  ♣ 9 8 5                          ♣ —
                ♠ A
                ♥ 8 6
                ♦ A K Q J 9 7 2
                ♣ A K Q
```

North-South vulnerable, South dealer, the bidding:

WEST	NORTH	EAST	SOUTH
			2♦
2♠	Pass	4♠	5♦
5♠	6♦	6♠	Dbl
All Pass			

It will be observed that West's only loser was the ace of trumps. Did South do something wrong when he doubled the slam contract?

FRED FRIENDLY AWARD. The annual Award given by the PROFESSIONAL TOURNAMENT DIRECTORS ASSOCIATION to the ACBL tournament director who best evidences the qualities of courtesy and friendliness to players. The award was named for Paul Stehly, whose nickname was Fred Friendly. For winners see PROFESSIONAL TOURNAMENT DIRECTORS ASSOCIATION.

FREE BID. A bid made by a player whose partner's bid has been overcalled by right-hand opponent. In such cir-

cumstances partner will have another chance to bid, so it would seem unnecessary to bid with minimum values. Traditional theory therefore prescribed elevated standards for all "free" actions, equivalent to perhaps an additional king.

However, experts have long since abandoned this requirement except when the bid is 1 NT.

There are three separate categories.

(1) 1 NT (e.g. 1♣-1♥-1 NT). The traditional range is 10-12 or 9-12, but many players reduce this by partnership agreement, sometimes to as little as 7-10. In that case the minimum would apply only when holding a double stopper in the opponent's suit.

(2) Suit Response (e.g.1♣-1♥-1♠). A minimum of 9 points according to old textbooks, but the modern expert style is to bid as if there has been no interference. There is a strong tendency for the free response, and this one in particular, to show a five-card suit (especially playing NEGATIVE DOUBLES), or at least a strong four-card suit. But in the ROTH-STONE SYSTEM, added values are necessary for a free bid; a negative double is used with weaker hands.

A free two-over-one response (e.g. 1♣ 1♥ 2♦) is usually held to show 11 points, or even 12; the standard should be slightly higher when the opener cannot rebid his suit at the level of two.

(3) Raises. In this category (e. g. 1♦-1♠-2♦) almost all experts have abandoned the idea that the raise shows greater strength than it would without the overcall. There is no disadvantage in raising exactly as if there had been no overcall, and there is a considerable tactical loss in adopting a waiting policy. See FREE RAISE.

FREE DOUBLE. A double of a contract which represents a game if undoubled. Usually confined to rubber bridge, when a partscore will convert an earlier partscore into game. If both sides have a partscore, judgment of a high level is required; all players may be straining their resources.

Doubles of game and slam contracts cannot properly be described as free. See PENALTY DOUBLE and SUCKER'S DOUBLE.

FREE FINESSE. A defensive lead which allows declarer to take a finesse without the risk of losing the trick, or a finesse which could not normally be taken at all.

FREE RAISE. A single raise of opener's suit after an overcall. The classical theory that a free raise implies extra strength (8-10 points) has been generally abandoned; most experts maintain the normal range (6-9 points) irrespective of the overcall. However, the overcall may make it necessary to relax the requirements for trump support, especially if the overcall is in the suit ranking immediately below opener's:

(a)	(b)
♠ A x	♠ x x
♥ x x	♥ A x x x
♦ x x x x	♦ Q x x x
♣ A J x x x	♣ K x x

In (a), a raise to 2♠ would be appropriate when 1♠ has been overcalled by 2♥. In (b), 1♣ should be raised to 2♣ after an overcall of 1♠. In each case the trump length is one card below standard. These examples assume that NEGATIVE DOUBLES are not being used.

FRENCH BRIDGE FEDERATION (FÉDÉRATION FRANÇAISE DE BRIDGE). The Federation was founded in 1935. Membership in 1992 was about 75,000. French victories in international events include four world team championships, one world pairs, 7 European Teams and 9 European Women's Teams. France has hosted four world championships and one European Championship. Officers 1993:

President, Jean-Claude Beineix
Vice-President, Jean-Paul Meyer
                  73 Avenue Ch. de Gaulle
                  92200 Neuilly France.
                  Tel 33 1 47 38 24 40
                  Fax 33 1 47 38 66 74

FRENCH CLUB. A simple 1♣ forcing system once in common use in France and other parts of the world.

FRENCH GUIANA (Comité de Bridge de Guyane).
President 1992
Jean-Noel Joffroy
Boite Postale 322
97310 Kourou
French Guiana

FRENCH SCORING. In tournaments sanctioned by the French Bridge Federation, the value of the fourth odd trick in notrump contracts is reduced to 20 points. Thus ten or more tricks will be scored the same in either notrump or a major suit.

If it is assumed that a major game should be preferred to a notrump game, this scoring eliminates the edge given to the notrump contract when both will produce the same ten or more tricks.

FREQUENCY CHARTS. Informational sheets produced for the players when computer scoring is used on across-the-field tops. The charts tell the number of times each score is achieved on each deal and also list the matchpoints each score is worth. Players use these charts to check their scores, but one drawback is that a player cannot tell whether or not he was credited with the correct result on any given board.

FRIEND AWARD. The annual award given by the AMERICAN BRIDGE ASSOCIATION to the player who earns the most ABA masterpoints in a calendar year.

FRIGID. See COLD.

FRONT OF CARD. A phrase indicating that a partnership responds to a one notrump overcall by partner as if partner had opened one notrump. An oddity occurs when the overcaller's partner appears to want to play in opener's major suit at the two-level, either by a non-forcing response or by a transfer response. Since this is improbable, many use such bids to show game-going values with a singleton or void in opener's suit.

FRUIT MACHINE SWISS. If responder has opening values and a fit in response to a major opening he can bid:

(1) Four clubs showing either: two aces and a singleton; three aces; or two aces and the trump king. After a 4♦ relay, the responder bids, respectively, the singleton, 4NT, or the trump suit.

(2) Four diamonds with two aces and none of the above.

FULFILLING CONTRACT. Taking as many tricks, in the play of the hand, as contracted for in addition to the book of six, i.e., eight tricks in a contract of two. A bonus of 50 points is awarded for a less-than-game contract in duplicate, 300 for a nonvulnerable game, and 500 for a vulnerable game.

FULWILER. A conventional asking bid. After the trump suit has been established, any bid by either partner at the lowest range in another suit asks for control in that suit. Responses are in steps:

no control	1 step
singleton	2 steps
void	3 steps
king	4 steps
ace	5 steps
ace and king	6 steps

For example:	WEST	EAST
	1♠	2♠
	3♣	3NT

3NT is four steps above 3♣ so the bid shows the ♣K. Subsequently the opener can ask about trump honors. See ROMAN ASKING BIDS.

G

GABARRET CUP. This Argentine award donated in memory of Adolfo Gabarret is the equivalent of the ACBL McKENNEY TROPHY. For winners, see Appendix IV.

GADGET. An artificial bidding device which can be grafted on to standard bidding methods but is not an integral part of any system. The term applies to nearly all the articles listed under ARTIFICIAL BIDS and SLAM CONVENTIONS.

GAMBIT. A deliberate sacrifice of a trick in order to gain additional tricks. The term is borrowed from chess.

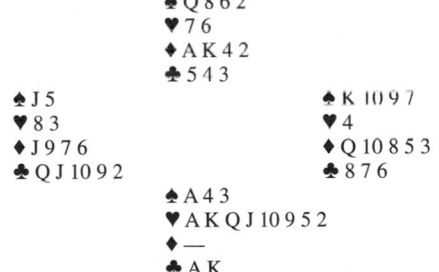

West leads the ♣Q against South's contract of 6♥.

Declarer, at trick two, must play one of his two small trumps and concede an otherwise unnecessary trick to the 8. This forces a trump entry to the dummy, and permits South to discard his two spade losers on dummy's diamond winners. A spade lead would have defeated the contract. See GREEK GIFT.

GAMBLING AT BRIDGE. Playing for stakes is quite common in social bridge games around the world, either in clubs or privately. The game is normally Chicago, or four deals, in North America, and traditional rubber bridge in Europe and other parts of the world such as Australia. Goulash games are common in France. In some countries, particularly the Scandinavian ones, duplicate play is normal and bridge for a stake is very rare.

In North America stakes are expressed in points, so that in a one-cent game 100 honors is worth one dollar. In Britain stakes are expressed in per-hundred terms, so that in a one-pound game 100 honors is worth one pound.

In a home game in North America the stake may be as little as 1/20th of a cent and is rarely more than three cents. In club games the lowest stake is usually one cent, and a game in New York City in which many of the players are millionaires is regularly played for 50 cents and sometimes as much as a dollar.

Gambling is prohibited in contests sanctioned by the American Contract Bridge League and other NCBOs. However a hybrid between social bridge and duplicate is popular in some clubs, particularly in New York City. A group of eight or more players cut to form teams and then play a short duplicate match for a predetermined stake. Losers pay winners according to the imp score. Then a fresh cut produces new teams.

GAMBLING THREE NOTRUMP. An opening bid based on a long, solid minor suit, a feature of the ACOL SYSTEM that has been adopted by many players using an artificial 2♣ forcing opening bid.

(a)	(b)
♠ A 5	♠ 7
♥ K 2	♥ Q 8 3
♦ J 3	♦ A K Q 8 4 3 2
♣ A K Q J 7 4 3	♣ J 3

The amount of outside strength required to make this bid varies with the individual partnership. In its original form stoppers were needed in at least two side-suits, as in (a). The modern tendency is to make the bid (except in fourth position) with little or no outside strength, as in (b).

Responses:

(1) 4♣ shows extreme weakness and a desire to play at the four-level in opener's suit.

(2) 4♦ is usually used artificially. A common arrangement is to use it as a singleton inquiry. Opener bids a major-suit singleton, bids 4 NT without a singleton, and bids his minor with a singleton in the other minor.

(3) 4♥ and 4♠ are natural, with a self-sufficient six-card suit or better.

(4) 4 NT is conventional, with responses downgraded because the opener has already shown an ace. A 5♦ rebid would therefore show two aces.

(5) 5♣ shows a desire to play in five of opener's suit - possibly for preemptive reasons.

(6) 5♦ is natural, implying that responder has a club honor and has therefore deduced that opener's suit is diamonds.

(7) 6♣ shows a desire to play a minor-suit slam. Defenses:

The most effective method of bidding against a gambling 3 NT opening bid is to use the RIPSTRA convention. Assuming adequate high-card strength, the bid of four of the better minor suit as a take-out for the majors gives the partnership the best chance of finding its best suit.

If 3 NT has become the final contract, the best chance to defeat the contract is usually for the opening leader to cash a winner in order to take a look at dummy and to

obtain information from his partner as to which hand controls which side suits.

GAME. The winning of 100 points below the line in bridge. Game can be attained by bidding and winning a succession of two or more partscores, or can be bid in one contract after it is determined that the partnership has sufficient values in the combined hands. The first team to win two such games wins the rubber and the premium. In CHICAGO, a game may be bid and scored on each of four deals and it is theoretically possible for a side to win four games in one CHUKKER.

GAME ALL. The situation when both sides are vulnerable. The term is rare in the United States but standard in England.

GAME BID. A bid for just enough odd tricks to complete the requirement for game in a particular suit or notrump. In duplicate bridge this is a bid for 3 NT, four of a major suit or five of a minor suit. In rubber bridge if a pair has a partscore, a game bid usually requires fewer tricks; a partscore of 40 points, for example, would make 2 NT, two of a major or three of a minor into game bids.

GAME CARDS. There are many games that are played with cards that are not the pack of playing cards. Authors, Rook, and Old Maid are examples of games designed principally for children. Flash cards, such as those used in teaching word recognition and foreign languages in schools, are other types. Dominoes and Mah-Jongg can also be played with cards in place of the blocks and tiles.

Major manufacturers of card games are located in the Massachusetts cities of Salem and Springfield, but games are produced by a wide variety of individual manufacturers, and most are covered by patents.

GAME CONTRACT. An undertaking of a contract which, if successful, will earn enough points in trick-score to make or complete the 100 required for a game. In notrump, three-odd, in hearts or spades, four-odd, in clubs or diamonds, five-odd tricks produce at least the 100 points necessary from a love score. With a partscore, lower contracts become game contracts. Some rubber bridge players will double a game contract more freely than below-game contracts, although such tactics are misconceived. See SUCKER'S DOUBLE.

GAME DEMAND BID. A bid which, once made, imposes an obligation upon the partnership to keep the bidding alive until game is reached or a satisfactory penalty inflicted upon the opponents. An obsolescent term. See FORCING TWO-BID.

GAME-FORCING BID. A bid which announces that the partnership should reach a game contract or higher, and thereby establishes a GAME-FORCING SITUATION.

GAME-FORCING SITUATIONS. A sequence of bidding which has committed both members of a partnership to reach a game contract. Many of these are listed under FORCING SEQUENCES.

GAME-GOING. A term applied to any hand or bidding

situation which promises to develop a game for the partnership.

GAME HOG. A player who habitually distorts his own bidding in the expectation that all hands should be played at a game contract.

GAME IN. A colloquial expression meaning vulnerable.

GAME INVITATION. See COMPETITIVE DOUBLE; DRURY; INVITATIONAL BID; JUMP RAISE BY RESPONDER; LIMIT JUMP RAISE; LIMIT JUMP RAISE TO SHOW SINGLETON; MAXIMAL OVERCALL DOUBLE; SHORT-SUIT GAME TRIES; TWO-WAY GAME TRIES; WEAK-SUIT GAME TRY.

GAME-TRY DOUBLE See MAXIMAL OVERCALL DOUBLE.

GAMMA TRUMP ASKING BIDS. Asking bids in the ROMAN and SUPER PRECISION systems concerned with the quality of responder's suit, which is inferentially agreed as trumps. The Roman responses are as follows:
1st step - Queen or worse
2nd step - King
3rd step - Ace
4th step - Two top honors
5th step - Three top honors

For responses in the SUPER PRECISION system, which are identical to the trump-asking responses in standard PRECISION CLUB, see PRECISION ASKING BIDS.

GARBAGE. A colloquial term for a minimum type of holding whose majority values are in unsupported queens and jacks.

GARDENER NOTRUMP OVERCALL. A two-way bid which may be either a natural notrump overcall with 16-18 points or a weak hand with a long suit. Partner usually bids 2♣ to find out which type of overcall was made, and the overcaller rebids 2 NT if he has the natural strong type. There is a technical reason for this procedure if strong jump overcalls are being used; a weak hand with a long suit has no convenient way to enter the auction. Devised by Nico Gardener, London. If the bid is always weak, it is referred to by the French as the Sans Atout Comique. See COMIC NOTRUMP.

GATHERING TRICKS. The taking in of tricks won by a side. The tricks taken by a side should be arranged in such a way that their number and sequence are apparent. See LAWS (Law 65).

GENERAL PURPOSE CUEBID. A bid of four notrump used as a general purpose slam try when a cuebid is not available or convenient. It may be difficult to distinguish this from Blackwood and similar bids, so it is rarely employed.

GENEVA. A method of showing any pair of unbid suits with an overcall of two notrump (or higher) by a player whose side has not yet bid. The bidder moves to his cheaper suit if his partner does not locate a fit. Many low-level doubles become penalty doubles. A danger is that the fit, if any, will be found at an excessively high level. Devised by Dr. William Konigsberger and Derrick Deane of Geneva, Switzerland.

GEORGE BURNS TROPHY. This trophy, inaugurated in 1993, is given annually to the ACBL Senior Player of the Year. It is named for George Burns, famous comedian who was still playing bridge daily at his country club into his late nineties. The first winner was Liane Slack of Kansas City MO.

GEORGIA BRIDGE FEDERATION, Republic of. Founded in 1991 following the break-up of the Soviet Union.
President 1992
Egons Lavendelis
Chvichia Str. 12/10
Tbilisi 380060
Georgia.
Fax: 43 1 602 9695 ext. 106

GERBER CONVENTION. A 4♣ bid to ask partner how many aces he holds. The responses are:
4♦ no ace 4♥ one ace 4♠ two aces 4 NT three aces
5♣ four aces
By analogy to the BLACKWOOD convention, 4♦ can be used instead of 5♣ to show the rare holding of four aces. As originally written (ROLLING GERBER), the 4♣ bidder uses the next available bid to ask for kings on the same principle, but cannot use the agreed trump suit for this purpose. For example, 4♠ asks for kings over a response of 4♥, unless spades is the agreed trump suit, in which case 4 NT becomes the king-asking bid. The modern tendency is to use 4♦ to show four aces along with 5♣ to ask for kings rather than the next higher bid. This helps remove ambiguity.

There may often be difficulty in distinguishing a conventional 4♣ bid from a natural one. Some players restrict the use of the convention to situations in which no suit has been genuinely bid (e.g., after a 1 NT or 2 NT opening, or a conventional 2♣ bid followed by 2 NT or 3 NT).

If 4♣ is to be used more generally, there are three possible rules a partnership can adopt:
(1) 4♣ is conventional unless it is a direct club raise.
(2) 4♣ is conventional unless clubs have been genuinely bid by the partnership.
(3) 4♣ is conventional if it is a jump bid, or if a suit has been specifically agreed. This is perhaps the best of these rules.

A partnership also has to consider how responder should act holding a void, or when there is interference bidding.

Treatment of similar situations is discussed under BLACKWOOD convention.

This convention, invented in 1938 by John Gerber is sometimes referred to as 4♣ Blackwood. The convention was devised earlier independently by Dr. William Konigsberger and Wim Nye, and published by them in Europe in 1936. See also ACE IDENTIFICATION; BLACK AND RED GERBER; CLARAC SLAM TRY; EXTENDED GERBER; KEY CARD GERBER; ROMAN GERBER; SUPER GERBER.

GERMAN BRIDGE LEAGUE (Deutscher Bridge-Verband). The League was founded in 1932 and by 1992 it had approximately 20,400 members. It hosted European Championships in 1963 in Baden-Baden and 1983 in Wiesbaden. Its Open Team won the Rosenblum Cup in 1990 and its Women's Team won the European Women's Teams in 1989. The League awards master points and publishes a monthly magazine "Deutsches Bridge Verbands-Blatt.

Officers 1992:
  President: Ulrich Wenning
  Vice-President: Detlev Piekenbrock,
  P.O. Box 2453 D-4900 Herford Germany.
  Tel (0 52 21) 8 36 63.

GESTURE. A mannerism that suggest a call, lead, play, or plan of play. See LAWS (Law 16).

GET A COUNT. To determine during the play the number of cards held in one or more suits by one of the hidden hands. See COUNTING THE HAND.

GHESTEM. A system of strong two-suited overcalls devised by Pierre Ghestem.
Over one club: 2NT shows the red suits
  2 ♦ shows the major suits
  3 ♣ shows diamonds and spades
  (This permits two clubs to be natural).
Over other suit openings:
  2NT shows the low-ranking suits
  3 ♣ shows the high-ranking suits
  Cuebid shows the top and bottom suits

GHOULIES. See GOULASH.

GIN. Colloquialism indicating total certainty of making a contract: "When the heart finesse won, I was gin."

GIVE COUNT. As a defender, to give a LENGTH SIGNAL to one's partner.

GLADIATOR. A method of responding to 1 NT, devised in New Zealand, and used in slightly modified forms in the ROMAN and CAB systems.
  A response of 2♣ is a relay, requiring the opener to bid 2♦. A minimum suit bid by responder then shows weakness, and the opener passes. Other rebids by the responder are limited.
  A response of 2♦ is a Stayman-type inquiry for major suits, and is forcing to game. A response of 2♥ or 2♠ is forcing, and higher suit responses are slam suggestions.
  The Gladiator idea can be used in other contexts. An example occurs after a weak-two is overcalled with two no-trump. Then three clubs can be used in this way, allowing for both weak hands, bidding three clubs, and forcing hands, making other bids.

GO DOWN. Synonym for failure to make a contract.

GO OFF. Fail to make a contract.

GOLD CUP. The Knockout Team Championship of Great Britain, contested under the auspices of the BRITISH BRIDGE LEAGUE. (See also VON ZEDTWITZ GOLD CUP.)

GO TO BED. Failure to take an obvious winner, usually an ace, and never taking a trick with it: "West went to bed with the ace of spades."

GO UP (or GO IN). To play a high and possibly winning

card when faced with a choice of playable cards.

GOING FOR A NUMBER, or a TELEPHONE NUMBER. Suffering a heavy penalty, presumably in four figures.

GOLD LIFE MASTER. An ACBL Life Master who has acquired at least 2500 masterpoints.

GOLD POINTS. Points awarded for section firsts and overall awards in regionally-rated or North American Championship events which have no upper masterpoint restrictions such as Open Pairs, Master Pairs, Men's and Women's Pairs, Mixed Pairs, Individual and Team events. One gold point is awarded to section winners in the annual ACBL Instant Matchpoint Game in sections of seven or more tables. Gold points are also awarded at regional events or regionally-rated events of two or more sessions which have a masterpoint limit of 750 or more points. The overall award in some restricted events at certain multiple-session North American Championships may contain a percentage of gold points.

GOLDEN AGE LIFE MASTER. A special category set up by ACBL to accommodate older players. There are two ways to qualify — (1) 70 years of age with 300 points of any color, or (2) 80 years of age with 100 points of any color.

GOLDEN RULE. The Golden Rule of bidding, as laid down by Alan Truscott, is that a suit should not be bid twice unless it has at least six cards. This applies to opener, responder, and the opponents of the opening bidder. Beginners do well to adhere to this rule, which is valid more than 90% of the time. Experienced players will be aware of some exceptions: (1) When a fit has been established, directly or by implication; (2) After a two-over-one response, guaranteeing a rebid in the modern style; (3) In a second suit. A player with 6-5 or 5-5 distribution can bid first suit, second suit and second suit again. See OPENER'S REBID.

GOLDWATER RULE. The satirical suggestion by Tournament Director Harry Goldwater that an opening lead out of turn should generally be accepted (see Law 53 for declarer's other options). The rationale is that a player who does not know whose turn it is to lead probably does not know the right lead either.

GOLF. As many bridge players also play golf, combined golf and bridge events are sometimes popular. An English plan conceived by David G. Clowes is to matchpoint the golf in the same way that a bridge event is scored (ten or more strokes on a hole counts as an automatic bottom or shared bottom). These scores are then divided by two, and the same pairs play a HOWELL or SCRAMBLED MITCHELL event to determine the winner on the combined scores.

GOOD. An adjective used to describe a hand which is better than the simple point-count would suggest, as in "a good 18". This may be owing to distributional factors, to the presence of body, to the location of honors in long suits, or to a combination of these items.

GOOD-BAD TWO NOTRUMP. See LEBENSOHL

APPLICATIONS.

GOOD CARDS. Cards which have been established during the play and which are winners that can be cashed. In a wide sense, a player of a partnership holding good cards has more than a fair share of the honor strength. But the term is sometimes used in a more precise technical meaning, referring to honor cards which have improved in value as a result of the auction. In a competitive auction, the improvement may arise because the significant honors are over the opponent who has bid the suit (see POSITIONAL FACTOR).

GOODWILL COMMITTEE. Organized by ACBL in 1955 with John E. Simon as chairman and Louise Durham as co-chairman. In 1957 the committee was made permanent, with two members, one man and one woman, being appointed from each district by the district director to hold permanent membership on the Committee. In 1963 three assistant chairmen were designated: Ethel Keohane (East), Louise Durham (Central) and Evelyn Piro (West). In 1972 John T. Murphy was added as another assistant chairman. The present committee consists of eight assistants — five in the United States, two in Canada (East and West) and one in Mexico.

In 1975 Jerome Silverman was named chairman, succeeding Simon who became Honorary Chairman Emeritus. In 1977 Kay Moody became chairman. She was succeeded in 1979 by Dr. John Pratt. In 1985, Aileen Osofsky, the present chairman, took the post. Under her tenure the committee has significantly expanded its endeavors, taking on promotion of Active Ethics, awareness of the hearing impaired, support of Junior, Youth and Charity programs, naming of a GOODWILL MEMBER OF THE YEAR and other projects.

GOODWILL MEMBER OF THE YEAR. An award begun in 1990 by Goodwill Committee chairman Aileen Osofsky to honor the ACBL member whose actions and philosophy embody the principles of goodwill: a promoter of bridge, a courteous and friendly opponent and a gentle and considerate partner. Recipients:

1990	Doris O'Grady, Highland CA.
1991	Julian Slager, Montgomery AL.
1992	Dorothy and Norman Edwardson, Springdale AR.
1993	Gladys Hodge, Pocatello, ID

GOREN AWARD. Endowed by Charles H. Goren until 1989, shortly before his death, this award for the Bridge Personality of the Year is presented annually by the INTERNATIONAL BRIDGE PRESS ASSOCIATION. It is made to the person deemed most worthy of recognition as an outstanding bridge personality. The Award is made annually but it is not restricted to achievement during the period in question: account may be taken of the entire bridge career of the nominee. For a list of winners See INTERNATIONAL BRIDGE PRESS ASSOCIATION AWARDS.

GOREN POINT-COUNT. See POINT-COUNT and DISTRIBUTIONAL POINT-COUNT.

GOREN SYSTEM. The bidding methods advocated by Charles H. Goren in many books from 1944 on. The method incorporated the Goren Point Count: to the basic Work Count, 4-3-2-1, he added a distributional count: a void counts for 3 points, a singleton for 2 and a doubleton for 1. The value of a hand is determined by adding the high card point total to the distributional total. 13-point hands are optional in the system, but 14-point hands must be opened. A third-hand opening can be made with as few as 11 points if the hand contains a fairly good suit. A fourth-hand opening bid should be made on 13 points, even though no good rebid is available. A different valuation system is used for the hand that figures to be dummy. High cards are counted at face value, and honors in partner's suit are promoted by a point each. One point is added for each doubleton, 3 for a singleton and 5 for a void if a fit has been established. A point should be deducted if dummy holds only three trumps, and another point should be subtracted if the dummy hand has a 4-3-3-3 distribution.

Using these methods, Goren determined that 26 points usually will produce game in a major, 29 game in a minor, 33 a small slam and 37 a grand slam.

The Goren System advocates opening 4-card majors as long as the suit is biddable–at least Q-x-x-x. When holding biddable touching suits of equal length, the higher-ranking should be the opening bid. When the two biddable suits of equal length are spades and clubs, the opening bid should be 1♣. In other combinations, the suit below the short suit should be the opening bid.

With balanced hands, responder should bid 1 NT with 6-10 points, 2 NT with 13-15 and 3 NT with 16-18. Responder should have the unbid suits stopped for the 2 NT and 3 NT bids. When responder has trump support, he should raise partner's suit to 2 with 7-10 points, to 3 with 13-16 points. Responder should jump shift with 19 or more points. He should respond in a new suit at the one level with 6 or more points. A two-level response in a new suit requires 10 points. With hands containing 11 or 12 points, responder should find two bids without forcing partner to game.

Opening two-bids in a suit should be made with a good five card suit and 25 points, with a good six-card suit and 23 points, and with a good seven card suit and 21 points.

Openings in notrump should be based on the following: 1 NT, 16-18 points; 2 NT, 22-24 points; 3 NT, 25-27 points. When evaluating for an opening notrump bid, a player should count only his high card values. A 2♣ response to 1 NT (also a 3♣ response to 2 NT) asks the opening bidder about his biddable major suits. With no four-card major, opener should rebid 2♦; with a four-card heart suit, 2♥; with a four-card spade suit or two four-card majors, 2♠.

This traditional Goren style closely resembled Culbertson methods, and is obsolescent in modern tournament play.

GOULASH. A deal in which the cards are not shuffled, and are dealt five to each player for two circuits, and finally three to each player. The name is apparently derived from Hungarian goulash, a highly spiced mixture of meat and vegetables, and is intended to suggest a spicy and unusual mixture.

Players sometimes agree to play goulash when a hand has been passed out, particularly in private or commuter games. Goulashes are standard in CUTTHROAT BRIDGE and TOWIE.

A more extreme form, known as the passing goulash,

achieved some popularity in the Twenties and Thirties. Each partner was permitted to pass six cards to his partner after the conclusion of the deal, usually three cards followed by two cards followed by one card.

A goulash is sometimes referred to as mayonnaise or hollandaise.

GRAND COUP. A play by which declarer deliberately shortens his trump holding by ruffing a winner in order to achieve a finessing position over an adverse trump holding in an end position.

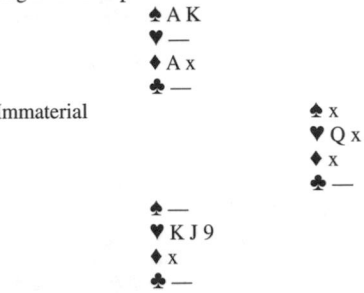

Declarer, in a heart contract, has discovered West to be void of hearts. With the lead in the dummy, declarer leads the ♠A and trumps it. He re-enters dummy with the ♦A to lead any card at trick 12. East must ruff and declarer overruffs.

GRAND LIFE MASTER. Highest rank in ACBL. It requires 10,000 masterpoints and at least one victory in a North American championship event that has no upper masterpoint limit.

GRAND MASTER. See WORLD BRIDGE FEDERATION PLAYER RANKINGS.

GRAND NATIONAL CHAMPIONSHIPS. (1) A series of annual championships first held in 1934 by the UNITED STATES BRIDGE ASSOCIATION and continued annually until 1937. See Appendix I.

(2) See GRAND NATIONAL TEAMS and NORTH AMERICAN OPEN PAIRS. See also CANADIAN NATIONAL TEAMS. See Appendix I.

GRAND NATIONAL FORTY-NINER PAIRS. See NORTH AMERICAN FORTY-NINER PAIRS and Appendix I.

GRAND NATIONAL PAIRS. See NORTH AMERICAN OPEN PAIRS and Appendix I.

GRAND NATIONAL ROOKIE PAIRS. A major ACBL pair championship 1979-1991. Since 1991, the NORTH AMERICAN FORTY-NINER PAIRS. See also NORTH AMERICAN ROOKIE PAIRS and Appendix I.

GRAND NATIONAL TEAMS. A major ACBL team championship, contested since 1973 for the MOREHEAD TROPHY. It is patterned in some respects after the USBA's event of the Thirties. The initial stages of the GNT are conducted over the course of several months in each ACBL district in the United States, Mexico and Bermuda, for members of units within the district to produce a district championship team. Canada originally participated in this event, but in 1980 Canada began con-

ducting its own national team championship parallel to the GNT. Through 1984 the district champions competed within eight Grand National Zones for the Zonal Championship. The final playoffs were contested as knockouts by the eight zonal champions at the Summer North American Bridge Championships. In 1985 the zonal stage was eliminated and the non-Canadian District Champions competed directly for the GNT title. At the same time the North American Teams Flight B was added for players with 0-500 masterpoints. Through 1991 the GNT champions were entitled to compete against the winners of the VANDERBILT CUP, the SPINGOLD TROPHY and the REISINGER TROPHY for the right to represent North America or the United States in the WORLD CHAMPIONSHIP two years hence. A new method, called the INTERNATIONAL TEAM TRIALS (ITT), was inaugurated in 1994. See INTERNATIONAL OPEN TEAM SELECTION. See NORTH AMERICAN TEAMS. Also see Appendix I.

GRAND OLD MAN OF BRIDGE. A term applied in the Twenties and early Thirties to MILTON C. WORK and in later years to SIDNEY LENZ. If the title belongs to those who have promoted the game at a great age, through writing and in other ways, there are other candidates for the title: R.F.Foster; George Beynon; Oswald Jacoby; B.Jay Becker; and Alfred Sheinwold.

GRAND SLAM. The winning of all thirteen tricks by the declarer. The bonus for a grand slam, 1,000 points when not vulnerable and 1,500 when vulnerable make a grand slam, bid and made, one of the best rewarded accomplishments at rubber bridge, and one of the more effective methods of SHOOTING at duplicate. While the general tendency among rubber bridge players is to avoid bidding grand slams except in ironclad situations, the mathematics of the game suggest rather freer acceptance of the risks involved in view of the large rewards.

See SLAM BIDDING for an explanation of methods of exploration suitable to bidding grand slams, and the percentage or odds that justify such bids. For a brief period (1932-35) the grand slam bonuses were higher than they are now: 1,500 non-vulnerable, 2,250 vulnerable.

GRAND SLAM FORCE. A method of locating the top trump honors when a grand slam is in view. It was devised by Ely Culbertson in 1936, was first described in a Bridge World article by Josephine Culbertson, and is often in consequence referred to in Europe as a Josephine.

A bid of 5 NT asks responder to bid a grand slam if he holds two of the top three trump honors. (This clearly does not apply if 5 NT is a natural notrump raise, or if it is used as part of another slam convention.) A jump to 5 NT fixes the last bid suit as trump unless another suit has been specifically agreed.

It is sometimes necessary to know whether responder has one of the top three honors. If the agreed trump suit is not clubs, one or more intermediate bids are available at the six-level for this purpose.

If diamonds are agreed, 6♦ should show one top honor. If a major suit has been agreed, several methods are in use, designed to permit a partnership to reach a grand slam missing Q-x-x in the trump suit.

One method is to divide the responses into four steps. The first step would show the weakest trump holding for the previous bidding (three or four small), the second step would show the queen, the third step the ace or king and the fourth step the ace or king with extra length. If hearts are agreed, the first and second steps are combined into one. If diamonds are the agreed suit, the first and second steps and the third and fourth steps are combined. For example:

```
               NORTH
               ♠ K 5 3 2
               ♥ 6 5 4
               ♦ 8 5 3
               ♣ 10 7 2

               SOUTH
               ♠ A 10 9 8 6 4
               ♥ A K
               ♦ A K Q 9 7
               ♣ —
```

SOUTH	NORTH
2 ♣	2 ♦
2 ♠	4 ♠
5 NT	6 ♥
7 ♠	

North's jump raise shows four spades, and his step response to the grand slam force shows the king. Since there is unlikely to be a trump loser, South bids the grand slam.

An alternate expert method, perhaps superior theoretically, is to sign off in the trump suit with the worst trump holding; other responses at the six-level are made inversely, the higher the bid the weaker the trump holding. In order to retain all four steps to show gradation of trump quality even when a suit other than spades has been agreed, some partnerships use jumps to five of the suit above the agreed trump suit, rather than to 5 NT as the grand slam force.

If clubs is the agreed trump suit, several methods are playable.

WEST	EAST
♠ A K J 3	♠ 7 2
♥ K 6	♥ A Q J 6
♦ A 5	♦ 9 4 2
♣ K 8 6 4 2	♣ A Q 5 3
1 ♣	1 ♥
1 ♠	3 ♣
4NT	5 ♥
5 ♠	5NT
6 ♣	7 ♣

West's unexpected bid of 5♠ forces East to bid 5NT. Then East can interpret the belated bid of 6♣, which logically suggests interest in a grand slam, as the Grand Slam Force.

The grand slam force can also be used in conjunction with Blackwood. The ROMEX system uses a bid of 5 NT as the grand slam force even after 4 NT has been used as Blackwood. It is more common, however, for partnerships to use the MALOWAN SIX CLUB CONVENTION to ask about trump honors. After the conventional response to Blackwood a bid of 6♣ is the grand slam force, providing clubs are not agreed.

In some systems, such as SCHENKEN, it is possible to agree on a trump suit and cue-bid first- and possibly second-round controls before 4 NT is reached. Richard Reed suggests that 4 NT should then be used to pinpoint trump honors. Partner returns to the agreed trump suit with none of the top three honors, bids the lowest-ranking side suit

with the king or queen, the next ranking side suit with the ace, the highest-ranking side suit with two of the top three honors, and 5 NT with full control of the trump suit.

The Grand Slam Force remains in the repertory of expert pairs; however, new methods to uncover trump honors, such as Roman Key Card Blackwood, have increasingly found favor. Furthermore, many expert pairs use a bid of 5 NT as a general inquiry: "Partner, pick a slam." See also BYZANTINE BLACKWOOD: TRUMP ASKING BIDS.

GRANO-ASTRO. A defense to one notrump in which double shows spades and another suit, and a minor-suit bid shows that suit and hearts.

GREEK BRIDGE FEDERATION (HELLENIC BRIDGE FEDERATION). The Federation was founded in 1965 by two clubs with about 320 members. By 1992 it had a membership of 1,724, and 21 clubs were affiliated. The Federation organized the 1971 European Championships in Athens.
Officers 1992:
President: Elias Skaleos
Secretary-General: George Economopoulos
13, Andinoros Str.
Athens 116 34 Greece
Tel: 01 72 30205
Fax: 01 72 20626

GREEK GIFT. A trick offered to the opponent which, if accepted, leads to disaster. The following example was played about 1930 with Lee Hazen in the East seat.

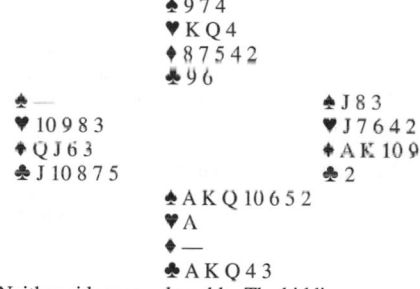

Neither side was vulnerable. The bidding:

West	North	East	South
Pass	Pass	1 ♥	2 ♥
4 ♥	Pass	Pass	6 ♠
Pass	Pass	Pass	

West led the ♥10 against 6♠ and South took his ace. He then made a tricky play by leading the ♠10. He assumed that somebody would win this, and he would be provided with the dummy-entry he needed to dispose of his club losers.

Hazen was about to take his jack, but paused to consider. Why was South being so generous? Was it a Greek Gift? It was clear from the bidding that South had no more hearts, so he must be trying to create an entry. The spade ten was allowed to win, and South did not look pleased. His next move was to lead the ace and king of clubs.

Now fully alive to the situation, Hazen refused to ruff, dooming South to defeat. If he tried for ruffs he would be overruffed, and if he did not West would score two club tricks.

Since the only danger for South was a bad split in both black suits, a better play would have been to play the top clubs at once. It would now have been more tempting for East to ruff, thus allowing the slam to score, but we are confident that Hazen would have resisted the temptation.

GREEN POINTS. A jocular term for tournaments in which the prizes are in dollars and therefore green. The Greater New York BA runs a Green Point Pairs annually in which cash prizes are awarded.

GREEN SUIT. The fifth suit in the American version of FIVE-SUIT BRIDGE, called Eagles. Prior to the introduction of five-suit bridge, the green suit was a nonexistent fifth suit. See HIPPOGRIFFS.

GROSVENOR GAMBIT. A humorous psychological ploy described by Frederick Turner of Los Angeles in The Bridge World in June 1973. A defender deliberately makes a clear error, giving the declarer an opportunity which he will refuse to take because he expects rational defense. The hope is that the declaring side will be demoralized on later deals. For example:

```
              ♠ 10 8
              ♥ J 3
              ♦ A 8 7 3
              ♣ J 8 7 6 4
♠ Q J 7 6 3 2              ♠ 9 4
♥ 7 5                      ♥ Q 8 4
♦ 10 6                     ♦ J 9 5 2
♣ A K 9                    ♣ Q 10 5 3
              ♠ A K 5
              ♥ A K 10 9 6 2
              ♦ K Q 4
              ♣ 2
```

Two top clubs are led against 6♥. South ruffs and plays spades, ruffing the third round in dummy. Instead of overruffing East discards. His trick comes back because South plays top trumps, sure that West has the queen.

GROUP SCORE. The score made by all the pairs in a group on a set of hands constituting a match. Competition between clubs and cities is sometimes based on a team of eight, twelve, or an even larger number of players. In such a game, each pair from one side meets each of the pairs on the competing side, all playing the same set of boards. The net score (plus and minus) of all pairs is included in the group score.

Also, in total point pair contests, the net score on a set of boards on which two particular pairs are in opposition.

GUADELOUPE BRIDGE COMMITTEE (Comité de Bridge de Guadeloupe). Founded about 1952, and in 1992 had a membership of 128 players, in three clubs. Hosted one zonal championship in 1979.
Officers 1993:
President: Joseph Boulogne
Secretary: Genevieve Biron
PO Box 380
Point a Pitre 97162
Guadeloupe.
Tel. (590) 93 89 18
Fax (590) 91 32 28

GUARD (or Stopper). An honor holding in a particular

suit which will or may prevent the opponents running the suit.
A guard may be:
(1) Positive: A, K-Q, Q-J-10, J-10-9-8.
(2) Probable: K-J-x, K-10-x, Q-J-x.
(3) Possible: Q-x-x, J-9-x-x.
(4) Positional: K-x.
(5) Partial: K, Q-x, J-x-x, 10-x-x-x.

GUARD SQUEEZE. A squeeze in three suits, in which an opponent holds guards in two suits, and his holding in a third suit prevents declarer from taking a winning finesse.

There are five basic endings, each of which resembles the basic double squeeze position. By contrast with the double squeeze, the guard squeeze takes place when the same opponent controls both isolated menaces, but as compensation the double menace contains finesse possibilities.

```
              ♠ —
              ♥ K
              ♦ K
              ♣ A x
♠ —                       ♠ x
♥ A                       ♥ —
♦ A                       ♦ —
♣ Q x                     ♣ J x x
              ♠ A
              ♥ —
              ♦ —
              ♣ K 10 x
```

South leads the ♠A, and West is squeezed in three suits. He must discard a club, but South leads a club to the ace (dropping the queen) and finesses the 10 on the way back.

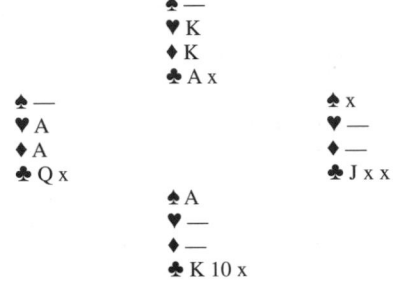

```
              ♠ A J
              ♥ —
              ♦ K
              ♣ x
♠ K x                     ♠ Q
♥ x                       ♥ K Q
♦ —                       ♦ A
♣ x                       ♣ —
              ♠ x
              ♥ A J
              ♦ —
              ♣ A
```

South leads the ♣A, and East is squeezed in three suits. If he discards a spade, South can lead that suit, and finesse the jack.

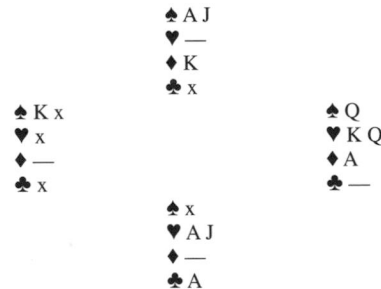

```
              ♠ K x
              ♥ A J x
              ♦ —
              ♣ —
♠ J x                     ♠ Q 9 x
♥ K Q                     ♥ x
♦ A                       ♦ —
♣ —                       ♣ x
              ♠ A 10 x
              ♥ —
              ♦ K
              ♣ A
```

South leads the ♣A and West is squeezed in three suits. If he discards a spade, South leads a spade to the king (dropping the jack) and finesses the 10 on the way back.

In each of the above positions the squeeze retains its effectiveness even if one of the isolated menaces is guarded by both opponents. This leads to a double guard squeeze whose constituents are a guard squeeze against one opponent and a simple squeeze against the other.

There are two other double guard squeeze positions:

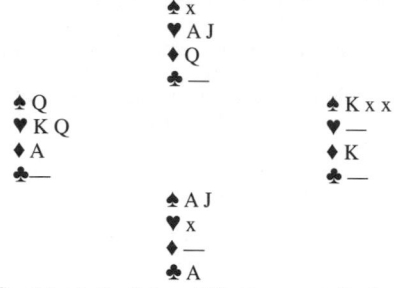

South leads the ♣A, and West is squeezed in three suits. He must discard a diamond. Now the ♥A squeezes East in spades and diamonds.

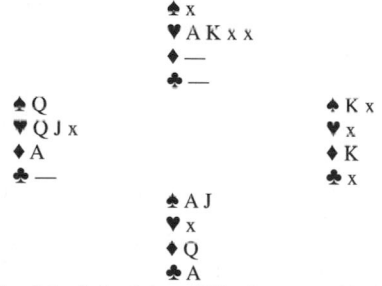

South leads the ♣A, and West is squeezed in three suits. He is forced to discard a diamond. South takes two top hearts, squeezing East in spades and diamonds. See SQUEEZES.

GUARDED HONOR or GUARDED SUIT. See GUARD.

GUIDE CARD. A card, usually printed, with prearranged instructions to each contestant, telling him which seat to occupy and which boards to play at each round. The guide card may also enable a contestant to check the positions and identities of his opponents.

Guide cards may be in the form of printed instruction cards remaining permanently at each table (suitable only for cyclic movements); or they may be in the form of separate cards to be hand-carried by each contestant (suitable for either cyclic or noncyclic movements).

Guide cards are used for HOWELL MOVEMENT pair games, team games, and individual contests.

H

HACKETT. A defense to weak two-bids in which 3♣ is a weak takeout request, with fewer than 16 points, and 3♦ is stronger, with 16 points or more.

HAITI BRIDGE ASSOCIATION (Association de Bridge de Haiti).
President 1992

Dr. Raymond Hippolyte
Cercle Bellevue
Case Postale 52
Port-au-Prince,
Haiti W.I.
Tel: 25685

HALF TABLES. An extra pair at a duplicate game. To accommodate the pair and still keep the game a fair contest requires a choice of methods by the director. The choice is based on the size of the game, the movement in use, and the time when it becomes known that a half-table situation exists.

If it is known in advance that a half-table situation exists, the director may consider that he has a full table and run the movement with a PHANTOM PAIR. Any pair scheduled to play the phantom pair will have a sitout for that round. However, such a movement should be used only if the game will have a complete movement. Otherwise there are serious problems with the scoring since pairs will have played different numbers of boards and boards will have different tops.

A better option, especially when confronted with the problem of adding a late-arriving pair, is to add a pair to the movement already in play. For Howell-like movements this pair will be added as an APPENDIX PAIR. For a Mitchell let the extra pair be a ROVER pair or shift into a PIVOT MITCHELL or a BUMP MITCHELL. This shift may be made unless the movement being used is a Relay Mitchell (with board sharing). This change in the movement can be effected as late as just before the move for the second round. Note that a Pivot Mitchell and a Rover Mitchell can be run in as many rounds as full tables, but a Bump Mitchell must have one fewer round than the number of full tables. All three movements may be curtailed at any time with no scoring problem.

The ACBL has guide cards for half-table games which are available upon request. Following are suggestions for half-table movements. No attempt has been made to include all the possibilities. However, it will be pointed out when one movement is clearly superior to the others.

2 1/2 tables. Use a three-table Howell movement. It is possible to shift to this movement if a two-table game has been begun and a fifth pair arrives late.

3 1/2 tables. If board method (a) or (b) is used, as given under THREE TABLES, use a rover pair with this movement: Out, EW2, NS2, EW3, EW1. If there is time to do so, it is better to switch to a four-table Howell.

4 1/2 tables. A five-table Howell is best if it is known that this will be the size of the game. If the half table comes in during the first round, use an appendix to the four-table Howell at any table other than Table 1. The new pair must be appended to a table that originally had two moving pairs.

5 1/2 tables. Run a five-table Howell with an appendix pair at any table without a stationary pair. If the size of the game is known early enough, a six-table THREE-QUARTER MOVEMENT can be used. With a Mitchell movement, a Rover pair will work well. Another reasonable possibility — set up a relay between Tables 1 and 6 with bye boards between Tables 3 and 4. The phantom pair should be North-South 6; East-West pairs will sit out when they reach Table 6.

6 1/2 tables. The best movement is the seven-table Howell — each pair meets every other pair and the sitout is only two boards long. If the half table comes in late and the movement is a six-table Three-Quarter Movement, append the pair to any table where there is no stationary pair. With a Mitchell movement, put out four boards at each table and have the pair at Table 7 sit out the first round. If the phantom pair is North-South, the East-West pairs will sit out when they arrive at Table 7. If the phantom pair is East-West, the North-South pairs will sit out when they are scheduled to meet East-West 7. If the game already has started when the extra pair arrives, use the Roving Pair method. (See ROVER).

7 1/2 tables. A number of possibilities cover this situation. If the movement is a seven-table Howell, add an appendix pair at any table that does not have a stationary pair. Alternatively an eight-table Three-Quarter movement may be used. If the movement is a Mitchell, the eight-table movement with a relay between Tables 1 and 8 with bye boards between Tables 4 and 5 will work out well. The phantom pair should be North-South 8 so that effectively there will be no board sharing. If a seven-table Mitchell already is in progress when the late pair arrives, the Rover movement may be used in either of two ways. The Rover may proceed from table to table, replacing either North-South pairs or East-West pairs in the usual progression. The problem here is that each sitout pair must sit out four boards. An alternative is to have the Rover replace first the East-West pair for two boards, then the North-South pair for the other two boards. By doing this every pair sits out two boards instead of half the field sitting out four and the rest playing all the boards. If this movement is used, the game will produce only one winner.

8 1/2 tables. If you know before the game starts that you have a half table, the best movement is a nine-table Mitchell. Put out boards on all tables and have one of the pairs sit out at Table 9. If the phantom pair is North-South 9 the East-West pairs will sit out when they reach Table 9. If the phantom pair is East-West, the North-South pairs will sit out when they are scheduled to play East-West 9. If the extra pair arrives after the game is under way, use the Roving Pair method. If you are using a Three-Quarter Movement, use the nine-table Three-Quarter or append to any table not having a stationary pair in an eight-table Three-Quarter.

9 1/2 tables. If the Mitchell movement is used, the best alternative, if time permits playing 10 rounds, is a relay between Tables 1 and 10 with bye boards between Tables 5 and 6. The phantom should be pair 10 North-South. The ACBL has a guide card movement for an East-West Roving Pair movement that works very efficiently — two East-West pairs have unusual progressions. A 10-table Mitchell with the phantom pair at North-South 10 and a skip after the fifth round is a possible alternative, but it is not recommended — both the boards and pairs must be factored, a headache for the director and a situation that is difficult to explain to the players' satisfaction. If a Three-Quarter movement is being used, use the 10-table Three-Quarter movement with a phantom pair or the nine-table Three-Quarter with an appendix at any table having two moving pairs.

10 1/2 tables. The Roving Pair movement works very well here. The Bump Mitchell also works well as long as no more than nine rounds are being played. A Three-Quarter movement is uncommon with this many tables but it is possible to set up for an 11-table Three-Quarter with a phantom pair or append a 10-table Three-Quarter at any table where there is no stationary pair.

11 1/2 tables. Best is the Roving Pair or Bump Mitchell. A good alternative is a 12-table game with a relay between Tables 1 and 12. The phantom pair is North-South 12. Put bye boards between Tables 6 and 7. The disadvantage to this game is that approximately half the field play only 22 boards. A Three-Quarter movement is not recommended, but it is possible to use the 12-table Three-Quarter with a phantom or to append a pair to the 11-table Three-Quarter.

12 1/2 tables. The best movement is to set up a 13-table Mitchell with a phantom pair at Table 13. If the phantom pair is North-South the East-West pairs sit out when they reach Table 13. If the phantom pair is East-West the North-South pairs sit out when they are scheduled to play against East-West 13. A Roving Pair will work very well and should be used if the half table comes in late. It is possible to append to a 12-table Three-Quarter at any table where there were originally two moving pairs.

13 1/2 tables. The best movement is a Roving Pair. A Bump Mitchell will work but the game must be curtailed after 12 rounds. It is also possible to play a 14-round game by setting up a relay between Tables 1 and 14 and bye boards between Tables 7 and 8. The phantom pair should be North-South 14. East-West pairs sit out when they reach Table 14.

14 1/2 tables. The best movement is the Roving Pair or Bump Mitchell. Either will work easily and well.

15 1/2 tables. The best movement is a Bump Mitchell. The Roving Pair is a reasonable alternative, but it requires special movements after certain rounds.

Olof Hanner recommends a simple method of adding a pair to a Scrambled Mitchell, whether with an odd number of tables or when using a Skip. Make the N-S Pair at the last table into a moving pair, and have an instruction on the last table as follows: E-W at last table sits out next, then plays N-S at last table, then E-W at table 1. This avoids factoring of boards even if the movement is curtailed, since each board is played once in each round. A Skip Mitchell with this extra pair can play a full number of rounds without repeating opponents. This technique can be used from the start, or before Round 2 starts.

Another general method is the 1 1/2-table Appendix Mitchell. 10 1/2 tables can play nine rounds. Give table 1-9 a set of boards each for a 9-table Mitchell. Table 10 shares boards with table 1 throughout. Moving pairs go to EW 9, then EW 10, then sit out, then EW 1. The basic movement can be a Skip Mitchell. There is no repetition of opponents.

HALF TRICK. An original holding in a suit that will win a trick by virtue of being a high card about half the time. A queen held in company with an ace of the same suit, or a king with a guard, is a half trick on original valuation. The position of adverse bids as the bidding progresses may add to or detract from such a valuation.

HALL OF FAME. A plan for commemorating the achievements of outstanding bridge personalities, suggested by Lee Hazen of New York and inaugurated in 1964 by Alphonse (Sonny) Moyse, editor and publisher of *The Bridge World*. The first three members elected were Ely Culbertson, Charles Goren and Harold Vanderbilt. In 1965 Oswald Jacoby, Milton Work and Sidney Lenz were named. Waldemar von Zedtwitz, Howard Schenken and Sidney Silodor were added in 1966. The plan is no longer in effect.

HAMILTON. A conventional system of defensive bidding over an opposing opening bid of 1NT. An overcall of 2♣ is a forcing bid showing a one-suiter and demanding a 2♦ response from partner — neither bid says anything about the suit mentioned. After the 2♦ response, the 2♣ bidder names his suit. Other overcalls in this system show two-suiters. Their meanings: 2♦ — spades and hearts; 2♥ — hearts and a minor; 2♠ — spades and a minor; 2NT — diamonds and clubs. If partner wishes to learn which minor after an overcall of either 2♥ or 2♠, he bids 2NT and the overcaller then names the minor. A double when using this convention is primarily for penalties. See CAPPELLETTI.

HAMILTON CLUB (London). One of the leading English card clubs, founded by Col. Henry M. Beasley, 1939, in association with Carl Repelaer, who continued to manage the club after Beasley's death in 1949. The club was closed in the early Seventies. See OLDEST CLUBS.

HAND. (1) A particular deal of 52 cards. (2) The cards held by one player. The term is also used to indicate the order in bidding rotation, as in "second hand" or "fourth hand."

HAND DISTRIBUTIONS. See HAND PATTERNS for general and specific distributions. See MATHEMATICAL TABLES for percentage frequency and distributions.

HAND HOG. A player who (often mistakenly) feels that he is the best qualified to manage the hands as declarer. The usual method of operation is to pass with minimum opening bids but to respond with jumps in notrump.

HAND PATTERNS. There are 39 possible hand patterns, ranging from the most balanced, 4-3-3-3, to the most unbalanced, 13-0-0-0. A player can hold specifically four spades, three hearts, three diamonds and three clubs in 13C4 ⟨⟩ 13C3 ⟨⟩ 13C3 ↔ 13C3 different ways, which computes to 16,726,464,040 or 2.634% of the 635,013,559,600 hands he could hold (see NUMBER OF POSSIBLE HANDS). This, of course, is not the percentage probability that he will have a 4-3-3-3 hand, because the four-card length need not be in spades, but could be in any of the four suits, so the chance of a 4-3-3-3 hand is 10.536%.

A rearrangement of the suits in a particular distributional pattern is termed a permutation of the pattern; 4-3-4-2 is a permutation of a 4-4-3-2 pattern. If we use the same letter of the alphabet to indicate the same length in a suit, there are three classes of hands: AAAB, such as 4-3-3-3 or 4-4-4-1, etc., which has 4 permutations; AABC, such as 4-4-3-2 or 5-5-2-1, etc., which has 12 permutations; ABCD, such as 5-4-3-1 or 7-3-2-1, etc., which has 24 permutations. Thus, the probability of five spades, four hearts, three diamonds and one club is .539%, but the probability of some 5-4-3-1 distribution is 24 times as great, or 12.931%. For all possible hand patterns, see MATHEMATICAL TABLES, Table 1.

HALL OF FAME. A plan for commemorating the achievements of outstanding bridge personalities, suggested by Lee Hazen of New York and inaugurated in 1964 by Alphonse (Sonny) Moyse, editor and publisher of *The Bridge World.* The first three members elected were Ely Culbertson, Charles Goren and Harold Vanderbilt.

In 1965 Oswald Jacoby, Milton Work and Sidney Lenz were named. Waldemar von Zedtwitz, Howard Schenken and Sidney Silodor were added in 1966. The plan is no longer in effect. However, the ACBL Board of Directors was checking into the possibility of beginning a new Hall of Fame in 1994.

HAND RECORDS. (1) Diagrams set up by the players after a deal in a major match is completed; (2) the sheets on which individual computer-dealt hands are printed for distribution to players for duplication; (3) the sheets distributed to players at the conclusion of a game on which all the hands from that session are printed.

In some tournaments, particularly in Europe, the players make a record of each hand after they have played it on the first round. This card is then placed with the hand in the pocket, and can be used by succeeding players to check whether the cards they hold are the ones that were originally dealt into that hand. Such hand records are known as CURTAIN CARDS.

HANDBOOK, ACBL. See ACBL HANDBOOK.

HANDICAPPED PLAYERS. A number of bridge players have overcome serious physical handicaps to become high-ranking players. There are a number of blind players who have earned life master status. Fred Snite played from an iron lung. Polio victim Robert Penn was transported to a Honolulu tournament in his wheelchair with a mechanical respirator attached. Morris Ribyat earned his LM Gold Card in 1962, 15 years after he became a victim of multiple sclerosis. Paralyzed from the neck down since a car accident in 1959, Life Master Walter Lewis of Pascagoula MS won all four events at an Alabama sectional in 1976.

Most outstanding among the players who participate from wheelchairs is Hermine Baron, who twice won the McKenney Trophy, setting a record in 1964. She represented the United States in international competition in 1968, 1978 and 1982 and was second on the list of ACBL members with the greatest total points in 1983 when she had 20,490 points.

Born armless, and with one leg, Life Master Mike Wilson of Vancouver plays bridge using his toes. Pat O'Brien, a Life Master with 3000 points and a certified director, is a hemophiliac.

A victim of kidney disease, Roberta Runion became a Life Master at a Wichita KS regional while taking three dialysis treatments a week.

Hugh Montague of N.Babylon NY continues to play at a high level several years after receiving a heart transplant. ACBL member Athan Cosmas devised cardholders to assist players with arthritic fingers and those who may have been injured.

A Potomac MD periodontist, Jay Slotkin, plays regularly in duplicate clubs and at tournaments despite the fact that he is almost totally incapacitated by amyotrophic lateral sclerosis (Lou Gehrig's disease). Slotkin cannot move or speak, but he played three sessions a day at the 1993 Summer NABC in Washington DC. Aided by nurses, Slotkin bid and played by blinking his eyes. He is affectionately known as "Doctor Double" for his aggressiveness at the table.

HANDICAPPING. A method of scoring in which each contestant is given a handicap (either plus or minus) based on previous performance or degree of competence. In the past in the ACBL, handicaps were used only to determine who won the JACKPOT — masterpoints were never based on handicaps. However, this was changed in 1980. At that time, the League strongly urged its member clubs to consider using a handicap method in order to create more interest among the less experienced and less talented players.

The plan most often used divides the masterpoints available for a club game into two, with half going to those who have the best raw scores and the other half going to those who have the best handicap scores. The most common form of handicap used is one based on an average of past performances matched against an almost unattainable par of .650.

This method requires additional work on the part of the club manager or director, but it is more equitable because the handicaps are based on results, avoiding claims of favoritism. This system is similar to the computation of averages in bowling, providing for a rapid change in handicap, up or down on the basis of recent result. The handicap is computed on the basis of 90% or 100% of the difference between the player's average performance and an artificial par established at 65% of possible.

It is also possible to handicap according to rank. Using this system, the sum of the handicaps of the partners constitutes the handicap for the pair. Because some players in such games do not hold ACBL rank, the ACBL recommends that the club manager or director arbitrarily assign such players to the Master classification.

Handicapping also is frequently used to make the sale of weaker teams more productive in a CALCUTTA tournament.

HANDLING CARDS. The handling of cards other than a player's own is improper. At duplicate, a player may ask to see his opponent's (or his partner's) card, and the player involved will turn it for him. There are some players who take a hand belonging to another player out of the board after play has been completed in order to discuss a matter of bidding or play. This practice is officially discouraged and is illegal if the opponents are not present. It is the cause of most fouled boards.

HANDS NOT PLAYED OUT. Hands can be concluded before the last trick for various reasons. Frequently declarer will table his hand and make a CLAIM, even as early as after the opening lead. He should then make a statement of how he would play if he actually continued the physical motions of doing so, and if the line he intends to follow seems reasonable to the opposition and is not susceptible of any challenge by them, then the cards can be thrown in, at rubber bridge, or returned to the board, at duplicate. See CLAIM OR CONCESSION.

HANNER MOVEMENTS. (1) Individual movements for up to 20 tables devised by Olof Hanner of Sweden, and detailed in his book on Duplicate Organization written in combination with Hans-Olof Hallén and Per Jannersten. See INDIVIDUAL MOVEMENTS. (2) A movement for a team-of-four contest in which each match is completed in two consecutive rounds. This provides for quick results without the board sharing necessary in a twinned movement. The movement may be played with an odd or even number of teams without any sit-out. The boards are either different for different matches, or in each

round played with the same boards at half the tables, which requires some duplication.

HEAD-TO-HEAD. A term used to describe any match in bridge of prearranged set opposition; that is, one team of four or more against another of four or more. Use of the term is restricted to two-team contests only.

HEART. The symbol ♥ for the second-ranking suit in bridge. Hearts are between spades and diamonds in value. The suit designation originated in France in the sixteenth century and takes its name from the shape of the pips used in designating card rank.

HEART SUIT. The second-ranking suit, with scarlet pips on each card in the shape of a heart. The suit ranks just below spades in bidding, and above diamonds.

HEARTBREAKER. A term applied to a hand that fails in a big way to live up to one's original expectations of it. It can be a defensive hand where one has, for example, been dealt cards that enable one to double a certain final contract with the assurance of setting the opponents badly. If, because of the distributional situations or highly expert card play by declarer, the contract is made, then surely the "heartbreaker" term would follow,

If, on the other hand, one is declarer at a contract that seems sure of success, and especially if the contract is a slam or a doubled or redoubled game bid, and is unable to make the hand or to avoid a large set in the process, then that hand is often called a "heartbreaker," too. Also applied to a session of duplicate which promises more than it achieves: in a head-to-head team match a pair may outplay their immediate opponents only to find their team score is negative.

The following deal was a heartbreaker for West.

```
                        NORTH
Vul: Both               ♠ Q J 8 5 4
Dlr: North              ♥ 5 2
                        ♦ —
                        ♣ K Q J 10 9 8
WEST                                        EAST
♠ —                                         ♠ 10 7 3 2
♥ A K Q 10 9 8 7 6                          ♥ J
♦ A K Q 4 2                                 ♦ J 9 8 7 3
♣ —                                         ♣ 4 3 2
                        SOUTH
                        ♠ A K 9 6
                        ♥ 4 3
                        ♦ 10 6 5
                        ♣ A 7 6 5
```

North	East	South	West
Pass	Pass	1 ♠	Dbl
4 ♠	Pass	Pass	5 ♥
5 ♠	Pass	Pass	6 ♥
Pass	Pass	Dbl	Redbl
Pass	Pass	6 ♠	7 ♥
Pass	Pass	7 ♠	Dbl
All Pass			

West could have bid an immediate 7♥, but he did not wish to push his opponents into 7♠. He began with a cunning takeout double, and then bid his hearts gently at the five-level and the six-level. This was good tactical bidding: The important thing for West was to be declarer, and the exact level was of secondary importance.

But at the six-level West became foolishly greedy. When he was doubled he should have been satisfied to make a doubled slam with an overtrick. Instead he redoubled, and Oswald Jacoby, in the South seat, worked out what was happening. He retreated to 6♠, and to West's considerable disappointment, carried on to 7♠ over 7♥.

West doubled in a bad temper, and could have cashed two heart tricks. But not unnaturally he thought that the ♦A was a better bet as an opening lead. Jacoby had a good clue to the distribution, and he made no mistake. He made the key play of ruffing with dummy's ♠8, leading the ♠4 and finessing the 6 — a remarkable way to play the first round of trumps in a grand slam.

A diamond was ruffed with the ♠J, and the ♠9 was finessed to reenter the closed hand. The last diamond was ruffed with dummy's last trump, and the closed hand was reentered with the ♣A to draw the missing trumps. Dummy's club winners gave Jacoby his doubled grand slam.

HEDGEHOG SQUEEZE. Hedgehog squeezes were named and analyzed by Hugh Darwen in the (British) *Bridge Magazine*, March 1968 and April 1968. A hedgehog squeeze is a squeeze of one opponent in two or three suits and a squeeze of the other opponent in three suits. These are the basic endings:

I. Single hedgehogs

1. Non-simultaneous guard hedgehog

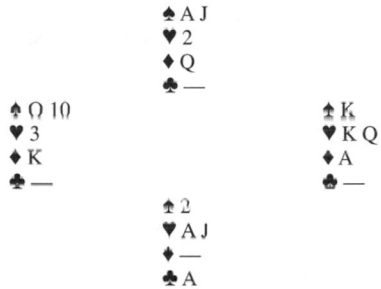

On the lead of the ♣A, West and North discard hearts, and East is squeezed out of the ♦A. Now the lead of the ♥A squeezes West in spades and diamonds.

2. Simultaneous guard hedgehog.

♠ K 2
♥ K
♦ Q
♣ —

♠ Q J   ♠ 10 8 7
♥ A   ♥ —
♦ A   ♦ K
♣ —   ♣ —

♠ A 9 3
♥ —
♦ —
♣ A

The lead of the ♣A squeezes West out of the ♦A, North discards the ♥K, and East is squeezed in spades and diamonds.

3. Blocked guard hedgehog

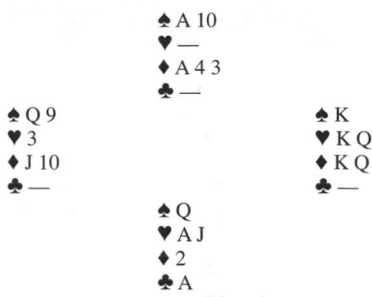

On the ♣A lead, West discards a heart, North discards a diamond, and East is squeezed out of a diamond. Now the lead of the ♥A squeezes West in spades and diamonds.

4. Automatic clash hedgehog

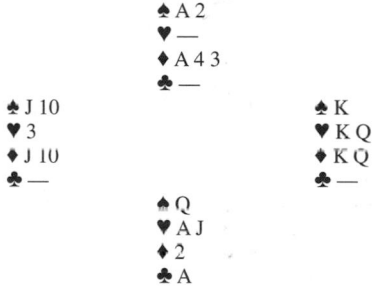

On the ♣A lead, West discards a heart, North discards a diamond, and East is squeezed out of a diamond. Now the lead of the ♥A squeezes West in spades and diamonds.

5. One-way clash hedgehog

♠ A 2
♥ A J
♦ 2
♣ —

♠ K   ♠ J 10
♥ K Q   ♥ 2
♦ K Q   ♦ J 10
♣ —   ♣ —

♠ Q
♥ 3
♦ A 3
♣ A

The lead of the ♣A squeezes West out of a diamond, while North and East discard hearts. Now a lead to the ♥A squeezes East in spades and diamonds.

II. Double hedgehogs (also known as "hexagon squeezes")

1. Double guard hedgehog

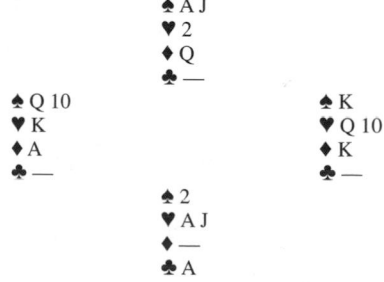

The lead of the ♣A squeezes West out of the ♦A, North discards the ♥2, and East is squeezed in three suits.

2. Double clash hedgehog

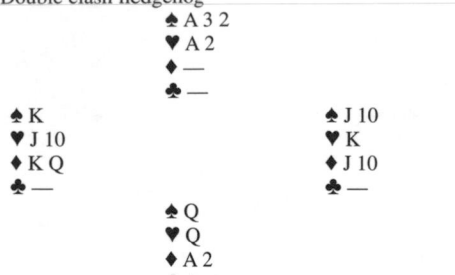

```
                ♠ A 3 2
                ♥ A 2
                ♦ —
                ♣ —
♠ K                          ♠ J 10
♥ J 10                       ♥ K
♦ K Q                        ♦ J 10
♣ —                          ♣ —
                ♠ Q
                ♥ Q
                ♦ A 2
                ♣ A
```

The lead of the ♣A forces West to discard a diamond, North discards the ♠2, and East is squeezed in three suits.

3. Hybrid double hedgehog

```
                ♠ A 2
                ♥ A J 3
                ♦ —
                ♣ —
♠ K                          ♠ J 10
♥ Q 10                       ♥ K
♦ K Q                        ♦ J 10
♣ —                          ♣ —
                ♠ Q
                ♥ 2
                ♦ A 2
                ♣ A
```

The lead of the ♣A forces West to discard a diamond, North discards the ♥3, and East is squeezed in three suits.

III. Progressive hedgehogs

1. Guard/guard progressive hedgehog

```
                ♠ A J 2
                ♥ A J 2
                ♦ —
                ♣ —
♠ Q 10 9                     ♠ K 8
♥ Q 10 9                     ♥ K 8
♦ —                          ♦ K 8
♣ —                          ♣ —
                ♠ 3
                ♥ 3
                ♦ A 2
                ♣ 3 2
```

When South cashes his clubs, West, North, and East must discard one card from each major. Now the ♦A squeezes West in the majors.

2. Clash/clash progressive hedgehog

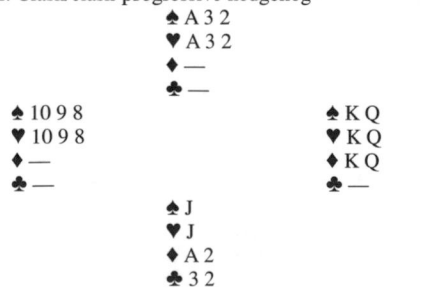

```
                ♠ A 3 2
                ♥ A 3 2
                ♦ —
                ♣ —
♠ 10 9 8                     ♠ K Q
♥ 10 9 8                     ♥ K Q
♦ —                          ♦ K Q
♣ —                          ♣ —
                ♠ J
                ♥ J
                ♦ A 2
                ♣ 3 2
```

The play is the same as in diagram 1.

3. Clash/guard progressive hedgehog (type 1)

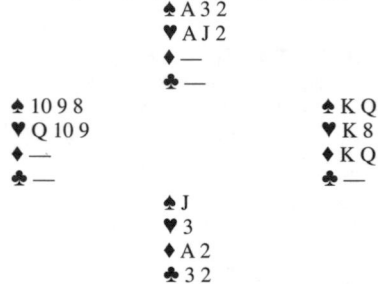

```
                ♠ 5 4
                ♥ A 2
                ♦ A J
                ♣ —
♠ K 2                        ♠ Q 3
♥ K Q                        ♥ J 10
♦ K Q                        ♦ 4 3
♣ —                          ♣ —
                ♠ A J
                ♥ 3
                ♦ 2
                ♣ 3 2
```

When South cashes his two clubs, West must discard a card in each major, North discards a spade then a diamond (unless West discards a diamond), and East discards two diamonds. Now the lead of a diamond to the ♦A squeezes East in the majors.

4. Clash/guard progressive hedgehog (type 2)

```
                ♠ A 3 2
                ♥ A J 2
                ♦ —
                ♣ —
♠ 10 9 8                     ♠ K Q
♥ Q 10 9                     ♥ K 8
♦ —                          ♦ K Q
♣ —                          ♣ —
                ♠ J
                ♥ 3
                ♦ A 2
                ♣ 3 2
```

When South cashes his clubs, East is compelled to discard a card in each major. Now the lead of the ♦A squeezes West in the majors. See CLASH SQUEEZE; HEXAGON SQUEEZE; OCTAGON SQUEEZE.

HELP SUIT GAME TRY. See WEAK SUIT GAME TRY.

HERBERT NEGATIVE. The idea that a negative response in a variety of situations can be made by making the cheapest possible suit response. It was advocated by Walter Herbert when he was a member of the Austrian national team in the 30s, and was applied in many ways in the Vienna System. Some of its many possible applications include: response to Forcing Two-Bid; response to Takeout Double; response to Acol Two-bid; as a second negative response to a strong forcing opening.

HERMAN TROPHY. This trophy is awarded to the player with the best overall individual performance record at the American Contract Bridge League Fall North American Championships. It was donated in 1951 by Sally Lipton, formerly Mrs. Lou Herman, of New York, in memory of her husband. For winners see Appendix II.

HESITATION. See HUDDLE.

HESITATION MITCHELL. A way to play one more round, or a few more, than in a Mitchell. The expansion is obtained by decreasing the number of stationary pairs and letting the moving pairs visit not only EW places but also the NS places at some table or tables. See REDUCED HOWELL.

HEXAGON SQUEEZE. A double guard squeeze in which each of the three menaces is protected by both opponents. (Analyzed and named by George Coffin.)

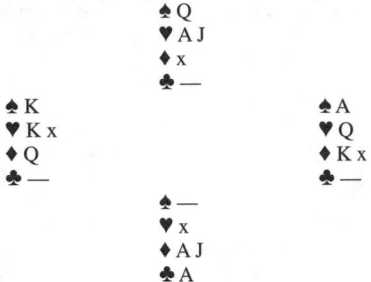

South leads the ♣A, and West must discard a spade. North discards a diamond, and East is squeezed in three suits. Once West discards his spade, East is caught in a standard guard squeeze. See also BARCO SQUEEZE, HEDGEHOG SQUEEZE, HEXAGON TRUMP SQUEEZE, OCTAGON TWO-TRICK SQUEEZE..

HEXAGON TRUMP SQUEEZE. A HEXAGON SQUEEZE in which both of the opponents are trump squeezed.

```
              ♠ A J
              ♥ A x x
              ♦ x
              ♣ —
  ♠ K x                    ♠ Q
  ♥ Q J x                  ♥ K x x
  ♦ Q                      ♦ K x
  ♣ —                      ♣ —
              ♠ x
              ♥ x
              ♦ A J
              ♣ J 10
```

South is on lead needing all the tricks; clubs are trumps. South leads the ♣J. West must discard a heart, dummy can discard a diamond, and East is squeezed in three suits. If East discards a spade, West can be finessed. East obviously cannot discard a diamond, and if he lets go a heart, the ♥A and a heart ruff will establish an extra heart trick.

Alternatively, when West discards a heart on the ♣J, suppose North and East both discard spades. South leads to the ♥A and ruffs a heart. A spade to the ace then squeezes East in hearts and diamonds. In this variation the squeeze of East occurs three tricks later than the squeeze of West.

HIDDEN ENTRY. A low card, usually in the dummy hand, by which an entry may be made, usually established as such through the play of unnecessarily high cards by the declarer. Thus, if dummy has A-Q-10-6 and declarer K-J-9-5, the 6 may be set up as an entry by playing the king to the same trick as the ace, the jack to the same trick as the queen, and the 9 to the same trick as the ten.

HIGH CARD. A ranking card; an honor card; a card that wins a trick by virtue of its being higher in pip value than the other three cards in the trick. A spot card which becomes the master card in the suit is said to be high.

HIGH CARD POINT PROBABILITIES. Average High Card Point (HCP) counts are easy to calculate. Before any cards are seen, the average HCP count for any

one hand is 10 and the average HCP count for a partnership is 20. (This is based on the popular count of ace = 4, king = 3, queen = 2, jack = 1.)

If a player has seen that his hand has x HCPs but has no information about the strength of any other hand, then on the average the remaining high card points are split equally among the other three hands, giving an average HCP count of (1/3) (40 - x) for each.

However, averages do not say very much because hands so often vary from the averages. Probabilities can be calculated for the various possible HCP counts, and the appended tables present the results of these calculations.

Table 1 is largely self-explanatory, but it is important to note that its probabilities apply only when there is no information about the strength of any hand. Many bridge players complain that it is hard to get a decent hand. Table 1 shows that the probability of 11 or fewer HCPs is 65.183%, so about 2/3 of all hands are too weak to open at the one level. Those opening 1 NT on 15-17 HCPs can see from Table 1 that the probability of an HCP count in this range is 4.424% + 3.311% + 2.362% = 10.097%.

Table 2 is also largely self-explanatory, but it is important to note that its probabilities apply only when there is no information about the strength of any hand. Table 2 shows that the probability of 26 or more HCP in a partnership's hands is 100%-87.354% = 12.646%, or about one deal in eight. Similarly, the probability of 33 or more HCP in a partnership is 100% - 99.652% = .348%, or about one deal in 300. Also, the probability of 37 or more HCP in a partnership is 100%-99.991% = .009%, or about one deal in 10,000. Readers can calculate the probabilities of other numbers of HCP for game or slam after allowing for their judgments of how many distributional points are present.

Table 1
Probabilities of High Card Point Counts
for One Hand

HCP	Percentage	HCP	Percentage
0*	.364	19	1.036
1	.789	20	.644
2	1.356	21	.378
3	2.462	22	.210
4	3.845	23	.112
5	5.186	24	.056
6	6.554	25	.026
7	8.028	26	.012
8	8.892	27	.0049
9	9.356	28	.0019
10	9.405	29	.00067
11	9.945	30	.00022
12	8.027	31	.00006
13	6.914	32	.00002
14	5.693	33	.000004
15	4.424	34	.0000007
16	3.311	35	.0000001
17	2.362	36	.000000009
18	1.605	37**	.0000000006

Table 2
Probabilities of High Card Point Counts
for a Partnership

HCP	Percentage	HCP	Percentage
0	.00005	21	8.047
1	.0005	22	7.566
2	.002	23	6.831
3	.006	24	5.907

4	.018	25	4.892
5	.043	26	3.883
6	.093	27	2.943
7	.196	28	2.124
8	.341	29	1.463
9	.588	30	.955
10	.955	31	.588
11	1.463	32	.341
12	2.124	33	.186
13	2.943	34	.093
14	3.983	35	.043
15	4.892	36	.018
16	5.907	37	.006
17	6.931	38	.002
19	7.566	39	.0005
19	8.047	40	.00005
20	8.222		

* The probability of a yarborough (no card higher than a 9) is 0.054703%. The probability of a square yarborough (4-3-3-3 suit distribution and no card higher than a 9) is 0.007744%.

** A hand cannot have more than 37 high card points without exceeding 13 cards.

HIGH CARD POINTS. A basis for determining the relative strength of a hand, especially for notrump contracts. The most common method for figuring high card points is as follows: ace = 4, king = 3, queen = 2, jack = 1. Many authorities also count an extra point for holding all four aces and a half a point for each 10. Most of the schemes for opening notrumps are based on this count.

The total of high card points, taking into consideration suit lengths, often is used as a basis for opening the bidding with a suit bid. Usually a hand that contains a total of 13 points in combined high card plus distributional points is considered an opening bid; a 12-point hand usually is considered optional.

Great efforts by Charles Goren, in many books and articles, popularized the point-count method of bidding. Bridge players everywhere suddenly found that they could estimate the strength of their hand reasonably accurately by using this method. Nowhere has this been more apparent than in notrump bidding. Goren told his students that 26 high card points in the partnership hands usually would be enough to produce game, and statistical studies have proved him correct.

The 4-3-2-1 method of evaluating high cards is not the only one that has been promulgated. Since it is acknowledged that the ace is somewhat undervalued using this count, there also have been adherents of a 6-4-2-1 count. Another that has had its share of popularity is the 3-2-1-° count. But the method used by the vast majority of players all over the world is the 4-3-2-1. Although it may not be the most accurate, it certainly is easy to use and is accurate enough to get a partnership to the correct bidding level the vast majority of the time. See POINT-COUNT.

HIGH GERBER. See SUPER GERBER.

HIGH-CARD TRICK. A term originally used to denote a trick won with an honor. The phrase had some currency in the OFFICIAL SYSTEM.

HIGH-LOW SIGNAL. Known also as echo or come-on, the high-low signal is probably the most important

single weapon that the defenders possess in their arsenal of aggressive warfare. In its normal, recurring application, the high-low signal in a suit expresses the desire for a continuation of that suit, or an interest in that suit being played when partner obtains the lead. For example:

Against South's 4♥ contract, West opens the ♠K, dummy plays the 5-spot, and East puts up the 10, South dropping the 6. West then continues with the ♠A, upon which East plays the 3-spot. Observing that East has played high-low, urging the continuation of the spade suit, West plays a third round of spades, East trumping. The ♦A is then cashed for the setting trick.

Unfortunately, as with all conventions, the high-low signal is often applied promiscuously, or misapplied, and is given merely because it is the "orthodox" thing to do. One sometimes forgets that the signal is given to get partner to continue the suit led only if it will attain an objective for the defenders. Here is an example of the misuse of the high-low signal.

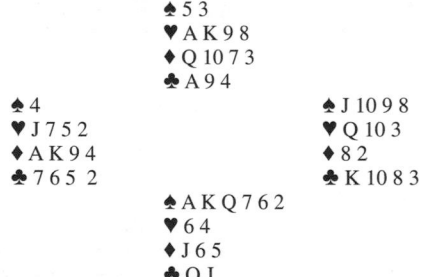

West opened the ♦K against South's 4♠ contract, and East mechanically played the 8-spot. West then continued with the ace, East dropping the 2, after which a third diamond was led, East ruffing. From here in declarer had no problem. He drew trumps, and discarded his ♣J on dummy's high ♦Q.

On the opening lead of the ♦K, East should have played the discouraging 2, not the 8. What did East have to gain by ruffing the third round of diamonds? Not a thing, since he possessed a natural trump trick which could never be taken away. Had he played the ♦2, West, at trick two, would unquestionably have shifted to a club. East would then have made his ♣K, and declarer would have lost his contract.

There is a conventional situation in which a high-low signal is given not to denote an interest in the suit, but to indicate an even number of cards in that suit. This convention is discussed and illustrated in the section entitled LENGTH SIGNALS, but a passing illustration at this point would not be out of order.

It is a rather simple convention, and is most useful when a defensive holdup play must be employed. The setup to which it is applicable is the following:

When it is obvious that declarer is trying to establish a long suit in dummy (which has no outside entries), and that second hand's partner (or second hand himself) is going to have a problem as to when he should take his ace, second hand (or his partner) gives a high-low signal when holding two or four cards of that suit; where second hand has three cards of that suit (say, 7-4-2), he plays his lowest card (the 2) on the first lead, and then follows up by playing the next highest (the 4).

In this latter case, partner will know that the signaler has exactly three cards in that suit, since with two or four he would have given a high-low signal.

Here is a practical application of this high-low convention:

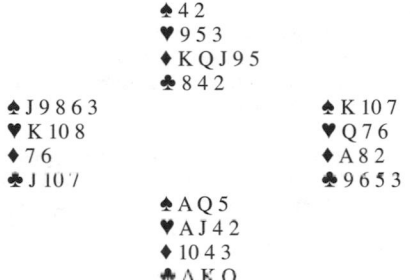

```
              ♠ 4 2
              ♥ 9 5 3
              ♦ K Q J 9 5
              ♣ 8 4 2
♠ J 9 8 6 3                    ♠ K 10 7
♥ K 10 8                       ♥ Q 7 6
♦ 7 6                          ♦ A 8 2
♣ J 10 7                       ♣ 9 6 5 3
              ♠ A Q 5
              ♥ A J 4 2
              ♦ 10 4 3
              ♣ A K Q
```

Against South's 3 NT contract, West opened the ♠6, East's king falling to declarer's ace. South then led the ♦10, West played the 7-spot, and North and East followed with low diamonds. Declarer then led the ♦4, West played the 6-spot, and dummy's 9 captured the trick when East properly declined to take his ace. Declarer now went down a trick, being unable to establish and cash dummy's diamonds.

West's high-low signal (7, 6) had told East that West had either two or four diamonds. That he had four became an impossibility when South led a second diamond, for if West had four diamonds then there were 14 in deck. Therefore East knew that West originally held precisely two diamonds, and that declarer still had a diamond left after the second diamond lead.

The best policy for the declarer is to "signal" as if he were a defender: Play high to encourage, low to discourage. This maximizes the chance to scramble the signals and cause the signaller's partner to misread the situation. See LORD HENRY BENTINCK. For alternative methods of signaling, see ODD-EVEN DISCARDS; UPSIDE-DOWN SIGNALS.

HIGH REVERSE. A non-jump bid in a third suit at the level of three in a lower ranking suit than that bid originally. For example, 1♥ -2♦-3♣. (This term is English usage, not current in the United States.) See OPENER'S REBID.

HIGHER BID. A bid higher in rank at the same level, or lower in rank at the next level, than the last previous bid; a sufficient bid. Usually a higher bid refers to a bid that is merely sufficient, i. e., does not use as much as a full level of bidding space. Where one or more levels of bidding space are used, it is termed a jump, skip, or preemptive bid.

HIGHEST SCORE. In ACBL competition, several pairs have produced remarkable scores in major North American Championship events. S. Garton Churchill and Cecil Head held the single-session record with a 77.4% game in the 1948 Life Master Pairs until 1963, when Eric Murray and Agnes Gordon scored 77.9% (506° match points on a 325 average) in the final session of the Fall NAC Mixed Pairs. This was subsequently beaten by Andrew Bernstein and Gene Neiger, who totaled 244 on a 156 average in the first session of the 1968 Spring NAC Open Pairs for 78.2%. For consistency in scoring, it is unlikely any pair can match the performance of Barry Crane and Dr. John Fisher in the 1970 Spring NAC Open Pairs. They averaged 69.5% in the two qualifying rounds and 63.4% in the two final sessions, the highest set of percentages ever for a four-session pair championship.

In regional competition, Paul Stern and Bob Webber, scored 257 (82.3%) in the Open Pairs at Great Lakes in 1973, only slightly below the 260 (83.3%) — highest on record for a 156 average game — scored by C. C. Wei and Ron Andersen in a single session at the 1974 New York Winter Regional.

The highest matchpoint score on record is 87.3%, by Bernard and France Marcoux in September 1991 at the Le Club de Bridge St. Adele in the Montreal area of Canada.

The highest score in an international championship scored by victory points occurred in the 1963 European Championships in Baden-Baden, Germany. The British team won with a score of 100 victory points out of a possible 102.

HINDSIGHT. Most bridge players are able to find the perfect bid, the correct line of play, and the killing defense after the hand has been misbid, misplayed, or misdefended at the table. Players who regularly indulge in long discussions of this sort are known as RESULT PLAYERS or second-guessers.

HIPPOGRIFFS. Sometime humorous name of a mythical suit; chiefly used in a celebrated anecdote about a man who dreamed he held a perfect notrump hand with 13 sure winners against a stranger (Satan), who was in the lead. The Devil then proceeded to run a 13-trick set against declarer by cashing all the cards of a weird greenish suit called hippogriffs.

HISTORY OF BRIDGE. Bridge can trace its ancestry at least to the early 16th century in England (first reference 1529 in a published sermon by Bishop Latimer) and through succeeding centuries when prototype forms of whist were played under such names as triumph, trump, ruff, slamm, ruff and honours, whisk and swabbers, whisk, and whist. "Whist" may have referred to the rapid action of sweeping up the cards after winning a trick, or "whist" to a call for silence. The game was popular under its modern name of whist by the middle of the 17th century, but it was not until 1742 that the first book devoted to whist appeared: EDMOND HOYLE'S famous "Short Treatise on Whist" (see BIBLIOGRAPHY, A). This rapidly became a best seller, and many pirated editions appeared immediately afterwards.

Whist maintained its popularity as a fashionable amusement, and in 1834 Lord Henry Bentinck invented the first signal. This was the forerunner of much research and writing by authorities on the game such as James Clay, Cavendish, Deschapelles and many others.

The first game of duplicate whist was apparently played in London in 1857 under Cavendish's direction. It was intended to demonstrate the advantage accruing to skillful play, and a team of supposedly good players was deliberately pitted against supposedly poor opposition (there having been no previous criterion for judging them). The "good" players won easily. Cavendish observed that this procedure all but eliminated the luck of the deal, but his pioneering effort was not followed for nearly a quarter of a century.

The United States was slightly ahead of England in extending the duplicate method. A duplicate whist game was played privately in Chicago in 1880 and in a club in New Orleans in 1882. The first interclub match was played in Philadelphia in 1883. The first duplicate match in the Old World was probably in Glasgow, Scotland, in 1888.

Duplicate offered the possibility of replacing private play by public contest. Major steps forward in 1891 were: the foundation of the American Whist League; the invention of the Kalamazoo tray (first duplicate board); and the first book on tournament organization, written by John T. Mitchell who devised the first movement for pair play and described the method of matchpointing which has been used ever since.

Although the American Whist League was to flourish for some 40 years, Bridge, the game which eventually led to its decline and fall, had come on the American scene early in the 1890s, at about the time it was also introduced in England. As chronicled by J. B. Elwell and R. F. Foster, the game reached New York in 1893, thanks to Henry Barbey, whose privately printed *Laws of Bridge* are dated 1892. In London, the Portland Club began to play bridge in 1894 at the instance of Lord Brougham who had learned it in India from some army officers. (W. Dalton in *Auction Bridge Magazine* of September 1927 states that Lord Brougham brought the game from Cairo.) But, according to a letter published in *Bridge Magazine* in 1932, Frank J. Nathan had played in the "first" English game in 1892 at St. George's Club, Hanover Square. It was introduced by a Colonel Studdy who said it was of Levantine origin and that he had learned it in the trenches at Plevna during the Russo-Turkish War of 1877-1878. (This was probably Col. T.C.J.A. Studdy of the Royal Artillery, who was a Captain in the Crimean War period.)

This earlier dating of the game and the probability that it was of Turkish or Russian origin is strongly supported by evidence uncovered in 1974-1975 by Robert H. True, who quotes from a 1904 issue of *Notes and Queries*, a letter from A. M. Keiley (nationality unknown): "I was in 1886 ... a member of the Khedival Club in Cairo, and bridge was the principal card game played there at my entry and, as members told me, had long so been." One of the names by which bridge was first known on the Riviera was Khedive, presumably because players had met it in Cairo. Turkey held Egypt almost without interruption from the early 16th century until World War I and "Khedive" was the official title held by the Turkish viceroy.

Further new evidence confirming Levantine origin and earlier dating of the game was presented by Bob van de Velde of The Netherlands in IBPA Bulletin #222. Sources for this evidence are *Daily Telegraph* (England, November 1932), *La revue du bridge* (France, December 1932) and *Bridge* (The Netherlands, February 1933). The primary source, *Daily Telegraph*, carried an article by a Mr. O. H. van Millingen who lived in Constantinople in 1879 or 1880 and remembered "a very interesting game called

Britch, a game that became very popular in all clubs and dethroned the game of whist." He included a letter, dated January 7, 1922, of his friend Edouard Graziani who at that time worked for the Italian Embassy as a translator and was one of the best bridge players of the Cercle d'Orient. In August 1873 Graziani played the game of bridge for the first time at the home of Mr. Georges Coronio, manager of the Bank of Constantinople. Also present at that game "in Buyukdere along the bank of the Upper Bosphorus" were Mr. Eustache Eugenidi and a Mr. Serghiadi, "a Rumanian financier" who taught the principles of bridge to the foursome. "After Constantinople," Graziani wrote, "bridge came first to Kairo, from where it conquered the Riviera, Paris, London and then New York."

A claim of even earlier existence of the game appears in the introduction to *Modern Bridge* by "Slam" published in London in 1901: "Bridge, known in Turkey as 'Britch,'...has been played in South-Eastern Europe ... ever since the early sixties."

Now we have, perhaps, a quantum leap backward to the period 1854-56. An Istanbul resident, Metin Demirsar, reports the following: "As part of a course on Ottoman history and architecture ... my guide mentioned that British soldiers invented the game bridge while serving in the Crimean War. The card game .... got its name from the Galata Bridge, a bridge spanning the Golden Horn and linking the old and new parts of European Istanbul, where they apparently crossed every day to go to a coffeehouse to play cards."

This does suggest a more plausible derivation for the name of the game than any previously offered. It is somewhat puzzling to comprehend why the game did not appear in England earlier than it did. Perhaps its creators were killed at Balaklava or Inkerman but their brainchild continued in action at the "Bridge" club.

Mrs. Marion Harding of the National Army Museum in London confirms that there was a considerable British presence — some 14,000 troops — concentrated around Constantinople in 1854, and a number of officers were there for considerable periods.

This explanation appears to supersede various explanations of the word "bridge" that connect it, implausibly, with some Russian and Turkish words, and with the early phrase "I bridge it" to partner when transferring the right to name the trump suit. The 1886 pamphlet in the British Museum entitled "Biritch or Russian Whist" is therefore a false trail. Sir James Paget, an English doctor, referred to playing "Bridge" in an 1843 letter, but that is a very faint clue. It is not even clear that he was playing a card-game.

An important change from whist was the exposure of one hand (dealer's partner) as the dummy, following the precedent of Dummy Whist, originated as a game for three players. According to one popular theory, this idea evolved from a game played first in India by three British officers so isolated they were unable to find a fourth. See THREE-HANDED BRIDGE; NEWGATE.

Another innovation was the introduction of the double and redouble. There was no limit to the number of redoubles, and this "gambling" feature of the new game, soon to be eliminated by the change to Auction Bridge, was one of the strong arguments against bridge adduced by whist devotees.

The prototypical game of bridge, or bridge whist, had a short life. A great step forward was taken in 1904, when the auction principle was introduced, traditionally in India, possibly in England. Auction bridge grew steadily in popularity until 1927, though only toward the end of this period were auction bridge tournaments organized. For some reason it was believed that the duplicate principle, long popular among whist players, was not suitable for bridge.

The next major change may have been developed in France, where the game of Plafond was played in 1918 and perhaps earlier. A similar game, S.A.C.C., was described by Sir Hugh Clayton as having been "invented" in India in 1912, and similar games had been tried in the United States before 1915. In all such games each side had to bid to its "plafond" or ceiling: only tricks bid and made counted toward game. This variation rapidly became the standard French game, but did not succeed elsewhere in spite of occasional experiments. In his slightly fictionalized memoirs of World War I entitled *Ashenden*, Somerset Maugham, who took bridge very seriously, reported a game in Switzerland: "The game was contract, with which I was not very familiar." In the early Twenties, two booklets entitled *Contract Bridge* were published, and an unsuccessful application was made to the Knickerbocker Club to prepare a code of contract rules.

Up to this point whist, bridge, auction, and plafond had simply grown, which is generally the way with card games. No individual can be given credit for inventing the dummy, the idea of bidding, the auction principle, or the ceiling principle of plafond. But in 1925 Harold S. Vanderbilt perfected a new form of the game, embodying the plafond principle but including the element of vulnerability and producing a scoring table that corrected the major faults in plafond. He succeeded so well that his game of "contract bridge' became the staple diet of card players everywhere. Afterward, he wrote:

Many years of experience playing games of the Whist family were, I think, a necessary prelude to acquiring the background and knowledge needed to evolve the game of Contract Bridge. Starting as a young boy about 70 years ago, I have played successively over the years Whist, Bridge, Auction Bridge, and Plafond.

... I compiled in the autumn of 1925 a scoring table for my new game. I called it Contract Bridge and incorporated in it, not only the best features of Auction and Plafond, but also a number of new and exciting features; premiums for slams bid and made, vulnerability, and the decimal system of scoring which by increasing both trick and game values and all premiums and penalties was destined to add enormously to the popularity of Contract Bridge.

An ideal opportunity to try out my new game presented itself while I was voyaging shortly after completing my scoring table with three Auction Bridge playing friends on board the steamship Finland from Los Angeles to Havana via the Panama Canal, a nine-day trip.

... At first, we were at a loss for a term, other than "game in," to describe the status of being subject to higher penalties because of having won a game. Fortunately for us, a young lady on board the Finland solved that problem by suggesting the word "vulnerable.". . .

We enjoyed playing my new game on board the Finland so much that, on my return to New York, I gave typed copies of my scoring table to several of my Auction Bridge playing friends. I made no other effort to popularize or publicize Contract Bridge. Thanks apparently to its excellence, it popularized itself and spread like wildfire.

No world-popular game in history — certainly none in the Whist family — can so accurately pinpoint its conception and the first time it was ever played. Recent research has established that the Finland reached Balboa on October 31, 1925, too late to proceed through the Canal or for passengers to go ashore. Francis Bacon III, in 1975 the then sole surviving member of Vanderbilt's foursome, recalled that on that night the lady who suggested "vulnerable" was allowed to join their game of plafond and attempted to suggest some exotic and impractical changes based on a game she said she had played in China. This so irritated Vanderbilt that the next day, while the Finland passed through the Canal, he worked out the scoring table for contract which, except for notrump tricks then being valued at 35 points each, remained virtually unchanged half a century later. On that night, November 1, the game became Contract Bridge, scored under Vanderbilt's new rules.

Within two years, three codes of laws had been produced for the new game. Those of Robert F. Foster and the Knickerbocker Whist Club (both 1927) were withdrawn in favor of the more authoritative code issued by the Whist Club of New York. In 1928 the game was adopted in the major New York clubs, and late that year the first National Championship was held, with the Vanderbilt Cup as the prize.

In 1929 the American Auction Bridge League dropped the word "Auction" from its title and it became clear that contract had supplanted auction. The established auction authorities struggled to achieve expertise in the field of contract, but for the most part unsuccessfully. Leadership in the new game went to Ely Culbertson, who founded the first contract magazine in 1929. The first issue of *The Bridge World* magazine advocated the promulgation of an international Code of Laws for Contract Bridge. Subsequently, committees representing the United States, England and France were appointed, and the first International Code became effective Nov. 1, 1932. See LAWS OF CONTRACT BRIDGE.

In September 1930, Culbertson published his *Contract Bridge Blue Book*, which became a best seller and which appeared in annual revisions for four years. This revolutionary work set out the principles of approach-forcing bidding which became the nucleus of all modern standard systems. (See BIBLIOGRAPHY). It was Culbertson, through his writings, his personality, his lectures and his organization, who was most responsible for the wide vogue the game quickly attained. The international publicity resulting from the famous CULBERTSON-LENZ MATCH in 1931 and the ANGLO-AMERICAN MATCHES in 1930, 1933, and 1934 made the new game of Contract Bridge a household word. Thanks to a thriving organization which exploited every phase of bridge activity and to his natural flair for publicity exhibited notably in the Culbertson-Lenz Match, Culbertson retained his leadership throughout the Thirties, untroubled by the tournament successes of the FOUR ACES.

Although Culbertson's was the first widely accepted system of bidding in Contract Bridge, it became outmoded, and numerous other systems of bidding have come to the fore since his day. The GOREN methods, based on POINT-COUNT valuation, which became standard in the United States after 1950, are based firmly on the foundations laid by Culbertson.

The growth of tournament bridge was hampered in the

Thirties by the simultaneous activity of three separate organizing bodies, the AMERICAN BRIDGE LEAGUE, the AMERICAN WHIST LEAGUE, and the UNITED STATES BRIDGE ASSOCIATION. But from 1937 onward the AMERICAN CONTRACT BRIDGE LEAGUE had the field to itself, and there followed a period of steady growth stimulated by the masterpoint plan. 1935 became the year of the first recognized World Championship, although several semiofficial international matches had been played earlier. Later landmarks on the international scene were the first of the postwar World Championship series in 1950, the foundation of the WORLD BRIDGE FEDERATION in 1958, and the first Team Olympiad in 1960.

The only major innovation in contract bridge during its first 40 years of existence was the development of CHICAGO, the four-deal game which displaced traditional rubber bridge in many clubs during the early Sixties. But this, like contract bridge itself, was a change in scoring rather than in structure, and there have been few radical changes in the game nor do any seem likely in the immediate future.

HISTORY OF PLAYING CARDS. The earliest known cards were used in China, at least as long ago as 979 A. D. The pack was divided into four suits, 14 cards in each, and was based on representations of coins. This discredits the pleasant story that they were invented in 1120 A. D. to amuse the concubines of the Emperor Suen-ho.

There is a tradition that a Venetian carried cards from China to his native city, the first place in Europe where they were known. This traveler may have been Niccolo Polo, who returned from China about 1269 with his brother Matteo, or it may have been Niccolo's son, the famed Marco, who accompanied his father and uncle on their second trip to that empire.

Some authorities favor India over China as the original source. A tenuous link has been suggested between early European cards and Ardhanari, the goddess of Hindu mythology. She was represented holding in her four hands a wand, a cup, a sword, and a ring (symbolizing money). Similar symbols appeared on some early European playing cards. One discredited theory suggests that cards were brought to Europe by the Gypsies, who may have belonged originally to an Indian race. They have been traced through Persia and Arabia into Egypt and then to Europe, and a body of over 100 entered Paris in August 1427 (Pasquier: *Recherches Historiques*).

However, this date is too late to be significant. Cards were manufactured in many parts of Europe, notably in Nuremberg, Augsburg, and Ulm, in the fourteenth century, and perhaps even earlier. The Italian Tarot cards may have predated the German cards: they are mentioned in an Italian manuscript dated 1299. Johanna, Duchess of Brabant, mentions cards in the Netherlands in 1379, and cards were known in Spain at least as early as 1371. The Moors or Saracens may have brought cards to Spain and Italy, but the attempt to show a resemblance between the Spanish word for cards (naipes) and the Arabic word (nabi, "a prophet") is not well founded.

In 1392 in France, the monarch Charles VI ordered a hand-painted deck to be made by Jacquemin Gringonneur, and this historical fact gave rise to the idea that cards originated in France. However, it seems clear that this order was for cards similar to others already in use. The royal treasurer, accounting for moneys paid out, mentions three packs of cards, painted "in gold and diverse colors, ornamented with many devices, for the diversion of our Lord, the King." Seventeen of these cards are on exhibition at the Bibliotheque Nationale (see COLLECTIONS OF PLAYING CARDS).

Cards probably reached England later than the other European countries. Chaucer, who died in 1400, never mentions cards, although he enumerates the amusements of the day: "They dance and they play at chess and tables." The reference to playing with four kings in the Wardrobe Rolls of Edward I in 1278 ("ad ludendum ad quattuor regis") almost certainly refers to some other game, perhaps a form of chess. The earliest clear-cut reference to playing cards in England dates from 1465, when manufacturers of playing cards petitioned Edward IV for protection against foreign imports, and were favored by an appropriate edict.

"There is a legend telling how the sailors with Columbus," writes Catherine Perry Hargrave in *A History of Playing Cards*, "who were inveterate gamblers, threw their cards overboard in superstitious terror upon encountering storms in these vast and mysterious seas. Later on dry land they regretted their rashness and in the new country made other cards out of the leaves of the copys tree, which greatly interested the Indians." This seems to be more than a legend, for Garcilaso de la Vega (*Historia de la Florida*, Madrid, 1723) tells that the soldiers of Spain played with leather cards in the 1534 expedition. Cards were known to the early Mexicans as amapatolli, from *amatl* meaning paper and *patolli* meaning game.

The present pack of 52 cards, arranged in two black and two red suits, probably derived from the early Italian Tarot packs, in which there were four suits with ten spot cards and four court cards — king, queen, cavalier, and knave. The queen was not included in early packs, and the chevalier still holds her position in some modern packs (see PACK).

The knave has been variously represented by a VALET, and still carries this name, although modern usage changes it to the jack. The chevalier, as apart from the queen, has been dropped from the 52-card pack.

The Chinese playing cards differ considerably from the occidental; they are long and narrow, usually 2 to 2° inches long and ° to 1 inch wide, early cards longer and even narrower. In number of suits and cards, both the Chinese and Hindu decks differ markedly from ours. One Hindu deck includes 144 cards with eight suits of 18 cards, another has 120 cards with 10 suits of 12 cards; one Chinese deck has only 30 cards, three suits of nine cards and three extra cards of supreme value, but four suits were normal.

Long before bridge was heard of, playing cards were used in many forms of gambling and in fortunetelling, and acquired an unsavory reputation, being associated with all vices. The DEVIL'S PICTURE BOOK and other names indicate the horror with which they were regarded by the virtuous and religious.

Playing cards, as a luxury, provided a source for much revenue in TAXES, first levied on them in England in 1615.

The modern authority on the history of playing cards is Stuart Kaplan.

For information about the MANUFACTURE OF PLAYING CARDS at the present time, see that heading.

HIT. Slang used as two distinct transitive verbs: (1) To double. (2) To ruff.

HOBSON'S COUP. See MERRIMAC COUP.

HOG. A player who attempts to become declarer as often as possible, or the action of one who does so: "to hog the bidding."

HOLD. (1) To possess (a certain card or cards). (2) To win or guarantee the winning of a trick (by the play of a certain card). Thus, if partner plays the king when you hold the ace, and no ruff is impending, the king is said to hold the trick unless you decide to overtake it.

HOLD OFF. To refuse to play a winning card. See DUCK and HOLD UP.

HOLD UP. The refusal to win a trick. The aim of a hold-up play is to keep control of a suit an opponent has led. The purpose is usually to break the opponents' communication.

This section deals only with hold-up play by declarer, but the defenders also hold-up (as when a defender refuses to take an ace to prevent the use of a long suit in dummy; see LENGTH SIGNALS). The hold-up play occurs at both suit and notrump contracts.

The following deal shows the basic hold-up play:

```
              ♠ Q 6 5
              ♥ K 8 4
              ♦ A J 9 8 3
              ♣ 8 3
♠ 10 7 2                    ♠ J 9 8 3
♥ Q 10 6 5                  ♥ J 9 3
♦ 7                        ♦ K 6 5
♣ K J 9 5 4                 ♣ Q 10 2
              ♠ A K 4
              ♥ A 7 2
              ♦ Q 10 4 2
              ♣ A 7 6
```

South plays 3NT, and West leads the ♣5. East puts up the queen. South must refuse to take the ace and hold up again when East returns the ♣10. If South wins either the first or second club, East will have a club to lead when he wins the ♦K, and the defenders will win four clubs and one diamond to defeat the contract. If South waits to win the third club lead, he makes game; the defenders' communication in clubs is broken, and West has no side entry.

Declarer can also hold up a winner other than an ace.

```
              ♠ K 6 4
              ♥ Q 6
              ♦ K 9 7
              ♣ A J 9 5 3
♠ Q 5                      ♠ J 9 7 3 2
♥ A 10 8 7 5 2             ♥ J 9
♦ J 6 5                    ♦ 10 8 4 3
♣ 7 4                     ♣ K 8
              ♠ A 10 8
              ♥ K 4 3
              ♦ A Q 2
              ♣ Q 10 6 2
```

South plays 3NT, and West leads the ♥7. If South puts up the ♥Q to win the first trick, he goes down; East will unblock the jack and return the ♥9 when he wins the

♣K. South should instead play low from both dummy and his own hand at the first trick, safeguarding the contract if West has six hearts and East has the ♣K.

```
Dlr: North      ♠ 10 8 4 3
Vul: N-S        ♥ K 4
                ♦ Q J 7 2
                ♣ A K 2
♠ J 7                           ♠ A K 9 6 5
♥ J 9 8 6 2                     ♥ 10 7 3
♦ K 8 6                        ♦ 5
♣ 10 9 8                       ♣ Q J 7 3
                ♠ Q 2
                ♥ A Q 5
                ♦ A 10 9 4 3
                ♣ 6 5 4
```

WEST	NORTH	EAST	SOUTH
	1 ♦	1 ♠	3 ♦
Pass	3 ♠ (1)	Pass	3NT
All Pass			

(1) Partial stopper

West leads the ♠J: 3, 6. South must play low to make the contract.

```
              ♠ 8 5 3
              ♥ A K 3
              ♦ 5 4
              ♣ A 10 9 4 2
♠ A J 9 4 2                 ♠ 10 7
♥ 8 6 4                    ♥ J 9 7 2
♦ J 9 6                    ♦ Q 10 8 7
♣ 8 5                     ♣ K 7 6
              ♠ K Q 6
              ♥ Q 10 5
              ♦ A K 3 2
              ♣ Q J 3
```

West leads the ♠4 against South's 3NT, and East plays the 10. To make the contract, South must follow with the 6.

The situation would be similar if the spade suit were:

```
              8 5 3
A 10 7 4 2              Q 9
              K J 6
```

After the lead of the 4 to the 3 and queen, South would need to play the 6.

```
              8
A 10 7 6 4              Q 9 5
              K J 3 2
```

After the lead of the 6 to the 8 and queen, South would follow with the 2 and play the 3 when East next led the 9.

```
              8
A 10 7 6 4              K 9 5
              Q J 3 2
```

If West leads the 6 to the king, and East returns the 9, South must play low. South must also play low if East makes the remarkable play of the 9 at the first trick.

As the examples above demonstrate, hold-up play is often linked with AVOIDANCE. Change the previous deal to:

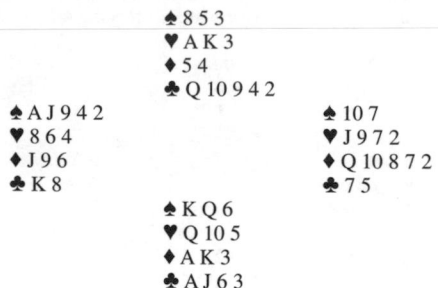

```
                ♠ 8 5 3
                ♥ A K 3
                ♦ 5 4
                ♣ Q 10 9 4 2
♠ A J 9 4 2                    ♠ 10 7
♥ 8 6 4                        ♥ J 9 7 2
♦ J 9 6                        ♦ Q 10 8 7 2
♣ K 8                          ♣ 7 5
                ♠ K Q 6
                ♥ Q 10 5
                ♦ A K 3
                ♣ A J 6 3
```

Since on this layout the club finesse may lose to West, South should win the first spade. He can then reach dummy with the ♥A and finesse in clubs. If West can win, South is safe, since his remaining holding in spades is safe from attack.

Sometimes declarer must guess whether to hold up.

```
Dlr: South       ♠ 8 4 2
Vul: Both        ♥ A J 6 4
                 ♦ K 10 6
                 ♣ Q 8 4
♠ A 10 7 6 3                   ♠ Q 9
♥ K 3                          ♥ Q 9 8 7 5
♦ A 5                          ♦ 8 3
♣ J 10 7 5                     ♣ 9 6 3 2
                 ♠ K J 5
                 ♥ 10 2
                 ♦ Q J 9 7 4 2
                 ♣ A K
```

WEST	NORTH	EAST	SOUTH
			1 ♦
1 ♠	Dbl (1)	Pass	2 ♦
Pass	3 ♦	Pass	3NT
All Pass			

(1) Negative

N-S bid aggressively to reach 3NT, and West leads the ♣6 to the 2 and queen. If East has the ♦A, South must hold up; if West has it, South should win, preserving a tenace in spades. South must recall the bidding. Since West's vulnerable overcall suggests high-card values, South should play West for the ♦A and win the first trick.

A holdup is often correct with two stoppers:

```
                ♠ A Q 7
                ♥ K J 6
                ♦ 10 9 8 2
                ♣ K 7 4
♠ 9 5                          ♠ 10 8 6 4 3
♥ 8 7 4 2                      ♥ Q 10 3
♦ K 6                          ♦ A 7 3
♣ Q 9 8 6 2                    ♣ J 10
                ♠ K J 2
                ♥ A 9 5
                ♦ Q J 5 4
                ♣ A 5 3
```

South plays 3NT, and West leads the ♣6. If South wins the first club and attacks diamonds, East will take the ace and lead his second club, establishing the clubs while West still has the ♦K. To make the contract, South must

play low from both hands on the first club.

A more testing example:

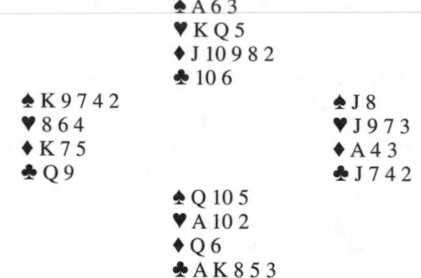

```
                ♠ A 6 3
                ♥ K Q 5
                ♦ J 10 9 8 2
                ♣ 10 6
♠ K 9 7 4 2                    ♠ J 8
♥ 8 6 4                        ♥ J 9 7 3
♦ K 7 5                        ♦ A 4 3
♣ Q 9                          ♣ J 7 4 2
                ♠ Q 10 5
                ♥ A 10 2
                ♦ Q 6
                ♣ A K 8 5 3
```

South plays 3NT, and West leads the ♠4 to the 3 and jack. If South impulsively grabs the queen, he is defeated. A hold-up play may be needed even with three stoppers:

```
                ♠ Q J 6
                ♥ 4 2
                ♦ K 9 3
                ♣ 9 7 5 4 2
♠ 7 5 4 3 2                    ♠ 10 9
♥ 9 5                          ♥ J 10 8 7 6
♦ Q 8 7 2                      ♦ J 6 4
♣ Q 3                          ♣ A K 6
                ♠ A K 8
                ♥ A K Q 3
                ♦ A 10 5
                ♣ J 10 8
```

South plays 3NT. Since West has few side entries, he leads the ♥9, trying to find East's long suit. To make the contract, South must refuse the first trick.

A hold-up may serve to ruin defenders' communication at a suit contract.

```
                ♠ Q 3
                ♥ K 9 8 2
                ♦ A Q 10 5 4
                ♣ K 6
♠ J 10 9 8 4 2                 ♠ K 7 6
♥ 5                           ♥ J 6 4
♦ 8 7                         ♦ K 3 2
♣ 10 5 3 2                     ♣ A Q 7 4
                ♠ A 5
                ♥ A Q 10 7 3
                ♦ J 9 6
                ♣ J 9 8
```

South plays 4♥, and West leads the ♠J, covered by the queen and king. South must not take the ace. If South instead wins, draws trumps and tries the diamond finesse, East wins and can put West in with a spade. Then a club shift defeats the contract.

A hold-up play is also proper to keep control.

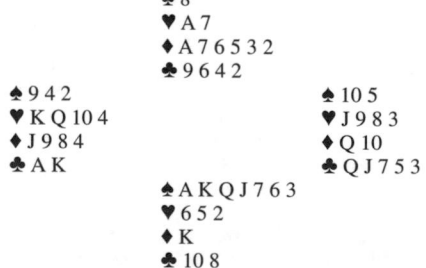

```
                ♠ 8
                ♥ A 7
                ♦ A 7 6 5 3 2
                ♣ 9 6 4 2
♠ 9 4 2                        ♠ 10 5
♥ K Q 10 4                     ♥ J 9 8 3
♦ J 9 8 4                      ♦ Q 10
♣ A K                          ♣ Q J 7 5 3
                ♠ A K Q J 7 6 3
                ♥ 6 5 2
                ♦ K
                ♣ 10 8
```

South plays 4♠, and West cashes the ♣AK and shifts to

the ♥K. South can safeguard the contract by holding up dummy's ace. If West shifts to a trump to stop a heart ruff in dummy, South can unblock the ♦K, reach dummy with the ♥A and win his tenth trick with the ♦A; if West leads another heart to force the ace before South unblocks in diamonds, South ruffs a heart in dummy.

In the following deal, timing requires a hold-up play.

```
              ♠ 8 4 3
              ♥ A 6 4
              ♦ A K 7 5 4
              ♣ 5 4
♠ Q 10 5                      ♠ J 9
♥ K 10 8                      ♥ J 9 5 2
♦ J 3                         ♦ Q 10 9 2
♣ K Q 10 9 3                  ♣ J 8 7
              ♠ A K 7 6 2
              ♥ Q 7 3
              ♦ 8 6
              ♣ A 6 2
```

South plays 4♠, and West leads the ♣K. South can expect four trump tricks in his hand, four top cards on the side and a club ruff in dummy. A long card in diamonds must provide the tenth trick, but South must take care with his entries. If he wins the first trick with the ♣A and returns a club, the defense can win and lead a third club, forcing South to use a dummy entry too soon.

South should therefore refuse the first trick. He wins the next club, cashes the ♠AK and proceeds with ♦AK, diamond ruff, club ruff, diamond ruff. (It makes no difference if West overruffs on one of the diamond leads.) South then goes to the ♥A to lead the good diamond and is sure of 10 tricks whether or not West ruffs.

Control is also the problem on the deal below.

```
              ♠ 6
              ♥ Q 8 7
              ♦ 7 6 5 4
              ♣ A K Q J 10
♠ K Q 10                      ♠ J 9 8 7 3
♥ 5 3                         ♥ A 6 4 2
♦ K 10 8 3 2                  ♦ J 9
♣ 5 3 2                       ♣ 6 4
              ♠ A 5 4 2
              ♥ K J 10 9
              ♦ A Q
              ♣ 9 8 7
```

South lands in 4♥, and West leads the ♠K. South's best play is to hold up the ace! If West continues spades, South ruffs in dummy and forces out the ♥A. South can win the next trick, draw trumps and take 10 tricks with the help of dummy's clubs. Other lines of play are likely to fail.

A hold-up play may be used in conjunction with avoidance and a LOSER-ON-LOSER play. In the deal below, the purpose is to establish a suit safely.

```
              ♠ Q J 4
              ♥ A 5
              ♦ A K 5 3 2
              ♣ 8 5 2
♠ 7 5                         ♠ 6 3
♥ K Q 10 4 3                  ♥ J 9 8 7 2
♦ 10 8                        ♦ Q J 9
♣ A 10 9 7                    ♣ Q J 3
              ♠ A K 10 9 8 2
              ♥ 6
              ♦ 7 6 4
              ♣ K 6 4
```

South plays 4♠ and West leads the ♥K. If South wins

the first trick, draws trumps and leads three rounds of diamonds, East wins and shifts to the ♣Q to defeat the contract. South does better to hold up the ♥A at the first trick. He wins the next heart, discarding a diamond, draws trumps, takes the ♦AK, ruffs a diamond and returns to dummy with a trump to throw two clubs on winning diamonds.

On some occasions, a hold-up play is ill-judged. Perhaps declarer cannot hold up long enough to accomplish anything; perhaps he cannot stop a dangerous defender from gaining the lead; perhaps a shift to another suit poses a greater threat. In the deal below, a hold-up play would let the defenders untangle their long suit.

```
              ♠ A 5
              ♥ K 6 4
              ♦ J 10 7 5 3
              ♣ J 8 4
♠ K J 8 6 3                   ♠ Q 7
♥ 10 8 2                      ♥ Q J 7 5
♦ A 2                         ♦ 9 8 4
♣ 7 5 3                       ♣ Q 10 9 2
              ♠ 10 9 4 2
              ♥ A 9 3
              ♦ K Q 6
              ♣ A K 6
```

South plays 3NT and West leads the ♠6. South is in no danger if spades are split 4-3. If West has five spades, East surely has at least one honor, since West would lead the king from K-Q-J-x-x. Thus, South cannot lose by taking the ♠A at the first trick. As the cards lie, this play blocks the spades; but if South instead plays a low spade, East wins the queen and returns a spade, and South goes down.

A hold-up play is generally wrong when it costs a winner. Still, the deal below shows an exception.

```
Dlr: East        ♠ 10 5
Vul: E-W         ♥ J 6 4
                 ♦ Q J 9 4
                 ♣ K J 9 3
♠ Q 9 8 6 2                   ♠ K 7 4
♥ 5                          ♥ Q 10 9 8 7 3
♦ 8 7 6                      ♦ A 2
♣ 8 7 5 2                    ♣ A 10
                 ♠ A J 3
                 ♥ A K 2
                 ♦ K 10 5 3
                 ♣ Q 6 4
```

WEST	NORTH	EAST	SOUTH
		1♥	1NT
Pass	2NT	Pass	3NT
All Pass			

West leads the ♠6, and East plays the king. East's opening bid marks him with most of the missing honors, but West probably has Q-x-x-x-x in spades. South should therefore refuse the first two spade leads and win the third spade. South then loses to the minor-suit aces, but makes his game.

If South takes the ♠A at the first trick (assuring two spade tricks) and leads a diamond, East wins the ace and returns a spade. West lets dummy's 10 win. When East gets back in with the ♣A, he leads his last spade, and West takes three spades.

A common reason to avoid a hold-up play is to preserve an exit card:

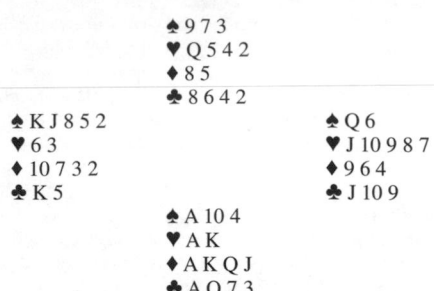

♠ 9 7 3
♥ Q 5 4 2
♦ 8 5
♣ 8 6 4 2

♠ K J 8 5 2   ♠ Q 6
♥ 6 3   ♥ J 10 9 8 7
♦ 10 7 3 2   ♦ 9 6 4
♣ K 5   ♣ J 10 9

♠ A 10 4
♥ A K
♦ A K Q J
♣ A Q 7 3

South plays 3NT and West leads the ♠5. South can refuse the first spade, but should win the second. South then cashes his top cards in the red suits and leads his last spade. West can take at most three spade tricks and then must lead a heart or club to South's advantage.

Hold-up play at matchpoint duplicate.

♠ 9 7
♥ A 8 3
♦ Q J 10
♣ A J 10 9 5

♠ A 4 3
♥ K 6 5
♦ A K 8 3
♣ Q 8 7

South plays 3NT and West leads the ♣6. East plays the queen. At rubber bridge or IMP scoring, South would hold up the ♣A twice before taking the club finesse, almost guaranteeing nine tricks. At matchpoint scoring, South's problem is more difficult; the contract is normal — every N-S pair will reach 3NT — and 12 tricks are available if West has the ♣K. If South gambles by winning the first or second spade, however, he may go minus if East has the ♣K.

Perhaps South's best play is to hold up once and see what spade East leads at the second trick. This play cannot cost, since South can take at most 12 tricks. If East returns the ♣2, South can assume that spades are split 4-4 or 6-2 and win the second trick. If East returns the ♠10 or ♠8, suggesting an original holding of three cards, South must consider holding up again. Obviously, the situation gives the defenders opportunity for deceptive play.

In his book *How to Win at Duplicate Bridge*, Marshall Miles posed this problem:

♠ x x x
♥ x x x
♦ A J 10 x x
♣ K Q

♠ A x x
♥ A K
♦ Q 9 x
♣ A J 10 x x

At matchpoints South opens 1♣, North responds 1♦, South jumps to 2NT and North raises to 3NT — a normal contract. West leads the ♠K. Miles showed that South's matchpoint expectation is greatest if he wins immediately. However, Miles' analysis assumed that the number of declarers who win the first, second and third spade are equal, and did not allow for the chance that West might have overcalled with five or more spades. See also BATH COUP, RULE OF SEVEN.

HOLDING. (1) The cards one is dealt in a particular

suit, as in the expression, "a club holding of king, queen, and two little." (2) A descriptive term used in reckoning one's entire hand, and often used in the question, "What would you bid holding five spades to the ace-queen, etc.?"

HOLLAND. See NETHERLANDS BRIDGE LEAGUE.

HOLLANDAISE. See GOULASH.

HOME STYLE BRIDGE. In the early 1970S Nate Silverstein devised a movement for a one-winner pair game. It is usually called a "Swiss Pair" game. The game gained popularity in some of the country clubs in Memphis. In 1979 the ACBL adopted most of the ideas and converted the game into an experimental Home Style bridge program.

The basic method of scoring is Chicago or "Four-Deal Bridge." Pairs are assigned seats at random by the director. When the game starts, and at the start of each round, the players cut for deal. Each round they play four hands. On the first hand no one is vulnerable, the second and third hands the dealer's side is vulnerable, and the last hand everyone is vulnerable. Partscores carry over, honors are scored. If you complete a hand when your side is vulnerable you score a bonus of 500; if you complete a game on a hand where your side is not vulnerable your bonus is 300 points. If you score a partscore on the last hand, and it does not complete a game, you receive a bonus of 100. All other scoring, overtricks, undertricks, doubles, redoubles, etc., are scored the same as in all other forms of bridge.

The only exception to playing four hands is if you have three or four tables. In this instance the director may opt to play six hands a round. In this instance no one would be vulnerable on the first two hands, the dealer's side vulnerable on the third and fourth hands, and both sides vulnerable on the last two hands.

At the end of the round the players total their points. The pair with the fewer points deduct their total from the greater. The difference is then converted into Victory Points. Following is a Victory Point schedule.

Difference in total points	Victory Points
0-40	10-10
50-140	11-9
150-240	12-8
250-340	13-7
350-540	14-6
550-740	15-5
750-940	16-4
950-1240	17-3
1250-1540	18-2
1550 or more	19-1

This is the ACBL Home Style formula. In the original method 1550-1940 was 19-1, and 1950 or more was 20-0. However, players in this type of game are discouraged by zeros - hence the change.

The easiest way to assign pair numbers is the pair starting at Table 1 North-South is assigned Pair #1, East-West at Table 1 is Pair #2, North-South at Table 2 is Pair #3, and so forth.

When the first round is completed and the Victory Point totals have been entered, the director gives each pair their second-round assignment. This is Swiss pairing where each pair plays against a pair with a score as close to theirs as is possible. The pair with the most Victory Points plays the pair with the next most Victory Points and so on. The one exception is that no pair can play another pair more than once. If the two pairs with the most Victory Points could not play because they had already played, the pair with the greatest total would play the pair with the third most points. This continues until all pairs have received a new assignment.

This is usually a fun kind of game and attracts players who are not interested in braving the rigors of duplicate bridge with the attendant restrictions and many conventions. It also appeals to the newcomer to competitive bridge. For these reasons Home Style Bridge is usually limited to the very basic conventions and understandings. Blackwood and Stayman are frequently the only conventions permitted. The use of understandings such as weak two bids, weak notrumps and preemptive jump overcalls is almost always barred. This is up to the director or, more specifically, up to those playing in the game. Any conventions could be permitted as long as they are determined beforehand.

Home Style Bridge is an interesting and enjoyable contest and has a strategy all its own. Once the players become familiar with the game they frequently become as devoted to the game as followers of other forms of bridge.

Home Style Bridge can be sanctioned for clubs and rating points issued on the same scale as for duplicate clubs. For more information contact The American Contract Bridge League, P.O. Box 161192, Memphis TN 38116.

HOME TOWN RULING. An action by the director which accepts the credibility of players personally known to him as opposed to others from distant parts; the type of ruling sometimes given by club directors in favor of regular participants in the games as opposed to occasional drop-ins comes in this category and is even less defensible. Application of the published rules from the rule book for any and all players must in the long run provide the fairest competition and the most enjoyable game.

HONEYMOON BRIDGE. A general name for two-handed bridge games, including the following.

(1) *Double-dummy.* Deal four hands, as in normal bridge, with the players sitting in adjacent seats, not opposite each other. Without seeing the dummies, the players bid, dealer first. A pass following a call ends the auction. The opening lead is made by declarer's opponent and both dummies are exposed. (In a variant, each player can see his dummy, using a rack, but not his opponent's dummy.) Scoring is normal.

(2) *Semi-exposed dummy.* Players are adjacent. Seven cards of each dummy are exposed, with six of them covering the face-down cards. When the bidding ends, play continues with face-down card exposed when the face-up card above it is played. Scoring is normal.

(3) *Draw bridge.* Players face each other, and receive 13 cards. The remainder form a stock. The non-dealer leads first, and play is in two-card tricks at notrump. After each trick the winner draws a card and then the loser. These tricks do not count in the score. When the stock is exhausted, there is a normal auction. The next 13 tricks are played, and scored in relation to the contract reached. See DUEL and DUOBRIDGE.

HONG KONG CONTRACT BRIDGE ASSO-CIATION. The Association was founded in 1951 by J.M. Remedios, E.M.Marchetti and Victor Zirinsky, with a nucleus of Hong Kong social clubs. By 1992 the membership was approximately 400. Hong Kong won the Far East Open Teams titles in 1960, 1965, 1973 and 1983, and hosted the Championships in 1959, 1960, 1976 and 1987.

1992 officers:

    Chairman: Anthony Ching
    Vice-Chairman: Ricky Chu
    G.P.O Box 1445, Hong Kong.

HONOR. One of the five top cards in a suit at bridge. An ace, king, queen, jack or 10 can properly be described as an honor.

HONOR CRASHING PLAYS. See CRASHING HONORS and DECEPTIVE PLAY.

HONOR LEAD. The lead of an honor, usually the top one of a sequence. The lead of an honor conventionally indicates possession of one or more lower touching honors, the exception being the lead of the king, which may be made from an A-K or K-Q holding. The purpose of the honor lead is usually to establish the cards directly beneath it. In the middle game the lead of an unsupported honor card is often correct.

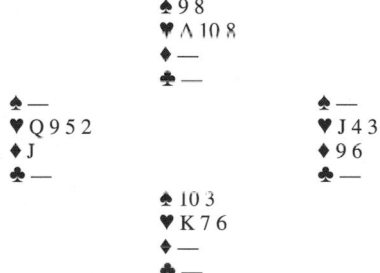

Spades are trump, and West is on lead and forced to open up the hearts. The queen is the proper play, for if he leads a low card, South simply plays the 8 from dummy, forcing the jack from East. On the next round he has a simple finesse position with dummy's A-10 over West's queen.

```
            DUMMY (N)
              K 9 8
   WEST
   J 6 4 3
```

West is on lead and has no further card of entry. Requiring three tricks from this suit, he must lead the jack, hoping that his partner has A-Q-10. See also INTERIOR SEQUENCE; JOURNALIST LEADS; OPENING LEAD; RUSINOW LEAD; ZERO OR TWO HIGHER LEADS.

HONOR SCORE. An extra bonus in rubber bridge and in Chicago scored above the line when claimed by a player (declarer, dummy, or defender) who held during the current deal any of certain honor card holdings in the trump suit as follows: For holding any four of the five top trump honors - 100 points. For all five trump honors - 150 points. For all the aces at notrump - 150 points. Honors are not scored at duplicate.

HONOR STRENGTH. The trick-taking value of a hand in honor tricks. This was of great importance as a basis for calculation of the power of a hand in the CULBERTSON SYSTEM.

HONOR TRICK. A unit of defensive valuation of honor cards and combinations. It is, of course, a combination which may also be expected to win a trick on the offensive. Valuations of combinations were made in accordance with the following table in the CULBERTSON SYSTEM:

2 HT	A-K
1° HT	A-Q
1 HT	A, K-Q, K-J-10
° HT	K-x, Q-J-x
+ values	any queen (but not a singleton)
(about ˇ HT)	any jack combined with another honor (but no singleton or doubleton, and not A-K-Q-J) any singleton or void (not more than one)

See DEFENSIVE TRICK and QUICK TRICK.

HONORARY MEMBERS. The title of Honorary Member, awarded by the American Bridge League and the American Contract Bridge League, is bestowed for long and meritorious service to the League. The ABL first gave the designation to Milton C. Work in 1927. The first person to be selected after the amalgamation of the ABL and the United States Bridge Association in 1937 was Ely Culbertson.

ABL

1927	Milton C. Work	1964	Jeff Glick
1928	Wilbur C. Whitehead	1965	Sidney B. Fink
1929	Maurice Maschke	1966	Harry J. Fishbein
1930	Eberhard Faber	1967	Oswald Jacoby
1931	Waldemar K. von Zedtwitz	1968	Frank T. Westcott
1932	E.J. Tobin	1969	Samuel M. Stayman
1933	A.E. Manning-Foster	1970	Julius L. Rosenblum
1934	P. Hal Sims	1971	Joseph J. Stedem
1935	Nathan S. Kelly	1972	Phyllis Smith
1936	Nate B. Spingold	1973	Kate Buckman
		1974	Louise Durham
ACBL		1975	Kay Moody
1937	Philip Steiner	1976	Charles S. Landau
1938	Ely Culbertson	1977	Fred B. Ensminger
1939	Henry P. Jaeger	1978	William A. Baldwin
1940	Cmdr. W.A. Corley	1979	Margaret Wagar
1941	Harold S. Vanderbilt	1980	Easley Blackwood
1942	Maj. Clarence Wyatt	1981	Judge Carl B. Rubin
1943	Russell J. Baldwin	1982	Ethel Keohane
1944	Gen. Alfred M. Gruenther	1983	Alfred Sheinwold
1945	Gen. Robert J. Gill	1984	Sol Seidman
1946	Albert H. Morehead	1985	Dave Treadwell
	Maureen O'Brien Bailey	1986	Ernie Rovere
1947	Benjamin M. Golder	1987	Kathie Wei
	Mrs. James C. Baird	1988	Vic Mitchell
1948	Shepard Barclay	1989	Dan Morse
1949	Alexander M. Sobel	1990	George Rosenkranz
1950	Dr. Louis Mark	1991	Bob Hamman
1951	James C. Baird	1992	Percy and Anne Bean
1952	R.L. Miles Jr.	1993	Edgar Kaplan
1953	Curt H. Reisinger	1994	Richard Goldberg
1954	Fred Snite Jr.		
1955	George W. Beynon		
1956	George Alderton II		
1957	Alvin Landy		
1958	Lee Hazen		
1959	Charles Goren		
	Dr. A.M. Dye		
1960	Tom Stoddard		
1961	Charles J. Solomon		
1962	John E. Simon		
1963	Max M. Manchester		
	Bertram Lebhar Jr.		

HONORS. The five highest ranking cards in each suit; specifically, for the purpose of scoring honor premiums, the ace, king, queen, jack, and ten of the trump suit, or the four aces at no trump, are honors. See LAWS (Law 84).

HOOK. Colloquialism for FINESSE.

HORSE AND HORSE. Slang term for both sides vulnerable.

HOSPITALITY. The general term for efforts by a host unit at a bridge tournament to make the players feel more comfortable and welcome. Among the forms that hospitality takes are souvenir programs and pencils; free orange juice (at Florida tournaments), coffee, or cokes; after-game refreshments; between-sessions buffets and even dinners; after-session dancing; morning tours to places of local interest; style shows and brunches; panel discussions; daily bulletins, etc.

Hospitality has other dimensions in international and world championships, often involving interpreting. A new high standard was set at the 1991 world team championships in Yokohama, Japan, where a team of Japanese ladies went to great lengths to ensure that players were met on arrival in Tokyo and were given all possible help in finding restaurants, confirming return flights, and in other ways.

HOUSE OF COMMONS. See BRITISH PARLIAMENT MATCHES.

HOUSE OF LORDS. See BRITISH PARLIAMENT MATCHES.

HOUSE PLAYER. A player at a bridge club who is available for making up tables and for joining tables when a member wishes to leave. Generally house players receive some compensation for their services to the club, but arrangements vary from club to club regarding winnings or losses at play. Some clubs have a few regular players who make themselves available to help in forming tables in exchange for remission of fees for their play.

HOUSE RULES. Additions or amendments to the Laws as required to meet conditions of play in a club or group. Proper subjects for house rules would be the posting of deposits to guarantee losses in rubber bridge games, clothing or dress rules, rules for cutting in to existent games, eligibility to play, pivoting regulations when time for play is limited, termination time of the game, etc.

HOUSTON AFFAIR. The January 1977 North American Team Trials competition that ended when the team captained by John Gerber was forced to forfeit when two members of his five-player team, Larry Cohen and Dr. Richard H. Katz, resigned from both the team and the American Contract Bridge League with 32 deals of the 128-board final still to be played. As a result, the 1976 Grand National Teams victors were declared the Trials champions and became eligible to represent North America in the 1977 Bermuda Bowl. They eventually won the world title.

The Gerber team, which also included George Rosenkranz, Roger Bates and John Mohan, had a 40-IMP lead, 221-181, after the 96th deal of the final concluded

Saturday evening's play. However, the start of the last 32-board set was held up on Sunday because the Tournament Committee was studying some charges concerning irregularities involving Katz and Cohen. Closed-door conferences consumed much of the day until an announcement was made by ACBL President Louis Gurvich that Katz and Cohen had resigned from their team and from the ACBL. This reduced the Gerber team to three members, forcing a forfeit.

In the following days, there was much media conjecture concerning the reasons for the sudden unexpected resignations. Various newspaper articles quoted "reliable sources" as saying that Katz and Cohen had been guilty of serious infractions against the Proprieties of bridge.

Soon after these accusations appeared in print, Katz and Cohen filed a $44 million lawsuit against the ACBL, Gurvich, Lew Mathe and Don Oakie. The suit alleged defamation of character, interference with business interests, false accusations of cheating, coerced withdrawal from the Houston Trials, and forced resignation from the ACBL. The suit demanded that Katz and Cohen be reinstated as ACBL members and that the Trials continue from the point where they were terminated. Gurvich, Mathe and Oakie all were members of the Tournament Committee at Houston, and all three were present during the events that took place on the final day.

Katz and Cohen later filed another suit in which they accused the ACBL of violation of federal antitrust actions.

The action finally was settled on February 23, 1982. The settlement consisted of the following:

1. Dr. Richard H. Katz and Lawrence Cohen are each readmitted, effective immediately, to membership in the ACBL with all privileges of full membership, except that they agree not to play together as a partnership.

2. Should Katz and Cohen desire to play together as a partnership, their request will be submitted to the National Board of the ACBL, to be decided under the rules and regulations of the ACBL. The ACBL will not entertain such an application prior to March 1, 1984.

3. The parties will be compensated by Commercial Union Assurance Company, insurer of the ACBL, for costs and attorneys' fees incurred with respect to this lawsuit: Katz and Cohen will receive the sum of $75,000 and the ACBL will receive an amount yet to be determined.

4. The lawsuit is dismissed. Katz, Cohen and the ACBL shall exchange mutual releases of all claims.

In an explanation of the settlement in the April 1982 *ACBL Bulletin*, ACBL President James Zimmerman wrote:

"This case was unique in that Katz-Cohen resigned from membership in the ACBL rather than face charges of improper communication and certain ejection from the ACBL should these charges be sustained. No matter how one may feel as to whether there was or was not improper communication, the fact remains that because of their resignations no evidentiary presentation of this charge was ever made.

"Those who were of the opinion that Katz and Cohen were guilty of exchanging information improperly have retained that opinion. I doubt that a resolution by a trial would have changed it, especially since that question would not have been the most relevant issue in the trial. Those who were on the other side were also vehement on behalf of Katz and Cohen — it is equally likely that their opinion would not have been changed by a trial.

"This matter has been before the ACBL Board of Directors for five years. Management has been continually required to furnish information to all lawyers. Katz and Cohen, by their resignations, have not been members of the ACBL nor have they played in ACBL-sanctioned events for five years.

"Estimates were that the trial would take five to eight weeks. A judge in Los Angeles County, therefore, made a most strenuous effort to dispose of this case without a trial.

"The basic position of the ACBL through all negotiations was that Katz and Cohen should not play together as a pair. Katz and Cohen would not accept this restriction. When there was movement by Katz and Cohen toward acceptance of restriction, this basic concession made it possible to find a ground whereby they could be considered for readmission. On February 23, 1982, Katz and Cohen were re-admitted, but they agreed not to play together.

"The Katz-Cohen lawsuit alleged a number of causes of action, all of which were terminated by this settlement. Payment of the plaintiffs' legal fees was made by the insurance company alone, a result of negotiations between the insurance company and the plaintiffs. No payments to the plaintiffs were made by the ACBL. (The amount of remuneration to the ACBL for legal fees is in litigation at this writing.)

"Is this settlement a precedent-setting case for any future law suit? Absolutely not! Each case will be dealt with individually."

HOWELL MOVEMENT. A method of producing one winner from a field at duplicate in which all pairs play each of the boards in play, with comparison in direct competition with other pairs on approximately half of the boards, and adverse comparison on the other boards. Because of the requirement that all pairs meet in head-on competition, the movement is not practical for many of the possible number of tables.

The four-table, five-table, and seven-table movements (requiring seven rounds of four boards, nine rounds of three boards, and 13 rounds of two boards, respectively)

Table 1		Table 2		Table 3		Table 4		Table 5		Table 6		Table 7	
Prs.	Bds.	Prs.	Bds.	Prs.	Bds.	Prs.	Bds.	Prs.	Bds.	Prs.	Bds.	Prs.	Bds.
8v1	1	3v6	4	2v7	6	5v4	7						
7v3	1	5v2	2	10v1	3	9v8	4	4v6	5				
5v12	1	2v4	2	9v10	3	14v1	4	8v13	5	7v11	6	6v3	7
8v13	1	2v5	2	9v11	3	14v1	4	6v7	5	4v10	6	3v12	7

provide excellent competition. Starting assignments for these movements are given below, and positions and boards for each round subsequent can be obtained by applying the following rules: the highest numbered pair remains stationary throughout; each other pair replaces the pair with the next lower number for their next seat, with number 1 replacing the pair with the next to the highest number. Boards progress so that each table plays the boards in ascending order.

Except in the four-table game, there are as many sets of boards in play during the session as there are rounds to be played. The extra sets are on a byestand behind the highest numbered table. From here they are fed into the last table, and the boards at the byestand are replenished from table 1. Note the special byestand layout with four tables.

For six tables, as well as eight to 12 tables, see RE-DUCED HOWELL.

At the bottom of the page is a chart showing the starting positions for four tables (1st line), five tables (second line) and seven tables (third line). The second seven-table movement (fourth line) is a revised schedule due to Olof Hanner. Using it, the balance is preserved if Pair 14 is a phantom in a six-and-a-half table set-up.

See THREE TABLES for the six-pair movement.

HUDDLE. A longer-than-usual pause preceding an action in the bidding (usually) or the play of a hand. If the huddle is followed by a positive action, usually no harm is done to the opponents. However, the ethics of the game (all information is to be conveyed by the bids made, not the manner of making them) require that the partner of the huddler not take cognizance of the information that the huddler "had a problem." See SLOW PASS.

One of the situations that used to cause difficulties was the problem that a player had after a preemptive bid on his right. Many hands seemed too good to pass but did not offer a clear-cut alternative action. A huddle followed by a pass created an ethical problem for the partner. Should he take action on some sort of miscellaneous holding or not? Partner's huddle has reduced the danger that the right-hand opponent holds a powerful defensive hand. This frequently recurring problem was answered in the United States by the "skip-bid warning rule", which puts the player following the preempter under the obligation to take a huddle at all times when a skip bid has been made so that his partner will have no ethical problem in connection with a valid huddle holding.

Players should strive for a rhythm in the tempo of bidding in order to obviate the necessity of huddling.

In the play, a hesitation by one defender will often reveal that he holds a key card. In that case his partner is not necessarily barred from making the indicated play, but should satisfy himself before doing so that he would have had sound technical reasons for playing in the same way without any hesitation.

A hesitation in the play when there is no possible reason to think (e. g., when playing a singleton, or when following suit with insignificant small cards) is an offense against the Proprieties. In such cases the director may award an adjusted score under Law 73. See RHYTHM and SKIP-BID WARNING.

HUM SYSTEMS. HUM is an acronym for Highly Unusual Methods, which are usually Strong Pass systems.

The World Bridge Federation decided in 1990 to bar HUM Systems from world championship play except in long matches: the Bermuda Bowl, or quarterfinal and subsequent stages of the Rosenblum Cup.

A HUM system was defined as one with one or more of the following elements:

(a) A pass in the opening position may or will show values normally understood to represent an opening bid at the one-level.

(b) An opening bid at the one-level is or may be weaker than a pass, and does not conform with the RULE OF EIGHTEEN. A 1NT opening which shows a balanced hand with a minimum below 9 HCP, or an unbalanced hand with a minimum below 17 HCP.

(c) An opening bid at the one-level with more than one potential meaning. Examples: a bid that shows length or shortage in the suit; a bid that is two-suited, with no suit specified; a bid that does not relate to a single specified suit. This does not restrict players using Strong Club or Strong Diamond systems.

Players using HUM Systems are usually required to give advance notice to their opponents.

HUNGARIAN BRIDGE FEDERATION (Magyar Bridzs Szövetség). Revived in 1963 to organize national championships and tournaments with international participation. In 1993 there were 1069 members. Before World War II, Hungarian teams won two European titles, in 1934 and 1938, and were second twice. Hungary returned to international competition in 1968. It publishes a monthly magazine, *Bridzsélet.*

1993 officers:

President, Géza Szappanos
International Secretary, Géza Homonnay.
1122 Budapest, Csaba u. 24/a Hungary.
Tel: 36 1 1553016
Fax: 36 1 175 3134

I

IBM NUMBER. See PLAYER NUMBER.

IBPA. See INTERNATIONAL BRIDGE PRESS ASSOCIATION.

ICELAND BRIDGE UNION (Bridgesamband Islands). The Union was founded in 1948 by six leading clubs. By 1992 there were about 3500 members and 48 clubs. Iceland won the Bermuda Bowl in 1991, the Nordic Open Championship in 1988 and the Nordic Women's Team Championship in 1990. Iceland has by far the highest membership per capita in the world. Polls have shown that 20% of the people know how to play bridge, and that 8%, or 20,000 people, play regularly.

Officers 1992:

President: Helgi Johansson
Secretary: Elin Bjarnadottir
Sigtun 9, 1S-105 Reykjavik, Iceland.
Fax: 354-1-689361.

ICY. See COLD.

IDAK (or IDAC). A defensive bidding system against strong artificial club sequences. IDAK stands for Instant

Destroyer and Killer, while IDAC means Instant Destruction Against a Club. The system is used when not vulnerable. WONDER BIDS are used when vulnerable.

The system works this way. If RHO opens an artificial club or responds artificially to a 1♣ opening:

1. If you have a long suit, bid the suit immediately below it at whatever level you deem appropriate (notrump shows clubs). This is not a transfer bid per se, for responder can pass the suit you bid. With two suits, "transfer" in one and rebid in the other.

2. 1♠ shows a 4-3-3-3 pattern (any) or a string of spades. Responder assumes you have the first type and bids his best suit at whatever level he wishes. If you really have a string of spades, you can always rescue him.

3. A jump in spades at any level shows the minor suits. Responder can ask for your better minor by bidding notrump.

4. A double shows a three-suited hand (any). If responder has: (a) a one-suited hand, he responds two suits below his real suit (i.e., spades shows diamonds) at any level. The original doubler bids the suit shown with support, and passes without it. (b) With both majors and an interest in preempting, responder bids 2 NT, for the doubler guarantees a major. (c) With both minors and interest in preempting, he bids three or more notrump. (d) With a constructive hand (9 + points) and two suits, responder bids 1 NT. The doubler now bids his suits up the line if there is no interference. If there is interference, the doubler should double again if short in the interference suit, and pass otherwise. (e) With specifically spades and diamonds, or hearts and clubs, responder can jump in either suit (which shows the other one), knowing that the doubler will have support for one of the suits.

IDIOT COUP. A defensive play with an indelicate name which works only if the declarer is naive. Consider this position:

```
                A K 10 x x
      J x                   Q x
                x x x x
```

In normal circumstances the top honors are played. But if South leads from his hand and West plays the jack, South may have to think after winning in dummy. Since it would be bad play for West to split with Q-J-x, South should not be tempted to take a second-round finesse. If he does so his partner may address him by the name of the Coup. If South continued with the ace, as any good player would, and finds that West began with Q-J-x, he has become the victim of a GROSVENOR GAMBIT.

This devious play requires more imagination when it is East who must attempt to divert declarer from an obvious winning line:

```
Vul: None        ♠ Q 5 4
Dealer: South    ♥ 9 6 3
                 ♦ A 9 6
                 ♣ 8 7 5 3
 ♠ K 9 8                      ♠ J 7
 ♥ J 7 2                      ♥ 10 8
 ♦ K 8 4                      ♦ Q J 10 7 3 2
 ♣ Q 9 6 2                    ♣ A J 4
                 ♠ A 10 6 3 2
                 ♥ A K Q 5 4
                 ♦ 5
                 ♣ K 10
```

WEST	NORTH	EAST	SOUTH
			1♠
Pass	1 NT	2♦	3♥
Pass	3♠	Pass	4♠
All Pass			

South won the diamond lead in dummy, led to the ♠A and misjudged by ducking a trump to East's jack. Another diamond was ruffed, and South cashed three heart winners. To reach the dummy he ruffed a heart winner in order to lead to the ♣K. But East confused the issue by throwing the ♣J. South fell into the trap by finessing the ♣10 to go down. Obviously East would not have thrown an honor from a queen-jack holding.

IDLE BIDS. Bids which have little or no natural function in a standard method of bidding, and which are therefore available for specialized use.

Bidding is a language with a limited vocabulary. If more bids can be added to a player's vocabulary without affecting other situations, efficiency tends to be increased. Theoreticians therefore search for idle bids, and try to assign useful meanings to them.

One example is a jump to 2 NT when the opener's suit bid has been doubled. This is idle because a player with a strong balanced hand would automatically redouble. Many players therefore use this bid conventionally to show a useful hand, probably 10-11 in high cards, with at least four-card support for the opener's suit. The immediate jump raise over the double can then be reserved for preemptive action. See TWO NOTRUMP RESPONSE (OVER OPPONENT'S TAKEOUT DOUBLE).

Another example is a response of 5NT to a 1NT opening. As 4NT is a natural invitation to 6NT, 5NT is not needed for that purpose. Expert players therefore use it as an invitation to 7NT, guaranteeing six. The same idea would apply to 2NT-5NT. See also IMPOSSIBLE BID.

IDLE CARD. See BUSY CARD.

ILLEGAL CALL. A call out of rotation, insufficient, or otherwise improper, during the bidding period of a hand.

ILLOGICAL BID. See IMPOSSIBLE BID.

IMP. Abbreviation for INTERNATIONAL MATCH-POINT. It is frequently used either as the three letters, or as the word imp in conversation.

IMP BRIDGE MAGAZINE. Dutch magazine for the better players, founded in 1990 by Jan van Cleeff. 8 issues annually: PO Box 156, 2394ZH Hazerswoude, Netherlands.

IMP SCORING. See INTERNATIONAL MATCH-POINTS.

IMP TACTICS. Bidding and play at IMPs is an intermediate stage between match points and rubber bridge. It is important to understand the mathematical factors that influence the bidding of games and slams.

The Odds

Bidding a close, non-vulnerable game can gain a swing of 250 points, 6 IMPS. If you go down, you may lose a swing of 190 points, 5 IMPS. So the odds are only 6 to 5 in your favor, without allowing for the badly-splitting hand on which you get doubled. It is about even money.

Vulnerable games, though, gain 10 IMPs and lose only 6. Here the odds are much more favorable. So, bid any vulnerable game that seems faintly possible; but bid a non-vulnerable game only with solid expectation of making it.

For example, suppose you hold:

> ♠ K 8 4
> ♥ A 10 2
> ♦ K 7 3
> ♣ Q J 10 5

After two passes, you open 1♣. Partner jumps to 2NT. Push on to 3NT if vulnerable, but pass if you are not.

Small slams are even-money bets at IMPS; you stand to gain or lose the same amount. However, tend to assume that any touch-and-go slam will not be bid at the other table. That is a fact of life. Thus, if you are comfortably ahead in the match, or playing a team you rate to beat easily, hold back; but if you are the underdog, play for the swing and bid. Actually, the best chance a weak team has to beat a stronger one is to bounce into slam whenever there seems to be a possibility of making.

Grand slams appear to have odds against them of only 15 to 11 non-vulnerable, or 17 to 13 vulnerable. These are not nearly so prohibitive as the 2 to 1 total-point odds — IMP scoring always reduces the big swing compared to the little one. But there is a hidden factor: at the other table, your opponents may not bid even a small slam. Then, going down in a grand slam vulnerable costs you 26 IMPS, the 13 you lose, plus the 13 you could have won: and making your grand slam gains only four IMPs extra. Perhaps you think it is next to impossible for the enemy to miss a small slam when you are thinking of a grand slam, but it has happened many times. So avoid grand slams unless you can count 13 tricks.

How does all this compare to matchpoint duplicate? There it probably pays to bid any game with a 45% chance. (You never get a tremendous score for staying out of a close game even when it should go down, for the defense is too often poor; and, after all, you are trying to get a big score and win the tournament.) This means that a duplicate buff playing at IMP scoring should be less willing than usual to bid a non-vulnerable game, but more ready to bid a vulnerable game. Slam bidding is much the same at IMPs as at pairs, but you are a little readier to bid a doubtful small slam at pairs, since you are more likely to need points urgently. In pairs, as at IMPS, you steer clear of doubtful grand slams, for a small slam bid and made is usually a good score.

One- and Two-Imp Swings

One major difference between IMPs and pair scoring is the relative insignificance of tiny swings; overtricks, and the extra points for notrump or major suits. Play these North-South hands at 3NT against the lead of the ♦2:

> ♠ 6 4
> ♥ 7 4
> ♦ A 8 3
> ♣ A K Q 7 5 2
>
> ♠ A K 10 5 2
> ♥ A J
> ♦ J 10 6 5
> ♣ 6 3

At matchpoint play, you should duck; this will probably allow you to make 11 tricks. Of course you will get a heart shift and will go down if clubs do not split, but you must try for the extra tricks. At IMP scoring, you

rise with the ♦A and concede a club, playing safe for your contract.

Now, suppose you ducked the diamond. Your heart stopper is knocked out; you test the clubs and they split 4-1. At matchpoints you take a diamond finesse and cash out for down one; it may even be a good score, for everyone is in the same spot. At IMPs, if you neglected to play safe, you would play a spade to your 10, trying desperately to make your contract, because an extra undertrick does not bother you.

Defense is very much simpler at IMPs than at matchpoint pairs, for your objective is always to defeat the contract, never to stop overtricks. For example:

> ♠ A J 4 2
> ♥ 10 6 3
> ♦ 5
> ♣ K Q J 9 5
>
> ♠ 8 5
> ♥ A Q 2
> ♦ 10 8 6 3
> ♣ A 8 7 2

South opened 1♠, North bid 3♠, South 4♠. You are East, and your partner leads the ♦K, won by declarer. Trumps are drawn and your ♣A is knocked out. At matchpoints, you cash your ♥A, or, if hungry for a good score, you lead the ♥2, hoping that declarer has ♥ K-x-x and will duck to ensure his contract.

At IMPs you have no choice; you lead the ♥Q. Clearly, your best chance to defeat 4♠ (not to hold it to four, but to defeat it) is to find declarer with king-third or fourth in hearts and partner with J-9. Declarer is then likely to go wrong, playing you for Q-J. Of course, most of the time you will lose your ace, declarer will hold K-J or K-x, or K-9; but then you never could have defeated the contract.

In bidding, also, you ignore tiny differentials at IMPs. Making your contract is your goal. Suppose you hold:

> ♠ Q 5
> ♥ Q 8 6 3
> ♦ 8 7
> ♣ A 10 7 4 2

Partner opens 1♣, you respond 1♥, partner rebids 1NT. At matchpoints, you might pass, hoping to make 120; at IMPs you bid 2♣. This must be safer, and you simply score 90 or 110 instead of 120 or 150.

Suppose you have the same hand when partner opens 1♠. You bid 1NT; partner rebids 2♣. At matchpoints it is surely right to give a false preference to 2♠; at IMPS, it is surely better to raise clubs. Plus 110 and plus 140 are, in effect, the same at IMPS, and you look for the safest, not the largest, plus. Obviously, this applies even more forcibly to game and slam contracts. You are perfectly willing to play in a minor suit if it is safer; you never strain to play notrump or major suit contracts simply for the few extra points. Of course, whatever the scoring, it is hard to make 5♣ and 5♦, so these are not common contracts. However, they should be played at IMPs much more often than at matchpoint pairs. The answer is: never even consider swings of one or two IMPS. Ignore them in your thinking about dummy play, defense or bidding. Of course, when your contract is secure (or when, on defense, you see that it is impossible to defeat the declarer), you can give yourself the pleasure of battling over the extra trick or tricks. But this is a frill. The business of IMP playing is making or setting contracts. The tiny swings almost always even out over a long match. And if your team goes out to win all the one-IMP and two-IMP swings, you are likely to lose the match.

Competing for Partscores

In many respects the fierce competition over partscore hands which characterizes matchpoint pairs should be carried over into IMPS. That is, you must do a lot of balancing; or, if you prefer, you must get into the auction early and very "lightly." One way or the other, you must not let the enemy buy a lot of contracts peacefully at the two-level. The difference between 2♥, making two, and 3♥ down one, is five IMPs, and a few swings like this can cost you a match.

Now, duplicate-oriented players usually do compete or balance at the two-level when playing IMPS. Where they tend to go wrong is in competing at the three-level. Here there is a big difference between the two games. This is a common dilemma in pairs.

WEST	NORTH	EAST	SOUTH
			1 ♠
Pass	2 ♠	Dbl	Pass
3 ♥	Pass	Pass	

You, South, hold:

      ♠ A Q 8 6 4
      ♥ A 8 5
      ♦ K 10 4
      ♣ J 8

If the cards lie favorably for your side, you might well make 3♠ — you cannot get a good result defending. Likewise, if the lie is unfavorable, the opponents might make 3♥; then you might do better to go down at 3♠. So at matchpoints you should consider bidding.

At IMPs though, you should certainly pass. Whether you are plus 140 or plus 100 is a matter of one IMP; the same is true of minus 100 or minus 140. However, if both 3♥ and 3♠ go down, not at all unlikely, the swing can be five IMPS. If your distribution were unbalanced, so that both contracts might make, then six IMPs might be gained by bidding. But with a flat hand you should expect that only one contract or the other can be made, according to whose finesses work. You cannot lose much by passing, only by bidding.

The key is to think about plus scores on partscore hands, not how big a plus or how small a minus. If both pairs can be plus on three-quarters of the small hands, the team can win almost any match. See LAW OF TOTAL TRICKS.

Sacrifice Bidding

One area of difference between the matchpoint and the IMP approach is in sacrificing against game contracts. Sacrificing can be very rewarding at matchpoints — it is a triumph to lose 300 rather than 420, or 500 rather than 620. At IMPs, though, for the swing of 120 points you earn three IMPS. And this is not a very good return on your investment, that is, for your gamble that the opponents could make their game. If you misjudge slightly, losing 800 to save 620, for example) this costs only five imps. But if you take a PHANTOM SACRIFICE of 500 points against an unmakable game, you lose 12 IMPS. So the odds are not nearly as good as in matchpoint scoring.

The other side of this picture is that you are much more prone at IMPs than you are at duplicate to double an enemy sacrifice, rather than push on to five in a major. In a pair game you are reluctant to accept 500 points in exchange for a vulnerable game; it can almost be a zero.

Playing IMPs though, you double a sacrifice bid unless you are a cinch for 11 tricks; the odds are greatly against bidding on.

Of course, this refers to the "matchpoint" type of sacrifice. In any game it pays to go for 100 or 300 against a vulnerable game. At any scoring it pays to bid on to five of a major on the chance you will make it when you feel that you may not beat the opponents by more than a trick. One should not say "never sacrifice" or "always double a sacrifice"; merely remember that the odds are quite different from those at matchpoints, so your normal tendencies must be different also.

Actually, one type of sacrifice is popular among experienced IMP competitors; this is a premature sacrifice made in the hope of stampeding the opponents to the five-level. Thus, it aims at a 12-imp, not a three-imp profit.

Suppose partner opens 3♥, not vulnerable against vulnerable, right-hand opponent doubles, and you hold:

      ♠ K 6
      ♥ A J 7 4
      ♦ Q 7 2
      ♣ 8 5 4 2

Jump to 5♥. You are likely to have to make this bid over 4♠, so bid it immediately. Your left-hand opponent, under pressure, may bid 5♠, down one.

Another time when a sacrifice aims at a large number of IMPs is when you save against a slam. Down five doubled, 1100, can gain eight IMPs if your partners make 1430.

Penalty Doubles

In almost all doubling situations at IMPs, the odds favor the coward, not the hero. Consider the position in which vulnerable opponents have crept up to 4♠ on a shaky auction. You can see that they are running into bad breaks and probably will go down, perhaps even two tricks, Then a double stands to gain 300 points for a two-trick set or lose 170 should the contract make; but the IMP odds are only 7 to 5. And if the opponent's contract is a silly one, your partners probably have stopped at a partscore; then a double stands to gain only an IMP or two, for you would have a handsome swing in your favor anyway.

This, actually, is quite similar to matchpoint thinking; why double the opponents if they have overbid when you are getting most of the points anyway? And maybe they have not overbid; and perhaps your double will allow them to make a contract which otherwise would go down; this is particularly disastrous at IMPS.

An entirely different situation is the one in which you are debating whether to double an enemy overcall or to bid your own game contract. At matchpoints the critical consideration is the vulnerability; can you score in penalties more than the value of your game? For example, suppose you hold as South:

      ♠ A 4 3
      ♥ 7 2
      ♦ 9 5
      ♣ K Q J 8 4 3

NORTH	EAST	SOUTH	WEST
1 NT	Pass	3 NT	4 ♠
Pass	Pass	?	

You are vulnerable and the opponents are not. Your partner is not sure about doubling and is leaving the decision to you. Should you bid 4 NT, which will probably score 630, or settle for a double. The double is likely to be worth 500, but might be 200 on a bad day or 800 on a good day.

The scoring should determine. Double at IMPs and make sure of a plus score. Bid 4NT at matchpoints, risking defeat, since 500 will be a poor score if there are many 600s and 630s.

The key question at IMPS, then, is whether or not your game is sure. With the first example, you can feel only that game is probable, so you are anxious to play for penalties. Holding the second example, you can hardly imagine a hand that partner can have which will not produce 10 or 11 tricks at notrump, so you are reluctant to double. In short, at IMPS, go for the surest, not the most sizable, plus score.

One big difference between proper matchpoint and IMP approach is in doubling enemy partscores on competitive auctions. If you have bid up to 3♥ in a pair game and vulnerable opponents contest with 3♠, you are likely to double any time you feel sure that your contract would make; you must try to get 200 instead of 100. Obviously, this is suicidal at IMPs. If you score 100 when 140 is made at the other table, you lose 1 IMP, and 200 would gain you only 2 IMPs. For this 3-IMP pickup, you are risking a loss of 12 IMPs when the doubled contract is made (and your teammates play it undoubled). At matchpoints, you would gain considerably by doubling such contracts even if one in three is made against you; at IMP scoring you would be a big loser.

Speculative lead-directing doubles (i.e., calling for a lead which does not ensure a set but merely increases your chances) are slightly better bets at IMPs than at total points. For example, suppose you double a non-vulnerable 3NT contract to get a favorable lead. At matchpoints you are gambling a top against a bottom, instead of settling for slightly below average; the odds are a little better than even money. To figure the odds at IMPS, assume that the game is bid and made at the other table. If you beat the contract, you gain 500 while if it makes, you lose 150; these total-point odds become 11 IMPs to 4. The chance of overtricks reduces this to about two to one in your favor. That is, you will break even if the lead you direct beats one game in three.

The odds become most attractive when it is a slam which you are doubling. Superficially, this does not seem to be so. If you double a non-vulnerable 6♠ contract you gain 1080 (15 IMPS) when you beat it, while you lose 230 (6 IMPS) if you do not. But this assumes that the contract is the same at the other table, and this is an unwarranted assumption in the case of a close slam (as distinct from a touch-and-go game which probably will be bid). If only game is reached at the other table, your loss from doubling a makable slam is 1 IMP; and when your double was necessary to defeat the slam, your gain is 22 IMPS. (You gain 11 instead of losing 11.) At odds of 22 to 1, it is hard to go wrong.

General Tactics

There is another area of difference, though, caused not so much by the scoring as by the objectives of the two games. At matchpoints, you are trying to beat some huge (and ever increasing) number of competing pairs. At IMPS, you are trying to beat one team (at a time). And, in a pair contest, the huge field usually means that a great number of poor and inexperienced players are your direct or indirect opponents. But in an IMP team game you are not likely to meet any really bad opponents. What this means is that it is probably the winning style at

matchpoints to try to beat par, to try for unusually good results; in contrast, at IMP scoring, this is not the winning style (unless you are far behind or a decided underdog).

Par bridge, i.e., taking everything which is yours without trying to steal what belongs to the enemy, will win almost any IMP match. Of course, you and your teammates are bound to make a few errors, but if you play a steady game and make fewer mistakes than your opponents, you will win. A 51% game is good enough. At matchpoints, 51% is a disaster; even 60% games will not win tournaments. You must take more chances (and this means make more bad bids) to win a pair game. One illustration of this is in preemptive bidding.

    ♠ 6
    ♥ K Q 10 8 6 4
    ♦ A J 10 6 3
    ♣ 2

At matchpoints one might open 4♥ as dealer with neither side vulnerable. At IMPs better heart spots would be desirable, and there is a greater chance that the hand should be played in diamonds, so open 1♥. At IMPS, there is less incentive to "steal."

Another illustration is in balancing in risky positions, i.e., when the opponents have not found a fit. Suppose that the auction goes as follows:

WEST	NORTH	EAST	SOUTH
1 NT	Pass	Pass	?

With neither side vulnerable, you hold, sitting South:

    ♠ K 10 8 4 3
    ♥ 5
    ♦ A 10 6 5
    ♣ Q 7 4

At matchpoints, bid 2♠. If you pass, you are settling for a normal, under-average score; it would be better to try to beat par with an unsound overcall. At IMPs, you should pass, accepting the fact that it is "wrong" to overcall. The risk of a disastrous result is one you do not have to take when trying to beat one team instead of 200 pairs.

In the bridge world there are quite a few famous players whose great strength is their tactical bidding. (A "tactical" is a bad bid which gets a good result.) These experts do very well at matchpoints, winning far more than their share of tournaments, killing the weak fields. But they do poorly in team games.

So, save your bad bids for matchpoints. When you play IMPs, try a cautious, cowardly style: leave the heroics to your opponents. Then, at the end of the match you can compliment them for some brilliant bid while they are congratulating you for winning.

IMP PAIR GAMES. The spread of computer scoring has made it practical to employ IMP scoring for pair contests on a regular basis. Since multiple comparisons are involved, scoring such events manually was impractical and slow. There are three types:

(1) The datum method, usually called Butler scoring after Geoffrey Butler. The two extreme scores are put aside and the remainder averaged to produce a datum score, or norm, or mean, against which all results are IMPed. This is unsuitable for a small number of tables. For a large number of tables, more than 12, it is wiser to eliminate two scores at each end of the spectrum.

(2) The full comparison method, used for example in the CAVENDISH INVITATIONAL CHARITY PAIRS. Each pair receives an IMP score by comparing with ev-

ery other table, subject to a 17-IMP maximum.

(3) Two experts play all the deals against each other, and their results constitute the datum, or norm, against which others are IMPed. This produces two sets of winners, one North-South and one East-West.

IMPERFECT PACK. A pack of playing cards which is incomplete or in which one or more cards are duplicated. See LAWS (Laws 11, 12), LAWS OF DUPLICATE (Laws 1, 14).

IMPOSSIBLE BID. Legally, an "inadmissible call" (see LAWS 36-39). A bid of eight is one example. A historic case was the double of "two cokes" ordered by the right-hand opponent. (It was suggested that this required a minimum holding of two Scotches.)

Technically, it is a bid which is inconsistent with previous bidding by the same player, and which therefore reveals that he is ignorant of bidding principles or has made a mistake.

For example, the bidding 1NT - 3NT - 4NT is impossible. If made by a good player, it would imply that the first bid was a mistake: probably there was an ace hidden when he looked at his hand originally.

However, some impossible bids become possible on closer examination. A bid which is forcing but limited can often be employed in a sense which appears impossible. Marshall Miles suggested a response of 2 NT to a suit bid (ostensibly 13-15) with a balanced hand counting about 19 points. The idea was to follow with a natural 4 NT bid, describing accurately a hand which is difficult to define by normal methods. See also IDLE BIDS.

IMPOSSIBLE NEGATIVE. A method of responding over a PRECISION CLUB opening in order to show 4-4-4-1 distribution. Responder first makes the negative response of 1♦, then jumps in his short suit in order to show that he did not have a negative hand after all. This was part of original Precision, but was modified in later versions.

IMPROPER CALL. A bid or double during the auction when the caller is under obligation to pass.

IMPROPER REMARK. Any statement or question by a player during the play or bidding of a hand which refers to a possible holding or interpretation of an action of the current hand. The proprieties of the game state that any information must be exchanged between partners by proper calls at a steady rhythm, or by the order of play of cards when a choice of possible plays is present. See PROPRIETIES and COFFEE-HOUSE.

IMPROPRIETY. A violation or breach of ethical conduct; also the failure to observe proper etiquette. See ETHICS; ETIQUETTE; LAWS (Proprieties, I-III).

IN BACK OF. A term describing the relationship of a player to the opponent on his right; i. e., a player who plays after the player on his right is said to be "in back of" that player. An equivalent term is "over."

IN FRONT OF. The phrase used to describe the relationship between a player and his left-hand opponent; i.e., the player who plays before another player is said to be "in front of" that player. An equivalent term is "under."

der."

IN THE RED. A seeming paradox in bridge terminology: in rubber bridge or CHICAGO it would mean being a loser, but in duplicate it describes a score good enough to earn masterpoints, because rankings that qualify for points used to be indicated in red on the recap sheet before computer scoring.

INADMISSIBLE CALLS. See LAWS (Laws 36-39).

INADMISSIBLE DOUBLE OR REDOUBLE. See LAWS (Law 36).

INADVERTENT CALL. See LAWS (Law 25).

INADVERTENT INFRINGEMENT OF LAW. A violation of the proper procedure without deliberate attempt to do so. It is assumed that all infringements of laws are inadvertent, and the penalties prescribed for such infringements are designed to indemnity the non-offenders against potential loss as a result of such inadvertence.

INCOMPLETE HAND. An original holding of fewer than 13 cards with the other three hands correct. The missing card or cards are deemed to have been part of the original hand providing attention is drawn to the irregularity during the bidding and play. See Law 14.

If the missing card is in one of the other hands and has been looked at, then the normal procedure is to award an artificial adjusted score under Law 13. This Law does, however, give the players an option of playing the board if the information gained is inconsequential.

INCOMPLETE PACK. A pack of cards from which one or more cards are missing. If a deal is made from an incomplete pack, the deal is void, if discovered within the legal time limits, and a new pack is substituted.

INCOMPLETE RUBBER. If a rubber is not completed, bonuses are awarded of 300 for a game already scored and 100 for a part-score already scored.

INCOMPLETE TABLE. (1) In club play, a table of four or five players in which there is room for a newcomer to cut in. Some clubs designate five players, some six, as a full complement of players. (2) In home play, two or three players in search of one or two. (3) In duplicate play, see HALF TABLE.

INCORRECT CARD. Any card played which is improper in that it may become a revoke, or is played out of turn.

INDEMNIFY. To give redress to a side that has been injured by an infraction of the laws by the other side. In duplicate bridge it is the duty of the tournament director to impose penalties for infractions. See LAWS OF DUPLICATE (Law 10). In rubber bridge a penalty may be imposed by agreement of the players, or by either member of the non-offending side (except dummy) so long as he does not consult his partner. See LAWS OF CONTRACT BRIDGE (Law 14).

INDIAN BRIDGE FEDERATION (Bridge Federation of India). The Federation was founded in 1958 by four state bridge associations: Andhra Pradesh, Maharashtra, South India and West Bengal. Its founder-president was Ramniwas Ramnarain Ruia of Bombay, who held the office until 1970 and died in 1978. There are now 30 member associations, some geographical entities and some government bodies such as the railways. There are about 7,100 registered players.

1993 officers:

President Emeritus: P.C.Goenka
President: Dr. N.S.Tibrewala
Hon. Secretary: Niranjan Ubhayakar
103/1, "Gurukrupa"
11th Cross, 10th Main
Malleswaram
Bangalore 560 003 India
Tel: 91 812 345 634

INDICES. Small identifying marks in the corners of playing cards, printed above the suit symbol.

The first use of indices is difficult to determine. Special packs of the seventeenth and eighteenth centuries (educational, heraldic, political, etc.) had so much of the card taken up with pictures and words that the identification consisted of a number or letter beside one pip in an upper corner. No one seems to have adapted this for use with regular playing cards for a long time. In the 1870s three American card makers tried different solutions to the problem. One put miniature cards in two corners (calling the style Triplicate); another used merely a letter or number and a small pip (called Squeezers, because they did not need to be fanned); the third put these in all four corners (Quadruplicate).

The use of double indices permits a hand to be fanned either right or left, and European cards today are usually so made; English and American players chose the single index at each end which is current today. In 1893 some packs were issued with a large corner pip, with a white index within it. Today some Swiss packs use no index pip, but put the index as a white numeral in the pip nearest the corner. Spanish and some Italian (trappola) packs have indices from 1 to 13, including both suit and court cards.

INDIVIDUAL MOVEMENT. The most popular individual movement is the RAINBOW, described separately.

The SHOMATE MOVEMENT also is possible for some games, but it is not recommended although it does provide for balanced comparisons of a sort. The Shomate involves many movement irregularities and is a major chore to score. Modern-day directors almost never use the Shomate.

Two tables with eight, nine and 10 players can be accommodated in an Individual tournament. The boards of each round are relayed between the two tables. The game can be curtailed at any point, as all boards are completed after each round. In all cases, the players are assigned numbers. They replace the player with the next lower number at the end of each round. (In the eight-player movement, player #8 is stationary, and #1 replaces #7.) Starting assignments are as follows:

	Table 1				Table 2			
	N	S	E	W	N	S	E	W
8 players	8	1	6	2	5	7	3	4
9 players	2	3	4	7	6	8	5	9
10 players	7	8	10	2	5	9	3	6

There is one (and essentially only one) cyclic move-

ment for 12 players with different board sets at the tables. Olof Hanner's variant allows terminating after any round, provided you have one round's warning. The four first rounds are:

N	S	E	W	bd	N	S	E	W	bd	N	S	E	W	bd
12	1	4	5	1	7	1	3	9	2	10	2	8	6	1
12	2	5	6	2	8	1	4	10	3	11	3	9	7	1
12	3	6	7	3	9	2	5	11	4	1	4	10	8	2
12	4	7	8	4	10	3	6	1	5	2	5	11	9	3

Except for the first round, where there is a board sharing between table 1 and 3, the tables play different board sets. In the round that you decide to be the last one, the eleventh or an earlier round if there is not time enough, you do not let table 2 start a new board set, but let this table share with table 1. All boards will then have been played three times and if the movement is played in 11 rounds, 22 boards, all players have met as partners.

The 13-player movement runs 13 rounds, two boards to a round. The tables play the boards in ascending order, the first set starting at table 1, sixth set at table 2 and 12th set at table 3. Seating assignments are as follows: table 1: 1, 3, 5, 6; table 2: 7, 12, 13, 4; table 3: 2, 9, 8, 11. All players replace the next lower numbered player for the next round, player #1 replacing player #13.

Movements for larger numbers of tables have been developed by Olof Hanner, and are set out in his book on Duplicate Organization, written with Hans-Olof Hallén and Per Jannersten.

INDIVIDUAL TOURNAMENT. A bridge competition in which each contestant plays with many different partners. Obviously it is impractical to have partnership understandings with so many players in the limited time available for discussion, so that bidding systems are kept simple and conventional bids are held to a minimum. In order to eliminate a certain amount of the luck involved in indiscriminate partnerships, it is frequently desirable to break the field by masterpoint holdings into two or more flights. For movements used, see RAINBOW, APPENDIX (Rainbow) TABLE, and others discussed under the appropriate number of TABLES and INDIVIDUAL MOVEMENTS.

INDONESIA CONTRACT BRIDGE ASSOCIATION (GABUNGAN BRIDGE SELURUH INDONESIA). The Association was founded in 1953, and by 1992 had a membership of 4,000. Its players have won the Far East Team title 10 times, and frequently represented the Far East zone in the Bermuda Bowl.

President 1992
Amran Zamzani
25 Cempaka Putih Raya
Jakarta Pusat 10510
Indonesia
Fax: 62 21 310 7027.

INFERENCE. A conclusion drawn from a call or play made by partner or an opponent. Though the ability to gather and assimilate the most delicate clues is the hallmark of a fine player, the bidding and play of many hands abound with inferences that can be drawn by the average performer provided that he is alert and knows what to look for. Note that an inference implies uncertainty. An inference leaving no room for doubt would be a deduction.

A declarer's task is frequently lessened when the opponents have been in the auction; apart from yielding specific information about the enemy suit(s), interference bidding generally assists the declarer to guess better in the play of a critical suit. For example in playing a common combination such as:

K J 10 9

A 8 7 6

Declarer has to catch the queen, and with nothing to guide him, he must sometimes guess wrong. See TWO-WAY FINESSE. Suppose, however, that in the course of the auction West has made a preemptive bid marking himself with shortages elsewhere; the odds now clearly favor a finesse against his partner.

In taking advantage of the information provided by the bidding, a declarer frequently must resort to unusual plays:

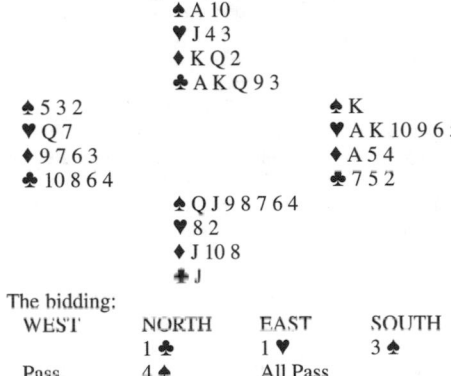

```
            ♠ Q 10 7
            ♥ 10 7 3 2
            ♦ K J 6
            ♣ K Q 10
♠ 5 4                      ♠ A 3
♥ K 8 6 5                  ♥ A Q J 4
♦ 10 5 4                   ♦ Q 7 3 2
♣ 7 5 4 2                  ♣ A 9 3
            ♠ K J 9 8 6 2
            ♥ 9
            ♦ A 9 8
            ♣ J 8 6
```

South is declarer in 4♠ after East has opened the bidding with 1NT. West leads a trump, and South, faced with three certain losers, has to avoid losing a diamond. The standard play of this combination is to finesse the jack, but in this instance declarer is fairly sure that East has the queen from his bid. His best chance is to take a backward finesse, leading the jack through East, and if covered, finessing against West for the 10 on the second round.

Sometimes the defenders find themselves in the unhappy position of guiding declarer's play through not bidding:

```
            ♠ K Q 4
            ♥ Q 6
            ♦ Q J 4 3
            ♣ A J 10 5
♠ 7 5                      ♠ J 9 2
♥ A K 4 3                  ♥ J 9 7 5 2
♦ K 7 6                    ♦ 10 9 8 5
♣ 8 7 4 2                  ♣ K
            ♠ A 10 8 6 3
            ♥ 10 8
            ♦ A 2
            ♣ Q 9 6 3
```

The bidding:

WEST	NORTH	EAST	SOUTH
Pass	1 ♣	Pass	1 ♠
Pass	2 ♠	Pass	4 ♠
All Pass			

West cashes two hearts and shifts to a trump, declarer drawing three rounds ending in dummy in order to take the diamond finesse. West wins and exits with a heart, South ruffing. The ♣K is now marked with East, for in the play West has shown up with the ♥A, ♥K and ♦K, and if he also held the ♣K he would have opened the bidding. Declarer's only chance is that the king is single-

ton. Accordingly, he plays a club to the ace, dropping East's lone king, winning both the contract and suspicious looks from the opposition.

Declarer has an even greater scope for making educated guesses based upon the play of the opponents' cards. This is particularly true when the defenders are forced to discard on a long suit, the order of their discards being most helpful to declarer. The accuracy of the inferences thus drawn varies with the skill of the opposition, for good players generally plan ahead in these situations, often leaving the declarer with little to go on. Nevertheless, it is the mark of a good player that he guesses the right play more often than not.

On rare occasions, the defenders are helpless to prevent declarer from gaining an inference.

```
            ♠ A 10
            ♥ J 4 3
            ♦ K Q 2
            ♣ A K Q 9 3
♠ 5 3 2                    ♠ K
♥ Q 7                      ♥ A K 10 9 6 5
♦ 9 7 6 3                  ♦ A 5 4
♣ 10 8 6 4                 ♣ 7 5 2
            ♠ Q J 9 8 7 6 4
            ♥ 8 2
            ♦ J 10 8
            ♣ J
```

The bidding:

WEST	NORTH	EAST	SOUTH
	1 ♣	1 ♥	3 ♠
Pass	4 ♠	All Pass	

West leads the ♥Q and continues the suit, East winning the king. After cashing the ♦A, East is in a cleft stick: if he returns a third heart, South will ruff high and West's failure to overruff will mark the ♠K. On the other hand, if he does not continue hearts, South's suspicions will be aroused and he is bound to diagnose the position.

The defending side is sometimes better placed to make deductions, for they have the advantage of being able to gather clues from both declarer's and partner's actions.

In a general way, the defenders can make certain assumptions about the nature of declarer's holding by his approach. For example, at a suit contract, if he plays a side-suit before broaching trumps, he probably has a shaky trump suit. On the other hand, if trumps are drawn immediately, it is safe to infer that declarer intends to utilize a side-suit to dispose of his losers. At notrump, when declarer makes no attempt to establish a strong suit, it is reasonably certain that the suit is ready to run.

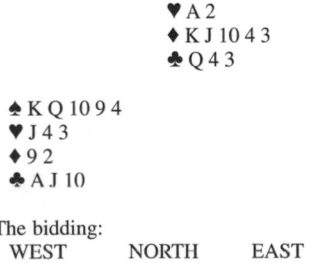

```
            ♠ 8 7 6
            ♥ A 2
            ♦ K J 10 4 3
            ♣ Q 4 3

            ♠ K Q 10 9 4
            ♥ J 4 3
            ♦ 9 2
            ♣ A J 10
```

The bidding:

WEST	NORTH	EAST	SOUTH
			1 NT
Pass	3 NT	All Pass	

West leads the ♠K, which declarer wins with the ace. To the second trick, South leads a club; West plays the ace and then the ♣Q, dropping declarer's jack, and takes three further spade tricks to set the contract. This was declarer's hand:

♠ A J
♥ K 9 7
♦ A Q 8 7
♣ K 9 5 2

West made two unusual plays: he rose with the ♣A in a position where it is customary to play low, and he continued spades at the risk of establishing the jack for declarer. The question is: how did he know? West reasoned that declarer could not have started with A-J-x of spades, for with that holding he would have surely refused the first spade, rendering the defense helpless. Either partner had the jack or, more likely, declarer had A-J alone. Further, declarer's failure to play on diamonds surely meant that the suit was solid, in which case, if declarer was permitted to steal a club, he would almost certainly have 9 tricks: one spade, five diamonds, one club, and two hearts (he was likely to have the ♥K for his bid).

Defenders are often misled into committing a blunder, basing their defense on the assumption that a declarer has adopted a reasonable line of play. Similarly, in deciding his play at a crucial point in a hand, a defender has to assume that his partner has played well. Terence Reese gives this example:

♠ Q 6
♥ A Q J 9 5
♦ J 9 4
♣ Q 7 4

♠ 10 5   ♠ J 9 4
♥ 8 6 2   ♥ 7 3
♦ A 5 2   ♦ K Q 10 7
♣ K 10 6 5 3   ♣ A 9 8 2

♠ A K 8 7 3 2
♥ K 10 4
♦ 8 6 3
♣ J

South plays in 4♠ and West leads the ♣5 to his partner's ace. East shifts to the ♦K and continues with the 7, declarer falsecarding with the 8. West is now faced with the problem of guessing whether to attempt to cash the third diamond or the ♣K. From his point of view, declarer might have well dropped the ♣J at trick one from J-x, and with apparently nothing to guide him he played the ♣K, giving declarer the contract. West failed to draw the proper inference from his partner's play: if East had held five diamonds, leaving declarer with two, he would have realized that the defense could take only two diamond tricks and would have played the ♦Q to hold the lead before shifting back to clubs. See also CARD READING and COUNTING THE HAND.

INFERENTIAL PROBLEM. A problem which requires the deduction of the lie of hidden cards through the use of information of a form not found in ordinary play.

Two examples of inferential problems follow. The first problem is of moderate difficulty and provides a good introduction to inferential problems. The second problem is a harder nut to crack with only one clue given as to the makeup of the concealed hands.

Big Casino and Little Casino*
by Jeff Rubens
*Reprinted from *The Bridge Journal*, Jan.-Feb. 1964.

♠ 3
♥ 9 6 4
♦ A 7 6
♣ K Q 9 5 4 2

♠ A Q 9 5 4
♥ 3 2
♦ K 9 5 3
♣ A 10

Contract: 6♦ by South
Clues:

(1) After the lead of any black card, South can make his contract by perfect play. However, after the lead of any red card, perfect defense can defeat the contract.

(2) A "spot card" is any card from 2 through 10. The sum of East's spot cards in hearts subtracted from the sum of his spot cards in diamonds is exactly one third of the sum of all his black spot cards.

(3) Neither defender is void of hearts, and neither defender holds both big casino (♦10) and little casino (♠2).

What are the exact East-West hands and how does South fulfill his contract after a favorable lead?

Solution to "Big Casino and Little Casino"

As neither defender is void of hearts, South must discard all his hearts before losing the lead. Further, he cannot lose a trick to one of the three missing low trumps. If diamonds are 3-3, no discards can be taken. Therefore, diamonds must be 4-2 with West holding two blank honors. In this way, declarer can obtain two discards on the clubs in dummy. These discards must be taken after two trumps are drawn; therefore one ruff must establish the spade suit. This places East with ♠K-J-10 and four clubs. East's four clubs must include the jack as the lead of a black card must help declarer by providing an entry for a black suit finesse. Since the sum of East's black spot cards is divisible by three, East must hold ♣J-8-6-3. Since West holds the ♠2, East's diamond honor is the 10. Therefore, East holds two hearts with a spot total of 15 and the East-West hands are:

♠ 8 7 6 2   ♠ K J 10
♥ A K Q J ? ?   ♥ ? ?
♦ Q J   ♦ 10 8 4 2
♣ 7   ♣ J 8 6 3

After a black suit lead, declarer wins cheaply. He cashes the ♦K and ♦A, takes the remaining black suit finesse, clears all the black-suit tops in the South hand, ruffs a spade in dummy and discards two hearts on good clubs. Clubs are now continued until East ruffs. If East ruffs low, South overruffs and leads good spades. If East ruffs high, South takes the balance easily. If East never ruffs, he is trump couped at trick 12.

East's two hearts must be 10-5, not 8-7, for if East held ♥ 8-7, the opening lead of ♥5 would not defeat the contract!

Inferential Problem*
By Terence Reese
*Reprinted from *The Bridge World.* Feb. 1950.

♠ 8 5 2
♥ J 6
♦ K 6 5 3 2
♣ 8 6 5

♠ K J 9 6
♥ K 7
♦ J 9 4
♣ Q 9 4 2

South played a contract of 3 NT. West led the ♠6. East

won with the ace and returned the 4. West won with the jack and played the king, on which East played the 3, and all followed. West then cashed the thirteenth spade. The contract was just made.

"Nicely played," said West to declarer at the end of the hand. "There was nothing we could do, was there, partner?"

"Well, yes," said East. "If, at the fourth trick, you had played any card except the thirteenth spade we could have put them one down."

Assuming that East was right, what was South's hand?

Solution to "Inferential Problem"

The key lies in realizing that the last spade, in addition to making the timing right for a squeeze, gives South a chance to unblock in diamonds. The diamond holding is A-Q-8-7, and the suit is blocked unless South can discard one of them. (The diamonds cannot be A-Q-10-8 or A-Q-10-7, for then a diamond lead by West would resolve the difficulty.)

Declarer has, at most, eight tricks on top. The ninth can come only from a squeeze in hearts and clubs. The hearts must be A-Q alone — if A-Q-x, the lead of ♥K would be fatal to the defense — and the clubs A-K-7-3, for if they are as good as A-K-10-x, the lead of ♣Q gives South three tricks in clubs, and enables him to endplay West. So the whole hand is:

♠Q 10 7   ♥A Q   ♦A Q 8 7   ♣A K 7 3

The play, when West leads the last spade, is to discard a heart from dummy and a diamond from declarer's hand. West exits with a diamond; declarer cashes the ♣A-K, and runs off the diamonds. The last diamond squeezes West in hearts and clubs.

A book of inferential problems is *Bridge: The Ultimate Limits* by Eric Mansfield. An example:

         ♠A Q J
         ♥ 10
         ♦A Q 5 3 2
         ♣ J 6 3 2

         ♠ 10 8
         ♥A K 8 7 3
         ♦ 10 6 4
         ♣ 10 5 4

South can make 5♦ against any defense. What are the East-West hands?

You must construct a hand in which you are lucky in spades and diamonds, and the defense cannot start by cashing three club winners. In addition West must have the intermediate hearts. The hand is this:

         ♠A Q J
         ♥ 10
         ♦A Q 5 3 2
         ♣J 6 5 2

♠9 7 6 5 4 3 2   ♠K
♥Q J 9   ♥6 5 4 2
♦K J   ♦9 8 7
♣A   ♣K Q 9 8 7
         ♠ 10 8
         ♥A K 8 7 3
         ♦ 10 6 4
         ♣ 10 5 4

West may or may not cash his ♣A. Whatever he does, South can take the ♣A and use a heart entry to finesse in diamonds. Eventually he will end in his hand by leading

to the ♦10. He cashes the ♥K throwing the ♠J. Then he leads the ♥8, throwing the ♠Q, and the ♠10 becomes the entry for the heart winners. See OCTAGONAL SQUEEZE.

INFORMATION, UNAUTHORIZED. See UNAUTHORIZED INFORMATION.

INFORMATORY DOUBLE. An early name for the TAKEOUT DOUBLE. More recently used by Robert Ewen in his book on doubles to encompass doubles designed to give the partner of the doubler a variety of options or information, such as the COMPETITIVE DOUBLE.

INFORMATORY PASS. See PENALTY PASS.

INHIBITORY DOUBLE. A psychic maneuver in a competitive auction aimed at intimidating the opponents. It may take the form of a double of a forcing bid after partner has made an overcall. For example:

WEST	NORTH	EAST	SOUTH
			Pass
1♥	2♣	2♠	Dbl

East's 2♠ bid is forcing in a standard style, and if South held a good hand with spades he would be well advised to wait for better things. The doubler, in fact, usually has a bad hand with support for his partner's suit, to which the latter retreats at his turn.

However, this double is now often used for takeout, showing moderate length in the fourth suit. See SNAPDRAGON and TAKEOUT DOUBLE.

INITIAL BID. The first bid of any deal. See OPENING BID.

INITIAL LEAD. The first lead of any deal. See OPENING LEAD.

INNER SEQUENCE. A sequence of which the top card is not the top card of the suit holding. In a holding Q-10-9-8, the inner sequence is the 10-9-8. See INTERIOR SEQUENCE.

INSPECTION OF TRICKS. (1) A trick may be inspected by any player until such player has turned his play to the trick face down. (2) Until play ceases, QUITTED TRICKS may not be inspected except at the director's specific instruction. (3) After play ceases, the played and unplayed cards may be inspected to settle, e. g., a claim of a revoke or of the number of tricks won and lost; but no player should handle cards other than his own. See LAWS OF DUPLICATE, Law 66.

INSTANT MATCHPOINTS. Games such as the EPSON in which the matchpoints are predetermined, based on the results of a previous competition using the same deals. The players discover their matchpoint score immediately after completing the play of a deal.

INSTINCT (or Intuition). A term loosely applied to one's inherent feeling about the right play, or less often the right bid, to make during a deal of bridge. Some players are said to be totally devoid of instinct or card sense (really sensitivity), and have to make calculations for any play involving percentages. The concept of "instinct" as such has been challenged by many authorities, but those who possess it or claim to possess it maintain its definite existence. See TABLE PRESENCE.

INSTRUCTIONS (director's). The announcements by the director by which a movement in a session of duplicate bridge is completed. At the end of each round, the director instructs the players as to their movement and the movement of the boards in play. At determined times, this movement may vary for one or more rounds. The ARROW SWITCH, Skip, and redistribution of boards are examples of such variations. Instructions are also given to the contestants for twinning of boards, methods of qualification, starting times for succeeding sessions, and other conditions of contest.

INSUFFICIENT BID. A bid which is lower in rank than a bid previously made in the same auction. For the penalties involved, see LAWS (Law 27). If the insufficient bid is conventional, the possibility of escaping penalty by making it sufficient in the same suit is not available.

INSULT. The 50-point penalty that the doubling side pays for doubling a contract that the declaring side makes. The insult bonus is 100 if the contract succeeds when redoubled.

INSURANCE BID. A high-level save made in spite of some expectation of defeating the opposing contract. The insurance bidder is willing to concede a small penalty to guard against the danger of a big minus score.

INTERCITY MATCH. Many intercity matches have been played in various parts of North America. Notable among these were the series between New York and Philadelphia which the latter won regularly. A series of matches were played from 1960 to 1973, usually preceding the Summer North American Championships.

INTERCOLLEGIATE BRIDGE TOURNAMENT. An annual event formerly contested by universities and colleges throughout the United States and Canada, organized by GEOFFREY MOTT-SMITH, 1949-1960, WILLIAM ROOT, 1961-1965, LAWRENCE ROSLER and JEFF RUBENS, 1966-1967, and subsequently by representatives of the Association of College Unions-International and the American Contract Bridge League. When the Charles Goren Foundation offered financial assistance in 1969 the tournament became known as the Charles Goren Intercollegiate Bridge Tournament. One year — in 1974 — the Celanese Corporation assumed full financial responsibility for the tournament.

A feature of the tournament in the early years was the use of par hands. The earliest matches were conducted as a face-to-face contest for 16 finalists, but in 1953 the procedure was changed to a mailing of par hands to each campus with the scorecards rated in New York. Under this plan, titles were awarded to the highest-scoring pair on the North-South hands and on the East-West hands. In 1965, the face-to-face final was restored and par hands were used in the qualifying round. Initially, the final was scored by matchpoints, but international matchpoint scoring was adopted in 1967, and the conversion of IMPs to Victory Points was introduced in 1968. Par hands were eliminated in 1969, and the tournament became a three-stage contest, with an on-campus qualifying round and a regional semifinal in addition to the final. The national final had the reputation of being a showcase tournament and a number of national champions emerged from these contests. The 37th and final contest in this series was held in Memphis in April, 1979 after which the ACBL withdrew technical and financial support. The contest was resumed in 1991 as a joint venture of ACBL and ACU-I. For a list of Intercollegiate winners, see Appendix 1.

INTEREST-SHOWING BIDS. Bids which can be used as an alternative to CUEBIDS when the opener and responder have agreed on a major suit at the level of three or four. Having been often suggested and played in the United States without achieving popularity, they were developed in 1948 by some Cambridge University, England, players (E.M.L. and J.R.A. Beale, and H. Peter F. Swinnerton-Dyer), and are an optional part of the ACOL SYSTEM. It can be considered an extension of TRIAL BIDS at a higher level.

If the bidding goes 1♠-3♠; 1♠-4♠; or similarly in hearts, a change of suit which would normally be a cue-bid is made in a suit in which some support is needed. For example:

(a)	(b)
♠ A K 10 5 3	♠ K Q 9 5 4
♥ Q J 7 3	♥ A K J 6
♦ A	♦ Q 7 3
♣ K Q 7	♣ A

The opening bid of 1♠ is raised to 3♠, a limit raise showing about 11 points or the equivalent counting distribution.

On hand (a) the interest-showing bid would be 4♥, indicating that the opener needs some help in the form of heart honors or a heart shortage.

The interest-showing bid may well be made in a three-card suit. On hand (b) the opener rebids 4♦ to ask for support in that suit.

In each of these cases a normal cuebid would leave the responder in doubt about how to evaluate his hand for slam purposes. For an alternative treatment, see ASKING BIDS.

INTERFERENCE BID. Any defensive overcall which is not attacking or strength-showing, but is designed to obstruct somewhat the path of the opponents, who have already opened the bidding. Sometimes interference is made with preemptive or jump-bid tactics. See NUISANCE BID and OVERCALLS.

INTERIM RESPONSE. See WAITING BID.

INTERIOR CARD. An intermediate card; formerly, the second card in sequence, as the jack in a holding of queen, jack, and others.

INTERIOR SEQUENCE. A sequence within a suit such that the top card of the suit is not a part of the sequence, as the Q-J-10 in a holding of A-Q-J-10, or the J-10-9 in a holding of A-J-10-9. Some experts play that the lead of the jack against notrump denies a higher honor, and therefore lead the 10 from A-J-10 and K-J-10. By extension, a lead of the 10 can promise a higher honor by partnership agreement. The 9 would then be led from a holding headed by 10-9. See JOURNALIST LEADS; RUSINOW LEADS; ZERO OR TWO HIGHER LEADS.

INTERMEDIATE CARDS. See BODY and SPOT CARDS.

INTERMEDIATE JUMP OVERCALL. A jump overcall promising a good six-card suit and better than a minimum opening. An ideal hand to make an intermediate jump overcall would be:

♠ x x ♥ A K J x x x ♦ A Q ♣ J x x

For alternative uses of the jump overcall, see JUMP OVERCALL, ROMAN JUMP OVERCALL, WEAK JUMP OVERCALL.

INTERMEDIATE TWO-BID. An opening bid of two in a suit to show a strong hand somewhat short of game strength. In the original version, introduced about 1930, responder could pass the intermediate two-bid with a worthless hand, and some experts still play it in this fashion. Most, however, play it as a one-round force, with 2NT or a HERBERT NEGATIVE the required weakness response. See ACOL TWO-BID.

INTERNAL BLOCK. See UNBLOCKING.

INTERNATIONAL BRIDGE. There have been international tournaments and challenge matches since the earliest years of bridge. (See ANGLO-AMERICAN MATCHES). The first officially sponsored international tournament was held in Vienna in June 1930 under the auspices of the AUSTRIAN BRIDGE FEDERATION. The first international organization was the INTERNATIONAL BRIDGE LEAGUE, founded in 1932 by a small group of European countries, which conducted European championships until 1939. After World War II, the EUROPEAN BRIDGE LEAGUE was formed to replace the IBL. Today there are a large number of regional international organizations or tournaments. See AMERICAN CONTRACT BRIDGE LEAGUE; BRIDGE FEDERATION OF ASIA AND THE MIDDLE EAST; CENTRAL AMERICAN AND CARIBBEAN BRIDGE FEDERATION; COMMON MARKET CHAMPIONSHIPS; EUROPEAN BRIDGE LEAGUE; FAR EAST BRIDGE FEDERATION; NORDIC CHAMPIONSHIPS; SOUTH AMERICAN BRIDGE CONFEDERATION; SOUTH PACIFIC.

The first official world championship was held in New York in 1935 between France, reigning European champions, and a team representing the AMERICAN BRIDGE LEAGUE. The only other prewar world championship was held in 1937 in Austria, hosted by the IBL. World championship play resumed in 1950 with the first of a series of contests for the BERMUDA BOWL. Since 1963 the Bermuda Bowl has been conducted by the WORLD BRIDGE FEDERATION, formed in 1958. The WBF also conducts WORLD PAIR CHAMPIONSHIPS, WORLD TEAM OLYMPIADS, VENICE CUP matches, ROSENBLUM CUP matches and McCONNELL CUP matches. For lists of winners, see Appendices III, IV and V.

INTERNATIONAL BRIDGE ACADEMY. Formed in 1965 by Jean Besse and Pierre Collet for the purpose of fostering the study of bridge as a science. The Academy held meetings and published articles on the scientific and technical aspects of bridge. World Bidding Contests were staged for many years. The Academy has been dormant since the mid-1980s.

INTERNATIONAL BRIDGE LEAGUE. A forerunner of the WORLD BRIDGE FEDERATION, founded on June 10, 1932, at Scheveningen, The Netherlands, by a small group of European countries. During the years 1932-39, the IBL organized annual championships, including a World Championship in Budapest in 1937.

INTERNATIONAL BRIDGE PRESS ASSOCIATION (IBPA). A worldwide organization of about 500 bridge writers, mostly professionals, whose reports and articles appear in newspapers and magazines and other periodicals in most countries where tournament bridge is played. Authors and radio and TV lecturers also are eligible for membership. The European Bridge Press Association, the father of the IBPA, was formed at the Oslo 1958 European Championships by the journalists present. At the first Olympiad, played in 1960 in Turin, many non-European bridge writers joined, so the name was changed to International Bridge Press Association.

The Presidents have been:

Guy Ramsey	1958-59
Ranik Halle	1960-64
Jack Kelly	1964-70
Richard Frey	1970-81
Alan Truscott	1981-86
Rene Ducheyne	1986-91
Tommy Sandsmark	1991-

Others who have made major contributions include Eloene Griggs, Nelson Rice and Berl Stallard.

Eric Jannersten was executive secretary-treasurer from the foundation of the organization until he resigned that post in 1975. At that time he was named senior vice president for life. He was editor of the IBPA monthly bulletins until 1967, when Rhoda Barrow (Lederer) assumed the editorial duties. Albert Dormer took over the editorship in 1973 and retained that position until he resigned in 1981. He was succeeded by Patrick Jourdain as editor and David Rex-Taylor as managing editor.

Herman Filarski took over as executive vice president in 1975 and was responsible for many promotions in which the IBPA was involved. These included the BOLS TIPS, which bridge writers throughout the world incorporated in their columns; the BOLS BRILLIANCY AWARDS, which are given at World Championships for outstanding articles by bridge writers about outstanding plays by competitors in the World Championships, the Philip Morris tournaments in Europe, which lead to a Grand Final in Monte Carlo each year; and the Heineken Fluke Award, which was given to the bridge writer who wrote the best story about a fluke during the 1980 World Team Olympiad in Valkenberg. The Bols Tips later were gathered together and expanded in a book for which Terence Reese was the editor. The Bols Brilliancy Prizes were awarded from 1976-1986, after which the series of Bols Tip contests was resumed.

The IBPA's functions have embraced negotiations with tournament organizers to improve working conditions and accessibility of information to the press; closer cooperation with national and international bridge organizations; publication of anthologies, such as *Bridge Writers Choice* (1964 and 1968) and *Bols Tips*; establishment and presentation of annual awards for accomplishments in various fields of bridge; the dissemination of news bulletins to members and associate members, and the sponsorship of bridge promotions.

Officers 1992:

President....................................Tommy Sandsmark
Exec. Vice-President................Per Jannersten
Organizational. VP...................Alan Truscott
Chairman.................................Jean Besse
Treasurer & Bus. Manager........Evelyn Senn
Secretary...................................Stuart Staveley
    Rhu-Na-Bid, Shieldaig, Strathcarron
    Ross-shire, Scotland IV54 8XN.

Other posts are held by:
Counsel..................................... William Pencharz
Bulletin Editor..........................Patrick Jourdain
Executive Editor.......................David Rex-Taylor
Awards Secretary......................Dirk Schroeder
Sponsorship Chairman..............José Damiani

INTERNATIONAL BRIDGE PRESS ASSOCIATION AWARDS.

These are presented at the world championship in the year following the one for which the award is given.

Personality of the Year
(Charles H. Goren Award until 1989)

1973	André Lemaître
1974	Julius L. Rosenblum
1975	Rixi Markus
1976	Herman Filarski
1977	Jaime Ortiz-Patiño
1978	Edgar Kaplan
1979	Amalya L. Kearse
1980	Deng Xiaoping
1981	Albert Dormer
1982	Oswald Jacoby
1983	Easley Blackwood
1984	Barry Crane
1985	José Damiani
1986	Kathie Wei
1987	Helen Lemaître
1989	Not awarded.
1990	Eloene Griggs
1991	Evelyn Senn-Gorter
1992	Hugh Kelsey

Sportsman of the Year
(John E. Simon Award now in abeyance)

1973	Omar Sharif
1974	Alan Sontag
1975	Donald A. Oakie
1976	Lord Glenkinglas, Sir Timothy Kitson, Rt. Hon. Harold Lever MP
1977	Maurits Caransa
1979	Steve Landen
1985	Irving Litvack and Joe Silver

Best Article or Series on a System or Convention
(C.C. Wei "Precision" Award)

1973	Charles H. Goren
1974	Eric Kokish
1975	George Rosenkranz
1976	Jeff Rubens
1977	Kit Woolsey
1978	Jeff Rubens
1979	Ed Manfield and Kenneth Lebensold
1980	Eddie Kantar
1981	Jeff Rubens
1982	Ed Manfield
1983	Bruce Neill

1984	Sven-Olov Flodqvist & Anders Morath

Subsequently awarded for Best Defense

1985	Bob Hamman
1986	Michel Lebel
1987	Primo Levi
1988	Dung Duong
1989	Valdis Pilenieks
1990	Geir Helgemo
1991	Mike Passell
1992	Bob Hamman

Best Played Hand of the Year
(Charles J. Solomon Award)

1973	José le Dentu
1974	Benito Garozzo
1975	Tim Seres
1976	Harold Ogust
1977	Dominique Pilon
1978	Maurizio Sementa
1979	Benito Garozzo
1980	Andrzej Wilkosz
1981	Zia Mahmood
1982	Not awarded
1983	Not awarded
1984	Wan Li
1985	Henri Szwarc
1986	Jon Stoevneng
1987	Trond Rogne
1988	Kerri Shuman
1989	Miss Raczynska
1990	Schmuel Friedman
1991	Liz McGowan
1992	Peter Shaltz

Best Bid Hand of the Year
(George Rosenkranz "Romex" Award)

1975	Matt Granovetter, Ron Rubin
1976	Gabino Cintra, Christiano Fonseca
1977	Eric Kokish, Peter Nagy
1978	Chip Martel, Lew Stansby
1979	Kyle Larsen, Ron von der Porten
1980	Knud-Aage Boesgaard, Peter Schaltz
1981	Not Awarded
1982	Zia Mahmood, Masood Salim
1983	Benito Garozzo, Giorgio Belladonna
1984	Steve Cooper, Wayne Timms
1985	Hugh Ross, Peter Pender
1986	Zia Mahmood
1987	Allan Graves, George Mittelman
1988	Sven-Akke Bjerregard, Anders Morath
1989	Andy Robson, John Pottage
1990	Edgar Kaplan, Brian Glubok
1991	Valta and Juuri-Oja
1992	Tom Sanders, Bill Pollack

The four annual awards serve a number of useful purposes: To confer distinction upon outstanding personalities in the world of bridge; to recognize excellence in bridge and to improve the standard of bridge journalism; to gain publicity for IBPA and for bridge.

INTERNATIONAL CHAMPIONSHIPS. See INTERNATIONAL BRIDGE. Also see Appendices III, IV and V for results.

INTERNATIONAL CODE. The Laws of Rubber Bridge or of Duplicate Contract Bridge.

INTERNATIONAL FUND PAIRS. One-session pair events held at the Spring and Fall North American Championships. These are in addition to the International Fund ACBL-WIDE GAMES held in May and July. The proceeds are used to defray the expense of North American participation in Bermuda Bowl competition. For results see Appendix IV.

INTERNATIONAL MATCH. A contest between two (or more) countries. See ANGLO-AMERICAN MATCHES; FRANCO-AMERICAN MATCHES; INTERNATIONAL BRIDGE; WORLD CHAMPIONSHIPS. Also see Appendices III, IV and V for results.

INTERNATIONAL MATCHPOINTS. A method of scoring used frequently in team events, and occasionally in pair events.

The procedure appears to have been invented in Vienna, and was first used at the international level in the 1938 European Championship in Oslo. IMPs were first used in the 1951 Bermuda Bowl.

The original name was EMP, or European Match Points. The original scale provided for a maximum gain of 12 points, as follows:

Point Diff.	EMP	Point Diff.	EMP
10- 30	1	400-490	7
40- 60	2	500-590	8
70-100	3	600-740	9
110-180	4	750-1490	10
190-290	5	1500-1990	11
300-390	6	2000 and up	12

A revised scale was adopted for the 1948 European Championships in Copenhagen, with a maximum of 15 points. A further revision in 1961, devised by a subcommittee of the World Bridge Federation, brought the maximum to 25 points. This had the effect of increasing the relative award to large gains, and brought the scale slightly nearer to total-point scoring. A further revision was made effective September 1, 1962. That scale is still in use.

1948 Scale		1961 Scale	
Point Diff.	IMPs	Point Diff.	IMPs
0- 10	0	0-10	0
20-60	1	20-40	1
70-130	2	50-80	2
140-210	3	90-120	3
220-260	4	130-160	4
270-310	5	170-210	5
500-740	6	220-260	6
750-990	7	270-310	7
1000-1240	8	320-360	8
1250-1490	9	370-420	9
1500-1990	10	430-490	10
2000-2490	11	500-590	11
2500-2990	12	600-690	12
3000-3490	13	700-790	13
3500-3990	14	800-890	14
4000 and up	15	900-1040	15
		1050-1190	16
		1200-1340	17
		1350-1490	18
		1500-1740	19
		1750-1990	20
		2000-2240	21
		2250-2990	22
		2500-2990	23
		3000-3490	24
		3500 and up	25

1962 Scale			
Total Points	Imps	Total Points	Imps
20-40	1	750-990	13
50-80	2	990-1090	14
90-120	3	1100-1290	15
130-160	4	1300-1490	16
170-210	5	1500-1740	17
220-260	6	1750-1990	18
270-310	7	2000-2240	19
320-360	8	2250-2490	20
370-420	9	2500-2990	21
430-490	10	3000-2490	22
500-590	11	3500-3990	23
600-740	12	4000-up	24

The purpose of introducing International Matchpoints was to eliminate the inherent defects of other methods: total-point scoring accentuated one or two big swing boards; board-a-match reduced all boards to equal status. The general effect of the graduated scale of International Matchpoints is to flatten the value of high scores and to heighten the value of partscore contracts.

In team games, the International Matchpoints are awarded after the net score of the team (North-South and East-West) has been computed. The points are awarded to the team with a positive net score.

In pair events, each pair is compared with an average score, and the International Matchpoints awarded may be positive (for a score better than average) or negative (for a score below the average). The average score is the arithmetic mean of all scores, except that the best and worst scores are usually omitted in computing the comparison value.

The purpose of this is to prevent one unusual result from influencing scores at other tables. The best and worst scores, however, are used in computing the difference for those pairs from the average. The net IMP scores on each match may be converted into victory points on a graduated scale.

This use of IMP scoring in pair events was originated by the British Bridge League under the chairmanship of Geoffrey Butler. It is sometimes called the Butler Method.

The most logical use of International Matchpoint scoring in pair competition is in connection with qualifying events for pairs to compete in team events, as it adapts pair play to team scoring results. However, this method of scoring has been used successfully at the club level.

INTERNATIONAL OPEN TEAM SELECTION. Many methods have been tried for selection of the North American team for Bermuda Bowl contests or of the United States team for World Olympiads. No method has proved satisfactory, but the following have been tried:

1950-60 — Team Performance

From 1950 to 1960, the ACBL selected the winners of the SPINGOLD, or the victors in a play-off between the Spingold and VANDERBILT winners. This had the advantage of producing a well-knit team, but it sacrificed the theoretical objective of fielding the "best" team: it is unlikely that the best six players, or the best three pairs, will form themselves into a voluntary team.

In 1960 the United States was entitled, by virtue of the size of the ACBL membership, to send four teams to the first World Team Olympiad. Two of the teams sent were the winners of the Vanderbilt and the Spingold. Each of the other teams consisted of three pairs selected by a committee (the five most recent ACBL presidents attending the 1959 Fall Nationals) from among the contestants remaining in the seventh or eighth round of the Vanderbilt and Spingold respectively. The four teams were:

Spingold winners: Oswald Jacoby, Ira Rubin, Victor Mitchell, William Grieve, Morton Rubinow, Sam Stayman; Benjamin O. Johnson, npc.

Vanderbilt winners: John Crawford, Sidney Silodor, B.J. Becker, Norman Kay, Tobias Stone, George Rapee; Julius Rosenblum, npc.

Spingold 2: Charles Goren, Helen Sobel, Howard Schenken, Harold Ogust, Lewis Mathe, Paul Allinger; R.L. Miles Jr., npc.

Vanderbilt 2: Leonard Harmon, Sidney Lazard, William Hanna, Meyer Schleifer, Donald Oakie, Ivar Stakgold; Harry Fishbein, npc.

1961 — Direct Selection

The ACBL International Team for 1961 consisted of three pairs selected by the ACBL Board of Directors from among the winners and runners-up in major national events. The direct selection method suffers from the disadvantage that it is virtually impossible to find selectors who are: technically competent; objective and unattached to particular players; not themselves candidates for the team. Italy solved this problem by appointing Carlo Alberto Perroux as "dictator" in charge of selection, but most countries would not accept this solution, even if a Perroux were available.

1962-69 — Trials by Pairs

In an effort to be fair and just, and to select pairs that are in effective current form, pairs trials were instituted in 1961 for the selection of the 1962 Team. From 1961 to 1966, the first three pairs in each trial were nominated as the international team for the following year, and the fourth-place pair became the alternate pair. Beginning with the 1967 trials, this automatic selection method was dropped and the non-playing captain was permitted to select any two of the top four pairs, and the third and alternate pair from among the remaining finalists. Julius Rosenblum exercised this option in 1967 when he named Edgar Kaplan and Norman Kay, who had finished fourth in the trials, to the team and Philip Feldesman and Ira Rubin, the third-place pair, as alternates, the only time the top three pairs were not selected as the international team.

The scoring method used in the trials is that described under INTERNATIONAL MATCHPOINTS.

1961 (Houston)
1. Charles Coon, Eric Murray
2. G. Robert Nail, Mervin Key
3. Lewis Mathe, Ron von der Porten
4. Norman Kay, Sidney Silodor

1962 (Phoenix)
1. James Jacoby, G. Robert Nail
2. Robert Jordan, Arthur Robinson
3. Howard Schenken, Peter Leventritt
4. Gerald Michaud, David Carter

1963 (Miami)
1. Robert Hamman, Don Krauss
2. Sam Stayman, Victor Mitchell
3. Robert Jordan, Arthur Robinson
4. Lewis Mathe, Edward Taylor

1964 (Dallas)
1. Howard Schenken, Peter Leventritt

2. Ivan Erdos, Kelsey Patterson
3. B. Jay Becker, Dorothy Hayden
4. Robert Hamman, Don Krauss

1965 (San Francisco)
1. Philip Feldesman, Ira Rubin
2. Lewis Mathe, Robert Hamman
3. Eric Murray, Sami Kehela
4. B. Jay Becker, Dorothy Hayden

1966 (Pittsburgh)
1. Eric Murray, Sami Kehela
2. Edgar Kaplan, Norman Kay
3. Al Roth, William Root
4. B. Jay Becker, Dorothy Hayden

1967 (Atlantic City)
1. Robert Jordan, Arthur Robinson
2. Al Roth, William Root
3. Philip Feldesman, Ira Rubin
4. Edgar Kaplan, Norman Kay

1968 (Atlantic City)
1. George Rapée, Sidney Lazard
2. Billy Eisenberg, Bobby Goldman
3. Robert Hamman, Eddie Kantar
4. Ira Rubin, Jeff Westheimer

1970 — Vanderbilt-Spingold Playoff

The Pair-Team trials were discontinued in order to allow selection of an entire team rather than individual pairs to comprise a team. The 1970 International Team was selected by a direct 180-board playoff between the winners of the 1969 Vanderbilt and Spingold. However, this did not prove entirely satisfactory since it limited the number of teams that could challenge for international representation and reduced the prestige of the Fall North American Championships, which previously had two events that qualified pairs for the trials.

1971-72 — Placing-Points Playoffs

Beginning with the 1969 Fall NABC, the ACBL adopted a playoff among the teams with the best records over the course of a year. Teams placing high in the three major team championships (Reisinger, Vanderbilt, and Spingold) were awarded points according to the following scale:

Vanderbilt and Spingold: 1st — 10 points; 2nd — 4; 3rd — 2. Reisinger: 1st — 6 points; 2nd — 4; 3rd — 2.

If a team accumulated 20 points it was to be automatically designated the International Team; otherwise teams with lesser numbers of points were to play off.

1973 — Vanderbilt, Spingold, Reisinger, Grand Nationals Winners Playoff

With the introduction of the GRAND NATIONAL CHAMPIONSHIPS in 1972, the selection of the North American international team became a simple matter of a four-team playoff among the winners of the ACBL's four major team events: the Vanderbilt, Spingold, Reisinger, and Grand Nationals.

1980 — Vanderbilt, Spingold, Reisinger, Grand National, Canadian National Winners Playoff

At the request of the CANADIAN BRIDGE FEDERATION, that section of the Grand National Teams that involved Canadian players was separated from the main event and changed into a Canadian National Teams Championship. The Canadian champions became a fifth entry in the trials in those years when a Bermuda Bowl team was being chosen. The trials start with a round-robin, with one team being eliminated. The usual knockout format is used from that point on, with a carryover formula applied.

1983 — Tri-Country Trials

In 1983, Canada was taken out of the international team trials by vote of the ACBL Board of Directors. At the same time, it was determined that, for Bermuda Bowl competition, Zone II would select one representative from the United States and that a second representative from Zone II would be chosen from among Canada, Mexico and Bermuda. Thus was established the tri-country trials which was still in use in 1994.

1983 — United States Bridge Championship

From 1983, the Bermuda Bowl selection process was known as the United States Bridge Championship and consisted of a four-team playoff among the winning teams in the Vanderbilt, Spingold, Reisinger and Grand National Teams. The event was played as a straight knockout, with a semifinal and final. In years when one team won more than one qualifying event, the doubly qualified team had a bye to the final. Here's how it went over the years:

1983　Five teams played off in Minneapolis to determine the two ACBL teams for the Bermuda Bowl in Stockholm, Sweden. For the first time the top team in Zone II was to be seeded in an automatic berth in the semifinals. One U.S. team (Slaner) was eliminated in the round-robin and San Francisco and Canada lost in the semifinals. The U.S. Aces (Spingold winners) defeated Grand National in the final. Winners: U.S. I: Bob Hamman, Bobby Wolff, Alan Sontag, Peter Weichsel, Michael Becker, Ron Rubin, npc Joe Musumeci; U.S. II: Mike Passell, Jim Jacoby, Eric Rodwell, Jeff Meckstroth, George Rosenkranz, Eddie Wold, npc Jim Zimmerman.

1985　Three teams competed for the the right to start in the Bermuda Bowl semifinals in São Paulo, Brazil, at trials in Memphis. Spingold defeated Reisinger in the one semifinal match as doubly qualified San Francisco (who had won both the Vanderbilt and the Grand National) had a bye to the final. Canada was playing for first time in tri-country matches with Bermuda and Mexico to determine the second Zone II team. See TRI-COUNTRY TRIALS. San Francisco defeated Spingold by 5 IMPs over the 128-board final. The winners: Chip Martel, Lew Stansby, Hugh Ross, Peter Pender, Bobby Wolff, Bob Hamman, npc Alfred Sheinwold.

1987　The four-team trials were won by the defending world champions (Grand National) who defeated the Spingold winners in the semifinals while the Vanderbilt winners eliminated Reisinger. In the 128-board final Grand National beat Vanderbilt to become Zone II's primary representative in the Bermuda Bowl in Ocho Rios, Jamaica. The winners: Chip Martel, Lew Stansby, Peter Pender, Hugh Ross, Bob Hamman, Bobby Wolff, npc Dan Morse.

1988　The Trials, previously labeled International, North American or United States, were designated the United States Bridge Championships in 1988. Three teams were eligible to compete for the right to represent the U.S. in the 8th World Team Olympiad in Venice, Italy. The Texan Grand National team defeated Spingold in the only semifinal match as doubly qualified San Francisco (Reisinger and Vanderbilt) enjoyed a pass to the final. In the final Grand National defeated San Francisco by 16 IMPs. The U.S. team: Seymon Deutsch, Jim Jacoby, Bob Hamman, Bobby Wolff, Jeff Meckstroth, Eric Rodwell, npc Dan Morse.

1989　Four teams competed for the right to compete in the Bermuda Bowl in Perth, Australia. Grand National defeated Spingold in one semifinal while Reisinger elimi-

nated Vanderbilt in the other. Grand National defeated Reisinger in the 128-board final. The winners: Chip Martel, Lew Stansby, Peter Pender, Hugh Ross, Mike Lawrence, Kit Woolsey, npc Dan Morse.

1991　Three ACBL teams were authorized as Zone II representatives for the NEC Bermuda Bowl in Yokohama, Japan. They were to be winner of the USBC, the winner of the tri-country trials and the top three pairs from the Pan North American Bridge Championships (PNABC). Twenty pairs qualified in specific NABC and certain regional IMP pair events for the PNABC, with the top three pairs making up the third Zone II team. The PNABC was held in Memphis alongside the USBC and NAWBTC. The winners constituted the youngest ACBL representatives in world championships since 1954. In the USBC, Grand National defeated Spingold in the semifinals while Vanderbilt eliminated Reisinger. In the final GNT defeated Vanderbilt 268-174. U.S.I (USBC): Bernard Miller, Alan Sontag, Robert Barr, Harold Stengel, Jeff Meckstroth, Eric Rodwell, npc Bob Rosen. U.S.II (PNABC): Steve Weinstein, Fred Stewart, Bart Bramley, Mark Feldman, Jeff Ferro, Alex Ornstein.

1992　In the battle for the U.S. World Team Olympiad berth in Salsomaggiore, Italy, the Spingold team (with five of the winners from Venice in 1988) defeated Grand National in the semifinal as Reisinger defeated Vanderbilt. In the final Spingold won by 3 IMPs. The U.S. team: Seymon Deutsch, Michael Rosenberg, Bob Hamman, Bobby Wolff, Jeff Meckstroth, Eric Rodwell, npc Dan Morse.

1993　The USBC was held in Memphis to select the Zone II representatives to the NEC Bermuda Bowl in Santiago, Chile. U.S.I: Russ Ekeblad, Ron Sukoneck, Bobby Levin, Peter Weichsel, Mike Becker, Ron Rubin, npc Jeff Wolfson. U.S.II: Larry Cohen, Dave Berkowitz, Eric Rodwell, Marty Bergen, Cliff Russell, Sam Lev, npc Bob Rosen.

1994 — International Team Trials

In 1994, the ACBL Board of Directors approved establishment of the International Team Trials Commission. The commission was to oversee a competition in early 1995 to select two teams to represent Zone II in the 1995 NEC Bermuda Bowl in Beijing, China. A third team would still be selected in the tri-country playoff involving Canada, Mexico and Bermuda.

Under the ITT Commission, the international team trials would be open to as many as 30 or 40 teams and would last for more than a week. The commission and new format were the brainchild of Bobby Wolff, World Bridge Federation president during 1993 and 1994. Wolff's idea was to expand the trials field beyond the usual so as to give more teams the chance to play in top-flight competition, a necessity for success at the world level.

The idea was not universally accepted, so there was some question whether the new trials format would endure beyond the initial competition in 1995. See also BERMUDA BOWL, WORLD TEAM OLYMPIAD. For results see Appendix III.

INTERNATIONAL POPULAR BRIDGE MONTHLY.
A magazine published in Great Britain dealing with bridge happenings around the world with emphasis on Great Britain. Editor: Tony Sowter. Address: Probray Press Ltd., 455 Alfreton Road, Nottingham, NG& 5LX England.

INTERNATIONAL WOMEN'S TEAM SELEC-
TION. The United States has sent women's teams to each of the World Women's Team Olympiads, each selected by a different method. For the 1960 event, a committee consisting of the five most recent ACBL presidents attending the 1959 Fall Nationals selected the team by choosing three pairs of women who finished first or second in any national championship event during 1959.

For 1964, a trial by pairs was held, similar to the trials held during that period for the INTERNATIONAL OPEN TEAM SELECTION. For 1968 a round-robin was held, for which four pairs qualified. Each pair played a 32-board match in partnership with each of the other pairs, and npc Margaret Wagar was empowered to select any three of the four pairs.

For 1972, women's teams were to earn points in the major national team championships and play off to determine the 1972 U.S. women's team. However, one team amassed so many points that it was designated without a playoff. The following were the U.S. women's teams in the first four Olympiads:

1960	1964
Agnes Gordon	Agnes Gordon
Dorothy Hayden	Muriel Kaplan
Malvine Klausner	Alicia Kempner
Helen Portugal	Helen Portugal
Sylvia Schwartz	Stella Rebner
Jo Sharp	Jan Stone
Charles J. Solomon (npc)	Paul Hodge (npc)
1968	1972
Hermine Baron	Mary Jane Farell
Nancy Gruver	Emma Jean Hawes
Emma Jean Hawes	Marilyn Johnson
Dorothy Hayden	Jacqui Mitchell
Suzanne Sachs	Peggy Solomon
Rhoda Walsh	Dorothy Hayden Truscott
Margaret Wagar (npc)	Margaret Wagar (npc)

For 1976, women were permitted to earn "selection points," either as teams or as pairs, on all-women teams in the Vanderbilt, Spingold, Reisinger, and Spring National Women's Team events. Available points ranged from 1 point for being runner-up in the Spring Women's teams to 28 for winning the Vanderbilt or Spingold. To be selected intact, a team must have won more qualification points than any individual pair, except that if there were only one higher pair, a four-person team plus the high-ranking pair would form the six-member team. After 1981 the WBF scheduled Venice Cup contests for odd-numbered years opposite the Bermuda Bowl. After skipping 1983 the new plan took effect beginning in 1985.

The selection of women's teams by qualification points was discontinued in 1989, and the North American Women's Bridge Team Championships (NAWBTC) were inaugurated. The 1989 winning team gained a bye to the Venice Cup semifinals in Perth, Australia, while the second-place team (Canada) had to compete in round-robin qualifications.

In 1991, three ACBL teams were selected for Yokohama, Japan — first and second in the U.S. Women's Trials and Canada, who won the playoff with Mexico for the third Zone II spot.

In 1992 the United States Women's Bridge Championships (USWBC) were held to select a team for the NEC World Team Olympiad in Salsomaggiore, Italy.

Zone II once again had three representatives for the Venice Cup in Santiago, Chile, in 1993. All of the trials through 1993 were played in Memphis. There was no women's team trials in 1994.

Automatic qualifiers for the women's trials include the reigning NEC Venice Cup champions, if the team is intact at the time of the trials; first and second in the Women's Knockout Teams; first in the Women's Swiss Teams; first in the Women's Board-a-Match Teams; any all-woman team reaching the semifinals of the Vanderbilt Knockout Teams or Spingold Knockout Teams; any all-woman team finishing first through fourth in the Reisinger Board-a-Match Teams. See also VENICE CUP, WOMEN'S TEAM OLYMPIAD. For results see Appendix III.

INTERVENING BID. An overcall.

INTERWOVEN HOWELL. Two Howell games of equal size, so arranged that each plays (at each round) the boards which are not in play in the other.

Since a Howell game of x tables requires 2x - 1 sets of boards, x - 1 sets are out of play at a given time. By proper arrangement these boards may be used in a parallel or "interwoven" Howell game; except that there must be one pair of relay tables at which the same set of boards is in play simultaneously in both games.

INTRA-FINESSE. A term introduced by Gabriel Chagas in a Bols Tip to describe certain finessing situation that call for successive finesses against both opponents. An example is:

$$♠A93$$
$$♠102 \qquad ♠QJ75$$
$$♠K864$$

A finesse of the nine loses to the jack or queen, and the declarer later cashes the ace and finesses against East's remaining honor.

INVERTED MINOR RAISES. A treatment, devised as part of the Kaplan-Sheinwold system, which became very popular with tournament players in the 80s. A single raise of opener's minor is strong and forcing, with at least 10 high-card points in principle, and a double raise is weak and obstructive. The combination affords more room for investigation on strong hands and has a preemptive effect on the weak ones.

$$♠A84$$
$$♥K4$$
$$♦643$$
$$♣KJ952$$

Raise 1♣ to 2♣. The bidding usually continues to game, but, barring special agreements, 2NT or 3♣ by either player may end the bidding. A bid of a new suit by opener is generally a probe aiming at 3NT.

$$♠K64$$
$$♥65$$
$$♦84$$
$$♣J96432$$

Raise 1♣ to 3♣. This is a minimum, and some players would expect slightly more.

$$♠52$$
$$♥A74$$
$$♦J853$$
$$♣K1053$$

After a 1♦ opening, this hand is unsuitable for a raise to two or three. 1NT is the least evil.

If the opponents intervene, the inverted meaning is abandoned and raises (1♦ 1♠ 2♦/3♦) are standard.

INVITATION, INVITATIONAL BID. A bid which encourages the bidder's partner to continue to game or slam, but gives him the option of passing if he has no reserve values in terms of high-card strength or distribution. The bidder announces that he can count about 23-24 points in the combined hands (including distribution).

In nearly all cases such bids are one level below the game or slam which is being suggested, so bids of 2 NT or three of a major suit often come in this category.

WEST	EAST	or	WEST	EAST
1 NT	2 NT		1 ♥	2 ♣
			2 ♥	2 NT

but a jump by responder (response or rebid) may be an exception, being forcing in traditional methods but invitational in a modern style.

A jump rebid by the opener is invitational:

WEST	EAST
1 ♥	1 ♠
3 ♥	

and so is a single raise from two to three in the later stages of the auction:

WEST	EAST	or	WEST	EAST
1 ♥	1 ♠		1 ♠	1 NT
2 ♥	3 ♥		2 ♥	3 ♥

For other sequences which are invitational in some styles but forcing in others, see JUMP REBIDS BY RESPONDER. See also conventions listed in GAME INVITATION.

INVITATIONAL PAIRS CHAMPIONSHIP. An invitational pair event that until January 1981 was sponsored by the *London Sunday Times* and called LONDON SUNDAY TIMES PAIRS. The field is usually limited to 16-22 leading pairs from many countries. See Appendix IV for results.

IRELAND, CONTRACT BRIDGE ASSOCIATION OF. The Association was founded in 1932 in Dublin to control the game in the Republic of Eire, the 26 southern counties of Ireland. In 1992 there were about 21,000 members organized through 445 clubs. The organization hosted the European Championships in 1967 and 1991. For international participation, see IRISH BRIDGE UNION. See also NORTHERN IRELAND BRIDGE UNION.

Officers 1993:
President: Graham Laird
General Secretary: Paul Porteous
41 Gledswood Avenue,
Clonskeagh, Dublin 14, Ireland.

IRISH BRIDGE UNION. Founded in 1955, the union consists of representatives from both the CONTRACT BRIDGE ASSOCIATION OF IRELAND and NORTH OF IRELAND BRIDGE UNION. It is responsible for selecting teams to represent the whole of Ireland in World Olympiads and European Championships (but not for CAMROSE TROPHY matches), and for organizing All-Ireland events for Teams-of-Four and Pairs. Membership, comprising the total of both integral bodies, was 3193 in 1993.
1992 Officers:

President: J.A. Hill
Joint Secretaries: Marie Gleeson
17 Beech Park, Athlone, Co. Westmeath, Ireland.
Tel. 0903 75549.
William M. Kelso, 9, Upper Malone Road. Belfast, Northern Ireland.
Tel.: Belfast 668279.

IRON DUKE, NOT THROUGH THE. An expression indicating that the user holds a very strong hand. The remark is an improper one, and is usually made when the player splits cards of equal value to prevent a finesse.

IRREGULAR LEAD. A calculated departure from normal procedure occurring in the play of the first card to any trick by a defender.

IRREGULAR RAINBOW. The regular RAINBOW MOVEMENT exists only for 5,7,11,13,17, etc. tables. For 8 and 9 tables H. Shomate constructed irregular variants. They were presented with stationary boards and completely irregular player progressions. They have been reorganized, however, so that, with one exception, the players and the board sets move regularly. They are therefore easily conducted with table guidecards. A similar 16-table Irregular Rainbow exists and one for 12 tables was constructed by P. Smith.

For 10 tables Shomate showed how to add 4 appendix players to his 9-table movement. Reorganized, this gives a smooth movement for 10 tables in 10 rounds.

Here are the starting assignments for the eight-table Irregular Rainbow.

	Table 1						Table 2				
Rd	N	S	E	W	b	N	S	E	W	b	
1	1	9	17	25	1	2	10	18	26	2	
2	8	14	23	27	1	4	11	21	30	2	
3	8	15	17	28	2	5	12	22	31	3	
4	8	9	18	29	3	6	13	23	25	4	
5	8	10	19	30	4	7	14	17	26	5	
6	8	11	20	31	5	1	15	18	27	6	
7	8	12	21	25	6	2	9	19	28	7	
8	8	13	22	26	7	3	10	20	29	1	

	Table 3						Table 4				
Rd	N	S	E	W	b	N	S	E	W	b	
1	3	11	19	27	3	4	12	20	28	4	
2	7	10	24	25	3	2	15	22	29	4	
3	1	11	24	26	4	3	9	23	30	5	
4	2	12	24	27	5	4	10	17	31	6	
5	3	13	24	28	6	5	11	18	25	7	
6	4	14	24	29	7	6	12	19	26	1	
7	5	15	24	30	1	7	13	20	27	2	
8	6	9	24	31	2	1	14	21	28	3	

	Table 5						Table 6				
Rd	N	S	E	W	b	N	S	E	W	b	
1	5	13	21	29	5	6	14	22	30	6	
2	6	16	18	28	5	5	9	20	26	6	
3	7	16	19	29	6	6	10	21	27	7	
4	1	16	20	30	7	7	11	22	28	1	
5	2	16	21	31	1	1	12	23	29	2	
6	3	16	22	25	2	2	13	17	30	3	
7	4	16	23	26	3	3	14	18	31	4	
8	5	16	17	27	4	4	15	19	25	5	

	Table 7					Table 8			
Rd	N	S	E	W	b	N	S	E	W	b
1	7	15	23	31	7	8	16	24	32	8
2	3	12	17	32	7	1	13	19	31	8
3	4	13	18	32	1	2	14	20	25	8
4	5	14	19	32	2	3	15	21	26	8
5	6	15	20	32	3	4	9	22	27	8
6	7	9	21	32	4	5	10	23	28	8
7	1	10	22	32	5	6	11	17	29	8
8	2	11	23	32	6	7	12	18	30	8

Note that the movement is regular except for the first round. From round 2 players 8, 16, 24, and 32 are stationary, as are the boards at table 8.

IRREGULARITY. A deviation from correct procedures set forth in the LAWS and PROPRIETIES.

ISOLATING THE MENACE. A maneuver in squeeze-play technique. A menace may be controlled by both opponents, in which case it is usually advantageous to have the full burden of guarding that suit imposed on one opponent. The term "isolating the menace" refers to declarer's efforts in that direction: he seeks to have the menace isolated so that it is protected by only one opponent.

$$
\begin{array}{ccc}
 & A K x x & \\
Q J x x & & 10 x x \\
 & x x &
\end{array}
$$

If the diagram illustrates the distribution of a side suit at a trump contract, then North's menace can be isolated by playing off the ace and king followed by a ruff on the third round. At any contract a first-round duck would ensure that the menace was isolated.

ISRAEL BRIDGE FEDERATION. The Federation was founded in 1940 as the Palestine Bridge Federation, and its present name was adopted in 1948. It had more than 6,000 members in 1993, in more than 40 branches. It hosted the 1974 European Championships in Herzlia and the 1980 European Team Championship in Tel Aviv. Israel teams have twice been second in the European Championships, and placed third in the 1985 Bermuda Bowl. The Federation sponsors an International Bridge Festival, held in Tel Aviv in February annually since 1966. Officers 1992:
President: David Bardach (now deceased)
General Manager: Zvi Ben Tovim
P.O. Box 9671, Haifa, Israel 31096.
Tel: 972 4 335333
FAX: 972 4 336343.

ITALIAN BRIDGE FEDERATION (FEDERAZIONE ITALIANA BRIDGE). Founded in 1936 by Paolo Baroni, Federico Rosa, and E. Pontremoli. Reactivated after World War II, with Carl'Alberto Perroux as president, and became an official body organizing regular national events. By 1993 there were more than 20,000 members in 250 affiliated bodies and 300 clubs. More than 15 national championships involving 8,000-9,000 players are organized annually, including Open, Women's and Mixed Teams and Pairs. The Knockout Team contest for the Italian Cup attracts more than 600 teams.

The record of the Italian BLUE TEAM is an extraordinary one that is unlikely to be equaled. The first Italian team to compete in the European Championships in 1938 was the predecessor of the invincibles who became European champions 1951, 1956, 1957, 1958, 1959, 1965, 1967, 1969, 1971, 1973, 1975, 1976, 1979 and 16 times World Champions (Bermuda Bowl 10 times from 1957-69, 1973-75, and World Olympiad winners 1964, 1968, 1972).

The F.I.B. has been host to eight world championships, second only to the United States, from Naples in 1951 to Salsomaggiore in 1992.
Officers, 1992:
President, Gianarrigo Rona
Secretary Romano Grazioli
Via Orti 3,
20122 Milano, Italy
Tel: 39 2 546 1643
Fax: 39 2 5518 1823

ITALIAN SYSTEMS. See BLUE TEAM CLUB; LEGHORN DIAMOND; LITTLE ROMAN CLUB; MARMIC SYSTEM; ROMAN SYSTEM; SUPER PRECISION.

J

JACK. The fourth ranking card in a suit. Also called knave. See COAT CARDS; COURT CARDS; VALET.

JACK, TEN, OR NINE SHOWING ZERO OR TWO HIGHER HONORS. See ZERO OR TWO HIGHER LEADS.

JACKPOT. Extra money beyond the entry fee collected from players for special prize purposes. Usually the pair or team taking part in the jackpot that places highest collects the jackpot money.

JACOBY INDIVIDUAL MOVEMENT. See RAINBOW INDIVIDUAL MOVEMENT.

JACOBY TRANSFER BIDS. Used in responding at the two-level to 1NT opening bids, or in responding at the three-level to 2NT openings. These transfers were introduced to the American bridge public by Oswald Jacoby in a *Bridge World* article in 1956, although they had been used in Sweden as early as 1953-54 as a result of a series of articles in *Bridge Tidningen* written by Olle Willner. 2♦ shows hearts and asks opener to bid 2♥. 2♥ shows spades, and asks opener to bid 2♠. This convention greatly increases the chance that the strong hand will be the declarer in a suit contract. It also solves the problems created by many hands of intermediate strength:

(a)	(b)
♠ Q 10 8 7 6 4	♠ 8
♥ K 6 3	♥ A 10 9 5 4
♦ 4 3	♦ 10 5
♣ 7 5	♣ K Q 10 5 3

On hand (a) the response is 2 ♥, and the rebid of 2♠ is raised to 3 ♠. This is a game invitation which the opener can pass if he wishes.

On hand (b) the response of 2♦ shows the heart suit, and responder continues with 3♣. This shows his two-suited hand, and leaves the next move to the opener. 3♣ is forcing, but might be made on a slightly weaker hand.

There are methods for extending transfers to the minor suits. See FOUR-SUIT TRANSFER BIDS and MINOR

SUIT STAYMAN.

If the bidding begins

Opener	Responder
1NT	2 ♥
2 ♠	

The normal rebid structure for responder is:

(1) Pass with no game prospects.

(2) 2NT, natural, invitational, balanced.

(3) 3♣ or 3♦, natural, forcing, possible slam interest.

(4) 3♥ at least 5-5 in the majors, game forcing.

(5) 3♠ invitational, 6-card suit.

(6) 3NT balanced, offering a choice of games.

(7) 4♠ sign-off, 6-card suit. (But a slam invitation if four-level responses are transfers.)

(8) 4NT. Natural slam invitation, balanced.

Rebids are similar after a transfer to hearts, but the sequence 1NT — 2♦ — 2♥ — 2♠ needs discussion.See PREACCEPTANCE.

JACOBY TWO NOTRUMP RESPONSE. A method of increasing slam-bidding accuracy, developed by Oswald Jacoby and used in conjunction with limit major-suit raises.

After a 1♥ or 1♠ opening, a jump response to 2NT by an unpassed hand is a forcing raise of opener's suit. Responder promises at least four trumps and suggests balanced distribution, but his strength is in theory unlimited. Opener rebids conventionally to clarify his strength and pattern:

New suit at the three level = singleton or void in the suit.

New suit at the four level = five-card suit.

Game in agreed trump suit = minimum hand, no slam interest.

Three of agreed trump suit = 16 or more points, slam interest.

3NT – sound opening, 14-15 points, no singleton or void.

Although many pairs use this schedule of rebids, variations are possible, especially in the meaning of the 3NT rebid.

Some structure is desirable when the opener shows a short suit, since his hand has a wide range. One possibility is to use a relay, the next available bid as a strength inquiry with the following rebids: First step: minimum with a singleton; Second step: maximum with a singleton; Third step: minimum with a void; Fourth step: maximum with a void.

An alternative, more complex, rebid structure:

3♣ = non-minimum, with a singleton or 5332.

3♦ = non-minimum, any 5422.

3♥ = unspecified void, any strength.

3♠ = minimum with a singleton.

3NT = non-minimum 6322 or 7222.

4 of lower-ranking suit = limited 5-5, good second suit.

4 of original major = minimum, no shortness.

After responses below 3NT, relay inquires further. Then one step shows club shortness, two steps diamond shortness, three steps other major shortness. (Except after 3♦ rebid, when the side length is shown similarly). After 3♣ rebid and 3♦ relay, 4♣ , 4♦ and 4♥ show doubletons in 5332 hands. This gives more distributional accuracy, but less definition of the strength of one-suited hands.

JAMAICA BRIDGE ASSOCIATION. The Association was founded in Kingston in 1944, and in 1993 had a memberships of 72 with eight affiliated clubs. Jamaica hosted the 1987 world championships in Ocho Rios. It hosted the CAC Championships in 1972 and 1982, and represented the zone in the 1983 Bermuda Bowl.

Officers 1992:

President: Noelle Chutkan

Secretary: Els Witte c/o Liguanea Club

Knutsford Boulevard , Kingston 5 Jamaica W.I.

Suite #18, 22

Trafalgar Road, Kingston 10, Jamaica.

Tel: (809) 967 0140

Fax: (809) 924 9120

JAPAN CONTRACT BRIDGE LEAGUE. Founded in Tokyo in 1953 with 11 members, by 1993 the membership had grown to more than 4,951 in 110 affiliated clubs, with branches in Osaka, Nagoya and Sapporo. Hosted 1991 Bermuda Bowl and Venice Cup in Yokohama, and the Far East Championships in 1958, 1964 and 1979. Hosted three Epson international tournaments 1983-4-5.

Officers 1992:

President: Kensuke Yanagiya

Secretary-General: Tetsuji Hikawa

Address: Room #101, Th-Samon-cho Bldg., 14 Samon-cho, Shinjuku-ku, Tokyo 160, Japan.

Telephone: 81-3-3357-3741

Fax: 81-3-3357-7444

JETTISON. The discard of a high-ranking honor, usually an ace or a king. The term was originated in England by A.E.Whitelaw in 1921. A typical example is the following:

```
              A 10 8 6 4 3
    Q 2                  J 9 5
              K 7
```

In a notrump contract, South leads the king in a position in which East needs an entry. West must drop the queen, for otherwise South will allow the queen to hold on the next round.

The play may be necessary to effect an unblock, to create an entry or to avert a ruff. See also ENTRY SQUEEZE.

JETTISON SQUEEZE. A form of ENTRY SQUEEZE.

JOKER. A fifty third card in decks of cards, sometimes used as a substitute or "wild" card, but not used in bridge. See TAROT.

JORDAN. See RESPONSES OVER OPPONENT'S TAKEOUT DOUBLE and 2NT RESPONSE (Over opponent's takeout double).

JORDANIAN BRIDGE ASSOCIATION.

Secretary: Ghassan Ghanem

PO Box 922498

Amman, Jordan.

JOSEPHINE. The GRAND SLAM FORCE, associated in Europe with the name of Josephine Culbertson, and therefore named after her. (Mrs. Culbertson was the first to write about the convention; it was devised by her husband, Ely Culbertson.)

JOURNALIST LEADS. A method of opening leads advocated by the *Bridge Journal* in 1964-1965. The details are as follows:

Against notrump contracts:

A, usually, from A-K-J-x (x-x) or A-K-10-x-(x-x). Third hand is requested to unblock a high honor if he can afford it, otherwise to give a length signal (high with an even number, low with an odd number of cards in the suit).

K from A-K or K-Q (assuming a high honor should be led).

Q from Q-J (or K-Q-10-9; third hand is requested to play the jack if he has it).

J from J-10. The jack denies a higher honor.

10 from A-10-9, K-10-9, Q-10-9, A-J-10, K-J-10. The 10 guarantees a higher honor (Q, K or A).

9 from 10-9. The 9 promises the 10 and no higher honor.

Second highest or highest from lower spot cards to discourage suit continuation.

Usually lowest card from a long suit headed by one or two honors to encourage suit continuation. The purpose of these leads is to make it easier for third hand to know whether to continue the attack on the suit led or to shift. The following hand shows what can happen when Journalist leads are not used.

Dir: North

		♠ A J 10 6 3	
Vul: Both		♥ 5	
Imps		♦ 7 4	
		♣ A K 10 7 2	

			♠ Q 9 5 2
			♥ Q J 10 4
			♦ A 6 3
			♣ Q 5

WEST	NORTH	EAST	SOUTH
	1 ♣	Pass	1 ♥
Pass	1 ♠	Pass	3 NT
All Pass			

Using standard leads, West led the ♦10 to East's ace, South playing the 2. Now if South started with a hand like: ♠K-x ♥A-K-x-x-x ♦Q-J-2 ♣x-x-x, East must continue diamonds. But if the 10 was West's highest diamond, a heart shift is called for.

East actually continued diamonds and found South with: ♠K-x ♥K-x-x-x ♦K-Q-J-x ♣ J-x-x. Declarer won the diamond, cashed ♣A-K (because he could hardly afford to lose a finesse to East and get a heart through) and made 10 tricks.

Using Journalist leads, West would have led the ♦9, and East would have shifted to a heart, defeating the contract.

Against suit contracts Journalist Leads follow a different pattern. From two touching honors the second highest is led; from spot cards the highest card below the 9 may be led to indicate a weak holding; otherwise, the third highest is led from an even number of cards or the lowest from an odd number of cards.

JUMP BID. A call of more than is necessary to raise the previous bid and made at any point after the auction has been opened. Bids of two or more than necessary are termed double jumps, etc. SKIP BID is a more general term, embracing jumps to any level.

JUMP CUEBID. A bid of a suit originally called by an opponent, but made at a higher level than necessary.

A jump cuebid is an unusual action, but modern bid-

known instance is the jump cuebid in response to a simple overcall:

WEST	NORTH	EAST	SOUTH
1 ♦	1 ♠	Pass	3 ♦

In most partnerships, South promises game-invitational values with spade support and a distributional hand; he has a hand suitable for a limit raise of an opening bid. South may hold:

♠ K J 6 4
♥ A J 5 2
♦ 9 7 5 2
♣ 2

Another instance is a jump cuebid of an opposing opening bid:

WEST	NORTH	EAST	SOUTH
		1 ♠	3 ♠

South promises a long, solid minor suit and asks North to bid 3NT if he can stop the spades. South may hold:

♠ 8
♥ Q 4
♦ A 10 5
♣ A K Q 9 8 5 3

Other partnerships use a jump cuebid to show specified two- suited hands.

In some circumstances, a jump cuebid may be a SPLINTER RESPONSE.

WEST	NORTH	EAST	SOUTH
1 ♦	1 ♠	Pass	4 ♦

or

WEST	NORTH	EAST	SOUTH
	1 ♠	2 ♦	4 ♦

South has a strong hand with an excellent spade fit and a singleton or void in diamonds. Slam is possible. South may hold:

♠ K 9 7 4 2
♥ K J 7 3
♦ —
♣ A J 7 3

JUMP OVERCALL. A suit overcall at a level one higher than necessary:

SOUTH	WEST		SOUTH	WEST
1 ♦	2 ♠	or	1 ♠	3 ♦

Three types are in common use, all based on good six-card suits, rarely longer.

(1) WEAK JUMP OVERCALL. A hand roughly equivalent to a weak-two opening, normally in the 6-10 point range, below the strength for a normal overcall. The strength requirement declines as vulnerability becomes more favorable.

(2) INTERMEDIATE JUMP OVERCALL. A hand about equivalent to a minimum opening.

(3) STRONG JUMP OVERCALL. A hand worth an opening bid followed by a jump.

The weak jump overcall, also called a preemptive jump overcall, is by far the most popular choice in North America. The intermediate jump has little to recommend it theoretically, since it deals with hands that can make a normal overcall.

Suit responses to all jumps are forcing. A 2NT response can, by agreement, ask for OGUST rebids.

See also separate entries, GHESTEM and ROMAN JUMP OVERCALL.

JUMP PREFERENCE. Returning to partner's original suit at a level one higher than necessary.

WEST	EAST
1 ♥	1 ♠ or 2 ♣ or 1 NT
2 ♦	3 ♥

See JUMP REBIDS BY RESPONDER.

If the opener gives jump preference, it is normally non-forcing:

WEST	EAST
1 ♣	1 ♥
2 ♣	2 ♦
3 ♥	

JUMP RAISE. See DOUBLE RAISE.

JUMP RAISE IN RESPONDER'S SUIT. See OPENER'S REBID.

JUMP REBID BY OPENER. See OPENER'S REBID.

JUMP REBIDS BY RESPONDER. These are jump bids short of game by responder at his second turn. The meanings of such bids vary widely. In traditional STANDARD AMERICAN all such jump bids were considered forcing, whether or not responder rebids his own suit, supports partner's suit or names a new suit. In the modern style all such secondary jumps are non-forcing unless they are in a new suit. Some players treat some as forcing and some as non-forcing. Partnership discussion is essential. See table below.

JUMP SHIFT. A new suit response at a level one higher than necessary:

WEST	EAST		WEST	EAST
1 ♥	2 ♠	or	1 ♥	3 ♣

In standard methods this shows a hand of great strength which can almost guarantee a slam (19 points or more including distribution). The hand is usually one of four types: a good fit with opener's suit; a strong single-suiter; a strong two-suiter; or a balanced hand with more than 18 points. However, the last type is not easy to handle with a jump shift, and an alternative method is described under IMPOSSIBLE BIDS.

Many experts have less elevated standards for a jump shift, making the bid with about 17 points including distribution; in ACOL, 16 points or less with a good fit or a good suit. In this last case the response may be made in a three-card suit, either because the hand is balanced or because there is a fit with opener but no side suit.

A theory advanced by Paul Soloway that is gaining adherence among experts is that jump shifts should be limited to three types of hands: (1) one-suiters, (2) semi-balanced hands, and (3) hands with a good fit for opener's suit. Responder clarifies his hand by his rebid. If he has a one-suited hand he rebids his suit. If he has a semi-balanced hand his next bid is in notrump. If he has a good fit for opener, he can have made a FRAGMENT bid in a new suit to show a singleton in the fourth suit, or he can return to opener's suit to deny having a singleton. This method of showing a singleton and support for opener's suit is workable only if it is agreed that the jump shift cannot be made with a two-suited hand; under this agreement responder's bid of a new suit at his second turn cannot show a real suit.

JUMP REBIDS BY RESPONDER		
2 NT	*Forcing Style*	*Non-forcing Style*
1 ♣ - 1 ♥	13-15	11-12. A 13-15 hand bids 3NT, or makes a fourth-suit bid.
1 ♠ - 2 NT	(An 11-12 point hand remains a problem)	
Jump Preference		
1 ♣ - 1 ♥	13 or more.	11-12; perhaps only three-card support if used
1 ♠ - 3 ♣		in combination with limit raises.
1 ♠ - 2 ♣	13 or more. Probably three-card support,	11-12; three-card support. But if 2 ♣ is a virtual
2 ♥ - 3 ♠	because of the failure to bid 3 ♠ originally.	game force, the range is 12+; the spades are strong.
1 ♦ - 1 ♠	12+, 6-card or longer	10-12; six-card suit
1 NT - 3 ♥	suit, forcing.	
1 ♥ - 1 ♠	12+, usually 3-card support	10-12; 3-card support
1 NT - 3 ♥		
1 ♦ - 1 ♠	12+, 4-card support or longer	10-12, probably four-card or longer support.
1 NT - 3 ♦		
Jump Raise		
1 ♣ - 1 ♥	13-15, 4-card support	10-12 and four-card support. A stronger hand
1 ♠ - 3 ♠		bids 4 ♠, or bids the fourth suit followed by 4 ♣ as a mild slam suggestion.
Jump Rebid		
1 ♣ - 1 ♥	Games values and a	10-11 and a six-card suit.
1 ♠ - 3 ♥	six-card suit	
Jump Shift		
1 ♣ - 1 ♥	No standard meaning in either method. Possible agreements are	
1 ♠ - 3 ♦	(a) 5-5 invitational; (b) 5-5 forcing; (c) splinter; (d) mini-splinter.	

Another use proposed by Albert Morehead called for a jump shift with a hand well-provided with controls but lacking suit substance, suggesting that the opening bidder, with a suitable hands, should use Blackwood.

Perhaps the most unusual treatment of the jump shift is that used by William Passell and David Strasberg. Their idea is that a jump shift shows a solid suit in the next higher-ranking suit, opener's suit excepted. For example, after a 1♣ opening, a jump to 2♥ shows a solid spade suit. Opener normally accepts the transfer, which permits responder to cuebid his other controls. If responder is unable to cuebid, he supports the agreed suit, and a subsequent bid of 4NT by opener is not Blackwood, but asks about the length of responder's suit.

Rebids by the opener after a jump shift are not standardized, but the opener should usually make the rebid he was planning after a non-jump response, only, of course, one level higher. There are two exceptions to this principle: a non-jump rebid of 3 NT would not promise extra values, nor would a reverse.

This idea was originated by Ely Culbertson, who called it "jump takeout" or "forcing takeout".

For a preemptive use of this response, see WEAK JUMP SHIFT RESPONSES. See also PASSED HAND.

JUMP SHIFT REBID. See OPENER'S REBID.

JUMP SHIFT TO 3♣. In order to keep the forcing raise at as low a level as possible, while reserving the jump to 2 NT for notrump-type hands, some partnerships use a jump shift to 3♣ as a forcing major suit raise. The jump says nothing about the responder's clubs. Opener rebids 3 ♦ if he has a singleton or a void. Without a singleton or void, opener should rebid as follows to describe his trump holding:

3 ♥ shows two of the top three trump honors.
3 ♠ shows one of the top three trump honors.
3 NT shows none of the top three trump honors.

JUMP TAKEOUT. See JUMP SHIFT.

JUMP TO GAME IN MAJOR SUIT. See OPENER'S REBID for jump to game in responder's major suit or in opener's major suit. See also TRIPLE RAISE.

JUNIOR. In international competition, a player under the age of 25.

JUNIOR CORPS. The ACBL established the Junior Corps as a part of its Junior program in 1990. Members of the Junior Corp are ACBL's elite Junior players who are the future of the organization. This group is charged with working together with Unit officials and tournament organizers to promote bridge among young people. New members inducted at the Junior Day receptions held at each of the three annual NABCs. As of 1993 the Corps had 58 members from 19 districts.

JUNIOR TEAM TRIALS. The method of selection of ACBL teams for the biennial World Junior Bridge Championships which were inaugurated by the World Bridge Federation in 1987.

1987   Representatives of six colleges, who had won their way to the North American Collegiate Bridge Championship final in St. Louis in March, 1987, competed for the right to play in the first World Junior Bridge Champi-

onships in Amsterdam, Netherlands. 244 students on 22 campuses participated in first-stage par contests. At St. Louis, two teams were eliminated in a round-robin and, after two knockout rounds, New York University was the victor. After one dropout and two augmentations, a five-person team was fielded at the WJBC. The first three were on the original NYU team. The North American team: Guy Doherty, Jon Heller, Asya Kamsky, Aaron Silverstein, Billy Hsieh, npc Matt Guagliardo.

1989   The selection process for the World Junior Championships was to approve the winning team at the North American College Bridge Championships in Reno, and to augment the four-man team to six at Junior Trials held in Memphis during the last three days of the United States Bridge Championships. The winning team also was to be sponsored to the European Junior Bridge Camp in Poland prior to the World Junior Championships in Nottingham, England, in August. The first four listed are the University of Tennessee champions who won the NACBC, the last two were the top pair at the Junior Trials. The North American team: Michael White, Mike Cappelletti, James Baker, David Williams, Michael Klein, David Rowntree, npc Bill Eisenberg. (When personal reasons forced Michael White to resign from the team he was replaced by Larry Hicks.)

1991   The ACBL was authorized three Junior teams at the World Junior Championships in Ann Arbor MI — two from the United States and one from Canada. U.S. I consisted of the top three pairs at Junior Trials held in Boston in July, 1990. Written examinations reduced the field of 65 candidates to 56 for the first rounds of the trials, conducted as IMP Pairs. Fourteen pairs qualified for the two-session final.

U.S. I: Brad Moss, Leni Holtz, Revindra Murthy, Mike Cappelletti, David Rowntree, Michael Klein, npc Bobby Wolff.

U.S. II: Jeff Ferro, Wayne Stuart, John Diamond, Brian Platnick, Martha Benson, Tricia Thomas, npc Chip Martel (Tricia Thomas was replaced by Debbie Zuckerberg when employment duties forced Thomas to withdraw from the team).

Canada: Mark Caplan, Eric Sutherland, Fred Gitelman, Geoff Hampson, Bronia Gmach, Mike Roberts, npc John Carruthers.

1993   A pair of Canadians topped the Junior Trials at Toronto in July 1992. The three top U.S. pairs were provisionally named to the team for the NEC World Junior Team Championships in Arhus, Denmark. In February it was announced that two teams would represent the United States and that a third ACBL team would represent Canada.

U.S. I: Eric Greco, Kevin Wilson, Jeff Ferro, Leni Holtz, Debbie Zuckerberg, Rich Pavlicek, npc Chip Martel.

U.S. II: Sam Dinkin, Michael Shuster, Albert Tom, Doug Hsieh, Eric Secan, John Fout, npc Jan Martel.

Canada: Geoff Hampson, Bronia Gmach, Eric Sutherlin, Mike Roberts, Jeffrey Blond, Nicholas L'Ecuyer, npc John Carruthers.

JUNK. A contemptuous term used to describe a hand or a holding felt to be particularly valueless by the person describing it. See BAD CARDS.

K

KAMIKAZE NOTRUMP. A bidding system devised by John Kierein of Boulder CO which incorporates a 1NT opener in first and second seat on 9-12 high-card points. Weak two-bids in hearts and spades show 9-11 HCP. A 2♦ opener shows 9-11 with 4-4-4-1 or 5-4-4-0 distribution (any singleton). The system also calls for frequent psychic bids in third seat after two passes.

Because the ACBL does not allow the use of conventions such as Stayman with any opening 1NT with a bottom limit below 10 high-card points, Kierein prepared an insert for his booklet recommending that players who employ the Kamikaze notrump adjust the range to 10-13.

KANTAR CUEBID. A specialized cuebid after an opponent's overcall suggested by Eddie Kantar. For example:

WEST	NORTH	EAST	SOUTH
1♠	2♦	3♦	

In this specialized usage, 3♦ shows a 5-4-4-0 or 4-4-4-1 hand with a shortage in the opponent's suit. The strength may be as little as 8-9 high-card points, but there is no limit.

For other uses of the cuebid, see CUEBID IN OPPONENT'S SUIT.

KANTAR THREE NOTRUMP. See THREE NOTRUMP OPENING.

KAPLAN-SHEINWOLD. A system devised by Edgar Kaplan and Alfred Sheinwold, based on the Weak Notrump and aimed at more precisely limiting the strength shown by all bids. The features of the system are:

(1) Weak notrump with 12-14 points. An 11-point hand may be opened with 2½-3 Quick Tricks, or a 15-point hand with less than two quick tricks. Responses of 2♦, 2♥, 2♠, 3♣ and 3♦ are weak signoff bids. A bid of 2♣ followed by a minor-suit rebid is strong and forcing. Other responses are standard, with non-forcing Stayman. A bid of 2♣ followed by a jump to 3♥ or 3♠ is forcing, and shows a more unbalanced pattern than an immediate jump. Whether doubled or not, responder runs from 1NT with fewer than 5 points, often into 2♣ or 2♦.

After an overcall, a double is negative and a new suit bid at the three level is forcing.

(2) Minor-suit openings are sound (but any hand with three quick tricks must be opened). If balanced, 15-20 points and possibly a three-card suit: 1NT rebid shows 15-17; and 2NT rebid shows 18-20. A single raise of responder's major shows 15-17; a double raise shows 18-19; a triple raise shows 20-21 (in each case the requirements are reduced as distribution improves). A maximum unbalanced hand reverses or jump shifts before raising.

Responder bids a major in response whenever possible. Opener's reverse is a one-round force. A 3NT rebid shows a solid minor with outside stoppers.

For single and double raises, see INVERTED MINOR SUIT RAISES. Single raises are forcing and double raises are preemptive. A response of 1 NT shows 5-8, and 2 NT 12-15. A balanced 9-11 point hand may respond in the other minor.

If the opening is doubled, takeouts retain their meaning, but all raises are preemptive (redouble is the strong raise).

Opener may raise responder's major with three-card support in competition.

(3) NEGATIVE DOUBLE.

(4) Jump shift by responder is preemptive in competition.

(5) FIVE-CARD MAJORS, which can be light: a 9-point hand with quick-trick and playing-trick strength is possible. Exceptionally, a strong four-card suit may be bid, with a balanced minimum with honors concentrated in two suits, or a touching lower-ranking, weak five-card suit. ONE NOTRUMP RESPONSE FORCING, but opener passes with the rare balanced minimum hand.

LIMIT JUMP RAISES are used. The jump raise preceded by 1NT shows three-card support and a more balanced hand. A 3NT response is used instead of the standard (strong) jump raise. A 2NT response is standard. A minor-suit response is 12-13 minimum unless followed by a rebid in the minor, showing only a semi-solid suit headed by the ace; a delayed raise for opener or a 2NT rebid is game-forcing.

After 1♥ - 1♠, opener rebids 1NT, 2♥ or 2♠ with a minimum. A bid of 2♣ or 2♦ would be more constructive. After 1♠ - 2♥ (minimum 10 HCP and a five-card suit), minimum hands bid 2NT, 3♥ or 2♠; maximum hands (18 or more) bid 3♣ or 3♦, which are the only forcing bids; other bids show 15-17.

(6) Opening psychics are lead-directing, containing a legitimate suit with a high honor (2-6 points). A jump shift forces the opener to rebid in his suit or notrump, whichever is cheaper. Psychics are recommended only when non-vulnerable; at imps, only non-vulnerable versus vulnerable; at Board-a-Match, never.

(7) WEAK TWO-BIDS need one and one-half to two quick tricks and a semi-solid suit in first and second position. A single raise is preemptive, and other responses by an unpassed hand are forcing; 2NT asks the opener to bid a side honor.

(8) 2♣ is the only forcing opening. After a 2♦ negative response, the bidding can stop short of game if the opener rebids 2NT or bids and rebids one suit.

(9) 3NT opening shows a 2NT hand (20-22) with a long solid minor.

(10) CUEBIDs are used under game to suggest a slam and over game to ask about an unbid suit. A subsequent 4 NT bid is a natural slam invitation, as in BLUE TEAM CLUB.

(11) GERBER over notrump bids.

(12) BLACKWOOD in other situations.

(13) GRAND SLAM FORCE.

(14) ROMAN ASKING BIDS.

(15) TAKEOUT DOUBLES emphasize distribution: there should be not fewer than three cards in each unbid suit. A cuebid is the only forcing response.

(16) Overcalls have the same range as an opening bid. Responder should seldom pass if he would have responded to an opening bid.

(17) WEAK JUMP OVERCALLS, usually with a maximum of one and one-half tricks.

(18) 1NT OVERCALL shows 17-19. A two-level takeout is a signoff, and a cuebid is Stayman.

(19) Optional features of the system include: SHORT-SUIT GAME TRIES; FLINT 3♦; UNUSUAL NOTRUMP; LANDY; FRAGMENT BIDS; MICHAELS CUEBID; ROMAN 2♦; WEAK JUMP SHIFT RESPONSES by passed hand; 3♣ as "prelude to signoff"

over a jump rebid of 2 NT; 2♦ as forcing Stayman; 2 NT over opposing takeout double as semi-preemptive raise; 3 NT after limit jump raise of major to ask for short suit.

KEEPING SCORE. The process by which a record is kept of the activity during a rubber of bridge or of CHICAGO, and of the result on a board in duplicate. There can be more than one scorekeeper among a group of rubber bridge players, but in duplicate the score is usually kept by North.

KEEPING THE BIDDING OPEN. For the strength needed to make a response, see ONE OVER ONE RESPONSE. For reopening action by the fourth player, see BALANCING.

KEM CARDS. The first successful plastic cards, manufactured in America since 1934. Each year several new designs are introduced. Lost or damaged cards will be replaced by the manufacturer. See PLASTIC CARDS.

KENYA BRIDGE ASSOCIATION. A group formed in 1963 with 140 members in 1993.
Officers 1993:
  Chairman: M.V.Shah
  Secretary: K.M.Shah
  PO Box 42914
  Nairobi
  Kenya
  Tel: 02542 228944
  Fax: 02542 331778

KEY CARD BLACKWOOD. A form of Blackwood in which the king of trumps is counted as a fifth ace. Responder bids 5♣ with no aces or four aces, 5♦ with one ace or five aces, 5♥ with two aces, and 5♠ with three aces. A subsequent bid of 5 NT by the Blackwood bidder may be used in various ways. It may ask for kings in the normal manner, except that the king of trumps would not be shown. Or it may ask for an additional feature in the Blackwood responder's hand. Although this method of ace-asking still is used in some areas, in general it has been replaced by ROMAN KEY CARD BLACKWOOD. See also BYZANTINE BLACKWOOD; CULBERTSON 4-5 NT; KEY CARD GERBER.

KEY CARD GERBER. A modification of the GERBER CONVENTION in which trump honors may be counted as aces. When only the trump king is to be counted as an ace, responder bids 4♦ with no aces or four aces, 4♥ with one ace or five aces, 4♠ with two aces, and 4 NT with three aces. Some partnerships agree to count both the king and queen of trumps as aces. Using this agreement responder's 4♠ bid would show two or six aces. SEE BYZANTINE BLACKWOOD; ROMAN GERBER.

KHEDIVE. An early name for bridge as played on the French Riviera, which lends support to the belief that the game is of Turkish origin. See HISTORY OF BRIDGE.

KIBITZER. An onlooker at bridge or other games.

KIBITZER'S MAKE. A hand which seems to have sufficient controls, enough high-card winners, and sufficiently few losers to be successful in a contract, but which

for reasons of entry problems, duplication of values, or lie of the cards is doomed. The term comes from the habit of some poorly-trained kibitzers to indulge in analyses that careful scrutiny shows to be fallacious.

KIBITZING. The act of watching a game from the sidelines. In serious play at top clubs, and at tournaments in America and Europe, the level of play is usually high, so there are unwritten, as well as written, rules concerning the deportment of any onlooker. See LAWS (Law 11 and 76). These onlookers know that it is extremely important for them not to give away any information about the nature of the hand or the holding that they are watching. In ACBL tournaments, kibitzers usually are permitted. However, one kibitzer may be removed at a player's request without cause. Any kibitzer can be removed for cause (failing to observe the proprieties for kibitzers). Numerous stories and legends have sprung up over the years about kibitzers and, although many of them are apocryphal, some are true, and others contain more than a germ of truth. Many of these tales are based on situations where the players are arguing vehemently about a bid or play, and it is decided that the matter be referred to the kibitzer for his opinion, with many varied and humorous endings.

The word "kibitzer" itself derives from the German word for a green plover, a highly inquisitive bird. The role of the kibitzer grew somewhat in stature and story as bridge itself expanded and progressed. In H. T. WEBSTER's regular series of bridge cartoons drawn for the *New York Herald Tribune*, the artist's attention was often turned to kibitzers, and the resulting drawings were among his most amusing. Some of the great humorists of the Thirties and Forties occasionally did pieces about kibitzers, and one of the wittiest was George S. Kaufman's "*The Great Kibitzers' Strike*." All the comic and semiserious articles reflected the general mores and customs of the times regarding kibitzers and attitudes toward them.

A classic story, and one of the few completely true ones, involved the players at a well-known New York club and their one kibitzer. The five-level contract was doubled, and with the opponents on lead to the tenth trick, declarer spread his hand, claiming the balance, just making the contract. The opposition agreed, and the cards were just about to be thrown in, when the kibitzer pointed out a defensive lead which would have defeated the contract at that point. Bitter harangue and confusion then ensued and the matter was at length referred to the card committee. The final decision was that declarer be credited with making the contract doubled, the defense be credited with defeating the contract one trick, and the kibitzer be ordered to pay the difference.

KICK IT. Colloquial term for "I double." Also a colloquialism for boosting the contract as a preemptive measure.

KICKBACK. A method of using ROMAN KEY CARD BLACKWOOD while saving space. It was proposed by Jeff Rubens in an article in the February 1981 *Bridge World* and has been adopted by many experts. The bid immediately above four of the agreed suit is used to ask for key cards, thus saving space in most cases. 4♦ is used with clubs agreed, 4♥ with diamonds agreed, and 4♠ with hearts agreed. With spades agreed, the normal 4NT bid is used. 4NT, if idle, is a cuebid in the Kickback suits.

Kickback followed by five of the Kickback suit suggests a grand slam, promises all the keycards and the trump queen, and asks for specific kings.

KILLED. (1) Captured, as in "The king was killed by the ace." (2) The fate of a player or pair playing well but scoring badly. At duplicate the term implies that the opponents have played luckily and well on a group of boards. At rubber bridge it would refer to a session of poor cards and bad breaks. The term is always born of frustration and frequently of a desire to avoid admissions of poor play to one's teammates or oneself. (3) Denuded of whatever entries it may have had, as "The spade lead killed the dummy."

KING. The second highest ranking card in a suit in bridge. See COAT CARDS and COURT CARDS.

KING OR QUEEN OF BRIDGE This honorary title is awarded annually to the graduating high school senior in the American Contract Bridge League with the best record in bridge. The winner is named by the International Palace of Sports Foundation and ACBL. The title carries with it the $1000 Homer Shoop/International Palace of Sports scholarship award. Earmarked for continuing education or as a career award, the scholarship is presented to the alma mater of the winner to be granted to a deserving student selected by the school from the same class.

Originally the winner was determined by total masterpoints, but over the years the winners have been cited for other bridge achievements and have been commended for deportment, demeanor and sportsmanship at the bridge table and for extra-curricular bridge activities such as teaching, directing, and Unit/District participation. For winners see Appendix II.

KING LEAD. See JOURNALIST LEADS; OPENING LEADS; RUSINOW LEADS.

K.I.S.S. An acronym for "Keep it simple, Stupid". It calls for a low-level system with no conventions, also called "momma-poppa".

KISS OF DEATH. A penalty of 200 points on a part-score deal in a pair contest; usually down two vulnerable, or down one doubled vulnerable.

KITCHEN BRIDGE A social game, perhaps within a family, with little emphasis on technique and skill.

KNAVE. The jack, the fourth highest ranking card of a suit. This term is obsolete in American usage, and obsolescent elsewhere, although it had considerable currency in England and Continental Europe until the Forties. One reason for the quick acceptance of the term "jack" instead of "knave" is that in reporting hands or in any abbreviated diagram or description of play the initial J can be used, whereas previously Kn had to be used, since a plain K would have been ambiguous. See COAT CARDS and COURT CARDS.

KNOCK. (1) An action, of doubtful propriety, consisting of hitting the table lightly instead of speaking the word "pass." While it is true that bridge laws technically condone passes executed in irregular style, provided the offender at least is consistent in passing that way all the time, the best practice and that most approved by top tournament directors remains the spoken word "pass." (2) An informal method of ALERTING.

These two meanings create ambiguity: A player who knocks intending an alert may be assumed by the next player to have passed. So knocking is a bad habit with any meaning.

KNOCK TOGETHER. See CRASHING HONORS.

KNOCKOUT SQUEEZE. A knockout squeeze is a squeeze in three suits, one of which is the trump suit. Declarer ruffs the fourth suit in the long trump hand, forcing the threatened defender to choose between establishing declarer's side suit or allowing him to score an extra trump trick. Example:

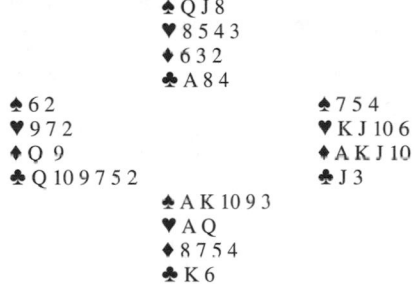

South is declarer in 4♠ after East opened the bidding and West showed club length. West leads a trump won by the ♠8 in dummy. A heart is led for a finesse of the ♥Q, and declarer continues with three rounds of clubs, ruffing the third round with the ♠K. On the third club, East is squeezed in three suits: a spade "discard" allows declarer to score an eventual diamond ruff in dummy, a heart discard allows declarer to establish and cash a long heart in dummy, while a diamond discard enables declarer to score a diamond ruff in dummy or establish and cash a long diamond in his hand, depending on the defense.

KNOCKOUT TOURNAMENT. An event (usually for teams of four) in which one team plays against only one opposing team in a given session. The losers are eliminated. The winners remain in the contest, new opponents at later sessions, until only one winning team remains.

In a DOUBLE KNOCKOUT event, a team must lose twice before being eliminated. After its first loss, a team is transferred to the "losers' bracket," from which teams are eliminated after each round, and to which teams losing in the second or later rounds in the winners' bracket are added. See also REPECHAGE.

Late night zip knockout events, with short matches and fast time limits, have acquired some popularity and are known as "lose and snooze."

KOCK-WERNER REDOUBLE. A rescue device invented by the Swedish partnership of Rudolf Kock and Einar Werner. When partner's low-level overcall has been doubled, a redouble is for takeout — the redoubler is very short in partner's suit. For example:

WEST	NORTH	EAST	SOUTH
			1 ♣
1 ♥	Dbl	Rdbl	

East shows that he has a singleton or void in hearts, and requests a takeout into another suit. The possibility of playing in 2♣ is not excluded: the best escape is often to a suit bid by the opposition.

Such redoubles are almost useless in a natural sense. If East is satisfied to play in 1♥ doubled, he simply passes.

This rarely applies, because in modern play the double is almost always negative. See also SOS REDOUBLE and ROSENKRANZ DOUBLE.

KOKISH RELAY. A maneuver, devised by Eric Kokish, to facilitate the bidding of very strong balanced hands. In this sequence:

OPENER	RESPONDER
2 ♣	2 ♦
2 ♥	2 ♠

2♥ is semi-artificial, promising either hearts or a strong balanced hand. 2♠ is forced, and opener bids 2 NT if he is balanced. Other rebids are natural, showing hearts. This is advantageous with the strong, balanced hands, too strong for an immediate, non-forcing 2NT rebid, because Stayman and transfers can be used conveniently at the three-level. This device loses ground when the opener is unbalanced with hearts, since responder loses the chance to use a second negative.

KUWAIT BRIDGE COMMITTEE. The game was introduced to Kuwait in 1950 and played in private clubs until 1981 when a national organization was founded. There are 90 members playing in one club.
1993 Officers:
President: Dr. Hassan Ali Al-Zaid
General Secretary: Sa'id Sulaiman Al-Saleh
P.O. Box 9226
61003 AHMADI - KUWAIT
Tel: 00965 3612101
Fax: 00965 3981585

L

LHO. Left-hand opponent, or the player on declarer's left.

LOL. An expression designating innocent-appearing bridge players who unexpectedly bid and play against you as though they were world champions. The letters originally designated "Little Old Ladies", and were used as a term of some opprobrium, but the frequency with which Little Old Ladies secured excellent results by simple commonsense action against pseudo-experts has caused the connotation to become more one of amusement and respect than of belittlement.

LAMB, Charles. See BATTLE, Sarah.

LANCIA TOURNAMENTS. A series of four challenge matches played in 1975, in which an Italian team sponsored by the Lancia division of Fiat opposed four American teams. The nucleus of the Italian team consisted of Walter Avarelli, Giorgio Belladonna, Pietro Forquet, Benito Garozzo and Omar Sharif. They won in Chicago,

but were defeated in New York, Los Angeles and Miami.

LANDY. A conventional overcall of 2♣ after an opposing 1NT opening as a request for a takeout to a major suit, devised by Alvin Landy. The overcaller promises at least four cards in each major suit and usually has five; some pairs agree that he guarantees five hearts. A Landy bidder is likely to be short in one or both minors, since with balanced distribution he would often double or pass. He seldom has more than 15 high-card points. By agreement, partnerships can use Landy in the direct position, the balancing position or both; over a strong notrump, a weak notrump or both.

RESPONSES to the Landy bid are not standardized but the following scheme had the endorsement of the inventor of the convention:

(1) 3♣ is a forcing response unrelated to clubs, and asks the Landy bidder to describe his hand further. The responder may have equal length in the major suits. This is the *only* forcing response.

(2) 3♠ and 3♥ are game invitations, often with a 3-card suit.

(3) 2NT and 3♦ are natural and encouraging but not forcing.

(4) 2♦ shows a weak hand with diamond length.

(5) Pass shows a weak hand with club length.

See DEFENSE TO ONE NOTRUMP and DEFENSE TO TWO-SUITED OVERCALLS.

LANGUAGE. (1) Symbolic: The art of communication between partners, as "the language of bidding" and "the language of signals". (2) Verbal: English is the international language of WBF and other international tournaments.

LAST TRAIN CUEBID A cuebid directly below game in the agreed suit. For example:

OPENER	RESPONDER
1 ♥	3 ♥
4 ♦	4 ♥

The responder squeezes in a cuebid, the only possible one short of going beyond game. Some use this, by agreement, to show some slam interest but not enough to venture beyond game. It shows nothing particular in diamonds. Also called Squeeze Cuebid.

LATE PAIR. A pair desiring to enter an event after it has started. An ingenious director can usually add one or more pairs to a game during the first round (or even later) without disrupting play for those who have already started. See APPENDIX TABLE; HALF TABLE.

LATE PLAY. Play, after completion of a session, of one or more boards which normally would have been played during an earlier round.

A late play arises when the director observes that a given table has one or more boards to play in a given round when the rest have finished and are ready to move. The director may instruct the contestants not to start another board, but to return at the end of the contest to complete their play.

LATVIAN BRIDGE FEDERATION
1992 President: Egon Lavendel
33, Sarkanannias Street, Riga, Latvia
Telephone: (0132) 373142

Fax (0132) 273787

LAVINTHAL SIGNAL. See SUIT PREFERENCE.

LAW OF BALANCED DISTRIBUTION. A general principle relating to suit distributions, stated as followed by John A. Tierney: The more symmetrical of two specific holdings is the more probable. Two equally symmetric holdings are equally probable. This does *not* mean that an even suit split is more likely than an uneven one, which is untrue with four cards (or a higher even number). It refers to specific layouts. If five cards are missing, the Q-J-4-3-2, all the following are equally probable: Q-4; 3-2; Q-4-3; 4-3-2. The following are less symmetric and therefore less probable: Q-2; Q-J-4-3; Q-4-3-2.

LAW OF SYMMETRY. A theory of distribution suggested by Ely Culbertson. His idea was that imperfect shuffles tend to produce a suit pattern equivalent to a hand pattern in the same deal. A player with 5-4-3-1 distribution should expect the outstanding cards in his long suit to be divided 4-3-1 more often than the mathematical odds would suggest. There is no mathematical or empirical basis for this theory.

LAWS. See LAWS OF CONTRACT BRIDGE and LAWS OF DUPLICATE CONTRACT BRIDGE. In this Encyclopedia, "LAWS" refers to both codes unless otherwise indicated. In general, Law numbers correspond in the two codes.

LAWS OF BRIDGE. In 1743, Edmond Hoyle published *A Short Treatise on the Game of Whist, Containing the Laws of the Game.* The Laws as codified there became so universally accepted that they guided whist players for more than 100 years. The Arlington and Portland clubs revised the code in 1864, and the Portland Club became the recognized authority in the newer game of bridge, the laws of this newer game appearing under the pen name of Boaz in 1895. Other clubs adopted their own versions, until in 1902 a committee representing many card clubs promulgated an American code. This set of laws was not received with universal acclaim, and gradually the laws of the Whist Club (New York) became standardized.

Bridge, which had succeeded in surpassing whist, was itself superseded by auction bridge, and in 1909 the Portland and Bath clubs in England framed a Code of Laws of Auction Bridge; The Whist Club followed with its Laws of Auction Bridge in 1910. These were revised in 1911, 1912, 1915, 1917 and 1926.

In the Twenties auction bridge began to be succeeded by the then new game of contract bridge, and in 1927 the Whist Club adopted a code based essentially on the 1926 Laws of Auction Bridge. This time the American clubs were ahead of their British counterparts, the Portland and other clubs adopting a code in 1929.

For several years thereafter, the Whist Club, the Portland Club, and the Commission Française de Bridge worked through their committees to make a code that would be international in scope, finally agreeing on one on October 19, 1932. This code was revised by equivalent groups in 1935, 1948 and 1963.

Meanwhile, the peculiar requirements of duplicate bridge, which was sweeping the country and most of the world, pointed up the necessity for a code to cover dupli-

cate. The first such code was the result of a committee of the American Bridge League, adopted in November 1928. The 1932 revision of the *Laws of Contract Bridge* necessitated a 1933 revision of the duplicate laws. In America a further revision in 1943 of the laws of duplicate led to an international effort (1948-49 by the Portland Club, the European Bridge League and the National Laws Commission of America) that revised the *Laws of Contract Bridge* and the *Laws of Duplicate Contract Bridge*. These laws remained in vogue throughout the world until the revision of both, under the same international groups, which became effective July 1, 1963.

The duplicate laws were revised again in 1975, and became a world-wide code with the involvement of the World Bridge Federation. They were revised again in 1986 under the auspices of the ACBL (with major contributions from Edgar Kaplan, Roger Stern, Karen Allison and Amalya Kearse) and the World Bridge Federation. They became effective March 31, 1987.

The contract bridge laws were revised again in 1992, by the same bodies, with major contributions on the American side from Edgar Kaplan, Karen Allison, Roger Stern, Ralph Cohen and Robert Wolff. They became effective January 1, 1993.

Representing the promulgating bodies in 1992 were the following:

LAWS COMMISSION (in 1993)
of the American Contract Bridge League
Edgar Kaplan (Co-Chairman)
Ralph Cohen (Co-Chairman)

Karen Allison	Jeff Polisner
Richard Goldberg	Eric Rodwell
Richard Hewitt	George Rosenkranz
Amalya Kearse	Roger Stern
Sami Kehela	Peggy Sutherlin
Chip Martel	Katie Thorpe
Robert Wolff	

LAWS COMMITTEE (in 1993)
of the World Bridge Federation
Edgar Kaplan (Chairman)
Grattan Endicott (Vice-chairman)

Jens Auken	Jaime Ortiz-Patino
Jean Besse	Jeffrey Polisner
Carlos Cabanne	Rebecca Rogers
Santanu Ghose	William Schoder
Denis Howard	Stuart Wheeler
Robert Howes	John Wignall
Ton Kooijman	James Zimmerman

Former members who have made substantial contributions include Geoffrey Butler, Colin Harding and Edgar Theus, all deceased.

LAWS COMMISSION OF THE AMERICAN CONTRACT BRIDGE LEAGUE. A committee of the American Contract Bridge League charged with formulating and promulgating the official Laws of Contract Bridge and Duplicate Contract Bridge.

In the preparation of international codes the Commission collaborates with other bodies. See Laws of Bridge.

Former members of the Commission who have made substantial contributions to the development of the Laws include: Walter Beinecke; B.Jay Becker; Easley Blackwood; John Gerber; Sam Gold; Charles H.Goren; Lee Hazen; Edward Hymes Jr.; Oswald Jacoby; Albert Morehead; William E. McKenney; Geoffrey Mott-Smith; Donald Oakie; George Reith; Harold Richard; Harold

Vanderbilt; Waldemar von Zedtwitz, all deceased, and Alfred Sheinwold.

In 1993 the members of the Commission were as shown above under LAWS OF BRIDGE.

LAWS OF CONTRACT BRIDGE.

The Scope of the Laws

The Laws are designed to define correct procedure and to provide an adequate remedy whenever a player accidentally, carelessly or inadvertently disturbs the proper course of the game, or gains an unintentional but nevertheless unfair advantage. An offending player should be ready to pay a prescribed penalty graciously.

These Laws do not deal with dishonorable practices; ostracism is the ultimate remedy.

The Proprieties

The object of the Proprieties is to familiarize players with the customs and etiquette of the game, generally accepted over many years; and to enlighten those who might otherwise fail to appreciate when or how they are improperly conveying information to their partners, or are acting on the basis of improper information.

Appendices

Most players will find the Laws and the Proprieties sufficient to their needs. Some, however, may wish to adopt procedures to reduce the risk that, unintentionally, extraneous information is given to partners, or proper information withheld from opponents. Possible procedures, very similar to those successfully used in competitive bridge, are set out in appendices 1, 2 and 3. Note that these appendices are not part of the Laws or the Proprieties of Rubber Bridge.

Part I

Definitions

Auction - 1. The process of determining the contract by means of successive calls. 2. The aggregate of calls made.

Bid - An undertaking to win at least a specified number of odd tricks in a specified denomination.

Call - Any bid, double, redouble or pass.

Contract - The undertaking by declarer's side to win, at the denomination named, the number of odd tricks specified in the final bid, whether undoubled, doubled or redoubled.

Deal - 1. The distribution of the pack to form the hands of the four players. 2. The cards so distributed as a unit, including the auction and play thereof.

Declarer - The player who, for the side that makes the final bid, first bid the denomination named in that bid. He becomes declarer when a legal opening lead is made, and the dummy is faced.

Defender - An opponent of declarer.

Denomination - The suit or notrump specified in a bid.

Double - A call over an opponent's bid increasing the scoring value of fulfilled or defeated contracts (see Law 19).

Dummy - 1. Declarer's partner. 2. Declarer's partner's cards, once they are spread on the table after the opening lead.

Follow suit - Play a card of the suit that has been led.

Game - A unit in scoring denoting 100 or more trick points scored on one deal, or accumulated over two or more

deals (see Laws 72 & 73).

Group - A number of players who have agreed to follow the same procedures.

Hand - The cards originally dealt to a player, or the remaining portion thereof.

Honor - Any Ace, King, Queen, Jack or ten.

Irregularity - A deviation from the correct procedures set forth in these Laws.

LHO - Left-hand opponent.

Lead - The first card played to a trick.

Odd trick - Each trick to be won by declarer's side in excess of six.

Opening Lead - The card led to the first trick.

Opponent - A member of the partnership to which one is opposed.

Overtrick - Each trick won by declarer's side in excess of the contract.

Pack - The 52 playing cards with which the game of Contract Bridge is played.

Partner - The player with whom one plays as a side against the other two players.

Partscore - 90 or fewer trick points.

Pass - A call specifying that a player does not, at that turn, elect to bid, double or redouble.

Penalty - An obligation or restriction imposed upon a side for violations of these Laws.

Penalty Card - A card prematurely exposed by a defender. It may be a major or minor penalty card (see Law 50).

Play - 1. The contribution of a card from one's hand to a trick, including the first card, which is the lead. 2. The aggregate of plays made. 3. The period during which the cards are played, starting immediately after the final pass.

RHO - Right-hand opponent.

Redeal - A second or subsequent deal to replace a faulty deal.

Redouble - A call over an opponent's double increasing the scoring value of fulfilled or defeated contracts (see Law 19).

Revoke - The play of a card of another suit by a player who is able to follow suit or to comply with a lead penalty.

Rotation - The clockwise order in which the right to deal, to call or to play progresses

Rubber - The scoring period that ends when one side had scored two games.

Side - Two players who constitute a partnership against the other two players.

Slam - A contract to win twelve tricks (called Small Slam) or thirteen tricks (called Grand Slam).

Suit - One of four groups of cards in the pack, each group comprising thirteen cards and having a characteristic symbol: spades (♠), hearts (♥), diamonds (♦), clubs (♣).

Trick - The unit by which the outcome of the contract is determined, regularly consisting of four cards, one contributed by each player in rotation, beginning with the lead.

Trump - Each card of the suit, if any, named in the contract.

Undertrick - Each trick by which declarer's side falls short of fulfilling the contract.

Vulnerable - The status of a side that has won a game and is therefore exposed to greater undertrick penalties and entitled to greater premiums.

Part II

PRELIMINARIES

LAW 1
THE PLAYERS - THE PACK
Contract bridge is played by four players with a pack of 52 cards of identical back design and color, consisting of 13 cards in each of four suits. Two packs should be used, of which only one is in play at any time; and each pack should be clearly distinguishable from the other in back design or color.

LAW 2
RANK OF CARDS
The suits rank downwards in order — Spades (♠), Hearts, (♥), Diamonds (♦), Clubs (♣). The cards of each suit rank in descending order: Ace, King, Queen, Jack, 10, 9, 8, 7, 6, 5, 4, 3, 2.

LAW 3
THE DRAW
Before every rubber, each player draws a card from a pack shuffled and spread face down on the table. A card should not be exposed until all the players have drawn.

Unless it is otherwise agreed, the two players who draw the highest cards play as partners against the other two players. When cards of the same rank are drawn, the rank of suit determines which is higher.

The player with the highest card deals first and has the right to choose his seat and the pack with which he will deal. He may consult his partner, but having announced his decision must abide by it. His partner sits opposite him. The opponents then occupy the two remaining seats as they wish, and having made their selection must abide by it.

A player must draw again if he draws more than one card, or one of the four cards at either end of the pack, or a card adjoining one drawn by another player, or a card from the other pack.

Part III

THE DEAL
LAW 4
THE SHUFFLE
Before the first deal of a rubber, the player to the dealer's left should shuffle the pack thoroughly*, without exposing the face of any card, in full view of the players and to their satisfaction. Thereafter, as each player deals, the dealer's partner shuffles the other pack for the next deal, and places the pack face down on his right.

A pack properly prepared should not be disturbed until the dealer picks it up for his deal, at which time he is entitled to the final shuffle.

No player other than the dealer and the player designated to prepare the pack may shuffle.

*It is recommended that the pack be shuffled at least five times.

LAW 5
THE CUT
The pack must be cut immediately before it is dealt. The dealer presents the pack to his RHO, who lifts off a portion and places it on the table toward the dealer. Each portion must contain at least four cards. The dealer completes the cut by placing what was originally the bottom portion upon the other portion.

No player other than the dealer's RHO may cut the pack.

LAW 6
NEW CUT - NEW SHUFFLE
There must be a new cut if any player demands one before the first card is dealt. In this case, the dealer's RHO cuts again.

There must be a new shuffle, followed by a cut:

(a) If any player demands one before the dealer has picked up the pack for his deal. In this case, the player designated to prepare the pack shuffles again.

(b) If any player demands one after the dealer has picked up the pack but before the first card is dealt. In this case only the dealer shuffles.

(c) If a card is turned face up in shuffling. In this case the player who was shuffling shuffles again.

(d) If a card is turned face up in cutting. In this case only the dealer shuffles.

(e) If there is a redeal (see Law 10).

LAW 7
CHANGE OF PACK
The two packs are used alternately, unless there is a redeal. A pack containing a card so damaged or marked that it may be identified from its back must be replaced* if attention is drawn to the imperfection before the last card of the current deal has been dealt.

A pack originally belonging to a side must be restored on demand of any player before the last card of the current deal has been dealt.*

*See Law 8

LAW 8
THE DEAL
The dealer distributes the cards face down, one at a time in rotation into four separate hands of thirteen cards each, the first card to the player on his left and the last card to himself. If he deals two cards simultaneously or consecutively to the same player, or fails to deal a card to a player, he may rectify the error, provided he does so immediately and to the satisfaction of the other players. The dealer must not allow the face of any card to be seen while he is dealing.

Players should not look at the face of any card until the deal is completed. A player who violates this provision forfeits those rights to a change of pack (Law 7) or redeal (Law 10).

LAW 9
ROTATION OF THE TURN TO DEAL
The turn to deal passes in rotation, unless there is a redeal. If a player deals out of turn, and attention is not drawn to the error before the last card has been dealt, the deal stands as though it had been in turn, the player who dealt the cards is the dealer (he makes the first call), and the player who missed his turn to deal has no redress; and the rotation continues as though the deal had been in turn, unless a redeal is required under Law 10.

LAW 10
REDEAL
A redeal cancels the faulty deal; the same dealer deals again, unless he was dealing out of turn; the same pack is used, unless it has been replaced as provided in Law 7; and the cards are shuffled and cut anew as provided in Laws 4 and 5.

There must be a redeal:

(a) If, before the last card has been dealt, it is discovered that

(i) a card has been turned face up in dealing or is face up in the pack or elsewhere;

(ii) the cards have not been dealt correctly;*

(iii) a player is dealing out of turn or is dealing with a pack that was not shuffled or not cut, provided any player* demands a redeal.

(b) If, before the first call has been made, it is discovered that a player has picked up another player's hand and has seen a card in it.

(c) If, before play has been completed, it is discovered that

(i) the pack did not conform in every respect to the requirements of Law 1, including any case in which a missing card cannot be found after due search;

(ii) one player has picked up too many cards, another too few;

(iii) two or more players on opposing sides have allowed any cards from their hands to be mixed together, following a claim that a redeal is in order.

*See Law 8.

LAW 11
MISSING CARD
When a player has too few cards and a redeal is not required by Law 10 (c), the deal stands as correct, and:

(a) If he has played more than once to a previous trick, Law 67 applies;

(b) If a missing card is found elsewhere, not in a previous trick, that card is deemed to have belonged continuously to the deficient hand and must be restored to that hand; it may become a penalty card, as provided in Law 23 or 49, and failure to have played it may constitute a revoke.

LAW 12
SURPLUS CARD
When a player has too many cards and a redeal is not required by Law 10 (c), the deal stands as correct, and

(a) If the offender has omitted to play to a trick, Law 67 applies.

(b) If the offender has picked up a surplus card from a previous trick, or from dummy's hand, or from the other pack, or elsewhere, such surplus card shall be restored to its proper place; and

(i) If the surplus card is in the offender's hand when it is discovered, there is no penalty.

(ii) If the surplus card has been led or played, or had been played to a previous trick, the offender must substitute for it a card from his hand that he can legally play to the trick, and, if possible, a card of the same suit as the surplus card. The offending side may not thereby win a trick it had lost, but it may lose a trick it had won. When attention is drawn to the offense before the lead to the next trick, either member of the nonoffending side may, without penalty, withdraw a play made subsequent to the offense, and substitute any legal play.

Part IV

GENERAL LAWS
GOVERNING IRREGULARITIES
LAW 13
PROCEDURE FOLLOWING AN IRREGULARITY

(Club Law 13)

When an irregularity has occurred, any player - except dummy as restricted by Law 43 - may draw attention to it and give or obtain information as to the law applicable to it. The fact that a player draws attention to an irregularity committed by his side does not affect the rights of the opponents.

After attention has been drawn to an irregularity, no player should call or play until all questions in regard to the assessment of a penalty have been determined. Premature correction of an irregularity on the part of the offender may subject him to further penalty (see Law 26).

LAW 14
ASSESSMENT OF A PENALTY
(Club Law 14)

A penalty may not be imposed until the nature of the irregularity to be penalized has been determined and the applicable penalty has been clearly stated; but a penalty once paid, or any decision agreed and acted upon by the players, stands and should not, except by agreement of all four players, be corrected even though at some later time it may be judged incorrect.

LAW 15
WAIVER OR FORFEITURE OF PENALTY
The right to penalize an offense is forfeited if

(a) both members of the nonoffending side waive the penalty;

(b) a member of the nonoffending side calls (Law 34) or plays (Law 60) after an irregularity committed by his RHO.

LAW 16
UNAUTHORIZED INFORMATION
(Club Law 16)

A player may be subject to penalty if he conveys information to his partner other than by a legal call or play.

Information conveyed by an illegal call, play or exposure of a card is subject to the applicable law in Part V or VI.

If a player conveys information to his partner by means of a remark or question or by an unmistakable hesitation or unwonted speed, special emphasis, tone, gesture, movement, mannerism or any other action that suggests a call, lead or plan of play; and if attention is drawn to the offense immediately, when the offending side has profited through the doubtful call or play so suggested, it should, in conformance with Proprieties 1, redress any damage done to the nonoffending side.

Part V

THE AUCTION
CORRECT PROCEDURE
LAW 17
DURATION OF THE AUCTION
The auction begins when the last card of a correct deal has been placed on the table. The dealer makes the first call, and thereafter each player calls in rotation. When three passes in rotation have followed any call the auction is closed, unless Law 34 applies.

LAW 18
BIDS

Each bid* must name a number of odd tricks, from one to seven, and a denomination. A bid supersedes the previous bid if it names either a greater number of odd tricks or the same number of odd tricks in a higher denomination. A bid that fulfills these requirements is sufficient; one that does not is insufficient. The denominations rank in descending order: notrump, spades, hearts, diamonds, clubs.

* Pass, double and redouble are calls, not bids

LAW 19
DOUBLES AND REDOUBLES

A player may double only the last preceding bid, and then only if it was made by an opponent and no calls other than pass have intervened.

A player may redouble only the last preceding double, and then only if it was made by an opponent and no calls other than pass have intervened.

A player should not, in doubling or redoubling, state the number of tricks or the denomination; but, if he states either or both incorrectly, he is deemed to have doubled or redoubled the bid as it was made. The only correct form is the single word "Double" or "Redouble".

All doubles and redoubles are superseded by a subsequent legal bid. If there is no subsequent bid, scoring values are increased as provided in Law 81.

LAW 20
REVIEW AND EXPLANATION

A player who does not hear a call distinctly may forthwith require that it be repeated.

At his own turn to call during the auction, a player (unless required by law to pass) may require a restatement of the auction in its entirety.

After the final pass, declarer before making any play, or either defender at his first turn to play, may require a restatement of the auction in its entirety.

A request to have calls restated should be responded to only by an opponent (dummy, or a player required by law to pass, may so respond).

All players, including dummy, should promptly correct errors in restatement.

A player may require an explanation of the partnership understanding relating to any call made by an opponent, but only at the player's own turn to call or play. A request for an explanation of a call should be responded to by the partner of the player making the call (see Proprieties 4).

LAW 21
CALL BASED ON MISINFORMATION

A player has no recourse if he has made a call on the basis of his own misunderstanding.

Until the auction is closed, a player may, without penalty, change any call he may have made as a result of misinformation given him by an opponent, provided his partner has not subsequently called. If he elects to correct his call, his LHO may then, in turn and without penalty, change any subsequent call he may have made.

LAW 22
PROCEDURE AFTER THE AUCTION IS CLOSED

After the auction is closed:

(a) If no player has bid, the hands are abandoned and the turn to deal passes in rotation.

(b) If any player has bid, the final bid becomes the contract and play begins.

IRREGULARITIES
LAW 23
CARD EXPOSED OR LED DURING THE AUCTION
(Club Law 23)

Whenever, during the auction, a player faces a card on the table or holds a card so that it is possible for his partner to see its face, every such card must be left face up on the table until the auction closes; and (penalty) if the offender subsequently becomes a defender, declarer may treat every such card as a penalty card (Law 50).

In addition:

(a) If it is a single card below the rank of an honor and not prematurely led, there is no further penalty.

(b) If it is a single card of honor rank, or any card prematurely led, or if more than one card is so exposed (penalty), the offender's partner must pass when next it is his turn to call.

(c) When the penalty under this or any other Law compels the offender's partner to pass, and offender could have known at the time of his infraction that the enforced pass would be likely to damage the nonoffending side, the offenders should redress the damage in accordance with Proprieties 1.

LAW 24
IMMEDIATE CORRECTION OF A CALL

A player may substitute his intended call for an inadvertent call, but only if he does so, or attempts to do so, without pause for thought. If legal, his last call stands without penalty; if illegal, it is subject to the applicable law.

LAW 25
CHANGE OF CALL
(Club Law 25)

When a call is substituted for a call made previously at the same turn, and it is too late for correction as provided in Law 24, then:

(a) If the first call was illegal, the substitute call is canceled and the offender is subject to the applicable law.

(b) If the first call was a legal one, the offender must either

(i) allow his first call to stand and (penalty) his partner must pass when next it is his turn to call; or

(ii) make any other legal call and (penalty) his partner must pass whenever it is his turn to call.

The offender's partner will also be subject to a lead penalty as provided in Law 26 if he becomes a defender.

Law 23C may apply to (b) (i) and (b) (ii).

LAW 26
CHANGE OF CALL - LEAD PENALTIES

When a player makes a call and subsequently changes it to another legal call (except as permitted under Law 24), then if he becomes a defender:

(a) if the changed call was in a suit, and the substituted call did not repeat that suit, declarer may* either require the offender's partner to lead, or prohibit him from leading, such suit when first the offender's partner has the lead (including the opening lead). A prohibition continues for as long as offender's partner retains the lead. When the irregular call artificially relates to a denomination other than the one actually named, "such suit" is the suit or suits to which the call relates.

(b) if the changed call was

(i) in notrump, and his final call at that turn was not, or

(ii) pass, double or redouble, other than an out-of-rotation call repeated in turn in accordance with Law 30(a) or 32(b)(i), declarer may* prohibit offender's partner from leading any one specified suit when first the offender's partner has the lead (including the opening lead). This prohibition continues for as long as offender's partner retains the lead.

*Declarer makes the decision at the time that offender's partner first has the lead.

LAW 27
INSUFFICIENT BID
(Club Law 27)
Any insufficient bid may be accepted (treated as legal) at the option of offender's LHO, and is accepted if that opponent calls.

An insufficient bid made in rotation must be corrected by the substitution of either a sufficient bid (not a double or redouble) or a pass*, unless the irregular bid is accepted.

If the call substituted is

(a) the lowest sufficient bid in the same denomination, the auction proceeds as though the irregularity had not occurred**.

(b) any other sufficient bid, or pass, (penalty) the offender's partner must pass whenever it is his turn to call, (Law 23c may apply) and the lead penalties of Law 26 will apply if he becomes a defender.

If the offender attempts to substitute a double or redouble, it is cancelled; he must pass at that turn and the offense is subject to the penalty provided in subsection (b) above.

If a player makes an insufficient bid out of rotation, Law 31 applies.

*The offender is entitled to select his final call at that turn after the applicable penalties have been stated, and any call he has previously attempted to substitute is cancelled, but the lead penalties of Law 26 will apply if he becomes a defender.

**Offender's partner must not base any subsequent calls or plays on information gained from such a withdrawn bid.

CALL OUT OF ROTATION
LAW 28
CALLS CONSIDERED TO BE IN ROTATION
A call is considered to be in rotation

(a) when it is made without waiting for the RHO to pass, if that opponent is required by law to pass.

(b) when it is made by the player whose turn it was to call, before a penalty has been imposed for a call out of rotation by an opponent; it waives any penalty for the call out of rotation and the auction proceeds as though that opponent had not called at that turn.

LAW 29
PROCEDURE AFTER A CALL OUT OF ROTATION
After a call out of rotation, offender's LHO* may either:

(a) make any legal call; if he chooses to do so, the call out of rotation stands as if it were legal (but if it is an inadmissible call, see Law 35), and the auction proceeds without penalty; or,

(b) require that the call out of rotation be cancelled. The auction reverts to the player whose turn it was to call. The offender may make any legal call in proper turn subject to Laws 30, 31, and 32.

*He alone exercises the option, although any player may draw attention to the irregularity.

LAW 30
PASS OUT OF ROTATION
(Club Law 30)
When a player has passed out of rotation;

(a) before any player has bid, or when it was the turn of his RHO* to call, (penalty) the offender must pass when next it is his turn to call.

(b) after any player has bid and when it was the turn of the offender's partner to call (penalty), the offender must pass whenever it is his turn to call; the offender's partner may make a sufficient bid or may pass, but may not double or redouble at that turn.

*After any player has bid, a call at the turn of offender's LHO is a change of call; Law 25 applies and not this section.

LAW 31
BID OUT OF ROTATION
(Club Law 31)
When a player has bid out of rotation:

(a) at the turn of offender's partner to call, or before any player has called when offender's LHO was the dealer, (penalty) the offender's partner must pass whenever it is his turn to call (Law 23C may apply), and the lead penalties of Law 26 will apply if he becomes a defender.

(b) at the turn of the offender's RHO* to call.

(i) if RHO passes, the bid out of rotation must be repeated, and there is no penalty (if the bid out of rotation was insufficient, it must be corrected as provided in Law 27);

(ii) If RHO makes a legal** bid, double or redouble, the offender may in turn make any legal call. If such call repeats the denomination of the bid out of rotation, (penalty) the offender's partner must pass when next it is his turn to call (Law 23C may apply). If the substituted call does not repeat the denomination, (penalty) the offender's partner must pass whenever it is his turn to call (Law 23C may apply), and the lead penalties of Law 26 will apply if he becomes a defender.

*After any player has called, a call at offender's LHO's turn is a change of call; Law 25 applies and not this section.

**An illegal call by that opponent may be penalized in the usual way, after which this subsection, (b) (ii), applies.

LAW 32
DOUBLE OR REDOUBLE OUT OF ROTATION
(Club Law 32)
When a player has doubled or redoubled out of rotation.**

(a) If it was the offender's partner's turn to call, (penalty) the offender's partner must pass whenever it is his turn to call (Law 23C may apply); the offender may not thereafter, in turn, double or redouble the same bid he doubled out of turn; and the lead penalties of Law 26(b) will apply if he becomes a defender.

(b) If it was the turn of offender's RHO* to call:

(i) If offender's RHO passes, the double or redouble

out of rotation must be repeated and there is no penalty.

(ii) If offender's RHO bids, the offender may in turn make any legal call, and (penalty) the offender's partner must pass when next it is his turn to call (Law 23C may apply), and the lead penalties of Law 26(b) will apply if he becomes a defender.

*After any player has called, a call of offender's LHO's turn is a change of call; Law 25 applies and not this section.

LAW 33
SIMULTANEOUS CALLS
A call made simultaneously with one made by the player whose turn it was to call is deemed to be a subsequent call.

LAW 34
RETENTION OF THE RIGHT TO CALL
When a call has been followed by three passes, the auction does not end when one of those passes was out of rotation, thereby depriving a player of his right to call at that turn. The auction reverts to the player who missed his turn. All subsequent passes are canceled and the auction proceeds as though there had been no irregularity.

LAW 35
INADMISSIBLE CALL CONDONED
(Club Law 35)
When, after an inadmissible call specified below, offender's LHO makes a call before a penalty has been assessed, there is no penalty for the offense (the lead penalties of Law 26 do not apply). If the inadmissible call was:

(a) a double or redouble not permitted by Law 19, that call and all subsequent calls are canceled, the auction reverts to the player whose turn it is to call and proceeds as though there had been no irregularity;

(b) a bid, double or redouble by a player required by law to pass, that call and subsequent legal calls stand; but if the offender was required to pass for the remainder of the auction, he must still pass at subsequent turns;

(c) A bid of more than seven, that call and all subsequent calls are canceled; the offender must substitute a pass, and the auction proceeds as though there had been no irregularity;

(d) a call after the auction is closed, that call and all subsequent calls are canceled without penalty.

LAW 36
INADMISSIBLE DOUBLE OR REDOUBLE
Any double or redouble not permitted by Law 19 is canceled, and the offender must substitute a legal call; and (penalty) the offender's partner must pass whenever it is his turn to call (Law 23C may apply), and the lead penalties of Law 26 (b) will apply if he becomes a defender.

If the right of the non-offending side to penalize is forfeited, Law 35 applies.

LAW 37
BID, DOUBLE OR REDOUBLE IN VIOLATION OF THE OBLIGATION TO PASS
A bid, double or redouble by a player who is required by law to pass is canceled, and (penalty) both members of the offending side must pass during the remainder of the auction (Law 23C may apply), and the lead penalties

of Law 26 will apply if they become defenders.

LAW 38
BID OF MORE THAN SEVEN
(Club Law 38)
No contract of more than seven is ever permissible. A bid of more than seven by any player is canceled, and (penalty) both members of the offending side must pass during the remainder of the auction (Law 23C may apply); and the lead penalties of Law 26 will apply if they become defenders.

LAW 39
CALL AFTER THE AUCTION IS CLOSED
(Club Law 39)
A call after the auction is closed is canceled, and:

(a) If it is a pass by a defender or any call by declarer or dummy, there is no penalty.

(b) If it is a bid, double or redouble by a defender, the lead penalties of Law 26 apply, unless the call has been condoned (see Law 35 d).

LAW 40
PARTNERSHIP AGREEMENTS
(Club Law 40)
A player may make any call or play (including an intentionally misleading call such as a "psychic bid", or a call or play that departs from commonly accepted or previously announced practice) without prior announcement, provided that it is not based on a partnership understanding. But a player may not make use of a bidding or play agreement unless:

(a) his side has disclosed its use of such a call or play beforehand, or

(b) it has been agreed beforehand that the use of partnership understandings be disclosed at the time they are used. His partner must then disclose it. In this case, partner's disclosure must be confined to an indication that a partnership understanding has been used; he should not offer any explanation unless requested to do so.

Any group may restrict the use of special partnership understandings in its games.

THE PLAY
CORRECT PROCEDURE
LAW 41
OPENING LEAD, REVIEW, QUESTIONS
After the auction closes* declarer's LHO makes the opening lead. After the opening lead, dummy spreads his hand in front of him on the table, face up, sorted into suits, the cards in order of rank in columns pointing lengthwise towards declarer, with trumps, if any, to dummy's right. Declarer plays both his hand and that of dummy.

Declarer, before making any play, or either defender at his first turn to play, may require a restatement of the auction in its entirety.

After it is too late to have previous calls restated, declarer or either defender is entitled to be informed what the contract is and whether, but not by whom, it was doubled and redoubled.

Either defender may require an explanation of the partnership understanding relating to any call made by an opponent (see Proprieties 4), but only at that defender's own turn to play. Declarer may at any time require an explanation of the partnership understanding relating to any call or play made by a defender.

*After the final pass, either defender has the right to ask if it is his opening lead.

LAW 42
DUMMY'S RIGHTS
Dummy is entitled to give information as to fact or law, but may not initiate the discussion; and provided he has not forfeited his rights (see Law 43) he may also:

(a) ask declarer (but not a defender), when he has failed to follow suit, whether he has a card of the suit led;

(b) try to prevent any irregularity* by declarer;

(c) draw attention to any irregularity, but only after play is concluded.

*He may, for example, warn declarer against leading from the wrong hand.

LAW 43
DUMMY'S LIMITATIONS
Dummy may not participate in the play (except to play the cards of dummy's hand as directed by declarer), or make any comment on the bidding, play, or score of the current deal; and if he does so, Law 16 may apply. During play, dummy may not call attention to an irregularity once it has occurred.

Dummy forfeits the rights provided in (a), (b) and (c) of Law 42 if he exchanges hands with declarer, leaves his seat to watch declarer play, or, on his own initiative, looks at the face of a card in either defender's hand; and if, thereafter:

(a) He is the first to draw attention to a defender's irregularity, declarer may not enforce any penalty for the offense.

(b) He warns declarer not to lead from the wrong hand, (penalty) either defender may choose the hand from which declarer shall lead.

(c) He is the first to ask declarer if a play from declarer's hand constitutes a revoke, declarer must substitute a correct card if his play was a revoke, and (penalty) unless Law 64d applies, one trick is transferred to the defending side.

LAW 44
SEQUENCE AND PROCEDURE OF PLAY
The player who leads to a trick may play any card in his hand.* After the lead, each other player in turn plays a card, and the four cards so played constitute a trick.

In playing to a trick, each player must follow suit if possible. This obligation takes precedence over all other requirements of these Laws. If unable to follow suit, a player may play any card.*

A trick containing a trump is won by the player who has contributed to it the highest trump. A trick that does not contain a trump is won by the player who has contributed to it the highest card of the suit led. The player which has won the trick leads to the next trick.

*Unless he is subject to restriction after an irregularity committed by his side.

LAW 45
CARD PLAYED
Each player except dummy should play a card by detaching it from his hand and placing it, face up, on the table where other players can easily reach and see it. Dummy, if instructed by declarer to do so, may play from his hand a card named or designated by declarer.*

A card must be played:

(a) If it is a defender's card held so that it is possible for his partner to see its face.

(b) If it is a card from declarer's hand that declarer holds face up, touching or nearly touching the table, or maintains in such a position as to indicate that it has been played.

(c) If it is a card in dummy deliberately touched by declarer except for the purpose of arranging dummy's cards or of reaching a card above or below the card or cards touched.

(d) If the player who holds the card names or otherwise designates it as the cards he proposes to play. A player may, without penalty, change an inadvertent designation if he does so without pause for thought; but if an opponent has, in turn, played a card that was legal before the change of designation, that opponent may, without penalty, withdraw any card so played and substitute another.

(e) If it is a penalty card, subject to Law 50.

A card played may not be withdrawn except as provided in Law 47.

*If dummy places in played position a card declarer did not name, the card must be withdrawn if attention is drawn to it before each side has played to the next trick, and a defender may withdraw (without penalty) a card played after the error but before attention was drawn to it (see Law 47).

LAW 46
PARTIAL DESIGNATION OF A CARD TO BE PLAYED FROM DUMMY'S HAND
When declarer instructs dummy to play a card from dummy's hand, as permitted by Law 45, but names only a suit or only the rank of a card, or the equivalent, without fully specifying the card to be played, declarer must complete his partial designation. Dummy must not play a card before declarer has completed his partial designation.

LAW 47
RETRACTION OF A CARD PLAYED
(Club Law 47)
A card once played may be withdrawn only:

(a) to comply with a penalty, or to correct an illegal play, or to correct the simultaneous play of two or more cards (see Law 58); if a defender's card which has been exposed is withdrawn under this sub-section, it becomes a penalty card (see Law 50); or,

(b) after a change of designation as permitted by Law 45(d), or

(c) after an opponent's change of play, to substitute a card for one played*, or

(d) to correct a play* after misinformation by an opponent. A lead out of turn may be retracted without penalty if the leader was mistakenly informed by an opponent that it was his turn to lead.

*The offending side must not base any subsequent plays on information gained from such a withdrawn play.

PENALTY CARD
LAW 48
EXPOSURE OF DECLARER'S CARDS
Declarer is not subject to penalty for exposing a card, and no card of declarer's or dummy's ever becomes a penalty card. Declarer is not required to play any card

dropped accidentally.

When declarer faces his cards after an opening lead out of turn, Law 54 applies. When declarer faces his cards at any other time, he may be deemed to have made a claim or concession of tricks, in which case Law 68 applies.

LAW 49
EXPOSURE OF A DEFENDER'S CARDS

Whenever a defender faces a card on the table, holds a card so that it is possible for his partner to see its face, or names a card as being in his hand, before he is entitled to do so in the normal course of play or application of the law, (penalty) each such card becomes a penalty card (Law 50).*

*Exposure of a card or cards by a defender who is making a claim or concession of trick is subject to Law 70.

LAW 50
DISPOSITION OF A PENALTY CARD

A card is a penalty card when prematurely exposed. It must be left face up on the table until it is played or until an alternate penalty has been selected.

A single card below the rank of an honor and exposed inadvertently (as in playing two cards to a trick or in dropping a card accidentally) becomes a minor penalty card. Any penalty card of honor rank, or any card exposed through deliberate play (as in leading out of turn, or in revoking and then correcting) becomes a major penalty card; when one defender has two or more penalty cards, all such cards become major penalty cards.

When a defender has a minor penalty card, he may not play any other card of the same suit below the rank of an honor until he has first played the penalty card. (However, he is entitled to play an honor card instead of the minor penalty card.) There is no further penalty, but the offender's partner must not base any subsequent play on information gained through seeing the penalty card.

When a defender has a major penalty card, such card must be played at the first legal opportunity, whether in leading, following suit, discarding or trumping. If a defender has two or more penalty cards that can legally be played, declarer may designate which is to be played. The obligation to follow suit, or to comply with a lead or play penalty, takes precedence over the obligation to play a penalty card, but the penalty card must still be left face up on the table and played at the next legal opportunity.

When a defender has the lead while his partner has a major penalty card, declarer may choose to impose a lead penalty at this point: he may require that defender to lead the suit of the penalty card, or may prohibit that defender from leading that suit (a prohibition continues for as long as he retains the lead). If declarer does impose a lead penalty, the penalty card is picked up at once. If declarer does not, the defender may lead any card; but the penalty card remains a penalty card. The defender may not lead until declarer has indicated his choice.

LAW 51
TWO OR MORE PENALTY CARDS

When a defender has two or more penalty cards in one suit, and declarer requires or prohibits the lead of that suit, the defender may pick up every penalty card in that suit and may make any legal play to the trick.

When a defender has penalty cards in more than one suit, declarer may prohibit the defender's partner from leading every such suit, or require him to lead one such suit; but the defender may then pick up every penalty card in every suit required or prohibited by declarer and may make any legal play to the trick.

LAW 52
FAILURE TO LEAD OR PLAY A PENALTY CARD

When a defender is required by Law 50 to play a penalty card, but instead plays another card, he must leave the illegally played card face up on the table and;

(a) declarer may accept the defender's lead or play, and must do so if he has thereafter played from his or dummy's hand, but the unplayed penalty card remains a penalty card; or,

(b) declarer may require the defender to substitute the penalty card for the card illegally played, in which case the illegally played card becomes a major penalty card.

LEAD OUT OF TURN

LAW 53
LEAD OUT OF TURN ACCEPTED

Any lead out of turn may be treated by an opponent as a correct lead. It becomes a correct lead if an opponent accepts it by making a statement to that effect, or if that opponent next to play plays a card to the irregular lead.*

However, the player whose turn it was to lead - unless he is the offender's partner - may make his proper lead subsequent to the infraction without his card being treated as played to the irregular lead. The proper lead stands, and all cards played in error to this trick may be withdrawn without penalty.

*When such a play is made by a defender who is not next to play after the irregular lead, Law 57 applies.

LAW 54
OPENING LEAD OUT OF TURN

When a defender makes the opening lead out of turn:

(a) Declarer may accept the irregular lead as provided in Law 53. Dummy's hand is spread in accordance with Law 41, and the second card to the trick is played from declarer's hand; but if declarer first plays to the trick from dummy's hand, dummy's card may not be withdrawn except to correct a revoke.

(b) Declarer must accept the irregular lead if he could have seen any of dummy's cards (except cards exposed during the auction, subject to Law 23). He is deemed to have accepted the irregular lead if he begins to spread his hand as though he were dummy and in so doing exposes one or more cards; declarer must spread his entire hand, and dummy becomes declarer.*

(c) Declarer may accept the irregular lead by spreading his hand and becoming dummy; his partner becomes the declarer.

(d) Declarer may require the defender to retract his irregular lead (except as provided in (b) above), and then Law 56 applies.

*If cards are so exposed from both declarer's and dummy's hands, the player who was regularly to become declarer remains declarer.

LAW 55
DECLARER'S LEAD OUT OF TURN

When declarer leads out of turn from his or dummy's hand;

(a) Either defender may accept that lead as provided in Law 53.

(b) Either defender may require declarer to retract that

lead. Then,

(i) if it was a defender's turn to lead, declarer restores the card led in error to his or dummy's hand, without penalty;

(ii) if declarer has led from the wrong hand when it was his turn to lead from his or dummy's hand, he withdraws the card led in error; he must lead a card from the correct hand.

(iii) if declarer adopts a line of play that could have been based on information obtained through his infraction, the offenders should redress the damage in accordance with Proprieties 1.

LAW 56
DEFENDER'S LEAD OUT OF TURN

When a defender leads out of turn:

(a) Declarer may accept that lead as provided in Law 53.

(b) Declarer may require the defender to retract that lead; the card illegally led becomes a major penalty card (see Law 50 - note that lead penalties are provided).

IRREGULAR LEADS AND PLAYS

LAW 57
PREMATURE LEAD OR PLAY BY A DEFENDER

When a defender leads to the next trick before his partner has played to the current trick, or plays out of turn before his partner has played, (penalty) declarer may:

(a) require offender's partner to play his highest card of the suit led; or

(b) require offender's partner to play his lowest card of the suit led; or

(c) prohibit offender's partner from playing any card of one different suit specified by declarer.

Declarer must select one of these options, and if the offender's partner cannot comply with the penalty selected he may play any card, as provided in Law 59.

When, as a result of the application of the penalty, the offender's partner wins the current trick, he leads to the next trick; and any card led or played out of turn by the other defender becomes a major penalty card (Law 50).

A defender is not subject to penalty for playing before his partner if declarer has played from both hands; but a singleton or one of two or more equal cards in dummy is not considered automatically played unless dummy has played the card.

LAW 58
SIMULTANEOUS LEADS OR PLAYS

A lead or play made simultaneously with another player's legal lead or play is deemed to be subsequent to it.

If a defender leads or plays two or more cards simultaneously, and if only one such card is visible, he must play that card; if more than one card is exposed, he must designate the card he proposes to play and each other card exposed becomes a penalty card (Law 50).

If declarer leads or plays two or more cards simultaneously from either hand, he must designate the card he proposes to play and must restore any other card to the correct hand. If declarer withdraws a visible card and a defender has already played to that card, such defender may, without penalty, withdraw his card and substitute another (see footnote to Law 47).

If the error remains undiscovered until both sides have

played to the next trick, Law 67 applies.

LAW 59
INABILITY TO LEAD OR PLAY AS REQUIRED

A player may play any otherwise legal card if he is unable to lead or play as required to comply with a penalty, whether because he holds no card of the required suit, or because he has only cards of a suit he is prohibited from leading, or because he is obliged to follow suit.

LAW 60
PLAY AFTER AN ILLEGAL PLAY

A play by a member of the non-offending side after his RHO has played out of turn, and before a penalty has been imposed, forfeits the right to penalize the offense. The illegal play is treated as though it were in turn (but Law 53 applies to the player whose turn it was). If the offending side had a previous obligation to play a penalty card or to comply with a lead or play penalty, the obligation remains at future turns.

When a defender plays after declarer has been required to retract his lead out of turn from either hand, but before declarer has led from the correct hand, the defender's card becomes a penalty card (Law 50).

A play by a member of the offending side before a penalty has been imposed does not affect the rights of the opponents and may itself be subject to penalty.

THE REVOKE

LAW 61
FAILURE TO FOLLOW SUIT -
INQUIRIES CONCERNING A REVOKE

Failure to follow suit in accordance with Law 44, or failure to lead or play, when able, a card or suit required by law or specified by an opponent in accordance with a penalty, constitutes a revoke. Any player may ask a player who has failed to follow suit whether he has a card of the suit led, and may demand that an opponent correct his revoke, except that dummy* may ask of declarer, but not of a defender. (A claim of revoke does not warrant inspection of quitted tricks, except as permitted in Law 66).

*Unless he has forfeited his rights, as specified by Law 43.

LAW 62
CORRECTION OF A REVOKE

A player must correct his revoke if he becomes aware of it before it becomes established (See Law 63). To correct a revoke, the offender withdraws the card he played in revoking and follows suit with any card. A card so withdrawn becomes a major-penalty card (Law 50) if it was played from a defender's unfaced hand. The card may be replaced without penalty if it was played from declarer's or dummy's hand* or if it was a defender's faced card. Each member of the non-offending side may, without penalty, withdraw any card he may have played after the revoke but before attention was drawn to it (see footnote to Law 47). After a non-offender so withdraws a card, the hand of the offending side next in rotation may withdraw a played card, which becomes a major-penalty card if played from a defender's hand.

On the twelfth trick, a revoke, even if established, must be corrected if discovered before the cards have been mixed together. If the revoke was committed by a defender before his partner has played to the twelfth trick, and if offender's partner holds cards of more than one suit, (penalty) declarer may then require the offender's partner to play to that trick either of the two cards he could legally have played.

*Subject to Law 43. A claim of revoke does not warrant inspection of quitted tricks except as permitted in Law 67.

LAW 63
ESTABLISHMENT OF A REVOKE

A revoke becomes established when the offender or his partner leads or plays (whether legally or illegally) to the following trick, or names or otherwise designates a card to be so played, or makes a claim or concession of tricks orally or by facing his hand. The revoke may then no longer be corrected (except for a revoke on the twelfth trick - see Law 62), and the trick on which the revoke occurred stands as played.

LAW 64
PROCEDURE AFTER ESTABLISHMENT OF A REVOKE

When a revoke has become established,

(a) If the offending player* won the trick on which the revoke occurred, (penalty) that trick and one of any subsequent tricks won by the offending side are transferred** to the nonoffending side (if no subsequent trick was won by the offending side, only the revoke trick is transferred);

(b) If the offender's partner won the trick on which the revoke occurred, (penalty) that trick is transferred** to the nonoffending side and, if the offending player himself won a subsequent trick with a card that could legally have been played to the revoke trick, one additional trick (but no more) is transferred** to the nonoffending side.

(c) If the nonoffending side won the trick on which the revoke occurred, and if the offending side won any trick after the revoke, (penalty)

(i) The first such trick is transferred** to the nonoffending side, and

(ii) If the offending side won two or more tricks after the revoke, any of which was won by the offending player with a card he could legally have played to the revoke trick an additional trick is transferred** to the nonoffending side;

(d) There is no trick penalty for the established revoke if,

(i) The offending side did not win either the trick on which the revoke occurred or any subsequent trick; or if,

(ii) The revoke was a subsequent revoke in the same suit by the same player; or if,

(iii) The revoke was made in failing to play any card faced on or belonging to a hand faced on the table, including a card from dummy's hand; or if,

(iv) Attention was first drawn to the revoke after all players had abandoned their hands and permitted the cards to be mixed together; or if,

(v) the revoke was on the twelfth trick (see Law 62).

N.B. When any established revoke, including one not subject to penalty, causes damage to the non-offending side insufficiently compensated by the law, the offending side should, under Proprieties 1, transfer additional tricks so as to restore equity.

* If declarer revokes, but wins the trick on which the revoke occurred in dummy, Section (b) applies

**For the scoring of transferred tricks, see Law 77.

TRICKS

LAW 65
COLLECTION AND ARRANGEMENT OF TRICKS

The cards constituting each completed trick are collected by a member of the side that won the trick and are then turned face down on the table. Each trick shall be identifiable as such, and all tricks taken by a side shall be arranged in sequence in front of declarer or of one defender, as the case may be, in such manner that each side can determine the number of tricks it has won and the order in which they were taken.

LAW 66
INSPECTION OF TRICKS

Declarer or either defender may, until a member of his side has led or played to the following trick, inspect a trick and inquire what card each player has played to it. Thereafter, until play ceases, quitted tricks may be inspected only to account for a missing or surplus card. After play ceases, the tricks and unplayed cards may be inspected to settle an allegation of a revoke, of honors, or of the number of tricks won or lost. If, after an allegation has been made, a player on one side makes verification of the allegation impossible, as by mixing the cards or merging the tricks, the issue must be decided in favor of the other side.

LAW 67
TRICK EITHER APPROPRIATED IN ERROR OR DEFECTIVE

A trick appropriated by the wrong side must, upon demand, be restored to the side that has in fact won it*.

A trick containing more or fewer than four cards is defective. When one player is found, during play, to have fewer or more cards than all the other players, the previous tricks should be forthwith examined, face down; if a defective trick is discovered, the player with a correspondingly incorrect number of cards is held responsible. The defective trick is inspected face up and

(a) Until the responsible player has played to a subsequent trick, the defective trick is rectified as follows:

(i) If the offender has failed to play a card to the defective trick, he adds to that trick a card he can legally play;

(ii) If the offender has played more than one card to the defective trick, he withdraws all but one card, leaving a card he can legally play;

(iii) the non-offending side may, without penalty, withdraw any cards played after the irregularity and before attention was drawn to it (see footnote to Law 47); but the offending side may not withdraw cards that constitute legal plays, and any cards they withdraw may become penalty cards (Law 50).

(b) After the responsible player has played to a subsequent trick, the ownership of the defective trick cannot be changed and

(i) If the offender has failed to play a card to the defective trick, he forthwith faces and adds a card to that trick, if possible one he could legally have played to it.

(ii) If the offender has played more than one card to the defective trick, he withdraws all but one card, leaving the highest card he could legally have played to that trick. A withdrawn card may become a penalty card (Law 50); such a card is deemed to have belonged continuously to the offender's hand and failure to have played it to an earlier trick may constitute a revoke.

*If calls have been made on a subsequent deal, see Law

78.

CLAIMS AND CONCESSIONS

LAW 68
DECLARER'S CLAIM OR
CONCESSION OF TRICKS

Declarer makes a claim or a concession whenever he announces that he will win or lose one or more of the remaining tricks, or suggests that play be curtailed, or faces his hand. Declarer should not make a claim or concession if there is any doubt as to the number of tricks to be won or lost.

LAW 69
PROCEDURE FOLLOWING DECLARER'S
CLAIM OR CONCESSION
(Club Law 69)

When declarer has made a claim or concession, play is temporarily suspended and declarer must place and leave his hand face up on the table and forthwith make a comprehensive statement as to his proposed plan of play, including the order in which he will play the remaining cards.

Declarer's claim or concession is allowed, and the deal is scored accordingly, if both defenders agree to it. The claim or concession must be allowed if either defender has permitted any of his remaining cards to be mixed with another player's cards; otherwise, if either defender disputes declarer's claim or concession, it is allowed. Then, play continues.

When his claim or concession is not allowed, declarer must play in, leaving his hand face up on the table. At any time, either defender may face his hand for inspection by his partner, and declarer may not impose a penalty for any irregularity committed by a defender whose hand is so faced.

The objective of subsequent play is to achieve a result as equitable as possible to both sides, but any doubtful point must be resolved in favor of the defenders. Declarer may not make any play inconsistent with the statement he may have made at the time of his claim or concession. And if he failed to make an appropriate statement at that time, his choice of plays is restricted thereby:

(a) If declarer made no relevant statement, he may not finesse* in any suit unless an opponent failed to follow in that suit before the claim or concession, or would subsequently fail to follow in that suit on any conceivable sequence of plays.

(b) If declarer may have been unaware, at the time of his claim or concession, that a trump remained in a defender's hand, either defender may require him to draw, or not to draw, the outstanding trump.

(c) If declarer did not, in his statement, mention an unusual plan of play, he may adopt only a routine line of play.

If declarer attempts to make a play prohibited under this law, either defender may accept the play, or, provided neither defender has subsequently played, require declarer to withdraw the card so played and substitute another that conforms to his obligations.

*For these purposes, a finesse is a play the success of which depends on finding one defender rather than the other with or without a particular card.

LAW 70
DEFENDER'S CLAIM OR CONCESSION

OF TRICKS

A defender makes a concession when he agrees to declarer's claim, or when he announces that he will lose one or more of the remaining tricks.

A defender makes a claim when he announces that he will win one or more of the remaining tricks, or when he shows any or all of his cards for this purpose. If:

(a) the claim pertains only to an uncompleted trick currently in progress, play proceeds normally; cards exposed or otherwise revealed by the defender in making his claim do not become penalty cards, but Law 16, Unauthorized Information, may apply to a claimer's partner.

(b) the claim pertains to subsequent tricks, play is temporarily suspended; the claimer must place and leave his hand face up on the table and make a comprehensive statement as to his proposed plan of defense. The claim is allowed, and the deal scored accordingly, if declarer agrees to it. If declarer disputes the claim, the defenders must play on with the claimer's hand face up on the table. Those cards do not become penalty cards. However, declarer may prohibit claimer's partner from making any play that could be suggested to him by seeing the faced cards.

LAW 71
CONCESSION WITHDRAWN

A concession may be withdrawn:

(a) If a player concedes a trick his side has, in fact, won; or if declarer concedes defeat of a contract he has already fulfilled; or if a defender concedes fulfillment of a contract his side has already defeated. (If the score has been entered, see Law 78).

(b) If a trick that has been conceded cannot be lost by any probable sequence of play of the remaining cards, and if attention is drawn to the fact before the cards have been mixed together.

(c) If a defender concedes one or more tricks and his partner immediately objects, but Law 16 may apply.

THE SCORE

LAW 72
POINTS EARNED

The result of each deal played is recorded in points, which fall into two classes:

1. *Trick Points.* Only declarer's side can earn trick points, and only by winning at least the number of odd tricks specified in the contract. Only the value of odd tricks named in the contract may be scored as trick points (see law 81). Trick points mark the progression of the rubber towards its completion.

2. *Premium Points.* Either side or both sides may earn premium points. Declarer's side earns premium points by winning one or more overtricks; by fulfilling a doubled or redoubled contract; by bidding and making a slam; by holding scorable honors in declarer's or dummy's hand; or by winning the final game of a rubber.* The defenders earn premium points by defeating the contract (undertrick penalty) or by holding scorable honors in either of their hands (see Law 81).

Each side's premium points are added to its trick points at the conclusion of the rubber.

*For incomplete rubber, see Law 80.

LAW 73
PARTSCORE - GAME

The basic units of trick points are partscore and game. A partscore is recorded for declarer's side whenever declarer fulfills a contract for which the trick points are less than 100 points. Game is won by that side which is the first to have scored 100 or more trick points either in a single deal or by addition of two or more partscores made separately. No partscore made by either side in the course of one game is carried forward into the next game.

LAW 74
THE RUBBER

A rubber ends when a side has won two games, At the conclusion of the rubber, the winners of two games are credited with a premium of the rubber, the winners of two games are credited with a premium score of 500 points if the other side has won one game, or with 700 points if the other side has not won a game.

The trick and premium points scored by each side in the course of the rubber are then added. The side with the larger combined total wins the rubber, and the difference between the two totals represents the margin of victory computed in points.

LAW 75
METHOD OF SCORING

The score of each deal must be recorded, and it is preferable that a member of each side should keep score.

Scores are entered in two adjacent columns separated by a vertical line. Each scorer enters points earned by his side in the left-hand column, and points earned by his opponents in the right-hand column.

Each side has a trick point score and a premium score, separated by a horizontal line intersecting the vertical line. All trick points are entered, as they are earned, in descending order below the horizontal line (below the line), all premium points in ascending order above the line.

Whenever a game is won, another horizontal line is drawn under all trick point scores recorded for either side, in order to mark completion of the game. Subsequent trick points are entered below that line.

LAW 76
RESPONSIBILITY FOR THE SCORE

When the play of a deal is completed, all four players are equally responsible for ascertaining that the number of tricks won by each side is correctly determined and that all scores are promptly and correctly entered.

LAW 77
TRANSFERRED TRICKS

A trick transferred through a revoke penalty is reckoned for all scoring purposes as though it had been won in play by the side to which it had been awarded.*

*Declarer plays in 3♥ and makes eight tricks. A revoke by a defender is found to have been established, with the defenders having won both the trick in which the revoke occurred and a later trick. Two tricks are transferred from the offenders to declarer, who therefore has ten tricks. Since he bid only 3♥, he scores 90 trick points, which count toward game, and 30 premium points for the overtrick.

LAW 78
CORRECTION OF THE SCORE

When it is acknowledged by a majority of the players that a scoring error was made in recording an agreed-upon result (e.g., failure to enter honors, or incorrect computation of score), the error must be corrected if discovered before the net score of the rubber has been agreed to. However, except with the consent of all four players, an erroneous agreement as to the number of tricks won by each side may not be corrected after all players have called on the next deal.

In case of disagreement between two scores kept, the recollection of the majority of the players as to the facts governs.

LAW 79
DEALS PLAYED WITH AN INCORRECT PACK

Scores recorded for deals played with an incorrect pack are not subject to change by reason of the discovery of the imperfection after the cards have been mixed together.

LAW 80
INCOMPLETE RUBBER

When, for any reason, a rubber is not finished, the score is computed as follows:

If only one game has been completed, the winners of that game are credited with 300 points; if only one side has a partscore or partscores in a game not completed, that side is credited with 100 points; the trick and premium points of each side are then added, and the side with the greater number of points wins the difference between the two totals.

LAW 81
TRICK SCORE

Scored below the line by declarer's side.
RUBBER, GAME, PART-SCORE, CONTRACT FULFILLED

	IF TRUMPS ARE			
	♣	♦	♥	♠
For each trick over six, bid and made				
Undoubled	20	20	30	30
Doubled	40	40	60	60
Redoubled	80	80	120	120

	AT A NOTRUMP CONTRACT		
	UNDBL	DBL	REDBL
For the first trick over six, bid and made	40	80	160
For each additional trick over six, bid and made	30	60	120

The first side to score 100 points below the line, in one or more hands, wins a GAME. When a game is won, both sides start without a trick score toward the next game. First side to win two games wins the RUBBER POINTS.

PREMIUM SCORE

Scored above the line by declarer's side.

For winning the RUBBER, if opponents have won no game	700
For winning the RUBBER, if opponents have won one game	500
For having won the only game in an UNFINISHED RUBBER	300
For having the only PARTSCORE in an unfinished game	100
For making any DOUBLED CONTRACT	50
For making any REDOUBLED CONTRACT	100

SLAMS

For making a SLAM,	Not Vulnerable	Vulnerable
Small Slam (12 tricks) bid and made	500	750
Grand Slam (all 13 tricks) bid and made	1000	1500

OVERTRICKS

For each OVERTRICK (tricks made in excess of contract)	Not Vulnerable	Vulnerable
Undoubled	Trick value	Trick value
Doubled	100	200
Redoubled	200	400

HONORS

Scored above the line by either side:

For holding four of the five trump HONORS (A,K,Q,J,10)
in one hand..100
For holding all five trump HONORS (A,K,Q,J,10)
in one hand..150
For holding all four ACES in one hand at a notrump contract 150

UNDERTRICK PENALTIES

Tricks by which declarer fails to fulfill the contract: scored above the line by declarer's opponents, if contract is not fulfilled.

	Not Vulnerable		
	UNDBL	DBL	REBDL
For first undertrick	50	100	200
For second and third undertrick	50	200	400
For each additional undertrick	50	300	600

	Vulnerable		
	UNDBL	DBL	REBDL
For first undertrick	100	200	400
For each additional undertrick	100	300	600

PROPRIETIES

1. GENERAL PRINCIPLES

These Laws cannot cover every situation that might arise, nor can they produce equity in every situation covered. Occasionally, the players themselves must redress damage. The guiding principle: The side that commits an irregularity bears an obligation not to gain directly from the infraction itself; however, the offending side is entitled to profit after an infraction, as an indirect result, through subsequent good fortune.*

*Two examples may clarify the distinction between direct gain through an infraction and indirect gain through good luck.

(a) South, declarer at 3 NT, will have nine tricks available if the diamond suit - six cards headed by the ace, king, queen in dummy opposite declarer's singleton - divides favorably; and the six missing diamonds are in fact split evenly, three-three, between East and West. However, West, who holds three diamonds headed by the jack, shows out on the third round of diamonds, revoking. Thus, declarer wins only three diamond tricks instead of six, for a total of six tricks instead of nine. The estab-

lished revoke is later discovered, so one penalty trick is transferred after play ends. But declarer is still down two.

Here, East-West gained two tricks as a direct consequence of their infraction. The players should adjudicate this result, scoring the deal as 3 NT, making three. (Note, declarer is not given a penalty trick in addition; the object is to restore equity, to restore the result likely to have occurred had the infraction not been committed.)

(b) South, declarer at 4♠, is entitled to require or forbid a diamond opening lead from West, because of an auction-period infraction committed by East. Declarer instructs West to lead a diamond - but West, having no diamonds, leads another suit. East, now aware that partner is void in diamonds, is able to find what would be, under normal circumstances, a most unnatural line of defense to give West two ruffs. Thereby, East-West defeat a contract that would almost certainly have been made but for the infraction.

Here, East-West profited only indirectly through their auction-period infraction; their gain was the direct consequence of declarer's decision to require a diamond lead, and of West's lucky void. So, the players should allow the result to stand. Declarer was damaged not by the infraction itself but by bad luck afterwards - and luck is part of the game of bridge.

To infringe a law intentionally is a serious breach of ethics, even if there is a prescribed penalty that one is willing to pay. The offense may be the more serious when no penalty is prescribed.

There is no obligation to draw attention to an inadvertent infraction of law committed by one's own side. However, a player should not attempt to conceal such an infraction, as by committing a second revoke, concealing a card involved in a revoke or mixing the cards prematurely.

It is proper to warn partner against infringing a law of the game: for example against revoking, or against calling, leading or playing out of turn.

2. COMMUNICATION BETWEEN PARTNERS

Communication between partners during the auction and play should be effected only by means of the calls and plays themselves, not through the manner in which they are made, nor through extraneous remarks and gestures, nor through questions asked of the opponents and explanations given to them. Calls should be made in a uniform tone without special emphasis or inflection, and without undue hesitation or haste. Plays should be made without emphasis, gesture or mannerism and so far as possible at a uniform rate.

Inadvertently to vary the tempo or manner in which a call or play is made does not in itself constitute a violation of propriety, but inferences from such variation may properly be drawn only by an opponent, and at his own risk. It is improper to attempt to mislead an opponent by means of a remark or a gesture, through the haste or hesitancy of a call or play (such as hesitation with singleton) or by the manner in which the call or play is made.

Any player may properly attempt to deceive an opponent through a call or play (so long as the deception is not protected by concealed partnership understanding). It is entirely proper to make all calls and plays in unvarying tempo and manner in order to avoid giving information to the opponents.

When a player has available to him improper information from his partner's remark, question, explanation, gesture, mannerism, special emphasis, inflection, haste or hesitation, he should carefully avoid taking any advantage that might accrue to his side.

3. CONDUCT AND ETIQUETTE

A player should maintain at all times a courteous attitude toward his partner and opponents. He should carefully avoid any remark or action that might cause annoyance or embarrassment to another player or might interfere with the enjoyment of the game. Every player should follow uniform and correct procedure in calling and playing, since any departure from correct standards may disrupt the orderly progress of the game.

As a matter of courtesy, a player should refrain from:

(i) Paying insufficient attention to the game (as when a player obviously takes no interest in his hand, or frequently requests a review of the auction).

(ii) Making gratuitous comments during the play as to the auction or the adequacy of the contract.

(iii) Detaching a card from his hand before it is his turn to play.

(iv) Arranging completed tricks in a disorderly manner, thereby making it difficult to determine the sequence of plays.

(v) Making a claim or concession of tricks if there is any doubt as to the outcome of the deal.

(vi) Prolonging play unnecessarily for the purpose of disconcerting the other players.

Furthermore, the following are considered breaches of propriety:

(a) Using different designations for the same call.

(b) Indicating approval or disapproval of a call or play.

(c) Indicating the expectation or intention of winning or losing a trick that has not been completed.

(d) Commenting or behaving during the auction or play so as to call attention to a significant occurrence, or to the state of the score or to the number of tricks still required for success.

(e) Showing an obvious lack of further interest in the deal (as by folding one's cards).

(f) Looking intently at any other player during the auction or play, or at another player's hand as for the purpose of seeing his cards or of observing the place from which he draws a card (but it is not improper to act on information acquired by inadvertently seeing an opponent's card).

(g) Varying the normal tempo of bidding or play for the purpose of disconcerting another player.

(h) Mixing the cards before the result of a deal has been agreed upon.

4. PARTNERSHIP AGREEMENTS

It is improper to convey information by means of a call or play based on special partnership agreement, whether explicit or implicit, unless such information is fully and freely available to the opponents.

It is not improper for a player to violate an announced partnership agreement, so long as his partner is unaware of the violation (but habitual violations within a partnership may create implicit agreements, which must be disclosed). No player has the obligation to disclose to the opponents that he has violated an announced agreement; and if the opponents are subsequently damaged, as through drawing a false inference from such violation, they are not entitled to redress.

When explaining the significance of partner's call or play in reply to an opponent's inquiry, a player should disclose all special information conveyed to him through partnership agreement or partnership experience; but he need not disclose inferences drawn from his general bridge knowledge and experience. It is improper for a player whose partner has given a mistaken explanation to correct the error immediately or to indicate in any manner that a mistake has been made. (He must not take advantage of the unauthorized information so obtained.)

5. SPECTATORS

A spectator, including a member of the table not playing, must not display any reaction to bidding or play while a hand is in progress (as by shifting his attention from one player's hand to another's). He must not in any way disturb a player. During the hand, he must refrain from mannerisms or remarks of any kind (including conversation with a player). He may not call attention to any irregularity or mistake, nor speak on any question of fact or law except by request of the players.

APPENDIX 1

Any group may specify that the Alert procedure be used in its games. Then, the partner of a player who makes a call to which the partnership attaches a special, unusual meaning, one with which the opponents may not be familiar, is required to say, "Alert."

N.B., no explanation should be volunteered. After the Alert, either opponent may, at his own turn to call, inquire as to the special meaning.

A partnership that does not want to be Alerted should so request; and this request should be honored.

APPENDIX 2

Any group may specify that the "Stop" or "Skip Bid" procedure be used in its games. Then, whenever a player opens the bidding at the two level or higher, or makes a bid higher than necessary to overcall the last preceding bid, he announces, "Stop," or "Skip Bid" (the group specifies the form to be used), before making the bid.

After this announcement, the opponent next to speak is required to hesitate for approximately ten seconds before making any call.

APPENDIX 3

Any group may specify that opening leads be made facedown in its games. If this opening lead is determined to be out of turn (before being faced), the leader returns the card to his hand without penalty.

When the face-down lead will be legal, dummy delays spreading his hand. Opening leader's partner asks any questions concerning the auction, including a review. Then, the lead is faced (opening leader may not withdraw it), dummy is faced, and play proceeds normally.

Part VIII
ALTERNATIVE CLUB LAWS

When bridge is played at a club, it is often practicable to designate an impartial and experienced person as "Arbiter" for the game. The Arbiter interprets and applies the Laws after an irregularity occurs, and generally assumes the role assigned to the "Director" in duplicate bridge. When such an Arbiter is available, certain laws can be modified so as to produce greater equity.

The "Club Laws" prescribe a somewhat different procedure after attention is drawn to an irregularity, and there is a different disposition for disputed claims. The principal changes, however, lie in the authority given to the Arbiter, after specified types of irregularity, to "adjust the score" of a deal once play is over. In adjusting a score, the Arbiter assigns a new result, the result he judges would have been achieved had the irregularity not occurred. The Arbiter should resolve any substantial doubt in favor of the non-offending side.

The alternative laws are in force only upon advance agreement by the players, or in accordance with the standing and published policy of a club. Any game may play under these Club Laws, so long as an Arbiter is nominated in advance; when there are more than four members of a table, a non-playing member can act as Arbiter.

CLUB LAW 13

The Arbiter must be called as soon as attention is drawn to an irregularity. Calling the Arbiter does not forfeit any rights to which a player may otherwise be entitled. Any player except dummy may draw attention to an irregularity and call the Arbiter. The fact that a player draws attention to an irregularity committed by his side does not affect the rights of the opponents.

After attention has been drawn to an irregularity, no player should call or play until the Arbiter has determined all matters in regard to rectification and to the assessment of a penalty. Premature correction of an irregularity on the part of an offender may subject him to further penalty.

CLUB LAW 14

The Arbiter assesses penalties when applicable. When these Club Laws provide an option among penalties, the Arbiter explains the options available.

The Arbiter may assign an adjusted score, but only when these Club Laws empower him to do so, or when the Law provides no indemnity to a non-offending contestant for the particular type of violation of law or propriety committed by an opponent. He may not assign an adjusted score on the ground that the penalty provided in the Law is unduly severe or unduly advantageous to either side.

CLUB LAW 16

If a player conveys information to his partner by means of a remark or question, or by an unmistakable hesitation, special emphasis, tone, gesture, movement, mannerism or any other action that suggests a call, lead or plan of play; and if attention is drawn to the offense and the Arbiter is called, the Arbiter should require that the auction or play continue, reserving the right to assign an adjusted score if he considers that the result could have been affected by the illegal information.

After play ends, he should award an adjusted score to redress damage caused to the innocent side, when an opponent chose from among alternative logical actions one that could reasonably have been suggested by his partner's tempo, manner, remark, etc.

CLUB LAW 23

(Regular Law 23 stands intact but with the following addition, which applies as well to a change of call, an insufficient bid, a call out of rotation and an inadmissible call.)

When the penalty for an irregularity, under this or any other Law, would compel the offender's partner to pass at his next turn, and when the Arbiter deems that this enforced pass will necessarily* damage the innocent side, the Arbiter may reserve the right to assign an adjusted score.

*The score should not be adjusted merely because the penalty happened to result in good fortune for the offending side. The word "necessarily" restricts score adjustment to those instances in which the offender could have known, at the time of his infraction, that it would be to his advantage to require partner to pass.

CLUB LAW 25

The penalties in Club Law 23 apply.

CLUB LAW 27

Regular Law 27 stands intact but with the following addition to sub-section (a).

If the insufficient bid conveyed such substantial information as to damage the non-offending side, the Arbiter may assign an adjusted score.

CLUB LAW 30

The provisions of Club Law 23 may apply.

CLUB LAW 31

The provisions of Club Law 23 may apply.

CLUB LAW 32

The provisions of Club Law 23 may apply.

CLUB LAW 35

The provisions of Club Law 23 may apply.

CLUB LAW 36

The provisions of Club Law 23 may apply.

CLUB LAW 38

The provisions of Club Law 23 may apply.

CLUB LAW 39

The provisions of Club Law 23 may apply.

CLUB LAW 40

If the Arbiter decides that a side has been damaged through its opponents' failure to explain the meaning of a call or play, he may award an adjusted score.

CLUB LAW 47

If a card retracted under sections (c) or (d) above gave substantial information to an opponent, the Arbiter may award an adjusted score.

CLUB LAW 64

Regular Law 64 stands, except that, when after any established revoke, including those not subject to penalty, the Arbiter deems that the non-offending side is insufficiently compensated by this Law for the damage caused, he should assign an adjusted score.

CLUB LAW 69

When declarer has made a claim or concession, play ceases (all play subsequent to a claim or concession must be voided by the Arbiter). Declarer must place and leave his hand face up on the table and forthwith make a comprehensive statement as to his proposed plan of play, including the order in which he will play his remaining cards.

Declarer's claim or concession is allowed, and the deal is scored accordingly, if both defenders agree to it. The claim or concession must be allowed if either defender has permitted any of his remaining cards to be mixed with another player's cards; otherwise, if either defender disputes declarer's claim or concession, the Arbiter must be called to adjudicate the result of the deal.

The Arbiter should adjudicate the result of the deal as equitably as possible to both sides, but any doubtful point should be resolved in favor of the defenders. He should proceed as follows:

(a) He should require the declarer to repeat the statement he made at the time of his claim. The Arbiter should then require all players to put their cards face up on the table and should hear the defenders' objections to the claim.

(b) When a trump is outstanding, he should award a trick to the defenders if

(i) in making his claim declarer made no statement about that trump, and

(ii) it is at all likely that declarer was unaware, at the time of his claim, that a trump remained in a defender's hand, and

(iii) a trick could be lost to that trump by any normal play (an inferior or careless play can be normal, but not an irrational play).

(c) He should not accept from declarer any proposed line of play inconsistent with his statement. If declarer did not make an appropriate announcement at the time of his original claim, the Arbiter should not accept from declarer any unusual line of play, or any proposed play that requires a finesse* in a suit, unless an opponent failed to follow in that suit before the claim or concession, or would subsequently fail to follow in that suit on any conceivable line of play.

*For these purposes, a finesse is a play the success of which depends on finding one defender rather than the other with or without a particular card

CLUB LAW 70

A defender makes a concession when he agrees to declarer's claim or when he announces that he will lose one or more of the remaining tricks.

A defender makes a claim when he announces that he will win one or more of the remaining tricks, or when he shows any or all of his cards to declarer for this purpose. If:

(a) the claim pertains only to an uncompleted trick currently in progress, play proceeds normally; cards exposed or otherwise revealed by the defender in making his claim do not become penalty cards, but Club Law 16, Unauthorized Information, may apply to claimer's partner.

(b) the claim pertains to subsequent tricks, play ceases (all play subsequent to the claim should be voided by the Arbiter). The defender must place and leave his hand face up on the table and make a comprehensive statement as to his proposed plan of defense. The claim is allowed, and the deal scored accordingly, if declarer agrees to it. If declarer disputes the claim, the Arbiter must be called to adjudicate the result of the deal. He does so as equitably as possible to both sides, but should award to the declarer any trick that the defenders could lose by normal play (an inferior or careless play can be normal, but not an irrational play).

CLUB APPEALS COMMITTEE

Whenever possible, a club should establish an Appeals Committee to review decisions of the Arbiter; and any game may designate a Committee to which appeals may be taken. If such a procedure has been agreed to or published in advance, any player may appeal any decision by the Arbiter. The Appeals Committee exercises all powers assigned by these Laws to the Arbiter, and may overrule any of his decisions.

When an Arbiter's decision is overruled on appeal, only the scoring of the particular deal is affected; subsequent scores stand as recorded. If the Committee's decision results in fulfillment of a contract originally recorded as defeated, or defeat of a contract recorded as fulfilled, then,

(a) for a contract now fulfilled: in addition to the other trick score and premium score, declarer's side received a premium of 50 points for a partscore that would not then have increased the below-the-line score to 100; and for any other contract, declarer's side received a premium according to vulnerability — 300 points if declarer's side was non-vulnerable, 400 points if declarer's was vulnerable and the defenders not, 500 points if both sides were vulnerable.

(b) for a contract now defeated, when the original scoring resulted in a game: in addition to the other premium score, the defenders receive a premium of 50 points if they alone had scored a partscore in that game; plus a premium of 500 points if declarer's side originally won two of two games, or 200 points if the defenders side originally won two of three games.

RULES FOR CLUB PROCEDURE

The following rules, governing membership is new and existing tables, have proven satisfactory in club use over a long period of years.

A. *Definitions*

Member — An applicant who has acquired the right to play at a table either immediately or in his turn

Complete Table — A table with six members

Incomplete Table — A table with four or five members.

Cut In — Assert the right to become a member of an incomplete table, or to become a member of a complete table at such time as it may become incomplete.

B. *Time Limit on Right to Play*

An applicant may not play in a rubber unless he has become a member of a table before a card is duly drawn for the selection of players or partners.

C. *Newly Formed Tables*

Four to six applicants may form a table. If there are more than six applicants, the six highest-ranking ones become members. The four highest-ranking members play the first rubber. Those who have not played, ranked in their order of entry into the room, take precedence over those who have played; the latter rank equally, except that players leaving existing tables to join the new table rank lowest. Precedence between those of equal rank is determined by drawing cards, the player who draws the highest-ranking card having precedence.

D. *Cutting In*

An application establishes membership in a table either forthwith or (if the table is complete) as soon as a vacancy occurs, unless applications in excess of the number required to complete a table are made at the same time, in which case precedence between applicants is established by drawing cards, as provided in the preceding rule.

E. *Going Out*

After each rubber place must be made for any member who did not play that last rubber, by the member who has played the greatest number of consecutive rubbers at that table. Cards are drawn for precedence if necessary. A member who has left another existing table must draw cards, for his first rubber, with the member who would otherwise have played. A player who breaks up a game by leaving three players at a table may not compete against them for entry at another table until each of them has played at least one rubber.

F. *Membership Limited to One Table*

No one can be a member of more than one table at the same time, unless a member consents, on request, to make a fourth at another table and announces his intention of returning to his former table as soon as his place at the new table can be filled. Failure to announce such intention results in loss of membership at his former table.

FOUR-DEAL BRIDGE

Four-Deal Bridge is a form of Rubber Bridge much played in clubs and well suited to home play. Long rubbers are avoided; extra players need wait no longer than the time (about twenty minutes) required to complete four deals. The game is also called Club Bridge or Chicago (for the city in which it originated).

A. *Basic Rules*

The Laws of Contract Bridge and Rules for Club Procedure are followed, except as modified by the following rules.

B. *The Rubber*

A rubber consists of a series of four deals that have been bid and played. If a deal is passed out, the same player deals again and the deal passed out does not count as one of the four deals.

A fifth deal is void if attention is drawn to it at any time before there has been a new cut for partners or the game has terminated; if the error is not discovered in time for correction, the score stands as recorded. A sixth or subsequent deal is unconditionally void and no score for such a deal is ever permissible.

If fewer than four deals are played, the score shall stand for the incomplete series and the fourth deal need not be played unless attention is drawn to the error before there has been a new cut for partners or the game has terminated.

When the players are pivoting,* the fact that the players have taken their proper seats for the next rubber shall be considered a cut for partners.

*In a pivot game, partnerships for each rubber follow a fixed rotation.

C. *Vulnerability*

Vulnerability is not determined by previous scores but by the following schedule:

First deal: Neither side vulnerable.

Second and Third deals: Dealer's side vulnerable, the other side not vulnerable.

Fourth deal: Both sides vulnerable.

D. *Premiums*

For making or completing a game (100 or more trick points), a side receives a premium of 300 points if on that deal it is not vulnerable or 500 points if on that deal it is vulnerable. There is no additional premium for winning two or more games, each game premium being scored separately.

E. *The Score*

As a reminder of vulnerability in Four-Deal Bridge, two intersecting diagonal lines should be drawn near the top of the score pad.

The numeral "1" should be inserted in that one of the four angles thus formed that faces the first dealer. After play of the first deal is completed, "2" is inserted in the next angle in clockwise rotation, facing the dealer of the second deal. The numerals "3" and "4" are subsequently inserted at the start of the third and fourth deals, respectively, each in the angle facing the current dealer.

A correctly numbered diagram is conclusive as to vulnerability. There is no redress for a bid influenced by the scorer's failure to draw the diagram or for an error or omission in inserting a numeral or numerals in the diagram. Such error or omission should, upon discovery, be immediately corrected and the deal or deals should be scored or rescored as though the diagram and the number or numbers thereon had been properly inserted.

F. *Partscores*

A partscore or scores made previously may be combined with a partscore made in the current deal to complete a game or 100 or more trick points. The game premium is determined by the vulnerability, on that deal, of the side that completes the game. When a side makes or completes a game, no previous partscore of either side may thereafter be counted toward game.

A side that makes a partscore in the fourth deal, if the partscore is not sufficient to complete a game, receives a premium of 100 points. This premium is scored whether or not the same side or the other side has an uncompleted partscore. There is no separate premium for making a partscore in any other circumstance.

G. *Deal Out of Turn*

When a player deals out of turn, and there is no right to a redeal, the player who should have dealt retains his right to call first, but such right is lost if it is not claimed before the actual dealer calls. If the actual dealer calls before attention is drawn to the deal out of turn, each player thereafter calls in rotation. Vulnerability and scoring values are determined by the position of the player who should have dealt, regardless of which players actually dealt or called first. Neither the rotation of the deal nor the scoring should be affected by a deal out of turn. The next dealer is the player who would have dealt next if the deal had been in turn.

H. *Optional Rules and Customs*

The following practices, not required, have proved acceptable in some clubs and games.

(i) Since the essence of the game is speed, if a deal is passed out, the pack that has been shuffled for the next deal should be used by the same dealer.

(ii) The net score of a rubber should be translated into even hundreds (according to American custom) by crediting as 100 points any fraction thereof amounting to 50 or more points: e.g., 750 points count as 800; 740 points count as 700 points.

(iii) No two players may play a second consecutive rubber as partners at the same table. If two players draw each other again, the player who has drawn the highest card should play with the player who has drawn the third-highest, against the other two players.

(iv) To avoid confusion as to how many deals have been played: Each deal should be scored, even if there is no net advantage to either side (for example, when one side is entitled to 100 points for undertrick penalties and the other side is entitled to 100 points for honors). In a result that completes a game, premiums for overtricks, game, slam, or making a doubled contract should be combined with the trick score to produce one total, which is entered below the line (for example, if a side makes 2♠ doubled and vulnerable with an overtrick, 870 should be scored below the line, not 120 below the line and 50, 500, and 200 above the line).

LAWS OF DUPLICATE CONTRACT BRIDGE.

The first Laws of Duplicate Contract Bridge were published in 1928; there have been successive revisions in 1933, 1935, 1943, 1949, 1963, 1975 and 1987.

Through the Thirties, the Laws were promulgated by the Portland Club of London and the Whist Club of New York. From the Forties onward, the American Contract Bridge League's National Laws Commission has replaced the Whist Club, while the British Bridge League and European Bridge League have supplemented the Portland Club's efforts. The 1975 Laws became international in fact as well as in name when the World Bridge Federation's Laws Commission joined the promulgating bodies. And these 1987 Laws reflect contributions from two dozen nations on six continents, coordinated by the World Bridge Federation.

This latest revision (which superseded the 1975 Code as of Oct. 1, 1987) comprises countless changes from the 1975 Code, mostly minor. Some of these changes have been dictated by the experience of the past dozen years; the increasing artificiality of bidding has required others. The trend toward reducing automatic penalties, evident in the '63 and '75 Codes, continues here. Most striking are the first changes in scoring since 1949: honors are dropped completely from the Duplicate scoring table; the bonus for making a redoubled contract is increased; doubled undertricks non-vulnerable cost more from the fourth undertrick on. Another significant change is the incorporation of the Proprieties into the Laws proper.

In earlier Codes, words such as may, should, shall and must were used without much discrimination; here they have been rationalized. When these Laws say that a player "may" do something ("any player may call attention to an irregularity during the auction"), the failure to do it is in no way wrong. A simple declaration that a player "does" something ("dummy spreads his hand in front of him.") establishes correct procedure without any suggestion that a violation be penalized. When a player "should" do something ("a claim should be accompanied at once by a statement."), his failure to do it is an infraction of law, which will jeopardize his rights, but which will incur a procedural penalty only seldom. In contrast, when these Laws say that a player "shall" do something ("No player shall take any action until the Director has explained"), a violation will be penalized more often than not. The strongest word, "must" ("before making a call, he must inspect the face of his cards"), indicates that violation is regarded as serious indeed. Note that "may" becomes very strong in the negative: "may not" is a stronger injunction than "shall not", just short of "must not."

A great deal of effort has been expended to make these Laws easy to use. References from one law to another have been made more explicit. The hundreds of headings and sub-headings can help a Director find the section of a law that is applicable to the facts of a case (these headings are for convenience of reference only; headings are not considered to be part of the Laws).

The format of these Laws was the idea of Donald Oakie, co-chairman of the ACBL Laws Commission, who died while this revision was in preparation. Another great loss was that of Geoffrey Butler of Great Britain, chairman emeritus of the WBF Laws Commission — these Laws bear the impress of his personality.

The Drafting Committee acknowledges with gratitude the efforts of Lawrence Berkley, who acted as its Secretary.

The Scope of the Laws

The Laws are designed to define correct procedure, and to provide an adequate remedy when there is a departure from correct procedure. An offending player should be ready to pay any penalty graciously, or to accept any adjusted score awarded by the Tournament Director. The Laws are primarily designed not as punishment for irregularities, but rather as redress for damage.

CHAPTER 1

Definitions

Adjusted Score — An arbitrary score awarded by the Director (see Law 12). It is either "artificial" or "assigned".

1. An artificial adjusted score is one awarded in lieu of a result because no result can be obtained or estimated for a particular deal (e.g., when an irregularity prevents play of a deal).

2. An assigned adjusted score is awarded to one side, or to both sides, to be the result of the deal in place of the result actually obtained after an irregularity.

Alert — A notification, whose form may be specified by a sponsoring organization, to the effect that opponents may be in need of an explanation.

Auction — 1. The process of determining the contract by means of successive calls. 2. The aggregate of calls made.

Average — The arithmetic median between the greatest and least awarded scores available.

Bid — An undertaking to win at least a specified number of odd tricks in a specified denomination.

Board — 1. A duplicate board as described in Law 2. 2. The four hands as originally dealt and placed in a duplicate board for play during that session.

Call — Any bid, double, redouble or pass.

Contestant — In an individual event, a player; in a pair event, two players playing as partners throughout the event; in a team event, four or more players playing as teammates.

Contract — The undertaking by declarer's side to win, at the denomination named, the number of odd tricks specified in the final bid, whether undoubled, doubled, or redoubled.

Convention — 1. A call that serves by partnership agreement to convey a meaning not necessarily related to the denomination named (for definition of conventional pass, see Law 30C). 2. Defender's play that serves to convey a meaning by agreement rather than inference.

Deal — 1. The distribution of the pack to form the hands of the four players. 2. The cards so distributed considered as a unit, including the auction and play thereof.

Declarer — The player who, for the side that makes the final bid, first bid the denomination named in that bid. He becomes declarer when the opening lead is faced (but see Law 54A when the opening lead is made out of turn).

Defender — An opponent of (presumed) declarer.

Denomination — The suit or notrump specified in a bid.

Director — A person designated to supervise a duplicate bridge contest and to apply these Laws.

Double — A call over an opponent's bid increasing the scoring value of fulfilled or defeated contracts (see Laws 19 and 77).

Dummy — 1. Declarer's partner. He becomes dummy when the opening lead is faced. 2. Declarer's partner's cards, once they are spread on the table after the opening lead.

Event — A contest of one or more sessions.

Follow Suit — Play a card of the suit that has been led.

Game — 100 or more trick points scored on one deal.

Hand — The cards originally dealt to a player, or the remaining portion thereof.

Honor — Any Ace, King, Queen, Jack or Ten.

International Match Point (IMP) — A unit of scoring awarded according to a schedule established in Law 78B.

Irregularity — A deviation from the correct procedures set forth in the Laws.

Lead — The first card played to a trick.

Matchpoint — A unit of scoring awarded to a contestant as a result of comparison with one or more other scores.

Odd Trick — Each trick to be won by declarer's side in excess of six.

Opening Lead — The card led to the first trick.

Opponent — A player of the other side; a member of the partnership to which one is opposed (RHO, right-hand opponent; LHO, left-hand opponent).

Overtrick — Each trick won by declarer's side in excess of the contract.

Pack — The 52 playing cards with which the game of Contract Bridge is played.

Partner — The player with whom one plays as a side against the other two players.

Part Score — 90 or fewer trick points scored on one deal.

Pass — A call specifying that a player does not, at that turn, elect to bid, double or redouble.

Penalty — An obligation or restriction imposed upon a side for violation of these Laws.

Penalty Card — A card prematurely exposed by a defender. It may be a major or minor penalty card (see Law 50).

Play — 1. The contribution of a card from one's hand to a trick, including the first card, which is the lead. 2. The aggregate of plays made. 3. The period during which the cards are played. 4. The aggregate of the calls and plays on a board.

Premium Points — Any points earned other than trick points (see Law 77).

Psychic Call — A deliberate and gross misstatement of honor strength or suit length.

Rectification — Adjustment made to permit the auction or play to proceed as normally as possible after an irregularity has occurred.

Redeal — A second or subsequent deal to replace a faulty deal.

Redouble — A call over an opponent's double, increasing the scoring value of fulfilled or defeated contracts (see Laws 19 and 77).

Revoke — The play of a card of another suit by a player who is able to follow suit or to comply with a lead penalty.

Rotation — The clockwise order in which the right to call or play progresses.

Round — A part of a session played without progression

of players.

Session — An extended period of play during which a specified number of boards is scheduled to be played before comparison of scores, and after which the ranking of contestants may be established.

Side — Two players who constitute a partnership against the other two players.

Slam — A contract to win six odd tricks (called Small Slam) or to win seven odd tricks (called Grand Slam).

Suit — One of four groups of cards in the pack, each group comprising thirteen cards and having a characteristic symbol: spades, hearts, diamonds, clubs.

Team — Two pairs playing in different directions at different tables, but for a common score (applicable regulations may permit teams of more than four members).

Trick — The unit by which the outcome of the contract is determined, regularly consisting of four cards, one contributed by each player in rotation, beginning with the lead.

Trick Points — Points scored by declarer's side for fulfilling the contract (see Law 77).

Trump — Each card of the suit, if any, named in the contract.

Turn — The correct time at which a player may call or play.

Undertrick — Each trick by which declarer's side falls short of fulfilling the contract (see Law 77).

Vulnerability — The conditions for assigning premiums and undertrick penalties (see Law 77).

CHAPTER II

Preliminaries

LAW 1

THE PACK — RANK OF CARDS AND SUITS

Duplicate Contract Bridge is played with a pack of 52 cards, consisting of 13 cards in each of four suits. The suits rank downward in the order Spades (♠), Hearts (♥), Diamonds (♦), Clubs (♣). The cards of each suit rank downward in the order Ace, King, Queen, Jack, 10, 9, 8, 7, 6, 5, 4, 3, 2.

LAW 2

THE DUPLICATE BOARDS

A duplicate board containing a pack is provided for each deal to be played during a session. Each board is numbered and has four pockets to hold the four hands, designated North, East, South and West. The dealer and vulnerability are designated as follows:

North Dealer	Boards	1	5	9	13
East Dealer	Boards	2	6	10	14
South Dealer	Boards	3	7	11	15
West Dealer	Boards	4	8	1	16
Neither Side Vulnerable	Boards	1	8	11	14
North-South Vulnerable	Boards	2	5	12	15
East-West Vulnerable	Boards	3	6	9	16
Both Sides Vulnerable	Boards	4	7	10	13

PRELIMINARIES

The same sequence is repeated for Boards 17-32, and for each subsequent group of 16 boards.

No board that fails to conform to these conditions should be used. If such board is used, however, the conditions marked on it apply for that session.

LAW 3
ARRANGEMENT OF TABLES
Four players play at each table, and tables are numbered in a sequence established by the Director. He designates one direction as North; other compass directions assume the normal relationship to North.

LAW 4
PARTNERSHIPS
The four players at each table constitute two partnerships or sides, North-South against East-West. In pair or team events, the contestants enter as pairs or teams and retain the same partnerships throughout a session (except in the case of substitutions authorized by the Director). In individual events each player enters separately, and partnerships change during a session.

LAW 5
ASSIGNMENT OF SEATS
A. *Initial Position.*
  The Director assigns an initial position to each contestant (individual, pair or team) at the start of a session. Unless otherwise directed, the members of each pair or team may select seats, among those assigned to them, by mutual agreement. Having once selected a compass direction, a player may change it only upon instruction or with permission of the Director.
B. *Change of Direction or Table*
  Players change their initial compass direction or proceed to another table in accordance with the Director's instructions. The Director is responsible for clear announcement of instructions; each player is responsible for moving when and as directed, and for occupying the correct seat after each change.

CHAPTER III

Preparation and Progression
LAW 6
THE SHUFFLE AND DEAL
A. *The Shuffle.*
  Before play starts, each pack is thoroughly shuffled. There is a cut if either opponent so requests.
B. *The Deal.*
  The cards must be dealt face down, one card at a time in rotation, into four hands of thirteen cards each; each hand is then placed face down in one of the four pockets of the board.
C. *Representation of Both Pairs.*
  A member of each side should be present during the shuffle and deal unless the Director instructs otherwise.
D. *New Shuffle and Redeal.*
1. Cards Incorrectly Dealt or Exposed. There must be a new shuffle and a redeal if it is ascertained before the last card is dealt that the cards have been incorrectly dealt, or that a player has seen the face of a card.
2. No Shuffle, or No Deal. No result may stand if the cards are dealt without shuffle from a sorted deck, or if the deal had previously been played.
3. At Director's Instruction. There must be a new shuffle and a redeal when required by the Director for any reason consonant with the Laws.
E. *Director's Option on Shuffling and Dealing*
1. By Players. The Director may instruct that the shuffle and deal be performed at each table immediately before play starts.
2. By Director. The Director may perform the shuffle and deal in advance, himself.
3. By Agents or Assistants. The Director may have his assistants, or other appointed agents, perform the shuffle and deal in advance.
4. Different Method of Dealing or Pre-dealing. The Director may require a different method of dealing or pre-dealing.
F. *Duplication of Board.*
  If required by the conditions of play, one or more exact copies of each original deal may be made under the Director's instructions.

LAW 7
CONTROL OF BOARD AND CARDS
A. *Placement of Board.*
  When a board is to be played, it is placed in the center of the table until play is completed.
B. *Removal of Cards from Board.*
  Each player takes a hand from the pocket corresponding to his compass position.
1. Counting Cards in Hand before Play
Each player shall count his cards face down to be sure he has exactly 13; after that, and before making a call, he must inspect the face of his cards.
2. Control of Player's Hand
During play each player retains possession of his own cards, not permitting them to be mixed with those of any other player. No player shall touch any cards other than his own (but declarer may play dummy's cards in accordance with Law 45) during or after play except by permission of the Director.
C. *Returning Cards to Board*
  Each player shall restore his original 13 cards to the pocket corresponding to his compass position. Thereafter, no hand shall be removed from the board unless a member of each side, or the Director, is present.
D. *Responsibility for Procedures*
  The North player is responsible for the proper observance of these procedures, and for maintaining proper conditions of play at the table. However, if the East-West pair alone is stationary, the responsibility becomes East's.

LAW 8
SEQUENCE OF ROUNDS
A. *Movement of Boards and Players*
1. Director's Instructions
The Director instructs the players as to the proper movement of boards and progression of contestants.
2. Responsibility for Moving Boards
The North player at each table is responsible for moving the boards just completed at his table to the proper table for the following round, unless the Director instructs otherwise.
B. *End of Round*
  In general, a round ends when the Director gives the signal for the start of the following round; but if any table has not completed play by that time, the round continues for that table until play has been completed and the score of the final board of the round has been confirmed and entered on the proper scoring form.
C. *End of Last Round and End of Session*
  The last round of a session, and the session itself, ends for each table when play of all boards scheduled at that table has been completed, and when all scores have been

entered on the proper scoring forms without objection.

CHAPTER IV

General Laws
Governing Irregularities

LAW 9
PROCEDURE FOLLOWING AN IRREGULARITY
A. *Calling Attention to an Irregularity*
1. During the Auction Period
Any player may call attention to an irregularity during the auction, whether or not it is his turn to call.
2. During the Play Period
  (a) DeclarerorEitherDefender
      Declarer or either defender may call attention to an irregularity that occurs during the play period.
  (b) Dummy (dummy's restricted rights are defined in Laws 42 and 43)
      (1) Dummy may not call attention to an irregularity during the play but may do so after play of the hand is concluded.
      (2) Dummy may attempt to prevent declarer from committing an irregularity (Law 42B2).
B. *After Attention Is Called to an Irregularity*
1. Summoning the Director
  (a) When to Summon
      The Director must be summoned at once when attention is drawn to an irregularity.
  (b) Who May Summon
      Any player may summon the Director after attention has been drawn to an irregularity (for dummy, see Law 43A1).
  (c) Retention of Rights
      Summoning the Director does not cause a player to forfeit any rights to which he might otherwise be entitled.
  (d) Opponents' Rights
      The fact that a player draws attention to an irregularity committed by his side does not affect the rights of the opponents.
2. Further Bids or Plays
No player shall take any action until the Director has explained all matters in regard to rectification and to the assessment of a penalty.
C. *Premature Correction of an Irregularity*
  Any premature correction of an irregularity by the offender may subject him to a further penalty (see the lead penalties of Law 26).

LAW 10
ASSESSMENT OF PENALTY
A. *Right to Assess Penalty*
  The Director alone has the right to assess penalties when applicable. Players do not have the right to assess (or waive) penalties on their own initiative.
B. *Cancellation of Payment or Waiver of Penalty*
  The Director may allow or cancel any payment or waiver of penalties made by the players without instructions.
C. *Choice after Irregularity*
1. Explanation of Options
When these laws provide an option after an irregularity, the Director shall explain all the options available.

2. Choice Among Options
If a player has an option after an irregularity, he must make his selection without consulting partner.

LAW 11
FORFEITURE OF THE RIGHT TO PENALIZE
A. *Action by Non-Offending Side*
  The right to penalize an irregularity may be forfeited if either member of the non-offending side takes any action before summoning the Director. The Director so rules when the non-offending side may have gained through subsequent action taken by an opponent in ignorance of the penalty.
B. *Call or Play before Imposition of Penalty*
  The right to penalize an irregularity is forfeited if offender's LHO calls or plays after the irregularity, and before a legal penalty has been stated and imposed.
C. *Irregularity Called by Spectator*
1. Spectator Responsibility of Non-Offending Side
The right to penalize an irregularity may be forfeited if attention is first drawn to the irregularity by a spectator for whose presence at the table the non-offending side is responsible.
2. Spectator Responsibility of Offending Side
The right to correct an irregularity may be forfeited if attention is first drawn to the irregularity by a spectator for whose presence at the table the offending side is responsible.
D. *Penalty after Forfeiture of the Right to Penalize*
  Even after the right to penalize has been forfeited under this law, the Director may assess a procedural penalty (see Law 90).

LAW 12
DIRECTOR'S DISCRETIONARY POWERS
A. *Right to Award an Adjusted Score*
  The Director may award an adjusted score (or scores), either on his own initiative or on the application of any player, but only when these Laws empower him to do so, or:
1. Laws Provide No Indemnity
The Director may award an assigned adjusted score when he judges that these Laws do not provide indemnity to the non-offending contestant for the particular type of violation of law committed by an opponent.
2. Normal Play of the Board is Impossible
The Director may award an artificial adjusted score if no rectification can be made that will permit normal play of the board (see Law 88).
3. Incorrect Penalty Has Been Paid
The Director may award an adjusted score if an incorrect penalty has been paid.
B. *No Adjustment for Undue Severity of Penalty*
  The Director may not award an adjusted score on the ground that the penalty provided in these Laws is either unduly severe or advantageous to either side.
C. *Awarding an Adjusted Score*
1. Artificial Score
When, owing to an irregularity, no result can be obtained, the Director awards an artificial adjusted score according to responsibility for the irregularity: 40% of the available matchpoints ("average minus") to a contestant directly at fault; 50% ("average") to a contestant only partially at fault; at least 60% ("average plus") to a contestant in no way at fault (see Law 86 for team play or Law 88 for pairs play). The scores awarded to the two sides

need not balance.

2. Assigned Score

When the Director awards an assigned adjusted score in place of a result actually obtained after an irregularity, the score is, for a non-offending side, the most favorable result that was likely had the irregularity not occurred, or, for an offending side, the most unfavorable result that was at all probable. The scores awarded to the two sides need not balance, and may be assigned either in matchpoints or by altering the total-point score prior to matchpointing.

LAW 13
INCORRECT NUMBER OF CARDS

When the Director determines that one or more pockets of the board contained an incorrect number of cards,* if a player with an incorrect hand has made a call, the Director shall award an artificial adjusted score, and may penalize an offender. If no such call has been made, then:

A. *No Player Has Seen Another's Card*

The Director shall correct the discrepancy as follows, and, if no player will then have seen another's card, shall require that the board be played normally.

1. Hand Records

When hand records are available, the Director shall distribute the cards in accordance with the records.

2. Consult Previous Players

If hand records are not available, the Director shall correct the board by consulting with players who have previously played it.

3. Require a Redeal

If the board was incorrectly dealt, the Director shall require a redeal (Law 6).

B. *A Player Has Seen Another Player's Card(s)*

When the Director determines that one or more pockets of the board contained an incorrect number of cards, and after restoration of the board to its original condition a player has seen one or more cards of another player's hand, if the Director deems:

1. The Information Gained Is Inconsequential

that such information will not interfere with normal bidding or play, the Director, with the concurrence of all four players, may allow the board to be played and scored normally.

2. The Information Will Interfere with Normal Play

that the information gained thereby is of sufficient importance to interfere with normal bidding or play, or if any player objects to playing the board, the Director shall award an artificial adjusted score and may penalize an offender.

C. *Play Completed*

When it is determined, after play ends, that a player's hand originally contained more than 13 cards with another player holding correspondingly fewer, the result must be cancelled (for procedural penalty, see Law 90).

*Where three hands are correct and one hand is deficient, Law 14, and not this Law, applies.

LAW 14
MISSING CARD

A. *Hand Found Deficient Before Play Commences*

When three hands are correct and the fourth is found to be deficient before the play period begins, the Director makes a search for the missing card, and:

1. Card Is Found

If the card is found, it is restored to the deficient hand.

2. Card Cannot Be Found

If the card cannot be found, the Director reconstructs the deal, as near to its original form as he can determine, by substituting another pack.

B. *Hand Found Deficient During Play*

When three hands are correct and the fourth is found to be deficient during play, the Director makes a search for the missing card, and:

1. Card Is Found

(a) If the card is found among the played cards, Law 67 applies.

(b) If the card is found elsewhere, it is restored to the deficient hand, and penalties may apply (see 3., following).

2. Card Cannot Be Found

If the card cannot be found, the deal is reconstructed as nearly as can be determined in its original form by substituting another pack, and penalties may apply (see 3., following).

3. Possible Penalties

A card restored to a hand under the provisions of Section B of this Law is deemed to have belonged continuously to the deficient hand. It may become a penalty card (Law 50), and failure to have played it may constitute a revoke.

LAW 15
PLAY OF A WRONG BOARD

A. *Players Have Not Previously Played Board*

If players play a board not designated for them to play in the current round:

1. Score Board as Played

The Director normally allows the score to stand if none of the four players have previously played the board.

2. Designate a Late Play

The Director may require both pairs to play the correct board against one another later.

B. *One or More Players Have Previously Played Board*

If any player plays a board he has previously played, with the correct opponents or otherwise, his second score on the board is cancelled both for his side and his opponents', and the Director shall award an artificial adjusted score to the contestants deprived of the opportunity to earn a valid score.

C *Discovered during Auction*

If, during the auction period, the Director discovers that a contestant is playing a board not designated for him to play in the current round, he shall cancel the auction, ensure that the correct contestants are seated and informed of their rights both now and at future rounds, and:

1. A Player Objects

Before a second auction begins, any player may require that the board be cancelled.

2. No Player Objects

If no player objects, a second auction begins. If any call differs from the corresponding call in the first auction, the Director shall cancel the board. Otherwise, play continues normally.

LAW 16
UNAUTHORIZED INFORMATION

Players are authorized to base their actions on information from legal calls or plays and from mannerisms of opponents. To base action on other extraneous information may be an infraction of law.

A. *Extraneous Information from Partner*

After a player makes available to his partner extraneous information that may suggest a call or play, as by means of a remark, a question, a reply to a question, or by unmistakable hesitation, unwonted speed, special emphasis, tone, gesture, movement, mannerism or the like, the partner may not choose from among logical alternative actions one that could reasonably have been suggested over another by the extraneous information.

1. When Such Information Is Given

When a player considers that an opponent has made such information available, and that damage could well result, he may, unless the regulations of the sponsoring organization prohibit (see page xxiv), immediately announce that he reserves the right to summon the Director later (the opponents should summon the Director immediately if they dispute the fact that unauthorized information might have been conveyed).

2. When Illegal Alternative Is Chosen

When a player has substantial reason to believe* that an opponent who had a logical alternative has chosen an action that could have been suggested by such information, he should summon the Director forthwith. The Director shall require the auction and play to continue, standing ready to assign an adjusted score if he considers that an infraction of law has resulted in damage.

B. *Extraneous Information from Other Sources*

When a player accidentally receives unauthorized information about a board he is playing or has yet to play, as by looking at the wrong hand; by overhearing calls, results or remarks; by seeing cards at another table; or by seeing a card belonging to another player at his own table before the auction begins: the Director should be notified forthwith, preferably by the recipient of the information. If the Director considers that the information could interfere with normal play, he may:

1. Adjust Positions

if the type of contest and scoring permit, adjust the players' positions at the table, so that the player with information about one hand will hold that hand; or,

2. Appoint Substitute

with the concurrence of all four players, appoint a temporary substitute to replace the player who received the unauthorized information; or,

3. Award an Adjusted Score.

forthwith award an artificial adjusted score.

C. *Information from Withdrawn Calls and Plays*

A call or play may be withdrawn, and another substituted, either by a non-offending side after an opponent's infraction, or by an offending side to rectify an infraction.

1. Non-offending Side

For the non-offending side, all information arising from a withdrawn action is authorized, whether the action be its own or its opponents'.

2. Offending Side

For the offending side, information arising from its own withdrawn action is authorized, after the payment of any penalty imposed by law. However, information arising from withdrawn actions of the non-offending side is unauthorized; then, a player of the offending side may not choose from among logical alternative actions one that could reasonably have been suggested over another by the unauthorized information.

*When play ends; or, as to dummy's hand, when dummy is exposed.

CHAPTER V

The Auction
PART I

CORRECT PROCEDURE
SECTION ONE

AUCTION PERIOD

LAW 17

DURATION OF THE AUCTION

A. *Auction Period Starts*

The auction period on a deal begins when a player makes a call on that deal. Even if no player has called, the auction period begins for a side when either partner looks at the face of his cards.

B. *The First Call*

The player designated by the board as dealer makes the first call.

C. *Successive Calls*

The player to dealer's left makes the second call, and thereafter each player calls in turn in a clockwise rotation.

D. *Cards from Wrong Board*

If a player who has inadvertently picked up the cards from the wrong board makes a call, the Director may cancel the board and must do so if any player of the non-offending side so requests (for penalty, see Law 90).

E. *End of Auction Period*

The auction period ends when all four players pass, or when, after three passes in rotation have followed any call, the opening lead is faced (when a pass out of rotation has been accepted, see Law 34).

LAW 18

BIDS

A. *Proper Form*

A bid names a number of odd tricks, from one to seven, and a denomination. (Pass, double and redouble are calls but not bids.)

B. *To Supersede a Bid*

A bid supersedes a previous bid if it names either the same number of odd tricks in a higher-ranking denomination or a greater number of odd tricks in any denomination.

C. *Sufficient Bid*

A bid that supersedes the immediately previous bid is a sufficient bid.

D. *Insufficent Bid*

A bid that fails to supersede the immediately previous bid is an insufficient bid.

E. *Rank of the Denominations*

The rank of the denominations in descending order is: notrump, spades, hearts, diamonds, clubs.

LAW 19

DOUBLES AND REDOUBLES

A. *Doubles*

1. Legal Double

A player may double only the last preceding bid. That bid must have been made by an opponent; calls other than pass must not have intervened.

2. Proper Form for Double

In doubling, a player should not state the number of odd tricks or the denomination. The only correct form is the single word "Double".

3. Double of Incorrectly Stated Bid

If a player, in doubling, incorrectly states the bid, or the number of odd tricks or the denomination, he is deemed to have doubled the bid as it was made. (Law 16 — Unauthorized Information—may apply.)

B. *Redoubles*

1. Legal Redouble

A player may redouble only the last preceding double. That double must have been made by an opponent; calls other than pass must not have intervened.

2. Proper Form for a Redouble

In redoubling, a player should not state the number of odd tricks or the denomination. The only correct form is the single word "Redouble".

3. Redouble of an Incorrectly Stated Bid

If a player, in redoubling, incorrectly states the doubled bid, or the number of odd tricks or the denomination, he is deemed to have redoubled the bid as it was made. (Law 16—Unauthorized Information—may apply.)

C. *Double or Redouble Superseded*

Any double or redouble is superseded by a subsequent legal bid.

D. *Scoring a Doubled or Redoubled Contract*

If a doubled or redoubled bid is not superseded by a subsequent legal bid, scoring values are increased as provided in Law 77.

LAW 20
REVIEW AND EXPLANATION OF CALLS
A. *Call Not Clearly Heard*

A player who does not hear a call distinctly may forthwith require that it be repeated.

B. *Review of Auction during Auction Period*

During the auction period, a player is entitled to have all* previous calls restated when it is his turn to call, unless he is required by law to pass; Alerts should be included in the restatement.

C. *Review after Final Pass*

1. Opening Lead Inquiry

After the final pass either defender has the right to ask if it is his opening lead (see Laws 47 E and 41).

2. Review of Auction

Declarer or either defender may, at his first turn to play, require all* previous calls to be restated (see Law 41B and 41C).

D. *Who May Review the Auction*

A request to have calls restated shall be responded to only by an opponent.

E. *Correction of Error in Review*

All players, including dummy or a player required by law to pass, are responsible for prompt correction of errors in restatement (see Law 12C1 when an uncorrected review causes damage).

F. *Explanation of Calls*

1. During the Auction

During the auction and before the final pass, any player, at his own turn to call, may request* a full explanation of the opponents' auction; replies should normally be given by the partner of a player who made a call in question (see Law 75, section C).

2. During the Play Period

After the final pass and throughout the play period, declarer or either defender (but Law 16, Unauthorized Information, may apply) at his own turn to play may request† such an explanation of opposing auction, and de-

clarer may request an explanation of the defenders' card play conventions.

*A player may not ask for a partial restatement of previous calls and may not halt the review before it has been completed.

†Law 16 may apply; and sponsoring organizations may establish regulations for written explanations.

LAW 21
CALL BASED ON MISINFORMATION
A. *Call Based on Caller's Misunderstanding*

A player has no recourse if he has made a call on the basis of his own misunderstanding.

B. *Call Based on Misinformation from an Opponent*

1. Change of Call

Until the end of the auction period (see Law 17E), a player may, without penalty, change a call when it is probable that he made the call as a result of misinformation given to him by an opponent (failure to alert promptly to a conventional call or special understanding, where such alert is required by the sponsoring organization, is deemed misinformation), provided that his partner has not subsequently called.

2. Change of Call by Opponent Following Correction

When a player elects to change a call because of misinformation (as in 1., preceding), his LHO may then in turn change any subsequent call he may have made, without penalty (unless his withdrawn call conveyed such substantial information as to damage the non-offending side, in which case the Director may assign an adjusted score). (For unauthorized information from withdrawn calls, see Law 16C.)

3. Too Late to Change Call

When it is too late to change a call, the Director may award an adjusted score (Law 40C may apply).

SECTION TWO

AUCTION HAS ENDED
LAW 22
PROCEDURE AFTER THE AUCTION HAS ENDED
A. *No Player Has Bid*

After the auction period has ended, if no player has bid, the hands are returned to the board without play. There shall not be a redeal.

B. *One or More Players Have Bid*

If any player has bid, the final bid becomes the contract, and play begins.

PART II

IRREGULARITIES IN PROCEDURE
LAW 23
IRREGULAR PASSES CAUSING DAMAGE
Reference will be made to this Law from many other Laws that prescribe penalties for auction-period infractions.

A. *Damaging Enforced Pass*

When the penalty for an irregularity under any Law would compel the offender's partner to pass at his next turn, and when the Director deems that the offender, at the time of his irregularity, could have known that the enforced pass would be likely to damage the non-offending side, he shall require the auction and play to continue, afterwards awarding an adjusted score if he considers that the non-offending side was damaged by the enforced pass.

B. *Damaging Pass at Partner's Turn*

When a player passes out of rotation at partner's turn to call, and when the Director deems that this pass may have damaged the non-offending side, the Director shall require the auction and play to continue, afterwards awarding an adjusted score if he considers that the non-offending side was damaged by the out-of-rotation pass.

SECTION ONE

EXPOSED CARD, AUCTION PERIOD

LAW 24

CARD EXPOSED OR LED DURING AUCTION

When the Director determines, during the auction, that because of a player's action one or more cards of that player's hand were in position for the face to be seen by his partner, the Director shall require that every such card be left face up on the table until the auction closes; and (penalty) if the offender subsequently becomes a defender, declarer may treat every such card as a penalty card (Law 50). In addition:

A. *Low Card Not Prematurely Led*

If it is a single card below the rank of an honor, and not prematurely led, there is no further penalty.

B. *Single Card of Honor Rank or Card Prematurely Led*

If the card is a single card of honor rank, or is any card prematurely led, (penalty) offender's partner must pass when next it is his turn to call (see Law 23A when a pass damages the non-offending side).

C. *Two or More Cards Are Exposed*

If two or more cards are so exposed, (penalty) offender's partner must pass when next it is his turn to call (see Law 23A when a pass damages the non-offending side).

SECTION TWO

CHANGES OF CALLS

LAW 25

LEGAL AND ILLEGAL CHANGES OF CALL

A. *Immediate Correction of Inadvertency*

A player may substitute his intended call for an inadvertent call but only if he does so, or attempts to do so, without pause for thought. If legal, his last call stands without penalty; if illegal, it is subject to the applicable Law.

B. *Delayed or Purposeful Correction*

If a call is substituted when section A does not apply:

1. Substitute Call Condoned

The substituted call may be accepted (treated as legal) at the option of offender's LHO*; then, the second call stands and the auction proceeds without penalty. If offender's LHO has called before attention is drawn to the infraction, and the Director determines that LHO intended his call to apply over the offender's original call at that turn, offender's substituted call stands without penalty, and LHO may withdraw his call without penalty.

2. Not Condoned

If the substituted call is not accepted, it is cancelled; and:

(a) First Call Illegal

If the first call was illegal, the offender is subject to the applicable law (and the lead penalties of Law 26 may apply to the second call).

(b) First Call Legal

If the first call was legal, the offender must either,

(1) Let First Call Stand

Allow his first call to stand, in which case (penalty) his partner must pass when next it is his turn to call (see Law 23A when the pass damages the non-offending side), or,

(2) Substitute Another Call

Make any other legal call, in which case (penalty) his partner must pass whenever it is his turn to call (see Law 23A when the pass damages the non-offending side).

(c) Lead Penalties

In either case (b) (1) or (b) (2) above, the offender's partner will be subject to a lead penalty (see Law 26) if he becomes a defender.

*When the original bid was insufficient, apply Law 27B.

LAW 26

CALL WITHDRAWN, LEAD PENALTIES

When an offending player's call is withdrawn, and he chooses a different* final call for that turn, then if he becomes a defender:

A. *Call Related to Specific Suit*

If the withdrawn call related to a specified suit or suits, and,

1. Suit Later Specified

If that suit was later specified by the same player, there is no lead penalty.

2. Suit Not Later Specified

If that suit was not later so specified, then declarer may (penalty) either require the offender's partner to lead the specified suit (or one particular specified suit) at his first turn to lead, including the opening lead; or prohibit offender's partner from leading the specified suit (or one particular specified suit) at his first turn to lead, including the opening lead, such prohibition to continue for as long as offender's partner retains the lead.

B. *Other Withdrawn Calls*

For other withdrawn calls, (penalty) declarer may prohibit offender's partner from leading any one suit† at his first turn to lead, including the opening lead, such prohibition to continue for as long as offender's partner retains the lead.

*A call repeated with a much different meaning shall be deemed a different call.

†Declarer specifies the suit when offender's partner first has the lead.

SECTION THREE

INSUFFICIENT BID

LAW 27

INSUFFICIENT BID

A. *Insufficient Bid Accepted*

Any insufficient bid may be accepted (treated as legal) at the option of offender's LHO. It is accepted if that player calls.

B. *Insufficient Bid Not Accepted*

If an insufficient bid made in rotation is not accepted, it must be corrected by the substitution of either a sufficient bid or a pass (the offender is entitled to select his final call at that turn after the applicable penalties have been stated, and any call he has previously attempted to substitute is cancelled, but the lead penalties of Law 26 may apply).

1. Not Conventional, and Corrected by Lowest Sufficient Bid in Same Denomination

(a) No Penalty

If the insufficient bid was incontrovertibly not conventional, and is corrected by the lowest sufficient bid in the same denomination, the auction proceeds as though the irregularity had not occurred (but see (b) following).

(b) Award of Adjusted Score

If the Director judges that the insufficient bid conveyed such substantial information as to damage the non-offending side, he shall assign an adjusted score.

2. Conventional, or Corrected by Any Other Sufficient Bid or Pass

If the insufficient bid may have been conventional, or is corrected by any other sufficient bid or by a pass, (penalty) the offender's partner must pass whenever it is his turn to call (see Law 23A when the pass damages the non-offending side; and the lead penalties of Law 26 may apply).

3. Attempt to Correct by a Double or Redouble

If the offender attempts to substitute a double or redouble for his insufficient bid, the attempted call is cancelled; and (penalty) his partner must pass whenever it is his turn to call (see Law 23A when the pass damages the non-offending side), and the lead penalties of Law 26 may apply.

C. *Insufficient Bid Out of Rotation*

If a player makes an insufficient bid out of rotation, Law 31 applies.

SECTION FOUR

CALL OUT OF ROTATION

LAW 28

CALLS CONSIDERED TO BE IN ROTATION

A. *RHO Required to Pass*

A call is considered to be in rotation when it is made by a player at his RHO's turn to call if that opponent is required by law to pass.

B. *Call by Correct Player Cancelling Call Out of Rotation*

A call is considered to be in rotation when made by a player whose turn it was to call, before a penalty has been assessed for a call out of rotation by an opponent; making such a call forfeits the right to penalize the call out of rotation, and the auction proceeds as though the opponent had not called at that turn.

LAW 29

PROCEDURE AFTER A CALL OUT OF ROTATION

A. *Out-of-Rotation Call Cancelled*

A call out of rotation is cancelled (but see B following), and the auction reverts to the player whose turn it was to call. Offender may make any legal call in proper rotation, but his side may be subject to penalty under Laws 30, 31 or 32.

B. *Forfeiture of Right to Penalize*

Following a call out of rotation, offender's LHO may elect to call, thereby forfeiting the right to penalize.

LAW 30

PASS OUT OF ROTATION

When a player has passed out of rotation (and the call is cancelled, as the option to accept the call has not been exercised—see Law 29):

A. *Before Any Player Has Bid*

When a player has passed out of rotation before any player has bid, (penalty) the offender must pass when next it is his turn to call (and see Law 23B when offender's partner was dealer).

B. *After Any Player Has Bid*

1. At RHO's Turn to Call

After any player has bid, when a pass out of rotation is made at offender's RHO's turn to call, (penalty) offender must pass when next it is his turn to call (if the pass out of rotation related by convention to a specific suit, or suits, thereby conveying information, the lead penalties of Law 26 may apply).

2. At Partner's Turn to Call

(a) Action Required of Offender

After any player has bid, for a pass out of rotation made at the offender's partner's turn to call, (penalty) the offender must pass whenever it is his turn to call, and Law 23B may apply.

(b) Action Open to Offender's Partner

Offender's partner may make any sufficient bid, or may pass, but may not double or redouble at that turn, and Law 23B may apply.

3. At LHO's Turn to Call

After any player has bid, a pass out of rotation at offender's LHO's turn to call is treated as a change of call and Law 25 applies.

C. *When Pass Is a Convention*

When the pass out of rotation is a convention, Law 31, not this Law, will apply. A pass is a convention if, by special agreement, it promises more than a specified amount of strength, or if it artificially promises or denies values other than in the last suit named.

LAW 31

BID OUT OF ROTATION

When a player has bid out of rotation (and the bid is cancelled, as the option to accept the bid has not been exercised—see Law 29):

A. *RHO's Turn*

When the offender has bid (or has passed partner's call when it is a convention, in which case section A2b applies) at his RHO's turn to call, then:

1. RHO Passes

If that opponent passes, offender must repeat the call out of rotation, and when that call is legal there is no penalty.

2. RHO Acts

If that opponent makes a legal* bid, double or redouble, offender may make any legal call (including pass); when this call

(a) Repeats Denomination

repeats the denomination of his bid out of rotation, (penalty) offender's partner must pass when next it is his turn to call (see Law 23A).

(b) Does Not Repeat Denomination

does not repeat the denomination of his bid out of rotation, the lead penalties of Law 26 may apply, and (penalty) offender's partner must pass whenever it is his turn to call (see Law 23A).

B. *Partner's or LHO's Turn*

When the offender has bid at his partner's turn to call, or at his LHO's turn to call if the offender has not previously called,† (penalty) offender's partner must pass whenever it is his turn to call (see Law 23A when the pass damages the non-offending side), and the lead penalties of Law 26 may apply.

*An illegal call by RHO is penalized as usual.

†Later bids at LHO's turn to call are treated as changes of call, and Law 25 applies.

LAW 32
DOUBLE OR REDOUBLE OUT OF ROTATION

A double or redouble out of rotation may be accepted at the option of the opponent next in rotation (see Law 29), except that an inadmissible double or redouble may never be accepted (see Law 35A if the opponent next in rotation nevertheless does call). If the illegal call is not accepted, it is cancelled, the lead penalties of Law 26B may apply, and:

A. *Made at Offender's Partner's Turn to Call*

If a double or redouble out of rotation has been made when it was the offender's partner's turn to call, (penalty) the offender's partner must pass whenever it is his turn to call (see Law 23A when the pass damages the non-offending side).

B. *Made at RHO's Turn to Call*

If a double or redouble out of rotation has been made at offender's RHO's turn to call, then:

1. RHO Passes

If offender's RHO passes, offender must repeat his out-of-rotation double or redouble and there is no penalty unless the double or redouble is inadmissible, in which case Law 36 applies.

2. RHO Bids

If offender's RHO bids, the offender may in turn make any legal call and (penalty) offender's partner must pass whenever it is his turn to call (see Law 23A when the pass damages the non-offending side).

LAW 33
SIMULTANEOUS CALLS

A call made simultaneously with one made by the player whose turn it was to call is deemed to be a subsequent call.

LAW 34
RETENTION OF RIGHT TO CALL

When a call has been followed by three passes, the auction does not end when one of those passes was out of rotation, thereby depriving a player of his right to call at that turn. The auction reverts to the player who missed his turn. All subsequent passes are cancelled, and the auction proceeds as though there had been no irregularity.

LAW 35
INADMISSIBLE CALL CONDONED

When, after any inadmissible call specified below, the offender's LHO makes a call before a penalty has been assessed, there is no penalty for the inadmissible call (the lead penalties of Law 26 do not apply), and:

A. *Double or Redouble*

If the inadmissible call was a double or redouble not permitted by Law 19, that call and all subsequent calls are cancelled. The auction reverts to the player whose turn it is to call and proceeds as though there had been no irregularity.

B. *Action by Player Required to Pass*

If the inadmissible call was a bid, double or redouble by a player required by law to pass, that call and all subsequent legal calls stand, but, if the offender was required to pass for the remainder of the auction, he must still pass at subsequent turns.

C. *Bid of More than Seven*

If the inadmissible call was a bid of more than seven, that call and all subsequent calls are cancelled; the offender must substitute a pass, and the auction proceeds as though there had been no irregularity.

D. *Call after Final Pass*

If the inadmissible call was a call after the final pass of the auction, that call and all subsequent calls are cancelled without penalty.

SECTION FIVE

INADMISSIBLE CALLS
LAW 36
INADMISSIBLE DOUBLE OR REDOUBLE

Any double or redouble not permitted by Law 19 is cancelled. The offender must substitute a legal call, and (penalty) the offender's partner must pass whenever it is his turn to call (see Law 23A when the pass damages the non-offending side); the lead penalties of Law 26 may apply. (If the call is out of turn, see Law 32; if offender's LHO calls, see Law 35A.)

LAW 37
ACTION VIOLATING OBLIGATION TO PASS

A bid, double or redouble by a player who is required by law to pass is cancelled, and (penalty) each member of the offending side must pass whenever it becomes his turn to call (see Law 23A when the pass damages the non-offending side). The lead penalties of Law 26 may apply. (If offender's LHO calls, see Law 35B.)

LAW 38
BID OF MORE THAN SEVEN

No play or score at a contract of more than seven is ever permissible. A bid of more than seven is cancelled, and (penalty) each member of the offending side must pass whenever it becomes his turn to call (see Law 23A when the pass damages the non-offending side). The lead penalties of Law 26 may apply.

(If offender's LHO calls, see Law 35C.)

LAW 39
CALL AFTER FINAL PASS

A call made after the final pass of the auction is cancelled, and:

A. *Pass, or Call by Declaring Side*

If it is a pass by a defender or any call by the future declarer or dummy, there is no penalty.

B. *Other Action by Defender*

If it is a bid, double or redouble by a defender, the lead penalties of Law 26 may apply. (If offender's LHO calls, see Law 35D.)

SECTION SIX

CONVENTIONS AND AGREEMENTS
LAW 40
PARTNERSHIP UNDERSTANDINGS

A. *Right to Choose Call or Play*

A player may make any call or play (including an intentionally misleading call—such as a psychic bid—or a call or play that departs from commonly accepted, or previously announced, use of a convention), without prior announcement, provided that such call or play is not based on a partnership understanding.

B. *Concealed Partnership Understandings Prohibited*

A player may not make a call or play based on a special partnership understanding unless an opposing pair may reasonably be expected to understand its meaning, or unless his side discloses the use of such call or play in accordance with the regulations of the sponsoring organization.

C. *Director's Option*

If the Director decides that a side has been damaged through its opponents' failure to explain the full meaning of a call or play, he may award an adjusted score.

D. *Regulation of Conventions*

The sponsoring organization may regulate the use of bidding or play conventions. Zonal organizations may, in addition, regulate partnership understandings (even if not conventional) that permit the partnership's initial actions at the one level to be made with a hand of a king or more below average strength (see page XXIV); Zonal organizations may delegate this responsibility.

E. *Convention Card*

1. Right to Prescribe

The sponsoring organization may prescribe a convention card on which partners are to list their conventions and other agreements, and may establish regulations for its use, including a requirement that both members of a partnership employ the same system (see page XXIV) (such a regulation must not restrict style and judgment, only method).

2. Referring to Opponents' Convention Card

During the auction and play, any player except dummy may refer to his opponents' convention card at his own turn to call or play, but not to his own*.

*A player is not entitled, during the auction and play periods, to any aids to his memory, calculation or technique.

CHAPTER VI

The Play
PART I

PROCEDURE
SECTION ONE

CORRECT PROCEDURE
LAW 41
COMMENCEMENT OF PLAY

A. *Face-down Opening Lead*

After a bid, double or redouble has been followed by three passes in rotation, the defender on presumed declarer's left makes the opening lead face down*. The face-down lead may be withdrawn only upon instruction of the Director after an irregularity (see Law 47E2); the withdrawn card must be returned to the defender's hand.

B. *Review of Auction, and Questions*

Before the opening lead is faced, the leader's partner and the presumed declarer each may require a review of the auction, or request explanation of an opponent's call (see Law 20). Declarer or either defender may, at his first turn to play a card, require a review of the auction; this right expires when he plays a card. The defenders (subject to Law 16) and the declarer retain the right to request explanations throughout the play period, each at his own turn to play.

C. *Opening Lead Faced*

Following this question period, the opening lead is faced, the play period begins, and dummy's hand is spread. After it is too late to have previous calls restated (see B, above), declarer or either defender, at his own turn to play, is entitled to be informed as to what the contract is and whether, but not by whom, it was doubled or redoubled.

D. *Dummy's Hand*

After the opening lead is faced, dummy spreads his hand in front of him on the table, face up, sorted into suits, the cards in order of rank, in columns pointing lengthwise towards declarer, with trumps to dummy's right. Declarer plays both his hand and that of dummy.

*Sponsoring organizations may specify that opening leads be made face up.

LAW 42
DUMMY'S RIGHTS

A. *Absolute Rights*

1. Give Information

Dummy is entitled to give information, in the Director's presence, as to fact or law.

2. Keep Track of Tricks

He may keep count of tricks won and lost.

3. Play as Declarer's Agent

He plays the cards of the dummy as declarer's agent as directed (see Law 45F if dummy suggests a play).

B. *Qualified Rights*

Dummy may exercise other rights subject to the limitations provided in Law 43.

1. Revoke Inquiries

Dummy may ask declarer (but not a defender) when he has failed to follow suit to a trick whether he has a card of the suit led.

2. Attempt to Prevent Irregularity

He may try to prevent any irregularity by declarer (he may, for example, warn declarer against leading from the wrong hand).

3. Draw Attention to Irregularity

He may draw attention to any irregularity, but only after play of the hand is concluded.

LAW 43
DUMMY'S LIMITATIONS

A. *Limitations on Dummy*

1. General Limitations

(a) Calling the Director

Dummy should not initiate a call for the Director during play.

(b) Calling Attention to Irregularity

Dummy may not call attention to an irregularity during play.

(c) Participate in or Comment on Play

Dummy may not participate in the play or make any comment, or ask any question, on the bidding or play.

2. Limitations Carrying Specific Penalty

(a) Exchanging Hands

Dummy may not exchange hands with declarer.

(b) Leave Seat to Watch Declarer

Dummy may not leave his seat to watch declarer's play of the hand.

(c) Look at Defender's Hand

Dummy may not, on his own initiative, look at the face of a card in either defender's hand.

B. *Penalties for Violation*

1. General Penalties

Dummy is liable to penalty under Law 90 for any violation of the limitations listed in A1 or A2 preceding.

2. Specific Penalties

If dummy, after violation of the limitations listed in A2 preceding:

(a) Draws Attention to Defender's Irregularity

is the first to draw attention to a defender's irregularity, declarer may not enforce any penalty for the offense.

(b) Warns Declarer on Lead

warns declarer not to lead from the wrong hand, (penalty) either defender may choose the hand from which declarer shall lead.

(c) Asks Declarer about Possible Irregularity

is the first to ask declarer if a play from declarer's hand constitutes a revoke or failure to comply with a penalty, declarer must substitute a correct card if his play was illegal, and the penalty provisions of Law 64 apply.

LAW 44
SEQUENCE AND PROCEDURE OF PLAY

A. *Lead to a Trick*

The player who leads to a trick may play any card in his hand (unless he is subject to restriction after an irregularity committed by his side).

B. *Subsequent Plays to a Trick*

After the lead, each other player in turn plays a card, and the four cards so played constitute a trick. (For the method of playing cards and arranging tricks see Law 65.)

C. *Requirement to Follow Suit*

In playing to a trick, each player must follow suit if possible. This obligation takes precedence over all other requirements of these Laws.

D. *Inability to Follow Suit*

If unable to follow suit, a player may play any card (unless he is subject to restriction after an irregularity committed by his side).

E. *Tricks Containing Trumps*

A trick containing a trump is won by the player who has contributed to it the highest trump.

F. *Tricks Not Containing Trumps*

A trick that does not contain a trump is won by the player who has contributed to it the highest card of the suit led.

G. *Lead to Tricks Subsequent to First Trick*

The player who has won the trick leads to the next trick.

LAW 45
CARD PLAYED

A. *Play of Card from a Hand*

Each player except dummy plays a card by detaching it from his hand and facing* it on the table immediately before him.

B. *Play of Card from Dummy*

Declarer plays a card from dummy by naming the card, after which dummy picks up the card and faces it on the table. In playing from dummy's hand declarer may, if

necessary, pick up the desired card himself.

C. *Compulsory Play of Card*

1. Defender's Card

A defender's card held so that it is possible for his partner to see its face must be played to the current trick (if the defender has already made a legal play to the current trick, see Law 45E).

2. Declarer's Card

Declarer must play a card from his hand held face up, touching or nearly touching the table, or maintained in such a position as to indicate that it has been played.

3. Dummy's Card

A card in the dummy must be played if it has been deliberately touched by declarer except for the purpose of arranging dummy's cards, or of reaching a card above or below the card or cards touched.

4. Named or Designated Card

(a) Play of Named Card

A card must be played if a player names or otherwise designates it as the card he proposed to play.

(b) Correction of Inadvertent Designation

A player may, without penalty, change an inadvertent designation if he does so without pause for thought; but if an opponent has, in turn, played a card that was legal before the change in designation, that opponent may withdraw without penalty the card so played and substitute another (see Law 47E).

5. Penalty Card

A penalty card, major or minor, may have to be played, subject to Law 50.

D. *Card Misplayed by Dummy*

If dummy places in the played position a card that declarer did not name, the card must be withdrawn if attention is drawn to it before each side has played to the next trick, and a defender may withdraw (without penalty) a card played after the error but before attention was drawn to it (see Law 47F).

E. *Fifth Card Played to Trick*

1. By a Defender

A fifth card contributed to a trick by a defender becomes a penalty card, subject to Law 50, unless the Director deems that it was led, in which case Law 53 or 56 applies.

2. By Declarer

When declarer contributes a fifth card to a trick from his own hand or dummy, there is no penalty unless the Director deems that it was led, in which case Law 55 applies.

F. *Dummy Indicates Card*

After dummy's hand is faced, dummy may not touch or indicate any card (except for purpose of arrangement) without instruction from declarer. If he does so, the Director should be summoned forthwith. The Director shall rule whether dummy's act did in fact constitute a suggestion to declarer. When the Director judges that it did, he allows play to continue, reserving his right to assign an adjusted score if the defenders were damaged by the play so suggested.

G. *Turning the Trick*

No player should turn his card face down until all four players have played to the trick.

*The opening lead is first made face down (unless the sponsoring organization directs otherwise). (See page XXIV.)

SECTION TWO

IRREGULARITIES IN PROCEDURE
LAW 46
INCOMPLETE OR ERRONEOUS CALL OF CARD FROM DUMMY

A. *Proper Form for Designating Dummy's Card*

When calling a card to be played from dummy, declarer should clearly state both the suit and the rank of the desired card.

B. *Incomplete or Erroneous Call*

In case of an incomplete or erroneous call by declarer of the card to be played from dummy, the following restrictions apply (except when declarer's different intention is incontrovertible):

1. Incomplete Designation of Rank

If declarer, in playing from dummy, calls "high", or words of like import, he is deemed to have called the highest card of the suit indicated; if he directs dummy to win the trick, he is deemed to have called the lowest winning card; if he calls "low", or words of like import, he is deemed to have called the lowest.

2. Designates Suit but Not Rank

If declarer designates a suit but not a rank, he is deemed to have called the lowest card of the suit indicated.

3. Designates Rank but Not Suit

If declarer designates a rank but not a suit:

(a) In Leading

Declarer is deemed to have continued the suit in which dummy won the preceding trick, provided there is a card of the designated rank in that suit.

(b) All Other Cases

In all other cases, declarer must play a card from dummy of the designated rank if he can legally do so; but if there are two or more such cards that can be legally played, declarer must designate which is intended.

4. Designates Card Not in Dummy

If declarer calls a card that is not in dummy, the call is void and declarer may designate any legal card.

5. No Suit or Rank Designated

If declarer indicates a play without designating either a suit or rank (as by saying, "play anything", or words of like import), either defender may designate the play from dummy.

LAW 47
RETRACTION OF CARD PLAYED

A. *To Comply with Penalty*

A card once played may be withdrawn to comply with a penalty (but a defender's withdrawn card may become a penalty card—see Law 49).

B. *To Correct an Illegal Play*

A played card may be withdrawn to correct an illegal or simultaneous play (see Law 58 for simultaneous play; and, for defenders, see Law 49, penalty card).

C. *To Change an Inadvertent Designation*

A played card may be withdrawn without penalty after a change of designation as permitted by Law 45C4(b).

D. *Following Opponent's Change of Play*

After an opponent's change of play, a played card may be withdrawn without penalty (but see 62C2) to substitute another card for the one played.

E. *Change of Play Based on Misinformation*

1. Lead Out of Turn

A lead out of turn may be retracted without penalty if the leader was mistakenly informed by an opponent that it was his turn to lead.

2. Retraction of Play

(a) No One Has Subsequently Played

A player may retract the card he has played after a mistaken explanation of an opponent's conventional call or play and before a corrected explanation, but only if no card was subsequently played to that trick.

(b) One or More Subsequent Plays Made

When it is too late to correct a play, under (a) preceding, Law 40C applies.

F. *Exposure of Retracted Card by Damaged Side*

If a card retracted under section C, D or E preceding gave substantial information to the offending side, the Director may award an adjusted score.

G. *Illegal Retraction*

Except as provided in A through E preceding, a card once played may not be withdrawn.

PART II

PENALTY CARD

LAW 48
EXPOSURE OF DECLARER'S CARDS

A. *Declarer Exposes a Card*

Declarer is not subject to penalty for exposing a card, and no card of declarer's or dummy's hand ever becomes a penalty card. Declarer is not required to play any card dropped accidentally.

B. *Declarer Faces Cards*

1. After Opening Lead Out of Turn

When declarer faces his cards after an opening lead out of turn, Law 54 applies.

2. At Any Other Time

When declarer faces his cards at any time other than immediately after an opening lead out of turn, he may be deemed to have made a claim or concession of tricks, and Law 68 then applies.

LAW 49
EXPOSURE OF A DEFENDER'S CARDS

Whenever a defender faces a card on the table, holds a card so that it is possible for his partner to see its face, or names a card as being in his hand, before he is entitled to do so in the normal course of play or application of law, (penalty) each such card becomes a penalty card (Law 50); but see the footnote to Law 68 when a defender has made a statement concerning an uncompleted trick currently in progress.

LAW 50
DISPOSITION OF PENALTY CARD

A. *Definition of Penalty Card*

A card prematurely exposed (but not led, see Law 57) by a defender is a penalty card unless the Director designates otherwise. The Director shall award an adjusted score, in lieu of the rectifications below, when he deems that the offender, at the time of his irregularity, could have known that exposing the card prematurely would be likely to damage the non-offending side.

B. *Penalty Card Remains Exposed*

A penalty card must be left face up on the table immediately before the player to whom it belongs, until it is played or until an alternate penalty has been selected.

C. *Major or Minor Penalty Card?*

A single card below the rank of an honor and exposed inadvertently (as in playing two cards to a trick, or in dropping a card accidentally) becomes a minor penalty card. Any card of honor rank, or any card exposed through deliberate play (as in leading out of turn, or in revoking and then correcting), becomes a major penalty card; when one defender has two or more penalty cards, all such cards become major penalty cards.

D. *Disposition of Minor Penalty Card*

When a defender has a minor penalty card, he may not play any other card of the same suit below the rank of an honor until he has first played the penalty card (however, he is entitled to play an honor card instead). Offender's partner is not subject to lead penalty, but information gained through seeing the penalty card is extraneous, unauthorized (see Law 16A).

E. *Disposition of Major Penalty Card*

When a defender has a major penalty card, both the offender and his partner may be subject to restriction, the offender whenever he is to play, the partner when he is to lead.

1. Offender to Play

A major penalty card must be played at the first legal opportunity, whether in leading, following suit, discarding or trumping. If a defender has two or more penalty cards that can legally be played, declarer may designate which is to be played. The obligation to follow suit, or to comply with a lead or play penalty, takes precedence over the obligation to play a major penalty card, but the penalty card must still be left face up on the table and played at the next legal opportunity.

2. Offender's Partner to Lead

When a defender has the lead while his partner has a major penalty card, he may not lead until declarer has stated which of the options below is selected (if the defender leads prematurely, he is subject to penalty under Law 49). Declarer may choose:

(a) Require or Forbid Lead of Suit

to require* the defender to lead the suit of the penalty card, or to prohibit* him from leading that suit for as long as he retains the lead (for two or more penalty cards, see Law 51); if declarer exercises this option, the card is no longer a penalty card, and is picked up.

(b) No Lead Restriction

not to require or prohibit a lead, in which case the defender may lead any card; the penalty card remains a penalty card.

*If the player is unable to lead as required, see Law 59.

LAW 51

TWO OR MORE PENALTY CARDS

A. *Offending Player's Turn to Play*

If a defender has two or more penalty cards that can legally be played, declarer may designate which is to be played at that turn.

B. *Offender's Partner to Lead*

1. Penalty Cards in Same Suit

(a) Declarer Requires Lead of That Suit

When a defender has two or more penalty cards in one suit, and declarer requires the defender's partner to lead that suit, the cards of that suit are no longer penalty cards and are picked up; the defender may make any legal play to the trick.

(b) Declarer Prohibits Lead of That Suit

If the declarer prohibits the lead of that suit, the

defender may pick up every penalty card in that suit and may make any legal play to the trick.

2. Penalty Cards in More Than One Suit

(a) Declarer Requires Lead of a Specified Suit

When a defender has penalty cards in more than one suit, declarer may require* the defender's partner to lead any suit in which the defender has a penalty card (but B1(a) preceding then applies).

(b) Declarer Prohibits Lead of Specified Suits

When a defender has penalty cards in more than one suit, declarer may prohibit* the defender's partner from leading every such suit; but the defender may then pick up every penalty card in every suit prohibited by declarer, and make any legal play to the trick.

*If the player is unable to lead as required, see Law 59.

LAW 52

FAILURE TO LEAD OR PLAY A PENALTY CARD

A. *Defender Fails to Play Penalty Card*

When a defender fails to lead or play a major penalty card as required by Law 50, he may not, on his own initiative, withdraw any other card he has played.

B. *Defender Plays Another Card*

1. Play of Card Accepted

(a) Declarer May Accept Play

If a defender has led or played another card when required by law to play a penalty card, declarer may accept such lead or play.

(b) Declarer Must Accept Play

Declarer must accept such lead or play if he has thereafter played from his own hand or dummy.

(c) Penalty Card Remains Penalty Card

If the played card is accepted under either (a) or (b) preceding, the unplayed penalty card remains a penalty card.

2. Play of Card Rejected

Declarer may require the defender to substitute the penalty card for the card illegally played or led. Every card illegally led or played by the defender in the course of committing the irregularity becomes a major penalty card.

PART III

IRREGULAR LEADS AND PLAYS

SECTION ONE

LEAD OUT OF TURN

LAW 53

LEAD OUT OF TURN ACCEPTED

A. Lead Out of Turn Treated as Correct Lead

Any lead faced out of turn may be treated as a correct lead. It becomes a correct lead if declarer or either defender, as the case may be, accepts it (by making a statement to that effect), or if the player next in rotation plays* to the irregular lead. (If no acceptance statement or play is made, the Director will require that the lead be made from the correct hand.)

B. *Wrong Defender Plays Card to Declarer's Irregular Lead*

If the defender at the right of the hand from which the lead out of turn was made plays* to the irregular lead, the lead stands and Law 57 applies.

C. *Proper Lead Made Subsequent to Irregular Lead*

If it was properly the turn to lead of an opponent of the

player who led out of turn, that opponent may make his proper lead to the trick of the infraction without his card being deemed played to the irregular lead. When this occurs, the proper lead stands, and all cards played in error to this trick may be withdrawn without penalty.

*But see C below.

LAW 54
FACED OPENING LEAD OUT OF TURN
A. *A Declarer Spreads His Hand*

After a faced opening lead out of turn, declarer may spread his hand; he becomes dummy, and dummy becomes declarer. If declarer begins to spread his hand, and in doing so exposes one or more cards, he must spread his entire hand.

B. *Declarer Accepts Lead*

When a defender faces the opening lead out of turn declarer may accept the irregular lead as provided in Law 53, and dummy is spread in accordance with Law 41.

1. Declarer Plays Second Card

The second card to the trick is played from declarer's hand.

2. Dummy Has Played Second Card

If declarer plays the second card to the trick from dummy, dummy's card may not be withdrawn except to correct a revoke.

C. *Declarer Must Accept Lead*

If declarer could have seen any of dummy's cards (except cards that dummy may have exposed during the auction and that were subject to Law 24), he must accept the lead.

D. *Declarer Refuses Opening Lead*

When declarer requires the defender to retract his faced opening lead out of turn, Law 56 applies.

LAW 55
DECLARER'S LEAD OUT OF TURN
A. *Declarer's Lead Accepted*

If declarer has led out of turn from his or dummy's hand, either defender may accept the lead as provided in Law 53, or require its retraction.

B. *Declarer Required to Retract Lead*

1. Defender's Turn to Lead

If declarer has led from his or dummy's hand when it was a defender's turn to lead, and if either defender requires him to retract such lead, declarer restores the card led in error to the proper hand without penalty.

2. Lead in Declarer's Hand or Dummy's

If declarer has led from the wrong hand when it was his turn to lead from his hand or dummy's, and if either defender requires him to retract the lead, he withdraws the card led in error. He must lead from the correct hand.

C. *Declarer Might Obtain Information*

When declarer adopts a line of play that could have been based on information obtained through the infraction, the Director may award an adjusted score.

LAW 56
DEFENDER'S LEAD OUT OF TURN

When declarer requires a defender to retract his faced lead out of turn, the card illegally led becomes a major penalty card, and Law 50E applies.

SECTION TWO

OTHER IRREGULAR LEADS AND PLAYS
LAW 57
PREMATURE LEAD OR PLAY BY DEFENDER
A. *Premature Play, or Lead to Next Trick*

When a defender leads to the next trick before his partner has played to the current trick, or plays out of turn before his partner has played, (penalty) the card so led or played becomes a penalty card, and declarer selects one of the following options. He may:

1. Highest Card

require offender's partner to play the highest card he holds of the suit led, or

2. Lowest Card

require offender's partner to play the lowest card he holds of the suit led, or

3. Card of Another Suit

forbid offender's partner to play a card of a different suit specified by declarer.

B. *Offender's Partner Cannot Comply with Penalty*

When offender's partner is unable to comply with the penalty selected by declarer, he may play any card, as provided in Law 59.

C. *Declarer Has Played from Both Hands before Irregularity*

A defender is not subject to penalty for playing before his partner if declarer has played from both hands, or if dummy has played a card or has illegally suggested that it be played. A singleton in dummy, or one of cards adjacent in rank of the same suit, is not considered to be automatically played.

LAW 58
SIMULTANEOUS LEADS OR PLAYS
A. *Simultaneous Plays by Two Players*

A lead or play made simultaneously with another player's legal lead or play is deemed to be subsequent to it.

B. *Simultaneous Cards from One Hand*

If a player leads or plays two or more cards simultaneously:

1. One Card Visible

If only one card is visible, that card is played; all other cards are picked up without penalty.

2. More Cards Visible

If more than one card is visible, the player designates the card he proposes to play; when he is a defender, each other card exposed becomes a penalty card (see Law 50).

3. After Visible Card Withdrawn

After a player withdraws a visible card, an opponent who subsequently played to that card may withdraw his play and substitute another without penalty (see Law 47F).

4. Error Not Discovered

If the simultaneous play remains undiscovered until both sides have played to the next trick, Law 67 applies.

LAW 59
INABILITY TO LEAD OR PLAY AS REQUIRED

A player may play any otherwise legal card if he is unable to lead or play as required to comply with a penalty, whether because he holds no card of the required suit, or because he has only cards of a suit he is prohibited from leading, or because he is obliged to follow suit.

LAW 60

PLAY AFTER AN ILLEGAL PLAY

A. *Play of Card after Irregularity*

1. Forfeiture of Right to Penalize

A play by a member of the non-offending side after his RHO has led or played out of turn or prematurely, and before a penalty has been assessed, forfeits the right to penalize that offense.

2. Irregularity Legalized

Once the right to penalize has been forfeited, the illegal play is treated as though it were in turn (but Law 53C applies to the player whose turn it was).

3. Other Penalty Obligations Remain

If the offending side has a previous obligation to play a penalty card, or to comply with a lead or play penalty, the obligation remains at future turns.

B. *Defender Plays before Required Lead by Declarer*

When a defender plays a card after declarer has been required to retract his lead out of turn from either hand, but before declarer has led from the correct hand, the defender's card becomes a penalty card (Law 50).

C. *Play by Offending Side before Assessment of Penalty*

A play by a member of the offending side before a penalty has been assessed does not affect the rights of the opponents, and may itself be subject to penalty.

SECTION THREE

THE REVOKE

LAW 61

FAILURE TO FOLLOW SUIT— INQUIRIES CONCERNING A REVOKE

A. *Definition of Revoke*

Failure to follow suit in accordance with Law 44, or failure to lead or play, when able, a card or suit required by law or specified by an opponent in accordance with an agreed penalty, constitutes a revoke (but see Law 59 when unable to comply).

B. *Right to Inquire about a Possible Revoke*

Declarer may ask a defender who has failed to follow suit whether he has a card of the suit led (but a claim of revoke does not automatically warrant inspection of quitted tricks—see Law 66C). Dummy may ask declarer. Defenders may ask declarer but, unless the zonal organization so authorizes, not one another.

NOTE: The ACBL Board of Directors, under the authority granted in the revised Law 61B, has ruled that in ACBL sanctioned events, a defender may inquire of his partner whether he has a card of the suit led.

LAW 62

CORRECTION OF A REVOKE

A. *Revoke Must Be Corrected*

A player must correct his revoke if he becomes aware of the irregularity before it becomes established.

B. *Correcting a Revoke*

To correct a revoke, the offender withdraws the card he played in revoking and follows suit with any card.

1. Defender's Card

A card so withdrawn becomes a penalty card (Law 50) if it was played from a defender's unfaced hand.

2. Declarer's or Dummy's Card, Defender's Faced Card

The card may be replaced without penalty if it was played from declarer's or dummy's hand*, or if it was a defender's faced card.

C. *Subsequent Cards Played to Trick*

1. By Non-offending Side

Each member of the non-offending side may, without penalty, withdraw any card he may have played after the revoke but before attention was drawn to it (see Law 47F).

2. By Partner of Offender

After a non-offender so withdraws a card, the hand of the offending side next in rotation may withdraw its played card, which becomes a penalty card if the player is a defender.

D. *Revoke on Trick Twelve*

1. Must be Corrected

On the twelfth trick, a revoke, even if established, must be corrected if discovered before all four hands have been returned to the board.

2. Offender's Partner Had Not Played to Trick Twelve

If a revoke by a defender occurred before it was the turn of his partner to play to the twelfth trick, and if offender's partner has cards of two suits, (penalty) declarer may require the offender's partner to play to that trick either of the two cards he could legally have played.

*Subject to Law 43B2C, when dummy has forfeited his rights. A claim of revoke does not warrant inspection of quitted tricks except as permitted in Law 66C.

LAW 63

ESTABLISHMENT OF A REVOKE

A. *Revoke Becomes Established*

A revoke becomes established:

1. Offending Side Leads or Plays to Next Trick

when the offender or his partner leads or plays to the following trick (any such play, legal or illegal, establishes the revoke).

2. A Member of Offending Side Indicates a Lead or Play

when the offender or his partner names or otherwise designates a card to be played to the following trick.

3. Member of Offending Side Makes a Claim or Concession

when a member of the offending side makes or acquiesces in a claim or concession of tricks orally or by facing his hand (or in any other fashion).

4. Attention is Illegally Drawn

when there has been a violation of law 61B.

B. *Revoke May Not Be Corrected*

Once a revoke is established, it may no longer be corrected (except as provided in Law 62D for a revoke on the twelfth trick), and the trick on which the revoke occurred stands as played.

NOTE: The new Law 63A.4 does not apply in ACBL sanctioned events.

LAW 64

PROCEDURE AFTER ESTABLISHMENT OF A REVOKE

A. *Penalty Assessed*

When a revoke is established:

1. Offending Player Won Revoke Trick

and the trick on which the revoke occurred was won by the offending player, (penalty) after play ceases, the trick on which the revoke occurred, plus one of any subsequent tricks won by the offending side, are transferred to the non-offending side;

2. Offending Player Did Not Win Revoke Trick

and the trick on which the revoke occurred was not won

by the offending player, then, if the offending side won that or any subsequent trick, (penalty) after play ceases, one trick is transferred to the non-offending side; also, if an additional trick was subsequently won by the offending player with a card that he could legally have played to the revoke trick, one such trick is transferred to the non-offending side.

B. *No Penalty Assessed*

The penalty for an established revoke does not apply:

1. Offending Side Fails to Win Revoke Trick or Subsequent Trick

if the offending side did not win either the revoke trick or any subsequent trick.

2. Second Revoke in Same Suit by Offender

to a subsequent revoke in the same suit by the same player.

3. Revoke by Failure to Play a Faced Card

if the revoke was made in failing to play any card faced on the table or belonging to a hand faced on the table, including a card from dummy's hand.

4. After Non-offending Side Calls to Next Deal

if attention was first drawn to the revoke after a member of the non-offending side has made a call on the subsequent deal.

5. After Round Has Ended

if attention was first drawn to the revoke after the round has ended.

6. Revoke on Twelfth Trick

to a revoke on the twelfth trick.

C. *Director Responsible for Equity*

When, after any established revoke, including those not subject to penalty, the Director deems that the non-offending side is insufficiently compensated by this Law for the damage caused, he shall assign an adjusted score.

PART IV

TRICKS

LAW 65

ARRANGEMENT OF TRICKS

A. *Completed Trick*

When four cards have been played to a trick, each player turns his own card face down near him on the table.

B. *Keeping Track of the Ownership of Tricks*

1. Tricks Won

If the player's side has won the trick, the card is pointed lengthwise toward his partner.

2. Tricks Lost

If the opponents have won the trick, the card is pointed lengthwise toward the opponents.

C. *Orderliness*

Each player arranges his own cards in an orderly overlapping row in the sequence played, so as to permit review of the play after its completion, if necessary to determine the number of tricks won by each side or the order in which the cards were played.

D. *Agreement on Results of Play*

A player should not disturb the order of his played cards until agreement has been reached on the number of tricks won. A player who fails to comply with the provisions of this law jeopardizes his right to claim ownership of doubtful tricks or to claim a revoke.

LAW 66

INSPECTION OF TRICKS

A. *Current Trick*

So long as his side has not led or played to the next trick, declarer or either defender may, *until he has turned his own card face down on the table*, require that all cards just played to the trick be faced for his inspection.

B. *Own Last Card*

Until a card is led to the next trick, declarer or either defender may inspect, but not expose, his own last card played.   •

C. *Quitted Tricks*

Thereafter, until play ceases, quitted tricks may not be inspected (except at the Director's specific instruction; for example, to verify a claim of a revoke).

D. *After the Conclusion of Play*

After play ceases, the played and unplayed cards may be inspected to settle a claim of a revoke, or of the number of tricks won or lost; but no player should handle cards other than his own. If, after such a claim has been made, a player mixes his cards in such a manner that the Director can no longer ascertain the facts, the Director shall rule in favor of the other side.

LAW 67

DEFECTIVE TRICK

A. *Before Both Sides Play to Next Trick*

When a player has omitted to play to a trick, or has played too many cards to a trick, the error must be rectified if attention is drawn to the irregularity before a player on each side has played to the following trick.

1. Player Failed to Play Card

To rectify omission to play to a trick, the offender supplies a card he can legally play.

2. Player Contributed Too Many Cards

To rectify the play of too many cards to a trick, Law 45E (Fifth Card Played to a Trick) or Law 58B (Simultaneous Cards from One Hand) shall be applied.

B. *After Both Sides Play to Next Trick*

After both sides have played to the following trick, when attention is drawn to a defective trick or when the Director determines that there had been a defective trick (from the fact that one player has too few or too many cards in his hand, and a correspondingly incorrect number of played cards), the Director establishes which trick was defective. To rectify the number of cards, the Director should proceed as follows.

1. Offender Has Too Many Cards

When the offender has failed to play a card to the defective trick, the Director shall require him forthwith to face a card, and to place it appropriately among his played cards (this card does not affect ownership of the trick); if

(a) Offender Has Card of Suit Led

the offender has a card of the suit led to the defective trick, he must choose such a card to place among his played cards, and there is no penalty;

(b) Has No Card of Suit Led

the offender has no card of the suit led to the defective trick, he chooses any card to place among his played cards, and (penalty) he is deemed to have revoked on the defective trick—he may be subject to the one-trick penalty of Law 64.

2. Offender Has Too Few Cards

When the offender has played more than one card to the defective trick, the Director inspects the played cards, and requires the offender to restore to his hand all extra cards*, leaving among the played cards the one faced in playing to the defective trick (if the Director is unable to determine which card was faced, the offender leaves the highest of the cards that he could legally have played to the trick). A restored card is deemed to have belonged continuously to the offender's hand, and a failure to have played it to an earlier trick may constitute a revoke.

*The Director should avoid, when possible, exposing a defender's played cards, but if an extra card to be restored to a defender's hand has been exposed, it becomes a penalty card (see Law 50).

PART V

Claims and Concessions

LAW 68

CLAIM OR CONCESSION OF TRICKS

For a statement or action to constitute a claim or concession of tricks under these Laws, it must refer to tricks other than one currently in progress*. If it does refer to subsequent tricks:

A. *Claim Defined*

Any statement to the effect that a contestant will win a specific number of tricks is a claim of those tricks. A contestant also claims when he suggests that play be curtailed, or when he shows his cards (unless he demonstrably did not intend to claim).

B. *Concession Defined*

Any statement to the effect that a contestant will lose a specific number of tricks is a concession of those tricks; a claim of some number of tricks is a concession of the remainder, if any. A player concedes all the remaining tricks when he abandons his hand. Regardless of the foregoing, if a defender attempts to concede one or more tricks and his partner immediately objects, no concession has occurred; Law 16, Unauthorized Information, and Law 57A, Premature Play, may apply, so the Director should be summoned forthwith.

C. *Clarification Required for Claim*

A claim should be accompanied at once by a statement of clarification as to the order in which cards will be played, the line of play or defense through which the claimer proposes to win the tricks claimed.

D. *Play Ceases*

After any claim or concession, play ceases. All play subsequent to a claim or concession shall be voided by the Director. If the claim or concession is acquiesced in, Law 69 applies; if it is disputed by any player (dummy included), the Director must be summoned immediately to apply Law 70 or Law 71, and no action may be taken pending the Director's arrival.

*If the statement or action pertains only to the winning or losing of an uncompleted trick currently in progress, play proceeds regularly; cards exposed or revealed by a defender do not become penalty cards, but Law 16, Unauthorized Information, may apply, and see Law 57A, Premature Play.

LAW 69

ACQUIESCENCE IN CLAIM OR CONCESSION

A. *When Acquiescence Occurs*

Acquiescence occurs when a contestant assents to an opponent's claim or concession, and raises no objection to it before his side makes a call on a subsequent board, or before the round ends. The board is scored as though the tricks claimed or conceded had been won or lost in play.

B. *Acquiescence in Claim Withdrawn*

Within the correction period established in accordance with Law 79C, a contestant may withdraw aquiescence in an opponent's claim, but only if he has acquiesced in the loss of a trick his side has actually won, or in the loss of trick that could not, in the Director's judgment, be lost by any normal* play of the remaining cards. The board is rescored with such trick awarded to the acquiescing side.

LAW 70

CONTESTED CLAIMS

A. *General Objective*

In ruling on a contested claim, the Director adjudicates the result of the board as equitably as possible to both sides, but any doubtful points shall be resolved against the claimer. The Director proceeds as follows.

B. *Clarification Statement Repeated*

1. Require Claimer to Repeat Statement

The Director requires claimer to repeat the clarification statement he made at the time of his claim.

2. Require All Hands to Be Faced

Next, the Director requires all players to put their remaining cards face up on the table.

3. Hear Objections

The Director then hears the opponents' objections to the claim.

C. *There Is an Outstanding Trump*

When a trump remains in one of the opponents' hands, the Director shall award a trick or tricks to the opponents if:

1. Failed to Mention Trump

claimer made no statement about that trump, and

2. Was Probably Unaware of Trump

it is at all likely that claimer at the time of his claim was unaware that a trump remained in an opponent's hand, and

3. Could Lose a Trick to the Trump

a trick could be lost to that trump by any normal* play.

D. *Claimer Proposes New Line of Play*

The Director shall not accept from claimer any successful line of play not embraced in the original clarification statement if there is an alternative normal* line of play that would be less successful.

E. *Unstated Line of Play (Finesse or Drop)*

The Director shall not accept from claimer any unstated line of play the success of which depends upon finding one opponent rather than the other with a particular card, unless an opponent failed to follow to the suit of that card before the claim was made, or would subsequently fail to follow to that suit on any normal* line of play.

*For the purposes of Laws 69, 70, and 71, "normal" includes play that would be careless or inferior for the class of player involved, but not irrational.

LAW 71

CONCESSION CANCELLED

A concession must stand, once made, except that:

A. *False Concession*

Within the correction period established in accordance with Law 79C, the Director shall cancel a concession:

1. Trick Cannot be Lost

if a player has conceded a trick his side had, in fact, won, or a trick his side could not have lost by any legal play of the remaining cards.

2. Contract Already Fulfilled or Defeated

if declarer has conceded defeat of a contract he had already fulfilled, or a defender has conceded fulfillment of a contract his side had already defeated.

B. *Implausible Concession*

Until the conceding side makes a call on a subsequent board, or until the round ends, the Director shall cancel the concession of a trick that could not have been lost by any normal* play of the remaining cards.

*For the purposes of Laws 69, 70, and 71, "normal" includes play that would be careless or inferior for the class of player involved, but not irrational.

CHAPTER VII

Proprieties

LAW 72
GENERAL PRINCIPLES

A. *Observance of Laws*

1. General Obligation on Contestants

Duplicate bridge tournaments should be played in strict accordance with the Laws.

2. Scoring of Tricks Won

It is improper for a player knowingly to accept either the score for a trick that his side did not win, or the concession of a trick that his opponents could not lose.

3. Waiving of Penalties

In duplicate tournaments a player may not, on his own initiative, waive a penalty for an opponent's infraction, even if he feels that he has not been damaged (but he may ask the Director to do so — see Law 81C8).

4. Non-offenders' Exercise of Legal Options

When these Laws provide the innocent side with an option after an irregularity committed by an opponent, it is appropriate to select that action most advantageous.

5. Offenders' Options

After the offending side has paid the prescribed penalty for an inadvertent infraction, it is appropriate for the offenders to make any call or play advantageous to their side, even though they thereby appear to profit through their own infraction.

6. Responsibility for Enforcement of Laws

The responsibility for penalizing irregularities and redressing damage rests solely upon the Director and these Laws, not upon the players themselves.

B. *Infraction of Law*

1. Intentional

To infringe a law intentionally is a serious breach of propriety, even if there is a prescribed penalty that one is willing to pay. The offense may be the more serious when no penalty is prescribed.

2. Inadvertent Infraction

There is no obligation to draw attention to an inadvertent infraction of law committed by one's own side (but see footnote to Law 75 for a mistaken explanation).

3. Concealing an Infraction

A player may not attempt to conceal an inadvertent infraction, as by committing a second revoke, concealing a card involved in a revoke, or mixing the cards prematurely.

LAW 73
COMMUNICATION BETWEEN PARTNERS

A. *Proper Communication between Partners*

1. How Effected

Communication between partners during the auction and play should be effected only by means of the calls and plays themselves.

2. Correct Manner for Calls and Plays

Calls and plays should be made without special emphasis, mannerism or inflection, and without undue hesitation or haste (however, sponsoring organizations may require mandatory pauses, as on the first round of auction, or after a skip-bid warning, or on the first trick).

B. *Inappropriate Communication Between Partners*

1. Gratuitous Information

It is inappropriate for communication between partners to be effected through the manner in which calls or plays are made, through extraneous remarks or gestures, or through questions asked or not asked of the opponents, through alerts and explanations given or not given to them.

2. Prearranged Communication

The gravest possible offense against propriety is for a partnership to exchange information through prearranged methods of communication other than those sanctioned by these Laws. The penalty imposed for infraction is normally expulsion from the sponsoring organization.

C. *Player Receives Unauthorized Information from Partner*

When a player has available to him unauthorized information from his partner's remark, question, explanation, gesture, mannerism, special emphasis, inflection, haste or hesitation, he must carefully avoid taking any advantage that might accrue to his side.

D. *Variations in Tempo*

1. Inadvertent Variations

Variations of tempo, manner, or the like may violate the Proprieties when the player could know, at the time of his action, that the variation could work to his benefit. Otherwise, inadvertently to vary the tempo or manner in which a call or play is made does not in itself constitute a violation of propriety, but inferences from such variation may appropriately be drawn only by an opponent, and at his own risk.

2. Intentional Variations

It is grossly improper to attempt to mislead an opponent by means of remark or gesture, through the haste or hesitancy of a call or play (as in hesitating before playing a singleton), or by the manner in which the call or play is made.

E. *Deception*

Any player may appropriately attempt to deceive an opponent through a call or play (so long as the deception is not protected by concealed partnership understanding). It is entirely appropriate to avoid giving information to the opponents by making all calls and plays in unvarying tempo and manner.

F. *Violation of Proprieties*

When a violation of the Proprieties described in this law results in damage to an innocent opponent:

1. Player Acts on Unauthorized Information

If the Director determines that a player chose from among logical alternative actions one that could reasonably have been suggested over another by his partner's remark, manner, tempo, or the like, he shall award an adjusted score (see Law 16).

2. Player Injured by Illegal Deception

If the Director determines that an innocent player has drawn a false inference from a deceptive remark, manner, tempo, or the like, of an opponent who could have known, at the time of the action, that the deception could work to his benefit, the Director shall award an adjusted score (see Law 12).

LAW 74
CONDUCT AND ETIQUETTE
A. *Proper Attitude*
1. Courtesy
A player should maintain at all times a courteous attitude.
2. Etiquette of Word and Action
A player should carefully avoid any remark or action that might cause annoyance or embarrassment to another player, or might interfere with the enjoyment of the game.
3. Conformity to Correct Procedure
Every player should follow uniform and correct procedure in calling and playing, since any departure from correct standards may disrupt the orderly progress of the game.
B. *Etiquette*
As a matter of courtesy a player should refrain from:
1. paying insufficient attention to the game.
2. making gratuitous comments during the auction and play.
3. detaching a card before it is his turn to play.
4. prolonging play unnecessarily (as in playing on although he knows that all the tricks are surely his) for the purpose of disconcerting an opponent.
5. summoning the Director in a manner discourteous to him or to other contestants.
C. *Breaches of Propriety*
The following are considered breaches of propriety:
1. using different designations for the same call.
2. indicating approval or disapproval of a call or play.
3. indicating the expectation or intention of winning or losing a trick that has not been completed.
4. commenting or acting during the auction or play so as to call attention to a significant occurrence, or to the number of tricks still required for success.
5. looking intently at any other player during the auction and play, or at another player's hand as for the purpose of seeing his cards or of observing the place from which he draws a card (but it is appropriate to act on information acquired by inadvertently seeing an opponent's card*).
6. showing an obvious lack of further interest in a deal (as by folding one's cards).
7. varying the normal tempo of bidding or play for the purpose of disconcerting an opponent.
8. leaving the table needlessly before the round is called.
*See Law 73D2 when a player may have shown his cards intentionally.

LAW 75
PARTNERSHIP AGREEMENTS
A. *Special Partnership Agreements*
Special partnership agreements, whether explicit or implicit, must be fully and freely available to the opponents (see Law 40). Information conveyed to partner through such agreements must arise from the calls, plays and conditions of the current deal.
B. *Violations of Partnership Agreements*
It is not improper for a player to violate an announced partnership agreement, so long as his partner is unaware of the violation (but habitual violations within a partnership may create implicit agreements, which must be dis-

closed). No player has the obligation to disclose to the opponents that he has violated an announced agreement; and if the opponents are subsequently damaged, as through drawing a false inference from such violation, they are not entitled to redress.
C. *Answering Questions on Partnership Agreements*
When explaining the significance of partner's call or play in reply to an opponent's inquiry (see Law 20), a player shall disclose all special information conveyed to him through partnership agreement or partnership experience; but he need not disclose inferences drawn from his general knowledge and experience.
D. *Correcting Errors in Explanation*
1. Explainer Notices Own Error
If a player subsequently realizes that his own explanation was erroneous or incomplete, he must immediately call the Director (who will apply Law 21 or Law 40C).
2. Error Noticed by Explainer's Partner
It is inappropriate for a player whose partner has given a mistaken explanation to correct the error immediately, before the final pass of the auction, or until play ends if he is a defender; nor is it appropriate for him to indicate in any manner that a mistake has been made. (He must not take advantage of the unauthorized information so obtained.) However, the player must inform the opponents, after calling the Director, that his partner's explanation was erroneous, at the earliest legal opportunity: after the final pass if he is to be declarer or dummy; after play ends if he is to be a defender.*
*Two examples may clarify responsibilities of the players (and the Director) after a misleading explanation has been given to the opponents. In both examples following, North has opened 1NT and South, who holds a weak hand with long diamonds, has bid 2♦, intending to sign off; North explains, however, in answer to West's inquiry, that South's bid is strong and artificial, asking for major suits.

Example 1—Mistaken Explanation
The actual partnership agreement is that 2♦ is a natural signoff; the mistake was in North's explanation. This explanation is an infraction of law, since East-West are entitled to an accurate description of the North-South agreement (when this infraction results in damage to East-West, the Director shall award an adjusted score).
If North subsequently becomes aware of his mistake, he must immediately notify the Director. South must do nothing to correct the mistaken explanation while the auction continues; after the final pass, South, if he is to be declarer or dummy, should call the Director and must volunteer a correction of the explanation. If South becomes a defender, he calls the Director and corrects the explanation when play ends.
Example 2—Mistaken Bid
The partnership agreement is as explained—2♦ is strong and artificial; the mistake was in South's bid. Here there is no infraction of law, since East-West did receive an accurate description of the North-South agreement; they have no claim to an accurate description of the North-South hands.
(Regardless of damage, the Director shall allow the result to stand; but the Director is to presume Mistaken Explanation, rather than Mistaken Bid, in the absence of evidence to the contrary.) South must not correct North's explanation (or notify the Director) immediately, and he has no responsibility to do so subsequently.
In both examples, South, having heard North's expla-

nation, knows that his own 2♦ bid has been misinterpreted. This knowledge is "unauthorized information" (see Law 16A), so South must be careful not to base subsequent actions on this information (if he does, the Director shall award an adjusted score). For instance, if North rebids 2NT, South has the unauthorized information that this bid merely denies a four-card holding in either major suit; but South's responsibility is to act as though North had made a strong game try opposite a weak response, showing maximum values.

LAW 76
SPECTATORS
A. *Conduct During Bidding or Play*
1. One Hand Only
A spectator should not look at the cards of more than one player, except by permission.
2. Personal Reaction
A spectator must not display any reaction to the bidding or play while a hand is in progress.
3. Mannerisms or Remarks
During the round, a spectator must refrain from mannerisms or remarks of any kind (including conversation with a player).
4. Consideration for Players
A spectator must not in any way disturb a player.
B. *Spectator Participation*
A spectator may not call attention to any irregularity or mistake, nor speak on any question of fact or law except by request of the Director.

CHAPTER VIII

The Score
LAW 77
DUPLICATE BRIDGE SCORING TABLE
TRICK SCORE
Scored by declarer's side if the contract is fulfilled

IF TRUMPS ARE	♣	♦	♥	♠
For each odd trick bid and made				
Undoubled	20	20	30	30
Doubled	40	40	60	60
Redoubled	80	80	120	120

AT A NOTRUMP CONTRACT

	UNDBLD	DBLD	REDBLD
For the first odd trick bid and made	40	80	160
For each additional odd trick	30	60	120

A trick score of 100 points or more, made on one board, is GAME.
A trick score of less than 100 points is a PART-SCORE.

PREMIUM SCORE
Scored by declarer's side
SLAMS

For making a slam	Not Vulnerable	Vulnerable
Small Slam (12 tricks) bid and made	500	750
Grand Slam (all 13 tricks) bid and made	1000	1500

OVERTRICKS

For each OVERTRICK	Not Vulnerable	Vulnerable
(tricks made in excess of contract)		
Undoubled	Trick Value	Trick Value
Doubled	100	200
Redoubled	200	400

PREMIUMS FOR GAME, PART-SCORE,

FULFILLING CONTRACT

For making GAME, vulnerable	500
For making GAME, not vulnerable	300
For making any PART-SCORE	50
For making any doubled, but not redoubled contract	50
For making any redoubled contract	100

UNDERTRICK PENALTIES
Scored by declarer's opponents if the contract is not fulfilled:

UNDERTRICKS
(tricks by which declarer falls short of the contract)

	Not Vulnerable			Vulnerable		
	Undbld	Dbld	Rdbld	Undbld	Dbld	Rdbld
For first undertrick	50	100	200	100	200	400
For each additional undertrick	50	200	400	100	300	600
Bonus for the fourth and each subsequent undertrick	0	100	200	0	0	0

LAW 78
METHODS OF SCORING
A. *Matchpoint Scoring*
In matchpoint scoring each contestant is awarded, for scores made by different contestants who have played the same board and whose scores are compared with his: two scoring units (matchpoints or half matchpoints) for each score inferior to his, one scoring unit for each score equal to his, and zero scoring units for each score superior to his.
B. *International Matchpoint Scoring*
In international matchpoint scoring, on each board the total point difference between the two scores compared is converted into IMP's according to the following scale:

Difference in points	I.M.P.	Difference in points	I.M.P.	Difference in points	I.M.P.
20- 40	1	370- 420	9	1500-1740	17
50- 80	2	430- 490	10	1750-1990	18
90-120	3	500- 590	11	2000-2240	19
130-160	4	600- 740	12	2250-2490	20
170-210	5	750- 890	13	2500-2990	21
220-260	6	900-1090	14	3000-3490	22
270-310	7	1100-1290	15	3500-3990	23
320-360	8	1300-1490	16	4000 & upwards	24

C. *Total Point Scoring*
In total point scoring, the net total point score of all boards played is the score for each contestant.
D. *Special Scoring Methods*
Special scoring methods are permissible, if approved by the sponsoring organization. In advance of any contest the sponsoring organization should publish conditions of contest detailing conditions of entry, methods of scoring, determination of winners, breaking of ties, and the like.

LAW 79
TRICKS WON
A. *Agreement on Tricks Won*
The number of tricks won shall be agreed upon before all four hands have been returned to the board.
B. *Disagreement on Tricks Won*
If a subsequent disagreement arises, the Director must be called. No increase in score may be granted unless the Director is called before the round ends as specified in

Law 8 (but Law 69 or Law 71 may supersede this provision when there has been an acquiescence or a concession).

C. *Error in Score*

An error in computing or tabulating the agreed-upon score, whether made by a player or scorer, may be corrected until the expiration of the period specified by the sponsoring organization. Unless the sponsoring organization specifies a later* time, this correction period expires 30 minutes after the official score has been completed and made available for inspection.

*An earlier time may be specified when required by the special nature of a contest.

CHAPTER IX

Tournament Sponsorship

LAW 80

SPONSORING ORGANIZATION

A sponsoring organization conducting an event under these Laws has the following duties and powers:

A. *Tournament Director*

to appoint the tournament Director. If there is no tournament Director, the players should designate one of their own number to perform his functions.

B. *Advance Arrangements*

to make advance arrangements for the tournament, including playing quarters, accommodations, and equipment.

C. *Session Times*

to establish the date and time of each session.

D. *Conditions of Entry*

to establish the conditions of entry.

E. *Special Conditions*

to establish special conditions for bidding and play (such as written bidding, bid boxes, screens—penalty provisions for actions not transmitted across a screen may be suspended).

F. *Supplementary Regulations*

to publish or announce regulations supplementary to, but not in conflict with, these Laws.

CHAPTER X

Tournament Director
SECTION ONE

RESPONSIBILITIES

LAW 81

DUTIES AND POWERS

A. *Official Status*

The Director is the official representative of the sponsoring organization.

B. *Restrictions and Responsbilities*

1. Technical Management

The Director is responsible for the technical management of the tournament.

2. Observance of Laws and Regulations

The Director is bound by these Laws and by supplementary regulations announced by the sponsoring organization.

C. *Director's Duties and Powers*

The Director's duties and powers normally include the following:

1. Assistants

to appoint assistants, as required to perform his duties.

2. Entries

to accept and list entries.

3. Conditions of Play

to establish suitable conditions of play, and to announce them to the contestants.

4. Discipline

to maintain discipline, and to insure the orderly progress of the game.

5. Law

to administer and interpret these Laws, and to advise the players of their rights and responsibilities thereunder.

6. Errors

to rectify any error or irregularity of which he becomes aware in any manner, within the correction period established in accordance with Law 79C.

7. Penalties

to assess penalties when applicable.

8. Waiver of Penalties

to waive penalties for cause, at his discretion, upon the request of the non-offending side.

9. Disputes

to adjust disputes, and to refer disputed matters to the appropriate committee when required.

10. Scores

to collect scores and tabulate results.

11. Reports

to report results to the sponsoring organization for official record.

D. *Delegation of Duties*

The Director may delegate any of the duties listed in 'C' to assistants, but he is not thereby relieved of responsibility for their correct performance.

LAW 82

RECTIFICATION OF ERRORS OF PROCEDURE

A. *Director's Duty*

It is the duty of the Director to rectify errors of procedure and to maintain the progress of the game in a manner that is not contrary to these Laws.

B. *Rectification of Error*

To rectify an error in procedure the Director may:

1. Award of Adjusted Score

award an adjusted score as permitted by these Laws.

2. Specify Time of Play

require or postpone the play of a board.

C. *Director's Error*

If the Director has given a ruling that he or the Chief Director subsequently determines to be incorrect, and if no rectification will allow the board to be scored normally, he shall award an adjusted score, considering both sides as non-offending for that purpose.

LAW 83

NOTIFICATION OF THE RIGHT TO APPEAL

If the Director believes that a review of his decision on a point of fact or exercise of his discretionary power might be in order (as when he awards an adjusted score under Law 12), he shall advise a contestant of his right to appeal.

SECTION TWO
RULINGS

LAW 84

RULINGS ON AGREED FACTS

When the Director is called to rule on a point of law or regulation in which the facts are agreed upon, he shall rule as follows:

A. *No Penalty*

If no penalty is prescribed by law, and there is no occasion for him to exercise his discretionary powers, he directs the players to proceed with the auction or play.

B. *Penalty under Law*

If a case is clearly covered by a law that specifies a penalty for the irregularity, he assesses that penalty and sees that it is paid.

C. *Player's Option*

If a law gives a player a choice among penalties, the Director explains the options and sees that a penalty is selected and paid.

D. *Director's Option*

If the law gives the Director a choice between a specified penalty and the award of an adjusted score, he attempts to restore equity, resolving any doubtful point in favor of the non-offending side.

E. *Discretionary Penalty*

If an irregularity has occurred for which no penalty is provided by law, the Director awards an adjusted score if there is even a reasonable possibility that the non-offending side was damaged, notifying the offending side of its right to appeal.

LAW 85
RULINGS ON DISPUTED FACTS

When the Director is called upon to rule on a point of law or regulation in which the facts are not agreed upon, he shall proceed as follows:

A. *Director's Assessment*

If the Director is satisfied that he has ascertained the facts, he rules as in Law 84.

B. *Facts Not Determined*

If the Director is unable to determine the facts to his satisfaction, he shall make a ruling that will permit play to continue, and notify the players of their right to appeal.

SECTION THREE

CORRECTION OF IRREGULARITIES
LAW 86
IN TEAM PLAY

A. *Average Score at IMP Play*

When the Director chooses to award an artificial adjusted score of 60% (see Law 84) to a non-offending contestant in IMP play, that score is 3 I.M.P.

B. *Non-balancing Adjustments, Knockout Play*

When the Director assigns non-balancing adjusted scores (see Law 12C) in knockout play, each contestant's score on the board is calculated separately. The average of the two scores is then assigned to both contestants.

C. *Substitute Board*

The Director shall not exercise his Law 6 authority to order one board redealt when the final result of a match without that board could be known to a contestant. Instead, he awards an adjusted score.

LAW 87
FOULED BOARD

A. *Definition*

A board is considered to be "fouled" if the Director determines that one or more cards were misplaced in the board, in such manner that contestants who should have had a direct score comparison did not play the board in identical form.

B. *Scoring the Fouled Board*

In scoring a fouled board the Director determines as closely as possible which scores were made on the board in its correct form, and which in the changed form. He divides the score on that basis into two groups, and rates each group separately as provided in the regulations of the sponsoring organization.

SECTION FOUR

PENALTIES
LAW 88
AWARD OF INDEMNITY POINTS

In a pair or individual event, when a non-offending contestant is required to take an artificial adjusted score through no fault or choice of his own, such contestant shall be awarded a minimum of 60% of the matchpoints available to him on that board, or the percentage of matchpoints he earned on boards actually played during the session if that percentage was greater than 60%.

LAW 89
PENALTIES IN INDIVIDUAL EVENTS

In individual events, the Director shall enforce the penalty provisions of these Laws, and the provisions requiring the award of adjusted scores, equally against both members of the offending side, even though only one of them may be responsible for the irregularity. But the Director, in awarding adjusted scores, shall not assess procedural penalty points against the offender's partner, if, in the Director's opinion, he is in no way responsible for the violation.

LAW 90
PROCEDURAL PENALTIES

A. *Director's Authority*

The Director, in addition to enforcing the penalty provisions of these Laws, may also assess penalties for any offense that unduly delays or obstructs the game, inconveniences other contestants, violates correct procedure, or requires the award of an adjusted score at another table.

B. *Offenses Subject to Penalty*

Offenses subject to penalty include but are not limited to:

1. Tardiness

arrival of a contestant after the specified starting time.

2. Slow Play

any unduly slow play by a contestant.

3. Loud Discussion

any discussion of the bidding, play, or result of a board, which may be overheard at another table.

4. Comparing Scores

any comparison of scores with another contestant during a session.

5. Touching Another's Cards

any touching or handling of cards belonging to another player (Law 7).

6. Misplacing Cards in Board

placing one or more cards in an incorrect pocket of the board.

7. Errors in Procedure

any error in procedure (such as failure to count cards in one's hand, playing the wrong board, etc.) that requires an adjusted score for any contestant.

8. Failure to Comply

any failure to comply promptly with tournament regulations, or with any instruction of the Director.

LAW 91
PENALIZE OR SUSPEND

A. *Director's Power*

In performing his duty to maintain order and discipline, the Director is specifically empowered to as sess disciplinary penalties in points, or to suspend a contestant for the current session or any part thereof (the Director's decision under this clause is final).

B. *Right to Disqualify*

The Director is specifically empowered to disqualify a contestant for cause, subject to approval by the Tournament Committee or sponsoring organization.

CHAPTER XI

Appeals
LAW 92
RIGHT TO APPEAL

A. *Contestant's Right*

A contestant or his Captain may appeal for a review of any ruling made at his table by the Director.

B. *Time of Appeal*

Any appeal for or of a Director's ruling must be made within the time period established in accordance with Law 79C.

C. *How to Appeal*

All appeals shall be made through the Director.

D. *Concurrence of Appellants*

An appeal shall not be heard unless both members of a pair (except in an individual contest), or the captain of a team, concur in appealing. An absent member shall be deemed to concur.

LAW 93
PROCEDURES OF APPEAL

A. *No Appeals Committee*

The Chief Director shall hear and rule upon all appeals if there is no Tournament or Appeals committee, or when a committee cannot meet without disturbing the orderly progress of the tournament.

B. *Appeals Committee Available*

If a committee is available,

1. Appeal Concerns Law

The Chief Director shall hear and rule upon such part of the appeal as deals solely with the law or regulations. His ruling may be appealed to the committee.

2. All Other Appeals

The Chief Director shall refer all other appeals to the committee for adjudication.

3. Adjudication of Appeals

In adjudicating appeals the committee may exercise all powers assigned by these Laws to the Director, except that the committee may not overrule the Director on a point of law or regulations, or on exercise of his disciplinary powers. The committee may recommend to the Director that he change his ruling.

C. *Appeal to National Authority*

After the preceding remedies have been exhausted, further appeal may be taken to the national authority (on a point of law, in ACBL the National Laws Commission, 2990 Airways Boulevard, Memphis, TN, 38116-3847).

ACBL REGULATIONS

The following regulations are in effect in ACBL through actions of the ACBL Board of Directors, under authority granted by the referenced laws.

LAW 16 A. 1.

At ACBL sanctioned events, competitors will not be allowed to announce that they reserve the right to summon the Director later. They should summon the Director immediately when they believe there may have been extraneous information available to the opponents resulting in calls or bids which could result in damage to their side.

LAW 40 D.

One notrump openings with fewer than eight high-card points are barred in all ACBL sanctioned events.

LAW 40 D.

An opening one bid in a suit which by partnership agreement could show fewer than eight high-card points is not allowed. This does not apply to an opening bid intended as a psych.

LAW 40 E. 1.

Both members of a partnership must employ the same system that appears on the convention card.

1. During a session of play, a system may not be varied, except with permission of the tournament director. (A director might allow a pair to change a convention, but would not allow a pair to change their basic system.)

2. At the outset of a round or session, a pair may review their opponents' convention card and alter their defenses against the opponents' conventional calls and preemptive bids. This must be announced to their opponents. The opponents may not vary their system after being informed of these alterations in defense.

LAW 41 A. & LAW 45 A.

Face-down opening leads shall be required at all ACBL sanctioned events.

LAW 61 B.

The restriction that otherwise would prohibit defenders from asking one another whether they have a card of the suit led shall not apply, unless otherwise specified by action of the ACBL Board of Directors.

LAW OF TOTAL TRICKS. The Law of Total Tricks is the theory that on any given bridge deal the total number of trumps will be approximately equal to the total number of tricks. The total number of trumps is obtained by adding North-South's longest trump fit to East-West's longest trump fit. The total number of tricks is the sum of how many tricks North-South would take if they played in their best fit, added to how many East-West would take in their best fit.

The "Law" is a most useful bidding tool for competitive auctions. The players often can deduce from the bidding how many trumps each partnership has, and then use the total-tricks formula as a guideline. Knowing the number of trumps gives the competitor an idea as to the number of tricks, and will often dictate the proper bidding decision. To use the "Law" to its best effect, it is necessary to take certain adjustment factors into account. Extreme distribution, possession of queens and jacks in the opponents' suits, and double-fits are some of the components that influence the accuracy of the Law of Total Tricks.

The Law was discovered in the 1950s by Frenchman Jean-René Vernes, but it didn't receive much attention until the 1990s when it was the subject of a book called to *To Bid or Not to Bid* by Larry Cohen.

LAY DOWN. Verb: (1) to put the dummy's cards on the table; (2) to play a (high) card with the assurance of winning that particular trick.

LAYDOWN. A colloquialism for a hand that can virtually be claimed for a successful contract as soon as the dummy is exposed. However, surprising things happen to laydown hands with disconcerting frequency. PIANOLA is a synonym.

LEAD. The first card played to a trick. See LAWS (Law 44). See LEADS.

LEAD-DIRECTING BID. A bid made primarily for the purpose of indicating a desired suit for partner to lead initially against an impending adverse contract. North holds, for example,

```
            ♠ 10 x x
            ♥ x x
            ♦ A K x x
            ♣ x x x x
```

and the bidding has proceeded:

WEST	NORTH	EAST	SOUTH
	Pass	1 ♥	1 ♠
2 ♥			

A bid of 3♦ by North in this position is a lead-directing bid. He has no intention of playing a diamond contract, and will retreat to 3 ♠ if doubled. He is merely maneuvering to secure a diamond opening lead if the final contract is in hearts.

LEAD-DIRECTING DOUBLE. The most frequent case is a double of a voluntarily bid contract at 3 NT by the player not on lead. In current practice the double requests in order of priority: (a) the lead of the opening leader's suit; (b) the lead of the doubler's bid suit; (c) the lead of the first suit bid by dummy. However, it may not be right to lead dummy's suit if it has been rebid; and some authorities leave to judgment the situation in which both defenders have bid a suit. See also FISHER DOUBLE.

The lead-directing double may occur at the partscore level:

(a)

WEST	NORTH	EAST	SOUTH
			Pass
Pass	1 ♦	Pass	2NT
Pass	Pass	Dbl	

(b)

WEST	NORTH	EAST	SOUTH
			1 ♦
Pass	1 NT	Pass	Pass
Dbl			

In each case the double is suggesting the lead of a dia-

mond.

A double of 3 NT when neither side has bid a suit implies that the doubler has a solid suit which can be run immediately. The opening leader will tend to lead a short major suit in which he has no honor.

A double of a conventional bid such as a response to Blackwood has obvious lead-directing implications. There is also a negative inference: a player who does not double such a bid is likely to prefer another lead.

Players often double FOURTH-SUIT ARTIFICIAL bids. Such doubles are not without risk, as this deal from the 1981 Vanderbilt Knockout Teams shows.

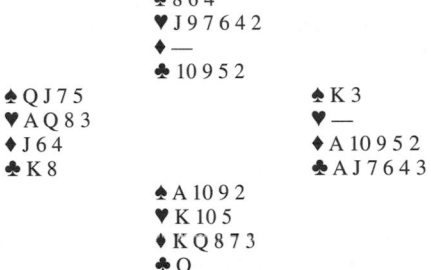

At one table East-West overreached to 6 ♦ after West opened 1♦ . At the other:

WEST	NORTH	EAST	SOUTH
1 ♦	Pass	2 ♣	Pass
2NT	Pass	3 ♦	Dbl
Pass	Pass	Redbl	Pass
3NT	All Pass		

Since the first West had managed nine tricks at his slam, the second West would have been well advised to stand for 3♦ redoubled. (3NT made, so he gained 11 IMPs anyway.) Note that South's double looked completely safe. See DOUBLES OF ARTIFICIAL BIDS FOR PENALTIES .

LEAD-DIRECTING RAISES. A method of suggesting a lead when partner's preemptive opening is doubled for take out.

NORTH	EAST	SOUTH	WEST
	2 ♥	Dbl	3 ♦

This shows, by agreement, heart support and a desire for a diamond lead if East is on lead. This applies in any unbid suit, and operates in the same way if the opening preemptive bid is at the three-level.

LEAD-INHIBITING BID. A tactical bid, in the nature of a semi-psychic call, which is designed to prevent the opponents from leading a specific suit. For example:

```
            ♠ K Q 6
            ♥ K J 7
            ♦ 8 5 2
            ♣ A Q 7 5
```

The normal opening bid should be 1♣ followed by a rebid of 1NT. An opening bid of 1♦ , made with the idea of discouraging a diamond lead against notrump, would be a lead-inhibiting bid.

Another common form of a lead-inhibiting bid:

```
            ♠ —
            ♥ K 7 6 5 2
            ♦ 9 5
            ♣ A K 8 5 3 2
```

After an opening bid of 1 ♦ by partner, one immediately thinks in terms of six or seven. A bid of 3♦ with this hand might stop the opponents from cashing the first two diamond tricks.

LEAD OUT OF TURN. An irregularity in play. See Law 54 for opening lead out of turn, Law 55 for declarer's lead out of turn, and Law 56 for defender's lead out of turn.

LEAD OUT OF WRONG HAND (by declarer). A lead out of turn by declarer, leading either from his or dummy's hand incorrectly. See Law 55.

LEAD THROUGH. To lead through a particular opponent is to initiate the lead in the hand to the right of that opponent, forcing that opponent to play to the trick before the leader's partner plays to it. See THROUGH STRENGTH; UP TO WEAKNESS.

LEAD THROUGH STRENGTH. See THROUGH STRENGTH.

LEAD UP TO. To lead, in defense, with the object of enabling partner's hand to win a trick because of weakness in the hand on the leader's right. Occasionally, a strong hand may be led up to, when the object is not necessarily to win the trick. A lead is always "up to" the hand on the leader's right. To "lead up to" is always leading "up to" the fourth hand. See UP TO WEAKNESS .

LEAD UP TO WEAKNESS. See UP TO WEAKNESS.

LEADER. The person or player who first plays to any given trick, "as opening leader."

LEADS. See ATTACKING LEADS; DESPERATION LEAD OR PLAY; DISCARDING; FORCING LEADS; HONOR LEAD; JOURNALIST LEADS; OPENING LEADS; RUSINOW LEADS; SHORT-SUIT LEADS; THIRD HIGHEST LEAD; THREE SMALL CARDS, LEAD FROM; TRELDE LEADS; TRUMP LEADS; UNDERLEAD; UP TO WEAKNESS.

LEAGUE. An organized association, which may be on a local, regional, national, or international scale. Members of the league may be individuals, clubs, teams, or other groupings. In this volume "the League" normally refers to the American Contract Bridge League. In England, "league" is commonly used as a synonym for ROUND-ROBIN.

LEAP. A bid missing several levels, generally to game or slam, either in support of partner or in a new suit, usually suggesting a final contract and inviting partner to pass at his next opportunity. Alternatively, a leap to a slam convention may be made.

LEAVE IN. See PENALTY DOUBLE.

LEAVES. One of the suits in early European PLAYING CARDS (a translation of German and Slavic words). See PACK.

LEBANESE BRIDGE FEDERATION (Federation Libanaise de Bridge).
The Federation was founded in 1949 by three Beirut

clubs and hosted the 1962 European Championships in Beirut. Lebanon was represented in most European Championships and World Olympiads in spite of the Civil War between 1975 and 1991. Membership in 1993 was 200. 1993 Officers:
President: Chucri Sader
Hon. Secretary: Gaby Merhy
P.O. Box 11-54 Beirut Lebanon
Tel: 384 511

LEBENSOHL. A convention first described by George Boehm of New York and attributed by him, wrongly, to Ken Lebensold. Sometimes, consequently, called Lebensold. It deals with the problem created for the partner of an opening notrump bidder following an overcall. The mechanism varies depending on whether the overcall shows one suit or two and whether it is made at the two level or three level. Over a natural two-level overcall, a double is for penalties, a two-level suit bid is nonforcing, a three-level suit bid is forcing and a 2 NT bid forces opener to rebid 3♣. Responder can pass opener's 3♣ bid if he has a weak hand with long clubs or can rebid. If he rebids a suit below the rank of the suit overcalled it is a signoff; if he rebids a suit above the rank of the suit overcalled, it is invitational to game. A cuebid is Stayman while a relay to 3♣ followed by a cuebid is also Stayman. The difference is that one shows a stopper in the opponent's suit and the other denies it. Direct jumps to 3NT and 3NT following a relay to 3♣ are similar raises to game with or without a stopper. It is up to the individual partnerships to decide which sequence shows the stopper and which denies. The modern tendency is to play SLOW SHOWS, FAST DENIES. Over a two-suited overcall such as LANDY, the double is penalty-oriented in at least one of the suits shown by the overcall. The two-level bid of a suit not shown by the overcall is not forcing, while the three-level bid of such a suit is forcing to game. Cuebids are generally forcing to game. Only when the overcall shows two specific suits and responder cuebids the cheaper may the partnership stop below game. Over a three-level overcall the double is a takeout for any suits not shown by the overcall. Suit bids at the three level are forcing to game.

Lebensohl has been modified to extend to other situations. See LEBENSOHL APPLICATIONS; ADVANCED LEBENSOHL.

LEBENSOHL APPLICATIONS. The Lebensohl idea can be used, and often is, in two other situations.

(1) *Responding to double of weak two-bids*: If a weak 2♣ bid is doubled, a suit response at the three-level has an uncomfortably wide range in standard bidding:

WEST	NORTH	EAST	SOUTH
2 ♠	Dbl	Pass	3 ♥

North cannot tell whether his partner has eight points or none at all. With a good hand he must guess whether to continue to game. Using Lebensohl the responder promises moderate values, perhaps 6-9 points or the equivalent. With a very weak hand he must bid 2NT, forcing a 3♣ bid from opener. Responder can pass 3♣ with length in that suit, or pick another suit. If the doubler is so strong that he hopes for game opposite a very weak South hand, he can disregard the instruction to bid 3♣.

(2) *Good-Bad two notrump.* In some competitive auctions a bid of 2NT has little value in a natural sense and

can be used to separate competitive actions from hands with serious game prospects. 2NT shows weaker hands.

South	West	North	East
1 ♦	Pass	1 ♠	2 ♥
?			

	(a)	(b)
♠	4 3	4 3
♥	5	5
♦	K Q J 8 5 4 2	K Q J 8 5
♣	A J 6	A Q J 10 4

2NT would, without agreement, suggest a hand with about 16-17 points, but that hand would presumably have opened 1NT. So 2NT can be used to show a competitive hand with one or both minors. If North bids 3♣, South reverts to 3♦ with hand (a).

With this agreement, 3♣ and 3♦ can clearly show invitational values, with perhaps a king more than the hands shown.

If the opponents open, or the bidding is at the one-level, the meanings are reversed: bids at the three-level are weak, and the rare strong hands bid 2NT.

LEBHAR TROPHY. For the NABC Mixed Team Championship. Donated by Bertram Lebhar, Jr., in 1948, in memory of his wife Evelyn; a replacement for the BARCLAY TROPHY. Contested at the Summer NABC, under which heading past results are listed. For results, see Appendix I.

LEBENSOLD. See LEBENSOHL.

LEBOVIC ASKING BID. A convention devised by Wolf Lebovic of Toronto, and publicized by Sami Kehela of Toronto; when two or three suits have been bid and a minor suit has been agreed as trumps, a double jump in an unbid suit asks about control in that suit. The last bid in each of the following auctions would be a Lebovic asking bid.

(a)		(b)	
SOUTH	NORTH	SOUTH	NORTH
1 ♣	1 ♥	1 ♣	2 ♦
1 ♠	3 ♣	3 ♦	4 ♥
4 ♦			

The responder to the asking bid answers as follows: with a singleton in the asked suit he bids six of the trump suit, with king doubleton or longer he bids 4NT, with the ace or a void he bids the asked suit, and with none of the above he makes the minimum bid in the trump suit.

One difficulty with this is that it is conflict with the popular SPLINTER BID.

LEDGER. See BACK SCORE.

LEFT-HAND PLAYER. The player on declarer's left. In assessing penalties there has been a differentiation between left- and right-hand opponents as respects power or right to invoke penalties. Generally, however, the term is restricted to use in describing situations on play. An alternative term is left-hand opponent, abbreviated to LHO. A colloquialism is "Lefty."

LEG. A colloquial rubber bridge term to indicate a game already won. Partners who have a leg are vulnerable.

LEGAL. Applied to any call or play not in contravention of the mechanics of the game as set forth in the laws.

A legal convention is one that is listed properly on the convention card that is either approved by the tournament committee or by the tournament director for use in that event. See LAWS, Sections 1, 11, and 111, and PROPRIETIES.

LEGHORN DIAMOND (LIVORNO) SYSTEM. Similar to the ROMAN SYSTEM, developed by Benito Bianchi and Giuseppe Messina and used successfully in many European Championships. The chief features are:

1 ♣ opening is forcing and may show any of four different types of hand: (1) 12-15 points, balanced distribution and no five-card major; (2) unbalanced with a long minor, 12-20 points, possibly with a side four-card major if the point range is 12 or 13; (3) unbalanced with a long major and no side four-card major or five-card minor, 16-20 points; or (4) a three-suiter with a singleton or void in a major, 12-13 points.

2 ♦ (natural) and 1 ♦ are both negative responses to 1♣, showing less than 8 points. 1♥ and 1♠ responses are positive, 8 points or more, and 1NT and 2NT deny a four-card major and are limited to 8-10 and 11-12 points respectively. Jump suit responses are natural and game forcing, except 3♣, which is forcing for only one round and suggests 3NT. A jump to 2♦ may be made on a four-card suit if responder intends to Canapé into a major.

The auction tends to develop naturally after the initial response. Minimum major-suit rebids by opener usually describe the weak balanced hand, but he may have the minimum major-minor two-suiter or the three-suiter. With either of the unbalanced hands, opener makes a simple rebid in a minor with 12-17, jumps to the two-level in a major with 16-17 or jumps to the three-level in any suit with 18-20. After a positive response, a jump rebid by opener to 2NT shows exactly 15 points. After responding in a major, responder's second suit is his long suit.

1 ♦ opening is forcing and shows either a balanced hand with 19 points or more, or an unbalanced hand that is about a trick short of game, possibly a three-suiter with at least 20 points.

Suit responses show controls by steps (king = 1 control, ace = 2 controls). 1♥ shows no controls, 1♠ shows 1 control, and so on. With no controls but scattered queens and jacks, responder bids 1NT with 5-6 points or 2NT with 7 or more.

A simple notrump rebid by opener describes a balanced hand with 19-21 points and a jump notrump rebid shows 22 points or more. If opener is unbalanced, he usually makes a minimum rebid in a suit, over which responder rebids conventionally by eight steps to show support. A new suit by opener is then a second asking bid, and the responses are on the same scale for that suit. After responder has made his support-showing step response to opener's second suit, a bid of the cheapest denomination by opener is a relay asking responder to choose between opener's suits.

1 ♥ and 1 ♠ openings are natural but show two different types of hand: (1) less than 16 points with a five-card or longer major; or (2) a two-suiter, usually a four-card major and a five-card or longer side suit, with 14-19 points. To distinguish between the two types, opener normally rebids his major with the first type of hand, even if he has a side four-card suit, and bids his second suit (jumping with 17-19 points) with hand type two.

1NT opening is standard (16-18) and denies a five-card major.

2♣ and 2♦ openings show three-suited hands (4-4-4-1 or 5-4-4-0 distribution) with 12-16 and 17-19 points respectively. Responses and rebids are similar to the Roman System.

2♥ and 2♠ openings show two-suited hands, the bid major and a four- or five-card minor, with 9-12 points.

2NT opening shows at least five cards in each minor with 14-16 high card points.

LENGTH. The number of cards held in a particular suit, usually referring to five or more; as opposed to STRENGTH, the high card values held in a suit. See DISTRIBUTIONAL VALUES.

LENGTH SIGNALS. See COUNT SIGNALS.

LENGTH OF SESSION. A session is generally 13 rounds of two boards each, and experienced players should complete this in about 3° hours. In no case may an ACBL tournament session consist of less than 22 or more than 30 boards in pair competition. One board to a round may be used only in certain one-session team events or in individual contests. In some team events, particularly in head-on knockout competition, late rounds may be more than 30 boards. See ACBL HANDBOOK.

LENGTH SIGNALS. See COUNT SIGNALS.

LESSON HANDS. Bridge teachers regularly offer prepared deals to their pupils, illustrating points in bidding and play covered by their lessons.

LEVEL. The "odd-trick" count in excess of the book, that is, each trick over six. Thus an overcall of 2 is a bid made at the two level and a contract to make eight tricks. A 4 opening bid is said to be made at the four level. See OVERCALLS.

LEVENTRITT TROPHY. For the Life Master Pairs consolation event; donated by PETER A. LEVENTRITT of New York in 1950. It was contested until 1972 at the Summer NABC.

LIECHTENSTEIN BRIDGE UNION
(Liechtensteinische Bridge Vereinigung).
1993 Membership 105.
Officers 1993
  President: D. Sprenger
  Vice-President: Vittorio Di Silvio
  Austrasse 27
  Postfach 183
  F1 9490 Vaduz
  Liechtenstein.
  Fax: 41 75 28862.

LIFE MASTER. Once the highest ACBL rank of player. (For qualification for this rank, see RANKING.) The category was created by the AMERICAN BRIDGE LEAGUE in 1936, and selection of the first Life Masters was based on national tournament successes, although a masterpoint program had been in effect since 1934. Initially, the rank was conferred on a group of 10 players, ranked in order according to the number and importance of their national victories, and an eleventh player was made Life Master shortly thereafter. There are now six separate categories of Life Master (see RANKING). The

first 100 players to achieve the rank were:

1.	David Bruce	1936
2.	Oswald Jacoby	1936
3.	Howard Schenken	1936
4.	Waldemar K. von Zedtwitz	1936
5.	P. Hal Sims	1936
6.	B. Jay Becker	1936
7.	Theodore A. Lightner	1936
8.	Richard L. Frey	1936
9.	Michael T. Gottlieb	1936
10.	Sam Fry Jr.	1936
11.	Merwin D. Maier	1936
12.	Charles S. Lochridge	1937
13.	Charles H. Goren	1938
14.	A. Mitchell Barnes	1938
15.	Harry J. Fishbein	1939
16.	Charles J. Solomon	1939
17.	Sally Young	1939
18.	Fred D. Kaplan	1939
19.	John R. Crawford	1939
20.	Walter Jacobs	1939
21.	Morrie Elis	1939
22.	Phil Abramsohn	1940
23.	Edward Hymes Jr.	1940
24.	Alvin Landy	1940
25.	Helen Sobel Smith	1941
26.	Sherman Stearns	1941
27.	Robert A. McPherran	1941
28.	Jeff Glick	1942
29.	Arthor Glatt	1942
30.	Dr. Richard Ecker Jr.	1942
31.	Albert Weiss	1942
32.	Lee Hazen	1942
33.	Peggy Solomon	1942
34.	Alvin Roth	1942
35.	Sidney Silodor	1943
36.	Olive Peterson	1943
37.	Margaret Wagar	1943
38.	Peter A. Leventritt	1943
39.	Edson T. Wood	1944
40.	Ralph Kempner	1944
41.	Arthur S.Goldsmith	1944
42.	Simon Becker	1944
43.	Stanley O. Fenkel	1944
44.	George Rapee	1944
45.	Ruth Sherman	1944
46.	Robert Appleyard	1945
47.	M. A. Lightman	1945
48.	Samuel Stayman	1945
49.	Edward N. Marcus	1945
50.	Charles A. Hall	1945
51.	Emily Folline	1946
52.	Joseph E. Cain	1946
53.	Harry Feinberg	1946
54.	Ambrose Casner	1946
55.	Samuel Katz	1946
56.	Jack Ehrlenbach	1946
57.	J. Van Brooks	1946
58.	Simon Rossant	1946
59.	Edward G. Ellenbogen	1946
60.	Sidney R. Fink	1946
61.	Bertram Lebhar Jr.	1946
62.	Meyer Schleifer	1947
63.	Louis Newman	1947
64.	Elinor Murdoch	1947

65.	Paula Bacher	1947	21.	Bob Hamman	17,461
66.	Florence Stratford	1947	22.	Peter Weichsel	17,197
67.	Jules Bank	1947	23.	John Fisher	17,096
68.	William McGhee	1947	24.	Kerri Sanborn	17,085
69.	Maynard Adams	1947	25.	Mark Itabashi	17,057
70.	Edith Kemp	1947	26.	Eric Rodwell	16,560
71.	David Carter	1947	27.	Glenn Lublin	16,309
72.	Jack Cushing	1947	28.	Chuck Said	16,212
73.	Dr. A. Steinberg	1947	29.	Joan Remey Moore	15,695
74.	Jane Jaeger	1947	30.	Howard Chandross	15,545
75.	Cecil Head	1947	31.	Gene Freed	15,537
76.	S. Garton Churchill	1947	32.	Lynn Deas	15,231
77.	Edward S. Cohn	1947	33.	Morris Portugal	15,223
78.	John Carlin	1947	34.	Alan Stout	15,195
79.	Lawrence Welch	1947	35.	David Siebert	15,057
80.	Frank Weisbach	1947	36.	Mike Cappelletti	14,996
81.	Charlton Wallace	1944	37.	Carol Sanders	14,919
82.	Dr. Louis Mark	1947	38.	Tom Sanders	14,731
83.	Edward Taylor	1947	39.	David Adams	14,702
84.	Dan Westerfield	1947	40.	Gerald Caravelli	14,676
85.	Tobias Stone	1947	41.	John Sutherlin	14,527
86.	Mark Hodges	1947	42.	Rhoda Walsh	14,367
87.	Leo Roet	1947	43.	Peter Boyd	14,240
88.	Sol Mogal	1947	44.	Kit Woolsey	14,226
89.	Herbert Gerst	1947	45.	Bob Glenn	14,149
90.	Lewis Mathe	1947	46.	John Anderson	14,105
91.	Ludwig Kabakjian	1947	47.	Jo Morse	14,086
92.	Gratian Goldstein	1947	48.	Allan Siebert	13,754
93.	Allen P. Harvey	1947	49.	John Mohan	13,663
94.	Lewis Jaeger	1947	50.	Edgar Kaplan	13,294
95.	Mildred Cunningham	1947	51.	David Berkowitz	13,255
96.	Elmer J. Schwartz	1947	52.	Robert Levin	13,069
97.	Linda Terry	1947	53.	Bill Passell	12,939
98.	Maurice Levin	1948	54.	David Ashley	12,724
99.	Dave Warner	1948	55.	Kathie Wei-Sender	12,632
100.	Ernest Rovere	1948	56.	Norman Kay	12,589
			57.	Helen Shanbrom	12,572
			58.	Dennis Clerkin	12,559

As of April 29, 1994, the ACBL has issued 55,496 Life Master cards. Of this number 46,686 were living. 13,885 Life Masters had 300-500 points; 19,228 were in the Bronze Life Master range (500-1000 points); 10,772 were Silver Life Masters with more than 1,000 points; 2,124 were Gold Life Masters with 2,500 or more points; 549 Diamond Life Masters had 5,000 or more points and 128 players were in the Grand Life Master range with 10,000 or more points. The top 100 masterpoint holders were:

1.	Paul Soloway	40,062	59.	Jan Janitschke	12,507
2.	Mike Passell	34,246	60.	Dennis Sorensen	12,488
3.	Ronald Andersen	32,467	61.	Richard Pavlicek	12,333
4.	Mark Lair	32,399	62.	Malcolm Brachman	12,319
5.	Eddie Wold	27,866	63.	Alvin Roth	12,311
6.	Grant Baze	24,525	64.	Ethel Keohane	12,268
7.	Jeff Meckstroth	23,685	65.	Phil Leon	12,238
8.	Hermine Baron	22,396	66.	Jan Weyant	12,155
9.	Gaylor Kasle	21,909	67.	Rick Henderson	11,987
10.	Mary Jane Farell	21,302	68.	Marc Jacobus	11,950
11.	Fred Hamilton	20,945	69.	Paul Ivaska	11,931
12.	Alan Bell	20,755	70.	Allan Cokin	11,882
13.	Bobby Goldman	19,682	71.	Frank Hoadley	11,853
14.	Michael Lawrence	18,160	72.	Betty Ann Kennedy	11,801
15.	Mike Shuman	18,017	73.	Charles Coon	11,694
16.	Bobby Wolff	17,985	74.	Robert Lipsitz	11,656
17.	Steve Robinson	17,933	75.	Marty Bergen	11,644
18.	David Treadwell	17,735	76.	John Zilic	11,591
19.	Garey Hayden	17,586	77.	Mark Blumenthal	11,587
20.	Zeke Jabbour	17,518	78.	Ross Rainwater	11,580
			79.	Sidney Lazard	11,546
			80.	Ronald Smith	11,515
			81.	Gail Greenberg	11,477
			82.	Ed Manfield	11,461
			83.	Frank King	11,444
			84.	Hugh Maclean	11,350
			85.	Clifford Russell	11,253
			86.	Bernie Chazen	11,065

87.	Erik Paulsen	11,063
88.	Roger Bates	11,016
89.	George Bloomer	11,003
90.	Jacqui Mitchell	10,949
91.	Beverly Rosenberg	10,896
92.	Steve Lawrence	10,890
93.	Jim Zimmerman	10,857
94.	Sydney Levey	10,816
95.	Marshall Miles	10,809
96.	Ron Smith	10,786
97.	George Rosenkranz	10,677
98.	Lew Stansby	10,676
99.	Michael Moss	10,636
100.	G. Robert Nail	10,607

LIFE MASTER MEN'S PAIRS, NORTH AMERICAN CHAMPIONSHIP. See APPENDIX I .

LIFE MASTER PAIRS, NORTH AMERICAN CHAMPIONSHIP. See APPENDIX I.

LIFE MASTER WOMEN'S PAIRS, NORTH AMERICAN CHAMPIONSHIP. See APPENDIX I.

LIFT. A term meaning "raise."

LIGHT (1) To go down in a contract. "He was two light." (2) To bid with insufficient values, especially in opening the bidding.

LIGHTNER DOUBLE. A lead-directing double of a slam contract. If competent opponents bid a slam voluntarily, it may be expected that they will fulfill their contract or fail by one trick. Thus a normal penalty double is unlikely to gain much. In 1929 Theodore Lightner devised a more useful interpretation of this bid. A double by the hand not on lead is conventional. Partner is requested to choose an unusual lead which may result in the defeat of the slam. A conventional double of this sort excludes the lead of a trump, a suit bid by the defenders, or an unbid suit. The player who doubles expects to ruff the lead of a side suit mentioned by the opponents, or else to win two top tricks in that suit. Some experts treat this double quite rigidly. They define the double to mean that partner must lead dummy's first-bid side suit. Other good players, including Lightner, interpret the bid more loosely. An unusual lead is requested and partner must deduce from the context which suit is required.

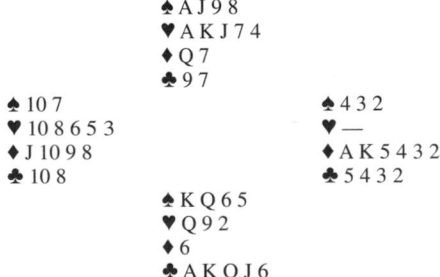

     ♠ A J 9 8
     ♥ A K J 7 4
     ♦ Q 7
     ♣ 9 7

♠ 10 7   ♠ 4 3 2
♥ 10 8 6 5 3   ♥ —
♦ J 10 9 8   ♦ A K 5 4 3 2
♣ 10 8   ♣ 5 4 3 2

     ♠ K Q 6 5
     ♥ Q 9 2
     ♦ 6
     ♣ A K Q J 6

 South plays 6♣, after opening 1♣ and getting a response of 1♥ . East doubles for an unusual lead. West leads a heart, East ruffs and cashes the ♦A for the setting trick. Without the double West would have led a diamond which declarer would have covered from dummy. East would be forced to win the only trick the defense could

take. See also LEAD-DIRECTING DOUBLES. For an alternative use of the double of a slam when the defenders have bid and raised a suit of their own, see DOUBLE FOR SACRIFICE.

LILIES. See ROYAL SPADES.

LIMIT. A bid which shows a maximum as well as a minimum range of values in the bidder's hand. Various limit bids are discussed in the following articles: DELAYED GAME RAISE; DOUBLE RAISE; INVERTED MINOR SUIT RAISES; INVITATIONAL BID; LIMIT BID; LIMIT JUMP RAISE; NOTRUMP BIDDING; 1NT RESPONSE; SINGLE RAISE; STRONG NOTRUMP AFTER PASSING; 3NT RESPONSE; TRIPLE RAISE; and 2NT RESPONSE.

LIMIT BID. A bid with a limited point-count range, usually fewer than 4 points. Although a traditional forcing jump raise (1 ♠ -3 ♠) is limited in the wide sense of the term, limit is normally applied only to nonforcing bids below the game level. With some exceptions, a bid is limited and nonforcing if it is in notrump, if it is a raise, if it is a preference, or if it is a minimum rebid in a suit previously bid by the same player. Opening notrump bids are invariably limited. Once we have decided that a certain bid is limited the vital question arises: how wide can the limits be? *The nearer the bidding is to game, the closer the limits must be.* When the bidding reached 2NT with the possibility of 3NT; or when the bidding reaches 3 ♠ , there is no longer any margin for exploration. So to give partner the chance of making an accurate decision, all such bids must have a range of only 2 points. Thus 1 ♥ -2NT by a passed hand shows 11-12, and 1 ♥ -1NT-2NT shows 17-18; similarly 1 ♠-3 ♠ by a passed hand shows 10-11, or the equivalent, and 1 ♥ -1 ♠ -3 ♠ shows 17-18, or the equivalent. All these are typical encouraging bids, indicating that the partnership has a minimum of 23-24 points and urging partner on to game if he has a little more than his promised minimum.

 Conversely, any bid of 1NT and any limited bid of two of a suit can afford a range of 3 or 4 points: there is still time for partner to make an encouraging bid below the game level. So 1 ♥ -1NT or 1 ♥ -2 ♥ are each 6-9 (and may have to stretch a little further at that), and 1 ♥ -1 ♠ -2 ♠ is 13-16, or the distributional equivalent. In the same way, opening 1NT bids usually have a range of 3 points (e.g., 16-18), but these could even be a point wider still without any disastrous loss of accuracy. See OPENER'S REBID, RESPONDER'S REBID, and RESPONSE.

LIMIT JUMP RAISE. Originally a feature of the ACOL and KAPLAN-SHEINWOLD systems, this is now standard in American tournament play and in most other parts of the world.

 A raise from 1 ♥ to 3♥ , for example, is nonforcing but strongly encouraging. It shows a hand with about 11 high-card points or the distributional equivalent.

 If the opening bidder has a minimum, he normally passes. If the nine-trick contract fails, it will often turn out that the opponents could have made a partscore or even a game.

 Limit jump raises were a part of the original CULBERTSON SYSTEM (to 1934) and were revived for minor suits only in 1948. A few players use limit jump raises in competition only, that is, after a suit overcall by an opponent; and nearly all players ascribe to them quite a low limit over an opponent's takeout double.

LIMIT JUMP RAISE TO SHOW A SINGLETON.
A part of the WALSH SYSTEM, using an immediate jump raise of opener's major suit opening to show three or four trumps, 10-12 points, and a singleton somewhere in the hand. If opener is interested in locating responder's singleton, he makes the cheapest bid over the limit raise (See MATHE ASKING BID.) This device can be used with other bidding styles if the partnership uses a forcing 1NT response to opening bids of 1 ♥ or 1 ♠. The forcing notrump followed by a jump to three of opener's suit can be used to show a balanced limit raise.

LIMIT RAISE.
A raise with closely defined limits of strength. Many such bids are limited in this way in standard methods, such as the single raise of opener's suit. The chief application is the jump raise from one to three (see LIMIT JUMP RAISE). The bid would indicate at least four-card trump support with 10-11 points or the distributional equivalent. The corollary is that a jump raise on the second round is invitational but nonforcing:

WEST	EAST	WEST	EAST
1 ♣	1 ♠	1 ♣	1 ♥
3 ♠		1 ♠	3 ♠

The second of these sequences is not clearly defined in traditional methods since 4♠ is also available. See JUMP REBIDS BY RESPONDER .

LIMIT RESPONSES.
The combination of LIMIT RAISES with limit responses in notrump, so that responses of 2NT and 3♠ to an opening bid of 1♠ , for example, are both encouraging but not forcing.

LINE.
The dividing horizontal marking on a score pad below which game and partial scores (trick scores) are written. See ABOVE THE LINE and BELOW THE LINE.

LITERATURE AND BRIDGE.
Several full-length novels have focused on bridge. *Tickets to the Devil*, by Richard Powell, deals with the activities at a Spring North American Championship, both at the tables and away from them. *Yarborough* by B. H. Friedman outlines the adolescence and young manhood of two precocious heroes. In one Agatha Christie mystery, *Cards on the Table*, the murder takes place during a bridge game and Hercule Poirot solves it by analyzing the score pad. Another British mystery and suspense writer, Georgette Heyer, also wrote about murder at a bridge game in *Duplicate Death*. A series of paperbacks by Don Von Elsner (*The Ace of Spies, The Jack of Hearts, The Jake of Diamonds, Kona Contract*, etc,) features a fictitious bridge pro, Jake Winkman, in a variety of adventures in tournament settings, in which the quality of the bridge hands is highly professional. Similarly, Frank Thomas, a veteran actor of stage, movies, radio and television, now a bridge teacher and editor of the ABTA Quarterly, has written two books about *Sherlock Holmes, Bridge Detective*, which combine good storytelling with excellent bridge hands. Author Terry Quinn relates the adventures of a strange foursome caught up in the world of tournament bridge and international intrigue in *The Great Bridge Conspiracy*. In Sinclair Lewis's *Main Street* the local bridge club is a barometer of the characters' accommo-

dation to the social life in Gopher Prairie MN. In Ian Fleming's *Moonraker*, James Bond rigged a variation of the DUKE OF CUMBERLAND'S HAND in dealing with the villain of that book. (See DISTRIBUTIONAL VALUES.)

Among famous writers who have used a bridge theme for short story purposes are: Somerset Maugham (*The Three Fat Women of Antibes, The Facts of Life*); Roald Dahl (*My Lady Love, My Dove*); Ring Lardner (*Contract, Who Dealt*); and George S. Kaufman (*The Great Kibitzers' Strike of 1926*). See Cole and Edwards, eds., *Grand Slam*, BIBLIOGRAPHY, B. In his long short story, *The Death of Ivan Ilych*, Leo Tolstoy made "vint", a Russian variation of bridge whist, the favorite leisure activity of his central character.

S. J. Simon, a European champion and bridge writer, made some minor references to the game in the delightful series of novels he wrote with Caryl Brahms. C. S. Forester made his naval hero, Horatio Hornblower, a whist expert. Jules Vernes' whist expert, Phileas Fogg, begins his incredible journey in *Around the World in Eighty Days* as a result of a wager made with his whist-playing associates.

For Charles Lamb's view of whist players, see BATTLE, SARAH.

LITHUANIA BRIDGE ASSOCIATION
Address 1992:
Viesulo 13 39
Vilnius
232050 Lithuania.
Tel: 0122 449164

LITTLE MAJOR SYSTEM.
An artificial system of bidding devised by Terence Reese and Jeremy Flint, London, in the early sixties and now obsolete. In principle, an opening of 1♣ denotes a heart suit and 1♦ denotes a spade suit. Strong hands are opened with 1♥ , and minor suit hands with 1♠ .

LITTLE OLD LADY. See LOL.

LITTLE ROMAN CLUB (ARNO) SYSTEM.
Developed by Camillo Pabis-Ticci and Massimo D'Alelio, and first used successfully in the 1965 Bermuda Bowl. The system is patterned closely on the principles of the ROMAN SYSTEM, especially the opening two-bids and structure of defensive overcalls. Its chief features are:

1♣ opening is forcing and shows either a balanced hand with 12-16 points, or a 17-20 point hand with a club suit or a two-suiter with at least four clubs. After a negative response of 1 ♦ (less than 10 points), opener rebids on the one-level to show the balanced minimum opening. A response of 1NT is forcing to game, showing 12 points or more, over which opener bids a suit on the two-level with 12-13 points or raises to 2 NT with 14-16 points. Jump responses are also forcing to game, and request opener to rebid conventionally by four steps to describe his strength and support for responder's suit.

1♦ , 1♥ and 1♠ openings are forcing and natural according to the Canapé principle with 12-20 points. The opening bid may be made in a three-card suit with a minimum of 15 points or if opener's longest suit is clubs. The next higher suit by responder (1NT over 1 ♠) is the conventional negative, after which opener makes a simple rebid with 12-16 points or a jump rebid with a stronger hand. After a positive response, a normal rebid by opener is forcing for one round, and responder creates a game-force if his rebid is a reverse, a jump in a new suit, a raise of opener's second suit if it is a major, or a jump raise of opener's first suit. A 1NT response, if it is not a negative, shows a balanced hand with at least 12 points and is forcing to game. If opener rebids in notrump after opening 1 ♦, he has a balanced hand with 17-20 points.

1NT opening is forcing and shows either a balanced hand with 21-24 points, or a powerful distributional hand that is forcing to game. Responder shows the number of aces he holds by steps and opener rebids 2 NT with the balanced hand or canapés in a suit with the unbalanced hand.

2♣ , 2♦ , 2♥ and 2♠ openings are as in the ROMAN SYSTEM. 2NT opening shows a minimum of five cards in both minors with 12-16 points.

LITTLE SLAM. See SMALL SLAM.

LIVORNO SYSTEM. See LEGHORN DIAMOND.

LOCAL TOURNAMENTS. See CHAMPIONSHIP TOURNAMENTS .

LOCK. A colloquial term, used principally in post mortems, to mean a 100% sure play or contract. For example, "4 ♠ was a lock." In certain ethical situations the term has a similar meaning: "After his partner's HUDDLE he had a lock to double."

LOCKED (IN OR OUT OF A HAND). To win a trick in a hand from which it is disadvantageous to make the lead to the next (or some later) trick is to be locked in. It usually refers to an endplay against a defender (see THROW IN) or to a declarer who is forced to win a trick in the dummy hand, when he has high cards established in his own hand which he is unable to enter. Locked out refers to situations in which established cards in the dummy cannot be cashed because an entry is not available.

LONDON SUNDAY TIMES PAIRS. See SUNDAY TIMES PAIRS and Appendix IV.

LONG CARDS. Cards of a suit remaining in a player's hand after all other cards of that suit have been played.

LONG HAND. The hand of the partnership which has the greater length in the trump suit, or, in notrump play, the hand which has winners that are or may be established. See AVOIDANCE.

LONG SUIT. A suit in which four or more cards are held. Frequently it is used in connection with a hand of little strength but with great length in a particular suit. For bidding on such a hand, see PREEMPTIVE BID .

LONG TRUMP. Any card of the trump suit remaining after all other players' cards of the suit have been played.

LOOSE DIAMOND. See SHORT DIAMOND.

LOSER. A card that must lose a trick to the adversaries if led, or if it must be played when the suit is led by an adversary. At notrump, all cards below the ace and not in

sequence with it are possible losers, but may become winners if the play develops favorably. At a suit contract, the same may be said with the exception that losers may possibly be ruffed if the suit is short in one hand. A distinction must be made between possible losers and sure losers. The former may be discarded on a setup suit, or ruffed, or perhaps discarded on a setup card cashed by an adversary. If a loser cannot be disposed of, it must, of course, lose a trick to the opponents.

LOSER ON LOSER. The act of playing a card that must be lost on a losing trick in some other suit. This technique can be valuable in many situations, the most common of which are:

(1) *To allow a safe ruff to produce a trick:*

	♠ 4 3 2
	♥ A J 6 5 2
	♦ 5 3
	♣ A 7 4

♠ 6 5	♠ 8 7
♥ Q 3	♥ K 10 8 7 4
♦ K Q J 9 8 6	♦ A 2
♣ Q 10 8	♣ J 5 3 2

♠ A K Q J 10 9
♥ 9
♦ 10 7 4
♣ K 9 6

WEST	NORTH	EAST	SOUTH
2 ♦	Pass	3 ♦	3 ♠
Pass	4 ♠	All Pass	

West leads the ♦ K. East overtakes with the ace, and continues the suit. West wins and plays a third diamond. South realizes that East will be able to overruff dummy. He therefore plays a loser on a loser by discarding a club from dummy. Declarer can later ruff a club in dummy safely.

(2) *To allow a safe re-entry:*

	♠ 5 4 3 2
	♥ A 3
	♦ 6 5
	♣ A 7 6 4 2

♠ A K 10	♠ Q J 9 6
♥ Q 5	♥ J 8 6
♦ Q 10 7 4 2	♦ J 9 8
♣ K J 10	♣ Q 5 3

♠ 8 7
♥ K 10 9 7 4 2
♦ A K 3
♣ 9 8

WEST	NORTH	EAST	SOUTH
1NT	Pass	Pass	2 ♥
Pass	Pass	2 ♠	Pass
Pass	3 ♥	All Pass	

West leads three rounds of spades against 3♥ , and declarer ruffs. Two rounds of diamonds are cashed and the third round is trumped in the North hand. After cashing the ♥A, declarer must now re-enter his hand to continue drawing trump. If he leads ace and another club, East will win and his spade continuation will create two trump tricks for the defense. Instead, declarer cashes dummy's ♣A and then leads a fourth round of spades, playing a loser on a loser by discarding his remaining club. The defense is now helpless. Declarer is fortunate in the distribution of the East-West minor suit cards but has nothing to lose by attempting this play.

(3) *To prevent a later overruff threat:*

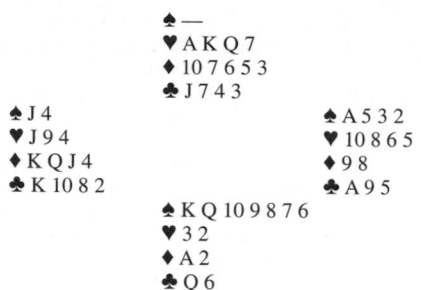

```
          ♠ —
          ♥ A K Q 7
          ♦ 10 7 6 5 3
          ♣ J 7 4 3
♠ J 4                      ♠ A 5 3 2
♥ J 9 4                    ♥ 10 8 6 5
♦ K Q J 4                  ♦ 9 8
♣ K 10 8 2                 ♣ A 9 5
          ♠ K Q 10 9 8 7 6
          ♥ 3 2
          ♦ A 2
          ♣ Q 6
```

With East-West vulnerable, South opens 4♠, and buys the contract. West leads the ♦K, which declarer wins. An immediate discard is necessary, so South takes three rounds of hearts, discarding his losing diamond. If South now fails to play the last heart, careful defense will obtain two clubs and two trump tricks. East will lead his last heart at a later stage, promoting West's jack of trump (see TRUMP PROMOTION). Instead, South uses the loser-on-loser technique. He leads dummy's remaining heart, discarding a club loser. East wins this trick, but the contract cannot be defeated.

(4) *To prevent a particular opponent from gaining the lead* (see AVOIDANCE):

```
          ♠ K J
          ♥ A K 4
          ♦ A 7 4 3 2
          ♣ J 10 6
♠ A 6 4 2                  ♠ 7
♥ —                        ♥ J 10 9 8 7 6 5
♦ J 10 9 8                 ♦ K Q
♣ A K Q 8 3                ♣ 5 4 2
          ♠ Q 10 9 8 5 3
          ♥ Q 3 2
          ♦ 8 6
          ♣ 9 7
```

WEST	NORTH	EAST	SOUTH
		3♥	Pass
Pass	Dbl	Pass	3♠
All Pass			

West leads the ♣K and (erroneously) continues with the A-Q. South observes that the bidding suggests West is void of hearts. He therefore plays a loser on a loser by discarding a diamond on the third club. If South ruffs the third club, West will shift to diamond after winning the second round of spades. South will then be unable to enter his hand without surrendering a heart ruff.

After South's discard on the third trick, his contract is safe.

(5) *To establish one or more tricks in the suit played:*

```
WEST                  EAST
♠ A K J               ♠ 5 4 3
♥ —                   ♥ K Q 4
♦ A 3                 ♦ 10 7 6 5
♣ A K J 10 9 8 7 3    ♣ Q 6 2
```

Against West's contract of 6♣, North leads the ♦K. West wins and draws two trumps ending in the East hand. He should now lead the ♥K from dummy, throwing a loser on a loser by discarding his diamond if South does not cover. If North wins the ♥A, the ♥Q will provide a discard for the ♠J. (Naturally, West has retained an entry to the East hand in clubs.) If South has the ace, either the ♥K will win or the ace will be ruffed out. Declarer can now try the spade finesse for an overtrick.

(6) *To help establish a side suit (see AVOIDANCE):*

```
          ♠ K Q 3
          ♥ J 9 7
          ♦ A 7 6 3 2
          ♣ 6 4
♠ 10                       ♠ J 9
♥ A K 10 8 5               ♥ Q 6 4 3
♦ 10 5                     ♦ Q J 9
♣ A Q 10 9 2               ♣ J 8 7 3
          ♠ A 8 7 6 5 4 2
          ♥ 2
          ♦ K 8 4
          ♣ K 5
```

WEST	NORTH	EAST	SOUTH
1♥	Pass	2♥	2♠
3♣	3♠	Pass	4♠
All Pass			

West leads the ♥K, and all follow. West, who has been reading this article, realizes that if he leads the ♥A, declarer will play a loser on a loser by discarding a diamond. This will allow the diamond suit to be established by ruffing and prevent East from gaining the lead to annihilate the ♣K.

West therefore shifts to a trump (a diamond has the same effect). Declarer wins in dummy, playing the four from his own hand. Anxious to execute the loser-on-loser play, he leads the ♥9 from dummy. East shakes off a yawn and rises with the queen to prevent the diamond discard. Declarer ruffs with the ♠5, returns to dummy by leading the ♠6 to the remaining honor in dummy. The ♥J is led from dummy. East cannot cover, and declarer sheds a low diamond. West wins and grudgingly cashes the ♣A to prevent an overtrick. Despite the best defense after the opening lead, declarer triumphs by continuing after his loser-on-loser play and careful unblocking in the spade suit (see UNBLOCKING.)

(7) *To avoid a force:*

```
WEST              EAST
♠ A K Q J         ♠ 10 8 5
♥ 3               ♥ 9 8 7
♦ A 4 3           ♦ 10 7 5
♣ A K J 9 5       ♣ Q 10 8 2
```

Against West's 4♠ contract, (Don't ask how he got there. It's a good contract, isn't it?) the defense begins with two rounds of hearts. To avoid weakening his trump holding, West should discard losing diamonds on the next two rounds of hearts. A fourth round of hearts can be ruffed in the East hand. If the trumps break 3-3 or 4-2, declarer romps home. If declarer ruffs a heart too early, a 4-2 trump break may defeat him, the defense taking four hearts and one trump trick.

(8) *To execute an endplay by creating a throw-in card:*

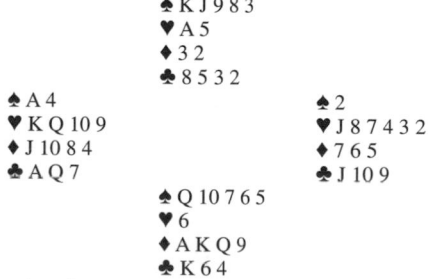

```
          ♠ K J 9 8 3
          ♥ A 5
          ♦ 3 2
          ♣ 8 5 3 2
♠ A 4                      ♠ 2
♥ K Q 10 9                 ♥ J 8 7 4 3 2
♦ J 10 8 4                 ♦ 7 6 5
♣ A Q 7                    ♣ J 10 9
          ♠ Q 10 7 6 5
          ♥ 6
          ♦ A K Q 9
          ♣ K 6 4
```

Against South's 4♠ contract, West leads the ♥K. Declarer wins with the ace, ruffs a heart, and leads a trump. West cautiously rises with the ♠A, and exits with a spade.

Declarer wins and tries to drop the ♦ J 10. On the third diamond, a club is discarded from dummy. South then leads the fourth round of diamonds. When West covers, declarer makes use of loser-on-loser technique by discarding another club from dummy. West is in, and must give away a trick.

(9) *To execute an endplay by forcing an opponent to remain on lead* (see RUFF AND DISCARD).

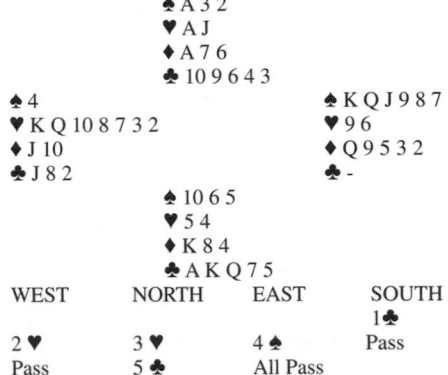

```
              ♠ A 3 2
              ♥ A J
              ♦ A 7 6
              ♣ 10 9 6 4 3
♠ 4                        ♠ K Q J 9 8 7
♥ K Q 10 8 7 3 2           ♥ 9 6
♦ J 10                     ♦ Q 9 5 3 2
♣ J 8 2                    ♣ -
              ♠ 10 6 5
              ♥ 5 4
              ♦ K 8 4
              ♣ A K Q 7 5
```

WEST	NORTH	EAST	SOUTH
			1♣
2♥	3♥	4♠	Pass
Pass	5♣	All Pass	

West leads the ♠4, which is won by North's ace. Declarer draws three rounds of trump and, placing West with seven hearts, cashes the two top diamonds and plays the ♥A and ♥J.

West is stuck on lead with only hearts remaining and must give up a ruff-and-discard. When he leads a heart, a diamond is thrown from dummy. South tosses a loser on a loser by discarding a spade from his own hand. West is forced to remain on lead. On the next heart, declarer ruffs in dummy and discards his last spade. He then crossruffs the balance of the tricks, having turned four losers into only two. West could counter brilliantly by permitting dummy's ♥ J to win, after which declarer would have no recourse.

(10) *To rectify the count for a squeeze.* This use of the loser-on-loser technique has many variations. Some of the most esoteric play problems revolve around declarer's attempt to correct the count for a squeeze by losing a trick in the correct suit. The following hand illustrates the method in a fairly complex setting.

```
              ♠ A K 3
              ♥ 8 4 3 2
              ♦ Q 4 2
              ♣ 6 5 3
♠ Q 10 7 2                 ♠ J 9 5
♥ 6                        ♥ 7
♦ A K 10 8 7 6 3           ♦ J 9 5
♣ 7                        ♣ Q J 10 9 8 4
              ♠ 8 6 4
              ♥ A K Q J 10 9 5
              ♦ —
              ♣ A K 2
```

WEST	NORTH	EAST	SOUTH
		3♣	4♥
5♦	5♥	Pass	6♥
All Pass			

West leads the ♦K, and South surveys the situation. He realizes that if neither opponent is short of spades (a reasonable assumption on the bidding) an elimination will fail, and the only chance for the contract is a double squeeze. The ♦Q is a menace against West, and declarer's third club threatens East. But the count is wrong. De-

clarer must lose a trick before the squeeze will operate.

Where can this trick be lost? Certainly not in spades or clubs, for the loss of a trick in either of these suits will destroy the essential menace cards. Therefore, a trick must be lost in diamonds. Furthermore, this trick must be lost *at once*. If declarer attempts to give up a diamond trick later on, the defense will play a third diamond, quashing the diamond menace. Therefore, declarer must throw a loser on a loser on the first trick. He discards a spade.

West has no effective defense. His best play is a spade. Declarer wins and runs winners until this ending is reached.

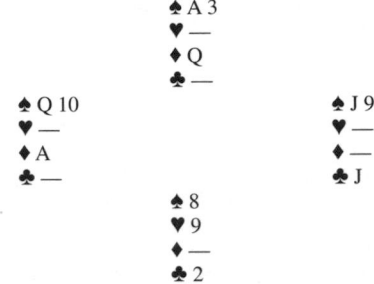

```
              ♠ A 3
              ♥ —
              ♦ Q
              ♣ —
♠ Q 10                     ♠ J 9
♥ —                        ♥ —
♦ A                        ♦ —
♣ —                        ♣ J
              ♠ 8
              ♥ 9
              ♦ —
              ♣ 2
```

When South leads the ♥9, West must surrender a spade. Dummy discards the ♦Q, and East is squeezed in spades and clubs.

LOSERS. A method of valuation for unbalanced hands used in the ROMAN and ROMEX Systems. Every missing ace, king or queen is counted as a loser unless shortness compensates. A doubleton king is one loser, but a doubleton queen is two losers. See LOSING TRICK COUNT and COVER CARDS.

LOSING-TRICK COUNT. A method of hand valuation. In 1934 the principle of assessing a hand in terms of "losers" was put forward by F. Dudley Courtenay in his book, *The System the Experts Play.* The general idea was this: when a suit fit came to light, you added the number of worthless cards in your hand to the number of losers revealed by your partner's bidding; the total was subtracted from 18, and the answer would tell you how many odd tricks the combined hands were likely to take.

After years of semi-obscurity the LTC was revived by Maurice Harrison-Gray and is now accepted as a reasonably accurate ready reckoner which pays due regard to the features that really matter.

This method of valuation is no longer treated with disdain by the expert. For instance, it is an integral part of the ROMAN SYSTEM, which has helped Italy to win seven world championships.

The Losing-Trick Count applies only to trump contracts. When a notrump contract is contemplated, the standard yardstick is the Milton Work Count.

Basic count of losers. With a void or singleton ace, count no loser in that suit; with any other singleton, or with A-x or K-x, count one loser; with any other doubleton, count two losers. In each suit of three or more cards, including the trump suit, count one loser for each missing high honor (A, K, or Q). Do not count more than three losers in any one suit. Count one loser only in a suit headed by A-J-10. Some distinction must obviously be made between A-x-x, K-x-x, and Q-x-x. The first is a better two-loser holding than K-x-x, and three losers must be counted in a queen-high suit unless: (a) it is the proposed trump suit; (b) the suit has been bid by the partner; (c) the queen is supported by the jack; (d) the queen is "balanced" by an ace in another suit.

The initial count. An opening bid of one is made with: (a) not more than seven losers; (b) adequate high-card values, including two defensive tricks; (c) a sound rebid. A response in a new suit is made with: (a) at the one-level not more than 9 losers (sometimes 10 with compensating values); (b) at the two-level not more than 8 losers (sometimes 9 with compensating values).

The count on the second rounds. Neutral rebids by opener (e.g., 1♥ -1♠ -2♥ , or 1♠ -2♣ -2♦ or 1♣ -1♠ -2♠) do not promise fewer than 7 losers.

A jump rebid by the opener in his original suit (e.g., 1♣ -1♠ - 3♣) shows 7 winners and (in most cases) only 5 losers.

A reverse rebid by the opener at the two-level (e.g., 1♣ -1♠ -2♦) shows five losers (sometimes six with a high point-count). A reverse at the three-level (e.g., 1♠ -2♥ - 3♣) shows not more than five losers.

A jump rebid by the responder in his original suit (e.g., 1♥ -1♠ -2♣ -3♠) shows 6 losers.

A responder's reverse at the two-level (e.g. 1♦ -2♣ - 2♦-2♥) shows 6 to 7 losers. A reverse at the three-level (e.g., 1♥ -1♠ -2♥ -3♣) shows not more than 6 losers.

It soon becomes second nature to adjust the original count of losers in the light of the bidding. Trump control is an important factor, and a loser should be deducted whenever the quota of aces and other key features, such as a king or a singleton in the right spot, is better than it might be on the bidding. The LTC will put a nonexpert player on the right track in a case like the following:

Dlr: South   ♠ Q 3
Vul: E-W   ♥ J 6
               ♦ A 7 4 3 2
               ♣ A 10 9 5

♠ J   ♠ 10 9 5 4
♥ A K 10 9 5 2   ♥ Q 8 4 3
♦ K J   ♦ 10 9 6
♣ J 8 7 2   ♣ K Q

            ♠ A K 8 7 6 2
            ♥ 7
            ♦ Q 8 5
            ♣ 6 4 3

The bidding:

SOUTH	WEST	NORTH	EAST
Pass	1 ♥	Pass	2 ♥
2♠	3 ♣	Pass	4 ♥
Pass	Pass	Dbl	Pass
Pass	Pass		

West had six losers, and East was marked with nine; 15 from 18 suggested that even 3♥ might fail through a dearth of top cards, but one of West's losers could be deducted for trump control, and a game try was in order. 3♥ would sound like mere contention, so he made a TRIAL BID in the spot where help was most needed. The onus was then on East, who saw two good reasons for jumping to game — his fourth trump and an ideal holding in the trial suit. The ♠ Q was led and West could not go wrong, in view of South's initial pass, when he came to tackle diamonds.

Application of the LTC would have averted an inelegant result on the deal below:

Dlr. South: ♠ J 10 8
Vul: E-W   ♥ K Q 3
             ♦ J 8
            ♣ A 10 9 7 2

♠ Q 6 3   ♠ 7 4
♥ 7 6 5 2   ♥ 10 8
♦ A K 4 3   ♦ 9 7 6 5 2
♣ 5 4   ♣ Q J 8 3

            ♠ A K 9 5 2
            ♥ A J 9 4
            ♦ Q 10
            ♣ K 6

The bidding:

SOUTH	WEST	NORTH	EAST
1 ♠	Pass	2 ♣	Pass
2 ♥	Pass	3 ♠	Pass
4 ♣	Pass	4 ♥	Pass
5 ♣	Pass	Pass	Pass

West could sit back and relax after cashing two diamonds. South made two common mistakes: his 17 points went to his head, and he read too much into a nonforcing preference bid. The LTC should serve as a halt sign. South has six losers, and his partner should have eight; if he deducts 14 from 18 he will see the futility of looking beyond 4 ♠ .

LOU HERMAN TROPHY. See HERMAN TROPHY and Appendix II.

LOVE. The state of the game, in rubber bridge, where there is as yet no score.

LOVE, TO PLAY FOR. To play rubber bridge without stakes.

LOVE ALL. A term, borrowed from tennis, used in some countries to describe that situation where neither side has made any score. Used in England at duplicate to indicate that neither side is vulnerable, but not used in the United States.

LOVE SCORE. Zero score; neither side vulnerable and no part-score.

LOW CARD. Not an honor; any card from the 2 to the 9, usually represented by an x in card or hand descriptions.

LOWER MINOR. See DEFENSE TO OPENING THREE-BID; SECOND NEGATIVE RESPONSE AFTER ARTIFICIAL FORCING OPENING.

LOWEST SCORE. The lowest score in major team-of-four play occurred in 1957, in the first Far East Team Championship at Manila. On the third set of eight boards in the match between Hong Kong and the Philippines, not one IMP was scored by either side. On each of the eight boards, both teams arrived at the same contract and made the same number of tricks. In a board-a-match team held at a Greater New York BA sectional tournament in 1975, one of the 74 teams entered scored only one-half board out of 26, a record that is unlikely to be broken, and if it is, it won't be by much. In pair play, the lowest recorded score is 13% (by opera star Lauritz Melchior). In head-to-head team play the record can be claimed for Eddie Kantar, Billy Eisenberg, Alan Sontag, Fred

Hamilton and Jim Cayne. In the first 16 deals of the 1983 Vanderbilt Knockout final in Hawaii they were outscored 68-2 by Bill Root, Richard Pavlicek, Edgar Kaplan and Norman Kay and were then penalized 10 IMPs for slow play. So they began the second quarter of the match with a score of minus 8 IMPs.

LUCK. A basic reason for the success of duplicate bridge is that it incorporates the optimum degree of luck. Although this means that the best players do not invariably win, it adds greatly to the fascination of the game and to the interplay of psychological factors. Par contests, where the luck element is removed, are much less popular.

Individual contests contain by far the largest element of luck and are less highly regarded as a test of skill than other forms of duplicate. The hazardous nature of an individual contest derives partly from the constant change of partners. Good luck may take the form of being teamed with a strong and compatible partner on critical deals which require accurate bidding or play; it would be bad luck to be teamed with an incompatible partner on such deals, and a player would prefer to reserve such a partner for a set of flat boards. Similarly, being teamed against incompatible players on swingy deals could be good luck, and a player might pick up a high matchpoint score without taking an active part.

After individual contests pair events contain the next highest proportion of luck. In a single-session event, a pair who are measurably stronger than the field will probably win less than half the time — but they will nearly always finish in the leading group. The greater the importance of a pair event, the greater the number of boards played, thus reducing the effect of luck.

Another facet of luck in pairs events is that toward the end of a contest an experienced pair who estimate that they have less than a winning score may adopt unusual tactics in an attempt to improve dramatically. Such tactics may take the form of bidding poor slams or games, or declining to bid good slams, in the hope that an improbable distribution of the cards will favor an unusual contract. Thus it is theoretically possible for a pair to have a comfortable lead with a few boards to go, to continue to bid and play perfectly, and yet be passed by a pair who have deliberately bid their way to faulty contracts or made imperfect plays. (See SHOOTING.) The fact that this is so has given rise to the misconception that the structure of pairs scoring is necessarily faulty; an alternate view is that it adds to the excitement and affords more scope for judgment and opportunism.

It is in team-of-four games - particularly those where the scoring is by International Match Points - that luck is reduced to a minimum; consequently these events carry most prestige and are the accepted medium for international competition.

At the same time, the structure of team games is such that luck, when it does occur, is both more recognizable and more dramatic than in pairs contests. This adds greatly to the ways in which skill may be manifested. For example, a player who at a critical stage of a close match is faced with the decision whether to bid an even-money slam may bring into the reckoning such factors as the personal idiosyncrasies of his counterpart at the other table, the bidding systems being played there, whether the players there will be able to judge the score as accurately as he and so on. Dramatic strokes of misfortune can also exert a profound psychological effect on the play-

ers and provide a stern test of character in the face of adversity.

Aside from close decisions, luck in team play may result in correct play being penalized by an unfortunate lie of the cards, while less sound play succeeds.

In team play an admitted but small mistake in technique can sometimes be penalized to an extent altogether out of proportion to the degree of error. Following were the cards in the crucial semifinal match between Britain and Italy in the second World Team Olympiad, held in New York City in 1964.

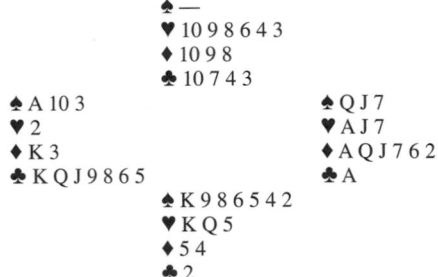

In the closed room the British bid to the best contract as follows:

WEST	EAST
Harrison-Gray	*Flint*
	2 NT
4 ♣	4 NT
7 NT	Pass

7NT was a spread, and the British scored 2220. When the deal was replayed on Bridge-O-Rama, the bidding was:

WEST	NORTH	EAST	SOUTH
Avarelli	*Reese*	*Belladonna*	*Schapiro*
	Pass	1 ♦	1 ♠
3 ♣	Pass	4 ♦	Pass
4 NT	Pass	5 NT	Pass
6 ♦	Pass	7 ♦	All Pass

This contract would be made unless North could ruff the opening lead or unless trumps were divided 5-0, the latter being only a 4% chance. Since 7♦ bid and made gives a score 2140, normal expectation would be a swing of 2 International Match Points to the team which bid 7NT. In fact the British South opened a low spade against 7♦ and his partner ruffed. The swing to Britain was thus 2320, or 20 IMPs. Although the Italian bidding was imperfect, one might say that they suffered ill luck to the extent of perhaps 18 IMPs. See also FORTUNE.

LUNCH-TIME BRIDGE. Popular, especially in large corporations that have teams belonging to the various commercial bridge leagues. In lunchrooms where there is sufficient space, one may find occasional foursomes of a serious or semi-serious nature, and these develop into groups of decent ability from time to time. If a person is willing to take a good chunk of time away from his rest or eating period to play a card game, it stands to reason there must be keen interest. In larger luncheon groups, there are even lunchtime matches, consisting of 6-board contests and lasting about 40 minutes.

LUXEMBOURG BRIDGE FEDERATION (FEDERATION LUXEMBOURGEOISE DE BRIDGE). The Federation was founded in 1979 and in 1993 had about 150 members, comprising 17 nationalities.

Officers 1993:
  President: Maryse Jeitz-Wolter
  Secretary: David Thompson
  12 Rue Massarette, L-2137 Luxembourg.
  Tel: 00352 43011
  Fax: 00352 459447

M

MACAO, ASSOCIAÇÃO DE BRIDGE DE
Officers 1993:
  President: Dr. Luis Serpa Soareo
  Secretary: Bob Da Motta
  Apta. 13A, Edif. Ka Vo, No. 30
  Praca Lobo d'Avila, Macau via Hong Kong
  Tel: 312085
  Fax: 312180

MACCABIAH GAMES. Games which celebrate athletic achievement held quadrennially in Israel and sometimes called "Israel Olympics". The Games were named after Judah Maccabaeus, a Hebrew religious zealot who fought against the encroaching Hellenization of Jewish life symbolized by the Greek Olympic-style games and the cult of the physical. The Games are open to amateur Jewish participants, all of whom must have Jewish mothers. Since its inception in 1932, the Games have included athletics, gymnastics, football, tennis and cricket. In 1977, for the first time, bridge and chess were accepted as competing sports. Gold medalists in bridge are:

1977	(Israel) David Birman, Michael Hochzeit, Capt. Kaufman, Yeshayahu Levit, Adrian Schwarz, Mori Stampf, Reubin Kunin (npc)
1981	(United States) Jim Cayne, Bill Eisenberg, Alan Greenberg, Eddie Kantar, Don Krauss, Neil Silverman

MACHINE-PREPARED HANDS. See COMPUTER HANDS.

MAGAZINES. See BIBLIOGRAPHY.

MAGNETIC CARDS. Cards made from a very thin sheet of metal. Though not themselves magnetic, the cards are attracted to and held onto a magnetized board which is part of the set.

The principal advantage of these cards is that play can take place alongside outdoor pools, on breezy patios, or at the beach. Manufacture began in 1962, and prices are comparable to those of plastic cards and bridge tables.

MAJOR. A major suit, i.e., hearts or spades.

MAJOR PENALTY CARD. Any card of honor rank prematurely exposed, or any card prematurely and deliberately exposed. If more than one card is thus exposed, each is a major penalty card. See Law 50C&E.

MAJOR SUIT. Either of the two highest-ranking suits, hearts and spades, so characterized because they outrank the third and fourth suits in the bidding and scoring.

MAJOR TENACE. An original holding of ace-queen (without the king) of a suit. After one or more rounds of

a suit have played, the highest and third highest remaining cards of the suit in the hand of one player are called major tenace (when the second highest remaining card is not held by the same player).

MAJORITY CALLING. The principle by which any bid outranks any other bid at a lower level, regardless of scoring value. The opposite principle, numerical calling, was standard in auction bridge, although abandoned in the United States in 1913. In this procedure 4♠, for example, could follow a bid of 5 ♣ because its scoring value was higher.

MAJORITY RULE. When you hold an eight-card fit missing the jack you usually play for the drop. But if one opponent has a preponderance of cards in two other suits, you might credit him with shortness in this suit and finesse his partner for the jack. The majority rule aids in determining when such a play is warranted.

The rule, first presented by Phillip Martin in *The Bridge World*, January, 1985, advises you to consider the implied lie of the fourth suit. If the hand with suspected length can hold four cards in the problem suit and still hold a majority of cards in the fourth suit, you should assume the bad break.

For example:

```
              ♠ Q 10 9 5
              ♥ A 7 6
              ♦ 9 6 5 3
              ♣ 10 4

              ♠ A 6 4 2
              ♥ K Q 10 9 8
              ♦ —
              ♣ A K 8 5
```

South plays in 6♠ after a diamond overcall by East. West leads a third-best ♦2. Declarer ruffs and plays a spade to the nine and king. East returns a diamond. Declarer ruffs with the ace and plays a spade to the jack and queen and cashes the ♠10. On the third spade, East follows, declarer pitches a club and West pitches a diamond. Both opponents follow to the ♣A and ♣K. Since East began with three spades and six diamonds, declarer is tempted to play him for heart shortness and run the ♥10. According to the majority rule, declarer should consider the implied lie of the club suit. A 4-1 heart break would leave West with four of the seven clubs, a majority. So declarer should indeed finesse. If West held one more diamond (or had shown up with three spades), a 4-1 break would leave West with three of the seven clubs and declarer should play for the drop.

MAKE. Used in bridge in four different senses. As a verb, it may mean (1) to shuffle the deck; (2) to succeed in a contract; (3) to win a trick by the play of a card. As a noun, it means (4) a successful contract but usually a hypothetical one in the postmortem: "5♦ would have been a make."

MAKE UP. To shuffle the cards.

MAKE UP A TABLE. A player who, with at least three others, forms a table for play at rubber bridge or Chicago, is said to make up a table.

MALAYSIAN CONTRACT BRIDGE ASSOCIA-

TION. Founded in 1961. In 1993 the Association had a membership of 109 in three branches and hosted the Far East Championships in 1968, 1986.

Officers 1993:
President: Norella Mohar
Treasurer: David Law
6th Floor,
3 Cangkat Raja Chulan
50200 Kuala Lumpur
Malaysia.
Tel: 60 3 2321834

MALOWAN SIX CLUBS CONVENTION. A variation of the GRAND SLAM FORCE originated by Walter Malowan. After Blackwood has been used, a 5 NT bid is not available as a grand slam force because it would be a conventional bid asking for kings. 6 ♣ is therefore used as a substitute grand slam force unless clubs is the agreed trump suit.

The responses to 6 ♣ must be influenced by the fact that the ace of trumps is already known. Marshall Miles suggests that the cheapest available bid should be used at the six level to show the best possible trump holding, with increasingly strong bids showing increasingly worse holdings.

MAMA-PAPA BRIDGE. A term applied to a simple bidding style uncluttered with conventions.

MANUFACTURE OF PLAYING CARDS. After the establishment of papermaking in America, several printers, including Benjamin Franklin, seem to have produced packs of cards as a sideline. The first man specifically listed as a manufacturer of playing cards was Jazaniah Ford of Milton MA, about 1800, followed by Thomas Crehore of Dorchester.

The fundamental principle of manufacture has changed little over the centuries. The standard "poker" card measures 2° x 3° inches, but bridge cards are a little narrower, 2˘ x 3°, to facilitate the holding of 13 cards in a player's hand. The stock on which the cards are printed consists of two thin sheets of paper pasted together with a black paste. (A single sheet of heavier paper would not suffice; if a player had a lamp at his back, the light would show what he had in his hand to the player across from him. The black paste makes the paper properly opaque.) Hence playing cards are sometimes called pasteboards.

One or two full packs of cards are printed at a time on large sheets of pasteboard. The individual cards are then stamped out, one at a time, with a sharp die that works like a household cookie cutter, but one that cuts about 36,000 cards per hour. Simultaneously, and synchronized to the infinitesimal fraction of a second in which the die descends, the edges of the cards are pressed into a knife-edge, almost invisible to the naked eye, but enough to permit each card to slip between two other cards during a shuffle, and this retards the fraying of the edges.

Delicate operations like this require special machinery, designed for this specific purpose. Modern refinements on traditional processes have not been disclosed in patents, and rate among the world's most jealously guarded trade secrets.

The demand for playing cards is not likely to outrun supply. It has been said that the largest playing-card plant could, without effort, supply the wants of the card-playing world.

Modern cardplayers are accustomed to the double-head card, which can be read from either end, and to the INDICES in the two corners, which permit one to recognize the card without seeing its entire face. Cards of this type did not become standard until the late 1870s. Until then a player had to look at a full face of the card, and hold it right-side up, to know what the card was.

Either superstition or habit prevents major changes in playing-card design. Unsuccessful attempts have been made to print the suits in four colors, to redesign the pips, to clothe the face cards in modern dress; and to introduce circular cards. Soviet Russia tried to replace the "anachronistic kings and queens" with revolutionary heroes, but so many packs were smuggled in that the conventional royalty cards were reinstated. (See also FIVE-SUIT BRIDGE.)

A more modest change reintroduced in 1964 and embodied in special decks used in the World Team Olympiad was to use a very pale blue-green tint instead of white for the background of the faces. This has been shown to reduce eyestrain.

For information on early cards and different packs, see HISTORY OF PLAYING CARDS; PACK; TAXES; TAROT. See also PLASTIC CARDS.

MARKED CARD. (1) A card that is known, from the previous play, to be in a particular hand. (2) A damaged card.

MARKED FINESSE. A finesse that is certain to win because the previous play has indicated the location of a crucial opposing card.

MARMIC SYSTEM. An Italian system, apparently obsolete, whose name is derived from the first names of the inventors (MARIO FRANCO and MICHELE GIOVINE). It is probably the most unusual system ever played in serious international competition by a major bridge country until the advent of HUM SYSTEMS (see WEAK OPENING SYSTEMS.) In some respects it was a forerunner of the ROMAN SYSTEM. The chief feature was that a player was expected to pass in first or second position with balanced distribution and 16°-19 points. The same principle applied after an opponent's opening bid, and in each case the passer's partner was expected to balance with 5 points or more. This opened the possibility of trap passing by the opponents, and the system was amended to provide an opening 1NT bid, instead of the strong pass, at unfavorable vulnerability.

MARX TWO CLUBS. An alternate name, especially in England, for the STAYMAN convention. Originated by Jack Marx approximately at the same time as the American counterpart devised by George Rapee.

MASTER CARD. The highest unplayed card of a suit. It can also be thus characterized while actually being played.

MASTER HAND. The hand which controls the situation—more particularly, the one which controls the trump suit, leading out high trumps to prevent adverse ruffs, and retaining a trump or two to prevent the adverse run of a long side suit. It is usually the declarer's hand, but sometimes, when the declarer's trumps are more valuable as ruffers, the dummy is made the master hand. See

DUMMY REVERSAL.

MASTER INDIVIDUAL, NORTH AMERICAN CHAMPIONSHIP. Formerly called World Master Individual or Life Master Individual. See STEINER TROPHY. For results see Appendix I.

MASTER KNOCKOUT TEAMS, NORTH AMERICAN CHAMPIONSHIP. See SPINGOLD TROPHY . For results see Appendix I.

MASTER MIXED TEAMS, NORTH AMERICAN CHAMPIONSHIP. See BARCLAY TROPHY and LEBHAR TROPHY. For results see Appendix I.

MASTERPOINT. The unit which measures bridge achievement in tournament play.

The term first arose when eligibles for the ABL's 1934 von Zedtwitz Master Pairs (later Life Master Pairs) were chosen from a list of players credited with masterpoints for winning tournaments run by the ABL and the AWL, as well as the Vanderbilt and Eastern Championships, which at that time were independent events. In the following year, winners of many smaller tournaments that had applied for ABL sanction became eligible. In 1936, to offset this rapid and somewhat haphazard inflation of masters the League created the rank of LIFE MASTER, then awarded only to those who had won their points in national championships or the equivalent. These point awards were tiny. At the outset, 10 points was the qualifying minimum, and a scheme for deducting points each year made it necessary for Life Masters to continue successful competition in order to retain their status. Deductions were discontinued in 1944.

Meanwhile, the USBA announced its own masterpoint program and appears to have been the first to extend the idea to the club level. Effective Sept. 1, 1935, City Masterpoints were awarded for duplicate games in USBA-affiliated clubs. These were convertible at 10 for 1 into State Masterpoints, awarded for citywide tournaments, which were in turn convertible at 10 for 1 into National Masterpoints, awarded for State tournaments. A legal dispute over the ABL's claim of exclusive right to award masterpoints was not resolved until 1937, when the USBA was merged into the ABL, becoming the ACBL. The ACBL introduced Rating Points (later called Fractional Masterpoints and even later Club Masterpoints), worth .01 of a masterpoint, into club games effective Jan. 1, 1938. The result was a rapid acceleration in the growth of ACBL membership, but it also led to the eventual need to distinguish among points won at local, regional and national levels.

Masterpoints are awarded at ACBL tournaments in amounts proportional to the size and classification of the event and the rating of the tournament. The basic point structure is based on open pairs. Since such events as mixed pairs, men's pairs, senior pairs, women's pairs and unmixed pairs are restricted to some extent, point awards for them are lower than for open pairs. In general, awards at a sectional tournament are higher than those at a local, and awards at a regional tournament are higher than those at a sectional. Awards for most North American Championships are fixed, and they are substantially higher than regional awards. Both the Vanderbilt Teams and the Spingold Teams award 150 masterpoints to the winners. This is the highest masterpoint award given by the ACBL.

Masterpoint awards at local, sectional and regional tournaments are given according to a formula in which the principal ingredients are the size of the event and the rating of the eligible players. In general, awards climb arithmetically up through 60 tables, and thereafter they follow a logarithmic curve which very much slows down the rate of increase.

England adopted a masterpoint scheme in 1956 and many other countries followed suit. In most of these schemes the award scale is less generous, and the achievement of high rank is usually slower. Points won in foreign bridge leagues may be converted to ACBL Masterpoints under certain conditions. Many nations also convert ACBL points to the national scale. See GOLD POINTS; MASTERPOINT PLAN; RED POINTS; REGIONAL AND NATIONAL POINTS; SILVER POINTS.

MASTERPOINT CERTIFICATE. See RATING POINTS.

MASTERPOINT PLAN. The method of awarding masterpoints in bridge tournaments at club, local, sectional, regional and national levels. Creation of the Masterpoint Plan in 1936 must be credited to William McKenney and Ray Eisenlord, with many others contributing to later developments. The details of the method by which the plan operates at the club level are set out in the HANDBOOK. The ACBL publishes a directory of clubs, which enables members to find bridge activity in any city they may visit.

Any club or group in the United States, Canada, Bermuda or Mexico may apply for a sanction to issue masterpoints at regularly scheduled duplicate games. The clubs are of four types: Open (to all comers); Invitational (restricted to members of the group and invited guests or restricted by expertise), Novice (restricted to players with not more than 20 masterpoints) and Bridge Plus+ (restricted to new players with not more than 5 masterpoints).

Club masterpoints must be awarded at every duplicate game conducted by a sanctioned club. Club masterpoints are hundredths of a full point. The scale for invitational clubs is slightly lower and novice and Bridge Plus+ clubs (or games) score at an even lower scale.

Once each calendar quarter a weekly club is entitled to a Club Tournament game with increased awards. Those clubs meeting less frequently are entitled to a Club Tournament for every 12 regularly scheduled sessions.

At club tournament level and higher, events can be of various types: Open Pairs, Mixed Pairs, Men's Pairs, Women's Pairs, Individual; and team events of various kinds. The scale of awards increases steadily through the various levels: club, local, sectional, regional and national. The highest award for any single event is given to the winners of the VANDERBILT and SPINGOLD championships (150) and the REISINGER championship, the Blue Ribbon Pairs championship and the Life Master Pairs championship (140 points). See also AMERICAN CONTRACT BRIDGE LEAGUE; DUPLICATE BRIDGE; DUPLICATE TOURNAMENT; SANCTIONED CLUBS; MASTERPOINT; RANKING OF PLAYERS.

Many other countries have adopted a masterpoint plan along similar lines. The WORLD BRIDGE FEDERATION also has such a plan, with GRAND MASTER as the premier rank.

MASTER TOURNAMENT. An event or series of events at a bridge tournament where the requirements for entry into the competition include the holding of a high masterpoint rating. For some of the championship events in the Spring, Summer and Fall North American Championships of the ACBL, some designated number of masterpoints is required for participation. Some events are restricted to Life Masters. See RANKING OF PLAYERS.

MATCH. A session or event of head-to-head competition between two pairs or two teams-of-four or more players.

The shortest matches in international competition were the 18-board qualifying round matches in the 1964 WORLD TEAM OLYMPIAD. The longest matches were played for the BERMUDA BOWL from 1951 to 1957, when there were only two teams in competition, and 224 to 256 boards were played. Even longer matches (300 boards) have been played on semi-official occasions. See ANGLO-AMERICAN MATCHES. The most famous of the nonofficial challenge pair matches of the Thirties were longer still. Both the CULBERTSON-LENZ MATCH (Dec. 1931-Jan. 1932) and the CULBERTSON-SIMS MATCH (March-April, 1935) were 150 rubbers. In the former, 879 hands were dealt, only 25 of which were passed out.

MATCH PLAY. A team-of-four contest in which two teams are competing for an appreciable number of boards. Tactics at match play are described in IMP TACTICS and STATE OF MATCH.

MATCH RECORDS. See HAND RECORD; BIBLIOGRAPHY.

MATCHPOINT. A credit awarded to a contestant in pair or individual events for a score superior to that of another contestant in direct competition.

The number of matchpoints available to a contestant is normally one less than the number of contestants in direct competition. For example, in a game of 13 rounds there are 13 North-South scores in direct competition and 13 East-West scores in direct competition. The highest score in each group beats the other 12 scores in that group and receives 12 matchpoints, the greatest number available to it.

Other pairs receive 11, 10, 9 points, etc., according to the number of pairs beaten in direct competition. The lowest pair in each group beats no pair in direct competition and receives 0 matchpoints.

When two or more pairs achieve identical scores, each pair receives ° matchpoint for each pair with which its score is tied (see Law 78, LAWS OF DUPLICATE) .

When matchpoint scoring is used in team games, the score that is obtained by a team on a board is 1 matchpoint if the combined score is plus, 0 if the score is minus, and ° if the team score is neither plus nor minus. (Each board is thus scored as a match in itself, hence "board-a-match" scoring.)

In tournaments in other sections of the world and in WORLD BRIDGE FEDERATION play, matchpoints are doubled to eliminate halves. A pair receives two matchpoints for each pair it beats and one for each pair it ties. See also DOUBLE TOP; SCORING ACROSS THE FIELD.

MATCHPOINT BIDDING. If bridge were played double-dummy (if one could see all four hands whenever one had to make a decision), the bidding and play would be exactly the same at matchpoint duplicate as at rubber bridge. A minor exception is caused by the scoring of honors at rubber bridge. If one could see only partner's hand, the bidding would usually be the same. The objective on any one hand is the same for both forms of bridge: to score the maximum number of points or to allow the opponents to score a minimum number. Yet successful matchpoint tactics are quite different from successful rubber bridge tactics. For example, suppose the bidding, with both sides vulnerable, has gone as follows:

WEST	NORTH	EAST	SOUTH
			1 ♥
Pass	2 ♥	Pass	Pass
?			

West holds: ♠ Q 9 8 x x
♥ x
♦ A x x x
♣ Q 10 x

The opponents' lack of enterprise marks East with at least 8 points, perhaps as many as 14. He may or may not fit West's hand. At either rubber or duplicate, West should bid 2 ♠ when East holds:

♠ K J x x
♥ x x x
♦ K J x
♣ K x x

West should pass when East holds:

♠ x
♥ K J 10 x
♦ J x x x
♣ K x x x

Since West does not know which type of hand his partner has, he must consider what he has to lose or gain by bidding. The best probable result from bidding is that East-West, instead of North-South, will make a partscore. This is equivalent to approximately a 250-point gain. A partscore is worth about an additional 50 points at rubber bridge, the same as at duplicate. The worst likely result is a 500- or 800-point penalty. Which is more likely to occur? Surely the former.

A reopening 2 ♣ bid would probably work out as follows: Four times in ten the opponents would bid and make 3♥, in which case the reopening bid would have neither lost nor gained.

Four times in ten it would gain. Perhaps East-West would be +140 instead of +100, +110 instead of –110, –100 instead of –110, or + 100 instead of –110 (because the opponents bid again).

The other two times the reopening bid would lose, perhaps quite heavily. The net loss from these two occasions would be greater than the gain from the other four.

In rubber bridge or IMP play it would not pay to reopen with a weak suit, because in the long run a reopening bid would lose points. In duplicate, a reopening bid is advisable. This is true whether most of the other West players would bid or not, but it is easier to demonstrate if the potential reopener were a lone wolf. Passing would result in an average score, 6 matchpoints out of 12. Whenever the reopening bid should gain, it would result in a top; whenever it should lose, it would result in a bottom. At rubber bridge, it is necessary to weigh the amount of gain against the amount of loss when considering any action. In duplicate, the main consideration is the frequency of gain or loss. The following hand illustrates a similar principle, except that the mystery is in regard to the opponents' holdings rather than partner's.

WEST	EAST
♠ A 10 x	♠ K Q x x
♥ 10 x	♥ x x
♦ A K J x	♦ Q 9 x x x x
♣ Q 10 9 x	♣ A

At rubber bridge, the bidding might well be as follows:

WEST	NORTH	EAST	SOUTH
			Pass
1 ♦	Pass	1 ♠	Pass
2 ♠	Pass	4 ♦	Pass
5 ♦	All Pass		

East has a good enough hand to be almost certain that 5 ♦ will be safe. Besides, a slam is still possible from his point of view. Consequently, he shows his excellent diamond upport while still allowing West to return to spades with four-card spade support.

At duplicate, the bidding should start the same way, but East would probably bid 4♠ over the raise to 2♠. A slam is unlikely, and with such a good four-card-spade suit, East would not want to "risk" a final diamond contract. Perhaps the word "risk" seems unusual here, but at duplicate 5♦ is a much poorer gamble, hence a greater risk, than is 4 ♠. At least 75% of the time, East-West will do better in spades than in diamonds; they cannot afford to "play safe" when the odds favor the more dangerous contract. This is true despite the fact that the gain in playing spades cannot exceed 20 to 50 points, while the loss, when the spades break badly or the opening diamond lead is ruffed, can be several hundred points.

It has been stated that the same contract usually would be chosen at duplicate as at rubber bridge if one could see partner's hand. The following is an exception. Even the reason for the exception is that bridge is not a double-dummy game.

WEST	EAST
♠ A x	♠ x x
♥ A x x	♥ x x
♦ K Q J x x	♦ A x x
♣ 10 8 x	♣ A Q J 9 x x

The ideal contract at rubber bridge is 7♣ — despite the fact that the odds are slightly against making it. To simplify this discussion, assume that the diamonds are not 5-0, and the slam depends merely upon the club finesse. Normally two-to-one odds are needed to justify a grand slam bid at rubber bridge, but these odds are based on the assumption that a small slam is safe. In this case, with a major suit lead, declarer will take either 11 or 13 tricks, never 12. By bidding seven, half the time declarer will score 1440 or 2140 points. At rubber bridge, a nonvulnerable game is worth approximately 300 points, even though no points are scored till the rubber is completed. When the club finesse fails, he will score -100 or -200. By bidding seven, he will average +670 not vulnerable or +970 vulnerable. This is better than he can score at any other contract.

Why is 7♣ not the ideal contract for duplicate also? The reason is that it will be very difficult, if not impossible, to get to any slam. The best contract is 6♣. Just bidding six, and making seven, will be good for a top board when no one else is in a slam. If the club finesse fails, down one may still be worth some points since the 3NT bidders may also be down one. It is time to move on

from theory to some practical applications.

WEST	NORTH	EAST	SOUTH
			1 ♥
Pass	1 NT	Pass	2 ♦
Pass	?		

What should North bid with the following?

♠ Q 10 x
♥ 10 x
♦ J 10 x x
♣ Q J x x

At rubber bridge or IMPs the answer is clear cut. Pass, for two reasons. 2♦ should be safer than 2♥. Also, if North bids 2♥, South may bid again, while a pass will prevent him from doing so. Surely 2♦ will be safer than 3♥. Since game is out of the question, one should stop in the safest contract.

With

♠ A x x
♥ Q 10
♦ K x x x
♣ x x x x

a false preference to 2 ♥ would be sound tactics at rubber bridge because game is still fairly likely.

At duplicate, a return to 2♥ is advisable on both hands. In the second case, the reason is the same as for rubber bridge: Game is still possible, and if opener has to pass, the hand may play as well (or within one trick as well) as hearts as at diamonds. In the first case, the reason is different. The hope is that opener will pass, and that he will pick up an extra 10 or 20 points in hearts. Quite frequently he will get too high or be defeated by a bad break, but the risk is justifiable because the odds are right.

WEST	NORTH	EAST	SOUTH
			1 ♥
Pass	1 ♠	Pass	?

What should South bid with:

♠ K x x
♥ A K x x x
♦ A 10 9 x
♣ x

At rubber bridge, the correct bid is surely 2♦. Unless North can bid again, there will be no game. If he does bid again, the delayed spade support will describe this hand perfectly: a pretty good hand, three-card spade support, and a singleton club. This sequence has the best chance to indicate whether the two hands fit, whether they belong in game, and what the best game (or slam!) contract will be. For example, with:

♠ A x x x x
♥ 10 x
♦ K J x
♣ x x x

North would pass a raise to 2♠, but would gladly bid four over the more descriptive sequence. Furthermore, responder would keep the bidding open by taking a false preference of 2♥ over 2♦ with the hand just described — at rubber bridge.

At duplicate, South should raise to 2♠ immediately. North might have to pass either a 2♠ or a 2♦ bid, and if so, 2♠ would surely be the better duplicate contract. The superior results at partscore contracts compensate for less efficient game and slam bidding since partscores are just as important as games or slams at duplicate. When each hand is worth as much as another, one cannot afford to adopt a style of bidding, which is bad for the partscore hands and good only for games and slams. Besides, there are hands such as the last example when responder would pass a 2♦ rebid at duplicate (rather than risk an inferior partscore contract by giving a false preference) even though he would always bid again at rubber bridge. There is more competitive bidding at duplicate. The first hand of this article illustrated a situation where it was advisable to reopen at duplicate and advisable to sell out at rubber bridge. It would be just as disastrous to let the opponents play 2♥ when one could make 2♠ as it would be to take an 800-point set.

Dlr.: North

Vul: Both

		♠ K J 5	
		♥ A 8 7	
		♦ Q 4	
		♣ J 8 7 4 3	
♠ A 10 6			♠ 3 2
♥ 10 5 4 3			♥ K Q J 6 2
♦ 10 9 7 2			♦ K J 6
♣ A 5			♣ K 9 6
		♠ Q 9 8 7 4	
		♥ 9	
		♦ A 8 5 3	
		♣ Q 10 2	

WEST	NORTH	EAST	SOUTH
	Pass	1 ♥	Pass
2 ♥	Pass	Pass	2 ♠
3 ♥	3 ♠	Pass	Pass
Dbl	All Pass		

East-West must defend carefully to defeat 3♠. As the cards lie, they can make 4♥. There are several interesting features about the bidding. The opening bid and raise were routine. So was the 2♠ bid — at duplicate. West properly bid 3♥ since he had a maximum raise. The first questionable bid was North's raise to 3♠. Usually, when the opponents are pushed one trick higher by a reopening bid, the percentage bid is to pass in all close situations. The reopener has already inferred from the opponents' bidding that his partner has high cards, and his partner has no business bidding again to show these same high cards. He should bid again only with good distribution or cards exceptionally well placed. The result from passing should be no worse than at other tables where someone failed to reopen, and it will be better when the opponents have been pushed beyond their depth. However, North's questionable bid would have gained him a top if West had not doubled. West knew that he would get a very poor score, perhaps 2 matchpoints out of 12, if North-South should make exactly 3♠. Consequently a double could not cost more than 2 matchpoints. On the other hand, if North-South should make exactly eight tricks, it would be extremely costly not to double. West has a good defensive hand, and is tempted to double anyway; he would double with a poorer hand than he actually has. At rubber bridge a double which could convert a partscore into game would need about seven-to-one odds in its favor.

In duplicate, a double is sometimes the percentage bid even when the odds are *against* defeating the contract. Suppose, for example, that East-West were to bid 4♥ over 3♠. North-South are doomed to get a bottom anyway, since presumably other pairs will not bid game. So a double will not cost them a thing. If the hands were changed slightly so that 4♥ could be defeated, a double would gain a few points, since +200 is better than North-South could do in spades. With nothing to lose and everything to gain, a double must be the right bid. If a double can lose only 2 points and may gain 9 or 10, it is a good

gamble, even when one expects the contract to be made.

Another way it pays to be more competitive in duplicate is taking sacrifices, but the attraction of the high-level save has diminished since the scoring table was modified. The more common dilemma is whether or not to take a sacrifice against a game contract. In rubber bridge, it is losing tactics to take deliberate 500-point sacrifice against a vulnerable game when there is any reasonable hope of defeating it. In duplicate, the sacrifice is correct if the contract is a normal one and a favorite to make.

MATCHPOINT DEFENSE. Defense at duplicate is often more difficult than at rubber bridge. In the latter, the objective is clear-cut: try to set the contract. It makes little difference when declarer makes an overtrick through an unsuccessful attempt to defeat him. At duplicate, the overtrick makes a great deal of difference.

		♠ K J 5	
		♥ 9 3 2	
		♦ A Q J 8 5	
		♣ Q 6	
♠ Q 8			♠ 7 6 3
♥ A 8 7 4			♥ K J 10
♦ 9 7			♦ 10 3 2
♣ K 9 7 5 2			♣ J 10 8 3
		♠ A 10 9 4 2	
		♥ Q 6 5	
		♦ K 6 4	
		♣ A 4	

WEST	NORTH	EAST	SOUTH
			1 ♠
Pass	2 ♦	Pass	2 ♠
Pass	4 ♠	All Pass	

West leads a small club, won by dummy's queen. Declarer plays the ♠K, then takes a losing trump finesse to West's doubleton queen. What should West do? At rubber bridge, he should lead a low heart. This play will set the contract whenever it can be set — when East has ♥ K-Q-x or K-J-10; also when he has ♥ J-10-9 and the ♦K. At duplicate the right play is not clear-cut, but cashing the ace is probably correct. It loses in only two situations, and it gains (a trick) much more frequently whenever declarer has the two red kings.

Suppose that West is on lead with:

       ♠ Q J 10 9
       ♥ A 8 7
       ♦ 9 5 3
       ♣ 7 5 2

after the following bidding:

WEST	NORTH	EAST	SOUTH
	1 ♣	Pass	2 ♦
Pass	2NT	Pass	3 ♣
Pass	3 ♠	Pass	5 ♦
Pass	6 ♦	All Pass	

North apparently has the ♥K; South probably has two hearts. The best chance to set the contract is to lead a low heart, and hope that East has the queen and that either North or South has the jack. If that situation exists, declarer may misguess. The low heart lead is not correct at duplicate because it stands too good a chance of giving away an overtrick. The opponents may have both the ♥ K-Q, or they may be missing the queen *and* jack (in which case declarer would have to play dummy's king).

The defense against unusual contracts may be just as interesting as the play of unusual contracts.

Another way in which the defense at duplicate varies from the defense at rubber bridge is that the defenders can take advantage of declarer's greed.

```
              ♠ 10 9
              ♥ 9 8 4
              ♦ A Q J 5
              ♣ A K J 7
♠ J 7                         ♠ 8 5 4 2
♥ Q 10 7 6 2                  ♥ A J 5
♦ 8 6                         ♦ K 10 7
♣ 10 8 4 2                    ♣ 6 5 3
              ♠ A K Q 6 3
              ♥ K 3
              ♦ 9 4 3 2
              ♣ Q 9
```

WEST	NORTH	EAST	SOUTH
			1 ♠
Pass	2 ♦	Pass	3 ♦
Pass	3 ♠	Pass	4 ♠
All Pass			

The bidding is not recommended, but that is the way it went. West led the ♣2, won by declarer's 9. He cashed three top spades and took the diamond finesse, which won. Dummy's clubs were now cashed for heart discards; East also discarded a heart on the last club. Declarer then ruffed a heart with his next-to-last trump in order to repeat the diamond finesse. This time the finesse lost. East cashed the good ♠8, and the defenders took the remaining tricks. Down one.

Did East make the right play in refusing the first diamond finesse, or was he just lucky? By playing cautiously, declarer could have made an overtrick after East's duck. However, East had a psychological factor working in his favor. Declarer risked his contract when he took the diamond finesse. If he wanted to play safe, he would have cashed his clubs first for heart discards. He did not play the hand this way because he was afraid of being stuck in the dummy unable to take the diamond finesse. Since declarer has risked his contract to take the diamond finesse, it would be inconsistent for him not to play to repeat the finesse, so as to make his apparently successful gamble pay off.

MATCHPOINT DUPLICATE, MATHEMATICS OF.
See MATHEMATICS OF MATCHPOINT PLAY.

MATCHPOINT PLAY.
In duplicate play, the test for deciding between various alternatives is not how much (in total points) a given play could gain or lose, but how many matchpoints it could gain or lose. (But see IMP TACTICS for a discussion of this specialized branch of duplicate play.) When the contract is a normal one, this means, "Does the play have better than a 50% chance of success?"

```
              ♠ 10 9
              ♥ J 5
              ♦ K Q 10 9 6 2
              ♣ A K 4


              ♠ A K J 8
              ♥ Q 10 9
              ♦ J 3
              ♣ J 10 9 6
```

WEST	NORTH	EAST	SOUTH

The opening lead is the ♥4 to East's king. West ducks the ♥7 return, playing the deuce. It is almost certain that three more heart tricks will be run by the opponents as soon as the lead is lost. Combined with the trick already lost and the ♦A, that is one too many. At rubber bridge, the proper play would be to try for four spade tricks and four club tricks without touching the diamonds. Declarer's chances would not be good, but it would be worth a try with so much to gain, so little to lose. In duplicate there is much more to lose. Down one should be almost an average board, while down two would surely be a cold bottom. The odds are greater than three to one that attacking the black suits will lose a trick rather than gain a trick, which means that playing to make the hand will result in three bottom boards for every top. When the odds are so unfavorable, it is better to play safe for eight tricks. The fact that the contract is for nine tricks is immaterial, since it is the contract everyone will reach.

Following is another example illustrating the same principle. In this case, however, declarer does not deliberately refuse to try to make his contract. He merely adopts a risky line of play which gives him a good opportunity for overtricks.

```
              ♠ 7 5
              ♥ K 4
              ♦ A K 10 9 7 6
              ♣ A J 4

              ♠ A 10 8
              ♥ A 10 7
              ♦ J 5
              ♣ 10 8 7 5 2
```

WEST	NORTH	EAST	SOUTH
	1 ♦	1 ♠	1 NT
Pass	3 NT	All Pass	

A spade is led, and declarer holds up until the third trick, upon which West discards a heart. The correct rubber bridge play would be to attack the diamonds by cashing the ace and king. If West has the queen, it is unnecessary to finesse, since West has no spade to return, and only five diamond tricks are needed. On the other hand, a losing finesse to East's singleton or doubleton queen would be disastrous. In duplicate, the better play is to take a first-round diamond finesse. This play will gain (a trick) approximately twice as often as it will lose (several tricks).

The finesse gains if West holds Q-8-4-3, Q-8-4-2, Q-8-3-2, Q-4-3-2, Q-8-4, Q-8-3, Q-8-2, Q-4-3, Q-4-2, Q-3-2 (10 distributions). The finesse loses if East holds Q, Q-8, Q-4, Q-3, Q-2 (5 distributions). Each 3-2 division is slightly more likely than each 4-1 distribution.

Both the contracts shown were quite normal. It is proper to jeopardize one's normal contract when the odds are favorable. When a contract is exceptionally good, it is proper to play safe, just as at rubber bridge.

A hard-to-reach game or slam, or a doubled contract, would be an example of a good contract. When just making the contract will be worth 10 matchpoints out of 12, only exceptionally good odds would justify jeopardizing the contract for an overtrick.

Some of the most interesting problems arise in the play

of unusual contracts at duplicate.

Dlr: North
Vul: N-S

♠ A 10 6 4 2
♥ 8 5
♦ Q 2
♣ Q 5 3 2

♠ K J 9 5
♥ 4 2
♦ A K 10 9 3
♣ 6 4

WEST	NORTH	EAST	SOUTH
	Pass	1 ♥	1 ♠
4 ♥	4 ♠	Pass	Pass
Dbl	All Pass		

North's 4♠ bid was a bit odd, considering the vulnerability, and many South players would not choose to overcall with a four-card suit. It is safe to say that 4♠ doubled will not be played at any other table, and down two will be a bottom, not even a tie for bottom. West leads the ♥Q, followed by the ♥J. Next he plays the ♣A followed by the ♣J to East's king (dummy playing low). East returns the ♦2, and West does not cover the 10. The only problem is how to play the trump suit for no losers. If the spades are split 2-2 and the diamonds no worse than 4-2 the opponents cannot make 4♥; consequently - 200 would be a bottom. Declarer must base his play on the assumption that 4♥ can be made, and a singleton spade is more likely than a singleton diamond. It appears that West has five clubs to his partner's two, so if anyone has a singleton spade, it will be West. The proper play is to lead to the ace and finesse East for the queen. This works, since the four hands are as follows:

♠ A 10 6 4 2
♥ 8 5
♦ Q 2
♣ Q 5 3 2

♠ 8
♥ Q J 7 6 2
♦ 5 4
♣ A J 10 9 8

♠ Q 7 3
♥ A K 10 4
♦ J 8 7 3
♣ K 7

♠ K J 9 5
♥ 9 3
♦ A K 10 9 6
♣ 6 4

Suppose that the four hands and bidding were changed slightly. The only difference in the bidding is that the 4♠ contract is not doubled.

♠ A 10 7 5 2
♥ 9 5
♦ Q J 8 7
♣ 8 3

♠ Q 8
♥ K J 6 2
♦ 5 4
♣ K J 10 7 2

♠ 4 3
♥ A Q 10 7 4
♦ 3 2
♣ A Q 9 4

♠ K J 9 6
♥ 8 3
♦ A K 10 9 6
♣ 6 5

The defenders take the first four tricks in hearts and clubs, then exit with a diamond. Should declarer play the same as before? The fact that he is not doubled enables him to make an unusual type of safety play. He should bang down the ♠A-K. If the queen does not fall, he does not care, because he knows that 4♥ is cold, and -200 will

be a good sacrifice. What he does not want to risk is a -200 when, as here, the opponents can make only 3♥. Minus 100 will beat all the -140 scores.

Dlr: South
Vul: E-W

♠ 7 6 5
♥ K 7 6 2
♦ K 5 4 2
♣ 5 2

♠ K 3
♥ A Q 4 3
♦ Q J 3
♣ J 8 6 3

South opens with a weak notrump, and the other players pass. West leads the ♠4 to East's ace. East returns the jack, and West plays the deuce. Before planning the play, declarer should evaluate his contract, and try to determine what other pairs in direct competition will be doing. If they buy the bid, most of them will be playing hearts. They will score 110 or 140, depending upon how the hand breaks. It is impossible to do as well at notrump as at hearts, no matter how badly the opponents defend, so the only hope to salvage the board is that the opponents can make something. Sure enough, North-South have a maximum of five defensive tricks against spades, and perhaps only three or four, depending upon the distribution. Since it is not possible to beat the pairs playing in hearts, the proper attitude is to forget about them and to concentrate on beating the pairs defending against spades. If North-South were vulnerable, it would be necessary to steal a diamond trick somehow — minus 200 would be no good at all. But not vulnerable, North-South can afford a two-trick set. Minus 100 should be just as good as - 50. The proper play is not to try to steal anything, but just to hope that the hearts will break so that five tricks can be cashed. The full deal is:

♠ 7 6 5
♥ K 7 6 2
♦ K 5 4 2
♣ 5 2

♠ Q 10 8 4 2
♥ 9 5
♦ A 7
♣ A 10 7 4

♠ A J 9
♥ J 10 8
♦ 10 9 8 6
♣ K Q 9

♠ K 3
♥ A Q 4 3
♦ Q J 3
♣ J 8 6 3

At most tables, South opens with a suit bid, and West plays 2♠ or 3♠, after an overcall and a raise by his partner. Minus 100 is an excellent result for North-South, but -150 would be a bottom.

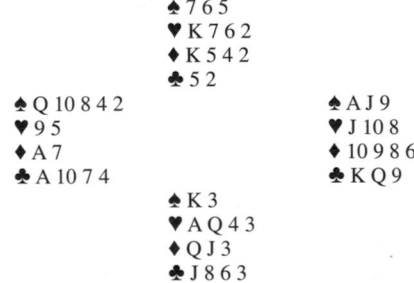

♠ 5 4 2
♥ A Q 6 4 3
♦ 10 9 3
♣ 4 2

♠ A J
♥ K J 10 7
♦ A K J 7
♣ Q 6 5

WEST	NORTH	EAST	SOUTH
			1 ♥
Pass			
	2 ♥	Pass	3 NT
All Pass			

tract? The first question is what will happen at the other tables. It seems quite likely that most of the field will be playing in 4♥. With the same spade lead, the declarers in 4♥ will either make five by discarding a club on the fourth diamond, or be down one if the diamond finesse fails. What are the prospects in notrump? To make 4NT or be down several if the diamond finesse fails. That is, down several if the finesse is attempted and fails. The only chance for a decent board is not to take the diamond finesse, and to hope that it does not work. If it does not work, down at 3NT will tie the field, which will be down one at 4♥. If the queen happens to be doubleton, offside, refusing the finesse will result in an overtrick and a top.

The opening lead can have an important influence upon the play of *normal* contracts.

```
            ♠ J 10 5 2
            ♥ 6 3 2
            ♦ K Q 10 6
            ♣ A 3

            ♠ A Q 7 4 3
            ♥ A 7 4
            ♦ J 3 2
            ♣ Q 2
```

WEST	NORTH	EAST	SOUTH
			1 ♠
Pass	2 ♦	Pass	2 ♠
Pass	3 ♠	Pass	4 ♠
All Pass			

Modern bidders would bid 1♠- 3♠, but North-South are traditionalists. West leads a club, a small card is played from dummy, and when East produces the jack, declarer wins with the queen. How should declarer play the spades? Normally he would take a finesse. However, the lead was very favorable. It gave declarer a trick he could never have won by himself. With a heart lead, declarer would have to be lucky to make four, and he would have no chance for more. Now he has a virtual cinch for his contract and an overtrick. Rather than risk a losing spade finesse and a heart return before the diamonds are established, declarer should cash the ♠A and knock out the ♦A. After the favorable lead, declarer should not jeopardize his advantage.

```
            ♠ 8 3 2
            ♥ 7 6 3
            ♦ A J 10 5 4
            ♣ Q 6

            ♠ A 7 6
            ♥ A K
            ♦ Q 9 3
            ♣ A K J 10 5
```

WEST	NORTH	EAST	SOUTH
			2 NT
Pass	3 NT	All Pass	

Surely every pair in the room will arrive at 3NT. West goes into a long study, and finally leads the ♠4. Apparently West had no clear-cut lead, but he made a good guess. Without a spade lead, declarer would be cold for 12 or 13 tricks, depending upon the diamond finesse. Should declarer hold up two rounds so as to shut out the thirteenth spade if the diamond finesse loses? Certainly not. If the diamond finesse loses, South is doomed to a poor result by West's fortunate lead. On the other hand,

if South wins immediately and if the diamond finesse works, he will still take 13 tricks. For that matter, the correct play at duplicate is probably to win the first trick even when West leads the king. Winning the first trick will always be worth a top or tie for top when the ♦K is onside. Therefore it is clearly the best play half the time. Even when the diamond finesse loses, declarer may tie with pairs who have held up, but not long enough. Holding up one round is best only when the finesse is off and East has a doubleton spade; holding up two rounds will lose to all other lines of play when the diamond finesse works, and it will be worth a top only if East has three spades with the ♦K.

MATCHPOINT SCORING. In duplicate tournaments matchpoint scoring makes each board of equal importance with any other board, whether the hand involved is a partscore competitive bidding situation or a grand slam. Most pair tournaments are scored by matchpoints. Most team contests and, occasionally, important pair events are scored by IMPs, which make larger swings possible on big hands, and approach the tactics of rubber bridge. See DUPLICATE SCORING for the details of scoring procedures. For a fuller discussion of the effect of matchpoint scoring on bidding and play tactics, see MATCHPOINT BIDDING; MATCHPOINT DEFENSE; MATCHPOINT PLAY; SHOOTING. See DUPLICATE BRIDGE for a full listing of the technical aspects of tournament organization. For the origins of the duplicate method, see HISTORY OF BRIDGE. See also LAWS OF DUPLICATE, Laws 77-79.

MATHE. A defense against strong 1♣ openings covered under DEFENSE TO STRONG ARTIFICIAL OPENINGS .

MATHE ASKING BID. A method of locating a singleton in a hand that has responded with a limit jump major raise, devised by Lew Mathe of Los Angeles. Used principally by partnerships that use limit jump raises to promise a side singleton, the Mathe Asking Bid is opener's rebid of the cheapest denomination after responder's limit raise. If the suit that has been established is spades, responder simply bids four of the suit in which he has a singleton. If hearts is the agreed suit, responder rebids 3NT if he has a singleton spade, or bids his minor-suit singleton. Mathe Asking Bids may also be used where the limit raise has not guaranteed a singleton.

MATHEMATICAL APPROXIMATIONS. When we deal with a quantity which can be expressed as a whole number we can express it exactly, so that we do not need to approximate. This does not mean that we never approximate. An example of an approximation is when we give the number of possible deals as 5.36×10^{28}. Rather than write out all 29 digits we express the quantity briefly with an error of less than 0.1% (itself an approximation). When we cannot express a quantity as a whole number, we can adopt one of two forms, vulgar fractions or decimal fractions. If we use vulgar fractions, we can always express a quantity (or number) precisely, e.g., °, 5 5/13 (I.E., FIVE AND FIVE THIRTEENTHS), 2/3, etc. We have, however, the disadvantage that when calculating with numbers of which two or more contain vulgar fractions we have to find the common denominator of such fractions, e.g.,

5 5/13 x 2/3 x 70/13 x 2/3 = 140/39 = 3 23/39

Further disadvantages are the space occupied and the greater possibility of error in calculating or writing down the numbers. When we use decimal fractions we frequently are able to express a number precisely, e.g., ° = 0.5. When we have a recurring decimal the number is still expressed precisely, e.g.,

1/7 = 0.142857 = 142857/999999 = 1/7

However, the great advantage when calculating with decimals is that we have a constant common denominator — the appropriate power of 10. When we have recurring decimals we may lose this advantage and either have to approximate or revert to vulgar fractions.

When our number is one which cannot be expressed precisely in decimal fractions, we are forced to approximate. The most widely-used quantity which can only be expressed as an approximation is the relationship (or ratio) between the circumference of a circle and the diameter of that circle, which is expressed by the Greek letter *pi*. We give this with the first 10 decimal places, i.e.,

3.14159 26535

It is customary to round up the last decimal figure we decide to use by increasing it by 1 if the following figure is 5 or more, e.g., our approximations for *Pi* would be
3.14   3.142   3.1416   3.14159   etc.
Our next problem is to decide how many decimal places we need in order to achieve our required degree of accuracy. If we wish to express a simple number, the choice is easy. We can choose quite arbitrarily and anyone who is given that number knows that it is accurate to within one-half either way of the last digit, e.g., 3.142 must lie between 3.1415 and 3.142499.

Our difficulty arises when we have to perform mathematic operations on one or more approximations. We may not achieve the degree of accuracy we require, e.g., we have
3.14 x 4 = 12.56
3.142 x 4 = 12.568 (or 12.57).
If we wish our answer to be accurate to *n* places of decimals, it will usually be sufficient if we approximate to *n* + *1* decimal places. If we want to be extra careful we can use *n* + *2* decimal places — no real problem if we have access to a modern calculator or computer. However, if we multiply by large numbers, any approximation error will be magnified and we should increase our number of decimal places when we make our original approximations.

We should try to use standard methods for similar problems. Failing this, we may find ourselves embarrassed by discrepancies. An instructive example appears in this encyclopedia. Although the articles we mention were first published in the encyclopedia in 1964, it was only in 1982 that the discrepancy was pointed out to the author by his friend, Dott. Ing. Bruno Burian, the well-known Italian bridge mathematician. Under the heading 'Mathematic Assumptions' the defenders hold Q-J-x-x of a suit. A comparison is made between the probabilities of a named defender holding the doubleton Q-J or the singleton J. These are given as

Q-J	52.17%	22C11
J	47.83%	22C12

Under the heading 'Probabilities a Posteriori' we compare the equivalent holding of a doubleton K-Q or the singleton K when the opponents have a combined holding of K-Q-x-x. The comparison is given as

K-Q	6.8%
K	6.2%

The percentages are based on 100% representing all possible divisions of the four cards, but the comparison is K-Q doubleton = 53.31% and singleton K = 47.69%.

In the first case our approximate ratio is 52:48 or 13:12, while in the second case it is 34:31. The discrepancy is shown more clearly if we use a common base
13:12 = 442:408   34:31 = 442:403
There is a discrepancy of over 1%. In fact the precise ratio between the holding of the doubleton K-Q (or Q-J) and the holding of the singleton K (or J) is the very simple one of 12:11. A comparatively easy method of making the calculation is given in the heading COMBINATIONS.

MATHEMATICAL ASSUMPTIONS. In all calculations of odds or probabilities, certain assumptions are made. The accuracy of an answer depends upon the validity of the assumptions. A condition that is taken for granted is that the pack has been sufficiently shuffled so that all possible deals are equally probable. Under the heading ODDS GOVERNING SPECIFIED CARDS, paragraph 7(b), is an example of another assumption that is specifically mentioned in the discussion.

Many controversies arise because the parties fail to mention the assumptions they make. By listing these clearly, the cause of dispute is often immediately apparent. An example is the following:

NORTH
5 4 3 2

SOUTH
A K 10 9 8

On the play of the ace, West plays the jack, and East the 6. Dummy is entered and the 3 is led, East playing the 7. Should the king be played or the finesse taken? Only two cases have to be considered:
(a) Where West originally held   Q-J   52.17%   22C11
(b) Where West originally held   J   47.83%   22C12
(the notation 22C11 can be read: the number of combinations of 22 things taken 11 at a time). We can make any of the following assumptions:

(1) With Q-J, West will always play the jack. In this case, playing for the drop is a 52% chance.

(2) With Q-J, West will always play the queen. In this case, the finesse is a 100% chance (a sure thing).

(3) With Q-J West will play either honor indiscriminately. This means that in the 52.17% of the cases when he held the Q-J, he will have played the queen 26% of the time, and the jack 26% of the time. When he has the singleton jack, he is bound to play it all 48% of the times. The odds are thus 24 to 13 in favor of the finesse. Assumption (3) is based on a postulate to Bayes's Theorem, published over two hundred years ago, providing that in the absence of knowledge to the contrary, we assume that all prior probabilities are equal. It is the assumption a player should make in normal circumstances. See OPTIMUM STRATEGY; RESTRICTED CHOICE; SUIT COMBINATIONS.

MATHEMATICAL TABLES. The tables below give a variety of information. When a percentage given is less than .0001th of 1%, the number of zeros before the first significant figure is indicated in parentheses. Thus 0.(6)3 should be read as .0000003.

TABLE 1
Probable Percentage Frequency of Distribution Patterns

This table may be used to determine percentages of various distribution patterns, both for hand patterns and suit patterns. Figures are expressed in percentage of hands. The percentage expectation of a particular pattern with the suits identified is given in the last column. For example, the chance that a given player has four spades, four hearts, three diamonds, and two clubs is 1.796%.

Pattern	Total	Specific
4-3-3-2	21.5512	1.796
4-3-3-3	10.5361	2.634
4-4-4-1	2.9932	0.748
5-3-3-2	15.5168	1.293
5-4-3-1	12.9307	0.539
5-4-2-2	10.5797	0.882
5-5-2-1	3.1739	0.264
5-4-4-0	1.2433	0.104
5-5-3-0	0.8952	0.075
6-3-2-2	5.6425	0.470
6-4-2-1	4.7021	0.196
6-3-3-1	3.4482	0.287
6-4-3-0	1.3262	0.055
6-5-1-1	0.7053	0.059
6-5-2-0	0.6511	0.027
6-6-1-0	0.0723	0.006
7-3-2-1	1.8808	0.078
7-2-2-2	0.5129	0.128
7-4-1-1	0.3918	0.033
7-4-2-0	0.3617	0.015
7-3-3-0	0.2652	0.022
7-5-1-0	0.1085	0.005
7-6-0-0	0.0056	0.0005
8-2-2-1	0.1924	0.016
8-3-1-1	0.1176	0.010
8-3-2-0	0.1085	0.005
8-4-1-0	0.0452	0.002
8-5-0-0	0.0031	0.0003
9-2-1-1	0.0178	0.001
9-3-1-0	0.0100	0.0004
9-2-2-0	0.0082	0.0007
9-4-0-0	0.0010	0.(4)8
10-2-1-0	0.0011	0.(4)4
10-1-1-1	0.0004	0.0001
10-3-0-0	0.00015	0.(4)1
11-1-1-0	0.(4)2	0.(5)2
11-2-0-0	0.(4)1	0.(5)1
12-1-0-0	0.(6)3	0.(7)3
13-0-0-0	0.(9)6	0.(9)2

TABLE 1A
Probable Frequency of High Card Content

This table gives the expectancies of having specific point counts, using the 4-3-2-1 count. Note that the chances of holding exactly one-fourth of the points — 10 — is the most probable, but only by a slight margin over 9. The chart also shows why many players prefer to use a lower range for an opening notrump, say 12-14, rather than the usual 15-17 or 16-18. The chance to use notrump as an opening bid comes up far more often. The chance of holding 12-14 points comes to 20.6345%, or one hand in five. The chance of holding 15-17 is only 10.0963%, or one hand in 10 — only about half as often as 12-14. Of course most of the hands with these counts will not be opened 1 NT for one reason or another — usually distribution.

Point Count	%	Point Count	%
0	.3639	16	3.3109
1	.7884	17	2.3617
2	1.3561	18	1.6051
3	2.4624	19	1.0362
4	3.8454	20	.6435
5	5.1862	21	.3779
6	6.5541	22	.2100
7	8.0281	23	.1119
8	8.8922	24	.0559
9	9.3562	25	.0264
10	9.4051	26	.0117
11	8.9447	27	.0049
12	8.0269	28	.0019
13	6.9143	29	.0007
14	5.6933	30	.0002
15	4.4237	31-37	.0001

TABLE 2
Probability of Holding an Exact Number of Cards of a Specified Suit

This table gives the probability (a priori, before dealing) of holding an exact number of cards in a specified suit. The number of times the specified number of cards can be expected in any suit in the course of 100 deals is four times as great.

Number of Cards	%
0	1.279
1	8.006
2	20.587
3	28.633
4	23.861
5	12.469
6	4.156
7	0.882
8	0.117
9	0.009
10	0.0004
11	0.(5)9
12	0.(7)8
13	0.(9)16

TABLE 3
Probability of Distribution of Cards in Three Hidden Hands

This table gives the probability of distribution of the remaining cards in a suit for a one-hand holding in column (a); among the other three hands, column (b); expressed as a percentage, column (c). For brevity, probabilities of less than half of 1% are omitted.

(a)	(b)	(c)
0	6-4-3	25.921
	5-4-4	24.301
	5-5-3	17.497
	6-5-2	12.725
	7-4-2	7.069
	7-3-3	5.184
	8-3-2	2.121
	7-5-1	2.121
	6-6-1	1.414
	8-4-1	0.884
1	5-4-3	40.377
	6-4-2	14.683
	6-3-3	10.767
	5-5-2	9.911
	4-4-4	9.347
	7-3-2	5.873
	6-5-1	4.405
	7-4-1	2.447
	8-3-1	0.734
	8-2-2	0.601
2	4-4-3	26.170
	5-4-2	25.695
	5-3-3	18.843
	6-3-2	13.704
	6-4-1	5.710
	5-5-1	3.854
	7-3-1	2.284
	7-2-2	1.869
	6-5-0	0.791
3	4-3-3	27.598
	5-3-2	27.096
	4-4-2	18.817
	5-4-1	11.290
	6-3-1	6.021
	6-2-2	4.927
	7-2-1	1.642
	6-4-0	1.158
	5-5-0	0.782
4	4-3-2	45.160
	5-3-1	13.548
	5-2-2	11.085

(a)	(b)	(c)
	3-3-3	11.039
	4-4-1	9.408
	6-2-1	4.927
	5-4-0	2.605
	6-3-0	1.390
5	3-3-2	31.110
	4-3-1	25.925
	4-2-2	21.212
	5-2-1	12.727
	5-3-0	3.590
	4-4-0	2.493
	6-1-1	1.414
	6-2-0	1.305
6	3-2-2	33.939
	4-2-1	28.282
	3-3-1	20.740
	4-3-0	7.977
	5-1-1	4.242
	5-2-0	3.916
	6-1-0	0.870
7	3-2-1	53.333
	2-2-2	14.545
	4-1-1	11.111
	4-2-0	10.256
	3-3-0	7.521
	5-1-0	3.077
8	2-2-1	41.211
	3-1-1	25.185
	3-2-0	23.247
	4-1-0	9.686
	5-0-0	0.671
9	2-1-1	48.080
	3-1-0	27.122
	2-2-0	22.191
	4-0-0	2.608
10	2-1-0	66.572
	1-1-1	24.040
	3-0-0	9.388
11	1-1-0	68.421
	2-0-0	31.579

		4-1	28.26	(10)
		5-0	3.91	(2)
7	6	4-2	48.45	(30)
		3-3	35.53	(20)
		5-1	14.53	(12)
		6-0	6.78	(2)
6	7	4-3	62.17	(70)
		5-2	30.52	(42)
		6-1	6.78	(14)
		7-0	0.52	(2)
5	8	5-3	47.12	(112)
		4-4	32.72	(70)
		6-2	17.14	(56)
		7-1	2.86	(16)
		8-0	0.16	(2)
4	9	5-4	58.90	(252)
		6-3	31.41	(168)
		7-2	8.57	(72)
		8-1	1.07	(18)
		9-0	0.05	(2)
3	10	6-4	46.20	(420)
		5-5	31.18	(252)
		7-3	18.48	(240)
		8-2	3.78	(90)
		9-1	0.35	(20)
		10-0	0.01	(2)
2	11	6-5	57.17	(924)
		7-4	31.76	(660)
		8-3	9.53	(330)
		9-2	1.44	(110)
		10-1	0.10	(22)
		11-0	0.002	(2)
1	12	7-5	45.74	(1584)
		6-6	30.49	(924)
		8-4	19.06	(990)
		9-3	4.23	(440)
		10-2	0.46	(132)
		11-1	0.02	(24)
		12-0	0.0003	(2)
0	13	7-6	56.62	(3432)
		8-5	31.85	(2574)
		9-4	9.83	(1430)
		10-3	1.57	(572)
		11-2	0.12	(156)
		12-1	0.003	(26)
		13-0	0.00002	(2)

TABLE 4
Probability of Distribution of Cards In Two Hidden Hands

This table gives the probability of distribution of cards in two given hands. Column (a) shows number of cards in the two known hands; column (b) shows the number of outstanding cards in the two hidden hands; column (c) the ways in which these cards may be divided; column (d) shows the percentage of cases in which the distribution in column (c) occurs, followed by a bracketed figure showing the number of cases applicable. By dividing the percentage in column (d) by the bracketed figure, the probability that one opponent will hold particular specified cards of that remainder can be obtained.

(a)	(b)	(c)	(d)	
11	2	1-1	52	(2)
		2-0	48	(2)
10	3	2-1	78	(6)
		3-0	22	(2)
9	4	3-1	49.74	(8)
		2-2	40.70	(6)
		4-0	9.57	(2)
8	5	3-2	67.83	(20)

TABLE 4A
Probability of Distribution of Two Residues between Two Hidden Hands

A residue is said to be favorably divided when it is divided as evenly as possible, e.g., 8 cards divided 4-4 or 7 cards divided 4-3. In this table, column (a) shows the number of cards outstanding in each of the two suits in the two hidden hands; column (b) shows the percentage of cases in which both residues will divide as evenly as possible; column (c) shows the percentage of cases in which at least one residue will divide favorably.

(a)	(b)	(c)
8-8	11.87%	53.57%
8-7	21.77	73.13
8-6	12.44	55.81
8-5	23.10	77.45
8-4	13.86	59.56
7-7	40.42	83.93
7-6	23.10	74.60

7-5	43.31	86.69
7-4	25.99	76.88
6-6	13.20	57.86
6-5	24.75	78.61
6-4	14.85	61.37
5-5	46.75	88.90
5-4	28.05	80.47
5-3	53.29	92.53

TABLE 5
Tables of Combinations (Values for nCr)

In making mathematic computations involving bridge (see MATHEMATICS OF BRIDGE), the formula nCr appears frequently. Since the formula involves factorial numbers, the computation is tedious (13! means 13 x 12 x 11 x 10 x 9 x 8 x 7 x 6 x 5 x 4 x 3 x 2 x 1). Values of nCr appear in the table below.

TOTAL NUMBER FROM WHICH
COMBINATIONS CAN BE TAKEN

r	2	3	4	5	6
2	1				
3	3	1			
4	6	4	1		
5	10	10	5	1	
6	15	20	15	6	1
7	21	35	35	21	7
8	28	56	70	56	28
9	36	84	126	126	84
10	45	120	210	252	210
11	55	165	330	462	462
12	66	220	495	792	924
13	78	286	715	1287	1716
14	91	364	1001	2002	3003
15	105	455	1365	3003	5005
16	120	560	1820	4368	8008
17	136	680	2380	6188	12376
18	153	816	3060	8568	18564
19	171	969	3876	11628	27132
20	190	1140	4845	15504	38760
21	210	1330	5985	20349	54264
22	231	1540	7315	26334	74613
23	253	1771	8855	33649	100947
24	276	2024	10626	42504	134596
25	300	2300	12650	53130	177100
26	325	2600	14950	65780	230230

	7	8	9	10
7	1			
8	8	1		
9	36	9	1	
10	120	45	10	1
11	330	165	55	11
12	792	495	220	66
13	1716	1287	715	286
14	3432	3003	2002	1001
15	6435	6435	5005	3003
16	11440	12870	11440	8008
17	19448	24310	24310	19448
18	31824	43758	48620	43758
19	50388	75582	92378	92378
20	77520	125970	167960	184756
21	116280	203490	293930	352716
22	170544	319770	497420	646646
23	245157	490314	817190	1144066
24	346104	735471	1307504	1961256
25	480700	1081575	2042978	3268760
26	657800	1562275	3124550	5311735

22C11 = 705432   25C11 = 4457400
23C11 = 1352078   25C12 = 5200300
23C12 = 1352078   25C13 = 5200300
24C11 = 2496144   26C11 = 7726160
24C12 = 2704156   26C12 = 9657700

24C13 = 2496144   26C13 = 10400600

TABLE 6
Sundry Odds

Various odds have been of interest to bridge players for many years. Below are a number of different possibilities, with odds computed.

Number of different hands a named player can receive
      52C13   635,013,559,600

Number of different hands a second named player can receive
      39C13   8,122,425,444

Number of different hands the third and fourth players can receive
      26C13   10,400,600

Number of possible deals
      52! $\div$ 13!^{4}
      53,644,737,765,488,792,839,237,440,000

Number of possible auctions with North as dealer, assuming that East and West pass throughout
      $2^{36} - 1 = 68,719,476,735$

Number of possible auctions with North as dealer, assuming that East and West do not pass throughout
      $(4 \times 22^{35} - 1) \rceil 3 = 128,745,650,347,030,683,120,231,$
926,111,609,371,363,122,697,557

Odds against each player having a complete suit
      2,235,197,406,895,366,368,301,559,999 to 1.

Odds against each player receiving identical hands except for difference of suit

♠ A K Q	♠ J 10 9	♠ 8 7 6	♠ 5 4 3 2
♥ J 10 9	♥ 8 7 6	♥ 5 4 3 2	♥ A K Q
♦ 8 7 6	♦ 5 4 3 2	♦ A K Q	♦ J 10 9
♣ 5 4 3 2	♣ A K Q	♣ J 10 9	♣ 8 7 6

    Approximately: 55,976,427,337,829,109,025 to 1.

Odds against receiving a hand
      A K Q   A K Q   A K Q   A K Q J
      the jack being in any of the four suits:
      158,753,389,899 to 1

Odds against receiving a perfect hand, a hand that will produce 13 tricks in notrump irrespective of the opening lead or the composition of the other three hands:
      169,066,442 to 1

Odds against a YARBOROUGH
      Approximately 1,827 to 1

Odds against both members of a partnership receiving Yarboroughs
      546,000,000 to 1

Odds against a hand with no card higher than 10
      274 to 1

Odds against a hand with no card higher than jack
      52 to 1

Odds against a hand with no card higher than queen
      11 to 1

Odds against a hand with no aces
      slightly more than 2 to 1

Odds against being dealt four aces
      Approximately 378 to 1

Odds against being dealt four honors in one suit
      Approximately 22 to 1

Odds against being dealt five honors in one suit
      Approximately 500 to 1

Odds against being dealt at least one singleton
      Slightly over 2 to 1

Odds against having at least one void
      Approximately 19 to 1

Odds that two partners will be dealt 26 named cards between them, e.g., all the red cards.

495,918,532,918,103 to 1 against

Odds that no players will be dealt a singleton or void

Approximately 4 to 1 against

Odds that four specified cards will be cut by the four players

270,724 to 1 against

MATHEMATICAL VALUE OF GAME. See VALUE OF GAME.

MATHEMATICAL VALUE OF PARTSCORE. See PARTSCORE BIDDING.

MATHEMATICS OF BRIDGE. The mathematics of bridge runs the gamut from simply counting the number of cards in one's hand up to involved problems of probability theory. Some examples of the application of mathematics to bridge are:

(1) Bidding systems, methods, and conventions. Use may be made of the frequency with which various patterns occur (see MATHEMATICAL TABLES, Table 1).

A bidder will also find it valuable to know the ways in which the outstanding cards are likely to be divided among the three hidden hands. We may wish to determine the probability that a trick will not be lost in a suit in which we have a particular holding. It can be determined from Table 3 that with A-K-Q-J-x-x there is a nearly 94% probability that no trick will be lost, but with A-K-Q-x-x-x-x, the probability is only 84%.

(2) Sacrifice bidding.

(3) Choice among part-score, game, and slam. These are dependent on EXPECTATION, and of course, on correctly estimating the value of the players' hands.

(4) Percentage play. This is shown in MATHEMATICAL TABLES, Table 4.

(5) Safety play. This is governed by expectation. See SUIT COMBINATIONS.

(6) Countering false cards (see DECEPTION, MATHEMATICS OF; FALSECARDING).

To express and solve such mathematic problems, the ordinary arithmetic symbols are used, and also the following two.

n! (read, *n* factorial), meaning that one multiplies all the numerals starting at 1, up to and including the number represented by *n*.

nCr (read, the number of combinations in which *n* things can be selected *r* at a time). Thus 52C13 is the number of different hands of 13 cards that can be dealt to a single player from a pack of 52 cards. The formula for finding this is:

n!/[(n-r)! x r!] or 52!/(39! X 13!)

Applications of this formula are, among others,

(a) NUMBER OF POSSIBLE HANDS. DEALS

(b) The number of cards held in a suit

(c) Hand patterns

(d) ODDS GOVERNING SPECIFIED CARDS

The following headings also cover facets of mathematics of bridge: CARDS, NEUTRAL AND POSITIVE; DECEPTION, MATHEMATICS OF; EXPECTATION; HAND PATTERNS; MATHEMATICAL ASSUMPTIONS; BIBLIOGRAPHY, M; MATHEMATICS OF MATCHPOINT PLAY; NUMBER OF POSSIBLE HANDS, DEALS; ODDS, IN BRIDGE; OPTIMUM STRATEGY; PERCENTAGE PLAY; PROBABILITIES, A POSTERIORI; PROBABILITIES, A PRIORI; PROB-

ABILITY OF SUCCESSIVE EVENTS; SUIT, NUMBER OF CARDS IN; VALUE OF GAME.

MATHEMATICS OF DECEPTION. See DECEPTION, MATHEMATICS OF.

MATHEMATICS OF MATCHPOINT PLAY. In duplicate, the bonus for making a non-vulnerable game is always 300 points, and the bonus for making a vulnerable game is always 500 points. The bonus for making a partial is always 50 points. When a contract is doubled and made, the bonus is always 50 points — 100 points when the contract is redoubled.

In rubber bridge, the value of winning a rubber with two games out of three is 500, of winning a rubber in two straight games 700, of winning the only game in an unfinished rubber 350, and of having the only partial in an unfinished game 100.

This is particularly applicable to SAFETY PLAYS. In matchpoint duplicate, a safety play is used only if the distribution to be guarded against has a probability of more than 50. Of course, if the contract is an excellent one that only a few other competitors will arrive at, any safety play that will ensure it is used; similarly, if the contract is a very bad one, the best chance to make a good score is that better contracts will be defeated by unusual distribution, so any possible safety play is used. For other considerations at matchpoint play, see MATCHPOINT BIDDING, MATCHPOINT PLAY and MATCHPOINT DEFENSE.

MAURITIUS BRIDGE LEAGUE The League was founded in 1960, and in 1992 had 200 members organized in seven clubs. It hosted the 1983 BFAME Championships, and its open team finished second in the 1987 championship.

President 1992:

Pierre Philogene

Alpha Bridge Club

Old Moka Road,

St. Jean, Quatre Bornes

Mauritius.

Tel: 626 2818

Fax: 637 3695

MAX or MAXIMUM. The greatest number of tricks which can be made with any holding. However, "to play for the maximum" may be used technically to indicate the line of play which will produce the maximum average number of tricks in the long run. The term is used in this sense in the article on SUIT COMBINATIONS. The word also can be used to describe a holding in high card strength or to justify a bid, e.g., "I had a maximum."

MAXIMAL OVERCALL DOUBLE. A type of COMPETITIVE DOUBLE used to invite game when the auction is too crowded for any other approach. The following situation is typical:

WEST	NORTH	EAST	SOUTH
			1 ♠
2 ♥	2 ♠	3 ♥	?

South may have a hand with which he wishes to sign off in 3♠ or a hand worth a game invitation. Either hand can be described if the maximal overcall double is used as a conventional bid inviting game and the 3♠ bid is reserved for use as a sign-off.

If the enemy competition is not in the maximum suit (the one just below South's), however, maximal overcall doubles are not needed if the partnership has agreed that opener's bid in the available side suit constitutes a general game try:

WEST	NORTH	EAST	SOUTH
			1 ♠
2 ♦	2 ♠	3 ♦	?

Here South can bid 3♥ (conventional, forcing) to invite game in spades and bid 3♠ to sign off, so some advocates of maximal overcall doubles prefer to use this double for penalties. See also COMPETITIVE DOUBLES.

MAYONNAISE. Variant of GOULASH.

McCABE ADJUNCT. See WEAK TWO-BIDS.

MCCONNELL CUP. In 1993, the World Bridge Federation established the McConnell Cup, a knockout teams event for women to be played at the World Bridge Championships alongside the competition for the Rosenblum Cup (an open event). The McConnell Cup, first contested at the NEC World Bridge Championships in Albuquerque NM in 1994, is named in honor of Ruth McConnell, former District 8 representative to the ACBL Board of Directors, and WBF treasurer from 1985 to 1990.

McKENNEY-BALDWIN MOVEMENT. One of a series of pair movements planned by William E. McKenney and worked out by Russell J. Baldwin, then respectively secretary and tournament director of the American Bridge League. The most widely used were two-session pair movements for 16 to 32 pairs, in which each pair played against each of the others in the course of two sessions, with approximately balanced comparisons. One session consisted of a Mitchell Movement using the APPENDIX TABLE concept, and the other of an INTERWOVEN HOWELL.

McKENNEY SIGNAL. Standard term in Great Britain for the SUIT PREFERENCE signal, named for William E. McKenney of the ACBL, who helped popularize it.

McKENNEY TROPHY. This trophy is presented to the ACBL member who has accumulated the most masterpoints during the calendar year. The trophy was put into play on January 1, 1938 by William E. McKenney, ACBL executive secretary. The previous year the AMERICAN BRIDGE LEAGUE awarded a trophy to Charles H. Goren for winning the greatest number of masterpoints in one year. Hence this competition dates back to 1937. Goren dominated the picture in the early years, winning eight times. The name of the masterpoint race was changed to the BARRY CRANE TOP 500 shortly after Crane's death in 1985. For winners see Appendix II.

MEAN SCORE. See IMP PAIR GAMES.

MECHANICS OF BRIDGE. Described in sections I, II, and III of the LAWS.

MEDIUM CARDS. The lower honor cards and the higher spot cards. Those which provide BODY in long suit holdings or in support of a partner's bid suit.

MEMBER. (1) Of a table: one of the players constituting a table at rubber bridge, whether actively playing or awaiting re-entry to the table for the next rubber or round of CHICAGO; (2) of a team: a player whose name was listed on the official entry blank whether actively playing or not (see RESERVE PLAYER); (3) of the ACBL: a person who has joined one of the geographical units chartered by the ACBL; see BYLAWS OF THE ACBL.

MEMBERSHIP LIMIT. Table membership is limited to six players, unless exactly seven players are present and no player may be a member of two tables simultaneously (LAWS, "Rules for Club Procedure," Section F). In order to make up tables with greater flexibility, many of the larger bridge clubs use HOUSE PLAYERS in order to be able to accommodate members as they arrive. For precedence in play at a table, see CUT IN.

MEMORY DUPLICATE. See REPLAY DUPLICATE.

MENACE. See THREAT CARD.

MEN'S BOARD-A-MATCH TEAMS, NORTH AMERICAN CHAMPIONSHIP. See GOREN TROPHY. For results see Appendix I.

MEN'S PAIRS. A pairs event in duplicate competition in which all the competitors are men. The ACBL no longer runs men's events at the North American level because such events often lead to participation in open world events such as the Bermuda Bowl and the World Team Olympiad. At the Spring NABC, what formerly was the Men's Pairs is now Open Pairs II, and it is run opposite the nationally-rated Women's Pairs. Men's Pairs events still take place with regional and lower ratings.

MEN'S PAIRS, NORTH AMERICAN CHAMPIONSHIP. See WERNHER TROPHY. For results see Appendix I.

MEN'S SWISS TEAMS, NORTH AMERICAN CHAMPIONSHIP. For results see Appendix I.

MEN'S TEAMS. Team events — Swiss, Knockout or Board-a-Match — in which all competitors are men. The ACBL no longer runs men's events at the North American level because such events often lead to participation in open world events such as the Bermuda Bowl and the World Team Olympiad. The former North American Men's Swiss Teams and the former North American's Men's Board-a-Match Teams now are open events. There was no nationally-rated Men's Knockout Teams. Men's team games of various sorts still take place with regional and lower ratings.

MENTAL PLAY. Hand valuation is mental play. To estimate the trick-winning value of his hand, a player must foresee the conditions that will prevail when the cards are actually played. The better the player, the more accurate his valuation; for he can foresee only those plays which he can actually execute.

MERRIMAC COUP. The deliberate sacrifice of a high card with the object of knocking out a vital entry in an opponent's hand, usually the dummy. Named after the Merrimac, an American coal-carrying ship sunk in 1898 in Santiago Harbor in an attempt to bottle up the Spanish fleet (often misspelled Merrimack, in confusion with the Civil War ironclad that fought the Monitor).

```
                    ♠ 4 3
                    ♥ 5 4 2
                    ♦ A 3
                    ♣ K Q J 10 9 3
♠ J 10 9 8 7                        ♠ A 5 2
♥ K 10 6                            ♥ Q 9 8 7
♦ 10 9 8 4                          ♦ K 7 2
♣ 6                                 ♣ A 5 4
                    ♠ K Q 6
                    ♥ A J 3
                    ♦ Q J 6 5
                    ♣ 8 7 2
```

South is the declarer at a contract of 3NT. West leads the ♠J which East wins with the ace. East at this point sees that the ♦A is dummy's only entry after the ♣A is knocked out, and East, realizing that this entry must be destroyed immediately, effectuates this by playing his ♦K at trick two. This defense holds declarer to eight tricks and defeats the contract. Occasionally called HOBSON'S COUP.

MEXICAN TWO DIAMONDS. A bid showing a balanced hand with 19-21 high-card points and 4-6 losers. A weak five-card major is permitted. Devised by George Rosenkranz as a cornerstone of the ROMEX SYSTEM.

Negative responses (0-4 points) are: pass with diamond length; 2♥ — transfer to 2♠ preparatory to a sign-off in clubs, hearts or spades (2♥ may also be a semi-positive with 5-6 points); 2♠ — transfer to 2 NT, planning to pass.

Positive responses (7 points or more and game forcing) include: TEXAS TRANSFERS; 2♠ — transfer to 2 NT with 7-9 points, balanced distribution; 2 NT — 10 points or more, normally balanced; three of a suit — at least 10 points with a broken six-card suit.

Responder's high-card requirements are reduced by 1 point for each five-card suit and by 2 points for a six-card major. In the modern version (1982) the bid is used differently. If balanced the opener must have 23-24 points, but he may also have an ACOL TWO-BID in a major suit or a strong three-suited hand.

MEXICO. An independent member of the WORLD BRIDGE FEDERATION whose teams compete separately in the World Bridge Olympiad. Nationally and locally, however, Mexico's organized tournament bridge is conducted by two Units of the ACBL, and Mexican players are eligible to compete to represent North America on ACBL teams for the BERMUDA BOWL.
Officers, 1982:
President: Dr. George Rosenkranz
Mexican National Federation of Bridge,
A.C., Parque Via Reforma 1730,
Mexico 10, D.F., Mexico

MICHAELS CUEBID The use of an immediate cuebid in the opponent's suit to show a two-suiter, devised by the late Mike Michaels of Miami Beach.

```
♠ J 10 9 4 3          ♠ K Q 6 4
♥ A J 10 6 2          ♥ J 10 7 6 4
♦ 6                   ♦ A 4
♣ 8 7                 ♣ 8 7
```

If an opponent opens with a minor suit, the cuebid is recommended with either of these hands unless the vul-

nerability is unfavorable. Over a minor suit the emphasis is on the major suits; there should be at least nine cards in the major suits and 6-11 points. The strength, however, is a matter of partnership agreement, and some would expect opening values unless the vulnerability is favorable. Greater strength is quite possible, intending further action.

Over a major suit the cuebid shows the unbid major suit and an unspecified minor suit:

```
♠ 7                   ♠ —
♥ Q J 10 9 5          ♥ 10 9 8 7 4
♦ 7 5                 ♦ A K J 6 2
♣ A J 10 6 2          ♣ Q 6 4
```

On each of these hands, 2♠ would be bid over 1♠. If partner does not fit the unbid major, he can bid notrump as a request to the cuebidder to show his minor suit.

The major-suit cuebid is unlimited in point-count: the cuebidder may have a strong hand and plan to take further action. Over either type of cuebid, partner will usually bid the full value of his hand if there is a known fit and in some circumstances he may put pressure on the opponents by making an advance sacrifice. He can also make use of a second cuebid to ask for further definition of the cuebidder's hand.

As with other devices which are partly obstructive, both the cuebidder and his partner have to watch the vulnerability. At unfavorable vulnerability, freakish distribution is needed to make the cuebid.

Michaels is often used, by agreement, in less obvious situations. Some of these are:

(i)	2♥	3♥		
(ii)	3♥	4♥		
(iii)	1♦	Pass	Pass	2♦
(iv)	1♦	Pass	1NT	2♦

For defense to Michaels, see DEFENSE TO TWO-SUITED INTERFERENCE.

MIDDLE CARD. The middle card of an original three-card holding. Generally referred to in connection with opening leads. See THREE SMALL CARDS, LEAD FROM.

MIDDLE GAME. The play, usually referring to the declarer's play, after the original lead or first few tricks won by the defenders, during which the plan of the play is developed, frequently leading to END PLAY positions or preparation for them. Aspects of the middle game are discussed in a number of articles listed under DEFENSE and DUMMY PLAY.

MIDDLE SUIT. See DOUBLE MENACE.

MIDNIGHT GAME. A contest staged after the main events of the day have concluded. Usually a midnight game is either an open pairs, a Swiss Teams or a Knockout Teams with abbreviated matches. Usually much shorter time limits on play are imposed so that the game will be finished and scored before 3 a.m. At sectionals the awards are in silver points. At regional and at North American Championships the awards are in red points.

MIDNIGHT SWISS. The most common type of midnight game. The game consists of five matches of five boards played at a rapid-fire pace — only 25 minutes is allowed per round, so that the average time spent on a board is only five minutes instead of the usual seven.

Sectional games pay in silver points, regional and North American in red points.

MILES CONVENTION.

See TWO NOTRUMP RESPONSE to opening suit bid of one.

MILES RESPONSES TO TWO NOTRUMP OPENINGS.

A method of responding to opening bids of 2 NT devised by Marshall Miles to facilitate safe exploration for slams, games, or partscores in any suit. The principal responses are as follows: 3♣ is STAYMAN; following a Stayman sequence, a 4♣ rebid by responder is GERBER, and a 4♦ rebid is a slam try that may be wholly artificial; JACOBY TRANSFER BIDS; jumps to the four level are natural, showing a broken suit with slam interest; 3 NT transfers to 4♣ and promises a good suit, after which responder may show a second suit if he has one; 3♠ transfers to 3NT, which responder may pass if he merely wanted to raise to game, or may continue with: (a) 4♣ to show a good diamond suit or a diamond-major two-suiter, (b) four of any other suit to show 4-4-4-1 distribution with shortness in the suit bid, or (c) 4 NT to show 5-5 or longer in the minor suits.

MILTON WORK COUNT.

See WORK POINT COUNT.

MINGLED MOVEMENT.

Individual movement, introduced by Olov Hanner, for one session with two or more groups of players, where the groups are mingled so that a player will have most of the other players during the contest either as partner or as opponent. The movements offer an alternative to letting each group play at their own tables with only the boards in common. Two useful examples:

6 tables, 2 groups,
12 rounds & board sets.
Starting positions:

Table	N	S	E	W	b
1	1	13	2	4	1
2	7	10	20	17	2
3	11	3	9	15	5
4	23	21	14	6	7
5	5	18	19	12	10
6	24	16	8	22	11

When changing to a new round #1 follows #12 and #13 follows #24. The remaining players follow the next lower numbered player.

10 tables, 3 groups
13 rounds & board sets.
Starting positions:

Table	N	S	E	W	h
1	40	1	14	27	1
2	16	20	4	35	2
3	10	2	13	19	3
4	12	23	32	33	4
5	39	9	8	37	5
6	31	7	36	30	6
7	24	29	15	17	7
8	21	28	3	6	10
9	34	18	26	38	11
10	22	5	25	11	13

#1 follows #13, #14 follows #26, #27 follows #39, #40 is stationary. The remaining players follow the next lower numbered player.

MINI-MCKENNEY.

The McKENNEY TROPHY was established in 1938 to recognize the ACBL member who won the most masterpoints during a calendar year. Today, players compete to win the BARRY CRANE TOP 500. In 1974, the ACBL Board of Directors voted to recognize masterpoint achievements among players below the rank of Life Master. Thus arose the Mini-McKenney races, honoring six categories — Rookie, Junior Master (Non-Master prior to 1987), Club Master (Master), Sectional Master (National Master), Regional Master (Senior Master) and NABC Master (Advanced Senior Master). At the Unit level, the winners in each category receive recognition and special medallions. For winners see Appendix II.

MINIMUM.

A holding which justifies an original bid, response, or rebid with no high-card strength or distributional values in reserve. See BORDERLINE OPENING BIDS.

MINI NOTRUMP

An opening notrump with 10-12 points. Other very weak ranges are sometimes used, but are often barred by organizing bodies. Lighter notrump openings are allowed by ACBL, but no conventional responses, not even Stayman, may be used.

MINI-SPLINTER

A variation of the SPLINTER bid, in which a jump shift, by opener or responder, shows a fit combined with shortage in the suit named. There are two types:

(1) A jump shift by a passed hand to show near opening values, a fit with opener, and a singleton or void in the named suit. If DRURY is being used, 3♣ will usually be natural since 2♣ is artificial. (Used by a few when responder is unpassed.)

(2) A jump reverse by opener after a one-level response. Example:

OPENER	RESPONDER
1♦	1♠
3♥	

If 2♥ is forcing, as it is in the modern style, then 3♥ is meaningless. As a mini-splinter, it shows a raise to 3♠ with a singleton or void in hearts. Responder can sign off in 3♠ if he chooses.

MINOR PENALTY CARDS.

A single card below honor rank that is exposed inadvertently is a minor penalty card. See Law 50C&D.

MINOR SUIT.

Either of the two lower-ranking suits, diamonds or clubs.

MINOR SUIT STAYMAN.

An artificial bid in response to an opening bid in notrump to explore for a minor suit game or slam or to determine whether or not notrump is playable. One such convention uses a 2♦ response to initiate the exploration. See TWO-WAY STAYMAN (2) . An alternative, when using transfer bids, is to use a 2♠ bid to ask about minor suits. If opener has four cards in one minor suit he bids that suit. If he has four cards in both minors he bids a major suit control, if he has no four card minor, he bids 3 NT if he has no interest in a minor suit slam or bids 2 NT if he can tolerate further investigation. If responder rebids in a major suit he shows a singleton in that suit.

MINOR SUIT SWISS.

A method devised by Albert Dormer and Terence Reese for use in conjunction with nonforcing minor suit jump raises, to show a strong hand in support of opener's minor suit without going past 3NT. In response to a 1♣ opening, a jump to 3♥ would show a very good club raise, and a jump to 3♦ would show a moderately good club raise. In response to a 1♦ opening, a jump to 3♠ would show the very good raise and a jump to 3♥ would show the moderately good raise. All these jumps are forcing either to 3 NT or to four of opener's minor suit. In determining which jump to make, principal emphasis is placed on the richness of responder's controls.

(a)	(b)
♠ x x	♠ A x
♥ K Q x	♥ x x x x
♦ K Q x x x	♦ K 10 x x x
♣ K x x	♣ A Q

Opposite a 1♦ opening, responder would jump to 3♥ with hand (a), and to 3♠ with hand (b). An alternative recommended by H. W. Kelsey is for responder not to attempt to distinguish between moderate and very good strength, but to choose among all three unbid suits and jump in the suit in which he holds the most secure stopper.

In American methods these jumps to the three level would be splinter bids.

MINOR SUIT TEXAS. See SOUTH AFRICAN TEXAS.

MINOR TENACE. An original holding of king-jack (without the ace or queen) of a suit. After one or more rounds of a suit have been played, the second and fourth highest remaining cards of the suit in the hand of one player are also called a minor tenace. See TENACE.

MIRROR DISTRIBUTION. See DUPLICATION OF DISTRIBUTION.

MIRROR MITCHELL. See MIRROR MOVEMENT.

MIRROR MOVEMENT. (Also called Mirror Mitchell). A team movement in which the teams of one group play against the teams of another group, both groups having the same odd number of teams. The start for 2 x 7 teams is:

Table	1	2	3	4	5	6	7
1st NS	A1	A2	A3	A4	A5	A6	A7
row EW	B4	B7	B3	B6	B2	B5	B1
2nd NS	B1	B2	B3	B4	B5	B6	B7
row EW	A4	A7	A3	A6	A2	A5	A1

In each row an ordinary Mitchell is played, EW up one table, boards down one table. The same boards are played at two parallel tables, either by sharing or duplicating. See Team-of-four movements.

MISBOARD. Replacement of hands in the wrong slots in duplicate play. If the next table is unable to play the board, the guilty pair or pairs may be penalized. A misboard may also occur in twinning.

MISCUT. An illegal cut; a cut that leaves fewer than four cards in either portion of the deck.

MISDEAL. An imperfect deal, owing to an incorrect number of cards being dealt to any player, a card being exposed during the deal, etc. See LAWS (Laws 8-12); LAWS OF DUPLICATE (Laws 6, 13, 14).

MISERE. A bad line of play that seems intended to fail. The name comes from solo and other card games in which it may be desirable to lose tricks. An alternative term is 'butcher'.

MISFIT. A term used to describe a situation where two hands opposite each other in any given deal are unbalanced, each containing two long suits and extreme shortages or voids in its third and fourth suits, and further, where these lengths are met by shortages in the partner's hand and the short suits correspondingly met by lengths in the reverse hand. Where not even one 4-4 or better trump fit can be found in a set of 26 cards, the deal may be said to be a misfit as respects those two hands.

MISHEARING. For mishearing of a bid or called card there is no recourse. If a player is not sure what a previous bid was, he may and should ask for a review of the auction when it becomes his turn to bid. If left-hand opponent bids 1♠, partner passes, and right-hand opponent bids 4♠, a call of 3♦ is insufficient, even though the caller may have thought that right-hand opponent had bid 2♠. The use of BID-BOXES helps to avoid such problems, especially for the hearing impaired.

In the play, dummy should not put a card in the played position until he has ascertained that the card was specifically named by the declarer, and it is the declarer's duty to see that any card he has named is the one actually placed in the played position by the dummy. See ACCIDENTS.

MISNOMER. A bid or play improperly called. If a player bids 1♥, for instance, when he meant to bid 1♠, he may substitute his intended call if he does so without pause for thought; otherwise his call, if legal, stands, and if illegal, is subject to penalty. Should a player change a call after a pause, he is giving information to his partner to which his partner is not entitled, and a penalty under this provision should be enforced. (LAW 25).

If a card is called by declarer from dummy in error, he may change the call if he does so without pause for thought, otherwise the called card, if a legal play, stands as the card played. (LAW 45).

MISPLACED BYESTAND. A byestand in a MITCHELL game with an even number of tables placed at a position other than equidistant from the sharing tables.

Adjustment can be made for a byestand too near the head table or too far from it. If the byestand is too near, the game can proceed without change until the halfway mark; the next round is the correction round, and players should be warned of an unusual move. The first set of boards is placed on the byestand, which is then placed in the proper spot. The highest set of boards does not move, but all other boards move down one table. East-West players make their normal move. The North-South players who have just finished playing the highest numbered boards, and the North-South players at the highest numbered table interchange for this round only (keeping their original table number after the correction round). During the correction round, and all subsequent rounds, the last two tables relay boards instead of the first and last tables. (During the correction round, the two interchanging North-South players play against the pair they met on the first round, unavoidably.)

If the byestand is too far, the adjustment is fairly simple. After half the rounds have been played, Table 1, which has been sharing boards with the highest-numbered table, shares boards with Table 2 for all but the last round. That is the only change during these rounds. The final round is an "adjustment" round. Table 2 and the table just beyond the halfway mark (for instance, Table 5 in an eight-table game) share the lowest-numbered set of boards. There will be two tables at which opponents will meet pairs they have played earlier - this cannot be avoided. For additional information, see Alex Groner's *Duplicate Bridge Direction*.

MISSING CARD. A card which is not in any of the four hands. If three of the four hands have a correct number of cards, and the fourth is deficient, and the fact is determined before play ends, a search for the card is conducted; if the card is located, it is deemed to have been in the hand which is deficient. In rubber bridge, if the card cannot be found, the hand is thrown out and a new deck of cards substituted. In duplicate, the director consults players who have played the board, and a new deck is used to supply the board. When the missing card has either been found, or its denomination established, it is deemed to have been a member of the deficient hand, and may either be an exposed card or establish a discard or ruff on a previous trick as a revoke. See LAWS (Law 11); LAWS OF DUPLICATE (Law 14).

MISSISSIPPI HEART HAND. A famous trick hand dating from the days of whist:

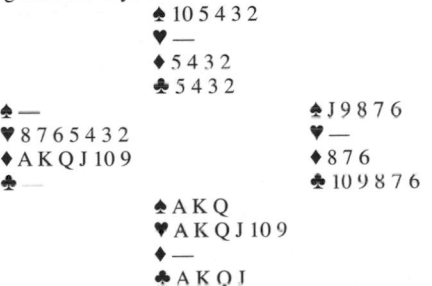

It will be seen that a diamond lead holds South to six tricks in a heart contract, and a game cannot be made in any denomination. South can make nine tricks in a spade contract or 10 tricks in a club contract.

An equivalent hand was given by Hoyle in 1747, and the modern version was given by Thomas Matthews in 1804. It was probably used by the cardsharps of the Mississippi River steamboats during the Civil War period, who hoped to persuade South to make a heavy bet on the odd trick with hearts as trumps. It grew in favor among the professional cheaters in the days of BRIDGE WHIST. As doubling and redoubling could continue indefinitely, the odd trick in a low-stake game could become worth $10,000 (or as much as the client was considered good for) with the help of sufficient redoubles. Charles M. Schwab is reported to have paid off not less than $10,000 on this hand.

MISSORTING HAND. See ACCIDENTS.

MR. AND MRS. An event at a bridge tournament in which entries are limited to married couples, playing together. In England such a tournament has the name FLITCH. When held, this event has been quite popular, particularly at tournaments held around St. Valentine's Day.

MITCHELL-HOWELL MOVEMENT. A two-session pair movement, in which one session is played as a SCRAMBLED MITCHELL and the other as a twin or

INTERWOVEN HOWELL.

MITCHELL-HOWELL movements are available at the ACBL office for 16 to 38 pairs, and for 42 pairs. Twinned 20's are used for 40.

Mitchell-Howell movements are especially valuable for two-session games of up to 5 tables. For instance, with 10 tables it's fairly simple to run a 10-table Mitchell in the first session and for the second session to put first-session North-South pairs into one five-table section and the East-West pairs from the first session into another section. Duplicate the boards and run two five-table Howells with a nine top.

Since there is an 8 top in the first session and a 9 top in the second, the second session must be factored down 1/9 to produce an overall winner. ACBL regulations require that the first session be used as the basis for factoring. Another possibility — use a Relay Mitchell in the first session, producing a 9 top in both sessions. This also provides a perfect contest — three-board matches against all 19 of the other competing pairs.

The same movement could be used with nine tables. In the first session run a Mitchell movement. In the second session you would have two 4°-table Howells. Let the sitout pairs play each other and avoid a sitout. Top in both sessions is 8 so no factoring is involved. The only problem here is that pairs will play one pair they played in the first session.

With 16 tables or more it's usually practical to play two Mitchell sections with a crossover for the second session.

MITCHELL MOVEMENT. A method of play for duplicate whist originated by John T. Mitchell which has been continued through auction and contract. In every pairs tournament, the movement has three basic components: boards, tables and pairs. In the Mitchell movement the pairs are in two groups, N-S and E-W, with the aim of having all N-S pairs meeting all E-W pairs and playing all the boards. Except for slight modifications with an even number of tables (skip mitchell or relay mitchell), E-W pairs move to the higher-numbered table, while boards move in the opposite direction to the next lower numbered table. N-S are always stationary. To produce one winning pair, see SCRAMBLED MITCHELL.

For an even number of tables, there are two alternatives: (1) The skip mitchell, in which E-W pairs skip one table after the half-way round. (2) The relay mitchell, which is normally used when it is desired to play as many rounds as there are tables. A set of boards is shared throughout between Table 1 and the high-numbered table. A spare set of boards is left on a byestand at the mid-point: between 4 and 5 for an 8-table game, 5 and 6 for a 10-table game and so on. Boards moving down after each round must include the byestand, so in an 8-table game they go from 5 to byestand to 4. This method has the advantage that all players play all boards and meet all opponents in the other line. It is not necessary that the relay and byestand be located as listed above. The following is the requirement: the byestand must be exactly halfway around the field from the relay. For instance if the relay in an eight-table game is between tables 1 and 2, then the byestand must be between tables 5 and 6.

MIXED PAIRS. An event at duplicate competition between pairs, each of which has one man and one woman member.

MIXED RAISE. See CUEBID IN OPPONENT'S SUIT.

MIXED TEAMS. In tournaments in the United States, a mixed team is composed of four (occasionally five or six) players, who are obligated to compete at all times as two mixed pairs, one member of each partnership being of each sex. In the U.S. formerly, and in some other countries still, a team is a mixed team if it has at least one member of the opposite sex.

MIXING CARDS AFTER PLAY. Illegal if a claim has been made to inspect the cards for a revoke, or to ascertain honors or the number of tricks won or lost. See LAWS (Law 66).

MNEMONIC DUPLICATE. See REPLAY DUPLICATE.

MONACO BRIDGE FEDERATION (Federation Monagesque de Bridge).
President 1992:
  Mr. Antoni,
  Centre de Congres Auditorium
  Boulevard Louis II
  9800 Monte Carlo,
  Monaco.
  Tel. 33 93 30 04 30

MONACO SYSTEM. A prototype relay system devised by Pierre Ghestem of France, and used by him very successfully in world championships in partnership with Rene Bacherich.

The 1♣ opening bid was not necessarily strong. The artificial relay bids available, usually by responder but sometimes by opener, were almost always in diamonds. After major-suit openings the minimum action (1♥ -1♠, or 1♠ - 1NT) was a relay. Most responses at the two level were transfers. See RELAY SYSTEMS.

MONITORS. Persons assigned to handle specialized chores at the table during high-level team events, occasionally at high-level pair events. Sometimes the monitor keeps track of how long each pair takes to make its bids and plays so that the tournament committee can make an informed decision concerning penalties for slow play. A monitor used to be the liaison between players on either side of the BIDDING SCREEN. The monitor noted the bids made on his side of the table, then called them aloud for the benefit of the players and monitor on the other side of the screen. This use became obsolete when the TRAY was introduced.

The monitor also frequently is called upon to keep complete bidding and play records of the action at his table.

MONSTER. A bridge hand of great trick-taking potential either because of a preponderance of high-card winners or because of concentrated strength in long suits and extreme shortness in weak suits. Also, a very big one-session score — a big game.

MONTY HALL TRAP. A common blind spot in probability problems in which the solver attributes undue significance to "new" information. The name alludes to the Monty Hall Problem: You are asked to choose one of three doors. One door conceals a prize; the other two conceal goats. So you have one chance in three of choosing the prize. Monty Hall, who knows the location of the prize, opens one of the remaining doors to reveal a goat.

Many people assume that your chance of having chosen the prize now increases to one in two. This would be true had Monty Hall opened a door at random. But since he always had a goat to show you, his revelation is meaningless. You still have one chance in three of owning the prize.

To avoid the trap, you must consider whether information you receive is random. When you learn a fact, you must ask yourself if it were equally possible for you to have learned the opposite fact.

For example:

$$\spadesuit\ A\ 5$$
$$\heartsuit\ 8\ 7\ 5$$
$$\diamondsuit\ J\ 5\ 3$$
$$\clubsuit\ K\ J\ 7\ 4\ 2$$

$$\spadesuit\ K\ 7\ 2$$
$$\heartsuit\ A\ 6\ 4\ 2$$
$$\diamondsuit\ A\ 7$$
$$\clubsuit\ A\ 10\ 5\ 3$$

After the auction 1 NT — 3 NT, West leads a spade. You hold up one round and the defense continues spades. It appears from the carding that spades have split five-three. Many players would finesse East for the ♣Q on the strength of the spade break. But this is falling for the Monty Hall Trap. West usually holds more cards than East in the suit he chooses to lead. So you cannot attribute full significance to the five-three break.

In fact, in this setting an even break would be abnormal. If West leads a four-card spade suit, you should reason that he holds fewer than his normal share and should finesse him for the ♣Q. For a more detailed discussion of "The Monty Hall Trap" by Phil Martin, see *Bridge Today*, May-June, 1989.

MOREHEAD TROPHY. Donated by *The New York Times* in memory of its longtime bridge editor Albert H. Morehead. The trophy was originally awarded to the winners of a special knockout team event that followed the Reisinger team contest at the Fall NABC in 1967, but was withdrawn when the event proved unpopular. The winners and runners-up were:

1967   1. Steve Altman, Michael Becker
            Charles Peres, Daniel Rotman
       2. Paul Deal, Noel Duvic, Frank Hoadley
            Gerald Kendal, Paul Munafo

Since 1973 the trophy has been awarded to the winners of the GRAND NATIONAL TEAMS. For results see Appendix I.

MORNING GAME. A contest played in the morning, usually geared to finish by noon. All morning games used to be SIDE GAMES, strictly secondary events. Many morning games still are side games, but far more are a major part of the tournament program. Most regional and all North American tournaments feature morning Knockout Teams which usually run over four consecutive mornings. These are championship events awarding gold points for overalls and red points for matches won. It is not at all unusual for more than 100 teams to enter a Morning Knockout.

MOROCCAN ROYAL BRIDGE FEDERATION (Federation Royale Marocaine de Bridge). Founded in

Casablanca by M. Tazi Mohamed, in 1957, after independence was achieved by Morocco, succeeding the Moroccan unit of the Federation Francaise de Bridge. Had 490 members in 1993.
Officers 1993:
President: Mah Abderrahman
Secretary: Bencherki Redouane
10 Rue Bendahan
Casablanca
Morocco.
Tel: 212 2 200027
Fax: 212 2 318931

MORTON'S FORK COUP. A maneuver by which declarer presents a defender with a choice of taking a trick cheaply or ducking to preserve an honor combination, only both decisions cost the defense a trick. If the defender wins the trick, he sets up another high card in the suit for declarer, while if he ducks, his winner disappears because declarer has a discard possibility. The name is derived from an episode in English history. Cardinal Morton, Chancellor under King Henry VII, habitually extracted money from wealthy London merchants for the royal treasury. His approach was that if the merchants lived ostentatiously, it was obvious that they had sufficient income to spare some for the king. Alternatively, if they lived frugally, they must be saving substantially and could therefore afford to contribute to the king's coffers. In either case, they were impaled on Morton's Fork.
Dorothy Truscott gives this example of the coup:

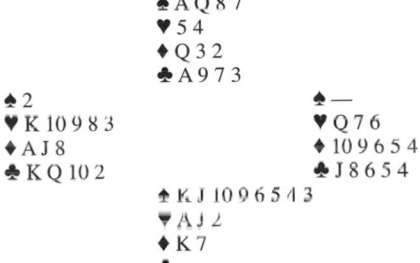

```
              ♠ A Q 8 7
              ♥ 5 4
              ♦ Q 3 2
              ♣ A 9 7 3
  ♠ 2                        ♠ —
  ♥ K 10 9 8 3               ♥ Q 7 6
  ♦ A J 8                    ♦ 10 9 6 5 4
  ♣ K Q 10 2                 ♣ J 8 6 5 4
              ♠ K J 10 9 6 5 4 3
              ♥ A J 2
              ♦ K 7
              ♣ —
```

South plays 6♠ after West has opened the bidding with 1♥ and receives the lead of the ♣K. Since South cannot profitably discard on the ♣A, he ruffs the first round, draws the outstanding trump and leads a low diamond toward the queen. If West goes up with the ace, declarer subsequently discards two hearts on the ♦Q and ♣A, while if West withholds the ♦A, declarer discards his losing diamond on the ♣A and loses only one heart trick. Alternatively, had declarer judged that East held the ♦A, he could have couped that defender by leading a low diamond toward his king.

MOSCITO. A system devised by Paul Marston and Stephen Burgess. The first four letters are an acronym for Major-Orientated Strong Club. It makes extensive use of the SYMMETRIC RELAY in auctions where the opening side has the balance of power.
It was originally a STRONG-PASS system, but in 1992 this is the opening-bid structure for the first or second position:
Pass: 0-5 points when not vulnerable; if vulnerable, you may also pass with 6-9 if not at least 5-4 in two suits.
1♣: 15-plus points, any shape
1♦: 10-14 points with no four-card major suit

1♥: 10-14 points, four or more hearts, fewer than four spades; may have a longer minor on the side
1♠: 10-14 points, four or more spades, fewer than four hearts; may have a longer minor on the side
1NT: 10-14 points, at least 4-4 in the majors; may be unbalanced
2♣: non-vulnerable: any 6-9 that isn't right for another of the two-openings
vulnerable: 6-9 with clubs and hearts
2♦: 6-9 with diamonds and spades
2♥: 6-9 with hearts and spades
2♠: 6-9 with clubs and spades
2NT: 6-9 with clubs and diamonds
If the responder has at least game ambitions opposite any of the opening bids, he makes a relay response. Otherwise he tries to consume as much bidding space as possible.
In the third and fourth positions, the point ranges increase because the responder's hand is so limited by virtue of his original pass.

MOSHER. The whimsical name for the "convention" in effect over the opponents' 1NT opening when all overcalls are natural: 2♣ shows clubs, 2♦ shows diamonds and so forth. Named for Robert Mosher.

MOTT-SMITH TROPHY. This trophy is awarded every year to the player with the best overall individual performance record in the American Contract Bridge League Spring North American Bridge Championships. Donated by friends in memory of Geoffrey Mott-Smith in 1961, it was made retroactive to 1958 to include all the winners. For winners see Appendix II.

MOVE. The change of seats in duplicate bridge after a round has been completed.

MOVEMENT. A schedule of progression for players, indicating the seat to be occupied and the boards to be played by each player at each round. The Tournament Director announces the movement to be followed, which is usually arranged to provide each contestant with different opponents at each round.
Specific movements in common use are listed under the following headings: AMERICAN WHIST MOVEMENT; HOWELL MOVEMENT; MITCHELL; SCRAMBLED MITCHELL; SHORT HOWELL; THREEQUARTER (Howell) MOVEMENT; WEB MOVEMENT; SHOMATE; RAINBOW.

MOVEMENT CARDS. Large plastic cards placed on the table during a pairs event, or perhaps an individual, indicating the player numbers and the board numbers for each round of play, with the movement of players at the end of the round. Essential for HOWELL movements and some others.

MOYSIAN FIT. A contract in which declarer's trump suit is divided 4-3, usually thus described when the selection is made deliberately. Named for Alphonse Moyse Jr. whose ardent advocacy of this choice was part of his case in favor of opening four-card majors and raising with three trumps.

MUD. A lead convention in which the original lead from three small cards is the middle one, followed in play by the higher. The name is the acronym of middle, up, down, the order in which the cards are played. See THREE SMALL CARDS, LEAD FROM.

MULTI. The Multi is a 2♦ opening bid showing a weak two-bid in either major, though some pairs tag on stronger types too, such as a big balanced hand, or a big 4-4-4-1, or a strong two-bid in a minor.

This opening made its first appearance at the end of the 1960s. It was devised by Terence Reese and Jeremy Flint, with input from such players as Robert Sheehan, Jonathan Cansino and Irving Rose.

Even if it is possible that the opener may have a strong hand-type, the responder assumes he is opposite a weak two-bid and makes his first bid based on his fit for the majors. His possible actions are:

a. 2♥: The responder wishes to play in 2♥ opposite a weak two-bid in that suit. The responder may be doing anything from passing to bidding a slam if the opener actually has spades. The key aspect is the strength of the responder's hand. If he has a good hand yet bids only 2♥, he must be short in hearts. If he has a weak hand, he might have length in both majors and does not wish to get to the three level.

b. 2♠: The responder wishes to stop in 2♠ opposite spades, but to bid at least 3♥ opposite that suit. Note that this bid strongly suggests shortage in spades and length in hearts. This is important to remember both when devising a defense and when defending if the responder should become the declarer.

c. 2NT: This is the forcing inquiry, similar to a 2NT response opposite a normal weak two-bid, except that the opener must describe not only his strength but also his suit. The bid is made with a hand willing to go to at least the three level opposite a minimum weak two-bid. But especially if the 2♦ opening bid cannot contain a strong hand, 2NT might occasionally be a semi-psychic response with length in both majors and a weak hand.

d. 3♣/♦: Either highly invitational or forcing, by partnership agreement.

e. 3♥/♠: Usually these bids are "correctable." In other words, the opener passes with the bid suit or corrects to the other suit at the minimum level (or, perhaps, jumps to 4♠ over 3♥ with a maximum).

f. 3NT: To play (though in the original Reese-Flint version it indicated a very strong minor two-suiter with at most four losers).

g. 4♣: Asking the opener to bid one below his suit: 4♦ with hearts and 4♥ with spades. This allows the responder to play in game in the suit.

h. 4♦: Asking the opener to bid his suit.

i. 4♥/♠: To play regardless of the opener's suit.

Note that a pair may have alternative interpretations for some of these bids.

Advantages of the Multi

One of the key pluses of the Multi is that the opponents do not always know the opener's suit. This makes defense more difficult than against a simple weak two-bid, especially when they have no cuebid available.

A strong responding hand may be able to become declarer in the major, protecting a side-suit king or tenace from immediate attack.

It is possible to play in 2♦ when this is a better contract than two of the major.

The opening 2♦ bid frees 2♥ and 2♠ openings for other meanings. Perhaps they could be ACOL TWO-BIDS,

removing some strain from the overloaded 2♣ opening in Standard; 2♥ could be FLANNERY, or like the PRECISION 2♦ OPENING; 2♠ could describe a minor two-suiter, or a weak preempt either in a minor or in any suit; the other two-bids may be used to show weak two-suiters with at least five cards in each suit.

Disadvantages of the Multi

The major drawback of the Multi is that sometimes the responder cannot make an immediate preemptive raise. For example, with a weak hand long in one major, the responder could jump to game in that major opposite a normal weak two-bid, but opposite a Multi he must assume his partner holds the other suit. Benito Garozzo says that he will not use the Multi as he is not willing to give up what he considers to be one of the best preempts in bridge: 2♠ - (Pass) -3♠.

By virtue of opening 2♦ rather than 2♥ or 2♠, the opponents have slightly more space to compete. And sometimes they will be able to double the major for penalties when they could not have done so against a normal weak two-bid.

Defenses to the Multi

This is complicated because all possible positions at the table must be considered. First of all:

Second Seat

There are several approaches that work. But there are two important aspects. First, you must act immediately with a decent hand. If you pass initially, waiting for the opener to define his suit, and then bid, your partner will assume you are balancing. Secondly, decide how you wish to play double, 2♥, 2♠ and 2NT; these choices will affect the rest of the structure.

Here are three workable schemes, which we will subhead under the meaning for an immediate double.

1. *Double is a takeout of a weak 2♠ opening*

Dbl: a takeout double of a weak 2♠ opening.

2♥: equivalent to a takeout double of a weak 2♥ opening.

2♠: natural.

2NT: balanced 16-19 points.

3 of a suit: natural (3♠ being stronger than 2♠, of course).

3NT: to play, probably based on a good minor: what is called a "tricks" hand.

4♣/♦: a strong hand with at least 5-5 in hearts and the bid minor.

4♥/♠: natural.

4NT: a big minor two-suiter.

With a minor two-suiter not strong enough to bid 4NT, either bid 3♦, planning to follow up with 4♣; or pass first and try to describe your holding later with an UNUSUAL NOTRUMP.

With a big spade-minor two-suiter, pass and bid four of your minor at your second turn. (If nervous, bid 2♥ immediately and hope to be able to express your two-suiter).

2. *Double shows a strong notrump*

Dbl: balanced 16-18 points, or perhaps a hand too strong for the non-forcing 2♥ and 2♠ bids.

2♥: equivalent to a takeout double of a weak 2♠ opener.

2♠: equivalent to a takeout double of a weak 2♥ opener.

2NT: minor two-suiter.

3 of a suit: natural.

3NT: to play: probably a "tricks" hand.

4♣/♦: a big major-minor two-suiter with the bid minor and either major.

3. *Double is two-way*

Dbl: either a balanced 13-16 points, announcing the values to contest the bidding but making no other guarantees, or a very strong hand: 19-plus points.

2♥/♠: natural.

2NT: balanced 16-18 points.

Rest: as above.

Fourth Seat

After the bidding begins (2♦)-Pass-(2♥/♠), fourth hand should remember that the responder has probably bid his shorter major. (As we saw above, this is definitely true if the response is 2♠ and probably true if it is 2♥.) The best approach is to make all simple bids including 2NT as natural (and four of a minor as above), except for one little ruse: a double should be two-way: it is either for takeout or for penalties. For example, after (2♦)-Pass-(2♠), fourth hand should double with either of these hands:

<table>
<tr><td>a.</td><td>♠ 3</td><td>b.</td><td>♠ K Q J 9 8 7</td></tr>
<tr><td></td><td>♥ K J 6 5</td><td></td><td>♥ 4</td></tr>
<tr><td></td><td>♦ A Q 8</td><td></td><td>♦ A Q 4</td></tr>
<tr><td></td><td>♣ K Q 9 8 5</td><td></td><td>♣ Q 10 9</td></tr>
</table>

This might appear to give the doubler's partner an insoluble problem, but it does not. The opener will clarify his suit by passing or correcting, and then the doubler's partner will know which double his partner has from his length in the opener's suit.

For example, it goes (2♦)-Pass-(2♠)-Dble-(Pass) and the responder holds either of these hands:

<table>
<tr><td>c.</td><td>♠ 3</td><td>d.</td><td>♠ K J 9 8 5</td></tr>
<tr><td></td><td>♥ 9 8 6 5 3</td><td></td><td>♥ 5</td></tr>
<tr><td></td><td>♦ A 7 6</td><td></td><td>♦ K J 7</td></tr>
<tr><td></td><td>♣ Q 9 7 6</td><td></td><td>♣ J 8 7 3</td></tr>
</table>

With hand c, it is obvious that partner has spades. The responder is short in spades and so are you. Just pass.

With d, though, you know partner has a takeout double. However, you are loaded with spades, so you pass, converting the double into one for penalties.

The only time the doubler's partner could have a problem is after (2♦)-Pass-(2♥)-Dbl-(Pass). The responder might have heart length in a weak hand. If unsure, the doubler's partner removes the double. If it was for penalties all along, the final result will probably be 3NT bid and made instead of 2♥ doubled and down some number.

Sixth Seat

You did not act immediately, but the bidding has returned to you, probably after (2♦) - Pass - (2♥/♠) - Pass (Pass). Now you are in a balancing position. Most actions will be natural, but there are two conventional bids you should consider. 2NT shows a minor two-suiter (and a particularly weak one if you could have bid an immediate 2NT as unusual). And three of a minor may be used to show a limited 5-5 in the bid minor and the other major. (Probably you should use these bids only if you couldn't bid an immediate 2 ♥ or 2♠ as natural.)

For example:

West	North	East	South
2 ♦	Pass	2 ♠	Pass
Pass	2NT: limited minor two-suiter		
	3 ♣: club-heart two-suiter		
	3 ♦: diamond-heart two-suiter		

Auction Continuations

In general, these are natural, except that over the 2♥ bid that acts as a takeout double of a 2♥ opening, it is logical to use a Lebensohl approach. An immediate response at the three-level promises values, and 3♥, either immediately or via the 2NT puppet, is a cuebid. (There is no

need to use Lebensohl over the double showing a takeout of spades because the doubler's partner — the advancer — has a 2♠ cuebid available.)

When the auction goes like (2♦) - 3♣ - (Pass), all bids by the advancer must be treated as natural. You have to pay off occasionally against the Multi.

MULTIPLICATING BOARDS. See TWINNING.

MURDER. See BENNETT "MURDER."

MURRAY CONVENTION. Devised by Eric R. Murray. See TWO-WAY STAYMAN.

N

NABC. North American Bridge Championships. See NORTH AMERICAN CHAMPIONSHIPS.

NAC. See NORTH AMERICAN CHAMPIONSHIPS.

NABC APPEALS COMMITTEE. The committee appointed at each North American Bridge Championship by the ACBL Board of Directors to hear appeals from rulings of directors or complaints as to conduct or ethics. The power and jurisdiction of this committee end with the end of the NABC tournament for which its appointment is made. See also COMMITTEE.

NAMYATS. A convention in which an opening bid of 4♣ promises a long heart suit and an opening of 4♦ promises a long spade suit. As most frequently used, opener promises a hand stronger than the normal direct opening of four of a major suit. Some pairs use the four-of-a-minor opening to show a weaker hand, or a hand with a solid major suit and nothing else.

Responder usually accepts the transfer by bidding four of opener's major. However, the bid of the next higher suit is available without getting the partnership beyond game, and can be used either as a retransfer, making opener the declarer, or as an asking bid.

The convention was devised as part of the Little Major system, and its name is a reversal of Stayman, who introduced the idea in the United States.

To defend against Namyats, players should discuss the meaning of a double, either of the Namyats bid or of a minimum response to it. It can be lead-directing, but it seems slightly better to use the double as take-out of opener's major, promising the other major.

For an alternative treatment see RUBIN TRANSFERS.

NATIONAL APPEALS COMMITTEE. See NABC APPEALS COMMITTEE and COMMITTEE .

NATIONAL AUTHORITY. The body which, in each country, has responsibility for sponsoring and promoting bridge in that country. For the names of such organizations, see entry under each country. Most national authorities are members of the WORLD BRIDGE FEDERATION. See NCBO. The national authority has jurisdiction over all competition in that country and APPEALS on matters of law and fact are taken to the group designated by the national authority to hear them. In the ACBL the national authority on matters of law is the LAWS

COMMISSION OF THE ACBL.

NATIONAL LAWS COMMISSION. See LAWS COMMISSION OF THE AMERICAN CONTRACT BRIDGE LEAGUE.

NATIONAL POINTS. See REGIONAL AND NATIONAL POINTS .

NATIONAL TOURNAMENT. A tournament which determines the winners of various events on a nationwide basis. In the ACBL there are three such tournaments held yearly, each with a different schedule of major events. In 1975 these were renamed North American Bridge championships. See CHAMPIONSHIP TOURNAMENTS; NORTH AMERICAN CHAMPIONSHIP.

NATIONAL TRUMP. The establishing by a governing body of a particular suit as trump at whist.

NATIONALS. A term for one of the NATIONAL TOURNAMENTS, now titled NORTH AMERICAN BRIDGE CHAMPIONSHIPS.

NATIONWIDE CHARITY GAME. See ACBL-WIDE GAMES. For results see Appendix IV.

NATURAL CALLS. Calls which reflect the character of the hand and suggest a possible final contract. A natural call is contrasted with an ARTIFICIAL CALL. However, some bids which have artificial meanings can be used as natural bids.

NATURAL FOUR NOTRUMP. See BLACKWOOD.

NATURALISTS. See SCIENTISTS.

NAVRATILOVA, Martina, tennis-player. On bridge: "Bridge is more than just a card game. It is a cerebral sport. Bridge teaches you logic, reasoning, quick thinking, patience, concentration and partnership skills." On winning: "Whoever said, 'It's not whether you win or lose that counts,' probably lost."

NCBO. National Contract Bridge Organization. A WBF term for any independent or self-governing country, in principle with at least 250 members. The membership of the WBF is 94 NCBOs.

NEAPOLITAN. A system devised principally by Eugenio Chiaradia, and played in many World Championship events by a group of Neapolitan players, which has included Pietro Forquet, Guglielmo Siniscalco, Massimo D'Alelio and Benito Garozzo. Since 1965 Garozzo, as the leading Neapolitan theorist, has gradually revised the system, renaming it the BLUE TEAM CLUB system. It is this version that became increasingly popular in the United States and was adopted as the official system of the SHARIF BRIDGE CIRCUS. See BLUE TEAM CLUB .

NEAPOLITAN FOUR DIAMOND CONVENTION. A form of delayed game raise used in the NEAPOLITAN SYSTEM. It is a jump bid which applies when a forcing jump in the intended trump suit is not available:

WEST	EAST	WEST	EAST	WEST	EAST
1♠	2♣	1♠	2♣	1♥	1♠
2♠	4♦	2♥	4♦	2♣	4♦
agrees spades		agrees hearts		agrees hearts	

See BLUE TEAM FOUR CLUBS-FOUR DIAMONDS CONVENTION.

NEAPOLITAN TWO DIAMONDS. See BLUE TEAM TWO DIAMONDS.

NEAR-SOLID SUIT. See SEMI-SOLID SUIT.

NEBULOUS DIAMOND see SHORT DIAMOND.

NEC SPONSORSHIP. At the 1989 World Championships in Perth, Australia, the World Bridge Federation decided, for the first time, to test corporate sponsorship of world championships in an effort to combat rising costs of staging the events. The Nippon Electric Corporation (NEC) of Japan, an international company specializing in communications and computer technology, was signed on for four years. The contract was later extended for two more years with a one-year option. Therefore in 1989, 1991, 1993 and 1995 the World Championships were designated NEC Bermuda Bowl and NEC Venice Cup World Championships. In 1992 the world championship events in Salsomaggiore, Italy, were named the NEC World Team Olympiad and the NEC World Women's Team Olympiad. In 1994 the world championship events in Albuquerque, New Mexico were designated the NEC World Championships. NEC sponsorship extended to world junior championships as well. The NEC World Junior Team championships were held in Ann Arbor, Michigan in 1991 and in Arhus, Denmark, in 1993.

NEGATIVE DOUBLE. The original name for a takeout double, in general use from 1915 to 1930, about which time the term informatory double became current, later superseded by the more descriptive take-out double. In 1957 Alvin Roth and Tobias Stone introduced a modern negative double into national championship play; what formerly was a penalty double of a suit overcall became a double for take-out. This feature of the Roth-Stone System was christened Sputnik, because the Russian space satellite dated from the same period, and the term is still sometimes used in Europe. The name was new but the idea was not; it had been used by Lou Scharf of the Bronx NY from 1937 on with various partners.

Almost all tournament players employ the negative double. The convention is simple and effective, and chances to use it occur frequently. The cost is negligible; it is still possible to penalize an opponent's overcall.

NORTH	EAST	SOUTH
1♦	1♥	Dbl
	or 1♠	
	or 2♣	

South has a hand on which no bid is satisfactory. He may lack the required length, strength or both to bid a suit at the two level.

A negative double can be made at the one level with as few as 7 points — after 1♦-1♥, on:

    ♠ K 6 4 2
    ♥ 7 4
    ♦ 7 4
    ♣ K J 7 4 2

A negative double may also be appropriate on a hand

worth an opening bid:

♠ A J 5 2
♥ 10 7 5 2
♦ K
♣ A Q 8 2

After 1♦-1♥, double and bid strongly later; hence, a 1♠ response can suggest a five-card suit (i.e., a suit that would welcome a raise on three-card support). Partnership agreement is a factor, however. Some players would bid 1♠ because a double would show length in the unbid minor only.

Following are auctions, with possible hands for the negative doubler:

NORTH	EAST	SOUTH
1♣	1♦	Dbl

♠ K 8 5 2
♥ A 8 5 3
♦ 7 5 4
♣ 7 4

Most pairs expect South to have at least four cards in any unbid major, and some require exactly four cards.

NORTH	EAST	SOUTH
1♦	1♠	Dbl

♠ 8 6 4
♥ A J 7 5
♦ 8 6
♣ K 10 7 4

♠ 8 6 3
♥ K J 10 5 3
♦ A 8 5
♣ J 4

♠ 9 6
♥ Q 10 8 6 4 2
♦ A 8 4
♣ Q 3

On the second and third hands, if North rebids in a minor, South can show hearts.

Although South promises heart length, not every South would have clubs, the other unbid suit, but South must be able to visualize a place to play whatever North rebids. South might avoid a negative double with:

♠ Q 7 5 4 2
♥ Q 8 5 3 2
♦ K
♣ J 4

because a 2♣ or 2♦ rebid by North would be uncomfortable.

NORTH	EAST	SOUTH
1♦	2♣	Dbl

♠ A J 8 4
♥ K J 8 3
♦ 8 6
♣ 8 5 3

♠ K J 9 6 4 2
♥ 8 5 3
♦ A 6
♣ J 5

South promises one or both majors, by partnership agreement. The second hand is an example of a one-suit negative double, but not all Souths would be willing to double with that hand. An opponent's overcall often makes it difficult for responder to handle one-suited hands. (See NEGATIVE FREE BID). But if South were a passed hand, he could comfortably bid 2♠.

NORTH	EAST	SOUTH
1♥	1♠	Dbl

♠ 8 6
♥ 8 5
♦ A J 8 3
♣ K 8 7 4 2

♠ 8 6
♥ 8 3
♦ K J 10 7 5 2
♣ A 7 4

South promises one or both minors, by partnership agreement. On the second hand, he can convert a club rebid by North to diamonds.

NORTH	EAST	SOUTH
1♣	2♥	Dbl

♠ K J 9 4
♥ 7 6
♦ A Q 7 3
♣ 8 6 4

♠ K J 10 6 4
♥ K 7
♦ K 7 5
♣ 8 6 4

NORTH	EAST	SOUTH
1♥	2♠	Dbl

♠ 7 6
♥ 8 5 2
♦ K 6
♣ A J 9 7 5 3

♠ 8 5
♥ 8 6
♦ K Q 8 3
♣ A J 9 5 3

Many Souths would bid 3♥ with the first hand.

NORTH	EAST	SOUTH
1♣	2♠	Dbl

♠ 7 6
♥ K J 9 2
♦ A Q 8 5 2
♣ 8 4

♠ 8 4
♥ A 10 8 5 2
♦ K 5
♣ K 8 4 2

Players should avoid a negative double when a good natural bid is available. South should bid 3♦ on:

♠ 7 5
♥ A J 8 5
♦ A K J 8 4 3
♣ 5

NORTH	EAST	SOUTH
1 ♦	2 ♥	Dbl

♠ 7 6
♥ 8 7
♦ A J 9 5
♣ K Q 8 5 3

♠ 8
♥ 8 5 3
♦ K J 10 7 5 3
♣ A 7 5

NORTH	EAST	SOUTH
1 ♥	3 ♣	Dbl

♠ Q 10 8 6 4
♥ 8 5
♦ A J 6 4
♣ K 5

In KAPLAN-SHEINWOLD, negative doubles are used after non-jump overcalls only and promise four cards in any unbid major. The strength is unlimited.

Most standard pairs use negative doubles only through the three level. Some use them after overcalls at higher levels, whether strong or preemptive, up to and including 4♦, or even 4♠. In these cases, the doubler is more likely to have general strength and less likely to guarantee length in the unbid suits. After:

WEST	NORTH	EAST	SOUTH
	1 ♣	3 ♠	?

some players would double with:

♠ 7 6 2
♥ A 6
♦ A K 9 4 2
♣ Q J 5

giving North-South a chance to reach 3 NT. (See CARD-SHOWING DOUBLE.) Opener is also more likely to pass a high-level negative double for penalty, since accuracy in constructive bidding is difficult. Therefore, if responder has support for opener's suit, he often prefers a shaded raise to a double.

Even at lower levels, experts are increasingly treating a negative double as an all-purpose flexible call rather than a call that promises specific suits. In 1990, a majority of experts thought that after 1♠-2♥, South should make a negative double on:

♠ K 6
♥ A 9 5 2
♦ 10 7 5 4 2
♣ A Q

rather than bid 3♦ or jump to 3NT.

A penalty double of an overcall is not available to responder if negative doubles are in effect. Responder may pass, however, in the hope that opener will reopen with a double (see below):

WEST	NORTH	EAST	SOUTH
	1 ♠	2 ♣	?

At equal or favorable vulnerability, South would pass with:

♠ 9 2
♥ A J 10
♦ Q 10 6 4
♣ K J 9 2

At unfavorable vulnerability, especially at matchpoint scoring, responder may decline to seek a penalty:

WEST	NORTH	EAST	SOUTH
	1 ♠	2 ♦	?

♠ Q 6
♥ J 8 3
♦ K 10 6 2
♣ A K 3 2

South would bid 3NT, expecting +630; prospects of beating 2♦ doubled four tricks for +800 are unclear.

By the same token, responder must strain to act when he is short in the overcaller's suit:

WEST	NORTH	EAST	SOUTH
	1 ♣	1 ♥	?

♠ K 9 5 3
♥ 8
♦ Q J 8 4 2
♣ 8 6 4

If South passes, West will probably raise hearts, making it harder for North-South to compete. Even if West passes, North may have heart length and hence sell out when North-South have a makable partial. South must tell his story with a double despite the slim values.

Reopening by the opening bidder:

WEST	NORTH	EAST	SOUTH
	1 ♠	2 ♣	Pass
Pass	?		

A common misconception is that North must not pass if North-South use negative doubles. North need not reopen with club length, since the possibility that South has a penalty double of 2♣ is ruled out; nor should North strain to reopen with a double if another action is more descriptive. In these examples, neither side is vulnerable:

♠ A J 9 5 3	Pass. South does not have clubs
♥ K 5	and did not raise spades or make a
♦ A 8	negative double.
♣ Q 10 8 3	

♠ A Q 8 5 2	Double. North has minimum high-
♥ K J 4	card values but ideal distribution.
♦ Q 9 5 2	
♣ 5	

♠ A Q 10 9 5	Cuebid 3 ♣.
♥ A K J 5	
♦ K Q 10 5	
♣ —	

♠ A K Q 9 6 3	Bid 2♠.
♥ K 5	
♦ J 8 5 2	
♣ 9	

♠ K Q 10 7 2	Bid 2 ♥.
♥ A Q 9 5 2	
♦ K 5	
♣ 4	

After a negative double, the opening bidder rebids according to the prospects of game. A cuebid is the only absolute force. A jump shift is invitational, not forcing.

With strength in overcaller's suit, opener can pass for penalty, but that action is rare, especially at a low level, since doubler's strength and distribution are unclear.

WEST	NORTH	EAST	SOUTH
	1 ♥	1 ♠	Dbl
Pass	?		

♠ 8 4 3
♥ A J 9 5 3
♦ A 6
♣ K Q 5
       Bid 2 ♣

♠ 8 4
♥ A K 8 5 3
♦ A 6
♣ K Q 8 3
       Bid 3 ♣, invitational.

♠ A J 5
♥ K Q 9 5 3
♦ A 5
♣ K J 9
       Bid 2 NT.

♠ 6 5
♥ A K J 5 2
♦ A K 7
♣ A J 3
       Bid 2 ♠

In the following auction, the meaning of North's second bid is open to debate:

WEST	NORTH	EAST	SOUTH
	1 ♣	1 ♠	Dbl
Pass	2 ♦		

Is North's 2♦ bid similar to a reverse, promising extra strength, or is it a simple placement of the contract? If South's double promises diamonds, North needs no extra strength to bid 2♦; if South promises only hearts, North needs a good hand. The answer also depends on North-South's opening-bid style; if South would always open 1♦ on a minimum hand with four cards in each minor, the 2♦ bid should suggest extra strength.

In Kaplan-Sheinwold, opener rebids as though responder had actually bid the indicated major:

WEST	NORTH	EAST	SOUTH
	1 ♦	1 ♥	Dbl
Pass	2 ♠		

North promises a minimum hand with four spades; to bid 1♠, North might hold only three spades; e.g.:

♠ A J 5
♥ 7 5 3
♦ A K J 3
♣ J 5 3

The negative double can be extended to many situations — for example, after a natural minor-suit overcall at the two or three level after a 1NT opening bid. A double would show support for one or both major suits, but would not be forcing to game (see LEBENSOHL).

In the following auction, most players would treat South's second double as for takeout.

WEST	NORTH	EAST	SOUTH
	1 ♥	1 ♠	Dbl
2 ♠	Pass	Pass	Dbl

South might hold:

♠ A 8 4
♥ 8 5
♦ A Q 7 3
♣ J 10 7 4

He has a good hand and wants to compete, but lacks a good bid. (See CARD-SHOWING DOUBLE.)

Defense against negative doubles

When right-hand opponent has made a negative double, the situation is similar to a bid over an opposing takeout double. A redouble shows high-card strength and may expose an opening psychic bid. A jump raise of overcaller's suit is preemptive. See also ROSENKRANZ REDOUBLE and PARKING LOT.

NEGATIVE FREE BID. A modern solution to a common bidding problem. Consider this situation:

WEST	NORTH	EAST	SOUTH
	1 ♣	1 ♠	?

South has:

♠ x x
♥ A Q x x x x
♦ Q x
♣ x x x

This is not strong enough in standard methods for a 2♥ bid, so the usual solution is to make a negative double, planning to bid hearts on the next round. But this may be difficult if spades are raised, and the negative double solution is not available if the suit is diamonds rather than hearts.

The alternative is to make a "negative free bid" of 2♥ on this hand, or of 2♦ if that suit is held. This is of course nonforcing. This obviously affects the use of the negative double. It is no longer needed for a hand that can make a negative free bid, but it is required for stronger hands that would normally make a forcing suit-response at a minimum level. Therefore a negative double followed by a new suit becomes forcing, indicating a hand with game values.

The negative free bid is not needed at the one level and is of dubious value at the four level. Many partnerships agree to use negative free bids at the two and three levels only.

NEGATIVE INFERENCE. Information deduced from a player's failure to take a specific action in the bidding or play. Though this type of inference is frequently available, it is often overlooked, the average player preferring to concentrate on more positive clues.

Here is a deal where the declarer was able to diagnose the location of a critical card based upon negative inferences gleaned from the bidding and play.

Dlr: South
Vul: N-S

	♠ A 10 8 2	
	♥ 8 4	
	♦ A Q 10 4	
	♣ J 6 4	

♠ K Q J 6 4		♠ 9 7 3
♥ A J 3		♥ K 10 6 5 2
♦ K 7 6 5		♦ 9 8 3
♣ K		♣ 9 3

	♠ 5	
	♥ Q 9 7	
	♦ J 2	
	♣ A Q 10 8 7 5 2	

The bidding:

WEST	NORTH	EAST	SOUTH
			Pass
1 ♠	Pass	Pass	2 ♣
2 ♦	3 ♣	3 ♠	4 ♣
Pass	5 ♣	All Pass	

West opened the ♠K, and the declarer won with dummy's ace. With the ♥A K to lose, declarer had to pick up both minor-suit kings. The percentages favor a finesse in the club suit; nevertheless he led a club to his ace at trick two, dropping West's king. A successful diamond finesse gave him 11 tricks.

Declarer *guessed* the club position well. He reasoned that if West had held both top hearts he would surely have led one in order to inspect the dummy and judge the best continuation. The absence of a heart lead therefore marked East with a high heart — if he held the ♣K in addition he would have responded on the first round. The only hope, therefore, was that West held a singleton king. See also INFERENCE.

NEGATIVE RESPONSES. Artificial responses that show weakness. Examples are: a 2NT response to a FORCING TWO or an ACOL TWO; a 1♦ or 2♦ response to an artificial 1♣ or 2♣ opening; or a 2♥ response to an artificial 2♦ opening. See also DOUBLE NEGATIVE; HERBERT NEGATIVE; SECOND NEGATIVE RESPONSE AFTER ARTIFICIAL FORCING OPENING. For natural negative responses, see WEAKNESS RESPONSE.

NEGATIVE SLAM DOUBLE. See DOUBLE FOR SACRIFICE .

NEPAL BRIDGE ASSOCIATION.
Secretary 1992:
   Dasarath Sports Complex
   Tripureswore
   Kathmandu, Nepal.

NET SCORE. The result of a rubber of bridge or of CHICAGO after the losing side's score is subtracted from the winning side's score. In rounding off to the nearest 100, 50 points counts as an extra 100 in the United States, but is dropped in England.

The term is also used in team matches to designate the difference between the scores of two teams at the end of a session or a match; it can be expressed in total points or in INTERNATIONAL MATCHPOINTS.

NETHERLANDS ANTILLES BRIDGE ASSOCIATION (Bridge Bond Nederlandse Antillen). The League was founded in 1963 to represent Curacao and Aruba, but Aruba has been a separate organization since 1985. There are 80 members in two clubs. The Association has hosted CAC Championships.
Officers 1993:
   President: Elly van Vliet
   Secretary: Siem van den Ende
   Brakkeout Ariba 4, Curacao, Netherlands Antilles.
   Telephone: (599) 9 674156
   Fax: same

NETHERLANDS BRIDGE LEAGUE (Nederlandse Bridge Bond). The League was founded in 1930 by the late A.J.E. Lucardie, and in 1993 had 88,320 members, 2nd largest in the world. The NBB is located in Utrecht, where it founded the National Bridge Centre. The League hosted the World Pair Olympiad in 1966, the World Team Olympiad in 1980, the European Championships in 1932, 1939 and 1955, the European Junior Championships in 1972 and the World Junior Championship in 1987. Dutch players have won two world titles, one European title, and won medals on 11 other occasions. Due largely to a beginners course based on a uniform, didactically sound bidding system, the League doubled its membership from

40,000 to 80,000 in the eighties. It organizes bi-annual courses for tournament directors and bridge teachers. Most international championships are under the technical control of Dutch supervisors.
Officers, 1993:
   President: André Boekhorst
   Secretary: Ybo Buruma
   Willem Dreeslaan 55, 3515 GB Utrecht,
   The Netherlands.
   Telephone: 31 30 71 26 44.
   Fax 31 30 71 14 82.

NEUTRAL CARDS. See CARDS, NEUTRAL AND POSITIVE .

NEUTRAL LEAD. See PASSIVE LEAD.

NEUTRAL SUIT. See ASTRO.

NEW DEAL. A fresh deal to take the place of a misdeal or to replace a deal voided for any reason.

NEW ENGLAND RELAY. See STAGGER MOVEMENT.

NEW MINOR FORCING (Unbid Minor-Suit Force). After opener's rebid of 1NT, responder often finds it useful to have available a low-level forcing bid, either to inquire about opener's support for responder's suit, or to make responder's description of his own hand flexible. Some pairs thus use a 2♣ rebid by responder as the only force after a 1NT rebid; others use a 2♣ rebid as Stayman on the second round. The most popular modern method, however, is the use of the unbid minor suit as responder's forcing call; when the opening bid was 1♣, this approach allows responder to sign off in his partner's suit.
   Suppose the auction is:

WEST	EAST
1 ♣	1 ♥
1NT	2 ♦

with 2♦ artificial and forcing. The meaning of West's third bid may depend on partnership agreement. One possible scheme:

   2 ♥ = minimum hand with three hearts.
   2 ♠ = minimum hand with fewer than three hearts, or natural if the 1NT rebid may have concealed a four-card spade suit.
   2NT = maximum hand, fewer than three hearts.
   3 ♣ = natural, five-card suit.
   3 ♦ = maximum hand, fewer than three hearts, no diamond stopper.
   3 ♥ = maximum hand with three hearts.
After a 1♠ response:

WEST	EAST
1 ♦	1 ♠
1NT	2 ♣

   2 ♦ = natural, five-card suit.
   2 ♥ = natural, four-card suit.
   2 ♠ = minimum hand with three spades; does not deny a four-card heart suit.
   2NT = fewer than three spades, no other attractive rebid.
   3 ♣ = maximum, fewer than three spades, no club stopper.
   3 ♠ = maximum hand with three spades.
Many pairs use the bid of the other minor on invita-

tional hands; others use it to create a game force, and then all second-round jumps by responder are invitational, not forcing. In the auction 1♦-1♠, 1NT-3♥, responder probably has a five-card suit.

For related devices, see COLE, CROWHURST CONVENTION, FOURTH SUIT FORCING, TWO-WAY STAYMAN AFTER ONE NOTRUMP REBID, NEGATIVE FREE BIDS, UNBID MINOR FORCING.

NEW SOUTH WALES SYSTEM. A variation of the VIENNA SYSTEM formerly used by Richard Cummings and Tim Seres and other Australians. The principal features are five-card openings in diamonds, hearts, and spades, strong 1NT openings, weak two-bids in the major suits. The 2♣ opening, which is used sparingly, is game forcing; the 2NT opening shows a strong minor two-suiter, and the 2♦ opening shows a balanced hand with at least 21 HCP. A forcing 1♣ opening is used for all other opening hands, e.g., long club suit, or a balanced hand worth 12-14 or 19-20, or a hand of any strength with 4-4-4-1 distribution. All responses in new suits are forcing, and jump shifts are used as modified CULBERTSON ASKING BIDS.

NEW ZEALAND CONTRACT BRIDGE ASSOCIATION. Founded by four clubs in 1936, and had 463 members by 1949. Now has 116 clubs with a total member ship of about 20,000. New Zealand has competed in five World Team Olympiads and four Bermuda Bowls, won Far East Teams 1990; Far East Women's Teams 1976, 1981, 1983; zonal "test match" against Australia 1979, 1981, 1983, 1985, 1987.

President A.G.Turner
Secretary Mrs. S.G.Truman
    P.O. Box 12116, Wellington, New Zealand.

NEW ZEALAND RELAY SYSTEM. See SYMMETRIC RELAY SYSTEM.

NEWGATE. A prison in London, England, where, prior to 1820, whist was played as a three-handed game with one hand exposed as the dummy.

NEWLY FORMED TABLES. These can be created with four to six players ranking according to precedence, this generally being established by order of entry into the playing room. Players leaving an existing table to cut into the new table have lowest precedence. See RUBBER BRIDGE.

NINE or NINE-SPOT. That card ranking sixth highest in a suit, and being between the 10 and 8 in position.

NINE TABLES. At duplicate, nine tables provide for competition among 36 players as individuals, 18 pairs or nine teams-of-four.

As an individual, the IRREGULAR RAINBOW is recommended. It is similar to the movement given under EIGHT TABLES, regular except for the first round.

As a pair event, MITCHELL, THREE-QUARTER (Howell) MOVEMENT or SHORT HOWELL movements may be used. In the Mitchell game, either eight or nine rounds of three boards each can be played.

A nine-table Mitchell, intending 27 boards, can be cut to 24 late in the play by instructing players to omit the first board on round 7, the second board on round 8, and

the third board on round 9.

As a team-of-four event, nine tables provide an excellent movement for meeting each of the other teams in an uninterrupted team-of-four progression, boards going to the next lower numbered table, and players skipping a table toward the lower number. The Swiss Team movement does not work well for nine tables. It requires three-way matches, and bad pairings may become necessary in the late rounds. For 8° or 9° tables, see HALF TABLES.

NO BID. A term meaning "pass", standard in England and some other English-speaking countries such as Australia and New Zealand where there is some likelihood of confusion in the enunciation of pass and hearts. The term has been generally accepted by custom, but does not appear in the official Laws and is subject to the warning (see LAW 74C) against use of different designations for the same call. Regulations for international play may specifically bar the term because it may be mistaken for another call, e.g., double.

NO CALL. An obsolete and inaccurate term occasionally used instead of PASS.

NONFORCING. A bid which does not require a response from partner.

NONFORCING SEQUENCES. A sequence which permits either member of the partnership to drop the bidding. A sequence starting with a suit bid can be assumed to be nonforcing unless it is listed under FORCING SEQUENCES.

Before passing a nonforcing sequence, a player should satisfy himself that a game contract is unlikely to be a sound proposition. He should also be sure that he cannot convert safely to a superior partscore.

NONFORCING STAYMAN. See STAYMAN.

NONMASTER PAIRS. See KEM CARD TROPHY.

NONMATERIAL SQUEEZES. Nonmaterial squeezes are squeezes against strategic values, rather than material values, such as winners or guards to winners. Nonmaterial squeezes operate against cards that are apparently idle, but actually perform a vital function, such as prevention of a throw-in, or protection of the defender's communications.

Dlr: East	♠ 7 4 2	
Vul: None	♥ A 8 6 5	
	♦ Q 3	
	♣ A Q 7 3	

♠ 5 3		♠ K J 10 8 6
♥ J 9 3		♥ Q 10 7 2
♦ K 9 6 5		♦ A 4 2
♣ J 6 5 2		♣ 9

	♠ A Q 9
	♥ K 4
	♦ J 10 8 7
	♣ K 10 8 4

WEST	NORTH	EAST	SOUTH
		Pass	1 ♦
Pass	1 ♥	1 ♠	1NT
Pass	3NT	All Pass	

Lead: ♠ 5

South wins the first spade, and he unblocks clubs by leading the ♣8 to dummy's ♣A. The ♣3 is returned to the ♣K, as East discards a diamond. Now the ♣10 is led and East is squeezed. If East throws a spade, it is safe to establish diamonds. A heart discard allows declarer to establish a long heart in dummy which can be reached with a fourth round club entry. And another diamond discard allows declarer to establish that suit, since East must take his now singleton ♦A before the spades have been established.

NONPLAYING CAPTAIN. See CAPTAIN.

NONVULNERABLE. The condition of a side that has not won a game in a rubber of bridge. In CHICAGO or four-deal bridge, each pair is nonvulnerable twice; that is to say, on the first deal and on either the second or third deal depending on local rules as respects dealer's vulnerability. In duplicate, deals or "boards" are marked according to vulnerability so that each tray clearly displays the vulnerability conditions, whether they be all nonvulnerable, or either side or neither side. When a pair is not vulnerable, it can bid with slightly more freedom than when vulnerable, because the schedule of penalties for undertricks is set up so as to levy more severe punishment on vulnerable pairs that incur penalties. Frequently then, it will be found that a nonvulnerable pair will "take a save" rather than allow the opposition to make a game, the premium for which can be quite high, especially, if, conversely, the team scoring the game is vulnerable. See LOVE ALL.

NORDIC CHAMPIONSHIPS. Organized in 1946 by delegates from the bridge federations of Denmark, Norway, Sweden and Finland, meeting at Copenhagen. The Nordic Championships represented one of the first postwar efforts to revive international bridge competition in Europe. The initial tournament was staged later the same year in Oslo, and the Championships were held on an annual basis until 1949. Iceland joined the competition in 1949 and has been a regular participant ever since. After the revival of the European Championships, the importance of a separate Nordic competition lessened, so the event became a biennial competition, except for a three-year lapse from 1959-62. It usually is played in Rottneros, Sweden. For results, see Appendix IV.

NORMAL EXPECTANCY. The holding in either high cards or distribution which a player might expect in partner's hand when he decides whether to open the bidding. For an unpassed partner, this can be roughly approximated as one-third of the missing high cards or high-card points, and one-third of the remaining cards in the suit. Partner's responses and future actions modify this concept as the bidding progresses. See SUIT COMBINATIONS and TRUMP SUPPORT for further treatment.

NORMAN FOUR NOTRUMP. A slam convention in which kings and aces are shown with one bid. An ace is counted as 1 point and a king as ° point, and responses are according to the following table:

5 ♣	less than 1° points
5 ♦	1° points
5 ♥	2 points
5 ♠	2° points
5NT	3 points, etc.

The 4NT bidder can usually determine which aces and kings are held by responder. This convention has been popular in England, where it is credited to Norman De Villiers Hart and Sir Norman Bennet, and was incorporated into the VIENNA SYSTEM. Several similar methods have been used in America, but only the SAN FRANCISCO convention achieved any substantial following. Similar responding principles are used in the BLUE TEAM CLUB System and by some players after an artificial 2♣ opening.

NORTH. A position in a bridge foursome or in a bridge diagram opposite South and to the left of West. In duplicate games the scoring is usually done by North, a matter designated by the Sponsoring Organization. In newspaper columns North is usually the dummy.

NORTH AMERICAN BLUE RIBBON PAIRS CHAMPIONSHIP. See CAVENDISH TROPHY; BLUE RIBBON PAIRS. For results see Appendix I.

NORTH AMERICAN CHAMPIONSHIP. The awards in major events at the three principal tournaments of the AMERICAN CONTRACT BRIDGE LEAGUE, which embraces the United States, Canada, Mexico and Bermuda, are the NORTH AMERICAN BRIDGE CHAMPIONSHIPS. Prior to 1975 they were known as NATIONAL TOURNAMENTS, with National champions. See also GRAND NATIONAL CHAMPIONSHIPS. The major championship events were allocated as follows in 1994.

Spring NABC events: VANDERBILT KNOCKOUT TEAMS, NORTH AMERICAN PAIRS FLIGHT A, NORTH AMERICAN PAIRS FLIGHT B, NORTH AMERICAN PAIRS FLIGHT C, OPEN PAIRS, OPEN PAIRS II (formerly MEN'S PAIRS), WOMEN'S PAIRS, MIXED PAIRS, OPEN SWISS TEAMS (formerly NORTH AMERICAN MEN'S SWISS TEAMS), NORTH AMERICAN WOMEN'S SWISS TEAMS, SILVER RIBBON PAIRS.

Summer NABC events: SPINGOLD MASTER KNOCKOUT TEAMS, WOMEN'S KNOCKOUT TEAMS, GRAND NATIONAL TEAMS, NORTH AMERICAN TEAMS, FLIGHT B, NORTH AMERICAN TEAMS, FLIGHT C. LIFE MASTER PAIRS, IMP PAIRS, MASTER MIXED TEAMS, RED RIBBON PAIRS, NON-LIFE MASTER SWISS TEAMS, NABC JUNIOR PAIRS, NORTH AMERICAN YOUTH PAIRS.

Fall NABC events: REISINGER BOARD-A-MATCH TEAMS, BLUE RIBBON PAIRS, LIFE MASTER OPEN PAIRS (formerly LIFE MASTER MEN'S PAIRS), LIFE MASTER WOMEN'S PAIRS, OPEN BOARD-A-MATCH TEAMS (formerly MEN'S BOARD-A-MATCH TEAMS), WOMEN'S BOARD-A-MATCH TEAMS, NORTH AMERICAN SWISS TEAMS, NON-LIFE MASTER PAIRS, NORTH AMERICAN 49ER PAIRS (NORTH AMERICAN ROOKIE PAIRS until 1991).

Winners of these events can be found under each tournament listing in Appendix I. Other events are held at each of the North American Bridge Championships that do not have major championship status, but for which the competition is no less keen.

NORTH AMERICAN BRIDGE CHAMPIONSHIPS. Name given in 1975 to the three AMERICAN CONTRACT BRIDGE LEAGUE CHAMPIONSHIP tournaments held each year for North America. (Formerly known as "NATIONALS.") Results are reported in Appendix I.

NORTH AMERICAN FORTY-NINER PAIRS. As the GRAND NATIONAL ROOKIE PAIRS (GNRP), this was a major ACBL pair championship established in 1979. In 1984 the GNRP became the North American Rookie Pairs. Competition was limited to ACBL members who had fewer than 20 masterpoints. The initial stage was conducted at the club level in the fall. Each district qualified one pair and a 26th pair was qualified at large to make 13 tables for a two-session final held during the Fall North American Bridge Championships. In 1991 the North American Rookie Pairs was changed to the North American Forty-Niner Pairs, open to ACBL members with fewer than 50 masterpoints. For winners see Appendix I.

NORTH AMERICAN GRAND NATIONAL PAIRS CHAMPIONSHIP. See GRAND NATIONAL PAIRS and Appendix I.

NORTH AMERICAN GRAND NATIONAL ROOKIE PAIRS CHAMPIONSHIP. See GRAND NATIONAL ROOKIE PAIRS and Appendix I.

NORTH AMERICAN GRAND NATIONAL TEAMS CHAMPIONSHIP. See MOREHEAD TROPHY and Appendix I.

NORTH AMERICAN LIFE MASTER MEN'S PAIRS CHAMPIONSHIP. See Appendix I.

NORTH AMERICAN LIFE MASTER PAIRS CHAMPIONSHIP. See VON ZEDTWITZ GOLD CUP and Appendix I.

NORTH AMERICAN LIFE MASTER WOMEN'S PAIRS CHAMPIONSHIP. See SMITH TROPHY and Appendix I.

NORTH AMERICAN MASTER INDIVIDUAL CHAMPIONSHIP. Formerly called World Master Individual or Life Master Individual. See STEINER TROPHY and Appendix I

NORTH AMERICAN MASTER KNOCKOUT TEAMS CHAMPIONSHIP. See SPINGOLD TROPHY and Appendix I.

NORTH AMERICAN MASTER MIXED TEAMS CHAMPIONSHIP. See BARCLAY TROPHY and LEBHAR TROPHY and Appendix I.

NORTH AMERICAN MEN'S BOARD-A-MATCH TEAMS CHAMPIONSHIP. See GOREN TROPHY and Appendix I.

NORTH AMERICAN MEN'S PAIRS CHAMPION-SHIP. See WERNHER TROPHY and Appendix I.

NORTH AMERICAN MEN'S SWISS TEAMS CHAMPIONSHIP. See Appendix I.

NORTH AMERICAN MIXED PAIRS CHAMPION-

SHIP. See ROCKWELL TROPHY and Appendix I.

NORTH AMERICAN NON-LIFE MASTER PAIRS CHAMPIONSHIP. See Appendix I.

NORTH AMERICAN NON-LIFE MASTER SWISS TEAMS. See Appendix I.

NORTH AMERICAN OPEN BOARD-A-MATCH TEAMS CHAMPIONSHIP. See REISINGER MEMORIAL TROPHY and Appendix I.

NORTH AMERICAN OPEN KNOCKOUT TEAMS CHAMPIONSHIP. See VANDERBILT CUP and Appendix I.

NORTH AMERICAN OPEN PAIRS. This has been a major ACBL open pairs championship since 1979. Originally known as the Grand National Pairs (GNP), initial stages were conducted over the course of several months at club, unit and district levels. Each district qualified three or four pairs (determined by total entry in the district at the unit level) to the North American Final held at the Spring North American Bridge Championships. In 1987 the GNP became the North American Open Pairs Flight A and the North American Non-Life Master Pairs was established. For the 1992 contest, Flight A (unlimited masterpoints) remained unchanged but Flight B was added for players with fewer than 1500 masterpoints. The configuration for the North American Non-Life Master Pairs was slightly changed for the 1994 contest when it was determined that non-Life Masters with more than 500 MPs would not be eligible for the third flight. For winners see Appendix I.

NORTH AMERICAN OPEN PAIRS CHAMPION-SHIP. See CAVENDISH TROPHY; SILODOR TROPHY. See Appendix I.

NORTH AMERICAN OPEN SWISS TEAMS CHAMPIONSHIP. See Appendix I.

NORTH AMERICAN ROOKIE PAIRS. A major ACBL pairs championship known as the GRAND NATIONAL ROOKIE PAIRS from 1979-1984. In 1991 the NARP became the NORTH AMERICAN FORTY-NINER PAIRS. For winners see Appendix I.

NORTH AMERICAN RUBBER BRIDGE CHAMPIONSHIPS. A form of nationwide bridge competition conducted in 1962 and 1963 by North American Van Lines of Fort Wayne IN, in connection with their sponsorship of the TV series *Championship Bridge with Charles Goren*. Entrants formed groups for home play. Local winners advanced by stages to a national final.

NORTH AMERICAN SENIOR AND ADVANCED SENIOR MASTER PAIRS CHAMPIONSHIP. See MILES TROPHY and Appendix I.

NORTH AMERICAN TEAM TRIALS. See INTERNATIONAL OPEN TEAM SELECTION and Appendix I.

NORTH AMERICAN WOMEN'S KNOCKOUT TEAMS CHAMPIONSHIP. See Appendix I.

NORTH AMERICAN WOMEN'S PAIRS CHAMPIONSHIP. See WHITEHEAD TROPHY and Appendix I.

NORTH AMERICAN WOMEN'S SWISS TEAMS CHAMPIONSHIP. See Appendix I.

NORTHERN IRELAND BRIDGE UNION. The organization, founded in 1932, is the controlling body of Northern Ireland. By 1992 there were about 40 clubs affiliated with a total membership of about 2000. The Union belongs to the British Bridge League and participates in the CAMROSE TROPHY. It hosted the 1952 European Championships in Dun Laoghaire. For international participation, see IRISH BRIDGE UNION.
Officers 1992:
President: M. O'Kane
Secretary-Treasurer: William M. Kelso,
9, Upper Malone Road. Belfast, Northern Ireland.
Tel.: Belfast 668279.

NORWEGIAN BRIDGE FEDERATION (NORSK BRIDGEFORBUND). The Federation was founded in 1932, and by 1992 had a membership of 15,489 organized in 630 clubs in 46 districts. The National Open Teams attracts an entry of about 530 teams, and the National Open Pairs has had an entry exceeding 9,000. Norway was second in the European Championship in 1938 and 1969, was third in the 1970 Bermuda Bowl, and won the European Junior Teams in 1980 and 1990. Norway hosted the 1938, 1958 and 1969 European Championships in Oslo.
Officers 1992:
President: Per Bryde Sundseth
Secretary: Rolf J. Olsen
Postboks 7648 Skillebekk 0205 Oslo, Norway.
Tel. 47 22 43 13 56
Fax: 47 22 55 17 01

NOTRUMP. A denomination in which a player may bid at bridge. Notrump is the ranking denomination during the auction, being just above spades in precedence. One is required to take only nine tricks for game at notrump, since the first trick over book of six counts for 40 points and the subsequent tricks for 30 points each as in a major suit. As the name implies, contracts at notrump are played without a trump suit; the play therefore is entirely different from that of suit contracts, one of the chief differences being that declarer while planning his line of play attempts to count winners rather than losers. At notrump, a primary concern of the side contracting for game or partial is that there be stoppers in the suits bid or held by the opponents. More game contracts are played at notrump than at any other denomination. In Britain it is normal to use two words and pluralize the second: "No trumps". The hyphenated form, "no-trump" is a rare compromise.

NOTRUMP BIDDING. The standard pointcount is particularly effective in its application to notrump bidding. A partnership aims to reach 3 NT with 26 points in high cards in the combined hands, and is prepared to play in game with 25. Similarly, 6 NT should be reached with 34 points, and 33 points will offer a fair play. Different aspects of this subject are under: DYNAMIC NOTRUMP; EXPECTED NUMBER OF CONTROLS IN BAL-ANCED HANDS; FIVE NOTRUMP OPENING; FOUR NOTRUMP OPENING; GERBER CONVENTION; GLADIATOR; JACOBY TRANSFER; ONE NOTRUMP OPENING; ONE NOTRUMP RESPONSE; OPENER'S REBIDS; RESPONDER'S REBIDS; SHARPLES; SIX NOTRUMP OPENING; SOUTH AFRICAN TEXAS; STAYMAN; TEXAS; THREE NOTRUMP OPENING; THREE NOTRUMP RESPONSE; THREE-QUARTER NOTRUMP; TWO NOTRUMP OPENING; TWO NOTRUMP RESPONSE; TWO-WAY STAYMAN; WEAK NOTRUMP; WEISSBERGER; WOODSON TWO-WAY NOTRUMP.

NOTRUMP DISTRIBUTION. A hand distribution suited to notrump play rather than a suit because of its balanced pattern. The three most common distributions are: 4-3-3-3, 4-4-3-2, 5-3-3-2. Occasionally 5-4-2-2 or 6-3-2-2 is considered a notrump pattern.

NOTRUMP OPENING. See ONE NOTRUMP OPENING; TWO NOTRUMP OPENING; THREE NOTRUMP OPENING; FOUR NOTRUMP OPENING; FIVE NOTRUMP OPENING; SIX NOTRUMP OPENING.

NOTRUMP OVERCALL. See ONE NOTRUMP OVERCALL; TWO NOTRUMP OVERCALL; THREE NOTRUMP OVERCALL; FOUR NOTRUMP OVERCALL; UNUSUAL NOTRUMP.

NOTRUMP PLAY. Play and defense in notrump contracts are discussed in many of the headings listed under DEFENSE and DUMMY PLAY.

NOTRUMP RESPONSES TO SUIT OPENINGS. See 1 NT RESPONSE; 2 NT RESPONSE; 2 NT RESPONSE OVER OPPONENT'S TAKEOUT DOUBLE; 3 NT RESPONSE.

NOT VULNERABLE. See NONVULNERABLE.

NOTTINGHAM CLUB. A system popular in the English Midlands. The chief features are:
(1) 1♣ opening bid with 16-21 points; negative response, 1♦ with less than 8 points.
(2) 1♦ with 12-13 points and no four-card major suit. Minimum suit responses are nonforcing and show 0-11 points.
(3) 1♥ and 1♠, 12-15 points with five-card suit.
(4) 1NT, 13-15 points.
(5) 2♣, 12-15 points with club length.
(6) 2♦, forcing opening with 22 or more points.
(7) 2♥ or 2♠, 12-15 points with eight playing tricks.

NOVELS. See LITERATURE AND BRIDGE.

NOVICE. A new or inexperienced player. In the ACBL, a player with fewer than 20 masterpoints.

NOVICE GAMES. A method of promoting duplicate bridge among inexperienced players that has proved very helpful in stimulating interest and building up membership in duplicate clubs and the ACBL. At sectional and higher-rated tournaments, the novice game is often conducted as a special event. It is normally limited to players with fewer than 20 masterpoints. Sometimes there is a pre-game talk on duplicate techniques.

The novice program received a boost in 1965 when the ACBL introduced analyzed sets of hands for novices with sufficient printed analysis sheets for distribution to all participants. The analysis sheet permits the novice to compare his result with what could have or should have been done on the board, and is often used as a reference for an increasingly popular post-game show where four experts replay four, six, or eight of the novice deals on VUGRAPH. Analyzed novice sets are available from ACBL HEADQUARTERS at a nominal charge.

When the ACBL revised its club regulations in 1969, novice games became a regular feature of many of the ACBL sanctioned clubs.

NOVICE TABLE. An appendix table at a duplicate contest, usually a club game, where inexperienced players remain stationary, getting their boards from a table in the regular competition, relaying with the table to which it is appended. The players at the novice table keep their own scores, which can be entered on the recapitulation sheet on a separate line, matchpoints being awarded in relation to the scores in the regular game. No harm is done if the novice table does not play all the boards, so the regular game is not appreciably slowed up. As players become more familiar with the techniques of duplicate, they join the regular game.

The pamphlet "Easy Guide to Duplicate Bridge," in which the use of novice tables and NOVICE GAMES is more fully described, is available from ACBL HEADQUARTERS.

NPC. Nonplaying captain. See CAPTAIN.

NUISANCE BID. A bid made to hinder the opponents and dislocate the flow of their bidding.

NUMBER. Used as in *going for a number*. Number as used here refers to the high numerical value of a set that a competitor sustains (*e.g.*, 500, 800 & 1100). A number usually represents a loss, because it exceeds the value of the score the opponents could have obtained on their own by declaring the contract plus any bonuses that might be connected to the fulfillment of their contract.

NUMBER OF POSSIBLE HANDS, DEALS.
(1) The number of hands any named player can have is
$$\frac{52!}{39! \times 13!} = 635,013,559,600$$
(2) The number of hands a second named player can have is:
$$\frac{39!}{26! \times 13!} = 8,122,425,444$$
(3) The number of ways the remaining 26 cards can be divided is:
$$\frac{26!}{13! \times 13!} = 10,400,600$$
(4) The total number of possible deals is the three above numbers multiplied together, or
$$\frac{52!}{(13!)^4} = 53,644,737,765,488,792,839,237,440,000$$
These rather simple-appearing mathematical formulas for the first three are the number of combinations in which 13 items can be combined from a supply of 52, 39 and 26 respectively. The fourth figure is, as mentioned, the product of the other three. In each case the symbol "!" (read

"factorial") means that the number preceding it is multiplied successively by each smaller number down to 1. A rather elementary program enables a computer of sufficient scope to handle the arithmetic problem in a matter of seconds.

O

OBJECT OF THE GAME. The object of the game is to do the best one can with the cards one has been dealt on a particular deal, so that at the conclusion of the hand, one can feel the result well warranted by the efforts put into the planning and strategy of the hand. It is sometimes said that the immediate object when playing rubber bridge is to score game and rubber, so as to receive the scoring advantages thereto pertaining. Likewise, in CHICAGO, games should be bid, as there are substantial bonuses accruing as benefits. In duplicate, the object of the game is to score points on a particular deal or board and various factors have to be weighed so as to determine the way to obtain the best score. Through the years, however, there has been one school of thought that has consistently maintained that the object of bidding in contract bridge should be to bid in such a way as to get the opponents into a contract they cannot make, and then double and set them. The points thus built up can attain significant proportions above the line. Of course this was largely a rubber bridge theory, and one that does not necessarily pertain to four-deal games or duplicate. Objectives may be affected by considerations of partnership psychology. See RUBBER BRIDGE TACTICS.

OBLIGATION TO PASS. When a player bids out of turn, the Laws may require as a penalty that his partner must pass when next it is his turn to call, or for the duration of the auction. This is an "obligation to pass." If a player under such an obligation to pass makes a bid, double, or redouble, then both members of the offending side must pass for the entire auction. OBLIGATION TO PASS references may be found in many of the Laws #27 to 40.

OBLIGATORY. A term characterizing a play which cannot lose but may win a trick, when the situation is such that not to make the play will gain nothing and will lose the opportunity of making a trick that might otherwise be sacrificed, as an obligatory duck, an obligatory finesse, etc.

OBLIGATORY FINESSE. The play of a small card on the second lead of a suit in the hope that the adversary yet to play holds only the commanding card of the suit. The object of the play is to limit the number of losers in the suit when only two of the five honors are held. It is usually made when the position of the master card is marked, and the adversaries originally held five cards of the suit. Thus, in the following situation:

$$♠\,Q\,7\,4\,2$$
$$♠\,A\,5 \qquad\qquad ♠\,J\,10\,9$$
$$♠\,K\,8\,6\,3$$

if South leads toward the North hand, and the ace is not played by West, he puts up the queen and wins the first spade trick, and leads a low spade from North. When East plays one of his equals, South must play a small card in the hope that West originally held only one guard to the ace. This play can lose nothing, since if the cards are otherwise distributed at least two tricks must be lost in spades in any event. Hence, an "obligatory" finesse is a play which cannot lose but may gain a trick.

OCTAGONAL TWO-TRICK SQUEEZE. The ultimate in squeeze complexity is the octagonal two-trick squeeze. The following example, perhaps the only example, was constructed by Eric Mansfield of England. South is playing 7NT, and must succeed against any defense.

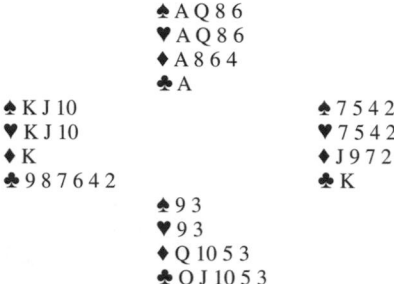

The following is Mansfield's analysis:

Whatever the opening lead, declarer's play is essentially the same and it is sufficient to follow the play after the lead of the ♣9. At Trick 2 declarer cashes the ♦A and finesses the ♦10 to reach this position:

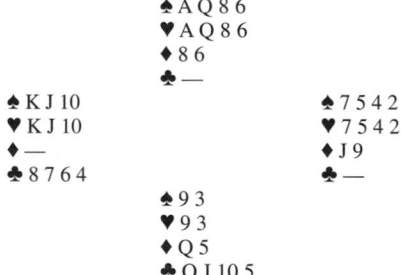

At this point all the opponents' cards are busy: the ♦Q would squeeze West and the ♣Q would squeeze East. The ♦Q lead is superficially the more attractive because West's discard immediately establishes another trick for declarer. However, a closer analysis shows that the ♦Q must be preserved a while because it is needed in its role of squeeze card and communication link. In the diagram position declarer therefore leads the ♣Q, discarding the ♦6 from dummy. East is squeezed: a diamond discard would immediately present declarer with an extra trick and enable him to operate a simple positional squeeze against West for his further trick. East therefore discards a major card which, because of their identical distribution, we may as well take to be the ♠2.

From declarer's viewpoint the continued presence of the ♠A-Q in dummy now becomes an encumbrance to his future plans and accordingly his next move is to finesse the ♣Q and cash the ♠A before returning to hand via the ♦Q to squeeze West in this position:

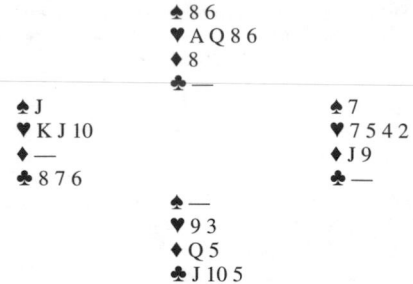

A spade discard by West would immediately present declarer with two extra tricks, while a club discard would enable declarer to squeeze him again in the major suits. West therefore discards a heart, thus promoting the ♥8 in dummy, and declarer continues by cashing his club winners to squeeze East again in this ending:

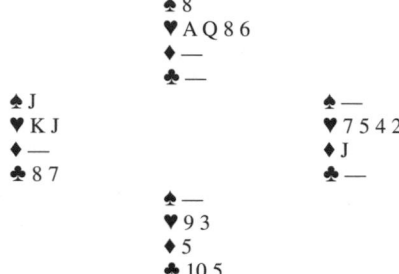

ODD-EVEN DISCARDS AND SIGNALS. A signaling method that assigns different meanings to odd- and even-numbered spot cards. An odd-card discard or signal encourages in that suit; an even-card discard or signal discourages and often doubles as a suit-preference signal (see SUIT-PREFERENCE SIGNALS).

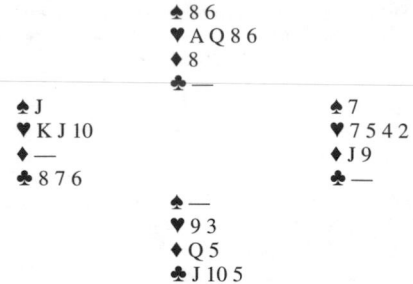

South is in 3NT, and West leads the ♠K. East plays the 8 to discourage and also (suit preference) suggests interest in diamonds instead of clubs.

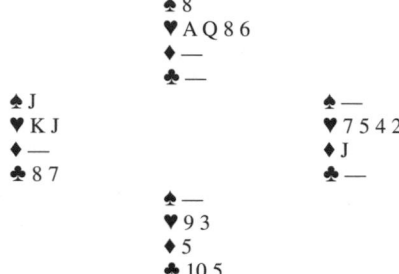

At matchpoint duplicate, South plays 4♠. West leads a trump, and South wins and draws trumps. On the second trump, East discards the ♥3 to encourage, and West will shift to a heart when he takes the ♣A.

Some partnerships use the odd-even concept in only limited circumstances; partnership agreement determines how extensive the use is.

Players using odd-even discards and signals hit a snag when no card is available to give the appropriate signal. The problem may be partially overcome by treating some even cards as more discouraging than others, and some odd cards as more encouraging than others. A 3, for example, may be a more encouraging signal than a 9; a 2 may be more discouraging than a ten.

Partnerships that use odd-even signals and discards (or any complex non-standard signalling method) must cultivate a high standard of ethics. A player must avoid taking advantage of information he receives from the speed or manner of his partner's play. See ETHICS and CONDUCT.

ODD TRICK. A trick won by the declarer, in excess of the first six tricks. The term is a holdover from WHIST, in which the winning of the odd trick was paramount.

ODDS, IN BRIDGE. Odds describe a ratio between two probabilities, the probability that an event (such as a player holding a particular card) will occur to the probability that it will not occur. If such a probability is expressed as a decimal, the alternate probability is the difference between totality (1), and that decimal. MATHEMATICAL TABLES, Table 4, shows the probabilities of distribution of cards between two hidden hands. It shows, for instance, that the probability that three outstanding cards will divide 2-1 is 78%. Expressing this probability in terms of odds on a 2-1 division are 78-22 or 39-11. The odds against a 2-1 division is the opposite (converse) of these figures, or 11-39, (which is the odds on a 3-0 division). Odds represent what would be a fair bet. Odds are often used to express the probability of two events that are mutually exclusive (cannot both happen at the same time, such as two winners in a prizefight). Thus in dealing with the division of four cards in a suit, Table 4 shows that the odds against a 2-2 division are 49.74 to 40.70 (approximately 5-4), provided that it is known that each opponent has at least one card of the suit. It should be noted that in this computation the possibility of a 4-0 split could be eliminated by one lead to test, and therefore odds could be expressed because there were left only two possible a priori divisions, 2-2 and 3-1. See MARBLES.

ODDS GOVERNING SPECIFIED CARDS. (For explanation of the notations used in this article, see MATHEMATICS OF BRIDGE, and SUIT, NUMBER OF CARDS IN.)

(1) A player can have $1C1 \times 51C12$ hands in which he holds the A. He can have the ace and three other spades in $1C1 \times 12C3 \times 39C9$ ways.

(2) If 26 cards are seen, of which n are spades, one of the other hands can have a singleton spade in $(13-n) C1 \times (26 = (13-n)) C12$ ways; that is, if six spades are seen, a singleton in an unseen hand can occur in $7C1 \times 19C12$ ways; he can have a named singleton, such as the Q, in $1C1 \times 19C12$ ways.

(3) A player can have n specified cards in $nCn \times (52-n) C (13-n)$ ways. He can, for instance, have the ♠A and the ♥K-Q in $3C3 \times 49C10$ ways.

(4) If 26 cards are known, the formula in (3) above, becomes $nCn \times (26-n)C(13-n)$.

(5) If there are an equal number of unknown cards in two closed hands, there is a 50% chance that a named card will be in one of those hands.

(6) When the entire distribution of a suit is known: (a) the probability that a named card in the suit is in a particular hand is proportional to the number of cards held in the suit; and (b) the probability that a named card of another suit is in a particular hand is proportional to the number of cards other than those of the suit whose distribution is known. As an example, if 10 spades are held by East-West, and East is known to hold six, and West, therefore, four, the chance that a named spade is with East is 60% (6 to 4). The chance that East holds a named card in some other suit is 43.75% (7 to 9), since there are seven vacant places (non-spades) in East's hand as against nine such vacant places in West's.

(7) The vacant places method (see [6] above) can be used in only two cases: (a) where the entire distribution of one or more suits is known; then the odds governing any of the other cards are accurately shown by this method; (b) where the play of an opponent shows RESTRICTED CHOICE. An example would be: with no defense bidding and an opening lead of the ♥Q from West. If we assume (see MATHEMATICAL ASSUMPTIONS) that this is from the ♥Q-J, and that West was certain to lead it, the odds on any other named card being with West are 11-13. (There are only 11 vacant places in the West hand, and 13 in East's.) In the above case, the assumption was made that declarer's side held the ♥A-K. If only the ♥A is held, then it must be assumed that East holds the ♥K, and there are only 12 vacant places in the East hand and the odds become 11-12 instead of 11-13. If East does not follow suit, the rule in (7)(a) applies because the exact distribution of hearts is known. If East follows suit with an insignificant heart, the odds change only very slightly, because it is possible to exclude only those distributions in which East was void of hearts. This is so small that the vacant places method is still accurate. A fallacy to be avoided is to argue that since East followed with a nondescript heart, there are only 12 vacant places in his hand, and the odds are 11-12 that a missing card is with West. The fallacy ignores the difference between significant and insignificant cards, for which see CARDS, NEUTRAL AND POSITIVE.

ODEN RULE, (from ODd-evEN). A rule devised by Alex Traub of South Africa to assist a declarer who must make a series of plays, often ruffs, and needs to end in a specific hand. If that is considered the master hand, the first trick must be won in the master hand if an odd number of plays must be made. If an even number of plays must be made, the first trick must be won in the non-master hand. Traub calls it the satellite hand, and gives the following example in his book "Trump Technique".

```
              ♠ J 9 4 3
              ♥ A J
              ♦ A 2
              ♣ A J 9 5 2
  ♠ 6 5 2                    ♠ 7
  ♥ 9 7 4 2                  ♥ K 8 6 5 3
  ♦ Q J 10 8                 ♦ 9 7 6
  ♣ Q 3                      ♣ K 10 8 6
              ♠ A K Q 10 8
              ♥ Q 10
              ♦ K 5 4 3
              ♣ 7 4
```

In 6♠, West leads the ♦Q and South wins with the ♦K. He finesses the ♣9, and East wins with the ♣10 and returns a diamond to dummy's ace.

South draws two rounds of trumps, and must then start a minor-suit cross-ruff. He wants to end up in his own hand to remove the missing trump, so the winning sequence of four ruffs must start with a diamond ruff. That conforms to the rule: an even number of plays must start in the non-master hand.

Similarly, if East returns a club at the third trick, South must win with the club ace and cash the diamond ace, enabling him to take the even number of ruffs and end in the master hand.

OFFENDER. The player who commits an irregularity. The laws assume that an offender commits the irregularity without doing so deliberately, and the penalties are devised in order to rectify such an error as equitably as possible. For a player to commit an irregularity, either with the intent of invoking a law to his advantage or with the intent of gaining or giving information improperly, is a violation of the proprieties of the game; it is unethical conduct and is not acceptable under any conditions. In duplicate bridge, Law 12 or Law 72 may be invoked.

OFFENSE. The attack. An offensive play or bid is an attacking move, as distinguished from a defensive play or bid. This is not to be confused with declarer or defender, since both of these must usually take offensive or defensive positions with certain suit holdings. Also, a breach of law.

OFFICIAL LAWS. See LAWS OF CONTRACT BRIDGE and LAWS OF DUPLICATE.

OFFICIAL SCORE. In duplicate bridge, the account prepared by the director (or under his supervision) which sets forth each contestant's score for each board, his score and rank for the session and for the event. The basis for the official score is the set of traveling scoreslips on which all the results for each board are recorded. Team scoreslips or other primary sources also can be used as the base for scoring. These primary sources are recorded on a recapitulation sheet, from which matchpoints and rankings are computed. It becomes the official score after the expiration of the correction period See LAWS (Law 79); PICK-UP SLIPS; RECAPITULATION SHEET; TRAVELING SCORESLIP.

OFFICIAL SYSTEM. A system of contract bridge bidding devised and endorsed by a group of leading American authorities in 1931-32. They opposed themselves to Ely Culbertson, while acknowledging their debt to him in certain areas of theory. Prominent among the group were Milton C. Work, Sidney S. Lenz, Wilbur C. Whitehead, Winfield Liggett Jr., and F. Dudley Courtenay. Other members of the Advisory Council included Shepard Barclay, Fred G. French, Henry P. Jaeger, Madeleine Kerwin and E.V. Shepard. Three of the principles which the Official System advocated in opposition to Culbertson have their place in the modern game: (1) the employment of the 4-3-2-1 count for notrump bidding; (2) the incorporation of an intermediate game invitation (nonforcing) suit bid of two; (3) the employment of an original opening forcing bid — the (artificial) TWO CLUB CONVENTION, designed not only for game but

also for slam bidding.

OFFSIDE. A card so placed that a finesse, if taken, will lose: "the king was offside."

OFFSIDE DOUBLE. A penalty double, usually of a game contract in a suit, based on an inference that the doubler's partner has trump length. The bidding must have made it clear that the declaring side is at full stretch, with borderline game values. For an example, see PENALTY DOUBLE.

OGUST REBIDS. See WEAK TWO-BIDS.

OLDEST CLUBS. The world's oldest clubs go back to the days of whist. The oldest is certainly the PORTLAND CLUB in London, England. It was founded before 1815 as the Stratford Club and reorganized under its present name in 1825. The second-oldest, and the oldest in the Western Hemisphere, appears to be the Hamilton Club in Bala Cynwyd PA, founded in 1887. The third-oldest seems to be the Continental Club in Amsterdam, the Netherlands, founded in 1889.

OLYMPIAD. Worldwide team competition at contract bridge, conducted by the WORLD BRIDGE FEDERATION. Contests have been held every four years since 1960. Two years after each Team Olympiad, beginning in 1962, an Olympiad is played with the main focus on pair play. See WORLD CHAMPIONSHIPS. The word "Olympiad" is a misnomer, since in Classical Greek it referred to a four-year period between Olympic Games. It is used in bridge to avoid any suggestion of connection to the modern Olympic Games. For results see Appendix V.

OLYMPIC. A name first applied in bridge in the sense of a contest of skill at contract bridge in which anyone may participate. The first AMERICAN BRIDGE OLYMPIC and WORLD BRIDGE OLYMPIC were promoted, sponsored and originated by Ely Culbertson in 1932. For results of this and other Olympics, see WORLD PAR CONTESTS and Appendix V. The term was modified to OLYMPIAD to describe WORLD CHAMPIONSHIP events conducted by the WORLD BRIDGE FEDERATION.

OLYMPIC PAR EVENTS. See WORLD PAR CONTESTS.

OMAR SHARIF WORLD INDIVIDUAL. The largest total purse ($200,000) in the history of bridge was at stake when the Omar Sharif World Individual bridge tournament was held in Atlantic City NJ May 7-10, 1990. This was the first time the ACBL sanctioned a cash-prize tournament. Winner of the $40,000 first place prize in the championship division was Zia Mahmood, Pakistani star who makes his home in New York and London. Fred Hamilton was second ($20,000) and P.O. Sundelin of Sweden was third ($12,000).

A swing of $28,000 occurred on this deal when Sundelin's partner pulled a wrong card, blowing a game contract and the first-place prize for Sundelin. Zia was North, Sundelin, West, and Peter Pender, a former world champion, was East.

Dlr: North	♠ 9 8		
Vul: N-S	♥ K 9 7 5		
	♦ A 3 2		
	♣ A Q 10 2		

♠ A K 5 4		♠ Q 10 6 3
♥ 8 4 3 2		♥ A J 10
♦ K Q 4		♦ J 9 8
♣ 9 5		♣ K 7 6

♠ J 7 2
♥ Q 6
♦ 10 7 6 5
♣ J 8 4 3

WEST	NORTH	EAST	SOUTH
	1 ♣	Pass	Pass
Dbl	Pass	2 ♣	Dbl
Pass	Pass	2 ♠	Pass
3 ♠	Pass	4 ♠	All Pass

South led a club and Pender, expecting Zia to win the ace, followed with a low club before he looked down and realized that — to maintain a link with his partner's hand — Zia had played the queen. Pender subsequently lost another club in addition to the expected heart and diamond tricks. Now the cold game, not bid by the majority of the field, was lost. Zia won the tournament and Pender's good friend and former winning NABC Men's Pairs partner, Sundelin, dropped from first place to third.

OMNIUM. A nationwide French tournament with many novel features, first played in 1963. The organizer was Irene Bajos de Heredia. Special decks with perforated edges were distributed to all playing centers, so that the players themselves could select the 13 cards needed for each deal by inserting a metal pin in the appropriate hole. The deals were pre-played but not "prepared". Scoring was on a basis similar to a PAR CONTEST, with awards for good and bad results in bidding and play according to the decisions of an expert panel.

ONE BID. A bid contracting to win one odd trick, or seven tricks in all. Articles appropriate to this heading are: BORDERLINE OPENING BIDS; CHOICE OF SUIT; ONE NOTRUMP OPENING; OPENING SUIT BID.

ONE CLUB ARTIFICIAL AND FORCING. Played in a variety of forms (see ONE CLUB SYSTEMS). The earliest in contract was Harold S. Vanderbilt's "Club Convention," although Robert F. Foster advocated a similar idea in auction.

ONE CLUB SYSTEMS. In an effort to reach the optimum contract, many players use systems which use an artificial opening bid of 1♣. Such systems discussed in this book are BANGKOK CLUB; BLUE TEAM CLUB; CANARY CLUB; CARROT CLUB; FRENCH CLUB; LITTLE ROMAN; MARMIC; ORANGE CLUB; PRECISION; RELAY; ROMAN; ROTH CLUB; SIMPLIFIED CLUB; TREFLE SQUEEZE; VANDERBILT; VIENNA.

ONE DIAMOND NEGATIVE RESPONSE TO ONE CLUB. In most bidding systems that use an artificial opening of 1♣ as a forcing bid, a 1♦ response is used to deny certain values. In some systems the 1♦ response denies certain point count; in others it denies a certain number of controls.

ONE DIAMOND STRONG ARTIFICIAL OPENING. See BIG DIAMOND SYSTEM; LEGHORN DIAMOND.

ONE NOTRUMP OPENING. The development of notrump bidding is discussed under APPROACH PRINCIPLE. Limit bidding and the Stayman convention combine to make one notrump a cornerstone of modern bidding methods. In considering an opening notrump bid, three aspects have to be reviewed.

(1) *Strength*. High-card points only are counted, but a five-card suit is worth a point, and the presence of tens can be taken into account. The standard range is 16-18, and alternatives are very rare at rubber bridge. In tournament play, on the other hand, the 16-18 range is obsolescent and there are many variations. These include: (a) 17-20. Used in the ROMAN SYSTEM. (b) 15-18. A relaxation of the standard range. (c) 15-17. The standard modern range. By including a 15-point hand the range for a 1NT rebid is reduced. The 18-point hand is then dealt with by a 2NT rebid (e.g., 1♣-1♥-2 NT). (d) 14-16. Once used in the LITTLE MAJOR SYSTEM, and now used in the modern style of PRECISION. (e) 13-15. Originally used nonvulnerable in the ACOL SYSTEM but now rare. An integral feature of the original version of PRECISION and some other BIG CLUB systems. 12-15 is sometimes used, allowing greater frequency but less accuracy. (f) 12-14. The usual range for a WEAK NOTRUMP, employed by many players using standard methods as well as the followers of the KAPLAN-SHEINWOLD and BARON systems. Some relax the requirements to include 11-point hands. (g) 10-12. A very weak notrump used most often in duplicate pairs tournaments. Some players use it only at favorable vulnerability, but others use it regardless of vulnerability. It is also the lower range of WOODSON TWO-WAY NOTRUMP. (h) 8-10. This extremely low range is called the KAMIKAZE NOTRUMP, and the bid is used only in duplicate pairs play. It is highly preemptive in nature. The ACBL Board of Directors has ruled that it is a conventional bid, and, no conventional bids, not even Stayman, can be used in conjunction with it. (i) Combinations. Two ranges, one weak and one strong, may be employed, depending on vulnerability and position at the table. The most common is 12-14 not vulnerable and 15-17 vulnerable, used in the Stayman System, the Acol System, and, with a different valuation method, in the original CULBERTSON SYSTEM. Some favor a weak notrump at all vulnerabilities in fourth position because a double is virtually impossible. See THREE-QUARTER NOTRUMP; WOODSON TWO-WAY NOTRUMP.

(2) *Distribution*. An orthodox notrump opening bid has one of the following distributions: 4-3-3-3; 4-4-3-2; or 5-3-3-2 with the five-card suit a minor. However, good players sometimes allow themselves the following exceptions: (a) 5-3-3-2 with a five-card major-suit, preferably in hearts. May be tried either because tenace holdings make a notrump contract particularly attractive, or because a 16-point hand is held. The latter is likely to create a rebid problem after a one-level response or a single raise. (b) 5-4-2-2. Two doubleton major-suit kings and a 16-point hand would be typical:

♠ K x
♥ K x
♦ K J x x
♣ A Q x x x

An opening bid in a minor suit would lead to a rebid problem after a major-suit response. (c) 6-3-2-2. In this case also the doubletons are likely to be strong, and the strength of the hand is likely to be a minimum or sub-minimum; 15 points is likely using a 16-18 range.

(3) *Location of strength.* There is a tendency to prefer a notrump bid holding tenaces, making it likely that the opening lead will be an advantage to declarer. Conversely, a notrump bid is unattractive with points concentrated in two suits:

♠ x x x   ♥ x x x   ♦ A K J   ♣ A K Q x

The concentration of honors in the minor suits would count against 1NT. On the other hand, a serious rebid problem will have to be faced after an opening of 1♣ and a one-over-one suit response. There is also a tendency, which some authorities make a rule, to avoid a 1NT bid holding a weak doubleton. The objection to this treatment is that it often creates a rebid problem:

♠ x x
♥ A J x
♦ A Q 10 x
♣ K Q x x

If the opening bid is 1♦ (or 1♣) the rebid will be difficult after any one-level response (except 1♣ - 1NT). For reasons of this kind many players open 1NT whenever the point-count and distribution are suitable, regardless of the location of the honor strength.

Responses to 1NT.

The structure of responses is independent of the range of notrump opening being used. There is one tactical exception when a weak hand faces a WEAK NOTRUMP opening. See WEAK NOTRUMP. The point-counts for following responses are based on a 15-17 notrump. When a different range is in use, the range for various responding bids must be adjusted accordingly.

(1) 2♣. Almost invariably STAYMAN. Occasionally, as when it is followed by a 3♣ bid, it proves to be natural after all. For subsequent bidding, see STAYMAN. See also GLADIATOR, PUPPET STAYMAN, and SKINNER RESPONSES TO A 1NT OPENING.

(2) 2♦. This bid is used frequently in both the natural and the conventional way. As a natural bid, it is not constructive, showing at least a five-card diamond suit and no interest in game. As a conventional bid, the two most popular methods are JACOBY TRANSFER BIDS and TWO-WAY STAYMAN. In the WALSH System, 2♦ also can be the beginning of a relay to show a strong minor.

(3) 2♥. A natural bid showing at least a five-card suit with no interest in game; but more often used in tournament play as a JACOBY TRANSFER BID.

(4) 2♠. Another bid that can be either natural or conventional. In a natural sense, it shows at least a five-card suit and no interest in game. Conventionally 2♠ can be MINOR SUIT STAYMAN, BARON, a transfer to 2NT or a transfer to 3♣ (FOUR-SUIT TRANSFERS). The transfer to 3♣ allows responder to pass and play there, to bid 3♦ as a signoff, or to make some other bid that would be forcing.

(5) 2NT. 8-9 points and relatively balanced if used naturally. The hand may contain a long minor suit, in which case the point-count requirement is reduced slightly. The 2NT bidder is unlikely to have a four-card major unless his hand is perfectly flat. The BARON System uses 2NT as a conventional forcing bid, asking partner to bid four-card suits up the line. 2NT is sometimes used as a takeout for the minors. See TWO NOTRUMP RESPONSE

(As a Relay to 3♣).

(6) 3♣. As a natural bid, 3♣ can be used three different ways — forcing, invitational or preemptive. Conventionally 3♣ can be a transfer to 3♦ or an EXCLUSION BID, showing shortness in clubs and support in all other suits — usually 4-4-4-1.

(7) 3♦. Like 3♣, this bid can have three meanings in a natural sense — forcing, invitational or preemptive. It also can be an EXCLUSION BID, probably showing a 4-4-1-4 distribution. It is also sometimes used as direct spinters showing 4-1-4-4, 4-1-5-3, 4-0-4-5, etc.

(8) 3♥ or 3♠. As natural bids, they can be either invitational or forcing, always showing at least a five-card suit. Opener usually bids game in either notrump or the major, choosing the major whenever he has three or more of the suit bid by responder. A rebid in a new suit at the four level is a slam try, showing an excellent fit for responder's suit, the ace of the suit bid and a maximum notrump. See also AUTOMATIC ACES; EXPECTED NUMBER OF CONTROLS IN BALANCED HANDS. But if transfer bids are being used, these bids are hardly needed, since a two-level transfer is normally the first move. Two special uses are: (a) 5-5 in the major suits, with 3♥ to show invitational values and 3♠ to show game values. (b) A long strong suit with slam interest and a void; opener must make a minimum bid, and responder shows his void, allowing opener to assess duplication. 1NT-3♥-3♠-3NT shows a spade void.

(9) 3NT. If responder's hand is balanced, his range is likely to be 10-14. But often he holds a long minor suit and less high-card strength. A minor suit of A-Q-x-x-x-x would justify a 3NT venture without any outside strength. A cautious player might use an invitational sequence to provide for the possibility that opener has a small doubleton, when game would no doubt depend on the success of a duck followed by a finesse.

(10) 4♣. This bid has no natural meaning. Conventionally it usually is GERBER, but it could also be SOUTH AFRICAN TRANSFER, requesting opener to rebid 4♥.

(11) 4♦. This bid also has no natural meaning. Conventionally it would be a TEXAS TRANSFER to hearts or a SOUTH AFRICAN TRANSFER to spades.

(12) 4♥ and 4♠. A bid closing the auction. Usually a six-card suit with at least 7-8 points but no slam interest. It might be a strong five-card suit if there is an outside singleton or void. 4♥ might be TEXAS, and if so 4♠ might be a freak minor two-suiter.

(13) 4NT. A balanced hand, usually 4-3-3-3 distribution, with 15-16 points. A natural slam invitation, and the opener may show suits at the five-level in the hope of locating a 4-4 fit.

(14) 5♣ or 5♦. A freak hand with a long, broken minor suit, probably seven or eight cards in length, and little honor strength. Bids of 5♥ and 5♠ are meaningless.

(15) 5NT. An IDLE BID in standard methods. Used by some experts as an invitation to 7NT, i.e., a hand slightly too strong to bid 6NT with 19-20. With a minimum, the opener must bid 6NT. Suits may be shown at the six level.

(16) 6NT. A balanced hand, probably 4-3-3-3 with 17-18 points. Closes the auction.

ONE NOTRUMP OVERCALL A direct overcall of 1NT shows a hand equivalent to a 1NT opening bid in standard methods: 16-18 points with balanced distribution. Individual partnerships may vary the range to 15-17, 15-18 or 16-19. A few play a range of 14-16 or lower.

Occasionally, a player may choose to overcall 1NT with unbalanced distribution:

♠ 5
♥ A Q 5
♦ A Q 7 3
♣ K J 6 4 2

If right-hand opponent opens 1♥, a 1NT overcall may be better than 2♣ or a trap pass on the hand above.

Since opener has suggested a long suit plus entries, a 1NT overcall is most attractive if overcaller has a source of tricks:

(a)	(b)
♠ J 6 3	♠ 10 6 3
♥ A Q 3	♥ A Q 5
♦ K J 6 3	♦ A 6
♣ A J 3	♣ K Q J 8 3

Hand (b) is a better 1NT overcall of 1♥ than hand (a). Overcaller also prefers secondary strength in opener's suit:

(a)	(b)
♠ K 6 3	♠ K 6 3
♥ A 6 3	♥ Q 10 6 4
♦ Q 10 6 4	♦ A 6 3
♣ A K 4	♣ A K 3

In (a), overcaller's heart stopper may be dislodged immediately, leaving the defenders with winners plus entries; the hand would make a more attractive 1NT overcall if the hearts were A-10-3. In (b), heart leads will actually help overcaller by setting up his secondary honors.

Responses by overcaller's partner. Partnerships should agree on one of the following methods:

(1) The cuebid in opener's suit takes the place of STAYMAN. A response of 2♣ is therefore natural and weak unless the opening bid was 1♣. A jump response in a suit is invitational to game, not forcing. In the absence of any discussion, these methods can be assumed.

(2) Overcaller's partner ignores the opening bid, responding exactly as he would have to an opening 1NT bid. 2♣ is always Stayman. A bid in opener's suit is natural and weak; if the opening bid was 1♦, responder may wish to bid 2♦ to play.

(3) Combining methods (1) and (2), overcaller's partner bids 2♣ as non-forcing Stayman and cuebids as forcing Stayman. Overcaller's side cannot play in clubs or in opener's suit, but overcaller has the tools to sign off, invite game or force to game.

(4) Overcaller's partner ignores the opening bid, responding as he would have done to 1NT, except when opener bid clubs. In that case, 2♦ is used as Stayman. This method permits overcaller's side to play in the opponent's minor suit, which may be desirable.

(5) Overcaller's partner uses transfer responses. A transfer into opener's suit takes the place of Stayman.

Action by the opening bidder's partner. A bid in a new suit at the two level is weak; responder is likely to have a fair five- or six-card suit with fewer than 9 high-card points. A jump to the three level in a new suit is weak and preemptive with a six- or seven-card suit. With most strong hands (9 or more points), a penalty double is appropriate. The only other strong action is a bid of 2NT (see CUEBID IN OPPONENT'S SUIT), which suggests a freakish hand, probably a two-suiter, unsuitable for defense.

When a 1NT overcall is doubled, the partnership can use whatever method it uses when a 1NT opening is doubled. See DEFENSE TO DOUBLE OF 1NT.

Some 1NT overcalls cannot logically be strength-showing. See UNUSUAL NOTRUMP and UNUSUAL 1NT OVERCALL. For 1NT overcalls by opener's right-hand opponent, see BALANCING.

ONE NOTRUMP REBID. A second call of 1NT by the opening bidder after a suit bid of one by responder. See OPENER'S REBID. For conventional actions by responder after the 1NT rebid see CROWHURST CONVENTION; STAYMAN ON SECOND ROUND; TWO CLUB REBID BY RESPONDER AS ONLY FORCE AFTER 1NT REBID; NEW MINOR FORCING.

ONE NOTRUMP RESPONSE. A bid of 1NT when partner has opened the bidding with a suit. The normal range for the bid is 6-9, but 10 is possible, particularly by a passed hand which does not wish to bid a four-card suit at the level of two. This assumes that 1NT is not forcing, but the subsequent developments are similar in the modern style. See ONE NOTRUMP RESPONSE TO MAJOR FORCING.

1♠ - 1NT, the most common situation, covers a wide range of hands. The responding hand may be quite unbalanced but unable to respond at the level of two:

♠ 3
♥ K 7 6 4 3
♦ K 10 8 7 2
♣ J 3

If the opener's rebid is 2♣, suggesting 5-4 distribution, responder should bid 2♦. (But see BART.) This does not exclude a heart contract, because the opener will continue to 2♥ with 5-3-1-4 distribution. If the opener rebids a lower-ranking suit at the two-level, responder should very rarely go beyond two of the original suit. When he does so, the reason is usually a fine fit for opener's second suit:

(a)	(b)	(c)
♠ 5	♠ 5	♠ 5
♥ A 8 5 4 2	♥ A 7 4 3	♥ K 7 5 3
♦ K 7 4 3	♦ K 8 6 2	♦ 8 7 3 2
♣ 10 7 6	♣ J 8 5 3	♣ K Q 7 4

After

| 1♠ | 1 NT | 2♥ |

Hand (a) can jump to 4♥. The five-card trump support, combined with the singleton spade and two useful honors, is enormously powerful. With (b), 3♥ is sufficient. Ten tricks may be out of reach if the opener has a minimum with a four-card heart suit. With hand (c) it would not be wrong to pass. If a try is to be made, some players would make it in clubs, showing a heart fit and some side strength in clubs. This helps the opener to make the right decision: with 5-4-3-1 distribution, for example, he will tend to sign off with a singleton club and bid game with a singleton diamond. This is a matter of partnership agreement; for many partnerships 3♣ would simply show club length. A 2NT rebid by responder is just conceivable in standard methods, but would be barred by some partnerships.

As the sequence

| 1 ♠ | 1 NT |
| 2 ♥ (or ♦ or ♣) | |

has a very wide range (10-18 in high cards), some experts make a jump rebid of 3♥ or 3♦ nonforcing. 3♣ then becomes an artificial game-force, unrelated to the club suit. The result is that the rebid at the level of two is more limited, and there is less temptation to try for game. (The same principle would be applied to other jump shifts in a lower ranking suit, such as

1 ♥	1NT
3 ♦	

encouraging but nonforcing).

Other strong rebids available to the opener include:

(1) 2NT:

1 ♠	1NT
2NT	

This shows about 17-18 points and probably a five-card or even six-card spade suit; the failure to open 1NT is significant. If responder bids a new suit, it is long, weak and nonforcing.

(2) A reverse:

1 ♥	1NT
2 ♠	

Traditionally encouraging with about 17-18 points. Shows four spades and five (or six) hearts. The modern style is for the reverse to be forcing, often with a three-card spade suit.

(3) A jump rebid:

1 ♠	1NT
3 ♣	

Encouraging but nonforcing, and roughly 16-17 points in high cards.

(4) Jump shift:

1 ♠	1NT
3 ♦	

Game-forcing, more than 18 points in high cards. Usually five spades and four or five diamonds, with a singleton or void in an unbid suit. (But see the alternative treatment above.)

(5) 3 NT.

1 ♠	1NT
3NT	

Usually a balanced distribution with 19-20 points, but might be somewhat less with a solid six- or seven-card spade suit.

(6) Jump rebid to game:

1 ♠	1NT
4 ♠	

An unbalanced hand with 8° or more playing tricks, and at least a six-card suit.

The lower the rank of the opening bid, the lower the frequency of the 1NT response. This is because minimum responding hands have alternative possibilities without going to the level of two. Over 1♥, 1NT traditionally denies a four-card spade suit. Some experts are prepared to conceal a weak four-card spade suit, and those using FLANNERY will conceal any 4-card spade suit. Similarly, the 1NT response to a minor suit denies a four-card major suit in principle and strongly suggests a balanced hand. Over 1♣, 1NT strongly suggests 4-3-3-3 distribution, and the four-card suit is normally a minor (see ONE NOTRUMP RESPONSE TO MINOR SUIT). See also DRURY; ONE NOTRUMP RESPONSE TO MAJOR, FORCING; STRONG NOTRUMP AFTER PASSING.

ONE NOTRUMP RESPONSE TO MAJOR, FORCING.
This response is used on a wide range of hands, including many which would qualify in standard systems for a single raise or a response at the two level in a new suit. The main purpose is to narrow the range for a single raise. In ROTH-STONE a single raise is strong (10-12 points), and one notrump followed by a preference at the level of two is weak (6-9 points). In other systems, such as KAPLAN-SHEINWOLD, EASTERN SCIENTIFIC, WALSH and PRECISION, a single raise is constructive, usually with four trumps, while a preference after a 1NT response is weaker, often with three-card support and occasionally with two-card support.

Since these systems usually guarantee five cards for a major-suit opening, it is assumed that the opener can take a further bid without strain. If he has a six-card suit, he rebids it. If not, he makes his rebid in another biddable suit or his lowest-ranking three-card suit. There are some inconvenient possibilities. If the opener's distribution is 4-5-2-2, the systems do not provide him with a rebid, and he may end up playing with six trumps in the combined hands. (This can also happen, for example, when the opener's distribution is 5-3-3-2 and responder has 1-3-3-6. The final contract may be 2♦.) In this rare situation some players would break the rule and open 1♠ if the spade suit was a strong one. This is one of the motivations for using FLANNERY.

An "impossible" sequence can develop:

Opener	Responder
1 ♥	1 NT
2 ♣ or 2♦	2 ♠

Responder cannot wish to bid spades naturally, so many partnerships use this to show a club raise stronger than a three-club bid would be. See BART.

ONE NOTRUMP RESPONSE TO MINOR SUIT.
Some systems lay down 8-10 points as the requirement for a response of 1NT to an opening of 1♣; in Goren, 9-11 are needed. This is because a weaker hand can usually find some other bid, perhaps a suit at the level of one, a raise to 2♣, or if need be a response of 1♦ based on a three-card suit. Some players treat a response of 1 NT to 1♦ in the same way, but this creates problems when responder has a weak hand including a club suit.

A modern tendency is to relax these requirements and respond 1NT to 1♣ with as little as 6 points. This has some preemptive value because the fourth player cannot bid at the one level; but it loses slightly in constructive efficiency.

In Kaplan-Sheinwold the range is 5-8 points, so that if opener was planning a 1NT rebid with 15-17 points, he may pass and not miss a game.

ONE-ODD. One trick more than six, the book. A bid of one odd is a bid to win seven tricks.

ONE-OVER-ONE RESPONSE. A suit response at the level of one to an opening suit bid. For example, 1♣ - 1♥. The usual minimum strength for this response is 6 points, but in some styles a response is permitted with 3 or 4 points and distributional features. The maximum is just below the level fixed for a JUMP SHIFT, i.e., about 17 points in standard methods and about 15 points in ACOL. For players using WEAK JUMP SHIFT responses, the one over one has no upper limit. The longest suit is usually chosen for the response, and if two five-card suits are held, the higher-ranking is given preference. However, a four-card suit that can be bid at the one-level is often preferred to a five or six-card suit which has to be bid at the two level when the strength of the hand does not justify a two-over-one response. Many modern players have adopted the Walsh idea that in response to 1♣ a four-card major is bid ahead of longer diamonds unless the hand is very strong. For other aspects of this response, see CHOICE OF SUIT, COURTESY BID, and UP THE LINE.

ONE-SPOT. A colloquial alternative for ACE.

ONE-SUIT SQUEEZE. A hybrid between a squeeze and a throw-in. Most squeeze situations involve two or more suits.

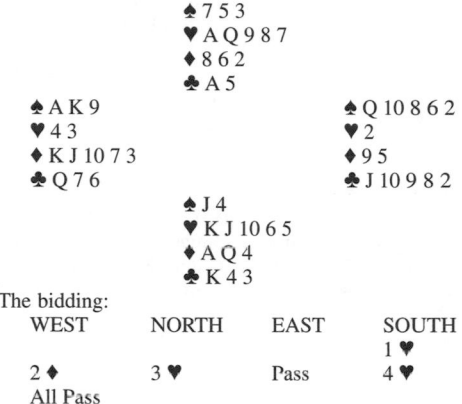

♠ 7 5 3
♥ A Q 9 8 7
♦ 8 6 2
♣ A 5

♠ A K 9   ♠ Q 10 8 6 2
♥ 4 3   ♥ 2
♦ K J 10 7 3   ♦ 9 5
♣ Q 7 6   ♣ J 10 9 8 2

♠ J 4
♥ K J 10 6 5
♦ A Q 4
♣ K 4 3

The bidding:

WEST	NORTH	EAST	SOUTH
			1 ♥
2 ♦	3 ♥	Pass	4 ♥
All Pass			

Spades are led three times and South ruffs. After ace, king, and a ruff in clubs and three rounds of trumps the position is:

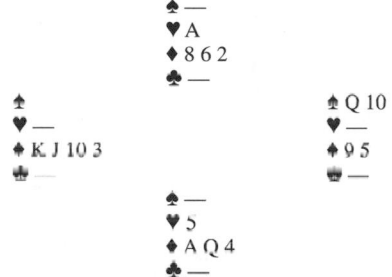

♠ —
♥ A
♦ 8 6 2
♣ —

♠ —   ♠ Q 10
♥ —   ♥ —
♦ K J 10 3   ♦ 9 5
♣ —   ♣ —

♠ —
♥ 5
♦ A Q 4
♣ —

♥A is led. If West discards the ♦3, South merely ducks a diamond. If West discards the ♦10, South leads the ♦6 from dummy. If East ducks, so does South. If East puts up the ♦9, South covers, creating a tenace position. For a related situation, see RUFF AND RUFF.

ONE-SUITER. A hand with a suit at least six cards long that contains no other suit with more than three cards.

ONE-TWO-THREE PRE-EMPTIVE. See PREEMPTIVE RE-RAISE.

ONSIDE. A card so placed that a finesse, if taken, will win: "the king was onside."

OPEN. (1) To lead to the first trick in the play of the hand. (2) The bidding: to make the first bid in a given auction. (3) Teams, pairs: tournament contests in which any pair, whether mixed (man and woman) or not, or any team of whatever constituency may play. (4) Room: that room in a championship event in which spectators may be present in somewhat substantial numbers as opposed

to a CLOSED ROOM that is limited as to both audience and accessibility. (5) Club: a game in which anyone may play.

OPEN BOARD-A-MATCH TEAMS CHAMPION-SHIP, NORTH AMERICAN CHAMPIONSHIP. See REISINGER MEMORIAL TROPHY. For results see Appendix I.

OPEN HAND. The dummy's hand, exposed on the table, as distinguished from the "CLOSED" HAND of the declarer.

OPEN KNOCKOUT TEAMS, NORTH AMERICAN CHAMPIONSHIP. See VANDERBILT CUP. For results see Appendix I.

OPEN PAIRS. An event of duplicate competition between pairs of players without regard to sex or masterpoint holding. When the event is scheduled for two or more sessions, there is often a qualifying and a final, with those eliminated eligible to compete in a consolation event. See CARRYOVER SCORES, QUALIFYING.

OPEN PAIR CHAMPIONSHIP, NORTH AMERICAN CHAMPIONSHIPS. See CAVENDISH TROPHY; SILODOR TROPHY. For results see Appendix I.

OPEN SWISS TEAMS CHAMPIONSHIP. For results see Appendix I.

OPENER'S REBID. The second bid by an opener who began with a suit bid of one is frequently the crucial point in the auction; judgment begins to be a factor. The following summary refers to standard methods (unless otherwise noted) and is limited to auctions in which responder made a non-jump bid in a new suit. Other rebids are separately dealt with under headings such as JUMP SHIFT, 1NT RESPONSE, 2NT RESPONSE, SINGLE RAISE and DOUBLE RAISE.

(1) After a ONE-OVER-ONE RESPONSE.

(a) *1NT rebid.* 13-15 is the standard range using a 16-18 notrump opening, but 12 is possible; if the opening notrump shows 15-17, the 1NT rebid shows 12-14. For users of a weak notrump, the notrump rebid promises a minimum of 15 (15-17 in KAPLAN-SHEINWOLD, 15-16 in ACOL). The sequence 1♥-1♠-1NT is given distinct treatment. In Kaplan-Sheinwold, it shows 12-14, equivalent to a 1NT opening; and an argument exists for treating the sequence as strong when a strong notrump is in use.

(b) *Rebid in first suit.* This suggests minimum strength and usually requires a six-card suit; opener avoids rebidding a five-card suit. A six-card suit is almost a certainty if the response was the most economical:

WEST	EAST	WEST	EAST
1 ♥	1 ♠	1 ♣	1 ♦
2 ♥		2 ♣	

In each case, West had four other minimum rebids at his disposal, but chose to rebid his first suit. Opener is more likely to rebid a five-card suit if the response consumed bidding space:

WEST	EAST
1 ♣	1 ♠
2 ♣	

West may have an unbid four-card suit that he could

not show without making a strength-showing REVERSE.

(c) *Rebid at the one level.* For example, 1♣-1♥-1♠. This is an unrevealing rebid, covering a wide range of hands. Opener has fewer than 19 high-card points; otherwise, he would have made a jump shift. His black-suit lengths remain a mystery: the clubs will often be longer; 5-4 and 6-4 are common distributions, and 6-5 possible. In a FIVE-CARD-MAJOR style, opener could be 4-3-3-3, but some players would prefer to rebid 1NT with that distribution. Even 5-3 and 6-3 are conceivable, since some experts might rebid 1♠ on:

    ♠ A K J
    ♥ 5
    ♦ K 6 4 2
    ♣ A 9 6 4 2

4-4 distribution is common. Opener could be 5-5, though many experts would then open 1♠ (see CHOICE OF SUIT). In exceptional cases, the spades may be longer:

    ♠ 7 5 4 3 2
    ♥ 7
    ♦ A 3 2
    ♣ A K Q 4

With this awkward hand, the lesser evil may be to open 1♣ and rebid 1♠ over 1♥. Similar considerations apply to the sequences 1♣-1♦-1♠ and 1♣-1♦-1♥, though in the latter case 5-5 distribution is unlikely. 1♦-1♥-1♠ is more precise, since a three-card diamond suit is improbable and so is 5-5 distribution.

(d) *Rebid in a lower-ranking suit at the two level.* Four sequences are possible, all consisting of a red-suit opening, a major-suit response and a minor-suit rebid. For example:

WEST	EAST
1♥	1♠
2♣	

West's most likely distribution is 5-4, but 5-5, 6-4 and 6-5 are possible. 4-5 and 4-4 are possible in some styles, but this course is risky since responder may wish to give preference on a doubleton. When opener's rebid bypasses 1NT in this way, responder can reasonably assume that opener's distribution is not balanced and his first suit is a five-carder. These sequences have a wide range in standard methods — 10-18 in high cards — and are therefore difficult to handle. (They are strong in ROTH-STONE and KAPLAN-SHEINWOLD, and in the latter system a 2♣ rebid rebid by opener after a 1♦ opening is forcing and virtually artificial.) However, when opener changes suits, he is more likely to hold extra strength. With:

    ♠ Q 6
    ♥ A K 7 5 3 2
    ♦ 5
    ♣ A Q 6 3

opener would rebid 2♣, since a 2♥ rebid would suggest a minimum hand. Furthermore, with:

    ♠ Q
    ♥ A Q 4
    ♦ A 10 6 3
    ♣ Q 9 6 4 2

opener might reject the popular notion of opening 1♦ and rebidding 2♣, since he distorts his distribution and leaves the strength of his hand poorly defined. Many players would open 1♣ and rebid 1NT over a 1♠ response (see CHOICE OF SUIT).

(e) *Reverse.* Opener's second suit is of higher rank than his first. For example:

WEST	EAST
1♣	1♠
2♥	

West's most likely distribution is 5-4. His reverse strongly suggests longer clubs than hearts, so alternative distributions are 6-4 and 6-5. A three-card heart suit is possible, especially if opener has spade support in reserve:

    ♠ K Q 5
    ♥ A K 4
    ♦ 5 4
    ♣ A Q 7 5 3

This atypical reverse is prompted by the weakness in the fourth suit. The same factor may even cause opener to ignore the principle that the first suit must be longer:

    ♠ K 5 3
    ♥ A K 4 3
    ♦ 6 5
    ♣ A K Q 6

Experts disagree on the high-card requirements for a reverse. One school is willing to reverse with hands worth only a trick more than a minimum; the other treats a reverse as equivalent to a jump shift. Most modern pairs accept a reverse as forcing on any normal response. See REVERSE.

(f) *Single raise in responder's suit.* For example, 1♦-1♠-2♠. This shows 12-15 points and an expectation of four-card trump support. However, a single raise with three-card support is common and is desirable unless the hand is completely balanced or the trumps are poor. Expert opinion is divided on the correct rebid when opener has three-card support and a six-card suit.

    ♠ K 10 3
    ♥ 4
    ♦ A 7 5
    ♣ A J 9 6 4 2

After 1♣-1♠, some experts would raise; others would rebid the clubs, hoping to support spades later.

(g) *2NT rebid.* The standard range is 19-20 using a 16-18 notrump range. Responder continues to game unless he has a minimum or subminimum response. The range is reduced to 18-19 for those using a 15-17 notrump, and is 17-18 in Acol. A rebid by responder in his own suit is forcing in standard methods. It would be a signoff in Acol, but forcing in Kaplan-Sheinwold, which uses a 3♣ rebid as preparatory to a signoff. (See WOLFF CONVENTION.)

(h) *Jump reverse.* For example, 1♣-1♠-3♥. Traditionally, this was simply stronger than a normal reverse and is still so for players who do not consider a reverse as forcing. In the modern style, with a simple reverse forcing, the sequence has no obvious meaning. It is often used as a mini-splinter, inviting game with a four-card fit for responder and a singleton in the suit shown.

(i) *Jump rebid in opener's suit.* For example, 1♣-1♥-3♣. This shows a good six- or seven-card suit and about 15-17 high-card points. The bid is encouraging, not forcing, and in a minor suggests 3NT. A new-suit bid by responder at the three level may show a stopper for notrump and not necessarily length. A raise of opener's suit is forcing.

(j) *Jump raise in responder suit.* For example, 1♦-1♠-3♠. This shows 16-18 high-card points, unbalanced distribution (since the opening bid was not 1NT) and four-card support. Three-card support is possible if the high-card strength is concentrated in the bid suits:

♠ A K Q
♥ 7 6
♦ A K J 4 3
♣ 7 5 4

Responder usually continues to game or slam, but may pass if his response was minimum.

(k) *Jump shift.* For example, 1♦-1♠-3♣. This shows unbalanced distribution and is forcing to game. Opener sometimes has a fit for responder's suit that he plans to show next.

(l) *3NT rebid.* The standard range of 21-22 has been abandoned by almost all experts, mainly due to the advent of weak two-bids and the strong 2♣ opening. The 3NT rebid is therefore rare. In Acol it shows 19-20 points. In standard methods it may show exactly 20 points with balanced distribution if the partnership has no other way to describe such a hand. Most pairs, however, use the sequence to show a hand strong in playing tricks with a solid or virtually solid minor and stoppers in the unbid suits. Opener will often have a singleton in responder's suit.

♠ 4
♥ A 10 2
♦ K 5
♣ A K Q 9 7 5 3

Open 1♣ and jump to 3NT if the response is 1♠.

(m) *Jump to game in responder's major suit.* 1♥-1♠-4♠. This shows four-card support and the values to justify game. The most common type of hand is relatively balanced with 19-20 points; a powerful unbalanced hand is likely to prefer a jump shift (see (j) above).

(n) *Jump to game in opener's major suit.* 1♥-1♠-4♥ is the only possible sequence. Many powerful hands with a seven-card suit or even an eight-card suit would qualify. A six-card suit is possible:

♠ Q 5 4
♥ A K Q J 10 4
♦ A J 3
♣ Q

In this case, the partial fit in spades improves opener's hand. (In Acol, the spade fit is indicated because many other hands with enough playing strength would qualify for a 2♥ opening.)

(o) *Double jump rebid.* This can be a jump to four of opener's suit, or responder's suit:

(a)		(b)	
WEST	EAST	WEST	EAST
1♣	1♥	1♣	1♦
4♣			4♦

Sequence (a) is often used to show a hand worth a raise to 4♥ with a long, solid club suit. A typical hand would be:

♠ 4
♥ K Q 5 4
♦ A 5
♣ A K Q 8 5 2

An alternative meaning for this sequence is to show a hand with a long minor, probably seven cards, and exactly three cards in partner's major.
Sequence (b) has no natural meaning.

(p) *A double jump shift rebid:*

WEST	EAST
1♣	1♥
3♠ or 4♦	

This is a SPLINTER for nearly all modern partnerships. In an earlier era it might have been a Culbertson Asking

Bid.
For other uses of these jump rebids, see ASKING BID, FRAGMENT BID, SPLINTER BID, VOID-SHOWING BID.

(2) After a TWO-OVER-ONE RESPONSE.

(q) *2NT rebid.* For example, 1♥-2♣-2NT. There are two schools among standard players. One school treats the bid as forcing, showing 15-17 points; players who adopt this treatment tend to avoid a 1NT opening with a five-card major. The other school is willing to rebid 2NT on a minimum balanced hand. In Roth-Stone (13-16) and Kaplan-Sheinwold (15-17), the bid is forcing. In a traditional style, with the rebid showing 12-14 and the responder promising only 10-11, the bid can be passed in theory but hardly ever is.

(r) *Rebid in first suit.* For example, 1♠-2♦-2♠. This shows a minimum opening bid with 10-14 or possibly 15 high-card points. The suit will usually be a six-carder, but occasionally may be a good five-card suit. The chance of a five-card suit is greatest when the response is in the suit ranking immediately below opener's: 1♠-2♥-2♠, 1♥-2♦-2♥ or 1♦-2♣-2♦. The sequence 1♠-2♣-2♠ suggests a six-card suit, since if opener had only five spades, he would often find a more descriptive rebid.
Many players would avoid rebidding a weak five-card suit that would play badly opposite a singleton.

♠ J 6 4 3 2
♥ A 5
♦ A Q 6
♣ Q 4 2

If the response to 1♠ is 2♣, some experts would rebid 2NT or raise to 3♣ if those actions promised no extra strength (see (s) below). Otherwise, the choice lies between 2♦, which may do no harm, and 2♠.
If the response to 1♠ is 2♥, 2NT is the best rebid if style permits; otherwise, opener must repeat the bad spades or support hearts on the doubleton.
The quality of the suit is more important in a traditional style, since the bidding may die. In the modern style, the partnership is committed to continue, normally to at least game.

(s) *Rebid in a lower-ranking suit.* For example, 1♠-2♣-2♦. Although in standard this sequence does not promise a strong hand (opener may have 5-5 with 11 high-card points), neither does it deny extra strength. Hence, responder, having bid at the two level, will not pass. A 2♦ rebid after a 2♣ response might occasionally be made with a strong tripleton.

(t) *Single raise in responder's suit.* For example, 1♥-2♦-3♦. There are two schools of thought. Many traditional textbooks class this raise as encouraging with about 15-16 high-card points; that makes it forcing in effect and leaves unsolved the problem of minimum hands on which a raise is the natural action. Other authorities regard the single raise as a non-forcing minimum rebid that promises no extra strength. The bid may then be passed, unless the response has promised further action.

(u) *Reverse at the two level.* For example, 1♥-2♣-2♠. The sequence is forcing in all methods and most players would regard the sequence as game-forcing. The first suit must be longer than the second; 5-4 is the expected distribution, with 6-4 or 6-5 possible. Players who raise a two-level response with a minimum may temporize with a reverse in a three-card suit:

♠A Q 4
♥A K 7 5 2
♦7 3
♣K J 3

After 1♥-2♣, a 2♠ rebid is best if a raise to 3♣ would be non-forcing.

(v) *Second suit at the three level (sometimes called a "high reverse").* For example, 1♥-2♣-3♣. This sequence is forcing in all methods and game-forcing in most. The distribution is usually 5-5 or 5-4; 5-5 may be less likely if the suits are spades and clubs, since some players would open 1♣. Opener's second suit may be a three-carder:

♠5 4
♥A Q 8 5 2
♦A J 5
♣A K 4

After 1♥-2♦, 3♣ would be the expert choice, especially if a raise to 3♦ is non-forcing.

(w) *Jump shift to the three level.* For example, 1♠-2♣-3♦. Many tournament players consider this sequence game-forcing. The sequence suggests five cards or more in each suit. However, some would treat it as a splinter.

(x) *Jump rebid in opener's suit.* For example, 1♠-2♦-3♠. This is game-forcing in standard methods (though not in Acol) and shows a good six- or seven-card suit with extra high-card strength.

(y) *Jump to game in opener's suit.* For example, 1♠-2♦-4♠. This shows a strong six-card or longer suit with the values for game, but no interest in a notrump contract. The bid also suggests a hand without controls in the unbid suits; hence, unsuitable for slam. After 1♠-2♦, a typical hand would be:

♠A K Q 10 5 4 2
♥J 7
♦7
♣K 6 4

In Acol, the bid implies a moderate fit for responder's suit because of the failure to open with a two-bid.

(z) *Jump raise in responder's suit.* This is forcing in a minor suit — for example, 1♠-2♦-4♦ — with four-card support. The bid is non-forcing by definition in Acol, but some pairs play it as forcing. 1♠-2♥-4♥ is a special case; it shows a hand only slightly too good for 3♥ (according to style), but with strong heart support.

(aa) *3NT rebid.* For example, 1♠-2♦-3NT. Equivalent to a 2NT rebid after a one-level response; therefore, 19-20 points. Some experts would make this bid, however, with 18 points or even 17. In a style where a two-over-one response forces to game, the bid may even suggest no extra strength.

(ab) *Double jump shift.* For example, 1♠-2♣-4♦. If 3♦ is a splinter, then 4♦ should be a splinter based on a void rather than a singleton. See GOLDEN RULE.

OPENING BID. The first call in the auction other than a pass. The treatment of opening bids is discussed in the following separate articles: ACOL TWO-BID; BENJAMIN; BIG CLUB; BLUE TEAM TWO DIAMONDS; BIDDABLE SUITS; BORDERLINE OPENING BIDS; CANAPE; CHOICE OF SUIT; DYNAMIC NOTRUMP; FIVE-CARD MAJORS; FIVE OF A MAJOR OPENING; FIVE NOTRUMP OPENING; FLANNERY TWO DIAMONDS; FLANNERY TWO HEARTS; FORCING TWO-BID; FOUR-CARD MAJORS; FOUR NOTRUMP OPENING; GAMBLING THREE NOTRUMP; KAMIKAZE NOTRUMP; MEXICAN TWO DIAMONDS; MULTI TWO DIAMONDS; NAMYATS; ONE NOTRUMP OPENING; OPENING SUIT BID; ORANGE CLUB; PREEMPTIVE BID; REVERSE FLANNERY; ROMAN TWO DIAMONDS; ROMEX TWO DIAMONDS; RUBIN TRANSFERS; SHORT DIAMOND; SIX OF A SUIT OPENING; SIX NOTRUMP OPENING; THREE NOTRUMP OPENING; TRANSFER OPENING PREEMPTS; TWO CLUBS STRONG ARTIFICIAL; TWO NOTRUMP OPENING; TWO NOTRUMP OPENING FOR MINORS; TWO UNDER TRANSFER PREEMPTS; TWO-WAY TWO-BIDS; WEAK TWO-BID.

OPENING BIDDER. The player at a deal of contract who makes the first bid of an auction.

OPENING CALL. The original call made by the dealer to start the auction. See OPENING BID.

OPENING LEAD. After the bidding has been concluded, the play of the hand commences by the declarer's left-hand opponent making an original or opening lead. For selection of opening leads, see OPENING LEADS.

OPENING LEADS. Defense is regarded as the most difficult aspect of bridge. Since the opening lead is the only defensive play made while the dummy is concealed, it requires a kind of detective reasoning and considerable analysis of the meaning of every call in the auction, as well as agreed conventional leads. The opening lead is frequently the source of substantial profits and losses.

Choosing the Card.

The card chosen for the opening lead should help pave the way for the defeat of the contract, insofar as this is possible, and should convey information to partner about the leader's holding in the suit. Some typical card choices, once the suit has been selected, are summarized in the accompanying table (See page 46-47).

The standard approach has a substantial number of critics, and one important controversy concerns the lead from a sequence of honors. With holdings like A-K-Q, K-Q-J, or Q-J-10, any of the honors can be led with equal trick-taking effect. The main concern is to inform partner about the opening leader's holding. The customary practice is to lead the king from A-K (unless it is doubleton, in which case the ace is led) and the top card from any other honor sequence. Similarly, the standard lead from holdings such as K-10-9-8 or Q-10-9-8 is the 10, the top of the interior sequence. However, standard leads create potentially costly confusion in certain instances. For example, the king is led from both A-K-4 and K-Q-4, so partner may have difficulty deciding whether to signal encouragement with J-8-2; and the 10 is led from both K-10-9-8 and 10-9-8-2, so partner may have difficulty deciding whether to return the suit when he gains the lead. Therefore, conventional nonstandard opening lead methods have become increasingly popular among experts, including ACE FROM ACE-KING; JOURNALIST LEADS; RUSINOW LEADS; and ZERO OR TWO HIGHER LEADS.

A second controversy has to do with the lead from three small cards against a suit contract. The top card is traditional, but all three possibilities have been recommended. See MUD, and THREE SMALL CARDS, LEAD FROM.

A third controversy concerns the standard fourth-best lead from a long suit. Against suit contracts, an increasing number of experts prefer to give count more accurately by leading the third-highest card from an even number, and the lowest card from an odd number. Against notrump contracts, some use a low spot card lead to encourage the return of the suit and lead a high spot card to discourage a return; others object to this because the leader's partner can no longer use the RULE OF ELEVEN. These modifications are an integral part of JOURNALIST LEADS.

Choosing the Suit.

Clues from the bidding. Regardless of the carding method that is used, no table or convention can indicate the right suit to lead; judgment and deduction must be applied to each situation. In particular, the auction can provide the astute opening leader with valuable clues:

(1) If the opponents are strong in certain suits, the opening leader should look elsewhere for his selection.

(2) If the opponents are weak in a particular suit, the opening leader should attack it. See ATTACKING LEAD.

(3) If one opponent is likely to be void in a certain suit (as when he bids two suits several times and supports a third suit), the opening leader should not lead that ace if the enemy ends up in a suit contract.

(4) If dummy holds a long and strong side suit that will provide numerous discards (as when he has rebid it several times), the opening leader should be aggressive and try to take tricks in a hurry.

(5) If the opponents have staggered into their contract with little strength to spare, the opening leader should be cautious and avoid giving away the fulfilling trick.

(6) If the opponents have strength to spare, (at rubber bridge or IMPs) an aggressive lead has little to lose save an unimportant overtrick.

(7) If partner has indicated a good suit to attack by bidding it (see LEAD-DIRECTING BID), it is usually safe to lead it.

(8) If partner has denied length and strength in a suit by refusing to make a cheap one-level overcall when given the opportunity, the opening leader should not try to hit him in that suit.

(9) If partner has indicated general high-card strength by making a takeout double, it is relatively safe to lead away from an unsupported honor.

(10) If partner has denied general high-card strength by making a preemptive bid, it is not advisable to lead away from an unsupported honor.

(11) If partner has requested the lead of a specific suit by making a LEAD-DIRECTING DOUBLE or LIGHTNER DOUBLE, it is usually advisable to lead it.

Clues from the strength of the opening leader's hand. If the opponents bid game and the opening leader has 13 or 14 high-card points, he should visualize the near-yarborough in partner's hand and reject any lead that requires substantial high-card help (such as the lead from an unsupported honor). When the opening leader's strength is mediocre, however, it is reasonable to expect some useful aid from partner. The location of the opening leader's strength is also important. If he holds finessable positions such as K-3-2 in front of suits bid by dummy, or a few small cards behind suits bid by declarer, the defenders are likely to be in trouble. Declarer's finesses rate to win, and the suits appear to be breaking well for the opponents. Holding length and weakness in dummy's long suit is also a bad sign, for declarer will probably be able to establish it with little difficulty. In such cases, an aggressive opening lead is often justified. But if the opening leader holds strength behind declarer's

bid suits, and if he can see that important suits will be breaking badly for the enemy, a more conservative strategy is preferable.

Clues from the strength of the opening leader's suit. Other things being equal, it is frequently desirable to lead from stronger suits. Leading from Q-10-4-3 is preferable to Q-4-3-2 because less help is needed from partner to build tricks (and avoid a disaster), while Q-J-10-9 is superior to both holdings. However, as the preceding sections indicate, other things are often not equal; and many opening leaders go wrong by using the strength of one suit as their sole guide while ignoring valuable information available from other sources.

Leads against notrump contracts.

Since declarer cannot ruff when he runs out of a suit, the defenders should usually try to establish length winners. Assuming that the bidding has not indicated the need for special action, the following guidelines apply:

(1) A five-card or longer holding in an unbid suit is usually an excellent choice, provided that the opening leader has at least one probable entry. For example, leading from A-Q-6-3-2 is ideal; even if declarer gets an undeserved trick with the king, three or four winners are likely to be established while the high cards are retained for use as entries.

(2) From a completely entryless hand, the opening leader should reject his own (weak) long suit and try to build length winners in partner's hand. An unbid major suit containing three cards or a strong doubleton is likely to be a good choice.

(3) From holdings such as J-10-9-x-x, Q-J-10-x-x, K-J-10-x-x, or A-J-10-x-x in a suit bid by the enemy, the fourth-best card should be led. This avoids blocking the suit when partner has a useful doubleton, and is likely to tempt declarer into a fatal error in situations such as:

$$Q ?$$

J 10 9 4 3   K 5

$$A 8 7 6$$

After the jack lead, South has two stoppers by covering. If a lower card is led instead, South inevitably plays dummy's queen.

(4) If no five-card or longer suit is held, a solid or nearly solid four-carder (such as Q-J-10-9 or J-10-9-3) is likely to build some winners without giving anything away.

(5) Leading from broken four-card suits is less desirable. Attacking from Q-10-4-2 in an unbid suit is not unreasonable, since the lead has a good chance to pay off if partner has even one of the missing honors. However, a suit like A-Q-3-2 should be avoided because the potential for length winners is too limited to justify giving declarer an undeserved trick.

(6) Against 3NT, leading an honor from A-K-2 in an unbid suit can be every effective (especially at rubber bridge or IMPs). Partner may turn up with five to the queen, or with five small cards and a side entry. Even the lead of an honor from A-Q-2 has at times paid similar dividends.

(7) If no attractive lead exists, a passive lead (as from three or four small cards) has the advantage of being relatively safe. Even the lead of a small doubleton may be advantageous (see SHORT-SUIT LEADS).

(8) In some instances, the opening leader may gain by disguising the length of his long suit. See FALSE-CARDING.

(9) After a 2NT opening bid, a passive lead gains more frequently. Declarer's hand contains most of his side's

strength, so he may have entry problems if left to his own devices.

(10) Against notrump partials, a passive lead gains more frequently. The strength is more evenly divided between the two sides, so the defenders are less likely to have to collect tricks in a hurry.

(11) After a GAMBLING 3NT opening bid has been passed out, it is desirable to lead an ace. Declarer is trying to score nine fast tricks with the aid of a solid minor suit, so losing the lead even once may be fatal.

Leads against suit contracts.

Here the defenders are less likely to gain by trying to build length winners, since declarer can simply ruff when he runs out of a suit. Assuming that the bidding has not indicated the need for special action, the following guidelines apply:

(1) Leading from solid or nearly solid honor sequences, such as A-K-J-5, K-Q-J-7-3, Q-J-10-2, or J-10-9-5, is likely to be both constructive and safe. Leading from weaker honor holdings like K-Q-7-3 or Q-J-9-2 can also be effective, but may cost a trick when partner is weak in the suit.

(2) Leads from long suits are safer but less likely to establish several tricks, while leads from short side suits are riskier but more likely to establish several tricks. If the defenders must rush to collect their winners (as when dummy's bidding shows a long side suit that will provide numerous discards), it is better to lead from Q-7-5 in an unbid suit than from Q-8-6-5. When safety considerations are more important, however, leading from length is preferable.

(3) When holding four or more trumps, it is particularly desirable to lead from a long suit. If declarer can be forced to ruff several times, his trumps may run out before the defenders' do and cause him to lose control of the hand. See FORCING LEADS.

(4) When no attractive lead exists, a passive lead (as from three or four small cards) has the advantage of being relatively safe.

(5) A trump lead is desirable in several situations: when the bidding indicates that declarer will try to ruff losers in dummy or crossruff; when the defenders hold substantial strength in all side suits, as when the opponents sacrifice against a contract that the defenders expected to make on power; when a one-level contract is passed out; and when a passive lead is indicated and the opening leader holds a few small trumps. A trump lead is mandatory when a one-level takeout double is passed out. However, a trump lead should be avoided when the opening leader's holding is too precarious to lead from; when the bidding indicates that the defenders must take their tricks in a hurry; when the opening leader is very long in a suit declarer plans to ruff in dummy, indicating that partner will be able to overruff; when the opening leader has a singleton trump; and when the opening leader has four or more trumps, in which case the forcing game is preferable. See TRUMP LEADS.

(6) A side-suit singleton is likely to be effective when the opening leader has some extra low trumps to use for ruffing and a probable entry in trumps, so long as the leader's partner rates to have an entry or two. However, singleton leads should usually be avoided when the opening leader has no excess low trumps to ruff with (as when holding A-Q or Q-J-3); when he has four or more trumps, in which case the forcing game is preferable; or when the singleton is a king or queen.

(7) Side-suit doubletons are considerably less likely to produce ruffs than are singletons, and should be led for this purpose only when holding a quick entry *in trumps*. A small doubleton may be a satisfactory passive lead, however. In some infrequent cases, leading from K-2 or Q-2 may be justified because the opening leader is truly desperate. See DESPERATION LEAD OR PLAY.

(8) With an otherwise worthless hand, leading the king from K-x-x-x in partner's bid suit can be effective. If the king holds the trick, the opening leader may now be able to make a profitable attack through dummy in a different suit; while if the opening lead is the normal small card and declarer has a singleton, no further leads through dummy will be possible.

(9) Underleading the ace is normally avoided, but can be a winning choice. The defenders may need tricks in a hurry, and declarer may also be missing the queen and misguess; or it may be urgent to put partner on lead for an attack through declarer's hand or to obtain a ruff. See UNDERLEAD.

Leads against slam contracts.

If the opponents reach a small slam and the opening leader holds K-Q and an ace, it is obvious that the king should be led. However, fate usually does not conspire to deal all the defenders' high cards to the opening leader, so he often has to decide whether to lead away from an unsupported king or queen in an unbid suit. Fortunately, slam contracts often involve considerable amounts of bidding, which offer more clues to the opening leader. Normally, the following guidelines apply:

(1) Against a small slam, an attacking lead is preferable when dummy's bidding indicates a long, establishable suit. A passive lead is more appropriate if both declarer and dummy appear to have balanced hands, whether or not the contract is at notrump.

(2) Against suit small slams, an ace lead is desirable if it is in an unbid suit and the opening leader holds a probable second winner elsewhere, or if the bidding suggests that the opponents might be off two fast tricks. Otherwise the ace lead is more debatable, and should normally be avoided if it is in a suit bid by the enemy.

(3) Against suit small slams, singleton leads are often effective. However, they should be avoided if both opponents have bid the suit, in which case the lead may help them overcome a bad break, or if the opening leader has a sure winner (or a relatively strong hand), in which case the slam will be defeated anyway if partner can take a trick.

(4) Against suit small slams, a trump lead is dangerous; it may pick up partner's queen and save declarer a crucial guess. However, a trump lead may work well if:

(a) the bidding plus the leader's holding indicates that partner has at most a singleton.

(b) the auction strongly suggests that declarer plans to do a great deal of ruffing in one or both hands.

(c) the trump holding is safe to lead from.

(5) Against a grand slam, without an immediate winner to cash, it is usually desirable to make a safe lead. Only one trick is needed to defeat the contract, so building winners in unnecessary. Trump leads are frequently desirable against suit grand slams, but should be avoided if partner may have the queen of trumps and a safe selection is available elsewhere.

Board-a-match and matchpoint considerations.

At board-a-match scoring, the opening leader must be careful to avoid losing a board that his teammates at the

Opening Leads: Some Typical Card
Choices Once the Suit Has Been Selected

(In general this table has been set up based on the basic opening lead policy of fourth-best from a holding of four or more cards in a suit. Many tournament players today have switched to leading third and fifth-best. This means that on those leads listed below where a lead is from fourth best in a four-card suit, the third-and-fifth player should lead third best instead of fourth if the usual lead would have been fourth best — otherwise there will be partnership confusion. When the suit chosen for the opening lead is at least five cards long, the lead from a third-and-fifth player should be the fifth best if ordinarily the lead would have been the fourth best.)

Suit Length	Holding in Suit	Lead vs. NT	Lead vs. Suits
Two Cards	Any non-trump doubleton	Top Card	Top Card
	Trumps: honor sequence or ace-any	—	Top Card[1]
	Trumps: any other doubleton	—	Low Card
Three Cards	9-8-7 or worse, not in trumps	Top Card	Low Card[2]
	Trumps: three small	—	2nd best[3]
	10-x-x, J-x-x, Q-x-x, K-x-x	3rd Best	3rd Best
	Q-10-x, K-10-x, K-J-x	3rd Best[4]	3rd Best
	10-9-x, J-10-x, Q-J-x, K-Q-x	Top Card	Top Card
	Trumps: J-10-x	—	3rd Best
	A-x-x, A-10-x	3rd Best[5]	Ace
	A-J-x, A-Q-x	2nd Best[6]	Ace
	A-K-x or better	King	King
Four Cards	9-8-7-6 or worse	4th best[7]	
	10-x-x-x, J-x-x-x, Q-x-x-x, K-x-x-x	4th Best	4th Best
	10-9-x-x, J-10-x-x, Q-J-x-x	4th best	4th best[8]
	Q 10-x-x, K-10-x-x, K-J-x-x	4th best	4th best
	Q-10-9-x, J-10-8-x, K-J-10-x	2nd best	2nd best
	A-10-9-x, A-J-10-x	2nd best	Ace[15]
	10-9-7-x, J-10-8-x, Q-J-9-x, K-Q-10-x	Top Card	Top Card
	10-9-8-x, J-10-9-x, Q-J-10-x, K-Q-J-x	Top Card	Top Card
	A-x-x-x-, A-10-x-x, Q-J-x-x, K-Q-J-x	4th best	Ace
	K-Q-x-x, K-Q-9-x, A-K-x-x, A-K-10-x	4th best	King
	K-Q-10-x, A-K-10-9, A-K-J-x, or better	King	King
Five Cards[14]	10-9-7-x-x, 10-9-8-x-x, J-10-8-x-x	4th best	
	10-9-7-6-x, 10-9-8-6-x, 10-9-8-7-x	Top Card	
	J-10-8-7-x, J-10-9-7-x, J-10-9-8-x	Top Card	
	Q-J-9-x-x, K-Q-9-x-x	4th best	
	J-10-9-x-x, Q-J-10-x-x, K-Q-10-x-x, K-Q-J-x-x	Top card or 4th best[9]	
	Q J 9 8 x, K Q 10-9-x	2nd best[10]	
	Q-J-10-8-x, Q-J-10-9-x, K-Q-J-9-x, K-Q-J-10-x	Top card	
	Q-10-9-x-x, K-10-9-x-x, A-10-9-x-x	4th best	
	Q-10-9-7-x, Q-10-9-8-x, K-10-9-7-x, K-10-9-8-x	2nd best	
	A-10-9-7-x, A-10-9-8-x	2nd best	
	K-J-10-x-x, A-J-10-x-x	2nd best or 4th best[11]	
	K-J-10-8-x, K-J-10-9-x, A-J-10-8-x, A-J-10-9-x		
	A-K-10-9-x	King or ten[12]	
	A-K-J-x-x	King or 4th best [12]	
	A-K-J-10-x	Ace[13]	

[1]An old chestnut is to lead the jack from Q-J or the nine from 10-9, hoping to induce declarer to misguess on the next round. However, this is unlikely to be necessary against a declarer familiar with RESTRICTED CHOICE.

[2]High and middle are also popular. See THREE SMALL CARDS, LEAD FROM.

[3]Followed by the smallest, thus denying a doubleton.

[4]In some cases, the jack from K-J-x is best in order to unblock.

[5]The ace is preferable if partner does not figure to have a side entry.

[6]The ace is correct is some cases.

[7]The top card or second best may be led to deny an honor; see text above.

[8]The queen from Q-J-x-x is correct in some cases.

[9]Fourth best is preferable when the goal is to establish the whole suit, rather than play safe, and when an opponent is likely to have four cards in the suit.

[10]Partner is expected to play the immediately lower honor if he has it.

[11]King from K-J-10-9-x-x is correct in some cases.

[12]The king is preferable when a sure side entry is held.

[13]Partner is expected to play an honor if he has one, and to signal his count (high-low for even, low-high for odd) if he does not.

[14]The rules for four card suits are frequently correct against suit contracts. Against notrump contracts, however, the degree of solidity of an honor sequence is particularly important.

[15]In general, leading from this holding is not recommended.

other table have all but won. At matchpoints, there are conflicting considerations. Notrump contracts based on shaky stoppers are more common at this form of scoring, so the opening leader is more likely to gain by trying to run a long suit. Yet conceding even one undeserved trick can result in a bottom score, so care must be taken to avoid presenting declarer with a gift that his counterparts at other tables will not receive. Thus an unusual attempt to defeat a contract, correct at rubber bridge or IMPs, may be wrong at matchpoints because it is too likely to concede the overtrick. See MATCHPOINT DEFENSE. Opening leads at matchpoints are a source of considerable complexity (and headaches). See also THIRD AND FIFTH and STRONG KINGS AND TENS.

OPENING ONE NOTRUMP BID. See ONE NOTRUMP OPENING.

OPENING SUIT BID. An opening of 1♣, 1♦, 1♥, or 1♠ has a normal range of 10-20 high-card points. It may sink below 10 in some freak cases — with 6-6 distribution, for example. It may rise above 20 with unbalanced hands, usually 4-4-4-1 or 5-4-3-1 patterns, unsuited to a 2NT opening and not quite strong enough for a forcing opening. For special factors affecting the opening bid, see BIDDABLE SUITS; BORDERLINE OPENING BIDS; CHOICE OF SUIT.

OPPONENT. A member of the adverse team at bridge. An opponent can be a member of an opposing team of two, four, five or six as well as merely a temporary adversary.

OPPONENT'S SUIT. A suit held or bid by one or both adversaries. In judging the bidding, a holding of three small cards in the opponent's suit is generally a danger signal. But if the opponent's suit is supported, a small tripleton may actually be better than a small doubleton because the chance of finding a singleton with partner is increased. For bids in the opponent's suit, see CUEBIDS IN OPPONENT'S SUIT.

OPPOSITION. (1) The opponents on a hand, set of hands or rubber; (2) The contestants in DIRECT COMPETITION; (3) The balance of the field; (4) The other team in a head-on team event.

OPTIMUM STRATEGY. Plans of play adopted by declarer or defender in the light of different tactics which may be adopted by the opposing side. The following, from Jean Besse, is one example of the complications which can arise in considering alternative strategies:

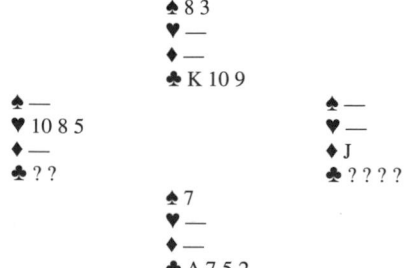

Spades are trumps. East has the lead. Further conditions are that West is marked with three hearts and East

with the ♦J. Declarer knows, therefore, that the critical club suit is divided 2-4, but he doesn't know where the Q and J are. Clubs are therefore designated with question marks on the diagram. Lest he give a ruff and discard, East must obviously lead a club, and, of course, declarer's aim is to make all the tricks. The problem is to analyze the optimum strategy both from declarer's and (more importantly) defender's point of view. The defender's clubs may break:

(1) x-x - Q-J-x-x .... 6 cases
(2) Q-x - J-x-x-x ....
    or
    J-x - Q-x-x-x .... 8 cases
(3) Q-J - x-x-x-x .... 1 case
                        TOTAL .... 15 cases

Let us examine East's possible tactics.

(a) The "naive" tactic. East is a weak player. He leads queen or jack in (1). He leads small in (2) and, perforce, in (3). Against such an opponent it is clear that South will lose only in (3). He will win 14 times out of 15.

(b) The "expert" tactic. East is a good player. He leads queen or jack whenever he has one (or both) of these cards.

Now declarer has to reverse his play. As (2) is more likely than (1), South should play for divided honors, i.e., cash the ace in hand and drop West's other honor next. So, South wins in (2) (8 cases) but loses in (1) (6 cases).

Declarer, however, takes a little revenge in case (3) as Terence Reese points out in his *Expert Game*. For South can easily divine case (3) from the very fact that East had led a small card (having no alternative). So South wins also in case (3) hence, in 9 cases out of 15.

To prevent this, East may lead sometimes small and sometimes high in case (2). Say 50% each. Which leads to:

(c) The shrewd tactic. East always leads an honor in (1), always small in (3), but in case (2) he leads half the time high and the rest small. Against this tactic, South does better to revert to his behavior against tactic (a), playing East for both honors whenever he leads high, and only then.

South thus wins the 6 cases from (1) and 4 of the 8 cases from (2), thus, on balance, 10 cases out of 15.

This shrewd tactic is therefore no improvement, but we may now figure out the correct optimum strategy as follows:

(d) The optimum strategy. East leads, of course, always an honor in (1), but in case (2) he leads exactly, but "at random", a small card 12°% of the time, i.e., once out of 8 times.

It is clear that declarer now has to play for split honors whenever East leads high (7 cases against 6). But if East leads small, declarer may:

(i) play for split honors. He will win in 0 + (7 + 1) + 0 = 8 cases (out of 15).

(ii) play for Q-J with West. He will win in 0 + (7 + O) + 1 = 8 cases (out of 15).

Thus according to whether the opponent's strategy is naive, expert, shrewd, or optimum, the declarer wins a trick in 14, 9, 10, or 8 cases out of 15. And he has no way to improve on those chances.

OPTIONAL. A term applied to a bid, play or point of law in which a player may have two or more choices; as distinguished from compulsory action or procedure strictly regulated by law.

OPTIONAL DOUBLE. A COOPERATIVE DOUBLE. shows a balanced hand with enough high cards to defeat the contract in all probability, and with support for any unbid suit, usually used against high-level contracts (at least the three-level). The partner of the doubler need not have a substantial trump holding in order to pass; he is expected to pass unless he has a good suit and unbalanced distribution. For example, the following hand would be appropriate for an optional double of a 3♥ opening pre-empt:

♠ A K 7
♥ A J 2
♦ 7 4 3
♣ A Q 6 5

Few experts use the cooperative double. 3NT would be the normal choice with this hand. See also DEFENSE TO OPENING THREE-BID; PENALTY DOUBLE; TAKEOUT DOUBLE.

OPTIONS. (1) Alternative actions available to a player in certain circumstances after an irregularity by the opposing side. An opening lead by the wrong defender is a case in which the declarer has four options. (See LAWS, Laws 53 and 54). (2) Alternative play possibilities available to a declarer. He should usually adopt a sequence of play which will "preserve options." A play which retains the possibility of trying for other possibilities is usually better than one which stands or falls on immediate success, even if the second is a better percentage chance.

OPTIONS TRADING. A popular occupation for bridge experts, especially on the Amex in New York City.

ORANGE CLUB. Strong club system used by James Jacoby and Bobby Wolff in the 1970, 1971 and 1972 World Championships, and subsequently by Wolff with Bob Hamman. The 1♣ opening promises 17 or more points; responses show controls. Other opening bids are limited and natural according to the CANAPÉ principle. A 1NT opening shows a balanced hand with 13-15 points with a 4- or 5-card club suit or 16-17 with any balanced distribution.

Other features include BLUE TEAM 2♦, FLANNERY 2♥, weak two bid in spades only; singleton- and void-showing forcing raises by a passed hand.

ORIGINAL BID. The first bid made in an auction. Reference is frequently made by a partner to one's "original bid" as having been in spades or notrump, etc., as for example: "I put you back to spades, since that was your original bid."

ORIGINAL HOLDING. The cards one has in a given suit at the beginning of play or at the beginning of the auction. Thus one might say, while describing the play of a hand, that one's original spade holding was five to the A-J-10, and that at a certain point one was down to the 10 and two small in the suit.

ORIGINAL LEAD. See OPENING LEAD.

OUR HAND. A colloquial expression indicating that a player thinks his side can make the highest positive score on a deal in which both sides take part in the auction. See BELONG.

OUT. A player who is a member of a table at rubber bridge, but not actively participating. The order in which players are out is established by cutting, the holder(s) of the lowest card or cards cut sitting out for the first rubber or chukker, other players going out in order.

OUT-OF-THE-BLUE CUEBID. An unusual bid of a new suit which cannot be taken as a suit bid, indicating support for partner's last bid suit, strength in the cuebid suit (often first-round control), and interest in reaching a high-level contract. The phrase was coined by Norman Squire, England, in his *Theory of Bidding*. See BLUE TEAM 4♣-4♦ CONVENTION.

OUT OF TURN. Not in rotation. For a call out of rotation, see LAWS (Laws 30-32). For a lead out of turn, see Laws 53-56. For a play out of turn, see Law 57.

OUT ON A LIMB. A phrase used to describe a player who has taken unusual or precipitate action during an auction and is in great danger of being doubled at a contract that is both risky and untenable. During the play of a hand, one may be said to be out on a limb as respects a situation, for example, when one is "wide open" in a suit at notrump, although the opposition may not be aware of this, or when one is playing at a trump contract and not only does not have control of the trump suit but is extremely vulnerable to attack in that area.

OVER. A term used to indicate one's position at the table in respect to one's right-hand opponent. One may be correctly said to be over that opponent if one is West to his South, for example. This term may be used in bidding situations as well as in play. See RIGHT-HAND PLAYER.

OVERBID. A call offering to undertake a contract for a greater number of tricks than is justified by the bidder's holding. Matters of system are often involved; a call may be an overbid in one system but an underbid in another. In competitive auctions, or auctions that are likely to become competitive, an apparent overbid may be an AD-VANCE SAVE. The term overbid is sometimes erroneously used in referring to an OVERCALL. See SACRIFICE.

OVERBIDDER. A player who consistently bids higher than his high-card and distributional strength justify. Playing with an overbidder, it is clearly necessary to be conservative, although this is no remedy holding extreme weakness. However, the overbidder must not be allowed to think that he is playing with an underbidder, or worse will follow. If the underbidder bids normally when he is due to be dummy he is little better off, because that is the situation in which the overbidder, vain of his dummy play, reaches for the moon.

OVERBOARD. The state of being (much) too high in a given auction. See SAFETY LEVEL.

OVERCALL IN OPPONENT'S MAJOR SUIT. 2♥ over 1♥, or 2♠ over 1♠, is most often used as a CUEBID IN OPPONENT'S SUIT, in which case it can have any of a number of agreed-upon meanings. The natural use of an overcall in an opponent's major suit is desirable if, and only if, the opponents use a CANAPÉ style of bidding, in which a major suit opening may frequently be made on a suit of only three cards.

OVERCALL IN OPPONENT'S MINOR SUIT. 2♣

over 1♣, or 2♦ over 1♦, is often used naturally instead of as a cuebid. Such treatment is most useful if the opponents are playing five-card majors, or any other method which requires frequent opening bids with prepared three-card (or shorter) minor suits. See also CUEBIDS IN OPPONENT'S SUIT.

OVERCALLS.

In a broad sense, the term overcall refers to any bid by either partner after an opponent has opened the bidding. The following discussion is limited to non-jump direct overcalls in a suit. A direct (or immediate) overcall is a bid at your turn immediately following a bid by your right-hand opponent.

In this heading, only minimum bids in a suit are considered.

As many as ten factors may influence a player's decision to overcall. In roughly descending order of importance, they are:

(1) *Suit length.* An overcall is nearly always based on a five- or six-card suit. A strong four-card suit may be sufficient if nonvulnerable at the one level, but obstruction (see [6] below) is a factor. A seven-card or longer suit will often qualify for action at a higher level. A vulnerable overcall at the two level is more likely to be based on a six-card suit.

(2) *Strength.* An average overcall is perhaps equivalent to a minimum suit opening bid, with about 13 points in high cards. The maximum with a five-card suit is likely to be 16-17 points — a hand just short of the strength required to double and then bid the suit.

Not vulnerable at the one level, a normal minimum is a king less than an opening bid. Even less strength is possible under some circumstances: if the overcaller passed earlier, he may overcall with little more than a good suit to direct a lead; if the opponents are vulnerable, the overcaller may bid spades on a weakish hand with good distribution, visualizing a 4♠ save against 4♥.

Some successful players practice an aggressive style of light overcalls; this style has advantages and drawbacks. In some circumstances, however — when vulnerable or at the two level — overcaller's partner can assume that overcaller has a sound hand.

(3) *Vulnerability.* A nonvulnerable bidder can afford to take more risk than a vulnerable player with a marginally sound hand (or a truly "unsound" one). The opponents will be less eager to double for penalties, and when they do so, they may have a poor bargain. This is particularly true at the part-score level with matchpoint scoring. For example, two down not vulnerable and undoubled is a frequent source of profit compared to part-scores of 110 or more in the other direction.

(4) *Level.* One-level overcalls are safer than two-level overcalls, which are easier to double for penalty.

(5) *Suit quality.* In close cases, the texture of the suit is a factor. Q-J-10-9-8-7 will be worth four tricks, Q-J-5-4-3-2 perhaps only two. An overcall on K-Q-10-9-5-2 can have lead-directing benefits, whereas one on Q-9-5-4-2 may cause disaster.

(6) *Obstruction.* An overcall that consumes the opponents' bidding space is attractive. 1♠ over 1♣, 2♣ over 1♦, 2♦ over 1♥, and 2♥ over 1♠ all have preemptive

value. (In each case, a single raise is the only bid available to the next opponent if he has a minimum responding hand; even if NEGATIVE DOUBLES are in use, the opponent's hand may be unsuitable.) Hence, these overcalls are often based on borderline values; but an overcall that consumes little space (e.g. 1♣- 1♦) implies more strength.

(7) *Opponents' skill.* Doubtful overcalls have less to gain against strong players, who will be quick to punish an indiscretion with a penalty double and defend accurately. Experts will also use inferences from an opposing overcall to judge the bidding and play.

(8) *Holding in opponent's suit.* Experts disagree on whether length in opening bidder's suit makes an overcall desirable. Suppose East opens 1♠, neither vulnerable, and South holds:

♠ K 9 5 2
♥ K 4
♦ A J 9 8 3 2
♣ 7

The traditional view is that South's length in spades indicates a misfit deal and dictates caution. Some authorities contend, however, that South's spade length suggests possible spade shortness in North's hand and therefore diamond support; hence, South should be more willing to act.

(9) *Opponents' vulnerability.* An overcaller must always be sensitive to the opponent's vulnerability as well as his own. At matchpoint duplicate and favorable vulnerability, an overcaller can show a profit by saving at 4♠, down three, against 4♥. At unfavorable vulnerability, he must exercise discretion. A 2♣ overcaller of 1♠ meets disaster if he is doubled and set two. To overcall in such circumstances requires a solid six playing tricks, and even that may not be sufficient.

(10) *Opponents' methods.* Overcalls can be made slightly more freely if the opponents use NEGATIVE DOUBLES. Overcalls of 1♠ over a minor suit can be made slightly more freely against opponents who play FIVE-CARD MAJORS, since there is a chance to prevent them from finding a heart fit.

Another factor is an overcaller's position at the table:

WEST	NORTH	EAST	SOUTH
1♣	Pass	1♠	?

After East-West open and respond, an overcall by South has less to gain and more to lose. The opponents have already exchanged some information (West knows, for instance, that East does not have four hearts and four spades); both opponents have values; South must overcall at the two level.

Responding to overcalls.

For actions by the opening bidder's partner after an overcall, see FREE BID.

Actions by overcaller's partner come under four headings: (*The Bridge World* magazine has suggested the term "advancer" for the partner of an overcaller to avoid confusion with "responder" of the opening bidder.)

(1) *Raises.* The traditional approach is for a single raise to be mildly encouraging, a double raise to be strongly encouraging (but not forcing), and for a raise to game to be natural and strong.

Consider an opening bid of 1♣ and a vulnerable overcall of 1♠. If advancer has spade support and normal distribution, he raises to 2♠ with 8-10 points; to 3♠ with 11-12; to 4♠ with 13-15. (If the overcall is non-vulnerable, the ranges are raised by about 2 points.) Note that three-card support is enough for any raise, and less support is possible, especially if opener's partner bids. If the bidding, with both sides vulnerable, is:

WEST	NORTH	EAST	SOUTH
1♥	1♠	4♥	4♠

South might hold K-x in spades and considerable strength in the minor suits.

A different treatment, proposed in the Sixties by Lawrence Rosler and Roger Stern, influenced modern theory. In this method, all raises of overcalls were preemptive, and cuebids in the opponent's suit were constructive raises at the appropriate level. After 1♣-1♠, responses of 2♣, 3♣ and 4♣ were sound raises to 2♠, 3♠ and 4♠ respectively.

WEST	NORTH	EAST	SOUTH
1♦	1♠	2♥	?

South would jump to 3♠ on:

> ♠ Q 9 7 4
> ♥ 4
> ♦ 8 5 3
> ♣ K 10 8 5 2

and directly to 4♠ on:

> ♠ Q 9 6 5 4
> ♥ 6 5
> ♦ 4
> ♣ A 10 8 4 2

North can hold many other hands that can produce game. Even if 4♠ doesn't make, it may be a fine save against the opponents' possible game.

The modern view of an overcall as a constructive action (as opposed to an obstructive or lead-directing action) has led most pairs to adopt methods that offer greater accuracy after an overcall. Many modern pairs retain preemptive raises, but use a cuebid to start the description of any hand with game interest. In this method, a cuebid is the only forcing response. A strong advancer must therefore be careful to avoid another response, since overcaller may pass. The advancer can clarify with his next bid whether he has a limit raise, a strong raise or perhaps a good suit of his own. (A bid of a new suit after the cuebid is forcing for one round, but not to game. Such a bid is sometimes used to show an unspecified singleton.)

A jump cuebid (1♦-1♠-Pass-3♥) also used showing limit with a singleton, somewhere is often used as a limit raise in the overcaller's suit, leaving the simple cuebid as a general-direction bid seeking further information.

After a cuebid, if overcaller rebids his suit, cuebidder may pass; but any other rebid by overcaller promises extra strength.

WEST	NORTH	EAST	SOUTH
1♦	1♠	Pass	?

South should cuebid 2♦ on:

> ♠ J 6 5
> ♥ K 8 4
> ♦ 5 3
> ♣ A K 8 4 2

South has a good offensive hand, but much depends on the strength of North's overcall. If North rebids 2♠, chances for game decline and South probably should pass.

(2) *Suit takeouts.* These may be forcing or non-forcing, by partnership agreement.

WEST	NORTH	EAST	SOUTH
			1♣
1♥	Pass	1♠	

In traditional methods, East has a spade suit (a good five-carder at worst) and is unlikely to have heart support. East expects West to pass, although game may still be reached if West has spade support. If East had bid 2♦, he would suggest a stronger hand.

Since the necessity to cuebid with a strong hand before showing a long suit is uneconomical, many pairs use a new-suit response by an unpassed hand as forcing. Some pairs differentiate between new-suit responses after overcalls at the one level and at the two level; they consider only two-level responses as forcing because a two-level overcall is usually equivalent to an opening bid.

The meaning of a jump shift is also a matter of partnership agreement. It may be forcing to game, forcing for one round, strongly encouraging or preemptive. A popular treatment is the fit-showing jump:

WEST	NORTH	EAST	SOUTH
1♣	1♠	Pass	3♦

South promises a spade fit with diamond length and strength. This information may help North make an accurate competitive decision if East-West sacrifice against 4♠.

(3) *Notrump responses.* These are constructive, but vary in strength with the level and vulnerability of the overcall. After a one-level overcall, the following ranges may apply:

	Not Vulnerable	Vulnerable
1NT	9-11	8-10
2NT	12-14	11-12
3NT	15-16	13-16

The 2NT ranges are reduced somewhat after a two-level overcall.

A 2NT response is non-forcing. After a 3NT response, overcaller seldom insists on game in his suit; advancer could have cuebid to investigate alternative game contracts. A few scientific pairs use a forcing 1NT response to an overcall.

(4) *Cuebid.* In addition to the references under, Raises above, see CUEBID IN OPPONENT'S SUIT.

For other aspects of overcalling see: BARON NOTRUMP OVERCALL; GARDENER NOTRUMP OVERCALL; GHESTEM; JUMP OVERCALL; MICHAELS CUEBID; ONE NOTRUMP OVERCALL; PREEMPTIVE OVERCALL; RESPONDING TO OVERCALLS; ROMAN JUMP OVERCALLS; THREE NOTRUMP OVERCALL; TWO NOTRUMP OVERCALL; UNUSUAL NOTRUMP; WEAK JUMP OVERCALL; WEAK NOTRUMP OVERCALL.

OVERLEAD. The Australian term for the traditional opening lead: higher of touching honors. RUSINOW leads of the second-highest honor are one type of UNDERLEAD.

OVERRUFF. To trump higher than the right-hand opponent after a plain-suit lead. An overruff is almost always good policy. The main exceptions occur when there is a possibility of achieving a trump promotion. A player who holds a certain trump trick together with a possibility of a second trick should usually refuse to overruff. This is an obvious position with spades as trumps:

> ♠ 4 3 2
> ♠ A J   ♠ 6 5
> ♠ K Q 10 9 8 7

If East leads a suit of which South and West are both void, South may elect to ruff with the king or queen. West then ensures two trump tricks by refusing to overruff.

OVERTAKE. To play a higher card than the one already played by partner for entry reasons. The objective may be suit establishment:

♠ A J 10 9 8 7

♠ K

If five tricks are needed from this suit in a notrump contract, and there is only one entry in the North hand, the king must be overtaken by the ace. The same would apply if South held the singleton queen and North's suit was headed by the ace or king. An alternative reason for overtaking would be an urgent need for an entry for finessing purposes.

WEST	EAST
♠ A 6	♠ 7 3
♥ K	♥ A J 5 3
♦ A J 8 4	♦ 9 7 3 2
♣ A Q J 6 5 3	♣ 10 9 2

North leads a spade against West's 3NT contract. The only hope is to run the club suit, so West overtakes his ♥K with the ace in order to take the club finesse. This sacrifices a heart trick, but makes the contract if the club finesse succeeds. Another common reason for overtaking is dealt with under UNBLOCKING.

OVERTAKING SQUEEZE. A specialized form of triple squeeze in which the squeeze trick can be won in either hand.

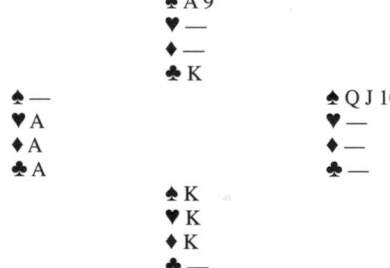

At notrump, South leads the ♠K, and West is squeezed in three suits. If he discards a red ace, North plays low and South cashes the red king. If West discards the ♣A, North overtakes and cashes the ♣K. South thus wins two tricks.

An analagous triple squeeze at a trump contract can give South all the tricks.

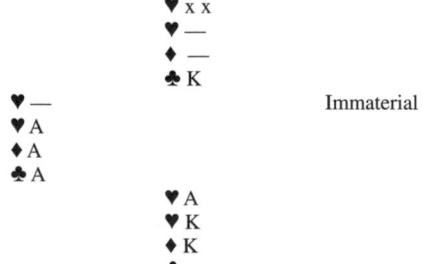

Spades are trump, and South leads the ace of that suit. This squeeze West in three suits, enabling South to all three tricks.

OVERTRICK. A trick taken by declarer in excess of the number of tricks required for his contract. If a player is in 4♠ and takes 12 tricks, he is said to have made two overtricks. If a contract is doubled or redoubled, and an overtrick or overtricks are taken, the premium accruing to declarer's side can be substantial. Under certain conditions redoubled overtricks can be worth more than the corresponding slam premium. At duplicate, the making of an overtrick can be all-important — it can actually win a board or even an entire tournament. This situation cannot occur in rubber bridge unless, again, the redoubled feature comes into consideration.

OVERTRUMP. See OVERRUFF.

P

PODI. See DEFENSE TO INTERFERENCE WITH BLACKWOOD.

PRO. Pattern Relay Organized. Also refers to a professional bridge player. See PRO SYSTEM, PROFESSIONAL PLAYERS.

PTDA. See PROFESSIONAL TOURNAMENT DIRECTORS ASSOCIATION.

PACIFIC BRIDGE LEAGUE. An organization founded by Tom Stoddard in 1933, and developed by him through the 15 years of its existence. The League included the 11 far-western states plus the territories of Hawaii and Alaska and the Canadian provinces of British Columbia and Alberta.

The League rapidly reached a four-figure membership. It promoted two major tournaments as well as many minor ones. The All-Western tournament was started in Los Angeles in 1935, and Bridge Week in 1936. The latter was held half in Los Angeles and half in San Francisco.

Collaboration between the ACBL and the Pacific BL began in 1940, when uniform masterpoint systems were agreed. A closer affiliation was planned in 1948, when the great services of Tom Stoddard to the Pacific BL were recognized. He was named President Emeritus of ACBL Western Division, with permanent status on the Executive Committee. The final merger between the ACBL and the Western Division became effective Jan. 1, 1956.

PACK. A group of a specific number of cards of consistent composition, sold and used as a unit. The makeup of a pack depends on the date and the country. In the Western world they are composed of four suits, with three FACE CARDS and up to thirteen SPOT CARDS, and have an extra card (JOKER) or cards. The tables below describe some of the many packs that have been in use. When ace is included with the face cards, it ranks high; when included with the spot cards, it ranks low and is called the ONE-SPOT.

(1) Pack with one of each card:

No. of cards	Game or Country	Face Cards	Spot Cards
62	500	A K Q J	*13 12 11 10 9 8 7 6 5 4 3 2
60	Fantan	K Q J	12 11 10 9 8 7 6 5 4 3 2 1
52	Bridge, Poker	A K Q J	10 9 8 7 6 5 4 3 2
48	Alouette	K C J †	9 8 7 6 5 4 3 2 1
48	Old German	K O U†	10 9 8 7 6 5 4 3 2

40	Trappola	K C J		7 6 5 4 3 2 1	
36	Schwerter (Ger.)	K O U		10 9 8 7 6	2
36	Russian	K Q J		10 9 8 7 6	1
36	Sixettes	A K Q J		10 9 8 7 6	
32	PiquetA	K Q J		10 9 8 7	
32	German	K O U		10 9 8 7	2
24	Schnaps	A K Q J		10 9 8	

(2) Packs with two of each suit:

64	Bezique	A K Q J		10 9 8 7	
48	Pinochle	A K Q J		10 9	
48	Gaigel	A K Q J		10	7

(3) With a group of extra cards not a part of the four suits called in various countries, atouts or atutti:

97 Minichiate taroc (Florence) 41 atutti, and each suit has four face cards and ten spot cards.

78 Lombard tarot (Venice) 22 atutti, and each suit has four face cards and ten spot cards.

62 Tarocchino (Bologna) 22 atutti, and each suit has four face cards and six spot cards (10 9 8 7 6 1).

54 Tarok (German) 22 atutti, and each suit had four face cards and four spot cards, black suits 10 9 8 7 and red suits 4 3 2 1.

64 Sicilian 22 atutti, K Q C J 10 9 8 7 6 5 of four suits and the ace and 4 of coins.

*Only two fo the 13 spot cards are used.

†C=Cavalier; O=Ober; U=Unter

For the 22 atutti, see TAROT.

For bridge purposes, the pack is a set of 52 standard playing cards divided into four suits (spades, hearts, diamonds and clubs) of 13 cards each, ranking in descending order from the ace to the deuce. See LAWS (Law 1). In the U.S., the term deck is often preferred. See also HISTORY OF PLAYING CARDS; PLAYING CARDS.

PACKET. A portion of the deck held together, as in gathering tricks, or in dividing the cards for shuffling purposes.

PAIR. A twosome or partnership of two players. All games at bridge come down to the basic competitive situation of pair versus pair, bridge being a partnership, or pair, game.

PAIRS. An event in which the players compete as pairs.

PAJAMA GAME. Duplicate session with many tops and bottoms.

PAKISTAN BRIDGE ASSOCIATION (PBA). Founded 1972, and competed in Far East Championships through 1979. Won five out of a possible six BFAME Championships, 1981, 1983, 1985, 1987 and 1991. Pakistan has twice reached world team championship finals, in the 1981 Bermuda Bowl and the Rosenblum Teams 1986. Pakistan hosted 1985 BFAME Championships.

Officers 1992:
President: S. Saeed Jafri
Secretary: Mohammad Aslam Sheikh
F-11/1 Moeen Steel Market Baba-e-Urud Road
Karachi, Pakistan.
Telephone: 92 21 241 7666
Fax: 92 21 773 7230

PALOOKA. A very poor player. The term was popularized by S.J. Simon.

PAMP PAR CONTEST. A feature of the 1990 world championships. The following is Alan Truscott's account in the *New York Times*:

Until recently, an expert asked to name the toughest test of cardplaying ability would have hesitated. But now the answer is clear: The Pamp Par Hands contest was the most difficult and challenging event in the history of bridge.

It was played during the World Championships in Geneva in October 1990. Twenty world-famous players were selected as the victims. The torture-master was Pietro Bernasconi of Switzerland, who is highly skilled in both bridge and computers, a rare combination.

The sufferers sat in front of a computer screen and were shown their own hand as declarer, the dummy, the bidding and the opening lead. There were only 12 deals to be played in two days, but such deals. Cover the East-West hands shown in the following diagram, and consider how you would tackle the play in six clubs, given that West has made a weak jump overcall in spades and then led the heart queen.

```
              ♠ 4 3
              ♥ 10 7 4
              ♦ 9
              ♣ A J 10 9 8 7 4
♠ K 10 9 7 6 2              ♠ Q 8
♥ Q J 9                    ♥ 8 6 5 3
♦ K 7 5 4                  ♦ Q J 10 6
♣ —                       ♣ Q 6 5
              ♠ A J 5
              ♥ A K 2
              ♦ A 8 3 2
              ♣ K 3 2
```

Neither side was vulnerable. The bidding:

South	West	North	East
1 ♣	2 ♠	5 ♣	Pass
6 ♣	Pass	Pass	Pass

West led the heart queen.

The computer is keeping track of the time you take, so you are working against the clock. If you make an error the computer will beep at you, charge you 250 points of an initial allowance of 1000, and allow you a second chance. And a third, and even a fourth. Many of the deals world champions were unable to solve even with four attempts.

South could look forward to an easy endplay against West if that player began with ♠K-Q and ♥Q-J, but with that hand West might well have led the ♠K. So the declarer must concentrate on finding a way to succeed if the ♠K-Q are in different hands.

The first move after winning the ♥K should be to cash the ♦A and ruff a diamond. Then cash the ♣A, since if anyone has a club void it is no doubt West. That proves to be right, for a spade is discarded. Now the ♣J is led for a marked finesse and the last trump is extracted.

A second diamond is ruffed, and the closed hand is re-entered with a spade to the ace to permit the final diamond ruff. The position then is:

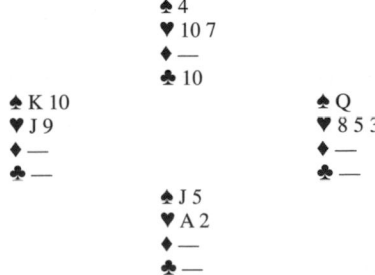

```
              ♠ 4
              ♥ 10 7
              ♦ —
              ♣ 10
♠ K 10                    ♠ Q
♥ J 9                     ♥ 8 5 3
♦ —                      ♦ —
♣ —                      ♣ —
              ♠ J 5
              ♥ A 2
              ♦ —
              ♣ —
```

As West has produced the ♦K the chance that he began with ♠K-Q, and would be exposed to a normal squeeze-endplay in the major suits, has vanished: If he had begun with 11 high-card points including a void club, he would have been far too strong for his preemptive jump.

But the lead of the last trump from the dummy succeeds in a more complex fashion. If East throws the ♠Q, West is in trouble as before so East must throw a heart. South throws a heart, and if West throws a spade South can develop his 12th trick in that suit.

So West throws a heart, and South cashes the ace, establishing the 10 in the dummy. Now the ♠5 is led, and West can decide whether to win and concede the last trick to the ♠J, or play low, in which case the ♥10 comes back to life.

The winner of the Pamp World Par Contest was Benito Garozzo, who won many world titles for Italy and now resides in the United States. Following him in the final rankings were Bob Hamman, United States; Pierre Ghestem, France; Chip Martel, United States; and Andy Robson, Britain.

Whether this event will ever be repeated seems doubtful. Even if Bernasconi makes the considerable effort required to prepare it, he may have trouble finding willing victims.

PANAMA. A defensive bidding system against the FORCING CLUB. Bids at the two-level show either a weak jump overcall in the suit bid or a three-suiter with shortage in the bid suit.

PANAMA BRIDGE ASSOCIATION (Association Panamena de Bridge). Founded in 1968.
President 1992:
   John Maduro
   PO Box 2178 Zona 9
   Panama
   Tel 66 2247 or 64 7560

PAN AMERICAN BRIDGE CHAMPIONSHIPS. The first-ever Pan American Bridge Championships and Pan American Games, sponsored by the World Bridge Federation and Texas World Bridge, were held in June, 1992, in Corpus Christi TX. Four premier events which required prior qualification were Open Teams, Women's Teams, Open Pairs and Women's Pairs. Every nation in North America, Central America and South America was entitled to field two teams and eight pairs, with the USA as host country allowed a double quota. Open to all comers were five other Pan American events, each four sessions, plus a full complement of regionally rated two-session games. ACBL and WBF points were awarded in most events of two or more sessions. United States competitors won the gold medals for first place in all four major Pan American championships. For results see Appendix III.

PAN AMERICAN INVITATIONAL CHAMPIONSHIPS. An invitational pair championship first held in 1974 in Mexico City, scored by IMPs. This competition was discontinued after 1977.

PAR. The result on a hand if both sides have done as well as possible.

PAR CONTEST. A tournament using prepared hands,

each of which embodies a predetermined optimum (par) result. The players' results are compared with par, rather than with each other. In an ordinary duplicate tournament, how you fare depends to a large degree on how well or poorly your opponents play against you. In a par contest, your skill alone determines the result. You may not profit by an opponent's blunder if you have already erred.

World Championships on a par basis were held in 1961 and 1963 by the World Bridge Federation which preferred the term par-point, perhaps because par can easily be confused with pair. Until 1966 the Intercollegiate Bridge Tournament was the only par contest held annually in the United States. The National Industrial Recreational Association Tournament was conducted in 1963 and 1964 as a par contest but then adopted matchpoint scoring.

The following hand (from the 1963 National Industrial Recreation Association Par Tournament) illustrates the fundamental difference between a par contest and an ordinary duplicate contest:

Dlr: North
Vul: Both

	♠ Q 3	
	♥ A 10 7	
	♦ J 10 8 7 5	
	♣ A Q 10	
♠ 4 2		♠ K J 8 7 6 5
♥ K 9 5 3		♥ J 6
♦ Q 6		♦ A 4 3
♣ 9 6 4 3 2		♣ 8 7
	♠ A 10 9	
	♥ Q 8 4 2	
	♦ K 9 2	
	♣ K J 5	

WEST	NORTH	EAST	SOUTH
	1♦	1♠	2NT
Pass	3NT	All Pass	

Opening lead: ♠4.

To earn par, East must not play an honor on the first trick, no matter what dummy plays. Then when West wins the ♦Q, he can play a spade, establishing East's suit while East still has the ♦A for entry.

In a duplicate tournament, many defenders would defeat the contract after playing an honor on the first trick, because South would play incorrectly and win the trick. In a par contest, these defenders would not be awarded par.

In 1963, the World Bridge Federation adopted an International Par Point Contract Bridge Code, drafted by Michael Sullivan and Robert Williams of Australia. This code deals with irregularities and penalties. The basic decisions about the format of the contest are left to the organizers. Some of the factors to be considered are discussed below.

Par-point scoring may be used for individual, pair, or team contest, (but only pair games are common). For a pair game, the par-setters should strive to ensure that the North-South pairs and East-West pairs will meet problems of equal difficulty. Such judgments are necessarily subjective, however, and it is better to choose the North-South and East-West winners separately.

(1) *The Bidding.* The bidding problems should be arranged so as not unduly to favor or penalize any common system or convention. As a rule, par points are awarded on the basis of the final contract reached, not on the actual auction. Minor awards may be given to inferior contracts. On some deals, players may be instructed (by a slip accompanying the board) to make specified preemptive bids, so that all pairs holding the other hands

will be presented with uniform bidding problems. Furthermore, players are instructed to refrain from psychics or other unwarranted or misleading bids. Nevertheless, all the vagaries of competitive auctions cannot be anticipated. Some players will inevitably face more difficult opposition bidding than others, and the par-setters may be called on to adjudicate. Despite this opportunity for redress, it is here that luck or the skill of one's opponent is most likely to affect one's score.

(2) *Before the Play.* So that all competitors face the same play or defense problem, it is usual to specify both the contract to be played and the opening lead. A traveling slip, accompanying the board for this purpose, is consulted after the bidding is over. The official contract need not be the same as the contract awarded maximum bidding par points, if a more interesting play problem is presented. The par-setters may also provide a guidance auction, from which the players can derive information needed during the play. They are instructed to ignore the actual bidding at their table (but there again, some luck enters).

(3) *The Play.* At the discretion of the par-setters, the traveling slip may inform the players before the play begins whether the par is for the declarer or the defenders. This saves time by eliminating long huddles by the non-involved side, but adds another artificial aspect to the event.

In addition to the opening lead, the play to one or more tricks may be directed, and declarer or defenders may receive public or private instructions. The primary purpose is to obviate the awarding of automatic pars, if the opponents should slip in advance of the anticipated problem. These instructions may also ensure the defeat of a misplaced contract or the fulfillment of a misdefended contract. This is of secondary importance, however, as the par would not be awarded in any case if the play at the table deviated from the prescribed line. Minor awards may be given for partially correct or slightly inferior lines of play or defense.

Note that an equitable two-way play par (that is, a separate par both for the declarer and the defenders on one deal) is almost impossible to arrange. For example, in the hand given above, South will not have a chance to make a par play (ducking the first trick) if East first makes his par play by ducking. Then that South would have to be awarded an unearned automatic par.

(4) *Movements.* Every player must play all the boards. No movement is necessary — a pair could well play the entire session against one pair of opponents, sharing the boards with the other tables. This arrangement also saves time, as the faster players need not wait for the slower ones to finish their boards each round. Nevertheless, for social and other reasons, some limited movements of the players is desirable.

It is recommended that a time limit for each group of boards be imposed. In important tournaments, the use of chess clocks should be considered. See PAMP PAR CONTEST.

PAR HAND. A hand prepared for use in a PAR CONTEST. By extension, a randomly dealt hand suitable for inclusion in such a contest because a single technical aspect of play or defense is dominant.

PAR POINT BRIDGE. See PAR CONTEST.

PARAGUAY BRIDGE ASSOCIATION. (Asociacion Paraguaya de Bridge)
It had a membership of 45 in 1993.
Officers 1993
President: Juan Pascual Burro
Secretary: Jose Maria Vidal
Estados Unidos No. 951
Asuncion
Paraguay
Tel: 595 21 441260
Fax: 595 21 213813

PARTIAL DESIGNATION. An incomplete request for a card to be played from the dummy. If the suit alone is named, the lowest card in the suit must be played. If a card is named but not a suit, and the card is ambiguous, the card must be taken from the suit previously led if possible.

PARTIAL ELIMINATION. A throw-in play depending on ruff-and-discard possibilities in which the stripping process is incomplete. In a perfect elimination the declarer eliminates all the suits which a defender may safely lead and saddles him with the choice of conceding a ruff and sluff or leading into a tenace. A partial elimination, on the other hand, is so called because the declarer only partially eliminates the suits which a defender may safely lead; now, whether the defender will have to lead to the declarer's advantage will depend on distributional hazards.

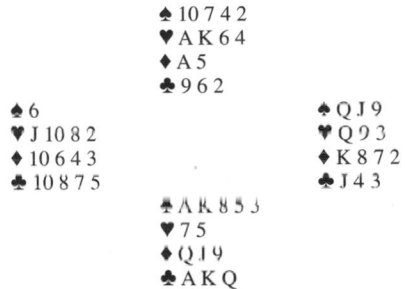

Playing in 6♠, South wins the heart lead and tests trumps. When West fails on the second round, South attempts an endplay to avoid taking the diamond finesse. He plays the second top heart, ruffs the third round in his hand, and takes his three top clubs before throwing the lead to East's master trump. East fortunately has no hearts or clubs left and has to lead away from the king.

South's maneuver is a partial elimination because he could only partially eliminate hearts. He did not have the entries to eliminate the hearts completely. This play had the added advantage that if East did have the 13th club as an exit card he might have been unwilling to give declarer a ruff-sluff and led a diamond anyway. The ruff-sluff could not possibly help South because he had only one trump left and could not ruff both the club return and dummy's last heart.

In the above example the critical suit — hearts — was eliminated from two of the four hands. When the distribution is favorable, a partial elimination may succeed even though the critical suit be eliminated from only one hand:

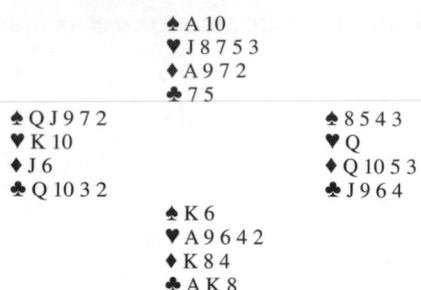

♠ A 10
♥ J 8 7 5 3
♦ A 9 7 2
♣ 7 5

♠ Q J 9 7 2   ♠ 8 5 4 3
♥ K 10   ♥ Q
♦ J 6   ♦ Q 10 5 3
♣ Q 10 3 2   ♣ J 9 6 4

♠ K 6
♥ A 9 6 4 2
♦ K 8 4
♣ A K 8

With hearts as trumps, South can make 12 tricks by means of partial elimination. He wins the spade lead, plays off the trump ace, and eliminates the black suits. He cashes the ♦ A-K and exits with a trump. West wins, but he is the only player without a diamond in his hand. He has to return a black suit, and South ruffs on the table, at the same time sluffing a diamond from the closed hand.

A partial elimination can also operate when one of the defenders still has a trump in his hand:

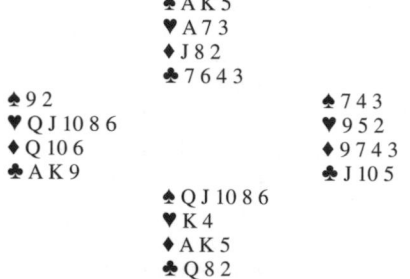

♠ A K 5
♥ A 7 3
♦ J 8 2
♣ 7 6 4 3

♠ 9 2   ♠ 7 4 3
♥ Q J 10 8 6   ♥ 9 5 2
♦ Q 10 6   ♦ 9 7 4 3
♣ A K 9   ♣ J 10 5

♠ Q J 10 8 6
♥ K 4
♦ A K 5
♣ Q 8 2

West opens the bidding with 1♥, and South reaches a contract of 4♠ instead of 3NT. After a heart lead, prospects are poor, but a partial elimination offers the best chance. However, it is essential to keep at least one trump in each hand to profit from a possible ruff and sluff; this means that South can afford to draw only two rounds of trumps, and must therefore rely on West's having no more than two trumps.

South wins the heart lead, plays off the ace and queen of trumps, and continues with a second and third round of hearts, ruffing. He then plays ace, king, and another diamond, throwing West into the lead. As expected, West has the outstanding high cards and has to offer a ruff and discard or concede a trick to the ♣ Q.

PARTIAL SCORE. See PARTSCORES.

PARTNER. The player with whom one is paired in a game of bridge.

PARTNER'S SUIT. The suit bid or rebid by the player seated opposite during an auction. It is usually advisable to support partner's suit when one can, as this builds firmness and reliability in a partnership. As respects defensive play situations, the leading of partner's suit raises many questions. Whether it should be led at all, and if so, which card of one's holding, etc., are all problems with which a good player constantly concerns himself.

PARTNERSHIP. Two players working as a unit, who must cooperate fully if they are to achieve good results.

PARTNERSHIP LANGUAGE. See SIGNALS and

SYSTEMS.

PARTNERSHIP MISUNDERSTANDINGS. All partnerships have misunderstandings about the meaning of bids, although these should be infrequent in a well-established expert partnership. Some advance consideration can reduce the frequency of such errors. Such misunderstandings fall into four general categories:

(1) *The strength of a bid.* For example, the range for a response of 1NT to 1♣: 5-8, 6-9, 7-10 and 9-11 are all in use.

(2) *The nature of a bid: sign-off, discouraging, encouraging, or forcing (for one round or to game).* A good example is a jump in a new suit over an opposing takeout double (see RESPONSES OVER OPPONENT'S TAKE-OUT DOUBLE). According to the partnership understanding, this bid can be preemptive, encouraging, forcing for one round, or fit-showing.

(3) *Artificial or natural quality of a bid.* Confusion can occur when a partnership has not specifically agreed whether a particular artificial device is being employed, such as LANDY over opposing notrump bids, especially with an unfamiliar partnership. Both players may normally use a convention, and be aware that the partner normally uses it, but still be in doubt about whether it is in use because it has not been discussed. A more common source of difficulty is doubt about whether a convention is applicable to a particular situation. It is sometimes difficult to diagnose, for example, whether 4 NT is natural or conventional; or whether a bid in the opponent's suit is a cuebid or an attempt to play in that suit.

(4) *The nature of a double.* There may be doubt about whether a double is for penalty, takeout, lead-direction, support, etc. A failure to agree on the use of RESPONSIVE or NEGATIVE DOUBLES would be an example of this problem. There are also situations, usually after the first round of bidding, in which the intentions of the doubler are not clear.

The nature of a pass may also be crucial, especially if a FORCING PASS is a possibility. No partnership can avoid misunderstandings altogether, but the following suggestions may help to reduce the incidence of disaster.

First, a regular partnership should have a detailed understanding.

Second, a player should avoid making an ambiguous bid when an unambiguous alternative is equally satisfactory.

Third, when an ambiguous bid is made, a partnership should apply some automatic rule. A reasonable rule is to take the weaker interpretation in each case, that is: the lower point range; nonforcing against forcing; natural as against conventional; and takeout rather than penalty double. The opposite rule is also playable, and so are a variety of hybrid rules. In any case, it is advisable to have some rule. This often avoids impending trouble, provided both players are aware of the possibility of trouble.

PARTNERSHIP PSYCHOLOGY. The art of keeping partner happy is worth more in terms of results than much advanced technical knowledge; but it is an art which many players, including some at the highest level never learn. At rubber bridge the player who encourages his partner instead of shouting at him, praising the occasional good plays instead of pointing out the obvious bad ones, earns large dividends. His partners then like to play with him, and play up to their capabilities. On the other hand, a player who is subjected to a barrage of criticism is likely to play below his best not only for the remainder of the rubber but on subsequent occasions.

In tournament play, two people who have agreed to be partners ought in theory to be compatible, but this is not always the case, and the same principles are applicable. Though some successful partnerships contain one player whose personality dominates, many long-lived partnerships consist of players who enjoy each other's company and have attained mutual respect. Egotists whose concern is to prove how brilliantly they themselves play and how foolishly their partners perform may have temporary successes, but they must find new partners regularly.

Since distance as well as respect may be a desirable partnership attribute, much has been written about the performance of partnerships — especially those with an emotional attachment. There is no standard; some otherwise affectionate couples seem to let all the tiny frustrations of their relationship surface at the bridge table, while the formidable marital problems of others may vanish. All that is clear is that emotional ties may oblige some partnerships to work harder to be effective.

Perhaps the simplest and best rule for all partners to remember is the "golden" one.

PARTNERSHIP RUBBER BRIDGE. A style of rubber bridge popular in England whereby two players play as partners throughout a session. Players agree in advance to play as partners, as they would in a duplicate event, and there is no game for unpaired individuals. This tends to raise the standard of the game by excluding those who, through inferior ability or character deficiency, find it difficult to get a partner.

PARTNERSHIP UNDERSTANDING. An agreement between partners that enables them to draw information or inferences from the bidding and play. Partnership understandings are of two types: explicit, describing agreements reached through discussion; and implicit, describing those not specifically discussed but arising through experience. The sum of a partnership's understanding comprises not only conventional bids and plays, but STYLE: a player's tendencies in exercising judgment.

In tournament play, pairs have a duty to see that understandings of which the opponents could not reasonably be aware are clearly and accurately stated on the CONVENTION CARD, alerted when required, and explained in response to a query. At rubber bridge, understandings are best announced to the opponents before play begins. In extended team events such as the Bermuda Bowl, pairs are required to provide their competitors with a summary of methods weeks in advance.

Partnership understanding is not to be confused with a PRIVATE CONVENTION, which is illegal and unethical. See ALERTING, EXPLANATION OF CONVENTIONAL CALL OR PLAY, STYLE, AND LAW 75.

PARTNERSHIPS. Either or both of the two sets of the players at a table, North-South and East-West. Players who play together frequently are considered an established partnership; players who pair up for a particular event, having played together either seldom or never, have a more casual partnership. Most of the bidding and play conventions were established as successful tactics by established partnerships; it is noteworthy that the use of these bids was carefully explained to opponents by their

developers, and they were quite well known even before their publication.

PARTSCORE. A partial; a trick score of fewer than 100 points. At RUBBER BRIDGE, a successful partscore counts toward game and enables one pair to make game by fulfilling an additional partscore or partscores. Sometimes a side that has a partscore must bid to the game level to buy the contract. If the contract is made, the entry on the scoring pad includes the total of both that score and the previous partscore or scores.

If, say, North-South score a game while East-West have a partscore, that frame ends, and both sides start anew in pursuit of game. (East-West's partial is wiped out.) But East-West still receive the trick score for their partscore when the full score, with all points won by each side above and below the line, is added together at the end of the rubber (or, in CHICAGO, after the fourth deal). See PARTSCORE BIDDING.

PARTSCORE BIDDING. Bidding by a side which possesses a partscore is a subject which is scantily treated by textbooks and produces considerable disagreement among experts. The following treatment is based on the opinion of a number of experts.

Forcing Bids. The most noticeable difference between partscore bidding and normal bidding results from the fact that many bids which would otherwise be forcing are no longer forcing when they complete the game. A new suit by responder, for example, is not forcing if it is sufficient for game. Similarly, a jump from one to three in a suit, or from one of a suit to 2NT may be passed. The jump shift remains forcing, however, regardless of the partscore.

Suit Bids. Because so many bids become nonforcing if they complete a partial, it is difficult for a partnership to conduct any lengthy bidding investigation. It is therefore of primary importance that whenever a partial exists, all suit bids should stress quality. Thus it would be poor policy to open a three-card minor with a partial. With 60 on score, holding ♠ A-K-J-x, ♥ x-x-x, ♦ x-x-x, ♣ A-J-x, a player should open 1♠, and pass partner's response (unless it is a jump shift). Similarly, responder should ignore a suit of doubtful quality. With 70 on score, holding ♠ K-x-x, ♥ Q-9-x-x, ♦ x-x, ♣ A-x-x-x, the response to 1♦ should be 1 NT, bypassing the poor heart holding. However, with ♠ K-x-x, ♥ x-x, ♦ x-x, ♣ Q-J-10-9-x-x, the response to 1♦ should be 2♣, this response at the two level does not promise as much high-card strength as at love score. Rather, it stresses the quality of the club suit. The opening bidder is expected to pass unless he has good reason to continue.

Notrump Bids. All notrump bids tend to have a slightly wider range when the bidder has a part score. Using a 16-18 point notrump range, with 60 on the score, it would be correct tactics to open 1NT holding either the 19-point hand (a) or the 15-point hand (b).

(a)		(b)
♠ A J x	or	♠ A J x
♥ K J x		♥ K J x
♦ A Q x x		♦ Q x x x
♣ K J x		♣ K J x

Some experts allow themselves more latitude than others in the range of their opening notrump, but taking the average approach of the experts consulted, standard expert procedure is to widen the range for an opening 1NT by about a point in either direction when a partscore is held.

There are two reasons for this increase in the notrump range. First, there is always a tremendous tactical advantage in opening with 1 NT. Partner is immediately in an excellent position either to place the contract or punish overzealous opponents. The opponents are unable to compete at the one level or may find it too dangerous to begin their search for a fit at the two level. To reopen in fourth seat after an opening notrump by opponents with a 60 partial is particularly dangerous, because opener's partner may pass with up to 13 high-card points, instead of being limited by his pass to seven or less.

Tactical advantages exist for opening 1NT frequently at no score also, but in this case the problem of whether to reach game or settle for a partial is paramount; widening the range of the notrump would be against the interests of accuracy. With a substantial partial, the question of whether to reach game or not is already solved, and tactical considerations become more prominent. Naturally the prospect of missing a slam is a deterrent to increasing the upper limit unduly. With 60 on score, and a passed partner, it is surely good tactics to open 1NT with 19 points regardless of the normal range, as slam can hardly be missed.

The second, and less obvious, reason for increasing the range, and thus the frequency of the notrump opening, goes back to the stress on quality for opening suit-bids. If the normal 1NT range is 15 to 17 points, and a partial of 40 is held, it would be proper to open 1NT holding ♠ K-x-x, ♥ A-x-x-x, ♦ A-x x-x, ♣ K-x. Ordinarily such a hand would be opened 1♥ or 1♦, depending on partnership attitude toward four-card majors. With the partscore, the suit-bid carries an added implication of quality. Partner will strain to raise the suit-bid, and the safer spot in notrump will be missed. If suit play is better, responder can choose the suit.

Other notrump bids are likewise affected by the partial. Most experts play 21-22 point opening 2NT bids. They increase this range, particularly the upper limit, when a partial exists. By far the most frequently used range (and, therefore, logically, the standard range) for an opening 2NT bid is 21-24 with a partial of 60 or more, and 20-24 with a lesser partial.

The opening strong 3NT bid becomes almost extinct in a partscore holding of 30 or more. It is better to open with 2♣, and rebid 2NT to a 2♦ response. After any other response a slam can be investigated with impunity.

Of all notrump bids, the simple response of 1NT is most affected by a partscore. Normally this bid shows 6-9 in Standard American, but with a partial it tends to become 4-12. The lower limit is reduced because of the strain to keep the bidding open when game is so near. The upper limit is increased because it keeps the bidding lower but in the game range on a hand where slam appears unlikely. The responses of 2NT and 3NT remain close to their usual ranges. The 13-15 range for a 2NT response increases to 13-16 with a partial, and becomes nonforcing, of course. The 3NT range moves from 16-17 to 17-18. It is a common practice among average players to avoid both these responses on some theory that it is unnecessary to get so high with a partial. This is a fallacy. There should be no danger at this level opposite an opening bid. More important by far is the fact that these bids are extremely useful when the opening bidder has slam aspirations.

Raising Partner's Suit. As responder, when holding a

fit with partner, it is imperative to show it immediately. The fact that one side has a fit increases the chances that the opponents have a fit and a profitable sacrifice. With a 90 partscore and an opening 1♠ bid by partner, holding Q-J-x-x, K-x, Q-x-x-x, x-x-x, bid 2♠ immediately. If opener's hand is such that 1 is the partnership limit, fourth hand will take some action, and the necessary 2♠ bid on the next round will come after the opponents have found their fit. Immediate action may keep the opponents out altogether. With a partscore, it is standard to give a single raise with 6-12 points. The lower limit may be reduced as far as three points if the raise is necessary to complete the game. With 13-16 points it is still standard to give a jump raise from one to three in a suit. With a stronger hand, a jump shift is in order.

Tactical Considerations. With a partscore, is it wise to open lighter or stronger than usual? What about when the opponents have a partial? Or when both sides are on score? This is an area of wide disagreement. No standard approach exists, but the various schools of thought are presented so the reader may form his own opinions.

One school holds that as long as fewer tricks are required to make a game, opening bids may be slightly weaker with a partial. A second school recommends using stronger opening bids with a partial. This group reasons: If the bidding is opened with a partial, the opponents are very apt to compete. Responder will fight for the partscore on the strength of the opening bid; if this bid is subminimum, responder may push too high, presenting the opponents with a very attractive double, or, even worse, he may decide to punish competing opponents, and double them into game. A third school suggests opening light with spades, but normally or slightly over without spades. Obviously the side with spades has an advantage in any bidding battle. Still a fourth school feels that the advantages and disadvantages of either stronger or lighter bids just about cancel each other out, maintaining that normal bids will work out best in the long run. A majority of the experts consulted recommended normal openings with a partial.

There are also various theories as to the best procedure when the opponents have a partial. A slight majority of the experts suggest opening light, believing that the best defense is an early offense. It is dangerous to overcall or balance against opponents who have a partial as they may have strength in reserve: hence the value of getting in first with the opening bid. Light takeout doubles and overcalls are also favored for the same reason. Many recommend the preemptive opening of 1♠ or 1 NT with a slightly lighter range than usual. Ely Culbertson, in his Contract Bridge Complete, says "Shade your bids downward if the opponents have a partscore and upward if you have the partscore." Then there are those who like to have stronger openings when the opponents have a partial; they would rather pass out a hand than open a minimum when they are at such a disadvantage in the score. Lastly there are those who stand steadfast for the normal opening.

A further point arising when the opponents have a partial is often overlooked. When in doubt whether to bid game or settle for a partscore, it is better to stretch a bit and bid game. The reason is that the value of success is substantially increased by the fact that the opponent's partial is wiped out. When both sides have a partscore, the experts are split into roughly two equal camps: those favoring lighter openings and those favoring normal openings. Reasons given are various combinations of those above.

The Value of a Partial. Experts have long been aware that a partscore at rubber bridge is worth far more than the 50 points awarded in the rules for a partial in an unfinished rubber. Because of the many imponderable factors involved, including the identity of one's opponents, mathematicians cannot agree on the correct way to calculate the value mathematically. However, Jean Besse kept a record or more than 1000 partscore situations. He compared the scores when a partial had just been achieved and again when the partial had been completed. Allowing 300 for any first game, 400 for the second game, and 500 for any third game, his results were as follows:

Values (over and above the trick score) of a nonvulnerable partial of 40 or more	100
Value of a vulnerable partial (opponents not vulnerable) of 40 or more	100
Value of a partial of 40 or more with both vulnerable	150

The tremendous value of a partial when both are vulnerable is attributed partly, of course, to the increased value of game but mainly to the increased difficulty encountered by vulnerable opponents in trying to defend.

In many bridge clubs in the United States, four-deal bridge Chicago has taken the place of rubber bridge. A partial must be worth somewhat less in this form of bridge, due to the limited time in which to capitalize on it. Naturally, a partial on the fourth deal is worth exactly the 100 points awarded for it in the rules.

PARTSCORE BONUS. In duplicate competition, 50 points are scored as a bonus for fulfilling a partscore contract. In CHICAGO, a bonus of 100 points is given for a partscore contract successful on the last hand. For the mathematical value of a partscore see PARTSCORE BIDDING.

PARTY BRIDGE. Private games consisting of at least two tables. The CHICAGO or four-deal method is customary. It is usual to give prizes to the players with the best scores and the player with the worst score may receive a booby prize. The manner of mixing partnerships varies widely; some hostesses use commercial tallies which give seating assignments to players, by which players enjoy four hands with all the other players or, alternately, all the other players of opposite sex. Another form, where excellence of bridge is to be rewarded, provides that, after each round, the winning pairs move to the lower numbered table, except at the head table, where the losing pair goes to the highest numbered table. Other possibilities are outlined under PARTY CONTRACT BRIDGE, LAWS OF.

At the end of a round each player enters on his tally only his net gain or loss — not his total score. At the end of the session these net gains and losses are totaled and the player's final score, plus or minus as the case may be, is entered at the bottom of his tally.

Some hostesses require players to record only plus scores and ignore minus scores. This compromises the quality of the game for serious bridge players, since it rewards wild doubling and redoubling.

PARTY CONTRACT BRIDGE, LAWS OF; DUPLICATE FOR HOME PLAY, AND COMPETITION

NOT IN DUPLICATE. The forms of Duplicate play described in the Laws are readily adapted to home play. Special games suitable to a small number of tables, or emphasizing the social above the competitive element, are described in the following pages.

For a single table, the available games are REPLAY DUPLICATE, COMPENSATION and PIVOT BRIDGE (non-duplicate). For two or three tables there are INDIVIDUAL MOVEMENTS, and MITCHELL or HOWELL PAIR MOVEMENTS, and TEAM-OF-FOUR MOVEMENTS. For a larger number of tables, where it is desired to emphasize the social element, the popular game is PROGRESSIVE BRIDGE.

In general, the Laws of Duplicate Contract Bridge apply to all forms of duplicate and multiple-table play — from the simplest replay contest to the most elaborate championship tournament.

Even in simple home games, such as Replay Duplicate, it is advisable to appoint one participant as Supervisor and to invest him with all the authority of a Tournament Director. Experience has shown that without a guiding hand even a social game is likely to be delayed or deadlocked by trivial irregularities.

Replay Duplicate is a contest between two pairs. It is played in two sessions, called the Original Play and the Replay. The players take places, one being designated North. The boards are shuffled, and are played with the arrows pointing North. Any number of boards is feasible. A separate scoreslip is kept for each board. At the close of the session the boards and scoreslips are laid aside where they will be undisturbed.

At some later time, the same four players take the same relative positions about the table. The boards are replayed with the arrows pointing East. Again a separate scoreslip is kept for each board.

The scoring may be by matchpoints, total points or imps. If the former method is used, each deal is treated as a separate match. The pair having the better net score on a deal is credited with 1 point. The final scores are the totals of these matchpoints. If total point scoring is employed, the two slips for each deal are compared, and the pair having the greater plus or lesser minus is credited with the difference. The next scores for all deals, so determined, are totaled, and the pair having the larger total wins the difference. Imp scoring is similar. Replay Duplicate has some limited popularity as a home game among foursomes that meet weekly for social bridge. It can easily be played in a continuous series of sessions. Half of the time in each session is devoted to the original play of new boards, and half to the replay of old boards.

The game tends to become a test of memory rather than of bridge skill. To check this tendency the following measures are recommended: 1. Do not play the boards in consecutive order. Choose the boards to be played next at random from the stack. 2. Avoid comment of any sort about the deal after its original play. 3. Allow at least a week to elapse between the original play and the replay.

It is sometimes desired to make the game a test of skill in play alone. The bidding during the original play is then recorded, and for the replay this bidding is read to fix the contract and declarer.

Individual Contests. In an individual game, each player plays once with every other as partner, and twice against every other as opponent. The initial seating of the players in games for two or three tables is shown below:

TWO TABLES

THREE TABLES

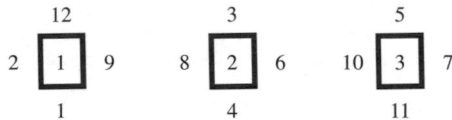

The game may be conducted without guide cards, as follows:

(1) Allow the players to take places at random. Reserve the North position at Table 1 for the Supervisor; this player is anchor, retaining his seat throughout the game.

(2) From this schedule inform each player of his number, and tell him who is the player of next-lower number.

(3) Announce that after each round, all players but the anchor will progress, each player taking the seat vacated by the player of next-lower number. (Player 1 follows Player 7 or 11 in the 2 or 3 table movements, respectively.) A new set of boards is played in each round. The set is played at all tables, the boards being circulated at convenience. The eight-player game requires seven rounds, with a total of 14, 21, or 28 boards. The twelve-player game requires 11 rounds, and the only feasible number of boards is 33.

The scoring of individual contests is explained in the Laws of Duplicate Contract Bridge. It is desirable to use Imps. With a 3-table movement, give two imp scores on each deal by comparing with the other tables. See PIVOT BRIDGE.

PASS. A call by which a player indicates that, at that turn, he does not choose to contract for a number of odd tricks at any denomination, nor does he choose, at that turn, to double a contract of the opponents or redouble a contract by his side that opponents have already doubled.

The proprieties require that only one term be used in passing. NO BID is an acceptable alternative (standard in England), but all calls must be made with uniform usage. See CALL, BID, PENALTY PASS, NO BID.

PASS OUT or THROW IN. A deal in which all four players pass on the first round of bidding. The score is zero. In duplicate, the hand is scored and returned to the board; in rubber bridge, the deal passes to the next player, but in CHICAGO a redeal by the same dealer is required. The term "pass out" is also applied to the action of the player who, after two passes, declines to reopen the bidding at a comparatively low level. He is said to be in the "pass-out seat" or the "pass-out position."

PASS OUT OF ROTATION. An irregularity in the auction. This can occur in three different circumstances: when each of the other three players is to call. Since damage to the opponents can vary in the circumstances, the prescribed penalties also vary. See LAWS (Law 30). A conventional pass out of rotation is treated under Law 31, Bid Out Of Rotation.

PASSED HAND. A bid by a previously passed hand usu-

ally carries with it the information that the hand is limited to below the requirements for a bid on the earlier round. (Exceptions are unusual passes such as TRAP PASSES and FORCING PASSES.) As a result of the added knowledge partner has about the bidder's lack of strength, the bidder who has passed previously can often safely be somewhat aggressive if his vaules, vulnerability and other factors warrant it.

When partner has opened the bidding in third or fourth seat, the problems of the responder may be rather special. There are two complicating factors: (1) a change of suit is no longer forcing, so responder must be prepared for a "sudden death" pass of his response; (2) partner may have opened a sub-minimum hand, to direct a lead or to try for a small plus score, and will then be annoyed if responder gets too high.

Since any response may be passed, one must be very wary of responding in anemic suits. In general, the higher the response the greater the chance that it will be dropped. This means that the responder can answer 1♦ to 1♣ with a weakish suit (four to the jack), since someone at the table will likely bail responder out. But if one responds 1♥ or, more particularly, 1♠, one should have a respectable four-card suit (at least four to the queen-ten). And if the response is at the two-level, one must be prepared to play opposite a doubleton — partner is now even money to pass. So responder would want to have a six-card suit or at least a husky five-carder. Suppose that one had passed this hand:

♠ K Q 2
♥ J 6 4 3
♦ A 9 6 3 2
♣ 7

If partner opens 1♣, respond 1♦. If, instead, he opens 1♦, respond 3♦ (not 1♥, as one might if it were forcing). If partner opens 1♥, one cannot temporize by answering 2♦, so 3♥ seems best. And if partner opens 1♠, one must still avoid the 2♦ response, for one belongs in spades, not diamonds — responder may choose between 2♠ or 3♠, and the jump raise is probably better in the long run. Suppose that one had passed this hand:

♠ K 6
♥ Q 10 4 2
♦ K 10
♣ K 9 6 3 2

Again, one must be careful about bidding suits. Should partner open with 1♦ a 1♥ response is preferable to 2♣. True, the hand is strong enough for a two-level response and a rebid; but (1) partner may pass before the second bid, and (2) partner is more likely to find a rebid if he can do so at the one-level, and (3) if partner does pass, one would rather be in the higher scoring major suit. What would be the response with the above hand if partner opened 1♠? Not 2♣, and certainly not 2♥. The best bet is 2NT, and this jump response could easily be right over 1♦ or 1♣ as well.

In contrast, if responder passed a hand that contains a strong suit, he can give himself a little more freedom in bidding at the two-level. For example, holding:

♠ Q 7 5 2
♥ 7 4
♦ 2
♣ K Q 10 8 6 3

one would respond 2♣ to a 1♦ opening if it was a passed hand, while 1♠ would be correct if it was not. What makes the difference? Once the responder passed, there is a fighting chance to play in 2♣ when the responder bids it; and if partner rebids 2♦, one can carry on with 2♠ without creating a forcing situation. What is more, it is dangerous to respond 1♠ — if partner passes there is no reason to believe that this is either the safest or most productive contract. Since the requirements for a two-over-one suit takeout are shaded down, there is a worry about missing game when holding the normal solid values for this response. Consider these hands:

♠ 8 3	♠ 7 4
♥ K Q 10 8 7 4 2	♥ 6 2
♦ A 10 5	♦ 8 5
♣ 5	♣ A K Q 10 9 6 5

If, for some reason that appealed to the time, either hand has been passed, jump shift over partner's opening. 2♥ or 2♣ in response to 1♠ is no longer nearly enough; one must jump to three. This puts partner on notice that there are game ambitions even opposite the bare minimum opening bid with which partner would pass a simple response.

But since few players would pass either of these hands, the traditional meaning of this jump shift has a very low frequency. The modern tendency is to use the jump shift with a fit in opener's suit.

Passed hand jump raises and jumps to 2NT entail considerable risk of a minus score. Consider these hands:

♠ K 8 6 2	♠ A Q J 9
♥ J 10 4	♥ 7 5 3
♦ A Q 7 5	♦ 10 2
♣ 7 3	♣ K 10 8 2

WEST	EAST
Pass	1 ♠
3 ♠	Pass

No one made a bad bid — East's third-hand opening is irreproachable, and West has the values for a passed-hand jump raise — but the final contract is dangerously high. Unless two finesses succeed, it will go down for a poor score. How do East-West get to 2♠? It is no solution for West to temporize with 2♦, as he might had partner opened in first seat, for he will be left in this unappetizing contract. Some players might bid only 2♠ with the West hand, fearing a light opening. This risks missing game opposite a sound minimum, for the range of the single raise becomes impossibly broad. Note that FIVE-CARD MAJORS bidding avoids the problem (Pass-1♣-1♠-Pass or 2♠). Here is a similar problem:

♠ J 8 7 3	♠ 9 6 2
♥ Q 10 4	♥ A K J 2
♦ K J	♦ Q 10 9 4
♣ A 9 4 2	♣ J 6

WEST	EAST
Pass	1 ♥
2NT	Pass

This contract is not likely to be a success. What went wrong? Surely West had to bid more than 1NT or 2♥; 3♥ is a possible response, but it is almost certainly down one. A response of 1♠ would be passed, and declarer can develop ulcers playing in a trump suit like that. Perhaps light third- and fourth-hand openings are undesirable.

Not really. One will show a big matchpoint profit in the long run by opening these hands. When partner has a normal minimum count, one will earn a small plus or at least impede the opponents or direct a good lead. The examples above are unlucky, but there is an answer for

them too.

A suggestion is to adopt the DRURY CONVENTION. When the bidding is opened in third or fourth seat with one of a major, the response of 2♣ by the passed hand, is artificial. It asks opener if he has a normal bid, or if he opened light. If opener has shaded his values, he rebids his suit. If he has a reasonable hand, he makes any other bid, and will often jump to game in his suit.

In the examples above, West would respond 2♣, Drury. East would rebid his suit and end the bidding. Let us see an auction where opener has his full bid:

♠ K 7 2	♠ A Q 10 8 4
♥ A Q 10 9	♥ K J 6 2
♦ Q 7 6 2	♦ 9 8
♣ 8 6	♣ A 5
WEST	EAST
Pass	1 ♠
2 ♣	2 ♥
4 ♥	Pass

Here, the advantage of Drury is in making it easy to find the essential heart fit; without it, West would likely jump to 3♠. However, the principal use of this convention is in staying at the two-level in case partner's hand is light.

♠ A J 9 8 4
♥ 6 2
♦ 9 8 4
♣ A J 5

The bidding then would be:

WEST	EAST
Pass	1 ♠
2 ♣	2 ♠

This is sometimes called REVERSE DRURY, because the original form of Drury called for a 2♦ rebid when opener is sub-minimum. That method fell out of favor in the Eighties. See also RULE OF SIXTEEN.

PASSIVE DEFENSE. A defense which aims principally to avoid establishing tricks for declarer, rather than principally to establish tricks for the defense. A defender's continuation of a suit already led either by declarer or the defense, rather than attacking a new suit, is a common type of passive defense. See PASSIVE LEAD.

PASSIVE LEAD. An opening lead which is unlikely to hurt the defending side, but is not expected to have a positive value. A lead from three or four small cards is a typical passive lead, but in certain circumstances a trump lead may be passive, or a lead in an opposing suit which is likely to be solid. See ATTACKING LEAD; OPENING LEAD.

PASSOUT SEAT. The position of a player who can end the bidding by passing.

PASTEBOARDS. A name given to playing cards because a coating of black paste between two paper layers gave the stock on which the cards were printed an opacity that made it impossible to see through them. See MANUFACTURE OF PLAYING CARDS.

PATTERN. See HAND PATTERNS.

PATTERN RELAY ORGANIZED SYSTEM. See PRO SYSTEM.

PEETERS, MARCEL CHALLENGE CUP. See IN-

TERNATIONAL BRIDGE ACADEMÝ.

PENAL INSTITUTIONS. See BRIDGE IN PRISONS.

PENALTY. Penalty can refer to rule violations and/or scoring of the hand.

(1) An obligation or restriction imposed upon a side for violation of the Laws of Bridge. In the language of the lawgivers, penalties are designed "... to provide an adequate remedy whenever a player accidentally, carelessly or inadvertently disturbs the proper course of the game. An offending player should be ready to pay graciously any penalty or adjusted score awarded by a Tournament Director."

(2) An amount scored above the line by the declarer's opponents when the declarer fails to make a contract. The penalty provisions of the score table are gauged so as to make competitive bidding a fine art. Many of the great stories in the anecdotage of the game are concerned with penalties. The biggest penalty in a championship tournament was reported from the Men's Pairs at the 1964 Summer North American Championships held at Toronto.

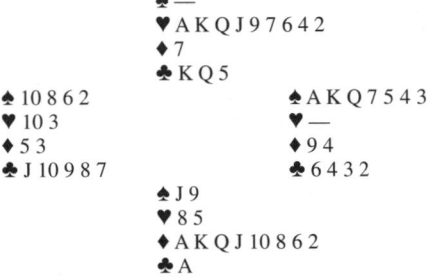

With both sides vulnerable, the par contract is a 7♠ sacrifice by East-West, which costs 1400 as compared with 2220 for the grand slam which North-South can make in hearts. (7♦ by South is defeated if West leads a heart.) At most tables the final contract was in fact 7♠ doubled, but at a number of other tables the North-South pairs refused to be outbid and overcalled 7♠ with 7NT, which was of course doubled and was usually redoubled. The auction at one such table, beginning with a strong two-bid, was:

WEST	NORTH	EAST	SOUTH
	2 ♥	2 ♠	3 ♦
Pass	4NT	5 ♠	6 ♣
Pass	7 ♥	7 ♠	7 NT
Pass	Pass	Dbl	Redbl
All Pass			

Spades were led, and West did not fail to unblock with the 8 and 10. East thus took the first seven tricks for a penalty of 4000. At another table the bidding was:

WEST	NORTH	EAST	SOUTH
	2 ♣	3 ♠	4 NT
Pass	6 ♥	Pass	7 NT
Pass	Pass	Dbl	Redbl
All Pass			

West, doubtless attributing some unusual lead-directing significance to his partner's double, led a club and the contract was made for a score of 2930. The spread between top and bottom score was 6930.

The biggest recorded penalty in tournament play resulted from a hand similar to the following:

Dlr: West
Vul: N-S

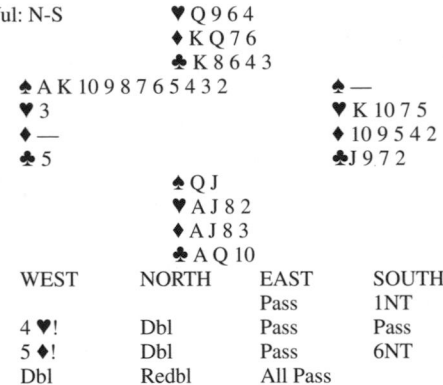

The deal was played at a Baltic Congress, with Andrzej Witkowski and Bogdan Swiatek of Poznan sitting East and West. East could have made 6NT, but this contract was ruled out by the opening bid.

West	North	East	South
3 NT	Pass	5 ♣	5 ♦
Dbl	Pass	Pass	Redbl
All Pass			

South tried to maneuver into a major, and 5♠ would have succeeded. But North did not realize that the redouble was an SOS. The defense did not score their spade ruff, but they had tricks to spare anyway. The score was 6400, not far short of the theoretical maximum of 7600.

This was exceeded in rubber bridge on the following deal, played in Megve, France in 1954.

Dlr: E
Vul: N-S

```
            ♠ —
            ♥ Q 9 6 4
            ♦ K Q 7 6
            ♣ K 8 6 4 3
♠ A K 10 9 8 7 6 5 4 3 2        ♠ —
♥ 3                             ♥ K 10 7 5
♦ —                             ♦ 10 9 5 4 2
♣ 5                             ♣ J 9 7 2
            ♠ Q J
            ♥ A J 8 2
            ♦ A J 8 3
            ♣ A Q 10
```

WEST	NORTH	EAST	SOUTH
		Pass	1NT
4 ♥!	Dbl	Pass	Pass
5 ♦!	Dbl	Pass	6NT
Dbl	Redbl	All Pass	

The ♠A was led. The result was down 12 for a penalty of 7000.

Probably the biggest penalty conceded by forgetting a convention occurred in Denmark. John Trelde forgot his own COPENHAGEN CONVENTION and went down nine tricks in 3♦ redoubled not vulnerable for a loss of 3400, pre-1987 scoring.

PENALTY CARD. A card that has been prematurely exposed by a defender, and must be left face up on the table until legally played or permitted to be picked up. If it is a LEAD OUT OF TURN, the declarer has several options, some of which permit the penalty card to be picked up; if it remains a penalty card on a lead out of turn, or is prematurely exposed in any other condition, it must be played at the first legal opportunity that the player may have to play it. See LAWS, Laws 24, 49-53, 55, 57, 58, and 62: LAWS OF DUPLICATE (Laws 23, 49-52, 54, 56-58, 62)

The 1987 Duplicate Laws and the 1993 Rubber Bridge Laws introduced a distinction between MAJOR PENALTY CARDS and MINOR PENALTY CARDS, which are explained under those headings.

PENALTY DOUBLE. The distinction between penalty doubles and takeout doubles is discussed under DOUBLES. Normal penalty doubles can be considered in three categories:

(1) **Positive doubles.** Suppose an opening bid is overcalled and doubled, and the opener's hand seems unsuited to defense. Should he stand the double or take it out? If the opening bid was of a sort which describes the hand within narrow limits, stand the double. If the opening bid is 3♠ with this hand:

> ♠ K J 8 7 6 4 3 2
> ♥ 3
> ♦ 2
> ♣ J 5 4

pass a double by partner of an overcall of 4♥. He does not expect the opener to have defensive strength

Having opened with a three-bid, a four-bid, a weak two-bid, or any notrump bid, pass partner's double of an overcall. These are all bids which describe a hand within narrow limits.

Opponents seldom argue with a game-forcing opening, but when they do, retaliation must be swift and sure and there must be no partnership misunderstanding. The responder should beware of doubling on hands which contain a feature outside the enemy suit.

> ♠ A J 6 5
> ♥ Q 8 7 4
> ♦ 5 4 3
> ♣ 7 2

After a 2♣ opening by partner, do not double an overcall of 2♠. (2NT is better). Too often the hand will belong in a heart contract. In any event, the hand must be useful in attack, and game must be there. Experience shows that the double is best reserved for hands like:

> ♠ Q 10 7 6 5
> ♥ 8 7 4
> ♦ 5 4 3
> ♣ 7 2

If this is the partnership understanding, opener will pass the double with:

> ♠ 4
> ♥ A K J 5
> ♦ A K J
> ♣ K Q J 8 3

If the double is made on both hands above, the opener has a very tough decision. He will never know, with the last hand, whether he is surrendering game or slam for poor recompense

Having opened with a game-forcing bid, opener should accept partner's double of an intervening call *unless holding game in hand with fewer than five defensive tricks.*

It is a mistake to double the only contract you can beat.

Dlr: East	♠ A Q 7 5 2	
Vul: None	♥ J 6 2	
	♦ Q 10 8 4 3	
	♣ —	

♠ 8 4		♠ K J 9
♥ A 9 8 7		♥ K Q 10 4
♦ J 7		♦ K 9 2
♣ J 8 7 5 3		♣ A 9 2

	♠ 10 6 3	
	♥ 5 3	
	♦ A 6 5	
	♣ K Q 10 6 4	

WEST	NORTH	EAST	SOUTH
		1NT	Pass
Pass	2♠	Pass	Pass
3♣	Pass	Pass	?

South should pass and take his plus. Even at matchpoint duplicate, a pass is better than a double, since the opponents are too likely to have a better spot. If South doubles, West will be nervous about his ragged suit and may run to hearts, where he can take nine tricks.

(2) **Low-level doubles.** Doubles after a suit opening and a suit overcall are almost invariably NEGATIVE in the modern style. If the double is not negative, the following applies: Stand a low-level double with three quick defensive tricks; pull it with fewer unless there is compensation in trump strength; pull the double nearly always with an unbid five-card suit. In a close decision, decide whether or not a lead or your bid suit will be crucial.

Two other opportunities for penalty doubles occur in these situations:

(a) A double of a one notrump overcall is made with almost any hand with 9 or more high-card points since the partnership is virtually certain to have the balance of strength.

(b) A double of an overcall of a one notrump opening depends on the strength of the one notrump opening. It shows that the partnership has the balance of strength, and that the doubler has at least three to an honor in the overcaller's suit. The double is more attractive at favorable vulnerability, unattractive at unfavorable.

(3) **Game doubles.** Doubles of game contracts in a competitive auction are usually aimed at taking the maximum penalty from opponents who have taken a save. However, the double may also act as a warning to partner not to proceed further. If a pass would be a FORCING PASS, then a double indicates a disinclination to go further. For this reason a player who anticipates disaster if his side bids further may double when his prospects of beating the opposing contract are not better than moderate.

Doubling a game contract which has been reached voluntarily without interference is very seldom good policy (unless the doubler suspects an advance save, for example, after 3♠-4♠).

Doubling a game on the basis of high cards only is a costly exercise. For the double to be worthwhile, both opponents must have limited their hands in such a way that it is clear that neither has any strength in reserve. For example:

WEST	EAST
1♣	1♥
2♥	2NT
3 NT	

In this auction it is clear that both players are straining to reach game, and either opponent may double if the honor strength, especially in clubs and hearts, seems well placed for the defense

The worst penalty doubles help declarer make a contract that would fail undoubled. Suppose declarer is playing 4♠ with this trump suit:

```
        ♠ Q 9 7 6 5 2
        ♥ 8
        ♦ A J 10 3
        ♣ K 4

        ♠ K 8
        ♥ A 4 2
        ♦ 9 7 4
        ♣ A Q J 6 5
```

If East passes, declarer will lead low to the king, intending to duck the next lead and hoping for A-x in East. But if East doubles, declarer may run the 9 through East, saving a trick.

When the deal is a freak and both sides have a double fit, a penalty double may be costly. In the long run, it is better to be declarer.

```
Dlr: East            ♠ A 10 7 5 3
Vul: E-W             ♥ 2
                     ♦ A Q 9 7 6 5 2
                     ♣ —

♠ Q 8 6                              ♠ —
♥ K Q 5 4 3                          ♥ J 10 9 7 6
♦ —                                  ♦ K 3
♣ A Q 9 8 6                          ♣ K 10 5 4 3 2
                     ♠ K J 9 4 2
                     ♥ A 8
                     ♦ J 10 8 4
                     ♣ J 7
```

WEST	NORTH	EAST	SOUTH
		Pass	Pass
1 ♥	2 ♥	4 ♣ (1)	4 ♠
Dbl	Pass	5 ♥	5 ♠
Pass	Pass	6 ♥	Dbl
All Pass			

(1) Clubs with heart support

This deal arose in the 1984 Vanderbilt Knockout Teams. In fairness to N-S, they received misinformation. East alerted 4♣ and interpreted the bid correctly for South, his screenmate. Meanwhile, West alerted and told North that 4♣ showed club shortness with a heart fit. Nevertheless, N-S paid dearly for failing to heed the "double-double" fit axiom: "When in doubt, bid one more". 6♥ doubled made for +1660, and 6♠ also would have made.

At the other table, South played 6♠ on a different auction and misguessed the ♠Q to go down one.

If the contract is a suit, a double becomes attractive if the declaring side has run into a bad trump split. It is sometimes possible to double with a void if the other defender is marked by the bidding with five trumps. But it is still necessary for both opponents to be limited, so that all possibility of a redoubled overtrick is excluded. DOUBLES OF NOTRUMP BIDS are listed separately. See also COOPERATIVE DOUBLE, DOUBLE FOR SACRIFICE, LEAD-DIRECTING DOUBLE, LIGHTNER DOUBLE, MAXIMAL DOUBLE, OPTIONAL DOUBLE, SUPPORT DOUBLE.

PENALTY EXCESS. See EXCESS POINTS.

PENALTY LIMITS. In social or progressive bridge, in order to prevent one hand from assuming overwhelming importance, it is customary to limit the plus score in premium points for doubled and redoubled undertrick penalties. Generally, 1000 points is the limit. In TOTAL POINT SCORING for pair events, a method that is ob-

solescent if not obsolete, a similar though somewhat smaller limit was set. See EXCESS POINTS.

PENALTY PASS. A pass by a player after a TAKEOUT DOUBLE from his partner and a pass by right-hand opponent. For example:

WEST	NORTH	EAST	SOUTH
1 ♦	Dbl	Pass	Pass

South's pass indicates considerable length and strength in diamonds; five cards headed by three honors would normally be the minimum diamond holding. Even holding five strong diamonds, a pass would be unwise with a two-suited hand because the declarer would be likely to score ruffs. After such a pass, North has an obligation to lead a trump, because South will wish to draw declarer's trumps.

After a minor-suit opening, a penalty pass may come into consideration with nothing but trump length at unfavorable vulnerability. If the contract succeeds, even with an overtrick, the resulting score may be less than the opener's side could have scored in other ways.

A penalty pass becomes more attractive if the doubler was in a balancing position. Q J x x of trumps may be a sufficient trump holding.

PEOPLE'S REPUBLIC OF CHINA. After a 30-year ban, bridge suddenly became the intellectual game for the whole of China. Early in 1979, the All China Sports Federation formed the All China Contract Bridge League. Within three months, bridge associations were established all over the country. Bridge is now being played at every level. Play is free — directors and other officials are volunteer workers. Within six months after the establishment of the ACCBL, an intercity tournament was staged. Later a team tournament was held in which there was a total entry of 176 teams. More recently, team events in Shanghai have attracted more than 400 teams with more turned away for lack of space. See CHINESE BRIDGE ASSOCIATION.

PERCENTAGE. A quotient obtained by dividing the actual matchpoint score of a contestant by the possible score of that contestant, which is then expressed as a percentage (of the possible score). Winning percentages tend to be higher (70 to 75%) in board-a-match team games than in pair games (60 to 64%)

PERCENTAGE PLAY. A play influenced by mathematical factors when more than one reasonable line of play is available. See PROBABILITIES A POSTERIORI, SUIT COMBINATIONS, and MATHEMATICAL TABLES (Tables 4, 4A). The following examples show how the above references can be used in bridge play.

(1) Neither the auction nor the play to the first trick has shown any marked UNBALANCED DISTRIBUTION in defenders' hands. Dummy has A-K-Q-J-4-3-2, and declarer is void in the suit. There is about 36% probability that the suit will be divided 3-3.

(2)   A K Q 10

                       4 3 2

The correct line of play, based solely on PROBABILITIES A PRIORI, is to play the A-K-Q unless East shows a singleton or void. From percentage play, probabilities are:

3-3 division   35.53%

J-x (J-9, J-8, J-7, J-6, J-5) either	16.15%	
J singleton either	2.42%	
J-9-8-7-6-5 with West	.74%	
J-x-x-x-x with West	6.05%	
Total	60.89%	

The alternative play of taking a finesse on the third round, unless the jack has been played, has the following probabilities:

J in West's hand	50.00%	
J-x with East	8.07%	
J singleton with East	1.21%	
Total	59.28%	

To make four tricks in the suit, the odds are slightly less than 61 to 59 on refusing the finesse.

(3)   A Q 10 7 3 2

                               9 8 5

Declarer disregards the safety play in favor of trying for the maximum number of tricks. He plans to finesse the queen and make six tricks if West holds both honors doubleton or if East holds the singleton jack. He may also have to decide on his action if West plays low and the finesse loses. Reference to MATHEMATICAL TABLES. Table 4 shows that the distribution

6-4 opposite K-J has a probability of 6.8%

J-6-4 opposite K has a probability of 6.2%

The odds are therefore 34 to 31 on playing the ace on the second round after the finesse has lost, as against taking a second finesse. Percentage play often requires calculations which, though not too difficult, require more involved operations. This may be valuable in subsequent analysis but not practical at the table.

In the following, two lines of play present themselves.

♠ —
♥ Q 3 2
♦ A K Q 10 4 3 2
♣ 7 5 4

♠ K Q J 6 3 2
♥ A K J 6 5 4
♦
♣ 3

South plays in 6♥. West leads the ♣Q, then a second club on which East plays the king. South ruffs. As West presumably has the Q-J and East the A-K, the play of this suit has not altered the ratio of the a priori odds, but in our more detailed calculations we must assume that East and West each originally held at least three clubs. South's best line of play depends upon the probability of the divisions of the two red suits. To determine this accurately it is necessary to calculate the appropriate combinations as explained in SUIT, NUMBER OF CARDS IN. For a satisfactory approximate answer apply the rule of multiplying PROBABILITY OF SUCCESSIVE EVENTS. (This is an approximation because the distribution of the two suits is interdependent, not independent. We note the discrepancy when we give the result of our detailed calculations later.) To the third trick South leads the ♥A, East and West both following. At trick four South can:

(a) lead the ♥K;

(b) lead a low heart to dummy's queen;

(c) lead the ♥J.

In each case we must consider the position if (i) West follows to the second round of hearts, and (ii) West does not follow.

(a) (♥K) will win whenever

hearts are 2-2	40%	
and diamonds are 3-3		36%
or doubleton J		16%
Total		52%

The probability that both will occur (hearts 2-2 and diamonds come home) is 40% of 52%, which equals 20.8%. If hearts actually divide 2-2, South leads the ♠K, and if this is covered his troubles are over. Assuming that West will cover half the time he holds the ace this gives another 4.8% (50% of 50% of 19.2%), bringing our total to 25.6%.

If West has three hearts (25%), South leads to dummy's ♥Q and makes his contract with the above division of diamonds (52%). This gives another 13%. Similarly, we have a further 13% if East has three hearts and there is the above diamond division.

Our grand approximate total for (a) is thus 51.6%.

(b)   (low heart) will win whenever

hearts are 2-2	40%	
diamonds 4-2		48%
diamonds 3-3		36%
singleton J		2%
any other division		
provided West has the ♠A		7%
Total		93%
or		
West has 3 hearts or	25%	
four diamonds and		
the ♠A		30%
East has 3 hearts	25%	
diamonds are 3-3		36%
doubleton ♦J		16%
East has five small diamonds		
and two low spades,		
or		
J-x-x-x and three low spades		2%
Total		54%

Our grand total for (b) is thus (40% of 93%) + (25% of [30% + 54%}), or 58.2%.

(c) (♥J) is obviously inferior to (b). If West follows to the second round of hearts and we overtake the ♥J we lose if West has three hearts and three diamonds even if he also has the A, South has to return to his own hand twice — once to take the ruffing finesse in spades and once to draw West's last trump. One entry has to be the ruff of a fourth diamond, and West will overruff. If the ♥J is not overtaken, the lead is not in dummy for the diamond suit to be led.

A more detailed calculation which takes account of the interdependence of the suit distributions gives us 48.99% for (a) and 52.62% for (b). We note that there is less difference between these two numbers than between our approximate calculations. This is due to the fact that (b) contains a larger number of unbalanced hands, the type on which approximate calculations give misleadingly high figures. See MARBLES. For a computer program that will make sophisticated percentage calculations, see BASE III.

PERCENTAGES. Because chance plays a considerable part in the distribution of cards at a bridge table, it is understandable that expert players are interested in the mathematical percentages applicable to different situations. Among the articles dealing with percentage are: MATHEMATICS OF BRIDGE, MARBLES, PERCENTAGE PLAY, SLAM BIDDING, SUIT COMBINATIONS,

VALUE OF GAME, and PARTSCORE. MATHEMATICAL TABLES also deals with various percentage situations. Bridge writers frequently use a variation of percentage, ODDS IN BRIDGE, in discussing situations yielding to mathematical treatment. For a computer program that will make sophisticated percentage calculations, see BASE III.

PERFECT BRIDGE HAND. A hand that will produce 13 tricks in notrump irrespective of the opening lead or the composition of the other three hands. A hand containing all 13 cards of a suit, therefore, does not qualify as a perfect hand, since such a hand will not take even a single trick if played in notrump. Although most players think of a hand containing four aces, four kings, four queens and a jack as the perfect hand, actually it is only one of many. Altogether there are 3,756 possible perfect hands, which break down as follows:

Hand Pattern				Number of Possible Hands
AKQJxxxxx	AK	A	A	1,512
AKQJ10xxx	AKQ	A	A	672
AKQJ10xxx	AK	AK	A	672
AKQxxxxxxx	A	A	A	480
AKQJ109x	AKQ	AK	A	168
AKQJ109x	AKQJ	A	A	84
AKQJ109x	AK	AK	AK	28
AKQJ109	AKQJ	AK	A	24
AKQJ10	AKQJ	AKQ	A	24
AKQJ109	AKQJ10	A	A	12
AKQJ109	AKQ	AKQ	A	12
AKQJ109	AKQ	AK	AK	12
AKQJ10	AKQJ10	AK	A	12
AKQJ10	AKQJ	AK	AK	12
AKQJ10	AKQ	AKQ	AK	12
AKQJ	AKQJ	AKQ	AK	12
AKQJ	AKQJ	AKQJ	A	4
AKQJ	AKQ	AKQ	AKQ	4
			Total	3,756

As there are 635,013,559,600 possible hands a player can hold, the odds against holding such a "perfect hand" are 169,066,442 to 1

PERIODICALS. See BIBLIOGRAPHY

PERMANENT TRUMP. At whist, a variation in which club card committees or other governing bodies declared a suit to be trump for all games under their jurisdiction. The rules of whist provided that the trump suit would be the suit of the last card dealt by the dealer to himself.

PERMUTATIONS. All the possible arrangements of the cards, usually the residue of a suit given the cards in two hands. See MATHEMATICAL TABLES.

PERUVIAN BRIDGE COMMISSION (PERU: COMISION NACIONAL DE BRIDGE). Founded in 1957. In 1992, the membership was about 200. Hosted South American Championships in 1956, 1961, 1974, 1981, 1991. Its women players won the South American women's team titles in 1963 and 1969.
Officers 1992:
President: Teresa Arosemena
Secretary: Carmen Rosa Lazarte
Av. Jorge Basadre 475
Lima 27, Peru
Tel. 51 14 41 99 95

PETER. A term used in Great Britain, but rarely elsewhere, to describe a high-low made in discarding, such

as high-low in any given suit. Originally, in whist, the use of the term was restricted to a highlow in the trump suit only. See HIGH-LOW SIGNALS and BLUE PETER.

PHANTOM PAIR. In a pair contest with an odd number of pairs, the pair which would (if present) complete the last table. The contestant scheduled to play against the phantom pair has a bye round.

PHANTOM SACRIFICE (or phantom save). A sacrifice bid against a contract which would have been defeated.

PHENOMENAL HANDS. See FREAK HANDS.

PHILIP MORRIS CHAMPIONSHIPS. The Philip Morris Corp. sponsors European bridge competitions — open pairs in odd-numbered years, mixed pairs and mixed teams in the even-numbered years. The competitions consist of several tournaments, and the overall performance of a pair or team determines their final standing. For results see Appendix IV.

PHILIPPINE CONTRACT BRIDGE LEAGUE. Organized in 1954. By 1992 the membership was about 120. The League hosted the 1977 world championships and the Far East Championships in 1957, 1962, 1967, 1974, and 1977.
Officers 1992:
President: Sylvia Alejandro
Secretary: Jimmy Soo
P.O. Box 1352 Makati M.M.
Philippines.
Fax: 632 831 4704.

PHONEY CLUB. See SHORT CLUB.

PHONEY DIAMOND. See SHORT DIAMOND.

PIANOLA. A hand at bridge which presents no problems to declarer, so easily playable that it almost plays itself. The name derives from the old player piano or "pianola" which would "play" itself.

PICK UP. To capture or drop an outstanding high card.

PICKUP BOY (GIRL). See CADDY.

PICKUP SLIP. A form devised for the recording of the result on the play of one board on one round. Information contained on the slip includes identifying numbers of the pairs; the board number; which pair was the declarer; the final contract and by whom whether doubled, redoubled, or undoubled; the result; trick-score; extra tricks; game or doubled bonuses; partscore bonus; slam bonus; or undertrick score. Usually the North (or South) player has the responsibility of making out the score, the East-West pair having responsibility for checking the entries and verifying the slip. After each round the pickup slips are collected and results of the round entered in a computer or on a recapitulation sheet by the director or a designated scorer.

PIN. The lead of a high card when the right-hand opponent has an unguarded card slightly lower in rank. The play can be made either by declarer or by a defender.

A 9 8 7 6

Q 10 5

If South must have five tricks from this suit, his best chance, a faint one, is to lead the queen and hope the singleton jack is on his right. The defenders can sometimes falsecard in an attempt to avert an impending pin:

♥ Q 10 3 2

♥ J 5 4   ♥ A K 8 7 6

♥ 9

South plays in a spade contract after East has bid hearts and West has raised them. If East plays in routine fashion to West's heart lead by winning with the king and shifting to another suit, South can establish a heart trick in the dummy by ruffing a low heart and later leading the queen, or vice versa. But if East wins the first trick with the ace and returns a low heart, South is likely to conclude that West started with K-x-x.

The term can be extended to some situations in which either opponent has an unguarded card slightly lower in rank:

♥ A 10 x

♥ Q x

The queen is led, intending to allow the king to win if played with a finesse of the ten to follow. This scores two tricks whenever the K-J is on the left, or if a singleton jack is on the right.

PINK POINTS. An obsolete term for REGIONAL POINTS. It was used to distinguish points won at a Regional tournament from those won at a National tournament (red points).

PINPOINT ASTRO. See ASTRO.

PIP. A small design indicating the suit to which a particular card belongs. The SPADE suit is indicated by a spearhead, the HEART suit by a heart, the DIAMOND suit by a diamond-shaped tile, the CLUB suit by a clover leaf. The spot cards have as many pips as the rank of the card indicates, from 1 to 10 in the standard deck, in addition to two INDICES, the lower half of which is a pip. In German cards, the pips of LEAVES and ACORNS usually have stems, and are often attached as if on a branch. In the trappola PACK, the pips often vary in size and design, and the SWORDS and CUDGELS are usually interlaced. See SUIT and INDICES.

PITCH. A colloquial term for DISCARD.

PITCH COUNT. An old name for the 4-3-2-1 POINT COUNT.

PITT COUP. A play by which the declarer places himself in a position to lead through his left-hand adversary in a suit in which the dummy holds a major tenace over the left-hand adversary's minor tenace. It frequently involves the unblocking of a trump suit in dummy, and also may include a deliberate higher-than-necessary ruff with an honor in the closed hand so as to be able to lead low through West.

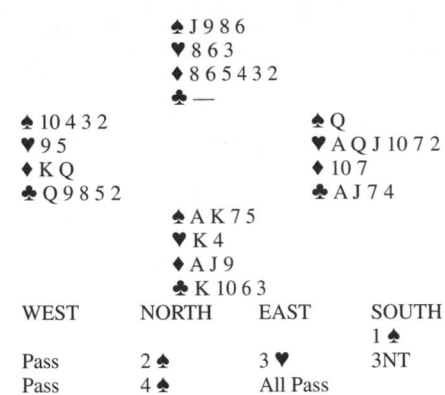

♠ J 9 8 6
♥ 8 6 3
♦ 8 6 5 4 3 2
♣ —

♠ 10 4 3 2   ♠ Q
♥ 9 5   ♥ A Q J 10 7 2
♦ K Q   ♦ 10 7
♣ Q 9 8 5 2   ♣ A J 7 4

♠ A K 7 5
♥ K 4
♦ A J 9
♣ K 10 6 3

WEST	NORTH	EAST	SOUTH
			1 ♠
Pass	2 ♠	3 ♥	3NT
Pass	4 ♠	All Pass	

West opened the ♥9, won by East who returned the suit. South won with the king. The ♠A was led, on which declarer called for the 8 from dummy (maintaining a two-way finesse situation against the 10). East's queen marked West with four spades to the 10. Declarer led ace and another diamond, hoping for and getting the 2-2 split in the suit. West won the second diamond, and returned a club, dummy discarding and East winning the ace. East returned the high heart, which declarer ruffed with the king. The lead of the ♠7 permitted South to take a finesse, playing dummy's 6; a further spade lead through West enabled declarer to unblock the high diamond from his hand on the fourth spade lead and win the balance of the tricks in dummy. The name is arbitrary, resulting from the use of Pitt, Chatham, etc., in whist literature to designate particular players.

PIVOT BRIDGE, LAWS OF. (A form of social bridge at home games where, instead of advancing from table to table as in party or progressive bridge, the players change or pivot among themselves at each individual table.) Pivot bridge is played by four (or five and sometimes six) players at a table. This form may be used for a single table or for large gatherings in which it is desirable to have each table play as a separate unit without progression by the players.

The game is so arranged that each player plays with each other player at his table both as partner and opponent. There are two methods of play: first, four deals may be played to a round, one deal by each player, and the players change partners at the end of each four deals. Second, rubbers may be played, and the players change partners at the end of each rubber.

If four deals to a round are played, the scoring is exactly the same as in Progressive Bridge; if rubbers are played, the scoring is exactly the same as in Rubber Bridge. The laws given below explain only the method of rotation in changing partners, not scoring, vulnerability, etc., which are covered elsewhere

DRAW FOR PARTNERS

1. The players draw cards for partners and deal, and for a choice of seats and pack. The player who draws highest is the first pivot; he deals first and has the choice of seats and packs. The player who draws second highest is the pivot's first partner; the player who draws third highest sits at the pivot's left during the first round; the player who draws fourth sits at the pivot's right; and if a fifth player is present, he does not participate in the first round or rubber.

CHANGING PARTNERS (FOR FOUR PLAYERS)

2. During the first three rounds or rubbers the players change positions as indicated in the following diagram:

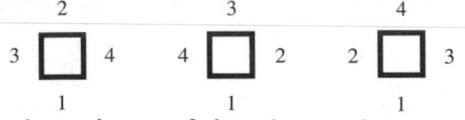

1st round   2nd round   3rd round

After the third round or rubber, the players again cut for position and partners.

CHANGING PARTNERS (FOR FIVE PLAYERS)

3. If five players desire to play at the same table, they may be accommodated in this manner: For the first round or rubber, the players take the positions indicated by their draw for position under law No. 1. For rounds one to five, they take the positions indicated in the following diagram:

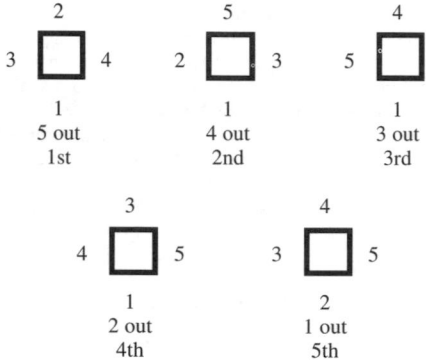

At the end of each five rounds, the players again draw for positions and partners.

COMMENT

This arrangement permits each player to play with each other player once as partner and once as opponent, and each player sits out one round in turn.

SIX PLAYER PIVOT

4. With six players at the same table, a complete pivot enabling each player to play once as partner and twice against each combination of opponents other than the player who is cut out at the same time, may be arranged by following this sequence of partnerships:

3-4	1-5	1-3	3-5	1-6	1-4	3-6	1-2
v	v	v	v	v	v	v	v
5-6	2-6	2-4	4-6	2-5	2-3	4-5	5-6

The player numbers correspond to the order in which they are cut out, with 1-2, 3-4 and 5-6 out simultaneously. If more than eight rounds are to be played, the pivot is resumed at round 3, or a new order may be determined by cutting so as to have different players out at the same time.

DETERMINATION OF THE WINNER

5. At the completion of each round or rubber, the player enters on his tally both his own score and that of his opponents. Each player totals his own and his opponents' scores separately and records the difference, plus or minus as the case may be, at the bottom of his tally. The player having the highest plus score is the winner and the others rank in descending order according to their scores.

PIVOT MITCHELL. A method of taking care of a half table in a MITCHELL game, particularly useful in a

SCRAMBLED MITCHELL. The last table will have no stationary pair and the moving pairs will pass this table in this way: play East-West, then sit out, then play North-South, then continue to E-W at table one. See BUMP MITCHELL and HALF TABLES.

PIVOT TEAMS. A team event in which each member of a team of four plays equally with each other member. Popular in Britain, and used in New York City in the Betty Kaplan Teams.

PLACE THE CARDS, PLACING CARDS. See ASSUMPTIONS, IN PLAY; CARD READING.

PLACING THE LEAD. See AVOIDANCE.

PLAFOND. A French card game which was the immediate predecessor of contract. Harold S. Vanderbilt, the originator of contract bridge, used *plafond* (which means "ceiling") as the basis for his approach to the new game.

PIERRE BELLANGER (*The Bridge World*, Sept. 1931) dates the origin of Plafond to 1918, where it was introduced at the Cercle Litteraire of Paris shortly after the Armistice. Only those tricks bid for and made were scored below the line and counted toward game. Tricks made above the bid scored 50 points above the line for each additional trick. Except for increasing the slam bonuses to 100 for a small slam and 200 for a grand slam, awarded whether the slam was bid or not, the trick scores and penalties were much as in auction. However, a bonus of 50 points was scored for making any contract successfully; the first game for either side received a bonus of 100; winning the rubber was worth an additional 400. Bellanger also claims authorship of the words "Contract Bridge," an appendix to his 1914 edition of *Legislation du Bridge aux Encheres* mentioning *Bridge avec Contrat*. But contract, as it was introduced in 1914 at the Automobile Club de France, was only an embryonic form of Plafond.

GEORGE F. HERVEY, bridge correspondent of *The Field*, cites a letter to that publication, dated February 8, 1941, in which Sir Hugh Clayton records that the contract principle was invented by four players in Poona (India) in 1912. The game was developed out of auction and named S.A.C.C., an acronym of the four men who invented it. On July 15,1914, the rules of this game were published by Sir Hugh in *The Times of India*, and there is evidence that the game was played in various parts of India from that date until some years after promulgation of the first official code of laws to govern contract bridge (December 1929).

MILTON C. WORK reported that similar games had been tried in the United States before 1914 but failed to become popular. Obviously, none of these games included the vulnerability feature and the scoring table devised by Vanderbilt, but it would appear that the "ceiling" principle of Plafond may have come to France from India or at least have originated there at an earlier date than reported by Bellanger. There was a Franco-American Plafond Match in 1930 which ended about even, and which employed many of the newly established contract bridge methods, but most players essaying both games tended to prefer the more precise and demanding contract.

PLAIN SUIT. A suit other than the trump suit.

PLAN OF PLAY, PLANNING THE PLAY. The mental process by which declarer decides on how to use the assets of the combined hands to fulfill the contract, and, secondly, to develop overtricks or to minimize penalties. Among the things to be considered is the management of the trump suit, development of long cards in side suits, maintenance of communication between the two hands, if and how to finesse, development of endplays, safety plays against adverse distributions. Declarer should mentally review these and other problems before playing to the first trick, even though such play may be automatic. Original plans should frequently be changed as more information about adverse holdings is developed, but the declarer should not require time to consider each play, and thus delay the tempo of the game. See NOTRUMP PLAY.

PLASTIC CARDS. Cards made of acetate cellulose or a vinyl or polyvinyl compound.

Since the wearing qualities of paper are limited, inventors searched for years for a substitute that would be more enduring. Success depended on two inventions, a method of making the thin material opaque so that no card could be identified from the back, and a formula for making ink that would adhere firmly to the plastic surface.

In 1932, Siegfried Klausner registered in Austria and other European countries a patent for making non-inflammable opaque plastic sheets and for making playing cards from them by coating the printed surfaces with a lacquer derived from the basic plastic. After manufacturing the cards under the trade name Mirakel, he sold domestic rights to Piatnik, the S. E. Europe monopoly, which took the cards off the market; but he retained U.S. rights and in 1934 founded the Kem Company with Ely Culbertson and others. The resulting KEM CARDS outwear paper cards, are resistant to soiling, and are easily cleaned.

Plastic cards are made by three companies in the United States, and by several in Japan and Europe. In spite of their proven superiority in many ways, they represent only about 2% of the number of packs sold yearly. See MANUFACTURE OF PLAYING CARDS.

PLASTIC VALUATION. One of the phrases popularized in the writings of Ely Culbertson to describe the mental processes of the bidder as he receives more information regarding the makeup of his partner's hand. REVALUATION, PROMOTION OF TRUMP HONORS, and DISTRIBUTIONAL COUNTS were all covered in the one phrase.

PLAY (of the hand). See NOTRUMP PLAY; TRUMP SUIT MANAGEMENT.

PLAY AFTER AN ILLEGAL PLAY. Such action forfeits (waives) any penalty incurred by the illegal play, unless the illegal play constitutes a revoke. This is in accordance with the principle that the nonoffending side may "condone" an offense. Such a play may be made only by the player to the left of the hand making the illegal play, and such right is not affected by partner calling attention to the illegality of the play. See LAWS (Law 60).

PLAY FROM EQUALS. When holding cards of equal rank in a suit, it is often very important which card is chosen to be played to a particular trick. A defender's card may provide partner with important information, or it may deceive the declarer. A declarer's card may confuse the defense, or at least avoid giving away information unnecessarily.

Defensive play from equals. On the opening lead, there is a standard table which usually requires that the higher of two equal honors be led. The only exception to this is that the king is usually led from ace, king, and others (see OPENING LEADS). However, when the honor combination is bare (no small cards) the lower honor is sometimes led to inform partner of the situation. For example, the normal lead from A-K-x against a suit contract is the king. From A-K alone, the usual lead is the ace. When this is followed by the king, the partner of the leader will know that the opening leader has exhausted the suit led (otherwise, the normal lead of the king would have been made).

This reversing order of plays can also be used later in the defense. Consider, for example, the deal below:

```
                    ♠ K 8 7
                    ♥ A Q J 10 8
                    ♦ Q 5
                    ♣ J 9 8
    ♠ 9 6 4                          ♠ 3 2
    ♥ 9 3                            ♥ 7 5 2
    ♦ J 10 9 8                       ♦ A 7 6 4 3 2
    ♣ A 4 3 2                        ♣ K Q
                    ♠ A Q J 10 5
                    ♥ K 6 4
                    ♦ K
                    ♣ 10 7 6 5
    SOUTH          NORTH
    1 ♠            2 ♥
    3 ♥            4 ♠
    Pass
```

Against South's 4♠ contract, West leads the ♦J.

East wins the ♦A and sees at once that the defense must look to clubs for the setting tricks. East should shift to the ♣Q, not the king. After the ♣Q wins and East continues with the ♣K, West should overtake to give East a club ruff. In this case, the deliberate play of the wrong honor from equals indicates no other cards in the suit led. If East had started with three clubs to the K-Q, he would have made the normal shift to the ♣K.

Sometimes the lower honor is led from equal cards for the purpose of deceiving the declarer.

In many situations a defender's play from equals should be the card he is known to hold. The most common situation in which this opportunity arises is:

```
                    ♠ A J 2
    ♠ Q 10 4                          ♠ 8 7 6
                    ♠ K 9 5 3
```

The declarer, South, leads the ♠3, and finesses dummy's jack. When the ♠A is cashed, West should drop the queen. This card ranks equally with the 10, but the cards are not equivalent, as West is known to hold the queen. If West drops the ♠10 under the ace, South must make four tricks in the suit. If West drops the queen on the second round, South is faced with a guess.

In some situations, the correct play from equals depends on the assumption of a possible distribution of the cards.

```
                    ♥ A J 3
    ♥ K Q 4 2                          Immaterial
                    ♥ 7 led
```

When declarer leads the ♥7, if West decides to split his honors, he should play the queen and not the king. It is possible that declarer is missing the 10, and can be put to a difficult guess on the second round of hearts. For example, the suit might be distributed:

♥ A J 3

♥ K Q 4 2   ♥ 10 6 5

♥ 9 8 7

After the queen loses to the ace, declarer will later lead the suit from his own hand once again. If West ducks, declarer must reckon with the possibility that he made a standard falsecard with an original holding of Q-10-4-2. Notice that the initial play of the king would not create this effect, as West could hardly afford to play the king from K-10-4-2, lest declarer hold the queen in the concealed hand.

In other situations, the defense can play from imaginary equal cards:

♣ A K 10 9 7 6

♣ J 8   ♣ Q 2

♣ 5 4 3

The declarer leads the ♣5 and West plays the jack. If the declarer suspects that West has split equals, he may later lose a trick to East's queen.

In choosing a deceptive card to play from equals, the best policy is to make the holding you are representing a believable one.

An opening lead from equal cards is often made in consideration of what dummy is likely to hold in the suit led. On lead against a suit contract with A-K-6-4 of a suit that dummy has bid strongly, the best lead is probably the ace. If the dummy's suit is headed by Q-J without the 10, and the declarer holds a singleton, he may later take a ruffing finesse against third hand's imaginary king instead of choosing a different (possibly successful) line of play.

Another occasion for a deceptive lead from equal cards is when it is desirable to misrepresent the potential entry position. Let us suppose that West is on lead against the auction:

SOUTH	NORTH
1NT	3NT

West holds Q-J-10-8-6-2. The best lead is the deceptive 10. East's first play will look like a high signal, and declarer may believe that West has hit East's suit. If this plan succeeds, South will probably take losing finesses into the West hand.

Third hand's standard play from equal honors is the lowest of touching cards. Declarer may sometimes be deceived by a change of strategy.

♠ 4 3

♠ 10 8 6 2   ♠ K Q 7 5

♠ A J 9

Against South's notrump contract, West leads the ♠2. If East believes he will obtain the lead first for the defense, he might well play the king as a deceptive move.

When East later leads the ♠5, South may decide his best chance is to hope that East has the 10.

When the declarer must guess which suit to attack, the defense can often mislead him with the play of an apparently unnecessarily high card from equals.

♠ A J 9 8 3

♠ 4 2   ♠ K Q 10 5

♠ 7 6

Declarer plays a spade to dummy's 9. If East wins with the 10 (equal with the king and queen on this trick), the declarer may look elsewhere for his tricks. If East wins with a high honor, however, declarer may continue the

suit at his next opportunity, thus losing time (and possibly tricks).

The defense often uses a play from equals as a suit preference signal. This frequently occurs when a defender is establishing a suit against a notrump contract, and has a choice of equal cards to use to knock out the declarer's last stopper. The use of a high card shows a possible entry in a high-ranking suit, and the use of a low card shows a possible entry in a low-ranking suit. A similar play from equals involves the play of a high honor from equals to show strength in a high-ranking suit and a low honor from equals to show strength in a low-ranking suit. See SUIT PREFERENCE SIGNAL.

Declarer's play with equals. The selection of declarer's play with equal cards is designed to misguide the defense as much as possible. The selection of which equal to play depends upon declarer's specific objective.

♦ 2

♦ K Q J 10 9

At a suit contract, declarer (South) must avoid a loser in diamonds (a side suit). If dummy holds a few trump cards, his best chance is to lead the ♦9 from his hand. If West holds the ace, he may duck on the assumption that East can win the trick cheaply.

Thus, declarer plays a low equal when he hopes the defense will not use their honor cards. If, in a similar situation, the declarer hopes to remove the ace quickly, he should play the king (or queen) on the first round.

At a notrump contract, the declarer is usually interested in concealing strength or feigning strength so that the defenders will not know whether or not they have hit a weak spot in declarer's armor.

♣ 4 3

♣ K Q 10

Against South's notrump contract, West leads the ♣5 on which East plays the jack. South should win with the king. By so doing, he may deceive West into believing that East holds the Q.

♣ 4 3

♣ A K Q

Declarer has a weak spot elsewhere, and hopes the defense will continue clubs. When West leads the ♣5 and East plays the jack, declarer should play the king.

Once again this play may lead West to believe that East holds the ♣Q. If declarer wins with the ace, West will know he has something else in clubs unless the unlikely situation of East holding K-Q-J exists. Thus, West may suspect some trickiness. (On the other hand, against an experienced West, the play of the ace may be a good double cross.)

If the declarer is afraid of a continuation of the suit led, he should put on a mock display of power.

♠ 4 3

♠ A K 8 5 2   ♠ 9 7 6

♠ Q J 10

On West's lead of the ♠5, East plays the 9. South might well gobble this up with the 10, making sure West knows that he holds the queen and jack as well. If South wins with a higher honor, West may tend to place East with more length because of the chance that the declarer lacks the ♠10.

When the declarer has a very powerful holding in the suit led, he can often paint a very misleading picture.

♥ Q 6 5
♥ 9 7 3 2 ♥ 10 8
♥ A K J 4

Against South's 3NT contract, West leads the ♥2. Dummy plays low and East plays the 10. To encourage the defense to continue the suit, South's best play is probably the king. In addition to concealing the jack, this play suggests to West that East may have started with A-J-10. The play of the ace may present the same type of picture, but if holding the ace, declarer might have played dummy's queen on the first trick to gain a tempo by raking in a fast winner.

In general, declarer's best idea is to keep the defense in the dark as much as possible about his holding. However, he sometimes plays with a specific objective in mind.

♠ 8 6 5
♠ A 2 ♠ 7 3
♠ K Q J 10 9 4

Spades are trumps. In drawing trumps, many declarers think it is amusing to lead the 8 from dummy and let it ride. This is a good way to let the dummy know the hand is not violently overbid, but it also gives away a lot of information. West may feel that declarer has taken a successful finesse and he may adopt an active defense in a desperate attempt to defeat the contract. If this is to declarer's benefit, then this method of playing the trump suit is correct. However, if the declarer fears an active defense, he should play a low spade to his king or queen. West may now hope his partner held J-10-x and that declarer must lose another trick in trumps. He may therefore play safe, assuming that if he does not give away a trick with an aggressive lead, the contract will probably be defeated.

(As with all of these deceptive plays which leave possibilities open, how well declarer knows his opponents is an important factor.)

The purpose of declarer's play from equals is often to locate the defensive honors in a suit.

♣ 4 3 2

♣ K Q 10

The declarer is anxious to discover the location of the ♣A. After he leads the suit from the dummy, his best play against inexperienced players is the king. Against more wary opposition, the queen may be more effective. In the first case, West may fear that the declarer holds the king as his only honor in the suit. However, a more experienced player may decide that the declarer is unlikely to start such a weak suit during the early play.

Declarer is anxious to have West take the ace if he holds it so that he will be able to take informed action on the second round of the suit.

In general, when declarer leads a suit, the play of his highest equal card will conceal his holding in the suit. For example, declarer might lead low to the queen with any of the following holdings:

NORTH	♦ 4 3 2	♦ 4 3 2	♦ 4 3 2
SOUTH	♦ A Q J	♦ Q J 10 6	♦ Q 6

In the last example, of course, the declarer is trying to stop the defense from leading this suit when it gets the lead later in the play.

In a suit contract, the declarer can often conceal a potential ruff from the defense by playing carefully from

equal cards.

♥ Q J 10 4 3
♥ 9 8 7 6 5 ♥ 2
♥ A K

West leads the ♥9 against a spade contract. By playing low from dummy and winning with the ace, South may lead West to believe that East holds the K. An alternate form of this deception is to play the queen from the dummy before winning with the ace. This makes it look as if South gave East the opportunity to go wrong.

Declarer can often conceal the possibility of taking a deep finesse by leading low from equals.

♠ Q 5

♠ A 10 9 8

By leading the ♠8 toward dummy's queen, declarer may induce West to pop in with his king, if he holds it. If the ♠10 or ♠9 is led, West may duck smoothly, being more likely to realize the possibility of a finesse against the jack.

♥ Q 3 2

♥ A 9 8 7 6

Declarer has a choice of plays in this situation. By leading the ♥6 toward the dummy, he may conceal from West the possibility of an immediate double finesse on the first round. If West ducks smoothly, declarer should probably let the 6 ride and make a good guess on the next round. In this way, he may avoid two losers when West holds J-x or 10-x in hearts (see SUIT COMBINATIONS).

The following situations are similar:

(a) ♦ J 5 4
♦ Q 10 2 ♦ K 3
♦ A 9 8 7 6

(b) ♦ J 5 4
♦ K 3 ♦ Q 10 2
♦ A 9 8 7 6

The declarer intends to lead toward dummy and play West for 10-x (unless he receives information through action at the table). By leading the 6, he can conceal the possibility of a finesse against the 10, and may find West jumping in with his king or queen (much to his subsequent embarrassment).

PLAY OF THE HAND. See NOTRUMP PLAY and TRUMP PLAY.

PLAY OUT OF TURN. A play is considered to be in turn if it is made after the player to the right has led or played, or if it is a lead by a player who has won the preceding trick or is the opening leader. Any other order constitutes a play out of turn, and is covered by the rule for a premature lead or play by a defender, or lead or play from the wrong hand by declarer. See LAWS (Laws 53, 54, 55 and 56).

PLAYED CARD. In duplicate each player except dummy plays a card by detaching it from his hand, and facing it on the edge of the table immediately before him. Declarer plays a card from dummy's hand by naming the card he proposes to play, after which dummy picks up the card, and places it face up on his edge of the table. (In playing from dummy's hand, declarer may, if he prefers, pick up the desired card, and place it in such position as to indicate that it has been played. However, this is not correct in duplicate play.)

In addition, a card must be played if it is a defender's card held so that it is possible for his partner to see its face; or if it is a card from declarer's hand that declarer holds face up in front of him with intent to play, and that is touching or near the table. Declarer must play a card in dummy that he touches for purposes other than arranging or in reaching for the card immediately above or below the card touched. Any player also plays a card by naming or otherwise designating it as the card he proposes to play. Also any penalty card must be played if it can be played legally (without revoking). See LAWS (Law 45).

PLAYER. A participant at a table of bridge, one of an active foursome engaged at bridge; one member of either pair playing against each other.

PLAYER NUMBER. A seven-digit number assigned by the ACBL to a member. The last digit is a self-checking device by which the computer throws out incorrect numbers. The method by which the checking digit is computed is interesting. Multiply the first six digits by 7, 6, 5, 4, 3, and 2 respectively; then add these products. Divide the total of the products by 11, and note the remainder. This remainder is then subtracted from the divisor, 11, and the resulting difference is the check digit. (If the net result of this work is a remainder of 1, then the number is not used.)

When a player achieves LIFE MASTER status, this is indicated by a change in his player number by the substitution of a letter for the first digit, alphabetically from J for 1 to R for 9.

Player numbers were instituted by the ACBL in July, 1961.

PLAYER OF THE YEAR. Each year the ACBL designates one of its members as Player of the Year. The player so designated is the one that earns the most masterpoints in North American championship events with no upper masterpoint limit. For winners see Appendix II.

PLAYING CARDS. The cards, usually pasteboard, used in playing various games. (See also MAGNETIC CARDS, PLASTIC CARDS.) The standard bridge pack (or deck) consists of 52 cards, arranged in four suits of 13 cards each. Among the principal games played in the U.S. are bridge, canasta, casino, chemin-de-fer, cribbage, gin and other rummy games, hearts, piquet, twenty-one (also called blackjack and pontoon), poker, and many varieties of solitaire and patience. Pinochle is played with a special deck, which can be formed from two decks of standard cards. (See PACK for non-standard packs and their makeup, and TAROT for a very special pack.) Each suit is divided into three COURT CARDS and 10 SPOT CARDS. Of the latter, the ACE, or one-spot, ranks highest in bridge (but not necessarily in other games). Below the ace in rank are the court cards — king, queen, and jack (which has replaced the older term, knave, almost completely) — followed by the spot cards — 10, 9, 8, 7, 6, 5, 4, 3 (or trey), and 2 (or deuce). The suits are identified by the symbols for spades, hearts, diamonds and clubs, they rank in descending order in bridge games. Today's cards have corner INDICES showing a letter or numeral above a PIP of the suit to which the card belongs, but this is a modern device. Cards lacked such an

index as late as 1870.

For other articles in this book referring to playing cards, see COLLECTIONS OF PLAYING CARDS; DEVIL'S PICTURE BOOK; FACE CARDS; FORTUNETELLING; HISTORY OF PLAYING CARDS; MANUFACTURE OF PLAYING CARDS; SUIT; TAXES ON PLAYING CARDS; 10 OR 10 SPOT and other-spot cards; TRANSFORMATION CARDS; and USES OF CARDS.

PLAYING KNOWN CARD. See FALSECARDING.

PLAYING TO THE SCORE. Risk taking in the bidding or play of a hand often is affected by vulnerability. The need to be aggressive or conservative often depends on the current standing of the pair or team involved. Variations from normal play in rubber bridge or CHICAGO are motivated by the pairs involved.

In rubber bridge, the net score is computed at the conclusion of each rubber. In Chicago the net score is computed at the conclusion of each four-board set. In each case the net score is rounded off to the nearest hundred. That means that it makes sense to play the final hand of CHICAGO or the rubber-deciding hand in rubber bridge with an eye to the score — if an extra trick means a number rounded off to a higher hundred, then declarer should go for it.

Decisions on whether or not to bid on also depend on the score. Sometimes it is possible in rubber bridge to take a sacrifice that would pay off in duplicate, but the problem is that the opponents still are more likely to get the rubber bonus if they have a game on.

Playing to the score also plays an important role in duplicate. In an event scored by barometer, the pairs know where they stand after each round. In the late rounds, pairs that are close to the leader are likely to take a few more chances in an attempt to get some good scores that will enable them to overtake the leaders. The same is true in Swiss Teams scored by VICTORY POINTS. Teams close to the top going into the last match know that a mere win will not be enough — they will shoot for big scores in their attempt to overtake the leaders. In KNOCK-OUT TEAMS, a team that is far behind after the first half will come out shooting in the second half, feeling this is their only chance to win the match.

PLAYING TRICKS. Tricks that a hand may be expected to produce if the holder buys the contract; attacking tricks or winners, as distinguished from defensive tricks or winners when the holder must play against an adverse contract. In estimating the trick-taking strength of a hand, the holder assumes that his long suit (or suits) will break evenly among the other three hands, unless the auction has indicated otherwise, and adds the number of tricks his long suit (or suits) is likely to yield to his quick-trick total of the other suits. For example, the following hand

♠ K 5 ♥ A Q J 8 6 2 ♦ A Q 7 ♣ 9 3

contains about seven playing tricks — five in hearts, ° quick trick in spades, 1° quick tricks in diamonds.

When the long suit is not solid or semi-solid, estimation of playing tricks becomes more difficult because a second factor must be considered — the position of the missing honor cards. Thus, this suit

♥ K J 8 6 5 3

is worth approximately 3° playing tricks. With normal distribution, the declarer might make four tricks if he can lead toward the suit or find the missing honors well placed, but could be limited to three tricks.

Assessment of playing tricks is particularly important when considering a preemptive bid or an overcall. See RULE OF TWO AND THREE.

PLAYS TO CONCEAL STRENGTH. See DECEPTIVE PLAY.

PLAYS TO CONCEAL WEAKNESS. See DECEPTIVE PLAY.

PLUS VALUE. An added feature of a hand or suit that should be weighed when one is planning a bid or series of bids. There are bidding developments which require evaluation of a hand on a fairly precise basis. Therefore, during a subsequent phase of the auction, if one has been somewhat rigid in describing his holding and does possess plus values such as J-10-9 combinations in suits otherwise protected or strengthened, or a guarded queen, etc., that may be felt to be of help to partner, one is sometimes more liberal in making a final placement of contract than without the aforementioned values.

The term was regularly used in counting HONOR TRICKS, but modern usage tends to include other factors such as spots and distribution.

POCKET. One of four rectangular areas in a duplicate board which hold the four hands, designated North, South, East, and West. See LAWS OF DUPLICATE (Law 2).

PODI. See BLACKWOOD AFTER INTERFERENCE.

POE, Edgar Allan (1809-1849), writer and poet. He said in 'Murders in the Rue Morgue": "Whist has long been known for its influence upon what is termed the calculating power; and men of the highest order of intellect have been known to take an apparently unaccountable delight in it. Beyond doubt there is nothing of a similar nature so greatly tasking the faculty of analysis — proficiency in whist implies capacity for success in all these more important undertakings where mind struggles with mind."

POINT-A-BOARD. British term for board-a-match.

POINT-COUNT. An almost universally used method of valuation. Many point-counts have become obsolete (see FOUR ACES, REITH and ROBERTSON). In general use is the high-card valuation introduced by Bryant McCampbell in 1915 and publicized by Milton Work after whom it was named:

Ace	4
King	3
Queen	2
Jack	1

This gives a total of 40 points in the pack, and makes an average hand worth 10 points.

The Work count is slightly less accurate mathematically than the Four Aces count, for example, but its simplicity favored its acceptance. It was regularly used by English experts in the Thirties, but did not find favor with American experts until it was adopted and publicized by Fred Karpin and Charles Goren in the late Forties. They supplemented the basic high-card count with valuation for distribution (see DISTRIBUTIONAL COUNTS).

All authorities recognize that the 4-3-2-1 count has some weaknesses and many recommend certain corrections:

(1) Aces are undervalued, so the presence or absence of aces materially affects the strength of a hand. Two methods are: add ° point for each ace; or deduct a point for an aceless hand, and add a point for holding four aces.

(2) Tens are valuable cards and are sometimes counted as ° point or a plus value. One expedient is to consider aces and tens as a group, and to count an extra point if the hand contains three or more such cards.

(3) Unguarded or insufficiently guarded honor cards may not be worth their full point value. An extreme case is a singleton king, which some authorities count as 1 point instead of 3, and a singleton queen, which is sometimes counted as worthless. It is more usual to deduct one point from the value of a singleton king, queen or jack. Even the singleton ace is not quite as good as it looks because it has little chance of capturing an opposing honor card and is inflexible in the play.

Stayman went to the extreme of recommending the deduction of a point for each of the following holdings: K-Q; K-J; Q-J; Q-x; J-x; Q-x-x; J-x-x. It is true that these holdings have a reduced value if partner has useless small cards in the suit. But if your side is destined to play the hand, there is a good chance that partner will hold a card which will combine effectively with the short honor holding.

(4) Honor combinations are slightly stronger than the same cards would be in different suits. For example, Q-J-x is more effective than Q-x-x in one suit and J-x-x in another suit. But so much depends on what partner can provide that it is better to make no adjustment in this respect unless there is reason to think that partner's hand will be worthless or nearly worthless; or unless the honor is in a suit bid by partner. For other methods of valuation, see BISSELL SYSTEM, HONOR TRICKS, and LOSING-TRICK COUNT.

POINTED. A term coined to describe the combination of the spade and diamond suits (for example a "pointed two suiter"), since both suits have pips that are pointed at the top. The converse is "rounded," to indicate hearts and clubs.

POINTING CARDS. When four cards have been played to a trick in duplicate, each player turns his own card face down on the edge of the table immediately before him. If his side won the trick, the card is pointed lengthwise toward his partner; if the opponents won the trick, the card is pointed lengthwise toward his opponents. Each player should arrange his own cards in an orderly overlapping row in the sequence played.

At the completion of the play, each player should have an accurate count of tricks won and lost; should there be a disagreement, the tricks can be inspected in turn, and the disagreement reconciled. Should any alteration of this order of play of the cards occur, the director must assume the possibility that the player whose cards are disarranged is in error. This order of play should never be disturbed until the director has been summoned in event of disagreement.

POINTS. (1) The score earned by a pair as a result of the play of a hand, including TRICK POINTS, PREMIUM SCORES, and BONUS. (2) A unit by which a hand is evaluated. See POINT-COUNT. (3) The holding of masterpoints that have been credited to a player-member in the ACBL.

POKER BRIDGE. An epithet attached to a style of bidding that relies heavily on stabbing boldly with bids calculated to produce SWINGS on every hand. Players who can legitimately be accused of using "poker" tactics in bridge are those who constantly overbid or take long chances, and in general try to inculcate many more gambling features into bridge than rightfully belong there.

A second and less unfriendly connotation is alternatively associated with the term POKER BRIDGE: it simply implies that some of the desirable strategies of poker players (such as bluffing) can be successfully adapted to the bridge table.

POLISH BRIDGE UNION. This Union was founded in 1956 and was known as the Contact Bridge Association of Poland during 1962 to 91. In 1992 the Union had about 6000 full members and about 4000 junior and associate members, organized in 1200 clubs. Its players have won two world team championships and two European Championships. The Union publishes Swiat Brydza and Przeglad Brydzowy. Training courses for bridge teachers are conducted at the Physical Education University. Bridge courses are given in schools starting at age 12, to more than 3000 children.
Officers 1992:
  President: Andrzej Orlow
  International Secretary: Andrzej Simon
  Zlota 9/4 Warsaw, Poland.
  Tel. 4822 272429
  Fax. 4822 269638

POLITICIANS. Many persons occupying high political or military offices also have been bridge players. U.S. President Dwight D. Eisenhower enjoyed a few hands of bridge during lulls in World War II, and he even made an appearance at the 1961 Summer North American Championships in Washington DC. He was accompanied by his wartime colleague, General Alfred Gruenther, who was the leading American tournament director prior to World War II. Gruenther's bridge exploits were overshadowed by his wartime services, his appointment as Supreme Allied Commander of NATO and his election to the presidency of American Red Cross.

Former Secretary of Agriculture Clinton P. Anderson was a prominent tournament player in the Thirties. Lynn Martin, Secretary of Commerce under President George Bush, was a member of the Congress team in its first match against Corporate America. Supreme Court Justice Paul Stevens is an ACBL Life Master. Federal District Court Judge Carl Rubin is a Life Master and a former president of the American Contract Bridge League. Many members of Congress are bridge players, and nearly a dozen have competed for Congress in its matches against Corporate America.

Deng Xiaoping, long a dominant force in the People's Republic of China, revived bridge in his country and plays regularly himself. He fostered team tournaments in his country and was instrumental in having his country join the World Bridge Federation. Several other senior members of the Chinese establishment are bridge enthusiasts. One of them is Wan Li, former Chairman of the People's Congress. He won the International Bridge Press Association's Hand of the Year Award in 1984, and was named the Association's Bridge Personality of the Year

in 1989.

In England, Winston Churchill was playing bridge when the news of Germany's 1914 declaration of war on Russia interrupted his game. Iain Macleod had been a top tournament player and was one of the most influential cabinet ministers as Chancellor of the Exchequer at the time of his death in 1970. The House of Lords and the House of Commons have an annual bridge battle that was inaugurated in 1975. See BRITISH PARLIAMENT MATCHES. One regular member of the House of Commons team, Dr. John Marek, has represented Wales in Camrose Trophy matches.

Former Greek Premier Sophocles Venizelos was a member of the French national team during the Thirties and was European champion in 1935. In Argentina, Ricardo Argerich was a player of international class until he retired to concentrate on his diplomatic duties.

POLYNESIA. Bridge is organized in this country by the District de Bridge de Polynesia.
  President 1992:
  Alain Cotti,
  B.P. 13038
  Punaavia
  Tahiti
  French Polynesia.
  Tel. 412393

POOL. The total amount of money that is distributed to winning entries at some duplicate games. To create the pool, the competing pairs may be auctioned off, as in a CALCUTTA, or they may contribute a set amount at the beginning of the game. See GAMBLING AT BRIDGE.

POPULAR BRIDGE MONTHLY. See INTERNATIONAL POPULAR BRIDGE MONTHLY.

PORTLAND CLUB OF LONDON. The principal bridge club of British gentry, nobility, and (at times) royalty; world-famous as promulgator of the laws used in many countries. Founded before 1815 as the Stratford Club, and reorganized in 1825, according to tradition, in order to be rid of one objectionable member. Bridge, introduced in 1894 by Lord Brougham, was given a code of laws in 1895, and with subsequent revisions at intervals, gave the Portland Club its reputation as a law-making body (see LAWS). Famous members of the Club in its whist days included James Clay, William Pole, William Dalton and HENRY JONES (CAVENDISH).

Stuart Wheeler, following the late Geoffrey Butler and the late Colin Harding, serves (1993) as the legal link between the Portland Club, the law-making body for Britain, and other law-making bodies, such as the European Bridge League, the American Contract Bridge League and the World Bridge Federation.

PORTLAND RULES. The laws of WHIST according to the English code, named after the PORTLAND CLUB, which officially issued them.

In the early days of CONTRACT BRIDGE and the later days of AUCTION BRIDGE, the use of bidding calls with conventional meaning (such as the Informatory Double of auction or the Vanderbilt Club Bid of contract) were decried by the card committee of the Portland Club, a staid, conservative, British stronghold, and barred in games held in their clubrooms. These rules were called

Portland Rules at that time.

PORTUGUESE BRIDGE FEDERATION (Federaçao Portuguesa de Bridge). The Federation was founded in 1961 by Conde de Mangualde and in 1993 had a membership of 855 in 7 regional circles. It hosted the 1970 European Championships and is scheduled to host the 1993 Common Market Championships.
1993 Officers:
  President: José Soares de Oliveira
  Secretary: Luiz Elso Marques
  R. dos Sapateiros, 173-4° Esq.
  1100 Lisboa Portugal
  Tel. (351) 1 3478892
  Fax (351) 1 3468044

POSITION. The place at a table occupied by a player. The various positions are called by the compass points, i.e., North, South, East, and West. Also, the term "position" can correctly be used to describe one's place in the order of bidding during a given auction. "Second" position means that position directly to the left of the dealer. "Fourth" position is the seat to the dealer's right. See SEAT.

POSITIONAL FACTOR. The value of honor cards during the bidding may improve or decline in accordance with the opposing bidding. A king becomes an almost sure trick when the suit is bid by the right-hand opponent, but is likely to be worthless if the suit is bid on the left, except as a notrump stopper if the holder of the king is declarer. See RIGHT SIDE.

Sidney Silodor gave the following example:

WEST	NORTH	EAST	SOUTH
	1 ♥	Pass	2 ♥
3 ♦	3 ♥	All Pass	

South holds:

  ♠ A J 7 3
  ♥ 10 6 3 2
  ♦ K 4 2
  ♣ 10 9

Although South has a relatively strong raise to 2♥, he should pass, because the ♦K has been devalued by the bid on the left. The decision to pass would be even clearer if the minor suits were interchanged and West bid 3♣. In that case North's failure to make the trial bid of 3♦ would imply a lack of interest in game. See COMPETITIVE DOUBLE.

POSITIONAL SQUEEZE. A squeeze which is effective against one opponent but not the other. This occurs when the hand opposite the squeeze card has nothing but busy cards; if that hand follows to the squeeze card before the opponent who is menaced, there can be no squeeze.

```
              ♠ A J
              ♥ K
              ♦ —
              ♣ —
  ♠ 7                    ♠ K Q
  ♥ 6                    ♥ A
  ♦ 2                    ♦ —
  ♣ —                    ♣ —
              ♠ 5
              ♥ 4
              ♦ A
              ♣ —
```

When the ♦A is led, the North hand is squeezed before East must play, so that the latter is in no difficulty; however, if the East and West hands were reversed, the squeeze would be effective. Positional squeezes are characterized by the fact that the one-card menaces lie to the left of the opponent threatened. See also AUTOMATIC SQUEEZE and SIMPLE SQUEEZE.

POSITIVE CARDS. See CARDS, NEUTRAL AND POSITIVE.

POSITIVE RESPONSE. A natural constructive response in a forcing situation where there is a bid available for an artificial negative or waiting response. See FORCING TWO-BID, TWO CLUBS STRONG ARTIFICIAL OPENING.

POSITIVE SLAM DOUBLE. See DOUBLE FOR SACRIFICE.

POST-MORTEM. A term applied to discussion of bridge hands after the conclusion of the play or any time thereafter. Some players aver that they object to constant post-mortems, but it can sometimes be pointed out with a degree of correctness that what they object to is being reminded of their own mistakes. Generally speaking, post-mortems can be of significant value when engaged in by experts, as points of great interest are sometimes highlighted by this type of discussion, and unusual features of a hand brought into better perspective.

In tournament play, long post-mortems should be indulged in only if time permits at the end of a round.

POSTING THE SCORE. Among the duties of the tournament director (and his staff) is the posting of the score as rapidly and conspicuously as possible, for the inspection of the players.

In club games, when TRAVELING SCORESLIPS are used, matchpoints are awarded on the traveling scoreslips, and these are posted. Sometimes the matchpoints are posted to a RECAPITULATION SHEET, where they are added and ranked. At no time is the score official until a PROTEST PERIOD has expired.

Posting of scores has been considerably speeded up, in both tournament and club play, since the introduction of COMPUTER SCORING.

POTTAGE. See CAPPELLETTI and HAMILTON.

POWERHOUSE. A descriptive term signifying a really huge (in point value) hand at bridge. A powerhouse could also, but considerably less frequently, be a strong distributional hand with outside aces or ace combinations, or possibly void features. An alternative term is "rock crusher."

PREACCEPTANCE This occurs in transfer auctions in two ways.
  (1) After a major-suit transfer response:

Opener	Responder
1NT	2♦ (=hearts)
3♣	

This shows maximum values, four good hearts, and a doubleton club, the suit bid.

This may take the partnership too high if partner is very weak. But in that case the opponents may have been deprived of a part-score.

(2) After a minor-suit transfer, when using four-suit transfers:

Opener	Responder
1NT	2 ♠ (=clubs)
2NT	

The usual practice is similar, using this to show a club fit and strong interest in game. However, the converse, with three clubs to show a fit and 2NT to deny one, has some advantages. It allows the partnership to handle weak minor two-suiters, for if the rebid is 2NT responder can bid 3♦ to close the auction.

PREALERT. In ACBL tournaments, players are required to explain to the opponents, or prealert, certain aspects of their methods. These are unusual bidding treatments that may require pre-discussion by the defense, and unusual carding methods such as upside-down, RUSINOW, LAVINTHAL and odd-even signals.

PRECEDENCE IN ENTERING A TABLE. In bridge clubs, precedence is given to that member who first appears in the playing room. The lowest priority belongs to a member leaving an existing table to join the new one. See HOUSE RULES.

PRECISION ASKING BIDS. The PRECISION CLUB system, in its standard version, allows the 1♣ opener to use asking bids for three purposes: (1) to find out about the length and quality of the trump suit, (2) to find out about responder's control of a particular suit, (3) to find out whether responder can fill in opener's SEMI-SOLID SUIT and what other aces he has.

Trump Asking. The most commonly used is the trump asking bid, which is initiated by the 1♣ opener's single raise of responder's positive suit response. The responses are as follows:

1st step	No top honor
2nd step	Five cards with one top honor
3rd step	Five cards with two top honors
4th step	Six cards with one top honor
5th step	Six cards with two top honors
6th step	Three top honors

These asking bids and responses are used also in the SUPER PRECISION system, which designates them Gamma Trump Asking Bids. For other trump asking devices see TRUMP ASKING BIDS.

Control Asking. After a trump asking bid has been made and responded to, a bid in a new suit by opener asks about responder's controls in a side suit. The controls shown may be either high card or distributional. The responses are:

1st step	No control
2nd step	Third-round control (Q or doubleton)
3rd step	Second-round control (K or singleton)
4th step	First-round control (A or void)
5th step	First- and second-round control (A-K or A-Q)

Opener may ask whether partner's control is a high card or distributional by rebidding the asked suit. Responder shows a high card by bidding the first step (next suit) and the distributional control by bidding the second step.

Ace Asking. The third type of asking bid asks whether responder has one of the top three honors in a particular suit. It is initiated by a jump shift rebid by the 1♣ opener after a positive response. The responses give informa-

tion about another suit as well as about the asked suit. The responses are:

Cheapest notrump	No top honor, no aces
Single raise	Top honor in asked suit, no other aces
New suit	Ace of bid suit, no top honor in asked suit
Jump in new suit	Top honor in asked suit, ace in suit jumped in
Jump in notrump	No top honor in asked suit, but two side aces
Jump raise	Top honor in asked suit with two side aces

See also ASKING BIDS; ROMAN ASKING BIDS; ROMEX TRUMP ASKING BIDS; SUPER PRECISION ASKING BIDS.

PRECISION CLUB. A system developed by C. C. Wei in 1963 with assistance from Alan Truscott. It was used successfully by the Taiwan team in the 1967, 1968, and 1969 Far East Championships, and attracted international attention during the 1969 Bermuda Bowl when Patrick Huang, M. F. Tai, C. S. Shen and Frank Hwang, all using the Precision Club, spearheaded Taiwan's drive into the final of the tournament. This was the closest a non-European, non-North American team had come to capturing the world team title. The Taiwan team reached the final again in 1970.

In the United States a number of top-level teams were sponsored by Wei to use and popularize the Precision System. One such team won three major ACBL knockout team events within a 19-month period. See PRECISION TEAM.

By 1972, when the Italian BLUE TEAM emerged from retirement to enter the World Team Olympiad, all three of its pairs were using versions of the Precision System. The version used by Giorgio Belladonna and Benito Garozzo was called SUPER PRECISION.

The chief features of the standard Precision System are as follows:

1♣ opening is forcing and artificial, and normally shows a minimum of 16 high-card points. Suit responses other than 1♦, which is the conventional negative, are positive, 8 points or more, guarantee at least a five-card suit and, in principle, are forcing to game. With a positive response and 4-4-4-1 distribution, there are two basic methods of responding. The partnership may agree to use the IMPOSSIBLE NEGATIVE: responder bids 1♦, then jumps in his singleton, or in notrump if his singleton is in opener's suit. Alternatively an UNUSUAL POSITIVE may be used: responder immediately jumps to 2♥, 2♠, 3♣, or 3♦ over 1♣ to show a singleton in the suit he jumps in, and four cards in every other suit. As a variation of the unusual positive, the jump can be made in the suit below the singleton, so that opener can economically cuebid the singleton to obtain additional information. Balanced hands are shown by responding either 1NT (8-10), 2NT (11-13, or 16 on up), or 3NT (14-15). After a negative response and a normal rebid, responder will usually bid again with 4-7 points.

If 1♣ is overcalled, responder: passes with fewer than five points; bids a five-card or longer suit, or makes a CARD-SHOWING DOUBLE with 5-8 points; jumps in notrump with the opponents' suit well stopped and 9-11 points; cuebids with a hand too strong for a card-showing double; or bids the cheapest notrump with an unbalanced, game-forcing hand. If 1♣ is doubled, normal responses are used, except that with a weak hand responder passes with clubs, bids 1♦ without clubs or redoubles with both major suits.

After a 1♦ negative response, opener rebids 1NT with 16-18 points, 2NT with 19-21, or 3NT with 25-27. A non-jump rebid in a suit is nonforcing; a jump rebid is forcing to game unless opener rebids his suit at the three level.

After a positive response, the auction develops naturally with one exception. A direct raise of responder's suit is an inquiry about the length of responder's suit and the number of top honors he holds, and subsequent suit bids by opener are asking bids. See PRECISION ASKING BIDS and SUPER PRECISION ASKING BIDS.

STAYMAN is used after all notrump responses and rebids.

1♦, 1♥, and 1♠ openings are natural and limited to a maximum of 15 points. Major-suit openings promise at least a five-card suit.

1NT response to a major-suit opening is forcing; 3NT is a strong balanced raise; double jumps are splinter bids, showing four-card support for opener's major and a singleton or void in the bid suit. Raises are limited and nonforcing, except after 1♦: 2♦ is forcing and 3♦ is preemptive. A jump response of 2NT shows 16 or more points.

1NT opening is weak, 13-15 points. 2♣ and 2♦ are nonforcing and forcing Stayman, respectively. However, many Precision experts prefer a stronger range, 14-16 or 15-17. In this case weaker balanced hands must begin with 1♦, which becomes a catchall, sometimes made with a doubleton.

2♣ is a natural opening, showing a six-card club suit (rarely five) and an unbalanced hand. 2♦ is a conventional response: with a minimum, opener bids a four-card major; with a maximum, opener jumps in a four-card major, raises to 3♣, or jumps to 3NT with a solid or semi-solid club suit. A rebid of 2NT shows two suits outside of clubs stopped. Responder may ask where the stoppers are by bidding 3♦; the responses are 3♥ to show hearts and diamonds, 3♠ to show spades and diamonds, and 3NT to show both major suits. A rebid of 3♣ by opener over the 2♦ response suggests a six-card club suit with one side suit stopped; over a 3♦ inquiry opener bids hearts or spades if that is where his stopper is, or bids 3NT if he has diamonds stopped.

2♦ is a specialized opening, describing a three-suited hand (4-4-1-4 or 4-4-0-5) with shortage in diamonds and 11-15 points. (4-3-1-5 and 3-4-1-5 were later included). A 2NT response requests opener to specify his exact distribution and point range of his opening bid. Other responses are limited and nonforcing.

2♥ and 2♠ openings are weak two-bids.

2NT opening is standard (22-24 points).

3NT opening is gambling, showing a long, solid minor with little side strength.

4♣ and 4♦ openings are NAMYATS.

The above describes traditional Precision, as set out in 1964 by C.C.Wei. The many experts who have adopted the system have modified it substantially in a variety of ways. The most important are:

(1) An opening one notrump with 14-16 points (or 15-17). Stronger hands open one club and rebid one notrump (17-19). Weaker hands open one diamond and rebid one notrump (11-13). This means that one diamond becomes

a catchall for hands that do not fit elsewhere, and is often made with a doubleton. (Some pairs permit a singleton). A two-diamond response to one diamond is then treated as a forcing two-over-one response with diamond length, rather than a raise.

(2) A rebid of one heart by a one-club opener (1♣ – 1♦ – 1♥) is forcing, with one spade as the usual rebid by responder, a waiting move. Notrump bids then show balanced hands, of 20 points or more, and other rebids show that one heart was natural.

(3) Two diamonds can have a variety of meanings. A MULTI is one popular choice.

(4) Two hearts is sometimes a substitute for Flannery, with four spades and five hearts.

See SUPER PRECISION.

PRECISION TEAM. A highly successful team of young experts from the New York City area sponsored by C. C. Wei to use his PRECISION CLUB system between 1970 and 1973. While there have been a number of teams using the Precision System and coached by Wei, the designation The Precision Team came to mean the team whose nucleus was Steven Altman, Thomas M. Smith, Joel Stuart and Peter Weichsel, and which won three of the four major ACBL knockout team championships held between August 1970 and March 1972.

With David Strasberg as a fifth member in 1970, the Precision Team defeated the World champion ACES to win the Spingold. With Eugene Neiger replacing Strasberg as the fifth member in 1971, the team successfully defended its Spingold title, becoming only the fifth team to do so since the event began in 1934. Adding Alan Sontag as a sixth member, the team won the Vanderbilt in 1972.

In January 1973 four members of the Precision Team entered the SUNDAY TIMES event. Altman-Sontag and Smith-Weichsel finished first and second, respectively, in the select 22 pair field, marking the first time a United States pair had ever finished higher than fourth.

After failing to defend its titles successfully in the 1972 Spingold and 1973 Vanderbilt, the team was disbanded in mid-1973. In the meantime many international stars adopted Precision, including members of the Italian BLUE TEAM, the South American champions from Brazil, and a group of British stars headed by Terence Reese. In 1992, many top-ranked pairs from different parts of the world were using Precision in WBF Championships.

PRECISION TWO DIAMONDS. See PRECISION CLUB.

PRE-DEALING. A method of (1) producing duplicated boards for play in more than two sections, or (2) producing deals prior to a match so that duplicates of the hand can be published and furnished to spectators or those who prepare slides or frames for exhibition.

Perhaps the first instance of pre-dealing occurred in Johannesburg, South Africa, in December 1962. The hands were pre-dealt and copies made for the spectators for an exhibition match between South African players and a visiting team from England. In modern times, predealing is done by computer. A program is devised so that a random mathematical setup is instilled in the computer, and the computer then distributes the cards to the four compass corners. Printouts then are made of the deals manufactured by the computer. These printouts are packaged and sealed and, in the case of the ACBL, sent to the ACBL Headquarters for storage until they are ready for use. The hand records are sent to the tournament, and kept intact and sealed until it is time for the game in which they will be used. Then, and only then, the tournament director opens the package and distributes the hand records to his fellow directors for distribution among the players. In addition, a special one sheet printout of all the hands is provided to the tournament. If the tournament officials wish, copies may be made of this master sheet for distribution to the players at the end of the session. This has proved very popular at American tournaments.

The same process makes it possible to have ACBL-wide and worldwide games involving the same deals. The hands are packaged and sealed, then mailed to the various areas where games are going to be held. The games are all held at approximately the same time, so that there is little chance of information being passed from one area to another.

PREEMPTIVE BID or SHUTOUT BID. An opening bid of three or more with a hand containing a long suit and limited high-card strength. The bid is defensive in purpose. The preemptive bidder hopes that opponents with strong hands will find it difficult to bid accurately when the auction has started at a high level.

The following considerations may influence the preemptive bidder.

(1) *Length of suit.* An opening three-bid is usually a seven-card suit or a strong six-card suit. An opening four-bid is usually an eight-card suit or a strong seven-card suit. An opening five-bid in a minor is usually a nine-card suit or a strong eight-card suit.

(2) *Vulnerability.* The traditional rule was to take the playing-trick strength of the hand and add three tricks when not vulnerable or two tricks when vulnerable. This is an over-simplification, and most experts make preemptive bids more freely than this two and three rule would permit.

In the most favorable circumstances, third-hand not vulnerable against vulnerable opponents, some experts would venture 3♠ with a hand as weak as:

♠ K J 10 8 6 4
♥ 4
♦ 3 2
♣ 7 6 5 3

When vulnerable against nonvulnerable, on the other hand, the preemptive bidder should be within two tricks of his bid in his own hand, and even then may lose 500 to save 420.

(3) *Position at the table.* The third player is best placed to preempt, because he knows that he cannot preempt his partner, and the fourth player is almost sure to have the best hand at the table. Preemptive bids by the dealer are also attractive. They run the risk of finding partner with a strong hand, and therefore giving him problems, but there are two opponents who may have strength, and the odds are that the hand belongs to them. Preemptive bids by the second player are less attractive, and should be slightly stronger than preempts by the dealer. Preempts by the fourth player are very rare, and should indicate a solid or near-solid suit if bid at the three-level.

(4) *Strength of suit, and outside strength.* The preemptive bidder prefers to have his honor strength concen-

trated in the suit bid. This automatically increases his playing strength, decreases the danger of suffering a substantial penalty, and decreases the chance of successful defense against an opposing contract. A doubleton queen in a side-suit is unlikely to play a part in attack, but may be an important factor in defense.

Some players make it a practice not to preempt when holding a four-card major side-suit but this rule is at best doubtful.

(5) *Bidding methods.* Opening three-bids tend to be weaker, and rarer, when using WEAK TWO-BIDS, which are a form of preemptive bid. The weak two is used with many hands which others players would open with three. The opponents' defensive methods also have to be taken into account. Opening four-bids tend to be weaker when the partnership is using artificial preemptive bids, which tend to be well-defined in strength and suit texture. More discretion must be exercised in opening three-bids against players who double for penalties than against players who double for takeout. See DEFENSE TO OPENING THREE-BID.

RESPONSES. Responses to opening three-bids are often of a tactical character, intended to reinforce the preemptive effect of the opening bid. If the dealer opens 3♠, for example, and the third player holds three-card spade support or better, he should rarely pass unless he has sufficient defensive honor strength to defend against 4♥. If the third player has a hand so weak that he fears an adverse slam, he may take more positive action by bidding 5♠, or 6♠, or venturing some psychic maneuver. This would have the character of an ADVANCE SAVE.

The following points relate to normal constructive responses to preemptive bids.

(1) *Raise to game in a major suit* (e.g., 3♠ – 4♠). Responder must take into account the vulnerability and other factors which influenced the opening bid. If vulnerable, he needs three sound playing tricks in the form of trump honors, aces, kings, and more ruffing values. Queens and jacks in side-suits must be discounted. If not vulnerable, he needs at least four playing tricks — more if circumstances favored a light preempt. But this raise is often made on a much weaker hand for the tactical reasons mentioned above.

(2) *3NT.* A bid which the opener should almost invariably pass. In response to a minor suit, it shows stoppers in at least two of the unbid suits, and probably a fitting honor in the opener's suit. In response to a major suit, it shows a hand capable of making nine tricks without using the opener's suit. Responder is likely to have a solid minor suit, and might be void in opener's suit.

(3) *Three of a higher-ranking suit* (e.g., 3♣ – 3♥). Forcing to game, showing that the preempt has found responder with a strong hand. The responder's suit should be a good five-card suit or better, and the opener should raise with any slight excuse. The opener should bid 3♠ if he has a spade stopper for notrump purposes; a rebid of 3 NT in this situation would show a diamond stopper.

(4) *Four of a lower-ranking suit* (e.g., 3♠ – 4♣; but not 3♠ – 4♥, which would be natural). A slam try, inviting the opener to cooperate. Spades are provisionally, but not definitely, agreed on as the trump suit. (The same applies to five of a lower-ranking suit after an opening four-bid.) These bids can be used as ASKING BIDS.

(5) *Five of opener's suit* (e.g., 3♠ – 5♠, or 4♠ – 5♠). Traditionally, a natural slam invitation, implying that responder is not worried about two losers in any side suit.

The quality of his trumps may decide opener's course of actions. The modern style after a three opening is for this bid to be preemptive, on a hand on which the opposition may have a slam.

See NAMYATS; RUBIN TRANSFERS; THREE NOTRUMP OPENING; TRANSFER OPENING THREE-BIDS; TWO UNDER TRANSFER PREEMPTIVE OPENINGS.

PREEMPTIVE JUMP OVERCALL. See WEAK JUMP OVERCALL.

PREEMPTIVE OVERCALL. A defensive overcall, usually a double or triple jump in a suit, aimed at obstructing the bidding by the opener's side. After an opening bid of 1♦, a jump to 3♥, 3♠, or 4♣ would be preemptive. Standards would be slightly higher than for opening preemptive bids at the same level, because the chance of seriously inconveniencing the opponents is reduced. A vulnerable jump to 3♠ suggests a hand with 7-8 playing tricks.

A jump to the game level is ambiguous. The overcaller is likely to have a preemptive hand, but may make the same bid with a strong hand prepared to abandon hopes of slam in view of the opposing opening. See also DOUBLE JUMP OVERCALL and WEAK JUMP OVERCALL.

PREEMPTIVE RAISES. A preemptive raise of a suit from the one-level to the four-level, usually in a major, has always been an element of standard bidding. In recent years there has been a tendency to use jumps to the three-level preemptively. See BERGEN RAISES and OVERCALLS.

PREEMPTIVE RE-RAISE. A three-level rebid by opener in his own suit which has been raised by responder, in order to make it more difficult for the opponents to bid rather than to try for game. Responder is expected to pass this rebid.

In order to try for game, partnerships using preemptive re-raises must bid notrump or bid a new suit either naturally or as a SHORT SUIT GAME TRY, a TWO-WAY GAME TRY, or a WEAK SUIT GAME TRY. See also TRIAL BID.

PREEMPTIVE RESPONSE. A new suit response to a suit opening at a higher level than would be required for a jump shift:

SOUTH	NORTH
1♥	3♠ or 4♣ or 4♦ or 4♠

North normally holds a seven-card suit or eight-card suit, but the exact playing strength varies with circumstances. He must take the vulnerability into account, and also the likelihood of the opponents entering the auction. The suit will be a broken one; with a solid or near-solid suit a simple response followed by a jump is more appropriate.

As these responses are rarely used, they can be given, and usually are given, conventional meanings. See ASKING BID, SPLINTER BIDS, SWISS, and VOID-SHOWING BID. For other preemptive responses, see INVERTED MINOR SUIT RAISES and WEAK JUMP SHIFT RESPONSES.

PREFERENCE. When a player bids two suits, and his partner returns to the original suit at the lowest possible level, he is giving simple preference. This is in no way strength-showing, and will usually be passed. Preference at an unnecessarily high level is termed jump preference, and is considered under RESPONDER'S REBID.

Simple preference can occur in five common situations:

(1) *After three bids at the one level (e.g., 1♣ - 1♥ - 1♠).* With a minimum responding hand (5-7 points) and three cards in clubs and spades, it is usually best to pass. If the opener has to play a 4-3 spade fit instead of a 5-3 club fit at a higher level, it is no great hardship. A preference to 2♣ would be appropriate with 8-9 points if diamond weakness rules out 1NT and responder wishes to give the opener another chance in case he has 17-18 points.

The most difficult situation arises when the responder has not more than a doubleton in each of the opener's suits, with exactly five cards in his own suit. A preference to 2♣ should never be given with a doubleton, so the choice lies between a pass, leaving the opener to play in a 4-2 fit with the prospect of a club ruff, or 1NT if the partnership method permits this to be weak.

(2) *When opener bypasses 1NT (e.g., 1♥ - 1♠ - 2♦).* Automatic preference to 2♥ is called for if the responder has equal red-suit length (3-3 or 2-2). There is a strong probability that the opener has a five-card heart suit (see OPENER'S REBID). Some authorities suggest a timid pass when the response is a minimum instead of giving preference, but this is born of fear that the opener may continue bidding without justification. With 8-10 points, two hearts and three diamonds, false preference to 2♥ may be appropriate in case the opener has a maximum rebid.

(3) *After a two-over-one response (e.g., 1♠ - 2♣ –2♥).* In traditional style, this was the way to give a strong raise to two spades with about 10 points and three or four spades. The four-card support was ruled out by the general adoption of the LIMIT RAISE. In the modern two over-one style, the sequence is forcing, suggesting three-card support with at least 12 points.

(4) *After a 1NT response (e.g., 1♠ – 1NT – 2♥).* The responder gives automatic preference, expecting the opener to hold five spades and four or five hearts. (If the opener has chosen this sequence with four spades and five hearts, the wrong contract is reached. But the popularity of FIVE-CARD MAJORS and FLANNERY has made this a rare problem.)

If the opener's two suits are a major and a minor, false preference with two of the original suit and three of the second suit may be appropriate, especially at matchpoints. This applies particularly after the sequence 1♠ - 1NT - 2♣, when the opener is likely to have shorter clubs. In the modern style, with a one notrump response forcing, opener may well have five spades and three clubs.

(5) *After a 1NT rebid (e.g., 1♥ – 1♠ – 1NT – 2♣).* A delicate situation, because the responder may hold a hand with four spades and five or six clubs which was not strong enough for an original response at the two level. The opener should usually refrain from giving preference, even if he holds three spades. (Alternatively, a partnership may agree that with only four spades, responder should pass 1NT, in which contract the minor suit may prove useful.) See NEW MINOR FORCING.

PREMATURE LEAD OR PLAY. A lead or play made before the proper time or before a player's proper turn. This irregularity may occur before or after the auction ends. Declarer incurs no penalty for a premature lead or play. See LAWS (Law 24 for a card led during the auction, Law 54 for a faced opening lead out of turn, and Law 57 for a premature lead or play by a defender); see also LEAD OUT OF TURN.

PREMATURE SAVE. See ADVANCE SAVE.

PREMIUM. A score made above the line. See BONUS.

PREMIUM SCORE. The score ABOVE THE LINE, consisting of extra tricks, making doubled contracts, rubber bonus, slam awards, honors, and premiums for defeating opposition contracts.

PREPARED CLUB. See SHORT CLUB.

PREPARED HANDS. See EPSON; INSTANT MATCH POINTS; MACHINE-PREPARED HANDS; PAR CONTESTS; PRE-DEALING; TWINNING.

PREPAREDNESS, PRINCIPLE OF. The idea, originally called "Anticipation" of looking forward to the next round of bidding when selecting a bid. It applies regularly to the opening bidder, but may also apply to the responder or to the opponents of the player who opened the bidding. Specific cases are considered under CHOICE OF SUIT.

PRESIDENTS. American Bridge League; American Contract Bridge League; and United States Bridge Association.

ABL

1927	Ralph R. Richards
1928	Henry P. Jaeger
1929	Robert W. Halpin
1930	Clayton W. Aldrich
1931	Capt. Fred G. French
1932	Waldemar K. von Zedtwitz
1933	Sir Derrick J. Wernher
1934	Ray H. Eisenlord
1935	Louis J. Haddad
1936	H. Huber Boscowitz

ACBL

1937	Gordon M. Gibbs
1938	Nate B. Spingold
1939	James H. Lemon
1940	Elmer J. Babin
1941	Robert J. Gill
1942	Morgan Howard
1943	Albert H. Morehead
1944	Richmond H. Skinner
1945	George A. Alderton, II
1946	Benjamin M. Golder
1947	J. McGrover
1948	Waldemar K. von Zedtwitz
1949	Dr. Louis Mark
1950	Rufus L. Miles, Jr.
1951	Julius L. Rosenblum
1952	Joseph Cohan
1953	Benjamin O. Johnson
1954	Peter A. Leventritt
1955	Jefferson Glick
1956	Rufus L. Miles, Jr.
1957	Joseph G. Ripstra
1958	Charles J. Solomon

1959	Winslow Randall
1960	Frank T. Westcott
1961	James P. Ferguson
1962	Max Manchester
1963	Jerry M. Lewis
1964	Leo Seewald
1965	Robin B. MacNab
1966	Eilif Andersen
1967	John W. Norwood
1968	Joseph J. Stedem
1969	Edgar G. Theus
1970	William A. Baldwin
1971	Carl Rubin
1972	Percy X. Bean
1973	Jerome R. Silverman
1974	Ruth McConnell
1975	Lewis L. Mathe
1976	Donald Oakie
1977	Louis S. Gurvich
1978	Walter K. O'Loughlin
1979	Leo J. Spivack
1980	Ira G. Corn, Jr.
1981	James E. Zimmerman
1982	Sydney A. Levey, Jr.
1983	William Gross
1984	Douglas Drew
1985	Chris Wilson
1986	Tommy Sanders
1987	Bobby Wolff
1988	Herb Smith
1989	Phyllis Smith
1990	Ed Gould
1991	David McGee
1992	Joan Levy Gerard
1993	Barbara Nudelman
1994	Virgil Anderson

USBA

1932-4	Milton C. Work
1935-7	Ely Culbertson

PRESSURE BID. An overbid made necessary by opposing action. Suppose this bidding:

WEST	NORTH	EAST	SOUTH
1♥	3♣	?	

North's 3♣ is a weak jump overcall, and East holds three-card heart support and 8 points in high cards. Although he could not have bid 3♥ in the ordinary way, even using LIMIT JUMP RAISES, he should bid 3♥ at this point under the pressure of the opposing bid. A pass would leave West to consider the possibility that East has a worthless hand. 3♥ is therefore less of an overbid than a pass would be an underbid.

In such circumstances 3♥ shows the upper range of a raise to 2♥ without interference. The opener allows for the pressure, and passes unless he would have considered a game after a single raise.

As a corollary, the responder must overbid similarly with a slightly stronger hand. If he would have made a limit jump raise to 3♥ in normal circumstances, he must jump to 4♥ over the bid of 3♣.

PRETEEN SCHOLARSHIP AWARD. In 1989 Homer Shoop, founder of the International Palace of Sports in North Webster IN, and long-time benefactor of ACBL youth programs, added the Preteen Scholarship to bridge and tennis scholarships previously established. Though Shoop died in 1991, the IPS survives as a public foundation and the scholarships Shoop established endure through the IPS Foundation. The pre-teen award is a 10-year maturity $5000 certificate to be used for academic or career training. Secured by zero coupon government bonds, the certificate can be used as collateral for a student loan or redeemed before maturity at a 10% annual discount.

ACBL members who have not celebrated their 13th birthday before July 1 of the contest year who have at least one full masterpoint on record are eligible for consideration. The winners:

1989 — Lisa Kow, 10, Concord CA
1990 — Joel Wooldridge, 10, Snyder NY
1991 — Vincent Molgat, 11, Red Deer AB
1992 — Bonnie Greco, 12, Annandale VA
1993 — Ari Greenberg, 12, Malibu CA

PRIMARY HONORS. Top honors, i.e., aces and kings. The king of a suit may instead be considered a SECONDARY HONOR when it is unaccompanied by the ace and when it is in a suit in which partner is known to be short. Primary honors usually carry more weight in suit contracts than in notrump.

PRIMARY TRICKS. A term first used by P. Hal Sims to describe high cards which will win tricks no matter who eventually plays the hand.

PRIMARY VALUES. Aces and kings, also called Hard Values.

PRISONERS OF WAR. See BRIDGE IN PRISON CAMPS.

PRISONS, PRISONERS. See BRIDGE IN PRISONS.

PRIVATE CONVENTION. A partnership understanding which is not made known to the opponents. The use of such a convention is a violation of the Laws and the Proprieties: "It is improper to convey information to partner by means of a call or play based on special partnership agreement, whether explicit or implicit, unless such information is fully and freely available to the opponents (see Law 40)." LAWS OF DUPLICATE (Law 75). This requirement is not easy to fulfill in tournament play. Many partnerships have elaborate understandings about the precise natural meaning to be allocated to certain bids and sequences. It is difficult to draw a hard-and-fast line to separate convention from style.

ACBL standards require that the opponents automatically be alerted to any conventional bid embodying an understanding that is not classified as a Class A Convention. See ALERTING. Other explanations should not be volunteered until the end of the auction. See also EXPLANATION OF CONVENTIONAL CALL OR PLAY.

PRIVATE CONVENTION CHANGE. See Law 75.

PRIVATE SCORECARD. Players competing in duplicate events usually wish to keep a written record of their performance. Cards that enable participants to keep such a record usually are given out by the host organization. The inside of the ACBL convention card is a private

scorecard. There are spaces for the contract, the declarer and the score, as well as matchpoints or imps. The ACBL card also lists an imp scale and two scales for Victory Point scoring.

PRIZES. For most of its history, the American Contract Bridge League had a regulation barring cash prizes at tournaments above the club level. Small cash prizes were permitted at club games. However, various types of prizes usually were given to winners — sometimes trophies, sometimes ACBL scrip that could be used to purchase ACBL products and to purchase tournament entries, sometimes merchandise. Those are the types of prizes still given at most ACBL events, but cash prizes no longer are totally forbidden. The ACBL conducted a cash-prize tournament in Las Vegas in 1993, and the OMAR SHARIF INDIVIDUAL cash-prize tournament in Atlantic City in 1990 was sanctioned by ACBL. The Greater New York BA now runs an annual Green Point event with high entry fees — the prizes are cash.

Many established tournament have permanent floating trophies for various events upon which each year's winners' names are engraved. Often these are held by the winner until a new winner is determined the following year. ACBL Headquarters in Memphis TN has display cases where trophies for North American Championships and various charity events are on display.

Many tournaments around the world offer cash prizes — this is especially true in Europe. Many of the European cash-prize tournaments draw competitors from all over the world.

PRO SYSTEM. A system formerly employed by some West Coast pairs. Many relay sequences allowed the stronger hand to control the auction and inquire about his partner's strength and pattern.

The principal features of PRO (Pattern Relay Organized): intermediate (14-16 HCP) notrump opening; forcing 1♣ opening promising either a club suit or a balanced hand with 17-20 points; nonforcing two over one responses and jump shifts; four-card major suit openings, with a 1NT response virtually game forcing; reverses based on distribution rather than on high-card strength. The principal slam gadget was the CLARAC SLAM TRY.

PROBABILITIES. See HIGH CARD POINT PROBABILITIES.

PROBABILITIES A POSTERIORI. See PERCENTAGE PLAY; PROBABILITY OF SUCCESSIVE EVENTS.
(1)

A Q 10 7 3 2

9 8 5

When dummy's queen is finessed and loses to East's king, there are two events. The first is that East has the K-J, or alternatively, that he has the singleton king. The second is that in both cases, he would play the king. The second is regarded as certain; resultant probabilities are 6.8% and 6.2%. Assumed is that West has the same choice in both cases, to play either the six or the four. On a second lead, with West following with the other of the small cards, percentage play (slightly) favors the play of the ace.
(2)

A J 10 7 3 2

9 8 5

The finesse of the 9 loses to East's king. The a priori probabilities of relevant distributions are:

6 4 opposite K Q	6.8%
Q 6 4 opposite K	6.2%

In the first case there is no certainty that East will win with the king: he can equally well play the queen. If he is a good player the chances are about equal that he will play either honor, as any other method will be likely to help declarer. While the probability of the first event (that East holds the K-Q) is 6.8%, the probability that he will play the king is 50%. Applying the rule for successive events, the probability that East will hold the K-Q, and play the king is 6.8% x 50% or 3.4%. The odds in favor of taking a second finesse are therefore 30 to 17. See RESTRICTED CHOICE.

(3)

A K Q J 4 3 2

void

Assume that on the ace and king, East plays the 7 and 8, and West the 5 and 6. The only possible distributions are:

WEST	EAST	A Priori Probability
5 6 9	7 8 10	1.78%
5 6 10	7 8 9	1.78%
5 6 9 10	7 8	1.61%
5 6	7 8 9 10	1.61%

All the outstanding cards are insignificant (see CARDS, NEUTRAL AND POSITIVE) in that they cannot take a trick. It can be assumed that defenders play insignificant cards at random, avoiding giving declarer information unnecessarily. There are three ways in which each defender can select two cards from both the first two cases. Thus the play of the four cards in question from these cases is 3.56% x 1/9 = .39%. There are only six ways in which the particular played cards could occur from the last two cases in the table, so the probability of the selected play is 3.56% x 1/6 = .54%. The a priori probability of a 4-2 against a 3-3 division is exactly the same as the ratio between these a posteriori probabilities, .54 to .39.

(4) But it is not always apparent to a player that his cards are insignificant.

4 3 2

J 10 9   Q 8 7

A K 6 5

West will appreciate that his cards are of equal value, but East will not know that his are. When West plays the 9 on South's ace, East is unlikely to play the queen. The probabilities of the possible distributions can be calculated only on an assessment of how defenders are likely to play from each. Before South attacks the suit (at an early stage, and after a neutral lead) the odds are about 49 to 36 on a 4-2 division as against a 3-3. Declarer's interpretation of the play of the first two rounds may cause him to change his original play. See MATHEMATICAL ASSUMPTIONS.

PROBABILITIES A PRIORI. Basic probabilities of a given distribution of cards is expressed as a fraction where the numerator is the total number of favorable cases, and the denominator the total number of (equally likely) pos-

sible cases. MATHEMATICS OF BRIDGE explains how these can be computed. Thus before the cards are seen (a priori), the probability a particular player will hold a 4-3-3-3 hand pattern is $\frac{66,905,856,160}{635,013,559,600}$.

See HAND PATTERNS and NUMBER OF POSSIBLE HANDS.

In bridge, probability is most commonly shown as a percentage (100 times the above fraction). Play based on a priori probabilities is therefore known as PERCENTAGE PLAY.

Probability of any distribution varies at different stages of the game. Before one has seen any cards, there is a probability (see TABLES, MATHEMATICAL, Table 1) of 10.58% that one will hold a 5-4-2-2 hand pattern. There is the same probability that a particular suit will be distributed 5-4-2-2 to the four players. After a player looks at his hand and sees a suit of five cards, the probability that this suit is distributed 5-4-2-2 among the four players is 21.21% (Table 3). Thus 5-4-2-2 is now less than twice as likely as 5-5-2-1 whereas it was more than three times as probable before any cards were seen. (A priori has become a posteriori). The difference is because it is now known that one player does have five of the suit, and concern is only with the distribution of the remaining eight cards.

Subsequently, if partner's hand is seen to contain a doubleton of the five-card suit, the probability of a 5-4-2-2 distribution of the suit rises to 48.45% (Table 4), and 5-4-2-2 is now more probable than 5-3-3-2 although the latter was more probable in the earlier stages. Concern is now with the distribution of the remaining cards of the suit in only the other two hands.

It is apparent that a priori probabilities take no account of INFERENCES in bidding or play. Use should be made of the former only where more accurate probabilities cannot be drawn from such inferences.

When the opening lead has been made, strict a priori probabilities no longer apply; but if the lead gives no material information, they are altered only very slightly or not at all. See CARDS, NEUTRAL AND POSITIVE.

PROBABILITIES OF DISTRIBUTION. See MATHEMATICAL TABLES, Tables 1, 3, 4, and 4A.

PROBABILITY OF SUCCESSIVE EVENTS. The probability that two events will occur is the product of the probability of each, the latter event's probability being calculated on the assumption that the former has taken place. See DECEPTION and PROBABILITIES A POSTERIORI and, for an unscientific, but practical application, the last example under PERCENTAGE PLAY.

PROBABLE TRICK. A playing trick that can be reasonably counted upon when attempting to forecast the play during the bidding. K-x of a suit bid voluntarily on the right is an example.

PROBLEMS. Usually of three types, SINGLE DUMMY PROBLEMS, DOUBLE DUMMY PROBLEMS, and INFERENTIAL PROBLEMS, which are listed in separate articles.

PROFESSIONAL PLAYERS (or PROs). Bridge professionalism takes several forms. The most common form consists of experts who are retained to play tournaments in partnership or on teams with lesser players. In addition, many experts teach bridge to pupils of all levels, and some give lessons by playing with the pupil in a tournament. Although bridge may be the full-time profession of writers, editors, and lecturers, they are not considered professional players.

Professionalism in the form of a pro playing with a client is a most controversial subject within the ACBL. Large numbers of members believe professionalism is an evil. They believe it is wrong for some players to hire professional players so that they will have a better chance to win gold points and become Life Masters or so that they can gain prestige by winning events and placing high in the TOP 500 race. These members believe that professionalism should not be allowed, that a player should have to earn his way to the top rather than paying a professional to help him along. On the other side of the coin are those that see positive advantages to professionalism. Playing with a professional partner and learning how an expert thinks can help an average player become a good one, their argument goes. They also believe that most persons who engage a professional do so in an attempt to learn more about the game, not to amass master points.

The ACBL Board of Directors has been addressing the problem of professional players for many years. Several committees have made various suggestions concerning regulating professionalism. The first major attempt to come to grips with professionalism came in 1975 when the Board set up regulations for Registered Players. Under these regulations, any player who accepted money or other remuneration, directly or indirectly, in excess of his actual expenses, as consideration for playing in an ACBL-sanctioned event, had to become a Registered Player. This policy was in effect for a time, but it did not work out to the satisfaction of its sponsors, and it finally was repealed. The professionalism committee then attempted to find some other avenue.

It was proposed in 1981 that the ACBL sanction certain professional organizations provided they met a set of strict requirements set down by the ACBL. These organizations are expected to maintain a high degree of responsibility and ethics among their members. At the same time, the Board passed a regulation that any player who accepted payment for playing professionally at a regional or North American Championship must be affiliated with one of these professional organizations. Several such organizations were formed, but were inactive a decade later.

Bridge has had its share of wealthy patrons who have sponsored expert bridge teams. In 1968, Dallas financier Ira Corn organized the ACES, the world's first full-time professional bridge team. This was an eminently successful venture, inasmuch as the Aces won the Bermuda Bowl World Championship in 1970 and 1971. One illustration of a successful sponsor is Malcolm Brachman, who led his team to victory in the International Team Trials of 1979 and thereby qualified to play in the Bermuda Bowl in Rio de Janeiro that year. Brachman and his team won the World Championhship that year, and Brachman played his share of the matches and thereby qualified for full world champion rating. Seymon Deutsch matched this feat by qualifying for, and then winning, the 1988 World Team Olympiad title. Bud Reinhold also led his team to victory in the Team Trials of 1981, and his team went on to win the Bermuda Bowl. However, Reinhold did not play the required number of boards in the final, so did not qualify as a world champion. In the Seventies, shipping magnate C. C. Wei sponsored several teams to popularize his Precision System. (See PRECISION TEAM).

In addition, some commercial concerns have sponsored teams in order to promote their products. The Lancia division of Fiat in Italy sponsored a team that made professional appearances in various cities in North America. Rothman's Cigarettes was the sponsor of the 1982 Canadian Team Championships. Philip Morris sponsors a series of tournaments leading to a grand champion in Europe each year.

Some professional players make their living, in whole or in part, by playing bridge for high stakes. This is usually in the form of rubber bridge at clubs, but occasionally it takes place in Calcuttas or tournaments at which substantial money prizes are at stake. Until the coming of accredited professional organizations, money-prize tournaments were extremely rare in North America. However, money tournaments are the rule rather than the exception in Europe.

PROFESSIONAL TOURNAMENT DIRECTORS ASSOCIATION (PTDA). A professional organization of persons who work for the ACBL as tournament directors at the hundreds of tournaments (as distinguished from club and local-rated events) conducted every year in North America. The principal objective of the PTDA is the development and maintenance of the highest possible standards for the conduct and operation of tournament bridge events.

The PTDA, officially organized in August 1968 at the Summer NABC in Minneapolis, and has a membership of approximately 100. The PTDA is governed by an executive committee consisting of seven regional vice presidents (one of whom is elected president), an executive secretary and a treasurer.

The PTDA conducts general membership meetings three times each year. The PTDA sends, at its own expense, a representative to each of the three yearly meetings of the ACBL Board of Directors for the purpose of representing the interests and opinions of the PTDA, providing technical advice in the area of Tournament Regulations and Direction and continuing an active liaison with the ACBL Board and Management.

Major activities of the PTDA have included a joint venture with ACBL Management to standardize the interpretation and application of the 1987 Code of the Laws of Duplicate Contract Bridge.

The *Tom Weeks Memorial Award* is presented annually to the PTDA member who demonstrates the greatest improvement in all facets of professional tournament direction. Weeks was an Associate National Director and first treasurer of the PTDA.

Past recipients of the award are: Sol Weinstein, 1972; Roger Putnam, 1973; Brian Moran, 1974; Fran Miller, 1975; Jerry Shakofsky, 1976; Roberta Shipley, 1977; Gary Blaiss, 1978; Thomas Quinlan, 1979; Robert Kitchel, 1980; Eleanor Kipperman, 1981; Jeff Alexander, 1982; Peter Mollemet, 1983; Chris Patrias, 1984; no award presented, 1985; Steve Bates, 1986; Butch Campbell, 1987; Doug Grove, 1988; Patty Johnson, 1989; Millard Nachtwey, 1990; Guillermo Poplawsky, 1991; Betty Bratcher, 1992, and Rick Beye, 1993.

In 1986, the *Fred Friendly Award* was created to honor the director who best exemplified the spirit of the late Paul Stehly, an Associate National Director who was legendary for his warmth and good cheer. Stehly's nickname was Fred Friendly.

Past recipients of the award are: Gus Ducheyne, 1986; Doug Grove, 1987; Margo Putnam, 1988; Betty Bratcher, 1989; Guillermo Poplawsky, 1990; Karl Hicks, 1991; Jack Mehrens, 1992, and Jackie Matthews, 1993.

The PTDA has honored two longtime tournament directors by awarding them lifetime membership in the PTDA. They are Phil Wood and Harry Goldwater.

Past presidents of the PTDA include Harry Goldwater, Henry Francis, Dale Egholm, William Weyant, Roger Putnam, William Schoder, Nelson Rowe, Roberta Shipley, Chris Patrias and Peter Mollemet.

PROGRESSION. (1) The movement of players in duplicate; (2) the movement of the boards in duplicate; (3) the movement of players in PROGRESSIVE BRIDGE.

PROGRESSIVE BRIDGE. A form of competition at Contract Bridge played in the home or among social groups. See PARTY CONTRACT BRIDGE.

PROGRESSIVE SQUEEZE (or Repeated Squeeze or Repeating Triple Squeeze). A sequence of two squeezes which results in a gain of two tricks. In rare instances three tricks may be gained (see #9 below). It is initiated by a triple squeeze which is followed by a simple squeeze, both against the same player. As in an ordinary triple squeeze, all but two of the remaining tricks must be in hand before pressure can be exerted. There are several types, of which (1) and (2) are most common.

(1) The requirements for a Type 1 progressive squeeze are:

(a) A one-card threat placed to the left of the opponent threatened.

(b) Two two-card menaces, one in each hand, for example:

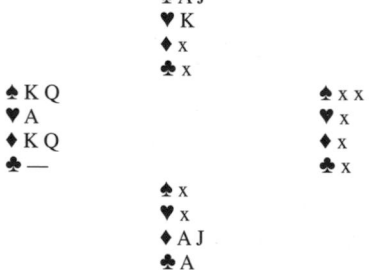

South leads the ♣A, and West is squeezed in three suits. If West discards a spade, South cashes two tricks in that suit which leads to an automatic squeeze against West in hearts and diamonds for the gain of a further trick. If West discards a diamond, South takes two diamonds, which results in a positional squeeze in the majors. Finally, if West discards a heart, South crosses to the ♠A in order to play the ♥K, which results in an automatic squeeze against West in spades and diamonds.

(2) The requirements for a Type 2 progressive squeeze are:

(a) A one-card threat placed to the right of the opponent threatened.

(b) The hand with the one-card threat has an entry in each of the other threat suits.

(c) The hand opposite the one-card threat contains the squeeze card, the remaining threat cards and entries in two of the three threat suits.

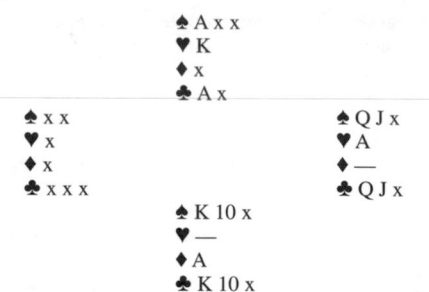

South leads the ♦A, and East is squeezed in three suits. Any discard costs a trick, and leads to a simple squeeze for the loss of another trick by East.

(3) A third form of progressive squeeze may arise, with these requirements:

(a) An extended two-card menace (also called a double threat).

(b) Two one-card menaces opposite the extended threat.

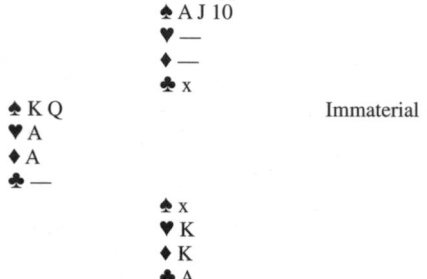

South leads the ♣A, and West is squeezed in three suits. If West discards a spade, it is at the cost of two tricks; if West discards a heart or a diamond, South continues with the king of that suit, effecting an automatic squeeze against West.

This squeeze is equally effective if the East and West cards are interchanged, so it is an automatic squeeze.

(4) (Described by Chien-Hwa Wang)

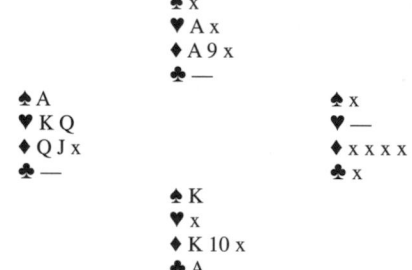

South leads the ♣A, and West is squeezed in three suits. If West discards a spade, then South leads the king of that suit, squeezing West in hearts and diamonds: a heart discard permits North to win his hearts, thereby squeezing West in spades and diamonds; if West discards a diamond, South cashes three diamonds, ending in his hand. The last of these squeezes West in the majors.

This is an automatic squeeze, since North's spade is an idle card. The requirements for this squeeze are as follows:

(a) A one-card menace placed to the right of the opponent threatened.

(b) A two-card menace in the hand opposite the one-card threat.

(c) A twin entry menace, with a menace card accompanying each winner.

The squeeze card lies in the same hand as the one-card menace.

(5)

```
              ♠ K 2
              ♥ K
              ♦ K
              ♣ x
  ♠ 7 x x                  ♠ Q J x
  ♥ x                      ♥ A
  ♦ x                      ♦ A
  ♣ —                      ♣ —
              ♠ A 8 x x
              ♥ —
              ♦ —
              ♣ A
```

The lead of the ♣A squeezes East in three suits, and South eventually wins all the remaining tricks. (Variation of #2)

(6)

```
              ♠ A J
              ♥ x
              ♦ K
              ♣ x
  ♠ x x                    ♠ K Q
  ♥ x x                    ♥ K Q
  ♦ x                      ♦ A
  ♣ —                      ♣ —
              ♠ x
              ♥ A J x
              ♦ —
              ♣ A
```

South leads the ♣A, and East is squeezed in three suits. The squeeze gains two tricks for South. (Variation of #2)

(7)

```
              ♠ J x x
              ♥ A
              ♦ A J
              ♣
  ♠ K Q                    ♠ x x
  ♥ K Q                    ♥ x x
  ♦ K Q                    ♦ x x
  ♣ —                      ♣ —
              ♠ A
              ♥ J x
              ♦ x x
              ♣ A
```

South leads the ♣A, and West is squeezed in three suits. A spade discard gives North two spade tricks; a heart discard enables South to take the ♥A, ♠A, and ♥J squeezing West in spades and diamonds; and a diamond discard leads to a crisscross squeeze.

(8) (Described by Clyde E. Love)

```
              ♠ 2
              ♥ 9 7 3
              ♦ A K 8 3 2
              ♣ A 10 9 5
  ♠ 9 8 4                  ♠ 7 6 5 3
  ♥ Q J 6                  ♥ 10 4
  ♦ Q J 10 4               ♦ 9 7
  ♣ K J 4                  ♣ 8 7 6 3 2
              ♠ A K Q J 10
              ♥ A K 8 5 2
              ♦ 6 5
              ♣ Q
```

South plays in 7♠ doubled by West. West makes his normal lead of the ♦Q. South starts life with only 10 top

tricks, but after he has won the diamond lead and cashed three spades this is the position:

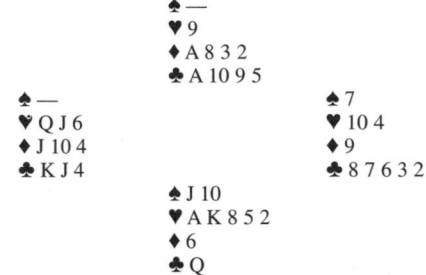

```
              ♠ —
              ♥ 9
              ♦ A 8 3 2
              ♣ A 10 9 5
  ♠ —                      ♠ 7
  ♥ Q J 6                  ♥ 10 4
  ♦ J 10 4                 ♦ 9
  ♣ K J 4                  ♣ 8 7 6 3 2
              ♠ J 10
              ♥ A K 8 5 2
              ♦ 6
              ♣ Q
```

When the fourth spade is led West cannot throw a heart or he will set up three tricks immediately. If West discards a diamond, a low club is discarded from dummy. Declarer then leads a diamond to the ace and ruffs a diamond to establish two tricks. The cashing of these two new winners squeezes West in clubs and hearts to promote a third trick. The result would be the same if West had discarded a club rather than a diamond. See also CLASH SQUEEZE; GUARD SQUEEZE; TRIPLE SQUEEZE.·

PROMOTION. See TRUMP PROMOTION.

PROMOTION OF TRUMP HONORS (in bidding). A higher value is given to an honor in a suit bid by partner than to a similar honor in a side suit. See GOOD CARDS.

PROPRIETIES. There are three different kinds of improper conduct: breaches of ethics, breaches of good manners, and cheating. Premeditated cheating is unforgivable; it is not dealt with by the Laws at all, for such a highly civilized game as bridge depends upon the assumption that players will not cheat.

Breaches of ETHICS or ETIQUETTE, however, are dealt with by the Laws. The proper code of behavior is set out in Laws 72-76. In the tournament world breaches of the Proprieties are punishable by the award of an adjusted score and by disciplinary penalties. In rubber bridge there is no way of adjusting the score except by agreement of the players or as provided in Law 16 (see LAWS).

PROTECT. (1) To guard with a small card, as an honor; (2) to make a bid in order that partner may have another opportunity to bid, thus "protecting" him if he has greater strength than his first call has implied (this usage is obsolescent); (3) in England, to balance; see BALANCING.

PROTECTED SUIT. See GUARD.

PROTECTION. An English term for BALANCING.

PROTEST PERIOD. The time specified by the sponsoring organization during which a director's ruling may be appealed. The term is also used, though not quite accurately, to designate the period in which scoring corrections may be accepted. See CORRECTION PERIOD and SCORING CORRECTIONS.

PROTESTS. See APPEAL; COMMITTEE.

PROVEN FINESSE. A finesse whose success is guaranteed. For example:

NORTH
♠ A Q J 7

SOUTH
♠ 10 9 5 3

The ♠10 is led and wins, while right-hand opponent discards. Subsequent finesses in the suit are proven or established. Also called a MARKED FINESSE, a slightly less absolute circumstance.

PSEUDO ELIMINATION PLAY. See THROW-IN PLAYS.

PSEUDO SQUEEZE. A play intended to induce a wrong discard by a defender who mistakenly believes he has been squeezed.

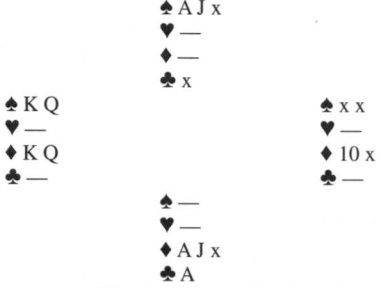

Suppose that West is not aware that South has no spades. South leads the ♣A, and West may discard a diamond hoping that East can protect that suit.

PSYCHIC BID. A bid that bears little or no resemblance to a logical choice for the hand in either a natural sense of as a conventional or systemic partnership agreement. Such bids are made primarily to make it more difficult for the opponents to find their optimum spot. The ACBL had defined such a bid as one which grossly misstates either the high-card count or the suit distribution. See PSYCHIC BIDDING. See also LAWS OF DUPLICATE BRIDGE (Law 40).

PSYCHIC BIDDING. A term coined in 1931 by Dorothy Rice Sims, generally meaning bluffing calls to create the illusion of strength or length in a particular suit or to conceal a weakness. From about 1931-34 a wave of blind enthusiasm for psychic bidding swept the country's bridge tables, making it appear that a malignancy was threatening to deform the game that was still in its infancy. Most of these early psychics were hit-or-miss affairs, the bidder never knowing until it was all over whether his ploy had been brilliant or catastrophic.

During this period Ely Culbertson, a keen strategist and psychologist who was not above making an occasional psychic himself, was categorically opposed to psychic bidding for the masses. His reasoning was simply that the techniques of the CULBERTSON SYSTEM were designed to create partnership harmony and confidence; any psychic bidding, unquestionably a unilateral and individualistic action, tended to destroy the precision his system was trying to create.

Fortunately the early passion for psychics quickly subsided. Some two decades later, around 1952, psychic openings re-emerged in a more disciplined form as parts of the ROTH-STONE, STAYMAN, KAPLAN-SHEINWOLD, and BULLDOG systems. In the opinions

of many experts, however, although the psychic opening had a tendency to force the opponents out of their familiar bidding patterns and into strange and uncomfortable situations, it was never terribly effective against sophisticated opponents, who would act positively when they had good cards in spite of the psychic. By 1964, the Roth-Stone system had eliminated the opening psychic because the complications it created outweighed the benefits it produced.

By and large the most effective psychic bids have been those that misdescribe the bidder's length in a particular suit. Sometimes these psychics promise extreme shortness in the suit; sometimes they promise considerable length in the suit. And when they find gaps in the opponents' defensive bidding conventions, the results can be extremely profitable. The least successful type of psychic bid tends to be one which attempts a bluff as to wholesale strength. The American Contract Bridge League has taken steps to reduce the usage of psychic bids. Don Oakie was commissioned by the ACBL Board of Directors to state the League's position in an article in the ACBL *Bulletin*. His article appeared in the February 1978 issue. Here are his conclusions:

"It is high time that we call all of our members' and directors' attention, especially at the club level, to the fact that while a psychic bid is legal, its indiscriminate use is not. People who employ psychic calls against less experienced players may be guilty of unsportsmanlike psyching and thereby be in violation of League regulations. People who psych against their peers may be guilty of frivolous psyching, or of having an unannounced partnership understanding. People who psych against more experienced players will probably get bad boards, and they may lose the few good boards they get by being judged to have indulged in unsportsmanlike psyching, or to have disrupted the game.

"What does this mean to you as a player? If you want to psych any call other than a forcing opening call, go ahead and do it — it's perfectly legal. If you psych on an average of once a month, no player or director is likely to say a word about it. If you can't resist the temptation to do it oftener, sooner or later you're going to run afoul of the Laws or League regulations."

Oakie made these observations about psychic bids in general:

"The excitement of using a psychic bid often exerts an almost irresistible attraction for a new duplicate player. An occasional jaded duplicateer will fall back on psychic bids as a means of having "fun" during a session marked by bad results in the early rounds or where few rating points are at stake. Expert players and the large majority of experienced club and tournament players seldom or never make a psychic bid.

"Psychic bids wear a high price tag. When employed against one's peers their chances of success are at best fifty-fifty. When they fail they can prove to be very costly and when they succeed, in a very short time the cost in loss of partnership confidence can far exceed any momentary advantage gained.

"By its nature, a psychic bid, successful or not, is remembered by the opponents as well as the user's partner. A player who becomes addicted to psychs is soon a marked man. Psychers live in a storm's eye of gloating or infuriated opponents, harried tournament directors and skeptical tournament committees . . . Win or lose, they tend to disrupt the events they enter and thus find the protection extended to them by the Laws is offset by their inability to prove they have not violated the Proprieties.

"An opening psychic bid that carried no conventional forcing meaning or implication is a legal bid. The Laws of Duplicate Contract Bridge state (see LAW 40). A player may make any call or play (including an intentionally misleading call — such as a psychic bid — or a call or play that departs from commonly accepted, or previously announced, conventional practice) without prior announcement, provided that such call or play is not based upon a partnership understanding."

The same Law continues. 'A player may not make a call or play based on a partnership understanding unless an opposing pair may reasonably be expected to understand its meaning or unless his side discloses the use of such call or play in accordance with the regulations of the sponsoring organization.'

"As this Law states, a psychic bid or other call is legal. At the same time nothing in this Law is to be construed as meaning that psychic bids may be used indiscriminately. The Law specifies that a call may not be made, if based on a partnership understanding, unless the opposing pair may reasonably be expected to understand its meaning, or unless the opponents have been Alerted.

"The ACBL recognizes that a psychic bid or call is legal. The right to regulate partnership understandings which arise from the usage of calls is specifically authorized by the Laws. Law 40 grants the sponsoring organization the right to regulate explicit partnership understandings (systemic or conventional calls). Law 75A clarifies that this right to regulate equally applies to implicit partnership understandings (understandings arrived at by usage and experience rather than discussion).

"League regulations do not in any way alter, infringe or nullify any right guaranteed by the Laws. The Laws are in accord with international agreements and cannot be changed unilaterally by the ACBL."

Oakie also stated that the regulations that any partnership understanding not readily available to the opponents must be alerted neither modifies, contravenes nor supersedes the opposing players' right to inquire as to the partnership understanding of an adverse call. The Alert procedure simply supplements the right to inquire. It provides a mechanism whereby a partnership that has failed to forewarn its opponents about either an explicit or implicit partnership understanding may do so while the auction is actually in progress.

Oakie continued: "Since players rarely think to disclose implicit partnership understandings prior to the situation actually arising during the auction - and for all possible situations it would be impractical to do so - the protection of the Alert procedure is invaluable where implicit understandings are involved. Where psychic bids are concerned, however, the nature of the bid or call is such that the need to disclose implicit understandings has the effect of practically preventing their use.

"Psychic bids are not soon forgotten by the user's partner. Since such a bid does grossly misstate either the strength or pattern of the hand, or both, the results obtained tend to be memorable where the partner is concerned. In this respect the psychic bid has the same effect as does an extraordinarily good guess by partner, either as declarer or defender, a particularly spectacular line of play or defense, or a sensationally successful or unsuccessful unilateral save by partner.

"But where the guesses, lines of play and saves are re-

membered as special cases, the psychic calls tend to become identified with the bidding situation in which they were used. When partner has psyched once, for many sessions to come every time a similar situation arises, his partner will remember and wonder.

"The partner who remembers and wonders is apt to test the water before he takes the plunge of an irreversible action predicated upon his partner's call. A player who thus displays caution may not be deemed to be simply prudent. His caution stems from prior knowledge and experience with this partner and thus constitutes prima facie evidence that an implicit partnership understanding exists.

"This caution is never quite as pronounced as it is in the deals that immediately follow the one where partner psyched. Accordingly, while a player's first psychic bid with a new partner is judged to be legal as far as the League regulations are concerned, a second psychic call by the same player during the same event, even in a radically different bidding situation, is judged to establish a pattern of psychic bidding that may well create an implicit partnership understanding.

"Since implicit partnership understandings are available to both members of a partnership, any further psychic bidding by either member, in the same event, might be presumed to be a violation of the Proprieties. The director would penalize the partnership accordingly unless the user could prove incontrovertibly that no partnership understanding existed."

Not everyone accepted Oakie's reasoning. A series of editorials in *The Bridge World* argued against the implicit message of Oakie's article: "It's all right to psych as long as you never do it." *The Bridge World* suggested that the proper course was not suppression of psychic bidding, but diligent enforcement of current ACBL regulations on psychics.

Oakie's definition of a psychic — a bid that deliberately and grossly misstates the bidder's high-card values or suit length — helps to distinguish true psychics from tactical bids.

North opens 1♠, and South tries to discourage a club lead by responding 2♣ on:

    ♠ J 8 3
    ♥ A J 9
    ♦ A Q J 2
    ♣ 9 6 2

South's 2♣ is a tactical bid. (However, if North never supports clubs with:

    ♠ A 10 7 4 2
    ♥ K Q 10
    ♦ 8
    ♣ A K J 5

evidence of an impropriety exists.)

Similarly, a first-hand 1♠ opening on:

    ♠ 8 4 2
    ♥ 10 7 6 3
    ♦ J 8 6 4 2
    ♣ 4

is psychic, but a third-hand 1♠ opening on:

    ♠ A K J 8
    ♥ 8 5
    ♦ 6 5
    ♣ 9 7 5 3 2

is without psychic intent.

In 1991, the ACBL's Board of Directors implemented a new measure to regulate psychics. At the Summer

NABC, pairs competing in regional-rated and higher events were required to report their own psychics in writing. The requirement was subsequently abandoned. See FIELDING A PSYCHIC. Following are some examples of various types of psychic bids:

A psychic that has long been almost so standard a part of the repertoire that it is thought hardly worth using any more is the 1♠ butt-in over an opponent's takeout double of partner's 1♥ opening. Yet it was used to good effect in the final of the 1966 Bermuda Bowl between Italy and North America.

Dlr: North
Vul: None

	♠ J 10	
	♥ A Q 5 4	
	♦ A 8 2	
	♣ 9 8 4 2	
♠ K Q 8 6 5		♠ A 4 2
♥ J 10		♥ K 9 8
♦ 10 6 4 3		♦ Q 9
♣ A Q		♣ K J 10 7 5
	♠ 9 7 3	
	♥ 7 6 3 2	
	♦ K J 7 5	
	♣ 6 3	

WEST	NORTH	EAST	SOUTH
Avarelli	Mathe	Belladonna	Hamman
	1 ♥	Dbl	1 ♠
1NT	Pass	2 ♣	Pass
2 ♦	Pass	2NT	All Pass

Hamman's psychic spade response found a flaw in the ROMAN SYSTEM. A double by Avarelli would have shown spade shortness rather than length. Still, the Italians could have recovered by bidding game in notrump. It was just as well that they did not, however, since after Mathe's opening ♠J was won by dummy's ace, Avarelli led a spade and covered Hamman's 7 with the 8, playing Hamman for a real suit, and lost a trick to Mathe's 10. Mathe wasted no time in shifting to a diamond to collect five tricks in all. In the replay West made 11 tricks in 4♠.

One of the most spectacularly successful psychics was an opening preemptive psychic by Martin Cohn in the Vanderbilt Teams at the 1967 North American Championships in Seattle.

Dlr: North
Vul: E-W

	♠ 10 8 7 6 4 3	
	♥ A 10 6	
	♦ K Q 6	
	♣ 7	
♠ A		♠ K Q 2
♥ K J 9 8 7 5 2		♥ Q 3
♦ A J		♦ 10 8 7 5 4 3 2
♣ A K 4		♣ 2
	♠ J 9 5	
	♥ 4	
	♦ 9	
	♣ Q J 10 9 8 6 5 3	

WEST	NORTH	EAST	SOUTH
Leventritt	MacCracken	Schenken	Cohn
	Pass	Pass	3 ♥
	All Pass		

Holding a weak hand and a shortage of hearts, Cohn opened the bidding with 3♥ and caught LHO Leventritt with a powerful hand including seven hearts. Leventritt could not double for penalties, so he passed, and 3♥ undoubled became the final contract.

Cohn suffered a six-trick penalty (he could have held it to five), but that still was a huge gain since this was the auction at the other table:

WEST	NORTH	EAST	SOUTH
	Pass	Pass	5 ♣
5 ♥	Dbl	All Pass	

North did not lead the ♥A and another, so West made an overtrick for 1050 and a 13-IMP gain.

PSYCHIC CONTROLS. Devices intended to avert a partnership disaster following a psychic bid.

Controls are usually related to the "disciplined psychic" used in KAPLAN-SHEINWOLD and the original ROTHSTONE. In such cases the opener has 3-6 points, mainly in the suit which he has bid.

Responses of 2NT and 3NT can be used to show powerful balanced hands. 2NT shows a hand with 21-22 points, and therefore interested in game even if the opener is psychic. 3NT shows a stronger hand that is sure of game even opposite a psychic.

The jump shift remains forcing, and the opener must take care with his rebid. If he has made a psychic opening, he must rebid his suit or rebid in notrump, whichever is the more economical. Conversely, he must avoid these rebids holding a genuine opening.

Psychic controls are disallowed in some countries, notably in England, on the theory that the psychic bidder must be prepared to take his chances along with the opponents.

Open to much greater ethical doubt are psychic controls of other actions, such as responses. These are not sanctioned by any leading authority.

PSYCHIC LEAD. See OPENING LEAD.

PSYCHIC PLAY. See DECEPTIVE PLAY.

PSYCHOLOGY. See DECEPTIVE PLAY; FALSECARDING; PARTNERSHIP PSYCHOLOGY.

PUDDING RAISE. A balanced raise based on high-card strength alone. (British).

PULLING TRUMP. See DRAWING TRUMPS.

PUMP. A colloquialism for FORCE. FORCING DECLARER TO RUFF is frequently referred to as pumping the declarer.

PUNCH. Verb: to cause a player (usually dummy or declarer) to use a trump for ruffing; to shorten; noun: the act of shortening in trumps. See FORCING LEADS.

PUNISH. Double for penalties.

PUPPET STAYMAN. A method of responding to 1NT devised by Kit Woolsey. Responder's 2♣ asks for a five-card major. With no five-card major, opener is forced to bid 2♦. Responder now bids the major he doesn't have, or notrump with both majors. Opener is now in a position to select the right denomination without revealing his distribution to the opponents. Puppet Stayman can also be used over 2NT openers with equal effectiveness.

PUSH. (1) A raise of partner's suit, usually at the partscore level, aimed at pushing the opponents to a level at which they may be defeated. For example:

WEST	NORTH	EAST	SOUTH
	1 ♠	2 ♥	2 ♠

Neither side is vulnerable and South holds:

♠ 6 5 3
♥ K 9
♦ A 8 4 2
♣ Q 7 3 2

It seems likely to West that both sides will make about eight tricks, so he bids 3♥. East is marked with, at worst, a good five-card suit. If North-South continue to 3♠, in which they will have more losers than they expect, they may be defeated, and West will have turned a minus score into a plus. The chance of being doubled in 3♥ is slight, and East should be wary of continuing to game.

(2) A board in a team match, in which the result is the same in both rooms (also STAND-OFF).

(3) A rubber in which the net score is zero after ROUNDING OFF.

PUZZLES. In bridge, puzzles are referred to as PROBLEMS, and are usually of three types, DOUBLE DUMMY PROBLEMS, SINGLE DUMMY PROBLEMS, and INFERENTIAL PROBLEMS. Examples of each type appear in this book. Crossword puzzles and acrostics using bridge definitions or texts have been published as bridge magazine features.

Q

QUACK. A term to indicate either the queen or the jack in situations where it is of no consequence which of the two cards is held or played. See RESTRICTED CHOICE.

QUALIFYING. Finishing high enough in a QUALIFYING SESSION to continue competing in the final session(s) of the event. See CONDITIONS OF CONTEST.

QUALIFYING SESSION. In an event of two or more sessions, one or more of them may be designated as qualifying sessions, to select contestants eligible for continued play in the remaining sessions.

QUALITY. See STRENGTH. Ely Culbertson stressed "quality" and "quantity" in discussing hand valuation. More modern usage concerns control cards, suit strength or the presence of intermediate cards, etc. See also WORKING CARDS.

QUANTITATIVE. A bid is quantitative if it is natural, limited, and non-forcing.

QUANTITATIVE FOUR NOTRUMP. A term covering a number of situations where 4NT is a natural bid. See BLACKWOOD .

QUANTITATIVE FIVE NOTRUMP. A raise of 1 NT or 2 NT, asking partner to bid 6NT with a minimum or 7NT with a maximum.

QUANTITY. See LENGTH.

QUEEN. The third highest card in a suit.

QUEEN OF BRIDGE. See KING OR QUEEN OF BRIDGE.

QUEEN FROM KING-QUEEN. See RUSINOW LEADS.

QUEEN LEAD. Traditionally, the lead of the queen from a long suit promises the jack and usually the 10 or 9 as well. See OPENING LEADS. In alternative methods the lead of the queen promises the king (see RUSINOW LEADS), or the ace and king. The JOURNALIST system of leads against notrump promises either the traditional holding headed by Q-J-10, or a holding of K-Q-10-9. The latter asks the partner of the opening leader to play the jack if he has it, enabling the opening leader to continue without fear of a BATH COUP by declarer.

QUEEN OVER JACK. The theory, or speculation, that the queen lies over the jack slightly more often than not is credited to Clagett Bowie. The assumption is based on the possibility that the queen may have captured the jack in the previous deal with the same deck, and that the cards may not have been separated in the shuffle. This assumption is valid only if declarer's holding in the suit is A-J opposite K-10. With K-J facing A-10, the chances are just as good that the king was used to capture the queen. However, the manner in which the trick is gathered is an important, and uncertain, influence. The theory has meaning only at rubber bridge, if it has any value at all. See TWO-WAY FINESSE.

QUESTIONS. For when to ask questions, see ALERTING; EXPLANATION OF ANY CALL OR PLAY, FACE DOWN LEADS.

QUICK TRICK. A high card holding that in usual circumstances will win a trick by virtue of the rank of the cards in either offensive or defensive play. Of course, in some distributional holdings, or FREAK HANDS, such defensive values evaporate. The accepted table of quick tricks is:

2 quick tricks	A-K of same suit
1 1/2	A-Q of same suit
1	A or K-Q of same suit
1/2	K-x

QUITTED TRICK. A trick is quitted, in rubber bridge, when the four cards played to it have been gathered together and turned face down in a packet in front of the side which contributed the winning card. Any player has the right to inspect a quitted trick until either he or his partner has led or played to a subsequent trick. In duplicate, a trick is quitted when all four players have played to it and turned their cards face down. A quitted trick may not be inspected except at the director's specific instruction. If a player wishes to inspect the cards just played to a trick, he may do so only if he has left his own card face up on the table, assuming neither he nor his partner has led or played to the next trick. See LAWS OF DUPLICATE (Law 66).

QUOTIENT. A device used to determine the winner in team competition if a ROUND-ROBIN ends in a tie either in won and lost matches, or in VICTORY POINTS won and lost. The total number of IMPs won by a team against all round-robin opponents is divided by the number lost to determine the quotient. Italy won two European Championships by quotient, over France in 1956 and over Great Britain in 1958.

R

RHO. Right-hand opponent. The opponent to the right of a player.

RABBI'S RULE. "When the king is singleton, play the ace. " A whimsical rule attributed to Milton Shattner, a New York attorney nicknamed "the Rabbi" because of his authoritative pronouncement of this and other convictions governing play.

RABBIT An inexperienced player (British).

RACK. (1) A device used by handicapped players for holding a hand of cards. (2) A device to hold traveling scoreslips for inspection by the players after the game has been scored (see CLOTHESLINE). (3) Colloq., (verb) to ruin opponents by holding exceptionally good cards; (noun) a player who holds such cards; also called a cardrack.

RAGS. A holding of only a few high cards, likely to be insignificant in the bidding or play of a hand. As "I had two rags in hearts."

RAINBOW INDIVIDUAL MOVEMENT. A movement for tournaments involving players competing as individuals, in which contestants are divided into groups corresponding to their original starting directions, with separate instructions for progressing to each group. The guide cards are often printed in different colors to make the groups more easily distinguished — hence the name Rainbow. This movement was devised by Oswald Jacoby and Shepard Barclay.

In a typical set of guide cards (ACBL 52-player Individual, a 13-table game), the North players receive blue cards and sit at the same table throughout. The East players receive yellow guide cards, moving two tables toward the higher number. South players receive white guide cards and move to the next higher-numbered table. West players receive pink guide cards and skip a table toward lower numbers, while the boards go to the next lower-numbered table. For identification purposes, players take a number: North, the table number; West, the table number plus 13; South, the table number plus 26; and East, the table number plus 39.

The movement in its regular form, as given above, will work when the number of tables is not divisible by two or three: 5, 7, 11, 13, 17, 19, 23, 25. For 8, 9, 12 and 16 tables see IRREGULAR RAINBOW. Tournament director Paul Marks devised a variation of this movement for prime number plus one tables (see EIGHT TABLES, TWELVE TABLES, FOURTEEN TABLES), which is based on the Rainbow. Tournament director Maury Braunstein devised special adaptations of the Rainbow for nine tables and 15 tables. He also devised a stanza movement for 14 tables.

A regular Rainbow can be carried out in any manner as long as it is remembered that there are five different movements for the four groups of players and the boards. As long as the groups and the boards have different progressions, and continue for succeeding rounds as they moved for the second, no difficulty is encountered. The number of rounds is equal to the number of tables, but can be cut short. If it is desired to increase the number of partnerships, the South and West players can interchange after the first boards in a two-board round, or the West player can travel around the table counter-clockwise for three boards to a round. In all cases the North player remains stationary. In no case do balanced comparisons result. Session awards are based on results as achieved in each direction.

RAISE. Noun: an increase of the contract in the denomination named by partner; verb: to make a bid increasing the contract in the denomination named by partner. See SINGLE RAISE; DOUBLE RAISE; TRIPLE RAISE. RAISE IN RESPONDER'S SUIT. See OPENER'S REBID.

RAISE IN RESPONDER'S SUIT. See OPENER'S REBID.

RAISER. The player who bids for a greater number of tricks in a suit first bid by his partner.

RANDOM FALSECARDS. See FALSE-CARDING.

RANK. (1) The priority of suits in bidding and cutting. Starting at the bottom, the suits rank in alphabetical order: clubs, diamonds, hearts and spades, with notrump at the top of the list.
(2) The trick-taking power of each card within a suit. The ace, king, queen, jack have priority in that order. The lower cards rank numerically.
(3) The status of a player in a masterpoint ranking system.

RANKING BRIDGE PLAYER. See LIFE MASTER, the highest basic category into which the ACBL ranks players (there are six Life Master ranks). The ranking of players by means of MASTER POINTS won cannot be construed as definitive as between any two players because of the difference in time during which points were earned, frequency of competition, ability to attend major regional and NORTH AMERICAN CHAMPIONSHIP TOURNAMENTS. Many other national organizations have set up similar systems to identify the more outstanding players.

RANKING. The position of a player, pair or team in the section or in the overall.

RANKINGS. Players in the American Contract Bridge League are ranked in 12 grades ranging from Rookie to Grand Life Master. Here are the requirements for each grade:

Rookie. 0-5 masterpoints.
Junior Master. 5-20 masterpoints.
Club Master. 20-50 masterpoints.
Sectional Master. At least 50 masterpoints, of which at least 5 must be silver.
Regional Master. At least 100 masterpoints of which 15 must be silver and 5 must be either red or gold.
NABC Master. At least 200 masterpoints, including at least 50 pigmented points of which at least 5 must be gold, at least 15 must be red and at least 25 must be silver.
Life Master. At least 300 masterpoints of which at least 50 must be silver, at least 25 must be gold, and at least another 25 must be either red or gold.
Bronze Life Master. Life Master status with 500-1000

masterpoints.

Silver Life Master. Life Master status with 1000-2500 masterpoints.

Gold Life Master. Life Master status with 2500-5000 masterpoints.

Diamond Life Master. Life Master status with at least 5000 masterpoints.

Grand Life Master. At least 10,000 masterpoints with at least one win in a North American championship event that has no maximum masterpoint restriction.

For the names of the top-ranking ACBL Life Masters, see LIFE MASTER.

Comparable masterpoint plans are in effect in many other bridge-playing countries, although rankings and requirements differ from country to country. See MASTERPOINT PLAN. In addition, the WORLD BRIDGE FEDERATION has adopted its own masterpoint plan for the ranking of players of international calibre. See WORLD BRIDGE FEDERATION RANKINGS.

RATING POINT CERTIFICATE. See CLUB MASTERPOINTS.

RATING POINTS. See CLUB MASTERPOINTS.

RAZZLE-DAZZLE. A bridge game derived from S.B.Fishburne's CUTTHROAT, which was devised in 1936 and has been played regularly since then at the Peninsular Club in Grand Rapids MI. It includes a nullo bid, which outranks notrump but has the same 40-30 etc. trick score. A bid of six nullos, for example, contracts to lose 12 tricks. The declarer at nullo can choose, before the opening lead, which hand will be exposed. Other rules:

(a) Opening bidder must have three quick tricks: AK = 2; AQ = 1°; A or KQ = 1; K x = °. Subsequent bids are unrestricted.

(b) When there are three consecutive passes, the last bidder becomes declarer. He then selects one player as his partner. That player may accept or reject, but in either case his cards become dummy. Either opponent may then double, and the declarer or an accepting dummy can redouble.

(c) A first game scores a 200 bonus, a second game 500. Other scoring is normal.

(d) Each player has an individual score.

(e) Partscores are not played and there is a redeal.

REBIDDABLE SUIT. A suit of six cards or more which can be bid twice. In some cases a five-card suit may be bid twice. See GOLDEN RULE, OPENER'S REBID and RESPONDER'S REBID.

REBIDS. See BELATED SUPPORT; CHANGE OF SUIT; CROWHURST; FORCING SEQUENCES; FOURTH SUIT ARTIFICIAL; GOLDEN RULE; JUMP PREFERENCE; JUMP REBIDS BY RESPONDER; NEW MINOR FORCING; ONE NOTRUMP REBID; OPENER'S REBID; PREEMPTIVE RERAISE; PREFERENCE; PUSH; RESPONDER'S REBID; REVERSE; SECOND NEGATIVE RESPONSE; SHORT-SUIT GAME TRIES; STRENGTH-SHOWING BIDS; THIRD-SUIT BID; THREE-CARD SUITS, BIDS IN; TRIAL BID; TWO-WAY GAME TRIES; WEAK-SUIT GAME TRY; WOLFF.

REBIDS IN ORIGINAL SUIT. See OPENER'S RE-

BID.

RECAPITULATION SHEET (RECAP). A large printed form on which the scores on pickup slips are posted at bridge tournaments, and on which matchpoints are assigned to scores, and totals computed. Recapitulation sheets are available in three forms, one for HOWELL MOVEMENT games or team-of-four play, one for MITCHELL MOVEMENT games and a third for SWISS TEAM events. All sheets have a heading where space is provided for names of players and their SEATING ASSIGNMENTS and PLAYER NUMBERS, their overall ranking, total score (for two or more session events or when FACTORING is involved), CARRYOVER SCORE for two or more session events and POINTS this session. These headings or copies thereof are the official records from which MASTERPOINTS are awarded by the NATIONAL AUTHORITY, and serve as permanent records. To the right of this heading are boxes in which the individual scores on boards 1-36 (subsequent sheets can be appended for more boards) are entered and MATCHPOINTS assigned. See also BURNER.

The recapitulation sheet in this form has been largely displaced in many nations by computer scoring.

RECIPROCAL SQUEEZE. A variant of the double squeeze. The squeeze card is not an established card in the fourth suit; rather each opponent is squeezed in turn by a winner in the suit guarded by his partner. These are the basic positions:

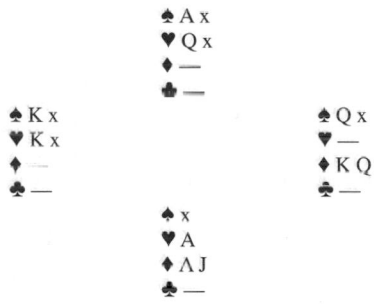

South leads the ♥A, which forces East to discard a spade. Now the lead of the ♦A squeezes West in the majors.

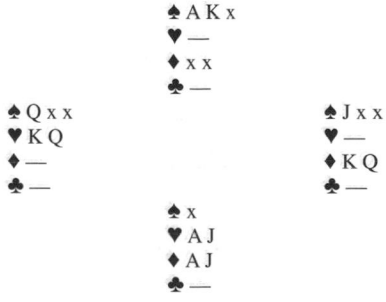

South leads the ♥A, which forces East to discard a spade. Now the lead of the ♦A squeezes West in the majors.

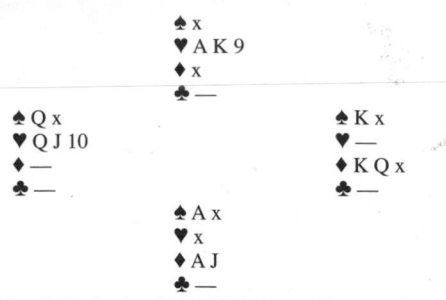

South leads the ♦A, which forces West to unguard spades. Now South leads hearts, and the second winner of that suit squeezes East in spades and diamonds.

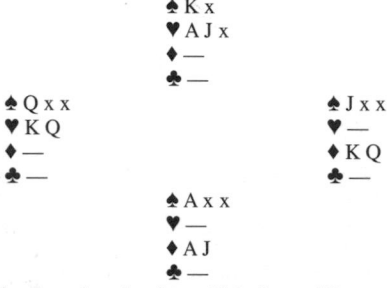

South cashes the ♦A, which forces West to unguard spades. A spade is led to the king followed by the ♥A, which squeezes East in spades and diamonds. A double squeeze may be played as a reciprocal squeeze by running off all declarer's winners in the fourth suit (which is not guarded by either opponent). This has a dual advantage: it allows more room for defensive error, and it enables declarer to obtain additional information regarding the outstanding cards.

RECORDING OF MASTERPOINTS. The results of each MASTERPOINT event are reported by the tournament director to the national organization, and points are recorded to the credit of the winners of club games and to those players placing in local, sectional, or higher rated tournaments.

The ACBL was first to develop a masterpoint plan, but similar plans are now in use by numerous other national bridge governing bodies.

RECORDING OF MATCHES. See BRIDGE-O-RAMA; HAND RECORD; VUGRAPH.

RECTIFICATION. An adjustment made to permit the auction or play to proceed as normally as possible after an irregularity has occurred. In the bidding stage, irregularities (other than violations of ethical procedure) are covered by specific penalties, as are most of the possible irregularities in the play. However, in the case of a failure to follow suit which is later corrected, it is possible that the offender inadvertently gains information that he is not entitled to under normal play; in this case, rectification is called for.

Occasionally the bidding will have started at a table when it is discovered that the traveling pair has come to the wrong table and should not be playing the board against that opponent. In this case the director may seat the proper pair at the table and have the bidding repeated. If no additional information is gained, the board is per-

mitted to stand; if the bidding progresses differently, then an adjusted score usually is given. See ALCATRAZ COUP and LAWS OF DUPLICATE BRIDGE (Laws 12 and 16).

RECTIFYING THE COUNT. The process of losing a trick or tricks in order to reach a certain number of remaining losers, thus enabling a desired ending to be reached. The most common use of the play is to reduce the number of losers to one, enabling a simple squeeze to be executed.

```
                    ♠ 3 2
                    ♥ A K 6
                    ♦ A Q 7 2
                    ♣ A K Q 5
    ♠ Q J 10 8                      ♠ K 9 7 6
    ♥ 3 2                           ♥ J 10 9 8
    ♦ 6 5                           ♦ J 10 9 8
    ♣ 9 8 7 4 3                     ♣ 2
                    ♠ A 5 4
                    ♥ Q 7 5 4
                    ♦ K 4 3
                    ♣ J 10 6
```

West leads the ♠Q against South's 6NT contract. South has 11 winners. The contract will succeed if either hearts or diamonds are favorably divided.

Another chance is a squeeze against an opponent holding guards in both red suits. This squeeze will operate only if South has but one loser remaining. If South wins the first trick, he can no longer make his contract. Instead, he should rectify the count by allowing West to hold the first spade. South wins any continuation and runs his black winners, squeezing East between the red suits. For another example, see LOSER-ON-LOSER.

RED. Colloquialism for vulnerable.

RED AND BLACK GERBER. See BLACK AND RED GERBER.

RED DOT. A small circle of red paper with a gummed back that duplicate players may paste on their CONVENTION CARD to indicate that they use nonstandard opening leads. The purpose is to alert the opponents that opening leads may not be what they seem.

REDEAL. A second or subsequent deal by the same dealer to replace his first deal. See LAWS OF CONTRACT BRIDGE, Part III Section 10. Hands are never redealt at duplicate except in special cases on the director's instructions.

REDOUBLE. A call, following an opposing double, that doubles all scores: penalties; trick scores, and overtrick premiums. When the contract succeeds, the bonus for making a doubled contract is also doubled, from 50 to 100.

Although the mathematics of the scoring table favor redoubles at high levels in rubber bridge and IMP play, redoubled contracts are rare when the standard of play is high. Ill-judged doubles of game or slam contracts may attract redoubles.

WEST	NORTH	EAST	SOUTH
	1♣	Pass	2♥
Pass	2NT	Pass	6♥
Pass	Pass	Dbl	?

♠ A J 2
♥ A K Q 8 6 4 2
♦ K 9 5
♣ —

East's double asks for an unusual lead, usually the lead of North's first-bid suit. East probably has the ♣AK or ♣AQ, since he is unlikely to be void when South is. If North's clubs are only fair, he must have strength in spades and diamonds. South should redouble.

In a high-level competitive auction, an expert may occasionally redouble as a bluff. He may expect his contract to fail by one trick, but he is prepared to sacrifice 100 or 200 points in the hope of inducing the opponents to continue in their own suit and go down.

A special situation arises when an artificial bid is doubled and redoubled. At a high level, when a CUEBID or response to BLACKWOOD is doubled, a redouble is generally regarded as control-showing. Whether the control shown is first- or second-round is usually a matter of partnership agreement, but the following situation is not ambiguous:

WEST	NORTH	EAST	SOUTH
	1 ♥	Pass	3 ♥
Pass	4 ♣	Pass	4 ♦
Dbl	Pass	Pass	?

♠ 8 3
♥ A J 9 2
♦ A K 5
♣ J 9 6 5

South can redouble to show first- and second-round diamond control.

At a low level, the situation is different:

WEST	NORTH	EAST	SOUTH
			1NT
Pass	2 ♣	Dbl	Redbl

South's redouble shows a desire to play at clubs; South may have a five-card club suit or a strong four-card suit.

Prior to 1987, making a redoubled contract was worth 50 extra points for the insult. This brought about some strange situations at high levels: Making 5♦ redoubled with an overtrick vulnerable was worth 1350, less than the value of 6♦ (1370); but making 5♦ redoubled with an overtrick not vulnerable (950) was worth more than making 6♦ (920). A scoring change in the 1987 edition of *The Laws of Duplicate Bridge* increased the bonus for making a redoubled contract to 100 points.

Tactical uses of the redouble

Redoubles are often used to show general strength:

WEST	NORTH	EAST	SOUTH
			1 ♣
Pass	Pass	Dbl	?

♠ A K 5
♥ A 8 3
♦ 9 3
♣ A K J 10 4

South should redouble to announce considerable extra strength, in this case at least 19 points.

WEST	NORTH	EAST	SOUTH
			1 ♣
Pass	1 ♥	Dbl	?

♠ A 8 3
♥ K 2
♦ Q 9 2
♣ A K Q 10 4

South should redouble. This call does not promise hearts; indeed, it tends to deny four-card support. It says that North-South have most of the high-card strength. If South held

♠ 6
♥ K J 9 3
♦ J 5 4
♣ A K Q 9 2

he would jump to 3♥ to preempt.

Another situation:

WEST	NORTH	EAST	SOUTH
	1 ♥	Pass	2 ♥
Pass	Pass	Dbl	?

♠ A Q 9 4
♥ 10 7 3
♦ Q 5
♣ J 9 8 4

South should redouble to show a maximum single raise and suggest playing for a penalty.

WEST	NORTH	EAST	SOUTH
			1 ♥
Pass	2 ♥	Dbl	?

♠ 10 5
♥ A K 7 4 2
♦ Q J 5
♣ A K 6

South should redouble, indicating that the deal belongs to North-South. If South later bids 3♥, he promises game interest.

There were some scoring anomalies involving high-level redoubled contracts. These have been removed by the increase of the bonus for making a redoubled contract from 50 to 100.

For other redoubling situations, see DOUBLES OF NOTRUMP BIDS, KOCK-WERNER REDOUBLE, RESPONSES OVER OPPONENT'S TAKEOUT DOUBLE, ROSENKRANZ REDOUBLE, SOS REDOUBLE, STRIPED-TAIL APE DOUBLE, SUPPORT REDOUBLE.

REDOUBLE OUT OF ROTATION. An improper bid when it is partner's or right-hand opponent's turn to call. If it is partner's turn to call, he must pass and continue to pass for the balance of the auction. If the partner of the offender has the opening lead, declarer may require or forbid him to lead a specified suit. Also the offender is not permitted to redouble the same bid which he redoubled out of turn.

If it is the turn of the right-hand opponent to bid, the redouble must be repeated if this opponent passes; if the opponent bids, the offender may make any legal call, but his partner must pass at his next opportunity. See LAWS (Law 32).

RED POINT. Masterpoints won in regional and NORTH AMERICAN CHAMPIONSHIP TOURNAMENTS are required for the advancement of players to NABC MASTER and LIFE MASTER status in the ACBL. To distinguish points won at these larger and more important events, the ACBL uses the term "red points". One hundred "colored," at least 50 silver and at least 50 red/gold of which at least 25 must be gold, are one of the requirements for promotion to Life Master status. See also GOLD POINT; RANKING OF PLAYERS; REGIONAL AND NATIONAL POINTS.

RED RIBBON PAIRS. An ACBL event with national rating held during the Fall North American Bridge Championships. Pairs earn qualification by placing first or second in regionally-rated events of at least Flight B status. Neither member of a qualifying pair may hold more than 1500 points at the time of qualification.

REDUCED HOWELL. When a HOWELL has too many rounds a Reduced Howell may be used. It has a reduced number of rounds, compared to the Howell movement for the same number of tables. The reduction comes from increasing the number of stationary pairs, hence decreasing the number of moving pairs, rounds, and board sets. The Reduced Howell may replace the play of a Howell with appendix table(s), but it also exists for an even number of rounds. With heavy reduction, when there are stationary pairs at most tables, it can be made very Mitchell-like.

The first movements of this kind were published in 1947 by Sam Gold for 8-12 tables and 13 rounds under the name Three-Quarter Howells. Another sequence, known as the Short Howells, was later constructed for 11 rounds.

With a computer it has been possible to construct Reduced Howells with much better balance than in the original movements and for other numbers of rounds. Note that since the Reduced Howells have several stationary pairs, it is necessary to arrow switch in certain rounds at these tables to get reasonable balance.

These are the starting positions, and the arrow switches, for 6 and 8-12 tables with good balance. In all movements the number of rounds is the same as the number of board sets and of moving pairs. The moving pairs follow the pair with the next lower number, #1 following the highest-numbered moving pair. Tables with stationary pairs switch as indicated.

Table	6 tables, 8 rounds NS EW b	6 tables, 9 rounds NS EW b	8 tables, 11 rounds NS EW b	8 tables, 12 rounds NS EW b	8 tables, 13 rounds NS EW b
1	9 1 1	10 1 1	12 1 1	13 1 1	14 1 1
2	10 6 2	8 12 2	13 6 2	14 8 2	16 6 2
3	11 4 3	5 11 3	14 8 3	11 6 3	9 5 3
4	12 2 4	7 3 4	16 10 4	15 9 4	2 15 4
5	8 7 5	6 9 5	7 4 5	16 4 5	13 12 5
6	5 3 6	2 4 6	2 3 6	3 7 6	11 3 6
7	9 NS in	10 NS in	15 5 7	2 5 7	10 8 7
8	all rds	all rds	11 9 8	10 12 8	7 4 8
	10 EW in rds 4-7	11 NS in rds 3,6,9	12-16 EW in rds 8,10,11	13 NS in all rds;	14 NS in all rds;
	11 EW in rds 4-8	12 NS in rds 2,5,8		14 EW in rds 2,3,6, 7,10,11	15 NS in rds 9-13
	12 EW in rds 5-8			15 EW in rds 3,4,7,8,11,12	16 EW in rds 8-12
				16 EW in rds 2,4,6,8,10,12	

Table	9 tables, 11 rounds NS EW b	9 tables, 12 rounds NS EW b	9 tables, 13 rounds NS EW b	10 tables, 11 rounds NS EW b	10 tables, 12 rounds NS EW b
1	12 1 1	13 1 1	14 1 1	12 1 1	13 1 1
2	6 4 2	8 4 2	4 10 2	13 11 2	14 7 2
3	13 10 3	14 10 3	9 6 3	14 10 3	15 2 3
4	14 9 4	15 5 4	15 11 4	15 9 4	16 11 4
5	15 2 5	2 9 5	16 2 5	16 8 5	17 8 5
6	16 5 6	16 11 6	17 5 6	17 7 8	18 3 6
7	17 8 7	17 3 7	8 3 7	18 6 9	5 9 7
8	11 3 8	7 6 8	12 13 8	19 5 10	20 12 8
9	18 7 9	18 12 9	18 7 9	20 4 11	19 10 9
10	12-18 EW in rds 8,10,11	13-18 EW in rds 7,8,12	14-18EW in rds 6,7,12,13	2 3 1 / 12-20 EW in rds 7,8,11	4 6 10 / 13-20 EW in rds 7,9,11,12

Table	10 tables, 13 rounds NS EW b	11 tables, 12 rounds NS EW b	11 tables, 13 rounds NS EW b	12 tables, 13 rounds NS EW b
1	14 1 1	13 1 1	14 1 1	14 1 1
2	15 10 2	14 12 2	15 7 2	15 13 2
3	16 5 3	15 11 3	2 10 3	16 12 3
4	17 8 4	16 10 4	16 6 4	17 11 4
5	18 11 5	17 9 5	17 13 5	18 10 5
6	2 3 6	18 8 7	18 4 6	19 9 6
7	19 6 7	19 7 8	19 11 7	20 8 9
8	9 13 8	20 6 9	20 9 8	21 7 10
9	12 7 9	21 5 10	12 5 9	22 6 11
10	20 4 10	22 4 11	22 3 10	23 5 12
11	14-20 EW in rds 5,8,9,13	2 3 12 / 13-22 EW in rds 7,8,9,12	21 8 11 / 14-22 EW in rds 7,10,12,13	24 4 13 / 2 3 1 / 14-24 EW in rds 6,8,11,13

RE-ENTRY. A card by which a player who has had the lead (including the opening lead) can regain it.

REFUSE. (1) Deliberate failure to win a trick because of reasons of strategy. (2) Used in the sense of refusing to finesse, i.e., not taking what was previously a winning finesse in order to ensure the contract. (3) An obsolete term formerly used in WHIST and AUCTION BRIDGE, the laws of which defined it as "to fail to follow suit". See DANGER HAND; DISCARD; DUCK; HOLD UP; RENOUNCE; REVOKE.

REGENCY WHIST CLUB (New York City). Formerly Regency Club, founded in 1936 and merged with the WHIST CLUB of New York in 1964. It has remained at 15 East 67th Street since it began its very successful career, with many of the outstanding bridge personalities among its members.

President 1992 Nicholas Barnes

Secretary John Hatsopoulos

REGIONAL TOURNAMENT. See CHAMPIONSHIP TOURNAMENTS.

REGRES. See WEAK OPENING SYSTEMS.

REID CONVENTION. See RESPONSIVE DOUBLE.

REISINGER MEMORIAL TROPHY. Donated by the Greater New York BA in 1965 in memory of CURT H. REISINGER and awarded to the winners of the Fall Open Teams Championships. It replaced the historic CHICAGO TROPHY. See INTERNATIONAL OPEN TEAM SELECTION.

REISINGER TROPHY. Donated by Curt H. Reisinger in 1930, for the Knockout Teams-of-Four contest in the Eastern States Championships, one of the world's oldest team events.

REITH ONE-OVER-ONE. A system of bidding described by George Reith in a series of five books published 1930-33. Approach bidding was used and four-card suits were bid freely. Responses and bids were kept to minimum levels, and third-hand openings were somewhat shaded. The essence of the system, a forerunner of methods considered as Standard by postwar writers, was the principle of emphasizing distribution in early bidding rounds as opposed to showing strength. The one-over-one response made it incumbent upon opening bidder to bid at least once more.

REITH POINT COUNT. An appraisal by George Reith of the relative values of high cards, primarily for notrump bidding. The values assigned were ace = 6, king = 4, queen = 3, jack = 2, ten = 1. See REITH ONE-OVER-ONE.

RELAY. (1) A minimum bid unrelated to the bidder's hand, aimed simply at keeping the bidding open so that the bidder's partner can describe his hand. An example is the LEBENSOHL rebid of 3♣, which is a forced bid. For the full development of this principle, see RELAY SYSTEM. (2) The practice of sharing boards at duplicate bridge, usually necessitated by a six-, eight-, or twelve-table MITCHELL MOVEMENT in which 24 boards are to be played. (3) In Britain, the equivalent of a BYESTAND.

RELAY MITCHELL. See MITCHELL MOVEMENT.

RELAY STAND. See BYESTAND.

RELAY SYSTEMS. Systems based on the idea that one player should make a series of minimum bids, or relays, until he has acquired sufficient information about his partner's hand to be able to fix the final contract. The first relay system was developed by Pierre Ghestem of France, about 1950, and was used by him very successfully in world championships, mainly with Ren Bacherich. In 1963 he played it with Claude Delmouly, using the name Monaco. This encouraged other European theorists to develop relay systems, notably Dr. Bertrand Romanet, with "Alpha", and Pierre Collet, with "Beta". Both these date from 1965.

An important impetus came with work done about 1972 by Dave Cliff. He can be considered the Father of modern relay methods, with Ghestem as the Grandfather. Cliff's ideas were adopted and refined by a group of young players including Matt Granovetter, Ron Rubin and Michael Becker. Their successes with the ULTIMATE CLUB attracted new interest in the relay principle and attracted imitators in many parts of the world who developed a series of relay languages. The most important of these is the SYMMETRIC RELAY SYSTEM.

RELAY TABLE. (1) One of the tables at which the players are sharing boards for that round with an adjacent table. (2) See BYESTAND.

RELAYS OVER WEAK TWO-BIDS. There are two ways of using a relay, one concerned with stoppers and the other with distribution.

(1) A method of responding to weak two-bids using the cheapest bid — either notrump if the opening bid was 2♠, or the next higher suit — as a relay bid. The relay asks opener to bid a stopper outside his suit if he has one. If his stopper is in the relay suit, he rebids in notrump. Lacking any stopper, opener rebids his own suit. Using this method, the relay bid is the responder's only forcing bid.

(2) The Symmetric Relay method, usable by any pair employing weak two-bids, uses 2NT to start a relay structure, whether the opening is 2♥ or 2♠. The opener bids 3♣ with a minimum, and makes other bids with a maximum. After 3♣, 3♦ is a relay. The following apply whether the opening bid is minimum or maximum:

(a) 3♥ shows a balanced hand. Then 3♠ asks opener to bid 3NT with two top honors, 4♣ or more with one.

(b) 3♠ shows a singleton in the unbid major.

(c) Four-level bids are void-showing.

Also:

(d) 3♦ shows a singleton in a minor; subsequent 3♠ shows it is diamonds, 3NT that it is clubs.

(e) 3♣ followed by 3NT shows a singleton in a minor. Later 4♦, shows it is diamonds, 4♥ that it is clubs.

(f) 3NT in response to 2NT is normal, showing a solid suit.

See WEAK TWO-BIDS.

REMAINDERS. The remaining cards of a four-card or longer suit, outstanding in the other three hands at the table. Two- and three-card remainders are called balanced remainders. One-card and four-card remainders, however, are called unbalanced remainders.

REMOVE. To bid on when partner has doubled for penalties.

RENEGE. Failure to follow suit when holding one or more cards of the suit led, a colloquial synonym for REVOKE. The term is borrowed from such games as two-handed pinochle and French whist in which it is permissible to revoke.

RENOUNCE. A term from AUCTION BRIDGE, meaning to fail to follow suit when able to do so; also (noun), the play involving such failure. See REFUSE.

REOPEN THE BIDDING. See BALANCING.

REPEATED SQUEEZE. See TRIPLE SQUEEZE

REPEATING TRIPLE SQUEEZE. See PROGRESSIVE SQUEEZE

REPECHAGE. A second chance after losing in a knockout competition. A repechage has been used in world championship events: the Rosenblum Cup Teams in 1978, 1982 and 1986. The knockout phase had three brackets. Teams that lost in the knockout moved into a Swiss competition. The five top teams in the Swiss at the time the three knockout survivors were determined joined the three losers of the last knockout round in a mini-knockout. The team winning the mini-knockout joined the knockout winners for the Rosenblum semifinals. In 1978, Poland, losers of an early knockout match, won the mini-knockout and went on to take the Rosenblum Cup. For the 1990 event, the repechage was discarded. See also DOUBLE KNOCKOUT; WORLD CHAMPIONSHIPS.

REPEATED FINESSE. See DOUBLE FINESSE.

REPLAY DUPLICATE. A form of duplicate in which just two pairs play against each other, playing the same boards but first in one position (i.e. North-South and then the other, East-West). Although this form of duplicate attained some currency in the Twenties, it quickly became obsolescent simply because a board could so easily be remembered by the players. Even the process of playing the boards one way one week and the other the next didn't work well.

REPO. See BLACKWOOD AFTER INTERFERENCE.

RE-RAISE. A colloquialism for opener's rebid of three of his suit after responder has raised to two:

1 ♠	2 ♠
3 ♠	

RESCUE. To bid another suit, or conceivably notrump, when partner has been doubled for penalties.

The most common rescuing situation arises when an overcall has been doubled for penalties, a rarer event than it was before negative doubles became popular.

There are three points for the overcaller's partner to consider:

(1) *His length in the doubled suit.* The more cards he holds, the less desirable a rescue becomes — it is rarely right with a doubleton, and virtually never right with more than two cards.

(2) *The level of the potential rescue.* Rescuing is more likely to be effective at the one-level, and may sometimes be attempted when holding a singleton or void in the doubled suit but no suit of more than five cards. See KOCK-WERNER REDOUBLE, SOS REDOUBLE. There is less case for rescuing if it must be done at a higher level.

(3) *The quality of the rescuer's suit compared with the likely quality of the doubled suit.* There must be a reasonable expectation that the rescuer's suit is more substantial than the doubled suit. In most circumstances a strong six-card suit or a seven-card suit is necessary.

Another common rescue situation occurs when a 1NT opening has been doubled. Here it is seldom right for responder to sit if he has no high-card strength or if he has a long suit. See DEFENSE TO DOUBLE OF 1NT.

RESCUE BID. A bid, based on a long suit, made with less than normal values because of a misfit with partner's bid suit after it has been doubled.

RESERVE. A back-up line of play: "He kept the heart finesse in reserve."

RESERVE ONE'S RIGHTS. In special circumstances, a player may announce "I reserve my rights." This applies when there is a possibility of an opponent having received unauthorized information. This option is not available in North America. In ACBL territory a player is required to call the tournament director immediately.

RESERVE PLAYER. In an event for teams of four or more members, any team member not currently playing.

A reserve player is eligible to replace an active member during the current or later sessions, but only under conditions announced by the director or published in advance. In major tournaments reserve players are barred from watching their teammates, and usually they are not permitted to watch play at an adjoining table.

RESOCK, REWIND. To redouble.

RESPOND. To answer in the language of bidding. A pass, however, is not a response.

RESPONDER. The player who responds, normally to an opening bid by his partner.

RESPONDER'S REBID. Many of responder's second bids are covered under separate headings: BART, DELAYED GAME RAISE, DELAYED SUPPORT, FOURTH SUIT FORCING, GOLDEN RULE, JUMP REBIDS BY RESPONDER, NEW MINOR FORCING, 1NT RESPONSE, PREFERENCE, REVERSE, SINGLE RAISE, STAYMAN ON SECOND ROUND, TRIAL BID, 2♣ REBID BY RESPONDER AS ONLY FORCE AFTER 1NT REBID, 2NT RESPONSE.

Other situations are discussed below:

(1) *After three suits at the one level:*

1 ♣	1 ♥
1 ♠	1NT

In most styles, the sequence suggests 6-10 points. Though responder usually has balanced distribution with strength in the unbid suit, exceptions arise.

(a)	(b)
♠ 5	♠ 6 4 2
♥ K 8 7 6 4	♥ A K 10 4
♦ K J 7 4 2	♦ J 4 2
♣ 9 3	♣ J 5 3

1NT is best on both hands: on (a) 2♦ fails to limit responder's strength; on (b) a 2♣ preference is risky, and though pass is an option, game is still possible.

> ♠ J 7
> ♥ A J 6 4 2
> ♦ K J 5
> ♣ J 8 4

A 2NT rebid is easy if that bid is non-forcing; if it is forcing, responder must underbid with 1NT or improvise a bid of 2♦.

1 ♣	1 ♥
1 ♠	2 ♠

Usually indicates four-card trump support and 7-10 high-card points. Occasionally, the raise is best with three-card support, even without a ruffing value:

> ♠ K 10 4
> ♥ A K 4 2
> ♦ 7 3 2
> ♣ 10 8 6

Other sequences are listed under FOURTH SUIT FORCING, PREFERENCE and JUMP REBIDS BY RESPONDER.

(2) *After three suits ending at the two level:*

1 ♦	1 ♠
2 ♣	2 ♠

Normally a six-card suit. If a jump to 3♠ would be forcing or if WEAK JUMP SHIFT RESPONSES are in use, the sequence is mildly encouraging; if 3♠ would be invitational, it is not encouraging.

1 ♦	1 ♠
2 ♣	2 NT

1 ♠	2 ♣
2 ♥	2 NT

At least one stopper in the unbid suit with 10-12 high-card points.

1 ♦	1 ♠
2 ♣	3 ♣

1 ♠	2 ♣
2 ♥	3 ♥

Encouraging but not forcing, showing 10-12 high-card points and four-card support (or, in the first sequence, possibly five-card support). The second sequence is forcing in a style where the 2♣ response forces to game.

Other sequences are listed under FOURTH SUIT FORCING, PREFERENCE and JUMP REBIDS BY RESPONDER.

(3) *After a 1NT rebid:*

1 ♦	1 ♥
1 NT	2 ♥

A six-card heart suit (possibly a strong five-card suit) and discouraging. Opener almost invariably passes.

1 ♦	1 ♥
1 NT	2 ♦

Discouraging, but game might still be possible if opener can give preference to hearts.

1 ♦	1 ♥
1 NT	2 ♣

In the absence of special agreements, non-forcing and neutral. Opener should not rebid 2NT, but may give preference to 2♥ or raise to 3♣, either of which actions might lead to game. Responder is likely to have five hearts and four or five clubs. With only four clubs, he should not automatically retreat from 1NT; with 3 5 1 4 distribution, a pass may be best, especially in a pairs event. This change of suit is forcing in ROTH-STONE. See also NEW MINOR FORCING.

1 ♦	1 ♥
1 NT	2 NT

Invitational to game. The strength depends on the range of opener's 1NT rebid, but responder indicates that the combined hands have a minimum of 23-24 points.

1 ♦	1 ♥
1 NT	2 ♠

See REVERSE.

1 ♦	1 ♥
1 NT	3 ♣

A jump shift, forcing to game, with unbalanced distribution and probable weakness in spades, the unbid suit. (In some styles, the sequence is used to sign off with a weak hand, four hearts and six or more clubs; see NEW MINOR FORCING.)

1 ♦	1 ♥
1 NT	3 ♦

Generally played as forcing (often, even when other jump preferences by responder are invitational), but non-forcing in ACOL and in standard methods by partnership agreement.

1 ♦	1 ♥
1 NT	3 ♥

At one time generally played as forcing, but the non-forcing treatment is logical and has gained popularity; a game-going hand with a six-card heart suit can jump to 4♥.

1 ♥	1 ♠
1 NT	2 ♥

A special sequence that suggests 9-11 points with three-card heart support; with less strength, responder would have raised to 2♥ originally.

1 ♥	1 ♠
1 NT	3 ♥

If the meaning of the previous sequence is accepted, this sequence is forcing, or strongly invitational with four-card heart support.

(4) *After a minimum rebid in the original suit:*

1 ♦	1 ♠
2 ♦	2 ♠

Normally a six-card suit. If a jump to 3♠ would be forcing or if weak jump shifts are in use, the sequence is more likely to be progressive; if 3♠ would be invitational, it is not encouraging. (With an extremely poor hand, responder could pass 2♦; at matchpoint scoring, however, he may wish to play in the higher-scoring strain.)

1 ♦	1 ♠
2 ♠	3 ♣

Forcing, probably with 5-5 or 5-4 distribution, but a probing rebid in a three-card suit may be necessary:

> ♠ A Q 5 4 3
> ♥ 8 4
> ♦ 8 5 3
> ♣ A K 5

1 ♦	1 ♠
2 ♦	2 ♥

Forcing, almost surely with five spades and usually with four or more hearts; rarely, with only three hearts.

1 ♦	1 ♠
2 ♦	2 NT

Encouraging but non-forcing. 10-12 points and presumably guards in both unbid suits.

1 ♦	1 ♠
2 ♦	3 ♦

Encouraging but non-forcing. Probably 10-12 points and weak in at least one of the unbid suits.

1 ♦	1 ♠
2 ♦	4 ♦

Forcing or, by partnership agreement, strongly invitational with a distributional hand.

(5) *After a single raise of responder's suit:*

1 ♦	1 ♠
2 ♠	2 NT

Encouraging but non-forcing. Stoppers in the unbid suits, 10-12 points, probably a four-card spade suit.

1 ♦	1 ♠
2 ♠	3 ♦

Game interest, forcing or non-forcing by partnership agreement. At least 10 points, probably only a four-card spade suit.

1 ♦	1 ♠
2 ♠	3 ♣

Forcing, maybe only a weak three-card club suit. Responder may be aiming for 3NT or trying to learn whether opener has extra strength for a spade game. See TRIAL BID.

1 ♦	1 ♠
2 ♠	3 ♠

Encouraging but not forcing. Responder has a long, strong spade suit without notable features in the unbid suits. Opener will pass or bid on depending on his overall strength and the quality of his trump support.

RESPONDING HAND. The hand, or player, facing the opening bidder; the partner of the initial bidder.

RESPONSE. Usually bid by a player whose partner has opened the bidding, but may be used to describe a response to an overcall, takeout double, cuebid, conventional bid, etc. See ACE-SHOWING RESPONSES; BERGEN RAISES; CHOICE OF SUIT; COURTESY BID; CRISSCROSS RAISE; DELAYED GAME RAISE; DOUBLE RAISE; DRURY; FLINT; FORCING RAISE; FOUR-SUIT TRANSFER BIDS; FREE BID; GLADIATOR; IMPOSSIBLE NEGATIVE; INVERTED MINOR RAISES; JACOBY TWO NOTRUMP RESPONSE; JACOBY TRANSFER BIDS; JUMP SHIFT; LIMIT JUMP RAISE; LIMIT RAISE; MINISPLINTER; NEGATIVE FREE BID; ONE NOTRUMP RESPONSE; ONE NOTRUMP RESPONSE; ONE NOTRUMP RESPONSE TO MAJOR FORCING; ONE NOTRUMP RESPONSE TO MINOR; ONE-OVER-ONE RESPONSE; PASSED HAND; PREEMPTIVE RESPONSE; RESPONSES OVER OPPONENT'S DOUBLE; REVERSE DRURY; ROMEX STAYMAN; SINGLE RAISE; SINGLE RAISE IN MAJOR CONSTRUCTIVE; STAYMAN; STAYMAN THREE CLUBS; STAYMAN FOR STOPPERS; STEP-SHOWING RESPONSES; STRONG NOTRUMP AFTER PASSING; TEXAS; TRANSFER BIDS; TRIPLE RAISE; TWO NOTRUMP RESPONSE; TWO NOTRUMP OVER TAKEOUT DOUBLE; TWO OVER ONE GAME FORCE; TWO OVER ONE RESPONSE; TWO-WAY STAYMAN; UP THE LINE; WEAKNESS RESPONSE; WEAK TAKEOUT.

RESPONSES OVER OPPONENT'S TAKEOUT DOUBLE.

Some aspects of bidding over an opponent's takeout double depend on partnership style. Popular treatments are as follows:

(1) A non-jump suit response may be forcing or nonforcing, by agreement. Many pairs use new-suit responses as forcing at the one level only; in that style, a two-level response suggests a six-card suit or strong five-card suit.

Any bid of a new suit logically suggests a fair suit. After 1♥-Dbl, for example, responder has little reason to mention a poor four-card spade suit, since doubler has implied spades. Also, since the auction has become competitive, responder should avoid suggesting a weak suit as trumps; he should instead take the opportunity to make a descriptive bid that will help his partner judge the bidding and defense.

(2) 1NT is mildly constructive, promising about 7-9 points with balanced distribution.

(3) A single raise is preemptive and may be slightly weaker than it would be without the double.

(4) A double raise is preemptive and shows a distributional hand with high-card weakness. After 1♠-Dbl, raise to 3♠ (at all but unfavorable vulnerability) with:

    ♠ K 10 6 4
    ♥ 5
    ♦ J 10 6 5 3
    ♣ 8 5 3

(5) A triple raise is preemptive with extra playing strength.

(6) A redouble may in theory show any hand with about 10 points or more. After a redouble, the doubler's side is seldom allowed to play the hand undoubled. Redoubler will usually have a defensive hand, and opener will not bid at his next turn unless he has a distributional hand

unsuited to defense.

With some strong hands, a redouble is tactically unsound. (See REDOUBLE.) If responder has a hand with offensive features, he should begin to describe his hand; to spend a bidding turn to redouble is shortsighted.

WEST	NORTH	EAST	SOUTH
	1 ♣	Dbl	?

  (a)   (b)
  ♠ 7 2   ♠ Q 9 2
  ♥ A K 10 6 2   ♥ J 7 3
  ♦ 9 3   ♦ K Q 8 2
  ♣ K 9 8 2   ♣ Q 9 4

(a) South should bid 1♥, planning to support clubs next. South wants to describe a fair hand with a heart suit and club support. If he redoubles, the bidding may continue 1♠ on his left, 2♠ on his right. Now South won't have room to show his hand below the four level, where he may take a minus.

(b) South's chances of penalizing the opponents are unclear. He should describe his hand with a 1NT response. Players who use the "omnibus redouble" on every 10-point hand are likely to encounter problems.

WEST	NORTH	EAST	SOUTH
	1 ♣	Dbl	Redbl
3 ♥	Pass	Pass	?

            ♠ K J 9 2
            ♥ 9 6 4
            ♦ A 10 7
            ♣ K 6 3

Neither side vulnerable. South is in an impossible situation; he would have done better to bid 1♠ over the double.

A redouble is also unattractive with four-card support or better for opener's suit, since the opponents are given a cheap opportunity to locate a fit for a possible sacrifice. A direct raise may be preferable, and there are also conventional possibilities:

(7) 2NT and 3NT have no natural meaning because a strong balanced hand would redouble. Most experienced players use 2NT to show a hand that would have made a LIMIT JUMP RAISE to three of opener's suit if there had been no double. This method, popularly known as Jordan, was developed by Alan Truscott. 3NT can be used to show a strong raise to game when the opening bid was 1♠ or 1♥. For other methods, see 2NT RESPONSE OVER OPPONENT'S TAKEOUT DOUBLE.

(8) A jump response in a suit (for example, 1♦-Dbl-2♠) shows length in the suit — often six or more cards — but the strength is a matter of style. There are four schools: (1) forcing to game; (2) forcing for one round; some pairs use conventional jump responses that indicate a fit for opener's suit as well as length and strength in the bid suit; (3) not forcing, a hand worth about 9 points; (4) preemptive, a hand such as:

         ♠ K J 10 8 5 2
         ♥ 7
         ♦ J 5 3
         ♣ 9 6 3

(9) Pass shows a hand unsuitable for positive action. But a pass followed by a bid on the next round can show a hand with fair defensive strength:

         ♠ A 5 3
         ♥ Q 6 4
         ♦ K 6 3 2
         ♣ 7 4 3

If partner's 1♠ opening is doubled, responder may pass

and bid 2♠ on the next round to suggest a maximum single raise.

A possible tactic is to trap-pass over a double with a good hand and shortness in opener's suit. After 1♠-Dbl, responder might pass with:

♠ 7
♥ A Q 9 3
♦ K J 3 2
♣ Q J 9 3

RESPONSES TO OVERCALLS. See OVERCALLS.

RESPONSIVE DOUBLE. (Originated by Dr. F. Field-ing-Reid). The use of a double for takeout when there has been an immediate raise to the two- or three-level over partner's takeout double. For example:

WEST	NORTH	EAST	SOUTH
1♦	Dbl	2♦	?

South holds:

♠ J 6 5 2
♥ Q 10 9 5
♦ 3
♣ Q 7 6 3

It would be cowardly to pass, and South is not nearly strong enough to make a cuebid of 3♦. He does not want to guess which suit to bid, so he makes a responsive double. In this situation, it is very seldom that South will wish to make a PENALTY DOUBLE. The double would also be used if East had raised to 3♦ instead- of 2♦. The doubler may have a balanced hand if his high-card strength is somewhat improved:

♠ 4 3 2
♥ A Q 9
♦ Q 8 5 2
♣ J 8 6

This would be ideal for a responsive double if an opening spade bid were doubled and raised to 2♠, and would be the most convenient action if the opposition had bid clubs, diamonds or hearts.

The minimum strength required for a responsive double varies slightly with the level of the auction. With a balanced hand, a double of 2♣ might be made with 6 points; a double of 3♣ would need at least 9 points.

The convention normally applies to any bid at the two- or three-level, but a few players use a double of 3♥ or 3♠ for penalties. An extension of the responsive idea can be used in the following situation:

WEST	NORTH	EAST	SOUTH
	1♥	2♣	2♥
Dbl			

A penalty double of a free raise is very seldom required, so by partnership agreement West's double can show length in spades and diamonds. Partnerships need to agree exactly how high this should apply. "Responsive through 4♦" is a common agreement. They must also consider whether it applies after a weak two-bid:

WEST	NORTH	EAST	SOUTH
2♥	Dbl	3♥	Dbl

RESTRICTED CHOICE. The play of a card which may have been selected as a choice of equal plays increases the chance that the player started with a holding in which his choice was restricted.

The Rule of Restricted Choice is a rule of card play which can enable the declarer to take the correct action in situations which used to be thought of as guesswork.

The underlying principles were first discussed by Alan Truscott in the *Contract Bridge Journal*. Later, these principles were unified by Terence Reese in his book, *Master Play*.

THE BASIC PRINCIPLE

Following is the sort of card combination which can call the Rule of Restricted Choice into operation:
Example 1:

NORTH (dummy)
♠ Q J 9
SOUTH (declarer)
♠ 4 3 2

South has to develop a trick in this suit. He leads low to dummy's queen and East wins with the king. Upon regaining the lead, South again leads toward the North hand. Should South play the jack or 9 from dummy? Is one play superior or is South faced with a guess? If either East or West now holds both the ace and 10, South's play is immaterial. The jack will score if West holds the ace and East holds the 10. The 9 is winning play if West holds the 10 and East holds the ace.

It is important to notice that this summary is sufficient, for when it comes time for South to make the final decision, he already knows that East held the king. Thus, South can exclude from the reckoning all distributions in which East does not hold the king.

The two possible distributions of the East-West honors given above are equally likely to occur, but the two plays are not of equal merit. To the statement," the two crucial defensive holdings are equally likely," should be added, "provided there is no information regarding the distribution of honor cards in the suit."

In fact, there is such information. There is a direct inference to be drawn from the fact that East won the first trick with the king. Consider the first possible honor holding given above. If this is the actual distribution of East-West honor cards, East was forced to play his ♠K on the first round; his choice was restricted. This is not true in the second case, where East had the option of winning the first trick with the ace instead of the king. His choice was not restricted.

It can be presumed that if East started with A-K, he would play the ace some percentage of the time. When East actually plays the king on the first round, the probability that he started with the A-K is diminished because with both honors he might have played the other one.

For the sake of argument, assume that East would play his equal honors with equal frequency, winning with the king 50% of the time and winning with the ace 50% of the time. It can be demonstrated that this is, in fact, East's best strategy.

Under this assumption, imagine that declarer is playing the Example I combination 200 times. On 100 of these deals, East starts with the K-10. On the other 100 deals, East starts with the A-K. Since, on the second 100 deals, East wins with the king only 50 times, certain things become clear.

East wins the king from an honor holding of K-10 on 100 occasions. But East wins the king from an honor holding of A-K on only 50 occasions. On the other 50 deals on which East holds A-K, he wins with the ace! From this one may conclude that the jack is the superior play on the second round of spades. In fact, it is exactly twice as good a play as the 9. The position is exactly the same if East wins the first trick with the ace and not the king.

The above conclusions may be checked by examining all possible honor distributions. If either defender holds all three honors, declarer will succeed or fail regardless of his plays, so these combinations can be omitted. This leaves the following possibilities, all equally probable before the suit is played for the first time:

	West holds	East holds
(a)	A K	10
(b)	A 10	K
(c)	K 10	A
(d)	A	K 10
(e)	K	A 10
(f)	10	A K

Each of the above situations is equally probable. Assume that each case occurs 100 times, 600 deals in all. Since East will (it is assumed) play equal honors with equal frequency, he wins a high honor on the first round on the following occasions:

	East wins with ♠A	East wins with ♠K
(a)	0	0
(b)	0	100
(c)	100	0
(d)	0	100
(e)	100	0
(f)	50	50
TOTAL	250	250

Thus, East will win with a specified honor 250 times. Of these 250 times, declarer triumphs automatically in cases (b) or (c); a total of 100. Of the remaining 150, the jack is the winning play 100 times in case (d) or (e), but the 9 is right only 50 times in case (f).

Thus declarer's play of a card combination such as Example 1, far from being a blind guess, is subject to very definite analysis.

The logic behind the rule is simple. If the player in question had a choice of plays, he might have elected the other option. Therefore, there is a presumption that he did not have the option. Thus, in Example 1, when East wins with the ♠K, the chances favor the play of the jack on the second round. The jack play caters to the situation in which East started with K-10, where he had no choice of plays on the first round, rather than the situation in which East had a choice of plays from A-K.

Other Card Combinations. The Rule of Restricted Choice can be applied to many more combinations:
Example 2:

NORTH (dummy)
♠ J 9 4
SOUTH (declarer)
♠ Q 3 2

South needs one trick, and is forced to attack the suit himself. He leads low to the queen, and West wins with a high honor. Later, South leads again toward the North hand. If West follows low, what should South do?

Applying the Rule of Restricted Choice, South should reason that if West held both high honors, he might have chosen the other one to capture the queen. But if West started with the high honor and the 10, his choice was restricted. The percentage play is the 9.
Example 3:

NORTH (dummy)
♠ K 10 9
SOUTH (declarer)
♠ 4 3 2

South leads toward the North hand and finesses the 9,

losing to a middle honor. On the next lead, South should finesse the 10.

A Mistake to Avoid. Care must be taken to avoid mistaken applications of the Rule of Restricted Choice. Example 4:

NORTH (dummy)
♠ K J 9
SOUTH (declarer)
♠ 4 3 2

South requires one trick here. He leads up to the North hand, and decides to play the jack. East wins with the queen. Declarer has gained no information whatsoever as to the distribution of the outstanding honors. On the next lead declarer is faced with a guess. There was no choice of plays involved for East, who would win the jack with the queen whenever he held that card. The Rule of Restricted Choice does not apply.
Example 5:

NORTH (dummy)
♠ A Q 10 7 6 5
SOUTH (declarer)
♠ 4 3 2

South hopes to take six tricks here, and leads a spade to North's queen, which East wins with the king. Later, South wants to pick up the remainder of the suit. Once again, there is no application of the Rule of Restricted Choice.

Lower Odds. In the above examples of the Rule of Restricted Choice, declarer was faced with a choice of plays, one of which was exactly twice as good as the other. Restricted Choice situations do not always give such good odds.

There is a large class of card combinations in which declarer's correct play under the Rule of Restricted Choice gives him less than two-to-one odds.
Example 6:

NORTH (dummy)
K 10 9 8 7 6
SOUTH (declarer)
A 3 2

South leads the ace from his hand, West follows with the 4 and East drops the QUACK. (We have already shown that from declarer's point of view it makes no difference whether East plays the queen or jack. Thus, terminology such as quack can be used to simplify both the discussion and the thinking.)

South leads toward the dummy, and West follows with the 5. Assuming (as always) no important inferences to be drawn from the play of other suits, how should South play? To answer that question, one starts by reflecting that the following distribution of East-West cards

	WEST	EAST
(a)	5 4	Q J

is slightly more probable (before the suit is played) than the following distribution:

	WEST	EAST
(b)	Q 5 4	J

Also, the chance of East holding Q-J is slightly more probable than the following distribution:

	WEST	EAST
(c)	J 5 4	Q

But East is less likely to have Q-J doubleton than he is to have a singleton quack. In other words, (b) and (c) together are greater than (a).

Thus, the correct play on the second round is to finesse. The odds favoring this play as opposed to the drop are slightly less than two to one.

Example 7:

> NORTH (dummy)
> A J 10 9 8 7
> SOUTH (declarer)
> 4 3 2

South wishes to take five tricks. The best play is to take two finesses. This fails to bring in the suit (if such was possible) only when East holds K-Q. It is easily seen that all other plays are inferior.

A common argument given about this combination is the following: It is best to take two finesses because it gains against more distributions than any other play. Once you have finessed the first time, you must follow through and finesse the second time.

This is an unfortunate way to get the right answer. According to the first part of this argument, if you finesse the jack and it loses to the king or queen when you lead up to the dummy the second time you have two possible combinations of cards:

	West holds	East holds
Case 1	6 5	K Q
Case 2 (a)	K 6 5	Q
(b)	Q 6 5	K

After the first trick, either Case 2 (a) or Case 2 (b) disappears, so only two relevant combinations remain, and the first is (initially) more probable. Therefore, the argument indicates playing for the drop on the second round.

The correct argument for the second finesse is that if East started with a singleton honor, his choice was restricted on the first round. Thus, the odds on the second finesse are almost two to one.

Another Mistake to Avoid. Some combinations are superficially similar to those in the last section, but do not admit exact application of the Rule of Restricted Choice.

Example 8:

> NORTH (dummy)
> A 2
>
> SOUTH (declarer)
> K Q 9 8 7 6

Declarer leads the 6 to the ace in dummy, and West plays the 10 or jack. According to the principles developed in the previous section, although an original West holding of doubleton J-10 is more likely than the holding of a particular singleton honor, it is now more likely that West had a singleton honor than two honors doubleton.

That is true so far as it goes, but declarer should not finesse on the second round. West may well have J-10-3!

Example 9:

> NORTH (dummy)
> A 2
> SOUTH (declarer)
> K 9 8 7 6

South needs three tricks before the defense makes two. He leads the 6 to the ace, and West plays the jack. If West has the singleton jack, South must finesse coming back. Declarer must avoid a mistaken application of the Rule of Restricted Choice. It is true that a singleton jack is more likely than either Q-J or J-10 doubleton. But the king is the right play if West has either of the two doubleton honor combinations, and these two together exceed the probability of a singleton jack.

Higher Odds. There are still other types of suit combinations that admit application of the Rule of Restricted

Choice. Sometimes the declarer can obtain even higher odds than two-to-one in favor of the correct play. The odds mount appreciably in the following three examples:

Example 10:

> NORTH (dummy)
> A K Q 10
> SOUTH (declarer)
> 4 3 2

Declarer plays off the A-K, and the jack fails to drop. He later leads toward the tenace in the North hand. If West follows with a small card, the percentage play is the queen. Assuming no relevant information about the side suits, East is a slight favorite to hold the jack.

Example 11:

> NORTH (dummy)
> A K Q 9
> SOUTH (declarer)
> 4 3 2

Dummy's holding is slightly weaker than in the previous example. Declarer cashes the A-K. West follows with two small cards, but East drops an honor. Best play is to enter the South hand and finesse. If West follows to the third round with a small card, it is slightly less than two to one that he holds the missing honor.

Example 12:

> NORTH (dummy)
> A K Q 8
> SOUTH (declarer)
> 4 3 2

Dummy's holding has been further debilitated, but the Rule of Restricted Choice is even more rewarding. When the ace and king are cashed, East drops two of the missing honors. Declarer's best play is to enter the South hand and finesse the 8.

The odds in favor of this play can be computed as follows. If East held J-10-9 originally, there were six ways in which he could have played two honors to the first two tricks. Only one of these ways was chosen; therefore the weight of this combination is only one-sixth its original chance. But if East held two blank honors originally, he still had two ways to play them and chose one of them. Therefore this combination carries only half its original weight. J-10-9 is slightly more likely than any particular doubleton (before any cards are played), but the finesse still has odds of almost three to one in its favor.

Following is an example of such a situation from actual play in a pair tournament:

Example 13:

> NORTH (dummy)
> 2
> SOUTH (declarer)
> Q J 8 7 6 5 4

Declarer entered the North hand, and led the singleton deuce. East followed with the 9. South contributed the jack, and West won with the king. South later regained the lead, and was forced to lead a trump from his own hand. Should he play the queen or the 8?

If the suit originally split 4-1, the card played at this stage is of no significance. Thus a 3-2 division can be assumed. If the doubleton was in the East hand, the 9 could have come from A-9 or 10-9 holdings which initially were equally likely. But if East had 10-9, he would presumably have played the 10 half the time. Furthermore, if East held 10-9, West must have started with A-K-3 and he might have won with the ace instead of the king. The Rule of Restricted Choice can be applied against both opponents in the same suit! Furthermore, the 9 could have come from 10-9-3.

Since the play of a small card on the second round caters to both applications of the Rule of Restricted Choice and guards against the falsecard, it is clearly the superior play.

The odds in favor of this play as opposed to the play of the queen can be computed as follows: Disregarding the falsecard, the odds in favor of the play of a small card are four to one. If East held A-9, the play of both opponents was restricted. There was only one way in which they could have played their cards. If East held 10-9, however, each opponent had a choice of two plays, giving them four different ways in which their cards could have been played.

Now consider the case in which East may have falsecarded from 10-9-3. This is another specific distribution of cards divided three and two, so it was originally equally likely as all the others. However, the weight of this double application of the Rule of Restricted Choice still applies. Thus, the correct odds are five to one.

Applications. An application of the Rule of Restricted Choice would have saved the United States team several IMPs on this deal from the 1958 Bermuda Bowl match against Italy.

Example 14:

        ♠ K 4 2
        ♥ 8 3
        ♦ K 9 3 2
        ♣ A K 8 7

        ♠ A 5
        ♥ Q 10 9
        ♦ A Q J 7 6 5
        ♣ 10 4

SOUTH	NORTH
1 ♦	2 ♣
2 ♦	2 ♠
2NT	3NT
Pass	

West led the ♥5 which East won with the king. A low heart was returned and South was faced with a guess. After consideration, he played the queen. This proved to be the wrong move as West had led from A-x-x. The consensus of expert opinion was that South's play was correct. *The Bridge World* commentator wrote: ". . . I think South's play is correct. If the hearts are 4-4, South's play makes relatively little difference; only if the lead was from three is it crucial. And a lead from three to the jack seems a little more attractive than from three to an ace."

This point — and psychological considerations — are important factors in deciding which card to play. But such factors have a lot of ground to make up. On the auction, a heart lead might be expected from any holding of three to an honor. And according to the Rule of Restricted Choice, the 10 is a two-to-one percentage favorite, for if East had started with five hearts to the A-K, he might have played the ace on the first round. With five hearts to the K-J, his choice was restricted to the play of the king. Another way of looking at it is that the combination of A-x-x and K-x-x in West's hand are together twice as likely as J-x-x.

Here is another situation in which the Rule of Restricted Choice should be applied when the defenders attack a suit.

Example 15:

        ♠ A K J 3
        ♥ Q
        ♦ 10 8 4
        ♣ A K J 10 5

        ♠ Q 10 9 8 6
        ♥ J 10 5
        ♦ K 3 2
        ♣ Q 9

At rubber bridge South is declarer at 4♠ with no East-West bidding. West leads a small heart which East wins with the ace. It is apparent that the contract will be made unless the defense takes three diamond tricks. East shifts to the quack of diamonds.

South knows that East is a good enough player to have shifted to the quack of diamonds from any of these holdings:

(1) ace, quack and small card(s)
(2) queen, jack and small card(s)
(3) quack and small card(s)

Even with restricted choice considerations put aside (which makes (2) less probable), playing low caters only to case (2) so South goes up with the king.

Naturally, West takes the ♦A and continues with a small diamond. Now the 9 becomes important. The only relevant holdings now are:

(4) East started with Q-J and small card(s) but not the 9. (If East led from Q-J-9, the game is over.)

(5) East started with quack-9 and possibly small card(s).

Q-J and quack-9 seem to be equally likely possibilities but, as usual, the Rule of Restricted Choice tells us that with (4) East might have selected the other honor to lead. And so the correct play is the 10.

Similar considerations can arise when the declarer attacks a suit.

Example 16:

        ♠ Q 10 9 7 6
        ♥ 4 2
        ♦ 5 3
        ♣ K 6 5 4

        ♠ A K J 8
        ♥ A K 3
        ♦ K 4 2
        ♣ 10 9 7

South plays in 4♠ at rubber bridge. West leads the ♦Q, East takes the ace, and returns the suit. South wins, ruffs his last diamond in dummy (East discarding a heart), plays a trump to the ace, and plays three rounds of hearts. West discards a diamond on the third round of hearts, which is ruffed in dummy. Now a spade to the king extracts both remaining trumps. Since both defenders have shown with two spades and 6-2 in the red suits, it is clear that both have three clubs, and the position is:

Example 17:   NORTH
        ♠ 10
        ♥ —
        ♦ —
        ♣ K 6 5 4

      SOUTH
        ♠ J 8
        ♥ —
        ♦ —
        ♣ 10 9 7

South needs one club trick (or a ruff and sluff) to make his contract. He leads the 9 (it can be verified that this is a superior play to the 7), and West plays the queen.

This play would be made from any of the holdings of A-Q-x, Q-J-x, or Q-x-x. Even with Restricted Choice set aside, the king is the best play. But East wins and returns a low club.

South must rely on the Rule of Restricted Choice and play the 10.

A little-known safety play shows that the Rule of Restricted Choice can be applied to spot cards as well as honors.

Example 18:

NORTH (dummy)
J 7 6 5
SOUTH (declarer)
A Q 9 8

South has adequate entries to both hands, and needs three tricks in this suit. The correct play is to lead low from the North hand and finesse the queen. If this loses to the king, South next plays the ace. It is easily verified that this play will fail to produce three tricks only when West holds the blank king.

Suppose it be asked: why, after West wins the king, should declarer play West for the remaining cards rather than East?

Suppose East played the 3 on the first round of the suit. If East started with 10-4-3-2, he had a choice of three low spots to play on the first round. He might equally well have played any of the low cards, therefore this holding can be counted only with a weight of one third. On the other hand, if East started with the singleton three, his choice was restricted.

To check this computation, notice that if declarer goes after the suit with the intention of playing the ace on the second round, he loses only when West starts with the singleton king (one distribution) but if he intends to play to the jack on the second round, he loses when East starts with the singleton 4, 3, or 2 (three distributions). As has been seen, the correct odds can always be discovered by returning to the original possibilities before any cards have been played (see Example 1).

The Rule of Restricted Choice may even be applied to the opening lead.

Example 19:

♠ A 4 3 2
♥ A K 4 3 2
♦ J 10
♣ J 2

♠ K Q J 10 9 8
♥ 6 5
♦ K Q
♣ A Q 10

SOUTH	NORTH
1 ♠	4NT
5 ♥	6 ♠

Against South's 6♠, West leads the ♦7 and East wins with the ace. East shifts to a low club. Should South finesse? There are two plays open to declarer. First, he can duck the club lead, hoping that East has the king. Second, he can rise with the ace, draw trump, and try to ruff out the heart suit. This play depends on a 3-3 heart split.

The chance of an even split in hearts is about 36%. The club finesse appears to offer a 50% chance and therefore

seems the better play. However, South must consider West's choice of opening leads. If East holds the ♣K, West started with a collection of small cards in each minor suit. If this was the case, he would have led a club about half the time. Since West did not lead a club, there is some presumption that his club-diamond holdings were not equivalent. If we assume West would lead a club half the time with equal minor suit holdings, the club finesse is only a 33% chance, and should therefore be rejected in favor of the attempt to split the hearts 3-3.

RESULT PLAYER (or result merchant). A partner (or kibitzer) who suggests a line of play that would have been successful after declarer has failed with a different line of play. Second guesser is a synonym.

RETAIN THE LEAD. To continue to lead the first card to a trick by virtue of having won the previous trick.

REUNION BRIDGE COMMITTEE. (Comit de Bridge de la Reunion)
It had 320 members in 1993.
Officers 1993
  President: Andr Metg
  Treasurer: Claude Pelloux
  24 Rue Theresien Cadet
  97490 Ste. Clotilde
  Ile De La Reunion
  France.
  Tel: 260 29 23 80

REVALUATION. The reassessment of a hand in the light of the bidding. Certain features of a hand may improve or deteriorate in value in the light of the bidding around the table. See DISTRIBUTIONAL COUNTS.

If partner shows a strong two-suited hand, secondary suit honors are of greater significance in those suits, but are probably useless in the other suits. A shortage in partner's side suit, together with a few trumps, is more valuable than a shortage in another suit which is likely to be duplicated.

Kings and queens in a suit bid by an opponent improve if the bid was on the right, and deteriorate if the bid was on the left (see POSITIONAL FACTOR).

A holding of three small cards in a suit bid by an opponent at a low level is a liability, but improves if the opponents raise the suit strongly to a high level. It is then reasonable to assume that partner has no more than a singleton. In such circumstances a doubleton is less attractive, because there is an increased chance that there will be two losers.

REVERSE. An unforced rebid at the level of two or more in a higher ranking suit than that bid originally — usually a strength-showing bid. The English definition of a reverse by the opener is slightly wider in scope: a bid of a third suit in an uncontested auction which prevents responder from returning to the original suit at the level of two. This allows for the situation described in England as a high reverse. The following are standard reversing sequences:

WEST	EAST	WEST	EAST
1 ♣	1 ♠	1 ♥	2 ♦
2 ♥		2 ♠	

Examples of reverses by responder:

WEST	EAST	WEST	EAST
1♦	1♥	1♣	1♦
2♦	2♠	1♠	2♥

All reverses, by opener or responder, show strong game possibilities — the combined strength is rarely less than 23 points. In most systems, reverses imply that the first-bid suit consists of at least five cards and the second is shorter.

There has been a change of thinking concerning reverses when the Two-Over-One forcing to game system is used.

WEST	EAST
1♥	2♣
2♠	

Since the two-level response to the opening bid already created a situation that called for reaching game under most circumstances, the reverse by opener does not necessarily show any additional strength beyond the opening bid.

In traditional methods reverses are not forcing after a one-level response. Many experts, particularly those of the scientific school, treat them as forcing. Whether this applies to 1♥-1NT-2♠ is a doubtful point.

If all four suits are bid, it is doubtful whether the term reverse should be applied, and the inference that the reverser's original suit is at least five cards in length is less strong. See FOURTH SUIT FORCING and LEBENSOHL CONVENTION.

In the modern style, the forcing quality of the reverse creates problems when the responder is weak. There is a tendency for partnerships to wander on to an unsound game when both players have a minimum. Regular partnerships discuss ways to put on the brakes. A common agreement is this:

With a minimum hand, responder (a) rebids his suit with five cards or more; or (b) makes the cheapest available other bid, which is either the fourth suit or 2NT. Although weak, this is forcing.

WEST	EAST
1♣	1♠
2♥	2♠

This shows at least five spades and a weak hand.

or

WEST	EAST
1♣	1♠
2♥	2NT

This shows a weak hand and denies five spades.

WEST	EAST
1♣	1♥
2♦	2♠

East denies a five-card heart suit and is likely to be weak. He may be hoping to play in 2NT, or three clubs or three hearts.

The corollary is that other rebids by East, such as 3♣ or 3♥, or in this situation 2NT, are game-forcing.

REVERSE COUNT. A method of giving count by playing low-high to indicate an even number of cards and playing high-low to indicate an odd number of cards. This was adopted in Sweden in the history of the game, and eventually spread elsewhere. It avoids the disadvantage of the standard signal, which forces a defender to waste a high card, such as 10 from 10-2, that he may not wish to spare.

REVERSE DISCARDS. See UPSIDE-DOWN SIGNALS.

REVERSE DRURY. The modern standard version of the DRURY convention. The original version became obsolescent in the Eighties. After a third or fourth seat opening of 1♠ or 1♥, a 2♣ response shows a strong raise of opener's suit, usually in the 9-11 point range. Then opener returns to his suit at the two-level with a minimum or sub-minimum hand. Other rebids are natural and forward-going. Opener will often jump to game in the agreed suit, ending the auction. The original version, in which 2♦ was an artificial weak action, is seldom used today.

REVERSE FLANNERY. An opening bid of 2♦ to show a minimum opening hand with four hearts and five spades. This convention is used almost solely by pairs that use CANAPÉ styles of bidding, e.g., BLUE TEAM CLUB, in which this distribution is difficult to show. Since such pairs usually use a 2♦ opening for some other purpose, the Reverse Flannery bid is usually 2♥.

REVERSE SEQUENCE LEAD. See RUSINOW LEAD.

REVERSE SWISS. The use of unusual jump shift rebids by opener to make a game raise of responder's suit, promising a wealth of high cards rather than just suitable distribution. For alternative uses of such jumps see FRAGMENT BIDS and SPLINTER BIDS.

REVERSING DUMMY. See DUMMY REVERSAL.

REVIEWING THE BIDDING. A player who does not hear a call distinctly may forthwith require that it be repeated. Any player may, when it is his turn to call, require that all previous calls be restated unless he is required by law to pass. In rubber bridge, after the auction is closed, any player may require such a review before his side has faced any cards. In duplicate, after the auction is closed, the declarer or either defender may require such a review at his own first turn to play. A review is not necessary, and should not be asked for or given, if the BID BOX is in use (unless one of the players has a vision handicap). See LAWS (Law 20); LAWS OF DUPLICATE (Law 20). See also FACE DOWN LEADS; EXPLANATION OF ANY CALL OR PLAY.

REVOKE. The play of a card of another suit by a player who is able to follow suit or comply with a lead penalty. Any player, including dummy if he has not forfeited his rights, may ask whether a play constitutes a revoke and demand its correction.

If a revoke by a defender is corrected, the card played in error constitutes a penalty card.

A revoke becomes established after either member of the offending side leads or plays to the next trick, or if the revoking side makes a claim or concession.

As a result of changes in the 1987 Duplicate Laws and the 1993 rubber bridge laws the penalties for revokes are the same in the two codes. The penalty is in general two tricks if the revoking side wins the revoke trick, and one trick if it does not. But a partnership cannot lose any tricks taken before the revoke trick. And the penalty is two tricks, not one, if the revoker subsequently takes a trick with a card he should have played to the revoke trick.

No player is ethically required to draw attention to his own revoke, but a player must not commit a second revoke to conceal the first offense. See LAWS (Laws 61-64).

REVOLVING DISCARDS. A method of discarding which assigns a suit preference meaning to the first discard on any hand. There are two possible procedures which are similar in effect but vary slightly in execution.

(1) A low card calls for the suit below the suit in which the signal is given, and a high card for the suit above. The suits are considered in a circle with spades below clubs. Thus a low club discard on a heart lead would call for a spade, and a high club would call for a diamond. This version was developed in England, primarily for notrump defense, and is credited to J. Attwood.

(2) A low card calls for the lower-ranking of the other two suits, and a high card for the higher-ranking. This was advocated by Hy Lavinthal, the inventor of suit preference by signaling, who gave this example:

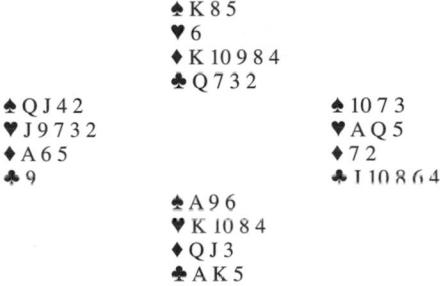

```
                ♠ K 8 5
                ♥ 6
                ♦ K 10 9 8 4
                ♣ Q 7 3 2
♠ Q J 4 2                        ♠ 10 7 3
♥ J 9 7 3 2                      ♥ A Q 5
♦ A 6 5                          ♦ 7 2
♣ 9                             ♣ J 10 8 6 4
                ♠ A 9 6
                ♥ K 10 8 4
                ♦ Q J 3
                ♣ A K 5
```

South plays in 3NT after opening 1NT. West leads the ♥3, and East correctly plays the queen. (After the play of the ace there would be no way to defeat the contract.) South wins the ♥Q with the king, and leads diamonds. West holds up the ace until the third round in order to get a signal from East. Normal signals would not help, because East cannot spare a heart, and a black-suit discard would be unenlightening. Using the Lavinthal discard signal the ♣4 asks for a heart, and the ♠10 would carry the same message. Using the revolving method given in (1), the ♠3 or the ♣J would be appropriate.

REX BRIDGE. A Swedish variation on contract in which any player may introduce a Rex call at any time, ranking between spades and hearts. It is a notrump contract except that the ace of each suit ranks below the deuce, and the king is the high card in each suit, other cards maintaining their rank with respect to the king.

RHO. Right-hand opponent.

R/H 4 NT CONVENTION. A nonjump bid of 4 NT after a trump suit has been established to ask about the three top trump honors. Partner responds to 4 NT by bidding five of the trump suit with none of the top three trump honors, 5 NT with all three honors, or a nontrump suit with one or two honors, as follows:

Lowest side suit = king or queen.
Middle side suit = ace.
Highest side suit = any two of the top three honors.

RHYTHM. Bidding and play at a uniform speed. The stress here is on uniformity and not on speed. An expert player attempts to foresee the possible problems that may evolve during the bidding of a hand before choosing his first action so that he may avoid the agony of a later HUDDLE. Since a good player knows that a huddle followed by a pass, or even a double, places the onus on his partner not to be influenced by the fact that he had a problem, he will try to solve his future problems before they occur rather than later.

In the play of the hand, the shrewd declarer will sometimes attempt to cause opponents to be careless in the defense by playing with unusual rapidity, as though the hand was practically a pianola. When confronted by a rapid tempo on declarer's part, a thoughtful defender will deliberately slow his own tempo so that he will have the opportunity to analyze declarer's play to see whether or not he has a problem.

In the play of the hand, too, the necessity for defenders to establish a rhythmic tempo to their play is important. In attempting to locate a particular card, such as an adversely held ace or queen, declarer is frequently put on the right track by applying the old adage "he who hesitates, has it. " While a declarer takes advantage of a hesitation at his own risk (see PRIORITIES), the opponent who hesitates before making a play with intent to deceive the declarer is guilty of unethical conduct.

RICHMOND TROPHY. The Richmond Trophy is awarded annually to the Canadian who wins the most points during a calendar year. See Appendix 2.

RIDE. (1) To take a finesse with, fail to cover; for example, "dummy's jack was led and declarer let it ride." (2) A large penalty, derived from underworld argot in which a victim is "taken for a ride" by his would-be murderers.

RIFFLE. A light shuffle of the deck; a flexing of the deck with the cards bent and held between the fingers so that a rapid motion ensues as the pack is straightened out.

RIGHT-HAND PLAYER. The player who, in rotation, acts before the given player. There are distinctions in the rules between irregular acts committed by the right-hand or left-hand player. The term is generally used, however, to refer to the player on declarer's right, after play commences. See RHO for a similar term.

RIGHT SIDE. The hand of the declaring partnership which can more successfully cope with the opening lead against the chosen contract. For example, assuming all other suits are adequately stopped, the hand holding A-Q-x opposite partner's x-x-x is the *right side* from which to play the hand. Sometimes there is no right or wrong side.

The *rightness* of one side and *wrongness* of the other may relate to factors other than the safety of the declarer's holding in the suit led; for example, the inability of one defender to lead the suit profitably (e.g., from K-x-x-x when the declaring side has the ace and queen), or the inability of one defender to diagnose the most effective lead whereas from his partner's hand the right lead would be obvious.

Sometimes it is impossible to know on the basis of the two hands of the declaring partnership which side is the right side. For example, when East and West have the following heart holdings

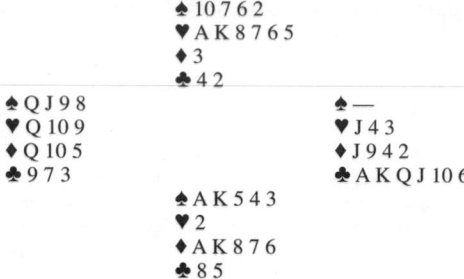

```
WEST            EAST
♥ Q x           ♥ A x
```

and a heart is led against 3NT, declarer does not know even upon seeing dummy whether or not the hand is being played from the right side. In this case the right side is the side that requires the hand with the ♥K to be on lead.

RIGHTS, PLAYER'S. A player does not forfeit his rights if a director is called when an irregularity occurs. Neither does an opponent of the violator lose any rights if the violator or his partner is the first to call attention to the irregularity.

RIGHTY. See RHO.

RIPO. See BLACKWOOD AFTER INTERFERENCE.

RIPSTRA. Over 1NT, the use of an overcall in a minor to show a three-suited hand, devised by J. G. Ripstra. The bid guarantees a shortage in the unbid minor:

```
(a)               (b)
♠ Q 4 3           ♠ A Q 8 4 3
♥ K J 6 2         ♥ K J 6 2
♦ K 10 6 3        ♦ 6
♣ 8               ♣ Q 6 3
```

On (a) bid 2♦; on (b) bid 2♣. The strength qualifications for the bid naturally vary according to vulnerability. It can be made freely at favorable vulnerability and should rarely be made at unfavorable vulnerability.

Some players use the convention with greater emphasis on the major suits, employing it with, for example, a 5-5-2-1 distribution. A disadvantage of the convention is that it has a relatively low frequency. It is more suited to matchpoint events than to rubber bridge or IMP scoring. It is, however, useful in defense against a GAMBLING 3 NT OPENING. See DEFENSE TO ONE NOTRUMP for alternatives.

ROBERT COUP. The unnecessary expenditure of a trump in order to preserve a plain suit card to lead later in the play (analyzed and named by Robert Darvas of Hungary).

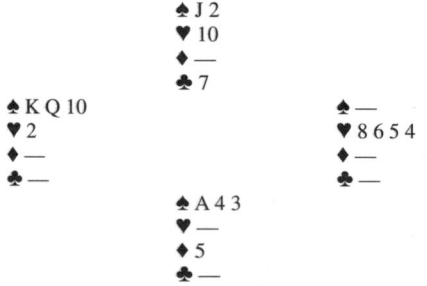

Spades are trump and East leads the ♥4. If South discards his diamond, his only other trick will be the ♠A. But if South ruffs and leads the ♦5, West will be limited to one trump trick.

The coup may be executed early in the play as in this example given by Jeff Rubens.

Against South's 4♠ contract, West leads the ♣9. East overtakes with the ♣10, cashes the ace and, unwisely, continues with a third round of clubs. South ruffs in the closed hand and plays the ♠K ; when the trump situation is revealed, declarer is obliged to play West for completely balanced distribution. The ♦A-K and a diamond ruff, followed by the ♥A-K and a heart ruff, leads to this end position:

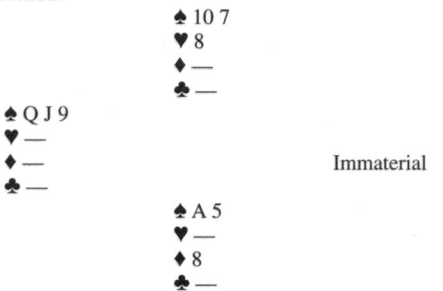

South produces his last diamond and West has no reply. The essential feature of the play was for South to reduce his trump holding by accepting the ruff and sluff in the long hand. The fifth spade could not be of use against any distribution but might get in the way if trumps broke badly. See also UNDERRUFF

ROBERTSON POINT-COUNT. A point count published by Edmund Robertson in 1904.

      Ace counts 7 points
      King counts 5 points
      Queen counts 3 points
      Jack counts 2 points
      10 counts 1 point.

A slight variation of this is the Bamberger point count used by the VIENNA SYSTEM, in which the jack counts one point and the 10 is not counted.

With a total of 64 points in the pack, if both hands are balanced, 39 points should produce a game in notrump or a major suit; and 52 points should produce a small slam.

ROBINSON. A defensive bidding system against the Forcing Club, devised by Kit Woolsey and named after his oft-times partner, Steve Robinson. Double is strong, showing 16+ HCP. A 1♦ overcall shows either a black two-suiter or a red two-suiter. A 1♥ overcall shows either a major two-suiter or a minor two-suiter. 1♠ is natural, but can be very weak. 1NT shows a club-heart two-suiter or a diamond-spade two-suiter. All bids of two of a suit are natural one-suited overcalls

ROBOT BRIDGE PLAYER. A Bendix G-15 computer was built in the shape of a bridge robot, into which Prof.

R. F. Jackson of The University of Delaware programmed bridge skills. It was displayed at a Western Regional in 1958, in a hand requiring a VIENNA COUP to make a grand slam. Opponents' plays were typed into Sputternik, as the robot was called, by the operator and Sputternik typed out his and the dummy's plays.

Three decades later this seems a very minor miracle. BASE III can work out double-dummy play of any hand, not just a particular one. See AUTOMATON BRIDGE PLAYER.

ROCKCRUSHER. A hand with tremendous trick-taking ability.

ROCKWELL TROPHY. For the North American Mixed Pair Championship, donated by Helen Rockwell in 1946; it replaced the HILLIARD TROPHY contested as a four-session event at the Fall North American Championships. For results see Appendix I.

ROLLING BLACKWOOD. A Blackwood variation in which the cheapest non-trump bid (rather than 5NT) is used to ask for kings. Also called Sliding Blackwood.

ROLLING BOX. See TRAY.

ROLLING GERBER. A Gerber variation in which the cheapest non-trump bid (rather than 5♣) is used to ask for kings. Also called Sliding Gerber.

ROMAN ASKING BIDS. A feature of the ROMAN SYSTEM which, in part, is also included in the 1969 version of the KAPLAN-SHEINWOLD SYSTEM. Both systems limit the use of the asking bids to jump bids that would otherwise be meaningless; so if an opening bid of 1♠ is raised to 3♠, 4♠ would be a cuebid and 5♣ would be an asking bid. The Roman responses are:

1st step	No control
2nd step	Singleton
3rd step	King
4th step	Ace
5th step	Void
6th step	A-K or A-Q (rare)

If responder cannot be short in the asked suit, the second and fifth steps are dropped.

An older and better known version of Roman asking bids which is a feature of the KAPLAN-SHEINWOLD SYSTEM, restricts the responses to four steps. First step shows no control; second step shows king or singleton; third step shows ace or void; fourth step shows A-K (rarely A-Q) or perhaps singleton ace. These are called ALPHA ASKING BIDS.

Roman asking bids are also used in certain specialized sequences, the most common of which occur after a 1♣ opening bid and a jump in a new suit by opener. Responder bids according to his holding in opener's suit as follows:

1st step	Two or three low cards
2nd step	Singleton or void
3rd step	A, K, or Q singleton or doubleton
4th step	A, K or Q third
5th step	Four low cards
6th step	A, K, or Q fourth
7th step	Two of the top three honors
8th step	Two of the top three honors fourth
9th step	Three top honors

These are called BETA ASKING BIDS. See also ASKING BIDS; PRECISION ASKING BIDS; ROMEX TRUMP ASKING BIDS; SUPER PRECISION ASKING BIDS; SPLINTER BIDS; VOID-SHOWING BIDS.

ROMAN BLACKWOOD. A 4NT convention which can help to determine which ace is missing if the partnership holds three. The responses are:

5♣	0-3 aces
5♦	1-4 aces
5♥	2 aces of the same color or rank
5♠	2 aces of unlike color and rank

A variation adopted by some BLUE TEAM CLUB users is to reverse the meanings of the traditional Roman responses of 5♣ and 5♠; the 5♣ response is used to show one or four aces in order to facilitate further non-Blackwood exploration of slam on the hands where slam is a more likely proposition.

A subsequent 5NT bid asks for kings in the same way.

The 4NT bidder can easily determine from the previous auction the meaning of a 5♣ or 5♦ response. 5♠ is also unambiguous, but a 5♥ response does not pinpoint the aces precisely. If, for example, a player with the ♥A receives the response of 5♥, he knows that his partner holds the ♣A and another ace.

A British variation is designed to avoid this ambiguity.:

5♥	2 aces of the same color
5♠	2 aces of the same rank
5NT	2 aces of unlike color and rank

This may, however, rule out the possibility of asking for kings. The general advantage of the convention is that it may be effective when the 4NT bidder has a void. If his partner has two aces, it is usually possible to tell whether the void is facing an ace.

When making a decision to go to the six-level, it is usually sufficient to know the number of aces possessed by the partnership. But for grand slam purposes, the identify of a missing king may be vital. For this reason some partnerships abandon the precise identification of the two aces held, using the 5♥ response to show two aces with no extra values and the 5♠ response to show two aces in a hand with extra values. Alternatively, there can be advantages in using these Roman responses in combination with other conventions. See ACE-SHOWING RESPONSES; BYZANTINE BLACKWOOD; ROMAN GERBER; ROMAN KEY CARD BLACKWOOD.

ROMAN DISCARDS, SIGNALS. Odd-numbered spot cards (3,5,7,9) are encouraging. Even-numbered spot cards (2,4,6,8) are discouraging, with a suit-preference message. This was originated as part of the ROMAN SYSTEM. Usually called ODD-EVEN SIGNALS.

ROMAN GERBER. A modified version of the GERBER FOUR-CLUB slam convention. A response of 4♦ shows three aces or none; 4♥ shows four aces or one; 4♠ shows two aces. If the 4♣ bidder continues with the cheapest bid, he asks for kings and subsequently queens in the same way. The next-cheapest bid asks for clarification of the previous response. With one or three of the specified honor cards, responder bids the control he has or does not have. With two honors to be identified, he makes the minimum bid if they are of the same color; the second possible bid if they are unmatched in color and rank; and the third possible bid if both are majors or minors. See

ACE IDENTIFICATION.

ROMAN JUMP OVERCALL. The use of a jump over-call to show a two-suited hand, specifically the suit bid and the next-higher-ranking suit excluding opener's suit. For example, if the opening bid is 1♦, an overcall of

2♥   shows ♥ and ♠
2♠   shows ♠ and ♣
3♣   shows ♣ and ♥

The strength shown is about the minimum for an opening bid or slightly more. Very strong two-suiters are shown by a conventional overcall of 2NT.

ROMAN KEYCARD BLACKWOOD. A form of BLACKWOOD in which the king of trumps is counted as a fifth ace. It has gained in popularity recently among American experts. The responses are similar in nature to ROMAN BLACKWOOD:

5♣   0 or 3 aces
5♦   1 or 4 aces
5♥   2 or 5 aces

In its original version (now obsolete), a response of 5♥ was reserved to show two aces with extra values. The modern interpretation uses 5♥ to show 2 or 5 aces without the queen of trumps while 5♠ shows 2 or 5 aces with the queen of trumps. A minor disadvantage of this method occurs when hearts are the agreed trump suit. If the Blackwood bidder holds only one ace without the queen of trumps he is well advised to not use the convention — a 5♠ response would prove most embarrassing.

An extension allows the 4NT bidder to ask for the queen of trumps after a response of 5♣ (if spades or hearts are trumps) or 5♦ (if spades are trumps). The bid of the next higher-ranking suit (5♦ after 5♣) asks for the trump queen. A signoff in the trump suit denies the queen. A jump to six of the trump suit indicates the queen, while a cuebid shows extra values along with the trump queen.

It is important that the partnership have a firm understanding of which suit is the trump suit before embarking on a keycard auction. A popular method sets the priorities as follows: (a) opener's suit if he opened with a strong forcing action; (b) the agreed trump suit; (c) responder's suit if he jump shifts and then bids keycard; (d) the last bid suit. Again, partnership agreement is most important.

Partnerships must agree how to respond when the 4NT bidder follows with 5NT. Most experts show specific side-suit kings, starting with the cheapest, but some show the number of side-suit kings on the Blackwood principle.

A modern variation, growing in poularity among experts, is to interchange the meanings of the 5♣ and 5♦ response. See KICKBACK.

ROMAN LEADS. See RUSINOW LEADS and FOURTH HIGHEST.

ROMAN MUD. A method of leading from four small cards. The opening leader leads the second highest from his four small cards, then he follows with the highest, then with the third highest and finally plays the lowest.

ROMAN SYSTEM. Developed by Walter Avarelli and Giorgio Belladonna, and used successfully in many World Championships The chief features are:

1♣ opening is forcing, and may show four distinct types of hands. It usually shows 12-16 points with 4-3-3-3 or 4-4-3-2 distribution. After a negative response of 1♦ (usually less than 9 points), the opener bids a major if he can, or 1NT. After a positive response in a suit (minimum of 8-11 points), the opener shows a minimum by a single raise, a rebid of 1NT, or a bid of a new suit on the same level.

Other positive responses are: 1NT, 12-16 points; 2NT, more than 16 points, over which opener rebids conventionally to show his exact point-count.

1♣ may also be bid with (1) 21-22 points and balanced distribution, in which case the rebid will be a jump in notrump; or (2) an unbalanced game-going hand, in which case the opener will jump rebid in a suit and responder rebids conventionally by six steps to show his holding in opener's suit; or (3) a two-suited hand with at least a four-card club suit and five cards in another suit and 17-20 points, in which case the opener will rebid in clubs.

If an opponent overcalls a 1♣ opening, an immediate cuebid by responder shows 12-16 points without a stopper and suggests a notrump contract.

1♦, 1♥, and 1♠ openings are natural (usually at least a four-card suit) and forcing, and guarantee at least one suit of more than four cards. With two suits, the shorter suit is opened (CANAPÉ principle), unless the shorter suit is clubs. With 5-3-3-2 distribution the opening bid is occasionally in the lower-ranking three-card suit other than clubs. A five-card suit may be opened and rebid with a minimum.

With fewer than 9 points, responder makes a single raise or makes the cheapest possible response, both of which are negative. Rebids are natural except for 1NT, which shows a minimum opening with five cards in the negatively bid suit. Other suit responses are positive, showing 9 points or more. Notrump responses are as over 1♣ (except 1♠ - 1 NT, which is negative).

1NT opening shows a balanced hand with 17-20 points. Responses of 2♣ and 2♦ are GLADIATOR. Responses of two of a major or three of a minor are forcing to game, and opener rebids by steps to show support and opening-bid strength; the first two steps show minimum openings with poor and good support respectively; the third and fourth steps show maximum openings with poor and good support respectively. Other responses are natural and limited.

2♣ and 2♦ openings show three-suited hands (4-4-4-1 or 5-4-4-0 distributions) with 12-16 and 17-20 points respectively. A response of 2NT is positive and asks the opener to show his short suit. Minimum suit responses are negative and may sometimes have to be made in a three-card suit. If the suit response strikes opener's shortage, he makes the cheapest possible suit rebid. See also ROMAN TWO DIAMONDS.

2♥ and 2♠ openings show at least a five-card suit, together with four or five clubs. A 2NT response asks opener to clarify his distribution by bidding a three-card suit with 5-4-3-1 distribution, 3♣ with 5-4-2-2, 3NT with 5-5-2-1, four of a minor with 5-5-3-0, or rebidding a six-card suit.

2NT opening shows a balanced hand with 23-24 points. Responses are as over 1NT.

Asking bids are used after a suit has been agreed, usually a jump in a new suit at the level of four or higher. If responder can be short in the asked suit, the responses are by six steps: the first step shows no control, second step shows a singleton, third step shows the king, fourth step shows the ace, fifth step shows a void, and the sixth step shows the ace-king, or occasionally the ace-queen. If responder cannot be short in the asked suit, the second and fifth steps are deleted. Different asking bids are also used in certain special situations. See ROMAN ASKING BIDS.

Overcalls are limited to a maximum of 12 points, and are normally made only on a good suit.

Takeout doubles show 12-16 points. If third hand passes, responder bids his shortest suit if he can do so at the level of one or two. See EXCLUSION BID. Otherwise, normal responses are given. If third hand bids, a double is for takeout.

1NT overcall is equivalent to a 1NT opening bid, although the distribution might be slightly unbalanced. Responses are as over a 1NT opening.

Jump overcall shows a two-suiter, the bid suit and the next higher-ranking, excluding the opener's suit. The distribution is usually 5-5 or 5-6 with a five- to six-loser hand.

2NT jump overcall shows a strong two-suiter, excluding the opener's suit. Responder bids the lower unbid minor and the overcaller bids an unbid suit, holding the bid suit and partner's conventionally named suit, or 3NT with both unbid suits.

Overcalls in the opponent's suit are natural. A jump cuebid shows a very strong three-suiter with a singleton or void in the opponents' suit and a four-loser hand. See also ROMAN BLACKWOOD

ROMAN TWO DIAMONDS. A bid showing a strong hand with 5-4-4-0 or 4-4-4-1 distribution. This feature of the ROMAN system can be used with standard methods. The original range of 17-20 is sometimes increased by one or two points. A 2NT response is positive, asking opener to bid his short suit. Other responses are natural and negative, but may be in an economical three-card suit. If the response is in opener's shortage he makes the minimum possible rebid.

An alternative method of responding, proposed by Marshall Miles, is to respond 2♥ on all weak hands. Other responses are natural and forcing to game. In all cases the opener bids his shortage on the second round, except that a notrump rebid shows a shortage in the suit bid by responder, whether naturally or artificially.

A version of the Roman 2♦ is also a part of BLUE TEAM CLUB. See BLUE TEAM 2♦.

ROMEX TRUMP ASKING BID. This can occur only after a 1NT or 2♣ opening bid. If a trump suit is agreed and the opener either raises the agreed suit below the level of game or bids a minimum number of notrump, it is a Trump Asking Bid (TAB).

Also, if the responder bids a natural 3♥ and 3♠, the opener may jump to 4NT as a TAB agreeing the responder's suit by inference.

The responses to a TAB are:
1st step: could not be worse for the previous bidding
2nd step: one of the top three honors but minimum length
3rd step: no top trump honor but at least one extra trump
4th step: one top honor and at least one extra trump
5th step: two of the top three honors but no extra length
6th step: two top honors and extra length
7th step: three top honors; or the best possible suit
Romex Control Asking Bid. When a trump suit has been agreed, either directly or by inference (perhaps via a splin-

ter bid), following an opening bid of 1NT or 2♣, the opener may make a Control Asking Bid (CAB) to check on his partner's holding in a side suit.

You can make only ONE CAB that asks about first-round control in a suit. Every subsequent CAB inquires only about third-round control.

If the responder's last bid was a raise of the opener's suit, a bid in a new suit is a CAB. If the responder bids a suit and the opener jumps in another suit, it is a CAB agreeing responder's suit by inference.

Here are the responder's replies to a CAB:
1st step: no control
2nd step: second-round control (king or singleton)
3rd step: first-round control (ace or void)
4th step: ace-king-third or longer
5th step: total control
Romex Special Trump Asking Bid. If a 2♣ opener, after receiving a 2♦ response (at most one control), jumps to 3♥ or 3♠, it is setting the suit as trumps and instigating an asking-bid auction. It is called a Special Trump Asking Bid (STAB).

The responder defines his length in the trump suit thus:
1st step: at most one card in the suit
2nd step: two cards
3rd step: three cards
4th step: four or more cards

If the opener bids the next step after the response, it asks for an honor in the suit.

If the responder made a one-step reply, he bids as follows:
1st step: a void
2nd step: low singleton
3rd step: singleton honor

If the STAB response was higher, the reply to the second inquiry follows this scheme:
1st step: no honor
2nd step: one honor
3rd step: two honors (this is *extremely* unlikely)

ROMEX AWARD. See ROSENKRANZ AWARD.

ROMEX STAYMAN. After an opening 2NT, or after second-round 2NT bids to show similar hands of slightly different strengths (see ROMEX SYSTEM), the Stayman inquiry includes a special rebid of 3NT to show both major suits. 3♠ shows a five-card spade suit; 3♥ shows four or five hearts; and 3♦ denies any of the preceding.

After a 3♦ rebid, 3♥ asks for a four-card spade suit, seeking a 4-4 fit.

After a 3♥ rebid, 3♠ asks for clarification, the opener rebidding 3NT with only a four-card heart suit.

This arrangement allows the partnership to locate 3-5 fits in the major suits.

ROMEX SYSTEM. A 2♣ system devised by George Rosenkranz. The distinguishing feature of the system is the use of the DYNAMIC NOTRUMP opening (showing a balanced hand with 19-20 points and six controls or an unbalanced hand just short of the requirements for a 2♣ opening) and the MEXICAN 2♦ opening (showing a balanced hand with either 21-22 points and seven controls or 27-28 points and 10 controls, or a unbalanced game-force with diamonds the longest suit, or a three-suited game-force).

One-bids and 2♣ (artificial, for all other very strong hands) are normal, except that one-bids are limited by the failure to open 1NT. The lack of a balanced notrump opening is compensated by the special one-bid limitation: opener, with a balanced hand, can make a minimum rebid in notrump with 12-16 points or jump in notrump with 17-18 points. An EASTERN SCIENTIFIC structure is used after major-suit openings.

Special methods include: special asking bids, in preference to cuebidding, after a strength- or weakness-showing opening; the Romex raise to show extra values through an otherwise impossible bid of 4NT by the responder; step responses to many strong bids and asking bids; emphasis on slam-bidding devices. See ROMEX TRUMP ASKING BIDS.

In the latest version of the system (1992), the balanced structure is as follows:

19-20	1NT followed by 2NT
21-22	2 ♦ followed by 2NT
23-24	2 ♣ followed by 2NT
25-26	2NT
27-28	2 ♦ followed by 3NT

On the next round, ROMEX STAYMAN is used, together with transfer bids.

Mexican 2♦ Opening. A bid showing a balanced hand with 21-22 points, or a game-forcing hand with diamonds the longest suit, or a game-force with any 4-4-4-1 distribution.

The responses are:

Pass: 0-4 points, relatively balanced

2 ♥: 5-10 points, any shape

2NT: 0-4 points, unbalanced

3 ♣ and higher: 11-plus points and assuming partner opened 2NT with 21-22 points (viz., 3♣ is Romex Stayman, 3♦ is a transfer to hearts, etc.). See TWO-WAY TRIAL BIDS.

RONF. An acronym for Raise Only Non-Force. Used as a response to WEAK TWO-BIDS.

ROPE and ROPI. See BLACKWOOD AFTER INTERFERENCE.

ROSENBLUM CUP TEAMS. A new event added to the World Pair Championships in 1978 in honor of Julius Rosenblum, former president of the WORLD BRIDGE FEDERATION. Although the event is primarily a knockout, it originally had an unusual feature — a defeated team got a second chance, or REPECHAGE. That was later eliminated. For results see Appendix V.

ROSENKRANZ AWARD. Endowed by George Rosenkranz, the Romex Award for the Best Bid Hand of the Year is presented annually by the International Bridge Press Association. It is made to the players who, in partnership, have produced the best bidding sequence. The Award is given only in respect of a hand which occurred in play, whether in a tournament, match or private play. The panel takes into account accuracy, originality and psychological factors. The result in play need not be a determining factor. See INTERNATIONAL BRIDGE PRESS ASSOCIATION AWARDS.

ROSENKRANZ DOUBLE. A convention invented by George Rosenkranz of Mexico to help an overcaller more accurately gauge his holding in light of partner's response. If a player overcalls an opening bid and the next player makes a bid, a double by the partner of the overcaller

shows a raise in partner's suit that includes the ace, king or queen of that suit. If the partner of the opening bidder makes a negative double over the overcall, then a redouble by the partner of the overcaller shows a raise with one of the top three honors. Conversely, if the partner of the overcaller, in either situation, merely raises the suit bid by the overcaller, this indicates that he does not hold one of the top three honors in partner's suit.

The alternative meaning for the double after three suits have been bid is for takeout, showing five cards in the unbid suit and moderate strength. See SNAPDRAGON.

ROTATION. The order in which actions take place at the bridge table. In the bidding stage, the dealer has the first action, followed in turn by the player on his left, his partner, and the right-hand opponent. In the play of the cards, the player to declarer's left has the initial lead. The duty of making the initial lead to each subsequent trick falls on the player whose card was the winning card played to the preceding trick. Any deviation from this clockwise rotation in bidding or play constitutes an irregularity; in tournaments, the director should be summoned when such an irregularity occurs.

ROTH ASKING BID. In response to a preemptive three-level opening, 4♣ asks for the following responses:

4 ♦ = bad suit, bad hand

4 ♥ = good suit, two of top three honors

4 ♠ = good hand, broken suit

4 NT = solid suit

Proposed by Alvin Roth.

ROTH DEFENSE TO ONE NOTRUMP.

Double = majors

2 ♣ = black suits

2 ♦ = diamonds and spades

2 ♥ = hearts

2 ♠ = spades

2NT = four hearts and a 6-card minor

3 ♣ = clubs and hearts

3 ♦ = red suits

Proposed by Alvin Roth.

ROTH POINT-COUNT. See DISTRIBUTIONAL COUNTS.

ROTH-STONE ASTRO. See ASTRO.

ROTH-STONE SYSTEM. Developed by Alvin Roth and Tobias Stone. Many of their ideas have been adopted by tournament players using standard methods. Since the publication of the 1953 book on the system, Roth has modified the system considerably, describing his new ideas in a second book published in 1958. Among the features of the revised system are:

(1) Sound opening bids in first and second position. The minimum requirement is 14 points, including at least 10 high card points, which is about one point more than in standard methods.

(2) Five-card majors in first and second position.

(3) ONE NOTRUMP RESPONSE TO A MAJOR, FORCING by an unpassed hand after a major-suit opening.

(4) A single raise in a major suit is constructive. It shows 10-12 points and is never passed by a first- or second-seat opener. With a void or singleton in a side suit and

10-12 points, responder, if he is an unpassed hand, jump raises to show shortness in the other major (e.g., 1♥-3♥ shows a singleton or void in spades), or jumps to 4♣ or 4♦ with shortness in the bid suit. A strong major raise is shown by a conventional jump to 3♣, which guarantees a minimum of four trumps and 13 points. Opener usually rebids conventionally to show whether or not he has a singleton, or, if not, the number of high trump honors he holds, but he may jump in a new suit as an asking bid.

(5) Two-over-one response (e.g., 2♣ in response to 1♠) normally shows at least 11 points. It is forcing for one round and guarantees that responder will bid again.

(6) Opening bids of 1♣ and 1♦ may be prepared with a three-card suit. After a major-suit response, opener jumps to four of his minor with a strong six-card suit and weak four-card support for responder's major, jumps to four of the major with strong four-card support and a weak minor suit, jumps to four of the other minor (or to 4♥ after a 1♠ response) with a singleton in the bid suit and a strong raise, or jumps to three of the other major with a strong, balanced hand and four-card support.

(7) Jump shift responses are weak, except by a passed hand in a non-competitive auction.

(8) Over one of a suit, a jump to 2NT by an unpassed hand is unlimited, at least 13 points, and a jump to 3NT is BABY BLACKWOOD.

(9) After a third- or fourth-seat major-suit opening, responder jumps to 3NT to show a strong, distributional raise, jumps to 4♣ to show a distributional raise with slightly fewer high cards, or jumps to 4♦ to show a strong raise with no singleton or void.

(10) 1NT opening is standard (16-18). Responses of 2♣ and 2♦ are forcing and slam-try STAYMAN respectively. 2NT forces opener to bid a minor; if responder then rebids a major, it shows a singleton. Jump responses to the three-level are weak, but mildly invitational in the major suits. TWO-WAY STAYMAN is also used over 2NT (21-23), except that 3♣ shows slam interest.

(11) TEXAS.

(12) GERBER over notrump openings.

(13) 2♣ opening is forcing to game. 2♥ is the conventional negative response and 2♦ is an artificial positive response, showing the equivalent of an ace and a king. Responses of 2NT and 3NT show balanced hands with 8-9 and 10-12 scattered points respectively.

(14) WEAK TWO-BIDS with 2NT the only forcing response by an unpassed hand. 2NT and a raise of opener's major are invitational by a passed hand.

(15) 3NT opening shows a strong preempt in one of the four suits. If responder bids 4♣, he warns opener not to bid game in a minor.

(16) NEGATIVE DOUBLES.

(17) RESPONSIVE DOUBLES only after an overcall (e.g., 1♣-1♠-2♣-double is responsive).

(18) WEAK JUMP OVERCALLS.

(19) UNUSUAL NOTRUMP.

(20) Bids in the opponents' suit are sometimes natural. After 1♣ - pass - 1♠, an overcall of 2♣ or 2♠ would be natural.

(21) A takeout double may be light, 10 high card points with 4-4-4-1 or 4-4-5-0 distribution. An immediate cuebid of opponent's suit is equivalent to a strong takeout double, 18 points or more.

(22) When an opponent overcalls 1NT, 2♣ is a weak takeout and double is a strong takeout, 8 points or more, but may be passed.

(23) When an opponent opens 1NT, 2♣ and 2♦ show the bid minor and spades, 3♣ and 3♦ show the bid minor and hearts, and double shows the major suits unless the notrump opening is weak, in which case it shows at least 15 high card points.

(24) After 1♥ or 1♠-pass-1NT, 2♣ and 2♦ overcalls show the bid minor and the unbid major.

(25) After 1♣ or 1♦-pass-1 NT, 2♣ and 2♠ overcalls show the unbid minor with spades or hearts respectively, and double shows the major suits.

(26) In a competitive auction where a sacrifice may be considered, a double of a slam contract at equal or favorable vulnerability shows no defensive tricks.

(27) A balancing bid of 2♣ is equivalent to a light takeout double.

After briefly experimenting with a Strong Club method, Roth added some new features and modifications to the system in *Picture Bidding* (1991):

(28) 1NT -3♦ promises game in a minor; 1NT-3♥ promises slam in a minor.

(29) 1NT-3♠ Strong 3-suiter, forces 3NT and responder shows short suit.

(30) 1NT-2♠ weak minors.

(31) 2NT-3NT weak with long minor.

(32) 2NT-3♠ weak minors, 4♠ good minors, 5♠ slam in minors.

(33) 1♣-2♣ shows 4-4-1-4 with 13-15.

(34) 1♥/1♠ -3♣ strong major-suit raise, slammish.

(35) 2♣-2♠ positive response.

(36) 4♣ good preempt in a major, solid suit plus outside length.

ROUND. A part of a session of bridge at a tournament during which the players and the boards remain at a table. When two boards are played during a round, its duration should be about 15 minutes. Three-board rounds require about 20 minutes; four-board rounds 25.

In rubber bridge, a round refers to the three or four rubbers (or double rubbers) during which each of the players plays with each of the other players as partners.

ROUND HAND. A colloquialism for a hand with BALANCED DISTRIBUTION, particularly 4-3-3-3. Flat and square are also used to describe such a hand.

ROUND-ROBIN. A form of competition in which each of the contesting groups (usually teams, though occasionally pairs) plays against each of the other groups entered in head-on competition. "League" is used as an equivalent term in England.

Round-robin team contests are increasing in popularity in individual playing areas, frequently requiring months to complete. KNOCKOUT TOURNAMENTS occasionally end up in a round-robin of surviving teams, or start with one. Round-robins frequently are used to determine semifinalists and finalists in WORLD TEAM CHAMPIONSHIPS. See CARRYOVER.

When a round-robin fails to establish a winner some tie-splitting device, such as QUOTIENT, must be used.

ROUNDED. A term used to describe the combination of hearts and clubs, these suits having pips rounded at the tops. The converse is POINTED to indicate spades and diamonds.

ROUNDING OFF. At rubber bridge, it is customary to

record the results of a rubber to the nearest 100 points. In America, 50 points are counted as an extra 100, but in Europe it is customary to ignore them. For maintaining a running record of the results of a rubber game, a BACK SCORE sheet is used, showing each player as plus or minus some number of hundreds of points, and this provides the basis of settling the game. Some players use a banker who distributes poker chips at the beginning of a game, and rubbers are settled at the end of each by passing the chips from losers to winners, and they are redeemed by the banker at the end of the session.

ROVER. A method of handling a half table in a MITCHELL MOVEMENT. The Rover is an alternative to the PHANTOM pair and the BUMP MITCHELL. The Rover pair may play in either direction, but North-South is preferable because the movement is easier to administer with a North-South sit-out.

The Rover pair is assigned a number, one higher than the number of full tables in play. After sitting out the first round the Rover pair enters the game by replacing one of the pairs playing in their direction. After playing the round at that table, the Rover pair moves to another table, usually skipping a table up the line. (There are exceptions when the number of full tables is divisible by three) Meanwhile the pair displaced for the previous round resumes its natural position and progression. This continues for as many rounds as there are in the game.

To start the game, boards are distributed only to full tables, as if there were no half table. This means that the boards never sit out, so all boards have the same top and the game can be curtailed at any point without having to factor boards. However, the pairs that sit out must be factored up.

This movement is good for almost all numbers of tables. In a game with an even number of full tables, there is an East-West skip after the halfway round. Although the usual move for the Rover pair is to skip a table up the line, there are exceptions when the number of full tables is divisible by three. The Rover movement for 9 1/2 tables is especially unusual. Guide cards for Rover pairs in most sizes of half-table games, including the 9 1/2, are available from the AMERICAN CONTRACT BRIDGE LEAGUE. The Rover movement can cause complications, the same as all half-table movements.

Here are suggested Rover movements for various size games:

8 1/2 - Out, 2, 4, 6, 3, 5, 7
10 1/2 - Out, 3, 5, 7, 9 ,4, 6, 8, 10
11 1/2 - Out, 3, 5, 7, 9, 11, 2, 4, 6
12 1/2 - Out, 2, 10, 8, 6, 4, 1, 11, 9, 5, 3
13 1/2 - Out, 3, 5, 7, 9, 11, 13, 2, 4, 6, 8, 10, 12
14 1/2 - Out, 3, 5, 7, 9, 11, 13, 4, 6, 8, 10, 12, 14
15 1/2 - Out, 2, 4, 6, 8, 10, 13, 15, 3, 5, 7, 9, 11
16 1/2 - Out, 2, 4, 6, 8, 10, 12, 14, 3, 5, 7, 9, 11

The above are for Skip Mitchells. The following are for Relay Mitchells:

6 1/2 tables: Out, 2, 5, 3, 6, 4
8 1/2 tables: Out, 1 6 2 7 3 8 4
10 1/2 tables: Out, 1 7 2 8 3 9 4 10 5
12 1/2 tables: Out, 3 9 4 10 5 11 6 12 7 1 8
14 1/2 tables: Out, 1 9 2 10 3 11 4 12 5 13 6 14 7

The movement for 9 1/2 tables involves use of a set of guide cards with East-West 10 as the Rover. Pairs 1 and 7 both have unusual moves. The movement for the Rover pair - Out, 3, 5, 7, 1, 4, 6, 8, 9. The movement for pair 1:

1, 2, 9, 4, 5, 3, 7, Out, 6. The movement for pair 7: 7, 8, 3, 1, 2, 6, 4, 5, Out. All other pairs move normally, going in at their normal table after their sit-out.

Both 8 1/2 and 12 1/2 tables lend themselves more satisfactorily to a PHANTOM pair. Pair 9 (or pair 13) in either direction is a phantom.

The Rover movement can be used for another purpose. One or more invited experts can be introduced into the game, using a Rover movement, so that each player plays one board with an expert and sits out one board while his partner does the same.

ROYAL SPADES (popularly LILIES). The spade suit when scored at nine points per trick, in an early phase of bridge whist.

RUBBER. A unit of measurement of games at home or club bridge, hence the expression, "rubber bridge." A rubber must consist of at least two games, but not more than three. The first side to win two games wins the rubber, and a premium is earned on the basis of whether the opponents have won any game. If they have not, the winning side's premium is larger (700 as against 500). If a rubber is stopped before either side has actually won two games, it is called an "unfinished rubber," and there is a somewhat smaller bonus (300) to the side having won one game. If no game has been won by either side but a partial does exist, there is a small premium (50) to the side having the partial.

The word "rubber" is probably borrowed from lawn bowls, which Sir Francis Drake was playing when the Armada was sighted in 1588. "We can finish the rubber and beat the Spaniards too," he is reported to have said. In 1749 Henry Fielding referred to "a rubber at whist" in *Tom Jones*.

RUBBER BRIDGE. The original and the most popular form of contract. However, DUPLICATE and CHICAGO bridge have increased in popularity. Rubber bridge is played for points, which sometimes may represent a monetary value per point.

Tactics at this type of bridge differ from those used at tournament or duplicate. The premium for winning a rubber of two games where the opponents have not won a game is high, and even in a three-game rubber, the premium is substantial. In rubber bridge, therefore, considerable effort is expended toward winning games, and risks in the bidding are taken to secure that end. (But see VALUE OF GAME.)

Penalties can be inflicted by the opponents if too little regard for safety has been observed by a side. These penalties become more severe when the incurring side has won a game, that is, when they become vulnerable. The competitive features of rubber bridge are sometimes overlooked by players who manifest their principal bridge endeavors in the tournament field. Many club players deplore the tendency toward Chicago and long for the days when rubber was the only game played. The disadvantage of rubber bridge is that a rubber may last more than an hour, a great inconvenience to players who are waiting to cut in. However, it has some psychological elements that are lost in Chicago: The rubber bridge player will strive to keep a good partner but get rid of a bad one. See PARTNERSHIP RUBBER BRIDGE and RUBBER BRIDGE TACTICS.

RUBBER BRIDGE TACTICS. Should one be willing to go two down at equal vulnerability to save game? At duplicate this is a matter of simple arithmetic. Each time the sacrifice will show a profit, for other things being equal, one concedes 300 to 500 against a game that is worth 400 or 600. At rubber bridge other things are rarely equal, and simple arithmetic is a poor guide. The issue is determined by the personal equation. With a good partner and mediocre opponents, there is always the risk of a phantom sacrifice, of going down to prevent them from going down.

Opponents may have a certain game, one that would be made in the other room. But there is no other room, and mediocre opponents miss a good many certain games.

Conversely, when partner is the weakest player at the table, the cheapest sacrifice may prove expensive, for what attraction can there be in prolonging a rubber when you start every hand at a disadvantage? Broadly speaking, there is little future in sacrificing at rubber bridge. The profit margin is too narrow, and it is generally best to leave this dubious pastime to the other side.

When the best slams are not so good. How about slams? At duplicate, the odds are clearly in favor of bidding a slam which depends on one of two finesses. At rubber bridge, the decision never rests with abstract figures, but always with concrete personalities.

Who will be declarer, you or partner? If it is partner and he goes down playing it his way, it will be poor consolation to know that he would have made it had he played it differently. It will be more painful still if on the next hand he concedes a needless penalty and then, through bad defense, allows opponents to bring home an impossible slam. Of course, when a good partner is in control, and opponents may be expected to slip in defense, you can bid slams with less than an even money chance. Faces alter cases, and it's the people, not the mathematical probabilities, that make the true odds.

Double the player, not the contract. If an overbidder calls 4♠, double him if there seems any reason for doing so. But if the 4♠ call was made by an underbidder, pass. When in doubt, you double the man rather than the contract.

The statistically minded can look at it from another angle. The overbidder's record shows that he often goes down. He is a bad risk actuarially, and doubling him offers favorable odds.

Not so the underbidder, who seldom gives away penalties. The best tactics against him are to open light, to intervene boldly, and to make a general show of strength. You may put him off, but you are not likely to score much above the line. The underbidder's main contribution to your welfare will come from the games and slams he makes but dares not bid

Confusion - for confusion's sake. Psychic bids can be most rewarding, yet here again everything depends on the uncertain quality of partner and opponents. Each player must be studied separately and treated strictly on his demerits.

In principle it pays to create confusion for confusion's sake, so long as you remain in control. With little defense against opponent's major, but support for partner's minor, you can bid notrump. With support for partner's major you can bid a nonexistent minor. If you are doubled, you have a ready-made escape, and meanwhile you may throw the other side off balance. Sometimes you will steal a hand that does not belong to you. Sometimes you will

mislead an opponent in the play of the hand. But you will draw your biggest dividends on all those occasions, the vast majority, when you bid honestly and are unjustly suspected of bluffing. For it is not psyching but the reputation of psyching which creates confusion in the adversary's mind.

Much the same is true of inhibitory bids. If you have decided to bid 6♠ over partner's 3♠, let us say, you may derive a twofold advantage from a spurious cuebid. Holding a worthless doubleton in clubs, call 4♣ on the way. It may discourage a club lead, which you do not want. Better still, it may induce the lead you do want next time, when you make your cuebid, deliberately, on A-K-J or A-Q or K-x. Of course, you must be careful to throw the bait to the same opponent. First develop suspicion, then exploit it. For it is the essence of rubber bridge to play the players as well as the cards. Every hand forms part of a pattern. In theory every hand must be treated in isolation, but in practice this is not true at all. At roulette red and black have equal chances every time the wheel spins regardless of how many reds or blacks have come up before. This is because the wheel is a purely mechanical device. As soon as the human element is introduced, this no longer applies. Every move is influenced by those that have preceded it, and neither emotion nor superstition can be left out of account.

If you have been doubled into game, you may take certain risks in partscore situations for the next half-hour or so provided that you are up against the same opponents. They will surely hang back, fearful of suffering the same ignominy twice in quick succession.

The partner problem. Handling a weak partner is, perhaps, the most difficult art at rubber bridge. Of course, you want to prevent partner from playing the hand, and of course you don't want him to know that you are trying to prevent him. Fortunately, weak players are singularly unobservant and with a little luck you will get away with it again and again.

On a balanced hand, intending to rebid notrump, there is a good case for opening a weak minor in preference to a strong major. That way you are likely to get the notrump bid in first. At the same time, you may discourage an unwelcome lead. Even a 1♦ opening on J-x-x may have something to commend it. It is a prepared bid - prepared to steer the contract into your own hand.

In defense, a little cynicism is seldom out of place. Opponents are in 3NT. What do you lead from K-7-6 in a suit bid by partner? The 6? Are you sure that he deserves the compliment? Perhaps he was brought up to believe that it is sinful not to lead the highest of partner's suit. Humor him. Never hesitate to do the wrong thing with the right partner. There are times when you can take advantage of partner's shortcomings, reversing on the sketchiest of values or falsecarding wantonly. Opponents may be misled with impunity when partner is not good enough to be deceived.

When not to concentrate. The key to success at bridge at every level lies in concentration. But whereas at duplicate, concentration can never be relaxed, at rubber bridge the good tactician takes an occasional breather, just as champions do at boxing or at tennis. If declarer can fulfill his contract of 2♦ he need not try too hard to make three or four. In terms of money the result will probably be the same, so why waste the effort? An extra ounce of mental energy may be all-important on the next hand or on the one after when the contract is a difficult game or slam. The winning player has his lapses, but he usually knows when he can afford to have them, and is quick to concentrate and to give of his best when the need arises. That is why when he nods the cards so often forgive him. See also PARTNERSHIP PSYCHOLOGY.

RUBBER DUPLICATE. A form of duplicate bridge using rubber bridge scoring. The boards are pre-duplicated by the director in preparation for a straight team-of-four match, and each deal is played simultaneously at the two tables. Play continues exactly as at rubber bridge, ignoring, of course, the vulnerability shown by the boards, until a rubber is scored at either table. The other table is then instructed to add its score as an unfinished rubber, counting the normal 300 for a game and 50 for a partscore. The table at which a rubber was completed is entitled to know whether a rubber was scored in the other room also, but not by which side it was scored.

The final score is calculated by adding the precise results of all rubbers (i.e., not rounded off to the nearest 100) including the unfinished rubber, if any, when play ends. It is usual to play the match in two equal halves, with a change of opponents at halftime.

The director must move constantly between the two playing tables to observe the possibilities that a rubber will be completed. Table 1, for example, must not be permitted to start Board 8 if there is a chance that Table 2 will complete a rubber on Board 7.

Two matches can be conducted simultaneously using the same boards. In a 16-board half-match, Match A would start with Board 1 while Match B started with Board 9. This introduces the possibility of a fouled board, and the director should have an extra pre-duplicated board available to meet this situation.

Rubber duplicate is rarely played except in England, where the Devonshire Club Cup, a knockout contest between leading London social clubs, is conducted on these lines. It has been won many times by the Royal Automobile Club.

RUBENS ADVANCES. A method of using transfer responses to overcalls, advocated by Jeff Rubens in the April 1981 issue of *The Bridge World*. Suit bids below two of the opponent's suit are natural and forcing. There are no transfers when the overcall has not used any space. Examples:

(a)

Opener	Overcaller	Responder	Advancer
1 ♦	2 ♣	Pass	2♦ = hearts
			2♥ = spades
			2♠ = raise

(b)

Opener	Overcaller	Responder	Advancer
1 ♠	2 ♦	Pass	2♥= hearts (forcing)
			2♠= clubs
			3♣ = raise

The responder's strength is undefined, as with normal transfer bids. A similar idea can be used by the responder following a weak jump overcall, with 2NT used as a transfer to clubs. See RUBINSOHL.

RUBINSOHL. A transfer method by responder following an overcall, introduced by Bruce Neill of Australia in a *Bridge World* article in May 1983. His ideas were based on earlier articles by Jeff Rubens, covering different situations, so he used the term Rubensohl. However, a similar idea to replace LEBENSOHL had been used much earlier in the United States by Ira Rubin, so Rubinsohl seems the appropriate name.
Examples:

(a)

Opener	Overcaller	Responder
1NT	2 ♠	2NT = clubs
		3 ♣ = diamonds
		3 ♦ = hearts
		3 ♥ = 4-card hearts
		3 ♠ = 3NT no stopper, no hearts
		3NT = 3NT stopper

(b)

Opener	Overcaller	Responder
1 ♦	2 ♠	2NT = clubs
		3 ♣ = diamonds
		3 ♦ = hearts
		3 ♥ = 4-card hearts
		3 ♠ = 3NT no stopper, no hearts
		3NT = 3 NT stopper.

The idea can be used similarly after simple overcalls. See LEBENSOHL and RUBENS ADVANCES.

RUBIN TRANSFERS. Devised by Ira Rubin as a method of preventing the opponents from finding a cheap sacrifice against a game or slam, and used in the 1966 BERMUDA BOWL.

4♣ opening describes a hand containing either a long, semi-solid major suit with 3½ to 4 honor tricks, or a long minor suit with 2½ to 3 honor tricks and no voids. Responder will usually bid 4♦ to allow opener to show his suit. Major-suit responses are slam tries, and minor-suit responses show a solid suit missing the king, queen, or jack, which opener may raise to slam with three first-round controls.

4♦ opening shows a strong major suit with 2½ to 3 honor tricks. 4♥ is the normal response, while 4♠ shows active interest in a heart slam, but only mild interest in a spade slam. Responses in the minors are cuebids, agreeing either major as trump, and 4NT is BLACKWOOD .

4NT opening shows a strong six-suit hand with one or more voids. Responder bids 5♠ or 5NT with three or four aces respectively.

Game openings in any of the four suits are weak preempts, denying much high-card strength. Alternatively, a hand with greater high-card or playing strength can be shown by an opening bid of one followed by a jump to game. See FOUR-CLUB AND FOUR-DIAMOND OPENING TRANSFERS.

RUFF. To trump a lead of a plain suit, other than the trump suit, winning the trick if no higher trump is played.

RUFF AND DISCARD (or Ruff and Sluff). When a defender leads a suit of which both declarer and dummy are void, the declarer gets a ruff and sluff; he can discard a loser from one hand and ruff in the other. This may be declarer's only way of making a contract when too many losers are present. To compel a defender to give a ruff and sluff, he must be placed in the lead after all his safe exit cards have been removed.

```
              ♠ A 10 9 2
              ♥ A 8 3
              ♦ A 8
              ♣ A Q 5 4
♠ 8                           ♠ Q 4
♥ K Q 10 9 6 4 2              ♥ 7
♦ Q 9 7 2                     ♦ K J 10 5 4 3
♣ 7                           ♣ J 10 6 3
              ♠ K J 7 6 5 3
              ♥ J 5
              ♦ 6
              ♣ K 9 8 2
```

West opens 3♥, North doubles, South jumps to 4♠ and North raises to 6♠. Owing to the unfortunate club break, declarer apparently has a club loser as well as a heart. The two suits are guarded by different opponents, so no squeeze operates, and the only way to make the contract is by compelling a defender to concede a ruff and discard.

The heart lead is won, trumps are drawn and clubs are tested. Finding that he has a club loser, declarer continues by ruffing out diamonds and playing off the remaining clubs, throwing East into the lead. As expected after West's opening three-bid, East has no more hearts and has to return a diamond. South throws the ♥J from his own hand, and ruffs in dummy.

A defensive weapon. It can be winning defense to present declarer with a ruff and sluff even when the defender has safe exit cards in other suits. The usual occasion is when declarer is short of trumps and has to lose the lead before he can develop a side suit:

```
              ♠ K 10 9 3
              ♥ A 9 7 3
              ♦ K J 7
              ♣ A 9
♠ 8 7                         ♠ A Q 6
♥ 10 3 2                      ♥ 6 4
♦ 8 5 4 3                     ♦ A 10 9
♣ J 7 5 3                     ♣ K Q 8 6 2
              ♠ J 5 4 2
              ♥ K Q J 8
              ♦ Q 6 2
              ♣ 10 4
```

East's 1♣ opening is passed to North, who doubles. South responds 2♥, and passes his partner's raise to three. West, with no clue to the killing spade lead, plays a club, which is won in dummy. After three rounds of trumps, South leads a spade to dummy's 10, and the queen wins, West starting an echo.

East may cash a club and exit passively with ace and another spade, expecting to beat the hand if West has the ♦Q, for then the declarer would eventually lose two diamonds. If East follows that reasoning, the contract is made because South has the ♦Q.

By forcing declarer with repeated club leads, East succeeds no matter who has the ♦Q and despite giving South a ruff and sluff. After the ♣Q, East plays a second and third round of clubs. It does not matter in which hand declarer ruffs, for when East comes in with the ♠A he plays another club, taking declarer's last trump. South has only eight tricks, East has three, and must make the ♦A and the long club.

The lesser evil. In the first example above the defender had no choice but to concede a ruff and sluff. Sometimes he has an option, albeit an unattractive one, such as leading into a tenace. If the situation does not lend itself to complete analysis, the defender should prefer to give a ruff and sluff rather than concede a trick in a side suit. This is particularly so when both declarer and dummy have four cards in the same side suit.

```
              ♠ J 8 2
              ♥ A K 9 5
              ♦ A 10 9 7
              ♣ A 8
♠ 9 5                         ♠ A 10 7 6 4
♥ 8 6 4                       ♥ 10 2
♦ 5 3                         ♦ K Q 6
♣ 10 9 7 6 5 4                ♣ K Q 3
              ♠ K Q 3
              ♥ Q J 7 3
              ♦ J 8 4 2
              ♣ J 2
```

East's 1♠ opening is passed to North, who doubles. South lands in 4♥, and the defense starts with two rounds of spades. Fearing a ruff, declarer pulls three rounds of trumps before touching the minor suits. South places East with all the missing high cards, and takes out the third round of spades before putting East on play with ace and another club. East counts declarer for four diamonds in his own hand as well as in dummy, so he gives him a ruff and sluff instead of leading a diamond. South still has to lose two diamonds, and is defeated, but had East returned a diamond the contract would have been made.

On the relatively few occasions when it is better to lead into a tenace than to concede a ruff and sluff, the usual reason is that a ruff and a sluff would enable declarer to establish a long card in a side suit. This suit will usually be distributed 4-3 between dummy and the declarer.

```
              ♠ Q 10 7 4
              ♥ A K 4
              ♦ Q 10 2
              ♣ K 10 9
♠ 9 2                         ♠ A J 3
♥ J 10 8 5                    ♥ 7 6 3 2
♦ 9 6 5 4                     ♦ A J 7
♣ Q 5 4                       ♣ J 7 2
              ♠ K 8 6 5
              ♥ Q 9
              ♦ K 8 3
              ♣ A 8 6 3
```

South opens 1♣ and after a forcing 2NT response lands in 4♠. West leads the ♥J, and South seeks to improve his chances by taking three rounds of hearts before leading a trump to the king and a trump back to dummy. East scores two trump tricks, but then has a choice of rotten apples. South had bid clubs, and if East plays the suit, declarer brings it in without loss and makes his contract. He has already discarded a diamond on the third round of hearts and now loses only to the ♦A. East's choice, therefore, lies between conceding a ruff and discard or playing a diamond.

Declarer had only eight ready tricks, so East willingly gives him a ninth by playing ace and another diamond. South still has to lose a club, and is defeated.

If East concedes a ruff and discard instead, South ruffs in hand and sluffs a club from dummy. The third round of clubs is ruffed on the board, a diamond led to South's king provides a ninth trick, and the long club is the tenth.

RUFF AND RUFF. A rare endgame situation described by Jean Besse, Switzerland, in which the declarer is offered a ruff and discard, and the only winning play is to ruff in both declaring hands.

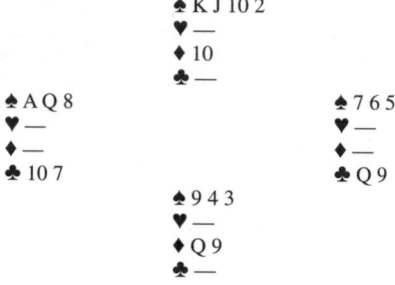

```
                ♠ K J 10 2
                ♥ Q J 8
                ♦ K 10 4 3
                ♣ K 3
♠ A Q 8                        ♠ 7 6 5
♥ 10 4 2                       ♥ K 7 6 5
♦ A J 6                        ♦ 7
♣ A 10 7 4                     ♣ Q 9 8 6 5
                ♠ 9 4 3
                ♥ A 9 3
                ♦ Q 9 8 5 2
                ♣ J 2
```

South plays in 3♦ after West has opened the bidding with 1♣, and the opening lead is the ♥2. The ♥8 forces the king, and the ace wins. A diamond is led to dummy's king, West naturally ducking, and dummy's two winning hearts are cashed.

A trump is continued, and West takes two trump tricks. He shifts to a low club, and South guesses right, putting up dummy's king. He returns a club, and West wins with the ace in this position:

```
                ♠ K J 10 2
                ♥ —
                ♦ 10
                ♣ —
♠ A Q 8                        ♠ 7 6 5
♥ —                            ♥ —
♦ —                            ♦ —
♣ 10 7                         ♣ Q 9
                ♠ 9 4 3
                ♥ —
                ♦ Q 9
                ♣ —
```

West returns a club, the best defense, and the only winning play for South is to ruff in dummy and overruff with his queen. He continues with the 9. If dummy discards any spade on the club lead, West can defend the position. For a related situation, see ONE-SUIT SQUEEZE.

RUFF AND SLUFF. See RUFF AND DISCARD.

RUFFING FINESSE. A play by which a finesse is successful if the missing honor lies behind the finesse holding. With a singleton opposite a holding of A-Q-J, a simple finesse may be taken by leading the singleton and playing the jack, thus providing immediate discard on the ace if this is needed. The other possibility, granting no problem of entry, is to play for the king to be behind the high card holding. In this case the ace is played at the first trick, and the queen led. If the queen is covered, the trick can be ruffed; if not covered a sluff is taken.

The bidding may give some clue to the missing king's location. When the declarer has no information to guide him, he should choose the ruffing finesse in preference to the simple finesse for the reason that the ruffing finesse will lose one less trick when it fails. If the 10 is missing, the ruffing finesse becomes less attractive:

```
            A Q J 3 2
            4
```

The play of the ace followed by the queen cannot produce more than three tricks in all, with the help of two ruffs. Entries permitting, it is slightly better to ruff a low card on the second round and lead the queen later.

The all-out play of finessing the queen on the first round offers the chance of four tricks, with the help of one ruff, if the left-hand opponent began with K-x-x.

Similarly, with a singleton opposite A-K-J-10-x, a first-round finesse must be taken if it is essential to make five tricks in the suit.

RUFFING SQUEEZE. See TRUMP SQUEEZE.

RUFFING TRICK. A trick won by ruffing; usually a ruffing trick is a trick won by a trump which would otherwise be of little or no value. See COUP EN PASSANT; ELOPEMENT. Exceptions are the CROSSRUFF, where both hands contribute to the ruffing values, and the DUMMY REVERSAL, where the normal method of play is reversed and the hand containing the long trumps is used for ruffing. In hand evaluation under the POINT-COUNT system the responding hand, after finding a trump fit with partner, may add substantially for shortness in a side suit. See DISTRIBUTIONAL COUNTS .

RULE OF EIGHTEEN. A rule employed by the World Bridge Federation to define the boundary between light opening bids and HUM (Highly Unusual Methods) methods in which bad hands are regularly opened. If the number of high-card points added to the total of the two longest suits totals 18, the bid is acceptable and not otherwise. Therefore 11 HCP are needed to open a 4-3-3-3 hand, or 8 HCP to open a 5-5-2-1. In England a similar Rule of 19 applies.

RULE OF ELEVEN. A mathematical calculation applicable when the original lead is construed as a FOURTH-HIGHEST one. It is sometimes possible to obtain an exact reading of the distribution in all four hands. The discovery of the rule is generally credited to Robert F. Foster, and was published by him in his Whist Manual. First put in writing in a letter from Foster to a friend in 1890, it is said to have been discovered independently by E.M.F. Benecke of Oxford at about the same time. The rule states: "Subtract the pips on the card led from 11; the result gives the number of higher cards than the one led in the other three hands. " Counting such cards in his own hand and in the dummy, both the leader's partner and the declarer can determine the number of such cards in the concealed hand of the other. The application of the rule is easier than stating it. For example:

```
                    DUMMY
                    K 5 2
    7 led                         A 10 9 3
```

If the lead of the 7-spot is a fourth-best lead, third hand subtracts 7 from 11 and knows that four cards higher than the 7-spot are held in his, dummy's, and declarer's hands. He has three and dummy one, therefore declarer has no card higher than the 7, which can be permitted to ride.

Frequently only the declarer gains from the application of this rule.

```
                    DUMMY
                    A Q 9 5 4
    6 led                         3 played
                    10 7 2
```

Since declarer sees in his own hand and the dummy five cards higher than the 6-spot, he can bring in the entire suit by successively finessing against the king, jack and 8-spot.

The Rule of Eleven often spots a singleton lead.

For example:

                    DUMMY
                    A 10 8 7 4
        5 led   K 9 3 2
                    DECLARER
                    Q J 6

If five is subtracted from 11, the third hand knows that this is the number of cards higher than the 5-spot held by himself, dummy and declarer. He sees six of them so declarer holds none if his partner's lead is a fourth best. Declarer ducks, the king is played, and declarer plays a seventh card higher than the 5. Third hand sees all cards lower than the 5; therefore the lead is not from a doubleton, and can be presumed to be a singleton.

The rule is based on an honest lead of fourth best in a suit. There is a modern tendency to be less revealing on the opening lead, with the lead of a small card indicating a suit whose return is desired and a middle card to indicate a suit to be abandoned. Care must therefore be taken not to apply the rule rigorously when the lead is not certainly a fourth best. See also RULE OF TWELVE, RULE OF FIFTEEN (2).

RULE OF FIFTEEN. (1) A rule of thumb as to whether or not the bidding should be opened in fourth seat. The rule states that fourth hand should open the bidding if the number of high card points and the number of spades totals 15 or more. The theory behind the rule is that if the high cards are likely very evenly divided between the two partnerships, fourth hand should open only with a spade suit that will facilitate his side's competing in the auction. (2) A generalization of the RULE OF ELEVEN which allows third hand to determine what numerical "rule" to apply in conjunction with various types of spot-card leads other than fourth highest. The type of lead employed and the rule to be applied always total 15. For example, the Rule of Eleven is applicable to fourth best leads; the RULE OF TWELVE is used with third best leads; a Rule of Ten would be applicable to fifth best leads. See RULE OF ELEVEN.

RULE OF N-MINUS-ONE. A rule for squeezes published in the *Red Book on Play* by Ely Culbertson. This is his definition:

Count the number of busy cards in plain suits held by one adversary. This number is represented by the symbol N. N-minus-one equals the number of uninterrupted winners the declarer needs for a squeeze.

This rule is applied at a time when the opponent to be squeezed has been stripped of all idle cards. At that point declarer must be capable of taking all but one of the remaining tricks. See RECTIFYING THE COUNT.

There are exceptions to this rule: see SQUEEZE WITHOUT THE COUNT; SECONDARY SQUEEZE; TRIPLE SQUEEZE.

RULE OF SEVEN. Devised independently by Robert Berthe of France and Gerald Fox of Napa CA. It is a guideline for declarer in holding up an ace. If he subtracts from seven the total number of cards in the suit in his own hand and the dummy, the answer is the number of times he should hold up. So with A x x opposite x x x, he should normally hold up once. Holding up twice may permit an effective shift to another suit.

RULE OF SIXTEEN. With borderline hands in fourth

position, the number of spades is crucial. The rule suggests that a bid should be made only if the number of points plus the number of cards in the spade suit totals 16 or more. However, this is on the cautious side. The RULE OF FIFTEEN has merit.

RULE OF TWELVE. A mathematical calculation applicable when the original lead is construed as a THIRD HIGHEST LEAD. The rule states, "Subtract the pips on the card led from 12; the result gives the number of higher cards than the one led in the other three hands." The application of the rule is similar to the application of the RULE OF ELEVEN. Example:

                    DUMMY
                    K 10 7
        6 led   A J 8 2

If the lead of the six-spot is a third-best lead, third hand subtracts 6 from 12 and knows that six cards higher than the six-spot are held in his hand, dummy's and declarer's hand. He has three and dummy has three, so if the lead was third highest, he will be able to win cheaply by topping whatever card is played from dummy. See RULE OF FIFTEEN (2).

RULE OF TWENTY-TWO. This is a way of determining, for players who believe in light opening bids, whether particular hands should be opened. It is based on the WBF RULE OF 18. Add the combined length of the two longest suits to the high-card point count. Always open if the total is 22 or more. Never open with 19 or fewer. Open with 20 or 21 if the hand has two defensive tricks. The disadvantage of this, as with any method that concentrates on long suits, is that 4-4-3-2 is equivalent to 4-4-4-1, 5-5-2-1 is the same as 5-5-3-0, and 5-4-4-0 is equal to 5-4-2-2. See DISTRIBUTIONAL COUNTS and ASSETS.

RULE OF TWO AND THREE. A guide to preemptive opening bids and overcalls. The player taking preemptive action cannot afford to be set more than 500 unless he is saving against a slam. He can therefore risk being defeated by two tricks doubled vulnerable or three tricks doubled not vulnerable.

A simple way of considering this matter is to assume that a vulnerable partner can make two tricks, and a nonvulnerable partner three tricks. Therefore, a player who opens 4♠ should have an eight playing trick hand if he is vulnerable, and a seven playing trick hand if he is not vulnerable.

These traditional requirements are often modified by position at the table, methods of scoring, and other circumstances. They have no mathematical validity, though they are sound psychologically. See PREEMPTIVE BID.

RULE OF X-PLUS ONE. A formula conceived by Ely Culbertson as an aid to planning the play at notrump. If it is desired to establish long cards in a suit, estimate the number of losing tricks in the suit before it can be established (X) and add one to this number. This is the number of stoppers in opponents' long suit needed to be able to cash the long cards.

RULING. An adjudication by the director after an irregularity has occurred at a bridge tournament; in rubber bridge, an application of an applicable law by agreement among the players.

RULINGS OUT OF THE BOOK. In all tournament play, whether at the club level or at the level of international competition, the director should carry a Law book (LAWS OF DUPLICATE BRIDGE) to the table where an irregularity occurs and quote the Law that applies directly from the book. The familiarity of the director with the provisions of the Laws is not in question, but the player is far more apt to accept a ruling against him graciously if the rule is read to him directly. Particularly does this practice avoid the dubious one of a club director giving home town rulings to his steady customers.

RUN. (1) Bidding: to take partner out in a different suit (or notrump) if he is doubled. (2) Play or run (a suit): to cash all the winning cards of an established or solid suit by playing them one after the other.

RUN OUT OF TRUMPS. To exhaust of trumps, usually by forcing the player to ruff. See CONTROL MAINTENANCE.

RUSINOW LEADS. The principle of leading the second-ranking of touching honors, devised by Sydney Rusinow and used by him, Philip Abramsohn, and Simon Rossant in the Thirties. These leads were barred in ACBL tournaments until 1964.

Ever since WHIST was the game, the standard lead from either A-K or K-Q has been the king. This ambiguity often gives third hand an unsolvable problem. Here is only one example of many:

```
              ♠ 6 5 2
♠ K                        ♠ J 10 4
              ♠ ?
```

Against a suit contract by South, West leads the ♠K. If he has K-Q, East wants to play the jack to encourage him to continue. But if he has A-K, East wants to play low to get him to shift. (If East plays the jack, West may try to give East a ruff, and even if he shifts a trick will be lost if South has Q-9-x.) Some players favor the lead of the ace from A-K. Unfortunately this practice substitutes one problem for another. Often an ace should be led against a suit contract without the king. But if this lead convention is used, a guessing situation is created - so much so that one is reluctant to lead an unsupported ace even when it might be right to do so.

A sound solution was proposed thirty years ago by Rusinow — the lead of the second highest from touching honors (king from A-K, queen from K-Q, etc.). Though endorsed by Ely Culbertson, these leads soon fell out of favor in America. They were adopted by many Europeans, however, notably the users of the ROMAN CLUB. The details are:

Ace denies the king (except with A-K doubleton — see next column).

King from A-K. Third hand should signal with the queen or a doubleton.

Queen from K-Q. Third hand should signal with the ace or jack, but not with a doubleton if dummy has three or four small. (Declarer may duck, and partner may continue into his A-J.)

Jack from Q-J; 10 from J-10, 9 from 10-9. Note that this blends nicely into MUD leads of second highest from three spot cards.

With more than two honors in sequence, the second highest is still led (queen from K-Q-J, etc.), followed by

a lower one in most cases. The Romans lead second highest from an interior sequence also (10 from K-J-10, 9 from K-10-9 or Q-10-9). This deserves more study; in any case, the problem is not too important, for the K-J-10 is not usually a desirable combination to lead from, and the fourth highest is perhaps a better choice from the other two holdings.

Rusinow leads are used only on the first trick against a suit contract in a suit which partner has not bid. Later in the hand, or in partner's suit, the highest card should be led from touching honors.

If the touching honors to be led are doubleton, the top card should be led. Then when you play the second honor, partner will know you have no more of the suit. On the following hand, this special feature of the Rusinow leads was crucial. Matchpoints.

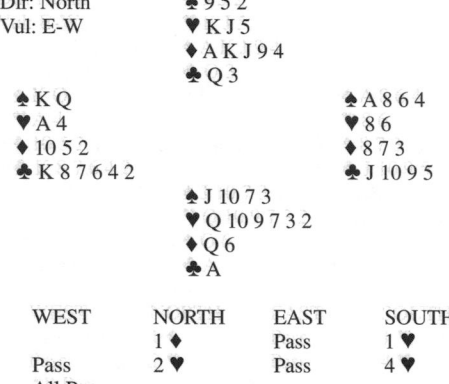

Dlr: North   ♠ 9 5 2
Vul: E-W   ♥ K J 5
             ♦ A K J 9 4
             ♣ Q 3

♠ K Q   ♠ A 8 6 4
♥ A 4   ♥ 8 6
♦ 10 5 2   ♦ 8 7 3
♣ K 8 7 6 4 2   ♣ J 10 9 5

             ♠ J 10 7 3
             ♥ Q 10 9 7 3 2
             ♦ Q 6
             ♣ A

WEST	NORTH	EAST	SOUTH
	1 ♦	Pass	1 ♥
Pass	2 ♥	Pass	4 ♥
All Pass			

Playing Rusinow leads, West opens the ♠K, which East instantly identifies as a doubleton (if it is a singleton, South has a hidden five-card suit). He plays the 8, then overtakes the queen, and returns a spade for West to ruff, setting the contract.

Playing standard leads, East has to guess. He cannot be sure that West would have led low to the second trick holding K-Q-x, for West might have been afraid East would shift to a club. Nor would it have helped West to have opened the spade queen, for East would surely have overtaken and tried for a club trick.

Against Notrump Contracts. If Rusinow leads work so well against suit contracts, should they be used against notrump also? Many think not, because the purpose of a lead against notrump is entirely different.

Against a suit, third hand has to know what specific honors the leader has, so the A-K ambiguity must be resolved. Against notrump, third hand has to know whether partner has led his side's best suit - that is, whether he has honors in the suit led, not which specific ones they are. See JOURNALIST LEADS.

RUSSIAN BRIDGE LEAGUE (VSEROSSIJSKAYA LIGA SPORTIVNOGOBRIDJA) Founded in 1989, by 1992 had a membership of about 2,000 organized in about 30 clubs.

Officers 1992:
President: Leonid Karetnikov
Tel. 095 213 52 26
Fax. 095 201 01 18

S

SAC. Colloquialism for SACRIFICE, as in "We took the sac".

S.A.C.C. A forerunner of PLAFOND, named for its originators and reported by Sir Hugh Clayton (probably one of the originators) in *The Times of India*, July 15, 1914, placing it five or six years earlier than Bellanger's dating of the advent of Plafond in Paris. It does not appear to have caught on outside India.

A side received credit toward game only for tricks for which they had bid. Bonuses for slams were of an order that made it worth running the risk of being set: 1,000 for grand slam, 500 for small slam, 250 for five odd. (This idea of a demi-slam bonus, at times suggested for contract bridge, has always been rejected as overrewarding a timid approach to slam bidding.) Tricks not bid for received no score. In addition to scoring game for tricks bid for to a value of 30 points, a game was credited to the side that, since completion of a previous game, scored a total of 500 by honors, penalties and points for slam. The avowed purpose of this rule was to discourage "flag-flying" and allow earlier completion of a rubber. From this distance in time, however, it would seem that the rule exaggerated one of the flaws in the auction scoring base used in S.A.C.C. and in Plafond – the penalties were already severe in ratio to a 250-point rubber bonus. See HISTORY OF BRIDGE.

SACRIFICE (or SAVE) Sacrifices over opponents' games can be much more profitable at matchpoint scoring than at rubber bridge. You'll never see a successful money player chortling in triumph after going down 500 to stop a vulnerable game; he has saved few if any points and would rather have had whatever small chance there was of defeating the opponents' game. Losing 500 instead of 620 at duplicate, however, can yield a high score.

Even at matchpoints, a sacrifice can earn a good score only when most of the field is bidding game with the opponents' cards. Suppose South holds this hand, not vulnerable against vulnerable:

    ♠ J 8 5
    ♥ 8 6 2
    ♦ J 7
    ♣ K 10 7 6 4

WEST	NORTH	EAST	SOUTH
		1 ♥	Pass
2 ♥	2 ♠	3 ♥	Pass
Pass	3 ♠	Pass	Pass
4 ♥	Pass	Pass	?

4♥ may make more often than not; South has too good a spade fit and too little defense to expect a set. Surely, 4♠ will go down 500 at most. Nevertheless, South should not sacrifice because the auction suggests that most East-West pairs will not reach game.

Say the deal is played in a partscore eight times, in 4♥ twice and in 4♠ doubled twice. If 4♥ makes, North-South score 1 point for letting it play or 3 points for saving; if 4♥ goes down, North-South score 11 points for letting it play or 1 point for saving. So a save stands to gain 2 points or lose 10, and the odds are nowhere near 5 to 1 that 4♥ will make.

Suppose South holds the same hand on this auction:

WEST	NORTH	EAST	SOUTH
		1 ♥	Pass
3 ♥	3 ♠	4 ♥	?

Now the whole field is likely to be in game. Suppose six pairs are allowed to play 4♥ while the other six double 4♠. A correct decision by South is worth 9 points, an incorrect one is worth 3. At those odds, the price is right for a sacrifice, since 4♥ will make perhaps three-quarters of the time.

The most important factor in sacrificing at matchpoints is the spirit of the enemy bidding. Be reluctant to save when the opponents stagger into game, even if you think they will make it; be alert to save against confident auctions when it appears that everyone else will also be in game.

Next in importance is the vulnerability. To be set more than the value of an enemy game is irritating at any scoring, but it is a disaster at matchpoints. Players seldom sacrifice when the vulnerability is unfavorable; if they outbid the opponents, it is with some idea that the contract may make or fail by one trick.

At equal vulnerability, one may loosen up, outbidding the opponents even when going down is certain. Here, there should be some hope of down one; otherwise, too much danger may exist of down three, for a zero. Players cannot be really frisky with sacrifices unless the vulnerability is favorable and down three is affordable. Suppose South holds:

    ♠ 2
    ♥ A Q J 8 4
    ♦ 8 5 2
    ♣ K Q 9 4

WEST	NORTH	EAST	SOUTH
			1 ♥
Dbl	2 ♥	4 ♣	?

It sounds as if East-West have reached a normal game, should South save?

If the vulnerability is unfavorable, South should pass; he has little chance for ten tricks. At favorable vulnerability, South can try 5♥; East-West can probably make game, but cannot defeat 5♥ doubled 800.

What about at equal vulnerability? The single most probable result is that East-West can make 4♠, while 5♥ is down two. Still, a pass is advisable. The combined chance of two events — 4♠ might fail or 5♥ doubled might go for 800 — outweighs the single most likely chance.

A hidden advantage of a sacrifice is that the opponents will push higher and go down. This possibility emphasizes the factor of vulnerability. On unfavorable vulnerability, the defenders are eager to double a save; at equal, they are willing to double; at favorable, they are reluctant and may well be pushed overboard.

At favorable vulnerability, the odds favoring saves are excellent. Players can consider a sacrifice against a confidently bid game whenever they have a trump suit and a little distribution. It is estimated that between one-third and one-half the time, a paying non-vulnerable sacrifice exists against a vulnerable suit game.

Players should avoid unilateral saves — solo flights of fancy. Although a preempt is a relatively descriptive action that makes it easy for partner to sacrifice, other actions are not as well defined:

WEST	NORTH	EAST	SOUTH
	1 ♦	1 ♠	?

♠ —
♥ Q 9 6 4 2
♦ K J 9 6 4 2
♣ 9 3

Only East-West are vulnerable. Perhaps South should bid 4♦, suggesting a save if East-West reach 4♠, but letting North decide.

WEST	NORTH	EAST	SOUTH
1 ♥	2 ♦	2 ♠	?

♠ A 6 4
♥ 8 4
♦ Q 10 7 4
♣ J 9 5 3

South should raise to 3♦. If East-West bid game, North can save with a shapely hand.

♠ 4
♥ J 9 8 4
♦ K 10 7 5 2
♣ J 10 3

Since South will save eventually, he should bid 5♦ *immediately*. If South prevents East-West from exchanging more information, they may land in the wrong major suit at the five level, miss a slam or misjudge by doubling. See ADVANCE SAVE.

♠ 8 7
♥ J 9 8 4
♦ K 10 7 4 2
♣ Q 5

South should bid a preemptive 4♦. (with a strong hand, South would cuebid). South suggests a save-oriented hand, but with slightly too much defense or too little distribution to save himself. See also ADVANCE SAVE and PHANTOM SACRIFICE.

SAFETY LEVEL. The maximum level a partnership is willing to reach, presumably without undue risk, in order to investigate a higher contract or compete against enemy bids.

At times, one partner may wish to suggest a slam. If his hand is not strong enough to guarantee a contract above the level of game, he must make a slam try below game. The game level is then his safety level. If his hand is strong enough to guarantee the safety of an above-game contract (such as 4NT or five of a major suit), he may, if he wishes, make a slam try above game. In this case, the safety level is 4NT, 5♠ or whatever.

When the bidding becomes competitive, the previous bids of a partnership often indicate they hold the strength to reach a certain level. This is their safety level and the contract should not be sold (undoubled) to the opponents below this level. See LAW OF TOTAL TRICKS. For example: South opens with a strong two-bid, forcing to game. If East-West enter the auction, North-South have a safety level at game, implicit in South's bid. North-South will not allow East-West to buy the contract below game unless they feel a satisfactory penalty will be obtained. See also FORCING BID; FORCING SEQUENCES; SLAM BIDDING.

SAFETY PLAY. For the safety play that applies to a specific SUIT COMBINATION, see that heading. This entry emphasizes applications of the safety-play idea.

In a broad sense, a safety play is any play by which declarer tries to reduce the risk of defeat. If the term were so defined, the best play of any hand would amount to a safety play. However, safety play invariably refers to the management of a specific suit; a safety play is the play of a suit to cope with an unfavorable break and minimize the danger of losing the contract.

Most types of safety plays are appropriate only at rubber bridge or IMP play. Since a safety play requires declarer to sacrifice possible overtricks, it is losing tactics at a normal contract at matchpoint duplicate, where overtricks have as much significance as the contract itself. See MATCHPOINT PLAY.

Many plays that are wrongly called "safety plays" only demonstrate good technique and hence are correct at any form of scoring:

(a) K Q 10 9 2   (b) K Q 9 8 3

A 6 4 3   A 5 4 2

In (a) declarer assures four tricks against any 4-0 break by cashing the king or queen first; in (b) declarer should take the ace first in case the left-hand defender has J-10-7-6. These are NOT safety plays. They are simply correct handling of suit combinations.

A true safety play is like an insurance policy: declarer pays a premium — one or more tricks — for protection against a break that would otherwise be fatal.

♠ 7 5 4 2
♥ K 4
♦ A 7 5
♣ A Q 7 5

♠ A Q 8 6 3
♥ 8 3
♦ K Q 6
♣ K 9 2

South plays 4♠, and West leads the ♥J. East takes two heart tricks and shifts to a diamond. South can afford to lose one trump trick, but not two. He therefore starts trumps by cashing the ace, guarding against a singleton king with West. South then reaches dummy to lead a second trump toward his hand; he holds the loss to one trick when possible.

At matchpoint scoring, South could not afford to play safe in this normal contract; he would try for an overtrick with a first-round finesse of the ♠Q.

Some safety plays merely improve declarer's chances; others offer him a sure thing.

♠ 7 6
♥ A Q 4
♦ 7 6 5 4
♣ K J 5 2

♠ A K
♥ K 3 2
♦ A 9 3 2
♣ A 9 4 3

South plays 3NT, and West leads the ♠Q. South counts eight top tricks; a third club trick will give him game. South should lead a club to dummy's king and return a club. If East discards, South can take the ace and lead toward the ♣J; if East follows low on the second club, South plays the 9. If West can win the trick, clubs have split 3-2, and South later takes the ♣A and a fourth club.

Suppose the North-South cards are:

♠ 7 6
♥ A Q 4
♦ 7 6 5 4
♣ K J 5 2

♠ A K
♥ J 10 3
♦ A 9 3 2
♣ A 9 4 3

Here, South can't tell immediately whether he should play safe. After winning the first spade, he should lead a heart to the queen. If the queen wins, South can count eight tricks and should employ the safety play in clubs. If East has the ♥K, South needs four club tricks; he should lead low and take a first-round finesse of the jack.

Some deals offer a chance for a partial safety play.

♠ 8 4
♥ Q 8
♦ A K J 7 5 3 2
♣ 7 5

♠ A Q 3
♥ J 9 4 2
♦ 6 4
♣ A K Q 6

South opens 1NT, and North raises to 3NT. West leads the ♠J: 4, king, ace. When South leads a diamond, West plays the 8. The true safety play, which South might consider at rubber bridge, is a low diamond from dummy, winning if West has Q-10-9-8. At matchpoints, South cannot afford this play, but he can compromise by finessing the ♦J. See also EXPECTATION.

SAINT CROIX. See VIRGIN ISLANDS.

SAN FRANCISCO CONVENTION. A 4NT convention, sometimes called the Warren convention, with responses showing aces and kings in one bid. Aces are counted as three points and kings as one point, and the responses are:

5 ♣	less than 3 points
5 ♦	3 points
5 ♥	4 points
5 ♠	5 points
5NT	6 points, etc.

By inspecting his own hand, the 4NT bidder can almost always judge what his partner's response represents in aces and kings. A response of 5♥ must show an ace and a king, or four kings. The convention results in some disadvantage if the responder's hand is strong. If he has three aces, the response of 6♥ may take his side too high. For a similar idea, see NORMAN FOUR NOTRUMP.

SAN MARINO BRIDGE LEAGUE (Sammarinese Bridge). In 1993 it had 75 members.
Officers 1993:
President: Filippo Filippi
Vice-President Fiorenzo Fiorini
Via G. Giacomini 73,
47031 Rep. San Marino,
Italy.
Tel: 39 549 992114
Fax: 39 549 990434

SANCTION. The permission given by the ACBL to a club, unit or district to hold a duplicate event within ACBL territory. In general a specific sanction to hold a tournament must be obtained from the ACBL well in advance of the date scheduled for the tournament. The ACBL sends the sponsoring organization a form suitable for use in reporting the results of the tournament and this report is used by the ACBL to record MASTERPOINTS won by the contestants.

SANCTIONED GAMES. More than 4000 bridge clubs in North America have been given the right to hold games sanctioned by ACBL. These clubs either give rating point certificates to those who place or transmit the masterpoint data to ACBL via disc or modem if they use computers to score their games.

SANCTIONS. Many thousands of bridge clubs exist in North America. Those that wish to do so may petition the American Contract Bridge League for sanctions to run games that award ACBL masterpoint awards. These sanctions allow clubs to run games awarding masterpoints at a given time on a given day for a year at a time. The game sanctions must be renewed each year.

SANDWICH. A term used in Europe to describe an overcall or bid made in fourth position after both opponents have bid. For example:

WEST	NORTH	EAST	SOUTH
			1 ♦
Pass	1 ♠	2 ♣	

The term emphasizes the danger of bidding in such circumstances.

WEST	NORTH	EAST	SOUTH
1 ♣	Pass	1 ♥	1 NT

A notrump overcall in sandwich is so dangerous that many players use if for take-out, showing at least 5-5 in the unbid suits. That would be the automatic meaning by a hand that passed originally.

SANDWICH DEFENSE, (also called a surrounding play). A group of defensive suit combination plays calling for the play of the second-highest card from particular broken holdings.

NORTH
J x x

EAST
A Q 10

NORTH
10 x x

EAST
A J 9 or K J 9

NORTH
9 x x

EAST
K 10 8 or Q 10 8

In each case dummy's highest card is "sandwiched" by the second and third cards held by East. East must lead his second card, the top of the sandwich, to neutralize dummy's card. The importance of the play can be seen by putting appropriate combinations in declarer's hand: in (1) K-x-x; in (2) Q-x-x (or A-Q-x), in (3) A-J-x.

The same plays must be made if these positions are turned 180 degrees, with the lead in the West hand and the card to be sandwiched hidden, but the play is less obvious.

For a similar play by the declarer, see BACKWARD FINESSE.

SANS ATOUT. Notrump. The term is French.

SAUDI ARABIA. See ARABIAN BRIDGE FEDERATION.

SAVE. See SACRIFICE.

SCANDINAVIAN CHAMPIONSHIPS. See NORDIC CHAMPIONSHIPS. For results see Appendix IV.

SCANIAN SIGNALS. A combination of standard signals and upside-down signals in an attempt to get the best of both worlds.

Use normal signals unless:

(a) Dummy has a finessable card:

```
              J 7 4 2
  A K 10 5                  Q 8 3
              9 6
```

After the lead of the ace or king, according to method, East signals upside-down with the three and West can lead the ten.

(b) The opener is known to be short or the signaller is known to be long:

```
              A J
  8 7 3                      K Q 10 4
              9 6 5 2
```

The 8 is led, top of nothing, and dummy plays the ace. Signal upside-down with the 4.

Devised by Anders Wirgren.

SCHENKEN SYSTEM (or SCHENKEN CLUB). An artificial 1♣ system devised by Howard Schenken, New York City, and played by him in World Championship competition in partnership with Peter Leventritt. The main features of the system are:

(1) 1♣ opening. Forcing, and used on almost all strong hands. It shows a minimum of 17 high-card points or the distributional equivalent. There are three types: balanced notrump type with 19-22; slightly unbalanced hand with 17 or more; strong distribution with 14 or more.

1♦ is the conventional negative response, usually 0-6 points. 2♣ is also artificial, showing a semi-positive response of 7-8 points, including at least one king or ace, and promising a rebid. Other responses are positive, natural, and forcing to game. After an overcall up to 3♦, a double is "positive," for takeout, and shows at least 9 points.

After a 1♦ negative response, showing in principle fewer than 7 points but perhaps 7 or 8 without the requirements for a 2♣ response: a non-jump suit rebid may be passed; a jump suit rebid is forcing for one round; a 1NT rebid shows 19-20; a 2NT rebid shows 21-22. STAYMAN is used after a 1NT response or rebid.

(2) One bids in other suits are limited, with a maximum of 16 points. Responder normally passes with less than 8 points.

All raises and notrump responses are limited and non-forcing. A jump to game in a major may be based on high-card strength or distribution, because the limited opening has excluded slam chances. 3♣ response to a major is equivalent to a strong raise (16-17 points including distribution) and requests opener to bid a singleton.

(3) 1NT opening is standard (16-18). 2♣ response is non-forcing STAYMAN. 2♦ shows an unbalanced responding hand (with a singleton or void), no four-card major, is game forcing and requests opener to show major suit stoppers.

(4) 2♣ is a natural opening with at least a good five-card club suit. A response of 2♦ asks opener to show a four-card major.

(5) 2♦. An artificial forcing opening bid used to locate specific honors. A 2♥ response denies an ace; other minimum responses are ace-showing, except that 2NT shows the heart ace. With two aces, responder jumps in the higher ranking ace with touching aces, 3NT with non-touching aces, or 4♣ with the black aces. The opener follows with minimum rebids to locate kings and queens in the same way.

A 2NT rebid over 2♥ shows 23-25, and may be passed. A 3NT rebid shows 26-27.

(6) 2♠ and 2♥ are weak two-bids, 8-12 points and a suit of reasonable strength. 2NT is the only forcing response.

(7) 2NT. Shows a minimum of five cards in each minor suit with 10-12 high card points not vulnerable, 13-16 high card points vulnerable.

(8) 3NT opening is based on a solid minor suit with 8-9 playing tricks and no side suit worse than Q-x.

(9) 3♣. A solid six- or seven-card suit, 10-15 points.

(10) Preemptive jump overcalls depending on the vulnerability.

SCHROEDER SQUEEZE. A triple trump squeeze without the count in a three-card position. This unique ending was executed in play by Dirk Schroeder of Wiesbaden, Germany.

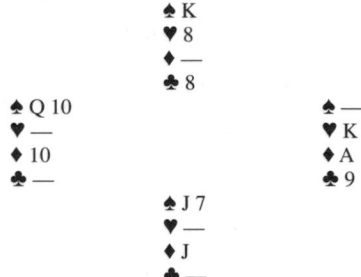

With spades trump, and the lead in North, on the lead of the ♠K East was squeezed. If he threw the winning heart or club South would have a winner to lead from dummy at the twelfth trick. If he threw the ♦A, South would ruff something and score his ♦J at the finish. The complete deal was:

In 3♠ doubled the defense led two rounds of clubs. South ruffed, entered dummy with a high spade, finessed the ♥10, and surrendered a diamond. After a third round of clubs was ruffed in the closed hand South ruffed a diamond, finessed the ♥Q, and led the ♥A. West ruffed and led a diamond which was ruffed in dummy to produce the ending shown.

SCHWAB CUP. For the World Pairs Championship, first contested in Cannes in 1962. Originally presented by Charles M. Schwab in 1933 for contest between the United States and England (see ANGLO-AMERICAN MATCHES). The trophy was redonated to the World Bridge Federation by the heirs of Ely Culbertson. For results of World Pairs, see Appendix V. For results of Anglo-American matches, see Appendix IV.

SCIENTISTS vs TRADITIONALISTS. Three matches have been held.

(1) New York 1965. Scientists (Roth-Stone; Mitchell-Stayman; Jordan-Robinson) defeated Traditionalists (Murray-Kehela; Becker-Hayden; Mathe-Schleifer) by 53 imps over 180 deals.

(2) London 1990. Scientists (Soloway-Goldman; Garozzo-Eisenberg) defeated Traditionalists (Zia, Chagas, Wolff, Forrester, rotating) by two sessions to one, although trailing in IMPs.

(3) London 1992. Scientists (Hamman-Wolff; Rodwell-Meckstroth;) defeated Traditionalists (Chagas-Branco; Forrester-Robson) by 70 imps over 128 deals, winning a $50,000 prize.

SCISSORS COUP. A play aimed at cutting the opponents' communications, usually in order to prevent a ruff (sometimes called less descriptively "the coup without a name").

```
                  ♠ A 10
                  ♥ J 9 7 3
                  ♦ J 2
                  ♣ K Q 10 7 6
♠ 8 7 5 2                          ♠ Q J 4 3
♥ 6 5                              ♥ A 8
♦ Q 6 3                            ♦ A K 10 8 5 4
♣ 9 8 5 2                          ♣ 3
                  ♠ K 9 6
                  ♥ K Q 10 4 2
                  ♦ 9 7
                  ♣ A J 4
```

South plays in 4♥ after East has opened the bidding with 1♦. South feels happy when it appears that there are only three losers, but feels much less happy when East wins the opening diamond lead with the king, and shifts to the ♣3. It is obvious that this is a singleton and that West has a diamond entry to give his partner a ruff.

South must try to cut the diamond communication, so he cashes the ♠ A-K and leads the ♠9. Dummy's diamond is discarded, allowing East to win, and the defense can make only one more trick. South's play succeeds whenever East has both missing spade honors, or if East has a tripleton queen and fails to unblock.

SCORE. (1) Noun: the number of game or premium points earned as a result of the bidding and play of a hand, rubber, or session of bridge. (2) Verb: to record the score.

There is slight difference, due to the nature of the games, between the scoring at rubber bridge, CHICAGO, and tournament bridge. The latter, too, has different scoring procedures and values, depending on the type of event.

See BOARD-A-MATCH SCORING; CUMULATIVE SCORE; INTERNATIONAL MATCH POINTS; LAWS (Laws 75 to 84); LAWS OF DUPLICATE (Laws 73, 74); MATCHPOINT; MATCHPOINT SCORING.

SCORECARD. See PICK-UP SLIP; SCORE PAD; RE-CAPITULATION SHEET. A personal (or private) scorecard used in tournaments is called a CONVENTION CARD; when used in PARTY or PROGRESSIVE BRIDGE, it is called a TALLY.

SCORE PAD. A printed tablet of sheets of paper used to keep a record of the scores in a game of rubber or Chicago bridge. Score pads come in various shapes and sizes, and some are imprinted with the name of the club at which they are used, but they are all ruled with printed lines, leaving spaces for entering game and partial score results and extra premiums such as undertrick penalties and slam and rubber bonuses and honors.

In North America each sheet of the pad will have a large cross at the top, like a letter X, so that players can keep track of the deal number at Chicago.

SCORE SHEET. In club games, the summary sheet on which the MATCHPOINTS won by a pair are entered for ease in totaling; in larger tournaments, the RECA-PITULATION SHEET, to which the scores are posted from the PICK-UP SLIPS. These are seldom used in tournaments any longer because most tournaments are scored by computer programs.

SCORER, OFFICIAL. See TOURNAMENT DIREC-TOR.

SCORESLIP. A printed form on which the results of a round of duplicate play are entered. Caddies collect the scoreslips after each round and give them to the director, who enters the scores either in the computer or on a re-cap sheet. See SCORING FORMS, TRAVELING SCORESLIP.

SCORING. Tallying the results of a game or event. At most tournaments throughout the world today, scoring is done by computer. Several excellent programs have been prepared, and scores are now available to the competitors within only a few minutes of the finish of the game. Whereas high tops on a board were extremely difficult to score when scoring was done manually, high tops are now common because they are child's play for computers. Today's sophisticated computer programs even allow the director or scorer to rearrange the movement if an irregularity forces changes.

Whether the scoring is done by computer or manually, the system of obtaining the results for each round is the same in general. In games where traveling scoreslips are used, the slips are picked up after the last time the board attached to that slip is played. In games where pickup slips are used, the slips are picked up after each round. With traveling slips, scoring is done during and after the last round. With pickup slips, the scores can be entered either on a recap sheet or on the computer after each round.

At many clubs scoring is still done manually. As each board comes out of play, the traveling scoreslip is matchpointed by the director, the scorer or a volunteer. The scores from each board are posted on a recap sheet.

When all the scores are posted, each board is matchpointed. When all the boards have been matchpointed, all the scores are added and crosschecked. If the scoresheet is in balance, then the rankings are assigned. Sometimes the starting positions for the next session also are placed on the scoresheet if the event is a multiple-session event. If pickup slips are used, the scores can be entered round-by-round, but the matchpointing, adding and ranking still must be done.

If the game is scored by computer, the scorer merely enters all the scores as they become available. When all the scores are entered, the scorer keys the necessary command and the computer does the rest — matchpointing, adding and ranking. The program is set up so that the computer also can provide printouts of the scoring of the event.

SCORING ACROSS THE FIELD. A method of scoring a multi-section MATCHPOINT event designed to prevent inequitable score comparisons when the results in one section are at extreme variance with the results in other sections. The score on each board is matchpointed not just against other contestants in the same section but against the contestants in all sections playing in the same direction.

SCORING CORRECTIONS. These are provided for in the regulations concerning tournament bridge. ACBL regulations in this area changed radically in 1994. At ACBL events, the score correction period for scorer and player errors expires at the announced starting time of the next session for PLAY-THROUGH events and one hour before the announced starting time of the session following a qualification. For the last (or only) session of an event, the correction period expires 24 hours after the completion of the event or 30 minutes after the completion of the last event of the tournament. Note that this is in effect for scorer errors as well as player errors. Once the correction period expires, no more score corrections can be made. This is a major change from the past — scorer's errors were subject to correction at any time through the end of the tournament.

The appeal period for or of a director's ruling expires 30 minutes after the completion of the session or at the announced starting time of the next session, whichever is earlier.

The correction period for scoring errors is set forth as follows in Law 79C of the LAWS OF DUPLICATE BRIDGE:

An error in computing or tabulating the agreed-upon score, whether made by a player or scorer, may be corrected until the expiration of the period specified by the sponsoring organization. Unless the sponsoring organization specifies a later time, this correction period expires 30 minutes after the official score has been completed and made available for inspection. An earlier time may be specified when required by the special nature of a contest.

Corrections are made by the scoring staff whenever the scoreslip is clearly in error - i.e., shows incorrect vulnerability, incorrect addition, etc., or when the slip has been incorrectly transcribed. When the correction involves a question of the results themselves — whether a contract was defeated one or two tricks, or whether extra tricks were scored — the correction may be made, within the limits of the correction period, only if there is reasonable

proof that a different score was achieved at the table. Entries on private scorecards of both pairs usually is considered satisfactory proof. See LAWS OF DUPLICATE, Law 75.

At rubber bridge, the rules set a time limit beyond which a correction may not be claimed — in most cases, after the score of the rubber has been determined and agreed upon.

SCORING FORMS. The most common scoring form, used at most clubs in North America and much of the rest of the world, is the traveling scoreslip. One such scoring form is inserted into each board during the first round of play. Each time the board is played, the North player enters the result and the pair numbers on the slip. At the conclusion of play, the slip is matchpointed in preparation for being copied onto the recap sheet or the computer.

The recap sheet, also known as the recapitulation sheet, is used when manual scoring is done. It is a large sheet wide enough to permit the entry of all boards in play and long enough to permit the entry of all pairs — or teams — in play. The recap sheet when a computer is used is printed upon command by the computer.

Another common scoring form is the pickup slip, used for entering the scores of a round at tournaments and some clubs. The pickup slip has spaces for the two or three board numbers for the round, the key pair numbers, the contracts, the fate of the contracts and the scores. These are collected at the conclusion of each round and immediately copied on the recap sheet or fed into the computer.

In team events of head-on competition, each pair keeps a running score of the results on the boards they play, and verification of these slips at each table makes it possible for each team to determine its own score, either in total point or IMP scoring. See PICKUP SLIPS, RECAPITULATION SHEET, TRAVELING SCORESLIP.

SCORING TABLE. The current scoring table is set out in LAWS (Law 81) and LAWS OF DUPLICATE (Law 77). See also FRENCH SCORING and SCORING VARIANTS. Today's scoring table includes few deviations from the original developed by Vanderbilt in 1925, having survived considerable tinkering, especially in the 1932 code. The 1927 Laws provided that each trick in a notrump contract was worth 35 points; that the premium for making a doubled contract was increased from 50 to 100 if vulnerable (if redoubled, the premiums were 100 and 200); and the penalties for undertricks increased as the tricks won fell farther short of contract, as follows:

PENALTIES

Undertricks (Scored in Adversaries' honor score):

	Points
If Undoubled (When Declarer is Not Vulnerable)	
per trick	50
If Undoubled (When Declarer is Vulnerable)	
for first trick	100
for subsequent tricks	200
If Doubled (When Declarer is Not Vulnerable)	
first two tricks, per trick	100
for third and fourth tricks, per trick	200
for subsequent tricks, per trick	400
If Doubled (When Declarer is Vulnerable)	
for the first trick	200
for subsequent tricks, per trick	400

Redoubling doubles the doubled premiums and penalties.

Partly on the theory that the higher scores were largely responsible for the enormous popularity of contract bridge, the 1932 Laws sharply increased slam bonuses and also increased penalties, with nonvulnerable undertricks as well as vulnerable undertricks punished on a rising scale.

Furthermore, the value of tricks made in notrump contracts alternated: first, third, fifth, and seventh trick were worth 30 each; the second, fourth, and sixth, 40 each. Also, the premium for making a doubled contract was dropped.

The distortions imposed by this inflated scoring were corrected within three years – the shortest period ever for the issuance of a new Laws code. In the forty years following the issuance of the 1935 code, the only change in scoring was the restoration in the 1943 Laws of a bonus for making a doubled contract, 50 points whether or not vulnerable. The current codes, established in 1987 for Duplicate Bridge and in 1993 for Contract Bridge, embody two changes:

(1) Non-vulnerable doubled penalties for defeats by four or more tricks became 800, 1100, 1400, etc. instead of 700, 900, 1100, etc. (Redoubled penalties are twice those numbers.)

(2) The bonus for making a redoubled contract was increased from 50 to 100.

In the contract bridge laws the bonus for having a partscore in an unfinished rubber was increased from 50 to 100.

SCORING VARIANTS. Several kinds of scoring variants have been introduced that are aimed at making tournament bridge or rubber bridge a better competition. Among the more important are: (1) FRENCH SCORING, to make four of a major and 4NT of equal value, (2) PENALTY LIMITS in TOTAL POINT SCORING and PROGRESSIVE BRIDGE to limit the SWING on one hand, (3) Different TOPS in final competition of multi-session events or all sessions of important tournaments. (4) IMPS FOR PAIR GAMES, to make conditions comparable to INTERNATIONAL MATCHPOINTS. (5) HYBRID SCORING to combine advantages of BOARD-A-MATCH and aggregate scores in team events.

SCOTTISH BRIDGE UNION. The Union is divided into six regional districts, and had a membership in 1992 of about 5,000. It is a member of the British Bridge League, and its players have often represented Britain in international events. Scottish victories in the CAMROSE TROPHY are listed under that heading. The equivalent event for women's teams, the Lady Milne Cup, was won by Scotland in 1980, 1984, 1986 and 1992.
1992 Officers:
President: Donald Falconer
Secretary: Tom Workman,
32, Whitehaugh Drive
Paisley PA1 3PG
Scotland.
Tel. 44 41 887 1903.

SCRAMBLED MITCHELL MOVEMENT. A modification of the MITCHELL MOVEMENT, used when it is desired to produce one winning pair. Pairs play some boards North-South and the rest East-West. This is ac-

complished by switching the arrows designating North so that they point to the original East simultaneously at the end of certain rounds. The original East-West pairs, having adopted a moving pattern, continue to move, and the original North-South pairs remain at their tables, even though the arrows have been switched and they are playing the East-West hands.

Arrow-switching arrangements devised by Russell Baldwin, George Beynon, Frank Farrington and Lawrence Rosler may be used but are obsolescent. Modern research by Olof Hanner, using computer analysis, recommends the following:

With odd number of tables:

Tables	Arrow East in rounds
7	6, 7
9	6, 8, 9
11	7, 8, 10, 11
13	7, 9, 12, 13
15	7, 10, 12, 14, 15

With even number of tables using relay-and-byestand:

Tables	Arrow East in rounds
6	5, 6
8	4, 7, 8
10	4, 6, 9, 10
12	5, 7, 11, 12
14	7, 9, 10, 11, 14

(But Table 1 does not switch. It is sharing with the last table).

With even number of tables using a skip:

Tables	Arrow East in rounds
6	5
8	2, 3, 5, 6, 7
10	2, 5, 6, 7, 8, 9
12	3, 5, 9, 10
14	4, 5, 10, 12

Frequent arrow-switching is a controversial matter. A mathematical paper by Dr. Ross Moore of Sydney, Australia, asserts that "Too many arrow-switches spoil the balance."

SCRAMBLING. (1) The art of maneuvering into a tolerable contract when the opponents are intent on collecting a low-level penalty. This often calls for the use of an SOS REDOUBLE. One of the commonest situations occur when 1NT is doubled for penalties.

Here is an example:

	WEST	EAST	
	♠ A Q 6 2	♠ J 5 4	
	♥ A K 7 6	♥ 4 3	
	♦ 8 5	♦ J 7 6 4 2	
	♣ J 9 4	♣ 6 5 2	

WEST	NORTH	EAST	SOUTH
1 ♣	Dbl	Pass	Pass
Redbl	Pass	1 ♦	Dbl
Redbl	Pass	1 ♠	Pass
Pass	Dbl	Pass	Pass
Pass			

The two redoubles are both SOS, and the best spot is reached. West will probably make six tricks. See DEFENSE TO DOUBLE OF 1NT.

(2) An attempt to score extra trump tricks by ruffing in the long trump hand with trumps that would otherwise be losers.

SCRAMBLING PLAYS, SCRAMBLING SIGNALS.

See DECEPTIVE PLAY.

SCRATCH. In pairs play, to place high enough in a section or overall standings to earn masterpoints. (colloq.)

SCREEN. An opaque barrier placed diagonally across the bridge table so that no player can see his partner. Perforce each player can see only one opponent. The screen has an opening in the center where the board in play is placed. Directly above the board is some sort of curtain arrangement that can be lifted or pulled aside once the bidding is complete and the opening lead has been made. This permits all players to see the cards being played, but the opening is shallow enough that the players still cannot see their partner's face. The screen extends to the floor, blocking partners' feet from each other, the result of a foot-tapping incident in the 1975 Bermuda Bowl (see BERMUDA INCIDENT). The bidding is done by BIDDING BOX.

Bids from one side of the table are revealed to the players on the opposite side by using a TRAY. Since both bids are "trayed" to the other side of the table simultaneously, it is usually difficult to discern who huddled.

Screens were used for the first time by the ACBL during the Vanderbilt Knockout Teams in 1974. The first appearance of screens at a world championship took place at the 1975 Bermuda Bowl in Bermuda. At first there was a great deal of controversy about the use of screens. Those who opposed their use felt that screens would create the public impression that a lot of cheating takes place in high-level bridge. They also felt that screens would be distracting and dehumanizing. Those in favor felt that screens would forestall charges of cheating (see CHEATING ACCUSATIONS).

However, screens received almost unanimous acclaim from the players who used them right from the outset. The players felt it made competing ethically much easier – they no longer had to worry about making facial expressions, they no longer had to bend over backward because of partner's huddle – they no longer knew when partner huddled. Certain rule violations, such as leads out of turn and bids out of turn became very rare because only one side of the table was involved at a time and such violations could be adjusted without any improper information being transmitted to partner. Cheating accusations have been virtually non-existent with screens in use. As a result of these benefits, screens are used in late rounds of almost all major team and some pair championships, and in all world and international championships. See FRANCO BOARDS.

SCREEN-MATE When screens are in use, the opponent on one's own side of the screen.

SCRIP. Financial certificates issued by the ACBL for use as prizes at tournaments. The certificates may be used to purchase bridge supplies, pay ACBL dues or pay for tournament entries.

SEAT. The position which a contestant takes at a table; usually designated by one of the four principal points of the compass, North, South, East, or West. The first two and the last two are partners, and each pair is the opponent of the other pair.

SEATING ASSIGNMENTS. At duplicate tournaments,

the ENTRIES sold to the players carry a section designation, a table number, and a direction. These are the seating assignments. For subsequent sessions of the same event, players either take their original seating assignments and await DIRECTOR'S INSTRUCTIONS, or pick up a new entry blank or GUIDE CARD for the subsequent session.

SECOND GAME. The second game of a rubber. Two games are required to win a rubber, and at the conclusion of a rubber a side may have won one, two, or no games, during that rubber. The winning of any second game immediately ends the rubber.

SECOND GUESSER. See RESULT PLAYER.

SECOND HAND. (1) The player to the left of the dealer. (2) The player who plays second to a trick.

SECOND-HAND PLAY. The old whist rule of *second hand low* is sound enough as a guide and gains in many positions:

```
              A 4 2
J 6                        K 10 8 3
              Q 9 7 5
```

South, the declarer, leads the 2 from dummy. If East plays the king, South can win three tricks; if East plays low, South wins two tricks.

```
              J 6
A Q 8 3                    9 4
              K 10 7 5 2
```

South leads the deuce from his hand; West gains by playing low.

In a suit contract, declarer leads a possible singleton toward a suit in dummy headed by K-Q or K-J. Unless the left-hand defender sees an obvious reason to grab the ace (such as having the setting trick to cash in another suit), he should duck promptly. To play the ace may benefit declarer, who avoids a guess if dummy has K-J or sets up two tricks if dummy has K-Q.

```
                    ♠ J 9 6 4
                    ♥ K Q 5 3
                    ♦ 7 5
                    ♣ J 6 4
    ♠ 5                              ♠ K 2
    ♥ A 10 7 2                       ♥ J 9 6 4
    ♦ Q 10 8 4 2                     ♦ A 9 3
    ♣ K 9 3                          ♣ Q 10 7 5
                    ♠ A Q 10 8 7 3
                    ♥ 8
                    ♦ K J 6
                    ♣ A 8 2
```

WEST	NORTH	EAST	SOUTH
			1 ♠
Pass	2 ♠	Pass	4 ♠
All Pass			

West leads the ♦4, and East wins the ace and returns a diamond to the king. South elects to cash the ♠A and next leads a heart. Even though declarer has a singleton, West can defeat the contract only by playing low.

A prompt duck is often best in the reverse situation:

when declarer leads a singleton from dummy.

Second hand low has many exceptions. Following are the most important reasons to play second hand high:

(1) To win a trick at no cost:

```
                  Q 5
       K J 9 4 2
```

Declarer leads low toward the Q-5. West should take the king unless he desperately wants East on lead or thinks East may have the singleton ace.

```
                  K 6 4 2
       A Q J 8
```

Declarer leads low toward the K-6-4-2. A duck by West is unlikely to gain and may lose the ace.

(2) To assure a later trick:

```
                  K 7 5
       Q J 4
```

Declarer leads the 5 from dummy. East should split his honors to assure one trick.

(3) To give partner information:

```
                  9 6 3
       A 4 2              J 10 8 7
                  K Q 5
```

Declarer leads the 3 from dummy. East should play the jack, promising a sequence. When West captures an honor with the ace, he can safely return the suit. See PLAY FROM EQUALS.

(4) To prevent a suit establishment:

```
                  A J 10 7 5
       K 8 3              Q 9 6
                  4 2
```

Dummy has no entry outside this suit. If South leads the deuce, West must play the king, and South can take only one trick. West would also play high from Q-8-3. If West instead plays low, South finesses the jack, and East must duck to stop South from winning four tricks.

(5) To block a suit:

```
                  K 9 6 5 3 2
       J 8 4              A 10
                  Q 7
```

South leads the 2 from dummy. If East plays low, South wins the queen and plays low from dummy on the next lead to establish the suit. By playing the ace at once, East blocks the suit.

(6) To gain time:

```
                  ♠ Q 6
                  ♥ K 10 6 3
                  ♦ 10 8 5 3
                  ♣ K Q 4
       ♠ K J 8 4 2              ♠ 10 7 3
       ♥ A 8 4                  ♥ 9 7 2
       ♦ J 6                    ♦ A 4 2
       ♣ 9 5 2                  ♣ J 10 7 3
                  ♠ A 9 5
                  ♥ Q J 5
                  ♦ K Q 9 7
                  ♣ A 8 6
```

WEST	NORTH	EAST	SOUTH
			1NT
Pass	3NT	All Pass	

West leads the ♠4 and dummy's queen wins. When South next leads a diamond, East should put up the ace to return a spade, establishing West's suit while West retains an entry. If East instead plays low, South scores a diamond trick and switches to hearts to establish nine

tricks.

(7) To break up an endplay:

```
                  ♠ K 10 3 2
                  ♥ A 5 2
                  ♦ A Q 7
                  ♣ K 5 3
       ♠ 7                      ♠ 8 5
       ♥ J 10 9 6               ♥ Q 8 7 3
       ♦ 10 8 4 2               ♦ K J 9 6
       ♣ J 9 7 6                ♣ Q 8 2
                  ♠ A Q J 9 6 4
                  ♥ K 4
                  ♦ 5 3
                  ♣ A 10 4
```

South plays at 6♠. He wins the first trick with the ♥K, draws trumps, takes the ♥A, ruffs a heart and leads a club to the king and another club. East must put up the queen on the second club; otherwise, he is thrown in on the third club to make a losing lead.

```
                  8 4 2
       A Q 10 5              J 7 3
                  K 9 6
```

At a trump contract, declarer has drawn trumps and eliminated the side suits. He then leads the 2 of this suit from dummy, planning to play the 9, forcing West to win and endplaying him. East can foil this plan by inserting the jack.

(8) To prevent a later RUFFING FINESSE:

```
                  ♠ A K 9
                  ♥ Q J 10 5 3
                  ♦ 5 4
                  ♣ 8 6 4
       ♠ 8 2                    ♠ 6 4
       ♥ A 8 6 2                ♥ K 7 4
       ♦ K J 8                  ♦ 10 9 6 3
       ♣ Q J 10 9              ♣ 7 5 3 2
                  ♠ Q J 10 7 5 3
                  ♥ 9
                  ♦ A Q 7 2
                  ♣ A K
```

West leads the ♣Q against South's 6♠. South wins the ace, leads a trump to the ace and returns the ♥3. South is unlikely to play this way with the singleton ace or A-x, so East should put up the ♥K, defeating the contract. See also COVERING HONORS.

SECOND NEGATIVE RESPONSE AFTER ART-IFICIAL FORCING OPENING. A rebid by a responder who has made a negative response to his partner's strong artificial opening bid, such as 2♦ in response to 2♣, that shows a hand worth about 0-3 points. Some partnerships use HERBERT NEGATIVE, the cheapest possible suit rebid by responder, as the second negative; others use the cheaper minor suit rebid. See also DOUBLE NEGA-TIVE; TWO DIAMOND ARTIFICIAL RESPONSE TO FORCING TWO CLUB.

SECONDARY EVENT. An event at a North American Championship held concurrently with a championship event. Such events, which are open to players eliminated from the major events and to new players, are usually two sessions long and carry regional rating. See CHAM-PIONSHIP TOURNAMENTS, SIDE GAME.

SECONDARY HONORS. The lower honors, i.e., queens and jacks. The king of a suit may also be considered a secondary honor when it is not accompanied by the ace. Secondary honors generally carry their weight better in notrump than in suit contracts, especially when they are not located in partner's long suits. See PRIMARY HONORS.

SECONDARY JUMPS. See JUMP REBIDS BY RESPONDER.

SECONDARY SQUEEZE. A squeeze in which the squeeze card is followed by the loss of one or more tricks to the opponents. (Also called SQUEEZE WITHOUT THE COUNT, or Strip -Squeeze.

(1) *Squeeze Establishment* (also called delayed duck squeeze by Dr. Clyde E. Love and squeeze suitout by George S. Coffin). A squeeze establishment has these characteristics: one opponent possesses a guard to a long menace and a winner in a suit which declarer seeks to establish. The preliminary squeeze forces him to discard an additional winner or a card which may be led to his partner's winner.

The endings are based on simple squeeze positions except that declarer has two losers with no convenient way to RECTIFY THE COUNT. Thus, in effect, the rectification of the count takes place after the lead of the squeeze card. Some typical positions:

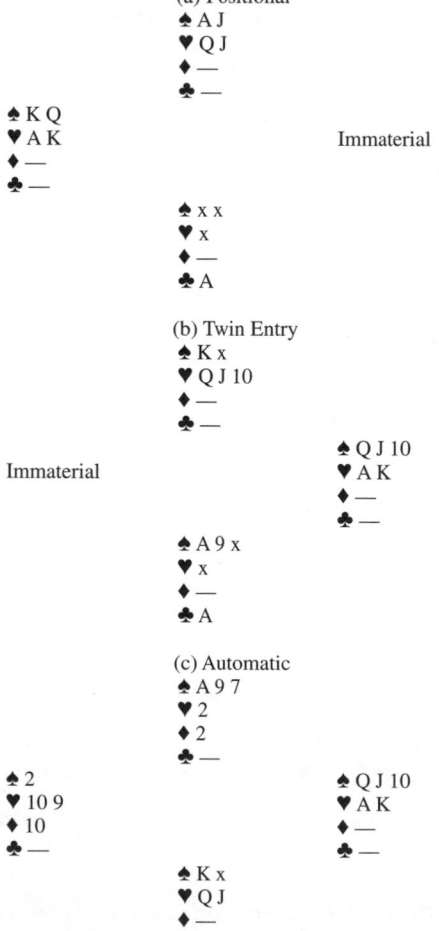

(a) Positional
- ♠ A J
- ♥ Q J
- ♦ —
- ♣ —

♠ K Q
♥ A K
♦ —
♣ —

Immaterial

- ♠ x x
- ♥ x
- ♦ —
- ♣ A

(b) Twin Entry
- ♠ K x
- ♥ Q J 10
- ♦ —
- ♣ —

Immaterial

- ♠ Q J 10
- ♥ A K
- ♦ —
- ♣ —

- ♠ A 9 x
- ♥ x
- ♦ —
- ♣ A

(c) Automatic
- ♠ A 9 7
- ♥ 2
- ♦ 2
- ♣ —

♠ 2
♥ 10 9
♦ 10
♣ —

♠ Q J 10
♥ A K
♦ —
♣ —

- ♠ K x
- ♥ Q J
- ♦ —
- ♣ A

(d) Automatic
- ♠ A J
- ♥ x x
- ♦ —
- ♣ x

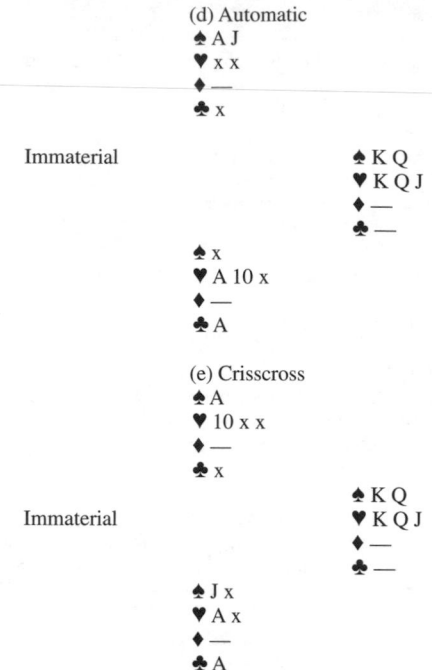

Immaterial

- ♠ K Q
- ♥ K Q J
- ♦ —
- ♣ —

- ♠ x
- ♥ A 10 x
- ♦ —
- ♣ A

(e) Crisscross
- ♠ A
- ♥ 10 x x
- ♦ —
- ♣ x

Immaterial

- ♠ K Q
- ♥ K Q J
- ♦ —
- ♣ —

- ♠ J x
- ♥ A x
- ♦ —
- ♣ A

In all the above cases, South leads the ♣A. Defender must discard a heart in order to protect his spade guard. South can then lead a heart in order to establish a trick for himself in that suit.

In (a) through (e) above, a defender was forced to discard a second winner in the suit which declarer sought to establish. In a minor variation (sometimes called a squeeze elimination [Romanet]), the opponent is squeezed out of a side winner or a card which may be led to partner's winner.

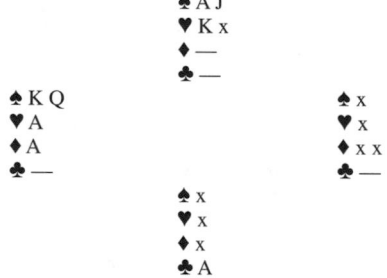

- ♠ A J
- ♥ K x
- ♦ —
- ♣ —

♠ K Q
♥ A
♦ A
♣ —

♠ x
♥ x
♦ x x
♣ —

- ♠ x
- ♥ x
- ♦ x
- ♣ A

South leads his ♣A, and West is squeezed in three suits. He must discard the diamond winner, and North discards a spade. Now South can concede a heart and establish North's king. Had the diamond winner been with East and a small diamond in the West hand, West would have been forced to part with his exit card to his partner's winner.

(2) *Squeeze Throw-In* (also known as a strip squeeze). An opponent guards a two-card menace which is in the form of a tenace combination, and he also holds a winner which corresponds to a low card in that suit held by declarer. Declarer intends to lead the low card, throwing the opponent into the lead to force a play into the tenace.

If the opponent has been stripped of exit cards in all other suits, he still may have too many winners in the throw-in suit. In that case, the preliminary squeeze reduces the number of surplus winners which the defender can hold in the throw-in suit.

A. Declarer has a major tenace, and the throw-in is followed by two tricks for declarer. Declarer may have two or more losers.

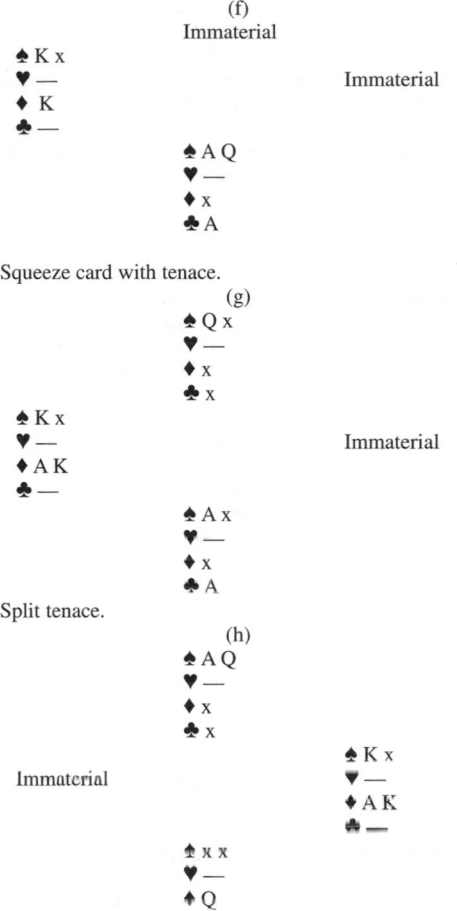

(f)
Immaterial

♠ K x
♥ —
♦ K
♣ —

Immaterial

♠ A Q
♥ —
♦ x
♣ A

Squeeze card with tenace.

(g)
♠ Q x
♥ —
♦ x
♣ x

♠ K x
♥ —
♦ A K
♣ —

Immaterial

♠ A x
♥ —
♦ x
♣ A

Split tenace.

(h)
♠ A Q
♥ —
♦ x
♣ x

Immaterial

♠ K x
♥ —
♦ A K
♣ —

♠ x x x
♥ —
♦ Q
♣ A

Squeeze card opposite tenace.

In (f) through (h), the ♣A is led, forcing the defender to part with a diamond winner. Now South leads the diamond, and the defender is thrown in to lead away from his ♠K. Note that the tenace may be with or opposite the squeeze card, or split between declarer and dummy.

B. Opponent has the major tenace, and the throw-in is followed by one trick for the declarer. Declarer has three or four losers.

(j)
♠ A 10
♥ x x
♦ —
♣ x

♠ K Q J
♥ A Q
♦ —
♣ —

Immaterial

♠ x x x
♥ K x
♦ —
♣ A

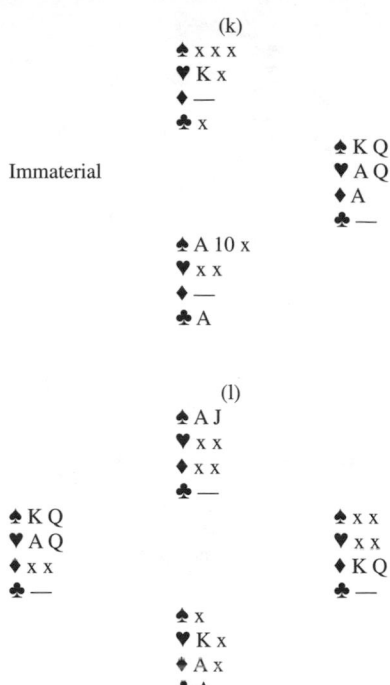

(k)
♠ x x x
♥ K x
♦ —
♣ x

Immaterial

♠ K Q J
♥ A Q
♦ A
♣ —

♠ A 10 x
♥ x x
♦ —
♣ A

(l)
♠ A J
♥ x x
♦ x x
♣ —

♠ K Q
♥ A Q
♦ x x
♣ —

♠ x x
♥ x x
♦ K Q
♣ —

♠ x
♥ K x
♦ A x
♣ A

South leads the ♣A, which forces the defender to discard a surplus winner – ♠J in (j), ♠J or ♦A in (k), or a potential exit card, the diamond, in (l). Now South takes his winner(s) and exits in spades, so that he ends up by taking a trick with his ♥K.

When a defender cannot afford to lead away from his stopper because declarer has a major tenace, then the endplay is effective when declarer has two losers, as shown in (j). The preliminary squeeze may force the defender to discard a surplus winner (as indicated) or an exit card. In this situation:

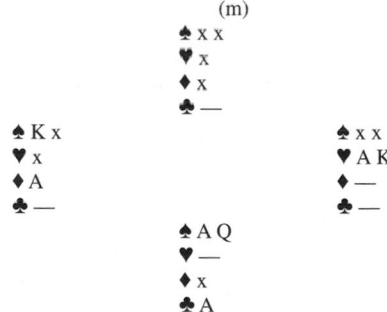

(m)
♠ x x
♥ x
♦ x
♣ —

♠ K x
♥ x
♦ A
♣ —

♠ x x
♥ A K
♦ —
♣ —

♠ A Q
♥ —
♦ x
♣ A

South leads the ♣A, and West is forced to discard his exit card in hearts. Now he can be thrown in with a diamond and be forced to lead a spade into declarer's tenace.

C. Three-suit variants: in the case where one opponent has guards in three suits, which include at least one vulnerable stopper (i.e., declarer has a major tenace in one of the suits), the squeeze works when declarer has three or more losers. Precisely three losers are required only if the defender has a potential exit card in one of the suits.

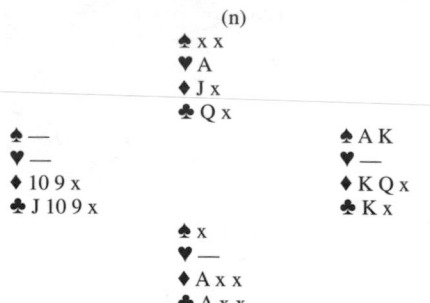

(n)

♠ x x
♥ A
♦ J x
♣ Q x

♠ —   ♠ A K
♥ —   ♥ —
♦ 10 9 x   ♦ K Q x
♣ J 10 9 x   ♣ K x

♠ x
♥ —
♦ A x x
♣ A x x

South has four losers, and the squeeze must fail since East has a potential exit card in diamonds. North leads the ♥A, and East throws a spade. Now East wins the next spade, and plays a high diamond to the ace. He wins the next diamond, but he can now play a low diamond to West's ♦10, so that the endplay is ineffective.

The squeeze establishment also has a three-suit variant which will gain a trick if declarer has three or more losers. Again, precisely three losers are required only if the defenders can kill one of the menace cards.

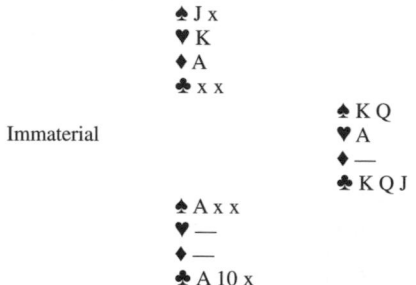

♠ J x
♥ K
♦ A
♣ x x

♠ K Q
♥ A
♦ —
♣ K Q J

Immaterial

♠ A x x
♥ —
♦ —
♣ A 10 x

South has three tricks on top. The ♦A is led from North and East is squeezed in three suits. He must discard a potential club trick. North leads a club, and declarer ducks in order to establish his 10, which furnishes him with a fourth trick.

In certain squeeze-establishment plays, declarer may duck two or even three times in order to establish a trick for himself; understandably such positions arise rarely in play.

In another rare variant, the secondary squeeze involving three suits may result in the gain of two tricks to declarer: with three losers in hand, a squeeze-establishment play concedes one trick to the opponents and adds one trick to declarer's stock. As a result, the count has been rectified, and declarer may be able to continue with a simple squeeze for the gain of another trick. For related squeeze situations, see STEPPINGSTONE SQUEEZE; VICE SQUEEZE; WINKLE SQUEEZE.

SECONDARY VALUES. Queens and jacks, also called soft values, as distinct from ace and kings, which are primary values or hard values.

SECTION. A group of contestants who constitute a self-contained unit in the competition in one event for one session of a tournament.

SECTION MARKERS. Signs at tournaments indicating the location of each group of tables forming a section.

SECTIONAL. An ACBL tournament run by a unit or by a club to which the unit has been given the authority to run the tournament. Silver points are awarded in all events at a sectional. Most sectionals run for three days, although some are longer and a few run for only two days. Sectionals draw their competitors mostly from the immediate area. Also see SECTIONAL AT CLUBS.

SECTIONAL AT CLUBS. An ACBL tournament with sectional rating staged at many clubs in a geographical area over a period of several days — up to seven days. Events are played at several clubs and results are transmitted to a central office manned by the director-in-charge. The director combines the results to determine the winners and overall placings. Points awarded are silver points.

SEED, SEEDING. The assignment of certain tables to particularly strong contestants when entries are sold so as to assure that there will be no preponderance of strong pairs in direct competition within any one section. It is desirable to seed weak pairs also to prevent an imbalance of weakness in a particular section. In pair events, tables 3 and 9 are usually reserved for seeded players, at national tournaments, tables 3, 6 and 9 usually are reserved. In board-a-match team competitions, adjacent pairs of tables such as 1 and 2, 9 and 10, 17 and 18, etc., are used for spotting the strongest teams through the field. In individual tournaments, an effort is made to assure that the North players, at least, are able to keep score. In a Swiss Team event, pairings are random for the opening match.

ACBL North American Championship knockout events (Vanderbilt and Spingold) utilize various formulas for seeding which include not only masterpoint holdings but recent performances by the players.

SEESAW SQUEEZE. See ENTRY-SHIFTING SQUEEZE.

SELECTION OF INTERNATIONAL TEAMS. See INTERNATIONAL OPEN TEAM SELECTION; INTERNATIONAL WOMEN'S TEAM SELECTION.

SEMIBALANCED. A hand with 5-4-2-2 or 6-3-2-2 distribution.

SEMIFINAL. (1) The round of four or six in a knockout team tournament. (2) In a pair, team or individual tournament, the round immediately following the qualifying round and immediately preceding the final round.

SEMI-PSYCHIC. A departure from normal bidding methods which is not a complete bluff but is still intended to deceive the opponents. The term usually refers to an opening bid well below minimum values, but LEAD-INHIBITING BIDS belong in the same category.

SEMI-SET GAME. A rubber bridge session involving five or more players in which one pair (sometimes two pairs), such as a husband and wife, play as partners except when one of them is cut out.

SEMI-SOLID SUIT. A suit of at least six cards which appears to contain only one loser, a suit that is one high card short of being a SOLID SUIT, for example,

AKJ10xx, AQJxxx, AKxxxxx, KQJxxxx.

SEND IT BACK. Redouble (colloquialism).

SENIOR PLAYER OF THE YEAR. The Senior Player of the Year contests recognizes the player 55 years or older who wins the most points each year in the American Contract Bridge League. In its inaugural year, only points won at senior regionals counted. Thereafter points won at senior events at other tournaments were counted as well. For winners see Appendix II.

SENIOR TOURNAMENTS. Competitions in which only players older than a specified age – usually 55 – may play. The first such tournament was a sectional staged at Sun City FL in 1977. The reaction from participants was so enthusiastic that regional tournaments for seniors only are now held. Senior events are included in almost all tournaments at the national and regional level.

SEQUENCE. Two or more cards in consecutive order of rank, as A-K-Q (three-card sequence) or Q-J-10-9 (four-card sequence). See PLAY FROM EQUALS .

SEQUENCE DISCARDS. The discard of an honor normally shows an honor sequence, of which the discard is the highest. Therefore the discard of a queen denies the king, and guarantees the jack and usually the 10.

The same principle applies in following suit when a top honor has already been played. This follows the more general principle of discarding the highest card which can be spared in transmitting a signal.

SEQUENCE OF ROUNDS. In a session of bridge the sequence of rounds is broken up for a few necessary irregularities. After about half the rounds have been played, the traveling pairs in a section with an even number of tables and no byestand must skip a table. In board-a-match team events there is often an irregularity at the halfway point where traveling pairs make an irregular progression as do the boards they have just played. When the number of teams is an even number, there are at least two, and sometimes three, irregularities. See PROGRESSION.

SEQUENCE RE-ENTRY. A type of suit preference signal. After leading a king against notrump from a combination headed by K-Q-J, the defender can follow with the queen or the jack at choice, in order to suggest a re-entry in a high- or low-ranking suit. See SUIT PREFERENCE SIGNAL.

SERES SQUEEZE. A rare triple squeeze in a three-card ending discovered by Tim Seres in 1965. Playing in 6♣, he arrived at the following ending with the lead in dummy:

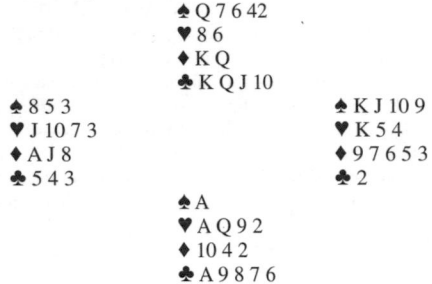

The ♠7 was ruffed, establishing the queen, and West

was triple squeezed. An unusual feature is that one of the three cards he is trying to retain is a trump loser. See BACKWASH SQUEEZE.

The complete deal was:

```
              ♠ Q 7 6 4 2
              ♥ 8 6
              ♦ K Q
              ♣ K Q J 10
♠ 8 5 3                      ♠ K J 10 9
♥ J 10 7 3                   ♥ K 5 4
♦ A J 8                      ♦ 9 7 6 5 3
♣ 5 4 3                      ♣ 2
              ♠ A
              ♥ A Q 9 2
              ♦ 10 4 2
              ♣ A 9 8 7 6
```

A club was led, and South won in dummy and finessed the ♥Q. He cashed the ♠A and led a diamond. West put up the ♦A and led a second trump. South won in dummy, ruffed a spade, and entered dummy with a diamond for another spade ruff. The ♥A and a heart ruff left the three-card ending shown above.

SERIES GAMES. Formerly duplicate sessions in a club which counted as a unit for points or prizes. As of January 1969, the ACBL discontinued sanctioned series games for point awards. ACBL reinstituted such games in 1993. Four or more sessions of play are required. The masterpoint bonus to the winning player is equal to .02 times the total number of tables in which the winner participated to a maximum of 1.5 points.

SERIOUS THREE NOTRUMP A slam move originated by Eric Rodwell. When an 8-card major-suit fit is located below 3 NT, a bid of 3 NT is a serious slam move, demanding a cuebid. A cuebid is only a mild slam try. Example:

NORTH	SOUTH
1 ♠	3 ♠

Then: (1) 3 NT is a serious, strong slam try.
(2) 4♣ or 4♦ is a mild slam try.
(3) 4♥ offers a choice of games.

Some experts play this in reverse — 3NT is a non-serious slam try and the cuebid is the serious slam try.

SERPENT'S COUP. When the serpent tempted Eve, she gave in and tried the forbidden fruit and then got Adam to do the same. This coup is similar – it tempts a defender – and the fruit looks very appealing.

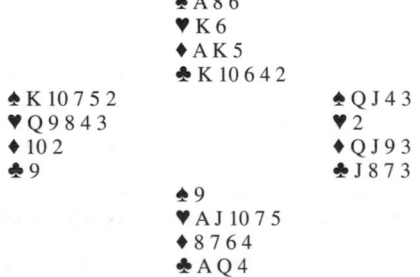

Against 4♥, West led the ♣9 which was won with the ace. A heart to the king was followed by a second heart. East showed out, playing the ♠3 and the 10 lost to West's queen. West returned the ♦2, and this was won with dummy's king.

At this point, declarer does not know whether the diamond suit is divided 5-1, 4-2 or 3-3. A club to the queen will lead to defeat if the diamonds are 3-3 and East has a diamond entry: Ace, king and another diamond will led to immediate defeat if East has four diamonds. The low diamond play at this point makes the contract legitimately if the diamonds are 3-3 and gives far greater temptation to East to give his partner a diamond ruff if they are 4-2 or 5-1. East would be loathe to give West a club ruff since that play establishes the club suit while there are still entries to dummy.

Alternatively, if the diamonds are 4-2, with East having the four diamonds, declarer has two heart losers and two diamond losers. Declarer cannot play the ♦A and trump a spade – West will have more trumps and be able to force declarer.

One play offers a better chance. At trick five declarer led a small diamond from the table. East won the jack and West followed with the 10.

East might hesitate to return a club since that would establish dummy's club suit and leave entries to it as well. But why not return a diamond? The worst that could happen is that West would trump the now bare ♦A.

East bit the apple and returned a diamond and West did trump it. The Serpent's Coup had worked.

West returned a spade, won by the ace in dummy. Declarer trumped a spade back to his hand. The ♥A pulled one of West's trumps and the ♥J followed in this position:

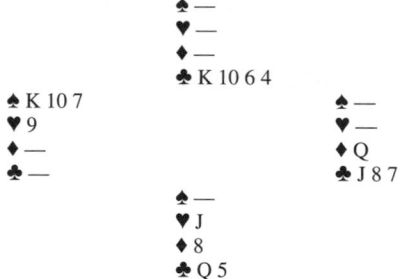

The Serpent's Coup ended with a two-suit squeeze.

SESSION. A period of play during which each contestant is scheduled to play a designated series of boards against one or more opponents. A session may consist of one or more rounds.

SET. Noun: the failure or defeat of a contract. Verb: to defeat a contract by at least one trick. Also, a set of duplicate boards, usually 32.

SET GAME. A pre-arranged match between two partnerships, with each pair almost always remaining the same for the duration of the contest. There have been set games where one of the players has been spelled for a while by some other player who had been waiting in reserve for such an instance. But generally set games involve only four people and last for several rubbers as previously agreed upon.

The CULBERTSON-LENZ MATCH was the most publicized set game in history. However, there also was wide interest in the match between the SHARIF BRIDGE CIRCUS and English experts Jonathan Cansino and Jeremy Flint (with Claude Rodrigue spelling Flint for part of the match), which was held in London in 1970. The stakes were enormous – 1 pound ($2.40) a point. Over the course of 80 rubbers, of which Sharif had agreed to play a minimum of 52, the Circus won by 5,470 points. See SCIENTISTS vs. TRADITIONALISTS.

SET UP. To establish one or more cards in the hand of the player himself, his partner, or an opponent.

SET-UP SUIT. See ESTABLISHED SUIT.

SEVEN or SEVEN-SPOT. The eighth-ranking card in a suit, located between the 8 and the 6.

SEVEN-ODD. Seven tricks over book, or 13 tricks in all.

SEVEN PLAYERS. See SHUTTLE DUMMY.

SEVEN TABLES. At duplicate, seven tables provide for competition among 28 players as individuals, 14 pairs or seven teams-of-four. This is an ideal number of tables – it provides a basic pattern for all numbers of tables up to 13 for pair contests, and is an excellent base for larger individual tournaments.

Since seven is a prime number, the RAINBOW MOVEMENT is suitable for an individual contest. Three boards to a round, with the West players moving counterclockwise around the table at the end of each board of the round, provides each player with 21 different partners. Six is top and 63 is average.

Thirteen rounds of two boards each makes the HOWELL MOVEMENT an ideal competition for pair events, each pair meeting every other pair, with almost perfectly BALANCED COMPARISONS throughout the field and at least 12 and no more than 14 direct comparisons between pairs. The MITCHELL MOVEMENT can also be used when two fields are desirable. Six rounds of four boards and seven rounds of three or four boards comprise the usual contest.

As a team event, the regular team-of-four progression, boards going to the next lower and traveling pairs skipping a table to lower numbers, provides six uninterrupted rounds for 24 boards, without any irregularities in the progression. A Swiss Team movement is not recommended. Three-way matches are necessary, and pairings are at best difficult after the second round. For IMP matches, use the team of-four progression and score each match on IMPs.

The following Reduced Howell for seven tables playing nine rounds is due to Olof Hanner. The starting positions are:

Table 1	2	3	4	5	6	7
NS	1	2	3	4	13	5	14
EW	6	7	8	9	10	11	12
Bd	1	2	5	6	7	8	9

Pairs 1-5 are stationary. Pairs 6-13 follow next higher number, and 14 follows 6. Boards go to next lower table, with two sets of boards on a byestand between 2 and 3. Short instruction on tables 5 and 7, telling pairs where to go, are sufficient. Use an arrow switch on rounds 6, 8, and 9.

For 6° or 7° tables, see HALF TABLES.

SEXTET BRIDGE. A seldom played bridge game for six players, playing as two partnerships of three each. Two new suits were introduced, called rackets and wheels.

SHADE, SHADED. A bid made on slightly less than technical minimum requirements.

SHAKE. A colloquialism meaning DISCARD.

SHARIF BRIDGE CIRCUS. A touring professional team of world class players, organized and headed by movie star Omar Sharif, to play a series of exhibition matches against leading European and North American teams.

The Circus made its debut late in 1967 when Sharif, Giorgio Belladonna, Claude Delmouly, Benito Garozzo, and Leon Yallouze, all playing the BLUE TEAM CLUB, defeated the Dutch international team in matches sponsored by newspapers and played in three Netherlands cities before enthusiastic audiences, who viewed the competition on BRIDGE-O-RAMA. Using this format – a match against a highly-rated team with the play-by-play displayed to the audience accompanied by expert commentary – the Circus made an extended tour in 1968. It defeated teams in Italy and London, lost its first matches to The Netherlands and Belgium in The Hague, and made a swing through six North American cities – Montreal, Toronto, Los Angeles, Dallas, New Orleans and New York – winning the majority of the matches. (Several of the American matches were three-cornered contests involving the Circus, the local team, and the ACES.) A second tour in 1970 received a spectacular sendoff when Jeremy Flint and Jonathan Cansino challenged Sharif and company to a 100-rubber pair game in London (later reduced by time pressure to 80 rubbers). The stakes were an unprecedented British pound ($2.40) per point, plus an additional bonus of $1,000 on the net result of each four rubbers. The match attracted wide newspaper and magazine coverage in the United States as well as in Europe. Sharif won by a margin of 5,470 points and collected more than $18,000. However, this was a comparatively small sum against the expenses of staging the match and taping the highlights for a series of television shows planned for later syndication.

This was immediately followed by a tour of seven North American cities – Chicago, Winnipeg, Los Angeles, St. Paul, Dallas, Detroit and Philadelphia. In addition to matches against powerful teams of local stars, the tour included a marathon 840-deal match against the Aces, who accompanied the Circus throughout the tour. The Circus defeated the all-star teams in Chicago, Winnipeg and St. Paul, but lost all its other matches, bowing to the Aces by 101 IMPs (1,793-1,692) after the lead had see-sawed excitingly from city to city. Pietro Forquet joined the Sharif team in Dallas but could not reverse the effect of the exhausting schedule, which included numerous personal appearances by Sharif.

Despite commercial sponsorship of more than $50,000 in 1970, neither of the American tours proved a financial success, although both resulted in wide publicity for bridge.

SHARING BOARDS. In some movements, it is necessary for two tables, and perhaps more, to "share" by playing the same set of boards in a single round. Boards may be played out of numerical order.

SHARK. An expert player, but more particularly one who specializes in playing for money and is adept at this type of competition.

SHARPLES. (1) A convention devised by James and Robert Sharples – a "natural" extension of the STAYMAN convention.

A responder who sees slam possibilities frequently faces a problem if he uses Stayman and does not find an immediate fit. If the responder has 4-4-3-2 or 4-4-4-1 distribution, he may wish to explore the possibility of a 4-4 fit in a minor suit.

Opposite a 16- to 18-point notrump, responder holds:

♠ K J 7 5
♥ 4
♦ A Q 5 2
♣ A 10 5 3

The Sharples idea is to bid four of a minor suit on the second round, showing specifically a four-card suit and sufficient strength to play in at least 4NT:

OPENER	RESPONDER
1NT	2♣
2♥	4♣

The opener rebids his hand naturally. If he has four-card club support, he raises to 5♣ or 6♣ in accordance with his estimation of slam prospects. If four-card club support is lacking, opener can make a natural suit bid of 4♦ or 4♠ (although in some styles a four-card spade suit may have been excluded by the 2♥ rebid). 4NT and 5NT would be natural bids announcing that the opener's distribution was 4-3-3-3.

All notrump bids at any stage should be regarded as natural.

Suppose responder holds:

♠ J 3
♥ K J 7 5
♦ A Q 5 2
♣ A 5 3

The bidding goes:

OPENER	RESPONDER
1NT	2♣
2♠	4♦

By jumping to 4♦, responder denies a four-card club suit, and keeps open the possibility of playing a slam in a red suit.

These sequences need partnership agreement. SPLINTER is the most popular choice.

(2) A defense to 1NT in which: an overcall of 2♣ shows a hand of unspecified shape but with at least four spades; an overcall of 2♦ shows a weak distributional hand with short clubs.

SHIFT (or switch). To change suit from one originally led on defense; alternatively, a change of suit by declarer in the development of his play. Shift can also be used to describe a bid in a new suit by either the opening bidder, his partner, or an overcaller or his partner, as JUMP SHIFT, ONE-OVER-ONE, etc.

SHOMATE MOVEMENT. For INDIVIDUAL TOURNAMENTS of 8, 9 or 10 tables. These movements are noncyclic and must be conducted with GUIDE CARDS. See IRREGULAR RAINBOW.

SHOOTING. The art of playing deliberately for an abnormal result. Occasionally near the end of a tournament, a couple of tops are needed in order to have any chance of winning. Two or three average results would be just as fatal to one's chances as bottoms. Under these circumstances, playing for abnormal results is justified.

Playing for top or bottom is called shooting.

Many players, quite wrongly, think of shooting as equivalent to overbidding. In fact, good shooting will consist of underbidding as often as overbidding. The aim should be to arrive at a contract which is wrong but only slightly wrong.

To bid a game or a slam which has a 30-40% chance of success is an intelligent "shot"; but it is equally sensible to stop short of game or slam which is a 60-70% chance. In each case the shooter is hoping for the less likely result.

But the best chance to shoot intelligently is in the play of the hand.

NORTH
♠ x x
♥ x x x
♦ x x
♣ A 8 x x x x

SOUTH
♠ A Q x
♥ A K x x
♦ A Q x
♣ K 9 x

West leads a spade against South's 3NT contract. Declarer wins East's king with the ace, and attacks clubs. Normally he would play the king, and then duck a round. This is the percentage play because the odds are slightly against a 2-2 club break. Obviously if declarer plays the king, then leads the nine to dummy's ace, his contract will be placed in jeopardy. For one who wishes to shoot, this is a wonderful opportunity. By playing the ace on the second round (unless West shows out), he can be almost certain of a top (or bottom).

SHORT CLUB. The short prepared or convenient club is an original opening bid made on a three-card club suit. It was first advocated by the FOUR ACES as a means of providing a comfortable rebid. In principle it requires a minimum of Q-x-x (to support a lead), and failing this, opener may choose instead to open with 1♦. It is most often used by the disciples of systems that require five cards for a major suit opening. For example:

♠ A 6 5 4
♥ A Q 3 2
♦ A 8
♣ 9 7 6

When playing FIVE-CARD MAJORS the hand is opened with 1♣. When the hand contains two clubs and three diamonds, an opening diamond bid is usually preferred. It is essential in these systems for responder to mention his four-card major holding, if at all feasible, in order to find the all-important major-suit fit. All players, even those who initiate weak major-suit bids, will at times resort to the Short Club.

Some specialized bidding systems use an artificial club opening as an introduction to a very strong hand (see BLUE TEAM CLUB, SCHENKEN SYSTEM, VANDERBILT CLUB), but it is to be understood that the short club, per se, is not a system but an opening bid to facilitate future rebids, and may be passed by partner. When otherwise used it is more properly announced as ONE CLUB ARTIFICIAL AND FORCING, and in such cases it does not promise any particular length or strength in the club suit itself.

Inexperienced players often assume that a 1♣ bid is likely to be short. Using standard methods it is very unlikely: A four-card or five-card suit is far more likely, and even a six-card suit is more likely than three. See also CHOICE OF SUIT.

SHORT DIAMOND. Many users of strong-club systems, particularly those such as Precision that employ five-card majors, employ a short diamond as a catch-all for hands that are not suitable for other bids. This must be alerted, and the explanation should include a minimum length: two, one or zero diamonds. A 2♦ response is natural and forcing.

Sometimes called the loose diamond, the nebulous diamond, or the phony diamond. The opponents should agree that against 1♦, a bid of 2♦ should be natural and not a cuebid.

A short diamond with three cards is a standard part of modern methods. It almost invariably is based on 4-4-3-2 distribution.

SHORT HAND. A term used to describe the hand of the partnership that contains the fewer cards in the trump suit, such as in the reference, "declarer (or the defenders) took the ruff in the short hand." Occasionally, the term may be applied to a hand that is short in a non-trump suit and therefore expects to ruff.

SHORT HOWELL MOVEMENTS. See REDUCED HOWELL.

SHORT SUIT. In an original hand of 13 cards, a suit containing two or fewer cards. In some contexts, a short suit would be defined as a singleton or a void. See SINGLETON, DOUBLETON.

SHORT-SUIT GAME TRIES. These were developed as part of the KAPLAN-SHEINWOLD system, but can be used effectively with any standard system. When the opening major-suit bid has been raised to two, the opener tries for game by bidding his shortest suit. For example:

♠ A K 6 5 3
♥ A 5 2
♦ 8
♣ K J 7 4

The bidding goes:

OPENER	RESPONDER
1♠	2♠
3♦	

This asks responder to go to 4♠ if his values are mainly outside diamonds. If responder rebids 3♥, that would also be a short-suit try, expressing doubt about game prospects.

This method gives a partnership a chance to judge whether strength is duplicated. A disadvantage is that it may help the opponents to find a cheap save. One defender may double the short-suit try, encouraging his partner to take the save. It may also provide a clue to the most effective lead and subsequent defense.

It is best to restrict these bids to the situations when a major has been raised and there has been no interference. The specific sequence 1♥ - 2♥ - 2♠ may need special consideration. The 2♥ rebid may be needed as a natural rebid, especially if the opening bidder has not guaranteed a five-card heart suit.

For alternative methods see TWO-WAY GAME TRIES, WEAK SUIT GAME TRY.

SHORT-SUIT LEADS. An opening lead of a singleton or a doubleton is often indicated when the leader examines his hand in the light of the bidding.

Against either notrump or a trump contract, a short-suit lead is normal when partner has bid the suit. (Partner's bid suit is less automatic as a lead with greater length; against a trump contract it may be necessary to aim quickly for tricks elsewhere.)

The short-suit lead is also indicated when there is a bidding inference that this is partner's suit, and that he will have the entries to make use of it.

```
                SOUTH
                ♠ Q 5 3
                ♥ J 8 6 2
                ♦ 7 4
                ♣ Q 7 6 3
```

After the bidding:

WEST	EAST
1 ♠	2 ♣
2NT	3NT

South should lead a diamond. The hand is too weak to hope to do much with hearts, so a diamond is led in the hope of hitting partner's strength. If South held the ♠A instead of the ♠3, a heart lead would be indicated.

A short-suit lead may be made for passive reasons, usually because other leads seem unattractive. This is most likely to be desirable if the bidding suggests that the declaring side has no long suit, and that therefore there is no urgent need to attack.

In a suit contract a short-suit lead is most desirable if the trump holding suggests that there are real prospects of obtaining a ruff. (A-x, A-x-x, or K-x-x would be ideal.) Conversely a short-suit lead, particularly of a singleton, may be a mistake when there is no ruffing prospect because it may help declarer to play a suit which would have presented problems. A singleton trump is usually a bad lead (but see TRUMP LEADS).

Against notrump, a short-suit lead is indicated when the opening leader is very weak and no entries are available to make use of a long weak suit. The leader should try to hit his partner's suit, although this may turn out to declarer's advantage. (For this reason the long weak suit may prove best as a passive lead.) A short-suit lead is required when the leader's partner has doubled notrump, and no suit has been bid:

WEST	NORTH	EAST	SOUTH
			1NT
Pass	3NT	Dbl	Pass
Pass	Pass		

SHORTEN. To force; to shorten in trumps by forcing to ruff. See FORCING LEADS.

SHOW OUT. To fail to follow suit for the first time during the play of that suit.

SHOW UP SQUEEZE. A squeeze which permits declarer to avoid a guess between a finesse and a play for a drop.

```
                K J x x x
    ? x x x                   ? x
                A x
```

If South can put pressure on West, forcing two discards in the vital suit, the ace and king can be cashed with confidence, knowing the queen will show up on one side or the other.

SHOWING PREFERENCE. See PREFERENCE.

SHUFFLE. Noun: the mixing together of the pack of cards prior to the next, or first deal. Several thorough mixings, or shuffles, are required as it is important that the deck be mixed completely from deal to deal. Verb: to mix the cards.

The most common shuffle is the riffle, in which the deck is divided into two approximate halves and then reunited by a flipping action so that the cards are roughly interleaved. A mathematician has calculated that seven riffles are needed to produce a good result, but few players bother with more than three or four.

SHUT-OUT BID. See PREEMPTIVE BID.

SHUTTLE DUMMY. This is a procedure to permit play with seven players at two tables, playing Chicago. One table starts, and dummy moves to the other table. This continues, with an individual score for each player maintained at each table.

SID. See STAYMAN IN DOUBT.

SIDE. A team of two in a rubber game or a CHICAGO game. The term can also describe a pairing in a duplicate contest, or, in team-of-four play, the entire team of whatever number.

SIDE GAME. A one-session event at a CHAMPIONSHIP TOURNAMENT, run concurrently with a championship event, and, at North American Championships, concurrently with SECONDARY EVENTS as well. At North American Championships, morning side games are held daily, and midnight ZIP Swisses are held frequently. Red points are awarded at NABCs.

SIDE SUIT. In bidding, a suit of at least four cards held by a player whose first bid is in another suit. In play, a suit of at least four cards other than trumps held by declarer in his own hand or dummy.

SIGNALS, SIGNALING. The language of defensive play by which defenders can legitimately exchange information about the makeup of their hands. Various methods of signaling are discussed under the following titles: COUNT; DISCARDING; ENCRYPTED; HIGH-LOW; LENGTH SIGNALS; ODD-EVEN DISCARDS; REVOLVING DISCARDS; SCANIAN SIGNAL; SMITH; SUIT PREFERENCE SIGNAL; TRUMP SIGNAL; UPSIDE-DOWN SIGNALS; VINJE SIGNALS.

SIGN-OFF BID. A bid which is intended to close the auction. These sometimes occur in partscore situations:

WEST	EAST	WEST	EAST	WEST	EAST
1 ♣	1 ♠	1 ♠	1NT	1NT	2 ♠
1NT	2 ♠	2 ♠			

In each case the player bidding notrump has limited his hand so partner can place the final contract. In each case, partner is saying that the values of the combined hands are not strong enough for game and that the best place to play probably is spades because the spade bidder has a long suit of spades – probably at least six and maybe more. (Five or more in the second auction, which assumes traditional responses to 1NT.) Other sign-off bids occur at the game level. The most common is the raise to 3NT by the partner of a player who opened 1NT. In general sign-off bids occur when a player names a contract after partner has severely limited his hand both as to point-count and distribution.

SILENCE. Observed during the play of important events, by consent of all, especially by the kibitzers. In the playing rooms of the top-level clubs, any noise or disturbance of the games is severely frowned upon, and should a disturbance occur, the officer of the day or other official will usually make the necessary remonstrance.

SILODOR TROPHY. For the Spring North American Open Pairs Championship. Presented in 1963 in memory of Sidney Silodor and made retroactive to include winners of the event since it started in 1958. For results see Appendix I.

SILVER POINTS. Masterpoints won at ACBL sectional tournaments. A player must earn at least 50 silver points as one of the qualifications for advancing to the rank of Life Master.

SILVER RIBBON PAIRS. An ACBL event with national rating for players 55 years of age or older. Pairs earn qualification by placing first or second in a regionally-rated senior event. For winners, see Appendix I.

SIMON AWARD. Endowed by John E. Simon, this award for the Bridge Sportsman of the Year was presented annually by the INTERNATIONAL BRIDGE PRESS ASSOCIATION. It has been in abeyance since 1986. It was awarded to the player deemed worthy of special mention for behavior showing a high degree of sportsmanship. For a list of winners, see INTERNATIONAL BRIDGE PRESS ASSOCIATION AWARDS.

SIMPLE. (as applied to an overcall or response). Non-jump; merely sufficient to overcall or respond.

SIMPLE FINESSE. A finesse for a single card held by the adversaries.

SIMPLE HONORS. A term used in auction bridge to denote three honors in the trump suit, for which 30 points were scored.

SIMPLE OVERCALL. A minimum overcall.

SIMPLE SQUEEZE. A squeeze which acts against one opponent in two suits. The minimum requirements are: (1) a two-card menace and a one-card menace, both guarded by the same opponent; (2) all the remaining tricks but one.

The card which forces the defender to discard a busy card is called the squeeze card. The squeeze card must be a winner played from the hand opposite the two-card menace, so that the two menaces and the squeeze card cannot all be in the same hand. The two-card menace contains a master card, which provides an entry to one of the menaces. The following are the basic endings for a simple squeeze:

(1) *Positional (or one-way) squeeze:*

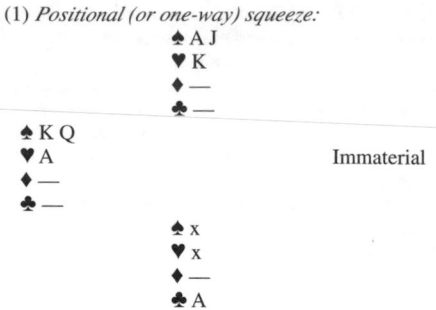

South plays the ♣A, and West is squeezed. When West discards one suit, North discards the other, and so takes the remaining tricks.

In this example, spades are the two-card menace and hearts the one-card menace. The squeeze card is the ♣A. Declarer has on top two of the remaining three tricks.

In this position both West and North have been reduced to busy cards, but West must discard first so that declarer can choose his discard accordingly, resulting in the gain of a trick. If, in this position, the East and West cards are interchanged, then the squeeze is inoperative.

(2) *Split two-card menace:*

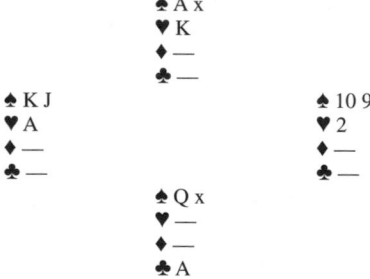

In this variation, the two-card menace is split between North and South. The North hand contains the master card (the ♠A this example), but the South hand contains the menace (here the ♣Q). The (split) two-card menace is still said to be opposite the squeeze card (here the ♣A) provided that a master card of that menace is properly situated, as here.

(3) *Automatic squeeze*

♠ A J
♥ —
♦ —
♣ x

♠ K Q   Immaterial
♥ A
♦ —
♣ —

        ♠ x
        ♥ K
        ♦ —
        ♣ A

(a) As usual, the two-card menace is opposite the squeeze card, but now the one-card menace accompanies the squeeze card. This means that the North hand has an idle card (see BUSY CARD AND IDLE CARD) which can be played on the ♣A; that is, North's discard does not depend on the opponent's play. As a result, the squeeze is automatic in that it operates against either opponent if the same opponent guards both menace cards.

(b) Twin-entry menace:

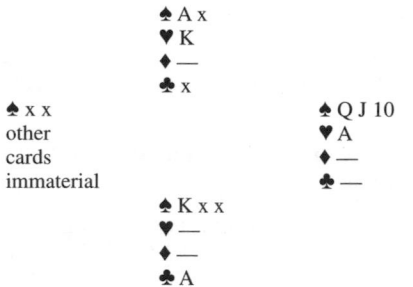

When South plays the ♣A, East is squeezed. The position is automatic; even though the one-card menace is opposite the squeeze card, there is compensation in the form of an extra winner in the long menace, which is now called a twin-entry two-card menace.

(c) Criss-cross squeeze:

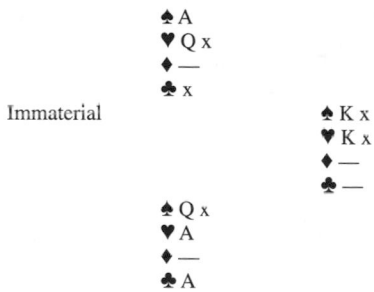

South leads the ♣A, which forces East to unguard one of his major suit kings. If East discards a spade, declarer takes the ace of that suit, dropping East's king, returns to hand with the ♥A to cash the ♠Q. If East can foresee the impending squeeze, he may be able to make a deceptive play, blanking one of his kings early, thereby presenting South with a guess.

SIMPLIFIED CLUB SYSTEM. Originated by Larry Weiss and played by him successfully in North American competition. It combines some of the features of the BLUE TEAM CLUB and the OMAN SYSTEM: (1) 1♣ shows 16 points or more, and responses show controls. A 2♣ rebid shows a stronger hand with game values, and the responses again show controls. A 2♦ rebid shows a strong three-suiter. (2) 1♦, 1♥, and 1♠ guarantee a two-suited hand, at least 5-4, and the shorter suit is bid first unless it is clubs. 1NT is an artificial positive response showing at least 10 points. The suit immediately above the opener's is an artificial negative, but the responder is not required to use it if he has some fit with the opener. (3) 1NT is 12-15 points. (4) 2♣ is 11-16 and three-suited. (5) Other two-bids show single-suited hands with 11-16 points. Club hands are shown by 2NT (14-17) or 3♣ (11-14).

SIMPLIFIED PRECISION. A version of the PRECISION CLUB system that differs from Standard Precision essentially in that (1) it uses no asking bids, (2) its 2♦

opening shows diamond length rather than diamond shortness, and (3) its four-level minor-suit openings are natural preempts. Compare also SUPER PRECISION.

SIMS-CULBERTSON MATCH. See CULBERTSON-SIMS MATCH.

SIMS SYSTEM. A system of contract bidding originated circa 1930-32 by P. Hal Sims. The system stressed strong first- and second-hand opening bids (with corresponding "protection" by third or fourth hand); strong four-card biddable suits, with the opening bid made in the lower ranking. All opening bids of two or three in a suit were forcing, both showing hands strong in honor value, but the three-bid showing length as well. Weak defensive bids were not made when vulnerable. The system also employed forcing overcalls and informatory doubles.

SIMULTANEOUS CALLS, LEADS, or PLAYS. Covered in appropriate sections of LAWS and LAWS OF DUPLICATE. The treatment is that, if one of the simultaneous acts is in legal rotation, that act stands; the other act, which is perforce out of rotation, is treated as a call, lead or play out of rotation and the penalty applicable to such act is invoked.

SIMULTANEOUS PLAY. The play of preduplicated boards at more than one table in a section at the same time, allowing instant scoring. See BAROMETER.

SINGAPORE CONTRACT BRIDGE ASSOCIATION. Founded in 1965, when Singapore left the Malaysian Federation. Hosted Far East Championships, 1972, 1986, 1990. Had 174 members in 1993.
1993 Officers:
President: Thomas Wong
Treasurer: Dr. A.K. Heng
P.O.Box 47, Newton Post Office
Singapore.
Tel: (65) 772 2731
Fax: (65) 779 4580 (Attn. A.K.Heng)

SINGLE COUP. A coup in which declarer shortens his hand once in trumps by ruffing a card from dummy, in order to reduce his trump holding to the same number held by his right-hand opponent. See COUP.

SINGLE DUMMY PROBLEMS. A solver is given the two hands of a partnership holding, approximating the conditions facing a declarer at the bridge table. Among the foremost inventors of these problems was Paul Lukacs of Israel, who presented these.

(a)

    ♠ 6 3 2
    ♥ Q J 4
    ♦ A Q 6 5 4
    ♣ 6 2

    ♠ A K 8
    ♥ 8
    ♦ K 8 2
    ♣ A K Q J 10 9

South plays 6♣ against the lead of the ♥5. East takes the first trick with the ♥A, and returns a low heart. Assuming that West holds the ♥K, South can claim the contract. Why?

♠ K 8 5
♥ 8 4 3 2
♦ 6
♣ A 10 9 8 7

♠ A Q 7
♥ K Q J
♦ K 10 9 8 4
♣ K 2

Against South's 3NT contract, West leads the ♣4. East's jack is taken by South's king. Next comes a successful club finesse, East following suit. What is the right continuation?

Solutions. (a) South trumps the heart return; then plays all his trumps (discarding one diamond and two spades from the dummy). The ♦A-K are cashed in that order. If both opponents follow, there is no problem. If West holds the diamond guard and the ♥K, he is squeezed in the two red suits on the second spade lead. If East holds the diamond guard, after the third lead of diamonds, West has the ♥K and East the diamond guard. Neither, then, has three spades, and declarer can claim the last three tricks in that suit. (b) The solution hinges on the continuation of the club suit; should declarer play the ace and then the nine, he has an impossible discard to make on the second play - discarding either a second diamond or a heart gives the opponents a chance to establish that suit, while a spade discard costs a trick in the suit.Therefore, the potential club loser must be lost immediately, by leading the nine at trick three, before leading the ace.

SINGLE GRAND COUP. A GRAND COUP in which the declarer shortens his hand once in trumps, to reduce his holding to the same number as held by his right hand opponent, by ruffing one winner from the dummy.

SINGLE RAISE. A raise of opener's one-level suit opening to the two-level. The normal range of the bid is 6-9 high-card points; but 10 is possible, and less than 6 is common when there is distributional compensation.

The higher the rank of the opener's suit, the less length is required for responder to raise. 1♠ tends to be a five-card suit in traditional methods, and can be raised freely with three-card support (and the five-card major-suit bidders might raise conceivably with a doubleton). 1♥ is often raised to two with three-card support, but a raise to 2♦ almost invariably indicates four cards or more This is a possible exception:

♠ 4 3   ♥ 5 2   ♦ A 5 2   ♣ Q 9 7 4 3 2

In reply to 1♣, even four-card support may not be sufficient. With a 3-3-3-4 hand, 1♦ or 1NT might be preferred to 2♣. (Se BIDDABLE SUITS.) For some special treatments of single raises see SINGLE RAISE IN MAJOR, CONSTRUCTIVE; INVERTED MINOR SUIT RAISES.

Rebids by the opener below the game level are almost always game invitations. (See SHORT-SUIT GAME TRIES; TRIAL BIDS; TWO-WAY GAME TRIES; WEAK SUIT GAME TRY.) But see PREEMPTIVE RERAISE. Many partnerships make an exception if the opener raises again; this can conveniently be regarded as a preemptive measure, especially if the suit is a minor. A rebid of 2 NT (1♥ -2♥ - 2NT) shows 17-18 points, and is not forcing. If responder then rebids a lower-ranking suit, he is showing a long suit and general weakness, and expects to be passed.

SINGLE RAISE IN MAJOR, CONSTRUCTIVE. In ROTH-STONE, a raise from 1♠ to 2♠ or 1♥ to 2♥ shows 10-12 points and is very rarely passed.

♠ K 5 4
♥ A 9 6 3
♦ Q J
♣ 8 4 3

See ONE NOTRUMP RESPONSE TO MAJOR, FORCING.

SINGLE RAISE IN RESPONDER'S SUIT. See OPENER'S REBID.

SINGLETON. An original holding of exactly one card in a suit (see WORTHLESS SINGLETON/DOUBLETON). Also called a STIFF. For valuation in a suit contract see DISTRIBUTIONAL VALUES.

SINGLETON-SHOWING BID. See SPLINTER BID;. SINGLETON SWISS.

SINGLETON SWISS. In response to a major-suit opening, 4♣ shows good controls, two aces and a singleton. The opener bids 4♦ to ask for the location of the singleton. A 4♦ response shows two aces without a singleton.

SIT, SIT FOR. To pass partner's PENALTY DOUBLE or TAKEOUT DOUBLE.

SIT OUT. (1) Miss a round of play in a duplicate game because there is an odd number of tables. (2) Waiting to cut in to a Chicago or rubber bridge game.

SITTING. Gerund: a session of bridge. Participle: descriptive term referring to one's position at the table, i.e., North, West, etc.; also used in a sentence to describe possession of a hand or a holding, in which case the exact holdings are always given. See SESSION, SEAT.

SIX or SIX-SPOT. The ninth highest card in a suit.

SIX NOTRUMP OPENING. A very rare opening bid showing a balanced hand with 12 sure tricks. Responder should raise if he holds an ace or a king. (To raise with a queen is doubtful.)

SIX OF A SUIT OPENING. The theoretical meaning of this bid is a 12-trick hand which is missing only the ace or king of trumps. Such a hand has such low frequency that the bid is idle. It is perhaps more sensible to reserve it for a freak hand, possibly a complete two-suiter, which is likely to offer some play for 12 tricks. This has the required preemptive value and does not encourage the opponents to save, as they would if the opener had guaranteed 12 tricks.

SIX-ODD. Six tricks over book or 12 tricks in all.

SIX TABLES. At duplicate, six tables provide for competition among 24 players as individuals, 12 pairs or six teams.

In addition, there is available a 25-player individual movement, which can be used for a one-session game using 30 boards, or a two-session game using only 25 boards per session.

As a pair contest, either the MITCHELL or HOWELL

MOVEMENT can be used. If a Mitchell is used, tables 1 and 6 share boards by relay throughout, with a byestand between tables 3 and 4, traveling pairs moving to higher numbered, and boards to lower numbered tables. The full six rounds must be played, usually four boards to the round. Top is 5, average is 60. If Howell movement is used, the full 11-round, 22-board movement is desirable for an early finish. For a longer game, the nine-round, three-boards-to-a-round THREE-QUARTER MOVEMENT is excellent. If you lack guide cards for this movement you may play a 5-table Howell with an Appendix Table.

For a team game the THURNER MOVEMENT is good. As an alternative you may start by having the moving pairs skip a table in the lower direction. After the first round have the moving pairs skip an extra table. After the second round the moving pairs move normally. After the third round the East-West pairs skip an extra table and the boards skip a table. For the last round tables 1 and 4, 2 and 5, 3 and 6 share the boards and relay. East-West Pair 1 follows these moves; 5, 2, 6, 3; then to 4 for the relay. A Swiss Team Movement is not practical for so few teams. For IMP matches use movement shown for a team-of-four and score each match on IMPs. The STAGGER MOVEMENT has considerable advantages. For 5° tables or 6° tables, see HALF TABLES. An individual movement for 12 rounds is available; for details, see MINGLED MOVEMENT. There is also a 25-player movement in 25 rounds.

SIXTEEN, RULE OF. See RULE OF SIXTEEN.

SKIP, SKIP MOVEMENT. An irregularity in the progression of the traveling pairs (or the boards) in a MITCHELL MOVEMENT pair game with an even number of tables, where it is not necessary that all contestants play every board in play. Skips also are used in certain forms of team movements, notably board-a-match events with an even number of tables. Skips also are employed in certain individual events, notably the 15-table movement.

SKIP BID. In a wide sense, any bid at a level higher than is required by the previous auction. In practice, a skip bid is used to refer to weak preemptive actions, whether as an opening bid, an overcall or a response. (See PREEMPTIVE BID, WEAK JUMP OVERCALL and PREEMPTIVE RESPONSE.) To avoid the ethical problems that may arise after preemptive action, the SKIP-BID WARNING is usually used in North America.

SKIP-BID WARNING. A notice given to the opponent by a player who is about to skip at least one level of the bidding. Such a player announces, "I am about to make a skip bid, please wait." The next player to make a call is expected to hesitate approximately 10 seconds before making his call.

The reason for this warning is that immediate actions by the player on the left of the player who makes a skip bid can give partner information to which he is not entitled. For instance, a quick pass could be construed as showing few if any values. A quick double could mean that the player has a very good hand. Long thought before finally making a call or a bid could easily indicate a hand on which no clear-cut action is called for.

All these actions could be perfectly ethical for the player who makes them. However, each one puts a very strong ethical burden on partner. Partner is not supposed to act on the basis that a quick pass shows very little strength, a quick double shows a lot of strength, and a slow pass or bid shows doubt as to whether the pass or the double should have been made. Since the skip-bid warning requires approximately a 10-second hesitation at all times by the next player to call, right-hand opponent should no longer have an ethical problem when left-hand opponent is forced to hesitate under all circumstances.

Sam Fry Jr. was the first to propose such a compulsory pause – he suggested it in 1938. The ACBL adopted this procedure in 1957.

When BIDDING BOXES are used in international matches where SCREENS are not in use, the player who is about to make a skip-bid places a sign saying "Stop!" on the table. He then makes his skip bid, and the next opponent to call must refrain from making his call until the skip bidder has picked up the "Stop" sign. Skip-bid warnings are not necessary when screens are in use because the two calls from one side of the screen come to the attention of the players on the other side at the same time.

SKIP MITCHELL. See MITCHELL MOVEMENT.

SLAM. The winning of 12 tricks (SMALL SLAM, previously called little slam) or all 13 tricks (GRAND SLAM) An original object in the earliest forms of WHIST (some of which were called "Slamm"), these results were rewarded by bonuses in BRIDGE-WHIST and auction bridge regardless of the declaration, so much so that in auction bridge a side that bid seven and won 12 tricks still received the 50-point premium for a small slam although the contract was down one. In contract bridge, however, slam bonuses are paid only when the slam is both bid and made.

SLAM BIDDING. The methods by which slam contracts are investigated. Accurate slam bidding is vital for a winning player; successful slams earn large bonuses, and those that fail are severely penalized (the undertrick penalty plus the value of the lost game). Ironically, the history of world championship matches is studded with failures in the slam zone.

The two vital ingredients of a successful slam are power and CONTROLS. A partnership must determine not only that it has the values to take 12 or 13 tricks in its best STRAIN, but that the defense cannot defeat the slam at the start. Hence, a large part of modern slam bidding machinery involves investigation of trump-suit solidity and first- and second-round controls. (See SLAM CONVENTIONS.)

The early creation of a game-forcing situation often provides the spark for slam investigation. (See FAST ARRIVAL, PRINCIPLE OF). Conventions have been devised to give slam information simultaneously with the announcement of a trump fit. (See JACOBY 2NT, SPLINTER BID, SUPER SWISS, UNBALANCED SWISS RAISE, VALUE SWISS RAISES.) Once a satisfactory trump fit is established, either player may start the search if he suspects the possibility of slam. Cuebidding may be approached in various ways.

Cuebidding a control, usually an ace, invites partner to cooperate, if his hand is suitable, by cuebidding a control in return or bidding slam. (Good players avoid initial cuebids on singletons and void suits. Doing so may induce partner to attach the wrong value to supporting kings and queens.)

WEST	EAST
♠ A K J 10 4	♠ 8
♥ K J 9 8	♥ A Q 10 6 5 2
♦ 6 2	♦ Q 5 4
♣ K 9	♣ A J 3

WEST	EAST
1 ♠	2 ♥
4 ♥	5 ♣
5 ♥	

By bidding 5♣, East shows the ♣A and asks West his opinion of slam. Having nothing to spare for his bidding, West signs off by returning to the agreed trump suit.

WEST	EAST
♠ A K 6 4	♠ 8 2
♥ K 6 5	♥ A Q J 9 2
♦ Q 6	♦ A K 5 3
♣ A 9 6 3	♣ 8 4

WEST	EAST
1NT	3 ♥
4 ♥	5 ♦
6 ♥	

East tries for slam with a 5♦ cuebid; West, with both black aces and fair trumps, accepts.

When a player invites invite slam with a cuebid, the partnership must clearly be in the slam zone.

WEST	EAST
1 ♥	2 ♥
3 ♣	

West does not promise slam interest; he may be trying for game.

Sometimes, however, slam tries are made below game:

WEST	EAST
♠ A K J 9 8	♠ Q 10 4 3
♥ 10 6	♥ K Q 9 7
♦ A 10 4	♦ K Q 2
♣ K J 9	♣ Q 2

WEST	EAST
1 ♠	3 ♠
4 ♦	4 ♠

Over East's forcing raise, West shows slam interest with 4♦, a convenient try that does not commit the partnership past game. East lacks controls and declines.

WEST	EAST
♠ A J 8	♠ K Q 10 6 3
♥ K 10 7 6	♥ A 3
♦ A Q 10 7	♦ 8 3 2
♣ K 9	♣ A 8 6

WEST	EAST
1NT	3 ♠
4 ♦	4 ♥
4 ♠	5 ♣
6 ♠	

West's 4♦ does not suggest an alternative trump suit; spades are agreed by implication, since without spade support, West would return to 3NT. The 4♦ bid is a slam try showing the ♦A, a maximum hand and good spade support. With two aces, East cooperates by showing the ♥A. West has nothing more to say, but when East makes a further try, West accepts. (See ADVANCE CUEBID.)

Slam auctions are invariably more accurate when the trump suit is agreed early:

WEST	EAST
♠ A K J 8 5 2	♠ 7
♥ A J 5	♥ K 4
♦ K J 4	♦ A Q 10 7 2
♣ 4	♣ K Q 9 5 2

WEST	EAST
1 ♠	2 ♦
3 ♠	4 ♣
4 ♥	4 ♠
5 ♦	6 ♦
6 ♠	

East thought 4♥ showed a suit and felt obliged to take a 4♠ preference on his singleton. West thought East's 4♠ had been a cuebid, preparatory to showing spade support. 6♠ went down when 6♦ was on. West could have avoided this result if he had set trumps by bidding 4♦ or 5♦ over 4♣.

After first-round controls are cuebid, subsequent cuebids in the same suit indicate second-round control:

WEST	EAST
♠ A 10 3	♠ K J 9
♥ A K 9 8 2	♥ Q J 10 6 5
♦ A 4 3	♦ 8
♣ K 7	♣ A Q 8 6

WEST	EAST
1 ♥	3 ♥
3 ♠	4 ♣
4 ♦	4 ♠
5 ♣	5 ♦
7 ♥	

The hands lend themselves to a smooth sequence where first- and second-round controls are shown in turn until West, having heard enough, bids the grand slam.

It is rare, but possible, to involve third-round controls:

WEST	EAST
♠ A K 9 8 5 2	♠ Q J 7 6
♥ A K 6 4	♥ 5 3
♦ A K 4	♦ Q 7 3 2
♣ —	♣ J 5 2

WEST	EAST
2 ♣	2 ♦
2 ♠	4 ♠ (1)
5 ♥	6 ♦ (2)
7 ♠	

(1) Good spades, but no side ace, king or singleton.

(2) Since East has denied any first- or second-round control, this bid shows third-round diamond control and, since it accepts West's slam try, implies third-round heart control. (See CUEBIDS TO SHOW CONTROLS.)

A Voluntary Bid Beyond Game is a slam try that usually asks about control of a specific suit.

WEST	EAST
♠ A K J 10 8 7	♠ Q 9
♥ Q 4	♥ 7 6
♦ A 10 7	♦ K Q 9 8 4
♣ K 6	♣ A Q 10 7

WEST	EAST
1 ♠	2 ♦
3 ♠	4 ♣
4 ♦	4 ♠
5 ♠	

West interprets East's sequence as a mild slam try. Since West has the minor suits under control, his 5♠ bid compels East to bid slam with as much as second-round control in hearts, the unbid suit. Though East holds a useful hand, he must pass.

WEST	EAST
♠ Q 7 6 4	♠ A K J 5 3
♥ A 6 5 4	♥ 8 6
♦ A 10 4	♦ 7
♣ 5 4	♣ A K Q J 2

WEST	EAST
Pass	1 ♠
3 ♠	4 ♣
4 ♦	5 ♠
6 ♥	7 ♣
7 ♠	

East's 5♠ bid asks West to bid slam with a control in hearts. Since West has the ♥A, he cuebids 6♥, and East-West reach the grand slam.

If the opponents have bid, a bid of five of the agreed trump suit asks partner to bid a slam if he controls the enemy suit, unless one member of the partnership has cuebid the suit.

WEST	NORTH	EAST	SOUTH
			1 ♥
2 ♠	3 ♥	Pass	5 ♥

South has a powerful hand, but losing spades.

WEST	NORTH	EAST	SOUTH
			1 ♥
1 ♠	3 ♥	Pass	3 ♠
Pass	4 ♥	Pass	5 ♥

South has spades controlled, but poor trumps. South probably has both minor-suit aces, since he would cuebid if he had one or the other.

The situation changes when the opponents' bidding *forces* the auction to the five level.

WEST	NORTH	EAST	SOUTH
			1 ♥
1 ♠	3 ♥	4 ♠	5 ♥

South has no slam aspirations, he feels that doubling 4♠ will not produce a satisfactory penalty and prefers to try for 11 tricks at 5♥.

Even a bid of 5♣ or 5♦ by South would not clearly be a try for slam. In a competitive auction, it is more practical to use new-suit bids to assist partner's judgment. South might bid 5♦ on:

```
♠ —
♥ A K J 6 5
♦ A J 10 5 4
♣ 6 5 2
```

to help North decide what to do if East-West go on to 5♠.

Cuebidding Style. One important cuebidding question a pair must answer is whether return cuebids below game are *cooperative* or *constructive*.

WEST	NORTH	EAST	SOUTH
			1 ♣
1 ♠	2 ♦	Pass	2 ♥
Pass	4 ♦	Pass	?

South holds:

```
♠ A J
♥ Q J 10 7
♦ A 3
♣ J 8 7 6 3
```

Although South has a minimum hand, some players would consider a 4♠ cuebid mandatory; others would

exercise judgment and bid 5♦.

Another matter of style:

WEST	EAST
1 ♠	3 ♠
4 ♦	5 ♣
5 ♠	6 ♠

The question is whether West's sequence *demands* slam if East has a heart control, as would surely be the case on *this* auction:

WEST	EAST
1 ♠	3 ♠
4 ♣	4 ♦
5 ♠	

Few players are willing to go *past game* to make a doubtful cuebid.

WEST	EAST
♠ K 3	♠ A Q 4 2
♥ A J 10 5 4	♥ K Q 3 2
♦ A K J	♦ 7 6 5
♣ J 4 3	♣ Q 6

WEST	EAST
1 ♥	3 ♥
4 ♦	4 ♥

Since East has a minimum, he refuses to cuebid 4♠.

With a choice of aces to cuebid, the usual choice is the cheapest ace to save bidding room.

WEST	EAST
♠ Q J 8 5 2	♠ A K 9 4
♥ A K 7 3	♥ 8 2
♦ 5	♦ A J 8 3
♣ A J 5	♣ K 4 3

WEST	EAST
1 ♠	3 ♠
4 ♣	4 ♦
4 ♥	5 ♣
5 ♥	6 ♠

Positional Slams. Occasionally slam can be made only from one side of the table. Thus, a player with a vulnerable holding tries to become declarer for protection from the opening lead.

```
              ♠ A K Q 9 7 6 5 2
              ♥ 8 5
              ♦ K
              ♣ J 2
♠ J 4 3                        ♠ 10
♥ J 6 2                        ♥ K 7 4 3
♦ J 8 4                        ♦ 9 7 3 2
♣ A Q 10 7                     ♣ 8 6 5 4
              ♠ 8
              ♥ A Q 10 9
              ♦ A Q 10 6 5
              ♣ K 9 3
```

This deal is from the 1962 Bermuda Bowl match between Great Britain and North America. In one room North America played 4♠, taking 11 tricks after a club lead. The British bidding was:

SOUTH	NORTH
1 ♦	2 ♠
3 ♥	4 ♠
4NT	5 ♦
6NT	

North's bidding showed a solid spade suit. Learning through BLACKWOOD that the ♣A was missing, South bid slam in notrump to protect his ♣K.

WEST	EAST
♠ A J 10 8	♠ K Q 7 3 2
♥ K	♥ A 10 8 3
♦ A Q 10	♦ J 8 7
♣ K Q J 10 2	♣ 6

WEST	EAST
1 ♣	1 ♠
4 ♠	5 ♥
6NT	

West accepts his partner's slam try, but bids 6NT; at 6♠, a diamond opening lead might break the contract. (See RIGHT SIDE.)

Asking About Controls. Since controls are a necessary feature of successful slams, conventions have been devised to determine how many aces and kings a partnership holds. The most prevalent is BLACKWOOD.

WEST	EAST
♠ A	♠ K 8
♥ K 10 8 7	♥ A Q 9 6 3 2
♦ A 5	♦ K Q 10
♣ A Q 9 8 7 6	♣ 10 3

WEST	EAST
1 ♣	1 ♥
4 ♥	4NT
5 ♠	5NT
6 ♦	6 ♥

The 4NT and 5NT bids are conventional, and West responds by showing aces and kings (5♠ = three aces, 6♦ = one king). Though East has a powerful hand, he must not venture beyond six, for he knows a critical king is missing.

Although Blackwood determines the total number of aces and kings a pair holds, it reveals nothing about power, trump quality or the fit in a key side suit; nor should a player use Blackwood if he must identify *specific* controls. West holds:

        ♠ A K Q 10 7 4 2
        ♥ 7
        ♦ 8 3
        ♣ A Q 4

West opens 1♠ and jumps to 3♠ over a 2♣ response by East. East raises to 4♠. West wants to be in slam if East has the ♦A, but if East instead has the ♥A, the defense may take the first two diamond tricks. Since a 5♦ response to Blackwood will leave West no wiser, he should cuebid 5♣, inviting East to cuebid an ace. If East then bids 5♦, West can jump to 6♠.

Variations of Blackwood are popular. See ROMAN KEY CARD BLACKWOOD.

ASKING BIDS inquire about controls in a specific suit.

WEST	EAST
1 ♠	3 ♠
5 ♣	

If asking bids are in use, West's 5♣ bid may conventionally ask East about his holding in clubs. East's responses would be conventional and confirm or deny controls.

WEST	EAST
4 ♥	5 ♣

East asks West whether he has a control in clubs. East might hold:

♠ A 5
♥ A 7
♦ A K Q 8 3
♣ 9 6 4 2

For details see ASKING BIDS.

Among the more scientific slam-bidding methods, RELAY SYSTEMS are known for their accuracy.

Distributional Slams. Well-fitting hands may produce slam with far fewer that 33 high-card points. If a player shows his distribution while committing to game, he suggests slam and lets partner judge the fit.

WEST	EAST
♠ K Q 10 8 4	♠ A J 6
♥ A 7 4 2	♥ 5
♦ 7 4	♦ K Q 8 3
♣ K Q	♣ A J 8 6 2

WEST	EAST
1 ♠	2 ♣
2 ♥	3 ♦
3NT	4 ♠
6 ♠	

If East were interested in game, he would bid 3♠ at his second turn. Since East stops to bid diamonds before supporting spades, he promises extra strength and heart shortness. If West had an unsuitable heart holding (such as K-J-4-2) or no help in clubs, he would avoid slam.

SPLINTERS BIDS are a popular slam-bidding tool with wide application. A splinter bid is an unusual jump to show support for partner's suit with shortness in the suit in which the jump is made. Partner can judge how well the hands fit. See SPLINTER BID.

Trump Suit Quality. If a grand slam is on the horizon, trump solidity is a critical factor. When a trump suit is agreed, a 5NT bid is available. This GRAND SLAM FORCE, asking responder to bid seven if he holds two of the top three trump honors. West holds:

        ♠ Q J 8 4
        ♥ A K Q 6 4 2
        ♦ —
        ♣ A K 6

West opens 2♣, strong and artificial, and East responds 2♠, natural and positive. West's only concern is the spade suit, and a bid of 5NT, agreeing spades by inference, will let East bid seven if he holds the A-K; otherwise, East will settle for a small slam.

Blasting. The success of slam contracts often depends on the opening lead. A player may resort to an adventurous approach when either he despairs of locating key cards in his partner's hand or feels that the opponents are more likely to profit from scientific investigation. South holds:

        ♠ K 7 4 3
        ♥ A K J 10 6 2
        ♦ —
        ♣ 6 4 2

North opens 1♠ and rebids 2♠ over South's 2♥ response. 6♠ must have an excellent chance without a club lead, and rather than tip off the opponents, South might blast into 6♠. In the same vein, a player may bid a nonexistent suit en route to a slam to discourage a possibly lethal lead. South holds:

        ♠ Q J 6 4 2
        ♥ —
        ♦ A K 10 6 4 2
        ♣ 3 2

If North opens 1♠, South might jump to 6♠ directly.

However, against ingenuous opponents, it may pay to bid a tactical 2♣ first in an effort to get a favorable lead. However, this tactic may induce a LIGHTNER DOUBLE. (See PSYCHIC BIDDING.)

WEST	EAST
♠ K J 7	♠ A Q 10 8 5 2
♥ A K J 4	♥ 3
♦ Q 8 6 3	♦ J 4
♣ Q 8	♣ A K J 4

WEST	EAST
1NT	3♠
4♠	5♣
5♥	5♠

This would be the auction if East-West used cuebidding; they would discover the lack of a diamond control and stop at 5♠. In real life, East might bash into 6♠ over 1NT. South must find the diamond lead to beat the contract.

Bidding slams at notrump is often easier, especially after an opening bid in notrump. Point count can evaluate balanced hands and reduce the matter to simple arithmetic: responder can add his points to opener's and place the contract. East holds:

♠ Q J 8
♥ A J
♦ K Q 3
♣ K J 8 4 2

If West opens 1NT, showing at least 16 points, East can leap to 6NT, counting at least 33 points in the combined hands.

With an in-between hand, responder needs his partner's cooperation and bids 4NT as an invitation. By going past game, East shows slam interest and asks West to continue with a maximum. (See EXPECTED NUMBER OF CONTROLS IN BALANCED HANDS.)

WEST	EAST
♠ A 8 4	♠ K 6 3
♥ J 6 4	♥ A K
♦ K J 3	♦ A Q 7 4
♣ A K 8 3	♣ Q J 6 4

WEST	EAST
1NT	5NT
6♣	7♣

East's 5NT bid forces to 6NT and invites a grand slam. West shows his strong four-card club suit on the way, and East-West reach a good grand slam.

Since in notrump sequences a 4NT bid has a quantitative meaning, Blackwood is unavailable. A bid of 4♣, the GERBER convention, is used instead to check on aces and kings.

Power slam auctions are also available when a trump suit is agreed. If South opens 1♠ on:

♠ A Q 9 6 4
♥ K 5
♦ A J 4
♣ A Q 7

and North raises to 3♠ (forcing), South can try 6♠. The power for slam is there, and controls are no problem.

Jump shifts. An immediate jump shift by responder suggests slam and implies that responder knows in what STRAIN the hand should play. Hence, responder may have great high-card strength for notrump, a solid suit or a fit for opener's suit. South has:

♠ 7
♥ K Q 5 4 3
♦ A K J 4 3 2
♣ 3

If North opens 1♥, South should jump to 3♦, intending to support hearts next.

On some strong hands, a jump shift is ill-prepared. South holds:

♠ A Q 10 5
♥ 5
♦ A K 5 4
♣ A Q 4 3

If North opens 1♥, South should respond 1♠. South needs bidding space to look for the best strain.

Slams at Duplicate. Because a minus score usually produces a poor result, matchpoint duplicate players tend to be conservative slam bidders. If good play is required to take 12 tricks, a good matchpoint score is available for +480 or +680. If most pairs in the field will bid a slam, however, players may prefer a higher-scoring strain even though a slightly superior slam is available in a minor suit.

Five-or-Seven Deals.

Dlr: North	♠ 8
Vul: None	♥ Q 5 2
	♦ A Q 8 7 6 5 2
	♣ K 9

♠ Q J 9 7 5 3	♠ A K 10 4
♥ 10 8 4	♥ A 9 3
♦ 10	♦ —
♣ 6 3 2	♣ A Q J 10 8 4

	♠ 6 2
	♥ K J 7 6
	♦ K J 9 4 3
	♣ 7 5

Table 1

WEST	NORTH	EAST	SOUTH
	1♦	Dbl	1♥
1♠	2♥	5NT	Pass
6♠ (1)	Pass	7♠	All Pass

(1) One top honor, extra length

Table 2

WEST	NORTH	EAST	SOUTH
	1♦	Dbl	1♥
1♠	2♦	3♦	4♦
Pass	5♦	6♠	All Pass

This deal arose in the 1986 Vanderbilt Teams. At table 1 East (Edgar Kaplan) thought he might as well bid seven. If South had held the ♣K, a heart lead would have beaten 5♠; as it was, 7♠ was cold.

Since East-West stopped in a small slam at the other table, Kaplan was getting excellent odds; he would gain 11 IMPs if the ♣K was right and lose 2 if it was wrong.

SLAM CONVENTIONS. Specialized methods adopted for slam exploration include the following conventions which are listed separately: ACOL DIRECT KING; ACOL FOUR NOTRUMP OPENING; ALPHA ASKING BIDS; ANTISPLINTER; ASKING BIDS; BABY BLACKWOOD; BARON SLAM TRY; BETA ASKING BIDS; BLACK AND RED GERBER; BLACKWOOD; BLACKWOOD AFTER INTERFERENCE; BLUE TEAM FOUR CLUB AND FOUR DIAMOND; BYZANTINE BLACKWOOD; CULBERTSON FOUR-FIVE NOTRUMP; DECLARATIVE-INTERROGATIVE FOUR NOTRUMP; DENIAL CUEBIDS; FRAGMENT

BID; GAMMA TRUMP ASKING BIDS; GERBER; GRAND SLAM FORCE; KEYCARD BLACKWOOD; KEYCARD GERBER; KICKBACK; LIGHTNER DOUBLE; MINOR-SUIT SWISS; NORMAN FOUR NOTRUMP; PRECISION ASKING BIDS; REVERSE SWISS; ROMAN ASKING BIDS; ROMAN BLACKWOOD; ROMAN GERBER; ROMAN KEYCARD BLACKWOOD; ROMEX TRUMP ASKING BIDS; SHARPLES; SINGLETON SWISS; SIX NOTRUMP OPENING; SIX OF A SUIT OPENING; SLIVER; SPLINTER; SUCKER DOUBLE; SUPER BLACKWOOD; SUPER GERBER; SUPER PRECISION ASKING BIDS; SUPER SWISS; SWISS; TRUMP ASKING BID; VALUE OF SLAM; See also topics such as EXPECTED NUMBER OF CONTROLS IN BALANCED HANDS; FAST ARRIVAL, PRINCIPLE OF; RIGHT SIDE; SAFETY LEVEL.

SLAM DOUBLE CONVENTIONS. See DOUBLE FOR SACRIFICE; LIGHTNER DOUBLE.

SLAM LEADS. Opening leads against slam contracts frequently involve some special considerations. The general principle is to make passive leads against grand slams and active leads against small slams, but there are many exceptions to this.

An attacking lead against a small slam is often necessary when the bidding indicates a long, establishable suit in the dummy. It may then be necessary for the defense to lead from a king or a queen, in the hope of establishing a trick in the suit led before dummy's suit can be established for discards. But if declarer and dummy both seem likely to have balanced hands, whether or not the contract is notrump, a passive lead is indicated. A deceptive lead is often appropriate, such as a third-best, a fifth-best, or the lower of touching honors. Misinforming the leader's partner is usually less important than misleading the declarer. Assessing the safety of a lead depends on the bidding as well as the suit holding. A low trump is safe from three small if the declaring side can be credited with at least nine trumps, but it would be unsafe against a likely eight-card trump fit, because partner may have Q-x.

The lead of an ace is right more often than some authorities indicate. Apart from the obvious advantage at matchpoint of preventing an overtrick, the ace lead is desirable if the opposing bidding has been crowded or rushed in such a way that two top losers are not unlikely. See also LIGHTNER DOUBLE.

SLIDING BLACKWOOD. See ROLLING BLACKWOOD.

SLIDING BOX. See TRAY.

SLIDING GERBER. See ROLLING GERBER.

SLIVER BID. An extension of the SPLINTER BID principle, devised by George Rosenkranz for use with weaker responding hands. With four- or preferably, five-card trump support for a major suit opening and fewer than 10 HCP, the standard response would be a jump to game. When such a hand includes a singleton or void and a minimum of three controls including at least one king (2 controls – ace or void; 1 control – king or singleton) possession of a "sliver" is indicated by a response of 3NT.

Opener's rebids: Sign off in the major with more than five losers and a hand poor in HCP and controls. With at least six high-card controls, or five controls and a singleton, 15 or more HCP and fewer than six losers, opener explores slam possibilities by bidding the suit where responder's singleton or void will represent duplication and be of least value.

Responder's rebids: Sign off by bidding game in agreed suit if singleton or void is opposite partner's "exclusion" rebid. With shortage elsewhere, rebid by steps: 1st step: Singleton in lower unbid side suit. 2nd step: Singleton in higher suit. 3rd step: Void in lower unbid suit. 4th step: Void in higher unbid suit. In counting steps, a game bid in the agreed trump suit – the sign-off – is omitted.

SLOVENIAN BRIDGE ASSOCIATION (Bridge Zveza Slovenije). The Association was founded in 1972, and joined the WBF in 1992 when Slovenia became independent.
Officers 1992:
President: Dr. Marjan Treppo
Secretary: Branislav Protega,
Novosadska 6,
61110 Ljubljana
Slovenia.
Tel. 0038 61 441 681
Fax: 0038 61 317 374

SLOW PASS. A pass at a slow tempo which reveals that the passer was considering an alternative action. This may be quite harmless; if the passer takes the final decision for his side and becomes the declarer or the dummy, no ethical problem can arise.

In other circumstances the slow pass is liable to convey improper information to the partner who must do his best not to be influenced by that information. Four particular cases are worth distinguishing:

(1) A player who considers making an opening bid and then passes has implied that he holds close to an opening bid. In such circumstances, after he has hesitated, the player should prefer a subminimum opening to a subethical pass.

(2) A slow pass may reveal ambitions at a higher level. If a player passes slowly when his partner raises 1♠ to 2♠, he has indicated faint game possibilities. Admittedly this information will not be significant unless an opponent indiscreetly balances.

(3) The slow pass is most revealing in competitive auctions. Some of the problems are solved by the SKIP-BID WARNING, but such situations often lead to protests. It is often difficult not to be influenced subconsciously. Some associations, notably the Greater New York BA, on the initiative of Edgar Kaplan, believe that adjustments should be made in such cases in the same way as offenses against the normal rules of the game. The slow-passing side is penalized in the same way that they would be for, say, a revoke, and there is no suggestion of unethical conduct. In order to provide standards and to avoid ad hoc judgments, some tournament protest committees apply a so-called 80% rule. If the committee finds that there was in fact a slow pass, it will ordinarily rescind the action taken by the partner of the slow passer if it believes such an action would normally be taken less than 80% of the time.

(4) A slow pass which ends the auction may be revealing when the passer's partner will be on lead. There may

be an indication that a LEAD-DIRECTING DOUBLE was contemplated.

In one special case a slow pass is quite harmless. A forcing pass at a high level by the side which is on the offensive does not convey information, because partner does not know whether the alternative contemplated was a bid or a double. See also HUDDLE.

SLOW PLAY. As opposed to careful or thoughtful play, slow play is discourteous not only to the opponents of the moment, but to all other competitors as well. In rubber bridge, it decreases the number of hands that can be played in a session; in duplicate tournaments, a consistently slow pair can delay the entire game by many minutes.

Contributing to slow play as defined here are some or all of these violations of the Proprieties of duplicate play: (1) delay in coming to the table after the round has been called; (2) discussion of boards previously played; (3) failure to pass at least one completed board promptly, or pass one board if the other has not been completed; (4) inattention during the bidding necessitating frequent reviews of the auction; (5) post-mortems, particularly those involving the player whose duty it is to score the board just played; (6) failure to accept a ruling from the director pleasantly and promptly in the event of an infraction; (7) blaming previous opponents for present tardiness instead of concentrating on finishing the present hand; (8) waiting for a miracle to change opponent's aces to deuces so that a bad contract will not receive its deserved result. The LAWS OF DUPLICATE specifically provide that as a matter of courtesy a player should avoid "Prolonging play unnecessarily for the purpose of disconcerting the other players." (Proprieties III.)

In national and international championships a team which repeatedly exceeds the time limit allowed for play is subject to penalties. The penalty may take the form of a matchpoint or victory-point "fine." It may be as extreme as exclusion of a team from an event. In team events, the penalty sometimes takes the form of barring offending pairs from playing as partners in later rounds.

There is a recurrent problem in controlling slow play in major national and international team play. If a table is slow players may ask for a monitor to keep track of the time use, but there is no record of the period during which the problem arose. A technological solution is a possibility. The software developed by NEC and the Japanese Bridge League for the 1991 world championships in Yokohama offered a possibility which was not utilized but may be in the future. The small terminals used to record bidding and play at the table can keep track of the time used by each player, giving an objective measure of time and therefore a basis for slow penalties.

SLOW SHOWS, DIRECT DENIES. The idea that a Lebensohl bid followed by a cuebid or 3NT promises a stopper in the opponent's suit:

WEST	NORTH	EAST	SOUTH
1NT	2 ♥	2 NT	Pass
3 ♣	Pass	3 ♥ or 3NT	

These bids show a heart stopper. Conversely, such bids made on the first round deny a heart stopper.

Some players prefer the converse: Slow denies, direct shows.

The same idea applies when Lebensohl is used in response to a double of a Weak Two-bid.

SLUFF. To discard a worthless card; to dispose of a loser by throwing it off on the lead of a suit not held by the sluffer. The word derives from slough, to cast off.

SMALL CARD. A card in a suit lower than the 6, although the 6 itself on occasion is considered a small card.

SMALL SLAM. The bidding and making of six-odd, or 12 tricks in all, for which the premium, scored above the line in rubber bridge, but in regular fashion in Chicago or Duplicate, is 500 points when not vulnerable and 750 points when vulnerable. See SLAM BIDDING for a mathematical treatment of percentage expectation of success for the bid. See also MATHEMATICAL VALUE OF GAME.

SMITH CONVENTION. (1) A club takeout as a DEFENSE TO OPENING THREE-BID, devised by Curtis Smith. (2) A 4NT slam convention devised by William S. Smith and Gertrude Smith of Waterbury CT, in 1935 and which was popular for many years. Identical in principle with the NORMAN 4NT, it is different in one detail. A response of 5♠ showed specifically one ace and three kings, while 5NT was used to show two aces and one king. (3) Also applied to the cheating device said to have been used at rubber bridge: holding a YARBOROUGH, one player announces that he has 14 cards, and his partner, also with a poor hand, announces 12, and rapidly mixes the two hands together. If partner has a good hand, he suggests a recount.

SMITH SIGNAL. An attitude signal given at the first opportunity by the partner of the opening leader against a notrump contract to indicate the degree of enthusiasm for the opening leader's suit. If defender's first spot card is low, this indicates he cannot stand a continuation in the opening leader's suit should opening leader regain the lead. Conversely, following with a high spot card pinpoints the desirability of a second lead in the original suit led. The opening leader can give the same kind of signal – a high spot card indicates a desire to have the opening suit continued should partner gain the lead; a low spot card suggests trying something else. The signal is sometimes attributed to T.R.H. Lyons of Great Britain, but I.G.Smith of Great Britain suggested virtually the same signal as early as the December 1963 issue of *British Bridge World.* Here is how the signal works:

```
              ♠ 9 7
              ♥ Q 10 2
              ♦ 7 6 5 4
              ♣ A K Q J
♠ A 10 8 4 2                    ♠ Q J 5
♥ 9 8 7                         ♥ K J 6 4
♦ K 3                          ♦ 10 9 8
♣ 9 7 3                        ♣ 10 8 2
              ♠ K 6 3
              ♥ A 5 3
              ♦ A Q J 2
              ♣ 6 5 4
```

SOUTH	NORTH
1 ♦	2 ♣
2NT	3NT

West leads the ♠4 against 3NT. Declarer wins East's jack with the king and leads a club to dummy. East should play the ♣10 on this trick, meaning please continue. Declarer takes the diamond finesse, and when West wins the king he cashes four spade tricks for one down. Now suppose the East and South cards had been slightly different:

```
            ♠ 9 7
            ♥ Q 10 2
            ♦ 7 6 5 4
            ♣ A K Q J
♠ A 10 8 4 2              ♠ J 6 5
♥ 9 8 7                   ♥ A J 6 4
♦ K 3                     ♦ 10 9 8
♣ 9 7 3                   ♣ 10 8 2
            ♠ K Q 3
            ♥ K 5 3
            ♦ A Q J 2
            ♣ 6 5 4
```

The bidding is the same and West, who has the same hand as before, makes the same opening lead and sees the same dummy. Again declarer wins the ♠J with the king and leads a club. This time, however, East cannot stand a spade continuation from partner, so he contributes the ♣2. Declarer takes a diamond finesse, losing to the king. West now knows he can't afford to continue spades from his side of the table, and he exits with the ♥9. East grabs the trick, returns the ♠6, and the contract fails by two tricks. Some use the reverse procedure.

SMITH TROPHY. Awarded to the winners of the Life Master Women's Pairs contested at the Fall North American Championships, under which heading past results are listed. Donated by Charles H. Goren in 1969 in memory of his longtime partner Helen Sobel Smith. For results see Appendix I.

SMOLEN TRANSFER. An adjunct to Stayman and Jacoby Transfer Bids for game-going hands, devised by Mike Smolen of Los Angeles, to allow the notrump opener to become the declarer in responder's long suit after responder has used Stayman with 5-4 or 6-4 in the major suits. Using Smolen Transfers, after the auction has started

NORTH	SOUTH
1NT	2♣
2♦	

South jumps to three of his four-card major suit, showing that he has more than four cards in the other major. If opener has three cards in the unbid major, he bids game in that major. If opener has only a doubleton he bids 3NT and, if responder has six cards in the unbid major, he continues by bidding four of the suit just below his unbid major, as a transfer bid.

After an opening 2NT bid, Stayman followed by 3♥ or 3♠ can be used similarly.

SMOTHER PLAY. A rare end position that permits capture of a defender's virtually certain trump winner.

```
            ♠ A 6 5
            ♥ K 5 4
            ♦ 8 7 6 5
            ♣ A Q 3
♠ K 7 4 3                ♠ 2
♥ J 9 7                  ♥ Q 10 8 3 2
♦ 9 4 2                  ♦ Q J 10
♣ 10 7 5                 ♣ J 9 4 2
            ♠ Q J 10 9 8
            ♥ A 6
            ♦ A K 3
            ♣ K 8 6
```

South plays 6♠. The contract appears doomed, for declarer must lose a diamond trick and West's trump king is sufficiently protected to elude capture by normal finessing. However, the opening lead of a diamond is won, and the ♠10 and ♠9 are finessed, West declining to cover. South continues with three rounds of clubs, and follows with the ace, king, and a heart ruff in his own hand. The ♦A is taken, leaving the following ending:

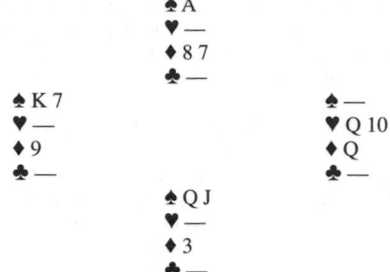

```
            ♠ A
            ♥ —
            ♦ 8 7
            ♣ —
♠ K 7                    ♠ —
♥ —                     ♥ Q 10
♦ 9                     ♦ Q
♣ —                     ♣ —
            ♠ Q J
            ♥ —
            ♦ 3
            ♣ —
```

East is thrown in with a diamond and has nothing but hearts to return. South ruffs with the queen, and West is helpless. Also known as the "disappearing trump trick." See also DEVIL'S COUP.

SNAP. Abbreviation for STRONG NOTRUMP AFTER PASSING. Frequently the initials are used as a word.

SNAPDRAGON A double by fourth hand when the first three players have each bid a different suit.

WEST	NORTH	EAST	· SOUTH
1♣	1♥	2♦	Dbl

The double shows a five-card suit and moderate values, probably with a doubleton heart. Players should discuss the levels at which this applies.

SOCIAL BRIDGE. Played in a home for moderate or no stakes, bridge can still be highly skillful and competitive. For larger gatherings, see PARTY BRIDGE and PROGRESSIVE BRIDGE. In expert circles, social bridge increasingly is taking the form of team-of-four competition, with a stake based on imps.

SOCK, SOCK IT. Obsolete slang for "double."

SOFT VALUES. Queens and jacks, which may well have no role in the play, as distinct from "hard values" which are aces and kings.

SOLID SUIT. A holding which is expected, at a trump or notrump contract, to win as many tricks as there are cards in the suit. Theoretically it should contain an many high cards as there are outstanding cards in the suit: A-K-Q-x-x-x-x-x might lose a trick if all four cards are in the same hand. Culbertson gave as his definition of reasonable expectancy of the solidity of a suit the rule of thumb that a suit was solid if half the outstanding cards were in one hand the entire suit could still be picked up by successive leads.

An alternative definition, similar in effect, is "a suit which can be expected to lose no tricks with a singleton in dummy, and may lose no tricks opposite a void." By this standard, A-K-Q-x-x-x-x, A-K-Q-10-x-x qualify, but A-K-Q-x-x-x does not.

SOLOMON AWARD. Endowed by Charles J. Solomon,

this award for the Bridge Hand of the Year is presented annually by the INTERNATIONAL BRIDGE PRESS ASSOCIATION. It is made to the player who has produced the best play of a hand, whether as declarer or defender, during the year in question. For a list of winners see INTERNATIONAL BRIDGE PRESS ASSOCIATION AWARDS.

SOLOMON TROPHY. A WBF trophy in honor of Charles J. Solomon awarded to the nation with the best overall victory-point record in the WORLD PAIR OLYMPIAD. The United States has won the trophy since it was put into play in 1966.

SOLOWAY JUMP SHIFT. See JUMP SHIFT.

SORTING THE HAND. The act of arranging the cards of a hand into suits and by order within suit after the cards have been dealt. Many fine players, after arranging their hand, then remove a couple of cards from a long suit and put them apart from the rest of the cards in the suit as a protection against an inadvertent glance of an opponent. Among the habits that experienced players develop are the placing of a singleton in the middle, rather than at an end of the hand, and the avoidance of rearranging a hand when a suit has been exhausted therefrom. It is a violation of the Proprieties to note from what part of a hand an opponent or partner draws a card in order to get a clue as to his holding or distribution.

SOS REDOUBLE. A redouble calling on partner to select another denomination. It applies whenever there is no possibility of the redouble being applied in a natural sense.

WEST	NORTH	EAST	SOUTH
			1 ♣
Dbl	Pass	Pass	Redbl

South may have opened on a short club suit. His redouble requests North to bid his best suit outside of clubs as a rescue. However, in a major suit such a redouble would be strength-showing, not an SOS. A double of an opening weak notrump bid often prompts an SOS redouble. For example:

WEST	NORTH	EAST	SOUTH
			1 NT
Dbl	2 ♣	Dbl	Pass
Pass	Redbl		

This sequence implies that North is planning to play in some other suit, and does not hold clubs. South should bid his lowest-ranking four-card suit, and if his only suit is clubs he should bid his lowest-ranking three-card suit. If South retreats into 2♦ and an opponent doubles, North might redouble again to ask South to select a major suit. Similar situations arise when the opening notrump bid is doubled and redoubled. It is the doubling side which is then on the run, perhaps using SOS redoubles in an attempt to find the best part-score fit at the level of two. In rare circumstances a player may redouble his partner's bid as an SOS instead of his own bid.

WEST	NORTH	EAST	SOUTH
			1 ♣
Pass	Pass	Dbl	Pass
Pass	Redbl		

If North could not respond to 1♣ he cannot wish to redouble naturally. The redouble therefore shows extreme shortage in clubs and begs South to pick another denomi-

nation. See also DEFENSE TO ONE NOTRUMP DOUBLED, KOCK-WERNER REDOUBLE, SCRAMBLING and WRIGGLE.

SOUND BIDDING. A bidding system stressing elevated standards for some opening bids and overcalls. ROTHSTONE opening bids in first or second position are examples of sound bids. A sound bidder refers to one whose bids, rebids and responses are fully justified by his holding, and who, when choices of bids are available, will choose the more conservative action.

SOUTH. One of the compass points used in describing the players at the table. South is partnered by North, and is OVER the East hand but UNDER the West hand.

SOUTH AFRICAN BRIDGE FEDERATION. The Federation was formed in 1954 and participated in all Olympiads 1960-80. It voluntarily withdrew from international competition 1981-91 because of international sanctions imposed on the country as a result of the Apartheid policies of the government in power. International play resumed in 1992. Membership reached 5000 in 1980, declined to 2000 in 1991 because of sanctions, then began to rise again. In 1993 there were 2399 members in 48 clubs, with Johannesburg the focal point. The SABF sponsors an 8 day national tournament in May and other events. The South African women players won silver medals in the 1968 and 1972 Team Olympiads and the 1974 Pairs Olympiad.

Officers 1992:
President: Julius Butkow
Secretary: Patsi Shefer
P.O. Box 87682
Houghton, Johannesburg
South Africa 2041.
Tel: 27 11 29 3007
Fax: 27 11 29 3007

SOUTH AFRICAN TEXAS. A special method of transfer bids at the level of four, now obsolescent. After an opening bid of 1NT or 2NT, a jump to 4♣ requires the opener to bid 4♥, and 4♦ asks for 4♠. This was the original form of David Carter's TEXAS convention, and was developed independently in South Africa. It was quickly abandoned in the U.S. in favor of red-suit transfer bids which permit the use of 4♣ as GERBER. The South African version has the psychological advantage that the responses do not sound natural, and the opener is protected from a lapse of memory.

SOUTH AMERICAN BRIDGE CONFEDERATION (Confederacion Sudamericana de Bridge). Founded in 1948, the Confederation consists of the bridge federations of 8 South American countries: Argentina, Bolivia, Brazil, Chile, Ecuador, Paraguay, Peru and Uruguay. South American Championships are organized, with the winning countries earning the right to represent the zone in world championships. (For past results, see Appendix III.)

President 1992:
Ernesto Velarde Arenas
Av. Jorge Basadre 475
San Isidro
Lima 27, Peru.
Tel 51 14 419995

Fax 51 14 457023

SOUTH PACIFIC ZONE. Zone 7 of the World Bridge Federation is the third-largest zone measured by registered players. There are six member countries: Australia; Cook Islands; French Polynesia; Fiji; New Zealand; Vanuatu. An annual championship is held for the island countries, beginning in 1991. The first two were won by Tahiti. Qualification for world championships (Bermuda Bowl and Venice Cup) was regularly by a "Test Match" between Australia and New Zealand. This was replaced in 1991 by a South Pacific Championship, with Australia the first winners in both open and women's divisions. For past results see Appendix III.
President 1993:
  John Wignall
  P.O. Box 2335
  Christchurch
  New Zealand
  Tel. 64 3 79 26 00
  Fax. 64 3 79 11 96

SOVIET UNION. Bridge was an "unofficial" game in the Soviet Union until 1986, but some internal tournaments were played, mainly in the Baltic states. International contacts began in Estonia about 1980, but full international participation did not begin until 1989. See RUSSIA, ESTONIA, LATVIA, UKRAINE.

SPADES. The highest ranking of the four suits at bridge. The 13 cards of the suit are indicated with a black symbol, ♠. In American and British decks, and some made for export to North America, the ace of spades usually carries a special design, trademarked by the manufacturer, on its face.

SPANISH BRIDGE FEDERATION. (FEDERACION ESPANOLA DE BRIDGE). Founded in 1941, by 1992 the Federation had about 4000 members. The Federation hosted the 1974 World Pair Olympiad in Las Palmas.
Officers 1992:
  President: Antonio Frances
  Secretary: Ignacio Jover de Castro
  Mallorca 290, Entlo 209
  08037 Barcelona, Spain.
  Tel: 34-3/207 20 98

SPECIFIED CARDS, ODDS GOVERNING. See ODDS GOVERNING SPECIFIED CARDS.

SPECIFIED SUIT. A suit of which the lead may be required or forbidden because of an irregularity earlier in the auction or play.

SPECTATOR. A person who watches a bridge tournament without actually taking part. This is differentiated from a KIBITZER, whose presence is limited to a particular table. The conduct of spectators is governed by the LAWS (Proprieties V). Misconduct by a kibitzer may result in a penalty against the side responsible for the kibitzer's presence. See LAWS OF DUPLICATE (Law 11).
  Some of the larger championship events and all of the international and inter-city matches draw large numbers of interested viewers for whom provision is usually made. Such provision is sometimes in the form of small raised

grandstands surrounding the table to accommodate more spectators than can be taken care of in chairs, and range up to the BRIDGE-O-RAMA or VUGRAPH facilities which enable hundreds of viewers to watch the play of all four hands simultaneously. The hand is shown on the screen and the bidding is added as it takes place. Each card is crossed off as played. Adding to the enjoyment of the spectators is the commentary offered by experts as the hands are bid and played. Of course the greatest number of spectators of a bridge match are the viewers of televised matches. From 1988 world championships have invariably used an electronic Vugraph, with bidding and play controlled by a computer. See TELEVISION .

SPEEDBALL. An event with an unusually fast time-limit, often a ZIP SWISS played at midnight or a daytime game that leaves the evening open for the competitors.

SPIDER MOVEMENT. See WEB MOVEMENT.

SPINGOLD TROPHY. For the NABC Master Teams Championship, donated by Nathan Spingold in 1934 for what was then called the World Championship Masters Team-of-Four and played originally as a separate knock-out event. In 1938 this event became a part of the Summer NABC (under which results are listed in Appendix I), superseding the CITY OF ASBURY PARK TROPHY event. In the Fifties and Seventies the Spingold helped select a number of U.S. international teams; it ranks with the Vanderbilt as the most highly prized trophy in the ACBL calendar. The Spingold is a major factor in selecting the American representatives in world championship play. See INTERNATIONAL OPEN TEAM SELECTION. For results see Appendix I.

SPIRAL. An idea introduced in SYMMETRIC RELAY and now used in other contexts. A player whose hand is already well-defined is asked to scan through the suits looking for high cards in a set order. A minimum step denies a top card in the longest suit. Minimum plus one shows a top card in the longest suit but denies one in the second-longest, and so on. When suits are of equal length the higher is scanned first. Used in the ROMEX SYSTEM following Blackwood and in other situations. See DENIAL CUEBIDS.

SPLIMIT RAISES. See MINI-SPLINTERS.

SPLINTER BID. A successor to the VOID-SHOWING BID idea, the splinter was devised by Dorothy Hayden Truscott in 1964. An unusual jump guarantees a fit for partner's last-named suit and shows a singleton or void in the suit in which the jump is made.
  The device can be used in a variety of situations. The most common are:

WEST	EAST
1 ♠	4 ♣

East shows a forcing raise which includes club shortage.

1 ♣	1 ♠
4 ♦	

Here West shows a powerful opening bid (willing to play 4♠ opposite what may be only 6 points) with 4-card support and diamond shortage.
  Splinters bids suggest slam, but on the basis of fit and

distribution rather than high cards. Over a 1♠ opening, responder would try 4♣ on as little as:

> ♠ Q J 7 4 2
> ♥ A 8 4
> ♦ A 10 5 2
> ♣ 8

Even if opener has a minimum hand, slam may have a good chance if he has no wasted strength in clubs: e.g.,

> ♠ A 9 8 5 3
> ♥ K Q 2
> ♦ K 4
> ♣ 9 5 2

Most experts also use splinters in the majors:

WEST	EAST
1 ♠	4 ♥

If East really had hearts he could bid 2♥ then 4♥.

1 ♥	3 ♠

If East really had a preempt in spades he could bid 1♠ then 2♠ then 3♠.

Other splinter sequences include:

1NT	2 ♣
2 ♥	4 ♦

1 ♠	2 ♦
2 ♥	4 ♣

1 ♥	1 ♠
2 ♥	4 ♣

This time East is showing only three trumps.

2 ♣ (1)	2 ♦ (2)
2 ♠	4 ♦

(1) Strong, artificial
(2) Negative, artificial

WEST	NORTH	EAST	SOUTH
	1 ♥	1 ♠	3 ♠

Splinters are very useful over a minor suit opening bid.

WEST	EAST
1 ♦	3 ♥

East denies a four-card major, but shows excellent diamond support (usually five cards), opening bid values and heart shortage. Perhaps ♠ A 5 3, ♥ 5, ♦ A 9 8 5 2, ♣ K J 9 7.

If West holds ♠ J 10 8, ♥ K Q 10, ♦ K J 7 6 3, ♣ A 2, he will bid 3NT. Reverse his major suit holdings and he should get to 6♦.

Be careful of this sequence:

1 ♣	2 ♣
3 ♦	

Is this a splinter agreeing clubs or a jump shift in a new suit? If 2♦ is forcing it is more flexible to use the jump to show shortness.

If the splinter bidder follows with a cuebid in the splinter suit he is showing a void (or a singleton ace).

WEST	EAST
1 ♥	4 ♦
4 ♠	5 ♦

A splinter at the five level which deprives the partnership of Blackwood should be used only with a void.

WEST	EAST
1 ♥	3 ♥
5 ♣	

East is being asked to evaluate his hand for slam in the light of partner's club void.

WEST	EAST
1 ♣	1 ♠
3 ♥ or 4♥	

As 2♥ would be forcing in the modern style, 3♥ and 4♥ are both available as splinters. Some play 3♥ shows a singleton and 4♥ shows a void. Others play 3♥ is a mini splinter (highly invitational but not forcing to game) and 4♥ is a full game force.

Defense to Splinters The usual agreement varies with vulnerability. If the vulnerability is favorable, the double shows length and suggests a save. At other vulnerability it is lead-directing. Some experts play that the double calls for a lead of the *lower* side-suit.

For alternative treatments, see ASKING BIDS, SWISS CONVENTION, VALUE SWISS RAISES, VOID-SHOWING BIDS, MINI-SPLINTER.

SPLIT. See BREAK.

SPLIT EQUALS. See PLAY FROM EQUALS.

SPLIT REGIONAL. A tournament with regional rating held at two widely separated sites within an ACBL district. Scores are compared between the two sites to determine winners of regionally-rated pair games. Swiss teams and knockout teams are separate events with different winners at each site.

SPLITTING HONORS. The play of an honor in second position from two or more sequential cards. A common position is:

> A J 9
> K Q 4   10 8 7 3
> 6 5 2

When South leads low, second-hand low by West would work well since South will probably finesse the nine. But if West plays high, the queen is slightly better than the king. If South takes the ace he may go wrong later: the queen is a plausible second-hand play from Q-10-x, but second-hand play of the king is much less plausible from K-10-x since South could have the queen.

Most partnerships make rules about whether to split high or low in such situations.

SPONSORING ORGANIZATION. The group which sponsors bridge tournaments conducted under the LAWS OF DUPLICATE (Law 80). Generally, this is a club or clubs for tournaments of local rating; a unit of the American Contract Bridge League for sectionally rated tournaments; a conference of units or a very large unit for regionally rated tournaments; and the American Contract Bridge League itself for the North American tournaments. See COMMITTEE. Outside North America, the sponsoring organization is usually an NCBO or a local organization delegated by the NCBO. In a wider sense, the sponsor may be a corporation or individual who is paying the expenses of the tournament in return for a public relations benefit.

SPONSORS. See PROFESSIONAL PLAYERS.

SPOT CARD LEADS. See JOURNALIST LEADS; OPENING LEADS; THREE SMALL CARDS, LEAD FROM.

SPOT CARDS. Cards ranking below the jack, from the 10 down to the 2. Of the 13 tricks which are won on each deal, approximately eight are won with aces, kings, queens, and jacks; the remaining five tricks are won with the lower cards. Generally speaking, a fraction more than five tricks is won by the lower cards in trump contracts, since the low trumps win tricks which are not available in notrump contracts. Through the years, all the emphasis on winning tricks has been on aces, kings, queens, and jacks (HONOR TRICKS, POINT-COUNT) and quite naturally so, since these cards are the leaders in the area of winning tricks. However, as can be observed from the above, the lower cards are not merely pawns in the trick-taking field.

SPREAD. (1) Verb: to spread the hand, either as a claim or as a concession of the remaining tricks. See CLAIM OR CONCESSION for the proper method of making such a claim. (2) Noun: the difference between the minimum and maximum values shown by a particular bid; in STANDARD AMERICAN, the range of values for an opening bid of 1NT is 16 to 18 high-card points, a spread of three, while an opening bid of one in a suit may have a high-card point-count spread of 11 to 24, or 14 points.

SPRING NORTH AMERICAN BRIDGE CHAMPI-ONSHIPS. Formerly called the Spring Nationals, this annual tournament of the American Contract Bridge League is held in March and was first convened in 1958. The most important event is the Vanderbilt Knockout Teams. In 1968 the tournament held in New York attracted a total of 13,535 tables, a record for the series until the Spring of 1989 when 13,808 were registered in Reno. For past results of Spring North American Bridge Championships, see Appendix I.

Spring North American Championships Attendance (an asterisk indicates the record was broken that year)

Year	Site	Tables
1958	Atlantic City	3,076
1959	Seattle	4,124
1960	Jackson MS	3,485
1961	Denver	4,910*
1962	Lexington KY	4,703
1963	St. Louis	6,556*
1964	Portland OR	6,950*
1965	Cleveland	8,128*
1966	Louisville KY	7,929
1967	Seattle	7,098
1968	New York City	13,535*
1969	Cleveland	8,958
1970	Portland OR	7,025
1971	Atlanta	9,706
1972	Cincinnati	9,495
1973	St. Louis	8,418
1974	Vancouver BC	8,329
1975	Honolulu	10,234
1976	Kansdas City	8,790
1977	Pasadena	12,713
1978	Houston	9,388
1979	Norfolk VA	8,273
1980	Fresno CA	9,669
1981	Detroit	8,221
1982	Niagara Falls	9,021
1983	Honolulu	11,698
1984	San Antonio	8,829
1985	Montreal	10,184
1986	Portland OR	9,222
1987	St. Louis	10,829
1988	Buffalo	9,157
1989	Reno	13,808*
1990	Fort Worth	11,303
1991	Atlantic City	11,279
1992	Pasadena	12,502
1993	Kansas City	10,132
1994	Cincinnati	11,003
1995	Phoenix	
1996	Philadelphia	

SPUTNIK. See NEGATIVE DOUBLE.

SQUARE HAND. Bridge geometry is peculiar; square hand, flat hand, and round hand all describe 4-3-3-3 distribution.

SQUEEZE. A play which forces an opponent to discard at a time when he would prefer not to do so. The forced discard will cost the opponent at least one trick, sooner or later. In most cases, a squeeze compels an opponent to discard a winner, a potential winner, or a guard to a winner The most familiar squeezes have the following requirements: a. Two threat (or menace) cards, at least one of which is accompanied by a winner in that suit. A threat card is any card that will take a trick provided the opponents unguard that suit. (When a threat card is accompanied by a winner in that suit, it is called a two-card threat.) b. The hand opposite at least one of the two-card threats contains a card in the suit of the threat card. This card provides a means of reaching the two-card threat in the opposite hand. c. The opponent to be squeezed holds no idle cards. This usually requires that the squeeze player can win all but one of the remaining tricks. (See RECTIFYING THE COUNT) When these conditions have been satisfied, the card played to the next trick forces an unwanted discard from at least one opponent. This card is called the squeeze card. It is usually a winner played from the hand opposite the two-card threat. If both menaces are in the same hand, only the opponent who is to the left of the squeeze card is affected. These are called positional (or one-way) squeezes. In an automatic squeeze, either opponent can be subjected to pressure. This occurs when the squeeze card is accompanied by a menace card, so that the hand opposite has one card which is immaterial and furnishes an automatic discard.

The term "squeeze" was coined by Sidney Lenz well after the operation of a squeeze had been recognized and analyzed. Originally a squeeze was simply called a coup. In the heyday of American whist it was known as "putting the opponent to the discard." Circa 1910 J. B. Elwell called squeeze play "forcing discards," and this term was in general use until Lenz in the middle Twenties, inspired by a squeeze play in a professional baseball game, introduced his new term. For various types of squeeze and aspects of squeeze play see ALTERNATE SQUEEZE; AUTOMATIC SQUEEZE; BACKWASH SQUEEZE; BARCO SQUEEZE; BONNEY'S SQUEEZE; BUSY CARD; CLASH SQUEEZE; COMPOUND SQUEEZE; COMPOUND TRUMP SQUEEZE; COUNT SQUEEZE; DEFENSE TO A SQUEEZE; DOUBLE SQUEEZE; ENTRY-SHIFTING SQUEEZE; ENTRY SQUEEZE; GUARD SQUEEZE; HEDGEHOG SQUEEZES; HEXAGON SQUEEZE; HEXAGON TRUMP SQUEEZE; KNOCKOUT SQUEEZE; NON-MATERIAL SQUEEZES; OCTAGONAL TWO-TRICK SQUEEZE; ONE-SUIT SQUEEZE; OVERTAKING SQUEEZE; POSITIONAL SQUEEZE; PROGRESSIVE SQUEEZE; PSEUDO-SQUEEZE; RECIPROCAL SQUEEZE; RECTIFYING

THE COUNT; SCHROEDER SQUEEZE; SECOND-
ARY SQUEEZE; SERES SQUEEZE; SHOW-UP
SQUEEZE; SIMPLE SQUEEZE; SQUEEZE; SQUEEZE
FINESSE; SQUEEZE MNEMONICS; SQUEEZE
WITHOUT THE COUNT; SQUEEZE POSITION; SUI-
CIDE SQUEEZE; THREAT CARD; THROW-IN
SQUEEZE; TRANSFER SQUEEZE; TRANSFERRING
THE MENACE; TRIPLE SQUEEZE; TRUMP
SQUEEZE; UNBLOCKING SQUEEZE; VICE
SQUEEZE; WINKLE SQUEEZE.

SQUEEZE FINESSE. Closely related to the GUARD
SQUEEZE. In each case, declarer threatens to take a successful finesse. In a guard squeeze, the opponents are not
equally threatened, whereas the squeeze finesse is characterized by the presence of a symmetric menace which
must be guarded with an equal number of cards by both
opponents.

(1) *Four-card squeeze finesse menaces:*

Triple tenaces

```
      K 9                           K 2
Q 8         10 5    or    Q 8             10 5
      J 2                           J 9
```

These positions may lead to a squeeze or throw-in of
either opponent.

Quadruple tenaces

```
      K 8                           K 2
Q 7         10 9    or    Q 7             10 9
      J 2                           J 8
```

In these positions, only West can be thrown in successfully.

(2) *Six-card squeeze finesse menaces:*

Triple tenaces

```
      K 9 x                         K 3 2
Q 8 x       10 5 x  or    Q 8 x           10 5 x
      A J 2                         A J 9
```

Either opponent may be thrown in.

Quadruple tenaces

```
      K 8 x                         K 3 2
Q 7 x       10 9 x  or    Q 7 x           10 9 x
      A J 2                         A J 8
```

Only West can be thrown in.

(3) *Squeeze-finesse positions (at notrump):*

(a)

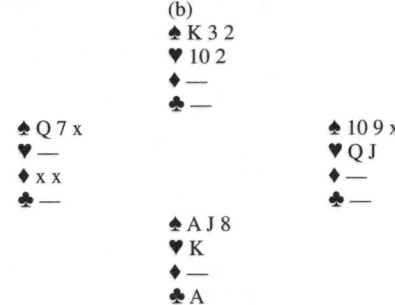

South has two of the remaining tricks. The ♣A is led
and East is squeezed in three suits. He must discard a

spade, and now South leads the ♠J to smother the 10. If
West's small diamond is exchanged for the king, this
merely opens up the possibility of a squeeze throw-in
against West.

(b)

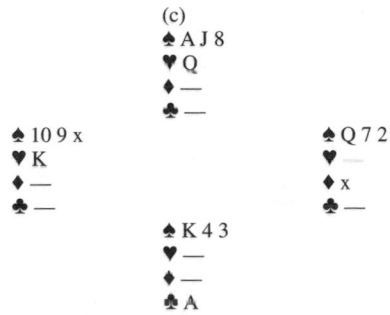

South has four of the remaining five tricks. The ♣A
squeezes East in two suits. He must discard a spade, but
declarer can now pick up three tricks in spades by leading the jack through West. The squeeze fails if the ♠8
and ♠2 are interchanged.

(c)

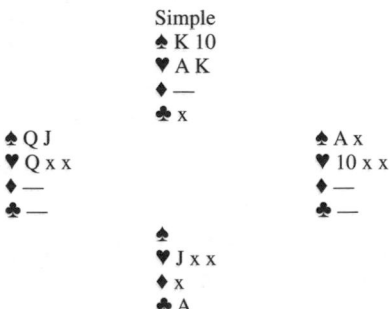

The ♣ A squeezes West in two suits. West discards a
spade, and declarer leads to the ♠ A, then runs the jack
through East to pick up the suit.

The ♠ 8 and ♠ 2 may be interchanged without affecting
the squeeze. East's small diamond may be exchanged
for the ♥ A, but the squeeze still works.

(4) *Squeeze Finesse at Trumps (also called simply
TRUMP SQUEEZE).*

Simple

```
      ♠ K 10
      ♥ A K
      ♦ —
      ♣ x
♠ Q J              ♠ A x
♥ Q x x            ♥ 10 x x
♦ —                ♦ —
♣ —                ♣ —
      ♠
      ♥ J x x
      ♦ x
      ♣ A
```

Diamonds are trumps. The ♣ A is led, putting the
squeeze on West. If he discards a heart, declarer cashes
the two top hearts, re-enters his hand by ruffing a spade
to cash the ♥ J. If West discards a spade, declarer can go
to dummy with a heart and lead the ♠K to ruff out the ace

and smother the queen, establishing North's 10.

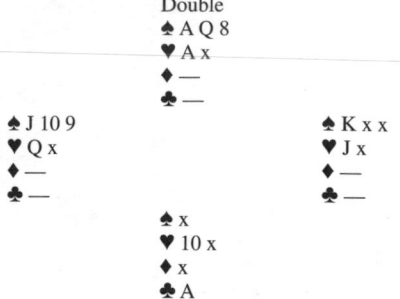

Diamonds are trumps. The ♣ A is led and West is squeezed. If he discards a spade, the ace and the queen of that suit are led, ruffing out the king and smothering West's honors. If West discards a heart, then North throws a heart and East is caught in a standard trump squeeze.

SQUEEZE MNEMONICS. An acronym or other set of initials used as a reminder of the ingredients necessary for the operation of a squeeze. Among the more well-known mnemonics are:

(1) Clyde Love's BLUE:
  B = Busy (one defender Busy in two suits)
  L = Loser (one Loser remaining)
  U = Upper (at least one threat in Upper hand)
  E = Entry (to the threat card)

(2) George Coffins's EFG (to Enter freedom, Force the Guards):
  E = Entry (to the threat card)
  F = Forcing card
  G = Guards (in one defender's hand)

(3) John Brown's STEM:
  S = Share-out or Substance
  T = Timing (count has been rectified)
  E = Entries (to the threat card)
  M = Menaces

SQUEEZE SUIT-OUT. A particular form of SECONDARY SQUEEZE.

SQUEEZE WITHOUT THE COUNT. An unusual variation of the squeeze. In order for a squeeze to be effective, declarer ordinarily must have all but one of the remaining tricks (see Rule of N-Minus-One). However, this is not invariably the case. In certain squeeze positions declarer gives up a trick after the squeeze. This is called "squeeze without the count" (see SECONDARY SQUEEZE).

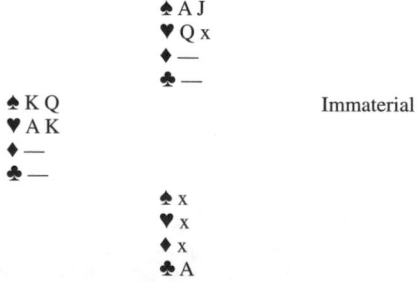

South leads the ♣ A which squeezes West, despite the fact that South has only two of the last four tricks. West must discard a heart; now South leads a heart to establish the queen.

SQUEEZED POSITION (PLAYING TO). In the development of the understanding of squeezes, Sidney Lenz invented the idea of a squeeze card, and this concept has dominated the analysis of squeeze play ever since. Indeed, some writers have even given special names, for example "reciprocal squeeze," where the actual squeeze card could not be identified.

  (1)

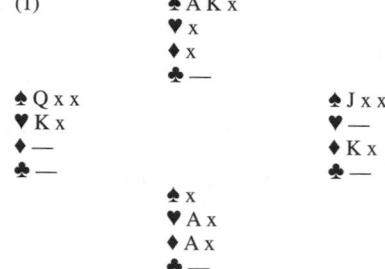

In this double automatic position, for instance, there is no separate and identifiable squeeze card. The two red aces are led, and each opponent is squeezed by the ace of his partner's suit. As more and more squeeze positions have been identified, the burden of remembering them for use in play has become impossible except for the most expert, and in trying to simplify the rules for the less expert players it has been found that, by abandoning the concept of a squeeze card, the number of end positions can be reduced, and, in particular, the more complex ones can be forgotten. This has probably always been the practice in expert circles, and was almost implied by Ely Culbertson in his *Red Book*.

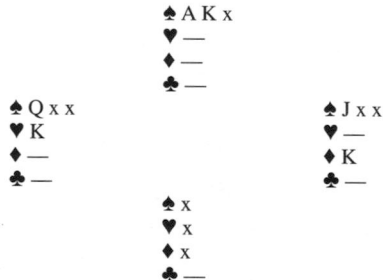

For example, in No. 1 above, if South cashes his red aces, he has achieved the "squeezed position". South is on lead, but East and West have yet to play. This position is true of all automatic double squeezes: squeeze cards, reciprocal squeeze, simultaneous and interrupted automatic double squeezes can all be forgotten.

The following are simple automatic squeezes:

  (2)

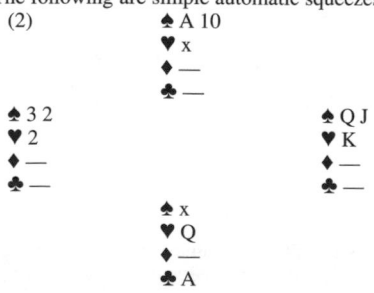

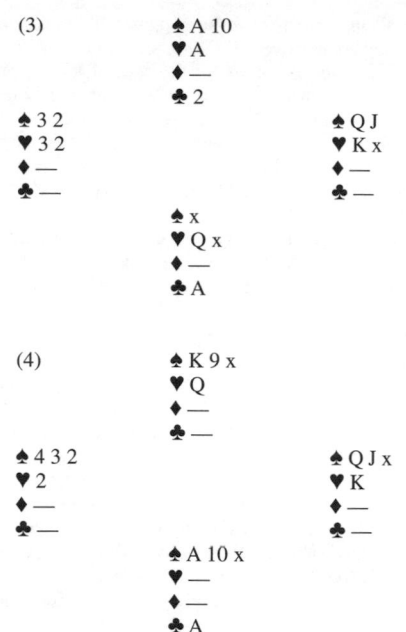

(3)

```
            ♠ A 10
            ♥ A
            ♦ —
            ♣ 2
♠ 3 2                    ♠ Q J
♥ 3 2                    ♥ K x
♦ —                     ♦ —
♣ —                     ♣ —
            ♠ x
            ♥ Q x
            ♦ —
            ♣ A
```

(4)

```
            ♠ K 9 x
            ♥ Q
            ♦ —
            ♣ —
♠ 4 3 2                  ♠ Q J x
♥ 2                     ♥ K
♦ —                     ♦ —
♣ —                     ♣ —
            ♠ A 10 x
            ♥ —
            ♦ —
            ♣ A
```

These three endings, Nos. 2, 3, and 4, can all be represented by one squeeze position, No. 5, with South on lead. North and South have both played, but the opponent with the high cards, either East or West, must now play and is squeezed. In No. 2 the ♣A squeezes either East or West, the ♥x being thrown from North. In No. 3 we first Vienna-Coup with the ♥A, and then the ♣A squeezes whichever opponent holds the high cards. In No. 4 we have to imagine North as South in No. 5.

(5)

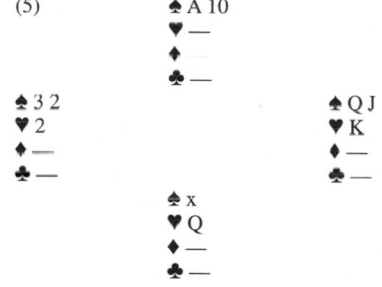

```
            ♠ A 10
            ♥ —
            ♦
            ♣ —
♠ 3 2                    ♠ Q J
♥ 2                     ♥ K
♦ —                     ♦ —
♣ —                     ♣ —
            ♠ x
            ♥ Q
            ♦ —
            ♣ —
```

Examples could be given for all varieties of squeezes but this would be tedious, so let the following suffice:

(6)

```
            ♠ A 10 9
            ♥ —
            ♦ x
            ♣ —
♠ Q J                    ♠ 2
♥ A                     ♥ x
♦ A                     ♦ x
♣ —                     ♣ x
            ♠ x
            ♥ K
            ♦ K
            ♣ A
```

(7)

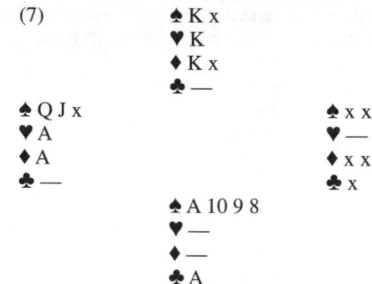

```
            ♠ K x
            ♥ K
            ♦ K x
            ♣ —
♠ Q J x                  ♠ x x
♥ A                     ♥ —
♦ A                     ♦ x x
♣ —                     ♣ x
            ♠ A 10 9 8
            ♥ —
            ♦ —
            ♣ A
```

Examples Nos. 6 and 7 are two triple squeeze positions, both automatic, in which the lead of the ♣A squeezes an opponent into promoting one of declarer's kings, then squeezing him a second time when that king is played— the other ace or the guard to declarer's long suit must be given up. Example No. 8 is either of these reduced to the squeezed position, with South on lead. No. 7 has to be turned upside down to get to No. 8, but as the position is automatic, this is of no consequence.

(8)

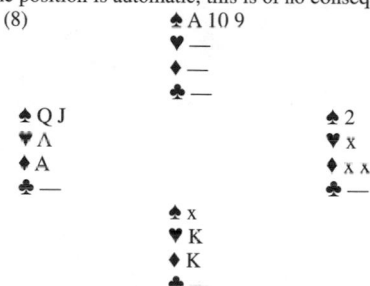

```
            ♠ A 10 9
            ♥ —
            ♦ —
            ♣ —
♠ Q J                    ♠ 2
♥ A                     ♥ x
♦ A                     ♦ x x
♣ —                     ♣ —
            ♠ x
            ♥ K
            ♦ K
            ♣
```

Finally, the simple trump squeeze. Although the three examples, Nos. 9, 10, and 11, all appear to be different, once one plays down to the squeezed position they all become the same.

(9)

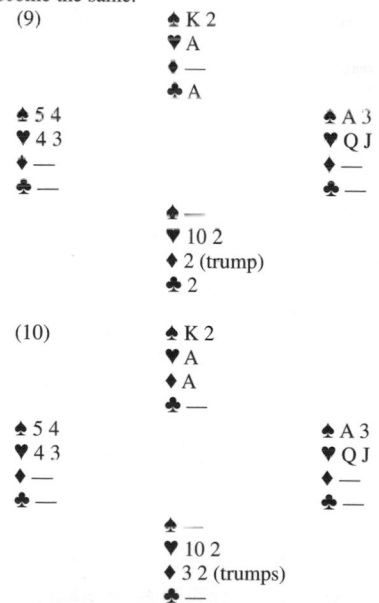

```
            ♠ K 2
            ♥ A
            ♦ —
            ♣ A
♠ 5 4                    ♠ A 3
♥ 4 3                    ♥ Q J
♦ —                     ♦ —
♣ —                     ♣ —
            ♠ —
            ♥ 10 2
            ♦ 2 (trump)
            ♣ 2
```

(10)

```
            ♠ K 2
            ♥ A
            ♦ A
            ♣ —
♠ 5 4                    ♠ A 3
♥ 4 3                    ♥ Q J
♦ —                     ♦ —
♣ —                     ♣ —
            ♠ —
            ♥ 10 2
            ♦ 3 2 (trumps)
            ♣ —
```

Trump squeezes are always automatic. In No. 9 the lead of the ♣2, or in No. 10 the lead of a trump, squeezes the opponent (in this case East) who holds the high cards. If he throws a spade the ♠2 is led and trumped, North is re-entered and the ♠K is cashed. If he throws a heart the ♥A is cashed, a spade is ruffed, and the last heart made.

(11)

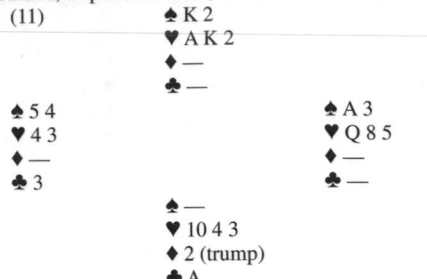

In No. 11 the ♣A is led and North's ♥2 discarded. If East throws a spade North is entered with a heart, the ♠2 is ruffed, and North re-entered to make the ♠K. If East throws a heart, North's ♥A-K are cashed and a spade ruff puts South in again to make the ♥10.

(12)

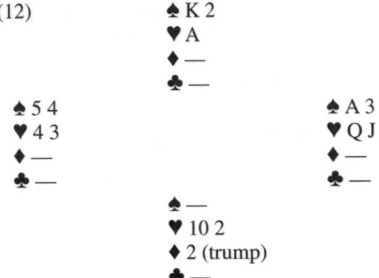

Each of the above three cases reduces to the squeezed position, No. 12, with East to discard and then North to lead. This is a much simpler position to remember – in fact it is all simple trump squeezes, and is one position instead of three.

SRI LANKA, BRIDGE FEDERATION OF
Hon. General Secretary 1992:
V.P.A.Perera
97 Castle Street
Colombo 8
Sri Lanka.

STACK, STACKED. (1) The cards are said to be stacked against one when a single opponent holds all or nearly all of the cards in a crucial suit. (2) To stack a deck is to arrange cards in an undealt deck in order to put predetermined holdings into one or more hands. See CHEATING.

STAGGER MOVEMENT. A movement for an even number of teams which permits scoring to start at the halfway mark. It is particularly useful for a two-session game.

Two parallel rows of tables are set up so that board-sharing is possible. For example, with eight tables the layout is:

1	5
2	6
3	7
4	8

The movement is the same as in an American Whist movement: boards up one table, sharing with the adjacent table (1&5, 2&6, 3&7, 4&8); East-West pairs up two tables. On reaching the end of a row, pairs must go to the start of the opposite line, 8 to 1 and 4 to 5.

When all the boards have been played, i.e. after n/2 rounds, they are removed. E-W pairs move up one, and start on a new set of boards for the start of the second half. This movement works for any even number of tables, and like the American Whist movement, can be shortened by eliminating the first and last rounds of either or both halves. A reduced number of boards can be played in the second half. See EIGHT TABLES and TEAM-OF-FOUR MOVEMENTS.

The two stanzas in the Stagger movement may be played intermingled, with half the board sets idle in each round. This method is known as the New England Relay.

STAKES. Rubber bridge is frequently played for stakes. Although it is a social game, the addition of stakes does provide an incentive to careful and accurate bidding and play. In major North American bridge clubs, where membership and card fees are considerable, stakes usually range from one-half cent to three cents per point, but higher stakes do occur, ranging up to 50 cents or even a dollar. In home and social games, stakes are usually much more modest and may be as little one-tenth of a cent.

In Britain and other parts of the world stakes are expressed on a "per hundred" basis. Therefore scoring 100 honors will be worth the announced stake in Britain, but 100 times the announced stake in North America.

STAND, STAND FOR. To pass one's partner's PENALTY DOUBLE or TAKEOUT DOUBLE.

STANDOFF. A colloquialism for either a rubber with no net score (after ROUNDING OFF); a hand in which HONOR SCORE balances undertrick penalties: or a deal in a team game (BOARD-A-MATCH, IMP or TOTAL POINTS) on which neither team gains.

STAND UP. In defensive play, a high card that wins a trick. A suit is said to stand until it is trumped by the declarer. On the offense or on the defense, too, a high card is said to stand up if it wins the trick, even though a higher card may be outstanding in the suit.

STANDARD AMERICAN. A nebulous term applied to the methods of bidding most commonly used in the United States. It approximates closely the methods formerly advocated by Charles Goren. Among serious tournament players the weak two-bid is standard, while some rubber bridge players continue to use the forcing two. Another debatable issue is the idea that jump bids by responder are always forcing. This is implicit in Goren's methods. In North America the trend has been toward expert methods which include limit bids, sign-off bids and nonforcing jumps.

In the 80s the Goren methods gradually fell out of favor in tournament play. A majority adopted methods which may be called EASTERN SCIENTIFIC or TWO-OVER-ONE GAME FORCE. The shift is continuing in the 90s, and traditional Goren, with four-card major openings and a 1NT response to a major opening non-forcing, is no longer than norm. But players continue to describe their methods as "standard" when they use a modern style which is far removed from traditional Goren.

STANZA MOVEMENT. A method of conducting a combined-section pairs game whereby the scoring of the first half the game can be completed while the second half is taking place. The method was devised by Maury Braunstein. The most common application takes place in twinned sections using a 25-top, usually with 14 tables in each section, although this is not necessary. Boards numbered 1-14 are distributed at tables 1-7 and tables 8-14 in each section. After six rounds, the boards are removed from one section and replaced with boards 15-28. After seven rounds, the boards are removed from the other section and replaced with boards 15-28. At this point, Boards 1-14 have been played the full complement of 26 times and are ready for matchpointing. When using this movement, great care must be taken in the original placement of boards and the switches during the sixth and seventh rounds – otherwise the resultant mixups consume more time than is saved by the early matchpointing. Since computer scoring now is the norm in tournament play, the Stanza Movement is almost never used.

STANZA HOWELL. A Howell-type movement for pairs or individuals which is split into several stanzas (or segments) usually played in several sessions with one stanza per session. When all sessions are played in a Stanza Howell for pairs, all pairs have met once. In a Stanza Howell for individuals, each player will have each other player as a partner once and an opponent twice.

STAR TEACHERS. Under the auspices of ACBL's Education Department, the number of accredited teachers grew by leaps and bounds in the 1980s. By early 1994, there were nearly 3000 ACBL-accredited bridge teachers. The Star Teacher designation was initiated in 1988 to those who use ACBL teaching materials — the *Club, Heart, Diamond* and *Spade Series* books. Any ACBL-accredited teacher who teaches 100 students using one or more of the ACBL manuals earns the designation of Star Teacher.

STARTING TIME. Events at bridge tournaments are announced in the advertising material, and it is a measure of a director's and tournament committee's efficiency to have the games start promptly as scheduled. At or near the end of each session, the director clearly announces the starting time for the next session. If it is a continuation of an event, the director may assess penalties for tardiness. After the scheduled starting time, late players may be added to the event if the director can do so without restarting or unduly delaying the game. Such late entries are accepted by the director at his discretion, and no player has an automatic right to be so accepted.

STATEN BANK. See CAP GEMINI WORLD TOP TOURNAMENT. For results see Appendix IV.

STAYMAN. The response of 2♣ to 1NT, or 3♣ to 2NT, asking opener to bid a four-card major suit. The Stayman convention was invented by George Rapee, but the first article on the convention (*The Bridge World*, June 1945) was authored by Sam Stayman, and the convention was named for the writer rather than the inventor. The device quickly became standard practice throughout the world, vying with the BLACKWOOD CONVENTION as the most popular. Rapee and Stayman were a strong, established partnership at this time. A similar convention was played in the early Thirties by Ewart Kempson in England and a group of Boston players headed by Lawrence Weiss. J.C.H. Marx of London, England, devised a simi-

lar 2♣ convention in 1939, but publication was delayed by World War II. It appeared in 1946, in the first issue of the *Contract Bridge Journal.* The Rapee and Marx ideas, independently generated, were identical. The original convention provided for opener to rebid 2♦ with a minimum hand and 2NT with a maximum. S.J. Simon suggested the simplification which became generally adopted: opener automatically rebids 2♦ if he does not have a major suit. The use of higher-level rebids by the opener (such as 3♣ to show both major suits) is frowned on by the leading authorities: such bids tend to give excessive information to the opponents and prevent responder from using Stayman with a weak unbalanced hand. The authorities are divided on the correct rebid for the opener holding both majors. It makes little difference and partnership agreement is not essential. Whether 2♥ or 2♠ is preferred, the opener can bid the other major if responder rebids 2NT or 3NT.

Responder has a wide range of possible rebids, many of which are subject to varying interpretations.

(1) *Two of a major suit.* This can be treated in four ways: (a) Forcing (usually described as forcing Stayman). The bidding must continue at least as far as 2NT. This permits a slow approach to the game and slam level with strong hands; but most experts reject this treatment because strong hands can be bid satisfactorily by bidding the suit at the three-level on the first or second round, by using a transfer bid. (b) Encouraging (usually described as non-forcing Stayman). This is the standard procedure. Responder indicates game possibilities, together with a five-card suit, or possibly a six-card suit. The use of transfer bids has diminished the need for this usage, since responder can transfer and then invite with a 2NT bid. (c) Weak. This shows an unbalanced hand and no game interest. The suit bid may be four cards only. If the opener has only a doubleton in the suit, he must make a further bid: over 2♥ he bids 2♠ with a three-card suit because responder presumably has spades; over 2♠ he bids 3♣ if he has a club suit; otherwise 2NT. (d) Modern. Use 2♥ as weak, inviting preference to 2♠, and 2♠ as invitational with a 4-card spade suit. In this treatment, opener must bid 2♥ with both majors, and 1NT 2♣ -2♥ -2NT denies four spades.

(2) *2NT.* This is encouraging, showing the same strength as an immediate raise to 2NT. If the opener showed a major, responder now implies that he holds the other major. If the opener rebid 2♦, responder simply indicates he has one or both majors. However, in many modern styles a direct raise to 2NT has an artificial meaning. Therefore a delayed 2NT, via Stayman, carries no information about major suits. See FOUR-SUIT TRANSFER BIDS. And see (1)(d) above.

(3) *Three of a minor suit.* The traditional treatment is for 3♣ to be weak, with a six-card or seven-card club suit with no game interest. 3♦ remains ambiguous, and can be treated as forcing or encouraging. (But see WEISSBERGER convention.) However, most experts use immediate jumps to 3♣ and 3♦ as preemptive (as in ROTH-STONE and KAPLAN-SHEINWOLD) in which case the delayed bid of 3♣ or 3♦ is forcing to game: responder is exploring the possibility of a minor-suit game or slam. These bids are usually encouraging when using FOUR-SUIT TRANSFER BIDS, since the transfer is employed with weak hands and strong hands.

(4) *Three of an unbid major suit (always a jump unless opener bid spades).* Forcing, showing a five-card or

longer suit, with an implication of four cards in the other major. See SMOLEN.

(5) *Raise to three of a major.* A natural invitation to game, showing four-card support for the major suit.

(6) *3NT.* A natural bid, implying that responder holds an unbid major (or possibly two unbid majors). The opener may continue in the unbid major if he has both.

(7) *Four of a minor suit.* When opener shows a major, 4♣ can be Gerber by partnership agreement. Many use these bids as a SPLINTER. A possible meaning is natural: A long, strong suit with a void and slam interest. Opener relays to ask for the void. See SHARPLES CONVENTION.

(8) *4NT.* An ambiguous bid, but most players who use Gerber would treat it as quantitative. A 4-3-3-3 hand would make an immediate raise to 4NT. (And a 4-4-3-2 hand could use the SHARPLES CONVENTION.) Other rebids by the responder are natural.

The above sequences apply to 1NT opening bids of any range. However, the employment of a weak notrump strengthens the argument for using nonforcing Stayman. See also GLADIATOR; ONE NOTRUMP OPENING; SMOLEN; TWO-WAY STAYMAN.

STAYMAN FOR STOPPERS. TWO-WAY STAYMAN may also be used in a way in which only the 2♣ bid searches for a 4-4 major suit fit. The 2♦ bid would then be used to discover whether the partnership has all suits sufficiently well-stopped to play in notrump. Responder normally reserves his 2♦ bid for a hand containing a singleton or a void. The bid asks opener to bid whichever major suit he has guarded. Suits containing four cards headed by the queen, or three headed by the queen and 10, are considered minimum sufficient stoppers. With both major suits guarded opener should bid 2NT. If opener does not have the responder's short suit stopped, responder can explore other game, or slam, possibilities.

STAYMAN IN DOUBT (S.I.D.) A British idea intended to deal with the difficulty presented by two hands with a four-four major-suit fit and identical 4-3-3-3 distributions. A three-diamond rebid by the Stayman bidder suggests this possibility, and asks the opener to decide between 3NT and a game in the major suit.

STAYMAN ON SECOND ROUND. This is standard in one situation:

SOUTH	NORTH
2 ♣ (artificial)	2 ♦
2NT	3 ♣

As no suit has been naturally bid, the responder can bid as he would opposite a 2NT opening, with the knowledge that the opener is slightly stronger. By partnership agreement this can be extended to other notrump rebids:

SOUTH	NORTH
1 ♣	1 ♥
1NT	2 ♣ (asking for a spade suit)

This checkback procedure permits the opener to conceal a four-card major suit on the second round if he wishes, but deprives the responder of some natural rebids. If the rebid is 2NT, 3♣ is not available for players who use it as preparation for a sign-off at the three level (see WOLFF CONVENTION). See CROWHURST CONVENTION; TWO CLUB REBID BY RESPONDER AS ONLY FORCE AFTER ONE NOTRUMP REBID; NEW MI-NOR FORCING.

STAYMAN THREE CLUBS. A Stayman response of 3♣ to 2NT, asking for a major-suit. The rebids are usually the same as after the normal Stayman 2♣ bid, but more sophisticated arrangements are possible taking advantage of the possibility of a 3NT rebid. The following rebid structure was devised by George Rosenkranz:

(1) 3♦ denies five spades, denies four or five hearts, denies both majors. A 3♥ relay asks for a four-card spade suit, and 4♠ shows that holding.

(2) 3♥ shows four or five hearts, and a relay of three spades asks for 3NT with four hearts.

(3) 3♠ shows five spades.

(4) 3NT shows four-four in the major suits.

STEP RESPONSES TO STRONG ARTIFICIAL TWO-BIDS. Responses to a TWO-CLUB STRONG ARTIFICIAL OPENING that show, by steps, how many controls responder holds, counting a king as one control and an ace as two. As described in *The Bridge Journal*, a 2♦ response shows 0-1 control, a 2♥ response shows 2 controls, a 2♠ response shows an ace and a king (3 controls), a 2NT response shows three kings (3 controls), a 3♣ response shows 4 controls and so on. The theory underlying using the 2NT response to show three kings is that if the hand is to be played in notrump it will more likely be played from the RIGHT SIDE. This method of responding is similar to that used in BLUE TEAM CLUB. See also NORMAN 4NT. A modification proposed by Edgar Kaplan requires responder to bid 2♦ with 0-6 points and 2♥ shows more than 6 points; both bids, however, show fewer than two controls. Most other responses are amended accordingly: a 2♠ response shows two controls, 2NT still shows three kings, 3♣ shows one ace and one king, 3♦ shows four controls, and so forth. See ACE-SHOWING RESPONSES.

STEPPINGSTONE SQUEEZE. A secondary squeeze in which the opponents must choose between a throw-in and a suit establishment play, each of which enables declarer to gain a trick. (Analyzed and named by Terence Reese).

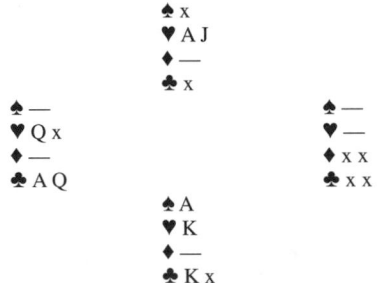

South leads the ♠A, and West is squeezed in two suits. In order to retain his guard in hearts, he must throw a club. If West discards the ♣Q, South takes the ♥K, and exits with a club, forcing West to lead a heart to North's ace; if West discards the ♣A, South's king is established. The blocked suit must include two winners, one in each hand, but the higher must be in dummy. South must have a one-card menace against the same player who protects the blocked suit. In the diagram position, if the East and West cards were reversed the squeeze would still be effective. See also ENTRY SQUEEZE and WINKLE

SQUEEZE.

STERN SYSTEM. See VIENNA SYSTEM.

STIFF. (1) Adjective or noun: Colloquialism for SINGLETON, frequently used in reference to a major honor (ace, king, or queen) without guards. (2) Verb: Colloquially, to blank; to discard the guards.

STONE AGE ACOL WITH PAKISTANI PRE-EMPTS. A system devised by Munir Ataullah of Pakistan. All opening bids from 2♣ through 4♦ have multiple meanings — some have as many as seven possible meanings. Subsequent bids identify the hand type, suit quality, etc. It is difficult to bounce quickly to the best spot because the type of hand opened must be determined first. It is also difficult to bid defensively against this complicated system.

STOP. See SKIP-BID WARNING.

STOP BID. A bid which fixes the final contract and commands partner to pass. Responses of 4♠ or 3NT to an opening notrump bid are examples. SIGNOFF BIDS are virtually stop bids, but in some cases the partner may have a reason to violate and continue with the auction. See PREEMPTIVE RERAISE.

STOPPER. A card which may reasonably be expected to or actually does stop the run of a suit. To be counted in the auction as a stopper, a high card, except an ace, must usually be accompanied by lower cards so that it will not have to be played on a higher one if the holder of the higher card decides to play for the drop. The number of low cards, or guards, needed is in inverse proportion to the rank of the honor. Thus, the king must ordinarily be accompanied by at least one guard, and the queen by at least two unless the bidding indicates that a higher ranking card is held by partner. Stoppers are particularly important at notrump contracts. See GUARD; NOTRUMP BIDDING. STOPPING BELOW GAME. The decision to "stop on a dime" in 2NT or three of a major may be influenced by a variety of factors: vulnerability, method of scoring and psychological reasons. It is usually considered advisable to reach for optimistic vulnerable games at rubber bridge and IMP scoring. A look at the mathematics involved (see VALUE OF GAME) indicates that this holds true for IMP scoring but not for rubber bridge. In matchpoint scoring, theory suggests that a game should be bid with a 50% chance, but in practice experts tend to be slightly conservative unless the opposition is weak. In such circumstances 3NT, down one, is likely to be a worse score than 2NT, made with an overtrick. It is desirable to make sure of a plus score.

STOPPING ON A DIME. Stopping one trick short of game (or perhaps slam) and making exactly the right number of tricks.

STRAIN. A term encompassing all four suits plus notrump. See DENOMINATION.

STRATIFIED PAIRS. A pair event that produces more than one set of winners. The field is divided into two or three strata, each with a predetermined masterpoint limitation. The tournament directors attempt to seed the field

in such a manner that approximately equal numbers of players from each strata are in each direction. All pairs are ranked in the top stratum; the pairs in the top stratum are eliminated in determining the ranks in Stratum B, and both the Stratum A and Stratum B scores are eliminated in determining the ranks in Stratum C. It is possible for Stratum B and C pairs to place in higher strat, but Stratum A pairs are eligible only for Stratum A awards. The stratum in which a pair plays is determined by the player who has the more masterpoints.

STRATIFIED TEAMS. A Swiss Team event that produces more than one set of winners. The event is run along exactly the same lines as an Open Swiss Teams — the only difference comes in the ranking. First overall rankings are determined for Stratum A by comparing all scores. Then Stratum A scores are eliminated to determine the placings in Stratum B. Then Stratum A and Stratum B scores are eliminated to determine the placings in Stratum C. It is possible for Stratum B and C pairs to place in higher strata, but Stratum A pairs are eligible only for Stratum A awards. The stratum in which a team plays is determined by the player who has the most masterpoints. This event has become quite unpopular because B and C teams that do well early find themselves playing strong A teams in later rounds. As a result Flighted Teams are held whenever the fields are large enough to accommodate flights.

STRATUM. An arbitrary division for a Stratified Pairs or a Stratified Teams event. All entrants are placed in groups determined by the masterpoint holding of the player with the most masterpoints. Common strata include 750 up, 300-750 and 0-300, or 20-50, 5-20 and 0-5.

STRENGTH. The top-card holding in a suit, either as stoppers in notrump, for drawing adversely held trumps, for trick-taking potential, or to set up LONG CARDS as winners.

STRENGTH-CONCEALING PLAYS. See DECEPTIVE PLAY.

STRENGTH-SHOWING BIDS. In some special situations a suit bid can be used to show strength rather than length or control. This applies particularly when exploring for a 3NT contract as an alternative to an obvious minor-suit possibility. The following are typical cases. The suit bid might conceivably be as weak as Q-J-x, but would usually contain at least 4 points.

(a)	WEST	EAST
	1♦	2♣
	3♣	3♥

(b)	WEST	EAST
	1NT	3♦ (forcing)
	3♥	

East can bid a strong three-card suit because West is unlikely to be interested in a major suit. This may reveal duplication if East is short in hearts, and permit a final contract of 3NT.

(c)	WEST	EAST
	1♦	3♦
	3♥	

(d)   WEST   EAST
            3 ♣   3 ♦
            3 ♥

The suit is unlikely to be raised. If it is, the choice lies between playing in a 3-4 fit and retreating to a minor suit.

STRIP PLAY. A method of play by which a chosen opponent is stripped of his cards in a certain suit with the purpose of later throwing the lead to that player and thus compelling him to lead a suit desired by the declarer. The term is also used for a method of play by which declarer exhausts the cards in a suit or suits in both his and the dummy's hands so that a later lead by a defender will give him a ruff-sluff. Often combined with endplay as in "strip and endplay". See ELIMINATION; ENDPLAY; SQUEEZE; THROW-IN.

STRIPED-TAILED APE DOUBLE. An inhibitory double of an opposing game contract made by a player who feels sure his opponents can make a slam. The doubled contract with overtricks scores less than the score for bidding and making the slam. So named by John Lowenthal and Samuel Scaffidi in a Bridge Journal article because the doubler flees like a striped-tailed ape in the face of a redouble. The same tactics can be applied at the small slam level if a grand slam can be made.

STRONG JUMP OVERCALL. See JUMP OVERCALL.

STRONG KINGS AND TENS. A British system of honor leads against a notrump contract whereby the lead of a king or ten suggests a strong holding and the lead of any other highcard suggests a relatively weak holding. Therefore:
  Ace from: A K x
  King from: A K Q, A K J, A K 10, K Q J, K Q 10
  Queen from: K Q x, K Q 9, Q J 10
  Jack from: J 10 x
  Ten from: A J 10, A 10 9, K J 10, K 10 9, Q 10 9
  Nine from: 10 9 x

STRONG MINOR RAISES. See INVERTED MINOR RAISES.

STRONG NOTRUMP. The traditional range for an opening bid of 1 NT is 16-18, but that fell out of favor in the Eighties. In tournament play 15-17 became standard, although 16-18 still is often used. Some players straddle, using a range of 15-18, or 15° to 17°. Sub-minimum hands in point-count may be opened 1NT if there is a five-card suit or a wealth of aces and tens.
    The distribution is expected to be 4-3-3-3, 4-4-3-2 or 5-3-3-2, but some experts will occasionally make the bid with 6-3-2-2 or 5-4-2-2 if the doubletons are strong, aiming to avoid a rebid problem after a suit opening.
    Traditionally, the notrump bidder was expected to have a stopper in a doubleton suit, but this guideline has been generally abandoned since it leads to a rebid problem with many hands. However, hands containing four spades and a four-card minor may choose to open in the minor when the doubleton is weak, since there will be no rebid problem.
    Even stronger 1 NT opening bids are advocated in some systems, notably ROMAN, SIMS, and VANDERBILT.

For strong notrump openings that are forcing for one round, see DYNAMIC NOTRUMP, LITTLE ROMAN CLUB SYSTEM, ROMEX SYSTEM.

STRONG NOTRUMP AFTER PASSING (abbreviated to SNAP). A response of 1NT by a passed hand as a strong bid, showing 9-12 points. This permits the bidding to stay in a comfortable low-level contract when the opener has a minimum or sub-minimum hand. The notrump bidder promises a relatively balanced hand and denies holding a five-card major suit which could have been bid at the level of one. The idea often gives an advantage in a partscore deal, and is therefore of most value in a matchpoint event. For a device with similar objectives, see DRURY.

STRONG PASS. Any of several systems used in various parts of the world whereby an opening pass indicates the values for an opening bid, while various opening bids indicate values less than sufficient for an opening bid in most other systems. Partner of the opening passer is usually required to open the bidding, and the process puts strong pressure on the opposition. Since the meaning of many ordinary sequences is reversed, the opposition must work out entirely new defensive bidding systems. Strong pass systems first gained popularity in Poland, but many partnerships throughout the world now employ some version of the strong pass. See FORCING PASS, MARMIC SYSTEM and WEAK OPENING SYSTEMS.

STRONG SUIT. A suit of four or more cards containing a minimum of six points.

STRONG TWO-BID. See FORCING TWO-BID.

SUBMARINE SQUEEZE. The concession of a trick by declarer in order to correct the count for a squeeze. If declarer gives up the trick on a lead by the opponents, he is said to be RECTIFYING THE COUNT; however, if the trick is conceded at a time when declarer holds the lead, some writers call this move a submarine squeeze.

SUBSTITUTE. (1) Call. When a player makes an illegal call, he may be required to substitute a legal call, with appropriate penalties against his partner. (2) Player. A player who, in rubber bridge, replaces a member of the table who is called away or must leave during or before the finish of a rubber. Such a substitute must be acceptable to all members playing at the table; and he would be assumed to have no financial responsibility unless agreed otherwise. (3) Player. In duplicate play, a player who is permitted by the director to replace a player who is unable to finish a session or play in a second or later session. Such substitution is at the discretion of the director, guided by the League regulations contained in the ACBL HANDBOOK in the United States, or other regulatory bodies for tournament competition. (4) Board. In team play, a board is introduced by the director at a table when an irregularity has occurred that makes a normal result impossible. Such a board is withdrawn after play, but reinstated when the teammates of the pairs who played it are scheduled to play that board. If the substitute board is needed on the replay (after the teammates have recorded a result), an offending side causing the substitution may be playing for at best a halved board.

SUCCESSIVE EVENTS, PROBABILITY OF. See PROBABILITY OF SUCCESSIVE EVENTS.

SUCKER DOUBLE. A double of a freely bid game or slam contract by a player who is relying solely on defensive high-card strength. Against good opponents such doubles rarely show more than a small profit. They can, however, show a disastrous loss, especially when the double helps declarer to make his contract. The probability is that the declaring side has distributional strength to compensate for the relative lack of high-card strength.

SUCTION. A defense to a 1NT opening. The overcall of any suit shows the next-higher suit, or the other two suits.

2 ♣ = diamonds, or hearts and spades
2 ♦ = hearts, or spades and clubs
2 ♥ = spades, or clubs and diamonds
2 ♠ = clubs, or diamonds and hearts

Partner of the suction bidder assumes the next-higher suit until he hears otherwise.

SUFFICIENT BID. A bid of the same number of a higher ranking denomination or of a greater number in a lower ranking suit or the same denomination. If the enforcement of a penalty permits a player to substitute a sufficient bid for an incorrect call, a double of an opponent's bid may not be substituted; even though such double is a legal call. See INSUFFICIENT BID.

SUICIDE SQUEEZE. A squeeze inflicted by a defender on his partner. (But as this name is hardly accurate, it is called by some the Cannibal Squeeze.) Inaccurate defense may lead to this position, but there are times when the opponents have no recourse.

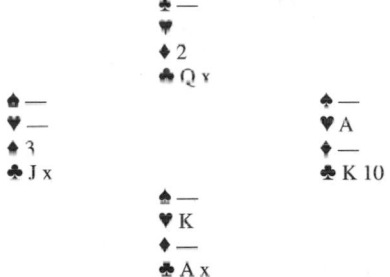

West, on lead, produces a suicide squeeze on his partner if he cashes the high diamond. If East discards the ♥A, South discards the low club, winning two tricks. If East discards the ♣10, South discards the ♥K. Proper defense calls for a club lead. If North were on lead, the small diamond lead would produce the simple squeeze against East. This is a simple squeeze position, with North on lead, but the squeeze card is a loser. Thus declarer must have all but two of the remaining tricks. In addition, the player who wins the squeeze card must have no other winner which he can cash. When these additional requirements are met, any simple squeeze ending may lead to a suicide squeeze, as can other squeeze positions.

SUIT. The group to which each card in a pack belongs. Modern packs have four suits. Until the 16th century, there was no agreement as to number; Hindu cards had 10, and packs of 5-11 suits were used in one country or another. In the Thirties there was a brief flurry of interest in a fifth suit, but it faded. Three different sets of sym-

bols have been developed which are in use today: International (British, American, French); spades, hearts, diamonds and clubs.

Trappola (Italy, Spain, Latin countries); cups, coins, swords and cudgels.

German (Germany, Austria, Bohemia, Poland, Hungary); hearts, leaves, bells and acorns, with the Swiss modification of blossoms and shields for the latter two. The club design is the cloverleaf of the French but the name is from the trappola deck; the diamond design is also French, but the name is an English descriptive term; the heart design is from the German pack; the spade design is the French pikehead, but the name is from the trappola deck. The suit names reflect the four orders of society — hearts for the church, spades for the military, clubs for the peasantry, and diamonds (tiles) for the merchants — was made long after the development of the suit names and symbols. See PLAYING CARDS.

SUIT, NUMBER OF CARDS IN. For notations used, see MATHEMATICS OF BRIDGE.

(1) A player can have x cards of a given suit in $13Cx \leftrightarrow 39C(13-x)$ ways. The percentage probability is found by multiplying this by 100 and dividing by 52C13. A player can have exactly five spades, then, in $13C5 \leftrightarrow 39C8 = 79,181,063,676$ ways. The percentage is

$$\frac{7,918,106,367,600}{635,013,559,600} = 12.469\%$$

(2) A player can have x cards of one suit and y cards of another suit in $13Cx \leftrightarrow 13Cy \leftrightarrow 26C(13-x-y)$ ways. He can have five spades and four hearts, then, in $13C5 \leftrightarrow 13C4 \leftrightarrow 26C4 = 13,757,064,750$ ways. The percentage is 2.166%.

(3) If 26 cards are known (such as after the dummy is exposed), of which y are the cards of the suit in question, a player can have x cards in that suit in $(13-y)Cx \leftrightarrow (26-13+y)C(13-x)$ ways. If four spades are seen (y), he can have five spades in $9C5 \leftrightarrow 17C8$ ways. This computes to 3,063,060 ways, or a percentage of 29.451%.

SUIT COMBINATIONS. The correct treatment of particular suit combinations by declarer is a highly complex subject. The classified analysis on the following pages is the first attempt in bridge literature at a comprehensive coverage. To find any particular combination, first count the number of high-card points held by the defense in the crucial suit. Find the appropriate section, which is subdivided according to the number of cards held by the declaring side. The play of each combination is considered in two ways. First from the angle of safety plays, the number of tricks required is given together with the appropriate play and the percentage prospects. Second, where no particular number of tricks is required, but declarer simply wants to do as well as possible, the indicated maximum play (abbreviated to MAX) is given, with the expectation of tricks if this line is followed. Whenever the symbol x is used, it should be assumed to be a completely insignificant spot card. In many cases the replacement of an x by an 8 or a 7 would affect the play or the percentages. Dummy is always assumed to have the greater length. When the same holding occurs the other way up, with the length in declarer's hand, the analysis and percentages are identical (except in very rare cases when psychological considerations apply).

Dummy Declarer	Tricks Required		% Chance of Success	Tricks per Deal

I. THE DEFENSE HAS NO POINTS

(a) Declarer Has Six Cards

1.	A K Q J 9 x	5	Cash top honors in the hope of dropping the ten	72	

(b) Declarer Has Seven Cards

2.	A K Q J 9 x x	6 5	Cash top honors Finesse the nine, in case East is void	86 99	
3.	A K Q J 9 x x	5	Cash top honors in the hope of dropping the ten	87	
4.	A K Q 9 x J x	5	Cash top honors in the hope of dropping the ten	87	
5.	A K Q J 8 x x	5	Cash top honors* (*But against defenders who would not false- card from 109x or 109xx, cash the jack and finesse the eight if the nine or ten appears from East)	84 85	
6.	A K Q 8 x J x	5	See (5) above	84	

(c) Declarer Has Eight Cards

7.	A K Q 8 x J x x	5	Cash the jack first in case East is void	98	

II. THE DEFENSE HAS ONE POINT

(a) Declarer Has Five Cards

8.	A K Q 10 x	4	Finesse the ten	50	

(b) Declarer Has Six Cards

9.	A K Q 10 9 x	5	Play off the top honors. This is fractionally better than the immediate finesse	36	
10.	A K Q 10 x x	5 4 Max	Finesse the ten Finesse the ten Finesse the ten	31 81	 4.12
11.	A K Q 10 x x	4	Cash the queen, and then finesse the ten	50	
12.	A K Q 9 x x	4	Finesse the nine; hope that West has both the jack and ten	24	
13.	A K 10 x Q x	4	Cash the queen, and then finesse the ten	50	
14.	A K 9 x Q x	4	Play off the queen, king, and ace, hoping that the jack and ten fall in three rounds* (*But against defenders who would not false- card from J10x, cash the queen and finesse the nine if East drops an honor)	11	

(c) Declarer Has Seven Cards

15.	A K Q 10 9 x x	6	Cash the top honors	54	

	Dummy Declarer	Tricks Required		% Chance of Success	Tricks per Deal
			II. THE DEFENSE HAS ONE POINT (cont'd)		
16.	A K Q 10 x x	6	Cash the top honors	52	
	x	5	Finesse the ten	91	
		4	Finesse the ten, in case East is void	99	
		Max	Cash the top honors		5.37
17.	A K Q 10 9	5	Play off the top honors	54	
	x x				
18.	A K Q 10 x	5	Play off the top honors	52	
	x x	4	Cash the ace, and finesse the ten	93	
		Max	Play off the top honors		4.39
19.	A K Q 9 x	5	Play off the top honors, hoping that the jack		
	x x		and ten drop in three rounds	39	
		4	Lead small to the nine, in case East has a void		
			or small singleton	90	
		Max	Play off the top honors*		4.23
			(*But against defenders who would not false- card from J 10 x, cash the ace and finesse the nine if East drops an honor)		4.24
20.	A K10 9 x	5	Play off the top honors	54	
	Q x				
21.	A K 10 x x	5	Play off the top honors	52	
	Q x	4	Cash the queen and finesse the ten	93	
		Max	Play off the top honors		4.39
22.	A K 9 x x	5	Cash the queen, king, and ace	54	
	Q 10	4	Cash the queen, and run the ten	100	
		Max	Cash the queen, and run the ten		4.44
23.	A K x x x	5	Finesse the ten	42	
	Q 10	4	Finesse the ten	92	
		Max	Finesse the ten		4.34
24.	A K 9 x x	5	Play off the top honors	39	
	Q x	4	Cash the queen, and finesse the nine if an honor drops from East	86	
		Max	Play off the top honors* (*But against defenders who would not false- card from J10x, cash the queen, and finesse the nine if an honor drops from East)		4.23 4.24
25.	A K Q 10	4	Cash the king and queen; if both follow, play the ace. This is 2% better than a third-round finesse	61	
	x x x				
26.	A K Q 9	4	Cash the queen and king; if an honor drops from East, finesse the nine next. This is 6% better than cashing the three top honors regardless	48	
	x x x				
27.	A K 10 x	4	See (25) above	61	
	Q x x				
28.	A K 9 x	4	See (26) above	48	
	Q x x				
29.	A K x x	4	Cash the ace, queen, and king, This is 4% better than a second-round finesse	55	
	Q 10 x				
30.	A 10 x x	4	See (25) above	61	
	K Q x				
31.	A 9 x x	4	See (26) above	48	
	K Q x				
32.	A x x x	4	Cash the king, queen, and ace. This is 4% better than a second-round finesse.	55	
	K Q 10				

(d)   Declarer Has Eight Cards

33.	A K Q 10 x x x 7		Play off the top honors	73	
	x	6	Finesse the ten, in case East is void	98	
		Max	Play off the top honors		6.70

	Dummy Declarer	Tricks Required		% Chance of Success	Tricks per Deal
			II. THE DEFENSE HAS ONE POINT (cont'd)		
34.	A K Q 9 x x x x	6	Play off the top honors* (*But against defenders who would not false- card from J10x, cash the ace and finesse the nine if an honor appears from East)	68 70	
		5	Lead small to the nine, in case East is void	98	
35.	A K Q 8 x x 10 x	6	Play off the top honors	73	
		5	Lead small to the ten	100	
		Max	Play off the top honors		5.70
36.	K Q 9 x x x A x	6	Play off the top honors* (*But against defenders who would not false- card from J10x, cash the ace and finesse the nine if an honor appears from East)	68 70	
37.	A K 9 x x Q 8 x	5	Cash the ace and queen (or the queen and ace) hoping for a 3-2 break or a singleton honor with East* (*But against defenders who would not false- card with J10x, cash the ace, and finesse the eight if West drops an honor)	73 76	
		4	Lead small to the eight or nine	100	
38.	A K 10 x Q 9 x x	4	Cash the ace. If the eight falls, play the next top honor from the hand on the left of the eight. Otherwise guess which honor to play next (*Assuming that the eight is not a false-card from J8xx)	92*	
39.	A K 9 x Q 8 x x	4	Cash the ace. If an honor appears, cash the next top honor from the hand on the left of the J or 10	79	
40.	A K 9 x Q x x x	4	Cash the queen, in case West has J10xxx	75	

(e) Declarer Has Nine Cards

	Dummy Declarer	Tricks Required		% Chance of Success	
41.	A K Q 8 x x x 9 x	7	Lead the nine, and play the ace whatever hap- pens. This saves a trick if West covers with J10xxx	90+	
42.	A K Q 7 x x 8 x x	6	Lead the eight, and play the ace whatever hap- pens. This saves a trick if West is lulled into covering with J109x	90+	
43.	A K 10 x x x Q 9 x	6	Lead the ace first in case either opponent is void	100	
44.	A K 9 x x x Q x x	6	Play the queen first, in case East is void	95	
45.	A K Q 7 x 8 x x x	5	Lead the eight, and play the ace whatever hap- pens. This saves a trick if West is lulled into covering with J109x	90+	
46.	A K 10 x x Q 9 x x	5	Cash the ace first, in case either opponent is void	100	
47.	A K 9 x x Q x x x	5	Cash the queen first, in case East is void	95	

III. THE DEFENSE HAS TWO POINTS

(a) Declarer Has Five Cards

	Dummy Declarer	Tricks Required		% Chance of Success	
48.	A K J 10 x	4	Finesse the jack. This line is 6% better than try- ing to drop the queen	11	

(b) Declarer Has Six Cards

	Dummy Declarer	Tricks Required		% Chance of Success	Tricks per Deal

III. THE DEFENSE HAS TWO POINTS (cont'd)

	Dummy Declarer	Tricks Req.		%	Tricks
49.	A K J 10 9 x	5	Finesse the jack	18	
50.	A K J 9 8 x	5	Lead small to the jack or nine, playing West for Q10x or Q10	5	
		4	Lead small to the jack	58	
		Max	Lead small to the jack		3.63
51.	A K J 9 x x	4	Finesse the nine; if this loses to the ten, finesse the jack	24	
		3	Finesse the jack and then the nine, *or* finesse the nine and then the jack	76	
52.	A K 9 8 J x	4	Run the jack; if it is covered, finesse the nine next. West must have Q10, Q10x or Qxxxxx	6	
		3	Lead the jack; if it loses, finesse the nine next	76	
53.	A K 9 x J x	3	Lead small to the jack. If this loses, finesse the nine	74	
54.	A J 9 8 K x	4	Cash the king and, unless an honor appears from East, finesse the jack	6	
		3	Cash the king, and unless an honor appears from East, finesse the jack or nine*	69	
		Max	Cash the king and, unless an honor appears from East, finesse the jack or nine* (*This line is only fractionally better than running the nine, which will be superior if West is likely to have fewer cards in the suit than East)		2.75
55.	A J x x K 9	3	Finesse the nine; if this loses to the ten, cash the king and ace	68	
56.	A K 9 J x x	3	Lead small to the nine, hoping that West has both the queen and ten	24	

57.	A K x
	J 9 8
		3	*Either* run the nine *or* run the jack. Guess
			  whether West has the bare queen or East the
			  bare ten*
			(*But against defenders who can be relied
			upon to cover the nine with the ten, lead the
			nine, and play the ace and king if it is not
			covered; if the nine is covered, run the jack
			next)
				24
				
				29	

(c) Declarer Has Seven Cards

	Dummy Declarer	Tricks Req.		%	Tricks
58.	A K J 10 9 x x	6	Finesse the jack. This line is 8% better than try- ing to drop the queen	27	
59.	A K J 9 8 7 x	6	Finesse the jack	19	

		5	Finesse the jack. This line is 2% better than
			  cashing the ace and king, and 1% better than
			  finessing the nine
				71	

60.	A K J 10 9 x x	5	Finesse the jack. Do not cash the ace first; Qxxx with West is more likely than Q with East	43	
61.	A K J 9 x x x	5	Finesse the jack, alternatively cashing the ace first	19	
		4	Finesse the nine; if this loses to the ten, cash the ace and king	73	

		3	Finesse the nine, and then the jack *or* finesse the
			  jack and then the nine, *or* cash the ace, and
			  then finesse the jack or nine
				94	

		Max	Finesse the nine; if this loses to the ten, cash the ace and king		3.85
62.	A K 9 8 x J x	5	Run the jack *or* lead small to the nine	9	
		4	Cash the ace and then run the jack	73	
		Max	Run the jack. If it is covered, finesse the nine; if it loses, cash the ace; if it holds, cash the ace		3.79

	Dummy Declarer	Tricks Required		% Chance of Success	Tricks per Deal

III.   THE DEFENSE HAS TWO POINTS (cont'd)

	Dummy Declarer	Tricks Required		% Chance of Success	Tricks per Deal
63.	A K 9 x x J x	5	Run the jack *or* lead small to the nine. West must hold Q10x	7	
		4	Lead small to the jack; if it loses, cash the ace and king	68	
		3	Lead small to the jack; if it loses, finesse the nine	99	
		Max	Lead small to the jack; if it loses, cash the ace and king		3.62
64.	A J x x x K 9	5	Cash the king, and then finesse the jack	18	
		4	Lead small to the nine	68	
		3	Cash the king, and then finesse the jack	94	
		Max	Cash the king, and then finesse the jack		3.74
64A.	K J 9 x x A x	5	Cash the ace and then finesse the jack. (If East plays the ten, play for the queen to drop unless East is capable of a falsecard from 10 x x.)	20.99	
		4	Cash the ace and then finesse the jack or the nine. If East plays the queen, finesse the nine	69.04	
		Max	Cash the ace and then finesse the jack.		3.84
65.	A K J 10 x x x	4	Cash the ace, and finesse the ten	51	
66.	A K J 9 x x x	4	Cash the ace, and finesse the jack	29	
		3	Cash the ace. Then lead toward dummy, and play the king if the ten fails to appear. Then lead up to the jack	85	
		Max	Cash the ace, and finesse the jack		3.07
67.	A K J x x x x	4	Cash the ace, and finesse the jack	18	
		3	Play off the ace and king, and then lead up to the jack	77	
		Max	Cash the ace, and finesse the jack		2.87
68.	A K 10 x J x x	4	Cash the ace, and then lead small to the ten. Don't lead the jack for the finesse; West may have Qx	28	
69.	A K 9 8 J x x	4	Run the jack; if this is covered, finesse the nine	25	
		3	Play the ace, and if no honor appears, run the nine; if it loses, run the jack through next* (*Assuming East would not duck with Qxx, this line only loses when West has 10x. If East is a very good defender, play the king if the nine loses to the ten)	94 84	
		Max	Run the jack; if this is covered, finesse the nine; if the jack loses, cash the ace and king		3.01
70.	A K 9 x J x x	4	Lead small to the nine, hoping that West has Q10 or Q10x	9	
		3 } Max }	Cash the ace and, unless the ten appears, lead small to the jack; if the jack loses, cash the king	84	2.88
71.	A K x x J 10 9	4	Finesse the jack	50	
		3	Finesse the jack *or* play the ace, and then finesse the jack	100	
72.	A K x x J 9 8	4	Run the nine and then the jack *or* run the jack and then the nine, hoping that West has Q10x or either Q or Qxxxx	8	
		3	Play the ace, and lead small to the jack	78	
		Max	Run the nine; if it loses to the ten, run the jack next		2.85

	Dummy Declarer	Tricks Required		% Chance of Success	Tricks per Deal

III. THE DEFENSE HAS TWO POINTS (cont'd)

	Dummy / Declarer	Tricks Required		% Chance	Tricks per Deal
73.	A K x x J 9 x	4	Play the ace, hoping that West has the singleton queen	1	
		3 } Max }	Play the ace, and then lead small to the jack or nine	78	2.79
74.	A K x x J x x	3 } Max }	Play the ace, and lead to the jack	69	2.69
75.	A J 9 8 K x x	4	Cash the king, and finesse the jack	29	
		3	Cash the king, and lead toward dummy, playing the ace unless the ten appears	85	
		Max	Cash the king, and finesse the jack		3.07
76.	A J 9 x K x x	4	Cash the king, and finesse the jack	29	
		3	Cash the king and ace; then lead to the jack	85	
		Max	Cash the king, and finesse the jack. If it loses, cash the ace		3.07
77.	A J x x K 9 x	4	Cash the king, and finesse the jack	19	
		3	Cash the king and ace; then lead to the jack	85	
		Max	Cash the king, and finesse the jack		2.98
78.	A J x x K x x	4	Cash the king, and finesse the jack	18	
		3	Cash the king and ace; then lead to the jack	77	
		Max	Cash the king, and finesse the jack		2.87
79.	K 9 x x A J x	4	Finesse the jack; then play the ace and king* (*Against defenders who would not falsecard from Q10x, finesse the nine if East drops the queen under the ace)	21 27	
		3	Lead small from dummy, and play the ace unless the ten appears. Then, unless West drops the ten, lead small to the jack	84	
		Max	Finesse the jack; then play the ace and king		3.03
80.	J 10 x x A K x	4	Cash the ace, and then run the jack. This line is only 1% better than cashing the two top honors	20	
81.	J 9 8 x A K x	4	Cash the ace and king, unless the queen drops from West* (*But if West is good enough to falsecard from Q10, we have to play the king, even if the queen falls under the ace)	12 11	
		3	Cash the ace and king; then lead to the jack	85	
82.	J x x x A K 9	4	Lead small to the nine, hoping that East has Q10 or Q10x	9	
		3 } Max }	Cash the ace and king; then lead to the jack	85	2.90

(d) Declarer Has Eight Cards

	Dummy / Declarer	Tricks Required		% Chance	Tricks per Deal
83.	A K J 10 9 x x x	7	Finesse the jack. This line is 4% better than playing off the ace and king	37	
84.	A K J 9 8 7 x x	7	Finesse the jack	34	
		6	Finesse the nine or, more profitably, finesse the jack	85	
85.	A K J 10 x x x x	6	Finesse the jack. Don't cash the ace first: Qxxx West is more likely than Q with East	48	
		5	Finesse the jack	98	
		Max	Finesse the jack		5.46

	Dummy Declarer	Tricks Required		% Chance of Success	Tricks per Deal

III.   THE DEFENSE HAS TWO POINTS (cont'd)

	Dummy Declarer	Tricks Required		% Chance of Success	Tricks per Deal
86.	A K J 9 x x x x	6	Finesse the jack, alternatively cashing the ace first*	37	
			(*Against defenders who would not falsecard from 10x, cash the ace, and play the king if the ten falls from East)	40	
		5 } Max }	Cash the ace, and finesse the jack	88	5.22
87.	A K J x x x x x	6	Finesse the jack, alternatively cashing the ace first	34	
		5 } Max }	Cash the ace, and then finesse the jack	85	5.17
88.	A K 9 8 7 x J x	6	Run the jack. If it is covered, guess whether to finesse for or drop the ten next	16	
		5 } Max }	Run the jack. If it loses, cash the ace and king; if it is covered, guess as above	87	5.03
89.	A K 9 8 x x J x	6	Run the jack. If it is covered, guess whether to finesse or cash the ace next	16	
		5	Lead small to the jack, and then cash the ace and king (which will be best if West is likely to be short in the suit) *or*		
			Run the jack, cashing the ace and king if it loses, and guessing if it is covered (which will be best if East is likely to be short in the suit)	85	
		Max	Run the jack, guessing what to do next if it is covered		5.01
90.	A K 9 x x x J x	6	Run the jack. If it is covered, finesse the nine *or* cash the ace	14	
		5	Lead small to the jack; then cash the ace and king	85	
		4	Lead small to the jack	100	
		Max	Lead the jack. If it is covered, finesse the nine next		4.94
91.	A J 8 x x x K 9	6	Play the king. If the queen drops from East, run the nine; otherwise finesse the jack	37	
		5	Cash the king, and then lead the nine, and finesse the jack	88	
		4	Lead small to the nine	100	
92.	A J x x x x K 9	6	Cash the king, and finesse the jack	34	
		5	Cash the king, and lead the nine, intending to finesse the jack	88	
		4	Lead small to the nine	100	
		Max	Cash the king, and finesse the jack		5.20
93.	A K 9 8 x J x x	5	Play the ace. Then play the king unless the queen has appeared from East	30	
		4	Play the ace, and unless an honor appears, lead low to the jack	96	
		Max	Lead the jack. If it is covered, finesse the nine; if it loses, cash the ace		4.14
94.	A K 9 x x J x x	5	Play the ace and king (unless the queen drops from East)	30	
		4	Play the ace, and if the ten fails to appear, lead small to the jack	96	
		Max	Play the ace and king		4.09

	Dummy Declarer	Tricks Required		% Chance of Success	Tricks per Deal

III.   THE DEFENSE HAS TWO POINTS (cont'd)

	Dummy Declarer	Tricks Required		% Chance of Success	Tricks per Deal
95.	A K 7 6 x J 9 8	5	Lead the nine to the ace. (This makes it harder for West to falsecard with queen from Q10, as it would help a declarer with J9.) If the queen falls, finesse accordingly; if not, cash the king Assuming no falsecard:	33	
		4	Play the ace, and if no honor appears, lead low to the jack	98	
		Max	Cash the ace and king* (*If West would not falsecard from Q10)		4.11 4.14
96.	A K x x x J 10 9	5	Finesse the jack. Don't cash the ace first: Qxxx with West is more likely than queen with East	48	
		4	Finesse the jack	100	
97.	A K x x x J 9 8	5	Cash the ace and king* (*But against defenders who would not false-card with Q10, finesse the nine if West drops the queen on the first round)	27 30	
		4	Play the ace, and lead small to the jack	88	
		3	Run the jack *or* lead small to the jack	100	
		Max	Cash the ace, and unless West is void, lead small to the king* (*If West would not falsecard with Q10)		4.01 4.04
98.	A K x x x J 9 x	5	Play the ace and king* (*But against defenders who would not false-card with Q10, finesse the nine if West drops the queen on the first round)	27 30	
		4	Play the ace, and lead small to the jack	88	
		Max	Play the ace and king		3.99
99.	A J 9 x x K x x	5 } Max }	Cash the king, and finesse the jack* (*But against defenders who would not false-card, it is fractionally better to play the ace if East drops the ten on the first round.)	40	4.27
100.	A J x x x K 9 x	5	Lead low to the jack* (*Against defenders who would not falsecard from Q10, finesse the nine next if the queen appears from West)	34 37	
		4	Play the ace, and unless an honor appears from West, lead low to the nine	96	
		3	Play either top honor	100	
		Max	Play the king, and finesse the jack		4.22
101.	A 9 x x x K J x	5	Finesse the jack. Don't cash the ace first, for East may have the singleton queen	37	
		4	Play the king, and unless the ten appears, lead low to the jack	96	
		3	Finesse the jack, and cash the king *or* play the king and lead small to the jack	100	
		Max	Finesse the jack		4.30
102.	J 9 8 x x A K x	4	Cash the ace, cross to dummy in another suit and lead the nine. If East shows out or covers, play the king. If not, run the jack.	96	
103.	A K J 10 x x x x	4	Play the ace, and finesse the jack	53	
104.	A K 9 x J x x x	4	Play the ace and king	30	
		3	Play the ace, and then lead small to the nine or jack	100	
		Max	Play the ace and king		3.21

	Dummy Declarer	Tricks Required		% Chance of Success	Tricks per Deal

III.   THE DEFENSE HAS TWO POINTS (cont'd)

	Dummy Declarer	Tricks Req.		%	T/D
105.	A K 8 x	4	Play the ace and king	27	
	J x x x	3	Play the ace; if the ten or nine appears from East, lead small to the jack	92	
		Max	Play the ace and king		3.14
106.	A K x x	4	Play the ace and king	33	
	J 9 8 x	3	Play the ace, and unless the ten appears from East, run the nine	100	
		Max	Play the ace and king		3.24
107.	A J x x	4	Finesse the jack	37	
	K 9 x x	3	Play the ace, and lead small to the nine	100	
		Max	Finesse the jack; if it loses, play the ace next		3.34
108.	A 10 8 x	4	Lead the jack to the ace *or* the ten to the king, and then take a second-round finesse. This gives the extra chance of a defender covering with Qx and Qxx		
	K J 9 x			53+	

(e) Declarer Has Nine Cards

	Dummy Declarer	Tricks Req.		%	T/D
109.	A K J x x x x x	8	Play the ace and king. This line is 8% better than a first-round finesse	53	
	x	7	Finesse the jack, in case East is void	95	
		Max	Play the ace and king		7.44
110.	A K J x x x x	7	Play the ace and king. This line is 2% better than a second-round finesse.	53	
	x x				
111.	A K 9 x x x x	7	Play the ace and king	53	
	J x	6	Lead low to the jack	100	
		Max	Play the ace and king*		6.44
			(*But againsst defenders who would always cover the jack, and would not falsecard with Q10, lead the jack, and play the ace whatever happens, finessing the nine next if East plays the queen)		6.48
112.	A J x x x x x	7	Play the king and ace	53	
	K 9	6	Lead small to the nine, in case West is void	100	
		Max	Play the king and ace		6.48
113.	A K J 10 x x	6	Play the ace and king	58	
	x x x				
114.	A K 9 x x x	6	Play the ace and king	53	
	J x x	5	Play the ace	100	
115.	A K 8 x x x	6	Play the ace and king	53	
	J x x	5	Lead small toward dummy, and cover whatever West plays	100	
		Max	Play the ace and king		5.48
116.	A K x x x x	6	Lead the jack to the ace; then cash the king	53	
	J 10 9				
117.	A K x x x x	6	Play the ace and king	53	
	J 9 8	5	Lead small to the jack *or* (best) run the nine	100	
		Max	Play the ace and king		5.48
118.	A J x x x x	6	Play the ace and king	53	
	K 9 x	5	Play the ace	100	
		Max	Play the ace and king		5.53
119.	A 9 x x x x	6	Play the ace and king	53	
	K J x	5	Play the king	100	
		Max	Play the king and ace		5.53

	Dummy Declarer	Tricks Required		% Chance of Success	Tricks per Deal
			III. THE DEFENSE HAS TWO POINTS (cont'd)		
120.	A K 8 x x	5	Play the ace and king*	53	
	J x x x		(*Against defenders who would always cover the jack, lead the jack, and play the ace whatever happens. If West covers and the ten or nine drops from East, finesse the eight next. This line will be better if East is likely to be short in the suit)	53	
		4	Lead small to the eight *or* small to the jack	100	
		Max	Play the ace and king		4.48
121.	A K x x x	5	Play the ace and king. This line is 2% better than a second-round finesse	58	
	J 10 9 x				
122.	A J 9 x x	5	Lead the jack to the king *or* lead the ten to the ace, and play for the drop on the second round. This gives the extra chance of a defender covering with Qxx	58	
	K 10 8 x				
123.	A J x x x	5	Play the king and ace, in case East is void	58	
	K 9 8 7	4	Play the ace, in case West is void	100	
124.	A J x x x	5	Cash the ace and king, preferably in that order	53	
	K 9 x x	4	Play the ace (best) *or* finesse the jack or nine	100	
125.	A 9 x x x	5	Play the ace and king in either order	53	
	K J x x	4	Play the king (best), *or* finesse the jack	100	
126.	A x x x x	5	Play the ace and king, in case West is void	58	
	K J 9 8	4	Play the king, in case East is void	100	
127.	J 10 9 x x	5	Play the ace and king; this line is 2% better than a second-round finesse	58	
	A K x x				
128.	J x x x x	5	Play the ace and king	53	
	A K 8 x	4	Lead small to the eight, in case West is void	100	
		Max	Play the ace and king		4.48

(f)   Declarer Has Ten Cards

	Dummy Declarer	Tricks Required		% Chance of Success	Tricks per Deal
129.	A K 9 x x x x x 8		Lead the jack, and play the ace whatever happens. This line succeeds against all 2-1 breaks and when West is lulled into covering with Q10x	78+	
	J x				
130.	A K 9 x x x x	7	See (129) above	78+	
	J x x				
131.	A J x x x x x	7	Lead the king, in case East is void	89	
	K x x				
132.	A K 9 x x x	6	See (129) above	78+	
	J x x x				
133.	A J x x x x	6	See (131) above	89	
	K x x x				
133A.	K x x x x x	6	Play the king, in case West is void* (*But if there is no side entry to dummy, play the ace, as the only way to avoid a suit block is to find a singleton queen)	26	
	A J 9 8				
134.	A K 9 x x	5	See (129) above	78+	
	J x x x x				
135.	A J 9 x x	5	Lead the ten to the ace, *or* lead the jack to the king. Guess who is most likely to be void	89	
	K 10 x x x				
136.	A J x x x	5	See (131) above	89	
	K x x x x				

Dummy Declarer	Tricks Required		% Chance of Success	Tricks per Deal

IV. THE DEFENSE HAS THREE POINTS
A. THE KING

(a) Declarer Has Five Cards

137.	A Q J 9	4	The only hope is that West has K10 doubleton	0.3	
	x	3	Lead small to the nine	52	
		Max	Lead small to the nine		2.53

(b) Declarer Has Six Cards

138.	A Q J 9 8	5	Finesse the queen. The only hope is that West has		
	x		K10 doubleton	1	
		4	Finesse the nine*	41	
		Max	Finesse the nine*		3.42
			(*The nine finesse is only 0.36% better than the queen finesse)		
139.	A Q J 9	4	Finesse the queen, hoping that West has K10 or		
	x x		K10x	5	
		3 }	Finesse the queen. If it holds, finesse the jack; if it		2.73
		Max }	loses, cash the ace and jack*	68	
			(*This assumes that East will duck the queen with Kx or Kxx. If not, it is better to finesse the nine if the queen loses)	76	
140.	A Q 9 8	4	Run the jack. If it is covered, finesse the nine		
	J x		next	5	
		3 }	Run the jack. If it losses, finesse the nine; if it		
		Max }	holds, finesse the queen*	76	2.81
			(*This assumes that West will cover the jack with Kxxxx or Kxxx, and that East will win with Kx or Kxx. If they would withhold the king in such circumstances, it is better to cash the ace and queen if the jack loses)	68	
141.	A Q 9 x	3	Lead small to the jack and finesse the nine next		
	J x		whatever happens	56	
142.	A Q 8 x	3	Lead the jack. If it holds, finesse the queen; if it		
	J 9		loses, cash the ace; if it is covered, run the nine*	68	
			(*The best defense is for East not to win with Kx or Kxx, and for West not to cover with Kxxxx or Kxxx)		
143.	A Q x x	3	Lead small to the nine, hoping that East has the		
	J 9		singleton ten or king*	50	
			(*Or that he will mistakenly play the king from Kx)	54	
144.	A Q 9	3	Lead small to the nine *or* (best) run the jack; if		
	J x x		it is covered, finesse the nine	24	
		Max	Run the jack; if it is covered, finesse the nine next		2.24
145.	A Q x	3	Run the nine *or* (best) run the jack; if it is cov-		
	J 9 8		ered, run the nine next	24	
		Max	Run the jack; if it is covered, run the nine next		2.24
146.	A x x	3	Lead the queen. If it is covered, play the jack, if		
	Q J 9		the queen holds, guess*	5	
			(*But against defenders who might cover un-necessarily—let us assume half the time—finesse the nine if the queen is covered and lead the jack next if the queen holds)	15	

	Dummy Declarer	Tricks Required		% Chance of Success	Tricks per Deal

IV. THE DEFENSE HAS THREE POINTS (cont'd)
A. THE KING (cont'd)

(c) Declarer Has Seven Cards

	Dummy Declarer	Tricks Required		% Chance of Success	Tricks per Deal
147.	A Q J 9 8 7 x	6	Finesse the queen. The only hope is that West has K10 doubleton	2	
		5 } Max }	Finesse the queen; then cash the ace	62	4.63
148.	A Q J 9 x x x	6	Finesse the queen, hoping that West has K10 doubleton	2	
		5	Finesse the queen; then cash the ace	58	
		4	Finesse the nine; then cash the ace	92	
		3	Finesse the nine; then cash the ace	99	
		Max	Finesse the queen; then cash the ace		4.46
149.	A Q J 9 8 x x	5	Finesse the queen; if it loses, cash the ace and jack	19	
		4 } Max }	Finesse the queen; if it loses, cash the ace and jack	71	3.91
150.	A Q 9 8 x J x	5	Lead small to the nine *or* (best) run the jack, finessing the nine next if it is covered	9	
		4 } Max }	Run the jack. If it loses, cash the ace; if it is covered, finesse the nine; if it holds, finesse the queen.	70	3.79
151.	A Q 9 x x J x	5	Lead small to the nine *or* (best) run the jack, finessing the nine next if it is covered	7	
		4	Lead small to the jack. If it holds, play the ace; if it loses, play the ace	58	
		3	Finesse the nine on the first or second round	93	
		Max	Run the jack. If it holds, finesse the nine; if it loses, cash the ace and queen; if it is covered, finesse the nine		3.54
152.	A Q x x x J 9	4	Lead small to the nine; if it loses, run the jack next*	49	
		3 } Max }	Lead small to the nine; if it loses, run the jack next*	93	3.42
			(*This line will also produce four tricks if East is tempted to play the king from Kx)	56	
153.	A Q x x x J x	4	Lead small to the jack, hoping that the suit divides 3-3 or that East has Kx	44	
		3	Play the ace, and lead small to the jack, in case West has the singleton king	86	
		Max	Lead small to the jack		3.29
154.	Q J 9 8 7 A x	5	Run the queen, cashing the jack next if it is covered	2	
		4	Play the ace, and lead to the queen	63	
		Max	Run the queen, cashing the jack next if it is covered*		3.63
			(*Playing the ace and leading to the queen makes only .004 tricks fewer, and will be the best line if West is more likely to be short in the suit)		
155.	Q J 9 x x A x	4	Play the ace, and lead to the queen	59	
		3	Play the ace, and lead to the nine	94	
		Max	Play the ace, and lead to the queen		3.49
156.	Q J x x x A 9	4	Lead small to the nine	50	
		3	Lead small to the nine	93	
		Max	Lead small to the nine		3.43

	Dummy Declarer	Tricks Required		% Chance of Success	Tricks per Deal

IV. THE DEFENSE HAS THREE POINTS (cont'd)
A. THE KING (cont'd)

	Dummy Declarer	Tricks Required		% Chance of Success	Tricks per Deal
157.	A Q J x	4	Finesse the queen, hoping that West has Kxx	18	
	x x x	3	Play the ace, and lead to the queen, in case East has the singleton king	69	
		Max	Finesse the queen		2.86
158.	A Q 10 x	4	Lead small to the ten, and then small to the queen. Do not lead the jack in case West has K or Kx	27	
	J x x				
159.	A Q 9 8	4 }	Run the jack. If it is covered, finesse the nine; if it holds, leads to the nine; if it loses, cash the ace and queen	25	3.03
	J x x	Max }			
		3	Finesse the queen. If it holds, run the jack; if it loses, cash the jack and ace	79	
160.	A Q 9 x	4	Lead low to the nine, hoping that West has K10 or K10x	9	
	J x x	3	Finesse the queen. If it loses, cash the jack and ace; if it holds, lead low to the nine	72	
		Max	Run the jack. If it is covered, finesse the nine; if it loses, cash the ace and queen		2.78
161.	A Q 8 7	4	Run the jack, hoping that East has the singleton nine or ten	2	
	J x x	3 }	Lead the jack. If it loses, cash the ace, and finesse East; if it holds, finesse the queen; if it is covered, finesse the eight and then the seven next* (*Assuming that West will not cover with Kxxx, K10xxx, or K9xxx)	59	2.61
		Max }			
162.	A Q 8 x	3	Lead small to the ace, then small to the jack. Then finesse the eight if possible. But if West plays the nine or ten, finesse the queen. (This assumes that West will play low with K 10 9 x or 10 9 x x. It is fractionally superior to the alternatives: Finesse the queen, and if it wins lead the jack (57%); small toward the jack (56%); or running the jack (53%).)	59	
	J x x				
163.	A Q x x	4	Run the jack, and then the nine (best) *or* run the nine. Hope that West has K10x or either Kxxxx or K	8	
	J 9 8	3 }	Lead the jack. If it loses, cash the ace; if it is covered, run the nine next	77	2.85
		Max }			
164.	A Q x x	4	Play the ace, hoping that West has the singleton king	1	
	J 9 x	3 }	Play the ace, and lead small to the jack	64	2.65
		Max }			
165.	A 9 8 7	4	Lead the queen. If it holds or is covered, lead the jack next	9	
	Q J x	3	Lead small to the queen. If it holds, lead small to the jack; if it loses, cash the jack and ace	83	
		Max	Lead the queen. If it loses, cash the jack and ace; if it holds or is covered, lead the jack next		2.88
166.	A 9 x x	3 }	Lead small to the queen. If it holds, lead small to the jack; if it loses, cash the jack and ace	83	2.83
	Q J x	Max }			
167.	Q J 9 x	4	Play the ace, hoping East has the singleton king	1	
	A x x	3 }	Play the ace and then lead to the queen and jack	78	2.79
		Max }			

Dummy Declarer	Tricks Required		% Chance of Success	Tricks per Deal

IV. THE DEFENSE HAS THREE POINTS (cont'd)
A. THE KING (cont'd)

168.	Q J x x	3	Play the ace, and lead low to the queen; then lead		
	A x x		low to the jack	69	
169.	J 9 8 7	4	Run the nine. If it is covered, run the jack	10	
	A Q x				
		3	Finesse the queen. If it holds, run the jack; if it		
			loses, cash the ace and jack*	78	
			(*This line offers extra chances if West is		
			tempted to win the queen with K10xxx)	83	
		Max	Run the jack. If it is covered, run the nine next		2.86
170.	J 9 8 x	4	Finesse the queen. If it holds, run the nine, hoping		
	A Q x		that East has K10, Kx, or K	9	
		3	Finesse the queen. If it holds, lead the jack; if it		
			loses, cash the ace and jack*	78	
			(*This line offers extra chances if West is		
			tempted to win the queen with K10xxx)	83	
		Max	Finesse the queen. If it holds, run the nine; if it		
			loses, cash the ace and jack		2.85
171.	J 9 x x	4	Finesse the queen, and then cash the ace, hoping		
	A Q x		that East has K, Kx, or K10	9	
		3	Lead small to the ace, unless the ten appears from		
			East; then lead to the queen and jack	69	
		Max	Finesse the queen, and then cash the ace		2.77
172.	J x x x	4	Lead small to the nine, hoping that East has		
	A Q 9		K10 or K10x	9	
		3	Lead small to the queen. If it holds, finesse the nine;		
			if it loses, cash the ace	71	
		Max	Lead small to the nine. If it loses, finesse the queen		2.77

(d) Declarer Has Eight Cards

173	A Q J 9 x x x	7	Finesse the queen, hoping that West has Kx or		
	x		K10	14	
		6	Play the ace, and lead the queen	79	
		5	Finesse the nine, in case East is void	98	
		Max	Finesse the queen		5.86
174.	A Q J 9 x x	6	Finesse the queen	34	
	x x	5	Finesse the queen; if it loses, cash the ace	85	
175.	A Q 9 8 x x	6	Finesse the queen, and run the jack if it holds *or*		
	J x		run the jack; if it loses, cash the ace; if it holds		
			finesse the queen; if it is covered, guess	14	
		5	As above	85	
176.	A Q 9 x x x	6	Finesse the nine *or* finesse the queen *or* lead the		
	J x		jack and guess next time	14	
		5	Run the jack. If it is covered, finesse the nine next	82	
		4	Safeguard against East being void by leading the		
			jack, leading to the jack or finessing the nine	98	
		Max	Run the jack. If it is covered, finesse the nine		
			next		4.94
177.	A Q x x x x	5	Lead small to the jack	76	
	J 9	4	Lead small to the nine, in case West is void	98	
		Max	Lead small to the jack*		4.72
			(*But against defenders who would play the		
			king from Kx as East, lead small to the nine		
			and run the jack next)		4.73

	Dummy Declarer	Tricks Required		% Chance of Success	Tricks per Deal

IV.   THE DEFENSE HAS THREE POINTS (cont'd)
A.   THE KING (cont'd)

177a	A Q 6 5 x x J 9	5	Run the jack. If West covers and East drops the seven, eight or ten, take the ace, return to hand and run the nine.	79	
178.	A Q x x x x J x	5 ⎱ Max ⎰	Play the ace. This succeeds if the suit divides 3-2 or there is a singleton king somewhere	73	4.70
179.	Q J 9 x x x A x	6	Lead the queen. If it is covered, finesse the nine, hoping East has Kx	10	
		5	Play the ace, and lead to queen	79	
		4	Play the ace; fails only if West is void	98	
		Max	Lead the queen, finessing the nine next if it is covered		4.83
180.	A Q 10 x x J x x	5 ⎱ Max ⎰	Finesse the queen. Don't lead the jack in case West has the singleton king	37	4.33
181.	A Q 9 7 6 J 8 x	5	Run the jack. If it is covered, finesse the nine next	25	
		4	Run the jack *or* finesse the queen	90	
		Max	Run the jack. If it is covered, finesse the nine next		4.14
182.	A Q 9 x x J 8 x	5	Finesse the queen. If it holds, guess whether to play the ace or the jack next* (*If West would not falsecard with K10, finesse the eight if the king appears on the first round)	16 19	
		4	Finesse the queen *or* run the jack *or* play the ace and lead small to the jack	88	
183.	A Q 9 x x J x x	5	Finesse the queen *or* run the jack. Guess whether West has K10x, Kxx, or Kx	14	
		4	Finesse the queen, and lead to the nine if it holds *or* play the ace, and lead to the jack	88	
		3	Finesse the queen	98	
		Max	Finesse the queen. If it loses, cash the jack; if it holds, lead to the nine		3.99
184.	A Q 8 x x J x x	5	Finesse the queen; if it holds, lead small to the eight* (*If East would not falsecard from 109x, lead the jack if the nine or ten appears on the first round)	14 17	
		4	Lead small to the ace, unless the nine or ten ap- pears from West; then lead low to the jack (best) *or* run the jack; if it is covered, lead low to the eight unless the nine or ten has dropped	79	
		3	Run the jack. If it is covered, lead low to the eight unless the nine or ten has dropped from East (best)	98	
		Max	Finesse the queen. If it holds, lead small to the eight		3.86
185.	A Q x x x J 9 8	5	Lead the jack. If it holds, finesse the queen; if it is covered, guess whether to run the nine or play the ace next	16	
		4 ⎱ Max ⎰	Lead the jack. If it loses, cash the ace; if it holds, finesse the queen; if it is covered, run the nine	85	4.01
		3	Lead the jack (best) or lead small to the jack	100	
186.	A Q x x x J 9 x	5	Finesse the queen. If it holds, guess whether to lead the nine or the jack next* (*If West would not falsecard from K10, finesse the nine if the king appears from West)	14 16	
		4	Play the ace, and lead small to the jack	79	
		3	Play the ace, or finesse the queen	98	
		Max	Finesse the queen, and cash the ace next		3.88

	Dummy Declarer	Tricks Required		% Chance of Success	Tricks per Deal

IV.   THE DEFENSE HAS THREE POINTS (cont'd)
A.   THE KING (cont'd)

	Dummy Declarer	Tricks Required		% Chance of Success	Tricks per Deal
186a	A Q 6 x x J 9 x	4	Run the jack. If West covers with the king, win the ace and lead to the nine.	85	
187.	A Q x x x J x x	5	Finesse the queen, and then play the ace	14	
		4	Play the ace, and lead toward the jack, in case East has the singleton king	73	
		Max	Finesse the queen		3.80
187a	A Q 7 x x J x x	4	Run the jack. If West covers and East drops the eight, nine or ten, win the ace, return to hand for the next lead.	76	
188.	A 9 x x x Q J x	5	Lead the queen. If it holds, lead the jack, hoping that West has Kxx or K10	14	
		4	Lead small to the queen. If it holds, lead to the jack	93	
		3	Lead small to the queen	100	
		Max	Run the queen. If it holds, lead the jack		3.96
189.	A x x x x Q J 9	5	Lead the queen. If it is covered, play the jack next; if it holds, lead the jack next* (*This assumes that West will cover with Kx about once in four times—best defense)	14	
		4	Lead small to the queen, and then small to the jack	85	
		3	Lead the queen *or* lead small to the queen	98	
		Max	Lead the queen. If it is covered, play the jack; if it holds, lead the jack next* (*The best defense is now for West never to cover with Kx		3.85
190.	Q J 9 x x A x x	5	Lead the Queen. If it holds, lead the jack; if it is covered, finesse the nine* (*This assumes that East will cover with Kx half the time; if he always covers, this line will produce five tricks)	15 20	
		4	Play the ace, and lead toward the queen	88	
		Max	Lead the queen. If it loses, play the ace; if it holds, play the ace; if it is covered, finesse the nine* (*But if West would not duck the queen with K10xx, lead the jack if the queen holds; and if East would always cover with Kx, lead the jack if the queen holds)		3.93 3.98 4.03
191.	J 9 8 x x A Q x	5	Finesse the queen. If it holds, guess whether East has Kx or Kxx	16	
		4 } Max }	Finesse the queen. If it loses, cash the ace; if it holds, run the nine	93	4.10
192.	J x x x x A Q 9	5	Finesse the queen *or* finesse the nine	14	
		4 } Max }	Finesse the queen. If it holds, lead small to the nine; if it loses, cash the ace	85	3.96
192a	J 7 x x x A Q 6	4	Run the jack. If West covers and East drops the eight, nine or ten. win and return to hand for next lead.	76	
193.	A Q J x x x x x	4	Finesse the queen	34	
		3	Play the ace, and lead to the queen	87	
		Max	Finesse the queen		3.18
194.	A Q 10 x J x x x	4	Finesse the ten. Don't lead the jack in case West has the singleton king	37	
195.	A Q 9 8 J x x x	4	Lead the jack. If it is covered, finesse the nine; if it holds, lead small to the nine	27	
		3	Lead small to the queen. If it loses, cash the ace; if it holds, lead to the nine	97	
		Max	Both the above lines produce		3.16

	Dummy Declarer	Tricks Required		% Chance of Success	Tricks per Deal

IV. THE DEFENSE HAS THREE POINTS (cont'd)
A. THE KING (cont'd)

	Dummy Declarer	Tricks Required		% Chance of Success	Tricks per Deal
196.	A Q 9 x J x x x	4	Finesse the queen *or* run the jack, guessing whether West has Kx or K10x	14	
		3 } Max }	Finesse the queen. If it loses, cash the jack; if it holds, finesse the nine	90	3.03
197.	A Q 8 x J x x x	4	Finesse the queen; if it holds, lead small to the eight* (*If East would not falsecard from 109x, lead the jack next if the nine or ten drops)	14 17	
		3	Lead the jack. If it is covered, lead small to the eight unless the nine or ten has appeared from East	81	
		Max	Finesse the queen; if it holds, lead small to the eight		2.90
198.	A Q x x J 9 8 x	4	Finesse the queen, hoping that West has K, Kxxx, K10, or Kx	19	
		3 } Max }	Finesse the queen. If it loses, play the ace; if it holds, run the nine	97	3.16
199.	A Q x x J 9 x x	4	Finesse the queen. If it holds, guess whether to lead the jack or play the ace	16	
		3	Play the ace, and lead small to the queen	90	
		Max	Finesse the queen, then play the ace		3.03
200.	A Q x x J x x x	4	Finesse the queen; then play the ace, hoping West has Kx	14	
		3	Play the ace, and lead small to either honor	73	
		Max	Finesse the queen, then play ace		2.84
200a	A Q 7 x J x x x	3	Run the jack. If West covers and East drops the eight, nine or ten, win with the ace and return to hand for the next lead.	76	
201.	A 9 8 x Q J x x	4	Lead the queen. If it is covered, cash the jack; if it holds, lead the jack. Hope that West has Kxx, K10, or Kxxx* (*It has been assumed that, if the queen is led, West will cover 1/3 of the time with Kx, and East will win 1/3 of the time with K10xx. This is the best defense)	16	
		3	Lead the queen (best). If it loses, cash the ace; if it holds, lead small to the nine *or* lead small to the queen. If it loses, cash the jack; if it holds, lead small to the nine	97	
		Max	Lead the queen. If it loses, cash the ace; if it is covered, run the nine; if it holds, lead small to the nine* (*It has been assumed that, if the queen is led, West will cover 1/3 of the time with Kx, and East will win 1/3 of the time with K10xx. This is the best defense)		3.10
202.	A x x x Q J x x	3	Play the ace, and lead to the queen. This fails only if East has a void or a small singleton	87	
203.	Q J 9 x A x x x	4	Lead the queen. If it holds, lead the jack; if it is covered, finesse the nine next* (*This assumes that East will cover 1/2 the time with Kx; if he always covers, this line will produce four tricks)	15 20	
		3	Play the ace and lead to the queen	90	
		Max	Lead the queen. If it holds, play the ace; if it is covered, finesse the nine* (*But if West would not duck the queen with K10xx, lead the jack next if the queen holds)		2.97 3.02

Dummy Declarer	Tricks Required		% Chance of Success	Tricks per Deal

IV. THE DEFENSE HAS THREE POINTS (cont'd)
A. THE KING (cont'd)

204.	Q J x x A 9 x x	4	Lead the queen. If it holds, lead the jack; if it loses or is covered, cash the jack	14	
		3	Lead small to the queen. If it loses, cash the jack; if it holds, lead small to the nine	97	
		Max	Lead the queen, and play the jack next whatever happens		3.00

(e) Declarer Has Nine Cards

205.	A Q J 10 x x x x x	8	Finesse the queen; Kx with West is more likely than K with East	27	
206.	A Q 9 x x x x J x	7	Finesse the queen	33	
		6	Run the jack *or* lead small to the jack	95	
		Max	Finesse the queen		6.23
207.	Q J x x x x x A x	7	Run the queen, hoping West has Kx	20	
		Max	Run the queen		6.11
208.	A Q 9 x x x J x x	6 }	Finesse the queen, hoping that West has Kxx, K10, Kx, or K	33	5.28
		Max }			
209.	A Q 8 x x x J x x	6	Finesse the queen	27	
		5	Lead the jack, in case East is void	95	
		Max	Finesse the queen		5.17
210	A Q 7 x x x J 9 8	6	Finesse the queen	33	
		5	Play the ace *or* finesse the queen	100	
		Max	Finesse the queen		5.33
211.	A Q x x x x J 9 8	6	Finesse the queen, hoping that West has Kxx, K10, Kx, or K	33	
		5	If West is more likely to be void, play the ace or finesse the queen; if East is more likely to be void, run the jack or lead small to the jack	95	
		Max	Finesse the queen		5.28
212.	A x x x x x Q J 9	6	Run the queen	27	
		5	Run the queen (best) *or* lead small to the queen	95	
		Max	Run the queen		5.22
213.	A x x x x x Q J x	6	Run the queen	20	
		5	Lead small to the queen, in case West is void	95	
		Max	Run the queen		5.11
214.	Q J 9 x x x A x x	6 }	Lead the queen. If it is covered, cash the jack	27	5.22
		Max }			
215.	Q J x x x x A x x	6	Run the queen	20	
		5	Play the ace, and lead to the queen	95	
		Max	Run the queen		5.11
216.	J 9 8 x x x A Q x	6	Finesse the queen	33	
		5	Finesse the queen *or* play the ace	100	
		Max	Finesse the queen		5.33
217.	A Q J x x x x x x	5	Finesse the queen	45	
		Max	Finesse the queen		4.40
218.	A Q 9 7 x J 8 x x	5	Finesse the queen. A singleton king with West is more likely than K10xx	33	
		4	Finesse the queen, in case West is void	100	
219.	A Q 9 x x J x x x	5	Finesse the queen	33	
		Max	Finesse the queen		4.28
220.	A Q 8 x x J x x x	5	Finesse the queen	27	
		4	Run the jack, in case East is void	95	
		Max	Run the jack. If it is covered, and the nine or ten drops from East, finesse the eight next		4.21
221.	A 9 8 x x Q J x x	5	Run the queen. If it is covered, cash the jack	27	
		4	Run teh queen (best) *or* lead small to the queen	100	
		Max	Run the queen. If it is covered, cash the jack next		4.27

	Dummy Declarer	Tricks Required		% Chance of Success	Tricks per Deal
			IV. THE DEFENSE HAS THREE POINTS (cont'd)		
			A. THE KING (cont'd)		
222.	A 9 x x x	5	Run the queen, hoping that West has Kxx, K10,		
	Q J x x		or Kx	27	
		4	Lead small to the queen	100	
		Max	Run the queen		4.22
223.	A x x x x	5 ⎫	Run the queen. If it is covered, cash the jack	27	4.22
	Q J 9 x	Max ⎭			
224.	A x x x x	5	Run the queen, hoping that West has Kx	20	
	Q J x x	4	Play the ace, and lead to the queen	95	
		Max	Run the queen		4.11
225.	Q J 9 x x	5 ⎫	Run the queen. If it is covered, cash the jack	27	4.22
	A x x x	Max ⎭			
226.	Q J x x x	5	20		
	A x x x	4 ⎫	See (224) above	95	
		Max ⎭			4.11
227.	J 9 8 x x	5	Finesse the queen; then cash the ace. Unless		
	A Q x x		West plays the ten	33	
		4	Finesse the queen (best) *or* cash the ace	100	
		Max	Finesse the queen, then cash the ace		4.33

(f) Declarer Has Ten Cards

	Dummy Declarer	Tricks Required		% Chance of Success	Tricks per Deal
228.	A J 9 x x x x x	8 ⎫	Run the queen	50	
	Q x	Max ⎭			7.50
229.	A Q J x x x x	7 ⎫	Finesse the queen	50	
	x x x	Max ⎭			6.50
230.	A J 9 x x x x	7 ⎫	Run the queen. Don't finesse the jack in case	50	
	Q x x	Max ⎭	East is void		6.50
231.	Q J x x x x x	7 ⎫	Run the queen	39	
	A x x	Max ⎭			6.39
232.	A Q J x x x	6 ⎫	Finesse the queen	50	
	x x x x	Max ⎭			5.50
233.	A J 9 x x x	6 ⎫	See (230) above	50	
	Q x x x	Max ⎭			5.50
234.	Q J x x x x	6 ⎫	Run the queen	39	
	A x x x	Max ⎭			5.39
235.	A Q J x x	5 ⎫	Finesse the queen	50	
	x x x x x	Max ⎭			4.50
236.	A J 9 x x	5 ⎫	See (230) above	50	
	Q x x x x	Max ⎭			4.50
237.	A x x x x	5 ⎫	Run the queen	39	
	Q J x x x	Max ⎭			4.39

(g) Declarer Has Eleven Cards

	Dummy Declarer	Tricks Required		% Chance of Success	Tricks per Deal
238.	A Q J x x x	6	Play the ace. The singleton king with East is 2%		
	x x x x x		more likely than Kx with West	52	

B. THE QUEEN-JACK

(a) Declarer Has Six Cards

	Dummy Declarer	Tricks Required		% Chance of Success	Tricks per Deal
239.	A K 10 9 8	5	Play the ace and king, hoping that the queen-		
	x		jack are bare	1	
		4	Lead small to the ten	45	
		Max	Lead small to the ten		3.46

	Dummy Declarer	Tricks Required		% Chance of Success	Tricks per Deal

IV. THE DEFENSE HAS THREE POINTS (cont'd)
B. THE QUEEN-JACK (cont'd)

240.	A K 10 9	4	Lead small to the ten, hoping that West has QJx or QJ	5	
	x x	3 Max	Finesse the ten; if this loses, finesse the nine next	76	2.81
241.	A 9 x x K 10	3	Lead small to the ten; then cash the king and ace	55	

(b) Declarer Has Seven Cards

242.	A K 10 9 x	5	Finesse the ten, hoping that West has QJx or QJ	9	
	x x	4	Finesse the ten; then finesse the nine	66	
		3	Play the ace, and then finesse the ten *or* finesse the ten and then the nine	94	
		Max	Finesse the ten; then finesse the nine		3.69
243.	A 10 x x x	4	Lead small to the nine	61	
	K 9	3	Lead small to the nine	92	
243A.	A 10 9 x x	5	Play the king, then the ace	3	
	K x	4	Play the king, then the ace (unless East shows out)	61	3.54
		Max			
		3	Play the king, then finesse the nine or ten	93	
244.	A K 10 9	4	Finesse the ten, hoping that West has both the queen and jack	24	
	x x x	3	Finesse the ten; if it loses, cash the ace, and finesse the nine (best) *or* play the ace, and then finesse the ten and nine	78	
		Max	Finesse the ten; if it loses, cash the ace, and finesse the nine		3.00
245.	A K 9 x	4	Finesse the nine, hoping that West has QJx or QJ	9	
	10 x x	3	Play the ace. If no honor drops from East, lead small to the nine next	72	
		Max	Finesse the nine		2.78
246.	A 10 9 x	4	Play the king. If an honor drops from East, finesse the nine	4	
	K 8 x	3 Max	Lead small to the eight. If it loses, run the ten next* (*This line fails only when West has QJ, QJx, or QJxx. In practical play, however, it might be better to lead small to the king, and then finesse the ten and nine: for East may split his honors with QJx, QJxx, etc.)	82	2.84
247.	A 10 x x	4	Play the ace anbd king, hoping that the queen and jack are doubleton	3	
	K 9 x	3 Max	Lead low to the nine; then cash the king and ace* (*This assumes that East would never split his honors from QJxx and longer; if this is not so, lead low to the king and then finesse the ten)	75	2.77
248.	A 10 x x K x x	3 Max	Play the king, and unless an honor appears from East, lead small to the ten* (*But if West might be tempted to split his honors, it might be better to play the king and ace and lead to the ten)	56	2.56

(c) Declarer Has Eight Cards

249.	A K 10 9 x x	6	Finesse the ten, hoping that West has QJ or QJx	14	
	x x	5	Play the ace. If an honor drops from East, play the king; otherwise finesse the ten	88	
		Max	Finesse the ten. If it loses, play the ace and king		4.94

	Dummy Declarer	Tricks Required		% Chance of Success	Tricks per Deal
			IV. THE DEFENSE HAS THREE POINTS (cont'd)		
			B. THE QUEEN-JACK (cont'd)		
250.	A 10 9 x x x K x	6	Play the ace and king, hoping that the queen- jack are doubleton	7	
		5 } Max }	Play the king, and unless an honor drops from East, lead small to the ten	88	4.92
251.	A 10 x x x x K 9	6	Play the king and ace, hoping that the queen- jack are doubleton	7	
		5	Lead small to the nine	82	
		4	Lead small to the nine	98	
		Max	Lead small to the nine		4.83
252.	A K 10 9 x x x x	5	Finesse the tne, hoping that West has QJxx, QJx, or QJ	22	
		4 } Max }	Finesse the ten. If it loses, cash the ace next	90	4.10
253.	A K9 x x 10 x x	5	Run the ten, hoping that West has QJ or QJx* (*Or will cover with Qxx or Jxx)	14	
		4	Play the ace. Unless an honor appears, run the ten next	88	
		3	Play the ace	100	
		Max	Lead small to the nine		3.96
254.	A K 8 x x 10 x x	5	Play the ace and king, hoping that the queen- jack are doubleton	7	
		4	Play the ace, and lead small to the ten	82	
		3	Lead small to the ten	100	
		Max	Play the ace, and lead small to the ten		3.78
255.	A 10 9 x x K x x	5	Play the king. If an honor falls from East, finesse the ten	9	
		4	Play the king, and finesse the ten	88	
		3	Play the king, and finesse the ten	98	
		Max	Play the king, and finesse the ten		3.95
256.	A 10 x x x K 9 x	5	Play the king and ace, hoping that the queen- jack are doubleton	7	
		4	Lead low to the nine; then cash the king	90	
		3	Play the king, or lead small to the nine	100	
		Max	Play the king, and unless an honor appears, lead low to the ten		3.94
257.	A 10 x x x K 8 x	5	Play the king and ace, hoping that the queen- jack are doubleton	7	
		4	Play the king, and unless an honor drops from East, lead small to the ten (best), *or* lead small to the ten; if an honor appears from West, lead small to the eight next. The latter method might be better if West is more likely to be short in the suit	82	
		Max	Play the king, and unless an honor appears from East, lead small to the ten		3.87
258.	A 10 x x x K x x	5	Play the king and ace, hoping that the queen- jack are doubleton	7	
		4	Play the king, and unless an honor appears from East, lead small to the ten	82	
		3	Play the king, in case East is void	98	
		Max	Play the king, and unless an honor appears from East, lead small to the ten		3.87
259.	A K 10 9 x x x x	4	Finesse the ten	24	
		3 } Max }	Finesse the ten; if it loses, cash the ace	90	3.14
260.	A K 8 x 10 x x x	4	Play the ace and king, hoping that the queen- jack are doubleton	7	
		3	Play the ace. Then either lead small to the		

Dummy Declarer	Tricks Required		% Chance of Success	Tricks per Deal
		IV. THE DEFENSE HAS THREE POINTS (cont'd)		
		B. THE QUEEN-JACK (cont'd)		
		eight, *or* if an honor has appeared from West, small to the ten	82	
	Max	Play the ace. Unless an honor appears from West, lead small to the ten next		2.85
261.	A 10 9 8	4	Play the ace, and run the ten if an honor appears, *or* cash the king and finesse the ten if an honor appears	9	
	K x x x	3 } Max	Run the ten. If an honor appears from East, finesse the eight next; if the ten loses, cash the king. Alternatively, if East is more likely to be short in the suit, finesse the ten first and cash the ace if it loses	94	3.00
262.	A 10 x x	4	Play the ace and king, hoping that the queen and jack will be doubleton	7	
	K 9 x x	3 } Max	Lead small to the ten, and then cash the ace, *or* lead small to the nine, and then cash the king; the latter line will be better if West is likely to be short in the suit	94	2.98
263.	A 10 x x	4	Play the ace and king, hoping that the queen-jack will be doubleton	7	
	K 8 x x	3	Lead small to the ten. If it loses, cash the ace; if West plays the jack or queen on the first round, lead small to the eight next	87	
		Max	Play the king, and unless an honor appears from East, lead small to the ten		2.91
264.	A 10 x x	4	Play the ace and king, hoping that the queen-jack will be bare	7	
	K x x x	3 } Max	Play the king, and unless an honor appears from East, lead small to the ten	84	2.91
(d)	**Declarer has Nine Cards**				
265.	A K 10 9 x x	6 } Max	Play the ace. If an honor drops from East, finesse the ten	46	5.42
	x x x				
266.	A K 8 x x x	6	Play the ace and king	41	
	10 x x	5	Lead small to the eight, *or* run the ten, *or* lead small to the ten	95	
		Max	Lead the ten, and play the ace whatever happens; then play the king		5.36
267.	A 10 x x x x	6	Play the ace, and finesse the nine if an honor appears from West, *or* play the king, and finesse the ten if an honor appears from East	46	
	K 9 x	5	Lead small to the nine or ten	100	
		Max	Play the ace, and finesse the nine, *or* play the king and finesse the ten		5.42
268.	9 8 7 6 x x	6	Play the ace and king	41	
	A K 5	5	Lead small to the five	95	
		Max	Play the ace and king		5.31
269.	A K 10 9 x	5 } Max	Play the ace. If an honor drops from East, finesse the ten next; otherwise play the king	46	4.42
	x x x x				
270.	A K 9 x x	5 } Max	Play the ace. If an honor drops from East, finesse the nine.	46	4.42
	10 x x x				
271.	A K 8 x x	5	Play the ace and king	41	
	10 x x x	4	Lead small to the eight, *or* run the ten, *or* lead small to the ten	95	
		Max	Lead the ten, and play the ace whatever happens; then play the king. This line saves a trick if West is tempted to cover with QJ9x.		4.31+

Dummy Declarer	Tricks Required		% Chance of Success	Tricks per Deal

IV. THE DEFENSE HAS THREE POINTS (cont'd)
B. THE QUEEN-JACK (cont'd)

272.	A 10 x x x K 9 x x	5	Play the ace (or king). If an honor falls, finesse the nine (or ten)	46	
		4	Lead small to the nine or ten	100	
		Max	Play the ace (or king). If an honor falls, finesse the nine (or ten)		4.42

(e) Declarer Has Ten Cards

273.	A K x x x 10 9 8 x x etc.	5	Lead the ten, and play the ace whatever hap- pens; this saves a trick when West is lulled into covering with QJx	78+	

V. THE DEFENSE HAS FOUR POINTS
A. THE ACE

(a) Declarer Has Five Cards

274.	K Q J 9 x	3	Finesse the nine	50	

(b) Declarer Has Six Cards

275.	K Q J 9 8 x	4	Play the king, queen, and jack	36	
		Max	Play the king, queen, and jack		3.36
276.	K Q J9 x x	4	Finesse the nine	31	
		3	Finesse the nine	82	
		Max	Finesse the nine		3.13
277.	K Q J 9 x x	3 }	Lead to the king; then finesse the nine	55	2.55
		Max }			
278.	K Q 9 x J 8	3	Lead to the jack, and run the eight next	51	
279.	K Q 9 x J x	3	Lead to the jack; then finesse the nine	51	
280.	K Q x x J 9	3	Finesse the nine	50	

(c) Declarer Has Seven Cards

281.	K Q J 9 x x x	5	Lead to the king; then play the queen and jack	52	
		4	Finesse the nine	92	
		3	Finesse the nine, in case East is void	99	
		Max	Lead to the king; then play the queen and jack		4.38
282.	K Q J 9 8 x x	4 }	Lead to the king; then lead to the queen	61	3.61
		Max }			
283.	K Q J 9 x x x	4	Lead to the king; then lead to the queen	58	
		3	Lead to the king; then finesse the nine	94	
		Max	Lead to the king; then lead to the queen		3.46
284.	K Q J x x 9 x	4	Lead to the king; then lead to the queen	44	
		3	Lead small to the nine, in case West has a void or small singleton	93	
		Max	Lead to the king; then lead to the queen		3.31
285.	K Q 9 x x J 8	4	Lead to the jack; then play to the king and queen	54	
		3	Lead small to the eight, or (best) lead to the jack and then run the eight	100	
		Max	Lead to the jack; then play the king and queen		3.49
286.	K Q 9 x x J x	4	Lead to the jack, and then lead to the king	52	
		3	Lead to the jack, and then finesse the nine	93	
		Max	Lead to the jack, and then lead to the king		3.40

	Dummy Declarer	Tricks Required		% Chance of Success	Tricks per Deal
			V. THE DEFENSE HAS FOUR POINTS (cont'd)		
			A. THE ACE (cont'd)		
287.	K Q x x x J 9	4	Finesse the nine. This offers a 5% better chance than hoping for a 3-3 break	42	
		3	Finesse the nine	93	
		Max	Finesse the nine		3.25
288.	K Q J 9 x x x	3	Lead to the king, to the queen, and to the jack. This is fractionally better than the third-round finesse	78	
289.	K Q 9 x J xx	3	Lead to the king, then to the jack, then to the queen. This is 2% better than the third-round finesse of the nine	62	
290.	K Q x x J 9 x	3	Lead to the king; then lead to the jack	56	
291.	KQ x x J x x	3	Lead to the king, and then to the queen. This is 8% better than leading to honors at randmon nad hoping for a 3-3 break	45	
292.	K 9 x x Q J x	3	Lead to the queen and then to the jack; play the king on the third round. This is 1% better than the third-round finesse of the nine	67	
293.	K x x x Q J 9	3	Lead to the queen and then to the jack	63	

(d) Declarer Has Eight Cards

	Dummy Declarer	Tricks Required		% Chance of Success	Tricks per Deal
294.	K Q J 9 x x x x	6	Lead to the king; then play the queen and jack	76	
		5	Finesse the nine, in case East is void	98	
		Max	Lead to the king; then play the queen and jack		5.72
295.	K Q J x x x 9 x	5	Lead to the king; then play the queen and jack	76	
		4	Lead small to the nine, in case West is void	98	
		Max	Lead to the king, and then play the queen and jack		4.72
296	K Q x x x x J 9	5	Lead to the jack, and then to the king	76	
		4	Finesse the nine, in case West is void	98	
		Max	Lead to the jack, and then to the king		4.72
297.	K Q 10 7 x J x x	4 ⎱ Max ⎰	Lead to the jack first; this fails only if West is void	98	3.98
298.	K Q 9 x x J 8 x	4	Lead to the king, and then to the jack	88	
299.	K Q 9 x x J x x	4 ⎱ Max ⎰	Lead to the king, and then to the jack	88	3.86
300.	K Q 8 x x J x x	4	Play to a high honor, and play the jack on the first or second round	76	
		3 ⎱ Max ⎰	Lead small to the jack. This fails only when West is void	98	3.74
301.	K Q x x x J 9 x	4 ⎱ Max ⎰	Lead to the king, and then to the jack, *or* lead to the jack and then to the king. The latter line is better if East is likely to be short in the suit	76	3.74
302.	K Q J 9 x x x x	3	Lead to the king first, in case West has the singleton ace	90	
303.	K Q 9 x J 8 x x	3	Lead to the king, and then to the jack. This fails only when West has a smal singleton	92	
304.	K Q 9 x J x x x	3	Lead to the king, and then to the jack. This fails only when West has a void or a small singleton	90	

	Dummy Declarer	Tricks Required		% Chance of Success	Tricks per Deal
			V. THE DEFENSE HAS FOUR POINTS (cont'd)		
			A. THE ACE (cont'd)		
305.	K Q 8 x J x x x	3	Lead low to the jack first, in case East is void	78	
306.	K Q 7 x J 9 x x	3	Lead to the king and then to the queen* (*But if East would not falsecard from A108x, lead to the king, and if the eight drops from East, lead to the jack next; otherwise lead to	87	
			the queen)	90	
307.	K Q x x J 9 x x	3	Lead to the king, and then to the queen	87	

(e) Declarer Has Nine Cards

308.	K Q 9 x x x J 8 x	5	Lead to the king	100	
309.	K Q 8 x x x J x x	5	Lead small to the jack. This fails only when West is void	95	
310.	K Q 9 x x J 8 x x	4	Lead small to the king	100	
311.	K Q 8 x x J x x x	4	Lead small to the jack, in case East is void	95	

B. THE KING-JACK

(a) Declarer Has Five Cards

312.	A Q 10 9 x	4	Finesse the queen, hoping that West has king- jack doubleton	0.3	
		3 } Max	Finesse the ten. If it holds, play the ace and queen	13	2.14
313.	A Q 10 x x	3	Finesse the ten, hoping that West has both the king and jack	24	
		2	Finesse the queen and then the ten, *or* (best) finesse the ten and then the queen	76	
		Max	Finesse the ten; if it loses, finesse the queen		2.00
314.	A Q 9 x x	2	Finesse the nine, and then finesse the queen	63	
315.	A 10 9 Q x	3	Lead the queen, hoping that East has the single- ton jack	0.2	
		2 } Max	Run the queen, finessing the ten next if it loses	76	1.76
316.	A 10 x Q x	2	Lead small to the queen. If it loses, finesse the ten	74	
317.	Q 10 9 A x	3	Play the ace, hoping that East has the singleton king	0.2	
		2 } Max	Play the ace, and guess whether to play the queen or ten next	53	1.53
318.	Q x x A 10	2	Finesse the ten	52	

(b) Declarer Has Six Cards

319.	A Q 10 9 8 x	5	Finesse the queen, hoping that West has the king-jack doubleton	1	
		4	Finesse the ten. If it holds, play the ace and queen	23	
		Max	Finesse the ten; then play the ace and queen		3.24

	Dummy Declarer	Tricks Required		% Chance of Success	Tricks per Deal

V. THE DEFENSE HAS FOUR POINTS (cont'd)
B. THE KING-JACK (cont'd)

	Dummy Declarer	Tricks Required		% Chance of Success	Tricks per Deal
320.	A Q 10 9 x x	4 3 } Max	Finesse the ten, hoping that West has KJ or KJx Finesse the ten; if it loses, finesse the nine	5 63	2.68
321.	A Q 10 8 x x	4 3 } Max 2	Finesse the ten, hoping West has KJ9 only Finesse the eight, and guess whether to finesse the ten or queen next, *or* finesse the ten and guess whether to finesse the queen or eight next Finesse the eight, ten, or queen, and guess which finesse to take next	1 33 86	2.19
322.	A Q 9 8 x x	3 2 } Max	Finesse the eight, and guess whether to finesse the nine or queen next Finesse the eight; if it loses, finesse the nine	24 86	2.09
323.	A 10 9 x Q x	3 } Max	Lead small to the queen, and finesse the nine next	24	2.24
324.	Q 10 9 8 A x	3	Run the ten. Then play the ace and queen* (*But if East might be tempted to cover with Kxx, the best practical chance is to lead the queen first)	23 27	
325.	Q 9 x x A 10	3 } Max 2	Finesse the ten, and then play the ace and queen Finesse the ten, *or* play the ace and run the ten	23 100	2.23
326.	Q x x x A 10	2 } Max	Finesse the ten. If it loses to the jack, cash the ace, and if the king fails to appear, play small from the queen	68	1.68
327.	A Q 10 x x x	3 2 Max	Finesse the ten Finesse the queen and then the ten, *or* (best) finesse the ten and then the queen Finesse the ten; if it loses, finesse the queen	24 76	2.00
328.	A Q 9 x x x	2 } Max	Finesse the nine, and then finesse the queen	63	1.63
329.	A Q x 10 x x	3 2 Max	Finesse the queen, hoping that West has king- jack doubleton Play the ace, and lead low to the queen Lead toward the ace-queen, and play the ace, unless the jack appears from West; then lead low to the queen	1 55 1.56	
330.	A Q x x x x	2 } Max	Lead small from the ace-queen, in case East has the singleton king; then finesse the queen* (*And if East panics into playing the king from Kx)	50 54	1.50
331.	A 10 9 Q x x	3 2 } Max	Lead the queen, hoping that East has the single- ton jack, *or* play the ace, hoping that West has the singleton king Lead small to the ten; if it loses to the jack, finesse the nine* (*But if East would play the king from Kx, run the ten first; if this loses to the jack, finesse the nine next)	0.5 76 78	1.77
332.	A 10 x Q x x	2	Lead small to the queen; if it loses, finesse the ten next	74	
333.	A x x Q 10 9	3 2 } Max	Lead the queen, hoping that East has the single- ton jack, *or* play the ace, hoping that West has the singleton king Run the ten; if it loses, run the queen* (*But if East would play the king from Kx, lead small to the ten; if this loses to the jack, run the queen next)	0.5 76 78	1.77

	Dummy Declarer	Tricks Required		% Chance of Success	Tricks per Deal

V. THE DEFENSE HAS FOUR POINTS (cont'd)
B. THE KING-JACK (cont'd)

(c) Declarer Has Seven Cards

	Dummy Declarer	Tricks		%	Tricks
334.	A Q 10 9 x x x	6	Finesse the queen, hoping that West has king- jack doubleton	2	
		5	Finesse the queen; then play the ace	40	
		4	Lead toward the dummy, and play the ace unless the jack appears from West; then lead the queen	89	
		Max	Finesse the queen; then play the ace		4.28
335.	AQ 10 9 x x x	5	Finesse the ten	9	
		4	Finesse the ten; if it loses, finesse the nine next	59	
		3	Finesse the queen, and lead to the ten if it holds *or* (best) finesse the ten	93	
		Max	Finesse the ten; if it loses, finesse the nine next		3.61
336.	A Q 9 8 x x x	4 } Max }	Finesse the nine, and finesse the queen next if it loses	33	3.09
		3	Finesse the nine, and finesse the eight next if it loses	82	
337.	AQ x x x 10 x	4	Play the ace, and lead to the queen, *or* finesse the queen and then cash the ace, *or* (best) lead small to the ten, and then finesse the queen	18	
		3	Lead small to the ten, and then finesse the queen* (*And there is the additional chance of East playing the king from Kx)	71 78	
		2 } Max }	Lead small to the ten, and then finesse the queen. This fails only when West has the singleton jack	99	2.88
338.	A 10 9 x x Q x	4 } Max }	Run the queen, and finesse the ten next if it loses, *or* lead small to the ten and run the queen next	36	3.23
		3	Play the ace	89	
		Max	Run the queen, and finesse the ten next if it loses, *or* lead small to the ten, and run the queen next		3.23
339.	Q x x x x A 10	4	Play the ace, and lead to the queen, *or* (best) finesse the ten	18	
		3	Lead small to the ten	68	
		2	Play the ace, and lead to the queen. This fails only when West has a void or a small single- ton	94	
		Max	Lead small to the ten		2.86
340.	A Q 10 9 x x x	4	Finesse the ten, hoping that West has both the king and jack	24	
		3	Finesse the queen, and then the ten, *or* (best) finesse the ten and then the nine	76	
		Max	Finesse the ten and then the nine		3.00
341.	A Q 10 8 x x x	4	Finesse the eight	11	
		3	Finesse the queen; then finesse the ten	53	
		2	Cash the ace, *or* (best) lead to the ten, and if it loses and the nine fails to appear on the second round, cash the ace next	91	
		Max	Finesse the eight. If it loses, finesse the queen. If that loses, cash the ace		2.51
342.	A Q 10 x x x x	4	Finesse the ten, hoping that West has KJx	7	
		3	Finesse the queen, and finesse the ten next	47	
		2	Play the ace on the first or second round. The best line is to finesse the ten and cash the ace next if it loses	85	
		Max	Finesse the ten, and finesse the queen next if it loses		2.36

	Dummy Declarer	Tricks Required		% Chance of Success	Tricks per Deal

V. THE DEFENSE HAS FOUR POINTS (cont'd)

B. THE KING-JACK (cont'd)

No.	Dummy Declarer	Tricks Required	Play	% Chance	Tricks per Deal
343.	A Q 9 8 x x x	3	Finesse the eight, and finesse the nine next if it loses	50	
		2	Finesse the eight. If it loses, (best) lead toward dummy and play the ace unless the jack or ten appears from West	91	
		Max	Finesse the eight. If it loses, finesse the nine. If that loses, cash the ace		2.39
344.	A Q 9 x x x x	3 } Max }	Finesse the nine, and finesse the queen next if it loses	32	2.08
		2	Play the ace, and lead to the nine, *or* (best) finesse the nine, and play the ace next	79	
345.	A Q x x 10 x x	3	Play the ace, and unless the jack appears from East lead small to the queen*	21	
			(*And if West would not falsecard from KJ, lead to the ten if the king appears from West on the first round)	22	
		2	Play the ace, and then lead low to the ten; then lead to the queen. This fails only when West has Jx	94	
		Max	Finesse the queen; if it loses, lead small to the ten. If the queen holds, play the ace*		2.05
			(*And if West would not falsecard from KJ, lead to the ten if the king appears from West on the first round. But if East would play the king from Kx, the best practical play is to lead low to the ten; if this loses, finesse the queen)		2.06 21.0
346.	A Q x x x x x	3	Play the ace, and lead to the queen, *or* finesse the queen	18	
		2	Lead low from dummy, then play the ace, and then lead to the queen	77	
		Max	Play the ace, and lead to the queen		1.87
347.	A 10 9 8 Q x x	4	Run the queen, hoping that East has the singleton jack	1	
		3 } Max }	Finesse the ten and then the nine, *or* (best) run the queen, and finesse the ten next if it loses	76	2.77
348.	A 10 9 x Q 8 x	4	Run the queen, hoping that East has the singleton jack	1	
		3	Run the eight, and then run the queen, *or* (best) run the queen, and then finesse the ten	76	
		Max	Run the queen, and finesse the ten next if it loses		2.77
349.	A 10 9 x Q x x	3 } Max }	Lead small to the ten. If it loses to the jack, lead small to the nine. If the ten loses to the king, cash the queen, and finesse the nine	68	2.68
350.	A 10 x x Q 9 x	3 } Max }	Lead small to the nine, and finesse the ten next if it loses to the jack. If East plays the king on the first round, finesse the nine next	52	2.52
351.	A 10 x x Q x x	3	Lead small to the queen, and finesse the ten next if it loses. If East plays the king on the first round, cash the queen and ace	28	
		2 } Max }	Play the ace, and unless the jack appears from West, lead small to the queen	94	2.16
352.	A x x x Q 10 9	3	Finesse the ten. If it loses to the king, finesse the nine. If the ten loses to the jack, run the queen next. If East plays the king on the first round, finesse the ten next*	50	
			(*And if West omits to falsecard with KJx)	57	
353.	Q 10 9 8 A x x	4	Play the ace, hoping that East has the singleton king	1	
		3 } Max }	Run the ten, and run the nine next if it loses	69	2.69

Dummy Declarer	Tricks Required		% Chance of Success	Tricks per Deal
		V. THE DEFENSE HAS FOUR POINTS (cont'd)		
		B. THE KING-JACK (cont'd)		
354. Q x x x	3	Finesse the ten, and finesse the nine next if it		
A 10 9	Max	loses	68	2.68
	2	Finesse the ten and then the nine (best), *or* play the ace and run the ten	100	
355. Q x x x	3	Lead small to the queen, and finesse the ten next		
A 10 x	Max	if it loses. If West plays the king on the first round, play the ace next	26	2.12
	2	Play the ace, and unless the jack appears from West, lead small to the ten. This fails only when West has J x	94	
356. 10 9 8 7	4	Run the ten, hoping that East has KJ or KJx	9	
A Q x	3	Finesse the queen. If it loses, run the ten; if the queen holds, run the ten	62	
	Max	Run the ten, and finesse the queen next		2.69
357. 10 9 x x	4	Finesse the queen, hoping that East has king-jack		
A Q x		doubleton	2	
	3	Finesse the queen. If it holds, play the ace; if the		
	Max	queen loses, run the ten next	47	2.48
(d) Declarer Has Eight Cards				
358. A Q 10 9 x x x 7		Finesse the queen, hoping that West has king-jack		
x		doubleton	3	
	6	Finesse the queen, in case East has the singleton		
	Max	jack	56	5.55
359. A Q 10 9 x x	6	Finesse the ten	14	
x x	5	Finesse the queen, and then the ten, *or* (best) finesse the ten and then the queen	71	
	4	Finesse the queen, *or* (best) finesse the ten	98	
	Max	Finesse the ten, and if it loses, finesse the nine		4.83
360. A Q x x x x	5	Play the ace, and then lead to the queen*	37	
10 x		(*But if East would play the king from Kx, lead to the ten, and then finesse the queen)	44	
	4	Lead small to the ten, and then finesse the queen	93	
	3	Lead small to the ten, in case either opponent is void	100	
	Max	Lead small to the ten, and then finesse the queen		4.27
361. A 10 9 x x x	5	Run the queen. If it loses, finesse the jack next	60	4.53
Q x	Max			
362. Q 9 x x x x	5	Play the ace, and then either run the ten or lead		
A 10		the ten to the queen	59	
	Max	Play the ace, and then either run the ten or lead the ten to the queen*		4.55
		(*The latter line is better against defenders who might cover the ten with Jxx)		
363. Q x x x x x	5	Finesse the ten	47	
A 10	4	Play the ace, and lead to the queen	88	
	3	Finesse the ten	100	
	Max	Finesse the ten		4.32
364. A Q 10 9 x	5	Finesse the ten and then the nine	22	
x x x	4	Finesse the ten and then the nine	76	3.96
	Max			
365. A Q 10 8 x	5	Finesse the ten	16	
x x x	4	Finesse the queen; if it loses, finesse the ten	66	
	Max	Finesse the ten; if it loses, finesse the queen		3.70
366. A Q 10 x x	5	Finesse the ten	14	
x x x	4	Finesse the queen; if it loses, finesse the ten	66	
	Max	Finesse the ten and then the queen		3.64

	Dummy Declarer	Tricks Required		% Chance of Success	Tricks per Deal
			V. THE DEFENSE HAS FOUR POINTS (cont'd)		
			B. THE KING-JACK (cont'd)		
367.	A Q 9 x x	5	Lead small to the nine, *or* run the ten	14	
	10 x x	4	Finesse the queen, in case East has the singleton jack	71	
		Max	Finesse the nine and then the queen, *or* run the ten, and finesse the nine if it loses. The latter line will be better if East is likely to be short in the suit		3.80
368.	A Q 9 x x	4	Finesse the nine and then the queen	50	
	x x x	3	Finesse the nine. If it loses, finesse the queen (best), *or* play the ace	87	
		Max	Finesse the nine and then the queen		3.35
369.	A Q x x x	5	Finesse the queen, hoping that West has king-jack doubleton	3	
		4	Play the ace, and unless the king appears from West, lead small to the queen	50	
		3	Play the ace, and lead small to the ten; this fails only if either opponent is void	96	
		Max	Lead to the ace, and unless West plays the king lead small to the queen* (*If West plays the jack on the first round, finesse the queen immediately; a good defender, however, will play the king from king-jack doubleton)		3.41
370.	A Q x x x	4	Finesse the queen, *or* (best) play the ace, and lead small to the queen	34	
	x x x	3 } Max }	Play the ace, and lead small to the queen	85	3.17
371.	A 10 9 x x	4 } Max }	Finesse the ten and then the nine, *or* run the queen, and finesse the ten next if it loses. The latter line is better if East is likely to be short in the suit	71	3.60
	Q x x				
372.	A 10 x x x	4	Play the ace, and lead small to the queen, *or* lead small to the queen, and if it loses, finesse the ten next	50	
	Q x x	3 } Max }	Play the ace, and lead small to the queen. This fails only if either opponent is void	96	3.46
373.	A 9 7 x x	5	Lead the queen, hoping that East has the single-ton jack	3	
	Q 10 8	4 } Max }	Lead the queen; if it loses, run the ten next* (*But if East would play the king from Kx, and West would not falsecard with KJ, lead low to the ten; if this loses to the jack, run the queen next)	76 83	3.79 3.83
374.	A 9 x x x	5	Lead the queen, hoping that East has the single-ton jack	3	
	Q 10 8	4	Lead the queen; if it loses, run the ten next* (*But if East would play the king from Kx and West would not falsecard with KJ, lead low to the ten; if this loses to the jack, run the queen)	74 83	3.77 3.83
		3	Lead the queen, *or* lead small to the ten, in case either opponent is void	100	
375.	A 9 x x x	4 } Max }	Lead small to the ten; if it loses to the jack, run the queen next* (*And there is the extra chance that East will play the king from Kx)	62 72	3.60
	Q 10 x	3	Lead small to the ten. This fails only if East is void	98	

	Dummy Declarer	Tricks Required		% Chance of Success	Tricks per Deal

V.   THE DEFENSE HAS FOUR POINTS(cont'd)
B.   THE KING-JACK (cont'd)

	Dummy Declarer	Tricks Required		% Chance of Success	Tricks per Deal
376.	A x x x x Q 10 9	4	Run the queen; if it loses, run the ten* (*But if West would not falsecard with KJ or KJx, lead small to the nine. If this loses to the jack, run the queen; if the nine loses to the king, finesse the ten And if East would play the king from Kx:)	60 62 72	
		3	Lead small to the nine	98	
		Max	Lead small to the nine; if it loses to the jack, run the queen through next* (*And if West would not falsecard with KJ or KJx, finesse the ten if the nine loses to the king)		3.57 3.60
377.	A x x x x Q 10 x	4 ⎫ Max ⎬	Play the ace, and then guess whether to lead to the queen or the ten	50	3.36
		3	Lead small to the ten. If it loses or holds, lead small to the queen next	90	
378.	Q 10 9 x x A 8 x	5	Lead small to to the ace, hoping that East has the singleton king	3	
		4 ⎫ Max ⎬	Finesse the eight. If it loses to the jack, run the queen next; if the eight loses to the king, run the ten next* (*But if West would play the king from Kx, lead low to the ten; if this loses to the jack, finesse the eight next)	71 72	3.74
379.	Q 10 9 x x A x x	5	Play the ace, hoping that East has the singleton king	3	
		4 ⎫ Max ⎬	Play the ace and lead small to the ten* (*But if West would play the king from Kx, lead small to the ten; if it loses to the jack, run the queen next)	67 72	3.68 3.70
380.	Q x x x x A 10 x	4	Play the ace, and unless the king appears from West, lead small to the queen	50	
		3	Play the ace, and lead small to the ten. This fails only if either opponent is void	96	
		Max	Lead small to the ten, and then cash the ace, or lead small to the queen, and finesse the ten next if it loses		3.41
381.	10 x x x x A Q x	5	Finesse the queen, hoping that East has king-jack only	3	
		4	Play the ace, and lead small to the queen, or finesse the queen, and then cash the ace	50	
		3	Play the ace, and lead small to the queen. This fails only if either opponent is void	96	
		Max	Finesse the queen, and then cash the ace		3.47
382.	A Q 10 9 x x x x	4	Finesse the ten	24	
		3	Either finesse the ten or finesse the queen; if it loses, finesse again	76	
		Max	Finesse the ten; if it loses, finesse the nine		3.00
383.	A Q 10 8 x x x x	4	Finesse the ten	16	
		3	Finesse the queen; if it loses, finesse the ten	68	
		Max	Finesse the ten; if it loses, finesse the queen		2.73
384.	A Q 9 x x x x x	3 ⎫ Max ⎬	Finesse the nine, and then finesse the queen	52	2.38

	Dummy Declarer	Tricks Required		% Chance of Success	Tricks per Deal

V. THE DEFENSE HAS FOUR POINTS (cont'd)
B. THE KING-JACK (cont'd)

	Dummy Declarer	Tricks Required		% Chance of Success	Tricks per Deal
385.	A Q x x 10 x x x	4	Finesse the queen, hoping that West has king-jack doubleton	3	
		3	Finesse the queen, *or* play the ace, and lead small to the queen	50	
		2	Play the ace, and lead small to the queen	100	
		Max	Lead small from the ten, and unless the jack appears, play the ace; then lead small to the queen		2.54
386.	A Q x x x x x x	3	Finesse the queen, *or* play the ace, and lead small to the queen*	34	
			(*But if East would not falsecard from Jx, play the ace, and duck on the second round if the jack appears from East)	37	
		2 } Max }	Play the ace, and lead small to the queen	87	2.21
387.	A 10 9 8 Q x x x	4	Lead the queen, hoping that East has the singleton jack, *or* play the ace, hoping that West has the singleton king	3	
		3 } Max }	Finesse the ten; if it loses to the jack, finesse the nine*	78	2.81
			(*But if West would not falsecard with KJxx, and East would play the king from Kx, run the ten. If the ten loses to the jack, finesse the nine; if the king appears on the first round, play the ace next)	84	2.84
388.	A 10 9 x Q 8 x x	4 3	See 387 above See 387 above	3 78	
389.	A 10 9 x Q x x x	3	Finesse the ten, and then finesse the nine, *or* lead the queen, and finesse the ten next if it loses. The latter line is better if East is likely to be short in the suit	73	
390.	A 10 x x Q 9 x x	3 } Max }	Play the ace, and lead small to the nine*	69	2.69
			(*But if East would play the king from Kx, lead small to the nine. If this loses to the jack, finesse the ten next; if East plays the king on the first round, play the ace next)	71	2.71
391.	A 10 x x Q x x x	3	Play the ace, and lead small to the queen (best), *or* lead small to the queen, and finesse the ten next if it loses, *or* lead small to the queen, and cash the ace next if it loses	50	
		2	Play the ace, and either lead to the queen (best) or to the ten	100	
		Max	Play the ace, and lead small to the queen		2.50
391A.	Q x x x A 10 8 7	4	Lead the queen, hoping that East has the singleton jack	2.83	
		3 } Max }	Lead the ace, followed by the seven or eight and guess whether to play the queen or duck in dummy. If East's first play is the nine, jack, or king, lead the ten on the second round intending to play low from dummy	61.62	2.62
		2	Play the ace	100	

	Dummy Declarer	Tricks Required		% Chance of Success	Tricks per Deal

V. THE DEFENSE HAS FOUR POINTS (cont'd)
B. THE KING-JACK (cont'd)

392.	A x x x Q 10 9 x	4	Play the ace, hoping that West has the singleton king	3	
		3 ⎱ Max ⎰	Play the ace, and lead low to the ten* (*But if East would play the king from Kx, lead small to the ten. If it lsoes to the jack, run the queen next; if the king appears on the first round, play the ace next)	69 74	2.72 2.74
393.	A x x x Q 10 x x	3 ⎱ Max ⎰	Play the ace, and lead small to the ten	64	2.53
		2	Play the ace, and then lead low to the ten (best) or low to the queen	90	

(e) Declarer Has Nine Cards

394.	A Q 10 9 x x x x x	8	Finesse the queen	20	
		7	Finesse the queen (best), or finesse the ten	72	
		Max	Finesse the queen		6.92
395.	A Q 10 x x x x x x	7	Finesse the queen, hoping that West has Kxx, KJ, or Kx	27	
		6	Play the ace, and lead small to the queen	78	
		Max	Finesse the queen; if it loses, cash the ace next		5.94
396.	A Q x x x x x 10 x	7	Finesse the queen	20	
		6	Lead small from the ten, and play the ace unless the jack appears; then lead to the queen	78	
		5	Lead small to the ten	100	
		Max	Finesse the queen		5.87
397.	A 10 9 8 x x x Q x	7	Run the queen, hoping that East has the singleton jack	6	
		6 ⎱ Max ⎰	Run the queen; if it loses, play the ace next	77	5.83
398.	A 10 9 x x x x Q x	7	Run the queen, hoping that East has the singleton jack	6	
		6	Run the queen, and play the ace next if it loses, or lead small to the queen, and play the ace next if it loses. The latter line is better if West is more likely to be short in the suit	72	
		Max	Run the queen; if it loses, play the ace next		5.78
399.	Q 10 9 x x x x A x	7	Play the ace, hoping that East has the singleton king	6	
		6 ⎱ Max ⎰	Play the ace, and lead to the queen	78	5.84
400.	Q x x x x x x A 10	6 ⎱ Max ⎰	Play the ace, and lead to the queen	78	5.73
		5	Finesse the ten	100	
401.	A Q 10 x x x x x x	6	Finesse the queen	27	
		5	Play the ace, and lead small to the queen	83	
		Max	Finesse the queen; if it loses, play the ace next		4.98
401	A Q 10 x x x x x x	5	Lead to the ace, then lead small to the queen. But finesse the queen if the jack appears originally.	83	
402.	A Q x x x x 10 x x	6	Finesse the queen	20	
		5	Play the ace, and lead small to the queen	78	
		Max	Finesse the queen		4.92
403.	A Q x x x x x x x	6	Finesse the queen	20	
		5	Play the ace, and lead small to the queen	72	
		Max	Finesse the queen		4.81
404.	A 10 9 x x x Q x x	6	Lead the queen, hoping that East has the singleton jack, or play the ace, hoping that West has the singleton king	6	
		5 ⎱ Max ⎰	Play the ace, and lead small to the queen	78	4.84

	Dummy Declarer	Tricks Required		% Chance of Success	Tricks per Deal
		V.	**THE DEFENSE HAS FOUR POINTS (cont'd)**		
			B. THE KING-JACK (cont'd)		
405.	A 10 x x x x Q x x	5 Max	Play the ace, and lead small to the queen	78	4.78
406.	A x x x x x Q 10 9	6	Lead the queen, hoping that East has the single- ton jack, *or* play the ace, hoping that West has the singleton king	6	
		5	Play the ace and lead small to the queen* (*But if East would play the king from Kx, lead small to the ten; if it loses to the jack, run the queen next)	78 89	
		4	Run the ten, *or* lead small to the ten, *or* run the queen, and play the ace if it lsoes	100	
		Max	Play the ace, and lead small to the queen		4.79
407.	A x x x x x Q 10 x	6	Play the ace, hoping that West has the singleton king	6	
		5 Max	Play the ace, and lead small to the queen	78	4.79
408.	Q 10 9 x x x A x x	6	Lead the queen, hoping that West has the single- ton jack, *or* play the ace, hoping that East has the singleton king	6	
		5 Max	Play the ace, and lead to the queen* (*But if West would play the king from Kx, lead small to the ten; if it loses to the jack, run the queen next	83 89	4.89
409.	Q 8 x x x x A 10 9	6	Play the ace, hoping that East has the singleton king, *or* lead the queen, hoping that West has the singleton jack	6	
		5 Max	Play the ace, and lead to the queen	83	4.89
410.	Q x x x x x A 10 x	5 Max	Play the ace, and lead small to the queen	78	4.78
411.	10 x x x x x A Q x	6	Finesse the queen	20	
		5	Play the ace, and lead small to the queen	78	
		Max	Finesse the queen		4.92
412.	A Q 10 x x x x x x	5	Finesse the queen	27	
		4	Play the ace, and lead to the queen	83	
		Max	Finesse the queen; if it loses, play the ace next		3.98
413.	A Q x x x 10 x x x	5	Finesse the queen	20	
		4	Play the ace, and lead to the queen	78	
		Max	Finesse the queen		3.92
414.	A Q x x x x x x x	5	Finesse the queen	20	
		4	Play the ace, and lead to the queen	72	
		Max	Finesse the queen		3.81
415.	A 10 9 x x Q 8 x x	5	Lead the queen, hoping that East has the single- ton jack, *or* play the ace, hoping that West has the singleton king	6	
		4 Max	Play the ace, and lead small to the queen* (*But if East would play the king from Kx, lead small to the eight; if this loses to the jack, run the queen next)	83 94	3.89
416.	A 10 9 x x Q x x x	5	Lead the queen, hoping that East has the single- ton jack, *or* play the ace, hoping that West has the singleton king	6	
		4 Max	Play the ace and lead small to the queen* (*But if East would play the king from Kx, run the ten; if this loses to the jack, run the queen next)	78 84	3.84

	Dummy Declarer	Tricks Required		% Chance of Success	Tricks per Deal

V. THE DEFENSE HAS FOUR POINTS (cont'd)
B. THE KING-JACK (cont'd)

417.	A 10 x x x Q 9 x x	5	Lead the queen, hoping that East has the single- ton jack, *or* play the ace, hoping that West has the singleton king	6	
		4 Max }	Play the ace, and lead to the queen* (*But if East would play the king from Kx, lead small to the nine; if this loses to the jack, run the queen next)	83 89	3.89
418.	A 10 x x x Q x x x	4	Play the ace, and lead small to the queen	78	
419.	A x x x x Q 10 9 8	5	Lead the queen, hoping that East has the single- ton jack, *or* play the ace, hoping that West has the singleton king	6	
		4 Max }	Play the ace, and lead to the queen* (*But if East would play the king from Kx, lead small to the ten, and run the queen next if it loses to the jack)	83 94	3.89
420.	A x x x x Q 10 9 x	5	Lead the queen, hoping that East has the single- ton jack, *or* play the ace, hoping that West has the singleton king	6	
		4 Max }	Play the ace, and lead to the queen* (*But if East would play the king from Kx, lead small to the ten, and run the queen next if it loses to the jack)	83 89	3.89

(f) Declarer Has Ten Cards

421.	A Q 10 x x x x x x x etc.*	5 Max	Finesse the queen Finesse the queen	39	4.28
422.	A Q x x x 10 9 8 x x etc.*	5 Max }	Lead the ten, and play the queen, giving an extra chance if West is tempted to cover with KJx	39	4.28
423.	A 10 9 x x Q x x x x etc.*	5 4 Max	Play the ace, hoping to drop the singleton king Lead small to the queen, *or* (best) lead small to the ten Play the ace	26 100	 4.15

(g) Declarer Has Eleven Cards

424.	A Q 10 x x x x x x x x etc.*	6	Play the ace. This line is fractionally better than the queen finesse	52	

*N.B. Similar principles apply if declarer's ten or eleven cards are distributed differently between his hand and dummy

VI. THE DEFENSE HAS FIVE POINTS
A. THE ACE-JACK

(a) Declarer Has Five Cards

425.	K Q 10 9 x	3	Finesse the ten	11	
426.	K Q 10 x x	2	Lead to the king, and whether it holds or loses, lead to the queen next* (*But this assumes that East will duck the king if he holds Ax (xxx), which is best defense. If he always wins with these holdings, lead to the king; if it holds, lead to the queen; if the king loses, finesse the ten next)	52 76	

	Dummy Declarer	Tricks Required		% Chance of Success	Tricks per Deal

VI.   THE DEFENSE HAS FIVE POINTS (cont'd)
A.   THE ACE-JACK (cont'd)

427.	K 10 x Q x	2	Lead to the queen, and then finesse the ten	50	
428.	K x x Q 10	2	Finesse the ten	50	

(b)   Declarer Has Six Cards

429.	K Q 10 9 8 x	4	Finesse the ten, hoping that West has AJx, Jxx, AJ, Jx, or J	18	
430.	K Q 10 9 x x	4	Finesse the ten	14	
		3	Lead to the king; then play the queen. This line gains a trick when East has AJ, Jx, or J	72	
		Max	Finesse the ten		2.82
431.	K Q 10 9 x x	3	Finesse the ten	50	
432.	K Q 9 8 x x	3	Finesse the nine, hoping that West has AJ10, J10x, or J10	5	
		2 } Max }	Finesse the nine. If this loses to the jack or ten, finesse the eight next* (*But if East would not duck with Ax, Axx, A10xx, or AJxx, lead to the king; if it holds, lead to the queen; if the king loses, finesse the nine)	79 81	1.85
433.	K Q x x 10 x	2	Lead small to the ten. If the ten loses, play to the king; if the king holds, play small from the queen	56	
434.	K Q 10 x x x	2	Lead to the king and whether it holds or loses, lead to the queen next* (*But if East would not duck the king if he holds the ace, lead to the king: if it loses, finesse the ten; if the king holds, lead to the queen)	55 76	
435.	K 10 x Q x x	2	Lead small to the queen, and then finesse the ten	51	

(c)   Delcarer Has Seven Cards

436.	K Q x x x x x —	5	Duck one round, and then play the king (best), *or* lead the king	36	
		4	Duck one round; then either duck again or lead the king	86	
		Max	Duck one round, and then lead the king		4.20
437.	K Q 10 8 x x x	5	Finesse the ten. If the jack appears from West, duck the next round	21	
		4	Finesse the ten or the eight	68	
		3	Finesse the ten or the eight	94	
		2	Finesse the ten or the eight	99	
		Max	Finesse the ten		3.82
438.	K Q 10 9 x x x	4	Finesse the ten* (*But if East would not duck with Axx, lead to the king; if it holds, lead to the queen; if the king loses, finesse the ten)	42 43	
		3	Finesse the ten	93	
		Max	Finesse the ten		3.35

	Dummy Declarer	Tricks Required		% Chance of Success	Tricks per Deal

VI.   THE DEFENSE HAS FIVE POINTS (cont'd)
A.   THE ACE-JACK (cont'd)

	Dummy Declarer	Tricks Required		% Chance of Success	Tricks per Deal
439.	K Q 9 8 x x x	4	Lead to the king; if it holds, lead to the queen	21	
		3	Lead to the king, and whether it holds or loses, lead to the queen next*	74	
			(*But if East would not duck with Ax, lead to the king; if it holds, lead to the queen; if the king loses, lead to the nine)	76	
		2	Lead to the king. If it loses, lead to the nine; if the king holds, lead to the queen or nine; *or* finesse the nine, and if it loses, finesse the eight	96	
		Max	Lead to the king, and whether it holds or loses, lead to the queen next*		2.90
			(*But if East would not duck with Ax, play to the nine if the king loses and to the queen if the king holds)		2.92
440.	KQ x x x 10 x	4	Lead small to the king; then lead to the queen	18	
		3	Lead small to the ten, and then lead to the king. This saves a trick when East has AJonly	61	
		2	Lead to the king and then to the queen, *or* lead small to the ten and then to the king. The latter line will be better if West is more likely to be short in the suit	93	
		Max	Lead to the king and then to the queen		2.71
441.	K Q 10 9 x x x	3	Lead to the king, and whether it holds or loses, finesse the ten next*	51	
			(*This assumes that East will duck about half the time with Ax and Axx, which is the best defense. If he always wins with these holdings, play to the queen if the king holds, and finesse the ten if the king loses.	54	
			Similarly, if East always ducks with Ax and Axx, play the queen if the king loses, and finesse the ten if the king holds)	52	
442.	K Q 9 8 x x x	3	Finesse the nine	24	
		2	Finesse the nine. If it loses, play to the king; if that loses, finesse the eight (best), *or* play to the king. If it loses, finesse the nine and, if necessary, the eight; if the king holds, play to the queen (best), or finesse the nine	89	
		Max	Finesse the nine. If it loses, lead to the king; if that loses, finesse the eight		2.13
443.	K 10 9 x Q x x	3	Lead small to the queen; then finesse the ten	53	
444.	K 10 x x Q 9 x	3 ⎫ Max ⎭	Lead small to the queen; then finesse the ten. This is better than leading to the king first, for there is time to discover whether the insertion of the ace by East is from AJdoubleton or A singleton	31	2.31
445.	K x x x Q 10 9	3	Finesse the ten	50	
446.	K x x x Q 10 x	3 ⎫ Max ⎭	Lead small to the ten and then small to the queen, hoping that East has AJ, AJx or Jxx	19	1.95
		2	Lead small to the queen and then small to the ten	77	
447.	10 9 8 7 K Q x	3	Lead to the king. If it holds, lead to the queen; if the king loses, cash the queen*	36	
			(*This assumes that West will duck with Axx, which is the best defense. If he always wins with this holding, lead to the king; if it holds, lead to the queen; if the king loses, run the ten next)	45	

Dummy Declarer	Tricks Required		% Chance of Success	Tricks per Deal

VI.   THE DEFENSE HAS FIVE POINTS (cont'd)
A.   THE ACE-JACK (cont'd)

(d) Declarer Has Eight Cards

448.	K Q x x x x x x —	6 ⎱ Max ⎰	Duck the first round, in case the ace is singleton; then play the king and queen	73	5.70
449.	K Q 10 x x x x x	6 5 4 Max	Finesse the ten Finesse the ten Finesse the ten Finesse the ten	34 85 98	 5.17
450.	K Q x x x x x x	6 ⎱ Max ⎰ 5	Lead to the king, hoping that West has the double- ton ace Play small from both hands, in case the ace is in- gleton; then play the king and queen	14 73	4.80
451.	K Q 10 x x x x x	5 ⎱ Max ⎰ 4	Lead to the king. If it holds, lead to the queen; if the king loses, cash the queen next* (*But if East would not duck with Ax, finesse the ten if the king loses and lead to the queen if the king holds) Lead to the king. If it loses, finesse the ten; if the king holds, guess which honor to play next	47 54 88	4.30 4.40
452.	K Q x x x x 10 x	5 ⎱ Max ⎰ 4 3	Lead to the king and then to the queen Lead to the king and then to the queen (best) *or* lead small to the ten Lead to the king *or* lead small to the ten. The latter line will be better if West is more likely to be short in the suit	34 85 98	4.17
453.	K Q 10 x x x x x	4 ⎱ Max ⎰	Lead to the king, and whether it holds or loses finesse the ten next* (*This assumes that East will duck about half the time with Ax. If he always ducks with this holding, finesse the ten if the king holds, and play the queen if the king loses. Similarly, if East always wins with Ax, finesse the ten if the king loses, and lead to the queen if the king holds)	55 59 57	3.43
454.	K 9 x x x Q 10 x	4 Max	Lead small to the queen. If it holds, finesse the nine; if the queen loses, either play the king or finesse the nine Lead small to the queen, and then finesse the nine	46 	 3.42
455.	K x x x x Q 10 9	4 3 2 Max	Finesse the ten Finesse the ten Finesse the ten (best), *or* lead to the queen Finesse the ten	48 98 100	 3.46
456.	K x x x x Q 10 x	4 ⎱ Max ⎰ 3	Lead small to the king, and then finesse the ten* (*The alternative is to lead small to the king or queen, playing the other top honor if it loses and ducking the next round if it holds, but this line is inferior against defenders who would not take the ace immediately) Lead small to the queen, and then lead small to the ten	37 88	3.20

Dummy Declarer	Tricks Required		% Chance of Success	Tricks per Deal

VI. THE DEFENSE HAS FIVE POINTS (cont'd)
A. THE ACE-JACK (cont'd)

457.	K Q 10 x	3	Lead to the king, and whether it holds or loses,		
	x x x x	Max	finesse the ten next*	57	2.47
			(*This assumes that East will duck about half the time with Ax. If he always ducks with this holding, finesse the ten if the king holds, and play the queen if it loses.	61	
			Similarly, if East always wins with Ax, play to the queen if the king holds, and finesse the ten if the king loses)	59	
458.	K 10 x x	3 ⎫	Lead to the queen, and then finesse the ten	40	2.27
	Q x x x	Max ⎭			
		2	Play small from both hands; then lead to the queen	90	
459.	K 9 8 7	3 ⎫	Lead to the queen, and then finesse the nine, hoping that East has 10, J, Ax, A10, AJ, or Axx;		
	Q x x x	Max ⎭	*or* lead to the king, and then run the nine. The latter line will be better if West is more likley to be short in the suit	23	2.12
		2	Finesse the nine. If this loses to the jack or ten. guess which honor to lead to next; if the jack or ten appears from West, run the eight, *or* run the nine. If this loses to the jack or ten, guess which honor to lead to next; if the jack or ten appears from East, finesse the eight	94	
460.	K x x x	3	Lead to the queen, and then run the ten, *or* lead		
	Q 10 9 8		to the king, and then finesse the ten	56	
461.	K x x x	3 ⎫	Lead to either honor, and duck on the next		
	Q x x x	Max ⎭	round, hoping to find the right opponent with the doubleton ace	14	1.84
		2	Play low from both hands, in case the ace is singleton, and then lead to either honor	73	

(e) Declarer Has Nine Cards

462.	K Q 8 x x x x	6 ⎫	Lead small to the king, and then small to the		
	10 x	Max ⎭	queen	72	5.67
		5	Lead small to the ten	100	
463.	K Q 10 9 x	4	Lead to the king; if it loses to the ace, lead		
	x x x x		to the queen next	77	
	etc.*				
464.	K 9 x x x	4	Lead to the king, and play the queen next if it		
	Q 10 x x		loses, *or* lead to the queen, and play the king		
	etc.*		next if it loses	59	
465.	K 9 x x x	4 ⎫	Lead small to the queen; if an honor appears		
	Q x x x	Max ⎭	from East, finesse the nine next	53	3.48
	etc.*	3	Lead small to the queen, in case East is void	95	
			*N.B. Similar principles apply, if declarer's nine cards are distributed differently between his hand and dummy		

(f) Declarer Has Ten Cards

466.	K 8 x x x x	5	Lead small to the king. This fails only if East is		
	Q 10 x x		void	89	
	etc.*				
			*N.B. Similar principles apply if declarer's ten cards are distributed differently between his hand and dummy		

Dummy Declarer	Tricks Required		% Chance of Success	Tricks per Deal

VI.   THE DEFENSE HAS FIVE POINTS (cont'd)
B.   THE KING-QUEEN

(a)   Declarer Has Five Cards

467.	A J 10 9 x	3	Finesse the jack; then play the ace	7	
468.	A J 10 x x	2	Finesse the jack; then finesse the ten	76	
469.	A J 9 x x	2	Finesse the nine; if it loses to an honor, finesse the jack next* (*If West inserts a high honor on the first round, still finesse the nine next, for West should falsecard with holdings like K10x, Q10x, etc. If he would not falsecard in this way, and would split high honors on the first round, finesse the jack next if the king or queen appears from West)	37 50	

(b)   Declarer Has Six Cards

470.	A J 10 x x x —	4	Play the ace, and then lead small from the jack- ten, hoping that the king-queen are doubleton or tripleton	10	
		3 } Max	Play the ace, and then lead small from the jack- ten, in case there is a doubleton honor	78	2.83
471.	A J 10 9 8 x	4	Finesse the jack, and then play the ace, hoping that West has xxxxx, KQx, KQ, Kx, Qx, K, or Q	14	
472.	A J 10 9 x x	3	Finesse the jack, and then finesse the ten	50	
473.	A J 9 x xx	3	Finesse the jack, hoping that West has KQ10 only	1	
		2 } Max	Finesse the nine. If it loses to the ten, play the ace and a small card; if the nine loses to a high honor, finesse the jack next* (*And if East omits to falsecard with KQ10)	41 42	1.42
474.	A J x x 10 x	2	Lead small to the ten; if it loses, play the ace, and lead small from the jack* (*But if East would play an honor from Qx, Kx, or Qxx, lead small to the ten, and finesse the jack next if it loses)	55 65	
475.	A J 10 x x x	2	Finesse the jack, and then finesse the ten	76	
476.	A J 9 x x x	2	Finesse the nine, and then finesse the jack. If West inserts a high honor on the first round, still finesse the nine next; West should falsecard with K10x, etc.* (*But if West would split high honors and would not falsecard, finesse the jack next if West plays the king or queen on the first round)	38 50	
477.	A J 8 10 x x	2	Lead small to the eight. If this loses to a high honor, finesse the jack next* (*And if West is tempted to split his honors from KQ and others)	39 51	
478.	A J x 10 x x	2	Lead small to the jack; then play the ace* (*But if East might be tempted to play an honor from Kx, Qx, or Qxx, lead small to the ten, and then finesse the jack)	33 41	
479.	A x x J 10 9	2	Run the jack, and then run the ten	76	

Dummy Declarer	Tricks Required		% Chance of Success	Tricks per Deal

VI. THE DEFENSE HAS FIVE POINTS (cont'd)
B. THE KING-QUEEN (cont'd)

(c) Declarer Has Seven Cards

Dummy Declarer	Tricks Required		% Chance of Success	Tricks per Deal
480. J 10 x x x x A	5	Play the ace, and then lead small from the jack-ten, hoping that the king-queen are doubleton	3	
	4	Play the ace, and then lead small from the jack-ten, in case there is a doubleton honor	65	
481. A J 10 9 x x x	5 } Max }	Finesse the jack, and then cash the ace	23	4.08
	4	Play the ace, and then lead the jack, in case East has a singleton honor	89	
482. A J 10 9 x x x	4 } Max }	Finesse the jack, and then finesse the ten	53	3.45
	3	Finesse the jack	92	
483. A J 9 x x x x	4 } Max }	Finesse the nine, and then finesse the jack	12	2.58
	3	Finesse the nine, and the jack	55	
	2	Finesse the nine, and the jack This fails only when West has a void or a singleton, or when East has a singleton ten	91	
484. A J 10 9 x x x	3	Finesse the jack, and then finesse the ten	76	
485. A J 10 x x x x	3 } Max }	Finesse the jack, and then finesse the ten	45	2.28
	2	Play the ace, and lead small to the jack, *or* finesse the jack, and then play the ace	85	
486. A J 9 8 x x x	3	Finesse the eight, and then finesse the nine	37	
	2	Finesse the eight, the nine, and, if necessary, the jack (best), *or* finesse the jack, the eight, and then the nine	89	
	Max	Finesse the eight, the nine, and, if necessary, the jack		2.26
487. A J 9 x x x x	3 } Max }	Finesse the nine, and then finesse the jack, hoping that East has x, xx, xxx, Qxx, Kxx, or void	22	1.89
	2	Play the ace, and lead to the nine, *or* finesse the nine and the jack, *or* finesse the jack and the nine	68	
488. AJ 8 x 10 x x	3	Lead small to the eight. If this loses to the king or queen, lead from the ten, and play the ace unless the nine appears from West*	26	
		(*And if West omits to falsecard with 9xx	28	
		And if West is tempted to split his honors with KQx)	33	
	2	Play the ace, and unless an honor appears from West, lead small to the ten. This fails only when West has Kx or Qx	90	
	Max	Lead small to the eight. If this loses to the king or queen, lead from the ten, and play the ace unless the nine appears from West. If the eight loses to the nine, lead small to the jack next*		2.15
		(*And if West omits to falsecard with 9xxx		2.16
		And if West splits his honors with KQx)		2.22
489. A J x x 10 x x	3	Lead small to the jack, hoping that West has KQ or KQx	9	
	2	Lead small to the ace, and unless an honor appears from West, lead small to the ten next. This fails only when West has Kx or Qx	87	

Dummy Declarer	Tricks Required		% Chance of Success	Tricks per Deal

VI. THE DEFENSE HAS FIVE POINTS (cont'd)
B. THE KING-QUEEN (cont'd)

	Max	Lead small to the ace, and unelss and honor appears from West, lead small to the ten*		1.90
		(*But if East would play an honor from Kx or Qx, lead small to the ten, and finesse the jack next if it loses to West)		1.93
490.	A 9 8 7	3	Run the nine. If this loses to the king or queen from West, run the jack next, hoping that East		
	J x x		has 10 or 10x*	6	
			(*But if East would not falsecard with 10x, run the nine; if the ten appears from East, play the ace next; if the king or queen appears from East or the nine loses to the king or queen from West, run the jack next.	8	
			And if East would play a higher honor from K10 or Q10, run the nine; if the king or queen appears from East, or the nine loses to the king or queen from West, run the jack next. This succeeds when East has 10, 10x, Q10 or K10)	9	
	2 Max	Run the jack. If it loses, finesse the nine next; if that loses, finesse the eight	89	1.90
491.	A x x x	3	Run the jack and then the ten	28	
	J 10 9	2	Run the jack and then the ten	100	
492.	J x x x	3 Max	Lead small to the ten, and then play the ace, hoping that East has KQ or KQx	9	1.93
	A 10 x	2	Play the ace, and unless an honor appears from West, lead small to the ten	87	

(d) Declarer Has Eight Cards

493.	A J 10 9 x x x x	6 Max	Finesse the jack, and then play the ace	43	5.39
494.	A J 10 x x x 9 x	5 Max	Lead small to the ten; then run the nine. Do not lead the nine for the first finesse: West may have a singleton honor	60	4.56
495.	A J 9 x x x x x	5	Finesse the nine, and then finesse the jack*	27	
			(*If West would not falsecard with 10xx, play the ace if the nine loses to a high honor, and the ten fails to appear on the second round)	31	
	4 Max	Finesse the nine, and then finesse the jack	79	4.04
	3	Finesse the jack or the nine in case East is void	98	
496.	A J x x x x 10 x	5	Lead small to the ten, and finesse the jack next, *or* run the ten and lead up to the jack next	24	
	4 Max	Lead small to the ten, and finesse the jack next	90	4.14
	3	Lead small to the ten	100	
497.	A 9 8 x x x J x	5	Lead small to the jack, hoping that East has K10 or Q10	7	
	4	Lead small to the jack and then to the nine, *or* play the ace, *or* run the jack, and finesse the nine next, *or* lead toward the ace, and play small unless an honor appears from West	85	
	3	Lead small to the jack	100	
	Max	Lead small to the jack. If an honor wins from East, run the jack next; if East plays the ten on the first round, cash the ace next		3.92

	Dummy Declarer	Tricks Required		% Chance of Success	Tricks per Deal

VI. THE DEFENSE HAS FIVE POINTS (cont'd)
B. THE KING-QUEEN (cont'd)

498.	A 9 x x x x J x	5	Lead small to the jack, hoping that East has K10 or Q10	7	
		4	Lead small to the jack; if the ten appears from East, finesse the nine next	73	
		Max	Lead small to the jack. If an honor wins from East, run the jack next; if East plays the ten on the first round, finesse the nine		3.76
499.	A J 10 x x x x x	4 } Max }	Finesse the jack, and then finesse the ten	63	3.50
		3	Finesse the jack, and then play the ace, *or* finesse the jack and then the ten (best)	90	
500.	AJ 9 x x x x x	4 } Max }	Finesse the nine, and then finesse the jack* (*If West would not falsecard from 10xx, play the ace if the nine loses to a high honor, and the ten fails to appear on the second round)	33 36	3.15
		3	Finesse the nine, and then finesse the jack	84	
501.	A J 8 7 x 10 x x	4 } Max }	Run the ten. If it is covered, lead to the eight next; if the ten loses to East, finesse the jack next* (*But if West would not falsecard with K9 or Q9, and would not split his honors with KQ9, lead small to the eight. If this loses to the nine, lead to the ten next; if the eight loses to a high honor, finesse the seven next; and if the king or queen appears from West on the first round, run the eight next. And if West would split his honors with KQx or KQ9)	42 44 47	3.35 3.37 3.40
		3	Lead small to the jack. If it loses, lead small to the ten next. This fails only if West is void.	98	
502.	A J x x x 10 x x	4	Lead small to the jack, and then cash the ace	37	
		3	Play the ace, and lead small to the ten. This fails only to a 5-0 break	96	
		Max	Lead small to the jack, and then cash the ace* (*But if East would play an honor from Kx or Qx, lead small to the ten, and then finesse the jack)		3.19 3.24
503.	A 9 8 7 x J x x	4	Run the nine. If it loses to the king or queen from West, run the jack; if the king or queen appears from East, either run the jack or cash the ace* (*This assumes that East will play an honor from K10 or Q10 about half the time, which is the best defense. If he would always play the high honor from these holdings, run the nine, and run the jack next if it loses to the king or queen on either side)	13 16	
		3	Run the nine. If this loses to the ten, run the jack next; if the nine loses to the king or queen on either side, lead small to the jack. This fails only when either opponent is void, or West has the singleton ten	93	
		Max	Run the nine. If this loses to the ten, run the jack next; if the nine loses to the king or queen from West, run the jack next; if the king or queen appears from East on the first round, lead small to the jack next		2.97

Dummy Declarer	Tricks Required		% Chance of Success	Tricks per Deal
		VI. THE DEFENSE HAS FIVE POINTS (cont'd)		
		B. THE KING-QUEEN (cont'd)		
504. A x x x x	4	Run the jack and then the ten	54	
J 10 9	3	Run the jack and then the ten	96	
	2	Run the jack	100	
	Max	Run the jack and then the ten		3.50
505. J 10 9 x x	4	Run the jack and then the ten	60	
A x x	3	Play the ace, *or* lead low to the jack. This fails only if West is void	98	
	Max	Run the jack and then the ten		3.56
506. A J 10 9	3	Finesse the jack and then the ten	76	
x x x x				
507. A J 10 x	3 ⎤	Finesse the jack and then the ten	65	2.54
x x x x	Max ⎦			
508. A J 9 x	3 ⎤	Lead small to the nine; then finesse the jack*	35	2.19
x x x x	Max ⎦	(*And if West would not falsecard with 10xx, play the ace if the nine loses to a high honor, and the ten fails to appear on the second round)	38	
	2	Play the ace, *or* take two finesses	84	
509. A J8 x	3	Run the ten. If it loses to East, finesse the jack next; if the ten is covered, finesse the eight next	44	
10 x x x	2	Lead small to the jack, and finesse the eight next if it loses (best), *or* play the ace, and lead small to the ten	100	
	Max	Finesse the jack; if it loses, finesse the eight next		2.37
510. A J x x	3 ⎤	Finesse the jack; then cash the ace	37	2.32
10 x x x	Max ⎦			
	2	Play the ace, and lead small to either honor	100	
511. A 9 8 7	3	Run the nine. If it loses to the king or queen from West, run the jack; if East plays an honor on the first round, cash the ace next* (*But if East would play an honor from K10 or Q10, run the nine, and run the jack next if it loses to the king or queen on either side)	13 16	
J x x x	2	Run the nine. If this loses, lead small to the eight next. This fails only when West has the singleton ten	97	
	Max	Play the ace, and then run the nine		2.05
(e) Declarer Has Nine Cards				
512. A J 10 9 x x x x	7 ⎤	Play the ace, *or* finesse the jack, and then play the ace	66	6.66
x	Max ⎦			
513. A J 10 9 x x x	6 ⎤	Finesse the jack and then the ten	76	5.76
x x	Max ⎦			
514. A J 9 x x x x	6	Play the ace, and lead to the jack, *or* finesse the jack* (*But if West would not falsecard with K10x, Q10x, or 10x, lead toward dummy, and play the ace unless the ten appears from West. And if West splits his honors with KQx)	53 59 66	
x x	5	Finesse the jack or the nine, in case East is void	95	
	Max	Finesse the jack* (*But if West would not falsecard with K10x, Q10x, or 10x, lead toward dummy, and play the ace if the ten fails to appear)		5.48 5.50

	Dummy Declarer	Tricks Required		% Chance of Success	Tricks per Deal

VI. THE DEFENSE HAS FIVE POINTS (cont'd)
B. THE KING-QUEEN (cont'd)

	Dummy Declarer	Tricks Required		% Chance of Success	Tricks per Deal
515.	A 8 7 x x x x J 10	6 ⎫ Max ⎬ 5	Run the jack, and then play the ace; this gains a trick when East has the singleton nine Run the jack, in case East is void	47 95	5.42
516.	A J 10 x x x x x x	5 ⎫ Max ⎭	Finesse the jack and then the ten	76	4.71
517.	A J 9 x x x x x x	5 ⎫ Max ⎭	Finesse the nine. If this loses to the king or queen, finesse the jack next* (*But if West would not falsecard with K10x, Q10x, or 10x, lead toward dummy, and play the ace if the ten fails to appear. And if West splits his honors with KQx	57 59 66	4.53 4.55 4.61
518.	A J x x x x 10 x x	5 ⎫ Max ⎭	Lead small to the jack, *or* play the ace, and lead small to either honor	66	4.66
519.	A 9 x x x x J x x	5 4 Max	Play the ace, and lead small to the jack Lead small to the jack Lead toward dummy, and play the nine if West follows small; otherwise play the ace, and lead small to the jack	53 100	 3.48
520.	A x x x x x J 10 9	5 ⎫ Max ⎭ 4	Run the jack and then the ten Run the jack	71 100	4.71
521.	A J 10 9 x x x x x	4	Finesse the jack and then the ten	76	
522.	A J 9 x x x x x x	4 ⎫ Max ⎭	Finesse the nine; if this loses to the king or queen, finesse the jack next* (*But if West would not falsecard with K10x, Q10x, or 10x, lead toward dummy, and play the ace if the ten fails to appear from West And if West splits hs honors with KQx)	57 59 66	3.53 3.55 3.61
523.	A J x x x 10 x x x	4 ⎫ Max ⎭	Finesse the jack, *or* play the ace, and lead small to either honor	66	3.66
524.	A 9 x x x J x x x	4 3 Max	Play the ace, and lead small to the jack Lead small to the jack, *or* lead small to the nine Lead toward dummy, and play the nine if West follows small; otherwise play the ace, and lead to the jack	53 100	 3.53
525.	A x x x x J 10 9 8	4	Run the jack and then the ten	76	

(f) Declarer Has Ten Cards

	Dummy Declarer	Tricks Required		% Chance of Success	Tricks per Deal
526.	A J 10 x x x x x x x etc.*	4 ⎫ Max ⎭	Lead to the jack, in case East is void *N.B. Similar principles apply if declarer's cards are distributed differently between his hand and dummy.	89	3.89

VII. THE DEFENSE HAS SIX POINTS
A. THE ACE-QUEEN

(a) Declarer Has Five Cards

	Dummy Declarer	Tricks Required		% Chance of Success	Tricks per Deal
527.	K J 9 x x	2 ⎫ Max ⎭ 1	Finesse the nine and then the jack, *or* finesse the jack and then the nine Immaterial: take two finesses	24 78	1.02

Dummy Declarer	Tricks Required		% Chance of Success	Tricks per Deal

VII. THE DEFENSE HAS SIX POINTS (cont'd)
A. THE ACE-QUEEN (cont'd)

(b) Declarer Has Six Cards

528.	K J 10 9 x x	3	Finesse the jack and then the ten	18	
529.	A J 9 8 x x	3	Finesse the eight, hoping that West has AQ10, Q10x, or Q10	5	
		2 } Max }	Finesse the eight: if this loses, finesse the nine next	63	1.68
530.	K x x x J 9	1	Lead small to the nine or jack; if this loses, lead to the king. Finessing the nine first will be better against East, who might be tempted to play an honor from AQ and others	75	
531.	K J 9 x x x	2 1 Max	Finesse the jack or the nine Immaterial: take two finesses Finesse the jack, and guess which to play next if the queen wins, *or* finesse the nine, and guess which to play next if the ten wins	25 79 1.04	
532.	K J x x x x	2 } Max } 1	Lead to the jack, hoping that West has both the ace and queen Lead to the jack and then to the king (best), *or* lead to the king and then to the jack	24 76	1.00
533.	K 9 8 J x x	2 1 } Max }	Lead small to the king, hoping that West has AQ doubleton or the singleton queen Finesse the eight; if this loses to the ten, guess whether to play the nine or king next* (*But if East would play a high honor from AQ and others, run the nine first; if this loses to the ten, lead to the king next)	1 80 88	0.81
534.	K x x J 9 x	2 1 Max	Lead small to the king, hoping that West has the ace-queen doubleton or the queen singleton Lead small to the king, and then back to the jack or nine (best), *or* lead to the nine and then to the king, *or* lead to the jack and then to the king. The last two lines will be better if East is more likely to be short in the suit Lead small to the king and then back to the jack or nine	1 76 0.77	
535.	K x x J x x	2 1 Max	Lead small to the king, hoping that West has the ace-queen doubleton Lead small to the king and then small to the jack (best), *or* lead small to the jack and then small to the king. The latter line will be better if East is more likely to be short in the suit* (*But if East would play an honor from AQ and others, lead small toward the jack, and duck whatever happens, then lead small to the king) Lead small to the king and then small to the jack	1 74 79 0.75	

(c) Declarer Has Seven Cards

536.	K J 9 8 x x x	3 2 Max	Finesse the eight, hoping that the queen and ten are both with West Finesse the eight; if this loses to the ten, finesse the nine next (best), *or* finesse the jack, and then finesse the eight Finesse the eight and then the nine	24 76 2.00	

	Dummy Declarer	Tricks Required		% Chance of Success	Tricks per Deal

VII.   THE DEFENSE HAS SIX POINTS (cont'd)
A.   THE ACE-QUEEN (cont'd)

	Dummy Declarer	Tricks Required		% Chance of Success	Tricks per Deal
537.	K 10 8 x J x x	3	Finesse the eight	20	
		2	Finesse the ten. If it loses to the queen, lead small to the jack and then to the king; if the ten loses to the ace, finesse the eight next	79	
		Max	Finesse the eight. If this loses to the nine, finesse the ten next		1.95
538.	K 10 x x J x x	3	Finesse the ten, hoping that West has AQ or AQx	9	
		2	Lead small to the king; then lead small to the ten	69	
		Max	Finesse the ten. If this loses to the queen, lead small to the king next		1.76
539.	K 9 8 7 J x x	3	Run the jack, hoping that East has the singleton ten	1	
		2	Run the jack, and then finesse the nine. If the ace appears from West on the first round, finesse the nine, and if necessary, the eight (best) *or* finesse the nine. If this loses to this queen, lead to the jack next; if the ace appears from West, finesse the nine next; if the nine loses to the ten, finesse the eight next*	76	
			(*But if West would not falsecard with AQ10 or AQ10x, run the nine. If this loses to the ten, finesse the seven next; otherwise run the eight.	77	
			And if East is tempted to play an honor from AQxxx)	78	
		Max	Run the jack. If it loses to the ace or queen from East, lead small to the nine next; if the ace appears from West on the first round, finesse the nine, and, if necessary, the eight		1.77
540.	Kx x x J 10 x	2	Lead small to the jack, and then small to the ten. This fails only when West has AQ doubleton, AQ and at least two others, or the singleton or doubleton queen	75	
541.	K x x x J 9 x	2	Lead small to the nine. If the ten or queen appears from East, lead small from the king next; otherwise lead small to the king	47	
		1 } Max }	Lead small to the nine, then small to the jack, and then small to the king. This fails only when West has the Q10 doubleton	98	1.36
542.	K x x x J x x	2 } Max }	Lead to the jack, and then, unless the queen appears from East, lead to the king, *or* lead to the king and then to the jack. The latter line will be better if West is more likely to be short in the suit	26	1.12
		1	Lead small from both hands; then, unless the queen has appeared from West, lead to the jack; then lead to the king. This fails only when West has Qx	94	

(d)   Declarer Has Eight Cards

	Dummy Declarer	Tricks Required		% Chance of Success	Tricks per Deal
543.	K 10 8 x x J x x	4	Run the jack. If this is covered, finesse the eight next	25	
		3	Finesse the ten, and run the jack if it loses to the ace (best), *or* lead small to the king, and then small to the jack	90	
		Max	Finesse the ten; if this loses to the ace, run the jack		3.12

	Dummy Declarer	Tricks Required		% Chance of Success	Tricks per Deal

VII.   THE DEFENSE HAS SIX POINTS (cont'd)
A.   THE ACE-QUEEN (cont'd)

	Dummy Declarer	Tricks Required		% Chance of Success	Tricks per Deal
544.	K 9 8 x x J x x	4	Lead small the king, hoping that West has the AQ only	3	
		3	Lead small to the eight. If it loses to the ten, finesse the nine next; if the ace appears from West on the first round, lead small to the jack	84	
		Max	Finesse the eight. If it loses to the ten, finesse the nine next; if the ace appears from West on the first round, lead small to the king		2.82
545.	K x x x x J 10 x	4	Lead small to the king, hoping that West has the AQ only	3	
		3 } Max }	Lead small to the jack, and then small to the ten	85	2.83
		2	Lead small to the jack. This fails only when East is void	98	
546.	K x x x x J 9 x	4	Lead small the king, hoping that West has the AQ doubleton	3	
		3 } Max }	Lead small to the nine, and then small to the king	63	2.58
		2	Lead small to the nine, and then small to the jack. This fails only if East is void	98	
547.	K J 9 8 x x x x	3	Finesse the eight	27	
		2	Finesse the eight and then the jack (best), *or* finesse the jack and then the eight, *or* lead small to the king	83	
		Max	Finesse the eight; if it loses to the ten, finesse the jack		2.10
548.	K 10 8 x J x x	3	Run the jack. If this is covered, finesse the eight next	27	
		2	Finesse the ten. If this loses to the queen, lead small to the jack; if the ten loses to the ace, run the jack (best), *or* lead small to the king, and then small to the jack	92	
		Max	Finesse the ten. If this loses to the queen, lead small to the jack; if the ten loses to the ace, run the jack		2.16
549.	K 9 8 7 J x x x	3	Lead small to the king, hoping that West has the ace-queen doubleton or the queen singleton	6	
		2 } Max }	Finesse the nine. If this loses to the queen, lead small to the jack; if the nine loses to the ten, finesse the eight	88	1.94
550.	K x x x J 10 8 x	3 } Max }	Run the jack. If the ace appears from West, run the ten next; if the jack loses to the ace from East, guess whether to lead small or run the ten next; if the jack is covered, guess whether to lead to the ten or to the eight next* (*This assumes that West will always play the ace from ace-queen doubleton and will cover with Qx about half the time, which is the best defense. If he always covers with Qx, lead to the eight if the jack is covered, lead the ten if the jack loses to the ace from East, and run the ten if the ace appears from West on the first round.	14 17	 2.01
			Similarly, if West never covers with Qx, lead small to the king if the jack loses to the ace from East, lead to the ten if the jack is covered, and run the ten if the ace appears from West on the first round)	17	2.01

Dummy Declarer	Tricks Required		% Chance of Success	Tricks per Deal

VII. THE DEFENSE HAS SIX POINTS (cont'd)
A. THE ACE-QUEEN (cont'd)

Dummy Declarer	Tricks Required		% Chance of Success	Tricks per Deal
	2	Lead small to the jack, and then small to the king. This fails only when East has a void or a small singleton	92	
551. K x x x	3	Lead small to the king, hoping that West has		
J 10 x x		AQ doubleton	3	
	2	Lead small to the king and then small to the jack, *or* lead small to the jack. The latter line will be better if East is more likely to be short in the suit	87	
	Max	Lead small to the king, and then small to the jack		1.90
552. K x x x	3	Lead small to the king, hoping that West has		
J 9 x x		AQ doubleton	3	
	2 } Max }	Lead small to the king and then small to the nine	70	1.71
	1	Lead small to the nine (best), *or* lead toward the king, and duck if West fails to play an honor, *or* lead small to the jack	100	
553. K x x x	3	Lead small to the king, hoping that West has		
J x x x		AQ doubleton	3	
	2	Lead toward the king, and duck if the queen fails to appear; then lead to the king (best), *or* lead to the king and then to the jack	50	
	1 } Max }	Lead toward the king, and duck if the queen fails to appear; then lead to the king and finally to the jack	100	1.54

(e) Declarer Has Nine Cards

Dummy Declarer	Tricks Required		% Chance of Success	Tricks per Deal
554. K J 9 x x	4	Lead small to the jack	33	
x x x x*	Max	Lead small to the jack		3.17
555. K J x x x	4	Lead small to the jack	33	
x x x x*	Max	Lead small to the jack		3.11
556. K 9 8 7 x	4	Lead small to the king	27	
J x x x*	3	Lead small to the nine (best), *or* run the nine	94	
	Max	Lead small to the king		3.16
557. K x x x x	4	Run the jack	50	
J 10 9 8*				
558. K x x x x	4	Lead small to the king	33	
J 10 x x*	3	Lead small to the king, in case West is void	95	
	Max	Lead small to the king		3.28
		*N.B. Similar principles apply if declarer's nine cards are distributed differently between this hand and dummy		

(f) Declarer Has Ten Cards

Dummy Declarer	Tricks Required		% Chance of Success	Tricks per Deal
559. K J x x x x	5	Finesse the jack	63	
10 x x x*				
560. K x x x x x	5	Run the jack	63	
J 10 9 x *				
		*N.B. Similar principles apply if declarer's ten cards are distributed differently between this hand and dummy		

Dummy Declarer	Tricks Required		% Chance of Success	Tricks per Deal

VII.   THE DEFENSE HAS SIX POINTS (cont'd)
B.   THE KING-QUEEN-JACK

(a)   **Declarer Has Five Cards**

561.	A 10 9 8 x	2	Finesse the ten, and then play the ace	25	

(b)   **Declarer Has Six Cards**

562.	A 10 9 8 x x	3 } Max	Finesse the ten, and then play the ace	16	1.99
		2	Play the ace, and then lead low from the 1098; this gains a trick when East has a singleton or doubleton honor	87	
563.	A 10 9 8 x x	2	Finesse the ten and then the nine	77	

(c)   **Declarer Has Seven Cards**

564.	A 10 9 8 x x x	4 } Max	Finesse the ten, and then cash the ace	65	3.55
		3	Finesse the ten, and then play the ace (best), *or* play the ace	91	
		2	Finesse the ten, in case East is void	99	
565.	A 10 9 8 x x x	3 } Max	Finesse the ten and then the nine; then play the ace	74	2.70
		2	Finesse the ten and then the nine (best), *or* play the ace	96	
566.	A 10 9 8 x x x	2	Finesse the eight, nine, and, if necessary, ten	89	
567.	A 10 9 x x x x	2	Finesse the ten and then the nine; then play the ace	68	
568.	A 10 x x 9 x x	2	Lead small to the nine. If this loses to West, finesse the ten next. If an honor appears from East on the first round, lead small to the nine again; if East shows out or plays another honor, finesse the ten next; otherwise play to the ace	51	

(d)   **Declarer Has Eight Cards**

569.	A 10 9 8 x x x x	5 } Max	Play the ace, in case East has a singleton honor	85	4.81
		4	Finesse the ten, in case East is void	98	
570.	A 10 9 8 x x x x	4 } Max	Finesse the ten and then the nine	90	3.88
		3	Finesse the ten and then the nine	98	
571.	A 10 9 8 x x x x	3 } Max	Finesse the ten and then the nine	92	2.90
		2	Finesse the ten and then the nine	98	
572.	A 10 x x x 9 x x	3	Play the ace, and lead small to the nine	85	
		2 } Max	Lead small to the nine and then small to the ten	100	2.82
573.	A 8 7 x x 10 x x	3 } Max	Run the ten, *or* lead small to the ten, in case East has the singleton nine	71	2.69
		2	Run the ten, *or* lead small to the ten, in case East is void	98	

	Dummy Declarer	Tricks Required		% Chance of Success	Tricks per Deal

VII. THE DEFENSE HAS SIX POINTS (cont'd)
B. THE KING-QUEEN-JACK (cont'd)

	Dummy Declarer	Tricks Required		% Chance of Success	Tricks per Deal
574.	A 10 9 8 x x x x	2	Finesse the ten and then the nine; this fails only when West has a void or a small singleton	92	
(e)	**Declarer Has Nine Cards**				
575.	A 10 9 8 x x x x x7 x	6 Max }	Play the ace, hoping for a 2-2 division Finesse the ten, and then play the ace	41 95	6.36
576.	A 10 9 x x x x x x x	6 5 Max }	Play the ace, hoping for a 2-2 division Finesse the ten, and then play the ace	41 95	5.36
577.	A 10 x x x x x 9 x x	5 4 Max	Play the ace Lead small to the ten, *or* lead small to the nine Lead small to the ten or nine; then play the ace	41 95	4.36
578.	A 10 x x x 9 x x x	4 3 Max	Play the ace, hopin g for a 2-2 division Lead small to the ten or nine Lead small to the ten or nine; then play the ace	41 95	3.36

VIIII. THE DEFENSE HAS SEVEN POINTS
A. THE ACE-KING

	Dummy Declarer	Tricks Required		% Chance of Success	Tricks per Deal
(a)	**Declarer Has Five Cards**				
579.	Q J 9 8 x	2	Finesse the eight. If it loses to the ace or king on either side, lead the queen and jack next	11	
580.	Q J 9 x x	1	Lead to the queen and then to the jack	78	
581.	Q 9 x J x	1	Lead small to the jack. If it loses to West, finesse the nine next	62	
582.	Q x x J 9	1	Finesse the nine	51	
(b)	**Declarer Has Six Cards**				
583.	Q J 9 8 x x	2	Finesse the nine	51	
584.	Q x x x J 9	1	Finesse the nine. If it loses to the ten, play the jack and then low from the queen* (*This is only fractionally better than leading small to the jack and then ducking two rounds, and the latter line might be better if East is more likely to be short in the suit)	56	
585.	Q J 9 x x x	1	Lead to the queen and then to the jack	79	
586.	Q 9 x J x x	1	Lead small to the jack. If it loses to West, finesse the nine next	64	
587.	Q x x J x x	1	Lead to either honor and then back to the other	49	
(c)	**Declarer Has Seven Cards**				
588.	Q J 9 x x x x	3 Max } 2 1	Lead to the queen and then to the jack Finesse the nine, and then lead to the queen Lead to the queen and then to the nine or jack (best), *or* finesse the nine, and then lead to the queen	38 80 96	2.12

	Dummy Declarer	Tricks Required		% Chance of Success	Tricks per Deal

VIII. THE DEFENSE HAS SEVEN POINTS (cont'd)
A. THE ACE-KING (cont'd)

	Dummy / Declarer	Tricks Required	Description	% Chance of Success	Tricks per Deal
589.	Q J x x x 9 x	3 Max	Lead to the queen and then to the jack	30	1.98
		2	Lead to the queen and then to the jack	73	
		1	Lead small to the nine. This fails only when West has the singleton ten	99	
590.	Q J 9 8 x x x	2 Max	Lead small to the queen. If it loses, finesse the nine next	63	1.63
591.	Q J 9 x x x x	2 Max	Lead small to the queen. If it loses, finesse the nine next	55	1.46
592.	Q J x x 9 x x	2 Max	Lead to the queen and then to the jack	49	1.38
		1	Lead small to the queen. If it loses, lead small to the nine and then small to the jack. This fails only when West has the doubleton ten	95	
593.	Q J x x x x x	2 Max	Lead to the queen and then to the jack	45	1.28
		1	Lead to the queen; if it loses, duck one round, and then lead to the jack (best) *or* duck one round, and then lead to the queen and jack	85	
594.	Q 9 8 x J x x	2	Lead small to the jack. If it loses to West, finesse the nine next; if an honor appears from East on the first round, lead to the jack again	56	
595.	Q x x x J 9 x	2 Max	Lead small to the nine. If it loses to a high honor from West, lead small to the queen; otherwise lead small to the jack	33	1.30
		1	Lead small to the nine and then small to the jack. This fails only if West has A10 or K10	97	
596.	Q x x x J x x	2	Lead small to the queen or jack, and then back to the other honor, hoping to find either opponent with AKx or the right opponent with AK doubleton	16	
		1	Lead toward the jack and duck; then lead to the jack and to the queen. This fails only when West has Kx or Ax	87	
		Max	Lead small to the jack. If it loses, duck the next round, and then lead to the queen		0.93

(d) Declarer Has Eight Cards

	Dummy / Declarer	Tricks Required	Description	% Chance of Success	Tricks per Deal
597.	Q J 10 6 x x 8 x	4 Max	Lead to the queen and then to the jack	85	3.83
		3	Lead small to the eight, in case West is void	100	
598.	Q J 9 8 7 x x x	3	Lead small to the queen. If it loses, finesse the nine	75	
599.	Q J x x x x x x	3 Max	Lead to the queen and then to the jack	63	2.50
600.	Q 10 9 6 x J x x	3 Max	Lead the jack, in case East is void	98	2.98
601.	Q x x x x J 9 x	3	Lead small to the queen. If it loses to East, finesse the nine next; if an honor appears from West on the first round, lead to the queen again	48	
		2 Max	Lead small to the nine and then small to the jack. This fails only if East is void	98	241
602.	Q J 9 8 x x x x	2	Lead small to the queen. If it loses, finesse the nine	77	

Dummy Declarer	Tricks Required		% Chance of Success	Tricks per Deal

VIII.   THE DEFENSE HAS SEVEN POINTS (cont'd)
A.   THE ACE-KING (cont'd)

603.	Q 9 8 7 J x x x	2	Lead small to the jack. If it loses to West, finesse the nine next	66
604.	Q 9 x x J x x x	2 ⎱ Max ⎰	Lead small to the jack. If it loses to West, finesse the nine next	64	1.58
		1	Finesse the nine (best), *or* lead small to the queen and them small to the jack, in case West has a bare honor	100
605.	Q x x x J x x x	2 ⎱ Max ⎰	Lead to the queen (or jack); if it loses, duck the next round	37	1.32
		1	Duck the first round, and then lead small to either honor	100

(e) Declarer Has Nine Cards

606.	Q J 7 x x x x 9 x	5 ⎱ Max ⎰	Lead small to the queen and then to the jack	84	4.79
		4	Led small to the nine, in case West is void	100
607.	Q x x x x x J 9 x	4	Finesse the nine. This only fails when West has AK10x, AK10, or 10	83
608.	Q J 8 x x 10 7 x x	3 ⎱ Max ⎰	Lead small to the queen, in case either opponent is void	100	3.00
609.	Q J x x x x x x	3 ⎱ Max ⎰	Lead small to the queen and then small to the jack	83	2.78
610.	Q 9 x x x J x x x	3	Lead small to the jack and then small to the queen, *or* finesse the nine. The latter line will be better if West is more likely to be short in the suit	83

B.   THE ACE-QUEEN-JACK

(a) Declarer Has Five Cards

611.	K 10 9 x x	1	Finesse the ten and then the nine	78
612.	K 10 x x x	1	Finesse the ten and then lead to the king	63

(b) Declarer Has Six Cards

613.	K 10 9 8 x x	2	Finesse the ten and then the nine	50
614.	K 10 9 x x x	1	Finesse the ten and then the nine	79

(c) Declarer Has Seven Cards

615.	K 10 9 8 x x x	2	Finesse the eight and then the nine	76
616.	K 10 9 x x x x	2 ⎱ Max ⎰	Finesse the nine and then the ten	61	1.51
617.	K 10 x x 9 x x	2 ⎱ Max ⎰	Lead small to the ten and then small to the king	37	1.25
		1	Lead small to the king, and then, unless an honor appears from West, small to the nine (best), *or* lead to the ten and then to the nine	90

	Dummy Declarer	Tricks Required		% Chance of Success	Tricks per Deal

VIII.   THE DEFENSE HAS SEVEN POINTS (cont'd)

B.   THE ACE-QUEEN-JACK (cont'd)

	Dummy Declarer	Tricks Required		% Chance of Success	Tricks per Deal
618.	K 10 x x x x x	2 } Max	Lead small to the ten and then small to the king	32	1.08
		1	Duck one round; then lead to the ten, and lead to the king	79	
619.	K 9 8 7 x x x	2	Lead to the nine and then to the king (best), *or* lead to the king, hoping that West has the ace and two other cards	18	
		1 } Max	Finesse the seven and then the eight. This fails only if West has xx, x, or a void	95	1.11
620.	K x x x x x x	2	Duck one round, and then lead to the king (best) *or* lead to the king, hoping that West has the ace and two other cards	18	
		1	Duck two rounds, and then lead to the king	77	
		Max	Duck one round, and then lead to the king		0.87

(d) Declarer Has Eight Cards

	Dummy Declarer	Tricks Required		% Chance of Success	Tricks per Deal
621.	K 10 9 x x x x x	3 } Max	Finesse the ten and then the nine	75	2.66
		2	Finesse the ten and nine (best), *or* lead to the king	92	
622.	K 10 x x x 9 x x	3 } Max	Finesse the ten, and then lead small to the king	63	2.56
		2	Finesse the ten. If it loses to the jack or queen, lead small to the nine next. This fails only if West is void	98	
623.	K 10 9 8 x x x x	2	Finesse the eight and then the nine	83	
624.	K 10 x x x x x x	2 } Max	Finesse the ten, and then lead to the king	52	1.38
625.	K x x x x x x x	2	Lead small to the king, preferably ducking one round first	34	
		1	Duck one round. Then either lead small to the king (best), *or* duck a second round	87	
		Max	Duck one round, and then lead small to the king		1.21

(e) Declarer Has Nine Cards

	Dummy Declarer	Tricks Required		% Chance of Success	Tricks per Deal
626.	K 10 9 x x x x x x	5	Lead small to the king, hoping that West has the doubleton ace	20	
		4 } Max	Finesse the ten. This gains a trick when East is void or has the singleton ace	89	3.98
627.	K 10 x x x x 9 x x	5	Lead small to the king, hoping that West has the doubleton ace	20	
		4 } Max	Finesse the ten, and then lead small to the king	89	4.03
628.	K 8 x x x x 10 x x	5 } Max	Lead small to the king, hoping that West has the doubleton ace	20	3.94
		4	Lead toward the king, and play the king if the nine fails to appear from West* (*But West should falsecard from QJ9)	84 78	
		3	Lead small to the ten	100	
629.	K x x x x x x x x	5 } Max	Lead small to the king, hoping that West has the doubleton ace	20	3.81
		4	Duck one round, and then lead small to the king	72	

Dummy Declarer	Tricks Required		% Chance of Success	Tricks per Deal

VIII. THE DEFENSE HAS SEVEN POINTS (cont'd)
B. THE ACE-QUEEN-JACK (cont'd)

630. K 9 x x x	4 ⎫	Lead small to the king, hoping that West has the		
x x x x	Max ⎭	doubleton ace	20	2.81
	3	Duck one round, and then lead small to the king	72	
631. K 8 x x x	4 ⎫	Lead small to the king, hoping West has the		
10 x x x	Max ⎭	doubleton ace	20	2.98
	3	Lead toward the king, and play the king if the		
		nine fails to appear from West*	84	
		(*But West should falsecard from QJ9)	78	

IX. THE DEFENSE HAS EIGHT POINTS
(a) Declarer Has Five Cards

632. Q 10 9 8	2	Finesse the ten, hoping that West has J, AJ, KJ,		
x		or Jx	2	
633. Q 10 x	1	Finesse the ten, and then lead to the queen	37	
x x				

(b) Declarer Has Six Cards

634. Q 10 9 8	2	Finesse the ten and then the nine	18	
x x				
635. Q 10 x x	2	Lead to the queen, hoping that West has the AKJ		
x x		only	1	
	1 ⎫	Lead to the ten and then to the queen	41	0.42
	Max ⎭			
636. Q 10 9	1	Finesse the ten and then the nine	51	
x x x				
637. Q 10 x	1	Finesse the ten, and then lead to the queen	38	
x x x				

(c) Declarer Has Seven Cards

638. Q 10 x x x	3 ⎫	Lead to the ten and then to the queen	12	1.58
x x	Max ⎭			
	2	Lead to the ten and queen	55	
	1	Lead to the ten and queen	91	
639. Q 10 x x	2 ⎫	Lead to the ten and then to the queen	22	0.89
x x x	Max ⎭			
	1	Lead to the ten and queen (best), *or* duck one		
		round and then lead to the ten and queen, *or*		
		lead to the queen and then to the ten	68	
640. Q 9 8 7	2	Lead small to the queen	7	
x x x	1 ⎫	Finesse the seven and then the eight	85	0.88
	Max ⎭			
641. Q x x x	2	Lead small to the queen, hoping that West has		
10 9 x		AKx or AKJ	7	
	1 ⎫	Lead small to the ten and then small to the nine.		
	Max ⎭	This fails only when West has AJ or KJ	97	0.97
642. Q x x x	2	Lead small to the queen, hoping that West has		
10 x x		AKx or AKJ	7	
	1 ⎫	Lead small to the ten. If an honor appears from		
	Max ⎭	East, lead small to the ten again; if the ten		
		loses to West on the first round, duck one		
		round, and then lead to the queen	70	0.70

(d) Declarer Has Eight Cards

643. Q 10 x x x	3 ⎫	Finesse the ten, and then lead to the queen	33	2.15
x x x	Max ⎭			
	2	Finesse the ten, and then lead to the queen, in		
		case East is void	84	

	Dummy Declarer	Tricks Required		% Chance of Success	Tricks per Deal
			IX. THE DEFENSE HAS EIGHT POINTS (cont'd)		
644.	Q x x x x 10 x x	3	Lead small to the queen. If the jack appears from West, cover with the queen, and duck the next round; if the ace or king appears on the first round, lead to the queen again	20	
		2 Max }	Lead toward the queen, and duck the trick. If an honor appears on the first round, lead small to the ten next; otherwise lead to the queen	90	1.95
		1	Lead small to the ten, in case West is void	100	
645.	Q x x x x x x x	3 } Max }	Lead small to the queen	14	1.88
		2	Duck one round, and then, unless the ace or king appears from East, lead small to the queen	82	
646.	Q 10 x x x x x x	2 } Max }	Finesse the ten, and then lead to the queen	35	1.19
647.	Q x x x 10 x x x	2 } Max }	Lead small to the queen, and then, unless the jack appears from West, lead small to the ten	20	1.15
		1	Lead small to the queen and then small to the ten, *or* lead from the ten, and duck unless the jack appears from West; then, unless the ace or king appears from East, lead small to the queen. The latter line will be better if East is more likely to be short in the suit	94	
648.	Q x x x x x x x	2	Lead small to the queen	14	
		1	Duck one round, and then lead small to the queen	84	
		Max	Lead small to the queen		0.92
(e)	**Declarer Has Nine Cards**				
649.	Q 10 9 x x x x x x*	3	Finesse the ten	70	
		Max	Finesse the ten		2.66
650.	Q x x x x x x x x*	3 } Max }	Lead small to the queen, *or* duck one round, and then lead small to the queen	53	2.48
			*N.B. Similar principles apply if declarer's nine cards are distributed differently between his hand and dummy		

X. THE DEFENSE HAS NINE POINTS

	Dummy Declarer	Tricks Required		% Chance of Success	Tricks per Deal
(a)	**Declarer Has Seven Cards**				
651.	J 10 8 x x x x	1	Lead to the jack, and then either lead to the ten or finesse the eight	73	
652.	J 10 x x x x x	1	Lead to the jack and then to the ten	68	
653.	J x x x 10 x x	1	Lead small to the ten. If it loses to West, duck the next round, and then lead small to the jack	69	
(b)	**Declarer Has Eight Cards**				
654.	J x x x x 10 x x	2 } Max }	Lead small to the ten. If it loses to West, lead small to the jack	88	1.88
		1	Lead small to the ten	100	
655.	J 10 x x x x x x	1	Lead small to the jack and then small to the ten	84	
656.	J x x x 10 x x x	1	Lead small to the jack (or ten). If it loses, lead small to the other honor	92	
					E.C.

SUIT DISTRIBUTION. There are 39 possible suit distributions. For the percentage play in handling any combination, see SUIT COMBINATIONS. For relative frequency of the occurrence of each pattern, see MATHEMATICAL TABLES, Table 1.

SUIT OPENING BID. See OPENING SUIT BID.

SUIT PATTERNS. For the 39 suit patterns, ranging from a balanced 4-3-3-3 to an outlandish 13-0-0-0, and the percentage frequency of each, see MATHEMATICAL TABLES, Table 1.

SUIT PLACING. The process of marking during the bidding the suit lengths around the table. See CARD READING; COUNTING THE HAND.

SUIT-PREFERENCE SIGNAL. A device whereby a defender may direct his partner to lead a specific suit. This method, devised by Hy Lavinthal in 1934, has had a greater effect on defensive play than any other development of this century and ranks with the distributional echo and HIGH-LOW SIGNAL of the 19th century. In various countries the suit-preference signal is known by the names of bridge writers, especially William E. McKenney and B. Jay Becker, who adopted and publicized it but did not otherwise contribute to it.

The signal never applies to the suit led, and never to the trump suit. The essence of the suit-preference signal is this: When a player has the lead and seems likely to switch suits, or when he may have a choice of suits when he next obtains the lead, the play of a conspicuously high card calls for a lead in the higher-ranking suit in question, the play of a conspicuously low card calls for a lead of the lower-ranking suit.

Properly used, the suit-preference signal does not interfere with signals that show ATTITUDE and LENGTH.

A common suit-preference application is seen in this deal:

```
                    ♠ K 9 6
                    ♥ 8 7
                    ♦ K 4 3 2
                    ♣ K 4 3 2
♠ 2
♥ 5 4 3 2
♦ J 10 9 8
♣ J 10 9 8
```

WEST	NORTH	EAST	SOUTH
			1 ♥
Pass	1NT	Pass	3 ♥
Pass	4 ♥	All Pass	

West leads the ♠2. East wins the ace and returns a spade. Which suit does West lead after he ruffs?

To help West, East signals with the rank of the spade he leads at the second trick. If East holds:

```
♠ A 10 7 4 2
♥ 9
♦ Q 7 6 5
♣ A Q 7
```

he returns the ♠2, his lowest, showing a desire for clubs, the lower ranking side suit. But if East holds:

```
♠ A 10 7 4 2
♥ 9
♦ A Q 7
♣ Q 7 6 5
```

he returns the ♠10, suggesting strength in diamonds, the

higher-ranking suit.

Suit preference can also indicate the location of an entry.

```
                    ♠ J 5
                    ♥ 6 5 3
                    ♦ A Q 10 7 6
                    ♣ J 6 5
♠ A 4
♥ Q 10 8 7 4 2
♦ 5 3
♣ 8 7 4
```

West leads the ♥7 against South's 3NT. East plays the king, ducked by South, and returns the ♥J to South's ace.

On the second heart West should follow with the queen. If East gets in with, say, the ♦K, he may be unsure which black suit to lead. A spade may look risky if he has the queen. West's striking play of the ♥Q must suggest an entry in the highest — ranking suit.

Suit preference is sometimes available on the opening lead:

WEST	NORTH	EAST	SOUTH
3 ♦	Dbl	4 ♦	4 ♠
All Pass			

West holds:

```
♠ 5 3
♥ J 8 4 2
♦ K J 10 8 7 4 2
♣ —
```

West would like East to win the first trick and return a club. East's most likely fast entry is the ♦A, but if West leads normally, he cannot expect East to shift to clubs. West should lead the ♦2. Since on the bidding this lead cannot be fourth highest, East should get the message.

```
Dlr: West           ♠ K
Vul: N-S            ♥ A J 7 6
                    ♦ Q 10 6 4
                    ♣ K Q 7 6
                                    ♠ Q 9 5 2
                                    ♥ 4
                                    ♦ A 7 5 3
                                    ♣ J 9 4 2
```

WEST	NORTH	EAST	SOUTH
3 ♠	Dbl	5 ♠	6 ♥
All Pass			

West leads the ♠A; East should jar partner by dropping the queen.

Suit preference is often abused and overused. Most authorities agree that attitude and length signals take priority over suit preference. A defender must not interpret a signal as suit preference if his partner may have sent a simpler message. A suit-preference signal is an unusual play of unmistakable significance.

```
                    ♠ K 4
                    ♥ Q 8 5 3
                    ♦ 7 4 2
                    ♣ A K Q 4
                                    ♠ J 9 5 2
                                    ♥ 7 4
                                    ♦ A Q 6
                                    ♣ 10 7 5 3
```

WEST	NORTH	EAST	SOUTH
1 ♠	Dbl	3 ♠	4 ♥
All Pass			

West leads the ♠A. East's play should show attitude as long as that is a conceivable message to send. East can get a shift (to diamonds) simply by following with the

♣2. West can look at dummy and see that diamonds is the logical switch.

East's play cannot ask for a club shift (especially since dummy has strong clubs). As long as East might merely want to signal for a spade continuation or a switch, West must interpret his play as attitude.

```
            ♠ K 4
            ♥ Q 8 5 3
            ♦ 7 4 2
            ♣ A K Q 4
                        ♠ J 9 5 2
                        ♥ A 4
                        ♦ 9 5 3
                        ♣ 10 7 5 3
```

The bidding and opening lead are the same. This time East should play the 9 to ask West to *continue spades*. (There is nothing illogical about a spade continuation although dummy can win. East may prefer a passive defense.) If East plays the ♠2, West will shift to a diamond, which may cost a trick.

```
            ♠ K 5 3
            ♥ 8 6 5 3
            ♦ Q 3 2
            ♣ Q 3 2
                        ♠ J 9 5 2
                        ♥ Q 4
                        ♦ K J 10
                        ♣ 8 6 5 4
```

WEST	NORTH	EAST	SOUTH
			1♥
1♠	2♥	2♠	4♥
All Pass			

West leads the ♠A, and East should play the jack. This is suit preference for several reasons. First, the jack is an unusually high spade when East clearly has a choice of plays. Also, a suit-preference signal is *needed*; since South is about to take a discard on the ♣K, the defenders need to cash out; but West has no obvious shift (as he would if dummy held good clubs and weak diamonds). An attitude signal is not enough.

```
            ♠ A K
            ♥ A 9 6 5 3
            ♦ 9
            ♣ A K J 8 6
♠ 7
♥ J 10 3
♦ A K 10 4 2
♣ 7 6 5 4
```

WEST	NORTH	EAST	SOUTH
	1♥	Pass	1♠
Pass	3♣	Pass	3♠
Pass	4♠	Pass	5♥
Pass	6♠	All Pass	

West leads the ♦A. East plays the 8, South the 3. West should continue with the ♦K. This is not a suit-preference situation, since there is no suit East can want led. A diamond continuation is possible, and East might want to use attitude to ask for it. In fact, East has ♣J 10 5 and wins a trump trick when dummy must ruff the second diamond.

Here are other applications of the suit-preference signal:

```
            ♠ A K Q 5
            ♥ Q 10 6 5
            ♦ 5 4
            ♣ 6 5 4
                        ♠ J 10 7 4 2
                        ♥ 4 3
                        ♦ A 9 4
                        ♣ J 3 2
```

WEST	NORTH	EAST	SOUTH
			1NT
Pass	2♣	Pass	2♥
Pass	4♥	All Pass	

West leads the ♠3, won in dummy. East should follow with the jack. West has led an obvious singleton and may have a reentry in trumps. The ♠J suggests an entry in diamonds. If East had an entry in clubs, he would play his lowest spade.

```
Dlr: West      ♠ Q J 7 5
Vul: None      ♥ A 8 5 2
               ♦ A 7 3
               ♣ 5 4
♠ A K 2                       ♠ 9 6 4 3
♥ K J 9 3                     ♥ Q 5
♦ Q 6                         ♦ 10 5 4
♣ A J 10 2                    ♣ Q 7 3 2
               ♠ 10 8
               ♥ 10 7 4
               ♦ K J 9 8 2
               ♣ K 9 8
```

WEST	NORTH	EAST	SOUTH
1♣	Dbl	Pass	1♦
Dbl	Pass	1♠	2♦
All Pass			

West leads the ♠A, and East plays the 9. This can't be attitude or length — West cannot be eager to cash his second spade. West should interpret East's play as suit preference and shift to a low heart.

```
Dlr: East      ♠ 6 5
Vul: N-S       ♥ K J 9 5
               ♦ 10 6 5
               ♣ K 10 9 5
♠ Q 9 3                       ♠ J 8
♥ 10 6 4 2                    ♥ A 8 7
♦ K J                         ♦ A Q 8 7 3 2
♣ J 8 6 2                     ♣ Q 4
               ♠ A K 10 7 4 2
               ♥ Q 3
               ♦ 9 4
               ♣ A 7 3
```

WEST	NORTH	EAST	SOUTH
		1♦	1♠
Dbl	Pass	2♦	2♠
3♦	3♠	All Pass	

West leads the ♦K and continues with the ♦J. East wins the ace and leads the ♦Q, ruffed low by South and overruffed. East had no chance for a suit-preference signal on the third diamond; he had to lead the queen to beat dummy's ten. However, East's play at the second trick was meaningful; when he won the ♦A instead of the queen, he suggested heart strength. West should lead a heart at the fourth trick, and East will win and lead another diamond, promoting a second trump trick for the defense.

In an expert partnership, suit-preference signals extend to many subtle situations; for example, a defender may signal as he discards in a side suit.

Dlr: East
Vul: Both

```
              ♠ K J 5 3
              ♥ J 7 3
              ♦ A 7 4
              ♣ A 8 3
♠ A 6 2                      ♠ 10
♥ K Q 9 5 2                  ♥ 10 8 6 4
♦ J 2                        ♦ K Q 10 6
♣ Q 9 6                      ♣ 10 7 5 4
              ♠ Q 9 8 7 4
              ♥ A
              ♦ 9 8 5 3
              ♣ K J 2
```

WEST	NORTH	EAST	SOUTH
		Pass	Pass
1 ♥	Dbl	2 ♥	4 ♠
All Pass			

West leads the ♥K, and East signals with the 8 (length). South wins the ace, leads a trump to the king and another trump. East would prefer not to discard a high diamond or low club, either of which could be costly; he can discard the ♥10 to suggest diamond strength.

```
              ♠ 7 5 3
              ♥ Q 8 5
              ♦ K Q J 8
              ♣ Q 7 6
                            ♠ 9 2
                            ♥ A K J 10
                            ♦ 10 5 2
                            ♣ 9 8 4 3
```

South opens 1NT, raised to 3NT. West leads the ♠J, and East plays the 2, discouraging. South wins the queen and leads a diamond to the king. East follows with the 2, length. South comes back to the ♠K and leads a second diamond. West's ace wins and East plays the ten (suit preference), suggesting a preference for hearts over clubs.

```
              ♠ 7 6
              ♥ Q 7 3
              ♦ J 6 3
              ♣ Q 10 8 4 2
♠ 5 4 3 2                    ♠ 10
♥ K 10 6 4                   ♥ A J 9 5
♦ 7 4 2                      ♦ Q 9 8 5
♣ 7 3                        ♣ K J 6 5
              ♠ A K Q J 9 8
              ♥ 8 2
              ♦ A K 10
              ♣ A 9
```

WEST	NORTH	EAST	SOUTH
Pass	Pass	Pass	2 ♠
Pass	2NT	Pass	4 ♠

West leads the ♣7: 2, jack, ace. South draws trumps, and West follows with the 5, 4, 3 and 2. South then leads a club. When East takes the king, he should shift to a low heart. West's trump plays can have no significance other than suit preference.

SUIT SIGNALS. See COUNT SIGNALS.

SUIT TAKEOUT. See RESPONSE.

SUMMARY SHEET. See RECAPITULATION SHEET.

SUMMER NORTH AMERICAN BRIDGE CHAMPIONSHIPS. Formerly called the Summer Nationals, this annual American Contract Bridge League tournament held since 1929 takes place in July or early August. These championships, usually the largest of the three North American Championships, were originally under the auspices of the American Bridge League, and since 1938 have been controlled by the ACBL. In the Thirties they were played at Asbury Park NJ and lasted eight days. In postwar years the program was gradually enlarged to nine days. In 1969 it became a ten-day tournament and in 1979 a pre-tournament Charity Gala was added. By 1991 this was a substantial bridge event with 156 tables in play on Thursday evening in the Charity Pairs and Charity Knockout Teams.

In 1930 the Knockout Team event (now the Spingold Master Knockout Teams) attracted an entry of 16 teams, and 22 pairs were entered in the Master Pairs for the von Zedtwitz Gold Cup (now the six-session Life Master Pairs). In the postwar years the size of the tournament expanded rapidly, partly as a result of the impetus given by the masterpoint scheme. A peak was reached in 1991 in Las Vegas with 24,221 tables, an all-time world record. For past results of Summer North American Bridge Championships, see Appendix I.

Summer North American Championships Attendance (an asterisk indicates the record was broken that year; table counts not available prior to 1952)

Year	Site	Tables
1929	Chicago	
1930-41	Asbury Park NJ	
1942-47	New York City	
1948-49	Chicago	
1950	Columbus	
1951	Washington	
1952	Cincinnati	3,093
1953	St. Louis	3,054
1954	Washington	4,496
1955	Chicago	4,619
1956	New York City	5,679*
1957	Pittsburgh	5,625
1958	Miami	4,068
1959	Chicago	6,939*
1960	Los Angeles	8,462*
1961	Washington	7,989
1962	Minneapolis	5,820
1963	Los Angeles	12,486*
1964	Toronto	11,150
1965	Chicago	14,511*
1966	Denver	10,112
1967	Montreal	10,926
1968	Minneapolis	9,857
1969	Los Angeles	11,470
1970	Boston	12,584
1971	Chicago	13,566
1972	Denver	11,449
1973	Washington D.C.	16,043*
1974	New York City	15,310
1975	Miami Beach	10,368
1976	Salt Lake City	10,722
1977	Chicago	13,170
1978	Toronto	18,408*
1979	Las Vegas	18,517*
1980	Chicago	11,889
1981	Boston	14,079
1982	Albuquerque	9,776
1983	New Orleans	10,520
1984	Washington D.C.	15,228
1985	Las Vegas	19,828*
1986	Toronto	21,075*

1987	Baltimore	17,052
1988	Salt Lake City	11,501
1989	Chicago	14,902
1990	Boston	15,325
1991	Las Vegas	24,221*
1992	Toronto	16,680
1993	Washington D.C.	18,270
1994	San Diego	
1995	New Orleans	
1996	Miami Beach	
1997	Albuquerque	
1998	Chicago	

SUNDAY TIMES PAIRS. An invitational pair event that until January 1981 was sponsored by the *London Sunday Times.* The field is usually limited to 16-22 leading pairs from many countries. The competition was in abeyance from 1982 to 1989. It was revived in 1990 with the *Sunday Times* and Macallan Malt Whisky as joint sponsors. For winners, see Appendix III.

SUPER BLACKWOOD. A method of asking for aces when 4NT would be a natural bid. Easley Blackwood listed three situations in which 4NT would be natural. (a) when the partnership has not bid a suit; (b) when no suit has been agreed, and the 4NT bidder has previously bid notrump; (c) when no suit has been agreed, and a notrump bid immediately preceded 4NT. In each of these situations Blackwood suggests that a bid of four in the lowest-ranking unbid suit should ask for aces with step responses. A subsequent 5NT bid asks for kings in the same way. The Super Blackwood bid will usually be 4♣ which lines it up with the GERBER convention.

SUPER GERBER. An ace-asking convention devised by Robert Goldman for use when a minor suit fit has been established, or when the last bid was 3NT, so that a 4NT call would be natural. The Super Gerber bid is the lowest possible bid in an unbid suit or in a suit that cannot be deemed trumps; if all suits are unavailable or ambiguous, the Super Gerber bid is a jump to 5♣. Over establishment of a minor suit fit, either expressly or by implication, the Super Gerber bid is a jump to four of the cheapest unbid suit:

(a)	(b)	(c)	(d)
1♦ 3♦	1♣ 3♣	1♦ 2♦	1♦ 1♥
4♥	4♦	4♣	3♦ 4♠

The last bid in each auction is Super Gerber. The use of Super Gerber in minor suit auctions is designed to allow 4NT to be used as a balanced general strength slam try, and to provide an ace-asking bid that does not risk getting the partnership beyond the game level with too few aces.

Responses as used by the ACES TEAM are in steps as follows:

1st step	0 or 3 aces
2nd step	1 or 4 aces
3rd step	2 aces
4th step	2 aces with extra value outside the trump suit
5th step	2 aces and a useful void
higher step	1 ace and a useful void

In showing one ace and a void, the void suit is bid if it ranks lower than the trump suit; the trump suit is bid if the void suit is higher ranking. This is sometimes called High Gerber, particularly when the bid is restricted to a five-club bid.

SUPER PRECISION. A version of the PRECISION CLUB system used by Giorgio Belladonna and Benito Garozzo in which there are many specialized bids and asking sequences. It differs from standard Precision in the following essential respects:

Notrump responses to 1♣ are revised: 1NT is enlarged to encompass hands worth 8-13 points. A 2NT response shows 14 or more points, with no upper limit. A 3NT response shows a solid seven-card suit, with or without a side suit stopper. Opener's rebids over 3NT ask about high card controls, or identification of responder's suit.

Over interference with 1♣, controls are shown (A = 2, K = 1). After a one-level overcall, a double shows 6 or more points with 0-2 controls, 1NT shows 3 controls and a stopper, 2♣ shows 3 controls without a stopper, 2♦ shows 4 controls, 2NT shows 5 or more controls; bids of 3♣, 3♦, and one, two, or three of a major are all natural, showing 0-2 controls.

Over a two level overcall the double shows a balanced hand with as many as 3 controls; 2NT shows 3 or 4 controls with a stopper; a cuebid shows 5 or more controls; suit bids are natural, showing unbalanced hands with 0-3 controls. Over a three level overcall the responses are similar.

2♦ opening may be 4-3-1-5 or 3-4-1-5 as well as 4-4-0-5 and 4-4-1-4. A 2NT response asks for clarification of distribution and strength. 3♣ and 3♦ rebids show hands with three spades and three hearts respectively; 3♥ and 3♠ rebids show 4-4-1-4 distribution of minimum and maximum strength; 4♣ and 4♦ rebids shows 4-4-0-5 distribution of minimum and maximum strength.

Super Unusual Positive is used in responding to 1♣ with 4-4-4-1 hands. An immediate jump to 3♣ shows a singleton in a black suit, a jump to 3♦ shows a singleton in a red suit; both show minimum high card values. Opener's bid of the next suit asks where responder's singleton is: responder bids the first step with the minor suit singleton, or the second step with the major suit singleton. Immediate jump responses of 3♥, 3♠, 4♣, and 4♦ over 1♣ show maximum values and a singleton in the next higher suit. Opener's bid of the next suit (responder's short suit) asks for controls — first step 4, second step 5, etc.

Three-level minor suit openings are offensive rather than purely preemptive. 3♣ shows a seven playing-trick hand with a semi-solid club suit and an outside entry. 3♦ shows any solid seven-card suit with an outside entry. In response to 3♦, 3♥ is a sign-off to play in opener's suit; 3♠ is a general constructive bid. Over 3♠ opener bids 3NT if he has a minor suit, 4♣ if his suit is hearts and he has a side void or singleton, 4♦ if his suit is spades and he has a side void or singleton; 4♥ and 4♠ are natural and deny a side void or singleton. Responder may ask opener where his shortness lies.

3NT opening shows a preemptive minor suit opening similar to standard openings of 4♣ or 4♦. Responder retreats with a weak hand by bidding 4♣ which opener passes if his suit is clubs, or corrects to 4♦.

Asking bids of several kinds are used after a 1♣ opening, each with its own series of responses. These include bids designated Alpha, in which opener asks about responder's support for opener's suit; Beta, in which opener asks about responder's length and strength in a particular suit; Gamma which asks about trump honors;

Delta, which asks about length and strength in a specific suit after a notrump bid or STAYMAN response. See SUPER PRECISION ASKING BIDS.

SUPER PRECISION ASKING BIDS. Any of a number of types of asking bids in the SUPER PRECISION system as played by Giorgio Belladonna and Benito Garozzo, used by the 1♣ opener to ask a variety of questions, such as trump suit quality, high card or distributional controls, and responder's support for opener's suit.

Alpha Support Asking Bids. After a positive response in a suit, a new suit bid by opener asks about responder's support for opener's suit and his overall controls. Support is defined as Q-x-x or better. A hand with 0-2 controls is considered minimum, four or more controls is maximum, and three controls can be considered in either category. The responses are in five steps:

1st step	no support, minimum
2nd step	no support, maximum
3rd step	support, minimum
4th step	support, maximum
5th step	four cards, maximum

Further definition of responder's support may follow.

Beta Suit Asking Bids. After a negative 1♦ response to 1♣, a jump to 2♥ or 2♠ by opener is a Roman-style asking bid inquiring about responder's strength and length in that suit. The responses are the first eight steps set out in ROMAN ASKING BIDS. See also Delta Suit Asking Bids below.

Gamma Trump Asking Bids. Initiated by the 1♣ opener's single raise of responder's positive suit response, the responses show trump quality and length as set forth in PRECISION ASKING BIDS. Delayed trump asking bids are also available.

Delta Suit Asking Bids. After a positive response in notrump, a jump in a suit by opener is used to determine the number of cards and honors held by responder in that suit. The responses are: 1st step no honors, doubleton or tripleton 2nd step doubleton honor 3rd step tripleton honor 4th step four headed by an honor 5th step two honors doubleton or tripleton 6th step four headed by two honors Control Asking Bids. After a suit fit has been established, a direct bid of 4♣ is control asking. If cuebidding has begun, 4♣ is a cuebid. There is one exception: if responder's first bid suit was clubs, then 4♦ is the control asking bid. Responses are in steps, with the first step showing none or one. See PRECISION ASKING BIDS. However, it may be agreed to vary the first step according to responder's previously shown strength.

Special Suit Asking Bids. After a Control Asking Bid, a new suit by opener asks responder to show his length and strength in the new suit as follows:

1st step	void or singleton
2nd step	doubleton
3rd step	tripleton
4th step	one of top three honors, any length
5th step	two of top three honors, any length
6th step	three top honors, any length

SUPER SWISS. An expansion of the SWISS CONVENTION recommended by Hugh W. Kelsey that allows responder to make a forcing raise of opener's major suit while announcing immediately whether he has a singleton, and whether he has a void, and if he has neither, showing whether he has good controls. Responder bids one of four steps, the first step being the bid next above a single jump raise (3♣ over 1♥, 3NT over 1♠):

1st step	void (unidentified)
2nd step	singleton (unidentified)
3rd step	two or three aces, denies a singleton or void
4th step	fewer than two aces, denies a singleton or void

After responder has shown a singleton or void, opener makes the cheapest bid to ask where responder's shortness lies; after the response, opener will usually be able to use Blackwood to ask about aces.

For alternative methods see CONGLOMERATE MAJOR RAISES, UNBALANCED SWISS RAISE, VALUE SWISS RAISES.

SUPERSTITIONS. Common as regards cards ever since games were first played. Some persons have the reputation of being good or bad cardholders. Substance is lent to such superstitions by the fact that a large number of instances is required to demonstrate the so-called law of averages. When tossing coins, it may require 1000 tosses to arrive at a point where there exists even a rough parity in the number of head and tail tosses. It is similar with cards. If one collates records on a series of several hundred hands held, one will find that the point-count holdings over the course will average about 10 points.

There are numerous superstitions occurring at or applying to bridge games, such as shuffling the cards in a certain way, or positioning the deck after the cut, or using a certain pencil for scoring but for no other purpose or getting up from one's seat and walking around one's chair or around the entire table "for luck" after a bad hand or a bad run of cards. A common superstition involves choices of seats or decks of cards after the cut for partners. Other players believe their luck will desert them if attention is drawn to it by calling them "lucky" or "the big winner," and so on, ad infinitum.

SUPPORT. Verb: to raise. Noun: (1) a raise; (2) whatever strength partner has in support of one's bid. See TRUMP SUPPORT.

SUPPORT DOUBLE. A conventional double used by the opening bidder at his second turn, after right-hand opponent overcalls, to show three cards in responder's suit.

WEST	NORTH	EAST	SOUTH
			1♦
Pass	1♥	1♠	?

South doubles on any of these hands:

♠ A 9	♠ 6 4	♠ 10 7 5 3
♥ A 4 2	♥ A Q 5	♥ A K Q
♦ K J 10 6 4	♦ A K J 5 3 2	♦ A K 5 4 2
♣ 7 5 3	♣ A J	♣ 4

Hence, a raise to 2♥ promises four-card support, and any other action denies three-card support.

Support doubles gain in many instances; the opening side can compete more freely, and competitive decisions are easier when responder knows how many trumps are present. The support double loses when opener really wants to double for penalties.

A support redouble operates similarly:

WEST	NORTH	EAST	SOUTH
			1♣
Pass	1♠	Dbl	Redbl

South shows exactly three-card spade support.

SUPPRESSING THE BID ACE. Ace-asking conventions such as BLACKWOOD are occasionally used when the responding hand is already known to have a particular ace. The holder may have made a cuebid or shown a solid suit. In such cases the partnership should agree whether the ace already identified should be shown when responding to the conventional bid. Similar questions arise when the partnership has used a VOID-SHOWING BID. It is preferable to agree that the ace of a suit in which partner is known to be void should not be shown. Lacking any agreement, however, the previous bidding should be disregarded and the number of aces shown in the normal way.

SURE TRICK. A trick that a player must win. For example: the ace of trumps, the guarded king of trumps when it is behind the ace, the ace of a suit you intend to lead against notrump. The lead of an ace against a suit contract, even though it be from a short suit not mentioned in the bidding, is not necessarily a sure trick, as declarer or dummy may be void. See HONOR TRICK, QUICK TRICK. The term is also used by George Coffin to describe single-dummy problems in which correct play will ensure the making of a specific number of tricks.

SURINAM BRIDGE LEAGUE (DE SURINAAMSE BRIDGEBOND)
Secretary 1992:
  Ur. P. Sonneveld
  PO Box 635
  Paramaribo,
  Surinam.
  Tel: 507 81418
  Fax: 597 81431

SURPLUS CARDS. A card in excess of 13 in a bridge hand before the play begins, or a card in excess of the number of tricks remaining to be played after play has commenced. See LAWS (Laws 12, 67), LAWS OF DUPLICATE (Laws 13, 67). See MISSING CARD.

SURROUND, SURROUNDING DEFENSE. See SANDWICH DEFENSE.

SUSPENSION. See DISCIPLINARY CODE; EXCLUSION.

SWEDISH BRIDGE LEAGUE (Sveriges Bridgeforbund). Founded in 1933, in 1993 it had about 15,200 members. Sweden won World Women's Teams 1968, European Teams 1939, 1952, 1977, 1987, European Women's Teams 1962, 1967. Sweden hosted: Bermuda Bowl 1970, 1983; World Pairs Olympiad 1970; European Championships 1936, 1956. National open team championships attract 400 teams, and national open pairs attract 4,500 pairs.
President 1993:
  Bo Appelqvist
Secretary, Ingvar Rune
  Gustavslundsv. 168
  161 36 Bromma
  Sweden.
  Tel: 46 8 704 3920
  Fax: 46 8 704 3970

SWIFT, Jonathan (1667-1745), author of Gulliver's Travels. His comment on luck: "I must complain the cards are ill-shuffled til I have a good hand."

SWINDLE, SWINDLING. Legitimate methods of attempting to get better than deserved results are discussed under DECEPTIVE PLAY, FALSECARDING, LEAD-INHIBITING BID, and PSYCHIC BIDDING. Also see CHEATING and CHEATING ACCUSATIONS.

SWINE (Sebesfi-Woods-1-Notrump-Escape). Developed in Australia. If 1NT is doubled, pass forces opener to redouble. Then responder may pass for penalties or bid the cheaper of touching suits. With a weak single-suited hand responder redoubles, requiring a 2♣ bid. A direct 2♣ shows clubs and hearts, 2♦ shows diamonds and spades. Direct 2♥ and 2♠ has moderate values; direct 2NT is strong and unbalanced.

SWING. The difference between the actual score made on a deal and "what might have been" were the bidding, play, or defense different. Thus if poor dummy play by declarer results in down one on a vulnerable 6♠ contract, the swing is said to be 1,530 points. The term is frequently used in team matches to name the actual gain or loss on a single hand. The term may be in total points or in imps. If North-South of a team make 3♠ for 140 points and their teammates defeat 4♠ by 50 points, the swing is 190 points or 5 IMPs. See SWING HAND.

SWING HAND. A term used to denote a hand on which a successful or unsuccessful result by a partnership produces a very decisive change in overall results of a rubber or a match. Consider this hand from a recent European championship:

Vul: N-S   ♠ Q 5 3
Dlr: South   ♥ A Q J
           ♦ K
           ♣ A Q J 9 4 3

♠ A 7 4   ♠ K 10 9
♥ 10 8 5 2   ♥ K 9 7 6 4 3
♦ 10 8 7 3   ♦ 4
♣ 6 5   ♣ 10 8 2

           ♠ J 8 6 2
           ♥ —
           ♦ A Q J 9 6 5 2
           ♣ K 7

WEST	NORTH	EAST	SOUTH
			1♦
Pass	3♣	3♥	4♦
4♥	4NT	6♥	Pass
Pass	6NT	Pass	7♦
Dbl	7NT	Dbl	Pass
Pass	Redbl	All Pass	

On the bidding above, East led a diamond, and North-South were plus 2,930 points. In the other room, North-South reached a contract of 6♣, down one, for a score of -100, a swing of more than 3,000 points on a single hand. See PENALTY.

SWISH. A colloquialism indicating that a bid is followed by three passes. A similar term is Float.

SWISS BRIDGE FEDERATION (Fédération Suisse de Bridge). The Federation was founded in Geneva in 1950, and by 1993 had 3,168 members in 66 affiliated clubs. The Federation hosted two European Championships, in

Montreux in 1954 and in Lausanne in 1979, and one World Championship, the Pairs Olympiad in Geneva in 1990.

Officers 1992:

President: Marcello Bardola
Secretary: Yves-Carol Mucha
Rue Bellefontaine 8
1003 Lausanne Switzerland.
Tel. 41 21 209095
Fax 41 21 209295

SWISS CONVENTION. A response of four in a minor suit to an opening of one in a major suit shows a standard forcing raise to the three-level. This is a strength-show-ing substitute used by players employing limit jump raises. (3NT is sometimes used for the same purpose, for example in KAPLAN-SHEINWOLD) . The usual high-card strength would be 13-15.

♠ A Q x x
♥ K J x x
♦ A x x
♣ x x

Over 1♥ or 1♠, the response is 4♣ or 4♦ to show a hand too strong in high cards to raise directly to game. It also suggests a relatively balanced hand because re-sponder would bid a side suit and raise to game on the second round with a two-suiter. The distinction between 4♣ and 4♦ is a matter of partnership agreement, but the trend is toward using 4♣ as the more forward-going bid. When 4♣ and 4♦ are the only forcing raises employed, one of the following treatments is usual:

(1) Trump quality: 4♣ shows (and 4♦ denies) four trumps headed by at least two of the top three honors, or five or more trumps headed by at least the ace or king.

(2) Controls: 4♣ shows (and 4♦ denies) three aces, or two aces and the king of trumps.

(3) Controls or Trumps: 4♣ emphasizes good controls, and 4♦ emphasizes strong trumps. Several methods have been developed which combine the jumps to four of a minor with other jump responses in order to allow for a finer distinction among types of strong raises. See CON-GLOMERATE MAJOR RAISES, FRUIT-MACHINE SWISS, SINGLETON SWISS, SUPER SWISS, UN-BALANCED SWISS RAISE, VALUE SWISS RAISES.

For other conventional uses of four of a minor in re-sponse to one of a major, see ASKING BID, SPLINTER BID and VOID-SHOWING BID.

SWISS MOVEMENT. A partial round-robin movement similar to the method used for many years in major chess tournaments when insufficient time is available for a com-plete round-robin.

The basic feature of a Swiss movement is that after the first round, winning teams (or pairs) are pitted against each other for the second round, and losers face each other. For each succeeding round, new pairings are made on the basis of the records of the matched teams (or pairs) with the added proviso that no two teams (or pairs) may play a second match against each other. Scoring is usu-ally by international matchpoints, although BOARD-A-MATCH and HYBRID SCORING are feasible.

Team events: Although many attempts at adapting the Swiss method to team contests have been made in the past, it was not until 1967 when John Hamilton and Marc Low developed the present method, which was first tried and proved successful at a Cincinnati Sectional, that Swiss

team contests became popular. The idea caught on quickly throughout the ACBL and resulted in a spectacular in-crease in team attendance at sectional and regional tour-naments, more than doubling the size of the previous board-a-match team events in many cases. The first North American Swiss team was held at the 1970 Spring North American Championships in Portland OR.

The team event is divided into a series of short, IMP-scored matches. Pairings for the first round are random.Pairings for each succeeding round are deter-mined by the won-loss or the Victory Point records of the teams. Since sufficient matches must be scheduled to produce a significant won-loss record, a minimum of two sessions of play usually is required. When possible, more matches are scheduled than needed to reduce the field to one undefeated team so that a team is not necessarily eliminated from a chance to win the event by a single loss.

An odd number of entries creates difficulties, but can be handled in various ways. The most common are short round-robins, lasting as long as one regular match, in which each winning team is given credit for half a match. The other common method is a three-team round-robin playing the full number of boards, so that a round lasts as long as two full matches. In either case, there is no com-parison of scores until the round-robin is completed.

An alternate method of scoring Swiss Teams is to con-vert IMP results into Victory Points. Pairings are then based on Victory Point totals, not wins and losses. The team with the most Victory Points is declared the winner.

Pair events: The ACBL introduced Swiss pair contests in 1970. As in the team event, the pairs play a series of short matches against each other, with each board IMPed against a computed average for the field. Pairings may be based on wins and losses or on VICTORY POINTS. Some of the difficulties encountered are:

(1) the boards must be duplicated for each round and

(2) since pair events attract larger fields than team con-tests, it may be difficult to determine an overall winner in two sessions.

SWISS PAIRS. Similar to Swiss Teams. After each short match pairs face those with similar scores.

SWISS POINTS. A method of breaking ties for prize purposes in Swiss Team events. The scores of all the teams that played against each team involved in the tie are added together. The team whose opponents' total is higher is declared the winner for prize purposes. Occasionally there is a refinement of this method — only those matches which take place in the second half of the contest are counted in totaling the Swiss Points.

SWISS TEAMS, NORTH AMERICAN CHAM-PIONSHIP. See Appendix I.

SWITCH. See SHIFT and ARROW SWITCH.

SWORDS. One of the suits in early PLAYING CARDS. Still used in the trappola deck (see SUIT).

SYMMETRIC RELAY. A modern relay system devel-oped by a group of New Zealand players. It was first de-scribed by Roy Kerr and first played successfully in in-ternational championships by Paul Marston and Malcolm Sims. A major difference between Symmetric and the

ULTIMATE CLUB is that almost all Symmetric responses to the strong club opening, other than the 1♦ negative, are natural. (This makes the system somewhat more acceptable to tournament committees and directors.) The responder describes his distribution, with sequences which usually end at the three-level. The opener can then relay to find the number of controls and the location of high cards. If the response is a negative 1♦ a relay of 1♥ asks responder to use the normal descriptive sequences but two steps higher than they would otherwise be. The general structure is based on five-card major openings (as opposed to Ultimate, which uses four-card majors.) In response to 1♦, 1♥ and 1♠, 1NT is used as a strong relay.

Here are some of the ways in which distribution is described:

(i) With two suits, bid the cheaper first regardless of length. 1♥ and then 1NT shows both majors.

(ii) After two suits are shown, 2♥ shows exactly four cards in the higher suit, longer in the lower; 2♠ shows at least 5-5. After one suit is shown, 2♥ shows a 4-card suit and longer diamonds. 2NT at any point shows shortage in the higher of the remaining suits, three clubs shows equal shortage.

(iii) After one suit is shown, 2♠ shows shortage in the high remainder suit, and 2NT shortage in the middle suit. See DENIAL CUEBIDS, RELAY SYSTEMS.

SYMMETRY. See LAW OF SYMMETRY.

SYNDICATED ARTICLES. See BRIDGE COLUMNS.

SYSTEM FIX. A bad result caused by one's own bidding methods.

SYSTEM ON (or system off). An agreement to apply (or not to apply) certain artificial methods in slightly changed circumstances. The commonest example occurs after a 1NT overcall. The partnership may agree to respond exactly as if the opening bid had been 1NT.

SYSTEMS. See BIDDING SYSTEMS.

T

TAB. See ROMEX SYSTEM.

TABLE. Four players, two pairs, or one team, in duplicate play, for individual, pair, and team movements suitable to a particular number of tables. See TWO, THREE, FOUR, etc., to FIFTEEN TABLES. The table most frequently used for bridge is a folding square table, about 30 inches on a side, and from 26 to 27 inches in height. The accoutrements should include two scorepads, two decks of bridge cards, two sharp pencils, ashtrays, coasters and four chairs.

Other meanings are:

(1) The dummy. "The lead is on the table."

(2) To face one's cards, either as dummy or in making a claim.

TABLE CARD. See TABLE GUIDE CARD.

TABLE FEEL. See TABLE PRESENCE.

TABLE GUIDE CARD. A large card placed under the boards in the center of a table, containing instructions for the players. See GUIDE CARD.

TABLE MANNERS. Bridge is a social game, and good manners at the bridge table are as necessary for full enjoyment of the game as in any other form of sociability. See ETIQUETTE, PROPRIETIES.

TABLE NUMBERS. Rectangular, large cards in the center of the table, which give the number of the table in the section. Sections are distinguished by the color of the table card.

TABLE PRESENCE. One of the features that make a good bridge player into an expert is the undefinable something that is referred to as table presence. It is a combination of INSTINCT; the drawing of correct inferences from any departure from RHYTHM by the opponents; the exercise of DISCIPLINE in bidding; the ability to coax maximum performance from partner, and the ability to make the opponents feel that they are facing a player of a higher order. Also called TABLE FEEL.

TABLE SPACING. The arrangement of tables for a duplicate tournament. For comfortable play tables should be spaced with nine-foot centers. When the available space does not permit the ideal arrangement, reduction to eight feet between centers is practicable. The minimum spacing permitting any degree of comfort is a trifle over seven feet between centers in a row. When the rows cannot be spaced at least eight feet apart, tables can be staggered in adjoining rows. If possible, the setup of tables within the section should put the last table in the section near the first so that boards and players have a minimum of movement. This can be done with a hairpin arrangement, utilizing two rows of seven, eight or nine tables.

TABLES, MATHEMATICAL. See MATHEMATICAL TABLES.

TACTICS. Various maneuvers in the play of the hand, bidding nuances and choices of action, taking into consideration the methods of scoring, quality of the competition and conditions of contests.

TAHITI. See POLYNESIA.

TAIWAN CONTRACT BRIDGE LEAGUE (National Contract Bridge League of Republic of China; designated by WBF for international purposes as Chinese Taipei). Founded in 1950 in Taipei, Taiwan. and by 1992 had a membership of about 3000. Taiwan hosted the 1971 Bermuda Bowl in Taipei, and has also hosted three Far East Championships. Its teams have twice finished second in the Bermuda Bowl, the best performance by any Far East country, and have won eight Far East Open Team titles and two Far East Women's Team titles. Its magazine, *Chinese Bridge* has been published for more than 30 years.

Officers 1992:

Chairman: Sam S.F.Tung

Executive Secretary: S.Y.Chang

P.O. Box 24-20 Taipei, Taiwan R.O.C.

Tel: (02) 772 4510.

TAKEOUT. A bid at a denomination other than one previously named by partner, as distinguished from a raise. See JUMP SHIFT and RESPONSE.

TAKEOUT DOUBLE. The use of a low-level double in certain circumstances as a request to partner to bid an unbid suit. This is a "natural" convention, because a penalty double of an opening suit bid of one can hardly exist; a player with great strength in the opponent's suit prefers to lie in wait (see TRAP PASS). The idea of doubling for a takeout appears to have been devised independently by Major Charles Patton in New York and Bryant McCampbell in St. Louis in 1912-13 and probably by others. For the problems involved in distinguishing a takeout double from a penalty double, see DOUBLE. By far the most common takeout double occurs when it immediately follows an opening bid of one in a suit. The doubler normally indicates a hand worth an opening bid with at least three-card support for all unbid suits. However, the respective vulnerability and the rank of the opener's suit may play a part in the decision.

> ♠ A Q x x
> ♥ x
> ♦ K x x
> ♣ J 10 x x x

At favorable vulnerability, a double of 1♥ can be ventured. If the doubler's partner can fit spades, a cheap save in 4♠ over 4♥ is likely to materialize. There would be less reason to double if the opener's suit were a minor, or if the doubler held only three spades. A player who doubles a major-suit opening tends to hold four cards in the unbid major, and this may be a factor in deciding to double. The high-card strength required for the double increases: (a) as the distribution becomes less suitable; (b) if the doubler is vulnerable; (c) if the opener's suit is spades, which will force a response at the two-level.

The following would be minimum vulnerable doubles of 1♠:

♠ x	♠ x x	♠ x x x
♥ A Q x x	♥ A J x x	♥ A Q x
♦ K J x x	♦ K Q x x	♦ A J x x
♣ K x x x	♣ K J x	♣ K J x

A non-vulnerable double would be justified in each case if a jack were removed.

The doubler should seldom ignore the requirement of at least three cards in each unbid suit unless his hand contains at least 17 high-card points.

> ♠ 7 5
> ♥ A Q 10 6 4
> ♦ A K 6
> ♣ K Q 4

Over 1♣, 1♦ or 1♠, a double followed by a minimum bid in hearts is appropriate; the hand is too strong for a simple heart overcall.

A takeout double is made with strong hands unsuitable for a 1NT overcall or a strength-showing suit overcall. The maximum for a double was once a hand just short of the requirements for a direct cuebid. However, many pairs have abandoned the direct cuebid as a strength-showing action because opportunities were rare; these pairs use conventional cuebids such as MICHAELS, in which case a takeout double has no upper limit. Most players would

double a 1♠ opening, planning to cuebid next, with:

> ♠ A 5
> ♥ A K Q 9 6 2
> ♦ 7
> ♣ A Q J 4

Subsequent bidding.

For action by the opener's partner, see RESPONSES OVER OPPONENT'S TAKEOUT DOUBLE. The following summarizes possible actions by the doubler's partner if the bidding starts:

    1♦   Dbl   Pass   ?

(1) *Minimum suit response* (1♥ or 1♠ or 2♣). A forced response which may have no high-card points. The normal maximum is 8 points, but see (3) following. Responder prefers a major suit to a minor, so 2♣ is more likely to be five cards than four. 1♥ is often bid with a three-card suit because there is no alternative: if responder's only suit is diamonds he has to invent an economical bid. Even 1♠ might be a three-card suit, with 3-2-5-3 distribution for example. In theory, 2♣ might be a 3-card suit with 2-2-6-3 distribution, but in that case a penalty pass would normally be the lesser evil.

The doubler passes these responses automatically if he has a minimum or near-minimum double. Further action shows that game is still possible in the face of responder's announced weakness. A raise of responder's suit or a bid in a new suit should show at least 17 points in high cards. A minimum rebid in notrump is very constructive, suggesting a hand too strong to overcall 1NT (i.e., 19-20 points). In one case responder may make an uneconomical response:

> ♠ A x x x
> ♥ K x x x
> ♦ x x x
> ♣ x x

1♠ is a better response than 1♥, as responder can then continue readily to 2♥ if, as is likely, the opponents contest with 2♣ or 2♦.

(2) *1NT response.* Indicates a relatively balanced hand with moderate strength and a stopper in opener's suit. The exact strength is a matter of style, and expert opinions vary. The conservative view is to use the bid for hands with 8-10 or perhaps 11 points, but this sets a problem when responder has a hand such as:

> ♠ K 9 4
> ♥ J 7 3
> ♦ Q 10 6 3
> ♣ 8 5 3

Many authorities recommend a range of 6-9. (Another factor is the rank of opening bidder's suit. If the opening was 1♣, responder has more options; hence, a 1NT response is more likely to show fair values; if the opening was 1♠, 1NT may be responder's indicated action with 6 points.)

(3) *Jump shift* (2♥, 2♠ or 3♣). Encouraging but not forcing. The high-card strength is likely to be 9-11, but might be eight with a five-card suit. (Playing this as forcing is an obsolete idea.) The jump in a major suit is often a four-card suit: in a minor at least five cards are desirable.

(4) *Cuebid* (2♦). Shows any hand which can guarantee game but cannot be sure of the final resting place. The bid is totally unrelated to the opener's suit. Some players use the cuebid slightly more freely:

♠ A Q x x
♥ K J x x
♦ J x x
♣ x x

Rather than make a nonforcing jump in one of the major suits, and perhaps pick the wrong suit, a possible treatment is to cuebid 2♦, intending to raise either major to the three-level. The doubler then passes with a minimum, because the responder would have bid game himself if he could.

(5) *2NT response*. Shows 11-12 points and at least a single stopper in the opener's suit. The strength will depend slightly on the range adopted for the 1NT response, in (3) preceding. If that is 6-9 the 2NT bid may be made with 10; if 1NT is 8-11, 2NT is likely to be 12.

(6) *3NT response*. Usually a double stopper in the opener's suit and 13-16 points. Alternatively, responder may have a single stopper and a long minor suit which he expects to run with the help of doubler's expected fit. With more than 16 points, responder may suspect that the opener or the doubler has psyched, and proceed more slowly with a cuebid.

(7) *Higher suit responses*. (3♥, 3♠, 4♣, 4♥, 4♠, 5♣). Natural limited bids based on a long suit (usually six cards or longer). Responder expects to make his contract if doubler has a minimum.

(8) *Pass*. Great length and strength in diamonds (see PENALTY PASS).

After action by opener's partner.

Action by third hand relieves the doubler's partner of his obligation to bid, but he should still make a "free" response if he has moderate values and can do so at a convenient level.

(9) *After a redouble*. A pass denies any opinion about a possible trump suit. (The idea that responder should ignore the redouble and therefore pass for penalty is virtually obsolete. But a few experts play that a pass after a minor-suit opening shows at least five cards in opener's suit. 1♣ or 1♦ redoubled may be the least evil for the doubling side, which may be in trouble otherwise.) Since responder is likely to have little strength — probably fewer than six points — doubler should not construe a suit bid as strength-showing. Responder should usually show a four-card suit if he can do so at the one level, and a five-card suit at the two level. Responder should always bid the cheapest suit if he can, for fear that doubler may run to a suit he cannot support. A jump response is weak and preemptive.

(10) *After a change of suit by opener's partner*. If responder can bid a suit of his own at the one-level, he should usually do so with five points, and make the normal encouraging jump with nine. Slightly more is needed to bid at the two-level but the free two-level response (1♦-Dbl-2♣-2♠) should be made more freely than the jump shift when third hand has passed.

(11) *After a raise by opener's partner*. The opener's partner is trying to shut out the doubler's partner, who must often strain his resources in order to avoid being shut out. For a treatment of hands which do not offer an obvious bid, see RESPONSIVE DOUBLE.

Other takeout doubles.

These can usually be identified by the general rule that a double of a suit bid below game is for a takeout when partner has not bid. The most important cases are as follows:

(12) *The balancing double*. See BALANCING.

(13) In standard practice, *the double of two suits* (1♣-Pass-1♥-Dbl) may range from a relatively weak distributional two-suiter to a strong, relatively balanced hand. However, when both opponents are bidding and partner is silent, there are obvious dangers in entering the auction. Many tournament players therefore dispense with a natural 1NT overcall in this position (or 2NT if the bidding is at the two-level) and treat a notrump bid as UNUSUAL. This takes care of the distributional two-suited hands, and the double can be reserved for relatively balanced hands, strong in high cards.

(14) *The double of a 1NT response* (1♥-Pass-1NT-Dbl). This is one of the few situations in which a double of a notrump bid is for takeout, but the takeout aspect is not very pronounced; partner will pass more often than he will pass any other takeout double. The double may have to be made with a strong balanced hand which would have overcalled 1NT if opportunity had offered.

(15) *The double of a raise* (1♥-Pass-2♥-Dbl). Vulnerability and the rank of opener's suit are important considerations here. At favorable vulnerability a double of 2♥ may be made lightly with suitable distribution because a save in 4♠ seems possible. A double of 2♠ commits the doubler's side to the three-level, and does not offer such good prospects of a save, so solid values are needed by the doubler. The double of a minor-suit raise emphasizes the major suits, and may be made freely; the probability that the doubling side has a fit is increased by the opening side's established fit.

(16) *The double of a suit response to a 1NT opening* (1 NT-Pass-2♥-Dbl). Here again vulnerability and the rank of the suit are important factors. If the suit is red, offering the possibility of play at the two-level, a nonvulnerable player may double with as little as 10 points and favorable distribution. He can rely on strength in his partner's hand because the opener's side has announced its intention of stopping at the two-level.

(17) *Doubles of weak two-bids and weak three-bids can be regarded as takeout*. See DEFENSE TO OPENING THREE-BIDS.

(18) When three suits have been bid around the table, a double by fourth-hand needs agreement:

WEST	NORTH	EAST	SOUTH
1 ♣	1 ♥	1 ♠	Dbl

It makes no sense for this to be penalty, as it would be on general principles since partner has bid. A common agreement is for it be takeout for the fourth suit. In this case the fourth player would have five diamonds and probably some tolerance for hearts. See SNAPDRAGON.

TALLEYRAND-PERIGORD, Charles Maurice de (1754-1838), French statesman and Napoleon's Foreign Minister. When a young man admitted that he did not play whist he was distressed: "Young man! You do not play whist? What a sad old age you reserve for yourself."

TALLIES. Prepared cards for the recording of results at the end of each round (four deals) in PROGRESSIVE or PARTY BRIDGE. These can be purchased at most gift and stationery stores.

TANK. A colloquialism in the phrase "go into the tank" meaning to fall into a protracted HUDDLE.

TANZANIA BRIDGE ASSOCIATION. Had 30 members in 1993.

Officers 1993:
Chairman: S. Soochak
Hon. Secretary: S.N.Pendharkar
PO Box 5104
Dar-es-Salaam
Tanzania.
Fax: 255 51 38760
Fax: 255 51 38293

TAP. (1) A colloquialism for shortening a hand in trumps by forcing it to ruff. See FORCE. (2) The Teacher Accreditation Program used by the Education Depatment of the ACBL.

TAP THE TABLE. (1) Give an informal ALERT. (2) Make an informal PASS. Both practices are undesirable, since they can be confused with each other and create problems.

TARDINESS. Late arrival at rubber bridge games curtails the length of time available for play and is inconsiderate of the host or hostess. At duplicate tournaments far more people may be inconvenienced when the start of a second session is delayed while the director seeks substitutes for no-shows. Purchase of an entry into an event obligates the players to abide by the conditions of play, including reporting on time for all following sessions of the same event. See TIME LIMIT ON RIGHT TO PLAY.

TAROT. The pack of 22 numbered cards without suit signs that were part of the first pack known to be used in Europe; or a pack containing these 22 atouts (atutti, trumps) plus 56 other cards divided into four suits, each with ten SPOT CARDS and four COURT CARDS. Not all packs are alike, but the basic cards were:

0   The fool (Il Pazzo or Il Matto), like a jester (most packs omit the numeral)
1   The juggler (Bagatto), wand or cup in hand, items of legerdermain on the table in front of him
2   The papess (La Papessa), double crowned, seated, book in hand
3   The empress (L'Imperatrice), singly crowned, scepter and shield
4   The emperor (L'Imperator), perhaps Charlemagne, scepter in hand
5   The Pope (Il Papa), crowned, carrying staff, seated before two columns
6   Love (Amore), Cupid aiming a double arrow at two of three persons
7   The chariot (La Carrozza), shows one driver and two horses
8   Justice (La Giustizia), a woman, sword in one hand, scales in other
9   The hermit (L'Eremita), an old man, lantern in right hand
10 Wheel of fortune (La Ruota della Fortuna), a crowned figure with sword above a wheel with one figure going up and another down
11 Force (La Forza), either a man opening the jaws of a lion, or a woman breaking a pillar
12 The hanged man (Il Penduto), suspended upside down by one foot
13 Untitled, picturing Death, a skeleton wielding a scythe over fragments of people
14 Temperance (La Temperanza), an angel pouring water from one jug into another
15 The devil (Il Diavolo), winged, with pitchfork and forked tail, threatening one or more figures
16 The tower (La Torre) being struck by lightning as two men fall
17 The star (La Stella), a nude woman pouring water from two jugs into a stream
18 The moon (La Luna), a profile face, riding over rooftops, with dogs baying below
19 The sun (Il Sole), full-face, shining on two boys in breech-cloths
20 The angel (L'Angelo), blowing a trumpet over people rising from the grave
21 The world (Il Mondo), a female in a wreath; an angel, a winged beast, a cow, and a lion are in each corner

The first tarot cards appeared in Italy, probably in the fourteenth century, and the original suits were cups, coins, swords and cudgels: the court cards king, queen, cavalier and knave.

The modern authority on Tarot is Michael Dummett of Oxford, England.

TARTAN TWO-BIDS. Devised by Hugh Kelsey and Tom Culbertson. 2♥ and 2♠ are multi openings, with clarification after a relay response. After a 2♥ opening and 2♠ relay: 2NT is 21-22 balanced; 3♣ is hearts and clubs, 3♥ is hearts and diamonds, 5-5 distribution with 6-10; 3H and higher are Acol two-bids with hearts. After a 2♠ opening and a 2NT relay, 3♠ and higher shows an Acol Two, lower bids show the suits bid, 5-5 with 6-10. 2♦ may be ROMAN TWO DIAMONDS, a strong three-suiter.

TAXES ON PLAYING CARDS. The first tax on playing cards in the United States was levied in 1862 to raise money for the War Between the States. The tax varied from 1 to 15 cents (or 15% of the cost, whichever was greater), until 1866 when it became 6 cents per pack. This tax was repealed in 1883 and not reinstated until the depression of Cleveland's second administration, when a 2-cents-a-pack tax was imposed under the Act of August 27,1894. Since that time it has been retained by the Federal Government as a constant source of revenue. The levy remained constant until the necessity of increased revenue following World War I caused an increase in 1920 to 8 cents a pack, increased to 10 cents in 1925, and to 13 cents in 1961. Revenues exceeded $5 million dollars in 1929, and more than $8 million in 1962. This tax was lifted on July 1, 1965. The first tax levied on playing cards, so far as the records show, was imposed in England in the reign of James I (1615).

TEACHING IN BRIDGE. The first teacher of games in the bridge family was also one of the most successful. The ladies of good family to whom EDMUND HOYLE taught whist were charged at the rate of one guinea an hour, equivalent to at least $50 an hour in modern terms. His celebrated *Short Treatise*, published in 1743, which became a best-seller for more than a century, was intended as a textbook for his students.

The first professional teacher of whist in America was Miss Kate Wheelock, who began teaching in Milwaukee in 1886. She achieved immediate success, touring the continent to lecture in all the principal cities. The whistograph which she invented for use in her classes was the forerunner of the VUGRAPH used by the ACBL in modern times. She was the first woman to be made an associate member of the American Whist League, and Cavendish called her, "The Whist Queen."

Whist teaching was a highly suitable occupation for ladies of some status and education who needed to supplement their incomes, and many others followed Miss Wheelock's example.

The first prominent male teacher was Charles Stuart Street of New York City, who began in 1890. The most successful teacher of BRIDGE WHIST, and of AUCTION BRIDGE up to the time of his death, was undoubtedly Joseph B. Elwell. Among his most prominent successors was Josephine Culbertson.

In the Twenties Milton Work and Wilbur Whitehead organized conventions for teachers, issuing certificates to those who had completed courses. A similar procedure was followed later by Ely Culbertson, and later still by Charles Goren, who was one of the highest-paid teachers of all time before he decided to concentrate on writing. The AMERICAN BRIDGE TEACHERS ASSOCIATION (ABTA), founded in 1957, holds an annual convention immediately preceding the ACBL's Summer NABC (North American Bridge Championships).

Many persons turned to bridge teaching as a temporary occupation during the Depression years, and at its peak the membership of the Culbertson National Studios totaled some 6,000. The number of bridge teachers dwindled markedly when prosperity returned, but increased again in the postwar years, particularly after Goren's point-count methods gained general currency.

In the Sixties and Seventies, the number of teachers continued to grow. Their ranks included many players of the highest quality. These teachers popularized the playing lesson for students with tournament ambitions. ABTA activities for bridge teachers flourished and certification by this organization was thought by many to be a prerequisite for professional bridge teachers.

In the late Eighties, ACBL contracted with Audrey Grant to write a series of beginning bridge textbooks and teacher manuals. Through a program known as the TAP, new bridge teachers were recruited and taught to teach bridge effectively using the ACBL materials. These teachers became known as ACCREDITED TEACHERS and numbered more than 3,000 by the mid-Nineties. See also ACBL TEACHING SERIES, AUTOBRIDGE, LESSON HANDS and E-Z DEAL CARDS.

In Europe, as in the United States, major steps have been taken to put major teaching programs to work. According to José Damiani, president of the European Bridge Federation, the French are probably leading the way at present with 500 bridge schools with 1000 instructors who had already trained 15,000 students as of the start of 1994. Damiani wrote as follows in the *European Bridge League Review*: "To make a success of such a challenge, a definite consistency between the minibridge taught to students and a complete teaching system of training for instructors was needed. Rigorous methods were used to obtain the magnificent results achieved by the French Bridge Federation."

In the Netherlands, a similar approach has produced excellent results. Two of the new world champions, Enri Leufkens and Barry Westra, are products of the Netherlands bridge schools.

Bridge leaders in Poland succeeded in setting up a school championship with more than 3000 finalists, contributing to the progress the EBL is making in its goal of organizing a Youth championship for under-20s in the near future.

Damiani and World Bridge Federation President Bobby Wolff suggested to Chinese leaders on a visit there that it might be worthwhile to begin teaching bridge in schools. The Chinese leaders thought this was an excellent idea and promised that they would begin such a plan as soon as possible.

Many other countries have outstanding teaching programs, and bridge is thriving in those countries — New Zealand, Norway, Denmark, Italy, Iceland and Australia to name a few.

TEAM. Four, five or six players competing as a unit in bridge tournaments. In mixed team events, no two members of the same sex are permitted to play as partners.

TEAM-OF-EIGHT MATCH. A four-table team contest in which each team has eight active players.

TEAM-OF-FOUR EVENTS. Contests between teams of four, five or six players. Such events are a standard part of duplicate tournaments at the sectional level or higher. At the sectional level most team events are SWISS TEAMS using the Swiss movement with imp — and sometimes Victory Point — scoring.

At the regional and North American levels, KNOCKOUT TEAMS have become more and more popular as a result of several changes — flighting, random pairings, bracketed sections, for example. Most regionals now feature at least one — sometimes more — morning Knockout events. At North American Championships there usually are two morning Knockouts as well as Knockouts for specified groups throughout the tournament (for Seniors, 0-2000, 0-750, 0-300, etc.) In addition NABCs start with a Charity Knockout that gets under way the night before the start of the NABC and continues through the next three mornings.

BOARD-A-MATCH was the most popular form of scoring prior to the late 1960s. Frequently the field is divided into two or more flights, divided by masterpoint limits. At regional tournaments, team contests limited to men, women, or mixed partnerships are frequently held in addition to open team events. Experienced duplicate bridge players generally consider that team-of-four competition is the most challenging and demanding. Most major international matches are team-of-four competitions. Specific conditions of contest vary from tournament to tournament as to type of scoring, number of members on a team (although only four play at any one time), and entry requirements. Other types of team-of-four contests have increased in popularity, but are not generally suitable for tournament play at the sectional level: (1) KNOCKOUT; (2) DOUBLE ELIMINATION; (3) ROUND-ROBIN. See also HYBRID SCORING, TOTAL POINT SCORING.

TEAM-OF-FOUR MOVEMENTS FOR BOARD-A-MATCH TEAMS. The basic movement for an odd number of teams is relatively simple. The movement is completed in one round less than the number of competing teams, and the progression is always the same. The traveling pairs (East-Wests) skip a table toward the lower number each round (5 to 3, 2 to the highest number, 1 to the next-to-highest number), and the boards move down one table. By omitting middle rounds two at a time, a large number of teams can be accommodated with an irregular movement of the boards at the midpoint. The traveling pairs return the boards they have just played to their home table, then go to their new table according to the director's instructions. If 12 rounds are being played, the pairs add 12 to their team number and go to that table. If 14 rounds are being played, the pairs add 14 to their team number. If the sum is greater than the highest-numbered table, subtract the number of teams in the event and move to the table number of the remainder.

For an even number of teams, special moves are necessary at a key point in the first half of the contest and at a second key point in the second half. To figure when the first special move takes place, divide the total number of teams by 4. If the result is fractional, the special move will take place during the round that matches the integer. If the number of tables was 14, dividing by 4 gives 3.5. Therefore the special move would be after the third round. However, if the quotient is an even number, then the special move occurs on the round before the integer. If the number of tables was 16, the quotient is 4, and therefore the special move would take place after the third round. On this round, the traveling pairs skip an extra table while the boards follow their natural progression. At the corresponding point in the second half, counting back from the end, there is another special move. If the special move in the first half occurred after the third round, then the special move in the second half would take place for the third round from the end. On this move, the traveling pairs skip two tables instead of one and the boards skip one table.

Other movements available for an even number of teams include the THURNER MOVEMENT, the INTERWOVEN HOWELL and the NEW ENGLAND RELAY.

TEAM-OF-FOUR MOVEMENTS FOR KNOCK-OUT TEAMS.

In general knockout matches are head-to-head affairs, with the winner advancing to the next round and the loser eliminated. However, special arrangements have to be made when the number of teams entered is not a power of 2.

Three-team matches have become quite common, with two outcomes possible. If the purpose is to eliminate one of the three, then the two with the better records advance. If each team wins one match, then the QUOTIENT method is used to determine which teams advance. If the purpose is to eliminate two of the three, then only the team with the best record advances. Once again the quotient method is used if each team wins one match. Three-way matches provide a good way to reduce the field to a power of 2. For instance, if the field should consist of 22 teams, the game could be set up with four head-to-head matches and six three-ways, with the top two advancing to the next round. The three-ways would provide 12 teams and the head-to-heads four — a total of 16, which is a power of 2.

Quotient works as follows: each team adds ALL of its imps for and against, then divides the imps won by the imps lost. This provides the quotient with which to compare with the other teams.

Frequently when large fields enter a knockout event, the teams are bracketed. The top 16 teams, usually determined by masterpoints, are placed in the first bracket, the next 16 in the second, etc.

Head-to-head matches usually are staged in halves. In a 28-deal match, boards 1-7 are given to one table and boards 8-14 to the other. When these boards are finished, the two tables exchange boards. After both tables finish 14 boards, the teams compare. Then they return to the tables to play boards 15-28 in the same fashion.

Three-way matches are somewhat more complicated. In a 28-board session, boards 1-7 are given to Table 1, boards 8-14 to Table 2 and boards 15-21 to Table 3. Upon completion of these boards, the East-West pairs bring the boards just played to their home table, then proceed to the table where they have not played. After 14 boards have been completed, the teams compare. They will have played seven boards against each of the other two teams. The same method is used for the second half, and at the end of the session each team will have 14-board match results against each of the other teams.

TEAM-OF-FOUR MOVEMENT FOR SWISS TEAMS.

Random pairings are made for the first round. After the first round pairings are made based on the present standings — in general, winners play winners and losers play losers with the proviso that no team plays another team more than once. If Victory Points are being used, pairings are based on the VP standings.

In some countries pairings are made two at a time to speed the movement. Each team has two random opponents for the first two rounds. Then when the matches are made after two rounds, each team is assigned matches for both the third and the fourth rounds.

TEAM OLYMPIAD. See WORLD TEAM OLYMPIAD. For results see Appendix V.

TEAM-OF-TWO PAIRS.

An event in which both of a team's two pairs sit in the same direction in two different sections. Both pairs of the opposing team sit in the opposite direction. Everyone plays a session of matchpoint duplicate — just like a pair game.

Of each team's two results on every board, only the better of the two is entered to determine the matchpoint score. Naturally, the score not used for your team is the "better" score for your opponent. This means it's possible to get a cold bottom on a board but still score a top because of your teammates' result on the same deal.

Strategy is necessary to maximize potential matchpoints. A team should not play or defend the same contract or make the same play at both tables. Here are some ways that teams use to maximize their results.

Bidding: Weak notrump at one table, strong at the other. Science at one table, natural at the other. Strong two-bids at one table, weak two-bids at the other. Sound opening bids at one table, open all 11-pointers at the other. Five-card major style at one table, four-card major style at the other.

Play: Agree in advance that, with a two-way guess for a queen, one pair always takes it one direction while the other takes it in the opposite direction. One pair should go all out for overtricks, the other should play safe for the contract. One pair for should play for even splits, the other for unusual distributions.

TEAM-OF-TWELVE (or more) MATCH. A team contest in which each team has 12 (or more) active players.

TEAM TRIALS. See INTERNATIONAL OPEN TEAM SELECTION. For results see Appendix III.

TEAMMATES. A term applied to the other members of a team of four (five or six). During the play of an event, the term is usually used to refer to the other pair, rather than including one's partner in the term.

TELEVISION. The importance of bridge players as an audience with high rating has been clearly demonstrated by television. Perhaps the first regular television show featuring bridge was by Robert Lee Johnson in Los Angeles. In a later program in Miami, William Seamon presented challenging pairs who played rubber bridge against the previous week's winners. Much the same format was developed nationally by Charles Goren in his nationally distributed, sponsored program, *Championship Bridge*.

The Goren TV program extended over a three-year period at the end of 1959. Alex Dreier, a well-known radio and TV commentator, acted as host and Charles Goren was the commentator. The program consisted of two pairs playing four hands. The winners were to receive $500. In actual practice, that money was split before the game.

KQED, Channel 9 San Francisco, in combination with KVIE, Channel 6 Sacramento, ran a TV bridge program designed by Ernest Rovere on Thursdays for 26 weeks. This was done in combination with the *San Francisco Chronicle*, which published a quiz based on the preceding night's program. Viewers were invited to mail their answers to the quiz show.

The first TV show sponsored by ACBL was the Mary McVey show out of Lexington KY. This show was only mildly successful.

However, the shows produced by Audrey Grant based on her beginning bridge books (*Club Series, Diamond Series, Heart Series*) have been highly successful. *The Bridge Class*, based on the *Club Series*, began airing on The Learning Channel on Jan. 1, 1991. The program was switched to public television in the fall of 1991. More than 175 PBS stations out of a total of 250 have aired the show.

The 26 shows produced by ACBL and WITF, known as *Play Bridge with Audrey Grant* and based on the *Diamond Series* and the *Heart Series*, were being shown on PBS in 1994. They were to be followed by 13 more shows, based on the *Spade Series*, scheduled for filming in late 1994.

Bridge on television also has proved popular in many other countries.

TEMPO. (1) The element of timing in card play, with special reference to the use of opportunities to make an attacking lead.

```
            ♠ 4 3
            ♥ 8 7 6 4
            ♦ K Q 3
            ♣ A 6 3 2
♠ Q 8 6 2                    ♠ 7 5
♥ A K Q 10                   ♥ 9 5 3 2
♦ 8 7                        ♦ 10 9 5
♣ J 9 7                      ♣ Q 10 5 4
            ♠ A K J 10 9
            ♥ J
            ♦ A J 6 4 2
            ♣ K 8
```

West leads two rounds of hearts against South's 4♠ contract. South should avoid losing a tempo by cashing the ♠A-K immediately and then starting his diamonds. The defenders can score the two remaining trumps but cannot damage the contract. If South loses a tempo by taking a spade finesse, the defense will continue hearts, reducing South's trumps to one fewer than West's. Should South allow this to happen, the defense will score a trick with a long heart and defeat the contract.

(2) The speed with which a bid or a play is made. Experienced players attempt to adjust the speed of their own

bidding and play so as always to use the same tempo and thus not convey information to partner or to the opponents. Players sometimes seek to force a rapid tempo of play, hoping to gain an advantage by encouraging an error by the opponents or by obtaining information from the opponents' pauses to think. The best defense against this somewhat unsporting tactic is to refuse to alter the tempo of one's own play, or even to slow the tempo down so as to protect one's partner. The term tempo, however, does not stretch to include deliberate hesitation when in fact a player has no problem.

TEMPORIZING BID. See WAITING BID.

TEN or TEN-SPOT. The fifth ranking card in each suit; at trump it is the lowest ranking honor card.

TEN TABLES. At duplicate, 10 tables provide for competition among 40 players as individuals, 20 pairs or 10 teams-of-four.

As an individual, use either the 13-round MINGLED MOVEMENT or the 10-round IRREGULAR RAINBOW.

As a pair game, the best contest is a MITCHELL. Three boards are given to each table, and a skip is called after the fifth round. This permits all pairs to play 27 boards — or fewer if desired since all boards are in play every round. If it is desired that all 30 boards be played, a byestand and relay setup can be employed. Boards should be relayed between tables 1 and 10, with the byestand between tables 5 and 6. The relay and byestand actually can be placed anywhere as long as they are exactly halfway around the game from each other.

The best movement for a one-winner game is the 10-table THREE-QUARTER. For an interesting variation, see BLACKPOOL MOVEMENT. Also see EXPANDED MITCHELL. For 9 1/2 tables and 10 1/2 tables, see HALF TABLES.

As a team contest you may use the INTERWOVEN HOWELL or play a Swiss Team movement. As an alternative play the standard team-of-four movement with two modifications. The East-West, or moving, pairs skip a table in the lower direction, while the boards move to the next lower table. After the second round the East-West pairs skip an extra table. After the sixth round the East-West pairs skip an extra table and the boards skip a table. East-West pair 1 moves, 9, 7, 4, 2, 10, 8, 5 and 3. If it is desirable to play a ninth round, East-West pairs 1 to 5 add five to their number and go to that table. East-West pairs 6 to 10 subtract five from their number and go to that table. 1 and 6, 2 and 7, 3 and 8, 4 and 9, and 5 and 10 relay newly shuffled boards during this final round. An important alternative is the STAGGER MOVEMENT.

TENACE. Two cards in the same suit of which one ranks two degrees lower than the other; the major tenace is A-Q; the minor tenace is K-J; more broadly, any holding of cards not quite in sequence in a suit.

TEXAS CONVENTION. A transfer bid, originated independently by David Carter of St. Louis and Olle Willner of Sweden. It is used after an opening 1NT or 2NT bid to make the strong hand declarer in a high suit contract. With a hand justifying a game contract, the responder jumps to 4♥ holding a six-card or longer spade suit; the opener is required to bid 4♠. Similarly, 4♦ requires the opener to bid 4♥. The convention is usually limited to those sequences in which the responder has a major suit. But 4♣ can be used in the same way to show diamonds, and 4♠ to show clubs. A South African variation uses 4♣ to ask for hearts and 4♦ to ask for spades. This has a psychological advantage, alerting an absent-minded partner who might otherwise pass a 4♥ bid that asked for spades, but it has the disadvantage of ruling out the use of the GERBER convention. As in the case of bidding against JACOBY TRANSFER BIDS, the fourth player can show a two-suited hand by previous partnership agreement. 4NT would show minor suits; a double would show the suit doubled and the non-touching suit; and a cuebid in responder's genuine suit would show two suits of the same color (COLORFUL CUEBID).

THAILAND, CONTRACT BRIDGE LEAGUE OF.
The Federation was founded in 1947 by Lt. William Howard Hunter, and in 1993 had 224 members in 13 clubs. Thailand won Far East titles in 1961, 1963, 1965 and 1966, and became the first Far East representatives in the Bermuda Bowl, in 1966 and 1967. Thailand won the Far East Women's Teams in 1964 and 1966, and 14 titles in the Asian Bridge Club Championships. It hosted Far East Championships in 1961, 1966, 1975 and 1982. Officers 1992:

President: Khunying C. Esther Sophonpanich
Secretary: Vallapa Svangsopakul
Address: 1508, 333 Silom Road,
Bangkok, Thailand
Telephone (66) 02 2755260-2
Fax: (66) 02 2753093

THEIR HAND. Term used by player who believes that his opponents can make the highest positive score.

THIN. An adjective used to describe (1) a hand without BODY; "a thin 15-count" indicates a hand with 15 high card points but lacking intermediates; (2) a makable contract with fewer than the expected HCP between the two hands.

THIRD. (similarly fourth, fifth, sixth, etc.). An adjective that, when used after naming a specific card, counts the number of cards held in the suit, e.g., ace-third denotes the holding of A-x-x.

THIRD AND FIFTH. During the 70s and 80s a majority of North American experts, and many in other parts of the world, abandoned the traditional fourth-best lead, which goes back to Edmund Hoyle, and adopted "third and fifth" -best leads. The idea is to lead the third card from a three or four-card suit, and fifth from five-card or longer suits. (Some lead "third and low" and would therefore lead the lowest from all suits of more than four cards).

If your partner leads, for example, the two from a presumed long suit, he is known to have three or five. This is easier for partner to judge than when using normal fourth-best leads when the two could be from a three-card or a four-card length. There is a corresponding disadvantage, however: The third-best card from a four-card suit may mean the wasting of a significant spot card. The lead of the nine from K J 9 2 may work out badly.

If the lead is third-best, the RULE OF TWELVE applies instead of the RULE OF ELEVEN. See also THIRD HIGHEST LEADS.

THIRD BEST. See THIRD HIGHEST LEAD.

THIRD HAND. In the bidding, the partner of the dealer; in the play, the partner of the leader to a trick. For considerations affecting the third hand in the bidding after two passes, see BORDERLINE OPENING BIDS and PASSED HAND.

THIRD-HAND BIDS. See BORDERLINE OPENING BIDS and PASSED HAND.

THIRD-HAND PLAY. The outcome of many deals is determined at the first trick, and correct play by the partner of the opening leader is often the key to a successful defense. Players should be familiar with the following elements of third-hand play. (If no mention is made whether the contract is at a suit or notrump, assume that third hand plays identically.)

I. *When partner leads low and dummy has low cards, the old whist rule of "third hand high" is usually right:*

```
                    NORTH (dummy)
                    9 4 3
        WEST                        EAST
        A 10 8 2                    K J 5
                    SOUTH
                    Q 7 6
```

Against notrump, West leads low. East must play the king.

If third hand has equal high cards, he plays the lower or lowest equal.

```
                    9 4 3
        K 8 7 2                     Q J 6
                    A 10 5
```

West leads low, and East plays the jack. The play of the jack denies the ten, but East may hold the queen.

II. *When not to play high when dummy has low cards.*
(1) With A-Q-x against notrump:

```
                    9 3
        J 8 7 6 2                   A Q 5
                    K 10 4
```

West leads low, and East plays the queen. If West has the king, no matter; if declarer has the king, the play of the queen prevents him from making a holdup play. This play works best when East expects to regain the lead before West; if West gets in first, he may think East lacks the ace and shift. A similar play is available with A-J-x, but it is dangerous since West may have K-10-x-x-x.

(2) To maintain communication with partner's hand at notrump:

```
                    7 5 4
        8 3                         A K 10 9 2
                    Q J 6
```

West leads the 8, and East does best to cover with the 9. If West has an outside entry, the defense can run the suit later.

```
                    5
        A 9 6 4 2                   K J 3
                    Q 10 8 7
```

West leads the 4. If East's hand is entryless, his winning play is the jack.

```
              ♠ A J
              ♥ A Q 5
              ♦ Q J 10 7 6
              ♣ A 7 6
   ♠ 9 4                      ♠ K Q 8 7 6
   ♥ 10 9 6 2                 ♥ J 8 7
   ♦ A 5 4                    ♦ K 3 2
   ♣ Q 10 8 3                 ♣ 9 5
              ♠ 10 5 3 2
              ♥ K 4 3
              ♦ 9 8
              ♣ K J 4 2
```

WEST	NORTH	EAST	SOUTH
	1 ♦	1 ♠	Pass
Pass	Dbl	Pass	1NT
Pass	2NT	Pass	3NT
All Pass			

West leads the ♠9, and dummy plays the jack. To defeat 3NT, East must follow with the 8, letting South win one of his two spade tricks while West still has a spade to lead.

(3) When declarer is known to have all the missing honors:

```
              4 3 2
   9 8                      K 10 6 5
              A Q J 7
```

Against a suit or notrump contract, West leads the 9. East should play low; since the lead marks declarer with A-Q-J, East has no reason to play the king. Indeed, the play of the king lets declarer win four tricks.

```
              ♠ Q 3 2
              ♥ K 7 2
              ♦ J 9 6
              ♣ 10 8 7 6
   ♠ 5 4                      ♠ 10 8
   ♥ J 9 6 3                  ♥ A Q 10 5
   ♦ A 8 7 5 3 2              ♦ Q 10 4
   ♣ 2                        ♣ Q J 5 3
              ♠ A K J 9 7 6
              ♥ 8 4
              ♦ K
              ♣ A K 9 4
```

WEST	NORTH	EAST	SOUTH
			1 ♠
Pass	1NT	Pass	2 ♣
Pass	2 ♠	Pass	4 ♠
All Pass			

West leads the ♣2, and dummy plays the 6. East must play low to defeat the contract.

(4) At a suit contract to make a discovery play:

```
              7 6
   10 8 3 2                 K J 5 4
              A Q 9
```

West leads low, and East knows that South has the ace (West will seldom lead low from the ace against a suit contract). To discover who has the queen, East plays the jack. If declarer wins the queen, East knows there is no future in the suit.

III. *When dummy has an honor and third hand has a higher honor.*

```
              Q 7 4
   10 8 6 2                 K 9 3
              A J 5
```

West leads the 2. If dummy plays low, East inserts the 9. The rule is that when third hand has an honor higher than dummy's honor, plus a middle card higher than the 8, he plays the middle card. With K-8-3, East should play the king if dummy plays low.

At suit play, this rule has exceptions when third hand has the ace and dummy has the queen.

```
              Q 7 5
   A 10 9
```

Against a suit contract West leads low and dummy plays low. East has a problem. If West is leading from the jack, it is usually right to play the 9 to deny declarer two tricks. If West is leading from the king, and declarer has the jack, it is usually right to play the ace.

If West is leading from K-J-x-(x), the play of the 9 saves a trick. There is no 100% answer. Third hand must judge from the dummy and the bidding.

```
              ♠ K 7 4
              ♥ 10 6 3
              ♦ A J 10 6 5 4
              ♣ 9
   ♠ 10 8 6 5 2                ♠ A J 3
   ♥ 5 2                       ♥ K Q J 9
   ♦ 8 7                       ♦ K 3
   ♣ 10 7 4 2                  ♣ J 8 6 5
              ♠ Q 9
              ♥ A 8 7 4
              ♦ Q 9 2
              ♣ A K Q 3
```

South plays at 3NT, West leads a low spade and dummy plays low. Clearly, in this case East must take the ♠A and shift to the ♥K.

Sometimes third hand can make no effort to win the trick:

```
              Q 10 2
   J 9 7 3                 K 6 4
              A 8 5
```

If West leads the 3 and dummy plays low, East must play low. If East plays the king, South takes three easy tricks; after East ducks, the third trick remains in contention.

The correct play may depend on entry considerations:

```
              Q 7 2
   J 9 5 3                 K 8 4
              A 10 6
```

West leads the 3, and dummy plays low. If East has no entry, he should play the 8 (West can then continue the suit safely). However, if East has an entry, he must play the king; later, he can continue the suit safely.

```
              ♠ J 9 3
              ♥ J 4
              ♦ K Q 10 6 4
              ♣ 7 6 5
   ♠ Q 10 6 5 2               ♠ K 8
   ♥ Q 6 5                    ♥ K 9 8 7
   ♦ 8 7 2                    ♦ A 5 3
   ♣ 4 3                      ♣ J 10 9 8
              ♠ A 7 4
              ♥ A 10 3 2
              ♦ J 9
              ♣ A K Q 2
```

South plays 3NT, West leads the ♠5 and declarer plays the 9 from dummy. East should play low to deny declarer a later entry to dummy's diamonds with the ♠J.

When third hand has one or two honors, and dummy has a higher honor, third hand often plays as if dummy had only low cards:

```
            A 8 4
J 7 3 2                 Q 9 6
            K 10 5
```

West leads low, and dummy plays low. East should play the queen.

IV. *Against a suit contract, when declarer is known to hold the ace.*

(1) When third hand has the Q-9 with or without lower cards:

```
            K J 5
10 8 6 2                Q 9 3
            A 7 4
```

West leads low and dummy plays low. East, knowing that South has the ace, plays the 9. (If West leads low in the middle game or end game, he may be underleading the ace; East must make an informed decision.)

(2) When third hand has J-8-x or J-7-x, and dummy has K-10-x or A-10-x.

```
            K 10 4
Q 9 8 2                 J 7 3
            A 6 5
```

West leads low and dummy plays low. East does best to play the middle card and hope it drives out the ace. With a weaker holding including the jack, East plays the jack and hopes declarer thinks he also has the queen. (Note that if West leads in this position after the first trick, it is usually right to attack with the 9.)

V. *More on third-hand play from equals.*

(1) When third hand has three or more equal honors, the proper order of plays is the lowest equal first, then the highest.

```
            7 6 3
8 4                     K Q J 10
            A 9 5 2
```

West leads the 8, and East plays the ten. East's second play in the suit is the king.

(2) Against notrump, with Q-J-10:

```
            5 4
A 9 8 7 6               Q J 10
            K 3 2
```

West leads low, and East should play the jack. If East plays the ten, West may think East started with J-10-x and South remains with Q-x; then West must wait for East to lead the suit.

However, if East plays the jack, West can safely continue the suit: either East has the queen, or South has K-Q-10, in which case it does not cost a trick to lead the suit again.

(3) Against notrump, with J-10-9:

```
            5 4
K 8 7 3 2               J 10 9
            A Q 6
```

West leads low, and East plays the ten and South wins the queen. West can safely continue the suit. Either East has the jack, or South has A-Q-J-9, in which case a tempo has been lost, but not a trick.

(4) With A-K-Q or A-K-Q-J to conceal strength:

```
            9 8
10 5 4 2                A K Q J 3
            7 6
```

If East wins the first trick with the ace and returns the queen, declarer may place West with the king. If East makes the normal play of the jack, South will know that East has 100 honors in the suit.

(5) With equal spot cards:

```
            Q 9 7 5
2                       K 10 8 6
            A J 4 3
```

West leads low and dummy plays low. East plays the 6 to limit South to two tricks.

(6) Third hand plays equal honors out of order to show a doubleton:

```
            J 8 6
Q 9 4 3 2               A K
            10 7 5
```

West leads low, and East wins the ace and cashes the king to show a doubleton.

```
            A 9 4
J 8 7 3 2               K Q
            10 6 5
```

West leads low and dummy plays low. East wins the king and returns the queen to show a doubleton. If East won the queen and led the king, West would assume that East had another card. (With equal doubleton honors, third hand should play them out of order only when he knows that he, not declarer, will win the trick.)

(7) At notrump, to ask for an unblock:

```
            7 6
Q 5 2                   A K J 8 3
            10 9 4
```

West makes the inspired lead of the 2 in an unbid suit. East wins the ace and leads the king, asking West to unblock the queen if he has it.

```
            J 10
9 8 2                   K Q 7 6 5
            A 4 3
```

West leads the 9, and East plays the king! When East leads the queen later, West unblocks the 8. Had East not wished an unblock, he would have played the queen first.

VI. *Deceptive plays.*

(1) At notrump, holding A-K-x-x:

```
            4 3
J 9 6 2                 A K 7 5
            Q 10 8
```

West leads the 2, and East places South with three cards in the suit. If South has both the queen and ten, a swindle looms. East wins the first trick with the ace and returns a low card, giving declarer a chance to misguess.

(2) At a suit contract, holding A-K-x-(x):

```
            10 6 3
J 9 7 2                 A K 5
            Q 8 4
```

West leads the two, and East wins the ace and returns the five. South may well play low and win no tricks.

(3) To feign a doubleton to encourage partner to continue a suit:

```
                    ♠ Q J 4
                    ♥ 6 4 2
                    ♦ A Q J
                    ♣ A Q J 6
♠ A K 9 5 3                         ♠ 10 7 6
♥ 9                                 ♥ A K
♦ 9 7 5 3                           ♦ 10 8 6 4 2
♣ 9 8 3                             ♣ 10 7 5
                    ♠ 8 2
                    ♥ Q J 10 8 7 5 3
                    ♦ K
                    ♣ K 4 2
```

South opens a vulnerable 3♥, and North raises to 4♥. West leads the ♠K. East can see that the only chance for the defense is to cash two spades. Accordingly, he plays the ♠10 to feign shortness. West continues with the ♠A, and the contract is defeated. If East plays his lowest spade at the first trick, West may shift to a minor suit and lose the setting trick.

(4) To feign a doubleton in the hope of conning declarer into trumping high in dummy unnecessarily:

```
              ♠ 3 2
              ♥ K Q 6 4
              ♦ A Q 10 6
              ♣ Q 8 3
♠ A K Q 7 6              ♠ 9 8 5
♥ 10 7 5 3              ♥ J 9 8
♦ J 8 4 2              ♦ 9 7 5 3
♣ —                    ♣ J 10 9
              ♠ J 10 4
              ♥ A 2
              ♦ K
              ♣ A K 7 6 5 4 2
```

After South opens 1♣ and West overcalls 1♠, South shows a strong hand and becomes declarer at 5♣. West leads two high spades, and East signals high-low to try to convince declarer that he has a doubleton. If West continues with a third spade, South may trump with the ♣Q and lose a trump trick.

VII. *Using the RULE OF ELEVEN.*

(1) To save a trick:

```
              ♠ A J 7
              ♥ K 5 3
              ♦ 7 3 2
              ♣ 7 5 4 2
♠ Q 10 8 6 3            ♠ K 9 2
♥ 10 7                 ♥ 8 4
♦ J 9 5                ♦ Q 10 8 6
♣ A 8 3                ♣ Q J 10 9
              ♠ 5 4
              ♥ A Q J 9 6 2
              ♦ A K 4
              ♣ K 6
```

South plays 4♥, and West leads the ♠6. If declarer plays low from dummy, the Rule of Eleven tells East that South has no spades higher than the 7. East can safely play the 9. If East incorrectly wins the king, South can finesse dummy's ♠J later for his tenth trick.

(2) To avoid an endplay:

```
              ♠ 10 4 3
              ♥ A K 4 2
              ♦ 6 4 3 2
              ♣ 7 4
♠ A Q 9 6 2            ♠ J 8 7
♥ 7 5 3               ♥ 10 9 8
♦ 9 7                 ♦ Q J 10 8
♣ K J 8               ♣ 10 5 2
              ♠ K 5
              ♥ Q J 6
              ♦ A K 5
              ♣ A Q 9 6 3
```

South plays 3NT, West leads the ♠6 and dummy plays low. East can tell that South has one spade higher than the 6; since it must be an honor, East does best to play the 7.

South runs his red-suit winners and exits with a spade, hoping West must win and lead a club. Because East re-

mains with the ♠J, however, no endplay is possible. Had East played the ♠J at the first trick, South could make his contract. (See RULE OF ELEVEN.)

VIII. *With the Q-J when partner leads from A-K-x-(x).*

When third hand plays the queen under the lead of the ace or king, he promises the jack or a singleton (unless the jack is in dummy; see subsequent example). Opening leader can underlead his remaining honor if he wants his partner on lead. The play of the queen is not a command to underlead; it simply shows the ability to win the next lead.

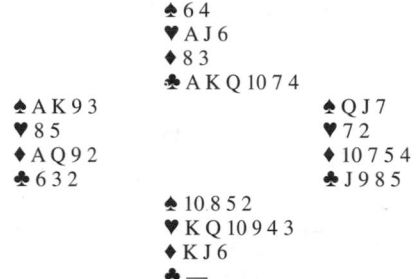

```
              ♠ 6 4
              ♥ A J 6
              ♦ 8 3
              ♣ A K Q 10 7 4
♠ A K 9 3              ♠ Q J 7
♥ 8 5                 ♥ 7 2
♦ A Q 9 2              ♦ 10 7 5 4
♣ 6 3 2               ♣ J 9 8 5
              ♠ 10 8 5 2
              ♥ K Q 10 9 4 3
              ♦ K J 6
              ♣ —
```

South plays 4♥ after West opens 1♦. West leads the ♠K, and East plays the queen, promising the jack. West has no trouble leading a low spade next, and East wins and returns a diamond. Down one.

If third hand has the Q-J doubleton and wants a ruff rather than a possible underlead, he plays the jack first.

IX. *With Q-x when partner leads from A-K-x-(x) against a suit contract.*

(1) Dummy does not have the jack:

```
              10 6 5
   A K 8 7              Q 2
              J 9 4 3
```

West leads a high honor, and East must play the 2. The play of the queen might induce West to underlead next.

(2) Dummy has the jack:

```
              J 6 5
   A K 10 4             Q 3
              9 8 7 2
```

West leads a high honor; East can play the queen to show a doubleton, and West cannot be misled.

X. *When partner leads a short suit against a suit contract.*

(1) Third hand has the ace and reads the lead as a doubleton:

```
              10 7 6
   9 5                  A 8 4 3 2
              K Q J
```

West leads the 9, and East judges from the bidding that the lead is top of a doubleton. If East has no side entry, he must signal with the 8 and hope West has an early entry. Then West can continue with the 5 and get a ruff.

(2) Third hand reads the lead as a singleton but cannot win the trick:

```
              ♠ Q J 5 4
   ♣ 6                  ♠ 10 9 8 3 2
              ♠ A K 7
```

Assume hearts are trumps, and West leads the ♠6, which East reads as a singleton. East's play should be a suit-preference signal to tell West where East's side-suit strength lies. If East has diamond strength, for example, he plays the ♠10 at the first trick; with club strength, East plays the ♠2. With equal strength in the minor suits, East plays a middle spade.

XI. *Other suit-preference plays at the first trick.*

```
            ♠ J 5 2
            ♥ K Q 6
            ♦ 8 5 2
            ♣ 8 6 4 2
♠ Q                        ♠ 8 6
♥ A 10 9 5 4 3            ♥ J 8 2
♦ K J 3                   ♦ A 10 9 4
♣ Q 7 5                   ♣ J 10 9 3
            ♠ A K 10 9 7 4 3
            ♥ 7
            ♦ Q 7 6
            ♣ A K
```

South plays 4♠ after West opened 1♥ and East raised to 2♥. West leads the ♥A, and both defenders know that a heart continuation cannot be right. East signals suit preference by playing the ♥J to show diamond strength. Had East not supported hearts, his first play would be count. See also SUIT-PREFERENCE SIGNALS.

```
            6 5 3
A 9                    K Q J 10 2
            8 7 4
```

At a suit contract or notrump, East has bid this suit, and West leads the ace. If East plays the king, he shows a solid suit. This is not a suit-preference play.

XII. *When partner leads a trump.*

(1) Third hand high may apply:

```
            6 2
J 9 3                  K 5 4
            A Q 10 8 7
```

West leads a low trump. If the bidding marks West with as many as three trumps, East should play the king, hoping to promote a lower honor.

(2) Third hand has A-x-x:

```
            J 5 4
3 2                    A 7 6
            K Q 10 9 8
```

If it is best to play two rounds of trumps quickly, third hand wins the ace and returns a trump. If it is best to play three rounds of trumps eventually, and third hand has no outside entry, he ducks the first trump. If opening leader has an early entry, he can lead a second trump, and third hand can win and lead a third trump.

(3) Third hand has an honor and wants to prevent dummy from gaining an entry:

```
            J 9 3
5 4                    K 7 6
            A Q 10 8 2
```

If East wants to deny declarer a later trump entry to dummy, he plays low regardless of which trump dummy plays at the first trick.

(4) When third hand has an honor he may use to overruff dummy:

```
            ♠ J 10 4
♣ 8 5                  ♣ K 2
            ♠ A Q 9 7 6
```

Assume spades is trumps, and both East and dummy have a doubleton heart. If West leads a trump, East plays low, saving the king for a possible overruff of dummy later.

XIII. *Overtaking. Third hand usually overtakes partner's honor lead with a higher doubleton honor:*

(1) When the queen is led, and third hand has K-x or A-x:

```
            9 4 3
Q J 10 8 7            K 5
            A 6 2
```

Against a suit or notrump contract, East overtakes the lead of the queen to unblock the suit. If dummy has 10-x-x, however, East establishes the ten if he overtakes.

(2) When the jack is led against notrump, and third hand has Q-x, K-x or A-x:

```
            7 4 2
J 10 9 6 3            Q 5
            A K 8
```

West leads the jack, and East plays the queen to unblock. (At a suit contract, East need not unblock with Q-x or K-x.)

```
            ♠ Q 7 5 2
            ♥ K J 4
            ♦ A 7 6
            ♣ 10 6 4
♠ J 10 9 8 4          ♠ K 3
♥ A 10 9             ♥ 8 7 6
♦ 10 3              ♦ Q 9 5 4 2
♣ A 9 2             ♣ 7 5 3
            ♠ A 6
            ♥ Q 5 3 2
            ♦ K J 8
            ♣ K Q J 8
```

South plays at 3NT, and West leads the ♠J. If dummy plays low, East must play the king to defeat the contract.

(3) When third hand has dazzling spot cards:

```
            9 4 3
J                    K Q 10 8 2
            A 7 6 5
```

West leads the jack, and East overtakes with the queen to prevent declarer from holding up. If the 9 were not in dummy, East could not afford this play. When partner leads an honor card from shortness, an encouraging signal indicates the inability to overtake.

```
            ♠ J 4
            ♥ A J 8 3
            ♦ A K Q 9 6
            ♣ 9 5
♠ 5                  ♠ A 9 7 2
♥ 10 7 5            ♥ Q 4 2
♦ 10 7 5 4 2        ♦ J
♣ J 10 8 6          ♣ A K Q 7 4
            ♠ K Q 10 8 6 3
            ♥ K 9 6
            ♦ 8 3
            ♣ 3 2
```

In the 1967 Bermuda Bowl final, South played 4♠ at both tables, and West led the ♣J. Both Easts overtook with the queen to return the ♦J. When East won the ♠A, he underled his remaining club honors to West's ten and got a diamond ruff to defeat the contract.

XIV. *Unblocking.*

(1) When partner leads the king against notrump, and third hand has J-x:

```
            8 4 3
K Q 10 7 6            J 2
            A 9 5
```

West leads the king, and East plays the jack. To play low denies a significant honor. Some partnerships lead the queen from K-Q-10-9 combinations and perhaps from K-Q-10; in this case, the lead of the queen compels third hand to unblock the jack if he has it.

When the king is led against a suit contract, East can afford to signal encouragement with J-x only if he knows that West has A-K.

(2) When partner leads the queen against notrump, and third hand has 10-x or 10-x-x:

	A 4 3	
Q J 9 7 2		10 6
	K 8 5	

West leads the queen, and regardless of dummy's play, East unblocks the ten. Unblocking is also safe from 10-x-x, provided West is not leading from Q-J-x. (Usually West will have Q-J-9; with Q-J-x-x, he would lead low.)

(3) When partner leads the ace against notrump, and third hand has the jack or high, he unblocks the honor:

	7 2	
A K J 10		Q 5 4
	9 8 6 3	

West leads the ace, and East unblocks the queen. (Some play that the lead of the king asks for an unblock, and the lead of the ace shows A-K-x or A-K-x-x.)

When third hand has no honor to unblock, he gives count.

	7 2	
A K Q 10 9		8 3
	J 6 5 4	

West leads the ace, and East plays the 8, count. West can deduce that South has the guarded jack.

(4) Miscellaneous positions:

	6 4	
A J 9 8		Q 7 5 3 2
	K 10	

Against notrump, West leads the 8. If East plays the queen, he blocks the suit.

	A 7	
K J 9 6 4		Q 2
	10 8 5 3	

Against notrump, West leads the 6, and declarer puts up the ace. If East unblocks the queen, he can lead the 2 later for the defense to run the suit.

XV. *Third hand middle.*

Third hand should be familiar with some seemingly strange plays with honor-9-x or honor-8-x.

	10 5	
K 8 3 2		A 9 4
	Q J 7 6	

West leads the 2 against notrump, amd dummy plays low. If East plays the 9, declarer takes one trick; if East plays the ace, declarer takes two tricks.

These plays do not come with a guarantee; they work most often when both leader and declarer have four cards and dummy has 10-x or J-x.

	10 2	
K 7 6 3		Q 8 4
	A J 9 5	

Against notrump, West leads the 3, dummy plays low and East saves a trick by playing the 8.

	9 2	
A 7 4 3		J 8 5
	K Q 10 6	

West leads low and dummy plays low. East saves a trick by playing the 8.

The play of the middle card also gains in this position:

	10 2	
A 9 7 5 3		Q 8 4
	K J 6	

West leads the 5 (fourth best), dummy plays low and

East saves a trick by inserting the 8. However, if West started with K-J-7-5-3, East must play the queen.

	10 5	
A 8 4 2		J 7 6
	K Q 9 3	

	10 3 2	
A 9 7 5 4		J 7 6
	K Q	

In both cases, West leads low, and dummy plays low. East can play the 6 to save a trick.

	10 5 2	
Q 9 8 7 3		J 6 4
	A K	

Against notrump, West leads the 7 and dummy plays low. If West will be first to regain the lead, it makes things easier if East plays low to the first trick. However, if East is first to regain the lead, his play at the first trick may not matter. And if the suit is:

	10 5 2	
K Q 9 7		J 6 4
	A 8	

to play low is disastrous.

	10 6 4	
Q 9 8 7 2		J 3
(K 9 8 7 2)		
	A K 5	
	(A Q 5)	

Against notrump, West leads the 7 and dummy plays low. If East has no entries and West is likely to get the lead first, East does best to play low.

XVI. *Spot-card signaling.*

(1) Third hand must not waste a valuable spot card to signal:

	J 8 7 6	
A K 2		Q 9 5 3
	10 4	

West leads a high honor, and East must content himself with the 5. To play the 9 sets up a fourth-round winner in dummy. Many partnerships use UPSIDE-DOWN ATTITUDE SIGNALS to overcome this problem.

	K 4 3	
Q J 7		A 9 8 2
	10 6 5	

Against a suit or notrump contract, West leads the queen, and dummy plays low. East signals with the 9, the higher equal, denying the ten. If West suspects the distribution, he does best to switch rather than continue and establish declarer's ten.

When third hand has three low cards, he should give count rather than play third hand high.

	♠ A 10 3	
	♥ 7 6 5	
	♦ Q 9 2	
	♣ K J 4 3	
♠ K J 7 5 4		♠ 8 6 2
♥ J 9 3		♥ Q 10 8 2
♦ A 8 6		♦ 4 3
♣ A 7		♣ 10 8 6 5
	♠ Q 9	
	♥ A K 4	
	♦ K J 10 7 5	
	♣ Q 9 2	

South opens 1NT and North raises to 3NT. West leads the ♠5, and dummy plays low. East should play the 2, giving count. South wins and knocks out the ♦A, but West will know to lead the ♠K next.

The same play may be made with 9-x-x (usually against a suit contract) when it is clear the 9 cannot drive out a significant card.

THIRD HIGHEST LEAD. The lead of the highest card but two. This is standard when holding three cards headed by an honor. When the suit is longer, the third highest is led as a matter of system by some players. In fact, more and more players are leading THIRD AND FIFTH. This type also may be used as a deceptive lead. A player who holds 10-5-4-2 and a weak hand may choose to lead the 4 followed by the 2. His purpose is to suggest a five-card suit, in the hope that declarer will make losing avoidance plays which are unnecessary, and which he would not have made if he had known that the opening leader's suit was a four-carder. For third-hand play when third highest leads are used, see RULE OF TWELVE. See also THREE SMALL CARDS, LEAD FROM; JOURNALIST LEADS.

THIRD-SUIT BID. A bid in a third suit at the one-level, is non-forcing except in the obsolete Baron System. If two suits are bid at the one level and a third at the two level, the situation is not forcing except when the second bid by opener is of higher rank than the first—e.g., 1♦-1♠-2♥. There is an exception in KAPLAN-SHEINWOLD: 1♦ followed by 2♣ is forcing. After a response at the two-level, a third-suit bid is forcing in any standard method.

THIRTEEN TABLES. At duplicate, 13 tables provide competition among 52 players as individuals, 26 pairs, or 13 teams-of-four. In the development of bridge tournament movements, it was early recognized that 13 rounds of two boards each, 3° hours of play approximately, came close to being the ideal game. For this reason, 13 tables is considered to be the ideal for section size because every player plays each of the boards in play.

For 13 teams it would be normal to use the NEW ENGLAND RELAY. See TEAM-OF-FOUR MOVEMENTS.

Since 13 is a prime number, the RAINBOW MOVEMENT is practical and is generally used for individual tournaments. This can be cut to 11 or 12 rounds for a shorter game without introducing any complications. To maximize the number of partnerships, South and West can exchange positions after the first board of each round.

For a pair game, the simple MITCHELL MOVEMENT is used.

For 12° and 13°, see HALF TABLES.

THIRTEENER. The card remaining in a suit when all other cards in that suit have been played on the first three tricks of the suit.

THREAT CARD (or menace). A threat card is a potential winner. It will take a trick provided that the opponent's holding in that suit can be weakened sufficiently. The term "menace" (or "threat card") may be used in one of the following specialized senses:

(1) Isolated menace: A menace consisting of one card, as the queen in the diagram.

```
              Q
   A                     K
              x
```

(2) Two-card menace: A two-card holding, consisting

of a winner in the suit accompanied by a menace, as in the diagram.

```
              A J
   K Q                   x x
              Q x
```

(3) Split two-card menace: A two-card menace in which the winner and the threat card are in opposite hands, as in this diagram:

```
              A x
   K J                   x x
              Q x
```

(4) Double menace: A threat card against both opponents (the diagram for a one-card menace, preceding, shows a double menace).

(5) Extended two-card menace: A two-card menace accompanied by one or more cards in that suit with the property that if the two-card menace is established, then the whole suit will run, e.g.:

```
              A J 10
   K Q                   x x x
              x x
```

In this diagram if West discards the queen (or king) he permits South to cash two additional tricks in the suit.

(6) Recessed menace: A menace card is accompanied by two (or more) winners in that suit, e.g.:

```
              A K 9
   Q J 10                x x x
              x
```

North's holding is a recessed menace against West.

(7) Twin entry menace: One hand contains a winner and one (or more) small card(s) while the opposite hands holds a winner, a menace, and one (or more) small card(s) in that suit, e.g.:

```
              K x
   Q J x
              A 10 x
```

This suit is a twin-entry menace against West.

THREE or THREE-SPOT. The second-lowest card in a given suit, ranking between the 2 and the 4, sometimes called "trey."

THREE-BID. See PREEMPTIVE BID.

THREE-CARD SUITS, BIDS IN. In many situations the most convenient bid available may be in a three-card suit. Some of the more common examples are:

(1) *In opening the bidding.* Most frequent is an opening bid of 1♣, to keep the bidding at a low level and avoid an opening in a poor four-card major suit. Less common is an opening of 1♦ with a three-card suit, although this is standard practice with 4-4-3-2 distribution using five-card majors. (Some bid 1♦ with 4-3-3-3 or 3-4-3-3 to avoid 1♣ with three small). Semi-psychic opening bids of 1♠ with a three-card suit are sometimes made, especially third-hand, nonvulnerable, with a subminimum opening. Opening bids in a three-card suit, of any rank, are often required in the ROMAN SYSTEM.

(2) *In responding.* A response in the lowest possible suit is sometimes made with a three-card suit, especially if the suit is strong, because no good alternative presents itself:

(a)	(b)
♠ J x x	♠ A K x
♥ x x x	♥ x x x x
♦ A K x	♦ x x x
♣ x x x x	♣ A Q x

(a) A response of 1♦ to 1♣ is slightly preferable to 1NT

or 2♣.

(b) In response to 1♠, 2♣ is the least evil unless 1NT forcing is available.

(3) *In rebidding*. See OPENER'S REBID.

(4) *In responding to a TAKEOUT DOUBLE*. See also FOURTH SUIT FORCING, FRAGMENT BID, INTEREST-SHOWING BID, TRIAL BID.

THREE-CLUB RESPONSE AS MAJOR RAISE. A convention devised by Alvin Roth to make a strong major suit raise while conserving space for exchange of information as to trump suit texture, singletons and controls below the game level. Over the 3♣ response, opener rebids 3♦ if he has any singleton; without a singleton he rebids 3♥, 3♠ or 3NT with two, one, or none of the top three trump honors, respectively. If opener has bid 3♦, responder can show his own trump texture in the same way. Four-level bids show high card or distributional controls.

THREE-CLUB RESPONSE TO ONE NOTRUMP. This bid is used in various ways, depending on the system. Possible are:

(i) Strong and forcing, the traditional meaning. Suggests slam interest.

(ii) Weak and preemptive, the standard modern meaning.

(iii) Invitational. Normal with four-suit transfers, since weak and strong hands can transfer via 2♠.

(iv) Transfer to diamonds.

(v) A prototype Stayman asking for a major. (Obsolete.)

THREE-CLUBS STAYMAN. See TWO NOTRUMP OPENING.

THREE-HANDED BRIDGE. Many three-handed versions of bridge have been devised. Apart from TOWIE, described separately, two games deserve consideration.

In the traditional cutthroat game, the players bid for a hidden dummy. The bidding continues until a bid, doubled or redoubled, is followed by two passes. The player on declarer's left leads, and the dummy is spread between the two opponents. The scoring is normal, declarer scoring a 700 rubber bonus only if neither defender has a game. Plus scores only are recorded for each player, and settlement is made on the net difference in scores. See CUTTHROAT.

An alternative game with a pre-exposed dummy was devised by George S. Coffin in 1932. It is sometimes called triangle contract or trio bridge. The laws are as follows:

(1) The three players are designated as North, South, and East. North and South bid as well as play as partners against East and his exposed dummy. There is no West player. Nor is there a second dummy, because North and South always play with closed hands, even if one or the other is declarer.

(2) To begin a game, the three players draw cards; the two players who draw the highest cards play as partners as North and South against East, who has the dummy for the entire rubber.

(3) For the first deal only, South shuffles either pack. Then East cuts and South deals while North shuffles the still pack. For the next hand, East cuts and North deals while South shuffles the still pack. Thereafter, North and

South continue to deal alternately.

(4) East never deals or shuffles, but always cuts.

(5) Dummy is exposed before there is any bidding. Hence, if any dummy card is faced up during the deal, it is not treated as an exposed card. If a card is turned up in any other hand, there must, of course be a new deal.

(6) South always calls first regardless of who dealt; North bids second. Dummy never bids, for East bids on the combined 26 East-West cards. If any player makes a bid, the auction continues indefinitely until two consecutive passes close it.

(7) As in four-handed bridge, the left-hand opponent (LHO) of declarer makes the opening lead. If South is declarer, dummy leads first; if North is declarer, East leads; or if East is declarer, South leads.

(8) If the revoke is established against East, he cannot be penalized for it unless South or North has called attention to East's failure to follow suit on the revoke trick. This special rule for three-handed bridge is called the courtesy of the table, and it is due to the fact that East has no partner to say "having none?" This service is rendered by North and/or South.

(9) Regular contract bridge scoring is used. After the net amount of a finished rubber has been computed, East wins or loses twice the net amount because he collects dummy's gain or suffers dummy's loss.

(10) At the end of each rubber, North shifts into the vacant chair on his right and becomes redesignated as South and his former partner as East. A weird variety calls for the dealer to play automatically in two notrump redoubled. See DUMMY BRIDGE.

THREE NOTRUMP. The lowest, quantitatively, bid that produces a game from a zero score; nine tricks without benefit of a trump suit.

THREE NOTRUMP OPENING. Traditionally this shows a balanced hand with 25-27 points. But with such hands most experts bid 2♣ followed by 3NT, or use KOKISH, and therefore prefer to use the 3NT opening for some other purpose, such as:

(1) GAMBLING 3 NT.

(2) Weak minor suit preempt, comparable to a standard 4♣ or 4♦ opening. This method is useful for those who use NAMYATS to show strong major suit hands.

(3) Solid major suit preempt with no side suit aces and at most one side king. This use, suggested by Edwin Kantar, is designed to ease responder's task of judging his side's game or slam prospects. The recommended responses are as follows: 4♣ asks opener to bid a side king if he has one; 4♦ transfers to opener's suit; 4♥ or 4♠ indicates that responder wants to be declarer and has tried to guess opener's suit (if he misguesses, opener should correct); 4NT asks about queens; 5NT asks opener to bid a grand slam if he can play opposite a void.

THREE NOTRUMP OVERCALL. An overcall at the game level, usually made on a strong balanced hand or one of a preemptive nature.

NORTH	EAST
3♠	3NT

In the above example East's hand might be:

 ♠ A J 9
 ♥ K 2
 ♦ A J 10 6 4
 ♣ K Q 2

It would be inadvisable for East to double 3♠ since he has poor support for the "other major." Normally, the double of one major suit invites partner to bid the other if he can. East therefore "gambles" on 3 NT. In these awkward situations it is generally a good idea arbitrarily to place 8 points in your partner's hand and proceed accordingly. An opponent's double or raise from partner will clarify the situation. In many situations the 3NT overcall is gambling and semi-preemptive in nature.

For example:

SOUTH	WEST
1 ♥	3NT

West is trying to "steal" 3NT. His holding might be:

♠ 6
♥ K 5
♦ A K Q 7 6 3 2
♣ 8 7 6

If an opponent doubles, it usually is incumbent upon partner of overcaller to run out to 4♣ if he has nothing of great value. A pass by partner would indicate a desire to play 3NT. This bid is usually made when not vulnerable.

THREE NOTRUMP REBID. See OPENER'S REBID.

THREE NOTRUMP RESPONSE to an opening suit bid of one. There are a number of treatments which can be adopted:

(1) *Standard*, traditional. Shows 16-18 points and any 4-3-3-3 distribution.

(2) *Limit*. Shows 13-15 points and any 4-3-3-3 distribution (ACOL SYSTEM).

(3) *Conventional*. Used with limit raises to show a standard forcing jump raise of 13-15 points when the opening bid was in a major (invented by Monroe Ingberman.) For alternative methods of solving this problem see DELAYED GAME RAISE and SWISS CONVENTION .

(4) *Distributional*. Shows a 13-15 point raise with a side suit singleton when the opening bid was in a major (ACES SCIENTIFIC SYSTEM).

(5) *Extra Strong or Distributional*. Shows one of a series of CONGLOMERATE MAJOR RAISES. In response to a 1♥ opening, 3 NT would show 17-18 points. In response to a 1♠ opening, 3NT would be as in (4) above.

(6) *Ace-asking*. See BABY BLACKWOOD.

(7) *Psychic Control*. Showing 23 points or more — a hand which offers a play for game opposite a psychic opening bid; this assumes a ROTH-STONE psychic with 3-6 points concentrated mainly in the bid suit. If the opening bidder has a normal opening he proceeds to a slam: the combined strength already suggests a grand slam.

(8) *Pre-emptive Major Suit Raise*. Similar to a direct raise to four of a major, but with some defensive value.

THREE-ODD. Three tricks over book or nine tricks.

THREE-QUARTER MOVEMENT. See REDUCED HOWELL.

THREE-QUARTER NOTRUMP. The use of a weak notrump in all situations except vulnerable against non-vulnerable. Players who combine this with a fourth-hand weak notrump at all vulnerabilities (safe because neither opponent can double and dummy must have some val-

ues) can be said to play 13/16ths.

THREE SMALL CARDS, LEAD FROM. There are three distinct schools of thought.

(1) *Top of nothing*. The traditional lead of the 8, for example, from 8-5-2, is advocated by many text-books. This has the advantage of advising partner immediately that no high honor is held, but it has some disadvantages. It clarifies the suit distribution for the declarer also; it leads to ambiguity on the second round because partner cannot be sure whether the lead was from three cards or two; and it may waste a significant card, especially if the lead is an unsupported 9. Partners using this treatment must agree which card should be played on the second round of the suit. Most experts believe in following with the middle card, whether leading or following suit. This identifies a doubleton with certainty if the second card is the lowest possible. There is no technical objection to the alternative of following with the lowest card, in which case a doubleton is identified if the second card played is the highest possible. Whether there is any partnership agreement, it is important to play in tempo. Hesitation clearly shows the three-card holding and is unethical.

(2) *Low Lead*. Most American experts now favor this, following the trend to THIRD AND FIFTH leads. This avoids the disadvantages of the top of nothing lead, but leaves partner in doubt whether the lead is from an honor. (An obvious exception occurs when the highest card is led in the suit that has been bid by partner and raised by the leader.)

(3) *Mud*. The lead of the middle card, usually to be followed by the top card. The term is derived from the initial letters of middle-up-down, and the lead is used by fewer and fewer pairs. It avoids most disadvantages, but may not be as clear to partner as the other methods.

A few expert partnerships have no clear-cut agreement, but use the method which seems best adapted to the particular situation. The top card is led if partner is likely to need to know about honors rather than length. The bottom card is led if length is the vital factor. And the middle card is chosen if it is desired to keep declarer in doubt.

THREE-SUITER. A hand with at least four cards in each of three suits, and therefore distributed 4-4-4-1 or 5-4-4-0. For opening the bidding with a three-suiter see BIDDABLE SUITS, BORDERLINE OPENING BIDS, and CHOICE OF SUIT. For specialized three-suiter conventions see BLUE TEAM TWO DIAMONDS, KANTAR CUEBID, PRECISION CLUB (2♦ opening), ROMAN SYSTEM (2♣ and 2♦ opening).

THREE TABLES. At duplicate, three tables provide for competition among 12 (or 13) players as individuals, five or six pairs, or three teams-of-four.

As an individual tournament, 11 rounds are required for 12 players, 12 for 13 players. Conduct of such a game is described under INDIVIDUAL MOVEMENT for 12 or 13 players.

As a pair contest, the HOWELL MOVEMENT is far superior to the MITCHELL, as it provides that each pair of players will meet with each other pair as opponents.

	Board			Board			Board		
Round	NS	EW	Sets	NS	EW	Sets	NS	EW	Sets
1	6	1	1	5	2	4	4	3	2
2	6	2	2	1	3	4	5	4	3
3	6	3	3	2	4	1	1	5	2

| 4 | 6 | 4 | 4 | 3 | 5 | 1 | 2 | 1 | 3 |
| 5 | 6 | 5 | 5 | 4 | 1 | 5 | 3 | 2 | 5 |

The usual method of handling this movement is to put five boards in a set. The first four sets will have been played by all six pairs by the end of the fourth round. During the fifth round the fifth set of boards i relayed among all three tables. In this manner every pairs plays 25 boards — five against each other pair. It is also possible to have the pairs share five boards each round.

A third possibility divides the game into 10 rounds. Each pair makes the circuit of all other pairs twice. If there are two boards per set, the game consists of 20 boards. With three boards per round, the game consists of 30 boards. A compromise by making sets 1 through 5 consist of two boards and sets 6 through 10 consist of three boards. Using this method, each pair would play 25 boards. Here is how the movement would work:

| | Board | | | Board | | | Board | | |
Round	NS	EW	Sets	NS	EW	Sets	NS	EW	Sets
1, 6	6	1	1, 6	5	2	4, 8	4	3	2, 10
2, 7	6	2	2, 7	1	3	4, 5	5	4	3, 6
3, 8	6	3	3, 8	2	4	1, 5	1	5	2, 9
4, 9	6	4	4, 9	3	5	1, 7	2	1	3, 10
5, 10	6	5	5, 10	4	1	7, 8	3	2	6, 9

The main advantage of this movement is that it offers nearly perfect balance whereas the prior two do not. The main disadvantage is the extra time made necessary by the five extra moves.

If the game consists of 2 1/2 tables, the easiest method to use is to eliminate the stationary pair. That way each pair sits out the round that matches their pair number.

A movement for three tables of players works out well as a team event. The following movement is used. If the plan is to play 24 boards, then 12 boards are placed at each table. The East-West pairs move to the next higher table (1 to 2, 2 to 3 and 3 to 1) and play those boards. The East-West players then return their boards to their home table and go back one table from their home table (3 to 2, 2 to 1 and 1 to 3). Without shuffling the players play the boards at their table. At the finish each team will have played a 12-board match against each of the other teams. For 3° tables see HALF TABLES.

THROUGH STRENGTH. The old whist idea that a defender should lead "through strength" is one of the least valuable rules of thumb. The implication is that a player on declarer's left should lead a suit in which dummy is strong. The rationale is that partner may hold any missing honors behind dummy; the defenders can profit by leading suits in which declarer's finesses will fail.

```
              ♠ 10 7 5 2
              ♥ J 9 3 2
              ♦ A Q 3
              ♣ J 2
  ♠ K J 6                    ♠ 9 8 3
  ♥ 8 4                      ♥ K 5
  ♦ 9 7 5                    ♦ K J 8 4
  ♣ K Q 10 7 5              ♣ 9 8 6 4
              ♠ A Q 4
              ♥ A Q 10 7 6
              ♦ 10 6 2
              ♣ A 3
```

South plays at 3♥; he wins the ♣K opening lead and leads a club back. When West takes the queen, he shifts to the ♦9 through dummy, since if East has diamond honors, they are well placed. If South ducks, East wins the

jack and leads the ♠9 in turn through declarer. Best defense defeats the contract.

Sometimes a lead through strength merely gives declarer time to establish the suit for discards. When dummy has a strong side suit, the defenders must often hasten to establish tricks elsewhere while they can. Even when a safe exit is a defender's goal, however, it may be safer to lead a suit in which dummy is weak.

In the following examples it is assumed that dummy is on the leader's left.

To lead from a worthless suit rarely costs a trick, though it may avoid a guess for declarer, but a defender must consider carefully before he leads from an honor. If dummy has A-K-x, for example, a lead from a queen is dangerous, but most other leads are safe. Other cases:

Dummy has A-x-x: A lead from J-9-x is safe; from J-x-x or Q-x-x more risky; from K-x-x, dangerous.

Dummy has A-Q-x or A-J-x: A lead from a king is dangerous; from the jack or queen, less dangerous. From K-J-9 or K-10-8, lead the middle card.

Dummy has K-Q-x: A lead from the jack is dangerous; from the ace or x-x-x, safe.

Dummy has K-J-x: A lead from the ace is safe; from the queen, dangerous, but for this reason declarer may be induced to misguess if he holds a low doubleton.

Dummy has K-x-x: All leads from single honors are risky.

Dummy has Q-x-x: A lead from the king is safest, since the king may win a later trick even if declarer has the ace; from the ace, dangerous.

Dummy has J-x-x: A lead from the ace is worst; it is better to lead from the king or queen.

Dummy has x-x-x: The lower the honor to be led from, the safer the lead. A lead from the jack is almost completely safe; from the queen loses only if declarer has A-K-J.

For a related situation, see UP TO WEAKNESS.

THROW AWAY. (1) To discard. (2) To defend or play so badly that a very poor score results.

THROW IN. (1) To make a THROW-IN PLAY. (2) In rubber bridge, to toss the cards into the center of the table, after four passes. Used in Great Britain as a synonym for PASS OUT.

THROW-IN PLAYS. When executing a throw-in play, an opponent is given the trick, but gaining the lead costs him a trick or more. There are three types of throw-in play, based on the way thre throw-in costs the defender his tricks.

(1) *Tenace Throw-in* (usually shortened to throw-in). An opponent is thrown in and forced to lead from a broken honor holding at the cost of a trick.

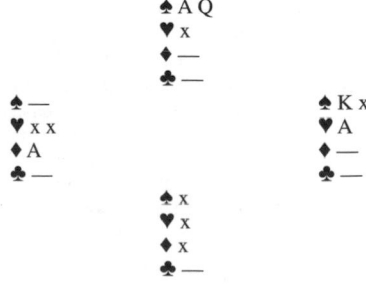

South has placed East with the ♠K. In order to avoid a losing finesse, a heart is led and East is forced into the lead. He must lead into North's spade tenace.

(2) *Trump Throw-in* (also known as an elimination play). An opponent is thrown in and forced to concede a ruff and discard.

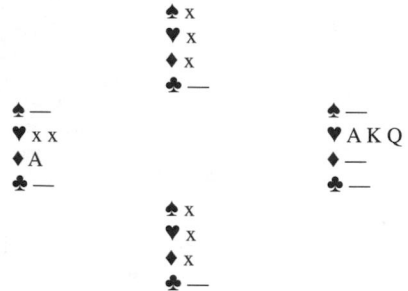

Spades are trumps, and South apparently has two unavoidable losers in hearts and diamonds. However, a heart is led, which forces East into the lead. He must continue a heart, permitting South to discard the losing diamond while ruffing the heart in the dummy. The distinction between these two types of throw-in does not rest on the contract, trump or notrump, but on the mechanism involved. Both types may occur at a trump contract. At a trump contract, the opponent who is thrown in may be faced with a choice of plays, each of which costs a trick; thus the various categories of throw-in may overlap.

(3) *Entry Throw-in.* The opponent who gains the lead must play a suit in which declarer has established tricks to which there is no entry.

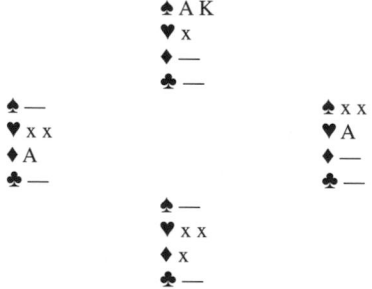

South has the lead in a notrump contract. North's two spade tricks are inaccessible. However, a heart lead saddles East with the necessity of leading a spade to the next trick, providing the entry to dummy's hand.

Proper execution of a throw-in play requires declarer to consider two factors: (a) the stripping, or elimination, process: this means that declarer must assure himself that, once thrown in, the defender has no safe lead; and (b) the throw-in card: at the judicious moment, declarer must be able to lose the lead to that opponent whose hand has been stripped of safe exit cards. Declarer may strip an opponent's hand by plain suit leads, by ruffing, or by a preliminary squeeze (see SECONDARY SQUEEZE). Sometimes a perfect elimination is not possible, and declarer must hope for favorable distribution.

South has become declarer at a 5♠ contract reached by trying for a slam. A club was led by West, won by the ace. The A♠ was cashed, followed by a club to the king and ruffing a third club (stripping both hands of clubs). Two top hearts were played declarer hoping to strip West of exit cards in that suit, followed by a spade, throwing West into the lead. Since West in fact had no more hearts, his choice was between a club or diamond, either of which would forfeit a trick. Certain suit combinations lend themselves to a throw-in. In the following combinations, the throw-in card is in the critical suit, which the defenders must return at the cost of a trick:

| A Q 9 | A J 10 | K 10 x | Q J x | K 9 x | A 10 x |
| x x x | x x x | x x x | x x x | J x x | J 9 x |

In each case, South leads low, and then simply covers the card played by West. Provided East has been stripped of all other exit cards, he will have to return this suit; in this way declarer can hold his losses in the suit to a minimum. There are other combinations in which an extra trick is guaranteed, provided the opponents must open up the suit. The throw-in card must be in some other suit.

| A 10 x | K x x | K 9 x | Q x x |
| J x x | J x x | Q 10 x | J x x |

There are certain combinations in which declarer's prospects are improved if the opponents can be forced to lead the suit. The throw-in card must be in some other suit:

| A 10 x | A x | A x x |
| K 9 x | Q x | J 9 x |

There are many suit combinations which can provide the means for a throw-in play. The most common is an eight-card holding, missing the king and queen, A-x-x opposite J-x-x-x-x. Declarer leads the ace, and then plays a small card in the suit after the elimination is complete. If either player holds K-Q, he can be thrown in; even if he holds K-x or Q-x, he may neglect to unblock, or else it may cost him a trick to do so. Many throw-in plays are named after the means employed to strip the hand or throw-in the opponents. One such would be a crossruff strip, and another a loser-on-loser elimination. The latter is commonly available, although often missed.

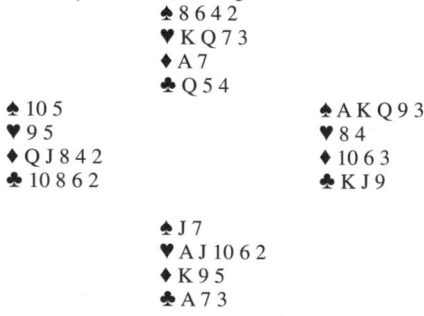

After East opened the bidding with 1♠, South became the declarer at 4♥. Spades are led and declarer ruffs high on the third round. Placing East with the ♣K for his opening bid, South draws trumps in two rounds, plays the A-K, followed by a diamond ruff, ending in dummy. So dummy's last spade is led, on which South discards a losing club, throwing East into the lead. East must concede a ruff and sluff, or lead from his club tenace. The throw-in usually follows the elimination, but this is not invariably the case.

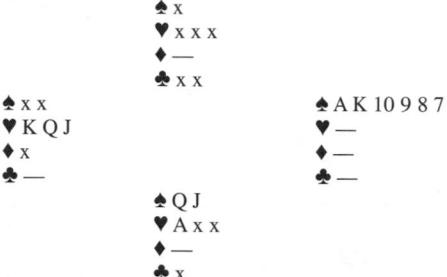

```
                    ♠ x
                    ♥ x x x
                    ♦ —
                    ♣ x x
    ♠ x x                        ♠ A K 10 9 8 7
    ♥ K Q J                      ♥ —
    ♦ x                          ♦ —
    ♣ —                          ♣ —
                    ♠ Q J
                    ♥ A x x
                    ♦ —
                    ♣ x
```

Clubs are trumps and South requires four of the remaining tricks, with only three in sight. A spade is led, won by East. On the spade continuation, North discards a heart. On the next spade, North discards another heart, while South ruffs. South can now lead the ♥A and win both of dummy's trumps for three more tricks. In a double elimination, either opponent may win the throw-in card, but the declarer gains a trick in either case.

(4) *Double Elimination.*

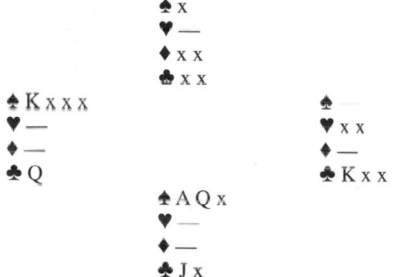

```
                    ♠ x
                    ♥ —
                    ♦ x x
                    ♣ x x
    ♠ K x x x                    ♠
    ♥ —                          ♥ x x
    ♦ —                          ♦ —
    ♣ Q                          ♣ K x x
                    ♠ A Q x
                    ♥ —
                    ♦ —
                    ♣ J x
```

Diamonds are trumps, and South requires four of the remaining tricks. A club is led which may be won by either opponent. If West's queen holds, he must lead into South's spade tenace; if East overtakes with the ♣K, South's jack is established. There are certain rare positions in which the declarer can bring off a repeating elimination, in which the same defender can be thrown in several times to make a losing lead.

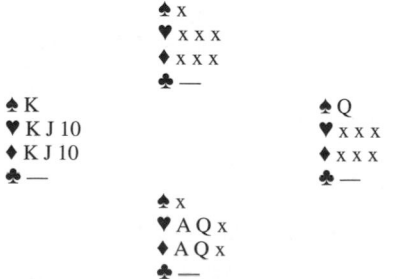

```
                    ♠ x
                    ♥ x x x
                    ♦ x x x
                    ♣ —
    ♠ K                          ♠ Q
    ♥ K J 10                     ♥ x x x
    ♦ K J 10                     ♦ x x x
    ♣ —                          ♣ —
                    ♠ x
                    ♥ A Q x
                    ♦ A Q x
                    ♣ —
```

Spades are trump. South leads a spade and West is thrown in. Whatever card he returns, South wins two tricks in that suit and throws West in again with the third round of the suit. West must now give declarer two tricks in the second suit. South, starting with two tricks, ends up with four.

(5) *Pseudo Elimination.* A defender may believe that he has been thrown in and must concede a trick, although this may not be the case. Usually this occurs when the defender fears to give declarer a ruff and sluff. This may not benefit declarer for either of two reasons: he may have concealed another card of that suit in his hand, or else the ruff and discard permits declarer to discard a card which was not a loser in any case.

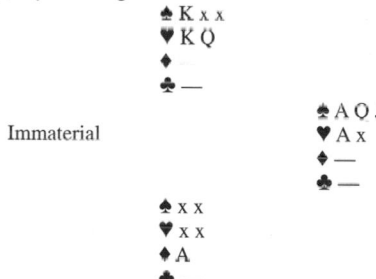

```
                    ♠ A 10
                    ♥ K Q 10 x
                    ♦ x x x
                    ♣ A 9 x x
    ♠ K Q J 9 8 7                ♠ x x x
    ♥ x x                        ♥ x x x
    ♦ K Q J                      ♦ x x x x
    ♣ J x                        ♣ Q x x
                    ♠ x x
                    ♥ A J x x
                    ♦ A x x
                    ♣ K 10 x x
```

South is declarer at 4♥. A spade is led, won by the ace. Trumps are drawn, the ♦A is taken, and the suit continued. West wins two diamonds and a spade. The only correct defense is a spade continuation, although South can discard a club in one hand while ruffing the spade in the other. South still has a club loser. However, if West is reluctant to give the ruff and sluff, he will lead a club, permitting South to avoid a loser in that suit.

(6) *Defense Against a Throw-in.* Often the defenders can foresee an impending throw-in. They have several ways of escaping the endplay.

(a) By retaining an Exit Card.

```
                    ♠ K x x
                    ♥ K Q
                    ♦
                    ♣ —
                                         ♠ A Q J
    Immaterial                           ♥ A x
                                         ♦ —
                                         ♣ —
                    ♠ x x
                    ♥ x x
                    ♦ A
                    ♣ —
```

At notrump, South leads the ♦A, throwing a spade from dummy. East must discard a spade, not the small heart. If he discards the heart, South can throw him in the lead with a heart, and East is forced to lead the spade. If he holds the small heart, he can exit with it after winning the ♥A, forcing the spade lead to come to him from North.

(b) By Unblocking.

```
                    ♠ x x x
                    ♥ A Q
                    ♦ —
                    ♣ —
    ♠ 10 x x                     ♠ Q J x
    ♥ x x                        ♥ K x
    ♦ —                          ♦ —
    ♣ —                          ♣ —
                    ♠ A K x
                    ♥ x x
                    ♦ —
                    ♣ —
```

South cashes the ♠ A-K on which East must unblock by playing his honors, so that West can win the third round of spades with the 10, returning a heart, to ensure a trick for East's king.

(c) By Playing Second Hand High.

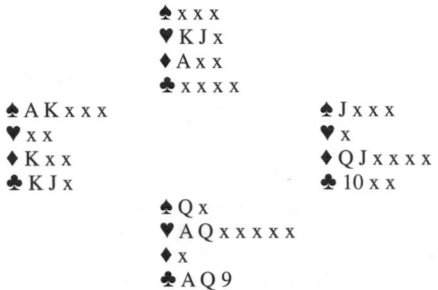

♠ A Q 8

♠ 10 x x   ♠ K J 9

♠ x x x

South leads small, intending to insert the 8. East can win with the 9, but then must lead into North's tenace. When South plays small, West must rise with the 10 to protect his partner from the endplay.

(d) By Refusing to Assist in the Elimination.

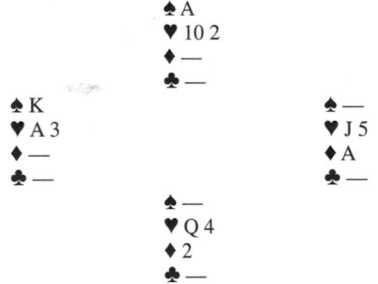

After West opened 1♠, South became the declarer at 4♥. West took two top spades. West must switch to hearts or diamonds. South does not have enough entries to dummy to ruff out spades and diamonds to strip the West hand before leading a club. See also ENDPLAY and PARTIAL ELIMINATION.

THROW-IN SQUEEZE A squeeze which operates as a trick is surrendered.

♠ A
♥ 10 2
♦ —
♣ —

♠ K
♥ A 3
♦ —
♣ —

♠ —
♥ J 5
♦ A
♣ —

♠ —
♥ Q 4
♦ 2
♣ —

In notrump, South leads his diamond.

THROWING THE LEAD (into a desired defender's hand). See THROW-IN PLAYS.

THURNER MOVEMENT. A team movement for a round-robin between an even number of teams. In each round there are two tables sharing boards. The movement exists for 6, 8, 12 and 14 tables. It is Mitchell-based with an appendix table.

Six teams. Tables 6 shares with each other table in turn, so it should be centrally situated.

Table	1			2			3			4			5			6		
Rnd	NS	EW	BD	NS	EW	BD	NS	EW	BD	NS	EW	BD	NS	EW	BD	NS	EW	BD
1	1	6	1	2	3	2	3	5	3	4	2	4	5	4	5	6	1	1
2	1	4	2	2	1	3	3	6	4	4	5	5	5	2	1	6	3	4

3	1	2	3	2	4	4	3	1	5	4	3	1	5	6	2	6	5	2
4	1	5	4	2	6	5	3	4	1	4	1	2	5	3	3	6	2	5
5	1	3	5	2	5	1	3	2	2	4	6	3	5	1	4	6	4	3

Eight teams.

Table and NS #	1	2	3	4	5	6	7	8
E-W #	8	4	7	3	6	2	5	1
Boards	1	2	3	4	5	6	7	1

N-S pairs remain stationary. E-W 1-7 move one table up, boards one table down. E-W 8 move two tables down: 1-6-4-2-7-5-3.

Twelve teams.

Table and NS #	1	2	3	4	5	6	7	8	9	10	11	12
E-W #	12	6	11	5	10	4	9	3	8	2	7	1
Boards	1	2	3	4	5	6	7	8	9	10	11	1

N-S pairs remain stationary. E-W 1-11 move one table up, boards one table down. E-W 12 move four tables up (five tables if home table 12 is encountered): 1-5-9-2-6-10-3-7-11-4-8

Fourteen teams.

Table and NS #	1	2	3	4	5	6	7	8	9	10	11	12	13	14
E-W #	14	7	13	6	12	5	11	4	10	3	9	2	8	1
Boards	1	2	3	4	5	6	7	8	9	10	11	12	13	1

N-S pairs remain stationary. E-W 1-13 move one table up, boards one table down. E-W 14 move four tables down (five tables if home table 14 is encountered): 1-10-6-2-11-7-3-12-8-4-13-9-5
See TEAM OF FOUR MOVEMENTS.

TICKETS. A colloquialism used in various ways to refer to (1) pick-up slips, (2) private score cards (tallies) (n.b. This will differentiate from private score cards used in tournaments which are called convention cards. See entry SCORECARD), or (3) the right high cards for a particular action — "He had the tickets."

TIE. Equality of result in a competition. (1) On a board; (2) In a knockout match. Additional boards must be played, in accordance with the conditions of contest, to determine a winner; (3) In overall standings or section standings. In ACBL contests, since 1992, any margin is a win.

TIERCE. A term, obsolete in bridge, used to describe a sequence of three cards, one or more of which usually has honor rank.

TIGHT. A colloquialism for SINGLETON or STIFF, particularly in describing a singleton high honor. Refers also to doubleton honors as in A-K or K-Q tight.

TIME LIMIT ON RIGHT TO PLAY. This is usually at the discretion of the director. In some tournaments the sponsoring organization sets a deadline beyond which purchase of additional entries depends on the need to fill in sections. In second and later sessions of multi-session events, the director must seek substitutes for pairs who are late to report.

TIME VALUATION. See TEMPO.

TIMING. An element in the play of a hand. The order in which trumps are pulled, losers are trumped, and side suits are developed are elements that enter into both declarer's and defenders' play.

The following example is given by Terence Reese:

```
                    ♠ 10 8 7 6 2
                    ♥ 7 6
                    ♦ 9 8 5 2
                    ♣ A K
♠ K 3                                   ♠ A Q J 9 5
♥ J 10 3 2                              ♥ K Q 9 8 4
♦ J 6 4                                 ♦ —
♣ Q 10 9 5                              ♣ 8 7 3
                    ♠ 4
                    ♥ A 5
                    ♦ A K Q 10 7 3
                    ♣ J 6 4 2
```

Spades are led against 5♦ and South ruffs the second round. If South makes the obvious play of drawing one round of trumps he will fail. He plays top clubs, returns to his hand with a diamond lead and ruffs a club. He returns to his hand with a heart and ruffs his last club. But he then lacks an entry to his hand and cannot prevent the defense from scoring a heart trick and also the ♦J, promoted by a spade play from East.

If South considers the danger of a 3-0 trump split, he can take precautions. He must take the slight risk of playing dummy's club winners before leading a round of trumps. Then he can maneuver the club ruffs and eventually draw West's last trump.

TOP. (1) On a board: the best score made in the play of a particular hand in a duplicate tournament; its value in matchpoint play is one less than the number of times the board was in competition. If one pair earns a top, their opponents must score zero points or a BOTTOM. (2) Score: the best score for a session of play among the contestants in direct competition (3) A card: to play a card higher in rank than the ones previously played by the second or third player to play to the trick; (4) The highest card in dummy's suit, as, declarer called for the top heart.

TOP AND BOTTOM CUEBID. An immediate overcall in the opponent's major suit to show the highest and lowest ranking unbid suits. See also MICHAELS CUEBID.

TOP OF INTERIOR SEQUENCE. See INTERIOR SEQUENCE.

TOP OF NOTHING. See THREE SMALL CARDS, LEAD FROM .

TOP SCORE. The highest number of matchpoints available to any contestant in direct competition. See MATCHPOINT; SCORING ACROSS THE FIELD; BAROMETER SCORING. In North America and some other areas of the world, top is one less than the number of times a board is in play. In Europe and some other areas, it is more common to make top two less than double the number of times a board is in play. The second method results in scores exactly twice as large as the first method, the major difference being that halves are eliminated. In American tournaments, fields are divided into sections and tops usually are figured within each section or, in some major events, combinations of sections. It is common in other parts of the world to score across the entire field, making for much larger tops. This has been easier to arrange since the advent of computers.

TORINO BULL. The trophy for the World Women's Team Olympiad, presented by the City of Turin, Italy, on the occasion of the 1960 Olympiad. See Appendix for winners.

TOTAL POINT SCORING. (British term is aggregate scoring.) Computation of scores based on points earned minus points lost, from the scoring table of contract bridge (see LAWS OF CONTRACT BRIDGE (Law 81), LAWS OF DUPLICATE (Law 77)); the scoring used at rubber bridge or CHICAGO. As a form of scoring in pair tournaments, total point scoring was complicated by the imposition of PENALTY LIMITS and the resulting EXCESS POINTS. It has been almost wholly eliminated, generally in favor of MATCHPOINT SCORING, but occasionally, in important matches, by IMPS FOR PAIR GAMES or scoring in team games by VICTORY POINTS. As a form of scoring in team games, it is adaptable particularly for match play in head-on contests. IMP scoring has largely replaced total point scoring. The Reisinger Trophy knockout teams in the Eastern States Regional was the last important knockout event in the United States to replace total point scoring with IMP scoring, doing so in 1965.

TOTAL TRICKS, LAW OF. See LAW OF TOTAL TRICKS .

TOUCHING CARDS. (1) Cards that are in sequence in the same suit, as the 10 and 9 in a holding of K-10-9-6. See SEQUENCE and PLAY FROM EQUALS. (2) With fingers: in duplicate bridge, it is illegal for any player to touch any cards other than his own, unless he is arranging the dummy's cards and so declares. See LAWS OF CONTRACT BRIDGE (Law 7).

TOUCHING HONORS. A holding of two or more honors that are in sequence. In a holding of Q-J-10-7 of a suit, the first three are touching honors.

TOUCHING SUITS. Suits that, within the order of ranking, are next to each other; spades and hearts, hearts and diamonds, and diamonds and clubs are touching suits. For some purposes, such as selecting the suit for an opening bid, clubs and spades are regarded as touching, with the clubs the "higher" suit.

TOURNAMENT. In the days of WHIST, gatherings of players for the purpose of competing at the game were termed "congresses", a term that is still current in Britain and Australia. As auction bridge replaced whist, the term "congress" gave way to tournament, as the accent shifted from sociability to competition. Club games among local groups up to competition at national and international level are all so described. The essentials of a tournament are the planning thereof by a SPONSORING ORGANIZATION, publicity and promotion, the programming of events, the competition itself, the SCORING and determination of winners, and the HOSPITALITY in connection therewith. Various aspects of tournament play and references to the results of important tournaments are treated in special articles in this book. See DUPLICATE BRIDGE and CHAMPIONSHIP TOURNAMENTS .

TOURNAMENT COMMITTEE. See COMMITTEE.

TOURNAMENT DIRECTOR. The official representative of the sponsoring organization, responsible for the technical management of the tournament, subject to the LAWS OF DUPLICATE BRIDGE and to supplementary regulations announced by the sponsor.*[1]

Classification of directors. ACBL tournament directors are ACBL employees. As such, ACBL hires, trains and assigns (as needed and required) TDs to officiate at ACBL sanctioned tournaments. Occasionally they will be assigned to direct at non-ACBL tournaments (such as World Bridge Federation Championships). They are ranked according to ability and experience. There were 27 tournament directors listed by ACBL in 1994 in its two top categories, National and Associate National tournament directors. Exclusive of club and local directors authorized to conduct games at affiliated duplicate clubs, there were approximately 200 more lower rated TDs.

As of January, 1995, directors were designated as follows in descending order of rank: National Director, Associate National Director, Tournament Director (formerly Regional Director), Associate Tournament Director (formerly Sectional Director), and Local Tournament Director (formerly Local Director). Trainee no longer will be a rank starting in 1995. As of 1995 only full-time or salaried directors will be assigned as directors-in-charge at regional tournaments.

Field Representatives. There are six National tournament directors who supervise the tournament directors residing in their geographical area. Each field representative is responsible for training and promotions of TDs, staffing of tournaments, communication with his area units and districts and members, and helping solve any problems which may develop. In 1994 the field representatives were:

Peter Mollemet	Tom Quinlan
Chris Patrias	Bill Schoder
Roger Putnam	Sol Weinstein

Other National Tournament Directors. Some are full-time salaried employees of the ACBL while the others, retired from the salaried staff, work various numbers of tournaments each year. All are qualified to provide top-flight direction at international, national and regional tournaments. When schedules permit, their services are also available as chief directors of sectionals, ensuring smooth conduct of these events as well as trained supervision of other directors of the staff. In 1994 the list included:

*Maurice Braunstein	Brian Moran
Henry Cukoff	Roberta Shipley
*Sid Davidson	*John Wiser
*Jack Hudgins	*Phil Wood

*retired, part-time

Associate National directors. Some, but not all, are full-time salaried ACBL employees. Members of this group are fully qualified to serve as chief directors at regional and national events. In 1994 the list included:

Jeff Alexander	Charles MacCracken
Steve Bates	Millard Nachtwey
Douglas Grove	Stan Tench
Max Hardy	Bill Weyant
Patricia Jackson	Tom Whitesides
Eleanor Kipperman	Walter Wilson
Robert Kitchel	

World tournament directors. Tournament directors from throughout the world were invited by the World Bridge Federation to work at the 1994 NEC World Bridge Championships in Albuquerque NM. Those selected were:

Max Bavin, England
Julius Butkow, South Africa
Claude Dadoun, France
Richard Grenside, Australia
John McGregor, Costa Rica
Hans Olof Hallén, Sweden
Zhou Qi, China
Yury Covalenko, Uzbekistan
Antonio Riccardi, Italy
Jan Louwerse, Netherlands
Viswanathan, India
Manuel Espinoza-Paz, Argentina

European tournament directors. In Europe directors are hardly ever employees of national organizations, though some make a living by combining working for their organization, teaching bridge and being a tournament director. For championships organized by the European Bridge League the best directors from all over Europe are invited. In 1987, when Harold Franklin, the chief tournament director for both the World Bridge Federation and the European Bridge League, retired, the EBL appointed four chief tournament directors: Max Bavin, England; Claude Dadoun, France; Hans-Olof Hallén, Sweden, and Ton Kooijman, Netherlands. Four assistant chief directors were also appointed: Nathalie van den Broeck, Belgium (now retired); Jan Louwerse; Netherlands, Claude Michaud, France, and Antonio Riccardi, Italy.

Since the beginning of the Eighties the EBL has organized a training course once every couple of years for tournament directors. It is attended by 50 to 60 tournament directors from all over Europe. All participants take an an examination at the conclusion of the course. The purpose is to recognize the EBL's best directors and to develop a higher standard of tournament directing.

*[1]*Note: Throughout this book, "Director," when capitalized, refers to a member of the Board of Directors of a governing body and not to a tournament director.*

TOWIE. A form of bridge devised for three players but intended to be played usually by four, five or more players, of whom only three play at one time but the others participate in the defenders' score against the declarer. The game was originated in Paris in 1931 by two Americans, J. Leonard Replogle and Paulding Fosdick, who were then living abroad. In 1935 Replogle, with the assistance of William Huske, sought to make towie a popular game in the United States, with only moderate success, though it is still played. The principal books on the game were written by Huske and by Stuyvesant Wainwright Jr.

The deal in towie conforms to that of certain earlier three-hand bridge games: After dealing four hands, the dealer turns up six cards of the dummy, after which the auction proceeds as in any three-handed game. Scoring is based on the 1932 INTERNATIONAL CODE, which differs from later codes in undertrick penalties and in the fact that notrump tricks count 35 each.

The three active players bid for the dummy. The high bidder becomes declarer. If he fulfills his contract, he collects from every other player, active or inactive; if he loses, he pays every such player. After each deal, one player is replaced by an inactive player, in order of precedence except that a player who is not vulnerable takes precedence over a vulnerable player.

If a game contract is not reached, the hands are thrown

in, and a GOULASH follows. See also THREE-HANDED BRIDGE.

TRADITIONALISTS. see SCIENTISTS.

TRAIN BRIDGE. See COMMUTER BRIDGE.

TRAM TICKETS. Very poor cards. (British colloquialism).

TRANCE. A protracted break in the tempo of the play during which a player attempts to solve a problem. Trances and huddles are frequent causes of ethical difficulties and disputes. See HUDDLE and SLOW PLAY .

TRANSFER BIDS. Bids aimed principally at making a strong hand declarer. It is often advantageous for the lead to come up to the stronger hand and for it to remain concealed. Transfer bids were first used in the United States by David Carter (see TEXAS CONVENTION) and subsequently developed by Oswald Jacoby (see JACOBY TRANSFER BIDS). These bids were independently devised by Olle Willner of Stockholm, Sweden, who discussed the use of transfers in a series of articles in *Bridge Tidningen* in 1953-54. See also FOUR-SUIT TRANSFER BIDS. The original form of transfer bid was the Texas Convention, and SOUTH AFRICAN TEXAS is a revised form. See also French RELAY SYSTEM. Another purpose of transfer bids is to distinguish between weak and strong opening preempts, to enable responder to judge whether to try for slam. See NAMYATS; FOUR NOTRUMP OPENING AS MINOR PREEMPT; FOUR-SUIT TRANSFER BIDS; RUBIN TRANSFERS.

TRANSFER OPENING PREEMPTS. See NAMYATS; FOUR NOTRUMP OPENING AS MINOR PREEMPT; RUBIN TRANSFERS; TRANSFER OPENING THREE-BIDS; TWO-UNDER OPENING PREEMPTS.

TRANSFER OPENING THREE-BIDS. A development of the TEXAS principle. They have three technical advantages. First, the lead comes up to the hand which is likely to be strong in the side suits. Second, the defense is more difficult because little is known about the declarer's strength and distribution. Third, the opening bidder may be able to show a freak two-suited hand by bidding his second suit on the second round. A technical disadvantage is that it is easier for the opponents to take action than it would be after a normal three-bid: a double and a cuebid in the opener's genuine suit are available as takeout bids of varying strength. Also, a preemptive bid in clubs cannot be made at the level of three. A practical disadvantage is that an absentminded partner may forget that the convention is being used. Also, it may gain an unfair advantage against opponents unfamiliar with the convention. Used in the World Championship by Pierre Ghestem and René Bacherich.

A complete method was devised in 1968 by Svend Novrup and Anders Laustsen of Denmark, and is called Verdi because the players make beautiful music with it. Three clubs, diamonds and hearts are transfers to the next-higher suit, with normal preemptive strength. Three spades shows a solid minor, allowing three notrump to be played from the correct side (unlike the gambling 3NT). Three notrump opening shows a semi-solid minor suit. NAMYATS is used with this structure. See TWO-

UNDER OPENING PREEMPTS.

TRANSFERS OVER DOUBLES OF ONE NOTRUMP. A four-suit escape method. A redouble is a transfer to clubs, 2♣ transfers to diamonds, 2♦ to hearts and 2♥ to spades. If responder redoubles and then bids 2♦ over the forced 2♣, he is asking opener to bid his better major.

TRANSFER OVERCALLS OF ONE NOTRUMP. Over one notrump:
  2 ♣ = diamonds
  2 ♦ = hearts
  2 ♥ = spades
  2 ♠ = clubs.
Responder normally accepts the transfer if he would have passed an overcall. Other actions are those he would have made in response to a normal overcall.

This idea was introduced as part of the BLUE TEAM CLUB and has gained favor in Europe.

TRANSFER SQUEEZE. A squeeze play which results from TRANSFERRING THE MENACE. The following hand was played by Alan Truscott in the 1958 European Championships:

```
                    ♠ 7 6 4 3
                    ♥ Q 8
                    ♦ Q 9 7 2
                    ♣ A J 8
        ♠ K                       ♠ 9 8 5 2
        ♥ 9 6 5 3                 ♥ K J
        ♦ J 10 8 5                ♦ K 6 4 3
        ♣ K 10 9 4                ♣ 5 3 2
                    ♠ A Q J 10
                    ♥ A 10 7 4 2
                    ♦ A
                    ♣ Q 7 6
```

West led the ♦J against 4♥, which was ducked around to the ace. A heart to the queen and king brought a spade return, and the finesse of the queen lost to the king. A heart was returned and won by South, who led a second round of trumps, revealing the bad split. A low heart was ruffed and overruffed, and East exited with his last trump. The ♣J was finessed, and the ♦Q was led to transfer the diamond menace. East covered, South ruffed, and two winning hearts squeezed West in the minor suits.

TRANSFERRED TRICK. A trick transferred to the non-offending side after a revoke has been established. See LAWS OF DUPLICATE (Law 64).

TRANSFERRING THE MENACE. The process whereby control of a suit is transferred from one opponent to the other.

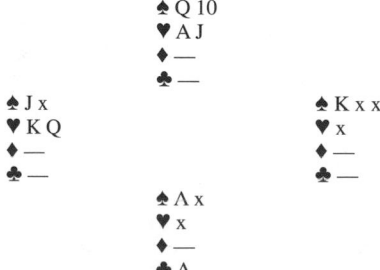

```
                    ♠ Q 10
                    ♥ A J
                    ♦ —
                    ♣ —
        ♠ J x                     ♠ K x x
        ♥ K Q                     ♥ x
        ♦ —                       ♦ —
        ♣ —                       ♣ —
                    ♠ A x
                    ♥ x
                    ♦ —
                    ♣ A
```

South has menaces in two suits, so that the material for a squeeze is present, but each opponent controls one menace, and neither can be squeezed. If the lead is in the North hand, the ♠Q is led forcing East to play the king which is taken by the ace. The spade menace is no longer the queen guarded by East's king but the ♠10 guarded by West's jack, so that West has BUSY CARDS in two suits, and he is squeezed by the lead of the ♣A. But if the lead had been in the South hand, the lead of the ♣A would have effected a GUARD SQUEEZE against West.

TRANSFERS OVER DOUBLES OF A PREEMPTIVE BID.

When a preemptive action is doubled, minimum actions can be used to show length in the next-higher strain, with or without a fit with opener. A transfer to opener's suit shows a fitting top honor.

TRANSFORMATION CARDS.

These are specially designed packs whose faces include the various pips on the suit cards as part of an overall design. During the last century, a number of artists tried their hands at creating pictures that would incorporate all of the pips, in their usual locations, into larger designs, generally of human or animal figures. The first such cards seem to have been made by J. G. Cotta, in Tubingen, Germany, in 1805, with several different packs produced by him in the next few years. English transformation cards appeared first in Ackerman's Repository in 1818, and several other packs soon followed. About 1850, sets of cards appeared in London, New York, Munich, Vienna and Paris, partially duplicates in design, some cards being different while others appear in three or four of the packs. Because of the widespread copying, it is difficult to know which versions were original. Grimaud and Hart put their names on packs, and some artists' initials can be found, but precise dating appears impossible. Issued in New York were the Eclipse Comic cards, designed by F. H. Lowerre in 1876, Tiffany & Company issued their Harlequin cards three years later; these same designs were used for the first series of Kinney Brothers Cigarette cards. A second Kinney series followed with all new designs. In 1895, the United States Playing Card Company published its own packs, called "Hustling Joe" and "Vanity Fair."

For more information, see "Transformation Cards" by Albert Field, published by U.S. Games Systems, Stamford Ct.

TRAP.

A defensive bidding system against the FORCING CLUB. Double indicates a heart suit and 1♦ shows a spade suit. 1♥ shows either a black two-suiter or a red two-suiter. 1♠ shows either both minors or both majors. 1 NT shows either a club-heart two-suiter or a diamond-spade two-suiter. All bids at the two level show either the suit bid or a three-suiter short in the suit bid. See TRAP WITH TWO LEVEL TRANSFERS.

TRAP BID

(or trap bidding). An inconsistent sequence of bids which traps partner by showing strength denied by an earlier bid. For example:

SOUTH	NORTH
1 ♣	1 ♠
3 ♠	4 ♠
5 ♥	

South's raise to 3♠ was encouraging but nonforcing. North accepted the invitation to bid game, perhaps straining his values to do so, and is now faced by a slam invita-

tion. South's bidding cannot be correct. If he is strong enough to bid 5♥, he must have been too strong to make the invitational bid of 3♠. His bidding means that his side must play below game or above game, but cannot stop in 4♠. See also IMPOSSIBLE BID and PRESSURE BID.

TRAP PASS.

A pass by a player holding a strong defensive hand, hoping that the opposition will bid themselves into difficulties. It is usually made by a player holding length and strength in the suit bid by the opener on his right:

♠ 6
♥ A Q 10 7 4
♦ K J 7
♣ A K 5 3

If the right-hand opponent opens the bidding with 1♥, there is no good alternative to a pass. There is strong evidence that the hand is a misfit, and that it will pay to defend. If 1♥ is passed out, the result should be reasonable. The same principle applies, only less forcefully, in a balancing position. A player with the above hand may consider passing if an opening bid of 1♥ is followed by two passes. This would certainly be sound tactics at matchpoint scoring against vulnerable opponents, as a score of 200 for the defense would beat all partscore results. A trap pass becomes a doubtful proposition when holding 18 or 19 high-card points, and is usually unwise with 20 or more. The danger of passing up a game in favor of a small penalty becomes too great.

Passes with strong hands by the player on dealer's right after an opening suit bid and a suit response are similar in principle, although the motive is slightly different: the prospect of a penalty is reduced, but the danger of taking action is greater. With a hand of exceptional strength, the fourth player should not necessarily rely on the fact that responder's bid is technically forcing. It is not at all unlikely that the dealer has made a psychic bid, and if he passes, the other defender cannot be expected to balance with a very weak hand. An unusual, and experimental, type of trap pass may sometimes be ventured by the partner of the opening bidder:

♠ 6
♥ K 8 5 3
♦ A J 4 2
♣ Q 10 5 4

If partner opens 1♠ and the next player passes, there is something to be said for a prompt pass if not vulnerable against vulnerable opponents. There is no certainty of a game, and if 1♠ is passed out the loss as a result of missing a game is unlikely to exceed 300. On the other hand, the fourth player may balance, in which case the penalty should not be less than 500 and might be 1,400. Such experiments should not be tried in matchpointed events (except when SHOOTING). See also MARMIC SYSTEM.

TRAP PLAY. See DECEPTIVE PLAY.

TRAVELING SCORESLIP (or TRAVELER).

The official score of each deal in a pair duplicate game may be recorded either of two ways: on a traveling scoreslip or an individual pick-up card. A majority of clubs and lesser championship events use the traveling scoreslip. This slip travels with the board, folded and inserted in a pocket so that the scores for the tables which have played it earlier are not visible until the slip is opened after the board has been replayed. The score at the new table is then entered. At the end of the session, when the board has been played at each table in the game, all the results will have been entered on the slip. The tournament director will then work out the matchpoints as shown here:

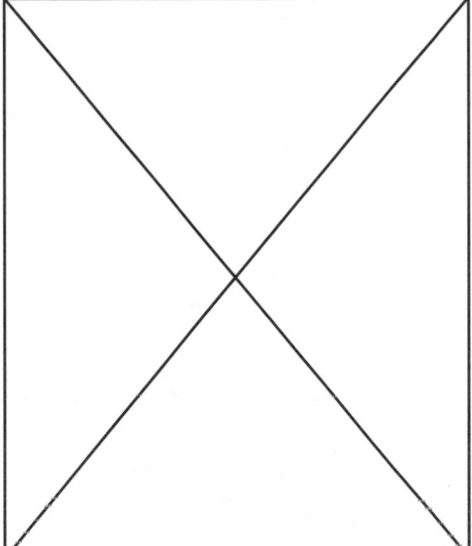

The completed traveling scoreslip gives you a full picture of how matchpoints are awarded. First the North-South scores are figured. Each score is awarded 1 point for every poorer score, half a point for every exactly equal score. It does not matter how much better one score is than another; the only thing that counts is how many pairs your score beats. Thus, the pair that bid and made 6♠ scored 530 points more than the next higher team, but got only one more Matchpoint. The pair that scored 450 for making five odd got only 30 points more than each of the four pairs that bid and made exactly four, but that 30 points turns out to be worth 2° Matchpoints more. The four pairs that got equal 420 scores were awarded 2° Matchpoints; 1 for the one pair they beat; ° for each of the three pairs they tied. The pair that was set at 6♠ got a zero. The East-West pairs might be figured exactly the same way. But the simple way is to give East-West the reciprocal of the North-South score: that is, deduct the N-S score from the possible top score, 6, and give East-West the difference. After several results have been entered, the contestants have an opportunity to compare their result with others previously recorded, and estimate an approximate final result. See CALIFORNIA SCORING, COMPARING SCORES, ESTIMATION, PICKUP SLIPS, SCORING FORMS.

TRAY (1) An obsolete term for a board. (2) The tray which slides under the SCREEN in major championships, carrying the bidding-box cards from one pair of opponents to the other pair. It was invented by Henny Dorsman of Aruba and introduced at the Central American and Caribbean Championships at Aruba in 1977. It was later improved under the supervision of Ernesto D'Orsi.

TREASURERS. Those who have held this position in the AMERICAN BRIDGE LEAGUE and the AMERI-

CAN CONTRACT BRIDGE LEAGUE are:

1927-28	Clayton W. Aldrich
1929	E. J. Tobin
1930-31	J. J. Laffeny
1932-34	Russell Baldwin
1935	David Burnstine (Burns)
1936	Gordon M. Gibbs
1937	J. N. S. Brewster, Jr.
1938-40	Gordon M. Gibbs
1941-42	J. H. Block
1943-44	Ralph W. Gresham
1945-47	Bertram Lebhar, Jr.
1949-51	Ralph W. Gresham
1952-66	Harry J. Fishbein
1966-69	Samuel Stayman
1969-70	Percy X. Bean
1970-72	Jerome Silverman
1973-74	Walter O'Loughlin
1975-76	Donald A. Moeller
1976-78	Lawrence Jolma
1979-80	Sydney A. Levey
1981	Lawrence Jolma
1982-83	Donald A. Moeller
1984	George Retek
1985-87	Herbert L. Smith
1988-94	Donald A. Moeller

TREATMENT. A natural bid that indicates a desire to play in the denomination named (or promises or requests values in that denomination), but that also, by agreement, gives or requests additional information on which further action could be based. A treatment thus differs from a CONVENTION, which is a bid that gives or requests information unrelated to the denomination named. For example, a LIMIT JUMP RAISE is a treatment; but a LIMIT JUMP RAISE TO SHOW A SINGLETON in a side suit is a convention. INVERTED MINOR SUIT RAISES and PREEMPTIVE RE-RAISES are other examples of treatments.

TRELDE LEADS (developed by John Trelde of the Netherlands). A method of leading from honor sequences to distinguish between a genuine sequence of three touching honors and a false sequence of only two touching honors. The principle is that from a genuine sequence the highest card is led and from a false sequence the second highest card is led. Partner should be able to determine which combination the lead is from by his and dummy's holding in the suit. Leads from A-K doubleton, a suit headed by A-K-Q and internal sequences follow accepted practices.

TREY. The 3 or three-spot of each suit.

TRIAL BID. A game suggestion made by bidding a new suit after a major suit fit has been located:

SOUTH	NORTH
1 ♥	2 ♥
3 ♣	

North-South have provisionally agreed to play a heart contract, although a final contract of 3NT is not completely excluded. However, it is completely impossible that the right contract could be clubs, so the club bid can only be an exploring maneuver. If North has no interest in game, he signs off with 3♥. If he wants to accept the invitation, he bids 4♥ or 3NT. As a rare alternative, he may bid an unbid suit in which he has strength, as a move toward 3NT. The usual practice is for South to make his trial bid in a suit in which he needs support, so it will generally contain at least three cards and at least two losers. Possible holdings would be: x-x-x, A-x-x, K-10-x-x, J-x-x-x, and many others.

The responder therefore takes his holding in the trial bid suit into account when making the decision whether to bid game. If his holding is neither maximum nor minimum in strength, he allows himself to be encouraged if he has honor strength or a shortage in the trial bid suit. Conversely, he should tend to reject the invitation if he has three or four small cards in the suit; a holding headed by the jack is only a slight improvement. In one special case, the final contract may be in a suit other than the one originally agreed on:

SOUTH	NORTH
1 ♠	2 ♠
3 ♥	4 ♥

4♥ may easily prove a superior contract to 4♠. If South holds four hearts, and North holds four, five, or six, spades will be an inferior landing place if the spade fit is 5-3.

There are two other situations in which bids of similar types are made.

SOUTH	NORTH
1 ♣	1 ♠
2 ♠	3 ♥

North's bid invites 4♠ and suggests some length in hearts, in which he would welcome support.

SOUTH	NORTH
1 ♣	2 ♣
2 ♥	

This is not a trial bid because no major suit has been agreed on. A heart fit is still possible, but it is very likely that the partnership will head for 3NT. South will tend to bid a suit in which he is strong, rather than a suit in which he is weak. His heart suit might be A-Q-x, but in no circumstances could it be x-x-x unless he was making a psychic effort to inhibit a lead.

Similarly:

SOUTH	NORTH
1 ♥	2 ♥
2 ♠	3 ♠

With three hearts and four spades in North, or with five hearts and four spades in South, the spade contract may be superior. However, restraint must be exercised. South's spade bid may be a three-card suit; hence a jump in spades by responder is unwise and unnecessary. See also INTEREST-SHOWING BID; PREEMPTIVE RE-RAISES; SHORT-SUIT GAME TRIES; SINGLE RAISE; TWO-WAY GAME TRIES; WEAK SUIT GAME TRY .

TRIATHLON. A three-event tournament, usually conducted over three days. The first event is a team of-four. Then the teams break down into pairs for a pairs contest. The final event is an individual. The winner is the player who has the best aggregate score. Since team events are scored differently from pair and individual events, the sponsoring organization has to set up a conversion scale that gives each event a proportional weight in the final standings.

TRICK. Consists of four cards played in rotation after an initial lead of one of the cards by the player whose turn it was to lead or to play first to the trick. A trick of four cards can be won by virtue of the winning card being highest in rank (number) of the four played; or because the card led is "long," that is, a remaining card in one's hand of a suit not held by any other player; or by having a trump card played to it either by declarer or dummy or either defender.

TRICK APPROPRIATED IN ERROR. A packet of the four cards played to a trick that has been gathered in by the pair of which neither contributed the winning card. Such a trick must be restored to the side that contributed the winning card if discovered in time. See LAWS OF CONTRACT BRIDGE (Laws 67 and 78).

TRICK POINTS. Points scored for fulfilled contracts toward the game. See BELOW THE LINE.

TRICK-SCORE. The value of the odd tricks of fulfilled contracts toward the winning of the game; in clubs or diamonds, 20 points each; in hearts or spades, 30 points each; at notrump, 40 points for the first and 30 for each subsequent trick. In French tournament play the fourth trick at notrump has been reduced to 20 points so that 4♥, 4♠, and 4NT each score 120 points. See FRENCH SCORING. Different trick scores operate in auction bridge and plafond.

TRI-COUNTRY TRIALS. Since 1985, a three-way playoff among Bermuda, Canada and Mexico has determined one of the Zone II teams for the Bermuda Bowl world championships. The tri-country trials are held every other year in odd- numbered years. (In even-numbered years, the three countries send their national champions to the World Team Olympiad or the World Pairs/ Rosenblum Teams championships.) In the tri-country trials, each team plays a 64-board match against the others. The team with the poorest record is dropped, while the other two play a 64-board final with full carryover from the first 64 deals. Canada, who had never participated in the Bermuda Bowl world championships before, won the first four tri-country trials to become one of the North American teams in the Bermuda Bowl. In 1993 Mexico won its first trip to the Bermuda Bowl by defeating Canada and Bermuda in the tri-country trials. See INTERNATIONAL OPEN TEAM SELECTION. For results see Appendix III.

TRINIDAD AND TOBAGO CONTRACT BRIDGE LEAGUE. Had 77 members in 1993.
President 1993:
Cyril Sancho
108 Cascade Road,
St. Anns
Port-of-Spain,
Trinidad.
Tel: 809 674 6720
Fax: 809 657 0556

TRIPLE COUP. A series of plays by the declarer in which he trumps three cards from the dummy's hand in order to shorten his own trump suit to the number held by his right-hand opponent. The purpose is to lead a card from the dummy at the eleventh or twelfth trick which the right-hand opponent must trump (being void of all other suits), and thus permit declarer to win the last two or three tricks by virtue of his own trumps being over those of his opponent. If the cards deliberately trumped by the declarer are side suit winners in their own right the coup is termed a grand coup. See COUP, TRIPLE GRAND COUP.

TRIPLE GRAND COUP. A grand coup in which the declarer shortens his hand three times in trumps, to reduce his holding to the same number as held by his right-hand opponent, by ruffing three winners from the dummy.

TRIPLE RAISE. A raise of partner's opening suit bid to the four-level. In a major suit the bid indicates that a fine distributional fit has been found, but that slam prospects are remote. A typical hand for responder would include an ace, a singleton, five trumps, and 7-10 points in high cards. None of these requirements is essential, but the hand should give promise of nine tricks opposite a minimum opening bid. The opener can assume that responder does not hold two aces, for he would then be likely to bid more slowly in case slam possibilities exist. See FAST ARRIVAL, PRINCIPLE OF; THREE NOTRUMP RESPONSE. In a minor suit the bid is rarer, and indicates an even more distributional hand. It is markedly preemptive in character, weaker in high cards than the major suit raise, and a typical distribution would be 6-5-2-0 with length in both minor suits. The raise of the major-suit opening to game can have a much wider range, up to perhaps 14 points in high cards, if the opening bid is limited as in the PRECISION, SCHENKEN and BLUE TEAM CLUB systems. See also DOUBLE RAISE and DELAYED GAME RAISE.

TRIPLE SQUEEZE. A squeeze against one opponent in three suits. It is a combination of three simple squeezes against the same opponent, which justifies the term. The term triple squeeze is often used to encompass squeezes which produce one trick and squeezes which produce two tricks. The latter is described under PROGRESSIVE SQUEEZE. See also BARCO SQUEEZE; CLASH SQUEEZE; COMPOUND SQUEEZE; GUARD SQUEEZE; HEXAGON SQUEEZE. The minimum requirements for a triple squeeze are two one-card menaces and a two-card menace with an entry opposite the squeeze card. These are the basic end positions:

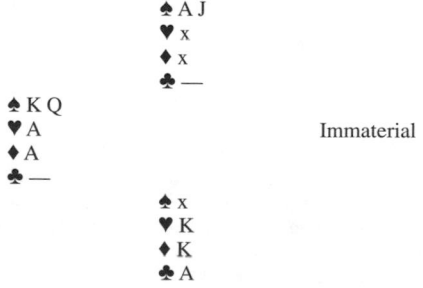

South leads the ♣A, and West must surrender a spade, establishing a trick for South in that suit. (Any other discard permits South to win all four tricks.) In this position the hand opposite the squeeze card has one menace. Since North has two idle cards, the position is automatic and either opponent may be squeezed.

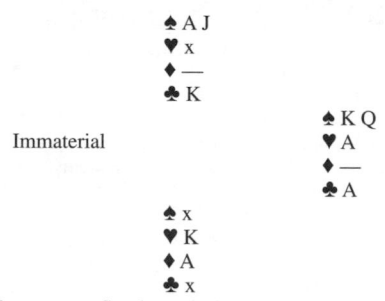

In notrump, South needs three tricks. He leads the ♦A, throwing a heart from the dummy, and East is squeezed in three suits.

In this position the hand opposite the squeeze card has two menaces. The ending shown is automatic and works equally well against either opponent.

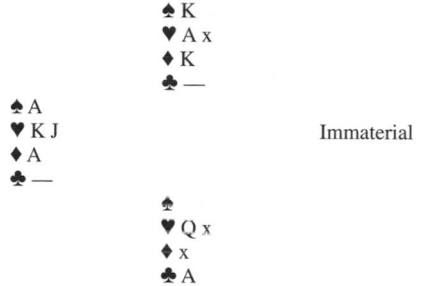

This is a variation of the above position, which is positional. If the East and West cards are transposed, the squeeze is ineffective. South leads the ♣A, and West is squeezed in three suits.

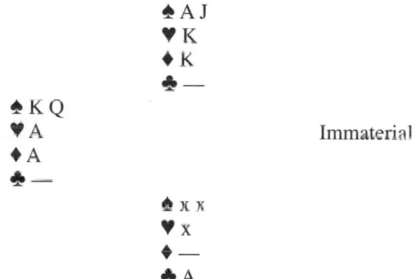

South leads the ♣A, and West is squeezed, permitting South to win two more tricks. In all these squeezes South has all but two of the remaining tricks. This is a characteristic of triple squeezes.

Fook H. Eng describes a situation where a gain of four tricks can be had in a progressive triple squeeze.

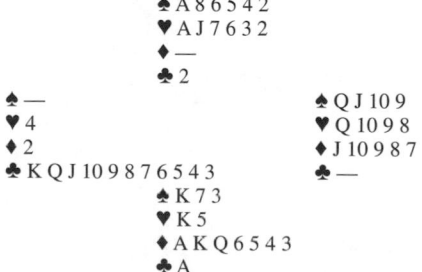

West leads the ♣K against an outrageous 6NT contract which has only eight top winners. However, on the very first trick East is already squeezed. No matter which suit he discards, that suit will immediately be conceded. It is not without complications, so let us examine the different cases.

If East discards a spade, a low spade is immediately conceded. If East returns a heart the free finesse provides us the balance already. Because of our immediate concession in the spade suit we have sufficient entries to pick them off in the right order. If East returns either a diamond or a spade, we simply win the trick and run the rest of the spades for a heart-diamond squeeze.

If East discards a heart, the A and K are taken and East is given his heart winner. If he returns a spade, the trick rides to the ace. The hearts are run and East is caught in a positional spade-diamond squeeze. If he returns a diamond, the three diamonds are cashed first just to tighten the hand. Then the A is cashed and the hearts are run for the same positional squeeze.

If East discards a diamond, a diamond is conceded. If a spade is returned, the A is won and either of the kings provide entry to run the diamond suit to squeeze East in hearts and spades. If a heart is returned, the free finesse provides the additional trick. If a diamond is returned, we simply run the suit to affect the spade-heart squeeze.

In rare situations the triple squeeze may win two tricks immediately. In the following position there are three two-trick threats:

```
              ♠ K Q
              ♥ A K 10 9
              ♦ —
              ♣ —
♠ A
♥ Q J x                    Immaterial
♦ K Q
♣ —
              ♠ x
              ♥ x
              ♦ A J 10
              ♣ A
```

South has only four tricks on top, but the ♣A squeezes West in three suits, and any discard costs him two tricks. Two two-trick threats (the VIENNA COUP)

```
              ♠ J 10 3
              ♥ A K Q J 3
              ♦ 5 2
              ♣ 7 4 2
♠ K 6                      ♠ 9 8 7 5 4 2
♥ 10 9 7 6 5               ♥ 8 4
♦ J 10 8                   ♦ K 9
♣ 8 6 5                    ♣ J 10 9
              ♠ A Q
              ♥ 2
              ♦ A Q 7 6 4 3
              ♣ A K Q 3
```

Clubs are led and South must take all the tricks in a notrump contract. South takes four club tricks, and West is squeezed in three suits. A discard of a spade or diamond costs two tricks, so West must throw a heart. South cashes the ♠A, and then runs the hearts, squeezing West in spades and diamonds. See also PROGRESSIVE SQUEEZE. For repeating triple squeezes, see BONNEY'S SQUEEZE; CLASH SQUEEZE; GUARD SQUEEZE; OVERTAKING SQUEEZE.

TRIPLETON. A holding of three cards in a given suit in a particular hand. The term is usually used to describe

an original, or dealt, combination; as, an ace-king tripleton in diamonds. For an opening lead from a small tripleton, see THREE SMALL CARDS, LEAD FROM .

TROPHIES. Those trophies competed for in International events are listed under the following headings: BERMUDA BOWL; CROWNINSHIELD TROPHY; CULBERTSON TROPHY; LENZ TROPHY; McCONNELL CUP; ROSENBLUM CUP; SCHWAB CUP; SOLOMON TROPHY; TORINO BULL; VANDERBILT CUP (2); VENICE CUP; WORLD BRIDGE FEDERATION TROPHY. ACBL Trophies are listed separately: CHICAGO TROPHY; FISHBEIN TROPHY; HERMAN TROPHY; MCKENNEY TROPHY; MOREHEAD TROPHY; MOTT-SMITH TROPHY; REISINGER MEMORIAL TROPHY; SPINGOLD TROPHY; VANDERBILT CUP (1); VON ZEDTWITZ GOLD CUP.

TRUMP. The suit named in the final bid, other than notrump. Such suit is the trump suit. and a card of the trump suit, when played, is a winner over any card of a plain (not trump) suit; if two or more trumps are played on the same trick, the highest trump card played wins the trick.

TRUMP ASKING BID. A convention used to inquire about key cards in the trump suit. As used in conjunction with ASKING BIDS as developed by Ely Culbertson a call of 4NT asked partner to describe his holding in the trump suit, as follows: 5♣ No ace, king, or queen; 5♦ One of three top honors; 5♥ Two of three top honors 5♠ All three top honors. If the 4NT bidder now bids 5NT, partner must show his trump length by a series of artificial responses. If the response to an asking bid is at the five level, 5NT can be used as a trump asking bid for honor cards but it is not possible to follow up by asking for trump length. See also BARON SLAM TRY; BYZANTINE BLACKWOOD; GRAND SLAM FORCE; KEY CARD BLACKWOOD; KEY CARD GERBER; MALOWAN SIX CLUBS CONVENTION; PRECISION ASKING BIDS; ROMAN KEY CARD BLACKWOOD; ROMEX ASKING BIDS.

TRUMP CONTROL. See CONTROL MAINTENANCE and TRUMP SUIT MANAGEMENT.

TRUMP COUP. See COUP.

TRUMP ECHO. See TRUMP SIGNAL

TRUMP KING. See conventions listed under TRUMP ASKING BID.

TRUMP LEADS. The opening lead of a trump is not a first-line lead, and it will prove costly if the particular deal happens to be one where it was necessary for the defenders to cash tricks in a hurry. Nevertheless, there are circumstances when an opening trump lead figures to be eminently proper. (Trump leads should not be made merely because one does not know what else to lead .)

Here are the major situations: (1) Where the bidding has indicated that dummy will be able to trump some of declarer's losing tricks; (2) Where the leader has reason to fear an aggressive lead in some other suit, lest it be beneficial to declarer; (3) Where there is a desire to mislead declarer as to the true state of affairs in the trump suit, as, for example, talking him out of taking a finesse that he figures to take if left to his own resources

The following hands illustrate some of the situations in which a trump opening should be made. Where the bidding has indicated that dummy will be able to trump some of declarer's losing tricks, a trump should be opened.

```
                    ♠ 9 8 3
                    ♥ 6 2
                    ♦ 10 9 8 4 3
                    ♣ 8 6 5
♠ A 5 4                            ♠ 7 2
♥ K J 9 8                          ♥ 4 3
♦ 7 5 2                            ♦ K Q J 6
♣ Q J 10                          ♣ 9 7 4 3 2
                    ♠ K Q J 10 6
                    ♥ A Q 10 7 5
                    ♦ A
                    ♣ A K
```

WEST	NORTH	EAST	SOUTH
			2 ♠
Pass	2NT	Pass	3 ♥
Pass	3 ♠	Pass	4 ♠
All Pass			

What could be more "normal" than to open the ♣Q? If made, this will be won by declarer and promptly he will bang down the ace and another heart. A belated shift by West to the ace and another trump permits South to trump one of his losing hearts with dummy's last trump; the closed hand is entered with the ♦A, picking up the last outstanding trump and conceding a further heart trick. Declarer makes 4♠. Based on the bidding, West should open the ace and follow with another trump. From the bidding it is apparent that South has a minimum of five spades and five hearts It is clear that North prefers spades (however mildly) to hearts as the trump suit. West should immediately make every effort to reduce dummy's ruff ing power and prevent dummy from ruffing hearts, especially since West has the ♥K-J-9-8 behind South's rebid suit. With the ace of trumps lead, followed by another trump (and a third trump when West regains the lead in hearts), declarer will be defeated, losing three heart tricks and a trump trick.

When you want to mislead declarer as to the true state of affairs in the trump suit; as, for example, talking him out of taking a finesse which he figures to take if left to his own resources, a trump lead may turn out to be the winning lead. A deal which illustrates this point arose in the Men's Pair Championship of 1956. The West defender was Dr. Richard Greene.

```
                    ♠ K 9 8 3
                    ♥ A 5 4
                    ♦ A Q 9
                    ♣ K J 7
♠ A Q 6 2                          ♠ J 10 5 4
♥ K 10                             ♥ 9
♦ J 7 5 2                          ♦ 10 8 3
♣ 8 6 5                           ♣ A Q 9 4 2
                    ♠ 7
                    ♥ Q J 8 7 6 3 2
                    ♦ K 6 4
                    ♣ 10 3
```

North-South vulnerable, North deals. The bidding:

WEST	NORTH	EAST	SOUTH
	1NT	Pass	4 ♥
Pass	Pass	Pass	

West opened the 10 of trumps on the reasoning: (a) On the bidding, North figured to have the ♥A, and South figured to have a long heart suit. (b) Even if South had something like an A-Q-J-x-x-x and dummy the x-x-x of hearts, West would still make his king, since declarer couldn't possibly diagnose the situation. (Upon winning the opening lead with the jack, declarer would enter dummy, and lead a low heart, finessing East for the king.)

What would you, as declarer, have played to the first trick? Probably the same as our declarer did: He went up with the ace in the hope that West was leading from the doubleton 10-9 and, hence, East had the singleton king.

Had Dr. Greene not opened a trump, declarer, upon obtaining the lead, would probably have made the standard PERCENTAGE PLAY of leading the queen of trumps and finessing. As it was, he was talked out of finessing, and thus went down, losing two clubs, one spade, and, of course, the king of trumps.

The following specific situations suggest a trump lead, although circumstances may indicate another selection:

(1) The opponents have bid three suits and ended up in a fourth.

(2) Declarer, raised in his suit, has bid notrump, and been put back to his suit.

(3) The declaring side appears to have a good fit (5-4 or 4-4) in one suit and a misfit in the other suits. For example:

WEST	EAST
1 ♣	2 ♦
2 ♥	4 ♥

(4) The bidding indicates that dummy has exactly three trumps.

(5) A takeout double has been passed for penalties.

(6) An opening suit bid of one has been passed out, and the opening leader has a weak hand. Partner's failure to balance suggests long, strong trumps.

(7) Your side has been doubled for penalties, and one opponent has removed the double.

(8) Your side has opened the bidding with a notrump bid.

(9) Against a high-level sacrifice bid, when the declaring side appears to have little high-card strength . Note also that a small trump is usually the desirable lead from holdings which would call for the highest in a plain suit: x-x-x, x-x; or J-10-x. See VINJE SIGNALS.

TRUMP PETER. See TRUMP SIGNAL.

TRUMP PICK-UP. A play that reduces trump loss by plain suit leads. It usually involves the lead of a side suit through an opponent in order to pick up his seemingly impregnable trump holding.

```
                    ♠ K Q
                    ♥ 3
                    ♦ K 4 3
                    ♣ A K Q 10 7 3 2
♠ 10 9 7 5 3 2                     ♠ J 6
♥ A 8 7 5                          ♥ K Q 10 2
♦ —                               ♦ J 9 7 6 2
♣ 8 6 4                          ♣ J 9
                    ♠ A 8 4
                    ♥ J 9 6 4
                    ♦ A Q 10 8 5
                    ♣ 5
```

Against South's 6 ♦ contract, West leads the ♥A and continues the suit in response to his partner's violent signal. Dummy ruffs and leads the ♦ K, revealing the trump break. Declarer would have had no difficulty in finessing East out of his jack of trumps if dummy had not been forced to ruff; as it is, however, he has to utilize the club suit for that purpose. At trick three declarer leads a diamond to his 8 and then starts the clubs. If East ruffs, declarer overruffs, draws trumps, and enters dummy with a spade to make the good clubs. If East refuses to ruff, South discards his spades and hearts until the following position is reached:

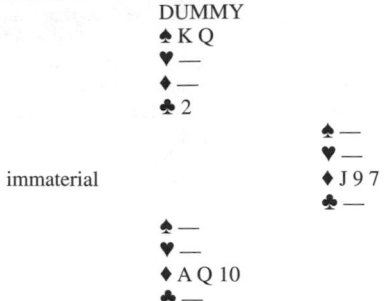

```
                  DUMMY
                  ♠ K Q
                  ♥ —
                  ♦ —
                  ♣ 2
                                    ♠ —
                                    ♥ —
  immaterial                        ♦ J 9 7
                                    ♣ —
                  ♠ —
                  ♥ —
                  ♦ A Q 10
                  ♣ —
```

Dummy is on lead, and East is helpless to prevent declarer from taking the balance. See COUP; DEVIL'S COUP; GRAND COUP; SMOTHER PLAY.

TRUMP PLAY. See the following headings: CONTROL MAINTENANCE; COUNTING TRUMPS; CROSS-RUFF; DRAWING TRUMPS; DUMMY REVERSAL; ELIMINATION; ELOPEMENT; PARTIAL ELIMINATION; RUFF AND DISCARD; RUFF AND RUFF; SMOTHER PLAY; TRUMP PICK-UP; TRUMP SUIT MANAGEMENT.

TRUMP PROMOTION. The creation of trump tricks by forcing the premature use of the trump cards of the opposition. There are several ways in which trump tricks can be promoted: (1) forcing ruffs (see FORCING DECLARER TO RUFF) so as to make trump tricks by length: (2) COUP EN PASSANT so as to make trump tricks by position (see also ELOPEMENT); (3) ruffing to force out (see UPPERCUT) so as to make trump tricks by force of cards; (4) threatening an overruff to force out so as to make trump tricks by force of cards. In the following examples, spades are trump, and East has led a plain suit of which both South and West are void. The best technique to promote trump tricks is to discard behind a player who has wasted a valuable card attempting to stop an overruff.

```
        WEST
        ♠ A J
                  SOUTH
                  ♠ K Q 10 9 8 7 6 3
```

South must ruff with the king or queen to shut out West's jack. West discards and now has promoted a second trump trick. Notice that West must not overruff.

```
        WEST
        ♠ K 10 2
                  SOUTH
                  ♠ A Q J 9 8 7 3
```

South must ruff with queen or jack to prevent West's 10 from winning. West discards and now makes two trump tricks.

```
        WEST
        ♠ J 3 2
                  SOUTH
                  ♠ A K Q 10 9 8 7
```

A trick is promoted for West's jack.

TRUMP-REDUCING PLAY. A play designed to reduce the number of trumps in a hand, usually as a preparation for the trump pick-up. The principal trump-reducing plays are the simple and grand coup, the preliminary throw-in to force the lead of a ruffable suit, and the play of a trump on a trick taken by a higher trump.

TRUMP SIGNAL. A play by defenders to indicate length of trump holding. The play of an intermediate card followed by a subsequent play of a lower card in the trump suit (HIGH-LOW SIGNAL) says a third trump is held. Such a signal is important if the player has a potential RUFFING TRICK. Note that the high-low trump signal to show a third card in the suit is the reverse of the meaning of an echo in a non-trump suit. Some players use the trump signal whenever they hold three trumps. But as the defenders can count declarer's trumps from the bidding far more often than vice versa, it is better to confine its use to situations in which there is a real prospect of a ruff. See also VINJE SIGNALS.

TRUMP SQUEEZE. A squeeze in which the ruffing power of the trump suit plays an essential part. Here is an example of the most common form of simple trump squeeze:

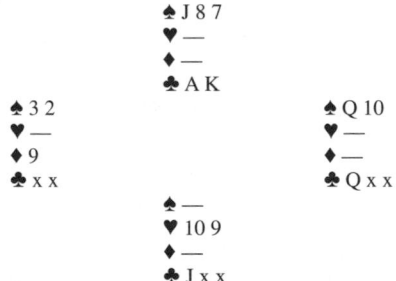

```
                  ♠ J 8 7
                  ♥ —
                  ♦ —
                  ♣ A K
  ♠ 3 2                            ♠ Q 10
  ♥ —                              ♥ —
  ♦ 9                              ♦ —
  ♣ x x                            ♣ Q x x
                  ♠ —
                  ♥ 10 9
                  ♦ —
                  ♣ J x x
```

Hearts are trumps, and South leads a trump, discarding a spade from dummy. East is squeezed. If he discards a spade, dummy is entered with a club, and the ♠Q is ruffed out. If East discards a club, then South cashes his winners in that suit, dropping the queen, and he returns to hand by ruffing a spade in order to cash the established ♣J. This squeeze is automatic, and it has a distinct resemblance to the CRISSCROSS SQUEEZE with a trump taking the place of an isolated master card in the other position.

These are the characteristic elements of the trump squeeze:

(1) A split menace, guarded on the right. But see BACKWASH SQUEEZE.

(2) A ruffing menace, also guarded on the right (a ruffing menace consists of two low cards in dummy, and a trick can be established by ruffing provided RHO weakens his guard in that suit).

(3) Dummy must have two entries either in the split menace (as above) or by means of an additional entry in a third suit. If both menaces are guarded on the left the trump factor is not essential and we have an ordinary simple squeeze against LHO. It is worth noting that the squeeze takes place while declarer retains a trump; in most squeeze positions the last trump must be played before the pressure is felt.

There are two more simple trump squeeze positions:

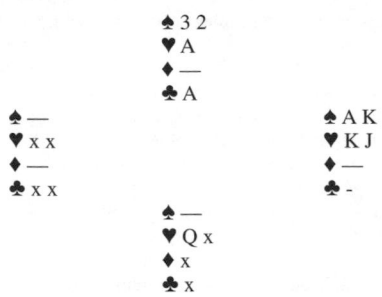

Diamonds are trumps. A club is led to the ace and East is squeezed. A spade discard enables South to ruff out East's spade guard and a heart discard permits North to cash the ace of that suit. The South hand is re-entered with a spade ruff and the ♥Q is cashed .

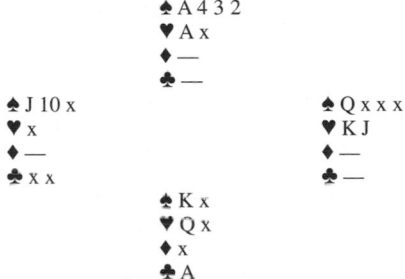

Diamonds are trumps. The ♣A is led and East is squeezed. A spade discard unguards his stopper which can be ruffed out; a heart discard establishes the queen once the ace is cashed.

Squeeze-Finesse at Trumps

Simple

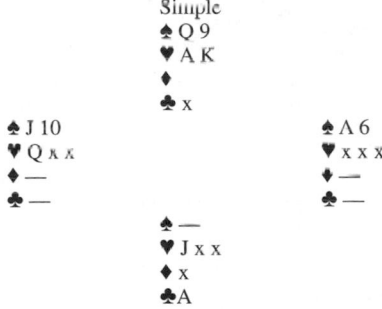

Diamonds are trumps. The ♣A squeezes West. If a heart is thrown the ace and king of that suit are cashed, South re-enters his hand by ruffing a spade in order to cash the ♥J. If a spade is thrown, a heart is led to North, and the ♠Q is led to ruff out the ace and establish the 9.

Double

♠ Q 9
♥ A K x
♦ —
♣ —

♠ J 10   ♠ A 6
♥ Q x x   ♥ J x x
♦ —   ♦ —
♣ —   ♣ —

♠ —
♥ 10 x x
♦ x
♣ A

Diamonds are trumps. South leads the ♣A, and West is squeezed. A spade discard enables South to ruff out East's stopper. If a heart is discarded, East is subjected to a simple trump squeeze.

Double

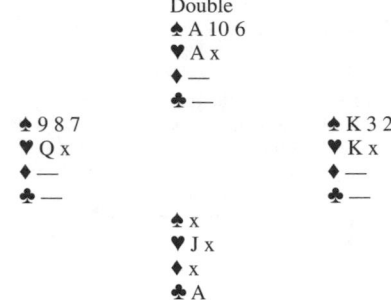

Diamonds are trumps. South leads the ♣A, and West is squeezed. A spade discard enables South to establish a spade by leading to the ace, and returning the 10. A heart discard places East in a simple trump squeeze.

Trump Guard Squeeze

Simple

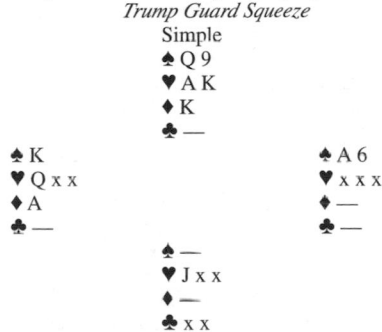

Clubs are trumps. A trump is led, and West is squeezed in three suits. A diamond discard establishes the king; a heart discard permits South to play ace and king of that suit, establishing the jack, with a spade ruff as re-entry; a spade discard allows South to lead a heart to the king, and lead a spade, to ruff out East's ace.

Double

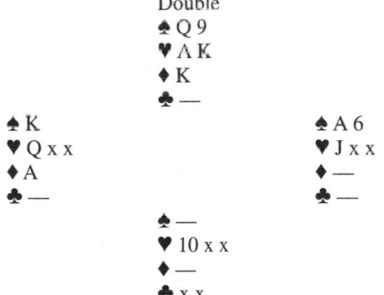

Clubs are trumps. A trump is led, and West is squeezed in three suits. A diamond discard establishes the king; a heart discard places East in a simple trump squeeze; a spade discard permits South to lead a heart to the king, and lead a spade to ruff out East's ace.

TRUMP SUIT. The principles governing the choice of a trump suit are well established. The following are basic rules, subject to certain exceptions.

(1) Eight cards or more between the partnership constitute a satisfactory trump suit.

(2) If the partnership can find an eight-card (or longer) fit in a major suit, the contract should usually be played

in that suit.

(3) If the partnership has values for game (i.e., 25-26 points), the contract should be 3NT if no major suit is available.

The following discussion centers on some of the exceptions.

When to play with fewer than eight trumps. Occasionally a trump suit in which the partnership has only seven cards may be the best bet, especially if the suit is strong (at least three of the top four honors) and one of the other suits appears to be weak. This type of hand is not uncommon:

♠ A Q 10 8 4	♠ K 6
♥ 8 7	♥ 9 3
♦ K 6 2	♦ A Q J 10 7
♣ K Q 3	♣ 10 8 6 4

These hands are on the borderline between partscore and game as far as values go. Clearly the only sound game contract is 4♠, which needs a 3-3 break in spades or the ♠J falling doubleton. Notice the symptoms which point to this seven-card trump suit: a strong trump suit and a marked weakness in another suit.

When the seven-card trump suit is split 4-3, a strong trump suit and a weak side suit are still the signs to look for, but there is a further and most important complication. For the contract to be a good one, it is usually necessary for the hand which is shorter in the trump suit to be able to ruff the weak suit.

♠ A K J 5	♠ Q 6 2
♥ 9 8 5	♥ 3
♦ K 10 5	♦ A Q J 9 2
♣ A 7 3	♣ 10 8 6 4

4 ♠ is a lay-down, barring very bad breaks, and on a heart lead West can certainly make 11 tricks and perhaps 12. Although the 5-3 fit in diamonds looks like a better bet than spades, 5♦ has no chance whatever. As the heart ruffs come in the long trump hand, 10 tricks are the limit. The fact that the heart shortage is with the spade shortage is doubly advantageous; there is a positive profit, in that the heart ruffs score extra tricks, and a negative profit in that heart ruffs do not weaken control of the trump suit. The converse position is much less attractive:

♠ A K J 5	♠ Q 6 2
♥ 3	♥ 9 8 5
♦ K 10 9 5 2	♦ A Q J
♣ A 7 3	♣ 10 8 6 4

If you play this hand in 4♥ and ruff the second heart lead, you are uncomfortably placed. It looks as though a 4-2 spade break will be fatal, but the play is interesting. West should cash his ♠ K-J, leaving two trumps at large, and then play diamonds. A defender ruffs and plays another heart, and now West can please himself whether he ruffs and continues diamonds, or simply discards a club loser. Is there a simpler way of dealing with West's problems? He should, of course, quietly discard his two club losers on the second and third rounds of hearts. Then a fourth heart can be ruffed in dummy.

So in this situation declarer has made 10 tricks by skillful play, and can never make more; while in the previous case, with the heart and spade shortages in the same hand, he makes 10 tricks without effort, and will often make more.

The moral is that a 4-3 fit in a strong suit will be satisfactory if the hand with three trumps has a shortage in the enemy suit. But if the hand with four trumps is going to be forced to ruff, the bidding should be more cautious:

there will certainly be problems of control which may be difficult to solve.

Seven trumps divided 6-1 or 7-0, on the other hand, will usually prove adequate, because declarer can accept ruffs without losing control. But here also it is better for the suit to be fairly robust, and if a six-card suit has only one high honor, there may well be a better spot to play the hand.

To play with six trumps is nearly always a mistake. It is true that a strong 6-0 fit will play well, and occasionally a strong 5-1 fit may be the best spot; it is even possible to construct hands on which the only game to be made is in a strong 4-2 fit. But for practical purposes we can rule out any deliberate intention of playing in a trump suit in which the opposition have the majority of cards. If, when dummy goes down, the combined hands prove to have only six trumps, then the bidding has probably failed.

When to reject an eight-card fit. There are three situations in which 3NT should be preferred to four of a major suit.

Type 1:

♠ K J 7	♠ A 4
♥ 9 7 6 3 2	♥ K 8 4
♦ Q 10 7	♦ K J 9
♣ A 3	♣ K Q J 9 6

Although there is a ruff to be had in dummy, both hands are balanced and the heart suit is very feeble. If East opens 1NT (strong), West should simply raise to 3NT, making no effort to play in hearts. If East has good hearts, the suit will pull its weight in notrump. It is easy to see that 3NT is a virtual certainty, while 4♥ needs a 3-2 heart break with the ace well placed.

Type 2:

♠ A 4	♠ 8 6
♥ A K Q J 8 3	♥ 10 6 2
♦ A 5	♦ J 7 4
♣ A 7 6	♣ J 9 8 4 3

Here the possible trump suit, far from being weak, is absolutely solid. But there are nine sure tricks in notrump and little chance of 10 in hearts, because the East hand has no usable ruffing value. This is, of course, easy for West to spot, because he can count nine tricks in his own hand; but the position will be difficult and perhaps impossible to diagnose if some of West's strength is transferred to East. If West has eight tricks in his hand, he can sometimes take the gamble that East will produce the ninth and that the opponents will not manage to cash five tricks.

To land this sort of contract the tricks have to be quick ones; aces in the side suits are essential, and the presence of minor honors will suggest that the suit contract is preferable. There is a paradoxical element in this: in a general way, the presence of aces normally suggests a suit contract, and the presence of minor honors suggests notrump.

Failure to recognize type 3 often does not show on the scoresheet, so it usually stays unrecognized.

Type 3:

♠ J 5 3 2	♠ A Q
♥ K J 7 5	♥ Q 6 3 2
♦ A Q	♦ K J 7 5
♣ Q J 4	♣ K 8 7

Suppose East opens 1NT (15-17). West should now reason along these lines: our combined count is about 30, so game is very easy, but there is no slam; even if there is a major-suit fit, the suit game may fail through a bad break, while 3NT is surely ironclad. So West raises to 3NT, which is impregnable, while 4♥ would fail with a little bad luck, a 4-1 trump break, and the ♠K with South. These tactics may cost 20 or 50 points aggregate, but this is good insurance except at matchpoint pairs.

In the slam zone there are other considerations which may cause us to reject a combined eight-card major suit holding. The most common symptom is a weak trump suit:

♠ A 8 6 3	♠ J 7 4 2
♥ A Q J 7	♥ K 3
♦ A K 6	♦ 4 2
♣ J 7	♣ A K Q 10 8

Twelve tricks are obviously a lay-down in clubs or notrump, but many players would arrive disastrously in 6♠, which needs the 7% miracle of doubleton K-Q. To avoid this type of trap often requires fine bidding judgment. This is another example in which the major suit has one loser only, but that denomination is still wrong:

♠ A 10 8 7 6 3	♠ K 5
♥ K Q 2	♥ 9 7 6
♦ A Q	♦ K 8 4
♣ J 6	♣ A K Q 10 8

6♠ again needs a miracle. 6NT is a good contract, with slightly better than an even chance: as well as the ♥A with South, we can hope for a lucky spade position or a squeeze against North if he holds all the major-suit honors. But far and away the best contract is 6♣, in which the twelfth trick may come from hearts or from ruffing out the spade suit. Again the strength of the trump suit proves more important than the length.

It may sometimes be advisable to reject an eight-card fit headed by the three trump top honors:

♠ A Q 7 5 4	♠ K 8 3
♥ K	♥ Q J 6 5
♦ A Q 9 3	♦ K
♣ K 9 4	♣ A Q 7 5 2

6♠ and 6♣ are obviously both sound contracts, depending on a 3-2 trump break. But with a lot of general strength, 6NT will often offer more chances. Here the notrump slam makes if either black suit breaks, or if a squeeze develops.

When to play in five of a minor. As it is much easier to make nine tricks than 11, contracts of five in a minor suit are rare. It is nearly always possible to play in 3NT, or in a seven-card major-suit fit.

This is particularly true in matchpoint duplicate events, when a successful contract of 5♣ or 5♦ usually scores badly: other pairs are likely to score slightly more by making 10 tricks in notrump or a major. To play in a minor-suit game with a 4-4 or 5-3 fit is very rare indeed. When it does happen, it is usually because *both* minor suits are held, and there is no seven-card fit in a major:

♠ x	♠ x x x x
♥ A x	♥ K x x
♦ A x x x	♦ K x x x
♣ A K x x x x	♣ x x

5♦ is the only possible game. It requires 3-2 breaks in both minor suits, representing a 46% chance.

This demonstrates two common symptoms of minor-suit games; a completely exposed suit, and obvious ruffing values (singleton or void) in each hand.

If a solid six-card minor suit is held opposite a balanced hand, 3 NT is usually right. But in some cases it may be possible to diagnose a serious weakness, and play in the minor suit:

WEST	EAST
♠ x x x	♠ A K x
♥ x	♥ x x x
♦ A Q x x x x	♦ K x x x
♣ A K x	♣ Q J x

The bidding may start:

WEST	EAST
1 ♦	2NT
3 ♣	3 ♠

after which the heart weakness is identified and the diamond game is reached. As is often the case when the choice lies between 3 NT and a minor suit, the players bid suits in which they have strength but not necessarily length (see STRENGTH-SHOWING BIDS). Interchanging East's rounded suits would produce a different contract:

WEST	EAST
♠ x x x	♠ A K x
♥ x	♥ Q J x
♦ A Q x x x x	♦ K x x x
♣ A K x	♣ x x x

In this case the first three bids would be the same, but East's second bid would be 3NT, showing stoppers in both major suits, and West would subside. Ten tricks in notrump are certain, and 11 are likely, while 5♦ needs a high heart lead or an endplay to succeed .

TRUMP SUIT FALSECARDING. See FALSECARDING .

TRUMP SUIT MANAGEMENT. The way in which declarer utilizes the trump suit in the play of the hand.

The proper technique in handling the trump suit varies, depending first upon the length and the division of the trump suit in the combined hands, i.e., declarer and dummy, and secondly the manner in which the outstanding trumps are distributed in the defenders' hands. Generally speaking, the minimum number of trumps required for a game contract is eight, and the most favorable distribution is four in the dummy and four in the declarer's hand, referred to as:

The 4-4 Fit. The main advantage of this division is that declarer can stand being forced to ruff twice in either hand, reserving the other for purposes of drawing trump. If one opponent holds four trumps, the situation will be much more satisfactory with a 4-4 than a 5-3 distribution; declarer must then take the precaution of looking to his side suits before tackling trumps:

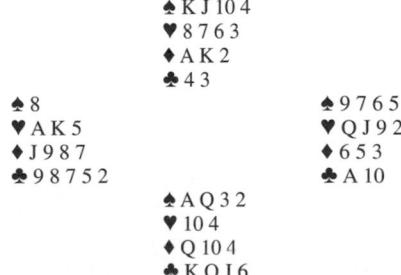

	♠ K J 10 4	
	♥ 8 7 6 3	
	♦ A K 2	
	♣ 4 3	
♠ 8		♠ 9 7 6 5
♥ A K 5		♥ Q J 9 2
♦ J 9 8 7		♦ 6 5 3
♣ 9 8 7 5 2		♣ A 10
	♠ A Q 3 2	
	♥ 10 4	
	♦ Q 10 4	
	♣ K Q J 6	

Against 4♠, West opens with the ♥K. If the defense continues hearts, declarer ruffs the third round and knocks out the ♣A. East leads his last heart and South ruffs with the ace, draws trump, and takes the rest. On any other defense, declarer makes 10 tricks by ruffing his losing club high in the dummy before drawing East's trumps.

The 4-4 distribution lends itself ideally to crossruffing; in this type of play the declarer must be careful to cash his side-suit winners before attempting to score his trumps separately.

```
                ♠ A 7 6 2
                ♥ A Q J 5
                ♦ —
                ♣ Q 10 6 3 2
♠ J 9 5 3                        ♠ Q 4
♥ —                              ♥ 9 8 4 3 2
♦ 10 7 6                         ♦ A J 5 4
♣ A K J 8 5 4                    ♣ 9 7
                ♠ K 10 8
                ♥ K 10 7 6
                ♦ K Q 9 8 3 2
                ♣ —
```

The contract is 4♥, against which West leads the ♣K. Declarer ruffs and is in a position to make 10 tricks in spite of the vile distribution, provided he makes the ♠A-K before he ruffs the third club. Failure to do so would give East an opportunity to discard a spade, and declarer would then be unable to enjoy both of his spade winners.

The 4-3 Fit. When the dummy holds only three trumps, facing four in declarer's hand, the play is unlikely to proceed favorably. These hands normally play better in notrump, especially at the higher levels; exceptionally (e.g., when the opponents have an established suit), 4-3 fits are the only ones available. These contracts frequently call for delicate handling.

The problem of control is critical, and declarer must often establish his side-winners before embarking on drawing trumps.

```
                ♠ K 4 3
                ♥ Q 10
                ♦ Q J 9 7 4
                ♣ K 3 2
♠ 6 5 2                          ♠ 10 8 7
♥ A K 7 4 3                      ♥ J 9 8 6 2
♦ A 3                            ♦ 6 2
♣ 10 5 4                         ♣ A 7 6
                ♠ A Q J 9
                ♥ 5
                ♦ K 10 8 5
                ♣ Q J 9 8
```

4♠ is the only possible game contract, and, as the cards lie, cannot be defeated. The defense does best to play hearts at every opportunity, and South ruffs the second round and plays diamonds. West plays a third round of hearts which is ruffed in dummy. Declarer now knocks out the ♣A and ruffs a further heart in dummy. Only now can he afford to draw trumps, and when they break he claims the balance with good diamonds and clubs.

Sometimes declarer can retain control of a shaky trump suit by refusing to ruff.

```
                ♠ K Q 10
                ♥ 4 3 2
                ♦ Q J 9 7
                ♣ A 10 4
♠ 8 7 6 4                        ♠ 9 5
♥ A K Q 8 5                      ♥ J 9 7
♦ 10                             ♦ 8 6 5 2
♣ Q 6 5                          ♣ J 9 8 7
                ♠ A J 3 2
                ♥ 10 6
                ♦ A K 4 3
                ♣ K 3 2
```

Against 4 ♠, West leads three top hearts. If declarer ruffs and draws trump, West will be left with a long spade which he will use to interrupt the run of the diamonds to cash his remaining heart winners. South can ensure the contract against all reasonable distributions by discarding his losing club on the third round of hearts. If the defense persists with a fourth round, he is able to ruff in dummy, preserving his own trump length, and is in a position to draw all West's trumps and take the rest of the tricks with minor-suit winners. A less obvious example from the same family:

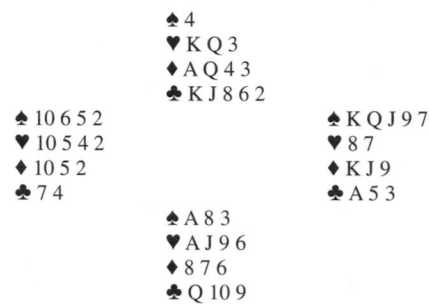

```
                ♠ 4
                ♥ K Q 3
                ♦ A Q 4 3
                ♣ K J 8 6 2
♠ 10 6 5 2                       ♠ K Q J 9 7
♥ 10 5 4 2                       ♥ 8 7
♦ 10 5 2                         ♦ K J 9
♣ 7 4                            ♣ A 5 3
                ♠ A 8 3
                ♥ A J 9 6
                ♦ 8 7 6
                ♣ Q 10 9
```

South plays in 4♥ after East has bid spades, and West leads the ♠2, East playing the jack. Declarer's best play is to let East hold the trick, ruffing in dummy if spades are continued. Declarer is now in a position to draw trumps and give up a club trick while still maintaining control of the enemy suit. Attacking the trump suit by forcing declarer to ruff is by far the most effective form of defense against 4-3 trump contracts. Curiously enough, declarer can often turn this to his advantage and succeed in an otherwise impossible contract

.

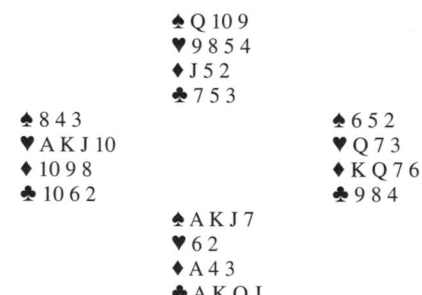

```
                ♠ Q 10 9
                ♥ 9 8 5 4
                ♦ J 5 2
                ♣ 7 5 3
♠ 8 4 3                          ♠ 6 5 2
♥ A K J 10                       ♥ Q 7 3
♦ 10 9 8                         ♦ K Q 7 6
♣ 10 6 2                         ♣ 9 8 4
                ♠ A K J 7
                ♥ 6 2
                ♦ A 4 3
                ♣ A K Q J
```

3NT is safe as the cards lie but, unsure of the heart suit holding, North-South settled reasonably enough in 4♠, West leading the ♥K. If West shifts at trick two, South has four inescapable losers — two hearts and two diamonds — and must go one down. A heart continuation looks tempting however, and South ruffs the third round with the ace, leads the ♠7 to dummy's nine, and ruffs the fourth round of hearts with the king. He now overtakes the ♠J to draw trump in dummy, discarding his losing diamond. Four club tricks plus the ♦A (in addition to the five trump tricks) round out the contract.

It is sometimes possible for declarer to counter the forcing game, utilizing a strong side-suit for the purpose of weakening the defender's trump holding.

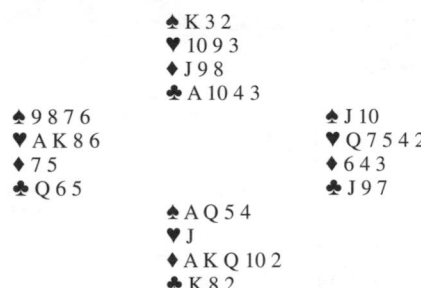

♠ K 3 2
♥ 10 9 3
♦ J 9 8
♣ A 10 4 3

♠ 9 8 7 6   ♠ J 10
♥ A K 8 6   ♥ Q 7 5 4 2
♦ 7 5   ♦ 6 4 3
♣ Q 6 5   ♣ J 9 7

♠ A Q 5 4
♥ J
♦ A K Q 10 2
♣ K 8 2

Against 4 ♠, West leads two top hearts, declarer ruffing the second round. If South attempts to draw all the outstanding trumps, the hand collapses. In order to succeed, he must draw only two rounds of trumps with the ace and queen, and then start the diamonds. If West ruffs the third diamond to lead a heart, South ruffs with his last trump, crosses to dummy's ♣A, and draws West's last trump with the king, making 11 tricks. After ruffing the diamond, West does better to lead his last trump, but declarer still makes 10 tricks.

TRUMP SUPPORT. A variable factor, depending on the nature of the bid which is being supported. (See BIDDABLE SUITS) In general, a player will be very ready to give support if he knows that his side has eight cards in the suit and may give a single raise when a combined seven-card holding is guaranteed and there are reasonable prospects of eight. In most situations in constructive bidding, a suit bid promises four cards, and therefore four cards are needed for any kind of raise. But many special cases should be noted.

(1) Five-card support may be desirable if there is a fair chance that the suit being raised consists of three cards only. This applies particularly to minor-suit raises when the five-card major rule is being used and the incidence of prepared minors is therefore high. KAPLAN-SHEINWOLD, for example, insists on five-card support for a preemptive jump raise of a minor suit, and a single raise in a minor may be avoided with four-card support if there is any convenient alternative. In standard methods, there is a tendency to avoid raising 1♣ with four-card support. With 3-3-3-4 distribution, an expert would often choose a response of 1♦ in preference to a raise to 2♣.

(2) Three-card support may be given to any suit which is known or expected to be of at least five cards (e.g., a five-card major opening; a response of 2♥ to 1♠; or an overcall).

Three-card support is normally considered adequate for a single raise of a major suit bid by opener or responder at the first opportunity. Many players prefer the three-card holding to be headed by a high honor, but consider the following cases:

(a)   (b)
♠ 4 3 2   ♠ 4 3 2
♥ 3 2   ♥ 3 2
♦ 4 3 2   ♦ A Q 2
♣ A Q 4 3 2   ♣ A Q 4 3 2

In (a) an opening bid of 1♠ should be raised to 2♠. Even if 4-card majors are in use, much more often than not the opener will hold more than four spades. The raise is a lesser evil than 1NT because of the weakness in hearts. The responder does not wish to play notrump, nor to allow a heart bid by the opposition at the level of two. Hand

(b) opens the bidding with 1♣ and gets a response of 1♠. A raise to 2♠ is again a lesser evil than a rebid of 1NT, for similar reasons. A jump raise or a raise of a secondary suit requires at least four-card support, but there are occasional exceptions on a least-evil basis:

(c)   (d)
♠ A Q 3   ♠ K 6 4
♥ 10 8 5 4 2   ♥ 4 2
♦ A 5 3 2   ♦ A Q 6 4 3
♣ 2   ♣ 5 4 2

Hand (c) has to respond to a fourth-hand opening bid of 1♠ and a jump to 3♠ is superior to a nonforcing bid of 2♥. (Better still, however, is DRURY.) Hand (d) has responded 1♦ to an opening bid of 1♣ and the opener has rebid 1♠. With the prospect of a ruffing value in hearts, responder is not unwilling to play in a 4-3 fit, and the mildly constructive raise to 2♠ is much better than a completely negative preference bid of 2♣.

(3) Two-card support may be given to any suit which is known or expected to be of at least six cards (e.g., any opening preemptive bid; a vulnerable overcall at the level of two; and almost any suit which has been bid twice (see OPENER'S REBID). In an emergency, a doubleton may be sufficient to raise a suit which is known to be of at least five cards:

(e)   (f)
♠ 7 5   ♠ K 7 6 5 3
♥ 2   ♥ A 4
♦ A 8 6 5 3   ♦ A Q 4 2
♣ J 7 6 5 2   ♣ 8 6

Hand (e) should raise 1♠ to 2♠ playing five-card majors, partly for preemptive reasons and partly because there is no good alternative (unless a 1NT response is forcing). The alternative is a pass.

Hand (f) opens 1♠, and the response is 2♥, showing at least a five-card suit. A raise to 3♥ is superior, some would think, to a rebid of the anemic spade suit.

(4) One-card support is usually adequate only when the suit has been bid so strongly as to indicate that support is not needed. An exceptional case is suggested by Terence Reese: South holds:

♠ Q J 6 2
♥ 8 6 5 4
♦ A K 4 3
♣ Q

Vul: None

WEST	NORTH	EAST	SOUTH
1 ♥	2 ♣	2 ♥	?

Reese's suggestion, endorsed by an expert panel, was to bid 3♣ (for a modern alternative, See SNAPDRAGON). With bidding all round the table, North's overcall is likely to be a distributional one based on a good six-card suit; 3♣ is likely to be the best contract for North-South; and East-West may be tempted to bid 3♥, which South can double effectively, and be surprised by the club situation. This is one case of a useful general rule: in competitive situations raises should be given more freely.

TRUMP SWISS CONVENTION. See SWISS CONVENTION.

TRUMP TRICK. A playing trick in the trump suit.

TRUNCATED HOWELL MOVEMENT. A shortening of the HOWELL MOVEMENT to terminate at the end of 13 rounds, 26 boards. Since this did not give balanced comparison, it is no longer used but has been replaced by the THREE-QUARTER MOVEMENT. See REDUCED HOWELL.

TRUSCOTT CARD. A card placed in the first board played in a session of team play, on which the players record their names, positions and table number. When the boards are exchanged, the new recipients can check, allowing for corrective action by the director if an error is discovered. Originated by Alan Truscott in 1976, following an episode at the World Team Olympiad: Because of an error in seating, a match between Brazil and Italy, the eventual gold and silver medal winners, was canceled and not replayed.

TRUSCOTT DEFENSE. A system of two-suited takeouts that can be used over strong artificial openings of 1♣, 2♣, 1♦ or 2♦ . See DEFENSE TO STRONG ARTIFICIAL OPENINGS.

TRUSCOTT TWO DIAMONDS. See TWO-WAY STAYMAN.

TUNISIA BRIDGE FEDERATION (FEDERATION TUNISIENNE de BRIDGE). It had 190 members in 1993.
President 1992
  Dr. Hosni Khaled
  20 bis, Rue Alain Savary
  BP 220, 1002 Tunis
  Tunisia
  Fax: 2161 782751 (Attn. Fauzia Belajouza)

TURGENEV. The Russian novelist, Ivan Turgenev, found playing cards useful. "You don't like walking, but you should force yourself to do it. I was once in prison — in solitary confinement — for more than a month: the room was small, the heat stifling. Twice a day I carried 104 cards (two packs), one by one, from one end of the room to the other ... that made 208 round trips; 416 a day, the round trip was eight paces, that made 3,300, nearly two kilometers! Let this ingenious calculation give you courage! The day I didn't take my walk all the blood went to my head!" (Letter to Gustave Flaubert 1879).

TURKEY (TURKEY GAME, TURKEY SHOOT). A colloquial term used to describe events in a tournament other than major championships, such as secondary events, consolation events and side games.

TURKISH BRIDGE FEDERATION (TURKIYE BRI FEDERASYONU). The Federation was founded in 1964, and by 1992 had a membership of about 3,000 players organized in 32 clubs.
Officers 1992:
  President: Server Serim
  Secretary: Halil Atalay
  PO Box 37, Bahariye, 81311
  Istanbul, Turkey.
  Tel: 90 1 40 84 16

TURN. (1) Noun: the appropriate moment for a player to make a bid or play; (2) verb: to quit a card at duplicate or a trick at rubber bridge after all four players have played; (3) verb: to take a trick, as "We turned six tricks against 3♠".

TWELVE, RULE OF. See RULE OF TWELVE.

TWELVE TABLES. At duplicate, 12 tables provide for competition among 48 players as individuals, 24 pairs or 12 teams-of-four.

As an individual, the obvious choice is the IRREGULAR RAINBOW. The alternative is the Appendix Rainbow devised by Paul Marks. Four stationary player seats are assigned: 12, North at table 1; 24, East at table 2; 36, South at table 3; and 48, West at table 4. Players numbered 1 to 11 sit North at the corresponding tables; numbers 13 to 23 sit East at tables 1 to 11; numbers 25 to 35 sit South at tables 1 to 11; and numbers 37 to 47 sit West at tables 1 to 11. (However, four of these players, one from each group, find their new seats occupied by the stationary players, 45 to 48). These players for the first round and their counterparts at every successive round play boards 23 and 24 at table 12. Otherwise, at the end of each round, North players skip a table to lower numbers, South players skip a table to higher numbers, East players go to the next higher number table, and West players skip two tables to higher numbers, boards going to next lower numbered tables. For purposes of progression and board numbers, table 12 is ignored, and is filled each round with players who find stationary players in the seats to which they are assigned. Each player thus plays 22 of the 24 boards in the 11 rounds. Ten is top and 110 average.

As a pair game, 22 boards can be played in 11 rounds, traveling players skipping a table after round 6. By inserting a byestand between tables 6 and 7, and relaying boards between 1 and 12, 24 boards can be played. It is also possible to give three boards to each table, skip after the sixth round and play nine rounds (27 boards) with an average of 108. The disadvantage is that all pairs will miss nine boards that most of the other competitors will play.

For team-of-four games a Swiss Team movement is a possibility. You can play an 11-round THURNER MOVEMENT. Alternatively you may start by letting the East-West pairs skip a table in the lower direction. After the first round you follow the normal team progression of the moving pairs skipping a table in the lower direction with the boards moving to the next lower table. After the second round the moving pairs skip an extra table. For the next six rounds the moving pairs follow the normal progression of skipping a table in the lower direction. After the eighth round the moving pairs skip an extra table and the boards skip a table. Following the 10th round, East-West pairs 1 through 6 add six to their number and go to that table number, and East-West pairs 7-12 subtract six from their number and go to that table. New boards are given out at tables 1 through 6 and, after being shuffled and dealt, are relayed with the table six numbers higher (1 and 7, 2 and 8, etc.)

The problem with an 11-round movement is that you will have 22 or 33 boards. By putting out three boards to a table and eliminating the relay round, 30 boards can be played in a session. The movement can be curtailed to 24 boards by eliminating the first and 10th rounds. At the start of the game East-West pairs 1 through 4 add eight to their number and go to that table; pairs 5-12 subtract four from their number and go to that table. After the first round, the moving pairs skip an extra table. After the seventh round , the moving pairs skip an extra table and the boards skip a table. For 11° and 12° tables, see HALF TABLES.

TWINNED MOVEMENT. To twin a movement is to set up two parallel rows, each playing the same movement with the same boards. If the boards are not duplicated, parallel tables share boards.

For a team contest you may twin any pair movement and reverse the compass direction in one of the rows. In each round each team will sit at parallel tables in different directions.

TWINNING. The process used to produce identical boards to be played in two (or more) sections. To twin the boards in a two-board movement (either for social purposes or for scoring with a multiple top), the odd-numbered boards are passed out, one to a table, in one section and the even-numbered boards are passed out in the other. As the boards are being shuffled and played, a second board of the same number is put on the table. After play is complete and the score is recorded, the twinning is done. There are several methods but this one works best. The cards in the second board are divided into suits, and each player picks up one suit. Each player faces the hand just played in front of him. Then each player distributes his suit to the four players to match the cards in front of them. Once all the cards from the second board are distributed, each player puts the hand actually played back in its original board, then puts the twinned hand in the second board. The director then picks up the twinned board and brings it to the correct table in the other section, where the board is played "as is", that is without being shuffled.

When boards are being twinned over three sections, one section is given the odd boards and another the even boards. The director then gives each table an additional two boards of the same number to duplicate. Meanwhile, the third section is patiently waiting. However, the first twinned board at each table is brought to the third section, so that the third section finishes first-round play at approximately the same time as the two sections where twinning took place.

Sometimes boards are twinned when three boards are being played per round. This can cause complications for the director, but concentration and care are all that are needed to make the method work .

In multi-section events, when it is desirable to have the same hands in play in all sections, computer-dealt hands usually are used. These are available in groupings of even numbers starting with two sections and going as high as needed. See COMPUTER-DEALT HANDS.

TWO or TWO-SPOT. The lowest-ranking card in any given suit. Sometimes referred to as the deuce, this card is just below the three in precedence.

TWO-BID. The bid of two in a suit as an opening bid is used in many different ways by various players. Specialized uses are referred to in the following articles: ACOL TWO-BID; BENJAMIN; BLUE TEAM TWO DIAMONDS; FLANNERY TWO DIAMONDS; FLANNERY TWO HEARTS; MEXICAN TWO DIAMONDS; ROMAN SYSTEM; ROMAN TWO DIAMONDS; TWO CLUBS STRONG ARTIFICIAL OPENING; WEAK TWO-BIDS.

TWO CLUBS ARTIFICIAL, BALANCING TAKEOUT. See BALANCING TWO CLUBS FOR TAKEOUT.

TWO CLUBS CONVENTIONS. *OPENINGS*: See TWO CLUBS OPENING AS MULTI-SUITER; TWO CLUBS SYSTEMS; TWO CLUBS STRONG ARTIFICIAL OPENING. *Responses and others:* See DRURY; GLADIATOR; STAYMAN CONVENTION; STAYMAN ON SECOND ROUND; TWO CLUBS REBID BY RESPONDER AS ONLY FORCE AFTER ONE NOTRUMP REBID. *TAKEOUTS*: SEE TWO-SUITER CONVENTIONS. TWO CLUBS OPENING AS MULTI-SUITER. The principal conventions that use a 2♣ opening bid to show a two-suited hand are features of the BIG DIAMOND, ROMAN, and SIMPLIFIED CLUB systems.

TWO CLUBS FOR MINORS, TWO DIAMONDS FOR MAJORS. See BECKER.

TWO CLUBS REBID BY RESPONDER AS ONLY FORCE AFTER ONE NOTRUMP REBID. A convention devised by Edwin Kantar to provide a full range of rebids by responder over a 1NT rebid by opener. Using 2♣ as the only forcing rebid by responder, all other two-level suit bids are discouraging and jump bids at the three level invite game. For example:

(a)	(b)
1♣ 1♥	1♣ 1♥
1NT 3♥	1NT 3♦

The last bid in each of the above sequences is nonforcing but invitational. See also CROWHURST CONVENTION; STAYMAN ON SECOND ROUND; UNBID MINOR SUIT FORCE.

TWO CLUBS RESPONSE TO NOTRUMP. See GLADIATOR; STAYMAN CONVENTION.

TWO CLUBS STRONG ARTIFICIAL OPENING. An artificial opening bid on powerful hands which is the cornerstone of many systems. A response of 2♦ is usually negative. See TWO DIAMONDS ARTIFICIAL RESPONSE TO FORCING TWO CLUBS OPENING. See also SECOND NEGATIVE RESPONSE AFTER ARTIFICIAL FORCING OPENING. The first use of the bid of 2♣ in this way is credited to David Burnstine at the Raymond Club, New York City, in 1929, but some experts soon used 2♣ for all strong hands, and this concept gradually superseded the FORCING TWO-BID in serious tournament play. It was part of the OFFICIAL SYSTEM which, although theoretically sounder, lost the public relations war with Ely Culbertson. It is usually used in combination with WEAK TWO-BIDS, but may be combined with INTERMEDIATE TWO-BIDS of various types. Originally the 2♣ bid was forcing to game. In modern practice many experts announce it as forcing to 2NT or three of a major (after a 2♦ response), to cover two common exceptions;

SOUTH	NORTH
2♣	2♦
2♥	2NT
3♥	

North may pass. This widens the use of the 2♣ opening to include a powerful one-suited hand where game may be missed if partner passes with 4-5 points, or slam may be missed because it becomes difficult for opener to show his strength clearly if he commences with a bid of one.

Another exception tightens the gaps in the structure of notrump bids:

SOUTH	NORTH
2♣	2♦
2NT	

North may pass. Under this method, instead of the traditional standard of 22-24 (or 21-23), a 2NT opener shows 21-22 (or 20-22) while 2♣ followed by 2NT shows 23-24 (or 22-24).

A semi-artificial rebid, the KOKISH RELAY, has some popularity:

SOUTH	NORTH
2♣	2♦
2♥	

This can be used to require a 2♠ rebid. Then opener can bid 2NT forcing with 25 points or more. Any other rebid shows that the 2♥ bid was natural. This gains on strong balanced hands, but deprives the responder of the chance to make a second negative.

Standard for a positive response to 2♣ varies, but most authorities insist on 1° quick tricks (an ace and a king, or three kings). Others are satisfied with an ace, or a good suit headed by king and queen with some plus values; these treatments have the advantage that positive responses can be given more frequently. 2NT can be regarded as an exception. Some players make this response with 8 points or more, irrespective of quick trick strength. Since this response often results in the weak hand becoming declarer, some avoid the bid altogether. It can be used artificially to show a weak minor two-suiter.

After a positive response, the opener will usually rebid as though the response had been negative. Therefore, 2♣-2♥-2NT, or 2♣-3♣-3NT, shows the balanced minimum hand with 23-24 points. Similarly, 2♣-2♥-3NT would show a balanced hand with 25-27.

In systems employing an artificial strength-showing bid of 1♣, a bid of 2♣ may be the equivalent of a standard 1♣ opening, including a long club suit and limited values. See also ACE-SHOWING RESPONSES; FORCING TWO-BID, KOKISH RELAY and TWO DIAMONDS ARTIFICIAL RESPONSE TO TWO CLUBS OPENING.

TWO CLUBS SYSTEMS. Many bidding systems use 2♣ as the opening bid with strong hands, irrespective of the holding in the club suit. Information on such systems is included in the following articles: ACE-SHOWING RESPONSES; ACOL; BARON; BENJAMIN; BULLDOG; CAB; KAPLAN-SHEINWOLD; OFFICIAL; ROMEX; ROTH-STONE; TWO CLUBS STRONG ARTIFICIAL OPENING.

TWO-DEMAND BID. See FORCING TWO-BID.

TWO DIAMONDS ARTIFICIAL OPENING. As a strong forcing opening bid, see BENJAMIN convention, ROMEX SYSTEM and SCHENKEN SYSTEM. As a two-suited or three-suited opening bid, see conventions listed in TWO DIAMONDS OPENING AS MULTI-SUITER.

TWO DIAMONDS ARTIFICIAL RESPONSE TO FORCING TWO CLUBS OPENING. In response to a

TWO CLUBS STRONG ARTIFICIAL OPENING a 2♦ response is usually negative, showing about 0-7 points but lacking the partnership requirements for a positive response. Alternatives are to use this response as:

(1) Automatic. The 2♦ bid is nondescriptive, but gives opener room to describe his hand.

(2) Positive. Responder's 2♦ shows 8 or more points, but says nothing about his distribution. All other responses are negative, showing 0-7 points with length in the suit bid. (2NT should show minor suits.)

(3) Double Negative. Responder's bid shows 0-3 points. With this treatment it is possible to use a 2♥ response artificially either to show specifically 4-7 points (see STEP RESPONSES TO STRONG ARTIFICIAL TWO-BIDS), or as a neutral bid showing at least 4 high-card points and allowing opener to describe his hand.

(4) ACE-SHOWING RESPONSE.

TWO DIAMONDS ARTIFICIAL RESPONSES TO ONE NOTRUMP OPENING. Conventions used in response to 1NT opening bids designed to solve particular notrump bidding problems. In conjunction with the various conventions so used, a substitute sequence may be required to show a weak hand with a long diamond suit: an immediate 3♦; or 2♣ followed by 3♦; or 2♦ followed by 3♦; or 2NT followed by 3♦. See FLINT 2♦; FOUR-SUIT TRANSFERS; GLADIATOR; JACOBY TRANSFER BID; TWO-WAY STAYMAN.

TWO DIAMONDS AS MULTI-SUITER. There are several conventions that use a 2♦ opening to show a two-suited or three-suited hand. The principal ones are BLUE TEAM TWO DIAMONDS, FLANNERY TWO DIAMONDS and ROMAN TWO DIAMONDS. In addition, a 2♦ opening shows a three-suited hand in the PRECISION CLUB system and a hand with both major suits in the BIG DIAMOND SYSTEM. See also MULTI.

TWO-HANDED BRIDGE. See BRIDGETTE, DUEL, DUOBRIDGE and HONEYMOON BRIDGE.

TWO NOTRUMP OPENING. This shows a balanced hand with 21-22 points, and might be made with 20 points. This is the standard expert treatment, although some weaken this to 20-22 or 20-21. The traditional range of 22-24 continues to be used by most players who use FORCING TWO-BIDS. See also TWO NOTRUMP OPENING FOR MINORS. Theoretically the distribution should be the same as for an opening notrump bid: 4-3-3-3, 4-4-3-2, or 5-3-3-2 with the five-card suit a minor. However, the 2NT opening often has to serve as a least evil choice with hands too strong to open with one of a suit and not strong enough for a forcing opening. 5-3-3-2 with a major suit is frequently opened with 2NT, and occasional departures such as 6-3-2-2 or 5-4-2-2 are permissible.

Responses are as follows:

(1) 3♣. Stayman, asking opener to bid a major suit. With no major he bids 3♦, and if responder then bids a major, he shows a five-card suit. Holding both majors, either suit may be bid by partnership agreement, and agreement is not essential. If responder then bids 3NT, the opener bids his second major.

A rebid of four in a major suit, other than a raise, can be used to show a club/major two-suiter with mild slam ambitions.

A rebid of 3NT by the opener virtually does not exist in standard methods. It can be used by partnership agreement to show a hand with no interest in a major-suit contract, perhaps a doubleton in each. (An alternative is to show a 5-card heart suit with this bid.) A variation popular in England (due to the BARON SYSTEM) is for the opener to bid all his suits up the line. 3♦ would show a diamond suit but would not deny a major. 3NT would show that the opener's only suit was clubs. This method facilitates minor-suit slam bidding but is somewhat inefficient when responder is 5-4 or 4-5 in the major suits.

For a more sophisticated structure, see ROMEX STAYMAN. And see SMOLEN.

(2) 3♦. The vast majority of American tournament players use this as a JACOBY TRANSFER, showing heart length, and 3♥ similarly to show spade length. See TWO NOTRUMP OPENING WITH TRANSFER RESPONSES.

A few use this as the FLINT convention. In a natural sense the bid shows at least five diamonds, and is a slam suggestion.

(3) 3♥ or 3♠. For 3♥, see TWO NOTRUMP OPENING WITH TRANSFER RESPONSES. Used naturally, these bids are forcing and show at least a five-card suit . The suit may be longer [see (6) below]. The responder is asking the opener to choose between the major suit game (with three-card support) or 3 NT (with a doubleton in responder's suit). However,the responder may have slam interests, so the opener makes a cuebid (2 NT-3♥-4♦) if he has good support and a suitable hand for slam purposes. See also AUTOMATIC ACES; EXPECTED NUMBER OF CONTROLS IN BALANCED HANDS; ROMEX STAYMAN.

(4) 3NT. A range of 4-10, although a thin 4-point hand may be passed. An occasional 3-point hand (K-x-x-x) may be worth a raise.

(5) 4♣ or 4♦. These bids are usually conventional (GERBER, TEXAS, or SOUTH AFRICAN TEXAS). In a natural sense they would show a strong suit, but are very rare. If 4♦ is Texas for hearts, it must be at least a 6-card suit with either no slam interest, or strong slam interest intending to head for slam subsequently, perhaps with some form of Blackwood.

(6) 4♥ or 4♠. In standard methods this shows a six-card suit with no slam interest. With mild slam interest, responder bids at the three level and then bids game. The traditional treatment, reversing these sequences, is obsolescent.

(7) 4NT. A natural invitation to 6NT, holding about 11 points. Responder's distribution is likely to be 4-3-3-3, but might be 4-4-3-2 or 5-3-3-2 if no major suit is held.

(8) 5♣ or 5♦. A very unbalanced weak hand. A seven-card suit and a void would be typical. The opener is expected to pass, but might bid six with a fine fit and excellent controls.

(9) 5♥ or 5♠. A strong invitation to bid six, based on a six-card suit.

(10) 5NT. An invitation to 7NT. With no interest in a grand slam, the opener bids 6NT.

(11) 6NT. A balanced hand, probably 4-3-3-3, *with* 12-14 points.   For an alternative system of responding, see MILES RESPONSES TO TWO NOTRUMP OPENINGS.

TWO NOTRUMP OPENING FOR MINORS. A convention using a 2NT opening bid to show a hand with

at least five cards in each minor suit. The strength and the meaning of responses in a major require agreement. This is usually part of a Strong Club system in which 2NT is not needed as a natural bid.

TWO NOTRUMP OPENING WITH TRANSFER RESPONSES. The vast majority of American tournament players, and many others around the world, use JACOBY TRANSFER responses to a 2NT opening, with 3♦ to show heart length and 3♥ to show spade length, at least five cards. The opener bids the next step, accepting the transfer and perhaps ending the bidding, unless he has an ideal hand, normally maximum values, a four-card fit with the major, and good controls. Possible rebids by responder are:

(a) Three spades (2NT-3♦-3♥-3♠). Four spades, heart length, forcing. May have slam interest.

(b) 3NT. Asks opener to choose between this contract and game in the major. He will almost always select the major when holding three-card or four-card support. Responder will have a five-card major, and will often have 5-3-3-2 distribution.

(c) New suit at four-level. Forcing, natural, and slam interest.

(d) Four of anchor suit. A mild slam invitation, since hands with no slam interest would bid game directly, or make a four-level Texas transfer with the same effect.

(e) 4NT is natural and invitational, usually 5-3-3-2 with borderline slam values.

A corollary is that three spades is used to show a minor-suit hand, usually at least 5-4 or 4-5, with slam interest. The opener bids 3NT with a fit in neither.

TWO NOTRUMP OVERCALL. Can be used in six different ways:

(1) *Natural.* To show a 2NT opening bid with about 22 points. This helps to define the range of a 2NT bid preceded by a takeout double, which would indicate 19-20. These two procedures can be interchanged by partnership agreement. STAYMAN would apply with partnerships that use it after a ONE NOTRUMP OVERCALL.

(2) *Unusual.* To show a specific two-suiter. The minimum strength would vary according to vulnerability. At favorable vulnerability, a 6-5 distribution with 6 points in the suits would usually be considered adequate. At unfavorable vulnerability both the hand and the suits should be distinctly stronger.

The suits are always clubs and diamonds if the opening is a major. If the opening is a minor, it is usual to play "Two Lower Unbid", and therefore it is red suits over 1♣ and rounded suits over 1♦.

One school of thought holds that the bid should either be weak, intending to pass partner's bid of 3♣ or 3♦, or strong, intending to bid on. Intermediate hands must overcall.

(3) *Preemptive.* To indicate a long broken suit lower in rank than the opening bid, justifying a preemptive bid at the level of three. Partner is expected to bid 3♣ if third hand passes, to permit his side to reach the appropriate suit; but third hand seldom passes. This is not needed playing WEAK JUMP OVERCALLS and has dubious value in any event since partner may be left in doubt when a save is possible.

(4) *Roman.* To show a strong two-suited hand in which the suits are not specified. Responder bids the lowest

unbid suit, and if the 2NT bidder shows a suit, he holds that suit and the suit in which responder made his artificial response. 3NT would show the two unbid suits. (For weaker two-suited hands, see JUMP OVERCALL.)

(5) *Modern.* To show a strong hand with a near-solid minor suit, for example:

♠ A 2
♥ K 5
♦ J 4 2
♣ A Q J 9 6 2

Responder may raise to 3NT, or bid 3♣ with no interest in game. In the latter case the overcaller passes or converts to 3♦. In borderline cases, responder is guided by possession of a key card in his partner's minor. With a diamond honor he bids 3♣, and converts a 3♦ rebid to 3NT. With a club honor he responds 3♦, giving the overcaller the choice between 3♦ and 3NT.

(6) *Artificial.* When an immediate cuebid in the opener's suit is given a specialized meaning (as in MICHAELS CUEBID), 2NT can be used to show a hand of game-going strength, with 3♣ as a conventional negative response.

TWO NOTRUMP REBID. See OPENER'S REBID.

TWO NOTRUMP RESPONSE (to Opening Suit Bid of One). There are five treatments which can be adopted.

(1) *Standard.* 13-15 points and game forcing. The opener raises with any balanced distribution. If he rebids at the three-level in a suit, it will usually show an aversion to notrump: he is likely to have a singleton or void. The responder must then move cautiously:

♠ Q 3
♥ A 8 6 2
♦ A Q J
♣ J 8 5 3

The bidding:

NORTH	SOUTH
1♠	2NT
3♣	3♦

The most useful bid South can make is a call at the three-level in a suit in which he holds considerable strength. If this corresponds to North's shortage, he will know that 3NT will be safe and that there would be duplicated values in a high suit contract. But if North's shortage is in an unbid suit, he will know that a suit contract will be preferable to notrump. Responder should avoid raising opener's secondary minor suit, although he may do so at a later stage if circumstances warrant it.

A possible additional use for the 2NT response, suggested by Marshall Miles, is for balanced hands with about 19 points. Whatever the opener rebids, the responder then suggests a slam, usually by rebidding 4NT. This makes it clear that responder cannot have the normal 2NT response.

(2) *Limit.* 11-12 points, encouraging but not forcing. The bidding can stop short of game in three ways: (a) an immediate pass by the opener, holding a minimum balanced hand; (b) after a rebid of his own suit by opener, showing a subminimum opening and, usually, a six-card suit (a typical ACOL signoff bid); (c) after a bid of a new suit by the opener and a preference bid at the three level by responder. The responder must give jump preference to 4♥ or 4♠ if his hand is particularly suitable for the suit game.

In choosing a rebid at the three-level, responder should

consider the possibility of bidding a strong suit, as in (1) above. The Miles variation for balanced hands with about 19 points is not available since 2NT is not forcing.

The limit 2NT response after minor suit openings became popular in the Eighties with players using modern methods. This solves some of the problems involved in a game-forcing 2♣ response to 1♦.

If responder has passed originally, a response of 2NT is always a limit bid (unless DRURY or SNAP is being used).

(3) *Baron.* 16-18 points and game forcing. In this system the responses of 2NT and 3NT are inverted. After 3NT (12-14) it is usually easy for the opener to select a suitable game; and the 2NT response leaves more room for exploration on hands on which a slam is likely.

(4) *Psychic Control.* 21-22 points, and therefore offering prospects of game if the opening bidder has a systemic ROTH-STONE psychic.

In all the cases listed, with the possible exception of (4), the 2NT response normally has a 4-3-3-3 distribution, or 4-4-3-2 with the doubleton in the opener's suit.

(5) *Conventional.* Used with limit raises to show a standard forcing jump raise when the opening bid was in a major (invented by Oswald Jacoby). See JACOBY TWO NOTRUMP RESPONSE.

TWO NOTRUMP (as a Negative Response to Strong Two-Bids). The traditional negative response to a strong opening two-bid, showing fewer than 7 or 8 points, counting high cards plus distribution.

TWO NOTRUMP RESPONSE (as a Relay to 3♣). A convention whereby a response of 2NT to a 1NT opening forces the opener to rebid 3♣. If the responder has a weak hand with a long club suit, he passes. If he has instead a weak hand with a long diamond suit, he bids 3♦, which opener is required to pass.

Some partnerships also use the relay when responder has a three-suited game-going hand with a singleton in one of the major suits. The responder shows this type of hand over opener's forced 3♣ bid by bidding the suit of his singleton.

TWO NOTRUMP RESPONSE (Over Opponent's Takeout Double). An artificial response of 2NT to an opening suit bid, devised by Alan Truscott and described in *The Bridge World* in Nov. 1954.

The bid shows a LIMIT RAISE in opener's suit, allowing the raise to the three-level to be preemptive. The 2NT bid is usually in the 9-11 point range, with some allowance for distribution. Stronger hands need partnership agreement: either 3NT to show 12-15, or 2NT, intending to continue following a signoff, are possible.

If the opening bid is a minor, some partnerships reverse the meanings of 2NT and the jump raise.

This convention is popularly called Jordan, in the mistaken belief that Robert Jordan originated it.

TWO-ODD. Two tricks over book or eight tricks in all.

TWO-OVER-ONE GAME FORCE. A method of bidding in which a two-level simple new-suit response to an opening suit bid is forcing to game, e.g., 1♠ - 2♣ or 1♥ - 2♦. When using this system, it is necessary to use the FORCING 1NT response to a major to handle certain types of intermediate hands. The method is used primarily in conjunction with FIVE-CARD MAJORS. When using this system, it usually is not wise to open the bidding with a minimum if the hand is flat or if the points are mostly queens and jacks. The two-over-one forcing response allows the partnership to test slam possibilities while the bidding level is still low.

Many partnerships allow one exception: If the responder bids and rebids a minor suit at a minimum level, he cancels the game-forcing message and opener may pass.

Many additionally allow a second exception: The bidding may end at four of a minor suit, although that introduces some ambiguity.

If there is interference the situation changes completely. Only a few diehards would insist that a sequence such as 1♥ - 2♣ (overall) 2♦ should be game-forcing.

Some partnerships restrict the game-forcing meaning to major-to-minor auctions, leaving 1♠-2♥ and 1♦-2♣ in traditional mode. See BRIDGE WORLD STANDARD, EASTERN SCIENTIFIC and WESTERN SCIENTIFIC.

TWO-OVER-ONE RESPONSE. A minimum response in a lower-ranking suit to an opening suit bid. For example, 1♥-2♣.

The minimum strength required for this response is 10 points in standard methods. Rather more is required in ROTH-STONE and KAPLAN-SHEINWOLD, when responder guarantees a second bid; rather less in traditional ACOL, although that system is now more conservative. The maximum strength tends to be just short of a JUMP SHIFT, i.e., about 17 points in standard methods or about 15 points in Acol. But many strong hands are unsuitable for a jump shift, so there is effectively no upper limit.

The longest suit is usually chosen for the response, and if two five-card suits are held, the higher-ranking is given preference. If the sequence is specifically 1♠ - 2♥, the responder virtually guarantees a five-card suit, and the opener can raise confidently with three card support or conceivably with a doubleton. Any response in the suit immediately lower in rank is likely to be at least five cards (1♥ - 2♦, or 1♠ - 2♣).

For other aspects of this response, see CHOICE OF SUIT and UP THE LINE.

TWO-SUITER. A hand with one suit of more than four cards and another suit of more than three cards. The term used to be confined to hands with at least five cards in each of two suits. A 5-4 distribution was called a semi-two-suiter. For opening the bidding with a two-suiter, see BORDERLINE OPENING BIDS and CHOICE OF SUIT.

TWO-SUITER CONVENTIONS. Several defensive two-suiter conventions are listed under the following headings: ASTRO, ASTRO CUEBIDS, BROZEL, COLORFUL CUEBIDS, COPENHAGEN, CRASH, DEFENSE TO STRONG ARTIFICIAL OPENINGS, GENEVA, GHESTEM, LANDY, MICHAELS, PANAMA, ROBINSON, ROMAN JUMP OVER-CALLS, TOP AND BOTTOM CUEBID, TRAP, TRAP WITH TWO-LEVEL TRANSFERS, TRUSCOTT, UNUSUAL NOTRUMP, UPPER SUITS CUEBID. Offensive-type two-suited conventions include BIG DIAMOND SYSTEM (2♣ and 2♦ openings); FLANNERY TWO DIAMONDS; FLANNERY TWO HEARTS; ROMAN SYSTEM (2♣ and 2♦ openings).

TWO TABLES. At duplicate, two tables provide for competition among eight (or nine) players as individuals, four pairs of players, or two teams of four. As an individual tournament among eight players, seven rounds are required so that each player will play with each other player as a partner. Conduct of this game is described under INDIVIDUAL MOVEMENTS for eight or nine players.

As a pair tournament, three rounds are required. In each round the boards are relayed between the two tables, and scores can be determined almost instantly by direct comparison. Pair 4 is North-South at table 1, facing pair 1 as East-West; at table 2, pair 2 is North-South, and pair 3 is East-West. The better score between the North-South pairs is awarded 1 point, the East-West players at the other table (having the better East-West score) also receiving a point.

New boards are brought in (or the same boards are reshuffled) for round 2, pair 3 replacing 2, 2 replacing 1 and 1 replacing 3 for positions. This is repeated for the third round with a third set of boards. Eight boards to a round give about a three-hour game. (This game also can be scored by IMPs.)

As a contest between two teams of four, the game may be divided into halves, if it is desired to have each pair of one team in head-on competition with both pairs of the other team. Otherwise it may be played straight through. In each half, one-quarter of the total number of boards to be played at each table are shuffled and played; the boards are then exchanged between tables. Scoring may be BOARD-A-MATCH, AGGREGATE (or total points), or scored by IMPs. The latter is preferred by most top players.

TWO-UNDER TRANSFER PREEMPTS. Preemptive openings of 3♣ and higher can be used to show the suit two steps higher than the one bid. For example:

(a)	(b)
♠ 6	♠ 6 5
♥ Q J 10 8 6 3 2	♥ K Q 10 8 6 3 2
♦ 8 7	♦ K 8 7
♣ 9 7 3	♣ 3

These are possible 3♥ bids, but are substantially different in playing strength. If 3♥ is bid with both hands, the responder will often have to guess. Bidding 3♣ to show a 3♥ opening allows the responder to bid 3♦ if he wishes to invite 4♥.

This has the usual advantage of transfer bids, in that partner becomes the declarer and the lead comes up to his possible tenace positions. A disadvantage is that it places less pressure on the opponents in the bidding: Second hand will have two opportunities to act. (Devised by Marty Bergen.) See TRANSFER OPENING THREE BIDS.

TWO-WAY FINESSE. A recurring type of situation in which a FINESSE may be taken through either opponent. For example:

(a)	(b)
NORTH	NORTH
A 10 3 2	K 10 2
SOUTH	SOUTH
K J 5 4	A J 3

The question, of course, is whom to play for the queen: East or West? In many cases, in the absence of any clues revealed during the bidding or the play, it becomes a pure guess. Quite a few players, in these circumstances, will finesse West for the queen, on the theory QUEEN OVER JACK. Of course, this method of taking a two-way finesse is rather on the unscientific side. In the absence of any external clues, a queen can frequently be located without resorting to guesswork. Here is such a case.

```
              ♠ K Q 3
              ♥ K Q 7 5
              ♦ K 10 9
              ♣ Q J 4
♠ 8 4 2                       ♠ 9 7 6 5
♥ 6 4 3                       ♥ 10 8
♦ 7                           ♦ Q 8 6 5 3 2
♣ 10 9 8 6 5 2                ♣ 7
              ♠ A J 10
              ♥ A J 9 2
              ♦ A J 4
              ♣ A K 3
```

South arrived at 7NT, against which West opened a club, dummy's jack winning. Declarer counted 12 tricks, and perceived that the thirteenth trick would be obtained only in the diamond suit. Whom to finesse for the ♦Q, East or West?

At trick two South cashed the ♣K, East discarding a diamond. Three rounds of spades were then taken, everybody following suit. Next, three rounds of hearts were played and declarer paused to take inventory.

West was known to have started with six clubs, three spades and three hearts. Hence he had, at most, one diamond. Dummy's ♦K was then played, and when West followed suit, all of his thirteen cards were accounted for. A diamond was now led off the board, and the ♦J was finessed successfully for declarer's thirteenth trick.

On occasion, when declarer is confronted with a two-way finesse, he can maneuver his play so that an opponent will lead that suit to him, thereby giving declarer a "free finesse." The deal which follows illustrates this point.

```
              ♠ Q J 8 5 2
              ♥ A Q 4
              ♦ A 10 6
              ♣ 7 5
♠ 10                          ♠ 7 4
♥ J 10 9 7                    ♥ 6 5 3
♦ 7 5 3                       ♦ Q 9 8 2
♣ K J 9 8 2                   ♣ Q 10 4 3
              ♠ A K 9 6 3
              ♥ K 8 2
              ♦ K J 4
              ♣ A 6
```

South arrived at a 6♠ contract. West opened the ♥J, dummy's queen winning. The opponents' trumps were picked up in two rounds, after which the ♥ A-K were cashed. Next came the ♣A, followed by another club, and this position was reached:

```
              ♠ Q J 8
              ♥ —
              ♦ A 10 6
              ♣ —
♠ —                           ♠ —
♥ 10                          ♥ —
♦ 7 5 3                       ♦ Q 9 8 2
♣ J 9                         ♣ Q 10
              ♠ 9 6 3
              ♥ —
              ♦ K J 4
              ♣ —
```

It mattered not which opponent won the trick. On a heart or a club return, declarer would ruff in dummy while simultaneously discarding the ♦4 from his own hand. If the winner of the club lead led a diamond, declarer would surely make three diamond tricks. The rules of thumb for taking two-way finesses for the queen fall under four headings. They all assume that other things are equal, which they very seldom are. In almost all cases, one defender will appear more likely to have missing honor cards, or to have greater length in the crucial suit.

(1) *Technical.* Play the left-hand opponent for the missing honor. Without the honor, he might have selected a passive opening lead in that suit. His selection of another opening lead is a slight indication that he may hold the missing queen.

(2) *Practical.* Declarer can often take advantage of the fact that the defenders are human.

```
              DUMMY
              ♥ A 10 8 4
              DECLARER
              ♥ K J 9 3
```

By leading the jack, South may induce West to cover with the queen (or think revealingly about covering). The cover would be necessary if South started with a doubleton jack (or with a tripleton jack, but in that case he would be unlikely to lead the jack). West has no temptation to cover if South has bid the suit, or if the 9 is visible in dummy as well as the 10. If West plays low without thought, South plans to put up dummy's ace and finesse on the way back. Note that this would be risky technically if dummy did not hold the 8. East would be able to make a trick from an original holding of Q-8-7-x.

(3) *Superstitious.* The QUEEN-OVER-JACK rule is such a slight indication that it virtually ranks with the Belgian rule-of-thumb that the younger player always has the queen. If it has any value, the king-over-queen and ace-over-king must be very slightly superior rules, because more significant cards are involved. Such rules normally have no applicability at tournament play, where the cards played to a trick are not gathered together. In England, however, it is habitual to sort the hand into suits at the end of each duplicate deal. If two adjacent honor cards were in the same hand on the previous deal and were not separated in the shuffle, the tendency will be for the jack to lie over the queen and the queen to lie over the king.

(4) *Psychological.* P. Hal Sims claimed that the first defender to speak, light a cigarette, order a drink or react in similar fashion could be expected to hold the queen. This would be an attempt to show nonchalant disinterest, but in fact betray nervousness.

Other two-way finesses:

(a)	(b)
DUMMY	DUMMY
♠ Q 10 5	♠ J 9 5
DECLARER	DECLARER
♠ K 9 7	♠ Q 8 4

(a) is a two-way finesse for the jack. (b) is a two-way finesse for the 10. For other specific situations, see SUIT COMBINATIONS .

TWO-WAY GAME TRIES. (devised by Robert Ewen). A method that combines both long-suit and short-suit game tries after a major-suit raise. If the auction starts 1♥-2♥, opener bids 2NT, 3♣ or 3♦ to make a short-suit try in spades, clubs or diamonds respectively. A 2♠ rebid by opener forces responder to bid 2NT, after which opener bids 3♣, 3♦ or 3♥ to make a long-suit try in clubs, diamonds or spades respectively. If the auction begins 1♠-2♠, a new suit by opener on the three-level is a short-suit try with the named shortage. A 2NT rebid by opener forces responder to bid 3♣, after which opener bids 3♦, 3♥ or 3♠ to make a long-suit try in diamonds, hearts or clubs respectively. Reraises of the major (1♥-2♥-3♥) are general-strength game tries. This method may be expanded to include raises of overcalls, or as a slam try after a forcing double raise. The converse procedure, in which direct bids are short-suit tries and delayed bids are long-suit tries, is recommended by George Rosenkranz.

TWO-WAY NOTRUMP. The use of two different point-count ranges for a 1NT opening bid. A popular treatment, especially in Britain, is the use of a WEAK NOTRUMP not vulnerable with a standard notrump vulnerable, and an alternative is the THREE-QUARTER NOTRUMP. WOODSON TWO-WAY NOTRUMP combines them in one bid.

TWO-WAY STAYMAN. Any of a variety of conventions that use a 2♣ response to a 1NT opening as STAYMAN and use a 2♦ response to 1NT as a supplement to Stayman. The following describe the principal uses of the 2♦ responses.

(1) *Double-barreled Stayman.* 2♣ is used for hands which cannot guarantee game, and 2♦ for hands which wish to force to game. After 2♣, the opener's rebids are normal, and the responder's rebids are all nonforcing. Since responder's second-round jump to 3♠, for example, would not be forcing, a two-level rebid can be regarded as weak. (See Stayman convention.) The meaning of 2♣ followed by a jump to the four-level is a matter of partnership agreement.

Over 2♦, the opener normally shows a major suit or rebids 2NT; but he can rebid at the three-level in a suit or in notrump if he wishes, showing a five-card suit, or a maximum 4-3-3-3 hand without a major. When there is a possibility of a minor-suit slam, a fit can be explored at the level of three because a forcing situation exists.

(2) *Stayman 2♦.* A forcing to game response showing an unbalanced minor-suit hand: no four-card major suit, and a singleton or a void is a necessary requirement. The opener rebids in a suit to show concentrated strength (e.g., A-K-J, not necessarily a four-card suit) and 2NT to show scattered strength. If the concentrated strength proves to be opposite responder's shortage, he will know that 3NT is playable and that there is duplication of values for a suit contract. The subsequent bidding is also aimed at determining whether there is a serious notrump weakness.

(3) *Roth 2♦.* A response that is forcing to game and invitation to slam. This convention allows slam exploration without getting past the game level.

Like Doubled-barreled Stayman, the 2♦ response asks opener about his four-card majors; unlike Double-barreled Stayman, the 2♣ response can be followed by rebids that are game-forcing as in simple STAYMAN. Opener's rebids show whether he has one or both four-card majors, or if he has none, whether he has a minimum or maximum notrump.

(4) *Murray 2♦* asks the opener to bid his longer major suit, bidding a three-card suit if necessary. With equal length (4-4 or 3-3) in the majors the opener bids 2♥. One advantage of the convention is that it permits responder

to bid weak unbalanced hands with 5-5 or 4-4 in the major suits. The responder does not promise any strength whatever, although he can have a strong hand. A rebid of 2NT by the responder asks the opener to bid four-card suits up the line.

The opener's rebid must be in a major suit unless he has two major-suit doubletons, in which case he bids a six-card minor suit or 2NT.

(5) *August 2♦*, developed concurrently with Murray 2♦ and patterned on similar principles, is also a takeout for the majors with the added proviso that any suit rebid by responder is a signoff. This permits responder to use the convention with a weak 4-5 major-minor two-suiter. If the opener rebids the wrong major, responder retreats to his minor. With a weak minor two-suiter, responder first bids 2♣ (Stayman), then rebids 3♣.

(6) *Truscott 2♦*, devised by Alan Truscott and used widely in Israel. After the 2♦ response, opener defines his distribution and responder uses relay bids, as follows: With 4-3-3-3 hands opener rebids 2NT and shows his suit after a 3♣ relay; with 4-4-3-2 hands, opener bids 3♦ with both minors; with a major and a minor, he bids the suits in that order; with both majors he bids 2♥ and then 2NT. In all cases after opener's two suits have been identified, the next relay by responder asks for a two-step clarification of opener's distribution; the first step shows that the doubleton ranks below the tripleton. With five hearts, spades, or clubs, opener bids the suit, and after a relay he rebids 3♥, 3♠, or 3NT to show the low, middle, or high ranking doubleton, respectively. If opener has a five-card diamond suit, he shows it and simultaneously identifies his doubleton by bidding 3♥, 3♠, or 3NT directly over 2♦. Responder can use a meaningless bid below the 3NT level to ask whether opener is minimum or maximum. This structure was later modified to make the remainder bids "numeric": 23 is shown before 32; 233, 323 and 332 in that order. See also BARON COROLLARY.

TWO-WAY TWO-BIDS. A method devised by Ira Rubin to open the bidding with a two-level bid with a strong, intermediate or weak hand. An opening bid of two in any suit usually is weak, showing a weak two-bid type hand in the suit just above the bid suit (2♣=2♦, 2♦=2♥, 2♥=2♠, 2♠=3♣). Both partner and the opponents assume at the start that the opening bid is weak, and partner is expected to make responses in line with a weak two-bid opener — opener's suit with a non-game hand, 2NT asking for a feature, etc. However, opener may have a *strong* hand, in which case his opening bid is either his suit in a one-suiter or one of his suits in a two-suiter. Here are typical rebids after opener bids 2♥ and responder, with a weakish hand, bids 2♠, the suit opener holds if his hand is weak:

OPENER	RESPONDER
2 ♥	2 ♠

3♥ - an excellent one-suiter, not enough for game, with values in the side suits; not forcing but highly invitational. 3♣/3♦ - a second suit; a one-round force.

U

USBA. Abbreviation for UNITED STATES BRIDGE ASSOCIATION, one of the predecessor organizations from which AMERICAN CONTRACT BRIDGE LEAGUE emerged. For tournament results see Appendix I.

USBA GRAND NATIONALS. For tournament results see Appendix I.

UKRAINIAN BRIDGE FEDERATION. The Federation was founded in 1991, following the break-up of the Soviet Union, with 500 players.
1992 Officers:
President: Sergei Kapustin.
Official Representative: Alexey Varfolomeyev
Soviet Ukraine place 7, 31003 Harkov-3, Ukraine
Telephone: (0572) 438293
Fax: (0572) 225571

ULTIMATE CLUB. The first totally integrated relay system to be substantially successful in tournament play. It is based on ideas propounded by Dave Cliff of Basking Ridge NJ, and was developed and refined by Matthew Granovetter, Ron Rubin and Mike Becker.

The advantage of this system, and of other relay methods, is that it greatly increases the number of meaningful auctions. The relay is a meaningless bid (usually but not invariably a minimum action) that asks partner to describe his hand further.

After a strong 1♣ opening, the responder describes his hand in three stages: the number of aces, kings and queens; the exact distribution; and the location of the high cards. In response to 1♦, 1♥ or 1♠, 2♣ by the responder is a relay, an artificial game force requiring a description by the opener. 2♦ in response to one of a major is an artificial invitation.

In response to 1NT, 2♣ is a relay requiring an exact description. See RELAY SYSTEMS.

UNASSUMING CUEBID. The use of a cuebid in response to an overcall to show a sound raise to the two-level. This makes it difficult to bid some strong hands, so it should be combined with the style in which new suits are forcing in response to an overcall.

UNAUTHORIZED INFORMATION. Information which is given to a partner by means other than a legal call or play. Such information may be conveyed by questions, tone of voice, special emphasis, mannerisms, grimaces, remarks, squirms, or huddles. If such information is received, a player should be governed by Law 16 of either rubber or duplicate bridge. See ALERTING; EXPLANATION OF ANY CALL OR PLAY .

At times in duplicate games a player may inadvertently overhear a remark by a contestant about a particular board which he has not as yet played. Such a fact should be reported to the director who will act in a manner as fair as possible to the player so reporting. See LAWS (Law 16).

UNBALANCED DISTRIBUTION. Referring to either the distribution of the suits in a hand or the distribution of one suit among the four hands, unbalanced is opposed to BALANCED DISTRIBUTION. Among the requirements for unbalanced distribution is the combination of one or more long suits and one or more singletons or voids.

UNBALANCED SWISS RAISE. Part of the ACES SCIENTIFIC SYSTEM, used in combination with VALUE SWISS RAISES to provide a full range of game-forcing raises in response to a major-suit opening. A jump response of three of the other major is used to show 10-12 with a singleton somewhere in the hand; a jump to 3NT shows 13-15 with a singleton.

Opener makes the cheapest bid to locate opener's singleton. Responder answers by bidding one of the next three steps; two of the steps will be natural and will show a singleton in the suit bid; the other step, either 3NT or four of the anchor suit, will show a singleton in the remaining suit. See also CONGLOMERATE MAJOR RAISES, SUPER SWISS.

UNBEATABLE. See COLD.

UNBID MINOR FORCING. (Often called New Minor Forcing.) After opener has made a rebid of 1NT, it is sometimes useful for responder to have available a low-level artificial forcing bid, either to inquire about opener's support for responder's suit, or to permit further action by responder.

WEST	EAST
1♣	1♠
1NT	2♦

If both majors have been bid, the cheaper minor is used: 1♥-1♠-1NT-2♣.

Opener's first duty is to show preference with 3-card support, second duty is to show an unbid major. (Other agreements are possible). Subsequent non-jump bids are invitational. See CROWHURST and TWO CLUBS REBID BY OPENER AS ONLY FORCE AFTER ONE NOTRUMP REBID.

UNBID SUIT. Suit which has not been bid by declarer or his partner during the auction. Frequently, without any attractive opening lead, a player will select a lead on the basis that a suit has not been bid. This applies particularly to a major suit against a notrump contract.

An unbid suit may be a useful waiting move in the auction. See FOURTH SUIT FORCING AND ARTIFICIAL.

UNBLOCKING. Throwing a high card in play in order to gain some advantage for the hand opposite.

```
                A 10 6 2
    J 9 8 3                  K 7 5
                Q 4
```

Dummy has no side entry. West leads the 3, won by East's king. South unblocks with his queen, permitting a later finesse of the 10 so that South makes two tricks. Similarly:

```
                A 9 5 3
    J 10 8 7                K 6 2
                Q 4
```

Dummy has no side entry. West leads the jack, won by East's king. South unblocks the queen, and makes two tricks by a later finesse of the nine.

```
                Q 10 5 3
    K 8 7 2                  6 4
                A J 9
```

If South needs a later entry to dummy in this suit, he must be careful to win the opening lead with the ace.

A blind spot for many players is the internal block:

```
        A K Q 4 3            A 7 6 4 2
                   or
```

```
        10 8 7           K Q 9 8
```
If one defender holds J x x, five tricks cannot be run without a side entry to dummy. Similarly:

```
              A 5 4 3 2


              Q J 10 9
```
If there is no side entry to dummy, this is never worth five tricks.

There are numerous unblocking situations for the defense.

```
              A 3 2
    Q 10 6 5 4           K 7
              J 9 8
```
If the five is led against 3NT and dummy plays the ace, East must unblock the king. If East has an entry, the defense will take four tricks. The declarer's play would be right if opening leader held the entry.

UNBLOCKING SQUEEZE. See JETTISON SQUEEZE.

UNCONSTRUCTIVE. A bid which is distinctly discouraging, but does not bar partner from making a further move.

UNDER. To the right of. Thus, South is under West, etc. A king or any other card may be said to be under another card if the positional factor applies as above.

UNDER THE GUN. A term borrowed from poker in which game the phrase refers to the hand betting immediately after the dealer. In bridge there are various meanings, both in bidding and play. The term can be used in bidding situations to cover the position where a hand or player can be said to be "under the gun" if he is bidding directly after a preemptive bidder and before a hand which has not yet been heard from. The term also can describe a position where a player has to meet a bid-or-double situation at the slam level. In play, it is used to describe the hand between dummy and declarer that has a high card or high cards that are finessable and are in a vulnerable position thereby.

UNDERBID. A bid lower than the value of the hand warrants. Although such bids are usually made because of inferior judgment, they may sometimes be made consciously and deliberately. One justification would be a tactical situation in which the opponents seem likely to save if the full value of the hand is bid. If the final contract is reached with, apparently, less assurance, the opponents may be deterred from saving. An underbid may also be made as an upside-down type of SHOOTING.

UNDERBIDDER. A player who regularly bids slightly less than the value his hand warrants. He is rarer, and easier to play with, than the overbidder. His psychological motivation is usually a reluctance to be set in any contract.

UNDERLEAD. The lead of a low card in a suit in which the master card or cards is held. This is routine in notrump contracts, but is unusual in trump contracts.

```
              K 7 2
    A 10 8 3           Q 9 6 5
              J 4
```
If West gains the lead early in the play and leads a low card, South should guess right. West would be unlikely to lead from the queen, giving South the chance for a trick he could not otherwise make. As the cards lie, one trick is all the defenders can make if they play passively.

But if West can find the lead of a low card originally, South is almost sure to go wrong and play low from dummy. Underleads of aces as the opening lead are distinctly daring, but may sometimes be risked if the bidding suggests strongly that dummy will have the king of the suit.

Another motive for an underlead is an urgent desire to get a particular lead from partner, perhaps for a ruff. The following celebrated example occurred in the 1958 Bermuda Bowl.

```
                ♠ A K 8 4
                ♥ A 7 6 3 2
                ♦ 5
                ♣ A J 8
    ♠ 10 6 5 3 2                ♠ Q J
    ♥ 9                         ♥ 10 5
    ♦ A J 10 8 7 4 3            ♦ K Q 2
    ♣ —                         ♣ K Q 6 5 4
                ♠ 7
                ♥ K Q J 8 4
                ♦ 9 6
                ♣ 10 9 7 3 2
```
Neither side was vulnerable.

WEST	NORTH	EAST	SOUTH
		1NT	2♥
2♠	3♠	Pass	3NT
5♦	5♥	Pass	Pass
Dbl	All Pass		

Pietro Forquet, West for Italy, judged that his partner's most likely entry was the ♦K. He therefore led the ♦3, a suit preference signal. East duly won and returned the ♣K. West ruffed, and East had to make a club trick to defeat the contract.

In the other room the ♦A was led against 5♥. The contract could not then be defeated. South was able to strip the hand and endplay East. See OVERLEAD .

UNDERRUFF, or undertrump. To play a low trump when a trick has already been ruffed with a higher trump. It can be the right play whether the previous ruff was by an opponent or by partner. The underruff, though unusual, is necessary in many situations.

(1) *To avoid a trump surplus (simple trump coup).* It is on occasion a disadvantage to hold too many trumps. When reduced to only trump cards you may be forced to ruff a trick belonging to your partner, and then lead away from or into a tenace position.

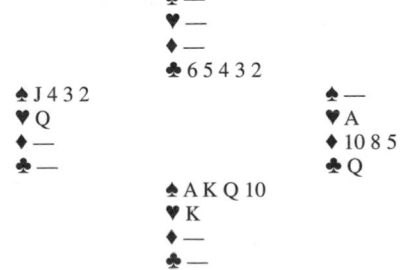

```
                ♠ —
                ♥ —
                ♦ —
                ♣ 6 5 4 3 2
    ♠ J 4 3 2                ♠ —
    ♥ Q                      ♥ A
    ♦ —                      ♦ 10 8 5
    ♣ —                      ♣ Q
                ♠ A K Q 10
                ♥ K
                ♦ —
                ♣ —
```
South is declarer at a spade contract and needs four tricks to make it. The lead is in North's hand. A club is led which East covers. South, knowing the trump posi-

tion, realizes his only chance is to ruff high. West must undertrump to avoid a trump endplay. If West discards, South will lead his losing heart. West must ruff and lead into a spade tenace. When West undertrumps, declarer is helpless. If he leads a heart, East will win and play a diamond through South's trump holding. (If South ruffs this high, West must undertrump perforce.)

(2) *To avoid a fatal discard in a plain suit.* In the following deal an underruff was necessary at the third trick because East could not spare any cards in the side suits.

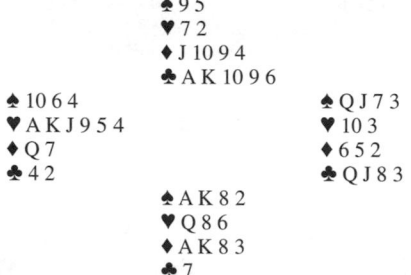

```
              ♠ 9 5
              ♥ 7 2
              ♦ J 10 9 4
              ♣ A K 10 9 6
♠ 10 6 4                    ♠ Q J 7 3
♥ A K J 9 5 4              ♥ 10 3
♦ Q 7                      ♦ 6 5 2
♣ 4 2                      ♣ Q J 8 3
              ♠ A K 8 2
              ♥ Q 8 6
              ♦ A K 8 3
              ♣ 7
```

South played in 5♦, and West led two high hearts. East played high-low, perhaps wrongly, and when the ♦J could not be overruffed at the third trick West was marked with the ♦Q. East had a discard problem which he solved by underruffing with the ♦2; any black suit discard would have made the play easy for South. The contract failed, although South could have succeeded by very accurate play. Two high spades, a spade ruff and four rounds of trumps would have squeezed East in the black suits.

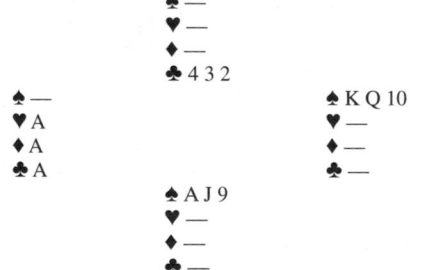

```
              ♠ —
              ♥ —
              ♦ —
              ♣ 4 3 2
♠ —                        ♠ K Q 10
♥ A                        ♥ —
♦ A                        ♦ —
♣ A                        ♣ —
              ♠ A J 9
              ♥ —
              ♦ —
              ♣ —
```

Again North is on lead with South the declarer at a spade contract. South needs two more tricks for the contract. When a club is led from dummy, East must ruff high to prevent South from scoring the ♠J.

South can now undertrump with the ♠9, leaving East to lead into an established tenace. If South overruffs, he must concede two spade tricks to East.

(3) *To be able to lead a plain suit card at a later time (ROBERT COUP).* In certain positions, it is profitable to be able to lead a plain suit card rather than a trump.

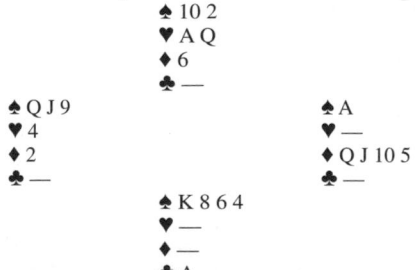

```
              ♠ 10 2
              ♥ A Q
              ♦ 6
              ♣ —
♠ Q J 9                    ♠ A
♥ 4                        ♥ —
♦ 2                        ♦ Q J 10 5
♣ —                        ♣ —
              ♠ K 8 6 4
              ♥ —
              ♦ —
              ♣ A
```

West leads against South's spade contract. South needs

three tricks to make the contract.

West leads the ♥4 which East ruffs with the ♠A. This appears to give West two natural trump tricks, but South underruffs! East returns a diamond and South ruffs again. South now leads the ♣A. West must ruff with a high honor to prevent dummy's ♠10 from winning this trick. Dummy discards and West must now lead away from his remaining spade honor.

If South does not preserve the ♣A to lead toward dummy, he will be defeated. When a low trump is led from the South hand, West wins with the jack and dummy must follow suit. West can now lead the ♠Q, smothering North's 10 and setting up the ♠9 for the setting trick.

(4) *To avoid a premature squeeze (anti-positional squeeze).* It is sometimes possible to avoid making a premature discard by undertrumping.

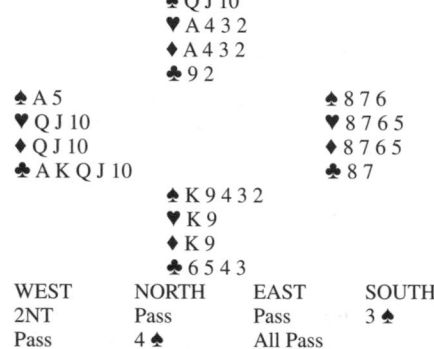

```
              ♠ Q J 10
              ♥ A 4 3 2
              ♦ A 4 3 2
              ♣ 9 2
♠ A 5                      ♠ 8 7 6
♥ Q J 10                   ♥ 8 7 6 5
♦ Q J 10                   ♦ 8 7 6 5
♣ A K Q J 10               ♣ 8 7
              ♠ K 9 4 3 2
              ♥ K 9
              ♦ K 9
              ♣ 6 5 4 3
```

WEST	NORTH	EAST	SOUTH
2NT	Pass	Pass	3♠
Pass	4♠	All Pass	

South's 3♠ bid had nothing to recommend it, but it happened that the contract was difficult to defeat. East had a poor hand but he played the star role. West led the ♣K and promptly shifted to ace and another trump. Dummy won and another club was won by West. West now shifted to the ♥Q which declarer won with the king.

When declarer ruffed a club in dummy, East had to undertrump to defeat the contract. If he discarded from a red suit, South would have been able to establish a trick in that suit in dummy by ruffing, and the contract would have been made. After East underruffed, declarer was helpless.

UNDERTRICK. Each trick by which declarer's side fails to fulfill its contract. For the penalties for each undertrick, see LAWS (Law 81), LAWS OF DUPLICATE (Law 77).

UNDERTRUMP. See UNDERRUFF.

UNDOUBLE. See DOUBLE FOR SACRIFICE.

UNFACED HAND. During the play, the hands of the declarer and both defenders. After the opening lead, the declarer's partner's hand is faced up on the table so that all players may see the cards (dummy's hand). Prior to the play, none of the hands is faced. A player in claiming or conceding tricks faces his hand in properly presenting his claim. See CLAIM OR CONCESSION; DEFENDING HAND; DUMMY.

UNFINISHED RUBBER. A rubber ended by agreement before either side has won two games. A side which has won one game is credited with a bonus of 300 points; a side which has the only partial is credited with a bonus of 100 points. (This was 50 until a change in the 1993

Code.)

UNINTENTIONAL. A violation of rules, ethics, or proprieties is assumed in bridge circles to be unintentional, not deliberate. It is the purpose of the LAWS to provide indemnities for the non-offending side to permit an accurate or fairly accurate result on the board or a hand. Any intentional violation contravenes the philosophy of the game as a contest involving ladies and gentlemen. An assumption that a violation is intentional by an opponent is as much a violation of ethics as such an intentional violation itself would be.

UNIT. A division of the American Contract Bridge League covering a relatively small area. Some units include only a city, but others include entire states. The unit supervises bridge activities at ACBL games in its territory and conducts tournaments at the local and sectional levels. Groups of units form ACBL districts, and officers and board members of units elect the district's representative to the ACBL Board of Directors.

UNIT-WIDE GAME. An ACBL game of Unit Championship rating held simultaneously at three or more locations in the Unit. Each Unit is entitled to hold one Unit-wide Championship a year for each full 200 members, up to a maximum of seven such championships. If more than one such game is held in a year, each game must be scheduled for a different day of the week. All masterpoint awards for unit-wide games are issued by the ACBL.

UNITED STATES BRIDGE ASSOCIATION. One of the predecessor organizations which merged to form the AMERICAN CONTRACT BRIDGE LEAGUE. The purpose of this association was to organize a national tournament in which participation would be based on skill alone, and which would be a thorough enough test so that its winners could be clearly recognized as national champions.

The Grand National Plan which this organization evolved was a pyramiding series of qualifying tournaments starting with open local tournaments, proceeding to city, state, and regional tournaments, and culminating in the Grand National.

In addition to the organization of tournaments truly national in scope, the United States Bridge Association was a charter member of the International Contract Bridge Union which was organized in 1934 under the joint sponsorship of the United States Bridge Association, the National Bridge Association of Great Britain, and the French Contract Bridge Association.

The American Bridge League (organized 1927) and the International Bridge League (headquarters at The Hague, Holland) existed concurrently, and some short-lived rivalry between the two organizations was eliminated in 1937 when the American Contract Bridge League resulted from the amalgamation of the two United States organizations.

For results see Appendix I.

UNITED STATES INTERNATIONAL REPRESENTATIVES. The names of players who have represented the U. S. or North America in international team events may be found under ANGLO-AMERICAN MATCHES, BERMUDA BOWL, FRANCO-AMERICAN MATCHES, INTERNATIONAL OPEN TEAM SELECTION, WORLD TEAM OLYMPIAD, INTERNATIONAL WOMEN'S TEAM SELECTION, VENICE CUP, ROSENBLUM CUP and WORLD CHAMPIONSHIPS.

UNITS OF THE ACBL. Units of the ACBL have been formed at different times and under different conditions, and they differ widely in background, scope, and membership. Some limit their activity to a given town or city, others comprise states.

The jurisdiction of a unit consists of a geographical area, bounded in its application and charter, and each unit has jurisdiction over its own members, while participating in the management of ACBL.

A new unit may be formed in any area where no unit exists, provided there are 100 or more members in the area to be organized. In the process of formation, a provisional charter may be granted with more than 50 members if a reasonable prospect of reaching the 100-member status exists.

The unit is expected to perform certain functions:

(1) Establish and maintain a membership of at least 100.

(2) Promote and stimulate interest in duplicate bridge among members and prospective members by providing an attractive program of bridge events.

(3) Expand and increase membership by interesting new players.

(4) Conduct or supervise tournament events at which masterpoints and rating points are awarded under ACBL regulations.

(5) Establish and maintain contact with neighboring units, supporting each other's activities.

(6) Conduct annual elections by popular vote for officers and/or Directors.

(7) Elect, in collaboration with other units in the district, a member of the National Board of Directors, a first and a second Alternate Director, and three representatives to the National Board of Governors.

(8) Adopt bylaws consistent with those of the ACBL, which must be filed with ACBL.

(9) Assume fiscal responsibility for funds collected on behalf of the ACBL, and membership dues from its members, submitting semi-annual financial reports to its officers; maintain accurate records.

UNLAWFUL. An action not in accordance with the mechanics of the game, as described in Parts I to III of LAWS.

UNLIMITED BID. A bid with wide limits in valuation. The bid with the widest limit of all is a STAYMAN response to a weak notrump, which could range from a worthless hand to a hand worth a forcing opening bid. Other unlimited bids are discussed under ONE OVER ONE, OPENING SUIT BID and TAKEOUT DOUBLE .

UNMAKABLE. A contract which cannot succeed unless the defense slips. Frequently an unmakable contract succeeds, however, because the defense is comparatively in the dark about the declarer's holding. Unmakable is the opposite of COLD (Unbeatable), and, like this term, is relative.

UNMIXED PAIRS. An event in which all pairs must consist of either two women or two men.

UNPENALTY DOUBLE. See DOUBLE FOR SACRIFICE.

UNSEEDED KNOCKOUT TEAMS. A method first tried in 1982 for improving the attendance at knockout team events. Random draws determine the pairings for all rounds leading up to the final. It is theoretically possible, but not too likely, that the two best teams in the field would meet each other in the first round. The event has proved quite popular.

UNUSUAL JUMP. See ASKING BIDS; FRAGMENT BID; GRAND SLAM FORCE; LEBOVIC ASKING BID; ROMEX TRUMP ASKING BIDS; SPLINTER BID; SUPER GERBER; SUPER SWISS; VOID SHOWING BIDS.

UNUSUAL NOTRUMP. A method of showing two-suited hands in competitive situations. The convention, which normally indicates length in the minor suits, was devised by Alvin Roth in 1948 and developed by him with Tobias Stone.

An overcall of 2NT after an opening bid of one of a major is normally used to show the minor suits. The overcaller may well be suggesting a sacrifice:

> ♠ 5
> ♥ 4
> ♦ K Q 9 5 2
> ♣ Q J 9 7 6 3

Overcaller might also have an extremely strong hand on which his next action will be a cuebid of opener's suit:

> ♠ A Q
> ♥ 2
> ♦ A Q 7 5 3
> ♣ A K J 8 4

See TWO NOTRUMP OVERCALL.

In many situations the Unusual notrump is a balancing move:

(a)

WEST	NORTH	EAST	SOUTH
			1 ♠
Pass	1NT	Pass	2 ♣
Pass	Pass	2NT	

(b)

WEST	NORTH	EAST	SOUTH
			1 ♠
Pass	2 ♦	Pass	Pass
2NT			

In both cases the Unusual notrump bidder wishes to contest the partscore and invites his partner to pick a minor. Case (b) is slightly safer than (a) because the known fit for North-South in spades increases the chance that East-West have a fit. The Unusual notrump may be used when the auction is still very much alive:

(c)

WEST	NORTH	EAST	SOUTH
			1 ♠
Pass	1NT	Pass	2 ♠ or 2 ♥
2NT			

(d)

WEST	NORTH	EAST	SOUTH
			1 ♥
Pass	1 ♠	Pass	2 ♠
2NT			

In (c) both North and South are limited and are unlikely to go beyond the level of two. West can rely on some strength from East, who should not entertain any hopes of game. In (d), North is not limited, but the North-South fit gives West some assurance of an East-West fit. If the vulnerability is favorable for East-West, 5♣ or 5♦ may prove a cheap save if North-South go to 4♠.

An original pass may serve to identify the Unusual notrump, as when the dealer overcalls 1NT after a fourth-hand major-suit opening bid. Many players apply the convention whenever the opponents have bid two suits:

(e)

WEST	NORTH	EAST	SOUTH
			1 ♣
Pass	1 ♥	1NT	

(f)

WEST	NORTH	EAST	SOUTH
			1 ♠
Pass	2 ♦	2NT	

It would seldom be right for East to make a notrump bid in a natural sense, because he would be laying himself open to a heavy penalty opposite a probably worthless dummy. With a strong defensive hand he would prefer to stay out of the auction, expecting to defeat any game contract.

So in this case, East's bid shows great length (at least 5- 5) in the unbid suits. This is one extension of the convention (optional by partnership agreement) to situations not limited to minor suits. Another is a direct 2NT overcall of a minor-suit opening, which many pairs use to show length in the two lower-ranking unbid suits. (However, since 1♣ openings are sometimes based on a three-card suit, some pairs use a 2NT overcall of 1♣ to show both minors.)

The Unusual notrump can be used when your side has already bid, and even when your side has opened the bidding:

(g)

WEST	NORTH	EAST	SOUTH
			Pass
3 ♥	Dbl	Pass	4NT

(h)

WEST	NORTH	EAST	SOUTH
			1 ♣
4 ♠	4NT		

In (g) South shows a good minor two-suiter, probably not far short of an opening bid. North may be able to jump to 6♣ or 6♦. In this case the Unusual notrump is an attacking weapon.

When the bidding has been seriously crowded by an opponent's preemptive action, 4NT is usually a takeout bid rather than BLACKWOOD. In (h) Sidney Silodor suggested the 4NT bid on this hand:

> ♠ —
> ♥ K Q 6 5 3
> ♦ A J 9 8 3
> ♣ 9 7 2

The bid indicates a desire to play at the five-level, with a free choice left to partner.

Partnerships must define the meaning of a 4NT overcall after a 4♠ or 4♥ opening. Most play that over 4♥, a double is a three-suit takeout and 4NT is for minors; over 4♠, a double is for penalties and 4NT is a takeout for all three suits.

The Unusual notrump can operate when the user has already bid a minor suit:

(i)

WEST	NORTH	EAST	SOUTH
			1 ♠
2 ♣	2 ♦	Pass	Pass
2NT			

(j)

WEST	NORTH	EAST	SOUTH
			1 ♣
1 ♥	Pass	4 ♥	4NT

In (i), West wishes to contest the partscore, and is likely to have five or six clubs and four diamonds. If his second suit were hearts he would double. In (j), South is likely to have five diamonds and six clubs: 4NT is his only way to indicate this distribution.

The Unusual notrump is usually made by the side which did not open the bidding. In (h) and (j) above, its use by the opener's side is shown, and here are two further examples:

(k)

WEST	NORTH	EAST	SOUTH
			1 ♦
1 ♠	Pass	4 ♠	4NT

(l)

WEST	NORTH	EAST	SOUTH
			1 ♥
1 ♠	Pass	2 ♠	Pass
Pass	2NT		

In (k), South's second suit must be hearts: with a minor two-suiter he would bid 5♣ to offer an easy choice at the level of five. In (1) North cannot wish to play 2NT when he could not bid over 1♥; clearly he has a weak minor two-suiter. See GENEVA CONVENTION.

UNUSUAL POSITIVE. A set of artificial jump responses to a Precision Club opening to describe 4-4-4-1 distribution.

UNUSUAL OVER UNUSUAL. See DEFENSE TO TWO-SUITED INTERFERENCE.

UP THE LINE. The practice of making the cheapest bid when responding or rebidding with two or three four-card suits, laid down as a principle by the BARON SYSTEM. The idea is employed in many bidding styles, with some reservations

    ♠ K 8 4 3
    ♥ K 8 4 3
    ♦ A J
    ♣ K 10 5

A 1♥ response to an opening bid in either minor suit gives the opener the opportunity to rebid in spades. If he fails to do so, responder can assume there is no spade fit and bid 3NT.

This idea has validity but there are many circumstances in which expert players would depart from the principle.

(1) If there is a great disparity in the strength of the suits:

    ♠ A Q J 3
    ♥ 8 4 3 2
    ♦ A J
    ♣ Q 10 5

The chief arguments in favor of bidding 1♠ in response to a minor-suit opening are that a heart response might lead to a notrump contract with an unguarded heart suit, and that a high heart contract might result in a weak trump holding. The opposing view is that 1♥ may inhibit a heart lead in notrump, and that a 1♠ response may exclude a 4-

4 fit in hearts.

(2) With two strong major suits:

    ♠ K Q J 3
    ♥ A Q 5 2
    ♦ 8 3
    ♣ 9 4 2

Some authorities recommend a response of 1♠ to an opening bid in a minor, with the intention of bidding hearts on the next round.

The choice of response is closely connected with the treatment of BIDDABLE SUITS. If the opener is not expected to rebid 1♠ with a bad four-card suit, the spade response is necessary to avoid missing a possible fit.

A disadvantage is that 1♠ followed by a heart bid strongly suggests a five-card spade suit. The "up the line" response of 1♥, used by players who do not impose standards for biddable suits, leads to a problem if the opener rebids his suit. In that case an eccentric reverse bid of 2♠ may be tried.

(3) With one major suit and one minor suit:

(a)	(b)
♠ Q J 7 3	♠ 8 2
♥ 8 2	♥ Q J 7 3
♦ Q J 7 3	♦ Q J 7 3
♣ J 7 2	♣ J 7 2

In each of these cases there is a good argument for rejecting the 1♦ response to 1♣ in favor of the major suit. The danger of 1♦ is that opposing intervention may shut out the major suit, which is a serious possibility in case (b). In case (a), 1♠ may work well by shutting out an opposing heart contract. But if the responding hand is stronger, there is less likelihood of intervention, and therefore less reason to prefer the major-suit response.

If the response is at the two-level, the minor-suit response is preferable. The chance of interference is slight, and a response of 2♥ to 1♠ is generally expected to show a five-card or longer suit. See CHOICE OF SUIT.

UP TO. (1) Toward the hand that will play last to a particular trick, as in UP TO WEAKNESS. (2) Toward a vulnerable third-hand holding such as K-x-x or K-Q-x, as opposed to leading away from such a holding.

UP TO STRENGTH. Traditional wisdom advises leading up to weakness but is silent about leading up to strength. If dummy is on your right, it is sometimes appropriate to lead a suit in which dummy is strong.

You should tend to avoid leading a suit in which you have an honor poised over an honor in dummy: ace over king or queen; king over queen or jack; queen over jack or ten. Leading in such circumstances will often give away trick.

If dummy on your right has two high honors, leading from a jack tends to be safer than leading from another honor:

♣ A K 2	♣ A Q 2
Dummy	Dummy
♣ J 4 3	♣ J 4 3
You	You
(a)	(b)

Leading from the jack can do no harm, but leading from any other honor may lose a trick.

UP TO WEAKNESS. The old whist maxim recommending a lead "up to weakness" is valid but not very helpful. It is quite true that a lead by declarer's right-hand opponent up to a completely worthless holding in dummy will never give away a trick, although it may help the declarer if he is short of entries to dummy.

The following discussion will consider defender's problems in this situation on the assumption that the suit in question is distributed evenly around the table. If one player is known to be short or is likely to be short, the prospects are of course altered. Crucial situations are classified in increasing order of dummy strength.

(1) Dummy has 9-x-x. Almost invariably a safe lead, but the defender should be careful to lead the 10 from holdings headed by K-10 or Q-10.

(2) Dummy has 10-x-x. The defender must lead the jack from holdings headed by A-J or K-J. If leading from a single honor, the higher the honor the safer the lead. A-x-x is completely safe, while J-x-x is the most dangerous.

(3) Dummy has J-x-x. Again, the higher the honor the safer the lead. A-x-x is relatively safe, while Q-x-x is very dangerous.

(4) Dummy has Q-x-x. A lead from the jack is virtually safe. A lead from the ace or king is very dangerous.

(5) Dummy has K-x-x. The lead from the ace is very dangerous. The lead from the jack or queen is almost completely safe.

(6) Dummy has A-x-x. All leads relatively safe, with J-x-x slightly the safest and Q-x-x the least safe.

The general principle applying in all the above cases is also applicable when leading through dummy. The defender should avoid breaking a suit in which an honor is poised over the honor ranking immediately below it. In other words, one should avoid leading from a jack up to a 10, a queen up to a jack, a king up to a queen, or an ace up to a king. Similarly, one should avoid leading from a jack through a queen, a queen through a king, or a king through an ace.

This applies also if dummy has two honors. It is obviously unwise to lead from a king up to A-Q, or a queen up to A-J or K-J. See also THROUGH STRENGTH.

UPPER SUITS CUEBID. An immediate overcall in the opponent's suit to show the two highest ranking unbid suits. See also MICHAELS CUEBID.

UPPERCUT. A ruff, usually by a defender, aimed at promoting a trump trick for partner.

$$\spadesuit\ 4\ 3\ 2$$
$$\spadesuit\ J\ 5 \qquad\qquad \spadesuit\ Q\ 6$$
$$\heartsuit\ A\ K\ 10\ 9\ 8\ 7$$

In a spade contract, West leads a suit of which East and South are void. East ruffs with his ♠Q, ensuring a trump trick for the defense. If South overruffs, the jack wins a trick.

A defender with a completely useless trump holding should usually ruff with his highest trump if he gets the opportunity. A ruff with a card as low as the six can possibly effect an uppercut and promote a trump trick for the defense.

UPSIDE-DOWN SIGNALS. The use of a low card in defense to encourage a continuation of a suit, or a shift to a suit, and a high card to discourage. The method is credited to Karl Schneider, but seems to have been first published by E.K. O'Brien in a *Bridge World* article in 1937.

The chief theoretical advantage of this procedure is that a player may not be able to spare a high card from a strong holding:

$$\spadesuit\ 10\ 7\ 6\ 3$$
$$\spadesuit\ J\ 5 \qquad\qquad \spadesuit\ K\ Q\ 9\ 2$$
$$\spadesuit\ A\ 8\ 4$$

West leads the ♠J against 3NT because his own suit has been bid by declarer. East has to drop the deuce because he cannot spare the 9. Using normal methods, it is now difficult for West to continue the suit when he gains the lead. But he continues happily using upside-down signals. Notice that if East had had a weak holding, such as Q-8-4-2, he could have spared the 8 as a discouraging card.

Other advantages claimed for this method are that it is harder for declarer to falsecard effectively, and that a one-card discard signal during the defense may be clearer than with normal methods.

As with standard signals, the appropriate counter for the declarer is to signal as if he were a defender: Play low to encourage, high to discourage. This gives the best chance to scramble the signals and confuse the signaler's partner.

For a different upside-down signal, which grew in popularity in the 80s, see COUNT SIGNALS. For a combination of standard and upside-down attitude signals, see SCANIAN SIGNALS.

URUGUAY BRIDGE ASSOCIATION (ASOCIACION URUGUAYA DE BRIDGE). The Association was formed in 1948 and has a membership of about 300. It hosted the South American Championships six times, and its players have won the South American Women's Teams four times.
Officers 1992:
President: Jorge Ucar Easton
Sarandi 584,
Montevideo, Uruguay.
Tel. 598 2 962424
Fax. 598 2 419393

USEFUL SPACE PRINCIPLE. When allocating bidding space under partnership agreements, assign it where it is most useful without reference to natural or traditional meanings of calls. This may involve deciding which tasks are most important to accomplish and arranging adequate space to perform those tasks efficiently. Techniques for allocating space include "lumping" (giving over all extra space to one function), "spreading" (giving increments of space to each of several functions, usually by removing most or all space from one task deemed less important), and making compromises (not making use of all available space in order to achieve some or all of a transcending objective).

According to Jeff Rubens in a series of articles in *The Bridge World*, several popular conventions and many standard methods are based on a misguided idea of simplicity. "They are not well-designed because they ignore the Useful Space Principle," he wrote. Rubens studied the BLACKWOOD convention, among others, to illustrate the principle. He pointed out that bidding the suit immediately above the agreed trump at the four-level (see KICKBACK) allows more room for control asking and trump length asking, while 4NT works perfectly well as the cuebid in the suit that initiates a Blackwood sequence. For example, if the auction has begun 1♥-3♥, then 4♠ would be Blackwood and 4 NT would be a spade cuebid. If the agreed suit is clubs, then 4♦ would be Blackwood and 4NT would be a diamond cuebid. However, if the agreed suit is spades, then 4NT is Blackwood. Specialized responses allow much more specific exploration of slam possibilities. Rubens also offered new structures for new-suit responses to overcalls and new methods for using the GRAND SLAM FORCE, while pointing out that many other applications also are possible.

USES OF CARDS. Although playing cards are made for the playing of games, individual cards have been used for other purposes. Since the backs were (until about 120 years ago) blank and unmarked, paper was scarce and expensive, and playing cards used the very finest quality paper obtainable, cards were practical to use for purposes where standardization was an asset.

Both handwritten and printed visiting cards were made on card backs, as were tickets and identifying passes. Workmen dismantling the Bastille carried such passes to distinguish them from the crowds of curious visitors who interfered with their work.

In France and in Canada, cards were used in emergencies as money. Several libraries used them for their original index cards. At one time it was fashionable to write social invitations on them. Advertisements were printed and written on them.

Old cards and sheets of cards were used to stiffen the covers of books, and some of our knowledge of early cards comes from discoveries of these fragments. And, of course, they are the building blocks for constructing a house of cards. See TURGENEV.

UTILITY. A British expression which summarizes the straightforward bidding methods used there in many rubber bridge clubs: strong notrump (16-18); 2♣ as the forcing opening; intermediate two bids; and 3NT for takeout over opposing three-bids.

UTILITY NOTRUMP RESPONSE. See CHURCHILL.

UZBEKISTAN, Bridge Federation of.
Founded in 1992.
President: Davijar Nuhraliev
Secretary: Yuri Covalenko
P.O.Box 4215 Tashkent - 115
Uzbekistan 700115
Fax: 3712 562 034

V

VALET. One of the court cards in decks of cards used centuries ago, decks that were ancestors of present-day cards. The term survives in French, meaning equivalent of English jack or knave. A knave, like a valet, is a male servant.

VALIDATION. In duplicate bridge, the certifying by the director of the correctness of an auction play; the approval of the opponents to a correction of the scoring of the results of a board of duplicate play; the initialing of a pair score in team play by the opponents of this pair on a set of boards.

VALUATION. Valuation of a hand is covered under particular types of valuation in the following articles: ACE

VALUES; ASSETS; BISSELL; BORDERLINE OPENING BIDS; DEATH HOLDING; FOUR ACES SYSTEM; LAW OF TOTAL TRICKS; LOSING TRICK COUNT; POINT COUNT; REITH POINT COUNT; REVALUATION; ROBERTSON POINT COUNT; RULE OF FIFTEEN; RULE OF EIGHTEEN; TRUMP SUPPORT; VALUE OF GAME; VALUE OF SLAM; WORK POINT COUNT.

VALUE OF GAME. At matchpoint play, a game bonus of 300 points is added to the trick score for non-vulnerable games and a bonus of 500 points is added to the trick score for vulnerable games. These values determine the mathematics of sacrificing against an opponent's game. For example, a better score results from going down three, doubled, non-vulnerable rather than letting an opponent make a vulnerable game. At matchpoints, any game should be bid with a 50% chance, all other things being equal.

In imp play, the values of the game and slam bonus are used to determine the probability of success needed to abandon a safe game for a risky small slam. For example, in a close team match with imp scoring, a 50% chance of success is needed to bid a vulnerable small slam vs. a sure game. At imps, games should be bid with a 37% chance vulnerable and a 45% chance non-vulnerable.

In rubber bridge, it has been shown that a game bonus of 500 points is appropriate for scoring the rubber game when both sides are vulnerable and a game bonus of 350 points is the correct value in all other combinations of vulnerability. This leads to the following decisions on the probability of success needed to bid a small slam in rubber bridge:

	Opponents vulnerable	Opponents non-vulnerable
Declarer vulnerable	50%	38%
Declarer non-vulnerable	55%	55%

Safety factors required for bidding grand slams in rubber bridge are 65% when declarer is vulnerable and the opponents are non-vulnerable and 68% in all other combinations of vulnerability.

The safety factor required for bidding a game can be shown to be 54% when declarer is vulnerable and the opponents are non-vulnerable and 49% in all other combinations of vulnerability. These factors are calculated using the values of the game bonus and the values of the partscore bonus of 100 or 150 points, depending upon vulnerability. See VALUE OF PARTSCORE.

Safety factors required for doubling an opponent's game bid are 63% to 77%, depending upon vulnerability. Safety factors required for doubling an opponent's partscore into game are 77% to 87%, depending upon vulnerability.

VALUE OF PARTSCORE. In matchpoint play, a bonus of 50 points if awarded for successful less-than-game contracts. In CHICAGO, a partscore remaining at the end of four deals is not rewarded except on the last deal where a partscore earned is worth 100 points. In rubber bridge, a partscore bonus has been shown to be worth 150 points when both sides are vulnerable and 100 points in all other combinations of vulnerability. For safety factors required to abandon a safe partscore and bid a game, see VALUE OF GAME.

VALUE SWISS RAISES. An expansion of the SWISS CONVENTION used in the ACES SCIENTIFIC SYS-

TEM to show a range of forcing balanced raises in responses an opening bid of 1♥ or 1♠. They deny a singleton or a good 5-card suit, and promise 4-card support or a tripleton with two top honors. The ranges shown, assuming a 1♠ opening, are as follows:

1NT forcing, then 4	
of opener's major	12-13 points
4♦	13-14
4♣	14-16
2NT then strong support	16-18

VANDERBILT CLUB SYSTEM. Harold S. Vanderbilt, who codified the game of contract bridge in 1925, was the first to advocate use of a 1♣ opening bid as an artificial bid to show a strong hand, and of a 1♦ artificial negative response to show a weak hand. He wrote three books, now long since out of print, on his Club Convention prior to 1934; and his Club Convention was very popular until his books were no longer available.

After a lapse of about thirty years, interest in 1♣ systems revived. The BLUE TEAM CLUB, which helped to win many World Championships for Italy, uses an opening 1♣ convention very like the Vanderbilt Club, and the SCHENKEN SYSTEM, used in two World Championships, is an even closer relation.

In 1964, Vanderbilt wrote a modernized version of his system entitled *The Club Convention Modernize*d, which may be summarized as follows:

(1) Opening bids of 1♦ (perhaps 3 cards), 1♥, 1♠, (both perhaps 4 cards), 2♣ (good 5-suit or better) are limited, usually fewer than 16 points.

(2) Opening bids of 1♣ show hands with 16 or more points. 1♦ is the negative response. Other minimum responses show two aces or their equivalent. 2♥ and other single jumps show solid 5-card suits. 3♥ and other double jumps show one-loser six-card suits. 1NT response is strong, with an honor in every suit.

(4) Opening notrump bids are: 1NT 16-18; 1♣ followed by 1NT with 19-20; 2NT with 21-22; 1♣ then 2NT with 23-24; 1♣ then 3NT with 9 tricks and all suits stopped.

(5) After interference over 1♣, double, redouble, and jump bids are positive and forcing. Minimum actions are encouraging but non-forcing.

(6) Other opening bids include weak two-bids, solid 3♣ and 3♦, sound 3♥ and 3♠.

VANDERBILT CUP. (1) For the National Knockout Team Championships presented by Harold S. Vanderbilt in 1928. The organizing body 1928-57 was the Vanderbilt Cup Committee. It was contested annually in New York until 1958 when it became part of the Spring North American Championships, under which heading past results are listed. The Vanderbilt often is used to help select United States and North American international teams. It ranks with the Spingold as the most highly prized trophy in the ACBL calendar. See INTERNATIONAL OPEN TEAM SELECTION. For results see Appendix I.

(2) For the World Olympiad Team Championship, presented by Harold S. Vanderbilt on the occasion of the first World Team Olympiad held in Turin, Italy, in 1960. For results see Appendix V.

The two events are among the few for which the winners receive individual replicas of the trophy, a practice initiated by the donor from the first running of the events, and perpetuated by a $100,000 trust fund administered by the ACBL under the terms of Vanderbilt's will.

VANIVA PROBLEM. One of the most famous of all DOUBLE-DUMMY PROBLEMS; composed by Sidney Lenz in 1928 in a contest promoted by Vaniva Shaving Cream.

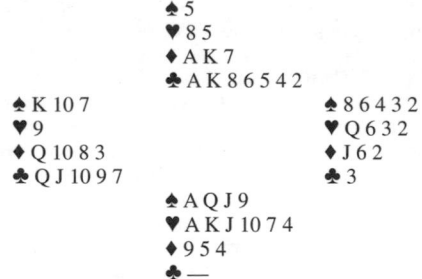

```
                  ♠ 5
                  ♥ 8 5
                  ♦ A K 7
                  ♣ A K 8 6 5 4 2
  ♠ K 10 7                         ♠ 8 6 4 3 2
  ♥ 9                              ♥ Q 6 3 2
  ♦ Q 10 8 3                       ♦ J 6 2
  ♣ Q J 10 9 7                     ♣ 3
                  ♠ A Q J 9
                  ♥ A K J 10 7 4
                  ♦ 9 5 4
                  ♣ —
```

South to make 7♥ after the lead of the ♣Q.

North wins the club opening, South discarding a diamond, and leads the other top club. Now:

(1) If East ruffs, South overruffs and takes a ruffing finesse in spades to kill West's king. A trump finesse gives South the balance.

(2) If East sheds a spade, South ruffs in hand and ruffs out the king of spades as before. He takes a trump finesse, cashes his spades, crosses to a diamond and ruffs a club. Then he crosses to another diamond and takes the last three tricks with the A-K-J of trumps over the queen.

(3) If East throws a diamond, South throws a spade and finesses in trumps. He crosses to a diamond, repeats the trump finesse, and runs all the trumps for a repeating squeeze against West in three suits.

VARIABLE NOTRUMP. An opening of 1NT which is weak non-vulnerable and strong vulnerable. Popular in Britain.

VENEZUELAN BRIDGE FEDERATION. (Federacion Venezolana de Bridge). The Federation was founded in 1958, and in 1993 had 740 members playing in 12 clubs. It competed in the South American Championships 1955-1978, winning the Open title 1963, 1965 and 1966 and representing the zone in the 1966 and 1967 world championships. It hosted the Championship 1963, 1970 and 1978. It hosted the CAC Championships in 1975, 1984, 1987 and 1991, and its players won the open team title 1973, 1977, 1984, 1985, 1986, 1987 and 1991 and the women's team title 1978-1987 inclusive, and in 1991. Officers 1993:
    President: Attilio Botto
    Secretary: Lilian Morganti
    c/o CBC 2 Calle De Campo Alegre
    Quinta Akeko
    Caracas Venezuela
    Tel. 58 2 2621160
    Fax: 58 2 2619948

VENICE CUP (or Venice Trophy). The event was first played in Venice in 1974, and continued in Monte Carlo in 1976, as a challenge between champion women's teams of Europe (in each case Italy) and the United States. It became a world championship in 1978, and the earlier events were retroactively recognized. Further events were played in 1981 and 1985, and subsequently biennially alongside the Bermuda Bowl. A new format was introduced in 1991 with an increased number of teams: four from Europe; three from North America; one from the

South Pacific and the host country; two from each other zone. Two groups of eight played a double-round robin, with four teams from each advancing to quarterfinal play-offs. For results see Appendix V.

VERDI. See TRANSFER OPENING THREE BIDS.

VERIFY (a score). In pair play, it is the duty of the North player to fill out the pick-up slip or traveling score and of the traveling pair or one of its members to verify (by initialing in a box provided on pick-up slips) the score as correct. In match play at teams-of-four, both pairs keep a record of their scores at each table, and each pair must verify the scoreslip of its opponents, from which the results of the match can be determined.

VICE SQUEEZE. A secondary squeeze that leads to a suit establishment play. (Analyzed and named by Terence Reese; the American spelling would be vise.)

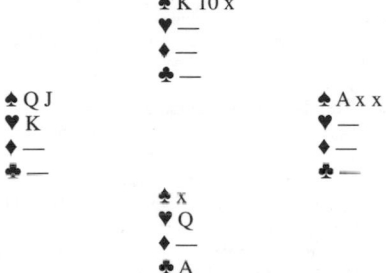

South leads the ♣A, and West is squeezed in two suits. If he discards the ♥K, then South's queen will take a trick; if he discards a spade, South can establish a trick in that suit.

The position looks like an automatic squeeze against West which has been modified in a particular way: instead of a two-card menace we have a vice menace consisting of the second-best card of the suit accompanied by a card which can be established if West weakens his second-round stopper.

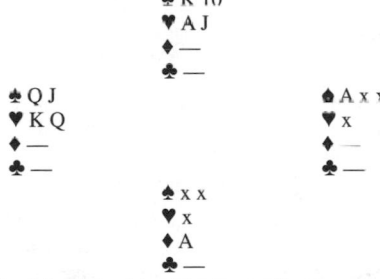

South leads the ♦A, which forces West to unguard hearts or to discard his second-round trick in spades.

This position is a modification of the simple positional squeeze. The vice menace does not provide an entry, so North's threat must be accompanied by a master card in the suit, which makes it a two-card threat.

In addition to the requirements stated above, East must have no trick to cash besides his stopper in the doubly-guarded suit.

VICTORY POINTS. In a contest among a great number of teams with a limited number of sessions, each team plays a relatively small number of deals against each of the other teams, ranging from 32 in the round-robin of the WORLD CHAMPIONSHIPS to as few as two deals in some smaller events. Various methods have been devised to counteract the excessive rewards to a 10- or 20-point swing in BOARD-A-MATCH SCORING, and to the slam contract made at one table and defeated at the other in IMP or TOTAL POINT SCORING.

The scoring method favored by many experts awards the IMP score on each board. The total IMP score on the boards of the match are then converted to victory points in accordance with a predetermined scale. This is the method most used in European Championships and in the round-robin portions of the Bermuda Bowl and World Team Olympiad.

The following scales were used in the 1992 World Team Olympiad in Salsomaggiore, Italy:

IMP DIFFERENCE	VICTORY POINTS
0 - 3	10 - 10
4 - 10	11 - 9
11 - 16	12 - 8
17 - 22	13 - 7
23 - 28	14 - 6
29 - 34	15 - 5
35 - 40	16 - 4
41 - 46	17 - 3
47 - 52	18 - 2
53 - 58	19 - 1
59 - 64	20 - 0
65 - 73	20 - (-1)
74 - 82	20 - (-2)
83 - 91	20 - (-3)
92 - 100	20 - (-4)
101 and more	20 - (-5)

VPs are used frequently in Swiss Team competitions and in round-robins with short matches. Here are the VP scales most often used in such competitions:

20-PT. VP SCALE			
IMPs	VPs	IMPs	VPs
0	10-10	14-6	16-4
1-2	11-9	17-19	17-3
3-4	12-8	20-23	18-2
5-7	13-7	24-27	19-1
8-10	14-6	28 +	20-0

30-PT. VP SCALE			
IMPs	VPs	IMPs	VPs
0	15-15	9-10	24-6
1	18-12	11-13	25-5
2	19-11	14-16	26-4
3	20-10	17-19	27-3
4	21-9	20-23	28-2
5-6	22-8	24-27	29-1
7-8	23-7	28 +	30-0

Even in win-loss type Swiss events, a form of victory points often is used in the ACBL. To receive credit for a full win, a team must win by 3 or more IMPs. A win by 1 or 2 IMPs constitutes a 3/4 win, with the losing team getting the other quarter of a point. However, the team winning the match receives the entire match masterpoint award. See ZIRINSKY FORMULA.

VIENNA COUP. An unblocking play made in preparation for a squeeze. Declarer plays off a master card which establishes a high card for an opponent. This clears the way for an automatic squeeze. Here is an example:

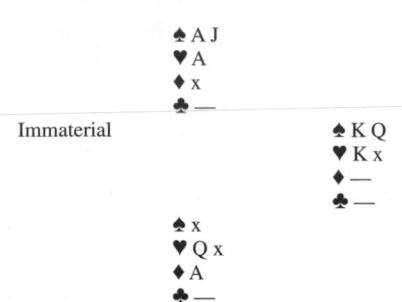

The menaces are correctly positioned for an automatic squeeze against East. Hearts should be a one-card menace, and spades the two-card menace. Therefore the ♥A should be played before the squeeze card, which is the ♦A.

If the ♦A is played prematurely in the diagrammed position East can discard a heart with impunity. Declarer can establish the ♥Q by crossing to the ace, but he cannot return to his hand to cash the queen.

VIENNA SYSTEM. Based on an artificial 1♣ bid for hands of normal strength and an artificial 1NT bid for strong hands. Devised in 1935 by Dr. Paul Stern, this was the first highly conventional system to achieve international success. (See WORLD CHAMPIONSHIPS.) Also known as the Austrian System, it has been played in many countries. In postwar years its main adherents have been in Iceland and Australia.

The Bamberger point count (7-5-3-1) was originally used, but many Vienna players have preferred the standard 4-3-2-1 point-count which is employed in the following system summary.

(1) 1♣ shows 11-17 points and no suit except clubs longer than four cards. 1♦ is the negative, or Herbert, response showing 0-7 points. With a six-card or longer suit, an alternative negative response is available: a negative jump to two of a major or three of a minor suit. Over 1♦ the opener rebids cheaply, as in the ROMAN SYSTEM.

Responses of one in a major or two in a minor are positive but limited, showing 8-11 points. The opener can pass or make a natural rebid: any jump rebid would be encouraging but not forcing.

The strongest response to 1♣ is 1NT, artificial, showing 12 points or more. This almost always leads to game, but the responder can pass if the opener rebids 2NT at any stage.

(2) 1♦, 1♥ and 1♠ shows a five-card suit with 11-17 points. Responses are standard except that 2NT is limit and nonforcing.

(3) 1NT shows 18 points at least, and is unlimited; any distribution is possible. With 0-7 points, the responder gives a negative response of 2♣ or a negative jump to 3♦, 3♥, or 3♠.

With 8 points or more, responder bids a five-card suit; but the jump to three is made only if the suit is very strong. With a broken five-card club suit, the response is sometimes 2NT, which denies a five-card diamond suit and also a total of five cards in the major suits. For other hands containing between five and eight cards in the major suits the response is 2♠, which is therefore a two-way bid.

After a negative response of 2♣, a rebid of 2♦ asks for a major suit. (A forerunner of the DYNAMIC NOTRUMP.)

(4) Two-bids were designed to be specialized asking bids, but most adherents of the system prefer standard methods.

(5) Three-bids in a minor are strong, with a powerful suit and an outside trick.

(6) Other opening bids are standard.

VIEW, TO TAKE A. To make decision in the bidding or play.

VINJE SIGNALS. Signals devised by Helge Vinje which pinpoint many distributions and situations that are ambiguous in standard signaling.

Distribution Signal: The length of a suit is shown by leading (counting lead) or by following suit or by discarding (counting signal) in this manner:

2-card suit:	high-low	
4-card suit:	next lowest - lowest	} even number
6-card suit:	third lowest - lowest	
3-card suit:	lowest - next lowest	
5 -card suit:	lowest - next lowest	} odd number
7-card suit:	lowest- third lowest	

The New Third-Hand Rule: On a counting lead from a long suit against a notrump contract, third hand should play high except in the following case: If dummy and third hand hold only spot cards in the suit, and the sum of leader's, dummy's and third hand's cards totals 11, third hand should play his lowest card.

The New Trump Signal: The new trump signal indicates the distribution type. High-low shows the hand has the distribution pattern of one suit with an even number of cards, three odd. Low-high shows the hand has the distribution pattern of one suit with an odd number of cards, three even.

Positive and Negative Signal: Positive or negative signals to show strength or weakness should be used generally on ace leads in situations where the defenders are obviously compelled to make their quick tricks immediately.

They should be used particularly on ace leads against slam contracts. The lead denies the king and asks primarily for the king in partner's hand. They should also be used on honor leads, in accordance with the rules for signaling on sequence leads against notrump contracts and against trump contracts. A positive signal is given by playing the lowest card in the suit. A negative signal is given by playing the third lowest card in the suit but the next lowest if the third lowest is an active card.

Suit Preference Signal: The suit preference signal should be used in situations where the defender in the lead is *obviously* compelled to switch to a suit other than the one played, and needs guidance from his partner. When partner plays an unusually high card he wants the higher ranking of the possible suits in return. When partner plays a low card he wants the lower ranking of the possible suits in return.

Combined Signaling: The use of a positive or a negative or a suit preference signal should be combined with a delayed distributional signal according to the following rules: The first signaling card indicates a positive or a negative or a suit preference signal, according to the respective rules. The second signaling card in the same suit is a delayed distributional signal indicating the remaining length in that suit.

New Table for Opening Sequence Leads Against Notrump Contracts:

Holding in suit	Lead	Reading
A K x (x-)	Ace	Partial sequence without other honors in the suit.
A K J (x-) K Q 10 (x-)	King	Incomplete sequence lacking the queen or the jack
A K Q (x-) Q J 10 (x-) Q J 9 (x-)	Queen	Two or no higher honors than the queen. Holding A-K-Q the second lead indicates the original suit length: king (13) shows an odd number; ace (14) shows an even number.
A Q J (x-) K Q J (x-) J 10 9 (x-) J 10 8 (x-)	Jack	Two or no higher honors than the jack.Holding K-Q-J the second lead or play indicates the original suit length: queen (12) shows an even number; king (13) shows an odd number.
A Q 10 (9-) A J 10 (x-) K J 10 (x-) 10 9 x	10	Two or no higher honors than the 10.With two higher cards the sequence is an interior one.
A 10 9 (x-) K 10 9 (x-) Q 10 9 (x-) 9 8 x	9	Two or no higher cards than the 9.With two higher cards the sequence is an interior one.

Appropriate signaling: Unblock with an honor second, unless this is likely to result in the loss of a trick. Use a counting signal when dummy holds at least three cards in the suit. Use any complementing card, followed by the next-lowest card, when the lead shows an incomplete sequence and dummy as well as partner holds exactly three cards in the suit. Use a positive or negative signal to show the existence or non-existence of a card touching the actual sequence, followed by a distributional signal on the next round, when dummy holds at most two cards in the suit.

New Table for Opening Sequence Leads Against Trump Contracts

Holding in suit	Lead	Reading
A K (x-)	Ace	When holding an even number ($A = 14$).
	King	When holding an odd number (K= 13). Exception: Against slam contracts the lead from A K (x) should always be the king, partner using counting signal.
K Q J (x-) K Q (alone)	King	Ambiguous: partner should read the lead as a counting lead from A-K with an odd number, unless dummy or partner has the ace. The second lead or play indicates the original suit length: queen (12) shows an even number; jack (11) shows an odd number.
A K Q (x-)	Queen	Ambiguous: partner K Q x (x-) should read the lead as K-Q-x. Holding A-K-Q the

second lead or play indicates the original suit length: king (13) shows an odd number; ace (14) shows an even number.

Holding	Lead	Reading
Q J x (x-)	Jack	Unambiguous.
J 10 x (x-) A J 10 (x-) K J 10 (x-)	10	Generally unambiguous.
10 9 x (x-) A 10 9 (x-) K 10 9 (x-) Q 10 9 (x-)	9	Generally unambiguous.
9 8 x (x-) K 9 8 (x-) Q 9 8 (x-) J 9 8 (x-)	8	Generally unambiguous.

Note: The lead from A-K-Q-(x) may alternatively be the ace or the king according to the rules for a counting lead from A-K-(x-).

Appropriate signaling:

1. On a counting lead from A-K-(x-) partner should: Use a counting signal if dummy has at least three cards, including the queen, in the suit. Use a trick counting signal on all other occasions by signaling as follows:
   - (a) Playing the lowest card (low-high) indicates that the defenders can make either one or three tricks in relation to declarer's closed hand. The three tricks may arise from a ruff or from the queen or from J-10-x.
   - (b) Playing the third lowest card, but the next lowest if the third lowest is an active card, means that the defenders can make two tricks in the suit, either because declarer has only two cards in the suit, or because partner cannot assist in making a third trick.
2. On a sequence lead showing K-Q-(J), with dummy or partner holding the ace, partner should use a counting signal if dummy holds the ace; use a counting signal or overtake when he himself holds the ace.
3. On a sequence lead showing K-Q-x or A-K-Q partner should use a positive or negative signal to show whether or not he holds the ace or jack; use a counting signal if dummy holds at least three cards, including the jack, or if dummy holds A-J.

Indicating a Sequence When Following Suit or When Discarding: A sequence is indicated by playing the lowest card in the sequence when the card has a possibility of influencing the trick; a sequence is indicated by playing the highest card in the sequence when the card will not influence the trick; a sequence is indicated by discarding the highest card in the sequence.

When holding a complete sequence, the sequence as well as the suit length may be indicated.

A K Q (x-)	The queen indicates the complete sequence. The next play may now indicate the length of the suit (original length): The king (13) indicates an odd number; the ace (14) indicates an even number.
K Q J (x-)	The jack indicates the complete sequence. The next play may now indicate the suit length (original length): The queen (12) indicates an even number; the king (13) indicates an odd number.

When holding A-K, the sequence as well as the suit length may be indicated:

A K (x-)   The ace followed by the king indicates an even number in the suit; the king followed by the ace indicates an odd number in the suit.

VIOLATION. (1) The disregard of a law of propriety. It is assumed that any violation that occurs is either through carelessness or ignorance. A penalty for a violation is enforced in an attempt to indemnify the nonoffending side, not to punish the offender. (2) A deliberate breach of a system agreement. Judgment may occasionally lead an expert player to pass a forcing bid or to continue bidding after a signoff bid, but such violations should be very rare if partnership confidence is to be maintained.

VIOLATION OF ETHICAL CONDUCT. An act of a player that deviates from the spirit or the form as described in the PROPRIETIES. Since there are no direct penalties for such violations, it is perhaps even more reprehensible than a deviation for which penalties are prescribed.

VIOLATION OF SYSTEM. A player is at any time entitled to violate his partnership agreement, and most players do so from time to time in minor ways. Major violations, such as passing a forcing bid, are very rare indeed among good players.

VIRGIN ISLANDS BRIDGE FEDERATION. Had a membership of 140 in 1993.
Officers 1993:
President: Alan J. Bronstein
Secretary: Jeffrey L. Resnick
P.O.Box 3485 Christiansted
St. Croix, Virgin Islands 00820.
Tel. (809) 773 0096
Fax (809) 778 8640

VISE SQUEEZE. See VICE SQUEEZE.

VOID. An original holding with no cards in a suit. "Chicane" is a much older term; "blank" is a synonym in current use.

VOID-SHOWING BIDS. The use of a jump bid which has no natural meaning to show a void suit. The idea was revived by E. M. L. Beale, of Cambridge University, England, about 1948, following a prototype idea once adopted briefly by Ely Culbertson.

According to this idea, the last bid in each of the following sequences would show specifically a void in the suit bid and, by inference, a good suit fit with partner.

	WEST	NORTH	EAST	SOUTH
(a)				1 ♥
	Pass	4 ♣		
(b)				1 ♣
	Pass	1 ♥	Pass	3 ♠ or 4 ♦
(c)				1 ♦
	1 ♠	3 ♠		

The following are examples of opportunities for using the bid at later stages in the auction:

Dlr. South
Vul: Both

```
           ♠ 10 6 2
           ♥ Q 8 7 5 4
           ♦ 4
           ♣ K 8 3 2
♠ A K J 9 5 3          ♠ 7
♥ J 2                  ♥ A 6 3
♦ A 10 9 6 5           ♦ K J 8 3 2
♣ —                    ♣ 10 6 5 4
           ♠ Q 8 4
           ♥ K 10 9
           ♦ Q 7
           ♣ A Q J 9 7
```

This deal was reported in *The Bridge World*, August 1951, from the Master Team-of-Four final. Both teams reached 5♦ played by East after this bidding, from the days of strong jump overcalls:

WEST	NORTH	EAST	SOUTH
			1 ♣
2 ♠	Pass	3 ♦	Pass
5 ♦	Pass	Pass	Pass

If East-West had been using void-showing bids, West could have used one over 3♦ by jumping to 5♣ and the grand slam would have been reached after a 5♥ cuebid by East. From West's angle, East's diamonds might be headed by queen-jack, but the finesse for the king would surely succeed.

Void-showing bids will sometimes make it possible to apply the brakes when duplication of values is present:

Dlr: South
Vul: E-W

```
           ♠ K Q 10 7 4
           ♥ 10 6 5 3
           ♦ —
           ♣ K Q J 2
♠ 9 5                  ♠ A 8 3 2
♥ 8 4 2               ♥ 9
♦ 8 5 4 2             ♦ 10 9 7 3
♣ A 9 7 3            ♣ 10 6 5 4
           ♠ J 6
           ♥ A K Q J 7
           ♦ A K Q J 6
           ♣ 8
```

In the 1953 Bermuda Bowl both the American and Swedish teams bid to 6♥ missing two aces. This is a not uncommon disaster when one side holds everything else in the pack except two aces. Ace-showing conventions are of limited value when a void is present, although Blackwood has some void-showing possibilities. (See also SUPRESSING THE BID ACE.)

Using a void-showing bid, the final contract should be 5♥.

SOUTH	NORTH
2 ♣	2 ♠
3 ♥	5 ♦
5 ♥	Pass

When North shows a void diamond, South puts on the brakes and North reluctantly accepts this decision.

The void-showing bid was an ancestor of the SPLINTER. For alternative treatments, see conventions listed under UNUSUAL JUMP.

VOLMAC. See CAP GEMINI WORLD TOP TOURNAMENT.

VOLMAC PRECISION. Strong club system developed

by Benito Garozzo for the training of the Dutch Volmac training group. A computer program of the system was demonstrated during the 1980 Olympiad in Valkenburg. The system continues to be played by the women's pair, Elly Schippers-Marijke van der Pas.

VOLUNTARY BID. See FREE BID.

VON ZEDTWITZ GOLD CUP. For the Life Master Pairs Championship, donated by Waldemar von Zedtwitz in 1930 for one of the most highly regarded pair events in the ACBL calendar. It is contested at the Summer North American Championships, under which heading past results are listed. Until Life Masters became numerous, the trophy was contested by master players who had qualified by winning a previous national championship. It was then a four-session event, and the field was limited to 64 pairs so that a complete movement could be played.

The trophy was originally presented on the basis that three wins by one player would secure him outright possession of the trophy, and this feat was achieved by Howard Schenken in 1934. The cup was subsequently put back into competition by the donor.

The cup was stolen in 1954 while in the possession of John Hubbell, who at that time held the Life Master Pairs title. The theft immediately followed a television appearance during which he had exhibited the trophy and given the address of his bridge club at which the cup was normally displayed. The trophy was not recovered and the present cup is an exact replica. For results see Appendix I.

VUGRAPH. (Often spelled viewgraph outside the United States.) A method of presenting an important match to an audience larger than can be accommodated around a bridge table. Until the computer was brought into the vugraph picture in the Eighties, a board was dealt, bid and played in the closed room, with a recorder at the table noting the bidding, opening lead, and result obtained. The board and record were sent to a copier, who wrote the hands, bidding, and play with wax pencil on a framed cellulose sheet, a form of hand record. The board was then sent to the open room where a microphone connected to the exhibition hall was used by a director in charge to relay the calls, leads, plays, and results to an operator in the exhibition hall. The frame was sent to the exhibition hall, where an operator, with a wax pencil, recorded the bids, plays, and results as announced from the open room on the frame which was put into an over-head projector, remaining visible to the audience in greatly enlarged form on a screen. Bidding was recorded in boxes on the printed frame, cards as played were crossed out from the hands, and results tabulated for further reference on the side of the screen.

Required for Vugraph presentation were a recorder in the closed room, a scribe, a director and commentator in the open room, and an operator at the projector who doubles as or is assisted by a commentator.

A more elaborate setup, used for many years in world championships and other major events was BRIDGE-O-RAMA. In the Eighties various electronic Vugraphs of considerable sophistication were introduced in Italy, Netherlands and elsewhere, with all the entries on the projected image controlled by a computer. These are regularly accompanied by closed circuit television, showing the players at work, and often by a screen showing the progress of the scores, perhaps in several matches.

In 1991, the ACBL commissioned Fred Gitelman, a Toronto programmer, to develop a computer vugraph program with a grant from the estate of Peter Pender. The vugraph was subsequently named the PenderGraph.

The PenderGraph debuted at the Summer NABC in Las Vegas, where the final of the Spingold Knockout Teams was shown to a huge audience. In 1993, Gitelman wrote a new PenderGraph program to work under the Windows operating system, enhancing and enlarging the graphics and adding features that distinguished the PenderGraph as the top program of its kind.

VULNERABILITY. The condition of being subject to greater undertrick penalties, and eligible to receive greater premiums as provided by the scoring table. In rubber bridge, vulnerability comes about by having won one game toward rubber. In duplicate bridge, vulnerability is arbitrarily assigned by board numbers. Vulnerability in duplicate is on a 16-board cycle, repeating for each succeeding 16 boards; boards 1, 8, 11 and 14 have no vulnerability; boards 2, 5, 12, and 16 have North-South vulnerable, East-West not vulnerable; boards 3, 6, 9 and 16 have East-West vulnerable, North-South not vulnerable; boards 4, 7, 10 and 13 have both sides vulnerable. This can be remembered fairly easily by the 16 letters forming this arrangement:

$$O\ N\ E\ B$$
$$N\ E\ B\ O$$
$$E\ B\ O\ N$$
$$B\ O\ N\ E$$

where O stands for no vulnerability, N for North-South, E for East-West and B for both.

In CHICAGO, a four-hand variation of rubber bridge, the vulnerability also is arbitrarily assigned in similar fashion; no vulnerability on the first hand; declarer vulnerable on the second and third hands; and everyone vulnerable on the last hand. A variation in a few clubs that is technically perhaps a slight improvement assigns the vulnerability on the second and third hands to the opponents of the dealer.

The feature of vulnerability gives rise to many variations in the strategy of bidding and play. These variations probably are foremost among the reasons for the great interest which contract bridge has stimulated.

VULNERABLE. A term applied to a side which has won a game and is thus exposed to greater under-trick penalties and entitled to greater premiums for slams and doubled overtricks. The term was suggested to Harold Vanderbilt by a woman passenger on the cruise on which Vanderbilt codified the game of contract bridge.

W

WBF. See WORLD BRIDGE FEDERATION.

WAITING BID. A temporizing bid by a player who aims to extract information from partner rather than give information about his own holding. This is usually made in a minor suit, perhaps in a three-card suit.

A prepared opening bid of 1♣ with a three-card suit is in a sense a waiting bid. For examples of waiting responses, see THREE-CARD SUITS, BIDS IN. The following is an example of a waiting rebid:

♠ A J 5
♥ A K 6
♦ Q 5 2
♣ K Q 7 3

After an opening bid of 1♣ and a jump shift response of 2♦, the best rebid is 2NT. The opener has no intention of stopping short of a small slam, and has thoughts of a grand slam, but his best move is to proceed cautiously, extracting more information from the responder before heading slamwards. For another type of waiting bid, see the 2NT response described under IMPOSSIBLE BIDS.

WAIVE A PENALTY. In rubber bridge, either member of a partnership, without consulting the other member, may waive a penalty (condone an irregularity); if either member so elects, the right to enforce a penalty is forfeited. In duplicate, players do not have the right to waive penalties on their own initiative, and the director may allow or cancel any waiver of penalties made by the players without his instructions. However, the right to penalize an irregularity may be forfeited. See LAWS (Law 15), LAWS OF DUPLICATE (Laws 10, 11).

WALES. See WELSH BRIDGE UNION.

WALLET. British name for a form of DUPLICATE BOARD in which each pocket is formed in the fold of a wallet-shaped receptacle. The board can be folded into one-half size for ease in carrying. Plastic wallet boards are popular in Europe. They date back to the 1932 World Bridge Olympics.

WALPURGIS DIAMOND. A convention used by John Collings and Paul Hackett of Great Britain in the 1981 Bermuda Bowl. As an opening bid, 1♦ shows either 0-8 high card points with any distribution, or 12-20 points with at least four diamonds, or any 4-3-3-3 with 20-22 points. It is used in conjunction with their specialized opening pass, which shows 9-12 points and any distribution.

WALSH SYSTEM. A style of bidding popular in the West, sometimes known as Western Roth-Stone or West Coast Scientific; its chief architect was Richard Walsh. The principal features are strong 1NT openings with nonforcing STAYMAN and JACOBY TRANSFER BIDS, five-card major suit openings with a forcing 1NT response, and usually some form of SWISS major suit raises. Direct limit raises promise a side-suit singleton; jump shift responses are preemptive. Minor suit raises are INVERTED (see INVERTED MINOR SUIT RAISES), and a 1♦ response to 1♣ usually denies a four-card major suit.

Two-over-one responses are game forcing. Over a 2♣ response to 1♦, opener has specialized responses: 2♥ or 2♠ shows a four-card suit and no extra values; 2NT shows 4-4-3-2 distribution and no extra values, and 2♦ usually shows five or more diamonds, but may be forced with 3-3-4-3 distribution and poor clubs.

Other methods include MATHE ASKING BIDS, COMPETITIVE DOUBLES, NEW MINOR FORCING, NAMYATS, NEGATIVE and RESPONSIVE DOUBLES, WANG TRUMP ASKING BIDS.

WANG TRUMP ASKING BIDS. Bids at relatively low levels to ask about trump honors. The responses are given in three steps as follows:

First step = none of the top three honors.
Second step = one of the top three honors.
Third step = two of the top three honors.

WAR ORPHANS SCHOLARSHIPS, INC. An educational foundation incorporated in 1943 in New York State by officers and governors of ACBL; in the eight years of its existence it awarded about $800,000 in scholarship benefits to sons and daughters of members of the U.S. armed services who in World War II suffered service-connected to battle-connected deaths. Tournament winners 1943-46 accepted printed certificates instead of prizes, the cost of trophies going to the scholarship fund, and special tournaments plus individual contributions and income from general solicitations made up the remainder of the fund.

WARNING PARTNER. A privilege of all players (including a dummy who has not intentionally looked at another hand) if the player feels that his partner is about to commit an irregularity. Examples: "It's not your lead, partner." "No hearts, partner?" "The lead is in the dummy, partner." It is not permitted during the auction to warn partner about a convention you or an opponent may be using, or to review the auction to apprise partner of a previous bid you think he may have misunderstood.

Defenders' questions to draw attention to a possible revoke ("having no hearts, partner?") can be controversial, since they can convey information. Such questions were barred by the 1987 Duplicate Code, but zonal bodies were later given authority to permit such questions. They are permitted in Zone 2 (North America) and Zone 7 (South Pacific) but not elsewhere. When questions are barred, an illegal question creates an automatic revoke penalty if partner has a card of the suit. See Law 61B and ALERTING.

WARREN. See SAN FRANCISCO.

WASHING LIST. See BACK SCORE.

WEAK JUMP OVERCALL. The use of a jump overcall in a suit as preemptive. A FOUR ACES innovation of the Thirties, credited to OSWALD JACOBY and embodied in ROTH-STONE and later systems.

Over a 1♦ opening, 2♥, 2♠ or 3♣ would show the equivalent of a WEAK TWO-BID — 6-12 points and a six-card or perhaps a seven-card suit. For many years, strong jump overcalls were a basic part of the Goren bidding system, which was the system used by the vast majority of players. However, the double values of the weak jump overcall — telling the whole story about a hand in one bid while throwing up a blockade against the opponents' bidding — caused Goren to incorporate the weak jump overcall into his standard bidding system.

The weak jump overcall must always take the vulnerability situation into account. Not vulnerable against vulnerable, a weak jump to the level of two could be made on a good five-card suit and little else. A vulnerable jump to the three-level against nonvulnerable would almost always be too dangerous with a weak hand. For this reason, Sam Stayman advised a strong jump overcall at unfavorable vulnerability.

The opening bidder's partner often faces a bidding problem after a weak jump overcall. If he makes his normal bid, but one level higher, he may easily be giving a wrong impression of the strength of his hand. If he passes, this could mean that the overcaller has achieved his objective — to buy the contract cheaply. Many players use the NEGATIVE DOUBLE against weak jump overcalls. The usual agreement is that the negative double shows a hand that would have responded with a natural bid at a lower level, but is not strong enough to make that natural bid at this higher level. The negative double can also show other types of holding. The next call by the negative doubler should make clear the type of hand he holds. Another possible solution is for minimum bids in a new suit to be nonforcing (NEGATIVE FREE BID). However, if this method is used, it becomes necessary to consider the use of a pass as a forcing call, in addition to a cuebid and a jump shift.

The partner of a weak jump overcaller may have sufficient values to be interested in game. A good agreement is to respond as to a weak two-bid. Thus those who use 2NT to ask for OGUST rebids can do so similarly after a weak jump overcall.

The weak jump overcall would not apply in the pass-out position, for there would be no object in preempting. In that situation a jump would be made with slightly less than the values needed for a strong jump. But if the opponents bid two suits, the jump retains its preemptive character. See also DOUBLE JUMP OVERCALL.

WEAK JUMP SHIFT RESPONSES. The use of a jump response in a new suit as a preemptive bid. After an opening 1♣, a response of 2♠ would be made by a player whose only asset was K-J-6-5-4-2. This works for the subminimum responding hands with a six-card or seven-card suit, but greatly increases the problem of bidding strong hands which would normally make a jump shift. The simple suit response becomes overloaded because it may be made with a hand of any strength from 6 points upwards.

Nevertheless, the weak jump shift response has merit in that it enables a player to describe his hand in just one bid while stealing a level of bidding from the opponents. The bid also makes it much easier for the opening bidder to assess his hand. He knows, as a result of a single bid, that his partner has a hand that probably will play best in his suit, and the opener also knows there is little hope for game unless he holds close to an opening force.

Like all preemptive bids, the weak jump shift response exerts pressure on an opponent with a good hand. The fourth player should bid as he would over an opening one-bid: double for a takeout, and bid 2NT on a hand which would open a strong 1NT, but with some flexibility, perhaps 15-19. See ROTH-STONE SYSTEM and OGUST REBIDS.

WEAK NOTRUMP. An opening 1NT with a minimum hand is an integral part of many systems. The usual range of the bid is 12-14 points, although 13-15 and 12-15 are in use, particularly in PRECISION. The usual corollary is that a rebid of 1NT shows a hand too strong to open with 1NT (15-17 in KAPLAN-SHEINWOLD, 15-16 in English systems).

Many modern tournament players have lowered the range to 10-12 points, in keeping with the philosophy that the side to strike first has the advantage in competitive auctions. Most players use the 10-12 1NT opener in the first three seats when not vulnerable, but some employ it at all vulnerabilities and in all positions with the rationale that the preemptive value of the bid is worth the risk of an occasional large penalty. Some experts recommend that a 10-12 notrump opener be a hand most other players would not open. This helps responder decide what to do with invitational values.

The 10-12 notrump works best in conjunction with a strong club system, but can be used by partnerships playing standard. Standard bidders employing the 10-12 notrump usually use semi-artificial minor-suit openings to distinguish between balanced hands of 13-14 points (1♣ followed by a notrump rebid) and 15-17 points (1♦ followed by notrump).

Each of these systems has some special features in response, but with a suitable adjustment of range any normal principles of responding to a strong notrump can be followed.

Some special tactical situations arise when 1NT by the dealer has been passed and the responder is very weak. The fourth player is almost certain to have a strong hand, and there is a danger of conceding a heavy penalty, so third hand may have to take evasive action:

♠ 6 2
♥ 9 7 4 3
♦ J 10 7 3
♣ 9 5 3

What the action should be depends on the methods in use. In a traditional style, natural weak 2♦ or 2♥ bids, purporting to show a 5-card suit are possible, since it will be difficult for the opposition to double for penalties. In a modern style, the least evil may be a 2♦ transfer to hearts with the probability of finding at least a 7-card fit. Stayman is not recommended, since a 2♠ rebid will leave the partnership in serious jeopardy, but would be a sensible choice if the black suits were reversed.

Some partnerships agree that a very weak hand must bid in response to 1NT, in which case a pass should be Alerted as denying a very weak hand.

Competitive bidding is much more common and much more critical when the weak notrump is being used. The opponents frequently need some conventional defensive arrangement such as ASTRO, BROZEL, CAPPELLETTI, EXCLUSION BIDS, HAMILTON, LANDY, or RIPSTRA. A double of a weak notrump should be for penalties, and partner should rarely remove the double: only a weak hand with a long suit would justify a takeout. The doubler should have a better hand than the notrump bidder, whether the double is made immediately or in the pass-out position. See also SWINE.

The action by fourth hand after a two-level response needs consideration. A double of a STAYMAN 2♣ response is usually taken to be an indication of a good club suit for lead-directing purposes. The modern tendency among some experts is to double 2♣ or any suit takeout at the level of two with a hand which would have doubled if responder had passed 1NT.

For other details about notrump bidding, see DEFENSE TO DOUBLE OF ONE NOTRUMP; MINI-NOTRUMP; ONE NOTRUMP OPENING; STAYMAN; TEXAS.

WEAK NOTRUMP OVERCALL. The use of an overcall of 1NT is the equivalent of a weak notrump opening. This permits a defender to enter the auction on many hands which he would normally pass, but the value is doubtful because the overcaller will often be doubled for penalties with no escape. The bid is sometimes confined to nonvulnerable situations. For matchpoint play, a 13-16 range has achieved some popularity.

The opener's partner follows the procedure for bidding over a normal strong notrump overcall. He usually doubles with 9 points or more, because his side is almost sure to have the balance of strength. With a weaker hand he can bid a five-card or longer suit at the two-level, which is unconstructive. And he can make a cuebid of 2NT with a strong unbalanced hand. See also BARON NOTRUMP OVERCALL.

WEAK OPENING SYSTEMS. The original work on Weak Opening Systems (WOS; also known as Forcing Pass) was done in Poland, primarily by Lukasz Slawinski. It took the theory behind a strong-club system one step further. The major difference is that if you pass with a good hand, you must open even with a yarborough. This weak bid, also called a FERT because of its affinity to fertilizer, normally shows 0-7 points. With 8-12 points, the most common point-range, you open with a different set of agreed-upon bids. And with 13 or more points, you pass.

These systems are known as *dominant* because they force the opponents into a defensive position on most deals. The opponents use their own bidding system only when they deal *and* the dealer opens. At all other times, the WOS pair dictates the form of the auction.

There are many weak opening systems. We will look at three from Poland, with the initial actions listed.

Regres
Pass: 13-plus points
1♣: 8-12 points and a catch-all opening for any hand that doesn't fit anywhere else
1♦: 0-7 points
1♥/♠: 8-12 with three or four cards in the bid suit; perhaps a five-card minor on the side
1NT: 8-12 with at least five cards in one of the majors
2♣/♦: 8-12 with at least five cards in the bid suit; no major
2♥/♠/NT/3♣: 8-12 with a 5-5 or 6-4 shape

No Name
Pass: 13-plus points
1♣: 8-12 points with at least 3-3 in the majors (at most 5-4 but not 5-3)
1♦: 0-7 points
1♥/♠: 8-12 with at most two cards or at least six cards in the bid suit
1NT: 8-12 with five hearts and four clubs or five spades and four diamonds
2♣: 8-12 with five hearts and four diamonds or five spades and four clubs
2♦: 8-12 with 5-3-3-2 shape and either five-card major
2♥/♠/NT/3♣: 8-12 with a 5-5 or 6-4 shape

Delta
In this unusual system, the opener shows his shortage before his long suit. This helps the responder to decide immediately how well the hands are fitting.
Pass: 13-plus points
1♣: 8-12 points and any hand with no singleton or void
1♦: 0-7 points
1♥: 8-12 and any hand with a singleton or void in hearts, or a singleton or void in clubs and either a long major or a 5-5 shape
1♠: 8-12 and any hand with a spade shortage
1NT: 8-12 with diamond shortage and either a long major or a 5-5 shape

2♣: 8-12 and all other hands with a diamond shortage
2♦: 8-12 with a club shortage and long diamonds
2♥: 8-12 and all other hands with a club shortage

It is possible to modify this system to avoid the forcing pass. Then, pass shows 0-11 points, 1♦ is any 17-plus pointer and the other bids are as above but with 12-16 points.

In all these systems, if the responder has a good hand, he continues the auction with a relay, the opener describing the complete shape of his hand. Then the responder has two choices: continue the relay with asking bids or employ the End Signal. The End Signal is a bid of 4♦. It asks the opener to puppet with 4♥, whereupon the responder names the final contract.

In Australia and New Zealand some modifications were introduced. The "bid of misery" varied with the vulnerability, going as high as 1♠ when non-vulnerable against vulnerable. And the systems all employed the SYMMETRIC RELAY rather than the Polish structures.

One of the earliest possibilities included using one-under opening bids: 1♦ was equivalent to a normal one-heart opening and 1♥ was equivalent to 1♠.

Whenever a relay system is employed, the ideal is that the known hand, the one that has been described, becomes the dummy, keeping the unknown hand hidden. This scheme tries to increase the chance that this will happen.

In the original form of MOSCITO, a 1♦ opening showed at least 4-4 in the majors. A opening of one of a major showed at least four cards in that suit, fewer than four cards in the other major, and maybe a longer minor. A 1NT opening showed a balanced hand without a four-card major (so Stayman asked for three-card majors!)

The above only scratches the surface of the subject. However, as these systems are dominant, they have been unpopular with officialdom. Nowadays, these systems are permitted in so few events that many pairs, unable to practice to their satisfaction, have abandoned them. See STRONG PASS.

WEAK SUIT. A suit which the opponents are likely to lead, and in which they can probably cash several tricks. Sometimes the term refers to an unstopped suit, but if a notrump contract is being considered it could also apply to a suit in which the opponents hold nine or more cards and in which only one stopper is held.

The weakness of a suit is relative to the auction. A small doubleton used to be regarded as a weak suit for the purposes of a 1NT opening, although there are two schools of thought, and few modern players would allow themselves to be deterred. For the purposes of a notrump rebid, a small doubleton in an unbid suit is unthinkable, and a small tripleton is highly unattractive. The chance that the opponents will lead the suit is increased, and the chance that partner can guard it is decreased.

If a side has bid three suits, a notrump bid requires at least one positive stopper and preferably two in the fourth suit.

Sometimes anything less than a double stopper would certainly represent a weak suit:

WEST	NORTH	EAST	SOUTH
			1♦
Dbl	Pass	3NT	

As West is likely to have a diamond shortage, the jump to 3NT shows a double diamond stopper. Anything less would constitute a weak suit, unless perhaps East held a single stopper with a long strong club suit.

WEAK SUIT GAME TRY.

WEAK SUIT GAME TRY. A rebid by opener in his weakest suit to try for game after responder has raised the major suit opening bid to two. Sometimes called a "help suit game try." For example if opener holds:

♠ A K x x x   ♥ x x x   ♦ x   ♣ A Q J x

the bidding goes

OPENER	RESPONDER
1 ♠	2 ♠
3 ♥	

Opener's 3♥ bid asks responder to bid game in spades if he has either strength or shortness in hearts. Responder might hold any of the following hands:

(a)	(b)	(c)
♠ Q x x	♠ Q x x	♠ Q x x
♥ J x x x	♥ A x x x x	♥ x
♦ A x x x x	♦ J x x x	♦ A J x x x
♣ x	♣ x	♣ x x x x

With hand (a) responder would sign off in 3♠ since he has no help for opener's anemic hearts. With hand (b) or hand (c), however, responder would bid game in spades since his strength in (b) and his singleton in (c) can take care of the heart situation.

A disadvantage of weak suit game tries is that they usually reveal to the opponents the vulnerable spot of opener's hand, and therefore the defenders' most advantageous point of attack. See SHORT-SUIT GAME TRIES and TWO-WAY GAME TRIES.

WEAK TAKEOUT. An English term for a natural unconstructive suit response to 1NT. The American colloquialism is "drop-dead bid". See WEAKNESS RESPONSE.

WEAK TWO-BIDS. The use of suit openings of 2♦, 2♥ and 2♠ as preemptive bids, in combination with TWO CLUBS STRONG ARTIFICIAL OPENING. A prototype of the weak two was used in auction bridge and adopted in the VANDERBILT CLUB SYSTEM. Subsequently Charles Van Vleck, New York, was responsible for an ultra-weak two-bid. Howard Schenken developed the modern weak two-bid along lines similar to Vanderbilt's. It was later incorporated into most modern American systems, and into the NEAPOLITAN and BLUE TEAM CLUB systems.

In modern tournament play the announced range for a weak two-bid is usually 5-10, 5-11, 6-10 or 6-11. Vulnerability and position at the table may be a factor in deciding whether to make a weak two-bid.

Responses. There are many schools of thought. The responses and rebids need precise partnership agreement.

(1) *Raise to four.* A two-way bid: perhaps a hand which expects to make game, or perhaps a preemptive action of the ADVANCE SAVE variety. The left-hand opponent may have a difficult decision with a strong hand.

(2) *Raise to three.* Originally a constructive invitation to opener to bid game, but modern players use the raise preemptively. In the latter case the responder's trick-taking expectation for the combined hands may vary from nine tricks to as few as six tricks at favorable vulnerability.

(3) *Suit takeout.* Normally natural and forcing. Psychic responses are sometimes used, especially at the level of two. An alternative treatment which has increased in popularity is to play suit takeouts as nonforcing and unconstructive, indicating that the responder has a misfit and expects a better result playing in his long strong suit. Responder must bid 2NT whenever he wishes to make a forcing bid when using this method.

(4) *2NT.* A one-round force with at least game interest. A rebid by opener in his own suit can be used to show a minimum; some players prefer to show a minimum by a 3♣ rebid. Using either agreement, a rebid in another suit shows a high-card feature (usually an ace or king, but a queen is possible) and better than a minimum hand. If responder then gives a mere preference to opener's original suit on the second round, the defenders should find out whether the opener is encouraged or permitted to continue: if not, a psychic should be suspected. Similarly, it is important for both the opener's side and the defenders to know whether the opener is permitted to rebid above the level of three in his original suit. A raise of 2NT to 3NT, if permitted, should show a solid suit.

(5) *Ogust.* A system of rebidding after a 2 NT response devised by Harold Ogust that requires opener to describe the strength of his hand and the quality of his suit by a series of artificial bids. They are as follows:

   3♣ minimum strength, poor suit
   3♦ minimum strength, good suit
   3♥ maximum strength, poor suit
   3♠ maximum strength, good suit.

A good suit is usually defined as one with two of the three top honors. (A solid suit would call for a 3NT rebid). In the original version devised by Ogust the meanings of the red-suit responses were reversed.

(6) *McCabe Adjunct.* Described by J.I. McCabe, Columbia SC, in *The Bridge World*, January 1955. This is a method of playing at the three-level in a new suit. After the 2NT response, the opener is required to rebid 3♣, irrespective of his holding. The responder can now play in his long suit at the three-level, either by bidding it or by passing 3♣. A preference to three of opener's suit is invitational.

(7) *Relays.* The cheapest response — either 2NT if the opening bid was 2♠, or the next higher suit. The relay asks opener to bid a stopper outside his suit if he has one. If his stopper is in the relay suit, he rebids in notrump. Lacking any outside stopper, opener rebids his own suit. Using this method, the relay is responder's only forcing bid.

(8) *Two Relays and a Transfer.* A single raise is constructive. 2NT is natural and not forcing. Almost all other responses are artificial and forcing for at least one round. The bid of the cheapest suit is a relay, forcing to game and asking opener to bid his lowest ranking feature (ace, king, singleton or void). Without a feature, opener rebids his suit. The bid of the second higher ranking suit, i.e., 2♠ over 2♦ or 3♣ over 2♠, is forcing and game invitational. This relay asks partner to show his point count. With a minimum (6-9), opener rebids his suit. With a maximum (10-12), opener makes the cheapest suit rebid. Since the direct raise is constructive, a transfer bid is used to make a preemptive raise. The bid of the suit just below the suit of the weak two-bid forces opener to rebid his suit.

For a more sophisticated responding method involving relays, see RELAYS OVER WEAK TWO-BIDS.

Defense. Standard procedure is to bid as over a one-bid: double for takeout, and bid 2NT on a hand which would qualify, loosely, for a strong notrump opening bid. But many other defensive arrangements are possible.

Nearly all American experts use a 2NT response to a double as Lebensohl, forcing 3♣. See LEBENSOHL APPLICATIONS

To combat players addicted to psychic suit responses to a weak two-bid, some players use a double of the response for penalty. But if the suit response is natural and nonforcing, the double should be a normal takeout action.

WEAKNESS-CONCEALING PLAYS. See DECEPTIVE PLAY.

WEAKNESS RESPONSE. A natural response which indicates a strong desire to close the auction at that point.

The most common case is the response of 2♠, 2♥, or perhaps 2♦ to an opening 1NT bid. Using traditional methods, with the STAYMAN 2♣ convention, responder shows at least a five-card suit and no desire to progress toward game.

In very rare circumstances the opener may make one further bid if he has a fine fit with responder, presumably four cards, and a maximum notrump opening consisting largely of top honors, usually including two of the three top honors in responder's suit. If opener raises to the three level and the contract fails, it may prove that the raise has forestalled a successful balancing action by the opponents.

If the opener bids a new suit 1NT-2♥-3♣ he implies a maximum with a fine fit for responder's suit. The clubs may be, by agreement, either a doubleton or concentrated strength.

Another example of a weakness response:

WEST	NORTH	EAST	SOUTH
			1♣
1NT	2♥		

North's failure to double 1NT marks him with a weak hand (less than 8 or 9 points) and heart length. South will rarely be strong enough to attempt a game, and should rarely rescue.

Weakness responses, which are natural, are sometimes confused with negative responses, which are conventional. Examples of these would be a negative 2♦ response to a conventional 2♣ bid, or a HERBERT NEGATIVE .

WEB MOVEMENT. The Web Movement was devised by National Tournament Director John "Spider" Harris in 1977 and is described by him as follows:

It is not uncommon to have, at least in small tournaments, sessions of from 16 to 22 tables in which a movement of reasonable technical adequacy is required, such as in a Master Pairs or an Open Pairs Final. In the past the standard procedure has been to use twinned 3/4 movements and combined match-pointing.

These movements are universally disliked by players and are not too popular with directors. They do have the purported advantage provided by rotating comparisons, but this is the subject of some disagreement. In all other respects the web movements are, in my opinion, superior.

In effect, these movements consist of two subsections in which the boards circulate independently, while the moving pairs progress to the other subsection after playing at the highest numbered table in one. In all cases, the traveling pairs move each round to the next higher numbered table, boards move next lower within each subsection. The 18-table game will be described in detail; the others will be understood by simply glancing at the Master Sheet and remembering what happened in the 18-table progression. (Master Sheets are available on request from ACBL Tournament Division.)

Basic Distribution of Boards. Tables 1-9 play one set ("A"), tables 10-18 another ("B"). Stationary pairs at 1-9 play the boards in ascending sequence, those at 10-18 in descending. Boards 1-2 start at Table 1, 3-4 at 2, etc. up to 17-18 at 9. The board order is inverted and displaced in the other sub-section: 25-26 start at Table 18, 1-2 at 17, 3-4 at 16, etc. to 15-16 at 10. Note that on round one, Boards 1-16 may be duplicated in the two sub-sections, 17-18 and 25-26 may either be duplicated at tables 9 and 18 respectively, or pre-duplicated (preferred). Boards 19-24 must be duplicated by the staff.

Movement of Boards and Players. Traveling pairs always move to the next higher numbered table. There is no skip. "A" boards move down until they reach Table 1 at which point they go to a bye-stand to re-enter at Table 9. "B" boards move down until they reach Table 10 at which point they go to the other bye-stand to re-enter at Table 18.

Seeded Tables. Assuming that Table 1 is to be seeded, the only suitable tables are:
Sixteen tables - 1, 5, 9, 13. Eighteen tables - 1, 7, 13. Twenty tables - 1, 9. Twenty-two tables - 1, 12.

Seating Assignments. In Open Pairs finals, two qualifying sections, the A qualifiers are simply made N-S, the B's E-W. For three qualifying sections, a schedule accompanies each Master Sheet for assigning pair numbers. It is assumed that the use of these progressions will never occur where there are more than three qualifying sections.

WEI AWARD. Endowed originally by C.C.Wei and after his death by Kathie Wei-Sender. The award was originally for the best article or series of articles, and is now for the best defensive play of the year. For a list of winners see INTERNATIONAL BRIDGE PRESS ASSOCIATION AWARDS.

WEISS CONVENTION. See DEFENSE TO OPENING THREE BIDS.

WEISSBERGER. A conventional extension of the STAYMAN convention to ask for three-card major suits, suggested by John Pressburger and developed by Alan Truscott and Maurice Weissberger. It is intended for use with English-style Stayman in which a secondary jump to 3♠ or 3♥ is invitational and not forcing. This is an optional feature of the ACOL system. Suppose the bidding proceeds:

OPENER	RESPONDER
1NT	2♣
2♦	3♦

The bid of 3♦ has little or no natural meaning in Acol. The Weissberger idea is to use it to inquire for three-card major suits. This helps the responder to solve three types of bidding problems:

(1) A game-going hand with five spades and four hearts.
(2) A game-going hand with five spades and five hearts.
(3) A hand with five spades and five hearts on which game is doubtful. As the responder is certain to have five spades, holding three spades the opener bids 3♠ with a minimum hand; 4♠ holding a maximum.

With only a doubleton spade, the opener bids 3♥ holding a minimum hand and 3NT holding a maximum. In all cases the responder has no problem in selecting the best final contract.

Notice that there are two other cases in which the convention is not needed:

(4) A game-going hand with four spades and five hearts. In this case the responder bids 3♥ immediately over 1NT, relying on the opener to show a four-card spade suit if he can.

(5) A hand with four in one major and five in the other on which game is doubtful. In this case the responder bids three of the five-card major suit over the opener's 2♦ rebid. This sequence is strictly non-forcing in Acol.

WELSH BRIDGE UNION. The Union was founded about 1934, combining three areas, North, West and East, and is affiliated with the British Bridge League. It conducts five national events and a masterpoint program. In 1993 the Union had 1500 members and 50 affiliated clubs. Officers 1993:

President: Diana Harris
Secretary: Mary Aherne
19 Pen-y-graig, Rhiwbina
Cardiff CF4 6ST
Wales U.K.
Tel: 44 222 611 652.

WEST. The player who sits at the left of South at a table of bridge. South is to his right and North to his left. He is the partner of East.

WEST COAST SCIENTIFIC. See WESTERN SCIENTIFIC.

WESTERN SCIENTIFIC. Also called WEST COAST SCIENTIFIC, or WESTERN ROTH-STONE, or WALSH. Originally devised by Richard Walsh in the 1960s and described in books by Max Hardy. Many of the elements are identical with those listed under Eastern Scientific. Distinctive features are:
(1) 1♦ response to 1♣ denies a 4-card major unless responder is strong.
(2) Limit raise promises a singleton.
(3) Swiss raises instead of splinters.
(4) After 1♦ - 2♣: (i) 2♦ may be 3-3-4-3 with poor clubs; (ii) 2♥ and 2♠ show minimum hands with a 4-card suit, denying the other major; (iii) 2NT shows 4-4-3-2 with minimum values.
(5) Mathe asking bids.

WALSH SYSTEM. See WESTERN SCIENTIFIC.

WESTERN CONFERENCE. Originally PACIFIC BRIDGE LEAGUE, founded by Tom Stoddard, it became known as the Western Division in 1948, and the Western Conference in 1956 when it merged with ACBL. Current member districts are 17, 20, 21 and 22. *Functions of Western Conference.* (1) Publishes *The Contract Bridge Forum*, a newspaper distributed to Western Conference members nine times a year. The *Forum* offers the members an opportunity to keep informed of activities throughout the Conference and provides the districts a means by which to communicate with their membership about unit and district affairs; (2) Assists member units in promotion of Novice and Junior games at regionals; (3) Schedules regionals, handled by the conference coor-

dinator.

The last president of the Western Division, the late Winslow Randall, was the first president of the Western Conference. Other presidents:

1956	Lewis Mathe	1976	David Tuell
1957	Robin MacNab	1977	George Clemens
1958	Hugh Edwards	1978	George Clemens
1959	C.F. Crossley	1979	Herbert Smith
1960	Roy Hislop	1980	Herbert Smith
1961	Tom Bussey	1981	Chris Wilson
1962	Lewis Mathe	1982	Chris Wilson
1963	Kelsey Petterson	1983	Robert Wingeard
1964	Lewis Mathe	1984	Robert Wingeard
1965	Max Manchester	1985	Syd Levey
1965	Donald Oakie	1986	Syd Levey
1966	Robin MacNab	1987	Roger Smith
1967	Eilif Andersen	1988	Roger Smith
1969	Paul Rhodes	1989	Chris Wilson
1970	Percy Bean	1990	Chris Wilson
1971	Maurice Hole	1991	Frank Sweeney
1972	Maurice Hole	1992	Mike Jones
1973	Alfred Gilpin	1993	Mike Jones
1974	Alfred Gilpin		and Frank Sweeney
1975	David Tuell		

WESTERN CUEBIDS. Generally, a cuebid of a suit bid by an opponent to ask about stoppers for notrump play, rather than promising such stoppers. SEE CUEBIDS IN OPPONENT'S SUIT; DIRECTIONAL ASKING BID .

WESTERN ROTH-STONE. See WESTERN SCIENTIFIC.

WETZLAR TROPHY. Awarded for distinguished services to bridge, this trophy was presented in memory of Edwin A. Wetzlar in 1935. The first winners were:

1935	H. Huber Boscowitz	1938	Alfred Gruenther
1936	Waldemar von Zedtwitz	1939	Nate Spingold
1937	Gordon Gibbs	1940	Harold S. Vanderbilt

After 1940 the Wetzlar was presented to ACBL HONORARY MEMBERS, under which heading the recipients are listed.

WHEEL. See CHUKKER.

WHISK. An alternative name for whist. It was an English lower-class term, according to Dr. Samuel Johnson, used until about the end of the eighteenth century.

WHIST. A game of cards of English origin gradually evolved from several older games such as triumph, trump, ruff and honors, swabbers, and whisk. Whist is played by four persons, two partners against two partners. A regular pack of 52 cards is dealt, 13 to each player. The last card dealt is turned face up on the table. Its suit becomes the trump suit. This card remains on the table until it is the dealer's turn to play to the first trick, when he may return it to his hand. The player at the left of the dealer makes the first lead, and the play proceeds as in bridge except that all four hands are concealed; there is no dummy. Six tricks taken make the BOOK. Each trick won over the book scores one point for the partners winning that trick. The range of possible scores for either set of partners is from one to seven. Any number of deals may be played. Scoring is by games. The English code of laws provides for rubber bonuses and honor bonuses. At the conclusion of play the side having the greatest number of points is the winner. The game of whist has, in general, been superseded in the United States by changing versions of the basic game — by BRIDGE, AUCTION BRIDGE and CONTRACT BRIDGE. It is still played in Great Britain and the U.S. See also AMERICAN WHIST LEAGUE; BIBLIOGRAPHY; CONTRACT WHIST.

WHIST CLUB. A club of men interested in whist and later in all successive forms of bridge, founded in New York 1893, merged with the REGENCY CLUB of New York 1964. Because nearly all of its members were men of great wealth and prominence (including bridge prominence, such as Harold S. Vanderbilt, J. B. Elwell, Milton Work, Ely Culbertson), unquestioned authority in the making of bridge laws for the U.S. was accorded to the Whist Club for more than 40 years. Two earlier codes of contract bridge laws were voluntarily withdrawn when in 1927 the Whist Club produced a code for contract bridge (formulated by a committee composed of Vanderbilt, H. C. Richard, Charles Cadley, Raymond Little and William Talcott).

Later the Whist Club's committees collaborated with the Portland Club of London and French Bridge Federation in producing the first and second international codes (1932, 1935), and Whist Club representatives served continuously on the NATIONAL LAWS COMMISSION for the laws of 1943, 1948, 1949, and 1963.

WHITEHEAD TROPHY. For the North American Championship Women's Pairs, donated by Wilbur Whitehead in 1930; contested at the Summer NABC until 1962 and subsequently at the Spring NABC, under which heading results are listed.

WHITE. Colloquialism for non-vulnerable. "With both white, I dealt .."

WHITFELD SIX. The father of all end-game problems, devised and published on January 31, 1885, by W. H. Whitfeld, mathematical tutor at Cambridge, England, who was Cavendish's successor as card editor of the *London Field*. (Sometimes known as the "Whitfield Six" through a common mispronunciation of the inventor's name.) Hearts are trumps. South must lead and make all the tricks.

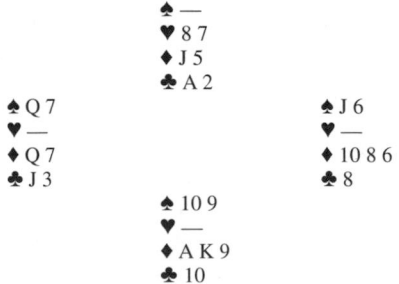

Solution. South cashes the ♦A, unblocking the jack from dummy. to prepare for a possible finesse. A spade is ruffed and the last trump from dummy is cashed, on which South discards the ♣10. The only temporary defense is for East to keep diamonds and the high spade, and for West to keep clubs and the ♦Q. The ♣A from dummy then squeezes East. The Whitfeld Six is a type of double guard squeeze.

WIDE OPEN. A phrase describing a suit in which declarer has no stopper or is extremely vulnerable to attack. For example, "Declarer was wide open in trumps."

WINKLE SQUEEZE. A secondary squeeze that forces the opponents to choose between a throw-in and an unblock, each of which costs a trick. (Analyzed and named by Terence Reese.) Declarer has enough winners for all but one of the remaining tricks, but he cannot take all his tricks because of entry problems.

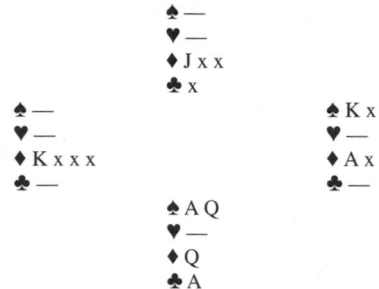

South leads the ♣A, and East is squeezed in two suits. A diamond must be discarded in order to protect the ♠K. If East discards a low diamond he will be thrown in to lead from his ♠K; if he discards the ♦A, South takes the ♣A, and then leads a diamond, eventually winning a trick with the jack.

The French names for a winkle is "crochet". The most famous example occurred in the 1963 International Team Trials in Miami Beach FL.

Vul: None

            ♠ Q 8
            ♥ 10 6 3
            ♦ A Q J 9 6
            ♣ A Q 4

♠ 5 4 3   ♠ J 10 7 2
♥ A 8 5   ♥ K Q 7 4
♦ K 5 3 2   ♦ 10 8 7
♣ 10 5 2   ♣ 7 6

            ♠ A K 9 6
            ♥ J 9 2
            ♦ 4
            ♣ K J 9 8 3

SOUTH	WEST	NORTH	EAST
(Becker)	(Stayman)	(Hayden)	(Mitchell)
1 ♣	Pass	1 ♦	Pass
1 ♠	Pass	3 ♣	Pass
4 ♣	Pass	4 ♠	Pass
6 ♣	Pass	Pass	Pass

3NT was the only good game, but was hard to reach with no heart stopper. A slight misunderstanding led to 6♣: South had forgotten a partnership agreement that 4♣ would always be Gerber after a minor-suit opening. South assumed that 4♠ indicated a singleton heart, and bid the slam.

West was also misled and chose a diamond lead. South, apparently calm, finessed the ♦J successfully. He threw a heart on the ♦A and ruffed a diamond. He crossed to the ♣A, ruffed another diamond to remove the king, and cashed the ♣K-Q.

The lead was in dummy in this position:

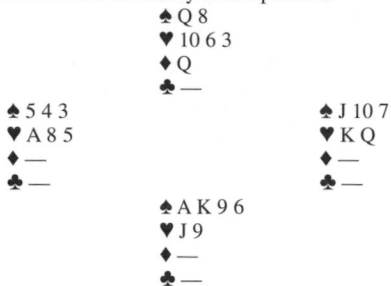

```
                    ♠ Q 8
                    ♥ 10 6 3
                    ♦ Q
                    ♣ —
    ♠ 5 4 3                        ♠ J 10 7 2
    ♥ A 8 5                        ♥ K Q
    ♦ —                            ♦ —
    ♣ —                            ♣ —
                    ♠ A K 9 6
                    ♥ J 9
                    ♦ —
                    ♣ —
```

On the ♦Q East perforce threw the ♥Q. South threw the ♥9, and West a spade. The ♠Q was cashed, and when the eight was played East covered with the ten. Now the ♥J was led and the defense was helpless. West chose to win and endplay himself, giving dummy two heart tricks. If he had played low, East would have been endplayed to give South two spade tricks. Interchange the ♥6 and ♥5 and the slam cannot be made, even with the favorable opening lead. See also ENTRY SQUEEZE and STEPPINGSTONE SQUEEZE.

WINNER. (1) A card that may reasonably be expected to win a trick in dummy or declarer's hand. On defense, a card that will win a trick during the play of a given hand may be termed a winner as well. (2) The player, the pair or team with the highest score in an event at a duplicate tournament.

WINNING CARD. The card that takes the trick. In a notrump declaration this is always the highest card played in the suit that has been led; it may be a LONG CARD, led in a suit to which the other players cannot follow. In suit declarations, the above will apply, except that on a trick where more than one trump is played it is the highest trump that will win the trick.

WINSLOW SYSTEM. See WINSLOW, Thomas Newby.

WITHDRAW CARD. It is not permitted to withdraw a card previously played except to correct a revoke, or a card played by an opponent after such a card was withdrawn. Declarer may insist that a card he had called to be played from dummy be substituted for a card actually put into the playing position by the dummy. In this case, too, the opponent may without penalty withdraw his card and substitute a different proper card. See, however, ALCATRAZ COUP for a possible situation that calls for a redress under the general powers of the director.

WOLFF SIGN-OFF. Devised by Bobby Wolff to allow responder to sign off at the three-level after opener has made a jump rebid of 2NT. Responder's rebid of 3♣ asks opener to bid three of responder's suit if he has three-card support, and otherwise to bid 3♦. Responder can then sign off by passing, by bidding 4♣, or by introducing a new suit of lower rank than his first suit; a rebid of 3NT by responder would be a mild slam try in clubs.

WOMEN'S INTERNATIONAL TEAM TRIALS. See INTERNATIONAL WOMEN'S TEAM SELECTION. For results see Appendix III.

WOMEN'S KNOCKOUT TEAMS, NORTH AMERICAN CHAMPIONSHIP, for the Coffin Trophy. Initiated in 1976 the event was played in the Spring NABC 1976-85 after which it was transferred to the Summer NABC. For results see Appendix I.

WOMEN'S PAIRS. An event at duplicate competition between pairs of women players. Awards are 20% lower than for events of comparable size and duration open to any players.

WOMEN'S PAIRS, NORTH AMERICAN CHAMPIONSHIP, for the Whitehead Trophy. Played at the Summer NABC 1930-62 and subsequently at the Spring NABC. For results see Appendix I.

WOMEN'S SWISS TEAMS, NORTH AMERICAN CHAMPIONSHIP. Played in the Spring NABC. For results see Appendix I.

WONDER BIDS. A defensive bidding system against strong artificial club sequences. They are used when vulnerable; IDAK (or IDAC) is commonly used when not vulnerable. If RHO opens an artificial club or responds artificially to a 1♣ opening:

1. Any nonjump suit bid shows that suit or the other three (let partner guess). Responder obviously can't raise blindly, but can: (a) bid 1NT with four or more cards in the Wonder suit (not forcing if the Wonder bidder has the three-suited hand); (b) bid two of any suit with four or more cards if he also has tolerance for the Wonder suit. The overcaller passes or returns to his real Wonder suit. The Wonder bidder redoubles for takeout if doubled in his short suit.

2. Double shows the major suits.

3. Notrump shows the minor suits.

4. A jump in diamonds shows diamonds and hearts, a jump in hearts shows hearts and clubs, a jump in spades shows spades and a minor (notrump asks which minor).

WOODSON TWO-WAY NOTRUMP. This requires an opening notrump bid holding a balanced hand with 10-12 points or 16-18 points. A 2♣ bid asks for clarification. It was devised by the late William Woodson.

WORK POINT-COUNT. A 4-3-2-1 point-count based on the Bryant McCampbell count of 1915, publicized and advocated by MILTON WORK, circa 1923. See POINT-COUNT.

WORKING CARDS. High cards which, on the basis of the auction, rate to mesh well with partner's hand for suit play. For example, a secondary honor or an unsupported king is usually discounted opposite a known singleton, whereas any top honor is likely to be "working" if it is in one of partner's suits. See also GOOD CARDS.

WORLD BIDDING CONTEST. See INTERNATIONAL BRIDGE ACADEMY.

WORLD BRIDGE FEDERATION (WBF). The World Bridge Federation was founded in August 1958 in Oslo, Norway, by delegates from Europe, the United States and Australia. In 1977 it was incorporated in New York State as a not-for-profit organization and new By-Laws were adopted.

In 1993 the membership consisted of 94 National Contract Bridge Organizations (NCBOs) with a total of about one million individual members. The Executive Council, meeting annually at world championships, consists of five delegates each from Europe (Zone 1) and North America (Zone 2), plus one delegate each from five other zones (South America; Asia and Middle East; Central American and Caribbean; Far East; South Pacific:) plus the president. A Management Committee transacts necessary business between meetings. A Congress, with one representative from each NCBO, meets biennially.

Major activities of the WBF include: promoting bridge throughout the world; coordinating periodic revision of the Laws; conducting world championships; publishing *World Bridge News*; maintaining WBF masterpoint records, maintaining the WBF Educational Foundation.

Member countries (NCBOs) must have a minimum of 250 individual members, and belong to the zonal organization if one exists.

The zones of the WBF are: (1) Europe, (2) North America, including Bermuda, (3) South America, (4) Asia and the Middle East, (5) Central America and the Caribbean, (6) Far East, (7) South Pacific, (8) General zone, for all countries not affiliated with any of the other zones.

The major world events are: NEC World Team Olympiad (held in 1992 and other years divisible by four); World Championships (held in other even-numbered years); NEC Bermuda Bowl and NEC Venice Cup (held in odd-numbered years); and NEC World Junior Team Championships (held in odd-numbered years).

The following world events are scheduled:
1994 World Championships..........Albuquerque, NM, USA.
1995 NEC Bermuda Bowl and
　　　NEC Venice Cup..................Beijing, China.
1996 World Team Olympiad.........Greece. (Probable).
Officers 1993:
　President: Robert Wolff
　　12340 Brittany Circle,
　　Dallas TX 75230. USA.
　　Tel: 1 214 458 88 57
　　Fax: 1 214 991 83 44
　General Manager:
　　Becky Rogers,
　　8300 Douglas, Suite 617
　　Dallas TX 75225 USA.
　　Tel: 1-214-750-4572
　　Fax: 1-214-750-4573.
　Secretariat: Carol von Linstow
　　29 bis, Residence les Roussets,
　　01210 Ornex, France
　　Tel: 33 5040 4131
　　Fax: 33 5040 4257
For a predecessor organization, see INTERNATIONAL BRIDGE LEAGUE.

WORLD BRIDGE FEDERATION PLACING POINTS.
Points, other than WBF MASTERPOINTS, awarded by the WORLD BRIDGE FEDERATION to winners and very high finishers in WBF tournaments and Zonal team championships. A certain number of placing points are needed to achieve the WBF rankings of Grand Master and World Life Master. See WORLD BRIDGE FEDERATION PLAYER RANKINGS.

WORLD BRIDGE FEDERATION PLAYER RANKINGS.
The ranking of players according to the world masterpoint plan of the World Bridge Federation. The three ranks, in descending order, are World Grand Master, World Life Master, and World Master.

The rank of World Grand Master is achieved by accumulating 10 or more WBF Placing Points and winning at least one World Champion title. The rank of World Life Master is achieved by winning 5 or more Placing Points. These titles are lifetime. A player who wins 150 WBF masterpoints becomes a World Master, but loses this rank if his total falls below 150 as a result of the annual percentage cut of 15%.

For listings, see WORLD OPEN RANKINGS and WORLD WOMEN'S RANKINGS

WORLD BRIDGE FEDERATION PRESIDENTS.
1958-1964	Robert de Nexon
1964-1968	Charles J. Solomon
1968-1970	Carl Bonde
1970 1976	Julius Rosenblum
1976-1986	Jaime Ortiz-Patino
1986-1991	Denis Howard
1991-1992	Ernesto d'Orsi
1992-	Robert Wolff

WORLD BRIDGE FEDERATION TROPHY. This trophy, for the World Women's Pairs Championship, first was contested in Cannes, France, in 1962. See Appendix V for results.

WORLD BRIDGE OLYMPIC. See WORLD PAR CONTESTS. For results, see Appendix IV.

WORLD JUNIOR TEAM CHAMPIONSHIP. This contest, sponsored by NEC, is for players 25 years or younger, and is played along Bermuda Bowl lines. For results, see Appendix V.

WORLD OPEN RANKINGS. (1) World Bridge Federation Open Career Rankings as at December 1, 1993. The following is a complete list of living Open World Grand Masters ranked by Placing Points won in Open events, which reflect career performance.

	NAME	NCBO	P.P.
1	Belladonna, Giorgio	ITALY	78.5
2	Garozzo, Benito	ITALY	75
3	Hamman, Bob	USA	66.5
4	Wolff, Bobby	USA	59.5
5	Forquet, Pietro	ITALY	58
6	D'Alelio, Massimo	ITALY	48
7	Pabis Ticci, Camillo	ITALY	36
8	Chagas, Gabriel	BRAZIL	28.5
9	Branco, Marcelo	BRAZIL	26.5
10=	Eisenberg, Bill	USA	25
	Goldman, Bobby	USA	25
12=	Lawrence, Mike	USA	23.5
	Soloway, Paul	USA	23.5
14=	Rodwell, Eric	USA	22
	Ross, Hugh	USA	22
16	Meckstroth, Jeff	USA	20.5
17	Stansby, Lew	USA	20
18	Martel, Chip	USA	19
19	Franco, Arturo	ITALY	18
20	Chemla, Paul	FRANCE	17.5
21=	Cintra, Gabino	BRAZIL	16.5
	Rubin, Ira	USA	16.5
23	Lebel, Michel	FRANCE	16

24	Perron, Michel	FRANCE	15.5
25=	Assumpção, Pedro Paulo	BRAZIL	14.5
	Pittala, Vito	ITALY	14.5
	Szwarc, Henri	FRANCE	14.5
28	Kantar, Eddie	USA	14
29	Schapiro, Boris	BRITAIN	13
30=	Hamilton, Fred	USA	12
	Passell, Mike	USA	12
32=	Martens, Krzysztof	POLAND	11.5
	Mello, Roberto	BRAZIL	11.5
34=	Branco, Pedro Paulo	BRAZIL	11
	Mouiel, Hervé	FRANCE	11
	Reese, Terence	BRITAIN	11
37=	Bacherich, René	FRANCE	10.5
	Ghestem, Pierre	FRANCE	10.5
39	Weichsel, Peter	USA	10
40	Kreijns, Hans	NETHERLANDS	9.5
41=	Bourchtoff, Gerard	FRANCE	7.5
	Delmouly, Claude	FRANCE	7.5
43	Rapee, George	USA	6.5
44	Stayman, Samuel	USA	5.5
45	Siniscalco, Guglielmo	ITALY	4

(2) World Bridge Federation current open rankings. The following are the top 50 as at December 1, 1993, based on diminishing masterpoints. (When possible, ties are split by Placing Points. WGM=World Grand Master, WLM=World Life Master, WM=World Master.)

	NAME	Rank	NCBO	M.P.
1	Hamman, Bob	WGM	USA	5139
2	Wolff, Bobby	WGM	USA	5003
3	Rodwell, Eric	WGM	USA	4976
4	Meckstroth, Jeff	WGM	USA	4671
5	Chagas, Gabriel	WGM	BRAZIL	3871
6	Stansby, Lew	WGM	USA	3808
7	Martel, Chip	WGM	USA	3808
8	Gawrys, Piotr	WLM	POLAND	3142
9	Branco, Marcelo	WGM	BRAZIL	2801
10	Ross, Hugh	WGM	USA	2669
11	Martens, Krzysztof	WGM	POLAND	2657
12	Perron, Michel	WGM	FRANCE	2561
13=	Berger, Heinrich	WLM	AUSTRIA	2397
	Meinl, Wolfgang	WLM	AUSTRIA	2397
15=	Balicki, Cezary	WLM	POLAND	2377
	Zmudzinski, Adam	WLM	POLAND	2377
17	Weichsel, Peter	WGM	USA	2363
18	Chemla, Paul	WGM	FRANCE	2332
19	Mouiel, Hervé	WGM	FRANCE	2289
20	Mello, Roberto	WGM	BRAZIL	2172
21	Sundelin, Per-Olov	WLM	SWEDEN	2155
22	Fucik, Jan	WLM	AUSTRIA	2035
23	Gullberg, Tommy	WLM	SWEDEN	2031
24	Fallenius, Björn	WLM	SWEDEN	2025
25	Lawrence, Mike	WGM	USA	1989
26	Göthe, Hans	WLM	SWEDEN	1989
27	Mahmood, Zia	WLM	PAKISTAN	1957
28	Terraneo, Franz	WLM	AUSTRIA	1805
29	Kaplan, Edgar	WLM	USA	1725
30	Flodqvist, Sven-Olof	WLM	SWEDEN	1725
31	Woolsey, Kit	WLM	USA	1708
32	Berkowitz, David	WM	USA	1664
33	Przybora, Tomasz	WLM	POLAND	1657
34=	Becker, Mike	WLM	USA	1649
	Rubin, Ron	WLM	USA	1649
36	Szwarc, Henri	WGM	FRANCE	1640
37	Camacho, Carlos	WLM	BRAZIL	1627
38=	Leufkens, Enri	WLM	NETHERLANDS	1596
	Westra, Berry	WLM	NETHERLANDS	1596
40	Branco, Pedro Paulo	WGM	BRAZIL	1568
41	De Boer, Wubbo	WLM	NETHERLANDS	1562
42	Forrester, Tony	WM	BRITAIN	1548
43	Tuszynski, Piotr	WLM	POLAND	1527
44	Lebel, Michel	WGM	FRANCE	1504
45	Muller, Bauke	WLM	NETHERLANDS	1503
46	Lévy, Alain	WLM	FRANCE	1456
47	Nagy, Peter	WLM	USA	1453
48	Fazli, Jan-e-Alam	WLM	PAKISTAN	1453
49	Silverman, Neil	WM	USA	1428
50	Lasocki, Krzysztof	WM	POLAND	1383

WORLD MASTER. See WORLD BRIDGE FEDERATION PLAYER RANKINGS.

WORLD OLYMPICS. See WORLD PAR CONTESTS.

WORLD PAR CONTESTS. International events using prepared deals (see PAR CONTESTS). The idea of a series of par tournaments conducted throughout the world was conceived by Ely Culbertson, and in 1932 the first World Bridge Olympic, using the par hand format, was held. Culbertson founded the National Bridge Association, a nonprofit corporation, in the same year, to conduct the tournaments. The bridge world's principal experts, regardless of their affiliation in the bridge politics of those times, constructed the prepared deals, and Culbertson's staff did the central management and scoring. Each contestant paid a fee of one dollar, of which half went to the game captain (who pre-arranged the hands and directed his game), and half was retained by the NBA. In 1932, both American and World Olympics were conducted: from 1934 on, only the World Olympics. In 1934 self-dealing cards (marked on their backs to show which player should receive each card for the particular deal) and folding duplicate boards (later called bridge WALLETS) were supplied without extra charge by the NBA. The World Bridge Olympic reached its peak in 1934 with 70 countries and nearly 90,000 players entered, but even in that year the NBA lost money. In 1938 the ACBL took over the management, with William McKenney in charge and Geoffrey Mott-Smith constructing the hands, but there were problems of foreign exchange, and World War II forced the abandonment after 1941.

The Olympic trophies were famous. For the American event, the two largest silver trophies in bridge history were provided. One of them is the McKenney Trophy; the other was lost in circumstances that had a lasting effect on insurance law. A winner, entitled to one year's possession only, pawned the trophy. A court ruled that since it was his honest intention to redeem it within the year, he was not liable although he found himself later without funds to redeem it, nor was the pawnbroker responsible for having sold it when the time for redemption had passed. The insurance underwriter paid its value to the NBA. The two World trophies each contained $5,000 worth of pure platinum but Culbertson, who donated them, never relinquished personal title to them and sold them for their value in platinum when the tournament was discontinued.

Individual prizes were given to all international and national winners and to state winners in the United States and provincial winners in Canada, both North-South and East-West, so the list of winners for each year was long indeed.

In 1951, the World Par Contest was revived by Australia and won by Dr. J. L. Thwaites and Dr. E.L. Field of Melbourne, Australia, in that year. It was held in 1961 and 1963 under the auspices of the World Bridge Federation. The WBF intended to hold this event biennially, but it has not been held since 1963. The organizers in 1961 and 1963 were Michael J. Sullivan and Robert E. Williams (Australia).

For winners, see Appendix IV.

WORLD TEAM OLYMPIAD. A WBF tournament conducted quadrennially starting in 1960, consisting of an open team event and a women's team event. In 1960 NCBOs having a very large number of members were allowed to enter more than one team. On this basis Sweden entered two teams and the United States entered four in the open event. Since 1960 each NCBO has been allowed to enter only one team in each event of the Olympiad. For results see Appendix. See INTERNATIONAL OPEN TEAM SELECTION and INTERNATIONAL WOMEN'S TEAM SELECTION. For results, see Appendix V.

WORLD TOP TOURNAMENT. See CAP GEMINI WORLD TOP tournament. For results, see Appendix IV.

WORLD WOMEN'S RANKINGS. (1) World Bridge Federation women's career rankings as at December 1, 1993. The following is a complete list of living Women World Grand Masters ranked by Placing Points won in Open events, which reflect career performance.

	NAME	NCBO	P.P.
1	Landy, Sandra	BRITAIN	23
2	Smith, Nicola	BRITAIN	21
3	Mitchell, Jacqui	USA	20.5
4	Wei-Sender, Kathie	USA	17
5	Radin, Judi	USA	16.5
6=	Davies, Pat	BRITAIN	16
	Sanborn, Kerri	USA	16
	Truscott, Dorothy	USA	16
9=	Deas, Lynn	USA	15
	Farell, Mary Jane	USA	15
11=	Greenberg, Gail	USA	14.5
	Kennedy, Betty Ann	USA	14.5
	Sanders, Carol	USA	14.5
14	Horton, Sally	USA	14.5
15	McCallum, Karen	USA	13
16	Bianchi, Marisa	ITALY	11.5
	Johnson, Marilyn	USA	11.5
	Valenti, Anna	ITALY	11.5
19	Palmer, Beth	USA	11
20	Capodanno, Luciana	ITALY	10.5
	D'Andrea, Marisa	ITALY	10.5

(2) World Bridge Federation Women's rankings. Top 50 as at December 1, 1993, based on diminishing master points. (When possible, ties are split by Placing Points.)

	NAME	Rank	NCBO	M.P.
1	Landy, Sandra	WGM	BRITAIN	2615
2	Sanborn, Kerri	WGM	USA	2461
3	Deas, Lynn	WGM	USA	2183
4	Smith, Nicola	WGM	BRITAIN	2088
5	Davies, Pat	WGM	BRITAIN	2088
6	Wei-Sender, Kathie	WGM	USA	2022
7	McCallum, Karen	WGM	USA	1900
8	Sanders, Carol	WGM	USA	1741
9	Radin, Judi	WGM	USA	1734
10	Horton, Sally	WGM	BRITAIN	1725
11	Kennedy, Betty Ann	WGM	USA	1724
12	Palmer, Beth	WGM	USA	1665
13	Vriend, Bep	WLM	NETHERLANDS	1519
14	Osberg, Sharon	WLM	USA	1458
15	Mitchell, Jacqui	WGM	USA	1403
16	Zenkel, Sabine	WLM	GERMANY	1383
17	Picus, Sue	WLM	USA	1382
18	Vogt, Waltraud	WLM	GERMANY	1375
19	Von Arnim, Daniela	WLM	GERMANY	1366
20	Gordon, Dianna	WM	CANADA	1329
21=	Caesar, Karin	WLM	GERMANY	1298
	Moegel, Marianne	WLM	GERMANY	1298
23=	Van Der Pas, Marijke	WLM	NETHERLANDS	1289
	Schippers, Elly	WLM	NETHERLANDS	1289
25	Delor, Elisabeth	WLM	FRANCE	1234
26	Erhart, Maria	WLM	AUSTRIA	1193
27	Schulle, Kay	WLM	USA	1161
28	Reus, Sharyn	WM	CANADA	1159
29=	Fischer, Doris	WLM	AUSTRIA	1150
	Weigkricht, Terry	WLM	AUSTRIA	1150
31	Bessis, Veronique	WLM	FRANCE	1129
32	Penfold, Sandra	WLM	BRITAIN	1111
33	Meyers, Jill	WLM	USA	1093
34	Palmund, Charlotte	WLM	DENMARK	1047
35	Lise, Colette	WM	FRANCE	1047
36	Kalkerup, Bettina	WLM	DENMARK	1039
37	McGowan, Elizabeth	WLM	BRITAIN	1026
38	Greenberg, Gail	WGM	USA	1023
39	Nehmert, Beate	WLM	GERMANY	1010
40	Willard, Sylvie	WLM	FRANCE	1001
41	Schaltz, Dorthe	WM	DENMARK	995
42	Arnolds, Carla	WM	NETHERLANDS	983
43	Gu Ling	WM	CHINA	970
44	Cimon, Francine	WM	CANADA	955
45	Zhang Yalan	WM	CHINA	928
46	Sun Ming	WM	CHINA	919
47	Allouche, Danielle	WLM	FRANCE	884
48	Ryman, Mari	WM	SWEDEN	869
49	Chevalley, Ginette	WLM	FRANCE	858
50	Ödlund, Bim	WM	SWEDEN	821

WRIGGLE. An intermediate step when escaping from an opposing penalty attempt at a low level.

♠ A 3 2
♥ A 3 2
♦ A 2
♣ J 5 4 3 2

You deal as South and the bidding is:

South	West	North	East
1 ♣	Pass	Pass	Dbl.
Pass	Pass	Redbl.	Pass
?			

West has the clubs stacked over you. Your partner's SOS redouble shows that he is short in clubs and prepared for any other suit. The least evil will be to play in one of a major suit, but which? You should wriggle by bidding one diamond, and then make an SOS redouble to force your partner to choose a major suit. See also DEFENSE TO DOUBLE OF ONE NOTRUMP and SOS REDOUBLE.

WRITTEN BIDDING. A variation in the bidding technique such that each bidder writes his bid on a sheet (designed to facilitate the placing of each bid in a proper box) which is passed to him as it becomes his turn to bid. The theory is that any extra time a player might take in a huddle can be construed as a review of previous bidding, as shown on the sheet, and no information can be conveyed to the partner by mannerism, gesture, or inflection, and the need for a review of the bidding at any time is removed. Another advantage, as against bidding boxes, is that it provides a written record for directors, journalists or others involved.

Written bidding is standard in Australia, New Zealand and China, has been used in Far East Championships and some other international events. See BIDDING BOXES.

WRONG BOARD. Occasionally the play of a wrong board is commenced before it is discovered that it is a wrong board. If this occurs, the director should be summoned and he will act under LAWS OF DUPLICATE, Law 15.

WRONG SIDE. The hand of the declaring partnership which is less well equipped to cope with the opening lead. See RIGHT SIDE.

X

X. (1) A symbol used in lower case in bridge literature to signify an insignificant small card in any suit, a card lower than a 10. Thus, K-x-x means the king and two low cards in that suit. (2) A capital X indicates a double, and is used in recording bidding, and in WRITTEN BIDDING, by hand in important matches. Similarly, XX means "redouble."

X PLUS ONE, RULE OF. See RULE OF X PLUS ONE.

Y

YARBOROUGH. Any hand at bridge containing no card higher than a nine, named after an English lord who customarily would offer to wager 1,000 pounds to one against the chance of such a hand being held by a player. The odds against holding a Yarborough are 1,827 to one, so he was giving himself a substantial edge. In post-mortem discussions the term "Yarborough" has gained currency to describe bad hands even if they do not meet the strict requirements.

YOUNGEST LIFE MASTER. The following players were the Youngest Life Masters at the time they achieved that status:

1952	Richard Freeman	18 yrs. 10 mos. 7 days
1961	Diane Barton-Paine	18 yrs. 12 days
1965	Kyle Larsen	15 yrs. 11 mos.
1968	Joseph Livezey	15 yrs. 5 mos.
1973	Bobby Levin	15 yrs. 4 mos.
1975	Michael Freed	15 yrs. 20 days
1976	Regina Barnes	14 yrs. 11 mos.
1977	Steve Cochran	14 yrs. 5 mos. 20 days
1980	Billy Hsieh	13 yrs. 7 mos. 15 days
1981	Andrew Kaufman	13 yrs. 4 mos. 15 days (June)
1981	Doug Hsieh	11 yrs. 10 mos. 4 days (Sept.)
1988	Sam Hirschman	11 yrs. 9 mos. 5 days
1990	Joel Wooldridge	11 yrs. 4 mos. 13 days

To become a Life Master is the dream of all serious bridge players. Some never make it in their lifetime; others seem to have a special gift for the game and become Life Masters within a very short time. To become a Life Master a player must win a specified number of masterpoints at different levels of play, including major

bridge tournaments, and accumulate 300 of these "colored" masterpoints. A masterpoint is the unit which measures bridge achievement in tournament play.

The first person to be recognized in the *Official Encyclopedia of Bridge* as the youngest Life Master, was John R. Crawford. He earned the title in 1939 when he was 23 years old and held this honored position for nearly thirteen years. (Crawford went on to become one of the most famous of bridge stars, winning many titles and championships during his career.)

In 1952 a former "Quiz Kid" of radio fame Richard Freeman became a Life Master at the age of 18. He once achieved notoriety for challenging and beating a computer in a race to score a bridge event. Freeman was definitely known as "The Fastest Pencil" in the days of manual tournament scorekeeping.

The first female to achieve the distinction of being the youngest Life Master was Diane Barton-Paine in 1961 just 12 days after her 18th birthday. The same year she became one of ACBL's youngest tournament directors.

Diane held the title of youngest female Life Master for 12 years, until Connie McGinley became a Life Master in 1973 at the age of 17 years, 5 months.

As more and more young players became seriously involved with the game of bridge, the age limit was quickly lowered. For example, the first female Life Master under the age of 17 was Regina Barnes. At 14 years and 11 months, she broke the record for both sexes in 1976. Six years later she was still the youngest female Life Master when her record was broken in 1982 by both Adair Gellman and Tricia Thomas. Adair was 14 years, 6 months and 4 days old, and Tricia was 14 years, and 26 days old. Tricia still holds the Youngest Female Life Master title and is listed as such in *Guinness Book of World Records.*

In 1965 Kyle Larsen became the first 15-year-old to become a Life Master. He was 15 years, 11 months. In 1968 he won the Reisinger Team trophy, thus becoming at 18 the youngest player ever to win a major NABC team title. In the years that followed he won half a dozen major championships.

Another 15-year-old, Bobby Levin, became the youngest Life Master in 1973. When he graduated from high school two years later he was named the *King of Bridge* by ACBL and the International Palace of Sports. In 1979 he won the Reisinger, Blue Ribbon and Lou Herman Trophies. In 1980 he won the Vanderbilt Knockout Team title. In 1981 he was a key member of the winning Bermuda Bowl team — the youngest player ever to capture that championship.

The players who became youngest Life Master in the Eighties have yet to make a substantial mark on the national and international scene — but they are younger than ever — with two preteens completing the prestigious list of a dozen Youngest Life Masters.

In 1980 Billy Hsieh became a Life Master at the age of 13 years, 7 months old. Then in 1981, Andrew Kaufman broke the record when he was 13 years, 4 months and 15 days old.

In 1981 Doug Hsieh astounded the bridge world by becoming a Life Master at the age of 11 years, 10 months and 4 days. Doug, younger brother of Billy Hsieh, is a member of a well-known bridge playing family of four ACBL Life Masters. When his achievement was announced by the ACBL one writer predicted that his record "is likely to stand well into the next century."

Doug held the title for almost seven years until Sam Hirschman came along in 1988. (Incidentally Sam's father Martin became a Life Master when he was 26.) Sam was 11 years, 9 months and 5 days old. His achievement received national recognition and was recorded in the *Guinness Book of World Records.*

It was felt that the record set by Sam Hirschman would never be broken, but on the final day of the 1990 Fall NABC in San Francisco, Joel Wooldridge of the Buffalo NY area assumed Hirschman's spot in the annals of bridge.

Wooldridge became a Life Master at the age of 11 years, 4 months and 13 days, breaking Hirschman's record by nearly five months. Wooldridge's accomplishment culminated a remarkable run for the precocious youngster. He hadn't seriously contemplated going for the Youngest Life Master crown until he and his mother, Jill, won the Mixed Pairs at the Toronto regional April 10, 1990.

Going from there and playing mostly with his mother, Joel earned his gold card in a breeze. Along the way, he was encouraged to go for the record by Martin Hirschman, Sam's father.

Wooldridge's record may seem impregnable, but in the Nineties there was increasing interest in bridge among young people. Beyond that, the ACBL's highly successful School Bridge Lesson Series, which had made inroads in elementary schools, could open doors for other, even younger players with a flair for the game. See also KING OR QUEEN OF BRIDGE and PRE-TEEN SCHOLARSHIP.

YOUTH PLAYER OF THE YEAR. The Youth Player of the Year award was established in 1990 by the American Contract Bridge League. The competition to determine the youth who wins the most masterpoints in a single year is restricted to contestants 19 or younger who had not reached their 20th birthday as of Dec. 31 of the previous year. For winners see Appendix II.

YUGOSLAVIA BRIDGE FEDERATION (BRIDGE SAVEZ JUGOSLAVIJE). Reactivated in 1967 in Belgrade, with approximately 250 members, the federation is located principally in Belgrade, Zagreb and Ljubljana. Prior to World War II, the League was an active member of the European Bridge League, tying for second place in the 1935 European Championships in Brussels, and finishing second in 1939 at The Hague.

Ninad Slipvecic
Gospara Vucica 4
11000 Belgrade
Yugoslavia
Fax: 38 11 444 3143

zero or two higher honors in the suit, while the lead of the jack denies any higher honors. Leads of the ace, king, and queen retain their standard meanings. These leads may be used against any contract or only against notrump, and may also be used throughout the deal. Proponents claim that the opening leader's partner usually has no trouble deducing the true situation, and that it keeps declarer in the dark better than do JOURNALIST LEADS or RUSINOW LEADS. Opponents consider that they give too much away to the declarer.

ZIMBABWE BRIDGE UNION. The Union was founded in 1967, a successor to the Central Africa Bridge Union. In 1992 there were six clubs and about 600 members.

Officers 1992:
Chairman: Don McDevitt
P.O. Box 1074,
Harare, Zimbabwe.
Tel. 263 4 709 076
Fax. 263 4 61881

ZIP SWISS. A special version of Swiss Teams designed to be finished in a short time, usually as a one-session event at the end of a day's championship play. The usual format is to conduct the game with five-board matches, five minutes per board, and five matches per game. These events are sometimes played in Australia, with even shorter time limits.

ZIRINSKY FORMULA. A method of determining victory points long used in Far East Championships. All "push" boards (with zero IMPs) are scored as one to each team. Then the winning score is multiplied by four and divided by the losing score, with a maximum of eight VPs. The losing team receives the balance of the eight points at stake. The "push board" provision was introduced by the inventor, Victor Zirinsky of Hong Kong, as a modification to the original idea which gave inequitable results in low-scoring matches.

Z

ZERO. The lowest score possible on a duplicate board, hence loosely, a very bad score. It also refers to a lost board in a team-of-four contest. Note that a score on a board of zero points (all four hands pass) may be any matchpoint score from none to top.

ZERO OR TWO HIGHER LEADS. An opening lead convention designed to eliminate the ambiguity of standard honor leads. The lead of the 10 or 9 promises either

LEADING BRIDGE PERSONALITIES

A

Å, Terje (b. 1961) of Norway, Post Office employee. Second Bermuda Bowl 1993, third European Teams 1993.

AABYE, Jon (b. 1952) of Oslo, Norway, accountant. Third World Teams 1980. Won Nordic Teams once. Won four national titles.

AARONS, Stephen H. (b. 1937) of Toronto, lawyer, graduated U of Toronto. Appointed Queen's Counsel 1978. Owner of thoroughbred race horses. Served on Unit 166 Bd. of Dir. 1965-80, chairman Unit Ethics Committee 1968-78, Chairman Dist 2 Ethics Committee 1979-85, served on National Appeals Committee 1975-83, District 2 director 1972-75. Placed 10th in World Mixed Prs 1978, was NPC of Canadian Team in Seattle 1984, placed second in 1989 Maccabiah Games. Won numerous regionals including Can-Am Open Tms 1969, Canadian Nat'l Mens Prs 1974, Dist. 2 GNT, Zone 1 1979, Gateway City Swiss 1981.

ABASS, Ahmed Zein (b. 1960) of Cairo, Egypt, electrical engineer. Runner-up Middle East Team Championship 1991, and represented Egypt in 1991 Bermuda Bowl. Has won three national team titles.

ABDEL BARI, Mohamed (b. 1954) of Cairo, Egypt, engineer. Middle East Team Champion 1989, and runner-up 1991. Has won five national titles, including open team three times.

ABDEL RAOUF, Walid El Ahmady (b. 1961) of Cairo, Egypt, engineer. WBF World Master. Middle East Team Champion 1989. Has won five national team titles.

ABDOU, Wafik (b. 1962 in Egypt) of Bakersfield CA, anesthesiologist, graduate of USC, enjoys chess. Winner of BAM Tms 1992. Won Golden State Swiss 1990, Spring secondary Open Prs 1992, Mid-Winter Holiday BAM Tms.

ABECASSIS, Michel (b. 1952) of Paris, France. Won European Pairs 1991, 1993, and represented France in one zonal championship.

ABEDI, Nishat M.H. (b. 1939) of Karachi, Pakistan, born in Allahabad, India, accountant. WBF World Master. Pakistan's top masterpoint winner. Second in two world championships, Bermuda Bowl 1981 and Rosenblum Teams 1986. Twice winner of BFAME zonal championship and has many Pakistani titles.

ABRAHAMS, Stanley J. (b. 1940 in Scotland), commercial manager. Represented New Zealand in two world championships and three Far East Championships. Third Far East Pairs 1981. National wins include Open Teams three times.

ABRAMS, Elsie of Pompano Beach FL, registered nurse

and certified director. Won Mixed Prs 1960 and placed second in Womens Tms 1963. Regional wins include New England Fall Mixed Tms 1958, KO Tms 1960; Southeastern Womens Tms 1962, 63, 64, 71.

ACKERMAN, Gerald W. (Jerry) (b. 1925) of New Bern NC, retired CPA and manager with Coopers & Lybrand, graduated magna cum laude Syracuse U. Served North Jersey BA as board member, vice president, auditor, and chairman of Conduct and Ethics Committee. Won Marcus Cup 1954, second 1956. Regional wins include Pocono Open Tms 1951.

ADAMCZYK, Wesley (Wes) (b. 1933) of Hammond IN, born in Poland, chemist with Lever Bros. since 1958 and senior tax consultant since 1970, educated at DePaul U. At age ten he and his family were deported to Russia — they escaped two years later. He lost both his parents during this period — his father was murdered in the Katyn Forest massacre. Moved from camp to camp for displaced persons, finally arriving in Chicago in 1950. Regional wins include Champaign Mens Prs, Mens Swiss, Pittsburgh Mens Swiss, Central St II Open Swiss, Swiss 1982; KOs, Spring NABC secondary Mens Prs, Wolverine Master Prs, Swiss 1987; Open Swiss, Mens Swiss, Masters Prs 1989; Open Prs, Swiss 1990.

ADAMS, Charles True (1900-1942) of Chicago, utilities attorney, a valuable contributor to the OFFICIAL SYSTEM. One of the first widely read authors on contract bridge, his *Contract Bridge Standardized* was published in 1928. Adams was co-editor-in-chief (with Milton Work) of *The Bridge Magazine*, and director of the AMERICAN AUCTION BRIDGE LEAGUE in 1927. See BIBLIOGRAPHY, C.

ADAMS, Bill R. (Tornado) (b. 1930) of Memphis TN, ACBL computer programmer, formerly a national tournament director since 1970.

ADAMS, Dee of Memphis TN, real estate broker, Diamond Life Master. Regional titles include St. Louis Womens Prs 1961, Memphis Open Swiss 1971, Hot Springs Womens Prs 1974, Memphis Master Prs 1983, Mexico City Womens Prs 1985, Gatlinburg Womens KOs 1988, 92; Paducah Swiss, Memphis Sr KOs 1989; Birmingham Womens Prs 1990, Monroe Womens Prs, Pine Bluff Womens Prs 1991; Jackson Womens Prs 1992.

ADAMS, Peggy (1900-1974) of New York City, an ACBL staff member who worked in the masterpoint department from 1948 to 1966 and wrote the feature *Club Corner* for the ACBL *Bulletin*. Under the stage name of Peggy Hart she was in vaudeville in her youth, playing the Keith Circuit and picture theaters. In 1950 she became Life Master #300. She won the Womens Tms 1955 and placed second in 1952.

ADAMS, Dr. Robert T. (b. 1923 in Japan) of Lafayette CA, retired manager and research chemist. Hobbies include tennis, genealogy research, table tennis, piano and organ. Roller skate dance champion 1968 & 69. Served on Oakland and Richmond Unit Bd of Dir. Authored a bridge column for the American Chemical Society magazine, *The Vortex*, 1967-78. Won Mixed Prs 1957. Regional wins include All-Western Masters Prs 1954, Open Tms 1960; Bridge Week Open Tms 1964, 73, KO Tms 1967; Oregon Trail Open Tms 1965, Pacific Southwest Open Tms 1969, CA Capital Mens Prs 1988, Santa Clara Sr KOs 1989, San Francisco Sr KOs 1991.

ADAMS, William E. (b. 1917) of Hamden CT, retired aeronautical, mechanical and product engineer, graduated Yale U., served on ACBL Board of Directors in the Sixties, Connecticut Unit Bd of Dir 1952-78 (past president), and District Bd of Dir 1955-70, chaired numerous sectional tournaments 1952-78, has been a certified director since 1968. Winner of National Sr Master Individual 1953. Won New England Open Tms 1961, NE Fall Mixed Tms 1961, 62, 69; Open Tms 1968; ESNC Tms 2nd Flt 1972.

ADLER, Betty (Mrs. Julian) (b. 1927) of Baltimore, bridge teacher since 1959, 1949-51, formally a social worker and did birth control surveys for Sinai Hospital. Avid tennis player. Maryland BA Bd member for 15 yrs, served as president twice, tournament chairman 1970-80 and member of National Goodwill Committee. A qualified director since 1981, directing mainly on bridge cruises. Placed second in Womens KOs 1980 and in Summer Master Mixed Tms 1970, 74, 78, represented ACBL in international play in Miami 1972. North American wins include Womens Prs 1959, Womens KOs 1977, 79. A Diamond Life Master, she has won numerous regionals including York Womens Prs, Mixed Prs 1955; Keystone Open Prs 1961, Mid Atlantic Mixed Prs, Summer Mixed Prs 1964, Winter Open Prs 1967, Womens Prs 1968; Labor Day Open 1979, Atlantic City Open Tms four years in a row, Mid Atlantic Sr Prs 1989.

ADLER, Julian (b. 1918) of Baltimore, retired CEO and Board Chairman, educated at Johns Hopkins and Harvard. Competed in Maryland Senior Olympics from 1980 to 1991 winning several swimming medals. Recipient of three Battle Stars in WWII. Served on Maryland BA Bd of Dir, placed second in Non-Master Prs 1961, Master Mixed Tms 1970, 74, 78. Won several regionals including Keystone Open Tms 1955, Open Prs 1961, Swiss 1971, 72, 73, 74; NY Individual 1958, Labor Day Open 1970, Norfolk Open Tms 1969, 70; Dist. 6 GN Tms 1975, Washington Bridge Week Swiss 1976, Pittsburgh Open Prs 1979, Mid-Atlantic Sr Prs 1989.

ADLER, Patricia. See SHEINWOLD, PATRICIA FOX

AFDAL, Darwin (Dar) (b. 1940) of Virginia Beach VA, U.S. Navy aviator for 21 years, currently in life insurance/financial services. Has held several executive positions including president on Unit and District level, member of Nat'l Bd of Gov since 1985, member Nat'l Goodwill Committee since 1986, currently serving on Nat'l Appeals Committee. Certified director since 1968. Writes column for Unit newsletter. Won Rocky Mtn Open Tms 1970, Pacific Northwest KOs 1973, Mid-Atlantic Mens Prs 1976, Open Swiss 1978, Mens Swiss, Open Prs 1979, KOs 1984, 86, Mens Prs 1984, Swiss 1989; Fall NABC secondary Win/Loss Swiss 1989.

AFSAR, Tugrul (b. 1949) of Ankara, Turkey, bridge teacher. Represented Turkey in two zonal championships. Four national wins include open teams three times.

AGUW, Maximilian (b. 1941) of Manado, Indonesia, police officer, former regional chess champion, represented Indonesia Bermuda Bowl 1973, 1974, 1981; World Team Olympiad 1976, 1980; Far East champion 1972, 1973, 1979, 1981; won many national pair and team titles.

AGRAN, Nathan (Nat) (b. 1908) of Sarasota FL, retired Philadelphia attorney, elected to three honorary societies. Was actively involved in many Philadelphia community activities. As general counsel of the Commonwealth of PA Commission on Human Relations (1960-73) he won landmark decisions before the Supreme Court of PA on de facto school segregation. Taught bridge during WW II to GIs and officers and later to disabled veterans with his late wife, Violet. Agran is Life Master #148. After retirement to FL he became active in local bridge and community activities. Won the Beynon Trophy 1948, Eastern States Mixed Prs 1951, Mid-Atlantic Open Prs 1955, Sun City Swiss, Central FL Swiss.

AHMED, Javed (b. 1947) of Karachi, Pakistan, business executive. WBF World Master. Won BFAME zonal title 1991 and represented Pakistan Bermuda Bowl 1991. Won many national titles.

AHMED, Nisar (b. 1936) of Karachi, Pakistan, accountant. WBF World Master. Second in two world championships, Bermuda Bowl 1981 and Rosenblum Cup 1986. Won BFAME zonal championship 1981, 1983, 1985, 1987. Second Far East Championship 1979. Won many national titles.

AKCA, Necmi (b. 1915) of Istanbul, Turkey, businessman. Represented Turkey in five world championships and seven zonal championships. Ten national wins include open teams twice.

AKTURK, Hans (b. 1932 in Turkey) of Tallahassee FL, manager systems programmer, educated at U. of Mich, enjoys playing chess and golf. Has more than 20 regional wins: Upper NY State Swiss 1973, Mixed Prs 1977, Master Swiss 1979, 1980; All-American Swiss 1975, Motor City Master Prs 1980,

ALBANO, Helen D. of Newark NJ, charter member of AMERICAN BRIDGE TEACHERS ASSOCIATION and its president in 1967, president and founder of *Bridge for the Blind,* a non-profit organization of some 118 volunteers who teach bridge to the blind throughout the United States, Canada, South Africa, Iran and Israel. Albano formerly wrote a column titled *Chuckles* for the ABTA *Quarterly* and is the author of the textbook, *Analysis and Practical Application of the Goren Method*. Her textbook was translated into braille, together with her program of lessons and techniques. See BIBLIOGRAPHY, C.

ALBARRAN, Pierre (1894-1960, born in West Indies) of Paris, France. The leading figure in French bridge until his death. Won European Teams 1935, and represented France that year in the first World Championship in New York. Represented France on 30 other occasions, and won 19 national titles, mainly in the 30s. Developed the canapé principle, short suit before long, which influenced many European players including Jaïs, Trezel and the Italian world champions. Also developed ACE SHOWING RESPONSES TO TWO CLUBS and a distributional point count. Author or co-author of nine books, five of them in collaboration with José Le Dentu. The most influential for the theory of bridge were *Notre Méthode de Bridge* with Robert De Nexon (1935) and *Le Canapé* (1946). Twice a member of the French Davis Cup tennis team.

ALBERSHEIM, Alberta G. (b. 1906) of Waban MA, former NY attorney. She has 19 grandchildren from her two natural children and six adopted foreign children. Now is virtually blind and has to carry her own boards with giant cards that enable her to continue to attend tournaments. At home and work she uses a machine called Optelec that magnifies up to 65 times. Served as a Board member of Eastern Massachusetts BA for ten years and was treasurer of the Summer NABC 1970, chaired a committee for Summer NABC 1981 and 1990. Member of National Goodwill Committee since the Sixties. A Diamond Life Master, she placed second in Womens Prs 1958. Regional wins include Eastern States Mixed Prs 1954, Mixed Tms 1967; New England Master Prs 1972, Fall NABC secondary Womens Prs 1980, Summer NABC secondary Open Prs 1981. Graduate of New York U Law School.

ALBERT, Mary (b. 1947) of Omaha NE, office manager for family-owned food brokerage business, competes in ballroom dancing pro-am tournaments four times a year, does demonstrations and exhibitions of partnership dancing, has won several dance awards. Chaired several sectionals and co-chaired Omaha and Iowa City regionals. Placed second in Womens Swiss 1982 and Life Master Womens 1983. Has won several regionals including three each Dist GN Prs and GN Tms.

ALCORN, Margaret. See GAER, MARGARET.

ALDER, Phillip D. (b. 1951) of New York, formerly of London, England, self-employed bridge journalist, succeeded Jim Jacoby as bridge columnist with Newspaper Enterprise Association. Educated at U College, where he was an honors student, and Institute of Education, both in London. Alder's other interests include Formula 1 Grand Prix racing, tennis, golf, cricket, baseball, American football, wine, travel, cats, West-End theatre and the stories of P.G. Wodehouse. Served as member of GNYBA Bd of Directors, member of ACBL National Appeals Committee, member of conventions working party of English Bridge Union. Life Master both in England and the US. At the time he became a Life Master in England he was the second youngest ever to attain that rank. He authored *You Can Play Bridge,* was a principal analyst on the *World Championship Books* for 1986, 87 & 88, has written and/or edited with Alan Truscott, Dr. George Rosenkranz, Bill Root and Zia Mahmood. Regular contributor to *ACBL Bulletin, New Zealand Bridge, The Bridge World, Australian Bridge, IBPA Bulletin,. Bridge d'Italia* and *Diversion* (a medical publication). Editor of *Bridge Magazine* 1980-85, editor at many World, European, Common Market and Zone 4 Championships. Contributing editor to *Bridge*

Encycleopedia. Author of *Get Smarter at Bridge.* Winner of a BOLs Brilliancy Prize for journalism in 1979 and Royal Viking Line Player of the Year (1986). Invented Alder Transfer Preempts. He has acted as a vugraph commentator at international events and coached teams from Egypt and Pakistan to prepare them for international competion. Represented England in the Camrose Trophy in 1980 and in the Jr. Camrose in 1971, 72, the Jr. European Championship 1972, Common Market Championships 1974, and the Jr Common Market Championships 1976. British national victories include Jr Prs Championship and Anglo-American Jr Prs Championship 1971, Jr Team Championship 1972, Two Star Prs 1973, Crockford's Cup 1984. In the U.S. his victories include Spring secondary Non-smoking Swiss 1987 and the Von Zedtwitz Double KO 1987.

ALDERTON, George A., II (1904-1982) of Detroit, probate and tax attorney, was ACBL president in 1945, ACBL vice-president, ACBL Honorary Member in 1956 and former president of the Midwest Conference and Michigan BA.

ALDRICH, Clarence (Clayton) (1871-1961) of Cleveland, furniture store owner, was active in forming the AMERICAN BRIDGE LEAGUE in 1927. President of the ABL in 1930 and a member of the executive committee in 1933.

ALIOTTA, Mike (b. 1943) of Oklahoma City, bridge professional, graduated from Western Michigan, vice chairman of the National Appeals Committee, president of Ethical Oversight Committee. He was second in the Men's BAM Tms 1981. Diamond Life Master with more than 30 regional titles.

ALLAN, Thomas W. (Tom) (b. 1951) of Broken Arrow OK, regional sales manager, graduate of U of Missouri, enjoys radio-controlled model airplanes. Won the Intercollegiate Championship 1975, Dist. 16 GN Prs winner three times, Spring NABC secondary Open Prs Flt B 1979, Texas Mid-Summer Swiss 1979, San Antonio Swiss, Dallas Swiss 1981; Wiesbaden KOs, Swiss, Masters Prs 1991.

ALLANA, A.R. (b. 1944) of Karachi, Pakistan, industrialist. WBF World Master. Won BFAME zonal championship 1991 and represented Pakistan in four world championships including 1991 Bermuda Bowl.

ALLEN, Ellen B. (Lulie) (Mrs. Larry C.) of Summerville SC, secretary/bookeeper and horse breeder, Diamond Life Master, won 17 Mid-Atlantic regional events including Summer Open Prs 1967, KO Tms 1977, Womens Prs 1979; Spring Open Prs 1969, Womens Prs 1972, KO Tms 1975, 79; Fall Swiss 1969, Womens Prs, Swiss 1971; Winter Womens Prs 1971, KO Tms 1976, 81, Master Prs 1977.

ALLEN, Larry C. (b. 1935) of Summerville SC, construction engineer, company president, Diamond LM, won 12 Mid-Atlantic regional events including Spring Open Prs 1969, Swiss 1971, KO Tms 1975, 79; Summer KO Tms 1977, Fall Swiss 1969, 71; Winter KO Tms 1976, 81, Master Prs 1977.

ALLINGER, Paul (1929-1988) of Alameda CA, accountant, won Mens Prs 1956, Mens Tms 1962, Chicago (since 1965 the Reisinger) 1962, Spingold 1958 and placed second in Open Prs 1957, Mens Tms 1956, Mens Prs 1961. Won numerous regional titles and was the co-inventer of ASTRO. Represented the U.S. in the World Tm Olympiad in 1960.

ALLISON, Karen R. of Jersey City NJ, formerly of Toronto, options trader, graduated Brooklyn College. Served on drafting committee for duplicate and rubber bridge laws revisions, Nat'l Appeals Committee vice-chairman, and past chairman GNYBA. Elected to Nat'l Laws Commission in 1982. Represented Canada in world competition in New Orleans 1978, Valkenburg 1980. She is WBF World Master and was the first woman to ever represent Canada in the Open Tms Monte Carlo 1976, where her team placed 13th in World Olympiad Open Tms. Placed eighth in the World Womens Prs 1990. Won Womens Tms 1968, Womens Tms 1969, Master Mixed Tms 1983, placed second in LM Womens Prs 1969, Womens BAM 1986. Numerous regional wins include Can-Am KO Tms 1972, Canadian Nat'l Womens Tms 1981.

ALLOUCHE, Danielle (b. 1956) of Paris, France. WBF World Life Master. Second World Women's Teams 1987, third 1985. Won European Women's Teams 1983, 1985, 1987. Represented France in two other world championships and won many national titles.

ALPAUGH, Nancy T. (formerly Mrs. Ray Zoller) of New Orleans, former bridge teacher, a Diamond LM, won the World Mixed Tms 1972, Womens KO Tms 1978, 84, Womens Swiss 1988, Womens Prs 1986; Master Mixed Tms 1977, 78, 79, North American Womens Swiss 1982, second in Womens KO Tms 1991; Womens BAM Tms 1990. She has many regional titles to her credit including Fall secondary Swiss 1981, Summer secondary Womens Prs 1979, 81.

ALPERN, Steven R. (The Dragon) (b. 1943) of San Diego, real estate investor, bridge professional, schooled at Western Illinois U. National Merit Scholar, represented college in chess and table tennis. Other interests are genealogy, classic cars, Oriental cuisine and stamp collecting. Certified director since 1972. Won Fall secondary Swiss 1979, Summer secondary Golder Prs 1974, Canadian Nat'l KOs 1975, Rockford BAM 1978, Central St. Swiss 1979, 80; Spring secondary Swiss 1993.

ALTAY, Andrew J. (Andy) (b. 1947 in Hungary) of Toronto, data processing manager, graduated U of Toronto. Has served on Unit 166 Bd of Dir and Bd of Dir of CBF, was national co-ordinator of Canadian National team championships for the first three years of its existence. Won Can-At Swiss, Fleur-De-Lys Swiss, Dist. 2 GN Tms, Sudbury Open Prs, Canadian National KOs (twice) and Syracuse KOs.

ALTER, William N. of Farmingdale NY, ACBL accredited teacher, graduated NYU, Alter pioneered in the field of teaching bridge to the hearing impaired.

ALTMAN, Steven B. (b. 1943) of Tenafly NJ, options trader, an original member of the PRECISION TEAM.

He coached the U.S. Bermuda Bowl teams in the 1973 and 1977 Bermuda Bowls (won in 1977). Won the Spingold 1970, 71; Vanderbilt 1972, Morehead Trophy 1967, *London Sunday Times* Prs 1973, placed second in the Reisinger 1967, Spingold 1968, 78. He also has won numerous regionals. Retired from tournament play in 1981.

ALTUS, Stephen S. (b.1969) of Stanford CA, graduate student, graduated from U of Michigan and Stanford U, collector of more than 3000 airline schedules, member of ACBL Junior Corps, collegiate coordinator of Youth Bridge Federation 1988-90 and a certified director. Won Summer NABC Jr Prs 1990, Bal Harbour Flt B Tms 1986, Tampa Open Tms, Denver Flt B KO Tms 1988, Southfield Mens Prs 1989, Rye Jr. regional Open Tms 1990.

ALUJAS, Gustavo (b. 1952) of Buenos Aires, Argentina, bridge teacher. WBF World Master. South American Champion 1981 and represented Argentina in the Bermuda Bowl the same year. 9 national titles won include open teams 3 times.

ALVAREZ, Jaime Carrera, (b. 1956) of Girardot, Colombia, teacher and computer programmer. Won CAAC Open Teams 1980, 1989, runner-up 1987. Runner-up South American Open Teams and Open Pairs 1985, Junior Teams 1979, 1980. Represented Colombia in one world championship, and is its top-ranked player, with wins in all national events.

AMARAL, Marcelo (b. 1949) of Sao Paulo, Brazil, engineer. Won South American Teams 1974, 1988, 1993, and represented Brazil in three world championships.

ANDERSEN, Eilif B. (1907-1977) of Los Angeles, president of the ACBL in 1966 and member of the Board of Directors from 1956-58 and 1961-67. Chaired the finance, building fund, headquarters site and other important committees, sponsored the ACBL's acceptance of the district organization plan. In the early Sixties Andersen founded and presided over the Association of Los Angeles County Bridge Units (ALACBU), and in 1967 was elected president of the Western Conference. He also founded and edited "Southern California Bridge News".

ANDERSEN, Ronald E. (Ron) (b. 1941) of Chicago, formerly of New York City and Dallas, options trader and professional bridge writer, player and teacher, one of the most successful American players. A WBF World Master and an ACBL Grand Life Master with more than 31,000 masterpoints, number three on the list of members with greatest total points. Involved in a host of bridge activities, he lectures, hosts panel shows and emcees bridge programs at NABCs, regionals all over North America and at international bridge tournaments throughout the world. For several years he has hosted and coordinated vugraph presentations at NABCs and has been the chief vugraph commentator at the European Championships. Placed sixth in World Open Prs 1978, eighth 1982, tied for fifth place in 1984 World Tm Olympiad. Finished third in the 1990 resumption of the *London Times Invitational*, won the *London Times* Charity Pro-Am event 1991, won the Proton Invitational

Tms in Taipei 1990. In 1981 Andersen played in the first international bridge tournament ever held in mainland China (Shanghai). He delivered a lecture at Chinese U in Shanghai with the aid of Katherine Wei as translator. He is the developer of DOOP and contributor to the development of the PRECISION SYSTEM. Editor-in-chief of Devyn Press's *Championship Bridge Series* and author of two pamphlets in the series titled *Killing Their Notrump* and *Matchpoint Tactics*. Edited four books on Precision, was associate editor of *International Precision Newsletter*, has written articles for the ACBL *Bulletin* and several other bridge periodicals throughout the world. He has authored *Where and How High, Lebensold* and is the co-author of *Matchpoint Precision, Making the Most of Your Limited Opening Bids, Profits From Preempts, Perfect Your Notrump Bidding*, and *Action for the Defense* and *Preempts from A to Z*. Was coach and acting captain of the U.S. Venice Trophy team that reached the finals in Rye NY 1981, and was npc of the Venice Trophy team that reached the semifinals in Yokohama 1991. In 1974 he won the Mott-Smith Trophy with a record 250 masterpoints. Four-time winner of *McKenney Top 500* (more than any other living player), he was the first to win more than 2000 masterpoints in one year (2009 MPs 1977, 2725 MPs 1980, 2994 MPs 1983). His national titles include Life Master Mens Prs 1970, Mixed Tms 1971, Mens Tms 1974, Blue Ribbon Prs 1978, Reisinger 1980, 92; Life Master Prs 1982, Spingold 1983, 88, 86; Mens Swiss 1989. He placed second in the Vanderbilt 1974, 77, 79, 80; Open Prs 1974, Blue Ribbon Prs 1975, Spingold 1990. Has won hundreds of regional events.

ANDERSON, A.T. Rex (b. 1945) of Coleraine, Northern Ireland, solicitor. WBF World Master. Third European Team Championship 1979, and represented Ireland on three other occasions and in two world championships. Represented Northern Ireland regularly in Camrose Trophy matches since 1971. National titles include open teams 11 times and open pairs 8 times.

ANDERSON, Janice (Jan) (b. 1952) of Regina SK, Canadian Bridge Federation coordinator, former parent aide with Social Services and teacher, graduate U of Regina. Involved with Canadian Foundation of Ileitis and Colitis, has been Unit 573 Sec/Treas since 1978, CBF Coordinator since 1989, certified director since 1979 and manager of Regina DBC 1991. Has been on numerous sectional committees and helped husband (RICHARD ANDERSON) when he chaired three regionals.

ANDERSON, John C. (Big John) (b. 1942) of Sixes OR, bridge professional, formerly taught school at both the elementary and college levels, certified director, Dist 20 Board member and director of district Player Education Program. One of the leading bridge personalities of the Northwest, a Grand Life Master with more than 13,000 MP. Won Master Mixed Tms 1971. His dozens of regional sucesses include four wins at Regina regional in 1971 (KO Tms, Swiss, Masters Prs, Open Prs) and 14 or more other multi-win tournaments.

ANDERSON, Richard G. (Dick) (b. 1940) of Regina SK, teacher, educated U of Saskatchewan and U of Regina. Recipient of Wilma Downing Award for coaching high-school athletics. Has served as Unit treasurer,

Unit president, Canadian Bridge Federation Bd member, CBF president and treasurer. Became member of ACBL Bd of Dir in 1992. Has chaired three regionals and numerous sectionals. A certified director since 1979 and a contributor to *WASUMI*. Winner of Winnipeg Swiss 1985 and Regina Swiss 1987.

ANDERSON, Virgil V. Jr. (b. 1924) of Springfield MO, ACBL president 1994, attorney and president of Anderson and Son, Inc. Educated at Drury College and U of MO Law School. Anderson's interests include photography, theater, travel and politics. Has acted in some 75 plays (college, community theater and professionally), is active in Springfield area Arts Council, former president Springfield Little Theatre, former member of Missouri House of Representatives and Springfield Chamber of Commerce. Directed summer camps for boys and served on Bd of Directors of the Gus Giordano Dancers. Has served as president of Dist. 15, MO Valley Conference, Unit 101; vice president of Dist. 15, member ACBL Bd. of Gov. and Chairman Tournament Committee 1991 International Team Trials. He is currently a member of ACBL Bd. of Directors (since 1989), Dist. 15 Bd of Directors, Unit 101 Bd of Directors. He won Silver Ribbon Prs 1994, also District 15 Flighted Open Prs, Open Prs 1988, Mens Prs 1989, Open Prs, KO Tms 1991.

ANDRESS, Patricia (Tricia) (b. 1968) (nee: Thomas) of Nashville TN, undergrad student at New Mexico SU 1986-91, currently working on master's in voice performance at Middle TN State U. Won New Mexico NATS competition 1990 (for singing). Enjoys all aspects of music, downhill skiing and active in church. Has played tournament bridge since age of 9, became youngest Life Master at 14 in 1982. While living in Scotland made it to the semifinals of Scottish Nat'l Prs at age 12. Qualified to be on Jr Team to play in World Jr Championship in 1991 but was unable to play. Has won Cincinnati Flt B Swiss 1984, Albuquerque Flt B KO and Flt B Open Prs, Champaign Womens Swiss, Lincoln Womens Swiss, Arlington Womens Prs, OK City Swiss 1985; Arlington KOs 1986, CO Spgs Open Prs, Fall NABC secondary Silver Trophy Prs 1987.

ANDREW, Mollie (b. 1936) of Belfast, Northern Ireland. Won Lady Milne Cup twice, and represented Northern Ireland more than 20 times in the contest against England, Scotland and Wales. Also represented N. Ireland in the Camrose Trophy and Ireland in the Europa Cup. Has won all N. Ireland national titles.

ANSAY, Nadine. See LIECHTENSTEIN, PRINCESS NADINE VON.

ANTHONISEN, Lorraine (Laurie) (nee: King, formerly Hathaway) of Altadena CA, teacher, graduated U of Kansas and U of Kansas Graduate School, interests include gourmet baking, ceramics and Siamese cat breeding. Went on a USO tour to Northeast Command while at U of KS. Has won many regionals including Pacific Southwest Womens Prs 1978, Open Prs 1983, Swiss 1990; Raincross Open Prs 1981, Bridge Week Open Prs 1987, 88, 91; San Bernardino Swiss 1991.

ANTHONISEN, Robert (Rob) (b. 1941) of Altadena CA, sales representative. Interests include golfing and sports, was editor of Diablo Valley District Newsletter for two years. Became certified director in 1971. Has dubious record of highest score on a board, +4600, and lowest score, -5800. Has won Golden Gate Swiss 1977, 78; Holiday Open Prs 1979, Raincross Open Prs 1981, Pacific SW Mens Prs 1981, Open Prs 1983, Swiss 1990; Bridge Wk Open Prs 1984, 87, 88, Mens Swiss 1985; Pasadena Winter Mayors Cup 1984, Open Prs 1986; Inland Empire Swiss 1991.

ANTUNE, Hugo Carve (b. 1943) of Montevideo, Uruguay, Procurator. Second South American Teams 1980 and represented Uruguay regularly in zonal championships since then. He has won 25 national titles.

ANTUNES, Manuel Costa (b. 1930) of Lisbon, Portugal, civil engineer. Represented Portugal in three European championships. National wins include open teams seven times and open pairs three times.

ARIMA, Keiichi (b. 1916) of Tokyo, Japan, company director. Flying officer Japanese Navy 1936-45. Chairman JCBL Board of Directors, and manager 1964 Far East Championships. Recipient Fourth Class Order of the Sacred Treasure.

APFEL, Dr. Kalman (1907-1988) of West Palm Beach FL, physician, won the Vanderbilt 1954, Spingold 1956. His regional wins include Summer secondary Golder Prs 1952, Non-Master Prs 1942, Sub-Senior Master Tms 1946, Eastern States KO Tms 1966, New York Winter Swiss 1974.

APFELBAUM, Jay M. (b. 1951) of Pittsburgh, Regional 1 director, graduate of Temple U, won the Blue Ribbon Prs 1976 and Mid-Atlantic Summer KO Tms 1974.

APPLEYARD, Robert (1909-1984) of New York City, bridge teacher and club director, won the Chicago (since 1965 the Reisinger) 1947, Vanderbilt 1948, Life Master Prs 1939, 45; placed second in Life Master Prs 1936, Fall Master Individual 1950, 56, Mens Tms 1950.

ARLAZAROV, Dr. Victor of Moscow, Russia, businessman. Represented Soviet Union, or C.I.S, in two world championships and one zonal championship. National wins include open teams once.

ARLINGHAUS, Dr. William Charles (b. 1944) of Ann Arbor MI, professor of math and computer science, educated Wayne St., Ph.D. U of Detroit, summa cum laude; graduate study U of Chicago and U of Toronto. Golfer with two holes-in-one. Listed in *Who's Who in the Midwest*. Served on Michigan BA Bd. of Dir. as president, chairman of board and tournament chairman. Chief scorer and co-chairman for hospitality WBF NEC World Jr Championship, Ann Arbor 1991. Occasional contributor to MBA newsletter, *Table Talk*, became certified director 1984. Won Great Lakes Swiss Team 1983, 89.

ARMSTRONG, John (b. 1952) of Formby, England, actuary and systems analyst. WBF World Master. Second Bermuda Bowl 1987. Won European Teams 1991, second 1987. Represented Britain in three other world championships, three other zonal championships and

England in 25 Camrose Trophy matches. Many national wins include Gold Cup four times.

ARNARSON, Gudmundur Pall (b. 1954) of Reykjavik, Iceland, publisher, teacher and writer. WBF World Master. Won Bermuda Bowl 1991. Represented Iceland in two other world championships, three European championships and two Nordic Championships. Four national wins include open teams twice and open pairs once. Publisher and editor of Icelandic bridge magazine. Writer of daily column for *Morgunbladid* and author of bridge books. Owner of Iceland's only bridge school.

ARNIM, Daniela von (b. 1964) of Wiesbaden, Germany. WBF World Master. Second Venice Cup 1993. Won European Women's Teams 1989, runner-up 1991. Represented Germany in Venice Cup 1989, 1991. Won ACBL Women's Swiss Teams 1990.

ARNOLD, Rodger S. (b. 1947) of Aurora CO, driver, once had a streak of 25 consecutive Swiss Team match wins with various partners. Regional wins include Wichita Swiss 1980, 1982; Rocky Mtn Open Swiss 1990, Pike's Peak Open Prs, Swiss 1991.

ARNOLD, Russell D. (b. 1927) of Miami, accountant and partner in a major appliance company, graduated U of Minnesota, enjoys tennis. Bermuda Bowl champion in 1981 and in 1986 competed in the Rosenblum Cup Tms. Life Master in the WBF and a Diamond Life Master in the ACBL. His nat'l wins include Spingold 1963, 85; GN Tms 1973, Reisinger 1979, Vanderbilt 1980, 93. He placed second in the Vanderbilt 1960, GN Tms 1980, and Spingold 1987. Has won more than 100 regional events including Florida KO Tms 1969, Mid-Atlantic KO Tms 1974, North Florida KO Tms, Mens Prs, Open Prs 1980.

ARNOLDS, Carla (b. 1960), of Tilburg, the Netherlands, bridge teacher and journalist. WBF World Master. Second Venice Cup 1989. Third World Women's Pairs 1990. Represented the Netherlands in three other world championships and two European Championships. National titles include Women's Pairs 1991. She is a columnist.

ARNTHORSSON, Orn (b. 1945) of Reykjavik, Iceland, pension funds manager. WBF World Master. Won Bermuda Bowl 1991. Represented Iceland in six other world championships, six European Championships and one Nordic Championship. Ten national wins include open teams five times and open pairs twice.

ARON, Adrien (1902-c.1970) of Paris, France, bridge writer. European Champion 1935. Represented France at Plafond against Ely Culbertson in 1933. Author of two books and many articles.

ARONSON, Sidney (b. 1911) of Pompano Beach FL, retired attorney and Deputy Assistant Inspector General, U.S. Department of Agriculture, graduate of Suffolk Law School. Has served as president and tournament chairman of New England BA and authored articles for *The Bridge World* in the Forties. Won the Chicago (since 1965 the Reisinger) 1949 and placed second in the Life Master Prs in 1959. Regional wins include New England

Mens Prs 1938, Open Prs 1941, Master Prs 1942, Mixed Prs 1949, Master Tms 1950; Mid-Atlantic KOs Fall 1971, Summer 1972, Winter Open Prs 1965, Open Tms 1966; Central FL Mens Prs 1988.

AROSEMENA, Carlos (b. 1924) of Lima, Peru, businessman. Represented Peru in one world championship and several zonal championships. Won several national titles. Bridge teacher.

AROSEMENA, Teresa (b. 1933) of Lima, Peru, bridge teacher. Represented Peru in two world championships and many zonal championships. Won many national titles. President of Peruvian Bridge Commission.

ARST, Frieda (1906-1985) of Chicago, bridge teacher, won Womens Tms 1966, Life Master Womens Prs 1973, second in Womens Tms 1972, numerous regional wins.

ARVEDON, Lloyd B. (b. 1953) of Medford MA, school fund-raising representative, graduated Boston State College, enjoys sports, politics and the psychic realm. Served on Eastern MA BA board 1985-87. A Diamond Life Master with more than 35 regional wins including Keohane Individual KO Tms, New England KO Tms, IMP Prs, Dist. 25 GN Prs three times.

ASBER, A. Joseph (b. 1932) of Behlehem PA. structural steel draftsman and checker, schooled at English-Moravian College. Past Pres, Unit 133, became certified club director 1962. Won Can-Am Open Prs 1955, Eastern States Open Prs, Goldman Pairs 1971; Mid-Atlantic Mens Swiss 1976, Dist, 4 GN Tms 1979, Zone II GN Tms 1991.

ASHLEY, David D. (b. 1941) of Las Vegas, expert bridge, backgammon and poker player, also enjoys bowling, wrestling and football handicapping, connoisseur of fine wines. Currently serving on the National Conduct and Ethics Committee. He is a certified director and directs on cruises. A Grand Life Master with more than 12,000 masterpoints, his national titles include Mens BAM Tms 1976, North American Swiss 1982. He placed second in LM Mens Prs 1987. Ashley has more than 100 regional wins including Rocky Mountain KO Tms, Mens Prs 1971; Bridge Week Mixed Tms 1970, BAM Tms 1972, KO Tms 1978; Pacific Southwest Open Prs 1969, 1970, Swiss 1976; Mid-Winter Holiday KO Tms 1974, Open Prs 1976, Swiss 1979, Mens Prs 1981; Gem State Flt. A Swiss 1980, Open Prs, Master Prs 1981; Sacramento KO Tms, Open Prs 1991.

ASMENIADIS, Nikos (b. 1931) of Thessaloniki, Greece, civil engineer. Honorary Vice-President of the Hellenic Bridge Federation and a member of its Board for nearly 20 years. International tournament director, with involvement in computerizing various bridge events. Founded the first club in Thessaloniki. Translated Edgar Kaplan's *Winning Contract Bridge* into Greek. Won several national events.

ASSOUAD-DOCHE, Marie Lucette (b. 1947) of Cairo, Egypt. Middle East Women's Team Champion 1991, runner-up 1989. Represented Egypt 1991 Venice Cup.

ASSUMPÇAO, Pedro Paulo Puglisi de (b. 1935) of Sao Paulo, Brazil, retired company director. WBF Grand Master. Won World Teams 1976, second 1978. Represented Brazil in 13 other world championships. Won South American Teams 1967, 1968, 1969, 1970, 1971, 1972, 1973, 1974, 1975, 1977, 1978. Won many national titles.

ÅSTRÖM, Lisbeth (Lisa) (b.1955) of Sweden, immigration camp manager. Third Venice Cup 1993. Won European Womens Teams 1993, Nordic Women's Teams 1982. Represented Sweden in two other zonal championships and won three national titles.

ATA-ULLAH, Munir Ahmed (b. 1940 in Pakistan) of London, formerly of Pakistan and Dubai, lawyer and managing director. (*Mooney*). WBF World Master. Second Bermuda Bowl 1981. Won BFAME zonal championship 1983, 1985 and 1987. Won many national titles. Inventor of "Stoneage Acol with Paki Preempts" system. Bridge theoretician who contributes to newspapers and magazines.

ATHANASSIADIS, Alexandros (b. 1954) of Thessaloniki, Greece, bridge teacher and journalist. National wins include Open Pairs 1986. Writes a daily newspaper column in Thessaloniki and a weekly one in Macedonia. Former vice-president of Hellenic Bridge Federation, and represents Northern Greece on its Board. Offers free classes for beginners, and occasionally promotes bridge on national television.

ATTAGUILE, Luis (b. 1926) of Buenos Aires, Argentina, clerk. World Life Master. South American Champion 1961, 1962, 1964, 1976, 1979, 1980. 1981, 1985. Represented Argentina in Bermuda Bowl 1962, 1963, 1965, 1977, 1985, in World Team Olympiad 1964, 1980. 15 national wins include Open Teams 11 times and Open Pairs once. Gabarret Cup 1961.

AUGUST, William J. (Bill) (b. 1926) of Palm Beach FL, bridge teacher, author, columnist, certified director and former bridge club owner. Was affiliated with Goren International 1962-76 lecturing on cruises and teaching classes for training teachers. Authored several pamphlets on bidding and directing, teaching texts, a duplicate bridge instructional club directors manual, articles for the International Bridge Press Association. Devised the August Two-Diamond Convention (see TWO-WAY STAYMAN). Former president and vice president of the New England Bridge Conference and vice-president of the ABTA. During the administration of Easley Blackwood was a special consultant to the ACBL regarding club matters, membership and club/unit/league relations. Created, with Blackwood, the method of formulating the present day masterpoint awards. Has won more than a dozen regional titles including Long Island Master Prs 1969, Southeastern Open Tms 1970, New England Master Prs 1974, Summer NABC secondary Mens Swiss 1990.

AUKEN, Jens (b. 1949) of Copenhagen, Denmark, lawyer. WBF World Master. Third World Teams 1984 and represented Denmark in one other world championship and four zonal championships. 20 national titles include open team five times and open pairs four times. Top Danish masterpoint winner five times. Won Nordic Club

Cup 1990 and European Club Cup 1990. Member EBL executive committee and a specialist in laws of bridge. Legal consultant for the Danish Federation.

AVARELLI, Walter (1912-1987) of Rome, Italy, judge. WBF Grand Master and fifth in world career rankings at the time of his death. Won World Teams 1964, 1968, 1972, Bermuda Bowl 1957, 1958, 1959, 1961, 1962, 1965, 1966, 1967, 1969. Won European Teams 1956, 1957, 1958, 1959. See BLUE TEAM and LANCIA TEAM.

AVELINO, Ronaldo (b. 1949) of Rio de Janeiro, Brazil, engineer. Won South American Teams 1986, 1987. Represented Brazil in two world championships.

AWAD, George L. (b. 1923 in Egypt) of Paris, France, systems computer analyst and former engineer, represented Egypt in the World Tm Olympiad 1964. Regional wins include All-Western Mixed Prs 1961, Florida Life Master Mixed Prs 1968, Long Island KO Tms 1969, Mixed Prs 1970; Fun City KO Tms 1970, Eastern States Reisinger KO Tms 1972.

AWAD, Marie (Mrs. George) (b. 1924) of Paris, France, born in Egypt, retired French teacher and tax consultant, represented Egypt in the World Team Olympiad 1964. Regional wins include All-Western Mixed Prs 1961, Florida LM Prs 1968, Long Island KO Tms 1969, Mixed Prs 1970; Fun City Tms KOs 1970, Eastern States Reisinger KO Tms 1972.

AYDIN, Ata (b. 1957) of Istanbul, Turkey, business administrator. Represented Turkey in two zonal championships. Seven national wins include open teams four times.

B

BABIN, Elmer J. (1902-1990) of Shaker Heights OH, attorney, ACBL president 1940, graduate of Harvard and Western Reserve Law School. Played first duplicate in March 1930, won Open State Prs championship the following month and won the AWL Open Prs two months later. Also won Western States Open Tms 1934, Open Prs 1939, before retiring from tournament play in 1951.

BABSCH, Andreas (b.1961) of Vienna, Austria, bridge teacher. Represented Austria in three world championships, two European open championships and seven other European events. Won national open teams twice, Life Master Individual twice, and Open Pairs. Youngest-ever Austrian Life Master.

BABSCH, Fritz (b. 1933) of Vienna, Austria, civil engineer, bridge journalist and tournament director. WBF World Life Master. World Pairs Champion 1970. Represented Austria in one World Team Olympiad and six European Championships. Won Caransa Tournament (Amsterdam). Won seven national team titles and one pair title. Chief organizer most Austrian tournaments since late 70s. Tournament Director several European Championships. Editor Austrian Bridge Magazine 1971-90. Bridge columnist of *Kurier*. He is an expert on Alpine flora.

BACH, Norman (1913-1971) of Bermuda, initiated and organized the first post-World War II World Championships held in Bermuda in 1950. These games are now known as the BERMUDA BOWL. Won the GOLD CUP for Great Britain in 1938 and was playing captain of the British team in the European Championships in 1938 and 1939.

BACHELDER, James Wallace (Bach) (b. 1946) of Columbus OH, tax auditor, graduated from Ohio State U. Hobbies are coin collecting, stock market and computers. A Vietnam veteran with 20 years in the Navy. Since 1985 has served as a board member of Unit 122 (past president) and Dist. 11 and as Unit GN Tms and NAOP Coordinator. Regional wins include Dayton Swiss 1986, Pittsburgh Mens Swiss 1988, Cincinnati Strat Prs 1990, Columbus KO Tms, Lexington KO Tms 1991; Dayton Swiss 1992, Cleveland Open Swiss 1993.

BACHERICH, René of Lille, France, retired merchant. WBF Grand Master. Won World Teams 1956 and 1960. Won European Teams 1953, 1955, 1962, second 1956, 1961. Represented France in four other world championships. National wins include Open Teams once. See RELAY SYSTEM.

BACON, Francis M. III (1899-1983) of New York City, stockbroker. In 1975, as the only surviving member of the first game of contract bridge played aboard the *S.S. FINLAND* on Nov. 1, 1925, he contributed much new information regarding the background of the origin of the game and helped to pinpoint its date.

BAER, Henry (b. 1930) of Dallas TX, born in Germany, attorney, graduate of Southern Methodist U. Served as executive secretary for Dist 16 since 1960. Member ACBL Goodwill Committee, Dist GN Tms and tournament coordinator. Received ACBL Presidential Citation for service in 1992. Regional wins include Hawaii Open Tms 1965, MO Valley Tms 1970, Texas Mixed Prs 1970, 71; Internat'l City Open Prs 1974, Texas Spring Swiss 1976, Mexican Fiesta Open Prs 1980, Masters Prs 1985.

BAFF, Charlotte (Char) (b. 1926) of Beachwood OH, graduated Ohio State U. Regional wins include Niagara Falls Sr Swiss, All American Womens Swiss 1985, 87; Babe Ruth Sr Swiss 1987, Knoxville Sr KO Tms, Sr Swiss 1989; Grand Rapids Sr Swiss 1989; Indianapolis Summer Sr Swiss 1990, Open Prs 1990, 92, KO Tms 1990, KO Tms 1991; Mid-Atlantic Sr KO Tms 1990, Callaway Gardens Sr Bracketed KO Tms 1991, 92, Williamsburg Sr KO Tms 1993, and six Senior Prs.

BAFF, Martin (Marty) (b. 1927) of Beachwood OH, founder and retired president of wholesale plumbing supply firm, graduate Ohio State U. Won all events at a 1985 sectional tournament. A Diamond Life Master with more than 50 regional wins including All American Swiss 1975, Mens Swiss 1979, 83, Mens Prs 1987, KO Tms 1984, 85, 87, Open Swiss 1991; Canadian Nat'l Mens Prs 1977, Dist 5 GN Tms, Zone IV 1981; Glass City Masters Prs 1984, Mens Prs 1986, Mens Swiss 1988; GN Prs 1985, 87; Pittsburg Labor Day Mens Prs 1987, Swiss 1989, Open Prs, Strat Prs, Open Prs 1992.

BAGUZIN, Dr. Sergei (b. 1961) of Moscow, Russia,

editor. Represented Soviet Union, or C.I.S, in two world championships and one zonal championship. National wins include open teams once. Editor of *Bridj*.

BAINS, Kenneth Richard (b. 1944) of Dallas TX, company president specializing in the financing of commercial income properties, educated at Texas Christian U and U of Texas. Won Hot Springs Masters Prs, Dallas Mens Tms 1974; Amarillo Swiss 1976, 80; San Antonio Swiss 1976; Houston Silver Trophy Open, OK City Swiss, Fort Worth Mens Prs, Wichita Swiss 1978; Tulsa Open Prs 1981.

BAIRD, James C. (1878-1963) Lived in a town named after him, Baird MS. Headed the Mississippi unit twice, ACBL Honorary Member in 1951. His wife, Mary Elizabeth Baird, was ACBL Honorary Member in 1947, the year she died.

BAKALISH, Robert (Bob) (b. 1957) of Sunnyvale CA, salesman, educated at San Francisco State U. Won San Francisco KO Tms 1977, San Jose Open Swiss 1980, 81; San Francisco Swiss 1983, Santa Clara Swiss 1990, Yakima Open Prs 1991.

BAKKER, Ellen (b. 1958), of Amsterdam, The Netherlands, systems analyst. WBF World Master. Second Venice Cup 1989 and represented the Netherlands in two other world championships and two European Championships. National titles include Women's Pairs 1991.

BALAILA, Jack (b. 1923) of Haifa, Israel, travel agent, represented Israel World Team Olympiad 1964, European Championships 1966. Born in Beirut, he played with Lebanese team before moving to Israel in 1954 where he was a member of the Israeli team in subsequent years. National successes include Open Pairs 1962.

BALDON, Suzanne (b. 1920) of Paris, France, was European champion 1953, 1954. Represented France World Women's Teams 1964, European Women's Championships 1957, 1967. National wins include Women's Teams several times.

BALDURSSON, Jon (b. 1954) of Reykjavik, Iceland, airline manager. Iceland's most successful player in recent years. WBF World Master. Won Bermuda Bowl 1991, Nordic Teams 1988. Second Cavendish Invitational 1990. Represented Iceland in six other world championships, five European Championships, four other Nordic Championships and one European Junior Championship. 15 national wins include open teams six times and open pairs four times.

BALDWIN, Robert H. (Bobby) (b. 1950) of Las Vegas NV, president and CEO of the Mirage Resort. Won four world championships in three different forms of poker and has written two books about poker. Won King Cotton KO Tms 1975, Land of Coronado Swiss, Missouri Valley KO Tms 1976; Oklahoma City Mens Swiss 1981.

BALDWIN, Col. Russell J. (1889-1969) of Norwalk CT, Army officer and expert on tournament procedure. Was active as organizer from the earliest days of contract bridge, became a director of American Bridge League and its treasurer shortly after it was founded in 1927. A member of the ACBL Laws Commission since its inception in 1933, Baldwin was primarily responsible for the first Duplicate Code issued in 1935 and played a considerable part in formulating subsequent codes. Authored the McKenney-Baldwin schedules for HOWELL MOVEMENTS and constructed other movements, devised a method to handle fouled boards. Was active as a tournament director 1927-41, after war service became ABCL business manager, 1946-51, was recalled to military service at the outbreak of the Korean War, returned to ACBL in charge of tournament scheduling 1958-63. Was ACBL Honorary Member in 1943. Wrote many magazine articles and was a contributing editor to the *Bridge Encyclopedia*.

BALDWIN, William A. (1907-1978) of Albuquerque NM, building and land developer. As 1970 ACBL president, was the person most instrumental in relocating national headquarters to Memphis. Was president of the Western Conference, trustee of the Charity Foundation, chairman of the ACBL Bd of Dir 1971, ACBL Honorary Member in 1978, ACBL representative to the WBF and treasurer of that body.

BALFE, Raymond A. (1895-1969) of New York City, enjoyed the distinction of winning national championships in both auction and contract bridge, taking the 1926 All-American Open Prs (auction) title with Waldemar von Zedtwitz as well as the 1936 USBA Grand Nat'l Mixed Tms (contract).

BALICKI, Cezary (b. 1958) of Wroclaw, Poland, bridge professional and chess instructor. WBF World Life Master. Second Bermuda Bowl 1991. Third World Open Pairs 1990. Won European Open Teams 1989. Represented Poland in three other world championships and two other zonal championships. Won Del Duca. Many national wins include Open Teams.

BALLANTYNE, Aldan (b. 1951) of Vancouver BC, born in Switzerland, consultant in environmental planning and private bridge teacher, educated at Simon Fraser U. Member of Canadian World Cup Ski Team (alpine) 1969-73, past president of Canadian Bridge Federation, member CBF Bd of Dir since 1985, member Unit 430 Conduct and Ethics Committee since 1983, member ABCL Goodwill Committee, certified director. Won Calgary Calcutta 1991, was NPC of Canadian team, 1991 Bermuda Bowl in Yokohama. Has won Peach City Masters Swiss 1978, Vancouver Mens Prs, Inland Empire KO Tms 1979; Emerald City Open Swiss 1983, Victoria Swiss 1984, Ocean Shores Open Prs 1987, Ottawa KO Tms, non-smoking Swiss 1988; Victoria Open Prs 1989, Red Deer Open Prs 1989, Vancouver KO Tms, Swiss 1990; White Hat Swiss 1991, Vancouver Open Swiss, KO Tms 1992.

BALLESTEROS, Carmen (b. 1922) of Rizal, Philippines. Won Far East Teams 1957. Represented Philippines in one world championship and two other zonal championships. National wins include open teams once.

BAMBERGER, Gabriele (b. 1953) of Vienna, bridge teacher. WBF World Master. Won European Women's Teams 1991, runner-up Venice Cup 1991. Represented

Austria in two World Team Olympiads and five other European events. Won three National Open Team titles, one Open Pair title and three Mixed Pair titles.

BAMBERGER, Johannes (b. 1946) of Vienna, publishing company employee. WBF World Master. Represented Austria in one World Team Olympiad and three European Championships. Won Caransa Tournament (Amsterdam). Won five National Open Team titles and three Mixed Pair titles.

BANDONI, Franco (b. 1942) of Toronto, born in Italy, represented Canada in the World Team Olympiad 1976. Regional wins include Canadian Nat'l KO Tms 1971, 80, Swiss 1971, 79, Master Prs 1974, Mens Swiss 1978, Open Prs 1981; Dist 2 GN Teams 1973, GN Pairs 1979, 80; All-American Master Prs 1976, Dist 5 Mens Swiss 1980.

BANK, Julius (b. 1913) of Chicago, CPA, attended NYU and John Marshall Law School. Bank became Life Master #63 in 1946 and was among the Top Ten players that year. He won Mens Tms 1946 and placed second in the Spingold 1948. Regional wins include Atlantic City Open Prs 1936, All-American Open Tms 1944, Central States Open Tms 1947, 56.

BAQAI, Iftikhar (b. 1946), of California. WBF World Master. Born in Pakistan, which he represesnted internationally. Won BFAME zonal championship 1987 and played in 1987 Bermuda Bowl.

BARAN, Boris (b. 1945) of Montreal, born in Switzerland, professor of computer information systems, educated at McGill U and Wayne State U. Plays organized softball and once was a nationally rated swimmer. Ranks third in lifetime masterpoints in Canada and is a three-time runner-up for the Richmond Trophy. WBF World Master and ACBL Diamond Life Master, has represented Canada in world championship competition six times, was a bronze medalist in the Rosenblum Cup Tms and a silver medalist in the Pan American Open Tms 1992. Won the Epson World Towers competition (E-W) 1990 and the Icelandair Invitational Prs in 1991, the NA Prs in 1991, North American Swiss 1992 and placed second in the GN Prs 1990. In Canada won the Canadian Nat'l Team Championship 1983, 85, 87, 89, 91; placed second in the CNTC 1986, 88, 90 and won the Canadian Open Prs Championship in 1985. His numerous regionals include Spring NABC secondary Swiss 1979, Canadian Nat'l KO Tms 1982, 83, 85, 89, 93, Open Prs 1981, 87, 90, 91; Dist. l GN Prs 1979, 85, 86, 87, 88, 90, 91, 93.

BARATTA, Franz (B. 1935 in Czechoslovakia) of Vienna, Austria, managing director. Represented Austria in two World Team Olympiads and four European Championships. Won National Open Team title. NPC winning Austrian team 1985 European Championship, and on many other occasions.

BARBEY, Henry I. (1832-1906) of New York City is credited with introducing bridge to New York in 1893. He is best remembered for writing the first code of laws for the new game, dated 1892.

BARBONE, Guido (b. 1925) of Italy, columnist and bridge writer, was npc of Italian Team Bermuda Bowl 1967, npc winning Women's Team in European Championships 1977, second-place Women's Team Venice Trophy 1978. Former president ITALIAN BRIDGE FEDERATION, member of executive committee of EBL, vice president of IBPA since 1981. Writings include *The Complete Book of Bridge, Funny Bridge* and *Complete Book of Duplicate Bridge*.

BARBOSA, Jose (b. 1936) of Rio de Janeiro, Brazil, engineer. Won South American Teams 1977, 1978, 1986, 1987, 1993. Represented Brazil in three world championships.

BARBOSA, Juliano (b.1950) of Lisbon, Portugal, civil engineer. Represented Portugal in one European Championship. National wins include open teams twice.

BARBOSA, Sergio Marinho (b. 1942) of Rio de Janeiro, Brazil, engineer and economist. Educational insurance executive. WBF World Life Master. Won World Teams 1976, second 1978. Won South American Teams 1971, 1983, 1984. Represented Brazil in six other world championships. National wins include open teams seven times.

BARBOUR, Kenneth R. (b. 1938) of Paradise Valley AZ, born in Scotland, computer executive, educated at Cambridge, England, represented Great Britain in the European Championships 1963, won the British Tm Trials 1962, Gold Cup 1963 and placed second in Master Mixed Tms 1970. Before his retirement from bridge he contributed to *The Bridge World*, *British Bridge World* and *Bridge Journal*. Regional wins include New England Mixed Prs 1966, 67, Mixed Tms 1967.

BARCLAY, Shepard (1889-1955) of New York City, was a bridge writer, publisher, lecturer and club director. Bought *Auction Bridge Magazine* in 1927 and sought to make it a mass magazine, featuring the editorship of Milton C. Work and Wilbur C. Whitehead. The magazine failed in 1929, but its mailing list was used by Ely Culbertson to start *The Bridge World*. Barclay conducted a bridge page in the New York *Herald Tribune*, 1929-34, also ranked the ten best players of each year annually for *Collier's* magazine. Conducted bridge clubs and duplicate games, wrote many books on bridge (see BIBLIOGRAPHY, E) and from 1932 until his death wrote a daily feature on bridge for King Features Syndicate. Was a member of the executive committees of the ABL and ACBL 1936-49 and was named ACBL Honorary Member in 1948.

BARDACH, David (1916-1993, born in Poland), book publishing executive and controller. Represented Israel in one world championship and one European Championship. Won Tel Aviv Teams 1977, runner-up in four national events. EBL Honorary Secretary since 1979; member EBL Management Committee. Member WBF Executive Council since 1981. President of Israel Bridge Federation and formerly its Secretary, Treasurer and Chairman of Executive Committee.

BARDOLA, Marcello (b.1925) of Zurich, Switzerland, mathematician. Represented Switzerland in four European Championships, and his national wins include five in Open Teams and four in Open Pairs. President of Swiss Bridge Federation since 1989.

BARE, Dorothy O. (Mrs Gerald) (b. 1923) of Pacific Palisades CA, travel agency owner since 1967, won Master Mixed Tms 1970. Regionals include Pacific Southwest Open Tms 1966, Disneyland Open Tms 1970, Mid-Winter Holiday Swiss 1979, Hawaii Sr Open Prs 1988, Pacific Southwest Sr Open Prs 1989, Fresno Sr Open Prs 1989.

BARE, Gerald W. (b. 1933) of Pacific Palisades CA, civil engineer, graduated from Washington State U. Tied for ninth in the Rosenblum Tms 1990. A Grand Life Master he won Master Mixed Tms 1970 and placed second in the Reisinger 1966. Has won more than 50 regional events including Oregon Trail Open Tms 1961, Bridge Week KO Tms 1973, 77, Swiss 1990; Las Vegas Swiss, Palm Springs Swiss Tms 1971; Pacific Southwest Open Prs 1972, Oil City Master Prs 1978, Los Angeles Winter KO Tms, Master Prs 1979, Open Prs 1980; Hawaii Mcns Swiss 1980.

BARNES, A. Mitchell (Mitch) (1906-1985) of New York City, former executive vice president of Travel With Goren. Became Life Master #14 in 1938. Won many USBA and AWL titles including USBA Grand Nat'l Open Tms 1936, AWL All-American Open Tms 1934, 35. Barnes won Open Prs 1937, Spingold 1941, Chicago (now the Reisinger) 1946 and placed second in Vanderbilt 1933, Spingold 1938, Chicago 1938, 41; Mixed Tms 1934, Mens Tms 1946, USBA Grand Nat'l Open Prs 1934, Mixed Tms 1936.

BARNETT, Harry (b. 1914) of Glasgow, Scotland, re tired bookkeeper/accountant, represented Scotland in nine international matches and was a member of victorious CAMROSE TROPHY team twice. National titles include Open Teams and Open Pairs twice. Reached Scottish Cup semifinal playing with his brothers Michael, Hymie and Sol.

BARNETT, Lewis B. (b. 1934) of Blacksburg VA, assistant Dean of Arts and Sciences, professor of biochemistry, educated at U of Kentucky and U of Iowa (PhD), contributed to The Netherlands' monthly bridge magazine *Bridge*, while a resident of that country. Won Netherlands Open Tms 1962, 63; Jewish Nat'l Fund Open Prs (The Netherlands) 1963. His regional wins are Mid-Atlantic Swiss 1973, 74.

BARNETT, Patricia (Patty) (b. 1951) of Gainesville FL, teacher, won Mixed Prs 1980.

BARNICLE, John F. (b. 1925) of Lutherville MD, educated at Harvard, retired management consultant. Active in bridge administration for more than 30 years, served as president of New Jersey BL, Delaware State BA and Maryland BA, teaches and directs on cruises. Regionals include New England Masters Tms 1950, Dist. 3 Open Tms 1963, 65; Asbury Park Open Prs 1968, Dist 6 Norfolk Open Prs 1976, 78; Dist 6 Open Tms 1976, Open Prs 1979; Dist 6 GN Tms 1980.

BARON, Hermine (Mrs. Arthur) of Los Angeles,

Grand Life Master with more masterpoints than any other woman (more than 22,000). Winner of the *McKenney Trophy* in 1964 and 1970, her winning total of 1370 masterpoints in 1964 stood as the all-time record until 1969. Nat'l titles include Womens Tms 1964, 68, Womens Prs 1968, 82; Life Master Womens Prs 1963; Life Master Prs 1966 and placed second in Spring Womens Tms 1967, 74; Womens Prs 1967, 75, 77, 80; Blue Ribbon Prs 1971. She has won well over 100 regional events. See also HANDICAPPED PLAYERS.

BARON, Leo (b. in England) of Bulawayo, Zimbabwe. High Court judge, at one time Chief Justice of Zambia. Co-inventor of the BARON SYSTEM. Retired from bridge, last heard of as a judge on the Zimbabwe Supreme Court.

BARON, Randall S. (Randy) (b. 1949) of Louisville KY, writer and publisher, graduate of U of Florida, owner and president of Baron Barclay Bridge Supplies, owner of Devyn Press, a certified director and member of Nat'l Goodwill Committee. Served as secretary of Dist 11 for five years, has authored more than 20 books and pamphlets on bridge, including ABTA Book of the Year, *The Bridge Book* with Frank Stewart. Baron is also the author of eight books on the history of baseball, basketball and horse racing. Was chairman and npc of 1993 U.S. Maccabiah bridge team. Regional wins include secondary Silver Trophy Prs Flt B 1977, Florida Mens Prs 1971, Dist 11 KO Tms 1974, 77; Midwest Fall Mens Swiss 1979, Central Florida Open Prs 1980, Great Lakes Master Prs 1981. See BIBLIOGRAPHY, C.

BARRETT, William K. (Billy) (1909-1981) of Atlanta, became one of the youngest players to win a nat'l championship when he and the late Johnny Rau captured the Chicago Trophy (now the Reisinger) in 1930. The two were credited in *Watson's Play of the Hand* and other souces as being the first to use psychic bids in a nat'l tournament. A lawyer, Barrett served two terms in the Georgia House of Representatives.

BARROW, James M. (Jim) (b. 1942) of Phoenix AZ, placed second in the *McKenney Trophy* race 1980, has won more than 50 regional events including North Florida Open Prs 1969, Mens Prs 1979, KO Tms 1980; Mid-South Mens Prs 1970, 71; Southeastern Swiss 1980, Mens Swiss 1975; Mississippi Valley Swiss 1978, 80; Mid-Atlantic Swiss 1978, 79, Open Prs 1982; All-Western Master Prs 1991, Rocky Mtn Bracketed KO Tms, Tulsa Open Swiss, Palm Springs Strat Open Prs 1992.

BARROW, Rhoda, see LEDERER, RHODA

BART, Leslie C. (Les) (b. 1947) of Olney MD, accountant for Marriott Corp., graduate of U of Rochester and George Washington U. Competes in tournament backgammon. Won Life Master Mens Prs 1972 and dozens of regionals including Mid-Atlantic Swiss 1973, Open Prs 1974, KO Tms 1977, 78; Fall KO Tms 1976, 77, 78. See also LANCIA Tms.

BARTON, Lionel Oscar (b. 1942) of Missouri City TX, born in Guyana, retired senior geophysicist with Chevron, educated at London U. Sectional VP of Southwest section of ABA, #1 in ABA masterpoints with more than

18,000 points as of December 1993, ACBL Life Master and a bridge teacher. Has won more than 200 regional ABA titles and more than 40 national ABA titles including 15+ KOs, Summer Open Prs 1980, Summer Open Tms 1981, Spring Open Tms 1982. Was Spring Nat'l "Player of the Year" 1976, 86; Summer Nat'l "Player of the Year" 1981, 85, 92; won the William A. Friend award (Player of the Year) six times 1978, 1982-85, 1992.

BARTON-PAYNE, Diane (Peanut) (b. 1943) of San Francisco CA, regional-3 ACBL director, former computer systems project manager, graduated San Francisco State U. At age of 6 taught herself chess, set a world's record at 8 by playing 20 games simultaneously in an exibition match. Both parents were directors and opened the first duplicate bridge club in San Francisco. Self-taught bridge at age 8 but didn't play seriously until 11. Became the youngest Life Master in 1961, also one of the ACBL's youngest tournament directors. Has been the subject of national magazine, radio and TV interviews including an article in *The Saturday Evening Post* and a guest appearance on *To Tell the Truth*. Won Golden State Prs 1975, Mid-Winter Holiday Womens Tms 1976.

BARTUSEK, Mark J. (b. 1955) of Fullerton CA, aerospace computer programmer for Hughes Aircraft, educated at U of Illinois. Won his high school chess conference 1973 and 74, was on intercollegiate chess, table tennis and bridge teams 1974 and 75, was the Mini-McKenney National Master of the Year 1978. Regional wins include Bridge Wk Mens Prs 1978, Swiss 1980, Super Open Swiss 1987, Secondary Swiss 1978, Raincross Swiss 1980, Spring secondary Swiss 1993.

BASEGGIO, Franco (b. 1970) of Concord MA, graduate of Harvard, varsity epeeist, National Merit Scholar 1988-92, president of Harvard Bridge Club and a certified director. Won North American College Bridge Championship in 1990, second in 1989.

BATCHELLER, John (b. 1941) of St. Petersburg FL, bridge club owner, certified director and teacher, member Nat'l Goodwill Committee, served as a member of Western Massachusetts Board for more than 20 years in several capacities including president Unit 196. A Diamond Life Master he has won Olympic Swiss, New England Summer Swiss, NE Masters Swiss 1976; Nat'l Capital Open Prs, Tri-State Winter Swiss 1977; New England Fall Swiss 1978, New England KO Swiss 1980, Dist. 25 GN Tms 1987, New England Summer KO Tms 1987, 88; Can-Am Swiss 1988, Dist. 3 Mens Swiss 1989.

BATES, Roger W. (b. 1947) of Mesa AZ, professional player, a WBF World Master and ACBL Grand Life Master with more than 10,000 MPs. Placed third in the World Championship Open Prs 1978, won the 1980 Cavendish Invitational Prs, the Mott-Smith Trophy 1975, 88, 92; Vanderbilt 1975, 76, 88, 92; Spingold 1976, Blue Ribbon Prs 1971, Mens Swiss 1986, North American Mens Swiss 1985, Fall Life Master Mens Prs 1985, North American Swiss 1982, 90. Placed second in Blue Ribbon Prs 1974, 89, Mens Tms 1975, Mens BAM 1985; GN Tms 1989. Has won more than 60 regional events.

BAUER, Keith Robert (b. 1955) of Buena Park CA, schooled at Cal St U and London School of Economics,

distributor and manufacturer of plastics products, lecturer and controller. Other interests include chess and racquetball. Regional wins include San Diego Standard Card Prs, Little Bridge Wk Swiss 1989; Spring secondary KO Tms 1990, Bridge Week Mens Prs, Strat Prs 1991; Fort Wayne Swiss 1991.

BAUSHER, Larry (b. 1939) of Hamden CT, biochemist, graduate of Franklin College, Marshall College and UCLA-Ph.D., engaged in biochemical and pharmacological research at Yale. A Diamond Life Master, his regional wins include secondary Swiss 1976, Can-At Master Prs, Long Island Swiss 1973; Tri-State Winter Swiss, NY Winter Swiss 1976; New England Master Swiss 1980, Fall Swiss 1978, 79; New England Summer KO Tms, Fall KO Tms 1982; Dist. 25 GN Tms 1985, GN Prs 1993; Dist 25 KO Tms, Open Swiss 1989.

BAXTER, Ken (b. 1939) of Edinburgh, Scotland, computer consultant. Won Gold Cup 1980. Represented Scotland nine times in Camrose matches. Many Scottish wins include Scottish Cup once.

BAZE, Diane (see HAYWARD, Diane)

BAZE, Grant Sheridan (b. 1943) of San Francisco, a leading professional player, also an expert rubber bridge player. Graduate of Stanford U. Won the Pan American Games the first two years of the event, captained the U.S. women's team in the 1988 Olympiad in Venice, placed ninth in the World Mixed Prs 1986 and 11th in the Rosenblum Cup Tms 1986. Nat'l titles include Reisinger 1969, Spingold 1975, Mens BAM 1983, North American Swiss 1984, Mens Swiss 1983, Fishbein Trophy 1975, Herman Trophy 1984; second in Reisinger 1971, Mens BAM 1972, Open Tms 1990. Winner of *Barry Crane Top 500* 1984, 85, 87, holds the record for the most masterpoints in a year, 3270 in 1984 -- the only player ever to surpass the 3000-point mark for a single year, ranks sixth in all-time masterpoint winnings with more than 22,000. WBF World Master, ACBL Grand Life Master, contributor of major articles to the ACBL *Bulletin*, has won more than 300 regional championships.

BAZE, Shaleen Notaro (b. 1948) of San Francisco, systems analyst, attended Georgia State U. Other hobbies include needlepoint, skiing and bowling. Has bowled in several national tournaments -- high game 233, high series 652. Has served Unit 114 as president, vice-president, secretary; served as secretary of Unit 506. Worked actively organizing NABC-Atlanta and was editor of District 7's *Pips 'n Tips* 1980-86 and Unit 114's *Pips 'n Tips* 1986-1989. Regional wins include Gatlinburg Swiss, Masters Prs; Nashville Open Prs, Atlanta Womens KO Tms, Central States Open Prs.

BEALE, Felicity (born in Yugoslavia) of Melbourne, Australia. WBF World Master. Won Far East Women's Teams 1973, 1984, 1990. Represented Australia in several world championships and several other zonal championships. Won many national titles.

BEAN, Anne (Mrs Percy X.) (b.1915) of Olympia WA, born in Poland, past president of Unit 441, assisted husband (late Percy Bean) on bridge cruises, first couple ever to receive Honorary Member as a pair, 1992. Regional wins include secondary Womens Swiss, Swiss 1976; Puget Sound Open Prs 1979.

BEAN, Percy X. (1916-1992) of Olympia WA, owned wholesale hardware business, was very active in his community where he was known as a businessman, fund raiser and civic leader, first recipient of Olympia's Man of the Year award 1968. On ACBL Bd 1964-1988, ACBL president 1972, chairman of the Board 1973, president of Charity Foundation 1974-81, member National Goodwill Committee and National Board of Governors, past president of his unit and general chairman of arrangements for World Team Olympiad in Seattle 1984. Bridge cruise director 1975-1991. Bean and his wife Anne were named ACBL Honorary Members for 1992, the first time that honor was bestowed on a husband-wife combination. Editor of *Mad, Mad World of Bridge*, a publication strongly championing players of less than expert class. Won many regional championships.

BEARD, Fran (b. 1929) of Dallas TX, owner of travel agency, graduated from U of Arkansas. Member of National Goodwill Committee and Ethics Committee. Competed in four world championships. Became a World Master in 1978 by placing fourth in the World Mixed Prs. A Diamond Life Master, she was second in Womens BAM 1973. Regional wins include secondary Womens Prs, Oswald Jacoby Memorial Swiss, Tulsa Open Prs, Bermuda Master Prs, Fall secondary Womens Swiss, Dallas Master Swiss, Dallas BAM Tms, Masters Prs 1992.

BEATTY, R. Stephen (Steve) (b. 1949) of Birmingham AL manages software development for Bell-South, graduate of U of South Alabama, soccer coach, zoo sponsor. Current Dist 10 recorder, past president of Birmingham BA, Diamond Life Master. Won ACBL-wide Royal Viking Instant Matchpoint Prs (N-S) 1992. Regional wins include Mid-South Swiss Tms 1976, 81; Mid-Atlantic Open Prs 1979, 86, Open Prs 1982, 86, Smoking Swiss 1984, Non-Smoking Swiss 1987, KO Tms 1988, Space City Open Prs 1984, Swiss 1988; Heart of Dixie KO Tms, Master Tms 1986.

BEAULIEU, Helene (b. 1932) of Sherbrooke PQ, secretary, former bridge club owner and certified director. Regional wins include Quebec Master Prs 1974, Halifax Mixed Prs 1979; Fredericton Swiss 1980, Fall secondary Flt B Swiss, Portland Open Prs 1981; Rockport Open Prs 1982; secondary Swiss, Open Prs, Miami Womens Prs 1984; Fall secondary Open Prs, Strat Prs, Chicoutimi Open Prs 1989; Bal Harbour Open Prs 1990.

BECKER, B. Jay (1904-1987) of New York City, attorney, bridge columnist and bridge teacher, born in Philadelphia where he trained as a lawyer at Temple Law School. One of the greatest players of all time, Life Master #6 and WBF Grand Master. Won a North American Championship in his first year of tournament play 1932, the Chicago Trophy (since 1965 the Reisinger), an event he won also in 1939, 42, 43, 50, 53, 54, 56. Also placed second in the Challenge Tms of Four (now the Spingold) and Mixed Prs 1932. Won Spingold seven times, 1936, 38, 44, 47 52, 57, 72 and the Vanderbilt eight times 1944, 45, 51, 55, 56, 57, 59, 81. His win in 1981 came at the age of 76; at that time no one had ever

won a major championship at a greater age (see JACOBY, Oswald). Becker had the best record of any player in the Master Individual Championship, winning in 1937 and 1948 and placing second in 1934, 41, 49, 55.

It is curious to note that he never won an NABC mixed pair or mixed team event, although his chief successes in the early Sixties were with Dorothy Hayden Truscott. In a two-year period, 1962-64, they won the three most important NABC pair championships -- Open Prs 1962, the Blue Ribbon Prs 1963 and Life Master Prs 1964. Becker's other wins include AWL All-American Open Prs, Open Tms 1935 and the Fishbein Trophy 1972. He was second in 27 NABC events, and his numerous regionals included Eastern States KO Tms 1935, 42, 71, 76.

Considered to be perhaps the most conservative of leading experts, Becker adopted very few bidding conventions, declining to play even the almost universally used Stayman convention. He was, however, among the first to adopt and recommend suit preference signals. Becker managed three New York clubs, the Cavendish 1942-47, the New York Bridge Whist Club 1948-50 and the Regency 1951-56. He was associated with the Card School of New York 1952-57 and became the bridge columnist for King Features Syndicate in 1956. He became a member of the ACBL Laws Commission in 1954. A contributor to *The Bridge World* and ACBL *Bulletin*, Becker was a member of the Editorial Advisory Board of the *Bridge Encyclopedia*. See also BUENOS AIRES AFFAIR, FAMILY.

BECKER, James W. (Jim) (1937-1994) of New York City, owner and manager of the Beverly Bridge Club in New York City, formerly an electrical engineer, educated at Columbia U., a certified director since 1970, member of Dist Bd since 1988, Unit Bd since 1980, vice-chairman of Nat'l Appeals Committee from 1985, first alternate to district Director from 1986. Authored *Biggest Little Bridge Book in the World* Grand LM, ranked 13th in all-time masterpoint holders 18,700. WBF World Master. Placed fifth in World Mixed Prs 1978, ninth in World Mixed Prs 1986 and 15th in Rosenblum Tms 1986. Won Intercollegiate Championship teams 1959, 60, second Mens Prs 1984, Vanderbilt 1987, Master Mixed Tms 1990 and Mixed Prs 1991. Won *Barry Crane Top 500* in 1991 with third highest total — 2916 points for one year. Won 39 regional events that year and has a lifetime total of more than 200.

BECKER, Judith (b. 1947) of Tenafly NJ, educated at U of Wisconsin. Won North American Swiss 1980, Harter Cup KOs 1980, Von Zedtwitz Tms, Winter Womens Prs 1982. See FAMILY.

BECKER, Michael M. (b. 1943) of Tenafly NJ, options trader, graduated Baruch College, involved in American Stock Exchange as Exchange official, arbitrator, disciplinary hearing panelist, chairman of the Option Market Makers Assn., partner and/or consultant to 50 ACBL members who became options traders, including 15 nat'l champions. He and father, B.Jay Becker, are the only father-son to play as teammates in a world championship (Brazil 1973). A Diamond Life Master and a WBF Life Master, became a world champion in 1983 when he won the Bermuda Bowl. Placed fourth in Bermuda

Bowl 1973; fifth in Rosenblum Tms 1986, 10th in 1982. North American championships include Morehead Trophy 1967, Spingold 1972, 80, 82, 92; Vanderbilt 1977, 81, 85, 89; USBC (Team Trials) 1972, 82; Life Master Prs 1990, Open Prs 1988. Placed second in Spring Mens BAM 1968, Spingold 1968, 88; Vanderbilt 1978, 88; Reisinger BAM Tms 1967, 83; USBC (team trials) 1980, GN Tms 1981, 92. Awarded GNYBA player of the year twice, team player of the year twice, recipient of the Fishbein Trophy 1990. A member of a famous bridge-playing family which boasts many Life Masters, he was introduced to the game at an early age. Won Teenyear Prs 1961 and just two years later became a LM at age 19. Regional wins include Hartford BAM 1968, Eastern States KOs 1971, 76; Swan Lake Swiss 1971, New York City Swiss 1972, Spring secondary Mixed Prs 1974, New York City Winter KOs 1980, Dist GN Tms 1984, Hofstra Mens Prs 1984. Has served on numerous committees of the Greater New York BA, including president and vice president. *The Bridge World* Master Solvers panelist since 1981, co-author of *Ultimate Club*. See FAMILY.

BECKER, R. Jay (Bob) (b. 1944) of New York City, actuary and stock options trader, schooled at Dartmouth and Harvard Law School, graduated cum laude and is a Fellow, Society of Actuaries. Won North American Swiss 1979; attained the rank of WBF Internat'l Master in 1979. Regional wins include Long Island Mens Prs 1969, 1972; secondary Swiss, Grossingers Mixed Prs 1971; New England Winter Swiss 1979, 1981; Dist 25 GN Tms 1979, Lancaster Master Prs, Newport Swiss 1979; Providence Swiss 1981, New York KO Tms 1991, NY Eastern States KO Tms 1992.

BECKER, Simon (Skippy) (1899-1987) of Philadelphia, born in Poland, retired court stenographer. A top checker player, was 1923 Pennsylvania champion. Won the Chicago (now the Reisinger) in 1944 and became Life Master #42 the same year. Placed second in Spingold 1944, Chicago 1946, Open Prs 1949, 60. His win in the 1964 Goldman Open Prs at the Eastern Regional set a record -- he and Eli Jaye had a 72% score. He was npc of the American team in the 1976 match with England held in Philadelphia. See FAMILY.

BECKER, Steve (b. 1937) of Cos Cob CT, syndicated bridge columnist for King Features, bridge teacher and certified director, graduated Queens College, executive editor of ACBL *Bulletin* 1970-1972, advertising manager and assistant editor 1964-1970, frequent contributor to ACBL *Bulletin*. Won North American Swiss 1980. Regional wins include New England Winter Open Tms 1968, Open Prs 1988, 89; NY Winter Swiss 1990, Goldman Open Prs 1992. See FAMILY.

BECKMAN, Terry L. (T) (b. 1947) of Eden Prairie MN, programmer analyst, graduate of U of Minnesota. Played in a strato-o-matic baseball league that lasted 15 years, executive board member of Minnesota State Chess Association, was co-director of U.S. Junior Chess Championship in 1972. Diamond Life Master and winner of several regional events including: Fargo Mens Prs 1972, Central States I Masters Prs, Sioux City KOs 1974; Thunder Bay Swiss and KOs 1976; Fargo KOs 1976, Gopher KOs 1978, 80, Swiss 1981, Master Prs 1984, Mens Prs 1987.

BEECHER, Martha (b. 1942) of Las Vegas NV. Member Bd of Gov since 1986, on Unit 373 Bd of Dir since 1976. Directs and teaches on cruises and writes a column for local newsletter. Co-chairman for largest NABC, held in Las Vegas 1991. Has been co-chairman for Las Vegas regionals and sectionals since 1984. Won Fall North American Swiss 1982. A Diamond Life Master with more than 50 regional titles including Pacific SW Swiss 1976, Cotton Boll KOs, Los Angeles Winter Master Swiss 1977; Raincross Master Prs, Mid-Winter Swiss 1979; Navajo Trail Swiss, Gem State Open Prs, Master Prs 1981; Wine Country KOs, Las Vegas Swiss 1982.

BEERS, Dale G. (Captain) (b. 1950) of Media PA, analyst/programmer, graduate Wesleyan U. Involved in amateur theater and varied sports activities, former semipro baseball player. Won Sr/Advanced Sr Master Prs 1974, Swiss 1980. Regional wins include Hartford KOs 1978, Boston KOs 1979, Providence Swiss 1981, Jeffersonville KOs 1984, Cherry Hill Swiss 1986 & 90, Dist 4 GN Tms 1988, Springfield KOs 1989.

BEERY, James L. Jr. (b. 1938) of Huntington NY, radio engineer, won the Grand National Tms 1973. Regional wins include Southeastern Mens Tms 1974, North Florida Fall Mixed Prs 1976, Mid-South Swiss 1975.

BEGIN, Jackie (b. 1917) of Montreal, retired stock broker and travel agent, educated at McGill U, professional football handicapper and poker player, avid sports fan. Life Master #234, she became the first woman Life Master in Canada in 1947. Represented Canada in internat'l competition three times. Before retiring from tournament play she won Womens Tms 1952 and many regional titles including Canadian Nat'l Open Tms 1963, Can-Am Open Tms 1956, 57, 65.

BEGUIN, Pierre (b. 1911) of Geneva, Switzerland, architect. Playing captain of the Swiss team in six consecutive European Championships 1951-56. 11 national wins include 5 in Open Teams and 3 in Open Pairs. He was the founder of the Swiss Bridge Federation.

BEILES, Roger (b. 1949) of El Cerrito CA, actuary for corporate pension plans and overseas compensation studies, educated at U of Rochester, awarded Fellowship in Society of Actuaries 1986. Placed second in Mens Prs 1989. Regional wins include Oakland Mixed Prs 1976, Eugene Unlimited KOs 1985, Reno Mens Prs, Open Prs 1986; Sacramento Open Prs, All-Western Swiss 1987; Santa Rosa BAM 1988, All-Western IMP Prs 1990.

BEINECKE, Walter (1888-1961) of New York City, corporate executive, was vice president of the Whist Club in New York and of the USBA, member of the Laws Commission from its formation in 1933, member of ACBL Board of Directors 1942, 1943. Placed second in the 1936 Vanderbilt.

BELL, Alan C. (b. 1925) of Fullerton CA, born in Windsor ON. Formerly electrical engineer and owner of harness race horses, currently a bridge professional. Graduate of U of Toronto and Northwestern U. Was member Bd of Dir, Chicago BA 1955-63, founded the

Emporium BC in Pennsylvania, long-time panelist for *The Bridge World*. Co-author and inventor of many currently popular conventions -- the SUPPORT PASS was printed with his name. Others were developed independently by several players, e.g. LANDY, CHECKBACK STAYMAN, and UNUSUAL VS. UNUSUAL. Bell is a regular on the Barry Crane Top 500 and placed second in the McKenney in 1958. Currently 11th in the standings of all-time masterpoint holders with more than 20,000 masterpoints. Has won more than 150 regionals including the Marcus Cup 1962, All-Western Master Prs 1969, Mens Swiss 1973; Summer Swiss 1976, Pacific Southwest KOs 1970, 71; Oregon Trail KOs 1975, 77, 78; Mid-Atlantic KOs 1976, 77; MS Valley KOs 1978, 80, Master Prs 1980.

BELL, Bruce C. (b. 1910) of Auckland, New Zealand, chartered accountant, industrialist and bridge writer, fourth World Par Olympiad champion 1963. Represented New Zealand Far East Championships 1964, 1972, npc 1973, 1974. National wins include Open Pairs 1950, 1957, 1958, 1966, Open Teams 29 times between 1947 and 1972. Writings include bridge articles for newspapers and magazines in New Zealand, United States, and United Kingdom. Member Most Excellent Order of the British Empire (M.B.E.), an honor awarded him by Queen Elizabeth in 1979 for services to the game of bridge, the second such award in the Commonwealth, the first being made to Rixi Markus of England. A Life Member and past president of New Zealand CBA, Bell founded the Auckland Bridge Centre which has some 20 affiliated clubs.

BELL, Leo A. (b. 1948) of Los Angeles CA, financial manager and administrator for Cal State U-Northridge, certified director and bridge teacher, educated at Wayne State and Cal State. Co authored *Two Over One Game Forcing* with Tom Oakley. Regional wins include Las Vegas Swiss 1984, San Diego Swiss 1988, Pasadena Masters Prs 1989, Strat Open Prs 1990; San Diego Swiss 1991, 93. Won Las Vegas Pro-Am Money Tournament in 1985.

BELL, Valerie of Christ Church, New Zealand. Won Far East Teams 1976 and represented New Zealand in two other zonal championships. Won several national titles.

BELLADONNA, Giorgio (b.1923) of Rome, Italy, retired public official. WBF Grand Master and #1 in world career rankings in 1992. Won World Olympiad Teams 1964, 1968, 1972, Bermuda Bowl 1957, 1958, 1959, 1961, 1962, 1963, 1965, 1966, 1967, 1969, 1973, 1974, 1975. Second Bermuda Bowl 1979, 1983. He is the only player who participated in all 16 Italian world victories. Won European Teams 1956, 1957, 1958, 1959, 1965, 1967, 1969, 1971, 1973, 1979. Many Italian victories include Open Teams 11 times. Won ACBL Men's Pairs 1971. Former columnist. A creative theorist, he was the primary inventor of the ROMAN SYSTEM, and collaborated in the invention of SUPER PRECISION. See BLUE TEAM, LANCIA TEAM and SHARIF BRIDGE CIRCUS.

BELLANGER, Pierre (1877-deceased) of Paris, France, was captain of the first French team to play an international match against an American team (1933; see FRANCO-AMERICAN MATCHES). He was ahead of his time as a theorist in card play, and his book on finesses, *Les Impasses au Bridge,* was a notable work. He formulated the doctrine which received general endorsement only after many years of debate, that PROBABILITIES A PRIORI are a reliable guide to the play after some cards have appeared. If declarer discovers, for example, that West started with five clubs and East with two clubs, the odds of 5-2 in favor of West's holding the missing queen are not affected by the fact that West has discarded three clubs. Bellanger also analyzed correctly a number of situations which were not generally understood until the principle of RESTRICTED CHOICE was formulated 20 years later. He was secretary general of the Commission Francaise de Bridge in the Thirties, and took an active part in formulating the 1935 Laws. Other writings included *Les 102 Donnes d'un Grand Match* as well as many magazine articles. See BIBLIOGRAPHY, D, G.

BELLE, Thomas (Tom) (b. 1948) of Andover MA, technician, tests computers in Air Force bases, graduate U of Maine, tennis player and golfer. Won secondary Class A Conventions 1975, New England Prs 1984, 89, Swiss 1984; Montreal Swiss 1984.

BEN TOVIM, Zvi (b. 1930) of Haifa, Israel, civil engineer. Senior tournament director, bridge teacher and journalist. General Manager of Israel Bridge Federation since 1989, earlier National Sports Captain. Edits IBF section in Israel's *Bridge Magazine*. Frequent NPC of Israel teams.

BENDERSKY, Marion F. (Mrs. Louis) (1928-1992) of Memphis TN, ACBL executive administrator. Earlier ACBL affiliations -- director of Board communications, director of elections, Club Department supervisor. Former bridge teacher, director and club owner, graduate of Louisiana State U.

BENEDICT, Gene (b. 1953) of Toledo OH, machinist, represents Dist 12 on Bd. of Gov. Won Dist. 5 GN Prs 1985, 87; Dist. 12 GN Tms 1989, All-American Tms 1985, Great Lakes Prs 1987, Open Swiss 1988; Labor Day Tms 1989, Columbus Prs, Southfield Horizontal Prs 1991, Buffalo Prs, Detroit Prs 1992.

BENEDICT, Commander J. Frederic (Fred) (b. 1910) of West Des Moines IA, retired security broker, graduated Colgate U. Past president Central NY BA, ACBL director 1945-55 and a member of Bd. of Gov. Mayor of Norwich NY 1948-52, Diamond Life Master. Won World Olympic and USBA Open Tms 1933, Gopher Open Tms 1972, Great Plains Mens Swiss 1979.

BENJAMIN, Albert L. (b. 1909) of Glasdow, Scotland, company director, former bridge writer and club owner, won Scottish Open Teams six times and represented Scotland 17 times in CAMROSE TROPHY matches, winning in 1964. Co-author of *Tournament Bridge for Everyone.* Other writings include regular contributions to *Bridge Magazine* and a daily bridge column 1937-1976. See BIBLIOGRAPHY, F.

BENJAMIN, Peter (b. 1939) of Culver City CA, retired budget analyst, currently part owner of print store.

Open Prs 1958.

Has served on various committees for tournaments including 1992 Spring NABC. Has been chairperson for Novice promotion, tournaments and ethics, and Unit Treasurer. Won Bridge Week Mixed Prs 1968, Tucson Mens Prs 1972, Bridge Week Swiss 1987, Bridge Week Masters Prs 1991, San Bernadino Swiss 1993.

BENNETT, Hamish (b. 1932) of Menlo Park CA, born in Scotland, retired financial executive educated at Oxford U. Captain winning Oxford bridge team 1955-56. Currently serving as Unit recorder and chairman Ethics committee, certified director and member ACBL Nat'l Goodwill Committee. Bridge correspondent for *San Mateo Times*. Placed second Mens Swiss 1982, North American Swiss 1984. A Diamond Life Master, his regional wins include Sacramento Mixed Prs 1979, BAM Swiss 1992; All-Western KOs 1979, Reno KO Tms 1988, 92; Albuquerque Masters Swiss 1989, Sacramento KOs 1990, Santa Rosa KOs, Phoenix Swiss 1991; plus more than 30 Sr regional events.

BENNETT, James E. Jr. (1936-1992) of Staten Island NY, insurance company supervisor, Diamond Life Master, won Amateur Swiss 1976 and placed second in Blue Ribbon Prs 1979. Regional wins include Eastern States KO Tms 1965, New England Individual KO Tms 1974, Masters Swiss 1975, Swiss 1976, Swiss 1979; Dist 3 Swiss 1977, Mens Swiss 1979, Open Prs 1980; Spring secondary Mens Prs 1979, Dist 25 GN Tms, Zone I 1980; New England KO Swiss 1982.

BENNETT, John G. see BENNETT MURDER

BENNETT, Randy (b. 1952) of St. John's Nfld, environmental health officer with Health and Welfare Canada, schooled at Ryerson Polytechnical and U of Queens. Hobbies -- golf, curling and computers. Certified director, writes bridge articles for local newspaper and the *Atlantic Bridge Line*. Won the Canadian National Team Competition and Royal Viking Prs 1989. Defeated Mexico and Bermuda in tri-country playoff 1991. Represented Canada in int'l play three times, placed 2nd in Yokohama Cup Prs. Regional wins include Halifax Open Prs 1985, Unmixed Prs 1987; Quebec City Swiss 1988, Ottawa KO Tms 1988, 89; St. John's Swiss, Mens Prs 1989.

BENNETT, Roy (b. 1940) of Falkirk, Scotland, teacher. Represented Britain in one world championship and Scotland in 22 Camrose matches. National wins include Gold Cup once and Scottish Cup once.

BENSON, Kirk W. (b. 1949) of Atlanta GA, computer programming manager, has written articles for the Toronto Unit magazine *The Kibitzer* and the Dist 7 *Pips and Tips*, certified director, Diamond Life Master. Won ACBL-wide International Fund Game 1975 and Florida Mens Prs 1975, Mid-Atlantic Open Prs 1977, KO Tms 1981; Nat'l Capital KO Tms, Mens Swiss 1978, Open Prs 1980; Spring secondary Swiss 1979, Mens Prs 1980; Dist 5 KO Tms 1980.

BENSON, Leo O. (1907-1979) of Chicago, bridge columnist, teacher and ABCL regional tournament director, was the first person to become both an ABA Life Master and an ACBL Life Master #3572. Won Gopher

BERAH, David (b. 1921 in Yugoslavia) of New York City, formerly of Venezuela, retired industrialist. Won South American Teams 1963, 1965, 1966. Represented Venezuela in 6 world championships and 12 other zonal championships. Many Venezuelan national wins include open teams 11 times. President Venezuela BF 1977-81, and at that time was #3 ranked player. Columnist and magazine contributor. Learned bridge as a British RAF pilot in the North African desert, serving with Montgomery against Rommel.

BERENBAUM, Carl (b. 1946) of Elkins Park PA, math teacher, graduate of Temple and Villanova, Unit 141 Bd member, bridge teacher. Regional wins include Long Island Swiss 1976, New York Swiss 1980, Dist 4 Master Prs, GN Prs 1981; secondary 0-2000 KOs 1984, Dist 4 GN Tms 1985, Cherry Hill Prs 1986, Port Chester Tms 1990, East Brunswick KOs 1990, 91; Smithtown Prs, Eastern States Bracketed KOs 1992.

BERGEN, Marty A. (b. 1948) of Farmingdale NY, bridge teacher, writer and bridge professional since 1976, graduated Albany State and State U at New Paltz. Won tennis championships in high school and college, still plays. Former member of Nat'l Appeals Committee. Has had a regular column in the Master Pointers section of the *ACBL Bulletin* since 1976 and *Bridge Today* since 1988. Author of two books, *Better Bidding with Bergen Volumes I & II*, assisted with several others. Well known for his development of new conventions and treatments, many of which are in common use. He also assisted with development of Law of Total Tricks, Support Doubles and 1NT Semi-Forcing. Bergen's aggressive preemptive bidding style prompted the ABCL to pass the 5-5 rule in 1984. He is a WBF World Master, placed 9th in Rosenblum Cup Tms, eighth in the 1986 World Simultaneous Prs. Grand Life Master. Has won ten nat'l titles — BAM Tms 1981, 84; Blue Ribbon Prs 1983, 88; Mens Prs, Life Master Mens Prs 1983; Spingold 1984, Reisinger Tms 1985, 91 and Life Masters Prs 1988. Some second places — GN Tms 1979, 91; Vanderbilt 1983, 90; Spingold, GN Prs 1984; Mens Prs 1986. His 60+ regional wins include secondary Sub-Senior Master Tms 1967, Upper NY State Open Prs 1970, Swiss 1974; Keystone Master Prs 1972, Mens Prs 1973; Tri-State Mens Prs 1977, Mens Swiss 1981, Mixed Prs 1982; New England Summer KOs 1979, Swiss 1980; Dist 3 Mens Swiss 1980, Mens Prs 1981. Won the Cavendish Invitational twice.

BERGER, Heinrich (b. 1952) of Vienna, Austria, merchant. WBF World Life Master. Runner-up Bermuda Bowl 1985, World Teams 1988, World Pairs 1986. Won European Teams 1985, European Pairs 1981, European Team Cup 1988. Won eight National Open Teams and three Open Pairs.

BERGER, Mark A. (b. 1927) of Fort Lee NJ, sales representative, graduated NYU, enjoys golf (varsity HS team), tennis (varsity NYU), flying and music. Used to fly to tournaments in his Cherokee 180. Plays oboe and piano and was oboist with the Queens Symphony Orchestra. Won the NY Tm-of-four 1961, Tri-State Mens Prs 1968, 70; NY-NJ Mens Prs 1975, placed second Mens Prs early Sixties and Master Mixed Tms 1974.

BERGOVOY, Bernie (b. 1930) of Oakland CA, president of a data processing company, won Mens Tms 1970 and several regionals.

BERGLUND, Sven Erik (b. 1936) of Stockholm, Sweden, auditor. Represented Sweden 1964 World Team Olympiad and two European Championships. National wins include open teams and mixed pairs.

BERISSO, Alberto (b. 1923) of Buenos Aires, Argentina, Doctor of Economics. World Life Master. South American Champion 1958, 1959, 1961, 1962. Represented Argentina in Bermuda Bowl 1959, 1962, 1965, in World Team Olympiad 1972. 28 national wins include open teams 7 times and open pairs twice. Won Gabarret Cup 1958, 1962, 1968, 1971.

BERKLEY, Lawrence (b. 1924) of New York City, editor. 10th in ABA rankings. Production editor of *The Bridge World*.

BERKOWITZ, David (b. 1949) of Old Tappan NJ, certified public accountant, member of Nat'l Goodwill Committee, past president of Greater New York BA and long-time member of its Board. A WBF World Master, placed 8th in World Open Prs 1982, 5th World Mixed Prs 1986; 6th Rosenblum Cup Tms 1986, 9th in 1990. In the 1992 Pan American Championships he won the Open Tms and placed third in the Open Prs. An ACBL Grand Life Master with more than 13,000 MPs as of 1993, he has won the Blue Ribbon Prs 1978, Mens Tms, Mens Prs, MOTT-SMITH TROPHY 1982; Mixed Prs 1986, 87; Life Master Prs 1987, Master Mixed Tms 1986, 1993; Reisinger, Open BAM, HERMAN TROPHY 1991, He has placed second in Spingold 1976, Blue Ribbon Prs 1977, Vanderbilt 1980, 84, 88, 90, 93; Open Prs 1983, 85; Life Master Prs 1991 Berkowitz is the winner of more than 60 regional titles.

BERKOWITZ, Lisa H. (Mrs. David) (b. 1952) of Old Tappan NJ, former CPA, educated at Cornell and Pace U, member of Nat'l Goodwill Committee. Placed fifth World Mixed Prs 1986, 14th World Womens Prs 1990, won 1992 Womens Tms in Pan American Championships, placed third in the Womens Prs. WBF World Master. Has won Nat'l Mixed Prs 1986, 87; Master Mixed Tms 1986, 1993; Womens BAM 1986, 88; Womens KO Tms 1990, Womens Swiss 1992; and numerous regionals.

BERNARD, Joan Ellen (b. 1925) of Sarasota FL, registered nurse and bridge teacher. Other interests are photography, gardening, oil painting and cats. Diamond Life Master. Regional wins include Mid-Atlantic Spring Open Tms 1965, MARCUS CUP, Florida Mixed Prs 1971; Southeastern Womens Tms 1973, 76; Mid-South Fall Masters Prs 1974, Mid-Atlantic Winter KOs 1975, 76; Sun City Womens Tms 1976, Puerto Rico Womens Prs 1980.

BERNASCONI, Pietro (b. 1932) of Geneva, Switzerland, data manager. WBF World Life Master. Represented Switzerland in five world championships and 15 European Championships. His national successes include Open Teams 11 times and Open Pairs three times. He created the Par contest at the 1990 world championship, an electronic test for world class players generally thought to be the most difficult playing challenge ever devised. He is in charge of recording WBF masterpoints.

BERNING, Dorothy E. (b. 1905) of Lake Worth FL, retired advertising traffic manager, was active for many years in GNYBA and in the organization of two NY nationals, was production manager for 13 years of *Post Mortem*. Placed second Senior and Advanced Senior Master Prs 1950, won Marcus Cup 1951, Eastern States Womens Prs 1960.

BERNSTEIN, Andrew J. (b. 1942) of Memphis TN, clinical psychologist, publisher and editor of bridge books -- Devyn Press 1979-87 and Pando Publications since 1988. Graduate of Hofstra U and U of Tennessee. Past President of GA Book Publishers Assn. Has served as Dist 7 Judiciary Committee chairman and on Nat'l Appeals Committee. Developed the two-way EXCLUSION BID overcall convention. Co-authored *Do You Know Your Partner*. Edited more than 50 bridge books including: *Bridge Conventions Complete* - Amayla Kearse; *Play These Hands With Me* - Terrence Reese; *The Devyn Press Book of Partnership Understandings* - Mike Lawrence; *101 Bridge Maxims* - Hugh Kelsey; *Bridge From the Top* - Marshall Miles; *Matchpoints* - Kit Woolsey; *The Devyn Press Book of Bridge Puzzles #1, #2, and #3* - Alfred Sheinwold; *Bidding Challenge* - Bobby Wolff. Published and edited *Teach Me to Play* -- Jude Goodwin and Don Ellison.

WBF World Master, placed fourth Bermuda Bowl in Guaraja, Brazil 1973. ACBL Diamond Life Master, won Spingold 1972. His numerous regional wins include Eastern States Open Prs (Goldman) 1969, Eastern States KOs 1971, Mid-Atlantic Fall Swiss 1970, 75; Swiss 2nd Flt, Spring Mens Prs 1975; Summer secondary BAM 1976; Swiss 1977, 80; Winter KOs 1977, Spring secondary Swiss 1981, Open Prs 1982.

BERNSTEIN, Dr. Cynthia G. (Cindy) (b. 1947) of Auburn AL, professor of English linguistics, educated at Cornell and Texas A & M, researches Southern American dialects. A certified director, she has been directing since 1968 and on cruise ships with her husband (Robert) since 1986. Placed fourth in Venice Cup, Jamaica, 1987. Won Womens KOs 1986, placed second Womens KOs 1984, Womens Swiss 1985, Womens KOs 1988, 89. Her many regional wins include Lone Star Mixed Prs, Dist. 3 Womens Swiss 1984, Lake Charles Womens Swiss, Womens KOs 1985; Liverpool Womens Swiss 1987, Albany Swiss 1989.

BERRY, Dolores (Dee) (b. 1934) of Kirkland WA, bridge teacher since 1959, wrote for *The Denver Post* in the Sixties, attended Bryn Maur College and was Phi Beta Kappa at U of Washington, antique collector. Active in the American Bridge Teachers Association, has held several executive positions. Dist 19 Education Liaison since 1989, initiated college and high school teaching programs in District 19. Has written more than 200 original lesson sheets and is a contributor to *ABTA Quarterly*. Named 1991 *Bridge Citizen of the Year* by the Seattle Unit. Diamond Life Master. Recent regional wins include Reno Open Prs, Edmonton Open Prs 1990; Nanaimo Sr Open Prs, Tacoma Sr Open Prs, Yakima Open Prs 1991; Vancouver Swiss 1992.

BESSE, Jean (b. 1914) of Geneva, Switzerland, program director and bridge writer. WBF World Life Master. Represented Europe in the 1954 Bermuda Bowl. Represented Switzerland in 10 world championships and 17 European Championships. Won *Sunday Times* 1969. Many national wins include Open Teams in both France and Switzerland. Won 1976 Bols Bridge Tips contest. Bridge columnist *Journal de Geneve* and author of many magazine articles. First Vice-President of IBPA. He is the originator of the Swiss Acol System, has been commentator at many world championships.

BESSIS, Veronique (b. 1950) of Paris, France, mathematics teacher. WBF World Life Master. Second World Women's Teams 1987, third 1985. Won European Women's Teams 1983, 1985, 1987. Represented France in three other world championships and four other zonal championships. Won many national titles.

BETHE, Henry (b. 1944) of Ithaca NY, senior financial strategy and planning officer for Chase Manhattan Bank, graduate of Columbia. Other interests include stamp collecting, hiking, baseball statistics and other mathematical recreation. Won the New York Triathlon 1979, 1980. Wrote a computer program for scoring IMP pairs. Became a certified director in 1967 and achieved rank of S4 during the time he was a tournament director (1967-73). Has served as vice chairman of Nat'l Appeals Committee, GNYBA president and board member; associate editor of *Post Mortem* for five years, contributing editor to *Bridge Encyclopedia*; has also contributed to *International Popular Bridge Monthly*, *Bridge Today*, *Bridge World* and *ACBL Bulletin*; established conditions for Cavendish Invitational Prs that are basically still used today, coached winning Venice Cup team in Perth 1989. Diamond Life Master. National wins include Life Master Mens Prs, Herman Trophy 1968; Swiss 1987, Open Prs 1991; has won more than 40 regionals including Canadian Nat'l Open Prs 1965, KO Tms 1977; Eastern States KO Tms 1988, 89.

BETHE, Kitty. See MUNSON, Kitty

BEYNON, George W. (1864-1965) an authority on tournament direction, born in Portage La Prairie MB and lived in St. Petersburg FL. Beynon studied at Wesley U, Winnipeg, and his first career was that of a professional hockey player. He made music his major occupation, studying at La Scala in Milan and later directing orchestras in Europe and America. After becoming an American citizen in 1904, Beynon developed a successful plan for synchronizing music with silent films. He was the musical director of *Birth of a Nation* (1915) and other early successes, retired to East Orange NY in 1917. Forced out of retirement by the 1929 crash, Beynon made a new career in bridge. After directing games in New Jersey and writing a Newark bridge column, he joined the Culbertson organization in 1935 as office manager and became secretary general for the USBA. He rapidly became an authority on MOVEMENTS and continued to report tournaments. After moving from New York to St. Petersburg in 1955, Beynon founded a successful correspondence school for directors and began writing a weekly bridge column for the *St. Petersburg Times*. When he celebrated his 100th birthday in September 1964, he was probably the oldest working newspaperman in America. His writings include *Bridge Director's Manual*, the standard work on duplicate organization (see BIBLIOGRAPHY, F), as well as many magazine articles. He was a contributing editor to the *Bridge Encyclopedia*.

BHATIA, Gena (Mrs. Kumar) of Pepper Pike OH, pharmaceutical sales representative, graduated U of Michigan. Regional wins include Great Lakes Masters Prs 1978, Womens Prs 81; Pittsburgh Labor Day Womens Swiss 1979, 80; Buffalo Womens Swiss twice, All-American Womens Swiss twice; Buffalo Open Prs 1986, 89; All American Womens Prs, Pittsburgh Labor Day Stratified Prs 1990.

BHATIA, Kumar (b. 1942) of Pepper Pike OH, grew up in India, pharmaceutical sales representative, graduated Nagpur U in India and Eastern Michigan U. Has served as president of Unit 125 and Dist 5; co-chaired All-America Regional 1974-1990. Has won more than 25 regionals including Wolverine Masters Prs 1978, All-American Open Prs, Swiss 1979, 93, KO Tms 1985, 86, 88.

BHAVNANI, Krishin H. (Kris) (b. 1930) of Carlisle MA, born in India, graduate of M.I.T., CEO of small software-based aerospace research company. Co-inventor of the American Relay and Super-Canape systems. Regional wins include Dist. 5 Open Prs 1960, Master Prs 1963; New England KO Tms 1967, California Capital Master Prs 1971, District 25 GN Pairs 1981, New England KO Swiss 1982.

BIANCHI, Benito (1924-1979) of Leghorn, Italy, furrier. WBF Grand Master. Won Bermuda Bowl 1973, 1974, European Teams 1965, 1967, 1969, 1971. Represented Italy in five other zonal championships, and won 7 Italy national titles including Open Teams once. Co-developer of LEGHORN DIAMOND.

BIANCHI, Marisa (Mrs. Benito) (b. 1928) of Leghorn, Italy, won World Women's Teams 1972, 1976, represented Italy in seven European Women's Championships, winning in 1970, 1971, 1973, 1974, 1977. WBF Grand Master. Won European Common Market Women's Teams 1971, 1973, Italian Mixed Teams twice and British Women's Teams 1973.

BIDDLE, John R. (b. 1928) of Columbus OH, won Open Prs 1965 and had many regional wins.

BIRD, David (b. 1945) of Eastleigh, England, systems analyst. Co-author of 12 books, many of them about the monks of St. Titus. Contributor to many magazines. Bridge columnist of *Mail on Sunday*.

BIRMAN, David (b. 1948 in Poland) of Tel Aviv, Israel, engineer-consultant in logistics and transportation. WBF World Master. Third Bermuda Bowl 1985, second European Teams 1985, second European Junior Teams 1972. Represented Israel regularly in world and European championships since 1977. Won Cavendish Teams 1991. Many national wins include open pairs three times and open teams five times. Chairman of IBF Youth Committee, and NPC and coach of junior team. Editor of Israel's *Bridge Magazine* since 1983.

BISHOP, Clifford W. (Cliff) (1921-1986) of Detroit, advertising executive, Bermuda Bowl champion 1954, represented U.S. in Bermuda Bowl 1955; won Spingold 1953, 54; and placed second Mens Prs 1951, Mens Tms 1953; won numerous regional titles.

BITMAN, Jack (b. 1922) of Denver won the GN Tms 1980 and several regional titles.

BITSCHENE, Jochen (b. 1958) of Heidelberg, Germany, computer programmer. WBF World Master. Won World Teams 1990, and won four national titles.

BITTERMAN, Dr. Robert A. (b. 1950) of Ann Arbor MI, faculty member U of Michigan, specialist in emergency medicine, has written for medical textbooks and publications, Fellow of the American College of Emergency Physicians. Authored column, *It's Your Bid*, in MBA *Table Talk*. Regional wins include Motor City Masters Prs 1982, 83, 86, Mens Swiss 1986, 88, Mens Prs 1987; Wolverine Open Prs 1985, Great Lakes BAM 1987, Glass City Swiss 1988, Open Prs 1992.

BJERKAN, Cheri of Elmhurst IL, graduate U of Illinois, former pension consultant and owner of folk art gallery. Active outside life — antiquing, spectator sports and children's activities — combined with job led her to restrict bridge life to NABCs and WBF events. Member of Nat'l Goodwill Committee, has served on the Conduct and Ethics Committee for Chicago Bd of Dir. WBF World Master, became a world champion in 1987 when her team won Venice Cup in Jamaica, fourth in Venice Cup 1991 in Japan and 10th in World Womens Prs, third in Womens Tms in Pan American Championships 1992. A Diamond Life Master Has won several national titles Womens Swiss 1984, 88, 91; Womens KO Tms 1989, 92; Womens BAM 1991 and Spring Womens Prs 1992. Seconds in Womens KO Tms 1978, 79, 81, 86, 90, 93; Womens Prs 1991. Regional wins include Spring secondary Swiss 1973, Dist. 13 GN Tms 1976, Central States II Womens Prs 1978, Women's Swiss 1979, Swiss, Open Prs 1980; Champagne Master Prs 1975, Swiss 1978, Women's Swiss 1979; Central States Womens Prs 1987, Womens KO Tms 1988, 90, Open Prs 1988, Womens BAM Tms 1992, Womens Swiss 1993.

BLACK, Robert A. (Bob) (b. 1954) of Beaumont TX, attorney, listed in *Who's Who in American Law* since 1987. When he became a certified director (1972) he was the youngest — 17 — in the country. Member of ACBL Bd of Gov and has served Unit 201 in various capacities including president. Author of bridge column since 1989. Has won Mexico City KO Tms 1985, Denver Masters Prs 1989, Houston Mens Prs, Cancun Open Prs 1990; Houston Master Prs 1991, El Paso KO Tms 1992.

BLACKSTOCK, Dr. Stephen (b. 1951) of Wellington N.Z., public servant. Far East Champion 1990. National wins include open teams twice, knockout teams once, open pairs four straight times. Member N.Z. Management Committee 1986-90. Bridge columnist *Wellington Evening Post*.

BLACKWOOD, Easley R. (1903-1992) of Indianapolis IN, one of the most famous bridge personalities in the world, most notable for his invention of the BLACKWOOD 4NT convention. A former insurance manager, since 1964 he had presided over Blackwood Enterprises which included a bridge club and bridge activies on 32 luxury ship cruises. Served as ACBL executive secretary 1968-71 and put the ACBL back on a sound financial basis. President of both the Midwest Conference and Central Indiana Unit; a history buff, chess player, singer and string player. Taught bridge and was in great demand as a lecturer; awarded Honorary Membership in the American Bridge Teachers' Assn. 1978; longtime member of the National Goodwill Committee and National Laws Commission; International Bridge Press Association Personality of the Year 1984. He was honored by the mayor of his city who proclaimed Oct. 28, 1977 *Easley Blackwood Day*. ACBL Honorary Member 1980. Writings include *Bridge Humanics*, *Blackwood on Slams*, *Winning Bridge with Blackwood*, *Play of the Hand with Blackwood*, articles for many magazines including the *ACBL Bulletin* and a syndicated newspaper column. Won Midwest Fall Mens Prs 1944, Southern Conference Open Tms 1962.

BLAIR, Jack (b. 1933) of Tulsa OK, oil executive. Won Mens Prs 1960, Mens Tms 1972, Life Master Prs 1973, Mott-Smith Trophy 1972; placed second in Open Prs 1961, 64; Reisinger 1973, Vanderbilt 1972. Diamond Life Master, has won numerous regionals. See FORTUNE.

BLAISS, Gary (b. 1943) of Memphis TN, national tournament director since 1979, became ACBL Chief Tournament Director 1993.

BLAKEY, Helen Margaret (b. 1945) of Baltimore, technical editor specializing in software manuals, test documents, involved in raising, breeding, showing and training Labrador Retrievers, also composes and is choir director. A certified director, has served Maryland BA as president, secretary and tournament chairman. Won GN Prs 1981. Regional wins include Summer secondary Mixed Prs 1975, Canadian Nat'l KO Tms, Washington Bridge Week Swiss, Fall secondary Womens Swiss 1976; Dist 4 Master Prs 1978, Mid-Atlantic Swiss 1975, Master Swiss, Womens Swiss 1980, Open Prs 1981.

BLAKEY, Robert C. (b. 1946) of Columbia MD, senior software engineer, won the Grand National Prs 1981, and many regionals.

BLAKSET, Knut (b. 1960 in Norway) of Copenhagen, Denmark, financial consultant. Member Danish team that lost 1992 World Teams quarterfinal by 2 imps to the eventual French winners. Won Nordic Teams 1986, Junior Teams 1983. Represented Denmark on many occasions including one zonal championship. Ten national titles include open teams three times and open pairs twice. Co-author of one book.

BLAKSET, Lars (b. 1961 in Norway) of Copenhagen, Denmark, bridge teacher. WBF World Master. Third World Teams 1988. Member Danish team that lost 1992 World Teams quarterfinal by 2 imps to the eventual French winners. Represented Denmark on many other occasions including three zonal championships. Won Nordic Teams 1986, Nordic Junior Teams 1983. 17 national wins include open teams four times and open pairs three times. Won Hoechst 1991. Contributor to theory in the area of systems and conventions, and author of official Danish book on the subject. Columnist of *Berlingske Tidende* since 1990 and magazine contributor.

BLANCHARD, Jillian Shane (b. 1961) of New York City, attorney, graduated U of Michigan and Columbia, a member of one of the outstanding bridge families. Instituted a highly publicized lawsuit in an attempt to force ACBL to allow women to play in high-level Men's Prs events. ACBL now runs women's events opposite some open events, and there are no men's events at the North American Championship level. WBF World Master, tied for 17th in the Rosenblum Tms Geneva 1990. Was second in the Reisinger 1989. Regional victories include Goldman Prs, New York Womens Prs, KO Tms, ABA KO Tms. (See FAMILY and BLANCHARD vs. ACBL)

BLANCHARD, Robert W. (Bob) (b. 1951) of New York City, manufacturer of electromechanical devices, graduate of Case Western Reserve and U of Oregon. Likes to sail, play tennis, cook and waterski. Chairman of Unit 128 and Dist 24 1992. ACBL Rookie of the Year 1975. WBF World Master, 13th Rosenblum Tms 1986, 17th 1990. In Cavendish Invitational Prs placed 6th 1981, 4th 1982, 3rd 1984. Placed second in Blue Ribbon Prs, Mens BAM 1982; Reisinger 1989. Regional wins include NY Winter Swiss 1979, Rye Mens Swiss 1980, Big Apple KO Tms 1981, 82, 86; Long Island Open Prs 1982, NY Goldmans 1984, NY Winter Swiss, Dist 3 Swiss 1986; Cromwell Swiss 1988, ABA Nat'l Summer KO Tms 1983. Blanchard was involved in fight for women's rights in bridge. See BLANCHARD vs. ACBL, BLANCHARD, JILLIAN and FAMILY

BLESSING, Leonard C. (b. 1920) of New Providence NJ, retired supervisor of science with Millburn NJ Bd of Education, past president NJ Science Teachers Assciation, has won several teaching awards, as track coach won 6 conference championships and two state championships, served on NJ Bridge League Board 1961-67. Wrote bridge column for *The Montclarion* and *The Hills-Bedminster Press*; author of *Crossing Your Bidding Bridges*. Won Swan Lake Sr. Charity Prs 1987.

BLOM, Britt. See Nordenson, Britt.

BLOOM, Betty of Duanesburg NY, Diamond Life Master, won Master Mixed Tms 1979 and many regional events.

BLOOM, Steven H. of Duanesburg NY, professor of math, Diamond Life Master, won Master Mixed Tms 1979 and many regional events.

BLOOMER, George Beale, Jr. of Pinehurst NC, retired comptroller, graduated U of North Carolina and Benjamin Franklin School of Accounting. Board member Northern VA BA 1972-82, board member Unit 119 since 1991. Has more than 10,000 MP and many regional wins including Dist. 4 Mens Tms 1981, Dist. 11 Mens Prs 1982, Summer secondary Super Bracket Tms 1984, Virginia Beach Sr Open Prs, Sr Swiss 1986; Mid-Atlantic Summer and Fall Swiss and more than a dozen other senior events.

BLOOMFIELD, Ruth (1925-1993) of Chicago IL, bridge teacher, certified director, ceramic jewelry maker. Winner of Life Master Womens Prs 1971. Regional wins include Bermuda Womens Prs 1976, Mixed Prs; Central States Womens Tms, Lake Geneva Open Prs.

BLOUQUIT, Claude (b. 1941) of Paris, France. WBF World Master. Third World Women's Pairs 1978. Third European Women's Teams 1989. Represented France in five other world championships and won several national titles.

BLUBAUGH, John E. (b. 1950) of Bowling Green IN, sales representative and graduate of Purdue. Enjoys archeology, natural history and collecting useless trivia. Has served as educational liaison, on the Nat'l Appeals Committee and ACBL Bd. of Gov. ACBL Rookie of the Year 1987, Senior Master of the Year 1988, has won more than 35 regional events. Regular contributor to *ACBL Bulletin*.

BLUHM, Louis E. (Lou) (1940-1990) of Atlanta, bridge professional, poker and gin expert. Was well known for his high standard of ethics and deportment. Placed third World Mixed Prs 1978, won Cavendish Invitational Prs 1981. Grand Life Master with 13,000 MPs. Only recipient to date of ACBL's Distinguished Player Award (an award originated for him). Won Reisinger 1972, Spingold 1974, 77; Vanderbilt 1979, 89; Blue Ribbon Prs, Mens Tms 1977; Spring Open Prs 1984, Life Master Mens Prs 1987; placed second in Vanderbilt 1978, 86; Spingold 1988, Mens Tms 1973, Grand National Tms, Mens BAM Tms 1983, 87. His 50 regional wins include Summer secondary Swiss 1979, Fall Swiss 2nd Flt, Open Swiss 1975; District 7 GN Tms 1974, 79, 80, 81, Zone III 1981; GN Prs 1979, 81 and many Mid-Atlantic regionals.

BLUMENTHAL, Lynn (1946- 1994) of Bellevue WA, elementary school teacher, company manager and tax consultant, graduate of U of California and U of Washington. Won Womens BAM Tms 1987, placed second North American Swiss 1993. Regional wins include Seattle Mixed Prs 1973, Masters Prs 1984; Vancouver Swiss 1986, Womens Prs 1990; Denver Swiss 1988, Hawaii Womens Prs 1990, Swiss 1991; Butte Swiss 1991, Victoria Prs 1991, Hawaii Prs 1993.

BLUMENTHAL, Mark E. (b. 1942) of Chicago, one of the leading American players until 1977 when complications arising from open heart surgery caused his retirement from active participation in tournament bridge, was a member of the Aces 1972-74. A WBF Life Master, placed second in the Bermuda Bowl 1973, 74, won Vanderbilt 1973, 77; Mott-Smith Trophy 1977; placed second in the Spingold 1976. ACBL Grand Life Master with more than 11,000 MP, has won numerous regionals.

BOARDMAN, Kathrin M. (Mrs. Peter R.) (b. 1949) of Auckland, New Zealand, university lecturer and school teacher, Far East Women's champion 1981. WBF World Master. Represented New Zealand World Women's Teams 1980. National wins include Interprovincial Teams 1978, 1979, 1980, 1981.

BOECK, Jens (b. 1916) of Copenhagen, Denmark, bridge writer. Columnist of *Jyllands-Posten* 1981-92. Former editor of *Dansk Bridge*, and a contributor. Author of several books.

BOEDER, John (b. 1943) of Roseville MN, designer of computer products for data communications networks, graduated U of Minnesota. Interests are outdoors, literature, and human rights (involved in Amnesty Internat'l). Contributor to *Gopher Bridge News*. Won All-American Swiss, Canadian Nat'l Swiss 1975; District 5 Swiss 1976, Roughrider Swiss 1979, Dist 14 GN Prs 1981.

BOEHM, George A. W. (1922-1993) of New York City, retired writer, editor, mathematician, graduated from Columbia. On staff of *Fortune*, *Newsweek* and *Scientific American*. Served many years as officer of Greater NYBA and was editor of *Post-Mortem* in the Sixties. Wrote several articles for *The Bridge World* including a two-part exposition of LEBENSOHL which he popularized. Won Eastern States KO Tms 1955.

BOEKHORST, André (b. 1934) of Utrecht, The Netherlands, chemistry teacher. Won National Pairs 1969 and represented The Netherlands in one zonal championship 1969. President of Netherlands Bridge League; Vice-President of European Bridge League; member WBF Executive. Secretary of Netherlands Bridge League 1978-90 and chief editor of its magazine *Bridge* 1971-1990. Columnist until 1990; author of one book and translator of some others.

BOER, Wubbo de (b. 1963) of Amsterdam, The Netherlands, application manager computer systems. WBF World Master. Won Bermuda Bowl 1993; Third World Teams 1992. World Junior Champion 1987, European Junior Champion 1986. Won national titles Open Teams 1992, Open Pairs 1991.

BOESGAARD, Knud-Aage (b 1950) of Copenhagen, Denmark, accountant. WBF World Master. Third World Teams 1984, second European Teams 1979, and represented Denmark on many other occasions including two world championships and four zonal championships. Won European Junior Teams 1970, Nordic Teams 1986, 20 national wins include open team six times and open pairs twice. Won IBPA Best Bidding Award 1980.

BOGAIR, Dr. Nahum (b. 1912) of Tel Aviv, Israel, pediatrician and lecturer, represented Israel in the European Championships 1965 and won Tel Aviv Open Teams 1964. Former president ISRAEL BRIDGE FEDERATION.

BOIVIN, Anna K. (b. 1932) of Laval PQ, bridge teacher for more than 15 years, club owner since 1972, Zone 2 Director for the Canadian Bridge Federation for three years, member of National Goodwill Committee, certified director since 1971. Represented Canada twice in world competition. Diamond Life Master with several regional wins including Can-Am Open Prs 1981, Womens Swiss 1984, 90, Womens Prs 1984; Ottawa Spring Womens Prs 1982, Fall secondary Silver Trophy Prs 1985, Bonaventure Prs 1989, CLTC Finals 1985.

BOLLS, Col. (ret) Larry R. (b. 1939) of Walnut CA,

Air Force officer, wrote a bridge column for both the NATO publication and an Italian newspaper for three years while stationed in Naples. Won Amateur Swiss 1977. Regional wins include CA Capitol Open Prs, Swiss 1981; Anchorage KO Tms, Swiss 1984, Wine Country KO Tms 1989.

BONDE, Count Carl (1897-1990) of Moerkoe, Sweden, landed estates owner, npc Swedish Open Team and Women's Team on many occasions. Served as president SWEDISH BRIDGE LEAGUE 1960-1965, president EUROPEAN BRIDGE LEAGUE 1965-1969, president of WORLD BRIDGE FEDERATION 1968-1970. An Honorary Member of the WBF, the EBL and the Swedish Bridge Federation.

BONGERS-LEJEUNE, Alphonsine (born in the Netherlands) of Curacao. Top-ranked woman player in the Netherlands Antilles, represented country in many world championships beginning in 1964. Won numnerous national titles.

BONNEY, C. Jack (1904-1982) of Ozona FL, accountant and bridge teacher. Organized the Westchester Contract BA and was its first president; also served as president of the Miami Bridge Club in the late Thirties. A bridge teacher and director in Westchester County NY from the Forties until 1975, he wrote several bridge teaching handbooks including *Master Bridge Teaching Guide*.

BORIN, Jim (b. 1935 in England) of Melbourne, Australia, bridge club owner and teacher. WBF World Life Master. Won Far East Teams 1970, 1971. Represented Australia in four world championships and other zonal championships. Won many national titles. Co-author of one book.

BORIN, Norma of Melbourne, Australia, bridge club owner, teacher, WBF World Master. Won Far East Open Teams 1970, 1971, Far East Women's Teams 1990. Represented Australia in four world championships and other zonal championships. Won many national titles. Co-author of one book.

BOTTEGA, Solange Bozzo de (b. 1952 in Chile) of Cochabamba, Bolivia, painter and jewelry designer. Won 1991 South American Open Pairs, 1988 South American Women's Pairs, and represented Bolivia in three other zonal championships. 13 Bolivian titles include Open Teams three times and Open Pairs five times. President Bolivian Bridge Association and Director of *Bridge para las Américas*.

BOSCOWITZ, Herbert (Hubie) (b. 1902) of New York City, first recipient of the Wetzlar Trophy, president of the American Bridge League 1935, was responsible for introducing the Masterpoint Plan, which became the basis of the ACBL's subsequent prosperity. Won AWL All-American Open Tms 1933, Master Mixed Tms 1932, placed second Vanderbilt 1934.

BOULENGER, Jean-Michel (1934-1985) of Paris, France, represented France World Team Olympiad 1964, 1976, Bermuda Bowl 1967, 1969, 1973, European Championships 1963, 1965. European champion 1966, 1970,

1974, runnerup 1967 and had many Franch titles. Won *London Sunday Times* Invitational 1977.

BOURBON, Philippe de (b. 1921 in U.S.A.) of Punta del Este, Uruguay, engineer. Regularly represented Paraguay 1980-87 and Uruguay from 1988 in zonal championships. Won 5 Uruguay national championships and ACBL regional titles.

BOURCHTOFF, Andree (Mrs. Gerard) (b. 1923) of Paris, France, European Women's champion 1953, 1954, represented France 1957, 1958. National wins include Women's Teams.

BOURCHTOFF, Gerard, (b. 1923) of Paris, France, company director, WBF Life Master, won World Team Olympiad 1960, represented France World Team Olympiad 1968, 1972, European Championships 1952, 1956, 1959 placing second 1956, 1959. National titles include Open Teams many times, Open Pairs 1959, English Master Pairs 1960.

BOURDILLON, Tom J.E. (b. 1938) of Harare, Zimbabwe, university lecturer. Represented Zimbabwe in one zonal championship, in many regional tournaments and won national titles. Chairman Zimbabwe Bridge Union 1979-80.

BOWIE, Clagett (Clag) (1907-1989) of Falls Church VA, mathematician, educated at Princeton and Harvard Law School. Credited with the queen-over-jack rubber bridge theory (see QUEEN OVER JACK and TWO-WAY FINESSE). Won several regional events.

BOYD, Lorraine of Auckland, New Zealand. WBF World Master. Represented New Zealand in two world championships and five zonal championships.

BOYD, Peter A. (b. 1950) of Silver Spring MD, systems analyst, graduate of Harvard. Has served as president Dist 6 and Washington Bridge League. Member Nat'l Goodwill Committee and Nat'l Appeals Committee. Won Rosenblum Tms 1986, WBF World Master, ACBL Grand Life Master with more than 13,000 masterpoints. National wins include GN Tms 1984, 88, 92; GN Prs 1985, Reisinger, Mens Swiss 1986; Vanderbilt 1987, 91; Mens BAM Tms 1989. Placed second in Blue Ribbon Prs 1982, GN Tms 1985, Life Master Prs 1987, Life Master Mens Prs 1988, Vanderbilt 1992, Spingold 1992. Has won more than 50 regionals including Spring secondary Silver Trophy Prs 1981, Upper NY KO Tms, Mens Prs 1974, Swiss 1975; Keystone Open Prs 1973, 75; Dist 5 Master Prs 1975, Washington Bridge Week KO Tms 1977, Dist 4 KO Tms 1981.

BOYE, Daniel (Dan) (b. 1951) of Syracuse NY, marketing consultant, graduated Syracuse U, likes to participate in sports and coaches soccer and Little League, served on Little League Bd of Dir. Certified director, won Dist. 4 Mens Swiss 1975, 76, 77, Open Prs 1990; Summer NAC secondary Mens Prs 1987, Dist. 5 Mens Prs 1988, Open Tms 1989; Capital District Open Swiss 1990, Springfield KO Tms 1992.

BOYLE, Brad (b. 1961) of Toronto ON, financial manager, graduate of U. of Western Ontario. Represented Canada in world play Bal Harbour 1986, Geneva 1990. Member of ACBL Junior team at Epson International bridge tournament in Tokyo 1984-85. Has won several Regionals including Canadian Nationals Men's Pairs, Swiss 1989; Canadian Nationals Swiss 1988-89; Frontier Swiss 1989.

BRACERAS, Jaime (1930) of Buenos Aires, Argentina, South American champion 1976; 9 national wins including open teams and open pairs once each.

BRACHMAN, Malcolm (b. 1926) of Dallas TX, independent oilman and company president, former physicist and life insurance executive, educated at Yale and Harvard (Ph.D.) ACBL Grand Life Master with more than 12,000 masterpoints and has international ranking in WBF. Won Bermuda Bowl 1979, 9th in Rosenblum Tms 1978, 1990. North American championships include Reisinger 1976, 80; Mens Tms 1976, Vanderbilt 1978, Spingold 1978, 83, 86. Placed second in Spring Mens BAM Tms 1984, Reisinger 1990, has won more than 100 regional events.

BRACHMAN, Minda (Mrs. Malcolm) (b. 1931) of Dallas TX, racehorse owner, president of Master Point Farm. Other interests include racing horses, hiking and horseback riding. Winner of Master Mixed Tms 1968, placed second Life Masters Prs 1971. Diamond Life Master with more than 45 regional wins including more than 30 KO Team titles, Pacific Southwest Mixed Prs 1977, King Cotton Master Prs 1980, Mount Shasta Open Prs 1981, Bridge Week KO, Central States KO, Gatlinburg KO and Texas Regional KO and Open Prs.

BRADY, Joseph L. (Joe) (b. 1926) of Upper Saint Clair PA, semi-retired financial consultant, former vice president of USX Credit Corp., graduated magna cum laude NYU. Served as Unit 188 president for two terms in the Sixties. Won Summer secondary Sr Swiss 1986, 92, Sr KO Tms 1991, 94, Spring Sr Swiss 1992, Sr KO Tms 1994; Pittsburgh KO Tms 1987, 88, 89, Mixed Prs 1987, Sr Swiss 1989, 91, 93; Dist. 5 GN Prs 1988, Sr KOs 1991; Erie Sr Prs 1989.

BRAHMACHARI, Ajoy (b. 1939) of Calcutta, India, engineer. Won Far East Open Teams 1977, third Far East Open Pairs 1978. Won two national titles.

BRALL, Carlyn (Mrs. Ira) (b. 1911) of New York City, editorial consultant, former editor of Greater New York BA's *Post Mortem* and editorial assistant to Waldemar von Zedtwitz and Albert Morehead, edited several bridge books including *Goren Answers the Bridge Problems*. Won Womens Tms 1955, 58 and several regionals.

BRAMLEY, Bart (b. 1948) of Chicago, stock options trader, graduated MIT, is a sports fan, especially baseball and specifically NY Yankees, Grateful Dead fan, likes word games and crossword puzzles, has written articles for The *Bridge World*. Once played ten consecutive days of national KO events at one tournament, placing second in both. WBF World Master, placed 11th Rosenblum Tms, 20th World Open Prs 1986; 9th Rosenblum Tms 1990 and 5th Bermuda Bowl 1991. ACBL Diamond Life Master. North American wins include Mens BAM 1980, Open Prs, Mens Swiss 1984;

Life Master Mens Prs 1987, Vanderbilt 1989, Open Swiss 1990; placed second in Mens BAM 1976, 87; Spingold 1981, 88; Mixed Prs 1981, Vanderbilt 1986, GN Tms 1988, Open Swiss 1991. Regional wins include Spring secondary Mens Swiss 1973, Summer secondary Open Prs 1974, Fall secondary Swiss 1979, New England KO Tms 1977, 84; Reno KO Tms 1985, Central States IMP Prs 1991. Was top E-W pair in US, 1990 Epson Prs (with Judy Wadas).

BRANCO, Marcelo Castello (b. 1945) of Rio de Janeiro, Brazil, computer engineer and government official. WBF Grand Master. Won World Teams 1976, World Open Pairs 1978, 1990, Bermuda Bowl 1989. He is the only player to have won the World Pairs twice, and one of eight to have won the TRIPLE CROWN of World Teams, World Pairs and Bermuda Bowl. Second World Teams 1978. Represented Brazil in 12 other world championships. Won South American Teams 1968, 1971, 1972, 1973, 1975, 1977, 1978, 1983, 1986, 1989, 1991 1993. National wins include open teams 10 times. Won Reisinger 1992. Won Sunday Times 1992, Cap Gemini 1993. See SCIENTISTS v. TRADITIONALISTS.

BRANCO, Pedro Paulo Castello (b.1940) of Rio de Janeiro, Brazil, insurance executive. WBF Grand Master. Won Bermuda Bowl 1989, South American Teams 1969, 1972, 1973, 1982, 1989, 1993. Represented Brazil in eight other world championships. 15 nationals wins include open teams four times.

BRATCHER, Robert L. (Bob) (b. 1930) of Vista CA, R4 regional tournament director, won Fall secondary Commercial and Industrial Prs 1962, Midwest Open Tms 1963, Mid-Atlantic Mixed Prs 1963, ABA National Open Tms 1962.

BRATTON, Paul Edward (b. 1943) of Indianapolis IN, buyer for GM, graduated U of Illinois. Won NABC Non-Life Masters Prs, second Red Ribbon Prs 1987. Won Dist 8 GN Tms 1985.

BRAUNSTEIN, Marion (Mrs. Maurice) (b. 1930) of Schenectady NY, retired auditor and regional tournament director, won Summer secondary Sub-Senior Master Tms 1956.

BRAUNSTEIN, Maurice (Maury) (b. 1914) of Schenectady NY, national tournament director, graduate of Columbia, formerly a computer processing director for the State of New York. Began his career as a tournament director in 1954 and soon found directing more of a challenge than playing. Became a national director in 1968 when he retired from his New York work, was in charge of all national-rated events at North American Championships 1973-1990. Made his debut as a World Bridge Federation director in 1972, was director-in-charge at the 1973 Bermuda Bowl in Guaruja, Brazil; also chief director for the world championships in Bermuda 1975, Bal Harbour 1986, Jamaica 1987, Venice 1988; assistant chief director at the world championships in 1974 and for all world championships 1976-1985. Originated several duplicate movements, including the STANZA MOVEMENT. Is known worldwide for his bow ties, his trademark at tournaments.

BRECHNER, Dora (Dosha) (b. 1920) of Tel-Aviv, Israel, born in Poland, owned and operated a nursing home in New York. A survivor of Auschwitz and Bergen Belsen, weighed only 76 pounds at liberation in 1945. Took up duplicate in 1961 and became a Life Master in one year. Resides most of the year in Israel but summers in US. Represented Israel from 1974-85 in the European Championships, World Womens Tms and World Womens Prs and became a World Master. When she retired from bridge in 1985 she hired two of the best teachers to teach the younger Israeli women. In 1991 her protegees won the European Community Championships. Besides her achievements in Israeli bridge she won Summer secondary Mixed Prs 1965, NY-NJ Womens Prs 1966, Keystone Womens Prs 1968.

BREED, Mildred (b. 1947) of Austin TX, purchasing agent, Diamond Life Master, represented ACBL in World Team Olympiad 1992. Won Womens Prs 1980 and placed second in Womens Tms 1975, Womens Prs 1984; has won many regional events.

BRENNER, Dr. Anne of Denver CO, has won Denver Masters Prs, Colorado Springs Open Prs, Salt Lake City Open Prs, Wichita Open Prs, Denver Pan-American Prs. Also won the Christchurch New Zealand Open Prs.

BRICKLIN, Albert R. (Al) (1913-1992) of Scottsdale AZ, club owner, automobile designer, engineer, educated at U of Pennsylvania, wrote bridge column for *Scottsdale Progress*. Diamond Life Master, won several regionals including Mid-Atlantic Swiss 1969, Fall NAC secondary Mens Swiss, Puerto Rico Mixed Prs 1972; Motor City Mens Prs 1974, Desert Empire Open Prs 1979.

BRIDSON, Edward W. (Edson) (b. 1951) of Unionville ON, born on Isle of Man, Great Britain, mathematics teacher, educated at U of Waterloo and U of Toronto. Winner of Canadian National Tm Championship 1991, placed second 1985. Placed second Pan American Open Tms 1992, CNTC 1993. Regional wins include Syracuse KO Tms 1975, District 2 GN Tms, Detroit Open Prs 1976; Reston Mixed Prs, Niagara Falls Swiss 1978; Buffalo Mens Swiss, Montreal Open Swiss 1980; North Bay Swiss, Open Swiss, KO Tms, Detroit Masters Prs 1981; Sudbury KO Tms 1983, Buffalo Open KO Tms 1985, District 2 GN Prs 1986, Liverpool Mens Swiss 1987, Toronto Mens Swiss 1989.

BRIER, Barbara S. (b. 1923) of Miami, bridge teacher, graduated from Cornell, frequent partner of Waldemar von Zedtwitz with whom she won World Mixed Prs 1970. Also placed high in World Womens Prs and World Mixed Tms twice. North American titles include Open Prs 1955, Mixed Tms 1965; placed second in Master Mixed Tms 1956, Mixed Prs 1963, Spring Womens Prs 1971. Regional wins include Marcus Cup 1958, Southeastern Womens Tms 1971, 74 and two subsequent times; Fall secondary Womens Swiss 1972, All-Conventions Prs 1986, Womens Tms 1989, Womens Prs 1990, Womens Prs, Sr. Swiss 1992; New York Summer Womens Prs 1972, Eastern States KO Tms 1973, 74; Sr Swiss 1993.

BRIGHTLING, Richard John (b. 1949 in New Zealand) of Sydney, Australia, bridge shop and club manager. Represented New Zealand in one world championship and one Far East Championship. Publisher of *Australian Bridge*.

BRILL, Laura (b. 1943) of White Plains NY, writer and consultant on business writing, co-owner of bridge club, educated at Smith College and Columbia. Her book, *Business Writing, Quick and Easy*, is in its second edition. Won more than 25 regional events including Summer secondary Womens Prs, Fall secondary Open Swiss 1985, Dist. 3 GN Prs 1986, 90, 91; Reno Open Prs, Summer Open Prs 1989; Dist. 3 Open Prs, Womens Swiss, Rye Womens Prs 1990; Mid-Atlantic Mixed Prs 1991, Spring secondary Open Prs 1992, Greater New York City Open Swiss 1993.

BRISSMAN, Jon C. (b. 1944) of Ontario CA, school principal, bridge professional and attorney, degrees from Parsons College, Northeast MO State and Western State (JD). Has competed in more than 70 10K runs, completed law school in 28 months with honors. Co-chairman Nat'l Appeals Committee 1983-88, chairman Conventions Committee 1986-87, coordinator of President's Advisory Committee 1986-87, ACBL National Recorder 1985-88. Was actively involved in setting up recorder program presently in effect at NABCs. Responsible for revision of ACBL Convention Chart, created or implemented many of the policies and procedures in effect at Nat'l Appeals Committee hearings and helped to create *ACBL Standard*. Has written for *ACBL Bulletin*, *Contract Bridge Forum* and *Southern California Bridge News*. Retired from active bridge 1988. A Diamond Life Master with 29 regional titles including Bridge Week Swiss, Pacific Southwest Mixed Prs 1978, Mid-Winter Holiday Open Prs 1979, Golden State Swiss, Raincross Swiss 1980, Mens Prs 1982.

BRITTON, Sonya (Mrs. John) of Dublin, Ireland, represented Ireland in the European Championships 1962, World Women's Tms 1972, 1976, World Women's Prs 1978; npc World Women's Tms 1980. National titles include Mixed Prs (twice), Women's Tms (four times), and National Team-of-Four. She has served as president of Contract BA of Ireland, as vice president of the IRISH BRIDGE UNION 1981-1982, and as IBU delegate to EUROPEAN BRIDGE LEAGUE.

BRKLJACIC, Miljenko (b.1943) of Zagreb, Croatia, data processing analyst, bridge writer and teacher. Represented Yugoslavia in two world championships and four European Championships. Won 15 national team titles and two open pair titles. He is the head of the CBF's tournament division, and organizes and directs its most important tournaments. Editor *Croatian Bridge Bulletin*.

BROCK, Raymond (b. 1940) of Heston, England, computer manager. WBF World Master. Runner-up 1987 Bermuda Bowl, 1987 European Teams. Played in more than 25 Camrose matches. Many national wins include Gold Cup 7 times. Technical director and planner of many bridge events, particularly the 1989 World Junior Championships and other initiatives for junior players. President British Bridge League 1986-88 and 1990-92, former chairman of its Selection and Finance Committees. General Manager of the English Bridge Union from 1992.

BROCK, Sally. See Horton, Sally.

BROCKMAN, Elaine B. (Mrs Charles C.) (b. 1914) of Issaquah WA, housewife, former dance teacher, graduated Met. Business College. Qualified director, ran lectures and bridge games on cruise ships for 15 years. Placed second Womens Tms 1965. Regionals wins include Portland Swiss 1971, Womens Prs 1973, Seattle Womens Prs 1975, Portland Womens Prs 1976, Yakima Swiss 1977, Boise Womens Prs 1978, 82; Penticton Womens Prs 1981, Seattle Sr Swiss 1992.

BRODY, Harvey D. (b. 1939) of San Francisco CA, graduated Western Michigan U, bridge professional, retired accountant, collector of paperback books. Has served on Nat'l Appeals Committee and treasurer of Dist 21 and 1990 Fall NABC. Winner of IMP Prs 1992, competed in Pan American Games 1992. Has won more than 40 regional events including All Western Open Prs 1972, Mens Prs 1978, Open Prs 1989, Open KO Tms 1991, Wine Country Master Prs 1982, Master Prs 1985, Swiss 1990, Prs 1992; Central CA Open Tms 1972, Swiss 1982, 83, Open Prs 1988, KO Tms 1991; Dist 21 GN Tms 1978, GN Prs 1979, 88, 91.

BROER, Lawrence ("Bertie") (b. 1923) of Johannesburg, South Africa, chartered accountant. Represented South Africa in World Team Olympiad 1968, 1972 and 1980, Maccabi Games 1977, 1981, 1985. 9 national wins include 4 in open teams.

BROGI, Giovan Battista (1920-1980) of Livorno, Italy, wholesale drug company manager, won Belgian Open Teams 1961, represented Italy European Championships 1961, 1962, placing second in 1962. National wins include Italian Cup 1955, 1957, 1961, Italian Open Teams 1961. Tournament director since 1961.

BRONSTEIN, Alan J. (b. 1941 in Bronx, U.S.) of Christianstedt, St. Croix, Virgin Islands, certified public accountant. Represented Virgin Islands in two world championships and 13 CAC zonal championships. President of Virgin Islands B.F. Bridge columnist of *St. Croix Avis*.

BRONSTEIN, Saul (Puppy) (b. 1949) of New York City, bridge director and teacher, formerly a comptroller, graduate of Pace U. Three-time Scrabble champion. General secretary Unit 155 (GNYBA) since 1979, has served on various other committees, directs on bridge cruises, associate editor GNYBA's *Post Mortem*. Won GNYBA Player of the Year and Team Player of the Year 1987, founder of Academy of Bridge (New York City). WBF World Master, eighth Rosenblum Tms 1986. In 1984 won Reisinger in famous four-way tie; won Cavendish Cup Tms 1989 and New York KO Tms 1990. Won Atlantic City Open Prs 1978, Long Island KO Tms 1981, Summer secondary BAM 1984, Eastern States KO Tms, Dist 24 GN Tms 1987.

BROOKS, Dorsey W. (b. 1926) of Stanwood MI, retired General Motors senior administrator, graduate of Wayne U. Played exhibition matches on team with Charles Goren and Harold Ogust. Placed second in Master Mixed Tms 1971, was Intercollegiate champion 1949. Regionals wins include BAM Swiss 1979; Canadian Nat'l Tms 1964, Great Lakes Open Prs 1965, Summer Leventritt Prs, Motor City Swiss 1970; Bermuda Mens Prs 1974, Motor City Mens Swiss 1977, Bermuda Swiss 1979, Mexican Nat'l Swiss 1981. Won two Industrial League par contests.

BROOKS, Zerrene (Mrs. Dorsey) of Stanwood MI, bridge teacher and recreational consultant, Girl Scout leader for 15 years. Placed second Master Mixed Tms 1971, second Intercollegiates 1950. Regionals include, Motor City Swiss 1970, Bermuda Swiss, Great Lakes Womens Prs 1979; Mexican Nat'l Swiss 1981. Won two National Industrial League par contests.

BROTMAN, Oscar J. (b. 1911) of Bayside NY, retired controller, graduated CCNY, won Spingold 1940, Eastern States KO Tms 1946. As a partner of Alvin Roth, he contributed to the early development of the ROTH-STONE SYSTEM. Won Maryland Masters 1939, 40, 41.

BROUILLET, Marsha E. (b. 1941) of Minneapolis, volunteer coordinator for Catholic charities, former social worker, graduate of Luther College, won Eau Claire Womens Swiss 1985, Thunder Bay Womens Prs 1986, Sioux City Womens Prs 1987, Gopher KO Tms 1988, Strat Womens Prs 1993.

BROWN, Dudley B. (b. 1935) of Grandview WA, Army Reserve technician, graduate of Washington State U. Member of Nat'l Bd. of Dir. since 1989, has served District 19 as president, Board member and chairman of various committees. Former executive editor of *The Dino Bridge Buff.* Diamond Life Master. Regional wins include Oregon Trail Men's Prs 1966, Intermountain Swiss 1972, Inland Empire Swiss 1973, Apple Tree Super Open Prs 1986.

BROWN, H. Sanborn (b. 1906) of Grosse Pointe Farms MI, architect, graduated U of Michigan, won Life Master Prs 1957, placed second in De La Rue International Pair Championship, London, England 1957, won Marcus Cup 1949, Midwest Spring Open Prs 1956. Served as ACBL Bd of Gov member 1942-66, Michigan BA Bd member 1942-66, Michigan BA president 1964-66.

BROWN, Jeffrey C. (b. 1955) of Albuquerque NM, attorney, graduated U of Illinois. Other interests include tennis and bicycling. Won Non-Life Masters Prs 1989.

BROWNE, John Charles (*Seamus*) (b. 1952 in New Zealand) of Sydney, Australia. Represented Australia in three world championships and three zonal championships.

BRUCE, Arthur Loring, See CROWINSHIELD, FRANK.

BRUCE, David (formerly Burnstine) (1900-1965) of Los Angeles, was Life Master #1. A tremendously successful player in early Thirties, he headed a group that made the Contract Bridge Club in New York the center of the most expert game of the times. Burnstine, the name by which he went during his bridge career, introduced the artificial 2♣ opening bid to show a strong hand (in-

cluding A-K, A-K, A), with other two bids not gameforcing, a method which became the most widely used among experts of the day and later developed into the cornerstone of ACOL.

Known as a soothing partner but an unsettling opponent, Burnstine played with Oswald Jacoby and Howard Schenken on the first of the outstanding teams, the FOUR HORSEMEN, captained by P. Hal Sims, and authored the first book on that team's system ("Four Horsemen's One Over One", 1932). In 1933, with Schenken, Jacoby and Richard L. Frey, and joined shortly afterward by Michael T. Gottlieb, he organized the FOUR ACES, the team that took the leadership in the field and held it, with several amendments in personnel, for the next decade. With his teammates he wrote *Four Aces System of Contract Bridge*, 1935. In the brief interlude between the reigns of the Four Horsemen and the Four Aces, Burnstine helped to organize and played on the BID-RITE TEAM.

An all-round star, Burnstine was rated by many of his teammates as the best bidder in the game. Brashly self-confident, Burnstine frequently locked horns with Culbertson and rarely came out second best. His impressive tournament record includes a victory in the first official World Championship in 1935 and many national championships including AWL All-American Open Tms (Contract) 1932, (Auction) 1931, 32, 33; USBA Open Tms 1934, 37; Open Prs 1936, ABL Challenge Tms 1931, 33, 37; Spingold 1934, 36, 38; Vanderbilt 1931, 34, 35, 37, 38; Master Mixed Tms 1931, 33; Life Master Prs 1931, 33, 36; Fall Mens Prs 1934, Master Individual 1933; also won the Eastern States Open Tms 1931-1934.

BRUELHEIDE, Frank E. (1884-1943) of Minneapolis, bridge book publisher, writer and lecturer. After graduating from Chicago Institute of Arts he entered the field of bridge and became an associate of Ely Culbertson; later became a director of the ACBL; organized Bridge League of Northwest; traveled throughout the U.S. lecturing, teaching and broadcasting over radio in the interests of bridge promotion; published and edited his own magazine, *Bridge Digest*, 1936-39. Writings include several articles for *The Bridge World* and other publications, pamphlets on bridge such as *Duplicate Bridge Guide* and the book *Party Bridge*.

BRUN, Johannes (1891-1977) of Oslo, Norway, army officer and bridge writer, founding member NORWEGIAN BRIDGE ASSOCIATION 1932 and president 1934. In 1937 became president of INTERNATIONAL BRIDGE LEAGUE, a forerunner of the WORLD BRIDGE FEDERATION. Was a founding member of EUROPEAN BRIDGE LEAGUE (1947) and was elected an honorary member in 1957. Represented Norway in European Championships six consecutive years and placed second in both pair and team championships in 1933. Awarded IBL prize for most distinguished player in 1934. Editor of *Aftenposten,* and contributor to several bridge publications.

BRUNNER, Michelle (b. 1953) of Manchester, England. WBF World Master. Won Venice Cup 1985. Second World Women's Teams 1988. Won European Women Teams 1977, 1979, second 1977. Won six national titles.

BRUNO, Steve (b. 1947) of Bellevue WA, state unemployment insurance adjudicator, graduate of U Washington. Captain and coach for womens team runner-up 1988 USWBC. Promoter of womens teams in Pacific Northwest and originator of NW Womens Intercity Team Challenge. Co-authored *Two-over-one Game Force – An Introduction*. Placed second North American Swiss 1993. Won Seattle Mixed Prs 1973, Master Prs 1984, KO Tms 1989; Victoria Prs 1989, Seaside Super Swiss 1986, 89; Hawaii Swiss 1991, Open Prs 1993. Bruno with partner Darrell Keel posted highest score reported to ACBL on two-session playthrough on 156 average for each session -- 452 1/2 on a 312 average (73%).

BRUNZELL, Anders (B. 1938) of Gothenburg, Sweden, mathematics and physics teacher. WBF World Master. Third Bermuda Bowl 1977, and represented Sweden in four other world championships. European champion 1977, and represented Sweden many other times. Nordic Champion 1968.

BRUSTUNOV, Witold (b.1944) of St. Petersburg, Russia, physicist and engineer. Chief organizer of tournaments in St. Petersburg (formerly Leningrad). Winner of several national titles.

BRYANT, Jack N. (b. 1934) of St. Louis, manager, systems development, Dept of Agriculture, educated at Southern Illinois U. Served as Unit 143 president, Bd. of Dir. member, treasurer and as member of Dist. 8 Bd. of Dir. Diamond Life Master. Regional wins include Dist. 8 GN Tms, Dist. 8 Swiss 1979, Dist. 8 GN Prs 1980, Champagne Open Prs 1982, Country and Creole Classic Swiss, Dist. 15 Fall Swiss 1986; Mid-South Swiss 1987, Kansas City Fall Swiss 1989, Indianapolis Summer Strat Prs 1990, Kansas City Summer Sr Prs, Mississippi Valley KOs 1991; Mississippi Valley KO Tms, Sr. Swiss, Champagne Swiss 1992; Music City Swiss 1993.

BUCHALTER, Ralph (b. 1958) of Berkeley CA, technical writer, graduated Oberlin College. Won IMP Prs 1991. Regional wins include Riverside Masters Prs 1987, Dist. 21 GN Tms 1988, Sacramento KOs 1990.

BUCHANAN, Dorothy (Mrs. Robert, formerly Kantor) of Minneapolis, retired, former owner and operator of full-time bridge studio, former office manager construction union. Other interests include travel, gourmet cooking and needlework. Has been active in all phases of bridge at unit level including president, chairman 1982 Fall NABC, chairman of many regionals and sectionals. Served on ACBL Bd. of Dir. 1972-81 and Nat'l Bd. of Governors. Wrote *Basic Bridge, New and Easy* revised 1985. Won Life Master Womens Prs 1982 and many regionals including Pheasant KO Tms 1970, 72; Canadian Prairie Master Prs 1970, Gopher Womens Prs, KO Tms 1971, Master Prs 1973; Tri-Unit Mixed Prs 1971, KO Tms, Iowa KO Tms 1972.

BUCHMEIER, Horst (b. 1942) of Vienna, Austria. Represented Austria in four world championships and three European Championships. Won Austrian Teams eight times, Open Pairs once. Now retired.

BUCHNER, Robert (Bob) (b. 1960) of Wheaton IL, software engineer, schooled at U of Illinois. Other interests include backpacking, sailing, country western dancing. Placed second in Flt B GN Tms 1985. Regional wins include Champaign Master Prs 1986, Central States II Smoking Swiss 1986, 88, Mens KO Tms 1988, Mens Swiss 1988; Central States I BAM Tms 1990, 93, Bracketed KO Tms 1992.

BUCKMAN, Harriette (b. 1935) of Lincolnwood IL, until 1984 a language arts and social studies teacher, currently teaches bridge. Graduated Northern Illinois U., former Girl Scout Community administrator. Other interests include needle arts and decorating. Member Nat'l Charity Committee, past president Chicago Contract BA, CCBA Bd member since 1984. S2 director, she directs on bridge cruises and has written articles for newcomers for CCBA *Kibitzer*. She once played a round with Charles Goren when she was a caddy. Her more than 30 regional wins include Central States Open Tms 1969, Womens Prs 1970, Womens Swiss 1992; Summer secondary Womens Prs 1980, Peoria Open Prs 1990.

BUCKMAN, Kate (b. 1902) of Toronto, bridge teacher, director and bridge club owner. Introduced duplicate to Vancouver shortly after WWII, opened bridge studio in Toronto 1959. Studio developed into the largest bridge club in Canada averaging 300 tables a week and 750 students a year. Many bridge stars and personalities such as Sami Kehela, Eric Murray, George Mittelman, Percy Sheardown, Bruce Elliott and Bruce Gowdy developed at this studio. Received the Edwin A. Wetzlar Memorial Award and was made ACBL Honorary Member 1973. Suffered a stroke 1983, sold Studio 1990, continues to visit and play occasionally. In 1982 the Metropolitan Toronto BA donated a trophy to Unit 166 to recognize special qualities to Unit 166 to honor Kate. She was its first recipient.

BUDIN, Barnett (d. 1964) of Philadelphia, printer, was ACBL director 1963-64 and past president of the Keystone Conference and Philadelphia Unit; co-authored *Bridge Players Digest of Conventions*.

BUDKIN, Diana (b. 1943) of Buenos Aires, Argentina, bridge teacher. WBF World Master. South American Women's Team Champion 1983, 1984, 1985, 1987, 1988. Represented Argentina in Venice Cup 1985, 1987. 3 national wins include open teams once.

BUFILL, Rafael (1927-82) of Barcelona, Spain, engineer. Represented Spain in two world championships and 11 zonal championships. Won many national championships. Former president of Spanish Bridge Federation.

BULLER, Lt. Col. Walter (1887-1938) of London, author and leading personality in British bridge in the Thirties, won first English National Pairs 1932; organized first ANGLO-AMERICAN MATCH 1930 and captained English team. Leading protagonist of *British Bridge* for direct methods of bidding without conventional forcing bids; bridge columnist; wrote several books including *Reflections of a Bridge Player, From Auction to Contract* and *How to Play Contract Bridge*. See BIBLIOGRAPHY E, G.

BURGER, Charles F. (Chuck) (b. 1936) of West

Bloomfield MI, attorney, WBF World Master and ACBL Diamond Life Master. Placed 9th Rosenblum Tms 1990. Won Life Master Mens Prs 1969, Blue Ribbon Prs 1970, Spingold 1985, 89, 90; Reisinger 1988, 92; Fall Mens BAM Tms 1988; placed second Reisinger 1981, GN Tms 1982, Fall Mens BAM Tms 1989, Master Prs 1969, 1973; co-winner of Herman Trophy 1970; has won numerous regional titles.

BURGER, Suzanne (Suzy, Mrs. Charles F.) of West Bloomfield MI, educated at Michigan State U., former social worker presently part time in law office and homemaker. Won Womens BAM 1989. Won District 12 GN Tms 1991 and several regionals.

BURGESS, Stephen (b. 1956 in New Zealand) of Sydney, Australia, options trader and bridge professional. WBF World Master. Third World Pairs 1986. Represented Australia in four other world championships and four zonal championships. Won many national titles in Australia since 1982 and before that in New Zealand. A leading practitioner of relay methods. See MOSCITO.

BURKA, Paul J. (b. 1942) of Austin TX, senior editor of *Texas Monthly*, former attorney, won Fall NAC secondary Open Prs 1970, Texas Fall Master Prs, Mens Prs 1973; editor of *Scorecard*.

BURKE, Phyllis (Phyl, Mrs. Wayne) of Pocatello ID, retired supervisor State of Idaho Dept. of Employment, beauty salon owner, operator; has owned and operated a number of local bridge clubs. Other interests include blackjack, golfing, bowling, fishing, hunting, sports and poker. Member of Nat'l Board of Directors for 10 years, ACBL president 1989, chairman of the Board 1990. Active locally in various community organizations including president of Golf Association, president of Soroptomist International and treasurer of Womens Nat'l Aeronautical Association. Member District 18 Bd. of Dir. for 18 years, including serving as president for three consecutive terms (1979-84); past president of her Unit; has served as chairman of many District 18 regionals and local sectionals. Through the course of her bridge career she played with eight novices until they achieved rank of Life Master. She feels her greatest accomplishment was the establishment of the ACBL Education Program. Won four regional titles.

BURN, David (b. 1956) of London England, systems programmer. Coach of five British teams. Regular contributor to British magazines.

BURNHAM, Dr. Charles (Charlie) (b. 1919) of Birmingham AL, physician, opthalmologist, educated at Mississippi College and Tulane. Fellow in Am. College of Surgeons, Am. Academy of Ophthalmology and Pan-Am Society of Ophthalmology. Held executive positions in Alabama BA in early Sixties, member Nat'l Goodwill Committee since 1960. Was partner for many years to Elinor Murdoch, one of the top women players of the Thirties. Won Open Tms 1960. Regional wins include Fall Southern Conf. Open Prs, Mens Prs 1962, Open Tms 1963; Mexican Nat'l Masters Prs 1965, Mid-South Fall Open Prs, Swiss 1974; Mid-Atlantic Winter Open Prs 1978, Huntsville Sr. Swiss 1992.

BURNS, Sanford R. (Sandy) (b. 1928) of Sarasota FL, retired real estate developer, former furniture manufacturer and owner of a chain of stores, graduated Wharton School and U of Pennsylvania. Was awarded Governor's Medal of the State of Florida for his bridge activities in 1983. His 13 regional wins include Sun City Open Prs 1983, Southeastern Mens Swiss 1984, North Florida non-Smoking Swiss 1986, Sunshine Sr KO Tms 1987, Lancaster Mens Prs 1988, Spring secondary Sr Prs 1989.

BURNSTEIN, Anne (Mrs. Robert) (d. 1988) of Las Vegas. Won Life Master Womens Prs 1963, Womens Tms 1951, 62, 79, Womens Prs 1979; Master Mixed Tms 1952, 53, Mixed Prs 1946, 52; placed second in Life Master Womens Prs 1962, Womens Tms 1955; won numerous regional titles. Burnstein was the sister of Edith Kemp-Freilich and William Seamon. See FAMILY.

BURNSTINE, David. See BRUCE, DAVID.

BURTON, Charles G. (Chuck) (b. 1950) of Ashland OR, tax preparer, bridge teacher and director. Won Santa Rosa Mens Prs 1981, Salem OR Masters Prs, Swiss 1986; Redding Swiss 1988, Open Swiss 1991; Yakima Super Open Prs 1991.

BUSTROS, Fady (1905-78) of Beirut, Lebanon, newspaper manager and bridge columnist. Represented Lebanon World Team Olympiad 1960, 1964, European Championships 1954, 1956, 1957, 1961, 1962. National successes include Open Team and Open Pairs six times each.

BUTCHER, Thomas D. (b. 1932 in Defiance, Ohio) of Tokyo, Japan, securities news editor and analyst. Represented Japan in eight Far East Championships, twice as playing captain. Won Far East Pairs 1964. Won many national team titles. Former editor *JCBL Bulletin*. Bridge columnist *Mainichi Daily News*. Chief director Far East Championships 1964 and 1979. He is a war-gamer, bridge system theorist, and advocate of total-point bridge.

BUTKOW, Hyman (b. 1927) of Johannesburg, South Africa, accountant. Represented South Africa in World Team Olympiad 1968, 1972, 1976. 20 national wins include 7 in open teams and four in open pairs.

BUTKOW, Julius ("Big Julie") (b. 1933) of Johannesburg, South Africa, chartered accountant. Represented South Africa at two world championships. Six national wins include two in open teams and one in open pairs. President of South African Bridge League since 1969 and organizer of all its national events. Editor of *Bridge S.A.* and a contributor. Bridge columnist *Business Day*. Member WBF Executive Council 1976, 1980. Tournament director Maccabi Games 1981, 1992.

BUTLER, David C. (b. 1949) of Keswick VA, comptroller, educated at U of Virginia. Has won more than 15 regional titles including Dist 6 GN Prs 1985, Mid-Atlantic Swiss 1977, 78, Open Prs 1978, 90, Open Prs 1979; Williamsburg KOs 1991.

BUTLER, Geoffrey (1898-1985) of London, England, journalist. Former member of WBF Executive and EBL Executive, then President Emeritus. Former president of

BBL, vice-president of EBU. Represented EBL and Portland Club in preparation of 1963 Codes of Laws. See BUENOS AIRES AFFAIR.

BUTLER, Dr. John (b. 1921) of Cardiff, Wales. Represented Wales in 58 Camrose Trophy matches between 1955 and 1982. 15 national wins include Welsh Teams 6 times. Formerly president WBU and vice-chairman BBL.

C

CABANNE, Carlos (b. 1917) of Buenos Aires, Argentina, dentist. WBF World Life Master. South American champion 1948, 1950, 1951, 1954, 1957, 1959, 1961, 1962, 1964, 1976. Represented Argentina in Bermuda Bowl 1958, 1962, 1965, 1977, in World Team Olympiad 1964, 1968, 1972, 1976, 1980. 40 national wins include open teams 12 times and open pairs six times. Won Gabarret Cup twice 1972, 1983. Named Honorary Member of the South American Bridge Confederation in 1980, he served as its secretary and president. He was director and president of the Argentine Bridge Association, a member of the World Bridge Federation executive committee 1961, 1962, 1964 and 1969-1977, and has been a member of its laws commission since 1970. Cabanne is a frequent contributor to bridge publications, the author of two books, *Bridge Razonada de A hasta Q*, and *Bridge después de la Q*. Member Editorial Board, *Bridge Encyclopedia*.

CABOT, Antonio (b. 1933) of Barcelona, Spain, bridge teacher. Represented Spain in four world championships and seven zonal championships. Won many national titles.

CABRAL, Francisco (b. 1943) of Lisbon, Portugal, technician. WBF World Master. Represented Portugal in one world championship and one European Championship. National wins include open team four times.

CACHO, Maxime (b. 1922) of Mandaluyong, Philippines. Won Far East Women's Teams 1967.

CAFFERATA, Mike (b. 1948) of Toronto ON, computer science and math teacher, represented Canada in world play 1982, 94. Won CNTC 1993, Canadian Open Prs 1991; has won more than 40 regionals including Can-At Swiss 1975, 80; Nickel City KO Tms, Swiss, Open Prs 1978; Canadian Nat'ls Master Prs 1988, Open Prs 1992; Cambrian Shield Open Prs 1992; London Bridge Open Prs 1993.

CAHN, Nell Bridge (b. 1935) of Shreveport LA, attended Stephens College and the U of Alabama, bridge teacher, accomplished oil painter, formerly restored old homes for resale, has an extensive collection of bridge memorabilia. Has represented Dist 10 on the Nat'l Charity Committee, National Board of Governors and the Nat'l Appeals Committee, served as president and VP of Unit 170. WBF World Master and ACBL Diamond Life Master. Won world championship Venice Cup 1991, represented U.S. in three other world championships and the 1992 Pan-American Games. North American championships include Life Master Womens Prs, Womens

BAM Tms 1988; Womens KO Tms 1991; placed second in Womens KO Tms 1983, Womens Swiss 1986, 90. Her 25-plus regional titles included Texas Spring Womens Prs 1967, Open Prs, Open Swiss 1976; Dist 10 GN Prs 1982, Reno Womens Prs 1984, Bridge Week Open Swiss 1986, Bermuda KO Tms, Jacksonville Womens Prs 1988; Nashville Womens Prs, Rocky Mountain Swiss, Monroe KO Tms 1991.

CAHN-SPEYER, Anton (b. 1918 in Austria) of Bogota, Colombia, public accountant. WBF World Master. Won CAC Teams 1968, and represented Colombia in six other zonal championships. Won eight national titles including Open Teams five times.

CALDWELL, Bobbye of Chicago, school teacher, bridge teacher. Columnist of *ABA Bulletin* and formerly its editor for 10 years.

CALE, Helen (1912-1990) of Glendale CA, bridge teacher and writer. Served as president of the ABTA, as president of ACBL Western Division and as chairman of the Los Angeles Unit. Won Barclay Trophy 1949, 1950 and placed second in Mixed Prs 1957. Regional wins include Bridge Week Open Tms 1948, Womens Prs 1954, Master Womens Prs 1971.

CALLAHAM, Thomas M. (b. 1934) of Wytheville VA, pharmacist. Won BAM Tms 1981. Regional wins include Rocky Mtn Open Tms 1969, Mid-Atlantic Fall Master Prs 1970, Swiss 1972, Spring Open Prs 1977, Master Prs 1976; Dist 11 Mens Prs 1978, Mens Swiss 1979.

CALVENTE, Ricardo (b. 1918 in Argentina) of Spain, trader. WBF World Life Master. Third World Teams 1958, 1959. Won South American Teams 1959, 1961, second 1963, 1967. Represented Argentina in three other world championships. In Spain since 1969, and represented Spain in one zonal championship.

CAMACHO, Carlos (b. 1946) of Rio de Janeiro, Brazil, engineer. WBF World Master. Won Bermuda Bowl 1989, South American Teams 1987, 1988, 1989, 1991, 1993. Represented Brazil in four other world championships.

CAMARA, Helen (Ninny) (b. 1907) formerly of Cairo, Egypt, born in Greece, WBF World Life Master, was World Women's Team champion 1960 and also represented Egypt in the World Women's Teams 1964, Women's European Women's Teams 1949, 1961, Open Teams 1956. Her national successes include Open Teams 1937, 1946, 1950, 1953, 1959, Interclubs 1931, 1934, 1947, Mixed Teams 1959, 1960, 1961. She has contributed to various bridge periodicals.

CAMBEROS, Hector R. (b. 1948) of Buenos Aires, Argentina, chemical engineer. WBF World Master. South American champion 1979, 1980, 1981, 1985, and represented Argentina in Bermuda Bowl 1977, 1981, 1985, World Team Olympiad 1984, 1988. 8 national wins include open teams five times. Won Gabarret Cup 1979. Editor *Bridge Para Todos* 1977-79.

CAMERON, Gail of Harare, Zimbabwe. Represented Zimbabwe in one world championship and one zonal championship. Represented Zimbabwe in many regional tournaments and won national titles.

CAMPBELL, Clifford V. (Cliff) (b. 1949) of Thunder Bay ON, store owner and bridge professional, attended Lakehead U. Placed second in Canadian Curling Championship 1979. Past president of Unit 228, Diamond Life Master, winner of Richmond Trophy 1985, 86, 92, 93; set Canadian record by winning more than 1500 points in 1992. Has won more than 60 regionals including Buffalo Mixed Prs 1977, Thunder Bay Swiss 1981, Canadian Nat'l Tms Zone 4 1982, St. Paul KOs 1982, 84; London KOs 1985, Green Bay KOs 1989, Thunder Bay KOs, Honolulu KOs, South Bend KOs 1990; Colorado Springs KOs, Nashville KOs, Montreal KOs 1991; Port Chester KOs, Dayton KOs, Pasadena KOs, Toronto KOs 1992.

CAMPBELL, Dr. Donald Keith (b. 1957) of Saskatoon SK, dentist, graduated U of Saskatchewan. Active in golf tournament play and administration. Has held several executive positions on local and Unit level including president and vice-president. Won National Open Prs 1990, competed in USBC 1991. Regional wins include Saskatoon Super Open Prs 1982, Regina KOs 1985, Saskatoon KOs 1988, Billings Masters Prs, Open Prs, Red Deer Open Swiss 1989; Butte Open Swiss 1990, Dist 18 NAOP 1991, Red Deer Swiss 1992.

CAMPBELL, Gordon (b. 1951) of Calgary AB, computer systems analyst, educated at Brunel U in London, England. British Jr. chess champion 1966, Alberta senior chess champion 1976. Past president Edmonton Unit 391 1981-83, served as tournament chairman 1979-81. Won Canadian National Tms 1984, represented Canada in tri-country playoffs and Bermuda Bowl Championship Sao Paulo 1985. Has won several Swiss Team events and one Mens Prs.

CAMPBELL, Dr. Hastings (b. 1949) of Belfast, Northern Ireland, property company director and lecturer in business and management. Represented Ireland once in the European Championship and Northern Ireland 32 times in Camrose Trophy matches.

CAMPBELL, Dr. Joe (1925-1992) of Union City TN, surgeon, graduated Vanderbilt and U of Tennessee, served as vice mayor of Union City. Won Ft Wayne Mens Swiss, St. Louis Swiss 1988; Hilton Head KOs, Paducah KOs 1989; Atlanta KOs 1990, Gatlinburg Open Swiss, Atlanta KOs 1991.

CAMPBELL, Dr. L. Andrew (b. 1942) of Manhattan Beach CA, research scientist, educated at Princeton, U of Paris and MIT, is interested in the Jacobian Conjecture and volunteers at Recording for the Blind. Placed second in Reisinger 1982. Regional wins include Pacific Southwest Mens Tms 1977, Barometer Open Prs 1981, Super Open Prs 1983, Mens Prs 1987, Swiss 1991; Dist 23 GNT 1981, Bridge Week Open Swiss 1982, Super Open Prs 1986, BAM Swiss 1988; Riverside Super Open Prs, Swiss 1987; Pasco Open Prs 1989.

CAMPBELL, Patricia L. (Mrs. Joe) (See Denger, Patricia) (b. 1932) of Union City TN, formerly a registered nurse and now a homemaker, graduated U of Tennessee, antique collector. Won Hilton Head Open KOs, Paducah KOs 1989; Atlanta KOs 1990, Spring NABC secondary Open Prs, Gatlinburg Open Swiss, Charlotte Strat Prs, Atlanta KOs 1991.

CAMPOS, Orlando (b. 1925) of Bombay, India, retired executive. WBF World Master. Represented India in seven world championships and two zonal championship. India's top masterpoint holder. 22 national wins include open teams twice and open pairs once. IBF treasurer 1970-85. Chief tournament director Far East Championships 1978.

CANESSA, Luciana R. of Rome, Italy, World Life Master, won World Women's Teams 1972, European Women's Teams 1970, 1971, 1973.

CANNELL, Douglas L. (b. 1924) of Winnipeg MB, architect, archeology-architect Rio Azul Archeological Project Guatemala for three field seasons, scuba diver. Awarded City of Winnipeg Community Services Award. First president and founding member Canadian Bridge Federation, past president Unit 181, chairman ACBL Canadian Charitable Foundation, chairman Omar Sharif Bridge Circus 1970, chairman 1985 Fall NABC. Represented Canada as president of CBF at World Olympiad in Deauville 1968. Won his first regional Open Prs in Winnipeg 1954.

CANNELL, Drew (Panama) (b. 1952) of Winnipeg MB, computer operations manager, bridge club assistant manager and bridge teacher, enjoys playing baseball and chess. Represented Canada (1974, 85, 90) and Panama (1978, 80) in WBF events. In 1978 won CAC Zonal team championship and represented CAC in World Championships. Was Canadian coach in 1984 and npc for Panama Venice Cup Team 1988. Cannell has competed in six World Championships since the Seventies, was youngest player at Las Palmas 1974, has won tournaments on five continents. Has been panelist on *International Popular Bridge Monthly* and *Bridge*; developed his own bidding system — the Panama Relay System. WBF World Master and Caribbean Grand Master. Was first Canadian (with partner G. Sekhar) to win Grand National Prs (1986), won Canadian Nat'l Tms Championship 1984, second in 1986 and was npc of winning team in 1985; placed second Zonal Grand National Tms 1974, Reisinger 1982, Open BAM Tms 1992; has won more than 100 sectionals and many regional titles.

CANNELL, Philip Drew (see CANNELL, Drew)

CANSINO, Jonathan (b. 1939) of London, England, former stock broker. Represented Britain in two zonal championships and England in Camrose matches. Eight national wins include Gold Cup.

CAPLAN, JoAnne (See CASEN, Jo Anne)

CAPLAN, Mark E. (b. 1965) of Toronto, interest rate swap trader at Bank of Montreal, graduated with honors from U of Western Ontario, contributor to *Canadian Masterpoint*. Won the Jr Collegiate Par Contest 1987, second in 1987 in the ACBL Intercollegiate Championships. Placed second in the World Jr Bridge Championships Ann Arbor 1991; won Toronto Swiss 1988, 89;

Buffalo Swiss 1988.

CAPODANNO, Luciana of Naples, Italy, won the World Women's Teams 1976, second Venice Cup 1978. WBF Grand Master. European Women's champion 1974, 1977.

CAPONI, Claudio (b. 1957) of Caracas, Venezuela, hydrologist. WBF World Master. Won CAC Teams 1984, 1985, 1987, 1991, CAC Pairs once. Represented Venezuela in four world championships and won many national titles. Bridge teacher and director.

CAPPELLETTI, A. Michael (b. 1942) of Alexandria VA, attorney with the U.S. Dept of Justice specializing in "complex litigation" (computers), graduate of MIT and Boston U. Is considered one of the world's leading authorities on Omaha poker, has written a bi-weekly column, *Cappelletti on Omaha*, for *The Card Player* magazine since 1989; wrote five plays which received local exposure in the Eighties. Has served on ACBL Bd of Governors, ACBL Nat'l Appeals Committee, as president of the Mid-Atlantic Conference and Washington BL. Wrote *Cappelletti over No-Trump* and *Cappelletti Over One-of-a-Major Doubled*; authored the same conventions and Cappelletti Two-Suited Cuebids. Grand Life Master with more than 15,000 MPs; placed third World Mixed Tms 1974, sixth World Open Prs 1978. Won Master Mixed Tms 1967, placed second in Mixed Prs 1967, Blue Ribbon Prs 1973, 77; Spring Mens Tms 1979, North American Swiss 1985, Mixed Prs 1988, Reisinger 1991. See FAMILY.

CAPPELLETTI, Katherine H. (Kathie). See WAL-VICK, KATHERINE H.

CAPPELLETTI, Michael D., Jr. (Mike Jr.) (b. 1965) of Knoxville TN, student and professional player, was National Merit Scholar finalist. Active in Junior bridge, became Life Master just prior to 16th birthday. Has won dozens of regionals -- his first in 1979 at age 14. Had highest pair score in Intercollegiates (Instant Matchpoints) 1990, won Dist 7 GN Prs 1991, NACBC (Inter-Collegiates) 1989. Placed second Reisinger 1991, participated in the Euopean Bridge League Jr Camp 1989, fifth World Jr Championships 1989, fourth 1991. See FAMILY.

CAPPS, Richard Aaron (b. 1944) of Baton Rouge LA, elementary school principal, educated at Northwestern State and Louisiana State. Has served as president and sec/treas for Unit 182, member of Nat'l Goodwill Committee. Placed second North American Swiss 1983; won Jackson Open Prs, Dallas Master Prs, New Orleans Master Prs, Atlanta Swiss, Gulf Coast Swiss, Shreveport Swiss, Monroe Swiss, Little Rock Swiss, Huntsville KO Tms, New Orleans Mixed Prs.

CAPRERA, David Anthony (Dave) (b. 1953) of Denver CO, tax attorney, degrees from Princeton and U of Chicago. Other interests include fly fishing, hunting mushrooms and most sports. Won Lansing Mens Tms, Denver KOs, Dist 17 Grand National Prs, Denver Master Prs, Denver Pan Am Prs, Wichita Open Prs, Salt Lake City Master Prs and Phoenix Swiss. Winner of Epson World-Wide Bidding Contest 1989 and Christchurch NZ Open Prs 1990.

CARACCI, Marcelo Lagos (b. 1949) of Santiago, Chile, engineer. Represented Chile in 10 zonal championships and won all national titles.

CARANSA, Maurits. See CONTINENTAL CLUB.

CARAVELLI, Gerald A. (Gerry) (b. 1943) of Des Plaines IL, accountant, graduated U of Illinois. Special interests include travel, movies, reading, classical music and opera. Member of Nat'l Goodwill Committee, has served as tournament chairman, president and vice president of Chicago CBA. Long-time panelist on *The Bridge World* Master Solvers Club. Grand Life Master with more than 14,000 points; won Mixed Prs 1974, Master Mixed Tms 1975, Mens Prs 1976, Grand National Tms 1978, Open Prs 1982; placed second in Senior and Advanced Master Prs 1964, Spring Mens Tms 1971, Mixed Tms 1980, Grand National Tms 1984, 88; North American Swiss 1979, 88, 89; Vanderbilt 1977, Open Prs 1984; won CAC Open Tms 1991. Has won more than 100 regionals including Spring secondary Swiss 1974, 77, Master Prs 1975, Open Prs A-D 1978; Central States KOs 1969, 72, 73; LM KOs 1979, Mens Swiss 1977, BAM Tms 1981.

CARGILE, Charles A. (Charlie) (b. 1940) of Toney AL, professional gambler and card player since 1970. Won his division in the Mini-McKenney two years in a row, Master 20-50 masterpoints 1985 and Advanced Sr Master 200-Life Master 1986; placed second Red Ribbon Prs 1986, 89. Regional wins include Atlanta Swiss, Portland Open Prs, Tulsa KOs, Little Rock KOs 1986; Nashville Bracketed KOs 1987, Gatlinburg Open Prs 1990, Bracketed KO Tms 1993.

CARINI-MAZZACCARA, Marchese Silvio (1907-1990) of Florence, Italy, wine industry executive, former member of executive committees of EUROPEAN BRIDGE LEAGUE, WORLD BRIDGE FEDERATION, ITALIAN BRIDGE FEDERATION, and of the Editorial Advisory Board, *Bridge Encyclopedia.*

CARLIER, Paul H. (b. 1931) of Brussels, Belgium, secretary-general of European consulting firms committee, former barrister. Vice-president of Belgian Bridge Federation, former president. Several national successes in Mixed Teams. Director of Brussels Chamber of Commerce.

CARLSON, Isabella S. (Mrs E. N.) (d. 1990) of Webster Grove MO, former bridge teacher, cruise conductor, club director, one of the early pioneers of bridge in the St. Louis area, helped organize the St. Louis Unit in the Thirties and the St. Louis Womens Bridge League, of which she was president for many years. Past president of the St. Louis Unit and former member of ACBL Bd. of Dir. and ACBL Charity Committee.

CARNS, Dr. Gail (b. 1941) of Export PA, systems analyst and mathematics professor, educated at U of New Mexico (PhD). Served Unit 142 as Bd member and president. Won Dist. 5 Grand National Tms 1983, 84, 86, 87, 90; Pittsburgh KOs 1984, Bermuda Open Prs, Pittsburgh Swiss 1990; Buffalo Swiss 1992.

CARRUTHERS, John (JC) (b. 1947) of Toronto, born

in England, research chemist, systems analyst, writer, graduated Mount Allison U. Outside activities are writing, music, travel, golf and reading. Has co-authored two books *Creating Effective Manuals* and *Ex-Etiquette*. Editor of Ontario *Kibitzer* for five years and has had articles published in *IBPA Bulletin*, *WBF News*, *Internat'l Popular Bridge Monthly*, ACBL *Bulletin*, *Australian Bridge*, New Zealand *Bridge Bulletin*, SABF *Bulletin*. WBF World Master, was npc of Canadian Bermuda Bowl team 1985 and Venice Cup team 1989 (placed third), Yokohama 1991, Womens Olympiad Salsomaggiore 1992; also World Jr. Championship team Ann Arbor 1991 (placed second), Denmark 1993. Competed for Canada in five world championships. Diamond Life Master. Was first recipient of the Richmond Trophy 1974; won Master Mixed Tms 1991; second Life Master Prs 1988; won Canadian Nat'l Team Championship twice and was second three times, won Canadian Open Prs Championship. Some of his many regionals are Motor City Open Prs 1972, Swiss Tms 1975; Canadian Nat'l Swiss 1973, KO Tms five times, Mens Swiss 1978, 79, 80; Buffalo Open Prs 1974, Bermuda Mens Prs 1978, Dist. 5 Open Prs 1979, secondary Silver Trophy Prs 1981.

CARSTENSEN, Svend (1899-1977) of Copenhagen, Denmark, bridge writer and journalist. Pioneered electronic computer scoring system. Founded one of the world's biggest pair tournaments. Columnist of *Berlingske Tidende* 1946-1969. As a journalist, had a world scoop in announcing the Nazi invasion of Denmark.

CARTER, David C. (1906-1989) of St. Louis, building and loan executive, past president of the Missouri Valley Conference and former vice president of the Midwest Conference. Originator of SOUTH AFRICAN TEXAS transfer bids (see also TEXAS), double-barreled variety of TWO-WAY STAYMAN. Was alternate for the 1963 North American Bermuda Bowl Team, won McKenney Trophy 1954, Life Master Prs 1954, Mens Tms 1950, Mens Prs 1957; placed second Spingold 1953, 62; Open Prs 1946, 53, 54, Mens Prs 1960; also won many regional events.

CARTER, Kay (b. 1921) of Seminole FL, insurance agency secretary/treasurer. Placed second Womens Prs 1962, Mixed Prs 1965; won Great Lakes Open Prs 1961, Mixed Prs 1962; Keystone Mixed Prs 1963, Mid-Atlantic Fall Open Prs 1968.

CASABAL, Leon (1892-1965) of Buenos Aires, Argentina, pioneer of Argentine bridge; was bridge columnist for *La Nacion* in the early Thirties; participated in a radio match against Ely Culbertson's team in 1936; authored *Bridge de Hoy* 1930.

CASEN, Drew (b. 1950) of Boca Raton FL, bridge professional, former accountant, educated at Baruch and Nassau Community Colleges, nine handicap golfer and expert holdem (poker) player. WBF World Master, placed second Rosenblum Tms 1990, 13th Rosenblum Tms 1986, 17th World Open Prs 1986. ACBL Diamond Life Master with more than 50 regional wins; won Cavendish Invitational Prs 1987; won Master Mixed Tms 1983, Open Swiss 1992; placed second in Mens BAM 1982, 88; Blue Ribbon Prs 1982, Mens Swiss 1986,

Vanderbilt 1987, Open Swiss, IMP Prs 1990; Open Prs II 1993. Casen met his wife at a regional, married at a World Championship, had son at an NABC.

CASEN, JoAnne (b. 1954) of Boca Raton FL, controller, graduate of Ohio State U. Finished 5th in the World Womens Prs 1986, won International Invitational Shanghai Bridge tournament 1981, North American Womens Prs 1985. Regional wins include Huntsville Womens Swiss 1984, Redcoat Open Swiss, Master Prs, Womens Prs, Swiss 1985; Houston Master Swiss, Bal Harbour Womens Swiss 1986; Cambridge KO Tms 1987.

CASEY, Jill (b. 1948) of Newport, Wales, teacher. Represented Britain in one Venice Cup and three Common Market Championships. Represented Wales in Camrose Trophy. Won Lady Milne Cup and four Welsh titles.

CASH, Ralph A. (b. 1904) of Phoenix, insurance agent, was the U.S. winner of the World Olympiad 1936. Was president of Western Division 1954, member of the Western Conference and ACBL executive committee, chairman of the Phoenix Unit and general chairman of the Fall NABC in Phoenix 1962. Won many regional titles.

CASIAN, Esteban (b. 1932 in Chile) of Spain, bridge teacher. Won South American Teams 1964. Represented Chile in three world championships and four other zonal championships. In Spain since 1978.

CASLAN, Dr. David F. (b. 1948) of Columbus IN, college professor, formerly an attorney, educated at Rose Hulman, Indiana State U, U of Louisville, Bellarmine and St. Louis U (PhD). Has done mountain climbing in the Himalayas, Europe and U.S., enjoys running in 10 Ks. Won Grand National Prs 1989, His 32 regional titles include Dist. 5 Open Prs 1972, Dist. 11 KOs 1974, 77; Great Lakes Mens Prs 1977, Central States Master Prs 1980, Midwest Fall Mens Swiss 1981.

CASTRO, Alejandro (1916-1989), of Lima, Peru, formerly of Buenos Aires, Argentina. World Life Master. Founder of the South American championships. Secretary of the South American Bridge Confederation 1955-1963. South American champion, for Argentina, 1948, 1953, 1954, 1957, 1958, and represented Argentina 1958, 1959, 1961 Bermuda Bowl. Later competed for Peru 1976-1981. President of Argentine Bridge Association 1948-1950 and 1952-1956. Won Gabarret Cup 1957 and won many national titles. Author of *Rebland System*.

CATON, Don J. (b. 1941) of Pensacola FL, attorney for the city of Pensacola, schooled at Florida State U and Stetson Law School; was Florida junior tennis champion and ranked 5th in the U.S. in singles and second in doubles in boys' division in the mid-Fifties; also a table tennis champion. Served as chairman and member of various rules and ethics committees at regionals. Placed second in Life Master Prs 1980 and Mens BAM Tms 1986. Regional wins include Mid-South Open Prs 1970, 73, Mens Prs 1970, 71; Azalea City Master Prs 1980, Jacksonville Open Swiss, Swiss 1984; Biloxi Open Swiss, Swiss 1988, Atlanta Open Prs 1989, Daytona Beach Open Swiss 1991.

CATZEFLIS, Georges (b.1931) of Lausanne, Switzerland, engineer. WBF World Life Master. Represented Switzerland in 5 world championships and 7 Championships. Won National Open Teams and Open Pairs nine times each.

CAVENDISH, pseudonym of **Henry Jones** (1831-1899), a famous London whist authority. Cavendish was the name of the club to which Jones belonged and the name under which he chose to publish his first book on whist in 1863. This book, *The Laws and Principles of Whist Stated and Explained, and Its Practice Illustrated on an Original System, by Means of Hands Played Completely Through*, became the most popular guide to the game of whist since Hoyle's *Short Treatise. Cavendish on Whist* (book spine title) went through many editions and revisions, incorporating Jones's latest and best theories. He was the author of a number of other books on whist, among them *Whist Developments, American Leads* and *The Plain-Suit Echo*, 1885, *Card Essays, Clay's Decisions* and *Card Table Talk*, 1890 and *American Leads Simplified*, 1891. With Nicholas Browse Trist he developed the system of whist play named by him the *American Leads*, which encountered rather violent opposition in some quarters, but nevertheless enjoyed great popularity in England and even greater in America. Jones attended the third Annual Congress of the AMERICAN WHIST LEAGUE, of which he was an honorary member.

CAYNE, James (Jimmy) (b. 1934) of New York City, investment banker. Placed second World Mixed Prs, World Mixed Tms 1974. WBF World Master and ACBL Diamond Life Master. Won Master Mixed Tms 1966, Life Master Mens Prs 1969, Reisinger BAM Tms (playing captain) 1977, 88, 92; Mens Tms 1969, Mens BAM Tms 1988, Spingold 1989, 90; npc Open BAM 1993; placed second Life Master Prs 1969, 73; Reisinger 1981, 93; Mens BAM Tms 1989; won many regional events. Won Maccabiah Games Tms 1981 as playing captain; won each of the three Corporate America vs Congress matches, was also a participant in the Corporate America vs. Hollywood Celebrities match.

CAYNE, Patricia (Pat) (b. 1939) of New York City, educational neuropsychologist; earned degrees from U of Pennsylvania and Columbia (PhD). Non-playing captain Chinese women's team 1993; started bridge program for New York League for Hard of Hearing 1989; authored *Hear I Am* for hearing impaired; member ACBL Educational Foundation; chairman Congress vs. Corporate America and Congress vs. Parliament matches; author of *Language Through Play*, a book for teaching language to language-impaired children.

CEARLEY, Boyce L. (1941-1982) of Fort Smith AR, dentist, tremendous asset to Arkansas bridge, organized duplicate games in Fort Smith and Fayetteville, trained directors, instituted a novice program, organized the first sectional in western Arkansas, was tournament chairman nine times. Cearley, a cancer victim, died in Niagara Falls after competing in the Grand National Prs finals. His many regional wins include Missouri Valley Mens Swiss, Master Prs 1978, Open Prs 1977; Mid-South KO Tms, Open Prs 1978.

CEDERBORG, Warren J. (b. 1945) of Visalia CA, sportswriter for Visalia *Times-Delta,* graduate of California State U at Hayward, a published poet. Frequent contributor to *Contract Bridge Forum,* author of *Coffee with Mary Jane Farell.* Won several regionals.

CHAGAS, Gabriel P. (b. 1944) of Rio de Janeiro, Brazil, financier and investment consultant. WBF Grand Master. Won World Teams 1976, Bermuda Bowl 1989, World Open Pairs 1990. He is one of just eight to have won the TRIPLE CROWN of world teams, world pairs and Bermuda Bowl. Second World Teams 1978, and represented Brazil in 23 other world championships, apparently a record. Won South American Teams a record 20 times in the period 1967-93, in 24 attempts. Won 26 national titles, and is the top-ranked South American player. Won Reisinger 1992. Won London *Sunday Times Pairs* 1979 and 1992; Cap Gemini 1993. Magazine contributor. Created the term INTRA-FINESSE. See SCIENTISTS v. TRADITIONALISTS.

CHAIKIN, Marla (b. 1944) of Sea Bright NJ, needlepoint shop owner, former interior designer, graduate of Skidmore College, GNYBA board member 1976-80. Placed second in Life Master Womens Prs 1990, was Staten Island Player of Year 1980, 81; NJ Woman Player of Year 1991, second in 1992. Regional wins include Fall secondary Open Prs 1982, Hofstra LI Open Swiss 1983, ParsippanyWomens Prs 1986, Womens Tms 1990; Stevensville Womens Tms 1986, Southeastern Master Prs 1987, Cherry Hill Womens Prs, Womens Tms 1989; Stamford Womens Tms, Rye Womens Prs 1989; San Juan Open Prs, Master Prs 1989; NJ Double KO Tms 1991.

CHAMBERS, Neil J. (b. 1946) of Schenectady NY, born in Regina SK, tax accountant, graduated U of Washington. Was coach for Canada during World Team Olympiad 1980, created the Chico 2 bid. Diamond Life Master, won North American Swiss 1977, Mens Tms 1978, 81; Vanderbilt 1992; placed second Spingold 1986, won numerous regional events.

CHAMBERS, Juanita of Schenectady NY, bridge professional. WBF Life Master, won world championship Venice Cup 1987, World Mixed Prs 1990, Pan-American Womens Prs 1992; placed 3rd in Pan-American Womens Tms 1992. ACBL Diamond Life Master, won Womens KO Tms 1985, North American Womens Swiss 1987, 91; Master Mixed Tms 1984, 89, 92, Womens KO Tms 1989, 92; Mixed Prs 1979, Womens BAM Tms 1991, 93; placed second Mixed Prs 1987, Womens KO Tms 1986, 90; has many regional wins.

CHAN, ANDY (b. 1962) of Kuala Lumpur, Malaysia, accountant. Represented Malaysia in one world championship. National wins include open teams.

CHAN, David Y. K. (b.1951) of Hong Kong, banking executive. WBF World Master. Won Far East Teams 1987, and represented Hong Kong in three world championships and two other Far East Championships. National wins include open teams and open pairs.

CHAN, Hin Cheung (b. 1918) of Kuala Lumpur, Malaysia, company director. Represented Malaysia in world and zonal championships. National wins include open teams.

CHAN, Lapt H. (b. 1963) of Woodside NY, manager of Manhattan Bridge Club, former baseball card dealer, collects autographed baseball bats. 1985 Rookie of the Year (0-5 points) in *Ace of Clubs* competition. Won Spring secondary Open Prs 1990, Tm of Two Prs 1992; Eastern States Open Prs (Goldman) 1987, NY Winter KOs 1987, Frank Westcott Open Prs 1987, Port Chester KOs 1988, Springfield Swiss 1990, Cherry Hill Open Prs 1992.

CHANDROSS, Howard (b. 1946) of Long Beach NY, tax accountant and bridge professional, graduate of Hofstra U. On Bd of Directors of Greater New York BA and Nassau Suffolk BA 1975-88. Member of Nat'l Bd of Governors and Goodwill Committee, past president and treasurer of NSBA. WBF World Master, placed 13th in Rosenblum Tms 1986. Placed second Vanderbilt 1987, Life Master Mens Prs 1984 and Master Mixed Tms 1990. An ACBL Grand Life Master with more than 15,000 masterpoints, won more than 100 regional events, including 35 in 1991.

CHANFRAY, Annie (d. 1981) of Lyons, France. WBF World Life Master. Second World Women's Teams 1960, third 1964.

CHANG, Godfrey (b. 1937) of Honolulu, supervisory computer systems analyst, graduate U of Hawaii. Practices Tai Chi, physical fitness, weight training, enjoys gardening. Served on Unit board and as tournament chairman. Diamond Life Master. Regional wins include Hawaii Mens Prs 1969, 82, 83, Mixed Prs 1972, Master Prs 1973, 81, 93, KO Tms 1976, 85, Open Prs 1983, 87, Open Prs 1984, 90, Swiss 1988, Unmixed Prs 1989; Dist. 20 Grand National Tms 1982, Rogue Valley Master Prs 1987.

CHANG, Hsi-Chung (b. 1939) of Taipei, Taiwan, art director. WBF World Master. Far East champion 1981, Far East Pairs champion 1977 and 1981. Represented Taiwan in three world championships. Won several national titles. Brother of Yin-Tsun Chang.

CHANG, Morris (b. 1931) of Santa Clara CA, born in China, educated at MIT and Stanford (PhD), semiconductor and computer executive at Texas Instruments. Placed second in North American Swiss 1992; won Big D Master Prs 1972, Swiss 1974, Open Prs 1978, 80; Mid-South Spring KOs 1973, Rocky Mountain Swiss 1977, Master Prs 1979; Austin KOs 1983, Master Prs, KOs Tms 1986; Secaucus Swiss 1984, Port Chester Swiss 1985, Houston Swiss 1986, 89, KO Tms 1986, 88; Albuquerque Open Prs 1987, NY KO Tms 1988, Houston Open Prs 1992.

CHANG, Yin-Tsun (b. 1945) of Taipei, Taiwan. WBF World Master. Far East champion 1981, Far East Pairs champion 1977 and 1981. Represented Taiwan in three world championships. Won several national titles. Brother of Hsi-Chung Chang.

CHARNEY, Gerald (Gerry) (b. 1933) of Toronto, barrister and solicitor, placed third World Olympiad Tms 1968, 72; fifth in Rosenblum Tms 1978; captained Canada in World Team Olympiad 1980. WBF Life Mas-

ter. Has won several regional events.

CHATTA, Patricia J. (Pat) (b. 1936) of Watertown MA, financial planner, cost analyst, technical writer, schooled at DePaul U and Aquinas. Won North American Rookie Prs 1981. Regionals wins are Smugglers Notch Swiss 1983, Hartford Swiss 1985.

CHATZINOFF, Kenneth (b. 1945) of Cinnaminson NJ, psychologist working in correctional institutions, graduate of U of Rochester and Pennsylvania State U; member Bd of Dir Unit 141 since 1980; chairman, Conduct and Ethics Unit 141 1983-1991. Won National Amateur Mens Prs 1976, Fall secondary Open Prs 1979, Mid-Atlantic Prs 1977.

CHAZEN, Bernard (Bernie) (b. 1942) of Tamarac FL, former teacher and systems analyst, won Mens Tms 1971, Mixed Prs 1973. Grand Life Master, has won numerous regional events.

CHEEK, Curtis (b. 1958) of Huntsville AL, aerospace engineer, active in bridge teaching and administration in Unit 232 and a past president. Diamond Life Master with numerous regional titles including Celebrity Mens Prs 1977, Mid-Atlantic Swiss 1988, Mens KOs 1989, 91; Mid-South Swiss 1982, 85, 91; Space-City Mens Swiss, Open Prs 1984, Swiss 1988, Champagne Swiss 1986, Dist. 10 KO Tms 1988, Derby City Masters Prs, Swiss 1991; Lexington Open Prs, Gatlinburg Open Prs 1991; San Diego Open Prs 1992. Represented Dist. 10 in Grand National Tms 1982, 86, 88, 91, 92; Grand National Prs 1985, 87, 89.

CHEMLA, Paul (b. 1944 in Tunis) of Paris, France, bridge professional, former literature lecturer. WBF Grand Master. Won World Teams 1980, 1992, second 1984. Won European Pairs 1976 and 1985. Represented France in many other world and zonal championships. Won *Sunday Times Pairs* 1991.

CHEN, Amy (b. 1949) of Taipei, Taiwan. WBF World Master. Far East champion 1988, 89. Represented Taiwan in three other zonal championships and three world championships.

CHEN, Chi-Ping (b. 1924 in China) of Taipei, Taiwan, retired judge. Far East champion 1967 and 1971. Managing director of Taiwan Bridge League since 1982 and former president of Taipei unit. Helped organize 1971 Bermuda Bowl, 1981 Far East Championships. Three of his children and one son-in-law have represented Taiwan in international competition.

CHEN, Chuan-Cheng (b. 1952) of Hsin Chu, Taiwan, mechanical engineer. WBF World Master. Won Far East Teams 1987, 1989, Far East Pairs 1987. Represented Taiwan in five world championships and two other Far East Championships. Won many national titles.

CHEN, Kuo Yong (b. 1944 in China) of Taipei, Taiwan, insurance manager. WBF World Master. Far East champion 1981, 1988 and represented Taiwan in two other zonal championship and two world championships. National titles include China Cup four times.

CHEN, Rongchang of Shanghai, China, technical employee. WBF World Master. Won Far East Teams 1991, second 1993. Represented China in three world championships and two other zonal championships. Five national wins.

CHEN, Zelan (b. 1959) of Beijing, China. Winner of many national championships. Deputy secretary Chinese Bridge Association, organizer for 1995 world championship.

CHENG, Kai Kwong (b. 1945) of Winnipeg MB, born in Guangdong Province, China. Engineer with the provincial power utility, educated at U of Manitoba. Other interests include backgammon, chess and travel. Regional wins include Buffalo Swiss 1978, 90; Saskatchewan KO Tms, Master Swiss 1979, Swiss 1980; Gopher Open Prs 1980, KO Tms 1981; Regina Open Prs 1987, Saskatoon Swiss 1988.

CHENG, Kuen Ren or **Conrad** (b. 1934) of Hsin Chu, Taiwan, land developer. World Life Master. Second Bermuda Bowl 1970 and represented Taiwan in two other Bermuda Bowls. Won Far East Teams four times and Far East Open Pairs three times. Writings include *Modern Bidding System and Theory* and *Z Convention*.

CHERNOFF, Victor B. (b. 1937) of Los Angeles, consulting actuary, former principal actuary with IRS. Educated Harvard and Bates College, college table tennis champion. Won numerous regional events including Eastern States Open Prs (Goldman) 1970 as non-Life Master. Diamond Life Master with other wins of York Harbor Open Prs 1960, Keystone Open Prs 1971, Mid-Atlantic Swiss 1973, LA Winter Swiss Tm 1975, Bridge Week KO Tms 1976, Master Mens Prs, Swiss 1981; Golden State KO Tms, Mens Prs, Open Prs 1980, Master Prs 1982; Raincross KOs 1980, Swiss 1981; Mid-Winter Holiday Swiss 1981, Wine Country Swiss 1982. Represented Dist. 23 in Grand National Tms 1980, 82, 89.

CHEVALLEY, Ginette (b. 1933) of Paris, France, retailer. WBF World Life Master. Second World Women's Teams 1987, third 1985. Won European Women's Teams 1983, 1985, 1987. Won European Women's Pairs 1991. Represented France in six other world championships and won many national titles.

CHEW, Henry of Sabah, Malaysia, lawyer. Represented Maylaysia in one world championship.

CHIARADIA, Eugenio (The Professor) (1917-1977) of Naples, Italy, professor of philosophy. Won Bermuda Bowl 1957, 1958, 1959, 1961, 1962, 1963. Won European Teams 1951, 1956, 1957, 1958, 1959, second 1952. Italian national wins included Open Teams five times. He devised the Neapolitan System, a cornerstone of the Italian rise to world championship victories, and was the leader of the team in its early days. After retirement from the Italian team he lived in Sao Paulo, Brazil, and coached the Brazilian team. Author of one book.

CHILCOTE, Mary J. (Mrs. William) (b. 1926) of Cleveland OH, educated at Smith College, teaches bridge. Her mother was a survivor of the Titanic. Has

served on Nat'l Bd. of Governors (1970-78) and Unit 125 Board (1975-80). Placed 15th in World Mixed Prs 1974. Diamond Life Master. Placed second in Mixed Prs 1970 and has won more than 40 regional events including Fall secondary Swiss 1970, Las Vegas KOs 1971, Desert Empire Womens Prs 1972, Spring secondary Mixed Prs, Navajo Trail Swiss 1973; Motor City KOs 1975, All-American Womens Swiss 1981.

CHILDS, Derrell W. (b. 1934) of Garland TX, CPA, educated at Texas Tech. Served the Dallas BA as president, treasurer, board member and National Charity Committee-Dist 16 representative. Won International City Mixed Prs 1974, Texas Mid-Summer Master Prs 1979, Republic of Texas Mens Prs 1981, Dallas Mens Prs 1985, Cancun Unmixed Prs 1986, San Antonio Open Prs, Dallas Swiss 1988; Lubbock KO Tms 1990.

CHILDS, Louise of Garland TX, served on Nat'l Charity Committee. Regionals wins are International City Mixed Prs 1974, San Antonio Master Prs 1979, Open Prs 1988; Dallas Swiss 1988; El Paso Open Prs 1992.

CHILDS, O. Allen Jr. (Al) (b. 1934) of Little Rock AR, bridge professional and glass shop owner, schooled at Southern Arkansas U, Oklahoma State U and U of Arkansas. Other interests are vegetable gardening and old homes, lives in converted 100-year-old livery stable, is a member of national champion dairy cattle judging team, does state champion beef and hog judging. Has served Unit 161 and Dist. 10 in various executive positions and as a member of the ACBL Bd of Gov. Editor of the *Mid-South Bridge Forum* since its inception. Diamond Life Master. Regional wins include Mid-South KO Tms 1976, 78, Swiss 1979, Open Prs 1979; Missouri Valley Open Prs 1977, Oklahoma City Open Prs 1981, Dist. 10 Grand National Tms 1977, 79, Zone IV 1977, 79.

CHIN, Lenan (b. 1931) of Kingston, Jamaica, business executive. Represented Jamaica in one world championship and four zonal championships. Won one zonal event and numerous national titles. Has represented Jamaica in international amateur golf.

CHIU, Karic P.K. (b. 1954) of Hong Kong, computer operations manager. WBF World Master. Far East champion 1987. Represented Hong Kong in four world championships and four other Far East Championships. National wins include open teams and open pairs.

CHMELIK, Neklan (b. 1940) of Augsburg, Germany, dentist. Represented Czechoslavakia until 1968, later Germany. Has won two Czech titles and 10 German titles.

CHMIELOWIEC, John (Big John) (b. 1942) of Michigan City IN, senior draftsman, restores 1964 Pontiac GTOs. Won Champagne Mens Prs 1967, Spring secondary Mens Prs, Wolverine Master Prs 1987, Midwest Open Prs 1989; Green Bay Open Tms, Mens Tms 1989; Champagne Tms, Cambrian Shield Tms, Midwest Fall KO Tms 1990.

CHNARIS, George (b. 1952 in Crete) of Athens, Greece. Represented Greece in European Championships 1987, 1989, 1991.

CHODOROW, Claire (b. 1924) of Kenmore NY, born in Toronto, club director, formerly a dental hygienist, 20-year volunteer as a Gray Lady, enjoys travel, knitting, entertaining and grandchildren. Has served Unit 116 as vice president for many years and is past president, current chairman of Unit Ethics and Laws Committee; for years scheduled all tournaments and chaired tournament, unit and charity games; contributing editor to *5th Column*. Won Upper New York State Womens Prs 1978, 79; Toronto Womens Prs 1977, Canadian Nat'l Womens Swiss 1980.

CHOKSI, Rita (b. 1938) of Delhi, India, export company director. WBF World Master. Won Far East Women's Teams 1978, BFAME Women's Teams 1983, 1985, second 1991. Second BFAME Open Pairs 1983. Represented India in three other zonal championships and four world championships. Won more than 11 national titles. Only woman to qualify for Indian Open Team.

CHONG, Antonio T. (Tony) (born 1927 in Canton, China) of Taipei, Taiwan, Chairman and CEO of petrochemical company. Far East champion 1989 and played in two world championships. NPC of Taiwan team in seven world championships and more than 10 Far East Championships. Won Hong Kong Inter-City tournament 1989, 1990. National titles include open teams more than 10 times and open pairs 4 times. Chief organizer of major events in Taiwan including Far East Championship and Proton International tournaments.

CHOY, Patrick (b. 1943 in Hong Kong) of Singapore, corporation president. Delegate of Far East BF to WBF. Member of WBF Executive Council, and member of several WBF committees including Youth, Zoning, Infrastructure, Finance. Chairman Hong Kong CDA 1986-89. Won national titles in Hong Kong and Singapore.

CHRISTENSON, Sharon L. (b. 1938) of Edina MN, advertising salesperson, graduated Central College, has won several national sales awards. Won Pheasant Open Prs 1972, Gopher Womens Prs 1973, Open Prs 1977; Dist 14 GN Tms 1974, Northwest Iowa Swiss 1978, secondary KO Tms 1985, Mid-Atlantic Continuous Prs 1992.

CHRISTIAN, Col. William F. (1914-1986) of Chipley FL, retired Army officer. In 1946 shared the distinction with his teammate, Capt. Mark Hodges, of being the first members of the military service on active duty to win a North American Championship. Was awarded the Bronze Star, Silver Star 1944; French Croix de Guerre 1945, 1st OLC Bronze Star 1951, Legion of Merit 1967, Air Medal 1967. Won Spingold 1946, Mens Prs 1960; placed second Life Master Mens Prs 1964; many regional wins.

CHRISTIANSEN, Leif (b. 1914) of Nordstradshogda, Norway. Won Nordic Teams 1946 and 1949. Represented Norway in seven European Championships. National wins include open teams 6 times and open pairs twice.

CHU, Nytt (b. 1944) of Singapore, chemical engineer. Represented Singapore in 4 zonal championships. National wins include open teams several times.

CHU, Y.M. (b. 1921) of Irvine CA, formerly of Hong Kong, businessman. Won Far East Open Teams 1959, second 1963, 1965, 1969, and represented Hong Kong on other occasions. 9 Hong Kong national wins include master teams three times and open teams four times.

CHU, Yung-Ming (b. 1922) of Irvine CA, formerly of Hong Kong, born in Shanghai, accountant. Won Far East Open Tms 1959, placed second in Open Tms 1963, 65, 69, Open Prs 1971; represented Hong Kong in Far East Championships 1963-71. North American wins include Master Tms 1960, 63, 68; Open Tms 1958, 62, 69, 70; Master Prs 1959, 71; Open Prs 1966, Mixed Prs 1968, 72; Individual 1958. Won Pasadena Open Prs 1976, Sr Open Prs 1989; Fall secondary Mens Tms 1978, Sr KO Tms 1990; Ventura Sr Swiss Tms 1990, Riverside Open Prs 1992, Pasadena Sr. Prs, Strat Prs, Palm Springs Sr. Swiss 1992.

CHUA, Cathy (b. 1959) of Sydney, Australia, historian. Won Far East Women's Teams 1990. Represented Australia in one other zonal championship. Wins include South Pacific Junior Teams and Pairs, national Open Teams and Grand National Teams. Has represented Australia at chess as well as bridge. Potentially, author of history of Australian bridge.

CHUA, Dr. Chee Peng (b. 1945) of Singapore, chemist. Represented Singapore in one world championship and 2 zonal championships.

CHUA, Stephen (1919-81) of Paranaque, Philippines, businessman. Won Far East Teams 1957, 1958, Far East Pairs 1970. Represented Philippines in three world championships and in Far East Championships regularly from 1958. Won more than 50 nationals titles including open teams 6 times.

CHUCK, Cecil (b. 1928) of Kingston, Jamaica, business executive. WBF World Master. CAC Team Champion 1983 and represented Jamaica 1983 Bermuda Bowl. Won numerous national titles.

CHUN, Peter H.L. (b. 1949) of Hong Kong, computer systems manager. WBF World Master. Won Far East Open Teams 1987, second Open Pairs 1984, 1988. Represented Hong Kong in three world championships and four other Far East Championships.

CHURCHILL, S. Garton (Church) (1900-1992) of Great Neck NY, retired attorney, one of the great American bridge players and personalities. Graduated from Ohio Wesleyan U and Harvard Law School. His bridge-playing activities were somewhat curtailed after 1944 due to his law practice and his desire to spend time with his family, but his interest in bridge never diminished. The originator of the CHURCHILL SYSTEM, he advocated ideas that were often scoffed at in the early Thirties but were generally adopted some 20 years later. These original theoretical ideas were set out in *Contract Bidding Tactics at Matchpoint Play* and articles in *The Bridge World*. Churchill won the Life Master Prs 1937,

48, setting two records in partnership with Cecil Head. They scored 65% as an average for four sessions and 77.4% in a single session. Churchill won the Chicago (since 1965 the Reisinger) 1932, placed second in 1933, 39, 41, 42; he was also second in Master Mixed Tms 1937, Asbury Challenge Tms 1931. His regional wins included Eastern States KO Tms 1937, 38, 39; New Jersey State Master Prs 1947, 59; secondary Senior Prs 1959.

CILLIE, Frank (b. 1943) of Pretoria, South Africa, development economist. Represented South Africa in 1992 World Team Olympiad. Five national wins include one open team title. Short-story writer and essayist.

CIMON, Francine A. (b. 1950) of Montreal PQ, high school teacher in charge of computer lab, former bridge club owner/manager, educated at U of Montreal and U of Quebec; enjoys foreign films and is actively involved in shows by students. Taught bridge on national television in Canada 1974-75. WBF World Master; represented Canada in World Tm Olympiads in Monte Carlo 1976, Valkenburg 1980, Seattle 1984, Venice 1988. Cimon was third in the Venice Cup 1989 and placed fourth in the World Womens Olympiad Tms 1976, 88, 7th in 1980, 9th in 1984; fifth in the Swiss Plate 1984. She represented Canada in World Pair Olympiads New Orleans 1978, Bal Harbour 86. Also represented ACBL in Venice Cup in Yokohama 1991. Won Canadian Open Prs Championship 1981, Canadian Womens Tm Championship 1979, 83, 84, 86, 87, 88, 89, 90, 91; was second Canadian Nat'l Tms Championship 1988. Her approximately 20 regional titles include secondary Silver Trophy Prs 1977, 81; Can-Am KO Tms 1978, Ottawa KO Tms 1980, Canadian Nat'l Tms Zone 2 1981, 82; Dist. 3 Open Prs 1981, Montreal Swiss 1982, 84, Open Prs 1983; Dist. 1 GN Prs 1982, Albany Open Prs 1985, Toronto Swiss 1988.

CINTRA, Gabino (b. 1942) of Rio de Janeiro, Brazil, IBM executive. WBF Grand Master. Won World Teams 1976, World Pairs 1978, a very rare double. Second World Teams 1978, and represented Brazil in 11 other world championships. Won South American Teams 1970, 1972, 1973, 1975, 1977, 1978, 1982, 1984, 1991. National wins include open teams 7 times.

CINTRA, Lia of Rio de Janeiro, Brazil. WBF World Life Master. Won South American Women's Teams 1971, 1972, 1973, 1981 and 1989. Represented Brazil in one world championship.

CLARK, Harry (b. 1932) of Sebring FL, retired ACBL national tournament director.

CLARK, Morris E. (Tom) (b. 1939) of Marble Falls TX, chemist and writer, educated at U of Texas and U of Houston (Ph.D). Author of *The Four-Leafed Club.*

CLARK, Sandi (b. 1944) of Sebring FL, graduate of MacAlester College. Clark was assistant manager of ACBL Education Dept. Assisted with first ACBL Junior Camp. Former tournament director, enjoys gardening, golf and raising parrots.

CLARKE, Angela (Gale) of McLean VA, bridge

teacher, loves cooking, square dancing and reading mysteries, member Nat'l Goodwill Committee, winner of Womens Prs 1969. Competed internationally in Sweden 1970 and placed 15th in the World Womens Prs. She won WBL Swiss 1989, Lancaster Sr Prs 1990, Hilton Head Womens Prs 1992,

CLARKE, Thomas (Tom), (b. 1946) of Lake Charles LA, insurance and financial services executive, Navy veteran, degree from McNeese St. U, likes sports, games, reading science fiction and computers. Has served Unit 221 and Dist. 10 in various executive positions. Won North American Swiss 1993; placed second in Life Master Prs 1993. His approximately 20 regional wins include Mid-South Unmixed Prs 1978, KO Tms 1979, 80, Master Prs 1979, 80, Master Swiss 1980; San Antonio Swiss 1979, Saskatoon KO Tms, Waterloo KO Tms 1980; Puerto Rico Mens Prs 1981, Tulsa Unmixed Prs 1981 and other wins in Vancouver, Regina, Houston, Pocatello, Gatlinburg and Acapulco.

CLARREN, David B. (1918-1989) of Minneapolis, insurance agent. He was a pioneer of bridge development in Minnesota, taught bridge for many years and lectured on TV for 52 weeks in 1960. He won the Vanderbilt 1947 and placed second in the Spingold 1949, 53; won numerous regional titles.

CLAY, James (1805-1873) of London, was leading British WHIST authority between HOYLE and CAVENDISH. His chief work was *Treatise on the Game of Whist* (1864).

CLAYTON, Sir Hugh Bayard (1877-1947) of India, born Queensland, was one of the inventors of S.A.C.C., the initials of four players living in India who developed an earlier prototype of PLAFOND about 1912. During World War I he served in the Intelligence Department, was Commissioner of Bombay (1919-1928), and was knighted in 1938.

CLERKIN, Dennis E. (b. 1950) of Bloomington IN, professional bridge player and instructor, a Grand Life Master with more than 11,000 MPs. He has won NAOP 1989, NAOT 1990, Master Mixed Tms 1992, placed second in Swiss 1977, Master Mixed Tms 1992. Clerkin has numerous regional wins to his credit.

CLERKIN, Gerald P. (Jerry) (b. 1952) of North Vernon IN, professional bridge teacher and player, placed second in Swiss 1977; Diamond Life Master with numerous regional wins.

CLIFF, David (Dave) (b. 1932) of Basking Ridge NJ, school teacher, principal and associate professor, educated at Harvard, Columbia, Boston State U and Rutgers. He is one of the earliest theorists in the field of relay bidding, which is a forerunner of modern scientific bidding and appears in one form or another in all world championships. Many top-ranked pairs use a RELAY SYSTEM with marked success. He is the originator of the SPLINTER BID, its corollary 3NT showing a forcing balanced raise, *Cliff Cross* and *Denial Cue Bidding.* Cliff won New England Master Tms 1956, 76, Open 1960 and KO Tms 1961.

CODY, Judi L. (b. 1949) of Annandale VA, court reporter, graduated U of New Hampshire and Strayer College. Outside interests are golf, tennis and antiques. Past president of Unit 195, member Bd of Gov 1976-88, she has chaired many tournaments. Represented ACBL in Biarritz 1982 and Geneva 1990 (placed 16th in World Womens Prs) and is a WBF World Master. In 1986 she won the Life Master Womens Prs, placed second in the GN Prs 1987, Womens BAM 1987, Womens Swiss 1992. Diamond Life Master with many regional wins including Upper NY Womens Swiss 1976, Fall secondary Swiss, Bermuda Swiss, Rye Womens Prs 1979; Tri-State Womens Prs 1980, N.E. Fall Open Prs, Prs 1981, Lancaster Womens Prs, Swiss 1985; Washington DC Masters Prs 1986, Morning KO Tms 1987; New England KO Tms, Bal Harbour Womens Swiss 1987.

COCHINWALA , A. Ghaffer (b. 1931) of Karachi, Pakistan, businessman. Won BFAME zonal championship 1981. Second Far East Championships 1978.

COCHINWALA, A. Sattar (b. 1934) of Karachi, Pakistan, businessman. Second Far East Championship 1978 and played in two world championships. NPC Pakistan team that placed second Bermuda Bowl 1981. Won many national titles.

COENRAETS, Philippe (b. 1951) of Huy, Belgium, civil engineer. WBF World Master. Represented Belgium in three world championships and five European Championships. Won Common Market Mixed Teams 1991. National wins include open teams three times and open pairs four times.

COFFIN, George S. (1903-1994) of Waltham MA, author, publisher and distributor of bridge books and supplies, won *The Bridge World* international problem solving contest 1930. His principal bridge work is *Bridge Play: Four Classics*, a 960 page compilation of his earlier works *Endplays*, *Bridge Perfect Plays* and *Match Point Ways* appended by *The Bridge Writer's Manual*. Coffin also wrote many volumes on games other than bridge (poker, pinochle, cribbage, etc.) and revised his publication on wild mushrooms. His other roles include co-founder of ABTA and first editor of its quarterly magazine; developer of THREE-HANDED BRIDGE; creator of many items of bridge equipment; publisher of many bridge books, including Beynon's *Bridge Director's Manual*, his own *Bridge Director's Logistics*, books by British writers; author of magazine and newspaper articles and of *Instant Bridge Bidding*; contributing editor, *Bridge Encyclopedia*.

COGAN, Evie (b. 1948) of Huntingdon Valley PA, professor of law, formerly a trial attorney with the Dept. of the Navy and the EEOC, graduated from Temple U. Won Master Mixed Tms 1988. Represented ACBL in Bal Harbour 1986. Has several regional wins.

COHAN, Joseph (1899-1958) of Wooster OH, born in Canada, businessman, president of ACBL in 1952, placed second in Mens Tms 1947, 49 and won All-American Mens Prs 1953, Mid-West Spring Mixed Prs 1949, Mississippi Valley Open Tms 1953.

COHEN, Barry. See CRANE, BARRY.

COHEN, Ben (1907-71) of Hove, England, bridge entrepreneur. He was an early pioneer of duplicate bridge, and published the first book on the Acol System. Wrote and published many others, including European edition of the *Official Encyclopedia of Bridge*, often in collaboration with Rhoda Barrow Lederer.

COHEN, David (1897-1982) of Belfast, Ireland, represented Ireland in European Championships 1956, Northern Ireland in more than 70 CAMROSE TROPHY matches, a record. In 1969-70 season won 11 of 15 major Irish tournaments at the age of 72, perhaps the best performance ever by a veteran player. President of IRISH BRIDGE UNION 1962-1963, chairman NORTH OF IRELAND BRIDGE UNION 1956.

COHEN, Harvey C. (b. 1935) of Encino CA, attorney, won Open Prs 1967. His regional wins include Bridge Week KO Tms, Open Tms 1964; Marcus Cup 1966. He was a member of the Los Angeles team which defeated the SHARIF BRIDGE CIRCUS 1970.

COHEN, Israel (b. 1913) of Washington DC, merchant, won Open Prs 1952 and placed second in the Chicago (since 1965 the Reisinger), Master Mixed Tms 1963, Open Individual 1956. He won Eastern States Mens Prs 1957, Keystone Conf. Mens Prs 1957, Open Tms 1959; NY-NJ Open Tms 1960.

COHEN, Janet (Jan) (b. 1934) of Los Angeles CA, accountant and business manager, Lakers fan, likes doing needlework and doublecrostics. Certified director, Unit 552 treasurer, Dist. 23 president, member National Goodwill Committee and National Bd of Gov. Member of Nat'l Ethical Oversight Committee and has been a member of President's Advisory Committee on Policy and Procedures from its inception. Represented ACBL in Biarritz 1982, Geneva 1990 (placed 20th in World Womens Prs) and Pan American Championship Womens Prs Corpus Christi 1992. Winner of Life Master Womens Prs 1992, Womens BAM 1993; placed second Womens Prs 1993. She has won more than 20 regional titles.

COHEN, Jay Richard (b. 1941) of Bethesda MD, senior vice-president of international real estate management and advisory company and executive vice-president of three real estate investment trusts. Educated at U of Pennsylvania, avid golfer, listed in *Who's Who in America*. Won Keystone Mens Swiss 1971, 72, KO Tms 1975; Mid-Atlantic Summer Open Tms 1972, Dist. 4 Mens Swiss, Swiss 1976, Washington Bridge Week KOs 1975, 76.

COHEN, Kenneth L. (Ken) (b.1948) of Philadelphia PA, bridge professional, placed first in Mixed Tms 1988, Mixed Prs 1990, Open Prs 1991. Came in second in Mixed Prs 1972, Life Master Prs and Spingold 1977. Won Fishbein Trophy 1977. Represented ACBL in WBF events New Orleans 1978 and Bal Harbour 1986. A Diamond Life Master with numerous regionals wins.

COHEN, Kenneth W. (b. 1943) of Brookline MA, real estate owner/manager, former social worker, graduate of Ohio Wesleyan U and NYU. Interested in sports and dancing. Won Pilgrim Open Prs 1981, secondary Open Prs 1982, Danvers Swiss 1986, Springfield Open Swiss

1987, Parsippany Mens Tms 1988, secondary Morning KOs 1989.

COHEN, Larry Neil (b. 1959) of Little Falls NJ, options trader, graduate of S.U.N.Y. He is the author of *To Bid or Not to Bid*, which was the best selling bridge book of 1992-1993. He is also a contributor to *The Bridge World*. Qualified for the USBC (team trials) 1986, 87, 92, 93; represented ACBL in Biarritz 1982 (placed 13th in Rosenblum Tms), Sao Paulo 1985 and Geneva 1990 (placed 9th in Rosenblum Tms) in WBF events. He won the Pan American Open Tms 1992 and placed 8th in the World Simultaneous Prs 1986. He has won the Spingold 1981, 84; Blue Ribbon Prs 1981, 83, 88; Reisinger 1985, 1991; Life Master Mens Prs 1983, Mens BAM 1984, Fall Open BAM 1991, Life Master Prs 1987, 88. He was second Open Prs 1979, NAOP 1980, 84; Spingold 1983, Fall LM Mens Prs 1986, 91; Vanderbilt 1990, 93; Fall Open BAM 1990; North American Open Tms 1991. Winner of the Cavendish Invitational Prs 1983, 88. At the 1991 Fall NABC in Indianapolis he won 356 masterpoints. He is an ACBL Diamond Life Master and has won numerous regional events.

COHEN, Lawrence (Larry) (b. 1943) of Palm Desert CA, pharmacist, graduate of U of Wisconsin where he was Intercollegiate champion in 1966. He is the co-author of *Breakthrough in Bridge*. A Grand Life Master, he has won Spingold 1973, 76; Reisinger 1973, GNT 1974, Vanderbilt 1975, 76; Blue Ribbon Prs 1968, Mens Prs 1976, Life Master Mens Prs 1989, Herman Trophy 1973, Mott-Smith Trophy 1976 and placed second in the Blue Ribbon Prs 1968, Mens Tms 1971, Vanderbilt 1973, 89; Fall NA Swiss 1992. Cohen has won numerous regional titles. See BIBILIOGRAPHY, C, HOUSTON AFFAIR and LANCIA Tms.

COHEN, Mark Allen (b. 1954) of New York City, elementary school teacher, bridge club owner, bridge teacher and director, theatrical producer, graduated Temple U. Delivers meals to homebound AIDs patients. Produced a one-man show about Bette Davis. Vice-Chairman ACBL Bd of Gov 1990-93 and served on Greater NYBA Bd and ACBL Bd of Gov 1984-93. Runs group tours and tournaments in Morocco, Spain and on cruises. Has won about 18 regionals including Southeastern Master Prs, secondary Morning KO Tms 1983; Rye Mens Swiss 1988, 89; Bermuda Open Swiss 1991.

COHEN, Mark D. (b. 1951) of Glen Ridge NJ, stock options trader, graduated Northwestern U. Other interests include rotisserrie baseball, his daughters and playing golf, basketball and baseball. Regular member of expert panel *Bridge World* Master Solvers club since 1983. He came in fifth in the Rosenblum Tms in Geneva 1990 and is a WBF World Master. Competed in other WBF events New Orleans 1978, Bal Harbour 1986. His nat'l titles are Master Mixed Tms 1979, 86; Mens Swiss 1984, 86. Placed second in NA Swiss 1979, Vanderbilt 1982, Spingold 1983, 89; Reisinger 1987, GN Prs 1988, USBC (Team Trials) 1989. Cohen is the husband of Stasha Cohen and they are one of the more successful husband-wife partnerships. A Diamond Life Master with more than 30 regionals including Cambrian Shield Open Prs 1976, Champaign KO Tms 1976, 77, Swiss 1977; Big Apple Prs 1978, Mixed Prs 1980, KO Tms 1981;

New England Fall Open Prs 1979, Summer Open Prs, Swiss 1980, Open Prs 1981, KO Tms 1987; Fun City Open Prs 1982, Spring secondary Open Prs 1984, Secaucus KO Tms 1986, secondary Stratified Prs, Eastern States KO Tms 1990.

COHEN, Nathan (Mr. Money Bags) (b. 1915) of Memphis, ACBL assistant treasurer and finance officer at North American Championships from 1948-1984, worked with Ely Culbertson as production manager of Autobridge sets 1936-46. In 1931 Cohen won 56 medals in various track events.

COHEN, Ralph (b. 1926) of Memphis TN, born in Montreal PQ, was Assistant Executive Secretary of the ACBL 1971-84, Executive Director of the ACBL 1984-86, consultant to the ACBL 1986-91. Cohen retired from the ACBL in 1991 and was manager of MA Lightman BC in Memphis for three years. Member ACBL Laws Commission since 1984, and is currently serving as co-chairman. Served on ACBL Laws Commission Drafting Committee for revision of rubber bridge Laws. He wrote *Ruling the Game* column for two years along with other contributions to the ACBL *Bulletin* and was a contributor to the Fourth Edition, *Bridge Encyclopedia*. Cohen represented Canada in the World Tm Olympiad 1964 placing fourth and has the rank of WBF World Master. In Bal Harbour 1986 and Geneva 1990 he represented the ACBL in WBF events. In 1990 his team was fifth in Rosenblum Tms. He won NABC IMP Prs 1990, was second in the Amateur Swiss 1977, North American Open Prs 1994; was a member of Montreal's winning Intercity Tm 1967, 68. Cohen is a Diamond Life Master with numerous regional wins including Can-Am Open Tms 1952, 54, 57, Mens Prs 1957; New England Open Prs 1965, 69, Open Tms 1969; Indian Summer Master Prs 1979, Nat'l Capital Open Swiss 1986, Memphis Open Prs, Open Swiss 1990; St. Louis Swiss 1991. See FAMILY.

COHEN, Rafael (1903-1986) of Budapest, Hungary, merchant. European Champion 1934, runner-up 1935, 1936. Hungarian Champion 1929-1935, and 1960. NPC of Hungarian teams 1963-1968.

COHEN, Stasha (Mrs Mark D., formerly Wroblewski) (b. 1954) of Glen Ridge NJ, civil trial attorney, formerly a computer programmer analyst with IBM, schooled at Rutgers School of Law and Barnard College. Student of Japanese flower arranging, enjoys gourmet cooking and theater. Has served on Board of Directors of GNYBA and New Jersey BA. WBF World Master; became a world champion in 1990 when she won the Venice Cup in Japan. In 1976 she was the Nat'l Master of the Year. She has won Womens KO Tms 1982, 91, 93; Womens Swiss 1982; Master Mixed Tms 1986. Was second in GN Prs in 1988, Womens BAM in 1986, 87. She and her husband Mark have one of the more successful husband-wife partnerships. Cohen won the first regional she ever played in, Fun City Swiss 1975. She has won more than 30 other regional titles including LI Womens Prs, Atlantic City Womens Swiss 1978; Big Apple KO Tms 1981, New England Summer Open Prs, Swiss 1980, Open Prs 1981, KO Tms 1987; Fun City Open Prs 1982, secondary Open Prs 1990.

COHEN, William E. (Billy) (b. 1958) of Las Vegas, born in Montreal, professional bridge player, Diamond Life Master, won Swiss 1978, Reisinger 1987, Open Swiss 1993; placed second in Spingold 1982, 86; Vanderbilt 1988. Cohen is the winner of many regional events. See FAMILY.

COHN, Janice. See HORWITZ, JANICE.

COHN, Bette L. of Clearwater FL, tax consultant, won Venice Cup 1974, placed 10th World Mixed Prs 1974. National titles include Mixed Prs 1966, Womens Tms 1967, Life Masters Womens Prs 1970. Regional wins include New England Master Prs 1965, Mexican Nat'l Mixed Prs 1967, Mid-Atlantic Womens Prs, Dist. 11 KOs 1969; Mid-Atlantic Open Tms 1970, Thanksgiving Womens Prs 1972, Mid-South Womens Prs 1974, Southeastern Womens Tms 1976, Puerto Rico Womens Prs 1980, Callaway Gardens Sr. Master Prs 1987, Fall Sr. Prs 1988, Tampa Sr. Open Prs 1989, Biloxi Sr. Womens Prs 1991.

COHN, Judith (Judy) (nee Orr) (b. 1942) of Ft. Thomas KY, aerodynamics engineering specialist, member Unit 124 Bd of Dir 1976-1991, co-chairman 1979 Fall NABC and past President Unit 124 and Dist. 11. She also served as VP of Dist 11 and editor Unit 124 newsletter, the *Alert*, member Natl Goodwill Committee, co-authored *Cincinnati Power Defensive Carding*. Won nine regionals including Spring 0-2000 secondary KOs 1987, secondary VP Swiss 1989, Louisville Swiss, Bowling Green Swiss 1990; Fall secondary Win-Loss Swiss 1991.

COHN, Martin J. (Marty) (b. 1923) of Sarasota FL, retired business executive, educated at U of Michigan and the Sorbonne, enjoys music especially Dixieland. Retired from tournament bridge in 1985 as a protest against cheating scandals. Won Life Master Prs 1957, Mixed Prs 1966; second in Mens Prs 1961, Mixed Tms 1964, Mens Tms 1969; placed second in the De La Rue International Pair Championship in London 1957. His numerous regional wins include: Mid-South Spring Mens Prs 1960, Dist. 5 Mens Prs 1961, 67, Open Tms 1965; Mid-Atlantic Fall Open Tms 1963, Texas Fall KO Tms 1964, Mexican Nat'l Open Tms, Mixed Prs 1967, Swiss 1972; All-American Open Tms 1968, Mississippi Valley Open Tms 1969, Mid-Atlantic Spring Swiss, Mens Prs 1970; Thanksgiving KO Tms 1973, Summer Mens Prs 1977, Sr. Mens Prs 1981, Southeastern KO Tms 1985, Mens Prs 1985.

COLBERT, David R. (b. 1952) of Etobicoke ON, department head in high school math department, graduate of U of Toronto, track and field champion, at one time held the Canadian record for indoor 800m relay. Won Canadian Nat'l Tms 1993, Canadian Nat'l Swiss 1975, Sudbury KO Tms, Open Prs 1978, Swiss 1983; Fredricton Open Prs, Swiss 1980; North Bay KO Tms 1981, Toronto Open Prs 1984.

COLCHAMIRO, Mel Alan (b. 1945) of Merrick NY, bridge teacher, writer, professional player and director, former Wall St economist and stock options trader, degrees from Hofstra U and U of Maine; movie collector; likes to play backgammon and golf. Past president Nassau-Suffolk BA, member Bd of Dir NSBA 1969-87; contributor to *The Islander* and *The Bridge World*. His 25 regional wins include New York City Swiss 1979, 82, 89; GN Prs 1983, 87, 88; New England Open Prs 1987, Swiss 1987, 90, 91, KO Tms 1990; Long Island Swiss 1989, New Jersey Swiss 1990, Eastern States Reisinger KOs 1992, Westchester Open Prs, KO Tms, Swiss 1993.

COLE, Dr. William D. (Bill) (b. 1963) of Cambridge MA, teaches medieval art and literature at Harvard, has played bridge professionally in U.S. and Spain, has written articles for *The Bridge World*, *Bulletin*, and *Popular Bridge*; described Fishhead Coup in *Fishheads* (1991). Founded Harvard Bridge Team 1985, still serves as coach and captain. Won North American Collegiate Championship 1990, second 1988. Has had many tournament wins in Spain; was the world record holder for egg-throwing (see *Guinness Book of World Records* 1981-83).

COLE, William P. (Bill) (b. 1950) of Silver Spring MD, engineer for Bell Atlantic, writes column for Washington BL. Developed with Lynn Deas Cole 2♣ Bid and Deas Over NT. Won Master Mixed Tms 1982, second 1981. Diamond Life Master. Regional wins include Open Prs 1980; Roanoke Prs, Morning KOs, Baltimore Swiss, Lancaster Flighted KO Tms 1988; Richmond Handicap KO Tms, Cherry Hill Swiss 1989; Washington DC Swiss 1990, Richmond and Bracketed KO Tms 1991.

COLKER, Dr. Richard E. (b. 1946) of Wheaton MD, psychology professor, psychology research investigator, recorder for ACBL Dist. 6, Appeals chairman for Washington Bridge League, vice chairman for Nat'l Appeals Committee, member Nat'l Ethical Oversight Committee, columnist for Washington BL *Bulletin* since 1988. Diamond Life Master with 29 regional wins including Baltimore Swiss 1979, Lancaster Mens Prs, Arlington Mens Prs, Richmond Mens Swiss 1981; Virginia Beach Open Prs, Arlington Swiss 1982; Toronto KO Tms 1986, Raleigh Mens Swiss, Washington DC Open Prs 1987; Parsippany KO Tms; Arlington KO Tms, Superflighted Open, Open Swiss 1991; Richmond Bracketed KO Tms, Handicap KOs 1991; Pittsburgh Open Swiss 1991.

COLLIER, Gladys W. (b. 1922) of East Hampton NY, mathematician, educated at Bryn Mawr and Columbia. Other interests are women's rights and animal rights. Won Master Mixed Tms 1989, second Life Master Womens Prs 1969. Regional wins include Atlantic City Mixed Prs 1967, Ft. Lauderdale Open Prs 1968, Montreal Swiss, Pasadena Swiss 1978; Washington DC Open Prs 1984, NY Sr Prs 1987, Lancaster Sr Swiss 1988, Dist 24 GN Prs 1989; Buffalo Womens Swiss 1990, Rye Sr Prs 1991.

COLLINGS, John D.R. (b. 1933) of London, England, retired bank officer. Second European Teams 1981. Represented Britain in one world championship and one other zonal championship. Also represented Switzerland in one world championship and one zonal championship, and England in Camrose Trophy. Six national wins include Gold Cup once. Won *Sunday Times* Pairs 1969.

COLLYER, Barbara. See KACHMAR, BARBARA.

COLSON, Sharon M. of Kirkland WA, CPA, controller, degrees from Central Washington U and U of Washington. Placed second Womens Swiss 1993, Womens BAM 1993. Regional wins include Oregon Trail Amateur Open Prs 1976, Open Prs (A-D) 1981, Open Prs 1992, 93; Indian Summer Open Prs 1981, Fall secondary Womens Prs 1987, Vancouver Womens Prs 1988, 90, Open Prs 1988; Emerald Empire Open Prs 1992.

COMPTON, Dane Christopher (Chris) (b. 1961) of Austin TX, bridge professional, certified director, graduate U of Houston, student U of TX School of Law; WBF World Master, placed 4th World Open Prs 1986. Diamond Life Master, had more than 5000 masterpoints by the time he was 24. Won Reisinger 1989, second Vanderbilt 1986 and Mens Prs 1987; has won more than 60 regional titles.

CONILL, Buenaventura (b. 1927) of Barcelona, Spain, engineer. Represented Spain in three zonal championships. Won many national titles.

CONLIN, David A. (b. 1923) of Phoenix AZ, retired real estate broker and developer, golfer. Won many regionals in 50's and 60's including Bridge Week Masters Prs 1960; Desert Empire Open Tms 1959, KOs 1967.

CONWAY, John T. (b. 1938) of Stuart FL, retired company vice president and physicist, graduate of NYU, Dist 5 representative to Bd of Governors for six years. Regional wins include Albany Mens Swiss 1974, Pittsburgh Masters Prs 1976, San Diego Swiss 1980, Spring secondary Swiss, San Diego Open Swiss 1981; Phoenix Swiss 1982, Toronto Open Prs 1984, 88; New York City Open Prs 1984; Buffalo Mens Prs, Master Prs 1985, Master Prs 1988.

COOK, Cecil Q. (b. 1932) of Long Beach CA, aerospace consultant, educated at Iowa State, UCLA and Cal State. Won the Volare Award for outstanding achievements in aircraft avionics, RTCA Citation for contribution to advancement of aeronautics. Started duplicate game in Guam 1958. President Dist 23 1975, Unit 554 president 1961, 63, helped organize Dist 23 (ALACBU) and was its first VP, organized and ran the ALACBU's prize plan, president 1975, VP for five terms, chairman and/or member Finance Comm. for 15 years, tournament manager of Dist. 23 1976, 77, member Dist. 23 regional committee for 15 years, treasurer ALACBU 1983-93, first alternate Director Dist. 23 1983-90, Dist. 23 representative to National Bd of Dir 1990-94. Member Nat'l Goodwill Committee. Won Spring secondary Senior Prs 1991, Dist. 23 Summer Sr Prs, Spring Sr Tms 1994.

COOK, Dorothy Jane (D.J.) of Asheville NC, bridge teacher and writer, former president and executive VP of ABTA; daughter of famed *Chicago Tribune* political cartoonist, Carey Orr; authored *Learn to Play Winning Bridge, Cook and Deal* and *Cook and Deal II*. Regionals wins include All-American Mixed Prs 1945, Central States Mixed Prs, Womens Tms 1947, Womens Prs 1948, Life Master Tms 1961.

COOK, Edward M. (Ed) (b. 1901) of Palo Alto CA, commercial real estate developer, physicist, graduated Haverford College, has done personal independent study on diet and vitamins for 25 years. Was occasional partner to Charles Goren, Captain Fred French, John Kunkel and Olive Peterson. Won Mens Prs 1935, 37. Regional wins include Los Angeles Mens Prs 1937, Philadelphia Team-of-Four 1937, 38; Philadelphia Prs 1938, Bridge Week Mens Prs 1958, Pacific Southwest Mens Prs 1967.

COOLIK, J. Samuel (b. 1943) of Atlanta GA, stock broker, graduated U of Georgia; has served on Unit 181 Bd of Directors, member of Nat'l Bd of Gov and Nat'l Appeals Committee. Regional wins include Texas Summer Mens Prs, Golden State Mens Prs 1969; Mid-South Summer Mens Prs 1971, 75; Mid-South Spring Mens Prs 1972, Swiss 1973; Mid-Atlantic Summer KO 1975, Mid-Atlantic Fall Swiss 1976, KO Tms 1978; Mid-Atlantic Winter Swiss 1977, Dist. 7 GN Tms 1979.

COOMBS, Norman D. (Norm, Stormin Norman) (b. 1934) of Brookville IN, graduated Ohio State U, company president, bridge professional, writer and teacher; likes to compose music. Invented Coombs Gambit--a defense to artificial club and diamond opening bids -- 1969. Won Life Master Mens Prs 1978. Winner of the first regional event restricted to Life Masters, 1969. Diamond Life Master with more than 100 regional wins including Midwest Spring Mens Prs 1970, Swiss 1982, Fall Mens Swiss 1977; Dist. 11 Master Prs, KO Tms 1977; GN Prs 1981. Won Senior Individual at the first ACBL cash prize tournament 1993.

COOMBS, William V. (Bill) (b. 1943) of Hamilton OH, educated at Kenyon, Columbia and U of Cincinnati, senior sales/use tax auditor for state of Ohio. Won Midwest Winter Swiss 1974, Fall Master Prs 1974, Swiss 1978, 1980; Dist. 11 Swiss 1974, KO Tms 1977; Winter Open Prs 1976, GN Tms 1979.

COON, Charles (b. 1931) of Gloucester MA, real estate broker and bridge teacher. WBF World Master; second Bermuda Bowl 1962, Rosenblum Tms 1990; won Team Trials 1961, Vanderbilt 1961, Master Mixed Tms 1962, Life Master Mens Prs 1964, Blue Ribbon Prs 1966, Mens Prs 1989; placed second Mens Tms 1964, 68; Reisinger 1961. ACBL Grand LM with more than 11,000 MPs, has won many regional titles.

COOPER, Martin J. (b. 1923) of Boynton Beach FL, retired pharmacist and owner of retail drug stores; directs bridge games on cruise ships. Won Southeastern Mixed Prs 1960, Open Prs 1961, Senior Prs 1989; Midwest Mixed Prs 1961, Bermuda Master Prs 1978, Summer secondary Sr. Swiss, Senior Prs 1989.

COOPER, Roslyn (Mrs Martin J.) (b. 1926) of Boynton Beach FL, directs bridge games on cruise ships. Won Southeastern Mixed Prs, Open Prs 1960, Senior Prs 1989; Midwest Mixed Prs 1961; Bermuda Master Prs 1978, Summer secondary Sr Swiss and Senior Prs 1989.

CORBIN, Helen (Mrs. Warren) of Menlo Park CA, born in Tokyo. Won Takamatsu Knockout Tms 1963, 64, represented Japan Far East Womens Tms 1963. Began ACBL competition in 1966. Regional wins include

Mid-Atlantic Masters Prs, Texas Open Prs 1968; Gem State Womens Prs 1981, Oregon Trail Open Prs 1982, Greatest Game on Earth Womens Prs 1988. During interims she resided in Indonesia and Jamaica and actively participated in duplicate bridge.

CORBIN, Jeff (b. 1948) of Wichita KS, partner in Wichita Shirt and Cap, former stockbroker and tennis instructor, graduated Wichita State U. Regional wins include Missouri Valley KOs, Swiss 1977; Dist. 15 GN Tms, Toast of Tulsa Mens Prs 1977; Mid-Atlantic KOs, Mid-South Spring Swiss, Summer Master Swiss, Fall KOs 1978; Wichita Swiss 1986.

CORMACK, Janas C. (Jan) (b. 1941) of Auckland, New Zealand, legal executive and journalist. WBF World Master. Won Far East Women's Teams 1981, second 1978. Represented New Zealand in three world championships and eight other zonal championships. Won five national titles. Bridge columnist of *New Zealand Women's Weekly*.

CORN, Ira G. Jr. (1921-1982) of Dallas, co-founder, executive and director of Michigan General Corp.; former assistant professor Southern Methodist U; organized, financed and captained the Aces (the world's first professional bridge team). He took America's constant losses in world play very personally. After Italy defeated America in the final of the 1964 World Team Olympiad, he decided to put his theories to the test. He signed six outstanding players to contracts and brought them to Dallas to live, practice and shape into a team that subsequently qualified to represent America in the Bermuda Bowl in 1969 and won the world championship in 1970 and 1971. The last Aces team Corn put together won the 1982 Spingold in July after his death in April. Bobby Wolff and Bob Hamman, longstanding members of the Aces, remarked, "Ira would have loved this. This was his team, he put the six of us together...just say we won one for Big Ira." That Aces team went on to win the International Team Trials and to defeat Italy in the final of the 1983 Bermuda Bowl.

A distinguished historian, in 1969 he purchased a copy of the Declaration of Independence in its first printing, then wrote and published *The Story of the Declaration of Independence* in 1977. A notable expert on World War II, he completed a book on the Normandy invasion that tells the story both from the Allied and the German side. Listed in *Who's Who in America* since 1971; author of *Play Bridge with the Aces*; wrote a daily syndicated column, *Aces on Bridge*.

Corn was reared in a Baptist home where no cards were permitted, but when, as a college student, he was invited to sit in a bridge game, he discovered it was much like a game he knew called Rook, which has colors instead of suits, numbers instead of face cards. "Rook is really Baptist Bridge," he said. He played social bridge until 1961 when he started playing tournament bridge. He was administrator and 1968 president of the Dallas BA, was tournament chairman 1966-1967, District Director from 1965 and ACBL president 1980. NABC wins include Mixed Prs 1963, Men's Tms 1968, Vanderbilt 1973; also won several regional titles. See also ACES TEAM.

CORNELL, Michael (b. 1947) of Auckland, New Zealand, accountant. WBF World Master. Second Far East Teams 1982, 1991, and also represented New Zealand in eight world championships and five other zonal championships. National wins include open teams four times and Australian open teams twice.

CORNELL, Vivien of Auckland, New Zealand, legal search agent. WBF Master. Represented New Zealand in two world championships and three zonal championships. Several national wins.

COROEIRO, José Antonio (1946-91) of Lisbon, Portugal. Represented Portugal in four European Championships. National wins include open teams twice and open pairs once.

COSTELLO, James Donn (b. 1926) of Seattle WA, engineer and retired regional director, educated at U of Washington; was responsible for design of exterior lights on 747 airplanes. Has been a contributor to *The Bridge World* and *Bridge Today*, member Unit 446 Bd. of Dir. Won Pacific NW BAM 1962, Swiss 1988; Kalispell Sr Prs, Fall secondary Sr Swiss 1988; Sun Valley Sr Prs 1989, Swiss, Open Swiss 1990; Ocean Shores Sr Swiss 1990.

COTTER, E. Patrick (b. 1904) of London, England, bridge writer and retired school teacher. Second European Teams 1938 and represented Britain in one other zonal championship. Represented England in several Camrose matches. Won Gold Cup twice, and other national titles. Bridge columnist of *Financial Times* and *Country Life*. Author of one book. Croquet champion.

COURT, Russell Asher ("Rusty") (b. 1928) of Johannesburg, South Africa, pharmacist and clinic manager. Won Namibian Teams 1991. Chief tournament director of South African Bridge Federation since 1982. Contributor to *Bridge South Africa*.

COURTENAY, F. Dudley (1892-deceased) of South Dennis MA, manufacturer of the first metal duplicate boards, was a major figure in the bridge battles of the early Thirties. Founded BRIDGE HEADQUARTERS and was a member of the group which produced the OFFICIAL SYSTEM in opposition to Ely Culbertson. Courtenay's chief contribution to theory was the development of the LOSING TRICK COUNT, an unusual and important method of hand valuation, which he described in his book *The System the Experts Play*. Other writings include *Standardized Code Of Contract Bridge Bidding*, *The Losing Trick Count*, *The Standard Manual on Play* and *Standardized Contract Bridge Complete*.

COURTNEY, Michael (b. 1959) of Sydney, Australia, professional bridge player. Won 10 national titles. Columnist for *The Melbourne Age*.

COVALCIUC, Valerie A. (Val) (b. 1946) of Omaha NE, chief copy desk editor, freelance technical writer/editor, bridge teacher (since 1972) and ACBL teacher-trainer (1987-93); graduate of Cornell; member ACBL Bd of Dir for Dist 14, member ACBL Goodwill Committee. Covalciuc has served in various executive positions on the Unit and Dist level, including president Unit 241 1986-87, Dist 14 president 1992. In 1986 she was named first Area Manager for ACBL Education Program. Some of her numerous regionals include Peach City Open Prs, Quad City Riverboat/Cornhusker Swiss, Dist 2 Split Strat Swiss 1992; Spring secondary Mixed Prs, Fall secondary Open Prs, Green Bay KO Tms 1993.

COWAN, Donald (Moo Cow) (b. 1931) of Toronto, general manager of entertainment and music agency, graduated Queen's U. Represented Canada in three WBF championships. Won All-American Open Tms 1960, Mixed Prs 1961; Can-Am Open Tms 1961; Canadian Nat'l Open Tms 1962, 71, 79, Mens Swiss 1978, 80; Upper NY State Mixed Prs 1967, Great Lakes Swiss 1970, Dist. 2 GN Tms 1973, London Sr. Swiss, Niagara Falls Sr. Open Prs 1991.

COWAN, Philip (Flip) (b. 1943) of New York City, founder and managing partner of law firm, educated at Cornell; actively involved NY State Bar Association and Copyright Society of USA, has served as VP and tournament chairman locally. Won North American Swiss 1980, placed second in Swiss 1984. Regional wins include Fun City Mens Prs 1970, Dist. 3 Open Prs 1973, Mens Swiss 1976, 78; Washington DC Open Prs 1980, Springfield Swiss 1984, Fall NABC secondary Swiss 1985, NY Winter Swiss 1990.

COYLE, William (Willie) (b. 1937) of Renfrew, Scotland, science and mathematics teacher. Third Bermuda Bowl 1976. Won Camrose Trophy once and represented Scotland in 14 Camrose Trophy matches. Won Gold Cup 1969, 1973. National wins include open teams twice.

COZIER, E.L. (Jimmy) (1912-90) of Bridgetown, Barbados, journalist. Founding president of CAC 1973. President Barbados Bridge League 1970-79, 1981-85.

CRAMER, Hector (1901-1974) of Buenos Aires, Argentina. South American champion 1954, 1957. Represented Argentina in Bermuda Bowl 1961. National wins include open teams 8 times and open pairs 4 times.

CRANE, Barry (1927-1985) of Studio City CA, television producer and director, considered by many to be the top matchpoint player of all time. He became the ACBL's top masterpoint holder (see LIFE MASTER) in 1968 when he replaced Oswald Jacoby who had held the record since 1962 when he passed Charles Goren. Crane steadily augmented his hold on the top spot and it was not broken until six years after his death when Paul Soloway, who was more than 11,000 points behind Crane in 1985, took the lead in 1991. On July 5, 1985, Crane was the victim of a brutal murder that has never been solved. He played every event in the annual Fourth of July Regional in Pasadena and had led his knockout team into the final. In a poignant aftermath to his death, Crane's knockout squad was allowed to substitute Kerri Sanborn (then Shuman) in his place and they went on to capture the title. When news of this team's victory was announced to the tournament on Saturday, the room, which had sunk into a listless silence on Friday, burst into applause.

As a fresh-faced 21-year-old from Detroit named Barry Cohen, Crane won his first big tournament in Chicago in 1949. He was 23 when he became Life Master No. 325 in 1951. (Though he never disclosed his age, it

is believed that he was born Nov. 11, 1927.) Crane's passion for bridge was equalled only by his passion for the career in motion pictures that was to come in the next decade. By 1954 Barry Cohen of Detroit had legally and officially become Barry Crane of Los Angeles. In the three decades between his first NABC title in 1953 and his last in 1983, Barry won a world championship and 16 NABC titles. He and Kerri Sanborn won the World Mixed Prs in New Orleans in 1978 by more than 500 points (61.9% over the four sessions on the 142 top). Won Open Prs 1964, 1970, 1971, 1972, 1974, 1977, 1983, Master Mixed Tms 1953, 1954, 1980, Mixed Prs 1975, 1977, 1982, North American Swiss Tms 1978, Men's Prs 1966, Men's Swiss Tms 1983. His 12 "silver medals" were bounded by performances in which he led his team to the finals of the Vanderbilt in 1951 and 1985. Placed second Mixed Prs 1953, 1955, 1969, 1971, 1974, Open Prs 1976, 1984, Men's Tms 1956, 1971, Open Swiss 1974; won *McKenney Trophy* 1952, 1967, 1971, 1973, 1975, 1978, and was second 1961, 1962, 1963, 1964, 1981, 1984. He so dominated the race that after his death it was renamed the *Barry Crane Top 500.* Won Mott-Smith Trophy 1970, 1971, Oeschger Trophy (West Coast McKenney) in 1961, 1962, 1963, 1967, Stoddard Memorial Trophy 1980. It is estimated that he won more than 700 pairs titles at the regional or higher level.

Despite his bridge addiction, Crane had an abiding passion for his work. His partners recognized that it never bothered him when he couldn't go to a tournament because of the job which was his prime interest. However, he was well established in Hollywood and usually could arrange his TV production schedule so he could attend most tournaments for a few days. As a habitual weekend commuter to tournaments, he mastered the art of sleeping on a plane and frequently said that he would travel anywhere within flying distance for a regional and anywhere within driving distance for a sectional. In Crane's *ACBL Bulletin* obituary, Frank Stewart recalled that S.J. Simon once wrote that there are two kinds of bridge players — the Parrots and the Naturals. "Barry Crane," he declared, "was a Natural. We shall not see his like again."

CRAWFORD, Carol (Mrs. John) (1934-1982) of New York City, won Mixed Prs 1958, Womens Tms 1966; placed second Womens Tms 1972, Master Mixed Tms 1974, 75; Life Master Womens Prs 1976. World backgammon champion in 1973, she was one of only three women ever to win the title.

CRAWFORD, John R. (1915-1976) of New York City, bridge teacher and writer. His total of 37 ACBL national titles up to 1964 exceeded any other player's record at that time. By winning three consecutive Bermuda Bowls 1950, 51, 53 and by other performances abroad, he established a solid international reputation; also represented U.S. Bermuda Bowl 1958, World Team Olympiad 1960. His 10 wins in the Chicago Trophy (since 1965 the Reisinger): 1937, 38, 39, 42, 46, 47, 53, 54, 56, 61, set a record. The first of these wins, at the age of 22, gave him his first national title at a younger age than any of the other great American players. Two years later he became Life Master #19, at that time much the youngest of a select group. Other national wins include Spingold 1943, 48, 50, 52, 57; Vanderbilt 1941, 46, 50, 51, 55, 56, 57, 59, 60; Mens Tms 1956, 61; Mixed Tms

1942, 45, 48, 57; Life Master Prs 1943, Mens Prs 1939, Mixed Prs 1945, 48, 49, 59; Master Individual 1956. His 23 seconds in national events include five in the Life Master Prs.

In 1957 he achieved a unique grand slam of national team titles by holding simultaneously the Vanderbilt, Spingold, Chicago, Men's and Mixed Team championships. He demonstrated his adaptability by achieving national successes with many different partners and earned a reputation for competitive repartee, table presence and psychological awareness. Expert on many card games and forms of gambling; lectured extensively during his war-time Army service in an attempt to help servicemen avoid being cheated; helped to found the New York Card School in 1950 and moved to New York City from Philadelphia in 1959. His writings include *Crawford's Contract Bridge, How to Be a Consistent Winner in the Most Popular Card Games*, books on canasta, samba and a column for the *The Elks Magazine*.

CRESSY, Sarah Anne of Cataumet MA, antique dealer, formerly a teacher and real estate broker; horse breeder and trainer. Won Distinquished Public Service Medal from the Dept. of Defense in 1990. Regional wins include Fall secondary Womens Prs 1983, Dist. 6 GN Prs, Cherry Hill Swiss, Womens Prs 1987, Open Prs 1988; Roanoke Womens Tms 1987, Richmond Womens Prs, Santa Rosa Swiss, VA Beach Swiss 1988, Lancaster Swiss, Williamsberg Womens Tms, Fallsberg Womens Tms 1990.

CROCKER, Anthony F. (b. 1957) of Glendale CA, actuary, graduate of Princeton. Won National Amateur Swiss 1977, Super Open Prs Flt B 1983, Super Open Swiss Flt B 1983.

CROMBIE, Dr. Dwayne Edward (b. 1960) of Auckland, New Zealand, consultant in community medicine. Far East champion 1990; represented New Zealand in two world championships and one other Far East Championship. Five national wins include open teams.

CRONIER, Philippe (b. 1953) of Paris, France, bridge teacher and writer. Third Bermuda Bowl 1983. Won European Teams 1983, second European Pairs 1987.

CROOKER, Jerry (b. 1947) of Midland TX, banker, educated at Kansas U, Vietnam veteran, won eight outstanding service medals, ribbons and distinguished marksmanship awards in Air Force; member high school championship basketball team. Past president of Unit 172. Regional wins include Capital City KOs 1977, Corpus Christi Swiss 1978, Big D Winter Mens Prs 1980, El Paso Bracketed KO Tms 1992. Crooker won the ACBL-wide International Fund Game 1984.

CROSSLEY, Dr. Clarence F. Jr. (Cap) (b. 1924) of Las Vegas, physician and anesthesiologist, former president of Dist. 17, Western Conference, Marin County CA and Nevada Units. Diamond Life Master. Regional wins include All-Western KO Tms 1955, Desert Empire Open Tms 1962, 63; Rocky Mtn Mens Prs 1963, Big D Bridge Week Swiss 1974, Oil City KO Tms, Master Swiss 1978; Pacific Southwest Swiss 1976, Mid-Winter Holiday KO Tms 1975, Pikes Peak Swiss, Master Prs 1980. See FAMILY.

CROSSLEY, Dr. David M. (b. 1948) of Las Vegas, anesthesiologist, won the Vanderbilt 1974. Regional wins include Rogue River Valley KO Tms 1973, Bridge Week Mixed Prs 1976, Golden Gate KO Tms 1974, Mid-Winter Holiday KO Tms 1974, 75; Dist. 17 GN Tms 1975, 76; Cotton Boll Swiss 1977. See FAMILY.

CROSSLEY, Robert E. (Bob) (b. 1951) of Corte Madera CA, bridge teacher, professional player, co-owner of bridge center, film producer, graduated from U of California, Berkeley. A semi-professional juggler performing on cruise ships and resorts. He is a judge for the International Juggling Association and has coached several professional acts including the 1986 IJA World Team Championship. In the Seventies traveled extensively for "Travel with Goren", teaching and directing bridge cruises. Started playing at age 7 and became a LM at age 16. Became the youngest player, age 23, to win a National KO, the 1974 Vanderbilt (since won by Bobby Levin, age 22). Has written two books, *Learn and Enjoy Bridge, Advanced Concepts in Bridge*, and numerous articles for *The Bridge World*. Developed the Crossley 2NT which was in use in the early '70s before Jacoby 2NT became popular. Has produced two promotional videos for ACBL. Diamond Life Master with more than 50 regional wins including Mid-Winter Holiday Open Prs 1968, KO Tms 1974; Dist. 20 KOs 1973, 74; Golden Gate KOs 1974, Open Tms 1981, 90, 92, Stratified Prs , Master Prs 1990; Swiss 1981, 91, KO Tms 1981, 86; Bridge Week KOs 1979, Pacific Northwest KO Tms 1979, Golden State KO Tms, Oregon Trail Open Tms 1981; Hawaii Open Prs 1988, Open Tms 1990, 91; won the Danish Albani Cup 1991. See FAMILY.

CROUNSE, Eleanor B. of Paducah KY, won Womens Tms 1962, Mixed Prs 1964, District 11 Womens Prs 1979, Champagne Open Prs 1970.

CROWHURST, Eric (b. 1935) of Reading, England, accountant, contributor to *British Bridge World, ACBL Bulletin*, and other periodicals; also contributed the unique SUIT COMBINATIONS section of the *Bridge Encyclopedia*. Inventor of CROWHURST CONVENTION, widely used by British tournament players; author of *Acol in Competition* and other books on British bidding.

CROWN, Ronald (b. 1927) of Boca Raton FL, formerly of London. Bridge teacher, teaching between 200-500 students per week. Was partner in the Card School of New York, contributor to *The Bridge World* and *ACBL Bulletin*, represented England in the Camrose Trophy match 1961, won the Tollemache Cup three times and the Richard Lederer Cup twice. Regional wins include New England Winter Open Tms 1968, Eastern States KO Tms 1969.

CRUZ, Joao Nuño Moreira (1936-89) of Lisbon, Portugal, lawyer. Represented Portugal in one world championship and five European Championships. National wins include open team five times, open pairs three times.

CUKOFF, Henry (b. 1949) of Montreal, national tournament director; avid baseball fan, has been to all major league parks. Director in charge of NABC events since 1990. Began directing 1973; directs mainly in Northeastern U.S. and Eastern Canada. Won New England Summer Open Prs 1972, Canadian Nat'l Open Prs, Can-Am Swiss 1973.

CULBERTSON, Ely (July 22, 1891-Dec. 27, 1955) America's foremost authority on contract bridge for many years. Credited with making the game an internationally popular pastime, Culbertson was also an author and lecturer on mass psychology and political science. He was born in Romania but was an American citizen from birth by registration with the U.S. consul, being the son of Almon Culbertson, an American mining engineer who had been retained by the Russian government to develop the Caucasian oilfields and who had married a Russian woman, Xenia Rogoznaya, daughter of a Cossack atamon or chief.

Culbertson belonged to a pioneer American family that settled near Titusville and Oil City PA, and later joined the Sons of the American Revolution to refute rumors that he had changed his name or falsified his ancestry. He attended gymnasia in Russia and matriculated at Yale (1908) and Cornell (1910), but in each case remained only a few months. Later (1913-14) he studied political science at l'Ecole des Sciences Economiques et Politiques at the U of Paris (Sorbonne) and in 1915 at the U of Geneva in Switzerland, but he was largely self-educated, and the erudition for which he was admired can principally be attributed to a self-imposed and invariable regimen of reading a book designed to improve his knowledge at least one hour before going to sleep each night. In this he was aided by an aptitude for languages. He conversed fluently in Russian, English, French, German, Czech, Spanish and Italian, had a reading knowledge of Slavic, Polish, Swedish and Danish-Norwegian, and a knowledge of classical Latin and Greek.

In 1907 Culbertson participated as a student in one of the abortive Russian revolutions. He pursued his revolutionary ideas in labor disputes in the American Northwest and in Mexico and Spain (1911-1912), serving as an agitator for the union and syndicalist sides. The foregoing biographical data, all of which is a matter of official record, is here given in detail because it has been disputed in various writings about Culbertson. After the Russian Revolution of 1917 wiped out his family's large fortune there, Culbertson lived for four years in Paris and other European cities by exploiting his skill as a card player.

In 1921 he returned to the U.S., almost penniless, and continued to derive his living primarily from winnings in card games. In 1923, having acquired some reputation as a bridge player, he married Mrs. Josephine Murphy Dillon (See CULBERTSON, JOSEPHINE), one of the highly reputed bridge teachers in New York City. Together they became a successful pair as tournament players and bridge authorities. Between 1926 and 1929, the then new game of contract bridge began to replace auction bridge, and Culbertson saw in this development an opportunity to overtake the firmly entrenched authorities on auction bridge. Culbertson planned a long-range campaign that included the construction of a dogmatic system; publication of a magazine to appeal to group leaders in bridge; authorship of a bridge textbook to serve as a "bible"; organization of professional bridge teachers; dramatization of himself and his wife as largely fictitious personalities; and expansion of the appeal of bridge by breaking down religious opposition to card playing.

The plan proved conspicuously successful. Culbertson founded his magazine, *The Bridge World*, in 1929, and through the same corporation published his earliest bridge books, all of which were best sellers; manufactured and sold bridge players' supplies including the introduction of Kem playing cards; maintained an organization of bridge teachers (Culbertson National Studios) which at its peak had 6000 members; and conducted bridge competitions through the United States Bridge Association and the World Bridge Olympics and American Bridge Olympics. In its best year, 1937, *The Bridge World* Inc. grossed more than $1,000,000, of which $220,000 were royalties payable to Culbertson before profits were calculated.

As a regular tournament competitor Culbertson had the best record in the earliest years of contract bridge. In 1930 he won the Vanderbilt and American Bridge League Knockout Team events, also the ABL Board-a-Match Team event, and finished second in the Master Prs. That year he led a team that played the first international match, in England, and defeated several teams there. In 1933 and 1934 his teams won the Schwab Cup. After 1934 Culbertson seldom played tournament bridge, but he was second in the ABL's 1935 matchpoint team contest and in the International Bridge League's first intercontinental tournament in 1937. Culbertson continued to play high-stakes rubber bridge until about two years before his death. The success of Culbertson's *Blue Book* in 1930 caused the established auction bridge authorities to join forces to combat his threatened domination of contract bridge. (See BRIDGE HEADQUARTERS and OFFICIAL SYSTEM.)

Culbertson countered by challenging the leading player among his opposition, Sidney Lenz, to a test match, offering 5-1 odds. Culbert-son's victory in this match, played in the winter of 1931-32, fortified his leading position (see CULBERTSON-LENZ MATCH). The great publicity accorded the match enriched Culbertson; he and his wife both acquired contracts for widely syndicated newspaper articles, he made a series of movie shorts for $360,000, and he received $10,000 a week for network radio broadcasts.

In 1935 Culbertson tried to recapture the magic of his match against Lenz by playing a similar match against P. Hal and Dorothy Sims (See CULBERTSON-SIMS MATCH), but although the Culbertsons won this match also, there was no such publicity advantage as accrued from the Lenz match. The publicity accorded Culbertson throughout his professional career can be attributed equally to his unquestioned abilities, his colorful personality and his flamboyant way of life. Culbertson lived in the grand manner, with total disregard of expense whether at the moment he happened to be rich or penniless. Once he strolled into Sulka's (then) on Fifth Avenue in New York and bought $5,000 worth of shirts. He smoked a private blend of cigarettes that cost him $7 a day. When he decided to buy a Duesenberg automobile in 1934 he did not sell his Rolls Royce but gave it away. His home for years was an estate in Ridgefield CT, with a 45-room house, several miles of paved and lighted roads, greenhouses, cottages, lakes, and an enclosed swimming pool with orchids growing along its periphery. He always had caviar with his tea and made special trips to Italy to buy his neckties. When he died in 1955, he owned five houses for his own use, four of them with swimming pools.

But Culbertson rationalized these extravagances as publicity devices. He actually lived in one small room with a cot and a table, and he spent most of his time pacing the floor and thinking. In 1933, when a newspaper reporter asked him, "Mr. Culbertson, how did you get ahead of those other bridge authorities?" he answered, "I got up in the morning and went to work."

Culbertson's contributions to the science of contract bridge, both practical and theoretical, were basic and timeless. He devised the markings on duplicate boards for vulnerability and the bonuses for games and partscores. He was the first authority to treat distribution as equal or superior to high cards in formulating the requirements for bids. Forcing bids, including the one-over-one, were original Culbertson concepts, as were four-card suit bids, limited notrump bids, the strong two-bid, and wholesale ace-showing including the 4NT slam try. These were presented in the historic *Lesson Sheets on the Approach-Forcing System* (1927) and in numerous magazine articles written by Culbertson in the Twenties and early Thirties. Specific bridge principles attributable to Culbertson, separately described, include among others *Asking Bids,* the *Grand Slam Force, Jump Bids,* and the *New-Suit Forcing* principle, which Culbertson first introduced and later repudiated.

In 1938, with war imminent in Europe, Culbertson lost interest in bridge and thereafter devoted his time to seeking some grand achievement in political science. To effect world peace he proposed international control of decisive weapons and a quota for each major nation in tactical forces. After formation of the United Nations, to which Culbertson's ideas made a discernible contribution, he persisted in a campaign to give it adequate police power. At one time 17 U.S. Senators and 42 U.S. Congressmen subscribed to a proposed joint resolution of Congress advocating Culbertson's proposals. But in the course of these activities Culbertson lost his position as the leading bridge authority; by 1950 or earlier, Charles Goren had surpassed him in the sale of books and other bridge writings and in the adherence of bridge teachers and players.

However, when a bridge Hall of Fame was inaugurated in 1964, nine years after his death, Culbertson was the first person elected. Though never an ACBL Life Master, he was named Honorary Member in 1938. Ely and Josephine Culbertson were divorced in 1938 and in 1947 Culbertson married Dorothy Renata Baehne, who was 35 years younger than he. There were two children by each of his marriages. Culbertson suffered in late years from a lung congestion (emphysema) and died at his last home, in Brattleboro VT, of a common cold that proved fatal because of the lung condition.

Minor works by Ely Culbertson, such as paperbound books and pamphlets, are literally too numerous to mention, and all or nearly all were written by members of Culbertson's staff, as also were most of the newspaper and magazine articles published under Culbertson's name from 1932 on. Earlier articles in bridge periodicals were written by Culbertson, as were the following of his major books, each of which was published in many editions: *Contract Bridge Blue Book,* 1930; *Culbertson's Self-Teacher,* 1933; *Red Book on Play,* 1934; *The Gold Book,* or, *Contract Bridge Complete,* 1936; and *Point-Count Bidding,* 1952. Culbertson's autobiography, *The Strange Lives of One Man,* was published in 1940. His principal works on political science were *Total Peace,* 1943, and *Must We Fight Russia?,* 1947. See Bibliography, C,D,E,G,K.

CULBERTSON, Josephine (Mrs. Ely) (February 2, 1898-March 23, 1956) stood in her own right as a renowned bridge teacher, player and writer. Born Josephine Murphy in Bayside NY (now part of New York City), she married James Dillon in 1919 and was widowed by his suicide shortly thereafter.

Her interest in bridge commenced when she became secretary to Wilber C. Whitehead. On June 11, 1923 she married Ely Culbertson and collaborated with him in the development and teaching of the Culbertson or Approach-Forcing systems of auction and contract bridge. During her teaching career, 1922-1930, she was reputedly the highest paid bridge teacher. Through the Twenties and into the Thirties, Culbertson was known as "the modern miracle — the woman who can play on even terms with the best men." She was the first woman to achieve highest championship caliber, and as such was unique in her times, before the advent of Helen Sobel and others.

As a member of *The Bridge World* team, with Waldemar von Zedtwitz as her partner and later Michael Gottlieb and Albert Morehead, she won several national and international championships including the Schwab Cup 1933, 1934. Paired with her husband she played many high-stakes set games, won international matches in England and France, and achieved national fame in the Culbertson-Lenz Match, 1931-1932. With Culbertson, she was co-founder of *The Bridge World* magazine, 1929, and inaugurated its *Pro et Contra* department, which appeared under her name until her death.

She was often on radio bridge shows, including two long series with her husband. She participated briefly in motion pictures made by her husband. Culbertson's great popularity was a natural reaction to her gentle ways, her gaiety and her good-natured approach to life. Culbertson was as glamorous as a movie star. The world of bridge was at her feet as was the world of fashion. Every newspaper, every smart magazine sang her praises and quoted not only her success at the bridge table, but also her beautiful clothes and the chic with which she wore them.

Josephine and Ely Culbertson were divorced in an uncontested action in 1938, though they continued as business partners and co-editors. She died March 23, 1956, of a cerebral stroke, 87 days after Ely's death. She won The ABL Open Challenge Team 1930, Vanderbilt 1930, and placed second in the Life Master Prs 1930, Open Prs 1928 (both of these events played for the first time on these dates), Chicago 1935, Women's Prs 1930.

At all times, Culbertson was an active editor of all books on the Culbertson System. She was co-author of the historic *Lesson Sheets on the Approach System* (1927) and made the first arrangement of material for Culbertson's *Summary* (1932), the largest-selling bridge book. However, her widely syndicated newspaper column, 1931-56, her department in *The Bridge World,* and the several books published under her name were largely prepared by *The Bridge World* technical staff; the best-known of these is *Contract Bridge for Beginners*, 1937. See Bibliography, E.

CUMMINGS, Michael Allan (Mike) (b. 1944) of Willowdale ON, data processing consultant. Represented Canada in internat'l play New Orleans 1978. Regional wins — Great Lakes Open Tms 1970, Can-Am KOs 1974, 77; Canadian Nat'l Swiss 1972, Mens Swiss 1977, 78, 80, KO Tms 1979; Dist. 2 GN Tms 1975.

CUMMINGS, Richard John (Dick) (b. 1932) of Sydney, Australia, bridge writer, teacher, WBF World Life Master. One of Australia's greatest players. Cummings had a long and successful partnership with Tim Seres. They helped Australia finish 3rd in the Bermuda Bowl in 1971 and 1979, and represented Australia on many other international occasions. He has won more than 20 national titles, in teams and pairs. He is the bridge columnist for the Sydney *Morning Herald* and the Sydney *Sun-Herald,* and edits *World Bridge Federation News.* He contributes to *The Australian Bridge* and World Championship bulletins, and is a member of the WBF Appeals Committee. Won BOLS Brilliancy player prize 1980.

CYPRES, Suzanne (b. 1946) of Brussels, Belgium. Won Common Market Mixed Pairs, Mixed Teams 1991. Won seven national titles.

D

D'ALELIO, Massimo (Mimmo) (b. 1916) of Rome, Italy, retired lawyer and advertising man. WBF Grand Master, 5th in world career listing in 1992. Won World Teams 1964, 1968, 1972, Bermuda Bowl 1957, 1958, 1959, 1961, 1962, 1963, 1965, 1966, 1967, 1969. Won European Teams 1956, 1957, 1958, second 1955, 1962, 1963. Many Italian national wins include Open Teams six times. See BLUE TEAM.

D'ANDREA, Baffi Marisa of Naples, Italy, won World Women's Teams 1976, placed second 1978, won European Women's Teams 1976, 1977. WBF Grand Master.

D'AVE, Adelstano P. (b. 1928) of Rio de Janeiro, Brazil, insurance broker. Won South American Teams 1967, 1968, 1971, 1982, 1984. Represented Brazil in four world championships. 16 national wins include open teams

D'ORSI, Ernesto (b. 1936) of São Paulo, Brazil, business consultant. Represented Brazil in seven world championships. National wins include open teams once. WBF president 1990-92, vice-president 1986-90, member of Executive from 1980, member of Committee of Honor 1986. Chief organizer of world championships in 1979, 1985, and member of organizing committee in 1973. CBB president since 1984, and member of South American Executive Council since 1978. Author of two books, and the specifications for Bermuda Bowl and Venice Cup organization. Magazine contributor.

D'UNIENVILLE, M. V. Robert M. (b. 1927) of Phoenix, Mauritius, mathematics teacher. Third European

Teams 1951, representing Britain. Represented Mauritius in one world championship and three zonal championships. Won ACBL National Senior Knockout Teams 1988.

DACOSTA, Donald (b. 1927 in United States) of Kingston, Jamaica, bridge teacher. Represented Jamaica in 1983 Bermuda Bowl and 4 CAC zonal championships. Won CAC Open Pairs and Open Teams, and numerous national titles. Former owner St. Clair Bridge Club, Toronto, Canada.

DAHL, Flemming (b. 1946), of Copenhagen, Denmark, engineer. Won European Junior Teams 1970 and Common Market Mixed Teams 1989. Has 65 caps after his debut in the Nordic Championships 1975. Represented Denmark in one world championships and on many other occasions. Won six national titles. Columnist of *Berlingske Weekend,* author of one book and a magazine contributor.

DAHL, Mark W. (b. 1950) of Richmond VA, stock and commodities broker. Has won approximately 15 regionals including Winston-Salem Swiss 1978, Baltimore Open Prs, Swiss 1978; Summer secondary Swiss 1984, Richmond Mens Swiss 1987, Open Prs 1991; Norfolk Swiss 1988, Open Prs 1990; Dist 6 GN Pairs 1986, 89; Richmond Swiss 1989, Williamsburg Top Bracket KO Tms 1991.

DAHL, Trine (b. 1954), of Copenhagen, Denmark. WBF World Master. Won World Women's Teams 1988. Represented Denmark in two other world championships, four zonal championhips and on many other occasions. Won 11 national titles.

DAHLER, Ivy Charlotte Marjorie (b. 1923 in England) of Toowoomba, Australia. Won Far East Women's Teams 1984 and several national titles.

DAIGNEAULT, Pierre (b. 1947) of Laval PQ, sociologist, director of research, graduate of McGill U, served as vice president of the Montreal BL for many years. Won many regionals including Can-Am Open Prs 1975, KO Tms 1978; Summer secondary Mens Prs 1978, Fleur-de-Lys KO Tms 1979, Nat'l Capital Swiss Tms, Dist. 5 KO Tms 1980; Dist 1 GN Prs 1981.

DALAL, Rajesh (b. 1953) of Bombay, India, chartered acountant and director of export company. WBF World Master. Second BFAME Open Teams 1985, 1989, Open Pairs 1985. Fourth World Open Teams 1988 and represented India in three other world championships. 10 national wins include open teams four times.

DALATI, Henri (died 1971) of Beirut, Lebanon. Represented Lebanon in World Team Olympiad 1960, 1964, European Championships 1954, 1956, 1957, 1961, 1962, 1963. Won many national titles. Former Secretary of Lebanese Bridge Dederation.

DALTON, Michael Edward (Mike) (b. 1949) of Glendale CA, POS\retail systems project leader, enjoys golf. Active rubber bridge player. Won Detroit Mens Swiss 1979, El Paso Master Pairs 1984, Phoenix Open Prs 1985, Sacramento Open Prs 1989, Santa Clara BAM

Tms 1990, Pasadena Morning KO Tms 1992.

DALTON, Roy S. (b. 1955) of Mississauga ON, chartered accountant, former bridge teacher and controller, currently a financial consultant, graduated U of Toronto. At age 18 (1974) was Canada's youngest Life Master. Representing Canada in world championship in New Orleans 1978, he finished 11th overall in the Rosenblum Teams, represented Canada in Geneva 1990, placed second in CNTC 1993. Has won approximately 10 regionals including Canadian Nat'l Swiss 1975, KOs 1981; Nickel City KOs, Swiss 1978; Dist. 2 GN Tms 1977, 78; Toronto KO Tms, Swiss.

DALY, Victor R. (1895-1986) of Washington DC, retired government deputy director and travel consultant, graduated Cornell, was one of the 36 founders of the AMERICAN BRIDGE ASSOCIATION at Hampton VA in 1932. For many years he was a prominent figure in the ABA, serving as its president from 1950-65, vice president 1941-49 and President Emeritus for many years. He was a member of the ACBL Goodwill Committee and a contributing editor, *Bridge Encyclopedia*. Daly received The Distinguished Service Award from the U.S. Dept. of Labor 1955, had two articles on labor problems entered into the Congressional Record and was listed in *Who's Who in America*, 1976.

DAM, Else (b. 1915) of Copenhagen, Denmark, bridge teacher. Won European Women's Teams 1948, 1949, second 1951, and represented Denmark on many other occasions. Won Danish open teams 1951 in a women's team, a unique circumstance, and won nine other Danish titles.

DAM, Villy (b. 1945), of Vejle, Denmark, bridge professional, bridge player, youth consultant for the Danish Bridge Federation. WBF World Master. Represented Denmark in one world championship, one zonal championship and on many other occasions. Won national open teams three times, open pairs once. Won Hoechst Teams 1991. Youth consultant for Danish Bridge Federation. Author of one book.

DAMIANI, José, (b. 1939) of Paris, France, industrialist. WBF World Master. President European Bridge League since 1987. WBF Vice-President since 1986. Chairman of several committees. Originator and organizer of Epson World Bridge Contest since 1986. Chairman INTERNATIONAL BRIDGE PRESS ASSOCIATION Sponsorship committee. Originator of Philip Morris Mixed Team and Pairs, and Generali European Individual Championships. President French Bridge Federation 1978-83, doubling the membership.

Chief organizer of world championships in Biarritz 1982 and Geneva 1990, greatly enlarging the role of sponsorship, computers and television. His initiatives in the period 1987-90 brought the former Soviet Union into the international bridge community. Won many national titles. NPC French World Champion team 1992.

DAMM, Otti (1918-1984) of Copenhagen, Denmark, bridge teacher. Third World Women's Teams 1960. Won European Women's Teams 1949, 1955, 1957, 1958, second 1951. Represented Denmark in one other world championship, five other zonal championships and many

other occasions including appearances for the Danish open team. She and her partner, Rigmor Fraenckel, were noted for fast play. In 1950 they won the first Danish Open Pairs, and in the following year with an all-women team won the Open Teams, a unique circumstance. Her 12 national victories included two other open team wins and the Open Pairs. She was the victim of a murder.

DANAS, Linda. See GORDON, Linda.

DANG, Douglas (b. 1942) of San Mateo CA, attorney, competed in the USBC Team Trials for qualification to the Bermuda Bowl 1991. Won Mid-Winter Holiday KO Tms 1977, Handicap KO Tms 1989; All-Western Swiss 1982, KOs Tms 1989; Sacramento Swiss 1982, BAM Tms 1992.

DARLING, Dean A. (1927-1991) of Eureka KS, retired chemical engineer, graduated Pittsburgh State U. Darling was a Diamond Life Master. He passed away in his sleep at a tournament while sitting out the first half of the afternoon session of the KOs. His team went on to win the event. Had numerous regional wins including: Mid-Atlantic Summer Mens Prs, Fall Mens Prs 1971, Master Prs 1974, Swiss 1975; Dist. 6 GN Tms 1976, Summer secondary Sr KOs, Sr Swiss, Sr Open Prs 1987; Summer secondary Sr Swiss (2), Sr Open Prs 1988; Arlington Sr Open Prs 1989, Myrtle Beach Sr KOs 1990, Oklahoma City Sr Swiss 1991, Summer secondary Sr Swiss (2), Sr Open Prs 1990; Fall secondary Sr Swiss, Sr Open 1990; Spring secondary Sr Swiss, Sr Open; Summer secondary Sr Swiss 1991.

DARVAS, Róbert (1903-1957) of Budapest, Hungary, bridge writer. He was the foremost bridge journalist in Hungary and contributed to many magazines. He created many interesting deals and composed bridge problems. Co-author of *Spotlight on Card Play* and the classic *Right Through the Pack*.

DARWEN, Hugh (b. 1943) of Warwick, England, computer programmer. The world's leading authority on double dummy problems. Conductor of double dummy column in *Bridge Magazine*, and successors, 1965-1990, and in *International Popular Bridge Monthly* 1990-. Author of one book. Expert on the theory and practice of relational data bases.

DASILVA, Lionel da (1911-89) of Manila, Philippines, insurance underwriter. Won Far East Open Teams 1957, 1958, and represented the Philippines in two world championships and five zonal championships. National wins include open teams once.

DAUTELL, Eugene G. (Duke) (b. 1921) of Los Angeles, bridge teacher, former insurance underwriter. Interested in all sports and was a table tennis champion in the Forties, past President Toledo Bridge Unit. Has been running 10-15 bridge classes weekly since 1964. Won Mens Tms 1951, Summer secondary Marcus Cup 1952, Midwest Open Tms 1957, Bridge Week Swiss 1974, Spring secondary Mens Prs 1977.

DAVID, Sharon H. of North Hollywood CA, born in Toronto, bridge teacher and professional. She served on San Fernando Unit 561 Board and as Assistant Chairperson ACBL National Goodwill Committee. Placed second in Life Master Womens Prs 1993; regionals include Mexican Nat'l Womens Prs 1982, Las Vegas Sr IMP Prs 1988, Pasadena Sr KO Tms 1989, 90; Palm Springs Sr Open Prs, Sr Prs 1989; Honolulu Sr Swiss, Reno Sr KO Tms 1989; Yosemite Sr KO Tms, Swiss 1991; Ventura Sr KO Tms 1992, San Diego Sr KO Tms 1993.

DAVIDSON, Sidney L. (b. 1918) of San Francisco, ACBL national director, began directing career 1956; achieved present rating 1972. He contributed to the simplification of fouled board calculations, carryover computations; evolved and modified various movements including the MIRROR MITCHELL TEAM MOVEMENT. Graduated from Medical College of Virginia; former dentist.

DAVIES, Pat (b. 1947) of Bristol, England, teacher. WBF Grand Master. Won Venice Cup 1981, 1985, European Women's Teams 1981. Second World Women's Teams 1984, 1988, 1992, Common Market Women's Teams 1977 and 1981. National wins include Gold Cup once.

DAVIS, Anita (Pidgeon) (b. 1924) of Beaumont TX, avid reader and football fan. Has served Unit 201 on various committees, as alternate for Nat'l Bd of Gov and served on Nat'l Rules and Ethics Committee. Davis has been a weekly bridge columnist for *Beaumont Enterprise* for more than 30 years. A Diamond Life Master, she placed second in Womens Tms 1975. Has numerous regional wins including Texas Conference Master Prs 1957, Womens Prs 1958, 68, Open Prs 1961; Mid-South Mixed Prs 1957, Swiss 1973, Womens Prs 1975, Womens Masters Swiss 1976; All-Western Womens Prs 1959, Mexican Nat'l Mixed Prs 1964, 71, Womens Prs 1966; Golder Prs 1966, Fall secondary Womens Prs 1968, 72; Capitol City Open Prs 1972, Spring secondary Womens Swiss 1984, Fall secondary Swiss 1992.

DAVIS, Chester P. Jr. (Chet) (b. 1922) of Vero Beach FL, former attorney and company president, educated at Harvard and Boston U. Past president Eastern Mass. Bridge Association; served for many years on Nat'l Appeals Committee. Diamond Life Master; placed second Blue Ribbon Prs 1979. Regional wins include Bermuda Swiss 1962, 72, Mens Prs 1962, 66; New England KO Tms 1963, 69, 73; Swiss 1971, 78, Swiss 1980; Southeastern Mens Prs 1967, Open Tms, Life Master Prs 1974; Fall secondary Master Prs 1973, Dist 25 GN Tms 1973, 75, 80, 83; Zonal 1973, 80; Manchester Strat IMP Prs 1991, also NAOP twice, Dist. 25 IMP Prs, Swiss Prs and three-time winner Dist. 25 Swiss.

DAVIS, Edgar F. Jr. (Ed) (b. 1942) of Seal Beach CA, systems analyst, graduated UCLA, USC; enjoys fantasy football and rotisserie baseball. Author of various ideas and methods including Octopus preempts. Grand Life Master with more than 10,000 masterpoints; placed second Mens Swiss 1985. Some of his numerous regionals include Fall secondary Mens Tms 1971, Spring Swiss 1975, 83, Open Prs 1976; Bridge Week Swiss 1968, 70, 79, 81, 87, Mixed Prs 1970, Open Prs 1975, 86; Orange County KO Tms 1974; Pacific Southwest Master Prs 1978, Open Prs 1989, Super Open Prs 1991; Dist. 23

GN Tms 1977, 79, 84, 90, Zone VIII 1979; Los Angeles Winter Swiss 1976, Master Prs 1979, Open Prs 1981, 91; Dist. 23 NA Prs 1985; Mid-Winter Holiday Life Master IMP Prs; Inland Empire Swiss 1988; Las Vegas Swiss 1990.

DAVIS, Victorine (Vickie) (b. 1922) of Dallas TX, home builder and land developer; elected Woman Builder of the Year in Dallas 1979. Has served in various capacities in local bridge. Won Mississippi Valley Master Prs 1968, Texas Swiss 1970, Int'l City KOs 1974, Mexican Nat'l Master Prs, Republic of TX Womens Prs 1973; Amarillo Womens Tms 1982, Dallas Ira Corn Prs 1985.

DAWKINS, George S. (Dr. Doom) (b. 1931) of Austin TX, professor of business, bridge professional, educated at Princeton and U of IL (PhD). Other interests include tennis, table tennis, backgammon, chess, literature. Has had two books of poetry published. Served on Houston and Austin boards, certified director, directs on bridge cruises. A Diamond Life Master, he won Mixed Prs 1970. He has won more than 50 regionals including Mid-South Spring Master Prs 1963, Summer Open Tms 1967; Big D KO Tms 1970, Republic of TX KO Tms 1970, Open Prs 1978; Texas Capital KO Tms 1975, Corpus Christi KO Tms 1978, Acapulco Fiesta Swiss 1980, Dist. 16 GN Tms, Zone VI 1976; Sr. Open Prs 1986; Houston Masters Prs 1986; Dist 16 GN Pairs, New Orleans Sr. KO Tms, Anaheim Sr Swiss, 1987; Corpus Christi KO Tms 1987, 90; Tulsa Sr Open Prs 1989, Reno Sr Swiss, Sr KO Tms 1989; Mesa Sr KO Tms, Sr Swiss 1989; Padre Island Sr Swiss 1990, Atlantic City Sr KO Tms, Sr Open Prs 1991; Austin Sr Open Prs 1991, Abilene Sr KO Tms, Hot Springs Sr Swiss 1992.

DAWSON, Dennis L. (b. 1946) of Reading MA, owner Dawson's Get Away Bridge Weekends since 1987, former bridge club owner and teacher, graduated U of Texas and U of Michigan, editor "Northeast Bridge" 1973-76. Won Spring secondary Mens Swiss 1973, Individual KO Tms 1974, 90; Olympic Masters Prs, Swiss 1975, Prs 1983; Can-At KOs 1975, Masters Swiss 1978; New England KO Swiss 1980, Masters Swiss 1981, Nat'l Capital Swiss, Labor Day Morning KOs, Tri-State Winter Morning KOs 1990; 4th of July Swiss 1991, Swiss 1992.

DE FALCO, Dano of Padua, Italy. World Life Master. Won Bermuda Bowl 1974, runner-up 1979, 1983. European team championship 1973, 1979, Common Market Teams 1977, 1979, and represented Italy on many other occasions.

DE LA PEÑA, Juan Ignacio (b. 1953) of Madrid, Spain, music critic. Represented Spain in one world championship. Won many national titles.

DE MIGUEL, Carlos (b.1949) of Buenos Aires, Argentina, industrialist. South American Champion 1985, and represented Argentina in Bermuda Bowl in the same year. 6 national titles include open teams once.

DEAS, Lynn (b. 1953) of Newport News VA, professional bridge player and teacher, graduated Catawba College. Coin collecter and has three dogs – Wishtrick, Finesse and IMP, that travel to tournaments with her.

Served as Conduct and Ethics chairman Unit 115. WBF Grand Master; three-time winner of Venice Cup 1987, 1989, 1991; placed second World Womens Prs 1982, fourth World Womens Pairs and World Mixed Prs 1990, third Pan American Womens Tms Championship 1992. ACBL Grand Life Master with more than 15,000 MPs (Dec 1993); has won many North American titles including Master Mixed Tms 1982, Life Master Womens Prs 1983, 85; Womens KO Tms 1985, Womens Swiss 1987, Womens BAM Tms 1992; placed second Master Mixed Tms 1984, 1990; Womens KO Tms 1986, 92; Life Master Womens Prs 1989, Womens BAM Tms 1991. Has numerous regional wins.

DEBONNAIRE, Carlos Augusto (b. 1940) of Lisbon, Portugal, commercial director. Represented Portugal in one world championship and five European Championships. National wins include open pairs four times, open pairs once.

DEBONNAIRE, José Antonio (b. 1940) of Lisbon, Portugal, technician. Represented Portugal in one world championship and five European Championships. National wins include open teams six times and open pairs three times.

DECSI, Leslie (Laslo) (1909 1969) of Sao Paulo, Brazil, born in Budapest; European champion 1934, second in 1935, 1936. Lived in Brazil after 1946; was South American champion 1955; represented Brazil in the World Team Olympiad 1964. Co-authored *The Limit System;* was a contributor to *European Bridge Review.*

DEDICHEN, Herman (Born in Norway, d. 1958) of Copenhagen, Denmark. Lived in France for 17 years before settling in Denmark in the Thirties. He was the man behind the reactivation of the European Championship in Copenhagen 1948, and honorary secretary of the EBL from 1947 until his death. For three decades, wrote column in the newspaper *Politiken* under the pen name "Mr Doubleton".

DEERY, Desmond (b. 1939) of Marbella, Spain, formerly of Belfast, Northern Ireland, solicitor, and club owner. Represented Ireland in one world championship and two European Championships. Represented Spain in one European Championship. National titles include open teams once and open pairs three times in Northern Ireland and open teams twice in Spain. Won Bridge Week Open Teams and Master Pairs 1964. Leading masterpoint winner in Ireland 1963-4. Former secretary of Irish Bridge Union and Northern Ireland Bridge Union.

DeHARPPORTE, Ronald E. (b. 1938) of Edina MN, company owner and president, schooled at U of Minnesota. Has served on Bd of Dir MN Civil Liberties Union and on Unit 179 Board. Regional wins include Gopher Master Teams 1968, 69, 71, Mens Prs 1978, 79.

DEIK, Adriana de Aguad (b. 1941) of Santiago, Chile, English teacher. Won South American Women's Teams 1977 and represented Chile in six other zonal championships and two world championships. Top-ranked Chilean woman, bridge teacher.

DEJARDIN, Florent (b.1937) of Brussels, Belgium,

bridge columnist. Represented Belgium in five European Championships and other international events. 14 national wins include open teams 7 times.

DELEVA, Nevena (b. 1959) of Sofia, Bulgaria, computer worker and mathematician. WBF World Master. Won European Women's Pairs 1987, third 1989. Third Olympiad Women's Teams 1988.

DEL GALLEGO, Tina (b. 1949) of Long Island, formerly of the Philippines, secretary. Won Far East Women's Teams 1979, 1982. Represented Philippines in one world championship and one other zonal championship. 7 national titles include open teams once.

DELMOULY, Claude (b. 1927) of Paris, France, bridge teacher and writer, WBF Life Master. Won World Team Olympiad 1960, represented France World Team Olympiad 1968, 1972, European Championships 1957, 1959, 1965. National wins include French Open Pairs 1959, Open Teams 1960, 1962, English Master Pairs 1960. Won London *Sunday Times* 1968. Authored six books including *Tous les Secrets de Bridge* and *Le Bridge d'aujourd'hui* with Pariente and is a contributor to various bridge periodicals.

DELOR, Elisabeth (b. 1945) of Paris, France. WBF World Master. Third World Women's Pairs 1978. Second European Women's Teams 1974. Represented France in six other world championships and won many national titles.

DeMARTINO, Richard A. (Rich) (b. 1939) of Riverside CT, insurance company executive, graduate of Lehigh U. Enjoys sports, waterskiing and boating. Has served as president of NY Metropolitan Commercial Bridge League and Stamford Bridge Club. In 1980 he won North American Swiss. Regionals include Eastern States Mens Prs 1967, 68, Mens Tms 1969, Goldman Prs, Bracketed KO Tms 1992; New England KO Open Prs 1971, Summer Prs 1986, Morning KOs 1991, Fall KO Tms, 1992; Long Island Prs 1986, Golder Master Prs 1987, Tri-State KOs 1988, Spring secondary KOs 1991, GNYBA Summer Open Swiss 1992; Tri-State Winter Strat Prs 1993.

DENBY, Charles W. D. (b. 1930) of Huntington NY, accountant, teaches adult education bridge courses. He won Mens Tms 1960.

DENG, Pu Fang (b. 1943) of Beijing, China, son of Deng Xiaoping, many time local champion. Chairman, Chinese Handicapped Association. Responsible for the improvement of facilities for handicapped people in China.

DENG, Xiaoping (b. 1904) of Beijing, China, Honorary President of Chinese Bridge Association. The chief architect of Chinese economic reform and modernization after the Cultural Revolution. Awarded IBPA "Man of the Year" title in 1980. WBF Golden Award 1989. Gold Medal winner 1993 from WBF. Winner of the ACBL Presidential citation 1993. Responsible for the rapid growth of bridge in China. Plays bridge several times each week.

DENNEHY, Daniel T. (b. 1949) of River Hills WI, attorney, educated at St Louis U (summa cum laude), U of Minnesota, Marquette. Enjoys dancing and volleyball, winner of dance awards for Irish folk dancing, gives employment and personnel seminars. Member Bd of Gov, 2nd alternate director Dist. 13, Nat'l Charity Committee; Unit 222 Player of the Year 1989, awarded Unit Goodwill and Sportsmanship award 1992. He won North American Non-Life Master Swiss 1983 and Oklahoma Flt B Swiss 1985, Spring secondary Morning KOs 1989.

DENNINGER, Tracy (b. 1924) of Altamonte Springs FL, formerly of Bermuda, retired condominium manager and consultant, Florida State cribbage champion 1986. Represented Bermuda in world championship competition in 1968, 72, 74, 76. Won Spring secondary Individual 1951, Bermuda Mens Prs 1972, Swiss 1977. Denninger monitored alleged cheating by the Italian team during 25th anniversary Bermuda Bowl in Bermuda 1975. Played his first game of bridge at age five.

DENNIS, Paul W. (b. 1952) of Winter Springs FL, claims adjuster, CPCU, graduated Stetson U. Music collector, baseball fan and history buff. Editor Unit 240 *Trumpet*, contributor to *Bridge Buffs Bulletin* and other publications. Volunteer Chairman Fall NABC 1992, member INTERNATIONAL BRIDGE PRESS ASSOCIATION. Won Southeastern Mens Prs 1977, All-Southern Non-Smoking Open Swiss 1983, 84; Tampa Non-Smoking Open Prs 1985, Orlando Masters Prs 1988.

DENNISON, Maureen of Isleworth, England, sales representative. Won Venice Cup 1981, European Women's Teams 1981, Common Market Women's Teams 1979, 1981. Contributor to *ACBL Bulletin* and other magazines.

DENNY, Jill (Mrs. Jack) (d. 1993) of Bradenton FL, bridge club owner, certified director and teacher, graduate Kent State U. Won Mississippi Valley Open Tms 1953, Master Prs 1959; MO Valley Open Tms, Mixed Prs 1955; Midwest Spring Womens Prs 1957, Open Tms 1958, Fall Open Tms, Mixed Prs 1960; Keystone Mixed Prs 1960, Dist 11 Open Tms 1962, All-American Open Tms 1967, Mixed Prs 1969; Southeastern Womens Swiss 1975, Northern FL Womens Prs, Womens Swiss 1977; Orlando Swiss 1982, Dayton Swiss, KO Tms 1984; Lake Charles Open Prs 1985, 86; Tampa Open Prs, Myrtle Beach Tms, Pittsburgh Open Prs 1987; Biloxi Open Prs, Swiss 1991.

DENNY, John W. (Jack) (1911-1993) of Bradenton FL, sales representative for Mahaffey Corp, bridge teacher and club owner (for 30 years). Lectured and ran bridge games on cruises. He won Mens Tms 1951, Spingold 1985 and was second in Open Prs 1961, Spingold 1987. Competed in USBC in 1987 and represented ACBL 1962. Diamond Life Master with numerous regional wins including Marcus Cup 1952, All-American Open Tms 1967, Mixed Prs 1969; FL KO Tms 1970, Southeastern Mens Swiss 1974, 77, Mens Prs 1977; FL BAM Tms, Master Prs 1976; Central FL KOs 1980, Mid-Atlantic KO Tms, Dist. 5 Mens Swiss 1981; Orlando KO Tms, Swiss 1982; Reno KO Tms 1983, Gatlinburg KOs 1984, Birmingham Mens Tms, Lake Charles Mens Tms 1985; Indianapolis Open Prs 1987, Tampa KO Tms 1988, Biloxi Open Prs, Swiss 1991.

DERBLAY, Dr. Paul, physician, of Mauritius. Second BFAME Teams 1987, and represented Mauritius in one world championship and three other zonal championships.

DERIVERY, Jean-Louis (b. 1939) of Gosier, Guadeloupe, businessman. Represents CAC on WBF Executive. President CAC 1983-87, 1989-91. President Guadeloupe BC 1979-85. Represented Guadeloupe in six world championships and 16 zonal championships.

DERMER, Dale (b. 1935) of Richmond VA, tax preparer, bookkeeper, bridge teacher and homemaker, educated U of Pennsylvania, member Unit Bd. Won Womens Prs 1985. A Diamond Life Master, she won Lancaster Womens Prs 1976, Buffalo Womens Swiss 1979, 82, Womens Prs 1983; Cleveland Swiss, Open 1983, Womens Swiss 1985, 88, Womens Swiss 1987; Pittsburgh Womens Swiss 1981, Womens Prs 1983, Mixed Prs 1987; Toronto Womens Swiss 1984, Nashville Womens Prs 1988, Richmond Standard Card Prs, Alexandria Swiss 1989; Baltimore KOs, Bracketed KOs, Norfolk Womens Swiss 1990.

DERUY, Claude (b.1927) of Vimy, Pas de Calais, France, bailiff and tournament director, represented France Bermuda Bowl 1961, World Team Olympiad 1964. Placed second European Championships 1961, won French Open Teams 1962. Author of *Bien jouer au Bridge*.

DESCHAPELLES, Alexandre Louis Honore Lebreton, sometimes referred to as Guillaume le Breton (1780-1847), a Frenchman of good family, was described by his contemporary, James Clay, English whist authority, as the finest whist player, "beyond any comparison, the world has ever seen." Deschapelles excelled at other games, among them billiards, Polish draughts and chess. Fighting in one of the many wars of his time, he lost his right hand, but continued to play whist, and, more remarkably, billiards. He invented the coup which bears his name (see DESCHAPELLES COUP) and a number of other coups. He published only fragments of a projected extensive work on whist. See BIBLIOGRAPHY, A.

DESCHENONE, Mercedes Guerrico de of Buenos Aires, Argentina. South American Womens Team champion 1948, 1949, 1950, 1951, 1953, 1961, 1962, 1977, 1979, 1981. 26 national titles won include open teams 3 times and open pairs once.

DESHPANDE, Dr. Aniruddha (b. 1961) of Glendale WI, born in India, physician of emergency medicine, educated at U of Wisconsin and Medical College of WI; enjoys chess and computers. He won Non-Life Master Swiss 1983. At time of first regional win was youngest person in Wisconsin history to win a regional title, age 16. Has won Wisconsin Flt B Swiss 1978, Oklahoma City Flt B Swiss.

DESPAIN, Elizabeth Patricia (Pat) of Los Angeles CA, retired; former ABA Western Section vice president, member ABA Bd of Dir 1974-77, Western Section coordinator 1990-91. Won manyABA national, sectional and regional events; ACBL Summer secondary Presidents Prs, Sub-Senior Master Tms 1963.

DESROUSSEAUX, Gerard (1927-1985) of Paris, France, bridge teacher and writer, won World Par Contest 1963, European champion 1962, represented France Bermuda Bowl 1963, 1969, World Team Olympiad 1964, 1968, European Championships 1965, 1967, 1979. WBF World Master, won *Sunday Times* Invitational 1966. National wins include Open Teams 1955, Open Pairs 1956, 1962, Mixed Teams 1960. Contributor to French periodicals and co-author of *Le Bridge d'Ecole Francaise.*

DEUTSCH, June A. of Williams Island FL, enjoys cooking, aerobics, traveling and reading. Represented ACBL in international play in New Orleans 1978 and Miami 1986. Placed second Pan American Championships Womens Prs 1992; has won each of the five womens national titles at least once -- Womens Tms 1966, Life Master Womens Prs 1973, Womens Swiss 1984, 85; Womens KO Tms 1981, Womens Prs 1990; placed second Womens Tms 1972, Life Master Womens Prs 1979, Womens KO Tms 1979. Diamond Life Master; has won more than 50 regional events and nine NABC secondary events.

DEUTSCH, Seymon (b. 1935) of Laredo TX, rancher and merchant, degrees from Trinity U. He quit bridge for 22 years to concentrate on home and business. He enjoys hunting, skiing and ranching. After layoff won World Team Olympiad Venice 1988 and placed second Salsomaggiore Italy 1992. Won GN Tms 1986, Spingold 1991, Vanderbilt 1994; placed second Vanderbilt 1990, 91; Spingold 1993; has won several regional events including Dist 16 GN Tms four times.

DEUTSCH, Tobi (Mrs. David Sokolow) of Austin TX, real estate broker, former social worker with degrees in sociology and biology. She loves to hike and run. Was Bd member and editor of newsletter in Phoenix Unit, currently active locally. Represented ACBL in World Championship play in Bal Harbour in 1986, Salsomaggiore Italy 1992. Won five NABC titles and placed second four times. Won USWBTC 1992 and competed in USBC 1991. She is a Diamond Life Master and has more than 65 regional wins and eight NABC secondary titles.

DE WITT, Joan. See McKEAN, Joan M.

DEWITZ, Egmont von (1907-1987) of Cologne, Germany, represented Germany World Team Olympiad 1960, 1964 and many European Championship since 1938. National titles included Open Teams 15 times.

DeYOUNG, Bernace A. (Bernie) (b. 1947) of Miami FL, attorney, graduate of Hope College and U of Miami. Was 1952 March of Dimes Poster Child. Second in Women's Pairs 1994. A Diamond Life Master, some of her regional titles include St. Petersburg KOs 1981, Jacksonville Prs 1982, Dist. 9 GN Pairs 1986, Orlando Open Prs 1984; Dayton Swiss 1986, Raleigh Womens Prs, Indianapolis Prs, Tms, Pasadena Prs 1990; Tampa Womens Prs, Sacramento Handicap KOs, Ft. Lauderdale KOs, Charlotte Womens Prs 1991; Peoria Swiss 1992; Dist 9 GN Pairs, Hunt Valley Womens Prs 1992; Nashville Swiss, Miami Swiss 1993.

DHERS, Alberto (b. 1932) of Caracas, Venezuela, professor of chemistry and mathematics. WBF World Master. Won CAC Teams 1973, 1986, 1991. Represented Venezuela in five world championships and won more than 30 national titles. CAC vice-president. Bridge teacher.

DI STEFANO, Franco (b. 1942) of Milan, Italy, journalist, and director of bridge school. European champion 1975. Has won several Common Market and national titles. Bridge columnist for *Il Giornale* and other newspapers. President of the Board of Italian Bridge Teachers.

DIAMOND, John (b. 1966) of College Park MD, systems engineer, graduated Duke U and U of Maryland, a member of the Junior Corp and a WBF World Master. He was a member of the winning World Junior Championship team in Ann Arbor 1991. He has won Arlington KO Tms 1989, Bracketed KO Tms 1990; Cherry Hill KO Tms, Open Swiss 1989; Williamsburg Prs 1991.

DIAZ-AGERO, Jaime (1926-1989) of Madrid, Spain, philatelist. WBF World Master. Fourth World Open Teams 1982 and represented Spain in three other world championships and four zonal championships.

DIBAR, Carlos F. (1911-1965) of Buenos Aires, Argentina, judge, was South American champion 1954, 1957. Represented Argentina in the Bermuda Bowl 1959, 1961. National wins include Open Teams 1937, 1938, 1956, Open Pairs 1947, Master Pairs 1962. Dibar served as secretary, Argentine Bridge Commission 1936, 1938, and director ARGENTINE BRIDGE ASSOCIATION 1962, 1963. He co-authored the Dibar system.

DIBBLEE, Carol of Salt Lake City UT, English teacher and director of Downtown Retail Merchants Association, graduate of U of Utah, currently working on PhD. Very active community organizations including Utah State Mental Health Bd. Member of ACBL Nat'l Charity and Goodwill Committees. Served on Dist. 18 Bd of Dir and is past president Salt Lake Unit, chairperson Salt Lake NABCs 1976, 88; contributor to Dist. 18 *WASUMI*, bridge reporter to *Salt Lake Tribune*, originated and edited SL Unit newsletter. Won Salt Lake Mixed Prs 1964, Open Prs; Idaho Womens Prs, Denver BAM Tms.

DICKENS, Charles (1812-1870), famed English novelist, describes Mr. Pickwick's discomfort after being inveigled into a WHIST game with three imposing women in Chapter 35 of *The Pickwick Papers.*

DILLON, Bettie (Mrs. Gene) (b. 1924) of Green Valley AZ, has won more than 20 regionals including Phoenix Open Prs 1981, Mesa Sr. Open Prs 1984, El Paso Open Swiss, Sr Swiss 1985; Sr KO Tms, Albuquerque Sr Prs, Spring secondary Sr Prs, Anaheim Sr Swiss 1987; Palm Springs Sr Master Prs, Reno Sr KOs 1989; Fall secondary Sr Prs 1990, Pasadena Sr Prs 1992.

DILLON, Gene D. (b. 1927) of Green Valley AZ, retired, graduated Oklahoma State, has been deaf since 1958 and severly disabled since 1972. Friends, other players and wife enable him to compete in tournament play. He has won more than 20 regionals including Phoenix Open Prs 1981, Mesa Sr Open Prs 1984, Sr Swiss

1985, Sr KO Tms 1987; El Paso Sr Open Swiss 1985, Albuquerque Sr Prs, Spring secondary Sr Prs, Anaheim Sr Swiss 1987; Palm Springs Sr Master Prs, Reno Sr KOs 1989; Fall secondary Sr Prs 1990, Pasadena Sr Prs 1992.

DING, Guan Gun (b. 1929) Deng Xiaoping's regular bridge partner. Represented China in 1982. Winner of many national titles. Adviser, Chinese Bridge Association. Member of politburo. One of the best players in China.

DIONISI, Antonio H. (Tony) (b. 1934) of New York City, formerly of Tokyo, banker, won Reisinger 1970, placed second in Mens Tms 1966, Reisinger 1971. He has several regional wins.

DISCHNER, Robert J. (Dish) (b. 1920) of Santa Ana CA, ACBL nat'l tournament director since 1972, began directing career in 1950.

DIXON, Christopher P. (b. 1944) of London, England, computer consultant. Second European Teams 1971. Represented Britain in one world championship and England in Camrose Trophy matches. Won Gold Cup twice.

DODDS, Leslie (1903-1975) of London, England, import-export merchant. Won Bermuda Bowl 1955, European Teams 1948, 1949, 1950, 1954. Represented Britain in three other zonal champions. Many national wins include Gold Cup four times.

DONAGHY, Ernest C. (1897-1986) of Mexico Beach FL, retired statistician, was one of the first six to be named ACBL associate nat'l director when that rating was created in 1963. Won Western States Open Tms 1938.

DONAGHY, George (b. 1928) of Memphis TN, ACBL employee since 1968, retired 1993, was assistant manager, tournament division, in charge of sanctioning regional and sectional tournaments and assigning tournament directors. Before joining ACBL staff he was a regional tournament director. He is a contributing editor, *Bridge Encyclopedia.* Avid fisherman.

DONATH, Andres (b. 1953 in Argentina) of Montevideo, Uruguay, industrialist. Second South American Teams 1979. Represented Uruguay regularly in zonal championships since 1978 and has won 36 national titles.

DONER, Cameron P. (b. 1954) of Richmond BC, professional bridge player, in real estate and construction, marketing and sales. Sports fan, loves movies, past member Nat'l Appeals Committee. Some of his numerous wins include Edmonton Open KO Tms 1987, Santa Clara Open KO Tms, Billings Open Swiss 1989; Dallas KO Tms, Open Prs, Santa Clara Open Prs, Pasadena Super Flt KO Tms, Salt Lake City Open Prs, KO Tms, Open Swiss, Honolulu KO Tms 1990; Amarillo Swiss, Bakersfield Open Swiss, Santa Clara Super Flt KO Tms, Pine Bluff KO Tms, Calgary Super Flt KO Tms 1991; Vancouver KO Tms 1992.

DONY, Gilbert (b. 1945) of Luxembourg, bridge teacher. Second Common Market Mixed Pairs 1979. Represented Luxembourg in several world, zonal and Common Market Championships.

DORFAN, Jacob (b. 1938) of Pretoria, South Africa, chartered accountant. Represented South Africa in two world championships and two Maccabi Games. 8 national wins include open teams and open pairs twice each. Competitive bowls player.

DORMER, Albert (b. 1925) of Scotland, bridge journalist and retired surveyor. WBF World Master. Won World Senior Pairs 1990, British Gold Cup twice. Bridge Editor of *London Times* since 1990. Editor *British Bridge World* 1962-64; associate editor *ACBL Bulletin* 1964-65. Editor *IBPA Bulletin* 1972-82. Editor *World Bridge News* 1971-87. Executive Assistant to WBF President 1982-1986. IBPA Personality of the Year 1981. Author and co-author of 10 other books including *The Complete Book of Bridge.* See Bibliography.

DORN, H. Charlie (b. 1919) of San Jose CA, retired naval aviator, placed second in Mixed Prs 1981. Diamond Life Master; regional titles include All Western KOs 1968, 71, BAM Tms 1968, Standard Card Prs, Sr Prs 1988; Intermountain KO Tms 1972, 73; Oregon Trail Mens Prs, Capital City KO Tms 1972; Northern CA KOs 1974, Golden Gate KOs 1977, Sr Swiss 1987.

DORSMAN, Henny B. (b. 1927) of Staunton VA, born in the Netherlands, formerly of Aruba, educator and retired director of technical/vocational school, writes weekly bridge column, enjoys soccer and tennis. Honored by the Queen of Holland for his social and educational accomplishments in Aruba. Was technical director of the Central American and Caribbean Bridge Federation 1977-83. Organizer of the first official Central American and Caribbean bridge tournament in 1977. Represented Netherland Antilles in Miami 1972, New Orleans 1978, Valkenburg 1980, Biarritz 1982. Also represented Netherland Antilles in numerous CAC championships. Inventor of the Dorsman-tray, a sliding bidding card-tray used in international play.

DOUGHTY, Richard E. (b. 1943) of Baton Rouge LA, started own industrial sales and service business in 1978, sold in 1990 but continues as manager, graduated Louisiana State U, fan of saltwater fishing. Won Mens Tms 1977 and placed second in the Reisinger 1975. Won Mid-South Swiss 1969, 1980, Open Prs 1974, Masters Prs 1975; Spring secondary Swiss 1972, Fall Mixed Prs, Summer Mixed Prs 1973.

DOWER, Jackie (b. 1949) of Sunrise FL, retired accountant, graduate of Springfield College, enjoys swimming and knitting, was Texas Woman of the Year 1989, 90, 91. Won Fall secondary Swiss 1988, Monterey Prs 1989, Honolulu KOs 1990, Detroit KOs, Quebec City KOs, Reno Handicap KOs, Topeka Open Swiss, Fallsburg Open Swiss, Daytona Open Prs, Master Prs 1991.

DOWNES, E(dwin) Hall (1897-1976) of Dover DE, was a bridge teacher, writer and educator. Graduate of Naval Academy; remained at Annapolis for three years as instructor to midshipmen; later received Master's degree in Education from Columbia U and served in that field for the rest of his life, not only in Delaware public schools but also in the Navy and with American industry abroad. In early Thirties promoted bridge through his books, radio and lectures; he was called "ace of Contract teachers". His writings included self-teachers and he was *Town and Country* editor for *The Bridge Magazine* (1931-33). A book by him on the Culbertson system provoked a lawsuit by Ely Culbertson, who had warned booksellers not to sell Downes' books on pain of legal action. Downes won both suits, the courts holding that the name of a system was public property. The case had permanent importance in legal history with respect to plagiarism and unfair practices.

DREW, Douglas A. (b. 1930) of Toronto, retired company vice-president and general manager, graduated U. of Saskatchewan. Has continuously served the interest of tournament bridge in elected office since 1958. Past president of Ontario Unit 166 and Dist. 2. Member ACBL Bd of Dir 1969-78 and 1981-1993, member ACBL Bd of Gov, served as President of ACBL 1984, ACBL Chairman of the Board 1985, chairman of various standing committees of the ACBL since 1969, member WBF Executive Council 1984-88. Drew initiated action to create the ACBL Education Program, was founding member of the Canadian Bridge Federation, originator of proposal creating all Canadian Districts within the ACBL. He has also won several regional titles.

DREYFUS, Jack (b. 1913) of New York City, founder of the Dreyfus Fund and "Wizard of Wall Street", reputed to be best American player of gin rummy. He won AWL Southern New England Open Tms 1937. Has played on the Corporate America bridge team and participated in the charity matches against Congress, Hollywood celebrities and Los Angeles Business. Author of *A Remarkable Medicine Has Been Overlooked*, a book about the drug Dilantin.

DRIVER, Gordon (b. 1947) of Johannesburg, South Africa, owner computer software company. Represented South Africa in World Team Olympiad 1972, 1976, 1980, 1992. Five national wins include Open Teams twice.

DRUCKER, Ned (1916-1983) of New York City, salesman, won the Vanderbilt 1952, 54 and placed second in the Life Master Prs 1951, Open Prs 1943. He won several regional titles.

DRUMEV, Christo (b. 1932) of Sofia, Bulgaria, president director general of the National Palace Culture. Formerly deputy cultural minister. Won Bulgarian Teams a record six times, 1980, 1981, 1983, 1988, 1989, 1990. Won Austrian Team Championship 1984, 1985, and several Open Pairs at Philip Morris grand prix tournaments including Athens 1982 and Vienna 1987. Npc bronze-medal winning Bulgarian Women's Team 1988 World Team Olympiad. vice-president Bulgarian Bridge Federation 1982-89, president since 1989. Author, columnist, and translator of books into Bulgarian.

DRURY, Douglas A. (1914-1967) of Sebastopol CA, stock broker, bridge teacher and club owner, was best known for his invention of the DRURY CONVENTION. A capable and popular bridge administrator, he served

as a member of the ACBL Bd of Gov, Systems and Conventions Committee and ACBL Goodwill Committee. He made his mark early as a tournament player while living in Toronto. He won Mens Prs 1954, 55; Master Mixed Tms 1956.

DU PONT, Lea C. (b. 1939) of Palm Beach FL, WBF World Master, placed 5th World Olympiad Womens Tms 1984; won North American Swiss 1984, placed second North American Swiss 1981, Mixed Prs 1983, Open Swiss 1993; has several regional wins to her credit. Regularly plays in major European championships, has won Coppa Italia 1977, Venice Open Prs 1978, Deauville Open Prs 1980.

DUBAY, William (Bill) (b. 1942) of Albany NY, fiscal research analyst, S2 tournament director, Syracuse U graduate, fan of sports, mystery novels and puzzles. Served as president and treasurer of Unit 115. Won New England KO Swiss 1976, Upper NY State Open Swiss 1977, Spring secondary Morning KOs 1988, Albany Open Swiss 1990, KOs 1991.

DUBOIN, Giorgio (b. 1959) of Turin, Italy, computer programmer and bridge teacher. Won European Junior Pairs 1980, and Common Market Pairs and Teams 1985, Teams 1987.

DUBRAU, Kenneth B. (b. 1943) of Chicago IL, program expeditor with city of Chicago, Dept. of Human Services, graduate Central Washington State U. Won Central States Swiss 1973, Champagne Mens Prs, Mens Teams 1982; Pittsburgh Mens Tms, Central States II Swiss 1982.

DUCHEYNE, René (1938-1991) of The Hague, The Netherlands, patent office employee. Head of Press Room at nearly all world and European Championships 1974-1991, assisted by his wife Elly. President INTERNATIONAL BRIDGE PRESS ASSOCIATION 1986-1991.

DUCHOVNI, Zeev (b. 1912) of Tel Aviv, Israel, export manager, represented Israel in World Team Olympiad 1964, European Championships 1965. Won several national titles.

DUDKA, Bette of Alexandria VA, administrative assistant to government official (Pentagon), and bridge teacher for 20 years. Dist 6 first alternate to Bd of Dir, past president of Mid-Atlantic BC, Unit Recorder, served on ACBL and Dist. 6 Bd of Gov, co-chairman 1984 Summer NABC, entertainment chairman Summer NABC 1973, 1993; has served in various other executive positions on Unit and Dist. level. Some of her wins are Summer secondary Womens Prs 1975, Mid-Atlantic Spring Womens Prs, Summer Open Prs, Virginia Beach Womens Swiss, Raleigh Open Prs.

DUMBOVICH, Miklós (b. 1949) of Budapest, Hungary, electrical engineer. The most successful Hungarian player of the 80s, winning many national titles. Represented Hungary in three world championships and eight European Championships. Won Caransa Teams twice and Venice Festival Teams once.

DUNCAN, Alexander H. (Sandy) of Dunfermline, Scotland, computer manager. Represented Britain in two world championships and the Common Market Championships. Represented Scotland in 19 Camrose Trophy matches. 14 national wins include Scottish Cup twice and open pairs three times.

DUNN, Suzanne E. (b. 1935) of Crystal Lake IL, bank director, former teacher, graduated U of Michigan. Won Lake Geneva Womens Swiss 1990, Nashville Bracketed KOs, Montreal KOs, Continuous Prs; Fort Wayne Open Prs 1991; Spring secondary Superflight A KOs, Swiss 1992, Toronto Bracketed KOs, Davenport Swiss, Sacramento Bracketed KOs 1992.

DUNN, Patrick (b. 1945) of Bellevue WA, state unemployment insurance tax administrator, graduate Washington St. U., Diamond Life Master. Has won many regionals including British Columbia Swiss 1973, 76, 93, KO Tms 1984; Puget Sound Swiss, Emerald Empire Swiss 1982, Super Open Prs 1992; Oregon Trail Mixed Prs 1984, Open Prs 1988, Open Prs 1992, 93; Puget Sound Mens Prs 1985, Dist. 19 GN Tms 1985, 87; Can-Am KO Tms, Swiss 1989; Dist. 19 NA Prs 1990.

DURHAM, Louise (Honeychile) of Durant MS, first Life Master in Mississippi; served as ACBL director and secretary, co-chairman of Goodwill Committee and WBF Friendship Committee; past president of Mississippi BA. ACBL HONORARY MEMBER 1974. Won several regionals including Central States Womens Prs 1951, Mid-South Open Tms 1957, Missouri Valley Womens Prs 1954.

DURRAN, Joan of Welwyn Garden City, England. WBF World Life Master. Won World Women's Pairs 1966, second World Mixed Pairs 1966. Won European Women's Teams 1961, 1966. Represented Britain in two other world championships and three other zonal championships. Won several national titles.

DYE, Dr. Arthur M. (1896-1980) of Charlotte NC, first blind bridge player to become an ACBL Life Master. A perfect sportsman, Dye never took advantage of his affliction; when he pulled wrong cards, he refused to allow opponents to let him retract his plays. When Dye made LM at the New Orleans Winter Nationals in 1956, he received a standing ovation. A charter member and long-time president of the Charlotte BA, he served as president of the Mid-Atlantic BC. Shared ACBL HONORARY MEMBER Award with Charles Goren 1959. See HANDICAPPED PLAYERS.

E

EARL, Christopher W. (Chris) (b. 1951) of Larkspur CA, violinist with Marin Symphony, computer programmer, violin teacher with interests in metaphysical studies, backpacking, chess and classical music; qualified director. Won Oregon Trail Swiss 1972, KO Tms 1975, 77; Dist. 20 GN Tms 1973, 74, Zone VII 1974; Peach Festival KO Tms, Puget Sound Swiss, Mt. Shasta Swiss 1974; Sacramento Open Prs 1990, Santa Rosa Swiss 1992.

EASON, Jane (b. 1939) of Memphis TN, graduated Memphis State U., antique dealer, casino dealer, former school teacher. Other interests include ice skating, collecting playing cards and early bridge memorabilia. Has served in various positions for New Jersey BL and Tennessee BA, member of Nat'l Goodwill Committee. Diamond Life Master. Regionals wins include Gatlinburg Womens Prs 1981, Womens KOs 1988, Womens Tms 1992; Oklahoma City Womens Prs 1983, 89; Summer secondary Womens Swiss, Louisville Womens Prs 1984; Mexican Nat'ls Womens Prs 1985, New Orleans Womens Prs, Paducah Womens Prs 1986; Memphis Master Prs, Birmingham Womens Prs 1990; Pine Bluff Womens Prs 1991.

EBER, Marilyn of Englewood CA, real estate business and art museum docent, Denver U graduate; appraiser and collector of Indian art, in particular Indian beads. Won Fall secondary Swiss 1978, Pikes Peak KO Tms 1980, Rocky Mountain KO Tms 1981, Denver Swiss 1990, Pikes Peak Master Pairs 1991.

EBER, Neville (b. 1944) of Johannesburg, South Africa, investment manager. Represented South Africa in World Team Olympiad 1972, 1976, 1992. 23 national wins include 11 in open teams and four in open pairs. Top South African masterpoint winner. Co-author *You Too Can Play Bridge Well* (1978). Winner of numerous international backgammon events.

EBERSON, Gertrude L. (d. 1992) of St. Petersburg FL, won Womens Tms 1949; placed second Master Mixed Tms 1954, Womens Prs 1960.

ECCLES, Bert (b. 1951) of Montreal, teacher and comedy writer, educated at McGill U. Won Nickel City Open Prs 1978, London Bridge Mens Swiss 1985, Nat'l Capital Swiss, Can-Am Prs 1988; Fall secondary KO Tms 1990, Fleur de Lys Swiss 1991.

ECKER, Wynne (Mrs. Richard H.) of New York City, won Womens Tms 1954; second Womens Prs 1956.

ECONOMIDY, Ann (Mrs. Byron) of Tucson AZ, won Womens Prs 1973 with her mother Vivian Williamson; placed second Life Master Womens Prs 1978.

EDELSON, Shirley M. of Redmond WA, bridge professional, teacher and lecturer, certified director since 1965; guided bridge groups in the Soviet Union in 1989-90 for three Friendship tournaments. Diamond Life Master; placed second in USBC 1988; won Womens BAM Tms 1987; has won 20+ regional events.

EDWARDS, Mary (1907-88) of Esher, England. Won European Women's Teams 1959 and several national titles. See FORTUNE.

EGHOLM, Dale (b. 1928) of St. Paul MN, ACBL associate national tournament director, has been tournament director since 1968.

EHLER, David F. (b. 1943) of Farmington CT, small business owner, former corporate laboratory director of "Fortune 500" company, educated at U of Wisconsin and Purdue (Ph.D.) Enjoys kayaking, skiing, hiking; first-place winner in national (Canon) photo contest. Has won New England Fall KO Tms 1977, Swiss 1978, 81, Masters KO Tms 1991; New England Summer Open Prs 1978, 81,

KO Swiss 1979, Summer KOs 1984; NY Eastern States KO Tms 1991.

EHRLENBACH, Julius (Jack) (1894-1979) of Los Angeles, bridge teacher, Life Master #56, became first Life Master on West Coast 1946. Won Barclay Trophy 1949, 1950 and scores of regional championships. Had a lifetime total of 5753 masterpoints and was on the list of the "Top 100" masterpoint holders from its inception through November 1977.

EIDI, Michel (b. 1956 in Egypt) of Athens, Greece, previously in Lebanon. WBF World Master. Represented Greece in 1988 World Team Olympiad, finishing fifth, the best performance ever by a Greek team. A musician and linguist.

EINHORN, Bolo of Amsterdam, The Netherlands., was deported by the Germans and died in a concentration camp during World War II. Regarded as the most brilliant Dutch player of the pre-war era. Second European Championship 1932, 1933, 1934 and represented The Netherlands 1935-39. Member of the CONTINENTAL CLUB team that drew a 232-board challenge match in 1938 against the Austrian world champions.

EISENBERG, William (Billy) (b. 1937) of Boca Raton FL, bridge professional, teacher, coach and vugraph commentator, former professional backgammon player. WBF Grand Master and ACBL Diamond Life Master. Won World Backgammon Championship 1974; is one of the official vugraph commentators for the WBF; was coach to the first ABCL Junior team to attend Junior Camp in Poland 1987; has coached and been teacher to many national teams around the world including Israel, Panama, Venezuela and the Netherlands. Has won five Bermuda Bowl Championships 1970, 71, 76, 77, 79 (with four different partners) and represented ACBL in three others 1969 (placed 3rd), 73, 75 (placed 2nd). Placed 7th in World Olympiad Tms 1976, 9th Rosenblum Tms 1978 and 17th in 1990. Has won numerous European tournaments including the prestigious *London Sunday Times* Pairs, Top 16-Italy, Mixed Pairs and Teams-Israel, Paris 600-Paris and Staten Bank-Holland (invitation only). Won Spingold 1969, 73; Vanderbilt 1971, 78; Reisinger 1970, 74, 76; GN Tms 1974, 76; Life Master Prs, Mens Tms 1968; has placed second many times including Spingold 1970, Vanderbilt 1966, 70, 73, 76, 83, 89; Reisinger 1968, 81, 83; Mens Tms 1969, Mens Prs 1981, Open Swiss 1993. Has numerous regional titles to his credit. See ACES TEAM.

EISENHOWER, Dwight D. (1890-1969) had a keen interest in bridge from the time he was a captain in the U.S. Army through his Presidency of the United States (1953-1961), and even after retirement. Nov. 7, 1942 was the day of the landing at Casablanca which constituted the first Allied invasion after the fall of France. During the nerve-racking period when the landing had begun and the first news had not yet come back to his headquarters, he relaxed in a celebrated bridge game with Mark Clark, Alfred M. Gruenther and Harry C. Butcher. He used bridge as a regular recreation before the Normandy invasion when he was Supreme Allied Commander, while he was NATO chief in Paris, and during his term of office in the White House. After his retire-

ment he was host at occasional games at his homes at Gettysburg PA and Palm Springs CA. Oswald Jacoby characterized his skill as "superior." Jacoby said Eisenhower was capable of holding his own in all but the most expert club games. When Eisenhower was asked whom he would choose as his NATO deputy in 1950 he said, "Al Gruenther — he's the best bridge player" (among the generals). When Gruenther called him from Chicago at 7 a.m. one day in 1960 to tell him to read the *New York Times* bridge column of that morning because it reported one of his hands, Eisenhower replied, "I've already read it."

EISENLORD, Ray H. (1884-1965) of Erie PA, accountant, was ABL president 1934 and one of the originators of the masterpoint plan.

EISENSTEIN, Lilyan P. (b. 1940) of Beverly Hills CA, bank founder, real estate and travel agent, member of ACBL Goodwill Committee. Eisenstein served as a trustee of the Nat'l Charity Foundation 1987-91. She is Unit 566 President and Bd. of Dir. member. Won Rogue River Valley Open Prs, Pacific Southwest Womens Prs, Gem State Swiss 1976.

EISENSTEIN, Robert A. (1933-1990) of Beverly Hills CA, film producer, attorney, president of property management company, Phi Beta Kappa graduate of NYU and a Harvard Law School graduate. He served on ACBL Nat'l Bd. of Dir. 1982-90, was president of Dist. 23. Served several terms as Unit president, served on the Nat'l Bd. of Gov., was a member of the Nat'l Goodwill Committee and was Dist 23 Judiciary and Bylaws Committee chairman.

EKEBLAD, Russell A. (b. 1946) of Providence RI, co-owner (with wife Sheila) of jewelry distributing firm, graduate of Brown U., other interests are golf and philosophy of politics. WBF World Master, third Rosenblum Tms 1990. Won Spingold 1992; Vanderbilt, Open Prs II 1993; Canadian Invitational Prs Calcutta 1990 and placed second 1991; placed third Cavendish Invitational Prs 1991. Diamond Life Master, has won more than 40 regional events and has represented Dist. 25 three times in GN Tms.

EL-RIEDY, Medhat Kotb (b. 1947) of Cairo, Egypt, professor of engineering. Runner-up Middle East Teams 1991; has won five national team titles.

EL KORDY, Adel Hassan (b. 1958) of Cairo, Egypt, executive. WBF World Master. Represented Egypt 1991 Bermuda Bowl.

ELIAS, Enrique (b. 1937) of Lima, Peru, professor of law. Former Peruvian Minister of Justice. Congress deputy. Represented Peru in two world championships and 10 zonal championships. Won many national titles.

ELIASSON, Hjalti (b. 1929) of Kopavogi, Iceland, electrician. Represented Iceland in four world championships, eight European Championships and two Nordic Championships. 17 national wins include open teams eight times and open pairs seven times. Frequently NPC. Built bridge-o-rama used to display major Icelandic events 1961.

ELIS, Morrie (1907-1992) of Lauderhill FL, retired company president, graduate of NYU. Assisted William E.

McKenney in formulating and establishing ACBL Charity Foundation 1933-37; constructed hands for Autobridge and wrote a column for *The Bridge World* 1936-40. In 1934 he represented U.S. in match against Bermuda team which U.S. won. Won *McKenney Trophy* 1938, 40; Vanderbilt 1949, Master Mixed Tms 1937, Life Master Prs 1938, 40; Fall Master Individual 1940, 50; placed second in Asbury Challenge Tms 1937, Spingold 1937, 38; Vanderbilt 1943, 54; Open Prs 1939, Master Individual 1946, Mens Prs 1934, 37, 38, 39, 40, 47; also won numerous regional titles. Elis was the 1932 NYC table tennis champion and semifinalist in National Table Tennis Championship.

ELKNER, Jeanne (b. 1940) of Clementon NJ, investigator for NJ Division of Public Welfare, bridge professional, founder and former manager South Jersey BC. Interests include travel, food, wine, cooking, music and art. Won Womens Prs 1989. Diamond Life Master with more than 30 regional wins including Lancaster Womens Tms 1978, Pittsburgh Mixed Prs 1979, Swan Lake Teams 1982, Charlotte KOs, Womens Tms 1986; Hunt Valley KO Tms 1986; Myrtle Beach KOs, Parsipanny KOs 1987; Arlington Womens Tms, Greenville KOs 1988; Rye KO Tms 1991, 92; Bethesda Womens Tms 1991.

ELLENBY, Milton Q. (b. 1923) of Skokie IL, actuary and physicist, was a physicist on the Manhattan Project for three years; was state and regional chess champion in mid-Forties. WBF Life Master; won Bermuda Bowl 1954, second 1955. Won Mens Prs 1951 (second in 1954), Spingold 1953, 54; Life Master Prs 1953, Open Prs 1955, Master Mixed Tms 1957, Fishbein Trophy 1953, Lou Herman Trophy 1955; won numerous regional titles.

ELLIOTT, C. Bruce (b. 1922) of Weston ON, estimator, WBF Life Master, represented Canada in World Tm Olympiad in Turin, Italy 1960, Deauville, France 1968. Won Spingold 1964, 65 and placed second in Life Master Prs 1964. Diamond Life Master; has had numerous regional wins.

ELLIOTT, Loren S. (b. 1923) of Clive IA, retired resource planning engineer for State of Iowa, formerly with the USDA-Soil Conservation Service, a certified director for 25 years, past president of Hawkeye Bridge Unit and former Board member. Won Summer secondary Masters Mens Prs 1972, Lincoln Swiss 1985, Des Moines Sr Swiss 1987, Mesa Sr Super Flt KOs 1988, 91.

ELLISON, Donald McLaren (b. 1949) of Rossland BC, residential designer and partner in planning and design firm, graduated U of Victoria and Selkirk College. He loves to cook and enjoys collecting and tasting wine, mountain biking, reading, art. Involved in local Chamber of Commerce, past president Unit 574, sectional chairman since 1981; editor, *Trump-It.* Co-authored with Jude Goodwin *Teach Me to Play, Teach Me to Play the Cards* and *Teach Me to Play Defense,* also beginner's and intermediate bidding manuals *Elwin: Module One and Two.* Won Zone VI Canadian National Team Championship 1987.

ELSTON, A. Roger (b. 1933) of Dix Hills NY, attorney, graduate Hofstra U and Brooklyn Law School. Won Long Island Swiss 1981, Swan Lake Master Prs 1982, Mens Prs 1986; Summer secondary Open Prs 1982, 85; Miami

Open Prs 1985; Cherry Hill Open Prs 1988, Port Chester Open Swiss 1989, 91, Sr Open Prs 1993; Lancaster Sr Swiss, Long Island Sr Prs 1992.

ELWELL, Joseph Bowne (1873-1920) was the principal American authority on the original game of bridge (bridge-whist) and on the early form of auction bridge. However, he is remembered chiefly as the victim of one of the most celebrated murder cases of the century. Born in Cranford NJ, Elwell began his bridge career about 1900 as a bridge teacher and quickly became a favorite of high society in NYC and Newport RI. He was a regular highstakes player at the Whist Club of NY and other clubs. He and his regular partner, Harold S. Vanderbilt, were considered the strongest American pair from about 1910 to 1920. Elwell amassed a considerable fortune, chiefly through speculation on Wall Street and at the time of his death owned more than 20 racehorses. His books, most of which went through several editions and sold in large quantities, included *Elwell on Bridge, Advanced Bridge, Practical Bridge, Bridge Axioms and Laws, Elwell on Auction Bridge,* and *Elwell's New Auction Bridge.* He also showed great skill at hand analysis.

On the morning of June 11, 1920, he was found in his home by his housekeeper. He had been fatally shot only about an hour earlier. Because none of the considerable amount of money or jewelry was touched, the motive could not have been robbery. At that time he was separated from his wife and several women had keys to his home. The case received wide publicity and has been the subject of several books and hundreds of articles. Offically the murder was never solved, though it is generally believed that the police knew the murderer but had insufficient evidence. Several novelists used the setting of the case for mystery novels in which they supplied their own solutions.

EMERY, Sue (b. 1920) of Memphis TN, formerly of Wichita Falls TX, Harding College graduate; former school teacher, newspaper reporter, bridge teacher and bridge club owner/operator. Editor of *ACBL Bulletin* 1972 to present, co-editor of the ACBL *Daily Bulletin* at North American Bridge Championships 1961 to present and co-editor of the World Championship *Daily Bulletin* 1972, 75, 78. Became a tournament director in the early Sixties and directed in many Texas tournaments with her husband, John W. "Big John" Emery (1926-72), a well-known ACBL associate national tournament director. She authored ACBL publication *No Passing Fancy* 1977, is a contributing editor of *Bridge Encyclopedia* and was associate editor of *Texas Bridge.* Won the International Bridge Press Assn. Romex Award in 1988 and WBF Epson Award for journalists in 1989; won Texas Mixed Pairs 1963, Open Teams 1965.

ENDICOTT, Grattan (b. 1924) of Liverpool, England, secretary to the Foundation for Sport and the Arts in England. President British Bridge League 1988-90. Chairman of EBL Laws Committee and vice-chairman WBF Laws Committee. Member EBL Executive Council, alternate delegate from EBL to WBF Executive Council. Former EBU treasurer and chairman of its Laws and Ethics Committee. Joint author of *EBL Commentary on 1987 Laws of Duplicate Bridge.*

ENG, Fook (b. 1925) of Monterey Park CA, retired astronautical guidance engineer with Rockwell Intl., worked on the space shuttle program, orbital tracking and analysis and on manned orbital lab missions; educated at Virginia Polytechnic Institute and U of California at Los Angeles (Ph.D.); airplane owner and hobbyist, plays the flute, recorder with Baroque ensemble groups. Author of what is considered to be one of the best books on squeezes, *Bridge Squeezes Illustrated*; has also been a contributor to *The Bridge World*.

ENGEL, Zvi (b. 1952 in Israel) of Brussels, Belgium, company manager. WBF World Master. Represented Belgium in one world championship and three European Championships. National wins include open pairs 4 times and open teams 3 times.

EPPERSON, William E. (b. 1931) of Sarasota FL, retired commercial airline pilot, former USAF officer, graduated Kansas State U and Penn State, enjoys golf and is member of Hole in One Club, docent at Mote Marine Aquarium. Won Fall Swiss 1980. Regional wins include Southeastern Mixed Prs 1975, Dist. 4 Open Prs 1978, Fall secondary Swiss 1979, Dist. 3 Mixed Prs 1980, Long Island Prs 1982, Southeastern Swiss 1986, Ft Lauderdale Smoking Swiss 1988, Orlando Open Prs 1992.

EPSTEIN, Mrs. Bert of Los Angeles, won Womens Prs 1959, Hawaii Womens Prs 1957, Golden State Womens Prs 1965, Summer secondary Womens Prs 1969.

EPSTEIN, Isadore (Eppy or Izzy) (1908-1992) of Tacoma WA, born in Grodno, Russia, graduate of U. of Washington, retired teacher; developed a one-handed typewriter keyboard for either hand for handicapped students. In 1932 defeated a renowned chess champion in both his games; devised a movement that allowed for one winner in a 16-plus table game -- it was replaced by the Mitchell movement in 1945. Won Pacific Northwest Mens Prs 1949, Open Teams 1956, Master Pairs 1957; Rocky Mountain Open Prs 1952, Inter-Mountain Open Teams 1958, Master Prs, Open Prs 1960.

EPSTEIN, Roberta E. (b. 1936) of South Orange NJ, computer science teacher, educated at Cornell and Columbia. Won Womens Tms 1960, 61; North American Womens Swiss 1986, Womens KO Tms 1990; placed second Womens Tms 1971, Womens Prs 1981, Womens KO Tms 1985, 87; Womens BAM Tms 1986, 88; has won many regional events.

ERDENBAUM, Israel (b. 1920 in Poland) of Tel Aviv, Israel, tournament director. Senior tournament director at 7 European Championships and 4 World Olympiads, and in charge at 4 Maccabia Championships. Won national teams once and NPC of 3 Israeli teams. Member EBL Laws Commission 1987-89. Editor Israel's *Bridge Magazine* 1981-82.

ERDOS, Ivan (1924-1967) edited the popular *Dupliquiz* column for *ACBL Bulletin*. A leading player, teacher and writer, Erdos also contributed to *American Bridge Digest* and wrote *Bridge A La Carte*; was bridge editor of *San Diego* magazine and several Southern California newspapers. Born in Budapest, Erdos lived in England from 1939 to 1951 before moving to Los Angeles, where he worked as a travel agent. Won World Mixed Prs 1966 and

represented North America in Bermuda Bowl in Buenos Aires 1965. Won Mens Tms 1959, Mens Prs 1962.

ERGUDEN, Garland I. (b. 1951) of Memphis TN, law student, former database administrator in a technical support group with "Fortune 500" company, graduate of Kennesaw State College. Has served as vice-chair Nat'l Appeals Committee, secretary Dist. 7, member National Goodwill Committee. Her 30-plus regionals wins include Bicentennial KO Tms, Swiss 1976; Mid-Atlantic Swiss, KO Tms 1977; North Florida Womens Prs 1978, secondary Swiss, Mid-South Holiday KOs, Open Prs 1979; Space City Womens Swiss, Azalea City KOs 1980; Florida Swiss 1981.

ERHART, Maria (née Kirner) (b. 1944) of Vienna, Austria. WBF World Life Master. European Women's Team champion 1991. Runner-up Venice Cup 1991. Represented Austria in four other world championships, twice in European Open Championship, and on many other occasions. Won European Women's Individual 1992. 13 national victories include Open Teams eight times. Won Caransa tournament (Amsterdam). Oriental carpet expert.

ERIKSSON, Karin (b. 1914) of Stockholm Sweden, WBF World Life Master. Won World Women's Teams 1968, Nordic Women's Teams 1957, 66, 68. National titles include Women's Pairs and Mixed Pairs.

ESBERG, William (b. 1935) of Elberon NJ, Columbia graduate, retired English teacher, currently bridge professional and teacher, learned bridge at age 9. Won Atlantic City Mens Prs 1972, Thunder Bay Open Swiss 1981, Summer secondary Open Prs 1982, Sioux St. Marie Mens Prs 1983, Reno Open Swiss 1985, New Brunswick Swiss 1991.

ESCUDE, Manuel (b. 1938) of Barcelona, Spain, businessman. Represented Spain in two world championships and six zonal championships. Won many national titles.

ETTER, Bob G. (b. 1954) of Sacramento CA, assistant math professor, educated at U of Georgia and Rice U. Placekicker for Atlanta Falcons 1968-69 and All-SEC football and baseball 1964-67. Won North American Swiss 1981, placed second North American Mens Swiss 1982, Master Mixed Tms 1986. Diamond Life Master; won several regional events.

ETTLINGER, Douglas M. (Duggie) (b. 1931) of Johannesburg, South Africa, retired trial lawyer. Represented South Africa in World Team Olympiad 1980, Maccabi Games 1977. 19 national wins include five in open teams and two in open pairs. Member WBF Executive Council 1970, 1974. Bridge columnist *Business Day*. Scorer at international cricket matches and an expert on the game.

EVANS, Donald S. (b. 1933) of Sydney, Australia, bridge teacher, represented Australia in the World Team Olympiad 1964 and won Australian Open Teams five times and the Individual 1963.

EVANS, Norah (Penguin) (1906-1977) of Bournemouth, England, bridge-club proprietor. Won European Women's Teams 1950, 1951, 1952, second 1939. Second Gold Cup once.

EVITT, Jane. See SKIPPER, Jane.

EVITT, John (b. 1946) of Auckland, New Zealand, sales director. Represented New Zealand in one world championship and two zonal championships. National wins include two team events. Former president of New Zealand CBA.

EWEN, Robert B. (Bob) (b. 1940) of Miami FL, self-employed author, formerly psychology professor with NYU and Florida International U, graduated Cornell U and U of Illinois (Ph.D.) Outside interests include family, religion and cats. Has written one book on psychology for the general public and two college psychology textbooks; is the creator of TWO-WAY GAME TRIES; author of articles for *The Bridge World*, including the popular bridge word puzzles, contributor to *ACBL Bulletin*, former associate editor of *Bridge Journal*, contributing editor to *Bridge Encyclopedia*. Has authored six bridge books -- *Opening Leads, Doubles For Takeout, Penalties and Profit in Contract Bridge, Preemptive Bidding, Contract Bridge: A Concise Guide, The Teenager's Guide to Bridge* and *The Defensive Bidding Quiz Book*. Won Eastern States KOs 1972, Mid-Atlantic KOs, Fun City Swiss 1973. See BIBLIOGRAPHY,

EYSTEINSSON, Björn (b. 1948) of Hafnarfjordur, Iceland, bank manager. WBF World Master. NPC and coach of Iceland's winning team in 1991 Bermuda Bowl. Represented Iceland in two other world championships and one European Championship. National wins include open teams twice.

EYTHORSDOTTIR, Hjördis (b. 1965) of Reykjavik, Iceland. Won Nordic Women's Teams 1990. Won ACBL Women's Swiss Teams 1994. Represented Iceland in two world championships and one other Nordic Championship. Eight national wins include Women's Teams five times, Women's Pairs twice.

EZEKIEL, David (b. 1948) of Paget, Bermuda, born in Darjeeling, India, company president, former partner in int'l accounting firm, educated in England. Enjoys tennis and is eight handicap golfer, was twice Bermuda backgammon champion. Has served as chairman of Bermuda regional twice, president Unit 198 and president of Bermuda BC for five years, received ACBL Presidential Citation for services to bridge. Bridge columnist *Mid-Ocean News* since 1980. Has represented Bermuda in int'l play New Orleans 1978, Valkenburg 1980, Biarritz 1982, Seattle 1984, Bal Harbour 1986, Tri-Country playoff 1987. Won ACBL-wide Charity game 1987; also won Bermuda Swiss 1980, Masters Prs 1983, 86, 91; Summer secondary Individual 1981. Winner of Norman Bach Trophy five times (top local masterpoint winner).

F

FACCHINI, Gianfranco (b. 1937) of Bologna, Italy, lawyer. Won Bermuda Bowl 1975, Sunday Times 1974. During the 1975 Bermuda Bowl he was accused of illicit communication through foot signals. See BERMUDA INCIDENT.

FAHS, Baha (b. 1938) of Saida, Lebanon. Represented Lebanon in 8 international championships. Won Gold Cup, Lebanese Festival 1971. Won more than five national titles.

FAIGENBAUM, Albert (b. 1946) of Paris, France, public relations executive. WBF World Master. Won World Teams 1982. Represented France in one other world championship and won several national titles.

FALAY, Faik (b. 1948) of Istanbul, Turkey, chemical engineer. Represented Turkey in three zonal championships. Eight national wins include open teams five times.

FALK, Allan (the Zookeeper) (b. 1947) of Lansing MI, attorney, commissioner of Michigan Court of Appeals, educated at Michigan State U, U.S. Army Air Defense School and Yale Law School (JD); attended Leningrad U 1968; is state director of Common Cause of Michigan, active in charity work, legislative draftsman and founder Opera Guild of Greater Lansing. Fought a 14-year legal battle with State Bar of Michigan that led to nationwide reforms in lobbying and other activities of state organizations for attorneys. Named to Outstanding Young Men of America 1975. Served on ACBL Bd of Gov 1982-88, past president Unit 195, Dist 12 Bd member, chairperson Bridge Center of Greater Lansing. Currently is member of Nat'l Goodwill Committee, ACBL Charity Foundation, Unit 195 Bd. Contributor to *IBPA Bulletin*; two-time winner World Bidding Contest. Co-inventor of Supersplinter, extended lebensohl and transfer response to preempt conventions. Authored *Spingold Challenge 1988, Team Trial 1992* and *The Bridge Player's Toolkit* (with the late Jim Jacoby). His numerous regional wins include Midwest Swiss 1973, Midland Swiss 1976, Summer secondary Silver Trophy Prs 1980, Chicago Open Prs 1982, Southfield KO Tms, Chicago Open Prs 1984; Grand Rapids Prs 1986, Summer secondary Mens Tms 1991; Dist 12 GN Tms 1991, 92, NA Prs 1991.

FALK, Charlotte F. (b. 1934) of Reno NV, graduate of U of Georgia, semi-retired from bridge in late Seventies. Won Fall secondary Swiss 1972, Spring Master Prs 1976; Southeastern Womens Swiss 1973, 76, 79; Celebrity Master Prs, North Florida Mixed Prs 1977.

FALLENIUS, Björn (b. 1957) of New York City, formerly of Malmö, Sweden, bridge professional and former controller. World Life Master. Representing Sweden, third Bermuda Bowl 1987, 1991, Rosenblum Cup 1986, World Team Olympiad 1988. European champion 1987. Won Reisinger 1991, Open Board-a-Match Teams 1991; second, Master Mixed Teams 1992, Vanderbilt 1993. Won Cavendish 1988.

FANG, Hien-Chee (b. 1911) of Fu-chien, China, telecommunications expert. Former Taiwanese director-general of telecommunications, vice-minister transportation. A founder of the Taiwan Bridge League, and NPC of Taiwan teams in two world championships and many Far East Championships. Chief organizer 1969 Far East Championship and 1971 Bermuda Bowl. Associated with Charles Wei in the promotion of the Precision System in Taiwan.

FARELL, Mary Jane (Mrs. Jules) of Los Angeles,

bridge teacher, WBF Grand Master, ACBL Grand Life Master. *Los Angeles Times* Woman of the Year in recognition of gaining first place among women in the all-time masterpoint rankings of the ACBL, displacing Helen Sobel Smith 1964. In January of 1992 held ninth place among all players and second place among women, behind Hermine Baron, in lifetime masterpoints. Farell won over 20,000 points in July of 1989 by winning a Womens Swiss in Pasadena. Won World Mixed Prs 1966, World Womens Prs 1970, Venice Cup 1978, World Womens Tms 1980. North American championships include Womens Tms 1968, 70, 72, 74, 75, 76 (second in 1967, 73); Womens Prs 1960, Master Mixed Tms 1949, 50, 55 (second in 1969, 89); Life Master Prs 1978, Womens KO Tms 1984, 90; North American Womens Swiss 1982; placed second Life Master Womens Prs 1965, 66, 67, 68; Womens KO Tms 1987, Womens BAM Tms 1988, Womens Tms 1990; has won more than 100 regional events.

FARIA, Octavio (b. 1920) of Rio de Janeiro, Brazil, business executive. Won South American Teams 1971. Represented Brazil in six world championships. National wins include open teams four times.

FARLEY, Joe R. (b. 1935) of Sacramento CA, president of insurance brokering firm. Won Portland KO Tms 1968, Open BAM Tms 1969; Denver Mixed Prs 1969, Sacramento KO Tms 1976, Mixed Prs 1978, Open Swiss 1980, Masters Prs 1982; San Jose Mixed Prs, Redding Master Swiss, Open Tms 1978; Reno Swiss 1985.

FARRINGTON, Frank (1908-1980) of Bolton, England, textile consultant. Three national wins include Gold Cup once. Played in Camrose Trophy match. Author of *Duplicate Bridge Movements*.

FAUCONNIER, Paul (b.1943) of Liège, Belgium, teacher. WBF World Master. Represented Belgium in four world championships and seven European championships. National wins include open teams 7 times and open pairs twice.

FAZLI, Jan-e-Alam (b. 1939) of Karachi, Pakistan, tax consultant. WBF World Life Master. Second in two world championships: Bermuda Bowl 1981 and Rosenblum Teams 1986. Played in several other world championships. Won BFAME zonal championship 1983, 1985 and 1987.

FEAGIN, Claudia (b. 1947) of Atlanta GA, teacher, graduated U of Michigan and Georgia State, enjoys aerobics and tennis, first person to win two categories on the MINI-MCKENNEY (Sectional Master 1975 and NABC Master 1976). Has won many regional titles as a Diamond Life Master including Jacksonville Swiss 1977, Gatlinburg Non-Smoking Open Prs 1984, KO Tms 1985, Womens KO Tms 1990, Handicap KO,Tms 1992; Atlanta Non-Smoking Swiss, Womens KO Tms 1984, 87, 89; Virginia Beach Open Prs 1984; Roanoke Open Prs 1985, Columbia Master Prs 1986, Greenville Swiss 1987, Washington Womens Prs, Charlotte Open Prs 1989; Dist 7 GN Tms 1992.

FEAGIN, Jack (b. 1948) of Atlanta GA, attorney, graduated U of Georgia (JD), enjoys tennis and golf. Has served in many capacities including president of Unit 114, Dist 7, the Mid-Atlantic Conference and COI (Committee for an Open and Improved ACBL). Served on ACBL president's Committee on Policies and Procedures, was chairman of Atlanta NABCs 1986 and 1995, co-editor of COI newsletter. Diamond Life Master; regional wins include Jacksonville Swiss 1977, Birmingham Mens Swiss 1978, Roanoke Mens Open Prs 1979, Gatlinburg non-smoking Open Prs 1984, KO Tms 1985, Handicap KO Tms 1992; Atlanta Non-Smoking Swiss 1984, Mens KO Tms 1988, 89; VA Beach Open Prs 1984, Washington Mens Swiss 1985, Roanoke Open Prs 1985, Nashville Mens KO Tms 1985, Columbia KO Tms, Master Prs 1986; Charlotte Open Prs 1989, Dist 7 GN Tms 1992.

FEATHERSTON, Norman D. (Norm) (b. 1934) of Redmond WA, retired electrical engineer, bridge teacher and bridge administrator, graduate U of Washington, enjoys hiking and music. Dist 19 recorder and past president Seattle Unit. Diamond Life Master, won Intermountain Open Tms 1966, Mid-Winter Holiday Open Tms 1977, 1986, Open Prs 1985; Puget Sound Masters Prs 1983, Open Prs 1992; Outlaw Open Prs 1983, KO Tms 1992; Apple Tree Mens Prs, Trails End Open Swiss 1986; Dist 19 GN Tms 1988, 1990; Dist 19 NA Prs, Seattle Summer Swiss 1989; Indian Summer Swiss, Open Prs 1991; Vancouver Island Super Swiss 1993.

FEICHTINGER, Kurt (b. 1954) of Linz, Austria, industrial manager. WBF World Master. Runner-up Bermuda Bowl 1985. Won European Open Teams 1985, European Team Cup 1988. Represented Austria in other world championships and 10 European team and pair championships. Won Coppo D'Oro (Paris) and CAC Open Pairs. Won four National Team titles and one Open Pairs.

FEIGUS, Jay T. (1892-1990) retired labor relations mediator, won Vanderbilt 1948, placed second Spingold 1942. Regional wins include Marcus Cup 1951, Eastern States KO Tms 1947, 49.

FEIN, Phyllis of Steamboat Springs CO, owner of data processing firm, former advertising director for the New York Nets, graduate Hofstra U. Active in local bridge and past president Unit 566, contributing editor *The Southern California Bridge News*. Author of *The Lighter Side of Bridge*. Wrote, directed and scored four bridge musicals; also scored two musicals for Unit 566.

FELD, Rena (b. 1915) of Brookline MA, retired payroll supervisor; Diamond Life Master; regional wins include New England Spring Open Prs 1959, Master Tms 1964, 70, Mixed Tms 1965, Open Prs 1993; Eastern States Mixed Prs 1965, Mixed Tms 1966; Long Island Open Prs 1970; Summer Secondary Women's Swiss 1988.

FEINGOLD, Dr. Adolph (b. 1920) of Edmonton AB, born in the Ukraine, retired manager design engineering division, former professor of engineering, graduate of U of Genoa Italy. A British officer in Special Operations during WW II, he parachuted into German-occupied France, also fought in the Independence War of Israel 1948-49. Has won several regionals including Canadian Nat'l Open Tms 1971, 73; Summer secondary Open Prs, Cambrian Shields KO Tms 1973; Fleur-de-Lys Open Tms 1974, Edmonton KO Tms 1990.

FELDESMAN, Phillip (1919-1986) of New York City, diamond merchant, represented U.S. in world championships 1962, 1966. Won Herman Trophy 1962, Mott-Smith Trophy 1965, 66; Vanderbilt 1965, 66; Reisinger 1969, Life Master Prs 1961, 62, 67; Master Mixed Tms 1973, Sr/Advanced Sr Master Individual 1957, Open Prs 1961, Men Prs 1961, 62; Mens Tms 1962, 63, 66; placed second in the Chicago (now the Reisinger) 1965; Spingold, Vanderbilt 1969; Mens Tms 1965, Open Prs, Blue Ribbon Prs 1967. Feldesman had numerous regional wins.

FELDHEIM, Harold (b. 1936) of Hamden CT, author, bridge professional, graduated Pratt Institute of Texas. Enjoys chess, golf, classical music; formerly chess master. Owned and operated bridge club 1975-86. Authored *The Weak Two-Bid in Bridge*, *Winning Swiss Team Tactics in Bridge*, *Negative and Responsive Doubles in Bridge*, *Five-Card Majors*, *Tactical Bridge*, chapter on Pressure Bidding in *Expert Bridge*, and *Charles Goren Teaches Bridge*, a computer program. Diamond Life Master with more than 60 regional titles including KO Tms, Open Prs 1988; Swiss, Flted KO Tms, Open Prs, IMP Prs, Open KO Tms 1990; Swiss, KO Tms, Flted Open Prs, Open Prs 1991; Open Prs, Swiss, Sr Open Prs, Sr KO Tms 1992; Swiss, Open Prs 1993.

FELDMAN, Lynne of Champaign IL, immigration and naturalization attorney, former municipal attorney in California, won Master Mixed Tms 1979, North American Womens Swiss 1986, Womens BAM Tms 1988; placed second Womens KO Tms 1985, Womens BAM Tms 1987; has numerous regional wins.

FELDMAN, Mark David (b. 1951) of New York City, economics professor at U of Illinois, educated at MIT and U of California at Davis (Ph.D.) In 1971 devised defenses to strong 1♣ and 1NT openings (SCREW) which later became known as CRASH; in 1975 invented the treatment of a jump to four of a minor over an opposing major suit weak 2-bid to show the bid minor and the other major. Feldman won Mens Tms 1974, Master Mixed Tms 1979; placed second in Vanderbilt 1974, 1980; GN Prs 1981, Spingold 1989; placed 5th-8th Bermuda Bowl 1991; is a WBF World Master and an ACBL Diamond Life Master with many regional wins.

FELDMAN, Ron L. (b. 1950) of Petaluma CA, business executive, inventor, entrepreneur and professional bridge player, graduate of California State U at Hayward, enjoys playing folk guitar. Listed *Who's Who in California* 1988 through 1993; former elementary school counselor; received Congressional recognition for his work with children; has directed more than 35 performances of his popular *Bidding Contest*, a vugraph show sponsored by entertainment committees of regionals and NABCs. President of the Association of Professional Bridge Players, Inc. (APBP Inc.), the first of the professional organizations recognized by the ACBL, 1981. Lifetime member of the Nat'l Goodwill Committee and served for more than ten years on Nat'l Appeals Committee. Is a major contributor to 2/1 Game Forcing; placed second in Life Masters Prs 1978 and Mens Tms 1979; successfully organized the largest cash prize corporate-sponsored tournament. Diamond Life Master with more than 40 regional wins. He is one of the few players ever to score a tournament "grand slam" (won all four events).

FELDMAN, Ronald W. (Larf) (b. 1948) of Redondo Beach CA, CPA, educated at U of Southern California. Placed second in IMP Prs 1991. Has won several regionals including Summer secondary Open Prs, Toast of Tulsa Swiss 1977; LA Winter KO Tms 1978, Bridge Week Master Swiss 1979.

FELDSTEIN, Harold F. (b. 1919) of Melbourne FL, retired computer systems analyst and ACBL nat'l tournament director, placed second Mens Prs 1948; won several regional events.

FELDSTEIN, Gretchen S. (Mrs. Harold) of Melbourne FL, won Womens Tms 1953, Womens Prs 1960; placed second Womens Prs 1953.

FELLER, Robert H. (Bob) (b. 1952) of Albany NY, attorney, won Grand National Prs 1980, has several regional wins.

FELLOWS, Barbara A. (Mrs. James E.) (b. 1938) of Omaha NE, ACBL accredited bridge teacher and director, graduate U of Nebraska at Omaha, has taught more than 400 youths since 1989. Unit 241 Bd member and Unit Education Liaison, member Nat'l Charity Committee. Won Womens Prs 1976. Regional titles include Iowa Swiss 1972, 81; Cornhusker Master Prs 1977, NW Iowa Womens Swiss, Pheasant Swiss 1978; Great Lakes Womens Swiss 1979 Tms.

FELLOWS, James E. (b. 1932) of Omaha NE, senior deputy attorney of Omaha, educated at Grinnell College and U of Iowa. Served as president on Unit and Dist level, editor of unit publication 1975-85. Diamond Life Master. His 30+ regional wins include Missouri Valley Open Tms 1967, Western Iowa Swiss 1975, Mens Swiss 1980; Dist 15 Spring KO Tms, Master Prs 1981.

FENKEL, Stanley O. (1902-1986) of Deerfield Beach FL, company vice president, former plastics manufacturer, Life Master #43. Placed second Spingold 1944, Chicago (now the Reisinger) 1946, Vanderbilt 1954. Fenkel was founder and former secretary/treasurer of the Cavendish Club of Philadelphia.

FENWICK, Thomas (b. 1928) of Geneva, Switzerland, company director. Represented Switzerland in four world championships and seven European Championships. National titles include Open Teams nine times.

FERER, Leland E. (b. 1927) of Miami Beach, import manager and bridge writer, former vice president of the Florida Unit and editor of its *Bridge News*. Won Master Mixed Tms 1958, placed second Master Mixed Tms 1967, Mixed Prs 1972, Blue Ribbon Prs 1966; had many regional wins.

FERGUSON, James P. (1907-1981) of North Palm Beach FL, candy manufacturer, ACBL president 1961 when ACBL was converting to a data processing system for masterpoints and memberships. Served three terms on the ACBL Bd of Dir.

FERNANDEZ, Carlos (b. 1958) of Barcelona, Spain, economist and enterprise manager. WBF World Master. Second European Junior Teams 1980 and represented

Spain in eight other zonal championships and three world championships. Won five national titles.

FERRE, Dr. George of Rockingham NC, physician and surgeon, certified director, taught bridge at Central Florida Community College. Won Yakima Open Prs 1977, Midwest Mens Swiss 1982, Greenville Mens Swiss 1985, Tampa Open Prs 1987, Fall secondary Sr Swiss 1990, Biloxi Sr Swiss 1991.

FERRO, Jeffrey (Jeff) (b. 1968) of San Francisco CA, ad agency production coordinator producing TV and radio commercials, Emory U graduate. Outside interests include music, skiing, exercise and tennis. Appointed Junior Liaison 1991. Became Life Master at age 15 and won his first regional. Currently a Silver LM, won 458 points in 1989 (more than any other Junior for that year); was on winning team at the World Junior Championships 1991 and is a WBF World Master. Playing on the USA II open team he competed in the Bermuda Bowl Yokohama 1991, tying 5th/8th. Won NABC Jr Prs 1991, GN Tms 1993; was second in 1st Annual "Expert Calcutta" in 1991.

FIELD, Albert (b. 1916) of Astoria NY, teacher, contributing editor, *Bridge Encyclopedia*, is a collector of playing cards with the largest collection in the world. Field has been the official cataloguer for Salvador Dali.

FIELD, Myron (formerly Fuchs) (1912-1974) New York stock broker, garnered four major national titles and placed second in 11 others, Field represented the USA in 1956 Bermuda Bowl.

FILARSKI, Herman W. (1913-1982) of Deil, The Netherlands, wine merchant, bridge teacher and journalist, learned to play bridge while in a German prison camp during World War II; placed second in World Mixed Teams 1962; represented The Netherlands in the World Open Pairs 1962, in many European Championships and other events 1947 to 1962. His many national successes included Open Pairs and Open Teams. He served several terms as executive vice-president of the INTERNATIONAL BRIDGE PRESS ASSOCIATION. He originated the idea of a *Daily Bulletin* for major championships in 1955, and he also was the author of the BOLS TIP and the BOLS BRILLIANCY competitions. Author of several books and an editor of *Nederlandse Bridge Bond;* was named IBPA Man of the Year in in 1977.

FINK, Jerold (Jerry) (b. 1941) of Cincinnati OH, tax attorney, listed in *The Best Lawyers in America* and *Who's Who in American Law*. Has won chess championships in Ohio and North Carolina. Co-authored *Power Defensive Carding*, introduced several bidding and defensive signaling innovations through articles published in *The Bridge World*". Developed and organized first intercity match between Cincinnati and Indianapolis 1988. Won Fall secondary 0-750 KO Tms 1986, Spring secondary 0-2000 KO Tms 1987, Pittsburgh Swiss 1988, Summer secondary Swiss, Dayton IMP Prs 1989; Louisville Swiss, Bowling Green Swiss 1990.

FINKEL, Lewis M. (Lew) (b. 1946) of Providence RI, attorney and CPA, educated at City College of NY and Harvard Law School (JD); Dist 25 judiciary chairman. Intercity champion (representing Boston) 1972. Has won

various team and pair events including Summer secondary Swiss 1971, Dist 25 GN Tms 1975, 79; New England KO Swiss 1979, 81.

FINTZ, Leora of Harare, Zimbabwe. Represented Zimbabwe in two world championships and one zonal championship. Represented Zimbabwe in many regional tournaments and won national titles.

FISCHER, Doris (b. 1959) of Vienna, Austria, teacher of history and German. WBF World Life Master. European Women's Team champion 1991. Runner-up Venice Cup 1991. Represented Austria in one other world championship and two other European events.

FISCHER, Norman H. (b. 1941) of Columbus OH, research mathematician, space systems analyst for DOD and NASA, graduate of Case Inst. of Technology and Ohio State U, head elder of his church since 1988. Served Unit 122 as president and Dist 11 as president and vice-president. Placed second Life Master Mens Prs, Mens Tms 1969. Diamond Life Master with numerous regional wins including Dist 11 GN Tms 1974, 76, 77, Zone III 1976; All-American Master Prs 1979, KO Tms 1980; Dist 11 GN Prs 1980, 81; Great Lakes Swiss, Mens Prs 1981; Spring Swiss 1981, 91; Opryland Open Prs, Swiss 1981; Spring secondary Mixed Swiss, Open Tms 1982.

FISHBEIN, Harry J. (1898-1976) of New York City, president of Mayfair Club, authored the FISHBEIN CONVENTION. Wore a beret as his trademark, Won 17 nat'l titles and placed second 19 times; represented U.S. Bermuda Bowl 1959, served as npc 1960 U.S. World Olympiad Tm. Treasurer of the ACBL 1952-1966; Honorary Member 1966.

FISHER, Arnold H. (Arnie) (b. 1938) of Clementon NJ, university instructor in German and Russian, owner foreign language typesetting company and bridge professional, graduate of U of Pennsylvania, enjoys travel, music and wine. Served as vice-chairman Nat'l Appeals Committee 1985-1990. Wrote *Solobridge* and *Bridge for Four*. WBF World Master, placed 15th Rosenblum Tms 1986. ACBL Diamond Life Master; has won 80+ regionals including Mid-Atlantic KO Tms 1974; Dist 4 Swiss 1977, 78; GN Tms 1978; GN Prs 1981; Rochester KOs Tms, Open Prs 1986; KO Tms, Open Prs 1990; Dist 4 Open Prs 1991, 92.

FISHER, Dr. John W. (b. 1925) of Dallas TX, physician, educated at Southern Methodist and Louisana State U School of Medicine (M.D.) Enjoys pro tennis, opera, European travel and the Italian language. Past president of Dallas BA, a member of Nat'l Goodwill Committee and inventor of the FISHER DOUBLE. Winner of the McKenney Trophy (now Barry Crane Top 500) 1972, a Grand Life Master with more than 17,000 MPs, ranks 20th in all-time masterpoint holders. WBF Life Master; placed second in World Open Prs 1966, 5th Olympiad Mixed Tms 1972. North American wins include Open Prs 1958, Master Mixed Tms 1964, Vanderbilt 1965, Open Prs 1970, 71, 72, 74; GN Tms 1975; placed second in Mens Tms 1954, 56, 71; Master Mixed Tms 1961, 67, 72; Open Prs 1976. His 100+ regional wins include TX Fall Open Prs 1952, 57, Mens Prs 1953, 57, Open Tm 1959, 60; Hawaii Open Tms 1969, 72, 79, Masters Prs 1969, 79; Texas Mid-

Winter Open Tms 1971, 73, 80, Master Prs, Swiss 1980; California Capitol Open Prs, Open Tms, Masters Prs 1979; Mid-South Spring Masters Prs 1991.

FISHER, Margaret L. (1912-1987) of Washington DC, technical writer, won Senior/Advanced Senior Master Prs 1953 and a few regionals. Was bridge columnist for *Washington Evening Star* 1948-1960; founder and secretary of Northern Virginia BA.

FISHER, Richard C. (Dick) (1921-82) of Tokyo, Japan, business manager. Won Northeastern Open Teams 1943 and became a permanent Japanese resident 1945. Represented Japan in several Far East Championships and won many national titles. Founded and directed two clubs, and a team event which led to the formation of the JCBL. Bridge columnist *Japan Times*.

FLADER, Michael F. (Mike) (b. 1947) of Hopkins MN, bridge club manager, teacher and director, educated at U of Minnesota. A good bowler carrying average of 190+, S4 director, tournament coordinator, education liaison, representative Unit 103 Bd of Gov, member Nat'l Goodwill Committee. Won Gopher Mens Prs 1976, Master Prs 1977, KOs 1990; Iowa Mens Prs 1978, Dist 14 GN Prs 1989.

FLANAGAN, Barbara J. (Mrs. Michael) (b. 1933) of Westlake Village CA, bridge teacher, enjoys gourmet cooking and needlepoint. Diamond Life Master, has won Bridge Wk Mixed Prs 1975, All Western Open Prs 1978, LA Winter Mixed Prs 1979, 88; Spring secondary Womens Prs 1980, CA Capitol Swiss 1981, Pasco Open Swiss, All Western Open Prs 1983; Tacoma Womens Prs 1984, Honolulu Womens Prs 1990.

FLANAGAN, Michael L. (b. 1939) of Westlake CA, statistician with U.S. Census Bureau, graduated U of Washington. Was U.S. Intercollegiate bowling champion in three events 1961. Diamond Life Master. Regional wins include Bridge Wk Mixed Prs 1975, Open Prs 1979, Mens Tms 1985; Dist 22 GN Tms 1978, All Western Open Prs 1978, Open Prs 1983; LA Winter Mixed Prs 1979, 88; Dist 22 GN Prs 1979, Honolulu Open Prs 1990, Summer Standard Card Prs 1991.

FLANNERY, William L. (b. 1932) of Sacramento CA, retired steamfitter, a specialist in installing sectional boilers, sports fan and enjoys making and refinishing furniture. Originator of FLANNERY TWO DIAMOND convention. Placed second in Chicago (since 1965 the Reisinger) 1963, Life Master Mens Prs 1967, Mixed Prs 1968. Has won more than 50 regional titles.

FLEET, Richard J. (b. 1953) of London, England, taxation manager. Second Common Market Junior Teams 1979. Several national wins. Frequent contributor to British magazines.

FLEISCHMAN, Dr. Richard K. (Dick) (b. 1941) of University Heights OH, professor and chairman, Dept of Accountancy; former professor of history U of Hawaii, educated at Harvard, State U of NY Buffalo (Ph.D.) Won *Excellence in Teaching* award, published one book and many articles on accounting and history. Past president of Buffalo and Hilo HI Units, treasurer Unit 125 from

1990, member Nat'l Goodwill Committee. Diamond Life Master. 25+ regional wins include Dist 11 KOs 1969, Can-Am KO Tms 1972, Peach Festival KO Tms 1974, Hawaii Master Prs, Swiss 1976, Presque Isle KO Tms 1977, Buffalo Masters Prs 1983, Black Swamp Swiss 1988, Wiesbaden Open Prs 1991.

FLEISHER, Martin E. (Marty) (b. 1958) of Northhampton MA, employee benefit attorney, graduate of Swarthmore College, NYU Law School (JD). Placed second GN Tms 1976, earning him the distinction of being the youngest (17 years, 10 months) ever to compete in the final of an NABC KO championship. Intercollegiate champion 1977 and runner-up in 78. Won Autumn Leaf Swiss 1977, Dist 3 Mens Swiss 1978, Tri-State Swiss 1979, 81; Long Island Swiss 1982, 85; Winter Swiss 1982, New England KO Tms 1990.

FLEMING, Ian (1908-1964), famous British novelist and creator of James Bond, pits 007 agent against the diabolical Drax in a high-stake bridge game in his short story *Bridge at Blades* which has been anthologized in *Grand Slam*. Bridge plays an important part in the plot of *Moonraker*, an 007 novel. See DISTRIBUTIONAL VALUES.

FLEMING, Irene (Dimmie) (b. 1911) of Heron's Ghyll, England, retired bridge supplies distributor. WBF World Life Master. Won World Women's Teams 1964, European Women's Teams 1951, 1952, 1959, 1963. Second European Open Teams 1953, the best performance ever by a woman and the only time a woman has represented Britain. Represented Britain in four other world championships. 11 national wins include Gold Cup once. Secretary of EBU 1956-75, then vice-president and honorary life member. Magazine contributor.

FLINT, Honor of London, England, represented Britain in three world championships and two zonal championships. Won five national titles and three ACBL regional titles.

FLINT, Jeremy M. (1928-1990) of London, England, bridge writer. WBF World Life Master. Second World Teams 1960 and Bermuda Bowl 1987. Won European Teams 1963, second 1987. Won Far East Open Pairs 1973. Represented Britain in seven other world championships and five other zonal championships. Won more than 10 British titles including Gold Cup twice. During a 1966 tour of the United States he won 13 regional titles and was runner-up in the McKenney Trophy. He became a life master in 11 weeks, a record that stood until 1989. He is a co-inventor of the MULTI TWO DIAMONDS, the LITTLE MAJOR system, and the Flint-Pender system, and inventor of several other conventions. He was bridge columnist of the *London Times* 1980-1990, and author of more than six books on bridge, as well as a book about horse-racing. Chief presenter of several televised series on bridge.

FLODQVIST, Ann-Margreth (Pyttsi) (b. 1948) of Stockholm, Sweden, chemical dependency counselor. Won European Womens Teams 1993, Nordic Women's Teams 1992 and represented Sweden in one other world championship and two other zonal championships.

FLODQVIST, Sven-Olov (Tjolpe) of Stockholm, Sweden, computer analyst and bridge editor. WBF World Life Master. Third Bermuda Bowl 1977, 1987, Olympiad Teams 1988, represented Sweden in five other world championships. European champion 1977, 1987, third 1989 and played on six other occasions. Won *Sunday Times* 1978, 1981. National wins include open teams six times. Bridge editor *Dagens Nyheter*. Author of book on Carrot Club System.

FLOREA, Harold R. (Happy) (b. 1914) of Winter Springs FL, retired engineering manager, graduate Stevens Institute of Technology. Won Golden Age Olympics tennis singles 1990. Inventor and patent holder of simulation devices used to train military pilots. Won Florida Mixed Prs 1969. Was one of first to introduce Swiss movement to bridge team play (while a director of a 27-team Long Island Industrial BL in 1962).

FLOURNOY, Carolyn Clay (b. 1924) of Shreveport LA, food columnist and cooking teacher, graduate of Centenary College and Northwestern U, delegate to Republican party convention for three Presidential elections, president of Mayor's Women's Commission and several other women's and philanthropic organizations; named to Sports Museum of Champions of Louisiana. Served on local Bd of Dir for many years, was tournament publicity chairman for more than 25 years, reports on NABC activities of area players for local newspaper and TV. Won Mixed Prs 1970. Regional wins include Texas Fall Open Tms 1957, 71, KO Tms 71; TX Mid-Winter Open Tms 1972, TX Summer KO Tms 1975.

FLOYD, Jason H. (b. 1908) of Gulfport MS, graduated U of Mississippi (JD), member of collegiate golf team, president of senior law class, representative in Mississippi State Legislature 1936-40. Past president of Unit 180, Life Master #471. Won Mid-South Spring Open Prs, Mixed Prs 1942, Summer Tm of Four 1962, Fall Open Prs 1989; Gulf Coast Tm of Four 1972.

FOLLINE, Emily (1907-1984) of Columbia SC, bridge studio owner, won Chicago (now the Reisinger) 1949, Spring Womens Tms 1943, 44, 45, 46; placed second Spring Womens Tms 1942, Mixed Tms 1946; had numerous regional wins.

FOLQUE, Luís (b. 1952) of Portugal, civil engineer. Represented Portugal in one world championship, one European Championship and two European Junior Championships. National wins include open team once and open pairs twice.

FONSECA, Christiano (b. 1940) of Rio de Janeiro, Brazil, financial executive. WBF World Life Master. Won World Teams 1976, South American Teams 1970, 1971, 1972, 1973, 1975. Represented Brazil in three other world championships. National wins include open teams six times.

FONTAINE, Walter J. (b. 1944) of North Providence RI, produces statisics and publications for the adult prison system for RI Dept of Corrections, authored *Use Your Imagination and Win at Bridge*. Won Buffalo KO Tms 1985, Swan Lake KO Tms 1986, Toronto Master Prs 1986, Morning Bracketed KO Tms 1992; Mens Prs 1987,

Super Flt KO Tms 1990; Ottawa Swiss 1987, Albany Open Mens Swiss 1990, KO Tms 1991; Summer secondary Open Prs, Thunder Bay Swiss 1990, New England Open Prs 1992.

FORQUET, Pietro (b. 1925) of Naples, Italy, banker. WBF Grand Master, third in world career rankings in 1992. At one time considered by many experts to be the world's best player. Won World Teams 1964, 1968, 1972, Bermuda Bowl 1957, 1958, 1959, 1961, 1962, 1963, 1965, 1966, 1967, 1969, 1973, 1974. Forquet established a reputation for calm, unruffled performances, apparently immune from the nervous tension that afflicted others. He employed the NEAPOLITAN CLUB, or BLUE TEAM CLUB, effectively with three partners, Guglielmo Siniscalco, Eugenio Chiaradia and Benito Garozzo. In three world championships 1972-74 he shifted to the PRECISION CLUB, playing with Garozzo and Benito Bianchi. He won his first European Teams title in 1951 at the age of 26, and won again in 1956, 1957, 1958, 1959. Author of one book, also a columnist. See BLUE TEAM, LANCIA TEAM and SHARIF BRIDGE CIRCUS.

FORRESTER, Anthony R. (Tony) (b. 1953) of Newmarket, England, chartered accountant and bridge professional. WBF World Master. Second Bermuda Bowl 1987. Won European Teams 1991, second 1987. Won European Junior Teams 1978, Common Market Teams 1981, 1983. Represented Britain in 5 other world championships and 3 other zonal championships, and England in 41 Camrose Trophy matches, a record. Won *Sunday Times* Pairs 1990. Numerous national titles include Gold Cup 6 times. Bridge columnist of the *London Daily Telegraph* from 1993 and frequent contributor to British magazines.

FORSTER, Dale E. (b. 1942) of Eugene OR, real estate broker, won Intercollegiate Championship 1964 and several regional events.

FOSTER, Robert Fredrick (1853-1945), world famous authority on card games, invented RULE OF ELEVEN. Born in Scotland; surveyor and prospector for gold; traveled the globe in this capacity. After making and losing two fortunes, he established himself as the world's leading authority on cards by writing *Foster's Complete Hoyle* (1897), a copy of which was inserted in the time capsule at the 1939 New York World's Fair. Although the Rule of Eleven is his chief theoretical contribution, he promoted numerous ideas in his *Vanity Fair* magazine column and in the *New York Sun*. His various writings traced the successive developments of bridge -- auction and contract. An AWL director, he later wrote the first set of laws for contract bridge. Up to age 85 he continued to lecture on games throughout the world and to teach and conduct games in NY. In addition to writing on various subjects, he wrote at least 50 books on card games.

FOURIEZOS, Bette L. See COHN, Bette L.

FOX, Betty (b. 1903) of Hove, England, bridge teacher and club owner. Won European Women's Teams 1966 and represented Britain in two other zonal championships. Many national wins included a sweep of all major women's events in 1964. Former training officer of EBU.

FOX G.C.H. (Foxy) (b. 1914) of Hove, England, bridge

writer, teacher. Won five national titles and represented England in a Camrose Trophy match. Bridge columnist of *Daily Telegraph* 1957-93, frequent magazine contributor and author of more than 8 books.

FOX, Dr. John H. (b. 1933) of Cathedral City CA, physicist and mathematician, served as consultant to U.S. and West German aerospace industries, owner Bacchus Press. Educated at UCLA and Penn State (PhD). Has authored a best-selling poker book *Play Poker, Quit Work and Sleep 'Til Noon*, authored other books on philosophy, humor and card play. Was a handball champion, directs bridge cruises, contributed to *British Popular Bridge*. In 1979 won four events in San Diego regional. Diamond Life Master, placed second North American Swiss 1987, winner of 80+ regionals including more than 10 NABC secondary Sr Prs and Tms, Dist 23 GN Tms 1980, Seattle GN Tms 1985.

FOX, Joseph L. (Joe) (b. 1937) of Mariposa CA, retired insurance company executive, currently a partner in a winery. Received degrees from U of California at Santa Barbara and Pepperdine U. Enjoys skiing, winemaking and concert piano. Won Mens Prs 1977. Regional titles include LA Winter Swiss 1988, Prime Time KOs 1991; Sacramento VP Swiss, Open Swiss 1989, Masters Prs 1990; Santa Clara Handicap KO Tms 1990, Modesto/San Bernardino Open Prs 1991, Anchorage Open Prs, Open Swiss, KO Tms 1991.

FOX, Robert S. (Bob) (b. 1919) of Boynton Beach FL, company vice president, graduate of Babson and Brown U. Past president New England BA and Rhode Island BA. Numerous regional wins include New England KO Tms 1953, 56, 59, 62, 63, Open Tms 1952, 54, 58, 62; Bermuda Open Tms 1970, 72.

FOY, Nancy W. (CMP) (b. 1956) of Memphis TN, meeting planner on staff of ACBL, graduate of Memphis State U, listed in *Who's Who Among Students in American Colleges and Universities*. Joined ABCL staff 1991.

FOZ, Mario (b. 1929) of Barcelona, Spain, physician and professor. Represented Spain in one world championship and two zonal championships.

FRAENCKEL, Rigmor (1909-1983) of Copenhagen, Denmark, bridge teacher. Third World Womens Teams 1960. Won European Womens Teams 1948, 1949, 1955, 1957, 1958, second 1951. Represented Denmark in one other world championship and three other zonal championships. She and her partner, Otti Damm, were noted for fast play. In 1950 they won the first Danish Open Pairs, and in the following year with an all-women team won the Open Teams, a unique circumstance. Her 16 national victories included another Open Teams and another Open Pairs.

FRANCES, Antonio (b. 1933) of Madrid, Spain, lawyer. President of Spanish Bridge Federation. Yachting captain and jazz musician.

FRANCIS, Henry G. (b. 1926) of Memphis, formerly of Nahant MA; graduate Boston College; writer, editor and news editor *Boston Herald* and *Boston Traveler* 1945-1972; bridge columnist and ACBL associate national tour-

nament director; executive editor of ACBL publications 1973-1992; editorial-publishing manager since 1992. Publications include *ACBL Bulletin, World Championship Books* (1973-1989), *Daily Bulletins* at World Championships (since 1977) and co-editor of *Daily Bulletins* at all North American Championships since 1972; editor of *Daily Bulletins* at first Far East Championships held in China 1987. Editor-in-chief of editions IV and V of the *Official Encyclopedia of Bridge*; regional vice president of INTERNATIONAL BRIDGE PRESS ASSOCIATION; weekly bridge columnist for *Boston Herald* and *Boston Herald-American*, 1965-1990. Began directing tournaments 1958, assisting at and running tournaments mostly in the Northeast and the Maritime provinces of Canada. Began bridge writing career in 1955 when he founded and became the first editor of *New England Bridge Bulletin*, 1955-1964 and 1967-1972. Has won several bridge-writing prizes. President of PROFESSIONAL TOURNAMENT DIRECTORS ASSOCIATION 1968-1972. Regional titles include New England Open Prs 1958, Can-At KO Tms 1968, 69, 70, Can-At Swiss 1981, Bermuda Master Prs 1986, Bermuda KO Tms 1990.

FRANCIS, Dorthy A. (Mrs. Henry G.) (b. 1940) of Memphis, bridge writer, co-editor of World Championship *Daily Bulletins* 1979-1987, has contributed to the *ACBL Bulletin*, ACBL North American Championship *Daily Bulletins*; assistant editor of *Daily Bulletins* at first Far East Championships held in China 1987; edited several *World Championship Books*. Won BOLS prize for best article on 1978 World Championships and several other IBPA bridge writing awards. Editor of *Fifth Edition, Bridge Encyclopedia*. Has won several regionals.

FRANCO, Arturo (b. 1946) of Milan, Italy, insurance agent. WBF Grand Master. Won Bermuda Bowl 1974, 1975, second 1976, 1979, 1983. (Two finals lost by 5 imps). Won European Teams 1973, 1975, 1979, second 1977, 1983. Many national wins.

FRANKEL, Arnold (Arnie) (b. 1931) of Laurel MD, retired CPA, graduated CCNY. Won Washington Bridge Wk Masters Prs 1974, Philadelphia Mens Prs, Roanoke Open Swiss 1979; Fall secondary Swiss 1980, Dist 4 Mens Prs 1979, Mens Swiss 1981; Baltimore Open Prs 1987.

FRANKEL, Jean (b. 1926) of New Orleans, bridge teacher and director, graduate of U of Wisconsin, secretary of Unit 134, Dist 10 for many years, certified director. Placed second Master Mixed Tms 1961, Womens Prs 1965, Womens Tms 1968. Regional wins include secondary Womens Prs 1965, Southern Conference Womens Prs 1958, Mid-South Open Tms 1962, 65, 67, 73, KO Tms 1973, Summer Mixed Prs 1962, 66, 70, Open Tms 1970; Mexican Nat'l Womens Prs 1962, Open Tms 1970, KO Tms 1973, Florida Womens Prs, Mixed Prs 1977; Celebrity Womens Prs, Womens Swiss 1977.

FRANKLIN, Harold (b. 1915) of Leeds, England, tournament director and bridge writer. Represented Britain in two zonal championships. National wins include Gold Cup twice. Former chief tournament director of WBF and EBU. Former member of EBL Laws Commission and WBF Tournament planning committee. Formerly a broadcaster, magazine contributor and bridge columnist of *Yorkshire Post*.

FRANKLIN, Marc S. (b. 1959) of Sherman Oaks CA, manages policy issue and financial analysis in insurance, former banker, educated Claremont McKenna College and Chicago Graduate School of Business. Avid traveler and scuba diver, has visited every continent, Eagle Scout, chairman of Southern CA Council-Jr Statesman since 1991. Organized and directed a duplicate bridge club for the five Claremont colleges during matriculation; was a National Merit Scholar; KING OF BRIDGE 1977. He and his brother (Matthew, King of Bridge - 1978) are the first siblings to have attained that title (see MOSS, Andrew and Brad). Franklin represented Great Britain in internat'l play in Europe, won British nat'l team event, the Spring Fours. All regional wins have been partnered by his brother, has won Midwinter Holiday Masters Prs 1976, Master Swiss 1977, Open Prs A-D 1981; Secaucus Masters Prs 1985. In 1979 he won $12,000 on *Wheel of Fortune* show. See FAMILY.

FRANKLIN, Matthew (b. 1961) of New York City, graduated Pomona College and U of California-Berkeley, doctoral student at Columbia U, collector of old bridge and whist books, enjoys designing games. AT & T Bell Labs PhD Scholar 1989-93. KING OF BRIDGE 1978 -- he and his brother Marc were the first siblings to attain that title (see MOSS, Andrew and Brad). In 1976 won Mid-Winter Holiday Master Prs with his brother, at ages 15 and 17. Other wins include Mid Winter Holiday Master Swiss 1977, Open Prs A-D Conventions 1981; Secaucus Master Prs 1984. See FAMILY.

FRASER, A. A. Douglas (b. 1940) of Mount Royal PQ, bridge club owner, has served on Canadian Bridge Federation board; represented Canada in Rosenblum Tms 1978, 82, 86, 90; won CNTC 1992. Won Master Mixed Tms 1981, Mens Swiss 1988; placed second Master Mixed Tms 1974. Diamond Life Master, has won numerous regionals.

FRASER, Brian (b. 1942) of Montreal PQ, born in England, accountant; won Can-Am Swiss 1976, Mens Swiss 1986, Swiss 1993; Spring secondary Open Prs 1983, Nat'l Capitol Swiss 1990.

FRÄSER, Renate (b.1951) psychologist. European Women's champion 1991, represented Austria in three other European events.

FRASER, Sandra E. (Mrs. Douglas) (b. 1944) of Mount Royal PQ, born in New Zealand, financial and administration manager, has served as vice chairman for Eastern Canada of the ACBL Goodwill Committee. WBF World Master, represented Canada in Rosenblum Tms 1982, 86, 90 and Womens Team Olympiad 1984 (placed 9th) and 5th in Swiss Plate. Diamond Life Master, won CNTC 1992 and Master Mixed Tms 1981; placed second Master Mixed Tms 1974, North American Womens Swiss 1983, 88; has won numerous regional events.

FRED, James David (Dave) (b. 1947) of South Bend IN, associate professor of accounting Indiana U, graduated with three degrees from Purdue U, enjoys golf, collecting trading cards and spectator sports, a certified director, treasurer of St. Joe Valley BA 1992-. Diamond Life Master. Regional wins include All-American Mens Prs 1975, Non-Smoking Swiss 1982, Swiss 1982, 83;

Midwest KO Tms 1978; Cambrian Shield Open Prs 1980, Master Prs 1982, KO Tms 1982, 85; Great Lakes KO Tms 1982, Nickel City Open Prs 1983; Dist 8 GN Tms 1984, GN Prs 1984, 85.

FREDD, Claudius G. (b. 1921) of College Park GA, retail liquor distributor, graduate of Tuskegee Institute, Phi Beta Kappa; has won more than 300 AMERICAN BRIDGE ASSOCIATION tournaments over four decades including ABA National Open Tms 1974. Former member of ABA Board, editor of *ABA Bulletin* and chairman of ABA Tournament Authority. Fredd is a former chess master.

FREED, Dr. Eugene (Gene) (b. 1930) of Los Angeles, plastic surgeon, specializing in ears, nose and throat, educated at San Diego State College and U of Southern California. In his profession has treated such Hollywood personalities as Mario Lanza, Maria Callas, Alfred Drake, Chita Rivera, Larry of the Three Stooges and Mickey Cohen. 11th World Open Prs 1990, 20th World Mixed Prs 1982; WBF World Master; ACBL Grand Life Master with more than 15,000 MPs. Won Mens BAM Tms 1986, IMP Prs 1988. In 1991 won three events a week in nine consecutive regionals partnered with Mike Passell. Regional wins include Summer secondary Mixed Prs 1977, Swiss 1979; All-Western Mens Prs, Cotton Boll Mens Prs 1977; Dist 17 Master Swiss 1978, California Capital Master Prs, Golden State Swiss 1981; ALACBU Sr KO Tms 1990, Mid-Atlantic Swiss, Open Prs 1991; Bakersfield Open Prs 1991. At the time his son Michael became a Life Master, he was the youngest at age 14.

FREEDMAN, Richard N. (Dick) (b. 1945) of Newton MA, computer programmer, educated at MIT and U of Western Ontario, former Western square dancer (challenge level), has performed in 12 Gilbert and Sullivan operettas. With his background as a player and a director, Freedman tired of waiting for scores so he developed the first scoring program. Its first official use was for a sectional in Lexington MA 1977. This program was subsequently used in North American Championships in Chicago, Atlanta and Houston, a couple of regionals in New England and then the World Prs Olympiad in New Orleans 1978. Regional wins include New England Masters Prs 1971, Summer KOs 1987, 88, Master Prs 1989, Summer IMP Prs 1991; Eastern States Goldman Prs 1972, Motor City Open Tms 1973, Dist 25 GN Prs 1979, 80; Dist 25 GN Tms 1987.

FREEDMAN, Robert P. (b.1926) of Buffalo NY, attorney, member of ACBL Board 1956-1957. Won Open Prs 1969, Master Mixed Tms 1956; placed second Master Mixed Tms 1955, Life Master Prs 1970. Member Nat'l Goodwill Committee, Diamond Life Master, has won numerous regional titles.

FREEMAN, Louise K. (Mrs. Richard, formerly Louise Robinson) of Atlanta GA, graduate Converse College, won Master Mixed Tms 1961. Regional wins include Canadian Nat'l Mixed Prs 1961, Mid-Atlantic Spring BAM Tms 1961, 62, 65, Fall BAM Tms 1962, 64, Fall Masters Prs 1965, Labor Day BAM Tms 1967, Spring Master Prs 1968; Southern Conference BAM Tms 1964.

FREEMAN, Richard A. (Dick) (b. 1933) of Atlanta GA,

senior vice-president Oppenheimer and Co., Inc., graduated U of Chicago and George Washington U (JD), interested in American and European history. Freeman was a "Quiz Kid" of radio fame 1942, 44, 45 with special emphasis on solving complex mathematical problems in his head; became ACBL's YOUNGEST LIFE MASTER in 1952 at age 18. Served on Bd of Gov 1976-80, directed from 1952-63 and was regionally ranked. Edited *Roth Stone System* and *Bridge is a Partnership Game*. Won Mens Tms 1955, 62, 66; Master Mixed Tms 1961, Vanderbilt 1979, Spingold, Reisinger 1993; placed second Spingold 1959, Mens Tms 1958, 77, 83; Reisinger 1965, Blue Ribbon Prs 1970, Vanderbilt 1975, GN Tms 1983. Diamond Life Master; regional titles include Mid-Atlantic BAM 1951, 56, 58, 61, 62, 65, 67, Mixed Prs 1956, Mid-Atlantic BAM Tms 1967, KO Tms 1975, 78, 88, Masters Prs 1975, Smoking Open Prs 1981, Mens KO Tms 1983, 86, Smoking Swiss 1984, IMP Prs 1990, Open Swiss 1992; Summer secondary Marcus Cup 1953, Swiss 1979, BAM Tms 1979; Eastern States Mens Prs 1957, KO Tms 1960, 61; Keystone Mens Prs 1957, Fall secondary KO Tms 1986.

FREILICH, Edith (formerly Kemp, nee Seamon) of Miami Beach FL, one of only two women (Helen Sobel Smith was the other) who have won all three major team championship events -- the Reisinger (formerly the Chicago), Spingold and Vanderbilt. Member of ACBL Nat'l Goodwill Committee and a Grand Life Master. WBF World Master; placed second in World Womens Prs 1966, 5th 1986, 18th 1982; second Venice Cup 1981, 5th Olympiad Womens Tms 1988. Her string of more than 30 North American titles began in 1941 and includes Chicago (now the Reisinger) 1946, 52; Vanderbilt, Spingold 1963; Master Mixed Tms 1947, 52, 53, 57, 74; Open Prs 1943, Womens BAM Tms 1951, 62, 65, 69; Womens KO Tms 1979, 80, 82, 84; NA Womens Swiss 1982, Womens Prs 1941, 42, 43, 46, 66, 79, 86; Life Master Womens Prs 1967, 77, 79, 81; placed second Spingold 1953, 72; Reisinger (Chicago) 1964, Master Mixed Tms 1942, 45, 48, 64; Womens BAM Tms 1948, 55, 71; Womens Prs 1957, 78; Life Master Womens Prs 1962, 73, 74, 80; GN Tms 1980, Life Master Prs 1962; won district and zonal GN Tms 1976, 1980 and the district 1982; has won numerous other regional rated events.

FRENCH, Capt. Fred G. (1893-1937) of Philadelphia, an Army officer, bridge teacher and writer, was 1931 president of ABL and a member of the Advisory Council which drafted and approved the OFFICIAL SYSTEM.

FRENCH, Marvin L. (b. 1927) of San Diego CA, retired senior engineer with General Dynamics Corp. A blackjack expert with many articles published under pen name "Marvin L. Master". Other interests are quantum physics, relativity, astrophysics and skiing. Member of Internat'l Society for Philosophical Enquiry, an organization restricted to those in upper 1/10 of 1% IQ score. Contributor to *The Bridge World*, *Contract Bridge Forum* and *Popular Bridge*. Author of many conventions and treatments including AmBIGuous Diamond System, Two Club Game Try, Stoplight, Defense against Precision One Diamond Opening, Unbalanced Heart Convention, Omnibus and Non-Jump Splinters.

FRENKIEL, Marian (b. 1919) of Warsaw, Poland, re-

tired journalist. WBF World Master. Won World Teams 1978 and represented Poland in many other world and zonal championships. Won many national titles. President of CBA of Poland 1973-1990. Member EBL Executive 1983-91.

FREW, David (b. 1943) of Edinburgh, Scotland, journalist. Represented Scotland 9 times in Camrose Trophy matches. Many national wins include Scottish Cup three tiems.

FREY, Mable (Mrs. Richard L.) (1905-1993) of New York City, editor, was recorder at many nat'l and int'l championships, won two consecutive Women's Prs in the Eastern States Regional in partnership with her mother, Gussie Planco, 1935-36; also won New England KO Tms 1936 and Bermuda Mixed Prs with husband Richard Frey.

FREY, Richard L. (Dick) (1905-1988) of New York City, writer, editor and champion player. Public relations chief and editor of *ACBL Bulletin* 1958-1970, editor-in-chief of the first three editions of the *Official Encyclopedia of Bridge* and edited 12 *World Championship Books*. Put together bridge exhibitions and TV shows and he had many salty performances as chief commentator at Bridge-o-rama or vugraph exibitions. After retirement in 1970, became president of INTERNATIONAL BRIDGE PRESS ASSOCIATION, serving in that post for 11 years. Freelance writer on diverse non-fiction subjects for major magazines; books on canasta published in 1950 and 1951 sold more than a million copies and his *According to Hoyle* in 1956 nearly three million. Author of *How to Win At Contract Bridge in Ten Easy Lessons* and several other books.

The new generation of bridge players who knew Frey as an editor and writer did not link him with personalities such as Ely Culbertson, Hal Sims, Harold Vanderbilt, Oswald Jacoby and Howard Schenken. But Frey was right there at the beginning of the heyday of contract bridge. The prestigious posts he filled later are attested to by honorary titles such as president emeritus of the IBPA, editor emeritus of *ACBL Bulletin* and editor emeritus of the fourth edition of the *Encyclopedia of Bridge*.

Was an original member of the BID-RITE TEAM and the FOUR ACES. The Bid-Rite team (David Burnstine, Charles Lockridge, Schenken and Frey) was forerunner of the original Four Aces, formed in 1933 when Oswald Jacoby broke free from a Culbertson commitment and replaced Lockridge. At age of 25 Frey had his first major tournament victory — the Goldman Prs. In a relatively short playing career he won both the Vanderbilt and the Spingold in the same year on two occasions (1934 and 1942) along with several other North American championships. Some of his other successes include Asbury Park Challenge Tms 1933, Master Prs, Grand National Tms (1934 and 35). He was second in seven other NABC events. He had the best tournament record of any player in 1934 with another good year in 1942.

He was No. 8 in the first group of players to be designated Life Masters when the category was created in 1936. For more than 20 years he had the highest percentage of North American Championship victories won out of events entered. In 1935 Frey resigned from the Four Aces to join the Culbertson organization as sales manager for KEM CARDS. He was an editor of *The Bridge World* magazine, technical consultant on the CULBERTSON

SYSTEM and a player on Culbertson teams, often as Culbertson's partner. After the sale of Kem in 1937, Frey returned to the advertising business. He had begun a daily newspaper bridge column in 1937, took over writing the Four Aces column in 1944 and in 1954 merged the two in collaboration with Howard Schenken. In 1970, when he turned the column over to Schenken, his was the longest continuously published syndicated bridge feature in the United States. From Culbertson to Charles Goren, Frey's writing frequently appeared under the byline of the bridge greats. He had the chameleon-like ability to change the style and flavor of his writing to fit that of the original. Following his retirement from ACBL, he became chairman of the Goren Editorial Board, editor of the *Precision Club Newsletter* and a consultant on a variety of bridge projects. Frey was boss and mentor to a number of bridge personalities he brought to ACBL -- Alan Truscott, Albert Dormer, Tannah Hirsch, Tom Smith, Steve Becker, Richard Oshlag and Sue Emery.

FRIEDBERG, Joel M. (b. 1954) of Scarsdale NY, attorney, real estate developer, options trader, broker and former regional tournament director. Degrees from Adelphi U and Benjamin Cardozo School of Law (JD). Won Pan American Games 1983, third Maccabiah Games 1977; Won Sr\ Adv. Sr Master Prs 1973, Mixed Prs 1977; placed second Mens Prs 1984, Fall Swiss 1988, 89. Diamond Life Master; won more than 50 regionals events.

FRIEDLAND, Dr. Peter (b. 1952) of Los Altos CA, chief of Artificial Intelligence Research and Applications at NASA Ames Research Center. Princeton and Stanford (PhD) graduate; interested in many fields of science and U.S. science policy; winner Westinghouse Science Talent Search 1970, University Scholar at Princeton 1970-74, captain of National Champion College Bowl Team-Stanford 1977, founder of two public corporations, IntelliCorp and Teknowledge. Served on both Unit and Dist Bds, contributor to *Palo Alto Kibitzer*. Won Golden State Open Prs 1975, KO Tms 1978, 84, Swiss 1979; All-Western Mens Prs 1977, KO Tms 1980, Master Prs 1984, Super Open Prs 1985, 88, Swiss 1986; Mid-Winter Swiss 1977, Wine Country Master Prs 1981, Dist 21 GN Tms 1989, 91; Dist 21 GN Prs 1991; placed second Continentwide Charity Game (1984) but was only second in his local club in same event.

FRIEDLANDER, Jerome (Thumbs, Jerry) (b. 1906) of Jupiter FL, ACBL Regional-4 tournament director since 1950; other interests are history and U.S. presidents. Was head director for CAVENDISH INVITATIONAL from its inception until 1978. Life Master #102; was awarded a scroll for 25 plus years as a tournament director in 1983; received honorary plaque in 1987 at 50-year anniversary of ACBL. Placed second Golder Cup Prs 1951. Regional wins include Eastern States Open Prs 1945, Open Tms 1947; Can-American Tms 1953, Canadian Nat'l Tms 1957, Upper NY State Tms 1960.

FRIEDMAN, Maurice (Mickey) (b. 1939) of Boca Raton FL, president of art gallery, estate consultant, bridge teacher and managing editor *Goren Bridge Newsletter*, graduated Brooklyn College. Enjoys stamp and coin collecting, chess, music, art and karate. Regional wins include Fall secondary BAM Tms 1980, Open Tms 1983; Summer secondary BAM Tms 1981, Spring secondary

Swiss 1982, Lancaster Open Prs, Norfolk Mens Swiss, Rye Mens Swiss, NYC Open Prs, Parsippany Open Swiss, Hofstra KO Tms.

FRIEDMANN, Marcel (b. 1924) of New York City, born in Belgium, bridge teacher, director and professional player, formerly a diamond dealer. Former Bd member of Greater New York BA, chairman of its Seeding Committee; founder and president of professional organization, CBPU; contributor to Unit 155 *Post Mortem*. Diamond Life Master; has won Eastern States Mens Tms 1967, Long Island Open Tms 1972, Mens Prs 1978; Sun City Sr Mixed Prs, Wisconsin KO Tms 1980; Sunshine State KO Tms 1986, NY Sr Open Prs, Southeastern Mens Swiss 1987; Long Island Sr Open Prs 1991.

FRISCHAUER, Edward (1895-1964) of Hollywood CA, criminal lawyer and real estate broker, was one of the greatest dummy players of all time. Born in Vienna, he served in the Austro-Hungarian army during World War I; emigrated to U.S. in 1938 after Austria was annexed by Germany. World champion 1937 as a member of the Austrian Team which played in Budapest; won BARCLAY TROPHY and placed second in Spingold 1953; had a host of regional wins.

FRUEWIRTH, Robert (b. 1968) of Melbourne, Australia, chemical engineer. Third World Junior Teams 1991. Won Far East Junior Teams 1990.

FRY, Sam, Jr. (1909-1991) of New York City, secretary of the REGENCY WHIST CLUB (NYC), represented North America in Bermuda Bowl 1959; Life Master #10 when that category was created in 1936 -- at 26 years old, was the youngest of the ten. Writings on bridge and other games include *How to Win at Bridge with Any Partner* and a modern edition of Watson's *Play of the Hand at Bridge*. Contributing editor of *The Bridge World* (1932-1966) and *Bridge Encyclopedia*. He won AWL Open Tms, Open Prs 1933, 34; USDA Open Tms 1936, ABL Asbury Challenge Tms 1933, Mens Prs 1934, Spingold 1937, 41, 45; Vanderbilt 1958; placed second Vanderblt 1933, 35, 42; Master Mixed Tms 1957, Life Master Prs 1940, Open Prs 1933, 47; won numerous regional titles.

FRYDRICH, Julian (b. 1937 in Poland), owner-manager of travel agency and journalist. WBF World Master. Third Bermuda Bowl 1976, 1985, second European Championships 1975 and 1985. Represented Israel in three other world championships and 12 other European Championships. Won more than 10 national titles. Edited Israel's *Bridge Magazine* 1971-72. Co-owner Israel's biggest club.

FUCIK, Jan (b. 1956 in Czechoslovakia) of Vienna, Austria, insurance clerk and bridge professional. WBF World Life Master. Top Austrian masterpoint winner. Runner-up Bermuda Bowl 1985, World Team Olympiad 1988. Won European Open Teams 1985, European Junior Teams 1976. Second, European Team Cup 1988, European Pairs 1985, and represented Austria on many other occasions. Second European Individual 1992. Won Statenbank 1987 and 1989. 12 national victories include 9 Open Teams.

FUKUSHIMA, Everett A. (b. 1944) of Aiea HI, attorney, graduated U of Hawaii and Golden Gate U School of Law (JD), enjoys golf and travel; retained as Hawaii State Senate Republican attorney since 1976. Past president Unit Bd, member Nat'l Goodwill Committee and Nat'l Appeals Committee; certified director; directs on cruise ships. Regional wins include Desert Empire Mens Prs 1972, Open Prs 1975; Mt Shasta Open Tms 1974, Hawaii KO Tms 1976, 86, Masters Prs 1985, Swiss 1990, 91; Polar Master Prs 1986; Bridge Week KO Tms 1986, Bracketed KO Tms 1990; Ocean Shores Open Swiss 1990, KO Tms 1991, 93; BAM Swiss 1993; All-Western KO Tms 1991; Yakima KO Tms, Super Swiss 1991; Redding Open Prs 1991; Emerald Empire KO Tms, Bracketed KO Tms, Open Prs 1992.

FULWILER, C. H. (1886-1980) of Albuquerque NM, investment and finance counselor, inventor of FULWILER; was president of Western Division ACBL 1940; served on ACBL Bd of Dir; had many regional wins.

FURBECK, Barbara W. (b. 1924) of Wilmington DE, retired research chemist with one patent, graduate of Salem College; sailed and raced 36-foot boat until 1982, also enjoys golf and bowling. Appointed by governor to state Bd of Pharmacy, has served as president of that body since 1987. Furbeck won Life Master Womens Prs 1976 and Lancaster Swiss 1982.

FURMAN, David B. (b. 1941) of Lansdowne PA, financial analyst and collection specialist, won North American Swiss 1980; also Fall secondary Swiss 1980, Texas Mid-Winter Swiss 1971.

FURNISH, Bradley J. (b. 1951) of North Kansas City MO, executive director of Heartland Institute (MO), a consulting economist and instructor of economics; degrees from U of Missouri at KC. Other interests in economics, politics and trout fishing. Won Omaha Open Prs 1971, Dist 15 GN Tms 1975, 89, 90, 92; Sioux City Masters Prs, KO Tms 1978; Kansas City Mens Swiss 1987, Topeka Swiss 1989, Dist 15 GN Prs 1990, 91.

FURR, William F. (Bill) (b. 1926) of New Orleans, retired professor of mathematics. Editor of *ABA Bulletin* from 1982. Instrumental in integrating bridge in New Orleans in the early Sixties, and later president of ABA Unit there. Certified director in ABA and ACBL, and head director for ABA in the Southwest. Life Master in both leagues.

G

GABARRET, Adolfo (1890-1956) of Buenos Aires, Argentina, writer and journalist, pioneer of bridge in Argentina. Long-time participant in the Argentine BA and its tournament affairs. GABARRET CUP was donated in honor of his memory. South American champion 1954; won Argentine Open Teams 1940, 1941, 1943. Participated in a radio match against Culbertson's team in 1936. Bridge columnist for both domestic and foreign magazines; authored several books and translations.

GABOS, Gábor (b. 1931) of Budapest, Hungary, concert pianist. Many times a national champion; represented Hungary in two world championships and two European Championships.

GABRIEL, Charles P. (Garp, Charlie) (b. 1933) of Irving TX, won GN Tms 1975. Regional wins include Texas Spring and Fall Open Tms 1961, Big D Winter Swiss 1974, 80, Master Swiss, Master Prs 1980; Fall secondary Swiss, Mid-South Swiss 1978; Missouri Valley Open Prs, Indian Summer Swiss 1979, Rocky Mountain Master Prs 1980.

GABRILOVITCH, Andrew (Andy) (b. 1925) of Vienna VA, retired director of administration for ITT, graduate of Columbia U, enjoys sports, played competitive table tennis in the Forties. Escaped from Paris the day before German occupation, did mine sweeping during World War II. Past president Washington Bridge League, honored with life member status by WBL. Heavily involved in the fight to desegregate WBL 1959-64. Retired from serious bridge in protest of cheating. Won Spingold 1961, second 1959. His approximately 20 regional titles include Eastern States KOs Tms 1960, 61; Keystone Conference Open Prs 1958, Mens Tms 1970, 71, 73, Fall Mens Prs 1971, KO Tms 1974; Bermuda Swiss 1978.

GAER, Gerald W. (Jerry) (b. 1934) of Scottsdale AZ, bridge teacher and professional player. Member Unit 354 Bd of Dir, local and Unit tournament chairman, appointed to Nat'l Appeals Committee 1991, regular contributor to Unit newsletter *Shuffle Deal and Play*. Diamond Life Master. Regional wins include Mid-Winter Holiday KO Tms 1970, California Capital KO Tms 1970, 71; Fall secondary Mens Prs 1971, Desert Empire KO Tms 1974, 81; Copper State KO Tms 1977, 88; Dist 17 GN Tms 1987, Dist 17 GN Prs 1989, 92; Western States Masters Tms 1990, Mesa Sr Tms 1990, 91, Open Prs 1991, El Paso Tms 1992.

GAER, Margaret (Maggie) (Mrs. Gerald W.) (b. 1921) of Scottsdale AZ, retired bridge teacher and professional player. Diamond Life Master, won Womens Tms 1959, Life Masters Womens Prs 1964, Womens Prs 1954, 1964; placed second Mixed Prs 1964. Regional wins include Mid-Atlantic Womens Prs 1953, Missouri Valley Mixed Prs 1959, Open Tms 1961; All-Western Open Prs 1962, Mixed Prs 1963, Womens Prs 1971; Mid-Winter Holiday KO Tms 1970, California Capitol KO Tms, Open Prs 1971.

GAINES, Joel. See KANSIL, PRINCE JOLI.

GALE, Bee. See SCHENKEN, BEE.

GALLAGHER, Jacqui. See MITCHELL, JACQUI.

GALLEY, Dwight (b. 1949) of Sugarland TX, network engineer for Southwestern Bell, graduate of U of Houston and Southern Methodist; served as chairman ABA Nat'l Appeals Committee 1992 and as chairman ABA Nat'l Tournament Committee 1986-88. Has won 18 major ABA national championships (including 7 KOs and 3 Open Prs), has had nine KO Tms and two Open Pair second places. Won William A. Friend Award 1980 and was first ABA player to win more than 1000 points in one year. Current lifetime ranking in ABA is seventh with 13,500 points. In the ACBL he has won Dist 16 GN Prs 1985, Houston Open Prs, Swiss 1987.

GANDHI, Mohandas Karamchand (1869-1948), world-renowned Indian spiritual leader and advocate of the philosophy of active non-violence, not only indulged in occasional games of bridge but even used bridge as a metaphor to illustrate a basic Hindu belief. Gandhi was trained as an attorney in England. During his years as a student, he emulated the British gentleman, taking dancing lessons, learning to play the violin and enjoying sessions of bridge. In fact, "Mahatma" (or "Great Soul," as he came to be called) insists that the very first occasion on which he felt the influence of God in his life came during a bridge game at an English resort. According to Gandhi, a female member of his foursome began making lascivious advances toward him. The lonely Gandhi, having left his bride at home in India, was about to succumb to temptation. Then the Hand of God stopped him. As he advanced spiritually, Gandhi never denigrated his bridge playing or other youthful experiences, looking upon them as formative. In fact, when he later developed firm theological beliefs, mostly based upon orthodox Hinduism, he used bridge to discuss the relationship between "kharma" (predetermined fate) and "dharma" (Man's action). Kharma is analagous to the hand dealt at bridge; Dharma is how man plays the hand. Man is not bound to a predetermined destiny because he may play his hand well or poorly and it is ultimately up to him whether he wins or loses. The final result of a man's life develops from his learning, striving and skill -- not just from the hand he is dealt.

GANDENBERGER, Dr. Kurt (b. 1951) of Pendleton SC, medical doctor, publishing company president and tree farmer, graduate of Duke U, enjoys music, playing piano, singing, gardening, racquet ball and weightlifting. Began playing bridge at age 4, has been a certified director since 1974. A Diamond Life Master and winner of more than 40 regionals since 1980 including Roanoke Open Prs, Swiss 1985; Long Island Prs, Swiss 1986; Atlanta Open Prs, Morning KO Tms 1990, Open Prs 1991; Charlotte Swiss, Columbia KO Tms 1991. Gandenberger has represented Dist 4 in the GN Tms and GN Prs seven times.

GANGULY, Sudhir (b. 1943) of Calcutta, India, clearing agency proprietor. Won Far East Open Teams 1977, second BFAME Open Teams 1985, won Far East Open Pairs 1979, and represented India in one other zonal championship. 16 national wins include open teams five times and open pairs once.

GARABELLO, Giuseppe (b. 1925) of Italy, businessman. World Life Master. Won Bermuda Bowl 1973.

GARBER, Keith E. (b. 1945) of New Rochelle NY, stock and options trader; other interests are raising twin sons, crossword puzzles and word games. Member of the original PRECISION TEAM, formed by C.C. Wei. Won Continentwide Charity Fund Game 1978 and won Goldman Prs twice. Regional wins include Keystone Swiss 1969, Fun City Mens Prs 1972, Eastern States Open Prs (Goldman) 1976, 80; New England Fall KO Tms, Swiss 1990; Cambridge Swiss 1991, Dayton Morning KO Tms, Eastern States KO Tms, Fall secondary Open Prs 1992; Rye Swiss, Morning KO Tms 1993.

GARCIA, Ribeyro Jaime (b.1942) of Lima, Peru, lawyer and bank president. Represented Peru in two world championships and 10 zonal championships. Won many national titles.

GARCIA, Roberto Casalegno (b.1945) of Santiago, Chile, lawyer. Represented Chile in three world championships and eight zonal championships. Second in Chilean rankings, and won all national titles.

GARCIA-HUIDOBRO, Enrique Toro (b. 1948) of Santiago, Chile, industrialist. Represented Chile in two world championships and seven zonal championships. Won all national titles.

GARDENER, Nico (formerly Goldinger) (1908-1989) of London, England, born in Latvia, bridge teacher and writer. Won World Mixed Teams 1962. Second World Teams 1960. Won European Teams 1950, 1961, second 1953. Represented Britain in two other world championships and two other zonal championships. Won *Sunday Times* Pairs 1970. National wins include Gold Cup. Founded and directed London School of Bridge. Co-author of two books. Devised GARDENER NOTRUMP OVERCALL. Won medals for ballroom dancing. See FAMILY.

GARDENER, Nicola. See SMITH, Nicola.

GARDENER, Patricia (1912-1988) of Canford Cliffs, England. Represented Britain in four zonal championships. Won several national titles. See FAMILY.

GARDINER, Jerre J. (Mrs. Henry) of Fort Worth TX, bridge teacher, club director, runs bridge seminars and bridge cruises. Enjoys horse racing, reading and travel; has served several times on Unit Bd of Dir in various positions. Regional wins include Big D Open Prs 1976, Capital City Swiss 1977, Fall secondary Womens Swiss 1978, Republic of TX Womens Prs, Oklahoma City Womens Swiss 1981; Fort Worth Masters Tms 1991, Houston Team of Two Prs 1992.

GARDNER, Craig (b. 1951) of Hanover Park IL, accountant-vice president in charge of finance, graduated Georgetown U, enjoys golf, bowling and computer strategy simulations. Coordinator for Chicago inter-city KO Tms 1988-92. Diamond Life Master. Regional wins include Champagne Master Prs 1981, Central States I Mens Tms 1983, BAM Tms 1987, 90, 93, Bracketed KO Tms 1992; Central States II Mens KO Tms 1984, 86, 87, Smoking Swiss 1987, Swiss 1987, Mens Tms 1988, Open Swiss 91; Grand Rapids Swiss 1986, Oconomowoc Swiss 1988, Summer secondary Prs 1989, Dist 13 GN Prs, Las Vegas Standard Card Prs 1990; Ft Wayne Dist 8 Swiss 1991, Cleveland Prs 1992.

GARDNER, James L. (b. 1946) of Lansing MI, data processing consultant. Diamond Life Master; placed second Mens Tms 1981; resigned in protest from tournament play with more than 30 regional wins including Midwest Spring Swiss, Dist 5 Swiss 1973; Great Lakes KO Tms 1979, Canadian Nat'l Open Prs, Wolverine Open Prs, Thunder Bay Swiss, Motor City Open Prs 1981.

GARDNER, Robert R. (Bob) (b. 1946) of Chicago, company vice president and chief financial officer, educated at Notre Dame and DePaul U; Diamond Life Master; has won Tri-Unit Mens Prs 1970, Mixed Prs 1973; Gopher Mens Prs 1972, Spring secondary Swiss 1973, Central States Swiss 1978, 87, BAM Swiss 1978, Masters Prs

1979, Open Prs 1987; Wisconsin KO Tms 1978, Masters Prs 1988; Kalamazoo Swiss 1986, Indianapolis Mens Prs 1987, Summer secondary Prs 1989, Dist 13 GN Prs 1990, Great Lakes Prs 1991.

GARDNER, Thomas W. (Tom) (b. 1921) of Southfield MI, company vice-president, graduated Purdue U, organizer (winner two years) of first University Team of Four championship (BAM), organizer of first Big Ten interuniversity league of four schools. Gardner has played with five generations of family from grandparents to grandchildren in tournament competition; had 41 bombing missions in WW II and was awarded Distinguished Flying Cross and seven other air medals; headed search for site of new Detroit Lions football stadium. First alternate for ACBL Bd of Dir; member of ACBL Bd of Gov and Nat'l Goodwill Committee; bridge instructor offering free classes. Diamond Life Master with many regional wins including Florida Swiss, Life Master Prs 1975; Veterans Day Swiss 1981, Buffalo Prs, Pittsburgh Swiss, Fall secondary KO Tms, Hudson Master Prs 1988; Lancaster KO Tms, Dayton Mixed Prs 1989; Saginaw Swiss 1991.

GARGRAVE, Jeffrey J. (Jeff) (b. 1949) of Pasadena CA, tax attorney, educated at Wright St U and U of Santa Clara. Won nat'l convention Battle Plan 1991. Involved in Nat'l and Dist committee work. Certified director, directs on bridge cruises. Diamond Life Master, has won more than 30 regionals including Great Lakes Swiss 1973, Mens Prs 1977; Music City Swiss, Motor City Master Prs, Swiss 1973; Dist 11 GN Tms 1973, 76, Zone III 1976; Dist 11 Swiss 1974, Midwest Spring Open Prs 1975, All-Western KO Tms 1991, 92; California Capitol Evening and Morning KO Tms 1993.

GARNER, Michael (b. 1940) of Bala Cynwyd PA, options trader. Was first of the now hundreds of bridge players to join an options exchange and trade listed options. Won Pittsburgh Open Tms 1966, Keystone Master Prs 1967, Mens Prs 1970, Master Prs 1973; Puerto Rico Mens Prs, Open Prs and Open Tms 1971; Mid-Atlantic Fall Master Prs 1971, Central States I KO Tms 1974.

GAROZZO, Benito (b. 1927) of Palm Beach FL, formerly of Rome, Italy, retired jewelry store owner, considered by many experts as the world's best player during his World Championship years.

Until 1976 he was never on a losing team in international competition. Garozzo and Pietro Forquet formed one of the great partnerships of the world through 1972.

From 1972 to 1976 he paired with Giorgio Belladonna in what many considered to be the best partnership in the world during those years. A WBF Grand Master, he ranked second in lifetime ratings in the world behind Belladonna as of 1993. He was a member of the LANCIA TEAM that toured the United States in 1975.

Co-creator (with Belladonna) of *Precision and Super Precision Bidding, The Blue Club* and *The Italian Blue Team Bridge Book* (see also BLUE TEAM). He won World Team Olympiad 1964, 68, 72; Bermuda Bowl 1961, 62, 63, 65, 66, 67, 69, 73, 74, 75, PAMP Individual Geneva 1990; placed second in World Open Prs 1970, Bermuda Bowl 1976, 79; placed 4th in World Open Prs 1966, 7th World Mixed Tms 1972, 6th Rosenblum Cup Tms 1982, 7th Olympiad Open Tms 1984; European champion 1969, 71, 73, 75, 79. Italian nat'l wins include Italian Open Tms

1958, 63, 67, 68 among others.

In ACBL has won Mens Prs 1971, North American Swiss 1984; placed second Mixed Prs 1983, Open Swiss 1993; has won several regional titles. He became a U.S. citizen in January 1994. See BLUE TEAM, LANCIA TEAM and SHARIF BRIDGE CIRCUS.

GARRELL, Shirley A. (Lucy) (Mrs. Burton, formerly Neilson) (1925-1984) of Agincourt ON, was a Regional 4 tournament director; won All-American Mixed Prs 1961, Canadian Nat'l Womens Prs 1961, Upper New York State Swiss 1971.

GARYN, Stephen (b. 1936) of Melville NY, CPA, tax accountant, graduate of Baruch College; 12 handicap golfer. Won Dist 24 GN Prs 1979, 81; Tri-State Mens Swiss 1980, Long Island Swiss 1981, Sr Open Prs 1992; Southeastern Open Prs 1985, Florida Flighted Open Prs, Lancaster Sr Open Swiss 1991.

GATES, Georgiana (b. 1945) of Houston TX, computer systems analyst, educated at Houston Baptist College, U of Houston and Rice U. Member City of Houston Electrical Board 1987-present, has contributed to *The Bridge World*; Diamond Life Master. Won Womens Prs 1988; placed second Womens KO Tms 1989. Regional wins include San Francisco Womens Swiss 1973, Redding Masters Prs, SF Mixed Prs, Reno Womens Swiss 1974; Kansas City Womens Swiss 1977, Corpus Christi Open Prs 1982, Dist 16 GN Tms 1984, Lake Charles Womens Swiss, KO Tms 1985; Houston Swiss 1987, Dist 16 NA Prs 1988.

GAULT, Gregory F. (Greg) (b. 1941) of Raleigh NC, high school psychology teacher, U of Arizona graduate; coach of golf team, enjoys bowling, is an expert in subliminal advertising. Was involved in local bridge in Tucson and currently assists wife running tournaments in Raleigh. Gault was a main witness in the Cokin/Sion case. Won International City Mens Prs 1971, Dist 7 GN Tms 1975, 89; Washington Bridge Week Mixed Prs 1977, Summer secondary Mixed Prs 1991.

GAWRYS, Piotr (b. 1955) of Warsaw, Poland, bridge professional and former architect. World Life Master. Won World Teams 1984, second Bermuda Bowl 1991. Won European Individual 1992, European Cup 1984. Won Cavendish 1990. Represented Poland in three other world championships and four zonal championships. Won many national titles.

GAZZARI, Paula (b. 1947) of Santiago, Chile, artist. Represented Chile in one world championships and eight zonal championships.

GELEERD, William L. Jr. (Bill) (b. 1930) of Highland Park IL, wine importer, broker and consultant, retired Army Reserve colonel --Intelligence Branch, graduate of Syracuse U and U.S. Army Command and General Staff College. Won Sr and Advanced Sr Master Prs 1971 and Central States BAM Tms 1989.

GELLMAN, Adair (b. 1968) of Rockville MD, computer systems analyst for Compucare, graduated U of Maryland, enjoys singing and reading mysteries. Vice president Youth Bridge Federation 1989-90, secretary of Washington BL 1992-94. Has represented Juniors to ACBL Bd of Dir and Bd of Gov, QUEEN OF BRIDGE 1985, became youngest female Life Master 1982 (14 yrs 6 mos 4 days). Placed second Mixed Prs 1990. Won Spring secondary BAM Tms 1982, Swiss 1984; Reno Mixed Prs 1988, Washington DC Womens Swiss, Swiss 1991; Cherry Hill Prs, Swiss 1992.

GENUD, Maury (b. 1940) of Tarzana CA, child psychologist and teacher, was ACBL analyst of the 1965 Team Trials report, former contributor to *The Bridge World* and columnist for *Los Angeles Bridge News*. Won Open Prs 1967 and many regional events.

GEORGE, Jan (formerly of Pittsburgh PA). See Shane, Jan.

GEORGE, Noldy (b. 1955) of Jakarta, Indonesia, company employee. Won Far East Teams 1991, 1992, represented Indonesia in one world championship.

GERARD, Joan Levy (b. 1935) of White Plains NY, former 1st grade teacher, administrator for private boys and girls camps, assistant to general manager of hotel handling personnel, purchasing, advertising; graduate of Smith College. Has served in all aspects of bridge administration starting at the Unit level, is a member of Nat'l Goodwill Committee. She was Unit 188 Sec 1969, tournament chairman 1975, president 1976; Dist 3 president 1976-85. In 1985 became Dist 3 representative to Nat'l Bd of Dir, served as ACBL president 1992 and chairman of the Board 1993. Won Keystone Master Prs 1974, Autumn Leaf Swiss 1979, Dist 9 KOs 1990, Tri-State Swiss 1991, Corpus Christi Open Prs 1992.

GERARD, Ronald (Ron) (b. 1944) of White Plains NY, pension attorney, graduated Harvard and Michigan Law School (JD), Likes classical music, tennis and college basketball. Contributor to *The Bridge World, Italian Bridge* and authored *1-2-3 Two-Bids*. WBF World Master, placed 13th Rosenblum Tms 1982; was 12th in world in World Simultaneous Prs 1988. Diamond Life Master; has won Spingold, Blue Ribbon Prs 1981, Mens Tms 1985, Vanderbilt 1990; placed second GN Tms 1976, GN Prs 1980, 83; Mens Tms 1983; Vanderbilt 1994. Some of his many regional wins are NY-NJ Open Prs 1973, 76; Keystone Master Prs 1974, Dist 3 Mens Swiss 1978, 79; Tri-State Mens Prs, Mens Swiss 1979; Dist 4 Swiss 1980, Dist 3 GN Tms 1975, 78, Zone II 1976, 78, 80.

GERBER, John (1906-1981) of Houston TX, famous as the inventor of the GERBER FOUR-CLUB ACE-ASKING CONVENTION; served for two years on the ACBL Bd of Dir and was a highly important and influential power in bridge politics. At North American Championships, an early riser, he could usually be found in a comfortable chair in the hotel lobby, collecting and dispensing information.

He was non-playing captain of North American Tms in the Bermuda Bowl competitions of 1962, 63, 65. He was in the eye of a storm on more than one occasion. In 1962 in New York he split the partnerships of Bobby Nail-Mervyn Key and Lew Mathe-Ron von der Porten, putting Mathe and Nail together as partners in an unusual move that worked well and almost capture the title from Italy.

The next year in St. Vincent, Italy, he again broke up a long established partnership, pairing Nail with Howard Schenken and benching Peter Leventritt and Jim Jacoby. This move was not successful and may have cost the Americans the championship.

It followed a little known incident that occurred at the time Gerber arrived at the Grand Hotel Bilia. An anonymous letter written in Italian was delivered to him. He secured a translator, but after the first paragraph was read to him, he asked the translator to stop; to deliver the letter to Italy's captain, Carl'Alberto Perroux and to explain that Gerber had listened only to the first paragraph. The writer had accused the BLUE TEAM of cheating.

Perroux, after reading the letter to his team, suggested that the match be played with screens running across the tables (this was 12 years before present-day screens were employed), but Gerber would have none of it. The goodwill engendered by this exchange inspired Perroux and his team to present their championship trophies to Gerber and the American team in what was described as the greatest act of sportsmanship in bridge history.

When Gerber's daring move to pair Schenken with Nail backfired, he faced a lot of flak, but the ACBL Board nevertheless appointed him captain of the next Bermuda Bowl team in 1965. That was the time when two members of his team brought cheating charges against a British partnership. (See BUENOS AIRES AFFAIR). Gerber spent 10 minutes in the grandstand watching the famous British pair who were accused of using finger signals to tell each other how many hearts were held. The 10 minutes were enough to convince him and he became one of the strongest witnesses against the pair when the World Bridge Federation suspended them.

A very strong captain, Gerber was a great player in his own right. He represented North America in the Bermuda Bowl in Buenos Aires 1961 and won the Chicago (now the Reisinger) 1964, Master Mixed Tms 1964, Mens Prs 1959, Mens Tms 1953; placed second Spingold 1954, 67; Chicago 1957, 59; Mens Prs 1957, Master Mixed Tms 1967, Mixed Prs 1953, 68; Life Master Mens Prs 1971. He also won many regionals.

GERONTOPOULOS, Panos (b.1949) of Athens, Greece, university lecturer, land surveyor, bridge writer and adminstrator. Member of WBF Executive Council and chairman of its Youth Committee. Member of EBL Executive and chairman of its Youth Committee and its Press and Publications Committee. Editor of *EBL News* and *EBL Review*. Chief organizer of 1991 Common Market Championships. Awarded EBL Silver Medal in 1991 for services to European bridge. Author in Greek of *Parabolic Victory Points Scales* and *On the Comparability of Pairs Movements*. Former bridge correspondent of *Messimvrini* and contributor to *Greek Bridge*. Member INTERNATIONAL BRIDGE PRESS ASSOCIATION Executive. Graduate of U of Thessaloniki, Greece, Oxford, and U of Graz, Austria.

GERSTMAN, Daniel M. (Dan) (b. 1948) of Buffalo NY, financial planner, won Open Prs 1981, Life Master Mens Prs 1982; placed second Open Prs 1982, 83. Diamond Life Master. His many regional wins include Syracuse Mens Prs, Fall secondary Open Prs 1972, All-American KO Tms 1976, 77, 88, 90, 93, Mens Swiss 1987, 88; Pittsburgh Labor Day Master Prs 1976, Mens Swiss 1980, 88, Mens Prs 1986; Rochester KO Tms 1978, Open Swiss

1982, Swiss 1984; Buffalo Mens Swiss 1980, 86, KO Tms 1984, 90, 92, Mens Prs 1985, Open Swiss 1992; Bowling Green Open Prs 1984, KO Tms 1988; Dayton Open Swiss 1986, Syracuse KO Tms 1987.

GIANERA, J. Howard (b. 1936) of Rancho Sante Fe CA, retired auto dealer, former mayor of La Crescenta CA, active locally in business and community organizations. Has served as Unit president and vice-president; won 14 unrestricted regional titles and five Flt B events.

GHAZI, Rashidul (b. 1948) of Karachi, Pakistan, bank executive. WBF World Master. Won BFAME zonal pairs championship 1985 and played in three world championships. Won many national titles.

GHESTEM, Pierre (b. 1929) of Lille, France, retired merchant; WBF Grand Master; Bermuda Bowl champion 1956; won World Team Olympiad 1960; European champion 1953, 1955, 1962, second in 1956, 1961; represented France in Bermuda Bowl 1954, 1961, 1963, European Championship 1965; won French Open Teams 1962, 1964; third PAMP Pairs 1990. National wins include open teams many times. Former world checker champion; former French chess champion. Inventor of complex MONACO SYSTEM with which he had many major successes in partnership with René Bacherich.

GHOSE, Santanu (b. 1948) of Calcutta, India, civil engineer, computer programmer and businessman. WBF World Master. Second BFAME Open Teams 1985 and 1989, Open Pairs 1985. Fourth World Open Teams 1988; represented India in three other world championships and one other zonal championship. 10 national wins include open teams four times and open pairs once. Won Epson Play Award 1987. Member WBF Laws Committee, Convention Card Committee and several Appeals Committees. Joint Secretary Bridge Federation of India 1981. BFAME *Daily Bulletin* editor 1991.

GHOSH, K. (Gora) of Calcutta, India, lawyer. Won Far East Teams 1977 and national open teams once.

GHOSH, Sukha Ranjan (b. 1935) of Calcutta, India, government servant. Won Far East Teams 1977; represented India in two other zonal championships and three world championships. 24 national wins include open teams 6 times and open pairs twice.

GIBBS, Gordon M. (1898-1968) of Rochester NY, had the unique distinction of serving as the last president of the ABL and the first president of the ACBL (1937); also served as ACBL treasurer seven years. His massive figure — he was a member of the New York Giants football team — was a familiar sight at early tournaments. He was the occasional partner and teammate of such luminaries as Charles Goren, Harry Fishbein, Helen Sobel and Sidney Silodor. His bridge victories included several regional titles.

GIELKENS, Ine (b. 1957), of Monnickendam, The Netherlands, mathematics teacher. WBF World Master. Second Venice Cup 1989; represented The Netherlands in two other world championships and two European Championships. Won National Women's Pairs 1991.

GILL, Brigadier General Robert J. (1889-1983) of Baltimore, retired attorney, ACBL president in 1941, chairman of ACBL Committee on Membership Eligibility 1952; named 1945 Honorary Member; served in both World Wars and received many military decorations; was appointed chief military counsel to Supreme Court Justice Robert Jackson at the War Trials in Nurenburg 1945.

GILPIN, Alfred B. (Big Al) (1915-1984) of Riverside CA, bridge teacher and club director, active member of ACBL Bd of Gov from 1964, vice chairman 1980-82, member of ACBL Bd of Dir 1969-75. Also served two terms as president of the Western Conference; was member of Western Conference assembly nine years; retired from U.S. Civil Service Commission where he had been project head for Navy Air-Launched Missile program; won Fall secondary Swiss 1976.

GINGRICH, James E. Jr. (Jim) (b. 1953) of Lansdale PA, actuary with U.S. Healthcare, graduate of Whitman College; fellow of Society of Actuaries, member of the Academy of Actuaries and winner of a National Science Foundation scholarship; contributor to *The Bridge World*. Won New York Swiss 1985, Cambridge Non-Smoking Open Prs 1986, Swiss 1986; Cromwell Swiss 1987; NY Swiss 1989, Manchester Swiss 1989, 92; Fall secondary Open Prs 1991.

GIOVINE, Michele (b. 1922) of Milan, Italy, car agent. Second European Teams 1952, 1955. Three Italian national wins include open teams once. Co-inventor of MARMIC SYSTEM, and co-author of a book on it.

GIRAGOSIAN, Robert P. (Bob) (b. 1950) of Bakersfield CA, general manager of Grimmway Farms, graduate California State U, Claremont Graduate School. Has served Dist 22 as Bd member and GN Tms co-ordinator, is member Nat'l Goodwill Committee. Won All-Western Life Master Prs 1973, Dist 22 GN Tms 1974, 85, 87; Raincross KO Tms 1978, Golden State Swiss 1981, Super Open Prs 1987; Dist 22 GN Prs 1986.

GITCHEL, Ronna (Roni) (b. 1951) of Pittsburgh PA, in epidemiological, cancer, drugs and alcohol research, educated U of Pittsburgh, enjoys jazz and other music. Unit president, member Bd of Gov and Executive Bd of Dist 5. Regional wins include Cleveland Womens Tms 1986, 87, 88; Pittsburgh Womens Tms 1986, Mixed Prs 1988; Arlington Open Prs 1988, Fall secondary Womens Prs 1988, Dist 5 GN Tms 1990, Toronto Womens Tms 1990.

GITELMAN, Fred (b. 1965) of Toronto ON, computer programmer specializing in bridge software. Creator of Base III, Bridge Master and Pendergraph Vugraph programs. Member ACBL Junior team, placed second World Junior Championships 1991; also represented ACBL Epson International bridge tournament Tokyo 1984, 85; represented Canada Maccabiah Games 1993. Won more than 15 regionals including Canadian Nat'ls Swiss 1988, 89, Bracketed KO Tms, Fltd KO Tms 1994; Frontier Swiss 1989.

GIUSSANI, John (b. 1931 in England) of La Paz, Bolivia, insurance company director. Represented Bolivia in 5 zonal championships. 12 national titles include 5 open teams and 6 open pairs. Tournament director and former president of Bolivian Bridge Association.

GLASER, Leo (The Leaper) (b. 1946) of Markham ON, born in Sweden, purchasing agent, enjoys photography and curling. Has won numerous regionals including Nat'l Capital Open Prs 1975, Mens Swiss 1980; Can-Am KO Tms 1978, 80, Swiss 1980; Gateway City Swiss, Dist 1 GN Prs, GN Tms Zone III 1981. Glaser has had double wins in Montreal, Ottawa, North Bay and Cornwall.

GLATT, Arthur (1909-1975) of Lincolnwood IL, financial consultant, technical adviser to the TV program *Championship Bridge*. Won Mens Prs, Mens Tms 1946, Open Prs 1951; was second in Chicago (now the Reisinger) 1936, Mixed Prs 1936, Spingold 1948, Life Master Prs 1949, 52; Spring Mens Tms 1962; won numerous regionals.

GLENN, Richard M. (Dick) (b. 1917) of Sarasota FL, retired stock broker, also founded and operated a large personnel placement service, educated at Princeton and Harvard Business School, U.S. Navy Reserve Lt. Cdr.; has received several commendations. Diamond Life Master; has won several regionals including Mid-Atlantic Spring Mens Prs 1956, 71; Summer secondary Commercial and Industrial Tms 1961, Mid-South Master Prs, Mens Prs 1974; Summer secondary Sr Tms 1991, several senior events in 1990 and 91. Won his first tournament on board the S.S. France at age 12 in 1930 and played with 27 different partners when they become Life Masters.

GLENN, Bob (b. 1948) of Chicago, professional bridge player since 1983, former vice president of management consulting firm, educated at Vanderbilt and U of Chicago, enjoys stock market and spectator sports. Grand Life Master with more than 14,000 masterpoints. Some of his more than 130 regional victories, which include wins in every ACBL district, are Summer secondary Silver Trophy Prs, Great Lakes Master Swiss, Central States II Master Prs 1978; Canadian Nat'l Mens Prs, Midwest Spring Open Prs 1981.

GLICK, Jefferson (Jeff) (1906-1985) of North Miami Beach, bridge administrator, was instrumental in organizing the Florida Unit, subsequently the largest unit of the ACBL. He was its president 1949-65 and was executive manager from 1965-79; served as chairman of two international tournaments and four North American Championships, all held in Miami. ACBL president 1955 and Honorary Member 1964. Npc of the U.S. team which placed second in the Bermuda Bowl 1956. Won Spingold 1949, Chicago (now the Reisinger) 1949, Mens Tms 1947, 48, 54, 58; Mixed Prs 1941, Asbury Challenge Tms 1934; placed second in Spingold 1934, 52; Chicago 1952; also won numerous regionals.

GLICK, Vera (Mrs. Jefferson) of Miami Beach, served as co-chairman of the 1975 Summer NABC held in Miami. She won Womens Tms 1953, Mixed Prs 1941 and many regional titles.

GLICKSTEIN, Earl H. (b. 1941) of Gaithersburg MD, programming manager for IBM, educated U of Maine, served on Unit 147 Bd of Dir 1980-85. Regional wins include Arlington Open Prs 1985, Open Conventions Prs 1988, KO Tms 1990; VA Beach Open Prs 1985, Mens Tms, Open Prs 1987, KO Tms 1989; Alexandria Master

Prs 1989, Greenville Mens KO Tms, Gatlinburg Swiss 1993; Cherry Hill KO Tms, KO Tms 1993; Charlotte Open Prs, Virginia Beach Handicap KO Tms 1993, Lancaster KO Tms.

GLUBOK, Brian (Gluby) (b. 1959) of New York City, bridge professional, novelist, rubber bridge player, graduate of Amherst College. Interests include writing, travel, cycling, rock music, current events, sports, history, literature, frisbee, backgammon, meditation and political science. Since 1985 he has divided time between New York and Sydney, Australia. In 1989 was granted residency status in Australia (in recognition of his bridge achievements) through the category "Special Talents - Sporting". Became Life Master at age 15 and his first major win was Eastern States KO Tms 1980 -- the youngest ever to win this event at 20, breaking the record of Kyle Larsen who first won it in 1973 at the age of 23. At 17 was a finalist in NABC Reisinger partnered by Oswald Jacoby. At 18 again partnered with Oswald Jacoby he competed in the 50th annual Goldman Prs. Jacoby, who had won the first Goldman in 1927, advised Glubok to "quit bridge and go back to college." Winner with Edgar Kaplan of the International Bridge Press Association ROMEX AWARD for best bid hand of 1990-91. A WBF World Master, he placed fourth in World Open Prs 1990, 17th Rosenblum Tms 1990. Won Spingold 1987, Reisinger 1991; placed second Spingold 1980, 83, 86; GN Tms 1981, Blue Ribbon Prs 1990; second Mott-Smith Trophy 1990; won Gold Medal in Maccabean Games 1983; won Australian Nat'l Open Tms 1990 (second in 1987). Has placed high in int'l money tournaments. A four-time winner of the Cavendish Tms, most recent 1993, 3rd 1990, 4th 1991; Canadian Invitational Prs 1st 1993, 2nd 1992; has had dozens of regional wins. A contributor to *The Bridge World, ACBL Bulletin, Popular Bridge, Australian Bridge, New Zealand Bridge*. He also writes on non-bridge subjects.

GLYNNE, Tony Christopher (b. 1947) of Portland OR, born in United Kingdom, formerly of Birmingham, England; professional bridge player, teacher and director, educated at Birmingham U. Does auctioneering for charitable organizations and enjoys cooking. Became education producer of Uganda TV in East Africa 1967 and while there climbed Mt. Kilimanjaro. From 1970 to 75 was the senior producer for BBC radio in Birmingham and interviewed a variety of entertainment stars. Represented England in 1975 in CAMROSE TROPHY match versus Wales, and represented ACBL in Pan American Championships 1992. Placed second Open Prs 1992. Diamond Life Master; has won more than 80 regionals since 1976.

GODFREY, Kerr M. (Deputy Dog) (b. 1951) of San Antonio TX, deputy constable, local and tournament director, graduated U of Texas, tournament backgammon player.Won San Juan Master Prs 1980, Tulsa Mens Swiss, New Orleans KO Tms 1981; Dallas Swiss 1982, El Paso Open Prs 1988, Mexico City Master Prs, Corpus Christi Masters Swiss 1990; San Antonio Open Prs, Ft Worth Masters Swiss 1991.

GOENKA, Prem Chand of Guwahati, India, managing director of carbon company. BFAME founder-president 1978 and continuing, with number of member countries increasing from 5 to 14. President of Indian Bridge Federation 1971-74, 1976-78, 1980-84. President Emeritus 1984-. During his presidency number of players rose from 430 to more than 12,000, and the number of organizations from 12 to 27. Pioneered carbon production in India. Chairman of Confederation of Indian Industries. President Assam Manufacturers Association. Former president of Table Tennis Federation of India.

GOKHALE, Avinash S. (b. 1947) of Pune, India, advertising agent. WBF World Master. Second BFAME Open Teams 1989. Fourth World Open Teams 1988 and represented India in three other world championships. 17 national wins include open teams twice. Joint secretary Bridge Federation of India 1980. INBA vice-president. BFAME *Daily Bulletin* editor 1983. Former editor of *Bridge Digest*.

GOLD, Don (b. 1919) of San Jose CA, born in England, served with British Royal Air Force during WWII; retired computer programmer; was member of Stanford Systems Programming Group since 1963. Has had four holes-in-one in golf, enjoys computer programming. Author of *Intermediate Two-Bids in Bridge*.

GOLD, Sam (1908-1982) of Montreal, retailer, tournament director, member of the Nat'l Laws Commission, was one of the leading Canadian players. In 1948 became Life Master #132, the second Canadian to achieve that rank. Represented Canada in 1964 World Team Olympiad; won Canadian-American Open Tms 1952, 54, 66, 67, Mens Prs 1956, 57; was member of Montreal Intercity Team which won the Congress Trophy in Montreal 1967 and in New York 1968. Charter member of the Montreal Bridge League in early Thirties and was instrumental in having the MBL affiliate with ACBL in 1946. Contributed many new tournament movements to the ACBL, the most notable being the THREE-QUARTER MOVEMENT now universally used for one-winner duplicate games.

GOLDBERG, Freddie (Mrs. Richard) of Nashville TN, formerly of Memphis, former bridge teacher. Her active bridge career proved a valuable background for her role as wife of the ACBL executive secretary. Member of the Nat'l Goodwill Committee; has won several regional events.

GOLDBERG, Richard L. (Dick) (b. 1922) of Nashville TN, formerly of Memphis, was ACBL executive secretary and general manager 1971-1984. His first official connection with ACBL was as a regional tournament director 1959 and a national tournament director 1961. He was brought to ACBL Nat'l Headquarters in New York to take over tournament scheduling in 1963 and was groomed for ACBL's top job by serving as assistant to the executive secretary 1965-71, when he succeeded Easley Blackwood. The smooth transition of ACBL Headquarters from Greenwich to Memphis was achieved under his aegis. Goldberg was active in WORLD BRIDGE FEDERATION affairs. Zone II representative in 1972, he was elected WBF secretary 1981; later became treasurer, then financial director of that body. Member of ACBL Laws Commission, ACBL Goodwill Committee. He is also a member of the World Bridge Federation Committee of Honor. Has won several regional events. ACBL Honorary Member 1994.

GOLDBERG, Steve of Miami, won Reisinger 1972, Spingold 1974; placed second Mens Tms 1973.

GOLDER, Colonel Benjamin M. (1894-1946) died the day before the close of his term as 1946 ACBL president. Member Pennsylvania State Legislature 1916-24; later elected to U.S. House of Representatives, where he served 1924-33; ACBL Homorary Member 1947. A trophy in his memory, the GOLDER CUP, was put into play 1947.

GOLDFEIN, Jerome R. (Jerry) (b. 1956) of Chicago, office manager for law firm, formerly an options trader; graduated Northern Illinois U; other interests are computers, sports and family. Teaches beginning bridge, became a Life Master at age 18 and won first national championship at 22. Diamond Life Master. Won GN Tms 1979, 91; placed second Vanderbilt 1982, Spingold 1983, GN Tms 1984, 88; North American Swiss 1988, 89; won more than 25 regionals.

GOLDMAN, Robert (Bobby) (b. 1938) of Highland Village TX, bridge professional, former vice president cable television company; interests include volleyball, tennis, basketball; was a high school singles tennis champion; as a freshman at Drexel U was captain of Mid-Atlantic Conference basketball champions 1957-58; served as an ACBL recorder 1986-88. Taught bridge classes, as many as 17 per week, in early 70s; wrote lesson plans, computer bridge practice hands, a computer program to evaluate bidding probabilities and TV scripts for *Play Bridge with the Experts*.

Is originator of SUPER GERBER (Kickback), EXCLUSION BLACKWOOD, Goldman after Stayman and other elements of ACES SCIENTIFIC SYSTEM. Author of *Aces Scientific* and *Winners and Losers at the Bridge Table*. Has been prominent in President's Advisory Committee activities, i.e.: Alerts, conventions, slow play, ethics, committee (appeals) precedent book.

Grand Master in both ACBL and WBF, ranks 13th on all-time ACBL masterpoint list with more than 18,500 points (as of May 1993) and is 11th (as of Feb. 1992) in all-time rankings on the WBF list. Was a member of first ACES team put together by Ira Corn 1968, remained a member of team until 1974. Won Bermuda Bowl 1970, 71, 79; World Mixed Tms 1972; also represented U.S. in Bermuda Bowl 1969, 73, 74; competed in other World Bridge Federation events 1972, 78, 84; placed 5-8th in the World Olympiad Tms in Seattle 1984; won both pair and team event at 1977 Pan-American Invitational Championships.

North American championships include Life Master Mens Prs 1964, Life Master Prs 1968, Open BAM Tms 1993; Mens Tms 1968, 89, 91; Spingold 1969, 78, 83, 86, 88; Reisinger 1970, 76, 80; Vanderbilt 1971, 73, 78; placed second Vanderbilt 1966, 70, 76; Spingold 1970, 90; Reisinger 1968, 86, 90, 93; Blue Ribbon Prs 1968, Mens Tms 1969, Life Master Prs 1968, Mens BAM Tms 1984. Had won three world championships, two NABC pair events and many NABC team events before ever winning his first regional pair event in 1974; since that time has won hundreds of regional events.

GOLDSMITH, Arthur S. (b. 1909) of Lyndhurst OH, retired attorney, Life Master #42, graduate of Yale and Western Reserve U Law School (JD) where he received

"Order of Coif". Other interests include photography and world travel. Won Spingold 1949, Chicago (now the Reisinger) 1949, Mens Tms 1947, 54, 58; placed second in the Spingold 1946, 52; Chicago 1952. Regional wins include All-American Open Tms 1953, Mens Prs 1978, Open Prs 1979.

GOLDSTEIN, Lin (b. 1962) of Butte MT, software engineer, won first Non-Life Master Prs 1981.

GOLDSTEIN, Rick (b. 1946) of White Plains NY, special education teacher, co-owner of Bridge Deck in Westchester, certified director, educated at Fairleigh Dickinson U and Manhattanville College. Enjoys stamp collecting. Diamond Life Master; has won more than 25 regionals including Summer secondary Mens Prs, Fall secondary Open Swiss 1985, Cherry Hill Swiss 1985, Dist 3 GN Prs 1986, 90, 91; Summer Open Prs, Reno Mixed Prs 1989; Dist 3 Open Prs 1990, Mid-Atlantic Mixed Prs 1991, Greater NY Open Swiss 1993, Spring secondary Open Prs 1992.

GOLDSTEIN, Abraham M. (Abe) (1902-1982) of Flushing NY, bridge teacher and director for more than 25 years, club owner for 10 years. Mentor of many young players who became successful, notably Bobby Levin. Authored *Common-Sense Bridge for the Intermediate Player*. Won Eastern States Master Prs 1943, 49, KO Tms 1949; Fall secondary Senior Master Individual 1950.

GOLDSTEIN, Barry (b. 1952) of Yonkers NY, attorney, served as ACBL area manager in Westchester for the education program and was a bridge professional. Before retiring from bridge he accumulated 18 regional wins including the first Jerry Machlin Open Prs 1983, Lancaster Mens Prs 1985, Thunder Bay Open Swiss 1990, Albany KO Tms 1991. In 1990 he won Albany Open Prs as his 85-year-old partner, Manny Dannet, was winning his first regional.

GOLDSTEIN, Gratian B. (b. 1919) of Coral Gables FL, retired, import business owner, Diamond Life Master. Won Womens Prs 1947, 48; Womens Tms 1948, 53; Life Master Womens Prs 1969, Master Mixed Tms 1955, 58; placed second Womens Prs 1953, Blue Ribbon Prs 1966, Womens Tms 1971, Mixed Prs 1972, Mixed Tms 1967. Had numerous regional wins in the Fifties and Sixties.

GOLDSTEIN, Stephen D. (b. 1947) of Cheverly MD, reporter and bridge columnist for *Washington Times*, graduated City College of NY, currently attending law school. Has written daily bridge column since 1982. Winner of Mens Tms 1974, placed second Vanderbilt and Reisinger 1974. His several regional titles include Eastern States Master Prs 1970, Fun City KO Tms 1972, New England KO Tms 1974.

GOLDWATER, Henry A. (Harry) (b. 1901) of Yonkers NY, ACBL national tournament director since 1957. Since 1962 has served as an adviser to ACBL Laws Commission and is a contributing editor to the *Bridge Encyclopedia*.

GOLDWATER, Robert A. (Bob) (b. 1924) of Hartsdale NY, formerly in public relations field with NBC and Xerox Corp, was sports information director of Fordham U and did promotion work with NY State Olympic Committee, graduate of U of North Carolina. Certified director (since 1976) and teacher. Has served on Unit 188 Bd of Dir since 1967 and held various executive positions including president, vice-president, tournament chairman; is member Nat'l Goodwill Committee. Has written Sunday bridge column for Gannett Suburban Newspapers since 1976. Won Summer secondary Senior Prs 1986, Dist 3 GN Prs 1987.

GOMEZ-DIAZ, Gala de Reschko de, of Las Palmas, Canary Islands, tournament organizer. Many national titles include open teams, women's teams and mixed pairs. Member of Spanish open team in one world championship and two European Championships. Represented Spain in women's and mixed play on 21 occasions including six other world championships. As delegate for Spain, proposed World Women's Team contest which became Venice Cup. She and husband "Juanfis" Gomez-Diaz were chief organizers of 1974 World Pairs Olympiad in Las Palmas.

GOODALE, Lyla (b. 1928) of Anaheim CA, retired teacher, educated at Mt. St. Mary's, U.S.C., traveled extensively around the world doing in-depth studies of many regions, directed and conducted tours. Diamond Life Master, member Nat'l Goodwill Committee. Top woman masterpoint winner for 1991. Has numerous regional wins including Portland Swiss 1986, Mesa Open Prs 1987, KO Tms, Swiss, Masters Prs 1988, 90; Ocean Shores Swiss, Open Prs, KO Tms, Master Prs 1987; Mexican Nat'ls Super Open Prs; Yakima Swiss, Open Prs 1988; Eugene Super Open Prs, KO Tms 1988; San Francisco KO Tms, Open Prs 1988, Open Prs 1989; Sacramento KO Tms, Saginaw KO Tms 1991; Pine Mountain KO Tms 1991; Yosemite KO Tms, Open Prs 1991.

GOODEN, George S. (1904-1981) of Carmel CA, bridge writer, lecturer, tour conductor, member of the ACBL Bd of Dir 1959, president of ABTA 1962-63; taught more than 250,000 pupils, lectured on radio and in department stores and authored many books and booklets for teaching purposes, including *Contract Bridge Bidding and Play: Self-Teaching Lesson Course for Beginning Players*, the first programmed bridge instruction book for beginners. He also co-authored *Sherlock Holmes, Bridge Detective*. In 1941 he won World Olympic par contest; also won several Pacific Coast regional events in the Thirties.

GOODMAN, Aaron (b. 1901) of Montreal, born in England, export/import businessman; served as treasurer and director of the CANADIAN BRIDGE FEDERATION and director and president of the Montreal BL. Won Mens Prs 1942 and several regional titles.

GOODMAN, Andy (b. 1946) of San Francisco CA, investment manager, previously founded and ran Professional Sports Publications, the nation's largest publisher of sports programs, educated at Yale. Has a 1500-bottle wine collection; is active member of Internat'l Wine and Food Society. Won his first and second regional titles on the same day (1988) and won four events at Wine Country regional in 1991. Won Vanderbilt 1992, placed second Red Ribbon Prs 1992. Regional wins include Pacific Southwest KO Tms, Open Prs 1988, All-Western KO Tms

1990; Wine Country KO Tms, Swiss, Team of Four and Two Prs, Open Prs 1991; Little Bridge Week Open Prs 1991.

GOODWIN, Jude (see HANSON, Jude Goodwin-)

GOPPERT, Clarence H. (b. 1908) of Valley Center CA, retired banker who has had control of or substantial interests in 20 banks, up to 17 at one time. Purchased his first "tiny" bank in 1941. Began horse racing business in 1982. A philanthropist who has been honored as "Donor of the Year" 1988, as "Kansas City Donor of the Year" 1991 and with honorary degrees from Wm. Jewell and Avila Colleges. Established the GOPPERT FOUNDATION in 1959. Didn't become Life Master until age 65 but then acquired more than 9000 points by age 73 to become a Diamond Life Master. Won McKenney Trophy (now Crane Top 500) in 1979 at age 71 after open-heart surgery and was second in 1976. His more than 90 regional titles include Fall secondary Swiss 1974, 1977; Summer Swiss 1977, 79 and many more Swiss and knockout team events.

GORDON, Agnes L. (1906-1967) Born in Ontario, she moved to Buffalo NY but remained a Canadian citizen for life. In world competition placed second World Womens Tms 1964; also represented U.S. in Turin, Italy 1969, New York 1962. Won 10 nat'l titles, six seconds and many regional victories. Her score of 506 1/2 on a 325 average with Eric Murray is one of the highest single-session scores ever recorded at an NABC.

GORDON, Dianna M. (b. 1944) of Toronto, travel agent, graduate Toronto U, won World Mixed Prs 1982, third Venice Cup 1989, fourth Olympiad Womens Tms 1976, 88, 7th in 1980, 9th in 1984; sixth in World Womens Prs 1986; 8th World Mixed Prs 1978; 5th Swiss Plate 1984; WBF World Master; also represented Canada in world competition Monte Carlo 1976, New Orleans 1978, Valkenburg 1980, Seattle 1984, Venice 1988, Yokohama 1991, Salsomaggiore, Italy 1992, Santiago, Chile 1993. Won North American Womens Swiss 1985; placed second Womens Tms 1981, North American Womens Swiss 1983. In Canada won Canadian Open Prs Championship 1982; second Canadian Open Prs Championship 1989; won all Canadian Womens Nat'l championships attended since 1975; has also won several regional titles.

GORDON, Fritzi (1916-1992) of London, England. WBF Grand Master; won World Women's Teams 1964, World Mixed Teams 1962, World Women's Pairs 1962 and 1974. Second World Women's Pairs 1970. Won European Women's Teams 1950, 1951, 1952, 1959, 1961, 1963, 1975. Represented Britain on 8 other occasions. Many national wins include Gold Cup twice. Partnership with Rixi Markus was once the best in women's play.

GORDON, Linda (b. 1944) of New York City, high school guidance counselor and member NYC Bd of Education, educated at Cornell U and Northwestern U. Won IMP Prs 1987. Won Pittsburgh Swiss, NY Barometer Prs 1986; Lake Geneva Swiss 1987, Chicago Master Prs, Hudson Swiss 1988; Dist 24 NA Prs 1990.

GORDON, Loula. See Zougheb.

GORDON, Robert M. (Robb) (b. 1956) of New York City, options specialist, interested in computer applications for bridge, a Michigan Competitive Scholar. Has served on local boards since 1979 and member of Nat'l Appeals Committee since 1983. Won IMP Prs 1987; second Open Prs 1986. Won Dayton Mens Prs 1979, Great Lakes Mens Swiss, Thunder Bay Swiss 1981; Hudson KO Tms 1983, Swiss 84, 86, 88; secondary KO Tms 1984, Pittsburgh Swiss 1986, Lake Geneva Swiss 1987, Central States Masters Prs 1988, Eastern States KO Tms, Dist 24 NA Prs 1990; Summer secondary Swiss 1991.

GORDY, Edward L. (1904-1979) of West Palm Beach FL, was for a long time a driving force in the AMERICAN BRIDGE TEACHERS ASSOCIATION, which he served as president in 1975 and as director-at-large in 1979. Gordy and wife Laura Jane devised valuable flash cards for teaching the play of the hand and a game kit to improve one's bridge playing ability, *Easy Bridge*. They also served as club directors and cruise directors. He produced the ABTA's *Standard American Report* for bridge teachers. Gordy was a member of the IBPA and contributed many articles to various bridge publications.

GORDY, Laura Jane (b. 1912) of West Palm Beach FL, bridge teacher and writer, with her late husband Edward devised flash cards, the *Easy Bridge* game and covered the Bermuda Bowl for the ABTA *Quarterly* in 1973. Served as regional vice president of the ABTA; is member of IBPA.

GOREN, Barry (Kid Zero) (b. 1960) of Chicago, options trader, former bridge teacher and professional, graduated NYU, other interests include skiing, reading and traveling. Goren lived in Tel Aviv, Israel 1970-79, graduated high school and learned to play bridge there. Played in Epson Tournament (collegiate team) Tokyo 1985, won several regionals including Hartford KO Tms 1980, Long Island Prs, Eastern States KO Tms 1982; NY Prs, Portland Prs 1983; Santa Rosa Prs 1988, Chicago Swiss, NY KO Tms, Chicago KO Tms, Hawaii Swiss 1991; Fall secondary Swiss 1991.

GOREN, Charles Henry (1901-1991) world's foremost bridge authority for most of this century. Known to millions as "Mr. Bridge." They bought his books. They attended his lectures. They took lessons from his accredited teachers. They "traveled with Goren" on bridge cruise ships. They collected cards and game accessories imprinted with his logo. They read his columns and the articles he wrote for *Sports Illustrated* and *McCalls* and for bridge magazines throughout the world.

Born in Philadelphia, Goren was a law student at McGill U when he learned to play bridge in a casual game. He earned an LLB in 1922 and a Masters degree in 1923, the year he was admitted to the Pennsylvania Bar. In his spare time he boned up on Milton Work's classics and laid out and studied hand after hand. When he felt he was ready he entered his first duplicate. He won his direction and was soon hooked.

Goren attracted the attention of Work, also a Philadelphian, and took a job as his technical assistant, helping to prepare books, lectures and columns. By 1931 Goren was playing tournament bridge. He won his first major events in 1933 — the United States Bridge Association and the American Bridge League's Open Teams of Four. He began to do some teaching on his own and in 1936 he published his first book, *Winning Bridge Made Easy. The Chicago Tribune* and the *New York Daily News* chose to syndicate his daily newspaper articles as a replacement for Ely Culbertson, who had moved to another syndicate. After 13 years as a member of the bar, Goren turned to bridge full time. Though still a member of the bar, he never practiced again.

Goren was a fine writer and analyst, an excellent speaker and a tireless worker. Starting in 1937 he won so many tournaments that he captured the *McKenney Trophy* for best performance on eight occasions, a record that still stands. Soon he took over the top of the masterpoint winners list and held that spot without interruption from 1944 to 1962.

His introduction of point-count valuation, adding points for distribution to high-card values of 4, 3, 2, 1 for ace, king, queen, jack, swept all other systems into the discard, and made his methods into what came to be called STANDARD AMERICAN. More important, because this valuation method proved much easier to learn, it helped make millions of new bridge players, giving the game a life it had not enjoyed since the first boom of the early Culbertson years.

The name of Goren became synonymous with bridge to the millions; his importance as a world figure was recognized when he was front-covered by *Time* magazine. His classic *Contract Bridge Complete* ran to 12 editions. His *Point Count Bidding* revolutionized bidding to the extent that "Goren" became a standard recognized worldwide. Culberton's honor-trick valuation died overnight. It is estimated that Goren books have sold more than 10 million copies. His writings have been translated into a dozen languages. His books include: *Better Bridge for Better Players; Standard Book of Bidding; Contract Bridge Made Easy; A Self-Teacher; Point-Count Bidding in Contract Bridge; Goren Presents the Italian Bridge System; New Contract Bridge In a Nutshell; Sports Illustrated Book of Bridge; Goren's Winning Partnership Bridge, Charles Goren's Winning Partnership Bridge, Charles Goren's Bridge Complete*; and *Goren on Play and Defense*.

Goren became a world champion in Bermuda in 1950 when the first of the Bermuda Bowl World Championships was staged. He was silver medalist to France in the World Championships of 1956 and to Italy in 1957. He was a member of the U.S. team that finished fourth in the first World Team Olympiad in Turin in 1960. He won the equivalent of 34 NABC championships and was runner-up on 21 occasions. His television show, *Championship Bridge with Charles Goren*, ran from 1959 to 1964. It was called the first successful bridge program on television and won an award as one of the best new television features.

A lifelong bachelor, Goren may genuinely be said to have been married to the game. In spite of his work as writer, lecturer, promoter, TV personality (unlike Culbertson, who grew bored with the game when he had become successful), Goren was devoted to tournament play. (He seldom played rubber bridge, and never for high stakes; he considered his playing status amateur and once turned over to the Damon Runyon Cancer Fund the full amount of a $1,500 purse which he won in a charity tournament played in Las Vegas.) Before his retirement from active competition in 1966, he captured virtually every major bridge trophy in U.S. tournament play. Goren was

named ACBL Honorary Member in 1959 and was one of the first three players elected to the Hall of Fame in 1963. He was a member of the ACBL Laws Commission from 1956. He was a contributing editor of *The Bridge World* and was a former member of the Editorial Advisory Board of the *Bridge Encyclopedia*. In 1973 he was awarded the honorary degree of doctor of laws by McGill U.

After retiring from the tournament scene in the late Sixties, Goren lived quietly at his home in Miami Beach and, for the last 19 years of his life lived with a nephew, Marvin Goren, in Southern California. Because of poor eyesight and failing health, he was seldom seen in the Seventies. There were rare appearances on the *According to Goren* panel shows at North American Bridge Championships and in 1972 he hosted a party for the press at his Miami Beach home during the Fourth World Bridge Olympiad. His personal record by events: BERMUDA BOWL 1st 1950, 2nd 1956, 1957. WORLD TEAM OLYMPIAD 3rd 1960. Vanderbilt 1st 1944, 1945; 2nd 1934, 1936, 1949, 1950, 1953, 1955, 1959, 1962; 1937: Challenge T-F Asbury Park Trophy 1st (later Spingold), 1937; Spingold Master KO Teams 1st 1943, 1947, 1951, 1956, 1960; 2nd 1939, 1950; Reisinger BAM Teams (formerly Chicago) 1st 1937, 1938, 1939, 1942, 1943, 1950, 1957, 1963; 2nd 1944, 1951; Master Mixed Teams 1st 1938, 1941, 1943, 1944, 1948, 1954; 2nd 1946, 1949, 1950. 1951; Men's Teams, 1st 1952, 1965; 2nd 1946, 1955; Life Master Pairs 1st 1942, 1958; 2nd 1953, Open Pairs 1st 1940; Mixed Pairs 1st 1943, 1947; 2nd 1934; Men's Pairs, 1st 1938, 1943, 1949; 2nd 1935; Masters Individual 1st 1945; McKenney Trophy 1937, 1943, 1945, 1947, 1948, 1949, 1950, 1951. See BIBLIOGRAPHY, B, C, D, E, H, J.

GOSLAR, Gerda (1912-87) of Johannesburg, South Africa, born in Germany. Runner-up World Women's Teams 1968, 1972, World Women's Pairs 1974. Also represented South Africa in World Open Teams 1960, World Open Pairs 1966, World Women's Pairs 1970. Five national titles. Founder Women's Bridge Association of South Africa.

GöTHE, Eva-Liss (b. 1941) of Stockholm, Sweden. WBF World Master. Runner-up 1990 World Mixed Pairs. 1989 European Women's Pair champion. Represented Sweden on 9 other international occasions.

GöTHE Hans G. (b. 1937) of Spånga, Sweden, computer expert. WBF World Life Master. Third 1987 Bermuda Bowl and 1988 World Team Olympiad and represented Sweden in many other world championships. European champion 1977 and 1987, third 1989, and played on six other occasions. Nordic champion 1968, 1984 1990. 9 national wins 1967-90.

GOUDSMIT, Fritz W. (1899-1971) of Amsterdam, The Netherlands, lawyer and bridge columnist; second in the European Championships 1932, 1933, 1934; represented The Netherlands on many other occasions. His many national wins included Open Teams 11 times between 1933 and 1956. He authored several books on bidding and play and translated several books from English into Dutch, including works by Ely Culbertson and S. J. Simon.

GOUGH, William L. (1951-1987) of Oreland PA, bridge teacher, was a board member of Unit 141 for several years. Won first regional and played in Blue Ribbon Prs in 1966 at the age of 15, placed first in ACBL in Epson Prs 1986, won many regionals.

GOULD, Lawrence E. (Larry) (b. 1942) of Raleigh NC, financial officer, won Spingold 1974, placed second Spingold 1977, Mens Tms 1973. Diamond Life Master with numerous regional titles.

GOULD, Edward A., Jr. (b. 1928) of Hooksett NH, sales representative, former president of Dist 25, served for 18 years on ACBL Board of Directors, 1973-91; was ACBL president 1990, chairman of the Board 1991. Was honored by the city of Manchester NH in 1990 and was presented the Key to the City. Won New England Open Prs 1991.

GOW, Robert D. (Bob) (b. 1942) of Midwest City OK, mathematician, educated at U of Oklahoma, was Merit Scholar as undergraduate (1960-64), enjoys reading and gardening. Won Tulsa Open Swiss 1979, OK City Open Swiss 1983, 85, Master Swiss 1989; Dist 15 GN Tms 1988, Kansas City Swiss 1991, Springfield Superflight KO Tms, Milwaukee Swiss 1992.

GOWDY, Bruce Douglas (B.G.) (b. 1930) of Toronto, chartered accountant, vice president of finance, store franchiser, graduate U of Western Ontario, enjoys Toronto Blue Jays, golf and travel. Former president Unit 166; became a tournament director in 1950 and scored sheets all over the country for Al Sobel, Alvin Landy and Russell Baldwin. WBF Life Master, placed third World Tm Olympiad 1972, also represented Canada in Turin, Italy 1960, New Orleans 1978 (11th Rosenblum Cup Tms), Monte Carlo 1976 (13th Olympiad Open Tms). Holds record for being the youngest player ever to win a major knockout event when he won the Spingold at the age of 19 in 1949; was second in the Spingold 1964; won Canadian Nat'l Open Tms 1949, 50, 51, 52, 53; numerous regionals won.

GRABEL, Ross D. (b. 1950) of Huntington Beach CA, company owner, 16th Rosenblum Tms 1986; WBF World Master. Won Mens Tms 1980, North American Mens Swiss 1982, Reisinger 1984, second Spingold 1989. Diamond Life Master; won numerous regionals.

GRACA, Ella (b. 1918 in China). Represented Hong Kong in one world championship and many Far East Championships. Top Hong Kong team winner in 1982, only woman ever to win this title.

GRAFT, Larry W. (b. 1934) of Sacramento CA, ACBL tournament director, began directing in 1963 and in 1979 advanced to Regional 4 rating; served as president of the Sacramento Unit 1963-64 and as a Board member of Dist 21 1964-81. Formerly sales executive, rocket engine test coordinator and navigator in the U.S. Air Force; a 2-handicap golfer.

GRANOVETTER, Matthew (Matt) (b. 1950) of Netanya, Israel, formerly of Ballston Lake NY, writer/publisher, graduate of Hunter College. Outside interests include family, Judaism, desktop publishing and music composition; has authored two children's musicals and several books -- *Murder at the Bridge Table, I Shot My Bridge Partner, The Bridge Team Murders* and co-authored *Tops and Bottoms, Conventions at a Glance* and

The Ultimate Club. Co-editor of *Bridge Today* magazine and the *ACBL Bulletin* column *Partnership Bridge*; bridge editor for the *Jerusalem Post* and writes a weekly column. One of the originators of the RELAY SYSTEM; was a member of the New York team that defeated the Lancia Team in 1975 (see LANCIA TOURNAMENTS). In 1981 he appeared in 13 episodes of *Grand Slam*, a TV challenge match made for BBC. Placed second World Mixed Tms Las Palmas 1974. Diamond Life Master; won Open Prs 1972, Mens Tms 1975, 1982; placed second Reisinger 1976, 77; has won numerous regional events. Won Cavendish Invitational Prs; Cavendish Invitational Tms 1993, New Orleans Money Tournament 1982, *Bridge Today* All-Star Game 1992, National Israel Open Prs, Mixed Prs, Open Tms 1993. Produces *Bridge Today* All-Star Games.

GRANOVETTER, Pamela (Pam) (b. 1953) of Netanya, Israel, formerly of Ballston Lake NY, writer; interests are mysteries, old movies, NY Mets, Judaism and family; member of ACBL Goodwill Committee; co-editor of *Bridge Today* magazine, the books *Tops and Bottoms, Conventions at a Glance* and *ACBL Bulletin* column *Partnership Bridge*; has co-produced four *Bridge Today* All-Star games. Represented Canada in world competition New Orleans 1978, Valkenberg 1980, U.S. in Bal Harbour 1986. Won Womens BAM Tms; placed second Womens KO Tms; won many regional events including the Eastern States (Reisinger) KO Tms. Won Cavendish Invitational Tms, Israeli Open Tms, Mixed Prs 1993; New Orleans Money Tournament 1983; placed second in Iceland Open Tms.

GRANT, Audrey (b. 1940) of Toronto, educator and author; graduate of U of McMaster; taught in Toronto school system for many years before concentrating on bridge; educational consultant for ACBL. Authored the ACBL teaching series -- *Club, Diamond, Heart* and *Spade*; co-authored with husband David Lindop *Joy of Bridge, Bridge Maxims*; founder and editor *Better Bridge* newsletter; producer of ACBL TV teaching series including *The Bridge Class, Play Bridge with Audrey Grant I, Play Bridge with Audrey Grant II*; produced many TV bridge shows in Canada starting in 1986.

GRANTHAM, John M. (b. 1944) of Amarillo TX, retail store owner, former commodity broker and professional bridge player, educated at Kansas U and West Texas State. Won Blue Ribbon Prs and Lou Herman Trophy 1971; has won numerous regional titles; brother of Becky Rogers, secretary to WORLD BRIDGE FEDERATION president.

GRAUPERA, Javier (b. 1958) of Barcelona, Spain, computer engineer and enterprise manager. WBF World Master. Second European Junior Teams 1980. Represented Spain in four world championships and seven other zonal championships.

GRAVES, J(ames) Allan (b. 1949) of Vancouver BC, family counselor, accountant, represented Canada in Las Palmas 1974, New Orleans 1978, Valkenburg 1980, Biarritz 1982, Seattle 1984, Bal Harbour 1986; third Rosenblum Tms 1982, 9th 1990; WBF World Master and ACBL Diamond Life Master. Won North American Swiss 1986; second Reisinger 1978; won Canadian Nat'l Tms Championship 1980, 81, 83; won numerous regionals.

GRAY, Charles (Charlie) (b. 1930) of Philadelphia, graduate of Drexel U, licensed professional engineer since 1967, semi-retired engineering consultant, served in various executive positions in Unit 141 and Dist 4 including president of both; was co-chairman of 1972, 80, 89 Fall NABCs. Directed first OMAR SHARIF BRIDGE CIRCUS visit to Philadelphia in 1968 and organized the first KO team event in Philadelphia bridge history, including a vugraph exhibition. Has won more than 30 regionals.

GRECO, Eric Alan (b. 1975) of Annandale VA, student, developed and plays his own system. Won Mini-McKenney NABC Master category 1991; became a Life Master at age 15 and won the Youth category (under 20) in 1991 amassing 557 points; was third in the Junior category (under 25). Was member of the Jr. team that competed in the World Jr Championships in Aarhus, Denmark 1993. Won North American Non-Life Master Prs 1991, GN Tms Flt B 1993 (both with his father, Philip). Won Youth Flight of Royal Viking/Instant Matchpoint Prs 1992. Regional wins include Charlotte 2nd Bracket KO Tms, NY 2nd bracket KO Tms, Reston Open Prs.

GREEN, Farrell B. (b. 1937) of Edina MN, financial controller, consultant and accountant. Has won Gopher Open Tms 1959, 61, 74, Open Prs 1960, 62, 67, 81; Intercity champion 1962, Mid-America Open Tms and various other events in Eighties and Nineties.

GREEN, Linda Joan (b. 1947) of Johannesburg, South Africa, clinical pathology technologist, calligrapher. Represented South Africa World Women's Teams 1992. Won National Mixed Pairs 1987. Chairman South African Women's Bridge Assn. 1987-91.

GREEN, Mary (Mrs. Roy G.) (b. 1930) of Memphis TN, formerly of Santa Barbara CA, former college math teacher, graduate of Henderson State U and U of Arkansas, wife of Roy G. Green, ACBL chief executive officer. Won several regionals including Jacksonville Women's Prs 1979; Orlando Open Tms 1980; Midland Open Pairs 1985; Bridge Wk Mixed Prs 1988; All-Western Open Sr Prs 1985; Bridge Wk Mixed Prs 1988; All-Western Sr Pairs 1990; ALACBU Winter Sr Pairs 1992.

GREEN, Roy G. (b. 1930) of Memphis TN, formerly of Santa Barbara CA, chief executive officer of ACBL, former banker, graduate of Henderson State U and U of Arkansas. A prominent banker and frequent public speaker, he was appointed by President Ford to Nat'l Commission on Electronic Fund Transfers. National president of U.S. League of Savings Institutions 1981-82; charter trustee and former chairman of Appraisal Foundation, Washington DC. Has been active over last 30 years in every aspect of bridge administration, long-time member of Nat'l Goodwill Committee; has won several regional events.

GREEN, Susan (Mrs. Michael Cappelletti, Sr.) (b. 1952) of Alexandria VA, technical editor/writer and consultant, graduate of U of Michigan, enjoys travel, reading and writing. Diamond Life Master; won Womens KO Tms 1991, placed second Mixed Prs, Womens BAM Tms 1988; won more than 75 regionals. See FAMILY.

GREENBERG, Byron (Beau) (b. 1927) of Las Vegas NV, retired restaurateur; interested in sports, golf and sports handicapping; has held executive positions several times in Oklahoma bridge. Won Open Prs 1953; placed second Spingold 1972, Reisinger 1973. Diamond Life Master. Recent regional wins include Gatlinburg KO Tms, Master Prs 1991; Albuquerque Swiss, Open Prs 1991; San Antonio Open Prs, Swiss 1991; Summer secondary Swiss 1991.

GREENBERG, Gail H. (b. 1938) of New York City, bridge teacher and professional player. World Grand Master and ACBL Grand Life Master with more than 10,000 MP. Vice-chairman Nat'l Appeals Committee; member of the Nat'l Goodwill Committee and the Nat'l Charity Committee; past president of Greater New York BA; former Dist 24 member of the ACBL Bd of Gov. Won Venice Cup 1976, 78 (second 1985); World Olympiad Womens Tms 1980, 84; second World Mixed Tms 1972; has represented ACBL in other world competition 1974 (4th Mixed Prs, 9th Womens Prs), 1976 (3rd Olympiad Womens Tms), 1978 (7th Mixed Prs, 8th Womens Prs), 1982 (17th Mixed Prs, 19th Womens Prs), 1986 (14th Mixed Prs), 1990 (17th Womens Prs). Won first Pan American Womens Tms Championship 1992. North American titles include Master Mixed Tms 1967, 72; North American Womens Swiss 1983, 92 (second 1985); Womens KO Tms 1983, 90, 93; Womens Tms 1971, 74, 75, 76 (second in 1973, 82); Mixed Prs 1978; placed second Womens BAM Tms 1986, 88. Has had numerous regional wins. See FAMILY.

GREENBERG, Julie (b. 1938) of Memphis TN, manager ACBL Education Dept, ACBL tournament director for 20 years achieving rank of associate national. Educated at Newcomb and Tulane, enjoys reading, oil painting and making scrapbooks; has 28-year collection of family scrapbooks. Authored *Duplicate Decisions*; wrote *ACBL Bulletin* column *Ruling the Game* for ten years; editor of ACBL newsletter, *The Bridge Teacher* and was first editor of *The Grapevine*; created the first Tournament Director manual; developed ACBL's student *Bulletin* supplements.

GREENBERG, Nate (b. 1910) of Scottsdale AZ, graduate U of Illinois, retired educator, interested in bird watching, ceramics, Indian jewelry and collecting stamps. He and wife Ruth had been married for 59 years as of 1993. Diamond Life Master. Regional wins include Navajo KO Tms 1969, Mens Swiss 1977, Open Prs 1981; Salt Lake KO Tms, Rocky Mtn KO Tms 1973; Palm Springs Mens Prs 1975, Lone Star Swiss 1987, Dist 2 Swiss 1989, Fall secondary Swiss 1990 Tms, Moose Jaw Swiss, Mid-Atlantic Swiss 1991, Pine Mtn Swiss 1992, Sacramento KO Tms, ABA Open Prs 1993.

GREENBERG, Ruth (Smiley) (Mrs. Nate) (b. 1914) of Scottsdale AZ, retired school teacher and camp director, graduated from Chicago Teachers College and Scottsdale Community College. Interests include bird watching, nature and rockhounding. Co-owner (with husband) of day camp and camp for boys. Her many regional wins include St. Louis Open Prs, Albuquerque Open Prs 1981, Lone Star Swiss 1987; Dist 2 Swiss 1989, Spring secondary Swiss 1990, Mid-Atlantic Swiss, Moose Jaw Swiss 1991, ABA Open Prs 1993.

GREENE, Richard P. (1910-1991) of New Orleans, dentist, a charter member and the second president of the Louisiana BA. He served as chairman or co-chairman of many regionals and of five North American Championships held in New Orleans. He won Mid-South Open Tms 1944, 48, 60, 63, Master Prs 1963, 64; Missouri Valley Master Prs 1973.

GRENSIDE, Richard (b. 1938 in England) of Lisarow NSW, Australia, tournament director. Chief director of Australian Bridge Federation since 1976. Chief director of Far East Bridge Federation since 1985. Senior director of World Bridge Federation at world championships since 1986.

GRESHAM, William Lindsay (1909-1962) of New Rochelle NY, noted American novelist, used the tarot pack as background material in his macabre story about carnival life, *Nightmare Alley*, from which an excerpt appears in *The Fireside Book of Cards*.

GRIEVE, William P. (Billy) (b. 1929) of White Plains NY, IBM system programmer and mathematician, educated at Boston U and NYU, enjoys computer hacking, tennis, chess and swimming. Retired tournament player; won Mens Prs 1958, Spingold 1959, Mixed Tms 1960, Reisinger 1969, 70. 71; Mens Tms 1975. Placed second in Open Prs 1959, Spingold 1960, 66, 69; Reisinger, Mens Tms 1972. He competed internationally in Turin, Italy 1960. His numerous regional titles include Mississippi Valley Open Tms 1951, New England KO Tms, Open Tms 1957; Mid-South Spring Open Tms, Eastern States KO Tms 1960.

GRIFFEY, Larry R. (b. 1944) of Jacksonville FL, mathematics professor, graduated Austin Peay State U, part-time bridge professional and teacher. Outside interests are basketball, teaching probabilities and statistics of gambling, collecting and tasting wine. Diamond Life Master, has won Dist 9 GN Prs nine times, GN Tms twice, Summer secondary KO Tms 1991, 15 Swiss, six Open Prs, three Mens Prs, two Mixed Prs, two Masters Prs and two KO Tms.

GRIFFIN, Estee (1931-1993) of New York City, systems manager, served as tournament chairman, vice president and president of the Greater New York BA and was former assistant editor of *The Bridge World*, associate editor of *Post Mortem* and promotion director of *The Bridge Journal*. Some of her wins include Eastern States Mixed Tms 1961, Fun City KO Tms 1971, Long Island KO Tms 1968, NY Winter Life Master Prs 1975, Tri-State Swiss 1980.

GRIFFIN, Edward Furnival (b. 1947) of Sydney, Australia, company director. Won Far East Open Pairs, and represented Australia in three zonal championships. Won New Zealand open teams and several Australian titles.

GRIGGS, Eloene T. of Washington DC, bridge teacher, former bridge club owner and director, graduate of U of Southern California. Served as general secretary of the IBPA (1973-1992) and has served in many executive positions in the AMERICAN BRIDGE TEACHERS ASSOCIATION, including president (1976, 77, 78), on editorial staff of *ABTA Quarterly*. She organized many service-connected womens clubs and has been a member of the National Council of Women since 1954. She is listed in *Who's Who of American Women, World's Who's Who of Women* and several other biographical dictionaries. Griggs was given Certificate of Appreciation for Advancement of Human Rights, honored by Business and Professional Womens Clubs as "Woman of the Year" -- 1986, was awarded certificate by U.S. Congressional Advisory Bd for Outstanding Services, made Honorary Citizen of New Orleans 1978, and awarded "Bridge Personality of the Year" 1990 at World Championships in Geneva.

GRISCOM, Dr. John H. (b. 1929) of Nashville TN, physician and associate clinical professor Vanderbilt Medical School, graduated Vanderbilt. Tennessee State Jr golf champion 1947, captain of collegiate golf team. Won GN Prs 1983 and competed in international competition in Bal Harbour 1986. Diamond Life Master; won more than 25 regionals including Mid-Atlantic Open Prs 1976, Mens Prs 1980, 81; Midwest Fall Open Prs 1978, Opryland KO Tms 1981, Dist 10 GN Tms, Zone III 1981; Albuquerque Swiss, Open Prs 1991; San Antonio Swiss, Open Prs 1991; Acapulco Open Prs, Open Prs 1991; Gatlinburg Super Flt KO Tms 1991.

GRISSOM, Bettye (B.J.) (b. 1922) of San Antonio TX, rancher, graduated National Park College, avidly interested in genealogy, active member of many historic and patriotic organizations. Was tournament chairman of Spring NABC in San Antonio 1984, member Nat'l Bd of Gov 1971-83, member of Nat'l Goodwill Committee from early 70's, assistant chairman-Southwest 1978-83. She held many executive positions on Unit and Dist level. She was a member Dist 16 Bd 1971-82 serving as president 1974, vice-president 1972, 73; member Ethics Committee 1972, 73, 74. Won Texas Summer Open Tms, Mid-South Fall Open Tms 1968; Spring secondary Womens Prs 1978.

GRODSKY, Mike J. (b. 1957) of Atlanta GA, computer programmer, graduate Brunswick College and U of Georgia, high school and college table tennis champion. Won Red Ribbon Prs 1990. His regionals include Atlanta Swiss, Prs 1987, Open Prs 1988; New Orleans Bracketed KO Tms, Jacksonville Open Swiss 1989; Ft Lauderdale KO Tms 1991.

GROMOV, Andrej (b. 1970) of Moscow, Russia, student. WBF World Master. Represented Soviet Union, or C.I.S, in two world championships. Many national wins.

GRONER, Alexander (Alex) (b. 1914) of Poway CA, retired journalist, former editorial writer for the *Cleveland Press*, correspondent for *Time, Life* and *Fortune* magazines, graduate Western Reserve U, Cleveland-Marshall Law School (JD). Creator of duplicate movements for Swiss pairs and multiple teams of multiple pairs. Wrote definitive work for club and tournament directors, *Duplicate Bridge Direction,* a must for ACBL tournament and club directors.

GRONER, Edward L. (Ed) (b. 1929) of Duncan OK, retired special products manager, educated U of Oklahoma, interested in golf, stock market and sports. Holds several patents on flow metering devices. Won Spring secondary Sr Prs, Ft. Worth Prs, Sr Swiss; OK City Swiss;

Tulsa Master Prs, Sr Swiss; Houston Sr Prs, Open Prs; Austin Sr KO Tms, Springfield Sr KO Tms, Wichita Sr Prs, Dist 15 GN Tms, Fall secondary Morning KO Tms, Sr Prs 1992; Hot Springs Sr KO Tms, Callaway Gardens Sr Swiss 1992; Pasadena Sr KO Tms, Salt Lake City KO Tms 1993.

GROSS, Steven H. (b. 1944) of Woodland Hills CA, attorney, security analyst and accountant, degrees from Stanford, Columbia, and U of W Los Angeles, played on high school and college golf teams, won many local tennis tournaments, also enjoys bowling. Placed second in Non-Life Masters Mens Prs 1965, competed in internat'l play New Orleans 1978, won PAC-10 Bridge Championship in 1965 playing for Stanford with Grant Baze. Diamond Life Master; regional wins include Pasadena Barometer Masters Prs 1976, Mens Prs 1989, Winter Open Prs 1988; Spring secondary KO Tms 1989, San Diego Swiss 1990, San Bernadino Swiss 1991, KO Tms 1993; Sacramento Open Prs, Bakersfield Open Prs 1991; Riverside Handicap KO Tms 1992.

GROSS, William M. (Bill) (b. 1930) of Harrisburg PA, attorney, executive director of ACBL 1987-1991, ACBL president 1983, served as ACBL Board member from Dist 4 (1972-87), member Bd of Gov and Nat'l Goodwill Committee; past president of Dist 4. Gross was co-chairman of the Fall NABC in Lancaster in 1972 and 1980. A former bridge columnist, he wrote regularly for the *Harrisburg Sunday Patriot-News*. Graduate of U of Pennsylvania and Harvard Law School, past president of the American Lung Association and served as a member of its Nat'l Bd of Dir. His interests include college football, white-water rafting and computers.

GROSSMAN, David L. (b. 1935) of Livingston NJ, senior director national programs-The House of Seagram, graduate Memphis State U, enjoys photography and movies. Won Non-Life Masters Tms 1984.

GROSSMAN, Sid (b. 1916) of Sun City AZ, retired general contractor, educated Cornell, enjoys computers and video taping, has won 18 regional events including Denver Master Prs 1983, Washington DC Open Swiss, Tacoma Mens Prs 1984; Tucson Master Prs 1985, Lake Geneva Master Prs, Mesa Sr. Master Prs 1991.

GROTHEIM, Glen (b. 1959) of Trondheim, Norway, engineer. Second Bermuda Bowl 1993. Third European Teams 1987, 1993.

GROVER, Kathleen M. (b. 1949) of Dharan, Saudi Arabia, club manager, director, and bridge teacher. Represented Saudi Arabia 1990 world championships. Secretary ARABIAN BRIDGE FEDERATION.

GROVER, Robert D. (b. 1946) of Dharan, Saudi Arabia, electric utility operations consultant. Founder ARABIAN BRIDGE FEDERATION. Represented Saudi Arabia 1990 World Championships.

GRUENTHER, General Alfred M. (1899-1983) of Washington DC, a recognized authority on duplicate contract bridge and the outstanding director of bridge tournaments in America in the Thirties, acted as chief referee in the CULBERTSON-LENZ MATCH 1931-32.

He authored *Duplicate Bridge Simplified*, *Duplicate Bridge Guide* and *Famous Hands of the Culbertson-Lenz Match*. He was Honorary president of the WORLD BRIDGE FEDERATION from the time of its inception in 1958 until he resigned from all bridge activities in 1978. Gruenther was awarded the WETZLAR TROPHY 1938, 44 and was named ACBL Honorary Member in 1944. He was a charter member of the ACBL Laws Commission and its Honorary Member 1948-78, chairman of the ACBL Charity Foundation 1964-65 and a former member of the Editorial Advisory Board of the *Bridge Encyclopedia*.

Gruenther served 38 years in the U.S. Army; his final military assignment was Supreme Commander, Allied Powers, Europe, 1953-56. He retired December 31, 1956 and from 1957 to 1964 was president of the American Red Cross. Besides awards from other countries for International Red Cross league activities (nine Red Cross Societies), he was decorated by 14 governments other than the United States. He was the recipient of the Distinguished Service Medal with two Oak Leaf clusters and the Legion of Merit from this country. He had honorary degrees from 31 American colleges and universities. See EISENHOWER, DWIGHT D.

GRUVER, Nancy G. (1931-1990) of Ellicott City MD, graduate of U of Maryland and a former elementary school teacher; past president of the Womens BL of MD and Board member of the Maryland BL, she served as co-chairman of the NABC Appeals Committee for many years and was elected to the ACBL Laws Commission 1982. A certified director and club manager in Baltimore, she gave private instruction on occasion and was an active member of BRIDGE PRO organization. She placed second in the World Womens Prs 1966, Venice Trophy 1981. She also represented the U.S. in 1968, 78, 82. She won Womens Prs 1965, Womens Tms 1966, 73, 78, 80, Master Mixed Tms 1975, Mixed Prs 1977, Life Master Womens Prs 1967, 79, 81; North American Womens Swiss 1982, Womens KO Tms 1984. She placed second in Master Mixed Tms 1969, Mixed Prs 1976, Life Master Womens Prs 1980. She won the USWBC (womens team trials) 1981, 87. Gruver was a Diamond Life Master and won numerous regional titles.

GU, Ling (b.1959) of Guangzhou, China, WBF World Master. Third Venice Cup 1991. Won Far East Women's Teams 1986, 1991, second 1987, 1988. Also represented China in 6 world championships. Winner of 3 Far Eastern zonal championships. Won many national titles.

GUAGLIARDO, Matthew T. (Matt) (b. 1945) of Memphis TN, financial management advisor and portfolio manager, former manager Education Department of ACBL. Was npc of the first ACBL Jr. team 1987. He was chairman of the 1980 Spring NABC held in Fresno, has also served as chairman of several regionals. He is the creator of many bridge hospitality functions including *The Bridge Gong Show*, *Bridge All-Star Challenge* and ACBL *Celebrity Squares*. Member ACBL Goodwill Committee and Charity Committee; has served in various executive positions in his former unit and district (22), including Dist president 1980, 81; has edited many regional *Daily Bulletins* on the West Coast, the Fresno Unit publication, Dist 22 news for the *Contract Bridge Forum* and has contributed to the *ACBL Bulletin*. He founded and was ex ecutive director of the PROFESSIONAL BRIDGE ASSOCIATION.

GUDGE, Anna (b. 1946) of Sudbury, England, bridge administrator. Secretary of BBL since 1986. Administrator at several world championships. Press Room manager 1991 world championships. Won EBU Women's Teams 1986.

GUERIN, Donald H. (Don) (b. 1942) of Sacramento CA, independent real estate appraiser, graduated U of Illinois, a distance runner and actively involved in YMCA. Has written articles for *The Bridge World*, *The Forum* and *Los Angeles Bridge News*. Diamond Life Master; placed second Senior and Advanced Senior Master Prs 1965; won Dist 11 Mens Prs 1966, Dist 22 KO Tms 1972, Masters Prs 1974; Golden State Masters Prs 1973, Los Angeles Winter Swiss, Las Vegas Swiss 1974; CA Capitol KO Tms 1976, All-Western Masters Prs 1980, Sacramento Open Prs 1986.

GUIVER, Harold B. (Squeezer) (b. 1925) of Long Beach CA, mortgage company co-owner, graduate of U of Southern California and was a member of its NCAA tennis championship team. His special outside interest is football. He was vice president of the Los Angeles Rams and assistant general manager of the New Orleans Saints. He was named Contract Negotiator of the Year in 1980 by *Sports Illustrated* for his role as an agent representing professional football players. Won the Chicago (Reisinger) 1962, Mens Tms 1962, Mens Tms 1962, Mens BAM Tms 1983 and placed second in the Chicago 1961, Vanderbilt 1961, 63; Mens Tms 1974, Spingold 1975. Diamond Life Master; has won numerous regionals.

GULLBERG S. Tommy (b. 1943) of Solna, Sweden, representative. World Life Master. Third Olympiad Teams 1988, Bermuda Bowl 1987, 1991. European champion 1987, second 1991, third 1989. European Junior champion 1968. Nordic champion 1984, 1990. Represented Sweden on many other international occasions. National tournament chairman 1971-73. Bridge columnist *Svenska Dagbladet*, contributor to *Bridgetidningen* and author of two teaching books.

GUMBY, Pauline (b. 1949) of Mosman, Australia, computer programmer, former mathematics teacher. Won Far East Womens Teams 1985. Represented Australia in four world championships. Won some national titles.

GUPTA, Subhash (b. 1947) of New Delhi, India, formerly of Calgary AB, mechanical engineer, represented Canada in Burmuda Bowl the first time a Canadian team qualified, Sao Paulo 1985, won tri-country playoff 1985. WBF World Master, has also represented Canada in Biarritz 1982, Bal Harbour 1986, Geneva 1990; represented India in world competition Salsomaggiore, Italy 1992. Won Epson Swiss in Japan 1984, Dubai 1990. He has won all major team events in India. Won Klondike Swiss 1978, Swiss 1980; Buffalo Swiss, Master Prs 1980; Dist 18 GN Tms, Zone VII 1979; Canadian Nat'l Team Zone 5 1981.

GURVICH, Louis S. (1921-1986) of Metairie LA, was president of a guard and detective agency. His interests included numismatics, philately, travel and tennis. He was president of the ACBL in 1977, chairman of the Board in 1978, chairman of the Bd of Gov 1967-71 and served on many committees prior to his presidency, including the committee that approved and refined the present-day convention chart and convention card. He was general chairman of the 1978 World Olympiad in New Orleans, a member of the WBF executive committee 1977, 79, co-chairman 1978. Gurvich was a former president of the Mid-South Conference and the Louisiana BA. He represented the U.S. in world play 1974; placed second in Mixed Tms 1961; won many regional events. Gurvich's daughter was one of the victims in the Jonestown tragedy.

GUSTAFSON, Helen R. (Mrs John) (b. 1923) of Des Moines IA, retired office manager, graduated U of Colorado; interests are traveling, reading and grandchildren. Has chaired numerous tournaments since 1973; Diamond Life Master; won Mixed Prs 1983, competed in WBF events in Bal Harbour 1986, placed 15th in World Sr Prs in Geneva 1990. Regionals wins include Summer secondary Swiss 1983, Lincoln Swiss 1985, Toronto Open Prs, St Louis Sr Open Prs 1987; Sioux Falls Womens Prs 1988, Iowa City Open Prs, Springfield Sr Open Prs, Grand Rapids Sr Open Prs 1989; Reno Mixed Prs, Summer secondary Sr Open Prs, Lake Geneva Sr Open Prs 1990; Cedar Rapids Swiss, Mexico City Sr Open Prs, Lincoln Sr KO Tms, Springfield Sr Open Prs, Fall secondary Sr Swiss 1991.

GUSTAFSON, Dr. John E. (b. 1924) of Des Moines IA, physician, medical director to five life insurance companies, educated at Columbia U College of Physicians and Surgeons (MD). Served Unit 116 and Dist 14 as president. Member Bd of Gov and vice-chairman ACBL Education Foundation. Won Mixed Prs 1983. Placed 15th in the World Sr Prs Geneva 1990, also represented ACBL in Bal Harbour 1986. A Diamond Life Master with numerous regional titles including Iowa City Open Prs, Lincoln Masters Prs, Omaha Sr Masters Prs, Springfield Sr Open Prs, Grand Rapids Sr Open Prs 1989; Reno Mixed Prs, Boston Sr Prs, Lake Geneva Sr Prs, Ft Worth Swiss 1990; Indianapolis Sr Swiss, Cedar Rapids Master Prs, Swiss 1991.

GUT, Enrichetta (b. 1935) of Milan, Italy. World Master. Second Venice Cup 1978. Won European Women's Teams 1979. Won numerous national titles.

GUTOWSKY, Ace Jr. (1909-1976) of Oklahoma City, won acclaim both as a bridge player and as a football star. On the gridiron Gutowsky played professionally from 1931-38 and was fullback for the Detroit Lions when they won the world championship in 1935. After his retirement from football he worked as an aircraft sales representative. His bridge victories came in the Fifties and included Mens Tms 1951. Ace was his given name.

GWOZDZINSKY, G. Margie (The Countess) of New York City, born in Poland, bridge teacher and business systems analyst. Member GNYBA Bd of Dir for 14 years; won Venice Cup team in Perth, Australia 1989. WBF World Master; represented ABCL Bal Harbour 1986, placing 16th in World Womens Prs. Won Womens Swiss 1984, Womens Swiss 1989, Womens BAM Tms 1993; placed second in Reisinger 1989; has won more than 20 regionals including Fall secondary Womens Prs 1971, Long Island Womens Prs 1972, Washington Bridge Week Womens Prs,

Eastern States Womens Prs 1976; Dist 4 Fall Open Prs 1981.

GYNZ, Detler von (b. 1944) of Munster, Germany, factory employee. Represented Germany in world and zonal championships from 1969-87. Won 22 national titles.

H

HABERMAN, Barbara (Bari) (Mrs. Sigmund, formerly Rappaport) (b. 1935) of New York City, options trader, former English teacher; one of the leading American women players in the late Sixties and Seventies, won Fishbein Trophy 1971, Life Master Prs 1971, 72; Life Master Womens Prs 1977; placed second in Womens Tms 1969, 71; Womens Prs 1978, Master Mixed Tms 1966, 74, 75; Life Master Womens Prs 1974. Diamond Life Master, won numerous regional titles. After sweeping the pair events in a sectional tournament, she was named honorary Mens Prs champion so that her record would not be flawed.

HABICHT, Velma (Val) (b. 1923) of Ft. Lauderdale FL, enjoys tennis, travel and ballroom dancing, certified director, served as president and vice president of Ft Lauderdale BC, president Gold Coast Unit 243 since 1981, tournament chairman of at least one tournament a year from 1955-72 while a member Bd of Dir—Eastern Massachusetts BA. Won Tri-State Womens Prs, Mixed Prs 1971; New England Individual 1972, Summer secondary Swiss Tms 1981, Dist 25 Sr Swiss 1989.

HACKETT, Paul D. (b. 1941) of Manchester, England, bridge professional. Second European Teams 1981, and represented Britain in two world championships. Second Common Market Pairs 1981. Several national wins, magazine contributor and author of two books.

HADDAD, Betty (formerly Windley) (1924-1984) of Arlington VA, painter, represented U.S. in international play 1962, won Mixed Prs 1954, Womens Prs 1961 and several regional events.

HADDAD, Louis J. (1900-1980) presided over ACBL 1935; insurance counselor, won many auction events 1928-1932 and the Hilliard Trophy 1935.

HADDAD, Said (b. 1916) of La Gorce Island FL, contractor, former director and treasurer of Washington BL; won Mixed Prs 1954; Baird Trophy 1956 and several regional events.

HAFFNER, Judy (b. 1940) of Pittsburgh PA, homemaker and bookkeeper; won Dist 5 KO Tms 1978, Womens Swiss 1981; All-American Swiss, Dist 5 GN Prs 1992, Hudson Womens Prs, Pittsburgh Womens Prs.

HAGEN, Paul W. (b. 1941) of Vancouver BC, computer analyst, graduate of British Columbia Institute of Technology and U of British Columbia. Won several regionals including Klondike Swiss Tms 1974, Dist 19 GN Tms 1974, 75; Dist 17 Fall KOs 1976, British Columbia Swiss Tms 1979, Canadian National Tms Zone 6 1981.

HAHN, Charlotte K. of Riviera Beach MD, directs lo-

cal bridge club, S1 director, former insurance underwriter, graduated Salisbury St College, novice chairman of Unit 135 since 1985, member Nat'l Goodwill Committee. Won Summer secondary Womens Prs 1975, Reno Womens Prs 1976, Canadian Nat'l Womens Prs, Dist 5 Womens Prs 1977; Mid-Atlantic Swiss Tms 1978, Rochester Spring Womens Prs 1986, Womens Swiss Tms 1989.

HALL, Clay (b. 1953) of Birmingham AL, computer programmer/analyst, schooled at Bucknell U, enjoys running, reading, bowling and sports. First alternate director for Dist 10 1991-96, held several executive positions in Unit and Dist including president of both, certified director, chaired several local sectionals and regionals. Was Intercollegiate campus winner 1975. Winner nationwide Instant Matchpoint Game (N-S) 1992. Won Birmingham KO Tms 1981; Spring secondary Open Prs 1982, Std Card Open Prs 1992, Open Swiss Tms 1993; Summer secondary KO Tms 1986; Charlotte Open Prs, Montgomery Swiss Tms, Fall secondary KO Tms 1986; Summer secondary Superflight KO Tms 1987; Dist 10 GN Prs 1989, Gatlinburg Open Prs 1990, Atlanta Handicap KO Tms 1992.

HALL, James M. (Jim) (b. 1940) of Minneapolis MN, insurance salesman, five handicap golfer. Placed second Reisinger 1988, Open BAM Tms 1991, 93. Has won more than 65 regionals; Diamond Life Master.

HALL, Jeffrey M. (b. 1951) of Schenectady NY, computer systems manager, degrees from Harvey Mudd College and State U of New York. In 1980 won GN Prs, placed second Sr and Advanced Sr Master Prs 1972; has won several regional events.

HALLE, Diana (b. 1924) of Boca Raton FL, lawyer, graduate of Cornell U and Brooklyn Law School. Won Amateur Womens Prs 1976.

HALLE, Ranik (1905-1987) of Oslo, Norway, editor and bridge columnist, represented Norway in the European Championships 10 times, placing second in 1938. Won 12 national championships. President INTERNATIONAL BRIDGE PRESS ASSOCIATION 1960-1964, honorary member and former president Norwegian Bridge Association. Former member Editorial Advisory Board, *Bridge Encyclopedia.*

HALLEE, Gerard F. (Jerry) (b. 1940) of Snohomish WA, president of software development and consulting company, graduated West Coast U, interested in state-of-the-art software development and use of personal computers, contributor to *Bridge World.* Won Vanderbilt 1969, Sr/Advanced Sr Master Prs 1963; placed second in Mens Prs 1969. Won Rocky Mtn Master Prs 1964, Bridge Wk Master Mens Prs 1967, KO Tms 1969, 70; Golden St Open Prs 1968, Seattle Mens Prs 1987.

HALLEN, Hans-Olof (b. 1929) Malmö, Sweden, tournament director. 1964 Nordic champion and 1964 Swedish team champion. One of four EBL Chief Tournament Directors. Awarded EBL Honor medal 1981. Co-author of *Tavlings-Ledaren,* a major work of directing and movements.

HALPERIN, Richard (Wizard of Odds) (b. 1940) of Skokie IL, real estate broker and mortgage loan originator, educated at U of Michigan. His nickname came from his facility to calculate odds instantaneously on almost any event. Unofficially known as World's Fastest Adder, he added 100 numbers in 30.3 seconds. Other interests are sports, gambling, movies, reading. Won Great Lakes Mens Prs 1963, Open Prs 1972; Florida KO Tms 1970, Champagne Open Prs 1975, KO Team 1976; Southeastern Mens Swiss Tms, MS Valley Open Prs 1976; Midwest Fall Swiss Tms 1977, Summer secondary Swiss Tms 1980.

HALPIN, Robert (1896-1972) of Chicago, printing company president, one of the founding fathers of the ABL and presided over that body in 1929. That same year he won the Chicago Trophy (now the Reisinger).

HAM, Esther of Montevideo, Uruguay. Won South American Womens Teams 1967, 1971, 1990. A regular member of the Uruguay Women's team in international competition and has won 66 national titles.

HAMAOUI, Steve (b. 1954 in Egypt) of Caracas, Venezuela, shirt manufacturer. WBF World Master. Won CAC Teams 1977, 1985, 1987, 1991, CAC Pairs once. Represented Venezuela in 10 world championships and won many national titles. President Venezuela Bridge Federation since 1990. Bridge teacher.

HAMILTON, John T. (b. 1933) of Columbus OH, graduate student, retired U.S. Air Force Lt. Col. and ACBL tournament director. A Rhodes Scholar, Hamilton was educated at the U.S. Military Academy at West Point, Balliol College, Oxford and Ohio State U. Current interests are applied mathematics and numerical analysis. Began directing full time 1965 and three years later was promoted to national director. Became director-in-charge at NORTH AMERICAN BRIDGE CHAMPIONSHIPS in 1976; served as treasurer of PROFESSIONAL TOURNAMENT DIRECTORS ASSOCIATION for more than 10 years; also served as director of the Miami Valley BA 1960-62, director and treasurer of the Central Ohio BA 1964-69, vice president of the Midwest Conference and chaired several regionals in mid 60s. With Marc Low he contributed to the SWISS TEAM MOVEMENT. Won Spring secondary Swiss 2nd Flt 1965, Mid-Atlantic Mens Prs 1975.

HAMILTON, Fred (b. 1936) of Encino CA, professional bridge player and teacher, WBF Grand Master. Won Bermuda Bowl 1976, placed second 1977; second World Tm Olympiad 1980; 4th Rosenblum Tms 1982, 5th World Open Prs 1978, 7th Olympiad Tms 1976, 4th Rosenblum Tms 1982, 5th World Open Prs 1978, 7th Olympiad Tms 1976.
Won Herman Trophy 1974, Reisinger 1974, 75, 78, 79; Vanderbilt 1977, Spingold 1979, Master Mixed Tms 1976, Team Trials 1975, 79; IMP Prs 1989; placed second Vanderbilt 1972, 81, 83; GN Tms 1974, Mens Tms 1980, 88; North American Swiss 1991, 92; Silver Ribbon Prs 1992; won Cavendish Invitational Pair Championship 1982, placed second Omar Sharif Individual 1990 and 3rd All-Star Individual 1992. ACBL Grand Master; has more than 20,000 MPs as of 1993; ranked 11th on all-time masterpoint list. Invented HAMILTON

OVER NOTRUMP; has won more than 200 regional events.

HAMMAN, Petra (Pete) (b. 1946) of Dallas TX, born in Germany, bridge teacher, former teacher and manufacturers representative, enjoys tennis. Member of the Bd of Governors and VP of Unit 176. Won Womens BAM Tms 1989, placed second Womens Swiss Tms 1992; won several regional events. See FAMILY.

HAMMAN, Robert D. (Bob) (b. 1938) of Dallas TX, company president, chartered life insurance underwriter, professional player; enjoys games, sports and backgammon. WBF Grand Master, has been the highest ranked player in the world since 1985. ACBL Grand Life Master with more than 17,500 masterpoints as of 1994.
World champion many times over, won the Bermuda Bowl 1970, 71, 77, 83, 85, 87; World Tm Olympiad 1988, World Open Prs 1974; placed second Bermuda Bowl 1966, 73, 74, 75; World Tm Olympiad 1964, 72, 80, 92; World Mixed Prs 1986, World Par Contest 1990; has had many other high finishes in world championship events. Won Team Trials (USBC) 1969, 71, 73, 77, 79, 85; Fishbein Trophy 1969, 83; Lou Herman Trophy 1978, 88; Player of Year in ACBL 1990, 93; was named Honorary Member 1991.
North American championships include Reisinger 1962, 70, 78, 79, 88, 93; Vanderbilt 1964, 66, 71, 73; Blue Ribbon Prs 1964, 86, 91, 93; Spingold 1969, 79, 82, 83, 89, 90, 93; GN Tms 1975, 77, 86; Life Master Prs 1980, 83, 92; Mens Prs 1986, Master Mixed Tms 1987, Mens BAM Tms 1988, Open Swiss Tms 1990. Placed second Reisinger 1968, Vanderbilt 1968, 70, 81; Spring Mens Tms 1969, 80; Spingold 1970, Life Master Mens Prs 1980, 81; Mens BAM Tms 1984, 89; Mens Prs 1985, Open Prs 1988, Open Swiss Tms 1992. See ACES TEAM and FAMILY.

HAMMERICH, Johannes J. J. (b. 1919) of Copenhagen, Denmark, lawyer and business executive. Resident of Caracas, Venezuela, for many years before moving back to his native country, Represented Venezuela in three world championships and three zonal championships. Nine Venezuelan national wins include open teams four times and open pairs twice. Co-founder Venezuelan Bridge Federation, and its vice-president 1960-78. Secretary General South American Bridge Confederation 1962-69. Member WBF Executive Council 1962-78, assistant secretary 1964-68, first vice-president 1968-78. Later president of Danish organization for brain sports, FIFO.

HAMMOND, Thomas E. (Tom) (b. 1933) of Redmond WA, structural engineer, educated U of Washington. Served Seattle Unit as Board member for four terms, bulletin editor for eight years and as vice-president. Diamond Life Master, placed second Goodwill Games 1990. Won Seattle KO Tms 1968, 69; Yakima Open Prs 1972, Edmonton Swiss Tms 1976, Dist 19 GN Tms 1977, 79, 90; Spring secondary Super Open Prs 1986, Penticton Super Open Prs 1987, Sr Open Prs 1990; Pasco Swiss Tms 1989, Vancouver Super Open Prs 1990; Spokane Sr Open Prs, KO Tms 1990; Nanaimo Sr Open Swiss Tms, KO Tms 1991; Dist 19 NA Prs 1991.

HAMPSON, Geoff (b. 1968) of Toronto ON, bridge

professional, member ACBL Junior Corps; placed second World Junior Championships 1991, Pan-Am Games Open Tms 1992. Won North American Swiss 1992, Mixed Prs 1994; CNTC 1991. His 30+ regional wins include Frontier Mens Swiss, Summer Fun Swiss 1989; Labor Day KO Tms, Open Prs, Bracketed KO Tms, Handicap KO Tms 1993; Lone Star Open Prs, Swiss 1994.

HAMUI, Jose J. (Johnny) (1935-1983) of Mexico City, company president and director, represented Mexico in world competition Monte Carlo 1976, New Orleans 1978, Maccabiah Games 1977. He was jai-alai champion 1955, 58, 62, 66 and a member of the Mexican jai-alai Olympic Team 1968. Served as president of Mexican Bridge Unit and treasurer of the MEXICAN BRIDGE FEDERATION; won Master Mixed Tms 1980 and several regional events.

HAN, Ittah (b. 1939) of Las Vegas NV, born in Indonesia, company president, has degrees from U of Colorado, U of California-Berkeley, U of Miami, U of Miami-Coral Gables, Whittier College School of Law (JD). Outside interests are reading, hiking, sightseeing, writing and foreign languages. He is listed in several *Who's Who* directories. Han has won Golden Gate Master Prs 1969, Golden State Open Swiss 1985, Master Swiss 1986; Desert Empire Open Swiss 1985, Rocky Mtn Open Prs 1986.

HANCOCK, John H. (Jack) (b. 1923) of Deming NM, mathematician, won Spring Mixed Teams, placed second Vanderbilt 1951; won several regional events.

HANDELSMAN, Lewis N. (b. 1948) of Harmon Cove NJ, computer programmer, stock options trader, directs and teaches on bridge cruises, graduate of CW Post, enjoys cooking and travel. Served on Nassau Suffolk BA Bd of Dir 1974-76. Wins include Summer secondary Mens Prs 1977, Washington Bridge Wk Swiss 1977, Tri State Mens Swiss 1978, Swiss 1979; Acapulco Fiesta Open Prs 1980, Mexican Nat'l Swiss 1981, Long Island Open Prs 1981, Spring secondary Std. Card Prs 1991.

HANDELSMAN, Rona (b. 1940) of Harmon Cove NJ, bridge teacher and director, directs and teaches on bridge cruises, graduate of Adelphi College, served on Nassau Suffolk BA Board, certified director. Regional wins include Long Island Womens Prs 1978, Dist 3 Womens Prs 1979, Mexican Nat'l Swiss Tms 1981, Dist 24 GN Tms 1980, GN Prs 1981; Cherry Hill Womens Tms 1985, Spring secondary Std Card Prs 1991.

HANDLEY, Michele V. (b. 1964) of London, England. WBF World Master. Second World Women's Teams 1992. Won Common Market Women's Pairs 1991, Teams 1993. Won ACBL Women's Swiss Teams 1992, the first foreign winner of a major ACBL team title. Won two national titles. Co-presenter, with Zia Mahmood, of 1991 British TV program *Play Bridge with Zia.*

HANLON, Ellie (b. 1936) of Lake Worth FL, bridge teacher and director, member of ABTA, has served on Unit 128 Board for nine years, member of Nat'l Goodwill Committee. Regional wins include Daytona Open

Swiss Tms 1990, Columbia Womens Prs 1991, Epson Prs Dist 9 1991, 92; Sunshine Sr Open Prs, Womens Prs 1992. Co-inventer of LAHAN.

HANN, Gary S. of Ann Arbor MI, real estate consultant, broker, appraiser, graduated U of Michigan, enjoys classical music, spectator sports and physical fitness. Served as member of ACBL Board of Dir 1988-89, member Nat'l Appeals Committee 1981-88, Board of Gov. 1980-88, 1990-, Chairman of Bd of Governors 1991-, co-chairman World Jr Championship Committee, contributing editor to Unit publication *Table Talk.* Diamond Life Master, placed second Mens BAM Tms 1979, has won more than 55 regional events.

HANNA, William J. (Bill) (b. 1931) of Bethesda MD, professor at U of Maryland, graduated UCLA (PhD), served as professor at institutions in Michigan, Nigeria, New York and Texas; currently doing study and work with people with physical disabilities and people without a home. One of the leading players on the West Coast until he retired from active play in 1961. Contributed many bridge articles to various publications including *The Bridge World,* wrote the monthly column *Western Dateline* for the *ACBL Bulletin,* co-authored *Precision Power Bidding* and the BULLDOG SYSTEM (see BIBLIOGRAPHY, C). Represented U.S. in int'l play Turin Italy 1960. Won Spingold 1958, Reisinger 1960; won numerous regional titles.

HANNER, Olof (b. 1922) of V. Frölunds, Sweden, retired professor of mathematics. Inventor and developer of many movements: PIVOT MITCHELL; STANZA HOWELL; movement for odd number of teams without bye; several perfectly balanced individual movements with each player having each other player as partner once and opponent twice. Co-author of *Tavlings-Ledaren,* a major work of directing and movements. Contributing editor of *Bridge Encyclopedia.*

HANSON, Jude Goodwin (b. 1953) of Vancouver BC, artist, illustrator, author, enjoys skiing, mountain hiking, cartooning, crafts, served as Unit 574 sectional co-chairman 1983-86. Author of *Table Talk Cartoons, Let's Play Cards,* co-authored *Teach Me to Play* and *Teach Me to Play, book two.* She has been the publisher of *Canadian Bridge,* editor of *Kootenay Trump-it, Vancouver Matchpointer, DINO Bridge Buff,* and Dist 19 Daily Bulletins; has done illustrations for *ACBL Bulletin* and Devyn Press. Her Table Talk cartoons have been published around the world in various bridge publications.

HANSON, Keith V. of Boca Raton FL, bridge teacher, former teacher, graduate of U of Iowa; has been certified director since 1973 and formerly taught college bridge classes for credit. Author of *Winning Bridge Intangibles* with Mike Lawrence, *Card Play Fundamentals* with Easley Blackwood, *Fingertip Bridge* and *The Art of Bidding.* Won Summer secondary Swiss Tms, Champagne Mens Prs 1971; Central States I Mens Prs 1972, Gopher Master Prs 1972, KO Tms 1979, 80, Open Prs 1980, Swiss Tms 1984; Dist 14 GN Tms 1973, Iowa Non-Mixed Prs 1976, Open Prs, Swiss Tms 1979; Zonal GN Tms 1983.

HARBIN, Rodger V. (Big D) (b. 1942) of Culver City CA, R2 tournament director since 1983, began directing in clubs 1972, tournaments 1979, former bridge professional and club owner; enjoys golf and fishing. Wins include Dist 23 GN Prs 1979, Reno Swiss 1983, 84, 85; Reno Mens Prs, Open Prs; Monterey Prs.

HARDY, Mary E. (Mrs. Max, formerly Senti) (b. 1936) of Las Vegas NV, bridge professional, former business manager for two radio stations, vice-chairman of Nat'l Appeals Committee. Worked on *Two-over-One Game Force-revised* with Max Hardy; competed in U.S. Women's Bridge Championship (Team Trials) 1991, placed second Womens BAM Tms 1989. Diamond Life Master, has won more than 60 regionals including Rocky Mtn Womens Prs 1969, Open Tms 1971; Spring secondary Open Prs 1977, Desert Empire Unmixed Prs 1981, Hawaii Mixed Prs 1981, Puget Sound Bracketed KO Tms, Peach City Womens Prs, Sr KO Tms 1992.

HARDY, Max L. (b. 1932) of Las Vegas NV, associate nat'l tournament director, bridge teacher and professional, graduated Chicago Musical College of Roosevelt U, former composer, conductor, singer and music teacher. Enjoys word games, sports and Lakers. Began directing 1961 and was assigned his present rating 1973. Former faculty member of Los Angeles Conservatory of Music which became California Institute of the Arts. Has served as vice-chairman of Nat'l Appeals Committee for five years; member of Nat'l Goodwill Committee. Hardy was an associate editor of *Popular Bridge* and was founding editor of *Southern California Bridge News*. He is the author of *Five Card Majors—-Western Style*, which went through four printings; the follow-up book was *Two over One Game Force*; other books include *Play My Card, Forcing NT, 4th Suit, New Minors, Splinters and other Shortness Bids, Two over One Game Force Revised*. Developed Hardy Adjunct to New Minor Forcing. Diamond Life Master; has won more than 70 regional events.

HARDY, William Thomas (Bill) (b. 1953) of Portland OR, sports cards and memorabilia retailer, former p.c. consultant and social worker for state of Oregon. Placed second in ABA Victor Daly Tms 1988, competed in 1989 Goodwill Games and finished second E-W in the U.S. in Epson Prs 1989. Won Seaside Open Swiss 1986, Dist 20 GN Tms 1989, Tacoma Strat Prs 1991, Portland Trail Swiss 1991, KO Tms 1991, 92, Prs 1992.

HARFOUCHE, Gaby (b. 1944) of Baabda, Lebanon, engineer. Represented Lebanon in 7 international championships. Won Gold Cup, Lebanese Festival 1973. Won more than five national titles.

HARKAVY, Harold (1915-1965) of Miami Beach, bridge club manager, one of the world's greatest at declarer play and a brilliant though unorthodox bidder; won Master Mixed Tms 1952, 53, 55, 57; Chicago (now the Reisinger) 1952, Vanderbilt 1963, Spingold 1956, 63; placed second Chicago 1945, Master Mixed Tms 1947, 64; Spingold 1953, Blue Ribbon Prs 1963.

HARKER, William C. (Bill) (b. 1942) of Santa Fe NM, writes scientific applications software, graduate of Colorado State U, enjoys running marathons. Won Dist 21

GN Tms 1975, 76, 89; California Capitol Swiss 1975, All Western Master BAM Tms 1975, KO Tms 1983; Mt. Shasta Open Prs 1981, Albuquerque Master Prs 1985.

HARMON, Leonard B. (b. 1919) of East Hampton NY, insurance company president, graduate of NYU, formerly served as president and treasurer of Greater New York BA and chairman of the Judiciary Committee in Dist 24. Retired from bridge in the Seventies; represented North America in Bermuda Bowl 1959 (placed second) and ACBL in first World Team Olympiad 1960; won *McKenney Trophy* 1958, Chicago (now the Reisinger), Vanderbilt, Open Prs 1958; Spingold 1962; placed second Spingold 1958, Master Mixed Tms 1959, Vanderbilt 1966; won many regional events.

HARPER, Barry C. (b. 1955) of Saskatoon SK, attorney, graduated U of Saskatchewan, member Unit Bd, Unit GN Tms and GN Prs coordinator; certified director; contributor to *Canadian Bridge Digest*. Won Open Prs 1990. Regional wins include Saskatoon Open KO Tms 1984, KO Tms 1988; Regina Open KO Tms 1985, Swiss, Mens Prs 1987, Open Prs 1991; Edmonton Open Swiss 1990; Red Deer Open Prs, Swiss 1992.

HARRIS, John T. (Spider) (1930-1994) of Houston, retired ACBL nat'l tournament director, began career in 1961; educated at Rice U and U of Houston. Intercollegiate champion 1952. See WEB MOVEMENT.

HARRIS, Laureen of Harare, Zimbabwe. Represented Zimbabwe in two world championships and one zonal championship. Represented Zimbabwe in many regional tournaments and won national titles.

HARRIS, Marguerite (Tommy) (1896-1987) of New York City, from 1946 to 1969 was an ACBL staff member in charge of the Club Department and writer of the *ACBL Bulletin* feature *Club Corner*. Won Womens Tms 1954; placed second 1952; won several regionals.

HARRIS, Shirlee (Mrs. Robert Cruise) (1934-1986) of Houston, former teacher; won Mixed Pairs 1960, 62 and several regional events in the late Fifies and the Sixties.

HARRISON-GRAY, Maurice ("Gray") (1900-1968) of London, England, bridge writer. Won European Teams 1948, 1949, 1950, 1963, second 1958. Represented Britain in three other world championships. National wins included Gold Cup seven times. A leader in developing the ACOL SYSTEM, and a protagonist of the LOSING TRICK COUNT. Bridge editor of *London Evening Standard, Country Life* and others. Author of two books.

HART, Norman de Villiers (1888-1976) of London, won English Inter-County Championship. Authored *Daily Telegraph Book of Contract Bridge, Bridge Player's Bedside Book,* and co-authored *Right Through the Pack, Vienna System of Contract Bridge,* and *Quintessence of CAB*. See BIBLIOGRAPHY, C, H.

HARTLEY, Patti (b. 1944) of Kirkland WA, self-employed in weight management and works for Doctor of Acupuncture, likes crossword puzzles, movies, dancing, singing and playing poker. Hartley works in local the ater groups and does volunteer work in the alcohol and drug addiction field. Was second Womens Swiss 1989; won Seattle Swiss 1982, KO Tms 1987, Swiss 1989; Penticton Master Prs 1982, Womens Prs 1985, KO Tms 1990; Wenotachee Open Prs 1986, Seaside KO Tms, Swiss 1986; Ocean Shores KO Tms, Swiss 1987.

HASSAN, Syed Ameer (b. 1936), retired business executive. NPC Pakistan Junior Team 1989. Bridge columnist and organizer.

HATHAWAY, Lorraine (nee: King). See ANTHONISEN, Lorraine.

HATHORN, John B. (1925-1964) of Houston TX. Though stricken by polio in 1954, he still achieved Life Master status in 1956; went on to become a bridge writer and leading bridge personality in the Southwest. Founded *Texas Bridge* 1959 which he published and edited until his death. Among his writings are several booklets on bidding and play, most written in collaboration with G. Robert Nail.

HATZIDAKIS, Manos (b. 1943 in Crete) of Athens, Greece, printer. Represents Greece in international events. National wins include open pairs twice, open teams twice and master teams five times. Formerly presented bridge on national radio and published a magazine that included eight pages about bridge. Publisher of *EBL News.*

HAUSE, Terry E. (The Reverend) (b. 1947) of San Jose CA, mathematics teacher, graduate U of Denver, selected for *Who's Who Among American Teachers*, enjoys travel and gardening. Qualified director; has been directing since 1971. Won Open Prs 1976, Spring secondary Swiss 1980, Bridge Week BAM Swiss.

HÄUSLER, Helmut (b. 1956) of Saarbrücken, Germany, mathematics and physics teacher. WBF World Master. Bronze medal 1980 European Pairs Championship and represented Germany frequently since 1974. Won more than 30 national titles. Vice-president of German Bridge Federation with responsibility for laws, regulations and selection.

HAVAS, Elizabeth (b. 1944) of Canberra, Australia, pharmacist. Won Far East Women's Teams 1977, and represented Australia in two world championships, six other zonal championships. Won one South Pacific playoff and five national titles.

HAVAS, George (b. 1947 in Hungary) of Brisbane, Australia, computer scientist and theoretical mathematician. Won Far East Open Pairs 1971, South Pacific playoff 1977. Runner-up Far East Teams and Far East Pairs 1976. Represented Australia in four world championships and one other Far East Championships. National wins include Open Teams twice, Open Pairs three times and Victor Champion Cup. Author of *The Australian Book of Bridge,* and bridge columnist of *The Australian* since 1973.

HAWES, Emma Jean (Mrs. David B) (d. 1987) of Fort Worth TX, graduated Cornell U at age 18, former president of Fort Worth Unit, was a member of ACBL Good-

will Committee and ACBL Bd of Gov. One of only eight women WBF Grand Masters; won Venice Trophy 1974, 76, 78, World Olympiad Womens Tms 1980; also represented U.S. in world competition Deauville, France 1968 (placed 3rd Womens Tms), Miami Beach 1972 (3rd Womens Tms, 5th Mixed Tms), Las Palmas 1974 (3rd Womens Prs), Monte Carlo 1976 (3rd Womens Tms). Won Open Prs 1958, Life Master Womens Prs 1966, 78; Womens Tms 1967, 70, 72, 74, 75, 76; Spring Womens Prs 1981, Master Mixed Tms 1964; placed second Life Master Womens Prs 1972, Womens Prs 1968, 76; Master Mixed Tms 1952, 67, 72; had numerous regional wins.

HAWKINS, Allen W. Jr. (Hawk) (b. 1949) of Birmingham AL, bank examiner, graduate Wake Forest U, is a 6 handicap golfer, won Dist 10 Swiss 1980, Mid-South KO Tms, Dist 10 GN Tms, Zone III 1981; Spring secondary Open Prs 1987, Huntsville Mens Prs 1987.

HAXTON, Owen V. (b. 1929) of Navato CA, retired math teacher and Army aviator, chairman ROTC Scholarship selection committee for Sixth Army, graduate of Kent State. Haxton began his career in bridge administration 1976 at the Unit level, became editor of Unit 508 *Double Dummy* and later served three terms as Unit president. He was also Unit secretary, tournament chairman, representative to the Dist. Member Dist 21 executive committee since 1981, district president 1985-87, member ACBL Bd of Dir since 1993; member ACBL Goodwill Committee.

HAYDEN, Dorothy. See TRUSCOTT, Dorothy Hayden.

HAYDEN, Garey (b. 1944) of Tucson, professional bridge instructor and player, owner of retail computer store, certified director since 1980. Grand Life Master with more than 17,000 masterpoints. Won Mens Tms 1973, Open Prs 1975, Mens Prs 1977, North American Swiss 1982, 85, 90; Fall Open BAM Tms 1992; placed second Blue Ribbon Prs 1972, Life Master Prs 1976, NA Swiss 1986; has won more than 150 regional titles; is one of a few people to have won five events at a regional.

HAYS, G. Gard (b. 1933) of Veradale WA, salesman, Dist 19 board member, Diamond Life Master, won Mens Prs 1961, Mens Prs 1964 and several regional events.

HAYWARD, Diane (b. 1936) of San Francisco, executive assistant, regional administration manager, Dist 21 *Forum* editor, graduated Hayward State U. Her avocation is genealogy and she is doing research for a book. Hayward edited the 4th edition *Bridge Encyclopedia* and is a contributing editor to the 5th Edition. Formerly assistant editor of *Contract Bridge Forum,* has been editor for many West Coast regional Daily Bulletins, Daily Bulletin assistant at NABCs and contributor to the *ACBL Bulletin*. She won Midwinter Holiday Swiss Flt B 1985.

HAZEN, Lee (1905-1991) of New York City, attorney, graduate of Columbia U and NYU Law School. Prior to graduating he played professional baseball for the Brooklyn Dodgers. Hazen was a driving force in modernization of ACBL in late Forties. ACBL director in 1940, served as ACBL counsel 1942-85, ACBL vice president 1945-47, named ACBL HONORARY MEMBER in 1958 and was a member of the ACBL Laws Commission from 1942 until 1973 when he resigned and was named member emeritus. He served as a trustee and treasurer of ACBL Charity Foundation, was founder and former vice president of Greater New York BA; contributing editor *Bridge Encyclopedia*. WBF Life Master; represented U.S. in Bermuda Bowl 1956, 59 (placed second both times); was designated npc of the winning North American team in 1971 Bermuda Bowl and the silver medal team in the World Tm Olympiad 1972. Won Spingold 1942, 47, 55; Chicago (now the Reisinger) 1945, 49; Vanderbilt 1939, 42, 49, 58; Mens Prs 1945, Master Individual 1941; placed second Spingold 1945, 58; Chicago 1941, 42; Vanderbilt 1944, 47; Master Individual 1940, Life Master Prs 1946.

HE, Zhenyi of China. Second Far East Teams 1993 and represented China in two world championships.

HEAD, Cecil (Cece) (b. 1910) of Fort Branch IN, retired attorney, educated at Harvard and Yale. Won Life Master Prs 1948; regional titles include New England KO Tms 1933, 34, 39, 41 (twice), 45, 46 (twice), 47, 51, 54, Mid-Atlantic Open Prs 1980, Myrtle Beach Sr Swiss 1989, Southern Indiana Open Prs 1992. (See S. Garton Churchill for records set by Head and Churchill when winning the Life Master Prs in 1948.)

HEITNER, Paul L. (the Whale) (1939-1988) of Bramalea ON, computer systems consultant, leading bridge theorist, co-developer with John Lowenthal of CANARY CLUB SYSTEM, co-founder and managing editor of *Bridge Journal*, now out of print. Won Life Master Prs 1970, Mens Tms 1976; placed second in Mens Prs 1972. Won numerous regional titles; also won events in South Africa in 1974.

HELGEMO, Geir (b. 1970) of Trondheim, Norway, bridge professional. WBF World Master. Second Bermuda Bowl 1993. Third European Teams 1993. Second World Junior Teams 1993. Won European Junior Teams 1990 and has represented Norway twice.

HELDRING, Ernst (b. 1904) of Amsterdam, The Netherlands, attorney, served European Bridge League as director 1952-1971, secretary 1958-1971. President Netherlands Bridge League 1949-1959, member Editorial Advisory Board, *Bridge Encyclopedia.*

HELLER, Max (Maxie) (b. 1916) of St Louis MO, public relations consultant. Heller was awarded the Distinguished Service Cross, the Silver Star and two Bronze Stars in WW II. Won Mississippi Valley Mixed Prs 1960, Mens Prs 1961, 67, 70; Midwest Fall Mens Prs 1962, Dist 8 GN Tms, Zone V 1975.

HELLER, Phyllis (Phyll) (b. 1934) of Pittsburgh PA, interviewer for Temple U, former sectional tournament director, graduate of U of Pittsburgh; served on Bd of Dir Pittsburgh BA, Dist 5 GN Tms coordinator for 10 years and chaired four Pittsburgh BA tournaments between 1958-88. Won Dist 5 Womens Prs 1968, Womens Swiss 1977, 81, GN Tms 1974; All-American Swiss 1975, 78.

HELMS, Gerald W. (Jerry) (b. 1950) of Charlotte NC, professional bridge player, club proprietor, teacher/trainer for ACBL, graduated East Carolina U; has served Unit 153 as vice president and president and Dist 7 as vice president. Certified director, contributor to *The Bridge Grapevine* and *The Bridge Teacher*, hand analyst for NA Collegiate Bridge Championship 1990, 91, 93 and Novice Championship 1992. As an ACBL teacher trainer he has trained more than 1200 teachers. Frequent lecturer at regionals and NABCs, member of Nat'l Appeals Committee, Nat'l Good Will Committee; Diamond Life Master. Has won more than 50 regionals including Eastern States Open Swiss 1977, Dist 7 GN Prs 1979, 80, 81, 87; Summer secondary Super Flight KO Tms 1989.

HELNESS, Tor (b. 1957) of Oslo, Norway, stock broker. WBF World Master. Second Bermuda Bowl 1993, Third World Teams 1980. Third European Teams 1993. Won Nordic Teams 1980 and 1982, European Junior Teams 1980. Represented Norway in 7 world and European Championships. Won 8 Norwegian titles.

HENG, Dr. Aik Koan (b. 1951) of Singapore, lecturer in computer science. Represented Singapore in one world championship and 6 zonal championships. National wins include open teams 6 times.

HENKE, Ron S. (b. 1943) of Yukon OK, retired research chemist educated at Northeastern State, certified director, now directs and teaches bridge at his bridge studio. Member Nat'l Charity Committee, former member of Dist 15 Bd of Dir; has been member of Sooner Unit Bd of Dir since 1971 and is past president. Served as Unit GN Tms and GN Prs coordinator since 1976 and is Dist coordinator every third year. Regional wins include Dist 15 Master Prs 1976, Swiss 1976, 80, 82; Toast of Tulsa Master Prs 1976, Open Prs 1980; Wichita Open Prs 1983.

HENKE, Chuck (b. 1934) of Aurora CO, safety coordinator with the Nat'l Child Safety Council, working with law enforcement agencies to promote child safety in the community; bonsai gardener. Was bridge professional, teacher and cruise director in the Sixties. Won Blue Ribbon Prs 1965; regional titles include Pacific Northwest Master Prs 1962, Rocky Mtn Mens Prs 1962, Master Swiss 1978; Inter-Mtn Open Tms 1965, Open Prs 1966; Oil City Master Swiss, Desert Empire Master Prs 1978.

HENNER-WELLAND, Christal (b. 1954) of New York City, vice president of financial services firm, graduate U of Illinois and attended graduate school at Fordham. Regional titles are New England Random Draw KO Tms 1988, Open Swiss 1990, KO Tms 1991, Open Swiss 1991; New England Winter Swiss 1991; Dist 24 GN Prs 1990; Mid-Atlantic KO Tms 1991, Port Chester Open Swiss 1992.

HENRIKSEN, John (b. 1959) of Copenhagen, Denmark, computer consultant. WBF World Master. 8th in the World Pairs 1992. Has won Copenhagen Pairs and Copenhagen Club Teams.

HENRY, Dr. Joseph L. (b. 1924) of Newton Centre MA, was top-ranking player of ABA for 12 years until his retirement from tournament competition. Became

ABA Life Master in nine months and won more than 20 ABA Nat'l Championships. He also won ACBL Mid-Atlantic Summer KO Tms 1962. Educated at Howard U, Xavier U, U of Illinois and Harvard; associate dean, professor and department chairman of Harvard School of Dental Medicine and chairman of the Board of Trustees, Illinois College of Optometry (the first non-optometrist to be named to this position); listed in *Who's Who in the World.*

HERBERT, Edmund J. (E.J.) (b. 1935) of Scottsdale AZ, retired from U.S. Army, bridge professional, blues fan, has written local bridge newsletters. Has won a regional event in each of last four decades. Regional wins include Desert Empire Swiss (twice), Master Prs (twice) and Mixed Prs; Rocky Mtn Swiss Tm, Pacific Southwest-Open Prs, Mens Prs; Bridge Week BAM, Inter-Mountain Mixed Prs.

HERBERT, Walter (1902-1975) of San Diego, conductor of the San Diego Opera, formerly general director of the Houston Opera Company, was the originator of the HERBERT CONVENTION, advocated by Herbert when he was a member of the 1937 Austrian team that defeated Ely and Josephine Culbertson, Helen Sobel and Charles Vogelhofer representing the U.S. to win the World Bridge Team Championship. The Herbert Convention was applied in many ways in the VIENNA SYSTEM.

HÉRÉDIA, Irènèe Bajos de (b. 1918) of Paris, France, chief tournament director French Bridge Federation, directed many international tournaments including World Pair Championships in Cannes 1962. Co-author with Desrousseaux of *Le Bridge d'Ecole Française* and originator and adviser of *Ominium.* Honorary chief French tournament director.

HERMANNSSON, Gudmundur Sv. (b. 1957) of Reykjavik, Iceland, journalist. WBF World Master. Represented Iceland in three world championships, one European Championship, three European Junior Championships and two Nordic Junior Championships. Four national wins include open teams once. Bridge columnist for *Morgunbladid.* Author of several bridge books. Vice-President Icelandic Bridge Union.

HERON, Dr. A. Douglas (Doug) (b. 1943) of Ottawa ON, surgeon; former pilot in Canadian Armed Forces (awarded Queen's Jubilee Medal), educated at Queen's U and U of Toronto. Owns his own float plane and enjoys flying, nature photography, golf, racquet sports and writing. Served as president of Canadian Bridge Federation 1991-, Unit 192 Pres, Dist 1 Judiciary chairman, Unit appeals chairman, member Nat'l Appeals Committee, Nat'l Goodwill Committee. Member INTERNATIONAL BRIDGE PRESS ASSOCIATION, regular contributor to *Canadian Bridge*, Unit newsletter and occasionally *The Bridge World.* Won the CNTC and the Tri-Country Playoffs 1990; competed internationally in Geneva 1990 and Yokohama 1991; has won more than 25 regionals.

HERR, Barbara Chase (b. 1920) of Wilmington DE, graduate Mount Holyoke College, appointed by governor of Delaware to chair Delaware State Commission for Women 1977-82, formerly a chemist, enjoys wild flower gardening, travel (has been to 47 states and 26 countries) and needlecrafts. Won Life Masters Womens Prs 1976 and Lancaster Womens Swiss 1982.

HERRINGTON, Gaye W. (b. 1938) of Redondo Beach CA, retired municipal court judge, graduated Washburn U and USC School of Law (JD), has served on several unit boards and ALACBU Bd; certified director and accredited teacher. Won Life Master Womens Prs 1987 and competed internat'ly Geneva 1990. Regional wins include Bridge Wk Mixed Prs 1970, San Francisco Mixed Prs 1971, Los Angeles Winter Womens Swiss 1976, Raincross Open Prs, Mid-Winter Holiday Swiss 1979; San Diego Womens Swiss 1982, Riverside Open Swiss 1992.

HERRMANN, John P. (b. 1945) of Franklin TN, bridge professional, former high school mathematics teacher, graduate of Vanderbilt, enjoys blackjack and major spectator sports. Has been a member of the Nat'l Goodwill Committee since 1988, served on Nat'l Appeals Committee 1983-91, has chaired many appeals committees since 1975 and since 1986 has lectured at NABCs. As a teacher he was nominated to his school's Hall of Fame. He placed second in the first North American Swiss 1977; Diamond Life Master; has won many regionals including Champagne Mens Prs 1972, Mid-Atlantic Mens Prs 1975, KO Tms 1981, Open Swiss 1991; Dist 11 Open Prs 1976, Mid-South Masters Prs 1976, Swiss 1982; Ft Wayne Mens Swiss, St. Louis Swiss 1988; Hilton Head Open KO Tms, Paducah KO Tms 1989; Lou Bluhm KO Tms 1990, 91.

HERTZBERG, Dr. Howard (b. 1936) of Alpine NJ, orthopedic surgeon, graduate of U of Pennsylvania and NY Medical College, enjoys golf and skiing. Has served city of Alpine as councilman and mayor. Placed second in Mens BAM Tms 1988. Regional wins include Savannah Open Prs 1964, Fall secondary Mens Swiss 1975, 80; Fall secondary Open Prs 1976, Summer secondary Superflight KO Tms, Hempstead Swiss 1990.

HERVEY, George F. (George John Frangopulo Hervey) (1897-1981), noted freelance British journalist and author; card correspondent of *The Field* (1940), bridge correspondent of *The Western Morning News* (Plymouth 1953), and contributor to *Bridge Magazine*; published six books on bridge, including *The Bridge Player's Bedside Book,* as well as other publications on card games and books on other subjects. See BIBLIOGRAPHY, B.

HESSEL, Dr. Ira Jay (The Iron Monkey) (b. 1946) of San Antonio TX, chemist, teacher, graduate of CCNY and U of Texas at Austin (PhD). On Bd of Dir Unit 172, editor of Unit newsletter. Regional wins include San Antonio Mens Prs 1979, Lake Charles Mens Prs 1985, Houston Masters Prs, Little Rock KO Tms 1986; Monroe Master Swiss 1987.

HESTHAVEN, Dennis G. (b. 1946) of Louisville KY, stock broker, graduate U of Wisconsin, enjoys travel and spectator sports, has served on Unit board including as vice president. Winner of North American Swiss 1991; regional wins include Hudson Masters Prs 1977, Dayton Mens Tms 1978, Columbus Open Tms 1980, Louiville Masters Prs 1981, KO Tms 1989, 90.

HETZER, Lloyd R. (b. 1946) of Memphis TN, bridge teacher and professional, former owner of record wholesale and export business. He made Advanced Sr Master and Life Master in the same week by increasing his MP total from 180 to more than 300 in one week. Regional wins include Fall secondary Blue Ribbon Prs 2nd Flt, Mid-Atlantic Open Prs 1970; Mid-South Swiss 1972, Dist 10 GN Tms 1973, 74, 89; Huntsville Open Prs, Jackson Open Prs 1988; Little Rock Stratified Prs, Gatlinburg Open Prs, Houston Open Prs, Zonal GN Tms 1989, Dist 10 GN Prs 1991, 92.

HEUSDEN, Willy van (1929 -1988) of Culemborg, The Netherlands. Represented The Netherlands in European Championships from 1963 to 1979. Her national titles include Open Teams 1969 (the first and only woman winner) and Women's Pairs 1973-77. She was married to Arie van Heusden (see CONTINENTAL CLUB).

HEWITT, Richard G. (Dick) (b. 1927) of New York City, attorney, educated at Williams College and Columbia U Law School, enjoys golf and serving on charitable boards. Hewitt has been very active in bridge administration for many years, having served on the ACBL Bd of Dir 1975-85, on ACBL Charity Foundation 1983-1991 (two terms as president), as president Westchester CBA, as president Dist 3 Co-ordinating Committee, member ACBL Executive Committee, treasurer of 1968 Spring and 1974 Summer North American Championships, chairman of the 1981 Bermuda Bowl Committee and as chairman of various other committees. He is currently 2nd alternate for ACBL Bd of Dir. Won Norwich Swiss, Tri-state Mixed Prs, three senior pairs and one senior Swiss teams.

HICKS, Karl S. (b. 1943) of Dominion NS, vice-principal and R-3 tournament director, graduated Mt. Allison U and College of Cape Breton; enjoys sailing and stamp collecting. Has served as Zone 1 director for CANADIAN BRIDGE FEDERATION, two terms as Unit 194 president and from 1974 to 84 was the Unit tournament chairman. Hicks is well-known for his repertoire of "stories". He is editor of *Maritime Bridge Line*. Was presented the "Fred Friendly" award at Summer NABC 1991. Placed first in North America and third in the world in the 1989 World-Wide Epson Prs.

HIJAB, Dr. Wasfi Ahmad (b. 1919) of Atlanta GA, born in Jordan, semi-retired, former university professor, graduate of Cambridge U (England), American U of Beirut, and U of Florida (PhD), father of quadruplets; columnist for Unit 114 *Pips and Tips*. Won Gatlinburg Morning KO Tms 1988, Sr Prs 1994; Fall secondary Morning Bracketed KO Tms 1989, Spring Sr Prs 1992; Keohane Individual 1993.

HILLIARD, Olga (1891-1979) of New York City, donated the ABL trophy for Mixed Prs, which is still given at the ACBL Spring NABC for a two-session event. She was victor of two national events and finished second twice.

HIN, Ong Keng (b. 1966) of Jakarta, Indonesia. Won Far East Teams 1992, represented Indonesia in one world championship.

HIRON, Alan M. (b. 1933) of Marbella, Spain, computer and games consultant. WBF World Master. Won World Senior Pairs 1990. Represented Britain in one zonal championship. Five national wins include Gold Cup once. Editor *Bridge Magazine* (1985-1990). Bridge correspondent *London Independent*.

HIRSCH, Harriette. see BUCKMAN, Harriette.

HIRSCH, Tannah (b. 1933) of Stamford CT, formerly of South Africa and Israel, bridge writer, editor and since 1978 president of Goren International, co-author of *Tournament Book of the 2nd World Olympiad Pairs*; edited Daily Bulletins at European Championships 1965, 74, was associate editor and editor of the *ACBL Bulletin* 1967-72; has contributed articles to bridge publications around the world. Won South Africa Congress Tms 1957, Natal Tms 1958, Jerusalem Prs 1962, 63, 64; ACBL Mid-Atlantic Summer Mens Prs 1968, Tri-State Swiss Tms 1970, 80; Bermuda Swiss Tms 1977, 78.

HIRSCHBERG, Ralph (1906-1962) of New York City, insurance broker, set a record by capturing the Eastern States Reisinger Trophy six times, including four consecutive wins, 1956-59. Won and placed second in numerous other events including Reisinger BAM Tms 1958 (second in 1945), Open Prs 1944, Mens Tms 1955.

HIRSCHHAUT, Fida (b. 1937 in Romania) boutique owner. WBF World Master. Won CAC Women's Teams 1979, 1980, 1981, 1985, 1987, 1991. Represented Venezuela in six world championships and won more than 10 national titles. Bridge teacher and director.

HIRSCHMAN, Samuel A. (b. 1976) of Southfield MI, student, enjoys computer and role-playing games. Became YOUNGEST LIFE MASTER at the time in July 1988, at age 11 years 9 months, 5 days. His feat was featured in *Sports Illustrated*. Won Bowling Green Swiss Tms 1992, Buffalo Flt B Prs 1992 (with Joel Wooldridge at ages 16 and 13). 1994 King of Bridge. See FAMILY.

HIRSCHMAN, Martin A. (b. 1949) of Southfield MI, bridge teacher and writer, retired attorney, former wire service newsman, editor Unit 137 *Table Talk* since 1987, member Unit Bd of Dir.; co-editor NEC World Jr Tm Championships *Daily Bulletin* 1991. Teacher and principal partner of son Sam during his successful campaign (1984-88) to become YOUNGEST LIFE MASTER. Has won about 15-20 regionals including Great Lakes Open Swiss Tms 1976, Open Prs 1992, Swiss Tms 1993; Motor City Mens Prs 1977, Open Prs, KO Tms 1990; Wolverine Mens Swiss Tms 1981, IMP Prs 1991, KO Tms 1993; Southeasterns Win-Loss Swiss Tms 1984, Cambrian Shield Prs 1987, KO Tms 1988; All-American KO Tms 1988, 90; Cornhusker Prs 1988, Midland KO Tms, Erie KO Tms 1989; Bowling Green Swiss Tms 1992, Buffalo KO Tms, Swiss Tms 1992. See FAMILY.

HIRSTY, Helen R. (b. 1927) of Wilmington DE, retired fingernail sculptress, has won Mid-Atlantic Womens Prs 1970, 81; Dist 4 Womens Swiss 1978, 91; Cherry Hill Womens Swiss 1987, 90, Womens Prs 1993.

HISATOMI, Hiroshi (b. 1946 in China) of Tokyo. Japan, bridge instructor and publisher. WBF World Master. Far East Champion 1985, and represented Japan in 11 other Far East Championships and seven world championships. Won 24 national team titles and two national pair titles. Author of *Five-Card Major Standard,* and *Seattle 84.*

HOADLEY, Frank M. (b. 1923) of New Orleans, retired professor of English, graduated U of Oklahoma (PhD), other interests are reading, tennis, travel and Barbou. Served several terms on New Orleans Board of Dir and is member of ACBL Nat'l Goodwill Committee. Grand Life Master with more than 11,000 points. Won Mens Prs 1960, placed second Spingold 1959, Reisinger 1975, GN Prs 1987. Some of his numerous regional titles are Keystone Open Tms 1959, Mid-South KO Tms 1970, Mens Prs, Master Prs, Open Prs 1973, Swiss Tms 1975, 76; MO Valley KO Tms 1975, 76; Crescent City KO Tms, Mens Prs 1977; Dist 10 GN Tms 1976, GN Prs 1979, 81; Dist 10 Open KO Tms 1988, Lone Star KO Tms, Summer secondary VP Swiss Tms 1991.

HOBLEY, Susan (b. 1952) of Sydney, Australia, systems computer analyst. Won Far East Women's Teams 1985 represented Australian in world championships and many national titles.

HOBSON, John (b. 1964) of London, England, stock broker. WBF World Master. Won World Junior Teams 1989. Won Gold Cup once.

HOCEVAR, Don of Southfield MI, won Marcus Cup 1970, Canadian Nat'l Tms 1971, Cambrian Shield KO Tms 1974, Presque Isle Swiss Tms 1977, Dist 12 GN Tms, Zone 1 1973.

HOCHZEIT, Michael (b. 1942) of Tel Aviv, Israel, building contractor and club owner. WBF World Master. Third Bermuda Bowl 1976, 1985. Represented Israel in 9 world championships, 5 European championships and 8 European Pairs Championships. Co-owner Israel's biggest club.

HODAPP, Thomas (b. 1942) of Cincinnati OH, advertising executive, won Life Master Mens Prs 1978, placed second Blue Ribbon Prs 1969. Grand Life Master with more than 10,000 masterpoints; has won numerous regional events.

HODGE, Paul (1910-1976), bridge teacher. Placed second 1961 Bermuda Bowl, also acted as npc of the U.S. Womens team in 1964 World Tm Olympiad. Frequently a commentator for ACBL vugraph presentations and panel shows. In 1955 captured both the Fishbein and Herman trophies. Won nine nat'l events, placed second eight times and had numerous regional wins.

HOERSCH, Joel J. (b. 1937) of La Jolla CA, newspaper composition programmer, educated at Yale, passionate about solving and creating word puzzles, particularly double-acrostics, has composed more than 100, about half with a bridge theme. Member San Diego Unit Bd of Dir and Nat'l Goodwill Committee for many years, currently a member Nat'l Appeals Committee, was chairman of Ethics and Conduct Committee San Diego Unit

through the 70's, contributor to *Contract Bridge Forum.* For 20 years has written, directed and acted in bridge skits and shows for regionals and NABCs. Placed second Reisinger 1981; has won more than 30 regionals including Pacific Southwest Master Prs 1969, Mens Swiss Tms 1976, 77, KO Tms 1975, Swiss Tms 1981; Bridge Week Open Prs 1972, BAM Tms 1976; Holiday Festival KO Tms, Swiss Tms 1979; Pikes Peak Swiss Tms 1980, Golden State Master Swiss Tms 1990, Oregon Trail Open Prs, Pacific Southwest Open Swiss Tms 1991, Palm Springs Swiss Tms 1992.

HOFFMAN, Arthur H. (b. 1935) of Maplewood NJ, credit insurance consultant, graduate U of Massachusetts, marathoner, golfer and tennis player, served as board member of Unit 140. His wins include Mens Prs 1988 and Summer secondary Commercial and Industrial Tms 1974, 75, 76, 83, 84; New Brunswick Sr Prs 1991.

HOFFMAN, Martin (b. 1932) of London, England, bridge writer and professional. WBF World Master. Winner of many European tournaments and one of the fastest analysts in the game. Author of *Hoffman on Pairs Play,* and occasional magazine contributor. He is a survivor of Auschwitz.

HOFFNER, David L. (Lion) of Potomac MD, croupier and entrepreneur, outside interests in nature and animals. Won Life Master Mens Prs 1977, placed second Life Master Mens Tms 1980. Diamond Life Master with many regional wins.

HÖIE, Erik (b. 1928) of Stavanger, Norway, tailor, represented Norway Bermuda Bowl 1970, European Championships 1959, 1961, 1965, 1969. Authored *Stavangergrangen,* a work on 1NT opening bids and responses.

HOLLAND, George T. (Georgio Bella Holland) (b. 1947) of Dartmouth NS, vice-president real estate development/brokerage firm. Served as local tournament chairman Units 194 and 166, two terms as president of Unit 194, chairman of Can-Am and Can-At regionals three times each, president Canadian Bridge Federation, regular contributor to *Maritime Bridge Line.* Won Fleur de Lys Swiss Tms 1974, Nat'l Capital Swiss Tms, KO Tms 1975; Can-At Open Prs 1981, 82, 83, 85, BAM Tms 1983.

HOLM, Cid F. (b. 1937) of Helsinki, Finland, data processing consultant. Represented Finland on seven occasions, including two world championships and three European championships. NPC on 12 occasions. 9 national titles include Open Teams once and Open Pairs once.

HOLT, Clarice K. (b. 1911) of Fort Worth TX, oil executive, won Womens Prs 1962, Mixed Prs 1962; placed second Womens Tms 1964. Diamond Life Master, has won numerous regional events.

HOMSY, Margueritte (b. 1951) of Cairo, Egypt, former bank official. WBF World Master. Middle East Team Champion 1987 and 1991, runner-up 1989. Represented Egypt 1991 Venice Cup.

HOOKER, Jim L. (b. 1937) of Los Angeles, independent oil operator, graduate of Southern Methodist U, won the GN Tms 1975 and numerous regional events in the Seventies.

HORN, Stormy (b. 1929) of El Paso TX, consultant-atmospheric physics, former research scientist at White Sands Missile Range, educated U of Texas and Columbia Pacific U (Ph. D.) Other interests are race horses and numismatics; is a pilot and science fair judge. Co-author of *The System* and *System Update*, authored *Bidding Magic* and did early presentations of several conventions including Reed/Horn 4NT, Integrated Major Raises, Mini-Splinters, Colorado Relays, Tricolor and StarWars. Has won more than 30 regionals including Rocky Mtn Mens Prs 1970, KO Tms 1975, Open Prs 1979, Swiss Tms 1981; International City Swiss Tms, Master Prs 1979; Texas Summer KO Tms 1974, Pikes Peak Master Prs 1976, Open Prs 1978; El Paso Swiss Tms 1992.

HORNING, Edmund M. (Ted) (b. 1940) of Willowdale ON, syndicated bridge columnist, bridge studio and travel agency owner, professional bridge teacher and player, served as vice chairman of the Canadian Bridge Federation Nat'l Championship Committee in 1977. Represented Canada in world championship play Stockholm 1970, New Orleans 1978. Diamond Life Master, placed second Blue Ribbon Prs 1978; has won numerous regional events.

HOROBETZ, Helen (1915-1989) of Chula Vista CA, bridge cruise director, lecturer and writer; struggled against the crippling effects of rheumatoid arthritis from the age of 18 months. With a background in journalism she came to the attention of ACBL which employed her in the Press Room at NABCs for 20 years. In between, she managed regional tournaments, edited Daily Bulletins at other tournaments, taught classes and devoted hours of volunteer work to advance bridge in the San Diego area. She instituted the District's regional Daily Bulletin which she edited, was a contributor to the *ACBL Bulletin*, *Southern California Bridge News*, *Contract Bridge Forum* and *ABTA Quarterly*. Member of AMERICAN BRIDGE TEACHERS ASSOCIATION since 1973, served as its regional vice president 1974-78, was a member of the committee that edited the Report of ABTA Committee on STANDARD AMERICAN. Held various executive positions in Unit 519 and Dist 22, was second alternate to the ACBL Bd of Dir, a member of the Bd of Gov, member of the Nat'l Goodwill Committee and ACBL Charity Committee. In 1987 at the celebration of the 50th anniversary of the ACBL she received a golden medallion for her lifetime of service to the game and its players, the only one so honored.

HORTON, Sally (formerly Sowter; now Mrs. Raymond Brock) (b. 1953) of Nottingham, England, typesetter. WBF Grand Master. Won Venice Cup 1981, 1985. Second World Women's Teams 1984. Won European Women's Teams 1979, 1981, Common Market Women's Teams 1979, 1981, 1993. Second Gold Cup twice. Former executive editor of *International Popular Bridge Monthly.*

HORWITZ, Janice C. (Jan) (b. 1924) of Butler PA and

Scottsdale AZ, bridge teacher, involved in charity work, tennis and gardening. Won Master Mixed Tms 1969; regional wins include Midwest Fall Womens Prs 1967, Gopher Open Tms 1973, Fall secondary Womens Tms 1975, Pittsburgh Labor Day Womens Prs 1984, Womens Tms 1991; Cleveland Womens Tms 1989, Sr Prs 1991; Summer secondary Sr Tms 1990. Horowitz won the World-Wide Epson Prs 1988, the only time ACBL members have won through 1993.

HOWARD, Denis (b. 1932) of Sydney Australia, solicitor, president WORLD BRIDGE FEDERATION 1986-1991. Represented Australia in Far East Championships in 1969, 71, 75; Bermuda Bowl 1971, 76, World Team Olympiad 1964, 68, 76 and was npc in 1979 and 1981. His nat'l titles include Australian Interstate Tms 1958, 59, 61, 62, 63, 64, 65, 67, 68, 69, 70, 75; Nat'l Open Tms 1976, Open Prs 1957, 61, 62, 64, 65, 71. Founding editor of *Australian Bridge* and was bridge columnist (15 years) of *The National Times*. Honor member of INTERNATIONAL BRIDGE PRESS ASSOCIATION. Howard was chairman of the New South Wales BA and president of AUSTRALIAN BRIDGE FEDERATION. From 1982-86 served on WBF Executive Council. In 1992 Howard served as the interim CEO of ACBL.

HOWARD, Laurence B. III (Bryan) (b. 1958) of Nashville TN, attorney, educated at U of California at Berkeley, Vanderbilt and U of Florida, member of Bd of Dir of Harold S. Vanderbilt Bridge Education Association. Won 20 regionals including Music City Master Prs 1977, Crescent City Master Prs 1981, Tampa KO Tms, Louisville Open Prs 1983; Paducah Masters Prs, Hot Springs Swiss Tms 1989; Nashville Master Prs 1991.

HOWARD, Laurence B., Jr. (Larry) (b. 1927) of Nashville TN, retired corporation board chairman, graduate VMI and Murdoch Business College. Has served in various executive positions on unit and district levels including as unit president. Won first legitimate (post litigation) victory by female in Mens Prs playing with his 13-year-old daughter. Howard has won regional events in Memphis 1964, New Orleans 1965, Chicago 1966, Lexington 1967, Monroe 1969, Houston 1975, Nashville 1976, Cincinnati 1977, Atlanta 1978, Huntsville 1979.

HOWARD, Morgan H. (1893-1965) of North Hollywood CA, for many years a top executive of the Hearst publishing enterprise in Pittsburgh and New York, was president of ACBL in 1942.

HOWELL, Edwin Cull (1860-1907) is credited with the invention of the HOWELL MOVEMENT in 1897. Born in Nantucket MA to clergyman George Howell and his wife Frances Sarah Cull, Howell attended prep school Charlier Institute in New York City prior to entering Harvard in 1877. He left in 1881 before completing his degree and taught in a private school in Asbury Park NJ. He returned to Harvard in 1883, graduated 11th in his class and took honors in math; taught math at John Hopkins U 1884-85 and in two private schools. After leaving the teaching field in 1887, Howell joined the staff of *The Daily News* in Baltimore. For 14 years beginning in 1889 he worked for the *Boston Herald*. He became assistant city editor in 1896 and assistant news editor in 1898. In July of 1903 he became assistant in the National Almanac Office of the U.S. Navy in Washington DC, a position he held until his death. Howell learned whist at Harvard and became its best player. He took a prominent part in the activities of the American Whist League and in 1896 published *Howell's Whist Openings: a systematic treatment of the short-suit game*, and in 1897 the *Howell Method of Duplicate Whist for Pairs*.

HOYLE, Edmond (1679-1769) a London, England, barrister, was the first authority on whist and other games and the first professional teacher of whist. His famous work was perhaps the best seller of the 18th Century and had the longest title of any book ever written on cards: *A Short Treatise on the Game of Whist, Containing the Laws of the Game, and also Some Rules Whereby a Beginner May, with Due Attention to Them, Attain to the Playing It Well*. It was published in 1742 and quickly went through several editions as well as being pirated extensively. Hoyle's technique was surprisingly modern. He introduced fourth-best leads and the idea of inferring the nature of unseen hands from the fall of the cards. He discussed matters of probability. He also included a Code of Ethics and Fair Play, which was embodied almost without change in the LAWS OF AUCTION nearly 200 years later. He was the first person to establish a tradition of law and order in card games, whence the phrase, now used to describe correct procedure in anything, "according to Hoyle". The book of laws by Hoyle was reprinted verbatim through the years. The prominent London Clubs eventually did make certain changes as to style and working from time to time, especially in the 19th century, but Hoyle's imprimatur remained on most editions. He achieved considerable fame during his lifetime and his name has since become a household word. Any collection of rules of card, table or board games is still termed a Hoyle.

HSIAO, Chi-han or **Elmer** (b. 1941 in China) of Taipei, Taiwan, English teacher. World Life Master. Runner-up Bermuda Bowl 1970 and represented Taiwan in two other Bermuda Bowls. Far East Champion 1969, 1976. Won many national titles.

HSIEH, Douglas (b. 1969) of New York City, corporate finance analyst, graduate of Dartmouth; loves skiing and taught between school terms. Hsieh became the YOUNGEST LIFE MASTER in 1981 at the age of 11 years 10 months and 4 days, a record that stood for seven years. He was also the youngest to win a regional event (age 9) and the youngest Jr Master (age 7). Representative of ACBL in World Jr Bridge Championships Denmark 1993; won Nat'l Youth Championship 1988 and Polar Mens Prs, Swiss Tms 1980. Hsieh believes, "The title of Youngest Life Master has been and will always be the measure of a family's strength and perserverance". See FAMILY.

HSIEH, William C. (Bill) (b. 1966) of San Francisco, investment banker, graduate of Dartmouth, YOUNGEST LIFE MASTER in 1980 at age 13 yrs 7 months. Hsieh placed third in the World Jr Championships in Amsterdam 1987, and was on the U.S. Jr team in the Epson International in Japan 1985. His regional wins include Space City KO Tms, Southeastern Mens Swiss

Tms, Polar KO Tms, Master Swiss Tms, Klondike KO Tms 1980. See FAMILY.

HSU, Jen Yuen (1914-83) of Taipei, Taiwan, born in China, textile merchant. Taiwan's "Father of Bridge". Won Far East Open Pairs 1959 and 1969, and represented Taiwan on six other occasions. Coordinator of 1971 Bermuda Bowl and three Far East Championships. Founded *Chinese Bridge Magazine* and edited it for 22 years. Taught widely, and coached first Taiwan Women's Team. Developed a system based on Goren Standard American, and translated more than 30 bridge books into Chinese.

HU, Jihong of Shanghai, China, technical employee. WBF World Master. Won Far East Teams 1991, second 1993. Represented China in three world championships and two other zonal championships. Won one national title.

HUANG, Kuang-Hui or **Patrick** (born 1943 in China) of Taipei, Taiwan, financial executive in plastics corporation. World Life Master, with the highest WBF ranking among Asian players. Runner-up Bermuda Bowl 1969, 1970 and represented Taiwan in 12 other world championships. Far East Teams champion seven times and pair champion five times in 20 appearances, the best record anywhere in zonal play. First played in the Far East Championship at age 15, the youngest to play anywhere at this level. Assisted Charles Wei in the development of the PRECISION SYSTEM, which has been used regularly by Taiwan teams.

HUDECEK, Carl J. (b. 1934) of Perrysburg OH, company president, former chief physicist of Owens-Illinois Glass Co, educated at U of Toledo and U of MI/Rutgers Institute. Author of many technical papers on glass and international expert on TV tube manufacturing. Served many times as president of Unit 105 and Dist 12, member Nat'l Goodwill Committee. His other interests are economics, glass science and golf. Member of *The Bridge World* Master Solver's Panel for more than 25 years. Regional wins include Midwest Open Tms 1957, 60, 74; Motor City Mens Swiss 1976, Wolverine Swiss Tms 1978, Dist 12 GN Tms, Zone IV 1980, 81. Won Master Mens Prs 1965 and Life Master Mens Prs 1966.

HUDGINS, John L. (Jack) (b. 1929) of Memphis TN, retired ACBL national tournament director, began directing in 1960 and achieved the rating of national director in 1968. Won Summer Sub-Senior Master Tms 1961, Mid-Atlantic Summer KO Tms 1962.

HUDSON, Robert R. (b. 1921) of Dunedin, New Zealand, company director and investment consultant, won New Zealand Open Teams 1966. Past president and Life Member of New Zealand CBA, former associate editor and long-time contributor to *New Zealand Bridge*.

HUGGARD, Marietta (b. 1935) of Naples FL, member of ACBL Nat'l Goodwill Committee, became a world champion when she won the Venice Cup 1974. Won Life Master Womens Prs 1970, Womens Tms 1971 (second in 1973), Master Mixed Tms 1972; has won numerous regional titles.

HULGAARD, Johannes (b. 1932) of Aarhus, Denmark, orthopedic surgeon. WBF World Master. Third World Teams 1988. Represented Denmark in two other world championships, nine zonal championships and on many other occasions. His 21 Danish titles include Open Teams 14 times and Open Pairs twice. A leading theorist, and co-author with Axel Voigt of several books on the Danish style of Acol.

HULGAARD, Lida (b. 1939) of Aarhus, Denmark, lawyer. Won Nordic Teams 1973. Represented Denmark in one world championship, five European Championships, three of them in the open series, and on many other occasions. Ten national wins include Open Teams six times and Open Pairs twice. Daughter of Axel Voigt.

HUME, L. Hampton (1924-1969) of Atlanta, represented U.S. in the World Open Prs 1962; won Open Prs 1961; placed second Master Mixed Tms 1964; had many regional wins; published *Modern Bridge* magazine in 1964.

HUMER, Norman D. (b. 1940) of Boston MA, scientific programmer, educated at MIT, enjoys backgammon. Humer retired from tournament play in protest against the way cheating situations were handled during the early Eighties. Regional wins include Spring secondary Mens Swiss Tms 1973, Tri-State Winter Open Prs 1973, Mens Prs 1974; New England KO Tms, Dist 25 GN Tms, Zone II 1973; Can-At Mixed Prs 1974, KO Tms 1975, Master Swiss Tms, Swiss Tms 1978; Can-Am KO Tms 1974, GN Prs 1981.

HUNTE, August J. (Augie) (b. 1928) of San Leandro CA, retired business manager, graduate of U of California at Berkeley; has played primarily rubber bridge since 1980. Has won All-Western KO Tms 1968, Mid-Winter KO Tms 1970, California Capitol Open Tms 1972, 73, Master Prs 1972; Golden Gate Master Prs 1977, Great Plains Mens Swiss 1979.

HUSKE, William H. (1879-1945) of New York City, a native of Quebec, spent 30 years in the newspaper business; was associated with International News Service as a reporter and later became district manager in Marion OH. From 1927 to 1929 was associated with the Cleveland *Plain Dealer* as its bridge editor. He covered the first famous "grudge" match between Ely Culbertson and George Reith who came from New York to play Carl Robertson, an editorial writer for the *Plain Dealer,* and Ralph R. Richards of Detroit. He became associate editor of *The Bridge World* and in 1932 was made editor. He was editor of *ACBL Bulletin* 1937-39 and wrote many articles on bridge and towie, the three-handed game he helped sponsor.

HUSSEIN, Ahmed D. (b. 1941) of New York City, born in Egypt, investment banker, graduate of Polytechnic U of NY (PhD), enjoys backgammon and chess. Given Cairo U Golden Medal for Social Services 1958, placed second in Egyptian Open Chess Championship 1959, awarded Fulbright in 1965. Represented Egypt in world play in New Orleans 1978; won Mixed Prs 1978; placed second Life Master Prs 1975; has several regional wins.

HUSTON, Michael B. of Joplin MO, labor arbitrator

and bridge professional, formerly an English professor, educated at Oberlin College and Western Michigan U. Member of Nat'l Appeals Committee since 1978, Diamond Life Master. Regional wins include Kalamazoo Open Prs 1979, Open Prs, Swiss Tms 1992; Sault Ste. Marie Swiss Tms 1987; Lansing Open Prs 1988; Cleveland KO Tms 1989, Southfield KO Tms, Open Prs 1989; Peoria KO Tms, Swiss Tms 1990; Bowling Green Swiss Tms 1990, Open Prs 1992; Corpus Christi KO Tms, Butte Open Prs, Cincinnati KO Tms 1990; Fort Wayne Swiss Tms 1991, 92; Lone Star Masters Prs, Nashville KO Tms 1993.

HUTCHINSON, Mary L. (b. 1916) of Lethbridge AB, company vice president. She and her husband celebrated their 57th wedding anniversary in 1992. Member Nat'l Goodwill Committee 1958-93 and one of the top women masterpoint holders in Canada, has won Hawaii Open Tms 1955, Pacific Northwest Master Prs 1959, 62, Mixed Prs 1959; Inter-Mountain Master Prs 1959.

HUTCHINSON, Robert (b. 1905) of Lethbridge AB, president of land company, retired farmer, graduate of Oregon State U, Diamond Life Master, ranks among top 20 masterpoint holders in Canada. Regional wins include Hawaii Mens Prs, Open Tms 1955; Rocky Mtn Mens Prs 1960, Edmonton Mens Prs, Canadian Mens Prs 1968.

HWANG, Dr. Frank K. (b. 1940 in Shanghai, China) of Warren NJ, research mathematician. World Life Master. Runner-up Bermuda Bowl 1969 and represented Taiwan in one other world championship. Won his first national title at the age of 17, and won 1992 national teams with an overseas Chinese squad. Coach of Far East champion Taiwan team in 1981. Represented Taiwan in the Far East Championship when he was 18 and his brother, Patrick Huang, was 15. This was the youngest international partnership ever on a major occasion.

HYLAND, Daniel A. (b. 1929) of Arlington Heights IL, president bank brokerage firm, enjoys handball and piano. In 1975 won Open Prs. Won Niagara Falls Swiss Tms 1982, Spring secondary Open Prs 1983, Lake Geneva Sr Swiss, Toronto Sr Prs 1986; Baltimore Open Prs 1987.

HYMES, Edward, Jr. (1908-1962) of New York City, attorney, was a colorful figure in the early days of contract bridge. Life Master #23, Hymes was one of the leaders among the "Young Turks" who gained their seasoning as members of the Deal Club group closely associated with P. Hal Sims at his summer home in Deal NJ. He won his first major national championship, the 1935 Fall Open Prs, with fellow Columbia alumnus Oswald Jacoby, then added one Vanderbilt and four Spingold wins. Hymes was a lifetime member and a former president of the CAVENDISH CLUB in New York.

I

ILYAS, Dr. Mohammad (b. 1921), retired World Health Organization official and Professor of Medicine. President of Pakistan Bridge Association. An organizer who has popularized duplicate bridge in Pakistan. NPC Pakistan team 1987 Bermuda Bowl.

IN DER MAUR, Gangolf (b. 1931) of Klagenfurt, Austria, lawyer. Represented Austria in five World Championships and five European Championships. Won Austrian Open Team seven times and Open Pairs twice.

INCE, Mehmet Ali (b. 1947) of Istanbul, Turkey, businessman. WBF World Master. Represented Turkey in one world championship and three zonal championships. Five national wins include open teams three times.

INGBERMAN, Monroe J. (1935-1985) of White Plains NY, college professor, graduate of U of Chicago and Northwestern U, inventor of the FRAGMENT BID, 3NT RESPONSE as a forcing major raise and for many years was a frequent contributor to bidding structure including SPLINTER BID, UNUSUAL OVER UNUSUAL, method for Inverted Minors, Structured Reverses, 3NT to ask for a singleton after a jump major raise (MATHE ASKING BID), modified Roman Keycard Blackwood. He was a columnist for the ACBL *Bulletin* and a contributing editor to *Bridge Encyclopedia*. Ingberman had several regional titles to his credit.

INGRAM, Henry St. John (1888-1974) of Farnborough, Kent, England, printer, bridge writer and editor, represented England in the SCHWAB CUP 1936, was captain of the British team in some prewar championships, and won the GOLD CUP 1936 in addition to other national successes. Editor *Contract Bridge Journal* 1950-1955, contributing editor for *Britannica* and *Chambers* encyclopedias, authored *How to Win at Bridge*. See BIBLIOGRAPHY, C, E.

INOUE, Shiro (b. 1915) of Tokyo, Japan, securities company adviser, former bank president. National titles include Princess Takamatsu Cup 1968, 1972, Prince Takamatsu Cup 1970, Fujiyama Cup 1970, Yamada Cup 1965, 1971, 1977. A life master in both U.S. and Japan. President JCBL 1969-72.

INOUE, Utako (Mrs. Shiro) (1914-1983) of Tokyo, Japan, former secretary. Played in Far East Womens Team Championships representing Japan 1964 and 1969, Philippines 1974. National titles include Yamada Cup 1971, Princess Takamatsu Cup 1968. A life master in three countries, Japan, U.S. and Philippines.

IRWIN, Florence (1865-1956) a well-known New York City novelist, bridge teacher and expert on auction bridge, she wrote one of the first books on contract bridge in 1927. In the early 1900's she was bridge editor of the *New York Times*.

ISAACS, E. Sydney (Syd) of London ON, retired U associate registrar, represented Canada in world play Monte Carlo 1976, New Orleans 1978. She won Spring secondary Mixed Swiss Tms 1975 and several regional events.

ITABASHI, Mark M. (b. 1954) of Murrieta CA, bridge teacher and professional, former computer analyst, graduate UC/Berkeley. Outside interests are tennis, skiing; is a former concert clarinet player. A Grand Life Master with more than 15,000 masterpoints, currently ranked in top 30 all-time ACBL masterpoint list. Won four events at several regionals — Portland, Santa Rosa,

Pasadena and Phoenix; placed second North American Swiss 1986, Master Mixed Tms, Mixed Prs 1987. His more than 150 regionals wins include Navajo Trail KO Tms 1977, Pacific Southwest Open Prs 1979, Riverside Swiss 1979, 80, 91; Raincross Swiss 1979, 80; Dist 23 GN Tms 1980, 88; Desert Empire Swiss, Bridge Wk Swiss 1981; Pasadena Masters Prs 1983, 84, 88, 91; Reno KO Tms 1985, 86, 87, 91; Santa Rosa Swiss 1986, KO Tms 1987, 88, 89, 90, 92; San Diego KO Tms 1987, 90, 91; Spring NABC secondary Open Prs 1988, Fall NABC Secondary Open Prs 1988, Swiss 1991.

IVANUS, Milan (1917-1987) of Ljubljana, Slovenia, government officer. First president of BZS. Founded several clubs and also major tournaments in Slovenia (Bled and Portoroz).

IVASKA, J. Paul Jr. (b. 1941) of Las Vegas NV, office manager, formerly a control systems engineer, designing and analyzing control and guidance systems for missiles and spacecraft; graduate of Stanford U. Sports and railroad fan, likes history, politics, travel and running. Has served Culver City and Las Vegas Units as president, Dist 17 Bd member in the early 80's and is Nat'l Goodwill Committee member. Competed in int'l competition in Biarritz 1982 (placed 18th in World Mixed Prs) and Geneva 1990. Won Amateur Swiss 1976, North American Swiss 1979; placed second North American Mens Swiss 1982, GN Tms 1989. Grand Life Master with more than 11,000 masterpoints; has won dozens of regional events including Bridge Wk Masters Prs 1967, Mens Prs 1971, KO Tms 1973, Open Prs 1975, Open Prs 1978, Master Swiss 1981, Open Swiss 1986; Pacific Southwest KO Tms 1973; Orange County KO Tms, Bakersfield Swiss 1974; Los Angeles Winter Swiss, Dist 23 GN Tms Zone VIII, Hawaii Mens Swiss 1980; Raincross Open Prs 1980, Mixed Prs, Master Swiss 1981; Desert Empire Swiss 1984, Rocky Mtn Swiss 1986, 89; State of Nevada Swiss 1989, Midwinter Holiday Swiss, Las Vegas Master Swiss 1990.

IVATURY, Uday B. of New York City, computer systems consultant, has won Port Chester Prs 1985, Mid-Atlantic KO Tms, New England Random Draw KO Tms 1991; Dist 24 GN Pairs, Port Chester Open Swiss 1992.

IVEY, Ernest (Ernie) (b. 1934) of Milpitas CA, software systems engineer, graduate of California State U, Interests are San Francisco 49ers, popular fiction, old movies, U.S. history and computers. He has served as Unit 503 representative to Dist 21 1981-87 and as Dist 21 Charity Committee chairman, vice president and president, a certified director. Won Open Prs 1976. Regional wins include Summer secondary Swiss 1976, All-Western Mixed Prs 1981, Standard Card Prs 1988.

IWASZKO, Anthony J. (Knute) (b. 1935) of Belmar NJ, sales manager; also owner/innkeeper of a seashore bed and breakfast, graduated Pennsylvania State U. Won Sub-National Masters Prs (under 50 pts) 1966.

J

JABBOUR, Zeke (Xique) of Boca Raton FL, professional player, enjoys theater, the arts, politics, writing, has won nat'l awards in theater, architecture, writing and community affairs. Has been associated with all aspects of the theater and has lent his expertise to variety shows at NABCs. A Grand Life Master with more than 16,000 masterpoints, he won 71 regional events in 1989, the year he won the *Barry Crane Top 500*. He won the Fishbein Trophy 1989, placed second Life Master Mens Prs, Spring Mens BAM Tms 1979. Has won hundreds of regional events.

JABES, Rina of Milan, Italy, won World Women's Teams 1972, 1976, European Women's Teams 1970, 1971, 1973, 1974. World Life Master.

JABON, Joseph A. (Joe) (b. 1925) of Seattle WA, owner of transportation company, graduated Tulane U, enjoys horse racing, hunting, golf and TV. Amateur playwright, producer and actor, he introduced musical entertainment at regionals using talent furnished by bridge players in the Sixties. He served two terms as president of Seattle Unit in the Sixties, was columnist for *Seattle Times* in the Sixties. Jabon was a member of the *Whiz Kids* team that included Sidney Lazard, Ron Dreyfus and Noel Duvic. Was one of the leading masterpoint holders in the Northwest until approximately 1975, when he began to pursue his career; competed sporadically until 1988 when he actively resumed tournament play. Diamond Life Master, won the Nat'l Open Individual 1959, second Individual 1950, Open Prs 1965, GN Prs 1992; has won numerous regional titles.

JACKSON, Jerry R. (b. 1946) of Chicago, member of Dist 13 board 1983-88; regional wins are Spring secondary ESC Open Swiss, Monterey Unmixed Swiss 1979; Milwaukee Open Prs 1982, Chicago Non-Smoking Open Prs 1986, Fall secondary Morning KO Tms 1990, Summer secondary Open Prs 1991.

JACKSON, Joan S. (b. 1947) of Dallas TX, financial manager, previously in corporate finance with a major retailer, graduate U of Texas. Represented ACBL in New Orleans 1978, Biarritz 1982 and Geneva 1990. Won Womens BAM Tms 1989, placed second in Nat'l Amateur Prs 1976, Womens Swiss, Life Master Womens Prs 1992. Some of her many regional wins include Oklahoma City Mixed Prs 1976, Shreveport Open Prs 1980, Ft Worth Open Prs 1981, Spring secondary Swiss 1984, Corpus Christi Swiss 1987, Dist 16 GN Prs 1988, Houston Open Prs 1990, 91; Ft Worth Swiss 1991.

JACKSON, Peter (b. 1940) of Pretoria, South Africa, scientist. Member of SABF Executive since 1971 and senior tournament director. Maintains masterpoint register and designs movements.

JACOB, Dan R. (b. 1951) of Burnaby BC, born in Romania, manager of fire protection engineering services/ government of Canada, graduate of Institute of Bucharest. Other interests skiing, tennis, cycling and is avid sports fisherman. He competed in world competition in Biarritz 1982 and Geneva 1990. Was Nat'l Master of the Year (see MINI McKENNEY) 1979, placed second Canadian Nat'l Tms Championship. Regional wins include Emerald Empire KO Tms 1979, British Columbia Mens Prs, Nat'l Capital KO Tms 1981; Portland Masters Prs, Puget Sound Mens Prs 1983; Seattle

Super Open Prs 1984, Spring secondary Swiss 1985, Penticton Swiss 1987, Vancouver KO Tms, Super Open Swiss, Strat Prs 1990.

JACOBS, Jos (b. 1947) of Amsterdam, The Netherlands. *Bulletin* editor at world and European Championship. Represented The Netherlands 1984 World Teams. National titles include Open Teams 1976. He contributes to *Bridge* as tournament directing expert. Speaks eight languages.

JACOBS, Walter L. (Wally) (1896-1985) of Bay Harbor Island FL, founder, president and chief executive officer of Hertz Rent-a-Car Corp. 1918-60. He was a recipient of the Horatio Alger award. Won Open Prs 1936, 39; and several regionals.

JACOBSON, Ann (b. 1940) of Stockton CA, staff accountant, won Swiss 1981 and several regionals.

JACOBSON, Rita (1911-1992) of Sydney, Australia, formerly of Johannesburg, South Africa. Runner-up World Womens Teams 1968, 1972, World Women Pairs 1974. Also represented South Africa World Team Olympiad 1964, 1976, 1980, World Pair Olympiad 1962, 1966, 1970, Maccabi Games 1977. Nine national wins included four in open teams and one in open pairs. Bridge columnist *The Star.*

JACOBUS, Marc S. (b. 1951) of Las Vegas, professional player, a Grand Life Master with more than 11,000 masterpoints, won Life Master Mens Prs 1972, North American Swiss 1986, placed second Reisinger 1974. He has won more than 100 regional titles.

JACOBY, James O. (Jim) (1933-1991) of Richardson TX, stock broker, graduate of Notre Dame. His outside interests included backgammon, sports and opera. Coauthor with his father (Oswald Jacoby) of JACOBY TRANSFER BID, JACOBY 2NT and a syndicated bridge column. He frequently served as a member of the ACBL Bd of Gov and was a past president of the Dallas BA. WBF Grand Master and an ACBL Grand Life Master with more than 25,000 masterpoints. He won the Bermuda Bowl 1970, 71; World Mixed Tms 1972, World Tm Olympiad 1988; placed second in the Bermuda Bowl 1963, 73; World Open Prs 1966, World Tm Olympiad 1972, World Mixed Prs 1978. Won the McKENNEY TROPHY 1988, Fishbein Trophy 1968 and many nat'l events including Spingold 1969, Chicago (now the Reisinger) 1955, Reisinger 1970, 77; Vanderbilt 1965, 67, 71, 82; Mens Prs 1956, Mens Tms 1968, 72, 73; Master Mixed Tms 1968, GN Tms 1981. He placed second in the Spingold 1957, 62, 70, 73, 76; Mens Tms 1954, 68; Mixed Prs 1963, Blue Ribbon Prs 1976, Life Master Prs 1968, 71; Mens Tms 1969, 88. Jacoby had dozens of regional titles to his credit.

JACOBY, Mary Zita (Mrs. Oswald) (1909-1987) of Dallas, a former tennis champion, one of two women whose husband and son have won world titles (see BECKER, B.J. or MICHAEL), she placed second in Master Mixed Tms 1935 and won several regionals in the Sixties.

JACOBY, Oswald (Ozzie, Jake) (1902-1984) of Dallas TX, bridge columnist, first achieved int'l preeminence as partner of Sidney Lenz in the CULBERTSON-LENZ MATCH, but he had already established himself as a champion at auction and contract. He next became a member of the famed FOUR HORSEMEN and FOUR ACES teams. His selection by Lenz over players of greater experience and with whom Lenz had practiced partnerships was early recognition of the brilliance and skill that were later to bring Jacoby to the top of the ACBL's list of all-time masterpoint winners.

Jacoby, born in Brooklyn on Dec. 8, 1902, left Columbia in his junior year to become an actuary, completing the examination of the Society of Actuaries in 1924 to become, at age 21, the youngest person ever to do so. After four years with Metropolitan Life, he went into business for himself, but his success was cut short by the 1929 stock market crash. Jacoby's victory-studded career includes many oddities. He played in (and won) his first auction tournament in July 1929, the Nat'l Team Championship of the AMERICAN WHIST LEAGUE. But he had already won the first big contract pair tournament ever played, the Goldman Pairs event in the Eastern States Championship held in February of that year.

Later on, he set a record by winning the GOLDMAN TROPHY three times in 20 years, the only occasions on which he entered. Afterward, he became a nat'l champion by winning two AWL pair and team events. After the Culbertson-Lenz match, Jacoby was secretary of the UNITED STATES BRIDGE ASSOCIATION for nearly two years, thus being associated with Ely Culbertson. Late in 1933, however, he helped to form the original Four Aces team, which dominated the bridge world for the next several years. During this period, in addition to American Bridge League triumphs, he won two pair championships and four team championships of the USBA. Jacoby had two months of Army service in World War I, when he was 15, and he was awarded the Victory Medal. On Dec. 7, 1941 he was playing in the Open Pairs in Richmond VA when the Pearl Harbor attack was announced. He immediately left the tournament and did not play again for four years. During most of that time he served as a specialist in the Navy, with the rank of lieutenant commander.

When he returned to competition in 1945, he found Charles Goren far ahead in the masterpoint rankings. He had done very little about returning to the top when he again returned to active duty in 1950 for service in the Korean War. He served as a commander in Intelligence and was a member of the original staff at the Panmunjom armistice conference. This return to service cost him his place on the American team in the first BERMUDA BOWL matches. However, he had represented the ABL in int'l competition as far back as 1935 when the Four Aces team defeated the French, champions of Europe, in the first official World Championship encounter. (See WORLD CHAMPIONSHIPS.)

Returning from two years of Korean service, Jacoby found he had dropped out of the top 19 masterpoint holders. By 1958 he had managed to move back into sixth place, still far behind Goren. At that time he decided to make a determined effort to regain the #1 position. By 1962, he had done so. Between 1959 and 1963, he won the *McKenney Trophy* four times in five years; the only player at that time older than 50 to win the trophy. He won it at ages 57, 59, 60 and 61. In 1963 he became the first player to acquire more than 1,000 points in a single year. His winning total that year was 1,034. In 1967, he surpassed the 10,000-point mark, at which time he retired from active competition for the McKenney Trophy. Almost exactly one year later he relinquished his position as top masterpoint holder to Barry Crane.

In 1950, Jacoby became the daily bridge columnist for Newspaper Enterprise Association, serving several hundred newspapers. He established a record on April 22, 1982 when his 10,000th article was printed. (Goren's name appeared on more than this number, but he had not written any columns for many years before his death in 1991.) Jacoby wrote books on poker, canasta, gin rummy and mathematical odds. He also continuously maintained a practice as a consulting actuary, served for six years as a member of the Board of Visitors of Harvard Observatory (for the last three, under the chairmanship of then Senator John F. Kennedy), became an expert on computers and was frequently consulted on questions of tournament movements, elimination schedules and scoring. He won a North American Championship (the Chicago in 1955) with his son, James Jacoby, and scored many victories with his wife of 50 years, Mary Zita Jacoby. He was hoping to add to his titles the missing one — most masterpoints owned by any husband and wife, regardless of when acquired. Jacoby was elected to the bridge HALL OF FAME 1965 and was named ACBL HONORARY MEMBER in 1967. As npc of the North American teams for 1969, 1970 and 1971, Jacoby captained the first North American Bermuda Bowl champion teams (1970 and 1971) in more than a decade.

His North American Championship titles are: Spingold 1934, 36, 38, 39, 45, 50, 59; Vanderbilt 1931, 34, 35, 37, 38, 46, 65; Chicago (now the Reisinger) 1955; Reisinger 1983; Master Individual 1935; Master Mixed Tms 1968; Life Master Prs 1936; Mens Tms 1952, 59; Open Prs 1935, 60, 64, Men's Prs 1934, 39, 49. He also won USBA Grand Nat'l Open Tms 1934, 35, 37, Open Prs 1936, 37; he won ABL Men's Tms 1931, 32, AWL Tm-of-Four 1929, 31, 33, Open Prs 1933, HERMAN TROPHY 1960. He placed second in many NADC events and won countless regional titles including the MARCUS CUP 1955. In 1973 he won the World Championship of Backgammon. Jacoby pioneered many bidding ideas, including FORCING 2NT, JACOBY TRANSFER BIDS and WEAK JUMP OVERCALLS. His innovations have included developments of GERBER and BLACKWOOD and a specialized use of TWO NOTRUMP and THREE NOTRUMP RESPONSES. His most recent innovations were the use of TWO-WAY STAYMAN in connection with Jacoby Transfer Bids after 2NT opening and after 2 -anything-2NT. He invented the use of 2♥ as a double negative response to 2♣ with 2NT a positive heart response and 2♦ the usual waiting bid. Among his writings are *The Four Aces System*, *What's New in Bridge*, *Win at Bridge with Oswald Jacoby*, *Win at Bridge with Jacoby Modern*, *The Backgammon Book* (with John Crawford). He also had many books on mathematics, gambling, poker and other card games, including canasta, in which he had the two best-selling books. See Bibliography, B, C, E, M, and FAMILY.

JADALI, Qumars (b. 1952 in Iran) of Vienna, Austria, programmer. Represented Austria in two European events. Won Austrian teams six times, Life Master Individual, Open Pairs once each. Represented Iran in two Chess Olympiads.

JAEGER, Henry P. (1888-1971) of Cleveland Heights OH, bridge writer and lecturer. Jaeger was a member of the group which promoted the OFFICIAL SYSTEM. He won trophies in whist, auction and contract bridge.

JAEGER, Jane (Mrs. Lewis M.) (b. 1914) of North Bay Village FL, she and her late husband were the first married couple to attain Life Master ranking, #74 and #94 respectively, in 1947. Currently semi-retired from competitive bridge. Won Open Prs 1945, Chicago (now the Reisinger) 1947, Master Mixed Tms 1951, GN Tms 1973; placed second in Vanderbilt 1956. Her regional titles include Eastern States KO Tms 1945, Mixed Tms 1946, Mixed Prs 1949, Womens Prs 1966; Southeastern Womens Prs 1966, KO Tms 1968; Fall secondary Womens Swiss 1977.

JAFRI, Mazhar (b. 1941) of Karachi, Pakistan. lawyer. Founder of the Bridge Federation of Africa and the Middle East (BFAME) in 1980 and its Secretary, Treasurer, and WBF representative since then. Chairman WBF Zoning Committee and Infrastructure Development Committee. Member of five other WBF Committees including Appeals and Credentials. WBF Vice-President since 1991. Senior Vice-President Pakistan Bridge Association. Helped China and other countries to form NCBOs and join WBF.

JAFRI, Syed Saeed (b. 1916) of Karachi, retired senior civil servant. As President of the Pakistan Bridge Association for 13 years, and President Emeritus, contributed to the promotiont of bridge in Pakistan, including the development of a strong national team. Was Vice-President of BFAME for 10 years.

JAÏS, Pierre (1913-88) of Paris, France, physician. WBF Grand Master. Won Bermuda Bowl 1956, World Teams 1960, World Pairs 1962, a unique triple in the three major open world championships at that time. Won European Teams 1955, 1970, second 1954, 1956, 1959. Won *Sunday Times* Pairs 1963 and many French national titles. His partnership with Roger Trézel was one of the world's strongest from 1950-70, and demonstrated the effectiveness of the *tendance canapé* (modified canapé). Author of more than 12 books, and a magazine contributor.

JAKOBSDOTTIR, Esther (b. 1944) of Reykjavik, Iceland, cashier. Won Nordic Women's Teams 1990. Represented Iceland in one world championship, two European Championships and five other Nordic Championships. 14 national wins include women's teams 8 times and women's pairs 3 times.

JALAVA, Matti (b. 1926) of Helsinki, Finland, salesman, represented Finland European Championships 1956, 1963, Nordic Championships 1962. National successes include Open Tms 1949, 1958, 190, 1962, 1963.

JALBUENA, Lydia (b. 1923) of Westbury NY, formerly of the Philippines, secretary. Won Far East Women's Teams 1982. Represented Philippines in four world championships and 11 other zonal championships. Over

20 national wins include open teams five times.

JAMES, Rex (b. 1942 in Antigua) of Kingston, Jamaica, banker. WBF World Master. CAC Team Champion 1982, 1983, and represented Jamaica on several other occasions including 1983 Bermuda Bowl. Numerous national wins.

JANITSCHKE, V. Craig (b. 1951) of Olympia WA, computer technical specialist for state of Washington, former professional bridge player (1977-84), graduated U of Colorado and St. Martin's College. Outside interests are computers, running, tennis, politics. He won a national award for a computer system that is currently in effect across the state of Washington. Was Colorado state champion pianist (junior high division) in 1966. He was the youngest Life Master in Colorado in 1971—a record that held for many years. Janitschke was a frequent partner of the late Barry Crane. He placed fourth in the World Open Prs in Biarritz 1982 and is a WBF World Master. He is an ACBL Grand Life Master with more than 10,000 MPs (as of Nov. 1993); won GN Tms, Life Master Mens Prs 1980; Open Prs 1981; was second in Mens Swiss. He has won dozens of regionals including Spring NABC secondary Open Prs 1980, California Capital KO Tms, Mens Prs, Swiss 1980; Mid-Winter Holiday Master Prs, Open Prs 1981; Los Angeles Winter Swiss, Master Prs 1981; Veterans Day Master Prs, Swiss 1981; Oregon Trail Mens Prs, Master Prs 1982; Portland Mens Prs, Masters Prs, San Diego Masters, Mens Swiss, Swiss 1982; Tacoma Swiss 1984, Seattle Swiss 1987, Tacoma Flighted Super Swiss 1991.

JANITSCHKE, Jan P. (b. 1947) of Littleton CO, bridge professional, graduated Colorado College, excellent pianist and violinist, performed as a soloist with several orchestras as a teenager. WBF World Master, placed fourth in World Open Prs Biarritz 1982. ACBL Grand Life Master with more than 12,000 points. His nat'l titles are GN Tms, Life Master Mens Prs 1980; North American Mens Tms 1982, GN Prs 1987. Regional wins include Mid-Winter Holiday KO Tms 1973, Missouri Valley Swiss 1974, Rocky Mtn Mens Prs 1977, 79, Swiss 1977, 1980; California Capital KOs, Swiss 1980; Acapulco Master Prs, Open Prs 1981; Rocky Mtn KO Tms, Wine Country KO Tms 1981; Desert Empire KO Tms, 1983; Pacific Southwest Super Open Prs 1984, Mid-Winter Holiday KO Tms 1986, Navajo Trail Master Swiss 1987.

JANNERSTEN, Eric (1912-1982) of Stockholm, Sweden, editor and publisher, represented Sweden on several occasions including European Championship 1951, won many national titles. Founder of INTERNATIONAL BRIDGE PRESS ASSOCIATION and its executive secretary-trasurer until his retirement in 1975. Founded, in 1939, *Bridgetidningen* Sweden's internationally acclaimed bridge magazine. Bridge columnist since 1940, Jannersten was editor and publisher of *European Bridge Review* 1949-1951, authored best-selling books on bridge, and published about 40 bridge books. He headed a bridge school from 1938, with an estimated 150,000 pupils. He introduced the bidding-box now used in all national and international events and in many clubs.

JANNERSTEN, Per (b. 1948) of Avesta, Sweden, publisher, printer and auditor. Owner of Jannersten Forlag, a major supplier of bridge books and equipment. Bridge columnist *Svenska Dagbladet.* Co-author of *Tavlings-Ledaren,* a major work of directing and movements. Contributing editor of this *Encyclopedia.*

JANSEN, Piet (b. 1957) of Groningen, the Netherlands, owner of bridge and chess pub. Won Bermuda Bowl 1993, EC Teams 1987.

JANSMA, Jan (b. 1962), of Nijmegen, The Netherlands, teacher. WBF World Master. World Junior Team Champion 1987. European Junior Champion 1986.

JANZ, Ricardo (b. 1948) of Rio de Janeiro, Brazil, engineer. WBF World Life Master. Won Bermuda Bowl 1989, South American Teams 1988, 1989, 1991. Represented Brazil in one other world championship.

JAQUES, Arturo (1923-1991) of Buenos Aires, Argentina, travel agent and bridge writer. South American champion 1958, 1959, 1961. Represented Argentina in Bermuda Bowl 1959, 1962, in World Team Olympiad 1964, 1972. 43 national titles won include open teams 13 times and open pairs 8 times. He won the Gabarret Cup 1959, 1960, and was the top Argentine master-point holder 1960-1975. A former editor of *Bridge Argentino,* and contributed to many bridge periodicals.

JARIGESE, Jacqueline L. (Jackie) (b. 1931) of Portland OR, co-owner Portland Bridge Club, former school teacher, graduate Portland State U. Enjoys reading, travel, bowling — she once had a 726 scratch series in league bowling. In 1990 she drove from Anchorage to Prudhoe Bay on the Arctic Ocean down to Valdez, following the pipeline and back to Anchorage, a feat few people have accomplished. Jarigese is a Diamond Life Master with numerous regional wins including Summer secondary Womens Prs Flt B 1980, Las Vegas Prs 1982, Seattle Swiss, Kalispell KO Tms, Victoria Open Prs 1983; Anchorage Womens Prs, Masters Prs 1984; Charlotte Swiss, Spokane Open Swiss 1984; Butte KO Tms 1986, Anchorage KO Tms, Ocean Shores KO Tms 1990, Columbia Prs 1991. She placed second in the ABA Victor R. Daly KO Tms Top Flight 1989 (equivalent to ACBL's Spingold).

JARIYANUNTINATE, Panjaroon (b. 1947) of Bangkok, Thailand, state employee. WBF World Master. Won Far East Open Pairs 1982. Runner-up Far East Open Teams 1985, and represented Thailand on seven other occasions and in three world championships.

JEFFERSON, Leonard A. Jr. (b. 1922) of Arlington TX, retired federal employee, teacher, social worker, bridge teacher, public relations consultant and convention planner. ABA Honorary Life Member, ABA Diamond Life Master with more than 10,000 masterpoints, represented U.S. in world championships Las Palmas 1974, New Orleans 1978. Won ABA Summer KO Tms 1969, Spring Round-Robin Tms 1978, 80, 84, 85; ABA KO Tms 1975-89; ABA Spring Nat'l Swiss, Open Tms, Nat'l Non-Mixed Prs 1993, Nat'l Swiss 1993. From 1946-1993 he has had more than 500 wins including more than 50 ABA nat'l championships, with wins in all major events. Member ABCL Bd of Gov 1962-68,

ACBL Nat'l Goodwill Committee, chaired ACBL regionals 1978, 91; consultant for ABA Nat'ls and has held many other bridge administrative postions.

JEITZ, Maryse (b.1942) of Luxembourg. President of Luxembourg Bridge Federation. Second Common Market Mixed Pairs 1979, and represented Luxembourg in several other Common Market events.

JELLINEK, Hans, born in Vienna, Austria, was deported by the Germans from Norway in 1940 and died in a concentration camp. World Champion 1937, European Champion 1936. His partnership with Karl Schneider was considered strongest in Europe in mid-Thirties.

JEMC, Tomaz (b. 1946) of Ljubljana, Slovenia, economist. Represented Yugoslavia in one zonal championship and one junior zonal championship. Represented Slovenia in one world championship. Won 10 national titles.

JENSEN, Nils E. (b. 1920) of Stockholm, Sweden, owner of Elfa, an electric supplies company. Represented Sweden in 7 world events. Runner-up Far East Pairs 1977. Jensen organized the 1970 Bermuda Bowl and World Pairs Olympiad in Stockholm, the 1974 World Pairs Olympiad in Las Palmas, and the 1983 Bermuda Bowl in Stockholm. President Swedish Bridge League 1965-70 and 1981-83. President European Bridge League 1981-1987, then President Emeritus. Delegate from Europe to WBF 1971-87. WBF Honorary Member 1982.

JEPSON, Tom (b. 1951) of Kirkland WA, won Seattle Swiss 1982, 89, KO Tms 1987; Penticton Master Prs 1982, KO Tms 1990; Wenatchee KO Tms, Open Prs 1986; Seaside KO Tms, Swiss 1986, Ocean Shores KO Tms, Swiss 1987; Portland Stratified Prs, Tacoma KO Tms 1988.

JERONIMIDIS, Elena D. (b. 1946) of Reading, England, editor, translator and theatrical producer. Editor of magazine *Bridge Plus* since 1989, bridge editor *Teletext* from 1993.

JESNER, George (b. 1925 in Scotland) of Canberra, Australia, master draper, bridge teacher and writer. Member of winning Scottish team in 1964 Camrose series. Won first South Pacific playoff and represented Australia on several other occasions. Won several national titles. Former ABF president and columnist for the *Australian.* Co-inventor of BENJAMIN.

JOELSON, Gail (b. 1954) of U Heights OH, programmer/analyst, graduate of Carnegie-Mellon U, enjoys computers, piano and tournament table tennis (she was the 1984 Ohio womens state champion). Member Unit 125 Bd of Dir. Won Non-Life Master Pairs 1992.

JOHANNSSON, Gudlaugur R. (b. 1944) of Hafnarfjordur, Iceland, certified public accountant. WBF World Master. Won Bermuda Bowl 1991. Represented Iceland in six other world championships, 6 European Championships and one Nordic Championship. National wins include open teams 5 times and open pairs twice.

JOHANNSSON, Helgi (b. 1951) of Reykjavik, Iceland, managing director. President of Icelandic Bridge Union since 1989 and promoter of many bridge events. Two national wins include open teams once.

JOHNSON, Benjamin O. (Ben) (1906-1976) counsel and member of the Executive Committee of the WBF, presided over the ACBL in 1953. An attorney from Spartanburg SC, Johnson served as npc of the U.S. Bermuda Bowl Tm in 1954 and as chairman of the ACBL Charity Foundation. Johnson won the Chicago (now the Reisinger) in 1949.

JOHNSON, Chester (Chet) (b. 1940) of Chicago, stock chaser, one of the leading ABA players, ranked 3rd in masterpoints with more than 17,600; some of his wins include the ABA Nat'l Open Tms 1977, KO Tms 1982, 83, 84, 86, 87, 89, 91; ACBL Central States I Mens Prs 1982, KO Tms 1984, 89; Fall secondary Open Prs 1986, Spring NABC secondary Open Prs 1987. Twice winner of William Friend Award.

JOHNSON, George W. (b. 1923) of Charlotte NC, U.S. Postal Service director of finance, won several American Bridge Association regional and nat'l titles. Has been active in ABA bridge administration since 1968 and served as president 1984. Member of ACBL Nat'l Goodwill Committee.

JOHNSON, Jane (b. 1933) of Memphis TN, manager of ACBL Club Membership Department since 1984, worked on Fourth Edition of *Bridge Encyclopedia*; editor of *Club Managers Newsletter*.

JOHNSON, Jared A. (b. 1948) of Golden CO, writer and lawyer, bridge columnist for *Denver Post* since 1977, graduated from Oglethorpe U, attended graduate school at Temple and U of Texas, graduate U of Denver; enjoys photography and world travel. Author of *Classic Bridge Quotes*, editor and writer for *The Contract Bridge Forum*, Dist 17 *Scorecard*, contributor to *Bridge World, Popular Bridge, Bridge Today* and *ACBL Bulletin*. Member International Bridge Press Association. Won Rocky Mtn Prs 1991 and other regionals.

JOHNSON, Jean of London England, formerly of Bermuda, has taught bridge, is a member of the Nat'l Goodwill Committee, has been very active in bridge administration for Bermuda and has served as vice president, ethics officer Unit 198; president BDA Bridge Club and chairman Bermuda regional 1988, 89, 90; has represented Bermuda in world competition in Biarritz 1982, Seattle 1984, Bal Harbour 1986, the Tri-Country playoffs 1989; won Norman Bach Trophy 1984. Won Bermuda Womens Prs five times, Open Prs and Open Tms twice, Mixed Prs and KO Tms once.

JOHNSON, Karl (b. 1924) of Sebring FL, retired ACBL nat'l tournament director. Directing career began in 1960; attained national ranking in 1967.

JOHNSON, Marilyn K. (b. 1928) of Houston, graduate of Wellesley College, WBF Grand Master. Won World Womens Prs 1970, Venice Cup 1978, World Womens Olympiad Tms 1980; represented U.S. in other world competitions 1972 (3rd Womens Olympiad Tms), 1974 (6th Womens Prs), 1976 (3rd Womens Olympiad Tms), 1978 (9th Womens Prs). She and Mary Jane Farell were the first women's pair ever to win the Life Master Prs (1978). ACBL Diamond Life Master. Other nat'l wins are Mixed Prs 1968, 73; Womens Tms 1974, 75, 76; placed second Womens Prs 1967, Mixed Prs 1969, Summer Master Mixed Tms 1969, Womens Tms 1973; has won numerous regionals.

JOHNSON, Patty (b. 1949) of Sebring FL, R-4 tournament director, secretary of Professional Tournament Directors Association, member of Nat'l Goodwill Committee; began directing in 1976; worked at world championships in Bal Harbour 1986 and Jamaica 1987.

JOHNSON, Perry L. (b. 1948) of Farmington Hills MI, company president, graduate of U of Illinois, enjoys golf, tennis and business. Author of *Keeping Score* and nine other books on quality. Won Open Prs I 1992, Open Swiss 1994, placed second in Mens Prs 1979. Regional wins include Wolverine Non-Master Prs 1978, Great Lakes Open Prs, Motor City Mens Prs 1980.

JOHNSON, Sallie B. of New York City, bridge teacher, represented U.S. in four Olympiads — Amsterdam 1966, Stockholm 1970, Las Palmas 1974, Miami Beach 1972 and won the Deauville Individual 1970. Won Womens Tms 1955, 58, 60, 61, 68; placed second in Womens Prs 1969, Master Mixed Tms 1957, 74; won many regional events.

JOHNSON, Walter D. (b. 1953) of Columbus OH, administrative officer in health care facility, graduate of Otterbien College, won Blue Ribbon Prs 1985, GN Tms 1990; placed second Reisinger 1987, USBC (team trials) 1989.

JOHNSTON, David Kyle (b. 1936) of Lurgan, Northern Ireland, solicitor. Represented Northern Ireland frequently in Camrose Matches from late 1960s and has won all major national titles.

JOLMA, Lawrence N. (Larry) (b. 1923) of Portland OR, a business broker, graduated U of Oregon; has been a member of ACBL Bd of Dir since 1966; has also served as ACBL treasurer, chairman of the Finance Committee, Dist 20 Bd member, Western Conference Bd member, is a Nat'l Goodwill Committee member and a past president of Unit 487. Won Mens Tms 1967. Regional wins include Oregon Trail KO Tms 1974, Spring secondary Mens Prs 1975, Rogue River Valley Mens Tms 1976, Emerald Empire Strat Open Prs 1989.

JONES, Dr. Arnold P. (Doc) of Chicago and Hilton Head NC, psychologist, educated at Western Michigan U, DePaul U and U of Illinois (PhD); enjoys jazz, formerly a professional entertainer. Served three terms as president of ABA 1972-74, 1977-81; was the first ABA president to be ranked in the top 25 list of ABA masterpoint holders; currently ranked 11th in the ABA; has won several ABA nat'l events including Open Prs, Mixed Prs, KO Tms, Swiss, Round-Robin and many lesser events.

JONES, Henry. See CAVENDISH.

JONES, Michael D. of Burlingame CA, bridge professional, former member of ACBL Bd of Dir, Diamond Life Master. Regional wins include Golden State Open Pairs 1970, Texas Capital Swiss 1975, Navajo Trail Open Prs 1971, Mens Prs 1975; Mid-Winter Holiday Swiss, Hawaii Mens Prs 1976; CA Capital Mens Prs 1976, Swiss, Mixed Prs 1980.

JONES, Robert G. (Bob) (b. 1949) of Auburndale NY, born in Lima, Peru, bridge professional as a player, teacher and director; graduated Queens College, member of American Philatelic Society, served on Unit 242 Bd. WBF World Master; placed fifth Rosenblum Tms 1990, won Australian Nat'l Mixed Tms 1989, he also competed in internat'l play in Bal Harbour 1986; placed second Mens Swiss 1986. Diamond Life Master; has won more than three dozen regional titles including Goldman Open Prs 1981, Dist 24 GN Prs 1984, GN Tms 1991.

JONSDOTTIR, Anna Thora (b. 1968) of Reykjavik, Iceland, teacher. Won Nordic Women's Teams 1990. Represented Iceland in one world championship and one other Nordic Championship. National titles include Women's Teams three times and Women's Pairs twice.

JONSSON, Thorlakur (b. 1956) of Kopavogur, Iceland, mechanical engineer. WBF World Master. Won Bermuda Bowl 1991, Nordic Teams 1988. Represented Iceland in three other world championships and in European and Nordic open and junior events. 4 national wins include open team twice, open pairs once.

JORDAN, John S. III (Big John) (b. 1939) of Washington DC, math teacher, former federal government economist, graduate of Queens College; ABA regional director and ACBL certified club director, frequent contributor to *ABA Bulletin*; ABA chairman of Nat'l Recommendations Committee. For more than 15 years has been listed as one of the ABA's top 10 players in total points, with more than 12,500. Won many ABA sectional (equivalent to ACBL regional) titles. ABA nat'l titles include KO Tms Flt B 1969, Summer KO Tms 1975, Mens Tms 1976, Mixed Tms 1979, Swiss 1980, Spring Open Prs 1982. He placed second in Summer Mixed Tms 1970, KO Tms 1978, 84, 88, 90; Spring Mixed Prs 1982, Swiss 1975, 88.

JORDAN, Robert F. (b. 1927) of Cincinnati OH, businessman, WBF Life Master; placed second World Tm Olympiad 1964, 68; also represented U.S. in world play New York 1962 (5th World Open Prs) and North America in Bermuda Bowl 1963 (second). He won the McKENNEY TROPHY 1960, Mott-Smith Trophy 1961, 62; Vanderbilt 1961, 68; Reisinger 1966, 67; Master Mixed Tms 1959, Open Prs 1960, 62; placed second Vanderbilt 1965, Chicago (now the Reisinger), Mixed Prs 1961; Mens Prs 1956. Jordan and Arthur Robinson, thought by many to be the best American partnership in the Sixties, came out of retirement to play in the *Bicentennial Bridge Match* against Great Britain in 1976.

JORGENSEN, Adalsteinn (b. 1959) of Reykjavik, Iceland, store owner. WBF World Master. Won Bermuda Bowl 1991. Second Cavendish Invitational 1990. Represented Iceland in one other world championship and four European Championships. 10 national wins include open team five times, open pairs twice.

JOTCHAM, Raymond G. (Ray) (b. 1941) of Scarborough ON, mathematics teacher and computer programmer, graduated Acadia U and York U, enjoys bowling, golf (8 handicap), computers, crossword puzzles and math problems. Has been directing since 1959 and has rating of R-l; placed second Spingold 1964, was Canadian Intercollegiate champion 1961. Regional wins include Eastern States (Goldman Prs) 1963, Can-Am Open Tms 1964, 67, 69, Master Prs 1974, Open Prs 1984; Dist 5 KO Tms 1980.

JOURDAIN, Patrick D. (b. 1942) of Cardiff, Wales, bridge journalist and teacher. Represented Wales more than 50 times in Camrose Trophy, and Scotland twice. Played in 5 world championships. Won Gold Cup 1976 and many Welsh titles. WBU President 1984-85. BBL Vice-President 1993. Editor *IBPA Bulletin* since 1982. Bridge correspondent of *London Daily Telegraph* since 1992. Author of two books.

JOYCE, David J. (b. 1942) of Chicago, commodity futures broker, attorney, won Open Prs, Bridge Wk Master Prs 1970, 74; Summer secondary Commercial Tms 1977.

JOYCE, Kay (b. 1949) of Raleigh NC, librarian, graduated U of North Carolina-Chapel Hill and NC Central U, has been secretary/treasurer of Unit 119 since 1978, was managing editor of Unit newsletter 1980-84 and editor-in-chief since 1984, appointed to ACBL Nat'l Goodwill Committee in 1978, served two terms as secretary of Dist 7, Unit tournament coordinator, as such has chaired eight sectionals and co-chaired one regional, Unit GN Prs and GN Tms coordinator. Diamond Life Master; has won Reston Womens Prs 1978, Roanoke Masters Prs 1982, Myrtle Beach Smoking Open Prs 1984, Raleigh Womens Swiss 1987, Washington DC Womens Prs 1988, Charlotte KO Tms, Bracketed KO Tms 1989; Myrtle Beach Swiss 1990, Columbia Open Prs, Williamsburg Bracketed KO Tms 1991.

JOYCE, Randolph (Randy) (b. 1947) of Raleigh NC, salesman, graduated U of North Carolina, enjoys bowling and fantasy league baseball and football. Has served Unit 119 as president, Dist 7 as recorder since 1986. Member ACBL Goodwill Committee and is alternate for Nat'l Bd of Gov. Diamond Life Master; placed second GN Tms 1983 and Open Prs 1990. Regional wins include Mid-Atlantic Fall Swiss 1968, 71, 73, 74; Mid-Atlantic Winter Open Prs 1979, 80, Swiss 1981; Washington Bridge Wk Open Prs, Swiss 1974, Super Flt Open Prs 1992; Dist 7 GN Tms 1977, 78, GN Prs 1981; Roanoke Masters Prs 1982, Charlotte KO Tms, Bracketed KO Tms 1989; Virginia Beach Open Prs 1990, Williamsburg Bracketed KO Tms 1991.

K

KACHMAR, Barbara (formerly Collyer) (1911-1982) of Beverly Hills CA, won USBA Mixed Prs 1936,

Womens Tms 1960, 61; Womens Prs 1962, placed second Master Mixed Tms 1934, Womens Tms 1963. Her writings includ many contributions to *Bridge World*, *Modern Bridge* and other periodicals.

KADIS, Elayne G. of Brookline MA, psychiatric social worker; chaired several Dist 25 regionals, member ACBL Goodwill Committee; her 18 regional wins include New England KO Tms 1978; Farmington Open Prs 1990; Cromwell Swiss 1992; Summer secondary Morning KO Tms 1992, Barometer Prs 1993.

KADIS, Kenneth L. (Ken) of Brookline MA, CPA, member Eastern MA BA board for over 20 years, member executive committee Dist 25 for 12 years, has served in various executive positions on Unit and Dist level including president of Dist 25; chaired several regionals; member ACBL Goodwill committee; 2nd alternate for Dist Director; member ACBL Bd of Gov; former member ACBL Charity Foundation and former editor Unit newsletter. Kadis has won 18 regional events including New England Fall Swiss Tms 1974, KO Tms 1978; Farmington Open Prs 1990; Cromwell Swiss 1992; Summer secondary Morning KO Tms 1992, Barometer Prs 1993.

KADLEC, Alfred (b. 1953) of Vienna, Austria, systems analyst. WBF World Master. Runner-up World Team Olympiad 1988, and represented Austria in one other world championship. European Junior champion 1976. Runner-up European Team Cup 1982. National wins include Open Teams five times and Mixed Pairs once. He is a cooking and cognac expert.

KAHN, Allen M. (b. 1952) of New York City, director of data processing, graduate of City College NY and NYU, interested in physical fitness, technology and science. Won New York Winter Mens Prs 1982, Swiss 1989, Summer Open Prs 1985, KO Tms 1987, BAM Tms 1991; Dist 24 GN Tms 1985, Port Chester Mens Swiss 1986, Eastern States (Goldman) Prs 1986, KO Tms (Reisinger) 1991; Long Island Swiss 1986, 88.

KAHN, Richard F. (1911-1987) of New York City, retired motion picture sales executive, graduated Columbia U, co-founder of the Card School of New York in 1950 and served both the CAVENDISH CLUB and the Greater New York BA for 10 years. Placed second Bermuda Bowl 1956; won Grand Nat'l Mixed Tms 1933, Mixed Prs 1939, the Chicago (now the Reisinger) 1949, Life Master Prs 1951, Vanderbilt 1953, Spingold 1955, Master Mixed Tms 1951; placed second in Open Prs 1951 and won many regional titles.

KALES, Dr. Eugene J. (b. 1946) of East Lansing MI, systems analyst, programmer; graduate of Wayne State U and Michigan State U (PhD). Member of Nat'l Goodwill Committee, Nat'l Education Foundation, ACBL Bd of Gov (Dist 12), Unit 195 board member and Education Liaison, faculty rep of MSU student club, chairman of Unit sectionalS since 1982, bridge director and teacher. Writer and editor of local bridge newsletters since 1981, he is the inventor of Lightning Prs super-zip event and a handicap scheme for team play. Won Motor City IMP Prs 1989.

KALES, Eugene L. (Gene) (b. 1943) of Arlington VA,

bridge teacher and CPA, graduated U of Iowa; won Dist 6, Zone III GN Tms 1973, Baltimore KO Tms 1975, Washington DC Open Prs 1987, Alexandria Masters Prs, Virginia Beach KO Tms 1989; Dist 6 GN Prs 1991.

KALKERUP, Bettina (b. 1963) of Copenhagen, Denmark, computer programmer. World Life Master. Won World Women's Teams 1988. Second World Women's Pairs 1986. Won Nordic Women's Teams 1988, Nordic Junior Teams 1985. Represented Denmark in one other world championship and three zonal championships. 13 national wins include Danish Cup.

KALOW, Gwenn (b. 1972) of New York City, student, placed first in North American Jr Prs 1990, second in 1991, won Fall secondary Womens Prs 1992.

KAMB, John G. (b. 1929) of Mount Vernon WA, attorney, former district court judge, graduate of Gonzaga U. Was presented *The Award of Merit* by Washington State Bar Association 1991; served for 18 years on the public school board, five times as chairman. Other interests are salmon fishing and thoroughbred horseracing. He has served as a member of ACBL Bd of Gov and as president of Unit 439; Diamond Life Master. Regional wins include Calgary Open Prs 1965, Puget Sound KO Tms 1968, 69; British Columbia Mens Prs 1970, Tri-Cities Open Prs 1975, Emerald Empire Open Prs 1977, Summer secondary Open Prs 1983, Reno Sr Prs 1984, Hawaii Swiss 1992.

KAMIYO, Takahiro (b. 1937) of Tokyo, Japan, oil company executive. Represented Japan in one World Olympiad and one Far East Championship. Won 10 national team titles and two national pair titles. JCBL librarian for 25 years, and member of its tournament committee 10 years.

KAMSKY, Asya (b. 1965) of Monterey CA, born in Leningrad USSR, computer programmer, bridge teacher and S3 tournament director, graduated from Cornell and NYU, enjoys rotisserie baseball. Member of Junior Corps, has served on Unit 497 Bd of Dir and GNYBA board, editor and publisher of *Youth Bridge Federation* newsletter. President and founder of Youth Bridge Federation, organizes and runs the annual Berkeley Calcutta; won North American Collegiate Tms 1987, placed second Master Mixed Tms 1991, was third in the World Junior Championships in Amsterdam 1989. As a Junior player she placed third in Life Master Open Prs 1992. Won Newton Flt B KO Tms 1987, Spring secondary Under 35 Prs 1988, Cherry Hill Open Swiss 1989, All-Western KO Tms 1991.

KANAZAWA, Masaji (b. 1935) of Tokyo, Japan, director and general manager of manufacturer. Represented Japan in five Far East Championships. Won more than 10 national titles. Bridge columnist.

KANNAVOS, Takis (b. 1956) of Athens, Greece, mathematician. WBF World Master. Represented Greece in 1988 World Team Olympiad, finishing fifth, the best performance ever by a Greek team. Many national wins include open team five times and open pairs once.

KANSIL, Prince Joli (formerly Joel D. Gaines) (b.

1943) of Honolulu, graduated Rutgers U and U of the Americas (Mexico City), enjoys travel and has visited 190 countries. Inventor of BRIDGETTE and many other card games, word games and board games that have been marketed nationally; author of *Backgammon Quiz Book;* held the Scrabble record for highest score on a single turn for 14 years; co-founder of the Eastern Collegiate Bridge League; retired from tournament bridge after college in 1964. He was personal assistant to the late Albert H. Morehead and a close friend of Waldemar von Zedtwitz, who co-authored the *Official Laws of Bridgette.*

KANTAR, Edwin B. (Eddie) (b. 1932) of Santa Monica CA, bridge teacher, writer and professional player, graduate U of Minnesota, enjoys racquet sports, languages and classical music. Minnesota state table tennis champion 1948 and competitor in World Table Tennis Championships in Stockholm 1957. A popular author of many bridge books including *Introduction to Declarer's Play, Introduction to Defender's Play, Bridge Bidding Made Easy, Bridge Conventions, Bridge Humor, Test Your Bridge Play (Vol. 1 and II), Gamesman Bridge, Improving Your Bidding Skills, Defend With Your Life, Kantar for the Defense (Vol. I and II), Complete Defensive Play, Kantar Lessons (Vol. I and II), Roman Key Card Blackwood, A Treasury of Bridge Tips, The Best of Eddie Kantar* and a video tape *Win at Bridge.* A regular columnist for the *ACBL Bulletin,* he is a frequent contributor to *Bridge World, Bridge Today, Le Bridgeur* and other periodicals around the world, contributing editor to *Bridge Encyclopedia.*

Kantar learned to play bridge at 11 and taught his first class at 17. His teaching is now confined mainly to cruises. WBF Grand Master, Bermuda Bowl champion 1977, 79 and runner-up 1975. He also competed in int'l play 1969 (3rd Bermuda Bowl), 1970, 1978 (9th Rosenblum Tms), 1982 (9th World Open Prs), 1986, 1990 (17th Rosenblum Cup Tms). He won MACCABIAH GAMES 1981, placed third 1977; won Pan-American Invitational Championships Open Tms 1977. An ACBL Grand Life Master with more than 10,000 masterpoints, he won Spingold 1961, 62, 74; Chicago (now the Reisinger) 1962, 65; Reisinger 1977, 81; Vanderbilt 1964, 88; GN Tms 1974, 76; Life Master Prs 1983, Mens Swiss Tms 1987; placed second Vanderbilt 1961, 68, 73, 76, 78, 83, 89; Reisinger 1968, 83, 92; Open Prs, Mens Prs 1962; Mens Prs 1967, Spingold 1991; also has won scores of regional events.

KANTOR, Dorothy. See BUCHANAN, Dorothy

KANTOR, Simon W. (b. 1925) of Agawam MA, born in Belgium, professor at U of Massachusetts, graduated New York City College and Duke U (PhD) Phi Beta Kappa. Listed in *Who's Who in America* since 1974, interested in math and chess clubs in colleges. Has more than two dozen U.S. patents on polymer science. Served on Capital District BA Bd 1967-72, Western MA Bridge Unit Bd 1989-92. Diamond Life Master; regional wins include New England Fall Mixed Tms 1959, Mens Prs 1960; Upper New York Open Tms, Open Prs 1968; Eastern States Master Prs 1969; Manchester KO Tms 1987, 88, 92, Random Draw KO Tms 1991, 92; Springfield Swiss 1988, Wm Keohane KO Tms 1989, 93; Sidney Cohen KO Tms 1989, 92; Stamford IMP Prs 1989;

Springfield Morning KO Tms 1990, Las Vegas Life Master Prs 1992.

KANZEE, Stephen (b. 1948) of San Francisco, certified bridge director since 1972, graduate of U of California, collects comic books and is interested in genealogy. Has served on Units 497 and 508 Bds and was vice-president for 497 1979-85. Diamond Life Master; placed second North American Swiss Tms 1984; regional wins include California Capital Unmixed Prs 1976, Golden State Open Swiss Tms 1978, 81, Swiss Tms 1984, Master Swiss Tms 1986, Open Prs 1990; Mid-Winter Holiday (non-smoking) Open Swiss Tms 1981, Open Prs 1986; All-Western Super BAM Tms 1985, Open Prs 1988; Emerald City KO Tms 1987.

KAPAIANNIDES, Thanos (b. 1963) of Athens, Greece. Won 1987 Common Market Junior Teams and also represented Greece in three European Championships. Won two national titles.

KAPLAN, Alain (b. 1940) of Brussels, Belgium, psychologist manager. WBF World Master. Represented Belgium in three European Championships and several Common Market Championships. National wins include open teams 6 times and open pairs twice.

KAPLAN, Betty (Mrs. Edgar, formerly Mrs. Alfred Sheinwold) (1913-1985) of New York City, was circulation manager of *The Bridge World,* former director of a music school, won Master Mixed Tms 1963, Life Master Womens Prs 1964, Mixed Prs 1965; Womens Tms 1965; placed second Master Mixed Tms 1959, Womens Prs 1962. She had many regional successes.

KAPLAN, Edgar (b. 1925) of New York City, bridge writer, teacher, has been editor and publisher of *The Bridge World* since 1967. Served as chief commentator for WBF Championships for more than a decade and is known not only for his expert analysis but his delightful wit. He is perhaps the world's greatest authority on the laws of duplicate and rubber bridge, has served as co-chairman of the ACBL Laws Commission since 1978 and is a member of the WBF Laws Commission. In 1979 Kaplan was named the Bridge Personality of the Year, a worldwide honor given by the INTERNATIONAL BRIDGE PRESS ASSOCIATION. He was named ACBL HONORARY MEMBER 1993. Represented District 24 (New York City area) on the ACBL Board for many years and is a former partner of the Card School of New York. He is co-inventor of the KAPLAN-SHEINWOLD system and the author of several books including *How to Play Winning Bridge* (co-author), *The Complete Italian System of Winning Bridge, Winning Contract Bridge Complete, Competitive Bidding in Modern Bridge, Duplicate Bridge: How to Play, How to Win* and is a contributing editor to the *Bridge Encyclopedia.*

Kaplan was assistant captain of the U.S. team in 1964 and was the coach many times to North American teams. The players on these teams benefited from his detailed knowledge of European systems. WBF Life Master; placed second in the World Tm Olympiad 1968, Internat'l Tm Trials 1966, USBC (team trials) 1987; also competed in world championships in 1966 (11th Mixed Prs), 1967 (second in Bermuda Bowl), 1971, 1978, 1982 (5th World Open Prs), 1986 (6th Rosenblum Tms), 1990

(4th World Open Prs, 17th Rosenblum Tms). ACBL Grand Life Master with more than 13,000 MPs; won McKENNEY TROPHY 1957 and has won North American championships in five decades - Vanderbilt 1953, 68, 70, 81, 83, 86; Spingold 1967, 68; Chicago (now the Reisinger) 1958, Reisinger 1966, 67, 71, 82, 83, 84, 90; Mens Tms 1955, 1966, Mixed Prs 1965; Master Individual 1957, Master Mixed Tms 1963, Mens Tms 1966, Open Prs 1966; Life Master Mens Prs 1973, Blue Ribbon Prs 1974; placed second Vanderbilt 1958, 65, 94; Mens Tms 1958, 61; Master Mixed Tms 1959, 68; Spingold 1965, 71, 78; Life Master Mens Prs 1965, Reisinger 1969, Mens Prs 1970, Mens Tms 1975, Open Swiss Tms 1991; won numerous regional titles.

KAPLAN, Michael David (b. 1943) of Marina del Ray CA, researches and writes books on American frontier history, graduated U of Denver and U of Colorado (PhD), has won several regionals including Mid-Winter Holiday KO Tms 1972, Rocky Mtn Master Prs 1973, Desert Empire KO Tms 1974, Navajo Trail Open Prs, Palm Springs Master Prs 1975; Pacific Southwest Open Prs 1978.

KAPLAN, Muriel (1920-1970) of New York City, won Womens Team Trials 1963, placed second World Womens Tms 1964.

KAPLAN, Natalie of Los Angeles, consumer advocate, trouble shooter for TV hotline, a jazz enthusiast, appeared in and co-produced with Eugenie Mathe many *Bridge Week* shows. Won Raincross Winter Womens Tms, Los Angeles Winter Womens Master Prs 1979, 85; Bridge Wk Mixed Prs 1983, Pasadena Winter Womens Prs 1990.

KARAMAN, Boris (b. 1931) of Zagreb, Croatia, professor of chemistry. Winner of 12 national team titles. Selector of national teams, and NPC of Yugoslav teams in many international events.

KARAMANLIS, Nikos (b. 1937) of Athens, Greece, lawyer and administrator. As first vice-president of the National Radio-TV network of Greece, played a major role in the acceptance of bridge by the mass media. First vice-president of the Hellenic Bridge Federation and its legal adviser. Tennis administrator.

KARAMOY, Walter D. (b. 1940) of Jakarta, Indonesia, company manager, represented Indonesia World Team Olympiad 1976, Bermuda Bowl 1974, 1981, Far East Championships 1977, 1978, 1981. Won national Open Teams 1973, Mixed Teams 1975, Intercity Teams 1975, 1976, 1980.

KARETNIKOVA, Natalya (b. 1955) of Moscow, Russia, economist. Represented Soviet Union in one zonal championship. National wins include open pairs.

KARLAFTIS, George (b. 1937) of Athens, Greece, civil engineer. WBF World Master. The leading Greek player, heading its masterpoint standings since the national Federation was founded in 1965. His partnership with Dimitrios Yialirakis was almost invincible in the 60s and 70s. A permanent member of the Greek team, which had a high point in finishing fifth in the 1988 World Team Olympiad. He is the only Greek with the rank of European Master, and has won every national title many times.

KARN, Willard S. (1898-1950) a member of the FOUR HORSEMEN, wrote *Karn's Bridge Service* as well as articles for *The Bridge World*. A New York executive, Karn won more than five nat'l championships.

KARP, Leonard (b. 1920) of Tenafly NJ, president and owner lecturers service and consulting firm, graduate of Stevens Institute of Technology, enjoys theater and entertainment. Past president and owner of bridge center, certified director since 1972, served as treasurer of Unit 106, has been New Jersey's *Player of the Year* six times. Diamond Life Master; regional wins include Marcus Cup 1954, Dist 3 Mens Swiss Tms 1977, Bermuda Mens Prs 1979, Bluenose KO Tms 1981, Dist 3 GN Tms, Zone II 1981.

KARPIN, Fred (1913-1986) of Silver Spring MD, bridge teacher, lecturer and writer. Pioneered development of the 4-3-2-1 POINT-COUNT method that eventually was popularized by Charles Goren. Bridge editor for *Washington Post* 1965-81 and a contributing editor to the *Bridge Encyclopedia*; ghosted books and newspaper columns for many of the game's greats. Some of his many books include *Contract Bridge: the Play of the Cards, Psychological Strategy in Contract Bridge, How to Play (and Misplay) Slam Contracts, Winning Play in Contract Bridge: Strategy at Trick One, The Finesse, The Art of Card Reading, Winning Play in Tournament and Duplicate Bridge: How the Experts Triumph, The Complete Book of Duplicate Bridge* (with Norman Kay and Bill Root). His cross-referenced file of hands was reputed to be one of the best in the world.

KARWASER, Willy Michel (b. 1946) of Toronto, born in Belgium, grocery specialist. Won several regionals in the Seventies and Cambrian Shield Open Prs 1989, 1991; Nat'l Capital Open Prs 1990, Syracuse Open Swiss, Fall secondary Morning KO Tms 1991.

KASDAY, Tony (b. 1936) of Las Vegas NV, owner direct mail business, former bridge club owner, certified director since 1966; collector of old movies, has 16,000 tapes. Won Open Swiss Tms 1993, placed second GN Tms 1989; Diamond Life Master; won at least 50 regionals including Bridge Wk Master Prs 1967, Can-At KO Tms 1974, 77, Swiss Tms 1974, Master Prs 1976; Mid-Atlantic Swiss Tms 1976, Open Prs 1977; Tri-State Winter Open Prs, Swiss Tms 1977; Wolverine KO Tms, Dist 4 KO Tms, Nat'l Capital KO Tms 1977; British Columbia Open Prs, Las Vegas Life Master Swiss Tms 1990; Lone Star Life Master Swiss Tms 1992.

KASLE, Barbara (Mrs. Gaylor) (b. 1939) of Boca Raton FL, former bridge club owner, won Las Vegas Open Prs 1973, Portland KO Tms 1974, Phoenix Open Prs 1990, Hawaii Swiss Tms 1991, Palm Springs Open Prs 1992, Miami Prs 1993. See FAMILY.

KASLE, Gaylor L. (b. 1941) of Boca Raton FL bridge professional since 1964, greatly responsible for professional bridge getting better and bigger in the middle Sixties and early Seventies. Grand Life Master with more than 21,000 masterpoints; ranks #9 (as of 1993) on the all-time masterpoint list. North American wins are Vanderbilt 1994, Mens Tms 1973, North American Swiss 1982, 85, 90; placed second in Reisinger 1978, North American Swiss 1986, GN Tms, Blue Ribbon Prs 1989, Open Prs I 1993. Won *Sunday London Times* Prs 1993. Some of his scores of regionals include Big D Winter KO Tms, Wine Country KO Tms 1982; Big D Master Prs 1983, Pikes Peak KO Tms, Open Swiss Tms 1984; Hawaii KO Tms 1984, Open Swiss Tms 1991, Swiss Tms 1987; Oregon Trail KO Tms 1984; All-Southern Smoking Swiss Tms 1985, Desert Empire KO Tms 1990, Mexican Nat'ls Swiss 1992. See FAMILY.

KASLE, Lee (Mrs. Sidney) (b. 1917) of Tucson AZ, mother of Gaylor Kasle, won Womens Tms 1959 a few months after becoming Life Master. She had a number of wins with her husband Sidney Kasle, who died in 1960, and in 1973 she won Dist 17 Womens Prs. See FAMILY.

KASS, Irving (Cookie) (1915-1993) of Hollywood FL, retired insurance agent who lectured and ran bridge games on cruise ships for 15 years. In 1952 he won the Vanderbilt, won several Southeastern team and pair events, von Zedwitz New York Double Elimination KOs the first and second years of its existence; also Eastern States KO Tms 1950, All-Southern Open Prs 1979, Southeastern Life Master Prs 1976.

KASSAY, Michael Bela (b. 1924) of Sarasota FL, born in Hungary, senior associate of engineering consulting firm, graduated Royal Hungarian U, enjoys competitive sailboat racing and pistol shooting. Lectures on energy conservation concepts and measures, listed in *Who's Who in the East*. He was involved in the Hungarian revolution of 1956 and moved to the U.S. afterward. He was part of a group that started the revival of organized bridge activities in Hungary after WWII. He held various positions in the organization including chairman of the rules and appeals committee. Was a member of the Hungarian National Tm in 1956 and won five Hungarian national titles 1954-56. ACBL regional titles include Eastern States Mixed Tms 1962, New England Open Tms 1965, 66; Big Apple Open Prs 1986, Southeastern Sr Swiss Tms 1990, Sr Prs 1992, Central FL Sr KO Tms, Sunshine KO Tms, Las Vegas Stratified Sr Prs 1992; St. Petersburg/Daytona Master Prs 1992; Sunshine State Open Prs 1993.

KATOPODIS, Spyros (b. 1941) of Athens, Greece, engineer. President of Hellenic Bridge Federation 1987-1990, and led successful Greek teams as playing captain or NPC. Translator of Greek and Spanish poetry.

KATZ, Emanuel B. (Manny) (b. 1915) of Snyder NY, retired real estate investor, enjoys golf, travel and grandchildren. Life Master #328, he has won several regionals including Canadian Nat'l Open Tms 1957, Can-Am Open Tms 1953, Upper New York Open Prs 1958, Mixed Prs 1958, 59, 61, 63, 65; Southeastern Open Prs, All-Southern Open Prs, Mens Prs 1979.

KATZ, Harold (b. 1935) of Memphis TN, proofreader for ACBL *Bulletin*, formerly a civil engineer, graduated

from U of Pennsylvania; ACBL staff member since 1973. Sectional director, has run local bridge games for more than 20 years. Won Mid-South Spring Swiss Tms 1971. His other interests are swimming, theater, opera, symphony, reading and television.

KATZ, Moshe (b. 1920) of Tel Aviv, Israel, retired sales manager. Represented Israel in six world championships and three European Championships. NPC twice. Several national wins.

KATZ, Ralph (b. 1957) of Burr Ridge IL, option trader, graduate of U of Stubenville, placed second in World Open Prs 1978, 13th 1982, 11th 1986; 5th 1990 in the Rosenblum Tms. WBF World Master and ACBL Diamond Life Master. He has won Fishbein Trophy 1981, Life Master Prs 1979, Master Mixed Tms, Spingold 1981; Mens Tms 1984, Open Prs 1985. Placed second GN Tms 1986, Reisinger 1987, Life Master Pairs 1989; has had scores of regional wins.

KATZ, Dr. Richard H. (b. 1942) of Rancho Mirage CA, physician, graduate of U of Wisconsin, enjoys tennis, high school state mathematics winner 1958, Intercollegiate champion 1966, co-author *Breakthrough in Bridge*. Winner of Fishbein Trophy 1973, 76; his nat'l wins include Open Prs 1967, Blue Ribbon Prs 1968, Reisinger 1973, Spingold 1973, 76; GN Tms 1974, Vanderbilt 1975, 76; Master Mixed Tms 1976, Life Master Prs 1989, BAM Tms 1992; placed second Blue Ribbon Prs 1969, Vanderbilt 1973. Diamond Life Master; has won many regional events. See BIBLIOGRAPHY C; HOUSTON AFFAIR and LANCIA TEAMS.

KATZ, Stanley B. (Steamer) (b. 1949) of Wheeling IL, controller, graduate U of Wisconsin, currently enrolled in Lake Forest Graduate School. He coaches youth football, enjoys golf and is involved with Lions Club International. Katz helped with the formation of high school bridge program in the Chicago area. Regional wins include Champagne Open Prs 1977; Midwest Spring Open Prs 1979, South Bend Non-Smoking Swiss 1983, Central States II Swiss Tms 1983, Mens Swiss Tms 1988; Central States I Mens Swiss 1987, Swiss 1991; Indianapolis Master Prs, Lake Geneva Swiss Tms 1987; Oconomowoc Open Prs.

KAUDER, Arnold J. (Arnie) (1908-1990) of Los Angeles, electronics engineer, graduate of UCLA, won Master Mixed Tms 1949, 50, 55; second Mens Tms 1953; won many regionals.

KAUDER, James S. (b. 1943) of Los Angeles, attorney, bridge writer, author of *The Bridge Philosopher* and formerly contributed *ACBL Bulletin* and *The Bridge World*. Son of Mary Jane Farell and Arnold Kauder. Won Eastern States Open Prs 1966, Golden State Swiss Tms 1971, Master Prs 1977; California Capital Open Prs 1972, Bridge Wk Mens Prs 1972, Unmixed Prs 1978; Los Angeles Winter Swiss Tms 1979, Navajo Trail Open Prs, Pikes Peak Open Prs 1980.

KAUFMAN, George S. (1889-1961) famous New York dramatist, was a prominent rubber bridge player. Kaufman was honorary member of the CAVENDISH CLUB and a member of CROCKFORD'S CLUB and

REGENCY CLUB. Many of his humorous writings about bridge appeared in *The New Yorker* and have often been reprinted. They include *Kibitzers' Revolt* and the ingenious suggestion that bridge clubs should post on the bulletin board the information that North-South (or East-West) are holding good cards.

KAUFMAN, István (b. 1922) of Budapest, Hungary, company manager. The most successful Hungarian player of the 60s and 70s, won national open teams 12 times between 1954 and 1979 and national open pairs 7 times between 1959 and 1975. Represented Hungary 150 times, including one world chammpionship and five European Championships.

KAWAKAMI, Kuniaki (b. 1940), computer software executive. Far East Champion 1985 and represented Japan frequently since 1964. NPC Japanese team Bermuda Bowl 1991. Won many national titles. Former member Japan Board of Governors.

KAY, Judy (Mrs. Norman) (b. 1934) of Narberth PA, owner and operator of wholesale baseball card business, former bridge teacher, graduate of Temple U, enjoys word games and writing lyrics, wrote the production for 1972 Lancaster NABC, served on PCBA in 70's. Has chaired several bridge game and dinner occasions for charities, once raised more than $25,000. Some of her many wins include Summer secondary Mixed Prs 1967, Keystone Conference Womens Tms 1972, Southeastern Womens Swiss 1978, Spring secondary Womens Prs 1986, 1992, Strat Womens Prs 1993; Fall secondary Womens Prs 1990, 93; Dist 4 Womens Tms 1989, Cherry Hill Sr Swiss Tms 1993, Eastern Mixed Tms, Philadelphia Swiss Tms, Atlantic City Womens Swiss, Washington Womens Tms.

KAY, Norman (b. 1927) of Narberth PA, retired account executive, in baseball card business since retirement, owned horses (harness) from 1970-87; co-author of *The Complete Book of Duplicate Bridge*. Served as active (and recent emeritus) member of PCBA for more than 30 years, was president of Keystone Conference in late 60's. Kaplan (Edgar)\Kay have had one of the most successful and longest lasting partnerships, spanning more than 40 years. He was named the top performance player for the double decade 1957-1977 (*ACBL Bulletin* Oct. 1977). Kay was honored by his Unit for outstanding achievement in bridge as well as being one of the finest gentlemen the game has known. WBF Life Master; placed second Bermuda Bowl 1961, 67; second Olympiad Tms 1968; third Olympiad Open Tms 1960; 5th World Open Prs 1982; 6th Rosemblum Tms 1986, 10th 1982; has represented U.S. in other world competitions. ACBL Grand Life Master with more than 12,500 MPs as of 1993; won McKENNEY TROPHY 1955, Master Individual 1955, Mens Prs 1958; Mott-Smith Trophy 1960, 68; Chicago (now the Reisinger) 1961, Vanderbilt 1959, 60, 68, 70, 81, 83, 86; Mens Tms 1955, 61, 66, Mens Prs 1962; Open Prs 1963, 66, Mens Tms 1966; Reisinger 1966, 67, 71, 82, 83, 84, 90; Spingold 1967, 68; Life Master Mens Prs 1973, Blue Ribbon Prs 1974; placed second in Vanderbilt 1958, 65, 94; Mens Tms, Mens Prs 1958; Chicago 1960, Spingold 1960, 61, 65, 71, 78; Mens Prs 1962, 65, 70; Mens Tms 1963, 75; Mens Tms 1967, Reisinger 1969, Open Swiss Tms 1991.

KAYE, Dorothy R. (b. 1923) of Denver, won Life Master Womens Prs 1968, Spring secondary Open Prs 1977; licensed helicopter pilot.

KAYE, Richard I. (b. 1923) of Denver, president of his fur company, chairman of the Denver Crime Commission and Colorado State Coordinating Bd. Won Mens Prs 1970 and several regionals.

KEARSE, Judge Amalya L. (b. 1937) of New York City, United States Court of Appeals circuit judge, attorney and former partner of Wall Street firm of Hughes, Hubbard and Reed; graduated from Wellesley College and U of Michigan Law School (JD cum laude). One of her professors called her "the best student, male or female, to come down the pike." She is the first woman to sit on the Federal Appeals court in Manhattan. She served the Greater New York BA as counsel to the Board 1970-79, Bd member 1966-75, Conduct and Ethics Committee counsel 1970-73, chairman 1973-79 and various other committees. She served the ACBL as member of the Bd of Gov 1970-76, member of the Nat'l Appeals Committee 1971-75 and as a member of the ACBL Laws Commission since 1975.

Kearse was the editor of the 3rd edition *Bridge Encyclopedia* and is a member of the Charles Goren Editorial Board. She authored *Bridge Conventions Complete, and Bridge at Your Fingertips* and was co-translator of *Championship Bridge* and *Bridge Analysis* with José LeDentu. Her non-bridge writings include several legal publications. She was editor of *Law Review* (at U of Michigan) and she has been listed in *Who's Who in America*. She was named Bridge Personality of the Year by the INTERNATIONAL BRIDGE PRESS ASSOCIATION in 1980.

She was taught to play bridge by her parents while in high school and took up duplicate in law school. WBF World Master, she won the World Womens Prs 1986, represented ACBL in other world play. ACBL Diamond Life Master; won U.S. Women's Bridge Championship 1992 and Womens Prs 1971, Life Master Womens Prs 1972, Womens KO Tms 1987, Womens BAM Tms 1990, North American Womens Swiss Tms 1991 and seven ABA nat'l championships 1972-73; placed second Womens KO Tms 1991; has many regionals titles.

KEEL, Darrell E. (b. 1940) of Aberdeen WA, senior account insurance agent, enjoys golf and travel, past president Unit 428, served as tournament chairman for sectionals and regionals, member ACBL Goodwill Committee, certified director since 1968. He and Steve Bruno are believed to hold the record for the highest two-session Flt A Pr event when they scored 452 ° on an average of 312. Was second North American Swiss Tms 1993; won Spring secondary Mens Prs 1970, British Columbia KO Tms 1979, Tri-Cities Swiss Tms 1979, Redcoat Swiss Tms 1982, Open Prs 1985; Oregon Trail Open Prs 1982, 86, Swiss Tms 1986, 89; Victoria Open Prs 1989.

KEHELA, Sami R. (Sammy) (b. 1934) of Toronto, born in Baghdad, semi-retired bridge journalist and teacher, enjoys wine and films. Former editor of *Ontario Kibitzer*, bridge columnist for *Toronto Life*, contributor to *ACBL Bulletin*, contributing editor to *Bridge Encyclopedia*.

Placed third in Olympiad Tms 1968, 72; Rosenblum Tms 1982; 4th Olympiad Tms 1964, 5th World Open Prs 1970, 5th Rosenblum Tms 1978; represented Canada in other world championships 1960, 66, 67, 72, 74, 76, 80, 86, 88, 90. He and partner Eric Murray are the only pair in the world to represent their country in the World Tm Olympiad since its inception in 1960 thru 1988 (missing only 1984). Their partnership lasted for more than 30 years. Kehela was coach for the North American team in the Bermuda Bowl 1962, 63, 65. Won Team Trials 1966, 73; Life Master Mens Prs 1963, Spingold 1964, 65, 68; Vanderbilt 1966, 70; Blue Ribbon Prs 1967, Life Master Prs 1969, Canadian National Teams 1980, 81; placed second Spingold 1963, Blue Ribbon Prs 1969, Reisinger 1969, 72. Some of Kehela's numerous regionals include Canadian Nat'l Open Tms 1959, 61, 65, 67, 70, KO Tms 1980, Mixed Prs 1959, 62; Summer secondary Swiss Tms 1978, Toronto Open Prs 1985, Mens Prs 1986.

KEHOE, Robert A. (Bob) (b. 1946) of Orange Park FL, contact representative, bridge professional, won Swiss Tms 1978.

KEIDAN, Bruce (b. 1943) of Monroeville PA, bridge columnist. Keidan was the first to notice unusual foot movements by one Italian pair during the 1975 Bermuda Bowl. Won Dist 4 GN Tms 1976, Dist 4 Mens Swiss Tms 1977, Pittsburgh Strat Prs 1990, Swiss Tms 1991, KO Tms, Open Tms 1992. See BERMUDA INCIDENT.

KELLER, Brenda (b. 1943) of Boise ID, professional player, Diamond Life Master, placed second Womens KO Tms 1983, North American Womens Swiss Tms 1983, 92; Life Master Womens Prs 1988; has won numerous regionals.

KELLY, Jack (1916-1970) of Sutton, Ireland was a government accountant, bridge writer and one of Ireland's greatest players. He represented Ireland in the World Team Olympiad 1960, 64; World Open Pairs 62, European Championships 54, 59, 65. National wins include every major event on the Irish calendar. Contributing editor, *Bridge Encyclopedia*. Kelly was IBPA president 1964-70.

KELLY, Nathan (1876-1959) of Boston MA, attorney and bridge teacher, prominent player of whist, auction and contract, invented KELLY SOLID SUIT SIGNALS. Kelly won many AWL national titles and several regional championships at contract.

KELNER, Louis (1907-1989) of Forest Hills NY, accountant, stockbroker and ACBL regional tournament director, won Spingold 1956, placed second Life Master Prs 1956.

KELSEY, Hugh Walter (b. 1926) of Edinburgh, Scotland, novelist and bridge writer. Represented Scotland 12 times in Camrose matches. Won Gold Cup 1969, 1980 and every major Scottish title many times. Bridge columnist for *The Scotsman*. Author of *Killing Defense in Bridge* and 44 other books. See BIBLIOGRAPHY.

KEMP-FREILICH, Edith. See FREILICH, Edith.

KEMPNER, Alicia (Mrs. Ralph) of Palm Springs CA, placed second World Womens Tms 1964; won Master Mixed Tms 1946, 54, 60; Womens Tms 1962, 69; placed second Mixed Prs 1955, Womens Prs 1965; won numerous regional titles.

KEMPNER, Ralph (deceased) of Los Angeles, stock broker, won Open Prs 1936, placed second Spingold 1948; also won numerous regionals.

KEMPSON, Ewart (1895-1966) of Gainford, England, army officer and bridge writer. In the Thirties he was the staunchest supporter of the WALTER BULLER method called *British Bridge,* or direct bidding without the use of forcing bids. His many tournament successes include English National Pairs. A prolific writer, Kempson authored 21 books on bridge including *Kempson on Contract, How to Win at Contract Bridge, More Bridge Quizzes, First Book of Bridge Problems, Second Book of Bridge Problems* (with PAUL LUKACKS), *Tournament Bridge for Everyone,* and co-authored *Quintessence of CAB, The CAB System of Bridge* and *Bridge Quiz.* He was editor and director of *Bridge* magazine from 1949 and a contributing editor, *Bridge Encyclopedia.*

KENDRICK, Boots K. (Mrs. J.O.) (b. 1925) of Anchorage AK, investment broker, assistant to Director of Institute of *Good Housekeeping* magazine, graduate of U of Mississippi. Placed second Master Mixed Tms 1961 and won Summer secondary Charity Prs 1960, Mexican Nat'l Open Tms 1960, Polar Open Prs 1971, Mixed Prs 1974; Midnight Sun Mixed Prs, Master Prs Open Prs 1977, Hawaii Open Prs 1991.

KENEDI, Tibor (born 1915) of Sao Paulo, Brazil, industrialist, represented Brazil in the World Olympiad 1964, South American Championships four times. National successes include Open Teams six times.

KENNEDY, Betty Ann of Shreveport LA, WBF Grand Master and ACBL Grand Life Master, has lectured on many bridge cruises and at many NABCs. Recipient of the 1985 Image Award. Inducted into Louisiana Sports Hall of Fame 1993 (only the second woman to be so honored). Member of Nat'l Goodwill Committee, NABC Appeals Committee, past vice-president of Unit 170, past member of Dist 10 Judiciary Committee, served on World Bridge Olympiad Appeals Committee 1992 and was for many years Chairman of Unit 170 Appeals Committee. A world champion several times over, she won Venice Cup 1974, 76; World Womens Prs 1982, World Womens Olympiad Tms 1984; placed second Venice Cup 1981, 85, World Womens Prs 1978; placed fifth World Womens Prs and sixth World Mixed Tms 1974. Won U.S. Women's Bridge Championship 1993. Her ACBL nat'l titles include Master Mixed Tms 1960, Womens KO Tms 1978, 80, 83, 87; North American Womens Swiss Tms 1983, Life Master Womens Prs 1990, Womens BAM Tms 1992, Womens Prs 1993; placed second Womens Prs 1960, Life Master Womens Prs 1971, 81; Womens KO Tms 1982, 92; North American Womens Swiss Tms 1985, Womens BAM Tms 1986, 91; Womens Prs 1990, 92. Kennedy has made many trips to China and won the Ambassador's Cup in Beijing 1988, Open Tms in Hong Kong 1981, Internat'l Bridge Tm

Championship in Beijing 1993 and placed third in the First International Invitational Chinese Bridge Tournament Open Tms 1981. Regional wins include Jackson Masters Prs 1958, Womens Prs 1969; New Orleans Open Prs 1970, 73; Houston Open Tms 1967, 83, Womens Prs 1976, 81, Masters Prs 1985, Super KO Tms 1992, Masters Swiss Tms 1993; Fort Worth Womens Prs 1970, 87, 89; Dallas Masters Prs 1974, 78, Open Tms 1980, Masters Swiss Tms 1980, Womens Prs 1988; Pine Bluff Open Prs 1991.

KENNEDY, John E. (Jack) (b. 1920) of Shreveport LA, industrialist, graduate of United States Military Academy, a retired U.S. Army colonel. In WW II he was awarded three U.S. and two foreign decorations and four campaign medals. Inducted into Louisiana Sports Hall of Fame; served on the ACBL Bd of Gov, as president of Unit 170 and as vice president of Dist 10; frequently has served as chairman of Mid-South regional and Shreveport sectionals and of their Rules and Ethics Committees. Diamond Life Master; placed sixth World Mixed Tms 1974 and competed in other world championshipsL: Miami 1972, New Orleans 1978, Bal Harbour 1986, Geneva 1990. Won Mens Prs 1973, Blue Ribbon Prs 1984; placed second in Mens Prs 1976. Kennedy won Open Tms in Hong Kong 1981 and was third in the First Invitational Chinese Bridge Tournament Open Tms 1981 and won the Open Prs in Shanghai 1987.

KENNY, Michael (b. 1964) of Toronto ON, systems analyst, former vice president Canadian Bridge Federation 1984-85, Unit 151 president 1984-85, member ACBL Bd of Gov 1983-85. Won CNTC 1993 and more than 20 regionals including Cambrian Shield Mens Prs, KO Tms, Swiss 1986; Can-Am Swiss 1986; Canadian Nat'ls Mens Swiss, Masters Prs 1988, Mixed Prs 1989; London Bridge Open Swis 1991.

KEOHANE, Ethel (Mrs. William H.) (b. 1901) of Wellesley Hills MA, retired administrative secretary, graduate of Midway College, enjoys gardening. Served as secretary of Eastern Massachusetts BA for 18 years, as assistant chairman of the Goodwill Committee for many years, was on the executive board of the New England BC. Named ACBL HONORARY MEMBER 1982, she was also honored in 1991 at the Spring NABC on her 90th birthday. Keohane, LM #151, is a Grand Life Master and has won more masterpoints than any other New Englander and is also among the leaders throughout the ACBL. She is still a strong competitor and plays in many regionals and at NABCs. In 1990 she won more than 250 points with many strong performances in NABCs and regional competitions. In 1981 she survived a car accident that killed her partner, Ida Bennett. Although practically every bone in her body was broken and she was not expected to live, she pulled through. She was told she would never walk again, but after months of exercise and going through physical rehabilitation she regained the use of her legs. She was on the winning Boston Inter-City Match team 1970, 71, 72, 73; placed second Womens Tms 1952, 77; has won numerous regionals in six decades starting in the Forties and continuing into the Nineties.

KERR, Robert A. (Bob) (b. 1935) of Los Angeles, supervisor of transportation pricing, graduate of Stanford

U, has appeared in several musical bridge productions, served on Unit ethics committees in the Seventies. Diamond Life Master; placed second Mens Prs 1971; won Bridge Wk Open Prs 1967, Mixed Prs 1980; Golden State Master Prs 1973, Los Angeles Winter Swiss Tms 1974, 84, Mixed Prs 1980; Pacific Southwest Swiss Tms 1975, Emerald Empire Swiss Tms 1977, Dist 23 GN Prs 1988.

KERR, Roy P. (b. 1934) of Christchurch, New Zealand, professor of mathematics, represented New Zealand Bermuda Bowl 1974. National successes include Open Teams 1971, Open Pairs 1973. A pioneer of relay methods described by him in *The Symmetric Relay*. Fellow of Royal Society, won Hughes Medal for mathematics.

KERWIN, Madeleine (1882-1965) introduced bridge in the CAVENDISH CLUB in 1926, was a bitter antagonist of Ely Culbertson. In 1931 she became second president of the ABL and helped codify the OFFICIAL SYSTEM, designed to replace Culbertson's as the public favorite. More successful than this effort was her theoretical work as one of the originators of the FORCING TWO-BID. Her writings include the first book on the Sims System (*The One Over One for Everyone*) as well as some five other books and numerous bridge articles.

KESSLER, Gary (b. 1953) of Springfield IL, store owner, graduated Bradley U and Eastern Illinois U, Springfield tournament co-ordinator; enjoys bowling, record collecting and the Jay Cees. Diamond Life Master; won Springfield Tms, Decatur KO Tms, Louisville Mens Swiss Tms, Dallas Master Prs, Pittsburgh Swiss Tms, Gatlinburg Swiss Tms, Bracketed Handicap KO Tms; Spring secondary Speedball Prs 1985, Fall secondary 0-1000 Swiss Tms 1978, Class A Convention Prs 1985, Swiss Tm 1986.

KESSLER, Mark N. (b. 1947) of Springfield IL, store owner, graduate of Simpson College, antique and jewelry collector. Won Central States Open Prs twice, Swiss Tms twice; St. Louis Mixed Prs, Peoria Swiss Tms.

KHAUTIN, Richard L. (1940-1993) of New York City, accountant, won Blue Ribbon Prs 1972.

KIATCHOKWIWAT, Adisorn (b. 1950) of Bangkok, Thailand, state employee. WBF World Master. Runner-up Far East Open Teams 1977, 1985, and represented Thailand in six other Far East Championships and four world championships.

KIJEWSKI, Wacek (b. 1940 in Poland) of Gaborone, Botswana, physics lecturer. Represented Botswana in two world championships. Won several national events.

KILSTRUP, Vivian (b. 1938) of Denver CO, born in Poland, bridge teacher, former bridge club owner. Regional wins include Spring secondary Open Prs 1980, Rocky Mtn KO Tms 1981, Oregon Trail KO Tms 1990, Fall NABC secondary Open Prs 1991, BAM Tms 1992; Bridge Wk Open Prs, Dist 4 Fall Open Swiss Tms 1992; Denver Bracketed KO Tms 1993.

KIMELMAN, Neil D. (b. 1954) of Regina SK, department manager, graduate U of Manitoba, past president and vice-president Unit 181 1975-78. Won Buffalo KO

Tms 1977, Open Prs 1977, 78, Master Prs 1987, KO Tms 1987, 89; Peach City KO Tms, Pheasant KO Tms 1978; placed fifth in Epson World-Wide Bidding Contest.

KIMOTO, Hidenobu (b. 1948) of Tokyo, Japan, bridge teacher and director. Represented Japan in World Team Olympiad 1976 and 1984 and in Far East Championships six times. Won 14 national team titles including Prince Takamatsu Cup three times. Won three National Pair events.

KIMURA, Rokuro (b. 1908) of Ashiya, Hyogo Pref., Japan. One of the 11 original members of the JCBL when it was founded in 1953. Vice-President 1972-81. Honorary Life Member 1981.

KINCAID, Arthur R. (b. 1911) of Liberty MO, attorney, graduated Jewell College and U of Missouri School of Law. Member of Missouri Legislature 1937-43 and city attorney 1945-51. Placed second in Spingold 1953. Regional wins include Mississippi Valley Open Prs 1951, Open Tms 1952; Missouri Valley Open Tms 1959, Open Prs 1961, Mens Prs 1961, 65; Springfield KO Tms 1980, Dist 15 Open Tms, Open Prs 1968; GN Prs 1981.

KING, David W. (b. 1951) of Omaha NE, systems engineer, Diamond Life Master; regional wins include Fall NAC secondary Open Prs 1982, Omaha KO Tms 1983, 90; Des Moines KO Tms 1983, 86; Topeka Masters Prs 1984, Iowa City KO Tms 1985, Waterloo KO Tms 1986, Spring secondary Master Prs 1987, Dist 14 GN Tms 1988.

KING, Frank P. Jr. (b. 1933) of Alexandria VA, bridge teacher and professional, retired from U.S. Air Force, graduate of U of Maryland. While on active duty was the leading masterpoint holder among members of the Armed Forces. Placed 9th in World Senior Prs 1990. Grand Life Master with scores of regional wins including Oregon Trail Mens Prs 1971, Keystone Master Prs, Open Prs 1973; Mid-Atlantic Master Prs 1974, Open Prs 1977, Swiss Tms 1978; Wine Country Swiss Tms 1981, Fall NABC secondary Senior KO Tms 1991.

KING, Fred M. (b. 1944) of Falls Church VA, economist at World Bank, graduated Stanford (Phi Beta Kappa) and Columbia (PhD). Spent two years in Ghana in the Peace Corps 1966-68. Won Fall secondary Flt A Swiss 1986, Raleigh Open Prs, non-Smoking Swiss Tms 1987; Roanoke Open Prs 1988, Arlington Midnite KO Tms 1989, 90.

KING, J. David (b. 1923) of Miami Beach FL, professional bridge player, graduate of U.S. Naval Academy. Life Master with more than 10,000 masterpoints. Won numerous regionals including Central States Life Master and Senior Master Prs 1960, Inter-Mountain Open Tms 1970, KO Tms 1973, Land of Coronado KO Tms 1974, Desert Empire Mens Prs, Swiss Tms 1973; Dist 9 GN Prs 1981, Fall NABC secondary Open Prs 1992, Spring NABC secondary Sr Prs 1993.

KING, Warren R. (b. 1958) of Albuquerque NM, sales representative, graduate of U of Dallas, won NABC Non-Life Master Prs 1989 and Tulsa Flt B Prs 1988,

Austin Bracketed KO Tms 1989, Dist 17 Flt B NA Prs 1992, Dallas Flt B Tms 1992.

KINSELLA, Jocelyn (deceased) of Wellington, New Zealand, property consultant. Won Far East Women's Teams 1981, second 1978. Also represented New Zealand in one world championship and two other zonal championships. Won several national titles. Was columnist for *New Zealand Sunday Times*.

KIRBY, Graham (b. 1955) of Warrington, England, researcher. WBF World Master. Second Bermuda Bowl 1987. Won European Teams 1991, second 1987. Represented Britain in three other world championships and three other zonal championships. Represented England in 25 Camrose matches and won several national titles including Gold Cup four times.

KIRKHAM, Corinne (b. 1936) of San Bernardino CA, computer programmer, systems analyst, project manager, graduate U of Maryland, Unit offical and tournament manager. Placed second in a regional event with 11-year-old daughter Adair Gellman. Gellman became YOUNGEST LIFE MASTER and QUEEN OF BRIDGE. Kirkham is a Diamond Life Master. Won Women's Pairs 1994, placed second IMP Prs 1988, Silver Ribbon Prs 1993. Regional wins include Fall secondary Open Prs 1984, 88; New York Barometer Open Prs 1987, Cherry Hill Masters Prs, Swiss Tms 1988; San Diego IMP Prs 1990, Summer secondary Superflight KO Tms 1991, Riverside Womens Prs, Open Swiss Tms, KO Tms 1992; San Diego Sr Swiss Tms, Sr KO Tms 1993.

KIRKHAM, Jim (b. 1936) of San Bernardino CA, retired U.S. Marine officer, graduated U.S Naval Postgraduate School and U of Missouri. Tournament manager, Dist 22 president, has served three terms as Unit president. While working full time in 1988 he won 1056 MPs. Invented Kirkham Over Big Bids (KOBB) and Modified Drury. Placed 17th World Mixed Prs 1986; Diamond Life Master; placed second IMP Prs 1988, Silver Ribbon Prs 1993. Regional wins include San Diego Open Swiss Tms 1978, 79, 80, IMP Prs 1990; Summer secondary Open Prs 1979, IMP Prs 1990, KO Tms 1991; Phoenix Open Prs 1979; Palm Springs KO Tms 1983; Fall secondary Open Swiss Tms, Masters Prs 1986; Washington DC KO Tms, St Louis Prs, NY Open Prs 1987; Baltimore KO Tms; Hilton Head KO Tms, Richmond Open Prs 1989; Riverside Open Swiss Tms, Bracketed KO Tms 1992; San Diego Sr Prs, Sr Swiss Tms, Sr KO Tms 1993.

KIRTLAND, Edith M. (Mrs. Sidney) (b. 1905) of Surfside FL, certified bridge teacher and club director, educated at U of Georgia, owner\operator of bridge clubs from 1962-1992. Began teaching in 1933 and is still teaching, served as manager of Greater Miami CBL for many years. Won Southeasterns Womens Tms 1957, Open Tms 1961, Florida Masters Prs 1961.

KIRTLAND, Cmdr. Sidney W. (1894-1990) of Miami FL, retired naval officer, graduate of U.S. Naval Academy. Life Master #462, he was the first to achieve this status while on active duty in the Navy. Won Southeastern Open Prs 1946, Open Tms 1950, 61, Mens Prs 1971.

KITCHEL, Robert H. (Bob, Kitch or Stanley) (b.

1931) of Union Grove AL, associate national tournament director, former stockbroker, graduate of Northwestern U, collects railroad timetables, enjoys travel and fishing. Served as PROFESSIONAL TOURNAMENT DIRECTORS ASSOCIATION representative to the ACBL Bd of Dir, adviser to Chicago CBA, tournament coordinator for Dist 10. Began directing career in 1962 and became full time in 1975. Placed second in President's Cup 1962.

KIVEL, Joseph (Joe) (b. 1934) of Corona del Mar CA, stock broker, formerly nuclear scientist, educated at New York U, U of Michigan, and Iowa State U (PhD). Diamond Life Master; placed ninth in Rosenblum Tms 1990, second in GN Tms 1990. Kivel has won more than 30 regional events including the GN Tms Dist 6 1974, Dist 22 1983, 86, 89, 90, 93.

KIVEL, Mickie of Potomac MD, technical writer, graduated U of Michigan, enjoys sailing, listed in *Who's Who in American Women* and *Who's Who in the East*. Placed 16th in World Womens Prs 1990, also competed in other world competition: New Orleans 1978, Bal Harbor 1986. Won Life Master Womens Prs 1986. Diamond Life Master; won Dist 6 GN Tms 1976 and approximately 30 other regionals.

KLAUSNER, Malvine (Mrs. Siegfried) (b. 1902) of Van Nuys CA, represented U.S. in int'l play Turin 1960; won Master Mixed Tms 1953; placed second Mixed Prs 1965; many regional wins.

KLAUSNER, Siegfried (1890-1949) of Beverly Hills CA, born in Vienna, was a leading Austrian player in the Thirties. In 1932 he invented plastic playing cards, those now manufactured in the Unites States under the name *Kem Cards.*

KLEINMAN, Danny (b. 1937) of Los Angles, computer programmer, bridge and backgammon teacher, songwriter, writer; graduate of Oberlin College, enjoys music, backgammon, political mathematics. Designed and programmed the first backgammon computer—Jack Gammon. His books on bridge include *Bridge Scandal in Houston, Understanding Bidding: Foundations, Understanding Bidding: Ramifications, Advice to the Bridgelorn, Bridge in the Real World, It's a Bidder's Game* and *Building Better Bridge.* Kleinman is the author of numerous conventions and of several other books on backgammon; won Intercollegiate Championship (E-W) 1957, Bridge Wk KO Tms 1976, Non-Mixed Prs 1974, Individual 1979; Los Angeles Winter Individual 1979 and others.

KLINGER, Ronald Denny (Ron) (b. 1941 in Shanghai, China) of Sydney, Australia, author, publisher, bridge teacher. Former U lecturer in law. WBF World Master. Won Far East Teams 1970, and Far East Open Pairs twice. Represented Australia in six world championships, and won almost every Australian national title. Author of more than 20 books, including *Guide to Better Card Play* which won award as 1991 Bridge Book of the Year. Won BOLS Brilliancy Prize as player in 1976 and as Journalist in 1980.

KLUKOWSKI, Dr. Julian (b.1939) of Warsaw, Poland,

mathematician. WBF World Life Master. Won European Teams 1981, 1989. Represented Poland in four world championships and nine other zonal championships. Won many national titles. Author of one book.

KNIEST, Thomas W. (Tom) (b. 1945) of Clayton MO, CPA, graduate of Southeast MO State U, enjoys classical music, pocket billiards, basketball. Placed second Life Master Prs 1986; has won more than 20 regionals including the first one he ever played in—the Mississippi Valley Open Prs 1969 with a score of 440. Other wins include Mississippi Valley KO Tms 1978, 80, Mens Prs 1980; Dist 8 GN Tms, Zone V 1974, Springfield KO Tms 1982, 87; Dist 8 GN Prs 1983, Indianapolis Open Prs 1985, St Louis KO Tms 1986, 89; St Charles KO Tms 1988; Louisville Master Prs 1990, Open Prs 1991; Dist 8 GN Tms 1991, Ft Wayne Open Prs.

KOCH-PALMUND, Charlotte (b.1965) of Copenhagen, Denmark, computer programmer. WBF World Life Master. Won World Women's Teams 1988. Second World Women's Pairs 1986. Won Nordic Women's Teams 1988, second Nordic Junior Teams 1985. Third Common Market Women's Pairs 1989. Represented Denmark in one other world championship and two zonal championships. 13 national titles include Danish Cup.

KOCH-PALMUND, Dennis (b. 1959) of Copenhagen, Denmark, clerk. Represented Denmark in one world championship and two zonal championships. 11 national titles include Open Teams and Open Pairs twice each.

KOISTINEN, Kalervo (b. 1958) of Helsinki, Finland, insurance mathematician. WBF World Master. Represented Finland eight times, including two world championships and three European championships. National wins include six Open Teams, one Open Pairs and three Open Knockout Teams.

KOISTINEN, Kauko K. (b. 1960) of Helsinki, Finland, advertisement designer and lithographic artist. WBF World Master. Represented Finland nine times, including three world championships and three European championships. 10 national titles include Open Teams six times, Open Pairs twice, and Open Knockout Teams twice. Bridge teacher and tournament director. Managing Director of Finland's largest club, Bridge-55.

KOKISH, Eric O. (b. 1947) of Montreal, bridge professional, writer, teacher, coach, former research analyst, graduate of McGill U, collector of rock and roll records and baseball cards, enjoys cooking; frequent traveler in his work with international teams, preparing them for world events. Has served as Dist 1 Judiciary chairman since the early Seventies, as Zone II CANADIAN BRIDGE FEDERATION representative, is a past president of Unit 151, Dist 1 GN Tms coordinator and is a member of the Nat'l Goodwill Committee. Has written large portions of the World Championship books 1979-85 and 1988-91. He is editor of Unit 151 *Melange de Bridge*, writes weekly bridge column for *Montreal Gazette*, is an associate editor *International Popular Bridge Monthly*, directs Master Solvers Club for *The Bridge World*, is a regular columnist for *ACBL Bulletin*, a regular contributor to *South African Bridge Bulletin, The Bridge World, IMP magazine* (Holland) and most leading bridge publications around the world.

Author of several conventions including KOKISH (Birthright), REJECT and the MONTREAL RELAY. Kokish won a BOLS BRILLIANCY prize 1980 and the ROMEX Best Bid Hand Award. Currently ranks 4th in Canada in masterpoint holdings and holds the rating of Life Master in the WBF. Placed second World Open Prs 1978, third Rosenblum Tms 1982, 90, 5th 1978, 9th 1986; has represented Canada in other world championships in 1974, 1978 (13th Mixed Prs), 80, 86. In other international competitions he has placed third Pan-Am Invitational in the Seventies, bronze medal MACCABIAH games 1981; won Deauville Tournament of Champions 1979, two world Intercity Tm tournaments in Tokyo, Calcutta (India) Int'l Tms 1985, CDN Int'l Prs 1989; has competed in all six Staten Bank\Cap Gemini Invitational Prs and in the *London Sunday Times* Prs 1981. ACBL Diamond Life Master; ACBL wins include Vanderbilt 1974, Mens Tms 1978; placed second Mens Tms 1974, Vanderbilt 1980, Spingold 1982, Reisinger 1982; has won the Canadian Nat'l Tm Championship 1980, 81, 85 and placed second 1984.

KOLKER, Larry M. (b. 1928) of St. Louis MO, rubber bridge club owner, professional bridge teacher and player, won Vanderbilt 1962 and numerous regional titles.

KONG, S.K. of Sabah, Malysia. Represented Malaysia in one world championship.

KONSTAM, Kenneth (1906-1968) of London, England, executive and journalist. Won Bermuda Bowl 1955. Won European Teams in 1948, 1949, 1950, 1954, 1961, 1963, and represented Britain in five other world championships and six other zonal championships. Many national wins included Gold Cup four times. Bridge editor *London Sunday Times.*

KONSTANTINOVSKY, Elias (Lucho) (b. 1934) of Mexico, bridge club owner and teacher, represented Mexico in int'l competition Las Palmas 1974, New Orleans 1978, Valkenburg 1980, MACCABIAH GAMES 1981; has contributed to Mexican bridge publications, has served as chairman of the 1982 Mexican Nat'ls and as a Board member of the MEXICAN BRIDGE FEDERATION. Won Master Mixed Tms 1980 and several regionals.

KOOIJMAN, Ton (b. 1941) of Gouda, The Netherlands, education inspector. WBF Operations Director since 1991.

KOPERA, Michael P. (b. 1953) of New York City, options trader, placed second North American Swiss Tms 1983. Won Dist 24 GN Tms 1981, 86; Lancaster Swiss Tms, Long Island Swiss Tms 1990; and numerous other regional events.

KORNFELD, Warren (b. 1939) of Jericho NY, owner of executive recruiting firm, graduate of Brooklyn College, stock market enthusiast. Has served North Jersey BA and Nassau\Suffolk BA in various capacities. Won Blue Ribbon Prs 1972 and had highest E-W score in North America in Epson Prs 1991. Regionals include Dist 3 Open Prs 1970, New York City Goldman Prs 1972,

Fall secondary Mens Prs 1980, Hunt Valley Mens Tms, Open Prs 1986.

KORTAY, Mehmet (d. 1988) of Istanbul, Turkey. Represented Turkey in three world championships and nine zonal championships. 23 national wins included open teams eight times.

KOSTAL, James J. (b. 1941) of Ajijic, Jalisco, Mexico, businessman, bridge teacher, bridge club owner, involved in charity work, was among first volunteers for the Peace Corps. Currently serving as president of Unit 205, Kostal has also served in various capacities including president for several southern California Units. Won Spring NAC secondary Silver Trophy Prs, Mexican Nat'l Mens Prs, Desert Empire Open Prs 1980.

KOUSSIS, Vassilis (b. 1942) of Athens, Greece, lawyer. Secretary-General of Hellenic Bridge Federation 1979-81 and organizer or co-organizer of six international bridge festivals. Teaches classes for beginners, and promotes bridge on national radio and television. His hobby is music.

KOVÅCS, Mihály (b. 1945) of Budapest, Hungary. Won many national titles, and represented Hungary in one world championship and five European Championships. Won Caransa Teams 1987.

KOVALENKO, Yuri of Tashkent, Uzbekistan. The leading tournament director in the former Soviet Union. Directed in one world championship.

KOYTCHOU, Boris (b. 1919) of New York City, born in Russia, retired bridge teacher and lecturer, co-founder and partner in the Card School, served as chairman of the Card Committee and Board member of the Regency Whist Club (New York City), represented France in European Championships 1948, 49, 50, North America in the Bermuda Bowl 1957, in Biarritz 1982; won three French national team championships and holds the WDF rank of World Master. Won Spingold 1956, 60; Chicago (now the Reisinger) 1963; placed second Vanderbilt 1955, 62, 65. Now enjoys competitive croquet.

KOZLOVE, Lawrence M. (Larry) (b. 1945) of Louisville KY, bank vice president, graduate U of Louisville, enjoys basketball, travel, theater, board games. Represented ACBL in Rosenblum Tms (placed 11th) 1978; won Mens Prs 1978; placed second Mens Prs 1975, Spingold 1977. Diamond Life Master with numerous regional wins.

KRANSBERG, Gladys (b. 1910) of North Miami Beach FL, placed second Fall Mixed Prs 1960; won New England Mixed Tms 1966, Womens Prs 1968; Southeastern Womens Swiss Tms 1977.

KRAUSS, Donald P. (b. 1937) of Los Angeles, stock broker, graduate of Stanford U, helped to organize the Corporate America vs. Hollywood Celebrities match 1992. WBF Life Master; placed second World Tm Olympiad 1964 and represented North America in the Bermuda Bowl 1971, the U.S. in New Orleans 1978; won the Team Trials 1963, International Playoff matches 1970, MACCABIAH GAMES 1981, Vanderbilt 1964, Chicago (now the Reisinger) 1962, Reisinger 1971,

Mens Tms 1970; placed second Spingold 1971, Mens Tms 1972, Life Master Mens Prs 1981; has won numerous regionals.

KREHBIEL, Carol (b. 1930) of Owensboro KY, bridge teacher, retired restaurant owner, graduated Indiana U, *Midwest Monitor* reporter, Unit Education Liaison. Won Spring secondary Open Prs, Fall Mixed Prs 1976; Rocky Mixed Prs, Dist 11 Master Prs 1976; Central Florida Swiss Tms, Midwest Womens Swiss Tms 1980; Mississippi Valley Womens Prs 1981, Lexington Master Prs 1985, South Bend Master Prs 1986, Orlando Swiss Tms 1988.

KREIJNS, Hans (b. 1925) of The Hague, The Netherlands, bridge tour conductor, former painting contractor. WBF Grand Master. Won World Open Pairs 1966, second European Teams 1965, 1966, third World Teams 1980. He represented The Netherlands regularly in international championships until 1987. Winner of 12 major national titles, including open teams five times, and top Dutch masterpoint winner.

KREKORIAN, James E. (Jim) (b. 1952) of New York City, options trader and bridge professional, graduated Duke U, enjoys sports and was three-time college track letterman, holds airline transport pilot rating. Grand Life Master with more than 10,000 masterpoints; won Life Master Mens Prs 1986, NA Pairs 1992; placed second Mens Swiss Tms 1986, Vanderbilt 1987, Mens Swiss Tms 1990. Won the Cavendish Invitational Prs 1987 and has had hundreds of regional wins.

KREMER, Norbert A. (Norb) (b. 1941) of Schenectady NY, tax preparer and partner in Neinor Corp with Neil Chambers, graduate of Washington U. Diamond Life Master, won Master Mixed Tms 1983; placed second GN Tms 1973, Master Mixed Tms 1981, Life Master Mens Tms 1985; has won many regional events.

KRISTJONSDOTTIR, Valgerdur (b. 1945) of Reykjavik, Iceland, editor and publisher. Won Nordic Women's Teams 1990. Represented Iceland in one world championship, two European Championships and four other Nordic Championships. National wins include women's teams 8 times and women's pairs twice.

KROJGAARD, Mads (b. 1962) of Aalborg, Denmark student. WBF World Master. Won Danish Cup 1988, Danish Club Teams 1992.

KROJGAARD, Niels (b. 1965) of Aalborg, Denmark. WBF World Master. Third European Junior Teams 1990, won Common Market Junior Teams 1991. Represented Denmark in two world championships. Won four national titles including Danish Clubs.

KUAI, Henry S.Y. (b. 1912) formerly of Hong Kong, engineer. Won Far East Open Teams 1959, 1960, second 1963, and represented Hong Kong in 1962. National wins include open teams, master teams and open pairs.

KUBAÇ, Nezih (b. 1961) of Istanbul, Turkey, mechanical engineer. WBF World Master. Represented Turkey in one zonal championship. Four national wins include open teams 3 times.

KUBAK, Fritz (b. 1949) of Vienna, Austria, croupier. WBF World Master. Second World Team Olympiad 1988. Represented Austria in 9 other world championships and 6 European events. Won Austrian Teams seven times and Mixed Pairs twice.

KUBISTA, Dr. Josef (b. 1931) of Sweden, formerly of Prague, Czechoslovakia, migrated to Sweden 1968, pediatrician, represented Czechoslovakia on many occasions, won Baltic Cup 1963. National titles include Open Teams 4 times, Open Pairs twice in the Sixties.

KUEHL, Florine W. See Walters, Florine W.

KUNDU, Oindrilla (1951-91), of Calcutta, India, actress and florist. Won BFAME Women's Teams 1985 and represented India in three world championships. Won two national titles. Only woman winner of West Bengal Open Pairs. BFAME Daily Bulletin Associate Editor 1991, and won journalist awards including Epson 1987. Child film star as *Tinkoo Tagore*, starring in best Indian movie of 1956. Related to Nobel laureate Rabindra Nath Tagore.

KUNGS, Egon (1912-1985) of Tallinn, Estonia, accountant. A driving force in the development of Estonian and Soviet bridge in the 60s and 70s. Won many Estonian titles and two Soviet titles.

KUO, Che-Kung (b. 1952) of Taipei, Taiwan. WBF World Master. Won Far East Teams 1976, 1968, 1981, 1986, Far East Pairs 1976. Represented Taiwan in four other zonal championships and eight world championships. Author of *Chinese Precision* and contributor to *Chinese Bridge Magazine*.

KURLANDER, Norman A. (b. 1938) of Flushing NY, co-owner of rubber bridge club and bridge teacher, former options trader, chairperson of Conduct and Ethics Committee for professional bridge union in NY, placed second Mens Tms 1973; won Long Island Mens Prs 1975, Swiss Tms 1982; NY\NJ Swiss Tms 1975, Eastern States Mens Prs 1977, Big Apple Swiss Tms 1978, Tri-State KO Tms 1993.

KUROKAWA, Akio (b. 1937) of Tokyo, Japan, bridge teacher, club owner, balalaika and mandolin player. Known as "ace-king-ten". WBF World Master. Far East Champion 1985. Represented Japan in many other Far East Championships. Won 28 national open team titles and 2 open pair titles. NPC Japanese Venice Cup team 1991. Author of *Introduction to Bridge Play, How to Improve in Bridge* and *Bridge for Beginners*.

KUSHNER, Jack B. (1903-1963) of Longmeadow MA, bridge teacher and writer, co-inventor of TNT system and author of *The Kushner System* and many booklets; won Open Prs 1950 and All-American Mens Prs 1950. Was president of New England Bridge Conference 1962.

KUTI, Richard Joseph (Dick) (b. 1946) of Neshanic NJ, senior cost analyst, graduate of Seton Hall U, enjoys college sports, politics, rock concerts. Won Richmond Non-Smoking Open Prs, Hempstead Open Prs 1984; Norfolk Mens Swiss Tms 1986, Roanoke Junior Prs,

Washington DC Swiss Tms 1988; Buffalo Mens Swiss Tms 1988, Open Swiss Tms 1990; Bowling Green KO Tms 1990.

KUZ, Robert Patrick (Bob) (b. 1953) of Selkirk MB, highway construction inspector, graduate of U of Winnipeg, Unit 181 vice president, zone coordinator of the Canadian National Team Championship since 1988; has won more than 25 regionals including Buffalo KO Tms 1977, Open Prs 1977, 78, Unmixed Prs, Master Prs 1978; Peach City KO Tms, Pheasant KO Tms 1978; Gopher KO Tms 1981.

KYRIAKIDES, Sosso (b. 1915 in Egypt) of Athens, Greece. Represented Egypt in international events 1937-62. Founded the Athens Bridge Club, one of two which initiated the Hellenic Bridge Federation in 1965. HBF Vice-President for ten years, and a regular member of its women's team in European Championships in the same period. Linguist.

KYRIAKOS, Costas (b. 1926) of Athens, Greece, journalist and retired Director-General of the Automobile Touring Club of Greece. Secretary-General of Hellenic Bridge Federation, and organizer of 1971 European Championships in Athens. Founded a club for junior players, and introduced computer scoring to Greece. Columnist for *Ethnos*, author of three bridge books, and translator-publisher of two Victor Mollo books. Established Kyriakos Trophy for yearly masterpoint winner.

L

LA SERNA, Agustín (1926-91) of Madrid, Spain, businessman. Represented Spain in three world championships and four zonal championships. Won many national titles.

LAANEMAE, Tiit, (b. 1953) of Tallinn, Estonia, engineer. WBF Master. Represented Estonia in two world championships and one zonal championship. Major titles include Soviet open teams 3 times, Soviet open pairs twice, Estonian open team 4 times, Estonian pairs 4 times. Editor of monthly bridge magazine *Bridzileht*.

LABINS, Stephen H. (b. 1933) of West Hartford CT, manufacturer's representative, graduate of Harvard, enjoys running and is a prison volunteer. Won numerous regionals including New England Mens Prs 1962, 67, Master Tms 1966, 70, 73, 74, KO Tms 1967, 70, 75, Master Mens Prs 1971, Open Prs 1976, Swiss 1977; New England Fall Mixed Swiss 1972, Dist 25 GNOT, Zone II 1973; Tri-State Winter Swiss 1974, NY\NJ Swiss 1974, New England Summer KO Tms 1979, Cromwell Winter Strat Open Prs 1993.

LACKLAND, Helen F. (b. 1910) of Cincinnati OH, consultant\librarian and bridge teacher, graduate of Arizona State U, enjoys music and theater, she has been a club director since 1951. Won Marcus Cup 1950 and Midwest Spring Womens Prs 1951.

LAFLEUR, Robert H. (Bob) (b. 1942) of Hampstead NH, computer consultant, enjoys golf, politics, flying, skiing; Dist 25 recorder 1986-90, has chaired New Hamp-

shire sectionals. His father was a tutor for Ely and Jo Culbertson's children. Won Dist 5 Open Prs 1967, Morning KO Tms 1985; Dist 25 smoking Open Prs, Open Swiss 1985, 0-1500 KO Tms 1985, 87, 88, 89, 90 (Jan), 90 (July), 0-1500 Swiss 1992; Motor City Open Prs 1986, Salt Lake City Morning KO Tms, Fall secondary KO Tms 1988.

LAFOURCADE, Jean-Pierre (b. 1952) of Liège, Belgium. WBF World Master. Represented Belgium in one world championship and three European championships. National wins include open teams three times.

LAGUARDIA, Carmen of Paranaque, Philippines. Won Far East Womens Teams, 1968, 1979, 1982 representing Philippines, and 1971, 1972 representing Singapore. Represented Philippines in several world and zonal championships.

LAI, Hui-Ping or **Jennifer** (b. 1961) of Taipei, Taiwan, system analyst. WBF World Master. Far East Womens Team champion 1989 and represented Taiwan in three other zonal championships and four world championships.

LAIR, Mark (b. 1947) of Canyon TX, bridge professional, collects sports cards with twin sons, Grand Life Master with more than 31,000 points as of 1993; ranked third on all time masterpoint list as of 1993. Competed to semifinals of Rosenblum Tms in 1982 (placed 4th) and quarterfinals in 1986; also competed in World Championships in Geneva 1990 (9th in Rosenblum Tms); WBF World Master. In 1990 he won the BARRY CRANE TOP 500 and placed second in 1979. Has won many nat'l championship events including Master Prs 1970, Master Mixed Tms 1977, 78, 79, 90; Vanderbilt 1979, Blue Ribbon Prs 1984, Fishbein Trophy 1986, Mens BAM Tms 1986, 88; Spingold 1986, 89; Reisinger 1988, 92; Open Swiss 1991, Open BAM Tms 1993. Placed second Blue Ribbon Prs 1972, Reisinger 1978, 80, 90, 93; Master Mixed Tms 1984. Lair has won more than 400 regional titles.

LAKATOS, Péter (b. 1961) of Budapest, Hungary, business manager. Won several national titles; represented Hungary World Team Olympiad 1988 and two European Junior Championships.

LALL, Hemant (b. 1951) of Nottingham, England, formerly of Houston, born in India, systems analyst. Represented Uttar Pradesh in the Nat'l Team Championships of India in 1971 at the age of 19. Won Life Master Prs 1992, placed second Mixed Prs 1980, Spingold 1993. Diamond Life Master; has won many regional events.

LAMB, Charles (1775-1834). See BATTLE, SARAH in General Information section.

LAMBARDI, Pablo (b. 1961) of Buenos Aires, Argentina, bridge teacher. WBF World Master. South American champion 1979, 1980, represented Argentina in World Team Olympiad 1984, 1988, Bermuda Bowl 1991. 10 national titles include Open Teams three times and Open Pairs once. Won Gabarret Cup 1980, 1984, 1986.

LAMBRINOS, Alex (b. 1950) of Athens, Greece, bridge teacher. WBF World Master. Represented Greece in 1988 World Team Olympiad, finishing fifth, the best performance ever by a Greek team; represented Greece in two European Championships. 16 national wins include five open teams and three open pairs.

LAMBRINOU, Sofia (b. 1958 in the then U.S.S.R.) Third 1989 Common Market Womens Teams and represented Greece on many other occasions. Five national wins include open pairs three times.

LAMPERT, Harry (b. 1916) of Deerfield Beach FL and Lenox MA, bridge teacher and author, worked in motion picture industry as an animation cartoonist 1933-53; later through 1953 he had cartoons in many leading magazines and newspapers. Lampert served as president of ABTA 1991-93. Authored *The Fun Way to Learn Serious Bridge, The Fun Way to Serious Bridge, The Fun Way to Advanced Bridge, Declarer Play and Opening Leads, A Fun Way Bridge Book* and *The Fun Way to Advanced Bridge*. Won Summer secondary Flt B Mens Prs 1977, Southeastern Individual 1980.

LAMPREY, Charles V. (Chuck) (b. 1938) of White Plains NY, WBF World Master; competed in world play 1986 (13th Rosenblum Tms) and 1990 (17th). Placed second GN Tms 1979, Mens Tms 1982. Diamond Life Master; has won numerous regionals.

LANDA, Sallie M. (b. 1925) of Boca Raton FL, former bridge teacher and professional player, past manager and originator of two duplicate clubs in Fargo ND and past president of the Fargo CBL. Became a director about 20 years ago and now directs on bridge cruises. Competed in World Womens Bridge Team Olympiad 1972; Diamond Life Master. Her 50-plus regional wins include Gopher Womens Swiss 1976, Gopher Womens Tms 1976, Rough Rider Womens Prs 1977, Buffalo Womens Swiss 1978, Southeastern Womens Swiss 1981, Summer secondary Swiss, Daytona Beach Open Swiss, Sunshine State Sr Open Prs, 1990.

LANDAU, Charles S. (1898-1981) of Mount Lebanon PA, former member of the Bd of Dir and longtime bridge administrator in the Pittsburgh area. He was ACBL HONORARY MEMBER 1976.

LANDAU, Eric (b. 1945) of Silver Spring MD, software developer, graduated from U of Rochester, other interests are science fiction and the Grateful Dead. Has contributed to *The Bridge World* and the *ACBL BULLETIN*. Author of *Every Hand an Adventure*, he codified and popularized the EHAA system. Won Upper NY State Swiss 1975, Canadian Nat'l Swiss 1976, KO Tms 1981; Dist 4 Swiss 1978, Dist 5 Master Prs 1978, Mens Prs 1979; Mid-Atlantic Master Prs 1987.

LANDAU, Judith (Judy) (b. 1947) of Palm Harbor FL, sales representative, graduate of U of Rochester, enjoys music, Bible study and is active in Messianic Judaism. Won Master Mixed Tms 1983; regionals include Summer secondary Swiss 1973, Upper NY Swiss 1975, Canadian Nat'l Swiss 1976, Dist 4 Swiss, Womens Swiss 1978; Reno Open Swiss 1978.

LANDEN, Stephen W. (b. 1952) of West Bloomfield MI, computer consultant and bridge professional, graduate of U of Michigan; interests are golf, backgammon and

PCs. Served on Unit 137 Bd of Dir and is a contributing editor to Unit *Table Talk*. In 1980 Landen was named "Sportsman of the Year" (see IBPA AWARDS). Diamond Life Master; won Open Prs 1990, placed second in GN Prs 1979, 91; GN Tms 1982. Regional wins include Spring secondary Non-Mixed Prs 1972, Summer Swiss 1974, BAM Tms 1976; All-American Swiss 1974, 76, Open Prs 1981; Motor City KO Tms 1977, Swiss 1978, Mens Prs, Master Prs 1980; Wolverine KO Tms 1980, Master Prs 1981.

LANDLEY, Wilson W. (1917-1990) of Orlando FL, retired US Civil Service employee, won Life Master Prs 1958.

LANDOW, Ellee. see LEWIS, Ellee

LANDOW, William (Billy) (b. 1940) of Cherry Hill NJ, options trader, graduated Temple U. Regional wins include Dist 4 Open Prs 1963, Open Prs 1969, Mens Swiss 1976, 80; Keystone Open Tms 1968, 73, KO Tms 1975; Hunt Valley Swiss, Pittsburgh Open Tms 1990; Summer secondary 2nd Sunday Swiss 1991.

LANDRETH, George H. (b. 1927) of San Antonio, consulting petroleum engineer and wild rice farmer, Non-Master of Year 1981; has won several regionals.

LANDY, Alvin (1905-1967) was ACBL top executive from 1950 until his unexpected death. Born in Cleveland, Landy graduated from Western Reserve U and received his law degree from that school in 1927. After serving in WW II, Landy joined ACBL as a tournament director and shortly thereafter became the League's business manager (1948). In his capacity as executive secretary, Landy was known for his temperance and wisdom. He was named HONORARY MEMBER of the ACBL in 1957. Landy's service to bridge took many forms. He was secretary of the ACBL Charity Foundation from the time of its inception, playing a key role in its creation and helping to build it into a quarter-million dollar annual project at the time of his death. Also a member of the ACBL Laws Commission, Landy acted as secretary of that body from 1956. He helped found and served as one of the original officers of the WBF — from 1958 to 1966 he was secretary-treasurer. Landy originated the convention bearing his name — 2♣ over opponents' 1NT, requesting partner to bid one of the majors. As a player he won several major titles, including the Spingold in 1949 and four victories in the Mens Tms. Landy was Life Master #24.

LANDY, Sandra (b. 1938) of Hove, England, university lecturer in mathematics and computing. WBF Grand Master, top woman in WBF 1992 current performance list. Won Venice Cup 1981, 1985; second 1976; second World Womens Teams 1976, 1984, 1988. 1992, third 1980; third World Womens Pairs 1982, 1986. Won European Womens Teams 1975, 1979, 1981; second 1969, 1977, 1985. Won five Common Market titles. Represented Britain in one other world championship and six other zonal championships. 21 national titles include Gold Cup once. Member BBL Council and chairman of its selection committee. Member EBU Board and its tournament and selection committees. Trustee of Educational Trust for British Bridge.

LÅNGSTRÖM, Linda, of Stockholm, Sweden, artist. Third Venice Cup 1993. Won European Womens Tms 1993, Nordic Teams 1992. Represented Sweden in one other world championship and two zonal championships. Has one national title.

LA NOUE, Jack (b. 1940) of New Orleans LA. Diamond Life Master; won GN Pairs 1990; placed second Reisinger 1975, GN Tms 1987. La Noue has won several regional events.

LAPIDES, Steven R. (b. 1943) of Towson MD, data processing sales and consultant, graduate of MIT, enjoys record collecting, golf and bowling. Won Life Master Mens Prs 1975, 89, and numerous regional events.

LARDNER, Ring (old) Wilmer (1885-1933) famous American author, wrote two short stories on bridge, both of which appear in anthologies: *Contract* in *Treasury of Gambling Stories* and *Who Dealt* in *Grand Slam*.

LARKIN, Jack A. (b. 1925) of Golden CO, retired general contractor; won Spring secondary Swiss 1976, Denver Masters Prs 1981, 86, Open Prs 1991; Fall secondary Swiss 1987.

LARSEN, Björn (1921-1991) of Bryn, Norway, inspector and bridge columnist. Won three Nordic Team titles and five Norwegian titles. Represented Norway twice in European Championship. Honorary Member NBF and formerly its secretary and president.

LARSEN, Kyle A. (b. 1950) of San Francisco CA, professional player; WBF World Master; has competed in several world championships. He was the youngest player ever to win a major North American Championship team title when he won the Reisinger in 1968 at the age of 18. He became a Life Master at age 15, the youngest player to do so at the time (see YOUNGEST LIFE MASTER). Diamond Life Master; won Mens Prs 1968, Reisinger 1977, Spingold 1980, GN Tms 1982; placed second Mens Tms 1970, Vanderbilt 1971; has won numerous regional titles.

LARSEN, Karl Christian (Chris) (b. 1941) of Costa Mesa CA, born in Norway, accountant, bridge teacher and club director, earned 3 college degrees in Norway, WBF World master, placed 9th Rosenblum Tms 1990; ACBL Diamond Life Master, placed second GN Tms 1990, has numerous regional wins with at least 9 Dist 22 GN Tms wins.

LARSON, Bernice E. (b. 1911) of Greenfield WI, bridge teacher, retired nursing administrator, graduate of Methodist Hospital School of Nursing, U of Wisconsin (Phi Beta Kappa), Columbia U, enjoys travel, reading and coin collecting. Larson has served as 1st alternate for Nat'l Bd of Dir, on the Nat'l Bd of Gov for many years, president of WI\Upper MI BA, Greater Milwaukee BA; member of Nat'l Goodwill Committee and has held various other executive positions. She has chaired many sectionals and regionals in Milwaukee. An annual unit award has been created in her name and is given for service and achievement. Won Life Master Womens Prs 1974. Diamond Life Master; won Gopher Womens Prs 1972, 81; Mississippi Valley Master Prs 1974, Midwest Fall Swiss 1978.

LASOCKI, Kryzsztof (b. 1940) of Warsaw, Poland, bridge professional. Second Bermuda Bowl 1991; third European Teams 1991. Won Toronto calcutta 1993; second Cavendish 1992.

LASUT, Henky (b. 1947) of Manado, Indonesia. WBF World Master. Won Far East Teams 1972, 1973, 1974, 1979, 1982, 1983, 1984, 1992, 1993. Represented Indonesia in 12 world championships and in other zonal championships.

LaTRAVERSE, Jean Joseph (b. 1939) of Dollard-des-Ormeaux PQ, executive search consultant, graduated Loyola and Canadian Institute of Chartered Accountants; other interests include gourmet cooking, playing the piano, golf, PCs; has private pilot's license. Member Nat'l Goodwill Committee; has been very active in administrative side of bridge; served as president of Dist 2, two terms as president of Unit 151, member of CBF Bd of Dir 1975-78, chairman of Dist 2 judiciary committee 1977-82; held several other executive positions; general chairman of 1985 NABC in Montreal. As a tournament director he achieved the rank of R-3.

LAURIA, Lorenzo (b. 1946) of Rome, Italy, insurance broker. World Life Master. Second Bermuda Bowl 1979, 1983, losing both finals by 5 imps. Won European Teams 1979, second 1977. Italian national wins include open teams once.

LAVALLEE, Paul E. (b. 1940) of Cumberland RI, insurance representative, graduated Bryn Mawr. Served as tournament chairman for Unit 45 and is past president. He won New England Fall Swiss 1976, 77, Summer Swiss 1979, Masters Swiss 1979; Can-At Swiss 1976, Capital District Fall KO Tms 1977, Bermuda Mens Prs 1980.

LAVENDEL, Egon (b. 1937), of Riga, university administrator. President Latvian Bridge Federation. Organizer of USSR Cities Cup. Latvian Bridge Federation president from 1989. Director of Latvian Technical U.

LAVINGS, Paul Warwick (b. 1945) of Sydney, Australia, bridge club manager. WBF World Master. Represented Australia in two world championship and six Far East Championships. Won South Pacific playoff 1991; won almost all national titles. Editor and consulting editor *Australian Bridge* 1985-90.

LAVINTHAL, Hy (1894-1972) invented the suit preference signal that bears his name in 1933-34. A retail store manager and innovative bridge teacher from Trenton NJ. Lavinthal also served as associate editor of *The Bridge World*. His book *Defense Tricks* explained all the stipulations of his theory of defense.

LAW, David of Petaling Jaya, Malaysia, accountant. Represented Malaysia in one world championship and several zonal championships. National wins include open teams several times.

LAWRENCE, Michael S. (b. 1940) of Berkeley CA, WBF Grand Master and ACBL Grand Life Master with more than 18,000 MPs as of 1993. Notable author; two of his books, *How to Read Your Opponents' Cards* and *The Complete Book on Overcalls in Contract Bridge* were named "Book of the Year" by Alfred Sheinwold and are generally considered to be classics. Some of his others are *Judgment at Bridge, The Complete Book on Balancing in Contract Bridge* and *Play a Swiss Team of Four with Mike Lawrence*. Won Bermuda Bowl 1970, 71, 87; placed second 1973, 89 and in World Tm Olympiad 1972; 5th Rosenblum Tms 1986, 9th World Open Prs 1982. Won Internat'l Playoff Match 1969, Herman Trophy 1965, Vanderbilt 1967, 71, 73, 77, 85; Spingold 1969, Reisinger 1965, 70, 77, 80; GN Tms 1978, 79, 87; Mens Tms 1964, 68; Mens Prs 1983, Life Master Prs 1984, Master Mixed Tms 1992. Placed second in Blue Ribbon Prs 1965, 68, 71, 83; Mens Tms 1969, Vanderbilt 1970, Spingold 1970, 76, 80 85; Vanderbilt 1970, Life Master Mens Prs 1978, Reisinger 1983; won numerous regional titles.

LAWRENCE, Richard M. (Dick) (b. 1903) of Ann Arbor MI, retired store owner, former holder of state record for 500-yard free-style for swimmers over 70; won Mens Prs 1967 and several regional events including Summer secondary Mixed Prs 1964, Champaign Mens Prs 1968.

LAWRENCE, Stephen J. (b. 1924) of Athens TX, retired from operations research at White Sands, graduate of U of Texas at El Paso; other interests — puzzles and stamps. A certified director, member of Nat'l Goodwill Committee, member Nat'l Bd of Gov 1970-86, has served Dist 16 and Unit 159 in various executive positions including president. ACBL Diamond Life Master with more than 10,000 masterpoints; regional wins include Republic of TX Mixed Prs 1972, Internat'l City KO Tms 1974, Unmixed Prs 1979; Los Angeles Winter Mens Prs 1978, Land of Coronado Master Prs, Open Prs 1982; Mexican Nat'l KO Tms 1989.

LAY, James E. (Spike) (b. 1944) of Daytona Beach FL, bridge teacher and club manager, former CPA, graduated U of Tennessee, certified director. Has won 15-20 regionals including Dist 11 Swiss 1971, Mid-Atlantic Swiss 1973, 77, 80, Open Prs 1985, Fall Open Prs 1969; North FL Swiss 1988, Central FL Swiss 1992, Holiday Open Swiss, Morning KO Tms 1992.

LAZARD, Sidney H. (b. 1930) of New Orleans LA, oil and gas producer. WBF Life Master;; represented North America in the Bermuda Bowl 1959 (2nd), 69 (3rd), US in Turin 1960, New Orleans 1978, Biarritz 1982, Bal Harbour 1986. Grand Life Master with more than 11,000 masterpoints; won Team Trials 1968, Spingold 1958, 68, Chicago (now the Reisinger) 1960, Vanderbilt 1970, Master Mixed Tms 1963, 77, 78, 79, 82; GN Prs 1990; placed second Spingold 1954, 66, 73; Vanderbilt 1967, Reisinger 1968, 69, 75; Mens Tms 1954, 56, 61, 65, Mens Prs 1967; Master Mixed Tms 1961, Mixed Prs 1959, North American Mens Swiss 1983, GN Tms 1987; has won numerous regionals.

LAZARD, Sidney Jr. (Squid) (b. 1958) of Metairie LA, computer consultant, enjoys bowling, sports events and statistical views of bridge. Became Life Master at age 16 and was the youngest Life Master that Louisiana had produced. Placed second in Mens Swiss 1983; won Monroe Swiss, Mobile KO Tms, Swiss; Baton Rouge Mens Swiss.

LAZARUS, Edmond P. (Ed) (b. 1937) of Baltimore MD, attorney, educated at Johns Hopkins U and U of Balti-

more (JD), has served as local tournament chairman and member Nat'l Appeals Committee. Diamond Life Master; won Mens Prs 1968 and numerous regional events.

LAZARUS-LERNER Shirlee (b. 1932) of Woodland Hills CA, placed second in Master Mixed Tms 1975 and won numerous regionals.

LEBEL, Michel (b.1944 in Rumania) of Nantes, France, bridge writer. WBF Grand Master. Won World Teams 1980, 1982. Won European Teams 1974, 1983, second 1973. Won European Pairs 1976. Represented France in three other world championships and four other zonal championships. Won 17 national titles. Columnist of *Le Point*. Author or co-author of many books.

LE BENDIG, Alan P. (b. 1948) of Los Angeles CA, property manager, former business owner, has served as member of Nat'l Bd of Gov since 1981, chairman 1984-87 (vice-chairman 1982-84), co-chairman Nat'l Tournament Appeals Committee since 1988, member of Nat'l Goodwill Committee, 1st alternate to Bd of Dir. Contributor to Southern CA *Bridge News* and *ACBL Bulletin*. Diamond Life Master; won North American Swiss 1993, placed second Life Master Prs 1993. His 50-plus regional wins include Big D Mens Swiss 1974, Biloxi Master Prs, KO Tms 1979; Shreveport Masters Swiss, KO Tms 1980; Sacramento KO Tms, BAM Swiss 1991; Spring secondary Strat Prs, Open Prs 1992.

LEARY, James Bolton (Jim) (b. 1936) of Pasadena CA, attorney, educated at Cornell U, U of Minnesota, Wm. Mitchell College of Law, avid baseball fan and comics collector. Diamond Life Master; won Silver Ribbon Prs 1992; regional wins include Mid-Am-Can Open Prs 1966, Summer secondary Swiss 1971, Central States Mens Prs 1972, Rough Rider Swiss 1975, 85; Dist 14 GN Tms 1976, Gopher Mens Tms 1976, KO Tms 1990; CA Capital Swiss 1991, KO Tms 1992; All Western Super Flt KO Tms 1991, 93; Dist 22 Swiss, Masters Prs, Handicap KO Tms 1991; Prime Time KO Tms 1992, 93; Reno Mid-Winter KO Tms 1992, Bridge Wk KO Tms, Wine Country Open Prs 1993; Pasadena Sr Swiss 1992, 93.

LEARY, Patricia L. of Livermore CA, graduate of NYU, won Womens Prs 1974; placed second Womens Tms 1980; won numerous regionals.

LEAVITT, Arnold K. (Arny) (b. 1932) of Lincolnwood IL won GN Tms 1979, placed second Open Prs; won numerous regional events.

LEAVITT, Carol (Toddy, formerly Mrs. J.J. Ruther) (b. 1936) of Chicago, bridge teacher, placed second Womens Tms 1965.

LEAVITT, Sandra (Sandi) (b. 1933) of Highland Park IL, retired editor, degrees from Northeastern U, loves taking nature trips, served as member Bd of Dir for CCBA in the Sixties, former associate editor and columnist of *The Kibitzer*; won Womens Tms 1981; placed second Mixed Prs 1975, Womens Tms, Life Master Womens Prs 1979. Diamond Life Master; has won every event (excluding men's events) at Central States regional at least once and scores of other regional events.

LEBENSOLD, Kenneth W. (b. 1947) of Oakland CA, mathematics professor, frequently credited with inventing the LEBENSOHL, but disclaims any connection with the convention. Won Fall secondary Mens Tms, Can-At Swiss 1969; Fun City KO Tms 1972, 75; New England Knockouts KO Tms 1974.

LEBHAR, Bertram, Jr. (1907-1972); under the name of Bert Lee, had a national reputation as a sportscaster and later as a bridge player and administrator. In private life owned radio and television stations in Florida. Perhaps his greatest achievements arose from his work as treasurer of the ACBL from 1945 to 1947 and as a member of the Steering Committee. In the late Forties, Lebhar was instrumental in the modernization of the ACBL. He was perhaps the first man to visualize the ACBL's vast potential for expansion. His farsighted efforts were recognized when he was made ACBL HONORARY MEMBER in 1963. Also one of the founders of the Greater New York BA and its first president in 1948, Lebhar donated the Lebhar Trophy to the ACBL. Won Spingold 1940, Master Mixed Tms 1946; placed second Mens Prs 1936, the Chicago (now the Reisinger) 1943, Life Master Prs 1945, Vanderbilt 1946, 47; Spingold 1953.

LEBI, Robert (b. 1951) of Toronto ON, computer programmer\analyst, graduated McGill U. Canadian Intercollegiate Pairs and Team champion 1972. Diamond Life Master; won Blue Ribbon Prs 1989; placed second Reisinger 1982; has won 25+ regionals including Montreal Open Prs 1972, KO Tms 1983, 84, Swiss 1984; Chicopee Swiss 1975, Canadian Nat'ls Open Prs 1979, KO Tms 1979; Detroit Open Prs 1980, Syracuse Swiss 1981, Sudbury KO Tms, Open 1983.

LEBIODA, Lukasz (b. 1943) of Krakow, Poland, chemist and crystallographer. Second European Teams 1970. Represented Poland in four world championships and five other zonal championships. Won Sunday Times and many national titles.

LEBOVIC, Wolf (Willy) (b. 1931) of Toronto ON, born in Czechoslovakia, builder and developer, enjoys tennis, golf, chess and backgammon. Originator of the LEBOVIC ASKING BID convention. He was npc of the Canadian Womens Tm in World Olympiad in Deuville 1968 and Canadian Mens Tms in Monte Carlo 1976; competed internat'lly in Amsterdam 1966, Geneva 1990; won Mens Prs 1963, Individual 1965; Blue Ribbon Prs 1967. Regional titles include Upper NY State Mens Prs 1965, Canadian Nat'l Master Prs 1974.

LEBOW, Howard A. (b. 1957) of Pittsburgh PA, biostatistician, graduated U of Pennsylvania, Intercollegiate Bridge Champion 1979; regional wins include Pittsburgh Mixed Prs 1973, Mens Swiss, Master Prs 1986, Swiss 1992; Cleveland Mens Swiss 1979, 87, Open Swiss 1989, KO Tms 1990, KO Tms 1992, Open Prs 1993, Morning KO Tms 1993; Dist 5 GN Tms 1987, Buffalo Mens Swiss 1987; Erie Mens Swiss 1988, Columbus Open Prs 1993.

LEIBENDERFER, Ralph J. (1881-1969) New York City attorney, one of the great players of auction bridge. Won Eastern Auction Open Tms 1927, 28 and was a regular member of the famous Knickerbocker Whist Club team which included Sidney Lenz, Winfield Liggett,

George Reith and P. Hal Sims; was associated with Ely and Josephine Culbertson in founding *The Bridge World*, acting as its counsel; was official referee for Culbertson in the CULBERTSON-LENZ MATCH. Wrote articles for *The Bridge World, Vanity Fair, Auction Bridge Magazine*, as well as book reviews and introductions to many books.

LEDERER, Anthony Richard (Tony) (1919-1976) of England, bridge player and administrator, won his first trophy when he was 14 and played on most of the winning teams captained by his father, Richard Lederer. He instituted the Richard Lederer Memorial Trophy in memory of his father, and with Jill Gatti founded the Charity Challenge Cup Simultaneous Pairs. With his wife, Rhoda Barrow Lederer, he was a prime mover in the formation of the EBU Teachers Association. He co-authored *Learn Bridge with the Lederers*.

LEDERER, Richard (1894-1941) of London, club owner and writer, first great figure in British bridge. He represented Britain in the 1934 SCHWAB CUP match and won the GOLD CUP 1933, 1934, 1939. At the end of the Thirties, Lederer's Club was the training ground for a group of players including Maurice Harrison-Gray, Kenneth Konstam, Adam Meredith and Terence Reese subsequently dominant in the British tournament game. Lederer's writings included *Lederer Bids Two Clubs*. See BIBLIOGRAPHY, C.

LEDERER, Rhoda (Mrs. Anthony, formerly Barrow) (d. 1990) of Chalfont St. Peter, England, bridge writer, columnist, teacher; was co-editor of *The Bridge Player's Encyclopedia* (British edition of the *Official Encyclopedia of Bridge*); co-author or author of many books including *Precision Bridge* (English version of the Eric Jannersten book), *Basic ACOL, ACOL-ite's Quiz, Conventions Made Clear, Opening Leads to Better Bridge* and *The ABCs of Contract Bridge*. Was editor of *IBPA Bulletin* 1967-1971 and co-editor (with Eric Jannersten) of two IBPA books; secretary of English Bridge Union Teachers Association, and Honorary Life Master teacher of the American Bridge Teachers Association; co-edited *Daily Bulletins* at the 1974 World Open Pairs and Bermuda Bowl. See BIBLIOGRAPHY, C, D, E.

LEE, Linda (b. 1947) of Toronto ON, systems management consultant, graduate of U of Toronto, publisher *Canadian Master Point* magazine since 1992, placed second Mixed Prs 1992 and won several regionals.

LEE, Ray (b. 1945) of Toronto ON, book publisher, holds PhD from U of Bradford (UK); bridge columnist for *Toronto Star* 1972-78; editor *Ontario Kibitzer* 1972-75; publisher *Canadian Master Point* magazine since 1992; contributor to other bridge publications; placed second Mixed Prs 1992 and has won several regionals.

LEE, Dr. Sidney (b. 1911) of London, physician and surgeon, was npc of winning British Womens Team in European Championships 1951 and of Great Britain's team in World Team Olympiad 1964. National successes include Gold Cup 1948, 1950, 1952, 1953, 1957, and multiple wins in CAMROSE TROPHY matches, Mixed Teams, Individual, Daily Telegraph Cup, Pachabo Cup.

LEENHARDT, François of Marseilles, France, banker.

WBF World Master. Third World Teams 1975. Won European Teams 1974. Represented France in two other world championships and won several national titles.

LeMAÎTRE, André (1911-1980) of Antwerp, Belgium, business executive, bridge organizer and writer, one of the greatest contributors to the cause of world bridge. Captained Belgian team 1959-1963, npc 1966, 1969-1973; won German Open Teams 1956, 1958, 1961, 1962, 1965, Mixed Pairs 1968, Open Pairs 1955, 1956, Belgian Teams II 1966, KO Teams 1961. Was president of European Bridge League, secretary of World Bridge Federation. Outstanding organizer and administrator for three decades, first for Germany, then for Belgium, then for Europe and finally for the world. LeMaître translated rules and established various tournament regulations for the German Bridge Federation. Newspaper columnist and contributor to various bridge periodicals; founder member of INTERNATIONAL BRIDGE PRESS ASSOCIATION; chosen IBPA "Man of the Year" 1973; contributing editor, *Bridge Encyclopedia*.

LEMING, John T. (b. 1938) of Port Hueneme CA, insurance broker and owner of insurance agency, enjoys scuba diving, has served in several executive positions including president of Oxnard Unit. Won Las Vegas Swiss 1987, Bridge Wk Masters Prs 1988, Swiss 1990; Spring secondary Open Prs, Penticton Strat Prs, Monterey Open Prs 1990; Santa Clara Swiss 1991, Riverside Open Prs 1992, Idaho Falls Open Prs, Strat Prs 1992.

LEMON, James H. (1903-1977), was ACBL president in 1939. He was a frequent golf partner of President Dwight Eisenhower, who honored Lemon by appointing him special ambassador for ceremonies celebrating the independence of the Republic of Ghana. As a bridge player, Lemon was director of Washington Bridge League and served for many years was a member of the ABL and ACBL Executive Committees.

LENT, Robin (formerly Grantham, nee Klar) (b. 1952) of Tempe AZ, bridge teacher, was youngest woman ever to win a major championship when she won Womens Prs 1970. Regional titles include Springfield IL Open Tms 1973, Land of Coronado KO Tms, Open Tms 1972.

LENZ, Sidney (Simon) (1873-1960), author and champion player at whist and all forms of bridge. He was an expert in many other games and sports as well. A series of coups in the lumber business had made him prosperous and by the age of 30 he was rich. He promptly retired and devoted the rest of his life to competition, writing, reading and travel. First he took up bowling and one of his records, an average of 240 over 20 consecutive games (1909), stood for nearly 20 years. In 1909 he became engrossed in whist and the next year he won the AMERICAN WHIST LEAGUE's principal national team championship (Minneapolis Trophy). Altogether he won more than 600 whist and bridge competitions, ranging from club duplicate games to 14 national championships. His Knickerbocker Whist Club auction bridge team (Lenz, Winfield Liggett, P. H. Sims, George Reith and Ralph J. Leibenderfer) was considered the strongest in the country. He won the last tournament he played in, the GOLDMAN CUP pairs at the Eastern Championships of 1932, then ranked as a national event.

Lenz had remarkable versatility in intellectual, coordinative and athletic competitions. He played chess against Jose Capablanca and tennis against "Little Bill" Johnston with small odds. He was scratch at golf and "shot his age" at 69. At table tennis he was of championship caliber. Professional magicians considered him the best amateur ever elected honorary member of the American Society of Magicians. His special skill at dealing seconds impelled him to refuse to play card games for stakes. However, whist and bridge were his greatest loves and he thought of himself primarily as a bridge player. Lenz wrote several books on auction and contract bridge; *Lenz on Bridge* (1926), is ranked as a classic. He wrote many short stories with bridge settings. As a part owner and associate editor of the former humorous magazine *Judge*, Lenz conducted double-dummy problem contests that greatly served to publicize bridge. He contributed articles on bridge to many other magazines including the bridge magazines, and occasionally wrote bridge columns for newspapers, including *The New York Times*.

In 1931 Lenz joined the advisory council of Bridge Headquarters and contributed to the OFFICIAL SYSTEM. He represented this group in the CULBERTSON-LENZ MATCH, from which he acquired lasting fame despite his loss. In his later years Lenz appeared frequently at major tournaments as an honorary referee. At whist he won the American Whist League Open Pairs Championship 1910, 18, 19, 20 representing the Knickerbocker Whist Club and the Mens Pairs 1914, 16, 30, 33, Open Teams 1929 and combination Open Teams and Pairs 1931; in auction in the American Whist League Championships he won Open Teams 1924, Open Pairs 1927, 28 representing the Knickerbocker Whist Club; in contract he won the Eastern States Open Pairs 1932.

The technical contributions of Sidney Lenz to contract bridge are hard to define. His effort to introduce a new call, the "challenge," to replace the takeout double, was unsuccessful. His bidding system at contract bridge, the one-two-three, gave way to the artificial 2♣ bid with intermediate (strong) two-bids in other suits. The Lenz echo, a distribution-showing high-low from a four-card holding, remains standard among experts, but Lenz disclaimed credit for it, saying that it was standard among whist experts and he merely taught auction players to use it. In 1965 he was elected to the Hall of Fame.

LEON, Philip H. (b. 1927) of Grosse Pointe Farms MI, retired but still does selective interior design projects, graduated U of Michigan, classical musical buff and enjoys oil painting. Member Nat'l Goodwill Committee, past president (two terms) of the Michigan BA, Leon served as an MBA and Nat'l Bd of Gov member for many years, vice-chairman of the NABC Appeals Committee for more than 20 years. A Grand Life Master with more than 12,000 MPs, he has won more than 35 regional titles including Dist 5 Open Teams 1968, Motor City Open Tms 1968, Master Prs 1978, Swiss 1989; Dist 11 KO Tms 1969, Open Prs 1979; Marcus Cup 1970, Canadian Nat'l KO Tms 1971, Great Lakes Mixed Prs 1971, Swiss 1981, 87, 89, KO Tms 1987; Cambrian Shield KO Tms 1972, 74, 80, Swiss 1980; Indy 500 KO Tms, Dist 12 GNT, Zone I 1973; Presque Isle Swiss 1977, Wolverine Master Swiss 1981, London ON KO Tms, Swiss 1988, Open Prs 1991.

LEONARD, William M. (Bill) (b. 1953) of Rancho Mirage CA, attorney, graduated from UCLA, Loyola Law School (JD). Won Edmonton KO Tms 1987, Golden State Open Swiss, KO Tms 1988; Hawaii Swiss 1990, Spring Southwest Swiss 1990.

LERENA, Raul (b. 1916) of Buenos Aires, Argentina, bank official, bridge columnist and writer; won Argentine Open Teams 1950, 1957, Master Individual 1952. Was Bermuda Bowl tournament director 1961, 1965; Edited *Bridge Argentino* since 1966.

LERNER, Lawrence I. (Larry) (b. 1935) of Warren NJ, attorney, graduated Newark College of Engineering and Georgetown U Law Center, served as adviser to ACBL Education Foundation 1987-90 and various executive positions on Unit and Dist level. Won NABC Non-Life Master Tms 1983 and Rye Open Tms 1992.

LERNER, Dr. Marcelo (b.1923) of Buenos Aires, Argentina, physician and surgeon. World Life Master. South American champion 1957. Represented Argentina in Bermuda Bowl 1958, 1962, 1965, in World Team Olympiad 1964, 1972. 21 national titles won include Open Teams six times, Open Pairs twice. Won Gabarret Cup 1964, 1965.

LESNIEWSKI, Marcin (b. 1948) of Zakopane, Poland, mathematician and bridge professional. WBF World Master. Won European Cup 1984, European Pairs 1989, European Mixed Pairs 1992. Represented Poland in three world championships and three zonal championships. Won many national titles.

LESTER, Claire (formerly Grigg) of Perth, Australia. Won Far East Womens Teams 1977 and represented Australia in three world championships and one other zonal championship.

LETIZIA, Marinesa (b. 1954) of Bloomington IN, professional bridge player, formerly critical care nursing supervisor, graduated Medical College of Georgia, she enjoys crafts, golf and all sports events. Won Master Mixed Tms 1990, 92, Womens KO Tms 1992. Grand Life Master with more than 10,000 MPs; has won more than 100 regional titles; won first four events at Montreal 1987.

LETIZIA, Ralph V. Jr. (b. 1952) of Louisville KY, systems analyst, graduate of U of Louisville, enjoys rotisserie baseball and basketball, golf and record collecting, has served on Unit Conduct and Ethics Committee for more than 11 years and is current chairman. Won North American Swiss 1991; regional wins include Louisville Mens Tms, KO Tms; Cincinnati Swiss, Indianapolis Swiss, Dist 11 GN Prs.

LETT, Carleton E. (b. 1949) of New York City, history teacher and owner/operator of games club, degrees from CUNY, interested in military history, poker and science fiction. Regional wins include Speedball Open Prs 1978, Rainbow Swiss 1982, Albany Open Prs 1982, Uniondale Open Prs 1983, Secaucus Mens Swiss 1985, Port Chester Mens Swiss 1986, Goldman Open Prs 1987.

LEUFKENS, Enri (b. 1963), of De Bilt, The Netherlands, automation expert. Won Bermuda Bowl 1993; WBF World Master. Third World Teams 1992. World Junior

champion 1987. European Junior champion 1986. Represented The Netherlands in two other world championships and two European Championships. National titles include Open Teams twice.

LEV, Sam (b. 1947) of Forest Hills NY. Placed third in the Bermuda Bowl 1976, 85; 7th Rosenblum Cup Tms 1978; WBF World Master; won Reisinger 1989, 91; placed second Blue Ribbon Prs 1990, Spingold 1991, Vanderbilt 1993.

LEVAN, Betty M. (b. 1918) of Bakersfield CA. Served several times on Unit Board; regional wins include Golden State Mixed Prs 1963, 64, 65; Hawaii Open Prs, Mixed Prs 1974, Womens Swiss 1977, 79, 89, Master Prs 1978, Womens Prs 1988, Womens Swiss, Open Prs, Swiss 1989; CA Capital Open Prs, Oil City Open Prs 1978; Pacific Southwest Womens Prs 1981, San Francisco Sr KO Tms 1987, LA Bridge Wk Womens Tms 1993.

LEVENE, Doug (b. 1963) of Birmingham AL, business owner, graduate of Birmingham Southern College, KING OF BRIDGE 1981, at the time he made Life Master (age 16) he was the 4th youngest in the country. Won Reston KO Tms, Huntsville Swiss 1980; Gatlinburg Open Prs 1981, Atlanta Open Prs 1986; Summer NABC secondary Open Prs 1987, Washington DC KO Tms 1988, Dist 10 GN Prs 1989.

LEVENKO, Vasily (b. 1950) of Tallinn, Estonia, mathematician. WBF World Master. Represented Estonia in two world championships and one zonal championship. Top Soviet masterpoint holder. Won Soviet open teams four times, Estonian open teams four times, Estonian open pairs five times. Official representative of Estonian Contract Bridge League.

LEVENTRITT, Peter A. (b. 1916) of NYC. ACBL president and assistant treasurer 1945-46; past president of Greater New York BA and the Card School of New York, which he co-founded. Pioneered the use of the SCHENKEN SYSTEM in partnership with its inventor. WBF Life Master; represented North America in Bermuda Bowl 1955 (npc), placed second 1957, 61, 63, 65; was coach of the South African Womens Tm in Deauville 1968. Won Spingold 1956, 60; Chicago (now the Reisinger) 1941, 49; Vanderbilt 1953, 64; Life Master Prs 1944, 51; Master Mixed Tms 1949, 50, 59; Mixed Prs 1950, Mens Tms 1966; placed second in the Chicago 1943, 53; Vanderbilt 1947, 48, 55, 59, 62, 67; Mens Tms 1955, Open Prs 1948, 51, Mixed Prs 1949; Master Mixed Tms 1947, Master Individual 1952. His many regional successes include events in Eastern States, Mid-South, New York-New Jersey and others.

LEVERONE, Anne Marie (b. 1947) of St. Louis MO, business manager, graduated St. Louis U, enjoys reading and nature hiking; placed second Life Master Womens Prs 1978, that same year she won her first sectional and regional events; has several other regional wins.

LEVEY, Sydney A. Jr. (b. 1927) of North Hollywood CA. CPA, graduate of U of San Francisco, ACBL president 1982, ABCL Treasurer 1979, 80, Chairman of the Board 1983 and was District 22 representative to the ACBL Bd of Dir from 1975-87. Served as chairman of

ACBL Systems and Convention Committee and as chairman of Finance Committee. A member of Western Conference Board 1962-65, Chairman of the Assembly 1965, president 1984-85; member of the Nat'l Bd of Gov and the ACBL Goodwill Committee; executive secretary of Bridge PRO. Competed in int'l competition Biarritz 1982, Bal Harbour 1986 (placed third in Swiss Plate Prs). Diamond Life Master with more than 10,000 MPs; placed second in North American Swiss 1983 and has won numerous regional events including Bridge Wk Open Tms 1960, 61, 88, Prs 1985, Victory Point Tms, BAM Tms 1987, Strat Prs 1991; Fresno KO Tms 1968, 78, Mens Prs 1978, Open Prs, BAM Tms 1981; San Francisco Life Masters Prs 1973, Sr KO Tms 1986, 88, 90; Sacramento Masters Prs 1974, Sr Open Prs 1991; Dist 22 GN Tms 1974, 84, Dist 22 GN Prs 1981; Reno Sr Open Prs 1986, Sr KO Tms 1989; Santa Clara KO Tms 1990, Primetime KO Tms 1991; Yosemite Sr KO Tms, Swiss 1991.

LEVIN, Muriel (Mutzie) (b. 1922) of Chicago, retired office manager, won Senior and Advanced Senior Master Prs 1965.

LEVIN, Robert J. (Bobby) (b. 1957) of Aventura FL, options trader, partner in real estate company, part-time bridge professional, enjoys outdoor sports, in particular tennis and swimming. WBF Life Master; won Bermuda Bowl 1981, the youngest player ever to win a world championship. Placed 6th World Mixed Prs and 9th Rosenblum Tms 1990. He won the Pan American Tms 1992; became Life Master in 1973, the youngest ever to do so at that time (see YOUNGEST LIFE MASTER), was KING OF BRIDGE in 1975. At the age of 13 he played in and won his first event, a sectional Mens Prs with his bridge teacher, the late Abe Goldstein. ACBL Grand Life Master with more than 12,000 MPs as of 1993; won USBC 1993 and the Lou Herman Trophy 1979. North American championships include Open Prs 1978, Reisinger, Blue Ribbon Prs 1979; Vanderbilt 1980, 89; Master Mixed Tms, Mens BAM Tms 1987; Life Master Mens Prs 1988, Life Master Prs 1989, Spingold 1992, Spring Open Prs I 1993. Placed second in GN Tms 1978, 92; Mens BAM Tms 1983, Vanderbilt 1984, Mens Prs 1986, Blue Ribbon Prs 1987, 88; Spingold 1988, 91; Open BAM Tms 1990; has won hundreds of regional events.

LEVIN, William K. (Bill) (b. 1925) of Nahant MA, bridge club director, won numerous regional titles including New England Spring Open Tms 1957, 59, 60, 61, Fall KO Tms 1961, Open Prs 1960.

LEVINSON, Delle (b. 1920) of Skokie IL, artisan and artist, won Senior and Advanced Senior Master Prs 1965, Life Master Womens Prs 1971.

LEVINSON, Michael A. (b. 1952) of Daly City CA, computer programmer, graduate of Union College and a former tournament chess player, won Life Master Mens Prs 1981.

LEVIT, Yeshayahu (b. 1943) of Tel Aviv, Israel, owner-manager of bridge club and bridge teacher. WBF World Master. Third Bermuda Bowl 1976, second European Teams 1975, and represented Israel on nine other occasions. Won several national team titles.

LEVITT, Evelyn (Mrs. Harold) (1919-1987) of Wilmington DE, bridge teacher, lecturer and director, a graduate of Temple U. Past president of Dist 4 and of Unit 190; former member of NABC Appeals Committee. WBF World Master; competed int'lly on a few occasions. North American wins include Womens Tms 1978, 81, Womens Prs 1983; Master Mixed Tms 1985, Womens KO Tms 1986; placed second Mixed Prs 1969, North American Womens Swiss 1985; won numerous regional titles.

LEVITT, Jerry (b. 1918) of Clayton MO, bridge teacher and columnist, won the Vanderbilt 1962 and placed second GN Tms 1973.

LEVITT, Paul A. (1939-1993) of Azle TX, life insurance management consultant, won Mixed Prs 1962, placed second Spingold 1966, Vanderbilt 1967.

LEVITZ, Jerry (b. 1943) of Ventura CA, attorney and businessman, graduated from UCLA and UCLA Law School (JD), active in Rotary International, past vice president Unit 547. Diamond Life Master; won Pasadena Open Prs, Fresno KO Tms, Swiss 1989; Portland Mens Prs 1989, Fltd KO Tms 1992, 30-hour KO Tms 1993; New Orleans Bracketed KO Tms; Spring NABC secondary Bracketed KO Tms, Swiss 1990, 92, Swiss 1993; Fall Bracketed KO Tms 1991, KO Tms 1992, Open Prs 1992; Redding Open Swiss, Bakersfield Swiss, Hawaii Swiss 1991; Riverside Fltd KO Tms, Santa Rosa KO Tms 1992; Emerald Empire Bracketed KO Tms, KO Tms, Swiss 1992; Palm Springs Bracketed KO Tms 1992; Vancouver Open Prs 1993, Summer secondary KO Tms 1993; Phoenix Strat Prs, Handicap KO Tms 1993.

LEVY, Alain (b. 1948 in Morocco) of Paris, France, bridge teacher and writer. World Life Master. Won World Teams 1992. Third European Teams 1981. Third European Individual 1992. Won Common Market Teams twice. Represented France in four other world championships and won many national titles.

LEVY, Alvin (b. 1940) of Stony Brook NY, research aerospace scientist, educated at The Cooper Union and Columbia U (PhD); numismatist, philatelist, enjoys golf; received a Special Achievement Award from NASA in 1981 and has been a visiting scholar at the U of Cambridge (England). President of Dist 24 Bd of Dir, has served as president and tournament chairman of Unit 242 and is a regular contributor to the *Islander*. Levy won Advanced Senior Prs 1967 and Long Island Swiss 1981, 91; Swan Lake Mens Swiss 1983, 84; Port Chester Mens Swiss 1985, Open Swiss 1990, Open Prs 1992; New York City Swiss, Summer secondary Open Prs 1985.

LEVY, David (b. 1934 in England) of Kingston, Jamaica, radiologist. Won CAC Teams 1982, 1983. Represented Jamaica in two world championships and four other zonal championships. Won numerous national titles. Past president of the Jockey Club of Jamaica.

LEVY, Louis (b. 1921) of Los Angeles CA, retired businessman, graduate of NYU, National Open chess co-champion 1972, US Senior chess champion 1984, US Senior co-champion 1991-92. Diamond Life Master; won Life Master Prs 1958 and has numerous regionals to his credit.

LEVY, Rose I. (nee Fadel) (b. 1930) of Santa Monica CA, born in Syria, graduate of Stanford and UCSF (PhD), college professor and bridge teacher, has served in various executive positions in Dist 23 and Unit 561. When DeGaulle came to Stanford, she was his interpreter; she speaks six languages. Regional wins include Reno Sr Swiss 1989; Ventura Sr KO Tms, Open Prs 1990, Swiss, Open Prs 1992; Pasadena Sr Prs, Sr Swiss, Sr KO Tms 1991; San Bernardino Sr Prs 1993, 94.

LEVY, William N. (b. 1941) of Voorhees NJ, lawyer, graduated U of Pennsylvania (JD). Won Fall NABC secondary Mens Prs 1975, Mid-Atlantic Swiss 1975, Mens Swiss 1979, 80; Washington Bridge Wk Mens Swiss 1976, Tri-State Winter Mens Prs 1976, Dist 4 Mens Swiss 1979.

LEWIS, Lt. Col. Edwin R. (Ed) (b. 1931) of Falls Church VA, bridge club owner/manager, teacher, certified director since 1975, graduate U of Nebraska and Air Force Inst. Tech. Member of Unit 218 Bd of Dir. Author of EXTENDED JACOBY TRANSFER and co-author of CAPPELLETTI OVER NT and CAPPELLETTI OVER ONE OF A MAJOR DOUBLED. Life Master #8 of Japan Contract Bridge League; represented Japan in Far East Championships 1961 (placed third); won seven Japanese Team Championships 1961-1963. Represented Nebraska U in first Big 8 bridge tournament 1950; won *The Bridge World* Chance-of-a-Lifetime contest 1968. Diamond Life Master; has won more than 60 regionals.

LEWIS, Ellee (b. 1934) of New York City, accountant for many leading Broadway shows, bridge professional; placed second Womens Swiss 1984, Master Mixed Tms 1990; regional wins include Los Angeles Mixed Tms (BAM) 1965, Hudson Womens Swiss, South Fallsbury Womens Swiss 1979; Swan Lake Womens Swiss, Lancaster Womens Swiss 1984; Arlington Womens Swiss 1985, Cherry Hill Womens Swiss 1986, 91; Parsippany Womens Swiss 1987, Fall secondary Masters Prs 1988, Horizontal Womens Prs 1992; Bal Harbour Open Prs 1990, New York Sr Prs 1991.

LEWIS, Harlow S. II (b. 1932) of Wynnewood PA, investment adviser, graduated Princeton U, enjoys golfing, past president of Philadelphia Whist Association (now Philadelphia Contract BA), member Nat'l Goodwill Committee. A *Bridge World* panelist and occasional contributor to *The Bridge World* and *Bridge Journal*. Won Life Master Mens Prs 1967, Mens Prs 1975, Reisinger 1970; placed second Mens Tms 1967, Reisinger 1971, Spingold 1974; won several regional titles including Intercollegiate Championship 1953.

LEWIS, Jerry M. (1895-1965). ACBL President 1963 and chairman of the Bd of Dir in 1962 and 1964. Served under General John Pershing in both the Mexican War and World War I and was decorated with a Distinguished Service citation. A Dallas sales executive, Lewis won several regional titles.

LEWIS, John Malcolm (b. 1943) of Sandwich, Kent UK, mathematics teacher, graduate of Queens College (ON), enjoys classical music, reading and stage lighting. Served on Bermuda Unit 198 including vice president 1975 and

on organizing committee for the Bermuda Bowl 1975. Represented Bermuda in world play Miami 1972, Monte Carlo 1976; Pan Americans 1975. Won the CROCKFORDS CUP 1991 (England) and Bermuda Open Swiss 1978. Lewis designed and made the first screens used in the Bermuda Bowl at the Silver Jubilee in 1975.

LEWIS, Linda Marie of Las Vegas NV, casino owner, former bridge professional and teacher, enjoys gambling and sports betting. Won the most number of MPs ever won in a year by a woman, 2715, in 1983. Won Master Mixed Tms 1981, placed second North American Womens Swiss 1983, 86; Womens KO Tms 1983, Womens BAM Tms 1989. Grand Life Master with more than 10,000 MPs; has won more than 200 regional titles including all the events at Portland ME regional 1983.

LEWIS, Paul J. (b. 1952) of Las Vegas NV, bank chairman, real estate developer, former professional bridge player and attorney, graduated U of South Dakota (JD), enjoys fine wines, thoroughbred horses and collecting antique glass paperweights. Diamond Life Master; has won Open Prs 1980, Master Mixed Tms 1981; placed second Reisinger 1982, Mens Swiss 1982, Open Prs 1988; has won more than 120 regional events.

LEWIS, Robert N. (b. 1937) of McLean VA, computer specialist, placed third World Mixed Tms 1974; won Keystone Fall Mens Swiss 1970, Mid-Atlantic Summer Open Tms 1971, Can-At KO Tms 1974.

LI, Lan Qing of Beijing, China. Vice premier. Winner of many VIP tournaments. Vice premier in charge of the Education & Economic program in China.

LIAO, Kuo Tang (b. 1948) of Singapore, education administrator. Represented Singapore in one world championship and 5 zonal championships. National wins include open teams 5 times.

LIARAKOS, Spyros (b. 1963) of Athens, Greece. Won 1987 Common Market Pairs while a junior. National wins open teams once and master pairs twice.

LICHTMAN, Edward L. (Ed) (b. 1949) of Winnipeg MB, chartered accountant, graduated U of Manitoba and U of Western Ontario; placed second Amateur Swiss 1976; won Winnipeg District Canadian National Teams Championship 1976, 86, 90; Saskatoon Masters Prs 1975, Thunder Bay KO Tms, Masters Prs 1979; Fargo KO Tms 1979.

LIGGAT, David of Edinburgh, Scotland, government servant; represented Scotland 9 times in Camrose Trophy matches. Many national wins include Gold Cup once and Scottish Cup three times.

LIGGETT, Cmdr. Winfield S., Jr. (1881-1937) executive officer of the U.S.S. Montana in World War I, retired from the Navy and became a bridge writer, teacher and lecturer. One of the leading pre-war American bridge personalities, Liggett partnered Sidney Lenz during the last part of the CULBERTSON-LENZ MATCH and won numerous national championships at whist, auction and contract. He was a member of the Advisory Council on the OFFICIAL SYSTEM and authored *Contract Bridge*

Summary and co-authored *Winning Leads at Contract Bridge*.

LIGGINS, Glyn (b. 1962) of London, England, editor. Represented Britain in one world championship and England in the Camrose Trophy. Editor of *Bridge* since 1990.

LIGHTMAN, M(alcolm) A. (1892-1958) of Memphis TN, was associated with the motion picture business. Won Life Master Prs 1945, Chicago (now the Reisinger) 1947.

LIGHTNER, Theodore A. (1893-1981) of New York City, a leading figure in bridge from the earliest days of contract. He was named Life Master #7 when the category was created by the AMERICAN BRIDGE LEAGUE in 1936. Born in Grosse Pointe MI, later a resident of Chicago and NYC, Lightner was a graduate of Yale and of Harvard Law School and had a seat on the NY Stock Exchange. He was a contributor to the development of the CULBERTSON SYSTEM and was the inventor of the LIGHTNER DOUBLE of slam contracts. His writings include *Highlights of the Culbertson System*, *Famous Hands of the Culbertson-Lenz Match* (co-author), and he made frequent contributions to *The Bridge World*. He partnered Ely Culbertson during a part of the CULBERTSON-LENZ MATCH and was a member of the Culbertson team which won victories over British teams in 1930, 33, 34 (see ANGLO-AMERICAN MATCHES). Won Bermuda Bowl 1953; won Spingold 1937, 39, 45; Chicago 1947, Vanderbilt 1930, Life Master Prs 1932, 35; Open Prs 1928; placed second Spingold 1941, Chicago 1932, 34; Vanderbilt 1937, 38, 39, 41, 45; Life Master Prs 1931, 47; won numerous regional titles.

LILIE, Harold J. of Las Vegas NV, WBF World Master, placed 6th in Rosenblum Tms 1986. ACBL Diamond Life Master; won Mens Tms, Mens Prs, MOTT-SMITH TROPHY 1982; Master Mixed Tms 1986; placed second Vanderbilt 1984; has won numerous regional events.

LILIE, Joyce of Las Vegas NV, retired schoolteacher, graduated Brooklyn College and Adelphi U, accomplished amateur pianist. Diamond Life Master; won Master Mixed Tms 1986, Womens BAM Tms 1986, 90; North American Womens Swiss 1991; placed second North American Womens Swiss 1985, Womens KO Tms 1989, 91. She has dozens of regional titles to her credit.

LIM, Dr. Teong (b. 1932) of Kuala Lumpur, Malaysia, virologist. Represented Malaysia in one world championships and more than 10 zonal championships. Several national wins include open teams.

LIN, Hsien Chu or **Harry** (b. 1939), bank auditor. World Life Master. Second Bermuda Bowl 1970; represented Taiwan in two other world championships. Far East champion 1967, 1970, 1976 and 1978. NPC Taiwanese Womens Team in three world championships and two Far East Championships.

LIN, Hung Shih or **Emerson** (b. 1956) of Taipei, Taiwan, textile entrepreneur. Far East champion 1981; represented Taiwan in two other Far East Championships and two world championships.

LIN, Mai-Li or **Phoebe** (b. 1956) of Taipei, Taiwan, mer-

chandiser. WBF World Master. Far East champion 1989; represented Taiwan in five other Far East Championships and three world championships. Has won 8 national titles.

LINAH, Mike (1942-1985) of Covina CA, formerly of New York City, became an ACBL associate national tournament director in 1975. In 1978 he was a member of the directing staff at the World Pair Olympiad in New Orleans.

LINCZMAYER, Lajos (b. 1942) of Budapest, Hungary, mechanical engineer. Many times a national champion; represented Hungary in three world championships and 10 European Championships. Won Caransa Teams 1987, Venice Festival Teams twice. Won IBPA 1981 Solomon Award for Hand of the Year.

LINDÉN, Johan C. (b. 1943) of Helsinki, Finland, electrical engineer. Represented Finland six times, including one world championship and four European Championships. National wins include Open Teams and Open Pairs three times each. Road-racing motorcyclist.

LINDÉN, Siv C. (b. 1932) of Helsinki, Finland, bridge organizer. Nordic Womens Team champion 1971; represented Finland on 13 other occasions including four world championships and five European Championships. Tournament director. Member EBL Ladies Committee and Board Member of Bridge League of Finland.

LINDKVIST, C. Magnus (b. 1958) of Lund, Sweden, bridge writer. World Life Master. Third in four world championships: Rosenblum Cup 1986, World Team Olympiad 1988, Bermuda Bowl 1987 and 1991. European champion 1987, third 1989. Won Cavendish Invitational Pairs 1988. Editor of *Bridgetidningen*. Bridge columnist for *Sydsvenskan*; author or co-author of four bridge books; chairman of Scania Bridgekonsult.

LINDKVIST, Jorgen (b. 1945) of Stockholm, Sweden, bridge writer. WBF World Master. European champion 1977. Represented Sweden in two world championships and five other European championships. National wins include open teams six times and open pairs twice.

LINDOP, David (b. 1946) of Toronto, born in England, business systems analyst, graduate of U of Toronto, past president Canadian Bridge Federation; represented Canada in world championships New Orleans 1978, Miami Beach 1986, Salsomaggiore 1992. Placed second Pan American Championships 1992, CNTC 1993. Chairman 1986 NABC in Toronto, at the time the largest NABC in history; member Unit board; co-author with wife Audrey Grant of *Joy of Bridge* and *Bridge Maxims*; technical editor of the ACBL *Club, Diamond, Heart* and *Spade* teaching texts; technical editor of *Better Bridge* newsletter; script writer for ACBL's video teaching series.

LINDSAY, Cameron A. (Cam) (b. 1940) of Surrey BC, realtor, graduated U of Western Ontario and York U. Regional titles include Can-Am Open Tms 1968, 72; Canadian Nat'l Master Tms 1969, Mixed Prs 1970, Master Prs 1975; Peach City Swiss 1978, Spokane Swiss, Open Prs; Victoria Masters Prs, Tacoma KO Tms, Seattle KO Tms.

LINDSAY, Ian (b. 1942) of Belfast, Northern Ireland,

chartered accountant. Represented N. Ireland in 15 Camrose Trophy matches. Won All-Ireland Clubs Pairs three times and other major national titles at least twice each. Past president of Irish Bridge Union.

LINDSEY, John H. II of Fort Myers FL, retired associate math professor, graduated CalTech and Harvard (PhD), won Bridge Week Open Prs 1971, Champagne Open Prs 1978, Central States Swiss 1979, 80; Mad City KO Tms 1979.

LING, Roger (b. 1951) of Hong Kong, accounting manager. WBF World Master. Won Far East Open Teams 1987; represented Hong Kong in four world championships and six other Far East Championships. National wins include open teams and open pairs.

LINHART, William James (Jim) (b. 1936) of New York City, professional bridge player, won Master Mixed Tms 1975. Diamond Life Master; has won numerous regional events.

LINZ, Rama (b. 1940) of Beverly Hills CA, born in Israel, designs jewelry, former building contractor, graduate of Israel Conservatory of Music, art and antique collector. Was the first to arrange sponsorships to promote tournament bridge in South Africa in 1971. WBF World Master; placed 8th World Womens Prs 1980; won Womens KO Tms 1985, Master Mixed Tms 1987; placed second Life Master Womens Prs 1985, 86; Womens KO Tms 1986; has won several regional events.

LINZNER, Temi of Pompano Beach FL, medical technician and interior designer, travel agent, certified bridge director and teacher; enjoys cooking, travel and collecting art; won Southeastern Womens Swiss 1982, Womens Swiss 1993; Orlando Open Swiss 1984, Hunt Valley Womens Prs 1988, 90; Mexican Nat'l Open Swiss 1989, Cherry Hill Womens Swiss 1990, Sr Prs 1990, 91, 93.

LIPKIN, Michael D. (b. 1958) of Ithaca NY, lecturer with department of physics at Cornell U, educated at MIT and U of Chicago (PhD). Author of *Invitation to Annihilation* and a regular contributor to CNYBA bridge bulletin. Won Flt B Morning KO Tms, Rochester Morning KO Tms, Parsippany/Albany Morning KO Tms 1988.

LIPMAN, James O. (Jimmy) (b. 1919) of Arlington VA, retired from US Library of Congress. ACBL regional tournament director for 20+ years, member Unit 218 Bd of Dir. Diamond Life Master; has won Durham Swiss, Keystone Conference Mens Prs 1971; Roanoke Open Prs 1979, Mid-Atlantic Independence Open Prs 1979, Swiss 1989; Richmond Swiss 1980, NVBA Swiss 1988, Fall secondary KO Tms 1988.

LIPSITZ, Robert H. (Bob) (b. 1942) of Annandale VA, computer analyst, Grand Life Master with more than 11,000 MPs; won World Mixed Tms 1974 and Rosenblum Cup Tms 1986; won Life Master Prs 1976, Fall Life Master Mens Prs 1982, GN Tms 1984, 88, 92; placed second Master Mixed Tms 1973, Reisinger 1976, 77; Life Master Prs 1977, 82; Vanderbilt 1978, GN Tms 1985; has won scores of regional titles.

LIPSKER, Aaron (b. 1918) of Olympia WA, retired real

estate and investment broker, Life Master #1400, club owner and certified director since 1967, has served as president of two Units, member of Nat'l Goodwill Committee, alternate director for Dist 18 for three terms beginning in 1956, won Rocky Mtn Mixed Prs 1959.

LIPTON, Dr. William V. (Bill) (1901-1977) of New York City, dentist; introduced the magazine *Post Mortem* and was widely thought to be the original author of its famous *Cynical Observer* column. Served as ACBL Board member 1956-1959; also presided over the Greater New York and the New York-New Jersey Bridge Associations. Won Vanderbilt 1953, Mens Prs 1942; placed second Chicago (now Reisinger) 1955.

LIU, Yiquian (b.1959) of Shanghai, China, assistant professor. WBF World Master. Third Venice Cup 1991. Won Far East Women Teams 1991. Represented China in three world championships and two other zonal championships. Won one national title.

LIVEZEY, Joseph C. (Joey) (b. 1937) of Paoli PA, realtor, bridge teacher and club director, his other interests are old homes and antiques. YOUNGEST LIFE MASTER in 1968, was first in North American Zone in Epson Prs 1986 and seventh in the world. Was a guest on the TV show *What's My Line* in 1969 as the youngest Life Master. Diamond Life Master; has won more than 70 regionals including Keystone Master Prs 1969, Swiss 1975, Open Prs 1991; Mid-Atlantic Swiss 1974, 81, Master Prs 1974, Open Prs 1975; secondary Swiss 1975, Open Prs 1979, BAM Tms 1981, KO Tms 1983; Spring secondary Swiss 1979, Fall secondary KO Tms 1984.

LIVINGSTON, Alene F. (Mrs. Milton M.) (b. 1908) of Paducah KY, won Womens Tms 1962; first certified director in Paducah.

LIVSHITS, Vitali L. (b. 1944) of Kharkhov, Ukraine, computer programmer. Won USSR Open Teams 1990, 1991, Ukrainian Open Pairs 1991. Represented Ukraine 1990 Goodwill Games.

LLOPART, Amadeo (b. 1954) of Barcelona, Spain, architect. Represented Spain in one world championship and two zonal championships. National wins include Open Teams many times.

LOBBEN, Mickey H. (formerly Rosenthal) (1933-1993) of Encino CA, psychologist, graduate of Skidmore College, placed second in Master Mixed Tms 1970 and won several regionals.

LOCKRIDGE, Charles (1905-1970) noted for the brilliance of his dummy play, was a member of the BID-RITE TEAM. President of a New York retailing company and a bridge teacher, Lockridge won five NABC championships and placed second several times.

LODGE, Steve (b. 1957) of London, England, electronics engineer. Second European Teams 1981. Won Junior European Teams 1978. Represented Britain in two world championships and one other zonal championship. National wins include Gold Cup four times.

LONG, Larry A. (b. 1942) of Canton OH, chemist and

manager, graduate of Marshall U, Unit 164 Board member and former bridge columnist. Diamond Life Master; has won 30+ regional events including Gatlinburg Masters Prs 1976, Spring secondary Open Tms 1981, Canadian Nat'l Mens Prs 1981, 84; Midwest Spring Open Prs Dist 5 Labor Day Master Prs 1981; Louisville Master Prs 1990, Open Prs 1991; Lexington Open Prs 1991.

LONG, May Belle (1901-1987) of El Paso TX, former physical education teacher and tennis coach, won Womens Prs 1961 and Navajo Trail Swiss 1971.

LOOBY, James V. (Jim) (b. 1947) of Burbank CA, tax attorney, educated at Harvard, Southwestern School of Law (JD), Emory U; won GNYBA Mens Prs 1973, Mid-Atlantic KO Tms 1973, 74, Mens Prs 1974; Puerto Rico Swiss 1974, Indianapolis KO Tms 1975, Winter Bridge Wk Swiss 1975, 82, Open Prs 1991; Bridge Wk KO Tms 1976, BAM Tms 1982, 83, Master Prs 1993; Riverside Mens Prs, KO Tms 1980; Dist 23 GN Tms 1982, 89, 92; Santa Rosa Master Prs, BAM Swiss 1982; San Diego Swiss 1982.

LOOKS, Harry A. (b. 1952) of St. Louis MO, president Edison Brothers Stores International. Won Senior and Advanced Senior Master Prs 1973.

LOPATA, Monte L. (b. 1919) of St. Louis MO, senior partner in accounting firm, graduate of Washington U, won gold medal for golf in Senior Olympics, chairman of Summer NABC 1963, won Mississippi Valley Mens Prs 1961, 70; Midwest Fall Mens Prs 1962, Dist 8 GN Tms, Zone V 1975.

LOPUSHINSKY, Jim E. (b. 1945) of Edmonton AB, tournament director, computer programmer, educated at U of Alberta and Northern Alberta Institute of Technology; developer of ACBLscore, served as Unit Manager Unit 391 1977-79, 1986-88. He first developed the scoring program in 1981, under the name Compu-Score. Its first testing was done in 1982 at club games. Over a course of 12 years the program has evolved into the one presently used. It was purchased by ACBL in 1990 and Lopushinsky was retained for enhancements and upgrades. ACBLscore is now used in all ACBL-sanctioned tournaments and at many bridge clubs.

LOPUSHINSKY, Patricia F. (b. 1944) of Edmonton AB, born in London, England, registered nurse and office manager, enjoys music and was member of a group for four years, former bridge club owner/operator. Won Calgary Open Swiss 1973, Womens Prs 1979; Saskatoon Open Swiss 1975, Edmonton Open Prs 1984, Womens Prs 1987.

LORD, Roger E. III (b. 1941) of St Louis MO, advertising executive, placed second GN Tms 1973; has won many regional events.

LORENTZ, Gabriel M. (Gaby) (b. 1937 in Hungary) of Sydney, Australia, solicitor and company director. Represented Australia in four world championships and two zonal championships. National titles include open teams twice.

LORER, Matilda (b. 1954) of Sofia, Bulgaria, micro-

electronic engineer. WBF World Master. Won European Womens Pairs 1987, third 1989. Third Olympiad Womens Teams 1988.

LORTZ, Henry A. (b. 1950) of Seattle WA, mathematician/computer scientist, graduate of U of Washington, Unit 446 and Dist 19 recorder, Dist Board member, member Nat'l Goodwill Committee. Diamond Life Master; regional wins include Inland Empire Open Tms, Master Prs 1973; Dist 19 GN Tms 1973, 86, Zone VII 1973; British Columbia Swiss 1973, Open Prs 1978, 79; Puget Sound Swiss 1976, Mens Swiss 1979, Mixed Prs 1980; Evergreen Swiss 1976, Oregon Trail Master Prs 1977, Open Prs 1990; Penticton Swiss Tm 1990.

LORVAN, Sidney (Sid) (b. 1933) of Pacifica CA, attorney, graduate Cornell U, Albany Law School (JD), former mayor and city councilman of Pacifica, placed second Mens Prs 1989, participant 1991 Pair Trials for USA Team #2 (internat'l) and won Upper NY State BAM Tms 1956, All-Western Open Swiss 1986, 89, IMP Prs 1990; Reno Handicap KO Tms 1989.

LOVE, Clyde E. (d. 1960) of Ann Arbor MI, professor of mathematics, specialist on squeeze plays. His writings include *Squeeze Play in Bridge*, *Bridge Squeeze Complete* and many magazine articles.

LOW, Marc E. (b. 1935) of Centerville OH, dean of College of Science and Mathematics Wright State U, educated at Oklahoma State U and U of Illinois (PhD), enjoys travel. With John Hamilton he adapted chess pairings to create the SWISS MOVEMENT in 1967. Diamond Life Master; placed second Mixed Prs 1989; has won numerous regional titles.

LOW, Sandra (Sandy) (b. 1932) of Centerville OH, enjoys sports, reading, cooking and travel; Diamond Life Master, placed second Life Master Womens Prs 1983, Mixed Prs 1989; has won 70+ regional events.

LOW, William S. (b. 1918) of New York City, retired attorney, author of *Graphic Guide to Duplicate Bridge Directing*.

LOWENTHAL, John (b. 1938) of New York City, computer software developer, enjoys computers, baseball and classical music, regular *Bridge World* Master Solvers panelist and author of numerous articles. Author of Borel computer program, a sophisticated hand-generator. Co-developer of the CANARY CLUB and the Ultra Club relay systems. Lowenthal also developed the computer system which reports US national election returns (1970). Won Mens Tms 1976; placed second GN Tms 1981; has won numerous regionals including New York Eastern States KO Tms twice.

LOWERY, Sylvester (1914-1985) of Longport NJ, builder and developer, won US Zone World Bridge Olympics 1940. Lowery was a past president of the Philadelphia CBA, Philadelphia Whist Association, Cavendish Club of Philadelphia, the Keystone Conference and chairman of the ACBL Conduct and Ethics Committee. He served as referee in the first Bermuda Bowl in 1950 and was npc of the Philadelphia women's team that played against the visiting British women's team in 1953. He placed second in Mixed Prs 1966 and won Keystone Conference Mixed Prs 1959, Texas Fall Open Prs 1962.

LUBLIN, Glenn A. (Iron Man) (b. 1951) of Silver Spring MD, professional bridge instructor and player, ACBL certified director and teacher. Diamond Life Master with more than 16,000 MPs; placed second North American Swiss, Life Master Mens Prs 1988, Open Prs 1990; has 200+ regional wins to his credit; has been Unit winner of Crane Top 500 for 13 years (1980-92).

LU, Frank (1925-1986, born in China) of Christchurch, New Zealand, professor of industrial administration. Represented New Zealand in one world championship. Seven national titles included open teams twice. President New Zealand CBA 1974-75.

LU, Yulin of Shanghai, China, technical employee. WBF World Master. Second Far East Teams 1984, 1987. Represented China in four world championships; won 15 national titles.

LUCARDIE, Anthonie J.E. (The Colonel) (1875-1954) of The Netherlands. Founder of the Netherlands Bridge Federation and one of the founders of the International Bridge League, forerunner of the World Bridge Federation.

LUCAS, Beverly of Youngstown, Ohio. Represented United States in two world championships. High-ranked ABA player. With husband, Sam, the top-ranked married couple in ABA for 40 years. Record number of wins in ABA national knockout events.

LUCAS, Michael H. (b. 1955) of Las Vegas NV, director management information service department, graduated Pennsylvania State U and Harvard Business School, computer hobbyist — enjoys building and repairing systems and programming. Won Open Prs II 1992 and New England Individual KO Tms 1987, 88; New England KO Tms 1988, El Paso Open Prs, Swiss 1992.

LUCAS, Sam of Youngstown OH. Represented United States in two world championships. High-ranked ABA player. With wife, Beverly, the top-ranked married couple in ABA for 40 years. Record number of wins in ABA national knockout events.

LUDEWIG, Bernhard (b. 1954) of Karlsruhe, Germany, market researcher. WBF World Master. Won World Teams 1990; won four national titles.

LUDWIG, R. J. (b. 1918) of Schenectady NY, modern languages teacher, placed second Fall Senior Master Individual 1954; won New England Master Prs 1954, Mens Prs 1955, 56.

LUND, Peter (b 1941) of Copenhagen, Denmark. Bridge teacher, author and journalist. Represented Denmark in one world championship and two zonal championships. National titles include Open Teams. Columnist for *Ekstra Bladet* since 1974 and author of several books.

LUO, Shaoxing of China. Second Far East Teams 1993; represented China in two world championships.

LURIE, Myrna J. (b. 1940) of Hamden CT, advertising and insurance sales, recruiting and training personnel, enjoys classical music, politics, travel and teaching bridge. Member of Nat'l Goodwill Committee and Nat'l Charity Foundation, past president of Dist 24 and has served in other executive positions. Regional wins include Dist 3 Womens Swiss 1977, Tri-State Womens Prs 1978, Fall secondary Womens Swiss 1980.

LUSK, Sue. Bridge teacher and bridge club manager. World Life Master, represented Australia in Venice Cup 1985, 87, 89, 91; Women's Team Olympiad 1992. Won Far East Women's 1985, 90; Zone 7 championship 1985, 87, 91; many Australia women's team championships and many South Australia titles.

LUSKY, John A. (b. 1951) of Portland OR, partner in law firm, graduated Harvard and Stanford Law School (JD), enjoys foreign travel and has climbed Mt. Kilimanjaro. Dist 20 Appeals Committee chairman 1983-present, Judiciary Committee chairman 1992-present. Winner of Portland Swiss 1979, 81, 82, 85, 88, 91, KO Tms 1982, 84, Open Swiss 1985, Open Prs 1988, Open Prs 1991; Eugene Mens Prs, KO Tms 1979; Richland Swiss 1979, Tacoma Swiss 1984, Open Prs 1991; Dist 20 GN Tms 1979, 84, 85, 87, 91, 92; Dist 20 GN Prs 1980.

LYON, Thomas P. (b. 1936) of Washington DC, bridge club owner/manager, certified bridge director since 1972; graduated Lycoming College and Georgetown U, enjoys reading, classical music and travel. Placed second in Open Prs 1969; won Dist 5 Open Tms 1966, Spring Mens Prs 1969, Independence Day Mens Prs 1970, Mid-Atlantic Open Prs, Open Prs 1981.

LYONS, Torrence B. (Ted) (1901-1989) of Pittsburgh, bridge teacher, certified director, lecturer and writer, graduate of U of Pittsburgh, served the AMERICAN BRIDGE TEACHERS ASSOCIATION in various executive positions, including president 1980-81. For many years he wrote the column *Lyons Den* for the *ABTA Quarterly* and was one of a few to be awarded a Master Bridge Teachers Certificate by the ABTA. He was a member of the IBPA.

M

MAAKESTAD, Bobbie of Northbrook IL, bridge teacher, graduate of Northwestern U; won Lake Geneva Womens Swiss 1984, 90; Chicago Womens Prs 1985, Rosemont Mixed Prs 1990, Open Prs 1992; Summer secondary Barometer Open Prs 1991.

MAAS, Anton (b. 1952) of Amstelveen, The Netherlands, bank manager. WBF World Life Master. Using DUTCH SPADE SYSTEM, second World Open Pairs 1982, after a scoring error made it appear that he had won. Third World Teams 1980. National wins include Open Teams six times and Open Pairs three times. Married to Bep Vriend.

MacCRACKEN, Charles M. (Charlie) (b. 1941) of Memphis TN, associate national tournament director and former ACBL tournament manager, is active in child abuse prevention and enjoys bicycling, tennis, fishing and travel. MacCracken began directing career in 1963 and had achieved R3 rating when he joined the ACBL headquarters staff in 1972, served as manager of ACBL Tournament Dept 1978-1989. He served ACBL on the Laws Commission for many years and was instrumental in developing ACBL's first computer scoring program. He was editor of the Northern California *Forum* 1970, 71 and technical editor of the *World Championship Book* 1977-83. Wrote hand analyses for continent-wide games 1974-87. Won Mixed Prs 1978. Regional titles include Oregon Trail Open Tms 1967, 68; Golden State Open Tms 1968; Hawaii Open Tms 1968, 69; Intermountain KO Tms 1968, 69, Open Prs 1971; Golden Gate KO Tms, Open Tms 1969.

MacHALE, J.P. (Joe) (b. 1922) of Dublin, Ireland, university secretary, represented Ireland in the World Open Pairs 1962, World Team Olympiad 72, European Championships regularly since 52. He has won every major Irish title.

MACHLIN, Gertrude (Trudy) (Mrs. Jerome) (b. 1918) of Silver Spring MD, bridge teacher and retired sectional director. Wife of retired national tournament director Jerry Machlin. Graduate of Hunter College, editor of Dist 6 and 7 Mid-Atlantic Insert. Won Mixed Prs 1967.

MACHLIN, Jerome S. (Jerry) (b. 1913) of Silver Spring MD, retired ACBL nat'l tournament director, graduated from City College of NY and State College for Teachers, PhD candidate Syracuse U. Began directing career in early Forties when his famous uncle, Al Sobel, asked him to assist at tournaments. Machlin became a full-time director in 1950 and retired in 1979. He served as Mid-Atlantic treasurer for many years and acted as ACBL tournament coordinator for Dist 6 and 7 for many years. He orginated the Dist 6 and 7 inserts, and is well known as the author of the Washington BL *Bulletin* column *The Poor Man's 30 (& 60) Days* and the book *Tournament Bridge: An Uncensored Memoir*. See Bibliography, L.

MACIESZCZAK, Andrzej (1940-86) of Warsaw, Poland, bridge professional and journalist. WBF World Life Master. Won World Teams 1978; represented Poland in one other world championship and five zonal championships. Won Del Duca and many national titles.

MACKENZIE, Greer (b. 1939) of Hillsborough, Northern Ireland, computer software engineer. Represented N. Ireland in more than 40 Camrose Trophy matches, and Ireland in World Team Olympiad, European Championship and Common Market Championship once each. Formerly president of the Irish Bridge Union, chairman of the Northern Ireland Bridge Union and Irish delegate to the WBF.

MacLEAN, Carole J. (b. 1942) of Eden Prairie MN, customer service representative, graduate of U of Minnesota; other interests are cooking, travel, golf and dancing. Served as president of Unit 103 1984-88 and Unit 178 1989-1990; member Dist 14 Bd, Nat'l Goodwill Committee and has worked in coordinating tournaments including co-chairman Fall NABC 1994. Won Wisconsin Womens KO Tms, Dist 14 Summer Swiss 1981; Gopher Womens Prs 1981, Swiss 1988; Cambrian Shield Swiss

1983, Canadian Prairie Open Prs 1984, Swiss 1986; Fargo Swiss 1990, 91; Fall secondary IMP Prs 1991.

MacLEAN, Hugh C. (b. 1938) of Bloomington MN, bridge professional and bridge club owner, interested in computers, military history and business. Dist 14 tournament coordinator. WBF International Master, represented US in Las Palmas 1974. ACBL Grand Life Master with more than 11,000 MPs; won Life Master Mens Prs 1970, Mens Tms 1974; placed second Advanced Sr Master Prs 1962, Open Prs 1974, Blue Ribbon Prs 1975, Vanderbilt 1977. His 80+ regional wins include Mid American-Canadian Tms 1962, 64, 65, Mens Prs 1963, Mixed Prs 1965, Master Prs 1966; Gopher Mens Prs 1966, 71, KO Tms 1967, 71, Master Prs 1973, 88, 89, Swiss 1973; Canadian Prairie Masters Prs 1970, 75, Mens Prs 1972, 86, KO Tms 1972, 76, Open Prs 1975, 76, 84, Mens Swiss 1976; Dist 14 GN Tms 1987, 88, Fargo Swiss 1990.

MacLEOD, Iain (1913-1970) of London England, cabinet minister and journalist, was one of the great British players. At his death was Chancellor of the Exchequer and considered a potential prime minister. One of the originators of the ACOL SYSTEM. By 1936 he was an international player and won the GOLD CUP the following year as a member of the famous Acol team (Maurice Harrison-Gray, Jack Marx, and S.J. Simon). Former bridge editor of the *London Sunday Times*; authored *Bridge Is an Easy Game*.

MacNAB, Robin B. (1915-85) of Bozeman MT, hotel owner, cattle rancher, ACBL president 1965, member of the ACBL Bd of Dir 1956-81, former member of the ACBL LAWS COMMISSION and past president of the WESTERN CONFERENCE. He also served on the executive council of the WORLD BRIDGE FEDERATION 1965-73. Graduate of Cornell U. Was a member of the US Olympic track and field squad in 1936. He won Inter-Mountain Master Prs 1957, Mid-Atlantic Fall Open Tms 1965.

MADDOX, Marilyn A. (b. 1929) of Pleasant Ridge MI, bridge teacher, member of Nat'l Goodwill Committee and a Diamond Life Master. She won ACBL-wide Charity Game 1992 and numerous regional events including Great Lakes Mixed Prs 1967, 68, Open Tms 1971, 74, Master Swiss 1978, Womens Prs 1981, 83, Sr Prs 1987, Sr KO Tms 1989, Sr Swiss 1991; Wolverine Master Swiss 1981, Sr Swiss 1988, 90, Womens Swiss 1989, Horizontal Sr Prs 1991, Sr Swiss 1991; Motor City Womens Swiss 1984, 85, 86, 90, Swiss 1988; Niagara Falls Sr Swiss 1987, Open Sr Prs 1989, Sr Open Prs 1989; Canadian Nat'l Sr Swiss 1989, Dist 4 Sr. Swiss, Fort Wayne Sr Swiss 1993.

MADDOX, Myles V. (b. 1925) of Pleasant Ridge MI, retired teacher, graduate of Eastern Michigan U. and Wayne State, board member Michigan BA 1958-62, president 1963. Diamond Life Master; won ACBL-wide Charity Game 1992; numerous regionals including Great Lakes Mixed Prs 1967, 68, Mens Prs 1970, Open Tms 1971, 74, Master Swiss 1978, Swiss 1981, Sr Prs 1987, Sr KO Tms 1989, Sr Swiss 1991; Spring NABC secondary Open Prs 1981, Wolverine Master Swiss 1981, Sr Swiss 1988, 90, Sr Horizontal Prs 1991, Sr Swiss 1991; Niagara Falls Sr Swiss 1987, 89; Motor City Swiss 1988,

London ON Sr Swiss 1988, Canadian Nat'l Sr Swiss 1989, Dist 4 Sr Swiss, Fort Wayne Sr Swiss 1993.

MAGEE, John (b.1939) of Bisley, England; promoter, now concentrates on bridge, calls self Mr. Bridge in promotional dealings, formerly was known as the Sandwich King, published *Dictionary of Bridge Terms, Bridge Plus*.

MAGEE, Lee T. (b. 1928) of Prairie Village KS, attorney for the IRS, graduate of U of Nebraska, Creighton U School of Law (JD), master chess player. Diamond Life Master; won numerous regional events including Mid-Am-Can Mens Prs 1967, Missouri Valley Open Tms 1968, KO Tms 1973; Dist 15 Open Tms 1968, Masters Prs 1981; Iowa Masters Prs 1977.

MAGERMAN, Paul (b.1929) of Schilde, Belgium, civil engineer. President European Community Bridge League (Common Market) 1983-85 and since 1989. President Belgian Bridge Federation since 1991. Represented Belgium in one zonal championship and several Common Market championships.

MAGYAR, Péter (b. 1946) of Budapest, Hungary. Won several national titles, represented Hungary in one world championship and three European Championships.

MAHFOOD, Sam (b. 1940) of Kingston, Jamaica, business executive. Represented Jamaica in one world championship and four CAC Championships. Won two zonal events and several national titles. Past president of Jamaica Bridge Association.

MAHMOOD, Zia (b. 1946) of New York and London, born in Pakistan, chartered accountant and company executive, one of the leading personalities in the bridge world. WBF World Life Master represented Pakistan in 1981 Bermuda Bowl and placed second; also second Rosenblum Tms 1986; represented Pakistan in world competition several other times; won BFAME zonal championship 1981, 83, 85, 87. Was ACBL Player of the Year 1991; won the Mott-Smith Trophy 1991; Reisinger 1987, 89; Life Master Open Prs 1990, 91; Spingold 1991, Open BAM Tms 1991; placed second Mens Prs 1987, Open Prs 1991, Open Swiss 1992; Vanderbilt 1988, 90, 91, 94; Spring Life Master Prs 1992, Spingold 1993. Inaugurated the Z TEAM concept, whereby star players partner deserving players in the charity events immediately preceding ACBL North American Championships. Won OMAR SHARIF INDIVIDUAL.

MAIA, Alcio (b. 1949) of Rio de Janeiro, Brazil, psychologist. Won South American Teams 1983; represented Brazil in three world championships.

MAIER, Merwyn D. (Jimmy) (1909-1942) of New York City, member of the FOUR ACES from 1937 to 1942, was a leading player of the pre-World War II era. Won Vanderbilt 1937, 38; Spingold 1938, 39; Master Individual 1939, Mens Prs 1940, Life Master Prs 1941; placed second Chicago (now Reisinger) 1934, Vanderbilt 1935, 41; Master Individual 1936, Spingold 1936, 41.

MAISON, Jacques (b. 1944) of Brussels, Belgium. WBF World Master. Represented Belgium in one world championship, four European championships and one Com-

mon Market championship. National wins include open teams four times and open pairs twice.

MALLANDER, Antha L. (b. 1917) of Houston TX, certified bridge teacher and director, received degrees from U of Denver, held various executive positions in the ABTA, including president 1976-78 and 1984-85. Member of IBPA; contributes articles to *ABTA Quarterly* and formerly for newspapers in Colorado and Texas. She is author of *Goren-Standard American Point Count Bidding System Student Manual* and *Standard American Bridge for All*. Mallander has actively promoted bridge as a college credit course.

MALOWAN, Walter (1882-1966) originator of the MALOWAN SIX CLUBS, was one of the leading players of the pre-World War II period. Born in Austria, Malowan moved to New York, where he was an exporter. He was secretary and honorary member of the REGENCY CLUB and secretary of CROCKFORD'S CLUB. Author of many articles, Malowan collaborated with Sidney Lenz on newspaper articles. Won AWL Open Tms 1933.

MANCHESTER, Max M. (1914-1969) of Portland OR, was executive secretary of the Oregon Public Employees Retirement System; ACBL president 1962, chairman of Board 1960, 61; named HONORARY MEMBER in 1963. Won Mens Prs 1961.

MANASSEH, Olga (b. 1922) of Beirut, Lebanon. Represented Lebanon in several European Womens Championships. Won more than five national titles.

MANDEL, Larry A. (b. 1947) of Van Nuys CA; won the 1974 Team Trials and several regional events.

MANDELL, Sidney (1907-1990) of Miami Beach, retired attorney, won the Vanderbilt 1952, 54; Florida Mens Prs 1972.

MANDELOT, Agota (b. 1941 in Hungary), of Brazil, artist. WBF World Master. Won South American Womens Teams 1975, 1980, 1981, 1982, 1986, 1989, 1991; represented Brazil in 10 world championships.

MANFIELD, Edward A. (Ed) (b. 1943) of Hyattsville MD, economist, professional bridge player, won Rosenblum Teams 1986, second in 1982. Grand Life Master with more than 11,000 MPs; won GN Tms 1984, 88, 92; Mens Prs 1985, Open Prs 1987, 89; Mens BAM Tms 1986, 89; Blue Ribbon Prs 1990, Vanderbilt 1991; placed second in Spingold 1979, 81; Reisinger 1980, Open Prs 1981, GN Tms 1985, Blue Ribbon Prs 1985, 86. Won the 1979 Cavendish Invitational Prs and numerous regionals. See also IBPA AWARDS.

MANFIELD, Jo Ann M. (b. 1950) of Philadelphia PA, regional sales manager, graduate U of Maryland, enjoys gourmet cooking, member Unit 141 board, ACBL Nat'l Goodwill Committee. Won Master Mixed Tms 1988, Mixed Prs 1990, 91; placed second Womens Tms 1984; has won numerous regionals.

MANGAN, Betty of San Antonio, bridge club operator, placed second in Life Master Womens Prs 1970.

MANHARDT, Peter (b. 1936) of Vienna, consultant. WBF World Life Master. World Pairs champion 1970. Represented Austria in one other world championship and eight European Championships. Dominated the European grand prix circuit in the 70s, winning the Philip Morris Bridge Cup four times and finishing second twice. Won Austrian Teams 11 times and Open Pairs and Mixed Pairs twice each. Headed Austrian masterpoint rankings for nearly 20 years.

MANLEY, Brent (b. 1947) of Memphis TN, managing editor *ACBL Bulletin*, co-editor *Daily Bulletins* at North American Championships since 1992; former city editor of *Houston Post*, graduate of Loyola U. Other interests include reading, running and sports. Regional wins include Nashville Swiss 1981, San Antonio Open Prs 1988, Reno Mixed Prs 1991, Huntsville Swiss 1992, Spring secondary Open Swiss 1993.

MANN, Timothy (b. 1949) of Scottsdale AZ, computer programmer/analyst; from 1979-85 was an archaeologist in the Sonoran Desert, graduate of U of Massachusetts. Served on Unit 354 board 1987-91, won Summer secondary Swiss 1979, Desert Empire Open Swiss 1980, 82, Horizonal Open Prs 1993; Dist 17 Open Prs 1991.

MANOS, Dr. John T. (b. 1924) of San Diego CA, retired psychiatrist/psychoanalyst, educated at Rutgers U and NYU School of Medicine (MD), won Eastern States Mixed Tms 1961; Upper NY State Mixed Prs 1962; New England Mixed Tms 1964; Bermuda Open Tms 1962, 70, 72.

MANNING-FOSTER, Alfred Edye (1874-1939) of London, one of leading pre-war bridge players. Founder of *Bridge Magazine* and its editor until 1939; foreign contributing editor of *The Bridge World* and bridge correspondent of the *Times* (London) for many years. Founder and first president of the British Bridge League (1931); named ABL Honorary Member 1933; writings include *Auction Bridge for All, Contract Bridge for All*, and *Baby Contract Book*. See BIBLIOGRAPHY, A, C.

MANRIQUE, Hector (b. 1936 in Ecuador) of Caracas, Venezuela, civil engineer. WBF World Master. Won CAC Teams 1977, 1987, 1991. Represented Venezuela in two world championships and won many national titles.

MANSELL, Petra (b. 1923) of Durban, South Africa, bridge teacher. WBF World Life Master. Runner-up World Womens Teams 1968, 1972, also represented South Africa World Olympiad Teams 1964, World Womens Teams 1960, 1976, 1992. 17 national wins include 8 in Open Teams and 3 in Open Pairs.

MARCUS, Edward N. (Eddie) (1895-1952) for whom the Marcus Cup is named, was a clothing manufacturer from Boston. Served as ACBL Board member and president of the New England BA. Won Chicago (now the Reisinger) 1949.

MAREK, Dr. John of Wrexham, Wales, Member of Parliament, chemist. Represented Wales in two Camrose Trophy matches, defeating England. Represented Wrexham in Parliament since 1983, and member of Parliament bridge team.

MARI, Christian (b. 1945) of Paris, France, bridge professional. WBF World Life Master. Won World Teams 1980, third Rosenblum 1978, Bermuda Bowl 1975. Won European Teams 1974, second 1973, 1989, third 1981. Won Common Market Teams 1973. Represented France in three other world championships and three other zonal championships.

MARIMON, Francisco (b. 1946) of Barcelona, Spain, financier. Represented Spain in one zonal championship and two zonal junior championships.

MARISCAL, Laura (Mrs. Elias Konstantinovsky) (b. 1939) of Mexico DF, bridge club owner and teacher, won Master Mixed Tms and several regionals.

MARK, Dr. Louis (1893-1954) in whose honor the Mark Memorial Trophy was donated, international authority on chest ailments. First Life Master in Columbus OH, ACBL president in 1949; HONORARY MEMBER 1950.

MARK, Louise Fu-Ming (Lulu) (b. 1934) of North York ON, born in Shanghai, China, senior systems analyst, represented Canada in World Womens Tms 1964, 1968. Won Womens Prs 1965.

MARKS, Paul N. (1908-1968) of Maywood IL, national tournament director from 1957, devised APPENDIX MOVEMENTS for 7-, 11- and 13-table RAINBOW INDIVIDUAL MOVEMENTS. Marks was an accountant as well as a teacher of mathematics and bridge.

MARKUS, Rika (Rixi) (1910-92) of London, England (b. in Romania). One of the greatest women players of all time, and the first to become a WBF Grand Master. She was the top woman in WBF rankings from the beginning (1974) until 1980. Won 14 international titles, more than any other woman: World Womens Teams 1937, 1964, World Mixed Teams 1962, World Womens Pairs 1962, 1974; European Womens Teams 1935, 1936, 1951, 1952, 1959, 1961, 1963, 1966, 1975. Pre-war wins were representing Austria, from which she fled to England in 1938. Other wins, mainly with Fritzi Gordon, were for Britain, including second World Mixed Pairs 1970 and World Womens Pairs 1970. Many national titles include Gold Cup once. Named IBPA Personality of the Year 1974, and awarded MBE for contributions to bridge by Queen Elizabeth 1975. Organizer of annual matches between House of Commons and House of Lords. Bridge editor of *The Guardian* 1955-92, and columnist of *Evening Standard* 1975-80. Contributor to many magazines and author of seven books. See BUENOS AIRES AFFAIR.

MARSAL, Reinhard (b. 1947) of Bonn, Germany, bridge teacher. Runner-up Common Market Teams 1985; represented Germany in one world championship and one European Championship. Won six national titles.

MARSH, Edward I. (Bud) (b. 1927) of Scottsdale AZ, retired businessman, enjoys tennis. Playing captain of Montreal's championship inter-city bridge team 1967, 68. Won Amateur Swiss 1977. Numerous regional titles include Canadian Nat'l Mixed Prs 1949, Open Prs 1951; Can-Am Mens Prs 1949, 75, Mixed Prs 1951, Open Tms 1949, 52, 54; New England Open Prs, Open Tms 1969; Spring secondary Swiss 1984.

MARSHALL, Cynthia (Cindy) of Knoxville TN, controller, graduate of U of Tennessee, won Fall secondary Swiss 1979, Gatlinburg Womens Prs 1980, 89, 91; Mid-Atlantic Womens Prs, Open Prs 1981; Louisville Swiss 1988, Washington 4th of July KO Tms 1989, Barometer Prs 1990.

MARSTON, Paul Hamilton (b. 1949 in New Zealand) of Sydney, Australia, bridge professional and club manager. WBF World Master. Won South Pacific playoff 1991. In world championships and Far East championships, represented New Zealand 8 times 1973-81 and Australia 7 times 1983-91. 13 national wins include Australian Open Teams 5 times. Columnist for *Financial Review*; author of 5 books. One of the world's leading authorities on strong pass and relay methods. See MOSCITO.

MARTEL, Charles U. (Chip) (b. 1953) of Davis CA, professor of computer science, educated at MIT and U of California at Berkeley, enjoys reading and bicycling. World Grand Master; was chairman of WBF System Rating Committee 1990. Won World Open Prs 1982 (the youngest player to win this event, age 29), Bermuda Bowl 1985, 87; placed second Rosenblum Tms 1982, Bermuda Bowl 89; placed 4th World Par Contest, 9th in World Open Prs and Rosenblum Tms 1990. In other int'l competitions he was second in EOE Optebeurs Netherlands 1990, third Sunday Times Prs 1991. Won the "Rosenkranz Best Bid Hand" award 1979 and the BOLS Tip competition 1991. Was captain and coach of the winning team in the World Jr Tms 1991 and captain of the bronze medal team in 1993. He won USBC 1985, 87, 89, second 88. Diamond Life Master; won Lou Herman Trophy 1981, Reisinger 1981, 85, 86; GN Tms 1982, 83, 85, 87, 93; Vanderbilt 1984, 87, 94; GN Prs 1988, Spingold 1990; placed second GN Prs 1981, Blue Ribbon Prs 1981, Vanderbilt 1992, Spingold 1992, 93. Numerous regional wins include Dist 21 GN Tms 1981, 82, 83, 84, 85, 86, 87, 90.

MARTEL, Jan F. (b. 1943) of Davis CA, retired attorney, educated at U of California at Berkeley (JD), enjoys horseback riding (in particular dressage), reading, gardening, cooking and cryptic crossword puzzles; was active in Forum for Women in Bridge 1985-1990. Competed int'ly New Orleans 1978, Bal Harbour 1986, Geneva 1992. Won Womens Prs 1974, Womens Swiss 1986, Womens BAM Tms 1987, GN Prs 1988; placed second Womens KO Tms 1979, 85, 87; Womens Prs 1988.

MARTENS, Krzysztof (b. 1952) of Rzeszow, Poland, retailer, chemical engineer and bridge professional. WBF Grand Master. Won World Teams 1984, 2nd Bermuda Bowl 1991, third 1981, 1989. Won European Teams 1981, 1989, third 1991. Represented Poland in five other world championships and two other zonal championships. Won many national titles. Author of one book.

MARTENSSON, Eva (b. 1924) of Stockholm, Sweden. World Life Master. Won World Womens Teams 1968, Nordic Womens Teams 1957, 1966, 1968. National wins include Womens Pairs five times.

MARTIN, Phillip (b. 1953) of Bronxville NY, stock options trader, graduate of Loretto Heights College, enjoys music composition. Placed second GN Tms 1981; numerous regional wins include Fun City Swiss 1975; Washington Bridge Week Swiss 1977; Dist 3 Mens Swiss 1979, Summer Open Prs 1984, 91, Swiss 1988, Tri-State KO Tms 1987, Tri-State Swiss 1990, Open Prs 1991; New England Fall Swiss 1980, Summer Swiss 1985; Eastern States Reisinger KO Tms 1981; Dist 24 GN Tms 1981, 83; Long Island KO Tms 1985, 87; Montreal Swiss 1988; New York Summer KO Tms 1991.

MARTINO, Michael J. (Mike) (b. 1936) of Hamilton ON, lawyer, executive, won Mens Prs 1969.

MASOOD, Tahir (b. 1956) of Karachi, Pakistan, hotel executive. Won BFAME zonal teams 1981 and BFAME zonal pair 1985. Represented Pakistan and finished second in 1991 Bermuda Bowl.

MASSO, Eugenio (b. 1929) of Madrid, Spain, physician. Represented Spain in six zonal championships. Won many national titles.

MASTERSON, Marcia W. of Pasadena CA, financial consultant, bridge teacher and professional player, graduate of Mount St. Mary's, Goucher College and U of Southern California, enjoys tennis and plays in amateur tournaments, competed int'ly in Biarritz 1982. Won Amateur Swiss 1977, Womens BAM Tms 1990; regional wins include Bridge Week Masters Prs 1974, San Diego Womens Tms 1976, Swiss 1981; San Jose Womens Prs 1977, Eugene OR Womens Prs, Swiss 1977; Pasadena Womens KO Tms 1984, Womens Prs 1989; Bakersfield Womens Prs 1986, Spring secondary Womens Swiss 1992.

MASTRON, Dr. Victor (1920-1992) of Sedona AZ, surgeon, graduate of U of California at Irvine and California College of Medicine (MD), member of Nat'l Goodwill Committee. As a navigator in WWII, he received the Distinguished Flying Cross and the Air Medal (8 oak leaf clusters). Won Inter-Mountain Mens Prs 1969, Canadian KO Tms 1970, Dist 18 KO Tms, Open Prs 1970; Mid-Winter Holiday Open Teams 1970, Golden Gate KO Tms 1971.

MATHE, Eugenie M. (Genie, Mrs. Lewis) (1925-1991) of Canoga Park CA, US Census Bureau survey clerk. Chairman of Publishing Committee of ALACBU from 1979; edited *Southern California Bridge News* 1979-82 and authored the popular monthly column *The LOL* from 1966. She was involved in writing and performing in many shows for bridge tournaments. She won the European Open Tms at Lake Balaton Hungary 1975, Master Mixed Tms 1970 (second in 1975), Mixed Prs 1971; also won several regionals.

MATHE, Lewis L. (Lew) (1915-1986) of Canoga Park CA, real estate appraiser and broker, WBF Grand Master, noted for his adaptability and table presence, was the leading exponent of the direct method of bidding favored on the West Coast. Originator of MATHE ASKING BID. ACBL president 1975, chairman of ACBL Board 1976, chairman of ACBL Bd of Gov 1968, WBF representative from ABCL and WBF treasurer 1977-82; three-time president of WESTERN CONFERENCE and ACBL Board member from Dist 23 1958-61 and 1970-1982. Won Bermuda Bowl 1954; represented North America in Bermuda Bowl 1955, 62, 66, 71; the US in the World Tm Olympiad 1960. Won International Playoff Match

1970, Herman Trophy 1957, Mott Smith Trophy 1959, 64, 67; Spingold 1954, Vanderbilt 1964, 66, 67; Chicago (now the Reisinger) 1959, 60, 62; Reisinger 1971, Blue Ribbon Prs 1964, Mens Tms 1957, 62, Open Prs 1957, Mixed Prs 1971; Open Prs 1959, Mens Tms 1970; Life Master Prs 1963, 67, Master Mixed Tms 1970; placed second Team Trials 1965, Spingold 1953, 71, 74; Reisinger 1966, Blue Ribbon Prs 1967, Master Mixed Tms 1953, Mens Prs 1961; Mixed Prs 1959, Open Prs 1964, 67, Mens Tms 1972; Life Master Mens Prs 1982. Won 1975 European Open Tms at Lake Balaton,Hungary, and a host of West Coast regional titles.

MATHIS, James L. (b. 1927) of Williamsville NY, retired bank executive, graduate of U of Buffalo; served on local board 1987-90 and on Nat'l Bd of Gov 1987-90, president of Unit in early Fifties. Won Open Prs 1969; placed second Life Master Prs 1970. Diamond Life Master, Mathis has had many regional wins.

MATTHEWS, Judge Ben G. (b. 1926) of Shelbyville KY, attorney, former city judge and bank president, educated at U of Virginia, US Navy, U of Virginia Law School and U of Louisville (LLB), enjoys college basketball, model railroads, gardening, had 300 in bowling 1963. Scored clean sweep of a sectional tournament in 1984 (four events). Regional wins include Midwest Mens Prs 1955, Open Tms 1971; Fall secondary Swiss 2nd Flt 1961, Dist ll Open Prs 1978, Fall secondary Charity Tms, Sr Swiss 1991.

MATTHEWS, Grace R. of Las Vegas NV, Western art dealer, runs Las Vegas Western Art Auction, loves skiing and reading, president Unit 373 1984 to present. Co-chairman of 1991 Summer NABC, largest in ACBL history with 24,221 tables; also co-chairman of Las Vegas Regionals in 1988, 90, 92. Some of her many regional wins include Pasadena Open Prs 1984, Womens Prs 1986, Mixed Prs 1986; Las Vegas Mixed Prs 1984, Santa Rosa Swiss 1985, 86, 90, Open Prs 1989, KO Tms 1990, 91; Penticton KO Tms 1987, Womens Prs 1990; Kalispell Swiss 1987, KO Tms 1988; Master Prs 1989, Swiss 1991; Sacramento Womens Prs, Salt Lake City Womens Prs, Phoenix KO Tms 1990.

MATTHEWS, Jackie A. (b. 1936) of Sacramento CA, S4 tournament bridge director; is in charge of all caddies at NABCs. Won Oregon Trail Womens Prs 1979, British Columbia Womens Prs 1979, Puget Sound Open Prs 1979, Gem State Womens Prs 1981, Wine Country Swiss 1982.

MATTHEWS, Lillian Munroe of Marbella, Spain, formerly of Toronto and Boston, journalist. Represented Spain in many world and zonal womens pairs and mixed pairs. Bridge columnist *Marbella Times* and hotel magazine *H*, magazine contributor. Organizer of Marbella Bridge Festival since 1980. Spanish delegate to EBL and WBF 1974-1982.

MATZ, Norma (b. 1916) of Miami Beach FL, investment counselor, won Womens Teams 1952, 54 and many regional titles.

MAUGHAM, (William) Somerset (1874-1965) famous novelist and short story writer, once called bridge "the

most entertaining and intelligent card game the wit of man has so far devised." He often used card playing in his settings. In *Three Fat Women of Antibes*, three middle-age women are looking for a congenial fourth, a story anthologized in *Grand Slam*. In his slightly fictionalized memoirs, *Ashenden*, he records playing contract bridge ("with which I was not very familiar") during World War I — one of the earliest references to the modern game in print. Maugham wrote the introduction to Charles H. Goren's book *The Standard Book of Bidding*. See CONTRACT BRIDGE.

His verdict on bridge is memorable. "If I had my way, I would have children taught bridge as a matter of course, just as they are taught dancing. In the end it will be more useful to them . . . You can play bridge as long as you can sit up at a table and tell one card from another. In fact, when all else fails – sport, love, ambition – bridge remains a solace and an entertainment."

On the requirements: "The essentials for playing a good game of bridge are to be truthful, clearheaded, and considerate, prudent but not averse to taking a risk, and not to cry over spilt milk. And incidentally those are perhaps also the essentials for playing the more important game of life."

MAVROMICHALIS, Brigitte (b. 1926) of Bridgetown, Barbados. President CAC 1987-89 and 1991-. President Barbados Bridge League 1986-88.

MAY, Walter R. (b. 1930) of Sarasota FL, bridge teacher, lecturer, director and former university official. Diamond Life Master; regional wins include Upper New York State Open Tms 1956, 75, 77; New England Fall Open Tms 1958, Master Prs 1959; Keystone Swiss 1974, 75; Dist 4 Open Tms 1975, 77, 78; GN Tms 1975, 78, Zone III 1975; Tri-State Mens Swiss 1977, Autumn Leaf Mens Swiss 1981, GN Prs 1982, Scranton Open Tms 1988, 89, Swiss 1988; Jacksonville Sr Swiss 1988, Tampa Sr Swiss 1989, 93; Orlando Sr Swiss 1990, Toronto Sr Swiss 1992, Hyannis Sr KO Tms 1993.

MAYADAS, Lina (b. 1935) of Bombay, India, plastics manufacturer and former journalist. WBF World Master. Won Far East Womens Teams 1978, BFAME Womens Teams 1983, 1985. Second BFAME Open Pairs 1983. Represented India in four world championships and two other zonal championships.

MAYER, EDWARD (1901-1980) of London, England, lawyer, represented Great Britain in SCHWAB CUP match 1933 and won unofficial matches against American teams 1954 and 1956; won GOLD CUP 1932 and English Open Tms 1948; served as Council Member of British Bridge League. Author of *Money Bridge;* bridge correspondent of *London Times* for more than 20 years.

McAVOY, James M. (b. 1950) of Victoria BC, partner in accounting firm, graduate of U of Victoria; European history and professional sporting events buff. Represented Canada in WBF events Bal Harbour 1986 and in Tri-Country playoff 1993; Zone VI CBF representative to the CNTC 13 times, won in 1992; regional wins include Vancouver KO Tms 1972, 87, Swiss 1981; Edmonton Masters Prs 1980, Open Prs 1993; Saskatoon Swiss 1984, Open Prs 1993; Calgary KO Tms 1985, 88, Super Open 1985, 88; Victoria KO Tms 1986, 88, 90, Swiss 1990;

Phoenix KO Tms, Swiss 1990.

MAYER, Malcolm (b. 1953) of Christchurch, New Zealand. WBF World Master. Won World Continuous Pairs 1990. Represented New Zealand in five other world championships and five zonal championships. Seven national wins include open teams once.

MAZZA, Dino (b. 1927) of Vigevano, Italy, journalist. General secretary of Italian Bridge Federation 1971-89. Bridge columnist of newspaper *La Republica*, contributor to *Bridge d'Italia*.

McCALLON, Dr. William R. (Bill) (b. 1929) of St. Augustine FL, retired epidemeologist; educated at Oklahoma State U and U of Maryland, has made two Atlantic crossings in his sailboat. Diamond Life Master; regional wins include Columbia Open Prs 1967, Washington DC BAM Tms 1968, Swiss 1982; Norfolk KO Tms 1968, Swiss 1980; Winston-Salem Open Prs 1976, Richmond Mens Prs, Masters Prs 1977; Baltimore KO Tms 1978; Raleigh Sr Open Prs 1987; Summer secondary Sr KO Tms 1987, Sr Swiss 1987, 88 (2), 90 (2), 91, Sr Open Prs 1987, 88, 90; Arlington Sr Open Prs 1989, 90 (2); Mexican Nat'l Master Prs, Sr Open Prs 1990; Birmingham Sr KO Tms 1990; Fall secondary Sr Swiss, Sr Open Prs (2) 1990; Myrtle Beach Sr Open Prs 1990; Daytona Beach Sr Swiss, OK City Sr Swiss 1991.

McCALLUM, Karen T. (Kate) (b. 1946) of Exeter NH, author and publisher, professional bridge player and teacher. Became a world champion when she won Venice Cup 1989; also won World Womens Prs 1990 and Venice Cup 1993; placed 5th Rosenblum Tms 1990. WBF Life Master; won North American Womens Swiss 1989, 90, 93; placed second North American Womens Swiss 1984, Summer Womens KO Tms 1987; has won many regional events.

McCAMPBELL, Bryan (d. ca 1930) of St Louis MO, claimed invention of the TAKEOUT DOUBLE as well as the 4-3-2-1 POINT-COUNT. There is no reason to doubt that he arrived at both ideas independently, though perhaps not first. McCampbell was one of the most successful players of auction bridge and author of perhaps the first book (*Auction Tactics*) to describe the strategy of the successful rubber-bridge player.

McCAMPBELL, Leavell (1880-1946) of New York City, was chairman of the Whist Club committee which produced the first generally accepted *Laws of Contract Bridge*; assisted in many later revisions of the Laws.

McCANCE, Ian (b. 1927) of Melbourne, Australia, senior lecturer in physiology. Represented Australia in one world championship. National titles include open teams four times, open pairs once, individual once. Former columnist *Melbourne Sun*. Devised Specific Trump Cuebids.

McCANDLESS, Dianne M. (b. 1942) of Thunder Bay ON, former teacher, accredited ACBL teacher, has served in a variety of positions on both the Unit and District level. Member of the Goodwill Committee, Dist 2 president 1993; member of Unit 228 board, Unit Education Liaison, Unit Hospitality chairman, Unit Novice chairman, Unit secretary and past president 1987-90. Regional wins include Gopher Womens Prs 1979, Thunder Bay Womens Prs 1979, Nat'l Capital Womens Prs 1981, Toronto Open Prs 1991.

McCONNELL, Ruth (Mrs. Lee W.) (b. 1918) of Columbia City IN, was ACBL's first woman president (1974), first woman Bd of Dir chairman 1975, first woman president of the ACBL Charity Foundation 1975; first woman elected, to WBF Executive Council (elected at Fall NABC 1984) 1985-93. Shortly after her election she was named WBF treasurer and served until 1990. McConnell was npc of the U.S. Womens Olympiad team in 1976, 80, Venice Cup team 1974, 76, 78 and was instrumental in upgrading the VENICE CUP to a WBF championship. It took five years but in 1978 it was designated a world championship event. She also established the first formal District Judicary Committee (1970)—now required by all Districts. She founded the *Midwest Monitor* and served as its editor 1963-67. Won Spring Continentwide Charity Game 1967, Dist 11 Mixed Prs 1968, Mississippi Valley Womens Prs 1970, 81; Spring secondary Olympiad Fund Prs 1980, Open Prs, Swiss 1986, Sr Swiss 1987.

McCRACKIN, Nancy P. (Mrs. M. R. McCrackin) (b. 1922) of Albuquerque NM, graduate of Mary Baldwin College; won Spring secondary Individual 1953, Arizona KO Tms, Open Prs 1953; Desert Empire Open Tms 1965, Womens Prs 1969, 71, Open Prs, Mixed Prs 1978.

McCRARY, Marilyn of Des Moines IA, won Master Mixed Tms 1971.

McDANIEL, Garner N. of Naples FL, realtor, Diamond Life Master; won Womens Tms 1963, 64, Womens Prs 1967; placed second Womens Tms 1962, Womens Prs 1963, 66; Master Mixed Tms 1963; has won many regionals.

McDEVITT, Don (b. 1932 in Ireland) of Harare, Zimbabwe, company director. Chairman of Zimbabwe Bridge Union since 1987. Represented Zimbabwe in two world championships.

McDONOUGH, James B. of Billings MT, attorney and former company president, graduate of Montana State U; won North American Swiss 1986 and Tri-City Mens Prs 1983, Edmonton Open Prs 1984.

McGARRY, Dennis J. (b. 1947) of Coconut Creek FL, small business owner, graduate of Case Western Reserve U, enjoys golf and biking. Diamond Life Master; placed second Sr and Advanced Sr Masters Prs 1970, Master Mixed Tms 1980; Life Master Mens Prs 1979. Has won more than 50 regionals including Dist 5 GN Prs 1980, 82; All-American Mixed Prs 1971, KO Tms 1976, 77, 78, Swiss 1982, 83; Dist 11 Masters Prs 1976, 77.

McGARRY, Linda (b. 1947) of Coconut Creek FL, bridge instructor and small business owner; won Buffalo Womens Swiss 1980, Houston Open Prs 1985, Holiday Adventure Masters Prs 1992, Open Prs 1993.

McGEE, David (b. 1939) of Mason City IA, a leading player and administrator for three decades; ACBL president 1991 and Chairman of the Board 1992; has served on Unit board since 1964 and is a past president. For many years he ran the Grand National events in Dist 14. Second alternate to the ACBL Board of Directors for six years and first alternate for nine before moving up to ACBL Board. Edited the *Iowa State Bridge Bulletin* for six years. Diamond Life Master; has won more than 20 regional titles.

McGERVEY, John D. (b. 1931) of Cleveland Hts OH, physics professor, graduated from U of Pittsburgh and Carnegie Mellon U (PhD). Won Keystone Conference Open Tms 1955, Central States Master Prs 1955, Dist 5 Open Tms 1960, Intercity Tms 1968, 71, Blue Ribbon Prs 1977, GN Prs 1983.

McGINLEY, Constance S. (Connie, Mrs. Larry Goldberg) (b. 1956) of Philadelphia, former business owner, became the youngest woman Life Master in 1973 at the age of 17. Won Keystone Swiss 1974, Mid-Atlantic Swiss 1975, Summer secondary Mixed Swiss, Swiss 1976, BAM Tms 1981. See YOUNGEST LIFE MASTER.

McGOWAN, Liz of Edinburgh, Scotland, teacher of Russian. WBF World Master. Second World Womens Teams 1988, 1992. Represented Britain in one other world championship, three European Championships and 4 Common Market Championships. Many national wins include British Mixed Pairs twice. Won IBPA Hand of the Year 1992.

McGROVER, Raymond J. (1905-1974) of New York City, attorney, ACBL president 1947, played a major role in the 1948 reorganization of the League and later assisted in the formation of the 1963 Laws. President of Long Island BL for seven years.

McHALE, J.P. (Joe) (b.1922) of Dublin, Ireland, university secretary. Represented Ireland in two world championships and a long string of zonal championships starting in 1952. Has won every national title.

McHANN, Annette (b. 1937) of Clinton MS, bridge teacher and small business owner, won continent-wide Royal Viking Instant Matchpoint Prs E-W 1993 and Mid-South Womens Prs 1974, Razorback Open Prs 1986, 89, Womens Prs 1992; New Orleans Swiss 1989, Dist 10 Swiss 1992, Summer secondary Open Prs 1993.

McINTYRE, Glenn (b. 1955) of Boston MA, computer programmer, professional player. Has documented some innovative bidding ideas including Advanced lebensohl. Numerous regional wins include Buffalo KO Tms 1985, Albany Mens Swiss 1988, Swiss 1988, 90, 93; Stamford Swiss, Nashville Open Swiss 1988; Columbus KO Tms 1991, Quebec City KO Tms 1991, Canadian Tms, Manchester Swiss 1992; Dist 25 GN Prs 1993.

McKEAN, Joan De Witt of Grosse Pointe MI, stockbroker and bridge teacher, graduate of Vanderbilt U, involved in numerous charities, president ACBL Charity Foundation 1987, 88, 91, 92, 93, 94; member ACBL Goodwill Committee. Represented ACBL in world play Biarritz 1982, Bal Harbour 1986, Geneva 1990; won Master Mixed Tms 1977, 78, 79, 82. Regional wins include Motor City Swiss 1972, 91, Womens Swiss 1987;

Mississippi Valley Womens Prs 1977, 1980; Central States Womens Prs 1980, 81; Tri-State Womens Swiss 1981, Tri-Unit Masters Prs, Womens Prs, Swiss 1982.

McKENNEY, William E. (1891-1950) whose memory the McKENNEY TROPHY (now the BARRY CRANE TOP 500) perpetuated; gained fame as bridge columnist, philanthropist and administrator; contributed daily bridge columns to Scripps-Howard newspapers from 1929-1950. So widely read was his work that in Europe the SUIT-PREFERENCE SIGNAL became known as the "McKenney Convention" instead of being attributed to its inventor, Hy Lavinthal. McKenney's dedication to bridge and its organizations extended well beyond the written word. In 1927 he helped found the American Auction Bridge League; became chairman of its committee on laws and then executive secretary in 1928; continued as secretary of both the ABL and ACBL until 1948. He founded the Nat'l Laws Commission in 1932, and chaired it from 1935-1948.

Several times McKenney contributed his privately earned income to the ABL and ACBL. For example, in 1929 he founded Bridge Supplies, Inc., which sold trophies, scoring supplies and other merchandise. In 1936 he donated this corporation to the ABL. He devoted nearly all his time to the interests of the successive bridge leagues. To a degree McKenney acquired a spirit of proprietary control which became increasingly inconsistent with the interests of ACBL as it became larger and more financially stable. The year 1948 found McKenney deposed in favor of democratic control of ACBL. McKenney founded both the ABL and the ACBL charity programs. Through these channels he led the League to endow the Children's Cancer Ward at Memorial Hospital in New York City and to establish WAR ORPHANS SCHOLARSHIPS. He won ABL Fall Nat'l Open Prs 1929.

McKINNEY, Lloyd V. (Jim) (b. 1935) of Springfield MO, business executive, played professional baseball for New York Yankees 1954-58. Served as district and unit president and is a member of nat'l Goodwill Committee. Regional wins include Dist 15 Masters Prs 1966, 75, Mens Prs 1971, KO Tms 1975, Sr KO Tms 91.

McKINNEY, Dr. Richard L. (Dick) (b. 1928) of Edmonton AB, professor emeritus of mathematics (U of Alberta), graduated from Syracuse U and U of Washington (PhD, Phi Beta Kappa). Won Inland Empire Swiss 1971, Intermountain Swiss 1975, White Hat Swiss 1977, Big Sky Super Open Prs 1979, Peach Bowl Mens Prs 1982, Edmonton KO Tms 1990.

McALEAR, Allen L. (b. 1928) of Bozeman MT, attorney, graduate of U of Montana (JD); enjoys golf and fishing; served as member of WESTERN CONFERENCE Bd 1964-68, Pres Dist 18 1969-74 and member Nat'l Bd of Gov 1982-present. Won Puget Sound Open Prs 1969, Inter-Mountain Swiss 1971, Dist 18 KO Tms, Open Tms 1971; Calgary Master Prs 1973, Dist 18 GN Prs 1987, Salt Lake Mens Prs, KO Tms.

McMAHAN, Robert F. (Bob) (b. 1930) of Columbia SC, bridge teacher, director and professional player, former stock and commodity broker, graduate U of South Carolina, enjoys golf, dancing, cooking. Has served on ACBL nat'l Bd of Gov, member nat'l Goodwill Committee, Dist 7 president, past president Unit 160 and served on Unit Bd of Dir 1975-1992; member of SC Bridge Hall of Fame. Diamond Life Master; won Spring Open Prs 1979, Columbia BAM Tms, Winston-Salem Swiss, Roanoke Swiss, Myrtle Beach KO Tms, Prs, Open Prs; Atlanta Mens Prs, Washington Mens Prs, Durham Mens Prs, Gatlinburg Open Prs, Hilton Head KO Tms; Fayetteville Prs.

McMAHON, Mary of Sydney, Australia, investor. Won Far East Open Teams 1970, Womens Teams 1973, 1974. Represented Australia in two world championships. National wins include Womens Teams nine times, Womens Pairs twice.

McNEELY, Brooks N. (b. 1946) of Knoxville TN, computer analyst, database specialist, graduate U of Tennessee, president Unit 165 1989-91, former chess and tennis champion. Won Fall secondary Swiss 1979, Mid-Atlantic Swiss 1972, Open Prs 1981, Open Prs 1990, Handicap KO Tms 1992.

McNEIL, Keith A. (1929-1993) of Adelaide, Australia, pharmacist. Received Medal of the Order of Australia for services to bridge. President of Australian Bridge Federation 1986-90, president emeritus 1990-93. McNeil held almost every committee position in the South Australian BF and became a Life Member 1984. Authored *Match Your Bidding Against the Masters*, a compilation of his articles as the moderator of *Bidding Forum in Australian Bridge*.

McPHERRAN, Robert A. (1915-1986) of New York City, won Spingold 1939, Vanderbilt 1940, 41; Master Mixed Tms 1936, Fall Master Individual 1946; placed second Vanderbilt 1939, Mixed Prs 1940. Numerous regional wins include Summer secondary Marcus Cup 1940.

MECKSTROTH, Jeffrey J. (Jeff) (b. 1956) of Reynoldsburg OH, professional bridge player, WBF Grand Master and ACBL Grand Life Master with more than 23,000 MPs as of 1993. He rose rapidly from KING OF BRIDGE in 1974 to Bermuda Bowl champion in 1981. Has represented ACBL in several world championships, won World Open Prs 1986, World Tm Olympiad 1988; is one of eight players in world who has won all three major world championships; placed second World Tm Olympiad 1992. Other int'l placings include 6th World Championship Open Prs 1982, 4th Bermuda Bowl 1983 and 5th in 1991; 5th Rosenblum Tms 1986. ACBL PLAYER OF THE YEAR 1992, won USBC (Team Trials) 1991, placed second 1985. Won Mott-Smith Trophy 1979, 80, 85; Lou Herman Trophy 1980, 82. His regular partner is Eric Rodwell — as a pair they are known as Meckwell. His many nat'l titles include Reisinger 1979, 85, 93; Life Master Mens Prs 1979, Open Prs 1979, Open Prs I 1992; Mixed Prs 1980, Vanderbilt 1980, 82, 85; Blue Ribbon Prs 1982, Spingold 1984, 88, 91, 93; Mens BAM 1984, Spring Mens Tms 1989, GN Tms 1990. Placed second Vanderbilt 1979, 91; Reisinger 1980, Life Master Prs 1983, Master Mixed Tms 1983, 92; Spingold 1985, 90; Life Master Mens Prs 1985, Life Master Open Prs 1992.

MEHTA, Anand J. (b. 1940) of Bombay, India, com-

pany director. WBF World Master. Second BFAME Open Teams 1989; represented India in one other zonal championship and four world championships. 18 national wins include a record 7 in open teams and open pairs twice.

MEINL, Wolfgang (b.1947) of Vienna, Austria, merchant. WBF World Life Master. Runner-up Bermuda Bowl 1985, World Pairs 1986, World Team Olympiad 1988. Won European Teams 1985, European Pairs 1981, European Team Cup 1988, European Junior Teams 1976. Austrian wins include Open Teams 13 times and Open Pairs five times. He has won the Caransa and Hoechst tournaments in the Netherlands. Bridge columnist *Die Presse*, conducts many seminars.

MELLO, Roberto Figueira de (b. 1950) of Rio de Janeiro, Brazil, engineer. WBF Grand Master. Won Bermuda Bowl 1989, South American Teams 1968, 1978, 1983, 1987, 1989, 1991. Represented Brazil in five other world championships. National wins include open teams three times.

MELLO, Sylvia Figueira (b. 1958) of Rio de Janeiro, Brazil, economist. WBF World Master. Won South American Womens Teams 1968, 1980, 1981. Represented Brazil in five world championships. Won two national titles.

MELMAN, Fredric L. (Fred) (b. 1935) of Agoura CA, bridge teacher and director, won Amateur Mens Prs 1976, Summer secondary Commercial and Industrial Tms 1974, 75, 76.

MELSON, Richard T. (Dick) (b. 1946) of Chicago IL, stock options trader, Diamond Life Master, placed second Mens Prs 1977, Mens Tms 1978; Reisinger 1988, Mens Open BAM 1991, 93.

MENG, Ching-Shan or **Gloria** (b. 1944 in China) of Taipei, Taiwan, bank employee. WBF World Master. Won Far East Womens Teams 1988, 1989, Far East Open Pairs 1988. Represented Taiwan in Far East Championships since 1969, and in six world championships. Has won 12 national titles.

MENGES, Cordelia Sykes (b. 1938) of New York City, bridge club owner and director, small business owner, graduate of Vassar, won Non-Life Master Prs 1992.

MERBLUM, Franklin P. (Frank) (b. 1949) of Bloomfield CT, actuary, graduated U of Hartford and U of Connecticut, won first regional at age 18 with his father. Other regionals include New England Fall Mens Prs 1967, Mixed Prs 1977, 78, KO Tms 1988, Swiss 1988, 91; Fall secondary Swiss 1972, New England Winter BAM Tms 1967, Swiss 1982, 87, Open Prs 1983, KO Tms 1989, 92; Rye Swiss 1988; New England Summer KO Tms 1989, 90; New England KO Tms 1992, Dist 25 GN Prs 1989, 90.

MEREDITH, Adam (1913-1976) of New York City, formerly of London; noted for his skill in dummy play, especially in making "unmakable" contracts and for unconventional bidding manuevers. Bermuda Bowl champion 1955; European champion 1949, 54; also represented Great Britain in European Championship 1955, 57, 59. British wins include GOLD CUP five times and

Master Prs 1960. Co-authored (with Leo Baron) *Baron System of Contract Bridge*.

MERHY, Gaby (b. 1928) of Beirut, Lebanon. Represented Lebanon in 12 international championships. Won more than five national titles. Secretary of Lebanese Bridge Federation since 1974. Bridge Editor of *Magazine Revue*.

MERRILL, James (J.) (b. 1955) of Potomac MD, first KING OF BRIDGE (1973); placed second Reisinger 1974 and won several regional events.

MERRY, Philip H. (b. 1924) of Tulsa OK, ACBL national tournament director since 1963, served as chairman of the Conduct, Deportment and Ethics Committee of the PROFESSIONAL TOURNAMENT DIRECTORS ASSOCIATION; contributing editor to *Bridge Encyclopedia*.

MESBUR, Adam (b. 1952) of Dublin, Ireland, chartered accountant. WBF World Master. Runner-up European Junior Pairs 1974, Common Market Pairs 1982. Represented Ireland regularly in world and zonal championships from 1975. Won more than 25 national titles. Columnist of *Sunday Tribune*.

MESSER, Alan W. (b. 1934) of Upper Montclair NJ, data processing consultant, won Mens Tms 1960. Messer pioneered the recorder system in the Greater New York BA. He is a tennis umpire at major professional tournaments and a marathon runner.

MESSINA, Giuseppe (b. 1926) of Florence, Italy. World Life Master. Won European Team Championship 1965, 1967, 1969, 1971, runner-up 1962, 1963.

METELLO, Jorge (b. 1955) of Portugal, systems analyst. Represented Portugal in three world championships and two European championships. National wins include open teams three times and open pairs once.

METHOL, Raquel of Montevideo, Uruguay. Won South American Womens Teams 1967, 1971, 1974, 1990. A regular member of the Uruguay Womens team in international competition and has won 14 national titles.

MEYER, Babe (Mrs. Frank H.) (b. 1908) of Virginia Beach VA, placed second Mixed Prs 1948.

MEYER, Mrs. Bert W. (1915-1993) of La Canada CA, won Amateur Swiss 1977. Her several regional titles include Golden State Mixed Prs 1969, Bridge Week Mixed Teams 1960, 63, Master Prs 1962, Womens Prs 1971; Los Angeles Winter Womens Prs 1974; Pacific Southwest Womens Swiss 1976; Golden Gate Womens Prs 1977.

MEYER, Jean-Paul (b. 1936) of Paris, France, bridge writer. WBF World Master. Won European Pairs 1987. Represented France in two world championships and two zonal championships. Editor *Revue Française de Bridge - Le Bridgeur* since 1978. Author of two books. Columnist of *L'Express*.

MEYER, Kenneth C. (Ken) (b. 1947) of Lititz PA, systems analyst, graduated Penn State and Kutztown U. Won

North American Swiss 1989 and Dist 4 GN Tms 1977, 81, 89, 90, Zone II 1981; Dist 4 GN Prs 1979.

MEYER, Maria del Carmen of Montevideo, Uruguay. Won South American Womens Teams 1971, 1974, 1990. A regular member of the Uruguay Womens team in international competition and has won 86 national titles.

MEYERS, Jill J. (Mrs. Sid Brownstein) (b. 1950) of Santa Monica CA, independent music supervisor in motion picture industry, graduated Tulane U and West Los Angeles School of Law (JD), enjoys travel, movies, music, animals and skiing. WBF World Master, won Venice Cup 1993, placed fourth 1991; won North American Womens Team trials (USWBC) 1991, placed second 1993; won Lou Herman Trophy 1987; nat'l wins include Life Master Womens Prs 1987, Summer Womens KO Tms 1989; Womens BAM Tms 1991, North American Womens Swiss 1991, 93; placed second NA Womens Swiss 1987, NA Swiss 1987, Womens KO Tms 1990, 93. Diamond Life Master; has won more than 50 regional events.

MICHAELS, Charles (1884-1962) of New York City, was active in promoting bridge among the younger group; introduced contract as a course of study at Queens College while a teacher there and later taught in the Manhasset and Great Neck high schools, stimulating juvenile interest in an unusual scientific manner. Founder of Barclay Bridge Supplies, Inc., Michaels co-authored *Ideal Student Textbook*.

MICHAELS, Michael N. (Mike) (1924-1966) of Miami Beach, bridge writer and lecturer, best known as the inventor of the MICHAELS CUEBID and for his longtime association with Charles Goren in various journalistic enterprises. Placed second Spingold 1959, Open Prs 1962; regional wins include Marcus Cup 1953.

MICHAELS, Terry (b. 1927) of Prairie Village KS, formerly of Washington DC, bridge teacher and director; established Bridge Center of Washington where she had the first club Swiss Team, the first computer scoring; started many duplicate players and directors including Harry Clark during the period 1968-78. WBF World Master; placed 14th World Womens Prs 1982 and competed in other internat'l events New Orleans 1978, Bal Harbour 1986, Geneva 1990. Won Master Mixed Tms 1955, Womens Tms 1963, 66, 73, 79; Womens Prs 1967; placed second Master Mixed Tms 1963,Womens Tms 1961, 62, 63, 66; Womens KO Tms 1984, 88. Diamond Life Master; has won numerous regionals.

MICHAUD, Gerald L. (b. 1929) of Derby KS, attorney, represented US Rosenblum Tms 1978 and was International Tm alternate 1963. He won Life Master Prs 1974, Life Master Mens Prs 1974, Open Swiss 1990; placed second Spingold 1962, Mens Tms 1962, Mens Swiss 1988; Intercollegiate champion 1951; Diamond Life Master.

MICHELL, Jean Ellen (b. 1925) of Orinda CA, bridge teacher, office management, graduate of U of California-Berkeley, enjoys tennis and reading; member Nat'l Goodwill Committee, Nat'l Charity Committee, Nat'l Bd of Gov; has served on Dist 21 board, Unit 499 president, vice-president, sectional tournament manager. Diamond Life Master; placed second Womens Swiss 1989; won Golden Gate Womens Prs 1972; Swiss 1977, 78, 80, Mixed Prs 1978, 79; All-Western Womens Prs 1981; Emerald Empire Open Prs, Swiss 1982.

MIDKIFF, David M. (b. 1953) of St. Louis MO, bridge professional, certified teacher and director; placed second IMP Prs 1992; won Champaign Swiss 1986, Mens Prs 1988; Great American Pyramid Swiss 1986; Fall secondary Swiss, Dist 8 GN Tms 1987; Spring secondary KO Tms 1988; Mid-Winter Festival Swiss, Mid-Atlantic Strat Prs 1991; Mississippi Valley KO Tms 1991, 92.

MIDSKOG, Caterina (Cat) (b. 1962) of Stockholm, Sweden, bridge teacher. Won European Womens Teams 1993, Nordic Womens Teams 1992. Represented Sweden in one other world championship and one other zonal championship. Won two national titles.

MIGNOCCHI, Mirette (b. 1926) of New York City, born in Austria, real estate manager, former bridge club owner and teacher. Won Great Gorge Swiss 1972, Mexican Nat'l Mixed Prs 1974, 75, Open Prs 1978; Puerto Rico Womens Prs 1986; awarded certificate of appreciation for outstanding services to the Greater New York BA.

MIKI, Sachi of San Jose CA; won Mid-Winter Holiday Masters Prs 1974, All-Western Open Swiss 1978, Sr Fall Fling Swiss 1987, 89, 91, Open Prs, Open Prs 1991; Wine Country Sr Open Prs, Sr Lark Open Prs 1992.

MILAVEC, Alexander (b. 1944) of Vienna, Austria, lawyer. WBF World Master. Represented Austria in three world championships and the European Junior Teams. Won Austrian Teams six times.

MILES, Betty (b. 1924) of San Bernardino CA, graduated Purdue U, columnist for District 22 *Bridge Forum* for several years; won Riverside KO Tms 1981; Pasadena Mixed Prs 1989, Sr Swiss 1989, 90; Ventura Sr KO Tms 1990, Anaheim Sr Swiss 1993.

MILES, Marshall (b. 1926) of San Bernardino CA, attorney and bridge writer, educated at Claremont Mens College and U of California-LA. Represented US in Cannes 1962; WBF World Master and ACBL Grand Life Master with more than 10,000 MPs. Books include *How to Win at Duplicate Bridge, All 52 Cards, Marshall Miles Teaches Logical Bridge, Bridge from the Top, Books I and II, Stronger Competitive Bidding*. Has written many articles for *The Bridge World, American Bridge Digest* and the *ACBL Bulletin;* contributing editor, *The Official Encyclopedia of Bridge*. Member of *The Bridge World* Master Solvers panel and bidding panel of *Australian Bridge*. Placed third in the world in World Bidding Contest and second in USA. Won Fishbein Trophy 1961, Spingold 1961, 62; Life Master Prs 1961, Lou Herman Trophy, Chicago 1962; Reisinger 1965; placed second Vanderbilt 1961, Open Prs 1962, Mens Prs 1962, 72. Regional successes include Marcus Cup 1960, Bridge Week KO Tms 1958, 59, 72, 74, 76, Open Prs 1953, 58, Open Swiss 1957, 61; Raincross Master Prs 1978, Swiss 1980, KO Tms 1981, Pasadena Mixed Prs 1989, Sr Swiss 1989, 90; Ventura Sr KO Tms 1990, Anaheim Sr Swiss 1993.

MILES, R(ufus) L. Jr. (Skinny) (1907-1984) of Virginia Beach VA, investment executive, ACBL president 1950, 56; member of many ACBL administrative committees for nearly two decades; Honorary Member in 1952. President of Mid-Atlantic Conference; npc of North American Bermuda Bowl team 1957 and US team in World Team Olympiad 1960. See also MILES TROPHY.

MILES, Sidsel K. (Cecile) (b. 1937 in Norway) of Adelaide, Australia, former secretary. WBF World Master. Won Far East Womens Teams 1975, 1977, 1990. Represented Australia in two world championships and one other Far East Championship. National wins include Interstate Teams three times.

MILLER, Arthur M. (b. 1924) of Beverly Hills CA, manufacturer and importer, placed second Vanderbilt 1956, Chicago (now the Reisinger) 1958.

MILLER, Bernard A. (Bernie) (b. 1940) of Boca Raton FL, retired attorney, enjoys sports, music and reading, past president Eastern Massachusetts BA, former member ACBL Bd of Gov, ACBL Rules and Protest Committee, Dist 25 Bd of Dir. WBF World Master, placed fifth Bermuda Bowl 1991, won USBC (Team Trials) 1991, GN Tms 1989, Open Prs II 1992. Diamond Life Master; has won 25+ regionals.

MILLER, Billy (b. 1956) of Las Vegas NV, writer, graduate of Claremont Men's College, attended New England Conservatory of Music at ages 3-5 (piano), taught guitar at age 10. He was the last person to play bridge with Barry Crane (Bridge Wk Master Prs), also a member of Crane's KO team that went on to win the event with substitute Kerri Sanborn. Has been columnist for *Western Contract Bridge Forum* since 1987 and the *ACBL Bulletin* since August 1993; has written and published a book based on his *Dear Billy* columns. Diamond Life Master; has won more than 40 Flight A events including Bridge Wk KO Tms, Wine Country Master Prs, Rocky Mtn Open Prs 1985; Hawaii KO Tms, Master Swiss, Open Prs 1985; Dist 21 GN Prs 1989, 90, GN Tms 1991; Reno Super Flt KO Tms, Bakersfield KO Tms, Santa Rosa KO Tms 1991.

MILLER, Charles (b. 1934) of Houston TX, investment executive, won Mens Tms 1964 and several regional events.

MILLER, Frances (Gerry) of Las Vegas NV, executive secretary, office manager, enjoys reading and travel; competed int'ly Biarritz 1982, Geneva 1990. Won Oregon Trail Swiss 1982, Reno Mid-Winter Holiday Master Prs 1984, Swiss 1989; Salt Lake City Swiss 1985, LA Bridge Wk Swiss 1986, Open Prs 1990; Phoenix Swiss 1986.

MILLER, Harvey H. (b. 1929) of Chicago, real estate broker and investor, won Amateur Mens Prs 1975, placed second in North American Swiss 1979 and won several regional events.

MILLER, James D. (Jim) (b. 1946) of Memphis TN, manager ACBL Membership Services Division, former retail store manager, graduate of U of Northern Colorado, enjoys reading and word games, past president North Colorado Unit.

MILLER, Jeffrey A. (b. 1948) of Naperville IL, research and computer modeling of equity options and other securities, professor U of Wisconsin; graduated Bowling Green U and U of Michigan (PhD); served on Upper Michigan BA Bd 1975-87, president 1981-83, current member Chicago Contract BA board. Diamond Life Master, regional wins include Tri-Unit Open Tms 1978, Open Prs, KO Tms, KO Tms 1990; Gopher Open Prs 1981, Open Prs 1983, 84; Bowling Green Master Prs 1984; Columbus Open Prs 1985; Central States II Master Prs 1985, 88, KO Tms 1993; Wisconsin KO Tms 1989; Spring Festival Swiss 1991; Mid-Atlantic Open Prs 1992; Central States I KO Tms 1993; Dist 13 NA Prs 1993.

MILLER, Joyce (b. 1946) of Bettendorf IA, served on Unit 163 Bd of Dir 1978-92, president 1990-92, member Nat'l Goodwill Committee; won Fargo Open Prs 1975, Gopher Swiss, Womens Prs 1980; Omaha Womens Tms, Swiss 1983; Bettendorf KO Tms 1992.

MILLER, Lauren A. (b. 1943) of Vancouver BC, postman, former school teacher and social worker, graduate U of California and U of British Columbia. Won Vancouver Open Swiss 1977, Swiss 1981; Dist 19 GN Tms 1978; CNTC Zone 6 1977, 80; Medford Open Swiss 1983; Victoria Open Prs 1984, 89; Penticton Open Swiss 1992.

MILLER, Martin E. (Marty) (b. 1937) of Rochester NY, college guidance counselor and social worker, former rubber bridge and backgammon club owner; graduate of Ohio State U, president of Unit 507 1978. Placed second Mixed Teams 1985 and won several regionals including Mid-Winter Holiday Master Prs 1968, Swiss 1981; Golden Gate Master Prs 1969, British Columbia Open Prs, Oregon Trail KO Tms 1970; Stockton KO Tms 1972, 73; California Capital KO Tms 1972, Dist 18 KO Tms 1975, Golden State Swiss 1981, Dist 22 Swiss 1992.

MILLER, Richard A. (Dick) (1911-1983) of York PA, account executive, bridge writer, one of the founders of the Keystone Conference (now Dist 4), member of its Board starting in 1951, was president 1960-61; one of founders of Unit 168; served as its president 1963; member ACBL Bd of Gov. Wrote weekly column for *The National Observer* 1962-77, *York Gazette and Daily* 1945-65 and prior to his death a monthly column for the *The American Way*, American Airlines' inflight magazine. One of the early exponents of the point-count method of evaluation, he wrote *Point Count Bidding* in 1947, the first application of point-count to suit bidding. Other works by Miller are *It's a Bidder's Game, Bridge Brilliance and Blunders* and *More Bridge Brilliance and Blunders*.

MILLERD, James A. (Jim) (b. 1927) of Dana Point CA, marketing director, enjoys golf and dancing, contributor to *The Bridge World* in Fifties. Life Master #753; has won events in five consecutive decades beginning in the Fifties including Bridge Wk Open Tms 1957, Summer secondary Leventritt Prs 1955, Mid-Am-Can Open Prs 1955, Pacific Southwest Master Prs 1970.

MILLION, Ruth (d. 1990) of Union City CA, won Master Mixed Tms 1951.

MILNES, Eric (1912-1984) of Bradford, York, England, customs and excise officer, won English Bridge Union Mixed Teams twice, Northern Pairs twice. Former editor *Bridge Magazine*; co-author of *Improve Your Dummy Play* and *Bridge Hands for the Connoisseur*. See BIBLIOGRAPHY, H.

MILONE, Corrado Di Fabio (b. 1943 in Italy) of Cochabamba, Bolivia, administrative manager. Won South American Open Pairs 1991 and two Bolivian titles.

MINKEN, Joanne (b. 1928) of Northridge CA, graduate of The Principia; won Southern CA Open Swiss 1974, 77; Cotton Boll Swiss 1977, Los Angeles Winter Open Prs 1980, Bridge Wk Swiss 1982, Fall secondary Master Prs 1984.

MINWALLA, Diniar (b. 1953 in India) of Gaborone, Botswana. Represented Botswana in 1990 world championships. Winner of many national events, and also events in Zimbabwe and Swaziland. Runner-up in Kenya Teams.

MINWALLA, Nancy (b. 1946 in U.S.A.) of Gaborone, Botswana. Represented Botswana in 1990 world championships. Winner of many national events, and also events in Zimbabwe and Swaziland. Runner-up in Kenya Teams.

MISK, Alexandre (b. 1952) of Minas Gerais, Brazil, engineer. Won South American Teams 1983 and represented Brazil in two world championships.

MITCHELL, Bill of Falkirk, Scotland, retired civil servant. Represented Scotland 14 times in Camrose Trophy matches. Won Gold Cup and Scottish Cup once each. Active as coach and administrator.

MITCHELL, George W. Jr. (Pretzel) (b. 1941) of Raleigh NC, retired businessman, graduate of Wake Forest U; regional successes include Florida Open Prs 1974, Mid-Atlantic Swiss 1980, 85, KO Tms 1982, 84, 91; Masters Prs 1987; Summer secondary Silver Trophy Prs 1985, KO Tms 1987; Dist 7 GN Tms 1985, North FL Prs 1988, Midwest KO Tms 1986, Fall secondary KO Tms 1986, Spring secondary Smoking Swiss 1987.

MITCHELL, Jacquelyn M. (Jacqui) (Mrs. Victor) (b. 1936) of New York City, bridge teacher, WBF Grand Master, ACBL Grand Life Master with more than 10,000 MPs as of 1993; won Venice Cup 1976, 78; World Olympiad Womens Tms 1980, 84; World Womens Prs 1986; placed second Venice Cup 1985, World Mixed Tms and World Mixed Prs 1974. Other years she represented the US in international competition are 1972 (3rd Olympiad Womens Tms, 5th Mixed Tms), 1974 (9th Womens Prs), 1976 (3rd Olympiad Womens Tms), 1978 (8th Womens Prs), 1982. As of 1993 had best lifetime record for a woman in WBF. Won USWBC 1983, 87. National titles include Womens Tms 1965, 70, 74, 75, 76; Womens Prs 1971, 75, 77, 84; Womens KO Tms 1983, 87; North American Womens Swiss 1983, 91; Womens BAM Tms 1990; placed second in Womens Prs 1962, 70, 74; Womens Tms 1973, 82; North American Womens Swiss 1985, Womens BAM Tms 1986, Master Mixed Tms 1989, Womens KO Tms 1991. Mitchell's numerous regional titles include Eastern States KO Tms 1962, 63, 64; New York Blue Ribbon Individual 1977; New York Player of Year 1958, her second year of tournament play.

MITCHELL, John Templeton (1854-1914) of Chicago, known as "Father of Duplicate Whist" because of the movements of boards and players he designed for tournaments. He invented many schedules for individual, pair and team contests, the most notable of which is the MITCHELL MOVEMENT. He helped to adapt the matchpoint scoring and used whist for the purposes of duplicate auction. See also HISTORY OF BRIDGE. Born in Glasgow, Scotland, Mitchell was a lineal descendant of Sir Roger Kirkpatrick, a famous Highland chieftain who supported Wallace and Bruce in the struggle for Scottish independence around 1350. In 1875, Mitchell emigrated to the United States and became a naturalized citizen. In 1888 he took up whist when he saw a clipping from the *London Field* regarding a duplicate whist match between two clubs in his native Glasgow, using James Allison's AUTOMATIC HAND REGISTERS. This interested Mitchell in duplicate whist and he formed the Chicago Duplicate Whist Club. He wrote the world's first book on duplicate whist, 1892, revised in 1896; joined the Hyde Park team-of-four in 1895 that won the fifth American Whist League Congress (nat'l championship). Mitchell, a director in the American Whist League, favored the long suit game; his modified American leads were published in *Whist*, 1896.

MITCHELL, Vi of Kilsyth, Scotland, teacher. Represented Britain in one world championship and one European Championship. Represented Scotland 4 times in Camrose Trophy matches. Many national wins include Scottish Cup three times.

MITCHELL, Victor (Vic) (b. 1923) of New York City, bridge teacher, WBF Life Master, placed second World Tm Olympiad 1964, World Mixed Teams 1974, 5th World Olympiad Tms 1960 and Mixed Tms 1972; eighth Rosenblum Tms 1986; represented US in other world championships. ACBL HONORARY MEMBER 1988 and ACBL Grand Life Master with more than 10,000 MPs as of 1993. Won Spingold 1956, 59; Life Master Mens Prs 1962, Mens Tms 1962, 63; placed second Life Master Prs 1954, 55; Chicago (now the Reisinger), Mens Prs 1955; Mens Tms, Life Master Mens Prs 1965; Vanderbilt, Spingold 1969; Mens BAM Tms 1988, Master Mixed Tms 1989; has had numerous regional successes.

MITTELMAN, George of Toronto, WBF World Master, won World Mixed Pairs 1982, placed third Rosenblum Tms 1982, 90; also represented Canada in international competition 1978 (5th Rosenblum Tms, 8th World Mixed Prs), 1980, 1984, 1986 (9th Rosenblum Tms). Diamond Life Master; won RICHMOND TROPHY 1981, North American Swiss 1986; placed second Reisinger 1978, 82; Mens Prs 1985; has won CNTC five times 1980, 81, 83, 85, 89; placed second 1990; has won many regional events.

MIYAISHI, Etsuko (b. 1942) of Tokyo, Japan, bridge teacher. WBF World Master. Second Far East Womens Teams 1989. Represented Japan in five world championships including Venice Cup 1991. Won more than 20 na-

tional titles.

MIZUTANI, Eizo (b.1933) of Tokyo, Japan, bridge teacher, writer and national tournament director. Represented Japan in Far East Championships 1962, 1965, 1968, 1969 and 1972. National wins include Knockout Teams five times, Round-Robin Teams three times. Co-author of *Contract Bridge Nyumon* and *Contract Bridge no Subete*.

MODLIN, Merle (b. 1940) of Johannesburg, South Africa, bridge teacher. Represented South Africa in World Womens Teams 1976, 1992. Won 3 national team titles. Represented South Africa in Maccabi games as a swimmer.

MOEGEL, Marianne of Hanover, Germany. WBF World Master. Second Venice Cup 1993. Won European Womens Teams 1989, second 1991. Second European Womens Pairs 1993 and has won 6 national titles. Represented Germany in other world championships.

MOELLER, Donald A. (b. 1925) of Dayton OH, banking executive and CPA, graduate of Northwestern U; holds numerous positions with ACBL, including District 11 Director since 1973, ACBL treasurer (1975, 76, 82, 83, 87-present), ACBL Charity Foundation trustee since 1986, ACBL Charity Foundation treasurer (since 1984), ACBL Pension trustee (since 1980). First president of Dist 11, treasurer *Midwest Monitor* beginning 1974, president Miami Valley BA, Unit 136 1969-70, 1990-present.

MOFFAT, John R. (b. 1949) of Bellingham WA, attorney, educated at Princeton and Duke U (JD); served as Unit 439 president 1978-85 and Dist 19 rep to ACBL Bd of Gov 1981-84. Regional wins include Inland Empire Master Prs 1975, Super Open Swiss 1983, Super Open Prs 1985, Mid-Winter Holiday Mens Swiss 1976, Pacific Northwest Master Prs 1978, Super Swiss 1986, Open Prs 1989; Oregon Trail Master Prs 1979, Super Open Prs 1984, Super Open BAM Tms 1987; Dist 19 GN Pairs 1981, Puget Sound Super Open Prs 1990.

MOETI, Dr. Justice Simon (b. 1926 in South Africa) of Gaborone, Botswana. Represented Botswana in two world championships. Chairman of Botswana Bridge Federation since its foundation in 1989.

MOGAL, Sol (1911-1989) of Croton-on-Hudson NY, import company president, won Spingold 1946, 49 (second 1952); Mens Prs 1947, Mens Tms 1947, 48, 54; the Chicago (now the Reisinger) 1949.

MOHAN, John A. (b. 1939) of Santa Monica CA, investment consultant, professional bridge player, graduate U of Chicago, enjoys tennis, paddle tennis and rotisserie baseball. ACBL Grand Life Master with more than 13,000 MPs as of 1993; WBF World Master; placed third World Open Prs 1978, represented US in several other events and in Bal Harbour 1986. Won So. African Nat'l Open Prs 1988, 89, Open Tms 1989, 90. Won ACBL Mixed Prs 1972, Vanderbilt 1975, 76, 88, 92; Spingold 1976, Life Master Mens Prs 1976, 85; Lou Herman Trophy 1977, North American Mens Swiss 1985; Spring Mens Swiss 1987; placed second Life Master Mens Prs 1977, Mens BAM Tms 1985, Life Master Prs 1990; has won hundreds of regional titles.

MOHR, Arne (b 1946), of Århus, Denmark, bridge teacher. WBF World Master. Won Nordic Junior Teams 1973, Hoechst 1991. Represented Denmark in one world championship and one zonal championship. Six national wins include Open Teams three times, Open Pairs twice.

MOHR, Mark D. (b. 1939) of Union NJ, attorney, won Sr/Advanced Sr Master Prs 1961; past president of New Jersey BL; former editor *The Declarer*.

MOLLEMET, Peter D. (b. 1943) of Williamsville NY, national tournament director, area field representative for Districts 2, 4, 5, 11 and 12; began his directing career 1975 and achieved nat'l ranking 1988. Won Canadian Nat'l Swiss 1975, Dist 4 Swiss 1977.

MÖLLER, Steffen Steen (b 1939), of Copenhagen, Denmark, lawyer. WBF World Master. Second European Teams 1969; represented Denmark in 11 other zonal championships and four world championships. Won 31 national titles including Open Teams 11 times and Open Pairs five times. Bidding theorist whose ideas are used widely in Denmark. Former columnist of *Berlingske Tidende*, author of several books, and magazine contributor.

MÖLLER, Kirsten Steen (b 1947), of Copenhagen, Denmark. WBF World Master. Won World Womens Teams 1988, Common Market Mixed Teams. Represented Denmark in two other world championships and seven zonal championships, with more international appearances than any other Danish woman. She has won 20 national titles.

MOLLO, Victor (1909-87) of London, England (b.in St. Petersburg), bridge writer. Best-known for characters he created as members of the fictional Griffins Club: the Hideous Hog, the Rueful Rabbit and others. They appeared first in *Bridge in the Menagerie*, and in many magazine articles which were collected in book form. Author of more than 25 books. Won four national titles. Editor in BBC European service 1939-69.

MOLOCHKO, Daniel Steele (b. 1955) of El Cerrito CA, data processing and business management consultant,. Won Open BAM Tms 1990, Spring secondary Swiss 1991.

MOLSON, Markland (Mark) (b. 1949) of Fenton MI, formerly of Montreal, professional bridge player, WBF World Master, has represented Canada in int'l competition several times, placed third Rosenblum Tms 1990. ACBL Grand Life Master with more than 10,000 MPs as of 1993; has won RICHMOND TROPHY 1979, 80, 82, 83, 84; Canadian Nat'l Prs 1985, Reisinger 1989, Blue Ribbon Prs 1989, North American Swiss 1992; placed second Spingold, Reisinger 1982; Open Pars II 1992. Molson and partner Boris Baran have the best record in the CNTC, having won it five times 1983, 85, 87, 89, 91, and come second three times 1986, 88, 90; has won numerous regional titles.

MONDOLFO, Renato (1916-1992) of Trieste, Italy. World Life Master. Won European Teams 1965, 1967, 1969, 1971. Italian national titles include open teams

twice.

MONK, Charles (1920-1991) of Brussels, Belgium, export manager and bridge columnist. Represented Belgium in five world championships and five European championships. National wins included open teams 3 times. Writings included *Système Complet des Enchères Modernes*.

MONSEGUR, Martín (b. 1941) of Buenos Aires, Argentina, lawyer. WBF World Master. South American champion 1985. Represented Argentina in Bermuda Bowl 1977, 1985, World Team Olympiad 1980, 1984, 1988. 9 national titles won include open teams four times. Won Gabarret Cup 1975, 1985, 1990.

MONZINGO, Ken (b. 1939) of San Diego CA, theatrical press agent for national touring shows, graduated North Texas State U, Dist 22 Bd of Gov representative, member nat'l Goodwill Committee, editor and publisher of *Contract Bridge Forum*; has served as Pacific Southwest Regional manager and *Daily Bulletin* editor for many West Coast regionals. Diamond Life Master; has won numerous regionals including Hawaii Mens Swiss 1977, Bridge Wk Master Swiss, Unmixed Prs 1979, Open Prs 1984; Raincross Open Prs, Mid-Winter Holiday Swiss; Pacific Southwest KO Tms 1980, Open Prs 1986, Swiss 1986, 1990; Fall secondary Open Prs 1981, Oregon Trail Swiss 1982, Navajo Trail Open Prs, Wine Country KO Tms 1990; Spring secondary Master Prs; San Bernardino KO Tms 1991, 93; Santa Rosa KO Tms 1991; Tucson KO Tms 1992, Albuquerque Prs, Sacramento KO Tms 1993; Phoenix Swiss, Open Prs 1993.

MOONEY, Guillermo (b. 1941) of Buenos Aires, Argentina, lawyer. South American champion 1985. Represented Argentina in Bermuda Bowl 1985, in World Team Olympiad 1984. 9 national titles won include open team four times and open pairs once. Won Gabarret Cup 1985, 1991.

MOORE, Dorothy H. (b. 1928) of Dallas, TX, retired corporate executive, graduate of Harvard (corporate executive MBA program), president ACES Internat'l 1968-82, listed by *Fortune Magazine* (1978) as one of the top 10 women in big business; edited the bridge column of the late Ira G. Corn Jr. and books published by the ACES TEAM; assisted Corn in forming and managing the Aces. Was deputy captain of the US Womens Tm at the World Team Olympiad 1980; won Mixed Prs 1963, Life Master Womens Prs 1975; regional wins include Bermuda Womens Prs 1975, Big D Mixed Prs 1976.

MOORE, Joan R. of Troy MI, retired social worker, educated at Mercy College and Eastern Michigan U; member of ACBL Bd of Dir representing District 12, member of Bd of Dir and past president of Michigan BA. Grand Life Master with more than 15,000 MPs; won Open Prs 1971, Master Mixed Tms 1987, Silver Ribbon Prs 1993; placed second Womens Tms 1960, 1965; Master Mixed Tms 1971, 75, 80; Womens Prs 1976, 77; has won more than 100 regionals since 1958 including Summer secondary Marcus Cup 1970.

MORAN, Brian J. (b. 1938) of Ellicott City MD, nat'l tournament director, graduate of Notre Dame, began di-

MORAN, John H. (1909-1977) of Camarillo CA, club director, former bridge instructor and cruise director, represented North America in Bermuda Bowl 1955; won Spingold 1954, Blue Ribbon Prs 1965; placed second in the Chicago (now the Reisinger) 1958, Mens Tms 1953, Mixed Prs 1954; won numerous regionals between 1950 and 1970 including the Marcus Cup 1957.

recting career in 1965 and was elevated to national status 1987; served as president of Virginia State BA 1972-77; won Mid-Atlantic KO Teams 1973, 74, 76.

MORATALLA, Marquesa de, (Sol Cabeza de Vaca-Leighton) of Lausanne, Switzerland, horse owner and breeder. WBF World Master. Fourth World Open Teams 1982, the best performance ever by a woman in the Rosenblum Cup. Also represented Spain in three other world championships and two zonal championships. Won two French national titles.

MORATH, Anders (Carrot) (b. 1944) of Järfälla, Sweden, computer services manager. World Life Master. Third Bermuda Bowl 1977, 1991; represented Sweden in many other world championships. European champion 1977, second 1991, and played on three other occasions. European Junior champion 1968. Won national open teams 8 times, and is top Swedish masterpoint holder. Co-author of Carrot Club System.

MORCOS, Josephine (b. 1923) of Heliopolis, Egypt. WBF World Life Master. World Womens Team Olympiad champion 1960, when the Egyptian team competed as United Arab Republic. Middle East Womens Team champion 1987 and 1991, runner-up 1985 and 1989. Represented Egypt regularly in World Womens Team Championship from 1964 to 1991, and is the highest Egyptian player in WBF rankings. Has won more than 30 national titles in Open Teams, Open Pairs and Mixed Pairs. Bridge columnist for *Cairo's*, a magazine.

MOREHEAD, Albert Hodges (1909-1966) of New York City; ACBL official, bridge author, writer and editor in general fields. Morehead was an officer and Director of the United States Bridge Association when that organization amalgamated with the American Bridge League in 1937. A governor of the ACBL 1937, president 1943, chairman of the Board 1943-45 and HONORARY MEMBER 1946; member ACBL Laws Commmission, was in charge of production of the Internat'l Laws of Contract Bridge in 1943 and subsequent years. Born in Flintstone GA and educated at Baylor and Harvard, he was only 25 when he played on the Culbertson team that defeated the British (1934) in the second international match for the SCHWAB CUP. He won or placed high in several national and regional tournaments. Ely Culbertson hired him in 1932 because of his outstanding ability as a player and analyst and made him technical editor of *The Bridge World* in 1933. He proved so invaluable that in 1934 he was made general manager of all Culbertson enterprises.

He relinquished tournament play in order to handle additional duties of editing (and in the case of the *Red Book on Play*, much of the writing) of Culbertson books, the *Bridge Encyclopedia* 1935, endorsements, the management details of Crockford's Clubs both in New York and Chicago and the executive direction of KEM Playing Cards, Inc., which he sold within four years for a profit of more than half a million dollars. Morehead was the first bridge editor of *The New York Times*, with a Sunday column from 1935 and a daily column from 1959. He resigned from the *Times* late in 1963 to devote full time to writing, editing and publishing of the dictionaries, encyclopedias and thesauruses that made him one of the foremost American lexicographers. His works also include many "Hoyle" books giving the rules of card games, on which he was the leading modern American authority. In 1946 he retired from *The Bridge World* except in an advisory capacity and as director of the Master Solvers' Club and devoted his time to other pursuits. He authored many bridge books, including *Bridge the Expert Way, Contract Bridge Summary*, and *Morehead on Bidding*, which won the IBPA "Bridge Book of the Year" award in 1966.

MORI, Lawrence K. (Larry) (b. 1948) of Charlton NY, raised in Tokyo, a licensed psychotherapist, currently administrator in family-owned business, professional bridge player, educated at Wayne State U and U of Michigan, enjoys golf, spectator sports, cooking, travel, music, computers. Intercollegiate champion 1976; Diamond Life Master; won North American Swiss 1990, Open Prs 1991, Mixed Prs 1992; placed second GN Prs 1979. His 50+ regional wins include All American Master Prs 1976, KO Tms, Swiss, Open Prs 1982; Summer secondary Open Prs, Midwest Mens Swiss 1976, Spring Open Prs 1978; Grand Rapids KO Tms 1976; Champagne KO Tms 1977, Motor City KO Tms 1990, Prs 1991; Montreal IMP Prs 1990, Tampa Open Swiss 1991, Summer secondary Swiss 1992.

MORLOCK, Ron (b. 1948) of Fargo ND, housing contractor; won Eau Claire Swiss, Thunder Bay Master Prs, St. Paul KO Tms 1981; Winnipeg KO Tms 1985, 87, 89, Swiss 1985, Open Prs 1987, 89; Fargo Open Swiss 1985, KO Tms 1991; Lincoln Mens Swiss 1985; Chicago Mens Tms 1988, Spring secondary Mixed Prs 1990, Winnipeg KO Tms, Swiss 1992.

MORRELL, Clinton D. (Clint) (b. 1945) of Marlborough MA, operations research analyst (USAF), graduate Boston College, enjoys golf, served on Unit 108 and Dist 25 Bd of Dir, chairman Unit Bylaws Committee. Placed second Life Master Prs 1991, won New England Master Swiss 1971, 72, 77, KO Tms 1978, 83, Swiss 1979, Individual 1980, 83, Mens Prs 1985; Dist 3 Open Prs 1979, 83, Swiss 1982; ESC Swiss 1982, KO Tms 1984, BAM Tms 1991; Dist 24 Swiss 1982; Dist 1 KO Tms, Mens Prs 1982; WSC Swiss 1990.

MORRIS, Robert F. (Tiger) (b. 1922) of Cincinnati OH, advertising agency field representative, graduated Vanderbilt and U of Cincinnati; placed second Blue Ribbon Prs 1969. Diamond Life Master with more than 10,000 MPs; won many regionals including Midwest Spring Mixed Prs 1956, All American Open Tms 1968; Albany KO Tms 1974; Blue Grass KO Tms 1975; Dist 5 Tms 1977, KO Tms 1990; Indianapolis KO Tms 1983; Albuquerque Master Prs 1986; Lancaster Swiss 1986; Paducah KO Tms 1986; Hudson KO Tms, Charleston Sr Prs 1988; Memphis Master Prs 1989, Fall secondary Sr Swiss 1990, 91, Charity KO Tms 1991; Louisville Swiss 1991.

MORRIS, Zelda (1915-92) of Hawkes Bay, New Zealand. Won Far East Womens Teams 1976; represented New Zealand in six other zonal championships. Won zonal playoff six times.

MORSE, Dan (b. 1938) of Houston TX, pharmacist, WBF World Master and ACBL Grand Life Master, placed third Rosenblum Tms 1978, 90; 7th World Open Prs 1986; npc of winning Bermuda Bowl team 1976, 87, Olympiad Tm 1988; second- place Bermuda Bowl Tm 1989, Venice Cup Tm 1985, Olympiad Tm 1992; Reisinger team winners in Teams Trials 1974, 75; Spingold team 1976. He was coach of the winners of the World Womens Team Olympiad 1984. He was named HONORARY MEMBER 1989 and replaced Bobby Wolff as ACBL District Director from Dist 16 1993. Morse has won Mixed Prs 1964, GN Tms 1977, Spingold 1977, Vanderbilt 1990, 93; Life Master Prs 1993; placed second Spingold 1967, Life Master Prs 1979, Blue Ribbon Prs 1980, Vanderbilt 1985, GN Prs 1989, Open Swiss 1991.

MORSE, Jo (b. 1932) of Tucson AZ, member Nat'l Goodwill Committee, served the Washington BL as Board member, secretary and treasurer. WBF World Master; won World Mixed Teams 1974, was captain of the winning Venice Cup team 1993; has represented ACBL in world competition several other times. ACBL Grand Life Master with more than 14,000 MPs as of 1993; ranks eighth among top women in masterpoints and is in the top 50 of all masterpoint holders. Won Womens Tms 1973, 77, 79, 81; Womens Prs 1983, Womens KO Tms 1986, Womens BAM Tms 1990; placed second Womens Tms 1980, North American Womens Swiss 1985, Womens KO Tms 1988, 89, 91; has won numerous regional events.

MORTELMANS, Ghislaine (b.1933) of Antwerp, Belgium. Represented Belgium in six world championships and four Common Market championships. Won three national titles.

MOSCA, Carlo (b. 1945) of Milan, Italy, bridge teacher. World Life Master. Runner-up World Olympiad Teams, 1976, Bermuda Bowl 1983. European champion 1975, second 1974, 1983 and represented Italy on many other occasions.

MOSHER, Dr. Robert E. (Bob) (b. 1937) of San Francisco CA, bank loan officer, author of mathematics texts, certified director, while living in Mexico he was bridge club manager 1979-82. Won New England Masters Prs, Master Tms 1962, Open Pairs 1964; Midwest Fall Open Teams 1965.

MOSS, Andrew B. (b. 1972) of New York City, student at U of Wisconsin, spent five weeks in 1990 as volunteer worker in refugee camps in Thailand. Youngest person ever appointed to ACBL Nat'l Goodwill Committee, member of the Junior Corps, *1991 King of Bridge*. Won Non-Life Master Swiss 1988 (he and Martha Benson at age 15 are the youngest players to win this event), North American Youth Tm Championship 1989, 0-2000 KO Tms; placed second in Summer Jr Prs 1991. See FAMILY.

MOSS, Mary (Mrs. John) (1920-1981) of London, England, won World Womens Teams 1964, European

Womens Championships 1963. WBF Life Naster; represented Great Britain in World Womens Pairs 1962; national titles include Mixed Pairs.

MOSS, Michael (b. 1935) of New York City, stockbroker, WBF World Master and ACBL Grand Life Master with more than 10,000 MPs as of 1993; placed second World Mixed Tms 1972, Rosenblum Tms 1990, 4th World Mixed Prs 1974; won Master Mixed Tms 1967, 72; Life Master Prs 1970, Mixed Prs 1965; Mixed Prs 1988, Mens Prs 1989; placed second Mens Prs 1966, Mens BAM Tms 1988; has won numerous regionals. See FAMILY.

MOSS, Michael Brad (Brad) (b. 1971) of Berkeley CA and New York City; when in NYC teaches bridge, when at school at Berkeley tends bar; a Nat'l Merit Scholar and member Junior Corps. 1989 KING OF BRIDGE; the youngest player to be NY Player of the Year 1991. Won 1990 World Jr Pr Trials, placed 4th in World Jr Championship 1991. Won Non-LM GN Prs 1988, Master Mixed Tms 1991; GN Tms, Life Master Open Prs 1993; placed second Blue Ribbon Prs 1992; has won many regional events. See FAMILY.

MOTT-SMITH, Geoffrey (1902-1960) of New York City, born in Honolulu, was co-chairman of ACBL Laws Commission, editor of *ACBL Bulletin* 1935-36, contributor to *The Bridge World*, writer and cryptographer. Mott-Smith was one of the first to operate a bridge club and to direct bridge tournaments. He was the director of the annual Intercollegiate Tournaments and other "par" bridge events. He worked with Ely Culbertson in the organization of the United States Bridge Association and with William E. McKenney in the early years of ACBL. During WW II, he served as chief instructor for the OSS in the training of cryptographers and cryptanalysts. He authored or co-authored more than 29 books on games and served as games consultant for the Association of American Playing Card Manufacturers. Mott-Smith was a great player, brilliant theorist and one of the soundest and most lucid of the early writers on contract bridge. See MOTT-SMITH TROPHY.

MOUAT, Andrew J. (1870-1956) of Evanston IL, was the leading personality in whist organization during the lifetime of the AMERICAN WHIST LEAGUE; was its chief tournament director for more than 40 years, serving as its president, secretary and tournament committee chairman; was editor of *Whist Review* 1915-1919; ACBL HONORARY MEMBER 1948.

MOUIEL, Hervé (b. 1949) of Paris, France, bridge professional. World Life Master. Won World Teams 1992, second 1984. Won European Teams 1983. Won Common Market Teams twice. Represented France 6 other world championships and won many national titles.

MOULIA, Simone (1913-1970) of Brussels, Belgium, typewriter saleswoman, represented Belgium World Womens Teams 1964; placed second European Womens Championships 1950, 1955, 1956, 1959; represented Belgium on several other occasions; placed third Cannes Mixed Teams 1962; won national titles in open, mixed, and womens events.

MOUSER, William S. (1912-1963) of Detroit MI, presumed dead when his private plane was lost over Lake Erie. He was a speech therapist and for 10 years the Sunday bridge columnist for the *Detroit News*; served as president and treasurer of the Michigan BA; member of ACBL Board 1963; wins include All-American Open Tms 1959. See MOUSER TROPHY.

MOWRY, Oris A. (b. 1936) of Longview WA, high school guidance counselor, former teacher, graduate of U of Utah and Indiana State U. Regional wins include Desert Empire Mixed Prs 1964, Klondike Open Prs, Puget Sound Open Tms 1972; LA Bridge Wk Non-Mixed Prs, Rogue River Valley Master Prs 1973; Dist 20 GN Tms, Tri-Cities Swiss 1979; Oregon Trail Swiss 1979, 81, 82; Dist 20 Swiss 1985, Summer secondary Swiss 1985.

MOYSE, Alphonse, Jr. (Sonny) (1898-1973), was publisher and editor of *The Bridge World* 1956-66, bridge author and champion player. Born in Summit MS, Moyse spent most of his boyhood in Cincinnati, then settled in NYC. When the crash of 1929 ended his career as a stockbroker, he adopted bridge as a profession. In 1934 he joined the organization of Ely Culbertson, partly as an associate editor of *The Bridge World* but chiefly as writer of syndicated newspaper articles that were published under the names of Ely and Josephine Culbertson. From that time until 1956 he wrote two bridge columns each day, a total of more than 20,000. In addition he did many magazine articles and editorial work on Culbertson books. Moyse was managing editor of *The Bridge World* 1939-43 and was publisher and chief editor 1946-56. On the death of Culbertson in 1955 he bought *The Bridge World*, Inc., from the Culbertson estate and was president and general manager until 1963 when he sold it to McCall Corp. He remained as publisher and editor until his retirement in 1966. Moyse was an original member of the Editorial Advisory Board of the *Bridge Encyclopedia*. In 1973, a few weeks before his death, he was selected as the first American to be named an IBPA Honorary Member. Perhaps Moyse's most admired writings were humorous articles about the bridge exploits of his wife, Jackie Moyse, whom he depicted as the typical member of ladies' luncheon-club bridge games. Though a comparatively infrequent contestant in tournaments, he won Mens Tms 1949, Mens Prs 1963 and several regional events.

MUELLER, Jane (Mrs. A. H.) of Cincinnati, former retirement consultant, represented US in World Womens Prs 1962. Won Womens Prs 1960 and several regional events.

MUHSAM, Gertrude (Mrs. Rudolf, formerly Brunner) (1909-1979) of New York City, born in Vienna, assistant manager of the CAVENDISH CLUB (New York) and an outstanding player. She was European Womens Tms champion 1935, 36, 37 and captain 1935-37.

MUKHERJEE, Kamal (b. 1945) of Calcutta, India, government employee. WBF World Master. Won Far East Open Teams 1977. Second BFAME Open Teams 1985. Fourth Open World Teams 1988 and represented India in three other world championships and two other zonal championships. Won 20 national titles including open teams four times and open pairs twice.

MULDER, André (b. 1951) of Alphen, The Netherlands, systems analyst. WBF World Master. Third World Team Olympiad 1980 and represented The Netherlands in six other world championships and two European Championships. National titles include Open Teams six times and Open Pairs three times.

MULLAMPHY, Matthew (b. 1966) of Townsville, Australia, entertainer. Third World Junior Teams 1991, won Far East Junior Teams 1990.

MULLER, Bauke (b. 1962) of Hoorn, Netherlands, psychologist. Won Bermuda Bowl 1993. Third World Teams 1992. National wins include Open Teams 1992 and Open Pairs 1991.

MULLINS, Carol Rae (formerly Ohmann) (b. 1934) of Sanford FL, bridge club manager, director and teacher, served on Unit 128 Board for several years and chaired several Daytona regionals. Won Southeastern Open Tms 1971, Womens Prs 1977; Florida Swiss 1976, 78, Open Prs 1977; Central FL Master Prs 1977; won the Mary Beth Hughes Trophy 1977.

MUNAFO, Dr. Paul M. (b. 1939) of Huntsville AL, chief metallurgist, NASA, designers of the space shuttle; his field is the prevention of premature structural failure in space vehicles. Educated at MIT and Tulane, Auburn (PhD). Enjoys fishing and Louisiana style gourmet cooking. Recipient of NASA Exceptional Service Medal 1991. Past president Dist 10, Unit 232, 143 and has served on unit and district boards for the past 25 years. Diamond Life Master; won North American Swiss 1988 (see also Morehead Trophy) and more than 50 regional events including Mid-South Master Prs 1966, 69, Mens Prs 1973, Open Prs 1992, 93, KO Tms 1992; Mid-Atlantic Swiss 1982, Mens KO Tms 1992, 93, Swiss 1993; Dist 10 GN Tms 1982, 92; Fall secondary Open Matchpoint Prs 1990.

MUNSON, Kitty (b. 1950) of New York City, computer systems analyst, graduated Harvard, enjoys gardening. Served on GNYBA Bd of Dir for several years, contributor to *International Bridge Monthly* and *Bridge International*; bridge teacher and certified director. Due to her appeal to the WBF, the rules governing the time period between representing different countries internationally were changed. WBF World Master; won Venice Cup 1989; also represented ACBL in Geneva 1990. Playing for Britain she placed 4th in World Mixed Prs in Bal Harbour 1986, won Common Market Mixed Tms and was 3rd in European Ladies Tms 1987. Her national titles are Advanced Senior Masters Prs 1975, North American Swiss 1987, 90; Womens Swiss 1989, Mixed Prs 1992; placed second Womens Swiss 1985, Womens BAM Tms 1988. Regional wins include Fall secondary Womens Swiss, NY-NJ Mixed Prs 1976; Can-At Open Prs 1977, NY Winter Womens Prs 1978, Mixed Prs, Dist. 3 Womens Swiss 1979; Eastern States Morning KO Tms 1991, Rye Winter Swiss, NY Morning KO Tms 1992; Cromwell KO Tms, Spring secondary Open Prs 1993.

MURDOCH, Elinor (1901-1986) of Birmingham AL, bridge teacher, Life Master #64; won Womens Prs, Mixed Prs 1931, Master Individual 1934; Master Mixed Tms; past president of Alabama BA; won numerous regional events.

MUNOZ, Rafael (b. 1927) of Madrid, Spain, lawyer and importer-exporter. WBF World Master. Fourth World Open Teams 1982 and represented Spain in four other world championships and six zonal championships. Won many national titles.

MURPHY, John T. (Jack) (1920-1992) of Calgary AB, retired locomotive engineer, served as Honor Guard for Pope John Paul II 1984, president of CANADIAN BRIDGE FEDERATION 1975-77; Canada's delegate to Bd of Gov to the WBF 1976, 80; served for 10 years on CBF Bd of Dir and CBF Charitable Trust; past president Unit 390 and chaired Calgary tournament 1967, 70, 73; in 1972 he became the first Canadian to be appointed assistant chairman ACBL Goodwill Committee 1972-80. Won Canadian Prairie Open Tms 1965.

MURRAY, David S. (b. 1921-1994) of Alexandria VA, retired statistician, graduate of U of South Carolina; was second Mixed Tms 1954; regional wins include Mid-Atlantic Fall Mens Prs 1953, 59, 63, Summer Mens Prs 1963; Keystone Conference Open Tms 1956; Washington Sr Swiss 1988, 89, 90; Life Master #381.

MURRAY, Eric R. (b. 1928) of Toronto, barrister and solicitor, represented North America in Bermuda Bowl 1962, 66, 67, 74, finishing second each time; Canada in other world competitions in 1960, 64 (4th World Teams Olympiad), 68 (3rd World Team Olympiad), 70 (5th World Open Pairs), 72 (3rd World Team Olympiad), 74 (17th World Open Pairs), 76 (13th World Team Olympiad), 78 (5th Rosenblum Tms), 80, 82 (3rd Rosenblum Tms), 88 (19th World Team Olympiad); won Team Trials 1966, Herman Trophy 1963, Vanderbilt 1961, 70; Spingold 1964, 65, 68; Mens Tms 1962, Life Master Mens Prs 1963, Mixed Prs 1963; Mens Prs 1945, 55, Master Mixed Tms 1956, 62, Life Master Prs 1969; placed second Master Mixed Tms 1954, the Chicago (now the Reisinger) 1961, Mens Prs 1965, Blue Ribbon Prs 1969, Reisinger 1969, 72. Has won Canadian National Tms (CNTC) 1980, 81, 87; placed second 1986, 88; won the Canadian Invitational Prs (Calcutta) 1993). Murray was the organizing chairman of the Summer NABC 1964, past president of Eastern Canadian BC and Ontario Unit, former director of Dist 2. He devised the MURRAY TWO DIAMOND convention and co-authored the DRURY convention; contributing editor to *Bridge Encyclopedia*; Grand Life Master; has won scores of regional events.

MURTHY, Ravindra (b. 1966) of Berkeley CA, graduate of U of California-Berkeley, member of Junior Corps, placed fourth World Jr Bridge Championship 1991, second Jr Tm Trials 1990; won GN Tms, Life Master Open Prs 1993; placed second Mixed Prs 1990, Blue Ribbon Prs 1992; has won more than a dozen regional events.

MURTINHO, Maria Elisabeth (Lizzie) (b. 1946) of Rio de Janeiro, Brazil, clinical psychologist. Won South American Womens Teams 1972, 1973, 1975, 1980, 1981, 1983, 1990. Represented Brazil in nine world championships. Former bridge editor of *Jornal do Brasil*.

MUSUMECI, Lt. Col. Joseph (b. 1921) of Richardson TX, retired Air Force officer, bridge teacher and writer. Musumeci was coach and trainer of the famed ACES team. He coached numerous US international teams from 1970-

84, captain of US team 1983; former president San Antonio BL. Associated with the late Ira Corn in the bridge column *Aces on Bridge* and ghost contributor to other Aces publications. Won Texas Conference Open Teams 1955, 61; Big D Swiss 1976, Mens Prs 1982, Master Prs 1989, Ira Corn Open Prs, Swiss 1990; San Antonio Unmixed Prs 1976, Ft. Worth Swiss 1981, Dist 16 GN Tms and Zonal GN Tms 1983.

MYRANS, Colette (b. 1915) of Deurle, Belgium, saleswoman, represented Belgium World Womens Teams 1964 and on several other occasions; placed second in the European Womens Championships 1955, 1956, 1959. National titles include Mixed Teams 1955, 1956, 1961, Womens Pairs 1954, 1955, 1960, 1963, Mixed Pairs, 1958.

N

NADAR, Kiran (b. 1951) of Delhi, India. WBF World Master. Won BFAME Womens Teams 1989, second 1991. Represented India in five world championships. Won three national titles.

NAGY, Edward A. (Ed) (b. 1946) of Oakland CA, attorney, won Master Mixed Tms 1979; placed second Open Prs 1989, Life Master Open Prs 1993; won numerous regionals.

NAGY, Peter I. (b. 1942) of Chicago IL, formerly of Montreal, options trader and professional bridge player, served as Dist 1 representative to ACBL Bd of Gov 1979-82. Born in Budapest, he escaped to Canada from Communist Hungary in 1957 with his uncle. He spoke neither French nor English, but by 1958 was at the top of his class and was valedictorian of his high school class in 1961. After graduating from Princeton in 1967, Nagy worked in the computer field until 1974. WBF Life Master; placed second in World Open Prs in 1978, 90; third Rosenblum Tms 1982, fifth in 1978, 90, 9th in 1986. On national level Nagy won Mens BAM Tms 1978, GN Tms 1991, Vanderbilt 1993; placed second Amateur Swiss 1977, Blue Ribbon Prs 1978, Vanderbilt 1980, 84; Spingold 1982, Mens Swiss 1989; won CNTC 1980, 81; won approximately 50 regional events. Nagy won IBPA Best Bid Hand of the Year Award 1977 and the BOLS Brilliancy Prize for the best defensive hand in World Tm Olympiad 1980. See also IBPA AWARDS.

NAGY, Zoltan (b. 1946 in Hungary), of Adelaide, Australia, public servant. Won South Pacific playoff 1974; represented Australia in nine Far East Championships. Winner of numerous national titles.

NAIL, Betty (Mrs. G. Robert) (b. 1923) of Houston TX, won Womens Prs 1958.

NAIL, G. Robert (b. 1925) of Houston TX, bridge teacher and writer, WBF Life Master; represented North America Bermuda Bowl 1962, 63 (placed 2nd). Originator of BIG DIAMOND SYSTEM, co-author of *Winning Duplicate, How to Play the Hand* and *Revolution in Bridge*. Won Team Trials 1962, Mens Tms 1965, Life Master Mens Prs 1974; Vanderbilt 1967, Life Master Prs 1974; placed second Mens Prs 1949, Spingold 1953, 62; Chicago (now the Reisinger) 1960, Mens Tms 1961, Mens Tms 1964, 88; Life Master Prs 1979, Blue Ribbon Prs 1980, Vanderbilt 1985, GN Prs 1989.

NAIMAN, Jeff (b. 1967) of New York City, radiology resident, graduate of Yale, founding member and president of Yale Student Bridge Club 1986-89; won Non-Life Master Prs 1990.

NAKAMURA, Yoshiyuki (b. 1944) of Tokyo, Japan, bridge teacher. Far East champion 1985. Represented Japan 12 other Far East Championships and one World Team Olympiad. Won many national titles.

NANDHABIWAT, Somboon (b. 1922) of Bangkok, Thailand, president of pulp and paper company. WBF World Master. Far East champion 1961, 1963, 1965 and represented Thailand, as player or captain, on 16 other occasions. Represented Thailand Bermuda Bowl 1966, 1967 and in five other world championships. Former president of the Far East Bridge Federation and the Contract Bridge League of Thailand. He originated the Bangkok Club System, and is Thailand's top masterpoint winner. With a career beginning in 1951, he won every national title including the Open Teams more than 10 times.

NARTIS, Evangelos (b. 1943 in Czechoslovakia) of Athens, Greece. WBF World Master. Represented Greece in 1988 World Team Olympiad, finishing fifth, the best performance ever by a Greek team. Won many national titles.

NASH, Garrett G. (b. 1919) of University City MO, former member of US International Table Tennis Team, was ranked #1 in US in 1939 and third in the world in 1948. Former professional baseball player and US Army officer. Won Vanderbilt 1962; has several regionals to his credit.

NASH, James L. (Jim) (b. 1946) of Omaha NE, professional bridge player, teacher and director, insurance company training supervisor, enjoys sports and collecting antiques. Diamond Life Master; won all six events at Omaha sectional 1991, staff writer for the Unit 241 bridge publication. Regional wins include Nebraska KO Tms 1973, Heartland Mens Swiss, KO Tms 1983, 90; Roughrider KO Tms 1985, 91; Iowa KO Tms 1985; Wichita KO Tms, Swiss, Master Prs 1988, KO Tms 1992; Springfield KO Tms, Open Prs 1988; Sunflower KO Tms 1989; Pot O'Gold Open Prs, KO Tms 1991; Lincoln Bracketed KO Tms, KO Tms, Swiss 1992; Omaha Open Prs, Swiss 1993; Cedar Rapids Bracketed KO Tms, Swiss 1993.

NATHAN, Marc W. (b. 1953) of Miami FL, personnel manager, won Open Prs 1981; placed second 1982.

NATHANSON, Neil L. (b. 1943) of Little Ferry NJ, pension fund auditor, placed second GN Tms 1976; won several regionals.

NATHER, Nola (b. 1919) of Christchurch, New Zealand. Won Far East Womens Teams 1976 and represented New Zealand in two other zonal championships.

NEEDHAM, Richard E. (1887-1956) of Greenville PA, bridge writer, tournament organizer and ABL tournament director, was one of the most active tournament promoters for many years in western Pennsylvania, Ohio, West Virginia and upstate New York. His writings included *Auction Bridge Sidelights, Contract Bridge Condensed* and *Tournament Tactics at Contract Bridge.*

NEHMERT, Ponyelle of Wiesbaden, Germany. Second Venice Cup 1993. Second European Womens Teams and Womens Pairs 1991.

NEIGER, Eugene J. (Gene) (b. 1936) of New York City, stockbroker, won Spingold 1971, Vanderbilt 1972; won numerous regional titles including the New York Blue Ribbon Individual 1979.

NEIKIRK, E. Bruce (b. 1944) of Louisville KY, born in England, attorney and CPA, graduate of Indiana U and U of Louisville (JD), won Champagne Masters Prs 1971, Dist 11 KO Tms 1974, 82; Midwest Spring KO Tms 1977, Fall Mens Swiss 1979, Dist 11 GN Prs 1982, 84; Derby City KO Tms 1988, 90.

NEILL, Bruce G. of Sydney, Australia, computer systems consultant. Represented Australia in two zonal championships. Won several national championships.

NELSON, Martin E. (b. 1944) of Annapolis MD, professor of nuclear engineering at US Naval Academy, graduated U of Wisconsin and U of Virginia (PhD). Won numerous regionals including Norfolk Open Prs 1973, Chicopee Swiss 1977, Reston Swiss 1980, Baltimore Open Prs 1980, 88; Arlington Swiss 1981, 90; Virginia Beach Master Prs 1982, Lancaster Swiss 1983, 89; Richmond Swiss 1984, Raleigh Master Prs 1985, Open Prs 1990; Cherry Hill Master Prs 1987, Roanoke Swiss 1988, Alexandria Open Prs 1989.

NELSON, Warren G. (b. 1940) of Pleasanton CA, sales and advertising manager, graduate of U of California-Berkeley, has served on unit boards of Sacramento and Oakland, columnist for Dist 21 publication; won Golden Gate Unmixed Prs 1976, Mt Shasta Open Prs 1978, Holiday Festival Swiss 1979, Mexican Holiday Fiesta Mens Prs 1988, All-Western IMP Prs 1991.

NEUBURGER, Frederic (b. 1944) of Liverpool NY, self employed tax preparer and certified financial planner, graduated Columbia U. and Syracuse U, former columnist and co-editor of the CNYBA Unit newsletter, member of judiciary committee. Has won Upper New York State Open Prs 1973, Swiss 1975, Mens Prs 1980; Syracuse Open Tms 1976, Nat'l Capital Master Prs 1977, Keystone Fall Master Prs 1979, Mens Tms 1981; Dist 5 Master Prs 1979, Dist 4 Mens Swiss 1981, 83, 84, 86, 88, Swiss 1985, 89, 90, Mens Prs 1989; Spring Mens Swiss 1982, Dist 3 Swiss 1986, Summer secondary Morning KO Tms 1992.

NEUFFER, Henry Happoldt (Hap) (b. 1950) of Columbia SC, store manager, graduate of U of South Carolina; won Mixed Prs 1993; regional wins include Mid-Atlantic KO Tms 1973, Swiss 1976, Mens Prs 1977, 81, Open Prs 1985, Open Prs 1989; Florida Open Prs 1974, Bicentennial Swiss 1976, Spring secondary Silver Trophy Prs 1979.

NEUMAN, Cyrus (b. 1921) of Miami, attorney, won Spingold 1958; placed second Spingold 1954.

NEUT, Jaap van der (b. 1959) of Amsterdam, Netherlands, bridge journalist. WBF World Master. Third World Teams 1992. Won National Open Teams 1991.

NEVINS, Emilie (b. 1912) of Ft. Lauderdale FL, retired social worker, graduate of Syracuse U, won Senior and Advanced Senior Master Prs 1956; placed second Womens Prs 1955. Regional wins include Upper NY State Womens Prs 1956, 58; Puerto Rico Master Prs 1973, Summer secondary Swiss 1974, Southeastern Womens Swiss 1975.

NEWELL, Peter (b. 1962) of Wellington, New Zealand, policy analyst. Won Far East Teams 1990, Far East Pairs 1991. Represented New Zealand two world championships and one other zonal championship. Won New Zealand pairs four straight years.

NEWLAND, Martin W. (b. 1945) of Ottawa ON, born in England, chartered accountant, a fellow in Institute of Chartered Accountants in both England and Wales. Won Red Ribbon Prs 1986; regional wins include Ottawa Mens Swiss 1981, 90, Mens Prs 1982; Albany Swiss 1982, Quebec Swiss 1985, North Bay Swiss 1991.

NEWMAN, Peter (b. 1966) of Sydney, Australia, computer programmer. Third World Junior Teams 1991, won Far East Junior Teams 1990, and represented Australia on three other occasions. Won several national titles.

NICHOLSON, Joyce (b. 1919) of Melbourne, Australia, journalist, author and publisher. Member of the Order of Australia for services to writing and the book-publishing industry. Won National Womens Individual 1983. Editor and publisher of *Australian Bridge* 1985-1989. Author of *Why Women Lose at Bridge*.

NICKELL, Frank T. (Nick) (b. 1947) of Raleigh NC, investment banker, graduated U of North Carolina, enjoys golf. Diamond Life Master; won Blue Ribbon Prs 1991, Spingold, Reisinger 1993; placed second GN Tms 1983; member of winning Corporate America Team in match vs. US Congress 1993; has also won numerous regional titles.

NIEBERDING, Joseph H. (b. 1908) of St. Louis MO, retired executive, won bridge events in seven decades beginning in 1930; regional wins include Midwest Fall Individual 1954; Mississippi Valley Mens Tms 1954, Mens Prs 1968, Sr Swiss 1989; Spring secondary Sr Swiss 1987.

NIEMEIJER, Chris (b. 1946) of Broek in Waterland, The Netherlands, project manager, computer systems. WBF World Master. Represented The Netherlands in three zonal championships. National titles include Open Teams and Open Pairs once each. A notable theorist, he developed the Biedermeier (Dutch) standard of bidding, based on a survey of 100 Dutch experts. Author of two books and contributor to *Bridge*.

NIKOLITS, Tamás (b. 1947) of Budapest, Hungary,, computer hardware engineer. Won many national titles;

represented Hungary in two world championships and six European Championships.

NIKOLOV, Ivan (b. 1927) of Sofia, Bulgaria, professor of sociology. Founded Bulgarian Bridge Federation 1979, served as president until 1989. Dismissed from Bulgarian Communist Party in 1988 after presiding over first public meeting of Bulgaria's dissident organization.

NILSLAND, Mats (b.1950) of Malmö, Sweden, flower wholesaler. WBF World Master. Third Bermuda Bowl 1991, third World Teams 1986. Represented Sweden in three other world championships. Second European Championship 1991. Second in Nordic Championships twice. Second Vanderbilt 1993. Won 3 Swedish titles. Author or co-author of 5 books on bridge.

NIPPGEN, Georg (b. 1950) of Karlsruhe, Germany, businessman. Won Rosenblum Teams 1990 and won five national titles. Member EBL Systems Committee.

NOLAND, Helen (Heitie) (1920-91) of Lake Charles LA, member of ACBL Goodwill Committee; Diamond Life Master; won World Mixed Tms 1972; placed second World Mixed Prs 1978, Womens Tms 1973; had numerous regional titles to her credit.

NOOYEN, Marcel (b. 1963) of Amsterdam, The Netherlands, chemist. WBF World Master. Third World Teams 1992. World Junior Team champion 1987. European Junior Team champion 1986. Won National Open Teams 1991.

NORANTE, Barbara of Butler PA, worldwide winner of the Epson Prs 1988 and winner of several regional events.

NORDBY, Harald (b. 1941) of Oslo, Norway, systems analyst. WBF World Master. Won Nordic Teams 1971, 1978 and 1982. Represented Norway in three world championships and seven European Championships. National wins include open teams 8 times and open pairs 3 times. Top Norwegian masterpoint holder. Pianist.

NORDENSON, Britt (formerly Blom, Nygren) (b. 1925) of Norrköping, Sweden. WBF Life Master. Won World Womens Teams 1968, European Womens Teams 1967, Nordic Womens Teams 1964, 1966, 1978, 1980, 1982, 1984. Won 14 national titles, including 12 Womens Pairs.

NORRIS, Georg (b. 1941) of Birkeröd, Denmark, engineer. WBF World Master. Won Common Market Mixed Teams 1989. Represented Denmark in two world championships, one zonal championships and on many other occasions. 9 national wins include Open Teams twice.

NORRIS, Judy (b. 1940) of Birkeröd, Denmark, correspondent. WBF World Master. Won World Womens Teams 1988, Nordic Womens Teams 1988, Common Market Mixed Teams 1989. Represented Denmark twice in world team championships, open series, and women's play in one other world championship, five zonal championships and on many other occasions. 17 national wins include Open Teams once.

NORTH, Frederick of Hove, England, bridge writer and teacher. Represented Britain in two world championships, and England in Camrose Trophy matches. Many national wins include Gold Cup 1962. Author and co-author of many books and magazine contributor.

NORWOOD, Barbara B. (Mrs. Robert) (b. 1938) of Austin TX, graduate U of TX-Austin (Phi Beta Kappa), has served in various executive positions on Unit and Dist level; won Womens Prs 1980; placed second Womens Prs 1984; has won several regional titles including Texas Capital Mixed Prs 1975, Acapulco Fiesta Swiss 1980, Republic of Texas Open Prs 1981, Dist 16 GN Prs 1981.

NORWOOD, John W., Jr. (b. 1908) of Greenville SC, attorney, graduated U of North Carolina and U of South Carolina Law School; ACBL president 1967, chairman of the Board 1968; member of WBF Executive Council in the Sixties and a member of the ACBL Bd of Dir 1961-76. Life Master #639; regional wins include Mid-Atlantic Summer Mens Prs 1960, 61, 66, Open Tms 1961, Open Prs 1964, Fall Master Prs 1962, Open Tms 1965.

NOSZKA, Gloria E. (1923-1983) of Pittsburgh, real estate agent, represented US in international competition Stockholm 1970, Las Palmas 74. She won ACBL Womens Prs 1969.

NOVAK, Ruth M. (b. 1909) of Salem IL, bridge teacher, member ACBL Goodwill Committee, Nat'l Charity Committee and served in varied positions on Unit and Dist level; received an Outstanding Service Award for her work for charity 1977. Won Womens Tms 1962; regional wins are Champagne Open Prs, Mississippi Valley Womens Prs 1970.

NOVAK, Phyllis (b. 1927) of Seattle WA, real estate investor, graduate of Antioch College, won Womens Prs, Mixed Prs 1958, Womens Tms 1962, and many regional events.

NUDELMAN, Barbara N. (b. 1931) of Chicago IL, retired advertising executive, graduate of U of Wisconsin, enjoys golf, charity work, travel and politics. President of ACBL 1993, chairman of Bd 1994, has served as a member of the ACBL Bd of Dir for Dist 13 since 1985; was chairman of ACBL Bd of Gov 1983, 84, president of ACBL Educational Foundation 1991-92, has served on many ACBL committees. She has held various executive positions in Chicago Contract BA (including president) since 1968. Has won several regional events.

NUNES, Jack (b. 1912) of London, England, company director. Represented England in numerous Camrose matches. Many national wins include Gold Cup four times. His book *Improve Your Bridge* was the basis for two instructional TV series.

NUTTING, Ann (formerly Jacobson) (b. 1940) of San Francisco CA, certified public accountant, Diamond Life Master, won Fall NAC Swiss Tms 1981 and numerous regionals.

NUTTING, Willard H. III (Bill) (b. 1945) of San Francisco CA, vice president and past president of Unit 197, former treasurer of Dist 21; won GN Prs 1982.

O

OAKEY, Larry B. (b. 1937) of Minneapolis MN, purchase and sales manager in brokerage firm, graduate of North Dakota State and Nebraska U, Dist 14 recorder 1985-present; R1 tournament director, contributor to *Gopher* and *Viking Bridge News*. Diamond Life Master; placed second Mens Tms 1978, played on Minneapolis Inter-City Match Team 1968 (won), 1969 (lost). Has won 40+ regionals including Summer secondary Leventritt Prs 1966, Canadian Prairie Mens Prs 1970, Open Prs 1971, Swiss 1972; Calgary KO Tms 1973, Mixed Prs, Master Prs 1975; Iowa Swiss 1970, 79, 80, KO Tms 1979; Gopher Swiss 1977, KO Tms 1980; Roughrider KO Tms 1977, 81, Mens Prs 1981; Dist 14 GN Tms 1985, 86, 87; Iowa Open Prs 1992, Dist 14 Open Prs 1993.

OAKIE, Donald A. (Don) (formerly Donald Akira Aoki) (1914-1983) of San Jose CA, first person of Japanese descent to win Bermuda Bowl (1954) and the first ACBL member to become a Life Master with all (300) red points. Represented US in int'l play Turin 1960. Won Spingold 1953, Chicago (now the Reisinger) 1958; placed second Mens Prs 1959; also won numerous regionals. For many years Oakie was involved with bridge administration; ACBL president 1976, chairman of the ACBL Bd of Dir 1977 and a Board member 1967-81, co-chairman of the ACBL Laws Commission from 1975, WBF Laws Commission 1974, president of the WESTERN CONFERENCE 1966. Oakie was the principal draftsman of the revised American format of the 1974 *ACBL Handbook* 1973, 74, 75; authored *Simplified Standard American Bridge Bidding*; was named "Sportsman of the Year" by the IBPA in 1976 (see IPBA AWARDS).

OAKS, Alan W. (b. 1938) of Germantown TN, ACBL MAD line director, former director for ACBL Member Services Dept, former secretary of ACBL Charity Foundation, graduate of U of Oregon. Frequent contributor to *ACBL Bulletin*. Regional wins include Oregon Trail Open Tms 1967, Pacific Northwest Open Prs 1967, Fall secondary Swiss 1979, Mens Swiss 1980; Summer secondary Golder Prs 1987, Spring secondary Morning KO Tms 1991.

O'BRIEN, Patrick L. (P.L.) (1943-1993) of Berkeley CA, counselor for the Hemophilia Foundation, retired bridge professional, graduate of San Francisco State and Yuba College. O'Brien, a hemophiliac, was a member of the Nat'l Hemophilia Society, an honorary member of the Royal Hemophilia Society, served as president of the Disabled Students Advisory Committee at Yuba College 1986. Won Pacific Northwest Spring Open Tms 1967, Palm Springs KO Tms 1971, Oregon Trail Open Tms 1973, Master Prs 1974; Mount Shasta Open Prs, Swiss 1974; Dist 20 Open Tms 1974, Bridge Wk KO Tms 1983. See HANDICAPPED PLAYERS.

ÖDLUND, Britt-Marie (Bim) (b. 1945) of Stockholm, Sweden, civil engineer. Third Venice Cup 1993. Won European Womens Tms 1993, Nordic Womens Tms 1982, 84. Represented Sweden in two other world championships and three other zonal championships. Won four national titles.

O'DOHERTY, Eileen of Dublin, Ireland, civil servant,

represented Ireland in the World Women's Pairs 1978 and in many European and Common Market Championships. National titles include Women's Pairs, Mixed Pairs, Women's Teams, Open Pairs, Open Teams.

O'DOWD, John (b. 1929) of Hamilton ON, computer operator and bookkeeper, enjoys reading and stamp collecting, served on Unit 166 Bd of Dir for five years; founder and first president of Hamilton and District BA 1966-72. Won Canadian Nat'l Open Tms 1958, KO Tms 1968, Sr Swiss 1991; Niagara Falls Sr Swiss 1989, Sr Prs 1991; London ON Sr Prs 1991.

OEST, John N. (Jack) (b. 1952) of Chicago IL, attorney, educated at Denison U and U of Wisconsin (JD). Diamond Life Master; won GN Tms 1991, second 1984, 88; has won 15-20 regional events. Oest was instrumental in putting together the Eric Rodwell - Jeff Meckstroth partnership.

O'GRADY, Angeline (Andy) of Miami FL, professional bridge teacher and player, enjoys swimming and water sports, finished second Womens BAM Tms 1988 and won the ACBL-Wide International Fund Game 1975. Diamond Life Master; has won 75+ regional titles.

OGUST, Harold A. (1916-1978) of New York City, plastics manufacturer, travel agent; the president and founder of Goren International, Inc., originator of OGUST REBIDS after WEAK TWO-BIDS. Represented US in Bermuda Bowl 1957, World Team Olympiad 1960; won Spingold 1956, 60; Reisinger 1957, 63.

OHMANN, Carol R., see MULLINS, Carol Rae.

OHNO, Kyoko (b. 1946) of Tokyo, Japan, computer systems engineer. WBF World Master. Runner-up Far East Women's Team Championship 1986 and represented Japan on many other occasions. Has won National Open Teams 11 times and National Open Pairs 14 times.

OKEN, Daniel (Dan) (b. 1917) of Ajijic, Mexico, retired real estate and land developer, graduate of NYU; certified director, has served as tournament chairman in two Units; member Bd of Dir for Unit 205. Has won 20+ regionals including Host Farms Masters Prs 1967, Keystone Fall Master Prs 1968, North Florida Fall Open Prs 1976, Swiss 1977; Southeastern Mens Swiss 1977, 1980; Daytona Beach Open Prs 1978; Headquarters Open Prs, Cincinnati Mens Swiss 1978; Gold Coast Mens Swiss 1981.

OKEN, Louise (Mrs. Daniel) (1937-1983) of Miami FL, real estate developer won Mixed Prs 1966 and several regional events.

OLIVER, Vince (b. 1959) of Manhattan Beach CA, gaming consultant, law student, graduate of U of Southern California; won Summer secondary Silver Trophy Prs Flt B 1977, Central States II Swiss 1978, All-Western Swiss 1978, Raincross Swiss 1980, Motor City Swiss 1990.

OLMEDO ZUMARAN, Alejandro (b. 1902) of Buenos Aires, Argentina, solicitor, South American champion 1951, 1953, 1957. National titles include Argentine Open Teams 1935, 1952, Open Pairs 1953, 1956, Interclubs 1947, 1951, 1952, 1957.

O'LOUGHLIN, Walter K. (1910-1989) of Towson MD, retired executive, graduated Catholic U; served as ACBL president 1978, ACBL Director 1962-65, 1971-80; ACBL treasurer 1973-75, president Maryland BA 1956, president Mid-Atlantic Conference 1970-72; won several regionals.

OLSEN, Jack (b. 1925) of Rollinsville CO, journalist and author, formerly wrote for *Sports Illustrated*; author of *The Mad World Of Bridge* and co-author of *A New Approach to Bridge*.

OLSON, Jeffrey A. (b. 1958) of Dallas TX, insurance agent and financial consultant, won Toast of Tulsa Open Prs 1979, Land of Coronado Open Prs 1982, Texas Fall Master Swiss 1988, Mid-Winter Open Prs 1990, Summer Open Prs 1991; King Cotton KO Tms 1990, Intern'l City Open Prs 1992, Magic Valley Handicap KO Tms, KO Tms 1993; Mid-winter Holiday Bracketed KO Tms 1993.

O'MALIA, Bernard E. (Barney) (1904-1994) of Kailua-Kona HI, casino owner, placed second Reisinger 1978; won numerous regional titles.

OMAN, Jacqueline N. (Jackie) (b. 1941) of East Lansing MI, has served on the Lansing BC Bd for 10 years and Unit 195 Board 1988-90. Won Hudson Swiss 1981, Spring secondary A-D Conventions 1982, Great Lakes Open Prs 1982, Master Prs 1989; Chicago Swiss 1982, Detroit Swiss 1987.

ONDERWYZER, Steven J. (b. 1941) of Marina del Rey CA, private investor, retired lingerie manufacturer, electrical engineer; graduated Michigan State and Stevens Institute. Won Monterey Open Prs, Portland KO Tms, Pasadena Open Prs, Santa Clara Super Open Prs 1990; Sacramento Handicap KO Tms, BAM Tms 1990; San Bernardino KO Tms 1991.

ONORATI, Mario (b. 1928 in Italy) of Caracas, Venezuela, insurance broker. WBF World Master. Won South American Teams 1963, 1965, 1966. Won CAC Teams 1973, 1977, 1984, 1985, 1986, 1987, 1991. Represented Venezuela in 11 world championships. Won many national titles, and is top-ranked Venezuelan player since 1970.

ONSTOTT, John H. (b. 1944) of New Orleans LA, finance company president, enjoys playing tournament tennis, served on ACBL Bd of Gov 1981-87, as vice-president of Louisiana BA, co-chairman of New Orleans NABC 1983. Placed second North American Swiss 1983 and GN Tms 1987. Diamond Life Master with more than 10,000 MPs; has won more than 50 regional titles.

OPPEN, Carol G.J. van (b.1935) of Amsterdam, The Netherlands, bridge-tour operator. WBF World Master. Third World Teams 1980 and represented the Netherlands in four other world championships and two European Championships. Won Common Market Teams. His national titles include Open Teams 10 times and Open Pairs twice. Author of four books.

OPPENHEIMER, Tom (b. 1949) of Ballwin MO, financial analyst with Anheuser Busch, graduate of Grinnell

College and U of Missouri-St. Louis; member of ACBL Nat'l Bd of Gov and Dist 8 Bd of Dir. Placed second IMP Prs 1992; won many regional championships including Dist 15 Fall Masters Prs 1986, Mid-South Swiss 1987, Dist 8 GN Tms 1988, Evansville Swiss, Rough Rider Swiss, Kansas City Swiss 1988; Indianapolis Strat Prs 1990, Mississippi Valley KO Tms 1991, 92; Oconomowoc Swiss 1991, Fall secondary Morning KO Tms 1992, Nashville Swiss 1993.

O'REILLY, Edward C. (Ed) (b. 1936) of Kingston ON, bridge club owner, teacher, director. Formerly a public health administrator. Executive member of Unit Bd for 15 years, Dist 1 treasurer for 5 years, member ACBL Bd of Gov 2 years. Founded Brockville DBC, assisted in founding three other clubs; writes weekly bridge column for *Kingston Whig-Standard*. Regional wins include Can-At KO Tms 1969, 70, Swiss 1970.

ORLOW, Andrzej (b.1941) of Warsaw, Poland, rehabilitation specialist, bridge trainer and theorist. President of Polish Bridge Union since 1990. Editor of bridge books and magazines.

OROCK, Lt. Col. Mary J. (b. 1939) of Fort Worth TX, bridge teacher, retired Air Force officer and Director of Nursing, served as a flight nurse during the Tet Offensive. Won Western Iowa Open Prs 1975, Rocky Mountain Swiss, Mid-Winter Holiday Open Prs 1977; Big Apple Womens Prs 1979.

ORTIZ-PATIÑO, Jaime (b. 1928) of Marbella, Spain, WBF World Life Master, has business interests throughout the world. President of WORLD BRIDGE FEDERATION 1976-86, president emeritus 1986-. WBF vice president 1974-75 and treasurer of EUROPEAN BRIDGE LEAGUE 1974-75. As WBF president he was instrumental in forming two new zones —CENTRAL AMERICAN-CARIBBEAN and ASIA AND THE MIDDLE EAST— and in adding many new countries to the WBF roster, including the People's Republic of China. General chairman of Geneva World Championships 1990.

He now has major interests in golf. His own golf course in Spain — Valderrama — will be the site of the 1997 Ryder Cup.

He was the prime force behind the introduction of bidding screens at international tournaments, despite strong opposition from world figures who insisted that screens would denaturalize and dehumanize tournament bridge. Screens were used for the first time in world competition at the Bermuda Bowl in Southampton, Bermuda, in 1975. The competitors were virtually unanimous in their approval. The screens allowed them to relax on their side of the curtain. They didn't have to fear that they might be transmitting unwitting messages to partner through body language. He also fostered, along with others, the use of bidding boxes, a move that cut the noise level tremendously. He attempted to do something about the destructive bidding systems that were invading international tournaments. He feels he was too late to stop the influx, but he helped design a complex convention card that makes it incumbent on all pairs to explain exactly what their system consists of, including follow-up bids. He also felt very strongly that international bridge should be on the highest possible ethical ground. He took major steps during his presidency to ensure the upgrading of ethics, and

he was eminently successful.

He represented Switzerland in World Team Olympiad 1964, 68, World Open Prs 1962, Rosenblum Cup 1982, European Championships 1955, 56, 59, 61, 62, 63, 65, 67. Placed fifth in the World Par Point Contest 1961. National titles include Open Tms 1953, 56, 59, 61, KO Tms 1955, 56, 60, 62, 63.

OSBERG, Sharon (b. 1949) of San Francisco CA, bank executive, graduate of Dickinson College, enjoys scuba diving and skiing, member Nat'l Appeals Committee since 1991. WBF World Master; won Venice Cup 1991, 93; was Venice Cup semifinalist 1987; placed 13th World Womens Prs 1986. She has placed second twice in USWBC. Won Master Mixed Teams 1979, Womens KO Tms 1986, 91; Womens BAM 1988; placed second Womens Prs 1986, Womens BAM 1987, Womens Swiss 1990; has several regional wins.

OSBORN, Florence (d. 1985) of Mount Carmen CT, bridge columnist and lecturer in the humanities, was bridge editor of *New York Herald Tribune* from 1936 until the newspaper was discontinued in 1966 and of *New York American*. Her writings include *How's Your Bridge Game?* Formerly conducted a bridge interview radio program and made many television appearances. She was stabbed to death in her home.

OSHLAG, Mary B. (b. 1942) of Germantown TN, ACBL headquarters staff member, graduate of Belmont College and Middle Tennessee State U, placed second Master Mixed Teams 1989; won Huntsville Open Prs 1978, 82; Paducah Swiss 1990; Dist 10 GN Prs, Monroe Womens Prs 1991; Gatlinburg Womens KO Tms, Jackson Womens Prs 1992.

OSHLAG, Richard J. (b. 1945) of Germantown TN, ACBL computer programmer/analyst, served as business manager for *ACBL Bulletin* 1969 to 1984, ACBL programmer 1984 to 1988, returned to ACBL as computer specialist 1993. Diamond Life Master; placed second Master Mixed Tms 1989. Regional wins include New York Winter Life Master Prs 1971, Mid-Atlantic KO Tms 1973, Mid-South Swiss 1974, Mens Prs 1975, Headquarters KO Tms 1978, Dist 10 GN Tms 1978, 88; Space City Open Prs 1980, 84; Dist 10 GN Prs 1986, 90, 91; Nashville Swiss 1988, Open Prs 1993; Memphis Swiss 1990, Mid-Atlantic Labor Day Mens KO Tms, Swiss 1993; Huntsville Open Prs 1992.

OSIE, Judith (b. 1936) of Joannesburg, South Africa, professional kaluki player. Represented South Africa in World Women's Teams 1976, 1980, Maccabi Games 1977. Six national wins include four in open teams and one in open pairs.

OSOFSKY, Aileen of New York City, has served as chairman of ACBL Goodwill Committee since 1985, as a director of ACBL Educational Foundation since 1989, for many years as a member of ACBL Bd of Gov. and for more than 10 years on the GNYBA Board. Won Dist 3 Womens Swiss 1979; Dist 4 Womens Prs 1980, Mexican Nat'l Womens Prs 1981, Spring secondary Womens Prs 1992.

OSTRICH, Dr. Nathan (b. 1928) of Lafayette LA, optometrist, founder of the SW Louisiana Unit; produced TV series *Play Bridge with the Experts*.

OSTROW, Albert A. (1910-1961) of Malverne NY, an authority on card games and the author of numerous books, among them, *The Complete Card Player* and *The Bridge Player's Bedside Companion*; consultant on card games to the Association of American Playing Card Manufacturers 1960-61.

OTSTAVEL, Ain (b. 1942) of Tartu, Estonia, economist. Won many Estonian and Soviet titles. Second Cavendish Invitational Pairs 1989. Devised Tartu Strong Pass System.

OTTLIK, Géza (1912-1990) of Budapest, Hungary, novelist, essayist and bridge writer. Co-author of *Adventures in Card Play* which introduced and developed many new advanced concepts: Entry Squeeze, Backwash Squeeze, Elopement, Elbow-room, Entry-shifting Plays, Non-Material Plays, Rio Finesse, and KO Squeeze. Author of many magazine articles, one which won IBPA's first *Article of the Year* Award in 1968. Represented Hungary in international matches 1936-38 and 1971-72. In Hungary he was known as the ultimate authority on Hungarian prose. His novel, *A School at the Frontier*, was translated into many languages, and in 1985 he received the Kossuth Prize for Literature.

OUDSHOORN, Nicolaus D. (Nico) (b. 1906) of Rijswijk, The Netherlands. Tournament manager of European Championships 1963, 1965, 1966, World Team Olympiad 1968, World Pair Olympiad 1974. Honorary EBL Tournament Director.

OUIMET, Jean G. (b. 1934) of Hollywood FL, born in Montreal, retired from US Air Force, has won 20+ regionals including Puget Sound Mens Swiss 1977, CA Capitol KO Tms, MO Valley KO Tms 1979.

OWEN, Ernest D., Jr. (b. 1942) of Warwick, Bermuda, permanent secretary, Ministry of Labor and Home Affairs, has served on ACBL Bd of Gov and Executive Committee of Bermuda BC; represented Bermuda in world play Miami 1972, 86; Monte Carlo 1976, Valkenburg 1980, Biarritz 1982; represented Bermuda in Pan Am games in Mexico City 1975; won the Bermuda Swiss 1976, 78, 80, Mens Prs 1983, Master Prs 1976, 83, 91; and has twice been the recipient of the Norman Bach Trophy.

OXLEY, John F. (b. 1945) of St. Joseph MO, company president, won Kansas City Mens Prs 1970, Open Prs 1989, Open Prs 1991, Swiss 1991; Cedar Rapids Swiss 1973; Dist 15 GN Tms 1986, 93, GN Prs 1991; Tulsa Open Prs 1986, Wichita Mens Prs 1986, Master Prs 1992; Topeka Mens Swiss 1989, Swiss 1991; Springfield KO Tms, Swiss 1992; Milwaukee Swiss 1992, Omaha Swiss, Oklahoma Swiss 1993.

ÖZDIL, Melih (b. 1948) of Istanbul, Turkey, bridge teacher. WBF World Master. Represented Turkey in three world championships and three zonal championships. Seven national wins include open teams once.

OZKAN, Serdar (b. 1957) of Istanbul, Turkey, bridge teacher. Represented Turkey in one world championship

and one zonal championship. Won national open teams three times.

OZORIO L.A. (b. 1911) of Hong Kong, businessman. Won Far East Open Teams 1959, 1960 and represented Hong Kong on two other occasions. National wins include open teams and open pairs.

P

PABIS-TICCI, Camillo (b. 1920) of Florence, Italy, engineer. WBF Grand Master, 7th in world career listings in 1992. Won World Teams 1964, 1968, 1972, Bermuda Bowl 1963, 1965, 1966, 1967, 1969. Italian national titles include Open Teams once. Columnist and magazine contributor.

PACHECO, Morella of Caracas, Venezuela. WBF World Master. Won CAC Women's Teams 1979, 1980, 1981, 1982, 1987, 1991. Represented Venezuela in eight world championships and won many national titles.

PADUA, Leticia de of Paranaque, Philippines, businesswoman. Represented Philippines in two world championships and one Far East Championship. As President of Philippines CBA, chief organizer of 1977 world team championships and Far East Championships.

PAGAN, Shirley (b. 1932) of Corpus Christi TX, Unit board member for many years; President Dist. 16 1993; member ACBL Education Foundation; member ACBL Goodwill Committee; chairman WBF Pan-American Championships in Corpus Christi 1992; chaired many Dist 16 sectionals and one regional.

PALMER, Beth (b. 1952) of Silver Spring MD, lawyer, WBF Life Master, won Venice Cup 1987, 89; placed second World Womens Prs 1982, 4th 1990. Diamond Life Master with many nat'l credits including Master Mixed Tms 1982, 92, 93; Life Master Womens Prs 1983, 85; Womens KO Tms, Mixed Prs 1985; North American Womens Swiss 1987, Womens BAM Tms 1993; placed second Womens KO Tms 1986, 92; Life Master Womens Prs 1989, Womens BAM 1991.

PAN, Kai Jian of Beijing, China, newspaper editor. WBF World Master. Won Far East Teams 1991, and represented China in 4 world championships and 2 other zonal championships. Fifth in the Rosenblum Cup 1990. Won 2 national titles. Coach of Chinese Open Team.

PANELEWEN, Sanje (b. 1956) of Jakarta, Indonesia. Won Far East Teams 1985, 1987, 1992.

PANG, Vern (b. 1950) of Honolulu HI, chief information officer, independant management and systems consultant; graduated U of Hawaii and Chaminade U, enjoys tennis. Regional wins include Fall secondary BAM 1971, Medford KO Tms 1973, Hawaii KO Tms 1975, 89, Mens Swiss 1981, Open Prs 1985, Swiss 1990, 91, Stratified Prs; Great Western Super Open Prs 1981, 83; CA Bridge Week Open Prs 1982, KO Tms 1986, 90; San Diego KO Tms, Open Swiss 1984, KO Tms 1989, Prime Time KO Tms 1990; Sacramento Swiss BAM, Fresno Super Open Prs 1989.

PAPP, Balint (b. 1921) of Sarasota FL, born in the Soviet Union, raised in Hungary, after a brief stint in the Hungarian Army he spent seven years as POW in the Soviet. After his release he worked as an interpreter and was Hungarian Nat'l Platform Diving Champion 1952, 53; coach of the Hungarian Olympic Diving Tm 1956. He defected to US in 1956. Diamond Life Master; has won Florida Tms 1973, Jacksonville Mixed Prs 1979, Miami Sr Swiss 1990, Sr Prs 1992; Orlando Sr KO Tms 1992, Tampa Sr KO Tms 1992.

PARENT, Henri F. (b. 1925) of Montreal, company president, served as an ACBL Director 1967-79, representative to the executive council of WBF, past president of Montreal BL, Dist 1; contributed to the organizing and sanctioning of a bridge club in a terminal patient hospital; won Canadian Nat'l Open Tms 1960, Can-Am Mens Prs, Open Tms 1967.

PARKER, Abner (Ab) (1902-1988) of Los Angeles CA, born in Russia, management consultant, former director of ACBL Charity Foundation, organized first District-wide Charity game.

PARKER, Joshua B. (b. 1956) of Briarcliff Manor NY, commodities and securities attorney, educated at Yale and NYU School of Law (JD). Served GNYBA as president and has been its general counsel since 1982. Won Mens BAM 1985 and numerous regional events.

PARKER, Steven J. (b. 1945) of Brookville MD, human resources director, graduate of U of Maryland and American U, enjoys racquetball, tennis and golf; served on Washington BL Bd of Dir 1967-77. Won World Mixed Teams 1974, Reisinger 1972, Mixed Prs 1969, 76; placed second Master Mixed Tms 1973, Reisinger 1976, GN Tms 1977. Diamond Life Master; has won 100+ regional events; has been WBL Player of Year three times.

PARKS, William C. (Bill) (b. 1949) of Butte MT, senior programmer/analyst, active in local bridge units, won Desert Classic Unmixed Swiss 1977, Open Prs 1979; Mid-Winter Holiday Swiss 1980, KO Tms 1984; Dist 18 GN Tms, Zone VI 1981.

PARTOS, George (1907-1986) of Miami Beach FL, retired bookkeeper, formerly owned one of the largest private collections of bridge books and periodicals; contributing editor, *Bridge Encyclopedia*.

PAS, Marijke van der (b. 1949) of Utrecht, The Netherlands, bridge journalist. WBF World Life Master. Second Venice Cup 1989, third World Women's Teams 1984, and represented Netherlands regularly since 1979. Second European Women's Teams 1983, 1989. Won European Women's Pairs 1980, second 1987. Won Netherlands Women's Pairs four times. Columnist, author and contributor to *Bridge*.

PASKIN, Stephen R. (Steve) (b. 1942) of South Bethlehem NY, senior research analyst, member Dist 3, Unit 115 Bd of Dir; contributes articles to *The Bridge World* and *Bridge Today*; won several regionals including Tri-State Swiss 1973, Upper NY State Master Prs 1974, 76; Capital Dist Fall Master Swiss 1977, Albany Swiss 1982, Life Master Prs 1984, Mens Prs 1991, LM

Mens Prs (only two times it was played); Stanford Swiss 1988.

PASQUINI, Paolo (b. 1944 in Italy) of Caracas, Venezuela, business executive. WBF World Master. Won CAC Teams 1977, 1984, 1985, 1986, 1987, 1991. Represented Venezuela in five world championships. More than 30 national titles include open teams 11 times and open pairs 7 times. Bridge teacher.

PASSELL, Michael (Mike) (b. 1947) of Dallas TX, professional player and computer programmer, enjoys family, sports and movies; learned to play bridge during high school vacations by watching his brother William teach bridge classes. Ranks #2 in all-time masterpoint holders; Grand Life Master with more than 33,000 MPs. WBF Grand Master; won Bermuda Bowl 1979, placed second 1977, 4th 1983; second World Tm Olympiad 1980, 4th Rosenblum Tms 1982, 9th 1978, 90; also represented US in Biarritz 1982. He and wife Nancy are one of only a handful of couples who are both world champions. Won *McKenney Trophy* (now the *Barry Crane Top 500*) 1976, Mott-Smith Trophy 1978, 83; Fishbein Trophy 1978. North American wins include Reisinger 1976, 88, 92; Vanderbilt 1978, 82; Spingold 1978, 86, 87; Open Prs 1978, 83; GN Tms 1981, Mens BAM 1986, 88, 93; IMP Prs 1988, Open Swiss 1991; placed second Vanderbilt, Life Master Prs 1976; Reisinger 1980, 90, 93; Mixed Prs 1982, Mens Prs 1983; has won several hundred regionals.

PASSELL, Nancy L. (b. 1949) of Dallas TX, professional bridge player, former teacher, graduate of Indiana U; WBF World Master, won Venice Cup 1991; she and husband Mike Passell are the only US couple to win Bermuda Bowl and Venice Cup. Won Life Master Womens Prs 1988, Womens KO Tms 1991; placed second Mixed Prs 1982, Womens KO Tms 1983; Womens BAM Tms 1988, North American Womens Swiss 1990; won numerous regional events.

PASSELL, William L. (Bill) (b. 1930) of Coral Springs FL, bridge teacher and certified director, Grand Life Master with more than 12,000 MPs; won Mixed Prs 1960, Master Mixed Tms 1972, Fishbein Trophy, Spingold 1985; placed second GN Tms 1980, North American Mens Swiss 1984; second World Bidding Contest 1969; has won 100+ regionals including 14 Florida and 6 Mexican Nat'l titles; Fall secondary Mens Tms 1968, Summer secondary Morning KO Tms 1985, Strat Open Prs 1991, Sr Prs 1993.

PATERSON, Jack of Edinburgh, Scotland, investment consultant. Represented Scotland 13 times in Camrose Trophy matches. Many national wins include Gold Cup and Scottish Cup once each.

PATIÑO, Jaime-Ortiz, See ORTIZ-PATIÑO, Jaime.

PATRIAS, Christopher (Chris) (b. 1949) of St. Louis MO, nat'l tournament director, tournament director field representative, former Director of Tournament Operations (ACBL) Headquarters, former ACBL Bridge Administrator, graduate of U of Minnesota. Won Sr/Advanced Sr Masters Prs 1972, Gopher Mens Swiss 1976, Black Hills Rodeo Swiss 1976, Dist 14 GN Tms 1979.

PATTERSON, Jean M. (formerly Wright) (b. 1947) of Memphis TN, graduate of Memphis State U, has served ACBL as a tournament coordinator, marketing coordinator, customer service supervisor, currently is manager of the ACBL Sales and Marketing Department; associate editor of *Bridge Builders Newsletter*.

PATTERSON, Lucille E. (Lucy) of Sacramento CA, secretary, won Womens Prs 1964. Diamond Life Master; regional wins include Pacific Northwest Mixed Prs 1955, Desert Empire Open Tms 1956, Inter-Mountain Open Tms 1958, Golden State Womens Prs 1967, All Western Womens Prs 1968, Bridge Week Mixed Prs 1969, Womens Prs 1972; CA Capital Swiss 1979, Rogue River Valley Mixed Prs 1976, Sacramento Womens Prs 1976, Swiss 1979, Master Prs 1987, Mixed Prs 1988, Sr Open Prs 1989; Medford Mixed Prs 1976, Redding Womens Prs 1981; San Mateo Swiss, Hawaii Womens Swiss, Santa Rosa Swiss 1987.

PATTON, Major Charles Lee (1851-1941) was a pioneer of bridge organization from 1906. Born in Mississippi, resident of New York City after 1888; originator of the Patton movement (see TEAM-OF-FOUR MOVEMENT) and one of those who claimed invention of the TAKEOUT DOUBLE.

PAUL, Abe (b. 1943) of Roswell GA, actuary, has served local unit as Appeals Committee chairman and recorder, board member. Diamond Life Master; regional wins include Bermuda Mens Prs, Nat'l Capital KO Tms 1978; Can-Am Open Prs 1980, Gatlinburg Swiss 1984, 87; Atlanta Swiss 1985, 88, Swiss 1985, 88.

PAUL, Mariana (Mary) of Toronto ON, born in Romania, accountant; WBF World Master, placed third Venice Cup 1989, 4th World Olympiad Womens Tms 1988, 7th 1980, 9th 1984; 5th Swiss Plate 1984, represented Canada in other World Championship events 1968, 72, 78, 82, 86, 91, 92. She was a member of the winning team of the first Canadian Nat'l Team Championship (CNTC) 1977, has subsequently won it 1993, second 1989. Former president of Montreal Team-of-Four BL.

PAUL, Maurice (Moose) (1923-86) of Toronto ON, born in Belgium, created the first team-of-four bridge league in North America, 1956 in Montreal. Served as member of ACBL Charity Committee, ACBL Goodwill Committee and NABC Appeals Committee. Besides his several regional wins he won the Intercity Championship (Montreal vs Chicago) 1967.

PAULS, Brian A. (b. 1940) of Winnipeg MB, attorney, graduate of U of Manitoba, legal counsel for CBF (pro tem), bridge editor for Winnipeg *Free Press* since 1962, contributing writer to *CBF News*. Won President's Cup Prs 1962, Mid-Am-Can Master Prs 1963; Summer secondary Leventritt Prs 1964, 66; Gopher Mens Prs 1966, Open Prs 1970; Winnipeg Open Prs 1966, 72, 75, Master Prs 1971, KO Tms 1972; Minneapolis Open Prs 1967, Dist 2 Tms 1974; Buffalo Mens Swiss 1976.

PAULSEN, Erik (b. 1926) of Upland CA, born in Norway, aerospace engineer, educated at Illinois Institute of Technology, College of the Armed Forces and UCLA; outside activities are golf, skiing, travel. WBF Life Master; ACBL Grand Life Master with more than 11,000 MPs as of 1993; won Bermuda Bowl 1976, second 1977; World Open Prs 1970, fourth World Tm Olympiad 1976. North American wins include Reisinger 1962, 68, 74, 75; Blue Ribbon Prs 1969; placed second Mens Prs 1959, Vanderbilt 1963, Reisinger 1966, Mens Swiss 1988; also has won many regional championships.

PAVLICEK, Richard (b. 1945) of Ft. Lauderdale FL, bridge teacher and writer; enjoys computer programming, pocket billiards and playing the organ. WBF World Master; placed 6th Rosenblum Tms 1986. ACBL Grand Life Master with more than 12,000 MPs as of 1993. Author of a variety of teaching texts and co-author of *Modern Bridge Conventions*; contributor to various bridge publications; past editor of *Gold Coast Bridge News* and *Florida Bridge News*; analyst for the Royal Viking Instant Matchpoint Prs 1987-93. Won GN Tms 1973; Reisinger 1982, 83, 84, 90; Vanderbilt 1983, 86; Open Swiss 1992; placed second Spingold 1978, GN Prs 1982, Mens Swiss 1984, GN Tms 1992.

PAVLIDES, Jordanis (1903-1985) of London, England, company director. Won Bermuda Bowl 1955, European Teams 1954. Represented Britain in one other zonal championship. National wins included Gold Cup.

PAVLOV, Anastas (b. 1927) of Sofia, Bulgaria, novelist and journalist. Devised the Apata system used by many Bulgarian players.

PAWLIK, Andreas (b.1950) of Augsburg, Germany, ophthalmologist. WBF World Master. Represented Germany in four world championships. National wins include Open Teams 8 times. Magazine contributor.

PEAKE, Lyle R. (the Rhinestone Cowboy) (1944-1994) of Culver City CA, crypto-translator, professional bridge player, teacher, director; interests include gemology and pool. Peake ran the first ACBL duplicate club in East Africa, founded the American Bridge College 1985, was appointed to Nat'l Goodwill Committee 1993. Diamond Life Master; won Western Celebrity Mens Swiss 1976, Bridge Week Master Swiss 1979, Master Prs 1989; Raincross KO Tms 1979, Las Vegas Open Swiss 1984, Pro-Am 1985; San Diego Open Swiss 1988, Super Swiss 1991, Swiss 1993; Los Angeles Stratified Prs 1990, Summer secondary IMP Prs 1991.

PEARSON, Don B. of Berkeley CA, won Mens Tms 1970; placed second Life Master Mens Prs 1968; won several regionals. Devised Pearson Point Count (see RULE OF 15) which states that fourth hand should open the bidding if the number of high card points and the number of spades total 15 or more. Fourth hand counts high card values plus one point for each spade. 13 pts = Pass, 14 is optional, 15 pts = an opener. Therefore, if you held a 10-point hand with five spades, you open; but with 12 points and one spade you pass.

PENCHARZ, William (b. 1945) of London, England, solicitor. Won four national titles including Gold Cup once. Member EBL Executive. IBPA General Counsel from 1991. Member WBF Laws Committee. Former EBL Laws Committee chairman and EBU vice-chairman.

PENDER, Peter A. (1936-1990) of Forestville CA, resort owner and executive director, served as commentator at numerous Team Trials and World Championships and as a member of numerous Appeals Committees including WBF. Pender was a United States Figure Skating Association and Canadian Figure Skating Association gold medalist and former figure skating coach. He was director of Human Rights Foundation 1977, president of Russian Business Association 1980 and an accomplished pianist. In 1966, Pender helped England's Jeremy Flint set a record by becoming a Life Master in 11 weeks. A multi-millionare, he bequeathed more than $2.26 million for AIDS research. Grand Life Master with more than 10,000 MPs; won Bermuda Bowl 1985, placed second 1989; was on 1987 Bermuda Bowl Team but was unable to play because of illness; placed second Rosenblum Cup Tms 1982; won the Pan-American Invitational Prs 1974, 75; won Team Trials 1985, 87, 89; won McKENNEY TROPHY 1966, Reisinger 1968, 70, 81, 85, 86; Life Master Mens Prs 1967, 84; GN Tms 1982, 83, 85, 87; Vanderbilt 1984, 87; placed second Mixed Prs 1964, Reisinger 1971, 83; Spingold 1974, GN Prs 1985. Was coach of U.S. World Womens Tm 1972, 76, Venice Cup team 1976; represented U.S. in Las Palmas 1974 and Biarritz 1982.

PENICK, Michael P. (b. 1947) of Dallas TX, attorney, author of *Beginning Bridge Complete* and *Beginning Bridge Quizzes* and pamphlet *Minor Suit Openings*. Won Nashville Open Swiss 1985; Dist 8 GN Tms 1985, St Louis Swiss 1993.

PENNARIO, Leonard (b. 1924) of Los Angeles CA, concert pianist, theater and film enthusiast and art collector; has performed as a soloist with all the major symphony orchestras of Europe and United States under conductors such as Fritz Reiner, Leopold Stokowsky, Otto Klemperer and Georg Solti; has played and recorded with Heifetz and Piatigorsky. Life Master; won open pairs event in Beijing, China, in 1991; placed second Fall secondary Swiss 1973, Spring secondary Open Prs 1980.

PENNINGTON, Lee H. (b. 1926) of Nashville TN, math teacher, won several ABA nat'l championships including KO Tms 1979, Open Prs Spring and Summer 1977, and several sectional (equivalent to ACBL regional) titles. An ABA tournament director since 1979, he served as NYC tournament committee chairman and as national coordinator of ABA point races.

PENROD, Dr. Darrell D. (b. 1936) of Crestview FL, professor of mechanical engineering, graduate of Northwestern, Washington State U, U of Illinois (PhD); Intercollegiate champion 1963; won Summer secondary Marcus Cup 1965, Atlanta Mens Prs 1979, Swiss 1983; Gatlinburg Open Prs 1984.

PERES, Charles (b. 1930) of Chicago, options and futures trader, won the MOREHEAD TROPHY 1967, Master Mixed Tms, Mens Prs 1969; GN Tms 1978; placed second Reisinger 1967, Open Prs 1973.

PERKINS, Frank K. (1891-1971) of Newton MA, civil engineer and bridge writer. For about 30 years he wrote daily bridge columns for the *Boston Herald*. He won wide acclaim for his chess and bridge-playing skills and writ-

ings as well as his expertise as a fly fisherman. He wrote numerous instructional texts on bridge, including *Vital Tricks at Contract Bridge, Modern Contract Standards*; served as bridge consultant to *Grolier's Encyclopedia* and the *American Heritage Dictionary*. Placed second Chicago (now the Reisinger) 1931; won New England KO Tms seven times. Founder of New England BL, he acted as its secretary, treasurer and tournament director until 1946.

PERLMAN, Howard M. (b. 1943) of Southfield MI, bridge and backgammon club owner, placed second Vanderbilt 1972 and GN Tms 1974; won many regionals.

PERLMAN, Linda M. (formerly Deaton) (b. 1945) of Bala Cynwyd PA, options trader. Diamond Life Master; won Master Mixed Tms 1987; placed second NABC Womens KO Tms 1988, 89; has won numerous regionals.

PERLMUTTER, Mark J. (b. 1960) of Redondo Beach CA, company president, degrees from U of Michigan and U of California-San Diego, won Mid-South Holiday Swiss 1979, Toast of Tulsa Master Prs 1980, Spring secondary BAM, Mid-Winter Holiday Swiss 1981; Bridge Wk Open Prs 1982, KO Tms 1983, 91; Grand Rapids Swiss 1984, Redding Mens Prs 1984; Bal Harbour Mens Prs 1988, Pasadena Winter Open Prs 1991, San Diego Strat Prs 1993.

PERLSTEIN, Lila E. (b. 1925) of Roslyn Heights NY, placed second Womens Tms 1976; won many regionals.

PERRIN, Wayne M. (b. 1952) of Gloucester ON, assistant municipal administrator, bridge teacher, held executive posts in Unit 192 1980-88, tournament chairman 1979-86, won Red Ribbon Prs 1986; won Ottawa Mens Prs 1979, North Bay Swiss 1991, Montreal Open Prs 1993.

PERRON, Michel (b. 1951) of Paris, France, bridge professional, WBF Grand Master. Won World Teams 1980, 1992. Won European Pairs 1985. Represented France in 6 other world championships and 4 other zonal championships. Won Sunday Times Invitational Pairs.

PERROUX, Carl Alberto (1905-77), trial lawyer. The most famous NPC in the history of bridge, leading the BLUE TEAM in record series of nine world championship wins from 1957 to 1966, and in five European Championship wins in the period 1951-59. He was celebrated for his tough team discipline, and was said to check that team members went to bed early and on their own. Players who violated his rules were benched, even when it hurt the team. Former president of Italian Bridge Federation. Author of *The Blue Team — Our Story of Bridge.*

PETERS, Aubrey (b. 1917) of Gweru, Zimbabwe, retired electrical engineer. Founder-member of Zimbabwe Bridge Union, and its Chairman 1968-69 and 1976. Represented Zimbabwe in many regional tournaments, and won national titles.

PETERS, Thomas J. (Tom) (b. 1943) of Houston TX, geophysicist, educated at Stetson U and U of Kentucky (PhD); has been active in local and district bridge administration since the Seventies including president of Louisana BA and Dist 16. Won Spring Open Pairs II 1994.

Placed second Open Prs, Swiss 1978. Diamond Life Master; regional wins include Midwest Mens Prs 1968, 70; Indianapolis Mens Prs 1969; South Texas Swiss 1974, San Antonio Open Prs 1975, Corpus Christi Swiss 1978, Master Prs 1983; Dist 16 GN Tms 1978, Dallas Swiss 1981, Jackson Swiss, Biloxi Open Prs 1988; Houston KO Tms 1991, Fall secondary Swiss 1992, New Orleans Swiss 1993.

PETERSON, Dr. Gary H. (b. 1946) of Louisville KY, radiologist, graduate of Ohio Wesleyan U and U of Louisville (MD); won North American Swiss 1991 and Louisville Open Prs 1992.

PETERSON, Linda, see LEWIS, Linda Marie

PETERSON, Harrison V. (Pete) (b. 1914) of Los Angeles CA, credit union general manager, retired; co-founder of ALACBU, first chairman of ALACBU Ethics Committee; set up a question and answer column in *Southern California Bridge News*; was president of the Los Angeles Unit 1959-61, 72, and 73. Regional wins include Pacific Southwest Mens Prs 1960, Open Tms 1966; Disneyland Open Tms 1970; Pasadena Sr Prs 1990, 91; Spring secondary Sr Prs 1992.

PETERSON, Olive A. (1894-1965) of St. Davids PA, outstanding player and teacher whose career spanned auction and contract bridge. She was closely associated with Milton C. Work with whom she won many auction and contract championships; she conducted one of the earliest bridge cruises with Work, 1933 on SS Carinthia. She was subsequently associated with Charles Goren. President Womens Nat'l Committee 1939, vice-president Womens Auxiliary of ABL 1936 and ACBL secretary 1951. Her National Auction Bridge titles include Womens Prs 1931, Womens Teams 1932. In contract she won Womens Prs 1930, 32, 45; Womens Tms 1938, 43; Mixed Tms 1940, 42, 43, 44; Mixed Prs 1943. Placed second in Womens Prs 1935, Womens Tms 1953. Her writings include *Work-Peterson Accurate Valuation System, 101 Celebrated Hands, Simplified Digest of Culbertson System* and *Common-Sense Contract*.

PETTERSON, Kelsey (1911-1983) of Las Vegas NV, retired attorney, member of ACBL Board of Directors 1967-70, former president and attorney of WESTERN CONFERENCE. Petterson was npc of the Los Angeles team in *Sports Illustrated* Trophy matches. Represented North America Bermuda Bowl 1965, won Mens Tms, placed second Vanderbilt; had numerous regional titles.

PETTIJOHN, Fran of Indianapolis IN, placed second Womens Tms; won many regionals.

PETTIT, Randall S. (Randy) (b. 1943) of Marietta GA, financial planner, president of Unit 114. Diamond Life Master; regional wins include Birmingham Mens Swiss 1977, Pine Mountain Open Swiss 1978, Roanoke Mens Prs 1979, Nashville Mens Swiss 1981, Gatlinburg Mens Prs, Open Prs (smoking) 1982; Atlanta Swiss, KO Tms 1982, Mens Prs 1987, Open Prs 1991; Columbia Open Prs (smoking), Norfolk Open Prs 1983; Dist 7 GN Tms 1991, 93, GN Prs 1992, Washington Open Prs 1993.

PFLUCKER, Alicia of Lima, Peru, psychiatrist. Won South American Teams 1969. Represented Peru in one world championship and many zonal championships, both open and women's divisions. Won many national titles.

PHILLIPS, Duncan R. (b. 1930) of Toronto, lawyer, WBF Life Master, placed third World Tm Olympiad 1973; represented Canada in international competition 1962, 66, 86; founder and first president of the Metropolitan Toronto BA.

PHILLIPS, Hubert (1891-1964) of London, England was editor of *British Bridge World* 1936-1939 and one of the pioneers of bridge organization in England. For many years he was internationally the most eminent author of intellectual and mathematical puzzles under the names "Caliban" and "Dogberry," and of cryptic crosswords. He authored some 70 books on various subjects including general knowledge quiz books and detective stories, and was the resident expert on Britain's most famous radio quiz program. Essayist and lead writer for the London *News Chronicle*, Phillips' many bridge writings include *Brush Up Your Bridge, The Elements of Contract, Bridge at Ruff's Club*, and *Bridge with Goren*. See Bibliography, E, H, L.

PHILLIPS, James L. (b. 1935) of Chicago IL, buyer, former president of Chicago CBA; Diamond Life Master. Won New England Master Tms 1961, Spring secondary BAM 1966, Swiss 1972; Fall Open Prs 1966, Midwest Spring Open Teams 1970, Motor City Open Tms, Hawaii Mixed Prs 1971; Pheasant Swiss 1972, Central States Master Prs 1973, Life Master KO Tms 1978, BAM 1981; Tri-Unit Mens Prs 1974, Dist 13 GN Tms 1976, Wisconsin Open Prs 1981, Swiss 1982.

PIASKI, E. John (b. 1945) of Raleigh NC, certified public accountant, graduate of North Carolina State U; won Mid-Atlantic Summer KO Tms 1973, Swiss 1975, Mens Swiss, Open Prs 1979, Fall KO Tms 1973, Swiss 1973, 75, Spring KO Tms 1975. Piaski's father competed with Jesse Owens in the early Thirties.

PICHLER, Ernst (b. 1950) of Weiz (Styria), Austria, entrepreneur. NPC Austrian women's team which won European Team 1991 and placed second Venice Cup 1991. Represented Austria in European Junior Teams 1974. Winner of European Simultaneous Pairs and runner-up Epson Pairs. Won Austrian Teams once and Open Pairs three times.

PICKETT, Randy (b. 1946) of Portland OR, attorney, graduated U of Arizona and U of Oregon (JD); won Oregon Trail Master Swiss 1979, Swiss 1980, Swiss 1981, 82, KO Tms 1982; Dist 20 GN Tms 1977, 79, 83, 84, 87, 91, 92; Dist 20 GN Prs 1981, 85, 91.

PICUS, Susan J. (Sue) (b. 1948) of New York City, computer scientist, graduate of NYU and U of Wisconsin; board member Greater NY BA 1990-present. WBF World Master; won Venice Cup 1991, 93; also competed internationally Las Palmas 1972, Bal Harbour 1986, Geneva 1990. Her nat'l titles include Master Mixed Teams 1971, Womens BAM 1972, North American Womens Swiss 1986, Womens KO Tms 1991; placed second in USWBC 1991, Womens Prs 1983, Womens KO Tms 1985, 91;

Womens Swiss 1990. Regional wins include Spring secondary Womens Swiss, Keystone Open Prs 1973; Roughrider KO Tms, Dist 15 Swiss 1975; Gopher Swiss 1976, Mad City Womens Swiss 1979, Puerto Rico Swiss 1978, 84, 85, Master Prs 1984; New York Winter Swiss 1988, 2-Day Swiss 1991; Rye Swiss 1992.

PIETRI, Luis (b. 1931) of Philadelphia PA, insurance salesman, one of the top-ranking players in the AMERICAN BRIDGE ASSOCIATION, won ABA Open Tms 1968, 70, 72, 78; Open Prs 1963, 66, 68, 72, 73 and all other major titles at least once. He has had a number of ACBL regional wins also.

PIGOT, David R. (1900-1965) of Dublin, Ireland, solicitor, was CBAI champion between 1936 and 1949, and represented Ireland in international events both as player and as npc. He served as president CBAI 1946, vice president 1955-65; member of WBC Executive Committee, member of EBL Executive Committee 1952-65 and chairman of EBL Tournament Committee 1957-65. He contributed to the revision of the IMP scale and to the preparation of 1964 Olympiad regulations. He was a member of the Editorial Advisory Board, *Bridge Encyclopedia*.

PIGOT, Peter (b. 1932) of Dublin, Ireland, economist, represented Ireland in the World Open Pairs 1962, 66; European Championships 65, 67, 69, 70, 71, 73, 74, 75. National wins include all major championships.

PILON, Dominique (b. 1950) of Paris, France, bridge teacher. WBF World Master. Won World Teams 1982. Won European Mixed Teams 1992. Represented France in three other world championships and won several national titles.

PILTCH, Howard J. of Andover MA, licensed real estate and insurance broker; member ACBL Bd of Dir for Dist 25; Diamond Life Master; regular lecturer at NABCs on *Shape, Beautiful Shape* and *Balance, Baby, Balance!* Author of many articles dealing with competitive and constructive bidding, developed Piltch Over NT. Placed second Mens BAM 1976; has won more than 100 regional events.

PINARD, Janet (b. 1949 in England) of Gaborone, Botswana. Represented Botswana in two world championships. Won several national events. Secretary of Botswana Bridge League and Editor of its newsletter. Writes for *Botswana Guardian, Midweek Sun* and formerly for *Newslink Africa.*

PINCUS, Carol (b. 1930) of Los Angeles CA, business school administrative assistant; interested in theater, concerts and reading. WBF World Master; finished 5th World Womens Olympiad Tms, sixth World Womens Prs, seventh World Mixed Prs 1982; represented ACBL São Paulo in 1985, Perth 1989. Diamond Life Master; has won Womens KO Tms 1984, 88; North American Womens Swiss 1988; finished second North American Womens Swiss 1986, North American Swiss 1987, Womens BAM 1989. Regional wins include Bridge Week Master Prs, Swiss, Womens Swiss.

PINTO, Rui (b. 1941) of Oporto, Portugal. WBF World Master. Represented Portugal in one world championship and four European Championships. National wins include open teams three times.

PIRO, Evelyn (d. 1990) of Federal Way WA, apartment house owner and manager, was one of the pioneers of bridge organization in the Northwest; responsible for starting several tournaments and various units and clubs. Chairman of the Seattle Unit 1949, 50, Portland Unit 1950, 51, co-chairman ACBL Goodwill Committee 1962, ACBL Director 1958-61, 1964.

PITTALA, Vito (b. 1927) of Turin, Italy, professor of mechanical engineering. WBF Grand Master. Won Bermuda Bowl 1973, 1975, second 1976, 1979. Won European Teams 1979. Italian national wins include open teams six times.

PLATNICK, Brian Scott (b. 1966) of Williamsburg VA, law student, former industrial engineer, graduate of Virginia Tech, became a certified club director at the age of 17 and was director and club manager of duplicate BC for two years while in high school. Member of Junior Corps, WBF World Master; won NEC World Jr Trn Championship 1991. Regional wins include Roanoke Master Prs 1985, Arlington non-smoking Open Prs, Columbia Swiss 1986; Cherry Hill Swiss, KO Tms 1989; Alexandria KO Tms 1989, Williamsburg Swiss 1991.

POE, Edgar Allan (1809-1849) American poet and critic, wrote a number of stories on mystery and occultism. He was interested in detection, cryptology and whist. In his famous detective story, *The Purloined Letter*, he embodied a fine analysis of the mental aspects of whist in the plot. He also discussed whist at some length in *The Murders in the Rue Morgue.*

POLAK, Ebi J. (1912-86) of Antwerp, Belgium, diamond dealer and bridge columnist. Represented Belgium in four world championships and 11 European Championships. Many national wins included open teams 8 times and open pairs 3 times.

POLAK, Gunther (b. 1933) of Chicago IL, insurance investigator. Placed second Blue Ribbon Prs 1964; won Golder Prs 1961 and many regional events.

POLAK, Milos (b. 1932) of Waterloo ON, born in Czechoslovakia, accountant, bridge club manager and teacher, represented Czechoslovakia in several int'l contests. His nat'l titles include Czechoslovakian Open Tms 1960, 61, 62, 63, 64, 65, 67, Open Prs 1961, 63, Mixed Prs 1962. Polak was the co-founder of the CZECHOSLOVAK BRIDGE ASSOCIATION in 1961, its vice president and secretary general 1961-68 and co-founder of the European Jr Championship 1968. He is the former editor of the Czechoslovak bridge magazine.

POLEC, Janusz (b. 1939) of Warsaw, Poland, mechanical engineer. WBF World Life Master. Won World Teams 1978. Represented Poland in one other world championship and five zonal championships. Won Del Duca and many national titles.

POLET, Guy (b. 1949 in Zaire) of Brussels, Belgium, civil engineer. Represented Belgium in three European championships and six Common Market Championships. National wins include open teams three times and open pairs once.

POLET, Valerie (b. 1961) of Brussels, Belgium. Won European Junior Teams 1984. Won Common Market Mixed Teams 1991 and represented Belgium on other occasions. National wins include open teams once.

POLISNER, Jeffrey D. (Jeff) (b. 1939) of Lafayette CA, attorney, became the counsel general of the ACBL 1985 and of the WBF 1992. He was president of Unit 499 1980, 81; president of Dist 21 1983-84, chairman of Dist 21 Judiciary and Conduct and Ethics Committee 1981. Was appointed to NABC Appeals Committee 1979 and ACBL Laws Commission 1982. WBF World Master; ACBL Diamond Life Master; was npc of winning GN Tms 1982, placed second Open Prs 1989, Life Master Open Prs 1993; won numerous regional events.

POLLACK, Dr. Rozanne (Mrs. William, formerly Marel) (b. 1948) of Englewood Cliffs NJ, sociologist, graduate of Radcliffe and Columbia (PhD); WBF World Master; placed third World Mixed Prs 1986, 14th World Womens Pairs 1990; placed second in *The Bridge World* Challenge of the Decade (with husband Bill); placed second USWBC 1985; Diamond Life Master; has won several nat'l competitions including Master Mixed Tms 1985, North American Womens Swiss 1986, Womens BAM 1988, Womens KO Tms 1990, 93; finished second Womens Prs 1981, Womens KO Tms 1985, Womens BAM 1986, 87; Master Mixed Teams 1991; has won dozens of regionals.

POLLACK, William L. (Bill) (b. 1951) of Englewood Cliffs NJ, computer software executive, graduate of Columbia U; served as co-chairman of NABC Appeals Committee 1984-90 and as a member of the Bd of Dir of the Greater New York BA. Was second in *The Bridge World* Challenge of the Decade (with wife Rozanne); became the youngest ACBL tournament director ever in 1967 at the age of 16. Placed third World Mixed Prs 1986; WBF World Master. On the nat'l level he was second in USBC (Team Trials) 1989, 91; won Master Mixed Teams 1985, Vanderbilt 1990; placed second Reisinger 1987. Winner of Romex Award for Best Bid Hand of 1992/93. Diamond Life Master; has won dozens of regional titles.

POLLARD, Evelyn represented Zimbabwe in two world championships and one zonal championship. Represented Zimbabwe in many regional tournaments and won national titles.

POLLENZ, Emmett (b. 1926) of East Meadow NY, manufacturers' representative, graduate of CCNY, member of Nassau/Suffolk BA Bd for more than 20 years. Won Eastern States Manhattan Prs 1964, IMP Prs 1992; New England Individual KO Tms, Westchester Swiss 1981; Dist 3 Split (Secaucus) Open Swiss 1990, Spring secondary Swiss 1991.

POLOWAN, Michael (b. 1958) of New York City, professional bridge player, graduate of New York U. Won Forbo (Netherlands) and placed second twice, won Prix des Nations in Luxembourg, won open pairs at Israeli National Bridge Festival, second twice in Icelandair

Teams, won first Green Point Pairs (cash prize tournament) in New York City, also has won more than 50 other regionals.

POLUNSKY, Harry (1895-1972) of San Angelo TX, was a food merchant who owned one of the largest private collections of books on playing cards and games played with them. He was a contributor to various magazines and a contributing editor to *Bridge Encyclopedia*.

PONTIOUS, Frances (Bitsy) (1911-1988) of Beaumont TX, former medical secretary; first president Unit 201 in 1957 and its executive secretary 1966-80; won Mixed Prs 1962.

POPLAWSKI, Mary McColl (b. 1945) of Endicott NY, bridge club owner and ACBL-accredited bridge teacher, graduate of U of Vermont, won GN Tms Flt B 1991 and Syracuse Womens Swiss 1985.

POPLAWSKI, Stanley M. (Stan) (b. 1940) of Endicott NY, computer programmer, graduate of Penn State; won GN Tms Flt B 1991 and Summer secondary Commercial and Industrial Tms 1973.

POPPER, Leslie A. (Les) (b. 1937) of Peabody MA, born in Hungary, computer scientist, graduated from West Virginia U and MIT. Past president of Dist 25 and Eastern Mass. BA. Diamond Life Master; won New England KO Tms 1965, 69, Master Prs 1974, Master Swiss 1977, Summer KO Tms 1982, Fall KO Tms 1982; Keystone Open Tms 1966, Fall Mens Prs 1969; Mid-Atlantic Spring Open Tms 1967, Canadian Nat'l Master Prs 1969, Fun City KO Tms 1972, Keohane KO Tms 1978, 79.

PORTER, Louise S., of Pasadena TX, retired real estate broker. Regional wins include; Billings Swiss 1985, Bermuda Open Swiss 1986, Baton Rouge KO Tms 1986, Anchorage Mixed Prs 1986, Saint John KO Tms 1989; New Orleans Swiss 1989, Daytona Beach KO Tms 1990, Spring secondary Sr KO Tms, Sr Swiss 1991; Sun Valley KO Tms, Swiss 1991; Bethesda Sr Prs, Sr Swiss 1991; Hawaii KO Tms 1992.

PORTUGAL, Helen (Mrs. Morris) (1919-1986) of Los Angeles CA. Placed second World Womens Tms 1964, represented U.S. in Turin 1960, Cannes 1962. Won Mixed Prs 1951, 53; Life Master Prs 1960, Life Master Womens Prs 1961, Master Mixed Tms 1962, Womens Tms 1969; placed second Womens Tms 1959, 63, 64; Womens Prs 1961, Vanderbilt 1964. See also LIFE MASTER.

PORTUGAL, Morris (Port) (b. 1916) of Los Angeles CA, professional bridge player/teacher, served on Los Angeles Unit Board 1947-48, Westwood Unit 1949-59, member of ACBL Goodwill Committee since 1960. Grand Life Master with more than 15,000 MPs; North American wins include Mixed Prs 1953, Mixed Tms 1954, Life Master Prs 1960; placed second Mens Prs 1947, Vanderbilt 1964, Mixed Prs 1965. Has had hundreds of regional wins including the first Los Angeles Bridge Wk 4-session Open Prs 1946. See also LIFE MASTER.

POTTAGE, John F. (b. 1964) of London, England, accountant, won World Jr Championship 1989, Common Market Jr Championship 1985, 89, represented England on many occasions in int'l competition; nat'l wins include the Crockford Cup, Spring Fours and Tollemache. Co-inventor of Pottage defense to 1 NT.

POTTAGE, Julian Y. (b. 1962) of Basingstoke, England, pension plan manager, photographer, bridge teacher and writer; won Pachabo Cup 1982, Jr Camrose Trophy 1984; captain of winning Cambridge team in the varsity match vs Oxford in 1983. Co-inventer of Pottage defense to 1NT; discovered COMPOUND GUARD SQUEEZE. Author of *Clues from the Bidding* and co-author with Terence Reese of *Positive Defense, Positive Declarer's Play* and *The Extra Edge in Play.*

POUZADA, José (1950-88) of Portugal, systems analyst. Represented Portugal in one world championship, one European Championship and one European Junior Championship. Won national open teams once.

POWELL, Richard P. (Dick) (b. 1908) of Fort Myers FL, novelist, graduate of Princeton; author of *Tickets to the Devil,* a bridge novel published in 1968; foreign editions have been published in England, Scandinavia, Germany and Italy. Powell, a certified director since 1970, is manager (since 1973) and past president of the Coconut DBC. A writer since 1930, he is the author of 19 published novels, four of which have been made into movies: *The Philadelphian,* filmed as *The Young Philadelphians; Pioneer, Go Home!,* filmed as *Follow That Dream; Don Quixote, U.S.A.,* filmed as *Bananas;* and *The Build-Up Boys* (published under the pen name Jeremy Kirk), filmed as *Madison Avenue.* See BIBLIOGRAPHY I.

PRALL, Jack W. (b. 1914) of Lakeland FL, retired postal clerk, one of founders of Dist 12, former president and vice president of Dist 12 and of the Northern Ohio BA; Dist 12 representative to ACBL Bd of Dir 1963-65.

PRATT, John M. (b. 1904) of Flint MI, scholar, retired teacher and General Motors executive; graduated from high school at age 16 as class valedictorian with the highest grades ever from that school, educated at Allegheny College, Boston U and Harvard (PhD), enjoys golf and travel. Pratt was named chairman of ACBL Goodwill Committee 1979 and served until 1984. He is a former president of Unit 200, Heart of America BC, and former vice president of the Hartford BC. Pratt organized other bridge clubs and has chaired sectional and regional tournaments and has taught bridge to thousands in the Flint area. In 1973 he did a series of 10 bridge lessons on TV.

PRICE, Robert J. (Bob) of Chicago IL, real estate broker, bridge professional, graduate of Alabama State U; enjoys singing gospel music and is a member of barber shop family quartet. Served as member Chicago CBA 1972-78, national vice president of AMERICAN BRIDGE ASSOCIATION 1988-89, president 1990-91. In 1978 for seven consecutive months he successfully "Challenged the Champs" in *The Bridge World.* #1 player in the ABA since 1965 with more than 19,000 MPs and has played for 25 years with the same partner, Joyce Williams. Won ABA Victor Daley KO Tms eight times, ABA Nat'l Open Prs 10 times, Mixed Prs nine times, Swiss seven times; won William Friend Award (equivalent to Crane Top 500) eight straight years 1972-79 and is annually one of the top finishers.

PRICE, Steven T. (b. 1951) of Safety Harbor FL, CFO, graduate of Swarthmore College, Southern Illinois U, Cal State; served as Dist 21 treasurer 1984-87. Placed second Blue Ribbon Prs 1993; won All-Western KO Tms, Master Tms 1977; Mid-Winter Holiday KO Tms 1977, Open Prs 1980, IMP Prs 1991; Dist 21 GN Tms 1980, GN Prs 1982, Sacramento Prs 1989, Santa Rosa Prs, Atlanta Prs 1992.

PRIDAY, Angela Jane (Mrs. Richard A., formerly Mrs. Jane Juan) (b. 1936) of London, England. WBF World Life Master. Won World Women's Teams 1964, World Women's Pairs 1966. Won European Women's Teams 1961, 1963, 1966, and represented Britain in one other world championship and four other zonal championships. Played in Camrose matches; seven national titles include Gold Cup 1972.

PRIDAY, Richard Anthony (Tony) (b. 1922) of London, England, chairman of hardwood company. WBF World Life Master. Third Bermuda Bowl 1962, World Teams 1976; Won European Teams 1961, second 1971. Represented Britain in two other world championships and six other zonal championships. Won *Sunday Times Invitational Pairs* 1970, and played in 28 Camrose matches. More than 15 national titles include Gold Cup seven times. Former British League chairman and held other executive positions. Columnist for *Sunday Telegraph.* See BUENOS AIRES AFFAIR.

PRISYON, Jerome B. (Jerry) (b. 1927) of Valley Stream NY, sales manager, bridge cruise lecturer, bridge administrator, Board member and former president of Greater New York BA; originated novice program for GNYBA which included printed hand analyses. This idea was later adopted and expanded by ACBL. Former regional tournament director.

PROMBOIN, Ronald L. (Ron) (b. 1945) of Chicago IL, economist, graduated Williams College and Stanford U (PhD) Phi Beta Kappa; former contributor to Palo Alto *Kibitzer;* won All-Western Mens Swiss 1973, Open Prs 1979, Hawaii Mens Prs, Swiss 1973; Dist 21 GN Tms 1974.

PROTHRO, James Thomason (Tommy) (b. 1920) of Memphis TN, football coach, graduated with three degrees from Duke U, in many "Halls of Fame" including the Nat'l Football Foundation, was named national Coach of the Year; was a blocking back for Duke and went on to coach football at Oregon State U, UCLA and subsequently for Los Angeles Rams and San Diego Chargers. He retired as executive vice president of Cleveland Browns in 1982. Regional wins include Rocky Mountain KO Tms 1969, Mexican Nat'l Swiss 1972, Golden Gate Mens Prs 1972.

PRUITT, Mitchell K. (Mitch) (b. 1955) of Chugiak AK, company president, graduate of Chapman College, has won 15-20 regional events including Anchorage Open Prs 1988, Swiss 1991, 93, KO Tms 1991, Master Prs 1993; Wichita Bracketed KO Tms 1992.

PRZYBORA, Tomasz (b. 1949) of Warsaw, bridge professional. WBF World Life Master. Won World Teams 1984. Won European Teams 1981, European Pairs 1989.

Represented Poland in five other world championships and one other zonal championship. Won many national titles.

PUIG-DORIA, Evelio (b.1924) of Barcelona, advertising executive. Former president Spanish Bridge Federation. Represented Spain in three world championships and six zonal championships. Won many national titles.

PUTNAM, Roger (b. 1942) of Redmond WA, national tournament director and TD field representative; began directing career in 1967, became associate nat'l 1977 and achieved present rating in 1985.

PUTTAERT, Louis (b. 1914) of Brussels, Belgium, bridge teacher. Represented Belgium in three world championships and six European championships. National wins include open teams four times.

Q

QUANTIN, Jean-Christophe (b. 1966) of Paris, France, bridge trainer. WBF World Master. French junior team organizer. Second World Junior Teams 1987, third 1989. Won European Pairs 1991, 1993. Second European Teams 1989. Won European Junior Teams 1988. Represented France three other world championships and won some national titles.

QUEEN, Frank C. (b. 1940) of Englewood CO, teacher, author of the monthly bridge column *It's Only a Game* in District 17 *Contract Bridge Forum*; has been member of District 17 Bd of Dir since 1985 and is a past president, served as a member of Unit 361 Bd of Dir 1979-88, president 1980-88, first alternate to ACBL Bd of Dir 1991 to present, member ACBL Bd of Gov 1991 to present, has been a member of ACBL Goodwill Committee since 1990 and is a member of ACBL Nat'l Charity Committee.

QUINLAN, Thomas J. (T.Q.) (b. 1942) of San Mateo CA, national tournament director, TD field representative, graduate of U of California-Berkeley and Cal State-Hayward; began directing career in 1964 and attained nat'l ranking 1987; has been director-in-charge at NABCs since 1991; past president of PROFESSIONAL TOURNAMENT DIRECTORS ASSOCATION; served as Dist 21 GN Prs and GN Tms coordinator 1974 to 1991; was editor of *Contract Bridge Forum* from 1970 to 1981 and of Dist 21 edition from 1967-81; won Gem State Mens Prs 1972.

QUINN, Anne of Dublin, Ireland, civil servant, has represented Ireland as a player and captain of the women's team from 1959. She won EEC Women's Pairs 1981. National titles include Women's Teams many times and Mixed Pairs, Women's Pairs, Open Pairs, Open Teams several times.

QUINN, Joe (b. 1950) of Irvine CA, chemical engineer, graduated Louisiana Tech, won North American Swiss 1993. Regionals include Fall secondary Open Swiss 1976, Bridge Wk Midnight Open KO Tms 1990, KO Tms 1990, 91, 93; Dist 22 GN Tms 1991, Denver Open Prs 1992, BAM 1993; San Bernardino KO Tms 1993.

QUINN, Terry (b. 1945) of Washington, novelist, former editor and ghostwriter, authored *The Great Bridge Conspiracy*.

QUIROGA, Sonia Ramirez de (b. 1939) of Cochabamba, Bolivia, secretary. Won South American Women's Pairs 1988 and several national titles. Represented Bolivia in 12 zonal championships. Organizer of 40th South American Championships. Former president Bolivian Bridge Association.

R

RABINOWITZ, Marc A. (b. 1949) of Hudson OH, auditor, graduate of U of Pittsburgh; won Pittsburgh Open Prs 1966, 73, 75, Swiss, KO Tms 1976; Spokane Open Prs 1974, Cincinnati Swiss 1974, KO Tms 1981; Washington DC Mens Prs 1978, Cleveland Swiss, KO Tms 1980; Columbus Swiss 1981, All-American KO Tms 1992.

RADIN, Judi (formerly Solodar, nee Friedenberg) (b. 1950) of New York City, bridge teacher and professional player, graduate of Columbia U. Contributing editor to *Precision Newsletter* and is co-author of *Precision Club*. World Womens Prs champion 1978, won the World Womens Team Olympiad 1984, Venice Cup 1987; placed second Venice Cup 1981, 85; World Womens Prs 1990. Ranked in the top five of women WBF masterpoint holders for the period of 1982-91; WBF Grand Master, ACBL Grand Life Master with more than 10,000 masterpoints. ACBL championships: Womens BAM 1971, Spring Womens KO Tms 1977, 80, 83; Womens Prs 1978, KO Tms 1987; Swiss 1983; placed second Reisinger 1974, Vanderbilt 1979, Womens KO Tms 1982, Master Mixed Tms 1983, Life Master Womens Prs 1984, Womens Swiss 1985, Womens BAM 1986, North American Swiss 1991.

RADIN, Michael (b. 1950) of New York City, attorney, graduated MIT and NYU School of Law (JD), Served on GNYBA Bd of Dir 1977-1983 and was vice-president 1981; placed 11th World Mixed Prs 1982, and competed in Bal Harbour 1986, Geneva 1990. Finished second Master Mixed Tms 1991; has won dozens of regional competitions including Eastern States KO Tms 1983, Dist 1 GN Tms 1985, Goldman Prs 1989.

RADJEF, Tarek Lucien (b. 1937) of Dallas TX, born in France, entrepreneur, formerly an electrical engineer, graduate of Oklahoma State U; won Mid-South Mens Prs 1969, Open Prs 1973, Swiss 1978; Motor City Swiss, Harvest Festival KO Tms, Lone Star Mens Prs 1977; Texas Labor Day Master Prs 1979.

RAENKHAM, Thawee (b. 1907) of Bangkok, Thailand, retired professor. Represented Thailand in six zonal championships, won all Thailand national titles in period 1951-81. President Thailand CBL 1951-66, and its #3 ranked player. Thailand's Deputy Minister of the Interior 1958-67.

RAFF, Dr. Barrett J. (b. 1938) of Johnson City NY, dentist, graduate of Brooklyn College of Pharmacy and U of Maryland-College of Dental School (DDS) won GN Tms Flt B 1991. Also won Stamford Open Prs 1988, Swan Lake

Swiss Flt B 1985.

RAGAZZO, Vincent L. (b. 1938) of Las Vegas NV, retired computer analyst, graduated U of Michigan; won Canadian Nat'l Open Tms 1972, 81; Can-Am Mens Prs 1976, Midwest Spring Mens Prs 1981, Mid-Atlantic Master Prs, Dist 12 Swiss 1984; Dist 4 Mens Prs 1985, Great Lakes Master Swiss 1986.

RAINWATER, Ross (b. 1948) of Portland OR, bridge club operator, former professional bridge player; has served as member of Portland Unit Bd 1987-1992. Grand Life Master with more than 11,000 masterpoints as of 1993; he has won more than 200 regional titles including Oregon Trail KO Tms 1977, 78, 80, Open Prs 1978; Fall secondary Master Prs 1978, Swiss 1981; Big Sky Swiss 1979, KO Tms 1981; Puget Sound Swiss, KO Tms 1981.

RALCA, Danilo (b. 1940) of Maribor, Slovenia, engineer and architect. He is the highest ranked Slovenian player, with 17 national wins and many international successes.

RALPH, Mark P. (b. 1946) of San Francisco CA, US Department of Defense investigator, graduated St. Mary's College, Cal State U Sacramento. Won Dist 22 GN Tms 1973, 76; Bakersfield Master Prs, Las Vegas Swiss 1974; California Capital Swiss, All Western Master Prs 1980; Sacramento Open Prs 1986, 92; Modesto Swiss 1992; Wine Country IMP/BAM Tms 1993.

RAMSEY, Guy (d. 1959) of London, England, was a journalist and author. His writings include *Aces All* and many magazine articles. Bridge editor for London *Daily Telegraph*, Ramsey was the first president of European (now International) Bridge Press Association (1958-1959).

RAND, Alfred (Al) (b. 1907) of New York City, investment manager, graduate U of Pennsylvania-Wharton School, enjoys philharmonic concerts, theater and golf; represented US in world competition Las Palmas 1974, New Orleans 1978, Bal Harbour 1986. Diamond Life Master; won Mens BAM Tms 1982, placed second Mens Swiss 1986 and has won more than 20 regionals.

RAND, Rita L. (Mrs. Alfred) of New York City, investor, graduate of Goucher College, has had poems published in the *New Yorker,* represented US in world competition Las Palmas 1974, New Orleans 1978, Bal Harbour 1986. Placed second in North American Swiss 1988, 89 and has won more than 20 regionals.

RANDALL, Winslow H. (1897-1983) of Redlands CA, was ACBL president in 1959; president of WESTERN CONFERENCE in 1955; served as ACBL Director for many years.

RANDEL, Judith C. (Judy) (b. 1936) of Albuquerque NM, certified bridge teacher and director, enjoys cross-country skiing and was a MIA wife for ten years, still active in Nat'l League of Families. Has served as a member of ACBL Bd of Gov since 1985, president of Unit 374 1976-77, Dist 17 recorder since 1986 and on ACBL Nat'l Bd of Appeals for 7 years. Diamond Life Master, has been top masterpoint holder in New Mexico since

1968. Won Womens BAM Tms 1990 and was 4th in Pan American Womens Prs 1992. Her many regionals include Albuquerque Master Womens Prs 1967, El Paso KO Tms 1974, Denver BAM Tms 1975, Dist 8 Womens Swiss 1985, Indianapolis Womens Swiss 1985, Rocky Mtn Open Prs, Unmixed Prs 1985; St. Louis Swiss 1985, Dist 17 GN Prs 1986, Lake Geneva Womens KO Tms 1986, Amarillo Swiss 1987, Central States Womens Swiss 1987, Desert Empire Swiss 1987, Navajo Trail KO Tms 1991.

RANDLES, Janice R. (b. 1934) of Redmond WA, bridge teacher, director and club owner. Won Womens BAM Tms 1987 and finished second in the USWBC (team trials) 1988. Randles has also won several regional events.

RANK, Peter C. (b. 1938) of Los Angeles, attorney and former California State Health director, graduate of Stanford and U of California School of Law at Berkeley. Retired from bridge in 1978. He was a member of the top masterpoint winning pair 1964-75 with BARRY CRANE. Rank won the McKENNEY TROPHY 1965 and won the Spring Mens Prs 1966, Open Prs 1977; Mixed Prs 1968; placed second in Master Mixed Tms 1969. He also won many regional titles. For more than two decades, he has produced fund-raising shows featuring many major celebrities such as Bob Hope, Betty Ford, Steve Allen, Tommy Tune and Gene Kelly. Rank is a former president of Dist 21 and was a commentator at NADCs and internat'l tournaments 1968 to 1980. He developed bridge musicals as entertainment for many NABCs. He has written, scored and produced five productions that were based on Broadway musicals: *My Fair Little Old Lady, The Lesser Vice (Guys and Dolls), Partnership! Partnership! (Kiss Me Kate), There Is Nothing Like a Game* and *Annie Bid Your Slam.*

RAPEE, George (b. 1915) of New York City, attorney and real estate investor, WBF Grand Master, ACBL Diamond Life Master, Life Master #44; inventor of the STAYMAN convention, which shares with BLACKWOOD the distinction of being the most widely played conventions throughout the world. Bermuda Bowl champion 1950, 51, 53; third in Rosenblum Tms 1990; also represented North America in Bermuda Bowl 1958, 59 and the U.S. in Turin 1960. He won the Team Trials and the FISHBEIN TROPHY 1968. Rapee had the best record of success in the three major team championships for the years 1942-80; winning 21 and finishing second in 18. Won the Spingold 1944, 48, 50, 52, 57, 68; Chicago (now the Reisinger) 1945, 47, 53, 54, 56; Reisinger 1970, 71; Vanderbilt 1946, 50, 51, 55, 56, 57, 59, 70; second in Vanderbilt 1942, 44, 52, 65, 67; Spingold 1943, 47, 55, 60, 61, 66, 76, 80; Chicago 1947, 48, 50; Reisinger 1968, 69, 72. His other national wins are Master Individual 1944, 49; Master Mixed Tms 1960; Mens BAM Tms 1975; placed second in Mens BAM Tms 1946, 48, 72; Mens Prs 1945, 50; Mixed Prs 1955; Master Mixed Tms 1952, 68.

RAPOPORT, Alexander J. (b. 1952) of Kharkov, Ukraine, mathematician. Won USSR Open Teams 1990, 1991, Ukrainian Open Pairs 1992. Represented Ukraine 1990 Goodwill Games.

RAPPAPORT, Barbara. See HABERMAN, Barbara.

RAPPLEYEA, Fred A. (b. 1918) of Houston TX, retired corporate executive, graduate of Villanova and U of Southern California; won All American Open Tms 1954, 57; Central States Open Tms 1956, Open Prs 1958; Great Lakes Open Prs 1959, Gopher Open Prs 1961, Rocky Mountain Open Prs 1965, Summer secondary Sr KO Tms 1990, Open Prs 1993; St Louis Open Prs 1991, Hot Springs Swiss 1993; and many other Swiss team events.

RASE, Davor (b. 1952) of Zagreb, Croatia, chemical engineer. Represented Yugoslavia in one world championship and three European championships. Won three national team titles. Founder president of Croatian Bridge Federation.

RASKIN, Raymond L. (b. 1943) of King of Prussia PA, chemist, graduated from St Joseph's and Temple; past president of Dist 4 and the Philadelphia CBA, served as Dist 4 recorder 1970-80 and chairman ACBL Appeals and Charges committee 1990, ACBL Bylaws and Regulations committee 1991. He served on the ACBL Bd of Gov 1983-86 and has been a member of the ACBL Bd of Dir since 1986. Won Keystone KO Tms 1973, Dist 4 GN Tms 1973, 79; Dist 4 Mens Swiss, Mens Prs 1978; Swiss 1979, Mens Swiss 1981, Spring Mens Swiss 1980, 82, KO Tms 1990; Fall secondary Swiss 1980, Spring Swiss 1993; recipient of Foering Trophy 1970, 71.

RASMIDATTA, Vibul (b. 1928) of Bangkok, Thailand, retired banker. Far East champion 1965, represented Thailand on four other occasions and in two world championships. He was the Epson winner in Thailand 1989, 1991, and has won all national titles.

RASMUS, Patricia A. (b. 1948) of Hamburg NY, school teacher, won Non-Life Master Swiss 1985.

RASMUS, Richard J. (b. 1942) of Hamburg NY, chemist, won Non-Life Master Swiss 1985.

RASMUSSEN, Arild (b. 1961) of Bergen, Norway, computer consultant. Second Bermuda Bowl 1993, third European Teams 1993.

RAU, John (1908-1982) of Walnut Creek CA, was one of the leading figures in the early days of contract bridge. In 1930 Rau and William K. Barrett caused a sensation at their first national tournament by extensive use of psychic bids and by winning the Open Team championship (now the Reisinger) as a pickup team with Ely Culbertson and W. James Carpenter. Rau won the National Open Prs Championship in 1934 and was second in the Vanderbilt (twice) and the Spingold as well as other major victories in important Eastern tournaments. He was protege and special assistant to P. Hal Sims in the early Thirties when the Sims mansion in Deal NJ was summer headquarters for all the principal bridge experts. When the category of Life Master was created by the American Bridge League in 1936, Rau was not included on the original list, having quit bridge to seek his fortune in the business world. Through the vagaries of the bridge league's bookkeeping system in those days, Rau's early exploits were never recognized with masterpoints, so when he moved to California and resumed playing bridge, he started a second bridge career and became a Life Master in three years. He was almost surely the only new Life Master to have finished first or second in such events as the National Open Prs, the Reisinger, the Vanderbilt and the Spingold.

RAUTENBERG, Lee H. (b. 1951) of Boca Raton FL, microcomputer systems programmer/designer, placed second in Mixed Prs 1976 and has won several regional events.

RAY, Debasish (b. 1956) of Calcutta, share-broker. WBF World Master. Second BFAME Open Teams 1989, fourth World Open Teams 1988, and represented India in one other world championship. Five national wins include open teams twice.

REBATTU, Maximiliaan J. (Max) (b. 1939) of Amstelveen, The Netherlands, bridge journalist and teacher. WBF World Life Master. Using DUTCH SPADE SYSTEM, second World Open Pairs 1982, after a scoring error made it appear that he had won. Represented the Netherlands in three other world championships and six European championships. He has won numerous national titles including open teams 10 times. Contributor to the biggest Netherlands newspaper *Telegraaf* and to *Bridge*. Introduced bridge on Teletext in 1980, and continues it.

REBNER, Stella (1910-1991) of Los Angeles CA, born in Austria, placed second World Womens Tms 1964; won Womens Team Trials 1963, Master Mixed Tms 1952, 53; Womens Tms 1957, 62; placed second in Mixed Prs 1959; won numerous regional titles.

REED, Broma Lou (formerly Harrison) (b. 1932) of Boulder CO, retired teacher, graduated U of Colorado, competed in world competition Biarritz 1982, Bal Harbour 1986, placed 20th World Mixed Prs 1990. Won Womens BAM Tms 1990, placed 2nd North American Womens Swiss 1993. Won Rocky Mtn Open Prs 1961, Womens Prs 1969, KO Tms 1975, Swiss 1981, Open Prs 1991; Canadian Open Prs 1969, Master Prs 1977, Swiss, KO Tms 1981; Navajo Trail Open Prs 1969, KO Tms 1991; MO Valley Swiss 1974, Desert Empire Swiss 1980, Pasadena KO Tms 1981, Womens Prs 1986; Montana Centenniel Open Prs 1989, El Paso Swiss 1992.

REESE, D. Ann (b. 1936) of Atlanta GA, professional bridge teacher/player, former teacher, model and TV show host; graduate of Jacksonville State U, U of Alabama; interests in drama and landscaping; novice coodinator for Dist 7, author of *Four Suit Transfers*, columnist Unit 114 *Pip 'n' Tips*. Diamond Life Master, won Mid-Atlantic Womens Prs, Swiss 1978, Womens Swiss 1979; Roanoke Open Prs 1982, Gatlinburg Smoking Open Prs 1983, Womens KO Tms 1989, Senior KO Tms 1992; Dist 7 GN Prs 1983, Atlanta Womens Prs 1985, Swiss 1990, Handicap KO Tms 1992; Charlotte Womens Prs 1986, 91; Sault Ste Marie KO Tms 1990, Tampa Womens Prs, Columbia Swiss, Ft. Lauderdale KO Tms 1991; Marco Island Swiss, Sr Open Swiss 1993.

REESE, J. Terence (b. 1913) of Hove, England, bridge writer. WBF Grand Master. Won Bermuda Bowl 1955, World Par 1961. Second World Teams 1960 and World Pairs 1962. Won European Teams 1948, 1949, 1954, 1963. Represented Britain in two other world championships and five other zonal championships. More than 20 national titles include Gold Gup eight times. Won Sunday Times Invitational Prs 1964. He was the first to write a book about the Acol System, which became standard in Britain. He conducted regular radio programs about bridge, and acted as commentator at international championships. Bridge columnist of *London Observer* and *London Evening News*, and other periodicals. Editor *British Bridge World* 1955-62. Author of more than 20 books of which two, *Reese on Play* and *The Expert Game*, are classics that made major contributions to the game. For the accusation of cheating made against him at the 1965 world championships, see BUENOS AIRES AFFAIR.

REICH, Louis I. (b. 1949) of Wheaton MD, computer programmer, Diamond Life Master, placed second Spring BAM 1976 and won numerous regional titles.

REICH, Peggy (Mrs. Louis, formerly Lipsitz, Parker) (b. 1941) of Potomac MD, bridge teacher, educated at American U, Greet Dramatic Academy and Johns Hopkins Medical School, volunteer at crisis centers and counsels battered women. Won the World Mixed Tms 1974 and Mixed Prs 1969, 76; finished second in the Master Mixed Tms 1973; has won many regional titles.

REICHMUTH, Eleanor A. (d. 1990) of Billings MT, bridge teacher and club director, a pioneer of bridge in Montana, she began directing in 1934 and was instrumental in starting many duplicate clubs. She received an ACBL Service Award for having directed a club continuously for 25 or more years (35 years as of 1981). She won Rocky Mtn Womens Prs 1949, Inter-Mtn Mixed Prs 1959.

REID, Felicity Cronk (b. 1942 in England) of Kingston, Jamaica, business executive and bridge teacher. Represented Jamaica in four CAC Championships. 4 national wins include open teams once. President of Jamaica Bridge Association. Organizer of world championships in Ocho Rios, Jamaica, 1987

REID, Martin Alexander (b. 1963) of Wellington, New Zealand, computer consultant. Won Far East Teams 1990, Far East Pairs 1991. Represented New Zealand in one other Far East championship and two world championships.

REINHOLD, Arthur E. (Bud) (b. 1913) of Highland Park IL, furniture industry consultant, former naval officer, graduate of U of Chicago Business School; WBF World Master; Bermuda Bowl champion 1981. He won the Spingold 1973, Reisinger 1973, 79; Vanderbilt 1980 and placed second in the Vanderbilt 1973, GN Tms 1978, IMP Prs 1989, Reisinger 1986. ACBL Diamond Life Master and has won many regional titles.

REISINGER, Curt H. (1891-1964) of New York City, was a principal patron of contract bridge and the American Contract Bridge League in the early years of both. Reisinger was a great-grandson of both Anheuser and Busch, the co-founders of the brewery from which he inherited great wealth. That wealth enabled him to become a stalwart financial supporter of the game, as well as a noted philanthropist on a far larger scale. Among the positions in which he served were Director of the UNITED STATES BRIDGE ASSOCIATION, president of the Greater New York BA and chairman of the ACBL. In 1953 Reisinger was named ACBL HONORARY MEMBER. See REISINGER TROPHY.

REITH, George (1876-1939) of Yonkers NY, bridge expert and writer. Reith took up bridge in 1927 after he retired from the brokerage business. In 1929 he won the first Eastern States Prs championship with OSWALD JACOBY. He won many titles including the CHICAGO TROPHY (now the Reisinger) 1932. Reith authored four books on bridge — *The Art of Successful Bidding, Contract, Accurate Contract* and *Reith's One-Over-One.* He was at one time chief exponent of the one-over-one system of bidding. Reith was chairman of the Knickerbocker Whist Club Card Committee for 15 years, president of Crockford's Club, executive vice-president of the USBA and ACBL Board member. He created and acted as chairman of the Eastern States Championships, which for many years was one of the largest regionals in the United States.

REMEY, Joan see MOORE, Joan R.

REITMAN, Dr. Nelson R. (b. 1911) of New Milford NJ, dentist, retired regionally rated tournament director, past president of NY/NJ Conference; won Eastern States Mixed Prs 1958, Mixed Tms 1960, Mens Prs 1961.

REMEY, Vincent O. (1911-1988) of Southfield MI, retired company executive; ACBL Life Master #341, Diamond Life Master with almost 9,000 MPs. A longtime member of the MI Unit 137 board, he founded and served as editor of the Unit newsletter *Table Talk.* Remey was first elected to the ACBL Bd of Dir in 1974 and served until his death. From 1981-83 he was an ACBL representative to the WBF. He won Open Prs 1971 and placed second in Life Master Prs 1948, Master Mixed Tms 1971, 75, 80. He won numerous regional titles.

RENGSTORFF, John C. (b. 1943) of New York City, stock options market maker, other interests are theater and antiques; placed second Open Prs 1986. Regionals include New York Winter Swiss 1974, Big Apple Swiss 1981, Hempstead KO Tms 1983, New England Fall Mens Prs 1983, Dist 3 Open Prs 1984, Montreal KO Tms, Open Prs 1985; Eastern States Swiss 1990, Summer secondary Swiss 1991.

RESNICK, Jeffrey L. (b. 1953 in Brooklyn, U.S.) of Christianstedt, St. Croix, Virgin Islands, federal magistrate. Represented Virgin Islands in two world championships and 11 CAC zonal championships. Secretary of Virgin Islands B.F.

RETEK, George (b. 1936) of Montreal PQ, born in Hungary, chartered accountant, graduate of Sir George Williams U. A member of the ACBL Board of Directors representing Dist 1 since 1979, primarily involved in finance, internat'l affairs and appeals committees; previously served as ACBL treasurer. Member of the WBF Executive Council since 1988, was elected to a four-year term as WBF treasurer 1990. Retek has won several regional events including Can-Am Open Tms 1976, Mens Swiss 1986, 88, Open Swiss 1993; Nat'l Capital Swiss 1990.

REUS, Sharyn (b. 1950) of St. Laurent PQ, office manager, accountant, software developer; enjoys reading and

Ma-Jong. Began playing in 1969 and by 1972 she was in her first Olympiad as the youngest player to represent Canada. Reus, a WBF World Master, placed third in the Venice Cup 1989, fourth World Womens Tm Olympiad 1976, 88, sixth 1980, seventh 1972; placed sixth in the World Womens Prs 1986. She also represented Canada in Monte Carlo 1976, New Orleans 1978, Biarritz 1982, Seattle 1984, Yokohama 1991, Salsomaggiore 1992, Santiago 1993. She placed second in the CNTC 1989 and won the secondary Golder Master Prs 1971 at her first NABC; has won numerous other regional events since.

REUSCHLEIN, Steven E. (b. 1947) of Middleton WI, CPA, graduate of U of Wisconsin; won MI Valley Swiss 1975, Wisconsin Mixed Prs 1976, Open KO Tms 1990; Dist 13 Swiss 1978, Central States Swiss 1982, Badger Swiss 1987, Reno Mens Prs 1987, Green Bay Swiss 1989.

REVELL, A. Richard (1913-1988) of Prospect Heights IL, accountant, won Mens Prs, Mens Tms 1950. He was director of the Chicago CBA 1961-65 and received its Sportsmanship Award.

REVILL, Colin (b. 1933) of Burlington ON, born in England, retired mathematics professor, commissioned in Her Royal Majesty's Navy; graduate of U of Sheffield (England); won Fall secondary Mens Prs 1985, Morning KO Tms 1989, Spring Morning KO Tms 1994; Rochester Swiss 1985; Saginaw Morning KO Tms, Mens Prs 1987; Midland Mens Prs 1989; Motor City Swiss 1992; Toronto Sr. Swiss 1992, KO Tms 1994.

REX-TAYLOR, David (b. 1947) of Feltham, England. Managing editor *IBPA Bulletin*; founder of Bibliagora Publishers and International Book Mail Order Co., Bridge Book Club and *Evening Standard* Bridge Congress; discoverer of word "bridge" from obsolete Russian word "biritch", meaning declarer. See INTERNATIONAL BRIDGE PRESS ASSOCIATION and BIRITCH.

REYES, Jose (1910-1980) of Pasay City, Philippines, attorney and planter. One of the founders of the Far East Bridge Federation and its president 1957-63. Delegate to the WBF. Won Far East Teams 1958. National titles include open teams three times.

REYES, Vicente (b. 1937) of San Bruno CA and Pasa City, Philippines, mechanical engineer and bridge columnist; was Far East Open Prs champion 1974. He also represented the Philippines in the World Team Olympiad 1960, 64; and the Far East Championships 1962-67, 1970-73, 1975. His nat'l titles include Philippines Open Tms 1958, 59, 60, 62, 71, 75; Open Prs 1961, 64, 70, 71; KO Tms 1971, 74; Master Prs 1964, 74, 75; Tuason Cup 1971, 72, 74; Intercommercial Tms 1976.

REYNOLDS, Robert (1925-1984) of Coral Gables FL, bridge teacher, represented US in Cannes 1962; won Master Individual 1960 and placed second Vanderbilt 1960, Life Master Prs 1961; also numerous regionals.

REYSA, Gloria (formerly Turner) (b. 1925) of Dallas TX, secretary; won Master Mixed Tms 1957, 61; placed second in Vanderbilt 1951, Master Mixed Tms 1953. Diamond Life Master; has won many regional events.

RHATIGAN, Jack K. (b. 1931) of Cottage Grove MN, pharmacist, graduate of U of Iowa; won Open Prs 1973. Diamond Life Master; regional wins include Gopher Master Prs 1977, Swiss 1979, 80; Iowa Mens Prs 1977, Swiss 1978; Buffalo Swiss 1974, Pheasant Mens Prs 1978; Sr Golden Get-Away Sr Prs, Sioux City Sr Prs 1987; Spring secondary Prs, Davenport/Omaha Sr Prs 1988; Cedar Rapids/Fargo Sr Prs 1989; Winnipeg Sr Prs, Sr Swiss 1991; Traverse City Sr Open Prs, Fltd Sr Prs, Sr Swiss 1992.

RHODE, George L. (b. 1949) of Duluth GA, retired U.S. Army drug and alcohol detoxification specialist, graduate of Southern Illinois U; served as Dist 8 college coordinator, Dist 7 GN Prs coordinator 1985-90, Unit 179 bridge school and has been a member the ACBL Nat'l Appeals Committee since 1986. He is a feature writer for *Pips and Tips* and the Dist 7, 9 and 10 *Bulletins*. Won Fall secondary Swiss, Mid-South KO Tms 1979; Opryland Mens Swiss, Florida KO Tms 1981; Atlanta KO Tms 1990, Dayton Super KO Tms 1991.

RHODES, Kathryn M. (Kay) (b. 1910) of Rohnert Park CA, formerly of New York City, an outstanding woman player with two unusual records — four consecutive wins in Womens Prs 1955, 56, 57, 58; seven consecutive seconds in Womens Tms 1952-58. Won the Chicago (now the Reisinger), Womens Prs 1949; placed second in Master Mixed Tms 1942, Womens Prs 1944; won numerous regionals.

RHODES, Lady Doris (1898-1982) of London, England, was European Womens champion 1951, 52; also represented Great Britain in European Women's Championships on four other occasions and England in the SCHWAB CUP 1933, World Women's Tms 1960.

RIBNER, Paula (formerly Bacher, Levin) (b. 1908) of Palm Beach FL, Life Master #65. Ribner and her teammates, (Jane Jaeger, Kay Rhodes, Sally Rhodes) won the Chicago (became the Reisinger 1966) in 1947, the only time in history the event has been won by an all-woman team. Also won Mixed Prs 1946. Placed second in Womens Prs 1944; Womens Tms 1946; Mixed Prs 1949, Open Prs 1952. Her numerous regional titles include Eastern States Mixed Tms 1943, 47, Womens Prs 1947; Southeastern Womens Prs 1953, 54, 66, Mixed Prs 1952, Womens Tms 1965, KO Tms 1968.

RICE, Betty K. (b. 1939) of Sante Fe NM, graduated Louisiana State U, was ACBL Rookie of the Year 1985 and ACBL Senior Master of the Year 1986 (set new record of 633 MPs). Won Cancun Open Prs, Open Swiss, Flt A Swiss 1986; St Louis Womens Swiss 1986, Lexington Open Prs 1986, Buffalo Master Prs 1986.

RICE, Shirley J. (b. 1925) of Clearwater FL, bridge teacher, certified director; has taught classes for qualified and certified directors. She was the first to author and record bridge lessons on cassette tapes *Anyone for Bridge?* Appointed to Nat'l Charity Committee in the Seventies, served two terms Unit 111 president and many terms Unit Bd of Dir, chaired GN Tms events Dist 5 for five years, served six years on Executive Committee of Dist 5 Bd of Directors. Won Cleveland Master Prs 1980; All American Mixed Prs 1984.

RICH, Pauline S. (Polly) (b. 1917) of Chattanooga TN, company executive, won many regional competitions including Nashville Swiss 1977; Atlanta KO Tms 1978, 80, 81 83, Open Prs 1980; Helena KO Tms; Seattle KO Tms 1980; Boise KO Tms, Swiss 1981; Pasadena KO Tms, Tulsa Swiss 1981; Rockton KO Tms 1982; Gatlinburg KO Tms 1982, 85, 86, 88, Swiss 1988, 91; Tampa KO Tms 1983; Oconomowoc KO Tms 1984; Edmonton KO Tms 1984; Birmingham KO Tms, St Louis KO Tms 1985; Penticton KO Tms, Monroe KO Tms, Winnipeg Swiss 1987; St Petersburg KO Tms, Open Swiss 1992.

RICHARDS, Ralph R. (1876-1943) of Detroit, accountant, founder and first president of the American Bridge League; also a bridge teacher, writer, lecturer and leading tournament player. Born in Chicago, Richards played bridge at the old Chicago Whist Club and won many honors at whist and auction bridge. He was an active member of the American Whist League and while attending the Congress at Hanover NH in the summer of 1927, he proposed an organization to sponsor, promote and develop the game of bridge. The American Auction Bridge League (subsequently American Bridge League) was the first national organization devoted entirely to bridge. At its initial tournament at Chicago in December of 1927, Richards and teammates Theodore A. Lightner, Waldemar von Zedtwitz and Ely Culbertson won the team-of-four championship. During the second meeting of the League held in Cleveland 1928, contract bridge was introduced for tournament play. In 1929, the tournament went back to Chicago and Richards and his partner, William E. McKenney, tied for first in the Open Prs. Richards authored *Championship Bridge* and co-authored *Common Sense Contract.*

RICHENS, Muriel W. of San Mateo CA, counselor, therapist, certified bridge director, retired educator, educated at U of California-Berkeley, San Francisco State, Oregon State. Member of the ACBL Goodwill Committee, involved with the organization of Fall NABC 1990, served on several Unit boards. Regional wins include Polar KO Tms 1974, Golden Gate Womens Prs 1978, California Capital Mixed Prs 1979, Open Prs 1993; Sr Fall Fling Open Prs 1986, Mixed Prs 1991; All-Western Sr Open Prs, Strat Prs, Swiss 1991; Modesto Swiss 1991, Mid-Winter Holiday Swiss 1992, Sr Prs 1993; Fall secondary Swiss 1993.

RICHMAN, Robert Alan (b. 1950 in Cleveland, Ohio) of Sydney, Australia, options trader. Won Maccabiah Games 1985 and represented Australia in one world championship. National wins include Open Teams four times and Open Pairs five times.

RICHMOND, David G. (1906-1980) of Winnipeg MB, pharmacist, represented Canada in World Open Prs 1962. He was active in promoting bridge in Canada and in 1974 donated the RICHMOND TROPHY, the Canadian equivalent of the BARRY CRANE TOP 500 (formerly the McKENNEY TROPHY).

RICHTER, Claude (b.1953 in Luxembourg) of Dunedin, New Zealand, interpreter. Won Oceania Teams 1991, 1992. Represented Luxembourg in several world, zonal and Common Market championships. Bridge tour operator.

RIEGLE, Jim E. (b. 1950) of Ottawa ON, economist, graduate of U of Toronto, Brock U; represented ACBL in world competition 1986; placed second in Canadian Nat'l Open Prs 1985. Riegle won a number of regionals including Ottawa Open Prs 1976, 87, 90, Mens Tm-of-Four 1980, KO Tms 1986, 89, Swiss 1987, 89; Montreal KO Tms 1978, 80, Swiss 1980; North Bay Swiss 1981, Swiss 1986, Mens Tms 1991; Dist 1 GN Prs, GN Tms Zone III 1981; Sudbury Swiss 1983, Mens Tm-of-Four 1989; Lancaster KO Tms 1987.

RIELY, Terry P. (b. 1943) of San Antonio TX, corporate executive, served as Unit 172 president 1985-90, president Dist 16 1986. Diamond Life Master, some of his wins include Texas Mid-Winter KO Tms, Master Prs 1973; Big D Open Prs 1974; Dist 16 GN Tms 1978; Navajo Trail Open Prs 1979; South Padre Island Open Prs, Swiss 1993.

RIGAL, Barry John (b. 1958) of London, England, oil tax accountant. WBF World Master. Won Common Market Mixed Teams 1987. Second European Junior Teams 1981. 10 national wins include Gold Cup once. Commentator at several world and zonal championships. Contributor to many periodicals.

RIGMAIDEN, Roscoe (b. 1918) of Philadelphia, retired US Postal superintendent, graduate of Prairie View College; first winner of ABA William A. Friend award for most masterpoints won in a year, and has been the leading AMERICAN BRIDGE ASSOCIATION masterpoint holder. He was top-ranked ABA player 1969-70, 1974-77 and won the leading player award in the ABA Summer Nat'ls 1966 and 1968, Spring Nat'ls 1969. He has won all major ABA titles including Open Prs six times and Open Tms four times. Rigmaiden is a former member of the ABA Executive Board, chairman of the Nat'l Ethics Committee and contributor to the ABA *Bulletin.*

RIMINGTON, Derek C. (b. 1927) of Beckenham, England, computer manager and bridge writer. Many national wins include Gold Cup 1956. Columnist for *Field* magazine and syndicated columnist. Contributor to many magazines. Author of one book and co-author of another.

RIPSTRA, Joseph G. (Rip) (1900-1982) of Wichita KS, investor, mechanical contractor; helped develop the Kansas State BA and was active on the national scene for many years. A member of the ACBL Bd of Dir 1945-58 and was instrumental in increasing the number of members on the ACBL Board from 8 to 23 when the ACBL merged with the WESTERN CONFERENCE. Ripstra was ACBL president 1957; invented RIPSTRA convention. He was npc of the US Bermuda Bowl team 1958, placed second in the Chicago (now the Reisinger) 1955, Mens Prs 1949 and won numerous regional titles.

RITZENBERG, James L. (b. 1957) of Bethesda MD, attorney, graduate of Yale and U of Virginia Law School (JD). Won Red Ribbon Prs 1987, Washington DC Swiss 1983, Northern Virginia KO Tms.

RIVAS, Santiago R. (b. 1955) of Bogotá, Colombia. WBF World Master. Winner CAC Open Teams 1980, 1981, 1989, runner-up 1985, 1987. Second South American Junior Championships 1979, 1980. Has won all national titles.

RIVERS, Loretta R. (b. 1938) of Monroe LA, investment company executive. Served several terms as president of Unit 211, chairman of many tournaments in Dist 10 in the Seventies and was a member of the ACBL Bd of Gov, Nat'l Goodwill Committee and Nat'l Charity Committee (representing Dist 10). Won Baton Rouge Mixed Prs 1969, Fall secondary Womens Swiss 1974; Mid-South Womens Prs 1975, Swiss 1976; Bermuda Swiss 1977.

ROBB, Linda Q. (b. 1934) of Altamonte Springs FL, retired administrative assistant, won several regionals including N. FL Womens Prs 1983, Summer secondary Swiss 1984, Womens Prs, Sr Swiss Tm 1991; Mid-Atlantic Womens Swiss 1988, Womens KO Tms 1989, 93; Mid-South Spring Sr KO Tms 1990, FL KO Tms 1992, Mid-South Sr Swiss 1992.

ROBB, Paul H. (b. 1923) of Altamonte Springs FL, bridge teacher and professional player, Diamond Life Master; his numerous regional wins include Summer Sr Swiss 1991; Gateway to Space Swiss, Sun City Open Prs 1982; Mid-Atlantic Open Prs 1982, Mens Swiss 1986, Open Prs 1986, Sr Swiss (2) 1988, Sr Master Prs 1990, Bracketed KO Tms 1992, Sr Swiss 1992; Mid-South Sr Master Prs 1985, Sr KO Tms 1990; Florida Open Swiss 1988, Sr Swiss 1989, 90; Florida KO Tms, Sr Open Prs, Sr Open Swiss 1992.

ROBBINS, Dr. Lawrence (Larry) (b. 1954) of Chicago, physician, won GN Tms 1979, 91; placed second 1984, 86. He won Intercollegiate Championship 1976; and Summer secondary Open Prs, Great Lakes KO Tms, Champaign Swiss, All-American Master Prs 1976.

ROBINSON, Arthur G. (b. 1936) of Villanova PA, bridge teacher, WBF Life Master, placed second Bermuda Bowl 1963, World Tm Olympiad 1964, 68; fifth World Open Prs 1962; also represented U.S. in Amsterdam 1966. He won the Team Trials 1967, finished second 1962; also won Vanderbilt 1961, 68; Open Prs 1962; Reisinger 1966, 67. Placed second in Fall Master Individual 1960; Chicago (now the Reisinger) 1961; Vanderbilt 1965; won many regional titles.

ROBINSON, Eric S. (b. 1956) of Scarsdale NY, attorney, graduate of Yale Law School (JD) and Harvard; won GN Prs 1979 and New England Swiss 1975; Long Island Swiss 1977; Dist 3 Swiss 1981.

ROBINSON, Frances E. (1908-1985) of Philadelphia, former teacher. In 1953 she was a member of one of the US teams that played against the visiting British women's team (which included Rixi Markus and Lady Doris Rhodes). Won Womens Tms 1947, 49 and had several regional successes. She was the mother of Arthur G. Robinson.

ROBINSON, Gary (b. 1943) of Lafayette CA, insurance broker, hypnotherapist; won KEM CARD TROPHY for Non-Life Master Prs 1965, Denver Mens Prs 1972, Fall secondary Swiss 1981, Sacramento Swiss 1983, San Diego KO Tms 1984. Inventor of anti-signaling bridge play-

ing cards.

ROBINSON, Louise K, see FREEMAN, Louise K.

ROBINSON, Maurice (b. 1918) of New York City, attorney and social worker, was president of the AMERICAN BRIDGE ASSOCIATION 1964-69 and one of its national tournament directors.

ROBINSON, Steve W. (b. 1941) of Arlington VA, U.S. Army computer specialist, graduate of U of Maryland; has been active in WBL since 1971, serving as a Board member 1971-78, 80, 87-88, treasurer since 1989, president Dist 6 1985, vice president 1982-85, was Dist 6 representative to the ACBL Bd of Gov 1975-81, 1st alternate to ACBL Bd of Dir (Dist 6) 1980-87. A WBF Life Master, won World Mixed Tms 1974, Rosenblum Cup 1986. Also represented US internationally in New Orleans 1978, Geneva 1990. ACBL Grand Life Master with more than 17,000 masterpoints and ranks 18th on all-time MP holders as of 1993. Co-inventor of the CRASH convention. Won the Herman Trophy, Mens Prs 1972; Reisinger 1972, 86; Blue Ribbon Prs 1973, 75; Mens BAM 1978, 89; GN Tms 1984, 88, 92; GN Prs 1985, Mixed Prs 1985; Mens Swiss 1986; Mott-Smith Trophy 1987; Vanderbilt 1987, 91. Placed second Life Master Mens Prs 1971, 72, Mens Tms 1973, 74; Mens Prs 1973, 74; Master Mixed Tms 1973; GN Tms 1977, 85; Spingold 1979, 92; Blue Ribbon Prs 1982; Life Master Prs 1987; Mens BAM Tms 1989; Vanderbilt 1992. His 50+ regional titles include Durham Master Prs 1967; Spartanburg Mens Prs 1969; Lancaster Mens Swiss 1970, Master Prs 1970, 71, Hex Open (N-S) 1981, 85; Norfolk Open Prs 1974, Master Swiss 1978, Open Prs 1979, KO Tms 1980, 83, Swiss 1983; Baltimore KO Tms 1976, Swiss 1980, 88; Arlington Mens KO Tms, Swiss 1985, Mens Prs, KO Tms 1988, Open Swiss 1990; Richmond KO Tms 1989, 91 Handicap KO Tms 1991.

ROBINSON, William A. (Bill) (1918-1992) of Campbellcroft ON, retired electrical engineer, graduate of U of Toronto; Unit 166 president 1967, CANADIAN BRIDGE FEDERATION president 1969, Dist 2 president 1972.

ROBISON, James R. (Jim) (b. 1942) of Los Angeles CA, bridge and poker professional, graduate of Ohio State U; WBF World Master, placed 7th World Mixed Prs 1982, 16th Rosenblum Cup 1986. ACBL Diamond Life Master, he won North American Swiss 1979, 90; Reisinger 1984, Open Prs 1985. Second in Open Prs 1981, Mixed Prs 1987; Mens Swiss 1982, Reisinger 1986. He has approximately 75 regional wins.

ROBLES, Jose Manuel Vasquez (b. 1949) of Santiago, Chile, engineer. Represented Chile in 12 zonal championships and won all national titles.

ROBSON, Andrew M. (Andy) (b. 1964) of London, England, bridge teacher. WBF World Master. Won World Junior Teams 1989, European Teams 1991, Sunday Times Invitational Prs and Statenbank Prs 1990. Frequent contributor to magazines, and author of one book.

ROCCHI, Egisto (1922-1984) of Buenos Aires, Argentina, wholesale furrier. World Life Master. South American champion 1959, 1961, 1964, 1976, 1979, 1980. Represented Argentina in Bermuda Bowl 1959, 1961, 1962, 1963, 1965, World Team Olympiad 1964, 1968, 1976. His 35 national titles won include Open Teams 10 times and Open Pairs 6 times. Won Gabarret Cup 1963, 1969, 1976, 1978, 1982. Was a director of the Argentine Bridge Association.

ROCK, Lawrence J. (b. 1945) of University Heights OH, pension consultant, graduate of Washington and Jefferson College; member Nat'l Appeals Committee 1984-present, Dist 5 Executive Committee 1987-89, Unit 125 president 1981-83; contributor to Dist 5 and Unit 125 publications. Won Mixed Prs 1984. Diamond Life Master; won Pittsburgh Mixed Prs 1977, Open Prs 1991; All-American KO Tms 1979, 92, Mens Prs 1983; Dist 5 GN Prs 1980, GN Tms 1992; Buffalo Prs 1983, Open Prs 1993; Cincinnati Master Prs 1984; Columbus Master Prs 1985, Erie Mens Swiss, Master Prs 1987; Wiesbaden KO Tms 1987, Open Prs 1987, 88; Fall secondary Continuous Prs 1990; Summer secondary Tm-of-Two-Prs 1991.

ROCKAWAY, Dr. Harold (Rocky) (1926-1993) of Houston, psychiatrist, won the Herman Trophy 1964, Open Prs, Mens Tms 1953; Chicago (now the Reisinger) 1964; placed second Fall Mens Tms 1956, Life Master Mens Prs 1964. Won many regional events.

RODRIGUE, Claude (b. 1930 in Egypt) of London, England, stockbroker. WBF World Life Master. Won World Par 1961, European Teams 1961. Represented Britain in seven world championships and nine other zonal championships. Represented Egypt in one zonal championship, and England in Camrose matches. Won Sunday Times Invitational Pairs 1967. Many national wins include Gold Cup three times. Magazine contributor.

RODRIGUE, Maria Elena Cucullu de (b. 1930) of Buenos Aires, Argentina. South American Women's Team champion 1957, 1961, 1962, and represented Argentina in World Women's Team Olympiad 1968, 1972. 19 national titles won include Open Teams and Open Pairs once each.

RODWELL, Eric V. (b. 1957) of West Lafayette IN, professional bridge player and writer, graduate of Purdue U; accomplished pianist, enjoys composing music. One of a very small group of players to have won all three major world championships; won Bermuda Bowl 1981, World Open Prs 1986, World Tm Olympiad 1988; finished second in World Tm Olympiad 1992, 5th in Rosenblum Cup 1988, 5th-8th in Bermuda Bowl 1991, 6th in World Open Prs 1982. Also won World Top Prs in Holland (second in 1994), Scientist vs Naturalist match in London and the Iceland Prs and Tms 1992, Pan-American Open Prs 1992, Notrump Challenge Match 1993; placed second in Sunday Times Invitational Prs 1993. An outstanding theoretician, he designed RM (Rodwell-Meckstroth) Precision System and invented SUPPORT DOUBLES. Co-author of *Joy of Bridge*, in collaboration with Audrey Grant, *The Joy of Bridge Companion* and *Bridge Maxims*; also a major contributor to the Teaching Series of books authored by Audrey Grant. WBF Grand Master and ACBL Grand Life Master with more than 16,000 MPs as of 1993. He won the Reisinger 1979, 85, 93; Open Prs 1979, Life Master Mens Prs 1979; Life Master Prs 1980, 86, 91; Mott-

Smith Trophy 1980; Vanderbilt 1980, 82, 85; USBC (Team Trials) 1981, 88, 91, 92; Blue Ribbon Prs 1982, 85; Lou Herman Trophy 1982, 85; Spingold 1984, 88, 91, 93; Mens BAM 1984, Mens Swiss 1989; GN Tms 1990, Fishbein Trophy 1991; placed second Spingold 1979, 85, 90; Reisinger 1980, Life Master Prs 1983, Mixed Tms 1983, Life Master Mens Prs, USBC 1985, 93; Life Master Open Prs 1992, Vanderbilt 1991. He has won well over 100 regional events.

ROET, Leo (b. 1903) of Hallandale FL, won Life Master Prs 1949, Master Mixed Tms 1951; Mens Tms 1949. Placed second in Open Prs 1945, 50, 52.

ROGASNER, Mrs. Ruth (b. 1919) of Baltimore MD, sports club manager; the co-creator of the Unmixed Prs event which was first implemented at Maryland BA games in 1967. Secretary of Maryland BA for 15 years, member Goodwill Committee; won Mid-Atlantic Womens Prs 1962 Dist 4 Master Prs 1966.

ROGERS, John R. (b. 1929) of Tucson AZ, regional-4 tournament director, retired USAF Lt. Col.; has won numerous regionals including Rogue River Valley Open Prs 1973, Golden State Mens Prs 1975, Unmixed Swiss 1976; Puget Sound KO Tms 1976, Pacific Southwest Mens Swiss 1976; LA Winter Open Prs 1980, Dist 17 GN Prs 1981.

ROGERS, Rebecca (Becky) (b. 1939) of Dallas TX, general manager and assistant treasurer of WORLD BRIDGE FEDERATION, ACBL nat'l tournament director (since 1979), former ACBL Director of Operations; graduated U of Kansas and U of Arizona. Coordinator of World Jr Championship 1991; npc of the US Womens Olympiad Tm Salsomaggiori 1992. Rogers was the second woman to ever achieve national rating as a director (see Weisbach, Dean). Served on several President's Advisory Committees in which were developed new convention charts, active ethics program, ACBL standard card. Won Navajo Trail Womens Prs, Open Prs 1973; Golden State Swiss, Los Angeles Winter Open Prs 1980; Fort Smith Womens Prs, Gatlinburg Womens Tms 1992.

ROGERS, Reece D. (b. 1951) of Cordova TN, member ACBL Nat'l Charity Committee, Diamond Life Master, placed second GN Tms 1974, GN Pairs 1994; has won several regional events.

ROHAN, Karl (b. 1934) of Salzburg, Austria, entrepreneur and prominent at world level as a bridge administrator. WBF World Master. Runner-up Bermuda Bowl 1985, third World Senior Pairs 1990, and represented Austria in three other world championships. European champion 1985, and played in four other European Championships. Won CAC Open Pairs, Copa d'Oro (Paris), and Tournoi de Champions du Monde (Deauville, France). Won Austrian Teams three times and Open Pairs twice.

ROHOWSKI, Roland (b. 1967) of Stuttgart, Germany, bridge teacher. WBF World Master. Won World Teams 1990, so becoming, at 22, the youngest world champion in the history of the game. Won five national titles.

ROMANSKI, Jacek (b. 1950) of Lublin, Poland, bridge professional. WBF World Life Master. Won World Teams

1984. Represented Poland in one other world championship and one zonal championship. Won many national titles.

ROMIK, Pinhas (b. 1946 in USSR) of Tel Aviv, Israel, physicist. Second European Teams 1975, European Junior Teams 1972. Represented Israel in one world championship and two other European championships. Won four National League titles.

RONA, Gianarrigo (b. 1940) of Pavia, Italy, lawyer. President of Italian Bridge Federation since 1986. Member of WBF Appeals Committee and of several EBL Committees. Chairman of organizing committees for 1988 and 1992 World Team Olympiads. NPC of many Italian teams.

RONCARELLI, Mimi (1909-1980) of Montreal, bridge club owner and outstanding player. Won Womens Tms 1947 and several regionals.

RONG, Gao Tang (b. 1909) of Beijing, China. President of Chinese Bridge Association, past chairman, China All Sports. Chairman of the Chinese organizing committee for 1995 World Championship.

RONG, Ledi of Beijing, China, NPC Chinese International Bridge team. Bridge partner of Wan Li. Second Epson 1990.

ROOSEN, Russell W. (b. 1908) of Hamden CT, formerly of Detroit; bridge club manager, one of Detroit's most prominent bridge figures in the early days of contract as a teacher, lecturer, problem composer and instructor via the radio. At exhibitions he demonstrated a remarkable memory by playing 10 separate hands simultaneously while blindfolded. Author of *When to Play Bridge and How*; was bridge columnist for the *Detroit Free Press*; a member of *The Bridge World* panel since 1956. Roosen won the Michigan BA "Player of the Year" award five times. Regional titles include All-American Open Tms 1955, Motor City Mixed Prs 1969, KO Tms 1974, Swiss 1979; Dist 12 GNT, Zone I 1973.

ROOT, William S. (Bill) (b. 1923) of Boca Raton FL, bridge teacher, lecturer and writer; served as national tournament director for the Intercollegiate Par-Hand Bridge Tournament 1959 to 1965 for about 400 colleges. During the same period he represented the Association of American Playing Card Manufacturers as its authority on card games. He is considered by many to be the foremost teacher on bridge and has taught tens of thousands of people in the past 35 years — probably more than any bridge teacher in history. He averages 7 classes of about 100 students each week. His bridge cruises have become legendary and are repeated by many. He organized many duplicate bridge clubs in the Greater New York area. He is a contributing editor to the *Cromwell-Collier Encyclopedia* and *The Official Encyclopedia of Bridge*. His most recent books are *Commonsense Bidding, How to Play a Bridge Hand, Modern Bridge Conventions* which he co-authored with Richard Pavlicek and *How to Defend a Bridge Hand*. His videos are *Bill Root Teaches Bridge, Volume 1 — Bidding, Volume 2 — The Play of the Hand, Volume 3 — Defense, Volume 4 — Open Leads, Volume 5 — Non-Competitive Bidding*. His playing expertise has been shown by his successes at the table, he placed sec-

ond in the Bermuda Bowl 1967, World Tm Olympiad 1968, 6th Rosenblum Cup 1986; second in USBC (Team Trials) 1987, 92; and is a WBF Life Master. An ACBL Diamond Life Master, won Mens Prs 1953, Chicago (now the Reisinger) 1957; Spingold 1961, 66, 67; Reisinger 1967, 82, 83, 84, 90; Vanderbilt 1968, 83, 86. Placed second in the Spingold 1963, 74, 78; Mens Tms 1963; Reisinger, Open Prs 1966; North American Mens Swiss 1984; GN Tms 1992. His numerous regional titles include Eastern States KO Tms 1960, 61, 66, 68, 88, 89.

ROSATI, Fabio (b. 1950) of Rome, Italy. World Master. Represented Italy regularly in world championships and other international events since 1986.

ROSE, Steven M. (b. 1949) of Des Plaines IL, data processing consultant, won more than 25 regionals including Great Lakes Swiss, Mississippi Valley Swiss 1974; Champaign Open Prs 1977; Dist 8 Swiss 1981.

ROSE, Albert (1908-1970) of London, England, textile converter. Second World Teams 1960, third Bermuda Bowl 1962. Won European Teams 1961, second 1953. Represented Britain in two other world championships and one zonal championship. National wins include Gold Cup four times.

ROSE, Irving N. (Ox) (b. 1938 in Scotland) of London, England, bridge club manager. WBF World Master. Third World Teams 1976. Second European Teams 1981. Represented Britain in two other world championships and five other zonal championships. Played frequently in Camrose Trophy matches, and won more than 15 national titles including Gold Cup.

ROSEN, Edward L. (Eddie) (b. 1929) of Los Angeles CA, controller, served as Board member of the Chicago CBA 1960-68. Diamond Life Master; won Life Master Prs 1959, Mixed Prs 1960, 62. His numerous regional titles include Central States Master Prs 1954, Mens Prs 1956, Open Tms 1958, Open Prs 1965, 69, KO Tms 1965, Life and Sr Master Tms 1960.

ROSEN, Eunice M. (b. 1930) of Highland Park IL, retired freelance editor, graduate of U of Chicago; Diamond Life Master, won Master Mixed Tms 1958, 66; finished second Womens BAM Tms 1972. She has won numerous regional competitions including Midwest Open Tms 1959, 67; Central States KO Tms 1964, 67, 77, Open Tms 1976, Womens KO Tms 1981, 86, BAM Tms 1982, 86, Womens Swiss 1982, Master Prs 1987, Open Prs 1991; Champagne Open Prs 1967, KO Tms 1981, Womens Tms 1986; Great Lakes Open Tms 1967, Master Prs 1980; Tri-Unit Womens Swiss 1979, Womens KO Tms 1982, 87; Wolverine Open Tms 1981; Dist 14 Open Tms 1983; Dist 13 Womens Swiss Tm 1986, 87, Womens KO Tms 1988.

ROSEN, Norman B. (Norm) (b. 1928) of Philadelphia PA, bridge teacher and certified director of the Cavendish Club of Philadelphia, graduate of Delaware Valley College; Unit 141 Bd and ABTA member since 1968; Unit recorder since 1970. Won Keystone Swiss 1973; Summer secondary Mixed Prs 1974; Dist 4 Master Prs 1979, Swiss 1981.

ROSEN, Robert (Bob) (b. 1941) of Delray Beach FL,

bridge professional, certified director and bridge club owner, graduate of C.W. Post; has served in various executive positions Unit 128 including president 1992, member ACBL Goodwill Committee, Dist 9 president, national recorder 1987-92. Rosen was npc of US Bermuda Bowl team Yokohama 1991 (tied 5th-6th); npc USBC (Team Trials) winners 1991 and the fourth-place Bermuda Bowl II team Santiago 1993. He has more than 60 regional wins.

ROSEN, Sondra (Sandy) (b. 1928) of Roslyn NY, high school math teacher, graduate NY City College, enjoys sculpting; numerous regional wins include Swan Lake Womens Prs 1985; Cherry Hill Open Prs 1987, Womens Prs 1989, Senior Prs 1991, 93; Stamford Womens Swiss 1988; Bal Harbour Womens Swiss 1990; Lancaster Open Prs 1991.

ROSEN, William A. (Billy) (b. 1928) of Highland Park IL, options trader, WBF Life Master; won Bermuda Bowl 1954, placed second 1955. He won the Bermuda Bowl at age 25, the youngest player ever to win that title until 1981 when the record was broken by Bobby Levin. Rosen, an ACBL Diamond Life Master, won the McKenney Trophy 1953, Mens Prs 1952, Spingold 1953, 54; Life Master Prs 1953, Master Mixed Tms 1958, 66 (second in 1965); GNT 1978, Mens Tms 1980. Has won numerous regionals.

ROSENBERG, Beverly of Sherman Oaks CA, bridge teacher and professional; graduate of Brooklyn College; WBF World Master, competed internationally New Orleans 1978, Biarritz 1982, Sao Paolo 1985, Venice 1988. She placed 5th Olympiad Womens Tms 1988, 7th World Mixed Prs 1986, second Pan Am Womens Prs 1992. ACBL Grand Life Master with more than 10,000 MPs as of 1993; won Womens Prs 1982, Womens KO Tms 1984, 88; North American Womens Swiss 1988; placed second Womens Tms 1973, Womens Prs 1977, 80, North American Womens Swiss 1987; North American Swiss 1987, Womens BAM Tms 1989. Rosenberg participates as a *Bridge World* Master Solver panelist and has won more than 50 regional events including Riverside Super Open Prs, Swiss 1984; Albuquerque Swiss 1985; Bridge Wk Super Open Prs 1985, 90, Superflight KO Tms 1990; Tulsa Swiss 1986; San Diego Swiss, Fresno Swiss 1987; LA Winter Open Prs 1987, Swiss 1990, 91; Bakersfield Open Prs 1991, Las Vegas IMP Prs 1992.

ROSENBERG, Michael (b. 1954) of New York City, formerly of Glasgow, Scotland, stock options trader, placed second World Tm Olympiad 1992; won the CAMROSE TROPHY 1974, 76, 77, three Jr Camrose Trophies, European Jr Championship 1978, London Sunday Times Prs (since 1981 Invitational Prs Championship) 1976, Cavendish Invitational 1992 (second 1978). A WBF World Master, he also represented Great Britain in the Common Market Championships 1975 and is the youngest person ever to win the British Gold Cup 1976 and Sunday Times Prs 1976 (age 21); also won Scottish Rayne Trophy 1972 and placed second in the British Tm Trials 1976, Scottish Tm Trials 1973. He won the Reisinger 1989; Spingold, Open BAM Tms 1991; Life Master Open Prs 1992, Blue Ribbon Prs 1993, Vanderbilt 1994; placed second in the Spingold 1980, 93; GN Tms 1981, Vanderbilt 1990, 91; Open Swiss 1992. Chairman (1993)

NY Cavendish Calcutta Invitational; represented Scotland in the World Student Chess Olympiad 1969, 71, 72, 80.

ROSENBERG, Milton (b. 1944) of Winfield IL, precious metals broker, Diamond Life Master, won GN Tms 1978, Mens Tms 1980, Mens Swiss 1984; placed second Vanderbilt 1977; has won more than 50 regional titles.

ROSENBERG, Mortimer (Monty) (b. 1923) of Belfast, Northern Ireland, retired furniture dealer. In a 36-year career has represented Northern Ireland more often than any other player in Camrose Trophy matches. Represented Ireland several times in world and European championships. Many wins in national open teams and open pairs. Northern Ireland BU competitions secretary and former chairman. Past president Irish Bridge Union.

ROSENBERG, Ronald (b. 1922) of Bronx NY, accountant and purchasing agent, won Spingold 1956, placed second Mens Tms 1951.

ROSENBLOOM, Edith L. (b. 1903) of Miami Beach FL, former high school teacher, won Mixed Prs 1951.

ROSENBLUM, Julius (1906-1978) of New Orleans, president of World Bridge Federation 1970-76 and of ACBL 1951. A native of Memphis, Rosenblum moved to New Orleans in 1935. He began playing duplicate bridge in 1943 and won his first major bridge championship, the Mid-South Open Tms, in 1944. He won many regionals after that and he won the Mens Prs in 1960. He captained the US team that defeated Italy in the 1951 Bermuda Bowl. He played briefly in that event, thus becoming the only person to have captained and played on a team that defeated the Italians. He also captained US internat'l teams in 1963, 66, 67, 68. Rosenblum became secretary-treasurer of the WBF in 1966 and a voting member of the WBF Executive Committee in 1968 when he was appointed to replace Waldemar von Zedtwitz, who retired. In 1974 he was elected to an unprecedented third term as president of the WBF and was elected to the WBF Committee of Honor. The International Bridge Press Association bestowed the Charles Goren "Man of the Year" award on Rosenblum in 1975. In 1977 the Australian Bridge Federation named him to Life Membership, the first non-Australian to be so honored. He was named ACBL Honorary Member in 1970.

ROSENBLUM, Michael (b. 1956) of Moscow, Russia, mathematician. Director of Association of C.I.S. national bridge organizations. Represented Soviet Union, or C.I.S, in two world championships and one zonal championship. National wins include open teams once and open pairs once. Contributor to *Bridj*.

ROSENBLUM, Robert D. (b. 1927) of San Diego CA, travel agency owner, graduate of Columbia and U of Wisconsin; past president of Unit 539 and Dist 22; co-chairman Fall 1984 NABC, chairman of several San Diego regionals; bridge columnist for the *San Diego Union* 1968-88, weekly bridge columnist Copley News Service 1975-81. Placed second GN Tms 1990; regional wins include Pacific Southwest Master Prs 1967; Dist 22 GN Tms 1975, 88, 89, 90, GN Prs 1980; Fall secondary Swiss 1984.

ROSENGREN, Kenneth (Ken) (b. 1920) of Phoenix AZ, retired attorney, graduate of Stanford and U of Arizona, has traveled in more than 100 countries. A Naval officer in WW II he was the commanding officer of a ship at the age of 23. A strong advocate of bridge education, Rosengren has conducted many bridge seminars. Some of his 30+ regional wins include San Diego Open Prs, Super Open Prs; Sacramento Sr Open Prs, KO Tms; Fresno Master Prs, Open Prs, Mens Prs; Denver KO Tms, Swiss; Colorado Springs KO Tms; Santa Clara KO Tms; Santa Rosa Swiss, Tm-of-Four and Two Prs 1992; Vancouver KO Tms, Houston Open Prs 1992.

ROSENDORFF, Hans-Gunther (1910-1983, born in Germany), retired librarian and bridge writer. Many times npc of Australian Women's Teams. National wins include Mens Pairs once, Individual twice. Held many executive positions. Columnist *West Australian* 1956-83 and *Weekend News* 1978-83.

ROSENKRANZ, Edith (Mrs. Jorge) (b. 1924) of Mexico DF, born in Austria; represented Mexico in World Olympiad 1962, 64, 66, 70, 74, 76, 78, 80, 82, 86, 90, and served as npc of the Mexican Olympiad Tm 1988. She is Mexico's leading female masterpoint holder, is Mexico's first female Life Master and a four-time winner of the John Pike Memorial Trophy for best overall performance at the Mexican Nat'ls. She won North American Womens Swiss and Master Mixed Tms 1990; placed second in Mixed Tms 1967, 84. She has won numerous regional events.

ROSENKRANZ, Dr. Jorge (George) (b. 1916) of Mexico DF, chemist and founding chairman of Syntex Corporation, he made scientific contributions in the field of steroid hormones, namely cortisone and birth control pills. The leading Mexican player and theorist, he has represented Mexico in world championships continuously (with three exceptions) since 1962, was npc of both Mexican teams 1964 and of a team in the USBC 1984. Represented North America in the Bermuda Bowl (1983) and reached the semifinals in Stockholm. ACBL Honorary Member 1990. He is a WBF World Master, ACBL Grand Life Master with more than 10,000 MPs and was Mexico's first Life Master. He established the Rosenkranz Award in 1975 and won the Precision Award in 1976 (see IBPA AWARDS). His writings include contributions to the *ACBL Bulletin* and other bridge periodicals. He has authored ten bridge books including *The Romex System of Bidding, Win with Romex, Bid Your Way to the Top, Trump Leads, Tips for Tops, More Tips for Tops, Bridge: The Bidders Game*, also *Modern Ideas in Bidding* and *Bidding on Target* with Alan Truscott and *Bid to Win, Play for Pleasure* with Phillip Alder. Rosenkranz invented DYNAMIC NOTRUMP, MEXICAN TWO DIAMONDS, ROSENKRANZ DOUBLES and is the author of the ROMEX SYSTEM. He served as president of the Mexican Federation of Bridge and the Mexican Unit of the ACBL and has served as a member of the ACBL Laws Commission since 1977. He won the Vanderbilt 1975, 76; Spingold 1976, 84; GN Tms 1981, Mens BAM Tms 1984, 87; Reisinger 1985, Master Mixed Tms, North American Swiss 1990; Mens Swiss 1991. Placed second Blue Ribbon Prs 1974, Mens Tms 1975, Vanderbilt 1978, Reisinger 1980, Team Trials 1982, Master Mixed Tms 1967, 84; Open BAM Tms 1990, Silver Ribbon Prs 1992. He has won countless regional titles and the John Pike Memorial Trophy for best overall performance at the

Mexican Nat'ls 12 times.

ROSLER, Dr. Lawrence (Larry) (b. 1934) of Palo Alto CA, senior scientist at Hewlett-Packard Labs, former physicist, graduate of Cornell and Yale (PhD), placed second in World Par Championship 1961; won North American Zone World Par Championship 1963; Mens Prs 1965. He is the former chairman of the Intercollegiate Par Tournament Advisory Committee and collaborated with Bill Root and Jeff Rubens in creating and judging par hands. He also served as vice president and president of the New Jersey BL 1967-1970. Rosler developed some team-of-four movements and helped introduce and popularize Swiss competitions. He co-authored *Journalist Leads* (with Jeff Rubens) and assisted in the writing of *Bridge Is a Partnership Game* and *Better Bidding in 15 Minutes*. He was editor of *The Bridge Journal* (no longer published). He contributes articles to *The Bridge World* and is a contributing editor to *The Official Encyclopedia of Bridge*. Rosler is co-inventor of JOURNALIST LEADS, ASTRO and ASTRO CUEBID.

ROSNER, Warren M. (b. 1944) of White Plains NY, systems analyst; WBF World Master, placed 13th Rosenblum Tms 1982, 86, 12th World Simultaneous Prs. Rosner won the Blue Ribbon Prs 1980, Mens Prs 1980, 81; Spingold 1981; placed second GN Tms 1979, Vanderbilt 1982. He won several regionals and posted an 84.7% game in the GN Prs qualifying game 1981.

ROSS, Harry (b. 1928) of Des Moines IA, born in Austria, salesman, member ACBL Goodwill Committee, served on unit and district boards, chaired regional and sectional tournaments, started or helped to start duplicate bridge in Mason City, Ottawa, LaSalle, Pontiac and Streator, all in Illinois. Diamond Life Master; contributed articles to *The Bridge World*; won many regionals including Nebraska KO Tms 1973, Iowa Swiss 1973, Gopher Swiss 1980, Waterloo BAM Tms 1984, Kansas City KO Tms 1985, Denver Open Prs 1986, Roughrider Swiss, Valley of the Sun Sr KO Tms 1991; Callaway Gardens Sr KO Tms 1992.

ROSS, Hugh L. (b. 1937) of Oakland CA, born in Montreal, systems analyst, graduate of McGill U, WBF Grand Master, won Bermuda Bowl 1976, 85, 87, placed second 1977, 89; second Rosenblum Tms 1982, seventh World Open Tms 1976. Was npc of Bermuda Bowl team USA II 1991. An ACBL Grand Life Master with more than 10,000 MPs, he won the Reisinger 1968, 74, 75, 81, 85, 86; Tms Trials 1975, USBC (Tm Trials) 1985, 87, 89; GN Tms 1982, 83, 85, 87, 93; Vanderbilt 1984, 87; Life Master Open Prs 1990, 91. Was second in the Reisinger 1966, 83; GN Prs 1985, Life Master Prs 1992. His numerous regional titles include the Marcus Cup 1963.

ROSS, John (b. 1948) of Brampton ON, corporate executive, graduate of U of Saskatchewan, founder of Flin Flon DBC and co-founder of the Northern Manitoba Unit, serving as its first president. Regional wins include Buffalo Master Prs 1976, Swiss 1979; Winnipeg Master Prs 1976, Swiss 1980, 83; Edmonton Open Prs 1978, 82, Swiss 1984, Mens Prs 1987, Open Prs 1990; Regina Master Prs 1978; Saskatoon KO Tms 1984, 88, Swiss 1988, Open Prs 1993; Fargo Swiss 1989; Ottawa Swiss 1993.

ROTH, Alvin L. (Al) (b. 1914) of Boca Raton FL, formerly of New York City, owner and manager of Mayfair Club, is generally considered the most original bidding theorist of his bridge generation. He represented North America in the Bermuda Bowl 1955, 58, 67; WBF Life Master, placed second in the World Team Olympiad 1968. Roth is co-inventor of the ROTH-STONE SYSTEM; his many contributions to bidding theory include UNUSUAL NOTRUMP, WEAK TWO BIDS, ONE NOTRUMP FORCING and NEGATIVE DOUBLE. Author of *The Roth-Stone System, Al Roth on Bridge* and *Picture Bidding*; co-author of *Bridge Is a Partnership Game, Modern Bridge Complete*, and *Bridge for Beginners*. On staff of *Bridge Today*, on the panel of *The Bridge World, Bridge Today, Australian Bridge*. ACBL Grand Life Master with more than 12,000 MPs as of 1993, won Spingold 1940, 56, 57, 63, 67; Open Prs 1942, Master Individual 1943, Vanderbilt 1943, 63, 68; Chicago 1946, 52; Lou Herman Trophy, Mixed Prs 1952; Master Mixed Tms 1952, 53, 55, 65; Mens Tms 1955, 61, 69, 71; Life Master Prs 1956, 71, 72; Open Prs 1960, Fishbein Trophy 1963, 65, 66; Reisinger 1967. Roth placed second in the Chicago 1937, 54; Spingold 1943, 45, 53, 61; Master Mixed Tms 1945, 63, 74, 75; Mens Tms 1957, 73, 77; Open Prs 1958; Life Master Prs 1965; Reisinger 1966; Team Trials 1967; Vanderbilt 1975. His numerous regional wins include Eastern States KO Tms (Reisinger) 1946, 60, 61, 66, 68, Open Prs (Goldman) 1961, 77, 78, 79; Spring secondary Mixed Prs 1959; Mixed Prs 1972. During his first World Championship appearance, Roth was declaring a two spade contract and felt he had played the hand before as a defender. The director, Al Sobel, did not believe him as the hands had been hand-dealt. Sobel made Roth call out all the cards in each hand, including the spots, before he threw the hand out. No one knows to this day how it happened.

ROTH, Daniel L. M. (b. 1946) of London, author of a number of bridge books, including *Clues to Winning Play, Signal Success in Bridge, Awareness The Way to Improve your Bridge*, and *Bridge — Groundwork in Play and Defence, Why Women Win at Bridge, Hand Reading in Bridge, The Expert Beginner, The Expert Improver, The Expert Advancer, The Expert Club Player*.

ROTHBLATT, Marc R. (1947-1993) of La Jolla CA, systems engineer, won more than 15 regionals, including Los Angeles Winter Swiss 1980, Pacific Southwest KO Tms 1989, Life Master Prs 1990; Summer secondary KO Tms 1989, California Capital KO Tms 1992.

ROTHFELD, Jessel M. (b. 1917) of Melbourne, Australia, born Dundee, Scotland, company director; marathon runner; Far East champion 1968, 1970; represented Australia Far East Championships 1967, 1969; npc of Australian team Bermuda Bowl 1971. Won Australian National Pairs 1970, ACBL Fall secondary Men's Teams 1969. Was president of the Australian Bridge Federation 1967-1971; organized the 15th Far East Championships 1971. Former member World Bridge Federation Executive Council.

ROTHLEIN, Robert R. (b. 1922) of Orlando FL, general contractor, former governor of Florida Unit, founder and president of Central FL Unit; won Spingold 1958, placed second 1954 and won many regionals.

ROTHWARF, Richard (Rich) (b. 1958) of Hi-Nella NJ, attorney, bridge professional and teacher; graduated LaSalle and Villanova (JD); member Unit 141 Bd of Dir, Unit recorder and education liaison. Won Dist 4 GN Tms 1985; Lancaster Mens Tms 1986; Port Chester Swiss 1990; East Brunswick KO Tms 1990, 91; Fall secondary Mens Prs 1991; Smithtown Open Prs 1992.

ROTMAN, Daniel (Danny) (b. 1932) of Aventura FL, bridge professional and retired businessman, graduated Bradley U, WBF World Master, placed fifth Rosenblum Tms 1990. A Diamond Life Master, has won Life Master Prs 1959, Morehead Trophy 1967, Mixed Tms 1969, 88; GN Tms 1978, Mens BAM Tms 1985, Spingold 1987; placed second in Open Prs 1963, 73; Mens Tms 1965, Reisinger 1967, Vanderbilt 1989, North American Swiss 1992.

ROTMAN, Florence (Flo) (b. 1931) of Aventura FL, retired stock options trader; won Mixed Tms 1969, Womens Prs 1978 and many regional titles.

ROTZELL, Peggy (1929-1969) was one of the leading bridge teachers of Philadelphia. Rotzell edited the *ACBL Bulletin* feature *Hand o' the Month* in the early Sixties and authored two books, *Bridge Play and Defense* and *Bridge Bidding Complete*. Her many victories included Womens Tms 1956, 58.

ROUDINESCO, Jean-Marc (b. 1932) of Paris, France, bridge writer, translator and theoretician. World Life Master. European champion 1966, 1970. Represented France in Bermuda Bowl 1967, 1971. National titles include four in open teams. Inventor of Two Clubs Roudi. Books include *La Majeure par 5* and *Comment Gagner en Tournoi par paires*. Contributor to *Revue Française de Bridge*.

ROUTMAN, Dr. Mark J. (b. 1944) of Cleveland MS, professor of sociology, earned his PhD at LSU, 1974. Author of *Club Level Duplicate Bridge: Which Strategies Win?*

ROVERE, Ernest (Ernie) of Carmel CA, journalist, author, director of Contract Bridge Cruises, ACBL Honorary Member 1986. Bridge editor for the *San Francisco Chronicle*, bridge columnist *San Francisco Call Bulletin* for 23 years and a commentator on radio and TV bridge programs in that city. Conducted one of the longest running TV bridge programs, 32 weeks on two PBS stations with 12,000 students. He was a pioneer in changing rules and laws restricting blacks and Jews from being included in the bridge community and served as a member of the ACBL Bd of Dir 1957-60. Rovere is a contributing editor to the *Bridge Encyclopedia* and the author of *Leads, Signals and Discards, Modern Point-Count Contract Bridge* and *Contract Bridge Complete*. Won Master Mixed Tms 1955 and numerous regional titles.

ROWE, Nelson G. (b. 1913) of Atlanta GA, associate nat'l tournament director, began his directing career in 1946. He served as president of the GA Unit for four terms and was an ACBL Board member 1956-57.

ROWLAND, Claude (b. 1922) of Wellington, New Zealand, retired marine engineer. Treasurer of New

Zealand CBA since 1976, and Life Member. Pilot in World War II.

ROWLANDS, Robert J. (Bob) (b. 1942) of London, England, government officer. Represented Great Britain in one world championship and one zonal championship. Played for England in some Camrose Trophy matches. Won several national titles. Magazine contributor.

ROY, N. Robi (b. 1931) of Calcutta, India, retired government officer. Represented India in three world championships. Won Far East Pairs 1979, 1980. 22 national wins include open teams five times, open pairs four times. Six wins came in 1982, a record.

ROYER, Barth E. (b. 1947) of Bexley OH, attorney, graduated Harvard and U of Michigan Law School (JD); Dist 11 judiciary chairman since 1989 and bridge columnist for the *Columbus Dispatch* 1981-93. Won Midwest Mens Swiss 1980, 81; Dist 11 GN Tms 1980, GN Prs 1981; Dist 11 Master Prs 1982, Mens Swiss 1984, Swiss 1990, Swiss, KO Tms 1993; All American Mens Prs 1982, 88, Mens Swiss 1986, 87; Midwest Spring Open Swiss 1991.

ROZEAUNU, Louis (b. 1912) of Haifa, Israel, professor of thermodynamics. Represented Israel in one world championship. National wins include open pairs once.

ROZECKI, Aleksander (1912-1975) of Warsaw, Poland, bridge writer and editor. Represented Poland in one world championship and one zonal championship. Won two national titles. Co-author of two books. Former executive editor of *Brydz*.

RUBBRA, Fredrick C. (Fred) (d. 1987) of Nassau, Bahamas, born in Canada, retired stockbroker, represented Bahamas in world play Stockholm 1970, Miami 1972, Monte Carlo 1976, Valkenburg 1980. Founder, honorary president and representative to the World Bridge Federation of the Bahamas Contract Bridge Club. Rubbra won many regionals.

RUBENS, Jeff (b. 1941) of Scarsdale NY, co-editor of *The Bridge World* since 1967, mathematician, computer scientist, educator, bridge writer and editor. He collaborated with Bill Root and Larry Rosler in creating and judging par hands for the Intercollegiate Par Hand Tournament. He edited *The Bridge Journal* (now defunct) 1963-66, was the Bols Tip competition winner 1977 and Precision Award winner twice (see IBPA Awards). He is the author of *Secrets of Winning Bridge*, *Swiss Match Challenge*, co-author of *Test Your Play as Declarer* (two volumes), *Modern Bridge Bidding Complete* and *Bridge for Beginners*, *Oddings and Endings* and is a contributing editor to the *Bridge Encyclopedia*. Rubens represented North America in the Bermuda Bowl 1973 and won the Team Trials 1972. Won Mens Tms, Mens Prs 1965; Spingold 1972, Intercollegiate Championship 1958 and many regional titles.

RUBIES, Pedro (b. 1949) of Barcelona, Spain, marine biologist. Represented Spain in one world championship and one zonal championship. Bridge teacher and journalist.

RUBIN, Judge Carl B. (b. 1920) of Cincinnati OH, attorney and since 1979 Chief Judge US District Court for the Southern District of Ohio, was ACBL president 1971. He was a member of the ACBL Bd of Dir 1966-73 and was named ACBL Honorary Member in 1981. A graduate of U of Cincinnati, he was a member of the Cincinnati Civil Service Commission 1960-66 (chairman 1964-66) and president of the Southwest Ohio Regional Transit Authority 1970-71.

RUBIN, Ira S. (b. 1930) of Paramus NJ, retired mathematician, computer analyst, consultant and instructor, has degrees from NYU School of Engineering and NYU Graduate School of Arts and Science and is the author of a digital computer textbook. Has other interests in stamp collecting (British Colonies) and digital computers (1953-65). Invented Rubin Transfers, Two-Way Two-Bids, Gladiator Responses to Notrump, and Extended Landy. WBF Grand Master, won Bermuda Bowl 1976, placed second Bermuda Bowl 1966, 77; 2nd World Tm Olympiad 1980, 4th World Open Prs 1970, 5th World Tm Olympiad 1960, 7th World Tm Olympiad 1976, 8th World Open Prs 1966. An ACBL Diamond Life Master he has won the Team Trials 1965, 75, 80; the Spingold 1956, 59, 66, 79, 85; Mens Prs 1958, 61, 62; Fishbein Trophy 1959, 62; Open Prs 1961, Life Master Prs 1962, Vanderbilt 1965, 66; Reisinger 1969, 74, 75, 78, 79; Lou Herman Trophy, Blue Ribbon Prs 1970; North American Mens Swiss 1983. He placed second in Life Master Prs 1954, 55, 63; Mens Prs 1955, Master Mixed Tms 1957, Spingold 1957, 69; Reisinger 1965, Vanderbilt 1968, 69, 71, 81; Mens Tms 1976, 80. Rubin has many regional titles to his credit.

RUBIN, Ronald D. (Ron) (b. 1948) of N. Miami Beach FL, stock options trader, became regional tournament director at the age of 18, WBF Life Master, won Bermuda Bowl 1983, placed 5th Rosemblum Tms 1986, 10th 1982. He also represented the ACBL in internat'l competition New Orleans 1978, Biarritz 1982, Bal Harbour 1986. ACBL Diamond Life Master, won Mens Tms 1975, Vanderbilt 1977, 81, 85, 89; Spingold 1980, 82, 92; USBC Team Trials 1980, 82; Open Prs 1988, Life Master Prs 1990. Placed second Vanderbilt 1978, Team Trials 1980, GN Tms 1981, 1992; Reisinger 1983, Spingold 1985, 88. He won *The Bridge World* "Challenge the Champs" competition 10 months in a row and the Rosenkranz Award in 1976. Rubin co-authored *The Ultimate Club*. Won world championship in backgammon 1983, finished second 1978, 89.

RUBINOW, Morton L. (1927-1962) of New York City, bridge teacher. A faculty member at The Card School, he was a pioneer in giving bridge lessons through phonograph records, *Play Bridge with Morton Rubinow* and *Advanced Bridge Conventions*. Rubinow represented the US in world play Turin 1960, won the Herman Trophy, Spingold, Open Prs 1959; Mens Prs 1961, as well as many regional events.

RUDMAN, William K., Jr. (Bill) (b. 1948) of Castro Valley CA, engineer, graduate of U of California-Berkeley; won CA Capital KO Tms 1975, Super Open Prs 1983, Master Prs, Swiss 1984; Mid-Winter Holiday KO Tms 1977; Golden State Open Prs 1981, Wine Country Mens Prs 1983, Super Open Prs 1993; All Western Super Open Prs 1984, IMP Prs 1990, 92; Dist 22 Split Super Swiss

1992.

RUDOLPH, Richard P. (Rudy) (b. 1938) of Pick-erington OH, retired engineer, graduated Otterbein College and Ohio U, was USAF tactical fighter pilot 1961-66. Won Summer secondary Open Prs 1977, Midwest Mens Prs 1972, 79, Open Prs 1975, Mens Swiss 1977, 80, 81; Blue Grass Open Prs 1975; District 11 Nonmixed Prs 1977, Columbus KO Tms, Swiss 1993; Louisville Swiss 1993.

RUPP, Henriette (Henree) (b. 1906) of Indianapolis IN, bridge director; one of the early organizers of bridge in Indianapolis area, Life Master #396; placed second in Womens Tms 1966 and won several regionals.

RUSH, Doris M. (Mrs. G. Rufus) (b. 1927) of Lubbock TX, won Texas Open Tms 1962, Womens Prs 1970; Dist 15 KO Tms 1968, Land of Coronado Womens Swiss 1978, Dallas Master Prs 1982.

RUSINOW, Sydney (1907-1953) of Newark NJ, businessman, silver mine owner; designer of a system of opening leads that bears his name (see RUSINOW LEADS). In 1933 he won the Vanderbilt and throughout the Thirties was the winner of several prestigious Eastern States and New England titles.

RUSKIN, Stanley C. (b. 1940) of Pittsburgh PA, CEO of packaging company, graduate of U of Pittsburgh, some of his many regional wins include Dist 5 Mens Prs 1966, Open Tms 1969, Mens Swiss 1978; Dist 5 GNT 1975, 78, 79, 80, Zone 1 1975; Fall secondary BAM Tms 1979.

RUSS, William (Bill) (b. 1945) of Zurich, Switzerland, born in New York City, EDP manager, graduate of U of Arkansas, U of Chicago, Oklahoma State U. Current coordinator of youth bridge in Switzerland, represented Switzerland in world competition Bal Harbour 1986, Geneva 1990; Europeans 1993. ABA Diamond Life Master with more than 30 regional and nat'l championships since 1967. Won several Swiss BF titles 1983-1993.

RUSSELL, Clifford (b. 1919) of Coral Gables FL, banker, builder and developer; graduate U of Arizona and past chairman of the Metropolitan Museum of Art (Coral Gables) and of the First National Bank of Hialeah. WBF World Master; placed 3rd Rosenblum Tms 1978; won Pan-Am Open Tms 1992; also represented ACBL in Bermuda Bowl in Santiago 1993. ACBL Grand Life Master with more than 11,000 MPS as of 1993, won Spingold 1963, 77; Vanderbilt 1963, 75, 79; GN Tms 1977, Reisinger 1991; placed second in Spingold 1954, 72, 91; Blue Ribbon Prs 1963, 70; Reisinger, Master Mixed Tms 1964; Mens Tms 1973, 77; Vanderbilt 1975, 84, 89, 93; GN Tms 1980, GN Prs 1982, Mens BAM Tms 1983, USBC (Team Trials) 1987. Russell has more than 150 regional wins.

RUST, Gail H. of Daytona Beach FL, bridge club co-owner and retired home economist, graduate of U of Miami; served for 20 years Dist 4 and Unit 148 Boards, member ACBL Goodwill Committee, ACBL Nat'l Appeals Committee, ACBL Bd of Gov. Diamond Life Master; won many regionals including Mid-Atlantic Womens Swiss 1978, 79; Dist 4 Womens Swiss 1980, Northeast FL Sr Swiss 1991, 93; Williamsburg Sr Swiss 1993, Spring sec-

ondary Open Prs (2) 1993, Summer Sr KO Tms 1993.

RUTSTEIN, Donald I. (b. 1927) of Evanston IL, salesman, former professional jazz musician, interests in thoroughbred racing and breeding. Won ABA Summer Nat'l KO Tms 1978. His ACBL titles include Beynon Trophy (Sr Master Individual) 1954; Central States Open Tms 1954, 72, KO Tms 1962, 77, Open Prs 1989; Great Lakes Open Tms 1965, Champaign Open Tms 1967, Tri-Unit Open Tms 1972; Mississippi Valley Open Tms, Open Prs 1972.

RYAN, Marion (1912-1988) of Indianapolis IN, placed second in Womens Prs 1950, Womens Tms 1966.

RYDER, Robert W. (b. 1935) of Caldwell NJ, consulting actuary, New Jersey BL Player of the Year 1968, 76, 91; Diamond Life Master; won Fall secondary Open Prs 1969, Mens Swiss 1980, Mens Prs 1974, Golder Master Prs 1980, Morning KO Tms 1990; Tri-State Open Tms 1967, Keystone Open Tms 1968, Mens Prs 1974; Eastern States Mens Prs 1973.

RYMAN, Mari (b. 1959) of Stockholm, Sweden, economist. Won European Womens Teams 1993 and represented Sweden in one world championship.

S

SABURI, Ken (1901-1985) of Tokyo, Japan, retired managing director of trading house. Former president and honorary president JCBL. Presided over Far East Championships 1964 and 1979. Contributor *JCBL Bulletin*.

SACHS, David S. (Dave) of Baltimore MD, actuary, former president of the Maryland BA, Diamond Life Master, placed second Open Prs 1969, Master Mixed Tms 1970, 74, 78; won numerous regional events.

SACHS, Edith of New York City, real estate broker, won Master Mixed Tms 1973.

SACHS, Suzanne H. (Sue) (Mrs. David S.) of Baltimore MD, travel agency owner, placed second World Womens Prs 1966, 3rd World Olympiad Womens Tms 1968, npc of US #1 Venice Cup Tm 1993, represented US in several other world championships. Sachs, WBF Life Master and ACBL Diamond Life Master, won Womens Prs 1965, Womens Tms 1966, 77, 79; Life Master Womens Prs 1967, Mott-Smith Trophy 1969; placed second Womens Tms, Open Prs 1969; Master Mixed Tms 1970, 74, 78; Womens KO Tms 1988.

SACKS, David L. (b. 1948) of Los Angeles, owner/operator of discount clothing stores. Placed second Life Master Prs 1978, Mens BAM Tms 1979, North American Mens Swiss 1985; won more than 25 regional events.

SACUL, Danny J. (b. 1948) of Jakarta, Indonesia, businessman. WBF World Master. Won Far East Teams 1974, 1979, 1983, 1984, 1992, 1993. Represented Indonesia in ten world championships and in other zonal championships.

SAID, Chuck (b. 1937) of Nashville TN, born in

Baghdad, professional bridge player and teacher, graduade of Eastern Michigan U; has more than 16,000 MPs as of 1993 to his credit. Before he left his native country in the late Fifties he had stories published in magazines and a collection of short stories published in a book; he was also an editor for a local newspaper. Said has won more than 175 regionals, some of his more recent include Space City Open Prs 1980; Reno KO Tms, Open Prs 1987, 90; St Louis KO Tms 1987, 88, 89, Open Prs 1990; Gatlinburg KO Tms 1989, 91, 92; Little Rock KO Tms, Open Prs, Strat Prs 1989; St. Charles KO Tms, Open Prs 1991; Atlantic City Open Prs (3), Williamsburg Swiss, Open Prs (2) 1991; Hot Springs KO Tms 1993, Albuquerque KO Tms 1994.

SAID, Elaine (b. 1946) of Nashville TN, flight attendant supervisor, graduate of U of Tennessee. Won Huntsville Womens Prs, Dayton Womens Prs 1988; Virginia Beach Womens Swiss 1989; Fall secondary Open Prs 1990, Summer Womens Swiss 1993; Daytona Beach Swiss 1990; Ft. Lauderdale KO Tms, Womens Swiss 1990; Raleigh Womens Swiss, Jackson Womens Swiss, Hunt Valley Womens Swiss 1992; Gatlinburg KO Tms, Atlanta Womens KO Tms 1993.

SAKURAI, Tsuneo (b. 1937) of Chiba Pref., Japan, company employee. Represented Japan in three Far East Championships. Won 20 national open team titles and three national open pair titles. JCBL tournament committee chairman for 10 years.

SALAVERRY, Dr. Martin (b. 1954) of Montevideo, Uruguay, veterinarian. Represented Uruguay in zonal championships regularly since 1979 and has won 12 national titles.

SALGADO, Alfonso Menchaca (b.1957) of Santiago, Chile, lawyer. Represented Chile in two world championships and five zonal championships. Has won all national titles.

SALGO, Gabor (b. 1917) of Budapest, Hungary, retired journalist. In the 70s and 80s, the link between Eastern European bridge players and the rest of the world, particularly the European Bridge League and IBPA. Edited Hungarian monthly *Bridzsélet* 1973-1981.

SALIM, Masood (b. 1940) of Karachi, Pakistan, businessman. WBF World Master. As partner of Zia Mahmood, second in Bermuda Bowl 1981, winner BFAME zonal championship 1981, 1983, 1985, 1987.

SALMENKIVI, Eero (b. 1958) of Espoo, Finland, philosopher and journalist. Second Nordic Teams 1984, and represented Finland on five other occasions, including one world championship and two European Championships. National wins include open teams seven times, open pairs twice and knockout teams twice. Editor of Finnish bridge magazine, *Bridge-Lehti*.

SALTSMAN, A. David (b. 1936) of Montreal PQ, stockbroker, placed second Open Prs 1975.

SALTSMAN, Barbara J. (b. 1936) of Montreal PQ, bridge teacher, represented Canada in world play Miami Beach 1972, Bal Harbour 1986, Chile 1993. placed sec-

ond Master Mixed Tms 1974. Her regional wins include Can-Am Womens Prs 1969, 70, 76; Southeastern Womens Swiss 1979; Fleur De Lys Womens Prs 1982, 85.

SALTZ, Jack B. (JBS) (b. 1936) of New York City, vice president Bear Stearns, graduate of U of Virginia, won varsity football state championship; placed second Master Mixed Tms 1974 and won many regionals.

SALVETTI, Sandro of Milan, Italy, npc of Italy's Bermuda Bowl champions 1973, 1974, 1975, npc Italy's European champions 1973, 1975, 1979, chose to continue to use Sergio Zuchelli and Gianfranco Facchini after the 1975 BERMUDA BOWL INCIDENT when the pair were reprimanded for foot-tapping.

SANBORN, Kerri (formerly Shuman) (b. 1946) of New York City, stock trader, formerly a bridge professional, she is actively involved in thoroughbred breeding and racing. WBF Grand Master and ACBL Grand Life Master with more than 17,000 MPs, ranks third among the top women all-time MP holders and in the top 25 of all MP holders as of 1993. Won World Mixed Prs 1978, (second 1986), Venice Cup 1989, 93; World Womens Prs 1990. Sanborn has had several other high placings in world events — 5th Olympiad Womens Tms 1988, Rosenblum Tms 1990; 8th World Womens Prs 1986. She also represented ACBL in the PAMP PAR CONTEST 1990 in Geneva. (This event was by invitation only, limited to about 10-15 players from throughout the world — she was the only woman.) She won the *McKenney Trophy* 1974; Womens Prs 1972, Womens Tms 1978; Mixed Prs 1975, 77, 82; North American Womens Swiss Tms 1989, 90, 93; Master Mixed Tms 1980, 87, 90; finished second Mixed Prs 1971, 74; Womens Tms 1974, Life Master Womens Prs 1975, 85, 86; North American Womens Swiss 1983, Womens KO Tms 1986, Blue Ribbon Prs 1987, Reisinger 1989. Sanborn has won scores of regional titles.

SANBORN, Steve (b. 1954) of Poughkeepsie NY, computer marketing analyst/consultant, won Mens Prs 1980 and several regional titles.

SANDERS, Carol L. (Mamma Bear) (Mrs. Thomas K.) (b. 1932) of Nashville TN, WBF Grand Life Master. In world competition she has won the Venice Cup 1974, 76; World Womens Prs 1982, Womens Tm Olympiad 1984 and was npc of winning Venice Cup team 1987. In addition she placed second in the Womens Prs 1978, Venice Cup 1981, 85. Other high placings in world events are 3rd World Mixed Prs 1978; 6th Olympiad Mixed Tms 1974, 7th World Mixed Prs, World Womens Prs 1974. She won the Israel Swiss Tm Championship and Beijing International Friendship Cup in 1986 and the Ambassador's Cup 1987. Sanders has represented the U.S. in world competition on many other occasions. She is an Honorary Lifetime Member of the Nashville Unit Board, a trustee of the ACBL Charity Foundation, vice chairman of the Nat'l Goodwill Committee. She has chaired or co-chaired many Nashville tournaments, has been a *Bridge World* panelist since 1963 and is a past member of the ACBL Appeals Committee. She is also a frequent bridge lecturer aboard cruise ships.

An ACBL Grand Life Master with more than 14,000 MPs as of 1993, she is in the top ten of all-time masterpoint holders among women and in the top 40 of all masterpoint holders. Sanders won Womens Prs 1962, 93; Womens Tms 1963, 78, 80; Open Prs 1964, Master Mixed Tms 1976, 82; Womens KO Tms 1978, 83, 87; North American Womens Swiss 1983, Life Master Womens Prs 1990, Womens BAM Tms 1992. She finished second Open Prs 1960, the Chicago 1961 (now the Reisinger), LM Womens Prs 1971, 81; Mixed Prs 1979, North American Womens Swiss 1983, Master Mixed Tms 1984, Womens KO Tms 1992, Womens BAM Tms 1986, 91; Womens Prs 1992. Sanders is a prolific winner on the regional circuit.

SANDERS, Thomas K. (Pappa Bear) (Tom) (b. 1932) of Nashville TN, investor, represented U.S. in world play Cannes 1962, Miami Beach 1972, Las Palmas 1974 (6th World Mixed Tms, 7th World Mixed Prs), New Orleans 1978 (7th Rosenblum Tms, 13th World Open Prs), Biarritz 1982, Bal Harbour 1986 (11th World Mixed Prs), Geneva 1990; was npc of the 1981 Bermuda Bowl champions and is a WBF World Master. An ACBL Grand Master with more than 14,000 MPs as of 1993, he ranks in the top 40 of all-time masterpoint holders. He has won the Mixed Prs 1961, Mens Tms 1962, 72; Spingold, Blue Ribbon Prs 1977; Vanderbilt 1979, 90, 93; Life Master Prs, Master Mixed Tms 1982; Mens BAM Tms 1983. He placed second in the Open Prs 1960, Chicago (now the Reisinger) 1961; Spingold, Mens Prs 1963; Reisinger 1973, 86; Vanderbilt 1978, 85; Mixed Prs 1979; North American Swiss 1982; USBC (Team Trials) 1990. He won the Israel Swiss Team Championship and the Beijing Internat'l Friendship Cup 1986 and the Beijing Ambassador's Cup 1987. He won the Cavendish Club Invitational Individual 1979, Open Prs 1981.

Sanders was a member of the ACBL Bd of Dir from 1980 to 1989. He is a lifetime member of the ACBL Bd of Gov, a past member of the ACBL and WBF Appeals Committees and a member of the ACBL Goodwill Committee. He is the only graduate of Vanderbilt U to win the Vanderbilt Trophy. Sanders was president of ACBL 1986 and chairman of the Bd of Dir 1987. He was a founder of the ACBL Educational Foundation, served as its first president (1987-1990), and was elected President Emeritus in 1990. He was chairman of the Fall NABC 1988 and has been a *Bridge World* panelist since 1963. He has also been a panelist for Italian and Turkish bridge magazines. He frequently lectures on bridge aboard cruise ships and has won an estimated 300 regional events.

SANDS, Norma (b. 1938) of Denver CO, bridge teacher, writer, member Nat'l Ethics Committee since 1991; author of *Standard American Bridge Updated, Playing the Cards* and *Bridge Helper*. She co-authored (with Jan Janitschke) the *Bridge Mini Series*, which included *Fine Tuning Your Bridge, Later in the Auction, Opening Leads Versus Suits, Double Trouble, Weak Two Bids, Competitive Bidding, Defensive Signals, Negative Doubles, Slam Bidding I, Slam Bidding II*. This series was awarded Book of the Year 1992 by the ABTA. Won Denver Womens Swiss 1989; Dist 17 GN Tms 1990; Colorado Victory Trophy 1989.

SANTAMARINA, Agustín (b. 1934) of Buenos Aires, Argentina, landowner. World Life Master. South American champion 1962, 1964, 1976, 1979, 1980, 1981. Represented Argentina in Bermuda Bowl 1967, 1977, 1981, 1991 in World Team Olympiad 1964, 1968, 1972, 1976,

1980, 1988. National titles won include open teams 13 times and open pairs twice. Won Gabarret Cup 1973, 1974, 1977, 1981.

SANTAMARINA, Marcos (b. 1931) of Buenos Aires, Argentina, landowner. South American champion 1962. Represented Argentina in Bermuda Bowl 1963, in World Team Olympiad 1988. 13 national titles won include open teams twice and open pairs once.

SANTIAGO, Rudisinda (b. 1931) of Makati, Philippines. Won Far East Womens Teams 1979, 1982. Represented Philippines in one other zonal championship.

SANTOS, Jorge Monteiro Dos (b. 1941) of Lisbon, Portugal, lawyer. Represented Portugal in three world championships and five European championships. National wins include open teams eight times and open pairs once.

SANTOS, Rui Silva (b. 1944) of Lisbon, Portugal, electrical engineeer. Represented Portugal in three world championships and four European championships. National wins include open team three times. President of Portuguese Bridge Federation 1984-86.

SAPIRE, Leon (b. 1910) of Johannesburg, South Africa, attorney. Npc South African teams World Team Olympiad 1960. Won Open Pairs 1955. Founder and editor of *Bridge Bulletin*. Honorary life vice-president of South African Bridge Federation. Formerly member of WBF Executive and vice-president of IBPA.

SAPIRE, Max (b. 1912) of East London, South Africa, retired business executive. Represented South Africa in World Teams Olympiad 1960. 7 national wins include two in open pairs. Contributor to *Bridge S.A.* and many other publications. Author of a book on Culbertson Asking Bids. Theoretical contributions include South African Texas.

SARAVIA, Alfredo (1908-1991) of Buenos Aires, Argentina, real estate official. South American champion 1964, represented Argentina in Bermuda Bowl 1963. 16 national titles won include open teams four times and open pairs twice. Former president of Argentine Bridge Association.

SARON, Robert (Bob) (1923-1990) of St. Petersburg FL, stockbroker, former company executive, Dist 9 representative to ACBL Bd of Dir from 1977-1990; four-time president of Unit 128, served more than 30 years as a member of its Board and served as president of Dist 9. Bridge editor of *St. Petersburg Times* and authored *Medical Directory of Good Bridge*. Won Fall secondary Commercial and Industrial Prs 1961, Swiss Tms 1979; Southeastern Open Tms 1962, Mens Swiss 1976; Florida Mens Prs 1974, Sr Swiss 1981, 82.

SARTORIUS, Barbara (b. 1941) of Lake Hiawatha NJ, professional bridge teacher/player, graduate of U of Miami, member NJBL Bd of Dir 1970-82. Won Open Prs 1969 and placed second Life Master Womens Prs 1990. A Diamond Life Master, her regional wins include Summer secondary Womens Prs 1967, Golder Prs 1980; Autumn Leaf Womens Tms 1985; Dist 3 GN Prs 1989; Dist 3 Summer Womens Prs 1990, Womens Swiss 1990, 91, Womens Prs, Swiss Tms 1991; Spring secondary Womens

Prs 1991, Summer Open Prs 1992. Won New Jersey BL Little McKenney 1992, 93.

SARWAT, Safeya (Sophie) (b. 1933) of Cairo, Egypt. WBF World Master. Won Middle East Womens Teams 1987 and 1991, second 1985. Represented Egypt in Venice Cup in 1987 and 1991. Has won many national mixed pair titles. Board member of the Egyptian Swimming Federation, holds many executive positions in the international organization of synchronized swimming.

SASSON, Esther (born in England) of Caracas, Venezuela. Won CAC Womens Teams 1979, 1981, represented Venezuela in 9 world championships. Won 24 national titles.

SAVEC, Herman (b. 1941) of Ptuj, Slovenia, electronic engineer. Represented Yugoslavia in some international events. Won 9 national titles.

SAWIRUDIN, Munawar (b. 1948) of Jakarta, Indonesia, staff secretary of Chamber of Commerce. Won Far East Teams 1979, 1982, 1984, 1992, 1993. Represented Indonesia in six world championships and in other zonal championships.

SAWYER, Victoria M. (Vicky) (b. 1975) of Occoquan VA, student, involved in athletic activities in school and volunteer work. In 1990 she was the fourth youngest female ever to achieve Life Master rating. She is the ACBL bridge lesson coordinator for her high school, a member of the Junior Corps and was been appointed Chairman for Junior Activities for the Summer NABC 1993. Sawyer won NABC Jr Prs 1992 and placed second NABC Youth Prs 1989, Youth Flt of the Viking Prs 1989, 90. She won Atlanta Open Midnight Swiss 1989; Buffalo Charity Prs 1988 and several other regional tournaments.

SAXE, Eugene G. (b. 1953) of Stamford CT, personnel consultant, vice president Dist 25 1994, member ACBL Charity Committee; won Dist 3 KO Tms 1988, Open Prs 1994; Mid-South Spring Swiss 1989; Long Island Open Prs 1991; New York Summer Swiss 1992, Winter KO Tms 1993; New England Summer KO Tms 1992, 93; Canadian-American Swiss 1993.

SAYED, Floyd E. (b. 1925) of Boca Raton FL, insurance agent, past president of the Michigan BA, served on its Board for more than 20 years. Diamond Life Master; won 20-25 regionals including Motor City Open Tms 1968, 79, Open Prs 1968, KO Tms 1974, Mens Prs 1975, 81, Mixed Prs 1976; Dist 12 GN Tms Zone I 1973; Marco Island Swiss 1993; Orlando Swiss, Sr Prs 1994.

SCAFFIDI, Sam (1935-1988) of Mingo Junction OH, social worker, won Midwest Fall Open Tms 1960, Great Lakes Open Tms 1962, Dist 5 Swiss 1970, All-American KO Tms 1978, Mixed Prs 1984. See STRIPED-TAIL APE DOUBLE.

SCANAVINO, Eduardo (b. 1941) of Buenos Aires, Argentina, bridge club manager and teacher. WBF World Master. South American champion 1976, 1979, 1980, 1981, 1985. Represented Argentina in Bermuda Bowl 1977, 1981, 1985, in World Team Olympiad 1976, 1980, 1984, 1988. 16 national titles won include open teams 7

times. He was a junior chess champion.

SCATASSA, Eva M. (Evi) (b. 1943) of West Nyack NY, born in Russia, administrative assistant, won Capitol Dist Fall Womens Prs 1977; Can-Am Open Swiss, Open Prs 1978; Dist 4 Womens Swiss 1981; Summer secondary Womens Prs 1984, Open Swiss 1985; Southeastern Womens Swiss 1988; Cambridge Open Swiss 1987; Puerto Rico Open Prs 1989; Gatlinburg Womens Prs, Las Vegas Womens Prs 1992.

SCHAAB, Gail K. (b. 1941) of Colorado Springs, former petroleum engineer, graduate Rutgers U. Won Womens Prs 1976; regional wins include Cornhusker Masters Prs 1977; Northwest Iowa Womens Swiss 1978; Pheasant Swiss 1978.

SCHAEFER, Lynne C. (b. 1955) of Southfield MI, vice-president for administrative services, graduate Michigan State U, won Womens BAM Tms 1989.

SCHÄFFER, Lauge (b. 1959) of Copenhagen, Denmark, a physician working in the field of diabetes research. WBF World Master. 8th World Pairs 1990. Won Copenhagen Pairs and Copenhagen Club Teams. Has contributed to bidding theory.

SCHALTZ, Dorthe (b 1956), of Odense, Denmark, medical secretary. WBF World Master. Won World Womens Teams 1988. Member of Danish open team which lost 1992 World Team quarterfinal by 2 imps to France, the eventual winner. This is the best performance ever by a woman in a World Team Olympiad. Also represented Denmark in one other world championship, one zonal championship and many other occasions, some in open play. Won nine national titles.

SCHALTZ, Lizzie (b 1923), of Copenhagen, Denmark, bridge teacher. WBF World Master. Third World Womens Teams 1960. Won European Womens Teams 1955. Represented Denmark in one other world championship and one other zonal championship. Three national titles include Open Teams once.

SCHALTZ, Peter (b. 1950) of Odense, Denmark, manager of a wine company. WBF World Life Master. Third World Teams 1984, second European Teams 1979. Won European Junior Teams 1970, Nordic Teams 1986. Represented Denmark in the 1992 World Open Teams, losing in the quarterfinal by 2 imps to France, the eventual winner. Also represented Denmark in two other world championships and four other zonal championships. 24 national titles include Open Teams seven times and Open Pairs three times.

SCHAPIRO, Boris (b. 1909) of London, England. WBF Grand Master. Won Bermuda Bowl 1955, second World Teams 1960, World Pairs 1962. Won European Teams 1948, 1949, 1954, 1963. Won Sunday Times Invitational Prs 1964, second 1991 at age of 81. Many national wins include Gold Cup 10 times. Author of two books, bridge columnist *London Sunday Times*. See BUENOS AIRES AFFAIR.

SCHAUFELBERGER, W.K.A. (Win) (1902-1972) of Sydney, Australia, chief director of New South Wales BA, captained the first Australian team to compete in an international contest, the World Team Olympiad at Turin 1960. Was playing captain of 11 N.S.W. teams and one Australian team; won 12 national titles, including Open Pairs 1954, 1959, and N.S.W. Open Teams, 1968. Served as treasurer of the Australian Bridge Federation, vice president of New South Wales BA.

SCHEINBERG, Martin R. (b. 1930) of New York City, systems engineer, won Mens Tms 1960. He was a pioneer in scoring tournament results and predealing hands by electronic data processing equipment. See COMPUTERS.

SCHEMEIL, Pierre (b. 1921 in Egypt) of Paris, France, former lawyer and finance counsel. The only person to have represented four countries (Lebanon, Egypt, Switzerland, France) in international competition. Won national titles in Lebanon, Egypt and France. Npc of two French world champion teams.

SCHENKEN, Bee (Mrs. Howard, formerly Bee Gale) (1916-1993) of New York City, one of the world's most successful women rubber bridge players, won Mixed Prs 1957, Fall Womens Tms 1958, 60, 61, 69; Spring Womens Tms 1964, 68; placed second Master Mixed Tms 1958, Spring Womens Tms 1963, 67; Reisinger 1966, Womens Prs 1969. She won numerous regional titles and several international titles including Deauville Open Prs eight times. She was an active fund raiser for various charities.

SCHENKEN, Howard (1905-1979) of New York City, real estate investor, bridge author and columnist, was considered by many to be the best player of all time. He is credited with introduction of several aspects of playing technique and deceptive play now standard, plus the WEAK TWO-BID, the forcing TWO-OVER-ONE, the prepared opening bid ("anticipation"), and other bidding devices. Schenken's Raymond Club team, 1927-1929, first successfully broke the reign of the established men's clubs in tournament competition. After occasional appearances with the Four Horsemen and Bid-Rite teams, Schenken was a founder of the Four Aces and participated in their long series of victories including victory over the French European champions in 1935 in the first official World Championship (see WORLD CHAMPIONSHIPS) and a winning tour of Europe in pair matches with Michael T. Gottlieb, the next year.

Bermuda Bowl champion in 1950, 51, 53; represented U.S. in World Olympiad 1960, and North America in World Championships 1961, 63, 65. He had five wins in the Life Master Pairs 1931, 33, 34, 41, 43; ten wins in the Spingold 1934, 36, 38, 39, 43, 45, 48, 50, 52, 60; ten wins in the Vanderbilt 1934, 35, 37, 38, 46, 50, 55, 56, 57, 64; each constitutes a record. Other national wins include Master Individual 1932, Mixed Tms 1935, Men's Tms 1949, Mixed Prs 1957, Chicago 1957, 63; Reisinger 1968. He was second in national events 19 times (See also USBA CHAMPIONSHIP.)

Schenken was an ACBL Board Member, and IBPA honorary member in 1973. His writings included *Four Aces System of Contract Bridge*, *Better Bidding in Fifteen Minutes* and *Howard Schenken's Big Club* (see Schenken System) and *Education of a Bridge Player*. He took over the Four Aces syndicated bridge column in 1943; in 1957 he merged it with Richard L. Frey's to become co-author of the longest continuously published nationally syndicated bridge feature. In 1970, he became the sole author of the column. He was a contributing editor *Bridge Encyclopedia*.

SCHERMER, John (b. 1948) of Seattle WA, painting contractor, won Swiss Tms 1977, Mens BAM Tms 1978, Vanderbilt 1992; placed second Spingold 1986. A Diamond Life Master, Schermer has won numerous regional events.

SCHEUER, Jerome (1889-1979) of Brookline MA, was an insurance broker, bridge writer and prominent lawn tennis official at the nat'l and internat'l levels. He won the New England KO Tms 12 times between 1938-54. His writing included contributions to *Bridge Magazine* and *The Bridge World*. He was a contributing editor *Bridge Encyclopedia*.

SCHICK, Dorothy E. of Mayfield Heights OH, won Dist 5 Womens Prs 1956, Summer secondary Goddard Prs 1957; Canadian Nat'l Womens Prs 1964, Mixed Prs 1981; All-American Mixed Prs 1967, Womens Swiss 1981, Womens Prs 1982; Great Lakes Womens Swiss 1981, Dist 5 GN Tms, Zonal.

SCHIPPERHEYN, Ton (b. 1933) of Amstelveen, the Netherlands, bridge writer and journalist. Assistant manager of the Netherlands Bridge League. Bridge columnist for regional syndicated newspapers and editor of *Bridge*. Author (with Cees Sint) of four TV courses and about 40 books, including *From Start to Finish*. (The first two volumes are the official beginners course of the Netherlands Bridge League.) More than a million copies of Sint/Schipperheyn's books have been sold.

SCHIPPERS, Elly (b. 1943) of Amstelveen, The Netherlands, systems analyst. WBF World Life Master. Second Venice Cup 1989, third World Womens Teams 1984. Second European Womens Teams 1983, 1989. Won European Womens Pairs 1980, second 1987. Represented Netherlands regularly since 1979. Won Netherlands Womens Pairs four times.

SCHLEIFER, Meyer (b. 1908) of Los Angeles CA, bridge teacher, won Life Master Prs 1966, Barclay Trophy 1947; a Diamond Life Master, he has won scores of regional events.

SCHLEPPEGRELL, Thorald W. (Terry) (b. 1953) of Anchorage AK, retail clerk, caught a 17-pound trophy rainbow trout in 1989, Unit treasurer and tournament chairmen. Won Polar Swiss 1974, Open Prs 1977, 80, KO Tms 1984, Masters Prs 1990, Mens Prs 1991; Hawaii Super Open Prs 1991.

SCHNEIDER, Karl (1904-1977) of Vienna, Austria, engineer, was one of the great players of the world. World champion 1937, European champion 1936. Represented France in Bermuda Bowl 1954, represented Austria five times in Europeans, placing second 1951, 57. Won first Austrian Teams in 1968 and then retired from play.

SCHNEIDER, Rebecca A. (b. 1977) of E Brunswick NJ, student. In 1991 became the youngest female (age 14) certified club director. She conducted novice bridge sessions at the Bethesda regional and at the Summer NABC 1991. She has directed at Rutgers U Duplicate Bridge Club and ran the North American College Bridge Championships there in 1991.

SCHODER, Lt./Col. William J. (Kojak) (b. 1932) of Tampa FL, chief tournament director for the World Bridge Federation (WBF), ACBL nat'l tournament director, ACBL Field Representative. Began his directing career part-time in 1959, in 1966 he achieved regional rating and in 1980 was promoted to associate nat'l. He contributes to the *ACBL BULLETIN, Florida Bridge News, Gold Coast Bridge News* and the *Trumpet*. Schoder is a past president of the PROFESSIONAL TOURNAMENT DIRECTORS ASSOCIATION. He serves as the chief tournament director for the Central American and Caribbean Bridge Federation (since 1972). He has been a World Bridge Federation director since 1972 and its Chief Director since 1987. A retired USAF pilot, he was awarded many decorations including the Distinguished Service Medal, the Distinguished Flying Cross, the Bronze Star, the Legion of Merit and 10 air medals. Schoder is a graduate of Queens College of the University of the city of New York. A linguist, he is fluent in Spanish, German and French. Also an accomplished pianist.

SCHOU, Steen (b. 1952), of Aarhus, Denmark, computer consultant, WBF World Master. Third World Teams 1984. Won Nordic Teams 1984. Also represented Denmark in one other world championship and two zonal championships. 4 Danish titles include Open Team twice.

SCHREIBER, Michael J. (b. 1952) of Fowler CA, investment syndicator; served for many years on ACBL Appeals Committee. Using the pseudonym Sol I. Taryman, he was the original moderator for the *Problem Solvers Panel* in the *Southern California Bridge News*. A Diamond Life Master, Schreiber won Open Prs 1980, was Intercollegiate champion 1973; placed second Mens Swiss 1987. Has won 40-50 regional titles including Bridge Wk Master Mens Prs 1980, Mens Prs, Master Prs 1981; Denver Super Open Prs, Master Prs 1982; Reno KO Tms 1986, San Diego Open Prs, Albuquerque KO Tms 1987; Eugene Super Swiss 1989, Tacoma KO Tms 1991, Portland KO Tms 1993.

SCHREIBER, William L. (Bill) (b. 1947) of Van Nuys CA, CPA, Intercollegiate champion 1973, has won many regionals events.

SCHROEDER, David A. (b. 1950) of Las Vegas, baseball handicapper, won Life Master Mens Prs 1977; backgammon champion.

SCHROEDER, Dirk (b. 1943) of Wiesbaden, Germany, bridge teacher, journalist and travel organizer. WBF World Master. Won three Common Market titles and 29 German titles. Represented Germany regularly since 1969, and headed German masterpoint standings since 1974. Developed first European Youth Camp 1975. Member of EBL Executive and its youth committee since 1989. Board member DBV 1983-89. IBPA awards secretary and member of its Executive. Columnist for *Deutsches Bridge Verbands-Blatt* since 1969. Theorist. See SCHROEDER SQUEEZE.

SCHROEDER, Kareen (b. 1947) of Wiesbaden, Germany, bridge teacher, journalist and travel organizer. WBF World Master. Third Venice Cup 1989; won European Womens Teams 1989, one Common Market title and 15 national titles. Member of German Womens Teams in many events since 1975 including five world championships. Columnist for *Deutsches Bridge Verbands-Blatt* since 1969.

SCHUETT, Jeffrey G. of Riverwoods IL, computer software developer, graduate of Northwestern U, other interests include gardening, photography, wildlife, solar energy. Designed and helped to build his passive solar home. Diamond Life Master; some of his more than 25 regional wins include Polar Open Prs 1982 84; Central States I Masters Prs 1987, BAM Tms 1990, Swiss 1991; Gopher Open Prs 1984, Swiss 1985; Central States II Swiss 1987, 92, 94, Master Prs 1988, 89, Open Prs 1989; St Louis Open Prs 1990; Spring secondary Morning KO Tms 1990, 91, Summer KO Tms 1991, Fall Morning KO Tms 1992; Fort Worth Open Prs 1991, Pheasant Run Open Prs 1993.

SCHUETT, Virginia (Ginny) of Riverwoods IL, high school and bridge teacher; graduated Northern Illinois U, Nat'l College of Education, collector of recipes, cards and crystal. CCBA Bd member since 1987, Unit Education Liaison since 1988, active in the ABTA. Won Central States II Womens Swiss 1981, Womens KO Tms 1988, Open Prs 1989; Milwaukee Womens Swiss 1982; St. Paul Open Prs 1984, Swiss 1985; Iowa City Swiss 1987; Oconomowoc Womens Swiss, Womens Prs, KO Tms 1988; Spring secondary Morning KO Tms 1990, 91; Grand Rapids Open Prs, Swiss Tms 1990; Summer Morning KO Tms 1991, St Louis Womens Prs 1991.

SCHULD, Diana K. (b. 1938) of Glen Head NY, graduated Augustana College, Hofstra U; retired elementary music teacher (34 years), co-owner/operator Vanderbilt BC, Unit 242 Bd member 1968-76; placed second Life Masters Prs 1967, won Eastern States Womens Prs 1970, Open Prs 1990; New England Fall Mixed Tms 1971; Fun City Womens Prs 1973; Summer secondary Open Prs 1973, Spring IMP Prs 1991, Fall Continuous Prs II 1992; Puerto Rico Womens Prs 1979, 81;

SCHULD, Frank P. Jr. (1927-1993) of Glen Head NY, co-owner/president Vanderbilt BC, bridge teacher and director, Civil War history buff. Schuld was a member of the committee that established Dist 24, Dist 24 Judiciary Committee and was instrumental in bringing about separate unit status for Nassau-Suffolk BA. Author of *The Simple Squeeze in Bridge*. Placed second Life Master Prs 1967 and won New England Fall Mixed Tms 1971, Summer secondary Open Prs 1973, Spring IMP Prs 1991, Fall Continuous Prs II 1992; Puerto Rico Mens Prs 1987. His 95-year-old father still plays regularly and runs a Senior Citizen weekly game.

SCHULLE, Kay (Mrs. John Mohan) (b. 1950) of Santa Monica CA; bridge professional, graduate of U of Washington; other interests are wildlife photography, paddle tennis and world travel. WBF World Master, won Venice Cup 1993, placed 4th 1991; won USWBC (Tm Trials) 1985, 91, second 1993; also competed internat'lly 1978, 86. An ACBL Diamond Life Master; won Womens KO Tms 1985, 89; Womens Prs 1987, North American

Womens Swiss 1991, 93; Womens BAM Tms 1991; placed second North American Womens Swiss 1988; Womens KO Tms 1990, 93; Life Master Prs 1990, Mixed Prs 1994. Has won more than 100 regional events and been USA Goodwill ambassador to South African Nat'ls 1985, 88, 89, 90, 91 where she won Nat'l Prs once and Nat'l Tms twice.

SCHUTZE, Kenneth R. (b. 1949) of Austin TX, staff attorney Texas Court of Criminal Appeals; won Life Master Prs 1979, GN Prs 1993, 94; placed second Fall Swiss Tms 1977, 79. Diamond Life Master, has won many regionals.

SCHWAB, Charles M. (1862-1939) of New York City, a noted financier, steel magnate and patron of bridge. He was president of the Whist Club of New York, played on its teams and was "ex officio" member of the committee that participated in the first International Code of Contract Bridge Laws 1932. See SCHWAB CUP.

SCHWAB, Irving W. (1903-1984) of Springfield MO, attorney, instrumental in the formation of the ACBL Goodwill Committee; won several regional events.

SCHWARTZ, Adrian (b. 1944) of Kiriat Ono, Israel, engineer, represented Israel World Team Olympiad 1968, 1972, 1980, European championships 1970, 1971, 1973, 1974, 1977, 1979, 1981; national wins include Open Pairs 1968, 1969, 1971.

SCHWARTZ, Elmer I. (b. 1903) of Shaker Heights OH, practicing attorney, Life Master #96; past president of Dist 5, *Bridge World* panelist in the Fifties. Won the Chicago (now the Reisinger) 1949, Mens Tms 1958; placed second in the Spingold 1946, Chicago 1952. His regional wins include Keystone Mixed Prs 1953; All American Open Prs 1964, Mens Prs, Mixed Prs 1965.

SCHWARTZ, Eugene (b. 1916) of Mercer Island WA, retired commercial pilot, graduate U of Illinois, has piloted all aircraft from DC-3 to B747; won Pacific Northwest Open Tms 1959, Master Prs 1960, 61, Open Prs 1982; Puget Sound Open Prs 1982, Oregon Trail Open Prs 1993.

SCHWARTZ, Peter L. (b. 1934) of Cote St. Luc PQ, corporate executive; won Can-Am Open Tms 1956, 57, Open Prs 1957, Mens Prs 1975, 77. A bridge teacher, Schwartz authored the book *K.I.S.S. (Keep it Simple, Stupid): A simplified Approach to Learning Bridge.* Previous owner, with Peter Pender, of Montreal School of Bridge, he became a Life Master in 1958 and at that time was the youngest in Canada.

SCHWARTZ, Richard C. (b. 1943) of E. Elmhurst NY, hotel owner and entrepeneur, graduate of Michigan State U; considered one of the country's most successful handicappers (horse racing). Won IMP Prs 1989, Open Swiss 1992; placed second IMP Prs 1990, Open Prs II 1993. His numerous regional wins include Great Lakes Mens Prs 1965; Summer secondary Commercial and Industrial Tms 1967; Tri-State Open Tms 1968; New York Winter Swiss 1991; Orlando KO Tms 1992; Ft Lauderdale Open Swiss, Swiss, KO Tms, Morning KO Tms 1992.

SCHWARTZ, Sylvia (Mrs. Elmer I.) (1907-1978) of Shaker Heights OH, represented US in Turin 1960, placed second Womens Prs 1959.

SCHWENCKE, John (Jack) (b. 1916) of N. Palm Beach FL, real estate developer, won NAC Swiss 1978, placed second Vanderbilt 1987. A Diamond Life Master; has numerous regional wins to his credit.

SCHWENKREIS, Tomas (b. 1942) of Frankfurt, Germany, corporate accountant. WBF World Master. Represented Germany regularly in world and zonal championships from 1973. Won several national titles. High-ranked German chessplayer.

SCHWERDT, Christian (b. 1958) of Schwäbisch Hall, Germany, lawyer. WBF World Master. Represented Germany in one world championship and two European Junior Championships. Won 7 national titles. Vice president German Bridge Federation with special responsibility for finance.

SCOPE, Ivan H. (b. 1934) of San Francisco, worker's compensation consultant. Diamond Life Master; won GN Prs 1982 and numerous regionals.

SCOTT, Gratz M. (1882-1935) of New York City, bridge teacher and president of the Cavendish Club of New York, was an outstanding figure in whist and bridge for 25 years. Scott and teammates Wilbur Whitehead, Edwin Wetzlar and Ralph Richards were co-winners of the first national contract bridge tournament ever held, the 1928 Board-a-Match competition for the Harold S. Vanderbilt Trophy. The following year he placed second.

SCOTT, Joe V. (b. 1947) of Rogers AR, director of administration, graduated U of Arkansas, past president Unit 247; won Dist 10 GN Tms 1977, 79, 83; Mid-South Open Prs 1978; Missouri Valley Mens Swiss, Master Prs 1978; Toast of Tulsa Swiss 1979; Oklahoma City Open Prs 1981; Dist 10 GN Prs 1981, 82, 84, 89, 92; Springfield Swiss 1982, 90; Pine Bluff Swiss 1991.

SEALY, Larry (b. 1955) of Huntsville AL, strategic defense systems analyst, graduate of U of Alabama, coaches youth basketball and baseball. His more than 20 regional wins include Nashville KO Tms 1977; Gatlinburg KO Tms 1980; Huntsville Mens Swiss 1980, 84, Swiss Tms 1980, KO Tms 1984; Dist 10 GN Tms 1982, 86, 88; Jackson Open Prs, Swiss Tms 1984; Memphis Swiss 1990.

SEAMON, Janice of N. Miami FL, attorney, bridge teacher, graduate of U of Florida, U of Kansas City, Nova U of Law (summa cum laude, JD); won Junior Master of the Year category 1976, her first year of playing. Won Womens KO Tms 1988, 92; Womens Prs 1992, Life Master Womens Prs 1993; placed second North American Womens Swiss 1988, Womens Prs 1989, Womens KO Tms 1989, 93; Life Master Womens Prs 1991. She has won more than 50 regionals including Central States Womens Swiss 1988, 89, 92, Womens KO Tms 1989, BAM Tms 1991, Open Swiss, Womens Prs 1992; Bonaventure Womens Prs 1990, Womens Swiss 1991, 92, Open Prs (2) 1991; Pointe Verde Open Prs, 1993. See FAMILY.

SEAMON, Michael E. (b. 1960) of Miami Beach FL, bridge teacher and professional player, a WBF World Master, he was second in Rosenblum Tms 1990. An ACBL Grand Life Master with more than 10,000 MPs, won Open Tms 1992, 93; placed second Spingold 1987, IMP Prs 1989; his more than 90 regional wins include Southeastern Masters Prs 1977; Florida Open Prs 1981; St Louis Swiss, Jacksonville Open Swiss 1987; Hollywood KO Tms 1988; Orlando Swiss, Hilton Head Swiss, San Antonio Prs 1989; Dist 9 GN Tms 1989; Nashville Swiss 1991; Columbia KO Tms 1991, Toronto KO Tms, Swiss 1991; Richmond Open Swiss, KO Tms 1991. See FAMILY.

SEAMON, Rita (Mrs. William E.) (b. 1924) of N. Miami Beach FL, bridge teacher and director; won Master Mixed Tms 1974; placed second Womens Prs 1961, 89. Diamond Life Master, numerous regional wins include Southeastern Mixed Prs 1959, 68, Womens Prs 1985; Central Florida Mixed Prs 1978, Puerto Rico Open Prs 1978; Gateway to Space Open Prs 1982; Dist 9 GN Prs 1980, GN Tms 1982. See FAMILY.

SEAMON, William E. (Billy) (1917-1992) of Miami Beach FL, retired banking executive, represented North America in the Bermuda Bowl 1957, was a contributing editor to *Bridge Encyclopedia* and a syndicated bridge columnist. Diamond Life Master; won Spingold 1956, 63; Vanderbilt 1963, GN Tms 1973, Master Mixed Tms 1974; placed second Fall Mens Tms 1952, Chicago (now the Reisinger) 1954, Vanderbilt 1960, Spring Mens Tms 1973, GN Tms 1978, 80. He won Israeli Mens Prs 1988 and numerous regional titles including Summer secondary Mixed Prs 1968 with his sister Edith Kemp-Freilich. See FAMILY.

SEARS, Richard C. (b. 1936) of Palisades NY, retired employee benefits consultant, attends 20-30 bullfights each year in Spain, youngest Fellow, Society of Actuaries since Oswald Jacoby. Won New England Fall Mens Prs in the late Fifties playing with a female fill-in (Connie Kemball). Regionals wins inclulde New England Fall Mixed Tms 1957, KO Tms 1958, 61, 64, Spring Open Tms 1959.

SEEWALD, Leo J. (1908-1991) of South St. Paul MN, retired teacher, ACBL president in 1964, a member of the ACBL Bd of Dir, Bd of Gov and chairman of the ACBL Masterpoint Plan Committee. He also served as president of the Minnesota Unit and as director of the Mid-American-Canadian Conference.

SEGANDER, Rut (b. 1917) of Karlsborg, Sweden, won World Womens Teams 1968, European Womens championships 1962, 1967, Nordic Womens championships, national Womens Pairs; WBF Life Master.

SEIDEL, Tilman (b. 1968) of Innsbruck, Austria, ecologist. Won European Junior Pairs 1991. Represented Austria in four other European events. Won Austrian Open Pairs. An active member of "Greenpeace".

SEIDMAN, Solomon (Sol) (b. 1909) of Brooklyn NY, retired social studies teacher and bridge lecturer, educated at NYU and City College of NY. Named ACBL Honorary Member 1984. Served as co-chairman of NABC Appeals Committee for many years and served on ACBL Bd of Dir 1974-1984. Former president of Dist 24 and has been associated with the Greater New York BA since 1952; has held every major office in that organization. He became chairman of the board of the GNYBA in 1984, succeeding Ira Zippert, who succeeded Seidman as Dist 24 director. Seidman was vice chairman of the Protest and Appeals Committee at the World Pair Championships in Biarritz 1982. Diamond Life Master. He has won just about every title at sectional and regional tournaments in the NY area, New Jersey and Philadelphia — including the Von Zedtwitz Tms, Goldman Prs and the Eastern States KO Tms.

SEIFERT, Bogumil (b. 1923) of Warsaw, Poland, economist. Helped found Polish Bridge Union and was its general secretary 1957-62. Helped establish Hungarian and Czechoslovak NCBOs. Bridge journalist and author of several books. Chief editor of Polish *Encyclopedia of Bridge*.

SELÇUK, Koray (b. 1938) of Istanbul, Turkey, businessman. Represented Turkey in one world championship and seven zonal championships. 12 national wins include open teams four times.

SELIGMAN, Barbara of Dublin, Ireland, company director, represented Ireland in the World Women's Olympiad 1992; World Women's Pairs 70, 74; European Championships 62, 63, 65, 67, 69, 71, 73, 74, 75. National wins include all major Irish titles.

SELLERS, Steve (b. 1954) of Arcata CA, real estate consultant, served as president of Dist 22 and member of ACBL Bd of Gov from Dist 22, placed second Masters Division Mini-McKenney 1980; won Sacramento Open Tms 1985, Hawaii Super Open Prs, Dist 20 GN Prs 1986; Spring secondary Open Prs 1987; Monterey Open Prs 1987.

SENDER, Elfreda (b. 1931 in Germany) of Irvine, Calif., formerly of Johannesburg, South Africa, retired secretary. Second World Womens Teams 1968, represented South Africa in two other world championships.

SENIOR, Brian R. (b. 1953) of Nottingham, England, bridge writer, teacher and director. WBF World Master. Represented both Britain and Ireland in world and zonal championships. Represented both England and Northern Ireland in Camrose Trophy matches. Author of 8 books and many magazine articles.

SERES, Thomas Peter (Tim) (b. 1925 in Austria), of Randwick NSW, Australia, horse-racing investor. WBF World Life Master. Third Bermuda Bowl 1971, 1979; represented Australia in 10 other world championships. Far East champion 1968, 1970; represented Australia on eight other occasions. 37 national wins include Inter-State Teams 21 times, Open Pairs 8 times. Contributor to several magazines. Honorary Member of ABF. Awarded Order of Australia for contributions to bridge. See SERES SQUEEZE.

SERF, Marianne (b. 1931) of Paris, France, bridge teacher, European Womens champion 1969, second World Womens Pairs 1962, represented France World

Womens Teams 1964, 1968, European Womens Championships 1963, 1967, 1981; won many national titles, WBF Life Master.

SERRAS, Jan (b. 1944) of Gent, Belgium, civil engineer. Bridge columnist for *Het Volk* and several other Belgian newspapers. Chief Belgian tournament director, worked at some international championships.

SERVER, Lenore (Len)(b. 1937) of River Vale NJ, elementary school teacher, certified director since 1971, she lectures and directs bridge games on cruise ships. Placed second Swiss Tms. Won Puerto Rico Womens Prs 1977; Dist 4 Womens Swiss 1981; Bluenose KO Tms 1981; Dist 3 Open Prs 1985.

SHAKOFSKY, Jerry (b. 1945) of Kew Gardens NY, graduate of Mannes College of Music, began directing bridge in 1969 and has attained the rank of Regional-3.

SHALLON, Marty (b. 1952) of Redondo Beach CA, accountant, placed second in Mens Tms 1974, Spingold 1975, IMP Prs 1991.

SHANAHAN, Dorothy of London, England, statistician, won the World Women's Teams 1964, and was European Women's champion 1961, 1966. Her national titles include English Women's Teams, Mixed Teams twice each, National Pairs 1956.

SHANBROM, Helen (b. 1919) of Tamarac FL, retired math teacher, educated at Western Kentucky Teachers College, U of Michigan, Wayne U, Boston College and Yale. ACBL Grand Life Master with more than 12,000 MPs as of 1994, contributor to *ACBL Bulletin*; member ACBL Goodwill Committee since the Fifties; LM #973 of the original 1000; won the ACBL Ace of Clubs Life Master category 1989, 90 (broke the record with 360 pts), 91, 92, 93. In 1970 she was a member of the Detroit team that beat the Italian Blue Team in a series of closed television sessions. Shambrom won Silver Ribbon Prs 1993, placed second in Womens Tms 1960. She has had numerous regional and sectional successes.

SHANE, Jan G. (b. 1942) of White Plains NY, former schoolteacher, graduated U of Nebraska and U of Michigan; past president of Dist 3, Pittsburgh regional chairman 1984-91, served on ACBL Bd of Gov, ACBL Charity Committee, is currently on the ACBL Appeals Committee and has served in other executive positions on the district and unit levels. Regional wins include Detroit Open Prs 1979, 86; Buffalo Womens Swiss 1980, 87, 93, Masters Prs 1982, Open Prs 1988; Toronto Swiss 1981, Womens Swiss 1985, 86, 90; Pittsburgh Open Prs 1990, KO Tms 1990, Womens Swiss 1992, 93; Hudson Open Prs 1988; Cleveland Open Prs 1991, Womens Swiss 1992; Long Island Open Tms 1994.

SHANE, Stephen H. (b. 1937) of White Plains NY, attorney, special assistant to the Commissioner of Housing for NY; graduate of U of Michigan and Columbia; won Mens Prs 1988; also several regionals including Lancaster Mens Swiss 1986; Rye Open Prs 1988; NY Swiss, Hempstead Swiss 1989; Puerto Rico Swiss, KO Tms 1990.

SHARIF, Omar (b. 1932) of Paris, France, formerly of Egypt, motion picture star, represented UAR World Team Olympiad 1964, playing captain of Egyptian team World Team Olympiad 1968. National wins include Interclubs 1960, 1962, 1963, 1964. Won 1963 Golden Globe Award, nominated for Academy Award 1963 as best supporting actor for performance in *Lawrence of Arabia*. One of the most active promoters of bridge, makes many public appearances on syndicated TV shows as a proponent of the game. His most famous quote: "Acting is my business — bridge is my passion." Organized Sharif Bridge Circus, participated in one of the highest stake set games in history (see SET GAMES), was a member, with many former members, of the BLUE TEAM, of the Lancia Bridge Team in 1975 (see LANCIA TOURNAMENTS), won SIMON AWARD 1974 (see IBPA AWARDS). Author of *Ma Vie au Bridge*; since 1975 co-author of Goren newspaper bridge column, since 1986 analyst of hands played in annual Epson world-wide bridge contest. See OMAR SHARIF INDIVIDUAL.

SHARP, Robert G. (1910-1990) of Miami Beach FL, real estate broker, former president of Midwest Conference, the Cincinnati BA and the Florida BA. Won Mens Tms 1959, Mixed Prs 1966, GN Tms 1973; placed second Blue Ribbon Prs 1964; won many regionals.

SHARPLES, Hendrik W. (b. 1954) of Portland OR, appraiser and custom jewelery designer, Dist 20 recorder 1988-91, Unit 487 recorder 1988 to present. Regional wins include B.C. Open Prs 1984, KO Tms 1988, 90; Oregon Trail Mens Prs 1984, 85, Open Swiss 1988, 90; Edmonton Open Swiss 1984; Seaside KO Tms 1986; Ocean Shores KO Tms 1987, Open Swiss 1993; Emerald Empire KO Tms, Red Deer Open Prs 1989; Rogue Valley Swiss 1990, KO Tms 1993.

SHARPLES, James (1908-85) of Caterham, England, retired bank officer. Second European Teams 1958; represented Britain in two other zonal championships. Represented England in more than 20 Camrose Trophy matches 1950-77. 21 national wins include Gold Cup six times. Twin brother of Robert.

SHARPLES, Robert (b. 1908) of Caterham, England, retired bank officer. Second European Teams 1958; represented Britain in two other zonal championships. Represented England in more than 20 Camrose matches 1950-77. 21 national wins include Gold Cup six times. Twin brother of James.

SHAUFEL, Elyakim (b. 1945) of Tel Aviv, Israel, born in Poland, European champion 1975, represented Israel World Team Olympiad, World Open Pairs, 1972, European championships 1966, 1967, 1969, 1971, 1973, 1974. WBF World Master. National titles include Open Pairs 1966, 1967, 1972, 1973, 1974.

SHAW, Shirlee R. (b. 1924) of Concord CA, legal assistant; past president Unit 499; won Non-Life Master Prs 1981; Sacramento Swiss 1988; Albuquerque Sr Prs 1991, Medford Swiss, Womens Prs 1993.

SHEARDOWN, Percy E. (Shorty) (1911-1993) of Toronto, bridge club owner/manager; Canada's first Life Master (1948) and greatest bridge player of the Thirties, Forties and Fifties. A brilliant card player, he was teacher and mentor of many of Canada's leading players. He began his bridge career while attending the U of Toronto in 1933 and was a consistent tournament winner before the days of masterpoints. He represented Canada internat'lly in Turin 1960, Deauville 1968; he won the Chicago 1936, 51; Spingold 1964, 65; Fishbein Trophy 1964; placed second in Life Master Prs 1964 and won many regional tournaments.

SHEEHAN, Robert M. (b. 1939) of London, England, animal physiologist, computer systems analyst, commodity broker, financial consultant. Second European Teams 1987, second Bermuda Bowl 1987. Represented Great Britain in World Team Olympiad 1972, 76, 80, European Championships 1971 (second), 73, 74, 75, 81; Bermuda Bowl 1981. Won Gold Cup 1972, Life Master Pairs 1982, Crockford's Cup.

SHEFCHIK, Charles Milton (b. 1939) of Las Vegas NV, advertising consultant, certified director since 1968; graduate of U of Colorado. Diamond Life Master; regional wins include Mid-Am-Can Open Tms 1965; Canadian Prairie Open Tms 1968; Gopher Master Prs 1969, KO Tms 1979, Swiss 1983; Iowa KO Tms, Swiss Tms 1979; Fargo KO Tms 1979; Eau Claire KO Tms 1981; Dist 14 GN Prs 1983; Colorado Springs Swiss 1984, 87, Open Prs 1987; Reno Open Prs; Dist 17 GN Tms 1988, KO Tms 1993.

SHEIKH, Mohammad Aslam (b. 1933) of Karachi, Pakistan, businessman. Secretary of the Pakistan Bridge Association and its chief tournament director. Supervises all major events in Pakistan, and officiated at 1990 world championships and many zonal championships. Npc Pakistan team 1980 and 1988 world championships. Represented Pakistan 1982 world championships. Editor of *Bridge Kibitzer.*

SHEIKH, Tufail Mohammad (b. 1939) of Karachi, Pakistan, businessman. WBF World Master. Won BFAME zonal teams 1991 and represented Pakistan in Bermuda Bowl 1991.

SHEINWOLD, Alfred (Freddy) (b. 1912) of Los Angeles, formerly of New York City, born in London, England, bridge author and columnist, one of the most successful player-writer personalities. During World War II he was the chief code and cipher expert of the OSS. He graduated from City College of New York in 1933. From 1945-1955 he sang with the Cantata singers. Sheinwold was npc of the runner-up North American team in the 1975 Bermuda Bowl when the Italians were accused of cheating. He captained the 1985 North American team that won the Bermuda Bowl. He won the Chicago (now the Reisinger) 1958, Men's Tms 1964; placed second in the Vanderbilt 1958, Chicago 1959. His regional titles are numerous.

He was editor of *The Bridge World* 1934-1963, successively as technical editor, managing editor and senior editor, and was editor of the *ACBL Bulletin* 1952-1958. He has been editor-in-chief of *Autobridge* since 1938. He is bridge editor of the *Los Angeles Times;* was a contributing editor of *Popular Bridge*, games editor for *Argosy* and is the current syndicated bridge and backgammon columnist for *Los Angeles Times* Syndicate. He pioneered bridge lessons on Pay TV 1963-1964.

Sheinwold served as chairman of the Laws Commission of the ACBL 1964-1975, as chairman of the Appeals Committee at North American Championships and as chairman of the ACBL Board of Governors 1970-1973. He was named ACBL Honorary Member in 1983. Co-inventor of the KAPLAN-SHEINWOLD SYSTEM, author of 13 bridge books, notably *Five Weeks to Winning Bridge,* (which has sold more than 1,000,000 copies), and a series of *Pocket Books of Bridge Quizzes.*

SHEINWOLD, Patricia Fox (formerly Mrs. Alfred, previously Mrs. Julian Adler) of New York City, author, retired from tournament play in the Mid-Sixties; won Womens Tms 1963, which made her one of only 16 women eligible for the first women's Olympiad team. She won secondary President's Cup Prs 1951, Keystone Conference Open Tms 1955. Served as president of Women's Bridge League of Maryland, board member Maryland BL, ACBL Goodwill Committee and Mid-Atlantic Conference; she has chaired Mid-Atlantic Regional. Sheinwold was a Pulitzer nominee for writing on subject of blindness; among her six published non-fiction books are *Husbands and Other Men I've Played With: Bridge, That Is* and the best seller, *Too Young to Die.* She is currently working on a novel.

SHELTON, Gary W. (Big Dog) (b. 1949) of Danvers MA, vice president of a computer software company that makes bridge-playing software (Base III); played violin in Carnegie Hall 1967; was a Mini-McKenney winner in 1991. Won Quebec City Morning KO Tms, KO Tms 1991; Montreal Open Swiss, KO Tms 1991; Lancaster Open Prs 1991; Cromwell Open Swiss 1992.

SHEN, Chun Shan (b. 1933 in China) of Hsin Chun, Taiwan, professor of physics and astrophysics, university administrator. Formerly at Purdue U. World Life Master. Runner-up Bermuda Bowl 1969. Far East champion 1976. Represented Taiwan in two other world championships and three other zonal championships. National wins include Open Teams six times, Open Pairs twice. Helped C.C. Wei develop the Precision System, and is a world class Go player.

SHENKIN, Barnet (b. 1950 in Scotland) of London, England, carpet importer. Represented Britain in one world championship, three European championships and three Common Market championships. Represented Scotland more than 40 times in Camrose Trophy matches 1974-92. Won *Sunday Times* Pairs 1976, 1980. Many national titles include Gold Cup 1973, 1977.

SHEPARD, Edward V. (1869-1937) of New York City, civil engineer, was one of America's leading authorities on the mathematics of bridge; he devoted many years to studying card probabilities. Called by Ely Culbertson, "a giant of the Old Guard;" Shepard was a pioneer in many areas of bridge. He was the first to establish a college for the teaching of bridge and the qualifying of bridge teachers, the first to teach bridge over the radio in 1923 and one of the first to teach and write on contract bridge in 1924 and 1925. A member of the advisory council of the ABL, he assisted in drafting and approving the OFFICIAL SYSTEM. He contributed articles to numerous magazines, had a syndicated newspaper column and authored several books including *Scientific Auction Bridge, Win* *at Bridge, Contract Bridge Standardized* and *Correct Contract Bridge.*

SHEPHERD, Richard of Pacific Palisades CA, won the Fishbein Trophy 1974, Spingold 1974 and numerous regionals.

SHERIDAN, John K. (b. 1948) of Indianapolis IN, attorney, graduated U of North Carolina and Indiana U (JD); national Merit Scholar 1966. Temporarily retired from bridge in 1984, won Mens Prs 1978; placed second Mens Prs 1975, Spingold 1977, 79. His more than 25 regional wins include Dist 11 Open Prs 1972, 74, KO Tms 1973, Swiss Tms 1974, 78, Mens Swiss, Mens Prs 1980; Dist 5 Swiss, Masters Prs 1974, Open Prs 1976; All American Open Prs 1972, 73, Mens Prs 1974, Swiss Tms 1976; Mid-Atlantic Summer Open Prs 1973, Winter Open Tms 1973; Dist 11 GN Tms 1974, 76, GN Prs 1979; Dist 8 Swiss 1975; Spring secondary Swiss 1978.

SHERMAN, Ruth T. (1903-1965) of New York City. Won Master Mixed Tms 1935, 45. She won a total of 10 major titles including the Chicago (now the Reisinger) 1944, Master Prs 1946, Vanderbilt 1953.

SHEVITZ, Dr. Henry A. (b. 1942) of West Bloomfield MI, physician practicing internal and nuclear medicine, graduate of U of Michigan, Wayne State U (MD); won Dist 5 Open Prs 1965; Motor City Open Tms 1967, Open Prs 1989; Great Lakes Swiss 1971, Open Prs 1979, Bloomfield Hills Open Prs 1979; Southfield Mens Tms 1991.

SHI, Shaomin of Hangzhou, China. Third Venice Cup 1991. Works as researcher in the coal ministry.

SHIBE, Harold of Lauderhill FL , certified director; member of highest scoring pair in 5th Epson Worldwide Bridge Contest in Zone II (US, Canada, Mexico, Bermuda) 1990; placed 25th in the world; won Summer secondary Swiss 1984.

SHIBE, Madelyn (Mady) of Lauderhill FL, bridge teacher and certified director; member of highest scoring pair in 5th Epson Worldwide Bridge Contest in Zone II (US, Canada, Mexico, Bermuda) 1990; placed 25th in the world; won Summer secondary Swiss 1984.

SHIELDS, Bruce of Arlington TX, bridge club owner, bridge teacher, director and professional player, teaches bridge in schools; member Bd of Dir Unit 183 1988-1994, tournament chairman and Education Liaison. Won San Antonio Open Prs; Dallas Mens Prs, Master Swiss, Open Prs 1992; New Orleans Mens Swiss; Lake Charles Swiss; Houston Mens Prs; and many other regional titles.

SHIMAMURA, Kyoko (formerly Mizutani) of Tokyo, Japan, psychologist with Association for Handicapped Children. Bridge teacher and club operator. WBF World Master. Far East champion 1985. Represented Japan in World Open Team Olympiad 1980, 1984; 9 other Far East Championships, Olympiad Womens Team 1988, and Venice Cup 1991. Won 18 national titles.

SHIPLEY, Roberta D. (Bobbie) (b. 1933) of Mundelein IL, ACBL national tournament director. A director since

1965, she received her associate national rating in 1981 and her national rating in 1987. Became involved in running NABCs in 1987 and is now assistant chief director at all NABCs. Won Iowa Master Prs 1969; Mid-Winter Holiday Womens Prs 1978; Great Lakes Womens Swiss 1979, 81; Midwest Spring Womens Swiss 1981.

SHIREY, Steven A. (b. 1958) of Ft. Worth TX, bridge professional and certified director. Diamond Life Master; regional wins include San Antonio Prs 1985; Corpus Christi Master Prs 1987; Houston Swiss 1988, 91; Austin Open Prs, Dist 16 GN Tms 1989; Las Vegas Master Tms, Open Prs 1990; Wichita KO Tms, Master Tms 1990; Summer Swiss, KO Tms 1993, Fall Open Prs 1993; Ft. Worth Master Tms, Williamsburg Open Prs, Amarillo Swiss, Denver Open Prs 1991; Abilene Master Tms 1993; South Padre Island KO Tms (2) 1993.

SHIVDASANI, Jaggy (b. 1958) of Bombay, India, chartered accountant, exporter and travel agent. WBF World Master. Won Spingold Teams 1987, making his U.S. debut and becoming the first non-American to win the event. Won Reisinger Teams 1988. Second BFAME Open Teams 1985 and 1989. Fourth World Open Teams 1988 and represented India in three other world championships. 12 national wins include open teams four times. Won open pairs twice, once at age 18, a record.

SHMUCKLER, Pauline (b. 1913) of Miami Beach FL, former bridge teacher, LM #114; placed second in Womens Tms 1946, 54; holds many regional titles including Mid-Atlantic Fall Mixed Prs 1952; Keystone Conference Open Tms 1952, 55, Open Prs 1959; Southeastern Womens Swiss 1978; Gold Coast Womens Swiss 1981. Shmuckler was on the Philadelphia womens team that played the British womens team in unofficial matches in 1953. She was forced to curtail her bridge-playing activities in 1954 due to an automobile accident.

SHNEIDER, Alma (1928-1986) of Durban, South Africa, bridge teacher. Second World Womens Teams 1968, 1972, represented South Africa World Womens Pairs. 11 national wins include five in open teams and two in open pairs.

SHOIB, Kamal (b. 1938) of Karachi, Pakistan, banker. Won BFAME zonal teams 1991 and represented Pakistan in Bermuda Bowl 1991.

SHOOP, Homer (1912-1991) of North Webster IN, retired banker, founder of the International Palace of Sports Youth Foundation which annually awards the KING OR QUEEN OF BRIDGE title. Placed second Life Master Prs 1980 and won numerous regional titles. Former tennis tournament player.

SHORT, Brian D. (b. 1944) of Edinburgh, Scotland, data processing manager. Represented Britain in two world championships and one Common Market Championship. Represented Scotland in 18 Camrose Trophy matches. National titles include Scottish Cup twice and open pairs three times.

SHORT, Karol K. (b. 1934) of Miami FL, tennis pro, won Southeastern Womens Prs 1969, Mixed Prs, Swiss 1972. Nicknamed Golden Goddess of Tennis, she was ranked the #5 woman player in the U.S. and #6 in the world in the Fifties. She was banned from playing at Wimbledon until she covered her gold lamé panties with white lace. Short turned pro in 1959 and toured with the Harlem Globe Trotters and Althea Gibson.

SHOUP, Russell O. (Mr. Bridge) (b. 1947) of Dayton OH, bridge teacher, club manager and professional player; competitive long distance runner and semi-professional basso. Diamond Life Master, finished second in Swiss 1979 and has won more than 40 regional titles including Dist 11 GN Tms 1973, 85, 86, GN Prs 1983, 91. Editor of *Valley Talley* since 1988, member MVBA Bd of Dir. Was once penalized for naming a dead man as non-playing team captain.

SHRAGE, Dr. Marcus (b. 1919) of Dublin, Ireland, physician, represented Ireland in the European Champions 1951, 54, 55, 57, 58, 63, 66, 67. National titles include IBU Open Teams, Mixed Pairs, CBA of Ireland Open Teams, Men's Teams.

SHUMAN, Kerri, See Sanborn, Kerri.

SHUMAN, Michael (b. 1931) of Pasadena CA, professional bridge player, owns and races thoroughbred horses; ran bridge cruises in the Sixties, has been a *Bridge World* Master Solvers panelist for 25 years. Grand Life Master with more than 18,000 MPs as of 1994, is 16th on all-time masterpoint list. Shuman is former managing editor of *Contract Bridge Forum*; his writings include *Dummy Play Technique* in *The Contract Bridge Forum* and contributions to *The Bridge World* and other magazines and tabloids. Won Mens Tms 1962; placed second in Mens Prs 1959, Chicago (now the Reisinger) 1961, Open Prs 1962, Mens Tms 1974, North American Mens Swiss 1985, North American Swiss 1991, 92. He has won scores of regional titles.

SIDELL, Steven G. (b. 1947) of Seattle WA, travel agent, graduate of Occidental College; former president of the Seattle Unit and of Dist 19. Won Puget Sound Mens Prs 1968, 81, Open Tms 1976, Swiss 1981; Oregon Trail KO Tms 1970, Open Prs 1972; Canadian Mens Prs 1970; Inland Empire Master Prs, Swiss 1973; Dist 19 GN Tms 1973, 83, 85, 87; Klondike Swiss 1974; Peach City Mens Prs 1978; Eugene Swiss 1982; Emerald City KO Tms 1985, 89; New York City Memorial Day Swiss 1988.

SIDES, William C. of Burbank CA, bank executive, placed second in Mens Tms 1974, Spingold 1975 and has numerous regionals. One of the top-ranking players of the American Bridge Association, he set a record at the 1969 ABA Summer Nat'ls by winning five major events and finishing second in another.

SIEBERT, Allan P. (b. 1942) of Little Rock AR, company president, graduate of Vanderbilt; he and brother (David) are the 2nd highest masterpoint brothers behind the Passells. A Grand Life Master with more than 13,000 MPs as of 1994; won North American Swiss 1988; placed second Life Master Prs 1985. Has won nearly 100 regional titles.

SIEBERT, David A. (b. 1940) of Las Vegas NV, company executive, graduate of Vanderbilt; served as member ACBL Bd of Gov Dist 10, past president of Unit 161, tournament chairman 1986, 89. Won North American Swiss 1988; placed second Life Master Prs 1985. Grand Life Master with more than 15,000 MPs as of 1994; has won more than 100 regionals.

SIEBERT, Ellen (nee Ostertag, formerly Pidhajecky, Gryka) of Little Rock AR, teacher, college professor and school principal; accredited bridge teacher and certified director; degrees from Northern Arizona U; involved in local/regional theater; served on ACBL Bd of Appeals and Bd of Dir Palm Springs Unit. Won more than 35 regionals including Palm Springs Masters Prs, Swiss 1983; Oklahoma City Womens Prs 1989; St. Louis Swiss, Monroe Swiss 1990; Nashville Womens Prs, Dallas Open Prs 1991; Summer secondary Open Prs, Mixed Tms 1993; Amarillo KO Tms, Swiss 1993; Pine Bluff KO Tms 1993.

SIEGEL, George I. (b. 1940) of Winnetka CA, engineer; won ACBL-wide Charity game (Summer) 1975 and many regionals including Pacific Southwest Open Prs, ABA KO Tms 1978; Raincross Swiss 1979; Golden State Swiss 1980; Los Angeles Winter KO Tms 1980; Northern VA BA Player of the Year 1969.

SIGURHJARTARSON, Karl (b. 1941) of Reykjavik, Iceland, manager. Won Nordic Teams 1988, 1992. Represented Iceland in two world championships, three European championships and two other Nordic championships. National wins include open team twice.

SIKORA, Thomas E. (b. 1938) of Charleston WV, engineering manager, graduated Case Western Reserve U. Won Roanoke Mens Swiss 1979; Dayton Swiss 1981; Toledo Open Swiss 1982; Columbus Swiss 1985, 91, KO Tms, Swiss 1993; Charleston Mens Prs, KO Tms 1988; Lexington Swiss, Fall secondary KO Tms 1991; Louisville Swiss 1993.

SILBER, Albert J. (Al) (b. 1912) of Birmingham MI, attorney, graduate of Wayne State U and U of Michigan (JD). At the age of 15 he lettered in track as a sophomore in college; at 20 he became the youngest ever law graduate from the U of Michigan and at 21 he was admitted to practice. In 1993 he was inducted into the Michigan Jewish Sports Hall of Fame. Past president Michigan BA, member ACBL Goodwill Committee; placed second Marcus Cup 1964, won All American Open Tms 1959, Mens Prs 1965; Great Lakes Open Prs 1966, Open Tms 1968; Motor City Mens Swiss 1976, 82, Sr Prs 1992, 93; Sun City Sr Mens Prs 1981, Open Tms 1982; Fall secondary Sr Prs 1987; Southern MI Sr Prs 1993. Silber was captain of the Dist 12 team that defeated the Sharif Bridge Circus in 1970.

SILBERSTEIN, David S. (b. 1951) of Medfield MA, reasearch assistant, won Summer Sr and Advanced Sr Master Prs 1974; New England Individual 1973.

SILBERWASSER, Roger (b. 1923 in Austria) of Brussels, Belgium, bridge club manager. Represented Belgium in four world championships and four European championships. National wins include open teams 4 times and open pairs twice.

SILBORN, Gunborg (b. 1924) of Norrkoping, Sweden,

WBF Life Master. Won World Womens Tms 1968, European Womens Championship 1967, Nordic Women's Championship 1964, 1966, 1978, 1980, 1982, 1984; also 11 national womens titles.

SILBY, Frances (b. 1916) of Ft. Lauderdale FL , retired psychiatric social worker; graduated U of Missouri and U of Kansas, does 5 miles of speed walking a day. Diamond Life Master, won Spring secondary Swiss 1973, Summer Swiss 1974; Puerto Rico Master Prs 1973; Bermuda Womens Prs 1974; Ft. Lauderdale Womens Tms, Sr Tms 1991.

SILODOR, Sidney (1906-1963) of Havertown PA, lawyer, bridge lecturer, writer and instructor. He was on the North American team that won the World Championship in the first Bermuda Bowl matches in 1950 and also represented North America in that event in 1958 and 61, as well as playing for the US in the World Olympiad of 1960. Silodor won the McKenney Trophy in 1946 and set a record when he won the Mixed Prs five times. He won more than 30 North American Championships, including the Vanderbilt eight times, the Spingold and the Mixed Teams three times each. At his death he was a member of the ACBL Board and holder of the Open Prs Championship, a title which he had first won in 1941 and again in 1945. He was third highest on the list of all-time masterpoint winners with a total of 6,450 — a figure great enough to hold that place until a year after his death when his total was surpassed by Norman Kay, who had been his regular partner. Silodor authored a newspaper column and wrote many articles for *The Bridge World*. His books included *Silodor Says*, *Contract Bridge According to Silodor and Tiernery* and *The Complete Book of Duplicate Bridge*.

SILVER, Joseph (b. 1941) of Montreal PQ, trial lawyer, graduate of McGill U; longtime active member of ACBL Bd of Gov. Represented Canada in world competition 1974, 78, 82, 90. Won Cavendish Invitational Prs 1985, but he and partner Irving Litvack withdrew and failed to defend in 1986 when an extra foreign pair from Great Britain showed up as a result of an invitation mixup. For that action he was awarded the John Simon Trophy for "Bridge Sportsman of the Year". Representing Montreal, won Epson Inter-City Team Championship 1983, 85. Contributor to *The Bridge World, Bridge Today, Australian Bridge, International Popular Bridge*. Diamond Life Master, won Vanderbilt 1974, Mens BAM Tms 1981, Open Prs 1985, North American Swiss 1986; placed second Mens Tms 1973, Master Mixed Tms 1974, CNTC 1984, North American Mens Swiss 1989. Silver has won more than 45 regional titles.

SILVERMAN, Gloria (b. 1948) of Toronto ON, born in Germany, educational program developer for Addiction Research Foundation of Ontario, graduate of York U; was invited in 1992 to present a paper at Internat'l Congress on Alcoholism and Addiction in Glasgow. WBF World Master, placed third Venice Cup 1989, fourth Womens Tm Olympiad 1988; also represented Canada in internat'l competition 1982, 86, 91, 92. Won Canadian Womens Team Championship 1986, 87, 88, 89, 91; placed second CWTC 1982, CNTC 1988; won Dist 2 GN Tms 1982, 94 and has many regional titles to her credit.

SILVERMAN, Jerome R. (Jerry) (1912-1985) of Mill Valley CA, retired attorney and account executive, graduate of Rutgers U School of Law; active in bridge administration for many years. ACBL president in 1973, ACBL treasurer 1970-72, chairman of ACBL Goodwill Committee 1975, ACBL representative to the WBF 1973-76, trustee of ACBL Charity Foundation 1974, president of ACBL Charity Foundation 1980-82, vice president of the WBF 1976-78, member of ACBL Bd of Dir 1966-75 and a member of the Laws Commission of the ACBL. He was a former president of the New Jersey BL, NY-NJ Bridge Conference and Dist 21. He served as npc of the North American team in the 1977 Bermuda Bowl.

SILVERMAN, Neil (b. 1949) of Ft. Lauderdale FL, options trader, former genealogical researcher. WBF World Master, won Rosenblum Tms 1986. Diamond Life Master, won Life Master Prs 1976, Mens Prs 1980; placed second Reisinger 1977, Mens Prs 1981, Open Prs 1990, Vanderbilt, Spingold 1992. Silverman won the gold medal at the Maccabiah Games; placed third in Invitational Prs Championship and made a 13-segment TV show on bridge for the BBC, all in 1981.

SILVERMAN, Shirley Seiner (Mrs. Harry J.) (1928-1992) of White Plains NY, bridge writer and administrator. Served as chairman of ACBL Bd of Gov 1975-78; as president, vice president, tournament chairman and publication editor for Unit 188. Formerly co-owner of bridge supply company; member of ABTA and IPBA. Author of *Five Card Major Bridge Teachers' Manual, Elementary Bridge Five Card Major Student Text, Intermediate Bridge Five Card Major Student Text, Play of the Hand as Declarer and Defender Student Text, Advanced and Duplicate Bridge Student Text, Chicago Bridge, Point Count Bidding Guide*. Editor of *Expert Bridge*.

SILVERSTEIN, Dr. Bruce M. (b. 1951) of Lancaster PA, physician, graduate of Brandeis U and Philadelphia College of Osteopathic Medicine, wine consultant and collector. Won North American Swiss 1989; approximately 10 regional events plus Dist 4 GN Tms five times, GN Prs three times.

SILVERSTEIN, Nate (1909-1992) of Memphis TN, born in Poland, bridge club manager, won dozens of regional titles in the Fifties, Sixties and Seventies and was a Diamond Life Master. For more than 30 years Silverstein was a devoted promoter of bridge. He was a member of the ACBL Bd of Dir 1968-71 and was largely responsible for the move of ACBL Headquarters to Memphis. He was a tireless worker for charity and because of his drive Unit 144 had the highest donations per capita for many years. He was president of his Unit many times and served as vice president of the ACBL Charity Foundation.

SILVERSTEIN, Philip J. (b. 1943) of Cote St. Luc PQ, financial consultant and accountant, graduate of Loyola; won Orlando Mens Prs 1984; Montreal Mens Swiss 1986, Mens Prs 1988; Ottawa Swiss 1987, 90.

SILVERSTONE, Victor (b. 1940) of London, England, formerly of Glasgow, Scotland, chartered accountant. Won Camrose Trophy once, and represented Scotland in 24 Camrose matches. National titles include open teams twice.

SIMMONDS, Alan (b.1940) of Cape Town, South Africa, journalist. Represented South Africa in one world championship and on other international occasions. Won three national titles. Editor of *S.A.Bridge Bulletin* 1974-81. Daily bridge columnist for *Cape Town Argus*, and is syndicated.

SIMON, Adaline (Mrs. John E.) (1901-1985) of St. Louis MO; won Womens Tms 1959 and numerous regional titles.

SIMON, Allan K. (b. 1945) of Calgary AB, systems analyst, McGill graduate; Zone V representative to CBF since 1991, was editor of the *Canadian Bridge Digest* 1985-90, chaired 1979 Calgary regional. Won 1988 Epson Bidding Challenge (5-card majors) and Edmonton Open Prs 1984, Swiss 1990; Red Deer Swiss 1989, 92; Calgary Swiss 1991; Ottawa Swiss 1992.

SIMON, Andrzej (b. 1934) of Krakow, Poland, chemical engineer and bridge journalist. Represented Poland in one world championship. Vice-president Polish Bridge Union. Former Secretary EBL Junior division. Former *IBPA Bulletin* editor and assistant secretary.

SIMON, Edith of Memphis TN, was ACBL librarian 1972-83 and administrative secretary for the Chicago CBA 1964-72; member of ACBL Goodwill Committee.

SIMON, Harold (Hal) (b. 1931) of Ventura CA, pharmacist, consultant to nursing homes; Wayne State graduate. Won Dist 12 Open Tms 1958; Desert Empire Open Tms 1960; Bridge Week Open Tms 1961, 62; Reno BAM Tms 1984.

SIMON, John E. (1897-1993) of St. Louis MO, limited partner in brokerage firm; named ACBL Honorary Member in 1962; LM #641, chairman of the ACBL Goodwill and Membership Committees, trustee of the ACBL Charity Foundation, president of the Midwest Conference and of the St. Louis Unit. He was the donor of the Simon Award (see IBPA AWARDS). Simon won Mens Tms 1972, 73; placed second in Open Prs 1961, won numerous regionals.

SIMON, S. J. (Simon, Skidelsky, or Skid) (1904-1948), novelist and bridge writer, was one of the best-loved British bridge personalities. One of the originators of the Acol System, he was European champion 1948 and also represented Great Britain in the European championships 1939. His many national wins include the Gold Cup 1937, 1947. His many successful humorous novels in collaboration with ballet expert Carol Brahms include *Bullet in the Ballet, No Bed for Bacon* and *Trottie True*. A contributor to *The Bridge World*, Simon wrote the classic *Why You Lose at Bridge, Design for Bidding*, and *Cut for Partners*. See Bibliography, C, E, H.

SIMPSON, Gene (b. 1942) of Anaheim Hills CA, advertising salesman, Grand Life Master with more than 10,000 MPs as of 1994; won North American Swiss 1983, placed second Mens BAM Tms 1986; has won scores of regionals.

SIMS, Dorothy Rice (1889-1960) of Deal NJ, was one of the leading personalities of the early days of bridge. She was the daughter of Isaac L. Rice, first manufacturer of the submarine and patron of chess and other recreational activities. From her teens she was active in competition and held the US motorcycle speed championship for women (1911). Sims was one of the first U.S. aviatrixes when she met and married P. Hal Sims. She was a noted sculptress and designed the City of Asbury Park Trophy. Her writings included several bridge books as well as work in fields other than bridge. She acquired her interest in bridge through her husband and became a successful player. Her wins included ABL Auction Womens Prs 1929; AWL Open Tms 1929, Open Prs 1930; Mixed Tms 1930. In 1935 she was her husband's principal partner in a 150-rubber match against Ely and Josephine Culbertson (see CULBERTSON-SIMS MATCH). She is widely credited with "inventing" the psychic bid, but probably initiated only the popular name for it; however, she wrote the first book on the subject, *Psychic Bidding*. After her husband's death, she toured the world several times as a political correspondent for various newspapers.

SIMS, P(hillip) Hal (1886-1949) of Deal NJ, was one of the great American players and his system had the largest expert following prior to 1935. Born in Selma AL, Sims represented U.S. banks in foreign countries from 1906-1916. While a member of the U.S. Army Air Corps in 1917 he met Dorothy Rice, a U.S. aviatrix in transport service, whom he married. After World War I Sims devoted himself chiefly to competitive sports, in which he excelled, and to bridge. He held a national trapshooting record and won the Artists' and Writers' Golf Tournament in 1937. In auction bridge he was a member of the highest-ranked team, the Knickerbocker Whist Club team, which included Sydney S. Lenz, Winfield S. Liggett, George Reith, and Ralph J. Leibenderfer. He was captain of the contract bridge team called the Four Horsemen whose other members were Williard S. Karn, Oswald Jacoby and David Burnstine. This team won most of the principal American tournaments 1931-1933.

The Sims System, a subjective approach based on Sim's desire to dominate every pair and team of which he was a member, left little impression on contract bridge methods used by experts from 1935 on; first- and second-hand opening one-bids were stronger than third- and fourth-hand bids; notrump bids were always strong but had wide limits; psychic bids were used freely; high preemptive bids were eschewed. In 1935 Hal and Dorothy Sims tested this system in a 150-rubber match against Ely and Josephine Culbertson, and were defeated (see CULBERTSON-SIMS MATCH).

Sims' books included *Money Contract, Master Contract* (his definitive work, largely by Sir Derrick Wernher) and several lesser works. Sims was one of the most colorful characters in bridge history. Called "The Shaggy Giant", Sims' commanding presence (6'4" in height, more than 300 pounds in weight, big-boned and muscular) augmented his claim to authority. For more than five years his mansion in Deal NJ was summer headquarters for the principal experts and the promising new players. He controlled the ABL for several years without holding formal office. He founded the Deal Club, a bridge club at which the principal U.S. and international experts played from 1930-1935. His skill as a raconteur and his personal charm were proverbial. He died of a heart attack while bidding a hand in a game at the Havana Country Club, where he and his wife spent their winters after 1946.

SINGHA, Govinda (b. 1934) of Calcutta, India. Won Far East Open Teams 1977, and represented India in two other zonal championships and three world championships. 14 national wins include open teams five times and open pairs once.

SINISCALCO, Guglielmo (b. 1921) of Naples, Italy, professor of civil engineering. WBF Grand Master. Won Bermuda Bowl 1957, 1958, 1959. Won European Teams 1951, 1956, 1957, 1958, second 1952.

SINT, Cornelis J. (Cees) (b. 1940) of Broek in Waterland, the Netherlands, bridge writer and journalist. WBF World Master. Represented the Netherlands in four world championships and seven zonal championships. His national titles include Open Pairs twice and Open Teams nine times. Author (with Ton Schipperheyn) of four TV courses and about 40 books, including *From Start to Finish*. (The first two volumes are the official beginners course of the Netherlands Bridge League). More than a million copies of Sint/Schipperheyn's books have been sold. Contributor to *Bridge* and to *Algemeen Dagblad*.

SITHISARIPUTRA, Boonita (b. 1946) of Bangkok, Thailand, company executive and director. Runner-up Far East Womens Teams 1979. Represented Thailand on 10 other occasions, and in two world championships. Won five ASEAN team titles. The first of her many national titles was the 1961 mixed pairs, at 17 the youngest winner in Thai bridge history.

SKAANNING-NORRIS, John (b.1964), of Copenhagen, Denmark, associated systems engineer. Son of Judy and Georg Norris, married to Lotte Skaanning-Norris, forming a family team with many wins. Won National Open Teams 1992 partnering his father.

SKAANNING-NORRIS, Lotte (b.1963) of Copenhagen, Denmark, computer programmer. WBF World Master. Second Nordic Womens Teams 1988 and 1992. Also represented Denmark in one world championship and one zonal championship. Won one national title.

SKALEOS, Elias (b. 1933) of Athens, Greece. Deputy mayor of Athens and former president of the Association of Greek Engineers. President of the Hellenic Bridge Federation, steering it in new directions. He is a water-sport enthusiast.

SKINNER, Lt. Col. Richmond H. (Dick) (1898-1986) of Dallas TX, ACBL president 1944 and a member of the ACBL Executive Committee from formation through 1944. Skinner also served as president of the Mid-Atlantic BA, Keystone Conference and New England BA. He was educated at MIT and California Institute of Technology. A civil engineer by training, he had a varied career; US Army officer, pipe organ builder and installer, pilot and flying instructor, top-flight tennis player and referee (awarded the McGovern Cup for national tennis umpire of the year 1972) and longtime member of the New Hampshire legislature. Invented SKINNER PSYCHIC CONTROLS, SKINNER RESPONSES TO A 1NT OPENING, SKINNER TWO-BIDS and originated a point-count method in 1932 in which an ace was assigned 5 points, king 3 points, queen 2 points and jack 1 point. Won Eastern States KO Tms 1940, New England Fall Mens Prs

1946, Mixed Tms 1947, 52, Mixed Prs 1947, 48, KO Tms, Master Tms 1948.

SKIPPER, Jane, (formerly Evitt) (b. 1949), of Christchurch, New Zealand, science and mathematics teacher. Won Far East Womens Teams 1981, second 1978. Represented New Zealand in one world championship and one other zonal championship. Top masterpoint winner in New Zealand 1978. Bridge teacher.

SKOLNIK, Mel of Newport Beach CA, real estate developer, investor and entrepreneur; graduate of U of Michigan and Columbia (JD); advocate of animal rights, protection of environment and free enterprise. Skolnik won the McKenney Trophy 1981 over Barry Crane in what was the hardest fought and most bitterly contested fight for that trophy in the history of ACBL. It went right down to the wire, including the midnight zip Swiss in the last tournament of the year — the Reno Regional. He won 38 regional events in 1981 — a record at that time. He also won 183 MPs at the Calgary Regional, another record for that time.

SKOROUPO, Roman (1900-1971) of Helsingfors, Finland, businessman and bridge writer, bridge administrator, for many years member of executive committee of European Bridge Federation and World Bridge Federation, on Appeals Committee at World Team Olympiads, secretary general of Finnish Bridge League, contributing editor *Bridge Encyclopedia*.

SKOTTE, Gulle (b. 1917) of Odense, Denmark. Third World Womens Teams 1960. Won European Womens Teams 1948, 1949, 1955, 1957, second 1951. Won Nordic Womens Teams five times. Represented Denmark in one world championship and one other zonal championship. 12 national title include open pairs once and open teams three times, one of these in an all-woman lineup, a unique circumstance. Known as one of the world's fastest women players.

SLAGER, Hilda K. (Mrs. Julian H.) (b. 1908) of Montgomery AL, won the international North-South Prs Championship in the 1933 World Bridge Olympic, the United States North-South Pair championship in the 1932 World Bridge Olympic and several regionals.

SLAGER, Julian H. (b. 1902) of Montgomery AL, ACBL Goodwill Member of the Year 1991, won New Orleans Sr. Swiss and several other regional events.

SLAVENBURG, Cornelis (Bob) (1917-1981) of Rotterdam, the Netherlands, merchant, WBF Grand Master, won World Open Pairs 1966, represented Netherlands Bermuda Bowl 1966, World Open Pairs 1970, European championships 1951, 1959, 1965, 1966, 1967; national titles include Open Teams four times, Open Pairs three times. Won London Sunday Times Invitational Prs 1971.

SLEMMONS, George W. of Bellevue WA, won Mens Prs 1974 and many regionals.

SLINGER, James W. (Jim) (b. 1938) of Fresno CA, professor of philosophy, U of Wisconsin graduate; past president Unit 522. Each summer Slinger takes a canoe/kayak trip in Alaska or northern Canada. Won California Capital Open Tms 1971, Open Prs 1992; Dist 22 GN Tms 1974, 81, GN Prs 1982, 85; Golden State KO Tms 1978; All-Western KO Tms 1990; Bridge Week Open Prs 1991.

SLOAN, Jesse (1913-1989) of Van Nuys CA, real estate loan broker, former bridge club owner, won Vanderbilt 1952.

SMART, Diana Frances of Melbourne, Australia, lecturer in psychology. WBF World Master. Won Far East Womens Teams 1984, 1990. Represented Australia in three world championships and other zonal championships. Won numerous national titles.

SMILDE, Roelof A. (b. 1930) of Sydney, Australia, bridge teacher, Far East champion 1968, 1970; represented Australia in World Team Olympiad 1964, 1968, 1972, Bermuda Bowl 1976. National titles include Open Teams 1958, 1961, 1962, 1963, 1965, 1974, Open Pairs 1974.

SMITH, Curtis (b. 1925) of Conroe TX, engineer, Grand Life Master with more than 11,000 MPs as of 1994; has been a contributor to the *ACBL Bulletin*, authored *Bidding Through Logic* and invented the Smith convention. Won Open Prs 1960, Spingold 1966, 77; GN Tms 1977; placed second in Open Prs 1953, Chicago (now the Reisinger) 1960, 64; Life Master Prs 1963, Life Master Mens Prs 1970, Spingold 1972. Smith has also won numerous regionals. See DEFENSE TO OPENING THREE-BID.

SMITH, David (b. 1949 in England) of South Yarra, Australia, computer manager. Won South Pacific playoff 1991. Represented Australia in one world championship and one Far East Championship. Three national wins include Open Teams once.

SMITH, David B. (b. 1951) of Lafayette CA, senior vice president, graduated St. Mary's College; won Golden Gate KO Tms 1974, Swiss Tms 1975, Open Prs 1978; All-Western KO Tms 1975, 78, Master Tms 1976; CA Capital Master Swiss 1977. Smith was a narrator for the Mike Lawrence bridge tapes; he dropped out of the bridge world at age 25 to pursue his career.

SMITH, David W. (Dave) (b. 1944) of Raleigh NC, computer programmer/analyst, Southern Illinois U graduate; represented Korea in the Far East Championships 1969. Diamond Life Master, placed second in GN Tms 1973 and has won about 50 regional events.

SMITH, Duncan H. (Syd) (b. 1948) of Victoria BC, bridge teacher and club director. Diamond Life Master; regional wins include Vancouver Mens Prs 1970, Open Swiss 1985, KO Tms 1986, Super Open Prs 1992; Dist 19 GN Tms 1978; Canadian Nat'l Tms, Zone 6 1981; Saskatoon Swiss, Mens Prs 1984; Victoria KO Tms 1986, Open Swiss 1989; Calgary KO Tms 1988; Phoenix KO Tms, Swiss 1991.

SMITH, Glenn F. (b. 1932) of Creve Coeur MO, retired senior vice-president, graduate of St. Louis U, computer hobbiest with other interests in family and travel. Dist 8 representative to ACBL Bd of Dir, member ACBL Goodwill Committee; has served on Unit 143 Board. Won

Springfield Mens Prs, Dist 8 GN Tms (twice), St Louis Sr Swiss, St Charles Sr Swiss, Marco Island Open Swiss.

SMITH, Hazel (Mrs. Fred R.) (b. 1914) of St. Petersburg FL, born in New Brunswick, retired math teacher, first Life Master in Saskatchewan. Won Canadian Prairie Womens Prs 1965; Navajo Trail Open Tms 1966; Can-At Mixed Prs, Tri-State Open Prs 1968.

SMITH, Helen of Philadelphia PA, insurance broker, placed second Mixed Prs 1973, Womens KO Tms 1976; won many regional events

SMITH, Helen Martin (Mrs. Stanley, formerly Mrs. Al Sobel and Mrs. Jack White) (1910-1969) of Detroit. Universally ranked as greatest woman bridge player of all time. Became Life Master #25 in 1941. Born in Philadelphia, after a long residence in New York City she moved to Miami Beach in 1963; after her marriage to Smith, she moved to Detroit. Smith enjoyed a brief stage career as a chorus girl and appeared in several stage shows including *Animal Crackers* with the Marx Brothers. Another chorus girl taught her how to play bridge and she rocketed to stardom at the card table.

In 1934, as Mrs. Jack White, she won the Women's Pairs championship, the first of her many titles. Shortly after her marriage to Al Sobel ended in divorce (1937-1945), she was invited by Ely Culbertson to represent the United States. She played with the Culbertsons and Charles Vogelhofer in a World Championship conducted by the International Bridge League (1937) in Budapest, which was won by Austria. This was tacit recognition that Culbertson, like many other experts, considered her the equal of any male player. That's the way Charles Goren saw it in 1940 when they won the North American Open Pair title, their first of many championships. This was to become one of the most enduring and successful partnerships in bridge history. Together they won the De La Rue International Invitation Pairs Tournament in London 1957, represented North America in the Bermuda Bowl 1957, the U.S. in the World Team Olympiad of 1960, and won many of the 33 national championships credited to Smith, including the Life Master Pairs twice.

Her 33 titles included the Spingold five times, the Chicago (now the Reisinger) four times, and the Vanderbilt twice. In addition to her many national and regional titles, Smith won the McKenney Trophy 1941, 42, 44, and the Fishbein Trophy 1958. By 1948 she had amassed the greatest number of masterpoints of any woman. She took over the top spot from Sally Young and held it uninterruptedly until 1964. She was the author of *All the Tricks* and several magazine articles.

SMITH, Herbert L. (b. 1932) of San Mateo CA, born in Austria, accountant, graduate of U of California-Berkeley, ACBL president 1988, Dist 21 representative to the ACBL Bd of Dir 1981-89; also served several terms as president of Unit 506, Dist 21 and the Western Conference, was tournament chairman of Fall NABC 1981, and served as ACBL treasurer for 2 1/2 years. Diamond Life Master; won more than 15 regional events.

SMITH, Ivy Mary (b. in New York City) of Caracas, Venezuela, teacher of English. WBF World Master. Won CAC Womens Teams 1980, 1981, 1985, 1991. Represented Venezuela in 8 world championships and won many national titles.

SMITH, Linda S. (formerly Linda George) (b. 1947) of Chattanooga TN, data processor, Diamond Life Master and past president of Unit 421. Won 148 MPs and five events at a Boise tournament. Some of her wins include Atlanta Swiss 1983, Open Prs 1984; Boise KO Tms, Swiss, Open Prs, Master Prs 1984; London KO Tms 1985; Tulsa Master Prs, Dayton KO Tms 1986; Richmond KO Tms 1987, Master Prs 1989; Fort Wayne KO Tms, Open Prs, Swiss 1988; Roanoke IMP Prs 1988; Memphis Open Prs 1990.

SMITH, Nicola P. (b. 1949) of London, England, bridge teacher. WBF Grand Master. Won Venice Cup 1981, 1985; second 1976; second World Womens Teams 1976, 1984, 1988, 1992, third 1980. Won European Womens Tms 1975, 1979, 1981, second 1969, 1977, 1985. Won five Common Market titles. Represented Britain in one other world championship and six other zonal championships. More than 20 national victories include Gold Cup twice. Director of the London School of Bridge since 1977.

SMITH, Paul C. (b. 1914) of Pacific Palisades CA, retired business executive, won Central States Open Prs 1940, Open Tms 1941; Bridge Week Master Prs 1955, Sr Prs 1990.

SMITH, Ronald (Ron) (b. 1950) of Chicago, professional bridge player, has performed as a concert pianist. Grand Life Master with more than 11,500 MPs. Won the Blue Ribbon Prs 1979, Reisinger 1987, North American Swiss 1993; placed second GN Tms 1973, Reisinger 1978, Vanderbilt, Blue Ribbon Prs 1988. He has won more than 100 regional titles.

SMITH, Dr. Ronald L. (b. 1947) of Chattanooga TN, mathematics professor, graduated U of California, Auburn (PhD); Grand Life Master with more than 10,000 MPs. Won Mens BAM Tms 1977 and finished second in GN Tms 1975. Has won more than 75 regionals including Mid-South Open Tms 1972, 74, Open Prs 1978, 79, Master Prs 1978; Atlanta Open Swiss 1983, Open Prs 1984, Open Prs 1988; Boise KO Tms, Open Prs, Master Prs, Swiss 1984; Richmond KO Tms 1987, Master Prs 1989; Fort Wayne KO Tms, Open Prs, Swiss 1988; Roanoke IMP Prs 1988; St. Charles Mens Swiss 1988; Memphis Open Prs 1990.

SMITH, Terry (b. 1936) of Los Angeles CA, general administrator, former regional tournament director, graduate of U of Chicago. Was ACBL tournament coordinator 1968-70, ACBL executive assistant 1970-74, member of the drafting committee of the 1975 Laws of Duplicate and ACBL organizer for the 1972 World Olympiad. Contributor to *ACBL Bulletin* and the *Bridge Encyclopedia*.

SMITH, Thomas M. (b. 1938) of Greenwich CT, bridge editor and writer, vice-president of Goren Internat'l; editoral manager second edition of *Official Encyclopedia of Bridge*, *World Championship Handbooks* 1966-72. Contributor to *ACBL Bulletin*, *Bridge Journal* and *The Bridge World*. Editor Greater New York BA *Post-Mortem* 1973-78, 1985-91. Business manager *ACBL Bulletin* 1970-72. Managed Cavendish Club 1973-87, elected

honorary member 1988 and president 1990. WBF World Master, placed 12th in Rosenblum Tms 1986. Diamond Life Master, was an original member of the Precision Team which won the Spingold 1970, 71; Vanderbilt 1972. Other NABC placings were second in the Life Master Mens Prs 1976; Spingold 1978, Mens BAM Tms 1982. Intercollegiate champion 1965. Regional titles include Canadian Nat'l Open Prs 1965; Eastern States Mixed Prs 1967, KO Tms 1988, 89; New England KO Tms 1968; Long Island KO Tms 1971, 72; New York Winter KO Tms 1993.

SMITH, William H. (Bill) (1909-1993) of Fort Meyers FL, retired teacher, was associate editor of *ACBL Bulletin* 1958-64. He became a tournament director in 1944 and directed bridge games on many cruises.

SMITH, William P. (Willie, Smitty) (b. 1948) of Endicott NY, won GN Tms Flt B 1991; and Stamford Open Prs 1989.

SMOLEN, Michael (Mike) (1940-1992) of Alamo CA, attorney and commodity trader; WBF World Master, placed 5th Rosenblum Tms, 13th World Open Prs 1990. ACBL Grand Life Master with a lifetime total of 17,421 MPs, he was #16 on the list of all-time MP holders at the time of his death. He devised the SMOLEN TRANSFER BID, was known for his ability to help develop new players and for being a good partner. Won Mens Tms 1976, Swiss Tms 1978, Mixed Prs 1979, Fishbein Trophy, Mens Swiss 1982; North American Mens Swiss, Reisinger 1984; placed second Mens Tms 1974, Open Prs, Open Swiss 1990; npc North American Womens Swiss 1982. Smolen had accumulated more than 100 regional titles.

SMOLEN, Steven F. (Steve) of Manhattan Beach CA, computer consultant, won Amateur Swiss Tms 1977.

SMOLSKI, Roman (b. 1950) of Yeovil, England, computer programmer. WBF World Master. Won European Teams 1991, Common Market Teams 1980. Represented Britain in five world championships and one other zonal championship. Represented England in 15 Camrose matches.

SNITE, Fred Jr. (d. 1955) of Miami Beach, lived the last 19 years of his life in an iron lung. He was a regular competitor in ACBL tournaments and was named ACBL Honorary Member in 1954. See HANDICAPPED PLAYERS.

SNOVEL, Edwin X. (E.X.) (b. 1933) of San Antonio TX, retired Air Force officer and Diamond Life Master. Won Capital City KO Tms 1977, Corpus Christi Swiss 1978, Big D Winter Mens Prs 1980, Master Swiss 1982; Harvest Festival Unmixed Prs 1981, Austin Open Prs 1986, Houston Swiss 1988, San Antonio Open Prs 1988, 89 (Sr).

SNYDER, Marion D. (formerly Weed) of Dallas TX, interior decorator, won Life Master Womens Prs 1975, Master Mixed Tms 1976 and many regional events.

SOBEL, Alexander M. (Al) (March 28, 1901-May 18, 1972) of New York City, was one of the leading bridge personalities. Sobel won his greatest fame as a director of bridge tournaments, but he was also noted as a writer, a quizmaster and a wit. He was the third person to be the North American Championships Tournament Manager for the ACBL, following Alfred M. Gruenther and Russell Baldwin. He held that position from 1942 until his retirement in 1969. Sobel, a graduate engineer of MIT, turned to bridge during the Depression "rather than sell apples." He directed tournaments from September 1934 in the U.S., Canada, Mexico, Argentina, France, Italy, England and Brazil, with guest appearances in Hong Kong, Tokyo and the Philippines. He also served at least once as director-in-charge in every state of the United States. His debut as manager of a major tournament was in 1935 when he substituted for Gruenther at the Eastern States Championships, then a national tournament.

He became the unofficial quiz master of the bridge players when the craze for quizzes resulted in the bridge experts playing a game similar to the popular, *Ask Me Another*, late at night after almost every tournament session. For three years, 1948-1951, he wrote the questions for the Bob Hawk radio quiz program. His commanding voice created a tournament directorial style; until the great crowds of the Fifties Sobel seldom needed a microphone. In 1937 he married Helen Martin White, the women unanimously acclaimed as the #1 woman bridge player of all time; they divorced in 1945. He became a member of the ACBL Laws Commission 1943, was the first Honorary Member of the Japan Contract Bridge League, and was ACBL Honorary Member in 1949. Sobel was one of a group of four talented writers who worked for Ely Culbertson in the early Thirties. Culbertson's summonses to "Al" regularly created confusion, since, in addition to Sobel, the others were Albert Morehead, Alfred Sheinwold and Alphonse Moyse Jr.

A former associate editor of the *ACBL Bulletin*, Sobel authored *60 Days*, a popular bi-monthly diary column for that publication, which became a monthly column *30 Days* and later returned to *60 Days*. He was also a former editor of the West Coast publication, *Contract Bridge Forum*, and a contributing editor to the *Bridge Encyclopedia*.

SOBEL, Helen Martin. See **SMITH, Helen Martin**.

SOKOL, Mike (b. 1948) of Fontana CA, city administration and travel consultant, president of Unit 521, has served on Board of Dist 22 and as its president. Vice-chairman ACBL Conduct and Appeals Committee; served on ACBL Bd of Gov and was named to both the Goodwill and Charity Committees. Sokol also teaches bridge and is a bridge professional. Regional wins include Riverside Swiss 1981; Mexican Fiesta Mens Prs 1983, 85, Unmixed Prs 1986, KO Tms 1992; Morning KO Tms 1986, Spring Swiss 1985; Palm Springs KO Tms, Swiss 1984; San Bernardino Swiss 1993.

SOLAR, Elizabeth (b. 1935 in Poland), of Venezuela computer and telcom consultant. Won CAC Womens Teams 1979, 1980, 1981, 1987. Represented Venezuela in 7 world championships and won many national titles.

SOLER, Rosa (b. 1920) of Barcelona, Spain. Represented Spain in 20 zonal championships and 6 world championships. Won six national titles.

SOLODAR, John (b. 1940) of New York City, director of systems and programming, was Bermuda Bowl champion 1981; WBF Life Master, placed 3rd Rosenblum Tms 1990, 11th 1986, 13th 1978; 14th World Mixed Prs 1978.

Solodar was New York manager for the Sharif Bridge Circus 1968. ACBL Diamond Life Master, won Life Master Mens Prs 1968, Vanderbilt 1980; placed second in the Spingold 1976, 1980; Mens BAM Tms 1983. Has numerous regional wins.

SOLOMON, Charles J. (1906-1975) of Philadelphia, attorney, bridge administrator, teacher and author, was one of the leading figures in the world of contract bridge. Life Master #16 in 1939, he amassed a lifetime total of 6594 masterpoints and won 12 national titles, including the Chicago (now the Reisinger) 1937, 1938, 1939, 1944; Mixed Tms 1949, 1950, 1959; Men's Tms 1952, 1965; Spingold 1955 and others, in addition to 16 second places and numerous regional wins. In 1956 he was a member of the U.S. International team, and he served as non-playing captain of the open team in 1959 and the U.S. women's team in 1960. He donated the Charles J. Solomon Trophy to the World Bridge Federation in 1966, to be given to the country with the best record in pair events at World Pair Championships. Solomon was ACBL president in 1958 and chairman of the Board in 1944, 1955 and 1957; ACBL Honorary Member 1961. On the international level, he was on the organizing committee and helped to found the World Bridge Federation. He served as WBF vice president 1958-1964, as president 1964-1968, as chairman of the Board 1968-1972, and as honorary chairman from 1972 until his death. He also served with distinction on the ACBL Laws Commission from 1940 to 1960 and was on the Editorial Advisory Board *Bridge Encyclopedia*. Solomon was the author of *Slam Bidding and Point Count* and *No Trump Bidding*; he was bridge editor of the *Philadelphia Inquirer* for 30 years. He sponsored the Solomon Award of the International Bridge Press Association, given annually for the best description of a bridge deal in the world press. See BUENOS AIRES AFFAIR.

SOLOMON, Eliezer N. (Ely) (b. 1944) of Riviera Beach MD, born in India, software engineer, placed second NAC Swiss Tms 1978 and has won several regionals.

SOLOMON, Peggy (Mrs. Charles J.) (b. 1910) of Philadelphia PA, one of the leading women players for three decades, Life Master #33. Won the Chicago (now the Reisinger) 1944, Master Mixed Tms 1949, 50, 59; Womens Tms 1957, 64, 68, 70; Womens Prs 1960; placed second Master Mixed Tms 1939, 40; Spingold 1944, Womens Tms 1948, 53, 54, 61, 67; Chicago 1953, Vanderbilt 1954, Mixed Prs 1961, Life Master Womens Prs 1965, 66, 67. Diamond Life Master, won numerous regionals.

SOLOWAY, Paul (b. 1941) of Bothell WA, professional player, WBF Grand Master, Bermuda Bowl champion 1976, 77, 79; placed second World Tm Olympiad 1972, 80; second Bermuda Bowl 1975, 4th 1973; 6th World Olympiad Tms 1984, 7th 1976; 9th Rosenblum Tms 1978. Represented ACBL in several other world competitions. Soloway has more masterpoints than any other member of the ACBL. He is a Grand Life Master with 40,000 MPs (as of February 1994). He won the Pan American Invitational Championship 1977, McKenney Trophy 1968, 69; Team Trials (now the USBC) 1975, 77, 79, 80, 84; Herman Trophy 1976, Life Master Mens Prs 1965, Master Mixed Tms 1966, 87; Vanderbilt 1969, 78;

Spingold 1978, 83, 86, 88; Reisinger 1976, 80; GN Tms 1974, 76; Mens Swiss 1989, Open Swiss 1991; placed second Mens Prs 1969, Mens Tms 1970, Vanderbilt 1971, 76; Spingold 1973, 90; Mens BAM Tms 1984, Reisinger 1986, 90, 93.

SONTAG, Alan (b. 1946) of Gaithersburg MD, professional player, was named "Sportsman of the Year" 1975 (see IBPA AWARDS). Author of *The Bridge Bum*, *Power Precision*, co-author of *Improve Your Bridge Fast*. WBF Life Master, Bermuda Bowl champion 1983, 5th 1991; placed 7th Rosenblum Tms 1978, 8th World Open Prs 1974, 78. Won USBC (Team Trials) 1983, 91; Mens Tms 1971, 79; Life Master Mens Prs 1971, Vanderbilt 1972, 88; Reisinger 1973, Life Master Prs 1977, Spingold 1980, 82; Mens Swiss 1985, 87; Master Mixed Tms 1989. Placed second in the Life Master Prs 1972, 84; Vanderbilt 1975, 81, 83, 89; Reisinger 1977, 92; Spingold 1984, 91; Mens BAM Tms 1985. ACBL Grand Life Master with more than 13,000 MPs as of 1994; won Invitational Prs Championship 1973, 75, the Cavendish Club Invitational 1976, 77, and numerous regional titles.

SOPHONPANICH, Khunying Chodchoy Esther (b. 1944) of Bangkok, Thailand, business executive. President of Far East Bridge Federation and Contract Bridge League of Thailand. Member of Thai women's team in two World Olympiads and 11 Far East Championships. Won 5 ASEAN Bridge Club championships.

SORENSEN, Dr. Dennis E. (b. 1946) of Gresham OR, bridge professional and owner of bridge supply company, graduated U of Illinois, U of Texas-Austin (PhD); serves on ACBL Conduct and Ethics Committee, past president Dist 20, coordinator of GN Tms and GN Prs events. Grand Life Master with more than 12,000 MPs (Feb 1994), won Crane Top 500 1992, Intercollegiate Bridge Championship 1978; finished second in North American Swiss 1991, Open Prs I 1993. His more than 150 regional wins include Dist 20 GN Tms, Zone VIII 1980; Charlotte Swiss, KO Tms 1991, Vancouver KO Tms, Calgary KO Tms, Phoenix KO Tms, Houston KO Tms 1991, Tacoma Open Prs 1991; Hawaii Swiss 1992; Reno Swiss, KO Tms, Open Prs, 30-Hr KO Tms 1993.

SORENSEN, Frederick A. (Fred) (b. 1926) of Pittsburgh PA, retired mathematician and statistician, graduate of Carnegie Institute of Technology (PhD), played chess at expert level 1945-72. Unit 142 president 1981-83; editor Dist 5 *5th Column* and co-editor of Unit 142 *Post Mortem* since 1986. Diamond Life Master, won Summer secondary Sr Swiss 1986, 92, Spring Sr Prs 1988, Sr KO Tms 1991, 94; Pittsburgh KO Tms 1987, 88, 89, Senior Prs 1991, Sr Swiss 1993; Dist 5 GN Prs 1988; All American Sr Swiss 1991; Canton Sr KO Tms 1991.

SORRI, Keijo (b. 1926) of Helsinki, Finland, represented Finland European championships 1953, 1954, 1957, 1962, 1965. Won national Open Teams eight times, Open Pairs 1951.

SOULET, Philippe (b. 1954) of Paris, France, bridge teacher. World Life Master. Won World Teams 1980, 1982. Won European Teams 1983. Represented France in three other world championships and one other zonal championship. Won many national titles.

SOWTER, Anthony P. (Tony) (b. 1946) of Nottingham, England. WBF World Master. Won European Teams 1991, second 1981. Represented Britain in 8 world championships. National titles include Gold Cup three times. Managing editor of *International Popular Bridge Monthly*. Editor of *World Championship Books* since 1990. Author of two books.

SPARKS, Jeffrey M. (b. 1948) of Rohnert Park CA, insurance claims auditor; served as president of Unit 169 for three terms; collector of political items, specializing in Richard Nixon buttons. Won Mid-Atlantic KO Tms, Mens Prs 1975, Master Prs 1977, Swiss Tms 1978, 80, 81, Open Prs 1978, 79.

SPIEGEL, Bernard M. (Buddy) (b. 1947) of Germantown TN, Zip code information manager for U.S. Postal Service; graduate of State U of NY, State Technical Institute of Memphis and U of Memphis. Former ACBL director of administration, ACBL tournament coordinator, ACBL associate national tournament director, secretary to the ACBL Laws Commission, author of *Ruling the Game* for *ACBL Bulletin*.

SPILIOPOULOS, Anna (b. 1925 in Egypt) of Athens, Greece. Third Common Market Womens Team Championships 1989, and a regular member of the Greek Womens Team since 1971. Played once in the Greek Open Team. Leading woman player in masterpoints won 1982-92.

SPILIOPOULOS, Nikos (b. 1913) of Athens, Greece, retired lawyer. Co-founder of Hellenic Bridge Federation in 1965 and its first president. Edited its first magazine (1966-69) and won several national titles. Deputy organizer 1971 European Championships.

SPINGOLD, Nathan B. (Nate) (1886-1958) of New York City, publicist, motion picture executive, patron of the arts, was the most influential man in bridge administration 1937-43. Born in Chicago, he became a reporter on the *The Chicago Examiner*, *The Chicago Record Herald* and *The Chicago Tribune*. Spingold's interest in show business brought him to New York City. In 1932 he joined Columbia Pictures in a public relations capacity and continued his association with the company until his death. In 1940 he was named to the board of directors and three years later was appointed vice president in charge of advertising, publicity and development. In 1954 he became vice president of the company. As leading art collectors, Nate and Frances Spingold owned an outstanding gallery of French impressionist paintings and contempory American art. Active in bridge from its earliest days, Spingold donated the prestigious trophy which bears his name and in 1936 he was named ABL Honorary Member. He was influential in effecting a peaceful merger between the American Bridge League and the United States Bridge Association in 1937 and became president of the newly formed American Contract Bridge League the following year. He served for many years on the League's Bd of Gov and Bd of Dir. Spingold was also president of the Cavendish Club in New York.

SPINN, Rosi (b. 1928) of Kitzbühel, Austria, retired English teacher. WBF World Master. Runner-up 1991 Venice Cup, and represented Austria in one other world championship and one European Championship.

SPIRIDONOV, Andrej (b. 1957) of Podolsk, Russia, computer programmer. Represented Soviet Union, or C.I.S, in two world championships and one zonal championship. National wins include open teams twice and open pairs once.

SPITALNICK, Richard L. (b. 1944) of Sunnyvale CA, CPA, degrees from Lafayette College and Rutgers U; treasurer Dist 21 1980-85, Fall NABC 1981; placed second in Amateur Swiss Tms 1977. Won the Rogue River Valley Master Prs 1976; Mid-Winter Holiday Mens Prs 1976, 77, 84, Swiss 1985, KO Tms 1990; CA Capital Mens Prs 1977; All-Western Mens Prs 1978, 79; Dist 21 GN Tms 1980; San Francisco Mens Prs 1982, 83, KO Tms 1985, 90; Dist 21 GN Tms 1991, 92.

SPITZ, Marshall R. (b. 1943) of Chestnut Hill MA, stockbroker, won New England Master Tms 1966, KO Tms 1967, BAM Masters 1967; Bretton Woods Mens Prs 1966, 67, 68; Long Island Open Prs, Swiss 1968; Summer secondary Golder Master Prs 1973.

SPIVACK, Leo J. (b. 1926) of Miami FL, formerly of Chicago, retired attorney and investment banker, educated at U of Chicago and Northwestern U. ACBL president 1979, member of Bd of Dir 1970-86, served as chairman of the ACBL Appeals and Charges Committee, 1974, 75, 77, 78, 82. He was chairman of the Board 1980, chairman of WBF Appeals Committee 1980-81. A Board member of Chicago CBA for many years, he served as its president 1968-70.

SPOONER, John Richard (b. 1965) of Canberra, Australia, systems administrator. Third World Junior Teams 1991, won Far East Junior Teams 1990, and represented Australia in one other world championship. Junior chess champion.

SPOTTS, Robert L. (b. 1937) of Oakley CA, project manager, placed second in Mens Tms 1967 and won several regional events.

SPRUNG, Danny (b. 1965) of Philadelphia PA, stock options trader, graduate of U of Pennsylvania; won Mixed Prs 1991; regional wins include Cherry Hill Mens Swiss, Standard Card Prs 1988, Swiss 1991; Stamford Open Prs 1989, New Brunswick Swiss 1990.

SPURWAY, Paul (b. 1926) of Melton Mowbray, England, accountant. Represented Britain in one world championship. Won 11 national titles. EBU vice-chairman 1968-73.

SQUIRE, Norman (1907-1991) of London, England, bridge writer. Won De La Rue international par tournament 1957. National wins include Gold Cup three times. Author of 12 books. Competition editor of *Bridge Magazine* for many years, and author of many magazine articles. He made important contributions to bidding theory, including FOURTH-SUIT FORCING and OUT-OF-THE-BLUE CUEBID.

ST. LUCE, Dr. Ralph (b. 1934) of Miami FL, formerly of Jamaica, physician, graduate of U of West Indies, Jamaica. Represented Jamaica in internat'l play Deauville 1968, CAC Championships 1971, 72, 73, 74 winning three times and placing second once; has won every major Jamaican title.

STACK, Don (b. 1939) of Overland Park KS, chemist and computer programmer, graduated Rockhurst College; recorder for Dist 15. Diamond Life Master, won more than 100 regionals, including Cornhusker Master Prs 1975; Indian Summer Mixed Prs, Open Prs 1979; Iowa Open Prs 1979; Dist 15 GN Tms 1979, 81, Zone V 1981, Master Prs 1980, GN Prs 1981, Spring Open Prs 1981; Dist 14 Summer Open Prs 1981; Oklahoma City Swiss, Omaha Swiss 1993.

STAKGOLD, Alice of Newark DE, (1924-1994) won Master Mixed Tms 1969.

STAKGOLD, Ivar (b. 1925) of Newark DE, born in Norway, mathematics professor, placed second Bermuda Bowl 1959; also represented US in Turin 1960. Won Mott-Smith Trophy, Chicago (now the Reisinger), Vanderbilt, Open Prs 1958; Spingold 1962; Leavintritt Prs 1964, Master Mixed Tms 1969; placed second in Mens Tms 1957, Spingold 1958, Open Prs 1963. He also won English Melville Smith Tms 1968 and placed second in Crockford's Cup 1968.

STALLARD, M. Berl (b. 1913) of Miles City MT, retired accountant, creator of FIRST UP, a method of bidding that uses no conventions. In the Seventies he hired professional players to play only his system in a regional in Helena MT, and his team beat out Barry Crane's team. He is the author of several books on this subject. He and his wife Helen also introduced Instant Bridge, a bridge-like game that requires no bidding. Stallard served as treasurer and business manager of IBPA, was voted Honor Member in 1991; treasurer ABTA for several years.

STANSBY, JAN, see MARTEL, Jan.

STANSBY, Lew (b. 1940) of Castro Valley CA, commodity trader; WBF Grand Master, won the World Open Prs 1982, placed 9th 1990; won Bermuda Bowl 1985, 87, placed second 1989; placed second Rosenblum Tms 1982, 9th 1990. ACBL Grand Life Master with more than 10,000 MPs as of 1994. Won Reisinger 1965, 81, 85, 86; Vanderbilt 1967, 84, 87; Spingold 1975, 90; GN Tms 1982, 83, 85, 87, 93; Mott-Smith Trophy 1984, 86; Open Prs 1986. Placed second Blue Ribbon Prs 1981, Reisinger 1983, Mens BAM Tms 1989, Open Prs 1991, Vanderbilt 1992, Spingold 1992, 93. Stansby won the Rosenkranz Romex Award in 1979 (see IBPA AWARDS).

STAPPENBECK, Harry A. (b. 1939) of Uniondale NY, bridge teacher, graduate of Hofstra College. Diamond Life Master; won Spingold 1987 and was second 1974. Has won more than 20 regional events. At 6 ft. 11 in., he is the world's tallest bridge expert.

STARK, Dr. Gary (b. 1931) of Portland OR, dentist, won NAC Mens Tms 1967.

STARK, Joshua G. (b. 1957) of Grayslake IL, his more than 20 regional wins include Chicago Swiss 1984, BAM Tms 1989; Great Lakes Open Swiss 1985, KO Tms 1989, Mens Prs 1991; Indianapolis KO Tms, Mens Swiss 1988; Lake Geneva KO Tms 1988; Green Bay KO Tms 1989;

Grand Rapids Masters Swiss 1990; Columbus KO Tms 1991.

STARR, Jeffrey C. (b. 1949) of Las Vegas NV, stock/ options trader and poker player; Diamond Life Master, placed second GN Tms 1974, 82; won more than 40 regionals including Spring secondary Mens Prs, Open Prs 1973; All-American KO Tms 1974, 75, Open Tms 1974, 76, Master Prs, Open Prs 1974; Summer secondary Mens Swiss 1989.

STARR, Robert E. (Bob) (b. 1919) of Centerville MA, retired merchandise manager, retired bridge club owner/ manager; Brown U graduate, very active in Rotary Club and an ardent antiquer. Won Summer secondary President's Prs 1947; New England Mens Prs 1951, 63, Open Tms 1952, 54, 58, 62, Mixed Tms 1953, 69, KO Tms 1956, 59, 62, 63, Open Prs 1970. Starr is a retired bridge columnist who wrote for several newspapers and magazines.

STARRATT, David M. (Dave) (b. 1947) of Lebanon OR, bridge teacher, won Medford Swiss 1978; Seaside Swiss 1988; Eugene Swiss 1989; Penticton KO Tms 1989; Santa Clara Open Prs 1990; Reno Open Prs 1990; Portland Swiss 1992.

STAUBER, Allan G. (b. 1944) of Cross River NY, collectables broker, WBF World Master and ACBL Diamond Life Master; won Blue Ribbon Prs 1980; Mott-Smith Trophy, Spingold, Mens Tms 1981; Mens Prs 1981, 83; North American Mens Swiss 1982, Reisinger 1984. Placed second GN Tms 1979.

STAYMAN, Josephine L. (Tubby, Mrs. Samuel) (b. 1924) of Palm Beach FL, former gift shop owner, placed second World Mixed Tms 1974 and won several regional events.

STAYMAN, Samuel M. (1909-1993) of Palm Beach FL, retired portfolio manager, investor and bridge author, Life Master #48, graduate of Dartmouth College and Tuck Business College. In the June 1945 issue of *The Bridge World* he described a convention, invented by his then partner George Rapee, which subsequently became known as the STAYMAN CONVENTION. He made other contributions to the theory of the game, including NAMYATS (Stayman spelled backwards). A WBF Grand Master, was Bermuda Bowl champion 1950, 51, 53 and placed second in the World Team Olympiad 1964, 5th 1960; 8th in Rosenblum Tms 1986. He also represented North America in several other world championships. An ACBL Diamond Life Master with more than 8,000 MPs at the time of his death, won the Spingold 1942, 44, 48, 50, 52, 55, 59; Vanderbilt 1942, 46, 50, 51; Chicago (now the Reisinger) 1945, 47; Fall Mens Tms 1952, 62; Open Prs 1959; Spring Mens Tms 1963, 80; Life Master Prs 1965, Reisinger 1984. He placed second in the Vanderbilt 1944, 45, 52, 69; Mens Prs 1945, Spingold 1947, 69; Fall Mens Tms 1948, 55; Chicago, Life Master Prs 1950; Spring Mens Tms 1965, Reisinger 1976, 77. He also won numerous regional titles, including Eastern States KO Tms 1939, 40, 51, 63. He was president of the Cavendish Club in New York and served as ACBL treasurer 1966-69 and as a trustee of the ACBL Charity Foundation. Stayman was named ACBL Honorary Member in 1969

and received the same honor from American Bridge Teachers Association in 1979. He is the author of *Expert Bidding, The Complete Stayman System of Contract Bidding*, and *Do you Play Stayman?* He was a contributing editor to the *Official Encyclopedia of Bridge*.

STEARNS, Sherman (1900-1965) of New York City, real estate broker, was one of the leading American players of the Thirties and a member of the Four Aces Team during its later years. Among his national championships were USBA Open Tms, Open Prs 1935; Vanderbilt 1938, 41; Life Master Prs 1938. He placed second in five national events and had numerous regional successes.

STEDEM, Joseph J. (1899-1983) of Palm Springs CA, retired executive vice president of the Hertz Corporation, was ACBL president 1968, a member of the Bd of Dir 1949-50 and 1964-69, president of the ACBL Charity Foundation 1973-74, trustee 1972-75 and was named ACBL Honorary Member 1971. He was a former president of the Midwest Bridge Conference and of the Chicago CBA. Stedem helped initiate the ACBL policy, begun in 1949, of holding North American Championships in many centers. Previously all such tournaments had been held in the greater New York area, but the experiment of attempting an NABC in Chicago in 1949 proved most successful. As a result, players in all sections of the ACBL have had the opportunity to play in NABCs at not too great a distance from their homes. He was also instrumental in the reorganization of the ACBL, working with Waldemar von Zedtwitz. Stedem placed second in the Senior Master Individual 1952 and won Midwest Spring Open Prs 1949, Central States Mixed Prs 1950.

STEEL, Les (b. 1957) of Edinburgh, Scotland, systems analyst. Represented Britain in one world championship and Scotland in 18 Camrose Trophy matches. Many national wins include Scottish Cup once.

STEEN, Douglas (b. 1927) of Los Angeles, division head with CIA, primary scientist to discover astropsychology via statistical studies in finance; WBF Life Master, was Bermuda Bowl champion 1954. Life Master #331; won Master Mixed Tms 1952, Spingold 1953 and placed second in Fall Mens Tms 1953, Mens Prs 1954. Co-inventor of the BULLDOG SYSTEM and co-author of *Precision Power Bidding*. Steen retired from bridge in 1956.

STEHLY, Paul E. (Fred, Fred Friendly) (1925-1985) of Minneapolis MN, associate national tournament director since 1968, formerly represented the tournament directors at the ACBL Bd of Dir meetings. After his death the FRED FRIENDLY AWARD was established in his honor. It is given to the tournament director who most epitomizes Stehly's character of friendliness and concern for the players.

STEIN, Ethan (b. 1946) of Irvington NY, attorney, bridge teacher, WBF World Master, placed 8th in Rosenblum Tms; Diamond Life Master, placed second in Sr and Advanced Sr Master Prs 1974, Mens Prs 1984, North American Mens Swiss 1986, North American Swiss 1988, 89.

STEIN, Joan S. (b. 1934) of River Hills WI, businesswoman and active in community affairs, graduate of Memphis State U, she represented ACBL in world competition 1982, 86, 90. Diamond Life Master, won Life Master Womens Prs 1974 and placed second 1983. Has won more than 70 regional events including Motor City Swiss 1981; Summer secondary Standard Card Prs 1988; Great Lakes Womens Prs 1989; Wisconsin KO Tms 1989; Dist 11 Fall Swiss 1989; Opryland Swiss, Womens KO Tms 1991, 93; Wiesbaden Open Prs, Central States II Seeded KO Tms 1993.

STEIN, Mark (b. 1935) of Montreal PQ, born in China, company president, graduate of Carleton U, represented Canada in international competition 1978, 86, as npc in 1988, 89, 90, Venice Cup team npc 1993; won CNTC 1985, npc of second-place teams 1988, 90. Stein won GN Prs 1991, North American Swiss 1992; placed second GN Prs 1990; won Epson Towers World 1990 and approximately 50 regional events.

STEIN, Sylvia A. (b. 1921) of Southfield MI, former bridge club owner, represented U.S. in World Womens Prs 1962, 70. Diamond Life Master, won Life Master Individual 1958; Lou Herman Trophy 1958, 69; Womens Prs 1962, Womens Tms 1965, 68; Life Master Womens Prs 1969; placed second Mixed Prs 1958; Womens Tms 1960, 65, 71; Master Mixed Tms 1960, 62, 65, 67; Life Master Womens Prs 1964.

STEINBERG, Jonathan (b. 1950) of Toronto ON, private investor, degrees from McGill U and U of Western Ontario, represented Canada in world play 1986, 90. Elected to ACBL Bd of Dir 1993, member Dist 2 and Unit 166 Bd of Dir; member ACBL Bd of Gov 1990-93. Diamond Life Master, placed second North American Swiss 1985; has won more than 20 regionals including London Bridge Mens Swiss 1985, KO Tms 1988, Open Prs 1991; Cambrian Shield KO Tms 1986, 91, Open Prs 1990, 92; Great Lakes KO Tms 1987; Nat'l Capital Swiss 1988, 93; Fleur-de-Lys Swiss 1991.

STEINER, Albert (1901-1977) of Cincinnati, president of a toy manufacturing company, won the Chicago (now the Reisinger) 1933, and Western States Mixed Prs 1935. He was co-donor of the Steiner Trophy.

STEINER, Carlyn J. (b. 1945) of Seattle WA, attorney, educated at Smith College, U of Chicago and U of Washington (JD); co-chairman Organizing Committee 1984 World Olympiad; community arts activist, board member and wine connoisseur. Placed second Womens Prs 1987; has won many regionals including Spring secondary Womens Swiss 1992, Fall Open Prs 1993; Dist 19 GN Tms 1985, 87.

STEINER, George M. (b. 1945) of Seattle WA, investment broker. Diamond Life Master, won Mens Prs, Life Master Prs 1985; Mens Prs 1987; placed second Vanderbilt 1994 and has won numerous regionals.

STEINER, Phillip (1901-1993) of Cincinnati OH, retired company executive, was ABL vice president 1936, a member of the Board 1930-38, committee chairman 1934, and ACBL Honorary Member 1937. He was the co-donor of the Steiner Trophy, which for more than a quarter century was one of the most important events on the ACBL calendar. Won the Chicago (now the Reisinger) 1933, Western States Mixed Prs 1935. With Albert and

another brother, Joseph, Steiner founded the toy-making firm Kenner Products in 1945.

STEINFELDT, Sherman I. (Irv) (b. 1918) of Minneapolis MN, company executive, U of Minnesota graduate; won Silver Ribbon Prs 1992. His numerous regional wins include Winnipeg Open Prs, BAM Tms 1963; Miami Beach Life Master Prs 1967; Sioux City Open Prs 1972; Minneapolis Swiss 1972, Sr Mens Prs 1988; Sioux Falls KO Tms 1972, 84; Milwaukee Mens Prs 1973; Indianapolis Mens Prs 1975; Palm Springs Sr Open Prs 1988, Spring secondary Sr Open Prs 1987.

STENGER, Dr. Charles A. (b. 1922) of Bethesda MD, retired clinical psychologist, was POW 1944-45 (Battle of the Bulge). He served as a member of the ACBL Bd of Dir (1980-1992) and is past president of District 6, Mid-Atlantic Conference and Washington BL. Chaired Dist 6 Judiciary Committee for many years and is a member of ACBL Goodwill Committee. Stenger is recognized as an international expert on hostages and POWs; he retired following a long career in the Veterans Administration, in which he served as national director of a staff of 1,400 psychologists. He was educated at Akron, Case Western Reserve U (PhD) and Vanderbilt. Diamond Life Master with numerous regional wins.

STENGER, E. Jeanne (Mrs. Charles A.) (b. 1924) of Bethesda MD, member ACBL Goodwill Committee, ACBL Charity Committee 1970-71; Diamond Life Master; her numerous regional wins include Mid-Atlantic Womens Swiss 1978, 79, 80, Swiss Tms 1980, Sr Prs 1990, 91; Fall secondary Sr Swiss 1990, Sr Prs (2) 1993; Daytona Beach Sr Swiss 1991, Richmond Sr Swiss 1993.

STEPHENS, Daisy W. (1907-1988) of Shreveport LA, won Amateur Womens Prs 1975 and several regionals.

STERN, Gerda (b. 1924 in Poland) of Sydney, Australia, interpreter. Represented Australia in one world championship, two South Pacific playoffs and four Far East championships. Won several national titles.

STERN, Roger D. (b. 1934) of New York City, financial corporation president, attorney, graduate of Columbia U and Columbia Law School; npc of Bermuda Bowl championship team 1977 and of the North American team in the 1973 Bermuda Bowl. He placed second in the World Par Contest 1961 and won the US Zone World Par Contest 1963, Mens Tms 1965, Mixed Prs 1969, Blue Ribbon Prs 1989. He was the first president of Dist 24 and served as president of the Greater New York BA. He served for many years as member of ACBL Bd of Gov, ACBL Laws Commission and as vice-chairman of the NABC Appeals Committee. Stern is the co-inventor of ASTRO and ASTRO CUEBID and co-author of several *Bridge World* articles, including a series outlining a modern style of defensive bidding.

STERNBERG, Dr. James H. (Dr. J.) (b. 1937) of Boca Raton FL, radiologist, graduate of Columbia College and U of Miami (MD); Rookie of the Year in 1977 and became a Life Master same year (see Mini-McKenney), won Mens BAM Tms 1979, placed second Spingold 1984. He has won 19 regional events including Fall secondary Open Prs 1977, Spring BAM Tms 1991; Roanoke Mens Swiss,

Albany Open Swiss 1977; Montreal Open Swiss 1978, 79, KO Tms 1979; Dist 9 GN Tms 1979, 90; Long Island KO Tms 1980; Miami Open Swiss 1982, Mens Prs 1983; Providence Swiss, Jacksonville Open Prs 1983; Halifax Open Swiss, Springfield KO Tms 1985; Tampa Swiss 1993.

STETTEN, Jacques (b. 1926) of Paris, France, builder, WBF Life Master, European champion 1962, second 1961, represented France Bermuda Bowl 1963, 1967, 1969, European championships 1966. Won French Open Teams 1961, 1963.

STEUER, Joseph B. of Memphis TN, placed second in Amateur Mens Prs 1975 and won several regional events.

STEUER, Marie Louise of Memphis TN, won Celebrity Swiss 1977; Spring secondary Open Prs 1978, Summer Womens Prs 1991; Headquarters Swiss 1978; Space City Womens Prs 1980; Mid-South Womens Prs, Gold Coast Swiss 1981; Southeastern Womens Tms, Swiss; Summer Women's Prs 1991.

STEWART, Frank R. (b. 1946) of Fayette AL, journalist, author, a major contributor to the Fifth edition of *The Official Encyclopedia of Bridge*; graduate of U of Alabama; represented South Korea in the 1968 Far East Bridge Championship while serving in the U.S. Army. He won several regional events but discontinued tournament play to devote full time to writing about bridge. Stewart served as co-editor of *The Contract Bridge BULLETIN* 1984-89, and continues to contribute to that publication through a column he began in 1981. He edited *ACBL World Championship Books* 1983-87 and was a principal contributor to those books 1986-89. Since 1986 he has worked with Alfred Sheinwold to produce the syndicated newspaper column *Sheinwold on Bridge*. Stewart has published hundreds of articles in most of the world's leading bridge magazines. Author of 17 books, among them *The Bridge Player's Comprehensive Guide to Defense, Better Bridge for the Advancing Player, The Devyn Press Bridge Teacher's Manuals and Student Texts, The Bridge Today 1001 Workbook, My Bridge and Yours*, and *A Christmas Stocking*. He frequently serves as an analyst for ACBL-wide and district-wide charity events and is known for his recall of bridge deals and facts. He is a low-handicap golfer, a bridge teacher, a former member of the NABC Appeals Committee, and a former professional player.

STEWART, Frederick M. (b. 1948) of Andes NY, stockbroker, WBF World Master, placed 5th Bermuda Bowl 1991, 14th World Open Prs 1986, also represented ACBL in international play 1982, 90. Won Pan-American Prs 1991 and Life Master Prs 1981, Reisinger 1984, Blue Ribbon Prs 1987, Open Swiss 1992; placed second GN Tms 1991. Won the Cavendish Invitational 1993. He has won many regionals including New England Summer Swiss 1981; Eastern States Open Prs (Goldman) 1982. See FAMILY.

STEWART, John G. (b. 1951) of Halifax NS, lawyer, bridge teacher and club manager, graduated Dalhousie U, placed second CNTC 1982; won Spring secondary Open Prs 1974, Dist 1 GN Tms 1978, Can-At KO Tms 1980. He is a founding member of *Halifax Bridge World*

and one of its contributors, he is a columnist for the *Halifax Daily News*.

STICKNEY, William L. (b. 1913) of Boynton Beach FL, retired company executive, a former director and president of the Chicago CBA and a contributor to its publication, the *Kibitzer*. Won All-American Open Prs 1942 (when playing duplicate for first time); Central States Open Prs 1943, Life and Senior Master Tms 1962; MS Valley Open Prs 1944; Florida KO Tms 1967.

STIEFEL, John D. (Jay) (b. 1944) of Wethersfield CT, actuary (Fellow of the Society of Actuaries), graduate of Yale and U of Michigan; Diamond Life Master, won Amateur Swiss Tms 1976 and more than 30 regionals including New England KO Tms 1974, 79, Summer Swiss 1976, Fall Swiss 1976, 78; Dist 25 GN Tms 1981, 88, 90, 92, GN Prs 1984, 85, 88, 90; Summer secondary BAM Tms 1985; Eastern States (Reisinger) KO Tms 1991. Wrote Sunday bridge column for the *Hartford Courant* 1979-84.

STIEFSOHN, Helga (b. 1959) of Vienna, Austria, social worker. European Womens Team champion 1991 and played in one other European Teams.

STOLITSA, Evgeny (1905-1985) of Sofia, Bulgaria, born in Russia, pianist and astrologer. Introduced duplicate bridge to Bulgaria and became its leading theorist, creating the natural bidding system "ERS" and Ultra-Texas.

STOBER, Ruth L. (b. 1935) of Great Neck NY, retired CFO and business manager, represented ACBL in world play New Orleans 1978, Biarritz 1982, Bal Harbour 1986, Geneva 1990. She has won a number of regionals including Philadelphia Swiss 1979; Puerto Rico Womens Prs 1981; Fall secondary Swiss 1982, 89; Cherry Hill KO Tms 1988, 89, 91, Sr Prs 1991; Atlantic City KO Tms 1989; Lancaster Swiss 1990; Mexico City 1991; Pan-Am Mixed Prs 1992; East Brunswick Prs 1992, Open Swiss 1993; Rye Womens Prs, Kiamesha Sr Prs 1993; Orlando Open Prs, Long Island Sr Swiss, New England Open Prs 1994.

STODDARD, Peggy (Mrs. Thomas W.) of Laguna Hills CA, retired real estate broker, assisted her husband in many Pacific Bridge League and ACBL Western Division activities. She was secretary of the PBL 1936-37 and a contributor to *The Contract Bridge Forum*. A member of the ACBL Goodwill Committee since 1952, she was awarded a silver card for "Outstanding Services to Bridge" by the ACBL in 1969. Won Pacific Southwest Mixed Prs 1953, All-Western Womens Prs 1966.

STODDARD, Tom (1896-1976) of Laguna Hills CA, "Father of Bridge on the West Coast," was one of the outstanding personalities of American bridge, a pioneer in bridge teaching and bridge club management, founder of the Pacific Bridge League, and former ACBL executive. In 1931 Stoddard owned a Los Angeles hotel at a time when most hotels were going bankrupt. He conceived the idea of making his hostelry a center for bridge lessons and duplicate games. The project was a sensational success — at its peak there were 11 teachers conducting games daily from 9:20 a.m. to midnight. Stoddard founded the PBL in 1933 and was responsible for the wildfire growth of bridge on the West Coast. The PBL included the 11 Far Western states, the territories of Hawaii and Alaska and the Canadian provinces of British Columbia and Alberta. It rapidly reached a membership in the thousands, promoting two major tournaments (the All-Western and Bridge Week) and many minor ones. Stoddard also founded the *Contract Bridge Forum* in the early Thirties; during its nearly 60 years of publication this news letter has been the voice of the PBL, the Western Division of the ACBL, and the Western Conference. Collaboration between the ACBL and the PBL began in 1940 when they agreed on a uniform masterpoint system. In 1946 Stoddard turned over his bridge business to his associates, and in 1948 he agreed to the amalgamation of the PBL and national organizations, an arrangement consummated in 1956. At this time he was elected President Emeritus of ACBL, Western Division, and ACBL Board member. He was named ACBL Honorary Member in 1960 and was also a member of the Goodwill Committee. In May of 1976 he was awarded the rare "Certificate of Service" citation by the ACBL Board of Directors for his long and devoted service to bridge and to the ACBL. Stoddard was a regional correspondent for the *ACBL Bulletin.*

STOLLER, Mildred (b. 1920) of Lauderhill, FL, retired model, buyer and piano teacher, member ACBL Charity Foundation and a gourmet cook. Won numerous regionals including St. Louis Swiss 1987; Richmond Master Prs 1987, Swiss 1993; Jacksonville Open Swiss 1987, Swiss 1988; Hilton Head Master Swiss, Bal Harbour Womens Swiss, Dist 9 GN Tms 1989; Bonaventure Swiss 1989, 92, Open Swiss 1991; Myrtle Beach KO Tms 1990; Nashville KO Tms, Swiss 1991, Open Prs 1993; Toronto KO Tms (2) 1991; VA Beach KO Tms (2), BAM Tms, Swiss 1992; Houston Swiss 1994.

STOLTZ, Eric (b. 1954) of Portland OR, computer scientist, won Tri-Cities KO Tms 1983, Oregon Trail Open Swiss 1985, 92, Open Prs 1985, Swiss 1993, 94; Emerald Empire Open Prs 1985; Penticton KO Tms, Swiss 1987; Reno Open Prs 1988; Dist 20 GN Tms 1989.

STONE, Barbara J. (b. 1942) of Framingham MA, former teacher and finance specialist; graduated U of Wisconsin and Fairleigh Dickinson U. Won Southeastern Womens Swiss 1980, Albany Womens Swiss 1980, 81, KO Tms 1986; Can-Am BAM Tms 1984, KO Tms 1988, New England Summer Swiss 1986, 91, Labor Day KO Tms 1986, Winter Swiss 1988, 91, KO Tms 1989, Fall KO Tms 1988, 91, Swiss 1990; Montreal Fall KO Tms 1986.

STONE, Janice G. (Jan) (Mrs. David H. Fulton) (1920-1992) of Miami Beach FL, formerly of New York City, became a Life Master in seven months, the first to attain that status in such a short time. She was also a backgammon champion. A radio and TV actress from childhood, she starred on many nationally prominent TV dramatic and variety shows. Between 1974-78 she was an executive in a family-owned mining operation. She was the former wife of Tobias Stone. The year after they married the couple finished first and second in the McKenney race. They were also the only married couple to win the New York City Goldman Prs (1957) in the 64-year history of the event. Stone placed second in World Womens Tms

1964 and won Womens Team Trials 1963. Her national wins included Womens Tms 1956, 69; Life Master Womens Prs, Master Mixed Tms 1965; placed second in Master Mixed Tms 1956, Spingold 1959, Womens Tms 1961, 62. She won numerous regional titles.

STONE, Kenneth (Sky King) (1910-1988) of Fort Worth TX, associate national tournament director since 1965, began directing in 1950. He was the owner/manager of an air and cruise travel agency.

STONE, Robert F. (Bob) (b. 1946) of Framingham MA, economist, won more than 20 regionals including Lexington Swiss 1971; Summer secondary Golder Master Prs, Upper NY State Mens Swiss 1972; New England Master Prs 1973, Summer Swiss 1986, 91, Labor Day KO Tms 1986, Winter Swiss 1988, 91, KO Tms 1989, Fall KO Tms 1988, 91, Swiss 1990; Dist 25 GN Tms 1975; Fall secondary KO Tms 1983; Can-Am Mens Prs, Swiss 1984, KO Tms 1988; Montreal Fall KO Tms 1986. Has contributed many articles to *The Bridge World.*

STONE, Tobias (Stoney) (b. 1921) of New York City, bridge author, WBF Life Master, placed second Bermuda Bowl 1958, third World Team Olympiad 1960, also competed internationally 1966, 72, 74. ACBL Diamond Life Master, he won the McKenney Trophy 1956, Open Prs 1942, Vanderbilt 1949, 59, 60; Chicago (now the Reisinger) 1952, 61; Master Individual 1953, Spingold 1956, 57; Fishbein Trophy, Life Master Prs 1956; Men's Tms 1961, 63; Men's Prs 1961, Master Mixed Tms 1965. He placed second in the Life Master Prs 1942, 65; Men's Prs 1952, Spingold 1953, 61, 63; Master Mixed Tms 1956; Fall Open Prs 1958, Spring Open Prs 1958, 1965; Men's Tms 1959, Vanderbilt 1969. Stone won dozens of regional titles including the Eastern States KO Tms 1942, 44, 61, 63, 67, 73, 74, Open Prs (Goldman) 1957, 1961; Marcus Cup 1960. He and partner Al Roth were the first Americans to win the Deauville Invitation pair event; they scored a record-breaking 82% game. He also is an international backgammon champion. Co-inventor of the ROTH-STONE SYSTEM, he has made many contributions to bidding theory. He is co-author of *Bridge Is a Partnership Game* and *The Bridge World* department *What Do You Play and Why?*

STOPPA, Dr. Jean-Louis (b. 1932) of Paris, France, physician. World Life Master. Second World Teams 1971. Won European Teams 1970. Represented France in six other world championships and three other zonal championships. Won many national titles.

STOTHART, C. David (Dave) (b. 1924) of Ottawa ON, director, senior management staffing (government of Canada), graduated U of New Brunswick, Princeton, Delft (Netherlands); inducted into New Brunswick Sports Hall of Fame (basketball). A Diamond Life Master, placed second CNTC 1981, Canadian Open Prs 1986; won Can-At KO Tms 1968; Fleur-de-lys Open Prs 1974; Can-Am Swiss 1979; Dist 1 GN Prs 1980.

STOUT, Alan F. (Herman) (b. 1949) of Cedar Rapids IA, field auditor for the State of Iowa, U of Iowa graduate; has more than 15,000 MPs as of 1994; has won more than 100 regionals including Pheasant KO Tms 1973; Gopher KO Tms 1977, 91, 92, Mens Prs 1990, Swiss

1991, Open Prs, Master Prs 1992; Dist 14 GN Prs 1981; Tri-Dist/Split KO Tms, Open Prs, Swiss 1993; Dist 10/Split KO Tms 1993. Stout has more than 790 sectional wins.

STRAFNER, Michael (b. 1952 in Austria) of Munich, Germany. WBF World Master. European Junior Team champion 1976. Represented Austria in three world championships and three European championships. Won Austrian Teams six times, Open Pairs three times; first-class badminton player.

STRASBERG, David I. (b. 1928) of Ft. Lauderdale FL, personnel agency owner, Diamond Life Master, won Spingold, Fishbein Trophy 1970; placed second in Chicago (now the Reisinger) 1958, Mens Prs 1968; Master Mixed Tms 1970, GN Tms 1980. See PRECISION TEAM.

STRICKLAND, Fred E., III (b. 1945) of Atlanta GA, bridge teacher, former attorney, graduated Florida State U and John Marshall U; past president Unit 114, Unit Player of the Year 1980. Diamond Life Master, won Mid-Atlantic Mens Prs 1970, Open Prs 1977, Celebrity Master Prs, Mens Swiss 1977; Fall secondary Swiss 1972, Open Prs 1974, Spring Master Prs 1976, Summer Mens Prs 1980; North Florida Mixed Prs 1977.

STUART, B. Wayne, III (b. 1965) of Raleigh NC, systems analyst, WBF World Master, won World Junior Team Championship 1991 and the NABC Junior Prs 1991. Member of the Jr Corps, won Raleigh Open Swiss 1986; Charlotte Open Swiss 1987; Columbia Open Swiss, Richmond BAM Tms 1991. He has Master ranking in US Chess Federation but no longer competes; enjoys playing pool.

STUART, Joel H. (b. 1927) of Rego Park NY, options trader, won Spingold 1970, 71; Vanderbilt 1972 and placed second Mens Tms 1968. See PRECISION TEAM.

STURM, Charlotte G. (Char) (b. 1927) of Whittier CA, bridge teacher, director on cruise ships, Diamond Life Master, placed second Senior Master Prs 1965. Won Pasadena Swiss 1974, Mixed Prs 1989, Womens Swiss 1991; Santa Rosa Open Prs 1982; Ventura Senior Open Prs 1984; Las Vegas Open Prs 1991; Bakersfield Swiss 1991. 1991-92 president of Unit 564. She and son (Steve Sturm) are one of the highest ranking mother/sons in total masterpoints.

STURM, Stephen F. (Steve) (b. 1951) of Whittier CA, mailhandler, Chicago Conservatory of Music graduate, won North American Swiss 1983. Also won Wine Country Open Prs 1982; Bakersfield Swiss 1991. Accomplished pianist, plays for entertainment at bridge tournaments. He and his mother (Charlotte Sturm) are one of the highest ranking mother/sons in total masterpoints.

SUEMATU, Shigehisa (b. 1910) of Tokyo, Japan, mathematics teacher. Lt. Colonel in World War II. First member of JCBL, and its first tournament director. Represented Japan first Japan-U.S.A. match 1950. Member JCBL Board of Directors for many years. Recipient Fifth Class Order of the Sacred Treasure.

SUGAR, Paul (b. 1928) of Chicago IL, attorney, CPA, former bank president, graduate of Roosevelt U, John Marshall Law School; placed second Mixed Prs 1975; won numerous regionals. Sugar was Chicago CBA Player of the Year 1962 and former director, treasurer and legal counsel of the Chicago CBA.

SUKONECK, Ronald M. (Ron) (b. 1949) of Annandale VA, legal administrator, U of Maryland graduate, member ACBL Appeals Committee 1977-1984. Sukoneck, a WBF World Master, placed third in Rosenblum Tms 1990; also represented ACBL in world play 1986 and in Bermuda Bowl in Santiago 1993; won USBC (Team Trials) 1993. ACBL Grand Life Master with more than 10,000 MPS, won North American Mens Swiss 1988, Spingold 1992; placed second Life Master Prs 1982, GN Prs 1987. He has won 50-75 regional titles.

SULGROVE, Kathleen J. (b. 1952) of Twinsburg OH, restaurant owner, U of Toledo graduate; won Mixed Prs 1984, also a number of regionals including Cincinnati Master Prs 1984; Chicago Smoking Swiss 1985; Hudson Womens Swiss 1985, 86, 87, 88, Mixed Prs 1987.

SULLIVAN, George R. (Maven) (b. 1953) of Longmeadow MA, business executive, graduated American Internat'l College and U of Maine; president Dist 25 1994, Unit 196 (1990-92), editor of Unit newsletter *Trumpeter*. Regional wins include Wm Keohane KO Tms 1982, 89, 93; Cambridge Open Prs 1983; Manchester Open Prs 1986, KO Tms 1991, KO Tms (2) 1992; Gatlinburg Open Prs 1987; Cromwell KO Tms 1992, 94; Springfield KO Tms 1990, 93 (2); Can-Am Swiss 1989; Albany Open Swiss 1991, KO Tms 1992.

SULLIVAN, Michael J. (Mick) (1894-1974) of Brisbane, Australia, accountant, did much to promote contract bridge in Australia, particularly in Brisbane, when it came on the scene in 1932. Co-founder of the World Bridge Federation 1958, chairman of its Constitution Committee, and a member of the WBF Executive Board. Organized 1951 Jubilee Year World Olympic, 1954 Bidding Championship, 1961 and 1963 WBF Global Par Championships; was joint formulator of Laws of Par Point Contract Bridge 1963 (International Code). World Par Zonal winner 1939, 1940, 1941. National titles include Par wins 1937, 1939, 1943, 1950, 1957. In 1974 was made the first Honorary Life Member of the Australian Bridge Federation. Contributed many double-dummy problems to British *Bridge Magazine*.

SUMMERS, Sylvia F. (b. 1954) of Long Beach CA, professional bridge player, degree from Penn State, other interests include sewing and acting. Senior Master of the Year 1982; won North American Swiss 1983, 88, and a number of regionals including Portland Open Swiss 1982; Hawaii Open Prs 1983; Palm Springs BAM Swiss 1985; Buffalo Womens Swiss 1988; Pasadena KO Tms 1989; Fort Worth KO Tms, Swiss 1990; Sacramento KO Tms 1990, 91, BAM Tms 1990; Detroit Swiss 1990.

SUN, Ming (b. 1955) of Beijing, China, commission employee. WBF World Master. Third Venice Cup 1991. Won Far East Womens Teams 1986, 1991,1993, second 1987, 1988. Also represented China in 6 world championships and 3 other zonal championships. Won four national titles.

SUNDBY, Robert D. (Bob) (b. 1925) of Madison WI, judge, author of *Breakthrough in Bridge*; *Bridge in the '80s*; past president Wisconsin/Upper Michigan BA.

SUNDELIN, Per Olof (PO) (b. 1937) of Stockholm, Sweden, computer analyst and consultant. World Life Master. Third in three world championships, Team Olympiad 1988, Bermuda Bowl 1987, 1991. European champion 1977 and 1987, 2nd 1991, third 1989. Represented Sweden in five other world championships and nine other European championships. National wins include open teams 7 times. Won *Sunday Times* Invitational Pairs 1978, 1981. Won 1984 North American Life Master Pairs; contributes to bridge magazines; vugraph commentator at many world championships.

SUNG, Leslie L. of Hong Kong, newspaper editor and lawyer. Represented Hong Kong in Far East championships four times. National wins include open teams and open pairs. Was chairman of Hong Kong CBA for 20 years.

SUSSEL, Andree (b. 1914) of Paris, France, antique dealer, WBF World Master, European Womens Team champion 1956, 1965, 1969; represented France European Womens championships 1958, 1959, 1962, 1966, 1975; won French Mixed Teams 1962

SUTHERLAND, Eric R. (b. 1972) of Waterloo ON, bridge teacher and student at U of Waterloo. Placed second World Junior Championship 1991. At 16 was one of the youngest Canadians to achieve Life Master status.

SUTHERLIN, John C. (b. 1936) of Dallas TX, WBF World Master, placed second World Mixed Prs 1982, 3rd Rosenblum Tms 1990, 7th World Open Prs 1986. ACBL Grand Life Master with more than 14,000 MPs, was second in Top 500 1990; national wins include Master Mixed Tms 1976, Spingold 1981, Mens BAM Tms 1983, Mott-Smith Trophy, Open Swiss 1990; Vanderbilt 1990, 93; Life Master Prs 1993; placed second in Mixed Prs 1962, 94; Mens Tms 1967, North American Swiss 1982, Vanderbilt 1985, Open Swiss 1991; npc Venice Cup team 1987; has had numerous regional wins.

SUTHERLIN, Peggy (nee Berry) (b. 1937) of Dallas TX, WBF World Master, placed second World Mixed Prs 1982, 4th Venice Cup 1987, 13th World Womens Prs 1986, also represented ACBL in Geneva 1990. Represented Dist 21 ACBL Bd of Gov 1988-91, member ACBL Laws Commission, and has been co-chairman ACBL Appeals Committee since 1990. ACBL Diamond Life Master, won Mixed Prs 1972, Master Mixed Tms 1976, Womens KO Tms 1986; placed second Mixed Prs 1962, Womens Prs 1986. Sutherlin is an amateur genealogist and it is in this capacity she was a contributing editor to the *The Official Encyclopedia of Bridge*.

SUTTON, Iona N. (b. 1911) of Wichita Falls TX, former bridge teacher; regional wins include Texas Fall Womens Prs 1959, 64, Spring Womens Prs 1958, Open Tms 1968; El Paso Womens Prs 1959, KO Tms 1961; Corpus Christi Swiss Tms 1959.

SVEINDAL, Jon (b. 1946) of Bergen, Norway. Second Bermuda Bowl 1993, third European Teams 1993. Has represented Norway on several other ocasions.

SVERRISSON, Sigurdur H. (b. 1953) of Reykjavik, Iceland. WBF World Master. Won Nordic Teams 1988. Represented Iceland in three world championships, two European championships, three European Junior championships, two other Nordic championships and one Nordic Junior championship. National wins include open teams three times and open pairs twice.

SWAN, Mary Margaret of Houston TX, publisher, won Mixed Prs 1964.

SWANDER, Shirley A. (b. 1930) of Mission KS, artist, won Womens Tms 1955 and several regionals.

SWANSON, John C. Jr. (b. 1937) of Mission Viejo CA, computer programmer, WBF Life Master, Bermuda Bowl champion 1977, second in 1975, 4th 1973; placed 5th World Open Prs 1978. He also represented North America in the Bermuda Bowl 1971. ACBL Diamond Life Master; won Mens Prs 1959, Vanderbilt 1969, 77; Mens Tms 1970, GN Tms 1974, 76; placed second Life Master Mens Prs 1968, Spingold 1973. Swanson has been a contributor to *Southern California Bridge News*, *The Bridge World* and *ACBL Bulletin*. He co-authored *Recap Bridge*, computer-dealt hands with analyses, and co-developed the WALSH SYSTEM.

SWANSON, Paul (b. 1932) of Morgantown WV, company president, Diamond Life Master, won Mott-Smith Trophy, Mens Tms 1972; Life Master Prs 1973, Master Mixed Tms 1976, Mens Prs 1979, 86; placed second in the Chicago (now the Reisinger) 1963, Life Master Mens Prs 1968, Vanderbilt 1972, Reisinger 1973, 80; Mens Prs 1978. Swanson has won numerous regional events.

SWANSTRÖM, Madeleine P.B. (b. 1942) of Solna, Sweden, district attorney. WBF World Master. Won European Womens Pairs 1989, Nordic Womens Teams 1980. Represented Sweden in two world championships and three European Championships.

SWEARINGEN, Gladys (b. 1913) of St. Louis MO, retired secretary, won NAC Womens Prs 1953.

SWEENEY, Frank Henderson Jr. (b. 1919) of La Jolla CA, retired CPA, graduate Wharton School, U of Pennsylvania; member ACBL Bd of Dir since 1988, ACBL Goodwill Committee; served on Dist 22 Board 1982-87, Western Conference president 1991; past president Unit 526.

SWIMER, Ralph (b. 1914) of London, England, company director. WBF World Life Master. Second World Teams 1960. Represented Britain in one other world championship and two zonal championships. National wins include Gold Cup once. See BUENOS AIRES AFFAIR.

SYDNOR, Mrs. Caroline of Alexandria VA, bridge teacher and writer, graduate of West Virginia U. Author of *Bridge Made Easy series*, *Book One (Basics)*, *Book Two (Intermediate)*, *Book Three (How to Win More Tricks)*,

Book Four (How to Set Your Opponents). Each volume has a special deck of cards coded to deal 40 lesson hands. *Book Three* won "Book of the Year" award from the American Bridge Teachers Association 1981; *Book Four* won in 1993. She also wrote *Teaching Bridge How To Do It Better* and *How to Set Your Opponents*.

SZURIG, Zbigniew (1938-1984) of Warsaw, Poland, bridge professional. Second World Par 1963. Represented Poland in three world championships and seven zonal championships. Won several national titles. Bridge theorist, editor and author of one book.

SZWARC, Henri (b. 1930 in Poland) of Paris, France, textile company director. WBF Grand Master. Won World Teams 1980, second 1984. Won European Teams 1966, 1970, 1974, 1983, second 1967. Represented France in six other world championships and seven other zonal championships. With J-M Boulenger, named best pair in Europe in 1966. Won Sunday Times Invitational Prs 1977. National titles include Open Teams many times.

SZYMANOWSKI, Marek (b. 1955) of Warsaw, Poland, economist and bridge professional. WBF World Master. Second Bermuda Bowl 1991, third 1989. Won European Teams 1989, third 1991. Represented Poland three other world championships. Won many Polish titles.

T

TAI, Min Fan (b. 1938) of Taipei, Taiwan, chemical engineer. World Life Master. Runnerup Bermuda Bowl 1969 and 1970 and represented Taiwan in 12 other world championships. Chief tournament director of several international events.

TAI TENQUEE, Ronald (b. 1933) of Kingston, Jamaica. CAC Team champion 1983, represented Jamaica in two world championships. Won numerous national titles.

TAKAHASHI, Satoru (b. 1913) of Tokyo, Japan, foreign service officer. Former ambassador to Spain. Represented Japan in Far East Championships. Won Takamatsu Cup 1958. Former president JCBL.

TAMMENS, Kees (b. 1950) of Amsterdam, The Netherlands, bridge journalist and barman. WBF World Master. Coach of Dutch junior team. Represented The Netherlands in three world championships and three European Championships. National titles include open teams three times and open pairs once. Columnist, staff member and contributor to *Bridge*.

TAMRES, Margery (Marge) (b. 1925) of Pittsburgh PA, retired bookkeeper. Diamond Life Master, won Dist 5 Womens Prs 1969, 80, Womens Swiss 1981; Keystone Fall Womens Prs 1971; All-American Swiss 1975, 79; Buffalo Master Prs 1982; Canadian Nat'l Womens Open Prs 1986.

TAN, Allen L. (b. 1947) of MetroManila, Philippines, represented Philippines World Tm Olympiad 1980; Asian Bridge Championships 1980, 88; Far East Bridge Championships 1990, 91, 93, 94. He invented and introduced MATCHPOINT TEAMS, a new form of duplicate,

authored article describing the system in *The Bridge World*.

TAN, Su Beng (b. 1956) of Petaling Jaya, Malaysia, engineer. Represented Malaysia in two world championships, several zonal championships and national wins.

TAN, Sze Guan (b. 1961) of Petaling Jaya, Malaysia, computer programmer. Represented Malaysia in one world championship and two zonal championships. National wins include open teams three times.

TANG, Hou Zou (b. 1935) of Shanghai, China, teacher. WBF World Master. Second Far East Teams 1984, represented China in four world championships and four other zonal championships. Won 12 national titles. Coach for Chinese womens team.

TANG, Ji Zou (b. 1940) of Shanghai, China, technical employee. WBF World Master. Second Far East Teams 1984, represented China in four world championships and four other zonal championships. Won 12 national titles. Coach for Chinese women's team.

TANNA, Dhiru (b. 1943 in Uganda) of Kingston, Jamaica, economist and executive director of conglomerate. Represented Jamaica in three world championships and one CAC championship. Won several national titles.

TARLO, Joel (1905-91) of Marbella, Spain, formerly of London, England, retired solicitor. Won European Teams 1960. Represented Britain in two world championships and four zonal championships. Represented Spain in a zonal championship at age of 82, perhaps a record. National wins include Gold Cup twice.

TARLO, Louis (b. 1911) of Hove, England, solicitor. Won European Teams 1950. Represented Britain in one world championship and 8 zonal championships. Former EBU chairman.

TAUBE, Richard of Marietta GA, attorney, graduated U of Virginia and U of Maryland (JD); Jr Nat'l Bowling champion 1949. As member of White House Commission on Emergency Medical Services 1969-79, he developed telemetry and roadside telephone emergency communication systems. Chairman of 1973 Summer NABC, member ACBL Nat'l Appeals Committee, has been active in bridge administration since 1965. Diamond Life Master; has won more than 65 regionals the most recent of which include Fall secondary KO Tms 1992, 93, Open Prs 1992, Summer KO Tms 1993; Pine Mountain Open Tms 1993.

TAXTE, Raimón (b. 1947) of Barcelona, Spain, engineer. Represented Spain in two zonal championships and two zonal junior championships. Won many national titles.

TAYLOR, Edward O. (1912-1984) of Glendale CA, marketing director, Life Master #83; won Fall Open Prs 1957, Chicago (now the Reisinger) 1959, 62; Mens Tms 1959, 62; Spring Open Prs 1959, Life Master Prs 1963; placed second Vanderbilt 1963.

TAYLOR, Eileen (1907-1990) of Auckland, New Zealand. Won Far East Women's Teams 1976, represented

New Zealand in four other zonal championships. National wins include open teams six times.

TAYLOR, Pauline J. of Detroit, retired decorative arts curator, was the first woman president of the American Bridge Association (1969-73). An active promoter of bridge since 1949, she was also president of the Detroit Unit 1956-61 and founder of the first womens duplicate club there. Her ABA nat'l titles include Mixed Tms 1952, Womens Prs 1957, Individual 1974.

TAYLOR, Tony (born in England) of Auckland, New Zealand. WBF World Master. Represented New Zealand in five world championships and two zonal championships. National wins include open teams once.

TCHAMITCH, Haig G. (b. 1951) of Don Mills ON, born in Lebanon, graduate of Haigazian College and American U of Beirut, semi-retired salesman. Won Lou Herman Trophy, Blue Ribbon Prs 1992; Lancaster KO Tms 1989, Spring secondary BAM Tms, Toronto KO Tms (2) 1992, Morning KO Tms 1993. In 1981 he was awarded a civilian citation by Metro Police in a hostage-taking incident.

TEAGUE, Terry (1904-1987) of Birmingham AL, insurance agent, member of ACBL Bd of Dir 1957-60; won several regional events.

TELFER, Roy L. (b. 1898, deceased) of Plymouth, England, retired army officer. A major contributor in the field of bridge mathematics, on which he wrote two books. Magazine contributor.

TEMMERMAN, Simone de (b. 1917) of Paris, France, musician, European Women's Teams champion 1956, 1965, 1969; represented France European Championships 1955, 1959, 1961, 1965, 1974; won French Mixed Teams 1960, Women's Teams 1955, 1960, Womens Pairs 1952, 1954, 1955, 1956, 1960, 1961.

TENCH, Stanley (Stan) (b. 1929) of Ottawa ON, retired director of government computer center, ACBL associate national tournament director; developed the Tench movement. Won Can-At KO Tms 1968, 69, 70.

TEPPER, Barbara (b. 1930) of Verona NJ, medical group administrator; Diamond Life Master, won Womens Tms 1969.

TERRANEO, Franz (b. 1953) of Vienna, Austria, project manager. WBF World Life Master. Runnerup Bermuda Bowl 1985, World Team Olympiad 1988. Won European Teams 1985, runnerup European Pairs 1985, European Mixed Pairs 1990. Won Statenbank Invitational (Netherlands) 1987 and 1989. Won Austrian Teams six times, Mixed Pairs twice.

TESSMER, Maxine F. (1912-1992) of Belton TX, was Far East Prs champion 1961, representing Japan.

TEUKOLSKY, Roselyn (Ros) (b. 1948) of Ithaca NY, born in South Africa, math and computer science teacher, graduate of U of the Witwatersrand and Cornell; author of *How to Play Bridge with Your Spouse...and Survive,* contributor to the *ACBL Bulletin* under the title *As I See It,* to *Bridge Today* under the title *Undertricks,* also contributes to *Canadian Masterpoint,* Dist 4 *4 Spot* and the *CNYBA Newsletter.* Had highest ACBL E-W score in Epson Prs 1988.

TEXEIRA, Carlos Spinola (b. 1939) of Lisbon, Portugal, company director. Represented Portugal in one world championship and five European Championships. National titles include open teams six times and open pairs twice.

THEIMER, Dr. Ernst T. (b. 1910) of Rumson NJ, retired company vice president, graduate of U of Cincinnati and NYU (PhD); former chess champion and North Woods tour guide. Served as president and tournament chairman of the New Jersey BL and for five years wrote a weekly bridge column for the *Newark News.* He is the author of *The Bridge Adventures of Androcles MacThick* and has contributed to *The Bridge World* and *Bridge Today.* Won Summer secondary Sub-Senior Master Tms 1945; NY-NJ Conference Mixed Prs 1967.

THEOBALDS, Vaughn (b. 1927 in Grenada) of Kingston, Jamaica, architect. Honorary secretary of CAC Bridge Federation, 20 years of service to bridge administration in Jamaica. Chairman, Organizing Committee 1982 CAC zonal championship.

THERON, Dr. Georges (1922-1970) of Paris, France, physician and bridge writer, European champion 1962, second 1967, represented France World Open Pairs 1962, Bermuda Bowl 1963, 1969; World Team Olympiad 1964, European Championships 1965. French Open Teams 1952, Open Pairs 1962. Contributed to Pierre Alberran's *Encyclopedia* and articles for French and foreign magazines. Translated into French Jack Olsen's *The Mad World of Bridge.*

THEUS, Edgar G. (1913-1994) of Oklahoma City OK, attorney, member of the ACBL Bd of Dir 1961-88; ACBL president 1969; chairman of the Board 1970, president emeritus since 1989. He served on the executive committee, the appeals and charges committee, the finance and tournament committees. He was also on the ACBL Laws Commission and was on the WBF Executive Council from 1969-86; served as 1st vice president of the World Bridge Federation; chaired the International Laws Commission; was co-captain of the defending Bermuda Bowl team in 1977 and was captain of the victorious North American Bermuda Bowl team in 1979. Theus placed second in Life Master Mens Prs 1966, won several regional titles.

THIENGTHAM, Sunai (b. 1936) of Bangkok, Thailand, managing director. WBF World Master. Twice runnerup Far East Open Teams. Represented Thailand in six other Far East Championships and two world championships.

THOMAS, D. Michael (Mike) (b. 1938) of Carnegie PA, company president, graduate of Vanderbilt; won All-American Mens Prs 1962, Mixed Prs 1963; Central States Mens Prs 1964, 65, 66; Texas Fall KO Tms, Mid-South Spring Open Prs 1964; Mississippi Valley Open Tms 1968, 69; Mid-Am-Can Open Prs 1967; Missouri Valley Open Tms 1965, 66; Midwest Open Tms 1967; Chicago Open Prs 1969, 70. Thomas was a member of the Chicago team that challenged the SHARIF BRIDGE CIRCUS.

THOMAS, E. Robert (Bob) (b. 1911) of Philadelphia PA, investments company executive, won his national events nearly 50 years apart, won Rothschild Team-of-Four 1940, Open Prs 1991, placed second in the Chicago (now the Reisinger). Thomas was 79 when he won the Open Prs, one of the oldest to win a national event. He has won several regionals.

THOMAS, Frank of Los Angeles, syndicated bridge columnist, former leading boy actor of stage and screen, playwright, scriptwriter, actor for radio and TV, retired from the theatrical side of the entertainment field in 1962 to begin bridge teaching in association with George Gooden, reaching as many as 18,000 students a year in department stores. Editor and publisher of the *ABTA Quarterly* since 1969. He writes a syndicated bridge column and is the author of several books including *Sherlock Holmes, Bridge Detective* (in collaboration with Gooden) and *Sherlock Holmes, Bridge Detective, Returns*. Thomas is a past president of the American Bridge Teachers Association.

THOMAS, Fred R. (Tommy) (b. 1925) of Leavenworth KS, retired, author of *Universal Club,"The" System for Everyone* and instant bidding guide for same.

THOMAS, James O. (b. 1938) of Olympia WA, cartographer; past president of Unit 441. Won Mid-Winter Holiday Master Prs 1971; Puget Sound Mens Prs 1972; Oregon Trail Mens Swiss 1976; City of Gardens Master Prs 1986; Peach City Open Swiss 1987.

THOMAS, Jayne (b. 1931) of Lutz FL, executive manager of Unit 128, retired 30-year math teacher, holds degrees from Stetson U and U of Florida. Other interests include slot tournaments, entertaining, backgammon; she is a gourmet chef. Represented ACBL the world championships 1978, 86, 90, Pan-Am Championship 1992. Diamond Life Master; won Silver Ribbon Prs 1994 and numerous regionals, two of which were Mens Prs (as a fill-in). She is a member of the ACBL Bd of Dir, the ACBL Educational Foundation (president twice, treasurer once), the ACBL Charity Foundation, and ACBL Goodwill Committee. She served for years as a member of the Bd of Dir of Dist 9 and Unit 128 and has served as president of both. She contributes to the *Florida Bridge Bulletin*.

THOMPSON, Benjamin John Polya (b. 1965 in California) of Melbourne, Australia, computer scientist. Third World Junior Teams 1991, won Far East Junior Teams 1990, and represented Australia in one other world championship. Won one national title.

THOMSON, Robert D. (Bob) (b. 1957) of Half Moon Bay CA, computer consultant and avid gardener; won North American Swiss 1981, BAM Tms 1990; placed second Master Mixed Tms 1991. Regional wins include Pacific Southwest Master Swiss 1979, All Western IMP Prs, KO Tms 1991.

THORBJORNSSON, Saevar (b. 1956) of Reykjavik, Iceland, civil engineer. Won Nordic Teams 1988, 1992. Represented Iceland in one world championship, two European Championships, two European Junior Championships, five other Nordic Championships and two Nordic Junior Championships. 5 national wins include

open teams twice and open pairs once. Chairman of Iceland's leading club, Bridgefelag Reykjavikur.

THORFINNSSON, Einar (1906-1980) of Reykjavik, Iceland, banker, represented Iceland World Team Olympiad 1960, European Championships 1950, 1951, 1958, 1971; Europe in Bermuda Bowl 1950; national titles include Open Teams 1953, 1954, 1957, 1962, 1965, 1970, 1971, 1972; Open Pairs 1956.

THORNTON, Susan M. (b. 1932) of Crescent Spring KY, placed second Master Mixed Tms 1977.

THORPE, Catherine C. (Katie) (b. 1948) of Toronto ON, born in England, data base administrator, graduate of McMaster U and U of Toronto Law School; Canadian Bridge Federation Zone III director since 1987, a member of the ACBL Goodwill Committee and ACBL Laws Commission; served as CBF president 1989-91, Unit 166 Board member 1976-81 (past president), member ACBL Bd of Gov, and as alternate Director Dist 2. WBF World Master; placed 3rd Venice Cup 1989, 4th Olympiad Womens Tms 1988, 9th 1984, 5th Swiss Plate 1984. She also represented Canada New Orleans 1978, Bal Harbour 1986, Geneva 1990, Yokohama 1991. Won Canadian Womens Team Championship (CWTC) 1984, 86, 87, 90, 91, Canadian Open Prs 1990, Master Mixed Tms 1991; placed second Canadian National Teams 1987. Won many regionals including Toronto Womens Swiss 1987, 88, 89.

THURRELL, Robert F. (Bob) (b. 1920) of Venice FL, retired insurance executive, graduate of Harvard; won Rocky Mountain Mens Prs 1948; New England Open Tms 1967, Open Prs, KO Tms 1970; member of Boston team that won Intercity Championship four consecutive years 1971-74.

TIBREWALA, N.S. (b. 1918) of Bombay, India, pediatrician. Represented India in four world championships and one zonal championship. Won Far East Pairs 1978. 11 national wins include open teams five times. President Indian Bridge Federation 1978-79 and 1990 on.

TIERNAN, Agatha D. (1884-1981) of Brandon VT, bridge teacher, writer and lecturer. As a director at the Cavendish Club (New York), she was granted the first club sanction for a monthly masterpoint game. She was named ACBL Honorary Secretary in 1960. Her playing achievements included second place in Womens Tms 1951.

TIERNAN, Mary Elizabeth (b. 1907) of Brandon VT, member ACBL Goodwill Committee; won Womens Tms 1956 and placed second 1951.

TIERNEY, Dr. John A. (b. 1917) of Ft. Lauderdale FL, retired USNA mathematics professor, member of the ACBL Goodwill Committee; co-author *Contract Bridge: According to Silodor and Tierney* and contributor to *The Bridge World*. Won Washington DC Mixed Prs 1970; Miami Sr Prs 1987; Jacksonville Sr Tms 1990.

TILLES, Jules (1907-1976) of New York City, bridge teacher, club owner and tournament director, was business manager of the Greater New York BA 1957-72. Placed second Mixed Prs 1952, won Eastern States Open

Prs 1943, 50, 54.

TING, Michael (b. 1935) of Singapore, engineer and company director. Represented Singapore in two world championships.

TINTNER, Leon (b. 1910) of Paris, France, born in Austria, publisher, European champion 1962, 1966, represented France Bermuda Bowl 1963, 1967, 1969; WBF Life Master; won *London Sun Times* Invitational 1971; many national championships include Open Teams twice, Interclubs twice.

TOBIN, E. J. (Ned) (1868-1953) of Miami and Chicago, was one of the founders of the American Bridge League. He served as its first secretary in 1927-28, became treasurer in 1929, and was made an Honorary Member in 1932. Tobin, a contributor to the Chicago *Record Herald* and the *Daily Journal*, was the holder of many whist championships. He was the author of *Sound Principles of Auction Bridge*.

TODD, Robert J. (Bob) (b. 1950) of Winnipeg MB, senior systems analyst; graduate of U of Manitoba; held several executive positions Unit 181 1977-1983 including president. Won Buffalo Individual 1976, KO Tms 1977, Unmixed Prs 1978, Swiss 1980; Peach City KO Tms, Saskatchewan Mens Prs 1978.

TOGORES, Antonio (1930-1984) of Barcelona, Spain, businessman. Represented Spain in two world championships and six zonal championships. Won many national titles.

TOH, Chee Kian (b. 1947) of Singapore, school teacher. Represented Singapore in seven zonal championships. National wins include open teams several times.

TOIBIN, Niall (b. 1959) of Dublin, Ireland, administrator of Irish aid to East Africa. WBF World Master. Won Common Market Open Pairs and Junior Teams 1981. Represented Ireland in two world championships and one zonal championship. Won 10 national titles.

TOLEDANO, John H. (Buster) (b. 1907) of New Orleans LA, bridge teacher, graduate of Tulane; with wife, Dotty, organized and developed Unit 134 and celebrated 50 years of continuous service with the Unit in 1992 -- they have been teaching and directing for 53 years. Toledano finished second Mens Tms 1956 and won Mid-South Open Tms 1944, 61, 62, Mens Prs 1944; Southern Conference Fall Open Tms 1960.

TOLSDORFF, Lore (b. 1921) of Wuppertal, Germany, bridge teacher and travel organizer. Represented Germany frequently since 1967 and won 11 national titles.

TOLSTOI, Count Lev Nikolaevich (1828-1910) famous Russian novelist, used the Russian game Vint, a form of bridge whist, as background for his long short story *The Death of Ivan Illych.* See HISTORY OF BRIDGE and BRIDGE LITERATURE.

TOLSTOY, Leo. See Tolstoi, Count Lev Nikolaevich.

TOM, Merle H. (b. 1935) of Cos Cob CT, attorney, Dia-

mond Life Master, won Open Prs 1972, Mens Tms 1974; placed second in Vanderbilt 1974, Mens Tms 1977.

TOMCHIN, Stanley of Orinda CA, won Master Mixed Tms 1973, placed second Vanderbilt 1975.

TOMCZYK, Gary (b. 1953) of Sunrise FL, Richmond Trophy winner 1987, 89 (Canadian equivalent of Top 500); Diamond Life Master with approximately 50 regional wins.

TORLANTANO, Anna Maria (b. 1930) of Pescara, Italy. Member of the Italian Bridge Federation Executive Committee. Member of the WBF and EBL Executive Committees, and heads the EBL Ladies and Ceremonies Committees.

TORNAY, Claire J. (C. Belle, Clara Belle) (b. 1940) of New York City, born in Belgium, graduated Barnard College, Pace U, Yeshiva U; currently pursuing new career as clinical social worker/therapist, formerly a teacher; has served as vice-chairman ACBL Appeals Committee since 1991. She was the first and only woman president of New York's Cavendish Club and was instrumental in 1989 in organizing the BATTLE OF THE SEXES. She served as president of the Greater NYBA from 1985-89 and has served on the WBF Appeals Committee. WBF World Master, placed 4th in World Womens Prs 1982 and also represented ACBL internationally Bal Harbour 1986, Geneva 1990. Won Womens Prs 1980, Mixed Prs 1988; placed second Swiss 1981, Womens Prs 1991; won numerous regionals.

TORNAY, George F. Jr. (b. 1936) of New York City, consulting actuary, graduated Miami U, he is a Fellow of Conference of Consulting Actuaries; WBF World Master, won Swiss Plate 1986, placed 8th Rosemblum Tms 1986, also represented ACBL in world competition Biarritz 1982, Geneva 1990. Won Sr and Advanced Sr Master Prs 1962, Mens BAM Tms 1980, Reisinger 1984. Has represented Dist 24 as GN Tms winner several times and won many regionals.

TORRENCE, Anita C. (b. 1942) of Bexley OH, bridge teacher and professional player, has served many terms on Unit and District boards including two terms as president of Central Ohio BA; member of the ACBL Goodwill Committee and ACBL Charity Foundation. Received outstanding service award for Central Ohio in 1988 for advancement in bridge. Won All-American Mixed Prs 1976, Womens Swiss 1979, 80, 90; Midwest Fall Womens Prs 1980, 82; Womens Swiss 1991; Charleston Master Prs 1982; Indianapolis Womens Prs, Womens Swiss 1983; Pittsburgh Womens Swiss 1986, 87, Womens Prs 1992; Cincinnati Womens Prs 1989, Mid-Winter Womens Prs 1992.

TOUCHTIDIS, Stelios (b. 1947) of Sherman Oaks CA, born in Greece, graduated Athens NTU and UCLA, advertising executive, with interests in archery, astronomy, comic book collecting and fine wines. WBF World Master, placed 7th World Mixed Prs 1986, was npc of US II Womens Tm 1985. Won Reisinger 1984, placed second Open Prs 1980, North American Mens Swiss 1982, North American Swiss 1987. ACBL Diamond Life Master, he has won more than 25 regionals including Reno

Superflt KO Tms 1978; Bridge Week Mixed Prs 1979, Open Prs 1979, 81, 85, 90, Swiss, Mens Prs 1981, KO Tms 1990; Pasadena Open Prs 1977, 87, KO Tms 1982, Swiss 1990, 91.

TOWNSEND, Mary B. (McBeth, MB) of Baton Rouge LA, bridge teacher and director, graduated Butler U and Southern Methodist U, records books for the blind in spare time. Member ACBL Goodwill Committee, secretary Dist 10. Diamond Life Master, placed second Womens Tms 1968. Regional wins include Missouri Valley Womens Prs 1958; Golder Prs 1966, South Texas KO Tms 1971; Mid-South Womens Prs 1973, Open Prs 1976; Music City Womens Swiss 1973, Lone Star Swiss 1977; Mississippi Valley Master Prs 1978; Spring secondary Sr Swiss 1990.

TRAANE, Nils (1925-1980) of New York City, engineer, composed many double-dummy problems published in *The Bridge World* and the British *Bridge Magazine*.

TRAUB, Alexander A. (Alec) (b. 1911) of Capetown, South Africa, wool merchant, bridge writer, won South African Par event 1953, Open Teams 1955, 1962, placed second 1956, 1957. IBPA Awards Secretary 1975-1982. Contributed to *Le Bridgeur,* translated *Mathematical Theory of Bridge,* authored *Point Count Expectancy Tables, Trump Technique,* co-authored *Probabilities Contract Bridge.* Editor of *Practical Odds at Bridge,* contributing editor to *Bridge Encyclopedia.*

TRAVIS, Barbara (b. 1959) of Adelaide, Australia. WBF World Master. Won Far East Women's Teams 1985 and represented Australia in five world championships and four other zonal championships. Won many national titles. Represented South Australia regularly as player and delegate. Youngest winner McCutcheon Trophy 1979, and first woman.

TREADWELL, David (b. 1912) of Wilmington DE, retired chemical engineer, graduate of MIT; WBF World Master, represented ACBL in world competition 1982, 86, 90. ACBL Honorary Member 1985; has served in various executive positions including chairman of ACBL Bd of Gov 1979, 80, 81, co-chairman ACBL Appeals Committee 1975-91, past president of Unit 190 and Dist 4. ACBL Grand Life Master with more than 17,000 MPs as of 1994, won North American Swiss 1982, Master Mixed Tms 1985; placed second Presidents Prs 1936; Mens BAM Tms 1960; Mixed Prs 1969. He also has won nearly 100 regional competitions.

TREDINNICK, Gerald A. (b. 1963) of Beckenham, England, WBF World Master. actuarial trainee. Won World Junior Teams 1989. Represented Britain in one zonal championship. Won one national title. Twin brother of Stuart.

TREDINNICK, Stuart P. (b. 1963) of Beckenham, England, computer programmer. WBF World Master. Won World Junior Teams 1989. Represented Britain in one Zonal championship. Won one national title. Twin brother of Gerald.

TREITEL, David H. (b. 1954) of New York City, transportation consultant, won Swiss Tms 1980; regional wins include Rumson Open Swiss 1990; NYC Open Prs 1992.

TRENT, Paul (b. 1936) of New York City, attorney, won Mens Tms 1969, 71; Intercollegiate Par champion 1957.

TREUIL, Pierre (b. 1934) of Ottawa ON, represented Canada in World Olympiad 1970; won Canadian Open Prs Championship 1992, 93; Ottawa Mens Swiss 1981, 87, 88, 89, Swiss 1987, 89; Montreal Swiss 1990, Open Prs 1991; North Bay Swiss 1991.

TRÉZEL, Roger (1918-1986) of Paris, France, journalist. WBF Grand Master. Won Bermuda Bowl 1956, World Teams 1960, World Pairs 1962, a unique triple in the three major open world championships at that time. Won European Teams 1955, 1970, second 1954, 1956, 1959. Won *Sunday Times* Invitational Pairs 1963 and many French national titles. His partnership with Pierre Jais was one of the world's strongest from 1950-70, and demonstrated the effectiveness of the tendance canapé (modified canapé). Author of a series of booklets later translated into English.

TROY, Anita E. of Henderson NV, retired purchasing agent; during her 35-year membership has held numerous executive positions in American Bridge Association including president 1992-95 and vice-president 1990-91, Great Lakes Section vice president 1973-74, Western Section vice-president 1986-89, nat'l tournament chairperson 1974, 1977 and consultant for 1986. ABA nat'l wins include Mixed Prs 1967, Womens Tms 1971, Flt B KO Tms 1971, 80, Swiss Tms 1982, 85, BAM Tms 1987, 90; placed second Womens Tms 1972, Womens Prs 1982, 92, Mixed Tms 1991.

TRUE, Robert H. (b. 1944) of San Francisco CA, systems analyst, mathematician, bibliographer; contributing editor to *Encyclopedia of Bridge.* His research (1974-75) contributed greatly to clarifying the early history of bridge, the probable origin of the name of the game, and the acquisition from Cambridge University Library of a copy of the 1886 pamphlet of BIRITCH, first recorded publication of rules of the game.

TRUSCOTT, Alan Fraser of New York City, born April 16, 1925 in England, is a leading international player-writer who came to the United States in 1962. Has been bridge editor for the *New York Times* since 1964, and was president of the INTERNATIONAL BRIDGE PRESS ASSOCIATION 1981-86. A frequent contributor to British *Bridge World, ACBL Bulletin,* and other magazines throughout the world. Truscott also has been executive editor of all five editions of *The Official Encyclopedia of Bridge.*

After serving as secretary of the BRITISH BRIDGE LEAGUE 1957-62, Truscott worked as associate editor of the *ACBL Bulletin* 1963-64. He was European champion in 1961 and represented Great Britain in the European Championships in 1951 and 1958. He represented Great Britain in the 1962 Bermuda Bowl, where he finished third. He has represented the United States in world competition in 1970, 72, 74, 78, 82, 86, 90.

He invented the TRUSCOTT CARD, now widely used to prevent seating errors in team play. He has authored several conventions, for which see DEFENSE TO STRONG ARTIFICIAL OPENINGS, TWO-NOTRUMP RESPONSE (over opponent's takeout double), and TWO-WAY STAYMAN. Contributions to theory include RE-

STRICTED CHOICE. He has written 9 books: *Contract Bridge, Bridge from First Principles, Practical Bridge, The Great Bridge Scandal, Master Bridge By Question and Answer, Teach Yourself Basic Bridge* (with Dorothy Truscott), *Grand Slams, Doubles and Redoubles, Basic Bridge in Three Weeks, On Bidding* (with Phillip Alder), *Intermediate Bridge in Three Weeks*. He was the co-translator of *Championship Bridge* (leDentu, *Bridge a la une*).

He was npc of the Bermuda team in the 1964 World Olympiad and of the Brazilian team in the 1971 Bermuda Bowl. British successes include Masters Individual 1953, 58. ACBL wins are Master Mixed Tms 1985, North American Swiss 1987, Mixed Prs 1989. He has won many regional titles. He was president of the Greater New York BA 1977-79 and president of Dist 24 1980-90. He has been president of the International Bridge Academy. He devised and organized the BATTLE OF THE SEXES. Truscott completed the 1986 New York Marathon when he was 61 and plays tennis. He was Oxford University chess champion and defeated several top-ranked British players while a student. See also BUENOS AIRES AFFAIR.

TRUSCOTT, Dorothy Hayden (Mrs. Alan) of New York City, bridge teacher, author, mathematician, WBF Grand Master, overtook Rixi Markus in 1980 to become the No. 1 woman player in world rankings. She has been selected 13 times to represent the United States in international competition including the first Womens Team Olympiad in 1960 (placed 5th). Truscott and Helen Sobel Smith are the only two women to have played on the North American team for the Bermuda Bowl. She won four world titles -- the Venice Cup 1974, 76, 78 and the World Womens Tms 1980. She finished second in the Bermuda Bowl in 1965 and placed third in the World Open Prs 1966 (the only woman ever to have finished in the top 10 in this event). She also was third in the World Womens Tms 1968, 72, 76, World Womens Prs 1962, 74; and placed 5th Olympiad Mixed Tms 1972. She won Pan-Am Womens Tms 1992 and was npc of the winning Venice Cup team in 1989.

Truscott has won 25 NABC titles (including four playing with partners with whom she had never played a session of bridge before): Mixed Prs 1959, 89; Womens Prs 1959, 61, 66, 78, 81; Open Prs 1962; Blue Ribbon Prs 1963; Life Master Prs 1964; Womens Tms 1967, 70, 72, 74, 75, 76, 82; North American Womens Swiss 1982, 84; Master Mixed Tms 1985, Womens BAM Tms 1986; North American Swiss 1987, 92; Womens KO Tms 1990, 93. She placed second in the Master Mixed Tms 1957, 60, 67, 72; Womens Prs 1961, 68, 72, 76, 88; Womens Tms 1963, 64; Vanderbilt 1964, Spingold 1965, 68; Womens KO Tms 1987; Womens BAM Tms 1988; and has won numerous regional titles.

Among her contributions to bridge theory are the UNUSUAL JUMP to show a singleton (now called the SPLINTER BID) and the responses to BLACKWOOD AFTER INTERFERENCE (now called DOPI). Truscott is the author of *Bid Better, Play Better, Winning Declarer Play* and co-author with Alan Truscott of *Teach Yourself Basic Bidding*. She contributes to various magazines and is a contributing editor to the *Encyclopedia of Bridge*. She also is writing a historical novel about New Amsterdam. See also BUENOS AIRES AFFAIR.

TSACNARIS, Francine (Fran) (b. 1923) of Los Angeles CA, bridge teacher, director and professional player. During the Seventies she wrote for the *Southern California Bridge News*, under the name I. Noalle. She has won many regional events dating back to the Forties, including Bridge Wk Mixed Tms 1966, 70, Womens Prs 1973, 76, Master Womens Prs 1977, 80; Los Angeles Winter Open Prs 1976, Master Swiss Tms 1978, Spring Womens Prs 1977, 83, 87, 89, 90.

TSCHEKALOFF, Alex (b. 1927) of Las Vegas NV, computer programmer, Diamond Life Master, won Life Master Mens Prs 1965, Blue Ribbon Prs 1969; placed second Mens Prs 1961; won numerous regional events.

TUBBS, Lewis G. (1902-1971) of Arlington VA, bridge instructor and club director, was an ACBL Board member 1965-68 and former president of Washington BA. Placed second Master Mixed Tms 1954; author of *How We Teach and Play Contract Bridge*.

TSIANG, George Y.C. (b. 1919) of Hong Kong, business executive. Far East champion 1959, second 1963. National wins include open teams and open pairs. Former vice-chairman of Hong Kong CBA, active in the Far East Bridge Federation.

TU, Ya Pin (b. 1950 in Taiwan) of San Francisco, computer software specialist. Far East champion 1978, represented Taiwan in two world championships and one other zonal championship.

TUASON, Severo (1909-1973) of Manila, Philippines, civil engineer. Represented Philippines in WBF Executive Council, was a leading adminstrator in the Philippines and Far East.

TUCKER, Alan J. (b. 1943) of Durham NC, bridge professional, served for 25 years on Bd of Dir Nassau/Suffolk BA, was president 1983-88; won Long Island Open Tms 1972; New York Open Tms 1979; Eastern States KO Tms 1986; Swan Lake Swiss 1986; New England Fall Smoking Open Prs 1987.

TUCKER, Judy (b. 1946) of New York City, bridge professional and travel agent; member of ACBL Goodwill Committee, 2nd alternate Dist 24, served for many years on Nassau/Suffolk BA Board and as a member of the NABC Appeals Committee. WBF World Master, she placed 5th in World Mixed Prs 1978, 8th World Womens Prs 1990; has also represented ACBL in world championships in 1982, 86, 90. She won the Pan Am Games Womens Tms and placed 3rd Womens Prs 1992. Diamond Life Master, won Womens Prs 1984, North American Womens Swiss 1992, Womens KO Tms 1993; placed second Womens BAM Tms 1986, 87; Mixed Prs 1991. Her numerous regional wins include Long Island Open Tms 1972, 80, Smoking Open Prs 1981; Keystone Conference Womens Tms 1974, 77, Womens Prs 1980; Tri-State Womens Prs, Womens Tms 1977; Upper New York State Womens Tms 1978, Open Tms 1980; Puerto Rico Open Swiss 1979, 80; Charlotte Swiss 1991.

TUDOR, Harry H. (The King) (b. 1951) of Miami FL, won dozens of regional events including Ft. Lauderdale KO Tms 1989, Swiss 1990, 91; Hilton Head Swiss 1990; Wiliamsburg KO Tms 1991; Southeastern Swiss 1992.

TUELL, David R. Jr. (Dave) (b. 1936) of Tacoma WA, lawyer, graduated U of Washington, professional bowler on Senior PBA Tour, has served in various executive capacities for Dist 19 and Unit 451 including president, also a former president of the Western Conference. Regional wins include Puget Sound Mens Prs, Southeastern Mixed Prs 1969; Las Vegas Mens Prs 1973, Oregon Trail Open Prs 1980, Indian Summer Swiss Tms 1981, Penticton Open Swiss 1986, Ocean Shores KO Tms, Open Prs 1988.

TUERAH, Donny (b. 1949) of Jakarta, Indonesia. Won Far East Teams 1982, National Open Teams 1992.

TUNG, Sam S.F. (b. 1917 in China) of Taipei, Taiwan, CEO engineering company. Former chairman of petrochemical company. Founder-member of KOR Team that won many national events in the 1950s and 1960s. President of the Taiwan Contract Bridge League since 1975.

TURK, Franc (b. 1938) of Maribor, Slovenia, textile technician. Former bridge teacher and pairs specialist. Won 5 national titles and some international events.
TURNER, Inez D. of Chicago, bridge teacher. Won ABA Merit Award 1992. Author of *...And Here's My Convention Card.*

TURNER, Alan George (b. 1947 in South Africa) of Tauranga, New Zealand, chemical engineer and high school mathematics teacher. Won zonal "test match" against Australia 1987. Represented New Zealand in one Bermuda Bowl and two Far East Championships. Won 10 national titles. Top masterpoint winner 1982, 1989. Former president New Zealand CBA.

TUSZYNSKI, Piotr (b. 1955) of Warsaw, Poland, transport engineer and bridge professional. WBF World Life Master. Won World Teams 1984. Represented Poland in two other world championships and one zonal championship.

TYLER, Frances (1897-1978) of Cincinnati, was one of the senior bridge columnists in the world. She began her long career in bridge as an instructor for the Culbertson studios in 1930. In 1933 she became a bridge columnist for *The Enquirer* and retained this position until six months before her death.

U

UKKONEN, Petri (b. 1960) of Helsinki, Finland, waiter. Represented Finland seven times, including one world championship and two European Championships. National wins include open teams once and knockout teams twice. Board member of Bridge League of Finland.

UNGER, Gavriel (b. 1943 in Israel) of Vienna, Austria, teacher. Represented Austria in several European Pair Championships. Won Austrian Teams five times and Open Pairs once. Editor of *Austrian Bridge Magazine.*

UNSON, Rosemarie (b. 1934) of Quezon City, Philippines, retired property owner. Won Far East Women's Teams 1979, and represented Philippines in one world championship and 8 other zonal championships.

UTEGAARD, Helen S. of Las Vegas NV, born in Beijing, China; WBF World Master, placed 5th World Womens Tms 1988, 6th World Olympiad Mixed Tms 1974, 7th in 1972. She also represented ACBL internationally in Sao Paulo 1985, Venice 1988, Santiago 1993. ACBL Grand Life Master with more than 10,000 MPs; won Womens Tms 1971, 73, 81; Mixed Prs 1974; Master Mixed Tms 1975, 88; Womens KO Tms 1984, 88; Fishbein Trophy, North American Womens Swiss 1988; Womens BAM Tms 1992; placed second Master Mixed Tms 1980; North American Womens Swiss 1987, Womens BAM Tms 1991; Womens KO Tms 1992; won numerous regionals.

V

VAKIL, Piyush (b. 1941 in India) of Wooster OH, chemical engineer, nationally ranked table tennis player in India during the Sixties; won Spingold 1975, placed second in GN Tms 1993. Regional wins include Palm Springs KO Tms 1967; All Western LM Tms 1971, Mixed Prs 1973; Dist 21 GN Tms 1974; Dist 5 GN Tms 1978, 79, Zone III 1979; Fall secondary Swiss 1979; Lake Geneva Swiss 1986; Rye KO Tms 1988.

VALENTI, Anna (Mrs. Paolo) of Leghorn, Italy. WBF Grand Master. Won World Women's Teams 1972, second 1980; second Venice Cup 1974, 1978. Won European Women's Teams 1970, 1971, 1973, 1974. Many other titles include EC Women's Teams twice and Italian Open Teams twice. See FAMILY.

VALENZUELA, Gonzalo (b. 1932 in Chile) of Montevideo, Uruguay, engineer. Second South American Teams 1979, 1989. Represented Uruguay regularly in zonal championships since 1980, and earlier represented Chile. Won 36 national titles.

VALENZUELA, Laly of Montevideo, Uruguay. Won South American Womens Teams 1967, 1971, 1974, 1990. A regular member of the Uruguay Women's team in international competition and has won 86 national titles.

VAN DE VEN, Alex J. M. of Galveston TX, represented the Netherlands Antilles in international competition Deauville 1968; New Orleans 1978, Corpus Christi 1992.

VAN VLECK, Charles Edward (1896-1950) of New York City, was a pioneer of new bidding methods in the Thirties. He originated the WEAK JUMP SHIFT RESPONSES subsequently adopted by the Roth-Stone System and advocated ultra weak WEAK TWO-BIDS. His system, which was based on the Vanderbilt Club System, was probably the first to use the Three-Quarter Notrump. Placed second Vanderbilt 1943.

VAN NESS, John P. (b. 1940) of Aspen CO, attorney, member of Aspen City Council 1977-81, graduate of Yale and NYU (JD); served on Dist 17 Bd of Dir for many years; won Amateur Prs 1976; Oil City KO Tms, Master Swiss 1978; New York City Open Tms 1985; Las Vegas Swiss 1988; Denver KO Tms 1991; El Paso Swiss 1992.

VAN ZANDT, Esta V. of Houston, born in India, bridge teacher, placed second in Far East Womens Championships (represented Okinawa) 1966. She won Master

Mixed Tms, Mixed Prs 1981; placed second in Womens Tms 1973. ACBL Diamond Life Master with numerous regional wins.

VAN GELDER, Jacques (Jacq) (1902-1993) of Ft Lauderdale FL, retired accountant, former billiards champion. Wrote the column *Mixed Masters* for the *ACBL Bulletin* and contributed to other bridge publications. Van Gelder directed bridge activities on more than 100 cruises starting in 1972. Won Southeastern Swiss Tms 1982.

VAN COURT, Wendell A. (Woody) (b. 1926) of Poland OH, high school teacher; member ACBL Goodwill Committee, president of Unit 111 1991-92. Won Canadian Nat'l Swiss 1972, 81, Mens Prs 1979, Mixed Prs 1981; Dist 11 Swiss 1979; Buffalo Mens Swiss 1983; Glass City Master Prs 1984, Swiss 1984, Mens Prs 1986, Mens Swiss 1988; Pittsburgh Mens Swiss 1986, Fltd Swiss 1991.

VAN DEN ENDE, Siem (b. 1925 in the Netherlands) of Curacao, Netherlands Antilles, civil engineer. Top-ranked masterpoint winner in the Netherlands Antilles, which he represented in many world championships. Won many national titles. Secretary and tournament director of the Netherlands Antilles BA.

VAN DEN BORRE, Jo (b. 1917) of Mariakerke, Belgium, engineer, public relations executive and journalist. Former chief tournament director of Belgium, directed in European and World Championships. Bridge reporter for numerous newspapers. Author of two books on bridge. Collector of European maps of 16th and 17th Century.

VAN SICHELEN, Sylvie of Brussels, Belgium. Represented Belgium in several world championships, zonal championships and Common Market championships. Won three national titles.

VANDERBILT, Harold Stirling (July 6, 1884 - July 4, 1970) of Newport RI, was a bridge authority whose revisions of auction bridge scoring principles created modern contract bridge, also a system-maker and a champion player. He was born at Oakdale NY into the richest and most famous American family of that time. His father, William Kissam Vanderbilt, died in 1920 leaving an estate of some $54.5 million. Vanderbilt graduated from Harvard Law School in 1910, then entered his family's railroad business, New York Central, founded by his great-grandfather, Commodore Cornelius Vanderbilt. For many years he was a successful business executive. His greatest fame in competitive fields is as a yachtsman. His revision of right-of-way rules are still known as the Vanderbilt Rules. Nevertheless, his lasting fame is more likely to come from his contributions to bridge.

Vanderbilt took up bridge seriously in 1906, and his partnership with J. B. Elwell was considered the strongest in the U.S. from 1910 to 1920. During that period the contract bridge principle — counting only bid tricks toward game — was often proposed and as often rejected, except for the limited success of PLAFOND (see HISTORY OF BRIDGE). Experimenting with the proposed new game while on a cruise late in 1925, Vanderbilt originated the factors of vulnerability and inflated slam bonuses. He produced a scoring table so balanced as to make nearly every aggressive or sacrifice bid an approximately even bet, allowing just enough differential to permit the exercise of nice judgment.

The rapid spread of contract bridge from 1926 to 1929 is largely attributable to Vanderbilt's espousal of it; his social standing made the game fashionable. Vanderbilt's technical contribution was even greater. He devised the first unified system of bidding, and was solely responsible for the artificial 1♣ bid to show a strong hand, the negative 1♦ response, the **strong** (16- to 18-point) notrump on balanced hands only, and the weak two-bid opening. These and his other principles were presented in his books, *Contract Bridge Bidding and the Club Convention*; *The New Contract Bridge*; *Contract by Hand Analysis*; and *The Club Convention Modernized*.

Vanderbilt was a member of the Laws Committee of the Whist Club of New York that made the American laws of contract bridge (1927, 1931) and the first international code (1932). He then became chairman of that committee, and largely drafted the international code of 1935, the American code of 1943, and the international codes of 1948 and 1949. He remained co-chairman of the National Laws Commission of the ACBL for the 1963 laws. In 1928 Vanderbilt presented the Harold S. Vanderbilt Cup for the national team-of-four championship now known as the Vanderbilt. This became, and still is, the most coveted American team trophy, mainly because the replicas were donated personally by Vanderbilt to the winners. In 1960 Vanderbilt supplied the permanent trophy for the World Bridge Federation's Olympiad Team tournaments, again adopting the policy of giving replicas to the winners.

As a player, Vanderbilt always ranked high. In 1932 and 1940 he won his own Vanderbilt Cup. He played by choice only in the strongest money games, and was a consistent winner. His regular partnership with Waldemar von Zedtwitz was among the strongest and most successful in the U.S. In 1941 he retired from tournament bridge, but he continued to play in the most expert rubber bridge games, in clubs and at home.

In 1968, Vanderbilt spent more than $50,000 to recreate the lost molds for the replicas of the American trophy and to provide a quantity of replicas of both trophies sufficient to last from 20 to 40 years. To perpetuate this practice of awarding individual replicas, Vanderbilt further bequeathed to the ACBL a trust fund of $100,000, a gift that wisely foresaw the possibility of inflation, but provided that excess funds, if any, can be donated in Vanderbilt's name to a charity of ACBL's choice. When last purchased, replicas of the American trophy cost $600; of the Olympiad trophy, $500.

In 1969, the World Bridge Federation made Vanderbilt its first honorary member. When a BRIDGE HALL OF FAME was inaugurated in 1964, Vanderbilt was one of the first three persons elected. Member Advisory Board *Bridge Encyclopedia*.

VANDERPORTEN, William S. (Bill) (1910-1991) of Sunrise FL, retired Job Corps coordinator; was associated in the founding of Long Island BL in the Thirties. Won Summer secondary Presidents Prs 1940, Eastern States Mens Prs 1958.

VAUCROSSON, Charles H. B. (b. 1934) of Pembroke Parish, Bermuda, attorney, graduated U of Western ON; Dist 2 Board member for five years and president Unit 198 for ten years. Represented Bermuda in world competition and in Tri-Country playoffs. Won Bermuda KO

Tms, Swiss Tms (3).

VAYANOU, Maro (b. 1944 in Cyprus) of Athens, Greece. Second-ranked woman in masterpoint standings, and a member of Greek women's team since 1973. National wins include open teams three times.

VELARDE, Cecilia (b. 1942) of Lima, Peru, bridge teacher. Represented Peru in one world championship and 15 zonal championships. Won many national titles.

VELARDE, Ernesto (b.1938) of Lima, Peru, lawyer. President of South American Bridge Federation since 1989, formerly vice president. Member WBF Executive Council since 1991. President Peruvian Bridge Commission 1984-89. Represented Peru in one world championship and two zonal championships.

VENTIN, Carlos (b. 1957) of Barcelona, Spain, actuary. Second European Junior Teams 1980. Represented Spain in two world championships, two zonal championships and three other zonal junior championships. Won many national titles.

VENTURINI, Maria of Rome, Italy, won World Women's Teams 1972, European Women's Teams 1970, 1971, 1973. World Life Master.

VERGARA, Osvaldo Gomez (b. 1945) of Santiago, Chile, civil engineer. WBF World Master. Represented Chile in four world championships and 12 zonal championships. Top-ranked Chilean player, has won all national titles.

VERGARA, Etelvina (1905-1983) of Buenos Aires, Argentina. South American Women's Team champion 1948, 1949, 1950, 1951, 1953, 1957, 1961, 1962, 1964. Represented Argentina World Women's Team Olympiad 1964, 1972. 8 national titles won include open teams and open pairs once each.

VERGOED, F.J.(Hans) (b. 1948) of Delft, The Netherlands, pharmacist. WBF World Master. Third World Teams 1980, represented The Netherlands in three other world championships and three European Championships. National titles include Open Teams five times and Open Pairs twice. Bridge columnist.

VRIEND, Bep (b. 1946) of Amstelveen, The Netherlands, secretary and bridge teacher. WBF World Life Master, has best record of any Dutch woman player. Second Venice Cup 1989, European Women's Tms 1989. Third World Women's Tms 1964, World Womens Prs 1990. A regular choice for the Dutch Women's Tm since 1979. National wins include Open Prs twice and Women's Prs six times.

VERNAY, Colby K. (b. 1942) of Lacon IL, basketball and baseball coach, graduate of Northwestern U; avid golfer, has had three holes - in-one. Was editor of the *Central Illinois Duplicate Bulletin* 1973-76, vice president of Unit 208 1975-76, and a member of ACBL Bd of Gov 1976-80. Diamond Life Master; has won more than 70 regional titles including Texas Fall Open Tms 1966; Summer Open Prs 1972; Mississippi Valley KO Tms, Mens Prs, Master Prs 1980; Dist 8 GN Prs 1982, 88, GN

Tms 1989, 91; Gatlinburg KO Tms 1992.

VERNE, Jules (1828-1905) famous French author of *Voyages Extraordinaires*, his 43-year output of 60-odd volumes, is called "The Father of modern science fiction". In his most successful "voyage" novel, *Around the World in Eighty Days*, his hero, Phileas Fogg, makes his extraordinary wager over the whist table at the Reform Club with his whist partners. Throughout the course of the voyage, Phileas Fogg plays whist with fellow travelers.

VERNOFF, Milton (1905-1989) of Los Angeles CA, retired attorney, won Master Mixed Tms 1938 and numerous regional events. Vernoff pioneered bridge on television in Florida and served as president of the Florida Unit.

VERNON, Francis (b. 1934) of Caracas, Venezuela, civil engineer. WBF World Master. Won South American Teams 1965, 1966, CAC Teams 1973, 1977, 1985. Represented Venezuela in nine world championships and won many national titles. Bridge teacher, writer and director.

VIEDMA, Rafael G. (b. 1934) of Saudi Arabia, formerly of Madrid, Spain, engineer. WBF World Master. Fourth World Open Teams 1982, represented Spain in two other world championships and two zonal championships. Won many national titles.

VIITASALO, Pekka (b. 1958) of Espoo, Finland, systems analyst. Second Nordic Teams 1984, represented Finland on seven other occasions including one world championship and four European Championships. Contributor to *Finnish Bridge Magazine*. Member Laws Committee of Bridge League of Finland and former member of EBL Systems Committee.

VINE, Frank (1927-1987) of Hamilton ON, attorney, won Mens Prs 1969 and was a contributor to *The Bridge World*, *ACBL Bulletin* and other publications.

VIOLIN, Roxy R. (b. 1929) of Tarzana CA, air conditioning engineer/consultant, graduate of UCLA and Northwestern (PhD); has served on ACBL Bd of Gov and Ethics and Appeals Committees and is a member of the ACBL Goodwill Committee. Won Mixed Prs 1970; placed second Life Master Mens Prs 1973. Has won more than 30 regionals.

VIVALDI, Antonio (b. 1942) of Turin, Italy. World Life Master. European champion 1973. National titles include open teams eight times.

VOGEL, Claude F. (b. 1942) of Chicago, mathematics teacher, Diamond Life Master, won GN Tms 1979; placed second Mens Swiss 1987; won numerous regionals.

VOGT, Waltraud of Kassel, Germany, lawyer. WBF World Master. Second Venice Cup 1993. Won European Women's Teams 1989, runner-up European Womens Teams and Women's Pairs 1991. Represented Germany in two other world championships and won one national title.

VOIGT, Axel (b. 1908) of Aarhus, Denmark, professor of mathematics and chemistry. Represented Denmark in one world championship and six zonal championships.

22 national wins include Open Teams 15 times and Open Pairs once. A bidding theorist who popularized a Danish form of Acol. Still playing successfully in 1992 at age 84.

VON DER PORTEN, Ronald P. (Ron) (b. 1936) of Orinda CA, computer programmer, WBF Life Master, represented ACBL in Bermuda Bowl 1962 and finished second in 1977. Diamond Life Master, won the Chicago (now the Reisinger) 1962; Vanderbilt 1967; Spingold 1975, 80; GN Tms 1982, Blue Ribbon Prs 1986; placed second Vanderbilt 1961, 63, 71; Blue Ribbon Prs 1965; Mens Tms 1970, Mixed Prs 1984. In addition he has won many regional titles. Von der Porten has been the comentator for some of the world's biggest bridge matches, including the CBS-TV match between the Aces Team and the Goren All-Stars, and he frequently directs bridge games on cruises. He is the author of *Introduction to Defensive Bidding*.

VON ELSNER, Don B. (b. 1909) of Hilo HI, bridge writer, lecturer, professional player, novelist, real estate broker and financial consultant, graduate of Temple College. He is the author of many mystery novels; in several of these bridge is featured, notably in *The Jake of Diamonds* (originally titled *How to Succeed at Murder Without Really Trying*) in which the setting is a Hawaii regional and several leading real-life experts play a part, the first book of the series featuring Jake Winkman as the hero. Von Elsner has been a member of *The Bridge World* Master Solvers' Panel for 40 years and has been a frequent contributor to *Popular Bridge*, *The Bridge World* and other publications. Won Hawaii Open Tms 1952, Mens Prs 1962, 68, Open Prs 1970.

VON ZEDTWITZ, Waldemar K. (May 8, 1896 - Oct 5, 1984) linguist and lexicographer, president emeritus of ACBL, one of the great players and personalities of all time. He was born in Berlin, the son of a German (Saxon) baron, to whose title he succeeded when his father died a few months after his birth, and of an American mother. He thereby acquired dual citizenship and after World War I he adopted United States citizenship, relinquishing his title.

He was ACBL president in 1948 and of its parent organization, the American Bridge League, in 1932. When dissension threatened to break up the ACBL in 1948, the contesting factions agreed to him as president and chairman with *carte blanche*, and he is credited with saving the ACBL. In 1949, after ACBL's rehabilitation, he immediately returned his *carte blanche* power of the presidency to the ACBL Bd of Dir.

He was a charter member of the ACBL Laws Commission and as co-chairman played an active role in preparing the international code in 1936. He helped found the World Bridge Federation, was a WBF director, chairman of its committee on International Match Points and chairman of the Rules Committee for the 1964 WBF Olympiad.

Von Zedtwitz was noted for versatility in playing with exponents of different systems. He was an early contributor to the CULBERTSON SYSTEM, a contributor and consultant in connection with the FOUR ACES SYSTEM, a member of the BRIDGE WORLD TEAM that won the first international matches (1930) in England and France. He had one of the most successful all-time partnerships with Harold S. Vanderbilt playing the club convention, and was a regular partner of P. Hal Sims, S. Garton Churchill, the FOUR ACES, Charles E. Van Vleck and many others. Later his regular partners included Harold Harkavy, Edith Kemp (now Freilich) and Barbara Brier. He was one of the first ten to be named Life Master (No. 4) when that category was created by the ABL in 1936.

Von Zedtwitz began his tournament bridge career in 1923 and won many national auction bridge championships and won nearly all the contract bridge championships. In 1930 he gave the GOLD CUP for Master Pairs (now Life Master Pairs) and won it the first year. His other tournament successes are World Mixed Prs 1970, USBA Grand National Teams, Mixed Prs 1936; Spingold 1937, 1941, 1947; Chicago (now the Reisinger) 1932, 1945; Vanderbilt 1930, 1932, 1940; Master Mixed Tms 1940, 1942, 1945, 1965; Life Master Prs 1930; Open Prs 1928, 1937; Mens Prs 1946; Master Individual 1936. He placed second in USBA Mixed Tms 1936; Spingold 1936, 1940, 1949, 1953, 1963; Chicago 1930, 1933, 1936, 1941, 1942; Vanderbilt 1937, 1938, 1943, 1945, 1960; Reisinger 1964, Mixed Tms 1933, 1935, 1956; Life Master Prs 1933, 1939; Open Prs 1935, Mens Prs 1938, 1953. His numerous regional titles included Eastern States KO Tms 1937, 1944, 1973, 1974.

A member of the Greater New York BA Board, he was elected to the ACBL Board in 1962. As such he organized the ACBL Charity Foundation (see CHARITY PROGRAM OF ACBL). He was a director of the WBF and chairman of its committee on INTERNATIONAL MATCHPOINTS, being largely responsible for the schedule adopted in 1961, and also chairman of its Rules Committee for the 1964 World Olympiad.

Von Zedtwitz won a major backgammon tournament in Hawaii at age 82. His other interests included Bridgette, travel, tennis and golf.

W

WADAS, Judith L. (Judy) (b. 1936) of Chicago IL, insurance company executive, co-founder Insurance Consumer Affairs Exchange; first president and co-founder of Forum for Women in Bridge; placed second Mixed Prs 1981, North American Womens Swiss 1988. Won ACBL-wide East-West Epson Prs 1990. Numerous regional wins include Summer secondary Swiss 1978, Spring Swiss 1979; Eastern States Womens Prs 1981; Dist 3 Swiss 1981; Gatlinburg KO Tms (2) 1994.

WAGAR, Margaret (April 6, 1902 - Jan. 6, 1990) of Delaware OH, formerly of Atlanta GA, bridge teacher and writer, served on the ACBL Bd of Dir 1960-72 and was named ACBL Honorary Member in 1979. Life Master #37 and one of the great American woman players of all time; npc of the U.S. World Womens Tms 1968 and 1972. With Kay Rhodes, she shared one of the most remarkable achievements in ACBL history -- they won the Womens Prs four straight times 1955, 56, 57, 58. Wagar won the same event in 1944. Her impressive record includes Womens Tms 1940, 43, 44, 45, 46, 64, 65; the Chicago (now the Reisinger) 1941; Master Mixed Tms 1942, 45, 48, 54, 64; Spingold 1946, 48; Open Prs 1947, 48; Mixed Prs 1948, 49; Life Master Womens Prs 1962. Wagar placed second Master Mixed Tms 1933, 49, 50, 62, 67; Life Master Prs 1943; Womens Tms 1952, 53, 54,

55, 56, 57, 58, 64. She also won the Hilliard Trophy 1933, 45 and the Marcus Cup 1958.

WAGNER, Willem M. (1926-1991) of Amsterdam, The Netherlands, chemist and marine biologist. Chief organizer 1980 World Team Olympiad. Appointed assistant chief tournament director of the European Bridge League in 1982. WBF Operations Director 1986-1991.

WAINWRIGHT, Stuyvesant (1891-1975) of New York City and Naples FL, stockbroker, avid sportsman and a descendant of Peter Stuyvesant. Member of Vanderbilt Cup Tournament Committee 1928-57, member of the Whist Club Committee on laws for international codes of 1932 and 1935 and vice president of Regency Club, New York. Placed second NAC Mixed Tms 1943. A promoter of the game TOWIE, he authored *Towie Tactics* in 1946.

WAINWRIGHT, Louise (Mrs. Stuyvesant) (1902-1986) of Southampton NY, former antique shop owner; in 1935 she donated a trophy in her name for the winners of the Eastern States Womens Prs. Placed second in Master Mixed Tms 1941; Hilliard Trophy 1939 and won Eastern States KO Tms 1941 (the first woman ever to win this prestigious event), Mixed Tms 1940, 41, 44.

WAKEFIELD, Joseph E. (Joe) (b.1943) of Southampton, Bermuda, born in England, attorney; represented Bermuda in Monte Carlo 1976, Valkenburg 1980, Seattle 1984, in the Tri-Country playoffs 1989 and 1991. Served as president of Bermuda Unit 1977-78 and tournament chairman 1975 and 76. Won Bermuda Open Tms 1978, Master Prs 1993, Open Prs 1994.

WAKEMAN, Robert P. (1913-1981) of Upper Montclair NJ, systems engineer, was a director of New Jersey BL and its former bridge editor as well as bridge editor of *Newark Evening News.* He was a contributing editor, *Bridge Encyclopedia.* Won Mens Tms 1960.

WAKEN, Harvard C. (Harv) (b. 1917) of Arcadia CA, company president, graduate Oklahoma State U, involved in thoroughbred horse racing, both as an owner and spectator; won North American Swiss 1983 and Riverside Swiss 1979.

WALDECK, Josias, Prinz zu (b. 1937) of Frankfurt, Germany, insurance instructor. WBF World Master. Represented Germany regularly from 1968 in world and zonal championships. Won several national titles.

WALDMANN, Arthur J. (b. 1933) of Rocky Hill CT, sales manager; Diamond Life Master, won Mens Prs 1975; placed second in the Spingold 1974, Mens Tms 1977.

WALETZKY, Niel (b. 1949) of Shaker Hts OH, wrote, directed and appeared in two Broadway-style bridge shows. Regional wins include All American KO Tms 1981, Mens Swiss, Open Prs 1988; Fall secondary Open Prs (2) 1982; Dist 5 GN Tms 1985, 89, 94; GN Prs 1982, 86, 93, 94; Bowling Green Swiss 1989.

WALKER, Karen S. (b. 1951) of Champaign IL, ad copywriter and college English teacher, graduate of U of Illinois; served on Unit 208 Bd since 1978 and Dist 8 *Advocate* editor since 1980; author of *Bridge for Beginners and*

Beyond. Placed second in Life Master Prs 1986. Her 15+ regional wins include Dist 8 GN Tms 1980, 90, 91.

WALLACE, Wilfred N.W. (b. 1908) of Summer Hill, NSW, Australia, chemist, was World Par champion 1937 with a 100% score. National titles include Interstate Open teams 1948, 1964, 1965, 1967, Open Pairs 1940, 1944, 1948, 1953, 1958, 1966.

WALLACE, Charlton (1904-1979) of Cincinnati OH, bridge writer, was a founder-member of the International Bridge Press Association and in 1978 was elected an honorary member of the IBPA. He was a bridge associate of Ely Culbertson, P. Hal Sims and other bridge greats. A director of the AWL, and Midwest president of the USBA in 1936, Wakeman was bridge editor of the *Cincinnati Post-Times-Star* from 1933 until his death. He was a contributing editor, *Bridge Encyclopedia.*

WALLACE, Jane V. (Mrs. Charlton) of Cincinnati OH, won Womens Tms 1947 and several regional events.

WALLACE, Barbara (b. 1947) of Miami FL, interior designer, won Summer secondary KO Tms 1988; Ft. Lauderdale KO Tms 1989; Orlando Womens Prs 1992, and a number of other regionals including Cherry Hill KO Tms; Daytona Beach, Ft. Lauderdale Womens Prs; Hilton Head, Tampa and Jacksonville Swiss.

WALLIS, Peter James (Jim) (b. 1965) of Brisbane, Australia. Third World Junior Teams 1991, won Far East Junior Teams 1990, represented Australia in one other world championship.

WALSH, Alan D. (b. 1945) of Sydney, Australia, systems analyst. Won Far East Open Pairs 1972 and represented Australia in four zonal championships. Won one national title.

WALSH, Rhoda of Los Angeles CA, attorney, former bridge professional, graduate of Loyola Law School (JD); WBF World Master, placed third World Womens Tms 1968, 5th 1988, 9th World Mixed Prs 1986. ACBL Grand Life Master with more than 14,000 MPS; #7 all-time masterpoint list for women; co-author of *Recap Bridge.* In 1968, Walsh won all three womens national events held that year, Womens Tms, Womens Prs, Life Master Womens Prs. Her other national titles include Womens Prs, Life Master Womens Prs 1972; Master Mixed Tms 1976; North American Swiss 1984, 85; North American Womens Swiss 1985, 88; Life Master Womens Prs 1989; placed second in Life Master Womens Prs 1982, North American Swiss 1986; North American Womens Swiss 1987. Walsh has won more than 100 regional events since 1974.

WALSH, Richard R. (b. 1936) of Zurich, Switzerland, commodities and currencies analyst, before retiring from tournament play was one of the leading American players and competed internationally. Diamond Life Master, he invented the WALSH SYSTEM; won the Vanderbilt 1969; Team Trials, Mens Tms, Mens Prs 1970; placed second Spingold 1959; had more than 50 regional wins.

WALSHE, Col. George Gordon J. (1873-1959) of London, England, represented his country in the ANGLO-

AMERICAN MATCH 1934 and was one of the referees in the Culbertson-Lenz Match in 1932. He was co-inventor of the CAB SYSTEM. Walshe wrote under the pseudonym of "Yarborough" for the *Sunday Times*, and authored *Count to Win at Bridge*, *Let's Play CAB*, and *Slams Made Simple*. With F. DUDLEY COURTENAY he wrote *The Losing Trick Count*, *Standard Manual of Play* and *Standardized Code of Contract Bridge*.

WALSHE, Pat (b. 1954) of Dublin, Ireland, computer analyst. WBF World Master. Second European Junior Teams 1974. Won Common Market Pairs 1981. Second Common Market Open Teams 1983, Mixed Teams 1989. Won more than 30 national titles.

WALTERS, Florine W. of Pittsburgh PA, real estate agent, former bridge club owner, director, teacher; graduate of Boston U; currently serving on Pittsburgh Bd as Ethics Chairman. Placed second in NAC Womens Tms 1978, 79; North American Womens Swiss 1985, GN Tms 1993. Won Champagne Open Prs 1972, 84, Swiss Tms 1978, Womens Swiss 1984; Southeastern Swiss 1973; Tri-Unit Open Tms 1975, Womens Swiss 1976, 78, 79, 88; Central States I Womens Prs 1976, Womens Swiss 1977, 79, 81; Mad City Womens Tms 1979; Missouri Valley Womens Swiss 1980; Dist 11 Womens Prs 1981, 83, Womens Swiss 1984; Dist 8 Womens Prs 1983; Mississippi Valley Womens Swiss 1988, Womens Prs 1990; All-American Open Prs, Dist 5 Womens Prs 1991.

WALUYAN, Ferdinand (b. 1946) of Jakarta, Indonesia, management consultant. WBF World Master. Won Far East Teams 1979, 1982, 1983, 1984. Represented Indonesia in four world championships and in other zonal championships.

WALVICK, Walter J. (Crab) (b. 1942) of McLean VA, attorney, graduate of U of Pennsylvania, Columbus School of Law (JD). WBF World Master placed 3th World Mixed Prs 1990, won the Swiss Plate 1986, also represented ACBL in world play New Orleans 1978, Biarritz 1982. ACBL Diamond Life Master, won Lou Herman Trophy 1975, Life Master Mens Prs 1975, 89; placed second Life Master Prs 1974; Mens Swiss 1988. Has numerous regional wins; former director and vice president of the Washington BL.

WALVICK, Katharine H. (Kathie) (Mrs. Walter J.) (b. 1942) of McLean VA, legal assistant, graduate of Wellesley College; WBF World Master, placed 3rd World Mixed Tms 1974, World Mixed Prs 1990, 4th World Womens Prs 1982. Walvick is the only woman to reach the finals of the World Championship Open Prs. She placed 15th in 1978 and 16th in 1974. Also represented ACBL in other world events 1986, 90. An ACBL Diamond Life Master, she has won Master Mixed Teams 1967; Life Master Womens Prs 1980; placed second in Mixed Prs 1967, Blue Ribbon Prs 1973, 77, Master Mixed Tms 1983; Womens Prs 1991. Her regionals include Mid-Atlantic Open Tms 1967, 70, 79, KO Tms 1972, 79, 83, Mixed Prs 1982, Open Prs 1983, Womens Prs 1988, 91. See FAMILY.

WAN, Samuel S.K. (b. 1951) of Hong Kong, executive recruitment consultant. WBF World Master. Won Far East Open Teams 1987. Represented Hong Kong in four world

championships and six other Far East Championships. National wins include open teams and open pairs.

WAN, Li of Beijing, China, retired Chairman of People's Congress. Won IBPA Solomon Award 1984. Second Epson 1990. Honorary president of Chinese Bridge Association. Winner of the Gold medal awarded by WBF 1993 and Presidential citation ACBL 1993. Chairman Wan was responsible for building the 12 famous architectural structures in 12 months, including the Great Hall of the People. Responsible for the rapid growth of bridge in China today.

WANG, Chia-Chi (b. 1925 in China) of Taipei, Taiwan, Air Force retiree. Represented Taiwan in two Far East Championships and won many national titles in the 1950s. Headed Taiwan's tournament committee since 1961, with organizing and directing responsibilities for many national and international tournaments. Manager of Taiwan's International Bridge Center. Author of *Natural Bidding System* and *Bridge for Beginners*.

WANG, Hanbin of Beijing, China. Vice chairman National Congress. Advisor Chinese Bridge Association. One of the leaders responsible for the growth of Chinese bridge.

WANG, Junren (b. 1947) of Shanghai, China, company employee. WBF World Master. Second Far East Teams 1984, 1987. Represented China in four world championships and three other zonal championships. Won 15 national titles.

WANG, Hongli Xian of China (b. 1965), physician. Second Far East Teams 1993.

WANG, Liping (b. 1962) of Hangzhou, China. Second Far East Teams 1993.

WANG, Ping of Hangzhou, China, employee. WBF World Master. Third Venice Cup 1991. Won Far East Teams 1991. Represented China in four world championships and two other zonal championships. Won two national titles.

WANG, Wenfei (b. 1968) of Shanghai, China. Second Far East Teams 1993.

WANUFEL, Christian (b. 1944) of Liège, Belgium, engineer. WBF World Master. Represented Belgium in two world championships and five European championships. National wins include open teams five times and open pairs twice.

WARADIA, Dadan (b. 1967) of Jakarta, Indonesia, government employee. Won Far East Junior Teams 1990, 1991. Won one national title.

WARDEN, Phillip J. (b. 1947) of Madison WI, painting contractor, graduate of U of Wisconsin; Diamond Life Master, has won more than 30 regionals including Tri-Unit Open Prs 1969; Mississippi Valley Swiss 1975; Wisconsin Swiss 1978, Open Prs 1980, Open Swiss 1991.

WARNER, David (1911-1987) of Bala-Cynwyd PA, stockbroker. Warner was a member emeritus, former

ACBL vice president and former president of Philadelphia CBA; placed second in Master Mixed Tms 1947, Mixed Prs 1957 and won a number of regional events.

WARNER, Janet M. (1901-1991) of Pampa TX, retired secretary, won NAC Womens Prs 1962.

WARREN, Emily (Mrs. Prescott) (1876-deceased) of Newton MA, daughter of Francis Edgar Stanley, inventor of the Stanley steam car. A prominent New England bridge teacher, bridge writer and radio lecturer in the Twenties and Thirties. She was a columnist for the *Boston Transcript* and authored several books on games including *Auction and Contract Bridge Condensed* and co-authored *Contract Bridge of 1930*.

WARREN, Ken R. (b. 1954) of Pickering ON, management accountant, graduated U of Toronto, represented Canada internationally 1987 (European Championships), Albuquerque 1994; Diamond Life Master, won Canadian Open Prs Championship (COPC) 1986, 91; and more than 35 regionals including Summer Fun KO Tms, IMP Prs, Open Prs 1989; All-American Swiss, Open Swiss, Open Prs 1992, Morning KO Tms, Fltd KO Tms 1993; Canadian Nat'ls Bracketed KO Tms 1992, 93.

WARSHAUER, Judge Bernard J. (b. 1920) of Sumter SC, family court judge, educated at The Citadel and U of North Carolina (JD); Dist 7 representative on ACBL Bd of Dir 1979-94 and past president of Unit 160. Warshauer has been a contributor to the Dist 7 newsletter, has a weekly column in *Sumter Daily Item* and was formerly the editor of Unit 160 newsletter. Diamond Life Master with more than 20 regional wins including Mid-Atlantic Fall Master Prs 1962, Winter KO Tms 1972, Spring KO Tms 1973, 79, Master Prs 1975, 76, Mens Prs 1977; Spring secondary Open Prs 1971.

WARSHAUER, Genie (Mrs. Bernard) (b. 1938) of Sumter SC, bridge teacher. Some of her numerous regional wins include Mid-Atlantic Master Prs 1975, 76, KO Tms 1979, 94, Womens Swiss 1979, Swiss 1980; Fall secondary Open Tms 1981.

WARZEK, Frank G. (b. 1931) of San Jose CA, nuclear engineer, graduate of Siena College; served as member Bd of Dir, Unit 507 and is a past president and vice president. Won Commercial and Industrial Tms 1969; regional wins include Golden Gate Mens Prs 1973; Mid-Winter Holiday Master Prs 1974; California Capital Open Prs 1975; All-Western Swiss 1978; Holiday Festival Master Prs 1979; Sr Fall Fling Swiss 1987, 89, 90, Open Prs, Strat Prs 1990; Wine Country Sr Open Prs, Sr Prs 1992.

WASHINGTON, Dr. Lawrence P. (Larry) (b. 1939) of Carmichael CA, dermatologist, past president of Unit 505, former member Dist 21 Bd of Dir; member of ACBL Bd of Gov, ACBL Goodwill Committee, and ACBL Charity Foundation. A Diamond Life Master, his wins include Monterey Mens Prs 1988; Wine Country Open Swiss 1989, KO Tms 1990; Bakersfield Open Prs 1991; All-Western KO Tms, BAM Tms 1993.

WATANABE, Fumio (b. 1917) of Kanagawa Pref., Japan. Formerly CEO of, and later adviser to, Tokyo Marine and Fire Insurance and Japan Air Lines. Represented Japan in first Japan-U.S.A. match 1950. JCBL president 1981-91. Worked for JCBL incorporation, for three Epson international tournaments, and the 1991 staging of the Bermuda Bowl and Venice Cup in Yokohama. JCBL Honorary Life Member. Recipient First Class Order of the Sacred Treasure.

WATSON, Louis H. (1907-1936) of New York City, was a leading player of the Thirties. *Collier's* magazine of March 24, 1934, ranked Watson as the fourth greatest player in the world on the basis of his tournament record. He won the AWL Open Tms and Open Prs 1933, 34; Asbury Challenge Tms 1932, Cavendish Club Individual 1933; and placed second in four major events including the Vanderbilt 1933. Watson was a widely followed analyst, acting as daily columnist for the *New York Post* and as technical editor for *The Bridge World*. His writings included the classic *Watson on the Play of the Hand* and *Contract Bridge*.

WATULINGAS, Giovani (b. 1956) of Jakarta, Indonesia. Won Far East Teams and National Open Teams 1992.

WEBBER, Robert F. (Bob) (b. 1946) of Waterford MI, CPA and financial planner; served as president and tournament chairman for the Michigan BA and currently serving as its treasurer and as executive secretary, treasurer and tournament coordinator for Dist 12. Diamond Life Master, he won Spring secondary Swiss 1973, 81, Summer Open Prs 1978; Motor City Open Prs 1974, KO Tms 1978; Dist 12 GN Tms 1975, 76, 87; Great Lakes Master Prs 1977, Open Prs 1983, Swiss 1993; All-American Master Prs 1981; Southfield Mens Swiss 1989, IMP Prs 1991, KO Tms 1993; Bowling Green Swiss 1992. See also HIGHEST SCORE.

WEBER, Lynne J. (formerly Pollenz) (b. 1955) of Redwood City CA, management consultant, graduate Cornell and Stanford U (PhD), won Womens Swiss 1986 and placed second in Womens Prs 1983. She has also won a number of regionals.

WEBSTER, Harold Tucker (1885-1952) noted syndicated cartoonist, was best known for the character "The Timid Soul," which he created. He used bridge as the topic of many of his humorous pictures. Born in West Virginia, he lived most of his adult life in New York City. He co-authored cartoon books on bridge with Ely Culbertson, Carswell Adams, Philo Clark Calhoun, William Johnston and authored *Grand Slams*.

WEED, Charles E. (Charlie) (b. 1931) of Shreveport LA, business consultant, served as president of the Dallas BA; won GN Tms 1975, NAC Swiss 1978. His over 50 regional wins include Mid-South KO Tms 1972, Swiss 1973, 78; Houston Mid-Winter Swiss 1973, Master Swiss 1981; Navajo Trail Master Prs, Swiss 1975; Rocky Mountain KO Tms 1981; Republic of Texas Master Swiss 1981.

WEED, Marion D. See SNYDER, Marion D.

WEESAKUL, Dr. Boonserm (b. 1933) of Bangkok, Thailand, university professor. WBF World Master. Runner-up Far East Championship 1988.

WEI, Charles C. (C.C.) (1914-Feb 20, 1987) of New York

City, born in Shanghai, China, shipbuilding magnate, graduate of Shanghai U; in the Mid-Sixties he devised the Precision bidding system which was used successfully by the Taiwan Team in the Bermuda Bowl 1969, 70, by the Precision Team in winning the Spingold 1970, 71, the Vanderbilt 1972, and by the Italian Team in winning World Team Olympiad 1972 and the Bermuda Bowl 1973, 74. Wei was a former trustee of the ACBL Charity Foundation. He was npc of the Taiwan team in the World Team Olympiad 1964, Bermuda Bowl 1969, and npc of the North American Venice Cup Team 1981. Wei authored many books and articles on Precision and Super Precision. Playing with Ron Andersen at the New York Winter regional 1974 he had the biggest game ever recorded in an ACBL regional on a 156 average -- 260, (83.3%)! He won Puerto Rico Open Prs 1970, Swiss Tms 1972; Mid-Atlantic Summer Swiss 1972; Metropolitan Open Prs 1974. See also HIGHEST SCORE, PRECISION CLUB, PRECISION TEAM, SPONSORS.

WEI, Stella (b. 1946 in China) of Taipei, Taiwan, computer network specialist for a bank. WBF World Master. Won Far East Women's Teams 1988, 1989, Far East Open Pairs 1988. Represented Taiwan in four world championships and 11 other Far East Championships. Has won 12 national titles.

WEI-SENDER, Katherine (Kathie) (formerly Mrs. Charles C. Wei) of Nashville TN, formerly of New York City, born in Peking, China. Writer and lecturer on the Precision Club system, graduate of Shanghai U School of Nursing, medical facility administrator for 15 years before retiring in 1972. Wei was appointed adviser to the Shanghai Bridge League while attending the first international bridge tournament ever held in China (March 1981). She makes frequent trips there to advise and assist in various bridge activities and endeavors. She is now the official adviser to the Chinese Bridge League and is the only United States citizen to hold minister rank in China. She also is Ambassador of Bridge for the World Bridge Federation. Wei, a WBF Grand Master, has won all three major world womens titles. Her first came in 1978 – World Womens Prs. She also won World Olympiad Womens Tms 1984 and Venice Cup 1987; placed second Venice Cup 1981, 85, Womens Prs 1990. Won the USWBC 1983, 87; and named ACBL Honorary Member in 1987.

She was co-captain and manager of the Taiwan team in the 1971 Bermuda Bowl (placed 2nd) and the 1972 World Team Olympiad; served as Board member of Greater New York BA, trustee and president of ACBL Charity Foundation; member of the ACBL Goodwill Committee. She is a contributor to various national and international bridge publications, with a regular weekly column with Alan Truscott in China's *People's Daily*; author of her biography *Second Daughter* and co-author of *Action for the Defense* and *One Club Complete*.

An ACBL Grand Life Master with more than 12,000 masterpoints as of 1993, #9 on all-time masterpoint list for women; her nat'l titles are Womens Tms 1971, 80; North American Womens Swiss 1983; Womens KO Tms 1983, 87; Womens BAM Tms 1992; placed second in Womens Tms 1973, 82; Vanderbilt 1974, 77, 79; Life Master Womens Prs 1984; North American Womens Swiss 1985; Womens BAM Tms 1986, 91; Womens KO Tms 1992.

WEICHSEL, Nancy E. (Mrs. Arthur Blaustein) (b. 1945) of Walnut Creek CA, former backgammon and bridge professional, won Master Mixed Tms 1976 and numerous regionals.

WEICHSEL, Peter M. (b. 1943) of Encinitas CA, professional bridge player, WBF Life Master, won the Bermuda Bowl 1983 and World Mixed Prs 1990. He also placed 5th in Rosenblum Tms 1986, 7th 1978, 9th 1990; 8th World Open Prs 1974, 78. He won the Pan-Am Tms 1992 and the International Team Trials 1982. An ACBL Grand Life Master with more than 17,000 MPs as of 1993, Weichsel is ranked in the top 25 of all masterpoint holders. He won the Spingold 1970, 71, 80, 82, 92; Life Master Mens Prs 1971; Vanderbilt 1972, 85, 89; Reisinger 1973; Master Mixed Tms 1976, 89; Life Master Prs 1977; Mens Tms 1979; Mens Prs 1980, 84; Mens BAM Tms 1987, Open Prs II 1993; placed second in Mens Tms 1968, Vanderbilt 1975, 81; Reisinger, Blue Ribbon Prs 1983; Spingold 1985, 88, 91; IMP Prs 1987; Life Master Mens Prs 1989; Open BAM Tms 1990. He won the Cavendish Club Invitational 1976, 77, *London Sunday Times* Prs 1975 (second in 1973). His more than 200 regional titles include Eastern States KO Tms 1977, 79. He once hitchhiked across the country from California to Queens NY in 56 hours. Also see LANCIA TEAMS and PRECISION TEAM.

WEIGKRICHT, Terry (b. 1958) of Vienna, Austria, mathematics and French teacher. WBF World Life Master. European Women's Team champion 1991 and runner-up Venice Cup 1991. Has represented Austria on several other occasions.

WEIK, Thomas W. (b. 1942) of Wyomissing PA, president of investment advisory firm, past member ACBL Bd of Gov, has served on two Dist Boards; placed second in Life Master Prs 1974; regional wins include Mid-Atlantic Open Tms 1968, KO Tms 1971, Open Prs 1991, Summer secondary BAM Tms 1974, Fall Open Prs 1989, Dist 4 GN Prs (twice).

WEIL, Elina (b. 1921) of Sacramento CA, teacher, bridge teacher and certified director, has run bridge on cruises for one-third of the year for more than 17 years, member ABTA and former member ACBL Charity Foundation; won All-Western Womens Prs 1968; CA Capital Womens Prs 1977; Hawaii Open Tms 1980.

WEIL, Lt. Col. Frank P. (b. 1918) of Sacramento CA, retired; founder and for 25 years the editor of the Unit 505 publication *The Overcall*; for 17 years was a columnist to *Contract Bridge Forum* and has been a contributor to *ACBL Bulletin*; certified bridge director, he has been directing bridge activities aboard cruise ships for 17 years. Member ABTA and ACBL Charity Foundation; won Reno Mens Prs 1972, Hawaii Open Tms 1980. Weil is the holder of five Air Medals and the Distinguished Flying Cross.

WEILAND, Alexander (b. 1947) of Skokie IL, born in Germany, accountant/tax preparer; regional wins include Central States I Open Tms 1972, KO Tms 1975, 80; Central States II Mixed Prs 1977, Open Prs 1984, Master Prs 1986; Tri-Unit Swiss 1972; Peoria Swiss 1976; Dist 13 GN Tms 1982.

WEINER, Barbara L. (b. 1930) of Joplin MO, retired secretary, won Womens Prs 1953. Her regional wins include Missouri Valley Womens Prs 1955, 59; Dist 15 Sr Swiss 1990, 91, Womens Prs 1991.

WEINER, Howard (b. 1944) of Southfield MI, attorney, graduated Wayne State U and Detroit College of Law (JD); member Dist 12 Judiciary Committee; Diamond Life Master; placed second GN Prs 1992. Weiner, two-time SOMBA Player of the Year, has won numerous regionals including Spring secondary Open Prs, Great Lakes Mens Swiss 1981; Motor City Open Prs 1981, 91, 93, Swiss Tms 1990; Dist 12 GN Prs 1980, 84, 91, GN Tms 1981, 82, 84, 85, 87, 88, 90; London ON Open Prs 1988, 91; Somba Mens Swiss, Open Prs 1991, 92, KO Tms 1993; Bermuda Open Prs 1992.

WEINER, Leo B. (1906-1993) of Chicago, retired insurance claims manager, club director and manager; LM #135 in 1948, first LM in Missouri and hosted the first TV show on bridge in St. Louis. Diamond Life Master; wins include Summer secondary Golder Master Prs 1966; Central States Open Prs 1943, 53, Life and Sr Master Tms 1957; Mississippi Valley Mens Prs 1951, 53, 56, Mixed Prs 1957, Open Tms 1962; Champaign Mens Prs 1977; Springfield Master Prs 1980.

WEINSTEIN, Arthur (Art) (b. 1927) of San Mateo CA, bridge teacher and certified director; author of *Bridge Poems for your Partner*, *Art of Bridge (Bridge Poems for your EX Partner)*, *Bridge the Gap*, *Art Weinstein Talks Bridge*. Former bridge columnist for several weekly newspapers, current bridge editor of Foster City *Progress*.

WEINSTEIN, Howard M. (b. 1953) of Chicago, stock options trader, graduate of U of Minnesota; member ACBL Ethical Oversight Committee, Appeals Committee since 1987; WBF World Master, placed 5th Rosenblum Tms 1990, second in USBC 1989. ACBL Diamond Life Master, won GN Tms 1991, Vanderbilt 1993; placed second GN Tms 1986, 88; Reisinger, Mens BAM Tms 1987; Life Master Prs 1988, 89. He has won more than 50 regionals.

WEINSTEIN, Sol (b. 1949) of Yonkers NY, born in Montreal; ACBL field representative and national tournament director, began directing 1969 and achieved his current rating in 1979. Served as ACBL chief tournament director 1992-93; currently serving as coordinator of tournament related computer activities and the ACBLscore program.

WEINSTEIN, Steven M. (b. 1964) of Upper Montclair NJ, stock options trader, graduate of NY State U; WBF World Master, placed 5th Bermuda Bowl 1991, 14th World Open Prs 1986; also represented ACBL internat'lly Biarritz 1982, Geneva 1990. At age 17 he was the youngest player ever to win an NABC event (Life Master Pairs) and is believed to be the youngest player ever to represent the U.S. in world competition (age 18); was King of Bridge 1982. Won Life Master Prs 1981, Reisinger 1984; Blue Ribbon Prs 1987; Open Swiss 1992; placed second GN Tms 1991. Won Pan Am Pair Trials 1991; won Cavendish Invitational Prs 1993, second in 1994. See also KING OR QUEEN OF BRIDGE; see FAMILY.

WEINSTEIN, Sue A. (b. 1938) of Glenview IL, administrative secretary for Chicago Contract BA (since 1975), former teacher of the blind and partially sighted, graduate of Michigan State U. WBF World Master, placed 10th World Womens Prs 1986. ACBL Diamond Life Master, won North American Womens Swiss 1984; Womens KO Tms 1988; Life Master Womens Prs 1991; placed second Womens KO Tms 1978, 79, 81. Her numerous regional wins include Tri-Unit Womens Prs 1980; Central States I Master Prs 1970, Open Prs 1981, Womens Swiss 1987, Open Prs 1991; Motor City Womens Swiss 1982, Wisconsin Womens KO Tms 1984; Central States II Womens Swiss 1977, 79, Womens KO Tms 1984, 89; St. Louis Master Prs 1985; Dist 8 Master Prs 1987, 88, Womens Swiss 1981, 88.

WEISBACH, Dean (Mrs. Frank) (b. 1911) of Redmond WA, ACBL Operations Division manager 1970-1976; was first women to ever achieve the rank of national tournament director 1956-1970.

WEISBACH, Frank (1906-1981) of Cincinnati OH, was a leading Midwest player and expert analyst. Life Master #80 in 1947, he was an active player for three decades. He won the Life Master Prs 1947, was second in the Spingold 1951 and won numerous regional events.

WEISS, Albert (Dingy) (1900-1981) of Miami Beach FL, won Open Prs 1939, 51; Mens Tms 1946; Vander-bilt 1963, 65; placed second Master Individual 1945; Life Master Prs 1949, 62; Mens Tms 1952; Spingold 1953, 72.

WEISS, David J. (b. 1944) of Pasadena CA, psychology professor, graduate of U of Pennsylvania and U of California-San Diego (PhD), was a Fulbright Scholar to India 1987-88; author of *BRIDGE: Parity Leads in Defence*; contributor to *International Popular Bridge Monthly*, *Bridge World*, *Southern California Bridge News*, and *Australian Bridge*. Weiss placed second Reisinger 1980 and won a number of regionals including San Diego Mens Prs, Master Prs 1969, Super Open Prs 1990; Anaheim KO Tms 1972, Open Prs 1983; Palm Springs Swiss 1973; Los Angeles KO Tms 1975, BAM Tms 1976, Swiss, Master Prs 1982; Monterey KO, Swiss Tms 1979.

WEISS, Larry A. of Vista CA, retired attorney, former ACBL photographer; author of several *Bridge World* articles and is the originator of the WEISS CONVENTION and SIMPLIFIED CLUB SYSTEM, which is described in his book *The Simplified Club*. Diamond Life Master, placed second Mixed Prs 1970; won many regionals including Fall secondary Swiss 1970, Open Prs A-D, Open Prs 1978, Spring Swiss 1979, Summer Goddard Prs 1966; All-Western Mens Prs 1975; Bridge Week KO Tms 1963, 65, Master Mens Prs 1975.

WEISS, Lawrence (1905-1979) of Brookline MA, attorney, chairman of the committee to revise ACBL by-laws in 1949. He is credited with devising administrative methods used by the ACBL since then. A former ACBL vice president and president of the New England Bridge Conference, he authored *Contract Bridge: The Bidding Structure*. He had numerous regionals wins to his credit.

WEISSMAN, Gloria L. (Mrs. William) of Bonita

Springs FL, distributor of video and audio tapes and other bridge supplies; bridge teacher, certified director, columnist and author of *Learn to Play Bridge the New Way*; hostess of a television series *Play Bridge with Gloria*. Won San Diego KO Tms 1987.

WEL, Rob van (b. 1962) of Sittard, the Netherlands, tax employee. WBF World Master. World Junior Team champion 1987. European Junior Team champion 1986.

WELCH, Lawrence J. (Larry) (b. 1895) of Indianapolis IN, retired realtor and appraiser, LM #79 in 1947; won the Chicago (now the Resinger) 1935 and many regionals.

WELLAND, Roy of New York City, computer systems consultant; regionals include Summer secondary Mens Prs 1987; New England Winter KO Tms 1988, Open Swiss 1990, 91, Fltd KO Tms 1991, Fall KO Tms 1988, 1991; Dist 24 GN Prs 1990; Mid-Atlantic KO Tms 1991; New York Winter Swiss 1991.

WELLS, Nell (formerly Childs) (d. 1987) of San Francisco CA, bridge teacher, LM #168 in 1949, first woman Life Master on Pacific Coast, won the Barclay Trophy 1946, 51, 55 and numerous regionals.

WELTMAN, Dr. Harold S. (b. 1931) of Kingston PA, dentist, past president of Unit 120 and Dist 4; placed second Amateur Mens Prs 1976; won Puerto Rico Master Prs 1976; Dist 4 Mens Prs, Open Prs 1977, Spring Open Prs 1979, Fall Mens Swiss 1979, GN Prs 1982; Spring secondary Open Prs 1978, Summer Swiss 1980,

WENDT, Edward G. Jr. (Jay) (b. 1928) of New York City, insurance company executive, placed second in the Chicago (now the Reisinger) 1961.

WENNING, Ulrich (b. 1949) of Bonn, Germany, lawyer. Represented Germany in two world championships and one European Championship. Won two national titles. President German Bridge Federation since 1989, formerly treasurer.

WERDELIN, Ole (b. 1933) of Copenhagen, Denmark, physician. Represented Denmark in four zonal championships and other events. Five national titles include Open Team three times.

WERDELIN, Stig (b. 1937) of Copenhagen, Denmark, supreme court lawyer. WBF World Master. Third in World Teams 1984. Second European Teams 1979, third 1961. Represented Denmark more often than any other player, including three other world championships and 10 other zonal championships. 38 national titles include Open Teams 16 times and Open Pairs eight times.

WERNZ, Timothy C. (b. 1943) of Minneapolis MN, commodities trader, editor of *Viking Bridge News*, contributor to *Gopher Bridge News*. Regional wins include District 14 GN Tms 1983, 89, Gopher Master Prs 1986, Open Prs 1991, Swiss 1984, 86, Bracketed KO Tms 1993; Roughrider KO Tms 1985, Master Prs 1985, Swiss 1972, 81; Pheasant KO Tms 1991; Duluth KO Tms 1990; Eau Claire KO Tms 1991; Thunder Bay KO Tms 1993.

WESTCOTT, Frank (1901-1974) of North Attleboro

MA, engineer and contractor. ACBL president 1960, Honorary Member 1968, a former member of the ACBL Board, president of the New England Bridge Conference and of the Eastern Massachusetts BA. Life Master #152, npc of the North American international team 1961, 64; placed second Mens Tms 1964. Won Inter-City matches 1970, 71, 72, 73 for Boston.

WESTERHOF, Jan (b. 1954) of the Netherlands, economics teacher. Won Bermuda Bowl 1993.

WESTHEIMER, Gerald J. (Jeff) (b. 1934) of New York City, commodity specialist, won Reisinger 1969, placed second Vanderbilt 1968, 69; Spingold 1969.

WESTRA, Berry (b. 1961) of Rotterdam, The Netherlands, bridge teacher. Won Bermuda Bowl 1993. WBF World Master. Third in World Teams 1992. World Junior Team champion 1987. European Junior Team champion 1986. Represented The Netherlands in one other world championship and three European Championships. National titles include Open Teams twice. He contributes to *IMP Bridge-magazine*.

WETZLAR, Edwin A. (d. 1934) of New York City, a leading personality in the early years of whist and bridge. He won Vanderbilt 1928, Master Mixed Tms 1933; placed second Vanderbilt 1929 and won AWL Open Prs 1931, 33. Wetzlar was a Board member of the American Whist League. See WETZLAR TROPHY.

WEYANT, William S. (Bill) (b. 1920) of Cincinnati, ACBL associate national tournament director, began directing in 1962 and achieved his current rating in 1972. A former scientist in charge of Antarctic atmospheric research, he was awarded a Congressional medal in 1960. Mount Weyant, Antarctica, was named for him.

WHALEN, Vivian (formerly Lavery) of Jupiter FL, bridge club owner, placed second Womens Tms 1976, North American Womens Swiss 1984; Master Mixed Tms 1990; won numerous regionals.

WHARTON, Frank H. (b. 1951) of London England, accountant, graduate of U of Exeter; represented Bermuda in international competition Seattle 1984, represented England in Geneva 1990; won Weisbaden Open Prs 1989, KO Tms 1990, Open Prs 1991; Spring secondary Morning KO Tms 1990, 92.

WHITE, C. Edward (b. 1937) of Grand Blanc MI, company president, graduated U of Tennessee. Won Rochester Swiss 1985; Fall secondary Mens Prs 1985, KO Tms 1989; Dist 12 GN Prs 1986; Saginaw KO Tms 1987; Midland Mens Prs 1989; Motor City Strat Swiss 1992; Toronto Sr Swiss 1992, KO Tms 1994.

WHITE, Effie L. (formerly Long) (1918-1989) of Mason TX, tournament director and Goren bridge teacher, associated with Charles Goren for many years, she conducted the Goren national forums in New York 1968-70 and numerous cruises 1965-77; was selected as coordinator of the Goren Teacher Society in 1965; co-authored with Goren *Introduction to Bridge* and was associate editor of *Goren Teacher Manual*. She was a past president of the ABTA and wrote articles for the *ABTA Quarterly*,

Popular Bridge, and was columnist for local newspapers. She won Eastern States Mixed Tms 1963.

WHITE, Charles H. (1908-1984) of Ft Lauderdale FL, retired advertising agency executive, won Open Prs 1949; ACBL Board member 1951-77, president of Florida Unit 1961, 63. Sunday columnist of *Ft. Lauderdale News* for many years and formerly edited and published *Florida Bridge News*.

WHITEHEAD, Wilbur C(herier) (1866-1931) of New York City, was one of the world's greatest bridge authorities. He was president of the Simplex Automobile Company, but bridge held such a fascination for him that he retired from business to devote his whole life to bridge in 1910. At that time he was living in France and wrote his first publication, *Royal Spades*. A second book was published in London in 1913. His first book appearing in America was *Whitehead's Convention of Auction Bridge* in 1914. He was the inventor of many of the outstanding conventions of bidding and play, the quick trick table of card values, the Whitehead system of requirements for original bids and responses, and the Whitehead table of preferential leads. He was instrumental in standardizing procedures in auction bridge and later in contract bridge. Whitehead was a member of the team which won the Vanderbilt in 1928, the first year it was put into play, and was second the following year. He was a contributing editor of *The Bridge World* and published several books, including *Auction Bridge Standards* which explained the Whitehead system.

WHITESEL, William F. (Bill) (b. 1940) of Couer d'Alene ID, bridge professional and club owner, member ACBL Goodwill Committee, past Unit president. Diamond Life Master with more than 30 regionals including Bridge Week KO Tms 1972; Mt. Shasta Swiss 1974; Richland KO Tms 1975; Spokane Swiss 1976; Helena Swiss 1979; Kalispell KO Tms 1983; Billings Super Swiss 1989; Salt Lake City KO Tms 1990; Ashland KO Tms, Super Swiss 1990.

WHITWORTH, George F. (Rick) (b. 1949) of San Ramon CA, systems programmer, graduate of U of California-Davis and U of Wisconsin-Madison; won Golder Master Prs 1979, CA Capital Master Prs 1980, Swiss 1982, Super Open Prs 1983, 88; Golden State Open Prs 1981, 83, Open Swiss 1985; Wine Country Mens Prs 1983, Swiss 1986, Fltd Prs 1993; All-Western Super Open Prs 1984, IMP Prs 1990; Modesto Swiss 1992.

WHOLEY, Jack (b. 1946) of Albany CA, attorney, graduate of Notre Dame, Stanford, Hastings College of Law (JD), Peace Corps volunteer to the Philippines 1968-70; won Open BAM Tms 1990.

WIDDER Dr. Lajos (1893-1979) of Budapest, Hungary, lawyer and author. European champion 1938, won five national open team titles between 1937 and 1957. Writings include *Tournament Bridge* and *The Technique and Tactics of Bridgeplaying*.

WIDENGREN, Britta (b. 1913 in Sweden) of Kitzbühel, Austria, retired managing director. WBF World Master. Runner-up Venice Cup 1991, represented Austria on three other occasions. Nordic Women's Team champion 1948.

Retired from bridge 1958-72, when she moved to Austria and resumed play. Her Venice Cup silver medal in Yokohama in 1991 seems to make her, at 78, the oldest person ever to finish first or second in a world championship.

WIEBE, Lavern E. (b. 1960) of Madison WI, student teaching assistant and technical writer, graduated U of Western ON; won Non-Life Master Swiss 1989; and Summer secondary Mens Prs 1993; Central States KO Tms 1994.

WIGNALL John (b. 1932 in England) of Christchurch, New Zealand, sharebroker. WBF World Master. Represented New Zealand in six world championships and several zonal championships. Many national wins. President Zone 7 (South Pacific) since 1986. Member WBF Executive Council and Laws Commission. Former President New Zealand CBA. Bridge correspondent *Christchurch Press* and *Otago Daily Times* since 1966.

WIJAYA, Yasin (b. 1940) of Jakarta, Indonesia, billiard center manager. Won Far East Teams 1972, 1979, 1984. Represented Indonesia in 6 world championships and more than seven other zonal championships. Won more than 9 national titles including open teams 4 times.

WILDAVSKY, Adam (b. 1960) of Jackson Heights NY, computer consultant, graduate of MIT, has held several positions on Dist 24 and 25 Boards; won Blue Ribbon Prs 1992; placed 5th Internat'l Lions Invitational tournament (for players under 25) in Italy 1984; won more than 25 regional events.

WILDY, Marion Edwin (1910-1978) of Aiea HI, bridge teacher and tournament director. He was the first black ACBL Life Master (#1225, 1956). Wildy was president of Honolulu Unit 1964.

WILEY, Charles E. (b. 1924) of Sun City FL, retired retail merchant, won Kansas City Open Prs 1951; Mississippi Valley Open Tms 1954, 55, 62, 73, was Player of the Year, St. Louis area 1973-74.

WILEY, Lois (Mrs. Kent) of Beverly Hills FL, chiropractic physician, the most successful blind player, she was a familiar sight at tournaments with her seeing-eye dog. Won numerous regional events. See HANDI-CAPPED PLAYERS.

WILKINS, Robert H. (Bob) (1911-1993) of Memphis TN, retired ACBL executive, served organized bridge in various capacities for many years. He became a tournament director in 1952 and held the rating of national tournament director in 1965 when he was appointed ACBL tournament coordinator. From 1968 to 1978 he was director of ACBL elections and director of communications for the ACBL Bd of Dir. He also served as executive secretary of the ACBL Charity Foundation 1969-1973. Wilkins contributed to many bridge publications, including the Chicago *Kibitzer* and the *ACBL Bulletin*. He was a past president of the CCBA. A librarian by profession, Wilkins was educated at Oberlin College and Western Reserve U; U of Chicago graduate fellow 1935-38.

WILKINSON, Charles D. (Chuck) (b. 1944) of

Ridgeland MS, investment adviser (CFA), bridge club owner/manager; graduate of U.S. Air Force Academy and Emory U; a member of the ACBL Bd of Dir, was the founder and editor of the Jackson Bridge Club newsletter, past president of Dist 10 and Mississippi Bridge Association. Wilkinson has won Dist 10 GN Prs 1985; Spring secondary Open Prs 1985, Summer Morning KO Tms 1991.

WILKOSZ, Andrzej (b. 1935) of Krakow, Poland, metallurgical engineer. WBF World Life Master. Won World Teams 1978. Second European Teams 1978. Represented Poland in five other world championships and 12 other zonal championships. Won many national titles. Author of one book.

WILKS, Betty E. (b. 1918) of Joplin MO, former bridge teacher, bridge columnist for *Joplin Globe* and Pittsburg *Morning Sun* for about ten years; past president of Unit 101 and a certified director. Regional wins include Missouri Valley Mixed Prs 1955, Womens Prs 1957, 77; Mississippi Valley Womens Prs 1956; Mexican Nat'l Master Prs 1978; Tulsa Sr Swiss, Overland Park Sr Swiss 1991.

WILLARD, Sylvie (b.1952) of Paris, France, bridge organizer. WBF World Life Master. Second World Women's Teams 1987, third 1985. Won European Women's Teams 1983, 1985, 1987. Represented France in three other world championships and four other zonal championships. Won many national titles.

WILLIAMS, Don R. (b. 1931) of Kansas City MO, economist, placed second in Mens Tms 1962.

WILLIAMS, Joyce of Chicago, retired schoolteacher. Represented United States in two world championships. Fourth in ABA overall masterpoint rankings. Top ABA woman player 13 times in masterpoint rankings, and the annual award is now named for her. Seven consecutive wins in *The Bridge World's* Challenge the Champs. Bridge teacher, often to children.

WILLIAMS, Dr. Mary C. (formerly Philley) (b. 1927) of Leander TX, retired attorney. In the Fifties she worked on the Nat'l Laws Commission with John Gerber, formulating the new Laws of Bridge, and with Emma Jean Hawes on the New Conventions Committee; former secretary and vice president of Dist 16 and was the first editor of its publication, *Scorecard*; served as first alternate to ACBL Bd of Dir from Dist 16 for many years; one of the founders and first vice president, The Forum for Women in Bridge. Recipient in 1991 of the Oswald and James Jacoby Service Award for Dist 16. Williams placed second in Master Mixed Tms 1964, Womens KO Tms 1984. Her numerous regional wins include Texas Fall Open Tms 1965, Womens Prs 1966; Houston Open Prs 1967; Mexican Nat'ls Womens Prs 1973; Dist 6 Bridge Week KO Tms 1974; Sand & Surf Srs Open Prs 1989, Swiss 1990; Texas Storm Sr Super Bracketed KO Tms 1991; Resort City Sr KO Tms 1992.

WILLIAMS, Phyllis (b. 1907) of London, England. Won European Women's Teams 1950, 1951, 1952 and represented Britain in six other zonal championships. Won several national titles.

WILLIAMSON, Mrs. Vivian (b. 1912) of Roswell NM, bridge teacher, won Womens Prs 1973, with her daughter, Ann Economidy, the only mother-daughter to have won this event. Former Board member of Unit 382.

WILLIS, Lt. Col. James T. (Tim) (b. 1913) of Houston TX, retired army officer and bridge club owner/manager; graduate of West Point, awarded the Silver Star, Bronze Star and Purple Heart in WWII; won Japanese Open Tms 1952; Spring secondary Open Prs 1978; Texas Fall Open Tms 1962, Open Prs 1979.

WILSON, Bert S. (b. 1915) of Clearwater FL, freelance writer, bridge columnist and lecturer, graduate of Temple U; bridge columnist for several newspapers, Travel with Goren cruise ship lecturer since 1965; served as a Board member of the Philadelphia CBA for many years; member of Mensa. Wilson is the co-author of *Hold our Bridge Hands* and the originator of Wilson 2♦; won Atlantic City Mixed Prs 1963.

WILSON, Chris H. of Phoenix AZ, served as ACBL president 1985, chairman of the Bd 1986; member of the ACBL Bd of Dir 1977-89; served as president of the Western Conference and Phoenix Unit for four terms each. One of the founders of Dist 17 Association in 1969, she was a member of its Board and executive committee until 1989. Member of the ACBL Goodwill Committee, ACBL Charity Committee and an adviser on the ACBL Education Foundation. Wilson served the longest term as president, presiding over four NABCs instead of three when the Board changed the time of the presidency. She was chairperson of the 1971 Fall North American Championships.

WILSON, Keith A. (b. 1949) of Louisville KY, corporate executive, graduate of U of Mississippi; won North American Swiss 1991; regionals include Richmond Open Prs 1983; Dist 11 GN Prs 1984; Indianapolis Open Prs 1988; Lexington Open Prs, Masters Tms 1991.

WILSON, Mike A. (b. 1950) of Vancouver BC, stockbroker, won Mid-Winter Holiday Swiss 1975; Puget Sound KO Tms 1976, Master Prs 1979; British Columbia Mixed Prs 1977. Wilson plays bridge with his toes. See HANDICAPPED PLAYERS.

WILSON, Robert W. (1909-1965) of New Kensington PA, aluminum company employee, organized and was active in the Pittsburgh Industrial League for 19 years. An authority on double-dummy proplems, he was a frequent contributor to many bridge magazines including the *ACBL Bulletin* and was a contributary editor *Bridge Encyclopedia*.

WILSON, Walter T. (b. 1910) of Auburndale FL, bridge teacher and writer, has been an ACBL associate national tournament director since the mid-Fifties.

WILTON, Herbert C. (b. 1933) of Cincinnati OH, born in Vienna; retired computer scientist, former president and secretary of the Cincinnati BA; placed second Master Mixed Tms 1958, Silver Ribbon Prs 1994. Won Great Lakes Open Tms 1962; Midwest Open Prs 1968; Louisville Swiss 1990, Open Prs, Sr Swiss 1991, KO Tms 1993; Atlanta Open Prs 1990, Open Prs 1993; Pittsburgh Open

Prs 1991, 92; Canton Sr Prs 1991; Cleveland Sr Prs, Evansville Sr Prs 1992; Pine Mtn Sr KO Tms 1993; Gatlinburg KO Tms, Sr Prs 1993.

WINGEARD, Robert O. (b. 1939) of Colorado Springs CO, assistant director, operations support, headquarters NORAD, graduate of Purdue U; member ACBL Bd of Dir since 1990, served as president of the Western Conference 1983-84, Dist 17 1976-79, Unit 360 1972-75, 1988. He has chaired several regionals and is a member ACBL Goodwill Committee and ACBL Charity Committee. Wingeard writes a regular column for the Dist 17 *Scorecard*, Western Conference *Forum* and served as editor of the *Peak Kibitzer* during the 1960s and 70s. He has won several Dist 17 regional events including Swiss Tms, Mixed Prs, Open Prs.

WINKLER, Dr. Peter (b. 1946) of Madison NJ, director of research group in mathematics and theoretical computer science for Bell Communications; discovered ENCRYPTED SIGNALS and has written a number of articles for *The Bridge World* and *Bridge Magazine*. Graduate of Harvard (summa cum laude) and holds a PhD in mathematics from Yale, former Navy cryptographer.

WINSLOW, Thomas Newby (1861-1942) of East Orange NJ, bridge author and system-maker. His system, introduced in a series of booklets beginning in 1930 and in the book *Win with Winslow*, anticipated the Four Aces System with its 1 1/2 - 1 - 1/2 point-count, also an early form of canapé in which the lowest four-card suit is bid first, regardless of the strength of that suit.

WIRGREN, Anders (b. 1951) of Lund, Sweden, bridge writer and editor. WBF World Master. Third 1986 Rosenblum Tms, and represented Sweden in three other world championships. Runner up 1976 European Junior Teams, 1973 Nordic Junior Teams, 1988 Nordic Teams Nine national wins include open team twice. Bridge columnist *Skånska Dagbladet* and *Aftonbladet*. Contributes to many bridge magazines and twice won IBA Award for best article of year. Author 8 bridge books and 2 chess books. Swedish junior chess champion 1968.

WISDOM, William E. (Ned) (b. 1949) of Salisbury NC, federal employee, past president of Unit 169. Diamond Life Master, has won Fall secondary Mens Prs 1977; Dist 7 GN Tms 1977, 78, GN Prs 1981, 84, 86, 88, 90; Mid-Atlantic Open Prs 1978, 81, 84, Swiss Tms 1981, 90; Labor Day Open Prs 1981; Dist 7 KO Tms 1989, Open Prs 1991.

WISEMILLER, James P. (b. 1943) of Fountain Valley CA, systems consultant; won Open Prs 1965.

WISER, John (b. 1926) of Beaconsfield PQ, bridge club owner, ACBL national tournament director 1979-1993, won Can-Am Mens Prs 1954. From 1961 1963 he was the director of a bridge TV show. Wiser began his bridge career in 1950, and with his even temper and quiet demeanor spent many years specializing in appeals at NABCs and other tournaments. He has been an accredited WBF tournament director since 1972. He has contributed several articles to *ACBL Bulletin* column *Ruling the Game*.

WITTES, Jon (b. 1942) of Downey CA, school psychologist, graduated Brown U and Cal State U; member ACBL Appeals Committee, WBF World Master, won World Mixed Prs 1986, placed 7th 1990. Wittes, an ACBL Grand Life Master with more than 10,000 MPs, won Reisinger 1984; placed second Mens Swiss 1982, 84; Spingold 1989; has won more than 35 regional events.

WITTES, Pamela S. (Pam) (b. 1944) of Huntington Beach CA, clothing store owner, WBF World Master, won World Mixed Prs 1986 (7th 1990), placed 4th in Venice Cup 1991, won Pan-Am Womens Tms 1992 . Wittes, an ACBL Diamond Life Master, won USWBC (Womens team trials) 1991; Womens KO Tms 1989, North American Womens Swiss 1991; placed second North American Swiss, Womens BAM Tms 1987; Womens KO Tms 1990.

WODNIANSKY, Alexander (Axi) (b. 1967) of Vienna, mathematician. European Junior Pair champion 1991. Represented Austria in European Teams 1991 and three other European events. Won Austrian Life Master Individual 1986, Mixed Pairs 1992.

WOHLIN, Jan (b. 1924) of Stockholm, Sweden, WBF Life Master, represented Sweden-Iceland Bermuda Bowl 1950, Sweden 1953; European champion 1952, placed second 1948, 1949, 1950; won many Scandinavian championships and 15 national titles. Co-inventor of EFOS System and co-author of *Winning Pairs Technique* and *Play Safe — and Win*.

WOLD, Edward M. (Eddie) (b. 1951) of Houston TX, bridge professional, graduate of Rice U, a pilot; WBF World Master, placed 3rd Rosenblum Tms 1978 (9th 1990); 4th Bermuda Bowl 1983, World Open Prs 1986; won *McKenney Trophy* (now the *Crane Top 500*) and the Int'l Tm Trials 1982, second in USBC 1985. ACBL Grand Life Master with more than 27,000 MPs, currently #5 in all-time masterpoint holders, Wold won the GN Tms 1977, 81; Spingold 1977, 84; Vanderbilt 1979, 82; Mens BAM Tms 1984, 87; Reisinger 1985; Mott-Smith Trophy 1989; Lou Herman Trophy, Master Mixed Tms 1990; Open Swiss 1991; placed second in the Reisinger 1980, 90; Master Mixed Tms 1984; Open BAM Tms 1990; Open Prs I 1993. He has won more than 500 regional events since 1976.

WOLF, Jack S. (b. 1934) of Stafford TX, insurance and financial planner. Regional wins include Missouri Valley Open Tms 1961, 62, Open Prs 1962, Mixed Prs 1971; Houston BAM Tms 1967; Texas Fall Unmixed Prs 1974, 79, KO Tms 1979, 81, GN Prs 1980.

WOLFE, Edward C. (1883-1972) of Cleveland OH, was a bridge expert writer whose success at whist and auction bridge helped make him one of the earliest of the recognized authorities on contract bridge. A member of the Advisory Council of Bridge Headquarters, he helped draft the Official System. After Culbertson's defeat of Lenz, he joined the Culbertson staff, organizing teachers' conventions and lecturing. A former contributing editor of *The Bridge World* and *British Bridge Magazine*, Wolfe authored *The Play of the Cards at Contract Bridge*.

WOLFF, Betsey Y. (b. 1937) of Dallas TX, consultant and bridge professional, graduate of North Texas State

U; won World Mixed Tms 1972; placed second Womens Prs 1971, 82; Womens Tms 1973; North American Womens Swiss 1988. She has won numerous regional events and has international rating.

WOLFF, Elizabeth. See WOLFF, Betsey.

WOLFF, Robert S. (Bobby) of Dallas TX, business consultant, professional bridge player, syndicated bridge columnist, author; graduate of Trinity U. The second most successful player over the past 10 years in international play (see HAMMAN, ROBERT). Grand Life Master in both the WBF (#8) and ACBL. With more than 18,000 MPs, he is in the top 20 of all-time ACBL masterpoint holders.

Wolff was a member of the ACBL Bd of Dir representing Dist 16 1981-1992 and served as ACBL president 1987, chairman of the Board 1988. He served on the executive council of the World Bridge Federation starting in 1988 and was president of that organization 1992-94. He has also served as tournament recorder at NABCs and is the author of the ACBL Active Ethics program.

He has won nine world titles — Bermuda Bowl 1970, 71, 77, 83, 85, 87; World Mixed Tms 1972; Open Prs 1974; Open Tms 1988. He is the only player to have won world championships in four different categories. He placed second World Open Tms 1972, 80, 92; Bermuda Bowl 1973, 74, 75; 3rd in Rosenblum Tms 1978, 1982 and has had other high finishes in world events.

He won the Pan-American Invitational 1974, 76, 77; the USBC (Team Trials) 1983, 85, 87, 92, 93; Spingold 1969, 79, 82, 83, 89, 90, 93; Reisinger 1970, 78, 79, 88, 93; Vanderbilt 1971, 73; Mens BAM Tms 1972, 73, 84, 88; Mott-Smith Trophy 1973; GN Tms 1975, 77, 86; Fishbein Trophy 1979; Blue Ribbon Prs 1984. He placed second in Life Master Prs 1960, 68; Reisinger 1964; Spingold 1967, 70; Mens Tms 1969, 80; Vanderbilt 1981; Mens BAM Tms 1989; Open Swiss 1992.

Wolff wrote, programmed and developed *Bridge Bidding* programs for use on home computers, and developed the WOLFF SIGN-OFF Convention. He has been on three TV bridge programs and contributed to *Play Bridge With the Aces* and *Winning Bridge*, and the video *Secrets of Successful Bridge*. See also ACES TEAM.

WOLFSON, Don of Aurora OH, won Open Individual (Baird Trophy) 1960 and Keystone Conference Open Tms 1956.

WOLKIN, Philip (b. 1948) of Philadelphia PA, options trader, has won many regionals including Canadian Nat'l Mens Prs 1977; Dist 5 KO Tms 1978; All-American Mens Swiss 1979; Great Lakes Swiss, Labor Day Swiss 1980.

WOLNY, Henryk (b. 1947) of Slupsk, Poland, bridge professional and teacher. WBF World Life Master. Won World Teams 1984. Represented Poland in three other world championships and two zonal championships. Won many national titles.

WOMACK, Paul K. (b. 1935) of Bella Vista AR, bridge professional and consultant, retired director of internat'l sales for U.S. Army troop support command; Diamond Life Master with more than 25 regional wins including Summer secondary Open Prs 1972, Fall Speedball Prs 1993; St Louis Swiss 1982, Open Prs 1991, KO Tms 1991,

92, Sr Swiss 1992; Springfield Swiss 1986; Memphis Swiss 1987; Evansville Swiss 1987; Oconomowoc Swiss 1990; Kansas City Sr Prs 1991; Detroit Swiss 1992; Paducah KO Tms, Indianapolis KO Tms 1993.

WOMACK, Shawn Y. (b. 1961) of Irvine CA, manufacturers representative, graduate of U of California and Western State U School of Law; certified director; other interests include gourmet cooking, gardening, piano. Womack won Life Master Womens Prs 1992; North American Swiss, Womens BAM Tms 1993; North American Womens Swiss 1994; placed second Womens Prs 1993. Regional wins are Bridge Wk Midnight KO Tms 1991, KO Tms 1990, 91, Early Bird KO Tms, Prime Time KO Tms 1993; Dist 22 GN Tms 1991; Denver Open Prs 1992, BAM Tms 1993; Little Bridge Wk Open Prs, Womens Prs 1992; San Bernardino KO Tms 1993.

WONG, John P. (b. 1928) of Rowland Hts CA, born in China, formerly of Japan and Taiwan, computer specialist, bridge teacher; graduated Soochow U (China); was the first Life Master in Japan. Wong is a former vice-chairman of Japan Contract Bridge League and former editor of its publication. He represented Taiwan in the World Olympiad 1964 and represented Japan in the Far East Championships from 1958, winning Far East Open Prs 1961 and placing second in Open Tms 1958, 64. He won the Takamatsu Open Tms 1955, 56, 62; *Japan Times* Cup 1959, 60, 61, 63, Mixed Prs 1960; Master Individual 1961, Trial Prs 1962. ACBL regional wins include Pacific Southwest Open Prs 1966, Sr Prs 1993, 94; Los Angeles Winter Mens Swiss 1976, Sr Prs 1993; Bridge Wk Open Prs 1976, Sr Open Prs 1989, Charity Prs 1993; Riverside Open Prs 1992; Anaheim Sr Prs 1993; San Bernardino Sr Prs 1993, Sr Swiss 1994.

WONG, Kok Leong (b. 1925) of Petaling Jaya, Malaysia, retired oil executive. Represented Malaysia in one world championship and 10 zonal championships. National events include open teams.

WONG, Dr. Maurice (b. 1932) of Larchmont NY, professor of mathematics; Diamond Life Master; won Hartford Swiss 1980; Arlington Open Prs 1983; Port Chester Open Prs 1984, Secaucus Mens Swiss 1985, Stamford Open Prs 1986, 89; Lancaster Mens Swiss 1988; Hyannis Sr Swiss 1993.

WONG, Thomas (b. 1943 in China) of Singapore, engineer. President Singapore CBA since 1983. Represented Singapore in one world championship and two zonal championships. National wins include open teams once.

WOOD, Nadine K. (b. 1935) of Silver Spring MD, caterer, bridge club director, member ACBL Bd of Dir representing Dist 6; member ACBL Bd of Gov and served as chairman 1988-90; member ACBL Goodwill Committee. She has served as president of the Mid-Atlantic Bridge Conference 1990-92, president Washington BL 1983-86, tournament chairman of Summer NABCs 1984 and 1993, and as tournament chairman for Washington BL since 1980. Wood has represented ACBL internationally 1982, 86, 90. Diamond Life Master; won Womens Prs 1989, placed second Womens Swiss 1982, North American Swiss, Womens Prs 1985. She has won more than 30 regional events.

WOOD, Philip A. (b. 1921) of Richmond BC, ACBL national tournament director, a former baseball writer and statistician, Wood began his directing career in 1954. In 1968 he became the first Canadian to achieve the rating of national tournament director. He has served as tournament manager for District 18 since 1971. Wood also manages country club bridge activity in greater Vancouver, averaging more than 400 tables per month. When manual scoring was the norm, many considered Wood the fastest adder in the business. A former member of the RCAF, he was awarded the Distinguished Flying Cross in 1944. Won Inter-Mountain Mixed Prs 1966.

WOODARD, William F. (Woody) (b. 1947) of Lilburn GA, computer systems consultant, past president of Unit 115. Won Upper NY State Open Prs 1970, Swiss 1974; Mid-Atlantic KO Tms, Keystone Mens Prs 1973; New England Fall Open Prs, Canadian Nat'l Open Prs 1974; Fleur-de-lys Master Prs 1975; Capital Dist Fall Mens Swiss 1977.

WOODS, Jo (1899-1977) of Little Rock AR, bridge teacher and writer, first president of American Bridge Teachers' Association; wrote many books and booklets for bridge teachers and students including *At the Bridge Table* and *Little Green Book*.

WOODSON, William B. (1921-1989) of Charlotte NC, computer consultant, served as member of ACBL Bd of Dir 1973-79, president of Mid-Atlantic BA for two terms, president and treasurer of Unit 153. He was a special consultant to the ACBL in 1967, was awarded a Certificate of Service by the Board in 1968 and was elected to the South Carolina Bridge Hall of Fame. He is the inventor of WOODSON TWO-WAY NOTRUMP and author of *Woodson Two-Way Notrump* and *Woodson Electronic Bidding System*. Won Southeastern Individual 1950; Mid-Atlantic Fall Open Prs 1954, Master Prs 1961, Open Tms 1965; Fall secondary Swiss 1977.

WOODWORTH, Robert M. (Woody) (b. 1911) of St. Petersburg FL, attorney, bridge lecturer, teacher, writer; bridge columnist for *St. Petersburg Times* for 20 years and a contributor to bridge publications. Woodworth was special agent, Counter Intelligence Corps ETO in World War II. Life Master #219 and past president of the Florida Unit, was awarded a prize for bridge articles by the IBPA. Diamond Life Master; earned his 8000th masterpoint at age 80. Regional wins include Florida Mixed Prs 1960, 63, 72, KO Tms 1967, Life Master Prs 1974; Mexican Nat'l KO Tms 1978; Sun City Swiss 1980, 81, Open Prs 1982; Mid Atlantic Sr Swiss 1989; Jacksonville Sr. Swiss 1989.

WOOLDRIDGE, Jill H. (b. 1939) of Buffalo NY, IRS employee, graduated U of Florida and U of Rochester; editor of Unit 116 *Bridge Buff*; was 2nd in ACBL and 5th world-wide in Epson Prs 1991; won Buffalo Open Prs, Womens Tms; Syracuse Womens Prs; Rochester Womens Prs, Summer secondary KO Tms 1990, Toronto Mixed Prs 1990 (with 10-year-old son Joel).

WOOLDRIDGE, Joel P. (b. 1979) of Buffalo NY, student, won Toronto Mixed Prs 1990, Dist 5 NLM-NA Prs 1991. At the age of 11 years and 4 months, Wooldridge became the youngest player ever to achieve the rank of Life Master (Dec. 2, 1990). He was the 1990 ACBL *Rookie of the Year* with the second highest total ever and believed to be the youngest player to make the *Top 500*. He also won the Homer Shoop youth scholarship in 1990. See YOUNGEST LIFE MASTER.

WOOLES, Kris G. (b. 1950) of Christchurch, New Zealand, solicitor. WBF World Master. Represented New Zealand in three world championships and one zonal championship. 12 national wins include open teams three times.

WOOLSEY, Christopher R. (Kit) (b. 1943) of Kensington CA, systems analyst, WBF Life Master, won Rosenblum Tms 1986, placed 2nd 1982; second Bermuda Bowl 1989, 6th World Mixed Tms 1974, 12th World Open Prs 1978; represented ACBL in other world events 1982, 86, 90; placed second in USBC 1989. Woolsey, an ACBL Grand Life Master with more than 14,000 MPs, is in the top 50 of all-time masterpoint holders. He won Blue Ribbon Prs 1978, 75, 90; Mens BAM Tms 1978, 86, 89; GN Tms 1984, Mens Prs 1985; Lou Herman Trophy, Mens Swiss 1986; Open Prs 1987, 89; placed second Life Master Mens Prs 1971, 72; Mens Prs 1973, 74; GN Tms 1977; Spingold 1979, 81, 92; Reisinger 1980; Open Prs 1981; Vanderbilt 1992. He has also won the Cavendish Invitational Prs 1979 and numerous regionals. Author of *Modern Defensive Signals*, *Partnership Defense in Bridge*, *Matchpoints* and co-author of *Clobber Their Artificial Club*. See IBPA AWARDS.

WORK, Milton C. (Sept. 15, 1864 - June 27, 1934) was the outstanding American authority on auction bridge, a noted player and authority on whist and contract bridge. He was born in Philadelphia and took three degrees at the U of Pennsylvania.

From 1887 to 1917 Work practiced law in Philadelphia. In 1917 he took a leave of absence to tour the U.S. with Wilbur C. Whitehead, organizing bridge competitions and lecturing on bridge, to promote the sale of Liberty bonds. The success of the tour, coupled with the fact that his bridge books were already selling in large quantities, induced him to quit the practice of law and adopt bridge as a career.

Work's whist career began as president of the U of Pennsylvania's whist club where he organized and played in the first duplicate whist team-of-four match ever held between clubs (1881). He helped found the American Whist League (1893), and was captain of the Hamilton Club team of Philadelphia, which won several whist tournaments. Work's first book, *Whist of Today* (1895), was published at his own expense for a gift to friends, but it demonstrated the clarity of style for which his later books were so admired. He turned to bridge and then to auction bridge as those games became preeminent. His first book on auction bridge (1913) began a series that outsold all other bridge books by a wide margin until the appearance of Ely Culbertson's *Blue Book* in 1930. From 1917 through 1931, Work was acknowledged the greatest bridge authority, with stature equivalent to that of Cavendish in whist before him and Culbertson and Charles H. Goren in contract bridge after him. In 1965, he was elected to the Bridge Hall of Fame.

Work became a member of the laws committee of the Whist Club (New York) in 1909. He largely wrote and controlled the 1915 auction bridge laws, which revolutionized the scoring, and the 1917 laws, for which the contract bridge principle was first considered and rejected. He was 1927 Honorary Member of the American Bridge League and Honorary Chairman of its Laws Committee. He was president of the United States Bridge Association (1933-1934).

Work became a founder and chief editor of the earliest auction bridge magazines, the *Work-Whitehead Auction Bridge Bulletin* (1924-1926) and its successor, the *Auction Bridge Magazine* (1927-29). Assisted by Whitehead, he served as chief authority on the first series of bridge games broadcast on radio (1926-29). In 1928 his fame was so great that he was paid $7,000 per week to give brief lectures on bridge in the course of vaudeville presentations.

Work's considerable fortune was substantially lost in the stock market crashes of 1929-30, and he resumed some bridge activities from which he had retired. In 1931 he participated in the founding of Bridge Headquarters and the promulgation of the Official System, being chief architect of the system and principal author of its official books. As a player he was not highly rated by his peers, but in 1933-34 he resumed tournament play in contract bridge and won five consecutive sectional tournaments as a member of a team that included Goren, Olive Peterson, and Fred French.

WRIGHT, Lionel (b. 1953 in England) of Auckland, New Zealand. WBF World Master. Won WBF Continuous Pairs 1990. Represented New Zealand in five other world championships and five zonal championships. Seven national wins include open teams once.

WU, Chin-Hsiang (b. 1954) of Taipei, Taiwan, chemical engineer. WBF World Master. Far East champion 1986, 1989, Far East Open Pair champion 1986. Represented Taiwan in six world championships and three other Far East Championships, Won many national titles.

WU, Tiak Pong (b. 1938) of Singapore, trader. Represented Singapore in three zonal championships. National wins include open teams several times.

X

XIAOPING, Deng. see DENG, XIAOPING.

XU, Hongjun of Shanghai, China, technical employee. WBF World Master. Won Far East Teams 1991, second 1993. Represented China in three world championships and two other zonal championships. Won one national title.

Y

YAMADA, Akihiko (b. 1946) of Tokyo, Japan, bridge teacher. WBF World Master. Far East champion 1985. Represented Japan 1991 Bermuda Bowl and many other international events. Won 32 national team titles and 16 national open pair titles.

YANAGIYA, Kensuke (b. 1924) of Tokyo, Japan, foreign affairs officer. Former ambassador to Australia. In 1992, with Japan International Cooperation Agency.

JCBL president from 1991.

YAÑEZ, Luis Schenstrom (b. 1923) of Santa Cruz de la Sierra, Bolivia, and Buenos Aires, Argentina. Won 1971 Argentine Open Teams and several Bolivian national titles.

YANG, K.T. (b. 1933) of Manila, Philippines, marine exporter. Won Far East Pairs 1974. Represented Philippines in 8 zonal championships. National wins include open teams 6 times.

YANKO, Richard F. (b. 1939) of Scottsdale AZ, attorney, graduate of Michigan State U and Detroit College of Law (JD); past president and chairman of the Bd of Dir of Unit 137. Diamond Life Master, placed second GN Tms 1974; has won numerous regionals.

YAP, Florence of Makati, Philippines, interpreter. Won Far East Teams 1957, Far East Women's Teams 1979, 1982. Represented Philippines in three world championships and six other zonal championships. National wins include open teams four times.

YAP, Robert (b. 1919) of Makati, Philippines, manufacturer. Won Far East Teams 1957. Represented Philippines in three world championships and many zonal championships. Many national wins include open teams six times.

YARINGTON, Richard B. (Dick) (b. 1952) of Seattle WA, property manager and bridge teacher, graduate of U of Washington; Diamond Life Master with numerous regional wins including Oregon Trail Mixed Prs 1975, KO Tms 1981; Reno KO Tms 1983; Tacoma KO Tms 1987, 89, 91, Swiss 1991; Penticton Swiss, KO Tms 1988; Vancouver Mens Prs 1988, KO Tms 1992; Portland BAM Tms 1988; Dist 19 GN Tms 1989; Yakima KO Tms 1991.

YAVITZ, Jerome A. of Bay Harbor Island FL, real estate developer, won Master Mixed Tms 1974, placed second 1964.

YELTON, Carey M. Jr. (b. 1934) of Glencoe IL, financial consultant and restaurateur. Intercollegiate champion 1953, 54.

YI, Hougao of Beijing, China. Executive vice-president Chinese Bridge Association and its active administrator. NPC 1993 Bermuda Bowl team. Chief organizer 1995 Bermuda Bowl and Venice Cup in Beijing.

YIALIRAKIS, Dimitrios (b. 1931 in Crete) of Athens, Greece, official of Greek Public Water Company. His partnership with George Karlaftis was almost invincible in national events in the 60s and 70s. Common Market Senior Team champion 1991. Author-publisher in 1969 of an encyclopedia of natural bidding. Marathon runner.

YODER, Frank E. III (b. 1944) of Fort Wayne IN, realtor; regional wins include Champaign Master Prs 1980; All-American Mens Prs 1981; Midwest Spring Mens Swiss 1981.

YOMTOV, Bernard D. (Bernie) (b. 1949 in Germany) of Nashville TN, private investor, graduate of Vanderbilt

U; edited *Partnership Defense*, *Matchpoints* and *Dynamic Defense* and assisted in the editing of the 1980, 81 *World Championship Book*. Won Non-Life Master Mens Prs 1969; placed second GN Tms 1975; regional wins include Dist 10 GN Tms 1981, Zonal 1975, 81.

YOST, E. Lowell (b. 1922) of Wichita KS, manufacturing company president, WW II Naval pilot; placed second Life Master Mens Prs 1970.

YOUNG, Sally (Mrs. R. C.) (1906-1970) of Narberth PA, was one of the great woman players of all time. Life Master #17, the first woman player to earn Life Master status. Between 1937 and 1958, she set a record by winning the Womens Tms seven times and finishing second three times. Among her other successes were four wins in the Chicago Trophy (now the Reisinger); four wins in the Womens Prs; five wins in the Mixed Tms, and one each in the Fall Open and Mixed Prs. Young's win of the Chicago in 1947 was the only time it was won by a team of all women. The others on that team were Paula Bacher, Jane Jaeger and Kay Rhodes. During the late Thirties she was among the favorite partners of Charles Goren.

YU KHE SIONG, Margaret (b. 1908) of Manila, Philippines, Far East Women's champion 1967.

YUDIN, Mark E. (b. 1947) of Montreal, bridge teacher and tournament director, past president of the Montreal BL. Won Can-Am Open Prs 1975, Mens Prs 1977; Nat'l Capital Swiss 1975, Dist 1 GN Prs 1982. Co-developer of the Sectional-in-Clubs idea.

YUE, Dr. Wen Y. (b. 1918) of Excelsior MN, born in China, anesthesiologist, won Sr/Advanced Sr Master Prs 1972.

Z

ZABEL, Gunnar of Copenhagen, Denmark, civil engineer. Member of EBL Executive from 1973. As Danish Bridge League president 1969-75 initiated masterpoints and bridge in adult education while increasing membership 50%.

ZAGAR, Ivan (b. 1943) of Maribor, Slovenia, technician. Won 15 national titles. Expert chess and Go player.

ZANALDA, David (b. 1932) of Buenos Aires, Argentina, court official. WBF World Master. South American champion 1981. Represented Argentina in Bermuda Bowl 1981, in World Team Olympiad 1968, 1972, 1976. National wins include open teams 7 times and open pairs 3 times. Won Gabarret Cup 1970. Bridge correspondent for newspaper *La Nacion*.

ZANANIRI, Marcel (1915-1990) of Kuwait, formerly of Egypt, chemist. Represented Egypt in two world championships and was that country's leading player in the 60s and 70s. Won many national titles and contributed to bridge periodicals.

ZÁNKAY, Dr. Péter (b. 1919) of Budapest, Hungary, retired catering manager. His book *Bridge*, published in 1937, revived bridge in Hungary in the face of the Com-

munist regime which regarded bridge as a capitalist game. This book, and his later works, caused Hungarian players to adopt Standard American bidding, which became normal in Hungary, with Precision gaining some ground later.

ZAWISZA, Jerzy (1908-1986) of Wilmington DE, retired bridge club manager, placed second Mens Tms 1960.

ZECKHAUSER, Richard J. (b. 1940) of Cambridge MA, professor of political economy, PhD from Harvard; won Blue Ribbon Prs 1966; placed second Mens Tms 1968; won Intercollegiate Championships 1961, Marcus Cup 1963; has had numerous other regional wins starting in the mid-Sixties and continuing into the Nineties.

ZEN, Derek W.P. (b. 1952) of Hong Kong, civil engineer. WBF World Master. Won Far East Open Teams 1975. Represented Hong Kong in three world championships and five other Far East Championships. National wins include open teams and open pairs.

ZENKEL, Sabine (b. 1965) of Germany, formerly of Chicago IL, options trader; WBF World Master. Zenkel has represented Germany internationally, placed 2nd Venice Cup 1993, 5th Venice Cup 1991, 7th World Womens Prs 1986, 11th World Womens Tms 1988. She also competed Geneva 1990, Salsomaggiore 1992. She won European Womens Tm Championship 1989 (this was the first time a German team ever won a European Team championship) (runner-up 1991); German Nat'l Womens Prs 1988, German Grand Nat'l Tms 1989, German Nat'l Open Tms 1992. Zenkel broke the late Jeremy Flint's record of becoming an ACBL Life Master in 11 weeks by three weeks; she won the first NABC event entered -- the Life Master Womens Prs 1989. She also won the North American Womens Swiss 1990 and the Life Master Womens Prs again in 1993; placed second Life Master Womens Prs 1992, Mixed Prs 1993; and has won more than 25 regional championships. She co-authored with Ron Andersen *Preempts A to Z* and has contributed to several international bridge publications.

ZEVE, Vic D. (1899-1985) of Wilton Manors FL, retired mortgage broker, won Open Prs 1952, Mens Tms 1958; served as president of Dist 9 in the Seventies; author of *Method Bidding*.

ZHANG, Yalan (b. 1957) of Guangzhou, China, company employee. WBF World Master. Third Venice Cup 1991. Won Far East Women's Teams, 1986, 1991, 1993 (same as Gu Ling) second 1987, 1988. Also represented China in 5 world championships and 3 other zonal championships. Won many national titles.

ZHOU, Jiahong of Shanghai, China, technical employee. WBF World Master. Won Far East Teams 1991. Represented China in two world championships and one other zonal championships. Won four national titles.

ZHU, Xiaoying (b. 1957) of Beijing, China, teacher. WBF World Master. Won Far East Women's Teams 1986, second 1987, 1988. Also represented China in 3 world championships. Winner of two zonal championships. Won four national titles.

ZIA, Mahmood. see MAHMOOD, ZIA.

ZIADIE, Victor (b. 1954) of Kingston, Jamaica, attorney. Won four CAC titles including Open Teams 1980, 1982. Represented Jamaica in one world championship and two zonal championships. Leading Jamaican masterpoint winner 1990, 1991. Caribbean badminton champion and comic book collector.

ZILIC, Mrs. Virginia A. (b. 1939 in Venezuela) of Houston TX, bridge club director and bridge teacher, co-chairman 1978 Houston NABC; placed second in North American Swiss 1978; won MO Valley Mixed Prs 1971; TX Fall Womens Prs 1971, Swiss 1974; TX Mid-Winter KO Tms 1973; Corpus Christi Swiss 1978.

ZILIC, John P. (b. 1939) of Houston TX, bridge professional, bridge club owner\manager, ACBL certified teacher, director and insurance underwriter; graduate of Northwestern U; has served more than 25 years for Dist. 16 and Unit 174 including 1978 Houston NABC co-chairman; an ACBL Grand Life Master with more than 12,000 MPs, won Open Prs 1966, 94; North American Swiss 1988; placed second in Swiss Tms 1978, Mens Swiss 1983; won more than 50 regionals.

ZIMMERMAN, James E. (b. 1942) of Shaker Hts OH, stockbroker/financial adviser, former attorney; graduate of Denison U and Case Western Reserve Law School (JD). Member ACBL Bd of Dir representing Dist 5, ACBL president 1981, chairman of ACBL Bd of Dir in 1982, ACBL representative to the WBF since 1983 and vice president since 1986. He also served as president of the Northern Ohio Unit 125 in 1973. As president of ACBL he led a group of ACBL members to the first major bridge tournament on Chinese soil in Shanghai. Zimmerman has represented ACBL in world play 1978, 82, 86, 90. ACBL Grand Life Master with more than 10,000 MPs; won Mixed Prs 1981, placed second in Life Master Mens Prs 1973, Master Mixed Tms 1975. He was npc of the Venice Cup winners 1984 and has more than 150 regional wins to his credit.

ZIPPERT, Ira (b. 1922) of Fort Lee NJ, business executive, graduated CCNY; district director for Dist 24 since 1984, served three terms as president of Unit 155, twice for Nassau/Suffolk BA before it became Unit 242; member of the ACBL Goodwill Committee.

ZIRINSKY, Victor J. (b. 1920) of Hong Kong, merchant. Won Far East Open Teams 1959, represented Hong Kong on other occasions. Co-founder of Far East Bridge Federation and Hong Kong CBA. Originator of ZIRINSKY FORMULA and some bidding conventions.

ZLOTOW, Tim (b. 1963) of Moscow, Russia, businessman. Represented Soviet Union, or C.I.S., in two world championships and one zonal championship. National wins include open teams once and open pairs once.

ZMUDZINSKI, Adam (b. 1956) of Katowice, Poland, electronic engineer and bridge trainer. WBF World Master. Second Bermuda Bowl 1991. Won European Teams 1989. Represented Poland in four other world championships and one other zonal championships. Won many national titles.

ZOLLER, Raymond G. (Ray) of Prescott AZ, won Life Master Mens Prs 1966. A panelist for *The Bridge World* Master Solvers' Club and *You Be the Judge* for many years. Zoller won numerous regionals including a BAM Team in which his team won 26 of 28 boards.

ZORLU, Nafiz (b. 1954) of Izmir, Turkey, businessman. Represented Turkey in two world championships and four zonal championships. Eight national wins include open teams four times.

ZOTOS, Loukas (b. 1951) of Athens, Greece. WBF World Master. Represented Greece in 1988 World Team Olympiad, finishing fifth, the best performance ever by a Greek team. Represented Greece regularly in junior and senior international events 1974-91. 15 national wins include open team 10 times and open pairs four times.

ZOUGHEB, Loula De, formerly Gordon (1918-1993) of Geneva, Switzerland. WBF World Life Master. Won World Women's Teams 1960. World Mixed Pairs 1974. Won many national titles in Egypt, Lebanon and Switzerland.

ZUCCHELLI, Sergio (b. 1934) of Bologna, Italy, pharmaceutical representative. Won Bermuda Bowl 1975, Sunday Times 1974. During the 1975 Bermuda Bowl he was accused of illicit communication through foot signals. See BERMUDA INCIDENT.

ZUCKERBERG, Debbie (b. 1968) of New York City, bridge teacher and professional player; member of the Junior Corps; served as a member Greater NYBA board and Education Liason to the ACBL. Zuckerberg won the World Junior Championship 1991, bronze medalist 1993. Zuckerberg won Cavendish Invitational Tms 1993 and was NYC Player of the Year 1992. Her regional wins include Manchester Swiss 1987, 88; New York KO Tms 1987; Rye Swiss 1989, Open Prs 1991; Parsippany Swiss 1989; Rye NY Jr Regional Open Prs, Swiss 1990, Dist 24 GN Tms 1992.

ZUMARAN, Ricardo (b. 1930) of Montevideo, Uruguay, farmer. Second South American Teams 1962. Represented Uruguay regularly since 1959 and has won 44 national titles.

ZWAAN, René (b. 1946) of Amsterdam, The Netherlands, bridge teacher and writer. Third World Teams 1980, represented The Netherlands in two European Championships. Won National Open Teams 1981. Columnist, contributor to *Bridge*.

APPENDIX I
NORTH AMERICAN CHAMPIONSHIPS
Spring Championships

VANDERBILT KNOCKOUT TEAMS. This originally was a double elimination Open Team event scored by international matchpoints; usually nine or ten sessions. In 1966 the double elimination method was replaced by three qualifying sessions (subsequently reduced to two), followed by single elimination knockout matches. The preliminary qualifying sessions were dropped in 1970. In 1928 it was scored by Board-a-Match, hence the tie.

1928	1-2.	Ralph R. Richards, Gratz M. Scott, Edwin A. Wetzlar, Wilbur C. Whitehead
	1-2.	Abraham Brown, Mrs. Sidney Lovell, Caroline Taylor, Nils M. Wester
1929	1.	Michael T. Gottlieb, Lee Langdon, Jean P. Mattheys, Harry B. Raffel
	2.	Ralph J. Leibenderfer, Gratz M. Scott, Edwin A. Wetzlar, Wilbur C. Whitehead
1930	1.	Ely Culbertson, Josephine Culbertson, Theodore A. Lightner, Waldemar K. von Zedtwitz
	2-3.	Winfield S. Liggett, Walter Malowan, George Reith, Howard Schenken
	2-3.	H. Huber Boscowitz, Oswald Jacoby, Willard S. Karn, P. Hal Sims
1931	1.	David Burnstine, Oswald Jacoby, Willard S. Karn, P. Hal Sims
	2.	Walter Malowan, Jean P. Mattheys, Howard Schenken, Sherman Stearns
1932	1.	Willard S. Karn, P. Hal Sims, Harold S. Vanderbilt, Waldemar K. von Zedtwitz
	2.	David Burnstine, Richard L. Frey, Charles S. Lochridge, Howard Schenken
1933	1.	Phil Abramsohn, Benjamin Feuer, Francis A. Rendon, Sydney Rusinow
	2.	A. Mitchell Barnes, Richard L. Frey, Sam Fry, Jr., Louis H. Watson
1934	1	David Burnstine, Richard L. Frey, Michael Gottlieb, Oswald Jacoby, Howard Schenken
	2.	H. Huber Boscowitz, Charles H. Goren, Charles S. Lochridge, Johnny Rau
1935	1.	David Burnstine, Michael T. Gottlieb, Oswald Jacoby, Howard Schenken, Sherman Stearns
	2.	Sam Fry, Jr., Edward Hymes, Jr., Merwyn D. Maier, Louis H. Watson
1936	1.	Phil Abramsohn, Irving Epstein, Harry J. Fishbein, Fred D. Kaplan
	2.	Walter Beinicke, Charles H. Goren, Lee Langdon, Jean P. Mattheys
1937	1.	David Burnstine, Oswald Jacoby, Merwyn D. Maier, Howard Schenken, Sherman Stearns
	2.	B. Jay Becker, Theodore A. Lightner, Charles S. Lochridge, Harold S. Vanderbilt, Waldemar K. von Zedtwitz
1938	1.	David Burnstine, Oswald Jacoby, Merwyn D. Maier, Howard Schenken, Sherman Stearns
	2.	B. Jay Becker, Edward Hymes, Jr., Theodore A. Lightner, Charles S. Lochridge, Waldemar K. von Zedtwitz
1939	1.	Melville Alexander, Sigmund Dornbusch, Syl Gintell, Lee Hazen, Harry B. Raffel
	2.	Wingate Bixby, Theodore A. Lightner, Robert A. McPherran, Mrs. S. W. Peck
1940	1.	Edward Hymes, Jr., Charles S. Lochridge, Robert A. McPherran, Harold S. Vanderbilt, Waldemar K. von Zedtwitz
	2.	Al Brodsky, Louis Lipschitz, Herbert Rosenzweig, Alexander Schultz
1941	1.	John R. Crawford, Myron Fuchs, Robert A. McPherran, Sherman Stearns
	2.	B. Jay Becker, Oswald Jacoby, Theodore A. Lightner, Merwyn D. Maier, Howard Schenken
1942	1.	Lester R. Bachner, Sigmund Dornbusch, Richard L. Frey, Lee Hazen, Samuel M. Stayman
	2.	Sam Fry, Jr., Benedict Jarmel, George Rapee, Helen Sobel
1943	1.	Harry Fagin, Harry J. Fishbein, Fred D. Kaplan, Alvin Roth, Tobias Stone
	2.	Phil Abramsohn, Morrie Elis, E. O. Keller, Charles E. Van Vleck, Waldemar K. von Zedtwitz
1944	1.	B. Jay Becker, Charles H. Goren, Sidney Silodor, Helen Sobel
	2.	Richard L. Frey, Lee Hazen, Charles S. Lochridge, George Rapee, Samuel M. Stayman
1945	1.	B. Jay Becker, Charles H. Goren, Sidney Silodor, Helen Sobel
	2.	Edward Hymes, Jr., Theodore A. Lightner, Howard Schenken, Samuel M. Stayman, Waldemar K. von Zedtwitz
1946	1.	John R. Crawford, Oswald Jacoby, George Rapee, Howard Schenken, Samuel M. Stayman
	2.	Samuel Katz, Bertram Lebhar, Jr., Peter A. Leventritt, Simon Rossant, Waldemar K. von Zedtwitz
1947	1.	David B. Clarren, Harry Feinberg, Harry J. Fishbein, Larry Hirsch, Joseph E. Low
	2.	Lee Hazen, Samuel Katz, Bertram Lebhar, Jr., Peter Leventritt
1948	1.	Robert Appleyard, Jay T. Feigus, William M Lichtenstein, Harry Sonnenblick, Albert Weiss
	2.	Ambrose Casner, Herman H. Goldberg, Fred Hirsch, Mrs. Ira Strasser, Albert Wolfe
1949	1.	Morrie Elis, Harry J. Fishbein, Lee Hazen, Larry Hirsch, Charles S. Lochridge
	2.	B. Jay Becker, Myron Field, Charles H. Goren, Oswald Jacoby, Helen Sobel
1950	1.	John R. Crawford, George Rapee, Howard Schenken, Sidney Silodor, Samuel M. Stayman
	2.	B. Jay Becker, Myron Field, Charles H. Goren, Helen Sobel
1951	1.	B. Jay Becker, John R. Crawford, George Rapee, Samuel M. Stayman
	2.	Barry Crane, Jack Hancock, Emanuel Hochfield, Gloria Turner, Hortense Evans
1952	1.	Ned Drucker, Irvin Kass, Sidney Mandell, Milton Moss, Jesse Sloan
	2.	B. Jay Becker, John R. Crawford, George Rapee, Howard Schenken, Samuel M. Staymen
1953	1.	Richard Kahn, Edgar Kaplan, Peter A. Leventritt, William V. Lipton, Ruth Sherman
	2.	Myron Field, Charles H. Goren, Alvin Roth, Sidney Silodor, Helen Sobel
1954	1.	Dr. Kalman Apfel, Francis P. Begley, Ned Drucker, Sidney Mandell, Milton Moss
	2.	Morrie Elis, Stanley Fenkel, Simon Rossant, Peggy Solomon, Charles S. Solomon
1955	1.	B. Jay Becker, John R. Crawford, George Rapee, Howard Schenken, Sidney Silodor
	2.	Charles H. Goren, Boris Koytchou, Peter A. Leventritt, Harold A. Ogust, Helen Sobel
1956	1.	B. Jay Becker, John R. Crawford, George Rapee, Howard Schenken, Sidney Silodor
	2.	Leonard Hess, Jane Jaeger, Lewis M. Jaeger, William M. Lichtenstein, Joseph E. Low
1957	1.	B. Jay Becker, John R. Crawford, George Rapee, Howard Schenken, Sidney Silodor
	2.	Rudolf Bortstiber, Raoul Lichtenstein, Ozzie J. Ray, Moe Rubenfeld
1958	1.	Harry J. Fishbein, Say Fry, Jr., Leonard B. Harmon, Lee Hazen, Ivar Stakgold
	2.	Ralph Hirschberg, Richard Kahn, Edgar Kaplan, Norman Kay, Alfred Sheinwold, Charles J. Solomon
1959	1.	B. Jay Becker, John R. Crawford, Norman Kay, George Rapee, Sidney Silodor, Tobias Stone
	2.	Charles H. Goren, Paul Hodge, Peter A. Leventritt, Harold A. Ogust, Howard Schenken,

Helen Sobel

1960 1. John R. Crawford, Norman Kay, Sidney Silodor, Tobias Stone
2. Russell Arnold, Edith Kemp, Robert Reynolds, William Seamon, Albert Weiss, Waldemar K. von Zedtwitz

1961 1. Charles Coon, Robert F. Jordan, Eric R. Murray, Arthur G. Robinson
2. Ollie Adams, Harold B. Guiver, Eddie Kantar, Marshall Miles, Ron Von der Porten

1962 1. Larry Kolker, Carolyn Levitt, Jerry Levitt, Garrett Nash, George de Runtz
2. Charles H. Goren, Boris Koytchou, Peter A. Leventritt, Harold A. Ogust, Howard Schenken, Helen Sobel

1963 1. Harold Harkavy, Edith Kemp, Alvin Roth, Clifford Russell, William Seamon, Albert Weiss
2. Harold B. Guiver, Lewis L. Mathe, Erik Paulsen, Ron Von der Porten, Edward O. Taylor

1964 1. Robert D. Hamman, Eddie Kantar, Donald P. Krauss, Peter A. Leventritt, Lewis L. Mathe, Howard Schenken
2. B. Jay Becker, Ivan Erdos, Dorothy Hayden, Kelsey Petterson, Helen Portugal, Morris Portugal

1965 1. Philip Feldesman, John Fisher, James Jacoby, Oswald Jacoby, Ira S. Rubin, Albert Weiss
2. Robert F. Jordan, Edgar Kaplan, Norman Kay, Boris Koytchou, George Rapee, Arthur G. Robinson

1966 1. Philip Feldesman, Robert D. Hamman, Sami R. Kehela, Lewis L. Mathe, Ira S. Rubin
2. Bill Eisenberg, Ivan Erdos, Bobby Goldman, Leonard B. Harmon, Tobias Stone

1967 1. James Jacoby, Michael S. Lawrence, Lewis L. Mathe, G. Robert Nail, Ron Von der Porten, Lew Stansby
2. Sidney H. Lazard, Peter A. Leventritt, Paul Levitt, George Rapee, Howard Schenken

1968 1. Robert F. Jordan, Edgar Kaplan, Norman Kay, Arthur G. Robinson, William S. Root, Alvin Roth
2. Robert D. Hamman, Eddie Kantar, Ira S. Rubin, Gerald J. Westheimer

1969 1. Gerald F. Hallee, Paul Soloway, John Swanson, Richard Walsh
2. Philip Feldesman, Victor Mitchell, Ira S. Rubin, Samuel M. Stayman, Tobias Stone, Gerald J. Westheimer

1970 1. Edgar Kaplan, Norman Kay, Sami R. Kehela, Sidney H. Lazard, Eric R. Murray, George Rapee
2. Bill Eisenberg, Bobby Goldman, Robert D. Hamman, James Jacoby, Michael S. Lawrence, Bobby Wolff

1971 1. Bill Eisenberg, Bobby Goldman, Robert D. Hamman, James Jacoby, Michael S. Lawrence, Bobby Wolff
2. Chuck F. Burger, Eddie Kantar, Kyle Larsen, Ron Von der Porten, Ira S. Rubin, Paul Soloway

1972 1. Steven Altman, Eugene Neiger, Thomas M. Smith, Alan Sontag, Joel H. Stuart, Peter Weichsel
2. Jack Blair, Fred Hamilton, Howard M. Perlman, Paul Soloway

1973 1. Mark E. Blumenthal, Bobby Goldman, Robert D. Hamman, Michael S. Lawrence, Bobby Wolff
2. Larry Cohen, Bill Eisenberg, Eddie Kantar, Dr. Richard H. Katz, Bud Reinhold

1974 1. David M. Crossley, Robert E. Crossley, Eric Kokish, Joseph Silver
2. Ron E. Andersen, Mark D. Feldman, Stephen Goldstein, Merle Tom, Kathie Wei

1975 1. Roger Bates, Larry Cohen, Dr. Richard H. Katz, John Mohan, George Rosenkranz
2. Richard Freeman, Alvin Roth, Clifford Russell, Alan Sontag, Stan Tomchin, Peter Weichsel

1976 1. Roger Bates, Larry Cohen, Dr. Richard H. Katz, John Mohan, George Rosenkranz
2. Malcolm Brachman, Bill Eisenberg, Bobby Goldman, Eddie Kantar, Mike Passell, Paul Soloway

1977 1. Mike Becker, Mark E. Blumenthal, Fred Hamilton, Michael E. Lawrence, Ron Rubin, John Swanson

2. Ron E. Andersen, Gerald Caravelli, Hugh C. MacLean, Milt Rosenberg, Kathie Wei

1978 1. Malcolm Brachman, Bobby Goldman, Eddie Kantar, Bill Eisenberg, Mike Passell, Paul Soloway
2. Mike Becker, Lou Bluhm, George Rosenkranz, Ron Rubin, Thomas K. Sanders

1979 1. Lou Bluhm, Richard Freeman, Mark Lair, Clifford Russell, Thomas K. Sanders, Eddie Wold
2. Ron E. Andersen, Dave Berkowitz, Jeff Meckstroth, Judi Radin, Kathie Wei

1980 1. Russ Arnold, Robert Levin, Jeff Meckstroth, Bud Reinhold, Eric Rodwell
2. Ron E. Andersen, Mark Feldman, Eric Kokish, Peter Nagy

1981 1. B. Jay Becker, Michael Becker, Edgar Kaplan, Norman Kay, Ron Rubin
2. Ira Corn, Robert D. Hamman, Fred Hamilton, Ira Rubin, Alan Sontag, Peter Weischsel, Bobby Wolff

1982 1. James Jacoby, Jeff Meckstroth, Mike Passell, Eric Rodwell, George Rosenkranz, Eddie Wold
2. Marty Bergen, Mark Cohen, Jerry Goldfein, Warren Rosner, Luella Slaner

1983 1. Bill Root, Richard Pavlicek, Norman Kay, Edgar Kaplan
2. Eddie Kantar, Bill Eisenberg, Fred Hamilton, Jim Cayne, Alan Sontag

1984 1. Chip Martel, Lew Stansby, Hugh Ross, Peter Pender
2. Cliff Russell, Robert Levin, Curtis Smith, Peter Nagy, Dave Berkowitz, Harold Lilie

1985 1. Eric Rodwell, Jeff Meckstroth, Ron Rubin, Mike Lawrence, Michael Becker, Peter Weichsel
2. Barry Crane, Bobby Nail, Dan Morse, Ira Chorush, Tom Sanders, John Sutherlin

1986 1. Edgar Kaplan, Norman Kay, Bill Root, Richard Pavlicek
2. Jim Whitaker, Chris Compton, Ira Corush, Bart Bramley, Lou Bluhm

1987 1. Peter Pender, Peter Boyd, Lew Stansby, Hugh Ross, Steve Robinson, Chip Martel
2. Jack Schwencke, Drew Casen, Jim Krekorian, Jim Becker, Howard Chandross

1988 1. Eddie Kantar, Alan Sontag, John Mohan, Roger Bates
2. Dave Berkowitz, Billy Cohen, Ron Smith, Zia Mahmood

1989 1. Ron Rubin, Michael Becker, Bart Bramley, Robert Levin, Lou Bluhm, Peter Weichsel
2. Eddie Kantar, Alan Sontag, Dan Rotman, Bill Eisenberg, Larry Cohen, Cliff Russell

1990 1. Dan Morse, John Sutherlin, Michael Kamil, Ron Gerard, Tom Sanders, Bill Pollack
2. Zia Mahmood, Michael Rosenberg, Seymon Deutsch, Dave Berkowitz, Larry N. Cohen, Marty Bergen

1991 1. Steve Robinson, Peter Boyd, Kit Woolsey, Ed Manfield
2. Zia Mahmood, Mike Rosenberg, Seymon Deutsch, Eric Rodwell, Jeff Meckstroth

1992 1. Andy Goodman, John Mohan, Roger Bates, John Schermer, Neil Chambers
2. Steve Robinson, Peter Boyd, Kit Woolsey, Neil Silverman, Chip Martel, Lew Stansby

1993 1. Howard Weinstein, Peter Nagy, Dan Morse, John Sutherlin, Tommy Sanders, Russ Arnold
2. Cliff Russell, Sam Lev, Dave Berkowitz, Bjorn Fallenius, Mats Nilsland, Larry N. Cohen

1994 1. Seymon Deutsch, Gaylor Kasle, Michael Rosenberg, Zia Mahmood, Chip Martel, Lew Stansby
2. Ron Gerard, George Steiner, Edgar Kaplan, Norman Kay, Sidney Lazard

NORTH AMERICAN PAIRS FLIGHT A.

This is a grassroots event, with the first stage conducted strictly at the club level. Qualifiers then advance to the Unit competition, and the qualifiers advance to the District finals. Two pairs qualify at the District level for the North American final, which is held just prior to the Spring North American Championships.

1979	1.	Arthur Moore, Eric Robinson
	2.	Steve Landen, Larry Mori
1980	1.	Bob Feller, Jeffrey Hall
	2.	Larry N. Cohen, Ron Gerard
1981	1.	Helen Blakey, Robert Blakey
	2.	Mark Feldman, Chip Martel
1982	1.	Bill Nuttig, Ivan Scope
	2.	Richard Pavlicek, Cliff Russell
1983	1.	John Griscom, Jim Felts
	2.	Ron Gerard, Stephen Sanborn
1984	1.	Steve Sion, Harold Stengel
	2.	Marty Bergen, Larry N. Cohen
1985	1.	Peter Boyd, Steve Robinson
	2.	Hugh Ross, Peter Pender
1986	1.	Drew Cannell, G. Sekhar
	2.	Craig Cordes, Tom Daniel
1987	1.	Jan Janitschke, Dick Reed
	2.	Ron Sukoneck, Judi Cody
1988	1.	Jan Martel, Chip Martel
	2.	Mark Cohen, Stasha Cohen
1989	1.	David Caslan, Dennis Clerkin
	2.	Bobby Nail, Dan Morse
1990	1.	Sidney Lazard, Jack La Noue
	2.	Mark Stein, Boris Baran
1991	1.	Mark Stein, Boris Baran
	2.	Pratap Rajadhyaksha, Steve Landen
1992	1.	Jim Krekorian, Rick Zucker
	2-3.	Joe Jabon, Harry Steiner
	2-3.	Howard Weiner, Robert Crafton
1993	1.	James Griffin, Kenneth Schutze
	2.	Iftikar Baque, Mitch Aunitz
1994	1.	James Griffin, Kenneth Schutze
	2.	Ralph Cohen, Reece Rogers

NORTH AMERICAN PAIRS FLIGHT B. A
grass-roots event conducted in the same way as Flight A — limited to players with 1500 masterpoints.

1992	1.	Peter Worley, Kevin Young
	2.	Kathie Blumenthal, Patricia Goldfein
1993	1.	Robert Sewell, Paul Janicki
	2.	Lawrence Gibbons, Gregory Jecker
1994	1.	Brendan Dempsey, Ian Crowe
	2.	Jack Kilby, Ernest Lambertsen

NORTH AMERICAN PAIRS FLIGHT C. A
grass-roots event conducted in the same way as Flight A -- open only to non-Life Masters.

1987	1-2.	Bill Thomas, David Deaderick
	1-2.	Bernard Pollack, Leo Austern
1988	1.	Brad Moss, Aaron Silverstein
	2.	Geoffrey O'Connor, Charles Bilick
1989	1.	Warren King, Jeffrey Brown
	2.	Sylvian Descoteauz, Guy Belisle
1990	1.	Philip Leung, Moske Harel
	2.	Deborah Hart, Nate Ward
1991	1.	Eric Greco, Philip Greco
	2.	Bruce Graff, Steve Castellino
1992	1.	Gail Joelson, Alan Kasner
	2.	J. Greg Fowler, Don Herring
1993	1.	Mark Michele, Everett Boyer
	2.	Gabrida Rabiega, Leszek Rabiega
1994	1.	Weizhong Bao, Jingdong Guo
	2.	Duane Tilden, Grace Jeklin

OPEN PAIRS. This four-session event consisting of two qualifying sessions and two final sessions is contested for the SILODOR TROPHY. It became Open Pairs I in 1992.

1958	1.	Leonard B. Harmon, Ivar Stakgold
	2.	Alvin Roth, Tobias Stone
1959	1.	Lewis L. Mathe, Edward O. Taylor
	2.	Harry J. Fishbein, Charles J. Solomon
1960	1.	Robert F. Jordan, Alvin Roth
	2.	Carol Sanders, Thomas K. Sanders

1961	1.	Mark Hodges, Hampton Hume
	2.	Jack Denny, John E. Simon
1962	1.	Robert F. Jordan, Arthur G. Robinson
	2.	Michael N. Michaels, Mike Shuman
1963	1.	Norman Kay, Sidney Silodor
	2.	Daniel Rotman, Ivar Stakgold
1964	1.	Barry Crane, Oswald Jacoby
	2.	Ivan Erdos, Lewis L. Mathe
1965	1.	John Biddle, James P. Wisemiller
	2.	Ivan Erdos, Tobias Stone
1966	1.	Edgar Kaplan, Norman Kay
	2.	Alvin Roth, William Root
1967	1.	Harvey Cohen, Maury Genud
	2.	Philip Feldesman, Lewis L. Mathe
1968	1.	Ronald Blau, Richard Spero
	2.	Harry F. Fishbein, Charles J. Solomon
1969	1.	Richard Freedman, James L. Mathis
	2.	David Sachs, Sue Sachs
1970	1.	Barry Crane, Dr. John Fisher
	2.	Gerald L. Michaud, G. Robert Nail
1971	1-2.	Barry Crane, Dr. John Fisher
	1-2.	Joan Remey, Vincent Remey
1972	1-2.	Barry Crane, Dr. John Fisher
	1-2.	Matt Granovetter, Merle Tom
1973	1.	Michael Hoffman, Jack Rhatigan
	2.	Charlie Peres, Daniel Rotman
1974	1.	Barry Crane, Dr. John Fisher
	2.	Ron E. Andersen, Hugh C. MacLean
1975	1.	Garey Hayden, Daniel Hyland
	2.	Don Piafsky, Dave Saltsman
1976	1.	Terry Hause, Ernest Ivey
	2.	Barry Crane, Dr. John Fisher
1977	1.	Barry Crane, Peter Rank
	2.	John Ashton, Troy Horton
1978	1.	Robert Levin, Mike Passell
	2.	Marty Arndt, Thomas Peters
1979	1	Jeff Meckstroth, Eric Rodwell
	2.	Larry N. Cohen, Dan Zirker
1980	1.	Paul J. Lewis, Michael Schreiber
	2.	Jim Robison, Stelios Touchtidis
1981	1.	Dan Gertsman, Marc Nathan
	2.	Ed Manfield, Kit Woolsey
1982	1.	Gerald Caravelli, V. Craig Janitschke
	2.	Dan Gertsman, Marc Nathan
1983	1.	Barry Crane, Mike Passell
	2.	Dave Berkowitz, Dan Gerstman
1984	1.	Lou Bluhm, Bart Bramley
	2.	Barry Crane, Gerald Caravelli
1985	1.	Jim Robison, Joey Silver
	2.	John Roberts, Dave Berkowitz
1986	1.	Lew Stansby, Ralph Katz
	2.	Robb Gordon, John Rengstorff
1987	1.	Ed Manfield, Kit Woolsey
	2.	Lyle Poe, Steve Carton
1988	1.	Ron Rubin, Michael Becker
	2.	Bob Hamman, Paul Lewis
1989	1.	Kit Woolsey, Ed Manfield
	2.	Ed Nagy, Jeff Polisner
1990	1.	Don Campbell, Barry Harper
	2.	Randy Joyce, Glenn Lublin
1991	1.	Ken Cohen, Bob Thomas
	2.	Jo Anna Stansby, Lew Stansby
		(became Open Pairs I)
1992	1.	Bernie Miller, Mike Lucas
	2.	Geoff Hampson, Mark Molson
1993	1.	Russ Ekeblad, Peter Weichsel
	2.	Richard Swartz, Drew Casen
1994	1.	Lloyd Arvedon, Allan Falk
	2.	Michael Rosenberg, Zia Mahmood

OPEN PAIRS II, formerly MEN'S PAIRS. This
four-session event consisting of two qualifying rounds and two final rounds is contested for the WERNHER TROPHY. From 1969 through 1971 it was contested as a three-session championship. In 1992 the event became Open Pairs II instead of Men's Pairs.

1934	1.	David Burnstine, Oswald Jacoby
	2.	Morrie Elis, George Kennedy
1935	1.	Edward M. Cook, Jr., Fred French
	2.	Charles H. Goren, Louis H. Watson
1936	1.	Dr. Richard H. Ecker, Fred D. Kaplan

	2.	Bertram Lebhar, Jr., Samuel Katz
1937	1.	Edward M. Cook, Jr., John C. Kunkle
	2.	Philip Abramsohn, Morrie Elis
1938	1.	B. Jay Becker, Charles H. Goren
	2.	Morrie Elis, Waldemar K. von Zedtwitz
1939	1.	John R. Crawford, Oswald Jacoby
	2.	Henry Chanin, Morrie Elis
1940	1.	Merwyn D. Maier, Robert A. McPherran
	2.	Morrie Elis, Harry J. Fishbein
1941	1.	Joseph E. Low, Simon Rossant
	2.	Joseph Davis, Sidney Silodor
1942	1.	Robert von Engel, Aaron Goodman
	2.	Murray Gross, Dr. William Lipton
1943	1.	Charles H. Goren, Charles J. Solomon
	2.	Dr. Richard H. Ecker, Jr., Fred D. Kaplan
1944	1.	Sigmund Dornbusch, Herman Goldberg
	2.	Ambrose Casner, Ralph Hirschberg
1945	1.	Sylvester Gintell, Lee Hazen
	2.	George Rapee, Samuel M. Stayman
1946	1.	A. Mitchell Barnes, Waldemar K. von Zedtwitz
	2.	Lewis A. Bernard, Jr., Frank Weisbach
1947	1.	Sol Mogal, Tobias Stone
	2.	Morrie Elis, Morris Portugal
1948	1.	Fred Hirsch, Samuel Katz
	2.	Lewis A. Bernard, Jr., Harold Feldstein
1949	1.	Charles H. Goren, Oswald Jacoby
	2.	G. Robert Nail, Joseph G. Ripstra
1950	1.	Phillip A. Briggs, A. Richard Revell
	2.	George Rapee, Sidney Silodor
1951	1.	Milton Q. Ellenby, Emanuel Hochfield
	2.	Clifford Bishop, Alexander Nusinoff
1952	1.	Arthur C. Grau, William A. Rosen
	2.	Harold Harkavy, Tobias Stone
1953	1.	Harold Harkavy, William Root
	2.	John R. Crawford, Waldemar K. von Zedtwitz
1954	1.	Douglas Drury, Eric R. Murray
	2.	Milton Q. Ellenby, Douglas Steen
1955	1.	Douglas Drury, Eric R. Murray
	2.	Ira S. Rubin, Victor Mitchell
1956	1.	Paul Allinger, James Jacoby
	2.	Robert F. Jordan, Robert Sitnek
1957	1.	David C. Carter, John W. Hubbell
	2.	John Gerber, Paul H. Hodge
1958	1.	William Grieve, Ira S. Rubin
	2.	Norman Kay, Sidney Silodor
1959	1.	Harry J. Fishbein, John Gerber
	2.	Erik Paulsen, Mike Shuman
1960	1.	Jack Blair, William Christian
	2.	David C. Carter, Paul H. Hodge
1961	1.	Philip Feldesman, Ira S. Rubin
	2.	Paul Allinger, Lewis L. Mathe
1962	1.	Philip Feldesman, Ira S. Rubin
	2.	Eddie Kantar, Marshall Miles
1963	1.	Sami R. Kehela, B. Wolf Lebovic
	2.	Alphonse Moyse, Jr., Thomas K. Sanders
1964	1.	Ed Don Weiner, G. Gard Hays
	2.	Darryl Pedersen, Don Nemiro
1965	1.	Lawrence Rosler, Jeff Rubens
	2.	Eric R. Murray, Norman Kay
1966	1.	Barry Crane, Peter C. Rank
	2.	Mark Blumenthal, Michael Moss
1967	1.	Richard Lawrence, Art Price
	2.	Eddie Kantar, Sidney Lazard
1968	1.	Kyle Larsen, Edmond Lazarus
	2.	William Passell, David Strasberg
1969	1.	Michael J. Martino, Frank Vine
	2.	Gerald Hallee, Paul Soloway
1970	1.	Richard Kaye, Richard Walsh
	2.	Edgar Kaplan, Norman Kay
1971	1.	Giorgio Belladonna, Benito Garozzo
	2.	Robert Kerr, Jay T. McKee
1972	1.	Stephen W. Robinson, Kit Woolsey
	2.	Paul Heitner, Marshall Miles
1973	1.	Jack E. Kennedy, David Hadden
	2.	Stephen W. Robinson, Kit Woolsey
1974	1.	George Slemmons, George Steiner
	2.	Stephen W. Robinson, Kit Woolsey
1975	1.	Harlow Lewis, Art Waldemann
	2.	Larry Kozlove, John Sheridan
1976	1.	Gerald Caravelli, Larry Cohen
	2.	Jack E. Kennedy, Bobby Wolff
1977	1.	Joseph Fox, Garey Hayden
	2.	David Lehman, Dick Melson
1978	1.	Larry Kozlove, John Sheridan
	2.	Roy Fox, Paul Swanson

1979	1.	Roy Fox, Paul Swanson
	2.	Perry Johnson, Michael Zerbini
1980	1.	Neil Silverman, Peter Weichsel
	2.	Warren Rosner, Stephen Sanborn
1981	1.	Warren Rosner, Allan Stauber
	2.	Bill Eisenberg, Neil Silverman
1982	1.	David Berkowitz, Harold Lilie
	2.	James Barlow, Chuck Carroll
1983	1.	Marty Bergen, Allan Stauber
	2.	Mike Passell, Ron Andersen
1984	1.	Mike Lawrence, Peter Weichsel
	2.	Joel Friedberg, Ethan Stein
1985	1.	Ed Manfield, Kit Woolsey
	2.	Bob Hamman, George Mittelman
1986	1.	Bob Hamman, Paul Swanson
	2.	Robert Levin, Fred Hamilton
1987	1.	Darryl Pedersen, George Steiner
	2.	Zia Mahmood, Chris Compton
1988	1.	Arthur Hoffman, Stephen Shane
	2.	Ken Kranyak, Harry Stratton
1989	1.	Mike Moss, Charles Coon
	2.	Robert Beiles, Sidney Lorvan
1990	1.	Steve Sion, Steve Landen
	2.	Neil Silverman, Mike Smolen
1991	1.	Larry Mori, Henry Bethe
	2.	Zia Mahmood, Fred Chang
		(became Open Pairs II)
1992	1.	Jeff Meckstroth, Perry Johnson
	2.	Tony Glynne, S. James Elliott
1993	1.	Gaylor Kasle, Robert Levin
	2.	Eddie Wold, Dennis Sorensen
1994	1.	Thomas Peters, John Zilic
	2.	Steve Beatty, Curtis Cheek

This event was held in the Summer North American Championships until 1963. A similar event was held at the Spring NABCs 1958-1962 with the following results:

1958	1.	Norman Kay, Sidney Silodor
	2.	Jack Denny, Richard Harrison
1959	1.	James Pestaner, John Swanson
	2.	Donald A. Oakie, Meyer Schleifer
1960	1.	Frank Hoadley, Julius L. Rosenblum
	2.	Harold Creed, S. Samuel Gould, Jr.
1961	1.	Morton Rubinow, Tobias Stone
	2.	Erik Paulsen, Alex Tschekaloff
1962	1.	Ivan Erdos, Philip Feldesman
	2.	Norman Kay, Sidney Silodor

WOMEN'S PAIRS. This four-session event consisting of two qualifying rounds and two final rounds is contested for the WHITEHEAD TROPHY. From 1969 through 1971 it was contested as a three-session championship.

1930	1.	Olive Peterson, Maud S. Zontlein
	2.	Josephine Culbertson, Elinor Murdoch
1931	1.	Vivi Hanson, Elinor Murdoch
	2.	Mary Clement, Olga Hilliard
1932	1.	Mrs. Jay S. Jones, Olive Peterson
	2.	Florence Fitch, Maud S. Zontlein
1933	1.	Doris Fuller, Mrs. Courtand Smith
	2.	Marie Black, Mary Clement
1934	1.	Helen Bonwit, Matie White
	2.	Ruth Sherman, Mrs. Thomas Stern
1935	1.	Bertine Teichman, Mable Ulbrich
	2.	Doris Fuller, Olive Peterson
1936	1.	Mrs. Jay S. Jones, Sally Young
	2.	Mable Ervin, Doris Fuller
1937	1.	Mable Ervin, Doris Fuller
	2.	Martha Lemon, Mrs. Martin R. West
1938	1.	Helen Sobel, Sally Young
	2.	Phyllis Gardner, Dorothy Roberts
1939	1.	Helen Sobel, Sally Young
	2.	Doris Fuller, Millicent Tansill
1940	1.	Edith Atkinson, Mrs. John Waidlich
	2.	Estelle Drescher, Gussie Planco
1941	1.	Mae P. Rosen, Edith Seligman
	2.	Ruth Horn, Gussie Planco
1942	1.	Mae P. Rosen, Edith Seligman
	2.	Helen Bonwit, Mrs. D. P. Hanson
1943	1.	Mae P. Rosen, Edith Seligman

	2.	Olga Hilliard, Evelyn Lebhar
1944	1.	Ruth Sherman, Margaret Wagar
	2.	Paula Bacher, Kay Rhodes
1945	1.	Peggy Golder, Olive Peterson
	2.	Ruth Sherman, Margaret Wagar
1946	1.	Edith Seligman, Sally Young
	2.	Anne Burnstein, Mrs. G. Rosenbaum
1947	1.	Gratian Goldstein, Josephine Gutman
	2.	Ruth Sherman, Helen Sobel
1948	1.	Gratian Goldstein, Josephine Gutman
	2.	Mildred Cunningham, Mrs. Harry Mason Smith
1949	1.	Kay Rhodes, Ruth Sherman
	2.	Mildred Cunningham, Mrs. Harry Mason Smith
1950	1.	Mrs. John Kelly, Dorothy Thompson
	2.	Reba Buck, Mrs. George P. Ryan
1951	1.	Alwina M. Dunphy, Mrs. Edward Minear
	2.	Mrs. Frank Fooshe, Mrs. Henry C. Wolfe
1952	1.	Shirley Fairchild, Elaine Lee
	2.	Mildred Betzler, Mrs. Michael Hoffman
1953	1.	Mrs. Harold P. Swearingen, Barbara Weiner
	2.	Gretchen Feldstein, Gratian Goldstein
1954	1.	Margaret Alcorn, Sally Neely
	2.	Paula Levin, Mrs. Max Ritter
1955	1.	Kay Rhodes, Margaret Wagar
	2.	Mrs. Carl I. Conklin, Paula Nevins
1956	1.	Kay Rhodes, Margaret Wagar
	2.	Wynne Ecker, Mrs. P. Halbestadt
1957	1.	Kay Rhodes, Margaret Wagar
	2.	Edith Kemp, Terry Michaels
1958	1.	Betty Nail, Phyllis Novak
	2.	Alberta Albersheim, Mrs. M. J. Root
1959	1.	Betty Adler, Dorothy Hayden
	2.	Agnes Gordon, Sylvia Schwartz
1960	1.	Mary Jane Farell, Peggy Solomon
	2.	Mabel Mahoney, Mrs. James Welch
1961	1.	Agnes Gordon, Betty Haddad
	2.	Mrs. Seymour Keith, Rita Seamon
1962	1.	Carol Sanders, Sylvia Stein
	2.	Betty Kaplan, Jacqui Mitchell
1963	1.	Mrs. K. L. Sargent, Mrs. Ray Tobin
	2.	Garner McDaniel, Terry Michaels
1964	1.	Margaret Alcorn, Lucille Patterson
	2.	Ruth Ballantyne, Mrs. Lloyd Scott
1965	1.	Nancy Gruver, Sue Sachs
	2.	Alicia Kempner, Helen Sobel
1966	1.	Virginia Heckel, Edith Kemp
	2.	Garner McDaniel, Terry Michaels
1967	1.	Garner McDaniel, Terry Michaels
	2.	Hermine Baron, Marilyn Johnson
1968	1.	Hermine Baron, Rhoda Walsh
	2-3.	Emma Jean Hawes, Dorothy Hayden
	2-3.	Gloria Cohen, Belle Kauffman
1969	1	Gale Clarke, Gloria Noszka
	2.	Sallie Johnson, Bee Schenken
1970	1.	Robin Klar, Tina Rockaway
	2.	Jacqui Mitchell, Gail Moss
1971	1.	Amalya L. Kearse, Jacqui Mitchell
	2.	Barbara Brier, Betsey Wolff
1972	1.	Kerri Davis, Rhoda Walsh
	2.	Gail Moss, Judi Solodar
1973	1.	Ann Economidy, Vivian Williamson
	2.	Mary Anderson, Pamela Eckard
1974	1.	Pat Leary, Jan Stansby
	2.	Jacqui Mitchell, Gail Moss
1975	1.	Jacqui Mitchell, Gail Moss
	2.	Hermine Baron, Carol Greenhut
1976	1.	Gail Schaab, Barbara Staton
	2.	Emma Jean Hawes, Dorothy Hayden Truscott
1977	1.	Jacqui Mitchell, Gail Moss
	2.	Hermine Baron, Beverly Rosenberg
1978	1.	Babs Charney, Flo Rotman
	2.	Edith Kemp, Barbara Rappaport
1979	1.	Anne Burnstein, Edith Kemp
	2.	Ann Roberts, Genne Winter
1980	1.	Mildred Boyce, Barbara Norwood
	2.	Hermine Baron, Beverly Rosenberg
1981	1.	Emma Jean Hawes, Dorothy Hayden Truscott
	2.	Roberta Epstein, Rozanne Marel
1982	1.	Hermine Baron, Beverly Rosenberg
	2.	Nancy Alpaugh, Betsey Wolff
1983	1.	Evelyn Levitt, Jo Morse
	2.	Lynne Pollenz, Sue Picus
1984	1.	Judy Tucker, Jacqui Mitchell
	2.	Mildred Breed, Barbara Norwood
1985	1.	Dale Dermer, JoAnne Caplan

	2.	Nadine Wood, Robin Taylor
1986	1.	Edith Freilich, Nancy Gruver
	2.	Peggy Sutherlin, Sharon Osberg
1987	1.	Tobi Deutsch, Kay Schulle
	2.	Carlyn Steiner, Janet Daling
1988	1.	Sally Wheeler, Georgiana Gates
	2.	Jan Martel, Dorothy Truscott
1989	1.	Nadine Wood, Jeanne Elkner
	2.	Janice Seamon, Rita Seamon
1990	1.	Tobi Deutsch, June Deutsch
	2.	Carol Sanders, Betty Ann Kennedy
1991	1.	Leslie Paryzer, Nancy Widman
	2.	Claire Tornay, Kathie Walvick
1992	1.	Cheri Bjerkan, Janice Seamon
	2.	Carol Sanders, Betty Ann Kennedy
1993	1.	Carol Sanders, Betty Ann Kennedy
	2.	Shawn Womack, Jan Cohen
1994	1.	Corinne Kirkham, Ann Kluewer
	2.	Bernace De Young, Ellasue Chaitt

This event was held at the Summer North American Championships until 1962. A similar event was held at the Spring NABC 1958-1962 with the following results:

1958	1.	Kay Rhodes, Margaret Wagar
	2.	Mrs. N. L. Cassibry, Ann Smith
1959	1.	Bert Epstein, Blossom Grossblatt
	2.	Betty Coombs, Malvine Klausner
1960	1.	Gretchen Feldstein, Jane Mueller
	2.	Gertrude Eberson, Mrs. M. Jones
1961	1.	May Belle Long, Effie Woods
	2.	Dorothy Hayden, Helen Portugal
1962	1.	Clarice Holt, Mrs. Greeley Warner
	2.	Kay Carter, Mrs. G. M. Sharum

MIXED PAIRS. This event is contested for the ROCKWELL TROPHY. It is a four-session event with two qualifying sessions and two final sessions.

1946	1.	Anne Burnstein, Alvin Roth
	2.	David C. Carter, Frances Carter
1947	1.	Evelyn Ansin, Charles H. Goren
	2.	John R. Crawford, Margaret Wagar
1948	1.	John R. Crawford, Margaret Wagar
	2.	Charles C. Johnson, Mrs. Frank Myer
1949	1	John R. Crawford, Margaret Wagar
	2.	Paula Bacher, Peter A. Leventritt
1950	1.	Peter A. Leventritt, Ruth Sherman
	2.	William Thiemann, Mrs. William Thiemann
1951	1.	Edith Rosenbloom, Sidney Silodor
	2.	Edward Burns, Shirley Fairchild
1952	1.	Anne Burnsetin, Alvin Roth
	2.	Ella Tilles, Jules Tilles
1953	1.	Jewel Hodge, Paul H. Hodge
	2.	John Gerber, Celeste Mounce
1954	1.	Said Haddad, Betty Windley
	2.	Zenobia Allen, John H. Moran
1955	1.	Sidney Silodor, Helen Sobel
	2.	Alicia Kempner, George Rapee
1956	1.	Sidney Silodor, Helen Sobel
	2.	Donald G. Farquaharson, Agnes Gordon
1957	1.	Bee Gale, Howard Schenken
	2.	Frances Carter, David Warner
1958	1.	Carol Ross, Edwin J. Smith
	2.	Louis J. Cohen, Sylvia Stein
1959	1.	John R. Crawford, Dorothy Hayden
	2.	Sidney H. Lazard, Stella Rebner
1960	1.	Elsie Abrams, William L. Passell
	2.	Peter Johnson, Gladys Kransberg
1961	1.	Art Comstock, Margaret Muirhead
	2.	Charles J. Solomon, Peggy Solomon
1962	1.	Clarice K. Holt, Paul Levitt
	2.	Peggy Jean Berry, John C. Sutherlin
1963	1.	Agnes Gordon, Eric R. Murray
	2.	Barbara Brier, Jerry Brier
1964	1.	Dan Morse, Mary Margaret Swan
	2.	Margaret Alcorn, Peter A. Pender
1965	1.	Betty Kaplan, Edgar Kaplan
	2.	Malvine Klausner, Morris Portugal
1966	1.	Robert G. Sharp, Louise Sharp
	2.	Gertrude Blasband, Sylvester Lowery
1967	1.	Gertrude Machlin, Kit Woolsey

 2. Kathie Cappelletti, Mike Cappelletti
1968 1. Marilyn Johnson, Peter C. Rank
 2. John Gerber, Carol Klar
1969 1. Peggy Parker, Steve Parker
 2. Evelyn Levitt, David R. Treadwell
1970 1. George S. Dawkins, Carolyn C. Flournoy
 2. Mary Chilcote, Larry Weiss
1971 1. Eugenie Mathe, Lewis L. Mathe
 2. Barry Crane, Kerri Davis
1972 1. John A. Mohan, Peggy Sutherlin
 2. Leland Ferer, Gratian Goldstein
1973 1. Bernie Chazen, Marilyn Johnson
 2. Kenneth L. Cohen, Helen Smith
1974 1. Gerald A. Caravelli, Helen Utegaard
 2. Barry Crane, Kerri Shuman
1975 1. Barry Crane, Kerri Shuman
 2. Sandi Leavitt, Paul Sugar
1976 1. Peggy Lipsitz, Steve Parker
 2. Nancy Gruver, Lee Rautenberg
1977 1. Joel Friedberg, Nancy Gruver
 2. Barry Crane, Kerri Shuman
1978 1. Ahmed Hussein, Gail Moss
 2. Dave McClintock, Janet McClintock
1979 1. Juanita Skelton, Mike Smolen
 2. Carol Sanders, Thomas K. Sanders
1980 1. Jeff Meckstroth, Patty Meckstroth
 2. Hemant Lall, Jan Lall
1981 1. Esta Van Zandt, James E. Zimmerman
 2-3. Charlie Dorn, Bonnie LaRochelle
 2-3. Bart Bramley, Judy Wadas
1982 1. Barry Crane, Kerri Schuman
 2. Mike Passell, Nancy Passell
1983 1. John Gustafson, Helen Gustafson
 2. Benito Garozzo, Lea duPont
1984 1. Kathy Sulgrove, Larry Rock
 2. Audrey Rennels, Ron Von der Porten
1985 1. Beth Palmer, Steve Robinson
 2. Patricia Hassett, Steve Garner
1986 1. Lisa Berkowitz, David Berkowitz
 2. Laurie Kranyak, Phil Becker
1987 1. Lisa Berkowitz, David Berkowitz
 2. Juanita Chambers, Jim Robison
1988 1. Claire Tornay, Michael Moss
 2. Susan Green, Mike Cappelletti
1989 1. Dorothy Truscott, Alan Truscott
 2. Sandra Low, Marc Low
1990 1. Jo Ann Manfield, Ken Cohen
 2. Adair Gellman, Ravindra Murthy
1991 1. Jo Ann Manfield, Danny Sprung
 2. Judy Tucker, Jim Becker
1992 1. Kitty Bethe, Larry Mori
 2. Linda Lee, Ray Lee
1993 1. Libby Fernandez, Happoldt Neuffer
 2. Sabine Zenkel, Ron Andersen
1994 1. Jillian Blanchard, Geoff Hampson
 2. Kay Schulle, John Sutherlin

OPEN SWISS TEAMS, formerly NORTH AMERICAN MEN'S SWISS TEAMS. This four-session event consists of two qualifying and two final sessions.

1982 1. Allan Stauber, Jan Janitschke, Ross Grabel, Mike Smolen
 2-3. Si Frome, Marc Renson, Hamish Bennett, Bob Etter
 2-3. Jim Robison, Stelios Touchtidis, Jon Wittes, Steve Cohen, Paul Ivaska, Paul Lewis
1983 1. Mike Albert, Ira Rubin, Grant Baze, Barry Crane
 2. George Ateljevich, Sidney Lazard, Sidney Lazard, Jr., John Zilic, Norb Kremer
1984 1. Bart Bramley, Mark Cohen, Milt Rosenberg, Ralph Katz
 2. Tom Mahaffey, Andy Bernstein, Richard Pavlicek, Bill Passell, Bill Root
1985 1. John Devine, Alan Sontag, John Mohan, Roger Bates
 2. David Ashley, David Sacks, Mike Shuman, Ed Davis, Jon Wittes, Steve Cohen
1986 1. Mark Cohen, Peter Boyd, Steve Robinson, Kit Woolsey
 2. Bob Jones, Jim Krekorian, Ethan Stein, Drew Casen, Al Rand
1987 1. Eddie Kantar, Alan Sontag, Roger Bates, John

  Mohan, John Devine
 2. Claude Vogel, David Lehman, Tom Fox, Michael Schreiber
1988 1. Ron Sukoneck, Doug Fraser, Kamel Fergani, Bill Pettis
 2. Jim Jacoby, Gerald Michaud, Bobby Nail, Fred Hamilton, Walt Walvick, Erik Paulsen
1989 1. Jim Mahaffey, Ron Andersen, Paul Soloway, Bobby Goldman, Jeff Meckstroth, Eric Rodwell
 2-3. Rob Stevens, Ron Powell, Sidney Brownstein, Mark Singer
 2-3, Jan Janitschke, Craig Janitschke, Marc Jacobus, Peter Nagy, Joey Silver
  (became Open Swiss)
1990 1. John Sutherlin, Bart Bramley, Gerald Michaud, Larry Richardson, Bob Hamman
 2. Grant Baze, Jim Krekorian, Drew Casen, Mike Smolen
1991 1. George Rosenkranz, Eddie Wold, Mark Lair, Mike Passell, Paul Soloway, Bobby Goldman
 2. Bart Bramley, Per Olov Sundelin, John Sutherlin, Dan Morse, Edgar Kaplan, Norman Kay
1992 1. Richard Schwartz, Drew Casen, Michael Seamon, Richard Pavlicek, Fred Stewart, Steve Weinstein
 2. Morris Chang, Bob Hamman, Bobby Wolff, Michael Rosenberg, Zia Mahmood
1993 1. Tony Kasday, Michael Seamon, Steve Sion, Bill Cohen, Ron Smith
 2. Martin Scheinberg, Benito Garozzo, Lea duPont, Bill Eisenberg
1994 1. Perry Johnson, Jeff Meckstroth, Chip Martel, Eric Rodwell
 2. Grant Baze, Tipton Golias, Hugh Ross, Bart Bramley, Mike Lawrence

NORTH AMERICAN WOMENS SWISS TEAMS. This four-session event has two qualifying and two final sessions with Victory Point scoring.

1982 1. Dorothy Truscott, Stasha Cohen, Edith Kemp, Nancy Gruver, Mary Jane Farell, Randi Montin, Mike Smolen (npc)
 2. Jo Ann Manfield, Nadine Wood, Marilyn Eber, Bonnie Smith, Jan Janitschke (npc)
1983 1. Kathie Wei, Judi Radin, Gail Moss, Jacqui Mitchell, Betty Ann Kennedy, Carol Sanders
 2. Dianna Gordon, Brenda Keller, Mary Albert, Sandra Fraser, Linda Peterson, Keri Shuman
1984 1. June Deutsch, Tobi Deutsch, Cheri Bjerkan, Margie Gwozdzinsky, Dorothy Truscott, Sue Halperin
 2. Karen McCallum, Ellee Lewis, Vivian Whalen, Kitty Bethe
1985 1. Sue Farino, Dianna Gordon, June Deutsch, Tobi Deutsch, Rhoda Walsh
 2-3. Kathie Wei, Jacqui Mitchell, Judi Radin, Gail Greenberg, Carol Sanders, Betty Ann Kennedy
 2-3. Jo Morse, Cindy Bernstein, Joyce Lilie, Evelyn Levitt, Sally Wheeler, Florine Kuehl
1986 1. Jan Martel, Rozanne Pollack, Lynne Pollenz, Lynne Feldman, Roberta Epstein, Sue Picus
 2. Sally Woolsey, Linda Peterson, Carol Pincus, Ann Jacobson, Nell Cahn, Kitty Poldosky
1987 1. Cheri Bjerkan, Juanita Chambers, Lynn Deas, Beth Palmer
 2. Helen Utegaard, Helene Gingiss, Rhoda Walsh, Jill Meyers, Beverly Rosenberg
1988 1. Helen Utegaard, Rhoda Walsh, Carol Pincus, Beverly Rosenberg
 2-3. Judy Wadas, Sandra Fraser, Janice Seamon, Renee Mancuso
 2-3. Tobi Deutsch, Betsey Wolff, Nancy Alpaugh, Kay Schulle
1989 1. Kerri Shuman, Kitty Bethe, Margie Gwozdzinsky, Karen McCallum
 2. Jean Michell, Patti Hartley, Shirley Blum, Janet Robertson
1990 1. Kerri Shuman, Karen McCallum, Edith Rosenkranz, Sabine Zenkel, Daniela von Arnim
 2. Nell Cahn, Sharon Osberg, Sue Picus, Nancy Passell

1991	1-2.	Jacqui Mitchell, Joyce Lilie, Amalya Kearse, Jo Morse
	1-2.	Ron Andersen (npc), Kay Schulle, Jill Meyers, Randi Montin, Pam Wittes, Juanita Chambers, Cheri Bjerkan
1992	1.	Gail Greenberg, Judy Tucker, Dorothy Truscott, Lisa Berkowitz, Sandra Landy, Michele Handley
	2.	Renee Mancuso, Brenda Keller, Joan Jackson, Petra Hamman, Judi Cody, Ellasue Chaitt
1993	1.	Kay Schulle, Jill Meyers, Kerri Shuman, Karen McCallum
	2.	Jean Anderson, Janet Daling, Sharon Colson, Broma Lou Reed
1994	1.	Juanita Chambers, Rhoda Kratenstein, Shawn Womack, Jan Cohen, Hjordis Eythorsdottir
	2.	Karen McCallum, Kitty Munson, Carol Simon, Sue Picus

SILVER RIBBON PAIRS. This event, consisting of two qualifying and two final sessions, is open only to players at least 55 years of age. Prequalification is required and may be earned by placing first or second in a regionally or nationally-rated senior event.

1992	1.	James Leary, S. Irving Steinfeldt
	2.	George Rosenkranz, Fred Hamilton
1993	1.	Joan Remey Moore, Helen Shanbrom
	2.	Corinne Kirkham, Jim Kirkham
1994	1.	Virgil Anderson, Jayne Thomas
	2.	Betty Wilton, Herb Wilton

Summer Championships

SPINGOLD MASTER KNOCKOUT TEAMS.
First known as the Challenge Knockout Teams, the event was contested for the ASBURY PARK TROPHY. The runner-up team in the regularly scheduled portion of the event had the right to challenge the winners to a playoff. This right was never utilized. In 1934, 1936 and 1937 the MASTERS TEAMS-of-FOUR and the Asbury Park Trophy were separate events, providing two sets of winners. In 1938 the event became the Spingold Master Knockout Teams. At one time the Spingold was a double elimination event scored by international matchpoints, usually lasting nine or ten sessions, restricted to players of Senior Master rank and higher. In 1965, the double elimination method was replaced by three qualifying sessions (subsequently reduced to two), followed by single elimination knockout matches. The preliminary qualifying sessions were dropped in 1970.

WINNERS ASBURY PARK TROPHY

1930	1.	Ely Culbertson, Josephine Culbertson, Theodore A. Lightner, Waldemar K. von Zedtwitz
	2.	Michael T. Gottlieb, Williard S. Karn, Lee Langdon, P. Hal Sims
1931	1.	David Burnstine, Oswald Jacoby, Williard S. Karn, P. Hal Sims
	2.	S. Garton Churchill, Travers J. LeGros, Dorothy Roberts, A. Phillip Stockvis
1932	1.	Michael T. Gottlieb, Oswald Jacoby, Theodore A. Lightner, Louis H. Watson
	2.	B. Jay Becker, Herbert D. Lent, George Reith, Anne Rosenfield
1933	1.	David Burnstine, Oswald Jacoby, Richard L. Frey, Howard Schenken
	2.	Sam Fry, Jr., Edward Hymes, Louis H. Watson, Waldemar K. von Zedtwitz
1934	1.	Aaron Frank, Jeff Glick, William Hopkins, Charles H. Porter
	2.	Josephine Culbertson, Theodore A. Lightner, Alphonse Moyse, Jr., Sherman Stearns
1935	1.	Sam Fry, Jr., Edward Hymes, Jr., Theodore A. Lightner, Merwyn D. Maier, Louis H. Watson
	2.	A. Mitchell Barnes, H. Huber Boscowitz, Charles S. Lochridge, Johnny Rau
1936	1.	Lewis A. Bernard, Louis J. Haddad, Alvin Landy, Matthew S. Reilly, Philip Steiner
	2.	E. Melvin Goddard, Sidney Silodor, Dr. Henry J. Vogel, Sir Derrick Wernher
1937	1.	David Burnstine, Charles H. Goren, Oswald Jacoby, Merwyn D. Maier, Howard Schenken
	2.	Phil Abramsohn, A. Mitchell Barnes, Henry H. Chanin, Morrie Elis, Fred D. Kaplan

WINNERS MASTERS TEAMS-of-FOUR

1934	1.	David Burnstine, Richard L. Frey, Michael T. Gottlieb, Oswald Jacoby, Howard Schenken
	2.	Aaron Frank, Jeff Glick, Louis J. Haddad, Charles

		A. Hall
1936	1.	B. Jay Becker, David Burnstine, Oswald Jacoby, Howard Schenken
	2.	Sam Fry, Jr., Edward Hymes, Jr., Merwyn D. Maier, Waldemar K. von Zedtwitz
1937	1.	Sam Fry, Jr., Edward Hymes, Jr., Theodore A. Lightner, Waldemar K. von Zedtwitz
	2.	Phil Abramsohn, Lewis Bernard, Morrie Elis, Harry Fishbein, Herbert Goldberg

WINNERS SPINGOLD KNOCKOUT TEAMS

1938	1.	B. Jay Becker, David Burnstine, Oswald Jacoby, Merwyn D. Maier, Howard Schenken
	2.	A. Mitchell Barnes, Morrie Elis, Fred D. Kaplan, Charles S. Lochridge
1939	1.	Oswald Jacoby, Theodore A. Lightner, Merwyn D. Maier, Robert A. McPherran, Howard Schenken
	2.	John R. Crawford, Myron Fuchs, Charles H. Goren, Charles J. Solomon, Sally Young
1940	1.	Oscar J. Brotman, Bertram Lebhar, Samuel Katz, Alvin Roth
	2.	Sam Fry, Jr., Myron Fuchs, Edward Hymes, Jr., Charles S. Lochridge, Waldemar K. von Zedtwitz
1941	1.	A. Mitchell Barnes, Sam Fry, Jr., Edward Hymes, Jr., Waldemar K. von Zedtwitz
	2.	B. Jay Becker, Oswald Jacoby, Theodore A. Lightner, Merwyn D. Maier, Howard Schenken
1942	1.	Sigmund Dornbusch, Richard L. Frey, Lee Hazen, Samuel M. Stayman
	2.	Jay T. Feigus, Charles Harvey, Samuel Katz, Edward Marcus
1943	1.	John R. Crawford, Charles H. Goren, Edward Hymes, Jr., Howard Schenken, Sidney Silodor
	2.	B. Jay Becker, Harry J. Fishbein, George Rapee, Alvin Roth, Helen Sobel
1944	1.	B. Jay Becker, George Rapee, Helen Sobel, Samuel M. Stayman
	2.	Simon Becker, Edward G. Ellenbogen, Stanley Frenkel, Peggy Golder
1945	1.	Sam Fry, Jr., Edward Hymes, Jr., Oswald Jacoby, Theodore A. Lightner, Howard Schenken
	2.	Harry Fishbein, Lee Hazen, Alvin Roth, Waldemar K. von Zedtwitz
1946	1.	William Christian, Mark Hodges, Sol Mogal, Margaret Wagar
	2.	Jeff Glick, Arthur S. Goldsmith, Alvin Landy, Elmer I. Schwartz
1947	1.	B. Jay Becker, Charles H. Goren, Lee Hazen, Helen Sobel, Waldemar K. von Zedtwitz
	2.	John R. Crawford, George Rapee, Howard Schenken, Sidney Silodor, Samuel M. Stayman
1948	1.	John R. Crawford, George Rapee, Howard Schenken, Samuel M. Stayman, Margaret Wagar
	2.	Julius Bank, Arthur Glatt, Robert W. Halpin, Oswald Jacoby, Ralph Kempner
1949	1.	Jeff Glick, Arthur S. Goldsmith, Bruce Gowdy, Alvin Landy, Sol Mogal
	2.	Henry H. Chanin, David Clarren, Oswald Jacoby, Jack Krause, Waldemar K. von Zedtwitz
1950	1.	John R. Crawford, Oswald Jacoby, George Rapee, Howard Schenken, Samuel M. Stayman
	2.	B. Jay Becker, Charles H. Goren, Sidney Silodor, Helen Sobel, Waldemar K. von Zedtwitz
1951	1.	Myron Field, Charles H. Goren, Sidney Silodor, Helen Sobel
	2.	Ambrose Casner, Charles A. Hall, Allen P. Harvey,

Frank Weisbach

1952 1. B. Jay Becker, John R. Crawford, George Rapee, Howard Schenken, Samuel M. Stayman
2. Jeff Glick, Arthur S. Goldsmith, Alvin Landy, Sol Mogal, Edwin J. Smith, Jr.

1953 1. Clifford Bishop, Milton Q. Ellenby, Donald A. Oakie, William Rosen, Doug Steen
2-5. Ed Burns, David Clarren, Bertram Lebhar, Sam Katz, Albert Weiss
2-5. F. Ayers Bombeck, David C. Carter, John W. Hubbell, Arthur Kincaid, G. Robert Nail
2-5. Harold Harkavy, Edith Kemp, Alvin Roth, Tobias Stone, Walemar K. von Zedtwitz
2-5. Ivan E. Erdos, Dr. Edward Fischauer, Lewis L. Mathe, Meyer Schleifer

1954 1. Clifford Bishop, Milton Q. Ellenby, Lewis L. Mathe, John Moran, William Rosen
2-4. F. Ayers Bombeck, David C. Carter, John Gerber, John W. Hubbell, Harold Rockaway
2-4. Eddie Burns, Ambrose Casner, Allen P. Harvey, Cliff Russell
2-4. Sidney Lazard, Cyrus Newman, Lewis Rosen, Julius L. Rosenblum, Robert Rothlein

1955 1. Myron Field, Lee Hazen, Richard Kahn, Charles J. Solomon, Samuel M. Stayman
2. B. Jay Becker, John R. Crawford, George Rapee, Howard Schenken, Sidney Silodor

1956 1-3. Charles H. Goren, Peter A. Leventritt, Boris Koytchou, Harold Ogust, William Seamon, Helen Sobel
1-3. Harold Harkavy, Victor Mitchell, Alvin Roth, Ira S. Rubin, Tobias Stone
1-3. Robert Abeles, Dr. Kalman Apfel, Francis P. Begley, Louis Kelner, Ronald Rosenberg

1957 1. B. Jay Becker, John R. Crawford, George Rapee, Alvin Roth, Sidney Silodor, Tobias Stone
2. Milton Q. Ellenby, Ivan E. Erdos, Emanuel Hochfeld, James Jacoby, Oswald Jacoby, Ira S. Rubin

1958 1. Paul Allinger, William Hanna, Sidney Lazard, Cyrus Neuman, Robert Rothlein
2. Harry Fishbein, Sam Fry, Jr., Leonard B. Harmon, Lee Hazen, Ivar Stakgold

1959 1. William Grieve, Oswald Jacoby, Victor Mitchell, Ira S. Rubin, Morton Rubinow, Samuel M. Stayman
2. Richard Freeman, Andy Gabrilovitch, Frank Hoadley, Mike Michaels, Jan Stone, Richard Walsh

1960 1. Charles H. Goren, Peter A. Leventritt, Boris Koytchou, Harold Ogust, Howard Schenken, Helen Sobel
2. B. Jay Becker, William Grieve, Ralph Hirschberg, Norman Kay, George Rapee, Sidney Silodor

1961 1. Andy Gabrilovitch, Eddie Kantar, Marshall Miles, William Root
2. John R. Crawford, Norman Kay, Alvin Roth, George Rapee, Sidney Silodor, Tobias Stone

1962 1. Leonard B. Harmon, Eddie Kantar, Marshall Mile, Ivar Stakgold
2. David C. Carter, John W. Hubbell, James Jacoby, Gerald Michaud, G. Robert Nail

1963 1. Russell Arnold, Harold Harkavy, Edith Kemp, Alvin Roth, Cliff Russell, William Seamon
2. Sami R. Kehela, Richard Kahn, William Root, Thomas K. Sanders, Tobias Stone, Waldemar K. von Zedtwitz

1964 1. Bruce Elliott, Sami R. Kehela, Eric R. Murray, Percy Sheardown
2. Marvin Altman, Bruce Gowdy, Fred Hoffer, Ray Jotcham

1965 1. Bruce Elliott, Sami R. Kehela, Eric R. Murray, Percy Sheardown
2. B. Jay Becker, Dorothy Hayden, Norman Kay, Edgar Kaplan

1966 1. William Root, Alvin Roth, Ira S. Rubin, Curtis K. Smith
2. William Grieve, Sidney Lazard, Paul Levitt, Harold Ogust, George Rapee

1967 1. Edgar Kaplan, Norman Kay, William Root, Alvin Roth
2. John Gerber, Paul H. Hodge, Dan Morse, George Rosenkranz, Bobby Wolff

1968 1. Sami R. Kehela, Edgar Kaplan, Norman Kay, Sidney Lazard, Eric R. Murray, George Rapee

2. Steve Altman, B. Jay Becker, Michael Becker, Dorothy Hayden

1969 1. Bill Eisenberg, Bobby Goldman, Robert D. Hamman, Michael S. Lawrence, James Jacoby, Bobby Wolff
2. Phil Feldesman, William Grieve, Victor Mitchell, Ira S. Rubin, Samuel M. Stayman, Jeff Westheimer

1970 1. Steve Altman, Thomas M. Smith, Dave Strasberg, Joel Stuart, Peter Weichsel
2. Bill Eisenberg, Bobby Goldman, Robert D. Hamman, James Jacoby, Michael S. Lawrence, Bobby Wolff

1971 1. Steve Altman, Eugene Neiger, Thomas M. Smith, Joel Stuart, Peter Weichsel
2. Edgar Kaplan, Norman Kay, Donald P. Krauss, Lewis L. Mathe

1972 1. B. Jay Becker, Michael Becker, Andy Bernstein, Jeff Rubens
2. Pat Brennan, Byron Greenberg, Edith Kemp, Cliff Russell, Curtis K. Smith, Albert Weiss

1973 1. Larry Cohen, Bill Eisenberg, Eddie Kantar, Richard H. Katz, Bud Reinhold
2. Minda Brachman, Sidney Lazard, James Jacoby, Paul Soloway, John Swanson

1974 1. Lou Bluhm, Larry Gould, Steve Goldberg, Richard Shepherd
2. Harlow Lewis, Lewis L. Mathe, Peter A. Pender, William Root, Harry Stappenbeck, Arthur Waldman

1975 1. Grant S. Baze, John Fejervary, Lew Stansby, Piyush Vakil, Ron Von der Porten
2. Ira Cohen, Harold Guiver, Marty Shallon, Bill Sides

1976 1. Roger Bates, Larry Cohen, Richard H. Katz, John Mohan, George Rosenkranz
2. Dave Berkowitz, Mark E. Blumenthal, James Jacoby, Michael S. Lawrence, George Rapee, John Solodar

1977 1. Lou Bluhm, Dan Morse, Cliff Russell, Curtis K. Smith, Thomas K. Sanders, Eddie Wold
2. Ken Cohen, Larry Gould, Larry Kozlove, John Sheridan

1978 1. Malcolm Brachman, Bobby Goldman, Eddie Kantar, Mike Passell, Paul Soloway
2. Steve Altman, Edgar Kaplan, Norman Kay, Richard Pavlicek, William Root, Thomas M. Smith

1979 1. Fred Hamilton, Robert D. Hamman, Ira S. Rubin, Bobby Wolff
2. Ed Manfield, Stephen W. Robinson, Eric Rodwell, John Sheridan, Kit Woolsey

1980 1. Mike Becker, Kyle Larsen, Ron Rubin, Alan Sontag, Ron Von der Porten, Peter Weichsel
2. Rich Freisner, Brian Glubok, Michael S. Lawrence, George Rapee, Michael Rosenberg, John Solodar

1981 1. Larry N. Cohen, Ron Gerard, Ralph Katz, Warren Rosner, Allan Stauber, John Sutherlin
2. Bart Bramley, Rich Freisner, Ed Manfield, Kit Woolsey

1982 1. Ron Rubin, Mike Becker, Bob Hamman, Bobby Wolff, Alan Sontag, Peter Weichsel
2. Mark Molson, Billy Cohen, Eric Kokish, Peter Nagy

1983 1. Malcolm Brachman, Bobby Wolff, Bobby Goldman, Bob Hamman, Paul Soloway, Ron Andersen
2. Luella Slaner, Marty Bergen, Brian Glubok, Larry N. Cohen, Mark Cohen, Jerry Goldfein

1984 1. George Rosenkranz, Eddie Wold, Jeff Meckstroth, Eric Rodwell, Marty Bergen, Larry N. Cohen
2. Alan Sontag, Allan Cokin, Jim Sternberg, Bernie Chazen, Steve Sion

1985 1. Tom Mahaffey, Jack Denny, Bill Passell, Russ Arnold, Ira Rubin, Chuck Burger
2. Ron Rubin, Jeff Meckstroth, Eric Rodwell, Mike Lawrence, Peter Weichsel

1986 1. Malcolm Brachman, Bobby Goldman, Ron Andersen, Mike Passell, Mark Lair, Paul Soloway
2. Brian Glubok, Billy Cohen, John Schermer, Neil Chambers

1987 1. Brian Glubok, Dan Rotman, Harry Stappenbeck, Jaggy Shivdasani
2. Tom Mahaffey, Jack Denny, Russ Arnold, Bernie Chazen, Roy Fox, Michael Seamon

1988 1. Jim Mahaffey, Ron Andersen, Paul Soloway,

Bobby Goldman, Eric Rodwell, Jeff Meckstroth
2. Ron Rubin, Michael Becker, Peter Weichsel, Bart Bramley, Robert Levin, Lou Bluhm
1989 1. Jim Cayne, Chuck Burger, Bob Hamman, Bobby Wolff, Mike Passell, Mark Lair
2. Jon Wittes, Ross Grabel, Mark Cohen, Mark Feldman
1990 1. Jim Cayne, Chuck Burger, Chip Martel, Lew Stansby, Bob Hamman, Bobby Wolff
2. Jim Mahaffey, Paul Soloway, Bobby Goldman, Ron Andersen, Jeff Meckstroth, Eric Rodwell
1991 1. Zia Mahmood, Michael Rosenberg, Seymon Deutsch, Jeff Meckstroth, Eric Rodwell
2. Cliff Russell, Peter Weichsel, Robert Levin, Sam Lev, Alan Sontag, Eddie Kantar
1992 1. Ron Rubin, Russ Ekeblad, Mike Becker, Ron Sukoneck, Robert Levin, Peter Weichsel
2. Steve Robinson, Peter Boyd, Lew Stansby, Kit Woolsey, Neil Silverman, Chip Martel
1993 1. Richard Freeman, Nick Nickell, Eric Rodwell, Jeff Meckstroth, Bobby Wolff, Bob Hamman
2. Zia Mahmood, Michael Rosenberg, Seymon Deutsch, Hemant Lall, Chip Martel, Lew Stansby

WOMENS TEAMS.

WOMENS TEAMS. This event is contested for the COFFIN TROPHY. Until 1976 it was a four-session event scored by Board-a-Match; contested as a three-session championship until 1972 and in 1975; held at the Fall North American Championships until 1963. In 1976 the event became a North American Championship Women's Knockout with Swiss qualifying.

1933 1. Mrs. Greene Fenley, Jr., Mrs. Richard Field, Mrs. John W. Friedlander, Jane Wallace
2. Mollie Funk, Ethel Gardner, Marguerite Hoffmeier, Marie White
1934 1. Gail Hamilton, Marguerite Hoffmeier, Helen Pendelton Rockwell, Anne Rosenfeld
2. Elizabeth Banfield, Phyllis Gardner, Eva Gross, Dorothy Roberts
1935 1. Doris Fuller, Angela Quigley, Florence Stratford, Helen White
2. Gail Hamilton, Marguerite Hoffmeier, Helen Pendelton Rockwell, Anne Rosenfeld
1936 1. Doris Fuller, Angela Quigley, Florence Stratford, Helen White
2. Marge Anderson, Mrs. J. A. Faulkner, Marjorie Haldeman, Mrs. G. Keedick
1937 1. Martha Lemon, Mrs. A. Philip Stockvis, Mrs. Martin West, Sally Young
2. Doris Fuller, Angela Quigley, Helen Sobel, Florence Stratford
1938 1. Mrs. Galloway Morris, Lillian Peck, Olive Peterson, Mrs. Donald B. Tansill
2. Mariquita Fullerton, Mollie Funk, Ann Rosenfeld, Lucille Schwarz
1939 1. Mabel Ervin, Doris Fuller, Helen Mitchell, Helen Sobel, Sally Young
2. Sylvia DeYoung, Margaret Katzen, Catherine W. Samberg, Florence Stratford
1940 1. Helen Levy, Adelaide Neuwirth, Margaret Wagar, Lottie Zetosch
2. Ruth Horn, Olga Hilliard, Marguerite McKenney, Gussie Planco
1941 1. Inez Buchannan, Mae Dickens, Mabel Scott, Linda Terry
2. Doris Fuller, Mrs. Joseph M. Rothschild, Helen Sobel, Sally Young
1942 1. Peggy Golder, Olga Hilliard, Olive Peterson, Ruth Sherman
2. Emily Folline, Doris Fuller, Ethel Gardner, Helen Sobel
1943 1. Emily Folline, Helen Sobel, Margaret Wagar, Sally Young
2. Eleanor Hirsch, Evelyn Lebhar, Marguerite McKenney, Florence Stratford
1944 1. Emily Folline, Helen Sobel, Margaret Wagar, Sally Young
2. Mrs. M. Godfrey, Mrs. C. W. Neeld, Dorothy Sullivan, Anne H. Todd
1945 1. Emily Folline, Helen Sobel, Margaret Wagar, Sally

Young
2. Josephine Gutman, Gratian Goldstein, Marjorie Perlmutter, Gretchen Schildmiller
1946 1. Emily Folline, Helen Sobel, Margaret Wagar, Sally Young
2. Paula Bacher, Marie Basher, Jane Jaeger, Pauline Shmukler
1947 1-2. Marge Anderson, Ruby Lyons, Mimi Roncarelli, Jane Wallace
1-2. Cass Illig, Frances Robinson, Alma Stewart, Carolyn Sondheim
1948 1. Ruth Gordon, Gratian Goldstein, Josephine Gutman, Charlotte Sidway
2. Ruth Gilbert, Olive Peterson, Edith Seligman, Ruth Sherman, Peggy Solomon
1949 1-2. Hortense Evans, Frances Robinson, Mrs. Henry Sabatt, Carolyn Sondheim
1-2. Marianne Boschan, Catherine Cotter, Gertrude Eberson, Katherine McNutt
1950 1. Marge Anderson, Mary Bowden, Ruth Gordon, G. Eloise Neil
2-5. Olive Peterson, Ruth Sherman, Helen Sobel, Margaret Wagar
2-5. Shirley Fairchild, Mrs. Ezra Feldman, Rose Groves, Luise Mathews, Claire Meyer
2-5. Margaret Byrd, Isabelle Garn, Virginia Ploehn, Billy Traveletti
2-5. Inez Buchanan, Zodie Glover, Sally Herman, Mabel Scott
1951 1. Paula Bacher, Anne Burnstein, Dolly Rosenfeld, Edith Seligman, Sally Young
2. Thelma Hathorn, Mollie Steiner, Agatha Tiernan, Clara Tiernan, Mary Elizabeth Tiernan
1952 1. Jackie Begin, Sally Herman, Jessie S. Moore, Norma Matz
2-3. Peggy Adams, Helen Baker, Marguerite Harris, Ethel Keohane
2-3. Kay Rhodes, Ruth Sherman, Helen Sobel, Margaret Wagar
1953 1. Gretchen Feldstein, Vera Glick, Gratian Goldstein, Lucille Schwarz
2-3. Mary Jane Kauder, Kay Rhodes, Ruth Sherman, Margaret Wagar
2-3. Elaine Lee, Olive Peterson, Roberta Sheronas, Peggy Solomon
1954 1. Wynne Ecker, Doris Fuller, Marguerite Harris, Norma Matz
2-5. Marguerite Bouldin, Lillian Hassler, Ann Jervis, Dorothy Payne
2-5. Marie Cohn, Olive Peterson, Pauline Shmukler, Peggy Solomon
2-5. Kay Rhodes, Ruth Sherman, Helen Sobel, Margaret Wagar
2-5. Margaret Alcorn, Louise Eisenman, Emily Folline, Sue Reith
1955 1. Peggy Adams, Carolyn Brall, Louise Eisenman, Shirley Johnson, Juanita Strich
2-4. Kay Rhodes, Ruth Sherman, Helen Sobel, Margaret Wagar
2-4. Ann Burnstein, Edith Kemp, Paula Levin, Ruth Steinberg, Sally Young
2-4. Ruth Gordon, Josephine Gutman, Evelyn Engleman, Margaret Katzen, G. Eloise Neil
1956 1. Peggy Rotzell, Jan Stone, Charlotte Sidway, Mary Elizabeth Tiernan
2. Kay Rhodes, Helen Sobel, Margaret Wagar, Sally Young
1957 1. Marie Cohn, Mary Jane Kauder, Stella Rebner, Peggy Solomon
2. Agnes Gordon, Kay Rhodes, Helen Sobel, Margaret Wagar
1958 1. Carolyn Brall, Bee Gale, Sally Johnson, Peggy Rotzell
2. Kay Rhodes, Helen Sobel, Margaret Wagar, Sally Young
1959 1. Margaret Alcorn, Lee Kasle, Josephine Sharp, Adelaide Simon, Garner McDaniel
2. Kay Dunn, Jane Herb, Malvine Klausner, Helen Portugal, Rose Reif
1960 1. Roberta Erde, Sally Johnson, Barbara Kachmar, Bee Schenken
2. Joan Remey, Helen Shanbrom, Sylvia Stein, Marge Stone
1961 1. Roberta Erde, Sally Johnson, Barbara Kachmar, Bee Schenken

2. Mary Jane Farell, Terry Michaels, Peggy Solomon, Jan Stone

1962 1. Anne Burnstein, Edith Kemp, Alicia Kempner, Stella Rebner, Teddie Warner
2. Muriel Kaplan, Terry Michaels, Garner McDaniel, Jan Stone

1963 1. Pat Adler, Terry Michaels, Garner McDaniel, Cora Sanders, Sylvia Stein
2. Dorothy Hayden, Barbara Kachmar, Agnes Gordon, Helen Portugal, Margaret Wagar

1964 1. Hermine Baron, Mary Jane Farell, Peggy Solomon, Bee Schenken
2. Agnes Gordon, Dorothy Hayden, Helen Portugal, Margaret Wagar

1965 1. Virginia Heckel, Betty Kaplan, Edith Kemp, Jacqui Mitchell
2. Debbie Polak, Joan Remey, Carol Ruther, Sylvia Stein

1966 1-2. Freida Arst, June Deutsch, Sylvia Stein, Carol Stoklin
1-2. Nancy Gruver, Garner McDaniel, Terry Michaels, Sue Sachs

1967 1. Dorothy Hayden, Emma Jean Hawes, Agnes Gordon, Margaret Wagar
2-3. Hermine Baron, Mary Jane Farell, Bee Schenken, Peggy Solomon
2-3. Dolores Bick, Jude Ballard, Ruth Needham, Viola Kirkwood

1968 1. Hermine Baron, Mary Jane Farell, Sally Johnson, Bee Schenken, Peggy Solomon, Rhoda Walsh
2. Jane Frankel, Teddy O'Brien, Mary Beth Townsend, Esta Van Zandt

1969 1. Karen Allison, Virginia Heckel, Edith Kemp, Alicia Kempner, Helen Portugal, Jan Stone
2. Nancy Gruver, Barbara Rappaport, Sue Sachs, Barbara Tepper

1970 1. Mary Jane Farell, Emma Jean Hawes, Dorothy Hayden, Marilyn Johnson, Jacqui Mitchell, Peggy Solomon
2. Dorothy Cowger, Diane Hawes, Florence Van Winkle, Freda Van Cleve

1971 1. Judi Friedenberg, Gail Moss, Marietta Passell, Helen Utegaard, Kathie Wei
2. Roberta Epstein, Gretchen Goldstein, Edith Kemp, Barbara Rappaport, Sylvia Stein

1972 1. Mary Jane Farell, Emma Jean Hawes, Dorothy Hayden, Sue Picus
2. Frieda Arst, June Deutsch, Eunice Rosen, Carol Stoklin

1973 1. Nancy Gruver, Terry Michaels, Jo Morse, Helen Utegaard
2-4. Nancy Alpaugh, Fran Beard, Heitie Noland, Betsey Wolff, Esta Van Zandt
2-4. Mary Jane Farell, Marilyn Johnson, Jacqui Mitchell, Gail Moss, Marietta Passell, Kathie Wei
2-4. Jean Christopher, Muriel Peterson, Beverly Rosenberg, Elaine Sternberg

1974 1. Mary Jane Farell, Emma Jean Hawes, Marilyn Johnson, Jacqui Mitchell, Gail Moss, Dorothy Hayden Truscott
2. Hermine Baron, Carol Greenhut, Trudi Nugit, Kerri Shuman

1975 1. Mary Jane Farell, Emma Jean Hawes, Marilyn Johnson, Jacqui Mitchell, Gail Moss, Dorothy Hayden Truscott
2. Anita Davis, Mildred Freedman, Robin Grantham, Carol Klar

1976 1. Mary Jane Farell, Emma Jean Hawes, Marilyn Johnson, Jacqui Mitchell, Gail Moss, Dorothy Hayden Truscott
2. Evelyn Levitt, Lila Perlstein, Helen Smith, Vivian Whalen

1977 1. Betty Adler, Jo Morse, Judi Radin, Sue Sachs
2. Ida Bennett, Mary Lou Cushner, Carole Felczer, Ethel Keohane

1978 1. Nancy Alpaugh, Nancy Gruver, Betty Ann Kennedy, Evelyn Levitt, Carol Sanders, Kerri Shuman
2. Cheri Bjerkan, Sue Halperin, Beverly Nelson, Florine Waters

1979 1. Betty Adler, Anne Burnstein, Edith Kemp, Terry Michaels, Jo Morse, Sue Sachs
2. Cheri Bjerkan, June Deutsch, Sue Halperin, Sandy Levitt, Beverly Nelson, Florine Walters

1980 1. Nancy Gruver, Edith Kemp, Betty Ann Kennedy, Judi Radin, Carol Sanders, Kathi Wei
2. Betty Adler, Pat Lapides, Pat Leary, Terry Michaels, Jo Morse, Jan Stansby

1981 1. June Deutsch, Pat Lapides, Sandy Leavitt, Evelyn Levitt, Jo Morse, Helen Utegaard
2. Karen Allison, Cheri Bjerkan, Lynn Deas, Dianna Gordon, Sue Halperin, Sharyn Kokish

1982 1. Stasha Cohen, Mary Jane Farell, Nancy Gruver, Edith Kemp, Randi Montin, Dorothy Hayden Truscott
2. Betty Ann Kennedy, Jacqui Mitchell, Gail Moss, Judi Radin, Carol Sanders, Kathie Wei

1983 1. Kathie Wei, Judi Radin, Jacqui Mitchell, Gail Moss, Carl Sanders, Betty Ann Kennedy, Jim Zimmerman (npc)
2. Brenda Keller, Linda Peterson, Nancy Passell, Patsy Arnett, Nell Cahn

1984 1. Edith Kemp Frelich, Nancy Gruver, Mary Jane Farell, Helen Utegaard, Beverly Rosenberg, Carol Pincus
2. Terry Michaels, Garner McDaniel, Mary Williams, Sally Wheeler, Cindy Bernstein

1985 1. Rama Linz, Beth Palmer, Kay Schulle, Barbara Hamman, Juanita Skelton
2. Roberta Epstein, Jan Martel, Lisa Berkowitz, Rozanne Pollack, Lynn Feldman, Sue Picus

1986 1. Jo Morse, Evelyn Levitt, Sharon Osberg, Peggy Sutherlin, Cindy Bernstein, Sally Wheeler
2. Rama Linz, Beth Palmer, Lynn Deas, Juanita Chambers, Kerri Shuman, Cheri Bjerkan

1987 1. Kathie Wei,.Judi Radin, Jacqui Mitchell, Amalya Kearse, Carol Sanders, Betty Ann Kennedy
2. Mary Jane Farell, Roberta Epstein, Jan Martel, Dorothy Truscott, Carol Simon, Karen McCallum

1988 1. Beverly Rosenberg, Helen Utegaard, Sue Weinstein, Janice Seamon, Carol Pincus, Pat Schor
2. Terry Michaels, Cindy Bernstein, Linda Perlman, Sue Sachs, Sally Wheeler, Jo Morse

1989 1. Juanita Chambers, Kay Schulle, Cheri Bjerkan, Randi Montin, Pam Wittes, Jill Meyers
2. Jo Morse, Joyce Lilie, Cindy Bernstein, Georgiana Gates, Janice Seamon, Linda Perlman

1990 1. Mary Jane Farell, Roberta Epstein, Dorothy Truscott, Gail Greenberg, Lisa Berkowitz, Rozanne Pollack
2. Juanita Chambers, Cheri Bjerkan, Kay Schulle, Jill Meyers, Pam Wittes, Randi Montin

1991 1. Nancy Passell, Nell Cahn, Sue Picus, Stasha Cohen, Susan Green, Sharon Osberg
2. Jacqui Mitchell, Amalya Kearse, Joyce Lilie, Jo Morse, Pamela Granovetter, Nancy Alpaugh

1992 1. Juanita Chambers, Cheri Bjerkan, Marinesa Letizia, Janice Seamon
2. Kathie Wei, Helen Utegaard, Carol Sanders, Betty Ann Kennedy, Lynn Deas, Beth Palmer

1993 1. Gail Greenberg, Dorothy Truscott, Judy Tucker, Stasha Cohen, Irinia Levitina, Rozanne Pollack
2. Kay Schulle, Jill Meyers, Cheri Bjerkan, Janice Seamon

GRAND NATIONAL TEAMS. The competition is contested for the ALBERT MOREHEAD TROPHY. The initial stages are contested over the course of several months. Originally this was a North American contest with all 25 ACBL districts participating. Now it is a United States event, with only the 23 U.S. districts participating. The district winners play off for the championship at the Summer North American Championships. In 1985 the event was subdivided into three separate events and this event became Flight A.

1973 1. Russell Arnold, James Beery, Jane Jaeger, Richard Pavlicek, William Seamon, Robert G. Sharp
2. Brian Economidy, Jerry Levitt, Roger Lord, Norb Kremer, Dave Smith, Ron Smith

1974 1. Larry Cohen, Bill Eisenberg, Eddie Kantar, Richard Katz, Paul Soloway, John Swanson
2. Chuck Burger, Fred Hamilton, Howard Perlman, Stanley Smith, Jeffrey Starr, Dick Yanko

1975 1. John Fisher, Charles Gabriel, Robert Hamman, Jim

Hooker, Charles Weed, Bobby Wolff
  2. Mike Cook, Jim Felts, Doug Hill, Reece Rogers, Ron Smith, Bernie Yomtov
1976 1. Bill Eisenberg, Eddie Kantar, Paul Soloway, John Swanson
  2. Marty Fleisher, Charlie Friedman, Ron Gerard, Halina Jamner, Archie McKellar, Neil Nathanson
1977 1. Robert Hamman, Dan Morse, Curtis Smith, Eddie Wold, Bobby Wolff
  2. Bobby Lipsitz, Steve Parker, Steve Robinson, Kit Woolsey
1978 1. Gerald Caravelli, Charles Peres, William Rosen, Milton Rosenberg, Dan Rotman
  2. Allan Cokin, Robert Levin, Bud Reinhold, William Seamon, Steve Sion
1979 1. Greg DeFotis, Jerry Goldfein, Arnold Leavitt, Larry Robbins, Claude Vogel
  2. Marty Bergen, Chuck Lamprey, Warren Rosner, Allan Stauber
1980 1. Jack Bitman, Jan Janitschke, Craig Janitschke, Dick Lesko
  2. Russell Arnold, Edith Kemp, William Passell, Cliff Russell, William Seamon, Dave Strasberg
1981 1. Ira Chorush, James Jacoby, Mike Passell, George Rosenkranz, Eddie Wold
  2. Mike Becker, Brian Glubok, John Lowenthal, Phillip Martin, Michael Rosenberg, Ron Rubin
1982 1. Ron Von der Porten, Hugh Ross, Chip Martel, Lew Stansby, Kyle Larsen, Peter Pender
  2. Steve Landen, Pratap Rajadhyaksha, Jeff Starr, Frank Bell, Chuck Burger
1983 1. Chip Martel, Hugh Ross, Peter Pender, Lew Stansby
  2. Lou Bluhm, Richard Freeman, Larry Gould, Randy Joyce, Nick Nickell
1984 1. Kit Woolsey, Ed Manfield, Peter Boyd, Bob Lipsitz, Steve Robinson
  2. Greg De Fotis, Larry Robbins, Jerry Goldfein, Hal Mouser, Jack Oest, Gerry Caravelli
1985 1. Chip Martel, Hugh Ross, Lew Stansby, Peter Pender
  2. Steve Robinson, Ed Manfield, Peter Boyd, Bob Lipsitz
1986 1. Seymon Deutsch, Bobby Wolff, Bob Hamman, Jim Jacoby
  2. Milt Rosenberg, Ralph Katz, Hal Mouser, Greg De Fotis, Larry Robbins, Howard Weinstein
1987 1. Chip Martel, Hugh Ross, Peter Pender, Lew Stansby, Mike Lawrence
  2. Frank Hoadley, Sidney Lazard, John Onstott, Jack LaNoue
1988 1. Steve Robinson, Ed Manfield, Peter Boyd, Robert Lipsitz
  2. Jack Oest, Steve Garner, Jerry Goldfein, Bart Bramley, Gerry Caravelli, Howard Weinstein
1989 1. Steve Sion, Robert Barr, Harold Stengel, Bernie Miller
  2. Tony Kasday, Paul Ivaska, Gaylor Kasle, Garey Hayden, Roger Bates
1990 1. Doug Simson, Walter Johnson, Jeff Meckstroth, Eric Rodwell, Dennis Clerkin
  2. Kay Larsen, Chris Larsen, Joe Kivel, Robert Rosenblum, Evan Bailey
1991 1. Larry Robbins, Jerry Goldfein, Jack Oest, Peter Nagy, Steve Garner, Howard Weinstein
  2. Marty Bergen, Fred Stewart, Larry Cohen, Steve Weinstein
1992 1. Steve Robinson, Peter Boyd, Robert Lipsitz, Ed Manfield
  2. Michael Becker, Ron Rubin, Richard Pavlicek, William Root, Robert Levin, Jeff Wolfson
1993 1. Ravindra Murthy, Brad Moss, Lew Stansby, Chip Martel, Hugh Ross, Jeff Ferro
  2. Brian Ellis, Asim Ulke, Florine Walters, Richard Finberg, Jay Apfelbaum, Piyush Vakil

NORTH AMERICAN TEAMS, FLIGHT B.

This event is a grass-roots competition, with games at various levels eventually leading to each of the 25 ACBL districts sending its champion to the Summer North American Bridge Championships to compete for the championship. It is open

only to players with fewer than 1500 masterpoints.
1985 1. Irving Goodman, Floyd Dyson, Leo Takefman, Tim McPhail, Louis Richardson
  2. Sally Grace, Linda Weinstein, Sharon Meng, Jennifer James, Jerry Poliquin, Robert Buchner
1986 1. Paul McGowan, George Towner, Winston Edwards, Regena Jones
  2. Ken Connell, Linda Connell, Carla Eisenhauer, S. K. Carruthers, Claire Jones, Dennis Nelson
1987 1. Dwight Hunt, Ed Horwitz, Ken Kadish, Claude LeFeuvre
  2. Bob Webb, Pat Webb, Kevin Chen, Joseph Blalock
1988 1. Steven Beck, Michael Camp, Win Allegaert, Fred Chang
  2. Jean Molnar, Michael Weber, Donn Holmer, Walter Riddle, Joseph Rubin
1989 1. George Runyan, Tim Joder, Iype Koshy, Robert Dupont
  2. Paul Nickerson, William Goldsmith, Denise Goldsmith, Cheryl Porter
1990 1. Judy Hughes, Karen Miller, Robert Seaholm, John Morano, Goutam Chakraborty, Krishnanand Maillacheruvu
  2. Jim Adams, John Edmunds, Dan Feldman, Larry Kahn, Usuf Ismail
1991 1. Mary Poplawski, Stanley Poplawski, William Smith, Barrett Raff
  2. Bruce Norman, Fred Gitelman, Sheri Winestock, Geoff Hampson
1992 1. Otto Rothenberg, Richard Baumer, Arthur Haley, Bert Kulic
  2. Nielih Cheng, Peter Kalat, Jeffery Allen, Carlos Munoz, L. P. Calahan, Bruce Platt
1993 1. Eric Greco, Philip Greco, Kefer Xu, Harry Zhou, David Better
  2. Jack Jessop, Morrie Kleinplatz, Barry Onslow, Elaine Morrison

NORTH AMERICAN TEAMS, FLIGHT C.

This event is a grass-roots competition, with games at various levels eventually leading to each of the 25 ACBL districts sending its champion to the Summer North American Bridge Championships to compete for the championship. It is open only to non-Life Masters with fewer than 500 masterpoints.
1991 1. Bob Fashingbauer, Kenneth Wolf, Thomas Dressing, David Marker
  2. Albert Tom, Dennis Erani, Valentin Carciu, Gary Gottleib
1992 1. Richard Unger, Charles Morrin, Andrew Ware, Martin Wewerka
  2. J. Michael Hill, Kevin Kadmus, Carol Wisemiller, Marty Lohdale
1993 1. Stephen Arshan, Richard Ross, Feng Liu, Steve Pessin, George Shamy
  2. Sardarsinh Gohel, Jack Shartsis, Joyce Bell, Nathan Banker

LIFE MASTER PAIRS. This six-session event

with two qualifying, two semifinal and two final rounds, restricted to Life Masters, is contested for the VON ZEDTWITZ GOLD CUP.
1930 1. P. Hal Sims, Waldemar K. von Zedtwitz
  2. Ely Culbertson, Josephine Culbertson
1931 1. David Burnstine, Howard Schenken
  2. Michael T. Gottlieb, Theodore A. Lightner
1932 1. Michael T. Gottlieb, Theodore A. Lightner
  2. David Burnstine, Howard Schenken
1933 1. David Burnstine, Howard Schenken
  2. P. Hal Sims, Waldemar K. von Zedtwitz
1934 1. Richard L. Frey, Howard Schenken
  2. Walter Malowan, Sydney Rusinow
1935 1. B. Jay Becker, Theodore A. Lightner
  2. Louis J. Haddad, Charles A. Hall
1936 1. David Burnstine, Oswald Jacoby
  2. Robert Appleyard, Isadore Epstein
1937 1. S. Garton Churchill, Charles L. Lochridge
  2. Doris Fuller, Dr. Henry J. Vogel

1938	1.	Morrie Elis, Sherman Stearns
	2.	John R. Crawford, Charles J. Solomon
1939	1.	Robert Appleyard, Harry J. Fishbein
	2.	Oswald Jacoby, Waldemar K. von Zedtwitz
1940	1.	Harry J. Fishbein, Morrie Elis
	2.	Sam Fry, Jr., Myron Fuchs
1941	1.	Merwyn D. Maier, Howard Schenken
	2.	John R. Crawford, Oswald Jacoby
1942	1.	Charles H. Goren, Helen Sobel
	2.	Philip Abramsohn, Tobias Stone
1943	1.	John R. Crawford, Howard Schenken
	2.	Sidney Silodor, Margaret Wagar
1944	1.	Samuel Katz, Peter A. Leventritt
	2.	Ambrose Casner, Ralph Hirschberg
1945	1.	Robert Appleyard, Malcolm A. Lightman
	2.	Bertram Lebhar, Jr., Simon Rossant
1946	1.	Sidney Silodor, Charles J. Solomon
	2.	Lee Hazen, Ruth Sherman
1947	1.	Allen P. Harvey, Frank Weisbach
	2.	John R. Crawford, Theodore A. Lightner
1948	1.	S. Garton Churchill, Cecil Head
	2.	Erik Coon, Vincent Remey
1949	1.	Ruth Gilbert, Leo Roet
	2.	Arthur Glatt, Albert Weiss
1950	1.	Manuel Sherwin, Dr. C. W. Yorke
	2.	Edward N. Marcus, Samuel M. Stayman
1951	1.	Richard Kahn, Peter A. Leventritt
	2.	Ned Drucker, Edgar Kaplan
1952	1.	William W. Jackson, William Joseph
	2-3.	Arthur Glatt, Albert Weiss
	2-3.	John R. Crawford, Howard Schenken
1953	1.	Milton Q. Ellenby, William A. Rosen
	2.	Charles H. Goren, Helen Sobel
1954	1.	David C. Carter, John W. Hubbell
	2.	Victor Mitchell, Ira S. Rubin
1955	1.	Ben Fain, Paul H. Hodge
	2.	Victor Mitchell, Ira S. Rubin
1956	1.	Alvin Roth, Tobias Stone
	2.	John R. Crawford, Sidney Silodor
1957	1.	H. Sanborn Brown, Martin Cohn
	2.	Francis P. Begley, Louis Kelner
1958	1-2.	Charles H. Goren, Helen Sobel
	1-2.	Wilson Landley, Louis Levy
1959	1.	Ed Rosen, Dan Rotman
	2.	Sidney Aronson, Larry Weiss
1960	1.	Helen Portugal, Morris Portugal
	2.	Curtis K. Smith, Bobby Wolff
1961	1.	Philip Feldesman, Marshall Miles
	2.	Paul Kibler, Robert Reynolds
1962	1.	Philip Feldesman, Ira S. Rubin
	2.	Edith Kemp, Albert Weiss
1963	1.	Lewis L. Mathe, Edward O. Taylor
	2.	Ira Rubin, Curtis Smith
1964	1.	B. Jay Becker, Dorothy Hayden
	2.	Bruce Elliott, Percy E. Sheardown
1965	1.	Victor Mitchell, Samuel M. Stayman
	2.	Alvin Roth, Tobias Stone
1966	1.	Hermine Baron, Meyer Schleifer
	2.	Morrie Freier, Robert Reynolds
1967	1.	Philip Feldesman, Lewis L. Mathe
	2.	Diana Schuld, Frank Schuld
1968	1.	Bill Eisenberg, Bobby Goldman
	2.	James Jacoby, Bobby Wolff
1969	1.	Sami R. Kehela, Eric R. Murray
	2.	Chuck F. Burger, James Cayne
1970	1.	Paul Heitner, Michael Moss
	2.	Robert Freedman, James Mathis
1971	1.	Alvin Roth, Barbara Rappaport
	2.	James Jacoby, Minda Brachman
1972	1.	Alvin Roth, Barbara Rappaport
	2.	Alan Sontag, Peter Weichsel
1973	1.	Jack Blair, Paul Swanson
	2.	Chuck F. Burger, James Cayne
1974	1.	Gerald Michaud, G. Robert Nail
	2.	Walter Walvick, Thomas Weik
1975	1.	Roy Fox, Eugene O'Neill
	2.	Michael Becker, Ahmed Hussein
1976	1.	Robert Lipsitz, Neil Silverman
	2.	Garey Hayden, Mike Passell
1977	1.	Alan Sontag, Peter Weichsel
	2.	Ken Cohen, Robert Lipsitz
1978	1.	Mary Jane Farell, Marilyn Johnson
	2.	Ron Feldman, David Sacks
1979	1.	Ralph Katz, Ken Schutze
	2.	Dan Morse, G. Robert Nail

1980	1.	Robert D. Hamman, Eric Rodwell
	2.	Don Caton, Homer Shoop
1981	1.	Fred Stewart, Steve Weinstein
	2.	Paul Lavings, Bob Richman
1982	1.	Tommy Sanders, Ron Andersen
	2.	Robert Lipsitz, Ron Sukoneck
1983	1.	Bob Hamman, Eddie Kantar
	2.	Eric Rodwell, Jeff Meckstroth
1984	1.	Mike Lawrence, Peter Weichsel
	2.	Alan Sontag, Steve Sion
1985	1.	George Steiner, Darryl Pedersen
	2.	David Siebert, Allan Siebert
1986	1.	Eric Rodwell, Douglas Simson
	2.	Tom Kniest, Karen Walker
1987	1.	Larry N. Cohen, Dave Berkowitz
	2.	Steve Robinson, Peter Boyd
1988	1.	Marty Bergen, Larry N. Cohen
	2.	Howard Weinstein, John Carruthers
1989	1.	Richard Katz, Robert Levin
	2.	Howard Weinstein, Ralph Katz
1990	1.	Ron Rubin, Michael Becker
	2.	John Mohan, Kay Schulle
1991	1.	Doug Simson, Eric Rodwell
	2.	Steve Sion, Clint Morrell
1992	1.	Bob Hamman, Hemant Lall
	2.	Hugh Ross, Zia Mahmood
1993	1.	Dan Morse, John Sutherlin
	2.	Tom Clarke, Alan LeBendig

IMP PAIRS. This event, consisting of two qualifying and two final sessions, is scored by International Match Points.

1987	1.	Robb Gordon, Linda Danas
	2.	Peter Weichsel, Richard Katz
1988	1.	Gene Freed, Mike Passell
	2.	Corinne Gellman, Jim Kirkham
1989	1.	Richard Schwartz, Fred Hamilton
	2.	Bud Reinhold, Michael Seamon
1990	1.	Ralph Cohen, Renee Mancuso
	2.	Richard Schwartz, Drew Casen
1991	1.	Harvey Brody, Ralph Buchalter
	2.	Ron Feldman, Marty Shallon
1992	1.	Vera Gama, Marcelo Branco
	2.	David Midkiff, Tom Oppenheimer
1993	1.	Bob Klein, David Ruderman
	2.	Win Allegaert, Gary Gottlieb

MASTER MIXED TEAMS. This event is contested for the LEBHAR TROPHY (originally for the BARCLAY TROPHY until 1945). A four-session Board-a-Match event, with two qualifying rounds and two final rounds, it is restricted to players who have won at least 100 masterpoints. In 1969 this event was played in three sessions.

1929	1.	Max M. Cohen, Mrs. M. K. Alexander, Rose Fleischer, R. Frankenstein
1930	1.	Cmdr. Winfield W. Liggett, Jr., Dorothy Rice Sims, P. Hal Sims, Sir Derrick J. Wernher
	2.	W. Cleveland Cogswell, J. Arnold Farrar, Doris Fuller, George Reith
1931	1.	Mrs. G. A. Bennett, Doris Fuller, Charles S. Lochridge, George Reith
	2.	E. M. Baker, Margaret Beech, William McKenney, Mrs. H. D. Stahl
1932	1.	Marie Black, H. Huber Boscowitz, Sam Fry, Jr., Olga Hilliard
	2.	Mrs. L. Bloomberg, Bernard Cone, A. Louis Gotthelf, Mrs. Thomas Stern
1933	1.	David Burnstine, Elinor Murdoch, Mrs. Ivan Stengel, Edwin A. Wetzler
	2.	Dorothy Rice Sims, P. Hal Sims, Margaret Wagar, Waldemar K. von Zedtwitz
1934	1.	Lester R. Bachner, Mrs. Lester R. Bachner, James H. Lemon, Martha Lemon
	2.	A. Mitchell Barnes, Barbara Collyer, Doris Fuller, Dr. Henry J. Vogel
1935	1.	Helen Bonwit, Howard Schenken, Ruth Sherman, Louis H. Watson
	2.	Mary Clement, Mary Zita Jacoby, Oswald Jacoby, Waldemar K. von Zedtwitz

1936 1. Hortense Evans, Louis J. Haddad, Robert McPherran, Elizabeth Whitney
     2. B. Jay Becker, Helen Bonwit, Howard Schenken, Sally Young
1937 1. Philip Abramsohn, Estelle Drescher, Morrie Elis, Ann Naiman
     2. S. Garton Churchill, Phyllis Gardner, Travers LeGros, Dorothy Roberts
1938 1. Doris Fuller, Charles H. Goren, Dr. Henry J. Vogel, Sally Young
     2. Eleanor Hirsch, John C. Kunkel, Helen Pendelton Rockwell, Milton Vernoff
1939 1. Robert Chatkin, Valerie Klein, Alvin Landy, Florence Stratford
     2. Edward G. Ellenbogen, Peggy Golder, Helen Mitchell, Charles J. Solomon
1940 1. Marie Black, Henry H. Chanin, Olive Peterson, Waldemar K. von Zedtwitz
     2. Edward G. Ellenbogen, Peggy Golder, Helen Mitchell, Charles J. Solomon
1941 1. Charles H. Goren, Sidney Silodor, Helen Sobel, Sally Young
     2. Oswald Jacoby, Louise Wainwright, Sherman Stearns, Mrs. William A. Tucker
1942 1. John R. Crawford, Olive Peterson, Margaret Wagar, Waldemar K. von Zedtwitz
     2. Philip Abramson, Kay Rhodes, Edith Seligman, Tobias Stone
1943 1. Charles H. Goren, Olive Peterson, Sidney Silodor, Helen Sobel
     2. Edith Hammond, Pat Lightner, Walter Malowan, Stuyvesant Wainwright
1944 1. Charles H. Goren, Olive Peterson, Sidney Silodor, Helen Sobel
     2. Marie Basher, Edward Cohn, John R. Crawford, Margaret Wagar
1945 1. John R. Crawford, Ruth Sherman, Margaret Wagar, Waldemar K. von Zedtwitz
     2. Morrie Elis, Harry J. Fishbein, Alvin Roth, Edith Seligman
1946 1. Samuel Katz, Alicia Kempner, Evelyn Lebhar, Bertram Lebhar, Jr.
     2. Charles H. Goren, Emily Folline, Sidney Silodor, Helen Sobel
1947 1. Harry J. Fishbein, Ruth Goldberg, Ludwig Kabakjian, Edith Seligman
     2-3. Emily Folline, Peter A. Leventritt, David Warner, Sally Young
     2-3. Harold Harkavy, Jane Jaeger, Lewis M. Jaeger, Mrs. O. Busser
1948 1. John R. Crawford, Charles H. Goren, Helen Sobel, Margaret Wagar
     2. Harry J. Fishbein, Ruth Goldberg, Ludwig Kabakjian, Edith Seligman
1949 1. Peter A. Leventritt, Charles J. Solomon, Peggy Solomon, Sally Young
     2. John R. Crawford, Charles H. Goren, Helen Sobel, Margaret Wagar
1950 1. Peter A. Leventritt, Charles J. Solomon, Peggy Solomon, Sally Young
     2. John R. Crawford, Charles H. Goren, Helen Sobel, Margaret Wagar
1951 1. Jane Jaeger, Ruth Kahn, Leo Roet, Ruth Sherman
     2. Myron Field, Agnes Gordon, Charles H. Goren, Helen Sobel
1952 1. Anne Burnstein, Harold Harkavy, Alvin Roth, Edith Seligman
     2. John R. Crawford, Emma Jean Hawes, George Rapee, Olive Peterson, Sidney Silodor
1953 1. Anne Burnstein, Harold Harkavy, Edith Kemp, Alvin Roth
     2. Emanuel Hochfeld, Mary Jane Kauder, Lewis L. Mathe, Gloria Turner
1954 1. Charles H. Goren, Sidney Silodor, Helen Sobel, Margaret Wagar
     2. Marianne Boschan, Gertrude Eberson, David Murray, Lewis Tubbs
1955 1. Gratian Goldstein, Harold Harkavy, Terry Michaels, Alvin Roth
     2. Mary Bowden, Douglas Drury, Richard Freedman, Agnes Gordon, Eric R. Murray
1956 1. Mary Bowden, Douglas Drury, Robert Freedman, Agnes Gordon, Eric R. Murray
     2. Barbara Brier, Jan Stone, Tobias Stone, Waldemar K. von Zedtwitz

1957 1. John R. Crawford, Milton Q. Ellenby, Harold Harkavy, Edith Kemp, Gloria Turner
     2. Sam Fry, Jr., Dorothy Hayden, Sally Johnson, Ira S. Rubin
1958 1. Leland Ferer, Gratian Goldstein, Eunice Rosen, William Rosen
     2. B. Jay Becker, Bee Gale, Betty Goldberg, Howard Schenken
1959 1. Peter A. Leventritt, Robert F. Jordan, Charles J. Solomon, Peggy Solomon, Sally Young
     2. Leonard B. Harmon, Edgar Kaplan, Peggy Rotzell, Alfred Sheinwold, Betty Sheinwold
1960 1. William Grieve, Alicia Kempner, George Rapee, Betty Ann Welch
     2. B. Jay Becker, Dorothy Hayden, Norman Kay, Sidney Silodor, Sylvia Stein
1961 1. Richard Freeman, Emanuel Hochfeld, Louise Robinson, Gloria Turner
     2. John Fisher, Jean Frankel, Lou Gurvich, Boots Kendrick, Sidney Lazard
1962 1. Charles Coon, Agnes Gordon, Eric Murray, Helen Portugal
     2. Norman Kay, Sidney Silodor, Sylvia Stein, Margaret Wagar
1963 1. Sidney Lazard, Betty Kaplan, Edgar Kaplan, Stella Rebner
     2. Israel Cohen, Garner McDaniel, Terry Michaels, Alvin Roth
1964 1. John Fisher, John Gerber, Emma Jean Hawes, Margaret Wagar
     2-3. Martin J. Cohn, Hampton Hume, Bernadine Jenkins, Mary Philley
     2-3. Harold Harkavy, Virginia Heckel, Edith Kemp, Clifford Russell, Jerome Yavitz, Jr.
1965 1. Barbara Brier, Alvin Roth, Jan Stone, Tobias Stone, Waldemar K. von Zedtwitz
     2. Burt Norton, Carol Norton, William Rosen, Sylvia Stein, Carol Stolkin
1966 1. James Cayne, Judy Dryer, Paul Soloway, Eunice Rosen, William Rosen
     2. Barbara Rappaport, Alvin Roth, Bee Schenken, Howard Schenken
1967 1. Mike Cappelletti, Kathie Cappelletti, Michael Moss, Gail Shane
     2-4. John Gerber, Norman Kay, Carol Klar, George Rosenkranz, Edith Rosenkranz
     2-4. B. Jay Becker, John Fisher, Dorothy Hayden, Emma Jean Hawes
     2-4. Leland Ferer, Gratian Goldstein, Fred Hamilton, Sylvia Stein
1968 1. Minda Brachman, James Jacoby, Oswald Jacoby, Helen Sobel Smith
     2. Betty Kaplan, Edgar Kaplan, George Rapee, Carol Stolkin
1969 1. Janice Cohn, Flo Orner, Charles Peres, Dan Rotman, Ivar Stakgold, Alice Stakgold
     2. Barry Crane, Jules Farell, Mary Jane Farell, Marilyn Johnson, Peter Rank
1970 1. Dorothy Bare, Gerald Bare, Eugenie Mathe, Lewis L. Mathe
     2-3. Ken Barbour, William Daly, Mickey Rosenthal, Helen Strasberg, Dave Strasberg
     2-3. Betty Adler, Julian Adler, Dave Sachs, Sue Sachs
1971 1. John Anderson, Ron E. Andersen, Marilyn McCrary, Sue Picus
     2. Dorsey Brooks, Zerrene Brooks, Joan Remey, Vincent Remey
1972 1. Gail Moss, Michael Moss, Marietta Passell, William Passell
     2. B. Jay Becker, John Fisher, Emma Jean Hawes, Alan Truscott, Dorothy Hayden Truscott
1973 1. Ellen Alfandre, Philip Feldesman, Edith Sacks, Stanley Tomchin
     2-5. Betty Adler, Julian Adler, Dave Sachs, Sue Sachs
     2-5. Doug Fraser, Sandra Fraser, Barbara Saltsman, Joe Silver
     2-5. Mark Berger, Sallie Johnson, Amos Kaminsky, Jack Saltz, Mona Stocknoff
     2-5. Carol Crawford, John R. Crawford, Barbara Rappaport, Alvin Roth
1974 1. Edith Kemp, Jerome Yavitz, Rita Seamon, William Seamon
     2. Robert Lipsitz, Jo Morse, Peggy Parker, Steve Parker, Steve Robinson
1975 1. Gerald Caravelli, Nancy Gruver, Jim Linhart,

Helen Utegaard
2-3. Shirlee Lazarus, Eugenie Mathe, Lewis L. Mathe, Joan Remey, Vincent Remey, James E. Zimmerman
2-3. Carol Crawford, John R. Crawford, Barbara Rappaport, Alvin Roth
1976 1-2. Richard H. Katz, Carol Sanders, Paul Swanson, Marion Weed
1-2. Fred Hamilton, John C. Sutherlin, Peggy Sutherlin, Rhoda Walsh, Nancy Weichsel, Peter Weichsel
1977 1. Nancy Alpaugh, Joan DeWitt, Mark Lair, Sidney Lazard
2. Ethel Dayboch, Morrie Freier, Richard Paulsen, Sue Thornton
1978 1. Nancy Alpaugh, Joan DeWitt, Mark Lair, Sidney Lazard
2. Betty Adler, Julian Adler, David Sachs, Sue Sachs
1979 1-3. Betty Bloom, Steven Bloom, Mark Cohen, Edith Sacks
1-3. Nancy Alpaugh, Joan DeWitt, Mark Lair, Sidney Lazard
1-3. Lynne Feldman, Mark Feldman, Ed Nagy, Sharon Smith
1980 1. Barry Crane, Jose John Hamui, Elias Konstantinovsky, Laura Mariscal, Kerri Shuman
2. Gerald Caravelli, Dennis McGarry, Joan Remey, Vincent Remey, Helen Utegaard
1981 1. Doug Fraser, Sandra Fraser, Ralph Katz, Paul Lewis, Linda Peterson, Esta Van Zandt
2. Bill Cole, Lynn Deas, Norb Kremer, Beth Palmer
1982 1-2. Tommy Sanders, Carol Sanders, Sidney Lazard, Joan DeWitt
1-2. Lynn Deas, Norb Kremer, Beth Palmer, Bill Cole
1983 1. Alan Kudisch, Judy Landau, Drew Casen, Karen Allison
2. Kathie Wei, Judi Radin, Eric Rodwell, Jeff Meckstroth
1984 1. Susan Sternberg, Bernie Chazen, Juanita Skelton, Allan Cokin, Barbara Sion, Steve Sion
2. Edith Rosenkranz, George Rosenkranz, Carol Sanders, Mark Lair, Lynn Deas, Eddie Wold
1985 1. Bill Pollack, Rozanne Pollack, Alan Truscott, Dorothy Truscott, Evelyn Levitt, Dave Treadwell
2. Rich Schmieder, Jyme Tropila, Martin Miller, Carole Dietz
1986 1. Mark Cohen, Stasha Cohen, Harold Lilie, Joyce Lilie, David Berkowitz, Lisa Berkowitz
2. Carol Simon, Bob Etter, Min Ross, Hugh Ross, Paul Kern, Claire Kern
1987 1-2. Jim Mahaffey, Linda Perlman, Joan Remey, Paul Soloway
1-2. Bob Hamman, Kerri Shuman, Rama Linz, Robert Levin
1988 1-2. Robert Radwin, Helen Utegaard, Flo Rotman, Dan Rotman
1-2. Ken Cohen, Jo Anne Manfield, Robert Woodard, Ev Cogan
1989 1. Alan Sontag, Peter Weichsel, Gladys Collier, Juanita Chambers
2-3. Marty Bergen, Dori Cohen, Mary Oshlag, Richard Oshlag
2-3. Chester Hirsch, Mary Jane Farell, Jacqui Mitchell, Victor Mitchell
1990 1. Edith Rosenkranz, George Rosenkranz, Eddie Wold, Marinesa Letizia, Kerri Shuman, Mark Lair
2. Jim Becker, Ellee Lewis, Howard Chandross, Vivian Whalen
1991 1. John Carruthers, Katie Thorpe, Brad Moss, Bronia Gmach, Jared Lilienstein
2. Robert Thomson, Asya Kamsky, Rozanne Pollack, Michael Radin, Marty Bergen, Dori Cohen
1992 1. Gabriel Chagas, Marinesa Letizia, Dennis Clerkin, Juanita Chambers, Mike Lawrence, Beth Palmer
2. Bjorn Fallenius, Kathy Anday, Shirlee Meckstroth, Jeff Meckstroth
1993 1. Lisa Berkowitz, David Berkowitz, Beth Palmer, William Pettis
2. Nancy Molesworth, Stephen Schneer, Robbie Hopkins, Joan Lewis

From 1946-1955 a separate event with national rating was held on the West Coast.
1946 1. Nell Wells, George Wells, Kay Dunn, James Dunn
1947 1. Rose Eidem, Meyer Schleifer, Betty Bysshe, Detmar Walther

1948 1. Alma Rosekrans, Waldemar von Zedtwitz, Maurice Seiler, Mrs. Maurice Seiler
1949 1. Arnold Kauder, Mary Jane Kauder, Helen Cale, Jack Ehrlenbach
1950 1. Arnold Kauder, Mary Jane Kauder, Helen Cale, Jack Ehrlenbach
1951 1. Ruth Smith, Casey Million, Nell Wells, John Hancock
1952 1. Don Oakie, Mrs. James Moffatt, Stella Rebner, Doug Steen
1953 1. Barry Cohen, Stella Rebner, Malvine Klausner, Dr. Eddie Frischauer
1954 1. Harriet Rethers, Clarence Strouse, Alicia Kempner, Barry Crane
1955 1. Arnold Kauder, Mary Jane Kauder, Nell Wells, Ernest Rovere

RED RIBBON PAIRS.

This event, with two qualifying and two final sessions, is open only to pairs that qualify by winning or placing second in two-session regional-rated events. Both members of the pair must have fewer than 2000 masterpoints.

1986 1. Wayne Perrin, Martin Newland
2. Hugh Ogle, Charlie Cargile
1987 1. Jim Gaarder, Jimmy Ritzenberg
2. Charles Moser, Paul Bratton
1988 1. Leni Holtz, Guy Green
2. Anthony Trafecanty, Michael Trafecanty
1989 1. Lu Kohutiak, Yvonne Hernandez
2-3. Warren Haynie, Charlie Cargile
2-3. Bill Goldberg, Bill McKenna
1990 1. Philip Gordon, Mike Grodsky
2. Rajendra Agarwal, Don Chillrud
1991 1. Dan Marthaler, Robert Johnstone
2. Steven Gaynor, Art Ardy Bakshian
1992 1. Duncan McCallum, Peter Peng
2. Andy Goodman, Steve Zolotow
1993 1. Ron Weinstock, John Gillette
2. Hank Meyer, Marty Graf

NON-LIFE MASTER SWISS TEAMS.

Two qualifying and two final sessions.

1982 1. Jay Feldman, Bill Carnes, David Rinehart, Gordon Grossetta, Norval Baran, Bill Brown
2. Donna Burtt, Ron Woodsum, Leonard Smith, John Shelley
1983 1. Ani Deshpande, Joel Guthmann, Dan Dennehy, Martha Benson
2. Rob Brown, Deborah Gattas, Jean Choi, Warren Fukushima
1984 1. Larry Lerner, David Grossman, Jackie Saltman, Brian Gunnell
2. Phil Articola, Harry Sapienza, Ken Harkness, Bill Anspach, Ben Brill, Paul McMullin
1985 1. Dorothy Shorts, John Shorts, Patricia Rasmus, Richard Rasmus
2-3. Dudley Hemphill, Phil Clayton, David Chyan, Bob Price
2-3. Charles Hopkins, Tom Smith, Esfandiar Khazai, Jo Schachner, Barbara Barnett, Edie Eastman
1986 1. Walter Bell, David Kresge, Bob Klotz, John Dickenson
2. Michael Chelst, Ellen Klosson, Lois Tenkin, Bob Bell
1987 1. Elaine Pettius, Judy Beul, Jim Beul, Steve Albin
2-3. Frances Schminky, Jane Baker, George Perry, Helen Perry
2-3. Michael Cheng, Ransone Price, John Diamond, David Cheng
1988 1. Andrew Moss, Amy Nellissen, Barry Margolius, Iain Abrahams
2. Chris Roberts, W. Aeschbacher, Candy Carlson, Roberto Scaramuzzi, David Marker, Mark Hunsaker
1989 1. Tom Gittings, Charles Sheaff, Lavern Wiebe, David Suplinski
2. Marcia Plonsker, Deanne Fox, Nancy Weil, Marilyn Kroll
1990 1. Wayne Oden, Daniel Jackson, Randy Paul, Larry Flowers

     2.   Thomas Courtney, David Pickering, Tommy Thompson, James Tieman

1991 1.   Steve Wood, Linda Wood, Beverly Whitehorn, Gene Nobles

     2.   Karen Berkowitz, Richard Clayton, James Raiford, Darl Brooks, Alan Hayman, Ernest Campbell

1992 1.   Dennis Hsu, Adam Weisz-Margulesku, Feng Lu, Xiadong Zhang

     2.   Darren Wolpert, Hazel Wolpert, M. Salamone, Sam Yoga

1993 1.   Douglas Crispell, Nicholas Straguzzi, Robert Browne, Paul Gorman

     2.   Michael Veve, Curtis Lending, Robert Zier, James Witting, Stephen Bunning

NABC JUNIOR PAIRS. Two sessions.

1991 1.   B. Wayne Stuart, Jeff Ferro
     2.   Andrew Moss, Gwenn Kalow
1992 1.   Vicky Sawyer, Chris Austin
     2.   Michael Roberts, David Gurvich

NORTH AMERICAN YOUTH PAIRS. Two sessions.

1991 1.   Daniel Kalish, Andrew Kalish
     2.   Itai Lourie, Oved Lourie

SENIOR AND ADVANCED SENIOR MASTER PAIRS.

This four-session event with two qualifying sessions and two final sessions was contested for the R. L. MILES TROPHY through 1975.

1950 1.   John Winsten, Mrs. John Winsten
   2-3. Dorothy E. Berning, Sims Gaynor
   2-3. Dorsey W. Brooks, Fred Gregorich
1951 1.   Ben Fain, Julius L. Rosenblum
     2.   Dorothy Glick, Aaron Ritter
1952 1.   Elaine Lee, Hary Feinburg
     2.   Betty Harding, Mrs. Allan E. van Ness
1953 1-2. Dr. Robert M. Lloyd, Elfric H. Martin
   1-2. Margaret L. Fisher, Kiffin Rockwell

1954 1.   Armand Fahrer, Richard B. Troxel
     2.   Richard G. Lesko, Paul A. Schwarz
1955 1.   Stanley Rappaport, Herschel Wolpert
     2.   Robert Sitnek, Betty Windley
1956 1.   Nat Gerstman, Mrs. Marshall Nevins
     2.   George Ateljevich, Robert E. Herb
1957 1-2. Arnold Levine, Harold Solof
   1-2. Daniel J. Conroy, William T. Dean
1958 1.   Fritz J. Hopf, Mrs. Fritz J. Hopf
     2.   Allan R. Cohen, Herbert C. Wilton
1959 1.   Victor Lohmann, Robert L. Muyres
     2.   Ira Ewen, Thomas C. Griffin
1960 1.   Lillian Hilbert, Forest Lowe
     2.   Ruth Row, Stephens Roe
1961 1.   Amos Brown, Mark D. Mohr
     2.   Dr. Ronald Forbes, Jack Howell
1962 1.   Leon Shore, George Tornay
     2.   Richard Dufour, Hugh C. MacLean
1963 1.   Gerald Hallee, Paul Soloway
     2.   Frank Adams, Max Neiman
1964 1.   Mrs. R. Gust, Jr., Mrs. Leslie Wilcox
     2.   Gerald A. Caravelli, Alan Levine
1965 1.   Muriel Levin, Belle Levinson
     2.   Don Guerin, Charlotte Sturm
1966 1.   Carla Gross, H. E. Pries
     2.   Steve Goldstein, Ron Rubin
1967 1.   Alvin Levy, Harold Thaw
     2.   Maryanne Drury, Kenneth Kadis
1968 1.   Henry Greenberg, John Landon
     2.   Howard Abrams, Jim Crumpacker
1969 1.   Col. William B. Foster, Bobbie Foster
     2.   Judy Carmena, Proctor Hawkins
1970 1.   Michael Krevor, James Lewis
     2.   Dennis McGarry, Louis Reich
1971 1.   William L. Geleerd, Jr., Marc S. Passman
     2.   Bert Newman, Dave Turner
1972 1.   Chris Patrias, Dr. Wen Y. Yue
     2.   Robert Bell, Jeff Hall
1973 1.   Joel Friedberg, Harry Looks
     2.   William Post, Alvin Swonger
1974 1.   Dale Beers, Dave Silberstein
     2.   Ethan Stein, Karen Swenson
1975 1.   Kitty Munson, Robert Schachter
     2.   John Brady, Patricia Murphy

Fall Championships

REISINGER BOARD-A-MATCH TEAMS.

This event is contested for the REISINGER TROPHY (originally the CHICAGO TROPHY until 1965). It is a six-session Open Team-of-Four event scored by Board-a-Match with two qualifying sessions, two semifinal sessions and two final sessions. It was contested as a four-session championship until 1966.

1929 1.   Max M. Cohen, Louis J. Haddad, Robert W. Halpin, Nils M. Wester
     2.   Carlton R. Drake, James Kelly, Paul D. Parcells, Charles Rilling
1930 1.   William K. Barrett, W. James Carpenter, Ely Culbertson, Johnny Rau
     2.   Mary Clement, Dorothy Rice Sims, P. Hal Sims, Waldemar K. von Zedtwitz
1931 1.   Elizabeth Banfield, Cmdr. Winfield S. Liggett, Jr., Frances Newman, George Unger
     2.   David Burnstine, Oswald Jacoby, Willard S. Karn, P. Hal Sims
1932 1.   B. Jay Becker, S. Garton Churchill, George Reith, Waldemar K. von Zedtwitz
     2.   Ely Culbertson, Michael T. Gottlieb, Oswald Jacoby, Theodore A. Lightner
1933 1.   Charles A. Hall, Albert Steiner, Philip Steiner, Richard M. Wildberg
     2.   B. Jay Becker, S. Garton Churchill, P. Hal Sims, Waldemar K. von Zedtwitz
1934 1.   Henry S. Dinkelspiel, Jr., Lewis Jaeger, Bernard Rabinowitz, Maurice Seiler
     2.   Theodore A. Lightner, Merwyn D. Maier, Jean P. Mattheys, Sherman Stearns

1935 1.   F. Roland Buck, Joseph E. Cain, Lawrence J. Welch, Edson T. Wood
     2.   Ely Culbertson, Josephine Culbertson, Richard L. Frey, Albert H. Morehead
1936 1.   Marge Anderson, Donald G. Farquharson, Mrs. J. A. Faulkner, Percy E. Sheardown
     2.   Arthur Glatt, Laura Heiner, John R. Smith, Albert Weiss
1937 1.   John R. Crawford, Charles H. Goren, Charles J. Solomon, Sally Young
     2.   Oscar J. Brotman, William Perry, Alvin Roth, S. S. Vorzimer
1938 1.   John R. Crawford, Charles H. Goren, Charles J. Solomon, Sally Young
     2.   A. Mitchell Barnes, Mary Clement, Benedict Jarmel, Waldemar K. von Zedtwitz
1939 1.   B. Jay Becker, John R. Crawford, Charles H. Goren, Charles J. Solomon, Sally Young
   2-4. Jay Cushing, Seymour Kaplan, Al Leibowitz, Edward N. Marcus
   2-4. Oswald Jacoby, Merwyn D. Maier, Robert A. McPherran, Waldemar K. von Zedtwitz
   2-4. Henry Auslander, Joseph Davis, Jacob D. Lindy, Catherine W. Samberg
1940 1.   Henry Feinberg, Jeff Glick, Maury J. Glick, Louis Newman
     2.   Alfred R. Dick, C. William Potts, James Sheern, Edward R. Thomas
1941 1.   Peter A. Leventritt, Simon Rossant, Helen Sobel, Margaret Wagar
     2.   A. Mitchel Barnes, S. Garton Churchill, Lee Hazen, Charles S. Lochridge, Waldemar K. von Zedtwitz
1942 1.   B. Jay Becker, Charles H. Goren, Sidney Silodor, John R. Crawford

	2.	S. Garton Churchill, Harry J. Fishbein, Lee Hazen, Waldemar K. von Zedtwitz
1943	1.	B. Jay Becker, Charles H. Goren, Sidney Silodor, Helen Sobel
	2.	Samuel Katz, Bertram Lebhar, Jr., Peter A. Leventritt, Simon Rossant
1944	1.	Simon Becker, Peggy Golder, Ruth Sherman, Charles J. Solomon
	2.	B. Jay Becker, Charles H. Goren, Sidney Silodor, Helen Sobel
1945	1.	Lee Hazen, George Rapee, Samuel M. Stayman, Waldemar K. von Zedtwitz
	2.	Ambrose Casner, Harold J. Harkavy, Ralph Hirschberg, Harold A. Ogust, Jack Shore
1946	1.	A. Mitchel Barnes, John R. Crawford, Alvin Roth, Edith Seligman
	2.	Simon Becker, Stanley O. Fenkel, Fred D. Karpin, Louis Newman
1947	1.	Paula Bacher, Jane Jaeger, Kay Rhodes, Sally Young
	2-3.	John R. Crawford, Theodore A. Lightner, George Rapee, Samuel M. Stayman
	2-3.	Robert Appleyard, Morris Berliant, Malcolm A. Lightman, Simon Rossant
1948	1.	George Boeckh, C. Bruce Elliott, Agnes Gordon, Charlotte Sidway
	2.	John R. Crawford, George Rapee, Sidney Silodor, Samuel M. Stayman
1949	1.	Lee Hazen, Larry Hirsch, Richard Kahn, Peter A. Leventritt, Jack Shore
	2-3.	Sidney Aronson, Emily Folline, Benjamin O. Johnson, Ludwig J. Kabakjian, Edward N. Marcus
	2-3.	Jeff Glick, Arthur S. Goldsmith, Alvin Landy, Sol Mogal, Elmer I. Schwartz
1950	1.	B. Jay Becker, Myron F. Field, Charles H. Goren, Sidney Silodor, Helen Sobel
	2.	John R. Crawford, George Rapee, Edward N. Marcus, Howard Schenken, Samuel M. Stayman
1951	1.	Corti Boland, C. Bruce Elliot, Micky M. Miller, Percy E. Sheardown
	2.	B. Jay Becker, Charles H. Goren, Myron F. Field, Sidney Silodor, Helen Sobel
1952	1.	Harold Harkavy, Edith Kemp, Alvin Roth, Tobias Stone
	2.	Edward H. Cohen, Jeff Glick, Arthur S. Goldsmith, Elmer I. Schwartz
1953	1.	B. Jay Becker, John R. Crawford, George Rapee, Samuel M. Stayman
	2.	Harry J. Fishbein, Peter A. Leventritt, Ruth Sherman, Charles J. Solomon, Peggy Solomon
1954	1.	B. Jay Becker, John R. Crawford, George Rapee, Sidney Silodor
	2.	Israel Cohen, Paul Kibler, Alvin Roth, William Seamon
1955	1.	Ben Fain, George Heath, Paul Hodge, James Jacoby, Oswald Jacoby
	2.	William V. Lipton, Victor Mitchell, W. Miller Nelson, Joseph G. Ripstra
1956	1.	B. Jay Becker, John R. Crawford, George Rapee, Sidney Silodor
	2.	Ben Fain, Paul Hodge, Oswald Jacoby, Dick Sutton
1957	1.	Charles H. Goren, Harold A. Ogust, William S. Root, Howard Schenken, Helen Sobel
	2.	Robert Y. Barrett, Ben Fain, Harry J. Fishbein, John Gerber, Paul Hodge
1958	1.	Leonard B. Harmon, Ralph Hirschberg, Edgar Kaplan, Alfred Scheinwold, Ivar Stakgold
	2.	Arthur M. Miller, John H. Moran, David Strasberg, Jay Wendt
1959	1.	Lewis L. Mathe, Donald A. Oakie, Meyer Schleifer, Edward O. Taylor
	2.	Harry J. Fishbein, John Gerber, Paul Hodge, Charles J. Solomon
1960	1.	Ollie Adams, William Hann, Sidney H. Lazard, Lewis L. Mathe
	2.	Oswald Jacoby, Mervin Key, G. Robert Nail, Curtis Smith
1961	1.	John R. Crawford, Norman Kay, Alvin Roth, Sidney Silodor, Tobias Stone
	2-3.	Charles Coon, Robert F. Jordan, Eric R. Murray, Arthur G. Robinson
	2-3.	Harold B. Guiver, Carol Sanders, Thomas K. Sanders, Michael Shuman
1962	1-2.	Paul Allinger, Harold B. Guiver, Lewis L. Mathe, Ron Von der Porten, Erik Paulsen, Edward O. Taylor
	1-2.	Robert D. Hamman, Eddie Kantar, Donald P. Krauss, Marshall Miles, Bill Eisenberg
1963	1.	Charles H. Goren, Peter A. Leventritt, Harold A. Ogust, Howard Schenken
	2.	Donald R. Faskow, William L. Flannery, Herbert Sachs, Paul Swanson
1964	1.	John Gerber, Paul Hodge, Mervin Key, Harold Rockaway
	2.	Harold Harkavy, Edith Kemp, Cliff Russell, Curtis K. Smith, Bobby Wolff, Waldemar K. von Zedtwitz
1965	1.	Eddie Kantar, Michael S. Lawrence, Marshall Miles, Lew Stansby
	2.	Michael Engel, Phil Feldesman, Richard Freeman, Ira S. Rubin
1966	1.	Robert F. Jordan, Edgar Kaplan, Norman Kay, Arthur G. Robinson
	2-3.	Gerald W. Bare, Harold B. Guiver, Lewis L. Mathe, Mike McMahan, Erik Paulsen, Hugh Ross
	2-3.	William S. Root, Alvin Roth, Bee Schenken, Howard Schenken
1967	1.	Robert F. Jordan, Edgar Kaplan, Norman Kay, Arthur G. Robinson, William S. Root, Alvin Roth
	2.	Steve Altman, Michael M. Becker, Charles Peres, Daniel Rotman
1968	1.	Kyle Larsen, Erik Paulsen, Peter A. Pender, Hugh Ross, Howard Schenken
	2.	Bill Eisenberg, Bobby Goldman, Robert D. Hamman, Eddie Kantar, Sidney Lazard, George Rapee
1969	1.	Philip Feldesman, William Grieve, Ira Rubin, Gerald Westheimer
	2.	Edgar Kaplan, Norman Kay, Sami R. Kehela, Sidney Lazard, Eric R. Murray, George Rapee
1970	1-2.	Bill Eisenberg, Bobby Goldman, Robert D. Hamman, James Jacoby, Michael S. Lawrence, Bobby Wolff
	1-2.	Grant S. Baze, Anthony H. Dionisi, William P. Grieve, Harlow S. Lewis, Peter A. Pender, George Rapee
1971	1.	William Grieve, Edgar Kaplan, Norman Kay, Donald P. Krauss, Lewis L. Mathe, George Rapee
	2.	Grant S. Baze, Anthony H. Dionisi, Harlow S. Lewis, Peter A. Pender
1972	1.	Lou Bluhm, Steve Goldberg, Steven J. Parker, Stephen W. Robinson
	2.	William Grieve, Sami R. Kehela, Eric R. Murray, George Rapee
1973	1.	Larry Cohen, Dr. Richard H. Katz, Bud Reinhold, Alan Sontag, Peter Weichsel
	2.	Jack Blair, Byron L. Greenberg, Thomas K. Sanders, Paul Swanson
1974	1.	Fred Hamilton, Erik Paulsen, Hugh Ross, Ira S. Rubin
	2.	Stephen Goldstein, Marc S. Jacobus, J. Merrill, Steve Sion, John Solodar
1975	1.	Fred Hamilton, Erik Paulsen, Hugh Ross, Ira S. Rubin
	2.	Richard E. Doughty, Frank M. Hoadley, Jack LaNoue, Sidney H. Lazard
1976	1.	Malcolm K. Brachman, Bill Eisenberg, Bobby Goldman, Eddie Kantar, Mike Passell, Paul Soloway
	2.	Matt Granovetter, Robert H. Lipsitz, Steven J. Parker, Samuel M. Stayman
1977	1.	Jim Cayne, Alan Greenberg, James Jacoby, Kyle Larsen, Michael S. Lawrence
	2.	Matt Granovetter, Robert H. Lipsitz, Neil Silverman, Samuel M. Stayman
1978	1.	Ira G. Corn, Jr., Fred Hamilton, Robert D. Hamman, Ira S. Rubin, Bobby Wolff
	2.	Allan Graves, Gaylor Kasle, Mark Lair, George Mittelman, Barney O'Malia, Ron Smith
1979	1-2.	Russ Arnold, Robert Levin, Jeff Meckstroth, Bud Reinhold, Eric Rodwell
	1-2.	Ira G. Corn, Jr., Fred Hamilton, Robert D. Hamman, Ira S. Rubin, Bobby Wolff
1980	1.	Ron E. Andersen, Malcolm K. Brachman, Bobby Goldman, Eddie Kantar, Michael S.

		Lawrence, Paul Soloway
	2-3.	Mark Lair, Jeff Meckstroth, Mike Passell, Eric Rodwell, George Rosenkranz, Eddie Wold
	2-3.	Roy Fox, Ed Manfield, Paul Swanson, Kit Woolsey
1981	1.	Chip Martel, Peter A. Pender, Hugh Ross, Lew Stansby
	2-3.	Roger Bates, Chuck F. Burger, Jim Cayne, Bill Eisenberg, Alan Greenberg
	2-3.	Evan Bailey, L. Andrew Campbell, Joel Hoersch, David J. Weiss
1982	1.	Bill Root, Richard Pavlicek, Edgar Kaplan, Norman Kay
	2.	Mark Molson, Eric Kokish, Paul Lewis, Robert Lebi, George Mittelman, Drew Cannell
1983	1.	Oswald Jacoby, Edgar Kaplan, Norman Kay, Bill Root, Richard Pavlicek
	2-3	Ron Rubin, Mike Becker, Bill Eisenberg, Eddie Kantar, Mike Lawrence, Peter Weichsel
	2-3.	Chip Martel, Lew Stansby, Peter Pender, Hugh Ross
1984	1-4.	Bill Root, Richard Pavlicek, Edgar Kaplan, Norman Kay
	1-4.	Fred Stewart, Steve Weinstein, Allan Stauber, Mike Smolen
	1-4.	Sam Stayman, Richard Reisig, George Tornay, Saul Bronstein
	1-4.	Jim Robison, Jon Wittes, Ross Grabel, Stelio Touchtidis
1985	1-2.	Chip Martel, Peter Pender, Hugh Ross, Lew Stansby
	1-2.	George Rosenkranz, Eddie Wold, Jeff Meckstroth, Eric Rodwell, Marty Bergen, Larry Cohen
1986	1.	Steve Robinson, Chip Martel, Hugh Ross, Peter Boyd, Peter Pender, Lew Stansby
	2.	Bud Reinhold, Ron Andersen, Tom Sanders, Paul Soloway, Bobby Goldman
1987	1.	Zia Mahmood, Jaggy Shivdasani, Billy Cohen, Ron Smith
	2.	Walter Johnson, Mark Cohen, Ralph Katz, Bill Pollack, Dave Berkowitz, Howard Weinstein
1988	1.	Jimmy Cayne, Bob Hamman, Mike Passell, Mark Lair, Chuck Berger, Bobby Wolff
	2.	Tom Fox, Dick Melson, Jim Hall, David Lehman
1989	1.	Zia Mahmood, Michael Rosenberg, Sam Lev, Chris Compton, Mark Molson
	2.	Jillian Blanchard, Robert Blanchard, Jon Greenspan, Kerri Shuman, Margie Gwozdzinsky, Glenn Eisenstein
1990	1.	Richard Pavlicek, William Root, Edgar Kaplan, Norman Kay, Brian Glubok
	2.	Malcolm Brachman, Mike Passell, Paul Soloway, Bobby Goldman, Mark Lair, Eddie Wold
1991	1.	Cliff Russell, Sam Lev, Larry N. Cohen, David Berkowitz, Marty Bergen, Bjorn Fallenius
	2.	Mike Cappelletti, Jr., Mike Cappelletti, Sr., Lawrence Hicks, Rob Crawford
1992	1.	James Cayne, Mike Passell, Mark Lair, Chuck Burger, Gabriel Chagas, Marcelo Branco
	2.	Jim Mahaffey, Alan Sontag, Eddie Kantar, Ron Andersen, Tony Forrester
1993	1.	Nick Nickell, Richard Freeman, Bob Hamman, Bobby Wolff, Jeff Meckstroth, Eric Rodwell
	2.	Jimmy Cayne, Chuck Burger, Mike Passell, Paul Soloway, Bobby Goldman, Mark Lair

BLUE RIBBON PAIRS. This event is contested for the CAVENDISH TROPHY. It is a six-session pair event with two qualifying sessions. Entry is restricted to winners and runners-up in regional championships and high finishers in North American Championships, members of current Grand National District Championship teams, members of current official teams representing the ACBL or member countries of the ACBL, together with the top 100 lifetime masterpoint holders.

1963	1.	B. Jay Becker, Dorothy Hayden

	2.	Harold Harkavy, Cliff Russell
1964	1.	Robert D. Hamman, Lewis L. Mathe
	2.	Gunther Polak, Robert G. Sharp
1965	1.	Chuck Henke, John H. Moran
	2.	Michael S. Lawrence, Ron Von der Porten
1966	1.	Charles Coon, Richard Zeckhauser
	2.	Leland Ferer, Gratian Goldstein
1967	1.	Sami R. Kehela, Baron Wolf Lebovic
	2.	Phil Feldesman, Lewis L. Mathe
1968	1.	Larry Cohen, Richard H. Katz
	2.	Bobby Goldman, Michael S. Lawrence
1969	1.	Eric Paulsen, Alex Tschekaloff
	2-4.	Sami R. Kehela, Eric R. Murray
	2-4.	Tom Hodapp, Robert F. Morris
	2-4.	Larry Cohen, Richard H. Katz
1970	1.	Chuck F. Burger, Ira S. Rubin
	2.	Richard Freeman, Cliff Russell
1971	1.	Roger Bates, John M. Grantham
	2.	Hermine Baron, Michael S. Lawrence
1972	1.	Richard Khautin, Warren Kornfeld
	2.	Garey Hayden, Mark Lair
1973	1.	Steve Robinson, Kit Woolsey
	2.	Kathie Cappelletti, Mike Cappelletti
1974	1.	Edgar Kaplan, Norman Kay
	2.	Roger Bates, George Rosenkranz
1975	1.	Steve Robinson, Kit Woolsey
	2.	Ron E. Anderson, Hugh C. MacLean
1976	1.	Jay Apfelbaum, Bill Edelstein
	2.	James Jacoby, David Berkowitz
1977	1.	Lou Bluhm, Thomas K. Sanders
	2.	Kathie Cappelletti, Mike Cappelletti
1978	1.	Ron E. Andersen, David Berkowitz
	2.	Ted Horning, Peter Nagy
1979	1.	Robert Levin, Ron Smith
	2.	James Bennett, Chester Davis
1980	1.	Warren Rosner, Allan Stauber
	2.	Dan Morse, G. Robert Nail
1981	1.	Larry N. Cohen, Ron Gerard
	2.	Chip Martel, Lew Stansby
1982	1.	Eric Rodwell, Jeff Meckstroth
	2-3.	Robert Blanchard, Drew Casen
	2-3.	Peter Boyd, Steve Robinson
1983	1.	Marty Bergen, Larry N. Cohen
	2.	Peter Weichsel, Mike Lawrence
1984	1-2.	Jack Kennedy, Bobby Wolff
	1-2.	David Funk, Mark Lair
1985	1.	Eric Rodwell, Walter Johnson
	2.	Kit Woolsey, Ed Manfield
1986	1.	Bob Hamman, Ron Von der Porten
	2.	Kit Woolsey, Ed Manfield
1987	1.	Fred Stewart, Steve Weinstein
	2.	Kerri Shuman, Mark S. Lawrence
1988	1.	Marty Bergen, Larry N. Cohen
	2.	Robert Levin, Ron Smith
1989	1.	Mark Molson, Robert Lebi
	2.	Gaylor Kasle, Roger Bates
1990	1.	Kit Woolsey, Ed Manfield
	2.	Brian Glubok, Sam Lev
1991	1.	Bob Hamman, Nick Nickell
	2.	Mark Tolliver, Marc Zwerling
1992	1.	Haig Tchamitch, Adam Wildavsky
	2.	Brad Moss, Ravindra Murthy
1993	1.	Bob Hamman, Michael Rosenberg
	2.	Martin De Bruin, Steve Price

LIFE MASTER OPEN PAIRS, formerly LIFE MASTER MEN'S PAIRS. It is a four-session event with two qualifying sessions and two final sessions, restricted to Life Masters. Before 1963 it was restricted to National Masters and players of higher rank. It was a men's event until 1990 when it became an open event.

1961	1.	G. Gard Hays, Max Manchester
	2.	Martin J. Cohn, Hampton Hume
1962	1.	Sam Fuoto, Victor Mitchell
	2.	Hal Kandler, Kelsey Petterson
1963	1.	Sami R. Kehela, Eric R. Murray
	2.	Harry J. Fishbein, Charles J. Solomon
1964	1.	Charles Coon, Bobby Goldman
	2-3.	Mervin Key, Harold Rockaway
	2-3.	Jack Blair, Col. William Christian
1965	1.	Paul Soloway, Alex Tschekaloff

	2.	Edgar Kaplan, Victor Mitchell
1966	1.	Carl J. Hudeck, Ray Zoller
	2.	Gaylor Kasle, Ed Theus
1967	1.	Harlow S. Lewis, Peter A. Pender
	2.	Donald R. Faskow, William L. Flannery
1968	1.	Henry Bethe, John Solodar
	2.	Don Pearson, John Swanson
1969	1.	Chuck F. Burger, James Cayne
	2.	Norman H. Fischer, Christopher G. Jeans
1970	1.	Ron E. Andersen, Hugh C. MacLean
	2.	Curtis K. Smith, E. Lowell Yost
1971	1.	Alan Sontag, Peter Weichsel
	2.	Stephen W. Robinson, Kit Woolsey
1972	1.	Leslie C. Bart, Marc S. Jacobus
	2.	Stephen W. Robinson, Kit Woolsey
1973	1.	Edgar Kaplan, Norman Kay
	2.	Roxy Violin, Ed Weiner
1974	1.	Gerald L. Michaud, G. Robert Nail
	2.	John Gerber, Daniel Kaim
1975	1.	Steve Lapides, Walt Walvick
	2.	Marc Culberson, Robert Visokey
1976	1.	Roger Bates, John Mohan
	2.	Steve Altman, Thomas M. Smith
1977	1.	David Hoffner, David Schroeder
	2.	Roger Bates, John Mohan
1978	1.	Norm Coombs, Tom Hodapp
	2.	Kevin Castner, Michael S. Lawrence
1979	1.	Jeff Meckstroth, Eric Rodwell
	2.	Zeke Jabbour, Dennis McGarry
1980	1.	V. Craig Janitschke, Jan Janitschke
	2.	Robert D. Hamman, Paul Swanson
1981	1.	Roger Abelson, Mike Levinson
	2.	Robert D. Hamman, Donald P. Krauss
1982	1.	Robert Lipsitz, Dan Gertsman
	2.	Lew Mathe, Harold Guiver
1983	1.	Marty Bergen, Larry N. Cohen
	2.	Mitch Chandler, Cliff Bishop
1984	1.	Per Olov Sundelin, Peter Pender
	2.	Jim Becker, Howard Chandross
1985	1.	John Mohan, Roger Bates
	2.	Eric Rodwell, Jeff Meckstroth
1986	1.	Jim Krekorian, Paul Kiefer
	2.	Marty Bergen, Larry N. Cohen
1987	1.	Bart Bramley, Lou Bluhm
	2.	Leslie West, David Ashley
1988	1.	Robert Levin, Larry Cohen
	2.	Glen Lublin, Peter Boyd
1989	1.	Steve Lapides, Walt Walvick
	2.	Peter Weichsel, Roger Stern

In 1990 the event became the LIFE MASTER OPEN PAIRS.

1990	1.	Zia Mahmood, Hugh Ross
	2.	Tommy Gullberg, Michael Polowan
1991	1.	Zia Mahmood, Hugh Ross
	2.	Larry N. Cohen, David Berkowitz
1992	1.	Mike Kamil, Michael Rosenberg
	2.	Jeff Meckstroth, Eric Rodwell
1993	1.	Brad Moss, Ravindra Murthy
	2.	Ed Nagy, Jeff Polisner

LIFE MASTER WOMENS PAIRS.

This event is contested for the HELEN SOBEL SMITH TROPHY. It is a four-session event with two qualifying sessions and two final sessions, restricted to Life Masters. Prior to 1963 it was restricted to National Masters and players of higher rank.

1961	1.	Dorothy Hayden, Helen Portugal
	2.	Gratian Goldstein, Jane Mueller
1962	1.	Barbara Kachmar, Margaret Wagar
	2.	Anne Burnstein, Edith Kemp
1963	1.	Anne Burnstein, Hermine Baron
	2.	Carrie Arnold, Neva L. Gray
1964	1.	Margaret Alcorn, Betty Kaplan
	2.	Agnes Gordon, Sylvia Stein
1965	1.	Ann Sheaber, Jan Stone
	2.	Mary Jane Farell, Peggy Solomon
1966	1.	Emma Jean Hawes, Dorothy Hayden
	2.	Mary Jane Farell, Peggy Solomon
1967	1.	Nancy Gruver, Edith Sachs
	2.	Mary Jane Farell, Peggy Solomon
1968	1.	Dorothy Talmage, Rhoda Walsh
	2.	Katherine Blanchard, Mary Jane Farell

1969	1.	Gratian Goldstein, Sylvia Stein
	2.	Karen Allison, Gladys W. Collier
1970	1.	Bette L. Cohn, Marietta Passell
	2.	Louise Krauss, Betty Mangan
1971	1.	Ruth Bloomfield, Della Levinson
	2.	Betty Ann Kennedy, Carol Sanders
1972	2.	Amalya Kearse, Rhoda Walsh
	2.	Emma Jean Hawes, Dorothy Hayden Truscott
1973	1.	Frieda Arst, June Deutsch
	2.	Edith Kemp, Barbara Rappaport
1974	1.	Bernice Larson, Joan Stein
	2.	Edith Kemp, Barbara Rappaport
1975	1.	Dorothy Moore, Marion Weed
	2.	Nancy Gruver, Helen Utegaard
1976	1.	Barbara Furbeck, Barbara Herr
	2.	Carol Crawford, Joan Remey
1977	1.	Edith Kemp, Barbara Rappaport
	2.	Bernadine Jenkins, Joan Remey
1978	1.	Emma Jean Hawes, Dorothy Hayden Truscott
	2.	Ann Economidy, Anne Leverone
1979	1.	Nancy Gruver, Edith Kemp
	2.	June Deutsch, Sandi Leavitt
1980	1.	Kathie Cappelletti, Claire Tornay
	2.	Nancy Gruver, Edith Kemp
1981	1.	Nancy Gruver, Edith Kemp
	2.	Betty Ann Kennedy, Carol Sanders
1982	1.	Dorothy Buchanan, Barbara Morris
	2.	Mary Albert, Rhoda Walsh
1983	1.	Beth Palmer, Lynn Deas
	2.	Sandra Low, Joan Stein
1984	1.	Karen Singer, Sharon Soules
	2.	Kathie Wei, Judi Radin
1985	1.	Lynn Deas, Beth Palmer
	2.	Rama Linz, Kerri Shuman
1986	1.	Mickie Kivel, Judi Codi
	2.	Rama Linz, Kerri Shuman
1987	1.	Jill Meyers, Gaye Herrington
	2.	Mary Ann Coyle, Jackie Hess
1988	1.	Nancy Passell, Nell Cahn
	2.	Brenda Keller, Renee Mancuso
1989	1.	Rhoda Walsh, Sabine Zenkel
	2.	Lynn Deas, Beth Palmer
1990	1.	Carol Sanders, Betty Ann Kennedy
	2.	Barbara Sartorius, Marla Chaiken
1991	1.	Sue Weinstein, Tobi Deutsch
	2.	Janice Seamon, Cheri Bjerkan
1992	1.	Shawn Womack, Jan Cohen
	2.	Sabine Zenkel, Joan Jackson
1993	1.	Janice Seamon, Sabine Zenkel
	2.	Sharon David, Trudi Nuget

OPEN BOARD-A-MATCH TEAMS, formerly MEN'S BOARD-A-MATCH TEAMS.

This four-session event consists of two qualifying and two final sessions. It was a men's event until 1990 when it became an open event. This event is contested for the GOREN TROPHY. It was contested as a three-session championship until 1972.

1946	1.	Maynard Adams, Julius Bank, Arthur Glatt, William McGhee, Albert Weiss
	2.	A. Mitchell Barnes, John R. Crawford, Charles H. Goren, George Rapee, Sidney Silodor
1947	1.	Jeff Glick, Arthur S. Goldsmith, Jack Kravatz, Alvin Landy, Sol Mogal
	2.	Joseph Cohan, Dr. Louis Mark, Dr. H. Russ Storr, George Unger
1948	1.	Jack L. Ankus, Jeff Glick, Alvin Landy, John H. Law, Sol Mogal
	2.	John R. Crawford, Edward N. Marcus, George Rapee, Samuel M. Stayman
1949	1.	Muriel Levin, Alphonse Moyse, Jr., Leo Roet, Howard Schenken
	2.	Joseph Cohan, Herbert J. Gerst, Jack L. Ankus, William Joseph, Dr. H. Russ Storr
1950	1.	Edward Burns, John F. Carlin, David Carter, A. Richard Revell
	2.	Robert Appleyard, Ned Drucker, Fred Hirsch, Milton Moss, Milton Vernoff
1951	1.	J. Van Brooks, Eugene Dautell, Jack Denny, Ace Gutowsky, Edwin J. Smith
	2.	Fred L. Bickel, Joseph J. Foreacre, Robert Lattomus, Ronald Rosenberg

1952	1.	Charles H. Goren, Oswald Jacoby, Sidney Silodor, Charles Solomon, Samuel M. Stayman
	2-3.	Samuel Katz, Charles Kuhn, William Seamon, Albert Weiss
	2-3.	Harry J. Fishbein, Harold Harkavy, Alvin Roth, Tobias Stone, Waldemar K. von Zedtwitz
1953	1.	Ben Fain, John Gerber, George Heath, Paul Hodge, Harold Rockaway
	2.	Clifford W. Bishop, Harry J. Fishbein, Arnold Kauder, John H. Moran, Douglas Steen
1954	1.	Aaron J. Frank, Jeff Glick, Arthur S. Goldsmith, Alvin Landy, Sol Mogal
	2.	Henry Chanin, Dr. John W. Fisher, James Jacoby, Oswald Jacoby, Sidney H. Lazard
1955	1.	Richard Freeman, Edgar Kaplan, Ralph Hirschberg, Norman Kay, Alvin Roth
	2.	Charles H. Goren, Peter A. Leventritt, Charles J. Solomon, Samuel M. Stayman
1956	1.	John R. Crawford, Ben Fain, Paul H. Hodge, Sidney Silodor
	2-3.	Paul Allinger, Dr. John W. Fisher, Emanuel Hochfeld, Oswald Jacoby, Sidney H. Lazard
	2-3.	Barry Crane, Harold Rockaway, Clarence Λ. Strouse, John H. Toledano
1957	1.	Lewis L. Mathe, Donald A. Oakie, Meyer Schleifer, Edward O. Taylor
	2.	Israel Cohen, Richard Freeman, John C. Kunkel, Alvin Roth, Ivar Stakgold
1958	1.	Jeff Glick, Arthur S. Goldsmith, Alvin Landy, Elmer I. Schwartz, Vic D. Zeve
	2.	Richard Freeman, Edgar Kaplan, Norman Kay, Ralph Hirschberg
1959	1.	Ollie Adams, Ivan Erdos, Oswald Jacoby, Robert G. Sharp
	2.	B. Jay Becker, John R. Crawford, Sidney Silodor, Tobias Stone
1960	1.	Charles Denby, Burrell I. Humphreys, Alan W. Messer, Marty Scheinberg, Robert P. Wakeman
	2-4.	Harry J. Fishbein, John Gerber, Paul H. Hodge, Charles J. Solomon
	2-4	Wilfred Dumas, Donald McGee, John Siverts, Jerzy Zawisza
	2-4.	James R. Hughes, Marvin Paulshock, Eli Reich, David R. Treadwell
1961	1.	John R. Crawford, Norman Kay, Alvin Roth, Sidney Silodor, Tobias Stone
	2.	Edgar Kaplan, Mervin Key, Sidney H. Lazard, G. Robert Nail
1962	1-2.	Phil Feldesman, Richard Freeman, Victor Mitchell, Eric R. Murray, Samuel M. Stayman
	1-2.	Paul Allinger, Harold G. Guiver, Lewis L. Mathe, Edward O. Taylor
1963	1	Phil Feldesman, Victor Mitchell, Samuel M. Stayman, Tobias Stone
	2.	B. Jay Becker, Norman Kay, William Root, Sol Rubinow, Sidney Silodor
1964	1.	Ivan Erdos, Harold B. Guiver, Michael S. Lawrence, Alfred Sheinwold
	2.	Charles Coon, G. Robert Nail, Robert Stucker, Frank T. Westcott
1965	1.	Harry J. Fishbein, Jeff Rubens, Charles J. Solomon, Roger D. Stern
	2.	Phil Feldesman, Sidney H. Lazard, Victor Mitchell, Daniel Rotman, Samuel M. Stayman
1966	1.	Philip Feldesman, Richard Freeman, Edgar Kaplan, Norman Kay
	2.	Anthony Dionisi, Jeremy Flint, Harlow S. Lewis, Peter A. Pender
1967	1.	Thomas E. Bussey, Jim R. Dunlap, Lawrence Jolma, Robert P. Patterson, Gary Stark
	2.	Edward J. Barlow, Phil Read, Robert Spots, John C. Sutherlin
1968	1.	Ira G. Corn, Jr., Bill Eisenberg, Bobby Goldman, James Jacoby, Michael S. Lawrence, Bobby Wolff
	2.	Michael M. Becker, Charles Coon, Joel H. Stuart, Peter Weichsel, Richard J. Zeckhauser
1969	1.	Chuck F. Burger, James Cayne, Alvin Roth, Paul Trent
	2-3.	Bill Eisenberg, Bobby Goldman, Robert D. Hamman, James Jacoby, Michael S. Lawrence, Bobby Wolff
	2-3.	Martin J. Cohn, Norman H. Fischer, Charles M. MacCracken, Bill Reister
1970	1.	Bernie Bergovoy, Donald P. Krauss, Lewis L.

		Mathe, Don Pearson, John Swanson, Richard Walsh
	2.	Eddie Kantar, Kyle Larsen, Paul Soloway, Ron Von der Porten
1971	1.	Bernie Chazen, Alvin Roth, Alan Sontag, Paul Trent
	2.	Gerald Caravelli, Larry Cohen, Barry Crane, Dr. John Fisher
1972	1.	Jack Blair, James Jacoby, John Simon, Paul Swanson, Bobby Wolff
	2.	Grant S. Baze, William Grieve, Donald P. Krauss, Lewis L. Mathe, Peter A. Pender, George Rapee
1973	1.	Garey Hayden, James Jacoby, Gaylor Kasle, John Simon, Bobby Wolff
	2-3.	Lou Bluhm, Steve Goldberg, Lawrence Gould, Stephen Robinson
	2-3.	John R. Crawford, Norm Kurlander, Alvin Roth, Clifford Russell, William Seamon
1974	1.	Ron E. Andersen, Mark Feldman, Stephen Goldstein, Hugh C. MacLean, Merle Tom
	2-3.	Eric Kokish, Stephen Robinson, Mike Shuman, Joseph Silver
	2-3.	Harold B. Guiver, Marty Shallon, William Sides, Mike Smolen
1975	1.	Matt Granovetter, William Grieve, George Rapee, Ron Rubin
	2.	Roger Bates, Edgar Kaplan, Norman Kay, George Rosenkranz
1976	1.	David Ashley, Paul Heitner, John Lowenthal, Mike Smolen
	2.	Bart Bramley, Marvin Herbert, Howard Piltch, Lou Reich, Ira S. Rubin
1977	1.	Lou Bluhm, Richard Doughty, Bruce Ferguson, Irv Kostal, Sidney H. Lazard, Ron Smith, Leslie West
	2.	Richard Freeman, Alvin Roth, Clifford Russell, Curtis K. Smith, Merle Tom, Art Waldmann
1978	1.	Neil Chambers, Eric Kokish, Peter Nagy, Stephen Robinson, John Schermer, Kit Woolsey
	2.	Steve Garner, Dave Lehman, Dick Melson, Larry Oakey
1979	1.	Allan Cokin, Steve Sion, Alan Sontag, Jim Sternberg, Peter Weichsel
	2.	Mike Cappelletti, Ron Feldman, Gary Hann, David Hoffner, Zeke Jabbour, David Sacks
1980	1.	Bart Bramley, Ross Grabel, William Rosen, Milton Rosenberg, Samuel Stayman, George Tornay
	2.	Ira Corn, Fred Hamilton, Robert D. Hamman, Ira Rubin, Bobby Wolff
1981	1.	Marty Bergen, Neil Chambers, Joseph Silver, Allan Stauber
	2.	Michael Ahota, Marc Culbertson, Jim Gardner, Bert Newman
1982	1.	Dave Berkowitz, Matt Granovetter, Harold Lilie, Al Rand
	2.	Robert Blanchard, Drew Casen, Chuck Lamprey, Thomas M. Smith
1983	1.	Tommy Sanders, Harold Guiver, Grant Baze, John Sutherlin
	2.	Cliff Russell, Robert Levin, Richard Freeman, Lou Bluhm, John Solodar, Ron Gerard
1984	1.	George Rosenkranz, Eddie Wold, Jeff Meckstroth, Eric Rodwell, Marty Bergen, Larry N. Cohen
	2.	Malcolm Brachman, Bobby Wolff, Bob Hamman, Paul Soloway, Ron Andersen, Bobby Goldman
1985	1.	Hal Mouse, Josh Parker, Ron Gerard, Dan Rotman
	2.	Roger Bates, John Mohan, Alan Sontag, John Devine
1986	1.	Gene Freed, Mike Passell, Ed Manfield, Kit Woolsey, Mark Lair
	2.	Don Caton, Robert Kehoe, Gene Simpson, Robert Teel
1987	1.	George Rosenkranz, Eddie Wold, Ira Chorush, Peter Weichsel, Robert Levin
	2.	Bart Bramley, Steve Garner, Howard Weinstein, Lou Bluhm
1988	1.	Jimmy Cayne, Bob Hamman, Bobby Wolff, Mike Passell, Chuck Burger, Mark Lair
	2.	Vic Mitchell, Albert Rahmey, Michael Moss, Drew Casen, Howard Hertzberg

1989	1.	Steve Robinson, Ed Manfield, Peter Boyd, Kit Woolsey
	2.	James Cayne, Chuck Burger, Bobby Wolff, Bob Hamman, Lew Stansby, Dave Berkowitz

In 1990 the Men's Board-a-Match Teams became the Open Board-a-Match Teams.

1990	1.	Mark Moss, Robert Thompson, Daniel Molochko, Jack Wholey
	2.	George Rosenkranz, Eddie Wold, Peter Weichsel, Robert Levin, Marty Bergen, Larry N. Cohen
1991	1.	Zia Mahmood, Michael Rosenberg, Jeffrey Wolfson, David Berkowitz, Larry N. Cohen
	2.	Jim Hall, Tom Fox, Dick Melson, David Lehman
1992	1.	Richard Katz, Garey Hayden, Wafik Abdou, Ira Cohen, Mike Whitman (npc)
	2.	Drew Cannell, Jeffrey Hand, Claudio Caponi, Steve Hamaoui
1993	1.	Paul Soloway, Bobby Goldman, Mark Lair, Mike Passell, Jimmy Cayne (npc)
	2.	Jim Hall, Tom Fox, Dave Lehman, Dick Melson

WOMENS BOARD-A-MATCH TEAMS. This four-session event has two qualifying and two final sessions.

1986	1.	Lisa Berkowitz, Dorothy Truscott, Joyce Lilie, Jan Martel
	2-4.	Eunice Portnoy, Halina Jamner, Genevieve Geiger, Madelynn Treitel
	2-4.	Kathie Wei, Judi Radin, Jacqui Mitchell, Gail Greenberg, Carol Sanders, Betty Ann Kennedy
	2-4.	Rozanne Pollack, Roberta Epstein, Judy Tucker, Stasha Cohen, Sue Picus, Karen Allison
1987	1.	Shirley Edelson, Donna Bailey, Lynn Blumenthal, Janice Randls
	2-3.	Rozanne Pollack, Randi Montin, Stasha Cohen, Pam Wittes, Judy Tucker
	2-3.	Lynne Feldman, Ellasue Chaitt, Sharon Osberg, Judi Cody
1988	1.	Lynne Feldman, Rozanne Pollack, Lisa Berkowitz, Sharon Osberg
	2-3.	Mary Jane Farell, Roberta Epstein, Dorothy Truscott, Gail Greenberg, Kitty Bethe, Susan Green
	2-3.	Elspeth Moore, Andy O'Grady, Nancy Passell, Nell Cahn
1989	1.	Lynne Schaefer, Suzy Berger, Petra Hamman, Joan Jackson
	2.	Beverly Rosenberg, Linda Lewis, Mary Hardy, Carol Pincus
1990	1-2.	Jacqui Mitchell, Amalya Kearse, Joyce Lilie, Nancy Alpaugh, Pamela Granovetter, Jo Morse
	1-2.	Judy Randel, Sally Woolsey, Broma Lou Reed, Marcia Masterson
1991	1.	Juanita Chambers, Cheri Bjerkan, Jill Meyers, Kay Schulle
	2.	Kathie Wei, Helen Utegaard, Betty Ann Kennedy, Carol Sanders, Lynn Deas, Beth Palmer
1992	1.	Kathie Wei, Helen Utegaard, Betty Ann Kennedy, Carol Sanders, Beth Palmer, Lynn Deas
	2.	Sally Woolsey, Karen Singer, Dori Cohen, Karen Allison
1993	1.	Juanita Chambers, Jan Cohen, Margie Gwozdzinsky, GerriAnne Klafter, Shawn Womack
	2.	Sharon Colson, Judy Pede, Jean Anderson, Carreen Hinds

NORTH AMERICAN SWISS TEAMS. This six-session event has two qualifying sessions, two semifinal sessions and a two-session final with Victory Point scoring.

1977	1.	Neil Chambers, Jim Donaldson, Bruce Ferguson, Clarence Goppert, John Schermer
	2.	Dennis Clerkin, Jerry Clerkin, John Herrmann, Ken Schutze
1978	1.	Barry Crane, Bob Kehoe, Mike Smolen, Charles Weed
	2.	Ira Chorush, Thomas Peters, Ely Solomon, John

		Zilic, Virginia Zilic
1979	1.	Hermine Baron, R. Jay Becker, Paul Ivaska, Jim Robison
	2.	Gerald Caravelli, Mark Cohen, Ralph Katz, Harvey Miller, Ken Schutze, Russell Shoup
1980	1-2.	Steve Becker, Philip Cowan, Rich DeMartino, Judy Rich
	1-2.	Dale Beers, William Epperson, Dave Furman, Dave Treitel
1981	1.	Ron Beall, Bob Etter, Ann Jacobson, Bob Thomson
	2.	Lea duPont, Benito Garozzo, Glenn Lublin, Claire Tornay
1982	1.	Gaylor Kasle, Garey Hayden, Garnet Snyder, Martha Beecher, David Ashley, Dave Treadwell
	2.	Andy Bernstein, Jim Foster, Tom Sanders, John Sutherlin
1983	1.	Sylvia Summers, Harve Waken, Robert Radwin, Gene Simpson, Steve Sturm
	2-3.	Philip Cowan, Michael Kapera, Alan Miller, John Heller, George Berger
	2-3.	Richard Capps, John Onstott, Dan Requard, Syd Levey
1984	1.	Grant Baze, Rhoda Walsh, Lea duPont, Benito Garozzo
	2.	William Laubenheimer, Stephen Kanzee, Marc Renson, Hamish Bennett
1985	1.	Jack Coleman, Rhoda Walsh, Jim Jacoby, Gaylor Kasle, Garey Hayden
	2.	Nadine Wood, Jonathan Steinberg, Eric Hochman, Mike Cappelletti
1986	1.	Marc Jacobus, Joey Silver, Jim McDonough, George Mittelman, Allan Graves
	2.	Jack Coleman, Rhoda Walsh, Mark Itabashi, Gaylor Kasle, Garey Hayden
1987	1.	Henry Bethe, Kitty Bethe, Alan Truscott, Dorothy Hayden Truscott
	2.	Jill Meyers, Beverly Rosenberg, Stelios Touchtidis, Steve Cohen, Pan Wittes, Carol Pincus
1988	1.	John Zilic, David Siebert, Allan Siebert, Sylvia Summers, Paul Munafo
	2.	Rita Rand, Gerald Caravelli, Joel Friedberg, Ethan Stein, Jerry Goldfein
1989	1.	Eugene Gardner, Kenneth Meyer, Ed Shapiro, Bruce Silverstein
	2.	Joel Friedberg, Rita Rand, Ethan Stein, Gerald Caravelli, Jerry Goldfein
1990	1-2.	Larry Mori, Kitty Bethe, Juanita Chambers, Jim Robison
	1-2.	George Rosenkranz, Miguel Reygadas, Gaylor Kasle, Garey Hayden, Roger Bates, John Grantham
1991	1.	Keith Wilson, Gary Peterson, Dennis Hesthaven, Ralph Letizia, Benton Wheeler
	2.	Jack Coleman, Judi Radin, Fred Hamilton, Dennis Sorensen, Mike Shuman
1992	1.	Lewis Kaplan, Boris Baran, Geoff Hampson, Mark Molson, Mark Stein
	2.	Jack Coleman, Mike Shuman, Larry Cohen, Dan Rotman, Fred Hamilton
1993	1.	Alan Le Bendig, Tom Clarke, Joe Quinn, Shawn Womack
	2.	Lynn Blumenthal, Steve Bruno, Loren Hawkins, Darrell Keel, Sue Lyski

NON-LIFE MASTER PAIRS. This four-session event has two qualifying and two final sessions.

1981	1.	Lin Goldstein, Shirlee Shaw
	2.	Ray Kuntz, Alex Stagner
1982	1.	Paul Bratton, Robert Bernhard
	2.	Yale Mallinger, G. LeBlanc
1983	1.	Moses Ma, Philips Santosa
	2.	Wally Weaver, Michael Lewis
1984	1.	Summer Steinfeldt, Nancy Muehter
	2.	Albert Rahmey, Jeanne Rahmey
1985	1.	Hank Hristienko, Zbigniew Radwanski
	2.	Linda Hendrickson, Wendy Haisley
1986	1.	Lanier Hurdle, Mike Hurdle
	2.	John Diamond, Andy Chesterton
1987	1.	Anthony Trafecanty, Michael Trafecanty
	2.	David Marx, Judy Levi
1988	1.	Sharon Tuggle, Tom Tuggle

	2.	Steve Clements, Nicholas Rogers
1989	1.	Jay Berke, Thomas Halton
	2.	Charles A. Carpenter, Edward Crane
1990	1.	Metin Uz, Jeffrey Naiman
	2.	Anlin Xu, Huichun Zhao
1991	1.	Daryl Hicks, Charles Papp
	2.	Sakiko Naito, Toru Amano
1992	1.	Cordelia Manges, Audrey Robb
	2.	Millie Huneycutt, Stuart Perlman
1993	1.	Bob Ehrlick, Clark Millikan
	2.	Jordan Lampe, Kingsum Chow

NORTH AMERICAN ROOKIE PAIRS.

This contest was designed exclusively for new recruits. To be eligible each player had to have fewer than 20 masterpoints. The winning pair from each of the 25 ACBL Districts and one pair at large competed for the title at the Fall North American Championships.

1979	1.	David Chen, Paul Chen
	2.	Walter Bell, David Kresge
1980	1.	Peter Ngan, Sunny Ngan
	2.	Thomas Sproule, Thomas Suman
1981	1.	George Berfield, Pat Chatta
	2.	John Kissell, John Levengood
1982	1.	Russell Boyle, Kent Ritchie
	2.	Richard Clark, Rose Allard
1983	1.	Anthony Cannaverde, Joseph Marciano
	2.	Carol Knechtges, Dorothy Vader
1984	1.	Peggi Brimacomb, Dick Brimacomb
	2.	Marc Labovitz, Magdy Maximos
1985	1.	Cindy Cummins, Kathy Gostin
	2.	John Nigrelli, Richard Grady
1986	1.	Fay Velquth, Judy Gaardner
	2.	Marcelle Cousineau, Joannine Charron
1987	1.	Jan Mozen, David Peters
	2.	Chris Roberts, Mark Hunsaker
1988	1.	Jeffrey Katz, Jeff Kallenback
	2.	Daniel Fox, Peter Fox
1989	1.	Peter Hudson, Terrance Hill
	2.	Josephine Peterson, Mary Voss
1990	1.	Mike Nadler, Ari Greenberg
	2.	Mark Weckworth, Perry Khakhar

NORTH AMERICAN 49ER PAIRS.

This event formerly was the North American Rookie Pairs. In 1991 it was changed so that all players with fewer than 50 masterpoints were eligible to compete for the chance to represent their district in the North American final at the Fall North American Championships.

1991	1.	Roy Johnson, Virginia Johnson
	2.	Bea Williamson, Billie Reece
1992	1.	Josh Shanes, Jordan Karol
	2.	Mike Boyle, Mick Riccio
1993	1.	Beverly Ballard, Donna Gilliam
	2.	Dennis Gamble, Gordon Murray

MASTER INDIVIDUAL.

This event was contested for the KARN TROPHY (1931-1933) and the STEINER TROPHY from 1934.

1931	1.	Willard S. Karn	2.	Richard L. Frey
1932	1.	Howard Schenken	2.	David Burnstine
1933	1.	David Burnstine	2.	Elinor Murdoch
1934	1.	Elinor Murdoch	2.	B. Jay Becker
1935	1.	Oswald Jacoby	2.	David Burnstine
1936	1.	Waldemar K. von Zedtwitz		
	2.	Merwyn D. Mayer		
1937	1.	B. Jay Becker	2.	George Unger
1938	1.	Richard Ecker, Jr.	2.	Harry Fishbein
1939	1.	Merwyn D. Maier	2.	Alvin Landy
1940	1.	Morrie Elis	2.	Lee Hazen
1941	1.	Lee Hazen	2.	B. Jay Becker
1942	1.	Harry J. Fishbein	2.	Olive Peterson
1943	1.	Alvin Roth	2.	Charles Solomon
1944	1.	George Rapee	2.	Robert D. Chatkin
1945	1.	Charles H. Goren	2.	Albert Weiss

1946	1.	Robert A. McPherran	2.	Morrie Ellis
1947	1.	Charles J. Solomon	2.	Jack Cushing
1948	1.	B. Jay Becker	2.	Myron Field
1949	1.	George Rapee	2.	B. Jay Becker
1950	1.	Morrie Elis	2.	Robert Appleyard
1951	1.	Sidney Silodor	2.	John Crawford
1952	1.	Harry J. Fishbein	2.	Peter Leventritt
1953	1.	Tobias Stone	2.	Larry Hirsch
1954	1.	Edward Burns	2.	F. Ayres Bombeck
1955	1.	Norman Kay		
	2-3.	Alvin Roth, B. Jay Becker		
1956	1.	John R. Crawford	2.	Robert Appleyard
1957	1.	Edgar Kaplan	2.	Dr. Ernest E. Karshmer
1958	1.	Sylvia Stein	2.	John Crawford
1959	1.	Leo Pressburg	2.	Frank L. Jackson
1960	1.	Robert Reynolds	2.	Arthur Robinson

UNITED STATES BRIDGE ASSOCIATION GRAND NATIONALS

OPEN TEAMS

YEAR	WINNERS	RUNNERS-UP
1934	Howard Schenken	Walter Malowan
	Michael Gottlieb	Lee Landon
	David Burnstine	Lester Bachner
	Richard L. Frey	Sydney Rusinow
1935	Howard Schenken	Walter Beinecke
	Michael Gottlieb	Jean (John) Mattheys
	Oswald Jacoby	Hugh Jackson
	Sherman Stearns	Charles Van Vleck
	Richard L. Frey	
1936	Josephine Culbertson	Edward Hymes
	Waldemar von Zedtwitz	B. Jay Becker
	Sam Fry	Merwyn Maier
	Mitchell Barnes	Charles Lochridge
1937	David Burnstine	Edward Burns
	Merwyn Maier	Stanley Sanders
	Howard Schenken	Morris Schoenfield
	B. Jay Becker	Len Reiter

MIXED TEAMS

YEAR	WINNERS	RUNNERS-UP
1935	John Sherman	M. Kalman
	Ruth Sherman	Richard L. Frey
	Richard Kahn	Gussie Planco
	Mrs. Fred Greenbaum	J. Arnold Farrer
1936	Mrs. George Harris	Doris Fuller
	Jean (John) Mattheys	Mitchell Barnes
	Mrs. Josiah Thaw	Barbara Collyer
	Raymond Balfe	Waldemar von Zedtwitz
1937	Henry Chanin	Mrs. S. A. Herzog
	Mary Clement	Doris Fuller
	Charles Lochridge	Robert Appleyard
	Mrs. N. Demarest	Jack Shore

OPEN PAIRS

YEAR	WINNERS	RUNNERS UP
1934	Howard Schenken	A. Mitchell Barnes
	Michael Gottlieb	Edward Hymes, Jr
1935	Merwyn Maier	Morris Elis
	Sherman Stearns	Fred Kaplan
1936	Oswald Jacoby	Sherman Stearns
	David Burnstine	Merwyn Maier
1937	Oswald Jacoby	Waldemar von Zedtwitz
	Lester Bachner	Merwyn Maier

MIXED PAIRS

YEAR	WINNERS	RUNNERS UP
1936	Waldemar von Zedtwitz	M. Lovejoy
	Barbara Collyer	Winfield Liggett
1937	Henry Chanin	Millie Tansill
	Mary Clement	Raymond Balfe

AMERICAN BRIDGE ASSOCIATION CHAMPIONSHIPS

OPEN TEAMS

1934 Egbert Clarke, J.C. Graham, Dr. Louis P. Rolerfort, D. Edward Smith
1935 Dr. E. Brandon, Lawrence Grant, Bernard Gray, George Gilmer, Dr. B. Withers
1936 Gilhooly F. Benoit, William A. Friend, Clyde L. Long, Allan L. Parkinson, Percy E. Thomas
1937 James P. Holt, Othello A. Moore, Lawrence Buser, Oliver Landry
1938 James P. Holt, Othello A. Moore, Lawrence Buser, Oliver Landry
1939 Gilhooly F. Benoit, William A. Friend, Albert E. Hawkins, Joseph Niles
1940 Lawrence Buser, James P. Holt, Oliver Landry, Othello A. Moore
1941 Roscoe Alexander, Caesar E. Barron, Leon A. Jones, Kermit D. Ross
1942 Caesar E. Barron, Dewey M. Carr, Kermit D. Ross, Allan L. Woolridge
1943 Robert Banks, Dr. William Richie, Glenn Stewart, Alvin Wilkes
1944 Zach H. Brooks, Kelly C. Brown, Louis Clay, Othello A. Moore, Lola Scales
1946 Kenneth F. Cox, Richard Cunningham, Charles Hanson, Samuel White
1947 Zach H. Brooks, Kelly C. Brown, Louis Clay, Othello A. Moore, Lola Scales
1949 Dorothy Alexander, Roscoe Alexander, Leon A. Jones, Caesar E. Barron, Morris Garrett
1950 Dorothy Alexander, Roscoe Alexander, Leon A. Jones, Caesar E. Barron, Morris Garrett
1952 Alfred A. Bishop, Kenneth F. Cox, James H. Smith, Samuel White
1953 William Chapman, Lyda Goggins, George Hall, Allan L. Woolridge, Mrs. Clyde Woolridge
1954 Howard M. Bowman, Martin Gertler, Kai Larson, Ruth Million
1955 Roscoe Alexander, Robert Friend, William A. Friend, Dr. Joseph Henry, Leon A. Jones
1956 Roscoe Alexander, Robert Friend, William A. Friend, Dr. Joseph Henry, Leon A. Jones
1957 Roscoe Alexander, Robert Friend, William A. Friend, Dr. Joseph Henry, Leon A. Jones
1958 Alfred A. Bishop, Kenneth F. Cox, James Garcia, Samuel White
1959 Caesar E. Barron, Oliver Cassell, Frederick O. Petite, Allan L. Woolridge, Mrs. Clyde Woolridge
1960 Caesar E. Barron, Oliver Cassell, Walter Mann, Frederick O. Petite
1961 Jim Becheley, Robert D. Hamman, William Hanna, Stella Rebner
1962 Robert Bratcher, Mary Cocherell, Dr. Guy Ginn, Robert Landry (tied with) Doris Brooks, Dr. Joseph Henry, Stanley Jarrett, Ronald Searcy
1963 Jean Haley, Andrew Mells, Charles Pyant, Janice Wilkins
1964 Roscoe Alexander, Dr. Joseph Henry, Leon A. Jones, Mrs. Clyde Woolridge
1965 Zenobia Allen, Andrew Mells, Samuel White, Bertram Hudson, Daniel Scrivens
1966 Zenobia Allen, Andrew Mells, Samuel White, Bertram Hudson, Daniel Scrivens
1967 Dr. Arthur R. Flowers, Glenn Fowlkes, George Hall, J. Herbert Kerr, Charles Pyant, Arthur Wills
1968 James Garcia, Dr. Guy A. Ginn, Luis Pietri, Roscoe Rigmaden, Ronald Smith, Hollis Steed
1969 Doris Brooks, Leonard Jefferson, Dr. William Lipton, J. Prisyon, Murray Schnee, Sol Seidman
1970 Dr. Arthur R. Flowers, Douglas Fullwood, Andrew Mells, Luis Pietri, Roscoe Rigmaden, William Sides
1971 Robert Becker, Mark Blumenthal, Oscar Cohen, William Landow, Harlow Lewis, Alan Sontag
1972 Dr. Arthur R. Flowers, Douglas Fullwood, Amalya Kearse, Andrew Mells, Luis Pietri, William Sides
1973 Zenobia Allen, Richard Halperin, Harvey Miller, Robert Price, Roscoe Rigmaden, Joyce Williams
1974 Zenobia Allen, Claudius G. Fredd, Robert Landry, Beverly Lucas, Samuel Lucas
1975 *1Herbert Bryan, Orlando Croft, John S. Jordan III, Robert Seymour
1976 *Douglas Fullwood, Beverly Lucas, Samuel Lucas,

Louis Sutherland
1977 Reginald Chapman, Leonard Jefferson, Chester Johnson, Arnold Jones (Spring)
Marv Dauer, Ed Davis, Al Okuneff, David Sachs, George Siegel, Perry Van Hook (Summer)
1978 Alfred Bishop, Douglas Fullwood, Samuel Lucas, Beverly Lucas, Luis Pietri, Louis Sutherland (Spring)
Richard Halperin, Harvey Miller, Paul Sugar, Don Rutstein, Claude Vogel, Carey Yelton (Summer)
1979 Dr. Arthur R. Flowers, Chester Johnson, Andrew Mells, Herbert Taylor, Arthur Wills (Spring)
Lawrence Berkley, Lee Pennington, Jeffrey Stroud, John Washington, William E. Williams (Summer)
1980 Kenneth Cox, Clinton Elmore, Charles Hanson, Leonard Jefferson, Robert Seymour (Spring)
Robert Canty, Theodore Griffith, Sandra Stevenson, Norma Sweeting (Summer)
1981 Paul Ivaska, Tony Kasday, William Sides, Eddie Thomas (Spring)
Lionel Barton, Dwight Galley, Samuel Lucas, Beverly Lucas, Robert Price, Joyce Williams (Summer)
1982 Lionel Barton, Dwight Galley, Samuel Lucas, Beverly Lucas, Robert Price, Joyce Williams (Spring)
1983 Bill Sides, Louis Sutherland, Luis Pietri, Chester Johnson (Spring)
David Berkowitz, Lisa Berkowitz, Ira Herman, Robert Blanchard, Jilliam Blanchard (tied with) William Russ, Eric Robinson, James Becker, James Hamilton, James Garcia, Jeffrey Stroud (Summer)
1984 Bob Price, Joyce Williams, Lionel Barton, Dwight Galley (Spring)
Daniel Page, Norma Sweeting, Vernette Wills, Robert Canty (Summer)
1985 Robert Price, Joyce Williams, Samuel Lucas, Beverly Lucas, Dwight Galley, Lionel Barton (Spring)
Robert Landry, Bobbye Caldwell, Dan Requard, Herbert Taylor, Bernice Laster, Joan Williams (Summer)
1986 Chester Johnson, Herbert Taylor, Joan Williams, Dan Requard (Spring)
Chester Johnson, Herbert Taylor, Dan Requard, Joan Williams (Summer)
1987 Chester Johnson, Herbert Taylor, Dan Requard, Joan Williams (Spring)
Bob Price, Joyce Williams, Beverly Lucas, Samuel Lucas, Bill Sides, Louis Sutherland (Summer)
1988 Robert Price, Joyce Williams, Louis Sutherland, Samuel Lucas, Beverly Lucas (Spring)
Luis Pietri, Dwight Galley, Lionel Barton, Sara Pearson (Summer)
1989 Roscoe Rigmaiden, Reginals Chapman, Sandra Stevenson, Clarice Reid, Dorothy Sides (Spring)
Chester Johnson, Herbert Taylor, Joan Williams, Luis Pietri (Summer)
1990 Sara Pearson, Dwight Galley, Mae Clark, Lela Wilson (Spring)
Chester Johnson, Herbert Taylor, Luis Pietri, Bill Sides (Summer)
1991 William M. Troy, Robert Friend, Edward West, Henry Bell (Spring)
Luis Pietri, Chester Johnson, Herbert Taylor, Joan Williams (Summer)
1992 Chester Johnson, Joan Williams, Herbert Taylor, Luis Pietri (Spring)
Dwight Galley, Lionel Barton, Sara Pearson, Luis Pietri, Eddie Thomas Jr., Bill Furr (Summer)

OPEN PAIRS

1934 Louis Collins, Mrs. Louis Collins
1935 Dr. A. Maurice Curtis, Dr. W. Wethers
1936 Lyda Goggins, Horace R. Milles
1937 James P. Holt, Othello A. Moore
1938 Leon A. Jones, James McDougald
1940 Hazel Facey, Lucius Fields
1941 Dr. A. Maurice Curtis, Allan I. Parkinson
1942 William A. Friend, Lyda Goggins
1943 Courtland Booker, Lewis White
1944 Eloise Landry, Elvert Marsh
1946 Roscoe Alexander, Leon A. Jones
1947 Kelly C. Brown, Louis Clay
1948 Elvert Marsh, Rexcell Watkins

1949	William A. Friend, Dr. Fred Slaughter
1950	Richard Cunningham, Zenobia Rucker
1951	Alexander Herndon, Evelyn Herndon
1952	William A. Friend, Dr. Fred Slaughter
1953	Louis Clay, Zenobia Rucker
1954	William A. Friend, Hollis Steed
1955	Robert Friend, William A. Friend
1956	James Garcia, Elvert Marsh
1957	Sandy Gholston, Marion Griffis
1958	Alfred A. Bishop, Dr. Joseph Henry
1959	Roscoe Alexander, Zenobia Hall
1960	James Lee, Carlisle Pratt
1961	Kenneth F. Cox, Samuel White
1962	Walter Hampton, Frank Tucker
1963	Luis Pietri, Roscoe Rigmaiden
1964	Alfred A. Bishop, Dr. Joseph Henry
1965	Bertram Hudson, Andrew Mells
1966	Luis Pietri, Roscoe Rigmaiden
1967	Robert Price, William Sides
1968	Luis Pietri, Roscoe Rigmaiden
1969	Lawrence Berkley, Arthur Wills (Spring)
	Dr. Milton Haley, Arthur Reid (Summer)
1970	Robert Canty, Sylvester Lee (*tied with*) Theodore Griffith, Ben Siegel (Spring)
	William Sides, Douglas Fullwood (Summer)
1971	F. Maxine Davis, James Dozier (Spring)
	Robert Price, Joyce Williams (Summer)
1972	Amalya Kearse, Luis Pietri (Spring)
	Dr. Guy A. Ginn, Theodore Griffith (Summer)
1973	Amalya Kearse, Luis Pietri (Spring)
	Dr. Felix Dunn, Sarah Dunn (Summer)
1974	Dr. Arthur F. Flowers, Andrew Mells (Spring)
	Vivian Banks, Franklyn Taylor (Summer)
1975	Reginald Chapman, Roscoe Rigmaiden (Spring)

	Dr. Arthur R. Flowers, Andrew Mells (Summer)
1976	Douglas Fullwood, Louis Sutherland (Spring)
	Bobby Caldwell, Robert Landry (Summer)
1977	Lee Pennington, William E. Williams (Spring)
	Lee Pennington, William E. Williams (Summer)
1978	James Garcia, Dr. Milton Haley (Spring)
	Taylor Cox, Vernette Wills (Summer)
1979	Reginald Chapman, Roscoe Rigmaiden (Spring)
	Reginald Chapman, Roscoe Rigmaiden (Summer)
1980	Douglas Fullwood, Louis Sutherland (Spring)
	Dwight Galley, Lionel Barton (Summer)
1981	Paul Ivaska, William Sides (Spring)
	Douglas Fullwood, Louis Sutherland (Summer)
1982	Mildred Anderson, John S. Jordan III (Spring)
1983	Leonard Jefferson, Arnold Jones (Spring)
	Not played (black out) (New York) (Summer)
1984	Robert Prince, Joyce Williams (Spring)
	Dwight Galley, Lionel Barton (Summer)
1985	Norm Coombs, Herbert Taylor (Spring)
	Chester Johnson, Herbert Taylor (Summer)
1986	Andrew Mells, Arthur Wills (Spring)
	Joan Williams, Dan Requard (Summer)
1987	Joyce Williams, Louis Sutherland (Spring)
	Dwight Galley, Lionel Barton (Summer)
1988	William F. Furr, James Garcia (Spring)
	Robert Price, Bill Sides (Summer)
1989	Melvin Rone, Harold Bickham (Spring)
	Joyce Williams, Louis Sutherland (Summer)
1990	Luis Pietri, Chester Johnson (Spring)
	Eddie Thomas, Sara Pearson (Summer)
1991	Joyce Williams, Robert Price (Spring)
	Arthur Wills, Julius Fields (Summer)
1992	George Johnson, Edna Cravanas (Spring)
	Reginald Chapman, Roscoe Rigmaiden (Summer)

CANADIAN CHAMPIONSHIPS

NATIONAL TEAM CHAMPIONSHIPS (CNTC)

The first official Canadian National Team Championship was held in Toronto in 1980. However, there were three previous playoffs to select a team for international competition.

1968	Eric Murray, Sami Kehela, Percy Sheardown, Bruce Elliott, Al Lando npc, Wolf Lebovic anpc
1971	Bruce Gowdy, Duncan Phillips, Gerry Charney, Bill Crissey
1977	Don Cowan, Mike Cummings, Maurice Paul, Mary Paul
1980	Allan Graves, George Mittelman, Eric Kokish, Peter Nagy, Eric Murray, Sami Kehela
1981	Allan Graves, George Mittelman, Eric Kokish, Peter Nagy, Eric Murray, Sami Kehela
1982	Nick Gartaganis, Zygmunt Marcinski, Gordon Crispin, Vojtech Pomykalski
1983	Mark Molson, Boris Baran, Allan Graves, George Mittelman, John Guoba, John Carruthers
1984	Subhash Gupta, Doran Flock, Gordon Campbell, Mike Chomyn, Bryan Maksymetz, Drew Cannell
1985	Boris Baran, Mark Molson, Eric Kokish, George Mittelman, Pascal Menachi, Mark Stein
1986	Michael Schoenborn, Harmon Edgar, Arno Hobart, Martin Kirr, Greg Carroll, David Turner, Laurie McIntyre npc
1987	Mark Molson, Boris Baran, John Guoba, John Carruthers, Eric Murray
1988	Maurice Larochelle, Jean Bernier, Andre Laliberte, Jacques Laliberte, Raymond Fortin, Kamel Fergani
1989	Mark Molson, Boris Baran, George Mittelman, Arno Hobart, Martin Kirr, Billy Cohen
1990	Doug Heron, David Willis, John Valliant, Mike Betts, Randy Bennett, Ed Zaluski
1991	Ed Bridson, John Gowdy, David Lindop, Geoff Hampson, Boris Baran, Mark Molson
1992	Jim McAvoy, Duncan Smith, Michael Strebinger, Peter Herold, Jim Dickie, Bruce Ferguson
1993	Mike Cafferata, Mike Kenny, Mary Paul, David Colbert, Michael Roche, Chris Hough

WOMENS TEAM CHAMPIONSHIPS (CWTC).

1984	Dianna Gordon, Sharyn Kokish, Francine Cimon, Sandra Fraser, Catherine Thorpe, Mary Paul, George Mittelman npc
1985	Anna Boivin, Renee Mancuso, Rhoda Habert, Beverly Kraft, Nancy Koffler, Barbara Saltsman
1986	Mary Paul, Francine Cimon, Katie Thorpe, Gloria Silverman, Sharyn Reus, Dianna Gordon
1987	Mary Paul, Francine Cimon, Katie Thorpe, Gloria Silverman, Sharyn Reus, Dianna Gordon, George Mittelman npc
1988	Mary Paul, Francine Cimon, Katie Thorpe, Gloria Silverman, Sharyn Reus, Dianna Gordon, George Mittelman npc
1989	Kathy Adachi, Ina Anderson, Pat Landau, Joyce Peters, Marge Neate, Alison Dorosh
1990	Mary Paul, Francine Cimon, Katie Thorpe, Gloria Silverman, Sharyn Reus, Dianna Gordon
1991	Mary Paul, Francine Cimon, Katie Thorpe, Gloria Silverman, Sharyn Reus, Dianna Gordon, John Carruthers npc
1992	Sharyn Reus, Dianna Gordon, Beverly Kraft, Rhoda Habert
1993	Judy Harris, Barbara Kupkee, Anne Pilon, Diane Christianson

OPEN PAIRS CHAMPIONSHIP (COPC)

1985	Boris Baran, Mark Molson
1986	Gary Whiteman, Ken Warren
1987	Maurice de la Salle, Mark Chalfin
1988	John Valliant, David Willis
1989	Ron Borg, Michael Strebinger
1990	Katie Thorpe, John Carruthers
1991	Michael Cafferata, Ken Warren
1992	Pierre Treuil, John Zaluski
1993	Pierre Treuil, John Zaluski

ROOKIE-MASTER GAME

1983	Reta Tobin, Toby Graser
1984	Rick Hodson, Gabriella Carr-Rollitt
1985	Gilles Boivin, Helene LaBreque
1986	Jacques Corbeil, Germaine Dion

1989   Eileen Howey, Dolores Holm
1990   Helen Finkle, Marlene Philp
1991   Gordon Braun, Peter Worby
1992   Herb Cronin, Nick Mogus

MEXICAN GRAND NATIONAL TEAMS

1986 1. Elisa Konstantinovsky, Alicia Duran, Laura
         Mariscal, Miguel Reygadas, George Rosenkranz
      2. Gonzalo Herrera, Odon Duran, Mauricio
         Epelbaum, Jacobo Podbilevich

APPENDIX II
ACBL MASTERPOINT CONTESTS

BARRY CRANE TOP 500

This trophy is presented to the ACBL member who has accumulated the most masterpoints during the calendar year. Originally the McKenney Trophy, it was put into play by William E. McKenney, ACBL executive secretary. It was known as the **McKenney Trophy** contest from 1937-1981. When the list was expanded to include the leading 500 players it was called the **Top 500** from 1982-1985. It became the **Barry Crane Top 500** in 1986. Cranc, who was murdered in July 1985, was ACBL's top masterpoint holder and was acknowledge by his peers to be unequalled as a masterpoint winner and a matchpoint player. His influence on the race was dominant for more than three decades. The winners from 1937 through 1947:

1937	Charles Goren
1938	Morrie Elis
1939	Merwyn Maier
1940	Morrie Elis
1941	Helen Sobel
1942	Helen Sobel
1943	Charles Goren
1944	Helen Sobel
1945	Charles Goren
1946	Sidney Silodor
1947	Charles Goren

The following are the victors since 1947, together with their point totals. An asterisk indicates the record was broken that year.

1948	Charles Goren	378
1949	Charles Goren	440*
1950	Charles Goren	399
1951	Charles Goren	457*
1952	Barry Crane	604*
1953	William Rosen	470
1954	David Carter	468
1955	Norman Kay	519
1956	Tobias Stone	791*
1957	Edgar Kaplan	808*
1958	Len Harmon	768
1959	Oswald Jacoby	784
1960	Robert Jordan	873*
1961	Oswald Jacoby	735
1962	Oswald Jacoby	713
1963	Oswald Jacoby	1034*
1964	Hermine Baron	1370*
1965	Peter Rank	1141
1966	Peter Pender	1282
1967	Barry Crane	1309
1968	Paul Soloway	981
1969	Paul Soloway	1434*
1970	Hermine Baron	1399
1971	Barry Crane	1443*
1972	John Fisher	1387
1973	Barry Crane	1562*
1974	Kerri Shuman	1619*
1975	Barry Crane	1547
1976	Mike Passell	1815*
1977	Ron Andersen	2009*
1978	Barry Crane	1790
1979	Clarence Goppert	2118*
1980	Ron Andersen	2725*
1981	Mel Skolnik	2421
1982	Eddie Wold	2016
1983	Ron Andersen	2994*
1984	Grant Baze	3270*
1985	Grant Baze	2209
1986	Ron Andersen	2521
1987	Grant Baze	1923
1988	Jim Jacoby	2223
1989	Zeke Jabbour	2468
1990	Mark Lair	2624
1991	Jim Becker	2914
1992	Dennis Sorensen	2745
1993	Jeff Meckstroth	1950

ACBL PLAYER OF THE YEAR

This recognition goes to the contestant who earn the most masterpoints at *nationally-rated* championships at the three NABC tournaments each year. The winners through 1993:

1990	Bob Hamman	451
1991	Zia Mahmood	616
1992	Jeff Meckstroth	342
1993	Bob Hamman	561

NORTH AMERICAN CHAMPIONSHIP TROPHY WINNERS

SPRING CHAMPIONSHIPS

MOTT-SMITH TROPHY. This trophy is awarded every year to the player with the best overall individual performance record in the Spring North American Bridge Championships. Donated by friends in memory of Geoffrey Mott-Smith in 1961, it was made retroactive to 1958 to include all the winners. The winners 1958 through 1968 are:

1958	Ivar Stakgold
1959	Lew Mathe
1960	Norman Kay
1961	Robert Jordan
1962	Robert Jordan
1963	Sidney Silodor died with Norman Kay
1964	Lew Mathe
1965	Phil Feldesman
1966	Phil Feldesman
1967	Lew Mathe
1968	Norman Kay

The following are the Mott-Smith Trophy winners since 1968 together with their point totals. An asterisk indicates the record was broken that year.

1969	Sue Sachs	168
1970	Barry Crane	155
1971	Barry Crane	135
1972	Paul Swanson tied	159
	with Jack Blair	159
1973	Robert Wolff	233*
1974	Ron Andersen	250*
1975	Roger Bates	203
1976	Larry Cohen	225
1977	Mark Blumenthal	200
1978	Mike Passell	250*
1979	Jeff Meckstroth	215
1980	Jeff Meckstroth tied	173
	with Eric Rodwell	173
1981	Allan Stauber	166
1982	Dave Berkowitz tied	198
	with Harold Lilie	198
1983	Mike Passell	214

1984	Lew Stansby	172
1985	Jeff Meckstroth	196
1986	Lew Stansby	207
1987	Steve Robinson tied	200
	with Peter Boyd	200
1988	Roger Bates	193
1989	Eddie Wold	167
1990	John Sutherlin	300*
1991	Zia Mahmood	183
1992	Roger Bates	186
1993	Michael Seamon	196
1994	Chip Martel	250

SUMMER CHAMPIONSHIPS

FISHBEIN TROPHY. This trophy is awarded every year to the player with the best overall individual performance record in the Summer North American Bridge Championships. The trophy, in memory of Sally Fishbein, was donated by ACBL in recognition of the untiring efforts of Harry Fishbein who served as Treasurer of ACBL and refused to accept the customary compensation. The winners 1952-1963 are:

1952	John Crawford
1953	Milton Ellenby
1954	David Carter
1955	Paul Hodge
1956	Tobias Stone
1957	John Crawford
1958	Helen Sobel
1959	Ira Rubin
1960	Boris Koytchou
1961	Marshall Miles
1962	Ira Rubin
1963	Alvin Roth

The following are the Fishbein Trophy winners since 1964 together with their point totals. An asterisk indicates the record was broken that year.

1964	Percy Sheardown	223*
1965	Alvin Roth	210
1966	Alvin Roth	186
1967	Phil Feldesman	177
1968	Jim Jacoby	205
1969	Robert Hamman	180
1970	Dave Strasberg	155
1971	Barbara Rappaport	187
1972	B.Jay Becker	179
1973	Richard Katz	199
1974	Richard Shepherd	162
1975	Grant Baze	176
1976	Richard Katz	219
1977	Ken Cohen	198
1978	Mike Passell	215
1979	Bobby Wolff	179
1980	Peter Weichsel	194
1981	Ralph Katz	236*
1982	Mike Smolen	221
1983	Bob Hamman	280*
1984	Steve Sion	271
1985	Bill Passell	225
1986	Mark Lair	187
1987	Danny Rotman	188
1988	Helen Utegaard	168
1989	Zeke Jabbour	198
1990	Ron Rubin tied	
	with Michael Becker	227
1991	Eric Rodwell	278
1992	Juanita Chambers	182
1993	John Sutherlin	233

FALL CHAMPIONSHIPS

LOU HERMAN TROPHY. This trophy is awarded to the player with the best overall individual performance record at the Fall North American Championships. It was donated in 1951

by Sally Lipton, formerly Mrs. Lou Herman, of New York, in memory of her husband. The recipients of this award 1952 through 1962 were:

1952	Al Roth
1953	John Crawford
1954	Paul Hodge
1955	Milt Ellenby
1956	Paul Hodge
1957	Lew Mathe
1958	Sylvia Stein
1959	Mort Rubinow
1960	Oswald Jacoby
1961	Phil Feldesman
1962	Marshall Miles

The following are the Herman Trophy winners since 1962 with their point totals. An asterisk indicates the record was broken that year.

1963	Eric Murray	211
1964	Harold Rockaway	180
1965	Mike Lawrence	211
1966	Charles Coon	144
1967	Sami Kehela	155
1968	Henry Bethe	144
1969	Sylvia Stein	150
1970	Ira Rubin tied	
	with Chuck Burger	154
1971	John Grantham	150
1972	Steve Robinson	181
1973	Larry Cohen	207
1974	Fred Hamilton	202
1975	Walt Walvick	171
1976	Paul Soloway	199
1977	John Mohan	160
1978	Bob Hamman	165
1979	Robert Levin	233*
1980	Jeff Meckstroth	225
1981	Chip Martel	224
1982	Jeff Meckstroth tied	
	with Eric Rodwell	191
1983	Marty Bergen	233*
1984	Grant Baze	200
1985	Eric Rodwell	365*
1986	Kit Woolsey tied	
	with Ed Manfield	212
1987	Jill Meyers	176
1988	Bob Hamman	270
1989	Mark Molson	254
1990	Eddie Wold	276
1991	David Berkowitz	357
1992	Haig Tchamitch	202
1993	Bob Hamman	355

ACBL MINI-McKENNEY CONTESTS

Rookie (0-5 Masterpoints)

1975	Robert Blanchard, New York NY	164
1976	Carolyn Behr, Orlando FL	176
1977	Jim Sternberg, Fort Lauderdale FL	377
1978	Bob Rosen, North Miami FL	216
1979	Cameron Cotton, Sacramento CA	190
1980	Alan Kleist, Cheverly MD	262
1981	Rick Purdy, Duluth MN	123
1982	Arif Janjua, San Jose CA	146
1983	Joe Barnard, Marysville OH	295
1984	Barbara Larson, Madison WI	116
1985	Elizabeth Rice, Huntington Valley OH	156
	Harry Falk, East Greenbush NY	156
1986	Richard Kennedy, East Cleveland OH	148
1987	John Blubaugh, Independence MO	141
1988	Norris "Pete" Peterson, Gaitherburg MD	119
1989	Donald Geerhart, Arlington VA	137
1990	Joel Wooldridge, Snyder NY	301
1991	John Cook, Gloucester ON	129
1992	Leslie Shafer, Silver Spring MD	181
1993	Niles Brown, New Orleans LA	328

Junior Master (5-20 Masterpoints)

1975	Jim Prentice, Santa Monica CA	161
1976	Janice Seamon, Gainesville FL	153
1977	Craig Harrison, Seattle WA	265

1978	Marc Arbour, Scarborough ON	201
1979	Elisabeth Brenhouse, Newport Beach CA	255
1980	Mary Wolf, Philadelphia PA	183
1981	George Landreth, Blackduck MN	388
1982	Alan Watson, Cambridge MA	291
1983	Robert Batoff, Philadelphia PA	148
1984	Paul Ford, Los Angeles CA	201
1985	Connie Hicks, Brentwood TN	167
1986	Yvonne Hernandez, Fort Lauderdale FL	224
1987	Michel Bertrand, Dorval PQ	133
1988	Manuel Urrizola, Los Angeles CA	204
1989	Tom Barlow, Little Rock AR	215
1990	John Fout, Fairfield CA	228
1991	Yann Ozenne, Bonsecours, France	159
1992	Charles Donahue, Glendora CA	289
1993	Nancy Freeman, El Cajon CA	226

Club Master (20-50 Masterpoints)

1975	Jeff Overby, St. Augustine FL	231
1976	Milton Stern, Dallas TX	306
1977	John D. Jones, Redondo Beach CA	364
1978	Ross Taylor, Hamilton ON	282
1979	Bruce Rogoff, Great Neck NY	223
1980	Bill Weakley, Nashville TN	237
1981	Robert Bobker, Wheeling IL	262
1982	Lele Dean, Greenville DE	166
1983	Moses Ma, Cambridge MA	335
1984	Cynthia Handy, Villa Park CA	254
1985	Charlie Cargile, Toney AL	205
1986	Robert Cohen, Minneapolis MN	239
1987	Sorin Samanta, Downey CA	190
1988	Earle Davidoff, New York NY	234
1989	Robert Cranor, Panorama City CA	166
1990	David Yang, Agoura Hills CA	313
1991	Sean Ganness, Ottawa ON	326
1992	Charles James, Salem OR	223
1993	Jeffrey Figgins, La Mesa CA	241

Sectional Master (50-100 Masterpoints)

1975	Claudia Zucker, Atlanta GA	214
1976	Stasha Wroblewski, Garnerville NY	365
1977	Lynn Deas, Norfolk VA	360
1978	Mark Bartusek, Anaheim CA	479
1979	Dan Jacob, Vancouver BC	296
1980	Keith Woolf, Mentor OH	422
1981	Andrew Kaufman, Bowie MD	304
1982	Charlie Ju, Rochester NY	309
1983	Mark Lewis, Charlotte NC	244
1984	Sharon Meng, Shaumburg IL	224
1985	Alan Benaroya, Kirkland WA	460
1986	Christopher Bohan, Berkeley CA	372
1987	Robert Crawford, Vancouver BC	401
1988	Michael Klein, Albany NY	357
1989	Jaf Chiang, South Windsor CT	350
1990	Hirsch Davis, Rockville MD	251
1991	Stephen Williams, Lawrenceville NJ	339
1992	Murray Johnstone, Chino Hills CA	289
1993	Marshall Hall, Boston MA	340

Regional Master (100-200 Masterpoints)

1975	Allan Feineman, St. Petersburg FL	508
1976	Shirley Boice, Cheyenne WY	359
1977	Jeff Corbin, Wichita KS	427
1978	Keith Balcombe, Oshawa ON	426
1979	Juanita Skelton, Dallas TX	628
1980	Chris Kaufman, Bowie MD	305
1981	Mary Wolf, Philadelphia PA	363
1982	Sylvia Summers, Santa Monica CA	356
1983	David Funk, Norman OK	321
1984	Robert Batoff, Philadelphia PA	322
1985	Andrew Greenberg, Ithaca NY	397
1986	Elizabeth Rice, Huntington Valley OH	633
1987	Brenda Wiseman, Lincoln NE	281
1988	John Blubaugh, Independence MO	329
1989	Jade Barrett, Reading MA	214
1990	Qiang Wang, Woodside NY	309
1991	Gary Brown, Philadelphia PA	644
1992	Vicki Smith, Morro Bay CA	278
1993	Mary Keeler, Basalt CO	396

NABC Master (200-Life Master)

1975	Troy Horton, Beaverton OR	493
1976	Claudia Zucker Feagin, Atlanta GA	442
1977	Fran Dolmage, Clovis NM	380
1978	Mike Hansen, Vancouver WA	342

1979	Ken Chen, Charlotte NC	401
1980	Elisabeth Brenhouse, Newport Beach CA	781
1981	Chris Hough, Ann Arbor MI	342
1982	Sally Alsfelder, Cincinnati OH	483
1983	Alan Kleist, Cheverly MD	540
1984	Emily Oglesby, Knoxville TN	473
1985	Jack Coleman, San Francisco CA	676
1986	Charlie Cargile, Toney AL	514
1987	Mary Keenan, Napa CA	548
1988	Dale Andersen, Busby AB	295
1989	Geoff Hampson, North York ON	464
1990	Lin-Huan Chen, Santa Monica CA	463
1991	Eric Greco, Annandale VA	557
1992	George Jacobs, Burr Ridge IL	482
1993	Donald Mamula, Kirkland WA	336

ACBL ACE OF CLUBS CONTESTS

Rookie (0-5 Masterpoints)

1984	Myrna Blaufarb, Culver City CA	60
1985	Lapt Chan, Woodside NY	72
1986	Roy Welland, New York NY	94
1987	Richard Gamble, Ottawa ON	87
1988	Norris Peterson, Gaithersburg MD	65
1989	Robert Kast, Fort Lauderdale FL	95
1990	Ralph Mastrangelo, Cranston RI	90
1991	Wayne Karson, Culver City CA	59
1992	Gregory Robbins, New York NY	80
1993	Rod Organt, Salt Lake City UT	109

Junior Master (5-20 Masterpoints)

1984	Alice Lahoud, Newport RI	60
1985	Charles Marsh, Venice FL	60
1986	Ralph McAuley, Sarasota FL	71
1987	Michel Bertrand, Dorval PQ	93
1988	Manuel Urrizola, Los Angeles CA	118
1989	Tom Koch, Pembroke Pines FL	93
1990	Tom Cannon, Clearwater FL	141
1991	Martin Saffian, Orange CA	60
1992	Martin Marinov, New York NY	113
1993	David Brown, Brookline MA	77

Club Master (20-50 Masterpoints)

1984	Donald Gifford, Seffner FL	80
1985	Manny Kussack, New York NY	91
1986	Ron Lucas, Long Beach CA	111
1987	Sorin Samanta, Downey CA	149
1988	Earle Davidoff, New York NY	118
1989	Jeffrey Baillet, Atlanta GA	89
1990	David Gurvich, New York NY	97
1991	Hugh Morrison, Harahan LA	92
1992	Greg Reich, New York NY	120
1993	Jeffrey Figgins, La Mesa CA	141

Sectional Master (50-100 Masterpoints)

1984	Jay Goldman, Thousand Oaks CA	99
1985	Esther Bigio, Miami Beach FL	102
1986	Marc Poupart, Longueuil PQ	117
1987	Sandra Nyman, Weston MA	106
1988	Paul Streigle, Clearwater FL	90
1989	Henry Barksdale, Riverview FL	131
1990	Madeleine Taeni, Cape Coral FL	112
1991	Tom Finley, Omaha NE	133
1992	Jack Chao, Vista CA	142
1993	Irving Klein, Montreal PQ	139

Regional Master (100-200 Masterpoints)

1984	Sadru Visram, Toronto ON	140
1985	John Sensale, Hyde Park NY	92
1986	Esther Bigio, Miami Beach FL	120
1987	Andrea Hayman, New York NY	149
1988	Morris Biale, Queens Village NY	160
1989	Joyce Collos, Pembroke Pines FL	149
1990	Joyce Collos, Pembroke Pines FL	172
1991	Ralph Mastrangelo, Cranston RI	201
1992	Hugh Morrison, Harahan LA	162
1993	Jackie Rowe, Sun City Center FL	161

NABC Master (200-Life Master)

1984	Aaron Brody, Riverdale NY	139
1985	Sadru Visram, Toronto ON	153
1986	Earl Ziskin, Los Angeles CA	138
1987	Marc Poupart, Longueuil PQ	176
1988	Malle Andrade, New York NY	191
1989	Morris Biale, Queens Village NY	158
1990	Alan Hayman, New York NY	188

1991	Dixie Hsu, San Luis Obispo CA	168
1992	Madeleine Taeni, Cape Coral FL	157
1993	Hugh Morrison, Harahan LA	183

Life Master

1984	Sallie Landa, Boca Raton FL	174
1985	Gayle Rubens, Bay Harbor Island FL	199
1986	Susi Katz, Orlando FL	231
1987	Hugh Montague, West Babylon NY	274
1988	Andy Tarkington, Dallas TX	254
1989	Helen Shanbrom, Tamarac FL	356
1990	Helen Shanbrom, Tamarac FL	371
1991	Helen Shanbrom, Tamarac FL	326
1992	Helen Shanbrom, Tamarac FL	351
1993	Helen Shanbrom, Tamarac FL	419
	(10,000+)	
	Frances Silby, Fort Lauderdale FL	291
	(5000-10,000)	
	Charles Drum, Dover MA	265
	(2500-5000)	
	Paul Kinney, Cambridge MA	289
	(1000-2500)	
	Christian Chantigny, Montreal PQ	220
	(500-1000)	
	Claude Rouleau, Ste. Adele PQ	165
	(300-500)	

Senior Players of the Year

1989	Homer Shoop, North Miami FL	233
1990	Homer Shoop, North Miami FL	819
1991	Mike Shuman, Pasadena CA	638
1992	Loren Lange, Hurley SD	616
1993	Liane Slack, Kansas City MO	547

SILVER LIFE MASTER OF THE YEAR
(1000-2500 masterpoints).

| 1993 | Paul Kinney, Cambridge MA | 867 |

GOLD LIFE MASTER OF THE YEAR
(2500-5000 masterpoints).

| 1993 | Jim Reiman, Mansfield OH | 1189 |

RICHMOND TROPHY

1974	John Carruthers, Toronto	522
1975	Mike Schoenborn, Toronto	524
1976	Bruce Ferguson, New Westminster BC	929
1977	Bruce Ferguson, New Westminster BC	671
1978	Bruce Ferguson, Calgary AB	610
1979	Mark Molson, Montreal	819
1980	Mark Molson, Montreal	599
1981	George Mittelman, Toronto	681
1982	Mark Molson, Montreal	689
1983	Mark Molson, Montreal	784
1984	Mark Molson, Montreal	679
1985	Cliff Campbell, Thunder Bay ON	552
1986	Cliff Campbell, Thunder Bay ON	493
1987	Gary Tomczyk, Parksville BC	1071
1988	Robert Crawford, Vancouver BC	1400
1989	Gary Tomczyk, Parksville BC	1214
1990	Robert Crawford, Vancouver	1399
1991	Cameron Doner, Richmond BC	944
1992	Cliff Campbell, Thunder Bay ON	1561
1993	Cliff Campbell, Thunder Bay ON	957

ACBL PLAYER OF THE YEAR. This recognition goes to the contestant who earns the most masterpoints at *nationally rated* championships at the three NABC tournaments each year. The winners:

1990	Bob Hamman	451
1991	Zia Mahmood	616
1992	Jeff Meckstroth	342
1993	Bob Hamman	561

JUNIOR PLAYER OF THE YEAR. The Junior Player of the Year award was established in 1990. The competition to determine the junior player who can win the most materpoints in a single year is restricted to contestants 25 or younger who had not reached their 26th birthday as of Dec. 31 of the previous year. The winners:

1990	Sabine Zenkel, Chicago IL	633
1991	Leni Holtz, Los Angeles CA	688
1992	Geoff Hampson, Toronto ON	658
1993	Eric Greco, Annandale VA	770

YOUTH PLAYER OF THE YEAR. The Youth Player of the Year award was established in 1990. The competition to determine the youth who can win the most masterpoints in a single year is restricted to contestants 19 or younger who had not reached their 20th birthday as of Dec. 31 of the previous year. The winners:

1990	Brad Moss, New York NY	385
1991	Eric Greco, Annandale VA	557
1992	Eric Greco, Annandale VA	608
1993	Eric Greco, Annandale VA	770

BRONZE LIFE MASTER OF THE YEAR
(500-1000 masterpoints).

| 1993 | Sean Ganness, Aventura FL | 997 |

APPENDIX III

ZONAL CHAMPIONSHIPS

EUROPEAN OPEN TEAMS (Zone 1)

Winners	Runners-up
1932 Scheveningen, Holland	
Austria	Holland
Dr. Paul Stern	Ernst C. Goudsmit
Edmond R. H. Pollak	Frits W. Goudsmit
Louis Urvater	Bolo Einhorn
Simon Fleischmann	Jacques Borel
	J. R. Cor van Bemmel Suyck
1933 London, England	
Austria	Holland
Simon Fleischmann	Ernst C. Goudsmit
Walter Herbert	Frits W. Goudsmit
Dr. Paul von Kaltenegger	Bolo Einhorn
Edmond R. H. Pollak	Jean de Kuyper
Dr. Paul Stern	
1934 Vienna, Austria	
Hungary	Holland
Emeric Alpar	Ernst C. Goudsmit
Rafael Cohen	Frits W. Goudsmit
Lasloo Decsi	Bolo Einhorn
Francis von Leitner	J. R. Cor van Bemmel Suyck
Andor Keleti	Sam van Houten
Laszlo Klor	Lion B. Zeldenrust
1935 Brussels, Belgium	
France	Hungary
Baron Robert de Nexon	Emeric Alpar
Pierre Albarran	Rafael Cohen
Adrien Aron	Laslo Decsi
Joseph Broutin	George Ferenczy
M. Georges Rousset	Laszlo Klor
Sophocles Venizelos	Andor Keleti
1936 Stockholm, Sweden	
Austria	Hungary
Hans Jellinek	Emeric Alpar
Dr. Paul von Kaltenegger	Rafael Cohen
Edmond R. H. Pollak	Laslo Decsi
Karl Schneider	Andor Keleti
1938 Oslo, Norway	
Hungary	Norway
G. E. Zichy	R. Abrahamsen
E. Bokor	Leif Christiansen
George Ferenczy	Ranik Halle
Laszlo Klor	Odd Larsson
A. Por	Jens Magnussen
Dr. Lajos Widder	Trygve Sommervelt
1939 The Hague, Holland	
Sweden	Yugoslavia
Rudolf Kock	Dr. Nicholas Singer
Jac Newmann	Dr. Josef Fischer
Tore Sandgren	Geza Klein
Dr. Einar Werner	Ing. Marjanovic
	G. Stern
	Julius Klein
1948 Copenhagen, Denmark	
Great Britain	Sweden
Leslie W. Dodds	Dr. Einar Werner
Kenneth W. Konstam	Rudolf Kock
Edward Rayne	Nils-Olof Lilliehook
Boris Schapiro	Jan Wohlin
Terence Reese	K. Sundin
S. J. Simon	Tom Wennberg
Maurice Harrison-Gary (capt.)	
1949 Paris, France	
Great Britain	Sweden
Kenneth Konstam	Rudolf Kock
Adam Meredith	Dr. Einar Werner
Boris Schapiro	Jan Wohlin
Terence Reese	Nils-Olof Lilliehook
S. J. Simon	P. Brome
Maurice Harrison-Gray (capt.)	J. Kjelldahl
1950 Brighton, England	
Great Britain	Sweden
John C. H. Marx	Rudolf Kock
Kenneth W. Konstam	Dr. Einar Werner
Leslie W. Dodds	Jan Wohlin
Nico Gardener	P. Brome
Louis Tarlo	J. Kjelldahl
Maurice Harrison-Gray (capt.)	

1951 Venice, Italy	
Italy	Austria
Paoli Baroni	Hans Eisler
Eugenio Chiaradia	Laszlo Gulyas
Pietro Forquet	Karl Klimt
Augusto Ricci	Dr. Max Reithoffer
Mario Franco	Karl Schneider
Guglielmo Siniscalco	
1952 DunLaoghaire, Ireland	
Sweden	Italy
Gunnar Anulf	Engenio Chiaradia
Rudolf Kock	Mario Franco
Robert Larsen	Michele Giovine
Dr. Einer Werner	Guglielmo Siniscalco
Nils-Olof Lilliehook	Paolo Baroni
Jan Wohlin	Celestino Zeuli
1953 Helsinki, Finland	
France	Great Britain
Jacques Amouraben	Leslie W. Dodds
Marcel Kornblum	Kenneth W. Konstam
Dr. F. Hervouet	Nico Gardener
Pierre Ghestem	Albert Rose
Robert Schiltz	Peter F. Swimmerton-Dyer
Rene Bacherich	Dimmie Fleming
1954 Montreaux, Switzerland	
Great Britain	France
Leslie W. Dodds	Pierre Jais
Kenneth W. Konstam	F. Bodier
Boris Schapiro	P. Figeac
Terence Reese	P. J. Guerin
Adam Meredith	Henri Svarc
Jordanis Pavlides	Roger Trezel
1955 Amsterdam, Holland	
France	Italy
Pierre Jais	Eugenio Chiaradia
Roger Trezel	N. Sabetti
Pierre Ghestem	Massimo d'Alelio
Robert Lattes	Mario Franco
Rene Bacherich	Michele Giovine
Bertrand Romanet	Augusto Ricci
1956 Stockholm, Sweden	
Italy	France
Walter Avarelli	Pierre Ghestem
Giorgio Belladonna	Rene Bacherich
Eugenio Chiaradia	Henry Svarc
Massimo d'Alelio	Gerard Bourchtoff
Pietro Forquet	Pierre Jais
Guglielmo Siniscalco	Roger Trezel
1957 Vienna, Austria	
Italy	Austria
Walter Avarelli	Dr. Max Reithoffer
Giorgio Belladonna	Hans Eisler
Eugenio Chiaradia	Karl Klimt
Massimo d'Alelio	Hans Hartwich
Pietro Forquet	Dr. Erich Gluttig
Guglielmo Siniscalco	Karl Schneider (capt.)
1958 Oslo, Norway	
Italy	Great Britain
Walter Avarelli	Terence Reese
Giorgio Belladonna	Boris Schapiro
Eugenio Chiaradia	James Sharples
Massimo d'Alelio	Robert Sharples
Pietro Forquet	Maurice Harrison-Gray
Guglielmo Siniscalo	Alan Truscott
1959 Palermo, Italy	
Italy	France
Walter Avarelli	Pierre Jais
Georgio Belladonna	Roger Trezel
Benito Bianchi	Gerald Bourchtoff
R. Manca	Claude Delmouly
Pietro Forquet	Dr. Jacques Pariente
Eugenio Chiaradia	Henri Svarc
1961 Torquay, England	
Great Britain	France
Nico Gardener	Pierre Ghestem
Albert Rose	Rene Bacherich
Claude Rodrigue	Louis Malabat
Kenneth W. Konstam	Claude Deruy
R. Anthony Priday	J. Herschmann
Alan Truscott	Jacques Stetten

1962 Beirut, Lebanon

France	Italy
Rene Bacherich	Giorgio Belladonna
Pierre Ghestem	Massimo d'Alelio
Gerard Desrousseaux	Benito Bianchi
Dr. Georges Theron	Giovan Battista Brogi
Jacques Stetten	Giuseppe Messina
Leon Tinter	Camillo Pabis-Ticci

1963 Baden-Baden, Germany

Great Britain	Italy
Jeremy Flint	Benito Bianchi
Maurice Harrison-Gray	Giovan Battista Brogi
Kenneth W. Konstam	Eugenio Chiaradia
Terence Reese	Massimo d'Alelio
Boris Schapiro	Dr. Giuseppe Messina
Joel Tarlo	Camillo Pabis-Ticci

1965 Ostend, Belgium

Italy	The Netherlands
Piero Astolfi	Moritz Blitzblum
Giorgio Belladonna	Pieter Boender
Benito Bianchi	J. T. M. (Hans) Kreyns
Vito Gandolfi	C. Leo Oudshoorn
Dr. Giuseppe Messina	Anton Rijke
Renato Mondolfo	Cornelis (Bob) Slavenburg

1966 Warsaw, Poland

France	The Netherlands
Jean-Michel Boulenger	Martijn Cats
Henri Svarc	Cornelis Kaiser
Jean-Marc Roudinesco	Jacobus C. Kokkes
Jacques Pariente	Jut Kramer
Jacques Stetten	Cornelis (Bob) Slavenburg

1967 Dublin, Ireland

Italy	France
Giorgio Belladonna	Henry Svarc
Renato Mondolfo	Jean-Michel Boulenger
Benito Bianchi	Jacques Pariente
Dr. Giuseppe Messina	Jean-Marc Roudinesco
Cesale Bresciani	Dr. Georges Theron
Oscar Bellentani	Gerard Desrousseaux

1969 Oslo, Norway

Italy	Norway
Giorgio Belladona	Eric Hole
Benito Bianchi	Tore Jensen
Paolo Frendel	Knut Koppang
Benito Garrozzo	Bjorn Larsen
Dr. Giuseppe Messina	Louis Andre Strom
Renato Mondolfo	Willy Varnas

1970 Estoril, Portugal

France	Poland
Jean-Michel Boulenger	Wit Klapper
Pierre Jais	Lukasz Lebioda
Jean-Marc Roudinesco	Janusz Nowak
Jaen-Louis Stoppa	Janusz Pietruk
Henry Svarc	Andrzej Wilkosz
Roger Trezel	Adam Zimnielski

1971 Athens, Greece

Italy	Great Britain
Giorgio Belladonna	Jonathan Cansino
Benito Bianchi	Chris Dixon
Benito Garozzo	Jeremy Flint
Dr. Giuseppe Messina	R. Anthony Priday
Frederico Meyer	Claude Rodrigue
Renato Mondolfo	Rob Sheehan

1973 Ostend, Belgium

Italy	France
Giorgio Belladona	Jean-Michel Boulenger
Dano de Falco	Charles Guiton
Arturo Franco	Pierre Jais
Benito Garozzo	Michel Lebel
Rodolfo Pedrini	Christian Mari
Antonio Vivaldi	Henry Svarc

1974 Herzliya, Israel

France	Italy
Jean-Michel Boulenger	Oscar Bellentani
Michel Lebel	Benito Bianchi
Francois Leenhardt	Cesare Besciani
Christian Mari	Giorgio Matteucci
Henry Svarc	Carlo Mosca
Edmond Vial	Silvio Sbarigia

1975 Brighton, England

Italy	Israel
S. Di Stefano	Julian Frydrich
Arturo Franco	Michael Hochzeit
Benito Garozzo	Schmuel Lev
Ottorino Milani	Yeshayha Levit
Carlo Mosca	Pinhas Romik
Silvio Sbarigia	Eliakim Shaufel

1977 Elsinore, Demnark

Sweden	Italy
Sven-Olov Flodqvist	Vittorio Fellegara
Per Olof Sundelin	Benito Garozzo
Hans Gothe	Giorgio Belladonna
Anders Morath	Vito Pittala
Anders Brunzell	Antonio Vivaldi
Jorgen Lingquist	Arturo Franco

1979 Lausanne, Switzerland

Italy	Denmark
Vito Pittala	Stig Werdelin
Loranzo Lauria	Steffen Steen Moller
Giorgio Belladonna	Peter Schaltz
Dano de Falco	Knud Aage Boesgaard
Benito Garozzo	Hans Werge
Arturo Franco	Eric Grande

1981 Birmingham, England

Poland	Great Britain
Alexander Jeziro	Irving Rose
Julian Klukowski	Robert Sheehan
Tomasz Przybora	John Collings
Krzysztof Martens	Paul Hackett
Andrzej Milde	Tony Sowter
Marek Kukla	Steve Lodge

1983 Wiesbaden, Germany

France	Italy
Michel Corn	Giorgio Belladonna
Philippe Cronier	Dano de Falco
Michel Lebel	Arturo Franco
Hervé Mouiel	Benito Garozzo
Philippe Soulet	Lorenzo Lauria
Henri Szwarc	Carlo Mosca

1985 Salsomaggiore, Italy

Austria	Israel
Heinrich Berger	Michael Hochzeit
Curt Feichtinger	David Birman
Jan Fucik	Julian Frydrich
Wolfgang Meinl	Eliakim Shaufel
Karl Rohan	Shalom Zeligman
Franz Terraneo	

1987 Brighton, England

Sweden	Great Britain
Magnus Lindkvist	John Armstrong
Bjorn Fallenius	Raymond Brock
Sven-Olov Flodqvist	Anthony Forrester
Hans Gothe	Graham Kirby
Tommy Gullberg	Robert Sheehan
Per-Olov Sundelin	Jeremy Flint

1989 Turku, Finland

Poland	France
Krzysztof Martens	Eric Eisenberg
Cezary Balicki	Christian Mari
Julian Klukowski	Dominique Poubeau
K. Moszczynski	Jean-Christophe
Marek Szymanowski	Quantin
Adam Zmudzinski	Maurice Salama
	Patrick Sussel

1991 Killarney, Ireland

Britain	Sweden
John Armstrong	Sven-Ake Bjerregard
Anthony Forrester	Bjorn Fallenius
Graham Kirby	Tommy Gullberg
Andy Robson	Anders Morath
Roman Smolski	Mats Nilsland
Tony Sowter	Per-Olov Sundelin

1993 Menton, France

Poland	Denmark
Cezary Balicki	Jens Auken
Krzysztof Lasocki	George Norris
Piotr Tuszynski	Peter Shaltz
Piotr Gawrys	Dennis Koch-Palmund

Wojoiech Olanski
Adam Zmudzinski

John Norris
Dorthe Shaltz

EUROPEAN WOMENS CHAMPIONSHIP (ZONE 1)

1935 Brussels, Belgium
Austria
Gertrude Brunner
Marianne Boschan
Ethel Ernst
Gretl Joseffy
Hella Mandl
Rixi Markus
1938 Oslo, Norway
Denmark
Mrs. K. Kolle
Mrs. E. Lundsteen
Mrs. A. Hillerup
Demly Wilming
1948 Copenhagen, Denmark
Denmark
Else Dam
Rigmor Fraenckel
Gurli Kieldsen
Vera Thostrup
Demly Wilming
1950 Brighton, England
Great Britain
Mrs. N. Renshaw
Phyllis M. Williams
Penguin Evans
Fritzi Gordon
Alison B. Crisford
Mrs. A. N. Carr
1952 Dun Laoghaire, Ireland
Great Britain
Penguin Evans
Fritzi Gordon
Dimmie Fleming
Lady Doris Rhodes
Rixi Markus
Phyllis Williams
1954 Montreus, Switzerland
France
Suzalle Baldon
Andree Bourctoff
Mrs. M. de Bries
Christianne Martin
Marie de Montaigu
Mrs. Morand
1956 Stockholm, Sweden
France
Mrs. C. Bedin
Christianne Martin
Mrs. M. de Vries
Simone de Temmermann
Esmerian Pouldjian
Andree Sussel
1958 Oslo, Norway
Denmark
Annelise Faber
Rigmor Fraenckel
Gerda Ljungberg
Otti Damm
Mis Nyholm

1961 Torquay, England
Great Britain
Fritzi Gordon
Rixi Markus
Jane Juan
Dorothy Shanahan
Joan Durran
Marjorie Hiron
1963 Baden-Baden, Germany
Great Britain
Dimmie Fleming
Fritzi Gordon
Jane Juan
Rixi Marcus
Mary Moss
Dorothy Shanahan

1936 Stockholm, Sweden
Austria
Gertrude Brunner
Marianne Boschan
Ethel Ernst
Gretl Joseffy
Hella Mandl
Rixi Markus
1939 The Hague, Holland
France
Moussia Behr
Marie de Montaigu
Christianne Martin
Esmerian Pouldjian
1949 Paris, France
Denmark
Rigmor Fraenckel
Otti Damm
Else Dam
Demly Wilming

1951 Venice, Italy
Great Britain
Penguin Evans
Fritzi Gordon
Dimmie Fleming
Rixi Markus
Lady Doris Rhodes
Phyllis M. Williams
1953 Helsinki, Finland
France
Suzanne Baldon
Mrs. M. de Vries
Andree Bourchtoff
Mrs. Morand

1955 Amsterdam, Holland
Denmark
Otti Damm
Lizzie Schaltz
Vibeke Peterson
Rigmor Fraenckel
Gulle Skotte

1957 Vienna, Austria
Denmark
Otti Damm
Mrs. Detlevsen
Rigmor Fraenckel
Vibeke Peterson
Gulle Skotte

1959 Palermo, Italy
Great Britain
Fritzi Gordon
Dimmie Fleming
Rixi Markus
Marjorie Whitaker
Mary Edwards
Mrs. G. R. Higginson
1962 Beirut, Lebanon
Sweden
Inga Lisa Larsson
Maj Rex
Rut Segander
Britta Werner
Elna Fribert
Lotty Saabye-Christiansen
1965 Ostend, Belgium
France
Mrs. de Gailhard
Christianne Martin
Esmerian Pouldjian
Andree Sussel
Simone de Temmermann
Jacqueline Velut

1966 Warsaw, Poland
Great Britain
Joan Durran
Fritzi Gordon
Betty Harris
Jane Juan
Rixi Markus
Dorothy Shanahan
1969 Oslo, Norway
France
Mrs. C. Brochot
Mrs. M. de Vries
Mrs. M. Kitabji
Marianne Serf
Andree Sussel
Simone de Temmermann
1971 Athens, Greece
Italy
Marisa Bianchi
Rina Jabes
Maria Antonia Robaudo
Luciana C. Romanelli
Anna Valenti
Maria Venturini
1974 Herzliya, Israel
Italy
Marisa Bianchi
Luciana Capodanno
Marisa D'Andrea
Rina Jabes
Maria Antonia Robaudo
Anna Valenti
1976 No Contest

(After 1975 held
only in odd years.)

1979 Lausanne, Switzerland
Great Britain
Nicola Gardener
Rita Oldroyd
Sally Sowter
Sandra Landy
Michelle Brunner
Rosemary Hudson
1983 Wiesbaden, Germany
France
Danielle Allouche
Colette Lise
Ginette Chevalley
Veronique Bessis
Sylvie Willard

1987 Brighton, England
France
Danielle Allouche
Ginette Chevalley
Helene Bordenave
Veronique Bessis
Sylvie Willard
Benedicte Cronier
1991 Killarney, Ireland
Austria
Gabriele Bamberger
Doris Fischer
Rosi Spinn
Maria Erhart
Terry Weigkricht
Britta Widengren

1967 Dublin, Ireland
Sweden
Britt Blom
Mrs. G. Jarpner
May Moore
Rut Segander
Gunborg Silborn
Britta Werner
1970 Estoril, Portugal
Italy
Marisa Bianchi
Rina Jabes
Antoinetta Robaudo
Luciana C. Romanelli
Anna Valenti
Maria Venturini
1973 Ostend, Belgium
Italy
Marisa Bianchi
Luciana Canessa
Rina Jabes
Maria Antonia Robaudo
Anna Valenti
Maria Venturini
1975 Brighton, England
Great Britain
Charley Esterson
Nicola Gardener
Fritzi Gordon
Sandra Landy
Rixi Markus
Rita Oldroyd
1977 Elsinore, Denmark
Italy
Marisa Bianchi
Luciana Capodanno
Marisa D'Andrea
Enrichetta Gut
Andreina Morini
Anna Valenti
1981 Birmingham, England
Great Britain
Pat Davies
Nicola Gardener
Sandra Landy
Sally Sowter
Maureen Dennison
Diana Williams
1985 Salsomaggiore, Italy
France
Veronique Bessis
Sylvie Willard
Danielle Allouche
Ginette Chevalley
Catherine Saul
Fabienne Pigeaud
1989 Turku, Finland
Germany
Daniela von Arnim
Sabine Zenkel
Waltraud Vogt
Kareen Schroeder
Karin Caesar
Marianne Moegel
1993 Menton, France
Sweden
Linda Langstrom
Pyttsi Flodqvist
Bim Odlund
Catharina Midskog
Mari Ryman
Lisa Astrom

EUROPEAN JUNIOR TEAMS (ZONE 1)

1968 (Prague)	Sweden
1970 (Dublin)	Denmark
1972 (Delft)	Poland
1974 (Copenhagen)	Sweden
1976 (Lund)	Austria
1978 (Stirling)	Great Britain
1980 (Tel Aviv)	Norway
1982 (Salsomaggiore)	Poland
1984 (Hasselt)	France
1986 (Budapest)	Netherlands

1988 (Plovdiv)   France
1990 (Neumunster)   Norway
1992 (Paris)   Italy

NORTH AMERICAN CHAMPIONSHIPS
(Zone 2)

BERMUDA BOWL QUALIFIERS

1950   John Crawford, Charles Goren, George Rapee, Howard Schenken, Sidney Silodor, Samuel Stayman
1951   B. Jay Becker, John Crawford, George Rapee, Howard Schenken, Samuel Stayman, npc Julius Rosenblum
1953   B. Jay Becker, John Crawford, Theodore Lightner, George Rapee, Howard Schenken, Samuel Stayman, npc Joseph Cohan
1954   Cliff Bishop, Milton Ellenby, Lew Mathe, Don Oakie, William Rosen, Douglas Steen, npc Benjamin Johnson
1955   Cliff Bishop, Milton Ellenby, Lew Mathe, John Moran, William Rosen, Alvin Roth, npc Peter Leventritt
1956   Myron Field, Charles Goren, Lee Hazen, Richard Kahn, Charles Solomon, Samuel Stayman, npc Jeff Glick
1957   Charles Goren, Boris Koytchou, Peter Leventritt, Harold Ogust, William Seamon, Helen Sobel, npc Rufus Miles
1958   B. Jay Becker, John Crawford, George Rapee, Alvin Roth, Sidney Silodor, Tobias Stone, npc J.G. Ripstra
1959   Harry Fishbein, Sam Fry, Leonard Harmon, Lee Hazen, Sidney Lazard, Ivan Stakgold, npc Charles Solomon
1961   John Gerber, Paul Hodge, Norman Kay, Peter Leventritt, Sidney Silodor, Howard Schenken, npc Frank Westcott
1962   Charles Coon, Mervin Key, Lew Mathe, Bobby Nail, Eric Murray, Ron von der Porten, npc John Gerber
1963   James Jacoby, Robert Jordan, Peter Leventritt, Bobby Nail, Arthur Robinson, Howard Schenken, npc John Gerber
1965   Howard Schenken, Peter Leventritt, Ivan Erdos, Kelsey Petterson, B. Jay Becker, Dorothy Hayden, npc John Gerber
1966   Phil Feldesman, Bob Hamman, Sami Kehela, Lew Mathe, Eric Murray, Ira Rubin, npc Julius Rosenblum
1967   Edgar Kaplan, Norman Kay, Sami Kehela, Eric Murray, William Root, Alvin Roth, npc Julius Rosenblum
1969   Bill Eisenberg, Bobby Goldman, Bob Hamman, Eddie Kantar, Sidney Lazard, George Rapee, npc Oswald Jacoby
1970   Bill Eisenberg, Bobby Goldman, Bob Hamman, James Jacoby, Mike Lawrence, Bobby Wolff, npc Oswald Jacoby
1971   Bill Eisenberg, Bobby Goldman, Bob Hamman, James Jacoby, Mike Lawrence, Bobby Wolff, npc Oswald Jacoby; Edgar Kaplan, Norman Kay, Donald Krauss, Lew Mathe, John Swanson, Richard Walsh, npc Lee Hazen
1973   Mark Blumenthal, Bobby Goldman, Bob Hamman, James Jacoby, Mike Lawrence, Bobby Wolff, npc Ira Corn; B. Jay Becker, Michael Becker, Andrew Bernstein, Jeff Rubens, Paul Soloway, John Swanson, npc Roger Stern
1974   Mark Blumenthal, Bobby Goldman, Bob Hamman, Sami Kehela, Eric Murray, Bobby Wolff, npc Ira Corn
1975   Bill Eisenberg, Bob Hamman, Eddie Kantar, Paul Soloway, John Swanson, Bobby Wolff, npc Alfred Sheinwold
1976   Bill Eisenberg, Fred Hamilton, Erik Paulsen, Hugh Ross, Ira Rubin, Paul Soloway, npc Dan Morse
1977   Fred Hamilton, Mike Passell, Erik Paulsen, Hugh Ross, Ira Rubin, Ron von der Porten, npc Jerome Silverman; Bill Eisenberg, Bob Hamman, Eddie Kantar, Paul Soloway, John Swanson, Bobby Wolff, npc Roger Stern
1979   Malcolm Brachman, Bill Eisenberg, Bobby Goldman, Eddie Kantar, Mike Passell, Paul Soloway, npc Ed Theus
1981   Russ Arnold, Robert Levin, Jeff Meckstroth, Bud Reinhold, Eric Rodwell, John Solodar, npc Thomas Sanders
1983   Michael Becker, Bob Hamman, Ron Rubin, Alan Sontag, Peter Weichsel, Bobby Wolff, npc Joe Musumeci; James Jacoby, Jeff Meckstroth, George Rosenkranz, Eric Rodwell, Mike Passell, Eddie Wold, npc James Zimmerman
1985   Bob Hamman, Bobby Wolff, Chip Martel, Lew Stansby, Peter Pender, Hugh Ross, npc Alfred Sheinwold; Canada Drew Cannell, Gordon Campbell, Bryan Maksymetz, Mike Chomyn, Doran Flock, Subhash Gupta, npc John Carruthers
1987   Mike Lawrence, Hugh Ross, Bob Hamman, Lew Stansby, Chip Martel, Bobby Wolff, npc Dan Morse; Canada Harmon Edgar, Michael Schoenborn, Arno Hobart, Greg Carroll, David Turner, Martin Kirr, npc George Mittelman
1989   Hugh Ross, Peter Pender, Chip Martel, Lew Stansby, Mike Lawrence, Kit Woolsey; Canada André Laliberté, Jacques LaLiberté, Raymond Fortin, Kamel Fergani, Maurice Larochelle, Jean Bernier
1991   Bart Bramley, Mark Feldman, Fred Stewart, Steve

Weinstein, Alexander Ornstein, Jeff Ferro, npc Hugh Ross; Robert Barr, Harold Stengel, Bernard Miller, Alan Sontag, Jeff Meckstroth, Eric Rodwell, npc Robert Rosen; Canada Doug Heron, Ed Zaluski, Mike Betts, David Willis, Randy Bennett, John Valliant, npc Dave Kent
1993   Mike Becker, Ron Rubin, Robert Levin, Peter Weichsel, Russ Ekeblad, Ron Sukoneck, npc Jeff Wolfson; Cliff Russell, Sam Lev, David Berkowitz, Larry Cohen, Eric Rodwell, Marty Bergen, npc Bob Rosen; Mexico Gonzalo Herrara, Miriam Rosenberg, Nancy Gerson, Alicia Duran, npc Beatriz Herrara

OPEN TEAM OLYMPIAD QUALIFIERS

1960   United States: John Crawford, Tobias Stone, B. Jay Becker, George Rapee, Sidney Silodor, Norman Kay, npc Julius Rosenbloom; Oswald Jacoby, Ira Rubin, Samuel Stayman, Morton Rubinow, Victor Mitchell, William Grieve, npc Ben Johnson; Charles Goren, Helen Sobel, Howard Schenken, Harold Ogust, Lew Mathe, Paul Allinger, npc R.L. Miles; Don Oakie, Meyer Schleifer, Leonard Harmon, Ivar Stakgold, Sidney Lazard, William Hanna, npc Harry Fishbein. Canada: Eric Murray, Percy Sheardown, C.B. Elliott, Harry Bork, Sami Kehela, Bruce Gowdy, npc N.M Burns
1964   United States: Bob Hamman, Robert Jordan, Donald Krauss, Victor Mitchell, Arthur Robinson, Samuel Stayman, npc Frank Westcott. Canada: Ralph Cohen, R. Forbes, Sam Gold, Jack Howell, Sami Kehela, Eric Murray, npc A.M. Lando. Bermuda: Norman Bach, Malcolm Martin, W.G. Rosner, Tony Saunders, Bill Tucker, Peter Willcocks, npc Alan Truscott
1968   United States: Robert Jordan, Norman Kay, William Root, Edgar Kaplan, Arthur Robinson, Alvin Roth, npc Julius Rosenblum. Canada: Bruce Elliott, William Crissey, Eric Murray, Gerald Charney, Sami Kehela, Percy Sheardown, npc Albert Lando. Bermuda: Mrs. Norman Bach, Hugh Barr, Thomas Lines, Norman Bach, Tracy Denninger, Malcolm Martin, npc Dudley Cooper
1972   United States: Bobby Goldman, Bob Hamman, James Jacoby, Mike Lawrence, Paul Soloway, Bobby Wolff. Canada: Gerry Charney, Bill Crissey, Bruce Gowdy, Sami Kehela, Eric Murray, Duncan Phillips, npc Al Lando. Bermuda: Tracy Denninger, H.B. Eve, M. M. Lewis, M.V.D. Martin, Ernie Owen, Tony Saunders, npc D.G. Cooper
1976   United States: Bill Eisenberg, Fred Hamilton, Paul Soloway, Ira Rubin, Hugh Ross, Erik Paulsen, npc Dan Morse. Canada: Bruce Gowdy, Karen Allison, Franco Bandoni, Don Cowan, Eric Murray, Sami Kehela, npc Baron Wolf Lebovic. Bermuda: Mal Martin, Tracy Denninger, Malcolm Lewis, Ernie Owen, Joe Wakefield, Colin Millington, npc Tony Saunders
1980   United States: Fred Hamilton, Bob Hamman, Mike Passell, Ira Rubin, Paul Soloway, Bobby Wolff, npc Ira Corn. Canada: Allan Graves, Sami Kehela, Eric Kokish, George Mittelman, Eric Murray, Peter Nagy, npc Gerlad Charney. Bermuda: Alan Douglas, David Ezekiel, Colin Millington, Ernie Owen, Charles Vaucrosson, Joe Wakefield, npc Jack Rhind.
1984   United States: Ron Andersen, Bob Hamman, Bobby Wolff, Malcolm Brachman, Bobby Goldman, Paul Soloway, npc Ed Theus. Canada: Mark Molson, Boris Baran, John Carruthers, John Guoba, George Mittelman, Allan Graves, npc Steve Aarons. Bermuda: David Ezekiel, Colin Millington, Alan Douglas, Charles Vaucrosson, Jean Johnson, Frank Wharton, npc Jack Rhind
1988   United States: Seymon Deutsch, Bob Hamman, James Jacoby, Jeff Meckstroth, Eric Rodwell, Bobby Wolff, npc Dan Morse. Canada: Boris Baran, John Carruthers, John Guoba, Sami Kehela, Mark Molson, Eric Murray, npc Mark Stein. Bermuda: Paul Below, John Burville, Alan Douglas, Ian Harvey, David Pereira, Charles Vaucrosson, npc Jack Rhind
1992   United States: Seymon Deutsch, Bob Hamman, Jeff Meckstroth, Eric Rodwell, Michael Rosenberg, Bobby Wolff, npc Dan Morse. Canada: Ed Bridson, David Lindop, Geoff Hampson, Jown Gowdy, Mark Molson, Boris Baran

VENICE CUP QUALIFIERS

1974   Bette Cohn, Emma Jean Hawes, Betty Ann Kennedy, Marietta Passell, Carol Sanders, Dorothy Truscott, npc Ruth McConnell
1976   Emma Jean Hawes, Betty Ann Kennedy, Jacqui Mitchell, Gail Moss, Carol Sanders, Dorothy Truscott, npc Ruth McConnell
1978   Mary Jane Farell, Emma Jean Hawes, Marilyn Johnson, Jacqui Mitchell, Gail Moss, Dorothy Truscott, npc Ruth McConnell
1981   Nancy Gruver, Edith Kemp, Betty Ann Kennedy, Judi

Radin, Carol Sanders, Kathie Wei, npc Ron Andersen
1985 North America I: Kathie Wei, Judi Radin, Jacqui
Mitchell, Gail Greenberg, Carol Sanders, Betty Ann Kennedy,
npc Dan Morse. North America II: Edith Freilich, Nancy
Gruver, Mary Jane Farell, Helen Utegaard, Beverly Rosenberg,
Carol Pincus, npc Stelios Touchtidis
1987 North America I: Jo Morse, Sue Sachs, Cindy Bernstein,
Sally Wheeler, Sharon Osberg, Peggy Sutherlin, npc John
Sutherlin. North America II: Lynn Deas, Beth Palmer, Juanita
Chambers, Cheri Bjerkan, Kathie Wei, Judi Radin, npc Carol
Sanders
1989 North America: Beth Palmer, Lynn Deas, Kitty Bethe,
Margie Gwozdzinsky, Karen McCallum, Kerri Shuman, npc
Dorothy Truscott. Canada: Dianna Gordon, Sharon Reus, Mary
Paul, Francine Cimon, Gloria Silverman, Katie Thorpe, npc
George Mittelman.
1991 North America I: Juanita Chambers, Cheri Bjerkan, Kay
Schulle, Jill Meyers, Pam Wittes, Randi Montin, npc Ron
Andersen. North America II: Lynn Deas, Stasha Cohen, Sharon
Osberg, Sue Picus, Nell Cahn, Nancy Passell, npc Kathie Wei.
Canada: Francine Cimon, Dianna Gordon, Mary Paul, Sharyn
Reus, Gloria Silverman, Katie Thorpe, npc John Carruthers
1993 North America I: Lynn Deas, Beth Palmer, Helen
Utegaard, Kathie Wei-Sender, Carol Sanders, Betty Ann
Kennedy, npc Sue Sachs. North America II: Jill Meyers, Kay
Schulle, Kerri Sanborn, Karen McCallum, Sharon Osberg, Sue
Picus, npc Jo Morse. Canada: Francine Cimon, Dianna Gordon,
Sharyn Reus, Barbara Saltsman, Rhoda Habert, Beverly Kraft,
npc Mark Stein.

WOMENS TEAM OLYMPIAD
QUALIFIERS

1960 United States: Malvine Klausner, Helen Portugal, Sylvia
Schwartz, Agnes Gordon, Dorothy Hayden, Jo Sharp, npc
Charles Solomon
1964 United States: Agnes Gordon, Muriel Kaplan, Alicia
Kempner, Helen Portugal, Stella Rebner, Jan Stone, npc Paul
Hodge. Canada: Cecile Fisher, Louise Mark, Joyce Philips,
Frances Pielsticker, Mimi Roncarelli, Helen Smith, npc Baron
Wolf Lebovic. Bermuda: Mrs. Colin Anderson, Mrs. Norman
Bach, Mrs. Brownlow Eve, Mrs. Roland Lines, Mrs. T.H.
Lines, Mrs. W.G. Rosser, npc Dudley Cooper
1968 United States: Hermine Baron, Emma Jean Hawes, Sue
Sachs, Nancy Gruver, Dorothy Hayden, Rhoda Walsh, npc
Margaret Wagar. Canada: Mary Bowden, Maureen O'Brien,
Mary Paul, Louise Mark, Jackie Begin, Vi Broad, npc Baron
Wolf Lebovic. Bermuda: Captain Mrs. Roland Lines, Mrs.
Hugh Barr, Mrs. Brownlow Eve, Mrs. James Murray, Mrs.
Dudley Cooper, Mrs. Thomas Lines
1972 United States: Mary Jane Farell, Emma Jean Hawes,
Marilyn Johnson, Jacqui Mitchell, Peggy Solomon, Dorothy
Truscott, npc Margaret Wagar. Canada: Jackie Begin, Moselle
Berger, Irene Hodgson, Sharyn Linkovsky, Mary Paul, Mrs.
David Saltsman, npc Aaron Goodman. Bermuda: Mrs.
Brownlow Eve, Mrs. F. Jackson, Mrs. B. Kahn, Mrs. Roland
Lines, Mrs. Thomas Lines, Mrs. W.A. Rosser, npc Arthur
Eccles
1976 United States: Mary Jane Farell, Emma Jean Hawes,
Marilyn Johnson, Jacqui Mitchell, Gail Moss, Dorothy
Truscott, npc Ruth McConnell. Canada: Dianna Gordon, Irene
Hodsdon, Sydney Isaacs, Marilyn Pearce, Sharyn Kokish,
Francine Cimon, npc Peter Nagy.
1980 United States: Dorothy Truscott, Emma Jean Hawes,
Gail Moss, Jacqui Mitchell, Mary Jane Farell, Marilyn
Johnson, npc Ruth McConnell. Canada: Karen Allison, Pamela
Bridson, Francine Cimon, Dianna Gordon, Sharyn Kokish,
Mary Paul, npc Georges Hania.
1984 United States: Gail Moss, Judi Radin, Kathie Wei, Betty
Ann Kennedy, Carol Sanders, Jacqui Mitchell, npc Jim
Zimmerman. Canada: Dianna Gordon, Mary Paul, Katie
Thorpe, Sharyn Kokish, Francine Cimon, Sandra Fraser, npc
Eric Kokish
1988 United States: Edith Freilich, Carol Pincus, Beverly
Rosenberg, Kerri Shuman, Helen Utegaard, Rhoda Walsh, npc
Grant Baze. Canada: Francine Cimon, Dianna Gordon, Mary
Paul, Sharyn Reus, Gloria Silverman, Katie Thorpe, npc
George Mittelman.
1992 United States: Jo Morse, Joyce Lilie, Jacqui Mitchell,
Amalya Kearse, Tobi Deutsch, Mildred Breed, npc Rebecca
Rogers.

WORLD JUNIOR TEAMS QUALIFIERS
1987 Guy Doherty, Jon Heller, Asya Kamsky, Aaron
Silverstein, Bill Hsieh, npc Matt Guagliardo

1989 Larry Hicks, Mike Cappelletti, James Baker,
David Williams, Michael Klein, David Rowntree, npc
Bill Eisenberg
1991 U.S. I Brad Moss, Leni Holtz, Revindra Murthy, Mike
Cappelletti, David Rowntree, Michael Klein, npc Bobby
Wolff; U.S. II Jeff Ferro, Wayne Stuart, John
Diamond, Brian Platnick, Martha Benson, Tricia
Thomas, npc Chip Martel; Canada Mark Caplan, Eric
Sutherland, Fred Gitelman, Geoff
Hampson, Bronia Gmach, Mike Roberts, npc John
Carruthers
1993 U.S. I Eric Greco, Kevin Wilson, Jeff Ferro, Leni
Holtz, Debbie Zuckerberg, Rich Pavlicek, npc Chip
Martel; U.S. II Sam Dinkin, Michael Shuster, Albert
Tom, Doug Hsieh, Eric Secan, John Fout, npc Jan
Martel; Canada Geoff Hampson, Bronia Gmach, Eric
Sutherlin, Mike Roberts, Jeffrey Blond, Nicholas
L'Ecuyer, npc John Carruthers

SOUTH AMERICAN CHAMPIONSHIPS
(Zone 3)

OPEN WINNERS	WOMENS WINNERS
1948 Buenos Aires, Argentina	
Argentina	Argentina
Ricardo M. Argerich	Celia M. de Basavilbaso
Alberto J. Blousson	Josefina M. de Cramer
Carlos Cabanne	Celia de Luro
Alejandro Castro	Sara R. de Pianentini
Carlos Ottolenghi	Etelvina S. de Vergara
Dr. Louis A. Schenone	Mercedes Guerrico
1949 Sao Paulo and Rio de Janeiro, Brazil	
Brazil	
Milton Alvarenga	
Mauricio de Couver	
Renato Cusano	
A. Figueredo	
Alacite Frigoli	
Dr. Samuel Leite Ribeiro	
1950 Montevideo, Uruguay	
Argentina	Argentina
Carlos Cabanne	Ines M. G. de Casado
Fernando de Corral	Mercedes Guerrico
Alejandro Zumarin Olmedo	Esther Perez Mendoza
Julio Quesada	Maria Elvira Quesada
Marcus Ugarte	
1951 Santiago, Chile	
Chile	Argentina
Alfonso Aguero	Ines M.G. de Casado
Antonio Carrasco	Maria Laura V. de Mihura
Carlos Doren	Etelvina S. de Vergara
Jorge Guzman	Elsa C. de Vidal
Arturo Herrera	Mercedes Guerrico
Jorge Ovalle	Esther Perez Mendoza
Jorge Suarez	
Julio Subercasseaux	
1953 Puenta del Este, Uruguay	
Argentina	Argentina
Ricardo M. Argerich	Ines M. G. de Casado
Carlos Cabanne	Maria Laura V. de Mihura
Alejandro Castro	Mercedes Guerro
Alejandro Olmedo	Esther Perez Mendoza
Dr. Luis A. Schenone	Leonor Vivot
	Etelvina S. de Vergara
1954 São Paulo, Brazil	
Argentina	Brazil
Miguel Alfredo Denedit	France Estella
Carlos Cabanne	Doris Machado
Alejandro Castro	Sylvia Salles Godoy
Hector Cramer	Lucia Stefani
Carlos F. Dibar	Dolores Vasconcellos
Adolfo Gabarret	Margarita Villalobos
1955 Buenos Aires, Argentina	
Brazil	Brazil
Eros Amaral	Marina Farias
Milton Alvarenga	Eddy Lessa Dos Santos
Laslo Desci	Doris Machado
Norberto Mandler	Rosa Fitueira de Mello
Joao Murtinho	Lucia Stefani
Carlos Soute	Dolores Vasconcelios
1956 Lima, Peru	
Brazil	Brazil
Milton Alvarenga	Marina Farias
Mario Giorgetti	Eddy Lessa Dos Santos
Caio Luis Pereira de Sousa	Doris Machado

Norberto Mandler
Nelson Martins
Joao Murtinho
1957 Santiago, Chile
Argentina
Alberto J. Blousson
Carlos Cabanne
Alejandro Castro
Hector Cramer
Dr. Marcelo H. Lerner
Alejandro Olmedo
1958 Punta del Este, Uruguay
Argentina
Alberto Berisso
Alberto J. Blousson
Alejandro Castro
Carlos F. Dibar
Arturo Jacques
Carlos Ottolenghi
1959 Santos, Brazil
Argentina
Alberto Berisso
Desidero Blum
Carlos Cabanne
Ricardo Calvente
Arturo Jacques
Egisto Rocchi
1960 Not Contested
1961 Lima, Peru
Argentina
Luis Attaguile
Alberto Berisso
Carlos Cabanne
Ricardo Calvente
Arturo Jacques
Egisto Rocchi
1962 Buenos Aires, Argentina
Argentina
Luis Attaguile
Alberto Berisso
Desidero Blum
Carlos Cabanne
Agustin Santamarina
Marcos Santamarina
1963 Caracas, Venezuela
Venezuela
Edgar Lloynaz
Manuel Gonzalez-Vaie
Mario Onorati
Renato Straziota
Roger Rossignol
David A. Berah
1964 Montevideo and Punta del Este, Uruguay
Argentina
Luis Attaguile
Desidero Blum
Carlos Cabanne
Egisto Rocchi
Agustin Santamarina
Alfredo Saravia
1965 Santiago, Chile
Venezuela
Roberto Benaim
David A. Berah
Mario Onorati
Roger Rossignol
Renato Straziota
Francis Vernon
1966 Sao Paulo, Brazil
Venezuela
Roberto Benaim
David A. Berah
Edgar Lloynaz
Jordao Roberto Romanelli
Roger Rossignol
Frank Vernon

Lucia Stefani
Dolores Vasconcelios

Argentina
Ines M. G. de Casado
Maria Elena C. de Rodrigue
Etelvina S. de Vergara
Esther Perez Mendoza
Maria Elvira Quesada
Leonor Vivot

Brazil
Sylvia Godoy
Eddy Lessa Dos Santos
Esther Rodrigues
Regina Schmieder
Lea Siguiera
Lucia Stefani

Brazil
Selda Almeida
Marina Faria
Rosa Figueira de Mello
Doris Machado
Ria Petzold
Dolores Vasconcellos

Argentina
Ines M. G. de Casado
Maria Elena C. de Rodrigue
Mercedes G. de Schnone
Etelvina S. de Vergara
Esther Perez Mendoza
Maria Elvira Quesada

Argentina
Ines M. G. de Casado
Maria Elena C. de Rodrigue
Mercedes G. de Schnone
Etelvina S. de Vergara
Maria Teresa de Espinosa Paz
Maria Elvira Quesada

Peru
Pauline de Alaez
Elena de Bozzo
Maruja de Foccaci
Elena de Carbone
Zita de Fleischman
Ana de Isnardi

Argentina
Esther Claret de Aguirre
Ines M. G. de Casado
Adela N. de Engel
Hildegaard S. de Lippstadt
Etelvina S. de Vergara
Maria Elvira Quesada

Brazil
Sybil Jung
Maria Elena Mirando Jordao
Yolanda Paez de Barros
Vera Sampaio
Lea Sequeira
Dolores Vasconcellos

Brazil
Teresa Chammas
Marina Farias
Marina Elena Mirando
Sylvia Figueira de Mello
Sylvia Salles Godoy
Dolores Vasconcellos
(tied with)
Uruguay
Marta Brito del Pino
Lola P. de Castillo
Esther M. de Ham
Raquel D. de Methol
Brigida Philipstal
Elena Maria G. de Zumaran

1967 Lima, Peru
Brazil
Pedro Paulo Assumpcao
Mario Giorgetti
George S. Golefarf
Eduardo Nahmias
Gabriel Pinheiro
Adelstano Porto D'Ave
1968 Bogota, Colombia
Brazil
Marcello Castelo Branco
Roberto Figueira de Mello
Decio Martins Coutinho
Pedro Paulo Assumpcao
Gabriel Pinheiro Chagas
Adelstano Porto D'Ave
1969 Buenos Aires, Argentina
Brazil
Pedro Paulo Assumpcao
Pablo Pino de Barros
Educado Bastos
Pedro Paulo Castelo Branco
Gabriel Pinheiro Chagas
Synesio Martina Ferreira
1970 Caracas, Venezuela
Brazil
Eros Amaral
Pedro Paulo Assumpcao
Gabriel Pinheiro Chagas
Gabino Cintra
Christiano G. Fonseca
Tibor Kenedi
1971 Montevideo, Uruguay
Brazil
Pedro Paulo Assumpcao
Adelstano Porto D'Ave
Sergio Barbosa
Marcelo Castelo Branco
Octavio G. de Faria
Christiano G. Fonseca
1972 Santiago, Chile
Brazil
Pedro Paulo Assumpcao
Marcelo Castelo Branco
Pedro Paulo Castelo Branco
Gabriel Pinheiro Chagas
Gabino Cintra
Christiano G. Fonseca
1973 Rio de Janeiro, Brazil
Brazil
Pedro Paulo Assumpcao
Marcelo Castelo Branco
Pedro Paulo Castelo Branco
Gabriel Pinheiro Chagas
Gabino Cintra
Christiano G. Fonseca
1974 Lima, Peru
Brazil
Eros Amaral
Pedro Paulo Assumpcao
Pablo Plinio de Barros
Gabriel Pinheiro Chagas
Nelson Martins Ferreira
Synesio Martins Ferreira
1975 Bogota, Colombia
Brazil
Pedro Paulo Assumpcao
Gabriel Pinheiro Chagas
Pedro Paulo Castelo Branco
Marcelo Castelo Branco
Gabino Cintra
Christiano G. Fonseca
1976 Buenos Aires, Argentina
Argentina
Luis Attaguile
Jaime Braceras
Carlos Cabanne
Egisto Rocchi
Agustin Santamarina
Eduardo Scanavino
1977 Montevideo, Uruguay
Brazil
Pedro Paulo Assumpcao
Gabriel Pinheiro Chagas

Uruguay
Marta Brito del Pino
Lola P. de Castillo
Esther M. de Ham
Raquel D. de Methol
Brigid Philipstal
Elena Maria G. de Zumarany

Colombia
Angela Echeverri Gonzalez
Marta Marulanda de Ferrer
Marta Olga Velez de Hortet
Maria Cristina Rivas de Rivas
Ana Pinzon de Soto
Emilia Osorio de Velez

Peru
Maria Delfina de Denegri
Zita de Fleischman
Blanca de Magnani
Eda de Piana
Alicia de Flucker
Pilar de Velarde

Colombia
Tania de Mandowsky
Rosario de Nunez
Marina de Prieto
Maria Cristina Rivas de Rivas
Ana P. de Soto
Olga de Zuloaga

Uruguay
Esther M. de Ham
Raquel D. de Methol
Maria del Carmen C. de Meyer
Marta Britto del Pino
Brigida Philipsthal
Lola de Pineyrua

Brazil
Lia Cintra
Gilda Leal
Doris Machado
Elizabeth Murtinho
Maria Helena de Oliveira
Dolores Vasconcellos

Brazil
Lia Cintra
Suzy Fujihura
Gerry Gramegna
Lucia Gil
Elizabeth Murtinho
Heloisa Nogueira

Uruguay
Vera B. de Beer
Raquel D. de Methol
Maria del Carmen C. de Meyer
Marta Brito del Pino
Brigida Philipsthal
Lola de Pineyrua

Brazil
Sylvia Figueira de Mello
Gertie Gramegna
Heloisa L. Nongueira
Agota Mandelot
Elizabeth Murtinho
Vera Schaffer

Colombia
Josefina de Bennet
Angela Echeverry Gonzalez
Marta Marulanda de Ferrer
Marta O. Velez de Hortet
Blanca de Jaramillo
Silva de Vazquez

Argentina
Delia C. de Biquard
Matilde I. de Espiasse

Gabino Cintra
Marcelo Castelo Branco
Jose Barbosa Oliveira
Roberto Figueira de Mello

Adriana C. Martinez de Hoz
Anke M.J. de Moirano
Mary Ann M. de Monsegur
Mercedes G. de Schenone

1978 Isla Margarita, Venezuela

Brazil

Pedro Paulo Assumpcao
Gabriel Pinheiro Chagas
Gabino Cintra
Marcelo Castelo Branco
Jose Barbosa Oliveira
Roberto Figueira de Mello

Chile

Adriana D. de Aguad
Odette Y. de Yanine
Samira B. de Awad
Dare Turenne
Carla P. de Pariatore
Sonia R. de Ready

1979 Santiago, Chile

Argentina

Luis Attaguile
Hector Camberos
Pablo Lombardi
Egisto Rocchi
Agustin Santamarina
Eduardo Scanavino

Argentina

Ana Maria G. de Alonso
Martha J. Matienzo
Clara Monsegur
Lurecia T. Monsegur
Mercedes G. de Schenone
Christina de Suaya

1980 Bahia, Brazil

Argentina

Luis Attaguile
Hector Camberos
Pablo Lombardi
Egisto Rocchi
Agustin Santamarina
Eduardo Scanavino

Brazil

Heloisa Nogueira
Gertie Gaamegna
Ana Maria Assumpcao
Agota Mandelot
Maria Elizabeth Murtinho
Sylvia Figueira de Mello

1981 Lima, Peru

Argentina

Gustavo Alujas
Luis Attaguile
Hector Camberos
Agustin Santamarina
Eduardo Scanavino
David Zanalda

Brazil

Agota Mandelot
Sylvia Figueira de Mello
Maria Elizabeth Murtinho
Susy Powidzer
Alice Saade
Maria Elena Brito E. Silva

1983 Buenos Aires, Argentina

Brazil

Alcio Maia
Sergio Barbosa
Marcelo Branco
Gabriel Chagas
Alexandre Misk
Roberto de Mello

Argentina

Marta Matienzo
Diana Budkin
Mary Ann Monsegur
Ines A. de Gonzalez Pini
Maria I. Iacapraro
Mercedes G. de Schenone

1984 Santiago, Chile

Brazil

Sergio Barbosa
Gabriel Chagas
Pedro-Paulo Assumpcao
Gabino Cintra
Adelstano Porto D'Ave
Marcelo Branco

Argentina

Diana Budkin
Maria T.B. de Diaz
Lucrecia Monsegur
Ana M. de Blum
Maria T.P. de Espinosa Paz
Grace C. de Camberos

1985 Uruguay

Argentina

Martin Monsegur
Eduardo Scanavino
Luiz Attaguile
Hector Camberos
Carlo de Miguel
Guillermo Mooney

Argentina

Maria Teresa Diaz
Diana Budkin
Marisu Llauro
Lucrezia Monsegur
Victoria Merdinger
Ana Maria de Alonso

1986 Beuenos Aires, Argentina

Brazil

Gabriel Chagas
Pedro-Paulo Assumpcao
Paulo Barbelos
Rolando Evelino
Marcelo Branco
José Barbosa Oliveira

Brazil

Heloise Nogueira
Agota Mandelot
Elizabeth Murtinho
Susy Powidzer
Sylvia F. de Mello
Vera Amaral

1987 Santiago, Chile

Brazil

Ronaldo Avelino
Eduardo Barcellos
Carlos Camacho
Gabriel Chagas
Roberto de Mello
Jose Barbosa Oliveira

Argentina

Marta Matienzo
Diana Budkin
Graciela Lucchini
Gloria de Rosenfeld
Lucrecia Monsegur
Monica Borstein

1988 Brazil

Brazil

Carlos Camacho
Marcelo Branco
Luis Fetter
Flavio Moreira
Sergio Aranha
Marcelo Amaral

Argentina

Diana Budkin
Marta Matienzo
Maria Iacapraro
Marisu I. De Lauro
Marta D. de Tiscornia
Charo Garateguy

1989 Bolivia

Brazil

Carlos Camacho
Marcelo Branco
Pedro Branco
Gabriel Chagas
Ricardo Janz
Roberto de Mello

Brazil

Lucia Gil
Vera Amaral
Suzy Powidzer
Agota Mandelot
Suely Sampaio
Lia Cintra

1990 Paraguay

Brazil

Gabriel Chagas
Pedro-Paulo Assumpcao
Marcelo Amaral
Sergio Aranha
Miguel Villasboas

Uruguay

Loly P. de Valenzuela
Raquel D. de Methol
Esther M. de Ham
Carmen A. de Meyer
Martha D. de Raffo
Ana C. de Castro

1991 Peru

Brazil

Carlos Camacho
Gabino Cintra
Marcelo Branco
Gabriel Chagas
Ricardo Janz
Roberto de Mello

Brazil

Agota Mandelot
Sylvia de Mello
Elizabeth Murtinho
Heloisa Noguera
Ana-Maria Assumpcao
Lia Cintra

1993 Brazil Colombia

Gabriel Chagas
Pedro-Paulo Branco
Marcelo Branco
Oliveira deBarbosa
Carlos Camacho
Roberto de Mello

Rina Klahr
Flor Macias
Tobina Croitoru
Celia Khoudari
Sara Wassermann
Patricia Ramirez

ASIA AND MIDDLE EAST CHAMPIONSHIPS (Zone 4)

Open	Womens
1981 Pakistan	
Nishat Abedi	
Nisar Ahmed	
Gatta Cochinnala	
Zia Mahmood	
Masood Salim	
1983 Pakistan	**India**
Nishat Abedi	Rita Choksi
Nisar Ahmad	Nina Bonerji
Munir Ataullah	Lina Mayadas
Jan-E-Alam Fazli	Ursula Garg
Zia Mahmood	Prabha Kanetkar
Masood Salim	Prabha Joshi
1985 Pakistan	**India**
Nishat Abedi	Lina Mayadas
Nisar Ahmad	Nina Bonerji
Munir Ataullah	Rita Choksi
Jan-E-Alan Fazli	Sheelu Thadani
Zia Mahmood	Kalpana Misra
Masood Salim	Olindrilla Kundu
1987 Pakistan	**Egypt**
Nisar Ahmad	Marguerite Homsy
Munir Ataullah	Lily Khalil
Iftikhar Baqui	Maud Khouri
Jan-E-Alam Fazli	J. Morcos
Zia Mahmood	Safia Sarwat
Masood Salim	Josephine Hanna
1989 Egypt	**India**
Samih Khalil	Shailaja Mahajan
Tarek Sadek	Snehlata Singha
Abdel Raouf	Nini Bonerji
Ashraf Sadek	Kirin Nadar
Ahmed Abass	Bimal Sicka
	Ursula Garg
1991 Pakistan	**Egypt**
Abdul Rehman Allana	Marguerite Homsy
Tahir Masood	Lily Khalil
Kemal Shoib	Maud Khouri
Javed Ahmed	J. Morcos
Tufail Mohammed Sheikh	Safia Sarwat
	Marie Assouad-Doche
1993 India	**India**
Avinash Gokhale	Shaila Mahajan
Alihas Vaidya	Bimal Sicka
Keshav Samant	Hilda Raymonds
Rajesh Dalal	Marianne Karmarkar
Ramamurthy Sridharan	Yvette Singapure
Ashok Vaidya	Greta Lakhani

CENTRAL AMERICA-CARIBBEAN TEAM (ZONE 5)

Open	Womens
1983 Jamaica	
Cecil Chuck	
Rex James	
Ronald Tai Tenquee	
David Levy	
Lenny Chin	
Don DaCosta	
1985 Venezuela	**Venezuela**
Claudio Caponi	Fida Hirschaut
Steve Hamaoui	Ivy Smith
Paulo Pasquini	Alice Lerch
Francisco Vernon	Rosario Nunez
Memo Danese	Juana Lawnern
Roberto Benaim	Lucy Rodriguez
1987 Venezuela	**Venezuela**
Ricardo Solomon	Fida Hirschaut
Claudio Caponi	Morella Pacheco
Steve Hamaoui	Elisabeth Solar
Hector Manrique	Maria-Grazia deBettini
Mario Onoratig	Guilia Fornari
Paulo Pasquini	Alice Lerch
1989 Colombia	**Colombia**
Jorge Barrera	Gloria deVargas
Anton Cahn-Speyer	Tobina Choitoru
Santiago Rivas	Flor Macias
J.C. Alvarez	Ana deSoto
	Gloria deArboleda
	Cilia Khoudari
1991 Venezuela	**Venezuela**
Claudio Caponi	Morella Pacheco
Alberto Dhers	Ivy Smith
Steve Hamaoui	Rosario Nunez
Hector Manrique	Gania Mandowski
Mario Onorati	Tania de Mandowsky
Paulo Pasquini	Alejandra Piontkowski
1993 Venezuela	**Venezuela**
Alejandro Bianchedi	Ayako Amano
Claudio Caponi	Tania deMandowsky
Alberto Calvo	Morella Pacheco
Steve Hamaoui	Alexandra Pointkowski
Mario Onorati	Elisabeth Solar
Paulo Pasquini	Esther Sasson
1994 Costa Rica	
Connie Almy	
Chuck Paparigian	
Lee Karam	
Richard Karam	

FAR EAST CHAMPIONSHIPS (ZONE 6)

OPEN	WOMENS
1957 Manila, Philippines	
Philippines	
Stephen Chua	
Antonio Zamora	
Lionel de Silva	
Robert Yap	
Carmen Ballesteros	
Florence Leung	
1958 Tokyo, Japan	
Philippines	
Jose J. Reyes	
Stephen Chua	
Lionel de Silva	
R. Hernandez	
Eligio Teehankee	
Vincent Reyes	
1959 Taipei, Formosa	
Hong Kong	
Y.T. Fong	
L.A. Ozorio	
Henry S. Y. Kuai	
Victor Zirinsky	
George Tsiang	
Y.M. Chu	
1960 Hong Kong	
Hong Kong	
Y.T. Fong	
L.A. Ozorio	
William Wong	
Dodge Chen	

Henry S.Y. Kuai
Andre Ouan

1961 Bangkok, Thailand	
Thailand	
Oei Keng Hian	
Tan Hok San	
M.W. Hasnam	
Mr. Djanwar	
Thio Oen Gei	
Tan Kiong Say	
1963 Taipei, Formosa	
Tailand	
Kovit Suchartkul	
Boontham Nantaterm	
Ua Isrankul	
Somboon Nandhabiwat	
Manoo Veeraburus	
Benno Gimkiewicz	

1964 Tokyo, Japan	
Indonesia	Thailand
Liem Hok Po	Saisawart Chang
Boris Hutagalung	Gladys Huang
P. Sanbudhi	Promari Pibulsonggram
K. Sudianto	Cherdsri Sooksawasdi
J. Alex Fraser	
Oey Tek Goan	
1965 Hong Kong	
Thailand	Malaysia
Kovit Suchartkul	Gladys Loh
Ananta Boonsupa	Dr. Lily Lim
Manoo Veeraburus	Mrs. R.G. Fraser
Vibal Rasmidatta	Mrs. G.W. Arnott
Patama Narabhallobh	Shirley Bradley
Ua Israngkul	Doreen Peddie

1966 Bangkok, Thailand	
Thailand	Thailand
K.W. Shen	Saisawart Chang
Benno Gimkiewicz	Gladys Huang
Reggie Gaan	Manee Dibavadi
Somboon Nandhabiwat	Inthira Chandarasomboon
Sara Pothisuwan	Cherdsri Sooksawasdi
Prakorb Vanigbandhu	Promari Pibulsonggram
1967 Manila, Philippines	
Taiwan	Philippines
Y.J. Hsi	Mrs. M. Cacho
Min-Fan Tai	Helen Small
Patrick Kuang-Hui Huang	R. Cacho
Harry T. Lin	Imelda Tubangui
C.W. Liaw	Helen Tobangui
	Margaut Yu

1968 Kuala Lumpur, Malaysia	
Australia	Philippines
Jessel Rothfield	Carmen LaGuardia
Nat Rothfield	Mrs. L. Galpert
Tim Seres	Mrs. C. Palmer
Roelof Smilde	Paz A. de Tuason
Wally Scott	Imelda Tubangui
Jim Borin	
1969 Taipei, Taiwan	
Taiwan	Singapore
Conrad K.R. Cheng	Josephine Crane
V. Chow	Lotta Pahverk
C. Hsois	Sybil Holloway
Patrick Kuang-Hui-Huang	Emily Hee
C. Lee	Jenny Han
Min-Fan Tai	
1970 Jakarta, Indonesia	
Australia	Indonesia
Ron Klinger	Joan Shariff
Mary McMahon	Indra Widowo
Jessel Rothfield	Netty Suparto
Tim Seres	E. Gontha
Roelof Smilde	A. Raturandang
	M. Djajawikadj

1971 Melbourne, Australia	
Taiwan	Singapore
C. Chen	Josephine Crane
Conrad Cheng	Lotta Pahverk
Ching-Po Huang	Sybil Holloway
Harry Lin	Carmen LaGuardia
C. Lu	Emily Hee
Min-Fan Tai	Jenny Han
1972 Singapore	
Indonesia	Singapore

Max Aguw
J. Alex Fransz
Hengky Lasut
Frank Manoppo
M.F. Manoppo
E. Najoan
Denny Sacul
Felix Walujan

1973 Hong Kong
Indonesia
Hengky Lasut
Max Aguw
Frank E. Manoppo
M.F. Manoppo
B. Mutagalune

1974 Manila, Philippines
Indonesia
Frank Manoppo
M.F. Manoppo
I. Arwin
Hengky Lasut
W. A. Montaga
Denny Sacul

1975 Hong Kong
Hong Kong
Leslie Sung
T.S. Lo
Anthony Chow
Raymond S.P. Chow
Derek Zen

1976 Auckland, New Zealand
Taiwan
Min-Fan Tai
Harry Shien-Chu Lin
Patrick Kuang-Hui Huang
Che Hung Kuo
Conrad Cheng

1977 Manila, Philippines
India
A. Brahmachari
S. Ganguly
S.K. Ghosh
S.R. Ghosh
Kamal Mukherjee
G. Singha

1978 New Delhi, India
Taiwan
Patrick Kuang-Hui Huang
Dr. Chun Shun Shen
Che-Hung Kuo
Conrad Cheng
Harry Lin
Ya Pin Tu

1979 Tokyo, Japan
Indonesia
Hengky Lasut
Max Aguw
Denny Sacul
Munawar Sawirudin
Felix Waluyan
Jasin Wijaya

1980 Not Contended
1981 Taipei, Taiwan
Taipei
Harry S.C. Lin
Patrick K.H. Huang
Yin-Tzun Chang
Che-Hung Kuo
K.R. Chen
H.T. Chang

1982 Bangkok, Thailand
Indonesia
Denny Sacul
Hengky Lasut
Felix Waluyan
Munawar Sawirudin
Donny Tuerah

1983 Hong Kong
Indonesia
Denny Sacul
Hengky Lasut

Josephine Crane
Lotta Pahverk
Sybil Holloway
Carmen LaGuardia
Emily Hee
Jenny Han

Australia
Felicity Beale
Ruth Eaton
Gerda Stern
Winsome Lipscomb
Mary McMahon
Gabay Tabak

Australia
P. Brown
Ruth Eaton
Gerda Stern
Winsome Lipscomb
Mary McMahon
Elaine Poulsen

Australia
Margaret Choate
Mary McMahon
Mrs. G. Reynolds
Cecile Miles
Val Cummings
Ivy Dahler

New Zealand
Eileen Taylor
Zelda Morris
Val Bell
Nola Mather
Marion Hill
Frances Ewington

Australia
Ivy Dahler
Elizabeth Havas
Fay Landy
Claire Lester
Barbara McDonals
Cecile Miles

India
Rita Choksi
Lina Mayadas
Suhhadra Krishna
Mrs. S. Thadami
Mrs. S. Mahajan
Jane Merma

Philippines
Helen Tubangui
Rose Unson
Florence Yap
Tina del Gallego
Rudi Santiago
Carmen LaGuardia

New Zealand
Kathy Boardman
Jane Evitt
Jan Cormack
Jocelyn Kinsella
Stella Secker
Rosalie Cunningham

Philippines
Tina del Gallego
Lydia Jalbuena
Carmen LaGuardia
Rudi Santiago
Helen Tubangui
Florence Yap

New Zealand
Kathy Boardman
Jan Cormack

FelixWaluyan
Munawar Sawirudin
Donny Tuerah
Max Aguw

1984 Macao
Indonesia
Denny Sacul
Hengky Lasut
FelixWaluyan
Munawar Sawirudin
Yasin Wijawa
E. Manoppo

1985 Sydney, Australia
Japan
Hiroshi Hisatomi
Kuniaki Kawakami
Akio Kurokawa
Yoshiyuki Nakamura
Kyoko Shimamura
Akihiko Yamada

1986 Panang, Malaysia
Taiwan
C.S. Chen
C.H. Kuo
Patrick Huang
M.F. Tai
C.H. Wu
C.C. Chen

1987 Shanghai, China
Hong Kong
David Chan
Karic Chiu
Peter Chun
Roger Ling
Samuel Wan

1988 Not contested.
1989 Jakarta, Indonesia
Taiwan
C.C. Chen
Patrick Huang
C.K. Shen
Min-Fan Tai
C.H. Wu
Antonio Chong

1990 Singapore
New Zealand
Stephen Blackstock
Peter Newell
Dwayne Crombie
Martin Reid
Malcolm Mayer
Lionel Wright

1991 Guangzhou, China
China
Zhang Weili
Hu Jihong
Xu Hong Jun
Zhou Jiahang
Chen Rongchang

1993 Indonesia
Henky Lasut
Danny Sacul
Sance Panelewen
Eddy Manoppo
Munawar Sawiruddin
Giovanni Watulingas

Lyn Bishop
Zelda Morris
Jane Evitt
Joyce Kerr

Australia
Rosemary Atherton
Margaret Drake
Lindy Vincent
Diana Smart
Felicity Beale

Australia
Pauline Gumby
Sue Hobley
Barbara Travis
Paula Schroor
Margaret Bourke
Sue Lusk

China
Gu Ling
Zhang Yalan
Li Manling
Lu Qin
Zhu Xiao Yin
Sun Ming

Japan
Kazuko Banno
Makiko Hayashi
Kyoko Mizutani
Setsuko Ogihara
Yukiko Yoshimori
Kaoru Kotani

Taiwan
Amy Chen
Jennifer Lai
Phoebe Lin
Gloria Meng
Stella Wei
Tze-Ying Chen

Australia
Norma Borin
Cathy Chua
Felicity Beale
Diana Smart
Sue Lusk
Cecile Miles

China
Gu Ling
Liu Yiquian
Sun Ming
Wang Ping
Zhang Yalan
Shi Shaomin

China
Sun Ming
Want Liping
Zhang Yalan
Wang Wenfei
Gu Ling
Wang Hongli

YOUTH TEAMS WINNERS
1989 Taiwan; 1990 Australia; 1991 China.

SOUTH PACIFIC (ZONE 7)

Open	Womens
	Australia
1981 Australia	Australia
Dick Cummings	Felicity Beale
Bill Jacobs	Sue Edwards
Paul Lavings	Barbara Travis
Gabby Lorentz	Pauline Gumby
Tim Seres	Sue Hobley
Davis Smith	Diana Smart
1983 New Zealand	
Michael Cornell	
Malcolm Mayer	
Tony Taylor	

John Wignall
Kris Wooles
Lionel Wright

1985 New Zealand	**Australia**
Michael Cornell	Pauline Gumby
Malcolm Mayer	Sue Hobley
Tony Taylor	Margaret Bourke
John Wignall	Paula Schroor
Kris Wooles	Sue Lusk
Lionel Wright	Barbara Travis
1987 New Zealand	**Australia**
Alan Turner	Felicity Beale
Bill Haughie	Claire Lester
Dwayne Crombie	Jill Courtney
Stephen Blackstock	Barbara Travis
Peter Newell	Sue Lusk
Martin Reid	Diana Smart
1989 New Zealand	**New Zealand**
Michael Cornell	Jan Alabaster
Tony Taylor	Rose Don
Andy Braithwaite	Tina McVeigh
Lionel Wright	Jenny Wilkinson
Pat Carter	Emma Barrack
Ken Yule	Shirley Newton
1991 Australia	**Australia**
Paul Lavings	Felicity Beale
Paul Marston	Sue Lusk
Terry Brown	Diana Smart
George Bilski	Norma Borin
Aldur Kaljo	Rae Branicki
Wally Malaczynski	Cecile Miles
1993 Australia	**New Zealand**
Ron Klinger	Jan Cormack
Terry Brown	Jan Alabaster
David Lilley	Jane Skipper
George Bilski	Shirley Newton
Warren Lazer	Rosie Don
Peter Gill	Jenny Wilkinson

APPENDIX IV
SPECIAL EVENTS

EPSON WORLDWIDE BRIDGE CONTEST
Worldwide and ACBL winners/high score %:

1986 — France (Worldwide) Francis Frainais, Jann Bouteille - 78.79
ACBL 1st Billy Gough, Joe Livezey - 76.58
ACBL 2nd Marty Bergen, Larry Cohen - 76.29
1987— Great Britain (Worldwide) Peter Thompson, Robin Stretch - 79.5
ACBL 1st David Harrison, Alan Roebuck, - 76.25
ACBL 2nd Frank MacEntee, William Isaacs - 75.33
1988 — USA (Worldwide) Jan Horwitz, Barbara Norante - 76.29
ACBL N/S Horwitz, Norante
ACBL E/W Roselyn Teukolsky, Saul Teukolsky - 74.95
1989— Poland (Worldwide) Wojciech Biegajlo, Dariusz Zembruzuski - 79.17
ACBL N/S Karl Hicks, Ron Macdonald - 78.19
ACBL E/W Marvin Schatz, Ronald Perry - 71.50
1990 — Denmark (Worldwide) Soren Godtfredsen, Sorin Lupan - 88.54
ACBL N/S Marilyn Shibe, Harold Shibe - 73.54
ACBL E/W Bart Bramley, Judy Wadas - 71.25
1991 — Poland (Worldwide) Miroslaw Kopowski, Wieslaw Maczkowski - 79.58
ACBL N/S Kay Harrison, John Gilliatt - 75.41
ACBL E/W Warren Kornfeld, Paul Markarian - 74.91
1992 — France (Worldwide) Patrice Baverel, Francois Hazard - 77.00
ACBL N/S Ralph Katz, Richard Halperin - 74.00
ACBL E/W Steve Garner, Gerald Caravelli - 73.12
1993 — China (Worldwide) Zho Bao Qi, Wang Zuo Lei - 78.17
ACBL N/S Julius Fields, Calvin Morris - 78.04
ACBL E/W Peter Gostovic, Jacques Cloutier - 71.17

ACBL-WIDE GAMES

	WINNERS	SCORE %
1962 (Summer)	Gertrude Wallendorf, J. Wallendorf	74.8
1963 (Spring)	Ruth Mellett, Mrs. E. G. Obie	75.6
(Summer)	Reva M. Ford, Doris Klein	74.4
(Fall)	Walter Kopacz, Wiltold Stauffer	79.5
1964 (Spring)	Leonard D. Hine, Frances Hull	74.2
(Summer)	James J. Boudreaux, Alma Inklebarger	78.5
(Fall)	Ken Barbour, Mickey Rosenthal	74.4
1965 (Spring)	Robert Bratzher, Russell Wall	75.6
(Summer)	Conrad O. Orr, Hannah Scholer	75.6
(Fall)	Katherine Cowing, Mildred Cunningham	79.5
1966 (Spring)	C. A. Duchene, Peter A. Marson	75.6
(Summer)	Carol Sanders, Thomas K. Sanders	76.2
(Fall)	Jack Meyer, Joan Meyer	72.9
1967 (Winter)	Mrs. Sam Cohen, Sam Cohen	75.0
(Spring)	Dr. Lowell Grant, Ruth McConnell	76.3
(Summer)	Mrs. S. B. Fishburne, S. B. Fishburne	75.8
(Fall)	Dennis Caro, Al Romm	75.3
1968 (Winter)	Mrs. Wlmer Dwyer, Dr. John Sheridan	73.8
(Spring)	Charles Bensinger, Julius Kozlove	76.1
(Summer)	Pauline Buechler, Lorayne Lang	75.9
(Fall)	Jerry Locks, William Odierna	79.9
1969 (Winter)	Joseph Panepinto, James Singmaster	73.8
(Spring)	Maurice A. Londry, Stewart Loyst	77.3
(Summer)	Terry Eiely, Leon St. Jean	74.4
(Fall)	Bonnie Lowe, Dean Lowe	76.5
1970 (Winter)	Mrs. A. L. Graham, Mrs. M. E. St. John	78.6
(Spring)	L. D. Hansen, Gary Polonsky	73.2
(Summer)	Howard Rosenkranz, Glenn Wiswell	78.3
(Fall)	Lucille B. Kessler, Raleigh K. Mayfield	75.0
1971 (Winter)	Joe Imholte, Stan Zabaglo	73.2
(Spring)	Mrs. Neal Moore, Neal Moore	83.0
(Summer)	Gus S. Afendoulis, Johnny Theodore	77.7
(Fall)	Hal Kandler, Bette Stutzer	77.5
1972 (Winter)	Sami R. Kehela, Eric R. Murray	80.0
(Spring)	Diana Scheinman, Marcie Wheatley	79.8
(Summer)	Dolly Caballero, Josefina De Costas	78.6
(Fall)	Tena Boutilier, Dolores MacNeil	81.4
1973 (Winter)	Michael Roberts, Jim Wood	78.0
(Spring)	Subhash C. Gupta, Hari Jagasia	73.5
(Summer)	Chris Nelson, Denis A. Sakoski	78.0
(Fall)	Joe Kivel, Richard Taube	77.4
1974 (Winter)	Michael Gore, Richard Wagner	75.9
(Spring)	Carrie Burge, Mary Shipton	77.7
(Summer)	Corrine Sturm, Walter Sturm	77.0
(Fall)	Mark Conn, Andy Wolff	79.8
1975 (Winter)	Kirk Benson, Angeline O'Grady	75.9
(Spring)	Ira Chorush, Tony Rosenstein	79.9
(Summer)	B. C. William, Grace Williams *tied*	73.8
	with Bernie Coleman, Jim McGrath	73.8
(Fall)	George Siegel, Pauline Tessier	79.0
1976 (Winter)	Edward Bibb, Jim Powell	75.0
(Spring)	Dr. Habib Bazyari, Duane Johnson	78.6
(Summer)	Bill Doherty, Robert Porteus	75.3
(Fall)	John Batcheller, Bill Henry	77.7
1977 (Winter)	Richard K. Fleishman, Linda Gorski	73.8
	tied with Bernie Coleman, Jim McGrath	73.8
(Spring)	Libby Fernandez, Leonard Spillman	81.2
(Summer)	Marie Filandro, Peter Filandro	75.0
(Fall)	France Allard, Michel Allard	78.6
1978 (Winter)	Bill Anderson, Eric Hautala	76.2
(Spring)	Keith Garber, Carl Lindenman	76.7
(Summer)	S. Chandra Mohan, Attilio Spaccarelli	74.7
(Fall)	Robert Gieselman, David Goblirsch	76.8
1979 (Winter)	Betty Caisse, Jeannette Kowalewski	77.4
(Spring)	Fannie Lee, Mary Melillo	74.4
(Summer)	Bill Doherty, Paul Walorz	81.9
(Fall)	Al McDonald, David Stothart	73.9
1980 (Winter)	Jan Briggs Yaple, Chuck Yaple	74.4
(Spring)	Roger Doughman, Lena Jelusich	75.6
(Summer)	Faye Harker, Berta Krop	75.0
(Fall)	Bob Schives, Karen Schives	77.0
1981 (Winter)	Norma Matthews, Roger Matthews	78.8
(Spring)	Ken Lowe, John Roblee	75.6
(Summer)	Frank Guzel, Parks King	73.5
(Fall)	David Gilbert, John Hazell	76.6
1982 (Winter)	Howard Clore, Ronald Hartwig	74.6
(Spring)	Arleen Lehman, William Kreps	76.9
(Summer)	Jeanette Mury, Juanita Brown	72.7
(Fall)	Jon B. Alder, Gary Jackoway	75.3
1983 (Winter)	Paul Kronfeld, Don Rothschild	74.1
(Spring)	William Esberg, Jonathan Vogel	75.4
(Summer)	Louis Glasthal, Howard Piltch	73.6
(Fall)	Janis Trussell, Susan Carle	79.8
1984 (Winter)	Brian McCartney, Colin Bruce	78.6
(Spring)	Katherine Smith, Carol Hoover	72.9
	tied with Bonnie and John Swenholt	72.9
(Summer)	Jerry Crooker, Diane Olson	77.7
(Fall)	Neil McQuarry, Bruce Langley	78.6
1985 (Winter)	Peg Moore, Suzanne Choulnard	75.9
(Spring)	Earle Fergusson, Russell Boyle	74.8
(Summer)	Micki Knable, Marie Holdbrook	70.8
(Fall)	Rose Watson, John Myers	73.8
1986 (Winter)	George Olivarri, Kim Cox	73.8
(Spring)	Rob Sewell, Sadru Visram	73.8
(Summer)	Suzanne Matte, Francois Laporte	73.8
(Fall)	Joe Godefrin, George Wood	76.1
1987 (Winter)	Virginia Waterfield, Jackie Ward	80.3
(Spring)	David Ezekiel, Colin Millington	73.5
(Summer)	Renee and Madeleine Thibaudeau	70.5
	tied with Larry Long, Joe Lux	70.5
(Fall)	Joe Godefrin, Terry Coleman	81.9
1988 (Winter)	Anita Porter, Bill Bray	77.7
(Spring)	Jim Bishop, Godfrey Chang	72.9
(Summer)	Linda Gordon, Robb Gordon	74.2
(Fall)	Frank Willsey, Mark Connell	81.3
1989 (Winter)	Donna Matulis, Edward Matulis	72.0
(March)	Don Pearsons, Bill Treble	81.3
(Spring)	Ursula Brasel, Gerry Krueger	75.0
(Fall)	Yvan Drolet, Jean Boyer	75.3
1990 (Winter)	Susan Ledford, Tanya Truax	71.3
(March)	Eleanor Saver, Sid Brody	78.0
(Spring)	George Retek, Mari Retek	82.2
(Summer)	Barbara O'Grady, Bill Hood	75.2
(Fall)	Leon Hammerman, Charles Boteler	76.0
1991 (Winter)	Stan Subeck, Suzi Subeck	75.5
(March)	Jean-Paul Roy, Paul Beaudoin	77.8
(Spring)	Aidan Ballantyne, Derek Ward	79.6
(Summer)	Larry Hyman, Victor Biezenski	72.3
(Fall)	Pattye Clark, Kathy Pace	76.7
1992 (Winter)	Elliott Kahaner, Howard Cowan	78.9
(March)	Myles Maddox, Marilyn Maddox	75.8
(Spring)	Shome Mukherjee, William Hunter	74.7
(Summer)	Mary Jane Leonard, Frank Leonard	75.8

(Fall)	Jane Moore, Adrienne Lissner		74.2
1993 (Winter)	Richard Goodwillie, Richard Becher		74.2
	tied with Mavis Cole, Jim Cole		74.2
	tied with Laura Bright, John Nickens		75.0
(March)	Gary Bernstein, Larry Pfefer		74.1
(Spring)	Richard Grant, Tom Thomsen		73.5
(Summer)	Patricia Thompson, Len McCarthy		78.4
(Fall)	Norinne Anderson, Richard Nelson		83.3

ACBL-WIDE INSTANT MATCHPOINT PAIRS

	Open winners	Score %
1987 1st	Grady Gravel, Bob Ayers	77.73
2nd	Helen Furbee, Maggie Wilson	74.38
1988 NS	Markland Jones, Howard Segel	80.50
EW	Robert Michaels, Robert Quinn	75.60
1989 EW	Gordon Ezekiel, Randy Bennett	79.64
NS	Robert Dolliver, Mike Inkpen	72.38
1990 NS	Bill Kass, Robert Bernstein	75.50
EW	Suzanne Lapierre, Marc Poupart	74.50
1991 NS	Bob Hill, Ken Cable	73.75
EW	Dr. Muin Haddad, George Laubacher	71.08
1992 NS	Clay Hall, Steve Beatty	75.50
EW	Raymond Lothian, Wilma Lothian	71.70
1993 NS	Jeanne Lathrop, Albert Rahmey	73.46
EW	Annette McHann, Bill Cook	73.38
	Youth Flight winners	
1989	Andrew Kalish, Daniel Kalish	56.14
1990	Andrew Kalish, Daniel Kalish	56.88
1991	Brian Denninger, Jonathan Rodney	62.50
1992	Eric Greco, Vicky Sawyer	71.50
1993	Brian Kregor, Diane Kregor	66.46

ACBL-WIDE SENIOR PAIRS

An annual game held in clubs throughout ACBL each February for players age 55 or older. All sections in each game play almost simultaneously and computer-dealt hands provide that all sections play identical deals. After the game players are provided with printed copies of the deals accompanied by expert analyses. ACBL compares scores from each game and determines a winner and runner-up on a best percentage score basis for each of the 25 ACBL Districts as well as winner and runner-up for the entire ACBL. Inaugurated in 1989, these are the winners through 1994:

1989	Gerry Fried-Bud Seidenberg, Buffalo NY	77.56%
1990	Ruth Thorpe-Audrey Johnson, Oswego NY	79.10%
1991	Frances Adams-Wallace Embrey, Lake Jackson TX	75.50%
1992	Hector Ferri-George Burlison, Monterey CA	81.48%
1993	Peggy Fritsch-Dale Bennett, San Antonio TX	77.08%
1994	Isadore Bronfein-Sylvia Bronfein, San Diego CA	77.38%

EUROPEAN COMMON MARKET CHAMPIONSHIPS

Also known as European Community Championships

TEAMS

Open	Women	Mixed	Junior
1991 Athens (Greece)			
France	Israel	Belgium	Denmark
Levy	Zur-Albu	V.Polet	Krojgaard
Mouiel	Porat-Levit	G.Polet	Jepsen
Duchon	Birman	Cypres	Caspersen
Bessis	Abramov	Coenraets	Clemmensen
Melech		Munksgaard	
Naveh		Bruun	
1993 Montechoro (Portugal)			
Israel	Gt.Britain	France	Israel
Birman	Landy	Willard	I.Herbst
Zeligman	Handley	Levy	O.Herbst
Frydrich	Smith	Mouiel	Levin

Hochzeit	Horton	Allouche	Hermelstein
Porat	Gaviard	Perlmutter	Fohrer
Barel			

PAIRS

1967 Overall: Italy
Open Monk-Silberwasser, Belgium; Women's Devries-Sussel, France; Mixed Peck-Schroeder, Germany
1969 Overall: France
Open Saulino-Zanasi, Italy; Womens Goldschmidt-Kover, Belgium; Mixed Deutsch-Gille, France
1971 Overall: Italy
Open Saulino-Zanasi, Itlay; Womens DeGailherd-Sussel, France; Mixed Valenti-Facchini, Italy
1973 Overall: Italy
Open Garozzo-Mayer, Italy; Womens Van Heusden-DeKater, Netherlands; Mixed Moscati-Sticotti, Italy; Junior Capri, Faina, Italy
1975 Overall: France
Open Aujaleu-Majoux, France; Womens Gardener-Landy, Great Britain; Mixed Schroeder-Schroeder, Germany; Junior Schoofs-Polet, Belgium
1977 Overall: Italy
Open Von Cirlacy-VonCirlacy, Germany; Womens Kennis-Segers, Belgium; Mixed Cyprés-Polet, Belgium; Junior Pattacini-Matson, Germany
1979 Overall: Italy
Open Lauria-Rosati, Italy; Womens Arrigoni-Felcini, Italy; Mixed Mondolfo-Belladonna, Italy; Junior Bellefroid-Schick, France
1981 Overall: Italy
Open Walshe-Tobin, Ireland; Womens Quinn-O'Doherty, Ireland; Mixed Van Mechelin-Rebattu, Netherlands; Junior Roger-Sahal, France
1983 Overall: Netherlands
Open Fauconnier-Wanuffel, Belgium; Womens Malcom-Mitchell, Great Britain; Mixed Pasman-Niemeyer, Netherlands; Junior Girollet-Eisenberg, France
1985 Overall: Italy
Open Duboin-Ferraro, Italy; Womens Moeller-Zenkel, Germany; Mixed Manara-Atttanasio, Italy; Junior Krijgsman-Ter Laare, Netherlands
1987 Overall: France
Open Duboin-Ferraro, Italy; Womens Lise-Delor, France; Mixed Nahmens-Solari, France; Junior Kapayannidis-Liarak, Greece
1989 Overall: Netherlands
Open Buratti-Bocchi, Italy; Womens Guillaumin-Saul, France; Womens Quevy-Zadikyan, Belgium; Junior Bilde-Larsen, Denmark
1991 Overall: France
Open Pietri-DiMaio, Italy; Womens Handley-Landy, Great Britain; Mixed Allouche-Gaviard, France; Junior Munksgaard-Bruun, Denmark
1993 Overall: Italy
Open Ricciarelli-DeFalco, Italy; Womens DaRos-Favas, France; Mixed Guillaumin-Quantin, France; Junior Versace-Nunes, Italy

ANGLO-AMERICAN MATCHES

Results of semi-official or unofficial matches:

London, 1930. America (Ely and Josephine Culbertson, Theodore A. Lightner, and Waldemar K. von Zedtwitz) beat England (Lt. Col. Walter Buller, Alice G. Evers, Cedric Kehoe, and Nelson Wood-Hill) by 4,845 total points over 200 boards.

London, 1933. For the SCHWAB CUP. America (Ely and Josephine Culbertson, Theodore A. Lightner, and Michael T. Gottlieb) beat England (Lt. Col. Henry M. Beasley, Gerald G. Domville, P.V. Tabbush, George Morris, Graham F. Mathieson, and Lady Doris Rhodes) by 11,110 total points over 300 boards.

London, 1934. For the SCHWAB CUP. America (Ely and Josephine Culbertson, Theodore A. Lightner, and Albert H. Morehead) beat England (Richard Lederer, William Rose, Henry St. John Ingram, and Stanley Hughes; with Col. George G. J. Walshe [capt.] and A. Frost as alternates) by 3,600 total points over 300 boards.

London, 1949. For the Crowninshield cup. England beat America by 330 total points, the net result of two matches. England (Maurice Harrison-Gray [capt.], Kenneth W. Konstam, Terence Reese, and Boris Schapiro) beat America (Johnny R. Crawford, George Rapee, Samuel M. Stayman, and Peter A. Leventritt) by 2,950 total points. The same American team beat England (Ewart Kempson [capt.], Rixi Markus, Kenneth W.

Konstam, Leslie Dodds, Edward Rayne, Jordanis T. Pavlides, and Graham F. Mathieson) by 2,620 total points. Both matches were of 96 boards.

London, 1954. England (Terence Reese, Boris Schapiro, Kenneth W. Konstam, Adam Meredith, and Edward Mayer) beat America (Clifford W. Bishop, Milton Q. Ellenby, Douglas Steen, Lewis L. Mathe, and Don Oakie; William Rosen was absent) by 81 IMPs over 100 boards.

Miami, 1955. America (Waldemar K. von Zedtwitz, Harold Harkavy, William S. Root, Albert Weiss, Edward Burns, William Seamon, Harold Vanderbilt, Charles Goren, and Charles Whitebrook) beat Great Britain (Terence Reese, Kenneth W. Konstam, Leslie Dodds, Adam Meredith, and Jordanis T. Pavlides) by 150 total points over 100 boards.

London, 1956. England (Terence Reese, Boris Schapiro, Kenneth W. Konstam, Leslie Dodds, and Edward Mayer) beat America (Samuel M. Stayman, Charles Goren, Charles J. Solomon, Myron Field, Lee Hazen, and Richard Kahn) by 79 IMPs over 100 boards.

Philadelphia, 1976. Bicentennial challenge match. The U.S. (Colonists) (Edgar Kaplan, Norman Kay, Bobby Goldman, Mark Blumenthal, Robert Jordan, Arthur Robinson with Simon [Skippy] Becker as npc) defeated Great Britain (Redcoats) (Claude Rodrigue, Tony Priday, Barnet Shenkin and Michael Rosenberg) 90 IMPs to 65 over 40 boards.

FRANCO-AMERICAN MATCHES

There have been 17 official meetings in world championship competition.

1936 New York	1968 Deauville, France
United States won	United States won
1954 Monte Carlo	1969 Rio de Janeiro
United States won	North America won
1956 Paris	1971 Taipei
France won	United States won
1960 Turin	1972 Miami
France won	United States won
1961 Buenos Aires	1974 Venice
North America won	North America won
1963 St. Vincent, Italy	1975 Bermuda
North America won	North America won
1964 New York	1976 Monte Carlo
United States won	France won
1967 Miami Beach	1980 Valkenburg
North America won	France won
	1992 Salsomaggiore
	France won

The following semiofficial or unofficial matches have been played:

(1) Paris 1930. United States (Ely and Josephine Culbertson, Theodore Lightner, Waldemar von Zedtwitz) drew with France (Pierre Bellanger, Pierre Alharran, A. B. de Puchesse, Robert de Nexon, Georges Rousset, Emanuel Tulumaris, Sophocles Venizelos). The match was played at PLAFOND, the forerunner of contract bridge, and, after a dispute, was abandoned as a draw shortly before the end when the scores were almost level.

(2) Paris 1954. France beat the United States (Cliff Bishop, Milton Ellenby, Lewis Mathe, Don Oakie, Doug Steen) by 17 IMPS.

PAN AMERICAN BRIDGE
CHAMPIONSHIPS

Held in Corpus Christi TX in 1992, the medal winners were:

OPEN PAIRS
1. USA: Eric Rodwell and Doug Simson
2. Brazil: Gabriel Chagas and Marcelo Branco
WOMENS PAIRS
1. USA: Marinesa Letizia and Juanita Chambers
2. USA: June Deutsch and Beverly Rosenberg
OPEN TEAMS
1. USA: Cliff Russell, Robert Levin, Sam Lev, David Berkowitz, Larry Cohen, Peter Weichsel
2. Canada: Ed Bridson, David Lindop, Geoff Hampson, John Gowdy, Mark Molson, Boris Baran
WOMENS TEAMS

1. USA: Gail Greenberg, Dorothy Truscott, Judy Tucker, Lisa Berkowitz, Randi Montin, Pam Wittes
2. Colombia: Tobi Croitoru, Flor Macias, Sara Wasserman, Cilia Khoudari, Zita Lechter, Deisl Gould

CAVENDISH INVITATIONAL PAIRS

1975	James Jacoby, Gerald Westheimer
1976	Alan Sontag, Peter Weichsel
1977	Alan Sontag, Peter Weichsel
1978	Roy Fox, Paul Swanson
1979	Roger Bates, Daniel Mordecai
1980	Lou Bluhm, Thomas Sanders
1981	James Cayne, Fred Hamilton
1982	Ed Manfield, Kit Woolsey
1983	Robert Lipsitz, Neil Silverman
1984	Marty Bergen, Larry Cohen
1985	Irving Litvack, Joseph Silver
1986	Matt Granovetter, Michael Rosenberg
1987	Drew Casen, Jim Krekorian
1988	Bjorn Fallenius, Magnus Lindkvist
1989	Marty Bergen, Larry Cohen
1990	Piotr Gawrys, Elyakim Shoufel
1991	Johan Bennet, Anders Wirgren
1992	Amos Kaminski, Shmuel Lev
1993	Fred Stewart, Steve Weinstein
1994	Kit Woolsey, Neil Silverman

SUNDAY TIMES PAIRS

1963	Pierre Jais, Roger Trezel (France)
1964	Terence Reese, Boris Schapiro (England)
1965	No contest
1966	Gerard Desrousseaux, Dr. George Theron (France)
1967	Claude Rodrigue, Louis Tarlo (England)
1968	Claude Delmouly, Leon Yallouze (France, Egypt)
1969	Jean Besse, John D. Collings (Switzerland, England)
1970	Nico Gardener, Richard Anthony Priday (England)
1971	Lukasz Lebioda, Andrezej Wilkosz (Poland)
1972	Steven Altman, Alan Sontag (U.S.A.)
1974	Gianfranco Facchini, Sergio Zucchelli (Italy)
1975	Alan Sontag, Peter Weichsel (U.S.A.)
1976	Michael Rosenberg, Barnet Shenkin (Scotland)
1977	Jean-Michel Boulenger, Henri Szwarc (France)
1978	Sven-Olov Flodqvist, Per Olof Sundelin (Sweden)
1979	Pedro Paulo Assumpcao, Gabriel Chagas (Brazil)
1980	Victor Goldberg, Barnett Shenkin (Scotland)
1981	Sven-Olov Flodqvist, Per Olof Sundelin (Sweden)
1990	Tony Forrester, Andrew Robson (England)
1991	Paul Chemla, Michel Perron (France)
1992	Gabriel Chagas, Marcelo Branco (Brazil)
1993	Robert Levin, Gaylor Kaelo (U.S.A.)
1994	Adam Zmudzinski, Cezary Balicki (Poland)

WORLD TOP INVITATIONAL PAIRS
(Also known as **Cap Gemini** and **Cup Volmac**
Pairs)

1987 — Jan Fucik - Franz Terraneo (Austria)
1988 — Jeff Meckstroth - Eric Rodwell (US)
1989 — Jan Fucik - Franz Terraneo (Austria)
1990 — Tony Forrester - Andy Robson (Great Britain)
1991 — Billy Eisenberg - Benito Garozzo (US)
1992 — Zia Mahmood (Pakistan) - Michael Rosenberg (US)
1993 — Gabriel Chagas - Marcelo Branco (Brazil)
1994 — Geir Helgemo - Tor Helness (Norway)

PHILIP MORRIS
EUROPEAN CHAMPIONSHIPS

Held in 1976 and 1980 as EUROPEAN BRIDGE PAIRS CHAMPIONSHIP. Philip Morris has been sponsor of this competition, held every two years, since 1985. Winners Open Pairs:

1976 *Cannes* Chemla-Lebel, France
1980 *Monte-Carlo* Kudla-Milde, Poland
1985 *Monte-Carlo* 1. Chemla-Perron, France; 2. Fucik-Terraneo, Austria; 3. Buratti-Mortabotti, Italy
1987 *Paris* 1. Meyer-Le Royer, France; 2. Cronier-Lebel, France; 3. Longinotti-Di Maio, Italy
1989 *Salsomaggiore* 1. Lesniewski-Przybora, Poland; 2.

Astore-Lanzarotti, Italy; 3. Engel-Buchlev, Germany
1991 *Montecatini* 1. Abecassis-Quantin, France; 2. Sjoerds-Wintermans, Netherlands; 3. Lévy-Mouiel, France
1993 *Bielefeld* 1. Abecassis-Quantin, France; 2. Meyer-Stretz, France; 3. Van Oppen-Rebattu, Netherlands

PHILIP MORRIS
EUROPEAN MIXED CHAMPIONSHIPS

1990 *Bordeaux* MIXED PAIRS 1. Saul-Quantin, France; 2. Terraneo-Terraneo, Austria; 3. Willard-Mouiel, France. MIXED TEAMS 1. France (Captain G. Chevalley); 2. Denmark (Captain K. Steen-Moller); 3. Italy (Captain Mrs. Lavazza)
1992 *Ostend* MIXED PAIRS 1. Harasimowiz-Lesniewsky, Poland; 2. Gebrandy-Jongejean, Netherlands; 3. Cronier-Bessis, France. MIXED TEAMS 1. France (Captain D. Pilon); 2. Italy (Captain M.T. Lavazza); 3. Netherlands (Captain Tammens)
1994 *Barcelona* MIXED PAIRS 1. Zenkel-Nippgen, Germany; 2. Feichtinger-Feichtinger, Austria; 3. Gaviard-Lévy, France; MIXED TEAMS 1. Netherlands (Captain van der Pas); 2. Denmark (Captain Norris); 3. France (Captain Gaviard)

NORDIC CHAMPIONSHIP

The Nordic Championships, contested by five Scandinavian countries, is one of the oldest international competitions. The winners are:

Year	Place	Open Winners	Women Winners
1946	Oslo	Norway	Sweden
1947	Copenhagen	Sweden	Denmark
1948	Stockholm	Norway	Sweden
1949	Helsinki	Sweden	Sweden
1950	Oslo	Norway	Denmark
1953	Arhus	Sweden	Denmark
1955	Bastad	Sweden	Denmark
1957	Helsinki	Sweden	Denmark
1962	Copenhagen	Sweden	Denmark
1964	Oslo	Sweden	Sweden
1966	Reykjavik	Norway	Sweden
1968	Goteborg	Sweden	Sweden
1971	Tavastehus	Norway	Sweden
1973	Alborg	Denmark	Norway
1975	Oslo	Norway	Sweden
1978	Reykjavik	Norway	Sweden
1980	Norrkoping	Norway	Sweden
1982	Helsinki	Norway	Sweden
1984	Helsinki	Sweden	Sweden
1986	Oslo	Denmark	Norway
1988	Reykjavik	Iceland	Denmark
1990	Torshavn	Sweden	Iceland
1992	Umea	Iceland	Sweden

GENERALI EUROPE
INDIVIDUAL CHAMPIONSHIP

1992 Men 1, Piotr Gawrys, Poland; 2, Jan Fucik, Austria; 3, Alain Lévy, France. Women 1, Maria Erhart, Austria; 2, C. Lise, France; 3, Nicola Smith, Great Britain.
1994 Men 1, Jon Baldursson, Iceland; 2, Christian Mari, France; 3, Jan Westerhof, Netherlands. Women 1, Nicola Smith, Great Britain; 2, Pyttsi Flodqvist, Sweden; 3, Bénédicte Cronier, France.

NORTH AMERICAN COLLEGE
TEAM CHAMPIONSHIPS

Competition began in 1987 at the Spring NABC in St. Louis and the winners (except Barry Goren, who was not eligible) represented ACBL in the first World Junior Championships in Amsterdam, the Netherlands. Guy Doherty, Jon Heller and Asya Kamsky -- joined by Bill Hsieh and Aaron

Silverstein -- finished third in the World Junior championships.

The championships were played at the Spring NABCs in 1988 and 1989. In 1990, the competition was moved to ACBL headquarters in Memphis where it was co-sponsored by ACBL and the Association of College Unions-International.

The competition moved back to the Spring NABC in 1991 but the following year it returned to Memphis, where it became a part of the annual "Memphis in May" festivities.

1987	New York University: Guy Doherty, Barry Goren, Jon Heller, Asya Kamsky.
1988	University of Illinois: Brian Blackmore, Dennis Carney, Justin Graver, Michael Steigmann.
1989	University of Tennessee: Jim Baker, Mike Cappelletti Jr., Michael White, David Williams.
1990	Virginia Tech: Shrikant Dixit, Chunming Duan, Venkateshwaran Sekharipuram, Xiandi Zeng.
1991	University of Virginia: John Miller, John Prince, Hank Strauch, Scott Tumperi.
1992	Rensselaer Polytechnic Institute: Scott Bieber, Brady Richter, Andrew Skolnick, Ron Sperber.
1993	Yale University: Matt Hastings, Douglas Koltenuk, Malik Madon-Ismail, Tony Tang.
1994	Harvard University: Mark Paltrowitz, Barry Piafsky, Michael Steigmann, Tom Rozinski.

NORTH AMERICAN COLLEGE
PAIR CHAMPIONSHIPS

1940	Radcliffe College
1941	Harvard University
1942	Princeton University
1943-45	(cancelled due to World War II)
1946	Cornell University
1947	University of California (first time on national basis)
	Charles W. Drake, Philip J. Smith
1948	Capital University, Columbus, OH
	Charles Krueger, Luther Schleisser, Jr.
1949	Wayne University, Detroit
	Clifford Bishop, Dorsey Brooks
1950	Massachussetts Institute of Technology
	Martin Cornish, Jr., Richard Lesser
1951	Washburn University, Topeka, KS
	Gerald Michaud, Bradley Post
1952	Rice Institute, Houston, TX
	John "Spider" Harris, Richard Sutton
1953	Purdue University (N-S)
	Frank McClure, Carey Yelton, Jr.
	Princeton University (E-W)
	David Bradley, Harlow Lewis
1954	Purdue University (N-S)
	Herman Rose, Carey Yelton, Jr.
	Dartmouth College (E-W)
	Harry Connaro, Robert Sokolsky
1955	Whitman College (N-S)
	William Click, Robert Luther
	University of Texas (E-W)
	Charles Callery, Charles Miller
1956	Harvard University (N-S)
	Franklin Bunn, Boyd Everett, Jr.
	Dartmouth College (E-W)
	Frank Barteaux, Jr., John Strong, Jr.
1957	Cornell University (N-S)
	Frank Goldring, Paul Trent
	Oberlin College (E-W)
	Danny Kleinman, Dick Recht
1958	University of Iowa (N-S)
	Terry Campbell, Peter Kemble
	Cornell University (E-W)
	Robert Ewen, Jeff Rubens
1959	Columbia University (N-S)
	James Becker, Sanford Reder
	Princeton University (E-W)
	John O'Neil, Willard Speakman
1960	Columbia University (N-S)

James Becker, Sanford Reder
North Carolina State College (E-W)
Robert Smith, Richard Stanton

1961 Harvard University (N-S)
Roman Weil, Richard Zeckhauser
Stanford University (E-W)
Mort Goerman, Roger Tippy

1962 University of Iowa (N-S)
Larry Friedman, Robert Pugh
Lake Forest College, Illinois (E-W)
Richard Berger, James Berg

1963 Lake Forest College, Illinois (N-S)
Richard Berger, James Berg
University of Illinois (E-W)
Robert Ewen, Darrell Penrod
     tied with
University of California at Berkeley
Bill Nutting, Hugh Ross

1964 University of Texas (N-S)
George Kirkwood, Dan Leightman
University of Oregon (E-W)
Dale Foster, Jeff Taylor
     tied with
State University of Buffalo
Richard Flieshman, Robert Lipsitz

1965 1. Cornell University
Thomas M. Smith, Emil Tobenfeld
2. University of Wisconsin
Larry Cohen, Richard H. Katz

1966 1. University of Wisconsin
Larry Cohen, RIchard H. Katz
2. University of Minnesota
Richard Dufour, Morrie Freier

1967 1. Rensselaer Ploytechnic Institute
Gerald Cohen, Tony Rosenstein
2. University of Colorado
Michael Copeland, Robert Wherry

1968 1. University of Maryland
Jeff Hand, John Richards II
2. University of Michigan
Ron Gerard, Daniel Suty
     tied with
Rensselaer Polytechnic Institute
Frank Hacker, Gary Weldin

1969 1. Rice University
Michael Finch, Delmas Parker
2. University of Utah
Reed Coray, Ron Rosenthal

1970 1. University of Virginia
E. Craig Kennedy, Jr., Bruce Platt
2. University of Florida
Markland Jones, Patricia Sprague

1971 1. Louisiana State University
Hennie Conlon, Charles Crosby
2. University of North Carolina
Douglas Stewart, William Wisdom

1972 1. State University of New York at Stoney Brook
Raghunath Khetan, Sheo Khetan
2. University of Washington
Neil Chambers, John Schermer

1973 1. Loyola University of Los Angeles
Bill Schreiber, Mike Schreiber
2. University of Alabama
Bob Dennard, Ann Hubmaier

1974 1. University of California at San Diego
Douglas DePoister, Barry Rothstein
2. University of Pennsylvania
Max Bazerman, Marc Nathan

1975 1. University of Missouri
Thomas Allen, Lee Goodman
2. Yale University
Jeff Juster, Andrew Markowitz

1976 1. University of Michigan
Larry Mori, Larry Robbins
2. University of Colordao
Stephen Strauss, Michael Zeitlin

1977 1. Swarthmore College in Pennsylvania
Marty Fleisher, Alan Heubert
2. Washington University in St. Louis
William Doroshow, Robert Alan Portnoy

1978 1. University of Texas
Charles Sterling Darrin, Dennis Sorensen
2. Swarthmore College in Pennsylvania
Marty Fleisher, Alan Heubert

1979 1. University of Pennsylvania

Saul Gross, Howard Lebow
2. University of Wisconsin
Jim Elliott, Mark Kinzer

WORLD PAR CONTESTS

International events using prepared deals. Par tournaments conducted throughout the world were initiated in 1932, and the event was called the World Bridge Olympic. The event was abandoned in 1941 because of World War II. The World Par Contest was revived by Australia in 1951, and the World Bridge Federation took over sponsorship in 1961, intending to run the event every two years. However, the event has not taken place since 1963.

1932 N-S Byrne Baldwin, Ruth Baldwin, East Orange, NJ
     E-W Lewis Frank, Robert Mayer, Detroit, MI
1933 N-S Hilda Slager, Fred Levy, Montgomery, AL
     E-W Leo Craine, J. Fredrick Benedict, Sherburne, NJ
     (tied with) Otto Krefting, Isak Nielson, Oslo, Norway
1934 N-S Dr Eugene Hilb, Robert Darvas, Budapest, Hungary
     E-W Mrs. Gene Hill, Mrs. George Whitaker, Winston-Salem, NC
1935 N-S Dr L.L. von Barkow, Mrs. C. von Kamensky, Dresden, Germany
     E-W Popy Lotou, Stephen Zotos, Athens, Greece
1936 N-S R. E. Horner, Alfred Harris, Ottawa, Canada
     (tied with) S Rivlin, Capt. W. H. Ricardo, Cardiff, Wales
     E-W Dr Paul Stern, Dr Paul Kaltenegger, Vienna, Austria
1937 N-S Dr O. P. Hampton, Jr, Walter Boeger, University City, MO
     E-W William Savery, Jr, J. E. Muckley, Seattle, WA
1938 N-S Tore Sandgren, Bertil Fant, Stockholm, Sweden
     E-W Irwin Fisher, Harold Karp, Baltimore, MD
1939 E-W Dr. W. Konigsberger and W. Nye, Netherlands.
1940 N-S I.M.Learmouth, E.Learmouth, Maracaibo, Venezuela
     E-W Mrs A. C. Bryant, Mrs. C. H. Drury, Ketchikan, AK
1941 N-S Robert Wilson, George Gooden, San Francisco, CA
     E-W Marjorie Foote, Charles Miller Jr, Phoenix, AZ
1961 Terence Reese, Claude Rodrigue, London, England
1963 Gerard Desrousseaux, Dr. Nernard Raomanet, Paris, France
     United States winners when not listed above were:
1934 N-S Elsieh Powell, Robert Powell, Freeport, TX
1935 N-S Cecile Guthrie, G A Smith, Conneaut, OH
     E-W Mrs. Theodore Ahronbeck Jr., M. O. McDonald, Houston, TX
1936 N-S Arthur Cowperthwait, Tucson, AZ, Ralph Cash, Phoenix, AZ
     E-W George Sherbaum, Memphis, TN, Larry Shurlds, Shelby, TN
1938 N-S Mr. and Mrs. W. H. Gharrity, Chippewa Falls, WI
1939 N-S Marcella Miller, Dr Mandel Shimberg, Leavenworth, KS
     E W Anton Bugge, Mrs. C. C. Covington, Houston, TX
1940 N-S G. R. Trimmer, Dell Keating, Glasgow, MT
1961 Lawrence Rosler, Murray Hill, NJ, Roger Stern, New York, NY
1963 Lawrence Rosler, Murray Hill, NJ, Roger Stern, New York, NY

GABARRET CUP

This Argentine award donated in memory of Adolfo Gabarret is the equivalent of the ACBL McKENNEY TROPHY or now the BARRY CRANE TOP 500. The winners:

1956 Carlos Ottolenghi	1975 Martin Monsegur
1957 Alejandro Castro	1976 Egisto Rocchi
1958 Alberto Berisso	1977 Agustin Santamarina
1959 Arturo Jaques	1978 Egisto Rocchi
1960 Arturo Jaques	1979 Hector Camberos
1961 Luis Attaguile	1980 Pablo Lambardi
1962 Alberto Berisso	1981 Agustin Santamarina
1963 Egisto Rocchi	1982 Egisto Rocchi
1964 Marcelo Lerner	1983 Carlos Cabanne
1965 Marcelo Lerner	1984 Pablo Lambardi
1966 Eduardo Diaz	1985 Martin Monsegur and

1967 Ricardo Calvente	Guillermo Mooney
1968 Alberto Berisso	1986 Pablo Lambardi
1969 Egisto Rocchi	1987 Alejandro Orzábal
1970 David Zanalda	1988 Rafael Benaderette
1971 Alberto Berisso	1989 Daniel González
1972 Carlos Cabanne	1990 Martín Monsegur
1973 AgustinSantamarina	1991 Guillermo Mooney
1974 Agustin Santamarina	

BRIDGE TODAY ALL-STAR GAMES

Game 1, Albany NY
1. Michael Rosenberg, tied with Zia Mahmood — $4500 prize split between them
Game 2, Boca Raton FL
1. Richard Pavlicek, $4000; 2, Zia Mahmood, $2000
Game 3, Albany NY
1. Dorothy Truscott, $3000; 2. Marcelo Branco, $2000
Game 4, Novato CA
1. Matt Granovetter, $4000; 2, Zia Mahmood, $2000

CAMROSE SERIES

This is an annual contest among England, Scotland, Wales and Northern Ireland. The Camrose Trophy was in play for the 50th time in 1993. England has been the winner 39 times, including 1994. Scotland has won 10 times -- 1964, 65, 67, 70, 71, 74, 76, 77, 79 and 89. England and Scotland tied for the title in 1972 and 1973.

The most successful player in the Camrose is Monty Rosenberg of Northern Ireland with 67 caps. Patrick Jourdain has been the most successful in Wales (56), Victor Goldberg in Scotland (49) and Tony Forrester in England (36).

LADY MILNE SERIES

This is an annual contest for women among England, Scotland, Wales and Northern Ireland. Over the 45-year history of the event, England has won 33 times, Scotland 7 (1956, 79, 80, 84, 86, 92 and 94), Wales 3 (1967, 68, 88) and Northern Ireland 2 (1981, 85).

The most successful player is Jessie Newton of Wales with 23 caps, closely followed by Mary Nimmons of Northern Ireland. Nicola Gardener-Smith has had nine caps for England, all wins.

JUNIOR CAMROSE AND
PEGGY BAYER SERIES

This is an annual contest for Junior players among England, Scotland, Wales and Northern Ireland. Over the past 23 years England has won 18 times and Scotland 5.

In 1990 an event for under-20s was added. Scotland won the first year, and England won the next four.

APPENDIX V
WORLD CHAMPIONSHIPS

BERMUDA BOWL

1950. Played in Bermuda. United States defeated Great Britain by 3,660 points and Sweden-Iceland by 4,720 points. UNITED STATES: John R. Crawford, Charles H. Goren, George Rapee, Howard Schenken, Sidney Silodor, Samuel M. Stayman. GREAT BRITAIN: Maurice Harrison-Gray (captain), Leslie Dodds, Nico Gardener, Kenneth Konstam, Joel Tarlo, Louis Tarlo. SWEDEN-ICELAND: Dr. Einer Werner (captain), Gunnar Gudmundsson, Rudolf Kock, Nils-Olof Lilliehook, Einar Thorfinnsson, Jan Wohlin.

1951. Played in Naples. United States defeated Italy by 116 IMPs. UNITED STATES: B. Jay Becker, John R. Crawford, George Rapee, Howard Schenken, Samuel M. Stayman, npc Julius Rosenblum. ITALY: Paolo Baroni, Eugenio Chiaradia, Pietro Forquet, Mario Franco, Augusto Ricci, Guglielmo Siniscalco, npc Carl'Alberto Perroux.

1953. Played in New York. United States defeated Sweden by 8,260 points. UNITED STATES: B. Jay Becker, John R. Crawford, Theodore A. Lightner, George Rapee, Howard Schenken, Samuel Stayman, npc Joseph M. Cohan. SWEDEN: Dr. Einar Werner (captain); Gunnar Anuldh, Rudolf Kock, Robert Larsen, Nils-Olof Lilliehook, Jan Wohlin.

1954. Played in Monte Carlo. United States defeated France by 49 IMPs. UNITED STATES: Clifford Bishop, Milton Q. Ellenby, Lewis Mathe, Don Oakie, William A. Rosen, Douglas Steen, npc Benjamin O. Johnson. FRANCE: Jacques Amouraben, Rene Bacherich, Jean Besse (Switzerland), Pierre Ghestem, Marcel Kornblum, Karl Schneider (Austria).

1955. Played in New York. Great Britain defeated the United States by 5,420 points. GREAT BRITAIN: Leslie Dodds, Kenneth Konstam, Adam Meredith, Jordanis Pavlides, Terence Reese, Boris Schapiro, npc Reginald Corwen. UNITED STATES: Clifford Bishop, Milton Q. Ellenby, Lewis Mathe, John H. Moran, William A. Rosen, Alvin Roth, npc Peter A. Leventritt.

1956. Played in Paris. France defeated United States 342-288 IMPs. FRANCE: Rene Bacherich, Pierre Ghestem, Pierre Jaïs, Roger Lattes, Bertrand Romanet, Roger Trezel, npc Baron Robert de Nexon. UNITED STATES: Myron Field, Charles H. Goren, Lee Hazen, Richard F. Kahn, Charles J. Solomon, Samuel M. Stayman, npc Jeff Glick.

1957. Played in New York. Italy defeated United States by 10,150 points. ITALY: Walter Avarelli, Giorgio Belladonna, Eugenio Chiaradia, Massimo D'Alelio, Pietro Forquet, Guglielmo Siniscalco, npc Carl'Alberto Perroux. UNITED STATES: Charles H. Goren, Boris Koytchou, Peter A. Leventritt, Harold Ogust, William Seamon, Helen Sobel, npc Rufus L. Miles Jr.

1958. Played in Como, Italy. Italy defeated United States 211-174 and Argentina 239-167. ITALY: Walter Avarelli, Giorgio Belladonna, Eugenio Chiaradia, Massimo D'Alelio, Pietro Forquet, Guglielmo Siniscalco, npc Carl'Alberto Perroux. UNITED STATES: B. Jay Becker, John Crawford, George Rapee, Alvin Roth, Sidney Silodor, Tobias Stone, npc J.G. Ripstra. ARGENTINA: Carlos Cabanne (co-captain), Alejandro Castro (co-captain), Alberto Blousson, Ricardo Calvente, Marcelo Lerner.

1959. Played in New York. Italy defeated United States 233-183 and Argentina 218-178. ITALY: Walter Avarelli, Giorgio Belladonna, Eugenio Chiaradia, Massimo D'Alelio, Pietro Forquet, Guglielmo Siniscalco, npc Carl'Alberto Perroux. UNITED STATES: Harry Fishbein, Sam Fry Jr., Leonard Harmon, Lee Hazen, Sidney Lazard, Ivar Stakgold, npc Charles J. Solomon. ARGENTINA: Alberto Berisso, Ricardo Calvente, Alejandro Castro, Carlos Dibar, Arturo Jaques, Egisto Rocchi, npc Dr. Luis Santa Coloma.

1961. Played in Buenos Aires. Italy defeated Argentina 422-282; France 371-261; North America 382-262. North America defeated Argentina, 411-284; France 262-236. France defeated Argentina 339-287. ITALY: Walter Avarelli, Giorgio Belladonna, Eugenio Chiaradia, Massimo D'Alelio, Pietro Forquet, Benito Garozzo, npc Carl'Alberto Perroux. NORTH AMERICA: John Gerber, Paul Hodge, Norman Kay, Peter A. Leventritt, Sidney Silodor, Howard Schenken, npc Frank Westcott. FRANCE: Rene Bacherich, Claude Deruy, Pierre Ghestem, José LeDentu, Roger Trezel, npc Baron Robert de Nexon. ARGENTINA: Jorge Bosco, Ricardo Calvente, Alejandro Castro, Hector Cramer, Carlos Dibar, Egisto Rocchi, npc Carlos Cabanne.

1962. Played in New York. Italy defeated Argentina 420-308; Great Britain 365-286, North America 331-305. North America defeated Argentina 400-242; Great Britain 345-332. Great Britain defeated Argentina 318-311. ITALY: Walter Avarelli, Giorgio Belladonna, Eugenio Chiaradia, Massimo D'Alelio, Pietro Forquet, Benito Garozzo, npc Carl'Alberto Perroux. NORTH AMERICA: Charles Coon, Mervin Key, Lewis Mathe, Eric Murray, G. Robert Nail, Ron Von der Porten, npc John Gerber. GREAT BRITAIN: Nico Gardener, Kenneth Konstam, Anthony Priday, Claude Rodrigue, Albert Rose, Alan Truscott, npc Louis Tarlo. ARGENTINA: Luis Attaguile, Alberto Berisso, Carlos Cabanne, Ricardo Calvente, Arturo Jaques, Egisto Rocchi, npc Desiderio Blum.

1963. Played in St. Vincent, Italy. Italy defeated Argentina 372-282; France 421-236; North America 313-294. North America defeated France 340-251; Argentina 496-261. France defeated Argentina 453-319. ITALY: Giorgio Belladonna, Eugenio Chiaradia, Massimo D'Alelio, Pietro Forquet, Benito Garozzo, Camillo Pabis Ticci, npc Carl'Alberto Perroux. NORTH AMERICA: James Jacoby, Robert Jordan, Peter Leventritt, G. Robert Nail, Arthur Robinson, Howard Schenken, npc John Gerber. FRANCE: René Bacherich, Gerard Desrousseaux, Pierre Ghestem, Jacques Stetten, Dr. Georges Theron, Leon Tintner, npc Baron Robert de Nexon. ARGENTINA: Luis Attaguile, Ricardo Calvente, Egisto Rocchi, Marcos Santamarina, Alfredo Saravia, Luis A. Schenone, npc Guillermo Malbran.

1965. Played in Buenos Aires. Italy defeated Argentina 325-237; Great Britain 354-233; North America 304-230. North America defeated Argentina 359-250; Great Britain (forfeit). Argentina defeated Great Britain (forfeit). ITALY: Walter Avarelli, Giorgio Belladonna, Massimo D'Alelio, Pietro Forquet, Benito Garozzo, Camillo Pabis Ticci, npcs Sergio Osella, Carl'Alberto Perroux. NORTH AMERICA: Howard Schenken, Peter Leventritt, Ivan Erdos, Kelsey Petterson, B. Jay Becker, Dorothy Hayden, npc John Gerber. ARGENTINA: Luis Attaguile, Egisto Rocchi, Carlos Cabanne, Agustin Santamarina, Marcelo Lerner, Alberto Berisso, npc Eduardo Marquardt. GREAT BRITAIN: Terence Reese, Jeremy Flint, Boris Schapiro, Kenneth Konstam, Maurice Harrison-Gray, Albert Rose, npc Ralph Swimer.

1966. Played in St. Vincent, Italy. Italy defeated North America 319-262; Venezuela 362-203; Netherlands 376-198; Thailand 486-143. North America defeated Venezuela 398-260; Netherlands 477-243; Thailand 359-234. Venezuela defeated Netherlands 331-247; Thailand 326-290. Netherlands defeated Thailand 293-230. ITALY: Walter Avarelli, Giorgio Belladonna, Massimo D'Alelio, Pietro Forquet, Benito Garozzo, Camillo Pabis Ticci, npc Carl'Alberto Perroux. NORTH AMERICA: Phil Feldesman, Robert Hamman, Sami Kehela, Lewis Mathe, Eric Murray, Ira Rubin, npc Julius Rosenblum. VENEZUELA: Roberto Benaim, David Berah, Mario Onorati, Roger Rossignol, Renato Straziota, Francis Vernon, npc Jean Albert. NETHERLANDS: Bob Blitzblum, Piet Boender, Hans Kreyns, Leo Oudshoorn, Robbie De Leeuw, Bob Slavenburg, npc G. Kramer. THAILAND: Anant Boonsupa, E.R. Gaan, Benno Gimkiewicz, Hasan Istenveli, Somboon Nandhabiwat, Thawee Raengkhan (captain).

1967. Played in Miami Beach. Italy defeated North America 338-227 in the final; in the playoff for third place France defeated Thailand 182-133. Qualifying round-robin scores were: Italy 170, North America 161, France 132, Thailand 73, Venezuela 64. ITALY: Walter Avarelli, Giorgio Belladonna, Massimo D'Alelio, Pietro Forquet, Benito Garozzo, Camillo Pabis Ticci, npc Guido Barbone. NORTH AMERICA: Edgar Kaplan, Norman Kay, Sami Kehela, Eric Murray, William Root, Alvin Roth, npc Julius Rosenblum. FRANCE: Jean-Michel Boulenger, Jacques Pariente, Jean-Marc Roudinesco, Jacques Stetten, Henri Svarc, Leon Tintner, npc René Huni. THAILAND: Anant Boonsupa, E.R.

Gaan, Benno Gimkiewicz, Somboon Nandhabiwat, K.W. Shen, Chord Sitajitt, npc H. Lau. VENEZUELA: Roberto Benaim, David Berah, Edgar Loynaz, Roberto Romanelli, Robert Rossignol, Francis Vernon.

1969. Played in Rio de Janeiro. Italy defeated Taiwan 429-182 in the final. In the playoff for third place North America defeated France 150-115. In the qualifying round-robin, the scores were: Italy 185, Taiwan 166, North America 141, France 126, Brazil 116. ITALY: Walter Avarelli, Giorgio Belladonna, Massimo D'Alelio, Pietro Forquet, Benito Garozzo, Camillo Pabis Ticci, npc Angelo Tracanella. TAIWAN: Frank Huang, Patrick Huang, C.S. Shen, K.W. Shen, Kovit Suchartkul, M.F. Tai, npc C.C. Wei. NORTH AMERICA: William Eisenberg, Robert Goldman, Robert Hamman, Edwin Kantar, Sidney Lazard, George Rapee, npc Oswald Jacoby. FRANCE: Jean-Michel Boulenger, Gerard Desrousseaux, Jacques Stelten, Henri Svarc, Georges Theron, Leon Tintner, npc René Huni. BRAZIL: Pedro Paulo Assumpcao, Marcelo Branco, Gabriel Chagas, Decio Coutinho, Roberto Mello, Adelstano Porto D'Ave, npc Paulo S. Brum de Barros.

1970. Played in Stockholm. United States defeated Taiwan 308-167. In the playoff for third place, Norway defeated Brazil 137-114. In the qualifying round-robin, the scores were United States 229, China 151, Brazil 136, Norway 118, Italy 105. UNITED STATES: William Eisenberg, Robert Goldman, Robert Hamman, James Jacoby, Michael Lawrence, Robert Wolff, npc Oswald Jacoby. TAIWAN: Conrad Cheng, Elmer Hsiao, Patrick Huang, Harry Lin, M.F. Tai, npc David Mao. NORWAY: Erik Hoie, Tore Jensen, Knut Koppans, Bjorn Larsen, Louis Andre Strom, Willy Varnas, npc Baard Baardsen. BRAZIL: Pedro Paulo Assumpcao, Paulo Barros, E. Bastos, Gabriel Chagas, Octavio Faria, Sinesio Ferreira, npc Eros Amaral. ITALY: Giuseppe Barbarisi, Enrico Cesati, Vittorio La Galla, Armando Morini, Bruno de Ritis, Riccardo Tersch, npc Angelo Tracanella.

1971. Played in Taipei. The Aces defeated France 243-181 IMPs. In the playoff for third place, Australia defeated Taiwan, 174-134. Brazil defeated North America in the clash for fifth place, 79-63 IMPs. In the qualifying round-robin the final Victory Point standings were: Aces 228, France 182, Australia 154, Taiwan 118, Brazil 103, North America 98. ACES: William Eisenberg. Robert Goldman, Robert Hamman, James Jacoby, Michael Lawrence, Robert Wolff, npc Oswald Jacoby. FRANCE: Jean-Michel Boulenger, Pierre Jaïs, Jean-Marc Roudinesco, Jean-Louis Stoppa, Henri Svarc, Roger Trezel, npc Rene Huni. AUSTRALIA: Jim Borin, Norma Borin, Dick Cummings, Denis Howard, Tim Seres, Roelof Smiide, npc Jessel Rothfield. TAIWAN: Conrad Cheng. Stephen Chua, Elmer Hsiao, Patrick Huang, Vicente Reyes, M.F. Tai, npc C.C. Wei. BRAZIL: Eros Amaral, Pedro Paulo Assumpcao, Gabriel Chagas, Gabino Cintra, Adelstano Porto D'Ave, Tibor Kenedi, npc Alan Truscott. NORTH AMERICA: Edgar Kaplan, Norman Kay, Donald Krauss, Lewis Mathe, John Swanson, Richard Walsh, npc Lee Hazen.

1973. Played in Guaruja, Brazil. Italy defeated the Aces 333-205 IMPs. In the qualifying round-robin the final Victory Point standings were: Aces 177, Italy 176, Brazil 148, North America 140, Indonesia 101. ITALY: Giorgio Belladonna, Benito Bianchi, Pietro Forquet, Benito Garozzo, Giuseppe Garabello, Vito Pittala, npc Sandro Salvetti. ACES: Mark Blumenthal, Robert Goldman, Robert Hamman, James Jacoby, Michael Lawrence, Robert Wolff, npc Ira G. Corn Jr. BRAZIL: Pedro Paulo Assumpcao, Marcelo Branco, Pedro Branco, Gabriel Chagas, Gabino Cintra, Christiano Fonseca, npc Adelstano Porto D'Ave. NORTH AMERICA: B. Jay Becker, Michael Becker, Andrew Bernstein, Jeff Rubens, Paul Soloway, John Swanson, npc Roger Stern. INDONESIA: Max Aguw, J.A. Fransz, Hengky Lasut, E. Najoan, Denny Sacul, Ferdinand Walujan, npc Ch. A. Bahasuan.

1974. Played in Venice. Italy defeated North America 195-166. Brazil defeated Indonesia in the playoff for third place, 182-181. In the qualifying round-robin the final Victory Point standings were: Italy 149, North America 148, Brazil 111, Indonesia 82. France 71, New Zealand 17. ITALY: Giorgio Belladonna, Benito Bianchi, Soldano de Falco, Pietro Forquet, Arturo Franco, Benito Garozzo, npc Sandro Salvetti. NORTH AMERICA: Mark Blumenthal, Robert Goldman, Robert Hamman, Sami Kehela, Eric Murray, Robert Wolff, npc Ira G. Corn Jr. BRAZIL: Pedro Paulo Assumpcao, Marcelo Branco, Pedro Branco, Gabriel Chagas, Gabino Cintra, Christiano Fonseca, npc Georges Vero. INDONESIA: Max Aguw, Wolter Karamoy, Hengky Lasut, Frank Manoppo, M.F. Manoppo, W.A. Moniaga, npc Dick B. Masengi. FRANCE: Jean-Michel Boulenger, Michel Lebel, Christian Mari, Henri Svarc, npc Claude Deruy. NEW ZEALAND: Stanley A.

Abrahams, Richard J. Brightling, Michael Cornell, Roy P. Kerr, Paul Marston, John R. Wignall, npc Frank P.S. Lu.

1975. Played in Bermuda. Italy defeated North America 215-189 in the final. In the semifinals, Italy defeated Indonesia 280-134 and North America defeated France 159-147. In the qualifying round-robin, the scores were: Italy 134, North America 116, France 105, Indonesia 90, Brazil 13. ITALY: Giorgio Belladonna, Gianfranco Facchini, Arturo Franco, Benito Garozzo, Vito Pittala, Sergio Zucchelli, npc Sandro Salvetti. NORTH AMERICA: William Eisenberg, Robert Hamman, Edwin Kantar, Paul Soloway, John Swanson, Robert Wolff, npc Alfred Sheinwold. FRANCE: Jean-Michel Boulenger, Michel Lebel, Francois Leenhardt, Christian Mari, Henri Svarc, Edmond Vial, npc René Bacherich. INDONESIA: I. Arwin, Hengky Lasut, Frank Manoppo, M. Manoppo, W. Moniaga, Denny Sacul, npc O. Wullur. BRAZIL: Marcelo Amaral, Pedro Paulo Assumpcao, Paulo deBarros, Gabriel Chagas, Sinesio Ferreira, Nelson Ferreira, npc Serge Apoteker.

1976. Played in Monte Carlo. North America defeated Italy 232-198 in the final. In the qualifying round-robin, the scores were: North America 131, Italy 119, Israel 114, Brazil 109, Australia 82 1/2, Hong Kong 32 1/2. NORTH AMERICA: William Eisenberg, Fred Hamilton, Erik Paulsen, Hugh Ross, Ira Rubin, Paul Soloway, npc Dan Morse. ITALY: Giorgio Belladonna, Pietro Forquet, Benito Garozzo, Arturo Franco, Vito Pittala, Antonio Vivaldi, npc Sandro Salvetti. ISRAEL: Julian Frydrich, Michael Hochzeit, Schmuel Lev, Yeshayahu Levit, Pinhas Romik, Elyakim Shaufel, npc Reuben Kunin. BRAZIL: Pedro Paulo Assumpcao, Marcelo Branco, Pedro Branco, Gabriel Chagas, Gabino Cintra, Christiano Fonseca, npc Adelstano Porte D'Ave. AUSTRALIA: Dick Cummings, Denis Howard, Ron Klinger, Les Longhurst, Tim Seres, Roelof Smilde, npc Eric Ramshaw. HONG KONG: Anthony Chow, Y.L. Chung, Raymond S.P. Chow, T.S. Lo, L.L. Sung, Derek Zen, npc Woo Tsing.

1977. Played in Manila. The North American challengers defeated the North American defenders 245-214.5 in the final. In the qualifying round-robin the final Victory Point standings were: Defending Champions 136.75, North American Challengers 119.75, Sweden 94.75, Argentina 91, Australia 79, Taiwan 68.75. NORTH AMERICA: William Eisenberg, Robert Hamman, Edwin Kantar, Paul Soloway, John Swanson, Robert Wolff, npc Roger Stern, Steve Altman (coach). DEFENDING CHAMPIONS: Fred Hamilton, Mike Passell, Erik Paulsen, Hugh Ross, Ira Rubin, Ron Von der Porten, npc Jerome Silverman, npc Ed Theus. ARGENTINA: Luis Attaguile, Carlos Cabanne, Hector Camberos, Martin Monsegur, Agustin Santamarina, Eduardo Scanavino, npc Alberto Berisso. TAIWAN: Conrad Cheng, Elmer Hsia, Patrick Huang, Che-Hung Kuo, Harry Lin, M.F. Tai, npc David Y.P. Mao. SWEDEN: Anders Brunzell, Sven-Olov Flodqvist, Hans Gothe, Jorgen Lindquist, Anders Morath, Per Olof Sundelin, npc Sven-Erik Berglund. AUSTRALIA: Jim Borin, Dick Cummings, George Havas, Jeffrey Lathbury, John Lester, Tim Seres, npc Roelof Smilde.

1979. Played in Rio de Janeiro. North America defeated Italy 253-248 in the final. In the qualifying round-robin the final Victory Point standings were: Italy 180, North America 176, Australia 166, Taiwan 127 1/2, Central America-Caribbean 123 1/2, Brazil 108. NORTH AMERICA: Malcolm Brachman, William Eisenberg, Robert Goldman, Edwin Kantar, Mike Passell, Paul Soloway, npc Ed Theus. ITALY: Giorgio Belladonna, Soldano de Falco, Arturo Franco, Benito Garozzo, Lorenzo Lauria, Vito Pittala, npc Guido Barbone; npc Sandro Salvetti. AUSTRALIA: Jim Borin, Norma Borin, Dick Cummings, Andrew Reiner, Bob Richman, Tim Seres, npc Denis Howard. TAIWAN: K.Y. Chen, Patrick Huang, Che-Hung Kuo, S.C. Liu, M.F. Tai, Y.P. Tu, npc A.T. Chong, C.K. Tau, coach. CENTRAL AMERICA-CARIBBEAN: Alberto Calvo, Alberto Dhers, Steve Hamaoui, Jeff Hand, John Maduro, Francis Vernon, npc J.L. Derivery. BRAZIL: Pedro Paulo Assumpcao, José Barbosa, Marcelo Branco, Gabriel Chagas, Gabino Cintra, Roberto Mello, npc Sergio Barbosa.

1981. Played in Port Chester, New York. United States defeated Pakistan 271-182 1/2. In the semifinals United States defeated Poland 178-119; Pakistan beat Argentina 174-113 2/3. The qualifying round-robin scores were: United States 160 1/2, Pakistan 151, Poland 146, Argentina 145, Great Britain 142 1/2, Australia 131, Indonesia 129. UNITED STATES: Russ Arnold; Robert Levin, Jeff Meckstroth, A.E. (Bud) Reinhold, Eric Rodwell, John Solodar; npc Thomas K. Sanders. PAKISTAN: Nishat Abedi, Nisar Ahmed, Jan-e-Alam Fazli, Munir Ata-Ullah, Zia Mahmood, Masood Salim, npc Sattar Cochinwala. POLAND: Alexsander

Jezioro, Julian Klukowski, Marek Kudla, Krzysztof Martens, Andrzej Milde, Tomasz Przybora, npc Marian Frenkiel. ARGENTINA: Gustavo Alujas, Luis Attaguile, Hector Camberos, Agustin Santamarina, Eduardo Scanavino, David Zanalda, npc Gonzalo Araujo. GREAT BRITAIN: John Collings, Paul Hackett, Steve Lodge, Irving Rose, Robert Sheehan, Tony Sowter, npc Gus Calderwood. AUSTRALIA: Dick Cummings, Bill Jacobs, Paul Lavings, Gabby Lorentz, Tim Seres, David Smith, npc Denis Howard. INDONESIA: Max Aguw, Wolter Karamoy, Hengky Lasut, Denny Sacul, Ferdinand Waluyan, Yasin Wijaya, npc Jack Rimbuan.

1983. Played in Stockholm, Sweden. United States 1 defeated Italy 413-408. In the semifinals U.S. 1 defeated U.S. 2, 440-338; Italy beat France 346-335. Under the new Bermuda Bowl format, the No. 1 teams from both North America and Europe automatically advanced to the semifinals, while the No. 2 teams from those continents had to battle through the round-robin. France won the European Championship. U.S. 1 won the North American Team Trials. The qualifying round-robin scores were: United States 2, 289, Italy 214, New Zealand 212, Sweden 211.51, Pakistan 208, Indonesia 195.75, Brazil 175.75, Central America-Caribbean 153. U.S. 1: Michael Becker, Robert Hamman, Ron Rubin, Alan Sontag, Peter Weichsel, Bobby Wolff, npc Joe Musumeci. ITALY: Giorgio Belladonna, Dano DeFalco, Arturo Franco, Benito Garozzo, Lorenzo Lauria, Carlo Mosca, npc Filippo Palma. FRANCE: Phillippe Cronier, Michel Corn, Michel Lebel, Hervé Mouiel, Phillipe Soulet, Henri Szwarc, npc Pierre Schemeil. U.S. 2: Jim Jacoby, Jeff Meckstroth, Mike Passell, Eric Rodwell, George Rosenkranz, Eddie Wold, npc Jim Zimmerman. NEW ZEALAND: Michael Cornell, Malcolm Mayer, Tony Taylor, John Wignall, Kris Wooles, Lionel Wright, npc C.L. Friis. SWEDEN: Bjorn Axelson, Anders Berglund, Hans Gothe, Tommy Gullberg, Gunnar Hallbers, Ake Sjoberg, coach Anders Morath, npc Bjorn Astrom. PAKISTAN: Nishat Abedi, Nisar Ahmed, Munir Ata-Ullah, Jan-e-Alam Fazli, Zia Mahmood, Masood Salim, npc Suleman Haider. INDONESIA: Hengky Lasut, Frank Manoppo, Denny Sacul, Munawar Sawiruddin, Felix Waluyan, Yasin Wijawa, npc Jack Rimbuan. BRAZIL: Sergio Barbosa, Marcelo Branco, Gabriel Chagas, Alcio Maia, Alexandre Misk, captain Octavio DeFaria. CAC: Alberto Calvo, Lennie Chin, Don DaCosta, Steve Hamaoui, Rex James, David Levy, npc Granville Gayle.

1985. Played in Sao Paulo, Brazil. United States defeated European champion Austria 399-324. In the semifinals the U.S. defeated Brazil 351-342 and Austria defeated Israel 434-346. In the playoff for third place, Israel defeated Brazil 174-142. Austria and the United States, champions of the WBF's two biggest zones, were automatically qualified for the semifinals. Taking part in a double round-robin to determine the other two semifinalists were Canada, second in North America; Israel, second in Europe; Argentina, South America; Venezuela, Central America-Caribbean; Indonesia, Far East; New Zealand, South Pacific, and Brazil, host country. Final standings of the round-robin: Brazil 252, Israel 237, Argentina 226, Indonesia 221, Venezuela 205, Canada 189.5, New Zealand 173. UNITED STATES: Bob Hamman, Bobby Wolff, Chip Martel, Hugh Ross, Lew Stansby, Peter Pender, npc Alfred Sheinwold. AUSTRIA: Heinrich Berger, Kurt Feichtinger, Jan Fucik, Wolfgang Meinl, Karl Rohan, Franz Terraneo, npc Franz Baratta. ISRAEL: David Birman, Julian Frydrich, Michael Hochzeit, Shmuel Lev, Shalom Zeligman, Eliakim Shaufel, npc Avrick Peleg. BRAZIL: Sergio Barbosa, Marcelo Branco, Pedro Paulo Branco, Fabio Sampaio, Gabino Cintra, Claudio Sampaio, npc Serge Apoteker. ARGENTINA: Luis Attaguile, Carlos de Miguel, Martin Monsegur, Guillermo Mooney, Hector Camberos, Eduardo Scanavino, npc Alfredo Suaya. INDONESIA: Ferdy Waluyan, Denny Sacul, Hengky Lasut, Eddie Manoppo, Sawiruddin Munawar, Yasin Wijaya, npc Amran Zamzami. VENEZUELA: Steve Hamaoui, Claudio Caponi, Paolo Pasquini, Memo Danese, Roberto Benaim, Francis Vernon, npc David Izaky. CANADA: Drew Cannell, Gordon Campbell, Bryan Maksymetz, Mike Chomyn, Doran Flock, Subhash Gupta, npc John Carruthers. NEW ZEALAND: Michael Cornell, Malcolm Mayer, Tony Taylor, John Wignall, Kris Wooles, Lionel Wright, npc R. Jacobs.

1987. At Ocho Rios, Jamaica. In the final United States defeated Great Britain 354-290. In the semifinals United States defeated Chinese Taipei 421-290 and Great Britain defeated Sweden 358-311. United States and Sweden won their continental championships and automatically qualified for the semifinals. Eight other teams competed in a round-robin to determine the other two semifinalists. Final standings in the round-robin: Chinese Taipei 258, Great Britain 249, Pakistan 239, Canada 230.5, Venezuela 225.5,

Brazil 175, New Zealand 170.5, Jamaica 104.5. UNITED STATES: Mike Lawrence, Hugh Ross, Bob Hamman, Lew Stansby, Bobby Wolff, Chip Martel, npc Dan Morse. GREAT BRITAIN: Tony Forrester, Graham Kirby, John Armstrong, Rob Sheehan, Jeremy Flint, Raymond Brock, npc Tony Priday. SWEDEN: Hans Gothe, Tommy Gullberg, Magnus Lindkvist, Bjorn Fallenius, Sven-Olof Flodqvist, Per-Olov Sundelin, npc P.D. Lindeberg. CHINESE TAIPEI: C.H. Wu, C.C. Chen, C.H. Kuo, M.F. Tai, Patrick Huang, C.S. Shen, npc Tony Chong. PAKISTAN: Nisar Ahmed, Zia Mahmood, Masood Salim, Jan-e-Alam Fazli, Munir Ata-Ullah, Itfikhar Baqai, npc M. Ilyas. CANADA: Harmon Edgar, Michael Schoenborn, Arno Hobart, Greg Carroll, David Turner, Martin Kirr, npc George Mittleman. VENEZUELA: Ricardo Salomon, Claudio Caponi, Steve Hamaoui, Mario Onerati, Paolo Pasquini, Manrique, npc Franco Gusso. BRAZIL: Eduardo Barcellos, Carlos Camacho, Jose Barbosa deOliviera, Roberto Figueira, Gabriel Chagas, Ronaldo Avelino, npc Sergio Peixoto. NEW ZEALAND: Alan Turner, Bill Haughie, Dwayne Crombie, Stephen Blackstock, Peter Newell, Martin Reid, npc Lionel Wright. JAMAICA: Cecil Chuck, Sam Mahfood, Victor Zaidie, Robert Carby, Dudley Holness, R. Tai Ten Quee, npc Rex James.

1989. Played in Perth, West Australia. Brazil defeated U.S.A. 442-338 in the final. In the semifinals Brazil defeated Poland 369-327 and U.S.A. defeated Australia 387-327. U.S.A. and Poland (Zonal champions) were automatically admitted to the semifinals. In the qualifying round-robin the final Victory Point standings of the other teams were: Brazil 280, Australia 240, Chinese Taipei 231, France 229, Egypt 202.5, New Zealand 200, Colombia 141.5, Canada 137. BRAZIL: Gabriel Chagas, Marcelo Branco, Pedro Branco, Roberto Mello, Carlos Camacho, Ricardo Janz. UNITED STATES: Hugh Ross, Peter Pender, Chip Martel, Lew Stansby, Mike Lawrence, Kit Woolsey. POLAND: Cezary Balicki, Adam Zmudzinski, Krzysztof Moszczynski, Julian Klukowski, Krzysztof Martens, Marek Szymanowski. AUSTRALIA: Gaby Lorentz, John Lester, Ron Klinger, David Lilley, Paul Marston, Stephen Burgess. CHINESE TAIPEI: Patrick Huang, M.F. Tai, C.C. Chen, C.H. Wu, C.K. Shen, H.S Lin; FRANCE: Christian Mari, Jean-Christophe Quantin, Eric Eisenberg, Patrick Sussel, Dominique Poubeau, Maurice Salama. EGYPT: Walid el Ahmady, Tarek Sadek, Sherif Naguib, Ashraf Sadek, Samir Salib, Samih Khazil. NEW ZEALAND: Michael Cornell, Tony Taylor, Andy Braithwaite, Lionel Wright, Pat Carter, Ken Yule. COLOMBIA: Tony Cahn-Speyer, Jorge Barrera, Jaime Carrera, Galileo Violini, Carlos Barrientos, Charles Weston. CANADA: André Laliberte, Jacques Laliberte, Raymond Fortin, Kamel Fergani, Maurice Larochelle, Jean Bernier.

1991. Played in Yokohama, Japan. Iceland defeated Poland 413-376 in the final. In the semifinals Iceland defeated Sweden 211-199 and Poland defeated Brazil 261-209. In the playoff for third place Sweden defeated Brazil 151-122. In the quarterfinals Iceland defeated USA II 271-184; Poland defeated Great Britain 282-195; Sweden defeated Argentina 224-198; Brazil defeated USA I 188-180. In the qualifying round-robin the final Victory Point standings of the teams were: Group E: Brazil 254, Sweden 252, Poland 240.35, USA II 233, Hong Kong 210, Canada 185, Pakistan 160.65, Surinam 123; Group W: Iceland 254.25, Great Britain 241, Argentina 217.25, USA I 213.5, Australia 194.25, Venezuela 189, Egypt 174.75, Japan 171. ICELAND: Orn Arnthorsson, Gudlaugur Johannsson, Gudmundur Arnarson, Thorlakur Jonsson, Jon Baldursson, Adalsteinn Jorgensen, npc Bjorn Eysteinsson. POLAND: Krzysztof Martens, Marek Szymanowski, Piotr Gawrys, Krzysztof Lasocki, Cezary Balicki, Adam Zmudzinski, npc Andnez Orlow. SWEDEN: Per Olof Sundelin, Tommy Gullberg, Bjorn Fallenius, Mats Nilsland, Anders Morath, Sven-Ake Bjerregard, npc Svante Ryman. BRAZIL: Gabriel Chagas, Marcelo Branco, Carlos Camacho, Ricardo Janz, Pedro Branco, Roberto Mello, npc Pedro-Paulo Assumpçao. UNITED STATES II: Bart Bramley, Mark Feldman, Fred Stewart, Steve Weinstein, Alexander Ornstein, Jeff Ferro, npc Hugh Ross. GREAT BRITAIN: Andy Robson, Tony Forrester, John Armstrong, Graham Kirby, Tony Sowter, Roman Smolski, npc Sandra Landy. ARGENTINA: Pablo Lombardi, Carlos Lucena, Hector Camberos, Eduardo Scanavino, Luis Attaguile, Agustin Santamarina, npc Alfredo Suaya. UNITED STATES I: Robert Barr, Harold Stengel, Jeff Meckstroth, Eric Rodwell, Bernard Miller, Alan Sontag, npc Robert Rosen.

1993. Played in Santiago, Chile. Netherlands defeated Norway 350-316 in the final. In the semifinals Netherlands defeated USA II 202-199 and Norway defeated Brazil 208-205. In the quarterfinals Netherlands defeated USA I 208-180; Norway defeated Poland 289-158; Brazil defeated China 312-134; USA II defeated Denmark 189-180. In the qualifying round-robin the final Victory Point standings of the teams were Group E: USA II 259, Netherlands 257, Poland 248.5, Brazil 233, South Africa 199, Indonesia 189, Mexico 147, Guadeloupe 124. Group W: China 240, Norway 237, Denmark 216.75, USA I 216.25, India 210.5, Australia 202.5, Venezuela 198, Chile 144. NETHER-LANDS: Bauke Muller, Wubbo deBoer, Piet Jansen, Jan Westerhof, Enri Leufkens, Berry Westra, npc Jaap Trouwborst. NORWAY: Glenn Groetheim, Terje Aa, Arild Rasmussen, Jon Sveindal, Geir Helgemo, Tor Helness, npc Runar Lillevik. UNITED STATES II: Cliff Russell, Sam Lev, David Berkowitz, Larry Cohen, Eric Rodwell, Marty Bergen, npc Bob Rosen. BRA-ZIL: Oliviera Barbosa, Marcelo Branco, Carlos Comacho, Pedro Paulo Branco, Gabriel Chagas, Roberto Mello, npc Pedro Paulo Assumpçao. UNITED STATES I: Mike Becker, Ron Rubin, Robert Levin, Peter Weichsel, Russ Ekeblad, Ron Sukoneck, npc Jeff Wolfson. POLAND: Cezary Balicki, Piotr Gawrys, Krzysztof Lasocki, Wojoiech Olanski, Piotr Tuszynski, Adam Zmudzinski, npc Andrzej Simon. CHINA: Hu Jihong, Xu Hongjun, Chen Rongchang, Zhou Jiahonk, Luo Shaoxing, He Zhenyi, npc Yi Hougao. DENMARK: Jens Auken, George Norris, Peter Schaltz, Dennis Kock-Palmund, John Norris, Dorthe Schaltz, npc Jens Kruuse.

Tomasz Przybora	Herve Mouiel
Piotr Gawrys	Henry Szware
Piotr Tuszynski	Fivo Paladimo
Marian Trnkiel (npc)	Felix Covo
	Pierre Schemeil (npc)

1988 Venice, Italy

UNITED STATES	AUSTRIA
Seymon Deutsch	Heinrich Berger
Jeff Meckstroth	Jan Fucik
Eric Rodwell	Alfred Kadlec
Bob Hamman	Friedrick Kubac
Jim Jacoby	Wolfgang Meinl
Bobby Wolff	Franz Terranao
Dan Morse (npc)	Franz Baratta (npc)

1992 Salsomaggiore, Italy

FRANCE	UNITED STATES
Paul Chemla	Bob Hamman
Michel Perron	Bobby Wolff
Herve Mouiel	Jeff Meckstroth
Alain Levy	Eric Rodwell
Pierre Adad	Michael Rosenberg
Maurice Aujaleu	Seymon Deutch
Jose Damiani (npc)	Dan Morse (npc)

TEAM OLYMPIAD

| OPEN WINNERS | OPEN RUNNERS-UP |

1960 Turin, Italy

FRANCE (16 V.P.)	GREAT BRITAIN (15 V.P.)
Pierre Jais	Terence Reese
Roger Trezel	Boris Schapiro
Gerard Bourchtoff	Albert Rose
Claude Delmouly	Nico Gardener
Rene Bacherich	Jeremy Flint
Pierre Ghestem	Ralph Swimer
Baron Robert de Nexon (npc)	Louis Tarlo (npc)

1964 New York, USA

ITALY	UNITED STATES
Walter Avarelli	Robert Hamman
Giorgio Belladonna	Robert Jordan
Massimo d'Alelio	Donald Krauss
Pietro Forquet	Victor Mitchell
Benito Garozzo	Arthur Robinson
Camillo Pabis Ticci	Samuel Stayman
Sergio Osella (npc)	Frank Westcott (npc)

1968 Deauville, France

ITALY	UNITED STATES
Walter Avarelli	Robert Jordan
Giorgio Belladonna	Edgar Kaplan
Massimo d'Alelio	Norman Kay
Pietro Forquet	Arthur Robinson
Benito Garozzo	William Root
Camillo Pabis Ticci	Alvin Roth
Angelo Tracanella (npc)	Julius Rosenblum (npc)

1972 Miami Beach, Florida, USA

ITALY	UNITED STATES
Walter Avarelli	Bobby Goldman
Pietro Forquet	Jim Jacoby
Massimo d'Alelio	Robert Hamman
Benito Garozzo	Paul Soloway
Giorgio Belladonna	Mike Lawrence
Camillo Pabis Ticci	Bobby Wolff
Umberto Barsotti (npc)	Lee Hazen (npc)

1976, Monte Carlo

BRAZIL	ITALY
Gabino Cintra	Giorgio Belladonna
Christiano Fonseca	Pietro Forquet
Marcelo Branco	Benito Garozzo
Pedro Paulo Assumpcao	Arturo Franco
Gabriel Chagas	Carlo Mosca
Sergio Barbosa	Silvio Sbarigia
Serge Apoteker (npc)	Sandro Salvetti (npc)

1980, Valkenburg, The Netherlands

FRANCE	UNITED STATES
Paul Chemla	Paul Soloway
Christian Mari	Ira Rubin
Michel Lebel	Robert Hamman
Michel Perron	Bobby Wolff
Henri Svarc	Fred Hamilton
Philippe Soulet	Mike Passell
	Ira Corn (npc)

1984 Seattle, Washington, USA

POLAND	FRANCE
Jacek Romanski	Paul Chemla
Krzysztof Martens	Michel Perron

VENICE CUP

1974. Played in Venice, Italy. United States defeated Italy 297-262. UNITED STATES: Bette Cohn, Emma Jean Hawes, Betty Ann Kennedy, Marietta Passell, Carol Sanders, Dorothy Hayden Truscott, npc Ruth McConnell. ITALY: Marisa Bianchi, Luciana Canessa, Rina Jabes, Antonietta Robaudo, Anna Valenti, Maria Venturini, npc Giovannl Pelucchi.

1976. Played in Monte Carlo. United States defeated Great Britain 395-211. UNITED STATES: Emma Jean Hawes, Betty Ann Kennedy, Jacqui Mitchell, Gail Moss, Carol Sanders, Dorothy Hayden Truscott, npc Ruth McConnell, Peter Pender (coach). GREAT BRITAIN: Charley Esterson, Nicola Gardener, Fritzi Gordon, Sandra Landy, Rixi Markus, Rita Oldroyd, npc Graham Cooke.

1978. Played in New Orleans, Louisiana. In the final the United States defeated Italy 229 1/2-140. Qualifying round-robin scores were: United States 71, Italy 65, Argentina 49, Australia 40, Philippines 35. UNITED STATES: Mary Jane Farell, Emma Jean Hawes, Marilyn Johnson, Jacqui Mitchell, Gail Moss, Dorothy Hayden Truscott, npc Ruth McConnell. ITALY: Marisa Bianchi, Luciana Capodanno, Marisa D'Andrea, Enrica Gut, Andreina Morini, Anna Valenti, npc Guido Barbone. ARGENTINA: Maria T.B. de Diaz, Maria Elena Iacapraro, Adriana C. de Martinez de Hoz, Marta Matienzo, Clara Monsegur, Mercedes G. de Schenone, npc Adolfo Campos. AUSTRALIA: Ivy Dahler, Elizabeth Havas, Fay Landy, Claire Lester, Barbara McDonald, Cecile Miles, npc Ian McCance. PHILIPPINES: Amy Austria, Winnie Monsod, Letty de Padua (captain), Helen Small, Helen Tubangui, Florence Yap.

1981. Played in Port Chester, New York. In the final Great Britain defeated the United States, 160 2/3-122. Qualifying round-robin scores were: United States 181 1/2, Great Britain 173, Brazil 170, Australia 144 1/2, Venezuela 100. GREAT BRITAIN: Pat Davies, Maureen Dennison, Nicola Gardener, Sandra Landy, Sally Sowter, Diana Williams, npc Derek Rimington. UNITED STATES: Nancy Gruver, Edith Kemp, Betty Ann Kennedy, Judi Radin, Carol Sanders, Kathie Wei, npc C.C. Wei, coach Ron Andersen. BRAZIL: Agota Mandelot, Sylvia Figueira de Mello, Maria Elizabeth Murtinho, Susy Powidzer, Alice Saade, Maria Lena Brito E Silva, npc Lia Cintra. AUSTRALIA: Felicity Beale, Sue Edwards, Barbara Gill, Pauline Gumby, Sue Hobley, Di Smart, npc Cecile Miles. VENEZUELA: Rosanna Bonanni, Fida Hirschaut, Morella Pietri, Esther Sasson, Ivy Smith, Elisabeth Solar, npc Agnesa Stern.

1985. Played in Sao Paulo, Brazil. In the final Great Britain defeated United States I 323-213. In the semifinals U.S. I defeated Chinese Taipei 342-246 and Great Britain defeated France 276-241. In the playoff for third place, France defeated Chinese Taipei 188-149. France and United States I, champions of Europe and North America respectively, automatically qualified for the semifinals. Competing in the round-robin for the other two semifinal spots were Great Britain, runner-up in the Europeans; Chinese Taipei, Far East; United States II, runner-up in North America; Australia, South Pacific; Argentina, South America; India, Mid-East; Venezuela, Central America-Caribbean, and Brazil, host country. Final standings in the round-robin: Great Britain 245, Chinese Taipei 239.5, United States ll 226, Australia 219, Argentina 207, Brazil 199, Venezuela 173, India 145. GREAT BRIT-

AIN: Sandra Landy, Sally Horton, Pat Davies, Nicola Smith, Gillian Scott-Jones, Michelle Brunner, npc Grattan Endicott. UNITED STATES I: Gail Greenberg, Kathie Wei, Betty Ann Kennedy, Carol Sanders, Judi Radin, Jacqui Mitchell, npc Dan Morse. FRANCE: Veronique Bessis, Danielle Gaviard, Ginette Chevalley, Fabienne Pigeaud, Catherine Saul, Sylvie Willard, npc Alain Lévy. CHINESE TAIPEI: Stella Wei, H.H.F. Wang, Joan Lin, Helen O'Yang, Phoebe Lin, Jenniter Lai, npc Harry Lin. UNITED STATES II: Edith Freilich, Nancy Gruver, Mary Jane Farell, Helen Utegaard, Beverly Rosenberg, Carol Pincus, npc Stelios Touchtidis. AUSTRALIA: Pauline Gumby, Sue Hobley, Margaret Bourke, Paula Schroor, Sue Lusk, Barbara Travis, npc Jay Greenfeld. ARGENTINA: Maria Susana de Llauro, Maria Teresa de Diaz, Diana Budkin, Victoria Merdinger, Lucrecia Monsegur, Ana Maria de Alonso, npc Graciela de Camberos. BRAZIL: Ana Maria Assumpcao, Lucia Gil, Agota Mandelot, Negra Miranda Jordao, Elisabeth Murtinho, Heloisa Nogueira, npc Lia Cintra. VENEZUELA: Fida Hirschaut, Alice Lerch, Ivy Smith, Morelia Pietri, Esther Sasson, Maria Grazia de Bettini, npc Armin Lerch. INDIA: Lina Mayadas, Nina Bonerjee, Sarain Thadani, Rita Choksi, Kalpana Misra, Olindrilla Kundu, npc Dr. N.S. Tibrewala.

1987. Played in Ocho Rios, Jamaica. In the final United States II defeated France 251-219. In the semifinals U.S. II defeated U.S. I 277-251 and France defeated Italy 276-227. France and U.S. I won their continental championships and automatically advanced to the semifinals. Eight teams played in the qualifying round-robin to determine the other two semifinalists. Final standings in the round-robin: U.S. II 285, Italy 271, Australia 239, China 212, Egypt 193, Argentina 174, Venezuela 163, Jamaica 113. UNITED STATES II: Kathie Wei, Judi Radin, Juanita Chambers, Cheri Bjerkan, Beth Palmer, Lynn Deas, npc Carol Sanders. FRANCE: Veronique Bessis, Helene Bordenave, Sylvie Willard, Benedicte Cronier, Danielle Gaviard, Ginette Chevalley, npc Gerard LeRoyer. ITALY: Luciana Capodanno, Marisa D'Andrea, Carla Gianardi, Marisa Bianchi, Anna Valenti, Gabriella Olivieri, npc Guido Resta. UNITED STATES I: Jo Morse, Sue Sachs, Cindy Bernstein, Sharon Osberg, Peggy Sutherlin, Sally Wheeler, npc John Sutherlin. AUSTRALIA: Felicity Beale, Claire Lester, Jill Courtney, Barbara Travis, Sue Lusk, Diana Smart, npc Jim Borin. CHINA: Lu Qin, Zhu Xiaoyin, Zhang Yalan, Sun Ming, Li Manling, Gu Ling, npc Gu Xuhai. EGYPT: Josephine Hanna, Renee Sidhom, Marguerite Homsy, Moud Khoury, Safeya Sarwat, Lily Khalil, npc Magdy Eskander. ARGENTINA: Marta Matieuzo, Gloria Iribarren, Lucrecia Monsegur, Monica Bornstein, Diana Budkin, Graciella Lucchini, npc Marta Tiscornia. VENEZUELA: Giulia Fornari, Maria Grazia Bettini, Fida Hirschhaut, Morella Pietri, Elizabeth Solar, Alice Lerch, npc Andres Carosio. JAMAICA: Rosemarie Mahfood, Muriel Fowles, Carol Coore, Marlene Fulford, Anne-Marie Bullis, Elizabeth Williams, npc Don DaCosta.

1989. Played in Perth, West Australia. U.S.A. defeated the Netherlands 353-319 in the final. In the semifinals U.S.A defeated Canada 344.5-197.5 and Netherlands defeated Germany 310-289. U.S.A. and Germany (Zonal champions) were automatically admitted to the semifinals. In the qualifying round-robin the final Victory Point standings of the other teams were: Netherlands 292, Canada 254, Australia 235, Chinese Taipei 221, Brazil 194, India 170, Colombia 156, New Zealand 154. UNITED STATES: Beth Palmer, Lynn Deas, Kitty Bethe, Margie Gwozdzinsky, Karen McCallum, Kerri Shuman, npc Dorothy Truscott. NETHERLANDS: Ellen Bakker, Ina Gielkens, Carla Arnolds, Bep Vriend, Marijke van der Pas, Elly Schippers. CANADA: Dianna Gordon, Sharyn Reus, Mary Paul, Francine Cimon, Gloria Silverman, Katie Thorpe. GERMANY: Sabine Zenkel, Daniela von Arnim, Waltraud Vogt, Karen Schroeder, Karin Caesar, Marianne Moegel. AUSTRALIA: Joan Butts, Elizabeth Havas, Sue Lusk, Barbara McDonald, Barbara Travis, Therese Tully. CHINESE TAIPEI: Gloria Meng, Stella Wei, H.S.F. Wang, Helen O'Yang, Amy Chen, Ying Chen. BRAZIL: Ana Maria Assumpcao, Lia Cintra, Lizzie Murtinho, Lucia Gil, Suzy Powidzer, Vera Gama. INDIA: Shailaja Mahajan, Snehlata Singla, Nina Bonerji, Kiran Nader, Rita Choksi, Bimal Sicka. COLOMBIA: Gloria deVargas, Tobina Choitoru, Flor Macias, Ana deSoto, Gloria deArboleda, Cilia Khoudari. NEW ZEALAND: Jan Alabaster, Rose Don, Tina McVeigh, Jenny Wilkinson, Emma Barrack, Shirley Newton.

1991. Played in Yokohama, Japan. USA II defeated Austria 360-258 in the final. In the semifinals USA II defeated USA I 219-125 and Austria defeated China 254-166. In the quarterfinals USA II defeated Great Britain 182-180; Austria defeated Germany 248-238; USA I defeated Japan 255-121; China defeated Chinese

Taipei 220-168. In the qualifying round-robin the final Victory Point standings of the teams were Group E: Austria 254.5, China 242.5, USA I 239, Great Britain 227, Argentina 194, Canada 186, Egypt 185, Martinique 126. Group W: USA II 237.5, Japan 229.5, Chinese Taipei 222.5, Germany 221, Netherlands 219, India 188, Venezuela 182, Australia 168.5. UNITED STATES II: Lynn Deas, Stasha Cohen, Sharon Osberg, Sue Picus, Nell Cahn, Nancy Passell, npc Kathie Wei. AUSTRIA: Maria Erhart, Gabriele Bamberger, Doris Fischer, Terry Weigkricht, Britta Widengren, Rosi Spinn, npc Ernst Pichler. UNITED STATES I: Juanita Chambers, Cheri Bjerkan, Kay Schulle, Jill Meyers, Pam Wittes, Randi Montin, npc Ron Andersen. CHINA: Gu Ling, Zhang Yaian, Wang Ping, Shi Shaomin, Sun Ming, Liu Yiquian, npc Yi Hougao. GREAT BRITAIN: Liz McGowan, Sandra Penfold, Jane Preddy, Vi Mitchell, Jill Casey, Kay Preddy, npc Mark Horton. JAPAN: Etsuko Miyaishi, Kazuko Banno, Mizuko Tan, Kyoko Shimamura, Makiko Hayashi, Misue Aoki, npc Akio Kurokawa. CHINESE TAIPEI: Gloria Meng, Stella Wei, H.S.F. Wang, F.W. Gong, Phoebe Lin, Helen O'Yang, npc C.K. Shen. GERMANY: Daniela von Arnim, Sabine Zenkel, Karin Caesar, Marianne Mogel, Beate Nehmert, Waltraud Vogt, npc Hans-Hermann Gwinner.

1993. Played in Santiago, Chile. USA II defeated Germany 304.5-240 in the final. In the semifinals USA II defeated Argentina 333.5-180 and Germany defeated Sweden 257-237. In the quarterfinals USA II defeated Italy 277-161; Germany defeated USA I 290-161; Argentina defeated Chinese Taipei 221-147; Sweden defeated Canada 205-190. In the qualifying round-robin the final Victory Point standings of the teams were: Group E: Sweden 262.25, USA II 231, Germany 214, Argentina 198.5, New Zealand 195, China 194, India 191.25, Colombia 184.5. Group W: Chinese Taipei 247, Canada 229, USA I 227, Italy 214, France 204.5, Venezuela 202.5, Chile 185, South Africa 156. UNITED STATES II: Kay Schulle, Jill Meyers, Kerri Sanborn, Karen McCallum, Sue Picus, Sharon Osberg, npc Jo Morse. GERMANY: Daniela von Arnim, Sabine Zenkel, Karin Caesar, Marianne Moegel, Beate Nehmert, Waltraud Vogt, npc Klaus Reps. ARGENTINA: Ana Blum, Marta Tiscornia, Marta Matienzo, Marilyn Hernandez, Christina Suaya, Gloria Rosenfeld, npc Gonzalo Valenzuela. SWEDEN: Linda Langstrom, Catharina Midskog, Pyttsi Flodqvist, Mari Ryman, Bim Odlund, Lisa Astrom, npc Kerst Strandberg. ITALY: Emanuelda Capriata, Cristina Colin, Francesca de Lucchi, Laura Rovera, Gabriella Manana, Caterina Ferlazzo, npc Riccardo Vandoni. UNITED STATES I: Betty Ann Kennedy, Carol Sanders, Katherine Wei-Sender, Helen Utegaard, Beth Palmer, Lynn Deas, npc Sue Sachs. CHINESE TAIPEI: Gloria Meng, Stella Wei, H.F. Wang, Helen O'Yang, Phoebe Lin, Fang Wen Gong. CANADA: Dianna Gordon, Sharyn Reus, Francine Cimon, Rhoda Hubert, Barbara Saltsman, Beverly Kraft, npc Mark Stein.

WOMENS TEAM OLYMPIAD

1960 Turin, Italy	1972 Miami Beach, Florida
UNITED ARAB	ITALY
REPUBLICS	Anna Valenti
Helen Camara	Marisa Bianchi
Alda Choucry	Rina Jabes
Samika Fathy	Antonietta Robaudo
Loula Gordon	Luciana Romanelli
Josephine Morcos	Maria Venturini
Suzanne Naguib	Giovanni Pelucchi (npc)
Sergio de Polo (npc)	

1964 New York City	1976 Monte Carlo
GREAT BRITAIN	ITALY
Irene (Dimmie) Fleming	Anna Valenti
Fritzi Gordon	Rina Jabes
Jane Juan	Maria Rabaudo
Rixi Markus	Luciana Capodanno
Mary Moss	Marisa D'Andrea
Dorothy Shanahan	Marisa Bianchi
Harold Franklin (npc)	Giovanni Pelucchi (npc)

1968 Deauville, France	1980 Valkenburg, the Netherlands
SWEDEN	UNITED STATES
Britt Blom	Dorothy Hayden Truscott
Karin Eriksson	Emma Jean Hawes
Eva Martensson	Gail Moss
Rut Segander	Jacqui Mitchell
Gunborg Silhorn	Mary Jane Farell
Britt Wilner	Marilyn Johnson
Lotty Saaby (npc)	Ruth McConnell (npc)

1984 Seattle, Washington

UNITED STATES	GREAT BRITAIN
Gail Moss	Nicola Smith
Judi Radin	Pat Davies
Kathie Wei	Sally Horton
Betty Ann Kennedy	Sandra Landy
Carol Sanders	Sarah Scarborough
Jacqui Mitchell	Gillian Scott-Jones
Jim Zimmerman (npc)	Hugh Kelsey (npc)

1988 Venice, Italy

DENMARK	GREAT BRITAIN
Kristin Moeller	Elizabeth McGowan
Dorthe Shaltz	Sandra Penfold
Bettina Kalkerup	Michelle Brunner
Charlotte Palmund	Nicola Smith
Trine Dahl	Pat Davies
Judy Norris	Sandra Landy
Inger Lindegaard, npc	Grattan Endicott (npc)

1992 Salsomaggiore, Italy

AUSTRIA	GREAT BRITAIN
Terry Weigkricht	Pat Davies
Doris Fischer	Michelle Handley
Maria Erhart	Sandra Landy
Barbara Lindinger	Elizabeth McGowan
Jovanka Smederevac	Sandra Penfold
Herta Gyimesi	Nicola Smith
	Mark Horton (npc)

ROSENBLUM CUP TEAMS

1978 Played in New Orleans, Louisiana. Poland defeated Brazil 164-80.

POLAND	BRAZIL
Marian Frenkiel	Gabriel Chagas
Andrzej Macieszczak	Pedro Paulo Assumpcao
Andrezej Wilkosz	Gabino Cintra
Janusz Polec	Marcelo Branco
	Roberto Taunay
	Sergio Barbosa

1982 Played in Biarritz, France. France defeated the United States 178-161.

FRANCE	UNITED STATES
Michel Lebel	Chip Martel
Philippe Soulet	Lew Stansby
Dominique Pilon	Peter Pender
Albert Feigenbaum	Hugh Ross
Pierre Schemeil (npc)	Kit Woolsey
	Ed Manfield

1986 Played in Miami Beach, Florida. United States defeated Pakistan, 357-207.

UNITED STATES	PAKISTAN
Neil Silverman	Nishat Abedi
Ed Manfield	Nisai Ahmed
Peter Boyd	Zia Mahmood
Steve Robinson	Jan-e-Alam Fazli
Bob Lipsitz	
Kit Woolsey	

1990 Played in Geneva, Switzerland. Germany defeated United States, 145-132.

GERMANY	UNITED STATES
Bernhard Ludwig	Mike Moss
Jocken Bitschene	Charles Coon
Georg Nippgen	Michael Seamon
Roland Rokowsky	Drew Casen

WORLD OPEN PAIRS

	Winners	Runners-up
1962	FRANCE	GREAT BRITAIN
	Pierre Jais	Terence Reese
	Roger Trezel	Boris Schapiro
1966	NETHERLANDS	UNITED STATES
	Bob Slavenburg	Dr. John Fisher
	Hans Kreyns	James Jacoby
1970	AUSTRIA	ITALY
	Fritz Babsch	Benito Garozzo
	Peter Manhardt	Frederico Mayer
1974	UNITED STATES	ITALY
	Robert Hamman	Leandro Burgay
	Bobby Wolff	Antonio Abato
1978	BRAZIL	CANADA
	Marcelo Branco	Eric Kokish
	Gabino Cintra	Peter Nagy
1982	UNITED STATES	THE NETHERLANDS

	Chip Martel	Max Rebattu
	Lew Stansby	Anton Maas
1986	UNITED STATES	AUSTRIA
	Eric Rodwell	Heinrich Berger
	Jeff Meckstroth	Wolfgang Meinl
1990	BRAZIL	UNITED STATES
	Gabriel Chagas	Ralph Katz
	Marcela Branco	Peter Nagy

WORLD WOMENS PAIRS

	Winners	Runners-up
1962	GREAT BRITAIN	FRANCE
	Rixi Markus	Fanny Pariente
	Fritzi Gordon	C. Serf
1966	GREAT BRITAIN	UNITED STATES
	Joan Durran	Sue Sachs
	Jane Juan	Nancy Gruver
1970	UNITED STATES	GREAT BRITAIN
	Mary Jane Farell	Rixi Markus
	Marilyn Johnson	Fritzi Gordon
1974	GREAT BRITAIN	SOUTH AFRICA
	Fritzi Gordon	Gerda Goslar
	Rixi Markus	Rita Jacobsen
1978	UNITED STATES	UNITED STATES
	Kathie Wei	Betty Ann Kennedy
	Judi Radin	Carol Sanders
1982	UNITED STATES	UNITED STATES
	Carol Sanders	Lynn Deas
	Betty Ann Kennedy	Beth Palmer
1986	UNITED STATES	DENMARK
	Amalya Kearse	Charlotte Palmund
	Jacqui Mitchell	Bettina Kalkerup
1990	UNITED STATES	UNITED STATES
	Kerri Shuman	Kathie Wei
	Karen McCallum	Judi Radin

WORLD MIXED PAIRS

	Winners	Runners-up
1966	UNITED STATES	GREAT BRITAIN
	Mary Jane Farell	Joan Duran
	Ivan Erdos	Maurice Weissberger
1970	UNITED STATES	GREAT BRITAIN
	Barbara Brier	Rixi Markus
	Waldemar von Zedtwitz	Georges Catzeflis
1974	SWITZERLAND	UNITED STATES
	Loula Gordon	Jacqui Mitchell
	Tony Trad	James Cayne
1978	UNITED STATES	UNITED STATES
	Barry Crane	James Jacoby
	Kerri Shuman	Heitie Noland
1982	CANADA	UNITED STATES
	Dianna Gordon	Peggy Sutherlin
	George Mittelman	John Sutherlin
1986	UNITED STATES	UNITED STATES
	Pam Wittes	Bob Hamman
	Jon Wittes	KerriShuman
1990	UNITED STATES	SWEDEN
	Juanita Chambers	Lars Anderson
	Peter Weichsel	Eva-Liss Gothe

WORLD MIXED TEAMS

1962	GREAT BRITAIN	THE NETHERLANDS
	Rixi Markus	Mme. Westerfield
	Fritzi Gordon	Mme. Hoogenkamp
	Boris Schapiro	Herman Filarski
	Nico Gardener	A. Kornlijnsliper
1974	UNITED STATES	UNITED STATES
	Jo Morse	Tubby Stayman
	Steve Robinson	Vic Mitchell
	Steve Parker	Jacqui Mitchell
	Bob Lipsitz	James Cayne
	Peggy Lipsitz	Matt Granovetter

WORLD JUNIOR TEAM CHAMPIONSHIPS

1987 Amsterdam, Netherlands
1. *Netherlands* -- Wubbo de Boer, Marcel Nooyen, Berry Westra, Enri Leufkens
2. *France* -- Christian Desrousseaux, Alexis Damamme, Frank Multon, Jean-Christophe Quantin, Bénédicte Cronier

1989   Nottingham, England
1. *England* — John Pottage, Andy Robson, Derrick Patterson, John Hobson, Gerald Tredinnick, Stuart Tredinnick
2. *Argentina* — Alejandro Bianchedi, Leonardo Rizzo, Claudio Varela, Marcelo Cloppet, Juan Martin Quitegui and Alexix Pejacsevich

1991   Ann Arbor MI, USA
1. *United States* — John Diamond, Jeff Ferro, Martha Benson (Katz), Brian Platnick, Wayne Stuart, Debbie Zuckerberg
2. *Canada* — Mark Caplan, Fred Gitelman, Bronia Gmach, Geoff Hampson, Michael Roberts, Eric Sutherland

1993   Arhus, Denmark
1. *Germany* — Klaus Reps, Markus Joest, Guido Hopfenheit, Roland Rohowsky
2. *Norway* — Lasse Aaseng, Geir Helgemo, Jorgen Molberg, Espen Kvam, Svein-Gunnar Karlberg, Knut-Ove Thomassen

SENIOR PAIRS
1990   GREAT BRITAIN
      Albert Dormer
      Alan Hiron

EARLY CHAMPIONSHIPS
1935 (the first official meeting between the champions of Europe and the American Bridge League.) The UNITED STATES defeated FRANCE by 2,810 points over 300 boards.

UNITED STATES	FRANCE
David Burnstine	Pierre Albarran
Michael Gottlieb	Baron Robert de Nexon
Oswald Jacoby	M. Georges Rousset
Howard Schenken	Emanuel Tulumaris

1937 (under the auspices of the International Bridge League) Budapest, Hungary, AUSTRIA defeated UNITED STATES by 4,740 points.

AUSTRIA	UNITED STATES
Karl von Bluhdorn	Ely Culbertson
Dr. Edward Frischauer	Josephine Culbertson
Walter Herbert	Helen Sobel
Hans Jellinek	Charles C. Vogelhofer
Udo von Meissel	
Karl Schneider	
Dr. Paul Stern (npc)	

WOMEN'S WINNERS

AUSTRIA	
Mariane Boschan	Lisi Klauber
Gertrude Brunner	Rixi Markus
Ethel Ernst	Ditta Riemer
Gretl Joseffy	Gertrude Schlesinger

BIBLIOGRAPHY

KEY: Many thousands of books have been written on bridge; this bibliography attempts to list those which have permanent value, under 17 subdivisions. In this category the books are listed alphabetically by author. All publishers, unless otherwise indicted, are American. If no place of publication appears after the publisher, it was published in New York City. Where there has been more than one edition, the earliest and latest dates are given when known. There may be slight variations in number of pages in different editions. No distinction is made between hardcover and paperback books.

A HISTORY Whist, Auction Bridge, Bridge

B ANTHOLOGIES

C BIDDING (including systems)

D PLAY

E BIDDING AND PLAY (in combination)

F DUPLICATE BRIDGE (bidding, play
   and tournament directing)

G MATCH AND TOURNAMENT RECORDS

H HAND COLLECTIONS

I FICTION

J PROBLEMS, QUIZZES, PUZZLES

K BIOGRAPHY

L HUMOR AND POETRY

M MATHEMATICS

N LAWS

O PERIODICALS

P ENCYCLOPEDIAS

Q BIBLIOGRAPHIES

Books of historic significance and books of importance for the purposes of a modern technical bridge library have been separately identified as follows:
* Books marked thus made a major contribution to the technical development of the game.

† Books marked thus are optional requirements for a modern technical bridge library

‡ Books marked thus are mandatory requirements for a modern technical bridge library.

AUTHOR	TITLE	PUBLISHER	PAGES	DATES
A HISTORY Whist, Auction Bridge, Bridge				
Ames, Fisher	A Practical Guide to Whist	Scribner's	92	1891-1907
Benham, W. Gurney	Playing Cards: History of the Pack	Ward, Lock (London & Melbourne)	196	1931
		Spring Books (London)	196	1957
Bruelheide, F. E.	Party Bridge	Buzza Co. (Minneapolis)	102	1927
Burney, Admiral James	*Treatise on the Game of Whist	Thos. & Wm. Boone (London)	87	1823
Butler, William	The Whist Reference Book	John C. Yorston Co. (Philadelphia)	568	1899
Cavendish (Henry Jones)	Card Essays, Clay's Decisions, and Card-Table Talk	Thos, De La Rue (London)	260	1879
Cavendish (Henry Jones)	*Cavendish on Whist	Thos. De La Rue (London)	107	1862-1902
Cavendish (Henry Jones)	Whist Developments	Thos. De La Rue (London)	181	1885-1891
Chatti, William Andrew	Facts and Speculations on the Origin and History of Playing Cards	John Russell Smith (London)	343	1848
Cotton, Charles	Compleat Gamester	Henry Brome (London)	232	1674-1726
Dalton, W.	Auction Bridge up to Date	Thos. De La Rue (London)	210	1909
Daniels, David	The Golden Age of Contract Bridge	Stein & Day	212	1980
Deschapples, Guillaume	Traité du Whiste	Perrotin (Paris)	328	1840
Elwell, Joseph B.	*Advanced Bridge	Scribner's	297	1904-09
Elwell, Joseph B.	Elwell on Bridge	Scribner's	136	1902-11
Elwell, Joseph B.	*Auction Bridge	Scribner's	170	1910-12
Emery, Sue	No Passing Fancy — Fifty Years of Contract Bridge	ACBL (Memphis)	128	1977
Ferguson, Wynne	Auction Bridge	Ferguson	64	1915-29

AUTHOR	TITLE	PUBLISHER	PAGES	DATES
Foster, Robert F.	*Foster on Auction*	Dutton	384	1918-25
Foster, Robert F.	*Foster's Bridge Manual*	Brentano's	200	1900-08
Hargrave, Catherine	*A History of Playing Cards*	Houghton Mifflin	468	1930
		Dover (Paperback)	462	1966
Howell, Edwin	*Whist Openings — A Systematic Treatment of the Short-Suit Game*	Pinkham Press (Boston)	206	1896
Hoyle, Edmund	**A Short Treatise on the Game of Whist*	T. Osborne (London)	86	1743-50
Hyde-Wollaston, A. (see Robertson, Edmond)	*Bridge Developments*			
Lenz, Sidney	**Lenz on Bridge*	Simon & Schuster	379	1926
Lenz, Sidney	*Lenz on Bridge,* volume II	Simon & Schuster	456	1927
Lenz, Sidney and Rendel, Robert	*How's Your Bridge?*	Simon & Schuster	224	1929
Manning-Foster. A. E.	*Auction Bridge for All*	Ernest Benn (London)	317	1928-30
Manning-Foster, A. E.	*Auction & Contract Bridge Made Clear*	Grayson & Grayson (London)	327	1933
Manning-Foster, A. E.	*Bridge — Plafond*	Ernest Benn (London)	93	1933
Mathews, T.	**Advice to the Young Whist Player*	Meyler & Son (England)	64	1806-25
Mitchell, John T.	*Duplicate Whist — Its Rules and Methods of Play*	McClurg (Chicago)	110	1891
Payne, William	**Maxims for Playing the Game of Whist with All Necessary Calculations*	Payne & Son (England)	67	1773-90
Pole, William	*Evolution of Whist*	Longmans (London & NYC)	269	1895
Pole, William	**Philosophy of Whist*	Thos. De La Rue (London)	218	1883-87
Portland (James Hogg)	*The Whist Table*	John Hogg (London)	472	1894
Reith, George	**The Art of Successful Bidding*	Doubleday	227	1928
Rendel, Robert (see Lenz, Sidney)	*How's Your Bridge?*			
Rheinhardt, Rudolf	*Whist Scores and Card-Table Talk with a Bibliography of Whist*	McClurg (Chicago)	310	1887
Robertson, Edmund and Hyde-Wollaston, A.	*Bridge Developments*	Brentano's	127	1904
Seymour, Richard	*The Compleat Gamester*	Curll & Wilford (London)	132	1734-54
Shepard, E. V.	*Expert Auction*	Harper & Bros.	245	1913-17
Shepard, E. V.	*Scientific Auction Bridge*	Harper & Bros.	241	1913-14
Singer, Samuel W.	*Researches into the History of Playing Cards*	Robert Triphook (London)	378	1816
Tilley, Roger	*A History of Playing Cards*	Crown	192	1973
Warren, Mrs. Prescott	*Auction and Contract Bridge Condensed*	Houghton Mifflin (Boston)	247	1927
Whitehead, Wilbur C.	**Auction Bridge Standards*	Stokes	188	1921-26
Whitehead, Wilbur C,	*Whitehead's Conventions of Auction Bridge*	Stokes	243	1914
Work, Milton	**Auction Bridge Complete*	J. C. Winston (Philadelphia)	500	1926-29

B ANTHOLOGIES

AUTHOR	TITLE	PUBLISHER	PAGES	DATES
The Bridge World	*The Bridge World: Best of the Sixties*	*The Bridge World*	48	1982
Frey, Richard (Editor)	*Bridge for Women*	Doubleday	221	1967
		Funk & Wagnalls	224	1970
Goren, Charles H.	*Bridge Is My Game: Lessons of a Lifetime*	Doubleday	190	1965
Goren, Charles H.	*The Sports Illustrated Book of Bridge*	Time, Inc.	520	1961
Hart, Norman de V.	*The Bridge Players' Bedside Book*	Eyre & Spottiswoode (London)	160	1939
Hervey, George F.	*The Bridge Players' Bedside Book*	Faber & Faber (London)	116	1964
Jacoby, Oswald and Morehead, Albert	*Fireside Book of Cards*	Simon & Schuster	365	1957
Jaïs, Pierre et al	*L'Aristocratie du Bridge*	Balland (Paris)	317	1973
Johnson, Jared	*Classic Bridge Quotes*	Devyn	119	1989

AUTHOR	TITLE	PUBLISHER	PAGES	DATES
Kleinman, Danny	The Bridge Weird Anthology	Kleinman (Los Angeles)	160	1981
Le Dentu, José (see Jaïs, Pierre)	L'Aristocratie du Bridge			
Le Dentu, José	Bridge à la Une	Fayard (Paris)	428	1964
Le Dentu, José	‡Championship Bridge (trans. by Alan Truscott and Amalya Kearse)	Harper & Row	308	1974
Mackey, Rex	The Walk of the Oysters	W. H. Allen (London)	197	1964
Mollo, Victor	Bridge Immortals	Faber & Faber (London) Hart	191 256	1967 1968
Morehead, Albert (see Jacoby, Oswald)	Fireside Book of Cards			
Olsen, Jack	The Mad World of Bridge	Holt, Rinehart & Winston	239	1960
Ostrow, Albert	The Bridge Player's Bedside Companion	Prentice-Hall (Englewood Cliffs NJ)	391	1955
Reese, Terence (ed.)	Bridge Tips from the Masters	Crown	234	1981
Stern, Milton and the Experts	Expert Bridge (edited by Shirley Silverman)	Max Hardy	136	1978
Truscott, Alan (see Jaïs, Pierre)	L'Aristocratie du Bridge			

C BIDDING (including systems)

AUTHOR	TITLE	PUBLISHER	PAGES	DATES
Albano, Helen	Analysis and Practical Application of Goren Method	Albano	27	1970
Alder, Phillip (see Truscott, Alan)	On Bidding (Revised & Updated "Morehead on Bidding")			
Amsbury, Joe	Bridge: Bidding Naturally	Batsford (London)	152	1979
Amsbury, Joe	Control Asking	Bridge Players Handbooks (Nottingham, England)	32	1980
Amsbury, Joe	Doubles in Competition	Nottingham, England	31	1985
Amsbury, Joe (see Payne, Dick)	TNT and Competitive Bidding			
Andersen, Ron	The Lebensohl Convention Complete in Contract Bridge	Barclay Bridge Supplies	107	1987
Andersen, Ron	Where and How High	Wisconsin Bridge Associates	92	1970
Andersen, Ron (see Wei, C. C.)	Bidding Precisely — Volume 2			
Andersen, Ron (see Wei, C. C.)	Bidding Precisely — Volume 3			
Andersen, Ron (see Wei, Katherine)	Action for the Defense — When the Enemy Opens the Bidding			
Andersen, Ron and Zenkel, Sabine	‡Preempts from A to Z	Magnus Books (Stamford CT)	290	1993
Anderson, Merrell (see Wolf, Murray)	The Subtle Club			
Anstett, Charles (see Winslow, T. N.)	Win With Winslow			
Avarelli, Walter (see Belladonna, Giorgio)	*The Roman Club System of Distributional Bidding			
Baker, Bob	The Swiss Convention	Bridge Players Handbooks (Nottingham, England)	31	1980
Bangs, Fred T.	Basic Bidding Contract Bridge	Phoenix Publishers (Phoenix)	128	1955
Barclay, Shepard	The Contract Bridge Guide	Bobbs-Merrill (Indianapolis)	266	1931
Baron, Leo and Meredith, Adam	*Baron System of Contract Bridge	Contract Bridge Equipment Co. (Leeds)	180	1948
Baron, Randy et al	Clobber Their Artificial Club	Baron Bridge Supplies (Louisville KY)	20	1979
Baron, Randy et al	Clobber Their Artificial Club (2nd edition, Revised)	Devyn (Louisville KY)	32	1983
Barrow, Rhoda	Acolites Quiz	George Allen & Unwin Ltd. (London)	197	1970
Barton, Major F. P.	The Barton System	Farrar & Reinhart	80	1934
Barton, Major F. P.	The "Barton" Variation	Joiner & Steele (London)	88	1933-42
Beasley, Lt. Col. H. M.	The Beasley Contract Bridge System	Assoc. Newspapers (London)	128	1935

AUTHOR	TITLE	PUBLISHER	PAGES	DATES
Bergen, Marty	Better Bidding with Bergen: Volume I — Uncontested Auctions	Max Hardy (Las Vegas)	199	1985
Bergen, Marty	Better Bidding with Bergen: Volume II — Competitive Bidding, Fit Bids & More	Max Hardy (Las Vegas)	149	1986
Becker, Mike et al	*The Ultimate Club	Ultimate Club (Livingston NJ)	126	1981
Belladona, Giorgio and Avarelli, Walter	*The Roman Club System of Distributional Bidding	Simon & Schuster	162	1959
Belladonna, Giorgio and Garozzo, Benito	‡Precision and Super Precision Bidding	G. P. Putnam's Sons	237	1975
Belladonna, Giorgio (see Wei, C. C.)	Summary of Super Precision			
Bird, David	All You Need to Know About Bidding			
Bissell, Harold	The Bissell System: Distributional Method of Bidding	Columbia University Press	316	1936
Blackwood, Easley	Blackwood on Bidding	Bobbs-Merrill (Indianapolis)	215	1956
Blackwood, Easley	Blackwood on Slams	Prentice-Hall (Englewood Cliffs NJ)	160	1970
Blackwood, Easley and Wallace, Charlton	*Blackwood Slam Bidding	Bruelheide (Minneapolis)	64	1941
Boland, Vincent and Law, John	Accurate Contract Bidding	Boland & Law (Cleveland)	84	1931
Borin, Jim	Bridge Borin Style (Baronized Acol)	Borin School of Bridge (South Yarra, Australia)		1978
Borin, Jim and Norma	Our Precision Style	D. W. Thorpe (West Melbourne, Australia)	72	1981
Bose Mullick, S. G.	The Relay Club	Allied (Bombay)	344	1975
Boyden, Elizabeth (see Warren, Mrs. Prescott)	Contract Bridge of 1929			
Braham, V. G. (see Smith, F. D.)	The Victorian Blackwood Slam Convention			
Brannon, Robert Means	The Incomparable Club Convention	News Printing House (Charlotte NC)	88	1935
Brashler, Ted	Sweep Q-Bids and Other Treatments	Brashler Enterprises (Glencoe IL)	289	1986
Bridge Headquarters	The Official System of Contract Bridge	Winston (Philadelphia)	236	1931
Bring, Liz	Bridge Bidding: The Golden Rules	Crowood Press (Swindon, England)	149	1991
Brown, John	Bidding Craft	Duckworth (London)	133	1962
Budin, Barnett and Kornfeld, Morris	Bridge Players Digest of Conventions	Budin Press (Philadelphia)	32	1962-63
Burgay, Leandro	Bridge: The Burgay Diamond	Burgay (Italy)	83	1979
Burns, Margery	The Nottingham System of Contract Bridge	Educational Productions (London)	107	1954-69
Burnstine, David (see Four Aces)	The Four Aces System of Contract Bridge			
Burnstine, David	The Four Horsemen's One-over-One Method of Contract Bidding	Walter J. Black, Inc.	118	1932
Butler, Geoffrey and Stern, Paul	Two Club System of Bidding	Faber & Faber (London)	300	1946
Cayley, Frank	Contract Bridge-bidding	Rigby (Australia)	64	1970
Champney, Ken (see Baron, Randy)	Clobber Their Artificial Club			
Champney, Ken (see Baron, Randy)	Clobber Their Artificial Club (2nd edition, Revised)			
Chiaradia, Eugenio and Perroux, Carl'Alberto	Il Fiori Napoletano	Federazione Italiana Bridge (Milano)	96	1956
Churchill, S. Garton	Churchill Natural Bidding Style at Contract Bridge	Churchill (Great Neck NY)	743	1979
Churchill, S. Garton and Ferguson, Albert	*Contract Bidding Tactics at Match Point Play	Ad Press	323	1936
Clark, Morris	The Four-Leafed Club	Tom's Technical Publications (Marble Falls, TX)	165	1983
Coffin, George	Acol and the New Point Count	Duckworth (London)	56	1953
Coffin, George	Natural Big Club	Coffin (Parsonsfield ME)	192	1969

AUTHOR	TITLE	PUBLISHER	PAGES	DATES
Coffin, George	*The Weak No Trump*	Eaton Press (Massachusetts)	32	1956
Coffin, George	*Winning Duplicate*	B. Humphries (Boston)	146	1933
Cohen, Ben and Lederer, Rhoda	*Current Conventions Made Clear*	Allen & Unwin (London)	161	1973
Cohen, Ben and Reese, Terence	**The Acol System of Contract Bridge (3rd ed.)*	Joiner & Steele (London)	84	1946
Cohen, Larry	*‡To Bid or Not to Bid: The Law of Total Tricks*	Platinum Press	272	1992
Collins, J. H.	*The Archer System*	Collins (Chicago)	303	1955
Courtenay, F. Dudley	*The Standardized Code of Contrct Bridge Bidding*	Bridge Headquareters	108	1937
Courtenay, F. Dudley	**The System the Experts Play*	Bridge Headquarters	94	1934
Cox, Jean	*Bridge With Jean Cox — The Bidding*	Cox (Pittsburgh)	66	1963
Crane, Joshua	*The Crane System of Modern Contract Bidding*	East Anglian Daily Times (London)	107	1948
Criticus	*Contract Simplicitas*	Jenkins, Ltd. (London)	332	1933
Cron, Bea & Rosen, Fern	*Advanced Bridge Five Card Major Student Text*	N. W. D. Enterprises (Torrance CA)	88	1985
Cron, Bea & Rosen, Fern	*Beginning Bridge Five Card Major Student Text*	N. W. D. Enterprises (Torrance CA)	78	1985
Cron, Bea & Rosen, Fern	*Intermediate Bridge Five Card Major Student Text*	N. W. D. Enterprises (Torrance CA)	74	1985
Crowhurst, Eric	*Acol in Competition*	Pelham (London)	383	1980
Crowhurst, Eric	*Precision Bidding in Acol*	Pelham (London)	240	1974
Crowhurst, Eric & Kambites, Andrew	*Understanding Acol: The Good Bidding Guide*	Victor Gollancz (London)	157	1990
de Satnick, Shelly	*Everyone's Introduction to Bridge Conventions*	Avon Books (NY)	137	1984
Culbertson, Ely	**Contract Bridge Blue Book*	The Bridge World	348	1930
Culbertson, Ely	*Contract Bridge Blue Book of 1933*	The Bridge World	599	1933
Culbertson, Ely	*Culbertson's Summary*	The Bridge World	47	1931
Culbertson, Ely	*Point Count Bidding*	J. C. Winston (Philadelphia)	171	1952
Culbertson, Josephine	*Contract Bridge Made Easy the Point Count Way*	J. C. Winston (Philadelphia)	148	1955
Danielson, Robert	*Danielson's Precision*	Danielson (Hackensack NJ)	26	1976
Danielson, Robert	*Relay Precision (5 booklets)*	Danielson (Hackensack NJ)	442	1977-79
Davis, Frank Maxie	*Precision Bridge*	Dorrance (Philadelphia)	425	1976
Desai, G. R.	*Contract Bridge and High Cards: A New Look*	Mehta (India)	144	1985
Desai, G. R.	*Revolution in Contract Bridge*	Ahmedabad, India	556	1982
Desai, G. R. & Mehta, Ravindra	*Contract Bridge Bidding Technique Through High Card and Pattern Points or Intrinsic Points Book I*	Mehta (India)	86	1988
Desai, G. R. & Mehta, Ravindra	*Contract Bridge Bidding Technique Through High Card and Pattern Points or Intrinsic Points Book II*	Mehta (India)	90	1988
Desai, G. R. & Mehta, Ravindra	*Contract Bridge Bidding Technique Through High Card and Pattern Points or Intrinsic Points Book III*	Mehta (India)	144	1988
Desai, G. R. & Mehta, Ravindra	*Elements of Modern Contract Bridge or Primer of Card Points and Pattern Points or Intrinsic Points*	Mehta (India)	117	1988
Dettman, H. V.	*Simplified Precision Bidding*	Dorrance (Philadelphia)	145	1972
Dewhurst, Victor	*The Two-Club System*	Faber & Faber (London)	220	1965
Disbrow, Bennett L. (see Solomon, Charles J.)	*Slam Bidding and Point Count*			
Dormer, Albert (see Reese, Terrence)	*The Acol System Today Blueprint for Bidding (American title)*			
Dormer, Albert	*†Powerhouse Hands*	Prentice-Hall (Englewood Cliffs NJ)	223	1975
Drury, Douglas	*The Drury Two Club Convention*	Drury	46	1969
Duke, J. Dan	*Advanced Basic Bidding*	Duke (Boone NC)	119	1991

AUTHOR	TITLE	PUBLISHER	PAGES	DATES
Duke, J. Dan	*Competitive Bidding*	Duke (Boone NC)	136	1988
Duke, J. Dan	*Modern Popular Conventions*	Duke (Boone NC)	148	1991
Duncan, John	*New Dimension Bidding in Contract Bridge*	Robert B. Luce Inc. (Washington DC)	308	1963
Eastgate, C. L. and McKillop, L. M.	*Modern Gladiator System of Bidding*	Whitcombe & Tomes (New Zealand)	67	1953
Eberling, Frederick J.	*Revolutionary Forcing Pass: The Eberling System of Bidding in Contract Bridge*	A B Publications (Sydney, Australia)	14	1984
Ewen, Robert	‡*Doubles for Takeout, Penalties and Profit*	Prentice-Hall (Englewood Cliffs NJ)	278	1973
Ewen, Robert	‡*Preemptive Bidding*	Prentice-Hall (Englewood Cliffs NJ)	162	1975
Feldheim, Harold	†*Weak Two-Bid in Bridge*	Barclay Bridge Supplies	105	1971-73
Feldheim, Harold	*Five Card Major Bidding in Contract Bridge*	Barclay Bridge Supplies	181	1985
Feldheim, Harold	*Negative and Responsive Doubles in Bridge*	Barclay Bridge Supplies	64	1980
Feldheim, Harold	*Negative, Responsive & Other Competitive Doubles*	C & T Bridge Supplies (Los Alamitos CA)	77	1993
Feldheim, Harold	*Tactical Bidding*	C & T Bridge Supplies (Los Alamitos CA)	228	1992
Ferguson, Albert (see S. Garton Churchill)	*Contract Bidding Tactics at Match Point Play*			
Fishbein, Harry	*The Fishbein Convention*	Crown	83	1960
Flannery, William	*The Complete Flannery 2 Diamond Opener*	Nella (Chicago)	16	1979
Flannery, William	*The Flannery Two Diamond Opening*	Devyn (Louisville KY)	190	1984
Flint, Jeremy & Sharp, Richard	*Competitive Bidding*	Cassell (London)	202	1980
Forquet, Pietro (see Garozzo, Benito)	‡*The Italian Blue Team Bridge Book*			
Foss, Frank	*Simplified Contract Bidding*	Gane & Son (Willimantic CT)	67	1935
Four Aces	*The Four Aces System of Contract Bridge*	Random House	302	1935
Fox, G. C. H.	†*Modern Bidding Systems in Bridge*	The Penguin Press (London) 2nd rev. ed.	333 424	1967 1973
Fox, G. C. H.	*Sound Bidding at Contract*	E. Arnold (London)	254	1954
Fransz, Alex & Klinger, Ron	*Medium Club Relay*	P T Pastaka Karya Graf; Katama (Jakarta, Indonesia)	231	1988
Frey, Richard L. (see Four Aces)	*The Four Aces System of Contract Bridge*			
Garozzo, Benito (see Belladonna, Giorgio)	‡*Precision and Super Precision Bidding*			
Garozzo, Benito and Forquet, Pietro	‡*The Italian Blue Team Bridge Book*	Grosset & Dunlap	274	1969
Garozzo (see Wei, C. C.)	*Summary of Super Precision*			
Garozzo, Benito and Yallouze, Leon	†*The Blue Club*	Faber & Faber (London)	170	1969
George, Leland E.	*Exactness in Bridge Bidding*	Carlton Press	79	1982
Gerber, John	*The Four Club Bid: A Slam Convention*	Gerber (Houston)	28	1942
Gerber, John	*The Gerber Four Club Slam Convention*	Texas Bridge (Houston)	24	1963
Gold, Don	*Intermediate Two Bids in Bridge*	Exposition Press	128	1982
Goldman, Bobby	†*Aces Scientific*	Goldman Max Hardy	250 169	1973 1978
Goodwin, Thomas	*A Natural Relay System*	Goodwin (Portland ME)	77	1982
Goren, Charles	*Advanced Bidding: A Tutor Text*	Doubleday	342	1963
Goren, Charles	*Goren Settles the Bridge Arguments*	Hart	429	1974
Goren, Charles	*Goren Presents the Italian Bridge System*	Doubleday	216	1958
Goren, Charles	†*Point Count Bidding*	Simon & Schuster	154	1949-58
Goren, Charles and Wei, C. C.	*Precisicon Bridge for Everyone*	Doubleday	155	1978
Goren, Charles	†*The Precision System*	Doubleday	228	1971
Goren, Charles	*The Standard Book of Bidding*	Doubleday	249	1944-49
Gorski, Andrew	*The Art of Logical Bidding*	Devyn (Louisville KY)	87	1985

AUTHOR	TITLE	PUBLISHER	PAGES	DATES
Gottlieb, Michael (see Four Aces)	*The Four Aces System of Contract Bridge			
Griffiths, D. C.	The Losing Trick Count	Probray (Nottingham, England)	32	1984
Hanna, William and Steen, Douglas	Precision Power Bidding: The Bulldog System	Coffin (Waltham MA)	104	1956
Hanson, Keith	The Art of Bidding	Hanson (Boca Raton FL)	224	1990
Hardy, Max	†Five Card Majors, Western Style	Hardy	94	1974
Hardy, Max	*Two Over One Game Force	Hardy	147	1982
Hardy, Max	New Minor — Fourth Suit Forcing — Forcing Notrump Responses	Hardy	81	1984
Hardy, Max	Splinters and Other Shortness Bids	Hardy (Las Vegas)	88	1987
Hart, Norman de V. (see Kempson, Ewart)	The Quintessence of CAB			
Hart, Norman de V.	Slams à la Culbertson	Joiner & Steele (London)	99	1937
Hart, Norman de V. (see Stern, Paul)	The Vienna System of Contract Bridge			
Hayden, Dorothy	‡Bid Better, Play Better	Harper & Row	196	1966
Heath, Forrest	*Seven-Eleven: A Manual of the Heath System	Heath (Upper Montclair NJ)	55	1933
Horn, A. C.	Limited Opening Bids	Horn (Dothan AL)	167	1977
Horn, Stormy (see Reed, Dick)	The System: Bidding Techniques of Reed-Horn			
Horton, Mark	Defences to a Strong Club	Probray Press (Nottingham, England)	32	1982
Horton, Sally	Responding to 2 NT	Probray Press (Nottingham, England)	32	1982
Howard, Denis (ed.)	The New South Wales System	Howard (NSW) Howard (NSW)	83 70	1964 1970
Husband, Pat & Kambites, Andrew	Task Masters Student Work Books by Master Teachers	Victor Gollancz (London)	24	1989
Husband, Pat & Klinger, Ron	Introduction to Acol Bidding: Task Masters Student Work Books by Master Teachers	Victor Gollancz (London)	24	1989
Husband, Pat (see Kambites, Andrew)	Strong Twos, Pre-Empts and Slams			
Ingram, H. St, John	The Ingram One Club	Eyre & Spottiswoode (London)	96	1935
Irwin, Florence	Contract Bridge	Stokes	23	1927
Jacoby, Oswald (see Four Aces)	*Four Aces System of Contract Bridge			
Jacoby, Oswald	Point Count Bidding Made Easy	Arrco (Chicago)	31	1960
Jacoby, Oswald	What's New in Bridge	Hanover House	158	1954
Janitschke, Jan	Weak Two-Bids	Rocky Mountain Books (Denver)	20	1992
Janitschke, Jan (see Sands, Norma)	Bridge — Competitive Bidding			
Janitschke, Jan (see Sands, Norma)	Bridge — Double Trouble			
Janitschke, Jan (see Sands, Norma)	Bridge — Later in the Auction			
Janitschke, Jan (see Sands, Norma)	Bridge — Negative Doubles			
Janitschke, Jan (see Sands, Norma)	Fine Tuning			
Janitschke, Jan (see Sands, Norma)	Slam Bidding			
Janitschke, Jan (see Sands, Norma)	Slam Bidding Part II			
Jannersten, Eric	†Precision Bridge	Allen & Unwin (London)	224	1972
Kambites, Andrew	Strategic Acol Bidding: Task Masters Student Work Books by Master Teachers	Victor Gollancz (London)	24	1989
Kambites, Andrew & Husband, Pat	Strong Twos, Pre-Empts and Slams	Victor Gollancz (London)	24	1990
Kambites, Andrew (see Husband, Pat)	Task Masters Student Work Books by Master Teachers			
Kantar, Edwin	Bidding	Kantar (Los Angeles)	52	1965

AUTHOR	TITLE	PUBLISHER	PAGES	DATES
Lawrence, Mike	*The Jacoby & Texas Transfer Convention*	Texas Bridge Supplies (Baytown TX)	22	1982
Lawrence, Mike	*The Lebensohl Convention*	Texas Bridge Supplies (Baytown TX)	24	1983
Lawrence, Mike	*The Complete Book on Hand Evaluation in Contract Bridge*	Max Hardy	194	1983
Lawrence, Mike	*The Complete Guide to Contested Auctions*	Lawrence & Leong (Oakland CA)	360	1992
Lawrence, Mike	*The Complete Guide to Passed Hand Bidding*	Lawrence & Leong (Oakland CA)	217	1989
Lawrence, Mike	*Mike Lawrence's Bidding Quizzes — Volume 1: The Uncontested Auction*	Lawrence & Leong (Oakland CA)	280	1990
Lawrence, Mike	*Mike Lawrence's Workbook on the Two Over One System*	Max Hardy (Las Vegas)	189	1987
Lea, Robert	*Bridge Is Easy with the Lea System*	R. H. Lea (Littleton CO)	144	1965
Lederer, Richard	**Lederer Bids Two Clubs*	Williams & Norgate (London)	220	1934
Lennon, Jacob	*Championship Defensive Bidding*	Lennon, n.p. (Indiana)	97	1987
Lenz, Sidney	*My System of Contract Bidding*	Simon & Schuster	93	1930
Lindelof, E. T.	*COBRA: The Computerized Bidding System*	Victor Gollancz Ltd. (London)	280	1983
Lindkvist, Magnus, Nilsland, Mats & Wirgren, Anders	*Notrump Bidding — the Scanian Way; Swedish Expert Methods — Volume Two*	Scandia Bridgekonsult (Lund, Sweden)	63	1990
Lindsay, Kenneth	*3-D and the MAFIA Club*	AIGA Publications (Baton Rouge)	228	1981
MacMillan, W. S.	*Simply Blue*	Bibliagora (Surrey, England)	256	1985
Manning-Foster, A. E.	*Contract Bridge for All*	Ernest Benn (London)	221	1930
Marchione, Richard	*Power Precision Updated and Expanded*	Barclay (Port Chester NY)	138	1982
McKillop, I. M. (see Eastgate, C. L.)	*Modern Gladiator System*			
McNeil, Keith	*Match Your Bidding Against the Experts*	Modern Bridge (Northbridge, Australia)	176	1991
Mehta, Ravindra (see Desai, G. R.)	*Contract Bridge Bidding Technique Through High Card and Pattern Points or Intrinsic Points Book I*			
Mehta, Ravindra (see Desai, G. R.)	*Contract Bridge Bidding Technique Through High Card and Pattern Points or Intrinsic Points Book II*			
Mehta, Ravindra (see Desai, G. R.)	*Contract Bridge Bidding Technique Through High Card and Pattern Points or Intrinsic Points Book III*			
Mehta, Ravindra (see Desai, G. R.)	*Elements of Modern Contract Bridge or Primer of Card Points and Pattern Points or Intrinsic Points*			
Meredith, Adam (see Baron, Leo)	*Baron System of Contract Bridge*			
Miles, Marshall	*Bridge From the Top — Book I*	Rondo Publications (Roswell GA)	299	1987
Miles, Marshall	*Bridge From the Top — Book II*	Tamarind Press (San Bernardino CA)	260	1989
Miles, Marshall	*Stronger Competitive Bidding*	Lawrence & Leong (Oakland CA)	317	1992
Miller, Richard A.	*Point Count Bidding*	R. A. Miller (York PA)	32	1947
Mollo, Victor	*Bridge: Modern Bidding*	Faber & Faber (London)	124	1961/78
Mollo, Victor	**Streamlined Bridge: or Bidding Without Tears*	Christopher Johnson (London)	256	1947-54
Monk, Charles	*Le Bridge: Système Complet des Enchères Modernes*	Albin Michel (Paris)	276	1970
Morehead, Albert	**†Morehead on Bidding*	Macmillan	374	1964
Morehead, Albert	*‡Morehead on Bidding (R. L. Frey, ed)*	Simon & Schuster	447	1974
Mott-Smith, Geoffrey	*Contract Bridge and Advanced Auction Bidding*	Minton, Bach	281	1927
Munday, Lindsay	*The Direct British System of Contract Bidding*	Rich & Cowan (London)	176	1932
Musumeci, Joe (see Wolff, Bobby)	*Jacoby Transfer Bids*			
Musumeci, Joe (see Wolff, Bobby)	*Limit Raises, Forcing Raises, Splinter Bids & the Forcing NT*			
Musumeci, Joe (see Wolff, Bobby)	*Negative Doubles, Responsive Doubles, Maximal Doubles*			
Nail, G. R. and Stucker, Robert	*Revolution in Bridge*	Naylor (San Antonio)	325	1965
Nilsland, Mats (see Lindkvist, Magnus)	*Notrump Bidding — the Scanian Way Swedish Expert Methods — Volume Two*			

AUTHOR	TITLE	PUBLISHER	PAGES	DATES
Kantar, Edwin	†*Bridge Bidding Made Easy*	Wilshire Books (North Hollywood CA)	256	1972
Kantar, Edwin	‡*Bridge Conventions*	Wilshire Books (North Hollywood CA)	108	1972
Kantar, Edwin	*An Expert's Guide to Improving Your Bidding Skills*	Wilshire Books (North Hollywood CA)	151	1980
Kantar, Edwin	*The Forcing Pass in Contract Bridge*	Barclay (Port Chester NY)	72	1983
Kantar, Edwin	*Roman Key Card Blackwood*	Granovetter Books (Ballston Lake NY)	128	1991
Kaplan, Edgar	†*Competitive Bidding in Modern Bridge*	Fleet	192	1965
Kaplan, Edgar	**Complete Italian System of Winning Bridge*	Washburn	159	1959
Kaplan, Edgar	*Kaplan-Sheinwold Updated*	The Bridge World	42	1972
Kaplan, Edgar and Sheinwold, Alfred	**‡How to Play Winning Bridge: Kaplan-Sheinwold System*	Fleet Collier	256 224	1958-63 1962-69
Karpin, Fred	**The Karpin Point Count System*	Kaufmann (Washington DC)	89	1949
Katz, Richard H. (see Cohen, Larry)	†*Breakthrough in Bridge*			
Kearse, Amalya	‡*Bridge Conventions Complete* (revised and expanded)	Hart	656	1975
Kearse, Amalya	*Bridge Conventions Complete* (revised and expanded)	Devyn (Louisville KY)	1121	1990
Kelsey, H. W.	*Slam Bidding*	Faber & Faber (London)	200	1973
Kempson, Ewart and Hart, Norman de V.	*The Quintessence of CAB*	Nicholas Kaye (London)	160	1959
Kennedy, George	*The Kennedy System of Bridge*	Arco	281	1965
Kerr, R. P. and Jones, W.L.	*The Symmetric Relay*	Kerr & Jones (Australia)	98	1980
Kerwin, Madeleine	*One Over One for Everyone*	Kerwin Co.	116	1932
Kierein, John	*Kamikaze No Trump*	Kierein (Boulder CO)	45	1977
Kleinman, Danny	*Understanding Bidding Volume 1: Fundamentals*	Kleinman (Los Angeles)	177	1981
Kleinman, Danny	*Understanding Bidding Volume 2: Ramifications*	Kleinman (Los Angeles)	144	1981
Kleinman, Danny	*Building Better Bridge*	Kleinman (Los Angeles)	210	1991
Kleinman, Danny	*Doubles: Sputnik and the Ax*	Kleinman (Los Angeles)	53	1992
Kleinman, Danny	*The Goldsmith Lectures: Slam Bidding*	Kleinman (Los Angeles)	62	1992
Kleinman, Danny	*It's a Bidder's Game*	Kleinman (Los Angeles)	192	1986
Kleinman, Danny	*Master Solvers Archives 1985-1987*	Kleinman (Los Angeles)	228	1988
Kleinman, Danny	*Master Solvers Archives 1988-1990*	Kleinman (Los Angeles)	234	1991
Kleinman, Danny	*PASS Is a Four Letter Word*	Kleinman (Los Angeles)	354	1992
Klinger, Ron	*5-Card Majors*	Houghton Mifflin (Boston)	126	1992
Klinger, Ron	*Acol Bridge Made Easy*	Victor Gollancz (London)	95	1987
Klinger, Ron	*Bidding to Win at Bridge — Book One: The Modern Losing Trick Count*	Modern Bridge Publications (Sydney, Australia)	122	1986
Klinger, Ron	*Bridge Conventions, Defences and Countermeasures*	Victor Gollancz (London)	144	1993
Klinger, Ron	*Cue Bidding to Slams*	D. W. Thorpe (Melbourne, Australia)	80	1983
Klinger, Ron	*Guide to Better Acol Bridge*	Victor Gollancz (London)	184	1988
Klinger, Ron (see Fransz, Alex)	*Medium Club Relay*			
Klinger, Ron (see Husband, Pat)	*Introduction to Acol Bidding: Task Masters Student Work Books by Master Teachers*			
Kornfield, Morris	*Bridge Player's Digest of Conventions*	Kornfeld (Warrington PA)	48	1962-68
Kushner, Jack	*The TNT System of Bidding*	Kushner	8	
Law, John (see Boland, Vincent)	*Accurate Contract Bidding*			
Lawrence, Mike	†*The Complete Book on Balancing in Contract Bridge*	Max Hardy	209	1981
Lawrence, Mike	‡*The Complete Book on Overcalls in Contract Bridge*	Max Hardy	202	1979

AUTHOR	TITLE	PUBLISHER	PAGES	DATES
Nilsland, Mats and Wirgren, Anders	*Major Suit Raises — the Scanian Way*	Scandia Bridgekonsult (Sweden)	53	1989
Noall, William	*Contract Bridge: The Australian One Club System*	Angus & Robertson (Sydney)	109	1959
Oakie, Don	*Simplified Standard American Bridge*	BPA (San Francisco)	339	1976
Pavlicek, Richard (see Root, William)	*†Modern Bridge Conventions*			
Pavlicek, Richard	*Competitive Bidding*	Pavlicek (Ft. Lauderdale FL)	14	1983
Pavlicek, Richard	*Standard Bridge*	Pavlicek (Ft. Lauderdale FL)	40	1985
Payne, Dick and Amsbury Joe	*Bridge: TNT and Competitive Bidding*	Batsford (London)	175	1981
Peche, George	*Interventions at the Bridge Table*	Peche (Dublin)	61	1986
Perkins, Frank	*Simplified Contract Standards*	Coffin (Fitzwilliam NH)	80	1939
Peterson, Olive (see Work, Milton)	*The Work-Peterson Accurate Valuation System*			
Radin, Judy (see Wei, Katherine)	*Precision's One Club Complete*			
Reed, Dick and Horn, Stormy	*The System — Bidding Techniques of Reed-Horn*	BPA (San Francisco)	51	1976
Reese, Terence	*‡Develop Your Bidding Judgement*	Sterling	254	1962
Reese, Terence	*Modern Bidding and the Acol System*	Nicholson & Watson (London)	128	1952-60
Reese-Terence (see Cohen, Ben)	*The Acol Systen of Contract Bridge*			
Reese, Terence and Dormer, Albert	**‡The Acol System Today*	E. Arnold (London)	163	1961
Reese, Terence and Dormer, Albert	**‡Blueprint for Bidding* (American title)	Sterling	163	1961
Reese, Terence	*What Would You Did?*	Faber & Faber (London)	160	1986
Reese, Terence & Bird, David	*All You Need to Know About Bidding*	Victor Gollancz (London)	128	1992
Reith, George	*Contract*	John Day	250	1929
Reith, Goerge	*Contract Bidding*	John Day	37	1930
Reith, George	*One over One System of Contract Bidding*	Knickerbocker	50	1932
Richards, Ralph (see Work, Milton)	*Common Sense Contract Bridge*			
Robinson, Steve	*"Washington" Standard*	Robinson (Arlington VA)	12	1991
Root, William	*Introduction to Bidding*	Prentice-Hall (Englewood Cliffs NJ)	151	1967
Root, William and Pavlicek, Richard	*†Modern Bridge Conventions*	Crown	244	1980
Root, William S.	*Commonsense Bidding*	Crown Publishers	216	1986
Rosen, Fern (see Cron, Bea)	*Advanced Bridge Five Card Major Student Text*			
Rosen, Fern (see Cron, Bea)	*Beginning Bridge Five Card Major Student Text*			
Rosen, Fern (see Cron, Bea)	*Intermediate Bridge Five Card Major Student Text*			
Rosenkranz, George	*Bridge: The Bidder's Game*	Devyn Press (Louisville KY)	489	1985
Rosenkranz, George	*Bid Your Way to the Top*	Chancellor Hall/Barclay	212	1978
Rosenkranz, George and Truscott, Alan	*†Modern Ideas in Bidding*	Devyn Press (Shelbyville KY)	236	1982
Rosenkranz, George	*The Romex System of Bidding*	World Publishing	325	1970
Rosenkranz, George	*‡Win With Romex*	Crown	402	1975
Rosenthal, Alvin S.	*Some Issues of Intermediate Bridge and the Montreal Relay Plus System*	Rosenthal (Silver Spring MD)	73	1992
Roth, Alvin	**Bridge Is a Partnership Game Revised Edition*	Granovetter Books (Ballston Lake NY)	251	1989
Roth, Alvin	**The Roth-Stone System*	Melville (Washington DC)	176	1953
Roth, Alvin and Rubens, Jeff	*†Modern Bridge Bidding Complete*	Funk & Wagnalls	512	1968
Roth, Alvin and Stone, Tobias	**‡Bridge Is a Partnership Game: the Roth-Stone System*	Dutton	237	1958

AUTHOR	TITLE	PUBLISHER	PAGES	DATES
Roth, Alvin	*Picture Bidding*	Granovetter Books (Ballston Lake NY)	317	1991
Rotzell, Peggy	*Bridge Bidding Complete*		43	
Rubens, Jeff (see Roth, Alvin)	*†Modern Bridge Bidding Complete*			
Ruminski, Stanislaw (see Slawinski, Lukosz)	*Introduction to Weak Opening Systems and Regres System*			
Sands, Norma	*Standard American Bridge Updated — Five-Card Majors*	Rocky Mountain Books (Denver)	85	1980
Sands, Norma & Janitschke, Jan	*Bridge — Double Trouble*	Devyn Press (Louisville KY)	24	1992
Sands, Norma & Janitschke, Jan	*Bridge — Competitive Bidding*	Devyn Press (Louisville KY)	24	1992
Sands, Norma & Janitschke, Jan	*Bridge — Later in the Auction*	Devyn Press (Louisville KY)	20	1992
Sands, Norma & Janitschke, Jan	*Bridge — Negative Doubles*	Devyn Press (Louisville KY)	21	1992
Sands, Norma & Janitschke, Jan	*Fine Tuning*	Rocky Mountain Books (Denver)	20	1992
Sands, Norma & Janitschke, Jan	*Slam Bidding*	Rocky Mountain Books (Denver)	24	1992
Sands, Norma & Janitschke, Jan	*Slam Bidding Part II*	Rocky Mountain Books (Denver)	23	1992
Sapire, Max	*Accurate Slam Bidding at Contract (Asking Bids)*	The Bridge World	63	1949
Schenken, Howard	**‡Better Bidding in Fifteen Minutes*	Simon & Schuster	192	1963
Schenken, Howard (see Four Aces)	**The Four Aces System of Contract Bridge*			
Schenken, Howard	*‡Howard Schenken's Big Club*	Simon & Schuster	224	1968
Senior, Brian	*The Multi-Colored 2♦*	Probray Press (Nottingham, England)	32	1982
Senior, Brian	*Balancing (after 1-level openings)*	Probray Press (Nottingham, England)	36	1986
Senior, Brian	*Bridge Conventions: Defending Against Pre-empts*	Probray Press (Nottingham, England)	32	1984
Senior, Brian	*Fourth Suit Forcing*	Probray Press (Nottingham, England)	32	1985
Senior, Brian	*The Transfer Principle*	Probray Press (Nottingham, England)	124	1986
Sharp, Richard (see Flint, Jeremy)	*Competitive Bidding*			
Sharif, Omar	*How To Play the Blue Team Club*	Stancraft Products (Minneapolis)	48	1969
Sheinwold, Alfred (see Kaplan, Edgar)	*Kaplan-Sheinwold System of Winning Bridge*			
Shepard, E. V.	*Correct Contract Bridge*	Doubleday	265	1929
Silodor, Sidney	*Silodor Says*	Pageant Press	240	1952
Silverman, Shirley (see Wei, C. C.)	*Official Precision Teacher's Manual*			
Simon, S. J.	*Design for Bidding*	Nicholson & Watson (London)	268	1949
Sims, Dorothy	*Psychic Bidding*	Vanguard Press	87	1932
Sims, P. Hal	**Master Contract*	Simon & Schuster	348	1934
Sims, P. Hal	**Money Contract*	Simon & Schuster	246	1932
Slawinski, Lukosz and Ruminski, Stanislaw	*Introduction to Weak Opening Systems and Regres System*	Slawinski (Warsaw, Poland)	102	1979
Slawinski, Lukosz	*The Singleton System "Delta"*	Slawinski (Warsaw, Poland)	30	1979
Smith, A. J. (see Stern, Paul)	*The Vienna System of Contract Bridge*			
Smith, Curtis	*Bidding Through Logic*	Curtis Smith (Houston)	185	1962
Smith, Curtis	*Bidding Throught Logic — Completely updated and conventionalized*	Baxter (Jefferson LA)	174	1981
Smith, F. D. and Braham, V. G.	*The Victorian Blackwood Slam Convention*	(Australia)	48	1939
Smokski, Charles	*Defenses to 1NT*	Probray Press (Nottingham, England)	32	1982
Solomon, Charles	*No Trump Bidding*	7 Stars (Woodstown NY)	49	1946

AUTHOR	TITLE	PUBLISHER	PAGES	DATES
Solomon, Charles Disbrow, Bennett	*Slam Bidding and Point Count*	Macrae Smith (Philadelphia)	281	1951
Sontag, Alan	*Power Precision*	Morrow	319	1979
Sowter, Sally	*Transfers After One No Trump*	Bridge Players Handbooks (Nottingham, England)	32	1980
Sowter, Tony	*The Takeout Double*	Bridge Players Handbooks (Nottingham, England)	32	1980
Squire, Norman	*Bidding at Bridge*	Penguin (London)	191	1965
Squire, Norman	*A Guide to Bridge Conventions*	Duckworth (London)	138 100	1958 1979
Squire, Norman	**†The Theory of Bidding*	Duckworth (London)	280	1957
Stallard, M. Berl	*Stallard's First Up* (presented by Terence Reese)	Berl & Helen Stallard (Miles City MT)	73	1978
Stayman, Samuel	**The Complete Stayman System of Contract Bidding*	Rinehart	223	1956
Stayman, Samuel	*‡Do You Play Stayman?*	Odyssey	207	1965
Stayman, Samuel	*Expert Bidding at Contract Bridge*	Wellington	144	1951
Stayman, Samuel	*Highroad to Winning Bridge* (reprint of *Do You Play Stayman?*)	Cornerstone Library	192	1970
Steen, Douglas (see Hanna, William)	*Precision Power Bidding: The Bulldog System*			
Stern, Paul	**The Stern Austrian System*	Harrap (London)	192	1938
Stern, Paul (see Butler, Geoffrey)	*Two Club System of Bidding*			
Stern, Paul et al	*The Vienna System of Contract Bridge*	Contract Bridge Equipment (Leeds)	249	1948
Stone, Tobias (see Roth, Alvin)	*Bridge Is a Partnership Game*			
Stucker, Robert (see Nail, G. R.)	*Revolution in Bridge*			
Sundby, Robert (see Cohen, Larry)	*†Breakthrough in Bridge*			
Sundby, Robert D.	*Bridge in the '80s*	Breakthrough Bridge Enterprises	571	1984
Truscott, Alan	*Doubles & Redoubles*	Times Books	152	1987
Truscott, Alan & Alder, Phillip	*On Bidding* (Revised & Updated "Morehead on Bidding")	Simon & Schuster	399	1990
Truscott, Alan and Dorothy	*Teach Yourself Basic Bidding*	Arco	270	1976
Vanderbilt, Harold	*†The Club Convention*	Scribner's	186	1964
Vanderbilt, Harold	**Contract Bridge: Bidding and the Club Convention*	Scribner's	251	1929
Vanderbilt, Harold	*The New Contract Bridge (Club Convention Bidding and Forcing Overbids)*	Scribner's	333	1930
Vickery, Ron	*The Hybrid Club, an Action System*	Vickery (Fountain Valley CA)	112	1981
Victor, A.D.J.	*Veejay System of Modern Bidding at Contract Bridge*	Devyn Press (Louisville KY)	268	1983
Von der Porten, Ron	*Introduction to Defensive Bidding*	Prentice-Hall (Englewood Cliffs NJ)	151	1967
Wallace, Charlton (see Balckwood, Easley)	*Blackwood Slam Bidding*			
Walshe, G. G. J.	*Count to Win at Bridge*	Ernest Benn (London)	147	1948
Walshe, G. G. J.	**Let's Play CAB*	Methuen (London)	71	1945
Warren, Mrs. Prescott and Boyden, Elizabeth	*Contract Bridge of 1929*	Garden City Press (Newton MA)	140	1928
Wei, C. C.	*Bidding Precisely*	Precision Headquarters	210	1974
Wei, C. C. and Andersen, Ron	*Bidding Precisely, Volume 2*	Monna Lisa Precision	159	1976
Wei, C. C. and Andersen, Ron	*Profits from Preempts: Bidding Precisely, Volume 3*	Monna Lisa Precision	162	1977
Wei, C. C. and Silverman, Shirley	*Official Precision Teacher's Manual*	Barclay	65	1972
Wei, C. C.	*†Precision Bidding in Bridge*	Barclay	112	1969

AUTHOR	TITLE	PUBLISHER	PAGES	DATES
Wei, C. C. (see Goren, Charles)	Precision Bridge for Everyone			
Wei, C. C.	The Simplified Precision System of Bridge Bidding	Precision Headquarters	64	1972
Wei, C. C. et al	Summary of the Super Precision System	Precision Headquarters	28	1974
Wei, Katherine and Andersen, Ron	Action for the Defense When the Enemy Opens the Bidding	Monna Lisa Precision	245	1980
Wei, Katherine and Radin, Judi	Precision's One Club Complete	Monna Lisa Precision	169	1981
Weiss, Larry	The Simplified Club	Weiss (Vista CA)	101	1989
Weiss, Lawrence	*Contract Bridge: The Bidding Structure	Garden Press (Newton MA)	376	1942
Winslow, T. N. and Anstett, Charles	Win with Winslow	Nascon	42	1933
Wirgren, Anders (see Nilsland, Mats)	Major Suit Raises — the Scanian Way			
Wirgren, Anders (see Lindkvist, Magnus)	Notrump Bidding — the Scanian Way; Swedish Expert Methods — Volume Two			
Wolf, Murray and Anderson, Merrell	The Subtle Club	Wand Books (Chelmsford MA)	187	1974
Wolff, Bobby & Musumeci, Joe	Jacoby Transfer Bids	Aces Publ. (Richardson TX)	26	1992
Wolff, Bobby & Musumeci, Joe	Limit Raises, Forcing Raises, Splinter Bids & the Forcing NT	Aces Publ. (Richardson TX)	23	1992
Wolff, Bobby & Musumeci, Joe	Negative Doubles, Responsive Doubles, Maximal Doubles	Aces Publ. (Richardson TX)	27	1992
Woodson, William	Woodson Electronic Bidding System	Greensboro Printing (NC)	63	1958
Woodson, William	Woodson Two-Way No Trump	Greensboro Printing (NC)	31	1953
Woolsey, Kit (see Baron, Randy)	Clobber Their Artificial Club			
Woolsey, Kit (see Baron, Randy)	Clobber Their Artificial Club (2nd edition, Revised)			
Work, Milton et al	Common Sense Contract Bridge	J. C. Winston (Philadelphia)	369	1931
Work, Milton and Peterson, Olive	The Work-Peterson Accurate Valuation System of Contract Bridge	J. C. Winston (Philadelphia)	101	1934
Wyman, Walter (see Work, Milton)	Common Sense Contract Bridge			
Yallouze, Leon (see Garozzo, Benito)	†The Blue Club			
ZYZ, Aba	Bridge Bidding Made Clear: Introducing the STEP System	Aba Zyz Books (Toronto)	359	1987

D PLAY

AUTHOR	TITLE	PUBLISHER	PAGES	DATES
Andersson, Ivar and Coffin, George	†Sure Tricks	Coffin (Fitzwilliam NH) David McKay	255 255	1948 1950
Baron, Randall &	The Bridge Student Text: Volume 4 — Defensive Play	Devyn Press (Louisville KY)	124	1990
Baron, Randall & Stewart, Frank	The Devyn Press Bridge Teacher's Manual: Volume 4 — Defense at Contract			
Baron, Randall (see Stewart, Frank)	The Bridge Book: Volume 4 — Defense at Contract Bridge (cover title "Defensive Play")			
Barrow, Rhoda (see Cohen, Ben)	Opening Leads to Better Bridge			
Barrow, Rhoda (see Cohen, Ben)	Your Lead, Partner			
Bellanger, Pierre and Roussière, C.	*Les Impasses au Bridge: Etude Scientifique et Solutions Pratiques de'apres une	Librairie Plon (Paris)	424	1936
Berthe, Robert and Lébely, Norbert	Bridge: Step by Step Card Play — No-Trumps (trans. by Barry Seabrook)	Batsford (London)	167	1981
Bird, David (see Reese, Terence)	Bridge — Tricks of the Trade			
Bird, David (see Reese, Terence)	The Hidden Side of Bridge			
Bird, David (see Reese, Terence)	How the Experts Do It: Improving your Bridge			

AUTHOR	TITLE	PUBLISHER	PAGES	DATES
Blackwood, Easley	†*The Complete Book of Opening Leads*	Devyn Press	475	1983
Blackwood, Easley	*Play of the Hand with Blackwood*	Pinnacle Books	458	1978
Blackwood, Easley & Hanson, Keith	*Card Play Fundamentals*	Devyn Press (Louisville KY)	114	1987
Brown, John	*‡Winning Defense*	Duckworth (London)	343	1952-60
Brown, John	*Winning Tricks*	Duckworth (London)	300	1947
Bruelheide, F. E.	*Fundamentals of Play*	Bruelheide (Minneapolis)	64	1939
Cayley, Frank	*Bridge Play Made Easy*	Reed (Sydney, Australia)	88	1980
Cayley, Frank	*Contract Bridge — Play*	Rigby (Australia)	64	1978
Cioffi, Raphael	*Bridge Endings*	Coffin (Boston)	127	1953
Coffin, George	†*Bridge Play Four Classics*	Duckworth (London)	960	1975
Coffin, George	*Bridge Play fron A to Z*	Faber & Faber (London)	352	1954
Coffin, George	**End Plays*	Duckworth (London)	212	1950
Coffin, George	*Endplays at Bridge Explained*	Bruce Humphries (Boston)	96	1932
Coffin, George (see Andersson, Ivar)	†*Sure Tricks*			
Cohen, Ben and Barrow, Rhoda	*Opening Leads to Better Bridge* (American Edition of *Your Lead, Partner*)	A. S. Barnes & Co.	96	1964
Cohen, Ben and Barrow, Rhoda	*Your Lead, Partner*	Allen & Unwin (London)	96	1964
Cohen, Ruth	*The Elements of Play*	Barclay	63	1958-61
Cohn, Judy & Fink, Jerry	*Power Defensive Carding*	Devyn Press (Louisville KY)	204	1988-89
Cotter, Pat and Rimington, Derek	*The Country Life Book of Bridge Play Technique*	Country Life Books (London)	176	1982
Courtenay, F. Dudley	*Standard Manual on Play*	Methuen (London)	95	1938
Cox, Jean	*Bridge with Jean Cox — The Play*	Cox (Pittsburgh)	54	1964
Culbertson, Ely	**Contract Bridge Red Book on Play*	J. C. Winston (Philadelphia)	616	1934
Culbertson, Ely	*How to Lead and Play: Self Instructor*	The Bridge World	64	1934
Donnelly, John	*Happiness Is a Squeeze*	Vantage	121	1972
Dormer, Albert (see Reese, Terence)	*The Play of the Cards*			
Duke, Dan J.	*Defensive Play of the Hand*	Duke (Boone NC)	152	1990
Duke, Dan J.	*The Play of the Hand*	Duke (Boone NC)	150	1990
Eng, Fook	†*Bridge Squeezes Illustrated*	Eng	185	1973
England, Frank and Reford, Hope	*The Play of the Cards*	Thos. De La Rue (London)	223	1934
Ewen, Robert	*‡Opening Leads*	Prentice-Hall (Englewood Cliffs NJ)	226	1970
Flint, Jeremy and Greenwood, David	*Instructions for the Defense*	Bodley Head (London)	125	1980
Flint, Jeremy and North, Freddie	*Match Your Skill against the Masters*	Stein & Day	208	1972
Fox, G. C. H.	*Bridge: The Elements of Play*	Robert Hale (London)	176	1980
Fox, G. C. H.	*Bridge: The Elements of Defence*	Robert Hale (London)	171	1984
Freehill, H. G.	*The Squeeze at Bridge*	Faber & Faber (London)	126	1949
Gardener, Nico (see Mollo, Victor)	‡*Card Play Technique*			
Goren, Charles	*Better Bridge for Better Players*	Doubleday	538	1942
Goren, Charles	‡*Goren on Play and Defense*	Doubleday	489	1974
Grant, Audrey	*ACBL Introduction to Bridge: Defense "Heart Series"*	ACBL (Memphis)	316	1989
Grant, Audrey	*ACBL Introduction to Bridge: Play of the Hand "Diamond Series"*	ACBL (Memphis)	224	1990
Hanson, Keith (see Blackwood, Easley)	*Card Play Fundamentals*			
Hathorn, John (see Nail, G. R.)	*How to Play the Hand*			

AUTHOR	TITLE	PUBLISHER	PAGES	DATES
Hathorn, John	It's Your Lead	Texas Bridge (Houston)	34	1958
Hathorn, John	Your Best Defense	Adams Press (Chicago)	40	1960
Hayden, Dorothy	Winning Declarer Play	Harper & Row	280	1969
Hoffman, Martin	Defense in Depth	Faber & Faber	144	1985
Husband, Pat & Klinger, Ron	Play Your Cards Right	Victor Gollancz (London)	24	1989
International Popular Bridge Monthly	The IPBM Book of Suit Combinations	Probray Press (Nottingham, England)	32	1984
Jannersten, Eric	†Cards on the Table Card Reading (American title)	Allen-Unwin (London) Hart	207 207	1972 1972
Janitschke, Jan (see Sands, Norma)	Defensive Signals			
Janitschke, Jan (see Sands, Norma)	Opening Leads Versus Suits			
Jourdain, Patrick (see Reese, Terence)	Squeeze Play Made Easy			
Kantar, Edwin	‡Complete Defensive Bridge Play	Wilshire Books (North Hollywood CA)	528	1974
Kantar, Edwin (see Reese, Terence)	Defend with Your Life			
Kantar, Edwin	Defensive Play	Kantar (Los Angeles)	47	1965
Kantar, Edwin and Stanley Jackson	Gamesman Bridge	Liveright	177	1972
Kantar, Edwin	Introduction to Declarer's Play	Prentice-Hall (Englewood Cliffs NJ)	147	1967
Kantar, Edwin	Introduction to Defender's Play	Prentice-Hall (Englewood Cliffs NJ)	153	1968
Kantar, Edwin	Play of the Hand Complete	Kantar (Los Angeles)	62	1965
Karpin, Fred Karpin, Fred	†The Art of Card Reading The Drawing of Trumps and Its Postponement	Harper & Row Max Hardy	232 178	1973 1981
Karpin, Fred	‡The Finesse	Prentice-Hall (Englewood Cliffs NJ)	273	1972
Karpin, Fred	How to Play and Misplay Slam Contracts	Harper & Bros	171	1962
Karpin, Fred	How to Play Slam Contrcts (reprint of How to Play and Misplay Slam Contracts)	Collier	191	1964
Karpin, Fred	‡The Play of the Cards	Bridge Quarterly (Chestnut Hill MA)	506	1958
Karpin, Fred	†Winning Play in Contract Bridge: Strategy at Trick one	Dell	288	1964
Kelsey, H.W.	*‡Advanced Play at Bridge	Hart	192	1968
Kelsey, H.W.	Countdown to Better Bridge	Devyn Press (Louisville KY)	184	1986
Kelsey, H.W.	Slam Bidding			
Kelsey, Hugh	Double Squeezes	Victor Gollancz (London)	125	1987
Kelsey, Hugh	Improve Your Partner's Defence	Victor Gollancz (London)	124	1988
Kelsey, Hugh	Simple Squeezes	Victor Gollancz (London)	120	1985, 1993
Kelsey, Hugh	Strip-Squeezes	Victor Gollancz (London)	120	1987
Kelsey, Hugh	Triple Squeezes	Victor Gollancz (London)	120	1990
Kelsey, Hugh (See Novrup, Svend)	First Steps in Card Play			
Kelsey, Hugh (see Ottlik, Géza)	*Adventures in Card Play			
Kelsey, H. W.	Bridge: The Mind of the Expert	Faber & Faber (London)	160	1981
Kelsey, H. W. and Glauert, Michael	*Bridge Odds for Practical Players	Victor Gollancz (London)	125	1980
Kelsey, H. W. and Matheson, John	Improve Your Opening Leads	Victor Gollancz (London)	124	1979
Kelsey, H. W.	*‡Killing Defense at Bridge	Hart	192	1967
Kelsey, H. W.	†More Killing Defense	Hart	92	1972
Kelsey, Hugh	The Tricky Game	Max Hardy	198	1982
Kelsey, Hugh	Winning Card Play	Victor Gollancz (London)	234	1979
King, Jack	Squeeze in Valhalla	Carlton Press	300	1964

AUTHOR	TITLE	PUBLISHER	PAGES	DATES
Klinger, Ron	*Bridge Without Error*	Victor Gollancz (London)	128	1981
Klinger, Ron (see Husband, Pat)	*Play Your Cards Right*			
Lampert, Harry	*Declarer Play & Opening Leads*	Lampert (Deerfield Beach FL)	207	1988
Lampert, Harry	*Teacher's Guide*	Lampert (Deerfield Beach FL)	11	1988
Lavinthal, Hy	*†Defense Tricks*	Coffin (Waltham MA)	192	1963
Lawrence, Mike	*Falsecards*	Devyn Press (Louisville KY)	215	1986
Lawrence, Mike	*How to Play Card Combinations*	Devyn Press (Louisville KY)	227	1988
Lawrence, Mike	*†Dynamic Defense*	Devyn Press (Louisville KY)	226	1982
Lawrence, Mike	*‡How to Read Your Opponent's Cards*	Prentice-Hall (Englewood Cliffs NJ)	175	1973
Lébely, Norbert (see Berthe, Robert)	*Bridge: Step by Step Card Play — No-Trumps*			
Love, Clyde	*‡Bridge Squeezes Complete*	Barclay / Dover	260 / 260	1959 / 1968
Love, Clyde	*Squeeze Play in Bridge*	R. R. Smith	183	1951
Mallon, John	*How to Play Your Cards When You Are the Declarer at Contract Bridge*	Chilton Book Co. (Radnor PA)	119	1976
Mallon, John	*Opening Leads and Signals in Contract Bridge*	Collier (London)	158	1969
Marston, Paul	*Contract Bridge: The Principles of Card Play*	Hamilton Pub. (Northbridge, Australia)	263	1986
Miles, Marshall	*All 52 Cards*	Exposition Press	142	1963-83
Miles, Marshall	*All Fifty-Two Cards*	C & T Bridge Supplies (Los Alamitos CA)	223	1992
Mollo, Victor and Gardener, Nico	*‡Card Play Technique*	Geo. Newnes, Ltd. (London)	381	1955-67
Nail, G. R. and Hathorn, John	*How to Play the Hand*	Texas Bridge (Houston)	73	1961
Nielsen, Aksel	*Focus on Bridge Defense*	Kaye & Ward (London)	196	1980
North, Freddie (see Flint, Jeremy)	*Match Your Skill against the Masters*			
Novrup, Svend and Kelsey, Hugh	*First Steps in Card Play*	Victor Gollancz (London)	64	1989
Ottlik, Géza and Kelsey, Hugh	*Adventures in Card Play*	Victor Gollancz (London)	285	1979
Parson, Donald	*Fall of the Cards*	Little, Brown (Boston)	280	1959
Pavlicek, Richard	*Play and Defense at Bridge*	Pavlicek	20	1976
Pavlicek, Richard	*Squeezes & Endplays*	Pavlicek (Fort Lauderdale FL)	22	1983
Payne, R.J.	*Bridge: Single Dummy Problems*	Robert Hale (London)	197	1984
Perkins, Frank	*Vital Tricks at Contract Bridge*	Joiner & Steele (London)	96	1953
Pottage, Julian (see Reese, Terence)	*Positive Declarer's Play*			
Pottage, Julian (see Reese, Terence)	*Positive Defence*			
Reese, Terence & Bird, David	*Bridge — Tricks of the Trade*	Victor Gollancz (London)	144	1989
Reese, Terence & Bird, David	*The Hidden Side of Bridge*	Faber & Faber (London)	136	1988
Reese, Terence & Bird, David	*How the Experts Do It: Improving your Bridge*	Faber & Faber (London)	215	1985
Reese, Terence & Pottage Julian	*Positive Declarer's Play*	Victor Gollancz (London)	128	1986
Reese, Terence & Pottage Julian	*Positive Defence*	Victor Gollancz (London)	128	1985
Reese, Terence and Trézel, Roger	*The Art of Defense in Bridge*	Frederick Fell	79	1979
Reese, Terence and Trézel, Roger	*Blocking and Unblocking Plays in Bridge*	Frederick Fell	64	1976
Reese, Terence and Kantar, Edwin	*Defend with Your Life*	Faber & Faber (London)	160	1981
Reese, Terence and Trézel, Roger	*Elimination Play in Bridge*	Frederick Fell	77	1977

AUTHOR	TITLE	PUBLISHER	PAGES	DATES
Reese, Terence	*‡The Expert Game Master Play (American title)	E. Arnold (London) Coffin (Waltham MA)	190 144	1958 1960
Reese, Terence and Trézel, Roger	Master the Odds in Bridge	Frederick Fell	79	1979
Reese, Terence and Dormer, Albert	The Play of the Cards	Penquin (Middlesex, England)	269	1967
Reese, Terence	*‡Play Bridge with Reese	Sterling	251	1960
Reese, Terence	*†Reese on Play	E. Arnold (London)	232	1947-75
Reese, Terence and Trézel, Roger	Safety Plays in Bridge	Frederick Fell	63	1976
Reese, Terence and Trézel, Roger	Snares and Swindles in Bridge	Frederick Fell	63	1977
Reese, Terence and Jourdain, Patrick	Squeeze Play Made Easy	Sterling	145	1980
Reese, Terence and Trézel, Roger	Those Extra Chances in Bridge	Frederick Fell	64	1978
Reese, Terence and Trézel, Roger	When to Duck, When to Win in Bridge	Frederick Fell	64	1978
Reford, Hope (see England, Frank)	The Play of the Cards			
Rimington, Derek (see Cotter, Pat)	The Country Life Book of Bridge Play Technique			
Romanet, Bertrand	*Le Squeeze au Bridge	Grasset (Paris)	414	1954
Root, William S.	How to Play a Bridge Hand	Crown Publishers	309	1990
Rosencrans	Squeezes, Coups, and End Plays	Rosencrans Publishing Co.	68	1965
Rosenkranz, George	Everything You Always Wanted to Know about Trump Leads and Were Not Afraid to Ask	Devyn Press (Louisville KY)	158	1986
Rosler, Lawrence & Rubens, Jeff	Journalist Leads	Pando Publications (Roswell GA)	198	1988
Roth, D. L. M.	Clues to Winning Play: Detective Work in Bridge	Victor Gollancz (London)	136	1987
Roth, Danny	Signal Success in Bridge	Victor Gollancz (London)	142	1989
Rotzell, Peggy	Bridge Play and Defense			
Roussière, C. (see Bellanger, Pierre)	Les Impasses au Bridge			
Rovere, Ernest	Leads, Signals and Discards in Contract Bridge	Call Bulletin (San Francisco)	36	1941
Sands, Norma	Playing the Cards: developing competence at the bridge table	Rocky Mountain Books (Denver)	127	1984
Sands, Norma & Janitschke, Jan	Defensive Signals	Devyn Press (Louisville KY)	23	1992
Sands, Norma & Janitschke, Jan	Opening Leads Versus Suits	Rocky Mountain Books (Denver)	20	1992
Schuld, Frank	The Simple Squeeze on Bridge	Drake	223	1974-77
Seabrook, Barry	Bridge: Expert Dummy Play	Batsford (London)	175	1981
Senior, Brian	Begin Declarer Play	Probray Press (Nottingham, England)	32	1985
Senior, Brian	Clever Bridge Tricks	Faber & Faber (London)	170	1988
Sheinwold, Alfred	Second Book of Bridge: The Play of the Hand	Sterling	159	1953
Sheinwold, Alfred	A Short Cut to Winning Bridge	Fleet	160	1961
Shows, George A.	Slam Bidding: Swinging Bridge Vol IV	Shows (San Fernando CA)	465	1987
Silverman, Shirley	Play of the Hand as Declarer and Defender	Baron/Barclay (Louisville KY)	64	1980
Smith, A. J.	Handbook of Safety Plays	Smith (England)	78	
Smith, Forrest G.	The Elementary Squeeze	The Canterbury Press (North Haven CT)	54	1989
Smith, Forrest G.	Sixty Hands Through the Mind of the Declarer	The Canterbury Press (North Haven CT)	92	1984
Sowter, Tony	Bridge: Improve Your Defense	Batsford (London)	168	1979
Squire, Norman	Contract Bridge Card Play Technique	Pitman (London)	145	1976
Squire, Norman	Contrct Bridge — Squeeze Play Simplified	Duckworth (London)	184	1979

AUTHOR	TITLE	PUBLISHER	PAGES	DATES
Stanley, Jackson (see Kantar, Edwin)	*Gamesman Bridge*			
Stewart, Frank	*The Bridge Player's Comprehensive Guide to Defense*	Dodd, Mead & Co. (NY)	404	1988
Stewart, Frank	*Winning Defense For the Advancing Bridge Player*	Prentice-Hall (Englewood Cliffs NJ)	324	1985
Stewart, Frank & Baron, Randall	*The Bridge Book: Volume 4 - Defense at Contract Bridge* (cover title *Defensive Play*)	Devyn Press (Louisville KY)	191	1990
Stewart, Frank (see Baron, Randall)	*The Bridge Student Text: Volume 4 - Defensive Play*			
Stewart, Frank (see Baron, Randall)	*The Devyn Press Bridge Teacher's Manual: Volume 4 - Defense at Contract Bridge*			
Sydnor, Caroline	*Bridge Made Easy — Book Four: How to Set Your Opponents*	Sydnor (Alexandria VA)	358	1992
Trézel, Roger (see Reese, Terence)	*The Art of Defense in Bridge*			
Trézel, Roger (see Reese, Terence)	*Blocking and Unblocking Plays in Bridge*			
Trézel, Roger	*Cahiers de Bridge*	Trézel (Paris)		1956-64
Trézel, Roger (see Reese, Terence)	*Elimination Play in Bridge*			
Trézel, Roger (see Reese, Terence)	*Master the Odds in Bridge*			
Trézel, Reese (see Reese, Terence)	*Safety Plays in Bridge*			
Trézel, Roger (see Reese, Terence)	*Snares and Swindles in Bridge*			
Trézel, Roger (see Reese, Terence)	*Those Extra Chances in Bridge*			
Trézel, Roger (see Reese, Terence)	*When to Duck When to Win In Bridge*			
Traub, Alec	*†Trump Technique*	Traub (Cape Town)	363	1981
Victor, A.	*Effective Defense at Contract Bridge*	Victor (New Delhi, India)	217	1982
Vinje, Helge	**Defensive Play in Bridge*	Sterling	184	1980
Walshe, G. G. J.	*Slams Made Simple — How to Use Cue Bids*	Methuen (London)	67	1938
Watson, Louis	**Play of the Hand at Contract Bridge*	Copeland	492	1934
Watson, Louis	*Watson's Classic Book on the Play of the Hand at Bridge* (edited and modernized by Sam Fry, Jr.)	Sterling	475	1958
Wolfe, Edward	*The Play of the Cards at Contract Bridge*	J. C. Winston (Philadelphia)	251	1932-34
Woolsey, Kit	*†Modern Defensive Signaling in Contract Bridge*	Barclay	64	1981
Woolsey, Kit	*‡Partnership Defense in Bridge*	Devyn Press	303	1980

E BIDDING & PLAY (in combination)

AUTHOR	TITLE	PUBLISHER	PAGES	DATES
Abrahams, Gerald	*Brains in Bridge*	Constable (London) Horizon Press	262 261	1964 1964
Adams, Charles True	*Contract Bridge Standardized*	Adams (Chicago)	73	1928
Albarran, Pierre	*Encyclopédie du Bridge Moderne*	Librairie Arthème Fayard (Paris)	800	1957
Albarran, Pierre and Jaïs, Pierre	*How to Win at Rubber Bridge*	Barrie Books (London)	191	1961
Albarran, Pierre and de Nexon, R.	*Notre Methods de Bridge*	Grasset (Paris)	313	1935
Alder, Phillip (see Rosenkranz, George)	*Bid to Win Play For Pleasure*			
Alder, Phillip	*You Can Play Bridge*	Thames Methiren (London)	214	1983
Bailey, Maureen O'Brien and Oeschger, Ivy	*Bridge for the Joneses*	Morrow	331	1947
Barclay, Shepard	*Learn Bridge Fast*	David McKay (Philadelphia)	125	1944-50
Baron, Randall & Stewart, Frank	*The Bridge Student Text: Volume I — For Beginning Players*	Devyn Press (Louisville KY)	127	1988

AUTHOR	TITLE	PUBLISHER	PAGES	DATES
Baron, Randall & Stewart, Frank	*The Bridge Student Text: Volume II — For Intermediate Players*	Devyn Press (Louisville KY)	143	1988
Baron, Randall & Stewart, Frank	*The Bridge Student Text: Volume III — For Advanced Players*	Devyn Press (Louisville KY)	127	1989
Baron, Randall & Stewart, Frank	*The Devyn Press Bridge Teacher's Manual: Volume I — For Beginning Players*	Devyn Press (Louisville KY)	142	1988
Baron, Randall & Stewart, Frank	*The Devyn Press Bridge Teacher's Manual: Volume II — For Intermediate Players*	Devyn Press (Louisville KY)	145	1988
Baron, Randall & Stewart, Frank	*The Devyn Press Bridge Teacher's Manual: Volume III — For Advanced Players*	Devyn Press (Louisville KY)	141	1989
Baron, Randall (see Stewart, Frank)	*The Bridge Book: Volume 1 — For Beginning Players*			
Baron, Randall (see Stewart, Frank)	*The Bridge Book: Volume 2 — For Intermediate Players*			
Baron, Randall (see Stewart, Frank)	*The Bridge Book: Volume 3 — For Advanced Players*			
Barrow, Rhoda (see Cohen, Ben)	*ABC of Contract Bridge*			
Bird, David (see Reese, Terence)	*Bridge: The Modern Game*			
Blackwood, Easley	*Bridge Humanics*	Droke House (Indianapolis)	255	1949
Blackwood, Easley	*How You Can Play Winning Bridge with Blackwood*	Pinnacle Books (Los Angeles)	281	1977
Bonney, Jack	*Master Bridge Teaching Guide*	Barclay	128	1957
Brannon, Robert Means	*Fool Proof Contract*	R. M. Brannon	169	1930-33
Buller, Lt. Col. Walter	*How to Play Contract Bridge*	*The Star* (London)	144	1932
Buller, Lt. Col. Walter	*Reflections of a Bridge Player*	Methuen (London)	197	1929
Cederborg, Warren (compiler)	*Coffee with Mary Jane (Farell)*	BPA (San Francisco)	197	1974
Chase, Stephen (see Gooden, George)	*Contract Bridge Advanced Lesson Course*			
Coffin, George	*Learn Bridge the Easy Way*	C. Branford (Boston)	128	1950
Cohen, Ben and Barrow, Rhoda	*ABC of Contract Bridge*	Anthony Blond (London)	288	1964
Cook, D. J.	*Cook and Deal*	D. J. Cook (Vero Beach FL)	210	1982
Cook, D. J.	*Learn to Play Winning Bridge*	D. J. Cook (Wilmette IL)	85	1962-67
Cook, D. J.	*Cook & Deal II — A collection of winning recipes and winning bridge hands*	Cook (Vero Beach FL)	28	1988
Cook, Mary	*Confessions of a Bridge Addict*	Mary Cook (Twin Falls ID)	215	1979
Cooper, Joan	*Bridge Basics*	Coles (Toronto)	152	1976
Cotter, E. P. C.	*The Financial Times Book of Bridge*	Robert Hale (London)	176	1977
Courtenay, F. Dudley	*Standardized Contract Bridge Complete*	Bartholomew	160	1941
Crawford, John	*Crawford's Contract Bridge*	Grosset & Dunlap	367	1953
Crawford, Richard	*Men, Women and Bridge*	Sterling	191	1978
Crawford, Richard	*People Play Bridge*	Vantage Press	167	1976
Cromelin, Paul	*Bridge Is Beautiful*	Cromelin (Savannah GA)	400	1977
Culbertson, Ely	**Contract Bridge Complete: Gold Book of Bidding and Play*	J. C. Winston (Philadelphia)	603	1936-54
Culbertson, Ely	*Contract Bridge for Everyone*	J. C. Winston (Philadelphia)	118	1948
Culbertson, Ely	*The Official Book of Contract Birdge*	J. C. Winston (Philadelphia)	399	1944
Culbertson, Josephine	*Contract Bride for Beginners*	J. C. Winston (Philadelphia)	221	1938-49
de Satnick, Shelly	*Bridge for Everyone: A Step-by-Step Text and Workbook*	Avon	152	1982
Dormer, Albert (see Reese, Terence)	*The Bridge Player's Alphabetical Handbook*			
Dormer, Albert (see Reese, Terence)	*‡Complete Book of Bridge*			
Dormer,. Albert (see Reese, Terence)	*†How to Play a Better Game of Bridge*			

AUTHOR	TITLE	PUBLISHER	PAGES	DATES
Ellison, Don (see Goodwin, Jude)	Teach Me to Play: a First Book of Bridge			
Erdos, Ivan	Bridge-a-la-Carte	American Press (Los Angeles)	232	1966
Ewen, Robert	The Teenager's Guide to Bridge	Dodd, Mead	214	1976
Ewen, Robert	Contract Bridge: How to Improve Your Technique	Franklin Watts	64	1975
Feldheim, Harold	Negative and Responsive Doubles In Bridge	Barclay	64	1980
Flint, Jeremy	Tiger Bridge	Simon & Schuster	192	1970
Flint, Jeremy and Gullick, John	The First Bridge Book	Pan Books (London)	223	1984
Flint, Jeremy and North, Freddie	Bridge: The First Principles	Pan Books (London)	224	1979, 1985
Forquet, Pietro	Bridge with the Blue Team	A. B. Publications (Sydney, Australia)	384	1983
Foster, Robert F.	Foster's Contract Bridge	Greenberg	121	1927
Fox, G. C. H.	Begin Bridge	Elliot Rightway (Surrey, England)	125	1973
Fox, Gerald (see Lawrence, Mike)	Introduction to Contract Bridge and Point Count Bidding			
Franklin, Harold (see Reese, Terence)	The Listener Book of Bridge — Best of Bridge on the Air			
Frey, Richard	How to Win at Contract in Ten Easy Lessons	Fawcett Pub.	288	1961-72
Fry, Sam Jr.	Better Bridge	Leisure League	109	1935
Fry, Sam Jr.	How to Win at Bridge with Any Partner	Golden Press	144	1960
Gardener, Nico (see Mollo, Victor)	Bridge for Beginners			
Goldstein, Abraham	Common-Sense Bridge for the Intermediate Player	Arco	80	1959
Gooden, George et al	Contract Bridge Advanced Lesson Course	Int'l Society of Bridge Teachers (Carmel CA)	138	1972
Gooden, George	Contract Bridge, Bidding and Play	G. S. Gooden (Carmel CA)	150	1969
Gooden George	Contract Bridge Lesson Course	G. S. Gooden (Carmel CA)	121	1960-78
Gooden, George	Contract Birdge Teacher's Blue Book	G. S. Gooden (Carmel CA)	200	1967
Goodwin, Jude	Let's Play Cards	Devyn Press (Louisville KY)	102	1989
Goodwin, Jude & Ellison, Don	Teach Me to Play: a First Book of Bridge	Pando Publications (Roswell GA)	195	1988
Gordon, Betty	Bridge Basics	Gordon (Winnetka IL)	42	1988
Goren, Charles	*Contract Bridge Complete	Doubleday	498	1951-57
Goren Charles	Contract Bridge in a Nutshell	Doubleday	128	1946-72
Goren, Charles	Contract Birdge Made Easy	Doubleday	96	1948
Goren, Charles	The Elements of Bridge	Doubleday	420	1960
Goren, Charles	‡Goren's Bridge Complete	Doubleday	562	1963
Goren, Charles (with Sharif, Omar)	Goren's Bridge Complete	Doubleday	706	1980
Goren, Charles	Goren's Easy Steps to Winning Bridge	Franklin Watts	287	1963
Goren, Charles	Goren's Winning Partnership Bridge	Random House	183	1961
Grant, Audrey	Bridge: Official American Contract Bridge League: Introductory Bridge Course "Club Series"	ACBL (Memphis)	240	1989
Grant, Audrey	Introduction to Bridge Bidding "Club Series" Teacher's Manual	ACBL Dept. of Education (Memphis)	132	1989
Grant, Audrey	Teacher's Manual for the ACBL "Club Series"	ACBL (Memphis)	106	1987
Grant, Audrey & Rodwell, Eric	Bridge Maxims: Secrets of Better Play	Prentice-Hall Press (NY)	239	1987
Grant, Audrey & Rodwell, Eric	The Joy of Bridge	Arco Publishing	322	1984
Grant, Audrey & Rodwell, Eric	The Joy of Bridge Workbook	Joy of Bridge (Toronto)	67	1984
Griffiths, David (see Lederer, Rhoda)	Winnning Ways at Bridge			

|--------|-------|-----------|-------|-------|
Gullick, John (see Flint, Jeremy)	*The First Bridge Book*			
Hanson, Keith (see Lawrence, Mike)	*Winning Bridge Intangibles*			
Harkness, Kenneth	*Invitation to Bridge*	Simon & Schuster	306	1950
Hathorn, John	*The Secrets of Tactical Bridge*	Texas Bridge (Houston)	85	1961
Hiron, Alan & Maureen	*Beginning Bridge*	Crowood Press (Swindon, England)	159	1989
Hiron, Alan & Maureen	*The 11+ Bridge Book (Young Master Series)*	Crowood Press (Swindon, England)	144	1983
Hiron, Maureen (see Hiron, Alan)	*Beginning Bridge*			
Hiron, Maureen (see Hiron, Alan)	*The 11+ Bridge Book (Young Master Series)*			
Ingram, H. St. John	*How to Win at Bridge*	Eyre & Spottiswoode (London)	126	1950
International Bridge Academy	**Annals (trans. by Alec Traub) — Volume 1* *— Volume 2*	(Brussels)	88 103	1966 1969
Jacoby, James	*Jacoby on Bridge*	Pharos Books	208	1987
Jacoby, James (see Jacoby, Oswald)	*Improve Your Bridge with Oswald Jacoby*			
Jacoby, Oswald & James	*Improve Your Bridge with Oswald Jacoby*	McGraw-Hill (NY)	140	1983
Jacoby, Oswald & James	*Win at Bridge with Jacoby and Son*	G. P. Putnam's Sons	222	1966
Jacoby, Oswald & James	*Win at Bridge with Jacoby Modern*	Enterprise Publications	128	1970
Jaïs, Pierre	*Apprendez à Mieux Jouer au Bridge*	Julliard (Paris)	582	1957
Jaïs, Pierre (see Albarran, Pierre)	*How to Win at Rubber Bridge*			
Jourdain, Patrick	*Play the Game: Bridge*	Ward Lock (London)	80	1990
Kantar, Edwin	*Kantar Lessons*	Kantar (Venice CA)	ca. 400	1988
Kantar, Edwin	*Kantar Lessons II*	Kantar (Venice CA)	ca. 400	1989
Kantar, Edwin	*A Treasury of Bridge Tips*	Harland Publishing (Santa Ana CA)	163	1992
Kantar, Edwin	*Beginner's Lessons*	Kantar (Los Angeles)	50	1965
Kantar, Edwin	*A Comprehensive Bridge Manual*	Kantar (Los Angeles)	143	1965
Kaplan, Edgar	**‡Winning Contract Bridge Complete*	Fleet	434	1964
Kaplan, Jim	*Raising Your Bridge*	Devyn Press (Louisville KY)	177	1993
Karn, Willard	*Karn's Bridge Service*	Long & Smith	361	1933
Karpin, Fred	*Psychological Strategy in Contract Bridge*	Harper	325	1960
Kearse, Amalya	*‡Bridge Conventions Complete*	Hart	624	1975
Kearse, Amalya	*Bridge at Your Fingertips*	Hart	320	1979
Kelsey, H.W.	*101 Bridge Maxims*	Devyn Press (Louisville KY)	209	1983
Kelsey, H. W.	*Improve Your Bridge*	Hart	191	1971
Kelsey, Hugh	*Start Bridge the Easy Way*	Victor Gollancz (London)	96	1988
Kempson, Ewart	*Contract Bridge, How to Play it*	Emerson Books (London)	164	1957
Kempson, Ewart	*Kempson on Contract — How to Win at*	Hodder & Stoughton (London)	180	1935
Kerwin, Madeleine	*Partnership Contract*	William Morrow	180	1934
Kleinman, Danny	*Advice to the Bridgelorn*	Kleinman (Los Angeles)	152	1981
Kleinman, Danny	*Bridge in the Real World*	Kleinman (Los Angeles)	217	1983
Kleinman, Danny	*Bridge in the Tower of Babel*	Kleinman (Los Angeles)	358	1989
Kleinman, Danny	*Bridge in Theory and Practice*	Kleinman (Los Angeles)	190	1986
Kleinman, Danny	*Drumming Bridge Basics into the Head*	Kleinman (Los Angeles)	156	1983
Kleinman, Danny	*Review, Please*	Kleinman (Los Angeles)	416	1987
Klinger, Ron	*100 Winning Bridge Tips*	Houghton Mifflin	128	1992
Klinger, Ron	*Bridge for Children Featuring the No-Frills* *System of Bidding*	Modern Bridge Publications (Northbridge, Australia)	96	1980
Klinger, Ron	*Bridge Made Easy*	Modern Bridge Publications (Sydney, Australia)	92	1985

AUTHOR	TITLE	PUBLISHER	PAGES	DATES
Klinger, Ron	*Improve Your Bridge Memory*	Victor Gollancz (London)	93	1984
Klinger, Ron	*Ron Klinger's Guide to Better Bridge*	Modern Bridge Publications (Sydney, Australia)	184	1987
Klinger, Ron	*Basic Bridge — A Guide to Good Acol*	Ward Lock (London)	127	1978
Klinger, Ron	*Bridge Basics*	Reldt (Australia)	118	1971
Lagron, E. M.	*Defensive Bridge*	Bobbs-Merrill (Indianapolis)	162	1933
Lampert, Harry	*The Fun Way to Learn Serious Bridge*	Hardel (Roslyn NY)	136	1978
Lampert, Harry	*The Fun Way to Advanced Bridge*	Simon & Schuster	158	1985
Lawrence, Mike	*Topics on Bridge*	Lawrence	347	1990
Lawrence, Mike and Fox, Gerald	*Introduction to Contract Bridge and Point Count Bidding*	Bridge-O-Matic (Inglewood CA)	32	1975
Lawrence, Mike	*Judgment at Bridge*	Max Hardy	151	1976
Lawrence, Mike	*Play a Swiss Teams of Four with Mike Lawrence*	Max Hardy	99	1982
Lawrence, Mike and Hanson, Keith	*Winning Bridge Intangibles*	Devyn Press (Louisville KY)	57	1985
Le Dentu, José	*Bridge Analysis* (trans. & ed. by Amalya Kearse)	Hart	287	1978
Le Dentu, José	*Bridge Facile*	Fayard (Paris)	446	1970
Lederer, Rhoda & Griffiths, David	*Winnning Ways at Bridge*	Unwin (London)	184	1987
Lederer, Richard	*Modern Contract & Duplicate*	Williams & Norgate (London)	149	1936
Lederer, Tony and Rhoda	*Learn Bridge with the Lederers*	Cassell (London)	202	1977
Lenz, Sidney	*Lenz on Contract Birdge*	Simon & Schuster	131	1927-29
Liggett, Winfield Jr	*Contract Dridge Summary: Official System*	Stokes	20	1931
Lipkin, Mike Lukacs, Paul (see Milnes, Eric)	*Invitation to ... Annihilation Learn to Play Bridge*	Devyn Press (Louisville KY)	144	1991
MacLeod, Ian	*Bridge Is an Easy Game*	Falcon Press (London) Victor Gollancz (London)	244 215	1952 1980
Markus, Rixi	*Common Sense Bridge*	Random House	171	1973
Markus, Rixi	*Improve Your Bridge*	Bodley Head (London)	104	1979
Markus, Rixi	*Play Better Bridge*	Octopus Books (London)	157	1979
Markus, Rixi	*The Rixi Markus Book of Bridge*		208	1985
Markus, Rixi (see Reese, Terence)	*Better Bridge for Club Players*			
Marston, Paul & Brightling, Richard	*The Bridge Workbook for Beginners*	Contract Dridge Supplies (Northbridge, Australia)	137	1985
Mayer, Edward	*Money Bridge*	Van Nostrand	258	1954
Mayer, Edward	*Winning at Rubber Bridge*	Batsford (London)	195	1975
McVey, Mary A.	*Bridge Basics*	KET (Lexington KY)	120	1982
McVey, Mary A.	*Play Bridge*	KET (Lexington KY)	196	1983
McVey, Mary A.	*Play More Bridge*	KET (Lexington KY)	229	1985
Melbourne, Howard (see Stubbings, Derrek)	*Bridge for Improvers*			
Miles, Marshall	†*Marshall Miles Teaches Logical Bridge*	Exposition Press	319	1967
Milnes, Eric and Lukacs, Paul	*Learn to Play Bridge*	Kaye & Ward (London)	153	1977
Mollo, Victor	*The Other Side of Bridge*	Methuen (London)	148	1984
Mollo, Victor	*Bridge Basics and Beyond*	Hart	155	1976
Mollo, Victor and Gardener, Nico	*Bridge for Beginners*	Barnes & Co.	160	1960
Mollo, Victor	*Bridge Course Complete*	Faber & Faber (London)	237	1977
Mollo, Victor	*Bridge with a Master*	Barnes & Co.	102	1960
Mollo, Victor	*Bridge Psychology*	Duckworth (London)	127	1958
Mollo, Victor	*Bridge Saga*	Hart	210	1976

AUTHOR	TITLE	PUBLISHER	PAGES	DATES
Mollo, Victor	*The Finer Arts of Bridge*	Faber & Faber (London)	210	1978
Mollo, Victor	*Success at Bridge*	Newnes (London)	125	1964
Morehead, Albert	*Bridge the Expert Way*	Bridge World Accessories	62	1943
Morehead, Albert	‡*Contract Bridge Summary*	Macmillan	126	1963
Nagel, Richard	*Play Bridge Like an Expert*	Nagel (Baltimore)	190	1983
Newman, John	*Beginner's Bridge*	Social Bridge Australia	76	1984
Newman, John	*Bridge for Developing Players*	Social Bridge Australia	72	1984
North, Freddie (see Flint, Jeremy)	*Bridge: The First Principles*			
Oeschger, Ivy (see Bailey, Maureen)	*Bridge for the Joneses*			
Pavlicek, Richard	*Modern Bridge*	Pavlicek	21	1975
Pavlicek, Richard	*Beginning Bridge*	Pavlicek	48	1984
Pearson, N. W.	*Chicago Bridge*	Cricket Press	61	1963
Penick, Michael	*Beginning Bridge Complete*	Devyn Press (Louisville KY)	172	1983
Phillips, Hubert and Reese, Terence	*The Elements of Contract* 2nd Rev. Ed.	*British Bridge World* (London) Eyre & Spottiswoode (London)	271 266	1937 1948
Phillips, Hubert	*Making Bridge Pay — How to Win at Rubber Bridge*	Max Parrish (London)	448	1962
Phillips, Hubert	*Thorne's Complete Contract Bridge*	Eyre & Spottiswoode (London)	257	1948
Pyros, Liberty Zabetakis	*Bridge and Baklava: A Complete Bridge Education For Beginning and Intemediate Players*	Pyros (Pittsburgh)	204	1987
Reese, Terence	‡*Advanced Bridge* (reprint of *Play Bridge with Reese* and *Develop Your Bidding Judgment*)	Sterling	464	1973
Reese, Terence	*Begin Bridge with Reese*	Sterling	128	1977
Reese, Terence	†*Bridge for Bright Beginners*	Sterling	151	1965
Reese, Terence and Schapiro, Boris	*Bridge Card by Card*	Hamlyn (London)	88	1969
Reese, Terence and Dormer, Albert	*The Bridge Player's Alphabetical Handbook*	Faber & Faber (London)	223	1981
Reese, Terence and Dormer, Albert	‡*The Complete Book of Bridge*	Dutton	486	1974
Reese, Terence (see Phillips, Hubert)	*The Elements of Contract*			
Reese, Terence and Dormer, Albert	†*How to Play a Better Game of Bridge*	Stein & Day	181	1969
Reese, Terence and Franklin, Harold	*The Listener Book of Bridge — Best of Bridge on the Air*	BBC (London)	176	1965
Reese, Terence	†*Precision Bidding and Precision Play*	Sterling	153	1973
Reese, Terence	*Your Bridge Questions Answered*	Jordan & Sons (London)	136	1951
Reese, Terence	*Bridge for Ambitious Players*	Victor Gollancz (London)	143	1988
Reese, Terence & Bird, David	*Bridge: The Modern Game*	Faber & Faber (London)	200	1985
Reese, Terence & Markus, Rixi	*Better Bridge for Club Players*	Victor Gollancz (London)	125	1989
Reese, Terence & Trézel, Roger	*The Mistakes You Make at Bridge*	Houghton Mifflin	168	1992
Rimington, Derek	*Learn Bridge from the Experts — 100 Lessons*	Pellham (London)	208	1981
Rodwell, Eric (see Grant, Audrey)	*Bridge Maxims: Secrets of Better Play*			
Rodwell, Eric (see Grant, Audrey)	*The Joy of Bridge*			
Rodwell, Eric (see Grant, Audrey)	*The Joy of Bridge Workbook*			
Romanet, Bertrand	**Les Bases du Bridge Moderne*	Albin Michell (Paris)	368	1958
Roth, Alvin and Rubens, Jeff	*Bridge for Beginners*	Funk & Wagnalls	216	1970
Rovere, Ernest	†*Contract Bridge Complete*	Simon & Schuster	834	1965

AUTHOR	TITLE	PUBLISHER	PAGES	DATES
Rovere, Ernest	*Point Count Contract Bridge Complete*	Random House	710	1954-64
Rubens, Jeff	**The Secrets of Winning Bridge*	Grosset & Dunlap	241	1969
Rubens, Jeff (see Roth, Alvin)	*Bridge for Beginners*			
Rosenkranz, Dr. George	*More Tips For Tops*	Devyn Press (Louisville KY)	210	1991
Rosenkranz, Dr. George	*Tips For Tops*	Devyn Press (Louisville KY)	224	1988
Rosenkranz, George & Alder, Phillip	*Bid to Win Play for Pleasure*	Devyn Press (Louisville KY)	428	1990
Schapiro, Boris (see Reese, Terence)	*Bridge Card by Card*			
Seabrook, Barry	*Bridge: From Average to Expert*	Batsford (London)	175	1979
Sheinwold, Alfred	*Complete Bridge Course* *First Book of Bridge* *Second Book of Bridge —* *Play of the Hand* *Third Book of Bridge —* *How to Bid and Play in Duplicate Tournaments* *Fourth Book of Bridge —* *How to Improve Your Game*	Sterling	640	1959
Sheinwold, Alfred	*First Book of Bridge*	Sterling Barnes & Noble	152 153	1952 1969
Sheinwold, Alfred	**‡5 Weeks to Winning Bridge*	Pocket Books Simon & Schuster	498 548	1960-75 1959-64
Shepard, E. V.	*Contract Bridge Standardized*	Cosmopolitan Book Corp.	209	1931
Silodor, Sidney and Tierney, John	*Contract Bridge According to Silodor*	Stanley Allan (Chester Hill NJ)	442	1961
Silverman, Shirley	*Advanced and Duplicate Bridge Student Text*	Baron/Barclay (Louisville KY)	64.	1976
Silverman, Shirley	*Elementary Five Card Major Student Text*	Baron/Barclay (Louisville KY)	48	1976
Silverman, Shirley	*Five Card Major Bridge Teacher's Manual*	Baron/Barclay (Louisville KY)	334	1976-80
Silverman, Shirley	*Intermediate Bridge Five Card Major Student Text*	Baron/Barclay (Louisville KY)	64	1976
Simon, S. J.	**†Why You Lose at Bridge*	Simon & Schuster	159	1946
Smith, Richard V.	*Let's Play Bridge*	Simon & Schuster	440	1987
Sobel, Helen	*All the Tricks* *Winning Bridge* (British title)	Greenberg Peter Davies (London)	245 253	1949 1950
Solomon, Charles and Dibrow, Bennett	*How to Bid and What to Lead*	Macrae Smith (Philadelphia)	128	1950
Squire, Norman	*Contract Bridge: How to Become a Champion*	Vikas Publ, (Delhi, India)	118	1976
Stewart, Frank	*The Bridge Today 1,001 Workbook — Duplicate and Tournament Edition*	Granovetter Books (Ballston Lake NY)		1990
Stewart, Frank & Baron, Randall	*The Bridge Book: Volume 1 — For Beginning Players*	Devyn Press (Louisville KY)	188	1988
Stewart, Frank & Baron, Randall	*The Bridge Book: Volume 2 — For Intermediate Players*	Devyn Press (Louisville KY)	189	1988
Stewart, Frank & Baron, Randall	*The Bridge Book: Volume 3 — For Advanced Players*	Devyn Press (Louisville KY)	191	1989
Stewart, Frank (see Baron, Randall)	*The Bridge Student Text: Volume I — For Beginning Players*			
Stewart, Frank (see Baron, Randall)	*The Bridge Student Text: Volume II — For Intermediate Players*			
Stewart, Frank (see Baron, Randall)	*The Bridge Student Text: Volume III — For Advanced Players*			
Stewart, Frank (see Baron, Randall)	*The Devyn Press Bridge Teacher's Manual: Volume I — For Beginning Players*			
Stewart, Frank (see Baron, Randall)	*The Devyn Press Bridge Teacher's Manual: Volume II — For Intermediate Players*			
Stewart, Frank (see Baron, Randall)	*The Devyn Press Bridge Teacher's Manual: Volume III — For Advanced Players*			
Stubbings, Derek & Melbourne, Howard	*Bridge for Improvers*	Crowood Press (Swindon, England)	176	1989
Sydnor, Caroline	*Bridge Made Easy* *Book One* *Book Two* *Book Three*	Sydnor (Alexandria VA)	 165 207 266	 1975 1977 1981

AUTHOR	TITLE	PUBLISHER	PAGES	DATES
Tait, J. W.	*Bridge Challenge*	Wolfe (London)	141	1974
Tait, J. W.	*Bridge Match*	Faber & Faber (London)	133	1976
Teukolsky, Roselyn	*How to Play Bridge with Your Spouse*	Granovetter Books (Ballston Lake, NY)	192	1991
Tierney, John (see Silodor, Sidney)	*Contract Bridge According to Silodor and Tierney*			
Thomas, Frank (see Gooden, George)	*Contract Bridge Advanced Lesson Course*			
Trézel, Roger (see Reese, Terence)	*The Mistakes You Make at Bridge*			
Truscott, Alan	*Bridge: Successful Play from First Principles*	Oldbourne (London)	159	1946
Truscott, Alan	The New York Times *Guide to Practical Bridge*	Golden Press	220	1970
Truscott, Alan	*Basic Bridge in Three Weeks: The Beginner's Day-by-Day Guide to Bridge Mastery*	Perigee Books, Putnam	224	1987
Truscott, Alan	*Contract Bridge*	Bantam Books	111	1983
Truscott, Alan	*Intermediate Bridge in Three Weeks: A 21-Day Guide to Bridge Mastery*	Perigee Boooks, Putnam	224	1990
Truscott, Alan	The New York Times *Bridge Series: Grand Slams*	Times Books	133	1985
Truscott, Dorothy Hayden	*Bid Better, Play Better*	Harper & Row	235	1988
Vanderbilt, Harold	*Contract by Hand Analysis*	*The Bridge World*	165	1933
Watson, Louis	*The Outline of Contract Bridge*	Grosset & Dunlap	333	1934
Whitehead, Wilbur	*Contract Bridge: What (to do) and Why*	Frederick A. Stoles	183	1931
Winokur, Lori Wiley	*Building Bridges to Bridge*	Goodwich Associates (Newtown CT)	45	1990
Woods, Jo	*Little Green Book, Artificial Bids, Leads, Signals*	Woods (Little Rock AR)	68	1968
Work, Milton	*Contract Bridge for All*	J. C. Winston (Philadelphia)	243	1929-31
Young, Ray	*Bridge for People Who Don't Know One Card from Another*	Follett (Chicago)	127	1964

F DUPLICATE BRIDGE (Bidding, Play, and Tournament directing)

AUTHOR	TITLE	PUBLISHER	PAGES	DATES
Andersen, Ron (see Wei, C. C.)	†*Match Point Precision*			
Benjamin, Albert (see Kempson, Ewart)	*Tournament Bridge for Everyone*			
Beynon, George	‡*Bridge Director's Manual* (6th ed., rev.)	Coffin (Waltham MA)	192	1944
Beynon, George	*Tournament and Duplicate Bridge*	Stuyvesant	270	1944
The Bridge World	*How Would You Rule?*	*The Bridge World*	52	1978
The Bridge World	*Appeals Committee Volume One*	*The Bridge World*	48	1981-1983
The Bridge World	*Appeals Committee Volume Two*	*The Bridge World*	48	1982-84
Bruelheide, F. E.	*Duplicate Bridge Guide*	Bruelheide (Minneapolis)	64	1938
Coffin, George	*Perfect Plays and Match Point Ways*	Coffin (Waltham MA)	160	1973
Culbertson, Ely	*Bidding and Play in Duplicate Contract Bridge*	J. C. Winston (Philadelphia)	271	1946
Dormer, Albert (see Reese, Terence)	*Bridge for Tournament Players*			
Farrington, Frank	*Duplicate Bridge Movements*	Farrington (England)	98	1960
Feldheim, Harold	*Winning Swiss Team Tactics in Bridge*	Barclay (Port Chester NY)	236	1976
Fox, G. C. H.	*Duplicate Bridge*	St. Martin's Press	160	1974
Fox, G. C. H.	*Duplicate Bridge, Its Procedures and Tactics*	E. Arnold (London)	143	1955
Grant, Audrey	*Introduction to Duplicate Bridge: "Spade Series"*	ACBL (Memphis)	305	1990
Greenberg, Julie	*Duplicate Decisions, A Club Director's Guide for Ruling at the Table*	ACBL (Memphis)	52	1982
Greenwood, David	*The Pairs Game*	Cassell (London)	150	1978
Groner, Alex	‡*Duplicate Bridge Direction*	Baron/Barclay (Louisville KY)	224	1967
Groner, Alex	‡*Duplicate Bridge Direction: A Complete Handbook*	Baron/Barclay (Louisville KY)	224	1972

AUTHOR	TITLE	PUBLISHER	PAGES	DATES
Gruenther, Alfred	*Duplicate Contract Complete	The Bridge World	328	1933
Hardy, Max (see Roney, Bill)	Play My Card			
Harrison-Gray, Maurice (see Squire, Norman)	*†Winning Points at Match-Point Bridge			
Harris, Larry	Bridge Director's Companion	Devyn Press (Louisville KY)	102	1988
Hasler, Alexander T.	Duplicate Bridge Simplified	Harrop (London)	134	ca.1935
Hathorn, John (see Nail, G. R.)	How to Play Championship Duplicate Bridge			
Hoffman, Martin	Hoffman on Pairs Play	Faber & Faber (London)	184	1982
Jannersten, Eric and Wohlin, Jan	Winning Pairs Technique (trans. by Hugh Kelsey)	Victor Gollancz (London)	160	1980
Jourdain, Catherine	ABC of Duplicate Bridge Direction	Coffin (Waltham MA)	96	1967
Kambites, Andrew	Duplicate Pairs for You	Victor Gollancz (London)	144	1991
Kaplan, Edgar	Director's Guide	ACBL (Memphis)	32	1976
Kaplan, Edgar	†Duplicate Bridge, How to Play, How to Win	Bantam Books Hearthside Press	149 148	1966 1968
Karpin, Fred (see Kay, Norman)	‡The Complete Book of Duplicate Bridge			
Karpin, Fred	Winning Play in Tournament and Duplicate Bridge. How the Experts Triumph	New American Library	241	1968
Kay, Norman et al	‡The Complete Book of Duplicate Bridge	G.P. Putnam Sons Barnes & Noble	496 496	1965 1969-72
Kelsey, H. W.	†Match Point Bridge	Faber & Faber (London)	239	1970
Kempson, Ewart and Benjamin, Albert	Tournament Bridge for Everyone	Faber & Faber (London)	200	1963
Klinger, Ron	50 Winning Duplicate Tips for the Improving Tournament Player	Victor Gollancz (London)	128	1991
Low, William	Graphic Guide to Duplicate Bridge Directing (charts, tables)	Low (NYC)	57	1978
McMullin, Edith	Adventures in Duplicate Bridge	ACBL (Memphis)	51	1989
McKinnon, Ian	Bridge Directing Complete (100 appendices)	Computer Accounting Services (Sydney, Australia)	182	1979
Miles, Marshall	*‡How to Win at Duplicate Bridge	Exposition Press	463	1957
Nail, G. R. and Hathorn, John	How to Play Championship Bridge	Texas Bridge (Houston)	69	1963
Nail, G. R. and Hathorn, John	Winning Duplicate	Texas Bridge (Houston)	28	1962
Needham, Richard	Tournament Tactics at Contract Bridge	Needham	16	1934
Parker, Allan	Let's Play Duplicate — Actual Duplicate in the Home	Miller Quarles (Houston) vol 1 vol. 2		1961 1962
Reese, Terence and Dormer, Albert	Bridge for Tournament Players	Robert Hale (London)	173	1968
Roney, Bill and Hardy, Max	Play My Card	Max Hardy	136	1980
Routman, Mark J.	Club Level Duplicate Bridge: Which Strategies Win?	Daring Books (Canton OH)	331	1986
Sheinwold, Alfred	Third Book of Bridge — How to Bid and Play in Duplicate Tournaments	Sterling	157	1954
Silodor, Sidney (see Kay, Norman)	‡The Complete Book of Duplicate Bridge			
Silverman, Shirley	Chicago Bridge: How to Play Four-Deal Contract Bridge	Baron/Barclay (Louisville KY)	16	1983
Squire, Norman and Harrison-Gray, Maurice	*‡Winning Points at Match-Point Bridge	Faber & Faber (London)	151	1959
Wei, C. C. and Andersen, Ron	‡Match Point Precision	Monna Lisa	195	1975
Weir, Richard Lloyd	Practical Duplicate Bridge (From your Convention Card)	CEO M/PIC of Dayton (Dayton OH)	20	1987
Wohlin, Jan (see Jannersten, Eric)	WinningPairs Technique			
Woolsey, Kit	*Matchpoints	Devyn Press (Louisville KY)	343	1982

G MATCH & TOURNAMENT RECORDS
Editor

AUTHOR	TITLE	PUBLISHER	PAGES	DATES
Albarran, Pierre (see Bellanger, Pierre)	*Les 102 Donnes d'un Grand Match*			
Aron, Adiene (see Bellanger, Pierre)	*Les 102 Donnes d'un Grand Match*			
Beasley, H. M.	*Beasley v. Culbertson*	Hutchinson (London)	288	1933
Bellanger, Pierre et al	*Les 102 Donnes d'un Grand Match*	Bernard Grasset (Paris)	189	1933
Buller, Walter and Kempson, Ewart	*The Buller Almacks Bridge Contest*	*Vail (London)*	*108*	*1934*
Buller, Walter	*Colonel Buller on the Beasley-Culbertson Bridge Contest*	*The Star* (London)	128	1933
Buller, Walter	*International Bridge Test*	*News-Chronicle* (London)	222	1930
Burn, David (see Senior, Brian)	*IPBM Book of the 1989 World Junior Team Championships*			
Culbertson, Ely	**Famous Hands of the Culbertson-Lenz Match*	*The Bridge World*	437	1932
Culbertson, Ely	*300 Contract Bridge Hands — First World Bridge Championship* (England vs U.S.)	*The Bridge World*	380	1933
Culbertson, Ely	*The 1932 World Bridge Olympic Hands*	*The Bridge World*	96	1932
England, Frank and Harris, A.F. Stapleton	*Experts at Contract: Crockford's Club v. the Dutch and German Teams*	Bodley Head (Lonndon)	104	1932
Flint, Jeremy and Rimington, Derek	*Grand Slam; 1983 BBC2 Television Tournament*	Country Life Books (Middlesex, England)	175	1983
The Foreign Affairs Recreation Association at the Department of State				1991
Francis, Henry	*1973 World Bridge Championships* (Brazil, Italy, North America, Indonesia, Aces)	ACBL (Memphis)	215	1973
Francis, Henry	*1974 World Bridge Championships* (Brazil, France, Indonesia, Italy, New Zealand North America)	ACBL (Memphis)	192	1974
Francis, Henry	*1975 World Bridge Championship* (Brazil, France, Indonesia, Italy, North America)	ACBL (Memphis)	205	1975
Francis, Henry	*1976 World Bridge Championships* (Bermuda Bowl, Venice Cup, Olympiad)	ACBL (Memphis)	191	1976
Francis, Henry	*World Championship '77* (Argentina, Australia, North America, Sweden, Taiwan, North America)	ACBL (Memphis)	187	1978
Francis, Henry	*V World Pair Olympiad* (Open Pairs, Women's Pairs, Mixed Pairs, Venice Cup, Rosenblum Cup)	ACBL (Memphis)	159	1979
Francis, Henry	*1979 World Championship* (Australia, Brazil, Italy, North America, Panama-Venezuela, Taiwan)	ACBL (Memphis)	238	1980
Francis, Henry	*1980 6th World Team Olympiad* (Open Series, Women's Series)	ACBL (Memphis)	190	1981
Francis, Henry	*1981 World Championships for the Bermuda Bowl* (Argentina, Australia, Great Britain, Indonesia, Pakistan, Poland, United States) *and the Venice Cup* (Australia, Brazil, Venezuela, Great Britain, United States)	ACBL (Memphis)	190	1981
Francis, Henry	*1982 VI Contract Bridge Pairs* (Knockout Teams, Women's Pairs, Mixed Pairs, Rosenblum Cup)	ACBL (Memphis)	176	1983
Francis, Henry	*1983 World Championship for the Bermuda Bowl* (Brazil, Central America-Caribbean, France, Indonesia, Italy, New Zealand, Pakistan, Sweden, USA1, USA2)		256	1984
Francis, Henry	*1984 7th World Team Olympiad* (Open Series, Women's Series)	ACBL (Memphis)	189	1985
Francis, Henry	*1985 World Championships for the 27th Bermuda Bowl and the 5th Venice Cup*	ACBL (Memphis)	238	1986
Francis, Henry	*1986 VII Contract Bridge World Bridge Pairs and Knockout Teams* (Open Pairs, Women's Pairs, Mixed Pairs, Rosenblum Teams Cup)	ACBL (Memphis)	144	ca. 1987
Francis, Henry	*1987 World Championships for the 28th Bermuda Bowl and the 6th Venice Cup*	ACBL (Memphis)	224	ca.1988

AUTHOR	TITLE	PUBLISHER	PAGES	DATES
Francis, Henry	*1988 8th World Team Olympiad* (Open Series, Women's Series)	ACBL (Memphis)	143	1989
Francis, Henry	*1989 World Championships* (Bermuda Bowl and Venice Cup)	ACBL (Memphis)	336	1990
Franklin, Harold (see Reese, Terence)	*World Bridge Championship 1955*			
Frey, Richard	*International Team Playoff*	ACBL	96	1969
Frey, Richard	*Team Trials*	ACBL		1964
Frey, Richard	*Team Trials*	ACBL		1965
Frey, Richard	*Team Trials*	ACBL	144	1966
Frey, Richard	*World Championship* (United States, Italy, and Argentina)	ACBL	158	1958
Frey, Richard	*World Championship* (United States, Italy and Argentina)	ACBL	160	1959
Frey, Richard	*1st World Bridge Olympiad* (France, Great Britain, Italy and United States)	ACBL	136	1960
Frey, Richard	*World, Championship* (Italy, North America France and Argentina)	ACBL	132	1961
Frey, Richard	*World Championship* (Italy, North America Great Britain and Argentina)	ACBL	118	1962
Frey, Richard	*World Championship* (Italy, North America, France and Argentina)	ACBL	120	1963
Frey, Richard	*2nd World Bridge Olympiad* (Italy, United States, Canada, Great Britain and 25 others)	ACBL	192	1964
Frey, Richard	*World Bridge Championship* (Italy, North America, Great Britain and Argentina)	ACBL	192	1965
Frey, Richard	*World Bridge Championship* (Italy, North America, Thailand, Venezuela and the Netherlands)	ACBL	224	1966
Frey, Richard	*World Bridge Championship* (Italy, France, North America, Thailand and Venezuela)	ACDL	224	1967
Frey, Richard	*3rd World Bridge Olympiad* (Italy, United States, Canada, the Netherlands and 29 others)	ACBL	192	1968
Frey, Richard	*World Bridge Championship* (Italy, North America, France, Taiwan and Brazil)	ACBL	224	1969
Gardener, Nicola et al	*Master Bridge*	Macmillan (London)	140	1983
Harris, A. F. Stapleton (see England, Frank)	*Experts at Contract: Crockford's Club v. the Dutch and German Teams*			
Herts, B. Russel (see Kerwin, Madeleine)	*Expert Misbidding* (Culbertson-Lenz 1931)			
Hirsch, Tannah	*1970 World Championship* (Italy, North America, Norway, Taiwan, Brazil)	ACBL	224	1970
Hirsch, Tannah	*1971 World Championship* (Aces, France, Australia, Taiwan, Brazil, North America)	ACBL	223	1971
Kempson, Ewart	*Bridge Match in Dublin*	Waddington (Leeds, England)	100	1958
Kempson, Ewart (see Buller, Walter)	*The Buller Almacks Bridge Contest*			
Kempson, Ewart	*Championship Hands*	Joiner & Steele (London)	59	1950
Kempson, Ewart	*Kempson versus Baron Exhibition Contest — 100 Hands*	Newcastle Chronicle (Newcastle)	104	1946
Kerwin, Madeleine and Herts, B. Russell	*Expert Misbidding* (Culbertson-Lenz 1931)	Covice-Friede	140	1932
Kleinman, Danny	*Bridge Internationalists, Famous and Infamous*	Kleinman (Los Angeles)	145	1988
Klinger, Ron	*The Australian Open Team at the Sixth World Team Olympiad* (Valkenburg, 1980)	Klinger (Australia)	50	1980
Klinger, Ron	*World Championship Pairs Bridge*	Victor Gollancz (London)	167	1983
Philip Morris	*Philip Morris 12th European Simultaneous Bridge Pairs*	Philip Morris & European Bridge League (Lausanne, Switzerland)		1986
McKenney, William	*Par Bridge-Hands for Replay National Intercollegiate Bridge Tournaments*	Barclay & Assoc. of American Card Manufacturers		1938

AUTHOR	TITLE	PUBLISHER	PAGES	DATES
Moyse, Alphonse Jr. and Sheinwold, Alfred	*World Championship, U.S. and Sweden*	ACBL	136	1953
	World Championship, U.S., France	ACBL	80	1954
	World Championship, U.S., Great Britain	ACBL	120	1955
	World Championship, U.S., France	ACBL	84	1956
	World Championship (United States, Italy)	ACBL	126	1957
Pigot, Peter	*Lausanne 1979* (Story of the Irish Bridge Team)	Pigot (Ireland)	194	1979
Reese, Terence and Franklin, Harold	*World Bridge Championship* (Great Britain v. United States)	Thos. De La Rue (London)	106	1955
Richards, Ralph	*Championship Bridge*	Greenberg	114	1928
Rimington, Derek (see Flint, Jeremy)	*Grand Slam; 1983 BBC2 Television Tournament*			
Senior, Brian	*1987 European Championships*	Probray Press (Nottingham, England)	96	1987
Senior, Brian & Burn, David	*IPBM Book of the 1989 World Junior Team Championship*	Probray Press (Nottingham, England)	112	1989
Smith, Thomas M.	*4th World Bridge Olympiad* (Italy, United States, Canada, France and 35 others)	ACBL	224	1972
Sowter, Tony	*1990 The VIIIth World Bridge Championships* (Mixed Pairs, PAMP Invitational Par Contest, Rosenblum Cup, Continuous Pairs, Senior Pairs, Women's Pairs, Open Pairs)		160	1991
Sowter, Tony	*1991 World Championships* (NEC Bermuda Bowl, NEC Venice Cup)	WBF (Nottingham, England)	192	1992
Sowter, Tony	*1992 9th World Team Olympiad* (Open Series, Women's Series)		176	1993
Stern, Paul	*Beating the Culbertsons*	T. Werner Laurie (London)	128	1938
Sullivan, Michael and Williams, R. E.	*World Par Hands*	World Bridge Federation	40	1961-63
Venizelos, Sophocle (see Bellanger, Pierre)	*Les 102 Donnes d'un Grand Match*			
Williams, R. E. (see Sullivan, Michael)	*World Par Hands*			

H HAND COLLECTIONS

The Bridge World	North American Collegiate Bridge Championship	ACBL & *The Bridge World*	(hands) 24	1986
Becker, B. Jay	Becker on Bridge	Grosset & Dunlap	128	1971
Bird, David (see Reese, Terence)	Miracles of Card Play			
Corn, Ira	*Play Bridge with the Aces*	Fawcett (Greenwich CT)	224	1972
Culbertson, Ely	*60 Contract Bridge Hands*	*The Bridge World*	160	1933
Darvas, Robert and Hart, Norman de V.	**Right Through the Pack*	Stuyvesant House	328	1947
Darvas, Robert and Lukacs, Paul	*†Spotlight on Card Play*	Barclay	160	1960
Flint, Jeremy	*Bridge with the Times*	Country Life Books (Middlesex, England)	175	1983
Flint, Jeremy & Reese, Terence	*Bridge with the Professional Touch*	Victor Gollancz (London)	141	1991
Forquet, Pietro	*Bridge with the Blue Team*	Victor Gollancz (London)	384	1987
Fox, G. C. H.	*The Daily Telegraph Book of Bridge*	Robert Hale (London)	237	1975
Fox, G. C. H.	*Master Play — The Best of International Bridge*	Robert Hale (London)	186	1976
Goren, Charles	*The Best of Championship Bridge*	American Van Lines	25	
Goren, Charles	*Bridge Mystery Deals*	Heines (Minneapolis)	64	1964
Goren, Charles	*Championship Bridge with Charles Goren*	Doubelday	255	1964
Goren, Charles	*Charles H. Goren's 100 Challenging Bridge Hands for You to Enjoy*	Doubleday	100	1976
Griffiths, John	*The Golden Years of Bridge* (Classic Hands from the Past)	Victor Gollancz (London)	127	1981
Harrison-Gray, Maurice	*Country Life Book of Bridge*	Hamlyn Gourp (London)	160	1972
Hart, Norman de V. (see Darvas, Robert)	**Right Through the Pack*			
Havas, George	*The Australian Book of Bridge*	Horwitz Publications (Hong Kong)	128	1979
Hoffman, Martin	*More Tales of Hoffman*	Faber & Faber (London)	187	1983

AUTHOR	TITLE	PUBLISHER	PAGES	DATES
Jannersten, Eric (see Mollo, Victor)	†The Best of Bridge			
Jannersten, Eric	Bridge Writer's Choice 1964	IBPA (Sweden)	177	1965
Jannersten, Eric	Bridge Writer's Choice 1968	IBPA (Sweden)	240	1968
Jelks, Edwards and Schmitt, Raymond	Trick Taking Potential	Jett (Normal IL)	80	1974
Kauder, James S.	Creative Card Play: The Cure for Unimaginative Bridge!	Lawrence & Leong (Oakland CA)	226	1989
Kauder, James	The Bridge Philosopher	Kauder (Los Angeles)	144	1972
Kelsey, Hugh	Bridge Hands for the Connoisseur	Victor Gollancz (London)	141	1991
Kempson, Ewart	Contract Bridge Hands	Faber & Faber (London)	96	1950
Le Dentu, José	120 Donnes et Problèmes du Bridge	Presses Pocket (Paris)	189	1975
Lukacs, Paul (see Darvas, Robert)	Spotlight on Card Play			
Lukacs, Paul (see Milnes, Eric)	Bridge Hands for the Connoisseur			
Markus, Rixi	Aces and Places	Bodley Head (London) Drake	140 140	1972 1973
Markus, Rixi	Bid Boldly, Play Safe	Blond (London)	212	1966
Markus, Rixi	Bridge Around the World	Bodley Head (London)	239	1979
Markus, Rixi	Best Bridge Hands	Unwin (London)	154	1985
McKenney, William	Contract Bridge (Bidding and Playing of over 750 Hands from Championship Tournaments)	American Merchandise Co.	108	1935
Miller, Richard A.	Bridge Brilliance and Blunders	Dow Jones (Princeton NJ)	222	1974
Miller, Richard A.	More Bridge Brilliance and Blunders	Dow Jones (Princeton NJ)	217	1975
Milnes, Eric and Lukacs, Paul	†Bridge Hands for the Connoisseur	Barclay Bridge Supplies	127	1974
Mollo, Victor and Jannersten, Eric	†The Best of Bridge	Faber & Faber (London)	223	1973
Nielsen, Aksel	Bridge with the Three Musketeers	Kaye & Ward (London)	233	1978
North, Freddie	Bridge with Aunt Agatha	Faber & Faber (London)	208	1983
North, Freddie	Aunt Agatha Plays Tournament Bridge	Faber & Faber (London)	181	1984
Peterson, Olive (see Work, Milton)	101 Celebrated Hands			
Phillips, Hubert	Bridge with Goren	Citadel Press	128	1960
Phillips, Hubert	Bridge at Ruff's Club	Batchworth Press (London)	248	1951
Phillips, Hubert and Reese, Terence	Bridge with Mr. Playbetter	Batchworth Press (London)	219	1952
Phillips, Hubert	Brush Up on Your Bridge	Dent (London)	119	1939
Phillips, Hubert	100 Contract Bridge Hands	Faber & Faber (London)	146	1932
Phillips, Hubert and Westall, F. C.	200 Hands from Match Play	Thos. De La Rue (London)	401	1934
Reese, Terence (see Phillips, Hubert)	Bridge with Mr. Playbetter			
Reese, Terence and Bird, David	Miracles of Card Play	Victor Gollancz (London)	160	1982
Reese, Terence (see Flint, Jeremy)	Bridge with the Professional Touch			
Reese, Terence	Do You Really Want to Win at Bridge?	Victor Gollancz (London)	159	1989
Saunders, P. F.	Bridge with a Perfect Partner	Ward Lock (London)	127	1976
Schapiro, Boris	Bridge Analysis	Sterling	187	1976
Schmitt, Raymond (see Jelks, Edward)	Trick Taking Potential			
Simon, S. J.	Cut for Partners	Nicholson & Watson (London)	128	1950
Smith, A. J.	Contract Chronicles	Grayson & Grayson (London)	52	1936
Smith, A. J. (see Stern, Paul)	Sorry Partner			

AUTHOR	TITLE	PUBLISHER	PAGES	DATES
Solomon, Charles and Wilson, Bert	Hold Our Bridge Hands	Lefax, Inc. (Philadelphia)	187	1976
Stern, Paul and Smith, A. J.	Sorry Partner	Faber & Faber (London)	141	1945
Stewart, Frank	My Bridge and Yours	Stewart (Fayette AL)	208	1991
Stewart, Frank	Two-Minute Bridge Tips	Stewart (Fayette AL)	191	1992
Truscott, Alan	†Master Bridge by Question and Answer	Quadrangle Books (Chicago)	252	1971
Tuite, Hugh	Contract Bridge for Iris	Geoffrey Bles (London)	125	1929
Tuite, Hugh	Mrs. Pottleton's Bridge Parties	Simon & Schuster	153	1928
White, Travis	Odd Tricks Reprinted	The Bridge World GBC Press (Las Vegas)	104 141	1934 1978
Whitehead, Wilbur	Championship Bridge Hands	Stokes	120	1929
Wilson, Bert (see Solomon, Charles)	Hold Our Bridge Hands			
Work, Milton and Peterson, Olive	101 Celebrated Hands	J. C. Winston (Philadelphia)	215	1933

I FICTION

AUTHOR	TITLE	PUBLISHER	PAGES	DATES
Ackerley, Chris	The Bridging of Troy or Tales from the Trojan Tournament	Victor Gollancz (London)	124	1986
Cole, E. R. and Edwards, James (eds.)	Grand Slam	Putnam	224	1975
Corbett, Andrea	Passionate Obsession	Healey Roman Associates (Natick MA)	155	1990
DeSerpa, Allan	The Mexican Contract	Max Hardy	148	1981
Edwards, James (see Cole, E. R.)	Grand Slam			
Flint, Jeremy(see Reese, Terence)	Trick 13			
Friedman, B. H.	Yarborough	World Publishing Co.	374	1964
Gooden, George and Thomas, Frank	Sherlock Holmes, Bridge Detective	Frank Thomas (Los Angeles)	122	1973
Granovetter, Matthew	The Bridge Team Murders	Granovetter Books (Ballston Lake NY)	400	1992
Granovetter, Matthew	I Shot My Bridge Partner	Granovetter Books (Ballston Lake NY)	370	1989
Granovetter, Matthew	Murder at the Bridge Table (or, Improve Your Duplicate Score Overnight)	Granovetter Books (Ballston Lake NY)	310	1988
Herts, Russell	Grand Slam: The Rise and Fall of a Bridge Wizard	Pratt	288	1932
Nicolet, C. C.	Death of a Bridge Expert	Simon & Schuster	235	1932
Powell, Richard	Tickets to the Devil	Scribner's	306	1968
Quinn, Terry	The Great Bridge Conspiracy	St. Martin's Press	196	1979
Reese, Terence and Flint, Jeremy	Trick 13	Weidenfeld & Nicolson (London)	172	1979
Theimer, Ernst T.	The Bridge Adventures of Androcles MacThick	E. T. Theimer (Rumson NJ)	247	1981
Thomas, Frank (see Gooden, George)	Sherlock Holmes, Bridge Detective	Frank Thomas		
Thomas, Frank	Sherlock Holmes, Bridge Detective, Returns	Frank Thomas (Los Angeles)	199	1975
Von Elsner, Don	The Ace of Spies	Award Books	192	1966
Von Elsner, Don	The Best of Jake Winkman	Max Hardy	117	1981
Von Elsner, Don	Cruise Bridge	Max Hardy	187	1981
Von Elsner, Don	Everything's Jake with Me	Max Hardy	105	1980
Von Elsner, Don	The Jack of Hearts	Award Books	188	1968
Von Elsner, Don	The Jake of Diamonds	Award Books	192	1963
Vourkas, Rudy	Pygmalion at the Bridge Table	Ginn Custom Publishing (Lexington MA)	87	1982

J PROBLEMS, QUIZZES AND PUZZLES

AUTHOR	TITLE	PUBLISHER	PAGES	DATES
The Bridge World	Bridge Movies & Post-Mortems	The Bridge World	48	1979

AUTHOR	TITLE	PUBLISHER	PAGES	DATES
The Bridge World	Challenge the Champs (Book I)	The Bridge World	52	1978
	(Book II)	The Bridge World	48	1974
	(Book III)	The Bridge World	48	1980
	(Book IV)	The Bridge World	48	1981
The Bridge World	Rate Your Own Game	The Bridge World	48	1981
The Bridge World	Challenge the Champs (Book VI)	The Bridge World	48	1988
The Bridge World	Challenge the Champs (Book VII)	The Bridge World	48	1990
Cohen, Ben	Playing Better Bridge (reprint of Test Your Bridge)	A. S. Barnes	227	1964
Cohen, Ben	Test Your Bridge	Arco (London)	227	1962
Cotter, Pat and Rimington, Derek	Bridge Quiz from a New Angle	Paperfronts Elliot Right Way Books (Surrey, England)	159	1972
Darwen, Hugh	†Bridge Magic	Faber & Faber (London)	213	1973
Dutta, Prabhat K.	Bridge Puzzle	N. E. Publishers (Calcutta, India)	131	1990
Ewen, Robert	The Defense Bidding Quiz Book	Monna Lisa Precision	105	1980
Foster, Robert F.	*Vanity Fair's Bridge Problems	Horace Liveright	198	1932
Fox, G. C. H.	The Daily Telegraph Bridge Quiz	Robert Hale (London)	115	1977
Fox, G. C. H.	The Second Daily Telegraph Bridge Quiz	Robert Hale (London)	122	1979
Goren, Charles	Bridge Quiz Book	Permabooks	184	1949
Hoffman, Martin (see Reese, Terence)	Play It Again, Sam			
Jannersten, Eric	Find the Mistakes: A Bridge Quiz (trans. & adapted by Hugh Kelsey)	Victor Gollancz (London)	160	1982
Jannersten, Eric	The Only Chance (trans. & adapted by Hugh Kelsey)	Bodley Head (London)	171	1980
Jannersten, Eric and Wohlin, Jan	Play Safe and Win (trans. by Hugh Kelsey)	Victor Gollancz (London)	160	1981
Kantar, Edwin	Kantar for the Defense: Volume I	Wilshire (N. Hollywood CA)	200	1983
Kantar, Edwin	Test Your Bridge Play	Wilshire (N. Hollywood CA)	201	1974
Kantar, Edwin	Test Your Bridge Play: Volume II	Wilshire (N. Hollywood CA)	234	1981
Kantar, Edwin B.	Kantar for the Defense: Volume II	Wilshire (N. Hollywood CA)	200	1984
Kantar, Edwin B.	A New Approach to Play and Defense	HDL Publishing (Costa Mesa CA)	204	1986
Kantar, Edwin B.	A New Approach to Play and Defense: Volume 2	HDL Publishing (Costa Mesa CA)	204	1987
Kelsey, Hugh	Test Your Card-Reading	Victor Gollancz (London)	80	1982
Kelsey, Hugh	Test Your Communications	Victor Gollancz (London)	80	1982
Kelsey, Hugh	Test Your Finessing	Victor Gollancz (London)	80	1981
Kelsey, Hugh	Test Your Match Play	Faber & Faber (London)	190	1977
Kelsey, Hugh	Test Your Trump Control	Victor Gollancz (London)	80	1981
Kelsey, Hugh	The Tough Game	Faber & Faber (London)	190	1979
Kelsey, Hugh	Challenge Match	Faber & Faber (London)	188	1983
Kelsey, Hugh	Test Your Card Play — 1	Victor Gollancz (London)	80	1990
Kelsey, Hugh	Test Your Card Play — 2	Victor Gollancz (London)	80	1990
Kelsey, Hugh	Test Your Card Play — 3	Victor Gollancz (London)	80	1991
Kelsey, Hugh	Test Your Card Play — 4	Victor Gollancz (London)	80	1991
Kelsey, Hugh	Test Your Card Play — 5	Victor Gollancz (London)	80	1992
Kelsey, Hugh	Test Your Card Play — 6	Victor Gollancz (London)	80	1992
Kelsey, Hugh	Test Your Defensive Play	Victor Gollancz (London)	80	1985
Kelsey, Hugh	Test Your Elimination Play	Victor Gollancz (North Pomfret VT)	80	1984
Kelsey, Hugh	Test Your Pairs Play	Victor Gollancz (London)	80	1985
Kelsey, Hugh	Test Your Percentages	Victor Gollancz (London)	80	1983
Kelsey, Hugh	Test Your Safety Play	Victor Gollancz (London)	80	1984
Kelsey, Hugh	Test Your Timing	Victor Gollancz (London)	80	1983
Kempson, Ewart and Ritch, J. H.	Bridge Quiz	Contrct Bridge Equipment Co. (Leeds)	215	1949

AUTHOR	TITLE	PUBLISHER	PAGES	DATES
Kempson, Ewart	*First Pocket Book of Bridge Problems*	Nicholas Vane (London)	79	1961
Kempson, Ewart	*More Bridge Quizzes*	Wm. Jackson (London)	109	1952
Klinger, Ron	*Playing to Win at Bridge — Practical Problems for the Improving Player*	Ward Lock (London)	125	1976
Klinger, Ron	*Winning Bridge — Trick by Trick*	Victor Gollancz (London)	127	1980
Lederer, Rhoda Barrow	*Acolites Quiz*	Allen & Unwin (London)	197	1970-74
Lukacs, Paul (see Milnes, Eric)	*Improve Your Dummy Play*			
Lukacs, Paul and Rubens, Jeff	*Test Your Play as Declarer*	Hart	189	1977
Lukacs, Paul and Rubens, Jeff	*Test You Play as Declarer — Volume 2*	Devyn Press	222	1982
Mansfield, Eric	*Bridge: The Ultimate Limits*	*Robert Hale (London)*	*208*	*1986*
Martin, Emerson	*Bridge Word Puzzles*	White Arts (Indianapolis)	140	1973
Milnes, Eric and Lukacs, Paul	*Improve Your Dummy Play*	Barclay	80	1969
Mollo, Victor	*Test Your Defense*	Prentice Hall (Englewood Cliffs NJ)	311	172
Mollo, Victor and Nielson, Aksel	*How Good Is Your Defense?*	Hart	256	1976
Mollo, Victor	*I Challenge You*	Methuen (London)	150	1984
Nielson, Aksel (see Mollo, Victor)	*How Good Is Your Defense?*			
Osborn, Florence	*How's Your Birdge?*	Faber & Faber (London)	212	1949
Osborn, Florence	*How's Your Bridge Game?* (American title)	McGraw-Hill	201	1948
Penick, Michael	*Beginning Bridge Quizzes*	Devyn Press (Louisville KY)	133	1989
Pottage, Julian	*Clues from the Bidding*	Victor Gollancz (London)	128	1990
Priest, Denis	*Problems in Play; First Book of Bridge Problems*	U. of Queensland Press (Australia)	167	1982
Priest, Denis	*Problems in Play: First Book of Bridge Problems*	University of Queensland Press (Australia)	167	1982
Priest, Denis	*Problems in Play: Second Book of Bridge Problems*	University of Queensland Press (Australia)	197	1983
Reese, Terence	*The Most Puzzling Situations in Bridge*	Sterling	160	1978
Reese, Terence	*Play These Hands with Me*	W. H. Allen (London)	195	1976
Reese, Terence & Hoffman, Martin	*Play It Again, Sam*	Devyn Press (Louisville KY)	158	1986
Rimington, Derek (see Cotter, Pat)	*Bridge Quiz from a New Angle*			
Ritch, J. H. (see Kempson, Ewart)	*Bridge Quiz*			
Roth, Danny	*Awareness: The Way to Improve Your Bridge*	Victor Gollancz (London)	128	1991
Roudinesco, Jean-Marc	*Play Bridge with Me — Forty Problems in Card Play*	Victor Gollancz (London)	95	1980
Rubens, Jeff (see Lukacs, Paul)	*Test Your Play as Declarer*			
Rubens, Jeff (see Lukacs, Paul)	*Test Your Play as Declarer — Volume 2*			
Rubens, Jeff	*Swiss Match Challenge*	Lawrence & Leong (Oakland CA)	234	1992
Sheinwold, Alfred	*The Pocket Book of Puzzles (Nos. 1-6)* reprinted	Pocket Books (6 vols) Devyn Press (3 vols.)	191 185	1970-71 1981
Sowter, Tony	*The First IPBM Book of Play Problems*	Probray Press (Nottingham, England)	32	1984
Stewart, Frank	*Better Bridge for the Advancing Player*	Prentice Hall (Englewood Cliffs NJ)	234	1984
Stewart, Frank	*Frank Stewart's Contract Bridge Quiz Book*	Prentice Hall (Englewood Cliffs NJ)	234	1986
Tait, Jimmy	*Tales of the Club Expert*	Faber & Faber (London)	116	1987
Wohlin, Jan (see Jannersten, Eric)	*Play Safe — and Win*			

K BIOGRAPHY

Clay, John	*Culbertson: The Man Who Made Contract Bridge*	Weidenfeld and Nicolson (London)	242	1985

AUTHOR	TITLE	PUBLISHER	PAGES	DATES
Culbertson, Ely	*Strange Lives of One Man	J. C. Winston (Philadelphia)	693	1940
Dunne, J. Patrick and Ostrow, Albert	Championship Bridge as Played by the Experts	McGraw-Hill Bodley Head (London)	251 188	1949 1952
Horton, Sally	A Fistful of Honours	Probray Press (Nottingham, England)	162	1985
Mahmood, Zia	Bridge My Way	Granovetter Books (Ballston Lake NY)	252	1992
Markus, Rixi with David Mountfield	A Vulnerable Game: The Memoirs of Rixi Markus	William Collins Sons (London)	153	1988
Mollo, Victor	Confessions of an Addict	Newnes (London)	199	1966
Ostrow, Albert (see Dunne, J. Patrick)	Championship Bridge as Played by the Experts			
Ramsey, Guy	Aces All	Museum Press (London)	204	1955
Reese, Terence	Bridge at the Top	Faber & Faber (London)	143	1977
Schenken, Howard	The Education of a Bridge Player	Simon & Schuster	286	1973
Sharif, Omar	Omar's Sharif's Life in Bridge	Faber (London)	146	1983
Sheinwold, Patricia Fox	Husbands and Other Men I've Played With	Houghton Mifflin (Boston)	196	1976
Sims, Dorothy Rice	Curiouser and Curiouser	Simon & Schuster	203	1940
Sontag, Alan	The Bridge Bum — My Life and Play	Morrow	240	1977

L HUMOR & POETRY

AUTHOR	TITLE	PUBLISHER	PAGES	DATES
Barclay, Shepard	Bridge Fun Verse and Worse	Walter Drey	95	1934
The Bridge	Bridge World Humor — 9 Short Stories	The Bridge World	48	1980
Bird, David & Klinger, Ron	Kosher Bridge	Victor Gollancz (London)	128	1992
Bird, David (see Reese, Terence)	Cardinal Sins			
Bird, David (see Reese, Terence)	Doubled and Venerable: Further Miracles of Card Play			
Bird, David (see Reese, Terence)	Unholy Tricks: More Miraculous Card Play			
Calhoun, Philo (see Webster, H. T.)	Who Dealt This Mess?			
Eber, Patty & Freeman, Mike	Have I Got a Story for You: An Anthology of Favorite Bridge Tales	Devyn Press (Louisville KY)	228	1984
Goldman, Bobby	Winners and Losers at the Bridge Table (illus. by Mary Grace)	Max Hardy	108	1979
Goodwin, Jude	Table Talk	Devyn Press (Shelbyville KY)	128	1982
Goren, Charles	Bridge Players Write the Funniest Letters	Doubelday	148	1968
James, Joe	What the Hell Is Trumps?	A. S. Barnes	91	1969
Johnston, William (see Webster, H. T.)	Webster's Bridge			
Kantar, Edwin	Bridge Humor	Wilshire (N. Hollywood CA)	151	1977
Kantar, Eddie	The Best of Eddie Kantar: Funny Stories from the Bridge Table	Granovetter Books (Ballston Lake NY)	213	1989
Kilpatrick, James J.	A Bestiary of Bridge	Andrews, McMeel & Parker (Kansas City MO)	119	1986
Klinger, Ron	The Bridge Player Who Laughed	Hutchinson Publ. Group (Victoria, Australia)	124	1984
Lawrence, Mike	True Bridge Humor	Max Hardy	61	1980
Lind, Betty	Psychotics, Neurotics and Bridge Players	Simons Pub. (Santa Fe NM)	58	1961
Machlin, Jerome	Tournament Bridge — An Uncensored Memoir	Max Hardy	120	1980
Mollo, Victor	Bridge in the Fourth Dimension	Faber & Faber (London)	160	1974
Mollo, Victor	Bridge in the Menagerie	Hawthorn	152	1967
Mollo, Victor	Masters and Monsters	Faber & Faber (London & Boston)	242	1979
Mollo, Victor	Destiny at Bay: The Latest from the Bridge Menagerie	Methuen (London)	207	1987
Mollo, Victor	Masters & Monsters: The Human Side of Bridge	Faber & Faber (London)	242	1979
Mollo, Victor	Bridge Club; Reprint of above	Simon & Schuster	242	1987
Mollo, Victor	You Need Neve Lose at Bridge: Happy Days in the Menagerie	Simon & Schuster	163	1987

AUTHOR	TITLE	PUBLISHER	PAGES	DATES
Mollo, Victor	Reprint of above	Simon & Schuster		1987
Natalie, George S.	*Dear Bridge Partner: A Book of Verses for the Bridge Table*	Natalie (n.p.)	(poems) 27	1985
Phillips, Hubert	*You Can Play and Laugh*	Faber & Faber (London)	269	1934
Reese, Terence & Bird, David	*Cardinal Sins*	Victor Gollancz (London)	156	1991
Reese, Terence & Bird, David	*Doubled and Venerable: Further Miracles of Card Play*	Victor Gollancz (London)	183	1987, 1993
Reese, Terence & Bird, David	*Unholy Tricks: More Miraculous Card Play*	Victor Gollancz (London)	160	1984
Rubens, Jeff	*Bridge in Muttropolis: Book 1*	*The Bridge World*	40	1968-1987
Rubens, Jeff	*Bridge in Muttropolis: Book 2*	*The Bridge World*	48	1987
Rubens, Jeff	*Bridge in Wonderland*	*The Bridge World*	40	1986
Saunders, P.F.	*Bridge with My Wife*	Probray Press (Nottingham, England)	143	1987
Smith, Marc	*Enterprising Tales*	Damien (Clifton NJ)	274	1990
Stewart, Frank	*A Christmas Stocking*	Stewart	64	1985
Webster, H. T. and Johnston William	*Webster's Bridge*	Stokes	112	1924
Webster, H. T. and Calhoun, Philo	*Who Dealt This Mess?*	Doubleday	174	1948

M MATHEMATICS

AUTHOR	TITLE	PUBLISHER	PAGES	DATES
Borel, Emile and Cheron, André	‡ *Mathematical Theory of Bridge* (trans. by Alex Traub)	Monna Lisa Precision	434	1975
Borel, Emile and Cheron, André	*Théorie Mathématique du Bridge	Gauthier-Villars (Paris)	424	1940-55
Frost, Frederick	†*Bridge Odds Complete*	Coffin (Waltham MA)	96	1971
Goren, Charles	*Go with the Odds*	Macmillan	308	1969
Jacoby, Oswald	*How to Figure the Odds*	Doubleday	215	1947
Kibler, Robert et al Levinson,	*Probabilities in Contract Bridge Science of Chance*	Frost Faber & Faber (London)	103	1963 1952
Northrop, Eugene and Stein, Arthur	*Mathematical Odds in Contract*	Vanguard	93	1933
Telfer, Roy	*Practical Odds at Bridge*	Traub (Cape Town)	114	1961
Telfer, Roy (see Kibler, Robert)	*Probabilities in Contract Bridge*			
Traub, Alec (see Kibler, Robert)	*Probabilities in Contract Bridge*			

N LAWS

AUTHOR	TITLE	PUBLISHER	PAGES	DATES
Whist Club, N.Y.	*The Laws of Contract Bridge*	J. C. Winston (Philadelphia)	54	1932
ACBL Laws Commission	*The Laws of Duplicate Contract Bridge*	ABL, USBA (Philadelphia)	64	1933
Whist Club, N. Y.	*The Laws of Contract Bridge*	J. C. Winston (Philadelphia)	51	1935
ACBL Laws Commission	*The Laws of Duplicate Contract Bridge*	J. C. Winston (Philadelphia)	91	1935
ACBL Laws Commission	*The Laws of Contract Bridge*	J. C. Winston (Philadelphia)	62	1943
ACBL Laws Commission	*The Laws of Contract Bridge*	J. C. Winston (Philadelphia)	47	1948
ACBL Laws Commission	*The Laws of Duplicate Contract Bridge*	J. C. Winston (Philadelphia)	67	1948
ACBL Laws Commission	*The Laws of Contract Bridge*	Crown	62	1963
ACBL Laws Commission	*The Laws of Duplicate Contract Bridge*	Crown	78	1963
ACBL Laws Commission	*Laws of Duplicate Contract Bridge*	ACBL (Memphis)	102	1975
ACBL Laws Commission	*Laws of Contract Bridge*	ACBL (Memphis)	55	1981
ACBL Laws Commission	‡*The Laws of Duplicate Contract Bridge*	ACBL (Memphis)	103 + XXIV	1990
Portland Club, EBL, ACBL, and WBF	*The International Laws of Contract Bridge 1981*	Bibliagora (Hounslow England)		1981

AUTHOR	TITLE	PAGES	DATES

O PERIODICALS

AUTHOR	TITLE	PAGES	DATES
Dollar, Stanley Kent, Walter	*The American Bridge Digest* (originally *California Bridge Digest*)	12	1962-63 1962-63
Coffin, George Shaw, Harold Thomas, Frank	*American Bridge Teachers' Quarterly* 7250 Franklin Ave. Los Angeles CA 90046	4	1961-63 1963-69 1969-
Howard, Denis Klinger, Ron	*Australian Bridge* Box 3805 GPO Sydney, NSW 2001, Australia	6 12	1970-71 1972-
Haremaker, R. N. Goudsmit, Frits Filarski, Herman Elffers, G. Boekhorst, Andre Schipperheyn, Ton	*Bridge* Nederlandse Bridge Bond Emmapark 9 2595 Es Den Haag The Netherlands		1930-34 1935-41 1946-56 1956-63 1963-71 1971-
Granovetter, Pamela & Matthew	*Bridge Today* 18 Village View Bluff Ballston Lake NY 12019	6	1988-
Grant, Audrey	*Audrey Grant's Better Bridge* 11684 Ventura Boulevard, Suite 426 Studio City CA 91604	4	1993-
Jeronimidis, Elena	*Bridge Plus* Ryden Grange, Bisley Surrey GV21 2TH, England	12	1989-
Lawrence, Mike	*Mike's Newsletter* 131 Alvarado Road Berkeley CA 94704	12	1988-
Paul Lavings & Joyce Nicholson	*Australian Bridge* P.O. Box 654, Split Junction NSW 2088, Australia		1985- 1989-
Richard Brightling and Stephen	*Lester*		1990-
de Togorco, Antonio Castellón, Joaquin Goded, Fredrico Francos, Luis Martorell, Juan	*Bridge* Edicones Bridge Castello, 45 Madrid-1, Spain	4	1961-
Jaques, Arturo Lerena, Raui	*Bridge Argentino* *Association del Bridge Argentino* Lavalle 1145 4 Piso B 1048 Buenos Aires, Argentina	6	1952-66 1966-
Mardulyn, Jean	*Bridge Belgium* Avenue Louis Lepoutre, 57 1060 Bruxelles, Belgium	6	1957-
Sachen, Bill	*Bridge Buffs' Bulletin* 927 Grand Avenue Waukegan IL 60085	4	1973
Firpo, Luigi Barbone, Guido	*Bridge D'Italia* Largo Augusto 3 20122 Milano, Italy	12	1943-75 1975-
Bruelheide, Frank	*Bridge Digest* 1645 Hennepin Avenue Minneapolis MN	12	1937-39
Gokhale, Avinash	*Bridge Digest* Ram Krópra, 17 Deccan Gymkhana Poona 414 004, India	8	1978-
Sandsmark, Tommy H. S. Stedding, Svein Thomas	*Bridge I Norge* Postboks 6765 St. Plass, Oslo 1, Norway	8	
Rubens, Jeff	*The Bridge Journal* 88-35 164 St. Jamaica 2, NY		1963-67
Shaikh, Mohammed Aslam	*The Bridge Kibitzer* 108 Motan Building, 2nd Floor M. A. Jinnah Road, Karachi-2, Pakistan		1983-
Manning-Foster, Alfred Edye Kempson, Cpt. Ewart Milnes, Eric Alder, Phillip	*Bridge Magazine* (not published during War) Wakefield Rd. Leeds 10, England	12	1926-39 1946-65 1965-80 1980-
Jannersten, Eric Flodquist, Sven-Olov	*Bridge Tidningen* Box 45 774 01 Avesta Stockholm, Sweden	10	1943-80 1980-

AUTHOR	TITLE	PAGES	DATES
Culbertson, Ely Moyse, Alphonse Jr. Kaplan, Edgar Rubens, Jeff	*The Bridge World* 39 W. 94th St. New York NY 10025	12	1929-55 1956-66 1967-
Phillips, Hubert Reese, Terence Dormer, Albert	*British Bridge World* 35 Dover St. London, W. 1 England	12	1932-39 1956-62 1962-64
Pomianowski, Jerz	*Brydz´* Ul. Widok 22 00-023 Warszawa, Poland		
Zankay, Peter	*Bridzselet* Buda 8 rsi ut 24 1118 Budapest, Hungary	12	Current
Cotzin, Sumner	*Communication* 10 Jamesbury Drive Worcester MA	12	1978-
Mott-Smith, Geoffrey Huske, William J. Benyon, George W. Sheinwold, Alfred Frey, Richard Becker, Steve Hirsch, Tannah Francis, Henry Emery, Sue Manley, Brent	*The Contract Bridge Bulletin* American Contract Bridge League 2990 Airways Blvd. P.O. Box 161192 Memphis TN 38186 Executive Editor Editor Managing Editor	12 16 16 40 80 88 148	1934-37 1937-39 1939-52 1952-58 1958-70 1970-72 1970-72 1972- 1972- 1989-
Harrison-Gray, Maurice Stern, Dr. Paul Ramsey, Guy Ingram, Henry St. John	*Contract Bridge Journal* 3 London Lane Bromley, Kent, England		1946-47 1947- 1947-50 1951-55
Nielsen, Aksel J. Pedersen, Leo Boeck, Jens Krause, Svend G. Boeck, Jens Lundby, Ib	*Dansk Bridge* Postboks 121 D-K 3400 Hillerod, Denmark	10	1941-47 1947-58 1958-64 1964-66 1966-73 1973-
Von Mutius, Erhard Schubert, Fritz Schubert, Vilma Borho, Volker	*Deutsches Bridge Verbands-Blatt* Teckstrasse 27 7238 Oberndorf, Germany	12	1952-64 1964-74 1974-79 1979-
Jannersten, Eric	*European Bridge Review* (in English)	12	1949-54
Neamtzu, Coriolan	*Expert Bridge* Victoe Manu 42, 73314 Bucarest, Romania	4-6	Current
Jannerstein, Eric Barrow, Rhoda Dormer, Albert Jourdain, Patrick	*IBPA Bulletin* The International Bridge Press Association Flat 8, Fein Wen, Rhiwbina, Cardiff, Wales CF4 6NW	10	1958-67 1967-72 1972-82 1982-
Amsbury, Joe Sowter, Tony	*International Popular Bridge Monthly* 12 Beech Avenue, Sherwood Rise Nottingham NG7 7LL.	12	1974-80 1980-
Walsh, P. F.	*Irish Bridge Journal* Northgate Street Athlone, Co Westmeath, Ireland	6	1979-
Hirsch, Tannah Frydrich, Julian	*Israel Bridge Magazine* 41 Weizmann St. Tel Aviv, Israel		1963-65 1966-67
Birman, David	*The Israeli Bridge Bulletin* 5 Bugrashov Tel Aviv, Israel		1980-
Wong, John Hikawa, Tetsuji	*Japan Contract Bridge League Bulletin* c/o Fudosan-Kaikan Room 705 3-5 Yotsuya Shinjuku-Ku, Tokyo 160		1963-80 1980-
Carruthers, John	*The Kibitzer* 65 Tiago Ave. Toronto ON, Canada M4B 2A2	4	Current
Kokish, Eric	*Melange de Bridge* 5050 Clanranald Ave. #406 Montrel PQ, Canada H3X 2S2	1	1975-
Freeman, Richard A.	*Modern Bridge* 1447 Peachtree St., N.E. Atlanta GA 30309	9	1964
Victor, Brig. A.D.J.	*News Bulletin* A-222 Defense Colony New Delhi 110 024, India	12	Current

AUTHOR	TITLE	PUBLISHER	PAGES	DATES
Fenton, H.E. Adams, Lindsay	*New Zealand Bridge* 49 Argyle St. Herne Bay, Auckland 2, New Zealand		6	1965-75 1975-
Wolenik, Bob	*Popular Bridge* 17337 Ventura Blvd. Encino CA 91316		6	1967-
Frey, Richard L.	*Precision Newsletter* 277 Park Avenue New York NY 10017		12	1973-81
Cardoso, Alinda Aranha, Sergio Barros, Ana C. M. Pinto, Sandra	*Revista Brasileira de Bridge* Caixa Postal 3334 São Paulo, Brazil		12	1975-
Bongrand, Michel Dreux, Emile Myer, Jean-Paul	*Revue Française de Bridge, Bridgeur* 28 Rue de Richelieu 75001 Paris, France		11	1958-
Sapire, Leon	*The South African Bridge Bulletin* South African Bridge Federation P.O. Box 10849 Johannesburg, South Africa 2000		11	1954-
Hathorn, John B.	*Texas Bridge* (last issue National Bridge)			1959-64
Marraro, Francesco	*Tutto Bridge* Roma Via della Scrofa 14 Milano, Italy		11	1980-
Dormer, Albert	*World Bridge News* 151 Blackheath Park London S. E. 3 OHA England		5-6	1971-

P ENCYCLOPEDIAS
Editors

AUTHOR	TITLE	PUBLISHER	PAGES	DATES
Cohen, Ben and Barrow, Rhoda	*The Bridge Player's Encyclopedia —* *International Edition* (British Edition of The Official Encyclopdeia of Bridge)	Paul Hamlyn (London)	674	1967
Culbertson, Ely	*The Encyclopedia of Bridge*	*The Bridge World*	471	1935
Francis, Henry and Truscott, Alan	*The Official Encyclopedia of Bridge* Diane Hayward (editor) 4th ed.	Crown	922	1984
Francis, Henry and Truscott, Alan	*The Official Encyclopedia of Bridge* Dorothy Francis, (editor) 5th ed.	ACBL (Memphis)	865	1994
Frey, Richard and Truscott, Alan	*The Official Encyclopedia of Bridge* Thomas Smith (editor) 2nd. ed. Amalya Kearse (editor) 3rd. ed.	Crown Crown Crown	691 793 858	1964 1971 1976

Q BIBLIOGRAPHIES

AUTHOR	TITLE	PUBLISHER	PAGES	DATES
Horr, Norton	*A Bibliography of Card-Games and* *of the History of Playing Cards*	Charles Orr (Cleveland)	79	1892
Jessel, Frederic	*A Bibliography of Works in English* *on Playing Cards and Gaming*	Longman's Green & Co.	311	1905
Parris, Leslie and Patricia	*Contract Bridge Books, an Annotated* *Bibliography for the British Isles* *1920-1969*	Wyvern House (Powys, Wales)	95	1975
Rather, John and Goldwater, Walter	*According to Hoyle...1742-1850* A Bibliography of editons by or based on the writings of Edmund Hoyle	Univeristy Place Book Shop	18	1983
Sachen, William	Bridge: A Guide to the Literature	Garland	171	1984